July 17-21, 2016
Pisa, Italy

Association for Computing Machinery

Advancing Computing as a Science & Profession

SIGIR'16

Proceedings of the 39th International ACM SIGIR conference on

Research and Development in Information Retrieval

Sponsored by:

ACM SIGIR

Association for Computing Machinery

Advancing Computing as a Science & Profession

The Association for Computing Machinery
2 Penn Plaza, Suite 701
New York, New York 10121-0701

Notice to Past Authors of ACM-Published Articles
ACM intends to create a complete electronic archive of all articles and/or other material previously published by ACM. If you have written a work that has been previously published by ACM in any journal or conference proceedings prior to 1978, or any SIG Newsletter at any time, and you do NOT want this work to appear in the ACM Digital Library, please inform permissions@acm.org, stating the title of the work, the author(s), and where and when published.

ISBN: 978-1-4503-4290-2 (Digital)

ISBN: 978-1-4503-4613-9 (Print)

Additional copies may be ordered prepaid from:

ACM Order Department
PO Box 30777
New York, NY 10087-0777, USA

Phone: 1-800-342-6626 (USA and Canada)
+1-212-626-0500 (Global)
Fax: +1-212-944-1318
E-mail: acmhelp@acm.org
Hours of Operation: 8:30 am – 4:30 pm ET

Printed in the USA

General Chairs' Welcome

It is our great pleasure to welcome you to SIGIR 2016, the 39th International ACM SIGIR Conference on Research and Development in Information Retrieval. SIGIR is back in Pisa, Italy, after exactly 30 years from the 1986 edition; at that time the proceedings were still in paper form, the conference did not have its own web page, Wi-Fi in the lecture rooms was not provided, and delegates tweeting about their impressions were still rare. Notwithstanding the lack of the modern commodities above, those who participated in that edition tell us stories of a lively and thoroughly enjoyable event; we hope to live up to that tradition and offer you five days of engaging scientific events, networking opportunities, and social fun.

The conference will start on July 17 with a day of (full-day and half-day) tutorials, plus the Doctoral Consortium. SIGIR 2016 will enter its main phase in the three days that follow, when the main conference (July 18-20) and the SIRIP Industry Track (July 20) will take place. The stimulating technical program set up includes two valuable and insightful keynote talks opening the first and the third day of the main conference:

- *Understanding Human Language: Can NLP and Deep Learning Help?* by Christopher Manning, Stanford University;
- *Big Data in Climate: Opportunities and Challenges for Machine Learning,* by Vipin Kumar, University of Minnesota.

The last day of the conference (July 21) will be entirely devoted to workshops.

We would like to take this opportunity to thank everybody who helped us in setting up SIGIR 2016. First of all, we would like to give heartfelt thanks to our sponsor, ACM SIGIR, and our corporate supporters: Baidu (Platinum Supporter), Appen, Bloomberg, Booking.com, eBay, Facebook, Google, Huawei, IBM, Microsoft, Yahoo! (Silver Supporters), and Yandex (Bronze Supporter). All of them provided generous sponsorship, which allowed us to keep the registration fees (believe it or not...) as low as possible and fund a lot of student travels. Thanks also to the National Research Council of Italy and to the Qatar Computing Research Institute for supporting our organizational work.

Putting everything together was a hard teamwork. We want to thank everybody involved in making SIGIR 2016 an exciting event. First and foremost, we want to thank our Program Chairs Javed Aslam, Ian Ruthven, and Justin Zobel, not only for chairing the selection of the full papers, but also for painstakingly overseeing the rest of the scientific program. Many thanks also to the Short Papers Chairs Ben Carterette, Carlos Castillo, and Jaana Kekäläinen, who had to deal with an inordinate amount of short paper submissions under tighter-than-usual time constraints; to the Tutorials Chairs Evangelos Kanoulas and Tie-Yan Liu; to the Workshops Chairs Aristides Gionis and Edie Rasmussen; to the Demo Chair Craig Macdonald; to the Doctoral Consortium Chairs Brian Davison and Kira Radinski; to the SIRIP Industry Track Chairs Jussi Karlgren and Gilad Mishne; to the Sponsorship Chairs Fabrizio Falchi and Jimmy Huang; and to the Awards Chair Norbert Fuhr. All of them went to great lengths to ensure the high quality of this conference. Quite aside from the people who held chairing roles, lots of other people contributed to the scientific success of SIGIR 2016: many thanks to the members of the Senior Program Committee, to the members of the first-tier Program Committee, to the mentors of the Doctorial Consortium Committee, and to all those who reviewed, in any capacity, full papers, short papers, tutorial and workshop proposals, demo papers.

Last but not least, we would like to thank all the members of the local organizing team at the National Research Council of Italy; in order to keep the registration fees as low as possible, no professional conference organization company was called in to help, and they took 100% of the organization upon them. We would thus like our two Local Chairs Andrea Esuli and Chiara Renso; our Treasurer Giulio Galesi; our Publications Chair Claudio Lucchese; our Publicity Chair Nicola Tonellotto; our Webmaster Franco Maria Nardini; our Student Volunteers Coordinators Alejandro Moreo Fernández and, again, Franco Maria Nardini. Thanks also to (in no particular order) Catherine Bosio, Matteo Catena, Francesca Donati, and Sara Montesi for helping in various phases of the organization. They all invested tremendous efforts into making SIGIR 2016 an exciting and enjoyable event. It is due to them that the organization of SIGIR 2016 was not just hard work, but also a pleasure.

We look forward to welcoming you in Pisa, Tuscany, possibly the most enchanting region of Italy, surely the richest of artistic heritage and landscapes. Due to its history and the extraordinary quality of food and wines, it is an unforgettable place to visit. We hope that you will be rewarded by the technical challenges of SIGIR 2016 but you will get also a chance to explore our region and enjoy its vibrant atmosphere!

Raffaele Perego
ISTI-CNR, Italy

Fabrizio Sebastiani
Qatar Computing Research Institute, HBKU, Qatar

SIGIR 2016 Program Chairs' Preface

Welcome to SIGIR 2016, the 39th Annual International ACM-SIGIR Conference on Research and Development in Information Retrieval, the premier conference in the area. We are grateful to all those who chose to submit their research papers to SIGIR 2016 and gave the Program Committee an opportunity to evaluate their work for potential inclusion in the program. We are also grateful to the 61 Senior Program Committee Members, 244 Program Committee Members, and many additional reviewers for providing significant time and effort to selecting this year's conference program. This pool of committed SIGIR volunteers comes from 24 countries and over 180 institutions.

The PC reviewed 341 papers for the full paper track, and accepted 62 with an acceptance rate of 18%. The top countries in terms of accepted papers (taking all author affiliations of each paper equally into account) were the U.S.A. (34%), and China (23%) with the most successful countries (as measured by how likely authors from that country were to have their papers accepted) were Russia (55% of authors had their paper accepted), Israel (50%), and Germany (45%). With 1236 authors overall, 313 were from the U.S.A and 283 from China; and 289 from the next six most represented countries combined.

As has been customary for many years, SIGIR 2016 employed a two-tier double-blind review process. At least three reviewers reviewed each paper, and then the Primary Area Chair of the paper led a discussion, which was used as the basis of the meta-review. The Secondary Area Chair assigned to each paper double-checked the reviews and discussion and, in some cases, provided an additional review. The PC chairs carefully examined the reviews and associated discussion, asking for additional reviews where necessary to provide a fuller discussion or additional expert opinion.

The SIGIR 2016 PC meeting operated as a virtual meeting, held over several days, in order to facilitate the involvement of as many Senior PC members as possible. Prior to the PC meeting the PC chairs proposed a list of "clear accepts" and "clear rejects" where the meta-reviews and reviews clearly indicated a decision. Over the four days of the PC meeting, the chairs indicated which undecided papers were open for discussion, led the discussion on these papers, and made the final decision when discussions moved towards completion; overall nearly half of the submitted papers were reviewed by the chairs or at the meeting. We are grateful for the involvement of the Senior PC members in supporting this PC meeting, especially those very committed members who participated in almost every discussion. The virtual PC meeting was supplemented by a small physical meeting of the Senior PC members who attended the ECIR 2016 conference, which took place during the same week.

The short paper track received 339 submissions and accepted 104 papers for what promises to be a strong short paper track. Thanks are due to Ben Carterette, Carlos Castillo, and Jaana Kekäläinen, the track chairs, for arranging and managing a thorough review process for so many papers – a huge effort for which we are very grateful.

The tutorial track reviewed 20 submissions and accepted 2 full-day tutorials and 10 half-day tutorials. We are grateful to Evangelos Kanoulas and Tie-Yan Liu for leading the selection of a diverse and high quality tutorial program.

The workshops track received 12 submissions and selected 7 workshop proposals. We thank Aristides Gionis and Edie Rasmussen for their efforts in producing a great set of workshops.

The demos track received 35 submissions of which 21 were accepted. Many thanks are due to Craig Macdonald for chairing this track and providing us with an array of interesting demos.

Brian D. Davison and Kira Radinsky organised the Doctoral Consortium, a vitally important part of the SIGIR program. Thanks to their efforts, the event received 23 submissions from doctoral students and accepted 15 of these for presentation and discussion at the consortium.

This year's industry track is the SIGIR Symposium on IR in Practice (SIRIP 2016) co-chaired by Jussi Karlgren and Gilad Mishne. Their efforts in organizing SIRIP and producing an interesting set of speakers from diverse backgrounds are gratefully acknowledged.

Finally, special thanks to Norbert Fuhr for chairing the panel to select the Best Paper and Best Student Paper.

We hope you find this program stimulating and thought provoking, and that the conference provides you with an opportunity to share ideas with other researchers, practitioners and students from institutions all around the world.

Javed Aslam
SIGIR 2016 PC Co-Chair
Northeastern University

Justin Zobel
SIGIR 2016 PC Co-Chair
University of Melbourne

Ian Ruthven
SIGIR 2016 PC Co-Chair
University of Strathclyde

Table of Contents

Volumn 1

Keynote I

Session Chair: Ricardo Baeza-Yates *(Universitat Pompeu Fabra)*

Keynote II

Session Chair: Susan Dumais *(Microsoft Research)*

Session: Evaluation I

Session Chair: Ben Carterette *(University of Delaware)*

Session: Speech and Conversation Systems

Session Chair: Gareth Jones *(Dublin City University)*

Session: Retrieval Models

Session Chair: Maarten de Rijke *(University of Amsterdam)*

Session: Learning-to-rank

Session Chair: Mattew Lease *(University of Texas at Austin)*

Session: Music and Math

Session Chair: Jaap Kamps *(University of Amsterdam)*

Session: Microblog

Session Chair: Mark D. Smucker *(University of Waterloo)*

Session: Web Search

Session Chair: David Hawking *(Microsoft Research)*

Session: Question Answering
Session Chair: Hideo Joho *(University of Tsukuba)*

Session: Learning
Session Chair: Emine Yilmaz *(University College London)*

Session: Efficiency I
Session Chair: Alistair Moffat *(University of Melbourne)*

Session: Recommendation Systems I
Session Chair: Oren Kurland *(Technion)*

Session: User Needs
Session Chair: Diane Kelly *(University of North Carolina at Chapel Hill)*

Session: Privacy, Advertising, and Products
Session Chair: Grace Hui Yang *(Georgetown University)*

Session: Novelty and Diversity
Session Chair: Charlie L.A. Clarke *(University of Waterloo)*

Session: Entities and Knowledge Graphs
Session Chair: Jamie Callan *(Carnegie Mellon University)*

Session: SIRIP I: Big companies, big data
Session Chair: Gilad Mishne *(Color Genomics)*

Session: Evaluation II
Session Chair: Tetsuya Sakai *(Waseda University)*

Session: Events
Session Chair: Fernando Diaz *(Microsoft Research)*

Session: SIRIP II: Small companies, big ideas
Session Chair: Gilad Mishne *(Color Genomics)*

Session: Recommendation Systems II
Session Chair: Josiane Mothe *(Institut de Recherche en Informatique de Toulouse)*

Session: Image and Multimodal Search
Session Chair: Gabriella Pasi *(Universitá degli Studi di Milano Bicocca)*

Session: SIRIP III: Modeling and Evaluation
Session Chair: Jussi Karlgren *(Gavagai & KTH)*

Session: Behavior Models and Applications
Session Chair: David Elsweiler *(University of Regensburg)*

Session: Efficiency II
Session Chair: Alistair Moffat *(University of Melbourne)*

Volumn 2

Session: Short Collection Papers

Session: Short Research Papers

Demonstrations

Session Chair: Craig Macdonald *(University of Glasgow)*

Doctoral Consortium

Tutorials

Workshops

SIGIR 2016 Conference Organization

General Chairs: Raffaele Perego *(ISTI-CNR, Italy)*
Fabrizio Sebastiani *(Qatar Computing Research Institute, HBKU, Qatar)*

Program Chairs: Javed Aslam *(Northeastern University, US)*
Ian Ruthven *(University of Strathclyde, UK)*
Justin Zobel *(University of Melbourne, Australia)*

Short Papers Chairs: Ben Carterette *(University of Delaware, US)*
Carlos Castillo *(Eurecat Technology Centre of Catalonia, Spain)*
Jaana Kekalainen *(University of Tampere, Finland)*

Tutorials Chairs: Evangelos Kanoulas *(University of Amsterdam, Netherlands)*
Tie-Yan Liu *(Microsoft Research, China)*

Workshops Chairs: Aristides Gionis *(Aalto University, Finland)*
Edie Rasmussen *(University of British Columbia, Canada)*

Demo Chair: Craig Macdonald *(University of Glasgow, UK)*

Industry Track Chairs: Jussi Karlgren *(Gavagai & KTH, Sweden)*
Gilad Mishne *(Color Genomics, US)*

Doctoral Consortium Chairs: Brian Davison *(Lehigh University, US)*
Kira Radinsky *(SalesPredict, Israel)*

Awards Chair: Norbert Fuhr *(University of Duisburg-Essen, Germany)*

Local Arrangements Chairs: Andrea Esuli *(ISTI-CNR, Italy)*
Chiara Renso *(ISTI-CNR, Italy)*

Sponsorships Chairs: Fabrizio Falchi *(ISTI-CNR, Italy)*
Jimmy Huang *(York University, Canada)*

Proceedings Chair: Claudio Lucchese *(ISTI-CNR, Italy)*

Publicity Chair: Nicola Tonellotto *(ISTI-CNR, Italy)*

Treasurer: Giulio Galesi *(ISTI-CNR, Italy)*

Volunteer Coordinators: Alejandro Moreo Fernández *(ISTI-CNR, Italy)*
Franco Maria Nardini *(ISTI-CNR, Italy)*

Webmaster: Franco Maria Nardini *(ISTI-CNR, Italy)*

Senior Program Committee:

Eugene Agichtein *(Emory University, USA)*
James Allan *(University of Massachusetts Amherst, USA)*
Leif Azzopardi *(University of Glasgow, UK)*
Krisztian Balog *(University of Stavanger, Norway)*
Peter Bruza *(Queensland University of Technology, Australia)*
Jamie Callan *(Carnegie Mellon University, USA)*
David Carmel *(Yahoo Research, Israel)*
Yi Chang *(Yahoo Research, USA)*
Charles L.A. Clarke *(University of Waterloo, Canada)*
Kevyn Collins-Thompson *(University of Michigan, USA)*
Nick Craswell *(Microsoft, USA)*
Fabio Crestani *(Università della Svizzera Italiana, Switzerland)*
Bruce Croft *(University of Massachusetts Amherst, USA)*
Ronan Cummins *(University of Cambridge, UK)*
Maarten de Rijke *(University of Amsterdam, The Netherlands)*
Arjen P. de Vries *(Radboud University, The Netherlands)*
Fernando Diaz *(Microsoft Research, USA)*
David Elsweiler *(University of Regensburg, Germany)*
Hui Fang *(University of Delaware, USA)*
Evgeniy Gabrilovich *(Google, USA)*
Jianfeng Gao *(Microsoft Research, USA)*
Shlomo Geva *(Queensland University of Technology, Australia)*
Marcos Goncalves *(UFMG, Brazil)*
Julio Gonzalo *(UNED, Spain)*
Claudia Hauff *(TU Delft, The Netherlands)*
Djoerd Hiemstra *(University of Twente, The Netherlands)*
Xian-Sheng Hua *(Alibaba Group, China)*
Jimmy Huang *(York University, Canada)*
Hideo Joho *(University of Tsukuba, Japan)*
Gareth Jones *(Dublin City University, Ireland)*
Jaap Kamps *(University of Amsterdam, The Netherlands)*
Diane Kelly *(University of North Carolina at Chapel Hill, USA)*
Wessel Kraaij *(Leiden University, The Netherlands)*
Oren Kurland *(Technion, Israel)*
Wai Lam *(Chinese University of Hong Kong, China)*
Matthew Lease *(University of Texas at Austin, USA)*
Hang Li *(Huawei Technologies, China)*
Stephane Marchand-Maillet *(University of Geneva, Switzerland)*
Massimo Melucci *(University of Padua, Italy)*
Donald Metzler *(Google, USA)*
Stefano Mizzaro *(University of Udine, Italy)*
Josiane Mothe *(Institut de Recherche en Informatique de Toulouse, France)*
Isabelle Moulinier *(Thomson Reuters, USA)*
Edleno S. Moura *(Institute of Computing - UFAM, Brazil)*
Vanessa Murdock *(Microsoft Research, USA)*

Senior Program Committee (continued):

Jian-Yun Nie *(University of Montreal, Canada)*
Douglas W. Oard *(University of Maryland, USA)*
Dan Pelleg *(Yahoo Research, Israel)*
Benjamin Piwowarski *(Université Pierre et Marie Curie, France)*
Tetsuya Sakai *(Waseda University, Japan)*
Mark Sanderson *(RMIT University, Australia)*
Falk Scholer *(RMIT University, Australia)*
Milad Shokouhi *(Microsoft Research, USA)*
Fabrizio Silvestri *(Yahoo Research, UK)*
Mark D. Smucker *(University of Waterloo, Canada)*
Andrew Trotman *(eBay, USA)*
Karin M. Verspoor *(University of Melbourne, Australia)*
Ellen M. Voorhees *(NIST, USA)*
Ryen W. White *(Microsoft Research, USA)*
Grace Hui Yang *(Georgetown University, USA)*
Emine Yilmaz *(University College London, UK)*

Program Committee:

Mikhail Ageev *(Moscow State University, Russia)*
Luca Maria Aiello *(Yahoo Research, UK)*
Elif Aktolga *(Apple, USA)*
Omar Alonso *(Microsoft Research, USA)*
Ismail S. Altingovde *(Middle East Technical University, Turkey)*
Robin Aly *(University of Twente, The Netherlands)*
Gianni Amati *(Fondazione Ugo Bordoni, Italy)*
Enrique Amigó *(UNED, Spain)*
Aris Anagnostopoulos *(Sapienza University of Rome, Italy)*
Avi Arampatzis *(Democritus University of Thrace, Greece)*
Ioannis Arapakis *(Eurecat Technology Centre of Catalonia, Spain)*
Jaime Arguello *(University of North Carolina at Chapel Hill, USA)*
Azin Ashkan *(Technicolor Labs, USA)*
Xiao Bai *(Yahoo Research, USA)*
Peter Bailey *(Microsoft Research, Australia)*
Niranjan Balasubramanian *(University of Washington, USA)*
Zhifeng Bao *(RMIT University, Australia)*
Steve Beitzel *(Applied Communication Sciences, USA)*
Michael Bendersky *(Google, USA)*
Fabrício Benevenuto *(Universidade Federal de Minas Gerais, Brazil)*
Klaus Berberich *(Max Planck Institute for Informatics, Germany)*
Bodo Billerbeck *(University of Melbourne and Microsoft, Australia)*
Lidong Bing *(Carnegie Mellon University, USA)*
Roi Blanco *(Yahoo Research, Spain)*
Toine Bogers *(Aalborg University Copenhagen, Denmark)*
Mohand Boughanem *(IRIT, France)*
Martin Braschler *(Zurich University of Applied Sciences, Switzerland)*
Chris Brew *(Thomson Reuters, UK)*

Program Committee (continued):

Marc Bron *(Yahoo, UK)*
George Buchanan *(City University London, UK)*
Iván Cantador *(Universidad Autónoma de Madrid, Spain)*
Rob Capra *(University of North Carolina at Chapel Hill, USA)*
Mark Carman *(Monash University, Australia)*
Claudio Carpineto *(Fondazione Ugo Bordoni, Italy)*
Marc-Allen Cartright *(Google, USA)*
James Caverlee *(Texas A&M University, USA)*
Soumen Chakrabarti *(IIT Bombay, Italy)*
Kevin C. Chang *(University of Illinois at Urbana-Champaign, USA)*
Ruey-Cheng Chen *(RMIT University, Australia)*
Yi Chen *(NJIT, USA)*
Ed H Chi *(Google, USA)*
Francisco Claude *(Universidad Diego Portales, Chile)*
Stéphane Clinchant *(Xerox Research Center Europe, France)*
Jack G. Conrad *(Thomson Reuters, USA)*
Gordon V. Cormack *(University of Waterloo, Canada)*
J. Shane Culpepper *(RMIT University, Australia)*
Tonya Custis *(Thomson Reuters, USA)*
Altigran S. da Silva *(Universidade Federal do Amazonas, Brazil)*
Jeff Dalton *(Google, USA)*
Van Dang *(Google, USA)*
Gianluca Demartini *(University of Sheffield, UK)*
Emanuele Di Buccio *(University of Padua, Italy)*
Giorgio Maria Di Nunzio *(University of Padua, Italy)*
Laura Dietz *(University of Mannheim, Germany)*
Shuai Ding *(Google, USA)*
Debora Donato *(StumbleUpon, USA)*
Dietmar H. Dorr *(Google, USA)*
Zhicheng Dou *(Renmin University of China, China)*
Doug Downey *(Northwestern University, USA)*
Andy Edmonds *(Adobe, USA)*
Miles Efron *(University of Illinois, USA)*
Carsten Eickhoff *(ETH Zurich, Switzerland)*
Yuan Fang *(Institute for Infocomm Research, Singapore)*
Yi Fang *(Santa Clara University, USA)*
Nicola Ferro *(University of Padua, Italy)*
Marcus C. Fontoura *(Microsoft, USA)*
Dayne Freitag *(SRI International, USA)*
Ingo Frommholz *(University of Bedfordshire, UK)*
Patrick Gallinari *(Université Pierre et Marie Curie, France)*
Debasis Ganguly *(Dublin City University, Ireland)*
Bin Gao *(Microsoft Research, China)*
Eric Gaussier *(Université Joseph Fourier, France)*
Lorraine Goeuriot *(Université Grenoble Alpes, France)*

Program Committee (continued):

Nazli Goharian *(Georgetown University, USA)*
Peter B. Golbus *(Wayfair, USA)*
Brigitte Grau *(LIMSI-CNRS and ENSIIE, France)*
Vincent Guigue *(Université Pierre et Marie Curie, France)*
Mustafa Ghulam *(University of Bedfordshire, UK)*
Jiafeng Guo *(Institute of Computing Technology, Chinese Academy of Sciences, China)*
Maxim Gurevich *(Bento Labs, USA)*
Cathal Gurrin *(Dublin City University, Ireland)*
Ido Guy *(Yahoo Research, Israel)*
Martin Halvey *(University of Strathclyde, UK)*
Allan Hanbury *(TU Wien, Austria)*
Sanda M. Harabagiu *(University of Texas at Dallas, USA)*
Morgan Harvey *(Northumbria University, UK)*
Ahmed Hassan *(Microsoft Research, USA)*
David Hawking *(Microsoft Research, Australia)*
Ben He *(University of Chinese Academy of Sciences, China)*
Daqing He *(University of Pittsburgh, USA)*
Jiyin He *(CWI, The Netherlands)*
Yunlong He *(Yahoo Research, USA)*
Liangjie Hong *(Yahoo Research, USA)*
Winston H. Hsu *(National Taiwan University, Taiwan)*
Jeff Huang *(Brown University, USA)*
Xuanjing Huang *(Fudan University, China)*
Samuel Huston *(Google, USA)*
Radu-Tudor Ionescu *(University of Bucharest, Romania)*
Adam Jatowt *(Kyoto University, Japan)*
Jiepu Jiang *(University of Massachusetts Amherst, USA)*
Jing Jiang *(Singapore Management University, Singapore)*
Joemon M. Jose *(University of Glasgow, UK)*
Min-Yen Kan *(National University of Singapore, Singapore)*
Mohan Kankanhalli *(National University of Singapore, Singapore)*
Evangelos Kanoulas *(University of Amsterdam, The Netherlands)*
Makoto Kato *(Kyoto University, Japan)*
Enver Kayaaslan *(Turgut Ozal University, Turkey)*
Heikki Keskustalo *(University of Tampere, Finland)*
Julia Kiseleva *(Eindhoven University of Technology, The Netherlands)*
Weize Kong *(University of Massachusetts Amherst, USA)*
Alexander Kotov *(Wayne State University, USA)*
Udo Kruschwitz *(University of Essex, UK)*
Anagha Kulkarni *(San Francisco State University, USA)*
Susana Ladra *(University of A Coruña, Spain)*
Dmitry Lagun *(Google, USA)*
Will Lamond *(Wayfair, USA)*
Sylvain Lamprier *(LIP6 - UPMC, France)*

Program Committee (continued):

Léa Laporte *(LIRIS - INSA Lyon, France)*
Ray R Larson *(University of California, USA)*
Martha Larson *(Delft University of Technology, The Netherlands)*
Dawn Lawrie *(Loyola University Maryland, USA)*
Chia-Jung Lee *(Microsoft Research, USA)*
Jochen L. Leidner *(Thomson Reuters, UK)*
Daniel Lemire *(Université du Québec, Canada)*
Liangda Li *(Yahoo Research, USA)*
Min Li *(Alibaba, China)*
Kewen Liao *(University of Melbourne, Australia)*
Christina Lioma *(University of Copenhagen, Denmark)*
Jialu Liu *(University of Illinois at Urbana-Champaign, USA)*
Tie-Yan Liu *(Microsoft Research, China)*
Yiqun Liu *(Tsinghua University, China)*
Claudio Lucchese *(ISTI-CNR, Italy)*
Robert WP Luk *(The Hong Kong Polytechnic University, China)*
Mihai Lupu *(TU Wien, Austria)*
Yuanhua Lv *(Microsoft Research, USA)*
Hao Ma *(Microsoft Research, USA)*
Andrew MacFarlane *(City University London, UK)*
Prasenjit Majumder *(DAIICT, India)*
Amin Mantrach *(Yahoo Research, USA)*
Ilya Markov *(University of Amsterdam, The Netherlands)*
Yosi Mass *(IBM Research Lab, Israel)*
Julian McAuley *(University of California San Diego, USA)*
Richard McCreadie *(University of Glasgow, UK)*
Gayle McElvain *(Thomson Reuters, USA)*
Kevin McGuinness *(Dublin City University, Ireland)*
Paul McNamee *(Johns Hopkins University, USA)*
Qiaozhu Mei *(University of Michigan, USA)*
Edgar Meij *(Yahoo Research, Spain)*
Mandar Mitra *(Indian Statistical Institute, India)*
Alessandro Moschitti *(Qatar Computing Research Institute, HBKU, Qatar)*
Yashar Moshfeghi *(University of Glasgow, UK)*
Franco Maria Nardini *(ISTI-CNR, Italy)*
Roberto Navigli *(Sapienza University of Rome, Italy)*
Michael L. Nelson *(Old Dominion University, USA)*
Chong-Wah Ngo *(City University of Hong Kong, China)*
Dong Nguyen *(University of Twente, The Netherlands)*
Alexandros Ntoulas *(Samsung Research America, USA)*
Pan Pan *(Alibaba Group, China)*
Laurence A.F. Park *(Western Sydney University, Australia)*
Gabriella Pasi *(Università degli Studi di Milano Bicocca, Italy)*
Virgil Pavlu *(Northeastern University, USA)*
Jan Pedersen *(Microsoft Research, USA)*

Program Committee (continued):

Vassilis Plachouras *(Thomson Reuters, UK)*
Barbara Poblete *(University of Chile, Chile)*
Martin Potthast *(Bauhaus-Universität, Germany)*
Kunal Punera *(RelateIQ, USA)*
Filip Radlinski *(Microsoft Research, UK)*
Fiana Raiber *(Technion, Israel)*
Karthik Raman *(Google, USA)*
Edie Rasmussen *(University of British Columbia, Canada)*
Yongli Ren *(RMIT University, Australia)*
Haggai Roitman *(IBM Research, Israel)*
Dmitri Roussinov *(University of Strathclyde, UK)*
Eric SanJuan *(University of Avignon, France)*
Rodrygo Santos *(Universidade Federal de Minas Gerais, Brazil)*
Jacques Savoy *(University of Neuchatel, Switzerland)*
Ralf Schenkel *(University of Passau, Germany)*
Anne Schuth *(Blendle, The Netherlands)*
Pavel Serdyukov *(Yandex, Russia)*
Chirag Shah *(Rutgers University, USA)*
Anna Shtok *(Technion IIT, Israel)*
Gianmaria Silvello *(University of Padua, Italy)*
Laurianne Sitbon *(Queensland University of Technology, Australia)*
Catherine L. Smith *(Kent State University, USA)*
Aya Soffer *(IBM Research, Israel)*
Alessandro Sordoni *(Université de Montréal, Canada)*
Laure Soulier *(Université Pierre et Marie Curie, France)*
Alessandro Sperduti *(University of Padua, Italy)*
Mingxuan Sun *(Louisiana State University, USA)*
Idan Szpektor *(Yahoo Research, Israel)*
S.M.M. Tahaghoghi *(Microsoft Research, USA)*
Jiliang Tang *(Yahoo Research, USA)*
Gabriele Tolomei *(Yahoo Research, UK)*
Anastasios Tombros *(Queen Mary University of London, UK)*
Dolf Trieschnigg *(Mydatafactory, The Netherlands)*
Manos Tsagkias *(904Labs, The Netherlands)*
Theodora Tsikrika *(Centre for Research and Technology Hellas, Greece)*
Emre Velipasaoglu *(OpsClarity, USA)*
Adriano Veloso *(Universidade Federal de Minas Gerais, Brazil)*
Rossano Venturini *(University of Pisa, Italy)*
Bin Wang *(Institute of Information Engineering, Chinese Academy of Sciences, China)*
Hongning Wang *(University of Virginia, USA)*
Jian Wang *(LinkedIn, USA)*
Jun Wang *(University College London, UK)*
Lidan Wang *(IBM Research, USA)*
Meng Wang *(Hefei University of Technology, China)*

Program Committee (continued):

Quan Wang *(Institute of Information Engineering, Chinese Academy of Sciences, China)*
Shuaiqiang Wang *(University of Jyväskylä, Finland)*
Ingmar Weber *(Qatar Computing Research Institute, HBKU, Qatar)*
Wouter Weerkamp *(904Labs, The Netherlands)*
Gerhard Weikum *(Max Planck Institute for Informatics, Germany)*
Ji-Rong Wen *(Renmin University of China, China)*
Robert West *(Stanford University, USA)*
Wei Wu *(Microsoft Research, China)*
Xuansong Xie *(Taobao, China)*
Chenyan Xiong *(Carnegie Mellon University, USA)*
Jun Xu *(Institute of Computing Technology, Chinese Academy of Sciences, China)*
Tan Xu *(AT&T Labs, USA)*
Xiaobing Xue *(Twitter, USA)*
Makoto Yamada *(Kyoto University, Japan)*
Zheng Ye *(Maluuba Research, Canada)*
Reyyan Yeniterzi *(Ozyegin University, Turkey)*
Xing Yi *(Yahoo Research, USA)*
Dawei Yin *(Yahoo Research, USA)*
Elad Yom-Tov *(Microsoft Research, Israel)*
Minoru Yoshida *(University of Tokushima, Japan)*
Dell Zhang *(Birkbeck, University of London, UK)*
Lanbo Zhang *(Twitter, USA)*
Min Zhang *(Tsinghua University, China)*
Qi Zhang *(Fudan University, China)*
Yi Zhang *(University of California Santa Cruz, USA)*
Le Zhao *(Houzz, USA)*
Xiaowei Zhao *(Alibaba Group, China)*
Ke Zhou *(Yahoo Research, UK)*
Mianwei Zhou *(Yahoo Research, USA)*
Nivio Ziviani *(Universidade Federal de Minas Gerais, Brazil)*
Guido Zuccon *(Queensland University of Technology, Australia)*

Program Committee additional reviewers:

Saeid Balaneshin-kordan *(Wayne State University, USA)*
Gianni Barlacchi *(University of Trento, Italy)*
Daniele Bonadiman *(University of Trento, Italy)*
Dongho Choi *(Rutgers University, USA)*
Yagmur Gizem Cinar *(Université Grenoble Alpes, France)*
Arman Cohan *(Georgetown University, USA)*
Eva D'hondt *(LIMSI-CNRS, France)*
Nan Du *(Georgia Institute of Technology, USA)*
Matthew Ekstrand-Abueg *(Northeastern University, USA)*
Mustafa Ghulam *(University of Bedfordshire, UK)*
Simon Gog *(Karlsruhe Institute of Technology, Germany)*

Program Committee additional reviewers (continued):

Parantapa Goswami *(Université Grenoble Alpes, France)*
David Graus *(University of Amsterdam, Netherlands)*
Artem Grotov *(University of Amsterdam, Netherlands)*
Longkun Guo *(Fuzhou University, China)*
Xiangnan He *(National University of Singapore, Singapore)*
Damien Jose *(Microsoft Research, USA)*
Denis Kotkov *(University of Jyväskylä, Finland)*
Will Lamond *(Wayfair, USA)*
Long Le *(Rutgers University, USA)*
Cheng Li *(Northeastern University, USA)*
Babak Loni *(Delft University of Technology, Netherlands)*
Xiaolu Lu *(RMIT University, Australia)*
Rui Luo *(University College London, UK)*
Craig Macdonald *(University of Glasgow, UK)*
Joel Mackenzie *(RMIT University, Australia)*
Maria Maistro *(University of Padua, Italy)*
Kleanthis Malialis *(University College London, UK)*
Stefania Marrara *(Università degli Studi di Milano Bicocca, Italy)*
Ziad Matni *(Rutgers University, USA)*
Corren McCoy *(Old Dominion University, USA)*
Avihai Mejer *(Yahoo Research, Israel)*
Pavel Metrikov *(Northeastern University, USA)*
Jun Miao *(York University, Canada)*
Matthew Mitsui *(Rutgers University, USA)*
Jose G. Moreno *(LIMSI-CNRS, France)*
Massimo Nicosia *(University of Trento, Italy)*
Fedor Nikolaev *(Wayne State University, USA)*
Joao Palotti *(Technical University of Vienna, Austria)*
Gaurav Pandey (*University of Jyväskylä, Finland)*
Denis Parra *(Pontificia Universidad Católica de Chile, Chile)*
Casper Petersen *(University of Copenhagen, Denmark)*
Giulio Ermanno Pibiri *(University of Pisa, Italy)*
Yuval Pinter *(Yahoo Research, Israel)*
Yongrui (Louie) Qin *(Univeristy of Huddersfield, UK)*
Adam Roegiest *(University of Waterloo, Canada)*
Yao Shen *(Nanjing University of Aeronautics and Astronautics, China)*
Martijn Spitters *(Blendle, Netherlands)*
Jian-Tao Sun *(Microsoft Research, USA)*
Xing Tan *(York University, Canada)*
Kateryna Timoshenko *(University of Trento, Italy)*
Gilad Tsur *(Yahoo Research, Israel)*
Antonio Uva *(University of Trento, Italy)*
Oscar Valdivia-Verdugo *(Cloner SpA, Chile)*
Marco Viviani *(Università degli Studi di Milano Bicocca, Italy)*
Sheng Wang *(RMIT University, Australia)*

Program Committee additional reviewers (continued):

Yao Wu *(Simon Fraser University, Canada)*
Yixin Wu *(University College London, UK)*
Yu Wu *(Beihang University, China)*
Chen Xing *(Nankai University, China)*
Lina Yao *(University of New South Wales, Australia)*
Aston Zhang *(University of Illinois at Urbana-Champaign, USA)*
Weinan Zhang *(University College London, UK)*
Yongfeng Zhang (*University of California Santa Cruz, USA)*
Jessie Zhao *(York University, Canada)*
Qi Zhao *(University of California Santa Cruz, USA)*
Masrour Zoghi *(University of Amsterdam, Netherlands)*

Short Papers Committee:

Jatowt Adam *(Kyoto University, Japan)*
Mikhail Ageev *(Moscow State University, Russia)*
Dyaa Albakour *(Signal Media, UK)*
Omar Alonso *(Microsoft Research, USA)*
Ismail S. Altingovde *(Middle East Technical University, Turkey)*
Jisun An *(Qatar Computing Research Institute, HBKU, Qatar)*
Paavo Arvola *(University of Tampere, Finland)*
KhudaBukhsh Ashiqur *(Carnegie Mellon University, USA)*
Mossaab Bagdouri *(University of Maryland, USA)*
Ashraf Bah Rabiou *(University of Delaware, USA)*
Rafael E. Banchs *(Institute for Infocomm Research, Singapore)*
Zhifeng Bao *(RMIT University, Australia)*
Bodo Billerbeck *(Microsoft Research, Australia)*
Danushka Bollegala *(University of Liverpool, UK)*
Gloria Bordogna *(Consiglio Nazionale delle Ricerche, Italy)*
Arbi Bouchoucha *(Yellow Pages Group, Canada)*
Mohand Boughanem *(IRIT, University Paul Sabatier, France)*
Leonid Boytsov *(Carnegie Mellon University, USA)*
Davide Buscaldi *(LIPN, Université Paris 13, France)*
Fidel Cacheda *(University of A Coruña, Spain)*
Rui Cai *(Microsoft Research, China)*
Fazli Can *(Bilkent University, Turkey*)
Cornelia Caragea *(University of North Texas, USA)*
Mark Carman *(Monash University, Australia)*
Marc-Allen Cartright *(Google Inc., USA)*
Praveen Chandar *(IBM Research Cambridge, USA)*
Francine Chen *(FX Palo Alto Laboratory, USA)*
Hsin-Hsi Chen *(National Taiwan University, Taiwan)*
Stefano Cresci *(IIT-CNR, Italy)*
Bin Cui *(Peking University, China)*
Sally Jo Cunningham *(University of Waikato, New Zealand)*
Emanuele Di Buccio *(University of Padua, Italy)*
Giorgio Maria Di Nunzio *(University of Padua, Italy)*

Short Papers Committee (continued):

Laura Dietz *(University of Mannheim, Germany)*
Bekir Taner Dincer *(Mugla University, Turkey)*
Carsten Eickhoff *(ETH Zurich, Switzerland)*
Tamer Elsayed *(Qatar University, Qatar)*
Yi Fang *(Santa Clara University, USA)*
Katayoun Farrahi *(Goldsmiths, Uni. of London, UK)*
Hakan Ferhatosmanoglu *(Bilkent University, Turkey)*
Nicola Ferro *(University of Padua, Italy)*
Luanne Freund *(University of British Columbia, Canada)*
Ingo Frommholz *(University of Bedfordshire, UK)*
Patrick Gallinari *(Université Pierre et Marie Curie, France)*
Debasis Ganguly *(Dublin City University, Ireland)*
Bin Gao *(Microsoft Research, China)*
Wei Gao *(Qatar Computing Research Institute, HBKU, Qatar)*
Susan Gauch *(University of Arkansas, USA)*
Tatiana Gossen *(Otto-von-Guericke University Magdeburg, Germany)*
Brigitte Grau *(LIMSI-CNRS and ENSIIE, France)*
David Graus *(University of Amsterdam, The Netherlands)*
Artem Grotov *(University of Amsterdam, The Netherlands)*
Morgan Harvey *(Northumbria University, UK)*
Ben He *(University of Chinese Academy of Sciences, China)*
Xiangnan He *(National University of Singapore, Singapore)*
Frank Hopfgartner *(University of Glasgow, UK)*
Jiepu Jiang *(University of Massachusetts Amherst, USA)*
Joemon Jose *(University of Glasgow, UK)*
Marko Junkkari *(University of Tampere, Finland)*
Nattiya Kanhabua *(Aalborg University, Denmark)*
Evangelos Kanoulas *(University of Amsterdam, The Netherlands)*
Bahar Karaoglan *(Ege University, Turkey)*
Liadh Kelly *(Trinity College Dublin, Ireland)*
Heikki Keskustalo *(University of Tampere, Finland)*
Yubin Kim *(Carnegie Mellon University, USA)*
Julia Kiseleva *(Technical University of Eindhoven, The Netherlands)*
Alexander Kotov *(Wayne State University, USA)*
Kriste Krstovski *(University of Massachusetts Amherst, USA)*
Udo Kruschwitz *(University of Essex, UK)*
Sanna Kumpulainen *(Tampere University of Technology, Finland)*
Hui Li *(University of Maryland, College Park, USA)*
Chenliang Li *(Wuhan University, China)*
Shangsong Liang *(University College London, UK)*
Christina Lioma *(University of Copenhagen, Denmark)*
Jiyun Luo *(Georgetown University, USA)*
Andrew MacFarlane *(City University London, UK)*
Takuya Maekawa *(Osaka University, Japan)*
Walid Magdy *(Qatar Computing Research Institute, HBKU, Qatar)*

Short Papers Committee (continued):

Maria Maistro *(University of Padua, Italy)*
Ilya Markov *(University of Amsterdam, The Netherlands)*
Mónica Marrero *(National Supercomputing Center, Spain)*
Paul McNamee *(Johns Hopkins University, USA)*
Edgar Meij *(Yahoo Rsearch, Spain)*
Aditya Mogadala *(Karlsruhe Institute of Technology, Germany)*
Alessandro Moschitti *(Qatar Computing Research Institute, HBKU, Qatar)*
Preslav Nakov *(Qatar Computing Research Institute, HBKU, Qatar)*
Michael L. Nelson *(Old Dominion University, USA)*
Dong Nguyen *(Twente University, The Netherlands)*
Daan Odijk *(University of Amsterdam, The Netherlands)*
Neil O'Hare *(Yahoo Research, Spain)*
Alexandra Olteanu *(EPFL, Switzerland)*
Jiaul Paik *(University of Maryland, College Park, USA)*
Dipasree Pal *(Indian Statistical Institute, Kolkata, India)*
Filipa Peleja *(Universidade Nova de Lisboa, Portugal)*
Casper Petersen *(University of Copenhagen, Denmark)*
Karen Pinel-Sauvagnat *(IRIT, France)*
Laura Po *(University of Modena and Reggio Emilia, Italy)*
Filip Radlinski *(Microsoft Research, UK)*
Zhaochun Ren *(University of Amsterdam, The Netherlands)*
Haggai Roitman *(IBM Research Lab, Haifa, Israel)*
Karankumar Sabhnani *(University of Delaware, USA)*
Maya Sappelli *(TNO, The Netherlands)*
Anne Schuth *(Blendle, The Netherlands)*
Jangwon Seo *(Google, USA)*
Jialie Shen *(Singapore Management University, Singapore)*
Michael Shuhmacher *(University of Mannheim, Germany)*
Gianmaria Silvello *(University of Padua, Italy)*
Yang Song *(Microsoft Research, USA)*
Ruihua Song *(Microsoft Research, China)*
Laure Soulier *(Université Pierre et Marie Curie, France)*
Damiano Spina *(RMIT University, Australia)*
Aixin Sun *(Nanyang Technological University, Singapore)*
S.M.M. Tahaghoghi *(Microsoft Research, USA)*
Carla Teixeira Lopes *(University of Porto, Portugal)*
James A. Thom *(RMIT University, Australia)*
Bart Thomee *(Yahoo Research, USA)*
Anastasios Tombros *(Queen Mary University of London, UK)*
Ricardo Torres *(University of Campinas, Brazil)*
Christophe Van Gysel *(University of Amsterdam, The Netherlands)*
Olga Vechtomova *(University of Waterloo, Canada)*
Suzan Verberne *(Radboud University, The Netherlands)*
Stephen Wan *(CSIRO, Australia)*
Changhu Wang *(Microsoft Research, China)*

Short Papers Committee (continued):

Hongning Wang *(University of Virginia, USA)*
Lidan Wang *(University of Illinois, USA)*
Wouter Weerkamp *(904Labs, The Netherlands)*
Xing Wei *(Inmobi Inc., USA)*
Christa Womser-Hacker *(University of Hildesheim, Germany)*
Tan Xu *(AT&T, USA)*
Zheng Ye *(Maluuba, Waterloo, Canada)*
Masaharu Yoshioka *(Hokkaido University, Japan*)
Xiaojun (Jenny) Yuan *(Univ. at Albany, The State Univ. of New York, USA)*
Mustafa Zengin *(University of Delaware, USA)*
Dong Zhou *(Hunan University of Science and Technology, China)*
Ke Zhou *(Yahoo Research, UK)*
Guido Zuccon *(Queensland University of Technology, Australia)*

Short Papers Committee additional reviewers:

Eva D'hondt *(LIMSI-CNRS, France)*
Maram Hasanain *(Qatar University, Qatar)*
K. Dilek Onal *(Middle East Technical University, Turkey)*
Rifat Ozcan *(Turgut Ozal University, Turkey)*
Jose Moreno *(LIMSI-CNRS, France)*

Demonstrations Committee:

Omar Alonso *(Microsoft Research, USA)*
Krisztian Balog *(University of Stavanger, Norway)*
Laura Dietz *(University of Mannheim, Germany)*
Dina Demner-Fushman *(NLM/NIH, USA)*
Henry Field *(Endicott College, USA)*
John Foley *(University of Massachusetts Amherst, USA)*
Ana Freire *(Universitat Pompeu Fabra, Spain)*
Grant Ingersoll *(Lucidworks, USA)*
Udo Kruschwitz *(University of Essex, UK)*
Sarvnaz Karimi *(CSIRO, Australia)*
Jochen Leidner *(Thomson Reuters, UK)*
Teerapong Leelanupab *(King Mongkuts Institute of Tech. Ladkrabang, Thailand)*
Richard McCreadie *(University of Glasgow, UK)*
Stefano Mizzaro *(University of Udine, Italy)*
Sean Moran *(University of Glasgow, UK)*
Iadh Ounis *(University of Glasgow, UK)*
Vassilis Plachouras *(Thomson Reuters, UK)*
Javier Parapar *(University of A Coruña, Spain)*
Jeremy Pickens *(Catalyst, USA)*
Rodrygo Santos *(Universidade Federal de Minas Gerais, Brazil)*
Jialie Shen *(Singapore Management University, Singapore)*
Luchen Tan *(University of Waterloo, Canada)*
Bin Wang *(Chinese Academy of Sciences, China)*
Tan Xu *(AT&T Research, USA)*
Guido Zuccon *(Queensland University of Technology, Australia)*

Doctoral Consortium Committee:

Eugene Agichtein *(Emory University, USA)*
Krisztian Balog *(University of Stavanger, Norway)*
Paul Bennett *(Ideo, USA)*
Kevyn Collins-Thompson *(University of Michigan, USA)*
Maarten de Rijke *(University of Amsterdam, The Netherlands)*
Susan Dumais *(Microsoft Research, USA)*
Debora Donato *(StumbleUpon, USA)*
Claudia Hauff *(TU Delft, The Netherlands)*
Jimmy Huang *(York University, Canada)*
Jaap Kamps *(University of Amsterdam, The Netherlands)*
Douglas Oard *(University of Maryland, USA)*
Filip Radlinski *(Microsoft Research, UK)*
Jie Tang *(Tsinghua University, China)*
Chengxiang Zhai *(University of Illinois at Urbana-Champaign, USA)*

Doctoral Consortium Mentors:

Paul Bennett *(Ideo, USA)*
David Carmel *(Yahoo Research, Israel)*
Kevyn Collins-Thompson *(University of Michigan, USA)*
Maarten de Rijke *(University of Amsterdam, The Netherlands)*
Fernando Diaz *(Microsoft Research, USA)*
Debora Donato *(StumbleUpon, USA)*
Susan Dumais *(Microsoft Research, USA)*
Claudia Hauff *(TU Delft, The Netherlands)*
Jimmy Huang *(York University, Canada)*
Jaap Kamps *(University of Amsterdam, The Netherlands)*
Oren Kurland *(Technion, Israel)*
Douglas Oard *(University of Maryland, USA)*
Filip Radlinski *(Microsoft Research, UK)*
Mark D. Smucker *(University of Waterloo, Canada)*
Pavel Serdyukov *(Yandex, Russia)*
Chengxiang Zhai *(University of Illinois at Urbana-Champaign, USA)*

Workshops Committee:

Roi Blanco *(Yahoo Research, Spain)*
Bruce Croft *(University of Massachusetts Amherst, USA)*
Norbert Fuhr *(University of Duisburg-Essen, Germany)*
Kal Jarvelin *(University of Tampere, Finland)*
Noriko Kando *(National Institute of Informatics. Japan)*
Diane Kelly *(University of North Carolina at Chapel Hill, USA)*
Josiane Mothe *(Institut de Recherche en Informatique de Toulouse, France)*

SIGIR 2016 Sponsors & Supporters

Sponsors: SIGIR Special Interest Group on Information Retrieval; Association for Computing Machinery (acm)

Platinum Supporters: Baidu 百度

Silver Supporters: appen™, Bloomberg, Booking.com, ebay™, facebook

Silver Supporters:

Google™

HUAWEI

IBM®

Microsoft

YAHOO!

Bronze Supporters:

Yandex

Institutional Supporters:

Consiglio Nazionale delle Ricerche

معهد قطر لبحوث الحوسبة
Qatar Computing Research Institute
عضو في مؤسسة قطر
Member of Qatar Foundation

Publisher Supporters:

M&C MORGAN & CLAYPOOL PUBLISHERS

now the essence of knowledge

Springer

Understanding Human Language: Can NLP and Deep Learning Help?

Christopher Manning
Stanford University
manning@stanford.edu

ABSTRACT

There is a lot of overlap between the core problems of information retrieval (IR) and natural language processing (NLP). An IR system gains from understanding a user need and from understanding documents, and hence being able to determine whether a document has information that satisfies the user need. Much of NLP is about the same thing: Natural language understanding aims to understand the meaning of questions and documents and meaning relationships. The exciting recent application of deep learning approaches in NLP has brought new tools for effectively understanding language semantics. In principle, there should be a lot of synergy, though in practice the concerns of IR on large systems and macro-scale understanding have tended to contrast with the emphasis in NLP on language structure and micro-scale understanding.

My talk will emphasize the two topics of how NLP can contribute to understanding textual relationships and how deep learning approaches substantially aid in this goal. One basic – and very successful tool – has been the new generation of distributed word representations: neural word embeddings. However, beyond just word meanings, we need to understand how to compose the meanings of larger pieces of text. Two requirements for that are good ways to understand the structure of human language utterances and ways to compose their meanings. Deep learning methods can help for both tasks. Finally, we need to understand relationships between pieces of text, to be able to do tasks such as Natural Language Inference (or Recognizing Textual Entailment) and Question Answering, and I will look at some of our recent work in these areas, both with and without the help of neural networks.

Keywords

Natural language processing, deep learning, word vectors, compositionality, natural language inference, recognizing textual entailment, question answering

SIGIR '16, July 17 - 21, 2016, Pisa, Italy.
ACM 978-1-4503-4069-4/16/07.
DOI: http://dx.doi.org/10.1145/2911451.2926732

Short Biography

Christopher Manning is a professor of computer science and linguistics at Stanford University. His Ph.D. is from Stanford in 1995, and he held faculty positions at Carnegie Mellon University and the University of Sydney before returning to Stanford. His research goal is computers that can intelligently process, understand, and generate human language material. Manning concentrates on machine learning approaches to computational linguistic problems, including syntactic parsing, computational semantics and pragmatics, textual inference, machine translation, and using deep learning for NLP. He is an ACM Fellow, a AAAI Fellow, and an ACL Fellow, and has coauthored leading textbooks on statistical natural language processing and information retrieval. He is a member of the Stanford NLP group (@stanfordnlp).

Big Data in Climate: Opportunities and Challenges for Machine Learning

Vipin Kumar
University of Minnesota
kumar@cs.umn.edu

ABSTRACT

This talk will present an overview of research being done in a large interdisciplinary project on the development of novel data mining and machine learning approaches for analyzing massive amount of climate and ecosystem data now available from satellite and ground-based sensors, and physics-based climate model simulations. These information-rich data sets offer huge potential for monitoring, understanding, and predicting the behavior of the Earth's ecosystem and for advancing the science of global change. This talk will discuss challenges in analyzing such data sets and some of our research results in mapping the dynamics of surface water globally as well as detecting deforestation and fires in tropical forests using data from Earth observing satellites.

Keywords
Big data; spatio-temporal data; predictive models for imperfect, incomplete, and heterogeneous data; rare class detection; monitoring global water dynamics; identifying tropical forest fires.

SIGIR '16, July 17 - 21, 2016, Pisa, Italy.
ACM 978-1-4503-4069-4/16/07
DOI: http://dx.doi.org/10.1145/2911451.2911550

Short Biography

Vipin Kumar is a Regents Professor at the University of Minnesota, where he holds the William Norris Endowed Chair in the Department of Computer Science and Engineering. Kumar's current research interests include data mining, high-performance computing, and their applications in Climate/Ecosystems and Biomedical domains. Kumar is the Lead PI of a 5-year, $10 Million project, "Understanding Climate Change - A Data Driven Approach" funded by the NSF's Expeditions in Computing program. This project is focused on the development of novel data driven approaches to help understand climate change and its impact. He has authored over 300 research articles, and has coedited or coauthored 10 books including two text books ``Introduction to Parallel Computing" and ``Introduction to Data Mining", that are used world-wide and have been translated into many languages. Kumar co-founded SIAM International Conference on Data Mining and served as a founding co-editor-in-chief of Journal of Statistical Analysis and Data Mining (an official journal of the American Statistical Association). Kumar is a Fellow of the ACM, IEEE and AAAS. He received the Distinguished Alumnus Award from the Indian Institute of Technology (IIT) Roorkee (2013), the Distinguished Alumnus Award from the Computer Science Department, University of Maryland College Park (2009), and IEEE Computer Society's Technical Achievement Award (2005). Kumar's foundational research in data mining and its applications to scientific data was honored by the ACM SIGKDD 2012 Innovation Award, which is the highest award for technical excellence in the field of Knowledge Discovery and Data Mining (KDD).

Statistical Significance, Power, and Sample Sizes: A Systematic Review of SIGIR and TOIS, 2006-2015

Tetsuya Sakai
Waseda University, Japan.
tetsuyasakai@acm.org

ABSTRACT

We conducted a systematic review of 840 SIGIR full papers and 215 TOIS papers published between 2006 and 2015. The original objective of the study was to identify IR effectiveness experiments that are seriously underpowered (i.e., the sample size is far too small so that the probability of missing a real difference is extremely high) or overpowered (i.e., the sample size is so large that a difference will be considered statistically significant even if the actual effect size is extremely small). However, it quickly became clear to us that many IR effectiveness papers either lack significance testing or fail to report p-values and/or test statistics, which prevents us from conducting power analysis. Hence we first report on how IR researchers (fail to) report on significance test results, what types of tests they use, and how the reporting practices may have changed over the last decade. From those papers that reported enough information for us to conduct power analysis, we identify extremely overpowered and underpowered experiments, as well as appropriate sample sizes for future experiments. The raw results of our systematic survey of 1,055 papers and our R scripts for power analysis are available online. Our hope is that this study will help improve the reporting practices and experimental designs of future IR effectiveness studies.

Keywords

effect sizes; evaluation; power analysis; sample sizes; statistical power; statistical significance; systematic review

1. INTRODUCTION

In experiments for retrieval effectiveness evaluation, the *de facto* standard is the practice of comparing the mean evaluation measure scores across topics by means of statistical significance tests such as the (paired and unpaired) t-test and Analysis of Variance (ANOVA). While alternative approaches to these standard tests exist (e.g., Carterette's Baysian inference [3], Robertson and Kanoula's view of *documents* as the source of variance [12], and Killeen's probability of replication for experiments in psychology [10]), so far they have not yet enjoyed the same popularity as the classical significance tests in the IR community.

SIGIR '16, July 17 - 21, 2016, Pisa, Italy

ISBN 978-1-4503-4069-4/16/07...$15.00

DOI: http://dx.doi.org/10.1145/2911451.2911492

In standard signifiance testing, the *test statistic* (e.g., the t statistic for the t-test and the F statistic for ANOVA) is a function of the *effect size* (i.e., the actual magnitude of the difference between systems) and the *sample size* (i.e., the number of topics, users etc.), even though what we are usually interested in is the effect size: is the difference "substantial"? However, due to the above relationship, increasing the sample size increases the value of the test statistic, which in turn decreases the *p-value* (i.e., the probability of observing the obtained result or something more extreme under the null hypothesis). Since we conclude a result to be statistically significant if, for a predetermined *significance level* α, we observe that $p\text{-}value \leq \alpha$ holds, we can make *anything* statistically significant by using a large enough sample. Conversely, if the sample size is too small, we might be missing differences that we really should be detecting. While α is the predetermined probability of Type I error (detecting a nonexistent difference), β is the probability of Type II error (missing a real difference), and the ability to detect a real diffrence, given by $(1 - \beta)$, is the *statistical power*. The combination $(\alpha, \beta) = (0.05, 0.20)$, known as *Cohen's five-eighty convention* (where "eighty" refers to 80% power), is often used as a standard setting for determining the sample size for an experiment [5, 15].

Recent statistically motivated studies have suggested that topic sets used in IR test collections should be substantially larger than they currently are in order to meet a clear set of statistical requirements. For example, Sakai's *topic set size design* results show that if researchers use the paired t-test for ad hoc IR and want to ensure Cohen's five-eighty convention for *any* system difference of 0.05 (or higher) in mean average precision, about 300 topics are required [15][1]. Urbano, Marrero and Martín conclude that "*in most cases a couple hundred*" topics are required for stable system rankings from their study based on the *Generalisability Theory* [20]. While these studies do not imply that all system comparison experiments based on 50 topics are invalid, they do suggest that some of the experiments may be *underpowered*: we may be missing a lot of real differences due to small sample sizes. On the other hand, the advent of web search engines brought with it the practice of using thousands or even millions of queries from their query log data for averaging; we suspected that some of such studies may be *overpowered*: even if the effect size is very small, statistically significant differences can be obtained due to large sample sizes. The original objective of this study was to identify IR effectiveness experiments that are extremely underpowered or overpowered.

We conducted a systematic review of 840 ACM SIGIR full papers and 215 ACM TOIS papers published between 2006 and 2015. SIGIR is considered by many to be the premier conference in IR,

[1]Over 700 topics are required if unstable measures such as expected reciprocal rank (ERR) is used [15].

while TOIS enjoys a similar status in the journal domain; this journal explicitly instructs authors as follows: "*When reporting statistics, the name of the statistic, the degrees of freedom, the value obtained, and the p-value should be reported, e.g.,* $F(3, 65) = 4.83, p < 0.01$"[2]. However, it quickly became clear to us that many IR effectiveness papers published in SIGIR and TOIS either lack significance testing or fail to report p-values and/or test statistics, which prevents us from conducting power analysis. Hence we first report on how IR researchers (fail to) report on significance test results, what types of tests they use, and how the reporting practices may have changed over the last decade. From those papers that reported enough information for us to conduct power analysis, we identify extremely overpowered and underpowered experiments, as well as appropriate sample sizes for future experiments. The raw results of our systematic survey of 1,055 papers are available online. We hope that this study will help improve the reporting practices and experimental designs of future IR effectiveness studies.

2. PRIOR ART

Two papers directly inspired us to conduct the present systematic review. The first is the study by Armstrong *et al.* [1]: they examined SIGIR papers in the period 1998-2008 and CIKM papers in the period 2004-2008 to investigate whether IR systems have improved over the years. A total of 106 papers, which contained IR effectiveness results using TREC test collections, were analysed in their survey. One of their main findings was that researchers often claim statistically significant results but use low baselines for comparison. The second is the study by Kelly and Sugimoto [9]: they analysed 127 journal and conference papers selected from 2,791 papers in the period 1967-2006 and investigated the evaluation practices in *interactive* information retrieval (IIR), including experimental designs, corpora and measures used. In the present study, we tried to follow Kelly and Sugimoto's description of *systematric reviews* to the best of our ability: "*Researchers articulate a plan for gathering and analyzing studies and attempt to be exhaustive with their coverage of the literature. Researchers also take a neutral position during analysis and attempt to create generalizations from findings. Systematic reviews adhere to strict scientific guidelines to minimize potential selection and interpretation biases to ensure replicability (and hence reliability).*" Like Armstrong *et al.* [1], we are primarily interested in *system* effectiveness studies that typically rely on averaging across a set of topics. However, as we shall see, some of the findings from the present study partially overlap with one of Kelly and Sugimoto's main finding from their systematic review of *IIR* studies: "*Because of the basic goals and design of these studies, the majority of researchers used either ANOVA or t-tests to analyze the results. [...] In some cases, the type of test conducted was not reported although statistically significant results were claimed and/or p-values were presented.*"

Sanderson and Zobel [16] report on a small-scale survey which is also relevant to our present study: they examined 26 system effectiveness papers from SIGIR 2003 and 2004 to see which significance tests and evaluation measures were used. Their findings, which are also in line with ours, are perhaps also worth quoting: "*We found that significance was not explicitly reported in 14 of the papers. In two it was implied such tests had been tried, but outcomes were not given. In three or four of these papers, the improvements were large and arguably a significance test was unnecessary. However, in at least six papers (23% of the sample) the reported improvements were small, sometimes no more than a few percent in relative MAP.*"; "*Among the 12 papers with significance tests, one used both ANOVA and the t-test, five each used either the t-test or Wilcoxon's test, and in one, the test was not identified.*"

In the present study, we manually examined 1,055 SIGIR and TOIS papers, and found that at least 862 of them appear to deserve statistical significance testing for performance differences; we then analysed these 862 papers further. This number is substantially higher compared to the above studies, although the numbers are not directly comparable due to differences in objectives and methods of analysis. More importantly, unlike prior art, we conducted power analysis for 133 papers that reported the p-value and/or the test statistic, and computed the achieved power as well as appropriate sample sizes for future experiments.

Table 1: Statistics of the ACM papers examined in this study.

Year	SIGIR	TOIS (Volume.Issue)	SIGIR+TOIS
2006	74	17 (24.1-24.4)	91
2007	85	23 (25.1-26.1)	108
2008	85	24 (26.2-27.1)	109
2009	78	18 (27.2-27.4)	96
2010	87	28 (28.1-29.1)	115
2011	108	16 (29.2-29.4)	124
2012	98	25 (30.1-30.4)	123
2013	73	22 (31.1-31.4)	95
2014	82	21 (32.1-32.4)	103
2015	70	21 (33.1-33.4)	91
Total	840	215	1,055

3. SURVEY METHOD

The primary purpose of this systematic survey is to examine how IR researchers, especially those working on improving IR *effectiveness*, use statistical significance tests, and to conduct power analysis wherever possible. We are interested, for example, in whether the topic set sizes are appropriate in test collection-based studies, and whether the number of participants or observations is appropriate in user-based studies. Table 1 shows the number of papers per year that we examined[3]. First, we created two lists of DOIs, one for SIGIR and the other for TOIS, on separate sheets in an Excel file, and we created columns in the Excel sheets according to a strict coding scheme as described below. Then, the author of this paper manually examined each paper at least twice. The coding started in February 2015, and was completed in October 2015. The pdf file of each paper was downloaded from the ACM digital library and was viewed on computer screen; for some papers that required careful interpretations of significance test results, hard copies were also used[4].

3.1 Coding Scheme

Each paper was coded in an Excel file as follows.

Step 1 Does the paper contain a table or figure of mean effectiveness, mean user performance, etc. that appears to deserve significance testing? If YES, select and record the name of one such table or figure, which we refer to as a *representative table* throughout this paper. No representative table was selected for papers that did not discuss IR effectiveness (e.g., those only discussing efficiency or theory). Note that we do not look at the magnitude of the difference in means here; Instead, Step 5 quantifies effect sizes wherever possible.

Step 2 Does the paper conduct a significance test? Assign exactly one category from (A)-(I) shown in Table 2. If multiple test types are used, pick a primary one, preferably from (A)-(E)

[2]https://tois.acm.org/authors.cfm visited April 12, 2016.

[3]TOIS published Volume 34 Issue 1 (6 papers) in October 2015. These papers are outside the scope of this study.

[4]The pdf files of three SIGIR papers were not searchable by Ctrl-F; for these cases also, hard copies were used.

Table 2: Paper categorisation scheme used in this study.

Category	
(A)	Unpaired t-test
(B)	Paired t-test
(C)	One-way ANOVA
(D)	Two-way ANOVA without replication
(E)	Two-way ANOVA
(F)	Other tests
(G)	Test type not specified
(H)	CIs used instead of significance tests
(I)	No significance tests

Table 3: Subcategories for papers that compare two systems

(Sub) category	significance test type
(A)	Unpaired t-test
(B)	Paired t-test
(F1)	Wilcoxon signed rank test
(F2)	Sign test
(F3)	Bootstrap test
(F4)	Randomisation test
(F5)	Wilcoxon rank sum test (Mann-Whitney U test)
(F6)	Other tests

to enable power analysis. Specifically, we searched for "statistical", "signi", "test" and "ANOVA" within the pdf file.

Step 3 If categorised as (I) in Step 2, check if the paper claims "significance" and record the exact expressions in an Excel popup comment. Section 4.2 provides more details.

Step 4 If categorised as (A)-(G) in Step 2, record whether the p-value and/or test statistic is reported. If only the p-value is reported, and if categorised as (A)-(E) in Step 2, compute the test statistic as described later (Eqs. 1-2).

Step 5 If the test statistic for categories (A)-(E) is obtained in Step 4 and the sample sizes actually used are indicated in the paper, conduct power analysis using tools described in Section 3.2 under Cohen's five-eighty convention ($\alpha = 0.05, \beta = 0.20$). If the achieved power is 0.99 or higher, label the paper as *overpowered*; else if the achieved power is 0.50 or below, label the paper as *underpowered*; otherwise, label it as *about right*. Also, record the effect size and the *future sample sizes* (i.e., recommended sample sizes for new experiments with similar purposes and settings) that are output by the tool. While the above power thresholds are arbitrary, note that the interested reader can easily apply different thresholds to our raw Excel file.

Step 6 In addition, copy and paste sentences from the paper that are relevant to power analysis (e.g., how exactly they report the p-values and test statistics). Save them as an Excel popup comment. Record the investigator's (i.e., the present author's) own comments in an Excel cell.

In Step 2, if the paper mentioned a t-test but did not indicate two sample sizes, we assumed that the test is paired (Category (B)) as this is the typical setting in test collection-based studies; if the paper did not indicate whether the test is two-sided or one-sided, we interpreted it as the more conservative two-sided test when conducting power analysis. Category (G) was chosen if the paper mentioned a significance level (α), a p-value, or just *statistical* significance, but did not specify the significance test used; Category (H) was chosen if the paper did not mention any significance testing *but* used CIs, boxplots, (often unexplained) error bars, or reported standard errors/deviations. Category (I) was chosen if the paper did not mention significance testing at all, even if it claimed "significant" improvements (without using the word "statistical").

In Step 4, we considered the p-value as "reported in the paper" if the *exact* p-value was reported. We did not regard "$p < 0.1, p < 0.05, p < 0.01$" as exact p-values; rather, we regarded them as the predetermined significance level α, which may or may not be substantially larger than the actual p-values. On the other hand, we count "$p < 0.001$" and smaller values as "reported in the paper" as such values should be accurate enough for power analysis. Whenever the test statistic t was not reported but the p-value and the sample sizes were, we deduced the test statistic as:

$$t = t_{inv}(\phi; p\text{-}value) \tag{1}$$

where $t_{inv}(\phi; P)$ is the critical t value for ϕ degrees of freedom and probability P, obtained with Microsoft Excel as $\texttt{T.INV.2T}(P, \phi)$ for two-sided tests, or $\texttt{T.INV}(1 - P, \phi)$ for one-sided tests[5]. For *paired* t-tests with sample size n, we let $\phi = n - 1$; for unpaired t-tests with sample sizes n_1 and n_2, we let $\phi = n_1 + n_2 - 2$. Similarly, for ANOVA results where p-values were reported but the F values were not, we computed them as follows whereover possible:

$$F = F_{inv}(\phi_1, \phi_2; p\text{-}value) \tag{2}$$

where $F_{inv}(\phi_1, \phi_2; P)$ is the critical F value for (ϕ_1, ϕ_2) degrees of freedom and probability P, or $\texttt{F.INV.RT}(P, \phi_1, \phi_2)$ with Microsoft Excel. The degrees of freedom are computed in accordance with ANOVA.

After coding each paper as described above, we focussed on papers labelled "(F) Other tests" and assigned a subcategory to each of them, for the purpose of examining the popularity of different significance tests for comparing two systems. The subcategories are shown in Table 3; (A)-(F5) are used in the analysis in Section 4.3. Category (F6) includes papers that used nonparametric tests for more than two systems.

Admittedly, even though our coding scheme is systematic, it is impossible to completely rule out the possibility that the present author has misinterpreted some of the papers. To accommodate correction, we have created a twitter account solely for this purpose[6]: if an assessment of a paper needs to be corrected, the author of that paper can point this out by using either `TOIS` or `SIGIR` followed by the last seven digits of the paper's DOI as the hashtag (e.g., `#SIGIR1148261`). Recall that our intepretation of each paper is available as a raw Excel file and therefore that it is easy to correct it. However, it is highly unlikely that these minor "bug reports" will affect the main conclusions of the present paper.

3.2 Power Analysis Tools

We conducted a power analysis for every paper in Categories (A)-(E) where the test statistic and actual sample sizes were obtained, based on modified versions of t-test and ANOVA power analysis tools provided by Toyoda [19]. The original R scripts of Toyoda, which simply rely on R's library `pwr`[7], are available at the publisher's website[8]; our own versions, which differ from Toyoda's only in input and output specifications[9], are available from our website[10], along with our raw systematic review results. We provide a function for each significant test type, for computing the

[5]For one SIGIR 2014 paper, the t statistic was computed by dividing the mean difference by the reported standard error of the mean. This paper is discussed in Section 4.6 (Table 7 Entry #12).

[6]http://twitter.com/IRsysrev

[7]https://cran.r-project.org/web/packages/pwr/pwr.pdf

[8]http://www.tokyo-tosho.co.jp/download/DL02065.zip

[9]The present author is solely responsible for the modifications and any errors introduced thereby.

[10]http://www.f.waseda.jp/tetsuya/data.html

effect size, achieved power and recommended future sample sizes. In what follows, we adhere to Toyoda's notations when we refer to effect sizes ($\hat{es}$ for t-tests; $\hat{f}$ and $\hat{f}^2$ for ANOVA).

3.2.1 *Unpaired (i.e., two-sample) t-test*

Our R function for unpaired t-tests is called `future.sample.unpairedt`, whose arguments are the t statistic (t), two sample sizes (n_1, n_2), whether the test is two-sided or one-sided (default: two-sided), α, and power ($1 - \beta$) (default: Cohen's five-eighty convention). The script computes first the sample effect size $\hat{es} = |t|\sqrt{(n_1 + n_2)/(n_1 n_2)}$ (which expresses the between-system difference in standard deviation units) and then the achieved power and the recommended sample size per group n' for future experiments, by calling the function `power.t.test` (if $n_1 = n_2$) or `pwr.t2n.test` (if $n_1 \neq n_2$). If a paper reports $n_1 + n_2$ but not n_1 and n_2 individually, we assume that $n_1 = n_2$.

3.2.2 *Paired t-test*

Our R function for paired t-tests is called `future.sample.pairedt`, whose arguments are the t statistic (t), the sample size (n), whether the test is two-sided or one-sided (default: two-sided), α, and power ($1 - \beta$) (default: Cohen's five-eighty convention). The script computes first the sample effect size $\hat{es} = |t|/\sqrt{n}$ and then the achieved power and the future sample size n', by calling `power.t.test`.

3.2.3 *One-way ANOVA*

Our R function for one-way ANOVA tests is called `future.sample.1wayanova`, whose arguments are the F statistic (F), number of groups being compared (m), number of observations per group (n), α, and power ($1 - \beta$) (default: Cohen's five-eighty convention). The script computes first the sample effect size $\hat{f} = \sqrt{\phi_A F/\phi_E}$ (where $\phi_A = m - 1, \phi_E = m(n - 1)$) and then the achieved power and the future sample size per group n', by calling `pwr.anova.test`. Here, $\hat{f}$ is an estimate of how large the between-group population standard deviation is compared to the within-group population standard deviation.

3.2.4 *Two-way ANOVA without Replication*

Our R function for two-way ANOVA (without replication) tests is called `future.sample.2waynorep`, whose arguments are the same as `future.sample.1wayanova`. The script first computes the sample effect size $\hat{f}^2 = \phi_A F/\phi_E$ (where $\phi_A = m - 1, \phi_E = (m - 1)(n - 1)$) and then the achieved power and the future sample size per group n', by calling `pwr.f2.test`. Note that this tool outputs $\hat{f}^2$ rather than $\hat{f}$ as the effect size, simply because that is what `pwr.f2.test` requires as an argument[11]. An equivalent way to express $\hat{f}^2$ would be $\hat{f}^2 = \eta_p^2/(1 - \eta_p^2)$, where η_p^2 expresses how much of the total variance (after removing other effects) is due to factor A; it can be computed as $\eta_p^2 = \frac{\phi_A F}{\phi_A F + \phi_E}$. Also, η_p is known as the *partial correlation ratio*.

3.2.5 *Two-way ANOVA*

Our R function for two-way ANOVA tests is called `future.sample.2wayanova`, whose arguments are the F statistics (F_A, F_B, F_{AB}), number of groups (m), number of cells per group (n), total number of observations (N), α, and power ($1 - \beta$) (default: Cohen's five-eighty convention). For example, A, B, AB could represent the system and topic effects and the interaction between them, respectively. Let the degrees of freedom for A, B, AB and the residual E be $\phi_A = m - 1, \phi_B = n - 1, \phi_{AB} = (m - 1)(n - 1), \phi_E = N - mn$. Then the sample effect size for A is given by $\hat{f}_A = \sqrt{\hat{\eta}_{pA}^2/(1 - \hat{\eta}_{pA}^2)}$, where $\hat{\eta}_{pA}^2 = \frac{\phi_A F_A}{\phi_A F_A + \phi_E}$; $\hat{f}_B$ and $\hat{f}_{AB}$ are computed similarly. The achieved power and the *total* sample size for future experiments N' are computed by calling `pwr.anova.test`.

[11] http://127.0.0.1:25552/library/pwr/html/pwr.f2.test.html

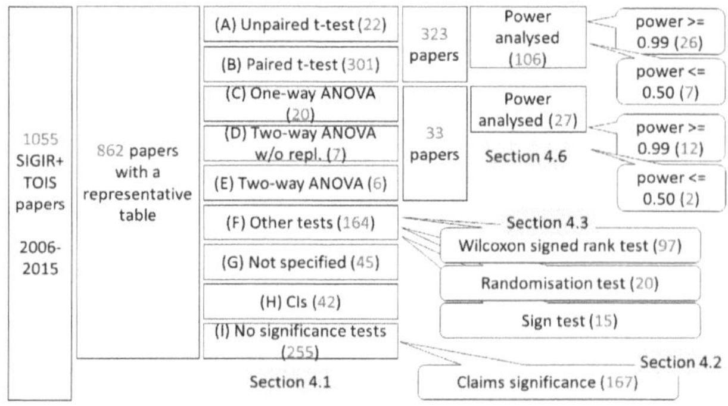

Figure 1: Number of papers concerning results reported in Sections 4.1, 4.2, 4.3, and 4.6 (SIGIR+TOIS).

4. RESULTS

In Step 1 of the coding scheme described in Section 3.1, a representative table was selected for 700 out of the 840 SIGIR papers (83%), and for 162 papers out of the 215 TOIS papers (75%). Thus, our view is that at least 862 papers out of the 1,055 papers that we examined may deserve statistical significance testing for comparing mean effectiveness scores and the like. Hereafter, we focus our attention to these 862 papers. Figure 1 provides an overview of some of the results reported in this section, in terms of paper counts.

4.1 Paper Distribution over Categories

Figure 2 shows the distributions of the aforementioned 700 SIGIR and 162 TOIS papers over the seven categories shown in Table 2. Paper counts are shown in addition to percentages. It can be observed that the distributions for SIGIR and TOIS are similar: 35-37% of the papers use the paired t-test (Category (B)); about 28-30% do not report significance test results even though these papers have a representative table (Category (I)); and about 18-24% use tests other than the t-test or ANOVA (Category (F))[12]. We shall examine Catgories (I) and (F) more closely in Sections 4.2 and 4.3, respectively.

Figure 3 shows the distribution of papers over the categories and across the timeline; the top graph shows the results for SIGIR; the bottom one shows the results obtained by summing the SIGIR and TOIS statistics. The number of TOIS papers alone per year is considered too small for our analysis and are not shown here. For each year, the number of papers in each category is divided by the total number of papers with a representative table for that year; the latter is shown below the x axis for each year. It appears that the the use of the paired t-test is now more common than a decade ago, and that we are also seeing fewer papers without statistical significance tests. In Section 4.4, we shall compare the results for 2006 and those for 2015 from this viewpoint.

[12] Recall, however, that we had to select exactly one significance test type per paper even if both t-tests and ANOVA were used in the same paper.

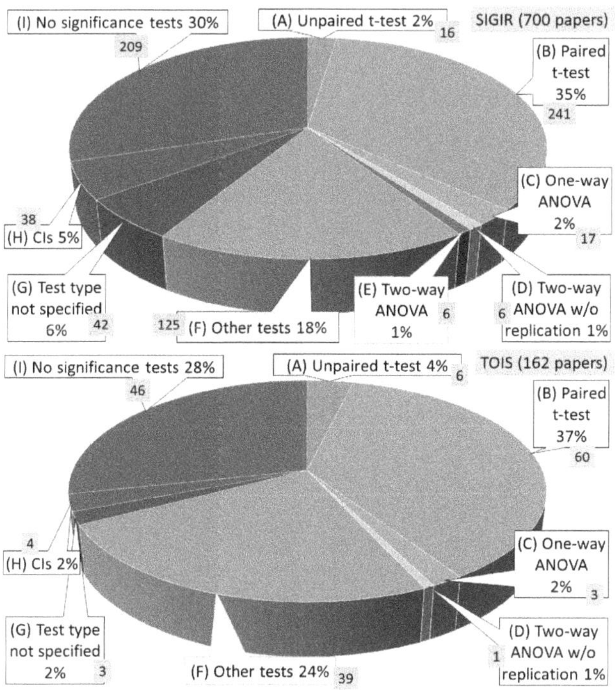

Figure 2: Distributions of papers with a representative table over categories.

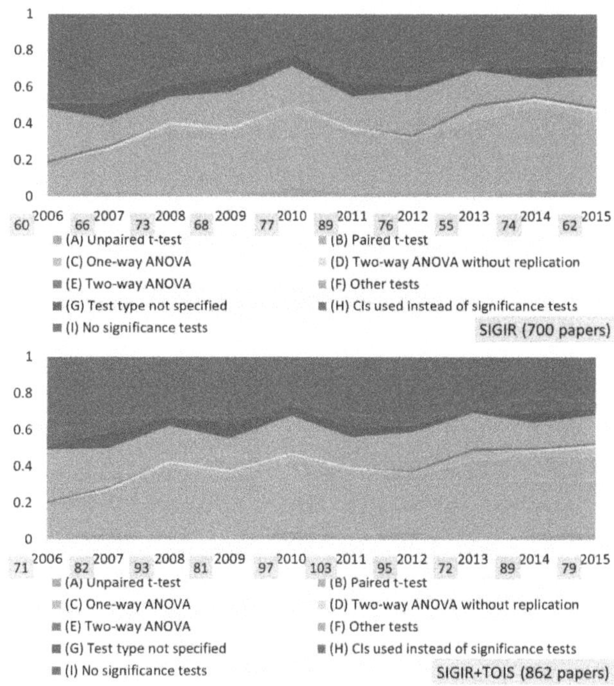

Figure 3: Distributions of papers with a representative table over categories across 10 years.

Table 4: Category (I) papers (no significance tests): Column (a) shows the number of papers that claim "significant" improvements and the like; Column (b) shows the number of papers that make no such claims. For the SIGIR and SIGIR+TOIS columns, the percentages are also shown, where the denominators are the paper counts shown in Figure 3.

	SIGIR		TOIS		SIGIR+TOIS	
	(a)	(b)	(a)	(b)	(a)	(b)
2006	**14** (23%)	12 (20%)	**1**	3	**15** (21%)	15 (21%)
2007	**21** (32%)	6 (9%)	**1**	1	**22** (27%)	7 (9%)
2008	**14** (19%)	8 (11%)	**0**	2	**14** (15%)	10 (11%)
2009	**15** (22%)	4 (6%)	**5**	1	**20** (25%)	5 (6%)
2010	**10** (13%)	6 (8%)	**5**	3	**15** (15%)	9 (9%)
2011	**13** (15%)	15 (17%)	**3**	1	**16** (16%)	16 (16%)
2012	**19** (25%)	8 (11%)	**6**	0	**25** (26%)	8 (8%)
2013	**7** (13%)	7 (13%)	**4**	1	**11** (15%)	8 (11%)
2014	**11** (15%)	4 (5%)	**4**	1	**15** (17%)	5 (6%)
2015	**10** (16%)	5 (8%)	**4**	0	**14** (18%)	5 (6%)
total	**134** (19%)	75 (11%)	**33**	13	**167** (19%)	88 (10%)

4.2 Claiming Significance without Providing Significance Test Results

Why are there so many papers without significance tests despite explicit instructions such as the ones from TOIS (Section 1)? Recall that all of these Category (I) papers have a representative table that appears to deserve significance testing. Possible good reasons include: (i) the authors consider statistical significance testing to be of limited or no value (e.g. [7, 8]); (ii) the authors judge that significance testing is unnecessary in their particular situations because either the sample size and/or the effect size is very large, or because the difference is not the central point the study. For example, one SIGIR 2012 paper (DOI: 10.1145/2348283.2348301) states: "*Since the present study does not aim to prove one retrieval method better than another, we report the findings without tests on significance of statistical differences.*" [2]. In Category (I), however, we did find some papers that use expressions such as "significant improvement" and "significantly outperform" in the context of discussing effectiveness even though *statistical* significance tests are never mentioned. Some of these claims are even made in the paper abstracts and conclusions. We argue that such practices are quite misleading and that the use of ambiguous expressions such as those mentioned above should be avoided. Table 4 breaks down the Category (I) papers from each year into papers that claim "significant" improvements and the like, and those that do not. It is worrying that 167 papers (19%) out of 862 papers with a representative table say "significant" without conducting significance tests, even if in some cases it may be clear from the context that the word is being used in the non-statistical sense.

4.3 Comparing Two Systems: Popular Tests

As was mentioned in Section 3.1, we used the subcategories shown in Table 3 to examine which significance tests are popular for comparing two systems. Historically, IR researchers in the 20th century were relatively reluctant to use parametric tests [14], but nowadays the robustness of the t-test (which is parametric) is recognised and the test is widely used. Savoy [17] and Sakai [13] advocated the use of the bootstrap test in 1997 and 2006, respectively, while Smucker, Allan and Carterette [18] advocated the randomisation test in 2007. Are these computer-based, distribution-free tests used more often now? Figure 4 breaks down 365 SIGIR papers and 99 TOIS papers that used a significance test for comparing two systems by test type. Again, the overall pictures are very similar for these two venues: 61-66% of these papers use the paired t-test; 20-23% use the Wilcoxon signed rank test[13]; 4-5% use the randomisation test; 3-4% use the sign test; only 1% use the bootstrap test. Recall, however, that we picked one primary test from each paper even if it utilised multiple test types. Figure 5 shows how the popularity of these tests have changed over the last decade; note that the bottom graph aggregates the statistics from SIGIR and TOIS as before. It appears that the paired t-test is now more popu-

[13]"Wilcoxon test" was always interpreted as the Wilcoxon signed rank test, not as the Wilcoxon rank sum test.

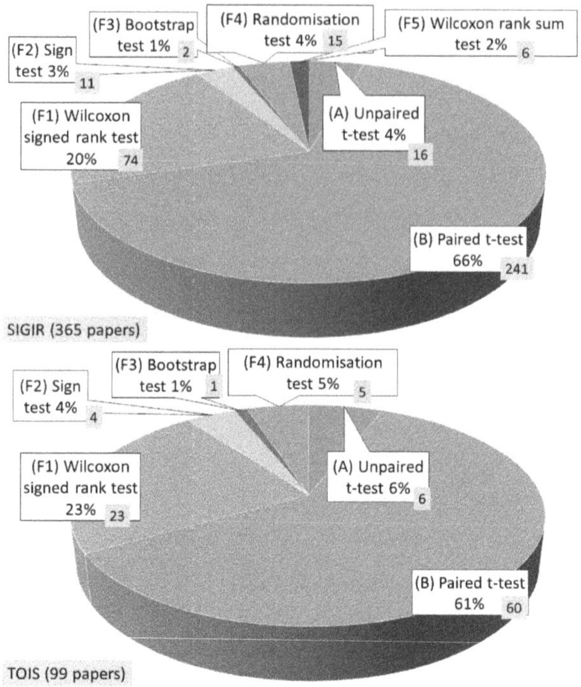

Figure 4: Distributions of papers over significance test types for comparing two systems.

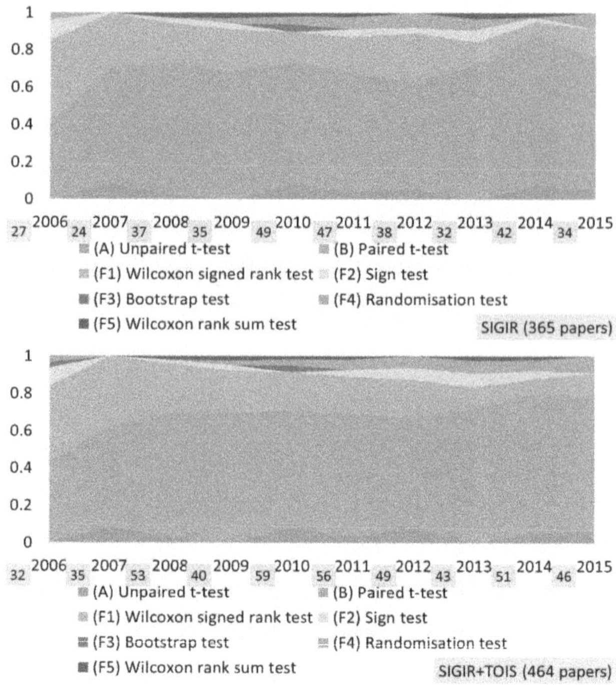

Figure 5: Distributions of papers over significance test types for comparing two systems across 10 years.

lar than it was 10 years ago, and that the Wilcoxon signed rank test is less so. In Section 4.4, we shall compare the results for 2006 and 2015 from this viewpoint.

We came across a few papers that explicitly discussed why a particular test type was chosen, although we did not conduct an exhaustive search for such comments. In a TOIS paper from 2012 (10.1145/2382438.2382445), the authors cite Sanderson and Zobel's SIGIR 2005 paper [16] and state: "*We report statistical significance test results using the nondirectional paired t-test at a confidence level of 0.01, since this test has been shown to be more reliable than the Wilcoxon and signed tests*" [6]; A SIGIR 2008 paper (10.1145/1390334.1390407) provides a similar argument. In a SIGIR 2015 paper (10.1145/2766462.2767700), the authors cite the aforementioned CIKM 2007 paper by Smucker *et al.* [18] as well as Sanderson and Zobel [16], and choose the randomisation test.

4.4 Have the Proportions Changed over the Last Decade?

Figures 3 and 5 suggest the following four clear trends: (1) In Figure 3, the proportion of Category (I) (no significance tests) papers is decreasing; (2) Similarly, the proportion of Category (B) (paired t-test) papers is increasing; (3) In Figure 5, the proportion of Category (F1) (Wilcoxon signed-rank test) papers is decreasing; (4) Similarly, the proportion of Category (B) (paired t-test) papers is increasing. Recall that Figure 3 considers all papers with a representative table, while Figure 5 only considers papers that used a significance test for comparing two systems. Ideally, these observations deserve a time series analysis, where an observation from a given year is modelled as a function of an observation from previous years along with some noise. However, this would not be very useful with our data with only ten data points. An obvious alternative is to regard the observation from each year as an independent sample to conduct standard significance testing, but in practice the independence assumption is highly unlikely to hold: for example, if many SIGIR paper authors use the t-test in 2014, those who submit a paper to SIGIR 2015 are also likely to do so, perhaps after reading some of the SIGIR 2014 papers. Due to the above considerations, we focus our attention on the comparison between 2006 and 2015, i.e., the leftmost and rightmost results in Figures 3 and 5, and conduct significance testing for two samples, each from a different population, under an independence assumption. Below, we describe our (two-sided) significance testing procedure for comparing two proportions (one from 2006 and the other from 2015) [11].

From the first population, we draw a sample of size n_1, and find that x_1 of them holds a certain property (e.g., lacks significance testing); the observed proportion is x_1/n_1. The observed proportion for the second population is defined similarly as x_2/n_2. The null hypothesis H_0 is that the true proportions are equal: $P_1 = P_2 = P$. Let $\hat{P}_1^* = \frac{x_1+0.5}{n_1+1}, \hat{P}_2^* = \frac{x_2+0.5}{n_2+1}, \hat{P}^* = \frac{x_1+x_2+0.5}{n_1+n_2+1}$, which are the estimates of the true proportions P_1, P_2, P with continuity corrections, respectively. Under H_0, it is known that the distribution of $\hat{P}_1^* - \hat{P}_2^*$ can be approximated by $N(0, P(1-P)(\frac{1}{n_1}+\frac{1}{n_2}))$. Hence a z-test can be performed using the following test statistic:

$$u_0 = \frac{\hat{P}_1^* - \hat{P}_2^*}{\sqrt{\hat{P}_1^*(1-\hat{P}_1^*)(\frac{1}{n_1}+\frac{1}{n_2})}} . \quad (3)$$

The point estimate for the true difference between the two proportions is given by $\hat{P}_1^* - \hat{P}_2^*$, whereas the margin of error (MOE) for computing the 95% CI is given by:

$$z_{\alpha/2}\sqrt{\frac{\hat{P}_1^*(1-\hat{P}_1^*)}{n_1} + \frac{\hat{P}_2^*(1-\hat{P}_2^*)}{n_2}} , \quad (4)$$

where $z_{\alpha/2}$ is the critical z value for probability $\alpha/2 = 0.025$ (since we want 95% confidence).

Our four null hypotheses, which correspond to the aforementioned trends (1)-(4), state that the population proportion computed for 2015 is equal to that for 2006. We denote them as $H_0^1, H_0^2, H_0^3, H_0^4$. Table 5 summarises the results of the significance tests; Part (a)

Table 5: Statistical significance test results: comparing the proportions from 2006 and those from 2015.

(a) SIGIR	H_0^1	H_0^2	H_0^3	H_0^4
n_1 (2006)	60	60	27	27
x_1 (2006)	26	11	12	11
n_2 (2015)	62	62	34	34
x_2 (2015)	15	24	5	24
p-value	0.028	0.015	0.013	0.023
$P_1^* - P_2^*$	0.188	−0.200	0.289	−0.289
95% CI	[0.023, 0.353]	[−0.357, −0.044]	[0.065, 0.513]	[−0.530, −0.048]
(b) SIGIR+TOIS	H_1	H_2	H_3	H_4
n_1 (2006)	71	71	32	32
x_1 (2006)	30	14	13	14
n_2 (2015)	79	79	46	46
x_2 (2015)	19	33	6	33
p-value	0.019	0.004	0.006	0.015
$P_1^* - P_2^*$	0.180	−0.217	0.271	−0.273
95% CI	[0.031, 0.329]	[−0.361, −0.074]	[0.073, 0.468]	[−0.489, −0.057]

uses data from the SIGIR papers only, while Part (b) uses both SIGIR and TOIS papers. It can be observed that all the p-values are below $\alpha = 0.05$, and that all of the above null hypotheses are rejected. More importantly, the 95% CIs for H_0^1 and H_0^3 are above zero, while those for H_0^2 and H_0^4 are below zero. Hence, we can conclude, for both Parts (a) and (b), as follows:

1. The proportion of Category (I) (no significance tests) papers among those with a representative table in 2015 is statistically significantly smaller compared to 2006;

2. The proportion of Category (B) (paired t-test) papers among those with a representative table in 2015 is statistically significantly larger compared to a 2006;

3. The proportion of Category (F1) (Wilcoxon signed-rank test) papers among those using a test for comparing two systems in 2015 is statistically significantly smaller compared to 2006;

4. The proportion of Category (B) (paired t-test) papers among those using a test for comparing two systems in 2015 is statistically significantly larger compared to 2006.

4.5 Do Researchers Report p-values and/or test statistics?

Next, we focused on papers (with a representative table) that did conduct significant tests, regardless of the test type. For 453 SIGIR papers and 112 TOIS papers in Categories (A)-(G), Step 4 described in Section 3.1 further categorised them into four classes: (i) both exact p-values and test statistics are reported; (ii) only exact p-values are reported (from which test statistics may be deduced if the sample sizes are known); (iii) only test statistics are reported; and (iv) neither is reported. Note that Class (iv) includes papers that specify a significance level α but does not report the exact p-values. Researchers (who accept and rely on classical significance tests) should report p-values and effect sizes. Saying "significant at $\alpha = 0.05$" leads to dichotomous thinking ("significant or not?") [5], and is not very informative for the reasons discussed in Section 1. Figure 6 visualises the proportion of Classes (i)-(iii) against Class (iv) papers for each year. It also contains a table of the actual number of papers. It can be observed that over one half of the papers with significance tests report neither p-values nor test statistics, and that the situation does not seem to be improving.

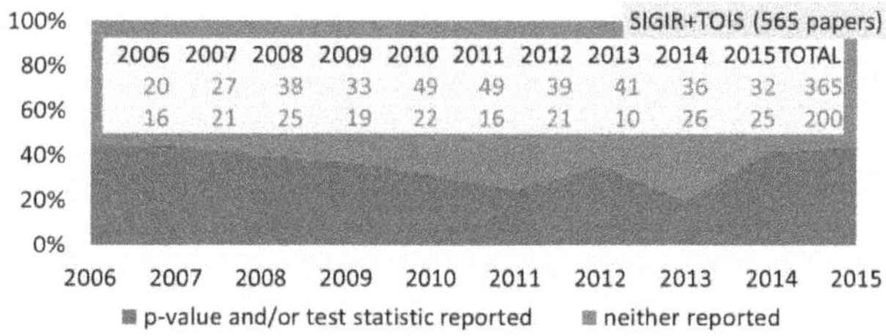

Figure 6: Proportion of papers (with a representative table) that report either p-values or test statistics (or both).

Table 6: Number of papers (with a representative table) with (a) an overpowered experiment (power ≥ 0.99); (b) an underpowered experiment (power ≤ 0.50); (c) "about right" experiment ($0.50 <$ power < 0.99).

	SIGIR			TOIS			SIGIR+TOIS		
	(a)	(b)	(c)	(a)	(b)	(c)	(a)	(b)	(c)
(A) Unpaired t-test	3	1	7	0	0	5	3	1	12
(B) Paired t-test	16	4	44	7	2	17	23	6	61
(C) One-way ANOVA	7	1	6	1	0	1	8	1	7
(D) Two-way ANOVA without replication	1	1	4	1	0	0	2	1	4
(E) Two-way ANOVA	2	0	2	0	0	0	2	0	2
total	29	7	63	9	2	23	38	9	86

4.6 Overpowered? Underpowered?

Among the 200 "good practice" papers indicated in Figure 6, we were able to conduct a power analysis for 99 SIGIR papers (75 with t-tests and 24 with ANOVA tests) and 34 TOIS papers (31 with t-tests and 3 with ANOVA test); the other 67 papers used other significance test types. Table 6 shows the paper counts for overpowered, underpowered, and "about right" papers for Categories (A)-(E). It can be observed that as many as 38 (29%) out of the 133 papers that went through power analysis are overpowered: the achieved power is 99% or higher for these papers. Whereas, only 9 (7%) papers were found to be underpowered: the achieved power is 50% or lower.

Hereafter, we focus on the power analysis results for SIGIR papers. Table 6 "SIGIR (a)" column shows that we found a total of 19 "overpowered" and 5 "underpowered" papers with t-tests (Categories (A) and (B)), as well as 10 "overpowered" and 2 "underpowered" papers with ANOVA tests (Categories (C)-(E)). Tables 7 and 8 provide complete power analysis results for these papers. Recall that n and n' denote the actual and future sample sizes *per group*, while N and N' denote the actual and future *total* sample sizes (Section 3.2). To quantify the gap between actual and future sample sizes, let us define *sample size ratio* as the actual sample size divided by the future sample size. Figure 7 plots sample size ratios against the achieved power; the baloons in the figure indicate which paper in Table 7 or 8 each dot corresponds to. For example, the top right balloon in Figure 7(a) indicates the third entry in Table 7, for which the effect size is $\hat{es} = 1.864$ (a "large" effect [4]) and the achieved power is 100%; although the actual sample size was $n = 192$, in fact $n' = 5$ is sufficient. The leftmost balloon in Figure 7(a) indicates the 24th entry in Table 7, for which $\hat{es} = 0.180$ (a "small" effect [4]) and the achieved power is only 15.2%; although the actual sample size was $n = 28$, in fact $n' = 244$ is needed to ensure 80% power. Similar relationships can be observed between Figure 7(b) and Table 8.

Table 7: SIGIR papers with overpowered (power ≥ 0.99) and underpowered (power ≤ 0.50) t-tests. Papers are sorted by achieved power, then by effect size.

#	year	doi (10.1145/*)	test type	t	actual sample size	effect size $\hat{es}$	achieved power	future sample size
1	2010	1835449.1835485	(B) Paired t-test	10.60	$n = 23$	2.209	1	$n' = 4$
2	2006	1148170.1148249	(B) Paired t-test	-25.27	$n = 182$	1.873	1	$n' = 5$
3	2009	1571941.1571991	(B) Paired t-test	25.83	$n = 192$	1.864	1	$n' = 5$
4	2007	1277741.1277784	(B) Paired t-test	5.68	$n = 45$	0.846	1	$n' = 14$
5	2010	1835449.1835518	(A) Unpaired t-test	-7.42	$n_1 = 486, n_2 = 114$	0.772	1	$n' = 28$
6	2014	2600428.2609577	(B) Paired t-test	11.41	$n = 234$	0.746	1	$n' = 17$
7	2008	1390334.1390407	(B) Paired t-test	7.46	$n = 100$	0.746	1	$n' = 17$
8	2010	1835449.1835459	(A) Unpaired t-test	7.40	$n_1 = n_2 = 605$	0.425	1	$n' = 88$
9	2008	1390334.1390352	(B) Paired t-test	7.51	$n = 600$	0.307	1	$n' = 86$
10	2012	2348283.2348313	(B) Paired t-test	8.26	$n = 7341$	0.096	1	$n' = 847$
11	2014	2600428.2609602	(A) Unpaired t-test	7.07	$n_1 = n_2 = 96762$	0.032	1	$n' = 15174$
12	2014	2600428.2609617	(B) Paired t-test	16.00	$n = 5352460$	0.007	1	$n' = 164107$
13	2008	1390334.1390412	(B) Paired t-test	5.07	$n = 8000$	0.057	0.999	$n' = 2441$
14	2007	1277741.1277821	(B) Paired t-test	5.03	$n = 25$	1.006	0.998	$n' = 10$
15	2006	1148170.1148214	(B) Paired t-test	4.90	$n = 20$	1.095	0.996	$n' = 9$
16	2011	2009916.2010052	(B) Paired t-test	4.61	$n = 11122$	0.044	0.996	$n' = 4105$
17	2015	2766462.2767712	(B) Paired t-test	4.42	$n = 3543978$	0.002	0.993	$n' = 1425634$
18	2014	2600428.2609586	(B) Paired t-test	4.51	$n = 30$	0.823	0.992	$n' = 14$
19	2008	1390334.1390370	(B) Paired t-test	4.46	$n = 60$	0.576	0.992	$n' = 26$
20	2007	1277741.1277778	(B) Paired t-test (one-sided)	1.55	$n' = 400$	0.077	0.461	$n' = 1032$
21	2014	2600428.2609632	(A) Unpaired t-test	2.60	$n_1 = n_2 = 100$	0.228	0.362	$n' = 303$
22	2010	1835449.1835536	(B) Paired t-test	1.56	$n' = 140$	0.132	0.342	$n' = 451$
23	2009	1571941.1571947	(B) Paired t-test	1.37	$n' = 48$	0.198	0.269	$n' = 203$
24	2012	2348283.2348343	(B) Paired t-test	0.95	$n' = 28$	0.180	0.152	$n' = 244$

Table 8: SIGIR papers with overpowered (power ≥ 0.99) and underpowered (power ≤ 0.50) ANOVA tests. Papers are sorted by achieved power.

#	year	doi (10.1145/*)	test type	F	actual sample size	effect size	achieved power	future sample size
1	2013	2484028.2484090	(E) Two-way ANOVA	$F_B = 68.01, m = n = 3$	$N = 82$	$\hat{f}_B = 1.365$	1	$N' = 18$
2	2015	2766462.2767746	(C) One-way ANOVA	$F = 243.42, m = 3$	$n = 2551$	$\hat{f} = 2.252$	1	$n' = 52$
3	2014	2600428.2609574	(C) One-way ANOVA	$F = 26.7m = 3$	$n = 12$	$\hat{f} = 1.272$	1	$n' = 4$
4	2014	2600428.2609596	(C) One-way ANOVA	$F = 56.52, m = 4$	$n = 1985$	$\hat{f} = 0.146$	1	$n' = 129$
5	2013	2484028.2484084	(C) One-way ANOVA	$F = 45.609, m = 2$	$n = 269$	$\hat{f} = 0.292$	1	$n' = 48$
6	2012	2348283.2348392	(C) One-way ANOVA	$F = 40, m = 7$	$n = 400$	$\hat{f} = 0.293$	1	$n' = 24$
7	2010	1835449.1835484	(C) One-way ANOVA	$F = 66.82, m = 5$	$n = 1100.2$	$\hat{f} = 0.221$	1	$n' = 51$
8	2010	1835449.1835486	(C) One-way ANOVA	$F = 31.77, m = 3$	$n = 173.3$	$\hat{f} = 0.351$	1	$n' = 28$
9	2014	2600428.2609620	(E) Two-way ANOVA	$F_B = 24.89, m = n = 2$	$N = 964$	$\hat{f}_B = 0.161$	0.999	$N' = 308$
10	2009	1571941.1572033	(D) Two-way ANOVA w/o replication	$F = 8.01, m = 4$	$n = 57$	$\hat{f}^2 = 0.143$	0.991	$n' = 35$
11	2008	1390334.1390362	(C) One-way ANOVA	$F = 1.28, m = 3$	$n = 12$	$\hat{f} = 0.279$	0.279	$n' = 43$
12	2015	2766462.2767719	(D) Two-way ANOVA w/o replication	$F = 0.63, m = 4$	$n = 17$	$\hat{f}^2 = 0.039$	0.183	$n' = 75$

4.6.1 Case Studies: Overpowered Experiments

There are a few extremely large sample sizes in the "overpowered" section of Table 7. The 12th entry in Table 7 (SIGIR 2014, 10.1145/2600428.2609617), a paper on personalisation from a search engine company, reported the difference in mean average precision (MAP) together with the standard error of the mean (SEM), which enabled us to compute the t-statistic by simply dividing the former with the latter. We chose the result with the largest difference ($MAP = 0.0224$, $SEM = 0.00140$) from one of their tables, which resulted in $t = 16.0$. The actual sample size (the number of impressions for averaging) was $n = 5352460$, but a recommended future sample size is $n' = 164107$. This situation is also visualised in Figure 7(a) (third balloon from the top). Note that the effect size is extremely small: $\hat{es} = 0.007$, although even such a small effect may possibly translate to a subtantial increase in profit for search engine businesses. The authors of the 17th entry in Table 7 (SIGIR 2015, 10.1145/2766462.2767712) are from academia, but they utilise commercial search engine logs, one of which contains 11,813,260 search sessions. As authors indicate that they used 30% of the above sessions for computing (mean) click entropy, we assumed that the sample size was $n = 3543978$ even though this exact number is not indicated in the paper. The authors report p-value $< 10^{-5}$, so the t statistic was computed as $t = t_{inv}(n-1; 10^{-5}) = 4.42$, and the future sample size obtained is $n' = 1425634$. Again, the effect size is extremely small: $\hat{es} = 0.002$. As for the 11th entry in Table 7 (SIGIR 2014, 10.1145/2600428.2609602), one of its authors works for the aforementioned search engine company. The authors use the unpaired t-test with large sample sizes ($n_1 + n_2 = 193524$, from which we assume that $n_1 = n_2 = 96762$) and report a p-value of $1.5 * 10^{-12}$. However, the purpose of employing this test in their study was to quantify the association between two different user search behaviour features rather than to compare retrieval effectiveness: one feature is used to split the data into two samples, and then the other is used to compare the two samples in terms of the unpaired t-test.

There were also two SIGIR papers (not included in the aforementioned 75 papers that went through power analysis) for which the sample sizes for unpaired t-tests were too large for our power analysis tool: A SIGIR 2010 paper (10.1145/1835449.1835537) used a sample of some 95.8M query-URL pairs per group; A SIGIR 2007 (10.1145/1277741.1277771) used two samples where the total sample size was approximately 60M. These papers are from two different search engine companies: the latter paper is from the same company as the aforementioned 11th and 12th entries in Table 7. All of the above papers should be commended (not condemned!) for providing enough information in their papers for post hoc power anal-

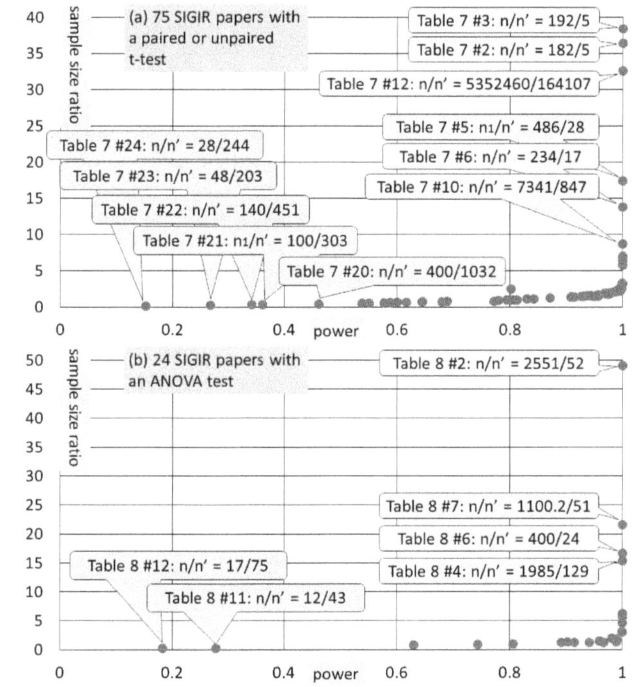

Figure 7: Summary of power analysis results: sample size ratio vs. achieved power.

ysis; however, recall that reporting p-values from an experiment with extremely large sample sizes without discussing effect sizes is generally not very informative, as was discussed in Section 1.

Next, let us examine a few overpowered *ANOVA* cases, using Table 8 and Figure 7(b). More specifically, we examine two papers indicated by the two top right balloons in Figure 7(b): The second and seventh entries in Table 8 (SIGIR 2015, 10.1145/2766462.2767746 and SIGIR 2010, 10.1145/1835449.1835484). These papers have a common first author, and the experiments in both papers utilise a commercial social media application suite for the purpose of item recommendation. In the second entry, a one-way ANOVA result is reported, where the number of groups is $m = 3$ (items rated "very interesting" vs. "interesting" vs. "not interesting"), the degree of freedom is $\phi = 7650$ and the F statistic is 243.42. Since our power analysis tool for one-way ANOVA recommends a per-group future sample size, we assume uniform group size for the analysis and let $\phi = m(n-1) = 7650$, which gives us the average group size $n = 2551$. As shown in Table 8 and Figure 7(b), this sample size is much larger than the required sample size $n' = 52$. Similarly, in the seventh entry, the authors report on a one-way ANOVA result with $m = 5$ (five recommendation systems), $\phi = 5496$. Again, if we assume equal group size for the purpose of power analysis, we obtain $n = 5496/5 + 1 = 1100.2$, whereas the future sample size is $n' = 51$. It can be observed in Table 8 that the effect size for the latter experiment is much smaller ($\hat{f} = 2.252$ vs. $\hat{f} = 0.221$). Again, let us emphasise that these are good papers which, unlike many other SIGIR papers, provide enough information for us to conduct post hoc power analysis. However, it is probably fair to say that many highly overpowered experiments come from industry, where data is abundant.

4.6.2 *Case Studies: Underpowered Experiments*

Arguably, extremely underpowered experiments may be more problematic than extremely overpowered experiments. Extremely overpowered experiments may conclude that some very small effects are statistically significant, and the small effects may or may not be *practically* significant. On the other hand, extremely underpowered experiments may hide away very important real differences forever.

First, let us have a look at two extremely underpowered paired t-test results indicated by the two leftmost balloons in Figure 7(a): the 24th and 23rd entries in Table 7. The 24th entry (SIGIR 2012, 10.1145/2348283.2348343) reports on many statistical significance results including ANOVA, but what we have selected for power analysis was a statistically insignificant result with a paired t-test, where $n = 28$ participants were involved (within-subjects design) and two systems were compared in terms of a *user experience sub-scale* called "focused attention." As Table 7 shows, the effect size is "small" ($\hat{es} = 0.180$) and the future number of participants is $n' = 244$, which is quite demanding for a user study. For this particular paper, we conducted additional power analyses for the other paired t-test results reported: "felt involvement" ($\hat{es} = 0.026, power = 0.052, n' = 12061$), "endurability" ($\hat{es} = 0.061, power = 0.061, n' = 2083$), "search effectiveness" ($\hat{es} = 0.111, power = 0.111, n' = 396$)[14]. It can be observed that the actual sample size ($n = 28$) was too small regardless of what user experience sub-scale is used, as the effect sizes are very small. The 23rd entry (SIGIR 2009, 10.1145/1571941.1571947) reports on a user study with 24 participants for comparing two algorithms (LAIR2 vs. Buckshot), but since each participants performed *two* tasks with each algorithm, we assumed that the sample size was $n = 48$ when the two algorithms were compared in terms of the F_1 measure. As Table 7 shows, $\hat{es} = 0.198, power = 0.269, n' = 203$. (Even if $n = 24$, the experiment is still underpowered: $\hat{es} = 0.280, power = 0.259, n' = 103$.) We would like to emphasise, however, that these papers are also examples of good papers, which provide enough details even for results that did not turn out to be statistically significant. This is what enables us to conduct post hoc studies, and the important question is how to design future experiments for similar studies.

Finally, we discuss the 12th and the 11th entry in Table 8, the two extremely underpowered cases indicated as the two leftmost balloons in Figure 7(b). The 12th entry (SIGIR 2015, 10.1145/2766462.2767719) reports on a statistically nonsignificant repeated-measures ANOVA result, where the relationship between four levels of search latency ($m = 4$) and Skin Conductance Responses (SCRs) were examined. This can be regarded as a two-way ANOVA without replication case, with $\phi_E = (m-1)(n-1) = 48$ and therefore the number of participants per group is $n = 17$. As can be seen at the bottom of Table 8, the effect size is $\hat{f}^2 = 0.039, power = 0.183, n' = 75$. Thus this experiment would have required 75 participants. The same paper also reports on statistically nonsignificant ANOVA results for examining the relationship between search latency and self-reported measures of engagement: if we apply the same R script to these results with $\phi_E = (m-1)(n-1) = 54, m = 4, n = 19$, we obtain $\hat{f}^2 = 0.042, power = 0.215, n' = 71$ for CSUQ (Computer System Usability Questionnaire), $\hat{f}^2 = 0.044, power = 0.222, n' = 68$ for FA (Focused Attention), $\hat{f}^2 = 0.052, power = 0.257, n' = 59$ for post-NAS (Negative Affect), and $\hat{f}^2 = 0.068, power = 0.332, n' = 46$ for post-PAS (Positive Affect). Thus, regardless of which ANOVA result we choose, relying on only $n = 17$ participants results in very low power, unfortunately. For the 11th entry (SIGIR 2008, 10.1145/1390334.1390362), we selected statistically nonsignificant one-way ANOVA results for comparing the

[14]For "perceived usability", the t statistic was zero, which suggests that there is no effect.

demographic characteristics of $m = 3$ participant groups, each with $n = 12$ subjects. As Table 8 shows, we would have wanted $n' = 43$ participants per group based on these particular results. However, these results do not constitute the main part of their study.

All of the "underpowered" papers discussed above are user study papers. This is not so surprising, as hiring good participants for experiments can always be difficult. Many such papers use statistical tests and report the results appropriately, but we argue that we should learn from past experiments as we have done in this study so that we can conduct better-designed experiments in the future.

5. CONCLUSIONS

We conducted a systematic review of 840 SIGIR full papers and 215 TOIS papers published between 2006 and 2015. Our main findings are as follows:

- Of the 862 papers that seem to deserve significance testing for comparison of means, 301 papers (35%) use the paired t-test; 255 papers (30%) lack significance testing (Figure 2).
- Of the 255 papers that lack significance testing, 167 papers (19%) make claims such as "significant improvement" and "significantly outperform" (Table 4).
- Of the 464 papers that report on a significance test for comparing two systems, 301 papers (65%) use the paired t-test; 97 papers (21%) use the Wilcoxon signed rank test (Figure 4).
- Compared to a decade ago, the proportion of papers that lack significance testing and the proportion of papers that rely on the Wilcoxon signed rank test have decreased; whereas, the proportion of papers that utilise the paired t-test has increased (Table 5). The differences are statistically significant according to two-proportions z-test.
- Of the 565 papers that report on significance test results, 365 papers (65%) report neither p-values nor test statistics (Figure 6).
- Of the 133 papers for which power analysis was possible, 38 papers (29%) were extremely overpowered ($power \geq 0.99$), while 9 papers (7%) were extremely underpowered ($power \leq 0.50$) (Table 6).
- We have observed extremely overpowered experiments in which proprietary data from industry (typically search engine companies) are utilised, as well as extremely underpowered user experiments in which the number of hired participants is limited.

To recap, p-values alone are not very informative as results of statistical significance testing, because one can obtain arbitrarily small p-values for any experiment by using a large enough sample [5, 14]. Hence, whenever researchers report on statistically significant differences based on overpowered experiments, it is vital that they report the effect sizes in addition to p-values. As for underpowered user experiments, researchers should conduct pilot studies first, or learn from similar studies in prior art about effect sizes and appropriate sample sizes.

One original question that is left unanswered in the present study is: are existing test collections with 50-100 topics good enough? Statistical requirements for comparing *any* systems suggest that test collection require many more topics [15, 20], but are current test collections actually serving the purpose for comparing *existing* systems? The question is left unanswered because, as we have seen above, many system effectiveness papers do not provide enough information for post hoc power analysis: recall that either an exact p-value or a test statistic (with a clearly stated sample size) is required for this. To make matters worse, there is the publication bias problem: researchers are often tempted not to report on statistically nonsignificant results. We already see some good reporting practices in interactive IR papers, complete with test statistics and effect sizes even for statistically nonsignificant results; we believe that similar practices are in order for the rest of the IR community as well.

Acknowledgement

We thank Professor Hideki Toyoda (Waseda University) for letting us modify his R code and distribute it.

6. REFERENCES

[1] T. G. Armstrong, A. Moffat, W. Webber, and J. Zobel. Improvements that don't add up: Ad-hoc retrieval results since 1998. In *Proceedings of ACM CIKM 2009*, pages 601–610, 2009.
[2] F. Baskaya, H. Keskustalo, and K. Järvelin. Time drives interaction: Simulating sessions in diverse searching environments. In *Proceedings of ACM SIGIR 2012*, pages 105–114, 2012.
[3] B. Carterette. Bayesian inference for information retrieval evaluation. In *Proceedings of ACM ICTIR 2015*, pages 31–40, 2015.
[4] J. Cohen. *Statistical Power Analysis for the Behavioral Sciences (Second Edition)*. Lawrence Erlbaum Associates, 1988.
[5] P. D. Ellis. *The Essential Guide to Effect Sizes*. Cambridge University Press, 2010.
[6] S. Gerani, M. Carman, and F. Crestani. Aggregation methods for proximity-based opinion retrieval. *ACM TOIS*, 30(4), 2012.
[7] J. P. A. Ioannidis. Why most published research findings are false. *PLoS Medicine*, 2(8):696–701, 2005.
[8] D. H. Johnson. The insignificance of statistical significance testing. *Journal of Wildlife Management*, 63(3):763–772, 1999.
[9] D. Kelly and C. R. Sugimoto. A systematic review of interactive information retrieval evaluation studies, 1967-2006. *Journal of the American Society for Information Science and Technology*, 64(4):745–770, 2013.
[10] P. R. Killeen. An alternative to null hypothesis significance tests. *Psychological Science*, 16:345–353, 2005.
[11] Y. Nagata. *Introduction to Statistical Analysis (in Japanese)*. JUSE Press, 1992.
[12] S. E. Robertson and E. Kanoulas. On per-topic variance in IR evaluation. In *Proceedings of ACM SIGIR 2012*, pages 891–900, 2012.
[13] T. Sakai. Evaluating evaluation metrics based on the bootstrap. In *Proceedings of ACM SIGIR 2006*, pages 525–532, 2006.
[14] T. Sakai. Statistical reform in information retrieval? *SIGIR Forum*, 48(1):3–12, 2014.
[15] T. Sakai. Topic set size design. *Information Retrieval Journal*, 2015.
[16] M. Sanderson and J. Zobel. Information retrieval system evaluation: Effort, sensitivity, and reliability. In *Proceedings of ACM SIGIR 2005*, pages 162–169, 2005.
[17] J. Savoy. Statistical inference in retrieval effectiveness evaluation. *Information Processing and Management*, 33(4):495–512, 1997.
[18] M. D. Smucker, J. Allan, and B. Carterette. A comparison of statistical significance tests for information retrieval evaluation. In *Proceedings of ACM CIKM 2007*, pages 623–632, 2007.
[19] H. Toyoda. *Introduction to Statistical Power Analysis: A Tutorial with R (in Japanese)*. Tokyo Tosyo, 2009.
[20] J. Urbano, M. Marrero, and D. Martín. On the measurement of test collection reliability. In *Proceedings of ACM SIGIR 2013*, pages 393–402, 2013.

Bayesian Performance Comparison of Text Classifiers

Dell Zhang
DCSIS
Birkbeck, University of London
Malet Street
London WC1E 7HX, UK
dell.z@ieee.org

Jun Wang
Dept of Computing Science
University College London
Gower Street
London WC1E 6BT, UK
j.wang@cs.ucl.ac.uk

Emine Yilmaz
Dept of Computing Science
University College London
Gower Street
London WC1E 6BT, UK
e.yilmaz@cs.ucl.ac.uk

Xiaoling Wang
Software Engineering Institute
East China Normal University
3663 North Zhongshan Road
Shanghai 200062, China
xlwang@sei.ecnu.edu.cn

Yuxin Zhou
Software Engineering Institute
East China Normal University
3663 North Zhongshan Road
Shanghai 200062, China
10122510216@ecnu.cn

ABSTRACT

How can we know whether one classifier is really better than the other? In the area of text classification, since the publication of Yang and Liu's seminal SIGIR-1999 paper, it has become a standard practice for researchers to apply null-hypothesis significance testing (NHST) on their experimental results in order to establish the superiority of a classifier. However, such a frequentist approach has a number of inherent deficiencies and limitations, e.g., the inability to accept the null hypothesis (that the two classifiers perform equally well), the difficulty to compare commonly-used multivariate performance measures like F_1 scores instead of accuracy, and so on. In this paper, we propose a novel Bayesian approach to the performance comparison of text classifiers, and argue its advantages over the traditional frequentist approach based on t-test etc. In contrast to the existing probabilistic model for F_1 scores which is unpaired, our proposed model takes the correlation between classifiers into account and thus achieves greater statistical power. Using several typical text classification algorithms and a benchmark dataset, we demonstrate that the our approach provides rich information about the difference between two classifiers' performances.

Keywords

Bayesian inference; hypothesis testing; performance evaluation; text classification

1. INTRODUCTION

Text classification (aka categorisation) [25] is a fundamental technique in information retrieval (IR) [19]. It has many important applications, including topic categorisation, spam filtering, sentiment analysis, message routing, language identification, genre detection, authorship attribution, and so on. In fact, most modern IR systems for search, recommendation, or advertising contain multiple components that use some form of text classification.

How can we know whether one classifier is really better than the other? Is it possible that they perform equally well? Sure we should be able to evaluate their classification performances on some benchmark datasets using some performance measures. However, given any finite amount of test results, we can never be completely certain that one classifier works better than the other or vice versa: the observed difference between their performance scores do not necessarily reflect their intrinsic qualities. The central question here is how to reliably tell if classifier A indeed outperforms classifier B, given a set of test results. Perhaps the simplest solution is to apply k-fold cross-validation [21] and then calculate the sample variance of performance scores over multiple "folds" of the dataset. This method tends to yield poor estimations though: the sample variance can approximate the true variance well only if we have a large number of folds, but when the dataset is divided into many folds, the size of each fold is likely to be too small to give a meaningful performance score (especially for complex multivariate performance measures like F_1 [26]). Hence it is desirable to derive the uncertainty of performance scores directly from all the atomic document-category classification results.

To address this problem, Yang and Liu defined in their seminal SIGIR-1999 paper [27] a suite of null-hypothesis significance testing (NHST) methods which aim to verify how strongly the experimental results support the claim that one particular classifier is more accurate than another classifier. That paper has been influential within and beyond the realm of text classification. Since its publication, it has received about 3,000 citations (according to Google Scholar). Today, it is almost compulsory for researchers to validate the superiority of their proposed text classification algorithms by means of NHST and report the p-values in their papers.

Although NHST has proven to be useful in assessing text classifiers and its adoption has greatly improved the rigour of performance evaluation in IR, such a frequentist approach has many inherent deficiencies and limitations which we shall elaborate on later. In this paper, we propose a novel approach to performance comparison of text classifiers based

SIGIR '16, July 17–21, 2016, Pisa, Italy

ISBN 978-1-4503-4069-4/16/07...$15.00
DOI: http://dx.doi.org/10.1145/2911451.2911547

on Bayesian estimation [15], and argue its advantages over the traditional frequentist approach based on t-test etc. Using a few representative text classification algorithms and a benchmark dataset, we demonstrate that the our approach provides rich information about the difference between two classifiers' performances.

2. RELATED WORK

2.1 Frequentist Performance Comparison

The traditional frequentist approach to comparing classifiers is to use NHST [21]. The usual process of NHST consists of four steps: (1) formulate the null hypothesis H_0 that the observations are the result of pure chance and the alternative hypothesis H_1 that the observations show a real effect combined with a component of chance variation; (2) identify a test statistic that can be used to assess the truth of H_0; (3) compute the p-value, which is the probability that a test statistic equal to or more extreme than the one observed would be obtained under the assumption of hypothesis H_0; (4) if the p-value is less than an acceptable significance level, the observed effect is statistically significant, i.e., H_0 is ruled out and H_1 is valid.

Specifically for performance comparison of text classifiers, the usage of NHST has been presented in detail by Yang and Liu in their SIGIR-1999 paper [27]. In summary, on the document level (micro level), sign-test can be used to compare two classifiers' accuracy scores (called s-test), while unpaired t-test can be used to compare two classifiers' performance measures in the form of proportions, e.g., precision, recall, error, and accuracy (called p-test); on the category level (macro level), sign-test and paired t-test can both be used to compare two classifiers' F_1 scores [26] (which are called S-test and T-test respectively).

In spite of being useful and influential, such a frequentist approach unfortunately has many inherent deficiencies and limitations [14, 15]. First, NHST is only able to tell us whether the experimental data are sufficient to reject the null hypothesis (that the performance difference is zero) or not, but there is no way to accept the null hypothesis. If we fail to reject the null hypothesis, we cannot conclude that it is true, but only recognise that the null hypothesis is a possibility. That is to say, it is impossible for us to use NHST to confidently claim that two classifiers perform equally well . Second, NHST will reject the null hypothesis as long as the experimental data suggest that the performance difference is non-zero, even if the performance difference is too slight to have any real effect in practice. Third, complex performance measures such as the F_1 score can only be compared on the category level but not on the document level, which seriously restricts the statistical power of NHST as the number of categories is usually much much smaller than the number of documents. Fourth, using sign-test, those pairs of identical classification outcomes are completely discarded, which is undesirable because the probability that the two classifiers are essentially equal would be substantially underestimated. Fifth, using unpaired t-test, the correlation between the classifiers in comparison are totally ignored, which is unreasonable because in reality both classifiers are likely to do well on "easy" test documents, and badly on "difficult" test documents, not to mention that those classifiers could be just different versions of the same machine learning algorithm.

The other NHST methods that have been applied to compare classifiers include ANOVA test [10], Friedman test [24], McNemar's test [6], and Wilcoxon signed ranks test [4]. Due to their frequentist nature, no matter which specific test they use, more or less they suffer from the above mentioned perils (especially the first three).

2.2 Bayesian Performance Comparison

It has been loudly advocated in recent years that the Bayesian approach to comparing two groups of data has many advantages over the frequentist NHST [14, 15]. However, to our knowledge, almost all the existing models of Bayesian performance comparison deal with continuous values (that can be described by Gaussian or t distributions) but not discrete classification outcomes, and they produce estimations for simple statistics (such as the average difference between the two given groups) but not complex performance measures (such as the F_1 score).

Probably the most closely related work is that of Goutte and Gaussier [8]. Their F_1 score model constructed using a couple of Gamma variates is not as expressive and flexible as ours. For example, generalising their model to the F_β measure ($\beta \geq 0$) [19, 26] with $\beta \neq 1$ would end up with a complex equation involving three Gamma variates, but that would be trivial in our approach. It seems that their model is restricted to a single F_1 score for binary classification with two classes only, due to its reliance upon the special properties of the Gamma distribution. In contrast, our approach is a *probabilistic graphical model* [13] which opens up many possibilities for adaptation or extension (see Section 5).

Our previous work on this topic [28, 29] has ignored any possible connection between the predictions from the two classifiers in comparison. Although this is totally fine when those two classifiers are evaluated separately each on a different test dataset, it is not the optimal solution in the common situation when those two classifiers are evaluated on exactly the same test dataset. In this paper, we extend such a simplistic "unpaired" model to the more general "paired" model which takes the correlation between classifiers into account, and demonstrate that the former has much less statistical power than the latter (see Section 4.1).

3. OUR APPROACH

3.1 Probabilistic Models

Let us consider a text classifier which has been tested on a collection of N labelled test documents, $\mathcal{D}$. For each document $\boldsymbol{x}_i$ ($i = 1, \ldots, N$), we have its true class label y_i as well as the predicted class label $\hat{y}_i$.

If this classifier is actually a Bayesian model, in principle there should be a direct way to assess the suitability of model $\mathcal{M}$ in explaining the experimental data by computing $\Pr[\mathcal{M}|\mathcal{D}] \propto \Pr[\mathcal{M}] \int_\Theta \Pr[\mathcal{D}|\Theta, \mathcal{M}] \Pr[\Theta|\mathcal{M}] \mathrm{d}\Theta$. However, here we would like to consider the general situation where the true and predicted class labels are the only information presumed to be available.

In the most basic setting, *binary classification*, a document belongs to either the positive class or the negative class. Without loss of generality, we use integer 1 as the ID of the positive class and integer 0 as the ID of the negative class. Furthermore, for the sake of clarity, we will also denote the true positive and negative classes using notations + and

Table 1: The classification results from one binary classifier.

y_i		$\hat{y}_i$	
$+$	μ	1	ρ^+
		0	$1-\rho^+$
$-$	$1-\mu$	1	ρ^-
		0	$1-\rho^-$

$-$ respectively which should be regarded as interchangeable synonyms of class IDs 1 and 0.

The test documents can usually be considered as "independent trials", so we regard both their true class labels y_i and their predicted class labels $\hat{y}_i$ as independent and identically distributed (i.i.d.) random variables.

Table 1 lists all the possible classification results and their corresponding probabilities for a test document using one binary classifier. It is worth noting that in our model a classifier is allowed to exhibit different prediction accuracies on documents from different true classes. This flexibility is necessary to reflect the reality and facilitate the estimation of complex performance measures that take class imbalance into account.

Given a test document $\boldsymbol{x}_i$, we use μ to represent the probability that its true class label y_i is positive. Obviously the probability that y_i is negative would therefore be $1-\mu$. This means that y_i follows a Bernoulli distribution with parameter μ: $y_i \sim \text{Bern}(\mu)$, i.e., $\Pr[y_i|\mu] = \mu^{y_i}(1-\mu)^{1-y_i}$. It would then be convenient to use the Beta distribution (which is conjugate to the Bernoulli distribution) as the prior distribution of parameter μ. More specifically, $\mu \sim \text{Beta}(\boldsymbol{\beta})$, i.e., $\Pr[\mu] = \frac{\Gamma(\beta^+,\beta^-)}{\Gamma(\beta^+)\Gamma(\beta^-)}\mu^{\beta^+-1}(1-\mu)^{\beta^--1}$ where the hyper-parameter $\boldsymbol{\beta} = (\beta^+,\beta^-)$ encodes our prior belief about each class's proportion. If we do not have such knowledge, we can simply set $\boldsymbol{\beta} = (1,1)$ that yields a uniform distribution, as we did in our experiments.

When a test document $\boldsymbol{x}_i$ with true class label y_i is classified, we anticipate that it will be classified as positive with a certain probability ρ^{y_i}, i.e., $\Pr[\hat{y}_i = 1|\rho^{y_i}] = \rho^{y_i}$. For example, ρ^- is the probability that a negative $(-)$ document is classified to be positive (1). Hence we can say that $\hat{y}_i$ follows a Bernoulli distribution with parameter ρ^+ when y_i is positive and ρ^- when y_i is negative. In other words, $\hat{y}_i \sim \text{Bern}(\rho^+)$ if $y_i = +$ and $\hat{y}_i \sim \text{Bern}(\rho^-)$ if $y_i = -$. It would then be convenient to use the Beta distribution as the prior distribution of parameter ρ^+ and ρ^-. More specifically, $\rho^+ \sim \text{Beta}(\boldsymbol{\alpha}^+)$, i.e., $\Pr[\rho^+] = \frac{\Gamma(\alpha_1^+,\alpha_0^+)}{\Gamma(\alpha_1^+)\Gamma(\alpha_0^+)}\rho^{+\alpha_1^+-1}(1-\rho^+)^{\alpha_0^+-1}$ where the hyper-parameter $\boldsymbol{\alpha}^+ = (\alpha_1^+,\alpha_0^+)$ encodes our prior belief about the classifier's prediction accuracy on positive test documents. In the same way, we have $\rho^- \sim \text{Beta}(\boldsymbol{\alpha}^-)$, where $\boldsymbol{\alpha}^- = (\alpha_1^-,\alpha_0^-)$. If we do not have any prior knowledge, we can simply set $\boldsymbol{\alpha}^+ = \boldsymbol{\alpha}^- = (1,1)$ that yields a uniform distribution, as we did in our experiments.

Once the parameters μ, ρ^+ and ρ^- have been estimated, it will be easy to calculate the contingency table of "expected" classification results: true positive (tp), false positive (fp), true negative (tn), and false negative (fn). For example, the anticipated number of true positive predictions of the classifier should be the number of positive test documents $N\mu$ times the rate of being predicted by the classifier as positive

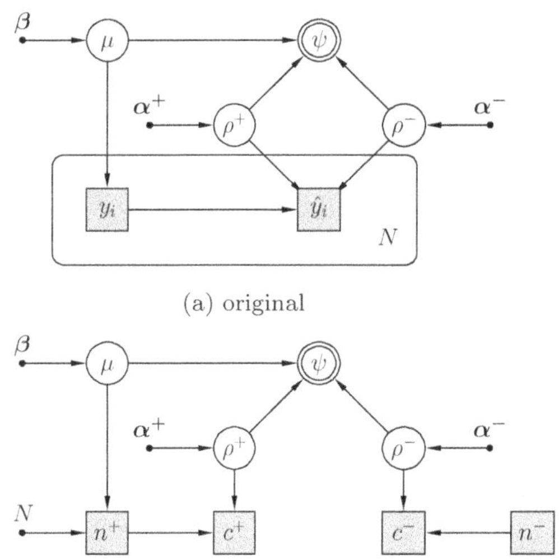

(a) original

(b) compact

Figure 1: The probabilistic graphical model for a binary text classifier's performance.

ρ^+. The equations to calculate the contingency table for a classifier are listed as follows.

$$tp = N\mu\rho^+ \qquad fp = N(1-\mu)\rho^-$$
$$fn = N\mu(1-\rho^+) \qquad tn = N(1-\mu)(1-\rho^-)$$

With the contingency table for a classifier available, we can compute not only the accuracy, but also more complex performance measures such as the F_1 score for that classifier. The precision P, recall R, and their harmonic mean F_1 score could be computed as follows.

$$P = \frac{tp}{tp+fp} = \frac{\mu\rho^+}{\mu\rho^+ + (1-\mu)\rho^-}$$
$$R = \frac{tp}{tp+fn} = \frac{\mu\rho^+}{\mu\rho^+ + \mu(1-\rho^+)} = \rho^+$$
$$F_1 = \frac{2PR}{P+R}$$

It can be seen that N is cancelled out in the calculation of the precision, the recall, and the F_1 score.

Such a model is quite general to accommodate various performance measures (see Section 5), though in this paper we focus on the F_1 score only to illustrate the usage of our model. Let ψ denote the chosen performance measure, then it is simply a function that depends on μ, ρ^+ and ρ^- only: $\psi = f(\mu,\rho^+,\rho^-)$.

This model describes a generative mechanism of a classifier's test results. It is summarised as follows, and also depicted in Figure 1a as a *probabilistic graphical model* [13] using common notations.

$$\begin{aligned}
\mu &\sim \text{Beta}(\boldsymbol{\beta}) \\
y_i &\sim \text{Bern}(\mu) \text{ for } i = 1,\dots,N \\
\rho^+ &\sim \text{Beta}(\boldsymbol{\alpha}^+) \qquad \rho^- \sim \text{Beta}(\boldsymbol{\alpha}^-) \\
\hat{y}_i &\sim \begin{cases} \text{Bern}(\rho^+) \text{ for } i = 1,\dots,N & \text{if } y_i = + \\ \text{Bern}(\rho^-) \text{ for } i = 1,\dots,N & \text{if } y_i = - \end{cases} \\
\psi &= f(\mu,\rho^+,\rho^-)
\end{aligned}$$

In the above model, each true class label y_i is regarded as an individual sampling event, and each prediction $\hat{y}_i$ is treated as an individual sampling event too. If we aggregate the occurrences of such individual sampling events into the counts of their occurrences, the model could be greatly simplified.

Let n^+ represent the total number of positive test documents and $n^- = N - n^+$ represent the total number of negative test documents, then n^+ is known to follow the Binomial distribution with parameters N and μ: $n^+ \sim \text{Bin}(N, \mu)$, i.e., $\Pr[n^+|N, \mu] = \binom{N}{n^+}\mu^{n^+}(1-\mu)^{N-n^+}$ where $\binom{N}{n^+} = \frac{N!}{n^+!(N-n^+)!}$ is the Binomial coefficient.

Let c^+ represent the count of positive predictions ($\hat{y}_i = 1$) produced on positive test documents ($y_i = +$), then c^+ is known to follow the Binomial distribution with parameters n^+ and ρ^+: $c^+ \sim \text{Bin}(n^+, \rho^+)$, i.e., $\Pr[c^+|n^+, \rho^+] = \binom{n^+}{c^+}\rho^{+c^+}(1-\rho^+)^{n^+-c^+}$. In the same way, we have $c^- \sim \text{Bin}(n^-, \rho^-)$.

The parameters μ, ρ^+ and ρ^- are the same as before and their prior distributions remain the same. The deterministic variable ψ also stays unchanged.

This compact model is equivalent to the original model, but it will be computationally much more efficient due to the drastic reduction of sampling events. So hereafter the compact model will be used instead of the original model for our work on performance comparison.

The compact model is summarised as follows and depicted in Figure 1b.

$$\begin{aligned} \mu &\sim \text{Beta}(\boldsymbol{\beta}) & & \\ n^+ &\sim \text{Bin}(N, \mu) & n^- &= N - n^+ \\ \rho^+ &\sim \text{Beta}(\boldsymbol{\alpha}^+) & \rho^- &\sim \text{Beta}(\boldsymbol{\alpha}^-) \\ c^+ &\sim \text{Bin}(n^+, \rho^+) & c^- &\sim \text{Bin}(n^-, \rho^-) \\ \psi &= f(\mu, \rho^+, \rho^-) & & \end{aligned}$$

The usage of conjugate priors (e.g., Beta for Bernoulli or Binomial) is not obligatory in our model. Actually any reasonable probability distribution can be used as the prior of μ, ρ^+ or ρ^-. If we insist on using conjugate priors, it is possible to simplify the model even further by computing the posterior probability distributions of our model parameters analytically and then sampling from the posterior probability distributions directly. However, this will only bring moderate improvement to computational efficiency, and more importantly it will make the model less flexible as some extensions to the model (such as hierarchical modelling) will be obstructed. So we shall not go down that direction in this paper.

3.1.1 Unpaired Model

In the unpaired model for performance comparison, the predictions from the two classifiers A and B being compared are assumed to be independent with each other [28,29]. Actually the two classifiers could be evaluated each on a different test dataset as long as the data come from the same distribution (e.g., with the same proportion of positive test examples). So we can simply pool the two probabilistic models for those two classifiers together, and introduce a deterministic variable δ to capture the difference between their performance scores ψ^{A} and ψ^{B}.

$$\delta = \psi^{\text{A}} - \psi^{\text{B}}$$

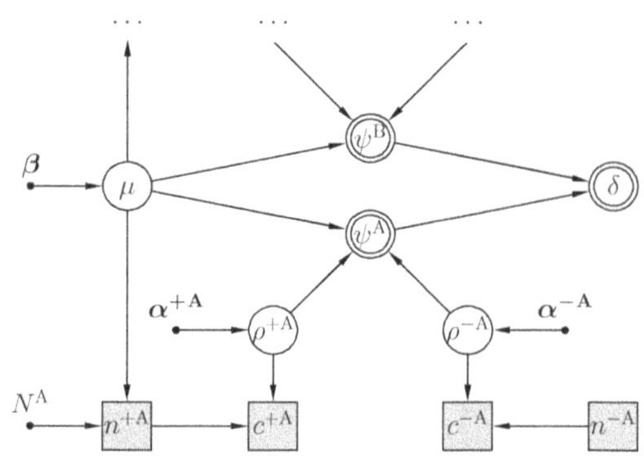

Figure 2: The unpaired model for performance comparison.

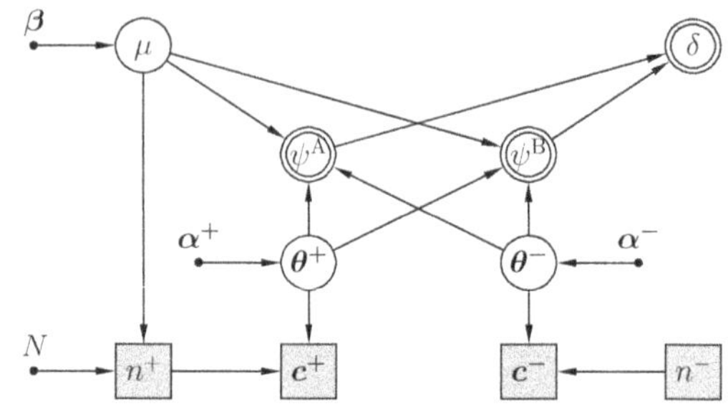

Figure 3: The paired model for performance comparison.

The unpaired model consisting of two separate sub-models for two classifiers A and B is depicted in Figure 2, where most of the sub-model for B is omitted as it is symmetric to that of A.

3.1.2 Paired Model

Although the unpaired model is simple and effective, its underlying assumption that the predictions from two classifiers A and B are independent of each other is unrealistic when those two classifiers are evaluated on the same test dataset. In contrast to the existing work for classification performance comparison (see Section 2), we would like to avoid this unrealistic assumption by modelling the two classifiers' predictions *jointly* as pairs. This is indeed crucial to assessing the real significance of the two classifiers' performance difference, as we demonstrate later in our experiments (see Section 4.1).

Considering two classifiers A and B evaluated on the same document collection, we have for each document $\boldsymbol{x}_i$ ($i = 1, \ldots, N$) a prediction outcome pair $\boldsymbol{o}_i = (\hat{y}_i^{\text{A}}, \hat{y}_i^{\text{B}})$ where $\hat{y}_i^{\text{A}}$ and $\hat{y}_i^{\text{B}}$ are the predicted class labels given by A and B respectively.

Table 2 lists all the possible classification results and their corresponding probabilities for a test document using two binary classifiers. Since for each of the two possible y_i values there are four possible $\boldsymbol{o}_i$ values $\{(1,1), (1,0), (0,1), (0,0)\}$, this table has $2 \times 4 = 8$ entries in total.

When a test document $\boldsymbol{x}_i$ with true class label y_i is classified by the two classifiers A and B, we anticipate that each possible prediction outcome pair $\boldsymbol{o}_i$ will occur with a certain probability $\theta_{\boldsymbol{o}_i}^{y_i}$, i.e., $\Pr[\boldsymbol{o}_i|\boldsymbol{\theta}^{y_i}] = \theta_{\boldsymbol{o}_i}^{y_i}$. For example, $\theta_{(0,1)}^{+}$ is the probability that a positive (+) document is classified to be negative (0) by the classifier A and positive (1) by

Table 2: The classification results from two binary classifiers.

y_i		$\hat{y}_i^{\mathrm{A}}$	$\hat{y}_i^{\mathrm{B}}$	$\boldsymbol{o}_i$	
+	μ	1	1	(1,1)	$\theta^+_{(1,1)}$
		1	0	(1,0)	$\theta^+_{(1,0)}$
		0	1	(0,1)	$\theta^+_{(0,1)}$
		0	0	(0,0)	$\theta^+_{(0,0)}$
−	$1-\mu$	1	1	(1,1)	$\theta^-_{(1,1)}$
		1	0	(1,0)	$\theta^-_{(1,0)}$
		0	1	(0,1)	$\theta^-_{(0,1)}$
		0	0	(0,0)	$\theta^-_{(0,0)}$

the classifier B. If we let $\boldsymbol{\theta}^+$ denote the vector of parameters $\theta^+_{\boldsymbol{o}_i}$ and similarly let $\boldsymbol{\theta}^-$ denote the vector of parameters $\theta^-_{\boldsymbol{o}_i}$, then we can say that $\boldsymbol{o}_i$ follows a Categorical distribution with parameter $\boldsymbol{\theta}^+$ when y_i is positive and $\boldsymbol{\theta}^-$ when y_i is negative. In other words, $\boldsymbol{o}_i \sim \mathrm{Cat}(\boldsymbol{\theta}^+)$ if $y_i = +$ and $\boldsymbol{o}_i \sim \mathrm{Cat}(\boldsymbol{\theta}^-)$ if $y_i = -$. It would then be convenient to use the Dirichlet distribution (which is conjugate to the Categorical distribution) as the prior distribution of parameter $\boldsymbol{\theta}^+$ or $\boldsymbol{\theta}^-$. More specifically, $\boldsymbol{\theta}^+ \sim \mathrm{Dir}(\boldsymbol{\alpha}^+)$, i.e., $\Pr[\boldsymbol{\theta}^+] = \frac{\Gamma(\sum_k \alpha_k^+)}{\prod_k \Gamma(\alpha_k^+)} \prod_k \theta_k^{\alpha_k^+ - 1}$ where the hyper-parameter $\boldsymbol{\alpha}^+ = \left(\alpha^+_{(1,1)}, \ldots, \alpha^+_{(0,0)}\right)$ encodes our prior belief about the classifier's prediction accuracy on positive test documents. In the same way, we have $\boldsymbol{\theta}^- \sim \mathrm{Dir}(\boldsymbol{\alpha}^-)$, where $\boldsymbol{\alpha}^- = \left(\alpha^-_{(1,1)}, \ldots, \alpha^-_{(0,0)}\right)$. If we do not have any prior knowledge, we can simply set $\boldsymbol{\alpha}^+ = \boldsymbol{\alpha}^- = (1, \ldots, 1)$ that yields a uniform distribution, as we did in our experiments.

Let $\boldsymbol{c}^+ = \left(c^+_{(1,1)}, \ldots, c^+_{(0,0)}\right)$ represent the counts of different types of prediction outcome pairs produced on positive test documents, then $\boldsymbol{c}^+$ is known to follow the Multinomial distribution with parameters n^+ and $\boldsymbol{\theta}^+$: $\boldsymbol{c}^+ \sim \mathrm{Mult}(n^+, \boldsymbol{\theta}^+)$, i.e., $\Pr[\boldsymbol{c}^+ | N, \boldsymbol{\theta}^+] = \frac{n^+!}{c^+_{(1,1)}! \cdots c^+_{(0,0)}!} \prod_k \theta_k^{c_k^+} = \frac{\Gamma((\sum_k c_k^+)+1)}{\prod_k \Gamma(c_k^+ + 1)} \prod_k \theta_k^{c_k^+}$. In the same way, we have $\boldsymbol{c}^- \sim \mathrm{Mult}(n^-, \boldsymbol{\theta}^-)$.

Once the parameters μ, $\boldsymbol{\theta}^+$ and $\boldsymbol{\theta}^-$ have been estimated, it will be easy to calculate, for each classifier, the contingency table of "expected" classification results as before by noticing the following facts:

$$\rho^{+\mathrm{A}} = \theta^+_{(1,1)} + \theta^+_{(1,0)} \qquad \rho^{-\mathrm{A}} = \theta^-_{(1,1)} + \theta^-_{(1,0)}$$
$$\rho^{+\mathrm{B}} = \theta^+_{(1,1)} + \theta^+_{(0,1)} \qquad \rho^{-\mathrm{B}} = \theta^-_{(1,1)} + \theta^-_{(0,1)}$$

Thus the performance scores ψ^{A} and ψ^{B}, as well as their difference δ could be estimated.

The paired model is summarised as follows and depicted in Figure 3.

$$\begin{aligned}
&\mu \sim \mathrm{Beta}(\boldsymbol{\beta}) && \\
&n^+ \sim \mathrm{Bin}(N, \mu) && n^- = N - n^+ \\
&\boldsymbol{\theta}^+ \sim \mathrm{Dir}(\boldsymbol{\alpha}^+) && \boldsymbol{\theta}^- \sim \mathrm{Dir}(\boldsymbol{\alpha}^-) \\
&\boldsymbol{c}^+ \sim \mathrm{Mult}(n^+, \boldsymbol{\theta}^+) && \boldsymbol{c}^- \sim \mathrm{Mult}(n^-, \boldsymbol{\theta}^-) \\
&\psi^{\mathrm{A}} = f(\mu, \boldsymbol{\theta}^+, \boldsymbol{\theta}^-) && \psi^{\mathrm{B}} = f'(\mu, \boldsymbol{\theta}^+, \boldsymbol{\theta}^-) \\
&\delta = \psi^{\mathrm{A}} - \psi^{\mathrm{B}} &&
\end{aligned}$$

3.2 Decision Making

3.2.1 Bayes Factor

Given a probabilistic model of the chosen performance measure, we can consider the comparison of two classifiers as a *model selection* problem and utilise the Bayes factor to address it [1,2].

In our context, the Bayes factor is the marginal likelihood of classification results data for the null model $\Pr[\mathcal{D}|\mathcal{M}_0]$ (where two classifiers perform equally well) relative to the marginal likelihood of classification results data for the alternative model $\Pr[\mathcal{D}|\mathcal{M}_1]$ (where one classifier works better than the other classifier): $\mathrm{BF} = \Pr[\mathcal{D}|\mathcal{M}_0]/\Pr[\mathcal{D}|\mathcal{M}_1]$. As the BF becomes larger, the evidence increases in favour of model $\mathcal{M}_0$ over model $\mathcal{M}_1$. The rule of thumb for interpreting the magnitude of the BF is that there is "substantial" evidence for the null model $\mathcal{M}_0$ when the BF exceeds 3, and similarly, "substantial" evidence for the alternative model $\mathcal{M}_1$ when the BF is less than $\frac{1}{3}$ [11].

Although for simple models the value of Bayes factor can be derived analytically as shown by [1,2], for complex models it can only be computed numerically using for example the Savage-Dickey (SD) method [5]. The SD method assumes that the prior on the variance in the null model equals the prior on the variance in the alternative model at the null value: $\Pr[\sigma^2|\mathcal{M}_0] = \Pr[\sigma^2|\mathcal{M}_1, \delta = 0]$. From this it follows that the likelihood of the data in the null model equals the likelihood of the data in the alternative model at the null value: $\Pr[\mathcal{D}|\mathcal{M}_0] = \Pr[\mathcal{D}|\mathcal{M}_1, \delta = 0]$. Thus, the Bayes factor can be determined by considering the alternative hypothesis alone, because it is just the ratio of the probability density at $\delta = 0$ in the posterior relative to the probability density at $\delta = 0$ in the prior: $\mathrm{BF} = \Pr[\delta = 0|\mathcal{M}_1, \mathcal{D}]/\Pr[\delta = 0|\mathcal{M}_1]$.

3.2.2 Bayesian Estimation

Instead of relying on the Bayes factor which is a single value, we can make use of the entire posterior probability distribution of δ, the performance difference between two classifiers, for their comparison. This Bayesian (parameter) estimation approach to performance comparison is said to be more informative and more robust than using the Bayes factor [14,15].

Given the posterior probability distribution of δ, we can then reach a discrete judgement (decision) about how those two classifiers A and B compare with each other by examining the relationship between the 95% Highest Density Interval (HDI) of δ and the user-defined Region of Practical Equivalence (ROPE) of δ [14,15]. The 95% HDI is a useful summary of where the bulk of the most credible values of δ falls: by definition, every value inside the HDI has higher probability density than any value outside the HDI, and the total mass of points inside the 95% HDI is 95% of the distribution. The ROPE of δ, e.g., $[-0.05, +0.05]$, encloses those values of δ deemed to be negligibly different from its null value for practical purposes. Using the HDI together with the ROPE, the performance comparison decisions could be made as follows:

- if the HDI sits fully within the ROPE (as illustrated in Figure 6), A is practically equivalent ($\approx$) to B;
- if the HDI sits fully at the left or right side of the ROPE, A is *significantly* worse ($\ll$) or better ($\gg$) than B respectively;

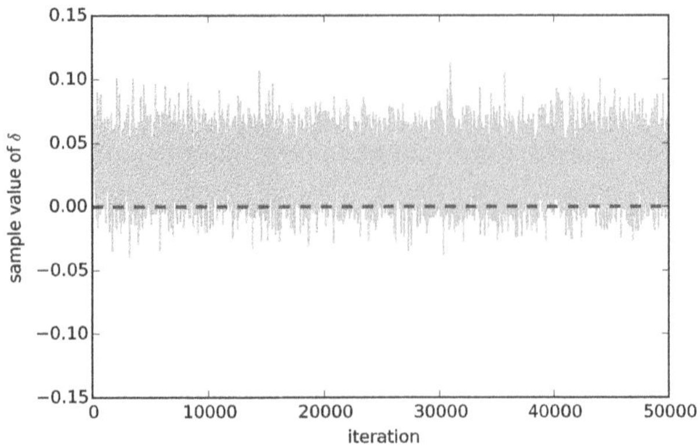

Figure 4: An example trace plot.

- if the HDI sits mainly though not fully at the left or right side of the ROPE, A is *slightly* worse (<) or better (>) than B respectively, but more experimental data would be needed to make a reliable judgement.

The need to specify the ROPE may sound like an extra burden on users compared to NHST, but in fact it is only making a hidden problem — how much performance difference would really matter for practical purposes (such as customer satisfaction and business profit) — explicit. The determination of the ROPE requires only knowledge about the application domain but not expertise in statistics. When the HDI is far away from or tightly surrounding the null value, the exact ROPE is inconsequential as any reasonable ROPE would lead to the same decision. Furthermore, in many situations, the exact ROPE can be left indeterminate. By reporting the HDI and other summary information about the full posterior distribution of δ, readers can apply whatever ROPE appropriate for them to make their own decisions.

3.3 Software Implementation

The purpose of building these models for classification results is to assess the Bayesian posterior probability of δ — the performance difference between two classifiers A and B. An approximate estimation of δ can be obtained by sampling from its posterior probability distribution via Markov Chain Monte Carlo (MCMC) [15] techniques.

We have implemented our models with an MCMC method *Metropolis-Hastings sampling* [15]. The default configuration is to generate 50,000 samples, with no "burn-in", "lag", or "multiple-chains". It has been argued in the MCMC literature that those tricks are often unnecessary: it is perfectly right to do a single long sampling run and keep all samples [13, 18]. In fact, the approximation accuracy of our program is very high: its Monte Carlo error (MC error) was usually close to 0 and never went beyond 0.002 in all our experiments (see Section 4). Figure 4 shows an example MCMC trace of our program in the experiments which clearly demonstrates the convergence of MCMC sampling.

In order to calculate the Bayes factor using the SD method (see Section 3.2.1), we approximate the posterior density $\Pr[\delta = 0|\mathcal{M}_1, \mathcal{D}]$ and the prior density $\Pr[\delta = 0|\mathcal{M}_1]$ by fitting a smooth function to the corresponding MCMC samples via kernel density estimation (KDE).

The program is written in Python 3 utilising the module `PyMC3`[1] [22] for MCMC based Bayesian model fitting. The source code is made open to the research community as online supplementary material[2]. It is free, easy to use, and extensible to more sophisticated models (see Section 5).

We should mention that this program for Bayesian performance comparison runs much slower than standard frequentist NHST techniques. On a machine with Intel x64 Core i7 CPU 2.30GHz, a sign-test or t-test would normally finish in less than 0.02 seconds, but our program could take up to 20 seconds for one comparison. Most of the time is spent on the computationally expensive MCMC sampling as it does require a decent number of samples to achieve high-fidelity approximation of probability distributions. Nevertheless, such a speed should be perfectly acceptable for the purpose of comparing classifiers because the classification experiments would usually take much longer time. Therefore the program is still very practical. Moreover, the program would be greatly accelerated if GPUs could be used by `Theano`, the underlying computational engine for `PyMC3`.

4. EXPERIMENTS

4.1 Synthetic Data

To demonstrate the advantage of our paired model over unpaired model, we perform power analysis using simulations. The statistical power is the probability of achieving the goal of a planned empirical study, if a suspected underlying state of the world is true [15]. As the power increases, there are decreasing chances of a Type II error aka the false negative rate β since the power is equal to $1 - \beta$.

We consider the following two scenarios where the two hypothetical classifiers A and B are somewhat correlated.
The scenario (a):
$\Pr[+] = \mu \quad = 0.5$
$\Pr[(1,1)|+] = \theta^+_{(1,1)} = 0.3$, $\Pr[(1,0)|+] = \theta^+_{(1,0)} = 0.3$,
$\Pr[(0,1)|+] = \theta^+_{(0,1)} = 0.2$, $\Pr[(0,0)|+] = \theta^+_{(0,0)} = 0.2$,
$\Pr[-] = 1 - \mu = 0.5$
$\Pr[(1,1)|-] = \theta^-_{(1,1)} = 0.2$, $\Pr[(1,0)|-] = \theta^-_{(1,0)} = 0.2$,
$\Pr[(0,1)|-] = \theta^-_{(0,1)} = 0.3$, $\Pr[(0,0)|-] = \theta^-_{(0,0)} = 0.3$,
It is easy to see that $F_1^{\mathrm{A}} = 0.6$ while $F_1^{\mathrm{B}} = 0.5$, so the goal here is to detect "A $\gg$ B".
The scenario (b):
$\Pr[+] = \mu \quad = 0.5$
$\Pr[(1,1)|+] = \theta^+_{(1,1)} = 0.3$, $\Pr[(1,0)|+] = \theta^+_{(1,0)} = 0.2$,
$\Pr[(0,1)|+] = \theta^+_{(0,1)} = 0.2$, $\Pr[(0,0)|+] = \theta^+_{(0,0)} = 0.3$,
$\Pr[-] = 1 - \mu = 0.5$
$\Pr[(1,1)|-] = \theta^-_{(1,1)} = 0.3$, $\Pr[(1,0)|-] = \theta^-_{(1,0)} = 0.2$,
$\Pr[(0,1)|-] = \theta^-_{(0,1)} = 0.2$, $\Pr[(0,0)|-] = \theta^-_{(0,0)} = 0.3$,
It is easy to see that $F_1^{\mathrm{A}} = 0.5$ and $F_1^{\mathrm{B}} = 0.5$, so the goal here is to detect "A $\approx$ B". Please note that this goal is infeasible using the frequentist NHST.

The power analysis results are shown in Table 3 and also Figure 5, which clearly indicate the superiority of the paired model to the unpaired model in terms of statistical power.

The reason why the unpaired model does not have as much statistical power as the paired model is because the former cannot tell whether the prediction differences (or

[1] http://pymc-devs.github.io/pymc3/
[2] http://www.dcs.bbk.ac.uk/~dell/publications/dellzhang_sigir2016_supp.html

Table 3: The power analysis of our models.

scenario	goal	dataset-size	power *unpaired*	power *paired*
(a)	A ≫ B	500	0.26	0.30
		1000	0.41	0.52
		1500	0.70	0.76
		2000	0.79	0.84
		2500	0.87	0.90
		3000	0.92	0.94
		3500	0.96	0.97
(b)	A ≈ B	500	0.00	0.00
		1000	0.01	0.22
		1500	0.26	0.58
		2000	0.63	0.81
		2500	0.72	0.87
		3000	0.88	0.96
		3500	0.92	0.99

agreements) between the two classifiers are consistent or not while the latter can. Inconsistent prediction differences yield a larger variability than consistent ones, and consequently more are required to exhibit statistical significance. Suppose that classifier A has a higher F_1 score than classifier B. If A almost always makes better predictions than B when they disagree, a relatively small amount of such consistent differences could give us enough confidence to assert statistical significance, which is recognised by the paired model but not the unpaired model.

4.2 Real-World Data

We have conducted experiments on a standard benchmark dataset for text classification, `20newsgroups` [16], of which the results are reported here. In order to ensure the reproducibility of our experimental results, we choose to use not the raw document collection, but a publicly-available ready-made "vectorised" version[3], as in [28, 29]. We have also done experiments on other "vectorised" datasets including the classic `Reuters-21578` [27], but due to the space limit those experimental results are reported only as online supplementary material together with our program's source code (see Section 3.3).

In the experiments, we have applied our proposed approach to carefully analyse the performances of two well-known supervised machine learning algorithms that are widely used for real-world text classification tasks: Naive Bayes (NB) and linear Support Vector Machine (SVM) [19]. For the former, we consider its two common variations: one with the Bernoulli event model (NB_{Bern}) and the other with the Multinomial event model (NB_{Mult}) [20]. For the latter, we consider its two common variations: one with the $L1$ norm penalty (SVM_{L1}) and the other with the $L2$ norm penalty (SVM_{L2}) [7, 30]. Thus we have four different classifiers in total. Obviously, the classification results of NB_{Bern} and NB_{Mult} would be highly correlated, and those of SVM_{L1} and SVM_{L2} as well. Among them, SVM_{L2} is widely regarded as the state-of-the-art text classifier [17, 25, 27]. It is also worth to notice that the NB algorithms will be applied not to the raw bag-of-words text datasets as people usually do, but on the vectorised `20newsgroups` dataset which has already been transformed by TF-IDF term weighting and document length normalisation.

We have used the off-the-shelf implementation of these classification algorithms provided by a Python machine learning library `scikit-learn`[4] in our experiments, again for the reproducibility reasons. The smoothing parameter α for the NB algorithm and the regularisation parameter C for the linear SVM algorithm have been tuned via grid search with 5-fold cross-validation on the training data for the macro-averaged F_1 score. The optimal parameters found are: NB_{Bern} with $\alpha = 10^{-14}$, NB_{Mult} with $\alpha = 10^{-3}$, SVM_{L1} with $C = 2^2$, SVM_{L2} with $C = 2^1$.

Table 4 shows the results of performance comparison between NB_{Bern} and NB_{Mult}, based on which we can confidently say that for most of the target categories, NB_{Bern} is outperformed by NB_{Mult}. Such results confirm the finding of [20] on this harder dataset.

Table 5 shows the results of performance comparison between SVM_{L1} and SVM_{L2}, based on which we can confidently say that for most of the target categories, SVM_{L1} and SVM_{L2} have no practical difference on classification effectiveness as measured by the F_1 score (given the ROPE $[-0.05, +0.05]$), though the former may have its advantages in terms of sparsity. Such results are complementary to those reported in [30].

Table 6 shows the results of performance comparison between NB_{Mult} and SVM_{L2} — the better performing classifiers from the NB and SVM camps. It can be clearly seen that for most of the target categories, the competition between NB_{Mult} and SVM_{L2} is too close to call: more test data would be needed to make a reliable judgement which one works better. Nevertheless, for six out of the eight target categories on which we can indeed make reliable judgements, NB_{Mult} and SVM_{L2} are practically equivalent (given the ROPE $[-0.05, +0.05]$). This phenomenon somewhat supports the claim of [23] that NB_{Mult}, if properly enhanced by TF-IDF term weighting and document length normalisation, can reach a comparable performance as SVM_{L2}.

On the micro (document) level, no NHST method exists for the comparison of F_1 scores. So in the above tables we show the results of using NHST to compare classification accuracies instead: the column "sign-test" and "t-test" contain the two-sided p-values of micro level sign-test (called s-test in [27]) and unpaired t-test (called p-test in [27]) respectively. The symbol $\star$ indicates that the accuracy difference between A and B is statistically significant ($p < 0.05$) according to NHST. When NHST fails to reject the null hypothesis that the two classifiers work equally well, no conclusion can be drawn from the comparison.

In all those tables, our proposed Bayesian performance comparison method has offered rich information about the difference between two classifiers' F_1 scores: in addition to the final judgement ("decision"), we have shown the posterior "mean", standard deviation ("std"), the Bayes factor estimated by the SD method ("BF_{SD}"), the percentage lower or greater than the null value 0 ("LG pct"), the percentage covered by the ROPE ("ROPE pct"), and the 95% "HDI". By contrast, the frequentist NHST would lead to a far less complete picture: it has only the p-values (and maybe also the confidence intervals) to offer. Furthermore, note that the judgements made by the Bayesian estimation on sev-

[3]http://scikit-learn.org/stable/datasets/twenty_newsgroups.html

[4]http://scikit-learn.org/stable/

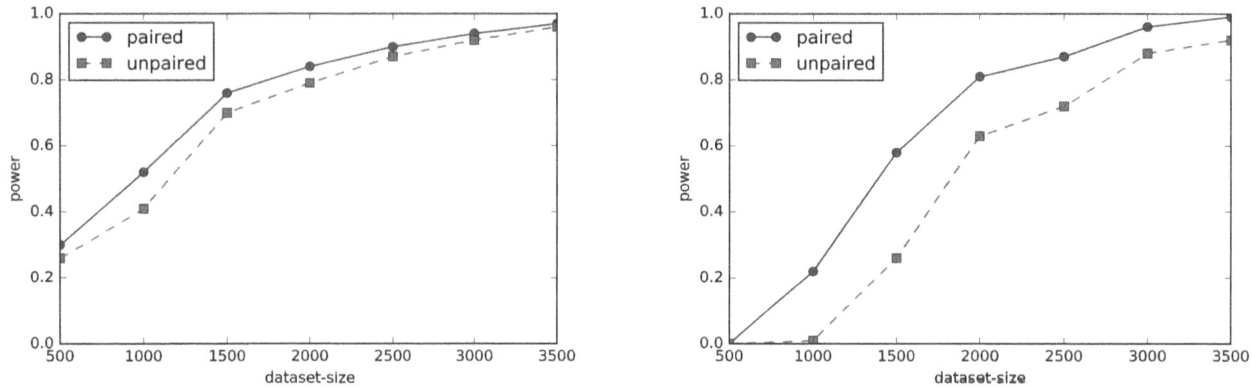

(a) example scenario: A $\gg$ B.

(b) example scenario: A $\approx$ B.

Figure 5: Comparing the statistical power of paired and unpaired models.

Table 4: The results of performance comparison between NB_{Bern} and NB_{Mult}.

category	frequentist		Bayesian						
	sign-test	t-test	mean	std	BF_{SD}	LG pct	ROPE pct	HDI	**decision**
0	⋆ 0.000	⋆ 0.008	−0.081	0.021	⋆ 0.003	100.0%<0<0.0%	6.6%	[−0.125, −0.041]	$<$
1	⋆ 0.000	⋆ 0.000	−0.114	0.017	⋆ 0.000	100.0%<0<0.0%	0.0%	[−0.148, −0.080]	$\ll$
2	⋆ 0.000	⋆ 0.000	−0.400	0.028	⋆ 0.000	100.0%<0<0.0%	0.0%	[−0.456, −0.345]	$\ll$
3	⋆ 0.000	⋆ 0.003	−0.095	0.016	⋆ 0.000	100.0%<0<0.0%	0.2%	[−0.126, −0.062]	$\ll$
4	⋆ 0.000	⋆ 0.000	−0.249	0.019	⋆ 0.000	100.0%<0<0.0%	0.0%	[−0.286, −0.211]	$\ll$
5	⋆ 0.000	⋆ 0.000	−0.101	0.017	⋆ 0.000	100.0%<0<0.0%	0.1%	[−0.135, −0.069]	$\ll$
6	⋆ 0.000	⋆ 0.000	−0.136	0.016	⋆ 0.000	100.0%<0<0.0%	0.0%	[−0.168, −0.105]	$\ll$
7	⋆ 0.000	⋆ 0.001	−0.092	0.016	⋆ 0.000	100.0%<0<0.0%	0.4%	[−0.123, −0.061]	$\ll$
8	⋆ 0.000	⋆ 0.000	−0.144	0.017	⋆ 0.000	100.0%<0<0.0%	0.0%	[−0.178, −0.111]	$\ll$
9	⋆ 0.000	⋆ 0.001	−0.080	0.013	⋆ 0.000	100.0%<0<0.0%	0.8%	[−0.105, −0.055]	$\ll$
10	⋆ 0.000	⋆ 0.000	+0.108	0.017	⋆ 0.000	0.0%<0<100.0%	0.0%	[+0.074, +0.142]	$\gg$
11	⋆ 0.000	⋆ 0.002	−0.092	0.016	⋆ 0.000	100.0%<0<0.0%	0.4%	[−0.125, −0.061]	$\ll$
12	⋆ 0.000	⋆ 0.002	−0.097	0.020	⋆ 0.000	100.0%<0<0.0%	0.8%	[−0.137, −0.058]	$\ll$
13	⋆ 0.000	⋆ 0.000	−0.115	0.016	⋆ 0.000	100.0%<0<0.0%	0.0%	[−0.147, −0.084]	$\ll$
14	⋆ 0.000	⋆ 0.000	−0.109	0.016	⋆ 0.000	100.0%<0<0.0%	0.0%	[−0.139, −0.079]	$\ll$
15	0.064	0.178	−0.027	0.016	♯ 3.132	95.7%<0<4.3%	92.2%	[−0.059, +0.004]	$<$
16	⋆ 0.024	0.151	−0.105	0.019	⋆ 0.000	100.0%<0<0.0%	0.1%	[−0.141, −0.068]	$\ll$
17	⋆ 0.000	⋆ 0.000	−0.102	0.016	⋆ 0.000	100.0%<0<0.0%	0.1%	[−0.134, −0.070]	$\ll$
18	⋆ 0.000	⋆ 0.034	−0.088	0.020	⋆ 0.007	100.0%<0<0.0%	2.9%	[−0.128, −0.049]	$<$
19	⋆ 0.000	⋆ 0.011	−0.040	0.030	2.389	91.3%<0<8.7%	62.9%	[−0.097, +0.022]	$<$

eral cases are different from those made by the frequentist NHST (e.g., at the significance level 0.05). So even if in some researchers' opinion the superiority of the former over the latter is still debatable, there is no doubt that the former can at least be complementary to the latter.

Figure 6 illustrates the visualisation of Bayesian performance comparison results produced by our program: the "posterior plot" sub-graph shows the posterior probability distribution of the performance difference variable δ; and the "factor plot" sub-graph shows the estimation of the Bayes factor by the SD method.

5. EXTENSIONS

The proposed Bayesian approach to performance comparison has been described above in the most basic setting for concreteness and simplicity, but it is in fact readily extensible to the following more general scenarios.

Multiple classes. It would be straightforward to extend our model to multi-class classification (either single-label or multi-label): we will need one μ parameter and a pair of $\boldsymbol{\theta}$ parameters for each class. Thus we are able to measure each classifier's overall performance using micro-averaged or macro-averaged F_1 scores [27], and compute their difference as the deterministic variable δ in the model [28]. Note that here δ is estimated using a large number of prediction outcomes for all test documents, rather than just a small number of F_1 scores for test categories as in [27] (see Section 2.1). It would be promising to go further to develop a Bayesian hierarchical model [15] where the classifier's parameters $\boldsymbol{\theta}_j$ for different classes are governed by a higher-level overarching hyper-parameter η (e.g., representing the overall probability of making correct predictions) and thus able to "share statistical strength" [29]. A potential problem, though, is the explosive growth of possible prediction outcome combinations along with the increase of class numbers, which in the worst situation may force us into backing off to the assumption of independence between classifiers so as to keep the model computationally tractable.

Other performance measures. To compare classifiers

Table 5: The results of performance comparison between SVM_{L1} and SVM_{L2}.

category	frequentist		Bayesian						
	sign-test	t-test	mean	std	BF_{SD}	LG pct	ROPE pct	HDI	**decision**
0	⋆ 0.049	0.299	−0.027	0.018	♯ 3.399	93.6%<0<6.4%	89.9%	[−0.063, +0.008]	<
1	0.523	0.706	−0.011	0.013	♯ 9.427	80.6%<0<19.4%	99.9%	[−0.038, +0.014]	≈
2	0.632	0.774	−0.007	0.014	♯ 12.058	68.3%<0<31.7%	99.8%	[−0.035, +0.020]	≈
3	0.270	0.542	−0.020	0.014	♯ 4.593	92.3%<0<7.7%	98.5%	[−0.047, +0.007]	≈
4	0.247	0.524	−0.022	0.014	♯ 3.781	94.8%<0<5.2%	97.4%	[−0.049, +0.005]	≈
5	1.000	0.960	−0.009	0.014	♯ 12.206	73.2%<0<26.8%	99.8%	[−0.035, +0.019]	≈
6	⋆ 0.000	⋆ 0.031	−0.053	0.013	⋆ 0.011	100.0%<0<0.0%	41.9%	[−0.078, −0.029]	<
7	⋆ 0.000	⋆ 0.000	−0.133	0.017	⋆ 0.000	100.0%<0<0.0%	0.0%	[−0.166, −0.098]	≪
8	0.221	0.457	−0.015	0.014	♯ 8.165	84.4%<0<15.6%	99.3%	[−0.042, +0.014]	≈
9	⋆ 0.000	⋆ 0.000	+0.126	0.017	⋆ 0.000	0.0%<0<100.0%	0.0%	[+0.094, +0.160]	≫
10	0.515	0.657	−0.013	0.011	♯ 9.261	87.7%<0<12.3%	99.9%	[−0.035, +0.009]	≈
11	0.771	0.837	−0.005	0.013	♯ 12.937	64.0%<0<36.0%	100.0%	[−0.030, +0.021]	≈
12	0.061	0.298	−0.033	0.016	1.209	98.2%<0<1.8%	84.7%	[−0.066, −0.003]	<
13	0.264	0.463	−0.019	0.015	♯ 5.513	90.2%<0<9.8%	97.9%	[−0.050, +0.009]	≈
14	0.733	0.814	−0.011	0.014	♯ 10.671	79.3%<0<20.7%	99.7%	[−0.036, +0.018]	≈
15	0.192	0.448	−0.035	0.013	⋆ 0.330	99.6%<0<0.4%	86.9%	[−0.062, −0.011]	<
16	0.065	0.355	−0.030	0.014	1.225	98.7%<0<1.3%	92.1%	[−0.057, −0.003]	<
17	0.105	0.333	+0.014	0.014	♯ 6.589	15.7%<0<84.3%	99.3%	[−0.015, +0.041]	≈
18	⋆ 0.014	0.192	−0.014	0.016	♯ 8.065	82.0%<0<18.0%	98.7%	[−0.045, +0.017]	≈
19	⋆ 0.033	0.265	+0.008	0.022	♯ 7.488	36.5%<0<63.5%	96.9%	[−0.035, +0.051]	>

Table 6: The results of performance comparison between NB_{Mult} and SVM_{L2}.

category	frequentist		Bayesian						
	sign-test	t-test	mean	std	BF_{SD}	LG pct	ROPE pct	HDI	**decision**
0	0.314	0.536	−0.001	0.022	♯ 8.542	50.5%<0<49.5%	97.7%	[−0.043, +0.042]	≈
1	0.386	0.521	+0.028	0.018	♯ 3.128	6.2%<0<93.8%	89.0%	[−0.007, +0.063]	>
2	0.056	0.205	−0.028	0.021	♯ 3.739	91.2%<0<8.8%	84.5%	[−0.069, +0.013]	<
3	1.000	1.000	+0.030	0.018	2.966	5.1%<0<94.9%	86.8%	[−0.006, +0.066]	>
4	0.840	0.853	+0.006	0.018	♯ 9.533	37.6%<0<62.4%	99.0%	[−0.031, +0.040]	≈
5	⋆ 0.017	0.089	+0.051	0.017	⋆ 0.075	0.2%<0<99.8%	48.0%	[+0.017, +0.083]	>
6	0.057	0.188	+0.013	0.016	♯ 8.805	20.6%<0<79.4%	99.1%	[−0.017, +0.046]	≈
7	0.180	0.312	+0.031	0.018	2.566	4.4%<0<95.6%	85.1%	[−0.005, +0.067]	>
8	1.000	1.000	+0.007	0.018	♯ 9.551	35.9%<0<64.1%	98.9%	[−0.028, +0.042]	≈
9	⋆ 0.000	⋆ 0.000	+0.215	0.019	⋆ 0.000	0.0%<0<100.0%	0.0%	[+0.180, +0.253]	≫
10	⋆ 0.000	⋆ 0.000	−0.115	0.017	⋆ 0.000	100.0%<0<0.0%	0.0%	[−0.149, −0.082]	≪
11	⋆ 0.024	0.102	−0.016	0.017	♯ 7.016	84.0%<0<16.0%	98.1%	[−0.048, +0.017]	≈
12	⋆ 0.000	⋆ 0.001	+0.073	0.020	⋆ 0.008	0.0%<0<100.0%	12.4%	[+0.034, +0.113]	>
13	⋆ 0.000	⋆ 0.009	+0.060	0.016	⋆ 0.004	0.0%<0<100.0%	26.1%	[+0.029, +0.090]	>
14	⋆ 0.038	0.129	+0.050	0.017	⋆ 0.194	0.2%<0<99.8%	50.7%	[+0.016, +0.082]	>
15	⋆ 0.009	0.064	−0.009	0.014	♯ 10.473	74.6%<0<25.4%	99.8%	[−0.037, +0.021]	≈
16	0.213	0.430	+0.041	0.017	0.650	0.8%<0<99.2%	71.1%	[+0.007, +0.074]	>
17	⋆ 0.010	0.070	+0.053	0.016	⋆ 0.058	0.0%<0<100.0%	43.2%	[+0.023, +0.085]	>
18	0.119	0.349	+0.015	0.019	♯ 6.927	22.2%<0<77.8%	96.5%	[−0.023, +0.053]	>
19	⋆ 0.021	0.179	−0.061	0.031	0.825	97.6%<0<2.4%	36.0%	[−0.119, +0.001]	<

using a performance measure different from the F_1 score, we would only need to replace the function $f(\mu, \boldsymbol{\theta}^+, \boldsymbol{\theta}^-)$ for computing ψ, as long as that performance measure could be calculated based on the classification contingency table alone [12]. For example, it would be straightforward to extend our model to handle the more general F_β measure ($\beta \geq 0$) [19,26] with $\beta \neq 1$: we just need to substitute the F_β formula for the F_1 formula in the function of ψ. For another example, the Area Under the ROC Curve (AUC) is essentially the proportion of correctly ranked document pairs [9, 12], so it could be modelled in a similar way.

Other tasks. More generally, the idea of building a Bayesian probabilistic graphical model to make comprehensive performance comparison could be applied to not just classifiers, but also search systems (see the ICTIR-2015 best paper [3]), recommender systems, and advertising systems.

6. CONCLUSIONS

This paper tries to address the problem of comparing text classifiers' performances by appealing to Bayesian reasoning. Although we ourselves believe that Bayesian statistics is "the way it should be", we understand that not everyone is a Bayesian or wants to become a Bayesian. Our argument is not whether being a Bayesian is philosophically better than being a frequentist, but that our Bayesian estimation based approach to performance comparison of text classifiers avoids all the aforementioned practical weaknesses of NHST (see Section 2.1) and it provides much richer information about the difference between two classifiers' performances than NHST does, therefore it can supersede or at least complement the currently popular frequentist approach.

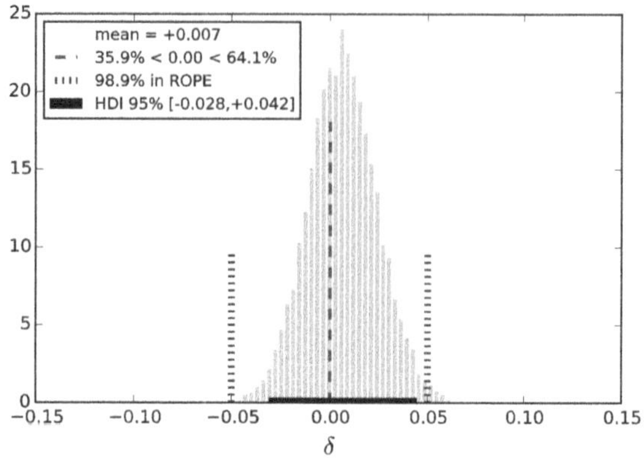

(a) posterior plot

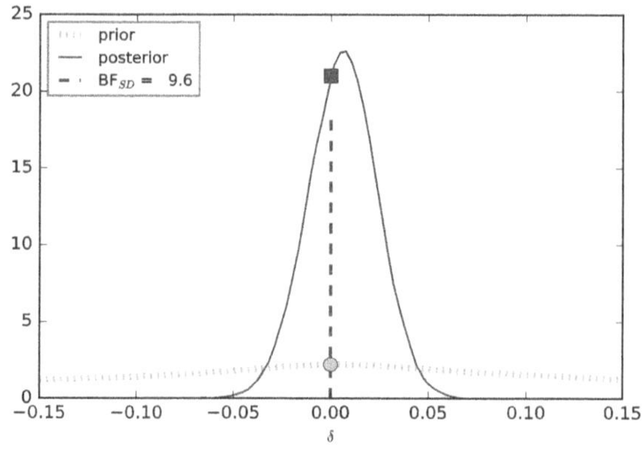

(b) factor plot

Figure 6: A ≈ B — NB_{Mult} is practically equivalent to SVM_{L2} for target category 8.

7. ACKNOWLEDGEMENTS

We thank the anonymous reviewers for their very helpful comments. This work was partly supported by the NSFC grants (61472141 and 61321064) as well as the Shanghai Knowledge Service Platform Project (ZF1213).

8. REFERENCES

[1] D. Barber. Are two classifiers performing equally? A treatment using Bayesian hypothesis testing. Technical report, IDIAP, 2004.

[2] D. Barber. *Bayesian Reasoning and Machine Learning.* Cambridge University Press, 2012.

[3] B. Carterette. Bayesian inference for information retrieval evaluation. In *Proceedings of the 2015 International Conference on the Theory of Information Retrieval (ICTIR)*, pages 31–40, Northampton, MA, USA, 2015.

[4] J. Demšar. Statistical comparisons of classifiers over multiple data sets. *The Journal of Machine Learning Research (JMLR)*, 7:1–30, 2006.

[5] J. M. Dickey and B. P. Lientz. The weighted likelihood ratio, sharp hypotheses about chances, the order of a markov chain. *The Annals of Mathematical Statistics*, 41(1):214–226, 1970.

[6] T. G. Dietterich. Approximate statistical tests for comparing supervised classification learning algorithms. *Neural Computation*, 10(7):1895–1923, 1998.

[7] R.-E. Fan, K.-W. Chang, C.-J. Hsieh, X.-R. Wang, and C.-J. Lin. LIBLINEAR: A library for large linear classification. *Journal of Machine Learning Research*, 9:1871–1874, 2008.

[8] C. Goutte and E. Gaussier. A probabilistic interpretation of precision, recall and *F*-score, with implication for evaluation. In *Proceedings of the 27th European Conference on IR Research (ECIR)*, pages 345–359, Santiago de Compostela, Spain, 2005.

[9] J. A. Hanley and B. J. McNeil. The meaning and use of the area under a receiver operating characteristic (ROC) curve. *Radiology*, 143(1):29–36, 1982.

[10] D. A. Hull. Improving text retrieval for the routing problem using latent semantic indexing. In *Proceedings of the 17th Annual International ACM SIGIR Conference on Research and Development in Information Retrieval (SIGIR)*, pages 282–291, Dublin, Ireland, 1994.

[11] H. Jeffreys. *Theory of Probability.* Oxford University Press, 3rd edition, 2000.

[12] T. Joachims. A support vector method for multivariate performance measures. In *Proceedings of the 22nd International Conference on Machine Learning (ICML)*, pages 377–384, Bonn, Germany, 2005.

[13] D. Koller and N. Friedman. *Probabilistic Graphical Models - Principles and Techniques.* MIT Press, 2009.

[14] J. K. Kruschke. Bayesian estimation supersedes the t test. *Journal of Experimental Psychology: General*, 142(2):573, 2013.

[15] J. K. Kruschke. *Doing Bayesian Data Analysis: A Tutorial with R, JAGS, and Stan.* Academic Press, 2nd edition, 2014.

[16] K. Lang. Newsweeder: Learning to filter netnews. In *Proceedings of the 12th International Conference on Machine Learning (ICML)*, pages 331–339, Tahoe City, CA, USA, 1995.

[17] D. D. Lewis, Y. Yang, T. G. Rose, and F. Li. RCV1: A new benchmark collection for text categorization research. *Journal of Machine Learning Research (JMLR)*, 5:361–397, 2004.

[18] D. J. C. MacKay. *Information Theory, Inference, and Learning Algorithms.* Cambridge University Press, 2003.

[19] C. D. Manning, P. Raghavan, and H. Schütze. *Introduction to Information Retrieval.* Cambridge University Press, 2008.

[20] A. McCallum and K. Nigam. A comparison of event models for Naive Bayes text classification. In *AAAI-98 Workshop on Learning for Text Categorization*, pages 41–48, Madison, WI, 1998.

[21] T. Mitchell. *Machine Learning.* McGraw Hill, 1997.

[22] A. Patil, D. Huard, and C. J. Fonnesbeck. PyMC: Bayesian stochastic modelling in Python. *Journal of Statistical Software*, 35(4):1–81, 2010.

[23] J. D. Rennie, L. Shih, J. Teevan, and D. R. Karger. Tackling the poor assumptions of Naive Bayes text classifiers. In *Proceedings of the 20th International Conference on Machine Learning (ICML)*, pages 616–623, Washington, DC, USA, 2003.

[24] H. Schutze, D. A. Hull, and J. O. Pedersen. A comparison of classifiers and document representations for the routing problem. In *Proceedings of the 18th Annual International ACM SIGIR Conference on Research and Development in Information Retrieval (SIGIR)*, pages 229–237, Seattle, WA, USA, 1995.

[25] F. Sebastiani. Machine learning in automated text categorization. *ACM Computing Surveys (CSUR)*, 34(1):1–47, 2002.

[26] C. J. van Rijsbergen. *Information Retrieval.* Butterworths, London, UK, 2nd edition, 1979.

[27] Y. Yang and X. Liu. A re-examination of text categorization methods. In *Proceedings of the 22nd Annual International ACM SIGIR Conference on Research and Development in Information Retrieval (SIGIR)*, pages 42–49, Berkeley, CA, USA, 1999.

[28] D. Zhang, J. Wang, and X. Zhao. Estimating the uncertainty of average F1 scores. In *Proceedings of the 2015 International Conference on the Theory of Information Retrieval (ICTIR)*, pages 317–320, Northampton, MA, USA, 2015.

[29] D. Zhang, J. Wang, X. Zhao, and X. Wang. A bayesian hierarchical model for comparing average F1 scores. In *Proceedings of the 2015 IEEE International Conference on Data Mining (ICDM)*, pages 589–598, Atlantic City, NJ, USA, 2015.

[30] J. Zhu, S. Rosset, T. Hastie, and R. Tibshirani. 1-norm support vector machines. In *Advances in Neural Information Processing Systems (NIPS) 16*, volume 16, pages 49–56, Vancouver and Whistler, Canada, 2003.

A General Linear Mixed Models Approach to Study System Component Effects

Nicola Ferro
Department of Information Engineering
University of Padua
Padua, Italy
nicola.ferro@unipd.it

Gianmaria Silvello
Department of Information Engineering
University of Padua
Padua, Italy
gianmaria.silvello@unipd.it

ABSTRACT

Topic variance has a greater effect on performances than system variance but it cannot be controlled by system developers who can only try to cope with it. On the other hand, system variance is important on its own, since it is what system developers may affect directly by changing system components and it determines the differences among systems. In this paper, we face the problem of studying system variance in order to better understand how much system components contribute to overall performances. To this end, we propose a methodology based on *General Linear Mixed Model (GLMM)* to develop statistical models able to isolate system variance, component effects as well as their interaction by relying on a *Grid of Points (GoP)* containing all the combinations of analysed components. We apply the proposed methodology to the analysis of TREC Ad-hoc data in order to show how it works and discuss some interesting outcomes of this new kind of analysis. Finally, we extend the analysis to different evaluation measures, showing how they impact on the sources of variance.

1. INTRODUCTION

The experimental results analysis is a core activity in *Information Retrieval (IR)* aimed at, firstly, understanding and improving system performances and, secondly, assessing our own experimental methods, such as robustness of experimental collection or properties of the evaluation measures. When it comes to explaining system performances and differences between algorithms, it is commonly understood [10, 17, 23] that system performances can be broken down to a reasonable approximation as

$$\text{system performances} = \text{topic effect} + \text{system effect} + \text{topic/system interaction effect}$$

even though it is not always possible to estimate these effects separately, especially the interaction one.

It is well-known that topic variability is greater than system variability [23, 26]. Therefore, a lot of effort has been put in better understanding this source of variance [17] as well as in making IR systems more robust to it, e.g. [25, 28], basically trying to improve on the interaction effect. Nevertheless, with respect to an IR system, topic variance is a kind of "external source" of variation, which cannot be controlled by developers, but can only be taken into account to better deal with it.

On the other hand, system variance is a kind of "internal source" of variation, since it is originated by the choice of system components, may be directly affected by developers by working on them, and represents the intrinsic differences between algorithms. Its importance is witnessed by the wealth of research on how to compare systems performances in a reliable and robust way [1, 2, 4, 9, 20–23, 27].

However, a limitation of the current experimental methodology is that it allows us to evaluate IR systems only as a kind of "black-boxes", without an understanding of how their different components interact with each other and contribute to the overall performances. In other terms, we consider system variance as a single monolithic contribution and we cannot break it down into the smaller pieces (the components) constituting an IR system.

In order to estimate the effects of the different components of an IR system, we develop a methodology, based on *General Linear Mixed Model (GLMM)* and *ANalysis Of VAriance (ANOVA)* [13, 18], which makes us of a *Grid of Points (GoP)* containing all the possible combinations of inspected components. The proposed methodology allows us to break down the system effect into the contributions of stops lists, stemmers or n-grams and IR models, as well as to study their interaction.

We experimented on standard *Text REtrieval Conference (TREC)* Ad-hoc collections and produced a GoP by using the Terrier[1] open source IR system [12]. This gave us a very controlled experimental setting, which allowed us to systematically fit our *General Linear Model (GLM)* and break down the system variance. Note that such a controlled experimental setting is typically not available in evaluation campaigns, such as TREC, where participating systems do not constitute a systematic sampling of all the possible combinations of components and often are not even described in such a detail to know exactly what components have been used.

We applied the proposed methodology to TREC 5, 6, 7, and 8 Ad-hoc collections and we employed different measures – AP, Precision at 10, RBP, nDCG@20, and ERR@20. This setup allows us not only to highlight how components contribute to the overall system variance but also to gain

[1] http://www.terrier.org/

SIGIR '16, July 17-21, 2016, Pisa, Italy

DOI: http://dx.doi.org/10.1145/2911451.2911530

insights on how different evaluation measures impact on system and component variances.

The paper is organized as follows: Section 2 presents related work; Section 3 introduces our methodology; Section 4 experiments the proposed methodology; and, Section 5 draws conclusions and discusses future work.

2. RELATED WORKS

The impossibility of testing a single component by setting it aside from the complete IR system is a long-standing and well-known problem in IR experimentation, as early remarked by [16]. Component-based evaluation methodologies [6–8] have tried to tackle this issue by providing technical solutions for mixing different components without the need of building a whole IR system. However, even if these approaches allowed researchers to focus on the components of their own interest, they have not delivered yet estimates of the performance figures of each component.

The decomposition of performances into system and topic effects has been exploited by [1, 23] to analyze TREC data; [4] proposed model-based inference, using linear models and ANOVA, as an approach to multiple comparisons; [10] used multivariate linear models to compare non-deterministic IR systems among them and with deterministic ones. In all these cases, the goal is a more accurate comparison among systems rather than an analysis and breakdown of system variance per se. [17] applied GLMM to the study of per-topic variance by using simulated data to generate more replicates for each (topic, system) pair in order to estimate also the topic/system interaction effect; however, they did not use real data nor did focus on breaking down the system effect.

The idea of creating all the possible combinations of components has been proposed by [7], who noted that a systematic series of experiments on standard collections would have created a GoP, where (ideally) all the combinations of retrieval methods and components are represented, allowing us to gain more insights about the effectiveness of the different components and their interaction; this would have called also for the identification of *suitable baselines* with respect to which all the comparisons have to be made. Even though [7] introduced the idea of a GoP and how it could have been central to the decomposition of system component performances, they did not come up with an full-fledged methodology for analyzing such data and breaking down component performances, which is the contribution of the present work instead.

More recently, the proliferation of open source IR systems [24] has greatly ameliorated the situation, allowing researchers to run systematic experiments more easily. This led the community to further investigate what *reproducible baselines* are [5, 11] and the "Open-Source Information Retrieval Reproducibility Challenge" provided several of these baselines, putting some points in the ideal GoP mentioned above. We move a step forward with respect to [11] since we propose an actual methodology for exploiting such GoPs to decompose system performances and we rely on a much finer-grained grid, in terms of number of components and IR models experimented.

3. METHODOLOGY

The goal of the proposed methodology is to decompose the effects of different components on the overall system performances. In particular, we are interested in investigating the effects of the following components: stop lists; *Lexical Unit Generator (LUG)*, namely stemmers or n-grams; IR models, such as the vector space or the probabilistic model.

We create a *Grid of Points (GoP)* on a standard experimental collection by running all the IR systems resulting from all the possible combinations of the considered components (stop list, LUG, IR model); we consider stemmers and n-grams as alternative LUG components, thus we do not consider IR systems using both stemmer and n-grams.

Given a performance measure, such as *Average Precision (AP)*, we produce a matrix Y, as the one shown in Figure 1, where each cell Y_{ij} represents a measurement on topic t_i of the system s_j. Note that the column average – i.e., $\mu_{\cdot j}$ – is the performance mean over all topics for a given system, e.g. *Mean Average Precision (MAP)*; the row average – i.e., $\mu_{i\cdot}$ – is the performance mean over all systems for a given topic.

A GLMM explains the variation of a dependent variable Y ("Data") in terms of a controlled variation of independent variables ("Model") in addition to a residual uncontrolled variation ("Error").

$$\text{Data} = \text{Model} + \text{Error}$$

The term "General" refers to the ability to accommodate distinctions on quantitative variables representing continuous measures (as in regression analysis) and categorical distinctions representing groups or experimental conditions (as in ANOVA). In our case, we deal with categorical independent variables, as for example different types of stemmers, which constitute the levels of such categorical variable. The term "Linear" indicates that the "Model" is expressed as a linear combination of factors, where the factors can be single independent variables or their combinations. In our case, we are interested both in single independent variables, i.e. the *main effects* of the different components alone, and their combinations, i.e. the *interaction effects* between components. The term "Mixed" refers to the fact that some independent variables are considered *fixed effects* – i.e. they have precisely defined levels, and inferences about its effect apply only to those levels – and some others are considered *random effects* – i.e. they describe a randomly and independently drawn set of levels that represent variation in a clearly defined wider population; a random factor is indicated by adding a single quote as superscript to the variable name. In our case, the different kinds of systems and components are fixed effects while topics are random effects.

The experimental design determines how you compute the model and how you estimate its parameters. In particular, it is possible to have *independent measures* designs where different subjects participate to different experimental conditions (factors) or *repeated measures* designs, where each subject participates to all the experimental conditions (factors). In our case systems and their components are the experimental conditions (factors) while topics are the subjects and, since each topic is processed by each system, we have a repeated measure design.

One advantage of repeated measures designs is a reduction in error variance due to the greater similarity of the scores provided by the same subjects; in this way, variability in individual differences between subjects is removed from the error. Basically, a repeated measure design increases the statistical power for a fixed number of subjects or, in other terms, it allows us to reach a desired level of power with less subjects than those required in the independent measures design.

A final distinction is between *crossed/factorial* designs, where every level of one factor is measured in combination with every level of the other factors, and *nested* designs, where levels of a factor are grouped within each level of another nesting factor. In our case, we have a crossed/factorial design because in the generated GoP we experiment each possible combination of components.

3.1 Single Factor Repeated Measures Design

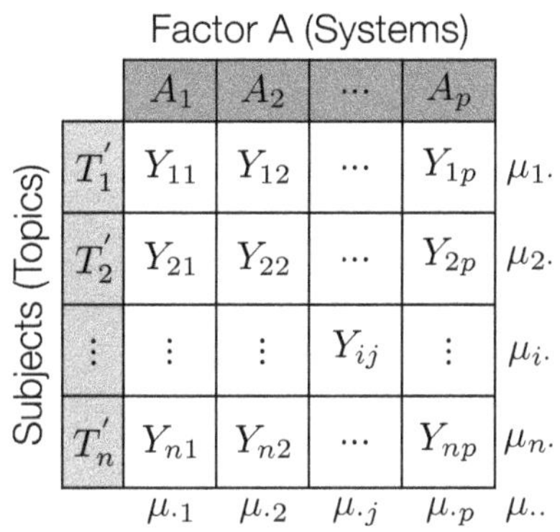

Figure 1: Single factor repeated measures design.

This design is the one typically used when ANOVA is applied to the analysis of the system performances in a track of an evaluation campaign, as in [1, 23], where the subjects are the topics and the factors are the system runs. Basically, in this context ANOVA is used to determine which experimental condition dependent variable score means differ, i.e. which systems are significantly different from others.

In our case, we are interested also in a second aspect, i.e. to determine what proportion of variation in the dependent variable can be attributed to differences between specific experimental groups or conditions, as defined by the independent variables. This turns into determining which proportion of variation is due to the topics and which one to the systems.

3.1.1 Model

The full GLMM model for the one-way ANOVA with repeated measures is:

$$Y_{ij} = \underbrace{\mu_{\cdot\cdot} + \tau_i + \alpha_j}_{\text{Model}} + \underbrace{\varepsilon_{ij}}_{\text{Error}} \tag{3.1}$$

where: Y_{ij} is the score of the i-th subject (topic) in the j-th factor (system); $\mu_{\cdot\cdot}$ is the grand mean; τ_i is the effect of the i-th subject $\tau_i = \mu_{i\cdot} - \mu_{\cdot\cdot}$ where $\mu_{i\cdot}$ is the mean of the i-th subject; α_j is the effect of the j-th factor $\alpha_j = \mu_{\cdot j} - \mu_{\cdot\cdot}$ where $\mu_{\cdot j}$ is the mean of the j-th factor; ε_{ij} is the error committed by the model in predicting the score of the i-th subject in the j-th factor. It consists of a term $(\tau\alpha)_{ij}$ which is the interaction between the i-th subject and the j-th factor[2]; and, a term ϵ_{ij} which is any additional error due to uncontrolled sources of variance.

3.1.2 Estimators

We have the following estimators for the parameters of the model above:

- grand mean: $\hat{\mu}_{\cdot\cdot} = \frac{1}{pn}\sum_{j=1}^{p}\sum_{i=1}^{n} Y_{ij}$
- mean of the i-th subject $\hat{\mu}_{i\cdot} = \frac{1}{p}\sum_{j=1}^{p} Y_{ij}$ and its effect $\hat{\tau}_i = \hat{\mu}_{i\cdot} - \hat{\mu}_{\cdot\cdot}$
- mean of the j-th factor $\hat{\mu}_{\cdot j} = \frac{1}{n}\sum_{i=1}^{n} Y_{ij}$ and its effect $\hat{\alpha}_j = \hat{\mu}_{\cdot j} - \hat{\mu}_{\cdot\cdot}$
- score of the i-th subject in the j-th factor $\hat{Y}_{ij} = \hat{\mu}_{\cdot\cdot} + \hat{\tau}_i + \hat{\alpha}_j = \hat{\mu}_{i\cdot} + \hat{\mu}_{\cdot j} - \hat{\mu}_{\cdot\cdot}$
- prediction error of the i-th subject in the j-th experimental condition $\hat{\varepsilon}_{ij} = Y_{ij} - \hat{Y}_{ij} = Y_{ij} - \hat{\mu}_{\cdot\cdot} - \hat{\tau}_i - \hat{\alpha}_j = Y_{ij} - (\hat{\mu}_{i\cdot} + \hat{\mu}_{\cdot j} - \hat{\mu}_{\cdot\cdot})$

3.1.3 Assessment

We can write the model of equation (3.1) introducing the estimated parameters as

$$\begin{aligned} Y_{ij} &= \hat{\mu}_{\cdot\cdot} + \hat{\tau}_i + \hat{\alpha}_j + \hat{\varepsilon}_{ij} \\ &= \hat{\mu}_{\cdot\cdot} + (\hat{\mu}_{i\cdot} - \hat{\mu}_{\cdot\cdot}) + (\hat{\mu}_{\cdot j} - \hat{\mu}_{\cdot\cdot}) + (Y_{ij} - (\hat{\mu}_{i\cdot} + \hat{\mu}_{\cdot j} - \hat{\mu}_{\cdot\cdot})) \end{aligned}$$

which leads to the following decomposition of the effects

$$\underbrace{Y_{ij} - \hat{\mu}_{\cdot\cdot}}_{\text{Total Effects}} = \underbrace{\hat{\mu}_{i\cdot} - \hat{\mu}_{\cdot\cdot}}_{\text{Subject Effects}} + \underbrace{\hat{\mu}_{\cdot j} - \hat{\mu}_{\cdot\cdot}}_{\text{Factor Effects}} + \underbrace{Y_{ij} - (\hat{\mu}_{i\cdot} + \hat{\mu}_{\cdot j} - \hat{\mu}_{\cdot\cdot})}_{\text{Error Effects}} \tag{3.2}$$

From equation (3.2), we can compute the sum of squares (SS), degrees of freedom (DF), and mean squares (MS) as follows:

- total effects $SS_{tot} = \sum_{j=1}^{p}\sum_{i=1}^{n}(Y_{ij} - \hat{\mu}_{\cdot\cdot})^2$ with mean squares $MS_{tot} = \frac{SS_{tot}}{df_{tot}}$ where $df_{tot} = pn - 1$ where df_{tot} comes from the fact that we are summing up pn scores and one degree of freedom is lost because of the grand mean $\hat{\mu}_{\cdot\cdot}$;
- subject effects
$$SS_{subj} = \sum_{j=1}^{p}\sum_{i=1}^{n}(\hat{\mu}_{i\cdot} - \hat{\mu}_{\cdot\cdot})^2 = \sum_{i=1}^{n} p\,(\hat{\mu}_{i\cdot} - \hat{\mu}_{\cdot\cdot})^2$$
with mean squares $MS_{subj} = \frac{SS_{subj}}{df_{subj}}$ where $df_{subj} = n-1$ where SS_{subj} considers that the quantity $\hat{\mu}_{i\cdot} - \hat{\mu}_{\cdot\cdot}$ is the same for all the p factors which the i-th subject experiences; df_{subj} is calculated by summing up n times the subject mean $\hat{\mu}_{i\cdot}$ where one degree of freedom is lost because of the grand mean $\hat{\mu}_{\cdot\cdot}$;
- factor effects
$$SS_{fact} = \sum_{j=1}^{p}\sum_{i=1}^{n}(\hat{\mu}_{\cdot j} - \hat{\mu}_{\cdot\cdot})^2 = \sum_{j=1}^{p} n\,(\hat{\mu}_{\cdot j} - \hat{\mu}_{\cdot\cdot})^2$$
with mean squares $MS_{fact} = \frac{SS_{fact}}{df_{fact}}$ where $df_{fact} = p-1$ where SS_{fact} considers that the quantity $\hat{\mu}_{\cdot j} - \hat{\mu}_{\cdot\cdot}$

[2] In order to calculate interaction effects, you need to have several scores (*replicates*) for each cell. The mean of the cell scores is taken as the best estimate of the cell score and is used to calculate interaction effects, with the discrepancy between the mean and the actual score providing the estimates of experimental error. If there is only one score per subject per factor, then a mean and its error cannot be calculated per subject per factor and without these estimates, the factor ϵ_{ij} cannot be separated from the interaction effect $(\tau\alpha)_{ij}$.

is the same for all the n subjects which experience the j-th factor; df_{fact} is calculated by summing up p times the factor mean $\hat{\mu}_{\cdot j}$ where one degree of freedom is lost because of the grand mean $\hat{\mu}_{\cdot\cdot}$;

- error effects

$$SS_{err} = \sum_{j=1}^{p}\sum_{i=1}^{n}(Y_{ij} - (\hat{\mu}_{i\cdot} + \hat{\mu}_{\cdot j} - \hat{\mu}_{\cdot\cdot}))^2$$

with mean squares $MS_{err} = \frac{SS_{err}}{df_{err}}$ where $df_{err} = (p-1)(n-1)$ where df_{err} is calculated by summing up n times the scores where one degree of freedom is lost in the subject scores because of the subject mean $\hat{\mu}_{i\cdot}$ and one degree of freedom is lost in the factor scores because of the factor mean $\hat{\mu}_{\cdot j}$.

Note that $SS_{tot} = SS_{subj} + SS_{fact} + SS_{err}$.

In order to determine if the factor effect is statistically significant, we compute the F statistics defined as:

$$F_{fact} = \frac{MS_{fact}}{MS_{err}} \quad (3.3)$$

and compare it with the distribution $F_{(df_{fact}, df_{err})}$ under the null hypothesis H_0 that there are not significant differences in order to estimate the probability (p-value) that F_{fact} has been observed by chance. We can set a significance level α (typically $\alpha = 0.05$) and, if p-value $< \alpha$, the factor effect is considered statistically significant.

As introduced above, we are not only interested in determining whether the factor effect is significant but also which proportion of the variance is due to it, that is we need to estimate its *effect-size measure* or *Strength of Association (SOA)*. The SOA is a "standardized index and estimates a parameter that is independent of sample size and quantifies the magnitude of the difference between populations or the relationship between explanatory and response variables" [15]. We use the $\hat{\omega}^2_{\langle fact\rangle}$ SOA:

$$\hat{\omega}^2_{\langle fact\rangle} = \frac{df_{fact}(F_{fact} - 1)}{df_{fact}(F_{fact} - 1) + pn} \quad (3.4)$$

which is an unbiased estimator of the variance components associated with the sources of variation in the design.

The common rule of thumb [14] when classifying $\hat{\omega}^2_{\langle fact\rangle}$ effect size is: 0.14 and above is a large effect, 0.06–0.14 is a medium effect, and 0.01–0.06 is a small effect. $\hat{\omega}^2_{\langle fact\rangle}$ values could happen to be negative and in such cases they are considered as zero.

When you conduct experiments, two types of error may happen. A *Type 1* error occurs when a true null hypothesis is rejected and the significance level α is the probability of committing a Type 1 error. A *Type 2* error occurs when a false null hypothesis is accepted and it is concerned with the capability of the conducted experiment to actually detect the effect under examination. Type 2 errors are often overlooked because if they occur, although a real effect is missed, no misdirection occurs and further experimentation is very likely to reveal the effect.

The *power* is the probability of correctly rejecting a false null hypothesis when an experimental hypothesis is true

$$\text{Power} = 1 - \beta$$

where β (typically $\beta = 0.2$) is the Type 2 error rate.

To determine the power of an experiment, we compute the effect size parameter:

$$\phi = \sqrt{n \cdot \frac{\hat{\omega}^2_{\langle fact\rangle}}{1 - \hat{\omega}^2_{\langle fact\rangle}}} \quad (3.5)$$

and we compare it with its tabulated values for a given Type 1 error rate α to determine β.

3.2 Factorial Repeated Measures Design

While single factor designs manipulate a single variable, factorial designs take into account two or more factors as well as their interaction. As an example a two factors repeated measure design can be defined extending the design described above, where we manipulated one factor (A), by adding an additional factor (B) and the interaction between them (AB).

We can therefore define a three factors design where we manipulate factors A, B and C which correspond to the stop lists, the LUG and the IR models respectively; with this design we can also study the interaction between component pairs as well as the third order interaction between them.

In Figure 2 we can see a table which extends to three factors the design presented in Figure 1 for a single factor. We can see that the systems are now decomposed into three main constituents: (i) factor A (stop lists) with p levels where, for instance, A_1 corresponds to the absence of a stop list, A_2 to the indri stop list, A_3 to the terrier stop list and so on; (ii) factor B (LUG) with q levels where B_1 corresponds to the absence of a LUG, B_2 to the Porter stemmer, B_3 to the Krovetz stemmer and so on; (iii) factor C (IR models) with r levels where C_1 corresponds to BM25, C_2 to TF*IDF and so on. We call this design a $p \times q \times r$ factorial design. Each cell of the table in Figure 2, say Y_{npqr}, reports the measurement (e.g., AP) on topic T'_n, for the system composed by the stop list A_p, the LUG B_q and IR model C_r.

The full GLMM model for the described factorial ANOVA for repeated measures with three fixed factors (A, B, C) and a random factor (T') is:

$$\begin{aligned} Y_{ijkl} = & \underbrace{\mu_{\cdot\cdot\cdot\cdot} + \tau_i + \alpha_j + \beta_k + \gamma_l}_{\text{Main Effects}} + \\ & \underbrace{\alpha\beta_{jk} + \alpha\gamma_{jl} + \beta\gamma_{kl} + \alpha\beta\gamma_{jkl}}_{\text{Interaction Effects}} + \underbrace{\varepsilon_{ijkl}}_{\text{Error}} \end{aligned} \quad (3.6)$$

where: Y_{ijkl} is the score of the i-th subject in the j-th, k-th, and l-th factors; $\mu_{\cdot\cdot\cdot\cdot}$ is the grand mean; τ_i is the effect of the i-th subject $\tau_i = \mu_{i\cdot\cdot\cdot} - \mu_{\cdot\cdot\cdot\cdot}$ where $\mu_{i\cdot\cdot\cdot}$ is the mean of the i-th subject; $\alpha_j = \mu_{\cdot j\cdot\cdot} - \mu_{\cdot\cdot\cdot\cdot}$ is the effect of the j-th factor, where $\mu_{\cdot j\cdot\cdot}$ is the mean of the j-th factor; $\beta_k = \mu_{\cdot\cdot k\cdot} - \mu_{\cdot\cdot\cdot\cdot}$ is the effect of the k-th factor, where $\mu_{\cdot\cdot k\cdot}$ is the mean of the k-th factor; and, $\gamma_l = \mu_{\cdot\cdot\cdot l} - \mu_{\cdot\cdot\cdot\cdot}$ is the effect of the l-th factor where $\mu_{\cdot\cdot\cdot l}$ is the mean of the l-th factor; ε_{ijkl} is the error committed by the model in predicting the score of the i-th subject in the three factors j, k, l. It consists of all the interaction terms between the random subjects and the fixed factors, such as $(\tau\alpha)_{ij}$, $(\tau\beta)_{ik}$ and so on, plus the error ϵ_{ijkl} which is any additional error due to uncontrolled sources of variance. As in the single factor design to calculate interaction effects with the subjects, you need to have replicates; when there is only one score per subject per factor the factor ϵ_{ijkl} cannot be separated from the interaction effects with the random subjects.

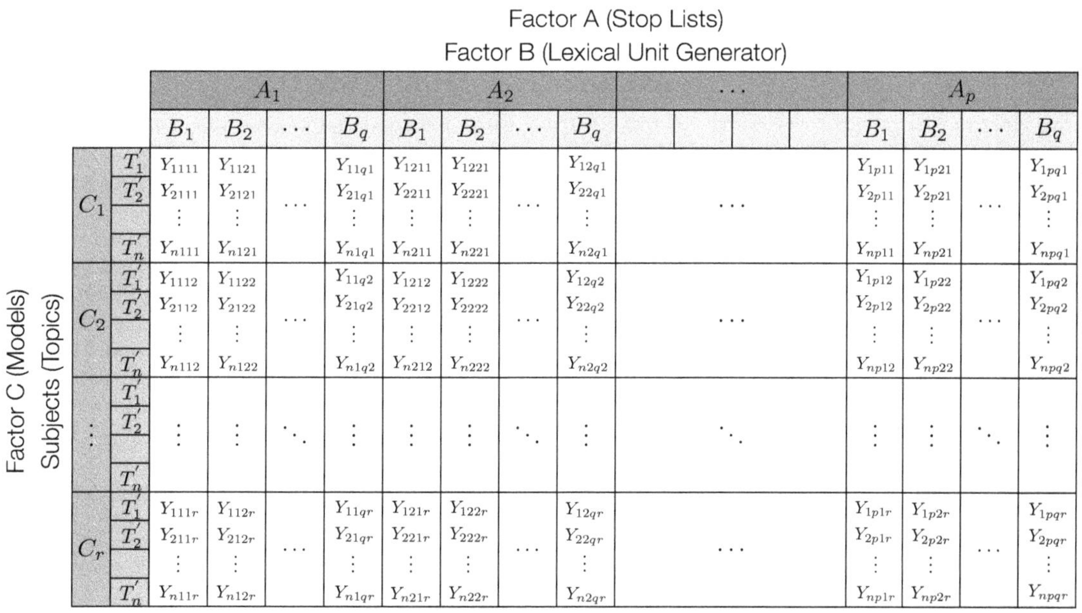

Figure 2: Three factors repeated measures design.

The estimators of the main effects can be derived by extension from those of the single factor design; for instance, the grand mean is $\hat{\mu}_{....} = \frac{1}{rqpn}\sum_{l=1}^{r}\sum_{k=1}^{q}\sum_{j=1}^{p}\sum_{i=1}^{n} Y_{ijkl}$, the mean of the k-th effect is $\hat{\mu}_{..k.} = \frac{1}{rpn}\sum_{l=1}^{r}\sum_{j=1}^{p}\sum_{i=1}^{n} Y_{ijkl}$ and its estimator is $\hat{\beta}_k = \hat{\mu}_{..k.} - \hat{\mu}_{....}$.

The estimators of the interaction factors are calculated as follows, let us consider $(\alpha\beta)_{jk}$:

$$\widehat{\alpha\beta}_{jk} = \hat{\mu}_{.jk.} - (\hat{\mu}_{....} + \hat{\alpha}_j + \hat{\beta}_k) \qquad (3.7)$$

where $\hat{\mu}_{.jk.} = \frac{1}{nr}\sum_{i=1}^{n}\sum_{l=1}^{r} Y_{ijkl}$; $\hat{\alpha}_j = \hat{\mu}_{.j..} - \hat{\mu}_{....}$; and, $\hat{\beta}_k = \hat{\mu}_{..k.} - \hat{\mu}_{....}$.

Similarly, we calculate the estimators for all the other interaction factors – i.e. $\widehat{\alpha\gamma}_{jl}$ and $\widehat{\beta\gamma}_{kl}$; $\widehat{\alpha\beta\gamma}_{jkl}$ is calculated by extending equation (3.7):

$$\widehat{\alpha\beta\gamma}_{jkl} = \hat{\mu}_{.jkl} - (\hat{\mu}_{....} + \hat{\alpha}_j + \hat{\beta}_k + \hat{\gamma}_l) \qquad (3.8)$$

where $\hat{\mu}_{.jkl} = \frac{1}{n}\sum_{i=1}^{n} Y_{ijkl}$ and $\hat{\gamma}_l = \hat{\mu}_{...l} - \hat{\mu}_{....}$.

In this design the error $\varepsilon_{ijkl} = Y_{ijkl} - \hat{Y}_{ijkl}$ contains the variance not explained by the main and interaction effects discussed above and it is composed by all the interactions of the subjects τ_j with the other factors in the model in addition to the uncontrolled sources of variance.

The sum of squares, mean squares and degrees of freedom of the main effects can be derived by extension form those of the one factor design. As an example, the degrees of freedom of factor A are $p-1$ and its sum of squares is:

$$SS_A = \sum_{l=1}^{r}\sum_{k=1}^{q}\sum_{j=1}^{p}\sum_{i=1}^{n} \hat{\alpha}_j^2 = rqn\sum_{j=1}^{p}(\hat{\mu}_{.j..} - \hat{\mu}_{....})^2$$

As an example of the computations for the interaction terms, we consider the term $A \times B$ whose degrees of freedom are $(p-1)(q-1)$ and whose sum of squares is:

$$SS_{A\times B} = \sum_{l=1}^{r}\sum_{k=1}^{q}\sum_{j=1}^{p}\sum_{i=1}^{n} \widehat{\alpha\beta}_{jk}^2$$

$$= rn\sum_{k=1}^{q}\sum_{j=1}^{p}(\hat{\mu}_{.jk.} - \hat{\mu}_{.j..} - \hat{\mu}_{..k.} + \hat{\mu}_{....})^2$$

As in the single factor design case, the mean squares of a factor (both main and interaction) are calculated by dividing its sum of squares by its degrees of freedom, the F-test is calculated with equation (3.3), the SOA measure with equation (3.4), and the power with equation (3.5).

4. EXPERIMENTATION AND DISCUSSION

We considered three main components of an IR system: stop list, LUG and IR model. We selected a set of alternative implementations of each component and by using the Terrier open source system we created a run for each system defined by combining the available components in all possible ways. The components we selected are:

stop list: nostop, indri, lucene, smart, terrier;

LUG: nolug, weak Porter, Porter, Krovetz, Lovins, 4grams, 5grams;

model: BB2, BM25, DFRBM25, DFRee, DLH, DLH13, DPH, HiemstraLM, IFB2, InL2, InexpB2, InexpC2, LGD, LemurTFIDF, PL2, TFIDF.

Note that the stemmers and n-grams of the LUG component are used as alternatives, this means that we end up with two distinct groups of runs, one using the stemmers and one using the n-grams; the `nolug` component is common to both these groups. The group using the stemmers defines a $5 \times 5 \times 16$ factorial design with a grid of points consisting of 400 runs; the group using the n-grams defines a $5 \times 3 \times 16$ factorial design with a grid of points consisting of 240 runs.

Table 1: Single factor, ANOVA table for TREC 08 (stemmer group) using AP.

Source	SS	DF	MS	F	p-value
Topics′	820.99	49	16.75	694.7235	0
Systems	36.44	399	0.09	7.4464	0
Error	88.20	19551	0.0045		
Total	945.63	19999			

We conducted single factor and three-factors ANOVA tests for both the groups on TREC 05, 06, and 08 collections, and by employing the following five measures: AP, P@10, nDCG@20, RBP and ERR@20. All the test collections are composed by 50 different topics and have binary relevance judgments; the corpus of TREC 05 is the TIPSTER disk 2 and 4 counting 525K documents, the corpus of TREC 06 is TIPSTER disk 4 and 5 counting 556K documents and the corpus of TREC 07 and 08 is the TIPSTER disk 4 and disk 5 (minus Congressional Record) counting 528K documents.

To ease reproducibility, the code for running the experiments is available at: http://gridofpoints.dei.unipd.it/.

4.1 Single Factor Repeated Measures Effects

We conducted 40 single factor ANOVA tests (4 collections × 5 measures × 2 run groups), so for space reasons we cannot report all the result; as an example, Table 1 reports the synthesis data of the ANOVA test for TREC 08 using the stemmer group of runs measured with AP.

From the sum of squares (SS) and the mean squares (MS), we can see that topics explain a large portion of the total variance. Nonetheless, the effect of the IR systems is statistically significant (p-value 0). We can also see that the sum of squares of the error is not negligible since it contains both the variance of the unexplained topics/systems interaction effect and the the other uncontrolled sources of variance. From this table we can calculate the statistical power of the experiment, which is 1 with a Type 1 error probability $\alpha = 0.05$, indicating that we are observing effects in a reliable way.

Table 2 reports the $\hat{\omega}^2_{\langle system \rangle}$ SOA measure and the p-value of the ANOVA test for the single factor models on all the test collections for all the considered evaluation measures. The "LUG" column indicates the runs group we are considering (stemmers or n-grams). This table shows that despite the high variance of the topics, the system effect sizes are generally large and this is consistent across all the collections and measures. Moreover, system effect sizes of stemmer runs group systems are large (> 0.14) for all the collections and measures with the solely exception of AP for TREC 05. Whereas, for the n-grams runs group we can see that the system effect sizes are consistently smaller than those of the stemmer group; this, supports the observation that "for English, n-grams indexing has no strong impact" [3].

Table 2 shows that measures impact on the amount of variance explained by the system effect. Generally, system effect sizes are higher when nDCG@20 is used, followed by RBP, P@10, AP and ERR@20. This could be related to two characteristics of the measures: their discriminative power and their user model. Indeed, if a measure is less discriminative than another one, it could be able to grasp less variance in the system effect; on the other hand, different user models mean looking at (very) different angles of system performances and this can change the explained variance.

To explore a bit this hypothesis, in Table 3 we report the discriminative power of the five considered measures over the test collections calculated by employing the paired bootstrap test defined in [19]. We can see that there is some agreement between the system effect sizes for a measure and its discriminative power; for instance, ERR@20 explains less system variance than the other measures and this can be explained by its discriminative power which is the lowest amongst all measures; similarly, RBP and nDCG@20 have both comparable discriminative power and close system effect sizes. The main exception is AP which typically has the highest discriminative power but the smallest system effect size; this could be due to the user model behind AP, which is quite different from the one of the other measures and may counterbalance the higher discriminative power leading to a final lower system effect size.

4.2 Three Factors Repeated Measures Effects

In Table 4 we report the ANOVA table of a three factors test for the stemmer group of runs on TREC 08 measured with AP.

We can see that the sum of squares of the topics is the same as the one determined with the single factor design, as well as the error and the total sum of squares. The main difference with the one factor design is that the variance of the systems is now decomposed into three main effects (stop list, stemmer and IR model) and four interaction effects. In this case all the main effects are statistically significant meaning that they have a role in explaining systems variance; in particular, the stop list explains more variance than the model and the stemmer is the component with the lowest impact in this design. Amongst the interaction effects, only the stoplist*model effect is significant explaining a tangible portion of the systems variance. The statistical power for the main effects is 0.97 for the stop list, 0.66 for the stemmer and 0.99 for the model with a Type 1 error probability $\alpha = 0.05$.

Table 5 reports the estimated ω^2 SoA for all the main and interaction effects and the p-values for all the ANOVA three-way tests we conducted; from this this table we can see that main and interaction effect sizes are consistent across the different collections.

Analyzing the main effect sizes reported in Table 5 we can see that for the stemmer group of runs the stop list has always a higher $\hat{\omega}^2$ than the IR model and the stemmer and, with the solely exceptions of TREC 05 for AP and ERR@20, the stop list has a medium effect size. Whereas, n-grams tend to reduce the stop list effect and to increase the IR model one; this can be also seen from the *n-grams**model* interaction effect which is small but statistically significant, differently from the *stemmer*model* effect which is never significant.

These observations cast a light on the importance of linguistic pre-processing and linguistic resources, given that the role of the stop list is significant in an IR system as well as choosing between stemmers or n-grams. We can further analyze these aspects by looking at Figure 3; the plot on the left reports the main effects for the TREC 08 stemmer group case and we show the marginal means (response means) described in Section 3.2 for the effect under investigation on the y-axis and the various components on the x-axis.

From the first plot we see that the presence or absence of a stop list affects the system performances because the line connecting "no stop" and "indri" is not horizontal, whereas

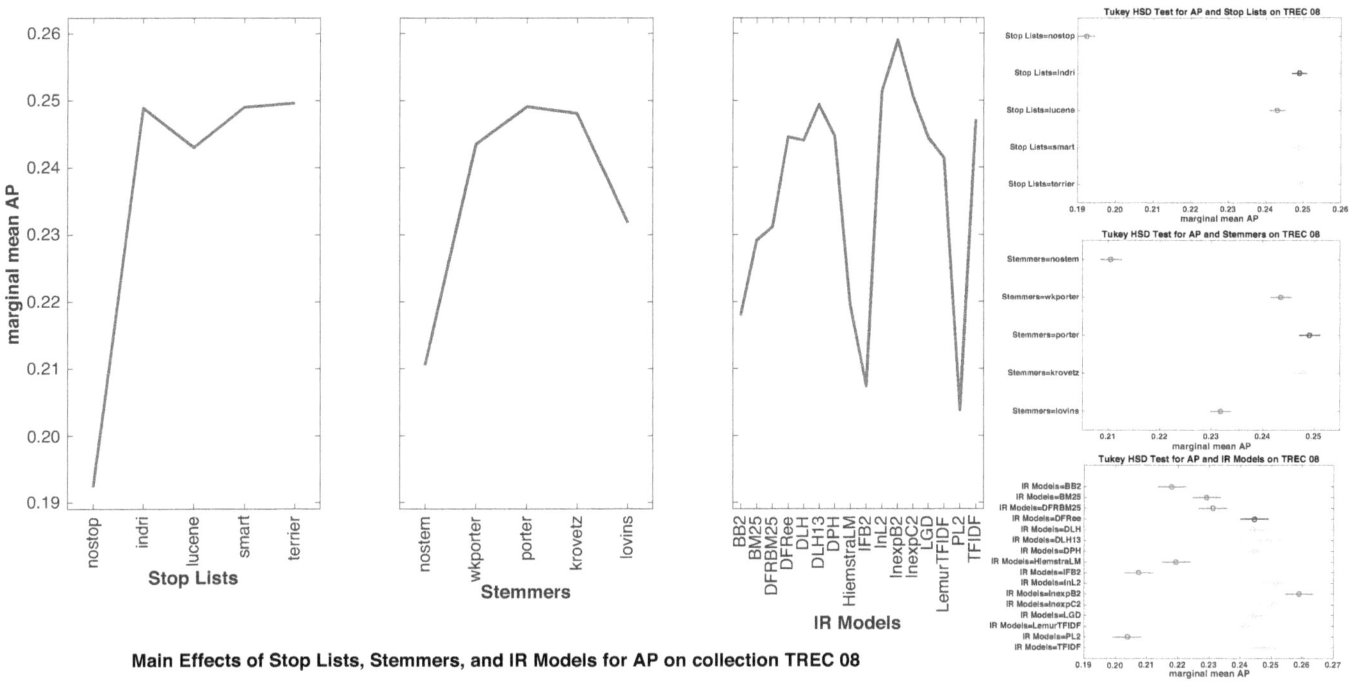

Figure 3: Main effects plots and Tukey HSD test plots for the stemmer group of runs on TREC 08 with AP.

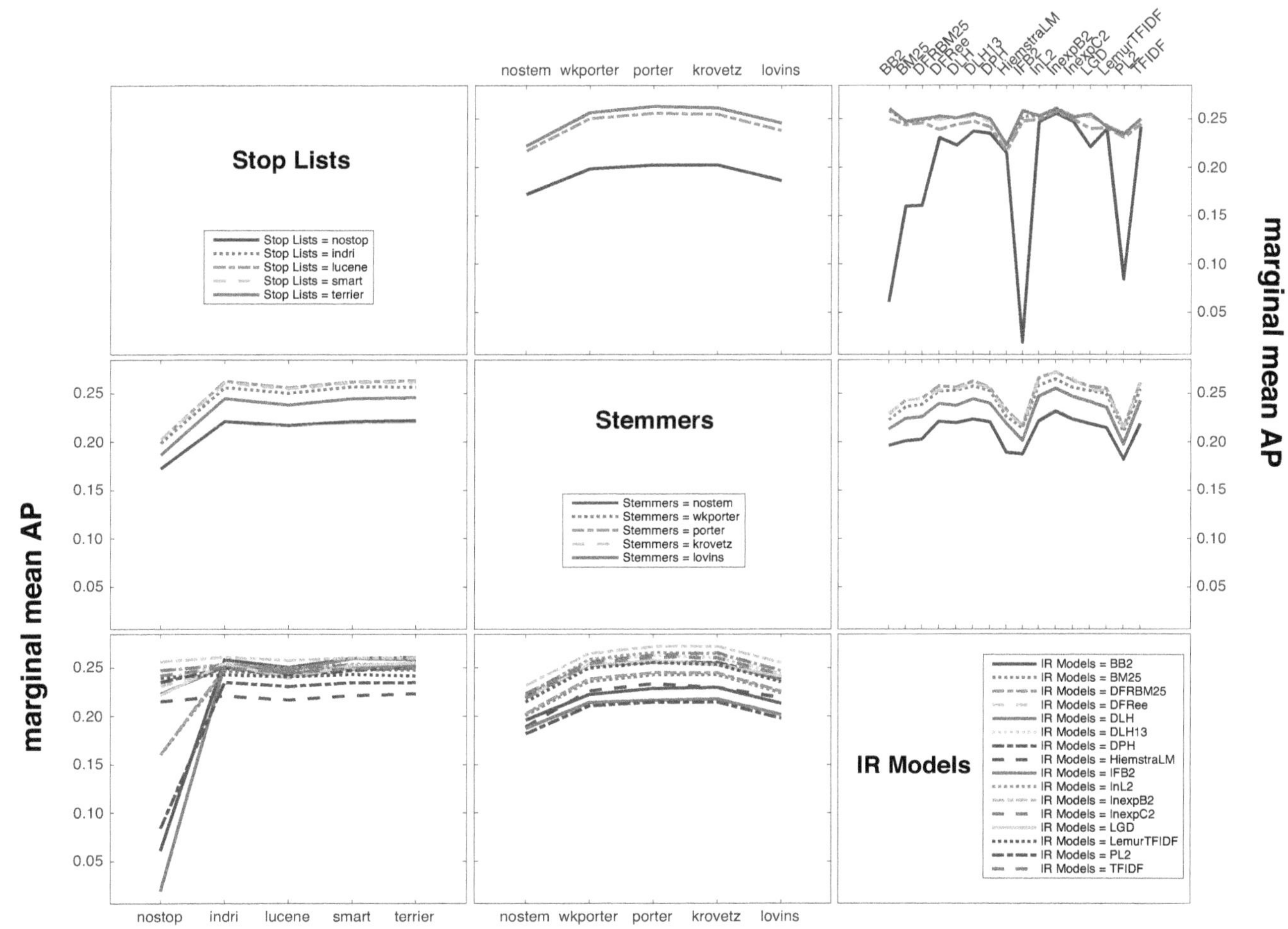

Figure 4: Interaction plots for the stemmer group of runs on TREC 08 with AP.

Table 2: Summary of single factor models on TREC collections. Each cell reports the $\hat{\omega}^2$ for the System effects and, within parentheses, the p-value for those effects. Large effect sizes ($\hat{\omega}^2_{\langle Systems \rangle} > 0.14$) are in bold.

Collection	LUG	Effects	AP	P@10	RBP	nDCG@20	ERR@20
TREC 05	Stemmers	$\hat{\omega}^2_{\langle \text{Systems} \rangle}$	0.1223 (0.00)	**0.2023** (0.00)	**0.1970** (0.00)	**0.1879** (0.00)	**0.1406** (0.00)
	n-grams	$\hat{\omega}^2_{\langle \text{Systems} \rangle}$	0.0794 (0.00)	0.1178 (0.00)	0.1349 (0.00)	0.1200 (0.00)	0.1063 (0.00)
TREC 06	Stemmers	$\hat{\omega}^2_{\langle \text{Systems} \rangle}$	**0.2108** (0.00)	**0.2458** (0.00)	**0.2716** (0.00)	**0.2742** (0.00)	**0.2377** (0.00)
	n-grams	$\hat{\omega}^2_{\langle \text{Systems} \rangle}$	0.1350 (0.00)	**0.1496** (0.00)	**0.1597** (0.00)	**0.1725** (0.00)	**0.1469** (0.00)
TREC 07	Stemmers	$\hat{\omega}^2_{\langle \text{Systems} \rangle}$	**0.2155** (0.00)	**0.2568** (0.00)	**0.2894** (0.00)	**0.2977** (0.00)	**0.2445** (0.00)
	n-grams	$\hat{\omega}^2_{\langle \text{Systems} \rangle}$	**0.1502** (0.00)	**0.1658** (0.00)	**0.1920** (0.00)	**0.1898** (0.00)	**0.1480** (0.00)
TREC 08	Stemmers	$\hat{\omega}^2_{\langle \text{Systems} \rangle}$	**0.2774** (0.00)	**0.2780** (0.00)	**0.3025** (0.00)	**0.3118** (0.00)	**0.2484** (0.00)
	n-grams	$\hat{\omega}^2_{\langle \text{Systems} \rangle}$	**0.1758** (0.00)	**0.1907** (0.00)	**0.2006** (0.00)	**0.2135** (0.00)	**0.1530** (0.00)

Table 3: Discriminative power of the evaluation measures on TREC 05, TREC 06, TREC 07 and TREC 08 for the stemmers and n-grams groups.

Group		TREC 05	TREC 06	TREC 07	TREC 08
stemmer	AP	3011	.2748	.3591	.4743
	P@10	.3774	.2687	.3222	.3171
	RBP	.3152	.2589	.3302	.3422
	nDCG@20	.3448	.2698	.3169	.3834
	ERR@20	.2014	.2235	.2096	.2388
n-grams	AP	.3180	.3553	.5184	.3498
	P@10	.3025	.2656	.3660	.2977
	RBP	.3852	.2539	.4193	.2797
	nDCG@20	.3260	.3130	.4292	.2938
	ERR@20	.2832	.1978	.2549	.2416

Table 4: Three factor, ANOVA table for TREC 08 (stemmer group) using AP.

Source	SS	DF	MS	F	p
Topics'	820.99	49	16.75	3713.90	0.00
Stop list	9.89	4	2.47	548.06	0.00
Stemmer	4.16	4	1.04	230.76	0.00
Model	5.16	15	0.3443	76.32	0.00
Stop list*Stemmer	0.05	16	0.03	0.67	0.83
Stop list*Model	17.01	60	0.28	62.84	0.00
Stemmer*Model	0.07	60	0.001	0.26	1.00
Stop list*Stemmer*Model	0.09	240	0.00	0.08	1.00
Error	88.20	19551	0.005		
Total	945.63	19999			

the lines connecting the different stop lists have much lower slope. In particular, we see that the choice of the stop list does not make a big difference with respect to use or not use a stop list; this can be further explored looking at the Tukey HSD test plot on the upper-right corner of the figure (in blue the selected component; in grey the components in the same group, i.e. not significantly different; in red the components in a different group, i.e. significantly different), where we can see that there are no significant differences between the "indri", "smart" and "terrier" stop lists, whereas the "lucene" stop list (which is composed by 15 words) is significantly different from the other three.

The main effect of the stemmer is always significant even though its size is quite small; nevertheless, the central plot of Figure 3 shows that there is a tangible difference between systems using or not using a stemmer. This can be seen also from the Tukey HSD test plot on the right; in particular, we can observe that there is no significant difference between the Porter and the Krovetz stemmer which are the stemmers with the highest impact on variance followed by the weak Porter and the Lovins ones.

Lastly, the plot on the right of Figure 3 reports the main effects of the IR models: they behave differently, as shown by several lines with high slopes, but the corresponding Tukey HSD shows that a many models are not significantly different one from the other. This can explain why the IR models effects are statistically significant but their effect sizes are not large.

For all the collections, consistently across the measures and both for the stemmer and the n-grams group, the higher effect size is reported by the *stop list*model* interaction effect which is always of medium or large size. This effect shows us that the variance of the systems is explained for the bigger part by the stop list and the model components. For the stemmer group of TREC 08, this can be seen in the plots on the upper-right and lower-left corners of Figure 4 where the lines of the interaction between the stop lists and the models intersect quite often. Indeed, the interaction plots show how the relationship between one factor and a response depends on the value of the second factor. These plots display means for the levels of one factor on the x-axis and a separate line for each level of another factor; if two lines (or segments) are parallel then no interaction occurs, if the lines are not parallel then an interaction occurs and the more nonparallel the lines are, the greater the strength of the interaction.

The *stop list*stemmer* interaction effects are always not significant as we can see from the p-values of Table 5 and the interaction plots in the upper-left part of Figure 4 where the line segments are parallel. A very similar trend can be observed for the *stemmer*model* interaction effect.

It is interesting to note that the second order interactions for the n-grams group are all statistically significant and that, in particular, we can see that n-grams, differently than the stemmers, have a bigger effect on the stop list than on the IR model.

We observe that different measures see the stop lists in a comparable way in terms of effect size and this is consistent with what we have seen in the one factor analysis. This is valid also for the stemmer, with the exception of ERR@20 for which it has an almost negligible effect size even though it is statistically significant. In Table 5 we can see that AP and ERR@20 weight the effects in a similar way as it happened in the single factor analysis reported in Table 2. For the n-grams group all the measures are comparable and ERR@20 is not as low as it happens for the stemmers.

Lastly, we can see that the third order interaction are never significant.

5. CONCLUSIONS AND FUTURE WORK

In this paper we faced the issue of how system variance contributes to the overall performances and how to break it down into some of the main components constituting an IR system. To this end, we developed an analysis methodology consisting of two elements: a *Grid of Points (GoP)* created on standard experimental collections, where all the combinations of system components under examination are considered; and, a GLMM model to decompose the contribution of these components to the overall system variance, paired with some graphical tools for easily assessing the main and interaction effects.

Collection	LUG	Effects	AP	P@10	RBP	nDCG@20	ERR@20
TREC 05	Stemmers	$\omega^2_{\langle \text{Stop Lists} \rangle}$	0.0432 (0.00)	**0.0632** (0.00)	**0.0638** (0.00)	**0.0605** (0.00)	0.0476 (0.00)
		$\omega^2_{\langle \text{Stemmers} \rangle}$	0.0178 (0.00)	0.0217 (0.00)	0.0116 (0.00)	0.0188 (0.00)	0.0000 (0.00)
		$\omega^2_{\langle \text{IR Models} \rangle}$	0.0219 (0.00)	0.0458 (0.00)	0.0452 (0.00)	0.0409 (0.00)	0.0311 (0.00)
		$\omega^2_{\langle \text{Stop Lists} \times \text{Stemmers} \rangle}$	-0.0005 (0.98)	-0.00 (0.46)	-0.0004 (0.97)	-0.0004 (0.94)	-0.0005 (0.99)
		$\omega^2_{\langle \text{Stop Lists} \times \text{IR Models} \rangle}$	**0.0632** (0.00)	**0.1118** (0.00)	**0.1145** (0.00)	**0.1047** (0.00)	0.0826 (0.00)
		$\omega^2_{\langle \text{Stemmers} \times \text{IR Models} \rangle}$	-0.0019 (1.00)	-0.00 (0.49)	-0.00 (0.48)	-0.0008 (0.95)	0.0009 (0.05)
		$\omega^2_{\langle \text{Stop Lists} \times \text{Stemmers} \times \text{IR Models} \rangle}$	-0.0115 (1.00)	-0.0099 (1.00)	-0.0109 (1.00)	-0.0107 (1.00)	-0.0102 (1.00)
	n-grams	$\omega^2_{\langle \text{Stop Lists} \rangle}$	0.0165 (0.00)	0.0272 (0.00)	0.0288 (0.00)	0.0256 (0.00)	0.0225 (0.00)
		$\omega^2_{\langle n\text{-grams} \rangle}$	0.0170 (0.00)	0.0105 (0.00)	0.0211 (0.00)	0.0288 (0.00)	0.0188 (0.00)
		$\omega^2_{\langle \text{IR Models} \rangle}$	0.0208 (0.00)	0.0341 (0.00)	0.0391 (0.00)	0.0275 (0.00)	0.0308 (0.00)
		$\omega^2_{\langle \text{Stop Lists} \times n\text{-grams} \rangle}$	0.0016 (0.00)	0.0015 (0.00)	0.0020 (0.00)	0.0019 (0.00)	0.0015 (0.00)
		$\omega^2_{\langle \text{Stop Lists} \times \text{IR Models} \rangle}$	0.0296 (0.00)	0.0544 (0.00)	0.0571 (0.00)	0.0483 (0.00)	0.0424 (0.00)
		$\omega^2_{\langle n\text{-grams} \times \text{IR Models} \rangle}$	0.0050 (0.00)	0.0047 (0.00)	0.0049 (0.00)	0.0050 (0.00)	0.0040 (0.00)
		$\omega^2_{\langle \text{Stop Lists} \times n\text{-grams} \times \text{IR Models} \rangle}$	-0.0063 (1.00)	-0.0040 (0.99)	-0.0034 (0.99)	-0.0056 (1.00)	-0.0048 (1.00)
TREC 06	Stemmers	$\omega^2_{\langle \text{Stop Lists} \rangle}$	**0.0750** (0.00)	**0.0852** (0.00)	**0.0904** (0.00)	**0.0932** (0.00)	**0.0673** (0.00)
		$\omega^2_{\langle \text{Stemmers} \rangle}$	0.0112 (0.00)	0.0082 (0.00)	0.0068 (0.00)	0.0126 (0.00)	0.0015 (0.00)
		$\omega^2_{\langle \text{IR Models} \rangle}$	0.0557 (0.00)	0.0596 (0.00)	**0.0692** (0.00)	**0.0696** (0.00)	**0.0638** (0.00)
		$\omega^2_{\langle \text{Stop Lists} \times \text{Stemmers} \rangle}$	-0.0007 (1.00)	-0.0007 (0.99)	-0.0007 (0.99)	-0.0004 (0.94)	-0.0001 (0.64)
		$\omega^2_{\langle \text{Stop Lists} \times \text{IR Models} \rangle}$	**0.1153** (0.00)	**0.1483** (0.00)	**0.1709** (0.00)	**0.1671** (0.00)	**0.1539** (0.00)
		$\omega^2_{\langle \text{Stemmers} \times \text{IR Models} \rangle}$	-0.0020 (1.00)	-0.0016 (0.99)	-0.0017 (1.00)	-0.0017 (1.00)	-0.0013 (0.99)
		$\omega^2_{\langle \text{Stop Lists} \times \text{Stemmers} \times \text{IR Models} \rangle}$	-0.0119 (1.00)	-0.0109 (1.00)	-0.0116 (1.00)	-0.0112 (1.00)	-0.0107 (1.00)
	n-grams	$\omega^2_{\langle \text{Stop Lists} \rangle}$	0.0241 (0.00)	0.0282 (0.00)	0.0305 (0.00)	0.0306 (0.00)	0.0296 (0.00)
		$\omega^2_{\langle n\text{-grams} \rangle}$	0.0340 (0.00)	0.0144 (0.00)	0.0126 (0.00)	0.0249 (0.00)	0.0104 (0.00)
		$\omega^2_{\langle \text{IR Models} \rangle}$	0.0404 (0.00)	0.0516 (0.00)	0.0563 (0.00)	0.0545 (0.00)	0.0494 (0.00)
		$\omega^2_{\langle \text{Stop Lists} \times n\text{-grams} \rangle}$	0.0026 (0.00)	0.0034 (0.00)	0.0036 (0.00)	0.0033 (0.00)	0.0032 (0.00)
		$\omega^2_{\langle \text{Stop Lists} \times \text{IR Models} \rangle}$	0.0465 (0.00)	**0.0628** (0.00)	**0.0673** (0.00)	**0.0746** (0.00)	**0.0646** (0.00)
		$\omega^2_{\langle n\text{-grams} \times \text{IR Models} \rangle}$	0.0058 (0.00)	0.0091 (0.00)	0.0111 (0.00)	0.0093 (0.00)	0.0080 (0.00)
		$\omega^2_{\langle \text{Stop Lists} \times n\text{-grams} \times \text{IR Models} \rangle}$	-0.0033 (0.99)	-0.0019 (0.94)	-0.0008 (0.72)	0.0004 (0.36)	-0.0010 (0.78)
TREC 07	Stemmers	$\omega^2_{\langle \text{Stop Lists} \rangle}$	**0.0747** (0.00)	**0.0830** (0.00)	**0.0997** (0.00)	**0.1023** (0.00)	**0.0802** (0.00)
		$\omega^2_{\langle \text{Stemmers} \rangle}$	0.0227 (0.00)	0.0157 (0.00)	0.0163 (0.00)	0.0146 (0.00)	0.0056 (0.00)
		$\omega^2_{\langle \text{IR Models} \rangle}$	0.0441 (0.00)	0.0525 (0.00)	**0.0601** (0.00)	**0.0653** (0.00)	0.0513 (0.00)
		$\omega^2_{\langle \text{Stop Lists} \times \text{Stemmers} \rangle}$	0.0001 (0.36)	0.0009 (0.00)	0.0004 (0.09)	0.0004 (0.08)	0.0002 (0.21)
		$\omega^2_{\langle \text{Stop Lists} \times \text{IR Models} \rangle}$	**0.1209** (0.00)	**0.1624** (0.00)	**0.1856** (0.00)	**0.1919** (0.00)	**0.1571** (0.00)
		$\omega^2_{\langle \text{Stemmers} \times \text{IR Models} \rangle}$	-0.0018 (1.00)	-0.0009 (0.95)	-0.0014 (0.99)	-0.0018 (1.00)	0.0007 (0.12)
		$\omega^2_{\langle \text{Stop Lists} \times \text{Stemmers} \times \text{IR Models} \rangle}$	-0.0113 (1.00)	-0.0103 (1.00)	-0.0111 (1.00)	-0.0110 (1.00)	-0.0107 (1.00)
	n-grams	$\omega^2_{\langle \text{Stop Lists} \rangle}$	0.0237 (0.00)	0.0344 (0.00)	0.0395 (0.00)	0.0362 (0.00)	0.0290 (0.00)
		$\omega^2_{\langle n\text{-grams} \rangle}$	0.0208 (0.00)	0.0059 (0.00)	0.0132 (0.00)	0.0154 (0.00)	0.0112 (0.00)
		$\omega^2_{\langle \text{IR Models} \rangle}$	0.0563 (0.00)	0.0552 (0.00)	**0.0623** (0.00)	**0.0663** (0.00)	0.0382 (0.00)
		$\omega^2_{\langle \text{Stop Lists} \times n\text{-grams} \rangle}$	0.00 (0.0001)	0.0014 (0.00)	0.0023 (0.00)	0.0025 (0.00)	0.0017 (0.00)
		$\omega^2_{\langle \text{Stop Lists} \times \text{IR Models} \rangle}$	0.0517 (0.00)	**0.0818** (0.00)	**0.0958** (0.00)	**0.0874** (0.00)	**0.0793** (0.00)
		$\omega^2_{\langle n\text{-grams} \times \text{IR Models} \rangle}$	0.0200 (0.00)	0.0126 (0.00)	0.0116 (0.00)	0.0145 (0.00)	0.0082 (0.00)
		$\omega^2_{\langle \text{Stop Lists} \times n\text{-grams} \times \text{IR Models} \rangle}$	-0.0055 (1.00)	-0.0044 (1.00)	-0.0031 (0.99)	-0.0030 (0.99)	-0.0034 (0.99)
TREC 08	Stemmers	$\omega^2_{\langle \text{Stop Lists} \rangle}$	**0.0986** (0.00)	**0.0913** (0.00)	**0.1000** (0.00)	**0.1006** (0.00)	**0.0799** (0.00)
		$\omega^2_{\langle \text{Stemmers} \rangle}$	0.0439 (0.00)	0.0165 (0.00)	0.0190 (0.00)	0.0268 (0.00)	0.0071 (0.00)
		$\omega^2_{\langle \text{IR Models} \rangle}$	0.0535 (0.00)	**0.0615** (0.00)	**0.0666** (0.00)	**0.0707** (0.00)	0.0521 (0.00)
		$\omega^2_{\langle \text{Stop Lists} \times \text{Stemmers} \rangle}$	-0.0003 (0.83)	-0.0005 (0.98)	-0.0005 (0.98)	-0.0006 (0.99)	-0.0004 (0.95)
		$\omega^2_{\langle \text{Stop Lists} \times \text{IR Models} \rangle}$	**0.1565** (0.00)	**0.1765** (0.00)	**0.1969** (0.00)	**0.2006** (0.00)	**0.1622** (0.00)
		$\omega^2_{\langle \text{Stemmers} \times \text{IR Models} \rangle}$	-0.0022 (1.00)	-0.0014 (0.99)	-0.0020 (1.00)	-0.0018 (1.00)	-0.0016 (0.99)
		$\omega^2_{\langle \text{Stop Lists} \times \text{Stemmers} \times \text{IR Models} \rangle}$	-0.0111 (1.00)	-0.0105 (1.00)	-0.0110 (1.00)	-0.0110 (1.00)	-0.0102 (1.00)
	n-grams	$\omega^2_{\langle \text{Stop Lists} \rangle}$	0.0396 (0.00)	0.0423 (0.00)	0.0445 (0.00)	0.0479 (0.00)	0.0304 (0.00)
		$\omega^2_{\langle n\text{-grams} \rangle}$	0.0037 (0.00)	0.0031 (0.00)	0.0008 (0.00)	0.0023 (0.00)	0.0093 (0.00)
		$\omega^2_{\langle \text{IR Models} \rangle}$	0.0550 (0.00)	0.0545 (0.00)	0.0548 (0.00)	**0.0637** (0.00)	0.0307 (0.00)
		$\omega^2_{\langle \text{Stop Lists} \times n\text{-grams} \rangle}$	0.0035 (0.00)	0.0023 (0.00)	0.0024 (0.00)	0.0029 (0.00)	0.0032 (0.00)
		$\omega^2_{\langle \text{Stop Lists} \times \text{IR Models} \rangle}$	**0.0928** (0.00)	**0.1129** (0.00)	**0.1231** (0.00)	**0.1277** (0.00)	**0.0940** (0.00)
		$\omega^2_{\langle n\text{-grams} \times \text{IR Models} \rangle}$	0.0080 (0.00)	0.0050 (0.00)	0.0059 (0.00)	0.0050 (0.00)	0.0040 (0.00)
		$\omega^2_{\langle \text{Stop Lists} \times n\text{-grams} \times \text{IR Models} \rangle}$	-0.0038 (0.99)	-0.0040 (0.99)	-0.0032 (0.99)	-0.0034 (0.99)	-0.0028 (0.99)

Table 5: Summary of three factor models on the TREC Ad-hoc collections. Each cell reports the estimated ω^2 SoA for the specified effects and, within parentheses, the p-value for those effects. Medium and large effect sizes are in bold; not significant effects are highlighted.

We conducted a thorough experimentation on TREC collections and used different evaluation measures to show how the proposed approach works and to gain insights on the considered components, i.e. stop lists, stemmers and n-grams, and IR models.

We found that the most prominent effects are those of stop lists and IR models, as well as their interactions, while stemmers and n-grams play a smaller role. Moreover, we have seen that stemmers produce more variation on system performances than n-grams. Overall, this highlights importance of linguistic resources.

Finally, measures explain system and component effects differently one from the other and not all the measures seem to be suitable for all the cases as it happens for ERR@20 which almost does not detect the stemmer effect. These insights can be useful to understand where to invest effort and resources for improving components, since they give us an idea of the actual impact of a family of components on the overall performances.

As far as future work is concerned, we plan to extend the proposed methodology in order to be able to capture also interaction between topics/systems and topics/components. Indeed, to estimate interaction effects, more replicates would be needed for each (topic, system) pair, as [17] simulated, and they are not possible in the present settings, since running more than once the same system on the same topics produces exactly the same results.

Moreover, we plan to further investigate the impact of the measures on the determination of effect sizes. A possible approach could be to conduct a four-factor analysis, using measures as additional factor. However, even if the measure scores are normalized in the range $[0, 1]$, they do not mean the exactly the same thing, i.e. $\text{AP} = 0.20$ is not exactly the same as $\text{ERR} = 0.20$ because of their different user models. A possibility for smoothing these differences and make the scores more directly comparable could be to normalize them by the maximum value achieved on the dataset, thus reasoning in term of ratios.

Lastly, an open challenge is how to run this kind of analysis on the systems which participated to past TREC editions. A first obstacle is that often there is no precise description of all the components used in these systems and so their metadata should be enriched in the way we suggested in [5]. A second obstacle is that the GoP would be very sparse and many combinations would be missing; therefore, we would need to rely on unbalanced GLMM and, probably, to consider the components as random factors.

6. REFERENCES

[1] D. Banks, P. Over, and N.-F. Zhang. Blind Men and Elephants: Six Approaches to TREC data. *Information Retrieval*, 1:7–34, May 1999.

[2] L. Boytsov, A. Belova, and P. Westfall. Deciding on an Adjustment for Multiplicity in IR Experiments. In *SIGIR 2013*, pp. 403–412, 2013.

[3] S. Büttcher, C. L. A. Clarke, and G. V. Cormack. *Information Retrieval: Implementing and Evaluating Search Engines*. The MIT Press, USA, 2010.

[4] B. A. Carterette. Multiple Testing in Statistical Analysis of Systems-Based Information Retrieval Experiments. *ACM TOIS*, 30(1):4:1–4:34, 2012.

[5] E. Di Buccio, G. M. Di Nunzio, N. Ferro, D. K. Harman, M. Maistro, and G. Silvello. Unfolding Off-the-shelf IR Systems for Reproducibility. In *SIGIR RIGOR 2015*, 2015.

[6] N. Ferro, R. Berendsen, A. Hanbury, M. Lupu, V. Petras, M. de Rijke, and G. Silvello. PROMISE Retreat Report – Prospects and Opportunities for Information Access Evaluation. *SIGIR Forum*, 46(2):60–84, 2012.

[7] N. Ferro and D. Harman. CLEF 2009: Grid@CLEF Pilot Track Overview. In *CLEF 2009*, pp. 552–565. LNCS 6241, 2010.

[8] A. Hanbury and H. Müller. Automated Component-Level Evaluation: Present and Future. In *CLEF 2010*, pp. 124–135. LNCS 6360, 2010.

[9] D. A. Hull. Using Statistical Testing in the Evaluation of Retrieval Experiments. In *SIGIR 1993*, pp. 329–338, 1993.

[10] G. K. Jayasinghe, W. Webber, M. Sanderson, L. S. Dharmasena, and J. S. Culpepper. Statistical comparisons of non-deterministic IR systems using two dimensional variance. *IPM*, 51(5):677–694, 2015.

[11] J. Lin, M. Crane, A. Trotman, J. Callan, I. Chattopadhyaya, J. Foley, G. Ingersoll, C. Macdonald, and S. Vigna. Toward Reproducible Baselines: The Open-Source IR Reproducibility Challenge. In *ECIR 2016*, pp. 357–368. LNCS 9626, 2016.

[12] C. Macdonald, R. McCreadie, R. L. T. Santos, and I. Ounis. From Puppy to Maturity: Experiences in Developing Terrier. *OSIR at SIGIR*, pp. 60–63, 2012.

[13] S. Maxwell and H. D. Delaney. *Designing Experiments and Analyzing Data. A Model Comparison Perspective.* Lawrence Erlbaum Associates, 2nd ed, 2004.

[14] K. R. Murphy and B. Myors. *Statistical power analysis: A Simple and General Model for Traditional and Modern Hypothesis Tests (2nd ed.)*. Lawrence Erlbaum, 2004.

[15] S. Olejnik and J. Algina. Generalized Eta and Omega Squared Statistics: Measures of Effect Size for Some Common Research Designs. *Psychological Methods*, 8(4):434–447, 2003.

[16] S. E. Robertson. The methodology of information retrieval experiment. In *Information Retrieval Experiment*, pp. 9–31. Butterworths, 1981.

[17] S. E. Robertson and E. Kanoulas. On Per-topic Variance in IR Evaluation. In *SIGIR 2012*, pp. 891–900, 2012.

[18] A. Rutherford. *ANOVA and ANCOVA. A GLM Approach.* John Wiley & Sons, 2nd ed, 2011.

[19] T. Sakai. Evaluating Evaluation Metrics based on the Bootstrap. In *SIGIR 2006*, pp. 525–532, 2006.

[20] T. Sakai. Statistical reform in information retrieval? *SIGIR Forum*, 48(1):3–12, 2014.

[21] J. Savoy. Statistical Inference in Retrieval Effectiveness Evaluation. *IPM*, 33(44):495–512, 1997.

[22] M. D. Smucker, J. Allan, and B. A. Carterette. A Comparison of Statistical Significance Tests for Information Retrieval Evaluation. In *CIKM 2007*, pp. 623–632, 2007.

[23] J. M. Tague-Sutcliffe and J. Blustein. A Statistical Analysis of the TREC-3 Data. In *Overview of TREC-3*, pp. 385–398. NIST, SP 500-225, 1994.

[24] A. Trotman, C. L. A. Clarke, I. Ounis, J. S. Culpepper, M.-A. Cartright, and S. Geva. Open Source Information Retrieval: a Report on the SIGIR 2012 Workshop. *ACM SIGIR Forum*, 46(2):95–101, 2012.

[25] L. Wang, P. N. Bennett, and K. Collins-Thompson. Robust Ranking Models via Risk-Sensitive Optimization. In *SIGIR 2012*, pp. 761–770, 2012.

[26] W. Webber, A. Moffat, and J. Zobel. Score Standardization for Inter-Collection Comparison of Retrieval Systems. In *SIGIR 2008*, pp. 51–58, 2008.

[27] W. J. Wilbur. Non-parametric significance tests of retrieval performance comparisons. *J. Inf. Science*, 20(4):270–284, 1994.

[28] P. Zhang, S. Dawei, J. Wang, and Y. Hou. Bias–variance analysis in estimating true query model for information retrieval. *IPM*, 50(1):199–217, 2014.

Searching by Talking: Analysis of Voice Queries on Mobile Web Search

Ido Guy
Information Systems Engineering Department
Ben Gurion University of the Negev, Beer Sheva, Israel
Yahoo Research, Haifa, Israel
idoguy@acm.org

ABSTRACT

The growing popularity of mobile search and the advancement in voice recognition technologies have opened the door for web search users to speak their queries, rather than type them. While this kind of voice search is still in its infancy, it is gradually becoming more widespread. In this paper, we examine the logs of a commercial search engine's mobile interface, and compare the spoken queries to the typed-in queries. We place special emphasis on the semantic and syntactic characteristics of the two types of queries. We also conduct an empirical evaluation showing that the language of voice queries is closer to natural language than typed queries. Our analysis reveals further differences between voice and text search, which have implications for the design of future voice-enabled search tools.

Keywords: mobile search; spoken queries; voice search

1. INTRODUCTION

The popularity of search from mobile devices (*mobile search*) has rapidly increased in recent years [34]. In fact, the number of mobile queries has already exceeded the number of those submitted from desktop devices in the United States and other countries [32]. A prominent characteristic of the advancement in mobile search is the emergence of *voice search*, allowing users to input queries in a spoken language and then retrieve the relevant entries based on system-generated transcriptions of the voice queries [19]. Recent developments in speech recognition, backed by high bandwidth coverage and high-quality speech signal acquisition, are enabling higher quality voice search [8]. Already in 2010, Google presented a case study stating that their goal is to make voice search ubiquitously available and that a level of performance was achieved such that usage is growing [30]. Since then, further enhancements to automatic speech recognition (ASR) for web search have been reported [31, 43], taking advantage of the large data that started to accumulate on voice search logs [8], and applying advanced learning methods [17]. The use of voice has also been promoted by the increasing popularity of voice-activated intelligent assistants, such as Siri, Google Now, and Cortana. These assistants provide context-based query-less personalized advice for mobile users, but also enable web search [18]. A recent survey of 1400 U.S. smartphone users found that 55% of the teenagers use voice search every day [3, 14]. It is therefore becoming important for information retrieval researchers and practitioners to understand this new medium of search and its differences from traditional *text search*.

Using voice as a means to search holds various potential advantages. Although typing usability has improved in recent years, querying by voice is still likely to be substantially easier and faster for the vast majority of mobile users. For users with visual or manual impairment, or with limited literacy skills, voice search may break down the entry barrier into web search. In addition, as searching by voice does not require visual attention or the use of hands, it can be performed in situations such as driving, cooking, or exercising, where typed search might be especially cumbersome, error-prone, and even dangerous. In the aforementioned survey, 78% of the teens who used voice search pointed out its usefulness for multitasking as a key motivating factor [14].

In spite of its growing popularity, the area of voice search has not received much attention in the IR literature. Early work compared voice and text queries in a laboratory study, however these did not represent typical web search queries, but rather complex long questions [10]. More recent work has mostly focused on voice recognition [1, 8, 27, 31, 38, 43] and query reformulation [3, 19, 33]. A few studies revealed more details about how voice search is performed on commercial search engines [30, 40], however we are not aware of a systematic log analysis of voice queries as of yet.

In this work, we perform a query log analysis of half a million voice queries, issued to the mobile application of a commercial web search engine, over a period of six months. The log includes English-only queries, from the United States, transcribed from voice to text using high-quality ASR. We compare the voice queries with a similar-size sample of mobile text queries, typed on the same mobile application. Our comparison inspects characteristics of context, clicks, sessions, and, primarily, the query text itself. We examine both semantic and syntactic features and compare them for voice versus text queries. In the final part of our analysis, we directly compare the similarity of the voice and text query language to natural language corpora, which include traditional news articles and the titles of questions in a large community question answering (CQA) website.

SIGIR '16, July 17-21, 2016, Pisa, Italy

DOI: http://dx.doi.org/10.1145/2911451.2911525

Our work has the following key contributions:

- To the best of our knowledge, we present the most comprehensive analysis of a web search engine voice query log.
- We combine a semantic analysis using novel methods, such as analyzing a broad set of triggered cards, with an in-depth syntactic analysis, to shed more light on the common and different between voice and text queries.
- We provide empirical evidence, based on language modeling, that voice queries are closer to natural language than text queries, yet are still distant from natural question language.

Our findings suggest different ways for search systems to enhance their support and take advantage of the unique characteristics of voice queries. We conclude the paper by summarizing the key findings and discussing their implications and future research directions.

2. RELATED WORK

Studies of mobile query log analysis have been published throughout the past decade, ever since mobile devices became ubiquitous. One of the early studies [20] compared search patterns on 12-key keypad cellphones, PDAs, and desktop (PC) computers. It found that the diversity of queries on mobile was substantially lower than on desktop and that the most popular query in each of the three device types was different. Baeza-Yates et al. [4] compared mobile and desktop search queries on Yahoo Japan and found that mobile queries included fewer characters, more queries in the Business category, and fewer in Art. Yi et al. [41] performed a large-scale query log analysis of the Yahoo OneSearch mobile service, and found that mobile query patterns were dynamic, as users were exploring how to use the devices. With the evolution of mobile devices into smartphones, mobile search has also been shown to change. Kamvar et al. [21] examined search behavior on iPhones and found it was more similar to desktop search than to search on basic mobile phones. Song et al. [34] performed a broad 3-month log analysis of Bing search on desktop, iPad, and iPhone. Due to the significant differences between user search patterns on the three platforms, they proposed a ranking system that considered platform-specific features.

With the advancement of speech recognition technologies, studies of mobile search using voice started to emerge. Many of the studies focused on voice recognition challenges. Wang et al. [38] defined voice search as *"the technology underlying many spoken dialog systems that provide users with the information they request with a spoken query"*, and reviewed key challenges, such as environmental noise, pronunciation variance, and linguistic issues. Acero et al. [1] described the architecture of the speech recognition interface of "Live Search for Mobile". Moreno-Daniel et al. [27] discussed the interleaving of ASR with IR systems and suggested to combine acoustic and semantic models to enhance performance. In recent years, alongside the enhancement of ASR technologies with deep learning [17], various studies suggested advanced methods for voice search ASR and reported further performance enhancements. Chelba et al. [8] leveraged the data on Google's voice search logs to enhance language modeling and achieved *"small but significant"* gains in speech recognition performance. Shan et al. [31] described a system for Mandarin Chinese voice search and reported *"excellent performance on typical spoken search queries under a variety of accents and acoustic conditions."* Zweig and Chang [43] found that the use of Model M (exponential n-gram language model) with personalization features improved the speech recognition performance on Bing voice search. In this work, we take advantage of the advancement in speech recognition, to explore a high-quality transcribed query log, but do not delve into speech recognition aspects.

Some of the recent work has focused on voice query reformulation, showing that users sometimes respond to voice recognition errors by different reformulation patterns, such as repeating a query or refining it [19]. Classifiers were built to predict and categorize voice reformulations, extending text-based approaches with features such as voice recognition time and confidence [3]. Researchers also found that users do not tend to switch between voice and text when reformulating queries [33]. While our study does not focus on query reformulation, we report related statistics for voice versus text queries in our session analysis.

Most closely-related to our research are three studies that directly referred to the comparison between voice and text queries. The first described a case study of the development of "Google Search by Voice" [30]. While most of the report is focused on describing the technology and the evaluation of the voice recognition component, a section is dedicated to evaluating the user experience based on a 4-week query log analysis. It was found that the query categories "food & drink" and "local" (e.g., place names or business listings) were more popular with voice searches. Also, short queries, in particular 1- and 2-word queries, were relatively more frequent in voice searches than in typed searches, while longer queries (5+ words) were far rarer. A poster by Yi and Maghoul [40] inspected the change in mobile search on Yahoo from 2007 to 2010 and provided a short comparison of 79K voice queries to typed mobile and desktop queries, which examined query length and categories. The most comprehensive comparison between voice and text queries was performed in a lab study from a decade ago (pre-smartphone era) [10]. The 12 participants were students from the local research lab, as voice search was in its infancy and required IR experience. They were asked to formulate 10 TREC topics as queries in a process that took 1 to 3 minutes per query. The resulting queries did not reflect typical web queries and were complex and long (23.1 words for an average voice query, 9.5 for text). Moreover, the study did not involve a search system and participants were not exposed to search results. In addition to query characteristics, such as length and typing duration, the retrieval effectiveness of typed versus spoken queries was evaluated. In our analysis, when relevant, we tie to the results reported in these three studies and discuss the common and different with our own findings.

3. RESEARCH SETTINGS

Our analysis is based on a random sample of 500,000 queries from the Yahoo mobile search application, performed by over 50,000 unique users of the voice interface along a period of exactly six months (April-October 2015) in the United States. The mobile search application transcribes a voice query into a text query using state-of-the-art ASR, and from this point onward treats it as a text query. In other words, the multi-modal interface allows inputting queries by voice, but returns results using the same information retrieval techniques and the standard mobile search user interface. For comparison, we collected an identical number of queries performed using the "regular" keyboard-based interface of the same mobile application. We refer to the former set of queries as *voice queries* and to the latter as *text queries*. The text queries were collected along the same period of six months for a similar number of users. Moreover, we sampled an identical number of voice and text queries in each day of the experimental period. When inspecting day-of-week distribution and session statistics, we compared all queries from all users in our voice sample with all queries from all users in our text sample, during two months of the experimental period, to allow suitable analysis.

Each query in the log, either voice or text, included, in addition to the query itself, a timestamp (adapted to the timezone in which it was performed), a location in the form of city and state, and, for logged-in users, the user's age and gender. In addition, for each query we had information about its associated clicks, if any were performed, including the corresponding URLs and ranks within the search results page (SERP).

Our analysis is organized as follows. Section 4 compares basic characteristics of voice and text queries, including context, query length, and session characteristics. Section 5 examines the query semantics by inspecting different categories as well as specific queries and terms. Section 6 looks into click behavior and distribution of clicked domains, reflecting on the findings in the query semantics analysis. Section 7 examines query syntax as reflected in characteristics of parsing and distribution of part-of-speech tags. The semantic and syntactic analyses reveal various differences between voice and text queries, of which many indicate that voice queries are phrased closer to natural language than text queries. The final part of our evaluation therefore explicitly compares the similarity of both types of queries to natural language corpora, and is described in Section 8.

4. BASIC CHARACTERISTICS

In this section, we compare basic characteristics of voice and text queries, including context aspects, basic query features, and session characteristics.

4.1 Context

We found similar contextual characteristics for voice and text queries in terms of searcher's age and geography (cities and states). There was a slight tendency towards male searchers in the voice log compared to the text log (up 3%).

The distribution across day-of-week was similar for voice and text queries: in both, there was a slight peak on weekends compared to weekdays (5% more searches on average). In contrast, there was a noticeable difference between voice and text queries with regards to time-of-day, as depicted in Figure 1. Voice queries were more frequent during day hours (from 8am to 8pm), while higher portions of the text queries (relative to voice) were performed during evening, night, and early morning hours (8pm to 8am). These differences were consistent during weekdays and weekends.

In our analysis, we inspected the results while controlling for factors that were found to be different between voice and text queries, including time-of-day and gender. When relevant, we report the influence of these factors on the results.

4.2 Queries

The average query length was significantly higher for voice queries at 4.2 (std: 2.96, median: 4, max: 109) versus 3.2

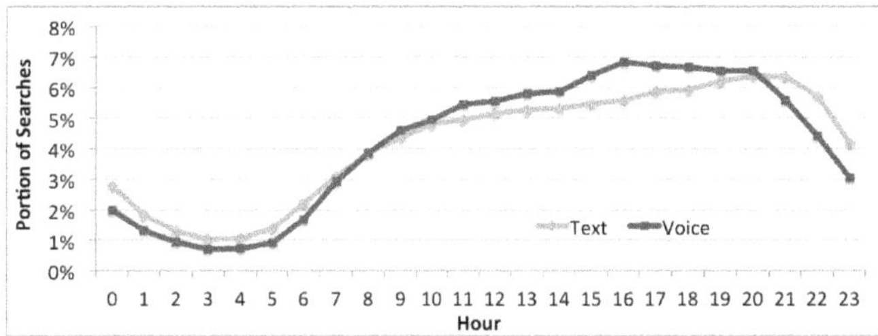

Figure 1: Query distribution by hour of the day.

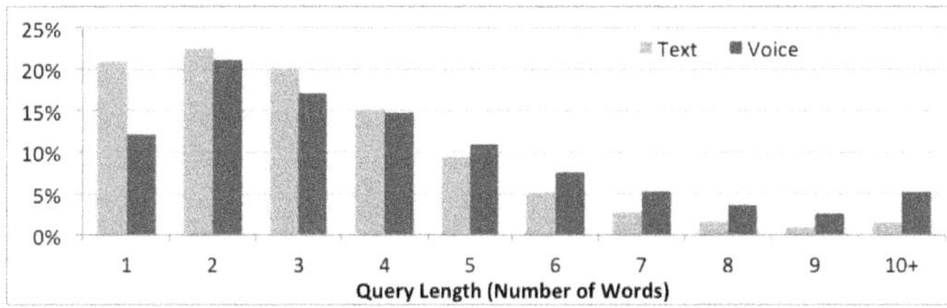

Figure 2: Query length distribution.

for text (std: 2.38, median: 3, max: 308). Query length was measured by the number of words, using white-space tokenization. The substantially higher maximum value in text queries is likely due to the use of the copy-paste feature, which does not exist for voice. Figure 2 shows the detailed distribution of voice versus text queries by length. It can be seen that one-word queries were particularly rarer on voice (12.2% vs. 21% for text), perhaps implying a lower portion of navigational queries. Voice queries were more common starting at queries of 5 words, which have been recently referred to as "verbose" queries [15]. Overall, 34.5% of the voice queries were of 5 words or more, compared to only 21.2% of the text queries. The length difference between voice and text queries has a major effect on query syntax, which we examine more closely in Section 7.

Previous work was somewhat inconsistent with regards to voice versus text query length. While a Google case study found that voice queries tend to be shorter than typed queries (2.5 versus 2.9 on average, respectively) [30], other studies found voice queries to be longer (e.g., 3.4 versus 2.2 on a Yahoo study) [10, 40]. Jiang et al. [19] pointed out this discrepancy and stated that *"further studies are needed to identify the characteristics of queries in voice search."*. Our findings evidently support voice queries being substantially longer than text queries (while also indicating a general trend of queries becoming longer on mobile search).

The portion of unique queries for voice was 73.9%, compared to 77.6% for text. This stands somewhat in contrast to voice queries being longer, as we would expect more repetition for shorter queries. We believe this finding stems from two main reasons. First, the lower query diversity for voice search characterizes search in its earlier stages, as has been the case for web and mobile search [40]. Second, the use of abbreviations, spelling variants, and punctuation marks, makes text queries more diverse. We will further demonstrate this in Section 5.

4.3 Sessions

A session is a series of queries issued by an individual user in close succession, often with all queries being related to the same topic. Using a common approach for defining sessions [35], we considered queries that occur in a sequence without 15 minutes of inactivity as part of the same session.

	Text	Voice
% 1-query sessions	65.1%	67.1%
Avg (std) session length	1.74(1.61)	1.77(2.03)
Avg (std) idle in seconds	174.4(207.9)	121.8(182.7)
Median idle in seconds	84	63.5
% identical queries	13.7%	15.1%
% refining queries	10%	7.6%

Table 1: Session characteristics.

Table 1 shows session statistics. The average session length on voice and text queries was very similar, with higher standard deviation for voice. About two thirds of the sessions, on both voice and text, included only one query. Average and median idle times were shorter on voice queries, likely as a result of the faster inputting enabled by voice. This gap may also reflect the fact that voice queries often focus on topics that require little interaction with the results, as our analysis will later demonstrate. Finally, we inspected the relation of a query in a session to its previous query (when such exists): the bottom of Table 1 shows the portion of identical and refining queries (a query q2 refines a query q1 if q1 is a prefix of q2, but not identical to q2). Overall, the numbers are similar, with somewhat higher portions of identical queries on voice and refining queries on text.

5. QUERY SEMANTICS

In this section, we compare voice and text query semantics. We first examine higher level query categories by inspecting the triggering of vertical cards. We then examine the query themselves more closely, by comparing the most popular queries and the most distinctive query terms.

5.1 Triggered Cards

The recent evolution of web search has introduced richer experience of the SERP, with cards (also referred to as 'oneboxes' or 'direct displays') showing results of verticals such as weather, direct factual answers, or live sport scores [32]. These cards extend organic search results ('ten blue links') by addressing a user's specific information need directly on the SERP [9], often sparing the need for a click [23]. Commercial search engines trigger cards upon the identification of a relevant user's intent. The card triggering technology largely relies on query pattern matching that provides high precision, since the presentation of a wrong card might substantially degrade the user experience and is therefore highly undesirable. In the following analysis, we examine the distribution of presented cards for voice versus text queries, relying on the search engine's technology for card triggering to shed light on semantic differences between the two types of queries. The card triggering technology allows us to build on the ability to capture clear and specific user intent based on different patterns of language. For example, the dictionary card is triggered by queries such as "what is <term>", "<term> definition", or "meaning of <term>".

Overall, the portion of queries for which at least one card was triggered was 43.3% for voice queries and 40.6% for text. The higher portion for voice may reflect a more frequent use for information needs that can be directly satisfied on the SERP and require less interaction from the user.

Table 2 presents the "triggering ratio" for 16 different cards (i.e., the ratio between the portion of voice queries for which the card was presented and the portion of text queries for which it was presented). We excluded very broad cards (news, shopping, and digital magazines) and cards that reflect a vague or ambiguous intent (e.g., company, which also includes websites such as Facebook or Amazon). The left side of the table shows the ratio for frequent cards, triggered for at least 0.5% of both voice and text queries, while the right side focuses on narrower less common cards that still appeared for at least 0.1% of either voice or text queries. Among the frequent cards, music videos, which are triggered by queries such as song names and singer names, were the most common for voice compared to text (highest triggering ratio). CQA cards, which include direct (inline) answers from community question answering sites, recipe cards, and map cards, were also more common for voice. On the other hand, sports and people cards were considerably more common for text queries. The latter is a particularly common card, triggered for celebrity names and sometimes a refining keyword such as age or height.

Inspecting specific queries that refer to popular celebrities, we indeed observed a ratio smaller than 1 between voice and text, which becomes particularly low for queries that only include the celebrity's name, without any refinements. For example, the voice/text ratio for queries that included "lebron james" was 0.85, but this ratio decreases to 0.57 when only considering the exact query "lebron james". Similarly, for "bruce jenner" these ratios were 0.97 and 0.47, respectively; for "kim kardashian" 0.63 and 0.48; and for "donald trump", 0.83 and 0.42.

Reviewing the less frequent cards, on the right side of table 2, the time card was largely more common on voice queries, with a triggering ratio of over 5.5. This card is typically triggered by queries that ask for the time in a specific location (e.g., "savanna time" or "what is the hour in chicago"). Countries (country names, sometimes with refinements such as "capital of" or "population"), dictionary, and weather, were also more popular on voice, whereas lottery and even more so horoscope were more popular on text. Overall, we see that many of the infrequent cards are more commonly triggered for voice. Additionally, it appears that cards with concise answers (time, definition, weather) are more commonly triggered for voice queries, while cards that require higher user engagement, as they present richer content or more likely to require interaction (horoscope, lottery), are more commonly triggered for text queries.

Some of the findings in this section coincide with the Google case study [30], which identified "food & drink" and "local" as the more popular categories for voice (out of a total of 8), corresponding with our findings w.r.t the "recipe" and "maps" cards. That study also found that the "online communities" and "adult" categories were less frequent for voice, to which we show support in the next section.

5.2 Popular Queries

Table 3 shows the most popular queries for text versus voice (popularity is measured by the number of unique users who issued the query at least once). The top query in each list is already different: "facebook" for text versus "youtube" for voice. The difference between the two is substantial: on text queries, "facebook" was issued by a number of users larger by a factor of 1.7 than the number of users who queried for "youtube", while on voice it was issued by less than half (0.44). It can also be seen that adult site queries ("porn", "xnxx", "redtube") appear only on the top text list.

Frequent Cards		Infrequent Cards	
Card Name	V/T Ratio	Card Name	V/T Ratio
Music Videos	1.32	Time	5.65
CQA	1.3	Countries	1.52
Recipe	1.3	Dictionary	1.43
Maps	1.27	Weather	1.19
Movies	1.13	Cars	0.95
Finance	1.02	TV	0.9
People	0.75	Lottery	0.56
Sports	0.73	Horoscope	0.36

Table 2: Voice(V)/text(T) card triggering ratio.

Text		Voice	
1. facebook	7. porn	1. youtube	7. yahoo
2. youtube	8. xnxx	2. yahoo mail	8. walmart
3. pornhub	9. yahoo	3. facebook	9. amazon
4. google	10. amazon	4. google	10. home depot
5. yahoo mail	11. redtube	5. hello	11. yahoo.com
6. craiglist	12. facebook login	6. craiglist	12. amazon.com

Table 3: Most popular queries.

On the other hand, the voice list includes more retail brands ("walmart", "home depot") and the query "hello", which is likely used for experimenting with the voice system. In addition, the voice list includes the use of the suffix '.com' for popular navigational queries, e.g., both "yahoo" and "yahoo.com" are on the top list for voice (and similarly for "amazon"). Across all queries, however, the '.com' suffix was less common on voice than on text (ratio of 0.6), likely due to substantially sparser use of full URLs on voice queries: the prefixes 'www' and 'http' appeared much more commonly on text queries, with a voice/text ratio of 0.07 and 0.01, respectively.

5.3 Distinctive Query Terms

To further inspect semantic differences, we set out to explore which terms mostly characterize voice versus text queries. To this end, we used Kullback-Leibler (KL) divergence, which is an asymmetric distance measure between two given distributions [6]. Specifically, we calculated the terms that contribute the most to the KL divergence between the voice and text query language models, for unigrams, bigrams, and trigrams[1]. Table 4 reports the terms with the highest KL divergence for text queries (w.r.t voice queries) and for voice queries (w.r.t text). Inspecting the unigrams, the terms on the voice list mostly include common function words (determiners, prepositions), question words, and pronouns. The only two nouns on the list are "end" and "number". For "end", closer inspection verified that this is due to the ASR often confusing it with the more common "and" (e.g., "can i eat onions end garlic while breast-feeding" or "the preacher end the bear song"). The text unigram list, on the other hand, includes site names (especially social media and adult) and common abbreviations (states, e.g., "tx", "ca", "nc"; and also "st", "vs"; "dr"), which are hardly ever used on voice.

For bigrams and trigrams, the text lists include website and entity names, sometimes with extending keywords such as "sign up", "login", "online", "2015", "news", or "scores". On the other hand, the voice list includes many common parts of natural language ("what is", "in the"), requests phrased in natural language ("show me", "take me to", "i'm looking for", "phone number for"), and also a few state names that appear in their standard form ("new york", "north carolina").

[1]We elaborate on the smoothing method in Section 8.

Unigrams		Bigrams		Trigrams	
Text	Voice	Text	Voice	Text	Voice
pornhub	the	yahoo mail	is the	facebook sign up	what is the
2015	is	facebook sign	what is	credit card login	how do you
xnxx	a	sign up	how do	fargo bank login	phone number for
tumblr	what	you tube	do you	bobbi kristina brown	do you spell
facebook	in	dear abby	in the	dicks sporting goods	how old is
redtube	you	online login	number for	online login site	how do i
tx	to	big tits	of the	drudge report 2015	what time is
ca	of	near me	phone number	yahoo mail inbox	where is the
st	how	mlb scores	north carolina	chase online login	i need the
login	end	schedule 2015	pictures of	wireless my account	time is it
vs	i	crossword clue	new york	verizon wireless my	what is a
nc	for	yahoo news	for the	scrabble word finder	what are the
craigslist	on	card login	what's the	online banking login	i want to
ny	do	horoscope 2015	where is	craigslist los angeles	take me to
dr	number	season 2	show me	toys r us	i'm looking for

Table 4: Most distinctive query terms.

Finally, we also used the KL analysis to examine distinctive unigrams positioned at the beginning and at the end of a query. The most distinctive words to open a voice query were the question words "what" and "how" and the most distinctive for text queries were the site names "pornhub" and "facebook". The most distinctive word to terminate a voice query was "please", again indicating the use of natural language, while for text it was "2015", perhaps as it is easy to write but relatively long to pronounce.

The difference in use of question words is one of the most prominent between voice and text queries. A recent study examined this form of "question queries", which *"take the form of natural language"* [39]. We used a similar methodology to identify this type of queries for voice and text. Overall, 9.9% of the voice queries begin with a wh-word (one of the 5W1H), compared to only 3.7% of the text queries (ratio 2.67). Adding yes/no questions (start with 'does', 'did', 'can', etc.), the portions grow to 11.9% and 4.7%, respectively (ratio 2.55). The two most popular question words, by a large margin, were "how" (3.6% of all voice queries) and "what" (3.5%); while for "what" the voice/text ratio was 3.1, for "how" it was lower at 2.3. The lowest ratio among the 5W1H was for "why" queries at 1.8 (these queries account for 0.4% of all voice queries), probably as these are more open-ended questions, often characterized by longer answers that require more exploration on the part of the user [37]. On the other hand, common prefixes for factoid questions were substantially more common on voice, e.g., "how old is" (ratio 5.74) or "who is the" (5.36) [16].

Thus far, we have seen many quantitative characteristics by which voice queries differ from text queries. Next, we show a few anecdotal examples of voice and text queries used to perform a semantically-similar search. To this end, we inspected queries in our voice sample that landed (i.e., resulted in a click) on CQA pages, as these often reflect a specific information need. For such queries, we matched text queries that landed on the same CQA page during a period of one week (our text sample did not contain such matches, thus we had to inspect a larger log). Table 5 presents seven examples of voice and text query pairs that landed on the same CQA page and express a similar information need. These examples nicely demonstrate some of the findings pointed out during this section. We note, however, that we cherry-picked examples where the voice query was especially different from the corresponding text query. In other cases, voice queries were similarly phrased to text queries. For instance,

voice query	text query
looking for a restaurant that serves oysters in san francisco	oysters restaurant sf
how many minutes are played in women's soccer	women soccer duration
what restaurant did colin farrell and vince vaughn have dinner at in brooklyn	colin farrell vince vaughn joint dinner
need to see old sites i visited	view browsing history
is priority shipping and standard shipping the same thing	priority vs standard shipping
if you're 65 years old do you need a fishing license	fishing license senior citizen
i need the phone number for walmart in canton connecticut please	walmart canton connecticut phone

Table 5: Example voice and text queries that landed on the same CQA page.

	Voice / Text Ratio
Click-through rate	0.78
Avg #clicks	0.83
MRR for all queries	0.78
MRR for clicked queries	0.97
% Unique domains (hosts)	0.71
% Top domain clicks	1.1

Table 6: Click statistics.

inspecting our original samples, 13.1% of the voice queries were completely identical to a query in the text sample.

6. CLICKS

Table 6 shows the ratio for various click characteristics between voice and text queries[2]. It can be seen that the click-through rate (CTR; the portion of queries for which at least one click was made) and average number of clicks per query were substantially lower for voice queries. We conjecture that voice queries are often conducted in a situation that allows less interaction with the device, including clicking on search results. The mean reciprocal rank (MRR) across all queries is also substantially lower for voice queries. The MRR across clicked queries only is similar for voice and text queries, indicating that the difference in the general MRR is mostly due to the lower CTR of voice queries.

Inspecting the clicked domains (a domain is determined by the 'host' part of the clicked URL), the portion of unique domains out of all clicks is substantially lower for voice queries, indicating lower diversity. Further analysis indicated that a higher portion of the voice clicks are performed on top domains, determined using a list of the 100 most commonly-clicked domains during our experiment's period.

Table 7 shows the top clicked domains for text and voice queries. The rightmost column shows, for each of the top voice domains, the "click ratio", i.e., the ratio between its number of clicks on the voice query sample and number of clicks on the text query sample. Differences emerge between the two lists from their top. While the most clicked domains for text queries are Wikipedia and Facebook, they are only 2nd and 5th, respectively, on the voice click list, with low click ratios, especially for the social network, at 0.51. Instead, the top of the voice query list is dominated by video domains: video.search.yahoo.com, with more than double the clicks as on text queries, and popular video sharing site

[2]We cannot disclose actual values due to business sensitivity.

	Text	Voice	
	Domain	Domain	Ratio
1	en.wikipedia.org	video.search.yahoo.com	2.05
2	facebook.com	en.wikipedia.org	0.81
3	pornhub.com	youtube.com	1.26
4	video.search.yahoo.com	answers.yahoo.com	1.26
5	youtube.com	facebook.com	0.51
6	answers.yahoo.com	pornhub.com	0.61
7	xvideos.com	local.yahoo.com	1.18
8	local.yahoo.com	maps.yahoo.com	1.99
9	xnxx.com	yellowpages.com	1.75
10	amazon.com	answers.com	1.76
11	redtube.com	amazon.com	0.76
12	imdb.com	xvideos.com	0.54

Table 7: Most clicked domains.

Youtube. Also higher on the voice list are CQA sites, such as Yahoo Answers at 4th (6th on text) and Answers.com at 10th (not among the top 12 for text). On the top voice list only, with high click ratios, are also maps.yahoo.com and Yellowpages, reflecting more specific information needs (we have already seen "phone number" is a distinctive term for voice queries). Another evident difference is with adult sites: while four (Pornhub, Xvideos, Xnxx, and Redtube) are on the top text domains, only two make the top voice domains, with low click ratios. As we saw, text queries are more popular during night hours, which could explain the difference. Inspecting the portions of adult site clicks by the hour of the day, we indeed observed a sharp increase during night hours compared to day hours, however, the gap between text and voice clicks persists throughout all hours of the day.

Further inspecting the lists of top clicked domains revealed differences towards voice queries in other CQA sites (e.g. wikiHow with a click ratio of 1.3), maps (MapQuest 1.75; appearances of "maps" within all clicked domain strings with a ratio of 1.74), weather (AccuWeather 2.22; "weather" string 1.48), dictionary (dictionary.reference.com 1.43; thefreedictionary.com 1.75, "dictionary" 1.35), recipes (allrecipes.com 1.58, "recipe" 1.53), video streaming (screen.yahoo.com 1.97; "screen" 1.77), and music (iTunes 1.88). On the other hand, more dominant on text queries were shopping sites (eBay 0.92, Craiglist 0.54, "shopping" 0.84), health (WebMD 0.88, drugs.com 0.77, nih.gov 0.64), news (news.yahoo.com 0.82, "news" 0.7), sports (sports.yahoo.com 0.72, espn.go.com 0.8, "sport" 0.83), finance (finance.yahoo.com 0.48, "finance" 0.56, "bank" 0.89), celebs (celebs.yahoo.com 0.63, "celeb" 0.81), and social network sites with a particularly low ratio between voice and text clicks (Twitter 0.17, Linkedin 0.37). Despite the differences in favor of voice clicks for audio and video results, there was no such difference for photo sites (Photobucket 0.97, Pinterest 0.65, "photo" 0.87).

7. QUERY SYNTAX

In Section 4.2, we saw that voice queries tend to be longer than text queries. In this section, we delve deeper into syntactic analysis of voice versus text queries. Our analysis includes two parts: we first inspect the characteristics of syntactic parsing of both types of queries and then examine the distribution of key part-of-speech (POS) tags. In our analysis, we used two corpora for additional comparison: the first is the Wall Street Journal (WSJ) corpus (sections 2-23) [26], which primarily includes business and financial news articles, broken into sentences (a total of 42,248 sentences). The second is a collection of 500,000 question titles in English, randomly sampled from the Yahoo Answers CQA website. We only considered question titles of one sentence (over 90% of all titles on the site).

7.1 Parsing Characteristics

For this analysis, individual sentences from each of the four corpora – WSJ, question titles, voice queries, and text queries – were tokenized, pos-tagged, and syntactically parsed using the Stanford parser[3]. The parser first generates an unlexicalized PCFG parse [22] and then produces typed dependencies by matching patterns on CFG trees [11].

Table 8 reports four measures of syntactic complexity (four middle columns) for each of the four corpora. The first column shows the median and average number of tokens per parsed item[4]. The second column depicts the median and mean dependency tree depth, defined as the number of edges in the longest path from the root node to a leaf in the tree. The third and fourth columns present the fraction of dependency tree root edges that go to tokens POS-tagged as nouns or verbs, respectively. We use these two measures as proxies to the syntactic category of the input text, with noun roots often indicating simple noun phrases and verb roots often indicating more complex syntactic forms [28]. Finally, the rightmost column of Table 8 presents the median and average length-normalized log probability score of the PCFG parse, which serves as a proxy for grammaticality (a more negative score reflects a lower probability of the parse).

These results indicate substantial differences between voice and text queries: voice queries have more tokens, higher tree depth, higher portion of root nodes that govern a verb, lower portion of root nodes that govern a noun, and higher parse score. All of these differences make voice queries more similar to question titles (which are, in turn closer to news articles), relative to text queries. This analysis suggests that on the scale where text queries are at one extreme (shorter, less grammatical) and natural-language news articles are at the other (longer, better-formed), voice queries are positioned somewhere in-between text queries and question titles.

7.2 POS Tagging

The second part of the query syntax evaluation focuses on the distribution of part-of-speech tags using the Stanford POS tagger[5] [36]. In our analysis, we removed all punctuation tokens. Mobile queries in general include very few punctuation marks: only 0.7% of the text tokens and 0.3% of the voice tokens were punctuation marks, compared to 12.4% and 12.8% for question titles and WSJ, respectively (largely due to the use of question marks at the end of question titles and periods at the end of WSJ sentences). We worked with a lower-case version of all four corpora, as all the voice queries and the vast majority of text queries were lower case in their original form.

Table 9 displays the portion of primary POS tags (as the portion out of of all tokens in the corpus) for the four corpora. The first row refers to nouns, which are prevalent in queries, as previously shown [5]. Yet, for voice queries the portion of nouns is substantially lower than for text queries (52.4% vs. 64.3%), although still considerably higher than for WSJ (34.5%) and question titles (30.6%). Adjectives are also somewhat more common for queries, with similar portions for text (9.9%) and voice (9.6%). For the other parts of speech, it can be seen that the portions for voice queries are higher than text queries, and closer to the portions for titles and WSJ, although not quite as high. These differences are consistent across all five lower POS types in the table, and especially salient, with more than a double ratio between voice and text, for determiners and pronouns.

The richer language used in voice queries is largely due to their length: as we saw, voice queries are a token longer on average than text queries. Yet, differences also emerge when comparing queries of the same length. Table 10 shows the POS tag portions for voice versus text across queries of 2-7 tokens. There is a clear general trend in POS distribution by query length: the portion of nouns decreases as the number of tokens increases, the portion of adjectives remains stable, while the portion of other POS types increases with the length of the query. For queries with a fixed length, differences can still be observed between voice and text in the number of nouns, on the one hand, which is higher for text queries, and verbs, prepositions, determiners, pronouns, and adverbs, which are higher for voice queries. These differences somewhat diminish as query length grows, yet such queries are quite rare, especially for text (e.g., only 2.7% of the text queries are of 7 tokens). The differences for determiners and pronouns remain solid even for queries of 7 tokens. Overall, we see that even for queries of the same length, there is a difference in POS distribution between voice and text queries, with more diverse language used in voice.

8. NATURAL LANGUAGE RESEMBLANCE

Our analysis so far has revealed semantic and syntactic differences between voice and text queries. In this section, we set out to validate that the language of voice queries is indeed closer to natural language than text queries. To this end, we built two natural language models (LMs). The first is based on the WSJ corpus (sections 2-23, 42,248 sentences). The second, marked QT, was built based on a random sample of 50M question titles from the Yahoo Answers CQA site, posted between 2006 and 2015. Yahoo answers is a large and diverse website, acting not only as a medium for sharing technical knowledge, but as a place where one can seek advice, gather opinions, and satisfy curiosity about a wide variety of topics [2]. We opted to use these two corpora since one (WSJ) represents classic formal language, commonly used in natural language processing research, while the other (QT) represents a more up-to-date web language contributed by the "crowd" in order to ask questions.

We built unigram, bigram, and trigram LMs, with Jelinek-Mercer smoothing [42], λ=0.8, as learned throughout our experiments[6]. Smoothing unknown unigrams was done using the standard ϵ of 1 over the vocabulary size.

For measuring the similarity to a natural language model we used perplexity, which is perhaps the most commonly used measure of model quality in speech, natural language processing, and information retrieval research [29]. Perplexity quantifies the error between the predicted probability of

[3]http://nlp.stanford.edu/software/lex-parser.shtml

[4]The number of tokens is slightly higher than reported in Section 4.2, due to the use of the Stanford tokenizer instead of white-space tokenization.

[5]http://nlp.stanford.edu/software/tagger.shtml

[6]In our experiments, we worked with λ=0.5, 0.6, .., 0.9. We only report the results with λ=0.8 for clarity of presentation, but note that the respective outcomes for other values of λ were very similar.

Corpus	Median (mean) token count	Median (mean) tree depth	$root \rightarrow NN*$ edges (%)	$root \rightarrow VB*$ edges (%)	Median (mean) parse score
WSJ	20 (20.41)	6 (6.5)	9.2	84.1	−6.2 (−6.3)
CQA question titles	10 (10.6)	4 (4.3)	16.7	75.0	−9.3 (−10.4)
Voice queries	4.3 (4)	3 (2.9)	55.7	37.1	−13.7 (−13.9)
Text queries	3.3 (3)	2 (2.4)	66.5	28.6	−15.3 (−15.6)

Table 8: Syntactic properties of four corpora.

	Text	Voice	Titles	WSJ
% Nouns (NN)	64.3	52.4	30.6	34.5
% Adjectives (JJ)	9.9	9.6	6.8	8.0
% Verbs (VB)	8.7	12.1	21.6	16.2
% Prepositions (IN)	5.5	7.6	8.9	11.8
% Determiners (DT)	2.0	4.5	7.5	9.8
% Pronouns (PR)	1.7	3.6	9.9	3.4
% Adverbs (RB)	2.2	3.5	6.4	4.6

Table 9: Part-of-speech distribution.

	2		3		4		5		6		7	
	T	V	T	V	T	V	T	V	T	V	T	V
NN	80.6	73.6	72.1	65.2	66.6	60.1	60.5	54.5	53.9	50.1	47.7	45.1
JJ	9.5	10.8	12.5	12.6	11.5	10.9	10.7	10.2	10.0	9.5	9.3	9.1
VB	5.8	7.4	6.3	8.3	7.5	9.8	8.7	11.2	10.5	12.4	12.8	13.5
IN	0.2	1.0	2.4	3.7	5.2	6.5	7.5	8.1	9.1	9.3	10.2	10.3
DT	0.3	1.1	0.8	1.9	1.3	2.6	2.0	3.6	2.9	4.6	3.6	5.6
PR	0.5	1.3	0.6	1.8	1.1	2.5	1.6	3.0	2.1	3.5	3.2	4.2
RB	1.1	1.7	1.0	1.7	1.2	2.2	2.1	3.2	3.2	3.7	4.2	4.5

Table 10: Part-of-speech distribution for text (T) vs. voice (V) by query length (number of tokens).

an event proposed by a language model, compared to the empirical probability of the event. In our case, we used perplexity to measure the quality of a natural language model (WSJ or QT) with regards to a corpus of queries (i.e., the events) from either voice or text. In other words, we measured how likely the set of voice versus text queries is to originate from the given language model.

More formally, given a language model LM and a set of observed probabilities P, the perplexity of LM is defined as $2^{H(P;LM)}$ where $H(P; LM)$ is the cross entropy of the probability model LM with respect to the observed probabilities P, summed over all events in P. The closer the estimated probabilities for each event to the actual probabilities, the lower the perplexity. In our case, each event is a query q in a corpus Q (either voice or text), with an observed probability $\frac{1}{|Q|}$. Therefore, the cross entropy can be calculated as:

$$H(Q; LM) = -\sum_{q \in Q} P(q) \cdot \log_2 LM(q) = -\frac{1}{|Q|} \sum_{q \in Q} \log_2 LM(q)$$

where $\log_2 LM(q)$ is the length-normalized log probability of the query q based on the language model LM. The perplexity itself is calculated by using the cross entropy as the exponent – the lower its value, the better is the language model for "predicting" the generation of the given query corpus.

The first two rows of Table 11 show the perplexity results for the WSJ and QT LMs. It can be seen that the perplexity for voice queries is considerably lower than for text queries, for unigrams, bigrams, and trigrams. The 'V/T' columns explicitly show the proportion between the two. It can also be seen that the ratio decreases, i.e., the gap between voice and text queries grows, when moving from unigrams to bigrams and then to trigrams, indicating that the difference is largely due to the structure of the voice query language, rather than merely due to its vocabulary.

The general perplexity values for bigrams and trigrams are substantially higher for WSJ than for QT. This can be either due to the WSJ language being less similar to query language than QT, or due to the large volume of training data for QT, which produced a better language model. To further explore this, we randomly sampled 42,248 question titles from the 50M QT corpus – identical to the number of sentences in the WSJ corpus – and trained unigram, bigram, and trigram LMs based on this smaller corpus. The lowest row of Table 11 shows the respective results. It can be seen that the bigram and trigram perplexity values are higher than for the massively trained QT model, but are still lower by roughly an order of magnitude for bigrams, and two orders of magnitude for trigrams, compared to the WSJ[7] . This gives a stronger indication that the queries are more likely to be generated from the QT LM than the WSJ. The differences between voice and text queries remain – the perplexity ratios are similar to the full QT LM.

While being longer is an inherent characteristic of voice queries, we set out to explore whether for queries of the same length, there are still differences in the perplexity between text and voice queries. Table 12 shows the results for both WSJ and QT, as measured for text and voice queries of length 3, 5, and 7 tokens. Generally, the perplexity values indeed decrease as query length increases, indicating, as conjectured, that longer queries are closer to natural language. For both WSJ and QT, the perplexity across all n-grams is still noticeably lower for voice versus text queries of the same length. While the ratio is not as sharp as for the general query population, the difference is still clear and the trend of decreasing ratio from unigrams to bigrams and from bigrams to trigrams persists. This indicates that when we take a voice query and a text query of the same length, the former will have a language closer to natural.

9. DISCUSSION AND IMPLICATIONS

Our study disclosed various differences between voice and text search. In this section, we summarize the key findings, discuss implications, and suggest directions for future work.

- **Query Categories.** Both our query semantics and click analysis revealed that voice queries are more focused on audio-video content, such as from music channels or video sharing websites. It seems that voice search is more often used when the result is also expected to include voice. In addition, we saw that higher portions of the voice queries triggered the "direct answer" card and yielded clicks on popular CQA sites. This may be a result of the fact that higher portions of the voice queries were phrased as ques-

[7]The unigram perplexity is substantially lower for the smaller training set. We suspect that the large training set adds many rare unigrams to the vocabulary that do not at all appear in the query sets, but reduce the probability of other unigrams that do appear in the queries.

Corpus	Unigrams			Bigrams			Trigrams		
	Text	Voice	V/T	Text	Voice	V/T	Text	Voice	V/T
WSJ	30,463	13,563	0.445	$11.9M$	792,952	0.066	$17.3B$	$133M$	0.008
QT	35,843	12,865	0.359	70,064	11,764	0.168	402,837	21,127	0.067
QT $42K$	12,667	6,665	0.526	466,428	83,924	0.18	$49.5M$	$2.89M$	0.058

Table 11: Perplexity of text (T) and voice (V) queries w.r.t natural language models.

	len	Unigrams			Bigrams			Trigrams		
		T	V	V/T	T	V	V/T	T	V	V/T
WSJ	3	$33.1K$	$17.4K$	0.53	$1.5M$	$519K$	0.35	$139M$	$33M$	0.24
	5	$16.2K$	$9.2K$	0.57	$169K$	$63K$	0.37	$4M$	$1M$	0.26
	7	$8.4K$	$5.4K$	0.65	$42.9K$	$19.1K$	0.45	$544K$	$181K$	0.33
QT	3	$43.4K$	$19.1K$	0.44	$40.8K$	$15.8K$	0.39	$112K$	$32.4K$	0.29
	5	$17.3K$	$9.5K$	0.55	$7.2K$	$3.7K$	0.51	$12.5K$	$5.5K$	0.44
	7	$6.7K$	$4.6K$	0.69	$2.3K$	$1.4K$	0.6	$3K$	$1.6K$	0.55

Table 12: Perplexity by query length for text and voice.

tions: White et al. [39] found that such "question queries" typically have informational intent and often result in visits to CQA sites. We also found evidence for higher portions of recipe-related queries and clicks, perhaps implying that voice search is used while cooking. On the other hand, lower portions of voice queries referred to social networking and adult sites, which may represent more sensitive or personal content [13]. These noticeable differences in query categories suggest that search services that build on query classification, such as vertical selection, card triggering, ad targeting, query expansion, and even result ranking, may need to be adapted when used for voice search. For example, as voice queries are often phrased as questions, the identification of CQA queries (e.g., for presenting a CQA vertical on the SERP) may need to change.

- **Device interaction.** Voice search tends to focus on topics that require less interaction with the device's touchscreen. This was reflected by a substantially lower number of clicks, higher portions of queries that triggered cards, and more queries that expressed a narrow information need (time, dictionary, weather, and phone numbers). We also saw this trend on celebrity queries, where the more open-style queries that only include the person's name, were relatively less common than queries that refer to a refined aspect, such as age or spouse. On the other hand, queries for research topics (e.g., health) and, as already mentioned, social network sites, which require higher level of engagement, were less frequent on voice. These results have two key implications. First, they suggest that voice search should enable voice-based result presentation, to support a complete hand-free interaction with the user. While short voice answers have started to emerge on commercial web search engines, we believe these capabilities should be further extended, to support interaction with more result types, exploration of different search results, query suggestion, and ultimately a complete dialogue with the user, as already done by intelligent assistants for personal advice [18]. The second implication relates to the IR evaluation process. Recent studies have argued that with modern search, especially on mobile devices, the merit of clicks as a primary evaluation measure decreases [23]. Other measurements, such as "good abandonment", have been proposed [24]. Our findings show that voice search clicks, as a form of interaction, are even rarer than text search clicks on mobile devices. Thus, new metrics for evaluating user satisfaction of voice queries should be developed.
- **Pronouncing vs. writing.** In our analysis, a variety of issues were observed that relate to the difference between speaking queries and typing them. We saw more frequent use of words that are easy to pronounce but hard to write (e.g., long state names), and on the other hand less frequent use of abbreviations or calendar years (2015), which are easy to type but harder to pronounce. Related to this is the absence of a copy-paste feature, reflected by the rare use of URLs in voice queries. In addition, some typing styles are "standardized" by the transcription process, e.g., the use of apostrophe for possession (on text, 's' is commonly used both with and without the preceding apostrophe) or the use of diacritical marks, such as in "beyoncé". Finally, the use of punctuation marks and upper case letters, which is infrequent on mobile search, is even rarer on voice search.
- **Voice query language.** Our syntactic analysis, based on parsing and POS tagging, showed that voice queries are not only longer, by a token on average, than text queries, but also use richer language. Our semantic analysis demonstrated this with the use of natural language phrases such as "i'm looking for", "take me to", and "please". The perplexity-based analysis showed that the language of voice queries is indeed closer to natural language, even when controlling for query length. While it has long been claimed that voice is a richer, more expressive media than written text [7, 10], our study demonstrates it for the domain of web search queries. Having said that, the language of voice queries was found to still be far from natural-language questions and even farther from news articles. We also saw that voice queries may often be as short and identically-phrased as text queries. These findings suggest that voice queries pose their own type of language, in-between traditional text queries and natural-language questions.

One question that follows, which we did not explore in this work, is how the length and richer language of voice queries can help improve the search process. Previous studies found that longer queries, closer to natural language, do not necessarily improve the retrieval effectiveness compared to typical keyword-based queries [10, 39]. On the other hand, taking advantage of the general growth of query length on web search, recent studies proposed various methods for applying linguistic analysis on long queries, including part-of-speech tagging, dependency parsing, and entity and relation extraction, in order to enhance search performance. Linguistic analysis can also be applied on the document side and matched against the query's analysis, to resolve ambiguity and further enhance query-document match calculation. A recent book on "verbose" queries (5 words or more; 34.5% of all voice queries) summarizes this body of research and explains that for such queries, not only is it more feasible to apply linguistic analysis, but it is also essential for the understanding of the specific intent and the relevance of the returned results [15].

Previous work has tried to automatically transform queries into questions, by adding missing functional words or using question templates [12, 25], motivated by a variety of reasons, such as helping with intent disambiguation, improving search over CQA archives, enhancing query expansion, and allowing to post a query directly as a question on a CQA site when the answer cannot be found. Since voice search queries are more often phrased as questions, they may directly enable these benefits.

There is plenty of room (and need) for further research, such as exploring the use of voice queries' phonetic characteristics, e.g., the speaker's stress, speed, and intonation for search personalization, or conducting user studies to gain in-depth understanding of the voice search process. Our analysis suggests that voice search is still in its early stages, as reflected by the smaller portion of unique queries and the lower diversity of clicked domains. Future research should follow the dynamics of voice search as it is poised to become ubiquitous and further evolve.

10. ACKNOWLEDGMENTS

My thanks to Alex Nus, Dan Pelleg, Yuval Pinter, and Gilad Tsur for their useful comments. Special thanks to Avihai Mejer for his useful advice throughout this research.

11. REFERENCES

[1] A. Acero, N. Bernstein, R. Chambers, Y. Ju, X. Li, J. Odell, P. Nguyen, O. Scholz, and G. Zweig. Live search for mobile: Web services by voice on the cellphone. In *Proc. ICASSP*, pages 5256–5259, 2008.

[2] L. A. Adamic, J. Zhang, E. Bakshy, and M. S. Ackerman. Knowledge sharing and yahoo answers: Everyone knows something. In *Proc. WWW*, pages 665–674, 2008.

[3] A. H. Awadallah, R. Gurunath Kulkarni, U. Ozertem, and R. Jones. Characterizing and predicting voice query reformulation. In *Proc. CIKM*, pages 543–552, 2015.

[4] R. Baeza-Yates, G. Dupret, and J. Velasco. A study of mobile search queries in japan. In *Query Log Analysis (WWW workshop)*, 2007.

[5] C. Barr, R. Jones, and M. Regelson. The linguistic structure of english web-search queries. In *Proc. EMNLP*, pages 1021–1030, 2008.

[6] A. Berger and J. Lafferty. Information retrieval as statistical translation. In *Proc. SIGIR*, pages 222–229, 1999.

[7] B. L. Chalfonte, R. S. Fish, and R. E. Kraut. Expressive richness: A comparison of speech and text as media for revision. In *Proc. CHI*, pages 21–26, 1991.

[8] C. Chelba and J. Schalkwyk. Empirical exploration of language modeling for the google.com query stream as applied to mobile voice search. In *Mobile Speech and Advanced Natural Language Solutions*, pages 197–229. 2013.

[9] L. B. Chilton and J. Teevan. Addressing people's information needs directly in a web search result page. In *Proc. WWW*, pages 27–36, 2011.

[10] F. Crestani and H. Du. Written versus spoken queries: A qualitative and quantitative comparative analysis. *JASIST*, 57(7):881–890, 2006.

[11] M.-C. De Marneffe, B. MacCartney, and C. D. Manning. Generating typed dependency parses from phrase structure parses. In *Proc. LREC*, pages 449–454, 2006.

[12] G. Dror, Y. Maarek, A. Mejer, and I. Szpektor. From query to question in one click: Suggesting synthetic questions to searchers. In *Proc. WWW*, pages 391–402, 2013.

[13] A. Easwara Moorthy and K.-P. L. Vu. Privacy concerns for use of voice activated personal assistant in the public space. *International Journal of Human-Computer Interaction*, 31(4):307–335, 2015.

[14] Google official blog. http://googleblog.blogspot.co.il/2014/10/omg-mobile-voice-survey-reveals-teens.html. [Accessed 2016-05-01].

[15] M. Gupta and M. Bendersky. Information retrieval with verbose queries. *Foundations and Trends in Information Retrieval*, 9(3-4):209–354, 2015.

[16] I. Guy and D. Pelleg. The factoid queries collection. In *PROC. SIGIR*, 2016.

[17] G. Hinton, L. Deng, D. Yu, G. Dahl, A. Mohamed, N. Jaitly, A. Senior, V. Vanhoucke, P. Nguyen, T. Sainath, and B. Kingsbury. Deep neural networks for acoustic modeling in speech recognition: The shared views of four research groups. *Signal Processing Magazine*, 29(6):82–97, 2012.

[18] J. Jiang, A. Hassan Awadallah, R. Jones, U. Ozertem, I. Zitouni, R. Gurunath Kulkarni, and O. Z. Khan. Automatic online evaluation of intelligent assistants. In *Proc. WWW*, pages 506–516, 2015.

[19] J. Jiang, W. Jeng, and D. He. How do users respond to voice input errors? lexical and phonetic query reformulation in voice search. In *Proc. SIGIR*, pages 143–152, 2013.

[20] M. Kamvar and S. Baluja. A large scale study of wireless search behavior: Google mobile search. In *CHI*, pages 701–709, 2006.

[21] M. Kamvar, M. Kellar, R. Patel, and Y. Xu. Computers and iphones and mobile phones, oh my!: A logs-based comparison of search users on different devices. In *Proc. WWW*, pages 801–810, 2009.

[22] D. Klein and C. D. Manning. Accurate unlexicalized parsing. In *Proc. ACL*, pages 423–430, 2003.

[23] D. Lagun, C.-H. Hsieh, D. Webster, and V. Navalpakkam. Towards better measurement of attention and satisfaction in mobile search. In *Proc. SIGIR*, pages 113–122, 2014.

[24] J. Li, S. Huffman, and A. Tokuda. Good abandonment in mobile and pc internet search. In *PROC. SIGIR*, pages 43–50, 2009.

[25] C. Y. Lin. Automatic question generation from queries. In *Workshop on the Question Generation Shared Task*, pages 156–164, 2008.

[26] M. P. Marcus, M. A. Marcinkiewicz, and B. Santorini. Building a large annotated corpus of english: The penn treebank. *Computational linguistics*, 1993.

[27] A. Moreno-Daniel, S. Parthasarathy, B. Juang, and J. Wilpon. Spoken query processing for information retrieval. In *Proc. ICASSP*, volume 4, pages IV–121–IV–124, 2007.

[28] Y. Pinter, R. Reichart, and I. Szpektor. Syntactic parsing of web queries with question intent: A distant supervision approach, 2016. Proc. NAACL.

[29] R. Rosenfield. Two decades of statistical language modeling: Where do we go from here? *Proceedings of the IEEE*, 2000.

[30] J. Schalkwyk, D. Beeferman, F. Beaufays, B. Byrne, C. Chelba, M. Cohen, M. Kamvar, and B. Strope. Your word is my command: Google search by voice: A case study. In *Advances in Speech Recognition*, pages 61–90. 2010.

[31] J. Shan, G. Wu, Z. Hu, X. Tang, M. Jansche, and P. J. Moreno. Search by voice in mandarin chinese. In *Proc. INTERSPEECH*, pages 354–357, 2010.

[32] M. Shokouhi and Q. Guo. From queries to cards: Re-ranking proactive card recommendations based on reactive search history. In *Proc. SIGIR*, pages 695–704, 2015.

[33] M. Shokouhi, R. Jones, U. Ozertem, K. Raghunathan, and F. Diaz. Mobile query reformulations. In *Proc. SIGIR*, pages 1011–1014, 2014.

[34] Y. Song, H. Ma, H. Wang, and K. Wang. Exploring and exploiting user search behavior on mobile and tablet devices to improve search relevance. In *Proc. WWW*, pages 1201–1212, 2013.

[35] J. Teevan, D. Ramage, and M. R. Morris. #twittersearch: A comparison of microblog search and web search. In *Proc. WSDM*, pages 35–44, 2011.

[36] K. Toutanova, D. Klein, C. D. Manning, and Y. Singer. Feature-rich part-of-speech tagging with a cyclic dependency network. In *Proc. NAACL*, pages 173–180, 2003.

[37] S. Verberne. Paragraph retrieval for why-question answering. In *Proc. SIGIR*, pages 922–922, 2007.

[38] Y. Y. Wang, D. Yu, Y.-C. Ju, and A. Acero. An introduction to voice search. *Signal Processing Magazine*, 25(3):28–38, 2008.

[39] R. W. White, M. Richardson, and W. Yih. Questions vs. queries in informational search tasks. In *Proc. WWW*, pages 135–136, 2015.

[40] J. Yi and F. Maghoul. Mobile search pattern evolution: The trend and the impact of voice queries. In *Proc. WWW*, pages 165–166, 2011.

[41] J. Yi, F. Maghoul, and J. Pedersen. Deciphering mobile search patterns: A study of yahoo! mobile search queries. In *Proc. WWW*, pages 257–266, 2008.

[42] C. Zhai and J. Lafferty. A study of smoothing methods for language models applied to ad hoc information retrieval. In *Proc. SIGIR*, pages 334–342, 2001.

[43] G. Zweig and S. Chang. Personalizing model m for voice-search. In *Proc. INTERSPEECH*, pages 609–612, 2011.

Predicting User Satisfaction with Intelligent Assistants

Julia Kiseleva[1,*] Kyle Williams[2,*] Ahmed Hassan Awadallah[3]
Aidan C. Crook[3] Imed Zitouni[3] Tasos Anastasakos[3]
[1]Eindhoven University of Technology, j.kiseleva@tue.nl
[2]Pennsylvania State University, kwilliams@psu.edu
[3]Microsoft, {hassanam, aidan.crook, izitouni, tasos.anastasakos}@microsoft.com

ABSTRACT

There is a rapid growth in the use of voice-controlled intelligent personal assistants on mobile devices, such as Microsoft's Cortana, Google Now, and Apple's Siri. They significantly change the way users interact with search systems, not only because of the voice control use and touch gestures, but also due to the dialogue-style nature of the interactions and their ability to preserve context across different queries. Predicting success and failure of such search dialogues is a new problem, and an important one for evaluating and further improving intelligent assistants. While clicks in web search have been extensively used to infer user satisfaction, their significance in search dialogues is lower due to the partial replacement of clicks with voice control, direct and voice answers, and touch gestures.

In this paper, we propose an automatic method to predict user satisfaction with intelligent assistants that exploits all the interaction signals, including voice commands and physical touch gestures on the device. First, we conduct an extensive user study to measure user satisfaction with intelligent assistants, and simultaneously record all user interactions. Second, we show that the dialogue style of interaction makes it necessary to evaluate the user experience at the overall task level as opposed to the query level. Third, we train a model to predict user satisfaction, and find that interaction signals that capture the user reading patterns have a high impact: when including all available interaction signals, we are able to improve the prediction accuracy of user satisfaction from 71% to 81% over a baseline that utilizes only click and query features.

Keywords: intelligent assistant, user satisfaction, user study, user experience, mobile search, spoken dialogue system

1. INTRODUCTION

Spoken dialogue systems have been thoroughly studied in the literature [37, 46–48]. However, it has only been in recent years that a new generation of intelligent assistants, powered by voice, such as Apple's Siri, Microsoft's Cortana, Google Now, have become common and popular on mobile devices. One of the reasons for the increased adoption is the recent significant improvement in accuracy of automatic speech recognition [38]. Intelligent assistants support multiple scenarios ranging from web search to proactive user recommendations [42]. In this work, we focus on dialogue mode of interaction with intelligent assistants. In this mode, a conversation takes place between the user and the intelligent assistant: the user speaks to the intelligent assistant, it responds and user speaks back, frequently referring to the subject of the previous request. This method of interaction is a more natural way for people to communicate and is often faster and more convenient (e.g., while driving) than typing. We call this type of interaction with intelligent assistants—*search dialogue.*

SIGIR'16, July 17–21, 2016, Pisa, Italy

ISBN 978-1-4503-4069-4/16/07...$15.00
DOI: http://dx.doi.org/10.1145/2911451.2911521

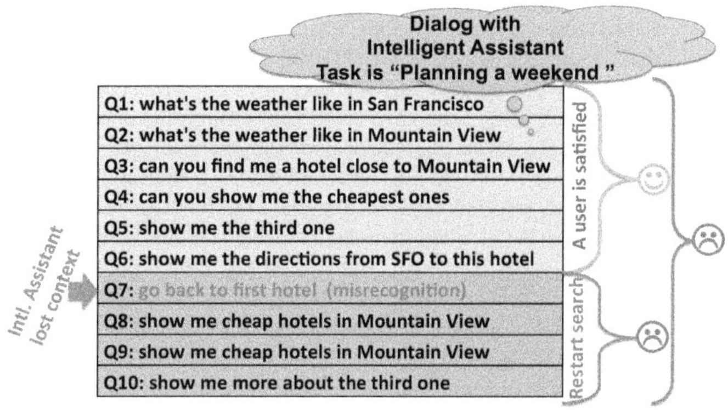

Figure 1: Example of search dialogue with intelligent assistant.

In search dialogue, users go through a sequence of steps in order to reach a desired goal: they solve one or more tasks, each of which consists of one or more search queries. As an example, consider the user dialogue in Figure 1: our user is trying to arrange a weekend in San Francisco. She has many tasks, from checking the weather to finding a hotel, or finding directions, etc. The user is engaged in a 'true' dialogue, i.e. the context is carried over across queries. When the intelligent assistant loses this context on Q_7, the user has to repeat some of the queries to rebuild the context and most probably gets dissatisfied with the intelligent assistant. So search dialogues are complex interactions, powered by voice control, with longer sessions consisting of different tasks and changes of focus within the same context. This is very different from traditional search in the query-response paradigm, and here session context becomes of crucial importance.

Clearly, evaluation of user satisfaction is an essential part of development of any intelligent assistant, as well as any traditional web search application. The ability to measure user satisfaction provides an understanding of the direction to take in order to improve the system. We can see from the example in Figure 1 that user satisfaction with search on intelligent assistants makes sense only for the entire dialogue, not as satisfaction with each query of a dialogue separately.

This prompts the need to better understand how users interact with search dialogue and how to define success and failure in terms of user experience—when are users (dis)satisfied? More specifically, we want to understand how we can measure and predict user satisfaction with search dialogue in ways that reflect perceived user satisfaction, and whether we can use traditional methods of offline and online evaluation or need to take other factors into consideration. The common practice for evaluating is to create a 'gold' standard (set of 'correct' answers) judged by editorial judges [22]. In the case of search dialogue, there may be no general 'correct' answer since the answers are highly personalized and contextualized (e.g. to a user's location or a user's past searches) to match better user-information needs. Another way to evaluate web search performance is through the use of implicit relevance feedback such as clicks, query length and landing page dwell time [2, 13, 17, 25, 26].

User satisfaction is widely adopted as a subjective measure of the quality of the search experience [27]. We know that user satisfaction for mobile web search is already very different when compared to desktop search [34]. The case of search dialogue is even more challenging for the measurement of user satisfaction [24]. Due to voice input-output to obtain answers directly from search dialogue without clicking, implicit relevance signals become far more important . The use of voice commands leads to a substantial increase in the length of queries: from 3.26 terms per query on average for mobile search to 4.48 for search dialogue, while also dramatically lowering the number of clicks per Search Engine Result Page (SERP): from 0.67 to 0.30[1]. Previous work [24] has modeled user satisfaction with intelligent assistants using generic explicit interaction signals (e.g. clicks, intelligent assistants request and response features, etc.) to simulate mobile search tasks, but the characteristics of more complex interactions and important touch-based signals were left unexplored. And [32] investigated self-reported user satisfaction in a related user study with a range of intelligent assistant tasks: device control, web search, and search dialogue. In this paper, we encompass all touch-based physical gestures that control the *mobile viewport location* (visible region on the mobile device), and screen taps (clicks), for the purpose of inferring user satisfaction with search dialogue. Concretely, our main research problem is:

> *How can we automatically predict user satisfaction with search dialogues on intelligent assistants using click, touch, and voice interactions?*

We breakdown our general research problem into three specific research questions.

> **RQ1:** *How can we define user satisfaction with search dialogues?*

As we show in Figure 1, a search dialogue is a sequence of user queries where each query is a step towards user satisfaction or frustration. We analyze interactions within search dialogue gradually increasing complexity of tasks and look at satisfaction with tasks.

> **RQ2:** *How can we predict user satisfaction with search dialogues using interaction signals?*

Clicks in web search have been extensively used to infer user satisfaction but clicks in search dialogue have lower significance due to the use of voice control and direct answers that does not require users to click. More insights can be gained by considering other interaction signals that characterize physical interaction with mobile devices. We investigate whether users' touch interactions provide useful signals for modeling user satisfaction for search dialogue and if they are more effective than using of general query, session, and click-based features.

> **RQ3:** *Which interaction signals have the highest impact on predicting user satisfaction with search dialogues?*

We analyze if touch-based features are important, while training an interaction-based predictor of satisfaction for search dialogue. Furthermore, we investigate which interaction signals are more important to predict user satisfaction by performing a correlation analysis between the interaction features. To answer our research questions, we set up a lab study with realistic tasks [5] for search dialogue derived from real user logs of a commercial intelligent assistant, measuring a wide range of aspects of user satisfaction. We use the outcome of the user study to understand and predict user satisfaction with intelligent assistants.

The remainder of this paper is organized as follows. Section 2 describes earlier work and background. We define user satisfaction though interaction signals for search dialogues in Section 3. Then, Section 4 introduces an approach for modeling user interaction with search dialogues. Section 5 provides a detailed description of the user study design to gather satisfaction labels. Finally, Section 6 reports our results, findings, and limitations. We conclude and discuss possible extensions of the current work in Section 7.

2. BACKGROUND AND RELATED WORK

This paper is relevant to three broad strands of research. First, we discuss research on spoken dialogue systems which are predecessors of the current intelligent assistants on mobile devices. Second, our work is related to evaluation of search quality because we propose a new model to evaluate user satisfaction with search dialogues. Third, our work is closely connected to the previous studies about user satisfaction in web search systems because we suggest a way to define and predict user satisfaction for search dialogues.

Spoken Dialogue Systems The main difference between traditional web search and intelligent assistants is their conversational nature of interaction. In the conversation mode of intelligent assistant, the technology can refer to the previous users' requests in order to understand the context of a conversation. For instance, in Figure 1 by asking Q_4 the user assumes that the intelligent assistant will 'know' that she is still interested in 'hotels in Mountain View'. Therefore, spoken dialogue systems [37] are closely related to intelligent assistants. Spoken dialogue systems understand and respond to the voice commands in a dialogue form; this area has been studied extensively over the past two decades [46–48]. Most of these studies focused on systems that have not been deployed in a large scale and hence did not have the necessary means to study how users interact with these systems in real-world scenarios, which led to most of the effort in evaluating spoken dialogue systems focusing on offline evaluation. Moreover, intelligent assistants on mobile devices support multiple scenarios of use compared with traditional spoken dialogue systems. For example, in addition to voice system response, intelligent assistants on mobile devices provide web search results, direct answers or proactive recommendations [42]. From these perspectives, intelligent assistants are similar to multi-modal conversational systems [20, 49].

This work is different from previous work on spoken dialogue systems in that, we study intelligent assistants on mobile devices and focus on analysis of user behavior that allows us to evaluate the system in an online setting, as well as identify instances of dissatisfaction with the system performance.

Search Quality Evaluation Historically, the key objective of information retrieval systems is to retrieve relevant information, typi-

[1]Statistics are calculated based on two weeks traffic of a commercial intelligent assistant in July 2015

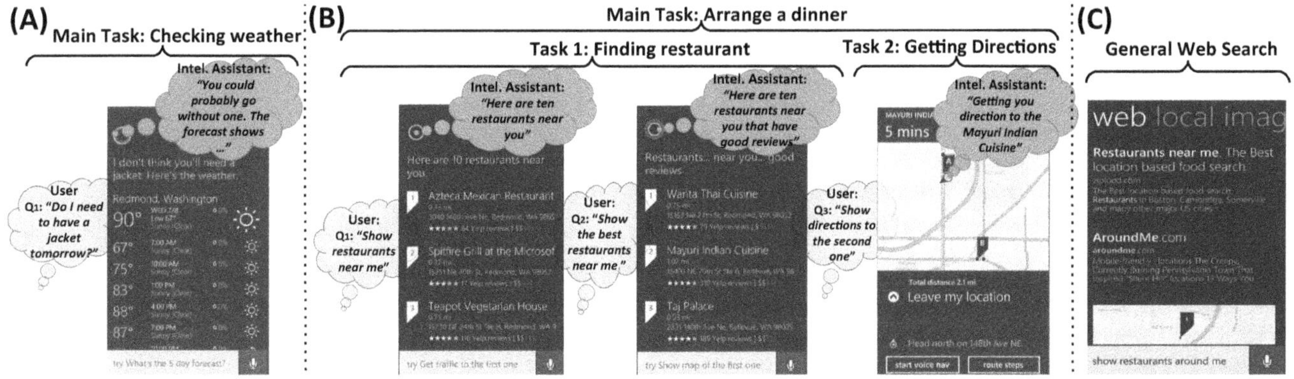

Figure 2: Examples (A) and (B) represent different types of intelligent assistant's response structured single task search dialogue and structured multi-task search dialogue accordingly. An example (C) represents a general SERP on mobile device.

cally in the form of documents or references to documents [40, 41]. In the simplest form, relevance can be defined as a score for a query-document pair. Given this query-document relevance score, many metrics have been defined, such as MAP, NDCG, DCG, MRR, P@n, TBG, etc. [22]. For such a setup, we have a collection of documents and queries that are annotated by human judges; such a setup is commonly used at TREC[2].

Recently online controlled experiments, such as A/B testing, have become widely used technique for controlling and improving search quality based on data-driven decisions [33]. This methodology has been adopted by many leading search companies such as Bing [7], Google [45], Facebook [4], and Yandex [10]. An A/B test is designed to compare two variants of a method (e.g. ranking on SERP, ads ranking , etc.) at the same time by exposing them to two user groups and by measuring the difference between them in terms of a *key metric* (e.g. the revenue, the number of visits, etc.), also known as an overall evaluation criterion. There are many existing studies towards better online evaluation which were devoted to inventing new metrics [9, 11] or improving existing ones [10]. The main goal of these studies was to make these metrics more consistent with the long-term goals [33]. User engagement metrics show different aspects of user experience. For instance, they can reflect **(1)** *user loyalty* – the number of sessions per user [43], **(2)** *user activity* – the number of visited web pages [35] or the absence time [11]. The periodicity engagement metrics of user behavior, which resulted from the Discrete Fourier transform of state-of-the-art engagement measures were applied in [9].

Our work is related to the online evaluation line of work since our objective is to build models that can be used to evaluate intelligent assistants, possibly in A/B testing settings. Our work is different in that we do not focus on how to run A/B experiments, rather we only focus on creating models that can be used to predict satisfaction.

User Satisfaction User satisfaction is widely adopted as a subjective measure of search experience. Kelly [27] proposes a definition: *'satisfaction can be understood as the fulfillment of a specified desire or goal'.* Furthermore, recently researchers studied different metrics reflective of user satisfaction, such as effort [52], and it has been shown that user satisfaction at the query-level can change over time [30, 31] due to some external influence. These changes lead to the necessity of updating the data collection. *Query-level* satisfaction metrics ignore the information about users' 'journey' from a question to an answer which might take more than one query [23]. Al-Maskari et al. [3] claim that *query-level* satisfaction is not applicable for informational queries. Users can run follow-up queries if they are unsatisfied with the returned results; reformulations can lead users to an answer – this scenario is called *task-level* user satisfaction [8, 17]. Moreover, Kelly et al. [29] have provided evidence that the most complex search tasks were similar to the work [6] characterization of complex tasks with respect to having multiple interdependent parts that needed to be addressed separately.

Previous research proposed different methods for identifying successful sessions. Hassan et al. [17] used a Markov model to predict success at the end of the task. Ageev et al. [1] exploited an expertise-dependent difference in search behavior by using a Conditional Random Fields model to predict a search success. Authors used a game-like strategy for collecting annotated data by asking participants to find answers to non-trivial questions using web search. On the other hand, situations when users are frustrated have also been studied. Feild et al. [12] proposed a method for understanding user frustration. Hassan et al. [18] and Hassan Awadallah et al. [19] have found that high similarity of successive queries is an indicator of an unsuccessful task. Our work is different from this line of work in that we focus on intelligent assistants while all these methods focus on analyzing user behavior when users interact with traditional search systems.

Most recently, user satisfaction for intelligent assistants on mobile devices started to gain attention [24]. Jiang et al. [24] focused on simulated tasks for device control and web search, and identify satisfactory and unsatisfactory sessions based on features used in predicting satisfaction on the web, as well as acoustic features of the spoken request. They do not focus on complex search dialogues and use use generic signals commonly used in Web search satisfaction modeling such as clicks and queries.

Sometimes, the information displayed on a SERP is sufficient to satisfy the users' information need. This phenomenon is called *good abandonment* [36, 44, 51] and was studied in [16] for mobile devices. The authors modeled viewing behavior based on touch interaction, and demonstrated the correlation of document relevance and *viewport* changing patterns on touch-enabled mobile devices. Recent research by Lagun et al. [34] extended this line of research to model the viewport for inferring user attention and satisfaction with SERPs. The absence of clicks is an emerging problem for intelligent assistants as well because they are frequently controlled by voice input.

Wildemuth et al. [50] reviewed over a hundred interactive information retrieval studies in terms of task complexity and difficulty, and found that the number of tasks and the number of facets were the main dimensions of task complexity. Recently, Kelly [28] linked perceived task complexity and effort, suggesting that user satisfaction may depend on the amount of effort to complete a complex task.

[2]Text REtrieval Conference: http://trec.nist.gov/

Our work focuses on modeling user satisfaction for intelligent assistants. We specifically focus on complex types of interaction —search dialogue. We show that interaction signals are essential to infer user satisfaction with search dialogue and demonstrate how they can be used in practice. We also focus on studying new interaction signals (such as touch and viewport changes) to model user's attention. We introduce a general notion of user satisfaction and exploit an extended list of interaction signals in order to predict user satisfaction with search dialogue

To summarize, the key distinctions of our work compared to previous efforts are: we studied a new method of user interaction with intelligent assistants on mobile devices, search dialogue, and we proposed a method to measure and predict user satisfaction for search dialogue using touch-interaction signals. Our metric is applicable to evaluation both online (e.g., introducing a new ranker or answer type for the intelligent assistant) and offline (e.g., mining search dialogues where users are dissatisfied).

3. DEFINING USER SATISFACTION

In this section we investigate **RQ1:** *How can we define user satisfaction with search dialogues?* In the case of search dialogue, the key distinction of this scenario is the ability of the intelligent assistant to maintain the context of the conversation. Moreover, responses provided by intelligent assistants can be either in the form of a structured answer or in the form of the usual mobile SERP. Figure 2 (A) and (B) illustrates examples of structured answers from a commercial intelligent assistant. Examples of tasks when this type of interaction is activated include requests about restaurants, hotels, travel, weather, etc. Structured answers differ significantly from the usual mobile SERP (e.g., Figure 2 (C)). We characterize different types of search dialogues based on our broad analysis of the logs from a commercial intelligent assistant (Section 3.1). We also present a generalized definition of user satisfaction with search dialogue using interaction signals (Section 3.2).

3.1 Search Dialogue Types

After intensive analysis of the logs of a commercial intelligent assistant, we split search dialogues into two types: single task search dialogues and multi-task search dialogues. Roughly 50-55% of interactions can be characterized as single task search dialogues, the rest as multi-task search dialogues.

Single Task Search Dialogue Single task search dialogue has one underlying atomic information need and mostly consists of one query and one answer. An example of a single task search dialogue is the weather-related information need shown in Figure 2 (A). Single task search dialogues are very similar to mobile web search and follow the query-response paradigm. We expect that they can be evaluated using *query-level* satisfaction.

Multi-Task Search Dialogue Multi-task search dialogue consists of multiple interactions with the intelligent assistant that lead towards one final goal e.g. 'plan a night out'. These long and complex interactions can be divided into a series of tasks. Obviously, multi-task search dialogues are more complex than other search dialogues because of a greater number of interactions whereby the user speaks to the intelligent assistant, the intelligent assistant responds, the user speaks back to it and so on.

An example of multi-task search dialogue is presented in Figure 2 (B): the intelligent assistant is used to arrange a dinner. The user makes the following transitions in this search dialogue:

- Q_1 : asking for a list of the nearest restaurants.
- Q_2 : sorting the returned list to find the best restaurants *(**During the transition** $Q_1 \rightarrow Q_2$, the intelligent assistant 'knows' that the user is referring to the list of restaurants from the previous query).*
- Q_3 : selecting a restaurant from the list and asking for the directions *(**During the transition** $Q_2 \rightarrow Q_3$ **:** the intelligent assistant 'knows' that the user is working with the sorted list of restaurants).*

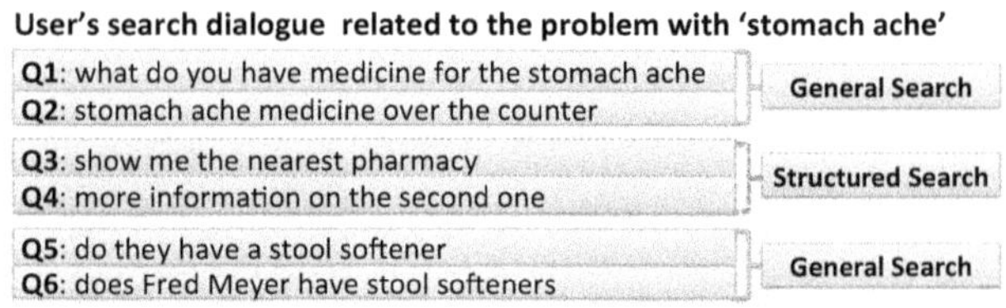

Figure 3: An example of the search dialogue where structured answer and general web SERP are used.

We notice that some user needs turn out to be too complex to answer with the structured interface. An example where a user needs help with a stomach ache that is shown in Figure 3. In this case, the intelligent assistant used both general web search and structured dialogue interface to respond to the user's requests. The intelligent assistant redirects a user to general search if the intelligent assistant deems that general SERP will satisfy the user's information needs better such as for queries: Q_1, Q_2, Q_5 and Q_6 in Figure 3.

A search dialogue is not just a sequence of $\langle Q, SERP\rangle$ pairs consisting of the SERP returned by intelligent assistant in response to the voice query Q. Search dialogue consists of one or more tasks, each of which consists of one or more queries. To better understand requirements for the user study setup, we divide search dialogues into single- and multi-task. Our hypothesis is that it is important for evaluation of user satisfaction with intelligent assistants if a response to a voice query Q can be either in a structured form ($SERP^{str}$, see Figure 2 (A) and (B)) or in a form of a general web search ($SERP^{web}$, see Figure 2 (C)).

3.2 User Satisfaction with Search Dialogues

Based on our analysis of a commercial intelligent assistant logs we hypothesize that much of the frustration happens when the intelligent assistant is not able to maintain the context and users need to start their search over in order to complete their tasks. As we present in the example in Figure 1, the intelligent assistant lost the context in the transition $Q_6 \rightarrow Q_7$ due to an automatic speech recognition error, and the user had to start over. Overall user satisfaction with the search dialogue decreases dramatically in this case despite the fact that the user seemed to be satisfied with the previous transitions: $Q_1 \rightarrow \cdots \rightarrow Q_6$. Furthermore, it is likely to be especially frustrating since the mistake happens at the end of the session.

Single task search dialogue has one main task T that can be represented as follows: $T = (\langle Q_1, SERP_1\rangle, \ldots, \langle Q_n, SERP_n\rangle)$. For any given task T, there are a set of interaction signals (e.g. touch, viewport change, etc.) that we denote as $I(T)$ and it can be defined as function f that combines all interactions for every $\langle Q, SERP\rangle$ pair in T:

$$I(T) = f\Big(I(\langle Q_1, SERP_1\rangle), \ldots, I(\langle Q_n, SERP_n\rangle)\Big). \quad (1)$$

In the case of multi-task search dialogue, the search dialogue has more than one task and can be viewed as a sequence of tasks: $T_1, \ldots, T_m$. Interaction signals within the search dialogue are defined through the function g that aggregates user interaction over tasks happening during search dialogue:

$$I(T_1, \ldots, T_m) = g\big(I(T_1), \ldots, I(T_m)\big). \quad (2)$$

Table 1: Description of implicit features per search dialogue

Feature Name	Feature Description
F_1 *NumQueries*	Number of queries
F_2 *NumClicks*	Number of clicks
F_3 *NumSATClicks*	Number of clicks (> 30 sec. dwell time)
F_4 *NumDSATClicks*	Number of clicks (≤ 15 sec. dwell time)
F_5 *TimeToFirstClick*	Time (seconds) until the first click
F_6 *MetaphoneLevenstein*	Levenstein similarity between pronunciation and writing
F_7 *MetaphoneSubstring*	Substring similarity between pronunciation and writing

Our objective is to define a function h that given a set of interaction signals would predict whether the user was satisfied or not. For multi-task search dialogues, h can be defined as:

$$SAT(T_1, \ldots, T_m) = h\big(I(T_1, \ldots, T_m)\big). \quad (3)$$

In the case of a single task search dialogue that consists of one task T, Equation 3 would be simplified to $SAT(T) = h\big(I(T)\big)$. If single task search dialogue consists of a single query, the equation can be further simplified to $SAT(T) = h\big(I(\langle Q, SERP \rangle)\big)$, like in standard query-level satisfaction.

In this section, based on extensive analysis of the logs of an intelligent assistant, we characterized search dialogues as single- and multi-task, divided queries as giving either a structured or a general web search response, and conceptually modeled user satisfaction with search dialogues. Additionally we illustrated that the overall user satisfaction with search dialogue cannot be reduced to the query or even task level satisfaction, because of the dependency between them and the expectation that the intelligent assistant maintains the context during the whole interaction within a dialogue.

4. MODELING USER INTERACTIONS

This section addresses **RQ2:** *How can we predict user satisfaction with search dialogues using interaction signals?* First, we describe used interaction signals that are logged as the following two types of features: (1) general *implicit features* which have been used in previous work on characterizing user behavior with general Web search [2, 13, 17, 25] and intelligent assistants [24] (Section 4.1), and (2) *touch and attention features* which, we believe, provide a different perspective for modeling satisfaction with search dialogues (Section 4.2). Note that some of these features were also shown to be useful for predicting the relevance of web search results [15, 16, 34]. These two types of features are used to define $I(\langle Q, SERP \rangle)$ which is a component of Equation 1. Finally, we present a method for modelling user interaction with the search dialogue task T to represent $I(T)$ from Equation 1 (Section 4.3).

4.1 Implicit Features

Queries and Click Features $(F_1, \ldots, F_5)$**:** In our case *click* means tapping a result item (e.g., the best answer from a list of candidates). We use the following features that are calculated across the entire search dialogue task: the number of queries (F_1) the number of clicks (F_2), the number of satisfied clicks, defined as clicks with dwell time $>$ 30 seconds (F_3), as well as the number of dissatisfied clicks, defined as clicks with dwell time $\leq$ 15 seconds (F_4), and the total time (seconds) before the first click in search dialogue (F_5). Note that previous work [13] has shown that long dwell time clicks ($>$ 30 seconds) are highly likely to indicate satisfaction while quick-back clicks ($\leq$ 15 seconds) are highly likely to indicate dissatisfaction.

Table 2: Description of touch features per search dialogue

Feature Name	Feature Description
F_9 *NumSwipes*	Number of Swipes
F_{10} *NumUpSwipes*	Number of up-swipes
F_{11} *NumDownSwipes*	Number of down-swipes
F_{12} *SwipedDistance*	Total distance swiped (pixels)
F_{13} *AvgNumSwipes*	Number of swipes normalized by time
F_{14} *AvgSwipeDistance*	Total distance divided by num. of swipes
F_{15} *DistanceByTime*	Total swiped distance divided by time
F_{16} *DirectionChanges*	Number of swipe direction changes
F_{17} *DurationPerAns*	SERP answer duration (seconds) which is shown on screen (even partially)
F_{18} *FractionPerAns*	Fraction of visible pixels belonging to SERP answer
F_{19} *ReadTimePerAns*	Attributed time (seconds) to viewing a particular element (answer) on SERP
F_{20} *1DReadTimePerPix*	Attributed time (seconds) per unit height (pixels) associated with a particular element on SERP
F_{21} *2DReadTimePerPix*	Attributed time (milliseconds) per unit area (square pixels) associated with a particular element on SERP

Acoustic Features (F_6, F_7)**:** We utilize acoustic feature to characterize voice interaction happening in search dialogues. More specifically, we use the phonetic similarity between consecutive requests to identify patterns of repetition. Metaphone representation [39] is a way of indexing words by their pronunciation that allows us to represent words by how they are pronounced as opposed to how they are written. Phonetic similarity is assessed by computing the edit distance between the Metaphone representation of two utterances. For example, a voice query *'WhatsApp'* may be incorrectly recognized as *'what's up'*, but their metaphone codes are both *'WTSP'*. In such cases, this phonetic similarity feature helps us detect repeated or similar requests that are missed by normal text similarity features based on recognized speech. As similarities metrics we use Levenstein Distance (F_7) and Substring (F_8). Table 1 lists the utilized implicit features: $(F_1, \ldots, F_7)$.

4.2 Touch Features

One of the main contributions of this work is the introduction of touch and attention features for detecting user satisfaction with search dialogues. We focus on touch-based features related to the way in which users interact with the screen and features based on elements visible to users. This serves as a surrogate for what the user is paying attention to on the page and how this changes throughout the search dialogue. Table 2 lists the used touch features. Capturing touch events is not easy in practice because of non-standard instrumentation [21]. We derive interaction features and the exact information that was displayed on the phone screen at any given time using *mobile viewport logging*. This allows us to record the portion of the answer/result currently visible on the screen, as well as bounding boxes of all results shown on the page. For instance, if an element is visible in the viewport at some point in time and then no longer visible, one can infer that a gesture must have taken place. Furthermore, if an element below the original element becomes visible, then one can infer that it must have been a downward swipe action. We use element-tracking in the viewport to infer features related to swipes happening during search dialogue: $F_9, \ldots, F_{16}$.

Lagun et al. [34] showed that there is strong correlation between the time for which a result is visible and its gaze time. Following this observation, we approximate how much attention different

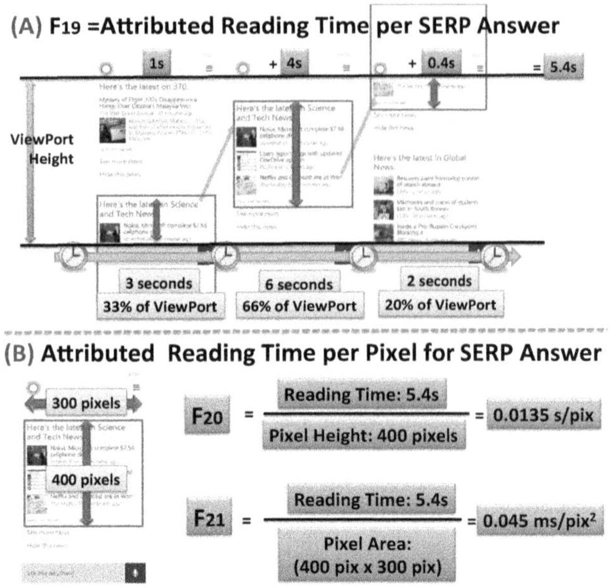

Figure 4: The illustration how to capture (A): F_{19} *ReadingTimePerAnswer* and (B): F_{20}, F_{21} *ReadingTimePerPixel.*

SERP elements get. Features F_{17}, F_{18} are used to characterize visibility of SERP answers. The feature F_{19} attempts to attribute the time the user spends looking at each stationary viewport to the different elements based on their area. Features F_{20} and F_{21} are responsible for reading time per pixel, they normalize the attributed reading time so that size of the content region does not introduce a systematic weight into the metric. Figure 4 illustrates how F_{19} is captured in the example (A) and how F_{20} and F_{21} are calculated in the example (B). To aggregate the features $F_{17}, \ldots, F_{21}$ at the $\langle Q, SERP \rangle$-level, we use four types of aggregation: average (Avg), maximum (Max), minimum (Min), and standard deviation ($Stdev$).

We presented a list of implicit and touch features that are collected on $\langle Q, SERP \rangle$-level during user interaction with search dialogues on intelligent assistants. We define $I(\langle Q, SERP \rangle)$ by the feature vector: $(F_1, \ldots, F_{21})$. Next, we will explain how to model user interaction on the task level—$I(T)$.

4.3 User Interactions over Search Dialogue

We showed that search dialogue tasks have underlying semantic structure and potentially can be divided into single task search dialogues and multi-task search dialogues. There is no automatic search dialogue analyser available so we cannot split search dialogues into tasks on the fly. The goal of this work is to deliver online metric for user satisfaction with search dialogues on intelligent assistants. Potentially, the semantic structure of a search dialogue task is not entirely flat and it might have a tree structure. Developing an automatic tool to mine the search dialogue structure is a promising direction for future work.

The intelligent assistant has two types of responses to a voice query Q: either in a structured form, $SERP^{str}$ as illustrated in Figure 2 (A) and (B), or in the form of a general web search, $SERP^{web}$ as illustrated in Figure 2 (C). Our hypothesis is that the type of response of intelligent assistants can be used to approximately divide search dialogues into the different types of tasks. Our assumption relies on the internal logic of the intelligent assistant that returns $SERP^{str}$ when tasks are about different types of locations (restaurants, hotels, pharmacies, shops etc.), directions to locations, or weather. If the intelligent assistant deems that information from general web is more suitable for a query then it returns $SERP^{str}$. This kind of intelligent assistant response still differs from general mobile search because it looks like a dialogue. For example, if a user voice query can be answered using the knowledge graph then, the intelligent assistant speaks the answer out aloud.

We define the function f from Equation 1 through aggregation. Further, in our experiment we use geometric mean as aggregation. We experimented with other aggregation functions, and they yielded similar or worse performance. We apply three techniques to define $I(T)$ for the search dialogue consisting of n queries in total, m queries resulted in $SERP^{str}$ and k queries resulted in $SERP^{web}$:

A_1**:** considering only interaction with $\langle Q, SERP^{str} \rangle$:

$$I(T) = \Big(\prod_{i=1}^{m} I(\langle Q_i, SERP_i^{str} \rangle)\Big)^{1/m}; \quad (4)$$

A_2**:** considering interactions with all $\langle Q, SERP \rangle$ equally:

$$I(T) = \Big(\prod_{i=1}^{n} I(\langle Q_i, SERP_i \rangle)\Big)^{1/n}; \quad (5)$$

A_3**:** separating interactions with $\langle Q, SERP^{str} \rangle$ and $\langle Q, SERP^{web} \rangle$ as two different tasks T^{str} and T^{web}:

$$I(T^{str}, T^{web}) = \Big[\Big(\prod_{i=1}^{m} I(\langle Q_i, SERP_i^{str} \rangle)\Big)^{1/m}, \Big(\prod_{j=1}^{k} I(\langle Q_j, SERP_j^{web} \rangle)\Big)^{1/k}\Big]. \quad (6)$$

In this section we introduced the list of features to model user interactions. We focused specifically on presenting interaction signals which are promising for modeling user interaction with intelligent assistants. Next, we will describe the set up for our lab study with real-world tasks for search dialogue derived from real user logs. The outcome of the study will be used to understand how important interaction signals are for modeling user satisfaction with search dialogue.

5. USER STUDY

This section describes the design of the user study to collect user interactions for search dialogues. The collected data is used to investigate our research questions: **RQ2–3**. While designing tasks for our user study, we rely on the following requirements: (1) the suggested tasks should be realistic; (2) following Borlund [5] we construct the tasks so that participants could relate to them and they would provide '*enough imaginative context.*'

Participants We recruited 60 participants to participate in the study. All participants were college or graduate students residing in the United States. They all had good command of English. 75% of participants were male and the remaining 25% were female. The average age of participants is 25.5 (± 5.4) years. They were reimbursed $10 gift card for participating in the study.

Tasks We analyzed over 400,000 search dialogues from the search logs of a commercial intelligent assistant to generate tasks for user study. Based on our analysis we generated **eight** tasks for the user study that were designed to cover approximately 70-80% of subjects queried by real users of the intelligent assistant. We formulate tasks in a free form in order to encourage query diversity and stimulate either genuine satisfaction or frustration with returned results. The final tasks for user study consist of:

- **one** single task search dialogue that is related to the weather e.g. **Task A:** *'Check if you need to wear a coat tomorrow?'*;

- **four** multi-task search dialogues that include two subjects e.g. **Task B:** *'You are planning night out. Pick a restaurant based on your preferences: cheap, best review, or closest. Find out driving directions to the selected restaurant.*;

- **three** multi-task search dialogues that require at least three switches within the same context e.g. **Task C:** *'You are planning vacation. Pick a place. Check if the weather is good enough for the period you are planning the vacation. Find a hotel that suits you. Find out driving directions to this place.*

For each task, we recorded an audio that verbally described the task objective. Following the study [24], we did not show the participants the written description while they were working on the task as it was demonstrated many participants directly used the sentences shown in descriptions as requests. We strongly wanted to avoid such outcome because our goal was simulate real user behavior.

Study Setup Participants performed the tasks on a mobile phone with a commercial intelligent assistant installed. If the task needed access to specific device resources, functions or applications (e.g. maps), they were pre-installed to make sure users would not encounter problems. The experiment was conducted in a quiet room, so as to reduce the disturbance of external noise. Although the real environment often involves noise and interruption, we eliminated those factors to simplify the experiment. While participants were doing the user study all their interactions were logged using an internal API.

The participants watched a 4 minutes video with instructions[3] that explained how to use the intelligent assistant. Then, participants worked on **one** training task and **eight** formal tasks. We instructed participants that they should stop a task when they had accomplished their goal or if they became frustrated and wanted to give up. After completing each task, participants were asked to answer the following four questions:

1. *Were you able to complete the task?*
2. *How satisfied are you with your experience in this task in general?*

   In case of multi-task search dialogue participants indicate their graded satisfaction e.g. for **Task C** questions were:

   2.1 *How satisfied are you with finding a hotel?*
   2.2 *How satisfied are you with finding a direction?*
3. *Did you put in a lot of effort to complete the task?*
4. *How well did the intelligent assistant recognize your voice?*

Except for the first question which required a Yes/No answer, all questions were answered using a 5 point likert scale. Additionally, to stimulate participants' involvement in search dialogues, we asked them to answer clarifying question(s) about task output. For example, if the task was about finding a restaurant the participant would need to indicate its name in the questionnaire. The total experiment time was about 30 minutes.

User Study Summary We stimulated participants' involvement by giving free form tasks. They needed to formulate their own goals for the task and it leads to satisfaction or frustration. For example, out of 60 responses for the **Task C** we extracted 46 references to unique places. As a result of free task formulation we obtained a diverse query set, characterized as follows: in total, participants perform 540 tasks that involved 2,040 queries in total of which 1,969 were unique; the average query length was 7.07. The single task search dialogue as **Task A** generated 130 queries in total, four multi-task search dialogues as **Task B** generated 685 queries, and three multi-task search dialogues as **Task C** generated 1,355 queries.

[3]Link to instructions withheld to preserve anonymity.

6. RESULTS AND FINDINGS

We now investigate our **RQ3:** *Which interaction signals have the highest impact on predicting user satisfaction with search dialogues?* We begin by introducing our results on the prediction quality of user satisfaction with search dialogues (Section 6.1). We conclude by presenting a correlation analysis between the interaction features and user satisfaction (Section 6.2).

6.1 Predicting User Satisfaction

The purpose of this study is to predict overall user satisfaction with search dialogues. Therefore we do not utilize graded satisfaction in this work but it would be useful for future research. In our user study, users reported overall satisfaction using a 5 point likert scale. Due to the large difference in rating distributions between the single- and multi-task search dialogue we consider the evaluation as a binary classification problem. We divide the labeled search dialogues into binary classes: satisfied (SAT) – users provided 5 or 4; dissatisfied (DSAT) – everything else. This resulted in the following proportion of positively and negatively labeled search dialogues: SAT – 64% and DSAT – 36%.

We formulate a supervised classification problem where, given a search dialogue, the goal is to classify it to SAT or DSAT. We train Gradient Boosted Decision Trees (GBDT) [14] as a satisfaction predictor h presented in Equation 3. We experiment with other classifiers (logistic regression, SVM), and they yield similar or worse performance. Hence we only report the results of GBDT. We use 10-fold cross validation. For each training fold, we use grid search to optimize for the number of leaves, tree depth, and number of leaves required to split. We train our predictors based on different subsets of features from $(F_1, \ldots, F_{21})$. For each experiment we report the overall accuracy (Acc), average F_1 score (Avg. F_1), area under the curve (AUC); and precision (P), recall (R) and F_1 score (F_1) for SAT and DSAT separately in Table 3.

The baseline is the classifier trained on queries and click features which are aggregated over a search dialogue using Equation 4. We observe that the baseline is overly optimistic with a low DSAT recall (30%) and high SAT recall (93%), showing that it is effective in picking up the imbalance in SAT/DSAT distribution but far less effective in distinguishing satisfaction from dissatisfaction. We train the predictor P_1 on an expanded feature set, adding the Methaphone features (F_6, F_7). From Table 3, we can see that the predictor P_1 shows statistically significant improvement ($p < 0.05$) in Acc , SAT P, DSAT R, DSAT F_1, Avg. F_1 and AUC when compared against the baseline. Next, we expand feature set by adding the touch signals from Table 2.

We use the three proposed techniques for feature aggregation over task(s) while training based on $(F_1, \ldots, F_{21})$: A_1 (Equation 4) for the predictor P_3, A_2 (Equation 5) for P_4, and A_3 (Equation 6) for P_5. Based on results in Table 3, we can infer that the predictors P_2, P_3 and P_4 demonstrate statistically significant improvements ($p < 0.05$) in Acc, SAT P, DSAT R, DSAT F_1, Avg. F_1 and AUC when compared against the baseline, indicating that the touch features incorporated in prediction models are fundamental to evaluation of user satisfaction with search dialogues. Also from Table 3, we can infer that the aggregation A_3 (when we separate user interactions: $SERP^{str}$ and $SERP^{web}$) is most beneficial one when compared against the baseline. In the next subsection,

Table 3: **Measurements of prediction quality based on different subsets of features. The relative improvements compared to the baseline are provided in parentheses. * indicates statistical significant ($p < 0.05$) using paired t-tests compared to the baseline.**

Features Description	Accuracy (%)	SAT (%)			DSAT (%)			Avg. F_1 (%)	AUC (%)
		Precision	Recall	F_1	Precision	Recall	F_1		
Baseline: $A_1(F_1, \ldots, F_5)$ (Eq. 4)	70.62	70.72	**92.91**	80.31	70.50	30.37	42.45	61.38	61.51
$\mathbf{P}_1$: $A_1(F_1, \ldots, F_7)$ (Eq. 4)	78.53* (+11.20)	81.81* (+15.68)	85.73 (-7.73)	83.72 (+4.25)	71.24 (+1.76)	65.55* (+115.84)	68.51* (+61.37)	76.11* (+24.00)	81.20* (+32.01)
$\mathbf{P}_2$: $A_1(F_1, \ldots, F_{21})$ (Eq. 4)	78.78* (+11.55)	80.98* (+14.51)	87.75 (-5.55)	84.23 (+4.88)	74.69 (+5.94)	62.61* (+106.16)	68.12* (+60.46)	76.17* (+24.10)	83.59* (+35.90)
$\mathbf{P}_3$: $A_2(F_1, \ldots, F_{21})$ (Eq. 5)	80.21* (+13.58)	82.55* (+16.73)	87.99 (-5.30)	**85.18 (+6.07)**	**76.28* (+8.20)**	66.07* (+117.55)	70.81* (+66.80)	78.00* (+27.07)	83.31* (+35.44)
$\mathbf{P}_4$: $A_3(F_1, \ldots, F_{21})$ (Eq. 6)	**80.81* (+14.43)**	**84.89* (+20.04)**	85.42 (-8.06)	85.15 (+6.03)	73.45 (+4.18)	**72.55* (+138.89)**	**73.00* (+71.95)**	**79.08* (+28.83)**	**85.62* (+39.20)**

Table 4: **Pearson correlations between satisfaction (SAT) and implicit features. Results are statistically significant ($p < 0.05$)**

Feature Type	Correlation
$F_7(Q_i, Q_{i+1})$ *[MetaphoneSubstring]*	0.45
F_4 *[NumDSATClicks]*	0.31
F_5 *[TimeToFirstClick]*	0.30
F_2 *[NumClicks]*	0.27
F_6 *[MetaphoneLevenstein]*	0.23
F_3 *[NumSATClicks]*	0.12
$F_7(Q_{i+1}, Q_i)$ *[MetaphoneSubstring]*	-0.16
F_1 *[NumQueries]*	-0.49

we present features analysis to characterize the relative importance of different features.

6.2 Features Analysis

To understand the impact of implicit features ($F_1, \ldots, F_7$) from Table 1, we calculate the Pearson correlation between the user satisfaction label (SAT) and each feature. The results are presented in Table 4. Feature $F_7(Q_i, Q_{i+1})$, which indicates that the subsequent query Q_{i+1} in the task contains prior query Q_i, is positively correlated with SAT. Expanding the query, or rather refining the query to better specify the intent, is a common user behavior and is expected to increase the probability of finding satisfactory content on the subsequent SERP. The complementary feature, $F_7(Q_{i+1}, Q_i)$, however, reflects the case where the subsequent query Q_{i+1} in the task is contained within the prior query Q_i; this feature is negatively correlated with SAT. Speech recognition errors in $Q_i \rightarrow Q_{i+1}$ can give rise to this type of feature, and the negative correlation is expected from such transitions. Our findings are similar to the previously reported results [24]. Based on relatively high correlation between click-based features ($F_2, \ldots, F_5$) we infer that clicks during search dialogues can be interpreted as a sign of user satisfaction. We find that the search dialogue length, in terms of F_1, is negatively correlated with satisfaction. Long conversations can be result from two types of behaviors: (a) multiple attempts of users to have their speech properly recognized, or (b) the loss of context by the intelligent assistant during the conversation, forcing users to restart the conversation; both of these explain the observed negative correlation.

Table 5 shows the results of correlation analysis for the touch features ($F_8, \ldots, F_{21}$) using aggregations A_2 and A_3. We present the top 5 positively correlated features and the top 5 negatively correlated features. To explain the correlations, we present three hypotheses:

Table 5: **Pearson correlations between satisfaction (SAT) and touch features. Results are statistically significant ($p < 0.05$)**

Feature Type	Cor.
A_2 **(Eq. 5) for aggregating Touch Features**	
$Stdev(F_{18})$ *[FractionPerAns]*	0.23
$Min(F_{20})$ *[1DReadTimePerPix]*	0.20
$Stdev(F_{19})$ *[ReadTimePerAns]*	0.19
$Avg(F_{20}))$ *[1DReadTimePerPix]*	0.19
$Max(F_{20}))$ *[1DReadTimePerPix]*	0.18
...	...
F_{10} *[NumUpSwipes]*	-0.10
F_9 *[NumSwipes]*	-0.12
F_{11} *[NumDownSwipes]*	-0.12
F_{12} *[SwipedDistance]*	-0.13
F_{15} *[DistanceByTime]*	-0.18
A_3 **(Eq. 6) for aggregating Touch Features Aggregation**	
$I(\langle Q, SERP^{str} \rangle)$: $Max(F_{18})$ *[FractionPerAns]*	0.35
$I(\langle Q, SERP^{str} \rangle)$: $Stdev(F_{18})$ *[FractionPerAns]*	0.34
$I(\langle Q, SERP^{str} \rangle)$: $Max(F_{19})$ *[ReadTimePerAns]*	0.32
$I(\langle Q, SERP^{str} \rangle)$: $Avg(F_{18})$ *[FractionPerAns]*	0.31
$I(\langle Q, SERP^{str} \rangle)$: $Avg(F_{19})$ *[ReadTimePerAns]*	0.31
...	...
$I(\langle Q, SERP^{web} \rangle)$: $Min(F_{20})$ *[1DReadTimePerPix]*	-0.35
$I(\langle Q, SERP^{web} \rangle)$: $Stdev(F_{18})$ *[FractionPerAns]*	-0.28
$I(\langle Q, SERP^{web} \rangle)$: $Min(F_{18})$ *[FractionPerAns]*	-0.32
$I(\langle Q, SERP^{web} \rangle)$: $Avg(F_{18})$ *[FractionPerAns]*	-0.35
$I(\langle Q, SERP^{web} \rangle)$:$Max(F_{18})$ *[FractionPerAns]*	-0.35

$\mathbf{H}_1$: The SERP for a query is ordered by a measure of relevance as determined by the system, then additional exploration is unlikely to achieve user satisfaction, but is more likely an indication that the best-provided results (i.e. the SERP top) are insufficient to address the user intent.

$\mathbf{H}_2$: In the converse case of $\mathbf{H}_1$, when users find content that satisfies their intent, their likelihood of scrolling is reduced, and they dwell for an extended period on the top viewport.

$\mathbf{H}_3$: When users are involved in a complex task, they are dissatisfied when redirected to a general mobile SERP, as opposed to receiving an explicit structured answer from the intelligent assistant (e.g. the transition $Q_4 \rightarrow Q_5$ in Figure 3). Unlike $\mathbf{H}_2$, the absence of scrolling on this landing page is an indication of dissatisfaction.

The features in Table 5 are explained in more depth below. A large $Stdev(F_{18})$ characterizes the situation where roughly half of the available answers are observed and the other half are not. This would occur when there is minimal or no scrolling behavior, since answers at the top of the SERP are visible and the answers toward the bottom are hidden from view. F_{20} is well-defined only for observable content, and when users do not scroll, this value will be identical for all items on the SERP. As such, in the absence of scrolling, $Min(F_{20})$ will be large, and therefore a positive correlation with SAT is consistent with our hypotheses. F_{19}, on the other hand, is well-defined for all answers, observed or not, but will be equal to zero for answers that are not observed. When there is minimal scrolling and a long dwell on the top viewport, F_{19} will be positive and large for the observed answers, and zero for the unobserved content, giving rise to a large $Stdev(F_{19})$. $Avg(F_{20})$ characterizes the same behaviour as $Min(F_{20})$ when users do not scroll at all, but, when users do scroll small distances, $Min(F_{20})$ would drop substantially whereas $Avg(F_{20})$ would remain relatively stable; a positive correlation with SAT is consistent with $\mathbf{H}_2$. A large $Max(F_{20})$ implies that users paused and dwelled on one portion of the page for an extended period, also consistent with $\mathbf{H}_2$.

Table 5 (A_2) shows that SAT is negatively correlated with (F_9, $\ldots$, F_{12}), which describe user swipes. Swipe down, up, or both are signs of exploration of the result set and a negative correlation of number of swipes and swipe-distance with SAT is consistent with $\mathbf{H}_1$. F_{15} provides a measure of the speed of exploration of the content. The observed negative correlation implies that fast swiping indicates dissatisfaction, and it is consistent with users who are skimming through and exploring the results without success, supporting $\mathbf{H}_1$. These results are consistent with the findings of [34], who concluded that scrolling is negatively correlated with SAT.

For the aggregation A_3 (Equation 6), we separate interaction with structured answers, $I(\langle Q, SERP^{str}\rangle)$, and interaction with general mobile SERP, $I(\langle Q, SERP^{web}\rangle)$. The correlation between SAT and F_{18}, F_{19} calculated though interaction with $SERP^{str}$ is even stronger. The same set of features calculated for interactions with $SERP^{web}$ is negatively correlated with SAT, which is consistent with $\mathbf{H}_3$. Users who are redirected to $SERP^{web}$ and does not scroll likely land there unintentionally, as a consequence of a voice-misrecognition or loss of context by the intelligent assistant. While Table 5 only shows the top features, the entire list of correlations for A_3 are consistent with the $\mathbf{H}_1$, in agreement with our previous finding for the aggregation A_2. Furthermore, we can see that swiping actions during interactions with $SERP^{web}$ have higher negative correlation than with $SERP^{str}$. Here, users are plausibly frustrated and perform quick swipes through $SERP^{web}$. The above observations lead us to the following conclusion—that users expect to find answers on the SERP without any 'additional effort' (e.g. scrolling), and users are not satisfied if the intelligent assistant cannot answer their request explicitly and redirects them to a general mobile SERP.

Although our paper shows that our method has a strong potential, there are at least two limitations that can be improved in future work. The first limitation is the collected data during user study which can be improved in terms of size and diversity. One way to do that is to monitor users as they do their normal tasks via additional instrumentation installed on their phones and prompt them to answer questions about their satisfaction. Another area of improvement is using data collected from multiple intelligent assistants. Most available intelligent assistants support search dialogues and the features we use are independent of the task subject and hence should be useful regardless of which tasks are supported by which assistants. Nevertheless, training and testing our models on data from different assistants can be very useful for proving their generality. This is particulate challenging though given the difficulty of performing third-party instrumentation on mobile devices.

To summarize, extensively experimenting with the user study data, we concluded that touch and attention based features are extremely helpful for predicting user satisfaction with intelligent assistants. Finally, we conducted feature analysis and concluded that active user interactions with the mobile device (e.g., scrolling) is the strong signal of user dissatisfaction with intelligent assistant.

7. CONCLUSIONS AND FUTURE WORK

The paper extends earlier work on desktop and general mobile search [16, 24, 34] and presents the first quantitative study for user satisfaction with the modern generation of intelligent assistants. Intelligent assistants allow for radically new means of information access: making a real dialogue with a context using voice commands and touch interactions. Evaluation of user satisfaction is crucial for intelligent assistants development. As the popularity of intelligent assistants rapidly grows, a strong need for better understanding and precise evaluating of user satisfaction grows correspondingly.

Our main research question was: *How can we automatically predict user satisfaction with search dialogues on intelligent assistants using click, touch, and voice interactions?* First, we studied **RQ1:** *How can we define user satisfaction with search dialogues?* We studied search dialogues by analyzing real logs of a commercial intelligent assistant and introduced two types of the dialogues: single task search dialogues and multi-task search dialogues. We also illustrated that the dialogue queries can lead to responses either in the form of a structured interface or in the form of general mobile search, when a request is 'out of scope' of the search dialogue. We defined user satisfaction with search dialogues in the generalized form, which showed understanding the nature of user satisfaction as an aggregation of satisfaction with all dialogue's tasks and not as a satisfaction with all dialogue's queries separately. The introduction of dialogue types and understanding which kinds of responses to queries exist helped us to set up a user study and make feature selection for answering the next research question.

Next we investigated **RQ2:** *How can we predict user satisfaction with search dialogues using interaction signals?* To predict user satisfaction, we used the following kinds of interactions: clicks (or 'taps' in terms of touches on mobile platforms), other touch interactions and voice features. The baseline was predicting user satisfaction using clicks and queries features. We showed that features derived from voice and especially from touch interactions add significant gain in accuracy over the baseline. To understand how to efficiently select features depending on different types of queries, we proposed three techniques: using only features of queries resulting in structured interface; calculating a single set of features for queries resulting in structured interface and queries resulting in general SERP; and calculating separate sets of features for each group of queries resulting in structured interface and queries resulting in general SERP. We showed that the third technique is the most accurate to model user satisfaction. This technique improves accuracy from 71% to 81% over the baseline.

Finally, we analyzed the prediction quality of the classifier trained on various selections of interaction features, answering **RQ3:** *Which interaction signals have the highest impact on predicting user satisfaction with search dialogues?* We conducted a feature analysis and concluded that users expect to find answers on the SERP directly without putting in any 'additional effort' (e.g. scrolling). Our analysis showed a strong negative correlation between user satisfaction and swipe actions. Additionally, we demonstrated that users are not satisfied if the intelligent assistant cannot answer their query explicitly and redirects them to a general mobile SERP.

Our general conclusion is that touch based features dramatically improve the prediction quality of user satisfaction with search dialogue. Research on intelligent assistants on mobile devices is a new area, and this paper addresses some of the first important and necessary steps. We proposed a method for evaluating user satisfaction with intelligent assistants which can be applied in online evaluation of ranking results, offline mining of user dissatisfaction and understanding directions for their future development.

Acknowledgments

We thank the help from Sarvesh Nagpal and Toby Walker for the help in collecting the internal API data for the user study.

REFERENCES

[1] M. Ageev, Q. Guo, D. Lagun, and E. Agichtein. Find it if you can: a game for modeling different types of web search success using interaction data. In *SIGIR*, pp. 345–354, 2011.

[2] E. Agichtein, E. Brill, and S. T. Dumais. Improving web search ranking by incorporating user behavior information. In *SIGIR*, pp. 19–26, 2006.

[3] A. Al-Maskari, M. Sanderson, and P. Clough. The relationship between ir effectiveness measures and user satisfaction. In *SIGIR*, pp. 773–774, 2007.

[4] E. Bakshy and D. Eckles. Uncertainty in online experiments with dependent data: an evaluation of bootstrap methods. In *KDD*, pp. 1303–1311, 2013.

[5] P. Borlund. The iir evaluation model: a framework for evaluation of interactive information retrieval systems. *Inf. Res. (IRES)*, 8(3), 2003.

[6] D. J. Campbell. Task complexity: A review and analysis. *The Academy of Management Review*, 1(13):40 – 52, 1988.

[7] A. Deng, T. Li, and Y. Guo. Statistical inference in two-stage online controlled experiments with treatment selection and validation. In *WWW*, pp. 609–618, 2014.

[8] A. Dong, Y. Chang, Z. Zheng, G. Mishne, J. Bai, R. Zhang, K. Buchner, and C. L. F. Diaz. Towards recency ranking in web search. In *WSDM*, pp. 11–20, 2010.

[9] A. Drutsa, G. Gusev, and P. Serdyukov. Engagement periodicity in search engine usage: Analysis and its application to search quality evaluation. In *WSDM*, pp. 27–36, 2015.

[10] A. Drutsa, G. Gusev, and P. Serdyukov. Future user engagement prediction and its application to improve the sensitivity of online experiments. In *WWW*, pp. 256–266, 2015.

[11] G. Dupret and M. Lalmas. Absence time and user engagement: evaluating ranking functions. In *WSDM*, pp. 173–182, 2013.

[12] H. A. Feild, J. Allan, and R. Jones. Predicting searcher frustration. In *SIGIR*, pp. 34–41, 2010.

[13] S. Fox, K. Karnawat, M. Mydland, S. T. Dumais, and T. White. Evaluating implicit measures to improve web search. *TOIS*, 23(2):147–168, 2005.

[14] J. H. Friedman. Greedy function approximation: A gradient boosting machine. *The Annals of Statistics*, 29(5):1189–1232, 2001.

[15] Q. Guo, H. Jin, D. Lagun, S. Yuan, and E. Agichtein. Towards estimating web search result relevance from touch interactions on mobile devices. In *CHI Extended Abstracts 2013*, pp. 1821–1826, 2013.

[16] Q. Guo, H. Jin, D. Lagun, S. Yuan, and E. Agichtein. Mining touch interaction data on mobile devices to predict web search result relevance. In *SIGIR*, pp. 153–162, 2013.

[17] A. Hassan, R. Jones, and K. L. Klinkner. Beyond DCG: user behavior as a predictor of a successful search. In *WSDM*, pp. 221–230, 2010.

[18] A. Hassan, X. Shi, N. Craswell, and B. Ramsey. Beyond clicks: query reformulation as a predictor of search satisfaction. In *CIKM*, pp. 2019–2028, 2013.

[19] A. Hassan Awadallah, R. W. White, S. T. Dumais, and Y.-M. Wang. Struggling or exploring?: disambiguating long search sessions. In *WSDM*, pp. 53–62, 2014.

[20] L. P. Heck, D. Hakkani-Tür, M. Chinthakunta, G. Tür, R. Iyer, P. Parthasarathy, L. Stifelman, E. Shriberg, and A. Fidler. Multi-modal conversational search and browse. In *SLAM@INTERSPEECH*, pp. 96–101, 2013.

[21] J. Huang and A. Diriye. Web user interaction mining from touch enabled mobile devices. In *HCIR Workshop*, 2012.

[22] K. Järvelin and J. Kekäläinen. Cumulated gain-based evaluation of ir techniques. *TOIS*, 20(4):422–446, 2002.

[23] K. Järvelin, S. L. Price, L. M. L. Delcambre, and M. L. Nielsen. Discounted cumulated gain based evaluation of multiple-query ir sessions. In *ECIR*, pp. 4–15, 2008.

[24] J. Jiang, A. Hassan Awadallah, R. Jones, U. Ozertem, I. Zitouni, R. G. Kulkarni, and O. Z. Khan. Automatic online evaluation of intelligent assistants. In *WWW*, pp. 506–516, 2015.

[25] T. Joachims. Optimizing search engines using clickthrough data. In *KDD*, pp. 133–142, 2002.

[26] T. Joachims, L. Granka, B. Pan, H. Hembrooke, and G. Gay. Accurately interpreting clickthrough data as implicit feedback. In *SIGIR*, pp. 154–161, 2005.

[27] D. Kelly. Methods for evaluating interactive information retrieval systems with users. *FTIR*, 3(1-2):1–224, 2009.

[28] D. Kelly. When effort exceeds expectations: A theory of search task difficulty (keynote). In *SCST@ECIR*, 2015.

[29] D. Kelly, J. Arguello, A. Edwards, and W. Wu. Development and evaluation of search tasks for iir experiments using a cognitive complexity framework. In *ICTIR*, pp. 101–110, 2015.

[30] J. Kiseleva, E. Crestan, R. Brigo, and R. Dittel. Modelling and detecting changes in user satisfaction. In *CIKM*, pp. 1449–1458, 2014.

[31] J. Kiseleva, J. Kamps, V. Nikulin, and N. Makarov. Behavioral dynamics from the serp's perspective: What are failed serps and how to fix them? In *CIKM*, pp. 1561–1570, 2015.

[32] J. Kiseleva, K. Williams, J. Jiang, A. H. Awadallah, I. Zitouni, A. Crook, and T. Anastasakos. Understanding user satisfaction with intelligent assistants. In *CHIIR*, pp. 121–130, 2016.

[33] R. Kohavi, A. Deng, R. Longbotham, and Y. Xu. Seven rules of thumb for web site experimenters. In *KDD*, pp. 1857–1866, 2014.

[34] D. Lagun, C.-H. Hsieh, D. Webster, and V. Navalpakkam. Towards better measurement of attention and satisfaction in mobile search. In *SIGIR*, pp. 113–122, 2014.

[35] J. Lehmann, M. Lalmas, G. Dupret, and R. A. Baeza-Yates. Online multitasking and user engagement. In *CIKM*, pp. 519–528, 2013.

[36] J. Li, S. B. Huffman, and A. Tokuda. Good abandonment in mobile and pc internet search. In *SIGIR*, pp. 43–50, 2009.

[37] M. F. McTear. Spoken dialogue technology: enabling the conversational user interface. *CSUR*, 34(1):90–169, 2002.

[38] M. Negri, M. Turchi, J. G. C. de Souza, and D. Falavigna. Quality estimation for automatic speech recognition. In *COLING*, 2014.

[39] L. Philips. Hanging on the metaphone. *Computer Language*, 7(12): 39–44, 1990.

[40] T. Saracevic. Relevance: A review of and a framework for the thinking on the notion in information science. *J AM SOC INF SCI TEC*, 26: 321–343, 1975.

[41] T. Saracevic, P. B. Kantor, A. Y. Chamis, and D. Trivison. A study of information seeking and retrieving. I. background and methodology. II. users, questions and effectiveness. III. searchers, searches, overlap. *J AM SOC INF SCI TEC*, 39:161–176; 177–196; 197–216, 1988.

[42] M. Shokouhi and Q. Guo. From queries to cards: Re-ranking proactive card recommendations based on reactive search history. In *SIGIR*, pp. 695–704, 2015.

[43] Y. Song, X. Shi, and X. Fu. Evaluating and predicting user engagement change with degraded search relevance. In *WWW*, 2013.

[44] Y. Song, X. Shi, R. White, and A. H. Awadallah. Context-aware web search abandonment prediction. In *SIGIR*, pp. 93–102, 2014.

[45] D. Tang, A. Agarwal, D. O'Brien, and M. Meyer. Overlapping experiment infrastructure: More, better, faster experimentation. In *KDD*, pp. 17–26, Washington, DC, 2010.

[46] G. Tür. Extending boosting for large scale spoken language understanding. *Machine Learning (ML)*, 69(1):55–74, 2007.

[47] G. Tür, Y.-Y. Wang, and D. Z. Hakkani-Tür. Techware: Spoken language understanding resources [best of the web]. *IEEE Signal Process. Mag. (SPM)*, 30(3):187–189, 2013.

[48] G. Tür, Y.-Y. Wang, and D. Z. Hakkani-Tür. Understanding spoken language. *Computing Handbook*, 3rd ed(41):1–17, 2014.

[49] W. Wahlster. Smartkom: Foundations of multimodal dialogue systems. *Springer*, 2006.

[50] B. Wildemuth, L. Freund, and E. G. Toms. Untangling search task complexity and difficulty in the context of interactive information retrieval studies. *Journal of Documentation*, 70:1118–1140, 2014.

[51] K. Williams, J. Kiseleva, A. Crook, I. Zitouni, A. H. Awadallah, and M. Khabsa. Detecting good abandonment in mobile search. In *WWW*, pp. 495–505, 2016.

[52] E. Yilmaz, M. Verma, N. Craswell, F. Radlinski, and P. Bailey. Relevance and effort: An analysis of document utility. In *CIKM*, pp. 91–100, 2014.

Learning to Respond with Deep Neural Networks for Retrieval-Based Human-Computer Conversation System

Rui Yan
Baidu Inc.
No. 10, Xibeiwang East Road,
Beijing 100193, China
yanrui02@baidu.com

Yiping Song
Baidu Inc.
No. 10, Xibeiwang East Road,
Beijing 100193, China
songyiping01@baidu.com

Hua Wu
Baidu Inc.
No. 10, Xibeiwang East Road,
Beijing 100193, China
wu_hua@baidu.com

ABSTRACT

To establish an automatic conversation system between humans and computers is regarded as one of the most hardcore problems in computer science, which involves interdisciplinary techniques in information retrieval, natural language processing, artificial intelligence, etc. The challenges lie in how to respond so as to maintain a relevant and continuous conversation with humans. Along with the prosperity of Web 2.0, we are now able to collect extremely massive conversational data, which are publicly available. It casts a great opportunity to launch automatic conversation systems. Owing to the diversity of Web resources, a retrieval-based conversation system will be able to find at least some responses from the massive repository for any user inputs. Given a human issued message, i.e., query, our system would provide a reply after adequate training and learning of how to respond. In this paper, we propose a retrieval-based conversation system with the *deep learning-to-respond* schema through a deep neural network framework driven by web data. The proposed model is general and unified for different conversation scenarios in open domain. We incorporate the impact of multiple data inputs, and formulate various features and factors with optimization into the deep learning framework. In the experiments, we investigate the effectiveness of the proposed deep neural network structures with better combinations of all different evidence. We demonstrate significant performance improvement against a series of standard and state-of-art baselines in terms of p@1, MAP, nDCG, and MRR for conversational purposes.

Categories and Subject Descriptors

H.3.3 [**Information Systems**]: Information Search and Retrieval; H.3.1 [**Information Storage and Retrieval**]: Content Analysis and Indexing; I.5.1 [**Pattern Recognition**]: Models—*Deep learning*

Keywords

Learning-to-respond; conversation system; contextual modeling; deep neural networks

SIGIR '16, July 17-21, 2016, Pisa, Italy

© 2016 ACM. ISBN 978-1-4503-4069-4/16/07...$15.00

DOI: http://dx.doi.org/10.1145/2911451.2911542

1. INTRODUCTION

To have a virtual assistant and/or chat companion system in open domains with adequate artificial intelligence has seemed illusive, and might only exist in Sci-Fi movies for a long time. Recently, the goal of creating an automatic human-computer conversation system, as our personal assistant or chat companion, is no longer an illusion far away. Due to easily accessible "big data" for conversations on the Web, we might be able to learn how to respond and what to respond given (almost) any inputs. It is likely to be a great timing to build data-driven, open-domain conversation systems between humans and computers.

Building conversation systems, in fact, has attracted much attention over the past decades. In early years, researchers have investigated into task-oriented conversation systems [44, 33, 36], which are basically for vertical domains. The conversational inputs are restricted and predictable; hence it would be easier—compared with open-domain systems—to design the logic, create the rules, prepare the data and construct the candidate replies to handle the particular task [23]. For instance, in a conversation system for flight booking or bus route inquiring, the computer side only needs to capture the origin, destination and flight/bus information, and then respond accordingly with templates [44]. One of the most obvious limitation of task-specific service is that the conversation cannot exceed the system topic scope. Illegible inputs will not be accepted, which is regarded as a hard constraint. The underlying system design philosophy is nearly impossible to generalize to the open domain.

It is only recently that researchers focus on non-task-oriented (i.e., open-domain) conversation systems for their functional, social, and entertainment roles in real-world applications [2, 26, 9, 35, 17, 31, 6]. Creating an open-domain conversation system to interact with humans is an interesting but notoriously challenging problem. Since people are free to say anything to the system, it is impossible to prepare the interaction logic and domain knowledge, which can be, in contrast, specified in task-specific systems before hand. Besides, the number of possible combinations of conversation status are literally infinite, so that conventional hand-crafted rules and templates would fail beyond any doubt [34].

Along with the maturity of Web 2.0, there has been an explosion in the number of people having public conversations on websites such as Bulletin Board System (BBS) forums, social media (e.g., Facebook[1], Twitter[2]) and community question answering (cQA) platforms (e.g., Baidu Zhidao[3], Yahoo! Answers[4]). These resources provide a unique opportunity to build collections of naturally occurring conversations that are orders of magnitude larger

[1] http://www.facebook.com
[2] http://www.twitter.com
[3] http://www.zhidao.baidu.com
[4] https://answers.yahoo.com

than those previously available. They also propel the development of retrieval-based techniques in the field of open-domain conversation research. The merit is that, owing to the diversity on the Web, the system will be able to retrieve at least some responses for any user input, and return a sensible response.

The big data era, however, seems like a double-edged sword. On one side, it brings the great opportunity, as mentioned above, to build practical human-computer conversation systems in open domain. On the other side, there are also challenges. Given a user-issued query, we ought to identify appropriate candidate replies from a very large volume of data. Besides, the proposed model should also be general and unified for different conversation scenarios. In a conversation system, usually there is additional information to use such as "contexts" (a.k.a. previous utterance sentences in a continuous conversation session). Therefore, capturing and integrating as much information as possible in a proper way is important for conversation systems.

In this paper, we propose a "deep learning-to-respond" framework for open-domain conversation systems. We create a huge conversational dataset from Web, and the crawled data are stored as an atomic unit of natural conversations: an utterance, namely a *posting*, and its *reply*. Each ⟨*posting-reply*⟩ can be regarded as a single-turn conversation. For a given query, we first apply traditional keyword-based retrieval methods and obtain a list of candidate replies; each reply is associated with its antecedent posting. We then enhance the current query by adding its contexts, i.e., one or more previous utterances in the current conversation session. Thus, we obtain a set of reformulated queries as well as the original query. A deep neural network (DNN)-based ranker thereafter tells how each candidate reply/post is related to a (reformulated) query, and yields a ranking list for each (reformulated) query. We merge the ranking lists corresponding to different reformulations. In this way, we are able to organically incorporate into the conversation system multi-dimension of ranking evidences including queries, contexts, candidate postings and/or replies, which is a novel insight.

The proposed reformulation approach and merging strategy provide a new means of conversation modeling, especially multi-turn conversations. By using previous utterances, we are aware of background information of the query, which might be informative. Moreover, different reformulations can capture different aspects of background information; their resulting ranked lists are further merged by a novel formula, in which we consider the relatedness between the reformulated queries (with context) and the original one.

The DNN ranker, serving as the core of "deep learning-to-rank" schema, models the relation between two sentences (query versus context/posting/reply). We use a bi-directional recurrent neural network to propagate information across words; a convolutional neural network layer further captures patterns of adjacent words. Then a matching layer combines the information in each individual sentence. Note that our DNN is a generic framework and applies to *Query-Reply*, *Query-Posting* and *Query-Context* in a unified way.

We conduct extensive experiments in a variety of conversation setups between humans and computers. In particular, we build the system upon an extremely large conversation resource, i.e., almost 10 million pairs of human conversation resources. We run experiments against several other rival algorithms to verify the effectiveness of the proposed DNN model. Our system outperforms standard and state-of-the-art baselines regarding a variety of evaluation metrics in terms of p@1, MAP, nDCG and MRR metrics. The result indicates that our conversation system is rather helpful to facilitate conversations between human and computer.

To sum up, our contributions are mainly as follows:

- We propose a "deep learning-to-respond" schema for automatic human-computer conversation systems with deep neural networks (DNNs). The deep learning model is general and well unified to adapt for various conversation scenarios.
- We propose a novel concept to model *context* in a continuous conversation session in multi-turns. The proposed query reformulation can capture different aspects of background information. We design an insightful framework to merge the ranking lists of candidates to all (reformulated) queries.
- We propose a new response ranking paradigm give each (reformulated) query, incorporating multi-dimension of ranking evidences: *Query-Reply*, *Query-Posting* and *Query-Context*, which is an adaption for conversational scenarios.

The rest of the paper is organized as follows. We start by reviewing related work. In Section 3, we describe the task modeling and proposed framework for conversation systems. In Sections 4 and 5, we introduce the detailed mechanisms of contextual query reformulation and the deep learning-to-respond architecture. We devise experimental setups and evaluations against a variety of baselines and discuss results in Section 6. Finally we draw conclusions in Section 7.

2. RELATED WORK

2.1 Conversation Systems

Early work on conversation systems is generally based on rules or templates and is designed for specific domains [33, 36]. These rule-based approaches requires no data or little data for training, while instead require much manual effort to build the model, or to handcraft rules, which is usually very costly. The conversation structure and status tracking in vertical domains are more feasible to learn and infer [44]. However, the coverage of such systems are also far from satisfaction. Later, people begin to pay more attention to automatic conversation systems in open domains [31, 6].

From specific domains to open domain, the need for a huge amount of data is increasing substantially to build a conversation system. As information retrieval techniques are developing fast, researchers obtain promising achievements in (deep) question and answering systems. In this way, an alternative approach is to build a conversation system with a knowledge base consisting of a number of question-answer pairs. Leuski *et al.* build systems to select the most suitable response to the current message from the question-answer pairs using a statistical language model in cross-lingual information retrieval [12], but have a major bottleneck of the creation of the knowledge base (i.e., question-answer pairs) [13]. Researchers propose to augment the knowledge base with question-answer pairs derived from plain texts [24, 3]. The number of resource pairs can be, to some extent, expanded, but are still relatively small while the performance is not quite stable either.

Nowadays, with the prosperity of social media and other Web 2.0 resources, such as community question and answering (cQA) or microblogging services, a very large amount of conversation data become available [35]. A series of information retrieval-based methods are applied to short text conversation using microblog data [9, 14, 17, 16]. Higashinaka *et al.* also combine template generation with the search-based methods [6]. Ritter *et al.* have investigated the feasibility of conducting short text conversation by using statistical machine translation (SMT) techniques, as well as millions of naturally occurring conversation data in Twitter [26]. In the approach, a response is generated from a model, not retrieved from a repository, and thus it cannot be guaranteed to be a legitimate natural language text.

Unlike previous work, we conduct a novel study of retrieval-based automatic conversation systems with a *deep learning-to-respond* schema via deep learning paradigm. We formulate the possible factors into a deep neural network architecture and further investigate the potential of combining different ranking evidences for the candidate responses. Deep learning structures are well formulated to describe instinct semantic representations.

2.2 Deep Neural Networks

In recent years, deep neural networks (DNNs, also known as *deep learning*) have made significant improvement in NLP [11]. DNNs are highly automated learning machines; they can extract underlying abstract features of data automatically by exploring multiple layers of non-linear transformation [1].

In NLP models, a word typically acts as an atomic unit. However, words are discrete by nature; it seems nonsensical to feed word indexes to DNNs. A typical approach is to map a discrete word to a dense, low-dimensional, real-valued vector, called an *embedding* [19]. Each dimension in the vector captures some (anonymous) aspect of underlying word meanings.

Prevailing DNNs for sentence-level modeling include convolutional neural networks (CNNs) and recurrent neural networks (RNNs). In CNNs, we have a fixed-size sliding window to capture local patterns of successive words [10], whereas RNNs keep one or a few hidden states, and collect information along the word sequence in an iterative fashion [38, 37, 39]. Socher *et al.* leverage sentence parse trees and build recursive networks [30]. Mou et al. [21, 20] propose syntax-aware convolution based on parse trees. However, conversational utterances are usually casual, and hence recursive models are less applicable in conversation systems. We prefer structure-insensitive models like CNNs and RNNs.

Beyond a single sentence, some studies are aimed to capture the relationship between two sentences—known as sentence pair modeling—with applications like paraphrase detection [5], discourse unit recognition [45], textual entailment recognition [27], etc. A sentence-pair DNN model is typically built upon underlying sentence-level models (CNNs/RNNs). Then two sentences' information is combined by matching heuristics like concatenation, cosine measure, or inner-product [5, 28]. Hu *et al.* develop word-by-word matching approaches [7], and obtain a similarity matrix between two sentences. Very recently, Rocktäschel *et al.* propose context-aware matching approaches [27], where the first sentence's information is available when modeling the second one. Such context-awareness interweaves individual sentence modeling and sentence matching, prohibiting pre-calculating the vector representation of a sentence; hence these methods are considerably more computational intensive, especially with multiple query reformulations in our scenario. For efficiency consideration, we leverage vector concatenation, which is simple yet effective.

Although the studies of sentence-pair modeling described above are similar to our DNN to some extent, the proposed learning-to-rank model is more than traditional ranking or matching. We have multiple query reformulations with "contexts". After computing the similarity between the query and reply/post/context, our DNN further merges the ranking results corresponding to different reformulated queries.

3. TASK MODELING

In this section, we provide a big picture of the proposed *learning-to-respond* schema for conversation systems. We illustrate the task modeling for conversations, and establish the pipeline with several processing procedures including data collection, search and retrieval, contextual query reformulation, DNN-based ranking with scoring, and ranked list fusion. We briefly go over through the pipeline and elaborate the details in the next section.

Table 1: An example of the original microblog $posting$ and the associated $replies$. Each posting might have more than one reply, e.g., $Reply_1$ and $Reply_2$. To create our database of conversation data, we separate different replies to a same post, and obtain ⟨*post-reply*⟩ pairs. We store two *Posting-Reply* pairs in the conversational dataset, i.e., $\langle Posting\text{-}Reply_1 \rangle$ and $\langle Posting\text{-}Reply_2 \rangle$. User accounts are anonymized.

$Posting$: 近视了需要戴眼镜...   (I need a pair of glasses because of the myopia...)
$Reply_1$: 我送你眼镜！   (I will offer the glasses for you!) $Reply_2$: 可以恢复的，别紧张 ...   (You will be recovered. Don't worry.)

Table 2: Part (I) indicates a real human (denoted by A) - computer (denoted by B) conversation scenario, while Part (II) indicates our proposed task modeling and formulations. A_2 is the current user-issued query. We have contexts and reformulated queries as listed. '⊞' is the literal concatenation action. Note that the selected response $Reply_1$ is associated with a $Posting$ in the conversational database shown in Table 1.

(I)

Human-Computer Conversation
A_1: 天哪一把年纪的人居然近视了   (OMG I got myopia at such an "old" age) B_1: 真的吗？   (Really?) A_2:嗯哪。求个眼镜做礼物！   (Yeah. Wish a pair of glasses as a gift.)
B_2:我送你眼镜！   (I will offer the glasses for you!)

(II)

Task Formulation
User query: $q_0 = A_2$ **Context information:** $\mathbb{C}=\{c_1=A_1, c_2=B_1\}$ **Reformulated queries:** $q_1=A_2 \boxplus A_1$, $q_2=A_2 \boxplus B_1$ $q_3=A_2 \boxplus A_1 \boxplus B_1, \ldots$
Top-1 ranked response: $r^\star = Reply_1$

Data collection. With the prosperity of Web 2.0, people interactively communicate with each other on the Web, which provides a huge thesaurus for conversation data. We collect a large amount of data samples from social media such as microblog websites, forums, cQA bases, etc. Users can publish a posting message visible to the public, and then receive one or more replies or comments in response to their posting. The communication can have a single turn as well as multiple turns. We illustrate an example in Table 1. Due to the heterogeneity of the sources, we treat each utterance, in multi-turn conversations, with its subsequent one as a posting-reply pair (i.e., our database is context-free). For a posting with multiply replies, we separate them and construct different $\langle p, r \rangle$ pairs. Table 1 shows the pre-processed samples in our dataset, applied to a real human-computer conversation illustrated in Table 2. In the sample shown in Table 1, the first message of a conversation is typically unique. There are many flexible forms to "respond" to a given message, which is exactly the nature of real conversations: various responses are all possibly appropriate, with different aspects of information to fulfill a conversation. We separate the posting and replies as a group of ⟨*posting-reply*⟩ pairs. The data repository is demonstrated to be a rich resource to facilitate human-computer conversations.

Search and retrieval. In the scenario of conversations, the user issues a query (q_0 in Table 2), which may be a sentence or a few terms. We apply a standard retrieval process via keyword search using traditional *tf.idf* weighting schema [18] on the conversation data-base (formatted as an inverted index prepared off-line) based on the light-weight search provided by Baidu[5]. Note that we treat each pair of posting and reply as a short *virtual document*, which is not a traditional process. In this way, the retrieved "virtual document" comprises two parts: the *candidate reply*, namely r, along with its antecedent *posting*, namely p.

Contextual query reformulation. A single query may not fully convey user intentions in (multi-turn) conversations, as illustrated in Table 2. Under such conditions, we usually have context information to use. We propose a novel insight to model the conversation task. In particular, we view previous utterances from both sides as *contexts*, denoted as $\mathbb{C}=\{c_i\}$. One or more utterances in $\mathbb{C}$ can be used to enhance q_0 so as to provide more information. We call this a *contextual query reformulation* process. Moreover, the context may comprise several sentences, and hence we have several strategies to reformulate the original query. Each reformulated query is denoted as q_i. More details will be given in Section 4.

DNN-based scoring, ranking, and ranked list fusion. We apply a deep neural network (DNN)-based model to rank optimization. In particular, we design a bi-directional long short term memory (LSTM) neural network to capture sentence-level semantics of a query q_0, candidate reply and the associated posting, i.e., $\langle p, r\rangle$, as well as context $\mathbb{C}$. A matching layer combines multi-dimensions of the sentence information, so that we know how candidate replies with associated postings are related to the query and contexts. Analogous to the traditional *Query-Document* matching, the relevance ranking can be measured via *Query-Reply* matching, the additional *Query-Posting* matching, as well as *Query-Context* matching. Intuitively, when a query and a posting look similar, they might share the same response (Tables 1–2). For each (reformulated) query, DNN ranks candidates replies with relevance scores from *Query-Query* and *Query-Posting*. We further merge all candidate ranked lists of all contextual reformulations using weighted fusion. The weight is controlled by the relevance between the original query and the reformulated one with contextual information, i.e., *Query-Context*. For continuous conversations, contexts can be used to optimize the response selection for the given query.

Table 3 summarizes the input and output of the proposed system with deep learning-to-respond schema. Given a query with context, the proposed model would return a response—which has the highest overall (merged) ranking score $\mathcal{F}(.)$—from the pre-constructed repository. We use DNN to assess the relevance between candidate replies, postings and reformulated queries with different combinations of contexts. The DNN also merges the ranking scores corresponding to different contextual query reformulations.

We apply hinge loss with negative sampling to train the network. Gradients can be back-propagated all the way back from merging, ranking, sentence pairing, to individual sentence modeling. Therefore, all these heterogeneous ranking evidences are integrated together through the proposed Deep Learning-to-Respond schema.

Table 3: Symbols and annotations for problem formulation.

q_0	the current query
r, p	candidate reply with the associated antecedent posting
$\mathbb{C}=\{c_i\}$	contexts (utterances before q_0). c_i is a utterance in $\mathbb{C}$
$\mathcal{Q}=\{q_i\}$	reformulated query: q_0 concatenates with some c_i
$f(.)$	matching metric for *Query-Reply*
$g(.)$	matching metric for *Query-Posting*
$h(.)$	matching metric for *Query-Context*
Input	Conversation repository: $\{\langle p, r\rangle\}$ Query: q_0 Context: $\mathbb{C}$
Output	Selected response: $r^* = \underset{r}{\operatorname{argmax}}\, \mathcal{F}(r \vert q_0, \mathbb{C}, \{\langle p, r\rangle\})$

4. CONTEXTUAL REFORMULATION

Generally, context information may be informative (but sometimes may be not) when modeling a query. It is non-trivial to explore different strategies to utilize context information for conversations. In this section, we describe the proposed contextual query reformulation approach.

The contextual query reformulation strategies are mainly inspired by the following observations:

- Some context utterances are informative, while others are not. As the example in Table 2 illustrates, the context utterance *"Really?"* should not be considered as informative as the context utterance *"OMG I got myopia at such an 'old' age"*. Therefore, we shall have different reformulations: we can add the contexts as a whole, or we can add the contexts one-by-one. The intuition is that context sentences are not equally informative, and they shall be used differently.

- Given a context of N sentences, the number of possible ways to concatenate the original query is theoretically 2^N. As a combinatory problem, the number of combinations will grow exponentially as N grows up. Hence we need to impose constraints on the contextual query reformulation strategies. An acceptable solution should be (at most) linear as N grows. We ought to use a subset of reformulations, and combine such strategies to approximate all possible reformulations. The results are then merged by DNN with different weights, analogous to Bayesian model average over different reformulations.

- Under the scenario of a continuous conversation, we observe that contexts, no matter from the *human* side or from the *computer* side, play a similar role to the future conversation. Therefore, we do not distinguish utterances from two sides in the context. Nevertheless, how relevant is a context with the current query is assessed by the *Query-Context* matching function, and the degree of relevance matters when DNN merges different ranked lists from reformulated queries.

Without loss of generosity, let us assume there are N sentences in the context $\mathbb{C}$, i.e., $c_1, \cdots, c_N \in \mathbb{C}$ being previous utterances in the current conversation session. We add one or more context sentences to the query q_0 and obtain a set of reformulated queries (each is denoted as $q_i \in \mathcal{Q}$). To reduce the explosive number of all possible 2^N combinations, we restrict the contextual query reformulation strategies in practice as follows:

- *No Context*: the simplest reformulation strategy is that no context information will be added, i.e., $\mathcal{Q}_{\text{No Context}} = \{q_0\}$.

- *Whole Context*: we do not distinguish different context sentences and hence incorporate the entire contexts as a whole, i.e., $\mathcal{Q}_{\text{Whole Context}} = \{q_0, q_0 \boxplus \mathbb{C}\}$.

- *Add-One*: we concatenate q_0 with one context sentence, one at a time, i.e., $\mathcal{Q}_{\text{Add-One}} = \{q_0, q_0 \boxplus c_1, \ldots, q_0 \boxplus c_N\}$.

- *Drop-Out*: we concatenate q_0 with the whole context while leave-one-out each context sentence, one at a time, i.e., $\mathcal{Q}_{\text{Drop-Out}} = \{q_0, q_0 \boxplus [\mathbb{C}\backslash c_1], \ldots, q_0 \boxplus [\mathbb{C}\backslash c_N]\}$.

[5]Baidu is the largest Chinese search engine provider. Some of the services are available at http://www.baidu.com.

- *Combined*: the combination of all strategies, i.e., $\mathcal{Q} = \mathcal{Q}_{\text{No Context}} \bigcup \mathcal{Q}_{\text{Whole Context}} \bigcup \mathcal{Q}_{\text{Add-One}} \bigcup \mathcal{Q}_{\text{Drop-Out}}$.

'$\boxplus$' refers to literal concatenation, where the order of context and the query is preserved. "$\mathbb{C} \backslash c_i$" indicates c_i is filtered out from $\mathbb{C}$. The benefits for all the contextual query reformulation strategies are that the cost is fixed (for $\mathcal{Q}_{\text{No Context}}$ and $\mathcal{Q}_{\text{Whole Context}}$) or linear (for $\mathcal{Q}_{\text{Add-One}}$ and $\mathcal{Q}_{\text{Drop-Out}}$) along as N grows. The intuition for *Add-One* and *Drop-Out* strategies is based on a finer-granularity: to incorporate relevant context sentences only, or to exempt one irrelevant context sentences. The last strategy combines all these strategies to approximate all possibilities.

5. DEEP LEARNING TO RESPOND

In this section, we describe the deep model for query-reply ranking and merging. Our model first determines the score of a candidate reply given the (reformulated) query, based on the candidate reply and its associated posting (Subsection 5.1). Then the model merges the score by summing over all query reformulations including the original query with a *gating* (product) mechanism (Subsection 5.2). In this way, all heterogeneous ranking evidence is combined organically in a differentiable manner.

5.1 Sentence Pair Modeling

As mentioned, our model first determines the relationship for *Query-Reply*, *Query-Posting*, and *Query-Context* matchings. The three scoring functions are defined as:

- $f(q, r)$: This scoring function directly judges the relatedness between a reply and the (reformulated) query. A larger score achieved means more relevance of the candidate reply.
- $g(q, p)$: If the associated posting of the reply is similar to the query, its subsequent reply is likely to be an appropriate response.
- $h(q, q_0)$: This scoring function tells how the reformulated query is correlated with the original q_0. A more relevant context, i.e., a larger $h(q, q_0)$, should leads to a more confident ranking result, and the scores from $f(q, r)$ and $g(q, p)$ will be credited with more weights for the final Sum fusion.

The scoring function $f(q, r)$ outputs a scalar in $\mathbb{R}$ (appropriateness or inappropriateness) in for a particular candidate reply, while the latter two functions serving as an adjustment or "*gate*", which are squashed by a logistic function into the $(0, 1)$ range. Nevertheless, all the above functions are computed by the same deep neural network architecture (except for the last activation function), but their parameters are different so that the three scoring functions can depict different meanings. In particular, the deep structure for sentence pair modeling includes the following components.

5.1.1 Word Embeddings

Traditional models usually treat a word as a discrete token; thus, the internal relation between similar words would be lost. Word embeddings [19] are a standard apparatus in neural network-based text processing. A word is mapped to a low dimensional, real-valued vector. This process, known as vectorization, captures some underlying meanings. Given enough data, usage, and context, word embeddings can make highly accurate guesses about the meaning of a particular word. Embeddings can equivalently be viewed that a word is first represented as a one-hot vector and multiplied by a look-up table [19].

In our model, we first vectorize all words using their embeddings, which serve as the foundation of our deep neural networks. Word embeddings are initialized randomly, and then tuned during training as part of model parameters.

5.1.2 Bi-Directional LSTM

We use a bi-directional long short term memory (Bi-LSTM) recurrent network to propagate information along the word sequence.

As reviewed in Section 2, a recurrent neural network (RNN) keeps a hidden state vector, which changes according to the input in each time step. As RNNs can iteratively aggregate information along a sequence, they are naturally suitable for sentence modeling.

LSTM is an advanced type of RNN by further using memory cells and gates to learn long term dependencies within a sequence [32, 25]. LSTM models are defined as follows: given a sequence of inputs, an LSTM associates each position with *input, forget*, and *output gates*, denoted as i_t, f_t, and o_t respectively. The vector l_t is used to additively modify the memory contents. Given an input sentence $S = \{x_0, x_1, \ldots, x_T\}$, where x_t is the word embedding at position t in the sentence. LSTM outputs a representation h_t for position t, given by

$$\begin{bmatrix} i_t \\ f_t \\ o_t \\ l_t \end{bmatrix} = \begin{bmatrix} \sigma \\ \sigma \\ \sigma \\ \tanh \end{bmatrix} W \cdot \begin{bmatrix} h_{t-1} \\ e_t \end{bmatrix} \tag{1}$$
$$\tilde{h}_t = f_t \cdot \tilde{h}_{t-1} + i_t \cdot l_t$$
$$h_t^s = o_t \cdot \tilde{h}_t$$

where $\tilde{h}$ is an auxiliary variable and can be viewed as the information stored in memory cell. $\sigma(\cdot) = \frac{1}{1+e^{-\cdot}}$ is a known as a sigmoid/logistic function.

A single directional LSTM typically propagates information from the first word to the last; hence the hidden state at a certain step is dependent on its previous words only and blind of future words. The variant Bi-LSTM [4] is proposed to utilize both previous and future words by two separate RNNs, propagating forward and backward, and generating two independent hidden state vectors $\overrightarrow{h_t}$ and $\overleftarrow{h_t}$, respectively. The two state vectors are concatenated to represent the meaning of the t-th word in the sentence, i.e., $h_t = \left[\overrightarrow{h_t}; \overleftarrow{h_t}\right]$.

5.1.3 Convolution

We further apply a convolutional neural network (CNN) to extract local neighboring features of successive words—i.e., discriminative word sequences can be detected—yielding a more composite representation of the sentences. The structure of CNN in this work is similar to [10], shown in Figure 1. Unlike RNNs, CNNs only impose local interactions between successive words within a filter (size m).

Concretely, we build a CNN upon the output of Bi-LSTM. For every window with the size of m in Bi-LSTM output vectors, i.e., $(H_t)_m = [h_t, h_{t+1}, \cdots, h_{t+m-1}]$, where t is a certain position, the convolutional filter $F = [F(0), \ldots, F(m-1)]$ will generate a vector sequence using the convolution operation "$*$" between the two vectors. More formally, the convolution results in a vector where each component is as follows:

$$o_F = \tanh\left[\sum_{i=0}^{m-1} h(t+i) * F(i)\right] \tag{2}$$

In practice, we also add a scalar bias b to the result of convolution. In this way, we obtain the vector o_F is a vector, each dimension corresponding to each word in the sentence.

Notice that the above equation describes a single "slice" of convolution. In fact, we may have multiple feature filters and thus

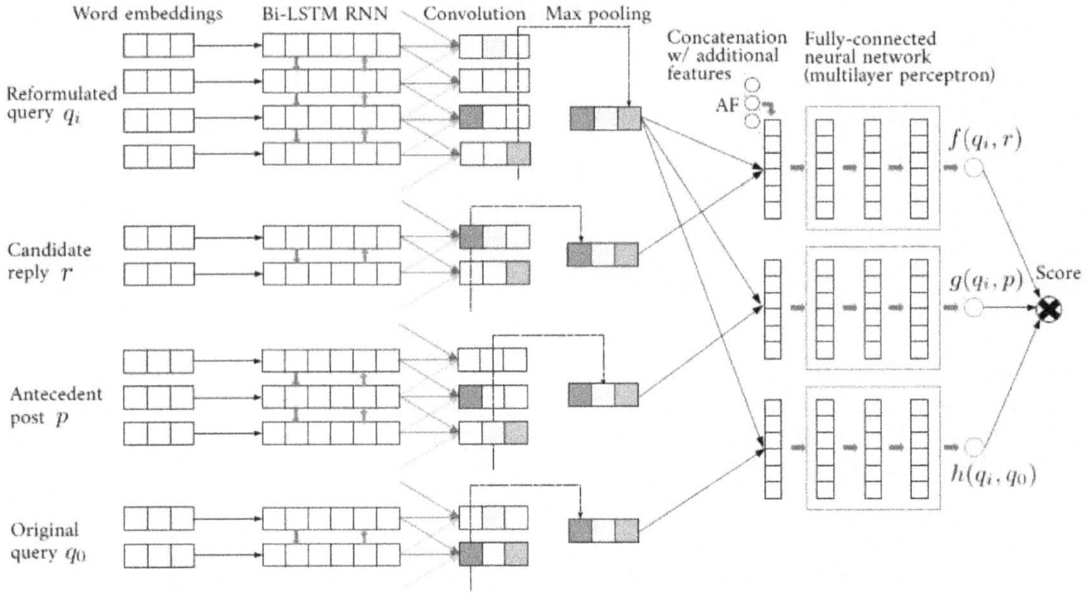

Figure 1: The deep neural network architecture for matching sentence pairs.

multiple feature maps. Different filters do not share parameters (F and b), so that they can capture different meanings.

5.1.4 *Pooling, Concatenation, and Matching*

On the basis of sentence representations using Bi-LSTM with CNN, we can model the interactions between two sentences. We apply pooling to aggregate information along the word sequence. In particular, a max pooling layer chooses the maximum value in each dimension in the feature maps after the convolution, indicating how much the feature is most satisfied along the sequence.

We concatenate two individual sentences' vector representations (with possible additional features), which are then fed to an ensuing network for further information mixing. Vector concatenation for sentence matching is also applied in other studies like [45, 22], which is effective yet of low complexity order, compared with other word-by-word matching [7], or attention methods [27].

The joint vector is then passed through a 3-layer, fully-connected, feed-forward neural network, also known as *multi-layer perception* (MLP) [1], which allows rich interactions between a sentence pair from one of the three components. The network enables to extract features automatically, starting from lower-level representations to higher-level ones.

Finally, a single neuron outputs the matching score of two sentences. As mentioned, $f(q, r)$ is in $\mathbb{R}$; hence the final scoring neuron is essentially a linear regression. For $g(q, p), h(q, q_0) \in (0, 1)$, we apply a sigmoid/logistic function given by $\sigma(\cdot) = \frac{1}{1+e^{-\cdot}}$.

5.2 Merging

In the previous subsection, we have described how the model captures the relation among sentence pairs. Now, we merge the scores of a particular candidate r in terms of different contextual query reformulations. As discussed in Section 5.1, if a posting is more related to the (reformulated) query and the reformulated query is more related to the original query, then $f(q, r)$ would be more reliable. Inspired by this observation, $g(q, p)$ and $h(q, q_0)$ as designed as two adjusting "gates". In particular, scores from different query reformulations are summed, weighted by these two gates. The overall ranking score of a candidate reply r and q_0 is defined as follows. The equation and spirit also appear similar to the integration of a $sum\text{-}product$ process, which combines the sum operations and $product$ operations:

$$\mathcal{F}(q_0, r) = \sum_{i=0}^{|\mathcal{Q}|} \left(h(q_0, q_i) \sum_{p} \left(f(q_i, r) \cdot g(q_i, p) \right) \right) \tag{3}$$

Here we propose to sum over all postings associated with the reply. Different data repository will have different settings: a candidate reply is possible to associate with more than one postings. In our data settings, each reply is associated with only one posting. However, Equation (3) is general and extensible.

Ranking problems can apply pairwise ranking loss such as hinge loss or cross-entropy loss. Here we apply hinge loss to train our DNN network. Given a triple $\mathcal{F}(q_0, r^+)$ in the training set, we randomly sample a negative instance r^-. The objective is to maximize the scores of positive samples while minimizing that of the negative samples. Concretely, we would like $\mathcal{F}(q_0, r^+)$ to be as least $\mathcal{F}(q_0, r^-)$ plus a margin Δ. Thus, the training objective is to

$$\underset{\Omega}{\text{minimize}} \sum_{q_0, r^+} \max\left\{0, \Delta + \mathcal{F}(q_0, r^+) - \mathcal{F}(q_0, r^-)\right\} + \lambda \|\Omega\|_2^2 \tag{4}$$

where we add an ℓ_2 penalty with coefficient λ for all the parameters $\Omega = \{\theta; \eta; \phi\}$ which are weight and bias values optimized by the network from multi-dimensions of ranking evidences, i.e., *Query-Reply*, *Query-Posting* and *Query-Context*, correspondingly.

5.3 Training

As our model is (almost) everywhere differentiable, the parameters of the networks are optimized with stochastic gradient descent using the back prorogation algorithm to compute the gradients. The gradients can be propagated all the way back through merging, gating, matching, and individual sentence modeling. In this way, heterogeneous information (ranking evidences) can be incorporated organically with our model under the unified deep architecture. Accordingly to the objective function to optimize $\mathcal{O}(.)$ in Equation (4), it is sufficient to learn the model by computing the gradients with respect to the model parameters θ, η and ϕ; that is, our goals

Table 4: Data statistics. Postings and replies are all unique.

Source	#Posting	#Reply	#Vocabulary
Zhidao	8,915,694	3,705,302	1,499,691
Douban	10,618,981	2,963,226	483,846
Tieba	4,189,160	3,730,248	1,046,130
Weibo	186,963	393,654	119,163
Misc.	3,056	1,548	4,297
Total	9,023,854	7,293,978	2,857,378

are to compute $\frac{\partial\mathcal{O}}{\partial\theta}$, $\frac{\partial\mathcal{O}}{\partial\eta}$ and $\frac{\partial\mathcal{O}}{\partial\phi}$ for *Query-Reply*, *Query-Posting* and *Query-Context*.

6. EXPERIMENTS AND EVALUATION

In this section, we evaluate our model for conversation task against a series of baselines based on a huge conversation resource. The objectives of our experiments are to 1) evaluate the effectiveness of our proposed deep learning-to-respond schema, and 2) evaluate contextual reformulation strategies and components of multi-dimension of ranking evidences for the conversational task.

6.1 Dataset

As mentioned, we collected massive conversation resources from various forums, microblog websites, and cQA platforms including Baidu Zhidao[6], Douban forum[7], Baidu Tieba[8], Sina Weibo[9], etc. We conducted data filtering and cleaning procedures by removing extremely short replies and those of low linguistic quality such as meaningless babblings according to the evaluation framework put forward in [40, 42], so as to maintain a meaningful, high-quality conversation record. In total, the database contains $\sim$10 million $\langle$*posting*, *reply*$\rangle$ pairs. Some statistics are summarized in Table 4.

We constructed the dataset of 1,606,583 samples to train the deep neural networks, 357,018 for validation, and 11,097 for testing. It is important that the dataset for learning does not overlap with the database for retrieval, so that we strictly comply with the machine learning regime. For each training and validation sample, we randomly chose a reply as a negative sample. Validation was based on the accuracy of positive/negative classification. For the test set, we hired workers on a crowdsourcing platform to judge the appropriateness of 30 candidate replies retrieved for each query. Each sample was judged by 7 annotators via majority voting based on the *appropriateness* for the response given the query and contexts (if any): "1" denotes an appropriate response and "0" indicates an inappropriate one.

6.2 Experimental Setups

6.2.1 Hyperparameters

In our proposed model, we used 128-dimensional word embeddings, and they were initialized randomly and learned during training. As our dataset is in Chinese, we performed standard Chinese word segmentation. We maintained a vocabulary of 177,044 phrases by choosing those with more than 2 occurrences.

The bi-directional LSTM has 128 hidden units for each dimension; CNN is 256 dimensional with a window size of 3. We used stochastic gradient descent (with a mini-batch size of 100) for optimization, gradient computed by standard back-propagation. Initial learning rate was set to 0.8, and a multiplicative learning rate decay was applied. The above parameters were chosen empirically. We used the validation set for early stopping.

[6]http://www.zhidao.baidu.com
[7]http://www.douban.com
[8]http://www.tieba.baidu.com
[9]http://www.weibo.com

6.2.2 Evaluation Metrics

Given the ranking lists (annotated by crowdsourced workers) for test queries, we evaluated the performance in terms of the following metrics: precision@1 (p@1), mean average precision (MAP) [31, 43], and normalized discounted cumulative gain (nDCG) [8, 41]. Since the system outputs the best selected reply, p@1 is the precision at the 1st position, and should be the most natural way to indicate the fraction of suitable responses among the top-1 reply retrieved. Besides, we also provided the top-k ranking list for the test queries using nDCG and MAP, which test the potential for a system to provide more than one appropriate responses as candidates. We aimed at selecting as many appropriate responses as possible into the top-k list and rewarding methods that return suitable replies on the top.

Formally, the metrics are computed as follows.

$$\text{nDCG@i} = \frac{1}{|\mathcal{T}|}\sum_{q\in\mathcal{T}}\frac{1}{Z}\sum_{i=1}^{k}\frac{2^{r_i}-1}{\log(1+i)}$$

where $\mathcal{T}$ indicates the testing query set, k denotes the top-k position in the ranking list, and Z is a normalization factor obtained from a perfect ranking. r_i is the relevance score for the i-th candidate reply in the ranking list (i.e., 1: appropriate, 0: inappropriate).

MAP is computed by

$$\text{MAP} = \frac{1}{|\mathcal{T}|}\sum_{q\in\mathcal{T}}\frac{1}{N_q}\sum_{i=1}^{k}P_i \times r_i$$

Here N_q is the number of appropriate responses selected, and P_i is the precision at i-th position for the query.

Since we use real conversations for testing, we also have the human response taken from the human-human conversation session as one of candidate replies ordered in the ranked list. Hence we include the Mean Reciprocal Rank (MRR) evaluation computed as:

$$\text{MRR} = \frac{1}{|\mathcal{T}|}\sum_{q\in\mathcal{T}}\frac{1}{rank(q)}$$

where $rank(q)$ is the position of the original response in the candidate ranking list. Unlike MAP and nDCG, which examine the ranks of all appropriate responses, MRR focuses on evaluating the capability of retrieval systems to find (perhaps) the best response. MRR is useful but does not test the full capability because there can be more than one appropriate responses to fulfill a conversation.

6.2.3 Algorithms for Comparison

To illustrate the performance of our approach, we include several alternative algorithms as baselines for comparison. The baselines can be divided into two categories, i.e., 1) generation-based methods and 2) retrieval-based methods for conversation systems from very recent studies. Since our proposed approach is technically a retrieval-based method, we mainly focus on the second category. For fairness we conducted the same pre-processing procedures and data cleaning for all algorithms.

Generation-based Conversation. For this group of algorithms, the conversation system will generate a response from a given input, i.e., a query from the user under the conversational scenario.

• *Statistical Machine Translation (SMT)*: SMT is a machine translation paradigm which translates one sentence in the source language to a sentence in the target language. If we treat queries and replies as separate languages, we can train a translation model to

Table 5: Retrieval performance against baselines with our proposed adaption of contextual reformulation. '⋆' indicates that we accept the improvement hypothesis of DL2R over the best baseline by Wilcoxon test at a significance level of 0.01. Performance of both generative methods and retrieval methods. For generative methods, they generate one response given each query. Hence the p@1 in fact refers to accuracy. Other metrics are not applicable.

Model	p@1	MAP	nDCG@5	nDCG@10	nDCG@20	MRR
SMT (Ritter et al., [26])	0.363					
LSTM-RNN (Sutskever et al., [32])	0.441					
NRM (Shang et al., [29])	0.465					
Random Match	0.266	0.246	0.247	0.289	0.353	0.083
Okapi BM25	0.272	0.253	0.337	0.302	0.368	0.169
DeepMatch (Lu and Li, [17])	0.457	0.317	0.419	0.454	0.508	0.275
LSTM-RNN (Palangi et al., [25])	0.338	0.283	0.330	0.371	0.431	0.228
ARC (Hu et al., [7])	0.394	0.294	0.397	0.421	0.477	0.232
DeepMatch w/ context adaption	0.603	0.378	0.555	0.584	0.628	**0.349**
LSTM-RNN w/ context adaption	0.362	0.296	0.354	0.395	0.453	0.237
ARC w/ context adaption	0.400	0.309	0.383	0.422	0.480	0.319
Deep Learning-to-Respond (DL2R)	**0.731**⋆	**0.416**⋆	**0.663**⋆	**0.682**⋆	**0.717**⋆	0.333

Table 6: Performance evaluations of different contextual query reformulation strategies.

	p@1	MAP	nDCG@5	nDCG@10	nDCG@20	MRR
No Context	0.522	0.340	0.476	0.509	0.559	0.296
Whole Context	0.698	0.404	0.635	0.657	0.696	0.327
Add-One	0.716	0.411	0.650	0.670	0.706	0.322
Drop-Out	0.720	0.413	0.656	0.675	0.711	0.328
Combined	0.731	0.416	0.663	0.682	0.717	0.333

Table 7: Performance evaluations of different components with multi-dimension of ranking evidences.

	p@1	MAP	nDCG@5	nDCG@10	nDCG@20	MRR
Query-Reply w/o Query-Context	0.522	0.340	0.476	0.509	0.559	0.296
Query-Posting w/o Query-Context	0.510	0.302	0.404	0.425	0.489	0.285
Query-Reply w/ Query-Context	0.596	0.366	0.528	0.561	0.603	0.327
Query-Posting w/ Query-Context	0.563	0.362	0.483	0.516	0.568	0.316
Full Combination	0.731	0.416	0.663	0.682	0.717	0.333

"translate" queries into replies. We implemented the phrase-based translation idea for conversation proposed in [26].

• *LSTM-RNN*: LSTM-RNN is basically a Recurrent Neural Network (RNN) using the Long Short Term Memory (LSTM) architecture. The RNN with LSTM units consists of memory cells in order to store information for extended periods of time. We use LSTM-RNN for both generation and retrieval baselines. For generation, we first use an LSTM-RNN to encode the input sequence (query) to a vector space, and then use another LSTM-RNN to decode the vector into the output sequence (reply) [32]; for retrievals, we adopt the LSTM-RNN to construct sentence representations and use cosine similarity to output the matching score [25].

• *Neural Responding Machine.* We implement the neural responding machine (NRM) proposed in [29], which is an RNN-based generation approach with a global-local attention schema.

Retrieval-based Conversation. The approaches within this group of baselines are based on retrieval systems, which return the best matched candidate reply out of the conversational repository given a particular query. Since our approach is retrieval-based, we select strong retrieval-based methods to make a thorough comparison.

• *Random Match.* The method randomly selects replies from the retrieved list for each query. Be aware it is not *true* random because it only randomizes the order of the retrieved results. The true random match is too weak to be included as a decent baseline.

• *Okapi BM25.* We include the standard retrieval technique to rank candidate replies. For each query, we retrieve the most relevant reply using BM25 model [18] from the corpus.

• *DeepMatch.* The DeepMatch method considers multiple granularity from the perspective of topics, obtained via LDA [17].

• *ARC.* The ARC approach is a CNN based method with convolutionary layers which construct sentence representations and produce the final matching scores via a MLP layer [7].

• *Deep Learning-to-Respond (DL2R).* We propose the DL2R system based on three novel insights: 1) the integration of multi-dimension of ranking evidences, 2) context-based query reformulations with ranked lists fusion, and 3) deep learning framework for the conversational task. There is actually a series of variants of DL2R model with different components and different context utilization strategies. We will first report the performance comparisons between DL2R against baselines and then show the details of components and strategies in Section 6.4.

6.3 Overall Performance

We compare the performance of all methods including baselines and our proposed DL2R model measured in terms of p@1, MAP, nDCG and MRR. In Table 5 we list the overall results against all baseline methods. Our proposed method DL2R shows clearly better performance than the baseline methods. On average, DL2R achieves an average +38.63% improvement (averaged on all metrics) compared with the strongest baseline group with context adaption (in Table 5). We then discuss the comparisons in details.

We illustrate the result from generative methods. Given one user query, the generative methods generally provide one generation as the response to output. Hence we do not compare MAP or nDCG@1 for this algorithm group. Note that the original response is not likely to be generated; thus it is infeasible to calculate the MRR. In general, the generative algorithms have relatively high p@1 scores, while LSTM-RNN and NRM perform better than the SMT method. The reasons can be ascribed to two aspects: firstly, SMT is not instinctively tailored for conversation systems and secondly, deep neural networks for LSTM-RNN and NRM will be more likely to learn a better representation for the queries and then return a better decoded generation as response. The generated responses are in general quite ambiguous or broad to answer a wide range of queries, but not specific enough. Such responses might be relevant but not appropriate enough to make a meaningful conversation, which have been raised as a problem in [15, 29].

We can see great improvement for DL2R against original retrieval-based baselines. *Random Match* is a lower bound for all baselines. As we mentioned, it randomizes the order of the retrieved results. Hence the result is comparable to that of BM25 but slightly worse. *Okapi BM25* represents the standard (and simple) retrieval system. The performance for BM25 is not as good as the other deep learning-based retrieval systems, which is not surprising. Deep learning systems are proved to have strong capabilities to learn the abstractive representation [1, 10, 30], while BM25 only utilizes the shallow representation of term-level retrieval. The deep learning algorithm groups clearly overwhelm shallow learning algorithms, yet it is interesting to see that DL2R still outperforms the other deep learning baselines in Table 5. The benefits might be due to the context information we have managed to use, while the other deep learning baselines are matching metrics for single turns only. For a more fair comparison, we adapt the original baselines into our proposed contextual reformulation framework to incorporate context information.

In Table 5, we can see with the usage of contextual reformulation, the performances for DeepMatch, ARC, and LSTM-RNN all get boosted, which greatly indicates the effectiveness of our proposed contextual query reformulation for conversation systems. It is a useful way to incorporate context information for conversational scenarios. Our proposed DL2R has obvious improvement against the modified baseline systems. The most probable credits come from the retrieval formulation: we frame the virtual document as a posting and reply, and we integrate multi-dimensions of ranking evidences to facilitate a better ranking list. The contextual DeepMatch method very slightly outperforms DL2R on MRR evaluation. As mentioned before, MRR is useful when trying the find the best response. Since conversations are open with more than one appropriate responses, MAP and nDCG scores indicate the full capacity of the retrieval systems.

Till now, we have validated that deep learning structures, contextual reformulations and integrations of multi-dimensions of ranking evidences are effective. Next we will come to a closer look at these strategies and components for further analysis and discussions.

6.4 Analysis and Discussions

We examine the relative contributions of different strategies and individual components of our proposed model. Other than the proposed deep neural network-based learning framework, we have two other contributions: 1) contextual query reformulation to utilize context information, and 2) integration of multi-dimension of ranking evidences. We now analyze the strategies and components.

6.4.1 Reformulation Strategies

As mentioned in Section 4, we have different ways to use contextual information via contextual query reformulation strategies: *No Context*, *Whole Context*, *Add-One*, *Drop-Out* and *Combined*. The *Whole Context* strategy incorporates context information in a coarse granularity, while the *Add-One* and *Drop-Out* strategies are in a finer-granularity. We illustrate the different performance with different strategies using the DL2R framework in Table 6.

We can see that the improvement from *No Context* to *Whole Context* is rather obvious, indicating that context information is quite beneficial to find better responses under the conversational scenarios. We also have an interesting observation that *Add-One* and *Drop-Out* strategies are better than the *Whole Context* strategy. *Whole Context* strategy is a coarse-grained method which uses context information without distinguishing irrelevant contexts from relevant ones. The results indicate a proper way to use context information is important. *Drop-Out* strategy is slightly better than the *Add-One* strategy, which confirms the exemption of irrelevant context information is necessary, and in most cases, there are more relevant context sentences than irrelevant ones. The combination of all strategies performs best since it balances both the coarse-grained and fine-grained context modeling. We combine the best approximations for all possible utilizations of contexts, avoiding explosive number of combinations.

6.4.2 Components Analysis

Since we have three major components from the multi-dimensions of ranking evidences, i.e., *Query-Reply*, *Query-Posting* and *Query-Context*, we examine the contributions of such components. Note that we can retrieve responses from the virtual document consisting of a *posting-reply* pair, from the *reply* side and/or the *posting* side. But we cannot directly retrieve the response using *Query-Context*. It is pointless to run solely on the *Query-Context* part.

The first group is to run only based on *Query-Reply* and *Query-Posting*. Neither of the two components incorporates *Query-Context* information. Without context information, the proposed framework might handle single-turn conversation well enough, while generally multi-turn conversation is beyond the capability of the system. With the incorporation of the contextual information, the performance of both components get boosted. It is not surprising that the combination of all three components yield to the best results: each component characterizes the appropriateness of the response from a different aspect, and all aspects should be integrated for scoring.

7. CONCLUSIONS

In this paper, we propose to establish an automatic conversation system between humans and computers. Given a human-issued message as the query, our proposed system will return the corresponding responses based on a *deep learning-to-respond* schema. There are 3 major contributions in this work: 1) we propose a contextual query reformulation framework with ranking fusions for the conversation task; 2) we integrate multi-dimension of ranking evidences, i.e., *queries*, *postings*, *replies* and *contexts*; 3) we establish the deep neural network architecture featured with above strategies and components. We launch the conversation system based on a massive repository ($\sim$10 million *posting-reply* pairs) and run experiments to validate the proposed paradigm.

We examine the effect of our proposed DL2R model with several baselines on a series of evaluation metrics. Our method consistently and significantly outperforms the alternative baselines in terms of p@1, MAP, nDCG, and MRR. Furthermore, we have investigated further experiments for component contributions and strategy analysis. In general, context information is demonstrated to be useful for conversations, especially multi-turn conversations and all dimensions of ranking evidences are helpful. This work opens to several interesting directions for future work with regard to automatic conversation between humans and computers. For instance, we can incorporate more additional features and more conversation-oriented formulations, such as dialogue acts, conversational logics, and discourse structures, etc.

8. ACKNOWLEDGMENTS

This work is supported by the National Basic Research Program of China (No. 2014CB340505). We thank all the reviewers for their valuable comments, and thank the support from the Deep Learning Platform in Baidu Natural Language Processing Department.

9. REFERENCES

[1] Y. Bengio. Learning deep architectures for AI. *Foundations and Trends in Machine Learning*, 2(1):1–127, 2009.

[2] F. Bessho, T. Harada, and Y. Kuniyoshi. Dialog system using real-time crowdsourcing and Twitter large-scale corpus. In *SIGDIAL*, pages 227–231, 2012.

[3] G. Cong, L. Wang, C.-Y. Lin, Y.-I. Song, and Y. Sun. Finding question-answer pairs from online forums. In *SIGIR*, pages 467–474.

[4] A. Graves, A.-r. Mohamed, and G. Hinton. Speech recognition with deep recurrent neural networks. In *Proc. Acoustics, Speech and Signal Processing*, pages 6645–6649, 2013.

[5] H. He, K. Gimpel, and J. Lin. Multi-perspective sentence similarity modeling with convolutional neural networks. In *EMNLP*, pages 1576–1586, 2015.

[6] R. Higashinaka, K. Imamura, T. Meguro, C. Miyazaki, N. Kobayashi, H. Sugiyama, T. Hirano, T. Makino, and Y. Matsuo. Towards an open domain conversational system fully based on natural language processing. In *COLING*, 2014.

[7] B. Hu, Z. Lu, H. Li, and Q. Chen. Convolutional neural network architectures for matching natural language sentences. In *NIPS*, pages 2042–2050, 2014.

[8] K. Järvelin and J. Kekäläinen. Cumulated gain-based evaluation of IR techniques. *ACM Trans. Inf. Syst.*, 20(4):422–446, 2002.

[9] Z. Ji, Z. Lu, and H. Li. An information retrieval approach to short text conversation. *CoRR*, abs/1408.6988, 2014.

[10] N. Kalchbrenner, E. Grefenstette, and P. Blunsom. A convolutional neural network for modelling sentences. *arXiv preprint arXiv:1404.2188*, 2014.

[11] C.-J. Lee, Q. Ai, W. B. Croft, and D. Sheldon. An optimization framework for merging multiple result lists. In *CIKM '15*, pages 303–312, 2015.

[12] A. Leuski, R. Patel, D. Traum, and B. Kennedy. Building effective question answering characters. In *SIGDIAL*, pages 18–27, 2009.

[13] A. Leuski and D. Traum. NPCEditor: Creating virtual human dialogue using information retrieval techniques. *AI Magazine*, 32(2):42–56, 2011.

[14] H. Li and J. Xu. Semantic matching in search. *Foundations and Trends in Information Retrieval*, 8:89, 2014.

[15] J. Li, M. Galley, C. Brockett, J. Gao, and B. Dolan. A diversity-promoting objective function for neural conversation models. *arXiv preprint arXiv:1510.03055*, 2015.

[16] X. Li, L. Mou, R. Yan, and M. Zhang. Stalematebreaker: A proactive content-introducing approach to automatic human-computer conversation. In *IJCAI*, 2016.

[17] Z. Lu and H. Li. A deep architecture for matching short texts. In *NIPS*, pages 1367–1375, 2013.

[18] C. D. Manning, P. Raghavan, and H. Schütze. *Introduction to Information Retrieval*. Cambridge University Press, 2008.

[19] T. Mikolov, K. Chen, G. Corrado, and J. Dean. Efficient estimation of word representations in vector space. *arXiv:1301.3781*, 2013.

[20] L. Mou, G. Li, L. Zhang, T. Wang, and Z. Jin. Convolutional neural networks over tree structures for programming language processing. In *AAAI*, pages 1287–1292, 2016.

[21] L. Mou, H. Peng, G. Li, Y. Xu, L. Zhang, and Z. Jin. Discriminative neural sentence modeling by tree-based convolution. In *EMNLP*, pages 2315–2325, 2015.

[22] L. Mou, M. Rui, G. Li, Y. Xu, L. Zhang, R. Yan, and Z. Jin. Recognizing entailment and contradiction by tree-based convolution. *arXiv preprint arXiv:1512.08422*, 2015.

[23] M. Nakano, N. Miyazaki, N. Yasuda, A. Sugiyama, J.-i. Hirasawa, K. Dohsaka, and K. Aikawa. WIT: A toolkit for building robust and real-time spoken dialogue systems. In *SIGDIAL*, pages 150–159.

[24] E. Nouri, R. Artstein, A. Leuski, and D. R. Traum. Augmenting conversational characters with generated question-answer pairs. In *AAAI Fall Symposium: Question Generation*, 2011.

[25] H. Palangi, L. Deng, Y. Shen, J. Gao, X. He, J. Chen, X. Song, and R. Ward. Deep sentence embedding using the long short term memory network: Analysis and application to information retrieval. *arXiv preprint arXiv:1502.06922*, 2015.

[26] A. Ritter, C. Cherry, and W. B. Dolan. Data-driven response generation in social media. In *EMNLP*, pages 583–593, 2011.

[27] T. Rocktäschel, E. Grefenstette, K. M. Hermann, T. Kočiský, and P. Blunsom. Reasoning about entailment with neural attention. *arXiv preprint arXiv:1509.06664*, 2015.

[28] A. Severyn and A. Moschitti. Learning to rank short text pairs with convolutional deep neural networks. In *SIGIR '15*, pages 373–382.

[29] L. Shang, Z. Lu, and H. Li. Neural responding machine for short-text conversation. In *ACL-IJCNLP*, pages 1577–1586, 2015.

[30] R. Socher, J. Pennington, E. H. Huang, A. Y. Ng, and C. D. Manning. Semi-supervised recursive autoencoders for predicting sentiment distributions. In *EMNLP*, pages 151–161, 2011.

[31] H. Sugiyama, T. Meguro, R. Higashinaka, and Y. Minami. Open-domain utterance generation for conversational dialogue systems using Web-scale dependency structures. In *SIGDIAL*, pages 334–338, 2013.

[32] I. Sutskever, O. Vinyals, and Q. V. Le. Sequence to sequence learning with neural networks. In *NIPS*, pages 3104–3112, 2014.

[33] M. A. Walker, R. Passonneau, and J. E. Boland. Quantitative and qualitative evaluation of darpa communicator spoken dialogue systems. In *ACL*, pages 515–522, 2001.

[34] R. S. Wallace. *The Anatomy of ALICE*. Springer, 2009.

[35] H. Wang, Z. Lu, H. Li, and E. Chen. A dataset for research on short-text conversations. In *EMNLP*, pages 935–945, 2013.

[36] J. Williams, A. Raux, D. Ramachandran, and A. Black. The dialog state tracking challenge. In *SIGDIAL*, pages 404–413, 2013.

[37] Y. Xu, R. Jia, L. Mou, G. Li, Y. Chen, Y. Lu, and Z. Jin. Improved relation classification by deep recurrent neural networks with data augmentation. *arXiv preprint arXiv:1601.03651*, 2016.

[38] Y. Xu, L. Mou, G. Li, Y. Chen, H. Peng, and Z. Jin. Classifying relations via long short term memory networks along shortest dependency paths. In *EMNLP*, 2015.

[39] R. Yan. i, poet: Automatic poetry composition through recurrent neural networks with iterative polishing schema. In *IJCAI*, 2016.

[40] R. Yan, M. Lapata, and X. Li. Tweet recommendation with graph co-ranking. In *ACL*, pages 516–525, 2012.

[41] R. Yan, C.-T. Li, H.-P. Hsieh, P. Hu, X. Hu, and T. He. Socialized language model smoothing via bi-directional influence propagation on social networks. In *WWW '16*, pages 1395–1405, 2016.

[42] R. Yan, X. Wan, J. Otterbacher, L. Kong, X. Li, and Y. Zhang. Evolutionary timeline summarization: A balanced optimization framework via iterative substitution. In *SIGIR '11*, pages 745–754, 2011.

[43] R. Yan, I. E. Yen, C.-T. Li, S. Zhao, and X. Hu. Tackling the achilles heel of social networks: Influence propagation based language model smoothing. In *WWW '15*, pages 1318–1328, 2015.

[44] K. Zhai and D. J. Williams. Discovering latent structure in task-oriented dialogues. In *ACL*, pages 36–46, 2014.

[45] B. Zhang, J. Su, D. Xiong, Y. Lu, H. Duan, and J. Yao. Shallow convolutional neural network for implicit discourse relation recognition. In *EMNLP*, pages 2230–2235, 2015.

Document Retrieval Using Entity-Based Language Models

Hadas Raviv
Technion, Israel
hadasrv@tx.technion.ac.il

Oren Kurland
Technion, Israel
kurland@ie.technion.ac.il

David Carmel
Yahoo Research, Israel
david.carmel@ymail.com

ABSTRACT

We address the ad hoc document retrieval task by devising novel types of entity-based language models. The models utilize information about single terms in the query and documents as well as term sequences marked as entities by some entity-linking tool. The key principle of the language models is accounting, simultaneously, for the uncertainty inherent in the entity-markup process and the balance between using entity-based and term-based information. Empirical evaluation demonstrates the merits of using the language models for retrieval. For example, the performance transcends that of a state-of-the-art term proximity method. We also show that the language models can be effectively used for cluster-based document retrieval and query expansion.

Categories and Subject Descriptors: H.3.3 [Information Search and Retrieval]: Retrieval models

Keywords: document retrieval; entity-based language models

1. INTRODUCTION

Most ad hoc document retrieval methods compare query and document representations. To address the potential vocabulary mismatch between a short query and documents relevant to the query, various semantic document-query similarity measures have been proposed [28].

Specifically, there is a growing body of work on retrieval methods that utilize information about *entities* in a repository (e.g., Wikipedia or Freebase) which appear in queries and documents (e.g., [46, 35, 39, 7, 13, 31, 45, 29, 33, 44]). Most of these methods expand the query with terms or entities related to those appearing (or marked) in it [46, 35, 39, 7, 13, 31, 45, 29]; other methods project queries and documents onto a latent or explicit entity space [14, 33, 44].

In this paper we take a step back, and address a more fundamental challenge regarding the use of entity-based information for document retrieval. We study whether using *surface level* entity-based query and document representations can help to improve retrieval effectiveness. By "surface level" we refer to representations based only on terms in the text and *markups* of entities in it, along with raw corpus-based occurrence statistics. This is in contrast to expansion-based and projection-based representations that utilize also terms and entities related to those (marked) in the text and which often use auxiliary information about entities from the entity repository; e.g., textual descriptions of entities, entities' categories and inter-entity relations [46, 35, 39, 7, 13, 31, 45, 29, 33, 44]. Put in simpler words, the question we address is *whether the markup of entities in a query and documents is, by itself, sufficient information for improving retrieval effectiveness.*

The reason for addressing the question just posed is two fold. First, it will shed light on the effectiveness of using entities in their most basic capacity; that is, special tokens marked in queries and documents. Indeed, findings in past work on ad hoc retrieval regarding the merits of using surface level entity-based representations are inconclusive [16, 42, 47, 3, 14]. Second, such representations can be naturally used in existing retrieval approaches and tasks to improve performance; e.g., query expansion and cluster-based document retrieval as we show in this paper.

There are various potential merits in using surface level entity-based representations. For example, these can help to cope with the vocabulary mismatch problem; e.g., the entity *United States of America* can have different expressions in the text, including, "U.S.", "USA", "United States" and more. Furthermore, expressions of entities in the text are variable-length n-grams that bear semantic meaning. Thus, entities can be used for effective modeling of term proximity information which goes beyond using fixed-length n-grams.

An important challenge in inducing entity-based representations is accounting for the uncertainty inherent in the entity-markup process (a.k.a. entity linking); that is, associating term sequences with entities in a repository. Specifically, a term sequence can potentially be associated with multiple entities; e.g., the term "Lincoln" can be associated with the U.S. president, the car, the 2012 movie, etc. The uncertainty in entity linking has significant impact on retrieval effectiveness as we show in this paper.

We present novel types of entity-based language models which consider *both* single terms in the text as well as term sequences marked as entities by an existing entity-linking tool. These language models are induced from the query and documents in the corpus and serve for retrieval in the language modeling framework. The main novelty of these language models is accounting, simultaneously, for (i) the uncertainty in entity linking — specifically, the confidence levels of entity markups; and, (ii) the balance between using

SIGIR '16, July 17-21, 2016, Pisa, Italy
© 2016 ACM. ISBN 978-1-4503-4069-4/16/07...$15.00
DOI: http://dx.doi.org/10.1145/2911451.2911508

term-based and entity-based information. We demonstrate the importance of accounting for the mutual effects of these two aspects. For example, we show that using high recall entity markup, which is quite noisy, can help to significantly improve retrieval effectiveness if the noise is "balanced" by sufficient utilization of term-based information.

Empirical evaluation demonstrates the merits of using our entity-based language models for retrieval. The performance significantly transcends that of a state-of-the-art term proximity method: the sequential dependence model (SDM) [36, 19]. Integrating the language models with SDM yields further performance improvements. The language models are also effective for two additional retrieval paradigms: cluster-based document retrieval and query expansion.

2. RELATED WORK

The work most related to ours is that on devising surface level entity-based document and query representations for document retrieval [21, 16, 42, 47, 3, 41, 14]. The findings about the merits of these representations have been inconclusive. The few cases where the representations were shown to be somewhat effective for retrieval were when entity markups were devised in extreme care and were of very high quality [47, 3, 14]. In contrast to this past work that focused on vector space models, we demonstrate the clear merits of using our entity-based language models for retrieval. Also, in contrast to previously proposed representations [21, 16, 42, 47, 3, 41, 14], our language models account simultaneously for the uncertainty in the entity-markup process, and the balance between using term-based and entity-based information. Consequently, a highly important aspect that further differentiates our approach from past work is the effective utilization of high recall, noisy, entity markups.

There is work on query expansion using entity-based information [43, 34, 30, 40, 8, 10, 18, 46, 6, 20, 7, 35, 39, 13, 31, 29, 45] and on projecting queries and documents onto an entity space to compare them [14, 33, 44]. There are two fundamental differences between all this past work and ours which focuses on surface level entity-based query and document representations. First, in these past methods, queries and documents are represented by external terms and entities which they do not contain[1]. Our surface level representations do not utilize such expansions. Second, auxiliary information about entities from the entity repository (e.g., textual descriptions of entities and their interrelations) is utilized in this past work, but not in our representations[2].

We show that our entity-based language models can be used to create effective expanded query forms by "plugging" them into an *existing* query expansion method: the relevance model [26, 1]. The resultant approach, which *simultaneously* expands the query with both terms and entities, is conceptually reminiscent of some methods recently proposed by Dalton et al. [13]. In their work, queries are expanded, independently, using terms and entities. The retrieval scores attained by using multiple term-only and entity-only expanded query forms are fused using a learning-to-rank method [13]. We show that our language models can be used to further improve the effectiveness of such expansion-based approaches by improving the quality of the pseudo relevant document list used for query expansion.

We also demonstrate the merits of using our language models for cluster-based document retrieval. Using entity-based representations for this task is novel to this study.

In some studies, concepts (entities) in verbose queries were automatically weighted [2, 22, 4, 5]. In contrast to our approach, weights (confidence levels) of entities in documents were not accounted for. We demonstrate the importance of accounting for the confidence level of entity markups in both queries and documents. Further tuning of entities' weights in our proposed language models, using some of these approaches [2, 22, 4, 5], is interesting future work.

There are language models that integrate word phrases and named entities based on their association with predefined classes [27, 23]. In contrast to our language models, which are not based on such classes, these language models were not designed and used for document retrieval.

3. RETRIEVAL FRAMEWORK

In what follows we present ad hoc document retrieval methods that rank documents in a corpus D in response to query q. The methods utilize information about entities mentioned in the query and in documents.

To mark entities in texts, we use *some* entity-linking tool that utilizes a repository (e.g., Wikipedia or Freebase) where entities have unique IDs. The entity-linking tool takes as input a text, query or document in our case, and marks variable length sequences of terms as *potential* entities in the repository. The entity markup of a term sequence is composed of entity ID and a confidence level in $[0, 1]$. The confidence level reflects the likelihood that the term sequence corresponds to the entity. The confidence level relies on the term sequence and its context; e.g., its neighboring terms or other term sequences marked as entities [15, 38]. Using high confidence level results in high precision entity markup while low confidence level results in high recall.

We assume that each position in a given text can be part of at most a single term sequence that is marked as an entity; i.e., the entity markups do not overlap. A specific occurrence of a term sequence in a text cannot be marked with more than one entity. Yet, a term sequence can appear several times in a text with different entity markups as the markups depend on the context of the sequence. Details of the entity linking tools we use are provided in Section 4.1.

The retrieval methods we present in Section 3.2 use entity-based query and document language models. We now turn to define these language models.

3.1 Entity-based language models

We define unigram entity-based language models over a token space $\mathcal{T}$; i.e., tokens are generated by the language model independently of each other. The token space,

$$\mathcal{T} \stackrel{def}{=} \mathcal{V} \cup \mathcal{E} \quad (1)$$

is composed of the set $\mathcal{V}$ of all terms in the corpus D and the set $\mathcal{E}$ of entities in the entity repository which were marked at least once in a document in D with *any* confidence level.

[1] Xiong and Callan [44] found that representing queries using only entities marked in them is of merit for their learning-to-rank approach. However, features describing the query-entities relations rely on auxiliary information from the entity repository that is not used by our methods.

[2] The entity-linking process could use auxiliary information from the entity repository. However, our proposed representations utilize the entity markups simply as tokens with confidence levels, and do not use auxiliary information.

The language models we devise rely on a definition of *pseudo counts* for tokens. Two definitions of pseudo counts will be presented in Sections 3.1.1 and 3.1.2. Let $pc(t, x)$ be the pseudo count of token t ($\in \mathcal{T}$) in the text or text collection x. We define the *pseudo length* of x as:

$$pl(x) \stackrel{def}{=} \sum_{t \in \mathcal{T}: pc(t,x)>0} pc(t, x).$$

The maximum likelihood estimate (MLE) of token t ($\in \mathcal{T}$) with respect to x is:

$$\theta_x^{MLE}(t) \stackrel{def}{=} \frac{pc(t, x)}{pl(x)}. \quad (2)$$

The MLE can be smoothed using Dirichlet priors [49]:

$$\theta_x^{Dir}(t) \stackrel{def}{=} \frac{pc(t, x) + \mu\theta_D^{MLE}(t)}{pl(x) + \mu}; \quad (3)$$

μ is a smoothing parameter.

We next describe two types of language models defined over $\mathcal{T}$ and induced using Equations 2 and 3. The language models differ by the definition of pseudo counts for tokens.

3.1.1 Hard confidence-level thresholding

The hard confidence-level thresholding language model, **HTLM** in short, is based on *fixing* a threshold τ ($\in [0, 1]$) for entity markups. Entity-based information is used only for entity markups with confidence level $\geq \tau$. In contrast, *every* term occurrence in a text, including those in entity markups with a confidence level $< \tau$, is accounted for.

To formally define a HTLM using Equations 2 and 3, we have to define pseudo counts for tokens from $\mathcal{T}$ in a text or text collection x. To that end, we lay down a few definitions. If t ($\in \mathcal{T}$) is a term, then $c_{term}(t, x)$ is the number of occurrences of t in x. Let $\mathcal{M}(x)$ denote the set of all entity markups in x; i.e., all occurrences of term sequences in x that were marked as entities with some confidence level. For a markup m ($\in \mathcal{M}(x)$), $E(m)$ is the entity and $\rho(m)$ is the confidence level. The equivalence relation $t_1 \equiv t_2$ holds iff the entity tokens t_1 and t_2 are identical (i.e., have the same ID). The pseudo count of t ($\in \mathcal{T}$) in x is based on (i) the raw count of t in x if t is a term; and, (ii) the number of entity markups of t in x with a confidence level $\geq \tau$ if t is an entity. Formally,

$$pc_{HTLM;\tau}(t, x) \stackrel{def}{=} \quad (4)$$

$$\begin{cases} \lambda c_{term}(t, x) & \text{if } t \in \mathcal{V}; \\ (1-\lambda) \sum_{m \in \mathcal{M}(x): E(m) \equiv t} \delta[\rho(m) \geq \tau] & \text{if } t \in \mathcal{E}; \end{cases}$$

λ ($\in [0, 1]$) is a free parameter which controls the relative importance attributed to term and entity tokens; δ is Kronecker's delta function: for statement s, $\delta[s] = 1$ if s is true and $\delta[s] = 0$ otherwise.

We note that using a Dirichlet smoothed HTLM (i.e., using Equation 4 in Equation 3) can still result in assigning zero probability to some tokens in $\mathcal{T}$. These are entities with no corresponding markup of a term sequence in the corpus with confidence level $\geq \tau$. We re-visit this point below.

If we set $\lambda = 1$ in Equation 4, then the resultant HTLM reduces to a standard unigram term-based language model. Setting $\lambda = 0$ results in **HTEntLM** which is a unigram language model that assigns non-zero probability *only* to entities: if the MLE from Equation 2 is used, then these are the entities with at least one markup in x with a confidence level $\geq \tau$; if the Dirichlet smoothed language model is used (Equation 3), then these are the entities with at least one markup in the corpus with a confidence level $\geq \tau$.

3.1.2 Soft confidence-level thresholding

A potential drawback of HTLM is committing to a specific threshold τ for entity markups. That is, information about entity markups with confidence level lower than τ is ignored. Furthermore, all entity markups with confidence level $\geq \tau$ are counted equally as their confidence levels are ignored.

Thus, we now turn to present a soft confidence-level thresholding language model, **STLM**. STLM accounts for all markups of an entity and weighs them by the corresponding confidence levels. Specifically, the pseudo count of t ($\in \mathcal{T}$) in the text or text collection x is defined as:

$$pc_{STLM}(t, x) \stackrel{def}{=} \begin{cases} \lambda c_{term}(t, x) & \text{if } t \in \mathcal{V}; \\ (1-\lambda) \sum_{m \in \mathcal{M}(x): E(m) \equiv t} \rho(m) & \text{if } t \in \mathcal{E}; \end{cases} \quad (5)$$

λ ($\in [0, 1]$) is a free parameter that, as in HTLM, controls the relative importance attributed to term and entity tokens. Thus, STLM addresses the uncertainty inherent in the entity linking process by using *expected* entity occurrence counts; the corresponding confidence levels serve for occurrence probabilities. These expected counts are then integrated with deterministic term counts.

If we set $\lambda = 1$ in Equation 5, then STLM reduces to a standard unigram term-based language model as was the case for HTLM. Setting $\lambda = 0$ results in **STEntLM**. This language model assigns a non-zero probability only to entities that have at least one markup (with any confidence level) in x when using the MLE (Equation 2) or in the corpus when using the Dirichlet smoothed language model (Equation 3). We note that in contrast to the case for HTLM, there is no token in $\mathcal{T}$ that is assigned a zero probability by a Dirichlet smoothed STLM.

3.2 Retrieval models

We rank document d by the cross entropy between the language models induced from the query (q) and d [25]:

$$CE(\theta_q \,||\, \theta_d) = -\sum_{t \in \mathcal{T}} \theta_q(t) \log \theta_d(t); \quad (6)$$

higher values correspond to decreased similarity.

Equation 6 is instantiated using the entity-based language models described in Section 3.1. Following common practice [48], we use an unsmoothed maximum likelihood estimate for the query language model (Equation 2) and a Dirichlet smoothed document language model (Equation 3). We obtain four retrieval methods : **HT**[3], **HTOEnt**, **ST** and **STOEnt**[4], which utilize the HTLM, HTEntLM, STLM and

[3] In HT, the *same* confidence-level threshold, τ_d, is used for all documents; the query threshold, τ_q, can be different from τ_d. Hence, an entity token assigned a non-zero probability by θ_q could be assigned a zero probability by θ_d; e.g., an entity marked in q with a confidence level $\geq \tau_q$ but with no markup in the corpus with confidence level $\geq \tau_d$. In these cases, we zero the probability assigned to the entity token by θ_q to avoid a $\log 0$ in Equation 6. This is common practice in addressing term tokens that appear in a query but not in any document in the corpus.

[4] HTOEnt and STOEnt rely only on entity tokens. If all entities in $\mathcal{E}$ are assigned a zero probability by the unsmoothed

Table 1: TREC data used for experiments.

corpus	# of docs	data	queries
AP	242,918	Disks 1-3	51 – 150
ROBUST	528,155	Disks 4-5 (-CR)	301 – 450, 601 – 700
WT10G	1,692,096	WT10g	451 – 550
GOV2	25,205,179	GOV2	701 – 850
ClueB ClueBF	50,220,423	ClueWeb09 (Cat. B)	1 – 200

STEntLM language models, respectively. HT and ST utilize entity and term tokens, while HTOEnt and STOEnt utilize only entity tokens, hence the "O" in the methods names.

3.2.1 Score-based fusion

The HTLM and STLM language models integrate term-based and entity-based information at the *language model level*. Hence, the query-document comparison in Equation 6 simultaneously accounts for the appearance of the query terms and entities in a document.

An alternative approach is integrating term and entity information at the *retrieval score level*. Inspired by approaches in the vector-space model [42], and in work on using a latent entity space [33], we consider a method that fuses document retrieval scores produced by utilizing, *independently*, term-only (θ_x^{term}) and entity-only (θ_x^{ent}) language models induced from text x. Document d is scored by:

$$\lambda CE\left(\theta_q^{term} \mid\mid \theta_d^{term}\right) + (1-\lambda) CE\left(\theta_q^{ent} \mid\mid \theta_d^{ent}\right); \quad (7)$$

the λ parameter balances the score fusion[5]. The query language models are unsmoothed maximum likelihood estimates (Equation 2) and the document language models are Dirichlet smoothed (Equation 3).

Instantiating Equation 7 with an entity-only language model, HTEntLM or STEntLM, and with a standard unigram term-based language model yields the **F-HT** and **F-ST** methods, respectively. These are conceptually highly similar to the HT and ST methods which integrate term-based and entity-based information at the language-model level. However, HT and ST use a single smoothing parameter for both term and entity tokens (see Equation 3) while F-HT and F-ST can use a different smoothing parameter for each as they utilize separately term-only and entity-only language models. We could have used different smoothing parameters for entity and term tokens under the same language model, e.g., by applying term-specific smoothing [17], but we leave this exploration for future work.

4. EVALUATION

4.1 Experimental setup

Experiments were conducted using the TREC datasets specified in Table 1. AP and ROBUST are mostly composed of news articles. WT10G is a small, noisy, Web collection. GOV2 is a much larger Web collection composed of high quality pages crawled from the .gov domain. ClueB is the English part of the Category B of the ClueWeb 2009 Web collection. ClueBF was created from ClueB by filtering from rankings suspected spam documents: those assigned a score below 50 by Waterloo's spam classifier [11].

Data processing. Titles of TREC topics served for queries. Tokenization and Porter stemming were applied using the Lucene toolkit (lucene.apache.org) which was used for experiments. Stopwords on the INQUERY list were removed from queries but not from documents.

Unless otherwise specified, the **TagMe** entity-linking tool (tagme.di.unipi.it) is used to annotate queries and documents. TagMe uses Wikipedia (a July 2014 dump) as the entity repository, and was shown to be highly effective and efficient in comparison to other publicly available entity-linking systems [12]. In Section 4.2.1 we also show the effectiveness of our methods using the **Wikifier** entity-linking tool[6] [9, 12]. Wikifier was applied with an efficient configuration claimed to yield baseline entity linking effectiveness.

TagMe and Wikifier cannot process very long texts. Thus, we split documents into non-overlapping term-window passages. We terminate a passage at the first space that appears at least 500 characters after the beginning of the previous passage. We let the tools mark the passages independently. The tools are applied on the non-stemmed and non-stopped queries and documents. Entity markup of a term sequence includes an entity ID and a confidence level (in $[0, 1]$). We scan each text left to right and remove overlapping entity markups so that each position can be part of at most a single markup. If two markups overlap, we select the one with the higher confidence level. We break ties of confidence levels by selecting the markup which starts at the leftmost position.

Baselines. We use standard term-based unigram language model retrieval [25], denoted **TermsLM**, for reference. This is a special case of the HT, ST, F-HT and F-ST methods with $\lambda = 1$. Documents are ranked by the cross entropy between the unsmoothed (MLE) query language model and Dirichlet smoothed document language models.

The **HTCon** method is a special case of HT with $\lambda = 0.5$ and $\tau_q = \tau_d = 0$ (τ_q and τ_d are the query and document thresholds, respectively). HTCon accounts *uniformly* for all entity mentions, and attributes the same importance to term and entity tokens. HTCon is conceptually reminiscent of methods representing documents and queries using concepts (e.g., from Wordnet) by concatenating with equal weights term-based and concept-based vector-space representations [41, 16, 42]. Accordingly, we consider **F-HTCon**: a special case of F-HT with $\lambda = 0.5$ and $\tau_q = \tau_d = 0$.

Additional baseline is the state-of-the-art sequential dependence model, **SDM**, from the Markov Random Field framework which utilizes term proximities [36, 19]. The comparison with SDM, and its integration with our STLM is presented in Section 4.2.3.

Evaluation measures and free-parameters. Mean average precision at cutoff 1000 (MAP), precision of the top 10 documents (p@10) and NDCG@10 (NDCG) serve as evaluation measures. Statistically significant performance differences are determined using the two-tailed paired t-test with a 95% confidence level.

query language model, then no documents are retrieved. This can happen for example when inducing HTEntLM from the query with a high confidence-level threshold or inducing a STEntLM from a query which has no entity markups.

[5]The λ in the score-based fusion model has a conceptually similar role to that of λ in STLM and HTLM: balancing the use of term-based and entity-based information.

[6]cogcomp.cs.illinois.edu/page/demo_view/Wikifier

Table 2: Comparison of methods instantiated from Equation 6 using term-only (TermsLM) and entity-based language models. Bold: the best result in a row. 't', 'h', 'o', 'c' and 's' mark statistically significant differences with TermsLM, HT, HTOEnt, HTCon and ST, respectively.

		TermsLM	HT	HTOEnt	HTCon	ST	STOEnt
AP	MAP	20.9	23.1^{t}	$15.6^{t,h}$	22.5_{o}	**$23.5^{t}_{o,c}$**	$17.5^{t,h}_{o,c,s}$
	p@10	39.1	**44.2^{t}**	36.0^{h}	43.4^{t}_{o}	43.8^{t}_{o}	$38.3^{h}_{c,s}$
	NDCG	40.4	45.3^{t}	37.6^{h}	44.7^{t}_{o}	**45.5^{t}_{o}**	$39.6^{h}_{c,s}$
ROBUST	MAP	25.0	**28.1^{t}**	$19.1^{t,h}$	27.4^{t}_{o}	**$28.1^{t}_{o,c}$**	$21.4^{t,h}_{o,c,s}$
	p@10	42.2	**45.5^{t}**	$35.7^{t,h}$	45.0^{t}_{o}	45.3^{t}_{o}	$38.0^{t,h}_{o,c,s}$
	NDCG	43.5	**47.1^{t}**	$36.9^{t,h}$	46.3^{t}_{o}	46.9^{t}_{o}	$39.2^{t,h}_{o,c,s}$
WT10G	MAP	19.1	21.9^{t}	$13.3^{t,h}$	21.4^{t}_{o}	**$22.9^{t,h}_{o,c}$**	$16.7^{h}_{o,c,s}$
	p@10	27.3	30.4^{t}	$21.6^{t,h}$	30.5^{t}_{o}	**31.6^{t}_{o}**	$25.3^{h}_{o,c,s}$
	NDCG	30.3	32.7	$21.2^{t,h}$	32.1_{o}	**$34.3^{t}_{o,c}$**	$25.4^{h}_{o,c,s}$
GOV2	MAP	29.6	32.1^{t}	$18.0^{t,h}$	30.6^{h}_{o}	**$32.2^{t}_{o,c}$**	$20.7^{t,h}_{o,c,s}$
	p@10	53.9	57.3^{t}	$39.4^{t,h}$	56.8_{o}	**57.7^{t}_{o}**	$44.0^{t,h}_{o,c,s}$
	NDCG	44.8	47.4^{t}	$32.7^{t,h}$	46.9_{o}	**47.9^{t}_{o}**	$35.7^{t,h}_{o,c,s}$
ClueB	MAP	17.1	18.7^{t}	$14.0^{t,h}$	18.5_{o}	**19.5^{t}_{o}**	$14.0^{t,h}_{c,s}$
	p@10	22.7	25.9^{t}	23.9	26.7^{t}_{o}	**27.4^{t}**	24.1
	NDCG	16.5	18.7^{t}	18.3	19.2^{t}	**19.3^{t}**	17.5
ClueBF	MAP	18.8	**20.5^{t}**	$14.4^{t,h}$	19.9_{o}	20.3^{t}_{o}	$14.4^{t,h}_{c,s}$
	p@10	33.6	37.9^{t}	29.2^{h}	**38.2^{t}_{o}**	37.9^{t}_{o}	$30.6^{h}_{c,s}$
	NDCG	24.3	**28.4^{t}**	22.2^{h}	**28.4^{t}_{o}**	27.5^{t}_{o}	$22.8^{h}_{c,s}$

The free parameter values of *all* retrieval methods are set using 10-fold cross validation performed over the queries in a dataset. Query IDs are used to create the folds. The optimal parameter values for each of the 10 train sets are determined using a simple grid search applied to optimize MAP. The learned parameter values are then used for the queries in the corresponding test fold.

The value of the Dirichlet smoothing parameter, μ, is selected from $\{100, 500, 1000, 1500, 2000, 2500, 3000\}$. The parameter λ, used in HTLM, STLM, F-HT and F-ST, is set to values in $\{0, 0.1, \ldots, 1\}$. The document (τ_d) and query (τ_q) entity-markup confidence level thresholds, used in HT, HTOEnt and F-HT, are set to values in $\{0, 0.1, \ldots, 0.9\}$.

4.2 Experimental results

4.2.1 Entity-based language models

Table 2 presents the performance of the methods that use entity-based language models to instantiate Equation 6. Our first observation is that the HT and ST methods outperform the standard term-based language-model retrieval, TermsLM, in all relevant comparisons (6 corpora × 3 evaluation measures); most improvements are substantial and statistically significant. Furthermore, HT and ST outperform to a substantial and statistically significant degree their special cases which use only entity tokens: HTOEnt and STOEnt, respectively. These findings attest to the merits of using our proposed language models, HTLM and STLM, which integrate term-based and entity-based information.

We also see in Table 2 that HT and ST outperform HTCon in most relevant comparisons; most MAP improvements for ST are statistically significant. Recall from Section 4.1 that HTCon represents past practice of concept-based representations: accounting uniformly for all entity mentions and attributing equal importance to entity and term tokens. Below we further study the importance of accounting for the confidence level of entity markups, and attributing different weights to term and entity tokens as in HT and ST.

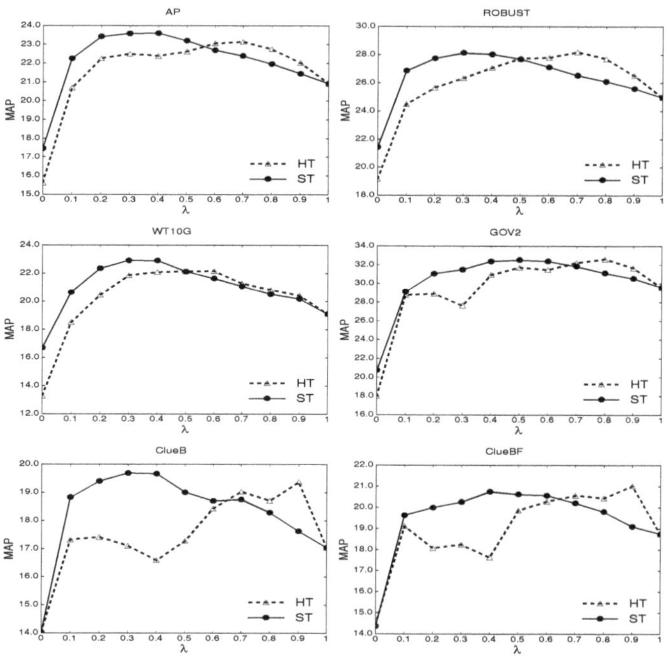

Figure 1: The effect of varying λ on the MAP of HT and ST. For $\lambda = 1$, the methods amount to TermsLM (term-based language model retrieval). For $\lambda = 0$, the methods use only entity tokens. The performance is reported for the test folds (i.e., all queries in a dataset) when fixing the value of λ and using cross validation to set the values of all other free parameters. Note: figures are not to the same scale.

Table 2 shows that ST outperforms HT in most relevant comparisons, although rarely to a statistically significant degree. In addition, ST posts more statistically significant improvements over HTCon than HT. We note that HT depends on four free parameters (λ, τ_q, τ_d and μ) while ST depends only on two (λ and μ). Furthermore, the values learned for τ_q and τ_d in HT using the training folds are very low, attesting to the merits of using high recall entity markup. (We revisit this point below.) Overall, these findings attest to the potential merits of using a soft-thresholding approach for the confidence level of entity markups (STLM) with respect to a hard-thresholding approach (HTLM); i.e., accounting for all entity markups in a text and weighing their impact by their confidence levels is superior to accounting, uniformly, for entity markups with a confidence level above a threshold.

Terms vs. entities. Figure 1 depicts the MAP performance of HT and ST as a function of λ. Low and high values of λ result in more importance attributed to entity-based and term-based information, respectively. For $\lambda = 1$, the two methods amount to TermsLM — i.e., standard term-based language model retrieval. For $\lambda = 0$, the methods use only entity-based information; specifically, HT reduces to HTOEnt and ST reduces to STOEnt.

We see in Figure 1 that optimal performance is always attained for $\lambda \notin \{0, 1\}$. This finding echoes those based on Table 2. That is, HT and ST outperform TermsLM,

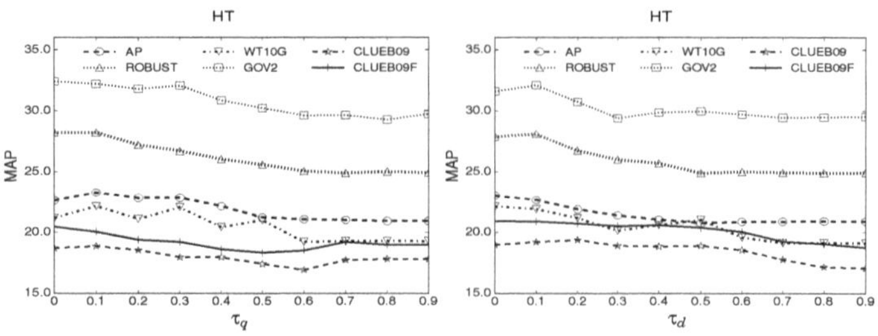

Figure 2: The effect of varying τ_q and τ_d on the MAP performance of HT. The values of free parameters, except for that in the x-axis, are set using cross validation as in Figure 1.

and HTOEnt and STOEnt, respectively. Thus, we find that there is much merit in integrating term-based and entity-based information for representing queries and documents.

Figure 1 shows that the optimal value of λ for HT is often higher than for ST. This can be attributed to the fact that HTLM, used to represent the query and documents in HT, uses a single confidence-level threshold for entity markups. Thus, potentially valuable information about entities is not utilized. As a result, HT calls for more reliance on term-based information to "compensate" for this potential information loss. In contrast, ST accounts for all entity markups, weighing their impact by their confidence levels. Hence, the "risk" in relying on entity-based information is lower[7].

To further explore the effect of using a hard threshold for the confidence level of entity markups in HT, we present in Figure 2 its MAP performance as a function of τ_q and τ_d — the query and document thresholds, respectively. Recall that low threshold corresponds to high recall markup. Figure 2 shows that low values of τ_q and τ_d lead to improved performance. This finding can be attributed to the fact that increasing the confidence-level threshold amounts to loosing potentially valuable information about appearances of entities in the query and documents. To compensate for the lower precision (i.e., noisier) markup caused by using a low threshold, more weight is put on term-based information as is evident in the relatively high optimal values of λ presented in Figure 1. Specifically, we note that the *learned values* of λ, τ_d, and τ_q, averaged over the train folds, for AP, ROBUST, WT10G, GOV2, ClueB and ClueBF are (0.6, 0.01, 0.11), (0.7,0.1,0.01), (0.55,0.1,0.2), (0.77,0.1,0.01), (0.7,0.15,0), and (0.81, 0.17, 0) respectively; namely, relatively high values of λ and low values of τ_d and τ_q lead to improved performance.

Entity linking. Our main evaluation is based on using TagMe for entity linking. In Table 3 we compare the retrieval performance when using the entity markups of TagMe and Wikifier. Having Wikifier annotate large-scale collections is a challenging computational task. Thus, we present results only for AP, ROBUST and WT10G. We report MAP and NDCG; the performance patterns for p@10 are the same.

Table 3 shows that using ST, our best performing method from above, with Wikifier, results in performance that transcends (often, significantly) that of the standard term-based language model (TermsLM) when using all queries in a dataset

[7]Setting λ on a per-query basis, in the spirit of work on fusing term-only-based and latent-entity-space-based retrieval scores [33], is a future direction we intend to explore.

Table 3: Comparing entity-linking tools. Either all queries in a dataset are used ("All Queries"), or only those marked with at least one entity by both TagMe and Wikifier ("Marked Queries"). Bold: best result in a column in a block; 't', 's', 'w' and 'e': statistically significant differences with TermsLM, TagMe-ST, Wikifier-ST and TagMe-STOEnt, respectively.

		AP		ROBUST		WT10G	
		MAP	NDCG	MAP	NDCG	MAP	NDCG
All Queries							
	TermsLM	20.9	40.4	25.0	43.5	19.1	30.3
TagMe	ST	**23.5**^{t}	**45.5**^{t}	**28.1**^{t}	**46.9**^{t}	**22.9**^{t}	**34.3**^{t}
Wikifier	ST	23.3^t	43.6	27.2^t	45.6^t	19.7^{t,s}	30.9^s
Marked Queries							
	TermsLM	22.2	41.7	25.4	43.9	21.4	34.2
TagMe	ST	**25.1**^{t}	**48.4**^{t}	**28.8**^{t}	**47.3**^{t}	**24.8**^{t}	**36.2**
Wikifier	ST	**25.1**^{t}	46.2^t	28.0^t	46.4^t	21.9^s	34.0
TagMe	STOEnt	18.5$^{t,s}_{w}$	41.4^s	22.9$^{t,s}_{w}$	41.1^s_w	18.1^s	28.1^s
Wikifier	STOEnt	17.5$^{t,s}_{w}$	39.1^s_w	19.4$^{t,s}_{w,e}$	34.8$^{t,s}_{w,e}$	12.6$^{t,s}_{w,e}$	21.8$^{t,s}_{w}$

(the "All Queries" block). However, the performance of using TagMe is consistently better.

TagMe marks more queries with at least one entity than Wikifier: for AP, ROBUST and WT10G, Wikifier marked no entities in 17, 34 and 26 queries, respectively; TagMe did not mark entities in 0, 1 and 3 queries. (For GOV2 TagMe marked all queries with entities and for ClueB/ClueBF all queries except for one.) Recall that for queries with no marked entities, ST relies only on term-based information.

To refine the comparison of TagMe and Wikifier, we report the performance of ST and STOEnt[8] — the latter relies only on entity tokens — with these two tools over only queries in which both marked at least one entity. As can be seen in the "Marked Queries" block in Table 3, TagMe still outperforms Wikifier in almost all relevant comparisons; for STOEnt, several improvements are statistically significant.

TagMe's superiority can be partially attributed to marking more entities (with confidence level > 0) on average than Wikifier: (2.4, 1.8, 2.0) with respect to (1.7, 1.2, 1.0) in queries over AP, ROBUST and WT10G; and, (157.2, 158.7, 207.0) with respect to (58.4, 50.5, 61.7) in documents.

To conclude, our methods are effective with both TagMe and Wikifier. Using TagMe yields better performance that can be partially attributed to higher recall entity markup.

4.2.2 *The score-based fusion methods*

Table 4 presents the performance of the F-HT and F-ST methods from Section 3.2.1 that perform score fusion of term-only-based and entity-only-based retrieval scores. The performance of TermsLM (term-only language model), HT and ST that integrate term and entity information at the language model level, and that of F-HTCon which is a special case of F-HT (see Section 4.1), is presented for reference. We see that F-HT and F-ST substantially outperform TermsLM. (F-ST posts the best performance in most relevant comparisons in Table 4.) Both methods also outperform F-HTCon in most relevant comparisons.

[8]For queries for which a tool does not mark any entities, no documents are retrieved with STOEnt. Thus, we do not report the performance of STOEnt using all queries as the results are inherently biased in favor of TagMe which marks many more queries with entities than Wikifier.

Table 4: Score-based fusion ("F-" methods). Bold: best result in a row; 't', 'h', 's', 'f' and 'c': statistically significant differences with TermsLM, HT, ST, F-HT and F-HTCon, respectively.

		TermsLM	HT	ST	F-HT	F-HTCon	F-ST
AP	MAP	20.9	23.1^{t}	23.5^{t}	23.1^{t}	22.5_{s}	$\mathbf{23.9^{t,h}_{f,c}}$
	p@10	39.1	44.2^{t}	43.8^{t}	$\mathbf{44.5^{t}}$	43.5^{t}	44.2^{t}
	NDCG	40.4	45.3^{t}	45.5^{t}	$\mathbf{46.2^{t}}$	45.1^{t}	45.8^{t}
ROBUST	MAP	25.0	28.1^{t}	28.1^{t}	28.1^{t}	27.7^{t}	$\mathbf{28.4^{t}_{c}}$
	p@10	42.2	45.5^{t}	45.3^{t}	45.7^{t}	45.2^{t}	$\mathbf{46.7^{t}_{s,c}}$
	NDCG	43.5	47.1^{t}	46.9^{t}	47.3^{t}	46.6^{t}	$\mathbf{47.8^{t}_{c}}$
WT10G	MAP	19.1	21.9^{t}	$\mathbf{22.9^{t,h}}$	22.2^{t}	21.6^{t}_{s}	$\mathbf{22.9^{t}_{c}}$
	p@10	27.3	30.4^{t}	31.6^{t}	30.0	30.4^{t}	$\mathbf{31.8^{t}}$
	NDCG	30.3	32.7	$\mathbf{34.3^{t}}$	32.7	33.1	33.7^{t}
GOV2	MAP	29.6	32.1^{t}	32.2^{t}	$\mathbf{33.5^{t,h}_{s}}$	$30.6^{h}_{s,f}$	$33.3^{t,h}_{s,c}$
	p@10	53.9	57.3^{t}	57.7^{t}	$\mathbf{58.6^{t}}$	57.0	58.0^{t}
	NDCG	44.8	47.4^{t}	47.9^{t}	$\mathbf{48.7^{t}}$	46.6	48.2^{t}
ClueB	MAP	17.1	18.7^{t}	19.5^{t}	$19.6^{t,h}$	19.3^{t}	$\mathbf{20.8^{t,h}_{s,f,c}}$
	p@10	22.7	25.9^{t}	27.4^{t}	26.4^{t}	27.5^{t}	$\mathbf{28.8^{t,h}_{f}}$
	NDCG	16.5	18.7^{t}	19.3^{t}	19.1^{t}	19.9^{t}	$\mathbf{20.5^{t,h}_{f}}$
ClueBF	MAP	18.8	20.5^{t}	20.3^{t}	$21.3^{t,h}$	19.7_{f}	$\mathbf{21.8^{t,h}_{s,c}}$
	p@10	33.6	37.9^{t}	37.9^{t}	$\mathbf{39.6^{t}}$	36.5_{f}	39.4^{t}_{c}
	NDCG	24.3	28.4^{t}	27.5^{t}	$\mathbf{29.5^{t}_{s}}$	27.6	29.2^{t}_{s}

Table 5: Comparison and integration with SDM [36]. Bold: the best result in a row. 't', 's', 'f' and 'm' mark statistically significant differences with TermsLM, ST, F-ST and SDM, respectively.

		TermsLM	ST	F-ST	SDM	SDM+STLM
AP	MAP	20.9	23.5^{t}	$\mathbf{23.9^{t}}$	21.6^{s}_{f}	$\mathbf{23.9^{t}_{m}}$
	p@10	39.1	43.8^{t}	$\mathbf{44.2^{t}}$	40.6_{f}	$\mathbf{44.2^{t}_{m}}$
	NDCG	40.4	45.5^{t}	$\mathbf{45.8^{t}}$	42.3_{f}	$\mathbf{45.8^{t}_{m}}$
ROBUST	MAP	25.0	28.1^{t}	$\mathbf{28.4^{t}}$	$25.7^{t,s}_{f}$	28.3^{t}_{m}
	p@10	42.2	45.3^{t}	$\mathbf{46.7^{t,s}}$	43.9^{t}_{f}	$45.7^{t}_{f,m}$
	NDCG	43.5	46.9^{t}	$\mathbf{47.8^{t}}$	$44.8^{t,s}_{f}$	$47.1^{t}_{f,m}$
WT10G	MAP	19.1	22.9^{t}	22.9^{t}	20.2^{s}_{f}	$\mathbf{23.1^{t}_{m}}$
	p@10	27.3	31.6^{t}	$\mathbf{31.8^{t}}$	27.7^{s}_{f}	31.6^{t}_{m}
	NDCG	30.3	$\mathbf{34.3^{t}}$	33.7^{t}	30.7^{s}_{f}	34.0^{t}_{m}
GOV2	MAP	29.6	32.2^{t}	$33.3^{t,s}$	32.1^{t}	$\mathbf{34.7^{t,s}_{f,m}}$
	p@10	53.9	57.7^{t}	58.0^{t}	58.3^{t}	$\mathbf{61.4^{t,s}_{f,m}}$
	NDCG	44.8	47.9^{t}	48.2^{t}	48.4^{t}	$\mathbf{50.6^{t,s}_{f,m}}$
ClueB	MAP	17.1	19.5^{t}	$20.8^{t,s}$	$18.2^{t,s}_{f}$	$\mathbf{21.5^{t,s}_{m}}$
	p@10	22.7	27.4^{t}	28.8^{t}	23.8^{s}_{f}	$\mathbf{30.8^{t,s}_{f,m}}$
	NDCG	16.5	19.3^{t}	20.5^{t}	16.9^{s}_{f}	$\mathbf{21.9^{t,s}_{m}}$
ClueBF	MAP	18.8	20.3^{t}	$21.8^{t,s}$	20.2^{t}_{f}	$\mathbf{22.7^{t,s}_{f,m}}$
	p@10	33.6	37.9^{t}	39.4^{t}	35.8^{t}_{f}	$\mathbf{42.8^{t,s}_{f,m}}$
	NDCG	24.3	27.5^{t}	$29.2^{t,s}$	25.9^{t}_{f}	$\mathbf{32.2^{t,s}_{f,m}}$

In most relevant comparisons, F-HT outperforms HT and F-ST outperforms ST, although most performance differences are not statistically significant. The improvements can be attributed to the fact that F-HT and F-ST use a different smoothing parameter value for terms and entities while HT and ST use a joint one. (See Section 3.2.1 for details.)

The potential effectiveness of using different smoothing parameters for term and entity tokens stems from the different number of terms and entity markups in a document. The average number of terms in a document for AP, ROBUST, WT10G, GOV2, and ClueB (ClueBF) is 455.4, 474.8, 588.2, 904.7 and 813.6, respectively. The average number of entity markups with a confidence level > 0 is much lower: 157.2, 158.7, 207.0, 291.9 and 307.8.

4.2.3 Comparison and integration with SDM

We next compare our entity-based approach with the sequential dependence model (SDM) [36] which scores d by:

$$S_{SDM}(d;q) \stackrel{def}{=} \lambda_S Sim_S(d,q) + \lambda_O Sim_O(d,q) + \lambda_U Sim_U(d,q);$$

the sum of the λ_S, λ_O and λ_U parameters is 1; $Sim_S(d,q)$, $Sim_O(d,q)$ and $Sim_U(d,q)$ are cross-entropy based similarity estimates of the document to the query, utilizing information about occurrences of unigram, ordered bigrams, and unordered bigrams, respectively, of q's terms in d; un-ordered bigrams are confined to 8-terms windows in documents.

Using entity tokens in our methods amounts to utilizing information about the occurrences of only *some ordered* variable-length n-grams of query terms in documents — i.e., n-grams which constitute entities. Thus, in contrast to SDM, our methods do not utilize proximity information for query terms which are not in entity markups nor proximity information for unordered n-grams of query terms.

In addition, we study the merit of integrating entity-based information, specifically, our soft-thresholding language model STLM, with SDM. To that end, we augment the SDM scoring function with an entity-based document-query similarity estimate, $Sim_E(d,q)$. For this estimate, we use the score assigned to d by the STOEnt method; i.e., we use an entity-only language model since term-based information is accounted for in $Sim_S(d,q)$. The resultant method, **SDM+STLM**, scores d by ($\lambda_S + \lambda_O + \lambda_U + \lambda_E = 1$):

$$S_{SDM+STLM}(d;q) \stackrel{def}{=} \lambda_S Sim_S(d,q) + \lambda_O Sim_O(d,q) + \lambda_U Sim_U(d,q) + \lambda_E Sim_E(d,q).$$

SDM+STLM can be viewed as a novel instantiation of a weighted dependence model (WSDM) [4] with a novel concept type (i.e., entity). If $\lambda_O = \lambda_U = 0$, SDM+STLM amounts to our F-ST method (see Section 3.2.1).

All free parameters of SDM and SDM+STLM: λ_S, λ_O, λ_U, λ_E and the Dirichlet smoothing parameter, μ, are set using cross validation as described in Section 4.1; λ_S, λ_O, λ_U, and λ_E are selected from $\{0, 0.1, \ldots, 1\}$ and μ is set to values in $\{100, 500, 1000, 1500, 2000, 2500, 3000\}$.

Table 5 shows that ST and F-ST outperform SDM, often statistically significantly, in most relevant comparisons (6 corpora $\times$ 3 evaluation measures). This implies that using variable length n-grams which potentially bear semantic meaning (entities) can yield better performance than using ordered and unordered bigrams which do not necessarily have semantic meaning. Recall that in contrast to SDM, ST and F-ST do not account for proximities between terms which do not constitute entities and for unordered bigrams.

In most relevant comparisons, SDM+STLM outperforms SDM and ST (which utilizes STLM) and is as effective as, and often posts statistically significant improvements over, F-ST — its special case that fuses unigram term-only and entity-only retrieval scores. The few cases where F-ST outperforms SDM+STLM could be attributed to potential overfitting effects due to the high number of free parameters of SDM+STLM and the relatively low number of queries.

We also found that effective weights assigned to entity-only similarities in SDM+STLM (λ_E) are much higher than those assigned to ordered (λ_O) and un-ordered (λ_U) bigram

Table 6: **Robustness analysis. Number of queries for which ST hurts (-) and improves (+) AP performance with respect to TermsLM and SDM.**

	AP		ROBUST		WT10G		GOV2		ClueB		ClueBF	
	-	+	-	+	-	+	-	+	-	+	-	+
ST vs. TermsLM	38	61	75	173	31	63	50	99	54	137	75	112
ST vs. SDM	35	64	87	161	33	60	74	75	79	112	89	97

term-based similarities. Furthermore, effective values of λ_O and λ_U are lower and higher, respectively, for SDM+STLM than for SDM. These findings further attest to the merits of using entity-based similarities with respect to (ordered and un-ordered) bigram similarities, and show that un-ordered bigram, in contrast to ordered bigram, similarities could be complementary to entity-based similarities.

4.2.4 *Further analysis*

We now turn to further analyze merits, and shortcomings, of using entity-based query and document representations. To that end, we focus on the ST method that utilizes STLM.

Table 6 presents performance robustness analysis: the number of queries for which ST improves or hurts average precision (AP) over TermsLM and SDM. In both cases, ST improves AP for more queries than it hurts; naturally, the differences with SDM are smaller than those with TermsLM.

One advantage of STLM is that it represents the query and documents using entities which constitute variable length n-grams with semantic meaning. A case in point, query #41 in ClueWeb, "orange county convention center", refers to the primary public convention center for the Central Florida region. TermsLM, SDM and ST ranked the Web home page for this entity second. However, at the third rank in the lists retrieved by TermsLM and SDM appears a Wikipedia page titled "list of convention and exhibition centers", which is not specific to the entity of concern. The average precision (AP) of TermsLM, SDM and ST for the query in the ClueB dataset was 9, 13, and 30, respectively, attesting to the merit of the correct identification of the entity in the query and its utilization by ST.

The ST method can suffer from incorrect entity identification in queries. For example, query #407 in ROBUST, "poaching, wildlife preserves", targets information about the impact of poaching on the world's various wildlife preserves. The entities identified by TagMe are "poaching", "wildlife" and "preserves"; the latter refers to fruit preserves instead of nature preserves. Such erroneous entity identification can be attributed to the little context short queries provide. Consequently, the AP of ST for this query is only 8 while that of TermsLM and SDM is 31.4 and 30.0, respectively.

4.3 Using entity-based language models in additional retrieval paradigms

We next explore the effectiveness of using our entity-based language models in two additional retrieval paradigms: cluster-based document retrieval and query expansion.

4.3.1 *Cluster-based document retrieval*

Let D_{init} denote the list of top-n documents retrieved by TermsLM (standard language-model-based retrieval). Following common practice in work on cluster-based document retrieval [32, 24], we re-rank D_{init} using information induced from nearest-neighbor clusters of documents in D_{init}.

Table 7: Cluster-based document re-ranking. Bold: the best result in a row; 't', 's', '$*$' and 'ψ' mark statistically significant differences with TermsLM, ST, C-Term-Term and C-Term-Ent, respectively.

		TermsLM	ST	C-Term-Term	C-Term-Ent	C-Ent-Ent
AP	p@10	39.6	42.5	43.2^{t}	44.3^{t}	$\mathbf{46.5}^{t,s}$
	NDCG	40.8	44.8^{t}	44.2^{t}	44.9	$\mathbf{46.8}^{t}$
ROBUST	p@10	42.2	44.3^{t}	43.1	46.0^{t}_{*}	$\mathbf{47.7}^{t,s}_{*,\psi}$
	NDCG	43.5	45.5^{t}	44.2	47.5^{t}_{*}	$\mathbf{49.1}^{t,s}_{*,\psi}$
WT10G	p@10	28.6	30.6	30.2	$33.7^{t,s}_{*}$	$\mathbf{34.8}^{t,s}_{*}$
	NDCG	31.2	33.4	32.1	35.4^{t}_{*}	$\mathbf{36.3}^{t,s}_{*}$
GOV2	p@10	53.4	57.0^{t}	55.1	$\mathbf{58.3}^{t}$	57.9^{t}
	NDCG	45.0	46.8	45.8	$\mathbf{48.9}^{t}$	47.8^{t}
ClueB	p@10	23.7	27.1^{t}	23.7	$\mathbf{33.0}^{t,s}_{*}$	$31.5^{t,s}_{*}$
	NDCG	17.2	19.1	17.2	$\mathbf{24.9}^{t,s}_{*}$	$22.9^{t,s}_{*}$
ClueBF	p@10	32.1	36.9^{t}	31.2^{s}	38.5^{t}_{*}	$\mathbf{39.0}^{t}_{*}$
	NDCG	22.9	27.8^{t}	23.1^{s}	$\mathbf{30.3}^{t}_{*}$	29.6^{t}_{*}

We use $Sim(x,y) \stackrel{def}{=} exp(-CE\left(\theta_x^{MLE} \mid\mid \theta_y^{Dir}\right))$ to measure the similarity between texts x and y [24]; θ_x^{MLE} is an unsmoothed MLE induced from x and θ_y^{Dir} is a Dirichlet smoothed language model induced from y. Each document d ($\in D_{init}$) and the $k-1$ documents d' ($d' \neq d$) in D_{init} that yield the highest $Sim(d,d')$ constitute a cluster.

We rank the (overlapping) clusters c, each contains k documents, by: $\sqrt[k]{\prod_{d \in c} Sim(q,d)}$ [32]. This is a highly effective simple cluster ranking method [24]. To induce document ranking, each cluster is replaced with its constituent documents omitting repeats; documents in a cluster are ordered by their query similarity: $Sim(q,d)$.

The document (re-)ranking procedure just described relies on the choice of the document language models used to induce clusters (i.e., in $Sim(d,d')$) and the choice of document and query language models used to induce document-query similarities ($Sim(q,d)$); the latter are used for ranking both clusters and documents within the clusters. We use **C-Term-Term** to denote the standard method that uses term-only language models for inducing clusters and document-query similarities [32, 24]. The **C-Term-Ent** method utilizes the same clusters used by C-Term-Term, but uses our entity-based language model, STLM, for inducing document-query similarities to rank clusters and documents in them. In the **C-Ent-Ent** method, STLM is used to both create clusters and induce document-query similarities. As a reference comparison, we re-rank D_{init} using the ST method that uses STLM but does not utilize clusters.

As the main goal of cluster-based re-ranking is improving precision at top ranks [32, 24], we report p@10 and NDCG@10 (NDCG). Free-parameter values are set using cross validation; NDCG is the optimization criterion. Specifically, n is selected from $\{50, 100\}$; k is in $\{5, 10\}$; and, λ (used in STLM) is in $\{0, 0.1, \ldots, 1\}$; the Dirichlet smoothing parameter is set to 1000. Table 7 presents the results.

We see that all cluster-based methods (denoted "C-X-Y") almost always outperform the initial term-based document ranking, TermsLM. C-Term-Ent substantially outperforms C-Term-Term. This attests to the merits of using STLM for inducing cluster ranking and within cluster document ranking. In most relevant comparisons, C-Ent-Ent outperforms (and is never statistically significantly outperformed by) C-Term-Ent, attesting to the potential merits of using

Table 8: Query expansion. Bold: the best result in a row. 't', 's', 'r', 'w', 'm' and 'n' mark statistically significant differences with TermsLM, ST, RM3, WikiRM, SDM-RM and RMST, respectively.

		TermsLM	ST	RM3	WikiRM	SDM-RM	RMST	RMST-ST
AP	MAP	20.9	23.5^{t}	24.1^{t}	24.0^{t}	24.9^{t}	24.6^{t}	**27.4**$^{\mathbf{t,s,r}}_{\mathbf{w,m,n}}$
	p@10	39.1	43.8^{t}	42.5^{t}	46.2^{t}	43.9^{t}	44.8^{t}	**46.8**$^{\mathbf{t,r}}$
	NDCG	40.4	45.5^{t}	43.2	**48.2**$^{\mathbf{t,r}}$	45.6^{t}	45.0^{t}	47.4^{t,r}
ROBUST	MAP	25.0	28.1^{t}	28.3^{t}	27.8^{t}	28.4^{t}	29.0^{t}	**30.5**$^{\mathbf{t,s,r}}_{\mathbf{w,m,n}}$
	p@10	42.2	45.3^{t}	43.6	44.6^{t}	43.2	45.9$^{t,r}_{m}$	**47.1**$^{\mathbf{t,s,r}}_{\mathbf{w,m}}$
	NDCG	43.5	46.9^{t}	43.8^{s}	46.1^{t,r}	43.6$^{s}_{w}$	46.5$^{t,r}_{m}$	**47.2**$^{\mathbf{t,r}}_{\mathbf{m}}$
WT10G	MAP	19.1	**22.9**$^{\mathbf{t}}$	19.6^{s}	21.9^{t,r}	20.0^{s}	22.7$^{t,r}_{m}$	22.8$^{t,r}_{m}$
	p@10	27.3	31.6^{t}	28.0^{s}	**34.2**$^{\mathbf{t,r}}$	28.6$_{w}$	31.7$^{t,r}_{m}$	31.1^{t}
	NDCG	30.3	**34.3**$^{\mathbf{t}}$	30.1^{s}	**34.3**$^{\mathbf{t,r}}$	30.5$^{s}_{w}$	32.9	31.8^{s}
GOV2	MAP	29.6	32.2^{t}	32.4^{t}	32.1^{t}	**33.7**$^{\mathbf{t}}_{\mathbf{w}}$	33.1^{t}	**33.7**$^{\mathbf{t,s}}$
	p@10	53.9	57.7^{t}	58.1^{t}	**60.1**$^{\mathbf{t}}$	58.0^{t}	59.6^{t}	58.5^{t}
	NDCG	44.8	47.9^{t}	48.0^{t}	**50.6**$^{\mathbf{t}}$	47.6	49.4^{t}	48.8^{t}
ClueB	MAP	17.1	19.5^{t}	19.3^{t}	21.9^{t,s,r}	20.9^{t,r}	20.7^{t,s,r}	**22.1**$^{\mathbf{t,s,r}}_{\mathbf{n}}$
	p@10	22.7	27.4^{t}	30.6^{t}	**35.3**$^{\mathbf{t,s,r}}$	32.2$^{t,s}_{w}$	32.2$^{t,s}_{w}$	34.9$^{t,s,r}_{n}$
	NDCG	16.5	19.3^{t}	22.6^{t,s}	26.1^{t,s,r}	24.3^{t,s}	25.1^{t,s,r}	**27.1**$^{\mathbf{t,s,r}}_{\mathbf{n}}$
ClueBF	MAP	18.8	20.3^{t}	20.4^{t}	21.0^{t}	21.8^{t,s,r}	20.8^{t}	**21.9**$^{\mathbf{t,s}}_{\mathbf{n}}$
	p@10	33.6	37.9^{t}	37.9^{t}	38.5^{t}	**39.7**$^{\mathbf{t,r}}$	38.2^{t}	38.4^{t}
	NDCG	24.3	27.5^{t}	28.1^{t}	28.2^{t}	29.8^{t,r}	28.5^{t}	**30.3**$^{\mathbf{t,s}}$

entity-based information to also create clusters. However, only two improvements are statistically significant.

Finally, Table 7 shows that in almost all relevant comparisons, ST outperforms TermsLM (often, statistically significantly) and C-Term-Term and is outperformed by C-Term-Ent and C-Ent-Ent. This shows that while there is merit in using STLM for direct ranking of documents as shown in Section 4.2.1, the performance can be further improved by using STLM for cluster-based document ranking.

4.3.2 *Query expansion*

As noted in Section 2, there is much work on expanding queries with terms and entities using entity-based information. In contrast, our entity-based language models, when induced from the query, utilize only query terms and entities marked in the query. Hence, we study the effectiveness of using our language models to perform query expansion.

We use the relevance model (RM3) [1] as a basis for instantiating expanded query forms. The probability assigned to *token* t by a relevance model RM is:

$$RM(t) \stackrel{def}{=} \alpha\theta_q^{MLE}(t) + (1-\alpha)\sum_{d \in L}\theta_d^{Dir}(t)\frac{S(d;q)}{\sum_{d' \in L} S(d';q)}; \quad (8)$$

α is a free parameter; L is a list of top-retrieved documents used to construct RM; $S(d;q)$ is d's score. Due to computational considerations, as in work on entity-based query expansion [13, 45] we use RM to re-rank an initially retrieved document list; $CE\left(RM \parallel \theta_d^{Dir}\right)$ serves for re-ranking.

Using only terms as tokens, and applying standard language-model-based retrieval (TermsLM) over the corpus to create L, yields the standard **RM3** [1]. Creating L by applying TermsLM over Wikipedia results in **WikiRM** [46], an external corpus expansion approach also used in [13, 45]. RM3 and WikiRM re-rank a document list retrieved by TermsLM. (WikiRM is the only model where the list from which RM is constructed, L, is not a sub-set of the list to be re-ranked.) In both methods, $S(d;q) \stackrel{def}{=} \exp(-CE\left(\theta_q^{MLE} \parallel \theta_d^{Dir}\right))$.

The **SDM-RM** model [13] is constructed from, and used to re-rank, lists retrieved by the sequential dependence model (SDM) [36]. θ_d^{Dir}, and the resultant relevance model constructed by setting $\alpha = 0$ in Equation 8, are term-based unigram language models; $S(d;q)$ is the exponent of the score assigned to d by SDM. Re-ranking is performed by linear interpolation of the SDM score assigned to d and $CE\left(RM \parallel \theta_d^{Dir}\right)$, using a parameter α. SDM-RM is, in fact, the highly effective Latent Concept Expansion method [37] without IDF-based weighting of expansion terms.

The next two relevance models, defined over $\mathcal{T}$ (the term-entity token space from Equation 1), are novel to this study. They utilize our STLM language model which integrates terms and entities at the language model level. **RMST** is inspired by methods proposed by Dalton et al. [13][9] by the virtue of using both terms and entities for query expansion. θ_q^{MLE} and θ_d^{Dir} are our STLM language models. $S(d;q) \stackrel{def}{=} \exp(-CE\left(\theta_q^{MLE} \parallel \theta_d^{Dir}\right))$. The TermsLM method is applied over the corpus to create the initial list to be re-ranked (cf. [45]) and from which L is derived.

RMST-ST is constructed as RMST using STLM. The difference is that our entity-based ST method, rather than TermsLM, is used to create the initial list to be re-ranked and from which L is derived. The formal ease of using STLM in the relevance model (Equation 8), yielding RMST and RMST-ST, attests to the merits of using a single language model defined over terms and entities with respect to the alternative score-based fusion approach from Section 3.2.1.

The free parameters of all methods are set using cross validation. The number of expansion terms (i.e., those assigned the highest probability by RM), the number of documents in L, and α are set to values in $\{10, 30, 50, 100\}$, $\{50, 100\}$ and $\{0, 0.1, \ldots, 1\}$, respectively. (Only for WikiRM, the number of documents in L is selected from $\{1, 5, 10, 30, 50, 100\}$ following [46].) All lists that are re-ranked contain 1000 documents. The values of the free parameters of ST and SDM are selected from the ranges specified in Section 4.1. The Dirichlet smoothing parameter, μ, is selected from $\{100, 500, 1000, 1500, 2000, 2500, 3000\}$; for relevance model construction (Equation 8) the value 0 is also used (yielding unsmoothed MLE). To reduce the number of free-parameter values configurations, we use the same value of μ for creating L, for re-ranking and for constructing the relevance model, unless 0 is used for relevance model construction.

Table 8 presents the performance. Our ST method, which does not perform query expansion, is competitive with the term-based relevance model (RM3). We also see that RMST is an effective expansion method which often outperforms RM3 and SDM-RM. This finding echoes those from past work [13, 45] about the merits of using both terms and entities for query expansion. The best performing method in most relevant comparisons is RMST-ST which uses STLM to (i) create an effective initial list for re-ranking; (ii) create an effective list, L, for relevance model construction; and, (iii) induce ranking using the entity-based relevance model as in RMST. We conclude that our STLM language model can play different important roles in query expansion.

Table 8 shows that expansion using Wikipedia as an external corpus (WikiRM) is effective. Our RMST and RMST-ST expansion methods (as well as ST) utilize entity tokens marked by TagMe (i.e., Wikipedia concepts), but do no use

[9]Various expansion methods, which utilize also auxiliary information about entities from the entity repository, were integrated in [13]. We do not use such auxiliary information.

the text on their Wikipedia pages in contrast to WikiRM. Thus, integrating WikiRM with our methods, e.g., using score-based integration [13], is interesting future direction.

5. CONCLUSIONS

We presented novel entity-based language models induced using an entity linking tool. The models simultaneously account for the uncertainty in the entity-linking process and the balance between using term-based and entity-based information. We showed the merits of using the language models for document retrieval in several retrieval paradigms.

Acknowledgments. We thank the reviewers for their comments. This paper is based upon work supported in part by a Yahoo! faculty research and engagement award.

6. REFERENCES

[1] N. Abdul-jaleel, J. Allan, W. B. Croft, O. Diaz, L. Larkey, X. Li, M. D. Smucker, and C. Wade. Umass at TREC 2004: Novelty and hard. In *Proc. of TREC-13*, 2004.

[2] J. Allan, J. P. Callan, W. B. Croft, L. Ballesteros, J. Broglio, J. Xu, and H. Shu. Inquery at TREC-5. In *Proc. of TREC-5*, pages 119–132, 1996.

[3] A. R. Aronson, T. C. Rindflesch, and A. C. Browne. Exploiting a large thesaurus for information retrieval. In *Proc. of RIAO*, volume 94, pages 197–216, 1994.

[4] M. Bendersky, D. Metzler, and W. B. Croft. Learning concept importance using a weighted dependence model. In *Proc. of WSDM*, pages 31–40, 2010.

[5] M. Bendersky, D. Metzler, and W. B. Croft. Parameterized concept weighting in verbose queries. In *Proc. of SIGIR*, pages 605–614, 2011.

[6] M. Bendersky, D. Metzler, and W. B. Croft. Effective query formulation with multiple information sources. In *Proc. of WSDM*, pages 443–452, 2012.

[7] W. C. Brandão, R. L. T. Santos, N. Ziviani, E. S. de Moura, and A. S. da Silva. Learning to expand queries using entities. *JASIST*, 65(9):1870–1883, 2014.

[8] G. Cao, J. Nie, and J. Bai. Integrating word relationships into language models. In *Proc. of SIGIR*, pages 298–305, 2005.

[9] X. Cheng and D. Roth. Relational inference for wikification. In *Proc. of EMNLP*, pages 1787–1796, 2013.

[10] K. Collins-Thompson and J. Callan. Query expansion using random walk models. In *Proc. of CIKM*, pages 704–711, 2005.

[11] G. V. Cormack, M. D. Smucker, and C. L. Clarke. Efficient and effective spam filtering and re-ranking for large web datasets. *Information Retrieval*, 14(5):441–465, 2011.

[12] M. Cornolti, P. Ferragina, and M. Ciaramita. A framework for benchmarking entity-annotation systems. In *Proc. of WWW*, pages 249–260, 2013.

[13] J. Dalton, L. Dietz, and J. Allan. Entity query feature expansion using knowledge base links. In *Proc. of SIGIR*, pages 365–374, 2014.

[14] O. Egozi, S. Markovitch, and E. Gabrilovich. Concept-based information retrieval using explicit semantic analysis. *ACM Transactions on Information Systems (TOIS)*, 29(2):8, 2011.

[15] P. Ferragina and U. Scaiella. Tagme: On-the-fly annotation of short text fragments (by Wikipedia entities). In *Proc. of CIKM*, pages 1625–1628, 2010.

[16] W. R. Hersh, D. H. Hickam, and T. Leone. Words, concepts, or both: optimal indexing units for automated information retrieval. In *Proc. of SCAMC*, page 644, 1992.

[17] D. Hiemstra. Term-specific smoothing for the language modeling approach to information retrieval: the importance of a query term. In *Proc. of SIGIR*, pages 35–41, 2002.

[18] M. Hsu, M. Tsai, and H. Chen. Combining wordnet and conceptnet for automatic query expansion: A learning approach. In *Proc. of AIRS*, pages 213–224, 2008.

[19] S. Huston and W. B. Croft. A comparison of retrieval models using term dependencies. In *Proc. of CIKM*, pages 111–120, 2014.

[20] A. Kotov and C. Zhai. Tapping into knowledge base for concept feedback: leveraging conceptnet to improve search results for difficult queries. In *Proc. of WSDM*, pages 403–412, 2012.

[21] R. Krovetz and W. B. Croft. Lexical ambiguity and information retrieval. *ACM Transactions on Information Systems (TOIS)*, 10(2):115–141, 1992.

[22] G. Kumaran and J. Allan. A case for shorter queries, and helping users create them. In *Proc. of NAACL*, pages 220–227, 2007.

[23] H.-K. J. Kuo and W. Reichl. Phrase-based language models for speech recognition. In *Proc. of EUROSPEECH*, 1999.

[24] O. Kurland and E. Krikon. The opposite of smoothing: A language model approach to ranking query-specific document clusters. *Journal of Artificial Intelligence Research (JAIR)*, 41:367–395, 2011.

[25] J. Lafferty and C. Zhai. Document language models, query models, and risk minimization for information retrieval. In *Proc. of SIGIR*, pages 111–119, 2001.

[26] V. Lavrenko and W. B. Croft. Relevance-based language models. In *Proc. of SIGIR*, pages 120–127, 2001.

[27] M. Levit, S. Parthasarathy, S. Chang, A. Stolcke, and B. Dumoulin. Word-phrase-entity language models: getting more mileage out of n-grams. In *Proc. of INTERSPEECH*, pages 666–670, 2014.

[28] H. Li and J. Xu. Semantic matching in search. *Foundations and Trends in Information Retrieval*, 7(5):343–469, 2014.

[29] R. Li, L. Hao, P. Zhang, D. Song, and Y. Hou. A query expansion approach using entity distribution based on markov random fields. In *Proc. of AIRS*, 2015.

[30] S. Liu, F. Liu, C. T. Yu, and W. Meng. An effective approach to document retrieval via utilizing wordnet and recognizing phrases. In *Proc. of SIGIR*, pages 266–272, 2004.

[31] X. Liu, F. Chen, H. Fang, and M. Wang. Exploiting entity relationship for query expansion in enterprise search. *Information Retrieval Journal*, 17(3):265–294, 2014.

[32] X. Liu and W. B. Croft. Evaluating text representations for retrieval of the best group of documents. In *Proc. of ECIR*, pages 454–462, 2008.

[33] X. Liu and H. Fang. Latent entity space: a novel retrieval approach for entity-bearing queries. *Information Retrieval Journal*, 18(6):473–503, December 2015.

[34] R. Mandala, T. Tokunaga, and H. Tanaka. Combining multiple evidence from different types of thesaurus for query expansion. In *Proc. of SIGIR*, pages 191–197, 1999.

[35] E. Meij, D. Trieschnigg, M. de Rijke, and W. Kraaij. Conceptual language models for domain-specific retrieval. *Information Processing & Management*, 46(4):448–469, 2010.

[36] D. Metzler and W. B. Croft. A markov random field model for term dependencies. In *Proc. of SIGIR*, pages 472–479, 2005.

[37] D. Metzler and W. B. Croft. Latent concept expansion using markov random fields. In *Proc. of SIGIR*, pages 311–318, 2007.

[38] D. Milne and I. H. Witten. Learning to link with Wikipedia. In *Proc. of CIKM*, pages 509–518, 2008.

[39] D. Pan, P. Zhang, J. Li, D. Song, J. Wen, Y. Hou, B. Hu, Y. Jia, and A. N. D. Roeck. Using Dempster-Shafer's evidence theory for query expansion based on freebase knowledge. In *Proc. of AIRS*, pages 121–132, 2013.

[40] C. Shah and W. B. Croft. Evaluating high accuracy retrieval techniques. In *Proc. of SIGIR*, pages 2–9, 2004.

[41] P. Srinivasan. Query expansion and medline. *Information Processing & Management*, 32(4):431–443, 1996.

[42] E. M. Voorhees. Using wordnet to disambiguate word senses for text retrieval. In *Proc. of SIGIR*, pages 171–180, 1993.

[43] E. M. Voorhees. Query expansion using lexical-semantic relations. In *Proc. of SIGIR*, pages 61–69, 1994.

[44] C. Xiong and J. Callan. EsdRank: Connecting query and documents through external semi-structured data. In *Proc. of CIKM*, pages 951–960, 2015.

[45] C. Xiong and J. Callan. Query expansion with Freebase. In *Proc. of ICTIR*, pages 111–120, 2015.

[46] Y. Xu, G. J. Jones, and B. Wang. Query dependent pseudo-relevance feedback based on Wikipedia. In *Proc. of SIGIR*, pages 59–66, 2009.

[47] Y. Yang and C. G. Chute. Words or concepts: the features of indexing units and their optimal use in information retrieval. In *Proc. of SCAMC*, page 685, 1993.

[48] C. Zhai. Statistical language models for information retrieval: A critical review. *Foundations and Trends in Information Retrieval*, 2(3):137–213, 2008.

[49] C. Zhai and J. D. Lafferty. A study of smoothing methods for language models applied to ad hoc information retrieval. In *Proc. of SIGIR*, pages 334–342, 2001.

Engineering Quality and Reliability in Technology-Assisted Review

Gordon V. Cormack
University of Waterloo
gvcormac@uwaterloo.ca

Maura R. Grossman*
Wachtell, Lipton, Rosen & Katz
mrgrossman@wlrk.com

ABSTRACT

The objective of technology-assisted review ("TAR") is to find as much relevant information as possible with reasonable effort. *Quality* is a measure of the extent to which a TAR method achieves this objective, while *reliability* is a measure of how consistently it achieves an acceptable result. We are concerned with how to define, measure, and achieve high quality and high reliability in TAR. When quality is defined using the traditional goal-post method of specifying a minimum acceptable recall threshold, the quality and reliability of a TAR method are both, by definition, equal to the probability of achieving the threshold. Assuming this definition of quality and reliability, we show how to augment any TAR method to achieve guaranteed reliability, for a quantifiable level of additional review effort. We demonstrate this result by augmenting the TAR method supplied as the baseline model implementation for the TREC 2015 Total Recall Track, measuring reliability and effort for 555 topics from eight test collections. While our empirical results corroborate our claim of guaranteed reliability, we observe that the augmentation strategy may entail disproportionate effort, especially when the number of relevant documents is low. To address this limitation, we propose stopping criteria for the model implementation that may be applied with no additional review effort, while achieving empirical reliability that compares favorably to the provably reliable method. We further argue that optimizing reliability according to the traditional goal-post method is inconsistent with certain subjective aspects of quality, and that optimizing a Taguchi quality loss function may be more apt.

Keywords: Technology-assisted review; predictive coding; electronic discovery; e-discovery; test collections; relevance feedback; continuous active learning; reliability; quality; systematic review.

*The views expressed herein are solely those of the author and should not be attributed to her firm or its clients.

SIGIR '16 July 17-21, 2016, Pisa, Italy

ACM ISBN 978-1-4503-4069-4/16/07.

DOI: http://dx.doi.org/10.1145/2911451.2911510

1. INTRODUCTION

A vexing question that has plagued the use of technology-assisted review ("TAR") is "when to stop"; that is, knowing when as much relevant information as possible has been found, with reasonable effort. We present a provably reliable method to achieve high recall using any search strategy that repeatedly retrieves documents and receives relevance feedback, continuing indefinitely until a decision is made to discontinue the review process. Amenable search strategies include traditional ranked retrieval,[1] interactive searching and judging [8], move-to-front pooling [8], and continuos active learning ("CAL") [5].

For the particular implementation of CAL supplied as the baseline model implementation ("BMI") [7] for the TREC 2015 Total Recall Track [13], we present two stopping procedures that achieve superior empirical reliability for comparable effort, and comparable empirical reliability for less effort, relative to our provably reliable method.

Our primary motivation is to provide quality assurance for TAR applications, including electronic discovery ("eDiscovery") in legal matters [5], systematic review in evidence-based medicine [10], and the creation of test collections for information retrieval ("IR") evaluation [14]. Since these applications generally require that a human review each relevant document, we assume for this study that the effort to provide relevance feedback for relevant documents is a sunk cost. On the other hand, the effort to assess and provide relevance feedback for non-relevant documents is wasted. We measure review effort in terms of the total number of documents reviewed, whether relevant or not. An ideal search would find all of the relevant documents with effort equal to precisely that number. An acceptable search would find most of the relevant documents with minimal wasted effort.

A reliable search method would achieve an acceptable search most of the time. More formally, if S is a random variable representing a search, and $acceptable(s)$ is an indicator function denoting whether a particular search s has an acceptable result, we define:

$$reliability =_{def} \Pr[acceptable(S) = 1] .$$

To this end, we define $recall(s)$ and $effort(s)$ to be the recall and effort associated with s. For simplicity, our primary

[1]To be amenable, a retrieval method must be able to rank the entire collection. Incomplete rankings or set-based results may be extended by adding the remaining documents in any order.

Collection	Source	Description	# Docs	# Topics	# Rel (R)
At Home	TREC 2015 Total Recall	Jeb Bush public email	290,000	10	227-17,135
At Home	TREC 2015 Total Recall	Hacker forums	465,147	10	179-9,517
At Home	TREC 2015 Total Recall	Local news	902,434	10	23-2,094
Kaine	TREC 2015 Total Recall	Tim Kaine non-public email	401,953	4	14,341-166,118
MIMIC II	TREC 2015 Total Recall	MIMIC II Clinical Database	31,538	19	180-19,182
RCV1-v2	Reuters	News subject categories	804,414	103	5-381,327
Filtering	TREC 2012 Filtering	NIST topics	804,414	50	12-610
Intersection	TREC 2012 Filtering	Conjunction of RCV1-v2 subject pairs	804,414	50	21-349
Robust-04	TREC 2004 Robust	Amalgam of TREC ad-hoc topics	528,256	249	4-161
Robust-05	TREC 2005 Robust	50 legacy topics, new dataset	1,033,461	50	17-376

Table 1: Ten Evaluation Datasets. In our experiments, the three At Home datasets are treated as a single test collection, for a total of eight test collections.

results use a *goal-post* definition [18] of acceptability:

$$acceptable(s) = \begin{cases} 1 & (recall(s) \geq 0.70) \\ 0 & (recall(s) < 0.70) \end{cases}.$$

Our primary results further assume that 95% reliability is sufficiently high.

The methods and results detailed in this work are:

- The *target method*: a provably reliable method that chooses ten random relevant documents as a target, and employs an independent search method to retrieve documents without knowledge of the target set, until each document in the target set has been retrieved. We prove that this method achieves 95% reliability for a minimum threshold recall of 70%.
- The *knee method*: a geometric stopping procedure, based on the shape of the gain (*i.e.*, recall versus effort) curve, that augments BMI to achieve similar empirical reliability to the target method, with substantially less effort. The knee method, in contrast to the target method, is practical regardless of the number of relevant documents in the collection.
- The *budget method:* a variant of the knee method that achieves superior empirical reliability to the target method, with similar effort.
- *Empirical validation*: we assess the effectiveness and reliability of our methods on eight archival test collections consisting of 555 topics and 4.5 million documents (*see* Table 1).
- *Quality evaluation*: As an alternative to binary relevance and fixed recall and reliability thresholds, we argue and provide evidence that quality loss functions [18] provide more nuanced measures that better reflect the tensions among consistency, effectiveness, and efficiency.

2. BACKGROUND

The modern literature on the effectiveness and reliability of high-recall retrieval is largely confined to the problem of constructing test collections for IR evaluation, and eDiscovery in legal matters. A 1985 study by Blair and Maron [2] showed that teams of lawyers and paralegals, using iterative Boolean searches, believed they had achieved 75% recall, when in fact they had achieved 20%. Blair [3] later described the difficulty of measuring high recall in general, and the use of targeted searching, systematically constructed Boolean queries, and stratified sampling to estimate recall for the Blair and Maron study.

The Text Retrieval Conference ("TREC") [21] first addressed the problem of IR evaluation for "large" datasets, which at the time of TREC's inception in 1992, contained on the order of 500,000 documents. TREC follows the Cranfield paradigm [20], which evaluates the results of subject systems against a gold standard that identifies every relevant document. For large datasets, the effort to render a human assessment for each document is prohibitive, thus occasioning the use of automated or semi-automated methods to limit the human review effort required to label the dataset. TREC saw the introduction of the "pooling method," which selects the top-ranked documents from a number of independent retrieval efforts for assessment, and deems all other documents to be non-relevant. A number of studies (*see* [19]) indicate that this method fails to identify a substantial number of documents, but even so, the resulting gold standard yields a stable evaluation of the relative effectiveness of candidate systems, as measured by Kendall's τ rank correlation. We are unaware of any studies that address the effectiveness of pool-based gold standards for evaluating high-recall retrieval, or for simulating interactive relevance feedback. Studies suggest that greedy or machine-learning methods to select the pool yield a more nearly complete gold standard [8, 14].

Interactive searching and judging ("ISJ"), in which a searcher repeatedly formulates queries and examines the top results from a relevance-ranking search engine, has been shown to yield gold standards with comparable quality to the pooling method, with considerably less effort [8]. Continuous active learning ("CAL") [5] is essentially the same as ISJ, but uses machine learning instead of, or in addition to, manually formulated queries to rank the documents for review. An approach similar to CAL was used in the TREC 2012 Filtering Track (*see* [17]) to construct the gold standard that was used for evaluation, and also to simulate relevance feedback. A subsequent study based on pooling showed that the CAL-like approach had achieved high recall, and high effectiveness, as measured by Kendall's τ [17]. CAL achieved superior results at the TREC 2009 Legal Track [4], and remains state of the art for eDiscovery.

The TREC 2015 Total Recall Track [13] represents the first study of high-recall human-in-the-loop retrieval in which all aspects of human intervention are simulated, and hence controlled. Fully automated or semi-automated retrieval systems were tested through their interaction with an evaluation server. At the outset, the evaluation server provided a document collection and a topic description, after which the system under test submitted potentially relevant documents from the collection to the evaluation server. In response, the evaluation server provided an assessment (derived from a pre-computed gold standard) for the submitted documents, and the process continued until the documents were exhausted or the system chose to stop.

Participants in the Total Recall Track were supplied with a CAL baseline model implementation[2] ("BMI") that, when connected to the evaluation server, performed all aspects of the task—other than deciding when to stop—without human intervention. Participating systems were allowed to run indefinitely, and were evaluated (primarily) on the quality of the ranking determined by the order in which the system presented documents to the server. Instead of actually terminating when they thought an acceptable result had been achieved, participants were invited to "call their shot" by indicating, in real time, when they would have stopped, had they been required to balance benefit with cost. The current study considers the addition of a call-your-shot mechanism to BMI, and, more generally, to any ranking system.

The TREC 2015 Total Recall Track contributed five fully labeled archival datasets. The *Jeb Bush*, *Hacker Forums*, and *Local News* datasets were used for the *At Home* task, in which participants ran their systems on their own platforms, connecting via the internet to the evaluation server, which was run by the track coordinators. The *Kaine* and *MIMIC II* datasets were used for the *Sandbox* task, in which participants encapsulated their systems as a virtual machine, which was run by the track coordinators, along with the evaluation server, isolated from the internet.

The reliability of methods for constructing gold standards for IR evaluation has typically been evaluated by how well the resulting gold standard ranks the relative effectiveness of precision-oriented retrieval systems, where the objective is to find as much relevant information as possible at low rank. For this purpose, a calibrated estimate is not required; it is sufficient to determine whether one system achieves higher recall than another, and the actual numerical value is ascribed little meaning. A number of studies (*see* [23]) eschew recall altogether, assuming that the user's information need will be satisfied by a tiny fraction of a vast sea of relevant documents. Zobel et al. [23] suggest that recall is a poor effectiveness measure, even for the "high-recall applications" where the user seeks "total recall," and that only an extensive ad-hoc effort using multiple queries and tools will satisfy the user that their information need has been met.

The reliability and effectiveness of TAR (also known as "predictive coding") is the subject of much interest in the legal community [9, 16]. A number of approaches to TAR, to deciding when to stop, and to quality assurance have been advanced, but no stopping procedure has previously been shown to be mathematically or empirically reliable. Perhaps the most commonly used approach to TAR involves the use of a supervised machine-learning algorithm trained using a set of documents from the collection (typically referred to as a "seed set") to partition the collection into a "review set," which is subject to human review, and a "null set," which is not. This approach is referred to as either simple passive learning ("SPL") or simple active learning ("SAL"), depending on whether or not the learning algorithm is involved in selecting the training documents [5]. Recently, CAL has been advanced as a superior alternative [5, 7].

Regardless of the TAR method used, the question remains of when to stop. For SPL and SAL, two questions must be answered: when to stop training; and how many documents should be included in the review set. For CAL, the sole question is when to stop. One approach that has been advanced is to draw a random hold-out set (referred to as a "control set") that is used to measure the effectiveness of the classifier, in order to determine when to stop training, and then to measure recall, so as to determine how many documents should comprise the review set. The control set must be large enough to contain a sufficient number of relevant documents to yield a precise estimate. Bagdouri et al. [1] note that the use of a control set constitutes sequential sampling, with the net effect that it yields a biased estimate of recall, and cannot be used for quality assurance. As an alternative, they propose "certified text classification," in which part of the review budget is set aside to conduct a frequentist acceptance test that will accept or reject the classifier. Bagdouri et al. are concerned with the problem of testing whether the classifier has achieved a threshold level of F_1; they do not consider recall, or how to proceed in the event that the classifier is rejected by the test.

The limitations of binary relevance may be of particular importance in evaluating the effectiveness and reliability of TAR systems. Binary relevance does not account for the differential importance of relevant documents, and there will necessarily be documents near the threshold about which competent assessors will disagree (*see* [19]). In evaluating the recall of a system against a gold standard, there will necessarily be uncertainty for some documents as to whether the system is correct, the gold standard is correct, or reasonable minds could disagree. If a system fails to meet a target recall threshold, is it because the system has missed important documents, because it has missed marginal documents about which reasonable minds could differ, or because it has missed documents that are incorrectly coded relevant in the gold standard? And, is the effort to remedy the shortfall proportionate to the importance of the missed documents?

Binary relevance and fixed recall targets are examples of traditional goal-post methods in quality engineering ([18]), where success or failure is a binary quantity, and reliability is the probability of success. In quality engineering, a quadratic loss function blends reliability and effectiveness into a single quality measure, with targets, but no arbitrary thresholds [18].

3. GUARANTEED RELIABILITY

Our *target method* involves drawing a target set T of k random relevant documents from the collection; for simplicity we fix $k = 10$, but a different number could be chosen. In order to draw T, we retrieve and review documents selected at random until k relevant documents are found, or the collection is exhausted. The underlying search strategy retrieves documents for review without knowledge of T, until every document in T has been found. This method achieves 95% reliability, as shown below.

Consider a document collection C and a function $rel(d)$ indicating binary relevance. The number of relevant docu-

[2] *See* `http://plg.uwaterloo.ca/~gvcormac/trecvm/`.

ments in the collection is $R = |\{d \in C | rel(d)\}|$. A search strategy is a ranking on C where $1 \le rank(d) \le |C|$ denotes the position of d in the ranking. It is important to note that the following argument holds for any such ranking, provided it is independent of T.

The retrieved set of the target method is the shortest prefix P of the ranking that contains T:

$$P = \{d | rank(d) \le \max_{d' \in T} rank(d')\}.$$

Now consider the ranking $relrank(d)$ of only relevant documents:

$$relrank(d) = \left|\{d' \in C | rel(d) \wedge rank(d') \le rank(d)\}\right|.$$

The last retrieved document d_{last} is necessarily in T:

$$d_{last} = \arg\max_{d \in T} rank(d) = \arg\max_{d \in T} relrank(d).$$

The recall of our method is:

$$recall = \frac{relrank(d_{last})}{R}.$$

Taking T to be a random variable, the method is reliable if:

$$R \le 10 \vee \Pr[\frac{relrank(d_{last})}{R} \ge 0.7] \ge 0.95.$$

Assuming large R, consider the problem of determining a cutoff c such that:

$$\Pr[\frac{R - relrank(d_{last})}{R} > c] = 0.05 \quad (1)$$

$$\Pr[R - relrank(d_{last}) > cR] = 0.05 \quad (2)$$

For the condition in Equation 2 to hold, it must be the case that the [numerically] top-ranked cR documents are absent from T, which occurs with probability

$$\left(1 - \frac{10}{R}\right)^{cR} = 0.05.$$

It follows that:

$$c = \frac{\log 0.05}{R \log\left(1 - \frac{10}{R}\right)}.$$

For all $R > 10$,

$$c < \lim_{R \to \infty} \frac{\log 0.05}{R \log\left(1 - \frac{10}{R}\right)} = 0.299573 < 0.3. \quad (3)$$

Combining (1) and (3), we have:

$$\Pr[\frac{R - relrank(d_{last})}{R} > 0.3] < 0.05$$

$$R \le 10 \vee \Pr[\frac{relrank(d_{last})}{R} \ge 0.7] \ge 0.95 \,\square.$$

Reliability is obtained at the cost of supplemental review effort inversely proportional to R, the number of relevant documents. The number of randomly selected documents that need to be reviewed to find k relevant ones is $k\frac{|C|}{R}$, on average for $R \ll |C|$. For $k = 10$ and prevalence $\frac{R}{|C|} \approx 1\%$, the target method entails a review overhead of about 1,000 additional documents. Lower prevalence entails substantially more overhead, while higher prevalence entails less.

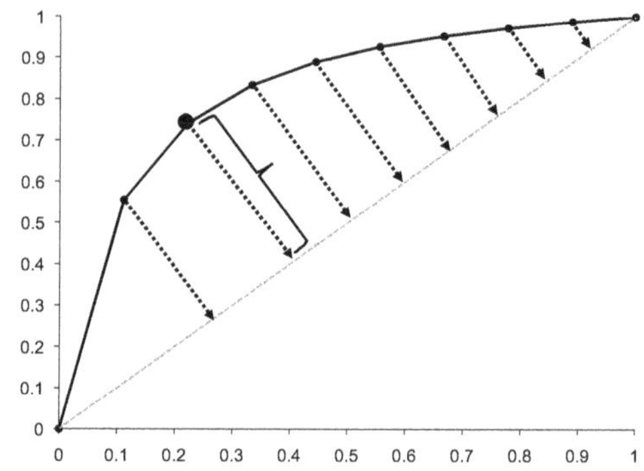

Figure 1: Knee Detection [15].

4. EMPIRICAL RELIABILITY

Our *knee method* relies on the assumption that CAL, in accordance with the probability-ranking principle, succeeds in ranking more-likely relevant documents before less-likely relevant documents. As a consequence, the gain curve plotting recall versus rank is assumed to be generally convex, with high slope (*i.e.*, "marginal precision") at the outset, and near-zero slope once nearly all relevant documents have been retrieved.

An ideal gain curve would have slope 1.0 until an inflection point corresponding to the rank at which all documents had been retrieved, and slope 0.0 thereafter. An actual gain curve typically diverges from the ideal due to limitations in probability ranking, random factors, and a noisy gold standard. Suppose that the retrieval method were able to achieve 70% recall and 70% precision at some rank r, as is typical for modern classifiers [11], or as might be achieved by exhaustive manual review [19]. The slope, up to that rank ($slope_{<r}$), would be 0.7, and the slope after that rank ($slope_{>r}$) would approach, but not equal 0. For small values of $R \ll |C|$, we would expect $slope \approx 0.0$, and for all R we would expect the "slope ratio" $\rho = \frac{slope_{<r}}{slope_{>r}} \gg 1$.

Based on our experience with non-public datasets, we observed that for $R \gtrsim 100$, $\rho \gg 6.0$ (with suitable smoothing) was a good indicator of high recall, achieving recall and reliability that compared favorably to that achieved by the target method. We formed the hypothesis that these thresholds were universal; that the same threshold would work for a wide variety datasets, including the ten that we subsequently used for our empirical evaluation (*see* Table 1).

4.1 Noise Abatement

If we were to stop at the minimum rank s, such that there exists an inflection point $1 < i < s$ such that $\rho \ge 6$, we would almost certainly stop prematurely due to chance. Moreover, this naïve approach would entail quadratic computational effort as a function of the size of the collection. To avoid both eventualities, we evaluate ρ only at values of s arising from the batches of documents selected by BMI. The number of batches is proportional to $\log |C|$, as the values of s are separated by an exponentially increasing interval. Relatively few of the candidate values for s will be viable, even by chance. Any residual sequential-testing bias is offset by a conservative choice of threshold for ρ.

For each value of s, we evaluate ρ at only one i, chosen using a geometric "knee-detection" algorithm [15], illustrated

Collection	Target Method			Knee Method			Budget Method		
	Reliability	Recall	*Effort*	Reliability	Recall	*Effort*	Reliability	Recall	*Effort*
At Home	1.00	0.91	*44,079*	0.93	0.93	*5,244*	0.97	0.97	*43,896*
Kaine	1.00	0.92	*119,644*	1.00	0.98	*172,774*	1.00	0.98	*172,774*
MIMIC II	1.00	0.89	*14,440*	1.00	0.97	*19,387*	1.00	0.97	*19,418*
RCV1-v2	0.96	0.88	*83,412*	0.99	0.94	*60,645*	0.99	0.94	*70,601*
Filtering	0.98	0.93	*133,788*	1.00	0.99	*3,857*	1.00	1.00	*143,798*
Intersection	1.00	0.92	*174,415*	0.98	0.96	*153,638*	1.00	0.99	*190,671*
Robust-04	0.89	0.94	*169,907*	1.00	1.00	*7,575*	1.00	1.00	*162,673*
Robust-05	1.00	0.92	*155,405*	1.00	0.96	*8,444*	1.00	1.00	*134,719*

Table 2: Reliability, Mean Recall, and Mean Effort for the Target, Knee, and Budget Methods.

in Figure 1. We draw a line from the origin to the recall achieved at rank s, and compute the maximum perpendicular distance from this line to the gain curve. Our candidate value of i is the projection to the x-axis of the intersection between the perpendicular and the gain curve. Our rationale in choosing this point was that it would correctly choose the inflection point for an ideal curve, and would avoid anomalies associated with points very close to the origin or to rank s, while capturing our intuitive notion of a genuine tipping point.

We calculated the slope ratio as:

$$\rho = \frac{\frac{|\{d|rank(d)\leq i \wedge rel(d)\}|}{i}}{\frac{1+|\{d|i<rank(d)\leq s\}|}{s-i}} .$$

Smoothing was accomplished by adding 1 to the number of relevant documents beyond the knee. This choice avoided the singularity of no relevant documents beyond the knee, and generally penalized situations in which the chosen inflection point was close to s. No smoothing was applied to the numerator, as we were not concerned with occasional underestimates.

4.2 Adjustment for Low Prevalence

The case of $R \lesssim 100$ is more problematic. Any correction for small R faces a dual problem:

1. the stopping procedure has no knowledge of the value of R, other than what can be estimated through relevance feedback from retrieved documents; and,
2. even if it were known that R was small, the sparsity of relevant documents compromises the reliability of our slope-ratio calculation.

The knee method relies entirely on the slope-ratio test, adjusted to compensate for low R. Initial tuning on the training collections from the TREC 2015 Total Recall Track indicated that a fixed lower bound β on the rank at which to stop, might be effective. For our submission to the TREC 2015 Total Recall At Home task, we conducted a parameter sweep of six combinations of $\beta \in \{100, 1000\}$ and $\rho \in \{3, 6, 10\}$. Our results showed that combinations involving $\beta = 100$ or $\rho = 3$ were unreliable, and we eliminated them from further consideration. Unsurprisingly, the combination of $\beta = 1000$, $\rho = 10$ proved most reliable, achieving the recall target for 29 of 30 topics (*reliability* $= 0.97$ [$0.830 - 0.999$ 95% c.i.]).

We observed that recall and reliability appeared to be lower for smaller R, while effort (especially for $\rho = 10$) appeared to be disproportionately higher for large R. This observation led us to seek more reliable methods for small R, and to choose $\rho = 6$ for large R. To aid in this endeavor, we used a non-public dataset consisting of about 300,000 documents reviewed by attorneys and labeled according to 63 criteria, with R ranging from 5 to 164,000 (median 431). Based on tuning experiments using this dataset, we calibrated the slope-ratio cutoff as a function of *relret*, the number of relevant documents retrieved at any given rank:

$$\rho = 156 - \min(relret, 150) .$$

In other words, we set the threshold for the slope ratio to be 150 when no relevant documents have been retrieved, 6 whenever at least 150 relevant documents have been retrieved, and use linear interpolation between these values.

We further observed that with this adjustment, the choice of $\beta = 100$ versus $\beta = 1000$ became less critical. The lower value occasionally achieved lower effort than the higher value, and occasionally failed when the higher value did not. We chose to retain the value of $\beta = 1000$ from our earlier experiments.

4.3 Effort Adjustment

A variant of our knee method—the *budget method*—adjusts for small R by stopping only when a review budget comparable to that of the target method has been expended, and the slope-ratio test $\rho \geq 6$ is also satisfied. This adjustment substantially delays termination for small R, thus ensuring reliability.

The approach is predicated on the hypothesis that the supplemental review effort entailed by the target method would be better spent reviewing more documents retrieved by CAL. The target method entails the supplemental review of about $\frac{10|C|}{R}$ documents in order to find 10 relevant ones. According to the probability-ranking principle, we would expect CAL to find more relevant documents than random selection, for any level of effort, up to and beyond $\frac{10|C|}{R}$.

While the supplemental documents retrieved by the target method provide a statistical estimate of R, the documents retrieved by CAL provide a lower bound for R, and therefore an upper bound for the expected effort entailed by the target method. At the outset, this upper bound is loose, but as the review progresses, it tightens. The budget method retrieves documents using CAL until review effort exceeds this upper bound *and* $\rho \geq 6.0$, or until $0.75|C|$ documents are retrieved.

For small R, the budget determines the stopping point. For large R, enough relevant documents will likely be discovered to bound the review budget to an insubstantial fraction of R, and the slope-ratio test will determine when to stop. In any event, the review stops at $0.75|C|$. This final cutoff is predicated on the probability-ranking principle: random

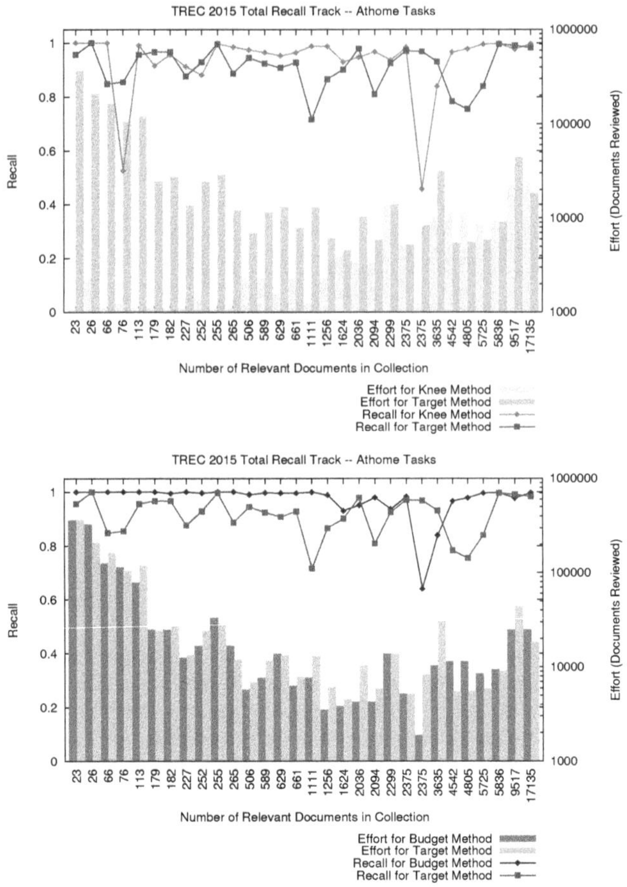

Figure 2: TREC 2015 Total Recall At Home Collection.

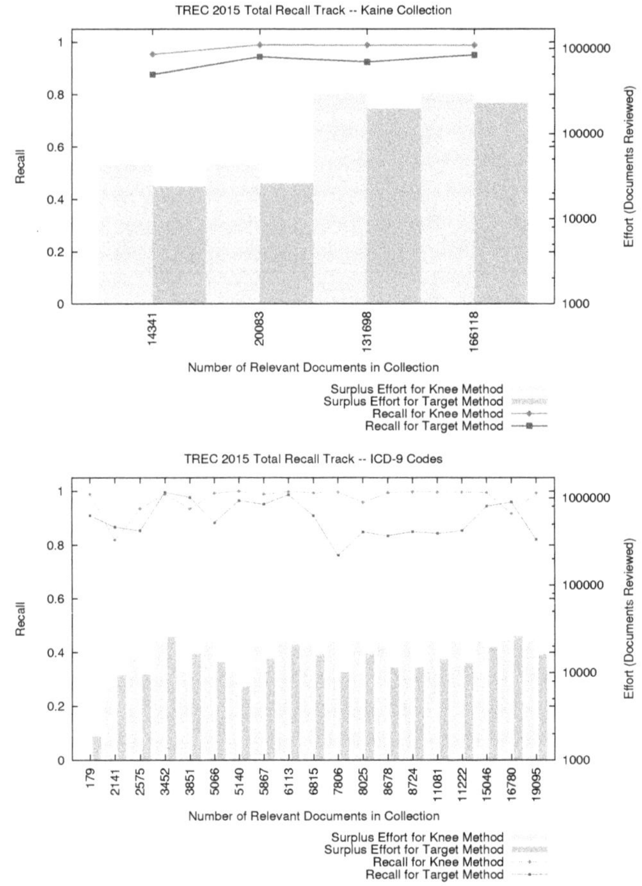

Figure 3: TREC 2015 Total Recall Sandbox Collections.

selection of 75% of the collection would, with high probability, achieve 70% recall; the top-ranked 75% should achieve even higher recall.

5. EXPERIMENTS

Testing the reliability of our stopping methods occasioned the use of "fully assessed" test collections, with a large number of topics and documents, where by "fully assessed," we mean that the pooling method, ISJ, or a rule base was used, and the resulting documents were labeled by a human assessor. From the limited number of collections that met these criteria, we selected the TREC 2015 Total Recall Track collections, the Reuters RCV1-v2 news dataset, the TREC 2002 Filtering Track collections, and the TREC 2004 and 2005 Robust Track collections, as detailed in Table 1. We used our Total Recall At Home participation to conduct an initial parameter sweep with six combinations, as well as final testing; the other datasets were used solely for testing.

The first phase of our experiments took place within the context of the TREC 2015 Total Recall Track, which had three distinct phases: training, At Home, and Sandbox. We conducted our initial development and tuning during the training phase, and submitted the knee method for evaluation in the At Home phase, but not the Sandbox phase. We captured the sequence of documents retrieved by BMI in both the At Home and Sandbox phases, and later used them to simulate the effect of the stopping methods whose results are presented here. After conducting further tuning on our non-public collection of 300,000 documents with 63 topics, we froze all parameters, and ran BMI on the other evaluation datasets, capturing the order in which the documents were retrieved. We then simulated our stopping methods by applying them to the ranking.

Summary results showing reliability, average recall, and average effort for all collections are shown in Table 2. The overall reliability of the target method, the knee method, and the budget method are substantially higher than the target of 0.95. Considering reliability, alone, there is little to choose among the methods; but the recall achieved by the knee and budget methods is substantially higher, while the effort expended by the knee method is, for some datasets, dramatically lower.

As illustrated in Figures 2 through 6, R (the number of relevant documents) appears to be the principal determinant of effort. For small R, effort for the target and budget methods approaches the size of the collection, while effort for the knee method, with one notable exception, generally diminishes with R, approaching the floor of $\beta = 1000$ that we chose for this study. On the other hand, for large R, the effort for all methods appears proportional to R.

The top panel of Figure 2 compares recall and effort for the knee and target methods, for each topic in the At Home col-

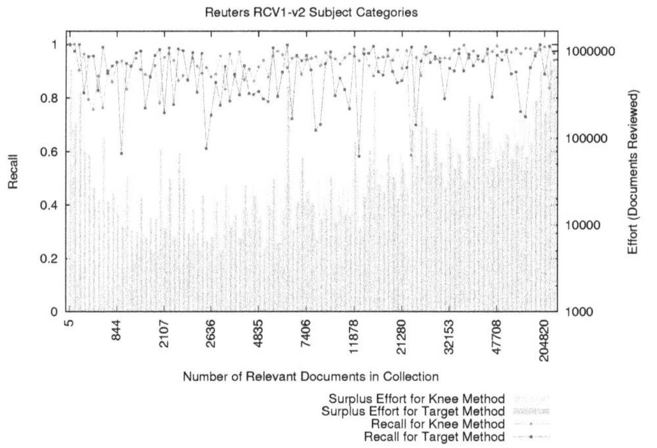

Figure 4: Reuters RCV1-v2 Subject Codes.

lection, ordered by R. We see that 28 of the 30 recall points for the knee method (shown by the green curve) fall above 0.7, indicating reliability of 0.93, while all of the points for the target method (shown by the red curve) fall above 0.7, indicating reliability of 1.00 for this collection. We also see that the most of the recall points for the knee method fall above those for the target method, indicating higher median recall, and the (signed) area between the curves is positive, indicating higher mean recall. Per-topic effort is shown as a bar graph on a logarithmic scale spanning three orders of magnitude. For small R, the knee method entails about 100 times less effort than the target method, while for large R, the effort is comparable.

The bottom panel of Figure 2 follows the same format, comparing the budget method (shown in blue) to the target method (shown in red). While the budget method achieves higher recall than the target method for nearly all topics, that superiority is not reflected in higher reliability. Effort for the two methods is very similar. The same observations apply to the results for the other collections: For low R, recall for the budget method exceeds that of the target method, while effort is indistinguishable; for large R, recall and effort are indistinguishable from the knee method. Both methods are reliable.

For brevity, we show graphical results comparing only the knee and target methods for the other collections. Tabular results for all methods are presented in Table 2.

Figure 3 shows results for the Sandbox task of the TREC 2015 Total Recall Track, which was notable in that participants had no prior access to the datasets or the topics, and their retrieval systems had to run fully autonomously. The top panel shows our results for the Kaine collection, which consisted of about 400,000 documents from Tim Kaine's eight-year tenure as Governor of Virginia. These documents had been previously reviewed and labeled by the archivist at the Library of Virginia according to four statutory categories: "record" (versus "non-record"), "open record," "restricted record," and "pertaining to the Virginia Tech shooting." Two of the topics had moderately high $R \approx 10^4$, and two had very high $R \approx 10^5$. For all topics, the knee method achieved higher recall at the expense of somewhat higher effort. The bottom panel shows our results for the MIMIC II collection, which consisted of about 30,000 medical records

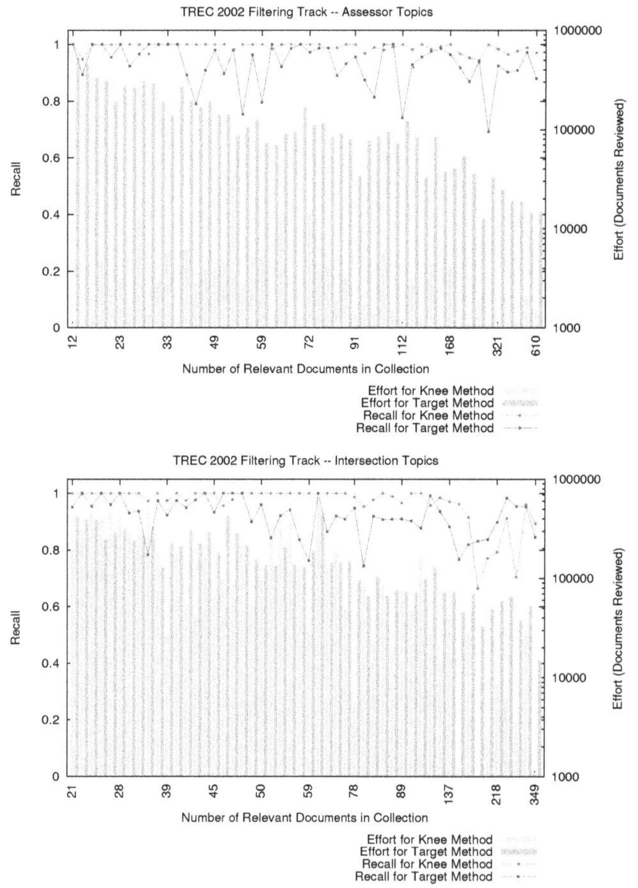

Figure 5: TREC 2002 Filtering Track Collections.

collected from a hospital intensive care unit. The documents consisted of nurses' notes, radiology reports, and discharge summaries. The "topics" consisted of ICD-9 diagnostic codes extracted from non-textual database records. With one exception ($R = 179$), all topics had moderately high R. The knee method generally achieved higher recall than the target method, at the expense of somewhat higher effort for most topics.

Figure 4 shows the results for the RCV1-v2 dataset, using the subject categories and descriptions published with the dataset as topics [11]. Over a very wide range $10^1 \lesssim R \lesssim 10^5$, we observe a familiar pattern: The knee method has somewhat higher recall and lower variance, with dramatically lower effort, for small R.

Figure 5 shows results for two sets of topics created for the TREC 2002 Filtering Track. The top panel shows results for topics that were created and assessed by NIST for the track. All topics had low $R \leq 610$; the majority had very low $R \leq 100$. For all topics, including those with the lowest $R \ll 100$, the knee method achieved near-perfect recall. Recall for the target method showed much higher variance, suggesting that its reliability is actually lower. The knee method entails order(s) of magnitude less effort. The lower panel shows results for intersection topics, each of which was the conjunction of two RCV1-v2 subject categories. If $rel_1(d)$ and $rel_2(d)$ indicate relevance for two RCV1-v2 topics, $rel_1(d) \wedge rel_2(d)$ indicates relevance for the intersection

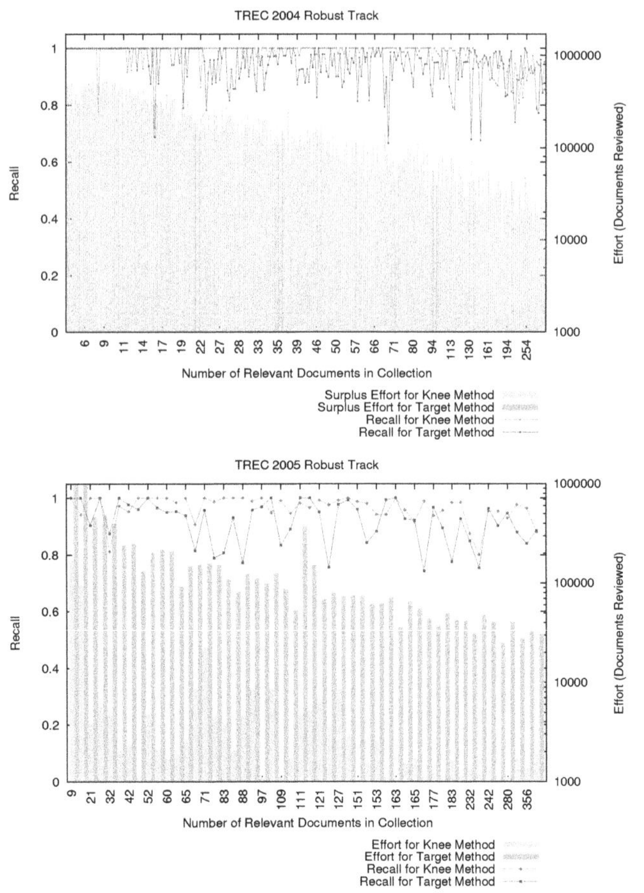

Figure 6: TREC 2004-2005 Robust Track Collections.

topic. The intersection topics were reported as a failed experiment [17], since no system achieved reasonable results on them. The results show that, while the effort to achieve high recall for these anomalous topics is inordinately large, our stopping methods are reliable.

Figure 6 shows results for the TREC 2004 and 2005 Robust tracks. In 2004, the Robust Track aggregated 150 topics developed for the TREC 6, TREC 7, and TREC 8 Ad-Hoc tasks, 50 topics developed for the 2003 Robust Track, and 49 new topics, for a total of 249 topics. For 2005, 50 of these topics—those deemed to be "difficult"—were reprised with a new dataset. The top panel reports our results for 2004; the bottom for 2005. The results further confirm that the target and knee methods both achieve high reliability, while the knee method entails dramatically less effort.

6. DIMINISHING LOSS

As evidenced by the results above, reliability does not capture certain important aspects of effectiveness or efficiency. Moreover, empirical measurements of reliability lack statistical power, while parametric estimates depend on assumptions regarding the distribution of recall values. Since the choices of acceptable recall and acceptable reliability are both somewhat arbitrary, bias due to incorrect distributional assumptions may be of little consequence. We suggest that reporting the mean μ and standard deviation σ of recall conveys more useful information, if not a provably accurate estimate of reliability. Such an estimate would have to be compared to one or more tacit thresholds to determine the reliability of the method; for example, assuming normality, any pair of μ and σ such that $\mu - 1.64\sigma \geq 0.70$ would be 95% reliable. More generally, the value of $Q = \mu - 1.64\sigma$ is a quantitative measure of quality, which may be used to determine the threshold level of acceptable recall for which 95% reliability may be obtained. Alternatively, by substituting the appropriate z-score in place of 1.64, a threshold of reliability different from 95% may be tested.

We suggest that reliability and recall should be supplanted by quality estimates based on loss functions, of which recall and reliability are special cases. We define $Q = 1 - \overline{loss}$, where $\overline{loss}$ is the mean value of a loss function over all topics. If

$$loss = 1 - recall\,,\ \ Q = \overline{recall}\,;\ \text{if,}$$

$$loss = \begin{cases} 0 & (recall \geq 0.7) \\ 1 & (recall < 0.7) \end{cases}\,,\ \ Q = reliability\,.$$

A quadratic loss function such as:

$$loss_r = (1 - recall)^2 \tag{4}$$

captures the desirability of consistently high recall, subsuming the roles of μ and σ in the previous discussion. Our aspirational goal is to achieve 100% recall. Any shortfall is penalized, and larger shortfalls are penalized more heavily.

Quadratic loss further generalizes to other aspects of quality, such as graded relevance, facet relevance [6], and efficiency. For example, let a_1, a_2, ..., a_n be categories of relevance, and $rel_a(d)$ be the indicator function for category a. Define:

$$recall_a = \frac{|\{d \in C | relret(d) \wedge rel_a(d)\}|}{|\{d \in C | rel_a(d)\}|}$$

$$loss_a = (1 - recall_a)^2$$

$$loss = \sum_{i=i}^{n} \alpha_i loss_{a_i}\,,\ \text{where } 1 = \sum_{i=1}^{n} \alpha_i\,. \tag{5}$$

The choice of weights α_i is not critical; the value $\alpha_i = \frac{1}{n}$ for all α_i will often suffice, as it rewards consistent recall over all categories, with the effect that documents belonging to rarer categories are afforded more influence.

Review effort may also be modeled as a category of loss, thus quantifying the notion of "reasonable effort." For the problem as we have framed it, an ideal method would entail *effort* $= R$. From the presentation of results in the TREC 2015 Total Recall Track Overview [13], we observe that a reasonable effort might entail *effort* $= aR + b$, where $a \approx 1$ represents effort proportional to sunk review cost, and $b \approx 0$ represents fixed overhead. We suggest that $a \leq 2$ and $b \leq 1000$ represent reasonable effort to achieve $recall \geq 0.70$ with 95% reliability. The use of a quadratic loss replaces the a and b thresholds by a soft target:

$$loss_e = \left(\frac{b}{|C|}\right)^2 \left(\frac{effort}{R+b}\right)^2\,. \tag{6}$$

$loss_e$ may be used to measure efficiency in its own right, or treated as a category loss in (5).

Collection	Target Method			Knee Method			Budget Method		
	$\sqrt{loss_r}$	$\sqrt{loss_e}$	$\sqrt{loss_{re}}$	$\sqrt{loss_r}$	$\sqrt{loss_e}$	$\sqrt{loss_{re}}$	$\sqrt{loss_r}$	$\sqrt{loss_e}$	$\sqrt{loss_{re}}$
At Home	0.0132	0.0090	0.0111	0.0197	**0.0000**	0.0099	**0.0056**	0.0108	**0.0082**
Kaine	0.0815	**0.0016**	0.0577	**0.0252**	0.0025	**0.0179**	**0.0252**	0.0025	**0.0179**
MIMIC II	0.1229	**0.0734**	0.1012	**0.0516**	0.0862	**0.0710**	**0.0516**	0.0866	0.0712
RCV1-v2	0.1475	0.0883	0.1216	0.0947	**0.0154**	**0.0678**	**0.0824**	0.0795	0.0809
Filtering	0.1011	0.2110	0.1654	0.0181	**0.0079**	**0.0140**	**0.0015**	0.2278	0.1611
Intersection	0.1057	**0.2499**	**0.1919**	0.0818	0.2740	0.2022	**0.0159**	0.2947	0.2087
Robust-04	0.0870	0.4136	0.2989	0.0430	**0.0481**	**0.0456**	**0.0025**	0.3865	0.2733
Robust-05	0.1141	0.2368	0.1858	0.0570	**0.0265**	**0.0445**	**0.0087**	0.1843	0.1305

Table 3: Root Mean Loss for Relevance, Effort, and Combined.

Target Method		Knee Method		Budget Method	
$\sqrt{loss_r}$	$\sqrt{loss_h}$	$\sqrt{loss_r}$	$\sqrt{loss_h}$	$\sqrt{loss_r}$	$\sqrt{loss_h}$
0.0837	0.0504	0.0134	0.0021	0.0007	0.0011

Table 4: Root Mean Loss for Relevance and High Relevance.

In Table 3, we report, for each collection, the root mean loss ($\sqrt{loss}$) over all topics for relevance loss as defined in (4); effort loss as defined in (6); as well as their unweighted average, $loss_{re} = 0.5 \cdot loss_r + 0.5 \cdot loss_e$. The results show conclusively the superiority of the budget method in terms of $loss_r$. They show the general superiority of the knee method in terms of $loss_e$, while calling to our attention three collections where the target method is more efficient. On inspection, we see that two of the three collections have exclusively or nearly exclusively topics with high prevalence. We further see that that the the target method's narrow margin of superiority in terms of $loss_r$ is offset by a wide margin of inferiority in $loss_e$, as reflected in $loss_{re}$. For the intersection collection, no system achieved acceptable $loss_e$.

The bottom line is that the quality loss results support our qualitative observation that the knee method affords the best balance between consistently high recall and consistently low effort; the budget method provides consistently higher recall at the expense of disproportionate effort for topics with few relevant documents; the target method, while provably reliable, yields empirical results that are generally inferior to the knee and budget methods.

To illustrate the use of quality loss for graded relevance, we used a subset of 84 topics from Robust-04, for which relevance assessments were available for the categories "highly relevant" and "relevant." Table 4 shows $\sqrt{loss_r}$ and $\sqrt{loss_h}$ for these categories, respectively. The knee and target methods have lower $loss_h$, than $loss_r$, indicating they retrieve highly relevant documents more consistently than merely relevant documents. The budget method shows the opposite effect, but even so, is markedly superior to the target and knee methods. While we cannot draw any firm conclusions from this small experiment, the results do not support the proposition that TAR methods achieve high recall by "bulking up" on marginal documents at the expense of important ones (*cf.* [12]).

7. DISCUSSION

To our knowledge, the target method is the first provably reliable method for TAR. The commonly used frequentist acceptance test (*see* [1, 9]) offers a p-value or confidence level which is a measure of the reliability of the *test*, not the reliability of the TAR method, not the probability that a given result is acceptable, and not the probability that a TAR method will pass the acceptance test. In eDiscovery, it is common to calculate a frequentist recall estimate, with a 5% margin of error and 95% confidence, and deem the result acceptable if the estimate exceeds 75%. Calculating such an estimate requires a sample of about 385 random relevant documents, entailing 38.5 times as much surplus effort as the target method.

Our proof of reliability does not require that the target sample T be chosen at the outset, as long as it is independent of the retrieval method. The target method could be used as an acceptance test, such that the consequence of failing the test would be to continue to retrieve documents without knowledge of T, until all the documents in T are retrieved.

Over test collections like the ones used in this study, there can be little doubt ($p \approx 0.00$) that the knee and budget methods are reliable, that the budget method is more reliable than both the knee and target methods, and that the knee method is the most efficient. As with any empirical work, the test collections constitute convenience samples and ongoing research is necessary to characterize the scope of TAR tasks to which our results may be generalized.

The target method is reliable regardless of the underlying review method; however, if the underlying method uses a human in the loop to formulate queries or to influence the selection of documents in any way, that human must be isolated from any knowledge of T. The simplest approach to accomplish this goal might be to complete all such human intervention before drawing T, and to rely on fully automated document selection thereafter. An alternative would be to establish an "information barrier" between those who draw T and those who conduct the search.

This work establishes the reliability of the knee and budget methods as applied to BMI. It remains to be determined how well these approaches would work—possibly with different tuning parameters—for other CAL methods, including hybrid systems in which a human is afforded influence in the selection of documents for review. It is not obvious how to adapt the knee or budget method to SPL or SAL, for which an essential question is when to stop training.

The target method, by design, targets less than 100% recall. It could be modified to continue past the point at which the last document in T is retrieved, thereby expending additional effort to increase the probability of achieving 100% recall. One might, for example, extrapolate from the distribution of $rank(d \in T)$. The knee method, on the other hand, does target 100% recall, and only incidentally optimizes reliability. It appears that loss functions better characterize the tension among consistency, effectiveness, and efficiency, as compared to goal-post methods. Regardless of which measure is chosen for evaluation, systems should be tuned to optimize their suitability for their intended purpose, not the measure itself (*cf.* [22]).

8. CONCLUSIONS

Reservations about the effectiveness and reliability of TAR have impeded its adoption for eDiscovery and other high-recall retrieval tasks. A primary area of concern has centered on the issue of "when to stop," or knowing with reasonable certainty—and being able to show an adversary or the court—that a particular TAR effort has identified an acceptable amount of relevant information. Many approaches to validation in common use today are simply invalid, or require disproportionate effort compared to the information they yield, and are often misunderstood and misapplied [9, 16].

We offer a method to determine when to stop that is guaranteed to be reliable, for the price of reviewing a number of random documents that is an order of magnitude less than acceptance tests that estimate recall, but neither determine when to stop nor guarantee reliability. We provide two other methods that entail no effort beyond that required by the underlying TAR method and, while not providing a guarantee of reliability, consistently demonstrate better reliability, and better recall, when evaluated on eight test collections, comprising 555 topics and 4.5M documents. Of particular interest is the knee method which, in contrast to the other methods, is demonstrated to be reliable and efficient when the collection contains few relevant documents.

While our primary results are demonstrated using measures derived from traditional goal-post methods—binary relevance, a recall threshold, and a reliability floor—we describe how loss functions may be formulated to capture the tension among consistency, degrees of relevance, facets of relevance, and efficiency. We apply these formulae to show insights into our results that might not have been readily apparent from the goal-post measures.

9. REFERENCES

[1] M. Bagdouri, W. Webber, D. D. Lewis, and D. W. Oard. Towards minimizing the annotation cost of certified text classification. In *SIGIR 2013*.

[2] D. Blair and M. E. Maron. An evaluation of retrieval effectiveness for a full-text document-retrieval system. *Commun. ACM*, 28(3):289–299, 1985.

[3] D. C. Blair. Stairs redux: Thoughts on the stairs evaluation, ten years after. *J. Am. Soc. Inf. Sci.*, 47(1):4–22, Jan. 1996.

[4] G. Cormack and M. Mojdeh. Machine learning for information retrieval: TREC 2009 Web, Relevance Feedback and Legal Tracks. In *TREC 2009*.

[5] G. V. Cormack and M. R. Grossman. Evaluation of machine-learning protocols for technology-assisted review in electronic discovery. In *SIGIR 2014*.

[6] G. V. Cormack and M. R. Grossman. Multi-faceted recall of continuous active learning for technology-assisted review. In *SIGIR 2015*.

[7] G. V. Cormack and M. R. Grossman. Autonomy and reliability of continuous active learning for technology-assisted review. *arXiv:1504.06868*, 2015.

[8] G. V. Cormack, C. R. Palmer, and C. L. A. Clarke. Efficient construction of large test collections. In *SIGIR 1998*.

[9] M. R. Grossman and G. V. Cormack. Comments on "The implications of Rule 26(g) on the use of technology-assisted review". *Fed. Cts. L. Rev.*, 7:285–312, 2014.

[10] C. Lefebvre, E. Manheimer, and J. Glanville. Searching for studies. *Cochrane Handbook for Systematic Reviews of Interventions*, 2008.

[11] D. D. Lewis, Y. Yang, T. G. Rose, and F. Li. RCV1: A new benchmark collection for text categorization research. *J. Mach. Learn. Res.*, 5:361–397, 2004.

[12] D. Remus and F. S. Levy. Can robots be lawyers? Computers, lawyers, and the practice of law. http://dx.doi.org/10.2139/ssrn.2701092, 2015.

[13] A. Roegiest, G. V. Cormack, M. R. Grossman, and C. L. A. Clarke. Notebook Draft TREC 2015 Total Recall Track Overview. In *TREC 2015*.

[14] M. Sanderson and H. Joho. Forming test collections with no system pooling. In *SIGIR 2004*.

[15] V. Satopää, J. Albrecht, D. Irwin, and B. Raghavan. Finding a "kneedle" in a haystack: Detecting knee points in system behavior. In *ICDCSW 2011*.

[16] K. Schieneman and T. Gricks. The implications of Rule 26(g) on the use of technology-assisted review. *Fed. Cts. L. Rev.*, 7:239–274, 2013.

[17] I. Soboroff and S. Robertson. Building a filtering test collection for TREC 2002. In *SIGIR 2003*.

[18] G. Taguchi. *Introduction to Quality Engineering: Designing Quality Into Products and Processes*. 1986.

[19] E. M. Voorhees. Variations in relevance judgments and the measurement of retrieval effectiveness. *Information Processing & Management*, 36(5):697–716, 2000.

[20] E. M. Voorhees. The philosophy of information retrieval evaluation. In *Evaluation of cross-language information retrieval systems*, pages 143–170. Springer, 2002.

[21] E. M. Voorhees and D. K. Harman. The Text REtrieval Conference. In E. M. Voorhees and D. K. Harman, editors, *TREC: Experiment and Evaluation in Information Retrieval*, pages 3–19. MIT Press, 2005.

[22] E. Yilmaz and S. Robertson. On the choice of effectiveness measures for learning to rank. *Information Retrieval*, 13(3):271–290, 2010.

[23] J. Zobel, A. Moffat, and L. A. Park. Against recall: Is it persistence, cardinality, density, coverage, or totality? In *ACM SIGIR Forum*, volume 43, pages 3–8. ACM, 2009.

A Sequential Decision Formulation of the Interface Card Model for Interactive IR

Yinan Zhang
Department of Computer Science
University of Illinois at Urbana-Champaign
Urbana, IL 61801
yzhng103@illinois.edu

Chengxiang Zhai
Department of Computer Science
University of Illinois at Urbana-Champaign
Urbana, IL 61801
czhai@illinois.edu

ABSTRACT

The Interface Card model is a promising new theoretical framework for modeling and optimizing interactive retrieval interfaces, but how to systematically instantiate it to solve concrete interface optimization problems remains an open challenge. We propose a novel formulation of the Interface Card model based on sequential decision theory, leading to a general framework for formal modeling of user states and stopping actions. The proposed framework naturally connects optimization of interactive retrieval with Markov Decision Processes and Partially Observable Markov Decision Processes, and enables the use of reinforcement learning algorithms for optimizing interactive retrieval interfaces. Simulation and user study experiments demonstrate the effectiveness of the proposed model in automatically adjusting the interface layout in adaptation to inferred user stopping tendencies in addition to user interaction and screen size.

1. INTRODUCTION

Formal modeling of information retrieval process is one of the most important fundamental research problems in information retrieval. It not only enables formalization of the retrieval task as a well-defined computation problem, which is required for designing any effective retrieval algorithm, but also provides a foundation for quantitative evaluation of a retrieval system.

The Probability Ranking Principle (PRP) was an early attempt to formalize the retrieval task as a problem of ranking documents for a query. It motivated and laid out a theoretical foundation for studying and deriving many traditional retrieval models to optimize ranking in the past few decades [21, 19, 18, 9, 1, 24, 6], as well as more recent works on learning to rank [11]. PRP also provides a foundation and justification for designing evaluation measures such as Mean Average Precision (MAP) and Normalized Discounted Cumulative Gain (nDCG) [10] to measure the accuracy of a ranked list of retrieval results.

SIGIR '16, July 17-21, 2016, Pisa, Italy
 ISBN 978-1-4503-4069-4/16/07 ...$15.00.
DOI: http://dx.doi.org/10.1145/2911451.2911543 .

However, PRP relies on two unrealistic assumptions: (1) independent utility/relevance of documents, and (2) sequential browsing, making it hard to study issues such as diversity (which requires "dependent relevance") or study how to optimize IR interface design within the PRP framework. To address the limitation due to assumption (1), a more general PRP for Interactive IR (namely PRP-IIR) was proposed [8], which captures the the dependency of the utility of documents examined later by a user on that of the documents already seen by the user in a theoretical framework. Such a framework also provides a theoretical justification for novel evaluation measures proposed for novelty and diversity (e.g., the α-NDCG [5]), and rank-biased precision [16]. The recent Interface Card Model (ICM) [26] further generalizes PRP-IIR to address the limitation due to assumption (2), and frames the retrieval problem as to optimize a sequence of "interface cards" to be presented to a user in an interactive manner so as to minimize the user's effort while maximizing the gain. The framework is shown to not only cover both PRP and PRP-IIR as special cases, but also enable automatic design of an interactive navigation interface in adaption to the screen sizes and the uncertainty about a user's information need [26]. From evaluation perspective, ICM implies that an evaluation measure should be "aware" of the actions taken by users on a retrieval result and the effort of taking an action, thus providing a justification for measures such as the time-based gain measure [23] where user effort is measured based on the time spent by the user.

ICM provides a high-level theoretical framework for optimizing interactive retrieval, but it does not specify a systematic way to instantiate it for solving a concrete interface optimization problem, leaving how to further refine this general framework an open challenge. In this paper, we address this challenge and propose a novel formulation of the Interface Card Model based on sequential decision theory, which leads to a general instantiation of ICM that can explicitly model user states and stopping actions in search in a formal framework. It naturally connects the optimization of interactive retrieval with Markov Decision Process (MDP) and Partially Observable Markov Decision Process (POMDP) [20], thus enabling the use of reinforcement learning algorithms for optimizing interactive retrieval interfaces in general. We refer to the new model as Interface Card Model with User States (ICM-US).

While the proposed ICM-US model remains a high-level framework, it has several important advantages over ICM. Firstly, ICM-US explicitly models user states, which can potentially include many relevant variables about a user that we want to model (e.g., patience, attention tendency, and readability) in optimizing retrieval results. In this paper, we will particularly examine the modeling of stopping actions which is related to a user's patience in search, and derive a framework to optimize the interface design with consideration of users' stopping tendencies. Secondly, ICM-US opens up many opportunities to use sequential decision theories and reinforcement learning algorithms to optimize interactive retrieval. In this paper, we will show that it is possible to use the ICM-US framework to define and solve the interface optimization problems studied in [26] in more elegant and more general ways. Specifically, we work out the "plain card" case in the sequential decision theory context and take the user stopping tendencies into consideration, and mathematically prove that a more general ranking principle is the solution to the Bellman Equation. In the "navigational card" case, we consider user stopping tendencies and define a more general interface optimization problem. The problem is proved to be NP-Hard and we conduct experiments to tackle it in two ways: (a) we conduct simulated experiments to solve the Bellman Equation under reasonable simplification assumptions; (b) we approximately solve the optimization problem in more general settings and conduct user studies to examine the empirical benefit of ICM-US. The results demonstrate that ICM-US is effective for automatically adjusting the interface layout in adaptation to inferred user stopping tendencies in addition to user interaction and screen size.

2. RELATED WORK

The proposed ICM-US framework is related to several lines of recent work on POMDP and reinforcement learning (e.g.,[13, 12, 22]) and economic IR models (e.g., [2, 3]), especially because all these works tend to also model user interactions formally. The main difference between ICM-US and these work is that ICM-US is based on the Interface Card Model, which is a very general framework for modeling retrieval process (framed as choosing optimally a sequence of interface cards), thus ICM-US can potentially model and optimize very complicated interaction interfaces, whereas the other works cannot optimize the design of an interface due to the restriction to mostly a ranking-based formulation of the retrieval problem. However, the specific techniques and models proposed in these existing work can all potentially contribute to further refinement of ICM-US to make it even more operational. For example, the economic IR work would enable ICM-US to incorporate a user decision model for refining the user actions (e.g., modeling how the user actions depend on the user state).

Our user action model characterizes how users make navigational decisions and stopping decisions in an information seeking process, which is related to Information Foraging theories [17], where models of user actions driven by information scent were proposed to describe how users navigate on the web following hyperlinks. Recent works in user search behavior analysis proposed and evaluated novel models for users' navigation actions [25], stopping actions [14], and for characterizing users' patience levels [16] in a search session. Our ICM-US framework is more focused on the "orthogonal" question of how to optimize interactive search interfaces given a learned user action model; such line of research and the existing works in user action modeling and analysis serve to complement each other and collectively lead to more effective search systems for users.

3. INTERFACE CARD MODEL WITH USER STATES

In [26], the authors proposed the Interface Card model for optimizing interactive retrieval interfaces in a general setting as follows. Let t be the interaction lap under consideration, q^t be an interface card the system could issue to the user, $a^{t+1} \in \mathcal{A}(q^t)$ be an action the user takes in the following lap as a response to q^t, [1] and f_c^t be the constraint function for q^t. Let c^t be the context accumulated till the current user action that starts from $c^0 = i$, the prior information the system has about the user, and is incrementally updated by the rule $c^{t+1} = (c^t, q^t, a^{t+1})$. Let $p(a^{t+1}|c^t, q^t)$ be the user action model for characterizing how likely the user issues action a^{t+1} given context c^t and card q^t. Let u^t be the estimated user surplus, which equals the difference between the user's reward and their cost for issuing an action. Then the Interface Card optimization problem is defined as:

Definition 3.1 (Interface Card Optimization). In each lap t, the interface system should play a card q^t that maximizes the expected surplus u^t given the current context and under the current constraint, where the expectation is taken with respect to the user action model:

$$\begin{aligned} \underset{q^t}{\text{maximize}} \quad & E(u^t|c^t, q^t) \\ & = \sum_{a^{t+1} \in \mathcal{A}(q^t)} p(a^{t+1}|c^t, q^t)\, u(a^{t+1}|c^t, q^t) \quad (1) \\ \text{subject to} \quad & f_c^t(q^t) \leq 0 \end{aligned}$$

Instead of directly extending Equation (1) as in [26], we first introduce its intrinsic relation to sequential decision theories, and then redefine and expand the instantiations in [26] in a more systematic way and derive new interesting results. In contrast to the typical practices adopted by other recent works in applying sequential decision theories in information retrieval (e.g., [13]), we are *not* deriving our framework based on sequential decision theories; all our derivation is self-contained and solely relies on the Interface Card model and our own assumptions, and the formalisms in sequential decision theories we observe at the end are natural consequences of the derivation.

We first relate the interface optimizations in consecutive laps using the notion of context surplus:

Definition 3.2 (Context Surplus). The *context surplus* is the maximum expected surplus across all possible cards q^t subject to the constraint under the given context:

$$E(u^t|c^t) = \max_{q^t} E(u^t|c^t, q^t) \quad (2)$$

subject to $f_c^t(q^t) \leq 0$.

Assumption 3.1 (Accumulative Surplus). The action surplus $u(a^{t+1}|c^t, q^t)$ takes the form of an arithmetic sum:

$$u(a^{t+1}|c^t, q^t) = u_0(c^t, q^t, a^{t+1}) + E(u^{t+1}|c^{t+1}) \quad (3)$$

[1] As in [26], we assume the action set $\mathcal{A}(q^t)$ is countable; the case of uncountable action set could be handled via trivial changes to the model.

The two components are: (a) $u_O(c^t, q^t, a^{t+1})$ - the *immediate action surplus* of action a^{t+1} given card q^t and under context c^t, which is the difference between the *immediate action reward* $r_O(c^t, q^t, a^{t+1})$ and the *immediate action cost* $s_O(c^t, q^t, a^{t+1})$; (b) $E(u^{t+1}|c^{t+1})$ - the context surplus in the next lap.

Conceptually, we assume that the user obtains surplus in an accumulative fashion: it is usually reasonable in real world cases, which is also the reason why it became a standard practice in reward modeling in sequential decision theories. However, there might also be cases where the user surplus takes a non-additive form. For example, certain future reward could be *conditioned* on some particular card in advance, e.g. some instructive cards at the beginning to help the user better understand the interactive interface. In such cases, our assumption would become invalid and we would need to step back to the more general form of the original Interface Card model; we leave it to future work.

There will always be a terminal lap in an interactive retrieval process, e.g. when the user fulfilled their information need or they could not find anything interesting and give up the interaction. To make our discussion more concise and modular, for the moment we assure that our proposed formulation could naturally characterize the case of terminal laps, and we will come back to this in Section 4.

In contrast to the diminishing reward model adopted in a large portion of sequential decision theories, where the future reward is multiplied by a discount factor $\gamma < 1$, we do not penalize future reward in the current most general form of our framework. Nevertheless, we will show in Section 4 that the diminishing reward model could be derived as a specialization of our framework to capture the user's stopping actions in the interaction process, which gives the diminishing reward model a much deeper and more principled reason of existence.

With Equation (2) and (3), we rewrite Equation (1) as:

Definition 3.3 (Interface Card Bellman Equation)**.** The expected surplus in consecutive laps satisfies:

$$E(u^t|c^t) = \max_{q^t} \sum_{a^{t+1} \in \mathcal{A}(q^t)} \Big(p(a^{t+1}|c^t, q^t) \cdot \big(u_O(c^t, q^t, a^{t+1}) + E(u^{t+1}|c^{t+1})\big) \Big) \tag{4}$$

and the optimal card the system should pick in lap t is:

$$q^t_{opt} = \operatorname*{argmax}_{q^t} \sum_{a^{t+1} \in \mathcal{A}(q^t)} \Big(p(a^{t+1}|c^t, q^t) \cdot \big(u_O(c^t, q^t, a^{t+1}) + E(u^{t+1}|c^{t+1})\big) \Big) \tag{5}$$

with q^t in both equations subject to $f^t_c(q^t) \leq 0$.

It is often convenient to define:

$$u_O(c^t, q^t) = \sum_{a^{t+1} \in \mathcal{A}(q^t)} p(a^{t+1}|c^t, q^t)\, u_O(c^t, q^t, a^{t+1}) \tag{6}$$

and transform Equation (4) to an equivalent form:

$$E(u^t|c^t) = \max_{q^t} \Big(u_O(c^t, q^t) + \sum_{a^{t+1} \in \mathcal{A}(q^t)} p(a^{t+1}|c^t, q^t)\, E(u^{t+1}|c^{t+1}) \Big) \tag{7}$$

Definition 3.3 forms the basis for all subsequent derivations in this paper. Due to space limitations, we will only write out derivations for Equation (4) or its equivalent form Equation (7) in most places; the part for Equation (5) could be trivially filled out in each case.

Now we propose a fundamental assumption underlying all our following derivations regarding the modeling of the user:

Assumption 3.2 (User State)**.** In each lap t, the user lies in a unique, unambiguous *user state* z^t that contains all the necessary information to determine the user action model and the immediate action surplus when given any interface card the system issues.

The user state is a general concept encapsulating many real world cases. For example, the user's information need could be one straightforward type of user state, and there could also be more subtle user states such as binary states indicating whether the user is in the exploration or exploitation stage of their information seeking process; it is at the will of the practitioners of our framework to decide on the type of user states they would like to model. We will be define the user state z^t in various forms in the following sections to fulfill diversified modeling needs.

The user state z^t is closely related to the context c^t in that they both characterize about the user for the system, but they are intrinsically different. There are two key insights we could obtain if we look back at Equation (4): (a) the user action model and the immediate action surplus are essentially all we need to fully carry out the computations in our framework; (b) it was the context that determined the user action model and the immediate action surplus when given the interface card, but its role is now fulfilled by the user state. More fundamentally, the context is always *explicit* to the system and contains *all* the information the system has at hand to speculate about the user, whereas the user state is intrinsic to the user and may or may *not* be known to the system, yet it is the *essential* information the system ever needs to know about the user. In other words, the user action model and the immediate action surplus are *independent* of the context given the user state - the user state serves as the sole linkage between the context and all the computational parts of our framework.

We first assume the user state is hidden from the interface system, and the interface system could only guess about the user state relying on the context.

Assumption 3.3 (Initial User State Distribution)**.** There exists an initial probability distribution over the user states, denoted by d^0, specifying how likely the user is in each user state at lap $t = 0$ that the system could estimate from the prior information i about the user, i.e. the initial context c^0. We write $p(z^0|d^0) = p(z^0|i) = p(z^0|c^0)$.

In cases where there is no prior information about the user, the system could naturally assume a uniform distribution over all possible user states.

When the interaction starts, we assume that the user states may probabilistically transition from lap to lap when the user observes an interface card:

Assumption 3.4 (User State Transition Function)**.** In each lap t, There exists a transition function $p^t_{\mathcal{T}}(z^{t+1}|z^t, q^t)$ that specifies the probability of the user transitioning from z^t to z^{t+1} when the user observes q^t.

Now, starting from $p(z^0|d^0) = p(z^0|c^0)$, we could estimate the user state distribution d^t inductively on t based on Bayes' rule:

$$\begin{aligned} p(z^{t+1}|d^{t+1}) &= p(z^{t+1}|c^{t+1}) = p(z^{t+1}|c^t, q^t, a^{t+1}) \\ &= p(z^{t+1}|d^t, q^t, a^{t+1}) = \alpha\, p(a^{t+1}|z^{t+1}, q^t)\, p(z^{t+1}|d^t, q^t) \\ &= \alpha\, p(a^{t+1}|z^{t+1}, q^t) \sum_{z^t} p(z^t|d^t)\, p_T^t(z^{t+1}|z^t, q^t) \end{aligned} \tag{8}$$

where $\alpha^{-1} = p(a^{t+1}|d^t, q^t)$ is computed by:

$$\begin{aligned} p(a^{t+1}|d^t, q^t) &= \sum_{z^{t+1}} p(a^{t+1}|z^{t+1}, q^t)\, p(z^{t+1}|d^t, q^t) \\ &= \sum_{z^{t+1}} p(a^{t+1}|z^{t+1}, q^t) \sum_{z^t} p(z^t|d^t)\, p_T^t(z^{t+1}|z^t, q^t) \end{aligned} \tag{9}$$

The context c^t now provides no useful information additional to our estimated user state distribution d^t for computational purposes, so it could essentially be replaced by d^t in all places. If we define $u_O(d^t, q^t, a^{t+1})$ as:

$$\begin{aligned} u_O(d^t, q^t, a^{t+1}) &= E(u_O|d^t, q^t, a^{t+1}) \\ &= \sum_{z^t} p(z^t|d^t)\, u_O(z^t, q^t, a^{t+1}) \end{aligned} \tag{10}$$

then Equation (4) becomes:

Definition 3.4 (Interface Card Bellman Equation (Partially Observable User States)).

$$\begin{aligned} E(u^t|d^t) = \max_{q^t} \sum_{a^{t+1} \in \mathcal{A}(q^t)} \Big(& p(a^{t+1}|d^t, q^t) \cdot \\ & \big(u_O(d^t, q^t, a^{t+1}) + E(u^{t+1}|d^{t+1})\big) \Big) \end{aligned} \tag{11}$$

subject to $f_c^t(q^t) \le 0$.

Equation (11) takes the exact same form as the standard Bellman Equation for Partially Observable Markov Decision Process (POMDP), where the user state z^t, the user state distribution d^t, the interface card q^t and the user action a^{t+1} respectively play the roles of state, belief state, action and observation (or often called evidence), and $u_O(d^t, q^t, a^{t+1})$ and $E(u^t|d^t)$ respectively serve as the the reward function[2] and the value function for belief states [20]; Equation (8) is the standard *forward* equation used for updating the belief state based on the action and the observation. In the language of POMDP, the state the interface system is interested in is the user state, and the actions the system could take are the interface cards it could issue to the user. However, since the user state is not fully observable, the system could only decide on the optimal action to perform according to the estimated distribution of user states, i.e. the belief state, and the estimation is computed based on the observations the system could collect about the user state, which are not surprisingly the user actions. We will see a concrete example of realizing Equation (11) to solve an interface optimization problem in Section 6.

Though the user states would usually be invisible to the system, we could often assume that the system is actually aware of the user states for the sake of modeling convenience, either by explicitly asking or confirming about the user states, or by interpreting that the user actions (e.g. queries or clicks) have exact mappings to user states. In such cases, the belief state d^t is collapsed into an observable user state z^t. With a series of simplifications (omitted here due to space limitations), Equation (11) becomes:

Definition 3.5 (Interface Card Bellman Equation (Fully Observable User States)).

$$\begin{aligned} E(u^t|z^t) = \max_{q^t} \sum_{z^{t+1}} \Big(& p(z^{t+1}|z^t, q^t) \cdot \\ & \big(u_O(z^t, q^t, z^{t+1}) + E(u^{t+1}|z^{t+1})\big) \Big) \end{aligned} \tag{12}$$

subject to $f_c^t(q^t) \le 0$.

Equation (12) takes the exact same form as the standard Bellman Equation for Markov Decision Process (MDP), which is not a surprise since MDP could be derived as a special case of POMDP if observations uniquely determine states. We will see an example of realizing Equation (12) to solve a concrete interface optimization problem in Section 5.

4. STOPPING ACTION MODELING

Definition 3.3 and its instantiations in the forms of Equation (11) and (12) have opened up enormous opportunities for research studies to apply the Interface Card model to a very wide range of real world problems via tools from sequential decision and reinforcement learning theories. In this work, as an initial step, we will utilize our new framework to study a basic yet nontrivial aspect of interactive information retrieval - stopping actions. We claimed in Section 3 that our framework could naturally characterize such cases, and we now establish the formalism, starting by making the following assumption:

Assumption 4.1 (User Stops Interaction). The interactive process is always ended by the user - the system would always respond to user actions with optimized cards whereas the user may or may not choose to continue the interaction.

Our assumption applies to most real world scenarios where the user may choose to stop the interaction either because of satisfaction of their information need or frustration due to lack of useful information. There might occasionally be cases where the system appears to be the one terminating the interaction, e.g. if the system determines that nothing in its database is interesting to the user and chooses to issue a "terminal card" that attempts to stop the interaction with some possible explanations. In such cases, the user is still free to choose between leaving the system and starting another round of interaction, and indeed many would choose the latter, so we could also model the termination as the user's choice when facing the system's "terminal card".

Definition 4.1 (Stopping Action). In each lap t, there is a *stopping action* $a_B^{t+1} \in \mathcal{A}(q^t)$ for any interface card q^t, and its estimated probability under the current context c^t, $p(a_B^{t+1}|c^t, q^t)$, is called the *stopping rate*. The expected future surplus of the the new context following the stopping action $E(u^{t+1}|c^{t+1}) = 0$, where $c^{t+1} = (c^t, q^t, a_B^{t+1})$.

[2]The reward function is defined on state-action-observation triples instead of on state-action pairs or just states as done in many studies which are special cases of our definition.

In the language of sequential decision theories, observing a user stopping action is analogous to entering a terminal state (or belief state for POMDP) for the system.

The stopping rate is typically dependent on the interface card the user faces: e.g., it would be smaller if the user is interested in certain content on the card, and larger if the content on the card does not look appealing to the user for the past couple of laps. However, for the sake of modeling and inference convenience, we may *sometimes* assume that the stopping rate is constant:

Assumption 4.2 (Constant Stopping Rate). The stopping rate is a constant determined by the prior information $c^0 = i$ of the user and is independent of the past interactions and the interface card; we denote it by: $\beta^0 = p(a_B^{t+1}|c^0) = p(a_B^{t+1}|c^t, q^t)$, $\forall c^t, q^t$, and we restrict that $0 < \beta^0 < 1$.

Assumption 4.2 is a "double-sided sword": in the language of bias-variance trade-off, it leads to a potentially large bias in exchange for less variance. In this work, we will be cautious and make use of it only to our own advantage: we will keep it for the rest of this section to derive one interesting theoretical result and continue to rely on it in Section 5 to simplify the computation, but we will discard it and resume the dependency of the stopping rate on the full context and the interface card in Section 6 for more realistic scenarios.

Now, with Assumption 4.2 in effect, if we define the *user continuation action model* as:

$$p_K^t(a^{t+1}|c^t, q^t) = \frac{p(a^{t+1}|c^t, q^t)}{1 - p(a_B^{t+1}|c^t, q^t)} = \frac{p(a^{t+1}|c^t, q^t)}{1 - \beta^0} \quad (13)$$

for all $a^{t+1} \neq a_B^{t+1}$, then Equation (7) becomes:

Definition 4.2 (Interface Card Bellman Equation (Constant Stopping Rate)).

$$E(u^t|c^t) = \max_{q^t} \Big(u_0(c^t, q^t) + (1 - \beta^0) \sum_{a^{t+1} \neq a_B^{t+1}} p_K^t(a^{t+1}|c^t, q^t)\, E(u^{t+1}|c^{t+1}) \Big) \quad (14)$$

subject to $f_c^t(q^t) \leq 0$.

We could further extend Equation (14) to derive its instantiated forms for the MDP and POMDP cases based on Equation (12) and (11); we omit such derivations here due to space limitations, but we will be developing concrete models as examples of these two forms in Section 5 and 6, respectively.

More interestingly, the term $1-\beta^0$ in Equation (14) clearly resembles the discount factor λ in a form of the standard Bellman Equation for MDP and POMDP frequently seen in sequential decision theories (as well as many recent works in applying sequential decision theories in information retrieval, e.g., [13]) for modeling diminishing reward, and the role of the (belief) state transition probabilities is here fulfilled by the user continuation action model. The resemblance is not a coincidence - it reveals a fundamental insight into the diminishing reward model in sequential decision theories. Traditionally, in addition to establishing an upper bound for the value function for mathematical conveniences, a major purpose for setting the discount factor is to express to the model our intuitive preference for quicker reward; in our case, we want to reduce the cost of excessive interaction laps for the user. In economic theories, every cost is intrinsically an *opportunity cost*, which is formally defined to be the value of the best alternative [7]. In the setting of interactive retrieval, when the opportunity cost is higher than the expected surplus of carrying on the interaction longer, the user is very likely to switch to their best alternative way of spending their time, e.g. working on something else or simply relaxing, and from the system's perspective, this is exactly the *stopping action* of the user. Therefore, our model for user stopping actions turns out to draw fundamental connections from economic theories to sequential decision theories by providing deeper explanations to the diminishing reward model. We could look even further into discrete choice models [15] in modern economic studies to derive more rigorous formalisms for user decision modeling, and we leave it to future works.

5. PLAIN CARD

As the first concrete extension of our proposed framework, we revisit the "plain card" setting in [26]. We augment it with stopping actions, and formally re-define the optimization problem based on our new sequential decision formulation for Markov Decision Process (MDP) defined in Equation (12). We will mathematically prove that a more generalized ranking principle with user stopping tendencies taken into consideration is the solution to the Bellman Equation.

In the "plain card" setting in [26], the main assumption is that each interface card q^t is an atomic choice e^t placed on a ranked list and that the user examines and either accepts or rejects the choices in a sequential manner. Now, we additionally allow that the user may also stop after examining each choice. We continue to use $p(e^t)$, $r(e^t)$, $s(e^t)$ to respectively denote the probability of the user's interest in accepting e^t, the immediate reward of accepting e^t and the immediate cost of examining e^t in lap t, and these quantities are assumed to be independent of the past user actions as long as they have all been reject actions. An accept action is regarded as a "satisfying" stopping action - it terminates the current interaction session and starts a new one with an updated set of parameters. We now formally define this framework in the MDP language, starting with defining the user state and the user action model:

Definition 5.1 (Plain User State). The *plain user state* z^t at lap t is defined to be the set of choices not yet examined by the user till the previous lap: $z^t = \{e : q^{t'} \neq e, \forall t' < t\}$.

Definition 5.2 (Plain User Action Model). The *plain user action model* for user state z^t and choice e^t is a distribution over the accept action a_0^{t+1}, the reject action a_1^{t+1} and the stopping action a_B^{t+1} defined under the constant stopping rate assumption as:

$$\begin{cases} p(a_0^{t+1}|z^t, e^t) = \mathbb{1}_{z^t}(e^t)\, p(e^t) \\ p(a_1^{t+1}|z^t, e^t) = 1 - \beta^0 - \mathbb{1}_{z^t}(e^t)\, p(e^t) \\ p(a_B^{t+1}|z^t, e^t) = \beta^0 \end{cases} \quad (15)$$

where $\mathbb{1}_{z^t}(e^t)$ is the indicator function for testing whether $e^t \in z^t$, and we assume $p(e^t) \leq 1 - \beta^0$, $\forall e^t$.

Essentially, the plain user action model claims that the user will always reject a choice they have rejected before (as long as no accept action has taken place in the middle), which is very reasonable in real world situations.

For technical conveniences, we define the *choice surplus* of a choice e: $u(e) = p(e)\,r(e) - s(e)$, and we assume: (a) the set of all possible choices is finite, so the cardinality of z^t, $||z^t||$, is also finite; (b) if the choice shown on the interface is the only element left in z^t, then the user's reject action is regarded as a "frustrating" stopping action; (c) $s(e) > 0$, $\forall e$, and (d) $u(e) \geq 0$, $\forall e$. Now, we could mathematically solve Equation (12) in closed form:

Theorem 5.1 (Optimal Plain Card). Let $z^t \neq \varnothing$. Define:

$$\eta(e) = \frac{u(e)}{p(e) + \beta^0} = \frac{p(e)\,r(e) - s(e)}{p(e) + \beta^0}, \; e \in z^t \quad (16)$$

Suppose $z^t = \{e_j\}_{j=1}^n = \{e_1, e_2, \ldots, e_n\}$ and e_j's satisfy:

$$\eta(e_j) \geq \eta(e_k), \; \forall 1 \leq j < k \leq n \quad (17)$$

Then e_1 is an optimal card for z^t and:

$$E(u^t|z^t) = \sum_{j=1}^{n} \left(\prod_{k=1}^{j-1} (1 - \beta^0 - p(e_k)) \right) u(e_j) \quad (18)$$

Further, the complete optimization solution is to sequentially show $e \in z^t$ to the user in descending order of $\eta(e)$.

Proof. We prove by induction on $||z^t||$:

1. $||z^t|| = 1$. Let $z^t = \{e_1\}$, then:

$$E(u^t|z^t, e^t) = \begin{cases} u(e^t), & \text{if } e^t = e_1 \\ (1 - \beta^0)E(u^t|z^t) - s(e^t), & \text{otherwise} \end{cases} \quad (19)$$

Since $E(u^t|z^t) \geq E(u^t|z^t, e_1) = u(e_1) \geq 0$, we have $E(u^t|z^t, e^t) < (1 - \beta^0)E(u^t|z^t) \leq E(u^t|z^t)$, $\forall e^t \neq e_1$, i.e. showing any choice other than e_1 is non-optimal. So, e_1 is an optimal card for z^t and $E(u^t|z^t) = u(e_1)$.

2. Suppose $n > 1$ and the theorem holds for all z s.t. $||z|| = n - 1$. Suppose $z^t = \{e_j\}_{j=1}^n$ and e_j's satisfies Equation (17). If $e^t \in z^t$, let $e^t = e_h, 1 \leq h \leq n$, then:

$$E(u^t|z^t, e_h) = u(e_h) + (1 - \beta^0 - p(e_h))E(u^{t+1}|z^{t+1}) \quad (20)$$

where $z^{t+1} = z^t \setminus \{e_h\}$. By induction hypothesis on z^{t+1}, we have $E(u^{t+1}|z^{t+1}) \geq 0$ from Equation (18). Thus, $E(u^t|z^t, e_h) \geq 0$, and $E(u^t|z^t) \geq 0$. Therefore, $E(u^t|z^t, e^t) = (1 - \beta^0)E(u^t|z^t) - s(e^t) < E(u^t|z^t)$, $\forall e^t \notin z^t$, i.e. showing any choice not in z^t is again non-optimal.

$E(u^{t+1}|z^{t+1})$ in Equation (20) is by induction hypothesis maximized from ranking $e \in z^{t+1}$ in decreasing order of $\eta(e)$. Thus, if $e^t = e_h \neq e_1$, then $e^{t+1} = e_1$. Let $z^{t+2} = z^t \setminus \{e_h, e_1\}$, $z_1^{t+1} = z^t \setminus \{e_1\}$, then:

$$\begin{aligned} E(u^t|z^t, e_h) &= u(e_h) + (1 - \beta^0 - p(e_h)) \cdot \\ &\quad (u(e_1) + (1 - \beta^0 - p(e_1))E(u^{t+2}|z^{t+2})) \\ &\leq u(e_1) + (1 - \beta^0 - p(e_1)) \cdot \\ &\quad (u(e_h) + (1 - \beta^0 - p(e_h))E(u^{t+2}|z^{t+2})) \\ &\leq u(e_1) + (1 - \beta^0 - p(e_1))E(u^{t+1}|z_1^{t+1}) \\ &= E(u^t|z^t, e_1) \end{aligned} \quad (21)$$

where the first inequality comes from $\eta(e_1) \geq \eta(e_h)$ and the second inequality comes from $E(u^{t+1}|z_1^{t+1}) \geq E(u^{t+1}|z_1^{t+1}, e_h)$. Therefore, $e^t = e_1$ is optimal and $E(u^t|z^t) = E(u^t|z^t, e_1)$, which expands to the right hand side of Equation (18). □

The definition for $\eta(e)$ in Equation (16) is identical to that of $\rho(e)$ in [26] except an additional multiplier involving β^0:

$$\eta(e) = \frac{p(e)}{p(e) + \beta^0}\left(r(e) - \frac{s(e)}{p(e)}\right) = \left(1 - \frac{\beta^0}{p(e) + \beta^0}\right)\rho(e) \quad (22)$$

If $\beta^0 \to 0$, i.e. when the user never abandons the search, then the two forms become equal. In the more general case where $\beta^0 > 0$, our new form of $\eta(e)$ may lead to a *different* ranking result where some choices with larger $p(e)$ values may be promoted because of the additional multiplier. Intuitively, when the user has a high tendency to stop, they would examine less choices on average, so by promoting choices with larger $p(e)$ values to higher places, the system could hope for a better chance of an accept action, and thus at least some reward, before the user leaves. Therefore, given a proper β^0 value (e.g. learned from user interaction logs), our new ranking principle defined by $\eta(e)$ could enable ranking with user stopping tendencies taken into consideration and form a basis for novel ranking algorithms on top of a richer user model.

6. NAVIGATIONAL CARD

In this section, we revisit the "navigational card" setting in [26] and formally re-define and solve the optimization problem based on our sequential decision formulation for Partially Observable Markov Decision Process (POMDP) defined in Equation (11). We will again incorporate stopping actions, but we will discard the constant stopping rate assumption and resume the more generalized and realistic setting: the stopping rate depends on the card and the full context. We will demonstrate that our new formalism leads to *automatic* interface adjustment based on users' stopping tendencies in addition to the context and the screen size.

The "navigational card" setting in [26] assumed the interface is backed by a set of information items denoted again by e (e.g. websites), each associated with some related tags (e.g. topics of websites), and the items and tags are respectively represented on the interface by item and tag blocks denoted by b. A card q^t could contain any combination of item blocks and/or tag blocks, as long as the total area they occupy does not exceed the screen area: $f_c^t(q^t) = \sum_{b \in q^t} w(b) - 1 \leq 0$, where $w(b)$ represents the space block b occupies relative to the entire screen size; the system may freely determine the layout of the interface by increasing or decreasing the number of item / tag blocks to display. Facing such a card q^t, the user may either select a displayed block or issue the "next card" action a_N^{t+1} if nothing on the card interests them, the probabilities of which follow an item action model that depends on the item the user is interested in. The interface system estimates the user action model as an expectation of the item action model taken with respect to the estimated probability distribution of the user's interest in each item based on the latest context.

In this work, we incorporate the stopping action a_B^{t+1} in all action set $\mathcal{A}(q^t)$. If the user finds an interesting item block and selects it, we consider it as a "satisfying" stopping action which triggers the interface system to jump to the item's corresponding page. We define the user interest as a hidden user state and assume it doesn't change across laps:

Definition 6.1 (User Interest State). A *user interest state* z^t denotes the user's interested item e^t in lap t: $z^t = e^t$.

Assumption 6.1 (Persistent User Interest). The user interest state does not change across laps: $p(e^{t+1}|e^t, q^t) = 1$ if $e^{t+1} = e^t$, 0 otherwise. From now on, we use $z^0 = e^0$ to denote the user interest state.

Essentially, Definition 6.1 implicitly assumes that the user's interest is focused on only one item within each lap, and Assumption 6.1 extends it to the whole interaction process. Both these two parts are sometimes inaccurate in reflecting real world scenarios, but they serve to exponentially reduce the complexity of our optimization problem.

With our simplification assumptions, Equation (8) and (9) respectively reduce to:

$$p(e^0|d^{t+1}) = \alpha\, p(a^{t+1}|e^0, q^t)\, p(e^0|d^t) \qquad (23)$$

$$\alpha^{-1} = p(a^{t+1}|d^t, q^t) = \sum_{e^0} p(a^{t+1}|e^0, q^t)\, p(e^0|d^t) \qquad (24)$$

In order to make the computations more tractable, we follow [26] and assume a constant immediate action cost s^0, a finite item set $E = \{e_1, e_2, \ldots, e_n\}$, and assume that we don't have any useful prior information so we start with a flat belief state d^0: $p(e_j|d^0) = 1/n$, $1 \le j \le n$. We further make the following two common assumptions before separating into the two experiment sections:

Assumption 6.2 (Uniform Item Reward). The reward to the user for selecting any item block in any lap is the same and is denoted by r^0.

Instead of modeling the actual expected reward of selecting an item block, r^0 could be regarded as measuring an eventual success in the interactive navigation, i.e. as the value of locating *any* interesting item to the user versus not finding anything at all.

Assumption 6.3 (Simple User Interest Action Model). Let $v(e, b)$ be a measure of the intrinsic relation[3] between item e and block b. Let $\varepsilon \ge 0$, $0 < \delta < 1$. Given a user interest state e^0 and an interface card q^t, the user issues an action based on the following *simple user interest action model*:

1. If the item block for e^0, b^0_e, is on q^t (i.e. $b^0_e \in q^t$), the user always selects it: $p(b^0_e|e^0, q^t) = 1$, $p(b|e^0, q^t) = 0$, $\forall\, b \in q^t, b \ne b^0_e$, and $p(a^{t+1}_N|e^0, q^t) = p(a^{t+1}_B|e^0, q^t) = 0$.
2. Otherwise, if q^t contains at least one tag block related to e^0 (i.e. $\exists\, b \in q^t$ s.t. $v(e^0, b) > 0$), the user will either select one of these tag block(s), select "next card" or stop: $p(b|e^0, q^t) = \alpha\, v(e^0, b)$, $\forall\, b \in q^t$, $p(a^{t+1}_N|e^0, q^t) = \alpha\, \varepsilon\, (1 - \delta)$, and $p(a^{t+1}_B|e^0, q^t) = \alpha\, \varepsilon\, \delta$, where $\alpha^{-1} = \sum_{b \in q^t} v(e^0, b) + \varepsilon$.
3. Otherwise, the user either selects "next card" or stops: $p(a^{t+1}_N|e^0, q^t) = 1 - \delta$, $p(a^{t+1}_B|e^0, q^t) = \delta$, and $p(b|e, q^t) = 0, \forall\, b \in q^t$.

The *uniform user interest action model* denotes the simple user interest action model where each $v(e, b)$ is either 1 or 0.

Conceptually, ε captures the chance the user misses to identify a related tag, and δ captures the user's stopping tendency given they have not identified any interesting block - either they missed one or there wasn't any indeed. Despite the fact that δ is treated as a constant, we are *not* assuming a constant stopping rate; the stopping rate is depending both on the card q^t and on the belief state d^t. With sufficient user interaction log data, we may apply reinforcement learning algorithms to learn a more refined user action model in the real world. In this study, we assume the simple user interest action model to reduce the learning complication and focus more on the modeling part.

[3]Please refer to [26] for a detailed explanation.

To apply our model in real problems, the only missing component now is the actual planning in the POMDP framework, and it is well known that planning in POMDP is NP-hard [20]. We reduce the planning problem to manageable forms via imposing additional assumptions on the cards in Section 6.1 and via employing planning heuristics in Section 6.2, and we leave explorations of general planning solutions to future work.

6.1 Simulation Experiments

In this section, we directly use the standard value iteration algorithm for POMDP in sequential decision theories [20] to explicitly solve our interface optimization problem defined in Equation (11). We assume the user follows the uniform user interest action model, and we set $\varepsilon = 0$: the user never misses a related tag. Similar to [26], we also assume a complete tag set: $\forall$ item subset $E' \subseteq E$, $\exists$ block b s.t. $v(e, b) = \mathbb{1}_{E'}(e)$, i.e. 1 if $e \in E'$, 0 otherwise. In addition, we make the following assumption on the card the interface system could issue in order to reduce to a *linear* belief state space:

Assumption 6.1.1 (Exclusive Blocks). Any item e is related to at most one block on any card q^t: $\forall e$, $\exists$ at most one $b \in q^t$ s.t. $v(e, b) = 1$.

Intuitively, this is a reasonable strategy for the system especially given that the system has access to a complete tag set: showing multiple blocks related to some item would not only confuse the user, but the system in turn would also be less precise in narrowing down into the item the user is truly interested in, ending up unnecessarily increasing the number of interaction laps.

More interestingly, this assumption guarantees that the belief state d^t is always a uniform distribution over a subset of the items, which could be trivially reasoned via induction (omitted here due to space limitations). Furthermore, due to the assumptions of uniform item reward and complete tag set, all belief states d^t over the same number of items would *appear* identical to the system in terms of planning: any optimal policy for a belief state d^t over e.g. items $\{e_1, e_2, e_3\}$ is completely reflective to one for a belief state d^t over items $\{e_4, e_5, e_6\}$ or any other item subset of size 3. Therefore, the belief state space has now been reduced from a high-dimensional continuous space all the way to a one-dimensional discrete space of size n. From now on, if d^t is over a set of n items, we say the *size* of d^t, $||d^t||$, is n.

We conducted simulation experiments to employ the standard value iteration algorithm to solve the Bellman Equation via dynamic programming. The experiments were performed for two screen sizes: a medium size (M) holding at most two item blocks or four tag blocks, and a small size (S) holding at most one item block or two tag blocks. We tested two values for δ: 0.02 for simulating a relatively patient (P) user, and 0.2 for a relatively impatient (I) user. In total, we had four settings abbreviated as "MP", "MI", "SP", and "SI". We found in our experiment runs that varying s^0 and r^0 within reasonable ranges did not affect the experiment

Figure 1: Value function of belief states

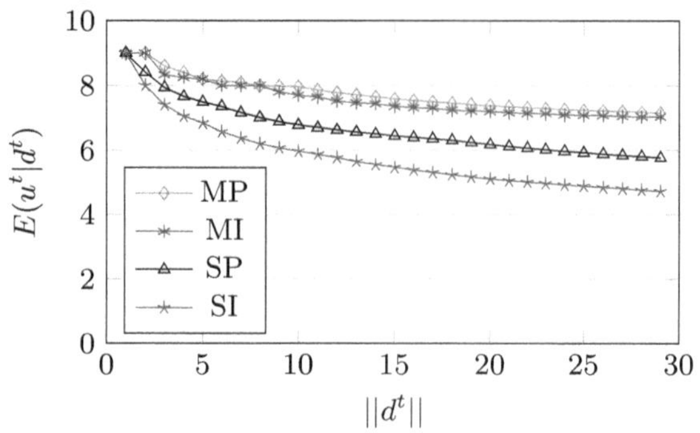

Figure 2: Optimal policy for belief states

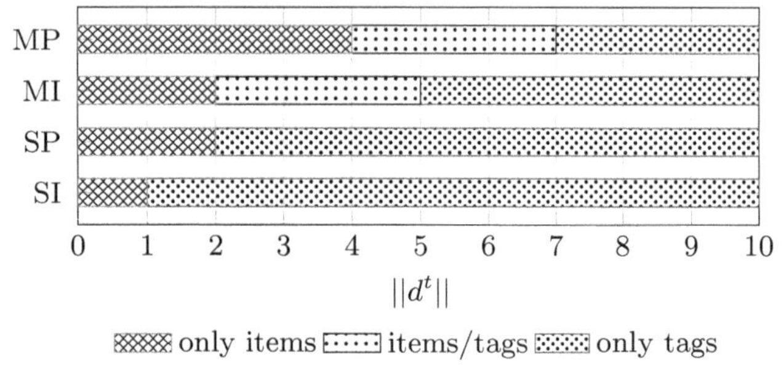

outcome in any fundamental way, and here we report the results we obtained when we set $s^0 = 1$ and $r^0 = 10$.

Figure 1 shows the value function of belief states as a function of their size. For all four settings, the value function decreases as the uncertainty of the belief state, i.e. their size, increases, and the decreasing rates are all diminishing, implying that the interface system could reduce the belief state size in an exponential manner through interacting with the user. It is also clear that the value function is higher for medium screens than for small screens, and higher for patient users than for impatient users: a larger screen naturally helps the user navigate to their interested items in less laps, and a more patient user is more likely to stick to the interaction until they obtain the reward. Further, the difference between the value function for patient and impatient users is much smaller on the medium screen compared to that on the small screen, suggesting that a larger screen is helpful in attracting the user to stick to the interaction by showing a wide variety of blocks to cater for the user's interest.

Figure 2 shows the optimal policy our model determined for each belief state size in terms of the interface layout. The interface is decided to be full of item blocks when the uncertainty of the belief state is low, and automatically changes to a combination of item and tag blocks and further to solely tag blocks as the uncertainty increases, which is a consequence of the tag blocks' advantage in more quickly narrowing down the belief state size using less screen space as compared to the item blocks. It is not possible to display both item and tag blocks in the small screen, so the layout directly "jumps" from all item blocks to all tag blocks, and the "jump" also takes place when the belief state size is relatively small as compared to the case on medium screen, reflecting the more urgent need for more space-efficient tag blocks on smaller screens. More interestingly, the layout is also automatically adaptive to user stopping tendencies: when the user is less patient, our model intelligently adjusts the layout to show more tag blocks on both small and medium screens - with the hope of a better chance to hold the user onto the interaction when they see a tag related to their interest. Therefore, our proposed novel formulation of the Interface Card model in the language of sequential decision theories successfully led to automatic interface layout optimization results which could not only adapt to user interest and screen size, but also better cater for both patient and impatient users.

6.2 User Study Experiments

In this section, we apply our theoretical framework to solve interface optimization problems in real world settings. The assumptions we made in Section 6.1 would hardly exist in the real world (e.g. the complete tag set assumption), so we are again facing a general NP-Hard POMDP planning problem. We continue to assume that the user follows the uniform user interest action model, but in contrast to Section 6.1, we now allow $\varepsilon > 0$, which permits the possibility of the user missing to identify a related tag as is often the case in the real world.

Instead of using other sophisticated planning algorithms, we employ a straightforward and widely adopted heuristic in sequential decision theories, the *dual-mode control* heuristic [4], which picks actions (i.e. interface cards in our case) that lead to a minimal expected entropy value of the belief state. We slightly modify the heuristic to accommodate user stopping actions:

Definition 6.2 (Entropy Heuristic (with stopping actions)).

$$q_{opt}^t = \underset{q^t}{\text{argmin}} \sum_{a^{t+1} \in \mathcal{A}(q^t)} \Big(p(a^{t+1}|d^t, q^t) \cdot \big(H(d^{t+1}) + \mathbb{1}_B(a^{t+1})\, r^0\big) \Big) \tag{25}$$

subject to $f_c^t(q^t) \leq 0$. ($H(d^{t+1})$ denotes the entropy of d^{t+1} and $\mathbb{1}_B(a^{t+1})$ is shorthand for the indicator function of testing whether $a^{t+1} = a_B^{t+1}$.)

The additional term $\mathbb{1}_B(a^{t+1})\, r^0$ we put into the dual-mode control heuristic measures the eventual reward of finding an interesting item if the user abandons the search (which we assumed to be uniform for all items and denoted by r^0).

In order to assess the effectiveness of our proposed model in automatically optimizing the interface layout of real interactive retrieval systems, we built prototype interface systems similar to those used in [26]: we fetched popular news articles (as items) from the New York Times *Most Popular API*[4] together with their associated keywords (as tags), and we used Amazon Mechanical Turk (AMT)[5] to conduct user studies. We employed a straightforward randomized algorithm similar to the one used in [26] to select the optimal interface card in each lap, but based on our new objective function defined in Equation (25). On the user side, we randomly partitioned the AMT workers into two groups, one being encouraged to stick to the interaction and thus playing the role of patient users, and the other being encouraged to freely give up the interaction and thus playing the role of impatient users; we refer to these two groups respectively as

[4]http://developer.nytimes.com/
[5]http://www.mturk.com

patient (P) and impatient (I) users. On the interface side, we varied the screen size and developed two sets of interfaces, one for a medium sized screen (M) being able to hold at most two item blocks or eight tag blocks, and the other for a very small screen (S) being able to hold at most one item block or four tag blocks. We again have four settings in total: "MP", "MI", "SP", and "SI".

We built two types of interfaces for each of the four settings for comparison. The first type is the baseline interface built based on the Interface Card Model (ICM) [26] without user stopping tendencies taken into consideration - it is essentially always assuming a "perfectly patient" user. The second type is based on our new Interface Card Model with User States (ICM-US) with user stopping tendencies being considered, and it employs a straightforward learning method to infer users' stopping tendencies. More specifically, in the uniform user interest action model, if we treat δ as the only free variable we would make inference about and all other parameters as given, then the Maximum Likelihood Estimate (MLE) of δ is:

$$\delta_{MLE} = \frac{\#(\text{stopping action})}{\#(\text{stopping action}) + \#(\text{next page action})} \qquad (26)$$

where "#()" denotes the number of occurrences of the enclosed action in the interaction log. In our experiment, we estimated that $\delta_{MLE} = 0.029$ and 0.145 respectively for the group of patient and impatient users. Ideally, we could learn δ_{MLE} for each individual user, but due to the limited amount of log data we could obtain, we decided to learn its value for each user group collectively. We noticed that our estimated δ_{MLE} value for both user groups differed within $\pm 8\%$ across the two screen sizes, implying that our uniform user interest action model is an adequately reasonable assumption for real world users.

We measure the effectiveness of the two types of interfaces using two metrics: (a) whether the users end up successfully finding an interesting article or not, referred as "*success?*", and (b) how many laps the user spent for reaching an interesting article, referred as "*#lap*". We use one-sided McNemar's test for comparing "success?" and one-sided Wilcoxon sign-ranked test for comparing "#lap". Table 1 shows the significance levels of our comparison tests for all four settings, where we adopt the convention in R [6] and use "$\cdot$", "$\star$" and "$\star\star$" to represent a p-value within the range of (0.05, 0.1), (0.01, 0.05) and (0.001, 0.01), respectively. It is clearly observed that our new interface is significantly better than the baseline interface at helping impatient users navigate to an interesting article without significantly increasing the number of laps they needed; the differences for patient users are not significant, which is also expected because the two types of interfaces would generate very similar optimization results due to a very small δ value used in our new interface.

Table 1: Significance levels of comparison tests.

Setting	Sample size	"Success?"	"#lap"
MP	25		
MI	25	$\star\star$	$\cdot$
SP	25		
SI	24	$\star$	

[6]https://www.r-project.org/

Figure 3: ICM interface after clicking "Colleges and Universities".

Figure 4: ICM-US interface after clicking "Colleges and Universities".

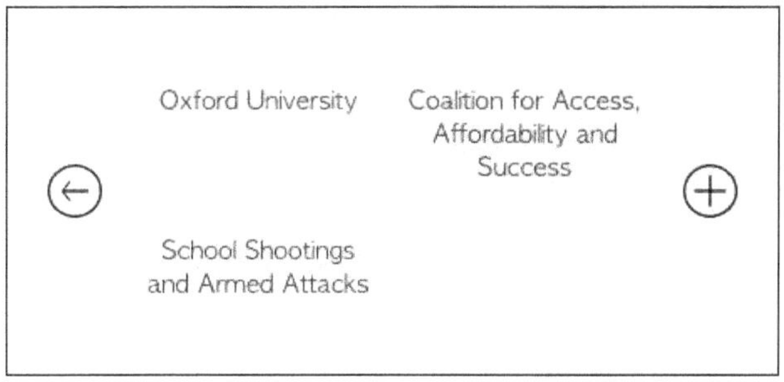

Interestingly, the differences in "success?" and "#lap" are both less significant on the very small screen than on the medium sized screen for impatient users, contradicting to our expectation that our new model should benefit smaller screens more which are in nature less effective in keeping users engaged with the system. We speculate that, on the very small screen, both the baseline and the new interface would decide that the very limited screen space is more suitable for the "keyword layout" in most of the laps where the system is still very uncertain about the user's interest, and the difference only occurs after the system could narrow down the user's interest to within a few articles (as was also observed in Figure 2).

To give better intuitions into the interface optimization outcomes of our proposed model, we show some example screens we observed when we used our interfaces ourselves. Figure 3 and 4 display the second screen we observed on the very small screen respectively in the baseline interface and in our new interface (fed with the δ_{MLE} value estimated from the group of impatient users), after we click the "Colleges and Universities" keyword on the first screen (where both interfaces chose to display four popular keywords due to the very limited screen space). Given that there are three news articles associated with the clicked keyword, the baseline interface decided to adopt the "article layout" and display the three articles one by one to the user (of which the first one is shown in Figure 3), with the hope that the user will thoroughly go over the three articles with the system. However, it is possible that an impatient user would stop if the first shown article does not interest them, and they would be even more likely to stop if they find the second shown article again not interesting. The new interface, on the other hand, considered user stopping tendencies in the optimization computation and thus chose to adopt the "keyword layout" and display three keywords within the same screen each corresponding to one of the three articles. Even an impatient user would likely identify a keyword related to their interest and continue on with the interaction by clicking it, and they would immediately reach their interested article in the next screen. It is also possible that the user might fail to recognize a related keyword, but the system determined that this would be a minor risk and would not affect the higher overall benefit of attracting an impatient user to stick longer to the interaction and eventually find something interesting. Note that all the reasoning above is only for our purpose to appreciate the intelligent layout decision of the interface system; the interface system is *not* built on top of any ad hoc logic to fulfill any part of our reasoning; its decision relies *only* on our optimization framework that elegantly captures all our intuitions in a single formulation.

Similar automatic layout decisions are observed on the medium sized screen as well, and the screen is even more capable in interface adaptations thanks to its additional intermediate layout choice of devoting half the space to an article and half to keywords, but we do not show the example screens here due to space limitations. The results demonstrate the clear effectiveness of our proposed model in automatically optimizing interface layouts according to users' stopping tendencies.

7. CONCLUSIONS AND FUTURE WORK

We proposed a novel refinement of the Interface Card Model based on sequential decision theory, i.e. ICM-US, that can facilitate formal user modeling and naturally connect optimization of interactive retrieval with Markov Decision Process and Reinforcement Learning (RL) in a general way, thus enabling the use of RL to solve potentially a wide range of problems of optimal interface design. ICM-US opens up many opportunities for formally modeling user behavior in interactive retrieval as well as incorporating user behavior models into an optimal retrieval algorithm, making the retrieval algorithm "sensitive" to user behavior.

An obvious future direction is to further explore the large space of specific refinements of ICM-US and apply ICM-US to many applications to optimize interactive search and interface design. Another very interesting direction is to use ICM-US to analyze interactive search log data for discovery of interesting user behavior patterns or testing hypotheses about users' search behavior.

8. REFERENCES

[1] G. Amati and C. J. Van Rijsbergen. Probabilistic models of information retrieval based on measuring the divergence from randomness. *ACM Trans. Inf. Syst.*, 20(4):357–389, Oct. 2002.

[2] L. Azzopardi. Modelling interaction with economic models of search. In *SIGIR '14*, pages 3–12, 2014.

[3] L. Azzopardi and G. Zuccon. An analysis of theories of search and search behavior. In *ICTIR '15*, pages 81–90, 2015.

[4] A. Cassandra, L. Kaelbling, and J. Kurien. Acting under uncertainty: discrete bayesian models for mobile-robot navigation. In *IROS '96*, volume 2, pages 963–972 vol.2, Nov 1996.

[5] C. L. Clarke, M. Kolla, G. V. Cormack, O. Vechtomova, A. Ashkan, S. Büttcher, and I. MacKinnon. Novelty and diversity in information retrieval evaluation. In *SIGIR '08*, pages 659–666, 2008.

[6] H. Fang and C. Zhai. An exploration of axiomatic approaches to information retrieval. In *SIGIR '05*, pages 480–487, 2005.

[7] R. Frank and B. Bernanke. *Principles of Microeconomics*. McGraw-Hill, 2009.

[8] N. Fuhr. A probability ranking principle for interactive information retrieval. *Information Retrieval*, 11(3):251–265, 2008.

[9] D. Hiemstra and W. Kraaij. Twenty-one at TREC-7: ad-hoc and cross-language track. In *TREC-7*, volume 500-242, pages 227–238, 1999.

[10] K. Järvelin and J. Kekäläinen. Cumulated gain-based evaluation of ir techniques. *ACM Trans. Inf. Syst.*, 20(4):422–446, Oct. 2002.

[11] T.-Y. Liu. Learning to rank for information retrieval. *Found. Trends Inf. Retr.*, 3(3):225–331, Mar. 2009.

[12] J. Luo, X. Dong, and H. Yang. Session search by direct policy learning. In *ICTIR '15*, pages 261–270, 2015.

[13] J. Luo, S. Zhang, and H. Yang. Win-win search: Dual-agent stochastic game in session search. In *SIGIR '14*, pages 587–596, 2014.

[14] D. Maxwell, L. Azzopardi, K. Järvelin, and H. Keskustalo. Searching and stopping: An analysis of stopping rules and strategies. In *CIKM '15*, pages 313–322, 2015.

[15] D. McFadden and K. Train. Mixed MNL models for discrete response. *Journal of Applied Econometrics*, 15(5):447–470, 2000.

[16] A. Moffat and J. Zobel. Rank-biased precision for measurement of retrieval effectiveness. *ACM Trans. Inf. Syst.*, 27(1):2:1–2:27, Dec. 2008.

[17] P. Pirolli and S. Card. Information foraging. *Psychological Review*, 106:643–675, 1999.

[18] J. M. Ponte and W. B. Croft. A language modeling approach to information retrieval. In *SIGIR '98*, pages 275–281, 1998.

[19] S. E. Robertson and K. S. Jones. Relevance weighting of search terms. *Journal of the American Society for Information Science*, 27(3):129–146, 1976.

[20] S. Russell and P. Norvig. *Artificial Intelligence: A Modern Approach*. Prentice Hall Press, 2009.

[21] G. Salton, A. Wong, and C. S. Yang. A vector space model for automatic indexing. *Commun. ACM*, 18(11):613–620, Nov. 1975.

[22] M. Sloan and J. Wang. Dynamic information retrieval: Theoretical framework and application. In *ICTIR '15*, pages 61–70, 2015.

[23] M. D. Smucker and C. L. Clarke. Time-based calibration of effectiveness measures. In *SIGIR '12*, pages 95–104, 2012.

[24] H. Turtle and W. B. Croft. Evaluation of an inference network-based retrieval model. *ACM Trans. Inf. Syst.*, 9(3):187–222, July 1991.

[25] W.-C. Wu, D. Kelly, and A. Sud. Using information scent and need for cognition to understand online search behavior. In *SIGIR '14*, pages 557–566, 2014.

[26] Y. Zhang and C. Zhai. Information retrieval as card playing: A formal model for optimizing interactive retrieval interface. In *SIGIR '15*, pages 685–694, 2015.

Generalized BROOF-L2R: A General Framework for Learning to Rank Based on Boosting and Random Forests *

Clebson C. A. de Sá Marcos A. Gonçalves Daniel X. Sousa Thiago Salles
Federal University of Minas Gerais
Computer Science Department
Belo Horizonte, Brazil
{clebsonc, mgoncalv, danielxs, tsalles}@dcc.ufmg.br

ABSTRACT

The task of retrieving information that really matters to the users is considered hard when taking into consideration the current and increasingly amount of available information. To improve the effectiveness of this information seeking task, systems have relied on the combination of many predictors by means of machine learning methods, a task also known as learning to rank (L2R). The most effective learning methods for this task are based on ensembles of tress (e.g., Random Forests) and/or boosting techniques (e.g., RankBoost, MART, LambdaMART). In this paper, we propose a general framework that smoothly combines ensembles of additive trees, specifically Random Forests, with Boosting in a original way for the task of L2R. In particular, we exploit out-of-bag samples as well as a selective weight updating strategy (according to the out-of-bag samples) to effectively enhance the ranking performance. We instantiate such a general framework by considering different loss functions, different ways of weighting the weak learners as well as different types of weak learners. In our experiments our rankers were able to outperform all state-of-the-art baselines in all considered datasets, using just a small percentage of the original training set and faster convergence rates.

Keywords

Learning to Ranking; Random Forests; Boosting

1. INTRODUCTION

Today, we live in an era of massive available information, with a never-seen-before (and increasing) rate of information production. It is not surprising that such a scenario imposes hard to tackle challenges. For example, the availability of massive amounts of data is not of great help if one is not able to effectively access relevant information that satisfies her information needs. Retrieval systems, such as search engines, question and answer, and expert search systems serve exactly this purpose: given an information need, expressed in the form of a query, and a set of possible information units (e.g., documents), the main goal is to provide an ordered list of information units according to their relevance with relation to the query. The desideratum is to increase the likelihood of satisfying an user's information need in an effective manner, which translates to maintain the truly relevant results on top of the less relevant ones.

One of the key aspects that influence retrieval systems is how they determine the relative relevance among candidate results in order to produce a ranked list based on their relevance with regard to some information need, posed in the form of a query. The quality of those rankings is thus paramount to guarantee efficient and effective access to relevant information (and, hopefully, the satisfaction of the user's information needs). Several approaches to generate such ranked lists do exist, being traditionally performed by the specification of a function that is able to relate some user's query to the set of known (indexed) information units. Usually, ranking functions consider several features, such as those that rely on the relatedness between query and possible results (e.g., BM25, edit distance, similarities in vector space models) or on link analysis information (e.g., PageRank, HITS). Such features must be somehow combined to provide accurate relevance scores (and, thus, a properly ranked list of results).

Unfortunately, to specify and tune ranking functions turns out to be a major problem, specially when the number of features becomes large, with non-trivial interactions. This motivates the use of supervised machine learning techniques to devise such functions, since machine learning techniques are effective to combine multiple pieces of evidence towards optimizing some goal. This is the direction pursued by Learning to Rank (L2R) techniques, the primary focus of this work.

More specifically, based on a set of query-document pairs with known relevance judgments, the goal is to learn a function $f(d, q)$ that is able to accurately devise the relevance scores for a document d, with respect to a query q. Due to its importance, several approaches for L2R have been proposed in the literature. Ensemble methods, such as RankBoost [7], AdaRank [32] and Random Forests [1] (and the variations thereof, such as [11]), are deemed to be the techniques of choice for L2R, achieving higher effectiveness in published benchmarks when compared to other algorithms [11, 3]. Both RankBoost and AdaBoost are based on boosting [26], an

*This work was partially funded by projects InWeb (grant MCT/CNPq 573871/2008- 6) and MASWeb (grant FAPEMIG/PRONEX APQ-01400-14), and by the authors' individual grants from CNPq, FAPEMIG, Capes and Google Inc.

SIGIR '16, July 17–21, 2016, Pisa, Italy.
© 2016 ACM. ISBN 978-1-4503-4069-4/16/07...$15.00
DOI: http://dx.doi.org/10.1145/2911451.2911540

iterative meta-algorithm that combines a series of weak-learners in order to come up with a strong final learner, focusing on hard-to-classify regions of the input space as the iterations go by. The strategies based on Random Forest rely on the combination of several decision trees, learned using bootstrapped samples of the training set, together with additional sources of randomization (such as random feature selection) to produce decorrelated-correlated trees—a requirement to guarantee its effectiveness.

In this work, we propose a general framework for L2R, named Generalized BROOF-L2R that explores the advantages of boosting and Random Forests, by combining them in a non-trivial fashion. More specifically, at each iteration of the boosting algorithm, a Random Forest model is learned, considering training examples sampled according to a probability distribution. Such probability distribution is updated at the end of each iteration, in order to force the subsequent learners to focus on hard to classify regions of the input space. In particular, the use of RF models as weak learners has its own advantages, since it is capable of providing robust estimates of expected error through out of bag error estimates and, by means of selectively updating the weights of out of bag samples, one can effectively slow down the tendency of boosting strategies to overfit (a well known phenomenon that becomes critical as the noise level of the dataset being analyzed increases).

As we shall detail in the next sections, the key aspects of the proposed Generalized BROOF-L2R have to do with how to update the probability distribution and how such update should be performed, as well as the underlying ranker to be used to produce the final set of results. In this work, we discuss a set of possible instances of the proposed general framework, in order to highlight the behavior and potential of the proposed L2R solution. In fact, the instances that makes use of out-of-bag samples and optimizes through gradient descent [12] over the residues is able to achieve the strongest results, in terms of Mean Average Precision (MAP) and Normalized Discounted Cumulative Gain (NDCG), with significant improvements over the explored adversary algorithms, considering 5 traditional benchmark datasets. Our alternative instances were also able to achieve competitive (or superior) results when compared to the baselines. Moreover, as our experimental evaluation shows, our approaches based on the proposed general framework are able to produce top-notch results with substantially less training samples when compared to the baselines. Such data efficiency is key to guarantee practical feasibility as obtaining labeled data is still a costly process.

To summarize, the contributions of this work are three-fold. We provide a general framework for L2R that is able to combine two strong methods (boosting and Random Forests) in an original way, which can be specialized in several ways and produce highly effective L2R solutions. We propose and discuss a set of alternative instantiations of such a framework, in order to highlight the behavior and effectiveness of each possible choice. Finally, we advance the state of the art in L2R by means of some instantiations of our proposed framework that are able to outperform top-notch solutions, according to an extensive benchmark evaluation considering five datasets and seven L2R baseline algorithms.

Roadmap: Section 2 discusses related work. Section 3 presents our proposed Generalized BROOF-L2R framework, as well as outlines our proposed set of possible instantiations of the proposed framework. We clarify our experimental setup and discuss the obtained results in Section 4. Finally, Section 5 concludes and highlights some future work.

2. RELATED WORK

Learn to Rank (L2R) [17] is the focus of active developments due to its cross-industry and society importance. Here, we review some relevant work on this topic, positioning our work in the literature.

L2R attempts to improve traditional strategies for ranking query results according to some relevance criteria, by exploring supervised machine learning algorithms to combine various relevance related features into a more effective ranking function, based on a set of queries and associated documents with relevance judgments. L2R have been successfully applied to a variety of tasks, such as Question and Answer [28], Recommender [29, 16] and Document Retrieval [14] systems.

Solutions specifically tailored to improve document retrieval have been extensively studied in the past years [4, 19]. In general, there are three major L2R approaches: the pointwise, pairwise and listwise approaches. Pointwise L2R algorithms are probably the simplest (yet successful) approaches, directly translating the ranking problem to a classification/regression one. In this case, the training set for the supervised learning algorithm consists of pairs $\langle q_i, (x_{i,j}, y_{i,j})\rangle$ of queries q_i and a list of associated documents $x_{i,j}$, each one with its relevance judgment $y_{i,j}$. In this case, each triple $\langle q_i, x_{i,j}, y_{i,j}\rangle$ is considered to be a single training example. The goal is to learn a classifier/regressor model capable of accurately predicting the relevance score of a document x', with relation to a query q_i, thus producing a partial ordering over documents. Pairwise algorithms, on the other hand, transform the ranking problem into a pairwise classification/regression problem. In this case, learning algorithms are used to predict orders of document pairs, thus exploring more ground-truth information than the pointwise approaches. Unlike both mentioned strategies, the listwise approaches essentially treat $\langle q_i, (x_{i,j}, y_{i,j})_j\rangle$ as a single training instance (that is, considering a ranked list of documents for a query q_i as a single training example), capturing more information from the training set (namely, group structure) than the previous alternatives. Of course, being able to better capture training data information when learning a ranking function comes with a price: usually, pairwise and mainly listwise approaches are harder to train, since they require more sophisticated (e.g. query-level) loss functions [17].

In terms of the state-of-the-art in L2R, methods based on Random Forests (RFs) and boosting were shown to be strong solutions according to already published benchmarks [22, 11, 3]. More specifically, RFs (and the variations thereof [11]) as well as boosting algorithms such as Gradient Boosted Regression Trees (GBRT) [9] and LambdaMART [33], are considered by many [3, 22, 18] to be the state of the art in L2R tasks. This work is based on both RFs and boosting strategies. Thus, in the following we briefly review some previous literature on them.

The RF algorithm was proposed in [1] as a variation of bagging of low-correlated decision/regression trees, built with a series of random procedures, such as bootstrapping of training data and random attribute selection. The popularity of RFs is highlighted by their successful application in several domains, such as tag recommendation [3], object segmentation [27], human pose recognition [30] and L2R [3, 22], to name a few. Thus, it is natural to expect several extensions to it, in order to improve its effectiveness even more. One such extension is the extremely randomized trees (ERT) model [10] and its application to L2R [11]. The ultimate goal of ERTs is to reduce the correlation between the trees composing the ensemble, a requirement to guarantee high effectiveness of RF models. This is achieved by modifying the RF algorithm in, essentially, two aspects: each tree is learned considering the entire training set, instead of bootstrapped samples. Furthermore, in order to determine the decision splits after the random attribute selection, instead of selecting a cut-point that optimizes node purity, ERTs simply select a random cut-point threshold. This ultimately reduces tree correlation, potentially improving generalization capability of the learned model. As a final remark, such RF based models can be regarded as nonlinear pointwise approaches for L2R.

Boosting strategies have also been shown to produce state of the art results on L2R tasks, with GBRT [9] (a.k.a, MART[1] (Multiple Additive Regression Trees) and Lambda-MART [33] as the two perhaps most widely used strategies. Both algorithms are additive ensembles of regression trees. GBRT learns a ranking function by approximating the root mean squared error (RMSE) on the training set through gradient descent. As with typical boosting algorithms, the goal of GBRT is to focus on regions of the input space where predicting the correct relevance score is a hard task. Since this algorithm aims at approximating the RMSE on the training data, it can be regarded as a pointwise approach. The Lambda-MART algorithm, on the other hand, is a listwise approach that directly optimizes the ranked list of documents according to some retrieval measure, such as NDCG (instead of simply approximating the RMSE of the training documents relevance scores in isolation). To this end, Lambda-MART learns a ranking function that generates a list of relevant documents to a query that is as close as possible to the correct rank. As GBRT, it is based on gradient descent to optimize such metric.

Due to the successful application of RFs and boosting in machine learning tasks (such as classification and L2R), some authors propose to use both strategies in order to come up with better learned models. For example, in [22] GBRTs and RFs are independently explored in order to learn better ranking functions. More specifically, the GBRT model is initialized with the residues of the RF algorithm, followed by the traditional iterations of a GBRT model. The main motivation behind this approach is that RFs are less prone to overfitting, being ideal to initialize the GBRT algorithm instead of the usual uniform initialization. According to the reported benchmark, such strategy was shown to be superior to the GBRT algorithm.

Unlike [22], in [21] the authors propose an enhanced RF model for classification by boosting the decision trees composing the ensemble. In this case, each tree is learned with training examples weighted by w_i, resembling boosting by re-weighting. In particular, training instances with higher weights influence more when determining the decision nodes (and cut-point threshold definition). Furthermore, each tree is evaluated according to this weighted training set, which enables the ensemble to focus on hard-to-predict regions. The observed effect of such combination is the ability to come up with high quality models with substantially reduced training sets. As we shall detail, our proposed framework is tailored for the L2R task and, instead of introducing boosting into random forests, we apply boosting to several RF models, which act as weak learners.

Differently from the aforementioned previous work, we base ourselves in a recent development for text classification, namely, the BROOF algorithm [25]. In BROOF algorithm, RF and boosting strategies are tightly coupled in order to exploit their unique advantages: by exploiting out of bag error estimates as well as selectively updating training weights according to out of bag samples, the BROOF model is able to focus on hard-to-classify regions of the input space, without being compromised by the boosting tendency to overfit. This ultimately leads to competitive results when compared to state of the art algorithms. In here, we generalize such approach specifically for L2R tasks in order to come up with better ranking functions: the Generalized BROOF-L2R. As we shall see, this general framework is flexible enough so that it can be instantiated in several ways, exploiting distinct characteristics of the ranking tasks being addressed. In special, with this general framework we are able to achieve state of the art results, with rankers superior to the top notch algorithms proposed so far in all evaluated cases.

3. GENERALIZED BROOF-L2R

In this section, we detail our proposed Generalized BROOF-L2R framework. Briefly speaking, this framework allows the definition of learners based on the combination of Random Forests and the Boosting meta-algorithm, in a non-trivial fashion. As we shall see, this framework establishes a set of operations to be performed during the boosting iterations, in a well defined order of application. The goal is to drive the weak learners towards hard to predict regions of the underlying data representation, in order to come up with an optimized additive combination of weak learners to form the final predictor. The extension points of the proposed framework can produce a heterogeneous set of instantiations that typically produces very competitive results for L2R. In the following, we present the generalized framework for L2R, as well as some pointwise instantiations. We stress that the set of instantiations discussed here is far from exhaustive, being possible to elaborate even better possibilities in future work.

3.1 Framework Description

Based on the BROOF algorithm, proposed in [25] to solve text classification tasks, we here extend the proposed ideas in order to exploit the combination of Random Forests and Boosting for the specific task of L2R. However, instead of directly adapting the original algorithm to a single L2R method, we here generalize it into an extensible framework that is flexible enough to permit a series of possible instantiations. The proposed framework, named Generalized BROOF-L2R is an additive model composed of several Random Forest models, which act as weak-learners. Each fitted model influences the final decision proportionally to its accuracy, focusing — as the boosting iterations go by — on ever more complex regions of the input space, in order to drive down the expected error. As usual in a boosting strategy, two aspects play a key role: (*i*) the influence β_t of each learner in the fitted additive model, and (*ii*) the strategy to update the sample distribution $w_{i,j}$ in each iteration t of the boosting meta-algorithm.

[1]From now on, we will use MART and GBRT as synonyms.

The basic structure of the framework is outlined in Algorithm 1, together with a brief explanation of what we call its extension points—the general functions exploited by the framework to determine how the optimization process works. There are 5 general functions whose purpose is to specify the weight distribution update process, the error estimation and the underlying input representation. Particularly, the use of the Random Forest classifier as a weak learner extends the range of possible instantiations of the framework, since it enables us to come up with better error rate estimates and a more selective approach to update the examples' weights, through the use of the so-called out-of-bag samples.

Let $Q_{trn} = \{(q_i, \{x_{i,j}, y_{i,j}\})|_{j=1}^{m_i}\}$ be the training set, descriptively the set of documents $x_{i,j}$, with associated graded relevance judgment $y_{i,j}$ with relation to a query q_i. Initially, associate a weight $w_{i,j}$ with each training example $x_{i,j}$ according to the general function INITIALIZEWEIGHTS. For each boosting iteration t, the input data representation may be updated, through the general function UPDATEEXAMPLES. This general function can considerably extend the range of possible implementations of the framework, allowing us for example, to instantiate a Gradient Boosting Machine algorithm [20, 12]. Then, a Random Forest regressor model RF_t is learned considering this data representation.

In order to evaluate the generalization capabilities of RF_t, predict $\hat{y}$ for a set of training documents given by VALIDATIONSET. The output of this step is paramount to guide the optimization process towards hard to classify regions of the input space. Although being of great importance to boosting effectiveness, this focus on hard to classify regions of the input space may also be harmful to the optimization process, specially when dealing with noisy data. As noted by [8, 13], boosting tends to increase the weights of few hard-to-classify examples (e.g., noisy ones). Thus, the decision boundary may only be suitable for those noisy regions of the input space while not necessarily general enough for general examples. In order to offer a greater robustness against such a drawback, our framework exposes an intermediary step related to how the examples weights get updates as the boosting iterations go by. The general function VALIDATIONSET serves the purpose of specifying which training examples should be used during error estimation and weights update. The main goal here is to provide some mechanism to slowdown overfitting as well as provide more robust estimates of error weight (to capture the generalization power of each weak learner and to determine how they should influence the final predictor).

The selected training examples are then used to compute both the error rate of the model and the influence β_t of the weak learner on the final model, through COMPUTELEARNERWEIGHTS. Finally, the training examples' weight distribution is updated by UPDATEEXAMPLEWEIGHTS. This update process should, ideally, take into account the generalization capability of the current weak learner RF_t, as well as how hard is to correctly predict the ranked lists of the validation examples. Validation examples whose outcome is hard to predict by an accurate learner should influence more in the following boosting iterations. An early stopping strategy is adopted, terminating the boosting iterations if the current learner has an estimated error rate greater than 0.5. The final prediction rule is then given by an additive combination of the weak-learners RF_t, weighted by β_t.

Instantiation	Description	
	Extension Point	Variation
$\text{BROOF}_{\text{absolute}}$	INITIALIZEWEIGHTS	**Uniform**
	UPDATEEXAMPLES	**Identity**
	VALIDATIONSET	**OOB**
	COMPUTELEARNERWEIGHTS	**Absolute**
	UPDATEEXAMPLEWEIGHTS	**OOB**
$\text{BROOF}_{\text{median}}$	INITIALIZEWEIGHTS	**Uniform**
	UPDATEEXAMPLES	**Identity**
	VALIDATIONSET	**OOB**
	COMPUTELEARNERWEIGHTS	**Median**
	UPDATEEXAMPLEWEIGHTS	**OOB**
$\text{BROOF}_{\text{height}}$	INITIALIZEWEIGHTS	**Uniform**
	UPDATEEXAMPLES	**Identity**
	VALIDATIONSET	**OOB**
	COMPUTELEARNERWEIGHTS	**Height**
	UPDATEEXAMPLEWEIGHTS	**OOB**
$\text{BROOF}_{\text{gradient}}$	INITIALIZEWEIGHTS	**Uniform**
	UPDATEEXAMPLES	**Residue**
	VALIDATIONSET	**OOB**
	COMPUTELEARNERWEIGHTS	**Constant**
	UPDATEEXAMPLEWEIGHTS	**Constant**

Table 1: Generalized BROOF-L2R: Possible instantiations.

3.2 Possible Instantiations

In this section, we describe a set of possible instantiations of the proposed framework. Due to space limitations, we here focus on four possible instantiations, stressing that this is far from being an exhaustive list of possibilities. In fact, we consider some representative alternatives that highlight the flexibility of the proposed framework to produce L2R solutions that typically produces very competitive results.

In order to induce a L2R algorithm based on the Generalized BROOF-L2R framework, one needs to specify the 5 generic functions discussed earlier. Our proposed instantiations can be found in Table 1. In that table, we specify which alternative was chosen for each generic function, providing details on how they are implemented.

As it can be observed, $\text{BROOF}_{\text{absolute}}$, $\text{BROOF}_{\text{median}}$ and $\text{BROOF}_{\text{height}}$ rely on out-of-bag samples in order to drive the boosting meta-algorithm further on hard to predict regions of the input space. Such samples are explored when estimating the weak-learner's error rate through out-of-bag estimates. Recall that in boosting, the usual way of assessing the errors is to use the training to measure the error. This is too optimistic, since the same data that was used to train the model is used as a measure of error. By using the out-of-bag samples we are able to produce better error estimates, since the out-of-bag are an independent set of samples that was left apart during the construction of the model. Thus, it is able to better approximate the expected error rate of the learner and is a more reliable measure than the usual training error rate [1].

In addition, the out-of-bag errors estimates are used to identify the weights' distribution that should be applied on following iterations of the boosting procedure; allowing the model to focus on hard to predict regions of the input space. We hypothesize that such selective update strategy can slowdown the algorithm's tendency to overfit. The major difference between them relates on how each weak-learner influence on the final predictor. The proposed instantiations can be found outlined in Algorithms 2 to 4. More specifically, we considered the absolute regression loss, $|y_{i,j} - \hat{y}_{i,j}|$, computed for the out-of-bag samples. We call

Algorithm 1 Generalized BROOF-L2R: Pseudocode

function FIT($Q_{trn} = \{(q_i, \{x_{i,j}, y_{i,j}\}|_{j=1}^{m_i}\}$, max_iter=$M$, num_trees=$N$, shrinkage=$\eta$)
  $w_{i,j}$ =INITIALIZEWEIGHTS(Q_{trn})
  $x'_{i,j} \leftarrow y_{i,j}$
  for each $t = 1$ **to** M **do**
    $x'_{i,j} \leftarrow$UPDATEEXAMPLES($Q_{trn}, x'_{i,j}$)
    $RF_t \leftarrow RF_{Regressor}$.FIT($\{(x'_{i,j}, y_{i,j})\}, N$)
    $\{(\hat{y}^t_{i,j}, y^t_{i,j})\} \leftarrow$VALIDATIONSET($RF_t, Q_{trn}$)
    $\langle e^t_{i,j}, \beta_t\rangle \leftarrow$COMPUTELEARNERWEIGHTS($RF_t, \{(\hat{y}^t_{i,j}, y^t_{i,j})\}$)
    if $\sum_{i,j} e^t_{i,j} w_{i,j} \geq 0.5$ **then**
      break
    end if
    $w_{i,j} \leftarrow$UPDATEEXAMPLEWEIGHTS($e^t_{i,j}, \beta_t, \{(\hat{y}^t_{i,j}, y^t_{i,j})\}$)
  end for
  return $\{(RF_t, \beta_t)\}|_{t=1}^{M}$
end function

Function	Description
INITIALIZEWEIGHTS	Initial weights associated to each example, ressambling boosting by re-weighting. **Uniform:** Equal weights for each example, $w_{i,j} = \frac{1}{\sum_{i,j} m_{i,j}}$. **Random:** Randomly initialized weights, $w_{i,j}$ =RANDOM(), $0 \leq w_{i,j} \leq 1$.
UPDATEEXAMPLES	Determines the underlying representation of the input data, directly defining what the algorithm should optimize for. **Identity:** Maintains the original representation of input data, $x'_{i,j} = x_{i,j}$. **Residue:** Optimizes for the residues: $x'_{i,j} = \begin{cases} x'_{i,j} - \eta\hat{y}^{t-1}_{i,j} & \text{if } t > 1 \\ y_{i,j} & \text{otherwise} \end{cases}$, where η is a shrinkage factor.
VALIDATIONSET	Determines which training data will be considered during weight update and error rate estimation, with direct influence on the algorithm robustness to overfitting. **OOB:** The set of out of bag examples OOB_t related to RF_t. **Train:** The entire training set Q_{trn}.
COMPUTELEARNERWEIGHTS	Determines how to compute the influence of the current weak learner on the final predictor. **Absolute:** $\beta_t = \eta\frac{\epsilon}{1-\epsilon}$, where $\epsilon = \sum_{i,j} e^t_{i,j} w_{i,j}$, $e^t_{i,j} = \lvert y_{i,j} - \hat{y}_{i,j}\rvert$ and η is a shrinkage factor. **Median:** Similarly to the above variant, $\beta_t = \eta\frac{\epsilon}{1-\epsilon}$ and $\epsilon = \sum_{i,j} e^t_{i,j} w_{i,j}$. However, the errors are given by $e^t_{i,j} = \lvert$MEDIAN$(R_{\hat{y}_{i,j}}) - \hat{y}_{i,j}\rvert$ where R_i denotes the list of predictions $\hat{y}_{i,j}$ associated to documents whose real relevance score is i. **Height:** Similarly to the variants above, both $\beta_t = \eta\frac{\epsilon}{1-\epsilon}$ and $\epsilon = \sum_{i,j} e^t_{i,j} w_{i,j}$. Unlike them, $e^t_{i,j} = \begin{cases} \#\text{ irrelevant documents above } x_{i,j} & \text{if } x_{i,j} \text{is relevant} \\ \#\text{ relevant documents below } x_{i,j} & \text{otherwise} \end{cases}$, in the ordered list of results. **Constant:** Produces constant coefficients, $\beta_t = \eta$.
UPDATEEXAMPLEWEIGHTS	Specifies how to update the training examples weights to be used in the next iteration. **OOB:** Updates the weights associated to the out of bag samples according to β_t and the difficulty involved in predicting the samples' outcomes. More specifically, $w_{i,j} = w_{i,j}\beta_t^{1-e^t_{i,j}}$ **Train:** Updates the weights associated to the entire training set. Similarly to the above variant, the update strategy considers both the coefficient β_t and the error $e^t_{i,j}$. **Constant:** Keeps the same weights during the boosting iterations, $w_{i,j} = w_{i,j}$.

this variant BROOF$_{\text{absolute}}$. We also considered two other alternatives, that rely on the position of documents in the predicted ranked lists. One alternative, named BROOF-L2R$_{\text{median}}$, relies on the intuition that documents with the same relevance judgment should be as nearer as possible to each other on the current ranked list. We thus consider as loss $\lvert$MEDIAN$(R_{\hat{y}_{i,j}}) - \hat{y}_{i,j}\rvert$ where R_i denotes the list of predictions $\hat{y}_{i,j}$ associated to documents whose real relevance score is i. The second alternative, named BROOF$_{\text{height}}$, is inspired on ideas of [5]. We define the height of a document $x_{i,j}$ as the total number of irrelevant documents ranked higher then $x_{i,j}$ if $x_{i,j}$ is relevant, or the total number of relevant documents ranked below $x_{i,j}$ if it is an irrelevant one.

Finally, in order to illustrate the generality of our proposed framework, we provide a fourth instantiation, BROOF$_{\text{gradient}}$, that resembles the gradient boosting machines (GBM), that optimizes through gradient descent [12] over the residues. More specifically, by a suitable combination of alternative implementations for each general function outlined in Algorithm 1, one can come up with an algorithm that could be named Gradient Boosted Random Forests (GBRF). This is achieved by considering an alternative representation of input data, that optimizes for the residues, such as $y - \hat{y}$, instead of the original input representation, updating them according to the negative gradient of the cost function (in this case, RMSE). Such alternative is outlined in Algorithm 5.

As we shall see in our experimental evaluation (Section 5), our proposed instantiations achieve very strong results compared to seven state-of-the-art baselines algorithms in five representative datasets. In particular, BROOF$_{\text{absolute}}$ and BROOF$_{\text{gradient}}$ were shown to be the strongest algorithms, obtaining significant improvements over the best baselines.

4. EXPERIMENTAL EVALUATION

We conducted extensive experiments in well-known L2R benchmarks. In the following, we describe the characteristics of the used datasets, the baseline algorithms, the experimental protocol/setup and the experimental results.

4.1 Datasets

The corpus we use are freely available online for scientific purposes. Such datasets can be divided into two groups

Algorithm 2 $\text{BROOF}_{\text{absolute}}$: Pseudocode

function $\text{FIT}(\{(q_i, \{x_{i,j}, y_{i,j}\}|_{j=1}^{m_i}\}, M, N, \eta)$
  $w_{i,j} = \frac{1}{\sum_{i,j} m_{i,j}}$
  $x'_{i,j} \leftarrow y_{i,j}$
  for each $t = 1$ **to** M **do**
    $x'_{i,j} \leftarrow x_{i,j}$
    $RF_t \leftarrow RF_{Regressor}.\text{FIT}(\{(x'_{i,j}, y_{i,j})\}, N)$
    $\{(\hat{y}^t_{i,j}, y^t_{i,j})\} \leftarrow RF_t.\text{OOB}$
    $e^t_{i,j} \leftarrow |y_{i,j} - \hat{y}_{i,j}|$
    $\epsilon \leftarrow \sum_{i,j} e^t_{i,j} w_{i,j}$
    $\beta_t \leftarrow \eta \frac{\epsilon}{1-\epsilon}$
    if $\epsilon \geq 0.5$ **break**
    $w_{i,j} \leftarrow w_{i,j} \beta_t^{1-e^t_{i,j}}$
  end for
  return $\{(RF_t, \beta_t)\}|_{t=1}^{M}$
end function

Algorithm 3 $\text{BROOF}_{\text{median}}$: Pseudocode

function $\text{FIT}(\{(q_i, \{x_{i,j}, y_{i,j}\}|_{j=1}^{m_i}\}, M, N, \eta)$
  $w_{i,j} = \frac{1}{\sum_{i,j} m_{i,j}}$
  $x'_{i,j} \leftarrow y_{i,j}$
  for each $t = 1$ **to** M **do**
    $x'_{i,j} \leftarrow x_{i,j}$
    $RF_t \leftarrow RF_{Regressor}.\text{FIT}(\{(x'_{i,j}, y_{i,j})\}, N)$
    $\{(\hat{y}^t_{i,j}, y^t_{i,j})\} \leftarrow RF_t.\text{OOB}$
    $e^t_{i,j} \leftarrow \text{MEDIAN}(pos(y_{i,j}) - pos(\hat{y}_{i,j}))$
    $\epsilon \leftarrow \sum_{i,j} e^t_{i,j} w_{i,j}$
    $\beta_t \leftarrow \eta \frac{\epsilon}{1-\epsilon}$
    if $\epsilon \geq 0.5$ **break**
    $w_{i,j} \leftarrow w_{i,j} \beta_t^{1-e^t_{i,j}}$
  end for
  return $\{(RF_t, \beta_t)\}|_{t=1}^{M}$
end function

Algorithm 4 $\text{BROOF-L2R}_{\text{height}}$: Pseudocode

function $\text{FIT}(\{(q_i, \{x_{i,j}, y_{i,j}\}|_{j=1}^{m_i}\}, M, N, \eta)$
  $w_{i,j} = \frac{1}{\sum_{i,j} m_{i,j}}$
  $x'_{i,j} \leftarrow y_{i,j}$
  for each $t = 1$ **to** M **do**
    $x'_{i,j} \leftarrow x_{i,j}$
    $RF_t \leftarrow RF_{Regressor}.\text{FIT}(\{(x'_{i,j}, y_{i,j})\}, N)$
    $\{(\hat{y}^t_{i,j}, y^t_{i,j})\} \leftarrow RF_t.\text{OOB}$
    $e^t_{i,j} \leftarrow \begin{cases} \#\text{ irrelevant documents above } x_{i,j} & \text{if } x_{i,j} \text{is relevant} \\ \#\text{ relevant documents below } x_{i,j} & \textit{otherwise} \end{cases}$
    $\epsilon \leftarrow \sum_{i,j} e^t_{i,j} w_{i,j}$
    $\beta_t \leftarrow \eta \frac{\epsilon}{1-\epsilon}$
    if $\epsilon \geq 0.5$ **break**
    $w_{i,j} \leftarrow w_{i,j} \beta_t^{1-e^t_{i,j}}$
  end for
  return $\{(RF_t, \beta_t)\}|_{t=1}^{M}$
end function

Algorithm 5 $\text{BROOF}_{\text{gradient}}$: Pseudocode

function $\text{FIT}(\{(q_i, \{x_{i,j}, y_{i,j}\}|_{j=1}^{m_i}\}, M, N, \eta)$
  $w_{i,j} = \frac{1}{\sum_{i,j} m_{i,j}}$
  $x'_{i,j} \leftarrow y_{i,j}$
  for each $t = 1$ **to** M **do**
    $x'_{i,j} \leftarrow \begin{cases} x'_{i,j} - \eta \hat{y}^{t-1}_{i,j} & \text{if } t > 1 \\ y_{i,j} & \text{otherwise} \end{cases}$
    $RF_t \leftarrow RF_{Regressor}.\text{FIT}(\{(x'_{i,j}, y_{i,j})\}, N)$
    $\{(\hat{y}^t_{i,j}, y^t_{i,j})\} \leftarrow RF_t.\text{OOB}$
    $e^t_{i,j} \leftarrow |y_{i,j} - \eta \hat{y}_{i,j}|$
    $\epsilon \leftarrow \sum_{i,j} e^t_{i,j} w_{i,j}$
    $\beta_t \leftarrow \eta$
    if $\epsilon \geq 0.5$ **break**
    $w_{i,j} \leftarrow w_{i,j}$
  end for
  return $\{(RF_t, \beta_t)\}|_{t=1}^{M}$
end function

considering the relevance judgments and their sizes. The two largest datasets contain ⟨query, document⟩ pairs with five relevance levels, ranging from 0 (completely irrelevant) to 4 (highly relevant). In this group we have one dataset from the "YAHOO! Webscope Learning to Rank Challenge", divided into three partitions for training, validation and test. The second largest dataset, WEB10K, consists of 10,000 queries released by Microsoft. In contrast to the YAHOO! datasets, the Microsoft dataset is partitioned into 5 folds for cross-validation purposes, with 3 partitions used for training, 1 for validation and 1 for test.

The second group of datasets corresponds to well-known LETOR 3.0 Topic distillation tasks, TD2003 and TD2004 (a.k.a., informational queries), of the Web track of the Text Retrieval Conference 2003 and 2004. These datasets contain binary relevance judgments. Similarly to the WEB10K benchmark, these datasets are partitioned into 5 folds to be used in a folded cross-validation procedure.

For comparative purposes, considering that the Microsoft and LETOR datasets were designed for a folded cross-validation procedure, we applied this same strategy to the YAHOO! dataset by merging the original partitions into a single set, and splitting the sorted queries into 5 folds, distributed using the same proportions: 3 folds for training, 1 for validation and 1 for test. We report results for both splits: the original one (called YAHOOV1S2) and the new 5-fold split (called YAHOOV1S2-F5).

4.2 Baselines

In our experiments we consider as baselines freely available implementations of state-of-the-art L2R methods, including AdaRank (with MAP and NDCG as loss functions), Random Forests, SVM^{rank}, MART, LambdaMART and RankBoost. We used the RankLib[2] (under the Lemur project) implementations of RankBoost, MART and LambdaMART. For AdaRank we used the implementation freely available at Microsoft Research[3]. For SVM^{rank}, we used the original implementation of [15][4]. Finally, for Random Forests, we used the implementation available in Scikit-Learn[24] library, which is also the basis of our implementations.

4.3 Experimental Protocol and Setup

To validate the performance of our approaches, we use two statistical tests to assess the statistical significance of our results, namely, the Wilcoxon signed-rank test and the paired Student's t-test. We consider the Wilcoxon signed-rank test since it is a non-parametric statistical hypothesis testing procedure that requires no previous knowledge of the samples distribution. In fact, some authors believe that it is one of the best choices for the analysis of two independent samples [6]. However, there is also some discussion in the literature favoring the Student's t-test when comparing L2R methods [23]. Due to the lack of consensus, we perform our

[2]http://sourceforge.net/p/lemur/wiki/RankLib/
[3]http://research.microsoft.com/en-us/downloads/0eae7224-8c9b-4f1e-b515-515c71675d5c/
[4]https://www.cs.cornell.edu/people/tj/svm_light/svm_rank.html

analysis with both tests, considering a two-sided hypothesis with significance level of 0.95% in both tests.

The statistical tests are computed over the values for Mean Average Precision (MAP) and the Normalized Discounted Cumulative Gain at the top 10 retrieved documents (hereafter, NDCG@10), the two most important and frequently used performance metrics to evaluate a given permutation of a ranked list using binary and multi-relevance order [31]. To compute these metrics we used the standard evaluation tool available for the LETOR 3.0 benchmark (for binary datasets), as well the tool available for the Microsoft dataset for all multi-label relevance judgment datasets [5]. For MAP, let Q be the set of all queries. These tools simply compute

$$MAP = \sum_{q \in Q} \frac{\text{AveragePrecision}(q)}{|Q|}.$$

Regarding NDCG, we assume that NDCG@p is 0 (zero) for empty queries, i.e., queries with no relevant documents. Some of the available evaluations tools (e.g., the one from YAHOO!) assume the value of 1 for these cases, which may lead to higher values of NDCG [2]. We chose to standardize this issue, using the same criterion used by most evaluation tools, e.g., those available for the Letor (3.0 and 4.0) and Microsoft datasets, in order to allow fairer comparisons. Accordingly, let $IDCG_p$ be the maximum possible discounted cumulative gain for a given query. These tools implement NDCG@p as follows:

$$NDCG@p = \frac{DCG_p}{IDCG_p}, \text{where } DCG_p = \sum_{i=1}^{p} \frac{2^{rel_i} - 1}{log_2(i+1)}.$$

In terms of algorithm tuning, we follow the usual procedure of tuning the hyper-parameters using training and validation sets. Considering the Random Forest based approaches we vary the number of trees ranging from 10 to 1000. We achieved convergence around 300 trees, We also optimized the percentage of features to be considered as candidates during node splitting, as well as the maximum allowed number of leaf nodes. The optimal values were 0.3 and 100, respectively.

For $\text{BROOF}_{\text{absolute}}$, $\text{BROOF}_{\text{median}}$ and $\text{BROOF}_{\text{height}}$, we limited the number of iterations to 500, reminding that the algorithms have an early stopping criterion that prevents further boosting iterations when the error rate exceeds 0.5. On average, our strategies converge at about 15 iterations on the LETOR datasets, and around 5 to 10 iterations on the multi-relevance judgment datasets. An exception was $\text{BROOF}_{\text{gradient}}$ which converged at about 100 iterations for the largest datasets.

Concerning the SVM^{rank} baseline, we favored the use of a linear kernel considering the fact that we verified in our analysis that a polynomial kernel is infeasible on large scale benchmarks such as WEB10K. The cost parameter C was calibrated using the training and validation sets with the explored values: 0.001, 0.01, 0.1, 1, 10, 100 and 1000. For the boosting methods Mart and LambdaMART, we tuned, always considering the validation set, the number of iterations ranging from one to a hundred, with a step of 1, and then scaling it up to 1000 iterations, with steps of 100. For the shrinkage factor of the predictive models, we tested the values of 0.025, 0.05, 0.075 and 0.1. The best found values for the MART and LambdaMART were ensembles of 1000 trees with shrinkage factor η of 0.1. For the AdaRank_{MAP}, $\text{AdaRank}_{NDCG@5}$ and for the RankBoost algorithm, similar procedures were performed in the validation set to configure the number of iterations.

Finally, we performed 5, 10 and 30 runs of the 5-fold cross validation procedure for WEB10K, YAHOO! and LETOR datasets, respectively. The differences in the number of repetitions are due to the size of the datasets and the need to properly address the variance of the results. The reported results on Tables 2 and 3 are the average of all these runs, being the statistical tests applied to these results.

[5]Reminding that, at the time of the writing of this paper, the evaluation tool used in the YAHOO! competition was not available online.

4.4 Results

In this section we analyze our proposals in terms of effectiveness, comparing them to the 7 explored baseline algorithms on the 5 described datasets. The results are reported on Tables 2 and 3.

We start by considering the MAP metric (Table 2). Briefly, the MAP results show that, overall, our proposed framework outperforms or ties with the strongest baselines in all cases. More specifically, with the TD2003 dataset, $\text{BROOF}_{\text{height}}$ outperformed the strongest baseline (RF) considering both statistical tests, with $\text{BROOF}_{\text{absolute}}$ and $\text{BROOF}_{\text{median}}$ as the winners according to at least one statistical test. In this dataset, $\text{BROOF}_{\text{gradient}}$ was statistically tied with the best baseline. Considering TD2004, $\text{BROOF}_{\text{absolute}}$ was considered the top performer amongst the proposed solutions, being tied with the strongest baseline – RankBoost – in this dataset. Regarding the WEB10K dataset, we can see that $\text{BROOF}_{\text{gradient}}$ was the top performer, according to both statistical tests, being superior to MART, the strongest baseline. Finally, in the YAHOOV1S2 dataset all four proposed algorithms were statistically superior to the strongest baseline (RF) according to both statistical tests, whereas in the YAHOOV1S2-F5 dataset $\text{BROOF}_{\text{gradient}}$ was the best approach. In sum, according to the MAP metric, our results clearly show that the proposed instantiations of the Generalized BROOF framework produced very competitive results as the best algorithm, being superior in the majority of the cases (and tying in the others) – a very significant result.

Turning our attention to the NDCG results, reported on Table 3, a similar behavior can be observed: our proposed instantiations are no worse than the strongest baselines in all cases, being superior in the majority of cases. Considering the TD2003 and TD2004 datasets, our solutions were no worse than any baseline, being statistically tied with the strongest one (RF, in both cases). $\text{BROOF}_{\text{gradient}}$ was the best algorithm in the three remaining datasets, according to both employed statistical tests. Furthermore, $\text{BROOF}_{\text{median}}$ was also superior to the best baseline (MART) in the YAHOOV1S2 dataset (according to the Student's t-test), with $\text{BROOF}_{\text{absolute}}$ and $\text{BROOF}_{\text{height}}$ tied with the MART algorithm. Again, this set of results highlights the effectiveness of the proposed approaches.

We now turn our attention to some behavioral aspects of our algorithms, namely, convergence and learning efficiency. In order to better understand the convergence rate of our proposals, we provide an empirical evaluation of our most effective solution (i.e., $\text{BROOF}_{\text{gradient}}$), by analyzing the obtained NDCG@10 as we vary the number of boosting iterations, contrasting these results with the boosting

	Algorithm	Datasets				
		TD2003	TD2004	WEB10K	YAHOOV1S2	YAHOOV1S2-5F
Baselines	Mart	0.192633	0.193744	0.352491	0.559721	0.568821
	LambdaMart	0.165181	0.169605	0.350263	0.5545	0.563694
	RF	$\underline{0.278644}$	0.2522	0.337702	0.563355	0.559019
	RankBoost	0.235189	$\underline{0.255467}$	0.316201	0.544887	0.547524
	AdaRank-MAP	0.2003	0.196801	0.294792	0.413846	0.480190
	Adarank-NDCG	0.121672	0.132435	0.304359	0.540243	0.538514
	SVM-Rank	0.257490	0.220392	0.324552	0.544887	0.551333
BROOF	$\text{BROOF}_{\text{absolute}}$	0.288039_{+}	$\underline{0.263288}$	0.342437	0.565486^{*}_{+}	0.563729
	$\text{BROOF}_{\text{median}}$	0.282427^{*}	$\underline{0.259941}$	0.347665	0.567696^{*}_{+}	0.567284
	$\text{BROOF}_{\text{height}}$	0.285937^{*}_{+}	$\underline{0.259058}$	0.340340	0.564774^{*}_{+}	0.557727
	$\text{BROOF}_{\text{gradient}}$	$\underline{0.280634}$	$\underline{0.252342}$	0.36251^{*}_{+}	0.572918^{*}_{+}	0.57656^{*}_{+}

'$*$': better than the strongest baseline, with statistical significance according to Wilcoxon Test
'$+$': better than the strongest baseline with statistical significance according to Student's t-test
'$\underline{\text{n}}$': statistically tied results considering both tests

Table 2: Mean Average Precision (MAP): Obtained results.

	Algorithm	Datasets				
		TD2003	TD2004	WEB10K	YAHOOV1S2	YAHOOV1S2-5F
Baselines	Mart	0.271274	0.263926	0.4404	$\underline{0.703757}$	0.714763
	LambdaMart	0.224536	0.237338	0.445437	0.69619	0.706287
	RF	$\underline{0.36346}$	$\underline{0.350582}$	0.424498	0.703139	0.702384
	RankBoost	0.31613	0.33399	0.397071	0.682478	0.681796
	AdaRank-MAP	0.271921	0.281035	0.35732	0.51767	0.607867
	AdaRank-NDCG	0.166241	0.182031	0.385761	0.66309	0.664115
	SVM-Rank	0.344177	0.303471	0.399902	0.682478	0.691064
BROOF	$\text{BROOF}_{\text{absolute}}$	$\underline{0.360802}$	$\underline{0.358146}$	0.434964	$\underline{0.70633}$	0.706954
	$\text{BROOF}_{\text{median}}$	$\underline{0.36798}$	$\underline{0.350466}$	0.436284	0.708538_{+}	0.709148
	$\text{BROOF}_{\text{height}}$	$\underline{0.368195}$	$\underline{0.355356}$	0.42882	$\underline{0.70383}$	0.701985
	$\text{BROOF}_{\text{gradient}}$	$\underline{0.368695}$	$\underline{0.348532}$	0.456081^{*}_{+}	0.717271^{*}_{+}	0.725129^{*}_{+}

'$*$': better than the strongest baseline, with statistical significance according to Wilcoxon Test
'$+$': better than the strongest baseline, with statistical significance according to Student's t-test
'$\underline{\text{n}}$': statistically tied results considering both tests

Table 3: Normalized Discounted Cumulative Gain (NDCG@10): Obtained results.

baselines. We here focus on the three largest datasets: YAHOOV1S2, YAHOOV1S2-F5 and WEB10K. Results can be found on Figure 1. As it can be observed, $\text{BROOF}_{\text{gradient}}$ share similar behavior with three explored boosting algorithms, namely, MART, RankBoost and AdaRank-NDCG: the four algorithms show fast convergence rates. The two key differences are: (*i*) our approach is able to achieve significantly better results at the initial boosting iterations and (*ii*) $\text{BROOF}_{\text{gradient}}$ converges to a higher asymptote than the other algorithms. On the other hand, the convergence rate of LambdaMART was significantly slower than the convergence rate of the mentioned algorithms. In sum, $\text{BROOF}_{\text{gradient}}$ enjoys faster convergence rates, with higher NDCG values at the initial boosting iterations and higher asymptote. This is paramount to guarantee practical feasibility of our solution: although high effectiveness is a requirement, achieving such high effectiveness with just a few boosting iterations is key to minimize running time.

Another aspect of direct impact on the practical feasibility of the solutions is to what extent the algorithms are "data efficient". That is, to what extent each algorithm is capable of delivering highly effective rankings with reduced training sets. We evaluate the solutions under this dimension by analyzing each algorithm's learning curve. To this end, we measure the effectiveness of each algorithm as we vary training set size. We randomly sample s% examples from the training set, selected at random. We vary s from 10% to 100%, with steps of 10%. The obtained results can be found on Figure 2. Considering the WEB10K dataset, we can observe a surprising result: $\text{BROOF}_{\text{gradient}}$ is able to outperform all algorithms with just 20% of the training set, even considering the other algorithms trained with larger training sets (including the entire training set). Also, it can be noted that $\text{BROOF}_{\text{absolute}}$ is no worse than the baseline algorithms, even with 10% of the training set. In fact, with about 40% of the training set $\text{BROOF}_{\text{gradient}}$ is able to achieve its maximum effectiveness, whereas for $\text{BROOF}_{\text{absolute}}$ 10% is enough. For the YAHOO datasets, a similar behavior was observed: with about 20% to 30% of the training set our approaches were able to outperform the baseline algorithms (or match, in the case of $\text{BROOF}_{\text{absolute}}$), even considering the baseline algorithms trained with the entire training set. In these datasets, our algorithms were able to achieve maximum effectiveness at 50% to 80% of the training set. Considering the TD2003 and TD2004 datasets, the RF baseline was a bit more competitive to our approaches, exhibiting a similar behavior in terms of effectiveness as the training set size varies. In these datasets, 50% to 60% of the training set was enough to produce the best effectiveness on the TD2003, while 40% was enough to surpass all baselines on TD2004. These findings have also a direct influence on the practical feasibility of our solutions. First, smaller training sets translates to smaller runtimes. Second, obtaining labeled data is critical but also costly. Clearly, being able to produce highly effective models from reduced training sets is an important characteristic of a successful approach.

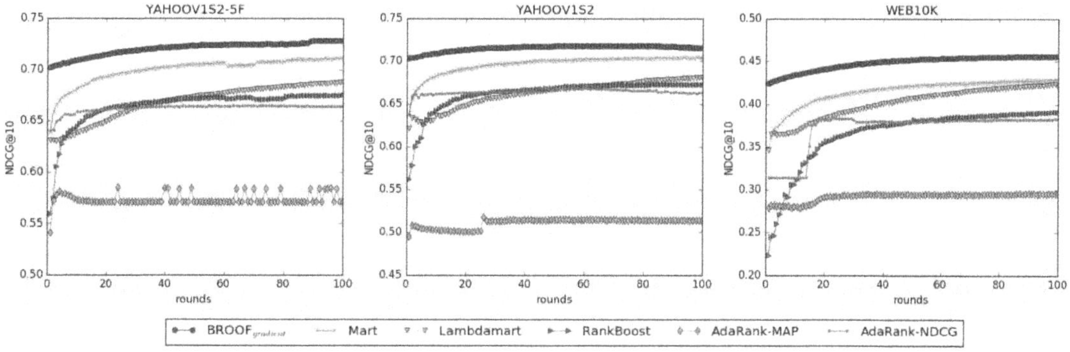

Figure 1: Convergence analysis: NDCG as the number of boosting iterations increases.

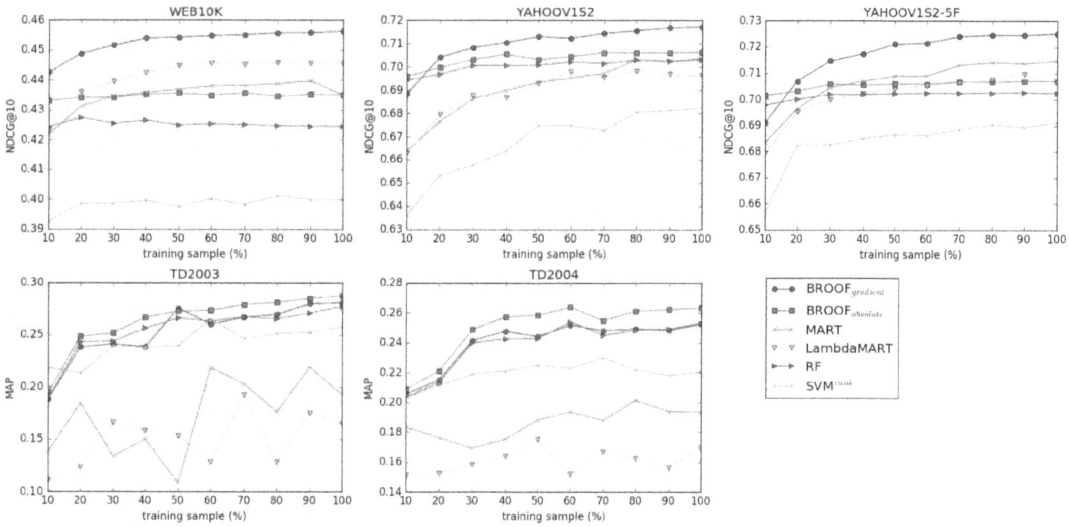

Figure 2: Learning curve analysis for the boosting algorithms.

Finally, we turn our attention to the effect of the use of out-of-bag samples by our approaches. Due to space restrictions, we here focus on $\text{BROOF}_{\text{gradient}}$, considering the WEB10K dataset. We analyze the effect of weak-learner error rate estimation through out-of-bag samples by contrasting it with a variant whose generic function VALIDATIONSET equals to **Train**. The effectiveness of $\text{BROOF}_{\text{gradient}}$ and the mentioned variation, as the boosting iterations go by, can be found on Figure 3. From that figure, it is clear that the out-of-bag error estimation produces more effective results than the simple training error estimate. In fact, for all boosting iterations, the $\text{BROOF}_{\text{gradient}}$ variation with VALIDATIONSET set to **OOB** produces better results than the results obtained with VALIDATIONSET set to **Train**. This highlights the importance of exploiting the out-of-bag error estimates in our proposed framework instantiations. As a final remark, as it can be observed in Figure 3, even the variant that uses the training error rate is able to outperform the explored baselines. This is also an important aspect that highlights the quality of the proposed framework.

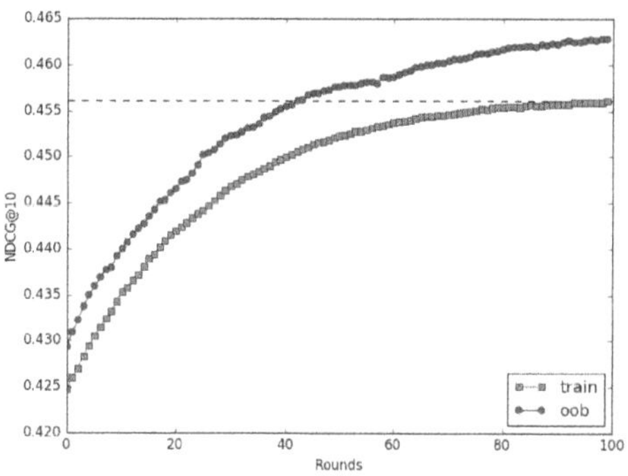

Figure 3: $\text{BROOF}_{\text{gradient}}$: Effect of out-of-bag samples versus entire training set.

5. CONCLUSIONS AND FUTURE WORK

In this work, we propose an extensible framework for L2R, called Generalized BROOF-L2R, which smoothly combines two successful strategies for Learning to Rank, namely, Random Forests and Boosting. Such combination, that uses Random Forests models as weak-learners for the boosting algorithm, relies on the use of the out of bag samples produced by the Random Forests to (*i*) determine the influence of each weak-learner in the final additive model and (*ii*) update the sample distribution weights by means of a more reliable error rate estimate. In fact, the framework is general enough to provide a rather heterogeneous set of instantiations that, according to our empirical evaluation, are able to achieve competitive results compared to state-of-the-art algorithms for L2R. We proposed four different instantiations. Three instantiations closely follows the ideas of a recently proposed algorithm for text classification, namely, BROOF. The fourth instantiation is based on gradient descent optimization, resembling gradient boosting machines. In fact, such instantiation can be seen as a gradient boosted random forests model. As our results show, despite the fact that all the four algorithms provide very competitive results, two of them are consistently the top-performers, highlighting the quality and effectiveness of our proposed framework. Also, our proposals have two properties that are paramount to guarantee their practical feasibility, namely, data efficiency and fast convergence rates.

The space of possible instantiations of the proposed general framework for L2R is rather large. This clearly makes room for further investigations regarding such possibilities. In fact, one can come up with improved instantiations of the framework, by means of extending the set of possible implementations for each generic function composing the framework. This is under investigation. We also plan to study a more comprehensive set of instantiations, in order to build a substantially larger catalog of algorithms based on the Generalized BROOF-L2R to better understand the effects of each choice on model effectiveness.

References

[1] L. Breiman. Random forests. *Mach. Learn.*, 45(1):5–32, 2001.

[2] R. Busa-Fekete, B. Kégl, T. Éltető, and G. Szarvas. Tune and mix: learning to rank using ensembles of calibrated multi-class classifiers. *Machine Learning*, 93(2):261–292, 2013.

[3] S. D. Canuto, F. M. Belém, J. M. Almeida, and M. A. Gonçalves. A comparative study of learning-to-rank techniques for tag recommendation. *JIDM*, 4(3):453–468, 2013.

[4] O. Chapelle and Y. Chang. Yahoo! learning to rank challenge overview. *JMLR - Proceedings Track*, 14:1–24, 2011.

[5] K. Christakopoulou and A. Banerjee. Collaborative ranking with a push at the top. In *WWW*, pages 205–215, 2015.

[6] J. Demšar. Statistical comparisons of classifiers over multiple data sets. *J. Mach. Learn. Res.*, 7:1–30, 2006.

[7] Y. Freund, R. Iyer, R. E. Schapire, and Y. Singer. An efficient boosting algorithm for combining preferences. *J. Mach. Learn. Res.*, 4:933–969, 2003.

[8] Y. Freund and R. E. Schapire. Experiments with a New Boosting Algorithm. In *ICML*, pages 148–156, 1996.

[9] J. H. Friedman. Greedy function approximation: A gradient boosting machine. *Annals of Statistics*, 29:1189–1232, 2000.

[10] P. Geurts, D. Ernst, and L. Wehenkel. Extremely randomized trees. *Mach. Learn.*, 63(1):3–42, 2006.

[11] P. Geurts and G. Louppe. Learning to rank with extremely randomized trees. In *Proc. of the Yahoo! L2R Challenge, held at ICML 2010, Haifa, Israel, June 25, 2010*, volume 14 of *JMLR Proceedings Track*, pages 49–61, 2011.

[12] T. Hastie, R. Tibshirani, and J. H. Friedman. *The Elements of Statistical Learning.* Springer, 2009.

[13] R. Jin, Y. Liu, L. Si, J. Carbonell, and A. G. Hauptmann. A new boosting algorithm using input-dependent regularizer. In *ICML*, 2003.

[14] T. Joachims. Optimizing search engines using clickthrough data. In *ACM SIGKDD*, pages 133–142, 2002.

[15] T. Joachims. Training linear svms in linear time. In *ACM SIGKDD*, pages 217–226, 2006.

[16] A. Karatzoglou, L. Baltrunas, and Y. Shi. Learning to rank for recommender systems. In *ACM RecSys*, pages 493–494, 2013.

[17] T.-Y. Liu. Learning to rank for information retrieval. *Found. Trends Inf. Retr.*, 3(3):225–331, 2009.

[18] C. Lucchese, F. M. Nardini, S. Orlando, R. Perego, N. Tonellotto, and R. Venturini. Quickscorer: A fast algorithm to rank documents with additive ensembles of regression trees. In *SIGIR*, pages 73–82, 2015.

[19] C. Macdonald, R. L. Santos, and I. Ounis. The whens and hows of learning to rank for web search. *Inf. Retr.*, 16(5):584–628, 2013.

[20] L. Mason, J. Baxter, P. Bartlett, and M. Frean. Boosting algorithms as gradient descent. In *In Advances in Neural Information Processing Systems*, pages 512–518, 2000.

[21] Y. Mishina, R. Murata, Y. Yamauchi, T. Yamashita, and H. Fujiyoshi. Boosted random forests. *IEICE Transactions*, 98-D(9):1630–1636, 2015.

[22] A. Mohan, Z. Chen, and K. Weinberger. Web-search ranking with initialized gradient boosted regression trees. *JMLR Workshop and Conference Proceedings: Proceedings of the Yahoo! Learning to Rank Challenge*, 14:77–89, 2011.

[23] L. a. F. Park. Confidence Intervals for Information Retrieval Evaluation. *Australiasian Document Computing Symposium*, 2010.

[24] F. Pedregosa, G. Varoquaux, A. Gramfort, V. Michel, B. Thirion, O. Grisel, M. Blondel, P. Prettenhofer, R. Weiss, V. Dubourg, J. Vanderplas, A. Passos, D. Cournapeau, M. Brucher, M. Perrot, and E. Duchesnay. Scikit-learn: Machine learning in Python. *J. Mach. Learn. Res.*, 12:2825–2830, 2011.

[25] T. Salles, M. Gonçalves, V. Rodrigues, and L. Rocha. Broof: Exploiting out-of-bag errors, boosting and random forests for effective automated classification. In *SIGIR*, pages 353–362, 2015.

[26] R. E. Schapire and Y. Freund. *Boosting: Foundations and Algorithms.* 2012.

[27] F. Schroff, A. Criminisi, and A. Zisserman. Object class segmentation using random forests. In *British Machine Vision Conf.*, pages 1–10, 2008.

[28] A. Severyn and A. Moschitti. Learning to rank short text pairs with convolutional deep neural networks. In *ACM SIGIR*, pages 373–382, 2015.

[29] Y. Shi, M. Larson, and A. Hanjalic. List-wise learning to rank with matrix factorization for collaborative filtering. In *ACM RecSys*, pages 269–272, 2010.

[30] J. Shotton, A. Fitzgibbon, M. Cook, T. Sharp, M. Finocchio, R. Moore, A. Kipman, and A. Blake. Real-time human pose recognition in parts from single depth images. In *CVPR*, pages 1297–1304, 2011.

[31] N. Tax, S. Bockting, and D. Hiemstra. A cross-benchmark comparison of 87 learning to rank. *Information Processing & Management*, 51(6):757–772, 2015.

[32] J. Xu and H. Li. Adarank: A boosting algorithm for information retrieval. In *ACM SIGIR*, pages 391–398, 2007.

[33] Z. E. Xu, K. Q. Weinberger, and O. Chapelle. The greedy miser: Learning under test-time budgets. In *ICML*, 2012.

An Optimization Framework for Remapping and Reweighting Noisy Relevance Labels

Yury Ustinovskiy, Valentina Fedorova, Gleb Gusev, Pavel Serdyukov
Yandex
Leo Tolstoy st. 16, Moscow, Russia
{yuraust, valya17, gleb57, pavser} @yandex-team.ru

ABSTRACT

Relevance labels is the essential part of any learning to rank framework. The rapid development of crowdsourcing platforms led to a significant reduction of the cost of manual labeling. This makes it possible to collect very large sets of labeled documents to train a ranking algorithm. However, relevance labels acquired via crowdsourcing are typically coarse and noisy, so certain consensus models are used to measure the quality of labels and to reduce the noise. This noise is likely to affect a ranker trained on such labels, and, since none of the existing consensus models directly optimizes ranking quality, one has to apply some heuristics to utilize the output of a consensus model in a ranking algorithm, e.g., to use majority voting among workers to get consensus labels.

The major goal of this paper is to unify existing approaches to consensus modeling and noise reduction within a learning to rank framework. Namely, we present a machine learning algorithm aimed at improving the performance of a ranker trained on a crowdsourced dataset by proper remapping of labels and reweighting of samples. In the experimental part, we use several characteristics of workers/labels extracted via various consensus models in order to learn the remapping and reweighting functions. Our experiments on a large-scale dataset demonstrate that we can significantly improve state-of-the-art machine-learning algorithms by incorporating our framework.

Keywords

Learning to Rank; IR theory; Consensus Models

1. INTRODUCTION

The fundamental problem faced by many of the of information retrieval systems is *learning to rank*. The aim of a ranking algorithm is to provide an ordered set of results, e.g., documents or recommendations, in response to a given query. In the last decade, various machine-learning techniques were applied to the construction of such rankers.

SIGIR '16, July 17-21, 2016, Pisa, Italy

DOI: http://dx.doi.org/10.1145/2911451.2911501

In the context of Web search, typically [1], ranking algorithms are trained with the use of supervised methods, i.e., methods employing a labeled set of query-document pairs. This makes labeling such a set an indispensable step in any learning to rank framework. In the classical setting, training and test datasets are manually labeled by professional assessors, who determine the relevance of each result retrieved in response to a given query. To achieve consistency of the labels, professional assessors are usually taught to follow very sophisticated and elaborated instructions. Although this approach provides high-quality training datasets and leads to an accurate evaluation of ranking algorithms, it does not scale well and turns out to be comparatively expensive.

Recent rapid take-up of crowdsourcing marketplaces, e.g., Amazon MTurk[1], provides an alternative way of collecting relevance labels. On these marketplaces, employers post labeling tasks to be completed by a large number of workers for a monetary payment. The human expertise in this scheme turns out to be much cheaper than in the scheme with hired professional assessors. However, labels collected via crowdsourcing have a number of serious shortcomings: (1) crowd workers are usually not provided with detailed instructions like those compiled for professional assessors, since the majority of them would either refuse or fail to follow complicated guidelines; (2) partly due to this, individual workers vary greatly in the quality of their assessments; (3) a large number of workers are spammers, answering randomly or using simple quality agnostic heuristics, see [22].

Label noise is likely to have a negative impact on machine learning algorithms. Traditionally, it is dealt with by various *noise reduction* techniques [6, 18]. For example, common approaches to noise reduction include *cleansing* and *weighting* techniques. Noise cleansing techniques are similar to outlier detection and amount to filtering out samples which 'look like' mislabeled for some reason. With the weighting approach none of the samples are completely discarded, while their impact on a machine learning algorithm is controlled by *weights*, representing our confidence in a particular label. In both approaches, one has to use certain heuristics or assume some underlying model for the noise generation.

In the setting of crowdsourced labeling, one can modify the labeling process in order to gain some evidence for each label being correct. Namely, the employers often: (1) provide facile labeling instructions, much simpler than in the case of professional assessors; (2) place 'honeypot' tasks, i.e., tasks with a known true label; (3) assign each task to multiple workers in order to evaluate and aggregate their answers.

[1]http://www.mturk.com/

The presence of honeypots and multiple labels for each query-document pair in the dataset allows one to use certain crowd *consensus models*, e.g, [5, 12, 23]. These models infer a single consensus label for each task, providing more accurate labels than those generated by individual crowd workers. Consensus models make additional assumptions on the distributions of errors among labels and workers and derive certain quantities that estimate the probabilities of labels being correct. The simplest examples of consensus models are 'majority vote' and 'average score', which assign the most frequent/average score to each query-document pair. In practice, crowd consensus models could be used to purify learning to rank datasets by substituting crowd labels with consensus labels or by discarding particular labels with low confidence in their quality. However, this approach is ad-hoc in its nature: the objective of a consensus model is *accuracy* of output labels, and optimizing the accuracy of labels, one does not necessarily optimize the quality of a ranker, trained on the dataset purified by the consensus model. In fact, our experiments in Section 6 demonstrate that a straightforward utilization of consensus labels within a learning to rank algorithm results in suboptimal rankers.

There is another aspect, which is usually not captured by the existing consensus models. Often, assessor instructions are simplified (e.g., a 5-grade scheme is reduced to a 2-grade scheme) to easier attract non-professional assessors from crowdsourcing platforms. Unfortunately, while such simplification allows to hire and quickly instruct more workers, it also introduces a bias into their judgements, as they become much less precise and expressive. For instance, some workers are more conservative than the others, thus their positive labels might imply higher relevance than the positive labels of workers who assign them less reservedly. We argue that in such cases it becomes important to have an additional pre-processing mechanism for putting crowd labels on the same more fine-grained scale.

To sum up, with the current state of consensus modeling within a learning to rank problem, many questions remain unsettled: (1) Which consensus model out of many should we use for a particular dataset? (2) How to utilize several aspects of 'quality' of crowd workers (e.g., experience, agreement rate with other workers, their parameters of the expertise inferred by the consensus models, etc) at once? (3) How to take into account variance in the workers' interpretation of the assessment instructions and put their labels on the same scale?

To address these questions, we propose a learning framework that automatically assigns to each learning sample (1) its relevance value and (2) its weight, which captures the confidence in this value. These two quantities are modelled as functions of *label features*, which may include the outputs of various consensus models, statistics on a given task, crowd label itself, etc. Our framework trains both functions (one for the relevance value and one for the weight). We assume that there is a background learning to rank algorithm which uses the assigned relevance values and the weights of samples. The proposed framework directly optimizes the ranking quality achieved by this background algorithm on the validation set. We refer to the two training steps as *label remapping* and *sample (re)weighting*.

With this paper we make the following contributions:

1. Utilize various approaches to consensus modeling and noise reduction in a single supervised framework;
2. Adopt the reweighting techniques to the problem of learning to rank with a crowdsourced dataset;
3. Introduce the *label remapping* step which assigns a relevance value to each label.

To evaluate our framework, we use two datasets. The first one is provided by Yahoo! within Learning to Rank Challenge[2] (LTRCD for short). LTRCD is one of common datasets for evaluation of learning to rank algorithms [3]. Since all samples in LTRCD are labeled by professional assessors, we were forced to adapt this dataset to our problem. We simulate errors by randomly corrupting some labels, see Section 6 for details. The second one (referred to as YD) is shared with us by a commercial search engine Yandex and precisely conforms to our problem statement. Experimental results demonstrate that our framework significantly outperforms various competitive baselines.

The rest of the paper is organized as follows. Section 2 reviews prior work related to our approach. The details on the YD dataset are provided in Section 3. Section 4 gives an overview of our framework and provides a rigorous formulation of the optimization problem we are solving. Section 5 describes the solution to this optimization problem in details and discusses possible extensions to a more general setup. In Section 6 we report the results of various experiments, showing that our approach significantly improves our baselines. Finally, in Section 7 we discuss some features of our framework and make recommendations for the directions of future research.

2. RELATED WORK

Reweighting of samples in a training dataset is a well-established method, applied in various contexts in machine learning. It is one of the classical approaches to the machine learning in the presence of noise and outliers, see [18, §3].

Sample reweighting is also extensively used in *transfer learning tasks*, when one tries to use a labeled dataset from a source knowledge domain in order to predict/classify/rank instances in a target domain. The samples in the source and target datasets are often differently distributed, so reweighting techniques are used to reduce this difference. In [8], Garcke and Vanck study inductive transfer with a dataset shift. They suggest supervised (DITL) and unsupervised (KLITL) instance reweighting algorithms. The idea of the reweighting optimization step in our framework is slightly similar to the supervised algorithm DITL, since it also tunes weights in order to improve the quality on the target dataset. However, as opposed to our approach, DITL does not address the problem of noise reduction and does not use any label features. In [4], Chen et al. use feature- and instance- transfer learning for cross-domain learning-to-rank. They propose a heuristic method for reweighting samples in the source set. Namely, the authors train a ranking function on a small portion of the target dataset and apply it on the source dataset. A query in the source dataset is assigned a weight proportional to the number of correctly ranked pairs of documents. This paper also does not deal with label noise and label features. Unlike the transfer learning task, in our case, samples in the source and target dataset are drawn from the same distribution and are represented by the same set of features.

[2]http://research.microsoft.com/en-us/um/beijing/projects/letor/yahoodata.aspx

While our framework solves a completely different problem, on the technical level, one of its optimization parts resembles the weights optimization method proposed by Ustinovskiy et.al. in [20]. This paper reweights clicks of users of a search engine in order to train a personalized ranker. Apart from tackling a different problem, our framework is also different in two important respects. Firstly, besides reweighting, our framework also includes a crucial *label remapping* step, which significantly advances the resulting quality. Secondly, the method from [20] has a serious shortcoming: it is targeted solely at simple linear background ranking algorithms. Whereas our framework is extended to a much wider class of background algorithms, including ensemble methods and neural networks.

As we are going to use labels collected via crowdsourcing, we give an overview of the literature on models for crowd consensus. A usual setting in crowdsourcing is the following: each sample is labeled by multiple workers (and each worker labels several samples), these labels are called noisy labels, and the goal is to infer the best consensus label of each sample, which is referred to as the consensus label. Two popular consensus models are Dawid and Skene model (DS) [5] and Generative model of Labels, Abilities, and Difficulties (GLAD) [23]. Dawid and Skene used latent confusion matrices for workers to model their class-specific mistakes. And in GLAD, the probability that a sample is labled correctly depends on both the worker's expertise and the sample's difficulty. We describe these two models in more details in Section 3.

There has been a number of interesting extensions of these two models. [11] imposed additional priors on confusion matrices and studied Bayesian version of DS model, later [21] extended it to model communities of workers with similar confusion matrices, which is useful in the situation when each worker provides only a few labels. Works [24, 25] extended the DS idea by introducing confusion vectors to encode samples difficulty, and proposed the minimax entropy principle for crowdsourcing. [16] describes a family of flexible consensus models (including DS and GLAD as special cases); models of this family can make use of additional features of samples and workers to model commonality among workers and samples. Another work [15] addresses the problem of learning a classifier when consensus labels are unknown: each sample is represented by a set of features and has multiple noisy labels, and the paper presents an approach to the joint estimation of workers' parameters, consensus labels within a classification problem. Unlike our approach, this method is unsupervised and relies on the fixed noise model for the workers. Similar set-up was used [13], where the authors aim at estimating class-conditional label noise via unsupervised techniques. For other details on crowdsourcing see recent surveys, e.g., [17, 14].

To the best of our knowledge, this paper is the first work that directly employs outputs of various consensus models within a learning to rank framework. In this framework, a noisy label is associated with a set of features, e.g., likelihoods of the noisy labels under various consensus models. In our empirical study, features for noisy labels are generated by the original DS and GLAD models, but any other consensus models can be used similarly.

3. DATA

Prior to formulating the problem considered in this paper, we describe the experimental data in real-world YD dataset. The structure of this data and its features reveal the motivation for the particular problem we are solving and clarify the main ideas behind our approach.

The first dataset consists of 132K query-document pairs. Each query-document pair is assigned three *binary* relevance labels from three crowd workers at a crowdsourcing platform YandexToloka[3]. The use of binary relevance labels allows to simplify assessment instructions and engage a larger number of workers. With these query-document pairs and crowd labels a dataset $\mathcal{X}^{\text{source}}$ consisting of $132\text{K} \times 3 = 396\text{K}$ samples is formed. One sample in $\mathcal{X}^{\text{source}}$ is a query-document pair together with one label assigned by one crowd worker. In particular, the same query-document pair may occur in $\mathcal{X}^{\text{source}}$ with different labels. Besides these query-document pairs, there are 1900 *honeypot* tasks completed by the same workers (each task is completed by several workers). These are query-document pairs labeled by professional assessors with the same instructions. Usually, honeypots are used to detect and penalize spammer workers. Query-document pairs corresponding to honeypots do not get into $\mathcal{X}^{\text{source}}$.

The second dataset $\mathcal{T}$ is collected in a standard manner for a learning to rank task. Namely, every query-document pair in the second dataset $\mathcal{T}$ consisting of 90K samples is judged once by one professional assessor and is endowed with a label, corresponding to one of the relevance classes {*Perfect, Excellent, Good, Fair, Bad*}. This is the dataset intended for evaluation and for supervised tuning of our framework.

Every query-document pair in both datasets $\mathcal{T}$ and $\mathcal{X}^{\text{source}}$ is represented by a feature vector $\boldsymbol{x} \in \mathbb{R}^N$. These are standard *ranking features*, including text and link relevance, query characteristics, document quality, user behavior features, etc. Our framework is quite general and any ranking features could be utilized within it. Hence, particular choice of these features is out of the scope of the paper.

Besides ranking features, the samples in the crowdsourced dataset $\mathcal{X}^{\text{source}}$ are endowed with a number of *label features*. These features comprise numerical information about the worker who assigned the label as well as about the task, and the label itself. Our framework is applicable to any set of label features, however we describe these features in detail, since their employment within a learning to rank algorithm is one of the main contributions of the paper. Intuitively, the purpose of label features is to provide evidence of the crowd label being correct.

To generate features for labels we utilize two classical consensus models. We describe these models assuming binary labeling tasks. For a sample in $\mathcal{X}^{\text{source}}$ let us denote by w the worker who labeled this sample, by $cl^{(w)} \in \{0, 1\}$ the crowd label itself.

Dawid and Skene model (DS) [5].

It is assumed that the ith sample has a hidden consensus label t_i, which is generated by the multinomial distribution with unknown parameters $\mathbf{p} = (p_1, p_2)$: $\Pr(t_i = c \mid \mathbf{p}) = p_c$. Each worker w has 2×2 confusion matrix $\pi^{(w)}$ whose rows describe distributions generating noisy labels for a given value of consensus label. Then a noisy label $cl_i^{(w)}$ assigned by worker w to sample i is generated by the multinomial distribution with parameters $\pi^{(w)}(t_i, \cdot)$: $\Pr(cl_i^{(w)} = k \mid t_i = c) = \pi^{(w)}(c, k)$. Assuming that noisy labels assigned by different

[3]http://toloka.yandex.com/

workers are independent given the value of consensus label and that samples are independently identically distributed, we can define the joint likelihood of observed noisy labels and hidden consensus labels as the product over all samples: $\Pr(\mathbf{cl}, \mathbf{t} \mid \mathbf{p}, \boldsymbol{\pi}) = \prod_{i=1}^{M} p_{t_i} \prod_{w=1}^{|W|} \pi^{(w)}(t_i, cl_i^{(j)})$ (bold characters $\mathbf{cl}$, $\mathbf{t}$, $\mathbf{p}$, $\boldsymbol{\pi}$ correspond to $\{cl^{(w)}\}$, $\{t_i\}$, etc). Then, to find the maximum likelihood estimates for $\mathbf{p}$ and $\boldsymbol{\pi}$ and consensus labels $\mathbf{t}$, we apply the Expectation-Maximisation (EM) algorithm. After this, we are able to evaluate the likelihood of each noisy label:

$$\Pr(cl_i^{(w)} \mid \mathbf{p}, \boldsymbol{\pi}, \mathbf{t}) = p_{t_i} \pi^{(w)}(t_i, cl_i^{(w)}).$$

This consensus model serves as the first source of label features.

Generative model of Labels, Abilities, and Difficulties (GLAD) [23].
Again, there is a hidden consensus label t_i of sample i generated from the multinomial distribution with parameters $\mathbf{p}$. Each worker w has parameter a_w, which is a real number representing the worker's expertise. And each sample i has parameter d_i ranging in $(0, +\infty]$ and representing the sample's difficulty. Then if worker w labels sample i, the probability that a noisy label $cl_i^{(w)}$ is correct is modeled as $\Pr(cl_i^{(w)} = t_i \mid a_w, d_i) = \frac{1}{1+\exp(-a_w d_i)}$. By imposing the same set of assumptions on the labeling process as in Dawid and Skene and applying the EM algorithm, we obtain estimates for $\mathbf{p}, \mathbf{a}, \mathbf{d}$ and consensus labels $\mathbf{t}$. Under this model the likelihood of each noisy label is computed as

$$\Pr(cl_i^{(w)} \mid \mathbf{p}, \mathbf{a}, \mathbf{d}, \mathbf{t}) = \begin{cases} \frac{p_{t_i}}{1+\exp(-a_w d_i)}, & \text{if } cl_i^{(w)} = t_i; \\ \frac{p_{t_i}}{1+\exp(a_w d_i)}, & \text{otherwise.} \end{cases}$$

This is the source for the second set of features that we used for noisy labels.

Besides the outputs of these two models we use several simple statistics on tasks and workers. For a worker w, let $n^{(w)}$ be the number of completed tasks, $n_0^{(w)}$ the number of zero-labeled documents. The complete set of raw label features is listed in Table 1. Given any raw feature f (except $cl^{(w)}$) we form two label features: $f_i \cdot I(cl^{(w)} = 1)$ and $f_i \cdot I(cl^{(w)} = 0)$, where $I(\cdot)$ is an indicator function. In total $M = 1 + 2 \times 14 = 29$ label features are constructed.

Some important details on the dataset are provided in Table 2

1	$cl^{(w)}$	the crowd label assigned by the worker
2-5	$\pi^{(w)}$	confusion matrix of the worker in DS model
6	a_w	worker's parameters in GLAD model
7-8	$\Pr(cl^{(w)} = t_i)$	probability the crowd label is correct under DS/GLAD model
9-10	$\Pr(cl^{(w)} = 1)$	probability of positive label under DS/GLAD model
11-12	$\Pr(cl^{(w)} = 0)$	probability of negative label under DS/GLAD model
13	$\log(n^{(w)})$	logarithm of the number of tasks, completed by the worker
14	$n_0^{(w)}/n^{(w)}$	fraction of negative labels, assigned by the worker
15	$f_{\text{hp}}^{(w)}$	fraction of correctly-labeled honeypots by a worker

Table 1: List of raw label features

$\mathcal{X}^{\text{source}}$	
# of queries	7200
# of query-document pairs	132K
# of samples	396K
# of workers	1720
average # of tasks per worker	233
# of unique honeypot tasks	1900
# of completed honeypot tasks	43300
$\mathcal{T}$	
# of queries	6600
# of query-document pairs (samples)	90K

Table 2: Statistics on YD dataset.

4. PROBLEM FORMULATION

In this section, we start with a general description of the problem we are solving. After this, we restrict the scope to a certain class of machine learning algorithms and provide the rigorous formulation within this specific class of algorithms.

4.1 General setting

As we discussed in the introduction, the subject of this paper lies on the intersection of (1) *learning to rank* and (2) *crowd consensus modeling* problems. The ultimate goal is to train, using the source crowdsourced dataset $\mathcal{X}^{\text{source}}$, a ranking function $\mathcal{F}$ of query-document features. The overall performance of a ranking function $\mathcal{F}$ on the dataset $\mathcal{T}$ is evaluated according to some fixed ranking performance measure $\mathcal{M}$ (e.g., DCG, ERR). This performance measure is calculated with the use of the labels assigned by professional assessors following a different (more complex) grading scheme. Slightly abusing the notation, we will write simply $\mathcal{M}(\mathcal{F})$ for the average of metrics $\mathcal{M}$ over all queries in $\mathcal{T}$, with documents ranked according to the ranking model $\mathcal{F}$.
Remark. Of course, one can use datasets labeled on a crowdsourcing platform both for training and the evaluation of a ranking model. However, in real-life applications, it is crucial to have an evaluation methodology which is as precise and comprehensive as possible. In particular, we want to use a single evaluation scheme for all possible rankers. It is known [10] that evaluation based on the graded relevance is more realistic and accurate. Therefore, employment of high-quality fine-graded assessor labels is essential. This potential difference between $\mathcal{X}^{\text{source}}$ and $\mathcal{T}$ is particularly evident in the experimental part, where we have only coarse *binary* relevance labels in $\mathcal{X}^{\text{source}}$ as opposed to the standard 5-graded relevance labels in $\mathcal{T}$.

The aim of our framework is to utilize the label features (not to be confused with the ranking features), while training a ranker $\mathcal{F}$, to directly maximize a selected quality performance measure $\mathcal{M}(\mathcal{F})$. The particular choice of label features is not essential for our learning framework, so we do not discuss any specialities of crowd consensus models here. Typically, before training a learning to rank algorithm with the use of crowd-labeled source set, one *processes* it in advance to reduce noise among the labels. This processing step may include filtration of samples with unreliable labels,

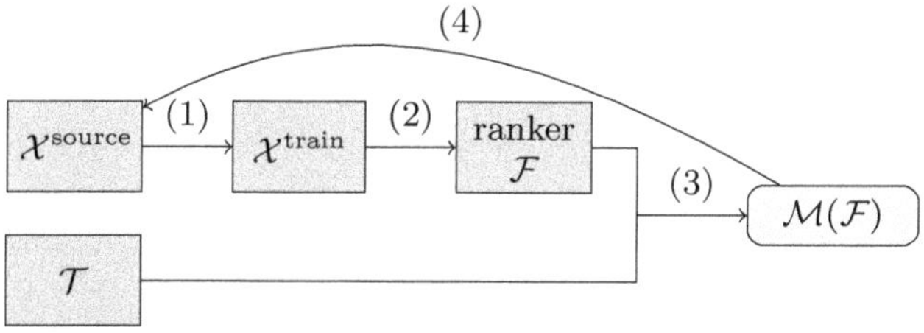

(1) Source dataset processing, $\mathbb{P}$ ← **our focus**
(2) Background learning to rank algorithm, $\mathbb{A}$
(3) Evaluation of the ranker on the target dataset
(4) Feedback for step (1) optimization ← **our focus**

Figure 1: General framework for learning to rank with a crowdsourced dataset.

aggregation of labels based on majority voting among workers, reweighting of samples, etc. To distinguish the initial source dataset $\mathcal{X}^{\text{source}}$ from the one actually used by the background learning to rank algorithm, we denote the processed dataset by $\mathcal{X}^{\text{train}}$.

The outline of the global learning scheme is depicted in Figure 1. We focus on step (1), namely, given a fixed learning to rank algorithm at step (2) and a fixed evaluation metric at step (3), e.g., DCG, we aim at direct maximization of the ranking metric by proper processing of the source dataset $\mathcal{X}^{\text{source}}$. More formally, let $\mathbb{A}$ be a learning to rank algorithm at the second step and let us denote the ranker $\mathcal{F}$, trained on the dataset $\mathcal{X}^{\text{train}}$ via the algorithm $\mathbb{A}$ as $\mathcal{F} = \mathcal{F}_{\mathbb{A}}(\mathcal{X}^{\text{train}})$. Finally, let $\mathbb{P}$ be a processing algorithm, with input $\mathcal{X}^{\text{source}}$ and output $\mathcal{X}^{\text{train}}$. With these notations defined, the optimization problem we are solving is

$$\widehat{\mathbb{P}} = \underset{\mathbb{P}}{\text{argmax}}\mathcal{M}(\mathcal{F}_{\mathbb{A}}(\mathcal{X}^{\text{train}})), \quad \text{where } \mathcal{X}^{\text{train}} = \mathbb{P}(\mathcal{X}^{\text{source}}). \tag{1}$$

We treat this problem as a *supervised* machine learning task. Namely, dataset $\mathcal{T}$ with its editorial labels is used to fit $\mathbb{P}$ by maximizing $\mathcal{M}(\mathcal{F}_{\mathbb{A}}(\mathcal{X}^{\text{train}}))$ on $\mathcal{T}$. To make sense of this optimization problem we have to specify the learning to rank algorithm $\mathbb{A}$ and the class of possible processing algorithms $\{\mathbb{P}\}$ we are solving (1) within. We discuss them in the next section.

4.2 Our approach

Let $\mathbb{R}^N$ be the space of 'query-document features', meaning that every sample in $\mathcal{X}^{\text{source}}$ and $\mathcal{T}$ is characterized by a vector $\boldsymbol{x} \in \mathbb{R}^N$. These are standard ranking features, including text and link relevance, query characteristics, document quality, etc.

In order to solve optimization problem (1) directly by gradient descent, we need to compute the partial derivatives of the output values of the ranking algorithm $\mathcal{F}_{\mathbb{A}}(\mathcal{X}^{\text{train}})$ with respect to the parameters of the processing algorithm $\mathbb{P}$. These derivatives do not necessarily exist and even their finite-difference approximation might be computationally expensive, since it requires additional trainings of the algorithm $\mathcal{F}_{\mathbb{A}}$. However, if there is a smooth closed-form expression for the ranker $\mathcal{F}_{\mathbb{A}}(\mathcal{X}^{\text{train}})$ in terms of the samples and features in the training set, the partial derivatives could be computed efficiently. We are aware of such closed-form expression only for a *linear*, *pointwise* machine-learning algorithm, so from now on we assume that:

- the i-th sample in the training set $\mathcal{X}^{\text{train}}$ is equipped with *relevance value* label l_i and *weight* w_i (as described below, the relevance value and the weight are the outputs of our data processing framework);
- the ranker $\mathcal{F}$ is a *linear function* of 'query-document features': $\mathcal{F}(\boldsymbol{x}_i) = \boldsymbol{x}_i \cdot \boldsymbol{b}$, where $\boldsymbol{b} \in \mathbb{R}^N$ is a column vector of coefficients and '$\cdot$' is the dot product;
- ranker $\mathcal{F}_{\mathbb{A}} = \mathcal{F}_{\text{WMSE}}$, trained via algorithm $\mathbb{A}$, minimizes L_2-regularized *weighted mean square error* (WMSE for short), here μ is the parameter of L_2 regularization:

$$\mathcal{F}_{\text{WMSE}} = \underset{\mathcal{F}|\mathcal{F}(\boldsymbol{x})=\boldsymbol{x}\boldsymbol{b}}{\text{argmin}} \sum_{i\in\mathcal{X}^{\text{train}}} w_i(\boldsymbol{x}_i\cdot\boldsymbol{b}-l_i)^2+\mu||\boldsymbol{b}||^2 \tag{2}$$

At the first glance, the minimization problem (2) appears to be non-conventional, since each query-document pair appears in the sum several times with presumably different labels. However, it, in fact, includes various standard baseline algorithms as special cases. For example, if we set each weight to 1 and each label l_i to the corresponding noisy crowd label $cl^{(w)}$, this minimization problem becomes equivalent to the 'average label' baseline, which predicts the average of labels assigned by different workers to a given query-document pair. Setting some weights to zero is equivalent to discarding corresponding crowd labels, i.e. to data filtration. Similarly, one can implement the 'majority vote' baseline and various weighting techniques within this minimization problem.

Remark It is well known (see [3]) that linear models are significantly outperformed by more sophisticated algorithms, e.g., neural networks, ensembles of trees, etc. In the next section, we show how our framework could be extended to cover these classes of learning models as well.

Let us now discuss two particular problems the processing algorithms $\mathbb{P}$: $\mathcal{X}^{\text{source}} \mapsto \mathcal{X}^{\text{train}}$ should solve. First, as we have discussed, the quality of crowd labeling significantly varies across different workers and tasks. Sometimes, it happens that our confidence in a particular crowd label in $\mathcal{X}^{\text{source}}$ is low, e.g., the worker who labeled this sample makes many mistakes on honeypots, or the label contradicts the two labels from the other workers, etc. In this case, we want it to have less impact on the trained ranker $\mathcal{F}$. In the WMSE algorithm this impact is controlled by *weight* w_i. So the larger our confidence in a label is, the larger should be its corresponding weight. Second, some workers turn out to be more conservative than the others. For instance, imagine workers w' and w'', such that w' assigns a positive label $cl^{(w')}$ only to 'perfect' query-document pairs and worker w'' assigns a positive label to each query-document pair, unless it is completely irrelevant. Clearly, in this case, the positive label of the first worker should have a greater *value*, than of the second. The *relevance value* of a sample for a ranker $\mathcal{F}$, minimizing WMSE, is reflected by l_i.

Recall that by the initial assumptions on the source dataset $\mathcal{X}^{\text{source}}$, its every labeled sample is equipped with an M-dimensional vector $\boldsymbol{y} \in \mathbb{R}^M$ of label features, see Table 1. Motivated by the above two issues, we consider the processing algorithms $\mathbb{P}$ assigning a weight w_i and a *relevance value* l_i to every sample i in $\mathcal{X}^{\text{source}}$, where w_i and l_i are now both functions of the label features $\boldsymbol{y}_i \in \mathbb{R}^M$ (not to be mistaken with the ranking features $\boldsymbol{x}_i \in \mathbb{R}^N$). Namely, let us put w_i and l_i to be sigmoid transforms of $\boldsymbol{y}_i$:

$$w_i = \sigma(\boldsymbol{y}_i \cdot \boldsymbol{\alpha}), \quad l_i = \sigma(\boldsymbol{y}_i \cdot \boldsymbol{\beta}), \tag{3}$$

where $\boldsymbol{\alpha} = (\alpha_1, \ldots, \alpha_M)^T$ and $\boldsymbol{\beta} = (\beta_1, \ldots, \beta_M)^T$ are parameter vectors of weight w and label l functions and $\sigma(x) = 1/(1 + e^{-x})$ is a sigmoid transform, which ensures that all weights and labels fall into the unit interval [0,1]. The computations of weights w_i and relevance values l_i are referred to as *reweighting* and *remapping* steps. The class of the processing algorithms under the consideration forms a $2M$-dimensional family with vectors of parameters $(\boldsymbol{\alpha}, \boldsymbol{\beta})$.

We stress out several important properties of this class of processing algorithms:

1. Sets of samples $\mathcal{X}^{\text{source}}$ and $\mathcal{X}^{\text{train}}$ are essentially the same, i.e., we do not need to explicitly filter out any samples;
2. The impact of an i-th sample on the trained ranker $\mathcal{F}_{\mathbb{A}}$ is controlled by weight w_i. In particular, by setting w_i to zero we completely discard the i-th sample;
3. Labels $cl^{(w)}$ assigned to samples in $\mathcal{X}^{\text{source}}$ by crowd workers might *differ* from relevance values l_i used in the train dataset $\mathcal{X}^{\text{train}}$.

Now let us reformulate problem (1) in terms of an optimization problem for parameters $\boldsymbol{\alpha}$ and $\boldsymbol{\beta}$ of processing step $\mathbb{P}$:

$$(\widehat{\boldsymbol{\alpha}}, \widehat{\boldsymbol{\beta}}) = \underset{(\boldsymbol{\alpha},\boldsymbol{\beta})}{\operatorname{argmax}} \mathcal{M}\big(\mathcal{F}_{\mathbb{A}}(\mathcal{X}^{\text{train}})\big), \quad \text{where } \mathcal{X}^{\text{train}} = \mathbb{P}(\mathcal{X}^{\text{source}}). \tag{4}$$

Since $\mathcal{M}$ is a locally constant function of the values of the ranker $\mathcal{F}$, this is a non-convex and non-differentiable optimization problem. In the next section we adopt well-established smoothing techniques (see [1, 19]) to reduce (4) to a differentiable optimization problem and solve it using gradient descent.

5. ALGORITHM

5.1 Reweighting and label remapping learning framework

We treat optimization problem (4) as a supervised learning task. To solve it directly via gradient descent, we need to compute the gradients $\partial\mathcal{M}/\partial\alpha_j$ and $\partial\mathcal{M}/\partial\beta_j$. Via the chain rule one has:

$$\begin{aligned} \frac{\partial\mathcal{M}}{\partial\alpha_j} &= \sum_{i\in\mathcal{T}} \frac{\partial s_i}{\partial\alpha_j}\frac{\partial\mathcal{M}}{\partial s_i} = \sum_{i\in\mathcal{T}} \boldsymbol{x}_i \cdot \frac{\partial \boldsymbol{b}}{\partial\alpha_j}\frac{\partial\mathcal{M}}{\partial s_i}; \\ \frac{\partial\mathcal{M}}{\partial\beta_j} &= \sum_{i\in\mathcal{T}} \frac{\partial s_i}{\partial\beta_j}\frac{\partial\mathcal{M}}{\partial s_i} = \sum_{i\in\mathcal{T}} \boldsymbol{x}_i \cdot \frac{\partial \boldsymbol{b}}{\partial\beta_j}\frac{\partial\mathcal{M}}{\partial s_i}, \end{aligned} \tag{5}$$

where $s_i = \mathcal{F}(\boldsymbol{x}_i) = \boldsymbol{x}_i \cdot \boldsymbol{b}$ is a score assigned by a linear ranker $\mathcal{F}$ to a sample $i \in \mathcal{T}$. To compute the derivatives $\partial\mathcal{M}/\partial s_i$ we, following the state-of-the-art approach to learning to rank, transform the objective metric $\mathcal{M}$ into a smooth one by a *smoothing procedure*. We have experimented with LambdaRank smoothing by Burges et al. [1] and SoftRank by Taylor et al. [19]. Our experiments have shown that these techniques result in a similar quality, while LambdaRank is a much faster algorithm, so, in what follows, we use only Lambda gradients. In order to alleviate notations, we will write simply $\partial\mathcal{M}/\partial s_i$, implying the LambdaRank gradient.

$\mathcal{X}^{\text{source}}$	dataset labeled via crowdsourcing platform
$\mathcal{T}$	dataset labeled by professional assessors
N	number of query-document features for samples in $\mathcal{X}^{\text{source}}$ and $\mathcal{T}$
M	number of label features for samples in $\mathcal{X}^{\text{source}}$
S	number of samples in $\mathcal{X}^{\text{source}}$
$\boldsymbol{x}_i$	row vector of ranking query-document features of a sample $i \in \mathcal{X}^{\text{source}}$ or $i \in \mathcal{T}$
$\boldsymbol{y}_i$	row vector of label features of a sample $i \in \mathcal{X}^{\text{source}}$
$\mathbb{P}$	algorithm processing raw source dataset $\mathcal{X}^{\text{source}}$ into $\mathcal{X}^{\text{train}}$
$\mathbb{A}$	background learning to rank algorithm, used at step (2) in Figure 1
μ	L_2-regularization parameter of WMSE algorithm
$\mathcal{X}^{\text{train}}$	output of processing step $\mathbb{P}$, used by learning to rank algorithm $\mathbb{A}$
$\mathcal{F}_{\mathbb{A}}$	ranker trained via $\mathbb{A}$
$\boldsymbol{\alpha}$	M-dimensional column vector of weight parameters of $\mathbb{P}$
$\boldsymbol{\beta}$	M-dimensional column vector of label parameters of $\mathbb{P}$
w_i	weight of a sample $i \in \mathcal{X}^{\text{train}}$
l_i	remapped label of a sample $i \in \mathcal{X}^{\text{train}}$
$\boldsymbol{X}$	$S \times N$ matrix of ranking features for $\mathcal{X}^{\text{source}}$
$\boldsymbol{Y}$	$S \times M$ matrix of *relevance value* label features for $\mathcal{X}^{\text{source}}$
$\boldsymbol{W}$	$S \times S$ diagonal matrix with weights w_i
$\boldsymbol{l}$	S-dimensional column vector of labels l_i
$\boldsymbol{b}$	N-dimensional column vector of parameters of a linear ranker

Table 3: List of notations.

To find the derivatives $\partial\boldsymbol{b}/\partial\alpha_j$ and $\partial\boldsymbol{b}/\partial\beta_j$ we need a bit of linear algebra. Let S be the number of samples in the source dataset $\mathcal{X}^{\text{source}}$ and let $\boldsymbol{X}$ be the $S \times N$ matrix with the i-th row $\boldsymbol{x}_i$, representing query-document features of the i-th sample. Similarly, let $\boldsymbol{Y}$ be the $S \times M$ matrix with the i-th row $\boldsymbol{y}_i$, representing label features of the i-th sample in $\mathcal{X}^{\text{source}}$. Finally, let $\boldsymbol{l}$ to be the column vector of labels $\{l_i = \sigma(\boldsymbol{y}_i \cdot \beta)\}$ in $\mathcal{X}^{\text{train}}$ and $\boldsymbol{W} = \operatorname{diag}(\{w_i\}_{i=1}^S)$ to be the diagonal $S \times S$ matrix. Note that, by the definition, datasets $\mathcal{X}^{\text{source}}$ and $\mathcal{X}^{\text{train}}$ have the same feature matrix $\boldsymbol{X}$. We summarize the notations in Table 3.

The minimizer of Equation (2) has the closed-form expression $\mathcal{F}_{\mathbb{A}}(\boldsymbol{x}) = \boldsymbol{x} \cdot \boldsymbol{b}$, where

$$\boldsymbol{b} = (\boldsymbol{X}^T\boldsymbol{W}\boldsymbol{X} + \mu\boldsymbol{I}_N)^{-1}\boldsymbol{X}^T\boldsymbol{W}\boldsymbol{l}. \tag{6}$$

Now set $\boldsymbol{Z} := (\boldsymbol{X}^T\boldsymbol{W}\boldsymbol{X} + \mu\boldsymbol{I}_N)$ and let $\widehat{\boldsymbol{l}} := \boldsymbol{X} \cdot \boldsymbol{b}$ be the column vector of values of the ranker $\mathcal{F}_{\mathbb{A}}$ on $\mathcal{X}^{\text{train}}$. Differentiating the equality $\boldsymbol{X}^T\boldsymbol{W}\boldsymbol{l} = \boldsymbol{Z}\boldsymbol{b}$ with respect to α_j one gets:

$$\begin{aligned} \boldsymbol{X}^T\frac{\partial\boldsymbol{W}}{\partial\alpha_j}\boldsymbol{l} &= \frac{\partial\boldsymbol{Z}\boldsymbol{b}}{\partial\alpha_j} = \frac{\partial\boldsymbol{Z}}{\partial\alpha_j}\boldsymbol{b} + \boldsymbol{Z}\frac{\partial\boldsymbol{b}}{\partial\alpha_j} = \\ &= \boldsymbol{X}^T\frac{\partial\boldsymbol{W}}{\partial\alpha_j}\boldsymbol{X}\boldsymbol{b} + \boldsymbol{Z}\frac{\partial\boldsymbol{b}}{\partial\alpha_j} = \boldsymbol{X}^T\frac{\partial\boldsymbol{W}}{\partial\alpha_j}\widehat{\boldsymbol{l}} + \boldsymbol{Z}\frac{\partial\boldsymbol{b}}{\partial\alpha_j}. \end{aligned} \tag{7}$$

Finally, a little manipulation with Equation (7) yields:

$$\frac{\partial \boldsymbol{b}}{\partial \alpha_j} = \boldsymbol{Z}^{-1}\boldsymbol{X}^T \frac{\partial \boldsymbol{W}}{\partial \alpha_j}(\boldsymbol{l} - \widehat{\boldsymbol{l}}) = \\ = \boldsymbol{Z}^{-1}\boldsymbol{X}^T \mathrm{diag}(\{y_j \sigma'(\boldsymbol{y}_i \cdot \boldsymbol{\alpha})\}_{i=1}^S)(\boldsymbol{l} - \widehat{\boldsymbol{l}}). \quad (8)$$

Computation of derivatives of $\boldsymbol{b}$ with respect to β from Equation 6 is a bit simpler, since only factor $\boldsymbol{l}$ depends on β:

$$\frac{\partial \boldsymbol{b}}{\partial \beta_j} = \boldsymbol{Z}^{-1}\boldsymbol{X}^T \boldsymbol{W} \frac{\partial \boldsymbol{l}}{\partial \beta_j}, \quad (9)$$

where $\partial \boldsymbol{l}/\partial \beta_j = \{y_j \sigma'(\boldsymbol{y}_i \cdot \boldsymbol{\beta})\}_{i=1}^S$

Plugging these expressions into equation (5), we get the derivatives of the objective function $\mathcal{M}$ with respect to parameters of the processing step $\boldsymbol{\alpha} = (\alpha_1, \ldots, \alpha_M)^T$ (and similarly $\boldsymbol{\beta} = (\beta_1, \ldots, \beta_M)^T$).

The algorithm for training the processing step $\mathbb{P}$ is summarized in pseudocode in Algorithm 1. The initial value $\boldsymbol{\alpha}^0 = (0, \ldots, 0)^T$ correspond to the all equal weights (corresponding to $\boldsymbol{W} = 1/2\, \boldsymbol{I}_N$) and the initial value $\boldsymbol{\beta}^0 = (1, 0, \ldots, 0)^T$ distinguishes the label feature $cl^{(w)}$.

Input: Crowdsourced dataset X^{source} and target dataset $\mathcal{T}$ labeled by professional assessors

Parameters: number of iterations J, step size regularization ϵ, parameter of L_2 regularization μ

Initialization: form matrices $\boldsymbol{X}, \boldsymbol{Y}$; set $\boldsymbol{\alpha} = \boldsymbol{\alpha}^0, \boldsymbol{\beta} = \boldsymbol{\beta}^0, \boldsymbol{l} = \{\sigma(\boldsymbol{y}_i \cdot \boldsymbol{\beta}^0)\}_{i=1}^S, \boldsymbol{W} = 1/2\, \boldsymbol{I}_N$

for $j = 0$ *to* J **do**
- $\boldsymbol{\alpha}^{j+1} = \boldsymbol{\alpha}^j + \epsilon\, \partial \mathcal{M}/\partial \boldsymbol{\alpha}$ (see (5));
- $\boldsymbol{\beta}^{j+1} = \boldsymbol{\beta}^j + \epsilon\, \partial \mathcal{M}/\partial \boldsymbol{\beta}$;
- update $\boldsymbol{W}, \boldsymbol{l}, \boldsymbol{b}$, (see (3), (6));

end

for $i \in \mathcal{X}^{\text{source}}$ **do**
- $w_i = \sigma(\boldsymbol{y}_i \cdot \boldsymbol{\alpha}^J)$;
- $l_i = \sigma(\boldsymbol{y}_i \cdot \boldsymbol{\beta}^J)$;

end

Output: $\mathcal{X}^{\text{train}}$

Algorithm 1: Steepest descend optimization of the processing algorithm $\mathbb{P}$.

5.2 Extension to other background learning-to-rank algorithms

So far, the background algorithm considered in our approach (Equation (2)) was assumed to be linear. This is a very strong and non-realistic assumption, since in the vast majority of regression/classification/ranking problems linear algorithms are outperformed by more sophisticated models, e.g., decision trees, ensembles of trees, neural networks, etc. We explain how to modify the learning scheme we have fixed in Section 4 in order to relax the linearity assumption and incorporate some of the more complicated models.

One of the main drawbacks of linear algorithms is their failure to leverage complex dependencies between individual features. To overcome it, we suggest improving algorithm (2) by transforming the feature space in order to make it more tractable for a linear model. To be more precise, let us consider any algorithm $\mathbb{A}$, which trains an *ensemble of weak learners*:

$$\mathcal{F}_{\mathbb{A}}(\boldsymbol{x}) = \sum_{j=0}^{T} f_j^{\text{weak}}(\boldsymbol{x}), \quad (10)$$

where each weak learner f_j^{weak} is a function on the feature space $\mathbb{R}^N$. Note that the class of models in Equation (10) includes boosted decision trees [7], polynomial models, neural networks as its special cases. The model $\mathcal{F}_{\mathbb{A}}(\boldsymbol{x})$ is trivially a linear transform of the T-dimensional vector $(f_1^{\text{weak}}(\boldsymbol{x}), \ldots f_T^{\text{weak}}(\boldsymbol{x}))$.

Let us substitute the initial feature vector $\boldsymbol{x} \in \mathbb{R}^N$ with the new one $\boldsymbol{x}^{\text{new}} = (x_1, \ldots, x_N, f_1^{\text{weak}}(\boldsymbol{x}), \ldots f_T^{\text{weak}}(\boldsymbol{x})) \in \mathbb{R}^{N+T}$. In what follows, this operation is referred to as *feature extension.*

Proposition 1. *Let $\mathcal{F}_{\mathbb{A}}$ be the ranker in Equation (10). Define ranker $\mathcal{F}_{\text{WMSE}}$ (respectively $\mathcal{F}_{\text{WMSE}}^{\text{new}}$) as the solution to the WMSE minimization problem (2) over the initial feature space $\mathbb{R}^N$ (respectively, over the new extended feature space $\mathbb{R}^{N+T}$) with L_2-regularization parameter $\mu = 0$. For a ranker $\mathcal{F}$, let $E(\mathcal{F})$ be the weighted error on the train dataset:*

$$E(\mathcal{F}) := \sum_{i \in \mathcal{X}^{\text{train}}} w_i (\mathcal{F}(\boldsymbol{x}_i) - l_i)^2.$$

Then one has the following bound:

$$E(\mathcal{F}_{\text{WMSE}}^{\text{new}}) \leq \min(E(\mathcal{F}_{\mathbb{A}}), E(\mathcal{F}_{\text{WMSE}})).$$

Proof. By its definition $\mathcal{F}_{\text{WMSE}}^{\text{new}}$ minimizes the error $E(\mathcal{F})$ among all the linear models of the form $\boldsymbol{x}^{\text{new}} \cdot \boldsymbol{b}^{\text{new}}$. Since the rankers $\mathcal{F}_{\mathbb{A}}$ and $\mathcal{F}_{\text{WMSE}}$ both have this form, the required bound holds. □

This proposition demonstrates that, in terms of $E(\cdot)$, the linear ranker $\mathcal{F}_{\text{WMSE}}^{\text{new}}$ trained with the use of the new, extended feature space is at least as good as $\mathcal{F}_{\text{WMSE}}$ or $\mathcal{F}_{\mathbb{A}}$. Although in the general scheme (see Figure 1) we are interested in a different quality measure on a different dataset, this proposition could be seen as an evidence of a possible benefit from the feature extension. In the experimental part we show that feature extension indeed significantly improves the quality of the trained ranker evaluated according to $\mathcal{M}$ on $\mathcal{T}$.

6. EXPERIMENTS

We conduct two sets of experiments. The first series of experiments uses the Yahoo! Learning to Rank Challenge dataset (LTRCD). This dataset is labeled by professional assessors and has neither noisy crowd labels, nor any label features. Hence, LTRCD does not suit our setup as is, so we are forced to simulate label noise and derive some label features. We use this simulated noise to demonstrate the actual weights and relevance values our algorithm is able to learn. There are no large-scale publicly available crowdsourced learning to rank datasets, so for the second set of experiments we use the proprietary dataset YD. This is the dataset described in Section 3 and it is used directly to evaluate various baselines and compare them with our processing framework. In both cases, we use *discounted cumulative gain* measure at positions $k = 1, 5, 10$, denoted by DCG@k [9], as the ranking quality metric. For both the datasets, graded relevance labels are mapped into the standard numerical gains $\{15, 7, 3, 1, 0\}$.

6.1 Simulated experiments

In Section 4.2, we motivated the introduction of the remapping and weighting steps in our framework by highlighting two specific shortcomings of crowd labels: the varying quality among the crowd workers and the inherent ambiguity of any labeling instructions. In the real world, both phenomena are difficult to observe as well as it is difficult to explicitly analyze their influence on the weights and the relevance values learned by our algorithm. For this reason, to illustrate the intuition behind our remapping and weighting steps, we design two simulated experiments with the *known* quality of the workers and interpretation of the instruction. With this setup, we demonstrate the particular label relevance values and weights our processing step learns.

Data.

We use the training and the validating dataset from the Set1 (see [3] for details) in LTRCD as the bases for our datasets $\mathcal{X}^{\text{source}}$ and $\mathcal{T}$. Namely, samples and features in $\mathcal{X}^{\text{source}}/\mathcal{T}$ are the same as in the training/validation dataset in LTRCD; labels in $\mathcal{T}$ also coincide with the ones in the validation dataset, while the labels in $\mathcal{X}^{\text{source}}$ are intentionally modified. Originally, samples in LTRCD are endowed with 5-graded relevance labels $\{4, 3, 2, 1, 0\}$ (corresponding to the gains $\{15, 7, 3, 1, 0\}$ in DCG@k respectively). In the simulated experiments, we treat each sample in $\mathcal{X}^{\text{source}}$ as one task completed by one virtual worker.

In the first simulated experiment, we assume that each worker w assigns a binary crowd label to each sample. This label depends on two quantities: the actual quality of the document, i.e., its label in the initial dataset $l \in \{4, 3, 2, 1, 0\}$, and the worker's *rigor* $r^{(w)} \in \{3, 2, 1, 0\}$. In this case, the worker assigns a crowd label:

$$cl^{(w)} := \begin{cases} 1, & \text{if } l > r^{(w)}; \\ 0, & \text{otherwise.} \end{cases} \tag{11}$$

In simple words, the most conservative workers with $r^{(w)} = 3$ assign the positive label only to the perfect result, the less rigorous workers with $r^{(w)} = 2$ assign positive labels to perfect and good documents, etc. This labeling scheme models a variable interpretation of labeling instructions by crowd workers. Intuitively, one expects that the more conservative the worker is, the higher actual relevance values her positive labels correspond to. To modify the initial dataset $\mathcal{X}^{\text{source}}$ in LTRCD, we assign each worker with a uniformly random rigor $r^{(w)}$ and compute each crowd label according to Equation (11). Moreover, in this experiment, we endow each sample with 4 binary label features:

$$\boldsymbol{y} := \{I(cl^{(w)} = 1 \& \ r^{(w)} = r) \text{ for } r \in \{3, 2, 1, 0\}\}.$$

The idea is that these features will help us to distinguish positive labels of different workers and remap them according to the worker's rigor.

In the second simulated experiment, we model this variable quality among workers. Namely, each worker is assigned with a random value $q^{(w)} \in \{0.0, 0.5, 0.75, 1.0\}$ reflecting her 'quality'. Further, we assume that each worker w makes a mistake with probability $1 - q^{(w)}$. We expect that the higher the quality of the worker, the higher our confidence in her labels and, therefore, the larger weight to the samples should be assigned by our framework. In this simulated experiment, we again endow each sample with 4 binary label features reflecting the quality of the worker:

$$\boldsymbol{y} := \{I(q^{(w)} = q) \text{ for } q \in \{0.0, 0.5, 0.75, 1.0\}\}.$$

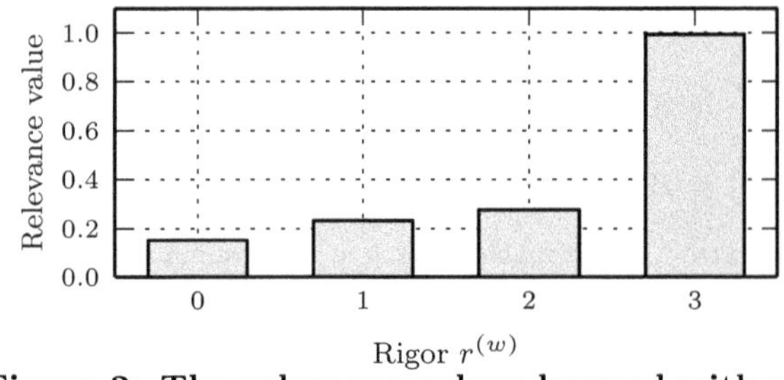

Figure 2: The relevance values learned with our algorithm in Simulated Experiment 1.

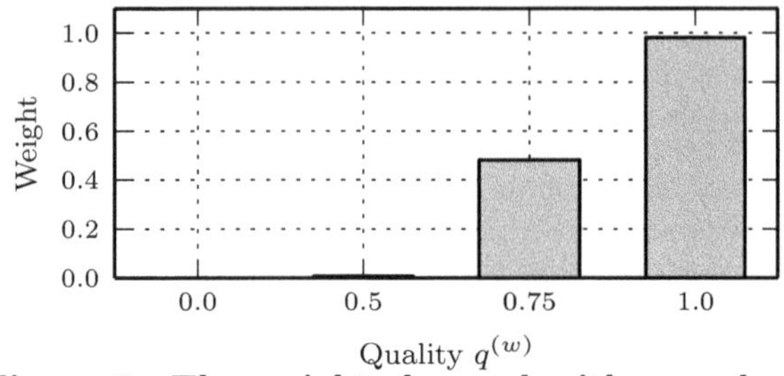

Figure 3: The weights learned with our algorithm in Simulated Experiment 2.

Results.

Simulated Experiment 1. For the first simulated experiment we learn only the relevance values, $l_i = \sigma(\boldsymbol{\beta} \cdot \boldsymbol{y}_i)$, see Equation (3), i.e., in Algorithm 1 only parameters $\boldsymbol{\beta}$ are tuned, while the vector $\boldsymbol{\alpha}$ is fixed. The resulting relevance values for the samples with positive crowd labels are depicted in Figure 2. As we have expected, the relevance value grows monotonically with the growth of the rigor of a worker $r^{(w)}$.

Simulated Experiment 2. In the second simulated experiment we, on the contrary, learn only the weights $w_i = \sigma(\boldsymbol{\alpha} \cdot \boldsymbol{y}_i)$ with $\boldsymbol{\beta}$ in Algorithm 1 fixed. Figure 3 demonstrates the resulting weights as the function of the worker's quality $q^{(w)}$. Again, the weights w_i grow with the growth of worker's quality. Surprisingly, the weight of workers with quality $q^{(w)} = 0.5$ is negligible, implying that the use of the corresponding samples within the background machine learning algorithm does not improve the ranking quality.

6.2 Experiments on the real-world data

Experiment design.

This set of experiments is conducted on the dataset described in Section 3. For a ranker $\mathcal{F}$ and a dataset $\mathcal{X}$, let us define DCG@k$(\mathcal{F}, \mathcal{X})$ to be the average of the values of the DCG@k metrics over all queries in $\mathcal{X}$, ranked according to the values of $\mathcal{F}$.

To evaluate our algorithm along with a number of baselines we perform 5-fold cross validation. Each time, the target dataset $\mathcal{T}$ is randomly split into 3 parts $\mathcal{T}^{\text{train}}$, $\mathcal{T}^{\text{validate}}$ and $\mathcal{T}^{\text{test}}$ on the basis of the unique query id. The part $\mathcal{T}^{\text{train}}$ is used to train Algorithm 1, specifically, to compute the LambdaRank-gradients ∂DCG@k$(\mathcal{F}, \mathcal{T}^{\text{train}})/\partial s_i$. The part $\mathcal{T}^{\text{validate}}$ is used to tune various hyperparameters of the background machine learning algorithm $\mathbb{A}$ and the pro-

Metric	Baselines									Our approach		
	Regression					LambdaMART						
	MV	Av	DS	GLAD	RD	MV	Av	DS	GLAD	**Rw**	**Rm**	**Rw+Rm**
ΔDCG@1	0%	2.49%*	2.58%*	-1.49%	-1.63%	11.61%*	13.03%*	13.56%*	9.53%*	9.76%*	12.46%*	**15.35%**†*
ΔDCG@5	0%	1.93%*	1.66%*	-1.03%	-0.74%	5.38%*	6.47%*	6.49%*	4.5%*	4.99%*	6.06%*	**7.30%**†*
ΔDCG@10	0%	1.58%*	1.38%*	-0.08%	-0.84%	4.27%*	5.16%*	5.32%*	3.64%*	4.05%*	4.80%*	**5.97%**†*

Table 4: Comparsion of various baselines with our framework. * denotes a significant improvement over the majority vote baseline with $p < 0.05$, † denotes a significant improvement over the best baseline with $p < 0.05$.

cessing step, i.e., L_2-regularization parameter μ; J and ϵ in our processing algorithm and the number of extended features T. The output of Algorithm 1 is the dataset $\mathcal{X}^{\text{train}}$ with samples corresponding to the elements in $\mathcal{X}^{\text{source}}$ and weights/labels given by (3). Finally, the third part $\mathcal{T}^{\text{test}}$ is used to evaluate the ranker trained via background algorithm $\mathbb{A}$ on $\mathcal{X}^{\text{train}}$ (our approach) and the baseline rankers.

Due to the proprietary nature of the data, we do not disclose the actual values of DCG@k metrics on the test dataset $\mathcal{T}^{\text{test}}$. Instead, we report the *relative improvement* over the 'majority vote' baseline, described further. We denote this relative improvement by ΔDCG@k.

Baselines.

Since the specific problem we formulate in this paper is novel, there are no baselines intended specifically for our setting. For this reason, we adopt various common approaches to noise reduction and consensus modeling. All of them are used at the processing step (see Figure 1). As the background algorithm for the baselines, we use the proprietary implementation of the Friedman's gradient boosted ensemble of decision trees [7]. We experiment with the standard *pointwise* regression regime and the state-of-the-art *listwise* algorithm LambdaMART [2] both trained on $\mathcal{X}^{\text{train}}$.

We use the following processing algorithms as the baselines:

1. MV, assigning the majority vote to every query-document pair;
2. Av, assigning the average of 3 crowd labels to every query-document pair;

3-4. DS/GLAD, assigning the most likely label to each task according to DS/GLAD model;

Besides these baselines, we experiment with the classical noise reduction technique, *reweighting by deviations* [6, §3.3.2], denoted by RD. This reweighting method does not take into account any label features, instead, it assigns to the i-th sample the weight $\min(1/\delta^2, 1/\Delta_i^2)$, where $\Delta_i = |l_i - \widehat{l_i}|$ is the absolute error of the background learning algorithm on the initial dataset $\mathcal{X}^{\text{source}}$ and $\delta \geq 0$ is a parameter.

Results.

One of the contributions of this paper is the introduction of the feature extension step (see Section 5.2). We first study the impact of the number of additional features T in the extended feature space $\mathbb{R}^{N+T}$. To construct the additional features, the ensemble of the gradient boosted decision trees on $\mathcal{X}^{\text{source}}$ is trained. Each individual tree in this ensemble is treated as a single extended ranking feature. We run remapping and weighting over the extended feature space with $T \in \{0, 100, 200, 400\}$ with $T = 0$ corresponding to no

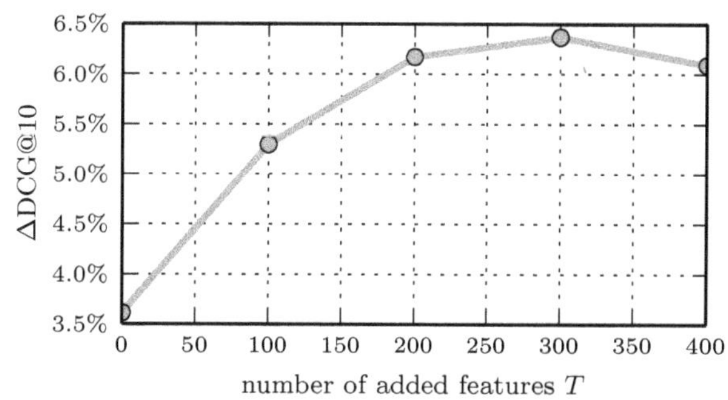

Figure 4: Performance of the feature extension step for different choices of T.

feature extension. All the resulting models are evaluated on $\mathcal{T}^{\text{validate}}$, see Figure 4. In accordance with the evidence provided in Section 5.2, the feature extension improves the quality of the linear background algorithm. However, with the growth of the number of the weak learners added, the background algorithm starts to overfit to the source dataset. Figure 4 suggests that the optimal number of trees is $T = 300$.

Next, using the optimal parameter $T = 300$ tuned on $\mathcal{T}^{\text{validate}}$, we evaluate all the baselines together with our approach on $\mathcal{T}^{\text{test}}$. We consider three versions of our framework: (1) the reweighting approach **Rw** which tunes only parameters $\boldsymbol{\alpha}$ in Algorithm 1; (2) the remapping approach **Rm** which tunes only parameters $\boldsymbol{\beta}$; (3) their combination **Rw+Rm** which tunes both $\boldsymbol{\alpha}$ and $\boldsymbol{\beta}$. Relative improvements of all these methods over the majority vote baseline (MV) are shown in Table 4. The remapping approach **Rm** alone turns out to be significantly better then the reweighting approach **Rw**, and both are outperformed by their combination. Note that, according to all three evaluation measures, **Rw+Rm** statistically significantly (with $p < 0.05$) outperform the best performing baseline, namely, LambdaMART trained on DS consensus labels.

Approach	Feature set		
	Basic + GLAD	Basic + DS	All
Rw	2.12%	3.29%	4.05%
Rm	3.20%	3.81%	4.80%
Rm+Rw	4.01%	5.38%	5.97%

Table 5: Feature sets and their performance.

The performance results of the baselines suggest that DS consensus model suits better for our dataset than GLAD model. We confirm this observation by analyzing the contribution of various types of label features into the model. Let us divide all features into three groups: (1) the features based on DS model; (2) the features based on GLAD model; (3) the remaining *basic* features (corresponding to the features 1,13-15 in Table 1). Feature importance is analyzed through the feature ablation, i.e., we train the whole framework on certain subsets of the full feature set and evaluate the resulting ranker according to ΔDCG@10 metric on $\mathcal{T}^{\text{test}}$. Similarly to our previous observations, on all the feature sets remapping **Rm** outperforms reweighting **Rw** and for all the algorithms GLAD features are outperformed by DS features.

7. DISCUSSION AND FUTURE WORK

In this paper we address the problem of learning to rank with the use of noisy labels, acquired via crowdsourcing, and aggregated with different consensus labeling models. Unlike the existing approaches to consensus modeling and noise reduction, the framework described in this paper leverages the label features (e.g., outputs of various consensus models, features of a worker and a task, etc) directly optimizing the quality of the ranker it produces. Its success prompts one to collect as much information about the worker (assessor), the task and the label as possible, e.g., track the actions of the worker/assessor in the browser, the time spent at a given task, the ranking features of query-document pair, etc. By transforming this information into a large label features vector $\boldsymbol{y}$, we are able to learn more refined weights and relevance labels. These, in turn, being fed to a background machine learning algorithm, will most likely lead to a better ranking function.

Also, we would like to make a remark about the role of the target dataset $\mathcal{T}$ in the framework. As we have discussed above, the samples in the target set are labeled by professional assessors and, therefore, are expensive and rare. Nevertheless, our framework is supervised and requires these high-quality labels. Since commercial search engines have to update their rankings algorithm often, it might be expensive to renew the target dataset every time. Luckily, it suffices to tune the weighting and remapping functions only once. After it, they can be used directly within a background machine leaning algorithm with the new datasets $\mathcal{X}^{\text{source}}$ to retrain the ranker $\mathcal{F}$.

In the future we are planning to apply the remapping framework to other problems. One of the promising directions is learning from the click-through data. Besides that, we intend to develop our algorithm on the technical level by extending it to deal with pairwise preferences.

8. REFERENCES

[1] C. Burges, R. Rango, and Q. Viet Le. Learning to rank with nonsmooth cost functions. *Proceedings of the Advances in Neural Information Processing Systems*, 19:193–200, 2007.

[2] C. Burges, K. Svore, P. Bennett, A. Pastusiak, Q. Wu, O. Chapelle, Y. Chang, and T. yan Liu. Learning to rank using an ensemble of lambda-gradient models. JMLR, pages 25–35, 2011.

[3] O. Chapelle and Y. Chang. Yahoo! learning to rank challenge overview. In *Yahoo! Learning to Rank Challenge*, pages 1–24, 2011.

[4] D. Chen, Y. Xiong, J. Yan, G.-R. Xue, G. Wang, and Z. Chen. Knowledge transfer for cross domain learning to rank. *Information Retrieval*, 13(3):236–253, 2010.

[5] A. P. Dawid and A. M. Skene. Maximum likelihood estimation of observer error-rates using the em algorithm. *Applied statistics*, pages 20–28, 1979.

[6] B. Frénay and M. Verleysen. Classification in the presence of label noise: a survey. *Neural Networks and Learning Systems, IEEE Transactions on*, 25(5):845–869, 2014.

[7] J. H. Friedman. Stochastic gradient boosting. *Comput. Stat. Data Anal.*, 38(4):367–378, 2002.

[8] J. Garcke and T. Vanck. Importance weighted inductive transfer learning for regression. In *Machine Learning and Knowledge Discovery in Databases*, pages 466–481. Springer, 2014.

[9] K. Järvelin and J. Kekäläinen. Cumulated gain-based evaluation of ir techniques. *ACM Transactions on Information Systems (TOIS)*, 20(4):422–446, 2002.

[10] J. Kekäläinen. Binary and graded relevance in ir evaluations-comparison of the effects on ranking of ir systems. *Inf. Process. Manage.*, 41(5):1019–1033, 2005.

[11] H.-C. Kim and Z. Ghahramani. Bayesian classifier combination. In *International conference on artificial intelligence and statistics*, pages 619–627, 2012.

[12] K. Lee, J. Caverlee, and S. Webb. The social honeypot project: Protecting online communities from spammers. In *Proceedings of the 19th International Conference on World Wide Web*, WWW '10, pages 1139–1140, New York, NY, USA, 2010. ACM.

[13] T. Liu and D. Tao. Classification with noisy labels by importance reweighting. *IEEE Trans. Pattern Anal. Mach. Intell.*, 38(3):447–461, 2016.

[14] J. Muhammadi, H. R. Rabiee, and A. Hosseini. Crowd labeling: a survey. *arXiv preprint arXiv:1301.2774*, 2013.

[15] V. C. Raykar, S. Yu, L. H. Zhao, G. H. Valadez, C. Florin, L. Bogoni, and L. Moy. Learning from crowds. *The Journal of Machine Learning Research*, 11:1297–1322, 2010.

[16] P. Ruvolo, J. Whitehill, and J. R. Movellan. Exploiting commonality and interaction effects in crowdsourcing tasks using latent factor models.

[17] A. Sheshadri and M. Lease. SQUARE: A benchmark for research on computing crowd consensus. In *First AAAI Conference on Human Computation and Crowdsourcing*, 2013.

[18] T. Strutz. Data fitting and uncertainty. *A practical introduction to weighted least squares and beyond. Vieweg+ Teubner*, 2010.

[19] M. Taylor, J. Guiver, S. Robertson, and T. Minka. Softrank: Optimizing non-smooth rank metrics. In *Proceedings of the 2008 International Conference on Web Search and Data Mining*, WSDM '08, pages 77–86, New York, NY, USA, 2008. ACM.

[20] Y. Ustinovskiy, G. Gusev, and P. Serdyukov. An optimization framework for weighting implicit relevance labels for personalized web search. WWW '15, pages 1144–1154, 2015.

[21] M. Venanzi, J. Guiver, G. Kazai, P. Kohli, and M. Shokouhi. Community-based bayesian aggregation models for crowdsourcing. WWW '14, pages 155–164, 2014.

[22] J. Vuurens, A. P. de Vries, and C. Eickhoff. How much spam can you take? an analysis of crowdsourcing results to increase accuracy. CIR '11, pages 21–26, 2011.

[23] J. Whitehill, T.-f. Wu, J. Bergsma, J. R. Movellan, and P. L. Ruvolo. Whose vote should count more: Optimal integration of labels from labelers of unknown expertise. NIPS '09, pages 2035–2043, 2009.

[24] D. Zhou, S. Basu, Y. Mao, and J. C. Platt. Learning from the wisdom of crowds by minimax entropy. NIPS '12, pages 2195–2203. 2012.

[25] D. Zhou, Q. Liu, J. Platt, and C. Meek. Aggregating ordinal labels from crowds by minimax conditional entropy. ICML '14, pages 262–270, 2014.

Learning to Rank with Selection Bias in Personal Search

Xuanhui Wang, Michael Bendersky, Donald Metzler, Marc Najork
Google Inc.
Mountain View, CA 94043
{xuanhui, bemike, metzler, najork}@google.com

ABSTRACT

Click-through data has proven to be a critical resource for improving search ranking quality. Though a large amount of click data can be easily collected by search engines, various biases make it difficult to fully leverage this type of data. In the past, many click models have been proposed and successfully used to estimate the relevance for individual query-document pairs in the context of web search. These click models typically require a large quantity of clicks for each individual pair and this makes them difficult to apply in systems where click data is highly sparse due to personalized corpora and information needs, e.g., personal search. In this paper, we study the problem of how to leverage sparse click data in personal search and introduce a novel *selection bias* problem and address it in the learning-to-rank framework. This paper proposes a few bias estimation methods, including a novel query-dependent one that captures queries with similar results and can successfully deal with sparse data. We empirically demonstrate that learning-to-rank that accounts for query-dependent selection bias yields significant improvements in search effectiveness through online experiments with one of the world's largest personal search engines.

Keywords

Personal Search; Selection Bias; Learning-to-Rank

1. INTRODUCTION

In the past several years, click-through data has become an indispensable resource for online information retrieval services. It provides a natural, abundant and continuously renewable source of user feedback. However, despite its tremendous value, click-through data is inherently biased and very noisy. Previous research shows that in order to reliably leverage click-through data one has to account for multiple sources of bias including: position bias [22], presentation bias [33], and trust bias [28]. Therefore, directly using click-through data may result in noisy and biased training data, which will negatively impact the downstream applications [21]. As a result, there has been a great deal of research on extracting reliable signals from click-through data [10].

Previous work has typically focused on click modeling to estimate relevance for individual query-document pairs. For instance, Craswell et al. [11] proposed the Cascade model, in which the conditional probability of a click on a document $\mathbf{x}$ given position i is predicated on the marginal probability of the document $\mathbf{x}$ being relevant to the query and the marginal probabilities of documents at positions $1, \ldots, i-1$ being non-relevant to the query. In order to estimate these marginals, the click models often assume access to large quantities of click data for each document $\mathbf{x}$ given the query [8, 11, 15]. Such models have generally proven to be successful in the context of web search, where this assumption holds. However, it is less clear how they can be applied in search scenarios where click data is highly sparse.

One such scenario that is the focus of this paper is *personal search*. Personal search is an important and well studied information retrieval task with applications such as email search [6], desktop search [13], and, most recently, on-device search [23]. One important difference between personal and web search is that in the personal search scenario each user has access only to their own *private* document corpus (e.g., emails, files, or mobile application data). Therefore, the vast majority of the existing click models that learn click probabilities from large quantities of clicks for individual query-document pairs are not applicable in the personal search scenario.

Another important challenge in the context of personal search is the collection of explicit relevance judgments. Collection of TREC-like document relevance judgments by third party raters (that are commonly used in other information retrieval tasks) such as LETOR data set [29] are difficult to obtain due to privacy restrictions. In addition, since each user will have their own unique set of information needs and documents that evolve over time (e.g., new emails arrive every day), explicit relevance judgments may be prohibitively costly to maintain. Therefore, development of ranking models in general, and specifically learning-to-rank models [26] that utilize click-through data as a *noisy and biased* source of relevance data becomes essential for personal search.

In this paper, we study the the problem of learning-to-rank from click data in personal search. Different from the majority of past click modeling work whose focus is on estimating the relevance for individual query-document pairs, we propose a novel *selection bias* problem in the context of the learning-to-rank from click data. The basic idea of the

SIGIR '16 July 17-21, 2016, Pisa, Italy

ACM ISBN 978-1-4503-4069-4/16/07.
DOI: http://dx.doi.org/10.1145/2911451.2911537

selection bias problem is that queries are under-sampled to different extents and thus biased when click data is collected to learn ranking functions. We propose several methods to estimate this bias. We begin with a *global* bias model and refine it to a *segmented* bias model. We show that such a segmented bias model gives rise to a general framework that defines a *query-dependent* bias, where every query (and its associated result set) can be associated with a potentially different bias model. This general query-dependent framework is especially powerful in the personal search scenario as it allows accurate bias estimation without explicit access to a large number of clicks for any given query-document pair. To the best of our knowledge, this is the first study that both proposes a theoretical framework for eliminating selection bias in personal search and provides an extensive empirical evaluation using large-scale live experiments.

Our primary contributions of this paper can be summarized as follows:

- We propose the problem of selection bias and address it when applying learning-to-rank to click data.
- We propose several novel bias prediction methods, including a query-dependent model that does not need a large quantity of click data for any given query-document pair.
- We propose a novel, unbiased and theoretically sound offline evaluation methodology for our problem.
- We verify the effectiveness of the proposed methods in the context of personal search through rigorous offline experiments and large-scale online experiments.

The remainder of the paper is organized as follows. In Section 2, we review previous related work. Our problem is formally defined in Section 3. Different methods of quantifying selection bias are described in Section 4. We present our extensive experimental study and our evaluation methodology in Section 5. Finally, we conclude and discuss future work in Section 6.

2. RELATED WORK

There is an abundance of prior work on interpreting clicks as implicit feedback from users. One of the seminal papers in the field by Joachims et al. [22] evaluates the reliability of click-through signals via a user study. The overall conclusion of the study is that clicks are indeed useful for implicit feedback interpretation as long as certain biases are accounted for, including "trust bias" (commonly referred to as "position bias" in later work) that leads to more clicks on higher-ranked results, and "quality bias" in which the click behavior is influenced by the overall quality of the ranked list.

Joachims et al. [22] also proposed five simple strategies to eliminate these biases, including the CLICK > SKIP ABOVE strategy, which gave rise to the well-known Cascade model [11]. Later work also introduced a variety of click modeling techniques including, among many others, a dynamic Bayesian network click model [8], click chain model [17], session utility model [14], whole page click model [9], multiple browsing model [15], and a general click model [36]. A recent survey by Chuklin et al. [10] provides a good overview of the latest advances in the field.

While both click models in prior work and selection bias estimation presented in this paper focus on deriving useful implicit feedback from click-through data, there are several important differences. First, while the majority of the past click modeling work focuses on estimating the degree of relevance between a query and a document, the main goal of this paper is to study the selection bias problem in which click data used in learning-to-rank may drift away from the true underlying distribution. Second, the existing click models assume that a sufficient amount of click data is available for each query-document pair in each position to reliably train the model parameters. While this assumption holds in the web search setting, it is not feasible in domains like desktop search, email search or enterprise search, where each user might have access to a different set of documents, and it is impossible to leverage the "wisdom of the crowds" to aggregate clicks across users. Third, the click models are generally evaluated using the perplexity between the estimated and observed clicks [9, 15]. In contrast, we directly evaluate the ranking effectiveness of our methods through offline evaluation and online live experiments.

Click data is extensively used in sponsored search where the main goal is to predict the click-through rate for ads (e.g., [30, 36]). Noticeably, our selection bias estimation methods are related to the position bias model in [30]. The main difference is that we use the estimated bias to address the selection bias problem, while the bias was used as the expected ads impressions when computing the click-through rate of ads using data from multiple positions. Furthermore, we also propose more advanced query-dependent bias models that are more tractable even in scenarios where training data can be scarce due to small sample sizes, low search volume or personal document collections.

Our bias estimation models rely on the randomized experimental data. Order randomization removes the position biases that are inherent to click data, and therefore one can view the proposed models as propensity score [31] estimates. Furthermore, randomized data is the basis for our proposed unbiased offline evaluator. Similar evaluation methodologies were proposed by Li et al. in prior work [24, 25]. The difference is that we also use the randomized data for selection bias estimation to improve ranking functions, which is not the case in the past work.

Order randomization also eliminates, to a certain degree, the selection bias inherent in many information retrieval applications that employ pooling of top retrieved results [27]. Previous work [5] proposed methods to avoid the selection bias in TREC-style evaluation settings. However, such approaches do not easily extend to the online evaluation case, which is addressed in this work.

The methods proposed in this paper can also be viewed as a novel extension of sample selection bias correction methods, which are well-studied in the context of regression and classification [20, 34, 32], in the online learning-to-rank setting. In contrast to previously proposed learning-to-rank models that make explicit assumptions about user behavior [19] or use heuristic-based method for document selection [1], we learn the selection bias directly from experimental data.

3. PROBLEM FORMULATION

In this section, we introduce the selection bias problem for learning-to-rank in personal search scenarios. We begin by briefly reviewing the general setting of learning-to-rank.

3.1 Learning-to-Rank

Let $Q = (q, \{\mathbf{x}_1, ..., \mathbf{x}_n\})$ denote a query string q and its set of result documents. We write $\mathbf{x} \in Q$ to indicate that $\mathbf{x}$ is in the result set of Q. Let $P(Q)$ denote the probability of observing query Q, based on the underlying distribution of queries in the universe $\mathcal{Q}$ of all possible queries that users can issue together with all possible result combinations. The goal of learning-to-rank is to find a scoring function $f(\mathbf{x})$ that can minimize the loss function defined as:

$$\mathrm{L}(f) = \int_{Q \in \mathcal{Q}} l(Q, f)\,\mathrm{d}P(Q) \qquad (1)$$

where $l(Q, f)$ is the incurred loss of scoring function f applied to query Q. Let $\mathbf{x}_i \succ_Q \mathbf{x}_j$ denote all pairs $\mathbf{x}_i, \mathbf{x}_j$ of result documents in Q for which $\mathbf{x}_i$ is more relevant than $\mathbf{x}_j$. An example of a pair-wise loss function used in [35] is defined as:

$$l(Q, f) = \sum_{\mathbf{x}_i \succ_Q \mathbf{x}_j} \max(0, f(\mathbf{x}_j) - f(\mathbf{x}_i))^2 \qquad (2)$$

The intuition behind this loss function is to penalize the out-of-order pairs when ranked by f.

In practice, the distribution of queries in $\mathcal{Q}$ is is unknown and the empirical loss defined over a uniformly random sample $\mathcal{U} = \{Q \in \mathcal{Q} : Q \sim P(Q)\}$ is used as the objective function for learning.

$$\mathrm{L}_{\mathcal{U}}(f) = \frac{1}{|\mathcal{U}|} \sum_{Q \in \mathcal{U}} l(Q, f) \qquad (3)$$

Most learning-to-rank algorithms differ in how the loss function $l(Q, f)$ is defined [26]. Generally, the state-of-the-art loss functions are pair-wise or list-wise. Practically, pair-wise loss functions tend to be more efficient for training and have been widely adopted by large search engines [4, 35]. Thus, in the rest of the paper, we make the assumption that a pair-wise loss function (e.g., Eq 2) is being used. However, it is important to point out that the methods described in this paper are general enough to be applied to list-wise loss functions as well.

3.2 Selection Bias Problem

The data set $\mathcal{U}$ in Eq 3 is the training data used to learn the scoring function $f(\mathbf{x})$. There are two commonly used approaches to obtain relevance estimates for $\mathcal{U}$. One way is to sample a set of queries and ask human raters to *explicitly* judge the relevance of the retrieved documents. The other way is to collect *implicit* relevance judgments such as click-through data. The click-through data approach has attracted the attention of the research community [21], as it is much cheaper to obtain than human-judged data, especially for major search engines. However, as we mentioned before, click data is biased and very noisy. For example, because of *position bias*, simple click counts can not be used directly to estimate relevance. A great deal of previous work (see Section 2) focuses on overcoming such bias to infer actual (or unbiased) relevance. Our focus is on the more general *selection bias* problem that arises when using click-through data to train learning-to-rank models.

Observation 1 *When using click-through data for learning-to-rank, queries without clicks provide no useful information when optimizing pair-wise loss functions.*

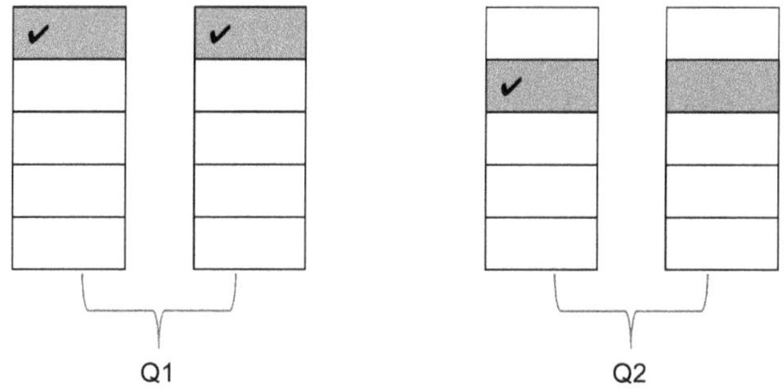

Figure 1: An illustration of selection bias in click data. The shaded documents are the relevant ones. A check mark means the document is clicked.

For example, consider Eq 2. When there are no clicks for query Q, the set $\mathbf{x}_i \succ_Q \mathbf{x}_j$ is empty since there is no way to derive preferences between any pairs of documents. Such an observation can be generalized to list-wise loss functions as well. In the following, we focus on the collection of queries with clicks and use $\mathcal{S}$ to denote this collection.

Observation 2 *The collection of queries $\mathcal{S}$ is biased. Formally, let $\hat{P}(Q)$ denote the probability mass of query Q in $\mathcal{S}$, then $\hat{P}(Q) \neq P(Q)$.*

We use an example to better explain this observation. In Figure 1, we have two queries Q_1 and Q_2 that both have equal probability of being issued by users, i.e., $P(Q_1) = P(Q_2)$ as they have equal probability in $\mathcal{U}$. The relevant document for Q_1 is at position 1 and is clicked every time the query is issued. On the contrary, the relevant document for Q_2 is at position 2 and is clicked half of the time when the query is issued. Thus, $\hat{P}(Q_2) = \frac{1}{2}\hat{P}(Q_1)$ in $\mathcal{S}$, which helps illustrate how selection bias may arise in click data. The problem illustrated in this example is rooted at the commonly known *position bias* and confirmed by eye tracking studies [22, 30] as well, which found that the users are less likely to see, and hence click on, lower-ranked documents.

3.3 Inverse Propensity Weighting

Selection bias is a widely known problem in many other scientific communities, such as the health care field in which the problem arises in clinical trial studies [31]. Many methods such as propensity matching, inverse propensity weighting, and doubly robust estimation have been applied in online settings [7] with the goal of comparing the effect of a treatment *vs.* its control (e.g., showing *vs.* not showing the ad). Some methods, including propensity matching, are specifically designed for comparison: given any individual in the treatment group, match it with another individual in the control group in the sense of their propensity scores being equal; the effect is obtained as the difference between the average of the treatment group and the matched individuals from the control group. It is not immediately clear how to adapt these methods to our use-case.

On the other hand, the inverse propensity weighting approach can easily be adopted to help overcome selection bias for learning-to-rank. With inverse propensity weighting, $\hat{P}(Q)$ is known as the *propensity score* of Q. Let $w_Q = P(Q)/\hat{P}(Q)$, i.e. the ratio between the probability of Q appearing in $\mathcal{U}$ and the probability that Q actually appears in

$\mathcal{S}$. Then the empirical loss function becomes:

$$\mathrm{L}_{\mathcal{S}}(f) = \frac{1}{|\mathcal{S}|}\sum_{Q\in\mathcal{S}}\frac{P(Q)}{\hat{P}(Q)}l(Q,f) = \frac{1}{|\mathcal{S}|}\sum_{Q\in\mathcal{S}} w_Q \cdot l(Q,f)$$

To the best of our knowledge, our work is the first to generally study selection bias to improve the effectiveness of learning-to-rank models. The problem of selection bias is especially important in the scenario of personal search where the personalized nature of information needs strongly biases the available training data.

To apply selection bias in practice, the primary challenge becomes estimating the inverse propensity weights w_Q. An open question is also whether such a weighting approach will have a significant impact on the effectiveness of learning-to-rank models. We address this challenge and answer this question in the following sections.

4. PROPOSED METHODS

Before we describe different methods of inverse propensity weighting estimation, we briefly describe our application scenario and the data set used to quantify the bias.

Application Scenario. Our application is a search engine for one of the world's largest commercial email and cloud file storage services. Given a query, the search engine provides instant results (i.e., the results refresh as the user types). These instant results provide an efficient way for the user to examine the results. There are up to n instant results *with no* pagination. The results are retrieved from a personal corpus (e.g. emails or cloud storage files) and therefore are generally unique to the user. Once the user detects a relevant result and clicks on it, the clicked document is immediately opened in the browser.

Our click data is obtained exclusively from the instant results. Therefore, for each issued query, there will be either no click or exactly one click. In the rest of the paper, we study the selection bias problem in this setting. While the methods presented here can easily be extended to the web search setting, it is beyond the scope of the current study.

Result Randomization. In order to quantify the position bias, which will be used for inverse propensity weighting estimation, we employ result randomization and collect user click data on the randomized result sets. Specifically, given a ranked result list of n documents returned for some query, instead of showing the original list, we permute the results uniformly at random and present the shuffled list to a small fraction of end users. We denote the collected randomized data by $\mathcal{R}$. As a special case, when $n = 2$, the randomization reduces to the previously proposed FairPairs algorithm [11, 33].

In the rest of this section, we present different methods to quantify the selection bias using the collected randomized data.

4.1 Global Bias Model

The global bias model can be viewed as the standard position bias model [11, 30]. It assumes that the bias is a function of the position within the ranked list itself. Formally, let $c^Q_{\mathbf{x}i}$ denote the probability of receiving a click when a document $\mathbf{x}$ is shown at position i for query Q, $r^Q_{\mathbf{x}}$ be the probability of relevance of $\mathbf{x}$ to Q, and b_i be the bias at position i (meaning how likely a user is to examine the document

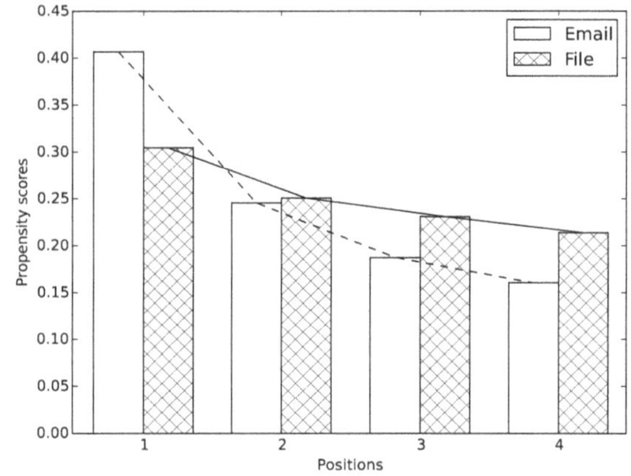

Figure 2: The position bias propensity scores for user emails and cloud storage files.

at this position), then it follows that:

$$c^Q_{\mathbf{x}i} = r^Q_{\mathbf{x}} \cdot b_i$$

Our goal is to estimate b_i for $1 \le i \le n$. Given query Q, $P(\mathbf{x}|Q,i)$ denotes the probability of showing result $\mathbf{x} \in Q$ at position i. In the randomized data, the probability of showing a given result $\mathbf{x} \in Q$ is the same for all positions, i.e., $P(\mathbf{x}|Q,i_1) = P(\mathbf{x}|Q,i_2)$ for all $1 \le i_1, i_2 \le n$. Thus, given Q, for all $1 \le i_1, i_2 \le n$:

$$\int_{\mathbf{x}\in Q} r^Q_{\mathbf{x}}\, \mathrm{d}P(\mathbf{x}|Q,i_1) = \int_{\mathbf{x}\in Q} r^Q_{\mathbf{x}}\, \mathrm{d}P(\mathbf{x}|Q,i_2)$$

Hence,

$$b_i = \frac{\sum_{Q\in\mathcal{R}}\int_{\mathbf{x}\in Q} c_{\mathbf{x}i}\, \mathrm{d}P(\mathbf{x}|Q,i)}{\sum_{Q\in\mathcal{R}}\int_{\mathbf{x}\in Q} r_{\mathbf{x}}\, \mathrm{d}P(\mathbf{x}|Q,i)} \propto \sum_{Q\in\mathcal{R}}\int_{\mathbf{x}\in Q} c_{\mathbf{x}i}\, \mathrm{d}P(\mathbf{x}|Q,i),$$

which is the total number of clicks at position i in the randomized data $\mathcal{R}$. In our application, every query in $\mathcal{S}$ has a single click. Let i be the clicked position for Q. Then b_i is proportional to the ratio between the probability of Q appearing in $\mathcal{S}$ and the probability of Q in the uniformly sampled collection $\mathcal{U}$, i.e., $\hat{P}(Q)/P(Q)$, and thus

$$w_Q = \frac{P(Q)}{\hat{P}(Q)} \propto \frac{1}{b_i}$$

We now show some empirical data for the global bias model. We ran our randomization experiments for two document corpora (user emails and cloud storage files) and collected their data. We set $n = 4$, normalize all b_i so that $\sum_i b_i = 1$, and plot the normalized b_i values in Figure 2. As the results show, there are clearly position biases in both the email corpus and the cloud file storage corpus. For example, b_1 in the email corpus is about 0.40 but b_4 is about 0.15, confirming the strong bias of clicking top positions. More interestingly, Figure 2 also shows that the emails and the cloud storage files have very different bias values: the bias for files is much more flat than that of the emails.

4.2 Segmented Bias Model

The global bias model quantifies the position bias solely based on the clicked position, which is a rather coarse estimate. Most of past work does not go beyond this. However, motivated by the bias difference shown in Figure 2, it is possible that even within a single document corpus (e.g., email), different segments of queries have different position biases. We thus propose a more fine-grained model called the *segmented bias model.*

The basic idea of the segmented bias model is to partition queries into a few segments and then apply the global position bias model separately within each segment. Thus, we have a specific bias model for each segment. There may be multiple application-specific ways of segmenting queries such as using a query classifier. In our application, we focus on the email corpus from now on, and rely on the categories or labels assigned to each email. There are several such labels available in our corpus such as *Promotional* or *Social.* Each email can be associated with multiple labels[1]. There are multiple emails in the result list for each query and our goal is to select a single label and treat it as the segment for the query.

Inspired by the inverse document frequency (IDF) metric, we compute the inverse query frequency (IQF) for each label. For a label t,

$$IQF(t) \propto \frac{1}{|\{Q : t \in Q\}|}$$

where $t \in Q$ means that label t is attached to some email retrieved for query Q and $|\{Q : t \in Q\}|$ is the total number of queries that have label t attached in the randomized data. Then the label $t(Q)$ of a query Q is:

$$t(Q) = \arg\max_{t \in Q}\{IQF(t)\}$$

A by-product is that this creates segments with more balanced size. Given all the queries labelled by t, we can then estimate the position bias b_i^t for this segment. Thus, for query Q, its inverse propensity weighting becomes:

$$w_Q \propto \frac{1}{b_i^{t(Q)}}$$

where i is the clicked position of Q. Though simple, we find that this method is quite effective in our experiments.

4.3 Generalized Bias Model

The segmented model goes a step further to model the bias in a more fine-grained manner. A natural question is how to generalize this even further. For example, is it possible to have a query-dependent bias model? In other words, each query can potentially have different position biases. Due to the large number of unique queries, such a formulation seems intractable. However, as we show in this section, result randomization makes it possible to formulate a generalized *query-dependent* bias model.

Specifically, to estimate the position bias for query Q, suppose that we can present a randomly shuffled list of documents every time the query is issued and that user clicks are independent. A similar approach to the global bias model can be applied on the randomized data specifically for query Q. However, this is not practically feasible for the following reasons. First, to be able to accurately estimate the position bias for the query Q, hundreds or thousands of data points are needed. This means most queries will be filtered out because of data sparseness. Second, in the private search scenario, as discussed here, documents are unique to an individual user. Even for the same query string, the retrieved documents will differ across users. In order to collect sufficient data for a query, we need to show different randomized results for the same user from time to time. This will not only annoy the users, but also miss the purpose of data randomization since the data independence assumption will be violated. Thus, the challenge is how to tackle the following prediction problem.

Definition 1 (Position Bias Prediction) *Given a query* $Q = (q, \{\mathbf{x}_1, ..., \mathbf{x}_n\})$*, the problem of* Position Bias Prediction *is to estimate the click probability at each position* i $(1 \leq i \leq n)$ *if we show the set of documents in a uniformly random order, specifically for* Q.

Recall that we have a set of queries in the randomized data. To solve the problem above, we propose a learning-based approach using multi-class logistic regression. We have n positions and thus n classes in the regression. For each query, we seek to estimate the probability of the query belonging to each class. Thus, we construct the training data from the randomized data and describe our approach as follows:

- **Labels**: For each query instance in the randomized data, we have the clicked position i. The label of this instance is class i. We use binary logistic regression as our algorithm and this query becomes a positive training example for class i and a negative example for all other classes.

- **Features**: For each query Q, we can construct a feature vector $\mathbf{v}(Q)$. In our setting, a feature can be query-dependent or user-dependent. For a feature which depends on documents, the feature should only depend on the "set" of retrieved documents, without dependency on the actual order in the randomized data. For example, $t(Q)$ in the segmented bias model is such a feature that only depends on the "set" of the emails.

- **Training**: We train n logistic regression models, each for a single position, based on the feature vectors and positive/negative training examples defined above. The logistic regression model for position i is parameterized by a vector β_i. For a feature vector $\mathbf{v}(Q)$,

$$b_i^Q = \frac{1}{1 + \exp(\beta_i \cdot \mathbf{v}(Q))} \quad (4)$$

  The parameter β_i can be obtained by maximizing the likelihood on the training data.

- **Prediction**: Given a query with its features, we can apply these n models and obtain n prediction values based on Eq 4. A value corresponding to position i is the click probability when the results are shown uniformly randomly and thus the position bias.

We call the above the *generalized bias model.* Indeed, both global and segmented models are special cases in this generalized bias model.

Proposition 1 *When the feature vector for each query has a single constant element* 1*, the generalized bias model is reduced to the global bias model.*

[1]The labeling algorithm itself is out of the scope of the paper, but the reader may refer to Grbovic et al. [16] or Bekkerman [2] for some prior work on the subject.

Proof Sketch. Let c_i denote the total number of clicks on position i and $C = \sum_i c_i$. When the feature vector for each query has a single constant element 1, b_i^Q only depends on i and the log likelihood of b_i in Eq 4 is

$$c_i \log(b_i) + (C - c_i)\log(1 - b_i)$$

which is maximized when $b_i = c_i/C$. □

Proposition 2 *The segmented bias model becomes a special case of the generalized bias model when we construct the feature vectors as follows. We create a binary feature for each segment, and a query has a value* 1 *in the feature corresponding to its segment and* 0 *elsewhere.*

Proof Sketch. The feature vector defined for the segmented model can partition the queries in the same way as the segmented model. The log likelihood of the whole data set can be separated into a few individual components, with each corresponding to a segment. Each component will be maximized similarly to Proposition 1 and thus the yielded biases are the same as the segmented bias model. □

As noted before, the generalized bias model is flexible to take any types of features such as query-specific or user-specific features. In our experiments we use a simple yet effective set of query length and query segment features described in Table 1. In Section 5, we will report some empirical results on the effectiveness of the generalized bias model based on these features.

5. EXPERIMENTS

In this section, we conduct experiments to compare different position bias prediction methods. All the methods that we compare are summarized in Table 2. In this table, NoCorrection means learning a scoring function without taking selection bias into account. It serves as the baseline to compare the other methods against. In the following, we first describe the experimental design and then present the experimental results.

5.1 Experimental Design

5.1.1 Data Sets

We use two data sets in this paper: regular click data and randomized click data.

- **Regular Data.** This is data collected from our click logs that is used for learning a scoring function. This data is made up of a random sample of email search logs from 2015-12-01 to 2015-12-07, resulting in 4 million queries with clicks. The training and test sets used in our offline evaluations are comprised of a 50/50 split of this data.

- **Randomized Data.** This is a randomized data set that is used to estimate bias in our proposed methods. To obtain randomized data, we randomly permuted the top search results returned for a a small fraction of email search queries (from 2015-11-18 to 2015-11-23), resulting in a total of 208K queries in total. To estimate position bias, we only retain the queries with exactly 4 results, which yields a data set with 148K queries.

Feature Type	Description
Query length	Binary indicator based on the bucketized number of query characters: $[0, 10)$, $[10, 20)$, $[20, 30)$, $[30, \infty)$.
Segment	Binary indicator based on category segment $t(Q)$, as described in Section 4.2.

Table 1: Generalized bias model features.

Name	Method Description
NoCorrection	No bias correction is applied. This serves as our baseline.
Global	The bias is estimated for each position globally.
Segmented	The bias is estimated for each position per segment.
Generalized	The bias is estimated for each position per query using logistic regression.

Table 2: List of position bias prediction methods.

5.1.2 Learning-to-Rank Algorithm

Our learning-to-rank algorithm is an adaptive one, in which we build a new model on top of the existing score. This is different from the standard approach, which learns a scoring function using the entire set of features. Instead, in the adaptive approach, we aim to train the adjustment $\delta(\mathbf{x})$ over the base score $s(\mathbf{x})$. The final scoring function becomes:

$$f(\mathbf{x}) = s(\mathbf{x}) + \delta(\mathbf{x})$$

We use the following ranking features to learn the adjustment $\delta(\mathbf{x})$:

- Email categories. This is the same set of categories used in the segmented bias model. An email can belong to multiple categories. For each category, we have a binary feature with 1 indicating that the email belongs to this category, and 0 otherwise.

- User interactions. We have a set of user interaction features logged for each email. For example, an interaction feature can be whether a user opened the email in the past or not.

This yields tens of ranking features. Although this may seem like a small number of features, the base score $s(\mathbf{x})$ is already highly optimized and includes hundreds of different features. The email category and user interaction features considered here add some additional information that is somewhat orthogonal to those used to compute the base score. For the NoCorrection baseline (see Table 2), we train $\delta(\mathbf{x})$ without applying any bias correction (i.e. $w_Q = 1$), and apply the respective selection bias weights during training for the Global, Segmented and Generalized models.

The additive nature in our adaptive model naturally fits the Multiple Additive Regression Trees (MART) learning algorithm [18]. In every iteration, MART trains a new tree to be added to the existing list of trees. In our setting, we start with our base score $s(\mathbf{x})$ and then train additive trees over it.

5.2 Experimental Results

In this section, we evaluate the position bias prediction models in a couple of different settings. Among them, the

	Uniform	Global	Segmented	Generalized
Mean	4.0	3.7360	3.7337	**3.7336**
95% CI	/	±0.0202	±0.0201	±0.0197

Table 3: Perplexity on the randomized data with 95% Confidence Interval.

online experiments serve as the ultimate ground truth, but are expensive because they need to run against live traffic. We thus explore cheap offline evaluation methodologies and discuss their strengths and weaknesses.

5.2.1 Perplexity on Randomized Data

The position bias prediction problem can be treated as a standard prediction problem and thus can be evaluated using techniques like cross-validation. We split the randomized data into 10 folds and use the leave-one-out strategy to evaluate the different prediction methods. For each query, a prediction method gives a distribution over all the positions. We can thus use *perplexity* as the evaluation metric, which is defined as:

$$perplexity = 2^{-\frac{1}{N}\sum_{o=1}^{N}\log_2 p_o} \tag{5}$$

where N is the total number of observations in the test data and p_o is the probability of observation o as predicted by the model to be evaluated. Perplexity measures how well a distribution predicts samples and is often used to evaluate or compare language models [3]. It is also used in recent work to compare click models [15]. In our case, each sample corresponds to a click at a position in the test data, and p_o is the predicted bias probability for that sample. A lower perplexity score means the model is better at predicting the observations.

In Table 3, we show the perplexity score and the 95% confidence intervals based on the cross-validation. In this table, Uniform is a non-informative baseline and corresponds to the uniform prediction that gives a 25% for each of the 4 positions. From this table, we can see that all the position bias methods outperform Uniform significantly. For example, the 95% confidence interval of Global is $[3.7158, 3.7562]$. The Uniform perplexity 4.0 is outside of this range and thus the difference is significant. Comparing across all the bias prediction methods, we can see that Generalized achieves the best score and Segmented is very close to Generalized. However, the difference among all the 3 methods showed in the table are not significant.

Perplexity is an intrinsic measure of a given method's prediction accuracy. However, from the practical perspective we are much more interested in extrinsic evaluations of how models trained using each approach perform in terms of retrieval effectiveness. In the following, we examine different options for directly evaluating search quality.

5.2.2 Offline Evaluation on Regular Data

The obvious way of evaluating the ranking quality offline is to apply our learnt scoring function to a held-out test data set. However, as we will show, such a method is not well-grounded. Let us consider the evaluation metric Mean Reciprocal Rank (MRR), which is defined as follows:

$$\text{MRR} = \frac{1}{|S|}\sum_{Q\in S}\frac{1}{\text{rank}_Q} \tag{6}$$

	Weighted MRR in Eq 7		
	Global w_Q	Segmented w_Q	Generalized w_Q
NoCorrection	1.0055	1.0055	1.0000
Global	1.0154	-	-
Segmented	-	1.0156	-
Generalized	-	-	1.0101
Improvement	0.9822%	0.9968%	1.0099%

Table 4: Offline evaluation on the regular data based on the weighted MRR. The number in this table is normalized by the smallest MRR.

where rank_Q is the rank of the first clicked document of query Q. In the context of selection bias, we need to incorporate the bias correction w_Q into the metric as well and thus get the weighted MRR:

$$\text{MRR} = \frac{1}{\sum_{Q\in S} w_Q}\sum_{Q\in S} w_Q\frac{1}{\text{rank}_Q} \tag{7}$$

Different position bias prediction models give rise to different w_Q values in Eq 7 and thus the MRR metric is not comparable across different w_Q weights. This means that even for the same data set and the same scoring function, we may get different MRR values. To illustrate this, Table 4 reports the weighted MRR on the test data set of the regular data. We normalize the raw MRR values by the smallest value in the table. The row denoted by NoCorrection corresponds to the evaluation results on the same data set with the same scoring function. Clearly, the table shows different values when different w_Q are used in the MRR metric. Though we can compute the relative improvement of different position bias correction models over the NoCorrection model, using the MRR with the corresponding w_Q, such improvement numbers are still not grounded as a reliable comparison metric. By changing the weight w_Q, one can artificially manipulate the improvement. For example, a high weight w_Q can be given to queries where the new model has a higher MRR.

5.2.3 Unbiased Offline Evaluator

In this section, we address the challenge of offline evaluation by proposing a novel *unbiased* offline evaluator based on the randomized data. Such a method directly evaluates the ranking quality and thus is more practically useful than perplexity. Furthermore, it is theoretically sound, unbiased, and can overcome the comparability issues that arise when using the regular data for offline evaluations.

Unbiased offline evaluators have been studied extensively in the setting of contextual-bandit problems [12, 25]. We adapt this strategy to our problem setting. Our proposed algorithm is detailed in Algorithm 1. This algorithm goes through every query in the randomized data set $\mathcal{R}$ and selects a matched subset $\mathcal{R}_s$ based on the provided scoring function $f(\mathbf{x})$. The matching condition is that the ranking recorded in our log data $\mathcal{R}$ is the same as that ranked by $f(\mathbf{x})$ for the top k documents. The metric value is then computed on the selected subset $\mathcal{R}_s$.

Theorem 1 *Given uniformly randomized data $\mathcal{R}$, Algorithm 1 gives an unbiased estimate of any metric M for any scoring function $f(\mathbf{x})$.*

Proof: This is a simplified version of Theorem 1 in [25] in that we have a static scoring function. We only prove the

Algorithm 1 Offline Evaluator

Input: scoring function f; randomized data $\mathcal{R}$; evaluation metric M on top k: M_k.
Output: evaluation value of f.

1: Set matched data collection $\mathcal{R}_s := \emptyset$
2: **for** $Q = (q, \langle \mathbf{x}_1, ..., \mathbf{x}_n \rangle)$ in $\mathcal{R}$ **do**
3: Let $\langle \mathbf{x}_{j_1}, ..., \mathbf{x}_{j_n} \rangle$ be $\langle \mathbf{x}_1, ..., \mathbf{x}_n \rangle$ re-ranked by f
4: **if** $\langle j_1, ..., j_k \rangle = \langle 1, ..., k \rangle$ **then**
5: $\mathcal{R}_s := \mathcal{R}_s \cup Q$
6: **end if**
7: **end for**
8: **return** $M_k(\mathcal{R}_s)$

case when $k = n$. Our goal is to show that $\mathcal{R}_s$ is an unbiased sample of events if we use $f(\mathbf{x})$ as the scoring function. Since all the rankings in $\mathcal{R}_s$ are the same as ranked by $f(\mathbf{x})$, we only need to prove that the marginal probability on the query string itself, $P(q)$, in $\mathcal{R}_s$ is unbiased.

$$P(q) = \sum_{\{Q: Q \in \mathcal{R}_s \text{ and } q \in Q\}} P(Q)$$

where $q \in Q$ means q is the query string of Q. This is the case because $P(q)$ in $\mathcal{R}$ is unbiased since we collect all the data and the probability of entering the if condition in Algorithm 1 is $\frac{1}{n!}$ for all the queries. □

One caveat of the above algorithm is that we only use queries with exactly n results. For queries with $j < n$ results, we can weigh them by $\frac{j!}{n!}$ when estimating the metric.

The full procedure for evaluating a position bias prediction method is as follows:

- Split the randomized data into training and test (e.g., via a 50/50 split).
- Train the bias prediction model using the randomized training data.
- Apply the learnt position bias model to the regular training data to obtain a scoring function.
- Evaluate the scoring function on the randomized test data based on Algorithm 1.

Using NoCorrection as the baseline, we report the relative improvement of different bias prediction models in Table 5. In this table, we show the MRR in Eq 6 evaluated on the top k results along with the size of $\mathcal{R}_s$. The results show that all position bias prediction methods outperform the NoCorrection baseline. For the position bias prediction methods, both Segmented and Generalized are better than Global, and Segmented is slightly better than Generalized, demonstrating the potential utility of advanced position bias models. However, the differences are not statistically significant, due to the high variance incurred by the small evaluation data set. For k, the expected size of $\mathcal{R}_s$ is about $\frac{(n-k)!}{n!}$ of the size of $\mathcal{R}$. A larger data set could be used to increase the statistical power of our proposed methods.

5.2.4 *Online Experiments on Live Traffic*

Online experiments are the ultimate litmus tests to evaluate different scoring functions. Our online experiments are in the form of A/B testing: we allocate a fraction of live traffic for each experiment. One half of the fraction is used as *control* (i.e., the NoCorrection model, as described in Section 5.1.2) and the other half is used as *treatment* (i.e., the one of the bias prediction methods). We create an online experiment for each of the methods listed in Table 2. We ran all four online experiments for a period of one week, collecting millions of clicks per experiment. Based on the click data, we compare the treatment and the control by computing the relative improvement in terms of our evaluation metric MRR (mean reciprocal rank of a click) in Eq 6. We also compute the relative improvement between two treatment methods using NoCorrection as the calibrator.

k	$\lvert\mathcal{R}_s\rvert$	Global	Segmented	Generalized
1	19.8K	0.94%	**1.01%**	0.97%
2	6.7K	1.08%	**1.28%**	1.20%
3	3.3K	1.58%	1.67%	**1.68%**
4	3.3K	1.37%	**1.44%**	1.41%

Table 5: Comparison of different position bias prediction methods using the unbiased offline evaluator. We report the relative improvement over the NoCorrection baseline.

MRR			
Baseline	Global	Segmented	Generalized
NoCorrection	0.67%***	0.88%***	0.79%***
Global	-	0.21%*	0.12%
CTR			
Baseline	Global	Segmented	Generalized
NoCorrection	0.46%***	0.71%***	0.62%***
Global	-	0.25%**	0.15%

Table 6: Comparison of different bias prediction methods using online experiments. We report the relative improvement over the NoCorrection baseline. Notation *, ** and * means the difference is significant at level 0.1, 0.05 and 0.01 respectively.**

Table 6 summarizes the results of our online experiments. In this table, we report the relative improvement in MRR compared with the NoCorrection and Global baselines. For the NoCorrection baseline, we can see that all our position bias methods yield statistically significant improvements at the 0.01 level. This confirms that selection bias in click data is significant and overcoming it can lead to significant quality improvement. From Global baseline, we can see that more fine-grained position bias models are capable of further improving our metric. For example, Segmented outperforms Global significantly at 0.1 level.

For the online experiments, we can also report the click-through rate (CTR). The CTR metric reflects how attractive the result section is as a whole. We also report the relative improvement in terms of CTR in Table 6. Our observations for the CTR metric parallel those for the MRR metric – the Global baseline significantly increases CTR, and Segmented and Generalized methods provide further improvements. Furthermore, Segmented model achieves significant improvement over Global at 0.05 level.

The results of the online experiments do not indicate a significant difference between Segmented and Generalized models, even though both outperform the Global baseline. As we showed before, Segmented is a special case of General-

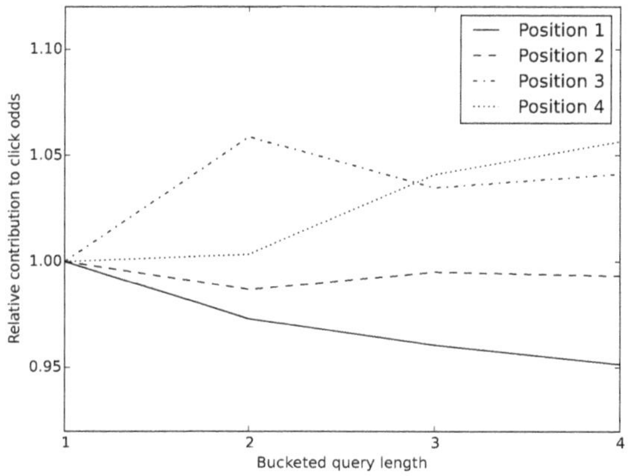

Figure 3: The importance of query length varied with positions.

ized when only the segmented features are used, suggesting the usefulness of the category segment feature, and the importance of feature engineering for further improvement of the generalized bias model.

5.2.5 *Regression Models Analysis*

The generalized bias model not only provides a flexible way for position bias prediction, but also enables us to understand the impact of different features in terms of their usefulness in modeling position bias. In this section, we analyze the features to distill additional insights.

We have two types of features in the regression models: segment features and query length features. The question is which group of features is more predictive. To answer this question, we compare 3 generalized models with different sets of features and observe the following changes in perplexity (as defined in Eq 5): segment and query length features (3.7336), segment features only (3.7337), and query length features only (3.7358). Clearly we can see that segment features are more useful than query length features in reducing the perplexity.

Furthermore, we can observe the impact of different lengths of query features. Our query lengths are bucketed as in Table 1 with larger bucket IDs corresponding to longer queries. For each position i and each query length bucket j, we have β_{ij} corresponding to the coefficient in the logistic regression model. Here, $e^{\beta_{ij}}$ represents the contribution of query length j to the odd of click on position i: $b_i/(1-b_i)$. We plot the relative contribution $e^{\beta_{ij}}/e^{\beta_{i1}}$ in Figure 3. For position $i = 1$, $e^{\beta_{ij}}/e^{\beta_{i1}}$ becomes smaller when j becomes larger. In other words, the odds of a click at position 1 *decrease* when the query is longer. In contrast, for position $i = 4$, $e^{\beta_{ij}}/e^{\beta_{i1}}$ becomes larger when j becomes larger, which means the odds of a click at position 4 *increase* as the query becomes longer. This makes sense intuitively, since when queries are longer, users have more refined needs and the position bias becomes flatter. This means that the users are more willing to examine the lower-ranked documents.

6. CONCLUSIONS

In this paper, we studied the problem of learning-to-rank with selection bias for personal search. We discussed the infeasibility of using existing click models in personal search and proposed a novel approach to overcome the inherent selection bias for this application. We proposed a few methods to estimate the selection bias and addressed it using inverse propensity weighting. In addition, we study offline and online evaluation methodologies and also propose a novel unbiased offline evaluator. Through extensive offline and online experiments, we show that the proposed methods for modeling selection bias can significantly improve the quality of learning-to-rank models that use click data for training.

There are a few interesting lines of future work. (1) We evaluate our methods in the context of personal search, but it would be interesting to see how applicable they are to web search. (2) Our experiments use queries with a single click. It would be interesting to extend the framework to the search scenarios that allow multiple clicks per query. (3) Given a different application, such as cloud storage files, what are the effective features in bias estimation? This could inspire lots of interesting feature engineering work in the research community. (4) The expensive part of our method is the dependency on randomized data. How to collect randomized data in a cheaper, less-intrusive manner is also worth studying. Furthermore, how to adapt our offline evaluator to improve its data utilization is also an interesting research problem.

7. REFERENCES

[1] J. A. Aslam, E. Kanoulas, V. Pavlu, S. Savev, and E. Yilmaz. Document selection methodologies for efficient and effective learning-to-rank. In *32nd Annual International ACM SIGIR Conference on Research and Development in Information Retrieval (SIGIR)*, pages 468–475, 2009.

[2] R. Bekkerman. Automatic categorization of email into folders: Benchmark experiments on Enron and SRI corpora. Technical report, University of Massachusetts Amherst, 2004.

[3] P. F. Brown, V. J. D. Pietra, R. L. Mercer, S. A. D. Pietra, and J. C. Lai. An estimate of an upper bound for the entropy of English. *Computational Linguistics*, 18(1):31–40, 1992.

[4] C. J. Burges. From RankNet to LambdaRank to LambdaMART: An overview. Technical Report MSR-TR-2010-82, Microsoft Research, 2010.

[5] S. Büttcher, C. L. A. Clarke, P. C. K. Yeung, and I. Soboroff. Reliable information retrieval evaluation with incomplete and biased judgements. In *30th Annual International ACM SIGIR Conference on Research and Development in Information Retrieval (SIGIR)*, pages 63–70, 2007.

[6] D. Carmel, G. Halawi, L. Lewin-Eytan, Y. Maarek, and A. Raviv. Rank by time or by relevance?: Revisiting email search. In *24th ACM International Conference on Information and Knowledge Management (CIKM)*, pages 283–292, 2015.

[7] D. Chan, R. Ge, O. Gershony, T. Hesterberg, and D. Lambert. Evaluating online ad campaigns in a pipeline: Causal models at scale. In *16th ACM SIGKDD International Conference on Knowledge Discovery and Data Mining (KDD)*, pages 7–16, 2010.

[8] O. Chapelle and Y. Zhang. A dynamic bayesian network click model for web search ranking. In *18th*

International Conference on World Wide Web (WWW), pages 1–10, 2009.
[9] W. Chen, Z. Ji, S. Shen, and Q. Yang. A whole page click model to better interpret search engine click data. In *25th AAAI Conference on Artificial Intelligence (AAAI)*, 2011.
[10] A. Chuklin, I. Markov, and M. de Rijke. *Click Models for Web Search*. Morgan & Claypool, 2015.
[11] N. Craswell, O. Zoeter, M. Taylor, and B. Ramsey. An experimental comparison of click position-bias models. In *1st International Conference on Web Search and Data Mining (WSDM)*, pages 87–94, 2008.
[12] M. Dudík, J. Langford, and L. Li. Doubly robust policy evaluation and learning. In *28th International Conference on Machine Learning (ICML)*, pages 1097–1104, 2011.
[13] S. Dumais, E. Cutrell, J. Cadiz, G. Jancke, R. Sarin, and D. C. Robbins. Stuff I've seen: A system for personal information retrieval and re-use. In *26th Annual International ACM SIGIR Conference on Research and Development in Information Retrieval (SIGIR)*, pages 72–79, 2003.
[14] G. Dupret and C. Liao. A model to estimate intrinsic document relevance from the clickthrough logs of a web search engine. In *3rd ACM International Conference on Web Search and Data Mining (WSDM)*, pages 181–190, 2010.
[15] G. E. Dupret and B. Piwowarski. A user browsing model to predict search engine click data from past observations. In *31st Annual International ACM SIGIR Conference on Research and Development in Information Retrieval (SIGIR)*, pages 331–338, 2008.
[16] M. Grbovic, G. Halawi, Z. Karnin, and Y. Maarek. How many folders do you really need?: Classifying email into a handful of categories. In *23rd ACM International Conference on Conference on Information and Knowledge Management (CIKM)*, pages 869–878, 2014.
[17] F. Guo, C. Liu, A. Kannan, T. Minka, M. Taylor, Y.-M. Wang, and C. Faloutsos. Click chain model in web search. In *18th International Conference on World Wide Web (WWW)*, pages 11–20, 2009.
[18] T. Hastie, R. Tibshirani, and J. Friedman. *The Elements of Statistical Learning*. Springer, 2001.
[19] K. Hofmann, S. Whiteson, and M. de Rijke. Balancing exploration and exploitation in learning to rank online. In *Advances in Information Retrieval – 33rd European Conference on IR Research (ECIR)*, pages 251–263, 2011.
[20] J. Huang, A. Gretton, K. M. Borgwardt, B. Schölkopf, and A. J. Smola. Correcting sample selection bias by unlabeled data. In *20th Annual Conference on Neural Information Processing Systems (NIPS)*, pages 601–608, 2006.
[21] T. Joachims. Optimizing search engines using clickthrough data. In *8th ACM SIGKDD International Conference on Knowledge Discovery and Data Mining (KDD)*, pages 133–142, 2002.
[22] T. Joachims, L. Granka, B. Pan, H. Hembrooke, and G. Gay. Accurately interpreting clickthrough data as implicit feedback. In *28th Annual International ACM SIGIR Conference on Research and Development in Information Retrieval (SIGIR)*, pages 154–161, 2005.
[23] M. Kamvar, M. Kellar, R. Patel, and Y. Xu. Computers and iPhones and mobile phones, oh my!: A logs-based comparison of search users on different devices. In *18th International Conference on World Wide Web (WWW)*, pages 801–810, 2009.
[24] L. Li, S. Chen, J. Kleban, and A. Gupta. Counterfactual estimation and optimization of click metrics in search engines: A case study. In *24th International Conference on World Wide Web (WWW) Companion*, pages 929–934, 2015.
[25] L. Li, W. Chu, J. Langford, and X. Wang. Unbiased offline evaluation of contextual-bandit-based news article recommendation algorithms. In *4th International Conference on Web Search and Web Data Mining (WSDM)*, pages 297–306, 2011.
[26] T.-Y. Liu. Learning to rank for information retrieval. *Foundations and Trends in Information Retrieval*, 3(3):225–331, 2009.
[27] T. Minka and S. Robertson. Selection bias in the LETOR datasets. In *SIGIR Workshop on Learning to Rank for Information Retrieval (LR4IR)*, pages 48–51, 2008.
[28] M. O'Brien and M. T. Keane. Modeling result–list searching in the world wide web: The role of relevance topologies and trust bias. In *28th Annual Conference of the Cognitive Science Society (CogSci)*, pages 1–881, 2006.
[29] T. Qin, T.-Y. Liu, J. Xu, and H. Li. Letor: A benchmark collection for research on learning to rank for information retrieval. *Inf. Retr.*, 13(4):346–374, 2010.
[30] M. Richardson, E. Dominowska, and R. Ragno. Predicting clicks: Estimating the click-through rate for new ads. In *16th International Conference on World Wide Web (WWW)*, pages 521–530, 2007.
[31] P. R. Rosenbaum and D. B. Rubin. The central role of the propensity score in observational studies for causal effects. *Biometrika*, 70(1):41–55, 1983.
[32] A. Swaminathan and T. Joachims. Counterfactual risk minimization: Learning from logged bandit feedback. In *32nd International Conference on Machine Learning (ICML)*, pages 814–823, 2015.
[33] Y. Yue, R. Patel, and H. Roehrig. Beyond position bias: Examining result attractiveness as a source of presentation bias in clickthrough data. In *19th International Conference on World Wide Web (WWW)*, pages 1011–1018, 2010.
[34] B. Zadrozny. Learning and evaluating classifiers under sample selection bias. In *21st International Conference on Machine Learning (ICML)*, page 114, 2004.
[35] Z. Zheng, K. Chen, G. Sun, and H. Zha. A regression framework for learning ranking functions using relative relevance judgments. In *30th Annual International ACM SIGIR Conference on Research and Development in Information Retrieval (SIGIR)*, pages 287–294, 2007.
[36] Z. A. Zhu, W. Chen, T. Minka, C. Zhu, and Z. Chen. A novel click model and its applications to online advertising. In *3rd International Conference on Web Search and Data Mining (WSDM)*, pages 321–330, 2010.

On Effective Personalized Music Retrieval by Exploring Online User Behaviors

Zhiyong Cheng Jialie Shen Steven C.H. Hoi
School of Information Systems, Singapore Management University, Singapore, 178902
jason.zy.cheng@gmail.com, jialie@gmail.com, chhoi@smu.edu.sg

ABSTRACT

In this paper, we study the problem of personalized text-based music retrieval which takes users' music preferences on songs into account via the analysis of online listening behaviours and social tags. Towards the goal, a novel Dual-Layer Music Preference Topic Model (DL-MPTM) is proposed to construct latent music interest space and characterize the correlations among (user, song, term). Based on the DL-MPTM, we further develop an effective personalized music retrieval system. To evaluate the system's performance, extensive experimental studies have been conducted over two test collections to compare the proposed method with the state-of-the-art music retrieval methods. The results demonstrate that our proposed method significantly outperforms those approaches in terms of personalized search accuracy.

Keywords

Topic Model, Semantic Music Retrieval, Personalized

1. INTRODUCTION

Over the past decades, empowered by fast advances in digital storage and networking, we have witnessed an ever-increasing amount of music data from various domain applications. Meanwhile, with the proliferation of mobile devices (e.g., mobile phones and laptops) and cloud-based music service, the development of personalized music information retrieval techniques has gained greatest momentum as a means to assist users to explore large-scale music collections based on "personal preference". In music information retrieval, there are two widely accepted and yet independent paradigms: content-based music retrieval [33] and text-based music retrieval [31, 28]. Due to a wide range of real applications, text-based music retrieval has been recently emerging as a popular paradigm. With this technique, users can compose several keywords to describe their music information needs and current contexts, with the expectation that the music search engine returns a list of suitable songs. However, existing methods in this paradigm only consider the relevance between songs and search keywords, while largely ignoring user's personal music preference. In fact, how an individual perceives a song is very subjective, heavily depending on his/her emotional and cultural background [30]. For example, given a query "*sad*", *whether a song is relevant* or *the relevance level of the song* with respect to "sad" is dependent on the user's personal perception on this song. Thus, for music retrieval, it is crucial to take user's personal music preference into account and effectively model the correlations among (user, song, term). In fact, the significance of leveraging user music preference has been widely recognized in the development of smart music information systems [8, 27]. However, few researches focus on 1) investigating the effects of user music preferences on search performance improvement; and 2) designing advanced schemes to catch and model such effects and exploit them in personalized music search systems.

Indeed, effective integration of user's music preference to improve retrieval performance generally requires a comprehensive understanding of user's music preference on songs with respect to search keywords. A naive approach is to leverage the assistance of end users to manually label songs with various music concepts. However, this approach could be very expensive in terms of time and expertise. In recent years, the rapid growth and popularity of online social music services such as Last.fm[1] and Pandora[2] provide excellent sources to harvest large-scale user behavior information. When interacting with the social music portals, users leave rich digital footprints, which contain the details of personal music listening history, such as *which song was played by which user at what time for how long*. Through analyzing user's listening behaviors, we could obtain comprehensive information related to user music preference or taste, e.g., *which songs are played frequently by a certain kind of users* and *what are the favorite levels of a user on different kinds of songs*. Besides, in those social music portals, songs are tagged by users with different types of concepts, which reveal the semantic contents of songs. The social tags in Last.fm almost cover all the concepts that users usually use to describe songs, and have been used for text-based music search [17, 22]. The listening history of users and social tags provide us reliable sources to learn the correlations among (user, song, term), which can be used to support music search at the personal level.

SIGIR '16, July 17–21, 2016, Pisa, Italy.

DOI: http://dx.doi.org/10.1145/2911451.2911491

[1]http://www.lastfm.com
[2]http://www.pandora.com/

Motivated by discussions above, in this work, we focus on designing a music retrieval system to facilitate personalized music search by jointly exploiting user listening behaviors and music tags extracted from popular social music portals. To achieve the goal, we propose a novel dual-layer topic model called *D*ual *L*ayer *M*usic *P*reference *T*opic *M*odel (DL-MPTM), which discovers two sets of latent topics - *latent music dimensions* and *latent semantic subtopics*. In this model, user's music preference is represented as mixtures of *latent music dimensions*, which are discovered based on the co-occurrence of songs in playlists and co-occurrence of *latent semantic subtopics* across songs. The latent semantic subtopics are represented as the mixtures of terms. Accordingly, the correlations among (user, song, term) can be captured by the associations of the two sets of latent topics. Based on the model, we further develop a personalized text-based music retrieval system. Comprehensive experiments have been conducted to examine the performance of the method by comparing with a set of competitors over two test collections. The results demonstrate the effectiveness and robustness of our proposed method on different types of queries and datasets. In summary, the main contributions of our work are as follows.

- Instead of conducting large-scale user study, we leverage online social music data (i.e., user listening history and music social tags) to study the problem of *personalized text-based music retrieval*, which has not been well studied in existing research.
- We propose a personalized text-based retrieval method based on a novel dual-layer topic model DL-MPTM, which captures user's music preference on songs with respect to a term via the connection of two latent semantic spaces.
- The proposed system has been fully implemented and tested. An extensive range of tests has been designed to investigate different factors that affect the performance of the proposed approach and its competitors. The results demonstrate the superiority of our method over other state-of-the-art approaches.

The remainder of this article is organized as follows: Section 2 gives an overview of related work. In Section 3, we introduce the proposed personalized music search system, including the DL-MPTM topic model and retrieval method. Section 4 introduces the experimental configuration, and Section 5 reports experimental results and main findings. Finally, Section 6 concludes the paper.

2. RELATED WORK

In this section, we review the literature in two closely related domains: personalized music retrieval and topic model.

2.1 Personalized Music Information Retrieval

Driven by numerous real applications, personalized information retrieval has attracted lots of research attentions in text retrieval community, and thus various approaches have been proposed in last decades [6, 19, 29]. However, very few works have been reported in the domain of personalized text-based music retrieval. Hoashi et al. [12] leveraged relevance feedback methods to refine users profiles for search performance improvement, while the method was designed for content-based music retrieval systems. In [34], Wang et al. proposed a tag query interface which enables users to specify their queries using multiple tags and with multiple levels of preferences. This method relies on user's efforts to specify the importance of query tags in each query session. In [30], Symeonidis et al. applied the high order singular value decomposition (SVD) method to capture the associations between $(user, tag, item)$. Based on the likeliness that user u will tag musical item i with tag t, musical items are recommended to user u. However, this method suffers from the high time complexity and thus is only applicable for small scale data. Hariri et al. [11] considered the problem of personalized text-based music retrieval, where users' history of preferences are taken into account in addition to their issued textual queries. The proposed system has not been compared with other music retrieval methods and evaluated under the standard information retrieval evaluation framework.

2.2 Topic Models

This section reviews hierarchical and multi-modal topic models, which are closely related to our work.

Hierarchical Topic Model. Latent Dirichlet Allocation (LDA) [5] is an unsupervised algorithm to discover the "latent topics" underlying a large scale of text collections. Each document is modeled as a mixture of the topics and each topic is a mixture of words. In recent years, several hierarchical topic models were proposed to gain the relations between topics, such as nested Chinese Restaurant Process (nCRP) [3], tree-informed LDA [15] and nHDP [23]. A common feature of these hierarchical topic models is that they all focus on modeling the parent-child and sliding relations between topics. In these models, all topics (parent topics and child topics) are represented as the mixture of words and thus in the same semantic space. Distinguished from these models, the proposed model in this paper discovers two sets of latent topics under two different latent spaces: the latent topics in a high-level latent space are the mixtures of the latent topics in a low-level latent space.

Multi-modal LDA. Due to the success of LDA in single modality scenarios, it is extended to support multi-modal case, such as mmLDA [1], Corr-LDA [4], tr-mmLDA [24], MDRF [14], and factorized multi-modal topic model [32]. The basic philosophy behind these multi-modal LDA models is the existence of shared latent topics that are the common causes of the correlations between different modalities. In mmLDA [1], the image and text words are generated from two non-overlapping sets of hidden topics. For an image, the two sets of topics follow the same topic distribution. Corr-LDA [4] was designed so that image is the primary modality and is generated first, and each caption word is forced to be associated with an image region and is generated based on the topic of this image region. Tr-mmLDA [24] uses a latent variable regression approach to learn a linear mapping between the topic distributions of two modalities. Factorized multi-modal topic model [32] and Multi-modal document random field (MDRF) [14] generalize the modeling of two modalities to multiple modalities. In our personalized music retrieval system, there are two modalities - audio and text. Besides, because social tags are usually incomplete, the text document (formed for a song) is not complete as a corresponding document to the audio content of the song. The Corr-LDA has the merits that the topics of text words are indeed a subset of topics that occur in the corresponding

Table 1: Notations and their definitions

Notation	Definition
v	audio term in the audio word vocabulary
t	text term in the text vocabulary
y	index variable - indicating a text word is associated with which audio word
υ, z	latent music dimension and latent subtopic
s, u	song and user
v_s, w_s	audio word and text word in documents
N_u^l	number of times observing $\upsilon = l$ in user u's profile
N_l^k	number of times observing subtopic k in $\upsilon = l$
N_l^s	number of times observing song s in $\upsilon = l$
N_k^v	number of times observing audio term v in $z = k$
N_k^t	number of times observing text term t in $z = k$
V, T	vocabulary size of audio and text terms
L, K	number of music dimensions and number of subtopics
N, M	number of users and number of songs
$\boldsymbol{\theta_u}$	music interest of user u characterized by multinomial distribution over music dimensions
$\boldsymbol{\theta_\upsilon}$	property of music dimension υ characterized by multinomial distribution over subtopics
$\theta_{u,l}$	probability of $\upsilon = l$ specific to user u
$\theta_{l,k}$	probability of $z = k$ specific to $\upsilon = l$
$\phi_{l,s}$	probability of song s specific to $\upsilon = l$
$\phi_{k,v}$	probability of audio term v specific to subtopic k
$\phi_{k,t}$	probability of text term t specific to subtopic k
$\boldsymbol{\alpha}, \boldsymbol{\gamma}$	Dirichlet priors to distributions θ_u and θ_υ
$\boldsymbol{\phi_s}, \boldsymbol{\phi_v}, \boldsymbol{\phi_t}$	multinomial distributions over songs, audio terms and text terms, respectively
$\boldsymbol{\beta_s}, \boldsymbol{\beta_v}, \boldsymbol{\beta_t}$	Dirichlet priors to multinomial distributions ϕ_s, ϕ_v, and ϕ_t, respectively

image (song in our context), and an audio segment could be associated with multiple text words, which is reasonable for the annotations of an audio segment. Thus, we use the Corr-LDA as a basic component in our model. Obviously, our model is very different from these multi-modal LDA models in terms of the dual-layer structure.

3. PERSONALIZED TEXT-BASED MUSIC RETRIEVAL SYSTEM

This section presents a detailed introduction of the DL-MPTM model and the associated retrieval method.

3.1 Dual-Layer Music Preference Topic Model

In this study, we aim at designing a personalized text-based music retrieval system for searching songs, which are not only relevant to the query but also effectively satisfy user's personal music information needs. Consequently, the core research problem is how to effectively model user's music preference on songs with respect to the search keywords. Users usually prefer different types of music tracks, which can be reflected from the songs they often listen to. Meanwhile, people's music preferences on songs are highly associated with the semantics embodied by the audio contents of songs. Based on the semantics, user's music preferences can be extracted by analyzing the semantics of songs listened by the users. Further, given that the semantics of songs are modeled by song's contents and user-generated annotations (e.g., social tags), the correlations among (user, song, term) can be estimated. To achieve the goal, we propose a dual-layer LDA model, which *characterizes the song's semantics based on the associations between audio contents and tags* and *models user's music interests based on the songs and their semantics*. To ease understanding of the model, we firstly introduce two important concepts.

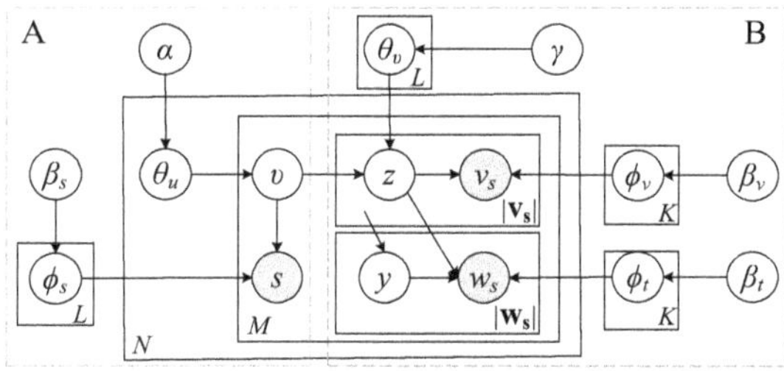

Figure 1: The graphical model representation of the DL-MPTM model. Note that the variable y are conditioned on V, the number of audio words.

- **Latent Semantic Subtopic:** Latent semantic subtopics (or subtopic for short) are the latent topics discovered (in the second layer - Part B in Fig. 1) based on the association between song's audio contents and annotations or text words. The subtopics are modeled using the multinomial distributions of audio words and text words. An audio word could be thought as a short audio segment (see Sect. 4.1).
- **Latent Music Dimension:** Latent music dimensions (or music dimensions for short) are a set of latent topics discovered (in the first layer - Part A in Fig. 1) based on co-occurrence of songs and their subtopic distributions. Users' music interests are modeled using the multinomial distributions of music dimensions. A music dimension is in turn a multinomial distribution of subtopics.

3.1.1 Model Description

Figure 1 illustrates the graphical representation of *D*ual *L*ayer *M*usic *P*reference *T*opic *M*odel (DL-MPTM). The model consists of two main components: Part A (the first layer) and Part B (the second layer). The second layer (Part B) is a Corr-LDA model [4], which discovers subtopics based on the co-occurrence of music contents (audio words and text words) in the same song. Besides, this model discovers the associations between audio contents and text words. The first layer (Part A) is a topic model to explore music dimensions υ based on the co-occurrences of songs in the same user's profile and the subtopics associated with these songs. Each subtopic z is represented by a multinomial of audio words and a multinomial distribution of text words; each music dimension υ is represented by a multinomial distribution of songs and a multinomial distribution of subtopics. The set of subtopics in the second level is shared across different music dimensions. These subtopics, which are represented by the distribution of text words or audio words, are used to characterize the music dimensions. User music interests are represented by the multinomial distribution of music dimensions. Because the music dimension is discovered based on the co-occurrence of subtopics of songs and the subtopics are discovered based on the co-occurrence patterns of songs' contents, the dual-layer topic model discovers the latent music dimensions and subtopics in a mutual reinforcement process.

From the generative perspective, a song s with text words $\boldsymbol{w_s}$[3] and audio words $\boldsymbol{v_s}$ preferred by a user u, namely, an

[3]In the paper, a notation in bold type denotes a vector or matrix.

observation of $(u, s, \boldsymbol{w_s}, \boldsymbol{v_s})$, is assumed to be generated by first choosing a music dimension υ (e.g., a certain music style) from music interest $\boldsymbol{\theta_u}$ of user u. Then based on the selected topic υ, song s is drawn according to $\phi_{\upsilon,s}$, which represents the likelihood for user u to select song s in the music dimension υ. The audio words $\boldsymbol{v_s}$ and text words $\boldsymbol{w_s}$ of song s are generated according to the subtopic distributions $\boldsymbol{\theta_\upsilon}$ of the music dimension υ. The generation process of audio words and text words is to firstly generate all the audio words, and then subsequently generate all the text words. Specifically, for each audio word v_s, a subtopic z is sampled and the audio word is generated accordingly based on ϕ_{z,v_s}. After obtaining all the audio words, for each text word, an audio word v_s is first selected and the text word w_s is generated, conditioned on the subtopic that generated the audio word. For details about the sampling process of the second layer (Part B), please refer to [4]. More formally, the process of user's profile generation is as follows:

1. For each music dimension $\upsilon \in \{1, ..., L\}$, draw a multinomial distribution $\boldsymbol{\phi_{\upsilon,s}} \sim Dir(\cdot|\boldsymbol{\beta_s})$;
2. For each subtopic $k \in \{1, ..., K\}$:
   (a) Draw a multinomial distribution $\boldsymbol{\phi_v} \sim Dir(\cdot|\boldsymbol{\beta_v})$;
   (b) Draw a multinomial distribution $\boldsymbol{\phi_t} \sim Dir(\cdot|\boldsymbol{\beta_t})$;
3. For each user u, draw a multinomial distribution $\boldsymbol{\theta_u} \sim Dir(\cdot|\boldsymbol{\alpha})$;
4. For each music dimension υ, draw a multinomial distribution $\boldsymbol{\theta_\upsilon} \sim Dir(\cdot|\boldsymbol{\gamma})$;
5. For each user u:
   - For each song $s \in \{1, ..., M\}$ in a user u's profile:
     (a) Draw a music dimension υ from the music interest distribution of user $\boldsymbol{\theta_u}$;
     (b) For each audio word $v_s \in \boldsymbol{v_s}$ in the song:
       i. Draw z from the subtopic distribution $\boldsymbol{\theta_\upsilon}$ of music dimension υ;
       ii. Draw v_s from the audio word distribution $\boldsymbol{\phi_v}$ from subtopic z ;
     (c) For each word w_s in the song (suppose there are n audio words in this song, and let z_i denote the sampled topic for the i-th audio word in previous step):
       i. Draw $y \sim$ Unif$(1, 2, ..., n)$[4];
       ii. Draw w_s from the text word distribution $\boldsymbol{\phi_t}$ from the subtopic z_y ;

Based on the connection of two layers of topic models, DL-MPTM thus specifies the conditional joint distribution on song s and a term t given a user u and the latent variables:

$$P(s, t|u, \boldsymbol{\theta_u}, \boldsymbol{\theta_\upsilon}, \boldsymbol{\phi_s}, \boldsymbol{\phi_v}, \boldsymbol{\phi_t}) = \sum_{\upsilon=1}^{L} P(\upsilon|u, \boldsymbol{\theta_u})P(s|\upsilon, \boldsymbol{\phi_s}) \sum_{z=1}^{K} P(z|\upsilon, \boldsymbol{\theta_\upsilon})P(t|z, \boldsymbol{\phi_t}) \tag{1}$$

This equation estimates how correlative user u, song s, and term t could be, and thus can be used for personalized text-based music retrieval, which is introduced in Sect. 3.2.

[4]Unif$(1, 2, ...n)$ denotes the sampling of a value from 1 to n with equal probability

3.1.2 Model Inference

In the DL-MPTM model, $\alpha, \gamma, \boldsymbol{\beta_s}, \boldsymbol{\beta_v}$, and $\boldsymbol{\beta_t}$ are Dirichlet priors and pre-defined. The parameters needed to be estimated include: (1) user interest (user-music dimension) distribution $\boldsymbol{\theta_u}$, (2) music dimension - subtopic distribution $\boldsymbol{\theta_\upsilon}$, (3) music dimension - song distribution $\boldsymbol{\phi_s}$, (4) subtopic-term distribution $\boldsymbol{\phi_t}$ and (5) subtopic-audio word distribution $\boldsymbol{\phi_v}$. Several algorithms have been developed to approximate the parameters in variants of LDA. In our implementation, collapsed Gibbs sampling [10] is used to estimate these parameters, as this method has been successfully applied in many large scale applications of topic models [9, 10]. Notice that in the learning of a model, Gibbs sampling iteratively updates each latent variable given the remaining variable until it converges.

Preliminary. Given a user music profile corpus D with user set U, for each user $u \in U$, a playlist $\{s_1, s_2, ..., s_n\}$ records his/her playing behaviors or music profile. Each song s contains a sequence of text words $\boldsymbol{w_s}$ and a sequence of audio word $\boldsymbol{v_s}$. In the Gibbs sampling process, the playlists of users are sampled in sequence. Let $\boldsymbol{S}$ be the sampling sequence in the Gibbs sampling process, which is the concatenation of songs in the playlists of all the users. Similarly, let $\boldsymbol{V}$ and $\boldsymbol{W}$ denote the corresponding sampling sequences of audio words and text words. $\boldsymbol{\Upsilon}$ and $\boldsymbol{Z}$ denote the set of latent music dimensions and subtopics corresponding to the song sequence and audio words sequence, respectively. Besides, $\boldsymbol{Y}$ is the assignment indicators of the word sequence $\boldsymbol{W}$. $\boldsymbol{S_{\neg i}}$ denotes $\boldsymbol{S}$ excluding the i-th song s_i in $\boldsymbol{S}$. Similar notation is used for other variables.

Music Dimension υ Sampling for a Song For the sampling of latent music dimension $\upsilon_i = l$ for s_i, the probability is

$$P(\upsilon_i = l|\boldsymbol{\Upsilon_{\neg i}}, \boldsymbol{S}, \boldsymbol{Z}, \boldsymbol{Y}, \boldsymbol{V}, \boldsymbol{W}) \propto \frac{\alpha_l + N^l_{u,\neg i}}{\sum_{l=1}^{L}(N^l_{u,\neg i} + \alpha_l)} \cdot \frac{\beta_s + N^s_{l,\neg i}}{\sum_{s=1}^{M}(N^s_{l,\neg i} + \beta_s)} \cdot PLS(l, s_i) \tag{2}$$

$$PLS(l, s_i) = \frac{\prod_{k=1}^{K}\Gamma(\gamma_k + N^k_l)}{\Gamma(\sum_{k=1}^{K}(N^k_l + \gamma_k))} \cdot \frac{\Gamma(\sum_{k=1}^{K}(N^k_{l,\neg i} + \gamma_k))}{\prod_{k=1}^{K}\Gamma(\gamma_k + N^k_{l,\neg i})} = \frac{\prod_{k=1}^{K}(\gamma_k + N^k_l - 1)!}{\prod_{k=1}^{K}(\gamma_k + N^k_l - n_{l,k,s_i} - 1)!} \cdot \frac{(\sum_{k=1}^{K}(N^k_{l,\neg i} + \gamma_k - n_{l,k,s_i}) - 1)!}{(\sum_{k=1}^{K}(N^k_{l,\neg i} + \gamma_k) - 1)!} \tag{3}$$

where N^l_u denotes the number of times that music dimension l is observed in u's playlist. N^k_l is the number of times that subtopic k is observed in music dimension l. Notice that the exclusion of $\upsilon = l$ will cause the changes of N^k_l for all $k = [1, K]$. $N^k_{l,\neg i}$ denotes the number of times latent subtopic k is observed in latent music dimension l by excluding l assigned to song s_i, and $N^k_{l,\neg i} = N^k_l - n_{l,k,s_i}$. n_{l,k,s_i} denote the number of times the subtopic k is observed in music dimension l due to s_i. $PLS(l, s_i)$ denotes the effects of the exclusion of $\upsilon = l$ on the distribution of subtopics in the music dimension l. $\Gamma(\cdot)$ is the Gamma function.

Subtopic Sampling of Audio and Text Word: Next we introduce the sampling of subtopic $z_j = k$ for an audio word $v_j = v$ in s_i and the sampling of all text words of the song s_i. Notice that the text words in s_i are sampled after sampling all the audio words in s_i, as the assignment of z_j to the words in a song is dependent on the subtopic sequence of audio words in this song. The probability of $z_j = k$ to an audio word $v_j = v$ is:

$$P(z_j = k|\boldsymbol{\Upsilon}, \boldsymbol{S}, \boldsymbol{Z}_{\neg j}, \boldsymbol{Y}, \boldsymbol{V}, \boldsymbol{W}) \propto \frac{\gamma_k + N^k_{l,\neg j}}{\sum_{k=1}^K (N^k_{l,\neg j} + \gamma_k)} \cdot \frac{\beta_v + N^v_{k,\neg j}}{\sum_{v=1}^V (N^v_{k,\neg j} + \beta_v)} \cdot PZ(k) \tag{4}$$

$$\begin{aligned} PZ(k) &= \frac{\prod_{t=1}^T \Gamma(\beta_t + N_k^t)}{\Gamma(\sum_{t=1}^T (N^t_{k,\neg j} + \beta_t))} \cdot \frac{\Gamma(\sum_{t=1}^T (N_k^t + \beta_t))}{\prod_{t=1}^T \Gamma(\beta_t + N^t_{k,\neg j})} \\ &= \frac{\prod_{t=1}^T (\beta_t + N_k^t - 1)!}{\prod_{t=1}^T (\beta_t + N_k^t - n_t - 1)!} \cdot \frac{(\sum_{t=1}^T (N^t_{k,\neg j} + \beta_t - n_t) - 1)!}{(\sum_{t=1}^T (N^t_{k,\neg j} + \beta_t) - 1)!} \end{aligned} \tag{5}$$

where N^v_k is the number of times that subtopic $z_j = k$ is assigned to audio word $v_j = v$. $N^t_{k,\neg j}$ denotes the number of times that t is assigned to subtopic k before assigning k to the j-th audio word of song s_i, and $N^t_{k,\neg j} = N^t_k - n_t$. n_t denotes the number of times that term t is assigned to the subtopic of the j-th audio word in the current song s_i. Notice that the exclusion of $z_j = k$ for audio word v_j may influence the assignment of $z_j = k$ to multiple text terms and multiple times. Similar to $PLS(l, s_i)$, $PZ(k)$ denotes the effects of the exclusion of $z_j = k$ on the distribution of text terms in the subtopic k.

Parameter Estimation. Based on the state of the Markov chain $\boldsymbol{\upsilon}$ and $\boldsymbol{z}$, we can estimate the parameters:

$$\theta_{u,l} = \frac{\alpha_l + N_u^l}{\sum_{l=1}^L (\alpha_l + N_u^l)} \qquad \theta_{l,k} = \frac{\gamma_k + N_l^k}{\sum_{k=1}^K (\gamma_k + N_l^k)} \tag{6}$$

$$\phi_{l,s} = \frac{\beta_s + N_l^s}{\sum_{s=1}^M (\beta_s + N_l^s)} \qquad \phi_{k,t} = \frac{\beta_t + N_k^t}{\sum_{t=1}^T (\beta_t + N_k^t)} \tag{7}$$

$$\phi_{k,v} = \frac{\beta_v + N_k^v}{\sum_{v=1}^V (\beta_v + N_k^v)} \tag{8}$$

3.2 Retrieval Model

The goal of the retrieval model is to search a subset of songs that are relevant to a particular query. Let $q = \{t_1, t_2, ..., t_n\}$ represent user u's query consisting of n terms. The retrieval algorithm aims at ranking songs based on their relevance to the query according to u's music preference on the songs. Notice that the relevance level of a song with respect to a query is dependent on user's music taste. Given a query q issued by user u, for a song s, $P(s|q, u)$ denotes the likelihood or probability of user u preferring this song s with respect to the query q. Thus, candidate songs can be ranked in the descending order of their probabilities $P(s|q, u)$ with respect to the user and query (u, q). According to Bayes rule, $P(s|q, u)$ can be computed as:

$$P(s|q, u) = \frac{P(q, s|u)P(u)}{P(q, u)} \propto P(q, s|u) \tag{9}$$

where $P(q, s|u)$ represents the relevance of song s to query q based on user u's opinions on the song.

With the posterior estimation of $\boldsymbol{\theta_u}$, $\boldsymbol{\theta_\upsilon}$, $\boldsymbol{\phi_s}$, and $\boldsymbol{\phi_t}$ in the DL-MPTM, we have:

$$\begin{aligned} &P(q, s|u, \boldsymbol{\theta_u}, \boldsymbol{\theta_\upsilon}, \boldsymbol{\phi_s}, \boldsymbol{\phi_t}) \\ &= \sum_{\upsilon=1}^L P(\upsilon|u, \boldsymbol{\theta_u}) P(q, s|\upsilon, \boldsymbol{\theta_\upsilon}, \boldsymbol{\phi_s}, \boldsymbol{\phi_t}) \\ &= \sum_{\upsilon=1}^L P(\upsilon|u, \boldsymbol{\theta_u}) \prod_{i=1}^n P(t_i, s|\upsilon, \boldsymbol{\theta_\upsilon}, \boldsymbol{\phi_s}, \boldsymbol{\phi_t}) \end{aligned} \tag{10}$$

where $P(\upsilon|u, \boldsymbol{\theta_u})$ is the probability of user u selecting music dimension υ, and $P(q, s|\upsilon, \boldsymbol{\theta_\upsilon}, \boldsymbol{\phi_s}, \boldsymbol{\phi_t})$ is the joint probability of query q and s in the music dimension υ. In the derivation, we assume the query terms are independent from each other under this specific music dimension. Given the music dimension υ, s and t are independent, the joint probability of term t_i and song s in the music dimension υ can be estimated by multiplying the the probability of s and t_i in the music dimension υ: $P(s|\upsilon, \boldsymbol{\phi_s})$ and $P(t_i|\upsilon, \boldsymbol{\theta_\upsilon}, \phi_t)$.

$$P(t_i, s|\upsilon, \boldsymbol{\theta_\upsilon}, \boldsymbol{\phi_s}, \boldsymbol{\phi_t}) = P(s|\upsilon, \boldsymbol{\phi_s}) \sum_{z=1}^K P(t_i|z, \boldsymbol{\phi_t}) P(z|\upsilon, \boldsymbol{\theta_\upsilon}) \tag{11}$$

The probability of term t_i in music dimension υ can be obtained by the generative probability of term t_i in the subtopic space: $\sum_{z=1}^K P(t_i|z, \boldsymbol{\phi_t}) P(z|\upsilon, \boldsymbol{\theta_\upsilon})$. Based on Eq. 10 and Eq. 11, the probability of user u selecting s for query q can be estimated:

$$\begin{aligned} &P(q, s|u, \boldsymbol{\theta_u}, \boldsymbol{\theta_\upsilon}, \boldsymbol{\phi_s}, \boldsymbol{\phi_t}) \\ &= \sum_{\upsilon=1}^L P(\upsilon|u, \boldsymbol{\theta_u}) \prod_{i=1}^n P(s|\upsilon, \boldsymbol{\phi_s}) \sum_{z=1}^K P(t_i|z, \boldsymbol{\phi_t}) P(z|\upsilon, \boldsymbol{\theta_\upsilon}) \\ &= \sum_{\upsilon=1}^L \theta_{u,\upsilon} \cdot \prod_{i=1}^n \phi_{\upsilon,s} \cdot \sum_{z=1}^K \theta_{\upsilon,z} \cdot \phi_{z,t_i} \end{aligned} \tag{12}$$

Intuitively, for a specific music dimension υ, $P(\upsilon|u, \boldsymbol{\theta_u})$ denotes the preference of user u in this dimension; $P(s|\upsilon, \boldsymbol{\phi_s})$ denotes the likelihood of song s in this dimension; $\sum_{z=1}^K P(z|\upsilon, \boldsymbol{\theta_\upsilon}) P(t|z, \boldsymbol{\phi_t})$ denotes the likelihood of a term t in this dimension. Thus, $P(\upsilon|u, \boldsymbol{\theta_u}) P(s|\upsilon, \boldsymbol{\phi_s}) \sum_{z=1}^K P(z|\upsilon, \boldsymbol{\theta_\upsilon}) P(t|z, \boldsymbol{\phi_t})$ indicates the likelihood for user u to consider song s is relevant to term t in this music dimension.

Algorithm 1 summarizes the whole procedure of personalized text-based retrieval method. DL-MPTM training process can be carried out in offline phase (line 1 - 2). Personalized music search is based on the obtained parameters in DL-MPTM, for a given query q, a rank list $\mathcal{L}$ can be returned (line 3 - 4).

Algorithm 1 DL-MPTM based personalized text-based music retrieval

Offline Phase: DL-MPTM model training
Input: User's music profiles: user-song documents, and song's contents
Output: $\theta_{u,\upsilon}$, $\phi_{\upsilon,s}$, $\theta_{\upsilon,z}$ and ϕ_{z,t_i}

1: Train the DL-MPTM model using the collapsed Gibbs sampling method
2: Estimate $\theta_{u,\upsilon}$, $\phi_{\upsilon,s}$, $\theta_{\upsilon,z}$, and ϕ_{z,t_i} using Eq. (6) - Eq.(8)

Online Phase: personalized music search
Input: A query $q = \{t_1, t_2, ..., t_n\}$
Output: A ranking list $\mathcal{L}$

3: Compute $P(q, s|u)$ using Eq. 12 based on the estimate parameters
4: Sort the songs into a ranking list $\mathcal{L}$ in the descending order of their probabilities $P(q, s|u)$

4. EXPERIMENTAL CONFIGURATION

In this section, we present the experimental settings for the performance evaluation, including test collections, query set with corresponding ground truth, competitors and performance metrics.

4.1 Test Collections

In order to achieve good repeatability of the experiments, test collections are developed based on two public datasets. Their details are as follows,

- **Taste Profile Subset (TPS)**[5] **[20]**: This dataset consists of more than 48 million triplets (*user, song, count*) gathered from user listening histories. Here, "(user, song, count)" refers to the number of times (*i.e., count*) the *user* played the *song*. It contains approximately 1.2 million unique users and covers more than 380,000 songs. From this dataset, we randomly select 10,000 users with their listening records for our experiments.
- **Lastfm-Dataset-1K (Lastfm-1K)**[6] **[7]**: This dataset contains (*user, timestamp, artist, song*) quadruples collected from the Last.fm using the public API. This dataset includes the listening history (until May 5th, 2009) of 992 users, 961,417 songs of 176,948 artists. Based on the quadruples records, we can also get the triplets (*user, song, count*) for this dataset.

In order to ensure the quality of test collections, the p-core filtering method [2] is used to filter users and songs. The p-core of level k has the property, that each song was listened to by at least k users and each user listened to at least k songs. In the experiments, k is set to 20. For the remaining songs, the 30 seconds audio samples were downloaded from 7digital[7], and their tags were crawled from Last.fm. Table 2 summarizes the details about the two datasets used in experiments. It is worth mentioning that two datasets have very different properties. Comparing with TPS, Lastfm-1K contains fewer users while each user has richer listening records. Thus, two datasets are used to examine the performances of personalized music retrieval systems in two scenarios: (1) with rich users' listening records available (Lastfm-1K), and (2) with limited users' listening records available (TPS), respectively.

Table 2: Details of two datasets used in experiments.

Dataset	#User	#Songs	#Artist	#Ave. Listened Songs per User
Lastfm-1K	992	7433	881	335.51
TPS	7022	2332	1094	15.96

The training of DL-MPTM model needs the played records of songs by users and the songs' contents, including textual content (e.g., textual words describing the song) and music content (e.g., audio words of the song). To facilitate the DL-MPTM training, we organize the related data into three types of documents. The description and generation process of the three types of documents are presented below.

User-Song Document For each user, a user-song document is generated based on his/her played records. The document is comprised by the concatenation of the songs (a "song" in a document is indexed by a unique ID) played by the users. For example, if a user u with profiles $(u, s_1, 2)$, $(u, s_2, 3)$, $(u, s_3, 1)$, the user's user-song document is $\{s_1, s_1, s_2, s_2, s_2, s_3\}$. It is worth noticing that the songs in the documents can be in any order of sequence. To accelerate the training process, the user-song document for each user is created by concatenating the songs that were played more than 2 times by the user, and each song only appears once. Thus, for each user, the user-song document is actually a playlist consisting of the songs that were preferred by the user in the past. For the users who are used as query users in experiments, half of the songs in their playlists are randomly selected as test songs and thus removed from the user-song document used in the training stage (see Sect. 4.1.1).

Song-Text Document The document contains the textual contents of the song, namely, the text words of a song used in the DL-MPTM. In our implementation, social tags are used to represent the text documents of songs. Our model is to capture the correlation of user, song, and term to facilitate personalized search. The tags of each song are collected from Last.fm using public API (Track.getTopTags). In our implementation, for each dataset, we filtered the tags that appeared in less than 10 songs. Besides, we also remove the tags which express personal preferences on the songs, such as "favorite songs", "favorite", "best song forever", etc. The remaining tags of a song are concatenated together and tokenized with a standard stop-list to form the text document for the song.

Song-Audio Document The document contains the audio content of a song, namely, the audio words used in the DL-MPTM. The audio contents of one song are represented by "bag-of-audio-words" document. An audio word is a representative short frame of audio stream in a music corpus. The general procedures to generate the audio words consists of three steps: (1) segment the audio track of each song in a corpus into short frames; (2) extract acoustic features from each short frame; and (3) apply a clustering algorithm (e.g., k-means) to group the short frames into n clusters based on their acoustic features. The cluster centers are the audio words generated for the corpus. By encoding each short frame of a song with the nearest cluster center (or audio word), then the song is indexed as a sequence of audio words. In our implementation, we segment each song into 0.05s short frames without overlapping. Also, each song is converted to a standard mono-channel and 22,050 Hz sampling rate WAV format. Mel Frequency Cepstral Coefficients (MFCCs) [18] feature is used to generate the audio words. For each frame, a 13-d MFCCs vector with its first and second instantaneous derivatives are extracted, achieving a final 39-d MFFCs feature. We use K-means to generate the audio words. And for each dataset, we generate a vocabulary of 4096 audio words.

4.1.1 User-Specific Query, Test Collection, Ground Truth

In personalized music retrieval, a positive result should not only be relevant to the query but also be preferred by the query user[8]. In other words, to evaluate personalized music retrieval systems, we need to know (1) whether the result is relevant to the query, and (2) whether the user prefers the result. Therefore, user's preferences on all the songs in the test collection should be available in the evalu-

[5]http://labrosa.ee.columbia.edu/millionsong/tasteprofile
[6]http://www.dtic.upf.edu/ ocelma/MusicRecommendation Dataset/lastfm-1K.html
[7]https://www.7digital.com/

[8]The user who submits the query is called the query user. In personalized information retrieval, user and query should be in pairs. Afterward, we use "query users" to refer to the users used in the search stage.

Table 3: Several examples for three types of queries.

1-Word Query	2-Word Query	3-Word Query
rock	chill, soft	00s, male, rock
metal	chill, mellow	00s, indie, mellow
piano	male, mellow	chill, mellow, rock
happy	drums, guitar	british, male, rock
rainy	country, guitar	melancholy, rock, sad
driving	danceable, harmonies	mellow, folk, tonality
energetic	alternative, guitar	guitar, rock, vocalists
romantic	emotional, romantic	chillout, mellow, rock

ation. To achieve the goal, we create the query set and the test collection specific to each individual user. Firstly, a set of users is randomly selected from the datasets (Lastfm-1K and TPS) as query users. Then, for each user, a set of text queries are generated and a test collection for this specific user is created by randomly sampling half of the songs from his/her user-song document. In the user-specific test collection, the played times of songs can be used to estimate the user's preferences on these songs. Specifically, the relevance levels of a song with respect to a user-specific query are defined as follows,

- Non-relevant (0): song's text document does not contain all the query terms *or* the user listened to the song only once.
- Relevant (1): song's text document contains all the query term, *and* the user listened to the songs for 2 to 5 times.
- Highly relevant (2): song's text document contains all the query term, *and* the user listened to the songs for more than 5 times.

The definitions of relevance levels are based on the assumption that more times a user listen a song, higher preference level the user have on the song. The evidence that a user listened to a song more than two times indicates that the user shows some interests in the song. The songs listened to only once are regarded as irrelevant, since it could be a variety of reasons why users listen to a song only once. Notice that for a user, his/her listened songs, which are used in the *user-song document* in the topic model training stage, are removed from the test collections in the retrieval stage.

To test the performance of queries used in real scenarios, three types of text queries are developed for evaluation purpose: one-, two- and three-word queries, as users seldom issue long queries for music search in reality [21]. This strategy is also often applied in previous text-based music retrieval studies [21, 31]. For the one-word queries in each dataset, the most frequently used words are used as candidates. For the two- and three-word queries, the most frequent co-occurrent two and three words in tags are used as candidates, respectively. The *query users* and *user-specific queries* are carefully selected from these candidates to ensure that, for each user, the user-specific test collection contains sufficient relevant songs for his/her queries (for the fair comparisons of different retrieval methods) [21]. The query words cover the commonly used music concepts, such as *genre*, *instrument*, *mood*, and *era*. Table 3 shows the query examples used in the experiments.

Since the average number of songs listened to by users in two datasets are very different, different numbers of users and queries can be generated in two datasets. The details about users and queries in both datasets are as below.

- **Lastfm-1K**: In this dataset, 124 users are selected as query users, and 96 different queries (30 one-word queries, 30 two-word queries, and 36 three-word queries) are selected. The selected queries are the same for all the users. The number of songs in this test collection of each user is at least 500. In total, there are 11,904 user-specific queries used in this dataset.
- **TPS**: Because the number of songs listened by users in this dataset is much smaller, few user-specific queries can be applied in order to make sure that there are enough positive songs (for each query) in the user-specific test collections. Finally, we select 20 users and 20 queries (8 one-word queries, 6 two-word queries, and 6 three-word queries) per user. Similarly, the queries of all the users are the same. The least number of songs in the test collection for each user is set to be 100. In total, there are 400 user-specific queries used in this dataset.

4.2 Experimental Setup

This section introduces the details about competitors, evaluation metrics and system parameters. To verify the effectiveness of the proposed personalized text-based music retrieval system, we compare it with popular and state-of-the-art text-based music retrieval methods, as well as the existing personalized music retrieval methods:

- **Text-based Music Retrieval (TMR)**: Based on the song-text documents, the standard tf-idf weighting scheme is used to compute the similarity between query and songs with the standard cosine distance in Vector Space Model (VSM) [26].
- **Weighted Linear Combination (WLC)**: Similar to the WLC described in [22], the first result returned by TMR is used as the seed for a content-based music retrieval (CBMR) method. Then the score of the TMR method and the CBMR method are linearly combined together to generate the final search results. In our experiment, the CBMR method described in [25] is used. Specifically, the "audio words" are treated as text terms, and then the standard VSM method is used to retrieve the music by using the seed song as query. The combination weights are carefully tuned to achieve the highest MAP in experiments.
- **Post-Hoc Audio-Based Reranking (PAR)** [16]: It was originally proposed to improve a text-based search engine that indexes songs based on related Web documents. Briefly, for each song s, the PAR approach computes a new score that combines the text-based rank of s, the text-based rankings of all the songs having s in their neighbourhoods, and the rank of s in all these neighbourhoods. The songs are then sorted according to this new score. In our implementation, the top 100 songs are re-ranked by the TMR method.
- **Personalized Retrieval Model (PRM) [11]**: To the best of our knowledge, this is the only scheme specially proposed for personalized text-based music retrieval in previous literature. It is an simple extension of LDA. The graphical representation of this model is illustrated in Fig. 2. This topic model captures the term associations based on their co-occurrences in the

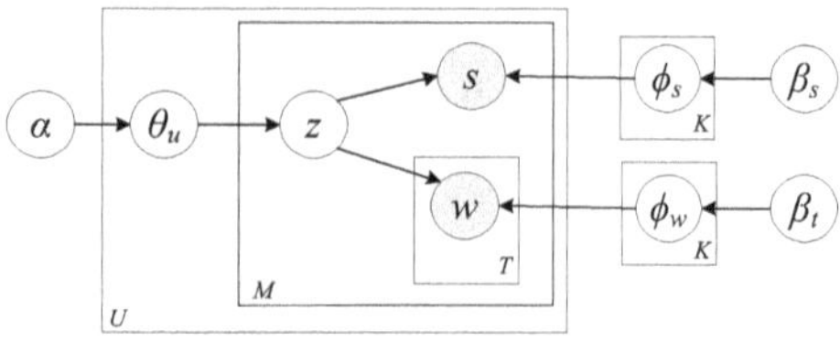

Figure 2: Graphical representation for PRM.

same song and the song associations based on their co-occurrences in the same user's profile under the same latent space. Each user's music preference is modeled as a multinomial distribution over a set of topics; and each topic has a distribution over the set of songs and terms. This model does not take the music contents into account.

Evaluation Metrics In information retrieval, users are more interested in results in the top positions. Therefore, we focus on the evaluation of top results in terms of accuracy. Several standard information retrieval metrics are used, including precision at k (Precision@k), Mean Average Precision (MAP) and Normalized Discounted Cumulative Gain at k (NDCG@k) [13]. The relevance levels (i.e., 0, 1, and 2) are used to compute NDCG. For Precision@k and MAP, both relevant (i.e., 1) and highly-relevant (i.e., 2) results are regarded as positive results.

Parameter Setting In our implementation, the Dirichlet hyper-parameters of both topic models (DL-MPTM and PRM) are empirically set: $\alpha = 1.0$, $\gamma = 1.0$, $\beta_s = \beta_t = \beta_v = 0.01$. We carefully tune the latent topic numbers in both topic models. In DL-MPTM, the number of latent music dimension is tuned in $\{5, 10, 20, 30, 40, 50, 60\}$ and the number of latent sub-topics is tuned in {20, 40, 60, 80, 100, 150}. The number of latent topics in PRM is tuned in {20, 40, 60, 80, 100, 150}. Besides, the combination weight w in WLC retrieval methods are both tuned from 0 to 1 in steps of 0.1.

5. EXPERIMENTAL RESULTS

This section reports the experimental results of our methods and other competitors on retrieval performance. The reported results of DL-MPTM and PRM are based on the optimal numbers of latent topics in each dataset. The reported results based on MAP and NDCG in all the tables are truncated at 10, namely, MAP@10 and NDCG@10. The symbol (*) after a numeric value denotes significant differences ($p < 0.05$, a two-tailed paired t-test) with the corresponding second best measurement. All the results presented in below are the average values of queries over all the users.

5.1 Retrieval Performance

Effectiveness Table 4 reports the retrieval performance on different queries composed of one, two and three words on the two datasets. As can be seen, the proposed model outperforms all the other algorithms over both datasets. Larger performance gain can be achieved when considering more results in the top positions; in particular, the improvements in P@10, MAP and NDCG are statistically significantly compared to other algorithms. After comparing the results gained using TMR, WLC, and PAR, it is easy to find that for Lastfm-1K dataset, the consideration of audio features with text can improve the search results. Besides, PAR obtains better results than WLC does. However, in TPS dataset, the performance decreases when using acoustic features for re-ranking. It is worth noticing that the results of WLC in TPS are the same to TMR. It is mainly because the best performance of WLC can be achieved by only using text feature in WLC. Notice that the search datasets of query users in Lastfm-1K is much larger than that of users in TPS (see Sect. 4.1.1). Generally, it is difficult for the content-based method to achieve better search results over a smaller dataset, because finding songs with similar contents in smaller datasets is harder. Thus the audio feature does not work well when being applied to support search over the TPS dataset.

On the other hand, PRM and DL-MPTM achieve much better performance than the other three methods (TMR, PAR, and WLC), which have not taken the personal music preferences into account. It demonstrates the importance of user's music preference in facilitating effective music retrieval. DL-MPTM's performance improvement over PRM on both datasets demonstrates the effectiveness of our proposed dual-layers topic model in capturing the correlation of user, song, and term. In PRM, the correlation is modeled using the same latent space, which is discovered based on both the co-occurrence of songs in playlists and the co-occurrence contents of songs. In DL-MPTM, the correlation is captured by two layers of connected latent spaces: the low-level latent space (constructed by *latent semantic subtopics*) is discovered based on the co-occurrence contents of songs, the high-level latent space (constructed *latent music dimensions*) is discovered based on the co-occurrence of songs in playlists and the co-occurrence of latent subtopics across songs.

Table 5 compares the performances of TMR, PAR, and DL-MPTM based on the top five search results in the ranking lists of one representative query in each type. The relevance level of each song in the top five positions is also shown. The results demonstrate that DL-MPTM achieves much better performance in task of searching user preferred songs with respect to the queries, comparing to TMR and PAR methods. For example, in response to the query "*guitar, pop*", DL-MPTM places three high-relevant songs at the top rank, compared with only one ranked by the TMR model at the 5th position and two ranked at the 3rd and 4th positions by the PAR model.

Robustness By comparing the results of different query types (one-, two- and three-word queries), we can observe that the search performance is slightly decreased when the query complexity increases. For different types of queries, DL-MPTM achieves significant and consistent improvement over all metrics, showing a superior robustness across multi-word queries.

Music is usually described by different categories of music concepts, such as *mood*, *instrument*, *genre*, and *vocals*, which have been widely studied in music retrieval related research, such as classification and annotation. We examine the search performance of our method over other methods on different categories of music concepts. Table 6 presents evaluation results. One-word queries are classified into different music concept categories as shown in the table. We focus on the one-word queries, since the two- and three-word queries could be the combination of different categories. The category "Other" contains queries, such as "*driving*", "*slow*", "*sexy*", which cannot be classified into other four categories.

Table 4: Retrieval performance for 1-word, 2-word, and 3-word queries

Dataset	Model	1-Word Query					2-Word Query					3-Word Query				
		P@3	P@5	P@10	MAP	NDCG	P@3	P@5	P@10	MAP	NDCG	P@3	P@5	P@10	MAP	NDCG
Lastfm-1K	TMR	.669	.671	.673	.668	.481	.664	.657	.664	.660	.483	.643	.647	.656	.649	.482
	WLC	.662	.654	.658	.669	.495	.652	.646	.653	.658	.489	.675	.669	.669	.650	.486
	PAR	.741	.735	.715	.728	.548	.734	.724	.713	.720	.541	.714	.710	.696	.704	.551
	PRM	.840	.818	.792	.824	.611	.839	.823	.795	.826	.602	.827	.814	.789	.819	.611
	DL-MPTM	**.842**	**.851***	**.858***	**.852**	**.663***	**.839**	**.845**	**.853**	**.846**	**.663***	**.846**	**.848***	**.848***	**.851***	**.664***
TPS	TMR	.550	.600	.557	.558	.434	.533	.575	.565	.564	.425	.490	.526	.533	.516	.412
	WLC	.550	.600	.557	.558	.434	.533	.575	.563	.565	.424	.490	.526	.531	.516	.411
	PAR	.492	.470	.455	.477	.365	.483	.495	.450	.468	.362	.486	.451	.443	.469	.363
	PRM	.648	.609	.583	.621	.492	.633	.565	.545	.595	.479	.567	.555	.557	.574	.486
	DL-MPTM	**.667***	**.640***	**.633***	**.645**	**.520***	**.658***	**.635***	**.629***	**.639***	**.534***	**.655***	**.625***	**.613***	**.619***	**.517***

Table 5: The top 5 songs in the ranking lists obtained by the TMR, PAR, and DL-MPTM models for 3 representative queries of a user "*user_000477*". The relevance level of each result is shown in the parentheses after each result, e.g., "(2)" indicates high relevance (see Sect. 4.1.1).

TMR	PAR	DL-MPTM
	metal	
System of a Down - thetawaves (1)	Rage Against the Machine - Bullet in the head (1)	**Rammstein - Du hast** (2)
System of a Down - I-E-A-I-A-I-O (1)	**Linkin Park - Valentine's day** (2)	A Perfect Circle - Over (1)
Linkin Park - Valentine's day (2)	Audioslave - Set it off (1)	**Nirvana - Smells like teen spirit** (2)
Korn - Did my time (1)	Goldfrapp - Cologne cerrone houdini (1)	Muse - Hysteria (1)
Metallica - Nothing Else Matters (1)	**Incubus - Anna molly** (2)	**AC/DC - Back In Black** (2)
	guitar, pop	
Dread Zeppelin - Misty mountain hop (0)	New Order - crystal (0)	**Oasis - Wonderwall** (2)
Dire Straits - Sultans of swing (1)	Dire Straits - Romeo and juliet (1)	**The Smashing Pumpkins - 1979** (2)
Dire Straits - Money for nothing (1)	**Linkin Park - Valentine's day** (2)	**The Cranberries - Zombie** (2)
Dread Zeppelin - Your time is gonna come (0)	**The Smashing Pumpkins - 1979** (2)	Blur - Song 2 (1)
Dire Straits - Brothers in arms (2)	Red Hot Chili Peppers - Mellowship slinky in b major (1)	Oasis - Live forever (1)
	guitar, rock, vocalists	
Lez Zeppelin - Communication breakdown (0)	The Smiths - Stretch out and wait (0)	**AC/DC - Back in black** (2)
Dread Zeppelin - Misty mountain hop (0)	New Order - Crystal (0)	**AC/DC - Highway to hell** (2)
Lez Zeppelin - Whole lotta love (0)	Interpol - The heinrich maneuver (0)	Dread Zeppelin - Heartbreaker (0)
Dire Straits - Sultans Of Swing (1)	Klaxons - Two receivers (0)	**The Cranberries - Zombie** (2)
Dire Straits - Money for nothing (1)	Dire Straits - Romeo and juliet (1)	**AC/DC - Hells bells** (2)

Table 6: Retrieval results for query categories. The best results for each category are indicated in bold.

Category	Modal	P@10	MAP	NDCG
Emotion	TMR	.684	.677	.487
	WLC	.659	.672	.498
	PAR	.721	.732	.550
	PRM	.790	.822	.606
	DL-MPTM	**.863**	**.858**	**.668**
Genre	TMR	.649	.639	.463
	WLC	.646	.644	.474
	PAR	.701	.718	.542
	PRM	.793	.831	.616
	DL-MPTM	**.852**	**.836**	**.647**
Instrument	TMR	.673	.665	.474
	WLC	.651	.669	.491
	PAR	.724	.735	.552
	PRM	.803	.835	.620
	DL-MPTM	**.871**	**.862**	**.673**
Vocals	TMR	.657	.651	.473
	WLC	.665	.672	.488
	PAR	.717	.720	.551
	PRM	.796	.830	.623
	DL-MPTM	**.842**	**.841**	**.648**
Others	TMR	.685	.687	.497
	WLC	.671	.683	.518
	PAR	.711	.729	.547
	PRM	.787	.808	.603
	DL-MPTM	**.850**	**.847**	**.666**

The significant improvements over other methods on P@10, MAP and NDCG show the effectiveness and robustness of DL-MPTM over different music concept categories.

Comparing the search performances of all the methods on the two datasets, they cannot achieve good performance when searching over the TPS dataset, because of the limited size of relevant results in each user's specific dataset. Notice that the number of training samples in the TPS dataset is also much smaller than that in the Last.fm-1K dataset. On the TPS dataset, the absolute performance gain achieved by DL-MPTM over other methods for all the metrics are at least comparable to those in the Lastfm-1K dataset. This demonstrates a strong robustness of DL-MPTM on relatively small training datasets.

5.2 Effects of Parameters

In this section, we investigate the effects of parameters on the proposed retrieval method. In topic models, it is hard to accurately pre-define the number of topics, which has important effects on the results. In the DL-MPTM model, there are two sets of latent topics: the number of latent music dimensions in the first layer, and the number of subtopics in the second layer. Fig. 3a and Fig. 3b illustrate the effects of the two parameters, respectively. From the results, it can be observed that the number of latent music dimensions has strong impacts on the final performance, and it is optimal to set the number of music dimensions to [5, 20]. In contrast, we can observe the minor effects of sub-topic number, especially for Lastfm-1K dataset. Fig. 3c shows the effects of weights in the combination of acoustic similarity and textual similarity. From the results, we can find that for Lastfm-1K, the combination of acoustic similarity and textual similarity can slightly improve the performance when w is set to [0.6, 0.8]. However, the performance degradation is observed when the same similarity combination is applied to the TPS dataset. Notice that in the WLC method, the acoustic similarity is computed based on the first search result of TMR. Thus, the accuracy of the first search result has an important impact on the WLC performance. When the search accuracy of TMR is relatively high, WLC can improve the TMR performance further, such as the results observed in the Lastfm-1K dataset. This also suggests that when searching music using both text and audio query examples (using relevance feedback), performance could be improved by the combination of acoustic similarity and text similarity.

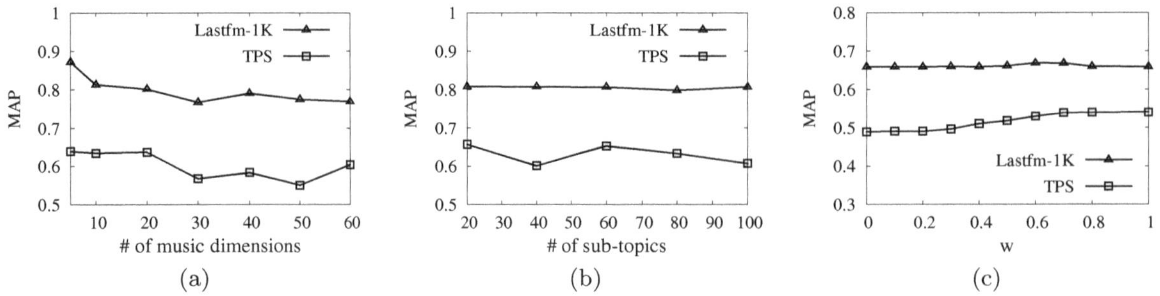

Figure 3: Effects of parameters in topic model based retrieval methods.

6. CONCLUSION

In this paper, we present a personalized text-based music retrieval system which exploits the user listening behaviors in social music services. The system can accurately estimate the relevance of a song with respect to a term subject to user's music preference. To achieve the goal, a Dual-Layer Music Preference Topic Model (DL-MPTM) is proposed to leverage the user listening logs and social tags to learn the interactions among (user, song, term), which are applied for personalized text-based music search. To evaluate the performance of the personalized retrieval system, comprehensive experiments have been conducted on two public datasets. The comparisons with the state-of-the-art text-based retrieval methods and existing personalized music retrieval methods in experiments show that our method can significantly improve the search performance in terms of accuracy. The results also demonstrate the importance of effective integration of personal music preference in developing high-performance music search engines, and verify the effectiveness of our proposed retrieval model.

7. REFERENCES

[1] K. Barnard, P. Duygulu, D. Forsyth, N. D. Freitas, D. Blei, and M. Jordan. Matching words and pictures. *The Journal of Machine Learning Research*, 3:1107–1135, 2003.

[2] V. Batagelj and M. Zaveršnik. Generalized cores. *arXiv preprint cs/0202039*, 2002.

[3] D. Blei, T. Griffiths, M. Jordan, and J. Tenenbaum. Hierarchical topic models and the nested chinese restaurant process. *Proc. of NIPS*, 16:17, 2004.

[4] D. Blei and M. Jordan. Modeling annotated data. In *Proc. of ACM SIGIR*, 2003.

[5] D. Blei, A. Ng, and M. Jordan. Latent dirichlet allocation. *Journal of Machine Learning Research*, 3:993–1022, 2003.

[6] F. Cai, S. Liang, and M. de Rijke. Personalized document re-ranking based on bayesian probabilistic matrix factorization. In *Proc. of ACM SIGIR*, 2014.

[7] O. Celma. *Music Recommendation and Discovery in the Long Tail*. Springer, 2010.

[8] Z. Cheng and J. Shen. Just-for-me: An adaptive personalization system for location-aware social music recommendation. In *Proc. of ACM ICMR*, 2014.

[9] Z. Cheng and J. Shen. On effective location-aware music recommendation. *ACM Trans. Inf. Syst.*, 34(2):13, 2016.

[10] T. Griffiths and M. Steyvers. Finding scientific topics. *PNAS*, 101(Suppl 1):5228–5235, 2004.

[11] N. Hariri, B. Mobasher, and R. Burke. Personalized text-based music retrieval. In *Workshops at the Twenty-Seventh AAAI Conference on Artificial Intelligence*, 2013.

[12] K. Hoashi, K. Matsumoto, and N. Inoue. Personalization of user profiles for content-based music retrieval based on relevance feedback. In *Proc. of ACM MM*, 2003.

[13] K. Järvelin and J. Kekäläinen. Cumulated gain-based evaluation of ir techniques. *ACM Trans. Inf. Syst.*, 20(4):422–446, 2002.

[14] Y. Jia, M. Salzmann, and T. Darrell. Learning cross-modality similarity for multinomial data. In *Proc. of IEEE ICCV*, 2011.

[15] D. Kim, G. Voelker, and L. Saul. A variational approximation for topic modeling of hierarchical corpora. In *Proc. of ICML*, 2013.

[16] P. Knees, T. Pohle, M. Schedl, D. Schnitzer, K. Seyerlehner, and G. Widmer. Augmenting text-based music retrieval with audio similarity. In *Proc. of ISMIR*, 2009.

[17] M. Levy and M. Sandler. Music information retrieval using social tags and audio. *IEEE Trans. Multimed.*, 11(3):383–395, 2009.

[18] B. Logan. Mel frequency cepstral coefficients for music modeling. In *Proc. of ISMIR*, 2000.

[19] A. Majumder and N. Shrivastava. Know your personalization: learning topic level personalization in online services. In *Proc. of WWW*, 2013.

[20] B. McFee, T. Bertin-Mahieux, D. Ellis, and G. Lanckriet. The million song dataset challenge. In *Proc. of WWW*, 2012.

[21] R. Miotto and G. Lanckriet. A generative context model for semantic music annotation and retrieval. *IEEE Trans. Audio, Speech, and Language Process.*, 20(4):1096–1108, 2012.

[22] R. Miotto and N. Orio. A probabilistic model to combine tags and acoustic similarity for music retrieval. *ACM Trans. Inf. Syst.*, 30(2):8, 2012.

[23] J. Paisley, C. Wang, D. M. Blei, and M. I. Jordan. Nested hierarchical dirichlet processes. *IEEE Trans. Pattern Anal. Mach. Intell.*, 37(2):256–270, 2015.

[24] D. Putthividhy, H. Attias, and S. Nagarajan. Topic regression multi-modal latent dirichlet allocation for image annotation. In *Proc. of IEEE CVPR*, 2010.

[25] M. Riley, E. Heinen, and J. Ghosh. A text retrieval approach to content-based audio retrieval. In *Proc. of ISMIR*, 2008.

[26] G. Salton, A. Wong, and C.-S. Yang. A vector space model for automatic indexing. *Communications of the ACM*, 18(11):613–620, 1975.

[27] M. Schedl and A. Flexer. Putting the user in the center of music information retrieval. In *Proc. of ISMIR*, 2012.

[28] J. Shen, H. Pang, M. Wang, and S. Yan. Modeling concept dynamics for large scale music search. In *Proc. of ACM SIGIR*, 2012.

[29] A. Singla, R. White, A. Hassan, and E. Horvitz. Enhancing personalization via search activity attribution. In *Proc. of ACM SIGIR*, 2014.

[30] P. Symeonidis, M. Ruxanda, A. Nanopoulos, and Y. Manolopoulos. Ternary semantic analysis of social tags for personalized music recommendation. In *Proc. of ISMIR*, 2008.

[31] D. Turnbull, L. Barrington, D. Torres, and G. Lanckriet. Towards musical query-by-semantic-description using the cal500 data set. In *Proc. of ACM SIGIR*, 2007.

[32] S. Virtanen, Y. Jia, A. Klami, and T. Darrell. Factorized multi-modal topic model. In *Proc. of UAI*, 2012.

[33] A. Wang. The shazam music recognition service. *Communications of the ACM*, 49(8):44–48, 2006.

[34] J. Wang, Y. Shih, M. Wu, H. Wang, and S. Jeng. Colorizing tags in tag cloud: a novel query-by-tag music search system. In *Proc. of ACM MM*, 2011.

Semantification of Identifiers in Mathematics for Better Math Information Retrieval

Moritz Schubotz[†], Alexey Grigorev[†], Marcus Leich[†], Howard S. Cohl[‡], Norman Meuschke[§], Bela Gipp[§], Abdou S. Youssef[♯‡] and Volker Markl[†]

[†]TU Berlin, Germany, [‡]National Institute of Standards and Technology, USA, [§]Universität Konstanz, Germany, [♯]The George Washington University, USA

schubotz@tu-berlin.de

ABSTRACT

Mathematical formulae are essential in science, but face challenges of ambiguity, due to the use of a small number of identifiers to represent an immense number of concepts. Corresponding to word sense disambiguation in Natural Language Processing, we disambiguate mathematical identifiers. By regarding formulae and natural text as one monolithic information source, we are able to extract the semantics of identifiers in a process we term *Mathematical Language Processing* (MLP). As scientific communities tend to establish standard (identifier) notations, we use the document domain to infer the actual meaning of an identifier. Therefore, we adapt the software development concept of namespaces to mathematical notation. Thus, we learn namespace definitions by clustering the MLP results and mapping those clusters to subject classification schemata. In addition, this gives fundamental insights into the usage of mathematical notations in science, technology, engineering and mathematics. Our gold standard based evaluation shows that MLP extracts relevant identifier-definitions. Moreover, we discover that identifier namespaces improve the performance of automated identifier-definition extraction, and elevate it to a level that cannot be achieved within the document context alone.

1. PROBLEM AND MOTIVATION

Mathematical formulae are essential in Science, Technology, Engineering, and Mathematics (STEM). Consequently, Mathematical Information Retrieval (MIR) continues to receive increasing research attention [13]. Current MIR approaches perform well in identifying formulae that contain the same set of identifiers or have a similar layout tree structure [2].

However, the ambiguity of mathematical notation decreases the retrieval effectiveness of current MIR approaches. Since the number of mathematical concepts by far exceeds the number of established mathematical identifiers, the same identifier often denotes various concepts [16]. For instance, 'E' may refer to 'energy' in physics, 'expected value' in statistics or 'elimination matrix' in linear algebra. Analyzing the identifier-based and structural similarity of formulae without considering the context of a formula can therefore lead to the retrieval of non-relevant results.

Ambiguity is a problem that mathematical notation and natural language have in common. Since words are also often ambiguous [6, 9, 16], *Word Sense Disambiguation* [15], i.e., identifying the meaning of an ambiguous word in a specific context [15], is an integral part of Natural Language Processing. Typical approaches for Word Sense Disambiguation replace a word by its meaning [34] or append the meaning to the word. For example, if the ambiguous word *man* has the meaning *human species* in a specific context, one can replace it by man_species to contrast it from the meaning *male adult*, replaced by man_adult. We transfer this idea to ambiguous mathematical identifiers. If the identifier E has the meaning *energy* in the context of physics, one could replace E by E_energy given one can determine that E is indeed used as energy in this context.

In this paper, we propose a method to semantically enrich mathematical identifiers by determining and assigning the context (namespace) in which the identifier is used, e.g., mathematics or physics. We determine the *namespace* of an identifier by analyzing the text surrounding mathematical formulae using Natural Language Processing (NLP) techniques. In software development, a namespace refers to a collection of terms that is grouped, because it shares functionality or purpose. Typically, namespaces are used to provide modularity and to resolve name conflicts [7]. We extend the concept of namespaces to mathematical identifiers and present an automated method to learn the namespaces that occur in a document collection.

Employing an analysis of natural language to enrich the information content of formulae is a new approach, which Pagel and Schubotz termed **Mathematical Language Processing** (MLP) [26]. Today's MIR systems treat formulae and natural language as separate information sources [2]. While current systems offer retrieval from both sources (formulae and text), they typically do not link them. For example, math-aware search systems allow to search in formulae by specifying a query using mathematical notation or specialized query languages. To search in the text, MIR systems support traditional keyword search [2].

We deem the MLP approach promising for two reasons. First, a large-scale corpus study showed that around 70 percent of the symbolic elements in scientific papers are explicitly denoted in the text [35]. Second, although almost all iden-

SIGIR '16, July 17 - 21, 2016, Pisa, Italy

ACM ISBN 978-1-4503-4069-4/16/07...$15.00

DOI: http://dx.doi.org/10.1145/2911451.2911503

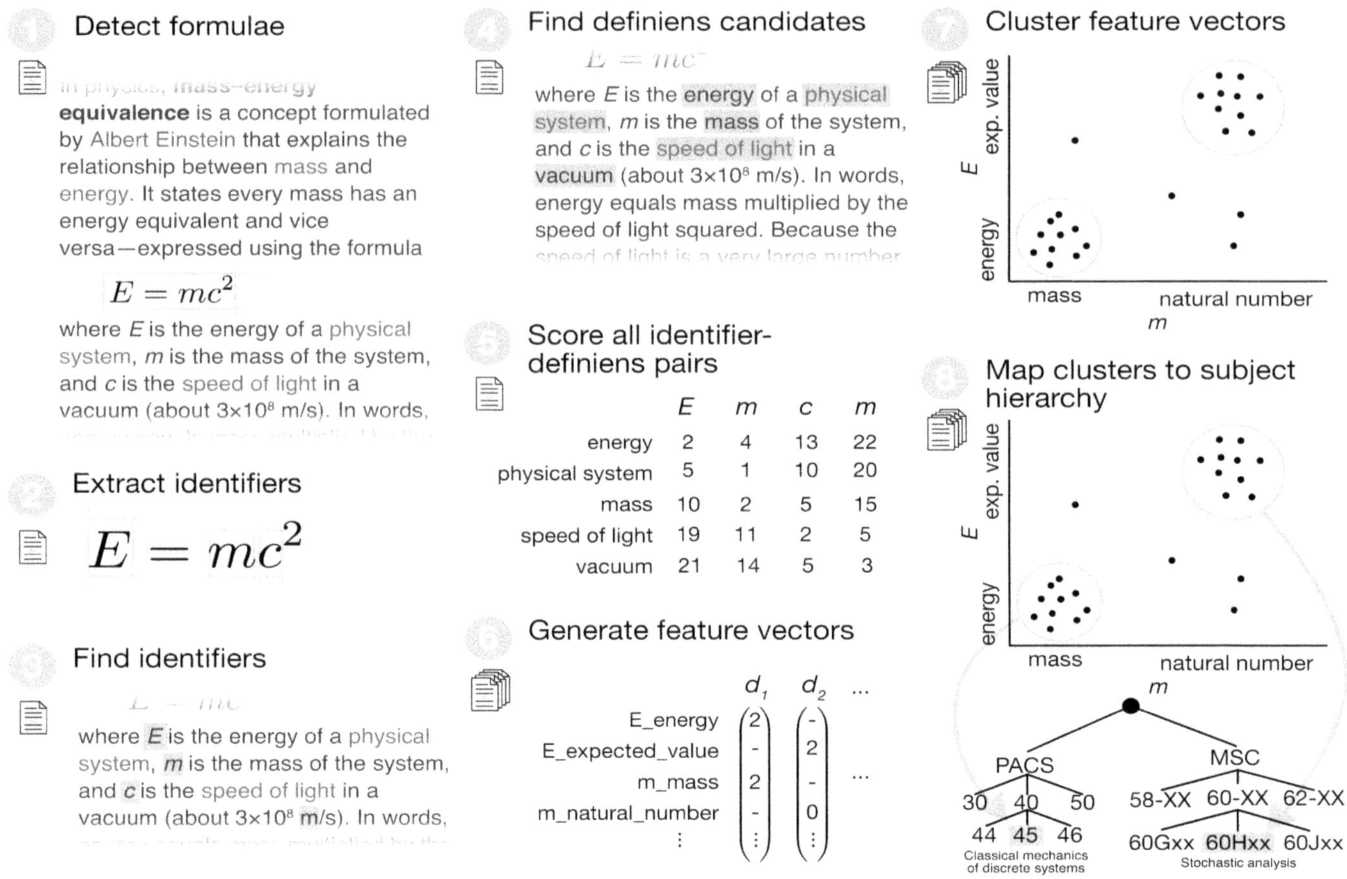

Figure 1: Overview of the document based Mathematical Language Processing pipeline (steps 1-5), and the corpus based namespace discovery pipeline (steps 6-8). For each step, a detailed description is available in the corresponding Subsection of Section 2.

tifiers have multiple meanings, mathematical notation obeys conventions for choosing identifiers [5, 16]. Therefore, we propose that identifying the namespace of identifiers can improve their disambiguation and the capabilities for machine processing mathematics in general. Improved machine processing of mathematics can benefit recommender [31] and plagiarism detection systems [8, 21] for STEM literature. Likewise, formula search engines, and assistance tools for authors and students could benefit.

In summary, the contributions we make in this paper are:

(1) a method to extract the semantic meaning of mathematical identifiers from the text surrounding mathematical formulae;
(2) a method to learn the set of mathematical namespaces occurring in a collection;
(3) a method that utilizes identified mathematical namespaces to improve the disambiguation of mathematical identifiers; and
(4) a large scale analysis of identifier use as part of the mathematical notation in different scientific fields.

Related Work

Several approaches extract information from the surrounding text to retrieve information about mathematical formulae [17, 36, 24, 26, 19, 11]. Quoc et al. [24] extract entire formulae and link them to natural language descriptions from the surrounding text. Yokoi et al. [36] train a support vector machine to extract mathematical expressions and their natural language phrase. Note, that this phrase also includes function words, etc. In [26], we suggest a Mathematical Language Processing framework - a statistical approach for relating identifiers to definientia, in which they compare a pattern based approach and the MLP approach with part-of-speech tag based distances. They find the MLP approach to be more effective. The findings of Kristianto et al. [17] confirm these findings.

Our approach is the first that uses the concept of namespaces to improve the extraction of semantics regarding mathematical identifiers. While other approaches only use one document at a time to extract the description of a specific formulae [17, 36, 19], we use a large scale corpus and combine information from different documents to extract the meaning of a specific identifier. In contrast, our task is more specific. We limit the extraction of mathematical expressions to identifiers and extract semantic concepts instead of descriptions.

2. OUR APPROACH

2.1 Mathematical Language Processing

The goal of Mathematical Language Processing is to extract identifier-definitions from a text that uses mathematics. Formally, a *definition* consists of three parts: *definiendum*, *definiens* and *definitor*. *Definiendum* is the expression to be defined. *Definiens* is the phrase that defines the definiendum. *Definitor* is the verb that links definiendum and definiens. An identifier-definition is a definition where the definiendum is an identifier.

According to ISO/IEC 40314: "Content *identifiers* represent 'mathematical variables' which have properties, but no fixed value." Identifiers have to be differentiated from *symbols*, that refer to 'specific, mathematically-defined concepts' such as the operator + or the sin function. Identifier-definiens pairs are candidates for identifier-definitions. Since we do not use the definitor, we only extract the definiendum (identifier) and the definiens (natural language term), and extract in the following, identifier-definiens pairs as candidates for identifier-definitions. To illustrate, we introduce the following running example:

Example 1: Mass-energy equivalence

The relation between energy and mass is described by the mass-energy equivalence formula $E = mc^2$, where E is energy, m is mass, and c is the speed of light.

This description includes the formula $E = mc^2$, the three identifiers E, m, and c, and the following identifier-definitions: (E, energy), (m, mass), and (c, speed of light).

In our approach (see Figure 1), we divide the MLP pipeline into the following steps:

(1) Detect formulae;
(2) Extract identifiers;
(3) Find identifiers;
(4) Find definiens candidates; and
(5) Score all identifier-definiens pairs.

(1) *Detect formulae*

In a first step, we need to differentiate between formulae and text. In this paper, we assume that all formulae are explicitly marked as mathematics and that everything marked as mathematics actually is mathematics. However, in real world documents such as conference papers, posters or Wikipedia articles, some formulae are typed using the unicode symbols instead of math mode. As this type of formula is hard to detect, we decided to exclude it from our analysis. Moreover, not all structures marked as formulae are really mathematical formulae. In some cases unmarked text like $\frac{work\ done}{heat\ absorbed}$ or chemical formulae $2\,H_2O \rightarrow 2\,H_2 + O_2$ are also marked as mathematics. One might develop heuristics to discover words and chemical structures within mathematical markup, but this is outside of the scope if this research.

(2) *Extract identifiers*

After having identified the formulae, we extract the list of identifiers from within the formulae. In the above example, this means to extract the identifiers E, m, and c from the formula $E = mc^2$. Mostly, identifiers (in formulae and text), are not explicitly marked as identifiers. Consequently, we develop a heuristic to extract identifiers by assuming the following characteristics: an identifier consists of one variable or a combination of a variable and one or multiple subscripts.

In the following, we will discuss advantages and limitations of this heuristic. In this process, we delineate four limitations (special notation, symbols, sub-super-script, incorrect markup), which we will quantify in the evaluation section. We observe that more complex expressions are sometimes used on behalf of identifiers, such as σ^2 for the 'variance', without mentioning σ and 'standard deviation' at all or ΔS for 'change in entropy'. In this work, we focus on atomic identifiers and thus prefer to extract the pair (S, entropy) instead of (ΔS, change in entropy). The disadvantage of this approach is that we miss some **special notation** such as contra-variant vector components like the coordinate functions x^μ in Einstein notation. In this case, we are able to extract (x, coordinate functions) with our approach, which is not incorrect but less specific than (x^μ, coordinate functions). In addition, we falsely extract several **symbols**, such as the Bessel functions J_α, Y_α, but not all symbols, i.e., we do not extract symbols that use **sub-super-scripts** like the Hankel function $H_\alpha^{(1)}$. Note that especially the superscript is not used uniformly (e.g., it may refer to power, n-th derivative, Einstein notation, inverse function). The most prominent example is the sin symbol, where $\sin^2 : x \mapsto (\sin(x))^2$ vs. $\sin^{-1} : \sin(x) \mapsto x$, for all $x \in [-1,1]$. Far less debatable, but even more common is the problem of **incorrect markup**. The one variable assumption tokenizes natural language words like *heat* into a list of four variables h, e, a, t.

Identifiers often contain additional semantic information, visually conveyed by special diacritical marks or font features. Examples of diacritics are hats to denote estimates (e.g., $\hat{w}$), bars to denote the average (e.g., $\bar{X}$) or arrows to denote vectors (e.g., $\vec{x}$). Regarding the font features, bold lower case single characters are often used to denote vectors (e.g., $\mathbf{w}$) and bold upper case single characters denote matrices (e.g., $\mathbf{X}$), while double-struck fonts are used for sets (e.g., $\mathbb{R}$), calligraphic fonts often denote spaces (e.g., $\mathcal{H}$) and so on. Unfortunately, there is no common notation established for diacritics across all fields of mathematics and thus there is a lot of variance. For example, a vector can be denoted by $\vec{x}$, $\boldsymbol{x}$ or $\mathbf{x}$, and the real line can be denoted either by $\mathbb{R}$ or $\mathbf{R}$.

To decide if two identifiers are identical, we need a comparison function that eliminates invariants in the input format. For example, the inputs `$c_0$` and `$c_{ 0 }$` produce the same presentation c_0 in LaTeX and therefore have to be considered as equivalent. In this work, we compare the identifiers based on abstract syntax trees, which eliminates most of the complications introduced by the invariants in the input encoding. We considered to reduce the identifiers to their root form by discarding all additional visual information, such that $\bar{X}$ becomes X, $\mathbf{w}$ becomes w and $\mathfrak{R}$ becomes R. The disadvantage of this approach is the loss of additional semantic information about the identifier that are potentially useful. For instance, $\mathbf{E}$ usually denotes the electric field, compared to E which is often used for energy. By removing the bold font, we would lose this semantic information. Therefore, we decided against unsing the root form in our approach.

(3) *Find identifiers*

In a next step, all identifiers that are part of the formulae have to be identified in the surrounding text. Therefore, we use mathematical formulae that only consist of a single identifier, or textual elements that are not marked up as mathematics (i.e., words) and are equivalent to one of the identifiers extracted in the formulae before. In the above example, the identifiers E, m and c have to be identified in the text: *'The relation between energy and mass is described by the mass-energy equivalence formula [...], where E is energy, m is mass, and c is the speed of light.'*

④ *Find definiens candidates*

We are not only interested in the identifier, but also in its definiens. Therefore, we extract identifier-definiens pairs (identifier, definiens) as candidates for identifier-definitions. For example, (E, energy) is an identifier-definition, where E is an identifier, and 'energy' is the definiens. In this step, we describe the methods for extracting and scoring the identifier-definitions in three sub-steps:

(1) Math-Aware Part-of-Speech Tagging;
(2) Part-of-Speech based distances; and
(3) Scoring of definiens candidates.

Pagel and Schubotz [26] found the MLP method with a Part-of-Speech based distance measure in a probabilistic approach to outclass a pattern based method. Thus, we use the Part-of-Speech based distances methods here to extract identifier-definitions. First, we define definiens candidates:

(1) noun (singular or plural);
(2) noun phrases (noun-noun, adjective-noun); and
(3) special tokens such as inner-wiki links.

We assume that successive nouns (both singular and plurals), possibly modified by an adjective, are candidates for definientia. Thus, we include noun phrases that either consist of two successive nouns (e.g., 'mean value' or 'speed of light') or an adjective and a noun (e.g., 'gravitational force').

Authors often use special markup to highlight semantic concepts in written language. For example in Wikipedia articles, Wiki markup, a special markup language for specifying document layout elements such as headers, lists, text formatting and tables, is used. In the Wikipedia markup processing, we retain inner Wikipedia links that link to another article that describes the semantic concept, which eliminates the ambiguity in the definiens itself. This link is an example for a definiens candidate of type special token. Part-of-Speech Tagging (POS Tagging) assigns a tag to each word in a given text [15]. Although the POS Tagging task is mainly a tool for text processing, it can be adjusted to scientific documents with mathematical expressions [29, 26]. Therefore, we tag math-related tokens of the text with math specific tags [29]. If a math token is only one identifier, an identifier tag is assigned rather that a formula tag. We introduce another tag for inner-wiki-links. For the extraction of definiens candidates, we use common natural language POS tags as well as the following three task specific tags:

(1) identifiers;
(2) formulae; and
(3) special tokens.

Generally, the Cartesian product of identifiers and definiens might serve as identifier-definition candidate.

⑤ *Score all identifier-definiens pairs*

To extract the definiens candidates, we make three assumptions, according to [26]:

(1) definiens are noun phrases or a special token;
(2) definiens appear close to the identifier; and
(3) if an identifier appears in several formulae, the definiens can be found in a sentence in close proximity to the first occurrence in a formula.

The next step is to select the most probable identifier-definition by ranking identifier-definition candidates by probability [26]. The assumption behind this approach is that definientia occur closely to their related identifiers, and thus the closeness can be exploited to model the probability distribution over identifier-definition candidates. Thus, the score depends on (1) the distance to the identifier of interest and (2) the distance to the closest formula that contains this identifier. The output of this step is a list of identifier-definiens pairs along with the score. Only the pairs with scores above the user specified threshold are retained.

The candidates are ranked by the following formula:

$$R(n,\Delta,t,d)=\frac{\alpha R_{\sigma_d}(\Delta)+\beta R_{\sigma_s}(n)+\gamma \mathrm{tf}(t)}{\alpha+\beta+\gamma}.$$

In this formula Δ is the number of tokens between identifier and definiens candidate, $R_{\sigma_d}(\Delta)$ is a zero-mean Gaussian that models this distance, parametrized with the variance σ_d, and n is the number of sentences between the definiens candidate and the sentence in which the identifier occurs for the first time. Moreover, $R_{\sigma_s}(n)$ denotes a zero-mean Gaussian, parameterized with σ_s, and $\mathrm{tf}(t)$ is the frequency of term t in a sentence, and the weights α,β,γ combine these quantities. Therefore, we reuse the values suggested in [26], namely $\alpha=\beta=1$ and $\gamma=0.1$.

We also tested a refined strategy, which takes into account that the same definition might be explained multiple times in a document and calculated a refined weighting $R_\Sigma=(\eta-1)^{-1}\sum_{i=1}^{n}\eta^{-i}R_i$. Thereby R_i iterates over all weightings from within one document that lead to one definition. However, this did not lead to a significant performance increase for the task at hand, so we dropped this approach. Note that the idea is revived in the Namespace Discovery section, where multiple documents are considered at the same time.

2.2 Namespace Discovery

In this section, we describe the adaptation of the idea of namespaces to identifier disambiguation and the process of namespace discovery to extract identifier-definitions in the following steps:

(1) Automatic Namespace Discovery;
(2) Document Clustering;
(3) Building Namespaces; and
(4) Building Namespace Hierarchy.

Automatic Namespace Discovery

Namespaces in well-defined software exhibit low coupling and high cohesion [18]. Coupling describes the degree of dependence between namespaces. Low coupling means that the dependencies between classes of different namespaces are minimized. Cohesion refers to the dependence within the classes of the same namespace. High cohesion principle means that the related classes should be put together in the same namespace. We define a notation $\mathcal{N}$ as a set of pairs $\{(i,s)\}$, where i is an identifier and s is its semantic meaning or definiens, such that for any pair $(i,s)\in\mathcal{N}$ there is no other pair $(i',s')\in\mathcal{N}$ with $i=i'$. Two notations $\mathcal{N}_1$ and $\mathcal{N}_2$ conflict if there exists a pair $(i_1,s_1)\in\mathcal{N}_1$ and a pair $(i_2,s_2)\in\mathcal{N}_2$ such that $i_1=i_2$ and $s_1\neq s_2$.

Thus, we can define a namespace as a named notation. For example, $\mathcal{N}_{\text{physics}}$ can refer to the notation used in physics. For convenience, we use the Java syntax to refer to specific entries of a namespace [10]. If $\mathcal{N}$ is a namespace and i is an identifier such that $(i,s) \in \mathcal{N}$ for some s, then $\mathcal{N}.i$ is a fully qualified name of the identifier i that relates i to the definiens s. For example, given a namespace $\mathcal{N}_{\text{physics}} = \{(E,\text{'energy'}), (m,\text{'mass'}), (c,\text{'speed of light'})\}$, $\mathcal{N}_{\text{physics}}.E$ refers to 'energy' – the definiens of E in the namespace 'physics'. Analogous to definitions in programming language namespaces, one can expect that (a) definiens in a given mathematical namespace come from the same area of mathematics, and (b) definiens from different namespaces do not intersect heavily. In other words, one can expect namespaces of mathematical notation to have the same properties as well-designed software packages, namely low coupling and high cohesion.

To precisely define these concepts for mathematical namespaces, we represent them via a document-centric model. Suppose we have a collection of n documents $\mathcal{D} = \{d_1,...,d_n\}$ and a set of K namespaces $\{\mathcal{N}_1,...,\mathcal{N}_K\}$. A document d_j can use a namespace $\mathcal{N}_k$ by implicitly importing identifiers from it. Note that real-life scientific documents rarely explicitly use import statements. However, we assume that these implicit namespace imports exist. In this document-centric model, a namespace exhibits low coupling, if only a small subset of documents uses it and high cohesion if all documents in this subset are related to the same domain.

We use the extracted identifier-definitions (see Section 2.1) to discover the namespaces. Since manual discovery of mathematical namespaces is time consuming and error prone, we use Machine Learning techniques to discover namespaces automatically.

We utilize *clustering methods* to find homogeneous groups of documents within a collection. Comparable to NLP identifiers can be regarded as 'words' in the mathematical language and entire formulae as 'sentences'. We use cluster analysis techniques developed for text documents represented via the 'bag-of-words' model for documents with math formulae that are represented by 'bag-of-identifiers'. Some definientia are used only once. Since they do not have any discriminative power, they are not very useful and are excluded. Once the identifiers are extracted, we discard the rest of the formula. As a result, we have a 'bag-of-identifiers'. Analogoe to the bag-of-word approach, we only retain the counts of occurrences of identifiers, but do not preserve any structural information.

⑥ *Generate feature vectors*

For clustering, documents are usually represented using the Vector Space Models [1, 25]. We apply the same model, but use identifiers instead of words to represent documents. As the vocabulary, we use a set of identifier-definiens pairs $V = I \otimes F$ which is an element of the vector product space of the identifier space I and the the definiens space F. We represent documents as m-dimensional vectors $\mathbf{d}_j = (w_1,...,w_m)$, where w_k is the weight of an identifier-definiens pair i_k in the document $\mathbf{d}_j$ and $m = \dim(I)\dim(F)$. We define an identifier-document matrix $\mathbf{D}$ as a matrix where columns represent document vectors and rows represent identifier-document co-occurrences. We evaluate three ways to incorporate the extracted definientia into the model: (1) we use only identifiers without definientia, which reduces the vocabulary to $V_1 = \mathcal{P}_I V$, where the projection operator $\mathcal{P}_I : I \otimes F \to I$ reduces the dimensions $\dim V_1 = \dim I$; (2) we use 'weak' identifier-definiens associations that include identifiers and definientia as separate dimensions, formally $V_2 = \mathcal{P}_{I \oplus F} V$ where the projector $\mathcal{P}_{I \oplus F} : I \otimes F \to I \oplus F$ reduces the dimension to $\dim V_2 = \dim I + \dim F$; and (3) we use 'strong' identifier-definiens associations that append a definiens to each identifier and thus $V_3 = V$.

	d_1	d_2	d_3
E	1	0	1
m	1	1	0
c	1	1	0

(a) identifier only.

	d_1	d_2	d_3
E	1	0	1
m	1	1	0
c	1	1	0
energy	1	0	1
mass	1	1	0
speed of light	1	1	0

(b) weak association.

	d_1	d_2	d_3
E_energy	1	0	1
m_mass	1	1	0
c_speed of light	1	1	0

(c) strong association.

Figure 2: Illustration of the identifier-document matrix $\mathbf{D}$ for the analyzed methods to create features from the identifiers and definientia, for the mass-energy equivalence example and three hypothetical documents $d_1 = \{E,m,c\}$, $d_2 = \{m,c\}$, $d_3 = \{E\}$.

There is some variability in the definientia: for example, the same identifier σ in one document can be assigned to 'Cauchy stress tensor' and in another to 'stress tensor', which is almost the same thing. To reduce this variability we perform the following preprocessing steps: we tokenize the definiens and use individual tokens to index dimensions of the space. For example, suppose we have two pairs (σ, 'Cauchy stress tensor') and (σ, 'stress tensor'). In the 'weak' association case, we will have dimensions (σ, 'Cauchy', 'stress','tensor'), while for the 'strong' association we only use the last term, i.e., (σ_tensor) as additional features.

⑦ *Cluster feature vectors*

At this stage, we aim to find clusters of documents that are reasonable namespace candidates. We vectorize each document using the following weighting function $\log(\text{tf})/(z\text{df})$, where tf denotes the *term frequency*, df the document frequency and z the normalization parameter, such that the length of each document vector is 1. In addition, we discard all identifiers with DF < 2. We further reduce the dimensionality of the resulting dataset via Latent Semantic Analysis (LSA) [6], which is implemented using randomized Singular Value Decomposition (SVD) [14], see [12]. After the dimensionality reduction, we apply Mini-Batch K-Means with cosine distance, since this algorithm showed the best performance in our preliminary experiments (refere to [12] for further details).

⑧ *Building namespaces*

Once a cluster analysis algorithm assigns documents from our collection to clusters, we need to find namespaces among these clusters. We assume that clusters are namespace-defining, meaning that they are not only homogeneous in the cluster analysis sense (e.g., in the case of K-Means it means that the within-cluster sum of squares is minimal), but also contain topically similar documents.

To assess the *purity* of the clusters, we use the Wikipedia category information, which was not used for clustering in the first place. Since each Wikipedia article might have an arbitrary number of categories, we find the most frequent category of the cluster, and thus define its purity C as

$$\text{purity}(C) = \frac{\max_i \text{count}(c_i)}{|C|},$$

where the c_i's are *cluster categories*. Thus, we can select all clusters with purity above a certain threshold and refer to them as namespace-defining clusters. In our experiments we achieved best results with a threshold of 0.6.

Afterwards, we convert these clusters into namespaces by collecting all identifiers and their definiens in the documents of each cluster. Therefore, we first collect all identifier-definiens pairs, and then group them by identifiers. During the extraction, each definiens candidate is scored. This score is used to determine which definiens will be assigned to an identifier in the namespace. We group the pairs by identifier. If an identifier has two or more identical definiens, we merge them into one. Thus, the score of an identifier-definiens pair is the sum of scores. There is some lexical variance in the definiens. For example, 'variance' and 'population variance' or 'mean' and 'true mean' are closely related definiens. Thus, it is beneficial to group them to form one definiens. This can be done by fuzzy string matching (or approximate matching) [23]. We group related identifiers and calculate the sum of their scores. Intuitively, the closer a relation is, the higher is the score. A high score increases the confidence that a definiens is correct.

In the last step of our pipeline, we label our namespace defining clusters with categories from well known classifications, effectively naming the namespaces we identified. We thus achieve two goals. First, we indirectly evaluate our dataset. Second, we ease the use of our dataset to improve MIR. We use the following official classifications:

(1) Mathematics Subject Classification (MSC2010) [3] [American Mathematical Society];
(2) Physics and Astronomy Classification Scheme (PACS) [4]; and
(3) ACM Computing Classification System [28] available as a Simple Knowledge Organization System (SKOS) ontology [22].

We processed the SKOS ontology graph with RDFLib. All categories can be found on our website [30]. After obtaining and processing the data, the three classifications are merged into one. We map namespaces to second-level categories by keyword matching. First, we extract all keywords from the category. The keywords include the top level category name, the subcategory name and all third level category names. From each namespace, we extract the namespace category and names of the articles that form the namespace. Finally, we perform a keyword matching, and compute the cosine similarity between the cluster and each category. The namespace is assigned to the category with the largest cosine score. If the cosine score is below 0.2 or only one keyword is matched, the cluster is assigned to the category 'others'.

Improve identifier-definition extraction

We used POS Tagging based distance measures (see Section 2.1) to extract identifier-definiens pairs from the text surrounding the formula. In a second step, we build namespaces of identifiers. This namespaces allows us to study the usage of identifiers in different scientific fields. Many, but not all definientia can be found in the text surrounding the formulae. Thus, the namespaces can additionally be used to identify the definiens in cases where the definiens is not mentioned in the text.

2.3 Implementation details

We use the Big Data framework Apache Flink, which is capable of processing our datasets in a distributed shared nothing environment, leading to short processing times. Our source-code, training, and testing data is openly available from our website [30].

For the MLP part, our implementation follows the open source implementation of the Mathematical Language Processing Project [26], with the following improvements: rather than converting the Wikipedia formulae via LaTeXML, we now directly extract the identifiers from the LaTeX parse tree via Mathoid [32]. Second, we include a link to Wikidata, so that Wikipedia links can be replaced by unique and language independent Wikidata identifiers (ids). These ids are associated with semantic concepts, which include a title, and in many cases a short description that simplifies disambiguation. For the POS Tagging, we use the Stanford Core NLP library (StanfordNLP) [20] for POS Tagging of natural language as well as additional math-aware tags (see Section 2.1). In summary, we use the following tags:

(1) identifiers ('ID');
(2) formulae ('MATH');
(3) inner-wiki link ('LINK');
(4) singular noun ('NN');
(5) plural noun ('NNS');
(6) adjective ('JJ'); and
(7) noun phrase ('NOUN_PHRASE').

For the Namespace Discovery step in our pipeline (Section 2.2), we use the following implementation to discover clusters that are suitable namespace candidates. Using 'TfidfVectorizer' from scikit-learn [27], we vectorize each document. The experiments are performed with $(\log \text{TF}) \times \text{IDF}$ weighting. Therefore, we use the following parameters: 'use_idf=False', 'sublinear_tf=True'. Additionally, we discard identifiers that occur only once by setting 'min_df=2'. The output of 'TfidfVectorizer' is row-normalized, i.e., all rows have unit length.

The implementation of randomized SVD is taken from [27] – method 'randomized_svd'. After dimensionality reduction, we apply Mini-Batch K-Means (class 'MiniBatchKMeans') from [27] with cosine distance. In our preliminary experiments, this algorithm showed the best performance. To implement it, we use the Python library FuzzyWuzzy. Using fuzzy matching we group related identifiers and then sum over their scores.

3. EVALUATION

3.1 Data set

As our test collection, we use the collection of Wikipedia articles from the NTCIR-11 Math Wikipedia task [33] in 2014. We choose this collection instead of the latest version of Wikipedia to be able to compare our results to previous experiments.

After completing the MLP pipeline, we exclude all documents containing less than two identifiers. This procedure results in 22 515 documents with 12 771 distinct identifiers that occur about 2 million times. Figure 3 shows that identifiers follow a power law distribution, with about 3 700 identifiers occurring only once and 1 950 identifiers occurring only twice.

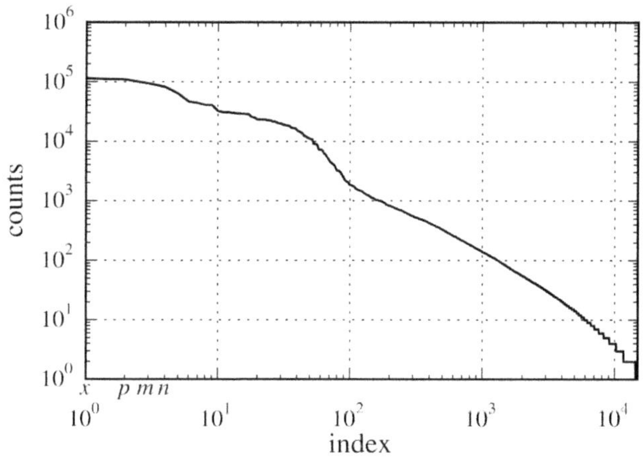

Figure 3: Distribution of identifier counts. The most frequent identifiers are x (125k), p (110k), m (105k), and n (83k).

The amount of identifiers per document also appears to follow a long tail power law distribution ($p < 0.001$ for KS test) as only a few articles contain a lot of identifiers, while most of the articles do not. The largest number of identifiers in a single document is an article with 22 766 identifiers, the second largest has only 6 500 identifiers. The mean number of identifiers per document is 33. The distribution of the number of distinct identifiers per document is less skewed than the distribution of all identifiers. The largest number of distinct identifiers in a single document is 287 followed by 194. The median of identifiers per document is 10. For 12 771 identifiers, the algorithm extracted 115 300 definientia. The number of found definientia follows a long tail distribution as well, with the median of definientia per page being 4. Moreover, we list the most common identifier-definiens pairs in Figure 3.

3.2 Gold standard

We created a gold standard from the 100 formulae patterns included in the NTCIR-11 Wikipedia task [33] and the following information:

(1) identifiers within the formula;
(2) definiens of each identifier; and
(3) links to semantic concepts on Wikidata.

We compared our results with that gold standard and calculated the three measures: precision, recall, and F1-score, to evaluate the quality of our identifier-definitions. In a first step, we evaluated the results acquired with the POS Tagging based distance measures (see Section 2.1). In a second step, we evaluated the results acquired by combining the POS Tagging based distance measures and the results of the namespaces (see Section 2.2)

The gold standard (cf. Figure 4) consists of 310 identifiers, with a maximum of 14 identifiers per formula. For 174 of those identifiers, we could assign the corresponding semantic concept in Wikidata. For 97, we assigned an individual phrase that we could not relate to a Wikidata concept. For an additional 27, we assigned two phrases. For example, for Topic 32 (cf. Figure 4), we assigned critical temperature in addition to the semantic concept of the critical point, since the critical temperature is more specific. The full list of assignments is available from our website [30]. Note, that the identification of the correct identifier-definition, was very time consuming. For several cases, the process took more than 30 minutes per formulae, since multiple Wikipedia pages and tertiary literature had to be consumed. The gold standard was checked by a mathematician from the Applied and Computational Mathematics Division, National Institute of Standards and Technology, Gaithersburg, Maryland, USA.

(1) Van der Waerden's theorem: $W(2,k) > 2^k/k^\varepsilon$

- W **Van der Waerden number**
- k **integer** : number that can be written without a fractional or decimal component
- ε **positive number** (real number. . .)

...

(31) Modigliani-Miller theorem: T_c

- T_c **tax rate** : ratio (usually expressed as a percentage) at which a business or person is taxed

(32) Proximity effect (superconductivity): T_c

- T_c critical temperature, **critical point** : critical point where phase boundaries disappear

...

(69) Engine efficiency: $\eta = \frac{work\ done}{heat\ absorbed} = \frac{Q1-Q2}{Q1}$

- η **energy efficiency**
- Q_1 **heat** (energy)
- Q_2 **heat** (energy)

...

(86) Lagrangian mechanics: $\frac{\partial L}{\partial q_i} = \frac{\mathrm{d}}{\mathrm{d}t}\frac{\partial L}{\partial \dot{q}_i}$

- L **Lagrangian**
- q_i **generalized coordinates**
- t **time** (. . .)
- $\dot{q}_i$ generalized velocities, **generalized coordinates**

Figure 4: Selected entries from the gold standard. Bold font indicates that the entry is linked to a language independent semantic concept in Wikidata. The descriptions in brackets originate from the English Wikidata label and have been cropped to optimize the layout of this figure.

4. RESULTS

In this section, we describe the results of our evaluation. First, we describe the quality of the MLP process in Section 4.1. Afterwards, we describe the dataset statistics and the results of the namespace evaluation in Section 4.2.

4.1 Mathematical Language Processing

4.1.1 *Identifier extraction*

Our gold standard consists of 310 identifiers to be extracted from the aforementioned 100 reference formulae. We were able to extract 294 identifiers (recall 94.8%) from the gold standard correctly. We obtained only 16 false negatives, but overall 57 false positives (precision 83.7%, F_1 89.0%). Falsely detected identifiers affect 22% of the reference formulae, showing that often several falsely extracted identifiers belong to one formula. In the following, we explain why the errors can be attributed to the shortcomings of the heuristics explained in Section 2.1.

Classical mechanics of discrete systems 45.00 (PACS)
Categories: Physics, Mechanics, Classical mechanics
Purity: 61%, matching score: 31%,
identifiers 103, semantic concepts 50, ⊘ 58, ✓ 4, ? 42, ✗ 1
Identifier-definitions:

Identifier	Definition	Score	Rating
m	**mass** (quantitative measure of a physical object's resistance to acceleration by a force ...)	$[s\approx 29]$	⊘
$\mathbf{F}$	**force** (influence that causes an object to change)	$[s\approx 25]$	⊘
$\mathbf{v}$	**velocity** (rate of change of the position of an object ... and the direction of that change)	$[s\approx 24]$	⊘
t	**time** (dimension in which events can be ordered the past through the present into the future)	$[s\approx 19]$	⊘
$\mathbf{a}$	**acceleration** (rate at which the velocity...)	$[s\approx 17]$	⊘
$\mathbf{r}$	**position** (Euclidean vector ...)	$[s\approx 14]$	⊘
i	particle	$[s\approx 12]$	✓
E	**energy** (physical quantity representing the capacity to do work)	$[s\approx 11]$	⊘
v	**speed** (magnitude of velocity)	$[s\approx 10]$	⊘
a	acceleration	$[s\approx 10]$	⊘
$\mathbf{V}$	velocity	$[s\approx 9]$	?
$\mathbf{u}$	**flow velocity**	$[s\approx 8]$	⊘
r	radius	$[s\approx 8]$	✓
...			
$\mathbf{E}$	**electric field** (... representing the force applied to a charged test particle)	$[s\approx 6]$	⊘
...			
c	**speed of light** (speed at which all massless particles and associated fields travel in vacuum)	$[s\approx 3]$	⊘

Stochastic analysis 60Hxx (MSC)
Categories: Stochastic processes, Probability theory
Purity: 92%, matching score: 62%, identifiers 54, semantic concepts 32, ⊘ 18, ✓ 0, ? 30, ✗ 0
Identifier-definitions:

Identifier	Definition	Score	Rating
a	**stochastic process** (... random variables)	$[s\approx 12]$	⊘
X	**stochastic process** (... random variables)	$[s\approx 10]$	⊘
...			
$\mathbf{E}$	**expected value**	$[s\approx 2]$	⊘
...			
$\mathbb{E}$	**expected value** $s<1$		
v	function $s<1$		

Theory of data 68Pxx (MSC)
Categories: Information theory, Theoretical computer science
Purity: 86%, matching score: 35%, identifiers 58, semantic concepts 10
Identifier-definitions:

Identifier	Definition	Score	Rating
R	rate	$[s\approx 12]$	⊘
X	**posterior probability**	$[s\approx 10]$	⊘
n	length	$[s\approx 8]$	⊘
...			
H	**Information entropy** (expected value of the amount of information delivered by a message)	$[s\approx 5]$	⊘
I	mutal information	$[s\approx 5]$	⊘
a	program	$[s\approx 5]$	⊘
...			
$\mathbf{a}$	codeword $s<1$		
$\mathbb{E}_X$	**expected value** $s<1$		

Table 1: Identifier-definitions for selected identifiers and namespaces extracted from the English Wikipedia, the accumulated score s and the human relevance rankings confirmed (⊘), partly confirmed (✓), not sure (?) and incorrect (✗). Discovered semantic concepts are printed using bold font. The descriptions were fetched from Wikidata. To improve readability of the table, we manually shortened some long description texts.

Incorrect markup. Errors relating to 8 formulae (33 false positive and 8 false negative identifiers), were caused by the incorrect use of LaTeX, especially the use of math mode for text or the missing usage of math mode for part of the formula. An identifier Q_1 that is falsely marked as $Q1$ (cf. Figure 4, Topic 69) in a formula, can easily be identified correctly by a human since it looks very similar in the output. As obviously Q_1 is meant in the formula, we took Q_1 as gold standard for this identifier. But in the MLP process it is impossible to extract the identifier correctly, as $Q1$ implies Q times 1.

Symbols. For 8 formulae (9 false positive identifiers), Mathoid [32] misclassified symbols as identifiers, such as d in $\frac{d}{dx}$. Two formulae (2 false positive identifiers) are substitutions (abbreviations that improve the readability of formulae without specific meaning).

Sub-super-script. Two formulae (3 false positive, 2 false negative identifiers), used sub-super-script such as σ_y^2.

Special notation. For 2 formulae (10 false positive, 2 false negative identifiers), use special notation like the Einstein sum convention.

We excluded incorrectly extracted identifiers from the following processing steps. Thus the upper bound for recall and precision are set by the identifier extraction step.

4.1.2 *Definition extraction*

In a first step, we only assess the definitions that matched exactly the semantic concepts materialized as Wikidata item in the gold standard. Thus, we found 88 exact matches (recall 28.4%), but also obtained 337 false negatives, which results in a precision of 20.7% (F_1 23.9%).

In addition, we evaluated the performance of partially relevant matches by manually deciding the relevance for each entry. For example, **integer** (number that can be written without a fractional or decimal component) would be classified as highly relevant, but the string `integers` was classified as relevant. Although this classification is mathematically incorrect, it provides valuable information for a human regarding the formulae. With this evaluation, we obtain 208 matches (recall 67.1%) and 217 false negatives (precision 48.9%, F_1 56.6%). To interprete these results, we differentiate between definitions that have not been extracted, although all necessary information is present in the information source, and definitions that do not completely exist in the information source. Wolska and Grigore [35] found that around 70% of objects denoting symbolic expressions are explicitly denoted in scientific papers. Since in our data source only 73% of the identifiers are explained in the text, 73% represents the highest achievable recall for systems that do not use world knowledge to deduce the most likely meaning of the remaining identifiers. Considering this upper limit, we view a recall of 67.1% that was achieved when including partly relevant results, as a good result. These results also confirm the findings of Kristianto et al. [17]. Although these overall results match with the results of Wolska and Grigore [35], we found major differences between different scientific fields. In pure mathematics, the identifiers usually do not link to a specific concept and the formulae do not relate to specific real-life-scenarios. In contrast, in physics the definientia of the identifiers are usually mentioned in the surrounding text, like in the mass-energy-equivalence example.

4.2 Namespace Discovery

The evaluation of the namespace discovery performance is twofold. First, we apply the same procedure as in the evaluation of the MLP process. In a second step, we perform a manual quality assessment of the final namespaces.

We obtain the following results with regard to the extraction performance. For the strict relevance criterion, the recall improved by 18% (0.048) to 33.2% (103 exactly correct definitions), and the precision declined only slightly with 420 false positives to 19.7% (F_1 24.7%). In the end, 30 identifiers (9.6%) reached the ultimate goal and were identified as a semantic concept on Wikidata. For the non strict relevant criterion, we could measure a recall performance gain of 19.4%, while maintaining the precision level. This exceeds the upper limit for recall achievable by exclusively analyzing the text of a single document of (73%) and extracts 250 definitions correctly (recall 80.6%) with only 273 false positives (precision 47.8%, F_1 60.0%).

The second part of the evaluation assesses the quality of the discovered namespaces. While a detailed performance evaluation of the clustering methods was already carried out in [12], we focus on the contents of the discovered namespaces here. For evaluating the Namespace Discovery, we evaluated 6 randomly sampled subject classes. Two independent judges rated the categorized identifier-definiens pairs regarding their assignment to subject classes using the four categories: 'confirmed' (✓), 'partly confirmed' (✓), 'not sure' (?) and 'incorrect' (✗), regarding their assignment to the subject class by two independent raters. All cases of disagreement (mostly ? vs. ✓) could be resolved in consensus.

With strong coupling and a minimal purity of 0.6, 250 clusters were obtained of which 167 could be mapped to namespaces in the official classification schemes (MSC 135, PACS 22, ACM 8). The purity distribution is as follows: 0.6-0.7: 98, 0.7-0.8: 57, 0.8-0.9: 44, 0.9-1.0: 51.

Those namespaces contain 5 618 definitions with an overall score >1, of which 2 124 (37.8%) link to semantic concepts. We evaluated the recall of 6 discovered namespaces exemplary. The purity of the selected namespaces ranged from 0.6 to 1, with an average of 0.8. They contained between 14 and 103 identifiers (with a score >1). Here, relevance means that the definition is commonly used in that field. This was decided by domain experts. However, since this question is not always trivial to judge, we introduced an unknown response (?). In total, 129 (43%) of the 278 discovered definitions matched the expectation (✓) of the implicit namespaces expected by the domain experts. For 7 definitions (3%), they were clearly wrong (✗), for 8 (3%), the definitor was not specific enough and for the remaining 144 (52%), the reviewers could not assess the relevance (?). Note that the quality of namespaces varied. For example cluster (33Cxx, Hypergeometric functions) had significantly more clearly wrong results, because symbols were classified as identifiers, compared to the investigated clusters in physics where the definition of specific symbols is less common.

In general, this result was expected, since it is hard to assess the namespaces that have not been spelled out explicitly before. Especially, the recall could not be evaluated, since to the best of our knowledge, there is no reference list with typical identifiers in a specific mathematical field. For details regarding implementation choices, visit our website [30], and contribute to our open source software mathosphere.

5. CONCLUSION AND OUTLOOK

We investigated the semantification of identifiers in mathematics based on the NTCIR-11 Math Wikipedia test collection using Mathematical Language Processing and Namespace Discovery. Previous approaches have already shown good performance in extracting descriptions for mathematical formulae from the surrounding text in individual documents.

We achieved even better performance (80% recall, while maintaining the same level of precision) in the extraction of relevant identifier-definitions. In cases where identifier-definitions were absent in the document, we used our fall back mechanism of identifier-definitions from the namespace that we learned from the collection at large. This way, we could break the theoretical limit for systems (about 70% recall cf. Section 4) that take into account only one document at a time. Moreover, the descriptions extracted by other systems are language dependent and do not have a specific data structure.

In contrast, we organized our extracted identifier-definitions in a hierarchical data structure (i.e., namespaces) which simplifies subsequent data processing tasks such as exploitative data analysis.

For about 10% of the identifiers, we were able to assign the correct semantic concept on the collaborative knowledge base Wikidata. Note, that this allowed extracting even more semantics beside a natural language description as spelled out in Table 1. Namely, one can find labels and descriptions in multiple languages, links to relevant Wikipedia articles in different languages, as well as statements. For example, for the identifier **speed of light**, 100 translations exist. As statements one can, for example, retrieve the numeric value ($3 \times 10^8 \mathrm{m/s}$), and the fact that the speed of light is a unit of measurement. We observed that identifier clusters in physics and computer science are more useful in the sense that they more often link to real-world semantic objects than identifier clusters in pure mathematics, which often solely specify the type of the variable.

During the construction of the gold standard, we noticed that even experienced mathematicians often require much time to manually gather this kind of semantic information for identifiers. We assume that a significant percentage of the 500 million visitors to Wikipedia every day face similar problems. Our approach is a first step to facilitate this task for users.

The largest obstacle for obtaining semantic information for identifiers from Wikidata is the quality of the Wikidata resource itself. For 44% of the identifiers in the gold standard, Wikidata contains only rather unspecific hypernyms for the semantic concept expressed by the identifier. We see two options to remedy this problem in future research. The first option is to use a different semantic net containing more fine-grained semantic concepts. The second option is to identify unspecific semantic concepts in Wikidata and to split them into more specific Wikidata items related to mathematics and science.

Our identifier extraction has been rolled out to the Wikimedia production environment. However, at the time of writing, incorrect markup is still a major source of errors. To overcome this problem, the implementation of procedures that recognize and highlight incorrect markup for Wikipedia editors is scheduled and will encourage editors to improve the markup quality. In addition, symbols falsely classified as identifiers have a noticeable negative impact on the quality of the clustering step. Improving the recognition of symbols is therefore an issue that future research should address. Moreover, in the future our method should be expanded to other datasets beside Wikipedia.

With regard to math information retrieval applications i.e., math search, we have shown that the discovered namespaces can be used to disambiguate identifiers. Exposing namespaces to users is one application of identifier namespaces. Using them as internal data structure for math information retrieval applications, such as math search, math understanding or academic plagiarism detection is another. Regarding MIR tasks, identifier namespaces allow for quiz like topics such as "At constant temperature, is volume directly or inversely related to pressure?". This simplifies comparing traditional word based question and answering systems with math aware methods.

In conclusion, we regard our namespace concept as a significant innovation, which will allow users to better express their mathematical information needs, and search engines to disambiguate identifiers according to their semantics. However, more research needs to be done to better understand the influence of each individual augmentation step of our presented pipeline for MIR applications.

6. REFERENCES

[1] C. C. Aggarwal and C. Zhai. A survey of text clustering algorithms. In *Mining Text Data*, pages 77–128. Springer, 2012.

[2] A. Aizawa, M. Kohlhase, I. Ounis, and M. Schubotz. NTCIR-11 Math-2 task overview. In *Proceedings of the 11th NTCIR Conference*, 2014.

[3] American Mathematical Society. AMS Mathematics Subject Classification 2010, 2009.

[4] American Physical Society. PACS 2010 Regular Edition, 2009.

[5] F. Cajori. *A history of mathematical notations. 1. Notations in elementary mathematics*. Open Court Publ. Co., Chicago, Ill., 1928.

[6] S. C. Deerwester, S. T. Dumais, T. K. Landauer, G. W. Furnas, and R. A. Harshman. Indexing by latent semantic analysis. *JAsIs*, 41(6):391–407, 1990.

[7] E. Duval, W. Hodgins, S. Sutton, and S. L. Weibel. Metadata principles and practicalities. *D-lib Magazine*, 8(4):16, 2002.

[8] B. Gipp. *Citation-based Plagiarism Detection - Detecting Disguised and Cross-language Plagiarism using Citation Pattern Analysis*. Springer Vieweg Research, 2014.

[9] A. Gliozzo and C. Strapparava. *Semantic domains in computational linguistics*. Springer Science & Business Media, 2009.

[10] J. Gosling, B. Joy, G. Steele, G. Bracha, and A. Buckley. *The Java ® Language Specification. Java SE 8 Edition*. Addison-Wesley Professional, 2015.

[11] M. Grigore, M. Wolska, and M. Kohlhase. Towards context-based disambiguation of mathematical expressions. In *ASCM*, pages 262–271, 2009.

[12] A. Grigorev. Identifier namespaces in mathematical notation. *arXiv preprint arXiv:1601.03354*, 2016.

[13] F. Guidi and C. Sacerdoti Coen. A survey on retrieval of mathematical knowledge. In *Intelligent Computer Mathematics*, pages 296–315. 2015.

[14] N. Halko, P. Martinsson, and A. Tropp. Finding structure with randomness: Stochastic algorithms for constructing approximate matrix decompositions. 2009.

[15] D. Jurafsky and J. H. Martin. *Speech & language processing*. Pearson Education India, 2000.

[16] M. Kohlhase and I. Sucan. A Search Engine for Mathematical Formulae. In *Proc. of AISC, number 4120 in LNAI*, pages 241–253. Springer Verlag, 2006.

[17] G. Y. Kristianto, A. Aizawa, and Others. Extracting Textual Descriptions of Mathematical Expressions in Scientific Papers. *D-Lib Magazine*, 20(11):9, 2014.

[18] C. Larman. *Applying UML and patterns: an introduction to object-oriented analysis and design and iterative development*. Pearson Education India, 2005.

[19] K. Ma, S. C. Hui, and K. Chang. Feature extraction and clustering-based retrieval for mathematical formulas. In *Software Engineering and Data Mining (SEDM)*, pages 372–377. IEEE, 2010.

[20] C. D. Manning, M. Surdeanu, J. Bauer, J. Finkel, S. J. Bethard, and D. McClosky. The Stanford CoreNLP natural language processing toolkit. In *ACL*, 2014.

[21] N. Meuschke and B. Gipp. Reducing Computational Effort for Plagiarism Detection by using Citation Characteristics to Limit Retrieval Space. In *JCDL*, 2014.

[22] A. Miles, B. Matthews, M. Wilson, and D. Brickley. SKOS Core: Simple Knowledge Organisation for the Web. In *COLING*, pages 1–9, 2005.

[23] G. Navarro. A guided tour to approximate string matching. *ACM computing surveys*, 33(1):31–88, 2001.

[24] M.-Q. Nghiem, K. Yokoi, Y. Matsubayashi, and A. Aizawa. Mining coreference relations between formulas and text using Wikipedia. In *COLING*, page 69, 2010.

[25] N. Oikonomakou and M. Vazirgiannis. A review of web document clustering approaches. In *Data mining and knowledge discovery handbook*. Springer, 2005.

[26] R. Pagel and M. Schubotz. Mathematical language processing project. In *WIP track at CICM*, 2014.

[27] F. Pedregosa, G. Varoquaux, A. Gramfort, V. Michel, B. Thirion, O. Grisel, and Others. Scikit-learn: Machine Learning in Python. *JMLR*, pages 2825–2830, 2011.

[28] B. Rous. Major Update to ACM's Computing Classification System. *Communications of the ACM*, 55(11):12, Nov. 2012.

[29] U. Schöneberg and W. Sperber. POS Tagging and its Applications for Mathematics. In *Intelligent Computer Mathematics*, pages 213–223. Springer, 2014.

[30] M. Schubotz. **mlp.formulasearchengine.com**.

[31] M. Schubotz, M. Leich, and V. Markl. Querying large collections of mathematical publications: NTCIR10 math task. In *NTCIR-10*, 2013.

[32] M. Schubotz and G. Wicke. Mathoid: Robust, scalable, fast and accessible math rendering for wikipedia. In *CICM*, pages 224–235, 2014.

[33] M. Schubotz, A. Youssef, V. Markl, and H. S. Cohl. Challenges of Mathematical Information Retrievalin the NTCIR-11 Math Wikipedia Task. In *SIGIR*, 2015.

[34] C. Stokoe, M. P. Oakes, and J. Tait. Word sense disambiguation in information retrieval revisited. In *SIGIR*, 2003.

[35] M. Wolska and M. Grigore. Symbol declarations in mathematical writing. In *Proceedings of the 3rd Workshop on Digital Mathematics Libraries*, pages 119–127, 2010.

[36] K. Yokoi, M. Nghiem, Y. Matsubayashi, and A. Aizawa. Contextual analysis of mathematical expressions for advanced mathematical search. In *CICLing*, 2011.

Multi-Stage Math Formula Search: Using Appearance-Based Similarity Metrics at Scale

Richard Zanibbi
Kenny Davila
Rochester Institute of Technology, USA
{rxzvcs,kxd7282}@rit.edu

Andrew Kane
Frank Wm. Tompa
University of Waterloo, Canada
{arkane,fwtompa}@uwaterloo.ca

ABSTRACT

When using a mathematical formula for search (*query-by-expression*), the suitability of retrieved formulae often depends more upon symbol identities and layout than deep mathematical semantics. Using a *Symbol Layout Tree* representation for formula appearance, we propose the *Maximum Subtree Similarity (MSS)* for ranking formulae based upon the subexpression whose symbols and layout best match a query formula. Because MSS is too expensive to apply against a complete collection, the Tangent-3 system first retrieves expressions using an inverted index over symbol pair relationships, ranking hits using the Dice coefficient; the top-k formulae are then re-ranked by MSS. Tangent-3 obtains state-of-the-art performance on the NTCIR-11 Wikipedia formula retrieval benchmark, and is efficient in terms of both space and time. Retrieval systems for other graphical forms, including chemical diagrams, flowcharts, figures, and tables, may benefit from adopting this approach.

Keywords

mathematical information retrieval (MIR), inverted index, query-by-expression, subtree similarity

1. INTRODUCTION

The Web is a rich repository of mathematical information, including large repositories of technical documents in online paper databases, tutorials and instructional materials, and other publications in mathematics and engineering. Numerous online resources are available for both experts and non-experts. Students may explore and review concepts using Wikipedia, MathPlanet, and the Khan Academy, while experts consult resources such as the On-Line Encyclopedia of Integer Sequences (https://oeis.org/).

While mature technologies for text search are readily available, search using formulae as queries *(query-by-expression)* remains an open research problem [8, 18, 28]. Interest in Mathematical Information Retrieval (MIR) has increased in recent years, as witnessed by math retrieval tasks at the NTCIR conferences [1, 2].

For the most part, large-scale search engines support formula search indirectly, e.g., through LaTeX strings as search terms. There is no wildcard support for formula subexpressions; for example, we cannot reliably locate expressions containing α with an unspecified exponent (α^*), or coefficient ($*\alpha$). This makes it difficult for users to browse for similar formulae in documents, clarify unfamiliar notation [25], or discover non-obvious connections between research papers based on their mathematical contents [27]. A recent report from the National Research Council (USA) considers developing a global library for mathematics research, and includes a discussion of limitations in existing search tools with regards to mathematical information [5].[1]

Math encodings are naturally hierarchical, defining formula appearance (through the arrangement of symbols on writing lines) in *Symbol Layout Tree (SLT)* encodings such as LaTeX or formula semantics in *Operator Tree (OT)* encodings such as Content MathML. Math symbol definitions are dialectic and context-dependent, and in general translating between appearance and semantic encodings is heuristic [28].

Both layout tree and operator tree representations have been used for query-by-expression (see Section 2). In the most general sense, query-by-expression involves tree matching for a class of SLTs or OTs. Open problems include defining appropriate similarity metrics, identifying what primitives to use for representing formula content, how to index and retrieve these primitives, and finally how to handle trade-offs between recall and both retrieval time and index size. In general, retrieval becomes more difficult when the best matches are less similar to the query formula (e.g., due to large expressions in the corpus with subexpressions similar to one or more parts of the query), and when wildcards are included in the query [10]. As SLT formula encodings are more common in practice, we focus on them in this paper.

Problem Statement. Create a formula search engine model that 1) effectively retrieves and ranks formulae based on formula appearance, 2) is fast enough to use in real-time with large corpora, 3) has index sizes and indexing speeds that are scalable, and 4) supports wildcards.

Contributions. This paper makes four primary contributions: 1) the *Maximum Subtree Similarity (MSS)* metric for ranking formulae using the best query match with unification and wildcard support (see Section 6), 2) an improved SLT model with consistent representation for lists, grids and matrices (see Section 4), 3) a novel, effective and efficient

[1]See p.28, "What is missing from the mathematical landscape?"

SIGIR 2016 July 18–20, 2016, Pisa, Italy
© 2016 ACM. ISBN 978-1-4503-4069-4/16/07... $15.00
DOI: http://dx.doi.org/10.1145/2911451.2911512

core engine for symbol pair-based retrieval (see Section 5), and 4) state-of-the-art performance on the NTCIR-11 formula retrieval benchmark: our method is efficient in terms of time and space, and produces effective formula search results (see Section 7).

2. RELATED WORK

In this section we provide an overview of existing techniques for formula retrieval. We categorize approaches to query-by-expression as *text-based*, *tree-based*, or *spectral* according to the primitives used to represent formulae.

Text-Based Approaches. In text-based approaches, math expression trees are linearized before indexing and retrieval. Common normalizations include defining synonyms for symbols (e.g., function names), using canonical orderings for commutative operators and spatial relationships (e.g., to group `a+b` with `b+a` and `x_i^2` with `x^2_i`), enumerating variables, and replacing symbols by their mathematical type (e.g., numbers, variables, and classes of operators) [19, 28].

Although linearization masks significant amounts of structural information, it allows text and math retrieval to be carried out efficiently by a single search engine. Most text-based methods use TF-IDF (term frequency-inverse document frequency) retrieval after linearizing expressions [14, 19]. In an alternative approach, the largest common substring between the query formula and each indexed expression is used to retrieve LaTeX strings [17]. This captures more structural information, but also requires evaluating all expressions in the index using a quadratic algorithm.

Tree-Based Approaches. These methods represent formula appearance or semantics directly as trees. Expressions are indexed as complete trees, along with their subtrees to support partial matching. Tree indices may be compressed by storing identical subtrees uniquely [10]. In addition to exact matching of trees and/or subtrees, tree-edit distances with early stopping have been used for fast retrieval [11]. The *substitution tree* [6] has been used to create indices for operator trees, with each path representing a series of subexpression variable substitutions [12]. The NII group from Japan has devised a hashing scheme to represent operator trees by a set of interdependent codes for all subexpressions [2, 18] (see Section 7 for results).

One method adapts TF-IDF retrieval for SLTs, using vectors of subexpressions, along with subexpressions where arguments are replaced by wildcards [13]. SLTs are modified, normalizing argument order for commutative operators and representing operator precedences. Text in the paragraphs preceding and following formulae are added to provide contextual features for improved ranking [24].

Spectral Approaches. These approaches use paths or partial subtrees rather than complete subtrees as retrieval primitives. This can improve recall through more flexible partial matching of expressions (e.g. in the SLT for x_a^2, x^2 is a subtree, but x_i^2 is not). Nguyen et al. convert operator trees to a bag of 'words' representing individual arguments and operator-argument triples [15]. A lattice is defined over generated word sets for formulae, and a breadth-first search starting from the query formula set is used to find similar formulae. Hiroya and Saito [9] use bags of paths from the root to each operator and operand in an operator tree, with an inverted index used for retrieval. The large number of possible paths from the root make this technique brittle.

The *Tangent-2* search engine uses the *relative* position of symbols to create a bag of symbol pairs [20], along with extensions to represent matrix and grid structures [16]. A *symbol pair* gives the location of symbol s_2 relative to an ancestor symbol s_1 in an SLT $(s_1, s_2, \delta x, \delta y)$, where $(\delta x, \delta y)$ are horizontal and vertical displacements along writing lines from s_1 to s_2. This representation supports partial matches well, while preserving enough information to return exact matches. Formula similarity is defined by the harmonic mean for the percentage of matched pairs in the query and a candidate (i.e., *Dice's coefficient*).[2] A Dice coefficient variant incorporating symbol pair frequencies was found to perform similarly [20]. This technique combined with keyword retrieval in Lucene produced the highest Precision@5 result for the NTCIR-11 math retrieval task (92%) [2].

Limitations of Symbol Pair-Based Retrieval. In Tangent-2, symbol pair matches may be scattered throughout a formula, and exact matches for small subexpressions in candidates produce low similarity scores. Wildcards match individual symbols, and pairs of wildcards are ignored to avoid performance problems. Non-wildcard symbols are not unified: symbol pairs that are equivalent after renaming are missed (e.g., x^2 does not match a^2). The Tangent-2 formula structure model is also inconsistent, with different groupings for roots, matrices, vectors and parenthesized expressions, and retrieval is very slow (see Section 7).

In this paper, we make improvements to the Symbol Layout Tree model used in Tangent, along with the symbol pairs data model. These changes reduce index sizes substantially while improving retrieval results. We also define a new engine for fast retrieval of symbol pair matches, and address limitations in wildcard handling and locality of matching through an additional re-ranking step.

3. FORMULA RETRIEVAL MODEL

The Tangent-3 formula search engine (i.e., the newest version of Tangent presented in this paper) employs a two-stage cascading search [23] for fast retrieval and intuitive rankings (see Figure 1).[3] Queries are parsed into a Symbol Layout Tree, which is then traversed from the root, generating tuples of the form $(s_1, s_2, R, \#)$ with ancestor symbol s_1, descendant symbol s_2, edge label sequence R from s_1 to s_2, and a count (#). Two parameters control the maximum path length between symbols in tuples (the window size, w) and whether to include tuples for symbols at the end of writing lines (EOL).

After parsing, the first retrieval stage (the *core engine*) ranks a given number of expressions k by matching query tuples, using an inverted index mapping symbol pair relationships to expressions and counts (see Section 5). Tuples with one wildcard are expanded, but tuples with two wildcards are ignored for efficiency. Iterator trees are used to process postings quickly. The initial ranking weighs matched vs. unmatched symbol pairs in the query and candidates. The second (*re-ranking*) stage re-scores matches using an approximate best matching subtree for the query in each candidate (see Section 6), addressing limitations of symbol pair-based retrieval described in the previous section.

Illustration. Table 1 shows queries processed using our two-stage method. For query 1, using MSS for re-ranking

[2]Given query tree T_q and candidate tree T_c with symbol pair sets F_q and F_c, Dice's coefficient of similarity is given by $\frac{2|F_q \cap F_c|}{|F_q|+|F_c|}$.
[3]Source code: http://www.cs.rit.edu/~dprl/Software.html.

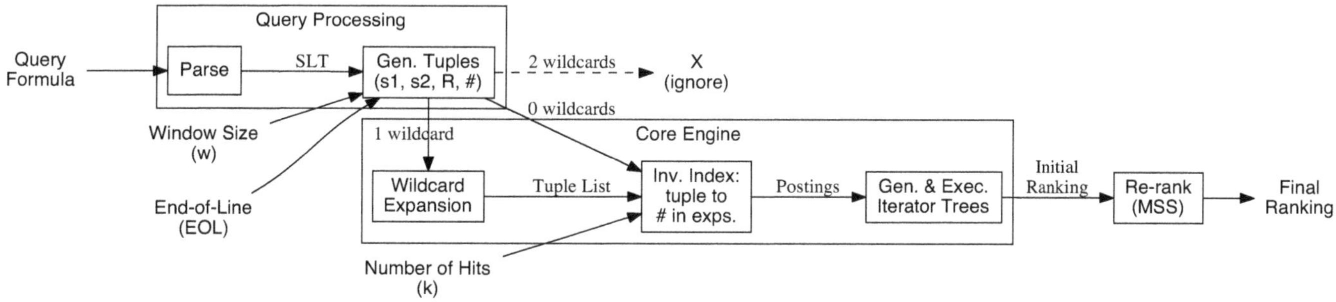

Figure 1: Tangent-3 Formula Retrieval Model. System parameters include maximum symbol pair distance (window size w), how end-of-line symbols are indexed (EOL), and the number of hits to return (k).

Table 1: Top-5 Results for Tangent-3 (k=100). Asterisks represent wildcards (e.g., $*$ or $*1*$).

	Query 1: $f_*(z) = z^2 + c$	
	Initial Ranking	Re-ranked (MSS)
1.	$f_c(z) = z^2 + c$	$f_c(z) = z^2 + c$
2.	$f_c(z) = z^2 + c.$	$\mathbf{P}_c(z) - z^2 + c$
3.	$f(z) = z^2 + c$	$f_c(\mathbf{x}) = \mathbf{x}^2 + c$
4.	$f_0(z) = z^2$	$f_c(z) = z^2 + c.$
5.	$f_c(z) = z * z + c$	$f(z) = z^2 + c$

	Query 2: $\sum_{*2*}^{*1*} * = \sum_{*2*}^{*1*} *$	
	Initial Ranking	Re-ranked (MSS)
1.	$E = \sum_i^N E_i$	$\sum_{i=1}^d a_i = \sum_{i=1}^d b_i$
2.	$G_{net} = \sum_i \sum_{i=1}^N$	$\sum_{i=1}^N d_i = \sum_{i=1}^N \lambda_i.$
3.	$\sum_i^{N_1} p_i = \sum_j^{N_2} p_j$	$\sum_{n=0}^\infty a_{\sigma(n)} = \sum_{n=0}^\infty a_n.$
4.	$\sum_{i=1}^n x_i k_i = \sum_{i=1}^n x_i$	$\sum_i^{N_1} p_i = \sum_j^{N_2} p_j$
5.	$= \sum_{k=1}^n a_k$	$\sum_{n=0}^\infty a_n = \sum_{n \in N} a_n.$

produces top-5 hits matching the query formula exactly after unifying identifiers (before re-ranking, only the top-3 match). For query 2, the numbered wildcards $*1*$ and $*2*$ should be identical when repeated. Before re-ranking only one hit matches the query exactly (rank 4), but after re-ranking the top-3 are exact matches for the query, and the remaining two hits are strong partial matches.

4. FORMULA STRUCTURE MODEL

The Tangent formula search engines use a Symbol Layout Tree (SLT) to represent formula appearance (see Figure 2). Whereas Tangent-2 based its encoding on a two-dimensional interpretation of formulas on a page, expressing symbol positions in terms of horizontal and vertical offsets (see Section 2), this revised SLT representation provides greater consistency and expressivity in representing relationships between symbols. In our representation, matrices are an integral part of formulas rather than auxiliary relational structures. Tangent-3 also includes a unified representation of all parenthesized subexpressions regardless of their interpretation (for example, as function arguments vs. parenthesized matrices). We also add a crude representation of type, which is critical for re-ranking using Maximum Subtree Similarity. We describe these in more detail below.

Node Labels and Types. Nodes in an SLT represent individual symbols and visually explicit aggregates, such as fractions, matrices, function arguments, and parenthesized expressions. More specifically, SLT nodes represent:

- typed mathematical symbols: numbers (N!n); identifiers such as variable names (V!v); text fragments, such as *lim*, *otherwise*, and *such that* (T!t)
- fractions (F!)
- container objects: radicals (R!); matrices, tabular structures, and parenthesized expressions (M!$frxc$)
- explicitly specified whitespace (W!)
- wildcard symbols ($*w$)
- mathematical operators

Because of their visual similarity, all tabular structures, including matrices, binomial coefficients, and piecewise defined functions are encoded using the matrix indicator M!. If a matrix-like structure is surrounded by fence characters, then those symbols are indicated after the exclamation mark. Finally, the indicator includes a pair of numbers separated by an x, indicating the number of rows and the number of columns in the structure. For example, M!2x3 represents a 2x3 table with no surrounding delimiters and M!()1x5 represents a 1x5 table surrounded by parentheses.

Importantly, *all* parenthesized subexpressions are treated as if they were 1x1 matrices surrounded by parentheses, and, in particular, the arguments for any n-ary function are represented as a 1xn matrix surrounded by parentheses.

Every node has a label, and a node's type (*number*, *variable*, *operator*, etc.) is reflected in its label. If a node's label includes an exclamation mark (e.g., V!), the type is the label prefix up to the (first) exclamation mark. Node labels starting with an asterisk (*) have type *wildcard*, and other node labels without exclamation marks have type *operator*. Using type V! for all identifiers simplies our SLT model, but sometimes leads to unexpected unifications (see Section 7).

Spatial Relationships. Labeled edges in the SLT capture the spatial relationships between objects represented by the nodes. With respect to a given object O, seven axes reflect the following relationships:

1. **next** ($\rightarrow$) references the adjacent object that appears to the right of O and on the same line
2. **within** ($\boxdot$) references the radicand if O is a root or the first element appearing in row-major order in O if it is a structure represented by M!
3. **element** ($\multimap$) references the next element appearing after O in row-major order inside a structure represented by M!
4. **above** ($\uparrow$) references the leftmost object on a higher

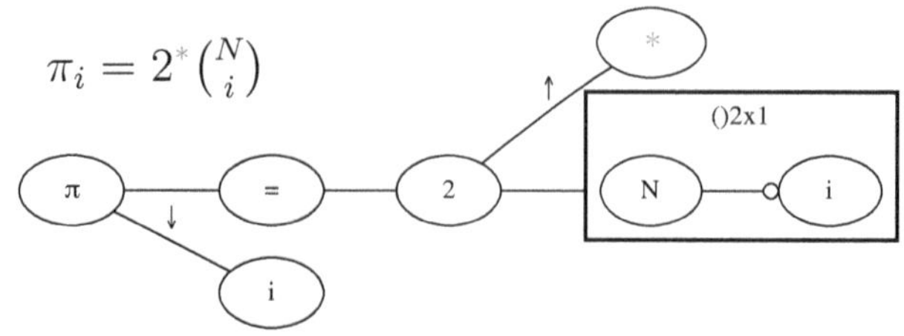

Figure 2: Query Formula with Corresponding SLT. The query has one wildcard, and a tabular structure.

line starting at the position above O (e.g., superscript, over symbol, fraction numerator, or index for a radical)

5. **below** (↓) references the leftmost object on a lower line starting at the position below O (e.g., subscript, under symbol, fraction denominator)
6. **pre-above** (⇑) references the leftmost object of a prescripted superscript of O
7. **pre-below** (⇓) references the leftmost object of a prescripted subscript of O

An SLT is rooted at the leftmost object on the main writing line of the formula it represents. Figure 2 shows an example of an SLT, where for simplicity, unlabeled edges represent the *next* relationship and the type prefixes are omitted. We do not distinguish vertical from scripted regions.[4] This causes $\hat{x}^2$ to be represented without an accent, but also represents limits uniformly: $\int_i^n$ and $\int\limits_i^n$ are equivalent.

Creating SLTs. SLTs can be created in linear time from Presentational MathML by a recursive descent parser. For other input formats, we assume that converters such as LaTeXML[5] exist to produce Presentational MathML.

In most circumstances, whitespace is not represented in an SLT. As a result, although unicode whitespace and related characters, such as "invisible times" (`U+2062`), occasionally appear as operators in Presentational MathML expressions, they are all ignored for the purpose of matching expressions in Tangent-3.

Tuple Representation for SLTs. An effective formula search engine must be able to find formulae that contain a query formula, appear within a query formula, or are in many ways only similar to a query formula. Thus high-quality search engines create indexes based on selected *features* of formulae found in a corpus and match queries based on those features. Previous versions of Tangent showed that pairs of symbols together with their relative inter-symbol distances in two dimensions are effective features to use [16], and we improve on this approach.

As described above, a node in an SLT can have up to seven labeled outgoing edges (with no edge label repeating for any node) corresponding to the seven defined axes. For a given SLT, Tangent-3 produces a set of tuples, each of which encodes the relationship between a pair of symbols occurring on some path from the root to a leaf. Given two nodes on such a path, we define the relative path between the nodes by the sequence of edge labels traversed from the ancestor node to the descendant. The features we use are tuples encoding pairs of labels occurring on ancestor and descendant nodes, together with their relative path and the number of times each such label-label-path triple occurs in an SLT. For example, the tuple ($V!x$,$N!2$,→↑→→,3) indicates that the corresponding formula includes three instances of a node representing the number 2 that appears "to the right, then above, and then twice to the right" with respect to some node representing variable x; for example, such a formula might include $...xy^{z+2}...$.

Tuple Generation Parameters. As seen in Figure 1, there are two parameters that control symbol pair tuple generation: the window size (w), and how symbols at the end of writing lines are included in the index (*EOL*).

To save both space and time, and following the practice of searching via n-grams [26], Tangent-3 extends the approach used in Tangent-2 by storing only those tuples for which the distance between symbols (measured by the number of edges separating them) is less than or equal to a specified window size w. For example, the tuple ($V!x$,$N!2$,→↑→→,3) will be included in the index only if $w \geq 4$.

In addition to symbol pairs, end-of-line information can be captured by introducing special tuples of the form (*symbol*, !0, →, *count*). Including these is likely to improve retrieval, particularly for very small expressions. However, wildcards as EOL symbols have very large wildcard expansions, increasing retrieval time. To alleviate this problem, we examine adding EOL symbols for small expressions with height two or less (*Sm-EOL*), adding all EOL symbols (*EOL*), and omitting EOL symbols (*No-EOL*).

5. CORE ENGINE

The core engine is the first retrieval stage in Tangent-3, quickly finding the top-k highly relevant matches for a formula query, which are later re-ranked (see Figure 1). The engine ranks these top-k formulae using a simple algorithm, along with a list of document locations for each formula.

Since runtime performance is a high priority, the core engine uses a customized inverted index data structure implemented in C++. In addition, the engine evaluates only a subset of the query language functionality to allow the use of a fast and simple ranking algorithm that can still find a good set of candidate results.

The input to the indexer is a set of document names and the extracted mathematical formulae found in each document, and the input to the search engine is a single query formula. Each formula is converted to a set of tuples (see Sections 3 and 4) that serve as index and search "terms."

Index Data Structures. At index time, an inverted index is built over the given document-formula-tuple relationships, using two main data structures: *dictionaries (D_*)* convert objects (such as strings or tuples) into a compact 0-based range of internal identifiers (integers) and *postings lists (P_*)* are lists of integer tuples ordered by the first integer in the tuple. The data structures listed below can be combined to produce compression, ease of storage, and fast access speeds.

D_f: formula → formID
D_t: tuple → tupleID
D_d: document → docID
D_w: wildcardtuple → wildcardtupleID
P_t: tupleID → (formID, count)$^+$
P_f: formID → (docID, position)$^+$
P_w: wildcardtupleID → (tupleID)$^+$

The index includes postings lists P_t that map each tuple

[4] This was later changed for *non-operator* symbols.
[5] http://dlmf.nist.gov/LaTeXML/

to all formulae containing that tuple. A query can thus be implemented by combining the corresponding tuples' postings lists using an OR operator. We store these postings lists as ordered lists of formula identifiers (integers), so that the lists can be easily combined using a merge algorithm. Dictionary D_f defines a consistent assignment of a formula to its identifier, and another dictionary D_t is used for tuples, thus saving both space and time in the engine.

In order to return document information for query results, the engine stores postings lists P_f mapping each formula identifier to the identifiers of the documents containing those formulae, along with their positions in documents. Dictionary D_d is used for document names.

Wildcards. The core engine supports limited wildcard functionality. As illustrated in Figure 1, query tuples containing a single wildcard are implemented as iterator expansions. The engine stores postings lists P_w that map each wildcard tuple to the set of tuple identifiers that match. Assigning tuple identifiers using a dictionary D_w again gives some compression benefits. Implementing even this restricted wildcard functionality can be expensive, since the iterator expansion can be quite large.[6]

Searching. Query processing follows the architecture shown in Figure 1. First, the query is parsed into an SLT, and tuples are extracted. Then wildcard tuples are expanded, the associated postings lists for each tuple are found, iterators over these lists are created, and an iterator tree that implements the query is formed. Next, the iterator tree is advanced along formula identifiers in order, the scores are calculated, and the top-k formulae are stored in a heap. During this process, non-wildcard iterators are advanced first so that wildcard iterators only match unallocated tuples. As optimizations, iterators may skip over some formulae based on thresholds and max-score calculations (*see below*). After the iterators are finished, matching formulae and scores are returned along with the associated document names.

The engine uses Dice's coefficient over tuples as a simple ranking algorithm, counting the number of tuples that overlap between the query and a candidate formula using the query iterators. The engine also stores the tuple count for each formula (the size of the formula) in an array A_s and uses these values in the ranking calculation:

$$A_s\colon \text{formID} \rightarrow \text{tuplecount}$$

Since wildcards can often match multiple tuples in a query and overlap with other wildcards, there could be multiple ways to count the tuples that overlap. The engine implements a greedy counting approach by simply assigning the matches for tuples when each of the iterators is advanced.

Optimizations. Even using simple dictionary and postings list implementations (i.e., std::maps and 32-bit arrays), the engine's data structures are small enough to be run in memory for the datasets being examined, so we do not consider compressing these data structures here. Nevertheless, query processing might still be slow, even though the data structures are in memory, ranking is fast, and using a dictionary avoids repeated processing of duplicate formulae. As a result, the techniques below are used to reduce query execution time (related results may be found in Section 7):

O_1: Avoid processing all postings by allowing skipping in query iterators. This functionality is implemented using doubling (galloping) search [3].

O_2: Skip formulae based on size thresholds. We use the current top-k candidate list to define a minimum score that defines minimum and maximum tuple size thresholds from the definition of Dice's coefficient. We also improve on the effectiveness of these thresholds by reordering formula identifiers: sort the formulae by size, split into quartiles $\{q_1, q_2, q_3, q_4\}$, and then reorder $\{q_2, \mathit{reverse}(q_1), q_3, q_4\}$.

O_3: Avoid formulae that match only wildcard tuples when the score threshold allows. This is similar to the max-score optimization [21], only at a coarser granularity.

O_4: Avoid processing all wildcard tuple expansions. If a tuple is matched to a wildcard for the next formula, do not process the remaining iterators for this wildcard.

O_5: Process iterators for large postings lists first. Evaluate the binary operator tree left-first and order tree operators descending by size when possible.

6. RE-RANKING BY MAXIMUM SUBTREE SIMILARITY

In this section we describe an alternative to Dice's coefficient that is particularly effective in ranking mathematical formulae. We first formalize matching of subtrees based on their structure and then on their consistent re-labelling, providing support for unification of identifiers and constants (which is absent in a direct application of Dice's coefficient to tuples). Next we define a metric based on such matched subtrees, and then apply the definition to score a candidate SLT against a query that may include wildcards.

Notation: The label on node n in SLT T is denoted $\lambda(n)$. The number of nodes in SLT T is denoted $|T|$. We also write $n \in T$ if n is a node in T and $(n_1, n_2) \in T$ if (n_1, n_2) is an edge in T.

Approximate matches of formulae might involve identifying corresponding parts of the SLTs that represent a query and a candidate match. We base such a correspondence on structural equivalence of those parts.[7]

Definition (*aligned SLTs*): SLTs T_1 and T_2 are *aligned* if there is an isomorphism f mapping nodes from T_1 onto nodes from T_2 such that for every edge $(n_a, n_b) \in T_1$, there is a corresponding edge $(f(n_a), f(n_b)) \in T_2$ that has the same label. (Note that *node* labels in aligned trees need not match.) For N a subset of nodes in T_1, we define $f(N) = \{f(n) \mid n \in N\}$.

Approximate matches might also involve simple replacements of symbols in one SLT by alternative symbols (e.g., x for y or 3 for 2). Naturally, a wildcard symbol can be replaced by any symbol.

Definition (*unified nodes*): Node n_1 in SLT T_1 can be *unified* with node n_2 in SLT T_2, denoted $n_1 \dashrightarrow n_2$, if any of the following conditions holds:

- Both n_1 and n_2 have type *variable name* (V!),

[6]The engine does not try to enforce wildcard variable agreement between tuples (wildcard joins), and it ignores multi-wildcard tuples. An initial implementation handling multi-wildcard tuples and wildcard joins was found to be approximately one hundred times slower for a small dataset.

[7]Formally, a "part" of an SLT T will be a *pruned subtree*: any connected subset of labelled nodes from T together with the labelled edges connecting those nodes. Thus a pruned subtree of T is itself an SLT, but it need not extend to the leaves of T. Henceforth, we will use "subtree" to mean "pruned subtree."

- Both n_1 and n_2 have type *number* (N!),
- Both n_1 and n_2 have type *matrix* (M!),
- n_1 has type *wildcard* (*), or
- $\lambda(n_1) = \lambda(n_2)$.

Next, when matching T_1 with T_2 and allowing substituted symbols, it is important that the substitutions are consistent when determining that T_1 and T_2 match approximately. We start by identifying candidate sets of nodes in T_1 that can be consistently relabelled.

Definition (*alignment partition*): Given T_1 and T_2, two aligned SLTs with isomorphism f from T_1 to T_2, an *alignment partition* is a subset of nodes N in T_1 such that $(x \in N \wedge y \in N) \Rightarrow (\lambda(x) = \lambda(y) \wedge x \dashrightarrow f(x) \wedge y \dashrightarrow f(y) \wedge \lambda(f(x)) = \lambda(f(y)))$ (i.e., the nodes have identical labels and their unified images have identical labels or identical SLTs). For node $n \in T_1$, we define $P(n)$ to be the alignment partition containing n if it exists and $\emptyset$ otherwise. (Note that $n \in P(n) \Leftrightarrow n \dashrightarrow f(n)$.) For alignment partition A, $\lambda(A)$ denotes the label common to all nodes in A and $\lambda(f(A))$ denotes the label that is common to all nodes in $f(A)$.

We can now choose a set of partitions that are consistent in their relabelling of nodes.

Definition (*matched set of nodes*): Given aligned SLTs T_1 and T_2 with isomorphism f from T_1 to T_2 and the set of all corresponding alignment partitions, we define a *matched set of nodes* M as

$$M = \{n \in T_1 \mid n \in P(n) \wedge \forall n' \in M$$
$$([\lambda(n') = \lambda(n) \vee \lambda(f(n')) = \lambda(f(n))] \Rightarrow n' \in P(n))\}$$

In preparation to preferring matches of large *connected* parts of SLTs, let $E(M) = \{(n_1, n_2) \mid n_1 \in M \wedge n_2 \in M \wedge (n_1, n_2) \in T_1\}$, the set of edges induced by M.

Note that there may be many possible matched sets of nodes for a given alignment, depending on which alignment partitions are chosen to be included.

Because the SLT for an arbitrary query formula will not necessarily align with the SLT for an arbitrary candidate match formula, we need to consider subtrees of the SLTs that can be aligned. In so doing, we need to allow (but penalize) situations in which superfluous or mismatched symbols might appear in the query or in the candidate match. We wish to balance the amount of structural match with the number of symbols that are identically preserved.

We suggest the following properties for a scoring function, as illustrated in Figure 3: alignments with more matched symbols, and especially identical symbols, in close proximity to each other score higher than those with fewer matched symbols or more disconnected matches; if two candidates score equally with respect to matched symbols and their proximity, the one with fewer superfluous symbols scores higher; and everything else being equal, alignments with more matched symbols that are identical scores higher. We employ such a scoring function:

Definition (*SLT score*): Given a query SLT T_q, an SLT T_c for a candidate match, and two aligned SLTs T_1 and T_2 where T_1 is a subtree of T_q and T_2 is a subtree of T_c, let M be a matched set of nodes for T_1 and T_2. Let S be the harmonic mean of the fraction of nodes from T_q preserved by M and the fraction of edges preserved by $E(M)$, i.e., $S = \frac{2}{\frac{|T_q|}{|M|} + \frac{|T_q|-1}{max(|E(M)|,0.5)}}$ if $|M| > 0$, otherwise 0; this is a

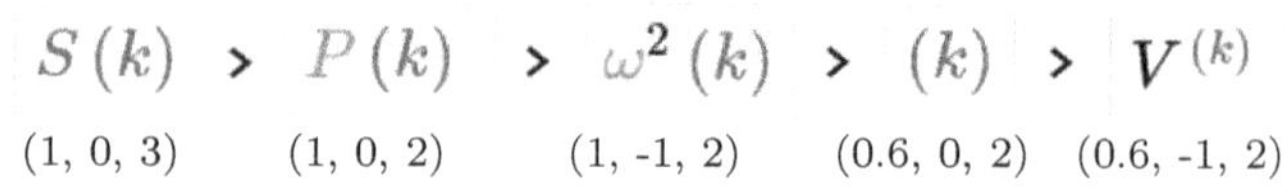

Figure 3: MSS Scoring for Query $S(k)$. Ranking triples contain MSS (1), and the number of candidate symbols that are unmatched (2) and match the query exactly (3). Parentheses count as one symbol.

measure of the size of the consistent structural part of the match. The *score* of T_c with respect to T_q, T_1, T_2, and M is denoted $s(T_q, T_c; T_1, T_2, M)$ and defined as the tuple composed of the following parts:

1. *structural match*: S (favor large matches).
2. *unmatched*: the negation of the number of unmatched nodes in T_c, i.e., $|M| - |T_c|$.
3. *exact match*: $|\{n \in M \mid \lambda(n) = \lambda(f(n))\}|$.

Scores assigned to any two candidate matches are compared lexicographically to determine which candidate ranks higher.

For aligned SLTs T_1 and T_2 with isomorphism f from T_1 to T_2 and the set of all corresponding alignment partitions, we want to choose a matched set of nodes M that produces a high score, but evaluating all matched sets induced by an alignment is too expensive. Therefore we use a greedy algorithm to select which partitions to include in the matched set of nodes, based on the properties used for scoring.

Algorithm 1 Greedy selection of matching subtree M

1. Let A_0 be the alignment partition containing the most nodes; if multiple partitions have the most nodes, let A_0 be one of those partitions where $\lambda(A_0) = \lambda(f(A_0))$ if it exists; otherwise let A_0 be any of the largest alignment partitions. Initialize M to include all nodes in A_0.
2. Repeatedly identify the largest alignment partition A_i such that $\lambda(A_i)$ does not label any node in M, and $\lambda(f(A_i))$ does not label any node unified with a node in M, choosing A_i where $\lambda(A_i) = \lambda(f(A_i))$ if it exists; replace M by $M \cup A_i$.
3. Stop if no more alignment partitions can be added to M.

If hash tables are used to record which node labels have been included in M and in $f(M)$, checking for duplicate labels can be performed in $O(1)$ time. Partitions can be considered one by one in decreasing order of size, which requires $O(|T_q| \log(|T_q|))$ time to initialize and then $O(|T_q|)$ to enumerate since the number of partitions cannot exceed the number of nodes in T_q.

Finally, to compare a query SLT T_q against a candidate SLT T_c, we choose a pair of aligned subtrees that maximizes the score for the candidate with respect to the query. Thus for each node n in T_q, we consider the score of the largest subtree rooted at n that can be aligned with some subtree in T_c. We start with a formal definition of the largest subtree.

Definition (*alignable and maximally similar subtree*): Given SLTs T_q and T_c and aligned SLTs T_1 rooted at r_1 and T_2 rooted at r_2 with isomorphism f from T_1 to T_2, where T_1 is a subtree of T_q and T_2 is a subtree of T_c, let $m = |\{n \in T_1 \mid n \dashrightarrow f(n)\}|$. Let $\frac{2m}{|T_1|+|T_q|}$ be a measure of similarity of T_1 to T_q with respect to T_2 (Dice's coefficient). T_1 is then *alignable and maximally similar* to T_q with respect to T_2 if r_1 can be unified with r_2 and there is no other SLT T_1' rooted at r_1 and T_2' rooted at r_2 with corresponding measure m', where T_1' is a subtree of T_q, T_2' is a subtree of T_c, $|T_1'| > |T_1|$, and $\frac{2m'}{|T_1'|+|T_q|} > \frac{2m}{|T_1|+|T_q|}$.

Definition (***Maximum Subtree Similarity score***)**:** Given SLTs T_q and T_c, consider pairs of nodes $n_{i_1} \in T_q$ and $n_{i_2} \in T_c$ such that n_{i_1} can be unified with n_{i_2}. Let T_{i_1}, rooted at n_{i_1}, be alignable and maximally similar to T_q with respect to tree T_{i_2}, rooted at n_{i_2}. The *Maximum Subtree Similarity* score $\text{MSS}(T_q, T_c)$ of T_c with respect to T_q is $\max_i s(T_q, T_c; T_{i_1}, T_{i_2}, M_i)$ over all such pairs, where M_i uses Algorithm 1 to chose matched sets of nodes.

THEOREM 1. *Computing Maximum Subtree Similarity for a candidate formula requires time* $O(|T_c||T_q|^2 \log(|T_q|))$.

PROOF. The number of pairs of aligned subtrees is at most $|T_q| * |T_c|$. For each pair, checking whether the roots can be unified takes $O(1)$ time, finding the largest alignable subtrees takes $O(|T_q|)$ time, and computing the score takes constant time plus time $O(|T_q| log(|T_q|))$ to choose M. □

MSS ranks more structurally similar subexpressions on a candidate higher, on the assumption they will be perceived as more relevant by users. Were this true, ranking by MSS would be consistent with the Probability Ranking Principle [22], that hits are ideally sorted by decreasing order of probable relevance, $P(c|q)$. In the next Section we show experimentally that the MSS similarity metric performs very well. In the future one might examine the correlation of MSS with $P(c|q)$ more directly.

7. EVALUATION

We now present experiments designed to observe the effect of system parameters on index size, retrieval time, and results, along with a human assessment of top-10 results.

Our main dataset is the NTCIR-11 Wikipedia collection with 30,000 articles totalling 2.5 GB and containing roughly 387,947 unique LaTeX expressions. In addition, we use the much larger NTCIR-11 arXiv collection to test the scalability of Tangent-3; this collection is 174 GB uncompressed, with 8,301,578 documents (arXiv article fragments) and 60 million formulae including isolated symbols.

7.1 Efficiency

Computational Resources and Parameters. We use a Ubuntu Linux 14.04 server with 24 Intel Xeon processors (2.93GHz) and 96GB of RAM. While some indexing operations were parallelized (as noted below), *all retrieval times are reported for single threaded processing.* Parallelization of query execution, and parallelizing re-rank scoring over matching formulas could be used to further speed up processing, and additional opportunities for decreasing runtimes are discussed below. All results reported for Tangent-3 in this Section were obtained using the top 100 formula from the core engine (i.e., $k = 100$).

Indexing. As seen in Table 2, index size increases roughly linearly from window sizes 1-4, with end-of-line tuples increasing storage by a constant amount. Adding EOL tuples just for small expressions (Sm-EOL; see Section 4) increases the index size modestly (by less than 500k for Wikipedia, and less than 10 MB for arXiv). The maximum Wikipedia index size is 503.1 MB on disk; in contrast, for the arXiv the maximum index size is 29 GB. For small window sizes storage is much smaller; for $w = 1$ with *No-EOL* and *Sm-EOL*, the index file is just over 64 MB for Wikipedia, and just under 5.4 GB for arXiv; these are much smaller than Tangent-2 (1.3 GB for Wikipedia, and roughly 36 GB for the arXiv dataset [16]). When these index files are loaded into memory, they consume 2 - 2.5 times their space on disk.

Table 2: Index Sizes for NTCIR-11 Collections.

	Index Sizes (*MB*)					
	WIKIPEDIA			ARXIV		
w	No-EOL	Sm-EOL	EOL	No-EOL	Sm-EOL	EOL
1	64.2	64.5	73.7	5,364	5,372	6,179
2	95.6	96.0	105.2	7,568	7,577	8,383
3	128.3	128.7	137.9	9,662	9,671	10,477
4	161.3	161.7	170.9	11,587	11,596	12,402
All	493.5	493.9	503.1	28,225	28,234	29,040

For the arXiv data, it took 43 hours to pre-process the documents (using 10 processes), and at most an additional 3.5 hours to generate the index (when $w = All$ and end-of-line tuples are included) using a single process. Wikipedia was much faster, requiring 260 seconds for preprocessing, and at most 95 seconds for index creation. As our document pre-processor is implemented in Python, we believe that a faster implementation (e.g., in C++) could reduce run times by a factor of 4-10 in both cases.

Retrieval Times. We ran the 100 NTCIR-11 Wikipedia formula queries over the large NTCIR-11 arXiv collection to test retrieval speed for the core engine. Larger window sizes increase index entries (see Table 2) and lead to longer query execution times. For example, when EOL tuples are ignored, retrieval times in milliseconds (given as (μ, σ, median)) increase from (372.95, 1649.24, 90.40) for $w = 1$ to (1932.41, 9332.54, 281.64) for $w = All$. Including EOL pairs has a much larger effect on performance: for $w = 1$, retrieval times increase to (4334.86, 16368.06, 584.94). Again using ($w = 1$, EOL), if we turn off the core optimizations O_1-O_5, the average retrieval time doubles and the standard deviation increases (9239.92, 23776.99, 681.79). Using the core optimizations again, for $w = 1$ with Sm-EOL retrieval times increase only a small amount over when no EOL pairs are used (435.55, 1626.48, 111.39).

When running the queries on the smaller NTCIR-11 Wikipedia collection, Tangent-2 requires 8 *minutes* to execute the 100 test queries using a parallelized index with nine sub-indices on Amazon Web Services [16]. In contrast, using a single process and the slowest configuration on our system ($w = All$, EOL), Tangent-3 requires only 8.48 *seconds* without re-ranking, and 106.14 seconds with re-ranking; in the fastest condition ($w = 1$, no EOL) this reduces to 0.57 seconds without re-ranking and 78.03 seconds with re-ranking.

Re-ranking times are consistent across w and *EOL* settings because the number of formulae re-ranked is fixed at $k = 100$. For the Wikipedia corpus, re-rank times are $(775, 3562, 72)$ milliseconds. The mean is skewed by a small number of outliers: for one query re-ranking takes 46 seconds, with retrieval from the core taking only 1.7 seconds ($w = All$, EOL). This query expression is very large (*Query 52*), with 16 wildcard symbols producing large candidates with many possible unifications. Re-ranking can be accelerated by recoding from Python to C++.

7.2 Effectiveness

The NTCIR-11 Wikipedia benchmark [18] includes 100 queries for measuring specific-item retrieval performance. Queries are associated with a single target formula in a specific document, ignoring identical formulae appearing within the same or different documents. These 100 queries are split

Table 3: NTCIR-11 Wikipedia Formula Retrieval Benchmark Results. 100 Queries: 65 Constant, 35 with wildcards (Variable). Metrics: % Recall@k for targets ($k = 10,000$) and Mean Reciprocal Rank (MRR in %).

	Recall@k						MRR					
	Documents			Formulae			Documents			Formulae		
System	Total	Const	Var	Total	Const	Var	Total	Const	Var	Total	Const	Var
TUW Vienna †	**97**	*100	91	**93**	98	83	**80**	80	79	***82**	86	75
NII Japan †	**97**	98	*94	**94**	97	89	**74**	79	74	**72**	*87	63
Tangent-2 ∘	**88**	91	83	**78**	78	77	**70**	68	75	**67**	65	72
Tangent-3 Core ∘												
w=1 No-EOL	**95**	97	91	**95**	97	91	**79**	80	77	**76**	76	76
Sm-EOL	**97**	*100	91	**97**	*100	91	**80**	*82	77	**77**	78	76
EOL	***98**	*100	*94	***98**	*100	*94	**81**	*82	79	**77**	78	76
w=All No-EOL	**95**	97	91	**95**	97	91	**79**	80	78	**76**	76	76
Sm-EOL	**97**	*100	91	**97**	*100	91	**80**	*82	78	**78**	78	76
EOL	**97**	*100	91	**96**	*100	89	**81**	*82	78	**77**	78	75
Tangent-3 Re-rank ∘												
w=1 No-EOL	**95**	97	91	**95**	97	91	**80**	80	*82	**77**	76	*80
Sm-EOL	**97**	*100	91	**97**	*100	91	***82**	*82	*82	**79**	78	*80
EOL	***98**	*100	*94	***98**	*100	*94	***82**	*82	*82	**79**	78	*80
w=All No-EOL	**95**	97	91	**95**	97	91	**80**	80	80	**77**	76	77
Sm-EOL	**97**	*100	91	**97**	*100	91	**81**	*82	80	**78**	78	77
EOL	**97**	*100	91	**96**	*100	89	***82**	*82	*82	**78**	78	78

†: uses Operator Tree (OT) formula representation (Content MathML)
∘: uses Symbol Layout Tree (SLT) formula representation (Presentation MathML)

into 65 *Constant* queries containing no wildcards and 35 *Variable* queries containing wildcards.

Search results are returned as a ranked list of (*documentId*, *formulaId*) pairs. *Document-centric* results are computed using the list of document identifiers in their order of appearance after removing duplicates. *Formula-centric* results are computed using the complete ranked list of matches.

Systems are evaluated using two metrics. First, by the *recall* (i.e., percentage of targets located at rank 10,000 or less) and second by the *mean reciprocal rank* (MRR) over all queries (assigning zero when not found). Note that a reciprocal rank of 50% indicates that on average, the target formula appears at rank two.

Summary of Results. At the top of Table 3, NTCIR-11 results from the two best systems and Tangent-2 are shown as fractions rounded to the nearest percentage [18]. A summary of participating systems is available [2]. The first two systems are *tree-based* approaches applied to Operator Trees encoded in Content MathML. As described earlier, Tangent-2 is a *spectral* approach, using symbol pair-based retrieval over Symbol Layout Trees encoded in Presentation MathML. TUW Vienna indexes individual symbols and linearized subexpressions. NII represents sub-expressions in Operator Trees by hash code sets (see Section 2).

Tangent-3 results are shown at the bottom of Table 3, split into core and reranked results. We include combinations of window sizes $w = \{1, 2, 3, 4, All\}$ (where *All* is all tuples) and End-of-Line symbol indexing settings (No-EOL, Small-EOL, EOL).

Using re-ranking, $w = 1$ and all EOL tuples, Tangent-3 obtains the highest document and formula recall (both 98% vs. 97% and 94%), the highest Variable (wildcard) formula MRR (80%) and the highest document MRR (82%) to date. In all Tangent-3 conditions, the mean rank of a target formula is just above the middle of ranks one and two (i.e., higher than an MRR of 75%). This is interesting, as previously the strongest results make use of Operator Trees rather than SLTs for retrieval. This supports the idea that choice of formula representation may be less important than the choice of primitives for retrieval. The higher formula recall obtained by Tangent-3 may be due to matching symbol pairs rather than complete subtrees (see Section 2).

Relative to Tangent-2, recall is increased 10% for documents, and 20% for formulae. MRR values are also 10% higher in Tangent-3 (all conditions) than Tangent-2.

Using *Sm-EOL* provides state-of-the-art performance comparable to *EOL*, but uses a smaller index size with faster retrieval times. With *Sm-EOL* we obtain document and formula recall of 97% (a reduction of only 1%) with unchanged MRR values. For the same parameter settings, formula MRR is 80% (the best reported value is 82%).

Window Size. Window size had little effect on performance, and so for space we show only results for $w = 1$ and $w = All$ in Table 3. Interestingly, recall in the top-10,000 actually decreases slightly when $w = All$ is used, missing two additional formula with wildcards (Var) and one document relative to $w = 1$. This may be because of noise introduced by the larger number of tuples, which may match anywhere in a candidate formula. Window size had no effect on MRR for queries without wildcards (*Const*), but we again see a small decrease for queries with wildcards for $w = All$.

End-of-Line Symbols. For $w = 1$, adding all EOL tuples increases the number of formulae retrieved by three (e.g., the query 's' produces no symbol pairs and thus requires an EOL tuple if it is to be matched). *Sm-EOL* gave fast queries and also retrieved two of the three formulae missed when EOL tuples are omitted. For $w = All$ using all EOL tuples decreases formula recall slightly relative to *Sm-EOL* (missing one query with wildcards), perhaps because of the numerous matches obtained using $w = All, EOL$. Adding the *Sm-EOL* tuples increases document and formula MRR slightly for non-variable queries.

Re-ranking. The re-ranker does not affect recall for Tangent-3, as the re-ranker only reorders hits returned by the core. Exact matches are represented well by the Dice coefficient over tuples, particularly for concrete queries without wildcards. However, the re-ranker does improve wildcard (variable) formula MRR by 4% for queries with wildcards

Table 4: **Likert Rating $\mu(\sigma)$ for Top-10 NTCIR-11 Wikipedia Hits (21 participants, 10 queries).**

	Rank/Position in Top-10 Hits									
	1	**2**	**3**	**4**	**5**	**6**	**7**	**8**	**9**	**10**
$w = 1$	4.54 (0.78)	3.79 (1.16)	3.48 (1.31)	3.23 (1.30)	2.83 (1.25)	2.94 (1.22)	2.65 (1.19)	2.78 (1.21)	2.78 (1.21)	2.85 (1.25)
$w = 2$	4.54 (0.78)	3.71 (1.22)	3.48 (1.30)	3.16 (1.28)	2.90 (1.26)	2.93 (1.20)	2.85 (1.25)	2.57 (1.18)	2.74 (1.22)	2.80 (1.13)
$w = All$	4.54 (0.78)	3.78 (1.19)	3.59 (1.23)	3.27 (1.16)	2.98 (1.25)	2.92 (1.23)	2.80 (1.17)	2.98 (1.24)	2.92 (1.21)	2.87 (1.17)
best	4.54 (0.79)	4.03 (1.07)	3.75 (1.12)	3.49 (1.13)	3.31 (1.20)	3.15 (1.16)	3.02 (1.17)	2.94 (1.17)	2.85 (1.19)	2.77 (1.19)

for $w = 1$, *Sm-EOL*. (80% with re-ranking, vs. 76% without). This is 5% higher than the best previous MRR results for formula MRR (75%).

On average, only 4.16 of the top-10 results (with standard deviation of 2.61) remain in the top-10 after re-ranking by MSS. MSS will not re-order exact or very nearly exact matches, hence constant queries have the same MRR values as the core engine, but the reranker is able to improve MRR values for variable queries where the core implements approximate wildcard handling.

Without re-ranking, the core engine produces comparable results using $k = 100$. For the core engine, increasing k produces perfect recall (100%) without substantially increasing query time. The reranker, however, cannot process a large number of results in a reasonable amount of time. The core engine also produces higher document-centric MRR values than the best published results, although limited handling of wildcards causes variable queries to underperform.

We now consider how well MSS-based rankings relate to human perceptions of formula similarity, using the top-10 results from 10 of the NTCIR-11 Benchmark queries.

Human Evaluation: Data. 10 queries were selected using random sampling from the Wikipedia queries. Five contained wildcards, and the other five did not. Some queries were replaced using a new randomly selected query to ensure a diverse set of expression sizes and structures.

To limit the number of hits for participants to evaluate, we chose to consider only $w = 1, 2$, and *All*. We used *No-EOL*, as none of the queries were a single symbol (the smallest query, Q8 is '$\alpha(x)$'), and we wished to observe the effect of window size using actual symbol pairs, without EOL tuples. Using the Wikipedia collection, for the three versions of the core compared ($w = \{1, 2, All\}$, *No-EOL*), we applied re-ranking to the top-100 hits, and then collected the top-10 hits returned by each query for rating.

Evaluation Protocol. Participants completed the study alone in a private, quiet room with a desktop computer running the evaluation interface in a web browser. The web pages provided an overview, followed by a demographic questionnaire, instructions on evaluating hits, and then familiarization trials (10 hits; 5 for each of two queries). After familiarization, participants evaluated hits for the 10 queries, and finally completed an exit questionnaire. Participants were paid \$10 each at the end of their sessions.

Participants rated the similarity of queries to results using a five-point Likert scale (Very Dissimilar, Dissimilar, Neutral, Similar, Very Similar). It has been shown that presenting search results in an ordered list influences relevance assessments [7]. Instead we presented queries along with each hit in isolation, with query presentation order randomized, and the presentation order for hits was also randomized.

Demographics and Exit Questionnaire. 21 participants (5 female, 16 male) were recruited from the Computing and Science colleges at RIT. Their age distribution was: 18-24 (8), 25-34 (9), 35-44 (1), 45-54 (1), 55-64 (1) and 65-74 (1). Their highest levels of education completed were: Bachelor's (9), Master's (9), PhD (2), and Professional (1). Their reported areas of specialization were: Computer Science (13), Electrical Engineering (2), Psychology (1), Sociology (1), Mechanical Engineering (1), Computer Engineering (1), Math (1) and Professional Studies (1).

In the post-questionnaire, participants rated the evaluation task as Very Difficult (3), Somewhat Difficult (10), Neutral (6), Somewhat Easy (2) or Very Easy (0). They reported different approaches to assessing similarity. Many considered whether operations and operands were of the same type or if two expressions would evaluate to the same result. Others reported considering similarity primarily based on similar symbols, and shared structure between expressions.

Similarity Rating Results. As seen in Table 4, Likert ratings are similar in all conditions. Average ratings increase from the 5th to 1st hits, and are close to the best obtained in the result pools ('best' in Table 4). On average Top-4 hits have some similarity with the query, with average ratings higher than 'Neutral' (3). For large formulae, strong matches for small subexpressions were sometimes perceived as dissimilar, and *exact* matches to the query were often rated as 'Similar' (4). Reading large formulae is difficult and may reduce perceived similarity; we wonder if highlighting matches would have increased these ratings.

The top-5 hits are largely identical across conditions (at least 4/5 match) with the exception of query 60:

$$p = \frac{-x \pm \sqrt{x^{*} - 4(*)(\frac{*}{*} - y)}}{2(\frac{-gx^2}{*})}$$

$w = All$ returns the best rated hits in the top-5, but $w = \{1, 2\}$ return only one of the best-rated matches in the top-5. $w = All$ generates more tuples for matching, compensating for wildcard pairs not being indexed by matching relationships between more distant symbols.

We produce ideal rankings by pooling top-10 hits and then sorting them by average Likert rating. Relative to this ideal, average nDCG@10 values increase and standard deviations decrease with window size ($w = 1$: 0.87 (0.1); $w = 2$: 0.88 (0.08); $w = All$: 0.90 (0.03)). Selecting the best window size for each query improves metrics further (*oracle*: 0.92 (0.02)). Interestingly, the highest nDCG values are obtained for six queries using w = 1; the additional symbol pair matches considered for larger window sizes sometimes lead to very scattered matches being returned in the top-k from the core engine, which $w = 1$ avoids.

Unification works well when most of a candidate matches the query (e.g., as in Table 1). In Tangent-3 all identifiers are unifiable, including greek letters, latin letters, and function names. At times high MSS scores are obtained for candidates with weak Likert ratings due to a large number of unifications, or unifying symbols of different types (e.g., x with π). Unifying or matching symbols associated with operators of different types appears to contradict some ratings (e.g., $a + b$ and $a \leq b$ may be perceived as dissimilar, while $a + b$ and $a - b$ perceived as similar).

To improve unification and MSS scores, one could expand

the set of symbol and operator types in the SLT model, annotate SLTs with semantic information [24], or modify MSS to be computed using matches in both Operator Tree and SLT formula representations. It should be straight-forward to adapt Tangent-3 to work with Operator Trees.

8. CONCLUSION

We have presented a new two-stage cascaded retrieval model for appearance-based formula retrieval. The Symbol Layout Tree and symbol pair retrieval models used in the first stage out-performs earlier versions, being more efficient in space and time. The second stage re-ranks the top-k matches by Maximum Subtree Similarity (MSS), producing state-of-the-art results for the NTCIR-11 Wikipedia formula retrieval task. Human similarity ratings agree substantially with formula rankings produced using MSS.

For future work, more human experiments are needed to identify features that affect the perception of formula similarity for mathematical experts and non-experts. Retrieval efficiency may be improved by compressing dictionaries and postings lists, and by using an implementation of weak-AND [4] or a more fine-grained implementation of max-score [21]. Retrieval effectiveness can be improved through changes to the SLT, unification models, and the MSS function and scoring vector. Additional opportunities include allowing wildcards to match subexpressions rather than single symbols, implementing additional query functionality in the engine, incorporating textual features and context [24], and integrating Tangent-3 with keyword search.

Acknowledgements

This material is based upon work supported by the National Science Foundation (USA) under Grant Nos. IIS-1016815 and HCC-121880. Financial support from the Natural Sciences and Engineering Research Council of Canada under Grant No. 9292/2010, Mitacs, and the University of Waterloo is also gratefully acknowledged.

9. REFERENCES

[1] A. Aizawa, M. Kohlhase, and I. Ounis. NTCIR-10 math pilot task overview. In *NTCIR*, 2013.

[2] A. Aizawa, M. Kohlhase, I. Ounis, and M. Schubotz. NTCIR-11 Math-2 task overview. In *NTCIR*, 2014.

[3] J. L. Bentley. An almost optimal algorithm for unbounded searching. *Inf. Process. Lett.*, 5(3):82–87, 1976.

[4] A. Z. Broder, D. Carmel, M. Herscovici, A. Soffer, and J. Zien. Efficient query evaluation using a two-level retrieval process. In *CIKM*, 2003.

[5] T. W. Cole, I. Debauchies, K. M. Carley, J. L. Klavans, Y. LeCun, M. Lesk, C. A. Lynch, P. Olver, J. Pitman, and Z. J. Xia. *Developing a 21st Century Global Library for Mathematics Research*. The National Academies Press, Washington, DC, 2014.

[6] P. Graf. Substitution tree indexing. In *RTA*, 1995.

[7] Z. Guan and E. Cutrell. An eye tracking study of the effect of target rank on web search. In *SIGCHI*, 2007.

[8] F. Guidi and C. S. Coen. A survey on retrieval of mathematical knowledge. In *CICM*, 2015.

[9] H. Hiroya and H. Saito. Partial-match retrieval with structure-reflected indices at the NTCIR-10 math task. In *NTCIR*, 2013.

[10] S. Kamali and F. W. Tompa. A new mathematics retrieval system. In *CIKM*, 2010.

[11] S. Kamali and F. W. Tompa. Structural similarity search for mathematics retrieval. In *CICM*. 2013.

[12] M. Kohlhase and I. Sucan. A search engine for mathematical formulae. In *AISC*, 2006.

[13] X. Lin, L. Gao, X. Hu, Z. Tang, Y. Xiao, and X. Liu. A mathematics retrieval system for formulae in layout presentations. In *SIGIR*, 2014.

[14] B. R. Miller and A. Youssef. Technical aspects of the digital library of mathematical functions. *Ann. Math. Artif. Intell.*, 38(1):121–136, 2003.

[15] T. T. Nguyen, S. C. Hui, and K. Chang. A lattice-based approach for mathematical search using formal concept analysis. *Expert Syst. Appl.*, 39(5):5820 – 5828, 2012.

[16] N. Pattaniyil and R. Zanibbi. Combining TF-IDF text retrieval with an inverted index over symbol pairs in math expressions: The Tangent math search engine at NTCIR 2014. In *NTCIR*, 2014.

[17] P. Pavan Kumar, A. Agarwal, and C. Bhagvati. A structure based approach for mathematical expression retrieval. In *MIWAI*. 2012.

[18] M. Schubotz. Challenges of mathematical information retrieval in the NTCIR-11 Math Wikipedia Task. In *SIGIR*, 2015.

[19] P. Sojka and M. Líška. Indexing and searching mathematics in digital libraries. In *CICM*, 2011.

[20] D. Stalnaker and R. Zanibbi. Math expression retrieval using an inverted index over symbol pairs. In *DRR*, 2015.

[21] H. Turtle and J. Flood. Query evaluation: strategies and optimizations. *Inf. Process. Manage.*, 31(6):831–850, 1995.

[22] C. J. van Rijsbergen. *Information Retrieval*. Butterworths, 2nd edition, 1979.

[23] L. Wang, J. Lin, and D. Metzler. A cascade ranking model for efficient ranked retrieval. In *SIGIR*, 2011.

[24] Y. Wang, L. Gao, X. Liu, and K. Yuan. WikiMirs 3.0: a hybrid MIR system based on the context, structure and importance of formulae in a document. In *Proc. JCDL*, pages 173–182, 2015.

[25] K. Wangari, R. Zanibbi, and A. Agarwal. Discovering real-world use cases for a multimodal math search interface. In *SIGIR*, 2014.

[26] P. Willett. Document retrieval experiments using vocabularies of varying size. II. Hashing, truncation, digram and trigram encoding of index terms. *J. Documentation*, 35:296–305, 1979.

[27] A. Youssef. Roles of math search in mathematics. In *Proc. Math. Knowl. Manage.*, pages 2–16. 2006.

[28] R. Zanibbi and D. Blostein. Recognition and retrieval of mathematical expressions. *Int. J. Document Anal. Recognit.*, 15(4):331–357, 2012.

Explainable User Clustering in Short Text Streams

Yukun Zhao[†*]
yukunzhao.sdu@gmail.com

Shangsong Liang[‡*]
shangsong.liang@ucl.ac.uk

Zhaochun Ren[§*]
z.ren@uva.nl

Jun Ma[†]
majun@sdu.edu.cn

Emine Yilmaz[‡]
emine.yilmaz@ucl.ac.uk

Maarten de Rijke[§]
derijke@uva.nl

[†]Shandong University, Jinan, China
[‡]University College London, London, United Kingdom
[§]University of Amsterdam, Amsterdam, The Netherlands

ABSTRACT

User clustering has been studied from different angles: behavior-based, to identify similar browsing or search patterns, and content-based, to identify shared interests. Once user clusters have been found, they can be used for recommendation and personalization. So far, content-based user clustering has mostly focused on static sets of relatively long documents. Given the dynamic nature of social media, there is a need to dynamically cluster users in the context of short text streams. User clustering in this setting is more challenging than in the case of long documents as it is difficult to capture the users' dynamic topic distributions in sparse data settings. To address this problem, we propose a dynamic user clustering topic model (or UCT for short). UCT adaptively tracks changes of each user's time-varying topic distribution based both on the short texts the user posts during a given time period and on the previously estimated distribution. To infer changes, we propose a Gibbs sampling algorithm where a set of word-pairs from each user is constructed for sampling. The clustering results are explainable and human-understandable, in contrast to many other clustering algorithms. For evaluation purposes, we work with a dataset consisting of users and tweets from each user. Experimental results demonstrate the effectiveness of our proposed clustering model compared to state-of-the-art baselines.

Keywords

User clustering; Short text processing; User topic modeling

1. INTRODUCTION

With the rising popularity of social media, hundreds of millions of active users are sharing short texts on microblogging platforms such as Twitter[1] and Sina Weibo.[2] A good understanding of users' dynamic preferences is important for the design of applications that cater for users of such platforms, such as personalized microblog search, twitter summarization, and computational advertising. In this paper, we study the problem of *user clustering in the context of short text streams*, where users are taken to be people who post messages on a microblogging platform. Our goal is to infer users' topic distributions over time and dynamically cluster users based on their topic distributions in such a way that users in the same cluster share similar interests while users in different clusters differ in their interests. In addition, we aim at making the clustering results explainable and understandable.

Previous work on user clustering [5, 18, 24] mainly clusters users who exhibit similar patterns when accessing information such as clicked documents. For instance, the user clustering method proposed by Mobasher et al. [24] constructs vector matrices for URLs and users and then utilizes K-means [16] to cluster users based on browsing vectors. These methods are designed to work with collections of static, long documents and they often make the assumption that users' interests do not change over time. Unlike previous work, we focus on clustering users at a certain point in time, in the context of streams of short documents.

Accordingly, we propose a dynamic multinomial Dirichlet mixture user clustering topic model, UCT for short, to tackle the problem of dynamic user clustering in short text streams. Traditional topic models such as probabilistic latent semantic indexing (PLSI) [12], latent Dirichlet allocation (LDA) [3], author topic models [31, 37] or the user interest topic model [21], have been widely used to uncover topics of documents and users. These topic models do not work well in the context of short text streams due to the problem of sparsity. How to utilize topic distributions for user clustering is still an open problem.

Inspired by previous work [5–7, 19, 20, 22, 28, 29], we extract word-pairs in each tweet and form a word-pair set for each user to explicitly capture word co-occurrence patterns. That is, UCT infers each user's interests with hidden topics while topics are captured from the word-pair set of the users. In addition, to track the dynamics of a user's interests, UCT infers a user's current interests by integrating the interests at previous time periods with newly observed data in text streams. It then utilizes users' current interests for clustering. Thus, the result of user clustering is time-varying and users in the same cluster share similar interests at the current

*These three authors contributed equally to the paper.

[1]http://www.twitter.com
[2]http://www.weibo.com

SIGIR '16, July 17 - 21, 2016, Pisa, Italy

ISBN 978-1-4503-4069-4/16/07. . . $15.00

DOI: http://dx.doi.org/10.1145/2911451.2911522

time, although their interests may differ at previous times. To the best of knowledge, we are the first to perform dynamic user clustering in short text streams based on the distributions of users' interests during a given time period.

Our main research questions are whether UCT outperforms state-of-the-art user clustering methods, and whether our clustering results are explainable and understandable in contrast to results of other methods. We conduct our experiments on a Twitter dataset and demonstrate the effectiveness of our UCT clustering model.

The main contributions of our work are:

(1) We propose the task of dynamically clustering users in the context of short text streams.
(2) We propose a dynamic multinomial Dirichlet mixture user clustering topic model, UCT, to address the user clustering task, where users' time-varying topic distributions can be captured.
(3) We propose a collapsed Gibbs sampling algorithm for the inference of dynamic users' topic distributions in the context of short text streams, where we tackle the problem of word co-occurrence sparsity.
(4) Our proposed clustering model can effectively cluster previously seen users as well as users who newly arrive in the stream.
(5) We provide a thorough analysis of UCT and of the impact of its key ingredients and parameters and find that it significantly outperforms state-of-the-art algorithms.

2. RELATED WORK

Two major types of research relate to our work: user clustering and text clustering, and topic modeling.

2.1 User clustering and text clustering

State-of-the-art research on user clustering mainly focuses on web user clustering [4, 18, 24, 32]. These papers study users' access information from logged server data including query and click data and then uncovers clusters of these users that exhibit similar information needs. For instance, Buscher et al. [4] cluster users based on user interaction information, including clicks, scrolls and cursor movements for search queries on long text documents. Another line of work, which mostly focuses on content-based similarity, has grouped users by expertise [1, 11]; recent advances in distributed representation learning have given rise to new types of joint topic and entity representations [34] but, so far, these have not been used for user clustering yet. To the best of our knowledge, existing content-based user clustering algorithms work with long documents and do not consider clustering users in the context of short text streams such as Twitter or Weibo. In this paper, we aim at dynamically clustering users in short text streams.

Another relevant line of work is text clustering. Yu et al. [40] and Huang et al. [13] propose a Dirichlet process mixture with feature selection model (DPMFS) and a Dirichlet process mixture with feature partition model (DPMFP) for normal document clustering, respectively. They compare DPMFP with four other clustering models: EM text classification (EM-TC) [25], K-means [16], LDA [3] and exponential-family approximation of the Dirichlet compound multinomial distribution (EDCM) [8]; they find that DPMFP performs best. In the context of short text documents, Rangrej et al. [27] compare three clustering algorithms including K-means, Singular Value Decomposition and Affinity Propagation [9] on a small set of tweets and find that Affinity Propagation outperforms the other two, but the complexity of Affinity Propagation is quadratic in the number of documents. Tsur et al. [33], Yin [38], and Yu et al. [40] focus on the problem of online clustering of a stream of tweets. They all use an incremental clustering framework that first groups a number of tweets into clusters, then assigns the newly arriving tweets to these clusters. Yin and Wang [39] introduce a collapsed Gibbs sampling algorithm for the Dirichlet multinomial mixture model for short text clustering in a static set of short documents. They do not model documents with a distribution of topics. Instead, they assign a single topic to each document, then cluster the documents based on the topic assignments. All of these algorithms aim at clustering short documents—the problem of dynamically clustering users in the context of short text streams has so far been ignored, however.

2.2 Topic modeling

Probabilistic topic models, such as PLSI [12] and LDA [3], aim to analyze latent topics of documents. Various LDA-type topic models have been proposed. The author topic model [31] has been proposed to uncover latent topics of authors; each author is associated with a multinomial distribution over topics and each topic is associated with a multinomial distribution over words. This suggests a method for clustering users in short text streams: model users as distributions over topics inferred from their tweets and then cluster users based on their topic distributions.

Various dynamic topic models have been proposed to track changes of topics in streams. The dynamic topic model (DTM) [2] analyzes the time evolution of topics in document collections, in which a document is assumed to have one timestamp. Since DTM uses a Gaussian distribution for the dynamics, the inference is intractable because of the non-conjugacy of the Gaussian and multinomial distributions. The dynamic mixture model (DMM) [36] considers a single dynamic sequence of documents, which corresponds to a single topic over time. The topic tracking model (TTM) [15] focuses on tracking time-varying consumer behavior, in which consumers' interests change over time. The topic over time model (ToT) [35] assumes that each topic is associated with a continuous distribution over timestamps, and the topic distribution of a document is influenced by both word co-occurrences and the document's timestamp. All of these models assume that the context of the documents is rich enough to infer a topic distribution for the documents, which may not work well for documents in short text streams.

Exploiting external knowledge to enrich the representation of short texts has been proposed to improve the performance of topic modeling for short texts. Phan et al. [26] train latent topics from large external resources. Jin et al. [17] learn hidden topics on short texts via transfer learning from auxiliary long text data. Ren et al. [30] apply a document expansion method that consists of entity linking and sentence extraction. Chen and Liu [6] retain the results learned in the past and using them to help future learning. Cheng et al. [7] extract bi-terms in each tweet to capture word co-occurrence explicitly for enhancing the performance of short text topic modeling. Again, unlike UCT, these algorithms aim at working with a static collection of documents only.

We work with short text streams and propose a dynamic Dirichlet multinomial mixture user clustering topic model, by which we capture a multinomial distribution of topics specific to each user over time in Twitter and then dynamically cluster users based on their dynamic topic distributions. To enhance the performance of the inference in our proposed Gibbs sampling for our topic model, we extract word-pairs in tweets and form a word-pair set for each user to explicitly capture word co-occurrence patterns. To the best of our knowledge, this is the first attempt to use a topic model to infer clusters of users in the context of short text streams.

3. PRELIMINARIES

In this section, we introduce the main notations and task to be addressed in this paper.

Table 1 summarizes our main notation. Term $u \in \mathbf{U}_t$ indicates a user, while $\mathbf{U}_t = \{u_1, u_2, \ldots, u_m\}$ is a set of users at time period $t \in \{\ldots, T-1, T\}$ with T being the most recent time period, and the length of each time period t can be a week, a month, a quarter, half a year, a year etc. Also, z is a topic and K is the number of topics we infer for our UCT model; w is a word in a tweet and b represents a word-pair extracted from a tweet.

Table 1: Main notation used in UCT.

Notation	Gloss	Notation	Gloss
u	user	t	time slice
z	topic	K	number of topics
w	word	b	word-pair
$\omega_{t,u}$	cluster user u belonging to at time t		
$\mathbf{U}_t$	a set of users at time t		
$\mathbf{D}_t$	a text stream at time t		
$\mathbf{D}_{t,u}$	texts published by user u at time t		
$\mathbf{B}_{t,u}$	a set of word-pairs published by user u at time t		
$\mathbf{B}_t$	a set of word-pairs published at time t		
α_t	the parameter of user Dirichlet prior		
β_t	the parameter of token Dirichlet prior		
$\theta_{t,u}$	multinomial distribution of topics specific to user u at time t		
$\phi_{t,z}$	multinomial distribution of words specific to topic z at time t		
$z_{t,u,b}$	topic assignment on b for user u at time t		
$m_{t,u,z}$	number of word-pairs published by u assigned to topic z at time t		
$n_{t,z,w}$	number of times word w is assigned to topic z at time t		

We extract a set of word-pairs $\mathbf{B}_{t,u}$ for each user u from their published tweets $\mathbf{D}_{t,u}$ at time period t, and we aggregate all users' word-pair sets as $\mathbf{B}_t$. We use $\mathbf{B}_t$ as input to monitor each user's interest in the UCT model. The parameters α_t and β_t are Dirichlet priors for our topic model at time t. $z_{t,u,b}$, $m_{t,u,z}$ and $n_{t,z,w}$, which are used in the topic model training process, represent the topic assignment on word-pair b for user u, the number of word-pairs published by user u assigned to topic z, and the number times of w is assigned to topic z, respectively. $\omega_{t,u}$ is a cluster to which user u belongs at time t, and the cluster $\omega_{t,u}$ can be changed over time as we assume the user's interest $\theta_{t,u}$ is time-varying.

The task we address is to dynamically track clusters of users over time in the context of short text streams such that users in the same cluster share similar interests. Specifically, for each time period t, given a set of users $\mathbf{U}_t = \{u_1, u_2, \ldots, u_m\}$ at time t and a short text stream $\mathbf{D}_t$ up to t, we focus on uncovering the clusters of users in $\mathbf{U}_t$, with $\omega_{t,u}$ being the cluster to which user u belongs at t.

4. METHOD

We start by providing an overview of our method in §4.1. We then detail each of our three main steps: preprocessing in §4.2, the user clustering topic model in §4.3, and user clustering in §4.4.

4.1 Overview

We use Twitter as our default setting of short text streams and provide a general scenario of our method for dynamically clustering users in tweet streams in Algorithm 1. We assume that each user's interest is represented by topics, and each user's interests may drift over time. Formally, given a time period $t \in \{\ldots, T-1, T\}$, the interest of each user $u \in \mathbf{U}_t$ is represented as a multinomial distribution $\theta_{t,u}$ over topics. The distribution $\theta_{t,u}$ is inferred from our proposed dynamic user topic model. Because documents in short text streams are short and sparse, we propose a preprocessing step to extract word-pairs (see step 1 in Algorithm 1), where a word-pair contains two words sharing the same topic. We enrich the context by considering co-occurring words in word-pairs instead of documents.

Algorithm 1: Overview of the algorithm for user clustering in short text streams.

Input : A set of users $\mathbf{U}_t$ along with their published tweets $\mathbf{D}_t$
Output: cluster of each user $\omega_{t,u}$
1 Extract a set of word-pairs $\mathbf{B}_{t,u}$ for each user u, see §4.2
2 Use UCT model to track each user's interests as $\theta_{t,u}$, see §4.3
3 Cluster users based on their interests distribution $\theta_{t,u}$, see §4.4

Next, we propose a dynamic Dirichlet multinomial mixture user clustering topic model (UCT) to capture each user's dynamic interests $\theta_{t,u}$, at time slice t, in the context of short text streams (see step 2 in Algorithm 1). Each user's interests $\theta_{t,u}$ is computed after sampling process has finished.

Based on the multinomial distribution $\theta_{t,u}$, we explore the cluster of users using K-means clustering [16] (see step 3 in Algorithm 1). With the time period t moving forward, the result of clustering users changes dynamically.

4.2 Extracting word-pairs

Traditional topic models [3, 15, 35] detect topics from a document based on word co-occurrences in documents. The topics are represented as groups of correlated words, while the correlation is revealed by word co-occurrence patterns in documents. In this paper, we do not use the words in tweets (our documents) to directly infer topics for users due to the limited length of tweets.

In order to tackle the lack of context in modeling users' interests, we explicitly consider word correlations via co-occurring words in a word-pair instead of a whole tweet, where a word-pair is a set of two order-exchangeable words being assigned to the same topic. Specifically, after removing stop words and apply Porter stemming, we obtain each user's tweet set $\mathbf{D}_{t,u}$ (the tweets user u published at the current time period t). Following [6, 7], we regard each tweet as an individual context unit, in which word-pairs in a tweet share the same topic. Then, the method to extract word-pairs from each tweet $d \in \mathbf{D}_{t,u}$ is as follows.

$$\mathbf{B}_d = \{(w_i, w_j) \mid w_i, w_j \in d, i \neq j\}, \tag{1}$$

Each word-pair $b \in \mathbf{B}_d$ contains two different words (w_i, w_j) in tweet d. For example, from the tweet "bananas and apples are all fruit" we extract three word-pairs, i.e., "banana apple", "banana fruit" and "apple fruit" after removing stop words and stemming. Then, we aggregate all word-pairs extracted from tweets $\mathbf{D}_{t,u}$ for user u:

$$\mathbf{B}_{t,u} = \bigcup_{d \in \mathbf{D}_{t,u}} \mathbf{B}_d, \tag{2}$$

Thus, for each user u, the set $\mathbf{D}_{t,u}$ of their published tweets at time period t is processed to a set of word-pairs $\mathbf{B}_{t,u}$.

We sample the topic assignment z for each word-pair instead of each independent word. In other words, the word correlation constructed to infer topics does not rely on the co-occurrence in tweets but in word-pairs. The next subsection shows how to use the word-pair set $\mathbf{B}_{t,u}$ to model the user's interests.

4.3 Dynamic user clustering topic model

In this subsection, we detail our dynamic multinomial Dirichlet mixture user clustering topic model (UCT). UCT captures a user's interests at time t as $\theta_{t,u}$, that is, as a distribution over mixtures of topics. We use $t \in \{\ldots, T-1, T\}$ to represent a time period, the length of which can be a day, week, month, quarter or even year.

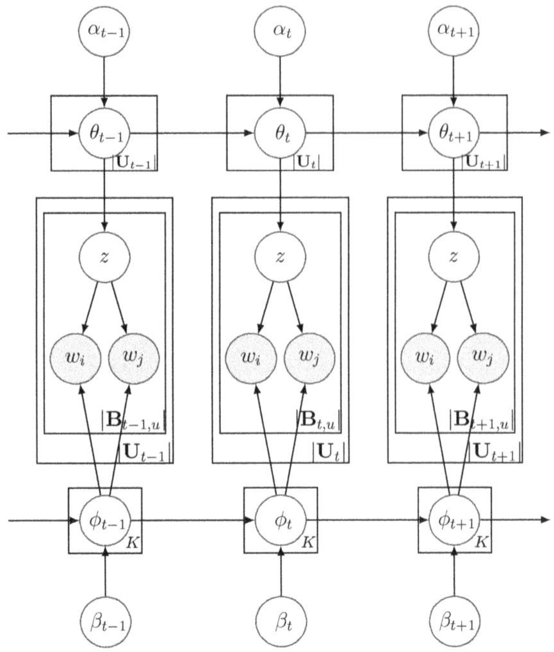

Figure 1: Graphical representation of our dynamic user clustering topic model, UCT. Shaded nodes represent observed variables.

Fig. 1 shows a graphical representation of our UCT model, where shaded and unshaded nodes indicate observed and latent variables, respectively. At t, we sample word-pairs $(w_i, w_j) \in \mathbf{B}_{t,u}$ for users $u \in \mathbf{U}_t$ based on the current topic-word distributions ϕ_t, and infer current users' interests θ_t. From Fig. 1, we see that a dependency is assumed to exist between two adjacent time periods.

We track the dynamics of a user's interests based on the assumption that a user's interests during the current time period t are the same as those during the preceding time period $t-1$ unless interests are changed by newly observed data at t. We model a user's interests by combining their topic distribution obtained during the previous time slice $t-1$ as prior knowledge and newly arriving observed data for inferring current model for the user's interests. In particular, we use both the user's previous interests $\theta_{t-1,u}$ and current Dirichlet prior α_t as a new Dirichlet prior. The K-dimensional variable $\theta_{t,u} = \{\theta_{t,u,z}\}_{z=1}^{K}$ has the following probability density:

$$P(\theta_{t,u} \mid \theta_{t-1,u}, \alpha_t) = \frac{\Gamma(\sum_z \theta_{t-1,u,z} + \alpha_{t,z})}{\prod_z \Gamma(\theta_{t-1,u,z} + \alpha_{t,z})} \cdot \prod_z \theta_{t,u,z}^{\theta_{t-1,u,z}+\alpha_{t,z}-1}, \tag{3}$$

where $\Gamma(x)$ is a Gamma function. In contrast with static topic models [3, 31], the Dirichlet prior changes from α to $\theta_{t-1,u}+\alpha_t$, where the added term $\theta_{t-1,u}$ represents the influence of previously inferred interests.

To model the dynamics of topics over words, we infer topic-word distributions $\phi_{t,z} = \{\phi_{t,z,v}\}_{v=1}^{V_t}$ at current time period t by using the following Dirichlet distribution:

$$P(\phi_{t,z} \mid \phi_{t-1,z}, \beta_t) = \frac{\Gamma(\sum_v \phi_{t-1,z,v} + \beta_{t,v})}{\prod_v \Gamma(\phi_{t-1,z,v} + \beta_{t,v})} \cdot \prod_v \phi_{t,z,v}^{\phi_{t-1,z,v}+\beta_{t,v}-1}, \tag{4}$$

The topic-words distributions are considered to be inferred through priors $\phi_{t-1,z} + \beta_t$. We estimate α_t and β_t for each time period instead of using simple symmetric priors. Given all users' word-pairs set $\mathbf{B}_t = \bigcup_{u \in \mathbf{U}_t} \mathbf{B}_{t,u}$, where $\mathbf{B}_{t,u}$ is the set of word-pairs specific to user u, from Fig. 1 we know that topic z is related with a distribution of words with the multinomial distribution $\phi_{t,z} = \{\phi_{t,z,w} \mid w \in \mathbf{V}_t\}$. In UCT, the multinomial distribution specific to the user u is used to select a topic, thereafter a word in a word-pair is generated according to the distribution $\phi_{t,z}$ specific to that chosen topic z. According to the graphical model, we sample each topic $z_{t,u,b}$ for each word-pair $b \in \mathbf{B}_{t,u}$. The distributions θ_{t-1}, ϕ_{t-1} at the previous time period and the priors β_t, α_t are utilized for inferring the current distribution θ_t and ϕ_t. The generative process is as follows:

i. Draw K multinomials $\phi_{t,z}$ from Dirichlet priors β_t and ϕ_{t-1}, one for each topic z;
ii. For each user u, draw a multinomial distribution $\theta_{t,u}$ from Dirichlet priors α_t and $\theta_{t-1,u}$; then for each word-pair b in the word-pairs set $b \in B_{t,u}$:
   (a) Draw a topic $z_{t,u,b}$ from multinomial $\theta_{t,u}$;
   (b) Draw a word $w_i \in b$ from multinomial $\phi_{t,z_{t,u,b},w_i}$;
   (c) Draw another word $w_j \in b$ from multinomial $\phi_{t,z_{t,u,b},w_j}$;

We sample word-pairs instead of words as shown in the above generative process. Then, the probability of generating a word-pair $b = (w_i, w_j)$ given a topic z at t is represented as:

$$P(b \mid t, z) = P(w_i \mid t, z) P(w_j \mid t, z), \tag{5}$$

and the probability of generating a word-pair b at t is represented as:

$$P(b \mid t) = \sum P(z \mid t) P(w_i \mid t, z) P(w_j \mid t, z). \tag{6}$$

Inference is intractable in this model. Following [3, 10, 15, 36, 39], we propose a collapsed Gibbs sampling method to perform approximate inference. We adopt a conjugate prior (Dirichlet) for the multinomial distributions, and thus we easily integrate out ϕ_t and θ_t, analytically capturing the uncertainty associated with them. In this way we facilitate the sampling, i.e., we need not sample ϕ_t and θ_t at all.

The proposed collapsed Gibbs sampling algorithm for the UCT model is shown in Algorithm 2 (recall that our main notation is shown in Table 1). The input of our Gibbs sampling algorithm is $\mathbf{B}_t$ (all users' word-pairs sets at time slice t) and the output consists of all users' interests distributions over topics at current time t. For the initialization of our Gibbs sampling, we randomly assign a topic $z = z_{t,u,b}$ to each word-pair $b \in \mathbf{B}_{t,u}$ and update $m_{t,u,z}$ and $n_{t,z,w}$ (to be defined below) accordingly.

In the Gibbs sampling procedure above at time slice t, we need to calculate the conditional distribution

$$P(z_{t,u,b} = z \mid \mathbf{B}_t, \mathbf{Z}_{t,-(u,b)}, \mathbf{U}_t, \mathbf{\Phi_{t-1}}, \mathbf{\Theta_{t-1}}, \alpha_t, \beta_t),$$

where $\mathbf{Z}_{t,-(u,b)}$ represents all topics assignments except the current word pair b from user u. We begin with the joint probability of the current word-pair set $\mathbf{B}_t$, the topic assignments $\mathbf{Z}_t$, and the user set $\mathbf{U}_t$ given the previous distributions $\mathbf{\Phi}_{t-1}$ and $\mathbf{\Theta}_{t-1}$, and two Dirichlet priors α_t and β_t. Using the chain rule, we obtain the conditional probability conveniently as follows:

$$\begin{aligned} &P(z_{t,u,b} = z \mid \mathbf{B}_t, \mathbf{Z}_{t,-(u,b)}, \mathbf{U}_t, \mathbf{\Phi_{t-1}}, \mathbf{\Theta_{t-1}}, \alpha_t, \beta_t) \\ &\propto \frac{(n_{t,z,w_i} + \phi_{t-1,z,w_i} + \beta_{t,w_i} - 1)}{(\sum_{v=1}^{V_t}(n_{t,z,v} + \phi_{t-1,z,v} + \beta_{t,v}) - 1)} \\ &\times \frac{(n_{t,z,w_j} + \phi_{t-1,z,w_j} + \beta_{t,w_j} - 1)}{(\sum_{v=1}^{V_t}(n_{t,z,v} + \phi_{t-1,z,v} + \beta_{t,v}) - 1)} \end{aligned} \tag{7}$$

Algorithm 2: Gibbs Sampling for UCT

```
Input  : K, N, t, B_t, Φ_{t-1}, Θ_{t-1}, α_{t-1}, β_{t-1}
Output: multinomial parameter θ_t and φ_t
Initialize z_{t,u,b}, m_{t,u,z}, n_{t,z,w} as zero and
for each user u ∈ U_t do
    for each word-pair b ∈ B_{t,u} do
        sample a topic z randomly:
        z_{t,u,b} ← z
        m_{t,u,z} ← m_{t,u,z} + 1
        while word-pair b contains two words w_i and w_j
        n_{t,z,w_i} ← n_{t,z,w_i} + 1
        n_{t,z,w_j} ← n_{t,z,w_j} + 1
Sampling Phase
for iter = 1, ..., N do
    for each user u ∈ U_t do
        for each word-pair b ∈ B_{t,u} do
            record the current topic, z = z_{t,u,b}
            m_{t,u,z} ← m_{t,u,z} − 1
            while word-pair b contains two words w_i and w_j
            n_{t,z,w_i} ← n_{t,z,w_i} − 1
            n_{t,z,w_j} ← n_{t,z,w_j} − 1
            draw z_b from P(z_{t,u,b} = z |
              B_t, Z_{t,−(u,b)}, U_t, Φ_{t−1}, Θ_{t−1}, α_t, β_t); see (7)
            update z_{t,u,b}, m_{t,u,z}, n_{t,z,w_i}, n_{t,z,w_j}
compute the parameters θ_t and φ_t using equation (8).
```

$$\times \frac{m_{t,u,z} + \theta_{t-1,u,z} + \alpha_{t,z} - 1}{\sum_{z=1}^{T}(m_{t,u,z} + \theta_{t-1,u,z} + \alpha_{t,z}) - 1},$$

where $m_{t,u,z}$ represents the number of word-pairs published by user u and assigned to topic z, and $n_{t,z,w}$ represents the number of times word w is assigned to topic z. The two Dirichlet priors α_t and β_t are estimated by maximizing the joint distribution

$$P(\mathbf{B}_t, \mathbf{Z}_t, \mathbf{U}_t | \mathbf{\Phi}_{t-1}, \mathbf{\Theta}_{t-1}, \alpha_t, \beta_t)$$

in the sampling at each iteration. We use the following updating rules in fixed-point iterations for obtaining these two Dirichlet priors,

$$\alpha_{t,z} \leftarrow \frac{\alpha_{t,z} \sum_u (\Psi(\Upsilon_1) - \Psi(\Upsilon_2))}{\sum_u \Psi \sum_z (\Upsilon_1) - \Psi(\sum_z \Upsilon_2)},$$

$$\beta_{t,v} \leftarrow \frac{\beta_{t,v} \sum_z (\Psi(\Upsilon_a)) - \Psi(\Upsilon_b))}{\sum_z \Psi \sum_v (\Upsilon_a) - \Psi(\sum_v \Upsilon_b)},$$

where $\Psi(x) = \frac{\partial \log \Gamma(x)}{x}$ is a Digamma function, and

$$\Upsilon_1 = m_{t,u,z} + \theta_{t-1,u,z} + \alpha_{t,z} - 1, \quad \Upsilon_2 = \theta_{t-1,u,z} + \alpha_{t,z},$$
$$\Upsilon_a = n_{t,z,v} + \phi_{t-1,z,v} + \beta_{t,v} - 1, \quad \Upsilon_b = \phi_{t-1,z,v} + \beta_{t,v}.$$

Once the Gibbs sampling has been done, with the fact that a Dirichlet distribution is conjugate to a multinomial distribution, we then conveniently infer the following distributions for $\mathbf{\Theta}_t$ and $\mathbf{\Phi}_t$, respectively:

$$\theta_{t,u,z} = \frac{m_{t,u,z} + \theta_{t-1,u,z+}\alpha_{t,z} - 1}{\sum_{z=1}^{K}(m_{t,u,z} + \theta_{t-1,u,z} + \alpha_{t,z}) - 1},$$
$$\phi_{t,z,w} = \frac{n_{t,z,w} + \phi_{t-1,z,w} + \beta_{t,w} - 1}{\sum_{w=1}^{V_t}(n_{t,z,w} + \phi_{t-1,z,w} + \beta_{t,w}) - 1}. \quad (8)$$

4.4 Clustering users

Clustering previously seen users. After we have determined each user's $u \in \mathbf{U}_t$ dynamic topic distribution at time t, $\theta_{t,u}$ (obtained by (8)), we use K-means [16] to compute the clusters of these users based on each user's topic distribution $\theta_{t,u}$. Obviously, as time progresses, the clusters of these users dynamically change.

Clustering previously unseen users. However, in some cases, we do not have users' interests $\theta_{t,u_{\text{new}}}$ for new arriving users $u_{\text{new}} \notin \mathbf{U}_t$. We then infer each new user's interests from their published tweets at time period t, where tweets are preprocessed into a word-pair set $\mathbf{B}_{t,u_{\text{new}}}$ as discussed in §4.2. We compute the probability of the user u_{new} being interested in topic z at t, i.e., $\theta_{t,u_{\text{new}},z}$, as:

$$P(z \mid t, u_{\text{new}}) = \prod_{b \in \mathbf{B}_{t,u_{\text{new}}}} P(z \mid t, b) P(b \mid t, u_{\text{new}}), \quad (9)$$

where $P(z \mid t, b)$ is computed as:

$$\begin{aligned} P(z \mid t, b) &= \frac{P(w_i \mid t, z) P(w_j \mid t, z) P(z \mid t)}{P(b \mid t)} \\ &= \frac{P(w_i \mid t, z) P(w_j \mid t, z) P(z \mid t)}{\sum_z P(z \mid t) P(w_i \mid t, z) P(w_j \mid t, z)} \\ &= \frac{P(z \mid t) \phi_{t,z,w_i} \phi_{t,z,w_j}}{\sum_z P(z \mid t) \phi_{t,z,w_i} \phi_{t,z,w_j}}, \end{aligned} \quad (10)$$

where $P(w \mid t, z)$ is the probability of word w associated with topic z at t, i.e., $\phi_{t,z,w}$, and $P(z \mid t)$ is the probability of topic z at t. We obtain $P(z \mid t)$ for (10) as:

$$P(z \mid t) = \frac{n_t(z, w)}{n_t(w)}, \quad (11)$$

where we use $n_t(z, w)$ and $n_t(w)$ to denote the total number of words assigned to topic z and the total number of words at time t, respectively.

Then we estimate $P(b \mid t, u_{\text{new}})$ in (9) as:

$$P(b \mid t, u_{\text{new}}) = \frac{n_{t,u_{\text{new}}}(b)}{\sum_b n_{t,u_{\text{new}}}(b)}, \quad (12)$$

where $n_{t,u_{\text{new}}}(b)$ is the frequency of word-pair b in $\mathbf{B}_{t,u_{\text{new}}}$.

Finally, after applying (10), (11) and (12) to (9), we obtain the new user's interests $\theta_{t,u_{\text{new}}}$. We then group this user into a cluster $\omega_{t,u}$ where they share most interests with other users in the cluster:

$$\omega_{t,u_{\text{new}}} = \arg\max_{\omega_{t,u}} \sum_{u \in \omega_{t,u}} \frac{\cos(\theta_{t,u}, \theta_{t,u_{\text{new}}})}{|\omega_{t,u}|}, \quad (13)$$

and update the user set $\mathbf{U}_t$ as $\mathbf{U}_t \leftarrow \mathbf{U}_t \cup \{u_{\text{new}}\}$.

5. EXPERIMENTAL SETUP

In this section, we describe our experimental setup; §5.1 lists our research questions; §5.2 describes our dataset; §5.3 and §5.4 list the baselines and metrics for evaluation, respectively;

5.1 Research questions

We list the research questions that guide the remainder of the paper:

RQ1 Does our dynamic user clustering method UCT outperform state-of-the-art baseline methods? (See §6.1)

RQ2 What is the impact of the different time slices in our dynamic user clustering method? (See §6.2)

RQ3 What is the quality of the topical representation inferred by our user clustering topic model? (See §6.3)

RQ4 Can we capture the dynamics of users' interests and make the clustering results produced by our proposed dynamic user topic model explainable? (See 6.4)

5.2 Dataset

In order to answer our research questions, we work with a dataset collected from Twitter. The data set contains 1,375 active users and their tweets that were posted from the beginning of their registration up to May 31, 2015. In total, we have 3.78 million tweets with each tweet having its own timestamp. The average length of the tweets is 12 words. Due to the crawling restrictions imposed by Twitter, we cannot obtain the follower-followee relationships for each user. So we ignore the possibility of using users' relationships to improve the performance; we leave this as part of our future work.

We use this dataset as our short text streams and manually judge the clusters of the 1,375 users based on the content of their published tweets. We obtain ground truth clusters for 5 different partitions of time periods, i.e., a week, a month, a quarter, half a year and a year. In the ground truth clusters for time periods of a week, the users are manually clustered through their published tweets during a week, resulting in 48 to 60 clusters. We also create ground truth for times periods of a month, a quarter, half a year and a year, with the number of clusters varying from 43 to 52, 40 to 46, 28 to 30 and 28 to 30, respectively.

For pre-processing, we remove stop words and apply Porter stemming using the Lemur toolkit.[3]

5.3 Baselines

We compare our proposed method UCT with the following baselines and state-of-the-art clustering strategies in our experiments:

K-means. This is a traditional clustering algorithm [16]. It represents users by TF-IDF vectors and categorizes them into different clusters based on their TF-IDF vector similarities.

GSDMM. This is a Dirichlet multinomial mixture model-based approach for short text clustering [39]. It represents each short document through a single topic and groups each user into a cluster that contains most of his tweets.

Latent Dirichlet Allocation (LDA). This model infers topic distributions specific to each document via the latent dirichlet allocation (LDA) model.

Author Topic Model (AuthorT). This model [31] infers topic distributions specific to each user in a static dataset, and then clusters the users into different clusters based on the similarities of their topic distributions.

Dynamic topic model (DTM). This model [2] utilizes a Gaussian distribution for inferring topic distribution of long text documents in streams.

Topic over time model (ToT). This model [35] normalizes timestamps of long documents in a collection and then infers topics distribution for each document.

Topic tracking model (TTM). This model [15] captures the dynamic topic distribution of long documents arriving during time period t in streams based on the content of the documents and the previous estimated distributions.

For the LDA, DTM, ToT and TTM baselines, we use the averaged topic distribution of all the documents a user posted before generated by LDA, DTM, ToT and TTM, respectively, to represent this user, and cluster users based on their topic distribution similarities. For static topic models, i.e., LDA and AuthorT, we set $\alpha = 0.1$ and $\beta = 0.01$. We set the number of topics $K = 50$ and the number of clusters equal to the number of topics.

[3] http://www.lemurproject.org

5.4 Evaluation metrics

Given the number of clusters P and the number of output clusters Q in the ground truth, we set $\mathcal{C} = \{c_1, \dots, c_j, \dots, c_P\}$ as a set of ground-truth clusters and $\Omega = \{\omega_1, \dots, \omega_i, \dots, \omega_Q\}$ as the set of output clusters at time slice t, respectively. We use the following metrics to evaluate our experimental results, all of which are widely used in the literature [7, 39].

Precision. At time slice t, each output cluster ω_i is assigned to a ground-truth cluster c_j *iff* the intersection of the two clusters $\omega_i \cap c_j$ owns the largest number of users. In case of a draw, we randomly assign the output cluster ω_i to one of the ground-truth clusters that call the draw, as the random assignment does not result in different evaluation performance. Then the *precision* of this assignment is measured by counting the number of user-pairs in the intersection correctly assigned and divided by the total number of user-pairs in the output cluster ω_i:

$$\text{Precision}(\mathcal{C}, \Omega) = \frac{1}{Q} \sum_{i=1}^{Q} \frac{\binom{\max_j |\omega_i \cap c_j|}{2}}{\binom{|\omega_i|}{2}},$$

where $\binom{|\omega_i \cap c_j|}{2}$ and $\binom{|\omega_i|}{2}$ are the number of 2-combinations from a given set $\omega_i \cap c_j$ and ω_i, respectively. Obviously, a higher precision indicates better user clustering performance.

Normalized Mutual Information (NMI) [23]. NMI is a measure that allows us to make the trade-off between the quality of the clustering and the number of clusters. It is an entropy-based metric that explicitly measures the amount of statistical information shared by the variables representing the output clusters and the ground truth clusters of users. Let $I(\Omega; \mathcal{C})$ denotes the mutual information of the output cluster set Ω and the ground-truth cluster set $\mathcal{C}$. NMI avoids the value biasing to large number of clusters by using entropy of Ω and $\mathcal{C}$, i.e., $E(\Omega)$ and $E(\mathcal{C})$:

$$\begin{aligned}\text{NMI}(\mathcal{C}, \Omega) &= \frac{I(\Omega; \mathcal{C})}{[E(\Omega) + E(\mathcal{C})]/2} \\ &= \frac{\sum_{i,j} \frac{|\omega_i \cap c_j|}{n} \log \frac{n|\omega_i \cap c_j|}{|\omega_i||c_j|}}{\left(-\sum_i \frac{|\omega_i|}{n} \log \frac{|\omega_i|}{n} - \sum_j \frac{|c_j|}{n} \log \frac{|c_j|}{n}\right)/2},\end{aligned}$$

where n is the total number of users. Note that when $\mathcal{C}$ is equal to Ω, NMI reaches 1, its maximum value. Larger NMI value indicate better clustering performance.

Adjusted Rand Index (ARI) [14, 23]. Consider clustering users based on a series of pair-wise decisions. If two users both in the same cluster are aggregated into the same cluster and two users in different classes are aggregated into different clusters, the decision is considered to be correct. The Rand index shows the percentage of decisions that are correct while the adjusted Rand index is the corrected-for-chance version of the Rand index [14]. The maximum value is 1 for exact match; larger values mean better performance for clustering. ARI$(\mathcal{C}, \Omega)$ is computed as follows, where n is the total number of users.

$$\text{ARI}(\mathcal{C}, \Omega) = \frac{\sum_{i,j} \binom{|\omega_i \cap c_j|}{2} - [\sum_i \binom{|\omega_i|}{2} \sum_j \binom{|c_j|}{2}]/\binom{n}{2}}{\frac{1}{2}\left[\sum_i \binom{|\omega_i|}{2} + \sum_j \binom{|c_j|}{2}\right] - \left[\sum_i \binom{|\omega_i|}{2} \sum_j \binom{|c_j|}{2}\right]/\binom{n}{2}},$$

The three metrics introduced so far are for evaluating the performance of user clustering, whereas the following metric is for evaluating the quality of topic representations of users in clusters.

H-score [7]. As our UCT model builds on topic modeling, we consider to evaluate the quality of the topic representation of each user using the H-score [7] metric, which is computed as:

$$\text{H-score}(\mathcal{C}) = \frac{\text{IntraDis}(\mathcal{C})}{\text{InterDis}(\mathcal{C})},$$

where the average intra-cluster distance $\text{IntraDis}(\mathcal{C})$ and average inter-cluster distance $\text{InterDis}(\mathcal{C})$ are computed as:

$$\text{IntraDis}(\mathcal{C}) = \frac{1}{P}\sum_{p}\sum_{\substack{u_i,u_j\in\mathcal{C}_p\\ i\neq j}}\frac{\text{dis}(u_i,u_j)}{\binom{|\mathcal{C}_k|}{2}},$$

$$\text{InterDis}(\mathcal{C}) = \frac{1}{P(P-1)}\sum_{\substack{\mathcal{C}_k,\mathcal{C}_{k'}\in\mathcal{C}\\ k\neq k'}}\left[\sum_{\substack{u_i\in\mathcal{C}_k\\ u_j\in\mathcal{C}_{k'}}}\frac{\text{dis}(u_i,u_j)}{|\mathcal{C}_k||\mathcal{C}_{k'}|}\right],$$

where $\text{dis}(u_i, u_j)$ is the symmetric Kullback-Leibler distance of topic distributions of user u_i and user u_j. The intuition behind the H-score is that if the average inter-cluster distance is small compared to the average intra-cluster distance, the topical representation of users reaches good performance.

We report the Precison, NMI and ARI scores of all eight methods listed above to evaluate clustering performance. Importantly, to evaluate the quality of topical representations, we report H-scores of all baseline methods except GSDMM. We cannot compute H-scores for GSDMM as it assumes each document to be a single topic; GSDMM clusters users based on topic assignments, not topic distributions. We evaluate the performance with the above metrics at each time period, and report the mean of the evaluation results.

6. RESULTS AND ANALYSIS

In the following subsections we report on our experimental outcomes and formulate answers to our research questions.

6.1 Effectiveness of UCT

To begin, we address research question **RQ1**. We evaluate the performance of our UCT model in the context of short text streams, and compare UCT with a traditional clustering method, K-means, GSDMM, which integrates a state-of-the-art clustering topic model for short documents in a static set, and three dynamic user clustering models, DTM, ToT and TTM (see §5.3). The training data we use for these eight models are all tweets published from the year 2013 to 2014, which we divide into two parts, each part containing tweets published during a year. We report the precision, NMI and ARI values of the eight methods by averaging the performance across the two parts.

Fig. 2 shows the performance of UCT and the baselines in terms of Precision, ARI and NMI. First, we see that UCT performs significantly better than K-means, GSDMM and the five topic models on all the metrics, which demonstrates the effectiveness of our model for user clustering. UCT and the other 5 topic models outperform K-means, which attests to the merit of utilizing topic models for user clustering. UCT and GSDMM, which infer topic distributions and infer single topic assignments for short documents, outperform all other baselines in most cases and on all three evaluation metrics. This finding demonstrates that considering documents representing users as short texts rather than as long documents during inference help to improve the performance on user clustering. UCT, ToT, TTM and DTM, which infer topic distributions for documents in streams, outperform AuthorT and LDA, which infer topic distributions in static sets of documents. This finding demonstrates that inferring dynamic topic distributions of documents in the context of streams can help to enhance the performance of user clustering over considering documents as a set of static ones for the inference.

Table 2: The average number of tweets a user published during a week, a month, a quarter, half a year, a year. Plus the average number of word-pairs extracted for each user.

	a week	a month	a quarter	half a year	a year
#tweets	16	111	220	418	744
#word-pairs	1012	3586	9199	14348	29810

UCT significantly outperforms all baselines, and this finding confirms that the way UCT infers dynamic topic distributions of short documents in streams improve the performance of user clustering.

6.2 Length of time periods

Next, we address research question **RQ2**. To understand the influence on UCT of the length of the time period that we use for evaluation, we compare the performance for different time periods: a week, a month, a quarter, half a year and a year, respectively. Fig. 3 shows the evaluation results in terms of Precision, ARI and NMI for time periods of different lengths; we average the scores over periods of six weeks, six months, six quarters, four semi-years and two years, respectively.

UCT always outperforms LDA, AuthorT, DTM, TTM, ToT, GSDMM for time periods of all lengths. This finding, again, confirms the fact that UCT, which infers topic distributions of short documents based on the previous distribution and arriving documents, works better than the state-of-the-art algorithms for user clustering in streams. When the length of the time period increases from a week to a month, both UCT and the baseline methods all obtain a big improvement, but UCT continues to outperform the other methods. Although the performance of UCT seems to level off on all three metrics when the length of the time period increases from a quarter to a year, it still significantly outperforms the baselines. These findings demonstrate that UCT's performance on the user clustering task is robust in the context of short document streams, and is able to maintain significant improvements over state-of-the-art algorithms.

To further understand why UCT and the baseline methods increase their performance when the length of the time period use for evaluation increases, we provide an analysis of word co-occurrence patterns in different time periods. Statistics of the number of tweets users published in different time periods are shown in Table 2. On average, a user only publishes 16 tweets per week, which indicates that there are 16×12 word co-occurrence patterns if we assume the average length of each tweet to be 12 words. The number 16×12 is not comparable with the number 1012, which is the number of word-pairs. A larger number of word-pairs help to better infer topic distributions in Gibbs sampling. The longer the time period, the more word-pairs can be utilized in our Gibbs sampling for the topic inference.

6.3 Quality of topical representations

We now address research question **RQ3**. To assess the quality of topics extracted by UCT, we compare UCT and the baseline methods. Fig. 4 shows the comparison of the performance of UCT and the baselines in terms of H-score. When compute the H-scores for evaluating the quality of topical representation in UCT and the baselines, we use the quarterly ground-truth user clustering results.

It is clear from Fig. 4 that UCT obtains a significantly smaller H-score compared to all other six models,[4] which indicates that the average inter-cluster distance is small compared to the aver-

[4]Recall that we cannot calculate the H-score for GSDMM as it assumes each document to be in only a single topic

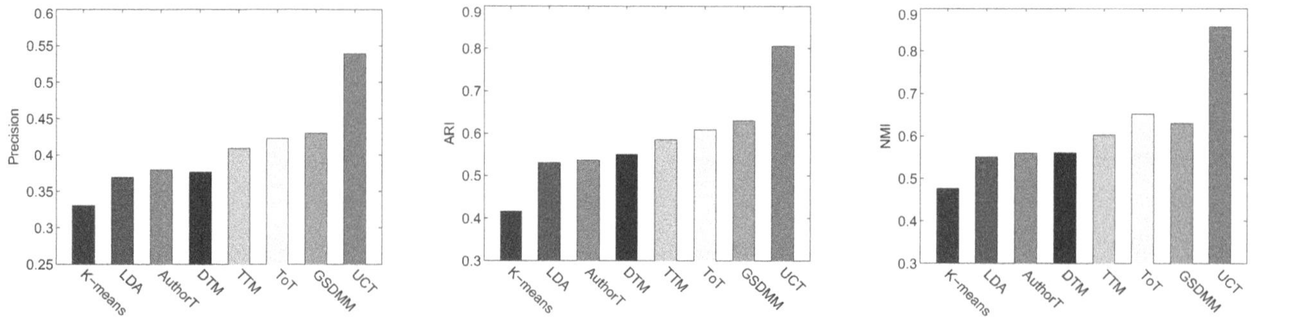

(a) Precision (b) ARI (c) NMI

Figure 2: Clustering performance of DCT and the baselines using a time period of a quarter. The performance is evaluated using Precision, ARI and NMI, respectively.

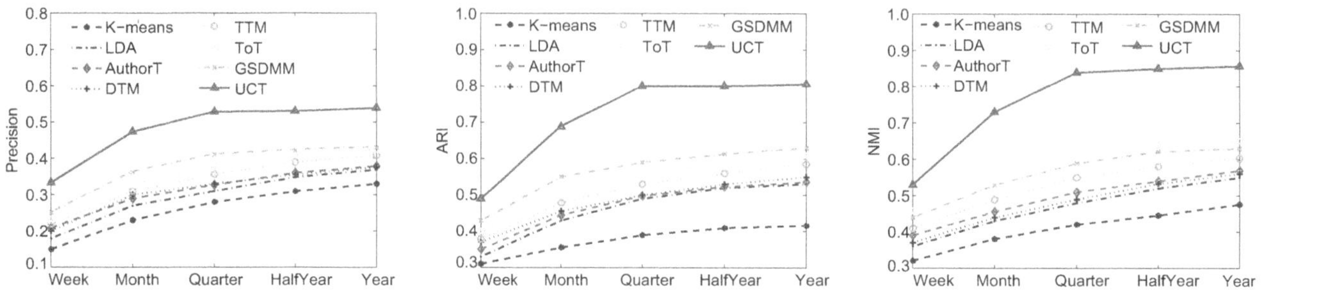

(a) Precision (b) ARI (c) NMI

Figure 3: User clustering performance of UCT and the baselines on time periods of a week, a month, a quarter, half a year, and a year. The performance is evaluated using Precision, ARI and NMI, respectively.

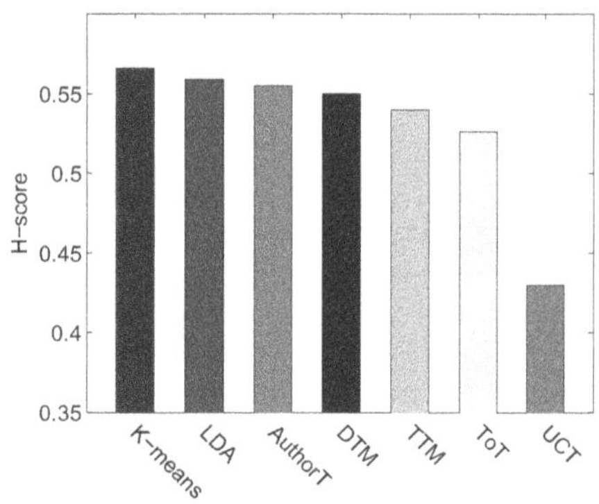

Figure 4: Evaluation results for the quality of topic representations for UCT and the baselines, using the H-score metric and time periods of a quarter.

age intra-cluster distance. A smaller H-score means that the topical representation of users is more similar to that labeled manually (each cluster in the ground-truth clusters of users has lower average intra-cluster distance and higher inter-cluster distance), which demonstrates a better quality of the topics represented by UCT in contrast to state-of-the-art clustering models.

To further illustrate the quality of topic representations in UCT, we display the top-N words for an output cluster and two users from this cluster. The top-N words of a user are generated as follows. First, we rank the words in decreasing order of the probability $P(w \mid t, z) \cdot P(z \mid t, u)$, i.e., $\phi_{t,z,w} \cdot \theta_{t,u,z}$, associated with the user; the words ranked within the top-N are then selected to represent the user. For generating the top-N words for a cluster, the words are ranked by the probabilities associated with the cluster, which is computed by $\frac{1}{|c|}\sum_{u \in c} P(w \mid t, z)P(z \mid t, u)$, i.e., $\frac{1}{|c|}\sum_{u \in c} \phi_{t,z,w} \cdot \theta_{t,u,z}$. Then, the top-$N$ words that obtain the highest probabilities are selected to represent the cluster. Table 3 shows the top 15 words extracted from a cluster and two users in this cluster. We use ToT as a representative topic model for comparison as it is the best baseline (GSDMM cannot obtain representative words for users' interests and clustering results). We see that the two users in the same cluster share more similar interests like "kids, immigration, community, education." UCT is able to obtain representative words for a cluster more accurately than ToT. This again, the explainable and human-understandable clustering results further illustrates that the quality of UCT's topic representation is better than that of the baseline methods.

6.4 Dynamic topic representation of users

Finally, we address research question **RQ4**. As UCT captures each user's dynamic topic distribution, we investigate the content of the users' interests. We conduct a qualitative analysis and see if the clustering result is explainable. As an example, we randomly choose two users and show their interests over five quarters. Specifically, we show each user's interests at each time period by using the top 15 words in Table 4, where the words are selected from the 10 most probable topics of the user and then the 20 most probable words for each topic.

As seen in Table 4, the first user is concerned with "book, promotion, prototyping, ios, etc." in the second quarter of 2014 and this is slightly changed to "app, store, browser, dialog, design, etc.", "prototype, android, web, internet, etc." in the following two quarters, respectively. As time moves on in 2015, their interests change to "Russia, government, designer, app, problem and etc." and "proto-

Table 3: Top 15 words representing a cluster and two users extracted by UCT and ToT, respectively. Words in the first row represent a cluster, while words in the second and third rows represent two users in the cluster, respectively. Words marked blue represent the most coherent words for topics; those marked orange represent less coherent words and others represent irrelevant words.

UCT	ToT
kid color community robbery spiritual immigration alert kicker education child violence star chocolate girl gay	media kid toast immigration dog campaign alert Mexico fan advertisement bet slide John image people
kid unit robbery ride arrest education star police civilian flat immigration internal rule city community	kid education internal photo fan media ad community game score rio toast process http process
immigration kid child kicker process community soccer color police officer rule city game violence gay	kid process soccer child media people dog Mexico reason score song education robbery fan star

type, apple, ios, music, mac etc.". The user's interests are almost stable and mainly focus on the design of apps. In contrast, during the second quarter in 2014, the second user is interested in "center, partner, WalMart, game, player, Oklahoma" that are about business, politics and some sports. Then they talk more about college football and feminism and equality with words like "TXST, star, game, campus, feminism, equality and etc." in the third quarter of 2014. In the next quarter, this user mostly enjoys college football as represented by words "ESPN, TXST, star, bowl, game etc." Then this user is concerned with politics and society with "TXST, state, feminism, government, university" and "violence, victim, responsibility" in 2015. This example illustrates how UCT captures dynamic topic distributions to represent the interests of each user and that the result of dynamic clustering is explainable and understandable in the context of short text streams.

7. CONCLUSION

We have proposed a content-based method for user clustering. Previous work on content-based user clustering has mostly focused on long documents. In contrast, we have studied the problem of dynamically clustering users in the context of streams of short documents. We have proposed a dynamic Dirichlet multinomial mixture user clustering topic model, UCT, to dynamically cluster both previously seen and previously unseen users based on their interests. To better infer the dynamic topic distribution specific to each user, we have proposed to extract word-pairs from each user and apply a Gibbs sampling algorithm for the inference.

For evaluation purposes, we have compared the performance of UCT to that of a traditional clustering algorithm, K-means, non-dynamic topic models, LDA, the author topic model, and state-of-the-art dynamic topic models, viz. DTM, ToT and TTM. Our experimental results demonstrate the clustering effectiveness of our model for user clustering in the context of short document streams. We have also found that UCT produces higher quality topic representations than competing methods, and it comes with the benefit of offering explanations of the clustering.

As to future work, we aim to incorporate other information such as users' social relations to collaboratively group users into clusters. Further research that we are keen to do concerns an evaluation of the similarity of topics, which can be used for automatic selection of K. Another line of work is to develop a more efficient user clustering model to utilize previously captured topic distributions of users for inferring a user's current interests, and to improve efficiency of the Gibbs sampling algorithm as the process is time-consuming.

Acknowledgements. We thank Juan Echeverría Guzman at UCL for collecting the dataset for us. This work was supported by the National Natural Science Foundation of China under Grant No. 61272240 and 61103151, the Big Data Institute, University College London, Ahold, Amsterdam Data Science, the Bloomberg Research Grant program, the Dutch national program COMMIT, Elsevier, the European Community's Seventh Framework Programme (FP7/2007-2013) under grant agreement nr 312827 (VOX-Pol), the ESF Research Network Program ELIAS, the Royal Dutch Academy of Sciences (KNAW) under the Elite Network Shifts project, the Microsoft Research Ph.D. program, the Netherlands eScience Center under project number 027.012.105, the Netherlands Institute for Sound and Vision, the Netherlands Organisation for Scientific Research (NWO) under project nrs 727.011.005, 612.001.116, HOR-11-10, 640.006.013, 612.066.930, CI-14-25, SH-322-15, 652.002.001, 612.001.551, the Yahoo Faculty Research and Engagement Program, and Yandex. All content represents the opinion of the authors, which is not necessarily shared or endorsed by their respective employers and/or sponsors.

8. REFERENCES

[1] K. Balog and M. de Rijke. Finding similar experts. In *SIGIR*, pages 821–822. ACM, 2007.

[2] D. M. Blei and J. D. Lafferty. Dynamic topic models. In *ICML*, pages 113–120, 2006.

[3] D. M. Blei, A. Y. Ng, and M. I. Jordan. Latent dirichlet allocation. *J. Machine Learning research*, 3(4–5):993–1022, 2003.

[4] G. Buscher, R. W. White, S. Dumais, and J. Huang. Large-scale analysis of individual and task differences in search result page examination strategies. In *WSDM*, pages 373–382. ACM, 2012.

[5] W. Chen, J. Wang, Y. Zhang, H. Yan, and X. Li. User based aggregation for biterm topic model. In *ACL*, pages 489–494, 2015.

[6] Z. Chen and B. Liu. Mining topics in documents: standing on the shoulders of big data. In *KDD*, pages 1116–1125. ACM, 2014.

[7] X. Cheng, X. Yan, Y. Lan, and J. Guo. A biterm topic model for short texts. In *WWW*, pages 1445–1456. ACM, 2013.

[8] C. Elkan. Clustering documents with an exponential-family approximation of the dirichlet compound multinomial distribution. In *ICML*, pages 289–296, 2006.

[9] B. J. Frey and D. Dueck. Clustering by passing messages between data points. *Science*, 315(5814):972–976, 2007.

[10] T. L. Griffiths and M. Steyvers. Finding scientific topics. *PNAS*, 101(suppl 1):5228–5235, 2004.

[11] K. Hofmann, K. Balog, T. Bogers, and M. de Rijke. Contextual factors for finding similar experts. *J. Am. Soc. Inf. Sci. Techn.*, 61(5):994–1014, May 2010.

[12] T. Hofmann. Probabilistic latent semantic indexing. In *SIGIR*, pages 50–57. ACM, 1999.

Table 4: Top 15 words representing two users' interests over time, covering five quarters from April 2014 to May 2015. The first row shows the top 15 words per quarter to represent a user whose interests center on the design of apps. The second row shows the top 15 words per quarter to represent another user's whose interests dramatically vary as time progresses. Words marked blue represent the most coherent words for topics; those marked orange represent less coherent words and others represent irrelevant words.

Apr. 2014 to Jun. 2014	Jul. 2014 to Sep. 2014	Oct. 2014 to Dec. 2014	Jan. 2015 to Mar. 2015	Apr. 2015 to May 2015
promotion book email battle html prototyping tweet feature ios team coding perspective lane motorway car	app kid store dog dialog browser design scenario book mobile element email programming night inspiration	prototype android web internet design house breakfast ios film tweet media social people Russia license	Russia government email designer app photo problem engineer mobile strategy smartphone product team hardware ios	prototype apple music ios mac video entrepreneur correlation point interaction task screen years amp reason
center partner WalMart TXST mall David belt offer game player improvement blue enforcement county Oklahoma	TXST star guy fan game night campus sports basketball member grace feminism equality score post	ESPN TXST starSports community StarOpinion StarNews student semester bowl game university star tonight traffic conference	TXST state respect feminism community Texas sexism opinion game campus podcast America nation government student	violence TXST victim responsibility police official opinion state campus respond columnist follow season lecture Texas

[13] R. Huang, G. Yu, Z. Wang, J. Zhang, and L. Shi. Dirichlet process mixture model for document clustering with feature partition. *IEEE Trans. Knowl. Data Eng.*, 8(25):1748–1759, 2013.

[14] L. Hubert and P. Arabie. Comparing partitions. *J. Classification*, 1(2):193–218, 1985.

[15] T. Iwata, S. Watanabe, T. Yamada, and N. Ueda. Topic tracking model for analyzing consumer purchase behavior. In *IJCAI*, pages 1427–1432, 2009.

[16] A. K. Jain. Data clustering: 50 years beyond k-means. *Pattern Recognition Letters*, 31(8):651–666, 2010.

[17] O. Jin, N. N. Liu, K. Zhao, Y. Yu, and Q. Yang. Transferring topical knowledge from auxiliary long texts for short text clustering. In *CIKM*, pages 775–784. ACM, 2011.

[18] I. Li, Y. Tian, Q. Yang, and K. Wang. Classification pruning for web-request prediction. In *WWW*. ACM, 2001.

[19] S. Liang and M. de Rijke. Burst-aware data fusion for microblog search. *Inf. Proc. Man.*, 51(2):83–113, 2015.

[20] S. Liang, Z. Ren, and M. de Rijke. Fusion helps diversification. In *SIGIR*, pages 303–312, 2014.

[21] S. Liang, Z. Ren, and M. de Rijke. Personalized search result diversification via structured learning. In *KDD*, pages 751–760. ACM, 2014.

[22] S. Liang, Z. Ren, W. Weerkamp, E. Meij, and M. de Rijke. Time-aware rank aggregation for microblog search. In *CIKM*, pages 989–998. ACM, 2014.

[23] C. D. Manning, P. Raghavan, and H. Schütze. *Introduction to information retrieval*. Cambridge university press, 2008.

[24] B. Mobasher, R. Cooley, and J. Srivastava. Creating adaptive web sites through usage-based clustering of urls. In *IEEE KDEX workshop*. IEEE, 1999.

[25] K. Nigam, A. K. McCallum, S. Thrun, and T. Mitchell. Text classification from labeled and unlabeled documents using em. *Machine Learning*, 2–3(39):103–134, 2000.

[26] X.-H. Phan, L.-M. Nguyen, and S. Horiguchi. Learning to classify short and sparse text and web with hidden topics from large-scale data collections. In *WWW*, pages 91–100. ACM, 2008.

[27] A. Rangrej, S. Kulkarni, and A. V. Tendulkar. Comparative study of clustering techniques for short text documents. In *WWW Companion*, pages 111–112. ACM, 2011.

[28] Z. Ren and M. de Rijke. Summarizing contrastive themes via hierarchical non-parametric processes. In *SIGIR*, pages 93–102, 2015.

[29] Z. Ren, S. Liang, and M. de Rijke. Personalized time-aware tweets summarization. In *SIGIR*, pages 513–522, 2013.

[30] Z. Ren, M.-H. Peetz, S. Liang, W. van Dolen, and M. de Rijke. Hierarchical multi-label classification of social text streams. In *SIGIR*, pages 213–222. ACM, 2014.

[31] M. Rosen-Zvi, T. Griffiths, M. Steyvers, and P. Smyth. The author-topic model for authors and documents. In *UAI*, pages 487–494, 2004.

[32] J. Srivastava, R. Cooley, M. Deshpande, and P.-N. Tan. Web usage mining: discovery and applications of usage patterns from web data. In *SIGKDD Explorations*, pages 12–23. ACM, 2000.

[33] O. Tsur, A. Littman, and A. Rappoport. Efficient clustering of short messages into general domains. In *ICWSM*, pages 621–630, 2013.

[34] C. Van Gysel, M. de Rijke, and M. Worring. Unsupervised, efficient and semantic expertise retrieval. In *WWW*, pages 1069–1079. ACM, 2016.

[35] X. Wang and A. McCallum. Topics over time: a non-markov continuous-time model of topical trends. In *KDD*, pages 424–433. ACM, 2006.

[36] X. Wei, J. Sun, and X. Wang. Dynamic mixture models for multiple time-series. In *IJCAI*, pages 2909–2914, 2007.

[37] S. Xu, Q. Shi, X. Qiao, et al. A dynamic users' interest discovery model with distributed inference algorithm. *IJDSN*, 2015:Article ID 280892, 2014.

[38] J. Yin. Clustering microtext streams for event identification. In *IJCNLP*, pages 719–725, 2013.

[39] J. Yin and J. Wang. A dirichlet multinomial mixture model-based approach for short text clustering. In *KDD*, pages 233–242. ACM, 2014.

[40] G. Yu, R. Huang, and Z. Wang. Document clustering via dirichlet process mixture model with feature selection. In *KDD*, pages 763–772. ACM, 2010.

Topic Modeling for Short Texts with Auxiliary Word Embeddings

Chenliang Li[1], Haoran Wang[1], Zhiqian Zhang[1], Aixin Sun[2], Zongyang Ma[2]
[1]State Key Lab of Software Engineering, Computer School, Wuhan University, China
cllee@whu.edu.cn,whrwhu@gmail.com,zhangzq2011@whu.edu.cn
[2]School of Computer Science and Engineering, Nanyang Technological University, Singapore
{axsun,zyma}@ntu.edu.sg

ABSTRACT

For many applications that require semantic understanding of short texts, inferring discriminative and coherent latent topics from short texts is a critical and fundamental task. Conventional topic models largely rely on word co-occurrences to derive topics from a collection of documents. However, due to the length of each document, short texts are much more sparse in terms of word co-occurrences. Data sparsity therefore becomes a bottleneck for conventional topic models to achieve good results on short texts. On the other hand, when a human being interprets a piece of short text, the understanding is not solely based on its content words, but also her background knowledge (*e.g.,* semantically related words). The recent advances in word embedding offer effective learning of word semantic relations from a large corpus. Exploiting such auxiliary word embeddings to enrich topic modeling for short texts is the main focus of this paper. To this end, we propose a *simple*, *fast*, and *effective* topic model for short texts, named GPU-DMM. Based on the Dirichlet Multinomial Mixture (DMM) model, GPU-DMM promotes the semantically related words under the same topic during the sampling process by using the generalized Pólya urn (GPU) model. In this sense, the background knowledge about word semantic relatedness learned from millions of external documents can be easily exploited to improve topic modeling for short texts. Through extensive experiments on two real-world short text collections in two languages, we show that GPU-DMM achieves comparable or better topic representations than state-of-the-art models, measured by topic coherence. The learned topic representation leads to the best accuracy in text classification task, which is used as an indirect evaluation.

Categories and Subject Descriptors

I.2.7 [**Natural Language Processing**]: Text analysis

Keywords

Topic Model, Short Texts, Word Embeddings

SIGIR '16, July 17-21, 2016, Pisa, Italy
© 2016 ACM. ISBN 978-1-4503-4069-4/16/07...$15.00
DOI: http://dx.doi.org/10.1145/2911451.2911499

1. INTRODUCTION

Short texts have become a fashionable form of information on the Internet. Examples include web page snippets, news headlines, text advertisements, tweets, status updates, and questions/answers, to name a few. Given the large volume of short texts available, effective and efficient models to discover the latent topics from short texts become fundamental to many applications that require semantic understanding of textual content, such as user interest profiling [38], topic detection [37], comment summarization [31], content characterizing [32], and classification [34].

Conventional topic modeling techniques, *e.g.,* pLSA and LDA, are widely used to infer latent topical structure from text corpus [2, 12]. In these models, each document is represented as a multinomial distribution over topics and each topic is represented as a multinomial distribution over words. Statistical techniques (*e.g.,* Gibbs sampling) are then employed to identify the underlying topic distribution of each document as well as word distribution of each topic, based on the high-order word co-occurrence patterns [29]. These models and their variants have been studied extensively for various tasks in information retrieval and text mining [14, 36, 42]. Despite their great success on many tasks, conventional topic models experience a large performance degradation over short texts because of limited word co-occurrence information in short texts. In other words, data sparsity impedes the generation of discriminative document-topic distributions, and the resultant topics are less semantically coherent.

Several ingenious strategies have been proposed to deal with the data sparsity problem in short texts. One strategy is to aggregate a subset of short texts to form a longer pesudo-document. Conventional topic models are then applied over these pesudo-documents. The aggregation is often guided by auxiliary metadata information. For example, in the context of Twitter, tweets can be aggregated based on their hashtags, users, locations, or timestamps before applying LDA [13, 19, 38]. However, a limitation of this strategy is that additional metadata may not be available always, *e.g.,* web page snippets. Another strategy is to restrict the document-topic distribution, such that each short text is sampled from a single topic, known as mixture of unigrams or Dirichlet Multinomial Mixture (DMM) model [26, 40, 42]. Given the limited content in a short text, this simplification is reasonable and it alleviates the data sparsity problem to some extent. It is reported to be a better alternative to conventional LDA models [39, 42]. The third strategy is to design a brand new topic model by explicitly incorporating additional word co-occurrence information. Examples include modeling word co-occurrence patterns [39] and using soft-clustering mechanism for further word co-occurrence augmentation [30]. However, the word co-occurrence information that can be captured by these models

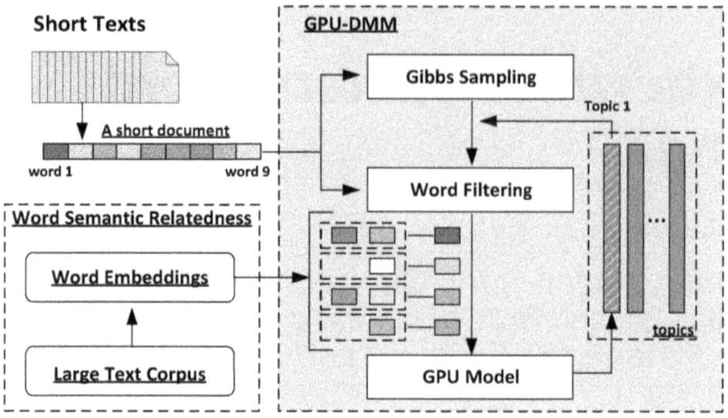

Figure 1: GPU-DMM Overview

is limited to the short text corpus itself. Given two words having strong semantically relatedness but rarely co-occurring in a short text corpus, these models can not fully capture the semantic relatedness between the two words.

When a human being interprets a piece of text, the understanding is not solely based on its content, but also her background knowledge, *e.g.,* semantic relatedness between words. It is also natural to exploit external lexical knowledge to guide the topic inference over short texts. Existing works in this line largely rely on either external thesauri (*e.g.,* WordNet) or lexical knowledge derived from documents in a specific domain (*e.g.,* product comments) [5–7]. The availability of such knowledge becomes vital for these models. This calls for a more generic model that can be effectively applied to short texts, without the need of manually constructed thesauri, and not limited to external documents in specific domains.

In this paper, we propose a new topic model for short texts, named GPU-DMM. GPU-DMM is designed to leverage the general word semantic relatedness knowledge during the topic inference process, to tackle the data sparsity issue. Effective learning of general word semantic relatedness is now feasible and practical with the recent development in neural network techniques, which have contributed improvements in many tasks in Information Retrieval (IR) and Natural Language Processing (NLP) [9, 10, 16, 17, 43]. Specifically, neural network language models, *e.g.,* Continuous Bag-of-Words (CBOW), Continuous Skip-gram model, and Glove model [20, 27], learn word vectors (also called *word embeddings*) with the aim of fully retaining the contextual information for each word, including both semantical and syntactical relations. The shallow neural network structure designed in these techniques is computationally effective on large text corpus. For instance, training skip-gram based word embeddings on a Google News corpus with 100 billion words takes less than one day on a modest computer.[1] That is, general word semantic relatedness knowledge can be efficiently learned from a very large text corpus, in any language. In fact, there are many pre-trained word embeddings learned from resources like Wikipedia, Twitter, and Freebase, publication available on the Web.[2]

Shown in Figure 1, the proposed GPU-DMM extends the Dirichlet Multinomial Mixture (DMM) model by incorporating the learned word relatedness from large text corpus through the *generalized Pólya urn* (GPU) model [18] in topic inferences. More specifically, GPU-DMM promotes the semantically relevant words under the same topic after sampling a topic for a short document. In this sense, GPU-DMM links the semantically relevant words together, even if they share very limited or no co-occurrences in the current collection of short texts being modeled. A filtering strategy is also introduced in GPU-DMM to guide the topic inference process, such that only appropriate external knowledge is exploited for the sampled topic. Because GPU-DMM takes in the word embeddings that have been learned from external documents, the model is *fast* and *flexible* in taking in word embeddings learned from any other large text collections. On two real-world datasets in two different languages (*i.e.,* snippets of an English search engine, and questions from Q&A service in Chinese), GPU-DMM discovers more prominent topics and achieves better classification accuracy than existing state-of-the-art alternatives. The main contributions of this paper are summarized as follows:

1. We develop a simple, fast, and effective topic model to learn the latent topic patterns over short texts. The model is flexible in directly taking in word semantic relations learned from large text corpus, which is domain free and ease to access. To the best of our knowledge, this is the first work for a topic model to incorporate the general word semantic relatedness knowledge based on word embeddings with GPU model.
2. On two real-world short text collections in two languages, we evaluate the proposed GPU-DMM against a few state-of-the-art alternatives for short texts. Experimental results demonstrate our model's superiority, in topic coherence, text classification accuracy, and learning speed.
3. We empirically study the impact of two document representation inference methods. Our results suggest that the summation over each word's contribution within a short document is more appropriate for topic-focused downstream applications, *e.g.,* text classification.

2. RELATED WORK

We review recent advances on learning better topic representations on short texts. We then focus on the models with word embeddings because our model uses word embeddings as external knowledge.

Topic Models for Short Texts. Conventional topic models such as pLSA and LDA are designed to implicitly capture word co-occurrence patterns at document-level, to reveal topic structures. Thus more word co-occurrences would lead to more reliable and better topic inference. Because of the length of each document, conventional topic models suffer a lot from the data sparsity problem in short texts, leading to inferior topic inferences. Earlier studies focus on exploiting external knowledge to help refine the topic inference of short texts. Phan *et al.* proposed to infer topic structure of short texts by using the learnt latent topics from Wikipedia [28]. Similarly, Jin *et al.* infer latent topics of short texts for clustering by using auxiliary long texts [15]. These models require a large regular text corpus of high quality, which may not be always available in some domains and/or languages.

Given the limited context information in short texts, many aggregation strategies have been studied by merging short texts into long pseudo-documents. Conventional topic modeling is then applied to infer the latent topics. In [38], the authors aggregate tweets from the same user as a pseudo-document before performing standard LDA model. Other metadata that have been used for short text aggregation include hashtags, timestamps, and named entities [13, 19, 42]. However, favorable metadata may not be available in some domains, *e.g.,* search snippets and news headlines. These studies suggest that topic models specifically designed for general short texts are imperative.

[1] https://code.google.com/p/word2vec

[2] Details are listed at https://github.com/3Top/word2vec-api

A simple and effective topic model, named Dirichlet Multinomial Mixture (DMM) model, has been employed to discover latent topics in short texts in many tasks [40,42]. DMM is based on the assumption made in the mixture of unigrams model proposed by Nigam *et al.* [26], *i.e.,* each document is sampled from a single latent topic. Given the limited content of short texts, this assumption is reasonable and is proven to be more effective than conventional topic models in many studies [30,39,42]. Yin and Wang [40] propose a collapsed Gibbs Sampling algorithm for DMM and show its effectiveness in short text clustering. Due to its simplicity and effectiveness, we develop GPU-DMM on the basis of DMM, as its name suggests.

Recently, many efforts have been spent towards intensifying the word co-occurrence information from the collection of short texts being modeled. Yan *et al.* propose a novel biterm topic model (BTM) to explicitly model the generation of word co-occurrence patterns instead of single words as do in many topic models [39]. Their experimental results show that BTM produces discriminative topic representations as well as more coherent topics for short texts. Inspired by the aforementioned aggregation strategies, Quan *et al.* propose a self-aggregation based topic model (SATM) for short texts [30]. SATM assumes that each short text is a segment of a long pseudo-document and shares the same topic proportion of the latter. The topic inference and the aggregation process is conducted in a mutual reinforcement manner, such that the aggregation is based on the topical similarity of the texts and vice versa. However, setting an appropriate number of long pseudo-documents in SATM is not an easy task. Further, the inference process involving both text aggregation and topic sampling is time-consuming.

Topic Models for Short Texts with Word Embeddings. Word embeddings, first introduced in [33], have been successfully applied in language models and many NLP tasks, such as named entity recognition and parsing [1,22]. Word embeddings are useful because they encode both syntactic and semantic information of words into continuous vectors and similar words are close in vector space.

Most relevant to ours is the work by Nguyen *et al.* [24]. They propose a topic model with word embeddings for short texts, called LF-DMM. Built based on DMM, LF-DMM replaces the topic-word multinomial distribution with a two-component mixture of a Dirichlet multinomial component and a continuous word embedding component. That is, each word in a short text is generated from either the Dirichlet multinomial distribution or the probability estimated by using word embeddings with respect to the sampled topic. A switch variable is utilized to decide which component is used to generate a word. Rather than using Bayesian parameter estimation, a simple and hard coded switch probability value is used for the switch variable in LF-DMM. This simple switch mechanism could incur some noise into the inference process. In order to estimate the word embedding component of each word, the topics are projected into the same latent continuous space as word embeddings by optimizing a regularized log-linear model. However, this optimization process is computational expensive. Similarly, Das *et al.* propose a LDA based topic model by using multivariate Gaussian distributions with word embeddings [11]. Our work differs significantly from these studies. GPU-DMM exploits the general word semantic relatedness knowledge provided by auxiliary word embeddings by using the generalized Pólya urn model in the topic inference of short texts. Compared with existing approaches of incorporating word embeddings in topic model, GPU reduces the computational cost significantly. To the best of our knowledge, GPU-DMM is the first attempt to combine word embeddings and GPU model for solving sparsity problem of short texts.

3. GPU-DMM

As its name suggests, the proposed GPU-DMM model is built upon the Dirichlet Multinomial Mixture (DMM). Given a short document, GPU-DMM samples a topic for it based on the conditional probabilities similar to DMM. The words that are highly relevant to the topic are then selected, and their semantically related words are extracted and promoted by using the GPU model [18]. As shown in Figure 1, the auxiliary word embeddings utilized in GPU-DMM is pre-learned using the state-of-the-art word embedding techniques from large document collections. Next, we present the details of the proposed model GPU-DMM.

3.1 Dirichlet Mixture Model

Dirichlet Mixture Model is a generative probabilistic model with the assumption that *a document is generated from a single topic* [26,40]. That is, all the words within a document are generated by using the same topic distribution.

Given a short text corpus of D documents, with a vocabulary of size V, and K pre-defined latent topics, each document d is associated with a specific topic k. Then the N_d words in document d $\{w_{d,1}, w_{d,2}, \ldots, w_{d,N_d}\}$ are generated by the topic-word multinomial distribution $p(w|z=k)=\phi_k$ by assuming independence of the words themselves. More formally, with the Dirichlet priors of α and β, the generative process of DMM is described as follows:

1. Sample a topic proportion $\theta \sim Dirichlet(\alpha)$
2. For each topic $k \in \{1, ..., K\}$
   Draw a topic-word distribution $\phi_k \sim Dirichlet(\beta)$
3. For each document $d \in \{1, ..., D\}$
   (a) Sample a topic $z_d \sim Multinomial(\theta)$
   (b) For each word $w \in \{w_{d,1}, ..., w_{d,N_d}\}$
   Sample a word $w \sim Multinomial(\phi_{z_d})$

The hidden variables in the generative process can be approximated by applying Gibbs sampling. Following the approach in [40], a topic z is sampled for each document in every iteration according to the following conditional distribution:

$$p(z_d = k|\vec{z}_{\neg d}, \vec{d}) \propto \frac{m_{k,\neg d}+\alpha}{D-1+K\alpha} \times \frac{\prod_{w\in d}\prod_{j=1}^{N_d^w}(n_{k,\neg d}^w+\beta+j-1)}{\prod_{i=1}^{N_d}(n_{k,\neg d}+V\beta+i-1)} \quad (1)$$

where N_d^w is term frequency of word w in document d, $m_{k,\neg d}$ is the number of documents assigned to topic k, $n_{k,\neg d}^w$ is the number of times that word w is assigned to topic k, and $n_{k,\neg d} = \sum_w^V n_{k,\neg d}^w$. Symbol $\neg d$ means that document d is excluded from the counting. The posterior distribution is calculated by using point estimation:

$$p(w|z=k) = \frac{n_k^w+\beta}{\sum_w^V n_k^w + V\beta} \quad (2)$$

3.2 Auxiliary Word Embeddings

Because of the length of short texts, the words with high semantic relatedness may not frequently co-occur in the same short texts. On the other hand, because the word embeddings are learnt with the aim to retain words' global contextual information, the learnt word embeddings capture the general word co-occurrence patterns. That is, words that are semantically or syntactically similar to

Table 1: Example words and their co-occurrences with semantically related words in the Snippet dataset.

Example (Freq.)	Word (Freq., #co-occur with example word)	
artworks (20)	paintings (17, 1)	artist (53, 3)
movie (333)	cinema (33, 10)	filmography (19, 7)
fiction (45)	book (142, 3)	literary (12, 2)
company (143)	business (431, 16)	industry (117, 4)
stock (131)	price (39, 1)	equity (15, 2)

each other are projected to be closer in the latent space. Next, we illustrate this point using some example words.

Table 1 lists 5 example words in the left-hand column (*i.e.,* "artworks", "movie", "fiction", "company", "stock"). The number following each word in paraphrase is the document frequency of the word in the Web snippet dataset. This short text dataset contains 12,340 Web search snippets (see Section 4.1 for more details). For example, "artworks (20)" means that the word "artworks" appears in 20 short documents in the Snippet dataset. In the right-hand column, for each word, we show two semantically related words obtained from pre-trained word embeddings. The word embeddings used here are learned from the aforementioned Google News corpus with 100 billion words of vocabulary size of 3 million. The two numbers following each word are (i) the document frequency of the word, and (ii) the number of co-occurrences with the example word on the left-hand side, in the Web snippet dataset. For instance, "movie" appears in 333 snippets, "cinema" appears in 33 snippets, and the two word co-occur in 10 snippets.

Shown in the table, the words obtained from word embeddings indeed show strong semantic relatedness with the example words. More importantly, the semantic relations provided by word embeddings are much broader than the limited lexical relations defined in an external thesauri (*e.g.,* synonymy, antonym and adjective-attribute relations in WordNet). The table also shows that semantically related words may not co-occur frequently in the short text collection. We therefore believe that incorporating auxiliary word embeddings learned from large corpus would significantly enhance topic modeling on short texts.

3.3 Incorporating Word Embeddings by GPU

It has been validated that the topic coherence measure based on word co-occurrence pattern is a reliable indicator of topic quality and is highly consistent with the human expert annotation [21]. Accordingly, it is reasonable that the words with high semantic relatedness should be clustered together under the same topic. In the following, we present how GPU-DMM achieves this through the generalized Pólya urn model [18].

Generalized Pólya Urn Model can be understood in terms of colored balls in a urn, where the probability of seeing a ball of each color is linearly proportional to the number of balls of that color in the urn. In a simple Pólya urn model, when a ball of a particular color is sampled from the urn, the sampled ball along with a new ball of that color is put back into the urn. This process is equivalent to the Gibbs sampling process utilized for the topic inference with Dirichlet-Multinomial distribution under the i.i.d assumption. In the generalized Pólya urn model, when a ball of a particular color is sampled, a certain number of balls of similar colors are put back along with the original ball and a new ball of that color. In this sense, the set of balls of similar colors are promoted as a whole from this iterative process. By analogy with the GPU model, in our case, given a ball of word w, the balls of similar colors refer to the semantically related words to word w. As the result, sampling a word w in topic t not only increases the probability of w itself under topic t, but also increases the association between the topic and w's semantically related words. Several existing works exploit the GPU model and the external thesauri or domain-specific knowledge for better topic inference of the standard LDA [5–7, 21]. However, these works rely on the specific domain knowledge, which may restrict their usage in a broader range. Here, we exploit the combination of GPU model and the global word relatedness knowledge, leading to a generic solution for short text topic modeling.

Formally, given pre-trained word embeddings, we measure the semantic relatedness between two words w and w' by the cosine similarity between their vector representations in the latent space (*i.e.,* the word embeddings of the two words). The semantic relatedness between the word pair is denoted by $sr(w, w')$. Then a word semantic relatedness matrix $\mathbb{M}$ can be constructed, consisting of all word pairs whose semantic relatedness score is higher than a predefined threshold ϵ, *i.e.,* $\mathbb{M} = \{\langle w_i, w_j\rangle | sr(w_i, w_j) > \epsilon\}$. The threshold ϵ is set to filter less semantic related word pairs.

Being a preliminary study on exploiting general word semantic relatedness knowledge based on word embeddings, we fix the amount of promotion μ for each semantically related word w' when working on word w. The promotion matrix $\mathbb{A}$ with respect to each word pair is defined below, where $\mathbb{M}_w$ is the row in $\mathbb{M}$ corresponding to word w. Note that $\mathbb{M}_w$ includes the word w itself.

$$\mathbb{A}_{w,w'} = \begin{cases} 1 & w{=}w' \\ \mu & w' \in \mathbb{M}_w \text{ and } w' \neq w \\ 0 & \text{otherwise} \end{cases} \tag{3}$$

The weight μ could be set based on the auxiliary word embeddings under use.

Incorporating the GPU model with DMM gives us the proposed GPU-DMM model. However, simply taking all word pairs in matrix $\mathbb{M}$ may not be the best choice for topic modeling in short texts, explained next.

Word Filtering. Based on DMM, GPU-DMM samples a short text from a single topic. All words in the short text are assigned to the same topic. Take a short text *"info website web cern consortium server project world copy first"* as an example. This document can be assigned to a computer related topic. However, words like *consortium* and *first*, along with their semantically related words, could be irrelevant to computer related topics. This scenario is prevalent in many short texts and could be harmful to DMM based topic models. In this sense, simply adopting GPU model for every word in a document to promote their semantically related words under the sampled topic could adversely affect the quality of the topic. This calls for an appropriate strategy to reinforce only the semantically related words if and only if a word has strong ties with the sampled topic. To this end, we propose a nonparametric probabilistic sampling strategy as follows:

$$\mathbb{S}_{d,w} \sim Bernoulli(\lambda_{w,z_d}) \tag{4}$$

$$\lambda_{w,z} = \frac{p(z|w)}{p_{max}(z'|w)} \tag{5}$$

$$p_{max}(z|w) = \max_k p(z = k|w)$$

$$p(z = k|w) = \frac{p(z = k)p(w|z = k)}{\sum_{i=1}^{K} p(z = i)p(w|z = i)} \tag{6}$$

In Equation 4, $\mathbb{S}_{d,w}$ indicates whether GPU is applied to word w given document d and topic z_d, where λ_{w,z_d} is defined in Equation 5. Observe from Equation 5, $\mathbb{S}_{d,w}$ is strongly related to the ratio of the conditional topic probability z_d given word w to its

Algorithm 1: GPU-DMM

input : Topic number K, α, β, μ, $\mathbb{M}$ and D short documents
output: The posterior topic-word distribution

1 **foreach** $d \in D$ **do**
2 $\quad z_d \leftarrow z \sim Multinomial(1/K)$;
3 $\quad m_z \leftarrow m_z + 1$;
4 $\quad \tilde{n}_z \leftarrow \tilde{n}_z + 1$;
5 $\quad$ **foreach** $w \in d$ **do**
6 $\quad\quad \tilde{n}_z^w \leftarrow \tilde{n}_z^w + N_d^w$;
7 $\quad\quad \mathbb{S}_{d,w} \leftarrow 0$;
8 **foreach** *iteration* **do**
9 $\quad$ UpdateWordTopicProb() ; /* See Eq. 6 and 8 */
10 $\quad$ **foreach** $d \in D$ **do**
11 $\quad\quad z \leftarrow z_d$;
12 $\quad\quad m_z \leftarrow m_z - 1$;
13 $\quad\quad$ **foreach** $w \in d$ **do**
14 $\quad\quad\quad$ UpdateCounter ($\mathbb{S}_{d,w}$, $\mathbb{A}$, d, w, $False$);
15 $\quad\quad z_d \leftarrow z \sim p(z_d = z|\vec{z}_{\neg d}, \vec{d})$;
16 $\quad\quad m_z \leftarrow m_z + 1$;
17 $\quad\quad$ **foreach** $w \in d$ **do**
18 $\quad\quad\quad$ UpdateGPUFlag ($\mathbb{S}_{d,w}$); /* See Eq. 4 */
19 $\quad\quad\quad$ UpdateCounter ($\mathbb{S}_{d,w}$, $\mathbb{A}$, d, w, $True$);

Algorithm 2: UpdateCounter ($\mathbb{S}_{d,w}$, $\mathbb{A}$, d, w, $promotion$)

1 **if** $promotion == True$ **then**
2 $\quad$ **if** $\mathbb{S}_{d,w} == 1$ **then** /* To apply GPU */
3 $\quad\quad$ **foreach** $w' \in \mathbb{M}_w$ **do**
4 $\quad\quad\quad \tilde{n}_z \leftarrow \tilde{n}_z + N_d^w \cdot \mathbb{A}_{w,w'}$;
5 $\quad\quad\quad \tilde{n}_z^{w'} \leftarrow \tilde{n}_z^{w'} + N_d^w \cdot \mathbb{A}_{w,w'}$;
6 $\quad$ **else**
7 $\quad\quad \tilde{n}_z \leftarrow \tilde{n}_z + 1$;
8 $\quad\quad \tilde{n}_z^w \leftarrow \tilde{n}_z^w + 1$;
9 **else**
10 $\quad$ **if** $\mathbb{S}_{d,w} == 1$ **then** /* GPU was applied */
11 $\quad\quad$ **foreach** $w' \in \mathbb{M}_w$ **do**
12 $\quad\quad\quad \tilde{n}_z \leftarrow \tilde{n}_z - N_d^w \cdot \mathbb{A}_{w,w'}$;
13 $\quad\quad\quad \tilde{n}_z^{w'} \leftarrow \tilde{n}_z^{w'} - N_d^w \cdot \mathbb{A}_{w,w'}$;
14 $\quad$ **else**
15 $\quad\quad \tilde{n}_z \leftarrow \tilde{n}_z - 1$;
16 $\quad\quad \tilde{n}_z^w \leftarrow \tilde{n}_z^w - 1$;

maximal topic probability. That is, if word w is highly relevant to topic z in terms of $p(z|w)$, GPU model is more likely to be applied to w when the sampled topic of its document is indeed z.

Because Gibbs sampling is a stochastic process (*i.e.,* the topic of a document is randomly sampled), there is a chance that an incorrect topic is sampled for a document. However, given the dominant topic of a document, the semantically related words of an irrelevant word are less likely to be promoted under the topic, because of the above probabilistic sampling strategy. The adverse impact of an incorrect sampled topic can not be aggravated by using GPU model. In the proposed word filtering strategy, calculating $p(z = k|w)$ (see Equation 6) for every word w of a document and topic k is very time-consuming. For efficiency purpose, we calculate $p(z = k|w)$ at the beginning of each iteration, and use these static values during the whole iteration, detailed next.

Model Inference. GPU-DMM and DMM model share the same generative process and graphical representation, but differ in topic inference process. In GPU-DMM, the *GPU-based Gibbs sampling* is applied during the topic inference process.

The GPU model is nonexchangeable, which suggests that the joint probability of the words under a specific topic is not invariant to the permutation of those words. This results in a more complex inference process. Following the work of Mimno *et al.* [21], we approximate the true Gibbs sampling distribution by treating each word as if it was the last word, ignoring its implications for subsequent words and their topic assignments. Accordingly, the conditional distribution for Gibbs sampling in Equation 1 is rewritten for GPU-DMM as follows:

$$p(z_d = k|\vec{z}_{\neg d}, \vec{d}) \propto \frac{m_{k,\neg d} + \alpha}{D - 1 + K\alpha} \times \frac{\prod_{w \in d} \prod_{j=1}^{N_d^w} (\tilde{n}_{k,\neg d}^w + \beta + j - 1)}{\prod_{i=1}^{N_d} (\tilde{n}_{k,\neg d} + V\beta + i - 1)} \tag{7}$$

In the Equation 7, $\tilde{n}_{k,\neg d}$ is the number of words associated with topic k, $\tilde{n}_{k,\neg d}^w$ is the number of balls of word w in the urn of topic k, $m_{k,\neg d}$ is the number of documents associated with topic k, symbol $\neg d$ means that document d is excluded from the counting, same as in Equation 1. The posterior distribution in Equation 2 for GPU-DMM is rewritten in Equation 8:

$$p(w|z = k) = \frac{\tilde{n}_k^w + \beta}{\sum_w^V \tilde{n}_k^w + V\beta} \tag{8}$$

The details of the Gibbs sampling process of GPU-DMM is described in Algorithm 1. At first, GPU-DMM initializes the topic assignment for each document with a uniform distribution without applying the GPU model (Lines 1-6). This initialization process is the same as in DMM. In each iteration of Gibbs sampling, we firstly calculate the conditional topic distribution, $p(z = k|w)$ for each k and w, based on Equations 6 and 8 (Line 9). These values will be used during the whole iteration. Then, the topic of each document d is resampled based on the conditional distribution in Equation 7 (Lines 10-14). During this process, GPU-DMM subtracts the corresponding counts for each word w based on the flag $\mathbb{S}_{d,w}$ in the previous iteration by calling the function *UpdateCounter()* (Line 14, Equation 4).

Shown in Algorithm 2, if $\mathbb{S}_{d,w} = 1$, meaning that the related words $\mathbb{M}_w$ for word w have been promoted in the last iteration, then the corresponding counts of each related word $w' \in \mathbb{M}_w$ are subtracted proportional to $\mathbb{A}_{w,w'}$ (Lines 11-13 in Algorithm 2). Recall that the semantic relatedness knowledge $\mathbb{M}_w$ of word w also contains w itself, *i.e.,* $w \in \mathbb{M}_w$ (see Equation 3). The substraction process is applied to both w itself and its semantically related words. Otherwise, if the related words were not promoted in the last iteration, then simple subtraction is applied to w as the same in DMM (Lines 15, 16 in Algorithm 2).

With the new sampled topic, the flag $\mathbb{S}_{d,w}$ for each word w is updated based on Equation 4 (Line 18 in Algorithm 1). Then the corresponding counts for word w are added based on the updated flag $\mathbb{S}_{d,w}$ through function *UpdateCounter()* (Line 19 in Algorithm 1). Similarly, if $\mathbb{S}_{d,w} = 1$, w and all its related words are promoted. Otherwise, simple update as in DMM is applied (Lines 2-8 in Algorithm 2)

This iterative process continues until the predefined number of iterations is reached.

Model Complexity. We now analyze the time complexity of GPU-DMM with reference to DMM. The time complexity of DMM in an iteration is $O(KD\bar{\ell})$, where K is the number of topics, D is the number of documents, and $\bar{\ell}$ is the average document length. Being extended with GPU model, GPU-DMM has a time complexity of $O(KD\bar{\ell}+D\bar{\ell}\tau+KV)$, where τ is a coefficient by considering the cost involved by applying the GPU model. The τ value depends on: (i) the average number of words for which GPU model is applied based on Equation 4, and (ii) the average number of semantically related words for each word appear in the short text corpus. KV is the computation required for calculating all $p(z=k|w)$.

Note that the size of the semantic relatedness knowledge $\mathbb{M}_w$ for word w obtained from auxiliary word embeddings could be large, but not all these semantically related words appear in the underlying short texts being modeled. In this sense, τ is expected to be relatively small. It is expected that $KV < KD\bar{\ell}$. Hence, GPU-DMM does not add too much computational cost to DMM.

4. EXPERIMENT

In this section, we conduct extensive experiments to evaluate the proposed GPU-DMM against the state-of-the-art alternatives.[3] The performance in terms of topic coherence and document classification are reported over two publicly available datasets, *i.e.,* an English Web search snippet dataset and a Chinese Q&A dataset. We also report the time taken per iteration for all models evaluated in our experiments. The experimental results show that our proposed model provides promising performance in both effectiveness and efficiency.

4.1 Datasets

BaiduQA dataset is a collection of 648,514 questions crawled from a popular Chinese Q&A website[4]. Each question is annotated with a category label by its asker. This dataset was prepared and has been previously used in [8, 39]. The dataset was preprocessed by the authors, *e.g.,* Chinese word segmentation and duplicate words removal. That is, every word has frequency of 1 in the question containing it. In our experiments, we removed the extremely short questions that contain only a single word.

Web Snippet (**Snippet** for short) dataset contains 12,340 Web search snippets. This dataset has been used in a few studies [4, 28, 35]. Each snippet belongs to one of 8 categories. We performed the following preprocessing on this dataset: (1) convert letters to lowercase; (2) remove all non-alphabetic characters and stop words[5]; (3) remove the words with fewer than 3 characters; (4) remove words with document frequency less than 3 in the dataset. As in the BaiduQA dataset, we further remove duplicate words within each snippet, reinforcing its data sparsity.

Statistics on the two datasets after preprocessing is reported in Table 2. Observe that the BaiduQA dataset is much more sparser with a larger vocabulary and much shorter documents compared to the Snippet dataset.

4.2 Experimental Setup

Word Embeddings. For the Snippet dataset, we use the pre-trained 300-dimensional word embeddings from the Google News corpus.[6] For the BaiduQA dataset, we train 100-dimensional word embeddings from 7 million Chinese articles crawled from Baike website,[7] using Goolge's Word2Vec toolkit with Skip-gram algorithm [20]. If a word has no embedding, the word is considered as having no word semantic relatedness knowledge.

[3] Our implementation is available at https://github.com/NobodyWHU/GPUDMM

[4] http://zhidao.baidu.com

[5] Stop word list is from NLTK: http://www.nltk.org/

[6] https://code.google.com/p/word2vec

Table 2: Statistics on the two datasets. #Label: the number of ground truth labels or categories; #Docs: the total number of documents; #Words: average number of words per document.

Dataset	#Label	#Docs	#Words	Vocabulary
Snippet	8	12,265	10.72	5,581
BaiduQA	35	179,042	4.11	26,560

As mentioned in Section 3.2, a parameter ϵ is required to determine the semantic relatedness knowledge provided by the auxiliary word embeddings. We employ a simple manual process to decide the value of ϵ. The value of ϵ is determined by manually examining some randomly sampled words. More specifically, a random set of 100 words are selected from the word embeddings, then the top-100 most related words to each of the selected words are computed based on the cosine similarity of their vector representations *i.e.,* $sr(w, w')$. These semantically related words are printed along with their cosine similarity scores to the selected word in descending order. Then we manually choose a reasonable ϵ after examining these related words. Based on the values, we set ϵ to 0.5 and 0.7 respectively for GPU-DMM over the Snippet and BaiduQA datasets. We argue that the optimal value of ϵ depends on both the external text corpus and the algorithm used in learning the word embeddings.

After setting ϵ, we observe that for some words, the number of semantic relatedness words (*i.e.,* the size of $\mathbb{M}_w$) is very large. For example, there are 129 words semantically related to word *houston*, including *dallas*, *altanta*, *orlando*, and *cleveland.* In fact, most of the 129 words refer to geographic areas like the word *houston* itself. Another example is word *carl*, which is highly related to many English names like *gordon*, *henry*, and *james*. Such words often refer to semantic relatedness in some specific domains (*e.g.,* geographical, temporal, or person names) rather than general concepts as the examples listed in Table 1. Hence, in our experiments, we simply disregard all the related words in $\mathbb{M}_w$ if $|\mathbb{M}_w| > 20$ [8].

As shown in the model overview in Figure 1, the preparation of word embeddings and $\mathbb{M}$ is independent of the proposed GPU-DMM model. The preparation can be done off-line.

Methods and Parameter Setting. We compare our GPU-DMM against the following four state-of-the-art topic models specific to short texts. For all the methods in comparison, we set the hyper-parameters $\alpha = 50/K$ and $\beta = 0.01$ unless explicitly specified elsewhere.

- **Biterm Topic Model (BTM)** learns the topics by directly modeling the generation of word co-occurrence patterns in the short text corpus [39]. In BTM, a *biterm* is an unordered word pair co-occurred in a short context.

- **Self-Aggregation based Topic Model (SATM)** assumes that each short text is sampled from a long pseudo-document unobserved in the current text collection [30]. It requires to set the number of pseudo-documents as a parameter. We tune the number of pseudo-documents from 100 to 1000 with a step of 100 in terms of classification accuracy over the two datasets (See Section 4.4) and set it to 200 and 700 respec-

[7] http://baike.baidu.com/

[8] The advanced filtering strategy is deferred to our future work.

tively, on the Snippet and BaiduQA datasets, for achieving the best classification results.

- **Dirichlet Multinomial Mixture (DMM)** assumes that each short document has only one topic, and works as the basis of our model [40].

- **Latent Feature model with DMM (LF-DMM)** integrates word embeddings into DMM by replacing the topic-word Dirichlet multinomial component with a mixture of two components: a Dirichlet multinomial component, and a word embedding component [24]. A hard constraint in LF-DMM is that all words in the short text corpus should have corresponding word embeddings. Therefore we remove all the words without the related word embeddings. We use the implementation provided by the authors and use the recommended settings with $\lambda = 0.6$, $\alpha = 0.1$, $\beta = 0.01$ as in their paper.[9]

As for GPU-DMM, we need to set the amount of promotion μ for each semantically related word. We empirically set μ to be 0.1 and 0.3 respectively for BaiduQA and Snippet datasets.

Note that [11] also proposes a LDA-based model by using multivariate Gaussian distributions with auxiliary word embeddings. Their model assumes a Multinomial topic distribution for each document, which has been proven to be inappropriate for short texts [13, 30, 42]. Hence, we exclude this model from the comparison.

We run Gibbs sampling for $1,000$ iterations and report the average results over 5 runs for all methods. The only exception is that $2,000$ iterations ($1,500$ iterations with baseline model $+$ 500 iterations with LF-DMM) are run for LF-DMM, as in its original paper [24]. We evaluate the performance of all models in terms of topic coherence and text classification. The statistical significance is based on the student *t-test*.

4.3 Evaluation by Topic Coherence

The topics generated by each model are evaluated by the *topic coherence* metric. Traditionally, topic models are evaluated using perplexity. However, as shown in [3], perplexity does not reflect the semantic coherence of a topic. It can sometimes be contrary to human judgments. Topic coherence measures the extent that the most probable words of a topic tend to co-occur together within the same documents. It has been shown to be a better metric to assess topic quality [21].

Following [8], we use the PMI-Score proposed in [23] to calculate topic coherence. Given a topic k and its top T words with highest probabilities $(w_1, \ldots, w_T)$, the PMI-Score of k is:

$$PMI(k) = \frac{2}{T(T-1)} \sum_{1 \le i < j \le T} \log \frac{p(w_i, w_j)}{p(w_i)p(w_j)} \quad (9)$$

In this equation, $p(w_i)$ is the probability that word w_i appears in a document, and $p(w_i, w_j)$ is the probability that words w_i and w_j appear in the same document. The overall topic coherence for each model is the averaged PMI-Score over all learnt topics. A higher topic coherence indicates the better learnt topics. Note that an external corpus is needed to calculate the PMI-Scores in Equation 9. In our experiments, we use 3 million English Wikipedia articles and 7 million Chinese Baike articles for the Snippet and BaiduQA datasets, respectively.

Figures 2 and 3 report the topic coherence of all models on the two datasets with number of top words per topic $T = \{5, 10, 20\}$ and number of topics $K = \{40, 60, 80\}$, respectively. On the Snippet dataset, GPU-DMM achieves the best topic coherence across all settings, and the improvement over other baseline models are statistical significance at the 0.01 level. BTM is the second best model in most cases, and always outperforms DMM and LF-DMM. On BaiduQA dataset, LF-DMM outperforms all other models in 6 out of 9 settings. GPU-DMM achieves the best performance in the rest 3 settings, and performs the second best overall. On both datasets, GPU-DMM significantly outperforms DMM at the 0.01 level.

Recall that the BaiduQA dataset was preprocessed with Chinese word segmentation by the dataset provider [8, 39]. For learning word embeddings and evaluating topic coherence, we used ICTCLAS[10], a Chinese word segmentation tool, to segment the words in the 7 million Chinese articles. The differences in Chinese word segmentation might introduce some performance variations.

4.4 Evaluation by Short Text Classification

With topic modeling, we can represent each document with its topic distribution $p(z|d)$. Hence, the quality of the topics can be assessed by the accuracy of text classification using the topic-level representation, as an indirect evaluation. A better classification accuracy means that the learnt topics are more discriminative and representative. Here, we employ a linear kernel Support Vector Machines (SVM) classifier in sklearn[11] with default parameter settings. The classification accuracy is computed through 5-fold cross validation on both datasets.

Methods for Topic-level Representation. Three models DMM, LF-DMM and GPU-DMM all assume only one topic for each short document. Estimating the topic distribution directly based on the topic assignment in the last Gibbs samplings for these models is inappropriate. It is reported that the post inference of document representation $p(z|d)$ based on $p(w|z)$ and $p(z)$ is important for the classification accuracy [30]. There are two ways to infer $p(z|d)$:

- Naïve Bayes (NB) rule:

$$p(z = k|d) \propto p(z = k) \prod_{i=1}^{N_d} p(w_i|z = k)$$

- Summation over words (SW):

$$p(z = k|d) \propto \sum_{w} p(z = k|w)p(w|d)$$

  where $p(w|d)$ is estimated based on the relative frequency of w in d.

Both the NB and SW representations have been used in earlier studies. BTM uses a variant of SW post inference by replacing w with *biterm* b [39]. However, in their comparison, they use NB method for DMM instead. SW method is used for DMM and LDA and proven to largely improve the classification accuracy in [30]. However, no studies have conducted a thorough comparison of the two methods.

Here, we first compare the two document representation methods by using DMM, GPU-DMM, and BTM on Snippet dataset. Table 3 reports the classification accuracy of using the two methods with different settings on the number of topics $K = \{40, 60, 80\}$. Observe that using SW method leads to large performance improvement over NB method in topic-level representation of short documents, regardless the number of topics or the underlying topic model. Table 3 also shows that GPU-DMM achieves the best classification accuracy over all settings, followed by DMM. Similar observations hold on BaiduQA dataset (results not shown).

[9] Authors' implementation is available at https://github.com/datquocnguyen/LFTM

[10] http://ictclas.nlpir.org

[11] http://scikit-learn.org/

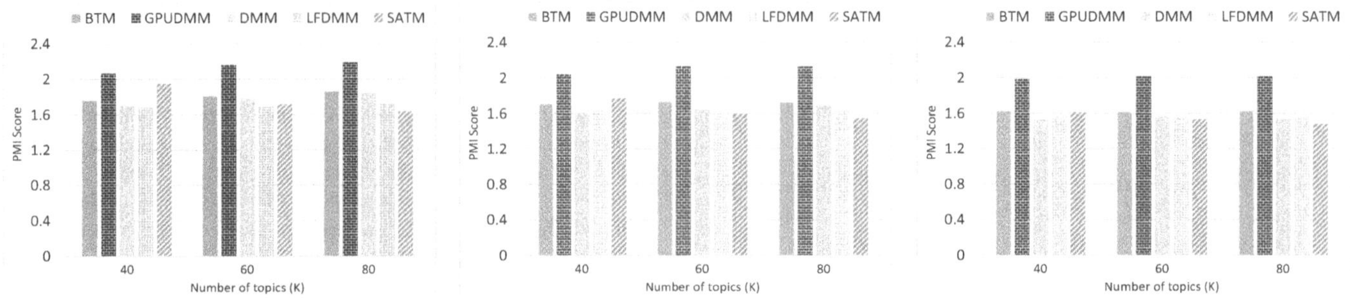

(a) Top-5 topic words (b) Top-10 topic words (c) Top-20 topic words

Figure 2: Topic Coherence on Snippet Dataset

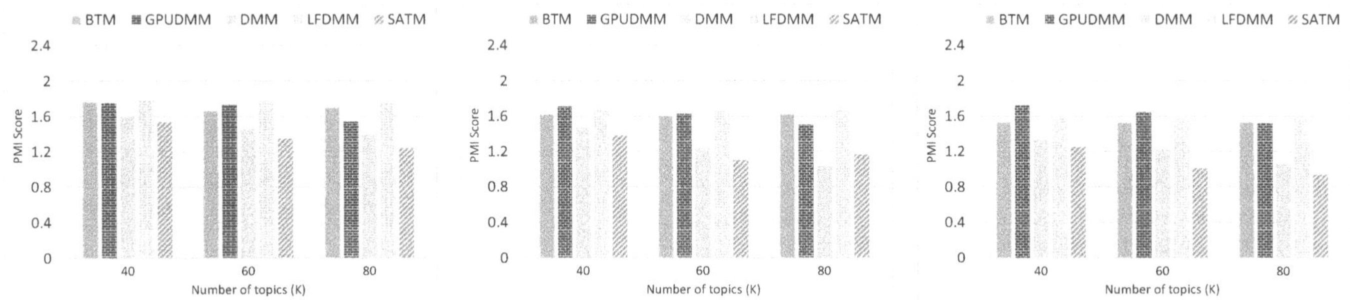

(a) Top-5 topic words (b) Top-10 topic words (c) Top-20 topic words

Figure 3: Topic Coherence on BaiduQA Dataset

Table 3: Classification accuracy of two post inference methods (NB and SW) on Snippet dataset. The best results are highlighted in boldface for each K setting.

Model	Method	K = 40	K = 60	K = 80
DMM	NB	0.7180	0.7590	0.7470
	SW	0.8298	0.8522	0.8479
GPU-DMM	NB	0.7510	0.7600	0.7650
	SW	**0.8539**	**0.8667**	**0.8722**
BTM	NB	0.7100	0.7120	0.6700
	SW	0.8100	0.8183	0.8272

Table 4: The top 3 topics and their proportions in an example document by using DMM.

Top	*SW*		*NB*	
	Topic Id	$p(z\|d)$	*Topic Id*	$p(z\|d)$
1	37	0.3187	37	0.9999
2	36	0.0820	27	2.92e-09
3	27	0.0760	36	4.57e-10

To better understand the big difference in classification accuracy by using the two different representation methods NB and SW, we show the top 3 topics with the corresponding $p(z|d)$ values for a random document in Snippet dataset by the two methods in Table 4. Observe that the top-3 topics for the document are the same (*i.e.*, topic Ids 27, 36, 37) inferred by both methods NB and SW. The relative proportions of each topic inferred by the two methods are tremendously different, particularly for the second and third topics. Using NB method, top-1 topic dominates the topic representation.

Table 5: Average classification accuracy of the 5 models on two datasets, with different number of topic K settings. The best results are highlighted in boldface on each dataset. † indicates that the difference to the best result is statistically significant at 0.01 level.

Dataset	Model	$K = 40$	$K = 60$	$K = 80$
Snippet	BTM	$0.8100^\dagger$	$0.8183^\dagger$	$0.8272^\dagger$
	DMM	$0.8298^\dagger$	$0.8522^\dagger$	$0.8479^\dagger$
	SATM	$0.8284^\dagger$	$0.8231^\dagger$	$0.8235^\dagger$
	LF-DMM	$0.7414^\dagger$	$0.7409^\dagger$	$0.7462^\dagger$
	GPU-DMM	**0.8539**	**0.8667**	**0.8722**
BaiduQA	BTM	$0.5098^\dagger$	$0.5336^\dagger$	$0.5486^\dagger$
	DMM	$0.5228^\dagger$	$0.5476^\dagger$	$0.5532^\dagger$
	SATM	$0.4872^\dagger$	$0.4567^\dagger$	$0.4605^\dagger$
	LF-DMM	$0.4240^\dagger$	$0.4486^\dagger$	$0.4868^\dagger$
	GPU-DMM	**0.5439**	**0.5637**	**0.5708**

Because NB method calculates $p(z|d)$ by a series of product of $p(w|z)$ over w, some irrelevant words could incur too much penalty for topic z. It was well studied that Naive Bayes makes unrealistic independence assumptions, push probabilities towards 0 and 1 [25]. As the result, NB method leads to extremely sparse topic distribution, equivalent to using the direct topic assignment. This is not a desired method for short texts. In the rest of this paper, we only report the classification accuracies by using the SW method.

Classification Accuracy. Table 5 reports the document classification accuracy on the two datasets by using the 5 models in comparison. We make the following observations.

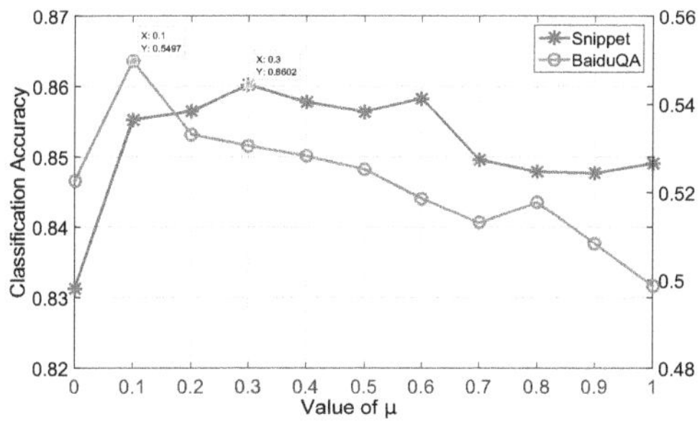

Figure 4: Effect of weight μ under $K = 40$

First, our GPU-DMM model significantly outperforms other state-of-the-art models on both datasets. Particularly, the significant performance gains of GPU-DMM with respect to DMM are achieved on all $K = \{40, 60, 80\}$ settings. This validates that incorporating general word semantic relatedness knowledge based on word embeddings with GPU models is beneficial for short text topic modeling.

Second, in our experiments, DMM is the second best performing model in the document classification task. Although BTM was shown to perform better than DMM in [39], as we discussed earlier, the NB based document representation was used for DMM in [39], which may be the reason for the poorer performance. By using the SW inference method, we show that BTM is inferior to DMM in this classification task on both datasets. This result suggests that generating biterms may bring little discriminative word co-occurrence knowledge, which is also observed in [30,41].

Third, SATM delivers mixed performance on the two datasets. On Snippet dataset, it performs slightly better than BTM when $K = 40$ and $K = 60$; it performs much poorer than BTM on BaiduQA dataset. Surprisingly, we observe that LF-DMM performs the worst among all models on both datasets even though it also exploits word embeddings. One possible reason for its modest performance is that harnessing the semantic relatedness via a two-component mixture may need a more complex mechanism. A simple switch mechanism with an indication variable used in LF-DMM may not optimally balance the two components.

Effect of the Promotion Weight μ. We now study the effect of weight μ in GPU-DMM (see Equation 3). Figure 4 depicts the classification accuracy of different μ settings under $K = 40$ on the two datasets. Note that, when $\mu = 0$, GPU-DMM is equivalent to the DMM model.

While GPU-DMM obtains significant improvements over DMM (*i.e.*, $\mu = 0$) with any positive μ values on Snippet dataset, it only achieves positive gains when μ is relatively small on BaiduQA dataset, *i.e.*, $\mu \leq 0.5$. Specifically, on BaiduQA dataset, the best accuracy is achieved when $\mu = 0.1$, further increasing μ results in performance degradation. Reported in Table 2, documents in BaiduQA is much shorter than that in Snippet dataset. Because of the very limited context information in such short document (4.11 words per document on average), that chance of sampling an incorrect topic for a document becomes high. Setting a larger μ means more related words in the wrongly sampled topic are promoted, leading to poorer results.

4.5 Efficiency

In the last set of experiments, we compare the running time of the models. We implement GPU-DMM, DMM, SATM and BTM models in Java, and use the Java implementation provided by its authors for LF-DMM.

Table 6: Time cost (in seconds) per iteration of each model on two datasets, with different settings on number of topics $K = \{40, 60, 80\}$. The best and the second best results are highlighted in boldface and underlined respectively.

Dataset	Model	$K = 40$	$K = 60$	$K = 80$
Snippet	BTM	0.572	0.832	1.121
	DMM	**0.042**	**0.069**	**0.088**
	SATM	0.392	0.451	0.478
	LF-DMM	5.209	7.234	9.702
	GPU-DMM	0.085	0.115	0.217
BaiduQA	BTM	1.411	2.042	2.603
	DMM	**0.355**	**0.566**	**0.843**
	SATM	10.120	10.345	11.711
	LF-DMM	13.028	20.493	31.822
	GPU-DMM	1.558	1.862	2.318

Table 6 reports the average run-time (in seconds) per iteration for each model. The simplest model DMM, is the most efficient one as expected. GPU-DMM is slightly slower than DMM, being the second most efficient model. This result is expected because GPU-DMM shares similar Gibbs sampling process with DMM. The extension of the sampling process by taking in semantically related words through GPU does not cost much in terms of computation. The average run-time of GPU-DMM is less than 3 times of DMM for different topic numbers K on both datasets. This observation is consistent with the analysis made in Section 3.3.

SATM is much faster than BTM on Snippet dataset, but requires much more time than BTM on BaiduQA dataset. As being described in [30], the computational cost of SATM is positively proportional to the number of pseudo-documents. Hence, the large difference in the run-time on the two datasets is due to the setting of the optimal number of pseudo-documents, *i.e.*, 200 and 700 respectively on the two datasets. LF-DMM is the slowest model in this comparison. As discussed in Section 2, LF-DMM estimates the word embedding component for each topic by projecting the topic into the vector space, where a regularized log-linear has to be optimized. This process is time-consuming.

In summary, our earlier results and the results in Table 6 suggest that GPU-DMM is a desired choice for short text topic modeling, with respect to both effectiveness and efficiency.

5. CONCLUSION

Unlike normal documents, short texts carry limited context information, causing severe sparsity problems when applying conventional topic models. In this paper, we propose a new topic model, named GPU-DMM, to leverage global word co-occurrence knowledge to help distil better topics over short texts. Instead of extracting word semantic relatedness knowledge from external thesauri, we propose to harness the knowledge from the results of the recent neural network language model techniques. GPU-DMM enhances the topic similarity for two semantically related words which rarely co-occur in short texts. We conduct extensive experiments on two real-world short text corpora. The experimental results show that GPU-DMM outperforms existing state-of-the-art alternatives in terms of effectiveness and efficiency. Nevertheless, there is still room to improve our model in the future. For example, we would like to adjust the promotion weight μ based on the topic and correlated word pair together, which is a fixed value in this work. Moreover, it is interesting to validate the effectiveness of using other word embedding techniques like Glove [27].

Acknowledgements. This research was supported by National Natural Science Foundation of China (No. 61502344), Natural Science Foundation of Hubei Province (No. 2015CFB337), Natural Scientific Research Program of Wuhan University (No. 2042015kf0014), and Singapore Ministry of Education Academic Research Fund Tier 2 (MOE2014-T2-2-066). Chenliang Li is the corresponding author.

6. REFERENCES

[1] Y. Bengio, H. Schwenk, J.-S. Senécal, F. Morin, and J.-L. Gauvain. *Neural probabilistic language models*. Springer, 2006.

[2] D. M. Blei, A. Y. Ng, and M. I. Jordan. Latent dirichlet allocation. *Journal of Machine Learning Research*, 2003.

[3] J. Chang, S. Gerrish, C. Wang, J. L. Boyd-Graber, and D. M. Blei. Reading tea leaves: How humans interpret topic models. In *NIPS*, 2009.

[4] M. Chen, X. Jin, and D. Shen. Short text classification improved by learning multi-granularity topics. In *IJCAI*, 2011.

[5] Z. Chen and B. Liu. Mining topics in documents: standing on the shoulders of big data. In *SIGKDD*, 2014.

[6] Z. Chen, A. Mukherjee, B. Liu, M. Hsu, M. Castellanos, and R. Ghosh. Discovering coherent topics using general knowledge. In *CIKM*, 2013.

[7] Z. Chen, A. Mukherjee, B. Liu, M. Hsu, M. Castellanos, and R. Ghosh. Leveraging multi-domain prior knowledge in topic models. In *IJCAI*, 2013.

[8] X. Cheng, X. Yan, Y. Lan, and J. Guo. BTM: topic modeling over short texts. *IEEE Trans. Knowl. Data Eng.*, 2014.

[9] R. Collobert and J. Weston. A unified architecture for natural language processing: Deep neural networks with multitask learning. In *ICML*, 2008.

[10] R. Collobert, J. Weston, L. Bottou, M. Karlen, K. Kavukcuoglu, and P. P. Kuksa. Natural language processing (almost) from scratch. *Journal of Machine Learning Research*, 2011.

[11] R. Das, M. Zaheer, and C. Dyer. Gaussian LDA for topic models with word embeddings. In *ACL*, 2015.

[12] T. Hofmann. Probabilistic latent semantic indexing. In *SIGIR*, 1999.

[13] L. Hong and B. D. Davison. Empirical study of topic modeling in twitter. In *The First Workshop on Social Media Analytics*, 2010.

[14] L. Hong, D. Yin, J. Guo, and B. D. Davison. Tracking trends: incorporating term volume into temporal topic models. In *SIGKDD*, 2011.

[15] O. Jin, N. N. Liu, K. Zhao, Y. Yu, and Q. Yang. Transferring topical knowledge from auxiliary long texts for short text clustering. In *CIKM*, 2011.

[16] T. Kenter and M. de Rijke. Short text similarity with word embeddings. In *CIKM*, 2015.

[17] M. J. Kusner, Y. Sun, N. I. Kolkin, and K. Q. Weinberger. From word embeddings to document distances. In *ICML*, 2015.

[18] H. Mahmoud. Polya urn models. *Chapman & Hall/CRC Texts in Statistical Science*, 2008.

[19] R. Mehrotra, S. Sanner, W. Buntine, and L. Xie. Improving lda topic models for microblogs via tweet pooling and automatic labeling. In *SIGIR*, 2013.

[20] T. Mikolov, K. Chen, G. Corrada, and J. Dean. Efficient estimation of word representations in vector space. *arXiv preprint arXiv:1301.3781*, 2013.

[21] D. Mimno, H. M. Wallach, E. Talley, M. Leenders, and A. McCallum. Optimizing semantic coherence in topic models. In *EMNLP*, 2011.

[22] A. Mnih and G. E. Hinton. A scalable hierarchical distributed language model. In *NIPS*, 2009.

[23] D. Newman, J. H. Lau, K. Grieser, and T. Baldwin. Automatic evaluation of topic coherence. In *HLT-NAACL*, 2010.

[24] D. Q. Nguyen, R. Billingsley, L. Du, and M. Johnson. Improving topic models with latent feature word representations. *TACL*, 2015.

[25] A. Niculescu-Mizil and R. Caruana. Predicting good probabilities with supervised learning. In *ICML*.

[26] K. Nigam, A. K. MacCallum, S. Thrun, and T. Mitchell. Text classification from labeled and unlabeled documents using em. *Machine Learning*, 2000.

[27] J. Pennington, R. Socher, and C. D. Manning. Glove: Global vectors for word representation. In *EMNLP*, 2014.

[28] X.-H. Phan, L.-M. Nguyen, and S. Horiguchi. Learning to classify short and sparse text & web with hidden topics from large-scale data collections. In *WWW*, 2008.

[29] I. Porteous, D. Newman, A. Ihler, A. Asuncion, P. Smyth, and M. Welling. Fast collapsed gibbs sampling for latent dirichlet allocation. In *SIGKDD*, 2008.

[30] X. Quan, C. Kit, Y. Ge, and S. J. Pan. Short and sparse text topic modeling via self-aggregation. In *AAAI*, 2015.

[31] Z. Ma, A. Sun, Q. Yuan, and G. Cong. Topic-driven reader comments summarization. In *CIKM*, 2012.

[32] D. Ramage, S. T. Dumais, and D. J. Liebling. Characterizing microblogs with topic models. In *ICWSM*, 2010.

[33] D. E. Rumelhar, G. E. Hinton, and R. J. Williams. Learning representations by back-propagating errors. *Cognitive Modeling*, 1988.

[34] B. Sriram, D. Fuhry, E. Demir, H. Ferhatosmanoglu, and M. Demirbas. Short text classification in twitter to improve information filtering. In *SIGIR*, 2010.

[35] A. Sun. Short text classification using very few words. In *SIGIR*, 2012.

[36] C. Wang and D. M. Blei. Collaborative topic modeling for recommending scientific articles. In *SIGKDD*, 2011.

[37] X. Wang, C. Zhai, X. Hu, and R. Sproat. Mining correlated bursty topic patterns from coordinated text streams. In *SIGKDD*, 2007.

[38] J. Weng, E.-P. Lim, J. Jiang, and Q. He. Twitterrank: finding topic-sensitive influential twitterers. In *WSDM*, 2010.

[39] X. Yan, J. Guo, Y. Lan, and X. Chen. A biterm topic model for short texts. In *WWW*, 2013.

[40] J. Yin and J. Wang. A dirichlet multinomial mixture model-based approach for short text clustering. In *SIGKDD*, 2014.

[41] X. Yunqing, T. Nan, H. Amir, and C. Erik. Discriminative bi-term topic model for headline-based social news clustering. In *AAAI*, 2015.

[42] W. X. Zhao, J. Jiang, J. Weng, J. He, E.-P. Lim, H. Yan, and X. Li. Comparing twitter and traditional media using topic models. In *ECIR*, 2011.

[43] G. Zheng and J. Callan. Learning to reweight terms with distributed representations. In *SIGIR*, 2015.

Interleaved Evaluation for Retrospective Summarization and Prospective Notification on Document Streams

Xin Qian, Jimmy Lin, and Adam Roegiest
David R. Cheriton School of Computer Science
University of Waterloo, Ontario, Canada

ABSTRACT

We propose and validate a novel interleaved evaluation methodology for two complementary information seeking tasks on document streams: retrospective summarization and prospective notification. In the first, the user desires relevant and non-redundant documents that capture important aspects of an information need. In the second, the user wishes to receive timely, relevant, and non-redundant update notifications for a standing information need. Despite superficial similarities, interleaved evaluation methods for web ranking cannot be directly applied to these tasks; for example, existing techniques do not account for temporality or redundancy. Our proposed evaluation methodology consists of two components: a temporal interleaving strategy and a heuristic for credit assignment to handle redundancy. By simulating user interactions with interleaved results on submitted runs to the TREC 2014 tweet timeline generation (TTG) task and the TREC 2015 real-time filtering task, we demonstrate that our methodology yields system comparisons that accurately match the result of batch evaluations. Analysis further reveals weaknesses in current batch evaluation methodologies to suggest future directions for research.

1. INTRODUCTION

As primarily an empirical discipline, evaluation methodologies are vital to ensuring progress in information retrieval. The ability to compare system variants and detect differences in effectiveness allows researchers and practitioners to continually advance the state of the art. One such approach, broadly applicable to any online service, is the traditional A/B test [12]. In its basic setup, users are divided into disjoint "buckets" and exposed to different treatments (e.g., algorithm variants); user behavior (e.g., clicks) in each of the conditions is measured and compared to assess the relative effectiveness of the treatments. As an alternative, information retrieval researchers have developed an evaluation methodology for web search based on *interleaving* results from two different comparison systems into a single ranked list [8, 17, 6, 15, 7, 3, 16, 19], as well as recent extensions to more than two system [20]. Instead of dividing the user population into disjoint segments, all test subjects are exposed to these interleaved results. Based on user clicks, it is possible to assess the relative effectiveness of the two input systems with greater sensitivity than traditional A/B testing [17, 3], primarily due to the within-subjects design.

This paper explores interleaved evaluation for information seeking on document streams. Although we focus on a stream of social media updates (tweets), nothing in our formulation is specific to tweets. In this context, we tackle two complementary user tasks: In the retrospective summarization scenario, which is operationalized in the tweet timeline generation (TTG) task at TREC 2014 [13], the user desires relevant and non-redundant posts that capture key aspects of an information need. In the prospective notification scenario, operationalized in the real-time filtering task ("scenario A") at TREC 2015 [14], the user wishes to receive timely, relevant, and non-redundant updates (e.g., via a push notification on a mobile phone).

The contribution of this paper is the development and validation of an interleaved evaluation methodology for retrospective summarization and prospective notification on document streams, consisting of two components: a temporal interleaving strategy and a heuristic for credit assignment to handle redundancy. Although we can draw inspiration from the literature on interleaved evaluations for web search, previous techniques are not directly applicable to our tasks. We face a number of challenges: the important role that time plays in organizing and structuring system output, differing volumes in the number of results generated by systems, and notions of redundancy that complicate credit assignment. Our evaluation methodology addresses these complexities and is validated using data from the TREC 2014 and 2015 Microblog evaluations. Specifically, we simulate user interactions with interleaved results to produce a decision on whether system A is better than system B, and correlate these decisions with the results of batch evaluations. We find that our methodology yields accurate system comparisons under a variety of settings. Analysis also reveals weaknesses in current batch evaluation methodologies, which is a secondary contribution of this work.

SIGIR '16, July 17 - 21, 2016, Pisa, Italy

ISBN 978-1-4503-4069-4/16/07...$15.00
DOI: http://dx.doi.org/10.1145/2911451.2911494

2. BACKGROUND AND RELATED WORK

We begin by describing our task models, which are illustrated in Figure 1. We assume the existence of a stream of timestamped documents: examples include news articles coming off an RSS feed or social media posts such as tweets.

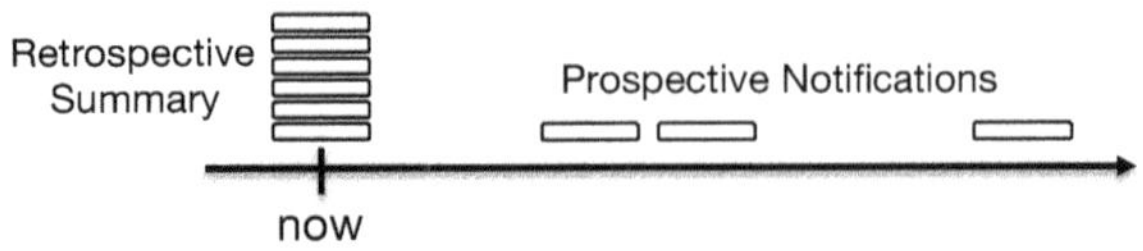

Figure 1: Illustration of our task models. At some point in time ("now"), the user develops an information need: she requests a retrospective summary of what has happened thus far and desires prospective notifications of future updates.

In this context, we consider a pair of complementary tasks: suppose at some point in time the user develops an information need, let's say, about an ongoing political scandal. She would like a retrospective summary of what has occurred up until now, which might consist of a list of chronologically-ordered documents that highlight important developments. Once she has "come up to speed", the user might wish to receive prospective notifications (on her mobile phone) regarding future updates, for example, statements by the involved parties or the emergence of another victim. Retrospective summarization and prospective notification form two complementary components of information seeking on document streams. In both cases, users desire relevant and novel (non-redundant) content—they, for example, would not want to see multiple tweets that say essentially the same thing. In the prospective notification case, the user additionally desires timely updates—as close as possible to the actual occurrence of the "new development". This, however, isn't particularly important for the retrospective case, since the events have already taken place.

In this work, we present and evaluate an interleaved evaluation methodology for the retrospective summarization and prospective notification tasks described above. Although there has been substantial work on interleaved evaluation in the context of web search [8, 17, 6, 15, 7, 3, 16, 19], we face three main challenges:

1. Temporality plays an important role in our tasks. In web search, ranked lists from different systems can be arbitrarily interleaved (and in some cases the relative ordering of documents swapped) without significantly affecting users' interpretation of the results. In our task, however, the temporal ordering of documents is critical for the proper interpretation of system output.
2. We need to interleave results of different lengths. In web search, most interleaving strategies assume ranked lists of equal length, while this is not true in our case—some systems are more verbose than others.
3. We need to account for redundancy. In our tasks the notion of novelty is very important and "credit" is only awarded for returning non-redundant tweets. This creates a coupling effect between two systems where one's result might "mask" the novelty in the other. That is, a system's output becomes redundant only because the interleaving algorithm injected a relevant document before the document in question.

Nevertheless, there is a rich body of literature from which we can draw inspiration. In particular, we employ a simulation-based approach that is well-established for validating interleaved evaluations [6, 7, 16].

Our retrospective summarization and prospective notification tasks are grounded in the Microblog track evaluations at TREC: specifically, the tweet timeline generation (TTG) task at TREC 2014 [13] and the push notification scenario ("scenario A") in the real-time filtering task at TREC 2015 [14]. Although there has been a substantial amount of work on developing systems that try to accomplish the tasks we study (see the TREC overview papers for pointers into the literature), our focus is not on the development of algorithms, but rather in evaluating system output. We adopt the framework provided by these tracks: relevance judgments and submitted runs are used in simulation studies to validate our interleaved evaluation methodology.

3. TASK AND METRICS

We begin by describing evaluations from TREC 2014 and 2015 that operationalize our retrospective summarization and prospective notification tasks.

3.1 Retrospective Summarization

Tweet timeline generation (TTG) was introduced at the TREC 2014 Microblog track. The putative user model is as follows: "At time T, I have an information need expressed by query Q, and I would like a summary that captures relevant information." The system's task is to produce a summary timeline, operationalized as a list of non-redundant, chronologically ordered tweets. It is imagined that the user would consume the entire summary (unlike a ranked list, where the user might stop reading at any time).

Redundancy was operationalized as follows: for every pair of tweets, if the chronologically later tweet contains substantive information that is not present in the earlier tweet, the later tweet is considered novel; otherwise, the later tweet is redundant with respect to the earlier one. Thus, redundancy and novelty are antonyms; we use them interchangeably in opposite contexts. Due to the temporal constraint, redundancy is *not* symmetric. If tweet A precedes tweet B and tweet B contains substantively similar information found in tweet A, then B is redundant with respect to A, but not the other way around. The task also assumes transitivity. Suppose A precedes B and B precedes C: if B is redundant with respect to A and C is redundant with respect to B, then by definition C is redundant with respect to A.

The TTG assessment task can be viewed as semantic clustering—that is, we wish to group relevant tweets into clusters in which all tweets share substantively similar information. Within each cluster, the earliest tweet is novel; all other tweets in the cluster are redundant with respect to all earlier tweets. The track organizers devised a two-phase assessment workflow that implements this idea. In the first phase, all tweets are pooled and judged for relevance. In the second phase, relevant tweets for each topic are then clustered. We refer the reader to previous papers for more details [13, 22], but the final product of the human annotation process is a list of tweet clusters, each containing tweets that represent a semantic equivalence class.

In TREC 2014, TTG systems were evaluated in terms of set-based metrics (precision, recall, and F-score) at the cluster level. Systems only received credit for returning one tweet from each cluster—that is, once a tweet is retrieved, all other tweets in the cluster are automatically considered not relevant. In this study, we performed our correlation analysis against recall, for reasons that will become apparent later. The track evaluated recall in two different ways: unweighted and weighted. In the relevance assessment process, tweets were judged as not relevant, relevant, or highly relevant. For unweighted recall (also called S-recall [23] and I-recall [18]), relevant and highly-relevant tweets were collapsed to yield binary judgments and all clusters received equal weight. For weighted recall, each cluster is assigned a weight proportional to the sum of relevance grades from every tweet in the cluster (relevant tweets receive a weight of one and highly-relevant tweets receive a weight of two).

3.2 Prospective Notification

In the real-time filtering task at TREC 2015 [14], the goal is for a system to identify interesting and novel content for a user in a timely fashion, with respect to information needs (called "interest profiles" but in actuality quite similar to traditional *ad hoc* topics). In the push notification variant of the task ("scenario A"), updates are putatively delivered in real time as notifications to users' mobile phones. A system was allowed to return a maximum of ten tweets per day per interest profile. The official evaluation took place over a span of ten days during July 2015, where all participating systems "listened" to Twitter's live tweet sample stream to complete the evaluation task; the interest profiles were made available prior to the evaluation period.

The assessment workflow was the same as the TTG task in TREC 2014 (see Section 3.1): relevance assessment using traditional pooling followed by semantic clustering. The task likewise used three-way judgments: not relevant, relevant, and highly relevant. We refer the reader to the TREC overview paper for more details [14].

The two metrics used to evaluate system runs were expected latency-discounted gain (ELG) and normalized cumulative gain (nCG). These two metrics are computed for each interest profile for each day in the evaluation period (explained in detail below). The final score of a run is the average of daily scores across all interest profiles.

The expected latency-discounted gain (ELG) metric was adapted from the TREC temporal summarization track [2]:

$$\frac{1}{N}\sum \mathrm{G}(t) \qquad (1)$$

where N is the number of tweets returned and $\mathrm{G}(t)$ is the gain of each tweet: not relevant tweets receive a gain of 0, relevant tweets receive a gain of 0.5, and highly-relevant tweets receive a gain of 1.0.

As with the TTG task, redundancy is penalized: a system only receives credit for returning one tweet from each cluster. Furthermore, per the track guidelines, a latency penalty is applied to all tweets, computed as $\mathrm{MAX}(0, (100 - d)/100)$, where the delay d is the time elapsed (in minutes, rounded down) between the tweet creation time and the putative time the tweet was delivered. That is, if the system delivers a relevant tweet within a minute of the tweet being posted, the system receives full credit. Otherwise, credit decays linearly such that after 100 minutes, the system receives no credit even if the tweet was relevant.

The second metric is normalized cumulative gain (nCG):

$$\frac{1}{\mathcal{Z}}\sum \mathrm{G}(t) \qquad (2)$$

where $\mathcal{Z}$ is the maximum possible gain (given the ten tweet per day limit). The gain of each individual tweet is computed as above (with the latency penalty). Note that gain is not discounted (as in nDCG) because the notion of document ranks is not meaningful in this context.

Due to the setup of the task and the nature of interest profiles, it is possible (and indeed observed empirically) that for some days, no relevant tweets appear in the judgment pool. In terms of evaluation metrics, a system should be rewarded for correctly identifying these cases and not generating any output. We can break down the scoring contingency table as follows: If there are relevant tweets for a particular day, scores are computed per above. If there are no relevant tweets for that day, and the system returns zero tweets, it receives a score of one (i.e., perfect score) for that day; otherwise, the system receives a score of zero for that day. This means that an empty run (a system that never returns anything) may have a non-zero score.

4. INTERLEAVING METHODOLOGY

The development of an interleaved evaluation methodology requires answering the following questions:

1. How exactly do we interleave the output of two systems into one single output, in light of the challenges discussed in Section 2?
2. How do we assign credit to each of the underlying systems in response to user interactions with the interleaved results?

4.1 Interleaving Strategy

We begin by explaining why existing interleaving strategies for web search cannot be applied to either retrospective summarization or prospective notification. Existing strategies attempt to draw results from the test systems in a "fair" way: In balanced interleaving [8], for example, the algorithm maintains two pointers, one to each input list, and draws from the lagging pointer. Team drafting [17], on the other hand, follows the analogy of selecting teams for a friendly team-sports match and proceeds in rounds. Both explicitly assume (1) that the ranked lists from each system are ordered in decreasing probability of relevance (i.e., following the probability ranking principle) and (2) that the ranked lists are of equal length. Both assumptions are problematic because output in retrospective summarization and prospective notification must be chronologically ordered: a naïve application of an existing web interleaving strategy in the retrospective case would yield a chronologically jumbled list of tweets that is not interpretable. In the prospective case, we cannot "time travel" and push notifications "in the future" and then "return to the past". Furthermore, in both our tasks system outputs can vary greatly in verbosity, and hence the length of their results. This is an important aspect of the evaluation design as systems should learn when to "keep quiet" (see Section 3.2). Most existing interleaving strategies don't tell us what to do when we run out of results from one system. For these reasons it is necessary to develop a new interleaving strategy.

After preliminary exploration, we developed an interleaving strategy, called *temporal interleaving*, where we simply interleave the two runs by time. The strategy is easy to implement yet effective, as we demonstrate experimentally. Temporal interleaving works in the prospective case because time is always "moving forward". An example is shown in Figure 2, where we have system A on the left and system B on the right. The subscript of each tweet indicates its timestamp and the interleaved result is shown in the middle (note that tweet t_{28} is returned by both systems). One potential

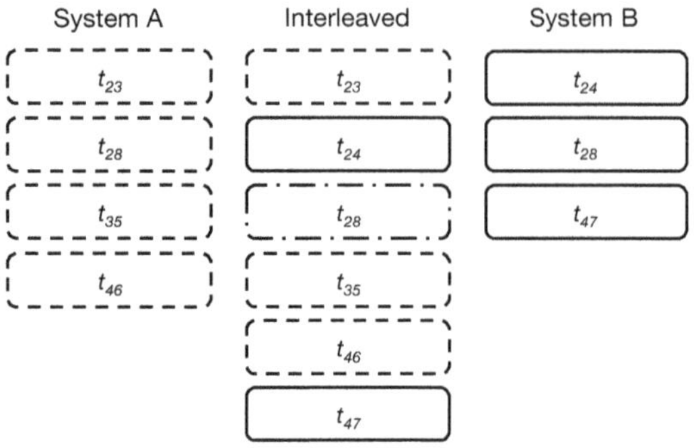

Figure 2: Illustration of temporal interleaving. Note that tweet t_{28} is returned by both systems.

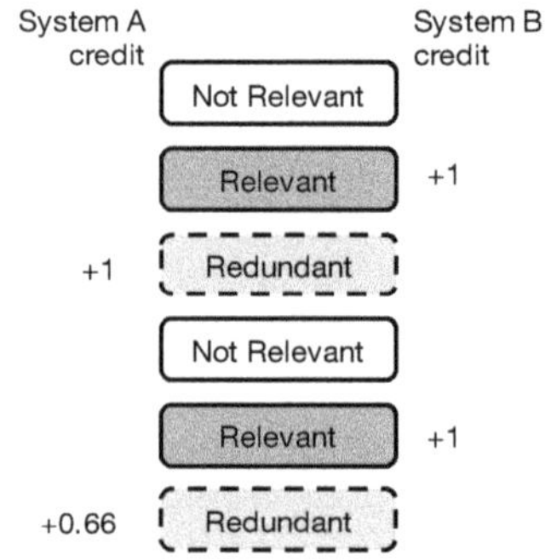

Figure 3: Example of interleaving credit assignment and redundancy handling.

downside of this strategy is that all retrieved documents from both systems are included in the interleaved results, which increases its length—we return to address this issue in Section 5.3.

Our simple temporal interleaving strategy works as is for TTG runs, since system outputs are ordered lists of tweets. For push notifications, there is one additional wrinkle: which timestamp do we use? Recall that in prospective notification there is the tweet creation time and the push time (when the system identified the tweet as being relevant). We base interleaving on the push time because it yields a very simple implementation: we watch the output of two prospective notification systems and take the output as soon as a result is emitted by either system. However, we make sure to apply de-duplication: if a tweet is pushed by two systems but at different times, it will only be included once in the interleaved results.

4.2 User Interactions and Credit Assignment

In our interleaved evaluation methodology, output from the two different test systems are combined using the temporal interleaving strategy described above and presented to the user. We assume a very simple interaction model in which the user goes through the output (in chronological order) from earliest to latest and makes one of three judgments for each tweet: not relevant, relevant, and relevant but redundant (i.e., the tweet is relevant but repeats information that is already present in a previously-seen tweet). This extends straightforwardly to cases where we have graded relevance judgments: for the relevant and redundant judgments, the user also indicates the relevance grade. In retrospective summarization, the user is interacting with static system output, but in the prospective notification case, output is presented to the user over a period of time. This is called the "simple task", for reasons that will become clear shortly. We assume that users provide explicit judgments, in contrast to implicit feedback (i.e., click data) in the case of interleaved evaluations for web search; we return to discuss this issue in Section 5.4.

Based on user interactions with the interleaved results, we must now assign credit to each of the test systems, which is used to determine their relative effectiveness. Credit assignment for the relevant label is straightforward: credit accrues to the system that contributed the tweet to the interleaved results (or to both if both systems returned the tweet). However, credit assignment for a tweet marked redundant is more complex—we do not know, for example, if the redundancy was actually introduced by the interleaving. That is, the interleaving process inserted a tweet (from the other run) before this particular tweet that made it redundant.

We can illustrate this with the diagram in Figure 3. A dotted border represents a tweet contributed by system A (on the left) and a solid border represents a tweet contributed by system B (on the right). Suppose the assessor judged the tweets as they are labeled in the figure. The second and fifth tweets are marked relevant, and so system B gets full credit twice. Now let's take a look at the third tweet, contributed by system A, which is marked redundant—we can confidently conclude in this case that the redundancy was introduced by the interleaving, since there are no relevant tweets above that are contributed by system A. Therefore, we can give system A full credit for the third tweet. Now let's take a look at the sixth tweet: generalizing this line of reasoning, the more that relevant tweets above are from system B, the more likely that we're encountering a "masking effect" (all things being equal), where the redundancy is an artifact of the interleaving itself. To capture this, we introduce the following heuristic: the amount of credit given to a system for a tweet marked redundant is multiplied by a discount factor equal to the fraction of relevant and redundant tweets above that come from the *other* system. In this case, there are two relevant tweets above, both from system B, and one redundant tweet from system A, so system A receives a credit of 0.66.

More formally, consider an interleaved result S consisting of tweets $s_1 \dots s_n$ drawn from system A and system B. We denote S_A and S_B as those tweets in S that come from system A and B, respectively. For a tweet s_i judged redundant, if $s_i \in S_A$, then we multiple its gain by a discount factor D_A as follows:

$$D_A(s_i) = \frac{|\{s_j | j < i \wedge I(s_j) \wedge s_j \in S_B\}|}{T(s_i)} \quad (3)$$

$$T(s_i) = |\{s_j | j < i \wedge I(s_j) \wedge s_j \in S_A\}| + |\{s_j | j < i \wedge I(s_j) \wedge s_j \in S_B\}| \quad (4)$$

where $I(s)$ is an indicator function that returns one if the user (previously) judged the tweet to be either relevant or redundant, or zero otherwise. On the other hand, if $s_i \in S_B$, we apply a discount factor D_B that mirrors D_A above (i.e., flipping subscripts A and B). If s_i is both in S_A and S_B, we apply *both* equations and give each system a different amount of credit (summing up to one).

We emphasize, of course, that this way of assigning credit for redundant judgments is a heuristic (but effective, from our evaluations). For further validation, we introduce an alternative interaction model that we call the "complex task": in this model, the user still marks each tweet not relevant, relevant, and redundant, but for each redundant tweet, the user marks the source of the redundancy, i.e., which previous tweet contains the same information. With this additional source of information, we can pinpoint the exact source of redundancy and assign credit definitively (zero if the source of redundancy was from the same run, and one if from the other run). Of course, such a task would be significantly more onerous (and slower) than just providing three-way judgments, but this "complex task" provides an upper bound that allows us to assess the effectiveness of our credit assignment heuristic.

One final detail: In the prospective task, we still apply a latency penalty to the assigned credit, as in ELG. Thus, in the case of a tweet that was pushed by both systems, but at different times, they will receive different amounts of credit. In the interleaved results, of course, the tweet will appear only once—from that single judgment we can compute the credit assigned to each system.

To recap: we have presented a temporal interleaving strategy to combine system output, introduced a model for how users interact with the results, and devised a credit assignment algorithm (including redundancy handling) that scores the systems based on user interactions. From this, we arrive at a determination of which system is more effective. Do these decisions agree with the results of batch evaluations? We answer this question with simulation studies based on runs submitted to TREC 2014 (for retrospective summarization) and TREC 2015 (for prospective notification).

5. SIMULATION RESULTS

5.1 Retrospective Summarization

To validate our interleaved evaluation methodology for retrospective summarization, we conducted user simulations using runs from the TREC 2014 TTG task. In total, 13 groups submitted 50 runs to the official evaluation. For each pair of runs, we applied the temporal interleaving strategy described above and simulated user interactions with the "ground truth" cluster annotations. Each simulation experiment comprised 67,375 pairwise comparisons, which we further break down into 63,415 comparisons of runs from different groups (inter-group) and 3,960 comparisons between runs from the same group (intra-group). Wang et al. [22] were able to elicit two completely independent sets of cluster annotations, which they refer to as the "official" and "alternate" judgments. Thus, we were able to simulate user interactions with both sets of clusters.

First, we ran simulations using binary relevance judgments. Results are shown in Table 1. When comparing simulation results (which system is better, based on assigned credit) with the batch evaluation results (unweighted recall), there are four possible cases:

- The compared runs have different batch evaluation results and the simulation was able to detect those differences; denoted (Agree, Δ).
- The compared runs have the same batch result and the simulation assigned equal credit to both runs; denoted (Agree, $\neg\Delta$).
- The compared runs have different batch evaluation results but the simulation was not able to detect those differences; denoted (Disagree, Δ).
- The compared runs have the same batch result and the simulation falsely ascribed differences in effectiveness between those runs; denoted (Disagree, $\neg\Delta$).

In the first two cases, the batch evaluation and interleaved evaluation results are consistent and the interleaving can be said to have given "correct" results; this is tallied up as (Agree, Total) in the results table. In the last two cases, the batch evaluation and interleaved evaluation results are inconsistent and the interleaving can be said to have given "incorrect" results; this is tallied up as (Disagree, Total) in the results table.[1]

With "official" and "alternate" clusters, there are four ways we can run the simulations: simulate with official judgments, correlate with batch evaluation results using official judgments (official, official); simulate with alternate judgments, correlate with batch evaluation results using alternative judgments (alternate, alternate); as well as the symmetrical cases where the simulation and batch evaluations are different, i.e., (official, alternate) and (alternate, official). Table 1 shows all four cases, denoted by the first two columns. Finally, the two vertical blocks of the table denote the results of the "simple task" (simulated user provides three-way judgments) and the "complex task" (simulated user additionally marks the source of a redundant tweet).

There is a lot of information to unpack from Table 1. Focusing only on "all pairs" with the "simple task", we see that our simulation results agree with batch evaluation results 92%-93% of the time, which indicates that our interleaved evaluation methodology is effective. The inaccuracies can be attributed to the credit assignment heuristic for redundant labels—this can be seen from the "complex task" block, where accuracy becomes 100% if we ask the (simulated) user to mark the source of the redundancy. Of course, this makes the task unrealistically onerous, so we argue that our credit assignment heuristic strikes the right balance between accuracy and complexity.

With the (official, official) and the (alternate, alternate) conditions, we are simulating user interactions and computing batch results with the same cluster assignments. With the other two conditions, we simulate with one set of clusters and perform batch evaluations with the other—the difference between these two sets quantifies inter-assessor differences. Results suggest that the effect of using different assessors is relatively small—this finding is consistent with that of Wang et al. [22], who confirmed the stability of the TTG evaluation with respect to assessor differences.

The inter-group and intra-group comparisons suggest how well our interleaved evaluation methodology would fare under slightly different conditions. Runs by the same group (intra-group) often share similar algorithms (perhaps varying in parameters), which often yield runs that are similar in effectiveness (or the same). This makes differences more difficult to detect, and indeed, Table 1 shows this to be the

[1] Methodologically, our approach differs from many previous studies that take advantage of click data. For example, Chapelle et al. [3] studied only a handful of systems (far fewer than here) but across far more queries, and hence are able to answer certain types of questions that we cannot. Also, most previous studies do not consider system ties, with He et al. [6] being an exception, but they do not explicitly break out the possible contingencies as we do here.

		Simple Task						Complex Task					
		Agree			Disagree			Agree			Disagree		
Simulation	Judgment	Δ	$\neg\Delta$	Total	Δ	$\neg\Delta$	Total	Δ	$\neg\Delta$	Total	Δ	$\neg\Delta$	Total
All Pairs													
official	official	89.6%	3.7%	93.3%	3.0%	3.7%	6.7%	92.6%	7.4%	100.0%	0	0	0
alternate	alternate	88.8%	3.6%	92.4%	3.5%	4.1%	7.6%	92.3%	7.7%	100.0%	0	0	0
official	alternate	88.4%	3.6%	92.0%	3.8%	4.2%	8.0%	89.2%	5.6%	94.8%	3.1%	2.1%	5.2%
alternate	official	88.7%	3.5%	92.2%	3.9%	3.9%	7.8%	89.2%	5.6%	94.8%	3.4%	1.8%	5.2%
Inter-Group Pairs Only													
official	official	91.1%	2.8%	93.9%	2.8%	3.3%	6.1%	93.9%	6.1%	100.0%	0	0	0
alternate	alternate	90.3%	2.7%	93.0%	3.3%	3.7%	7.0%	93.6%	6.4%	100.0%	0	0	0
official	alternate	89.9%	2.7%	92.6%	3.6%	3.8%	7.4%	90.7%	4.4%	95.1%	2.9%	2.0%	4.9%
alternate	official	90.2%	2.6%	92.8%	3.7%	3.5%	7.2%	90.7%	4.4%	95.1%	3.2%	1.7%	4.9%
Intra-Group Pairs Only													
official	official	65.8%	18.1%	83.9%	5.8%	10.3%	16.1%	71.6%	28.4%	100.0%	0	0	0
alternate	alternate	65.1%	17.8%	82.9%	6.5%	10.6%	17.1%	71.6%	28.4%	100.0%	0	0	0
official	alternate	64.3%	17.9%	82.2%	7.3%	10.5%	17.8%	65.3%	24.0%	89.3%	6.3%	4.4%	10.7%
alternate	official	64.7%	17.6%	82.3%	7.0%	10.7%	17.7%	65.3%	24.0%	89.3%	6.3%	4.4%	10.7%

Table 1: TTG simulation results for both the "simple task" and the "complex task". The "Agree" columns give the percentages of cases where the simulation results agree with the batch evaluation results, when the runs actually differ (Δ), and when the runs don't differ ($\neg\Delta$). The "Disagree" columns give the percentages of cases where the simulation results disagree with the batch evaluation results, when the runs actually differ (Δ), and when the runs don't differ ($\neg\Delta$).

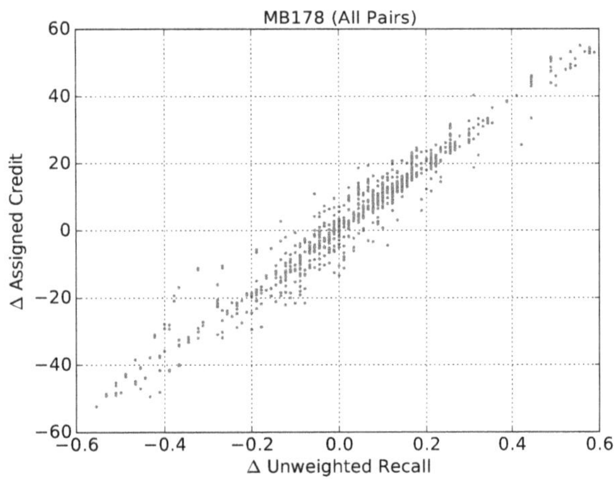

Figure 4: Scatterplot showing batch vs. simulation results for topic MB178.

case (lower agreement). In contrast, differences in effectiveness in runs between groups (inter-group) are slightly easier to detect, as shown by the slightly higher agreement.

To help further visualize our findings, a scatterplot of simulation results is presented in Figure 4 for a representative topic, MB 178, under the all-pairs, (official, official) condition. Each point represents a trial of the simulation comparing a pair of runs: the x coordinate denotes the difference based on the batch evaluation, and the y coordinate denotes the difference in assigned credit based on the simulation. We see that there is a strong correlation between simulation and batch results. Plots from other topics look very similar, except differing in the slope of the trendline (since credit is not normalized, but recall is).

The previous results did not incorporate graded relevance judgments. Our next set of experiments examined this refinement: relevant tweets receive a credit of one and highly-relevant tweets receive a credit of two. The simulated user now indicates the relevance grade for the relevant and redundant cases. There is, however, the question of which batch metric to use: the official TREC evaluation used weighted recall, where the weight of each cluster was proportional to the sum of the relevance grades of tweets in the cluster. This encodes the simple heuristic that "more discussed facets are more important", which seems reasonable, but Wang et al. [22] found that this metric correlated poorly with human preferences, suggesting that cluster size is perhaps not a good measure of importance. We ran simulations correlating against official weighted recall: the results were slightly worse than those in Table 1, but still quite good. For example, we achieved 90% accuracy in the (official, official) condition on the simple task, as opposed to 93%.

However, given the findings of Wang et al., these simulations might not be particularly meaningful. As an alternative, we propose a slightly different approach to computing the cluster weights: instead of the sum of relevance grades of tweets in the cluster, we use the highest relevance grade of tweets in the cluster. That is, if a cluster contains a highly-relevant tweet, it receives a weight of two; otherwise, it receives a weight of one. This weighting scheme has the effect that scores are not dominated by huge clusters. The results of these simulations are shown in Table 2.

From these experiments, we see that accuracy remains quite good, suggesting that our interleaved evaluation methodology is able to take advantage of graded relevance judgments. One important lesson here is that capturing "cluster importance" in TTG is a difficult task, and that it is unclear if present batch evaluations present a reasonable solution. Without a well-justified batch evaluation metric, we lack values against which to correlate our simulation outputs. Thus, these results reveal a weakness in current batch evaluations (indicating avenues of future inquiry), as opposed to a flaw in our interleaved evaluation methodology.

5.2 Prospective Notification

For prospective notification, we validated our interleaved evaluation methodology using runs submitted to the TREC 2015 real-time filtering task ("scenario A"). In total, there

		Simple Task						Complex Task					
		Agree			Disagree			Agree			Disagree		
Simulation	Judgment	Δ	$\neg\Delta$	Total	Δ	$\neg\Delta$	Total	Δ	$\neg\Delta$	Total	Δ	$\neg\Delta$	Total
All Pairs													
official	official	89.9%	3.1%	93.0%	4.1%	2.9%	7.0%	93.3%	5.5%	98.8%	0.7%	0.5%	1.2%
alternate	alternate	89.0%	3.0%	92.0%	4.7%	3.3%	8.0%	92.9%	5.7%	98.6%	0.8%	0.6%	1.4%
official	alternate	88.6%	3.0%	91.6%	5.1%	3.3%	8.4%	89.9%	4.4%	94.3%	3.8%	1.9%	5.7%
alternate	official	88.7%	3.0%	91.7%	1.3%	3.0%	8.3%	90.0%	4.4%	94.4%	4.0%	1.6%	5.6%
Inter-Group Pairs Only													
official	official	91.3%	2.2%	93.5%	3.9%	2.6%	6.5%	94.6%	4.2%	98.9%	0.6%	0.5%	1.1%
alternate	alternate	90.4%	2.2%	92.6%	4.5%	2.9%	7.4%	94.2%	4.5%	98.7%	0.7%	0.6%	1.3%
official	alternate	90.0%	2.1%	92.1%	4.9%	3.0%	7.9%	91.4%	3.3%	94.7%	3.5%	1.8%	5.3%
alternate	official	90.2%	2.1%	92.3%	5.0%	2.7%	7.7%	91.5%	3.3%	94.7%	3.8%	1.5%	5.3%
Intra-Group Pairs Only													
official	official	66.5%	17.2%	83.7%	7.4%	8.9%	16.3%	72.5%	25.0%	97.5%	1.4%	1.1%	2.5%
alternate	alternate	65.8%	16.8%	82.6%	8.2%	9.2%	17.4%	72.6%	25.0%	97.6%	1.4%	1.0%	2.4%
official	alternate	64.7%	17.0%	81.7%	9.3%	9.0%	18.3%	66.3%	21.9%	88.2%	7.7%	4.1%	11.8%
alternate	official	65.3%	16.9%	82.2%	8.6%	9.2%	17.8%	66.3%	22.0%	88.3%	7.6%	4.1%	11.7%

Table 2: TTG simulation results with graded relevance judgments, organized in the same manner as Table 1.

were 37 runs from 14 groups submitted to the official evaluation. This yields a total of 33,966 pairwise comparisons; 32,283 inter-group pairs and 1,683 intra-group pairs.

Simulation results (with graded relevance judgments) are shown in Table 3 for correlations against ELG and in Table 4 for correlations against nCG. The table is organized in the same manner as Tables 1 and 2, with the exception that we only have one set of cluster annotations available, so no "official" vs. "alternate" distinction.

Results of the simulation, shown under the rows marked retaining "quiet days", are quite poor. Analysis reveals that this is due to the handling of days for which there are no relevant tweets. Note that for days without any relevant tweets, there are only two possible scores: one if the system does not return any results, and zero otherwise. Thus, for interest profiles with few relevant tweets, the score is highly dominated by these "quiet days". As a result, a system that does not return anything scores quite highly; in fact, better than most submitted runs [14]. To make matters worse, since 2015 was the first year of this TREC evaluation, systems achieved high scores by simply returning few results, in many cases for totally idiosyncratic reasons—for example, the misconfiguration of a score threshold.

This property of the official evaluation is problematic for interleaved evaluations since it is impossible to tell without future knowledge whether there are relevant tweets for a particular day. Consider the case when system A returns a tweet for a particular day and system B does not return anything, and let's assume we know (based on an oracle) that there are no relevant tweets for that day: according to our interleaved evaluation methodology, neither system would receive any credit. However, based on the batch evaluation, system B would receive a score of one for that day. There is, of course, no way to know this at evaluation time when comparing only two systems, and thus the interleaved evaluation results would disagree with the batch evaluation results. The extent of this disagreement depends on the number of days across the topics for which there were no relevant tweets. Since the interest profiles for the TREC 2015 evaluation had several quiet days each, our interleaved evaluation methodology is not particularly accurate.

We argue, however, that this is more an artifact of the current batch evaluation setup than a flaw in our interleaved evaluation methodology per se; see Tan et al. [21] for further discussion. As the track organizers themselves concede in the TREC overview paper [14], it is not entirely clear if the current handling of days with no relevant tweets is appropriate. While it is no doubt desirable that systems should learn when to "remain quiet", the current batch evaluation methodology yields results that are idiosyncratic in many cases.

To untangle the effect of these "quiet days" in our interleaved evaluation methodology, we conducted experiments where we simply discarded days in which there were no relevant tweets. That is, if an interest profile only contained three days (out of ten) that contained relevant tweets, the score of that topic is simply an average of the scores over those three days. We modified the batch evaluation scripts to also take this into account, and then reran our simulation experiments. The results are shown in Table 3 and Table 4 under the rows marked discarding "quiet days". In this variant, we see that our simulation results are quite accurate, which confirms that the poor accuracy of our initial results is attributable to days where there are no relevant tweets. Once again, this is an issue with the overall TREC evaluation methodology, rather than a flaw in our interleaving approach. These findings highlight the need for additional research on metrics that better model sparse topics. In order to remove this confound, for the remaining prospective notification experiments, we discarded the "quiet days".

Our credit assignment algorithm is recall oriented in that it tries to quantify the total amount of relevant information a user receives, and so it is perhaps not a surprise that credit correlates with nCG. However, experiments show that we also achieve good accuracy correlating with ELG (which is precision oriented). It is observed in the TREC 2015 evaluation [14] that there is reasonable correlation between systems' nCG and ELG scores. There is no principled explanation for this, as prospective notification systems could very well make different precision/recall tradeoffs. However, there is the additional constraint that systems are not allowed to push more than ten tweets per day, so that a high-

	Simple Task						Complex Task					
	Agree			Disagree			Agree			Disagree		
Condition	Δ	¬Δ	Total	Δ	¬Δ	Total	Δ	¬Δ	Total	Δ	¬Δ	Total
Retaining "quiet days"												
All Pairs	45.6%	16.6%	62.2%	37.7%	0.1%	37.8%	45.6%	16.6%	62.2%	37.6%	0.2%	37.8%
Inter-Group Pairs	46.4%	15.3%	61.7%	38.2%	0.1%	38.3%	46.5%	15.3%	61.8%	38.1%	0.1%	38.2%
Intra-Group Pairs	29.0%	41.4%	70.4%	29.1%	0.5%	29.6%	29.5%	41.7%	71.2%	28.6%	0.2%	28.8%
Discarding "quiet days"												
All Pairs	56.7%	34.8%	91.5%	8.4%	0.1%	8.5%	56.8%	34.8%	91.6%	8.3%	0.1%	8.4%
Inter-Group Pairs	58.0%	33.9%	91.9%	8.0%	0.1%	8.1%	58.1%	33.9%	92.0%	7.9%	0.1%	8.0%
Intra-Group Pairs	32.0%	52.7%	84.7%	14.8%	0.5%	15.3%	32.5%	53.0%	85.5%	14.3%	0.2%	14.5%

Table 3: Results of push notification simulations, correlating against ELG.

	Simple Task						Complex Task					
	Agree			Disagree			Agree			Disagree		
Condition	Δ	¬Δ	Total	Δ	¬Δ	Total	Δ	¬Δ	Total	Δ	¬Δ	Total
Retaining "quiet days"												
All Pairs	52.8%	16.7%	69.5%	30.0%	0.5%	30.5%	52.8%	16.8%	69.6%	30.0%	0.4%	30.4%
Inter-Group Pairs	53.5%	15.3%	68.8%	30.7%	0.5%	31.2%	53.6%	15.4%	69.0%	30.6%	0.4%	31.0%
Intra-Group Pairs	38.3%	43.8%	82.1%	17.3%	0.6%	17.9%	37.8%	44.1%	81.9%	17.8%	0.3%	18.1%
Discarding "quiet days"												
All Pairs	62.5%	35.2%	97.7%	2.1%	0.2%	2.3%	62.7%	35.3%	98.0%	2.0%	0	2.0%
Inter-Group Pairs	63.7%	34.1%	97.8%	2.1%	0.1%	2.2%	63.8%	34.3%	98.1%	1.9%	0	1.9%
Intra-Group Pairs	41.2%	55.4%	96.6%	2.9%	0.5%	3.4%	40.9%	55.8%	96.7%	3.3%	0	3.3%

Table 4: Results of push notification simulations, correlating against nCG.

	Summarization	Notification
All Pairs	92.8%	96.9%
Inter-Group Pairs	94.0%	97.9%
Intra-Group Pairs	73.7%	76.5%

Table 5: Lengths of interleaved results as a percentage of the sum of the lengths of the individual runs.

volume low-precision system would quickly use up its "daily quota". Additionally, we suspect that since TREC 2015 represented the first large-scale evaluation of this task, teams have not fully explored the design space.

5.3 Assessor Effort: Output Length

We next turn our attention to two issues related to assessor effort: the length of the interleaved system output (this subsection) and the effort involved in providing explicit judgments in our interaction model (next subsection).

One downside of our temporal interleaving strategy is that the interleaved results are longer than the individual system outputs. Exactly how much longer is shown in Table 5, where the lengths of the interleaved results are shown as a percentage of the sum of the lengths of the individual runs. The lengths are not 100% because the individual system outputs may contain overlap, and comparisons between runs from the same group contain more overlap. Nevertheless, we can see that temporal interleaving produces output that is substantially longer than each of the individual system outputs. This is problematic for two reasons: first, it means a substantial increase in evaluation effort, and second, the interleaving produces a different user experience in terms of the verbosity of the system.

There is, however, a simple solution to this issue: after temporal interleaving, for each result we flip a biased coin and retain it with probability p. That is, we simply decide to discard some fraction of the results. Figure 5 shows the results of these experiments. On the x axis we sweep across p, the retention probability, and on the y axis we plot the simulation accuracy (i.e., agreement between simulation credit and batch results). The left plot shows the results for retrospective summarization using unweighted recall and the (official, official) condition; the rest of the graphs look similar and so we omit them for brevity. In the middle plot, we show accuracy against ELG for prospective notification and against nCG on the right (both discarding quiet days). Since there is randomness associated with these simulations, the plots represent averages over three trials.

We see that simulation results remain quite accurate even if we discard a relatively large fraction of system output. For the prospective task, accuracy is higher for lower p values because there are many intra-group ties. At $p = 0$, accuracy is simply the fraction of "no difference" comparisons. Based on these results, an experiment designer can select a desired tradeoff between accuracy and verbosity. With p around 0.5 to 0.6, we obtain an interleaved result that is roughly the same length as the source systems—and in that region we still achieve good prediction accuracy. It is even possible to generate interleaved results that are shorter than the input runs. Overall, we believe that this simple approach adequately addresses the length issue.

5.4 Assessor Effort: Explicit Judgments

Another potential objection to our interleaved evaluation methodology is that our interaction model depends on explicit judgments for credit assignment, as opposed to implicit judgments (i.e., clicks) in the case of interleaved evaluations for web ranking. This issue warrants some discussion, because the ability to gather implicit judgments based on be-

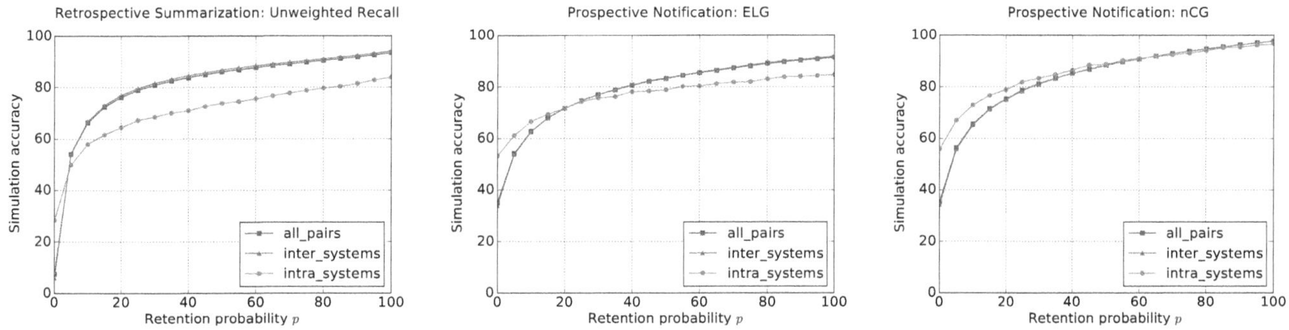

Figure 5: Simulation accuracy as a function of retention probability p for unweighted recall on retrospective summarization (left); ELG (middle) and nCG (right) for prospective summarization.

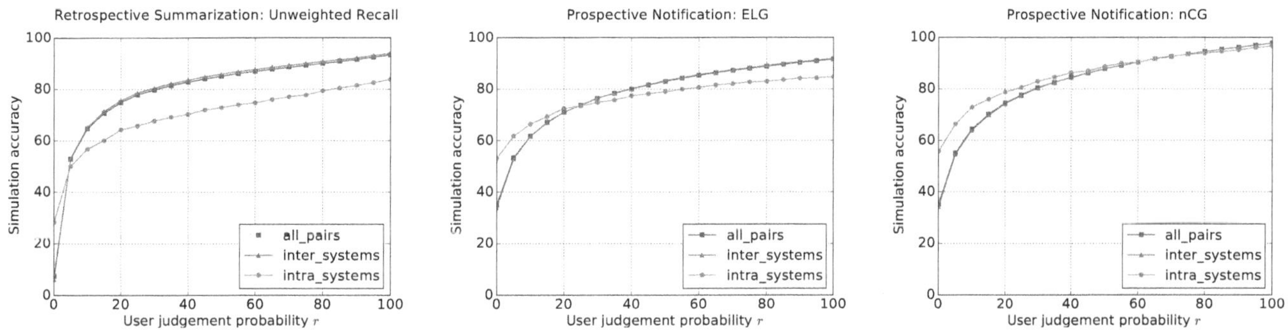

Figure 6: Simulation accuracy as a function of user judgment probability r for unweighted recall on retrospective summarization (left); ELG (middle) and nCG (right) for prospective summarization.

havioral data greatly expands the volume of feedback we can easily obtain (e.g., from log data).

We have two responses: First, it is premature to explore implicit interactions for our tasks. For web search, there is a large body of work spanning over two decades that has validated the interpretation of click data for web ranking preferences—including the development of click models [1, 4], eye-tracking studies [5, 9], extensive user studies [10], and much more [11]. In short, we have a pretty good idea of how users interact with web search results, which justifies the interpretation of click data. None of this exists for retrospective summarization and prospective notification. Furthermore, interactions with tweets in our case are more complex: some tweets have embedded videos, images, or links. There are many different types of clicks: the user can "expand" a tweet, thereby showing details of the embedded object and from there take additional actions, e.g., play the embedded video directly, click on the link to navigate away from the result, etc. Not taking any overt action on a tweet doesn't necessary mean that the tweet is not relevant—the succinct nature of tweets means that relevant information can be quickly absorbed, perhaps without leaving any behavioral trails. Thus, any model of implicit interactions we could develop at this point would lack empirical grounding. More research is necessary to better understand how users interact with retrospective summarization and prospective notification systems. With a better understanding, we can then compare models of implicit feedback with the explicit feedback results presented here.

Our second response argues that in the case of prospective notifications, an explicit feedback model might not actually be unrealistic. Recall that such updates are putatively delivered via mobile phone notifications, and as such, they are presented one at a time to the user—depending on the user's settings, each notification may be accompanied by an auditory or physical cue (a chime or a vibration) to attract the user's attention. In most implementations today the notification can be dismissed by the user or the user can take additional action (e.g., click on the notification to open the mobile app). These are already quite explicit actions with relatively clear user intent—it is not far-fetched to imagine that these interactions can be further refined to provide explicit judgments without degrading the user experience.

Nevertheless, the issue of assessor effort in providing explicit judgments is still a valid concern. However, we can potentially address this issue in the same way as the length issue discussed above. Let us assume that the user provides interaction data with probability r. That is, as we run the simulation, we flip a biased coin and observe each judgment with only probability r. In the prospective notification case, we argue that this is not unrealistic—the user "pays attention" to the notification message with probability r; the rest of the time, the user ignores the update.

Figure 6 shows the results of these experiments (averaged over three trials). On the x axis we sweep across r, the interaction probability and on the y axis we plot the simulation accuracy. The left plot shows the results for retrospective summarization using unweighted recall and the (official, official) condition. In the middle plot, we show accuracy against ELG for prospective notification and against nCG on the right (once again, discarding quiet days in both cases). Experiments show that we are able to accurately decide the relative effectiveness of the comparison systems even with limited user interactions.

The next obvious question, of course, is what if we combined both the length analysis and interaction probabil-

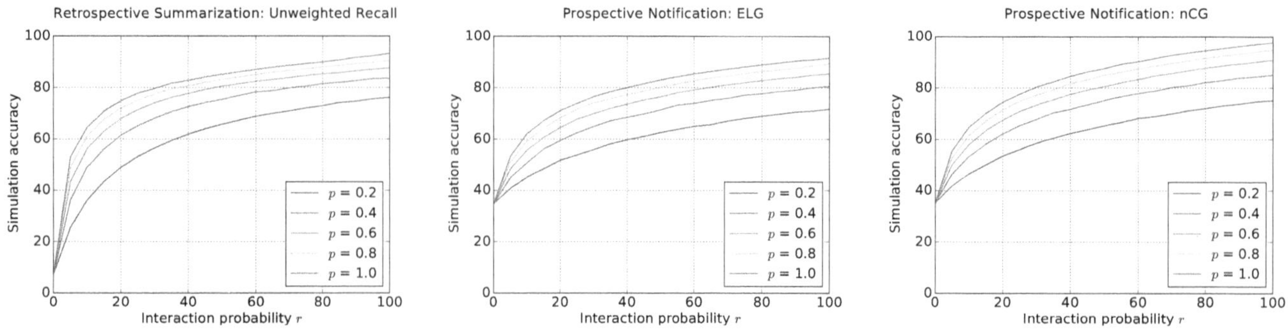

Figure 7: Simulation accuracy combining both retention probability p and interaction probability r.

ity analysis? These results are shown in Figure 7, organized in the same manner as the other graphs (also averaged over three trials). For clarity, we only show results for all pairs. The interaction probability r is plotted on the x axis, with lines representing retention probability $p = \{0.2, 0.4, 0.6, 0.8, 1.0\}$. As expected, we are able to achieve good accuracy, even while randomly discarding system output, and with limited interactions. Given these tradeoff curves, an experiment designer can strike the desired balance between accuracy and verbosity.

6. CONCLUSIONS

In this paper, we describe and validate a novel interleaved evaluation methodology for two complementary information seeking tasks on document streams: retrospective summarization and prospective notification. We present a temporal interleaving strategy and a heuristic credit assignment method based on a user interaction model with explicit judgments. Simulations on TREC data demonstrate that our evaluation methodology yields high fidelity comparisons of the relative effectiveness of different systems, compared to the results of batch evaluations.

Although interleaved evaluations for web search are routinely deployed in production environments, we believe that our work is novel in that it tackles two completely different information seeking scenarios. Retrospective summarization and prospective notification are becoming increasingly important as users continue the shift from desktops to mobile devices for information seeking. There remains much more work, starting with a better understanding of user interactions so that we can develop models of implicit judgment and thereby greatly expand the scope of our evaluations, but this paper takes an important first step.

7. ACKNOWLEDGMENTS

This work was supported in part by the U.S. National Science Foundation (NSF) under awards IIS-1218043 and CNS-1405688 and the Natural Sciences and Engineering Research Council of Canada (NSERC). All views expressed here are solely those of the authors. We'd like to thank Charlie Clarke and Luchen Tan for helpful discussions.

8. REFERENCES

[1] E. Agichtein, E. Brill, S. Dumais, and R. Ragno. Learning user interaction models for predicting web search result preferences. *SIGIR*, 2006.

[2] J. Aslam, M. Ekstrand-Abueg, V. Pavlu, F. Diaz, R. McCreadie, and T. Sakai. TREC 2014 Temporal Summarization Track overview. *TREC*, 2014.

[3] O. Chapelle, T. Joachims, F. Radlinski, and Y. Yue. Large-scale validation and analysis of interleaved search evaluation. *ACM TOIS*, 30(1):Article 6, 2012.

[4] O. Chapelle and Y. Zhang. A Dynamic Bayesian Network click model for web search ranking. *WWW*, 2009.

[5] L. Granka, T. Joachims, and G. Gay. Eye-tracking analysis of user behavior in WWW search. *SIGIR*, 2004.

[6] J. He, C. Zhai, and X. Li. Evaluation of methods for relative comparison of retrieval systems based on clickthroughs. *CIKM*, 2009.

[7] K. Hofmann, S. Whiteson, and M. de Rijke. A probabilistic method for inferring preferences from clicks. *CIKM*, 2011.

[8] T. Joachims. Optimizing search engines using clickthrough data. *KDD*, 2002.

[9] T. Joachims, L. Granka, B. Pan, H. Hembrooke, F. Radlinski, and G. Gay. Evaluating the accuracy of implicit feedback from clicks and query reformulations in web search. *ACM TOIS*, 25(2):1–27, 2007.

[10] D. Kelly. Understanding implicit feedback and document preference: A naturalistic user study. *SIGIR Forum*, 38(1):77–77, 2004.

[11] D. Kelly and J. Teevan. Implicit feedback for inferring user preference: A bibliography. *SIGIR Forum*, 37(2):18–28, 2003.

[12] R. Kohavi, R. M. Henne, and D. Sommerfield. Practical guide to controlled experiments on the web: Listen to your customers not to the HiPPO. *KDD*, 2007.

[13] J. Lin, M. Efron, Y. Wang, and G. Sherman. Overview of the TREC-2014 Microblog Track. *TREC*, 2014.

[14] J. Lin, M. Efron, Y. Wang, G. Sherman, and E. Voorhees. Overview of the TREC-2015 Microblog Track. *TREC*, 2015.

[15] F. Radlinski and N. Craswell. Comparing the sensitivity of information retrieval metrics. *SIGIR*, 2010.

[16] F. Radlinski and N. Craswell. Optimized interleaving for online retrieval evaluation. *WSDM*, 2013.

[17] F. Radlinski, M. Kurup, and T. Joachims. How does clickthrough data reflect retrieval quality? *CIKM*, 2008.

[18] T. Sakai, N. Craswell, R. Song, S. Robertson, Z. Dou, and C. Lin. Simple evaluation metrics for diversified search results. *EVIA*, 2010.

[19] A. Schuth, K. Hofmann, and F. Radlinski. Predicting search satisfaction metrics with interleaved comparisons. *SIGIR*, 2015.

[20] A. Schuth, F. Sietsma, S. Whiteson, D. Lefortier, and M. de Rijke. Multileaved comparisons for fast online evaluation. *CIKM*, 2014.

[21] L. Tan, A. Roegiest, J. Lin, and C. L. A. Clarke. An exploration of evaluation metrics for mobile push notifications. *SIGIR*, 2016.

[22] Y. Wang, G. Sherman, J. Lin, and M. Efron. Assessor differences and user preferences in tweet timeline generation. *SIGIR*, 2015.

[23] C. X. Zhai, W. W. Cohen, and J. Lafferty. Beyond independent relevance: Methods and evaluation metrics for subtopic retrieval. *SIGIR*, 2003.

Learning Query and Document Relevance from a Web-scale Click Graph

Shan Jiang[†], Yuening Hu[‡], Changsung Kang[‡], Tim Daly Jr.[‡], Dawei Yin[‡], Yi Chang[‡], Chengxiang Zhai[†]

[†]Department of Computer Science
University of Illinois at Urbana-Champaign
Urbana, IL, 61801
{sjiang18,czhai}@illinois.edu

[‡]Yahoo Research
Sunnyvale, CA, USA
{ynhu,ckang,timjr,daweiy,yichang}@yahoo-inc.com

ABSTRACT

Click-through logs over query-document pairs provide rich and valuable information for multiple tasks in information retrieval. This paper proposes a vector propagation algorithm on the click graph to learn vector representations for both queries and documents in the same semantic space. The proposed approach incorporates both click and content information, and the produced vector representations can directly improve ranking performance for queries and documents that have been observed in the click log. For new queries and documents that are not in the click log, we propose a two-step framework to generate the vector representation, which significantly improves the coverage of our vectors while maintaining the high quality. Experiments on Web-scale search logs from a major commercial search engine demonstrate the effectiveness and scalability of the proposed method. Evaluation results show that NDCG scores are significantly improved against multiple baselines by using the proposed method both as a ranking model and as a feature in a learning-to-rank framework.

Categories and Subject Descriptors

[**Information retrieval**]: Information retrieval query processing—*Query log analysis*; [**Information retrieval**]: Retrieval models and ranking—*Similarity measures*

Keywords

Click-through bipartite graph, vector propagation, vector generation, Web search, query-document relevance

1. INTRODUCTION

Incorporating user feedback is one of the most effective ways to improve a search engine. For a commercial search engine with a large audience, this can be done by logging user actions – the queries they issued, the results they saw, the clicks they made, and so on. This behavioral data can be used to create a training target for a machine learned ranking function, or turned into features to improve the performance of the ranking function. In fact, click-based features are used as one of the primary sources to improve the ranking quality for popular queries.

However, the click information is sometimes *noisy*, and the coverage of clicks is quite limited compared to all possible relevant query-document pairs, which produces *sparsity* for the click-based features [9]. The sparsity and noise problems impact the overall quality of click-based features, especially for less popular queries.

To deal with these problems, an effective way is to learn a vector representation for both queries and documents in the same space [12, 25, 27]. Traditional methods typically learn low-rank vectors in a latent space. Though the low rank embedding of queries and documents has its own advantages, it also has some weaknesses. For example, it hurts interpretability and debuggability of the ranking function because individual dimensions in the latent space are hard to interpret. In comparison, using word features gives a more interpretable representation. However, direct text matching methods, e.g. BM25 [22] and the language models [28], suffer from the lexical gap between queries and documents which is shown to exist by previous study [20].[1] Thus, how to represent both queries and documents in the same semantic space and explore their relevance based on the click logs, remains a challenge.

Moreover, we need an approach that can be generalized to represent the queries and documents that have never been observed in the search logs. This is especially important in real applications because new queries and documents are emerging every day. However, purely click-based features are limited by the range of previous logs, and improving their coverage is a challenge.

Finally, though a Web-scale click graph provides us with unprecedentedly rich information, it also brings in great challenge of how to consume the entire click log efficiently rather than focus on a small sample. As a result, we need

SIGIR '16, July 17-21, 2016, Pisa, Italy
© 2016 ACM. ISBN 978-1-4503-4069-4/16/07... $15.00
DOI: http://dx.doi.org/10.1145/2911451.2911531

[1]Lexical gap means that the query terms are different from the corresponding terms in relevant documents in terms of string matching.

an efficient and scalable approach that can be easily applied to large scale click logs.

To solve all these challenges in a unified framework, this paper proposes a propagation approach to learn vector representation based on both content and click information (Section 2). The vector representation learned by our algorithm can directly improve the ranking performance for queries and documents that have been observed in the click log. For queries and documents that are not in the click graph, which are referred as *click-absent* queries and documents, we further propose a two-step vector estimation algorithm which generates a representation based on their association with the vectors that are already created by propagation on the click graph (Section 3). This generalization significantly improves the coverage of our vectors, which is particularly important for long-tail queries in web search.

This whole framework is very efficient and scalable, especially compared to matrix factorization-based methods [12, 25, 27]. Since a search engine click log can grow by many millions of new entries in a single day, this scalability is essential. In the experiments (Section 4), we collect click-through log data from a major commercial search engine, which contains 25 billion query-document pairs in total, and demonstrate the effectiveness of our proposed approach used as an individual ranking model and a feature in the learn-to-rank framework. More analysis and case study about why and how the proposed approach improves ranking are discussed in Section 5.

To summarize, our main contributions include:

- A unified approach, which generates the semantic representations for both queries and documents in an explicit and interpretable way.
- A generalized method, which estimates vector representations for any unseen queries and documents.
- A scalable and efficient framework, which is easy to implement and works effectively in a real commercial search engine.

2. VECTOR PROPAGATION ON THE CLICK GRAPH

Click-through data provides a soft indicator of relevance between queries and documents, and click-based features are one type of the most important and effective features in ranking task. However, purely click-based features highly rely on the users' behavior, and it sometimes suffers from sparsity and noise in the click data, especially for less popular queries. On the other hand, content-based features capture the intrinsic relevance embedded in the text content, and they are independent of other resources such as click logs. However, the lexical gap between queries and documents and the fact of missing users' feedback make the content-based features less effective in real ranking problems.

This paper bridges the two information resources and proposes a vector propagation algorithm which makes use of both click and content information to learn the vector presentation of queries and documents. This algorithm not only introduces new words from the relevant queries and documents through the propagation, but also smoothes the term weights based on the click information. Besides, the sparsity and noise are also reduced during this process thus better quality of the vector representations is guaranteed. Once we obtain the vectors for queries and documents, similarity functions such as cosine similarity can be applied to compute the query-document relevance.

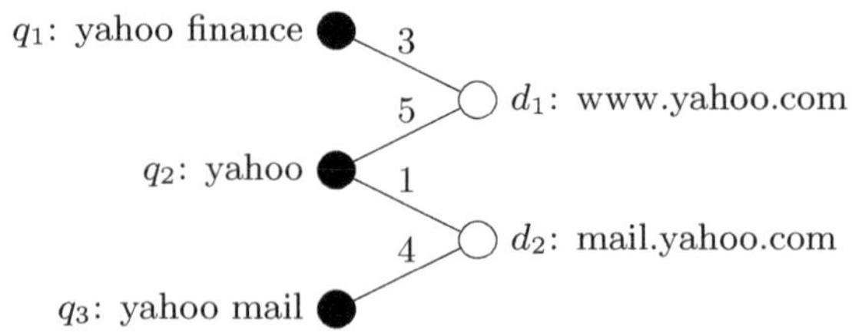

Figure 1: An example of click-through bipartite graph.

2.1 Preliminaries and Notations

Click-through data consists of queries and documents with their co-click information[2]. Let $\mathcal{D}oc$ be the set of documents and $\mathcal{Q}uery$ be the set of queries. We construct the click graph $\mathcal{G}$ with the node set $\mathcal{V} = \mathcal{D}oc \cup \mathcal{Q}uery$. For a document $d \in \mathcal{D}oc$ and a query $q \in \mathcal{Q}uery$, if there is at least one co-click between them, i.e., at least one user clicked on d when he or she searched for query q, an edge is built between them. The weight of the edge is set to be the number of co-clicks. The set of edges in the graph is denoted as $\mathcal{E}$. An example of the click graph is shown in Figure 1. Documents are denoted as open circles and labeled by the corresponding URL, while queries are represented as solid circles.

The adjacency matrix of the graph is denoted as C where the entry in the i-th row and j-th column ($C_{i,j}$) equals to the weight of the edge between query q_i and document d_j. If there is no edge between them, $C_{i,j}$ is 0.

We denote Q as the matrix where i-th row Q_i is the vector representation of query q_i. $Q^{(n)}$ is the query vector matrix at the n-th iteration. If the vocabulary size is V, then the size of Q is $|\mathcal{Q}uery| \times V$. Similarly we denote D as the document vector matrix and its size is $|\mathcal{D}oc| \times V$.

2.2 Vector Propagation Algorithm

The goal of this vector propagation algorithm is to learn the representation of queries and documents in the same semantic space (either the query space or the document space). It starts with the content information initialized as vectors on one side of the click graph, and propagates the vectors to the connected nodes on the other side of the click graph. Co-clicks between queries and documents are used to weight the vectors so that the important terms stand out while less informative terms are gradually filtered out. More details are introduced as follows.

We first choose one side of the click graph (either side) and initialize the vectors based on the content information, e.g., the query words on the query side, or the titles and abstracts on the document side. This initialization keeps the word-level information in the vectors. Words can be considered as human-designed features and past studies have repeatedly shown that keeping the word-level representation is very helpful. In traditional content-based models such as VSM [23], vocabulary from query and document is merged together. Though it makes the vector representation easier and more natural, it may also bring in the lexical gap between queries and documents [20]. Our method starts with

[2]If a document is clicked by a user for a proposed query, it is referred as a co-clicked query-document pair in this paper.

one vocabulary space, and learns the vectors for queries and documents based on one consistent vocabulary space (either query vocabulary or the document vocabulary). Thus the lexical gap is reduced.

In the next step, vectors are propagated through the click graph. Our basic idea is to represent queries based on their relevant documents and vice versa. Queries that are co-clicked with a lot of common documents should have similar representations, and documents sharing many co-clicked queries should also be close in the vector space. Moreover, the click information is a soft indicator of relevance and the confidence of relevance is positively correlated to the number of clicks. Thus, co-clicked pairs that have a higher frequency should dominate the vectors. The propagation starts from the side where vectors are initialized, then the initialized vectors are weighted by the clicks and propagated to the connected nodes on the other side of the click graph. For example, if we start from the query side, the document vectors are calculated by aggregating all query vectors that are co-clicked with them. In the next iteration, vectors are propagated in the opposite direction, and this process is conducted repeatedly until convergence.

We take starting from the query side as an example. In the initialization, each query is represented by its own words. Words are weighted in proportion to their frequency and normalized by the $\mathcal{L}2$ norm. The initialized vector matrix is denote as $Q^{(0)}$. In the n-th iteration ($n \geq 1$), we first compute document vectors $D^{(n)}$ by a weighted summation of their co-clicked queries where the weights depend on the number of clicks. Formally, given the j-th document d_j, its vector representation $D_j^{(n)}$ is calculated as:

$$D_j^{(n)} = \frac{1}{||\sum_{i=1}^{|\mathcal{Q}uery|} C_{i,j} \cdot Q_i^{(n-1)}||_2} \sum_{i=1}^{|\mathcal{Q}uery|} C_{i,j} \cdot Q_i^{(n-1)} \quad (1)$$

where $Q_i^{(n-1)}$ is the vector representation for the i-th query in the (n-1)-th iteration. $D_j^{(n)}$ is also normalized by $\mathcal{L}2$ norm. Then the query vectors in $Q^{(n)}$ are updated based on their co-clicked document vectors:

$$Q_i^{(n)} = \frac{1}{||\sum_j^{|\mathcal{D}oc|} C_{i,j} \cdot D_j^{(n)}||_2} \sum_{j=1}^{|\mathcal{D}oc|} C_{i,j} \cdot D_j^{(n)} \quad (2)$$

Through this propagation process, we learn the vectors for both queries and documents using the query vocabulary. Without the lexical gap, better query-document relevance can be achieved. Similarly, if we start from the document side, document vectors (denoted as $D^{(0)}$) are initialized by using their content words, and the vector propagation starts from the document side to the query side in each iteration:

$$Q_i^{(n)} = \frac{1}{||\sum_j^{|\mathcal{D}oc|} C_{i,j} \cdot D_j^{(n-1)}||_2} \sum_{j=1}^{|\mathcal{D}oc|} C_{i,j} \cdot D_j^{(n-1)} \quad (3)$$

$$D_j^{(n)} = \frac{1}{||\sum_{i=1}^{|\mathcal{Q}uery|} C_{i,j} \cdot Q_i^{(n)}||_2} \sum_{i=1}^{|\mathcal{Q}uery|} C_{i,j} \cdot Q_i^{(n)} \quad (4)$$

Take the click graph in Figure 1 as an example. If we start from the query side, Q_1, Q_2 and Q_3 are initialized as {yahoo:$\frac{1}{\sqrt{2}}$, finance:$\frac{1}{\sqrt{2}}$, mail:0}, {yahoo:1, finance:0, mail:0} and {yahoo:$\frac{1}{\sqrt{2}}$, finance:0, mail: $\frac{1}{\sqrt{2}}$} respectively. Then document vectors are derived from the co-clicked queries. For instance, the vector representation for d_1 (D_1) is calculated as $(\frac{3}{8}Q_1 + \frac{5}{8}Q_2)/||\frac{3}{8}Q_1 + \frac{5}{8}Q_2||_2$. If we start from the document side, we first initialize the document vectors by their titles: "Yahoo Finance - Business Finance, Stock Market, Quotes, News" and "Yahoo" for d_1 and d_2 respectively.[3] Then the document vectors are propagated to the query side and the query vectors are generated in a similar way. Because of the lexical gap between queries and documents, the learned vectors starting from different sides are indeed different, and in fact they complement each other in the real ranking system. More analysis is in Section 5.

The proposed vector propagation is similar to the importance propagation in HITS algorithm [14]. In HITS algorithm, mutual reinforcement bonds the authority and hub scores through the Web link structure, while our propagation algorithm aims at mutual improvement of query and document vector representations. Instead of propagating importance scores, we propagate the feature vectors which are derived from the text content. In this way, both content and click information are encoded in the learned vectors.

In practice, we represent each vector in a sparse way (only keeping the terms with non-zero weights), which helps to increase the computational speed. However, a potential problem in this propagation algorithm is the rapid growth of the non-zero entries, which leads to a considerable increase in time and space consumption in a Web-scale scenario. However, if we rank the terms in a vector according to their weights, we can clearly see that the vectors have long tails: the weights drop significantly after the first few terms, and the remaining terms in the vector have very small weights (examples can be found in Section 5.1). Thus we can simply keep the top K terms with the highest weights for both query and document vectors in each iteration to further reduce both time and space consumption.

3. VECTOR GENERATION FOR CLICK-ABSENT QUERIES AND DOCUMENTS

Though the vector propagation algorithm proposed in Section 2 enables us to get the relevance feature for any query-document pair in the click graph, it still cannot handle queries or documents that have no click information. As a matter of fact, the ability to deal with click-absent queries and documents is of great importance in real applications, since we can always see new queries and documents that are not included in previous logs.

An intuitive way is to use bag-of-words model to generate their vector representations, e.g., use the query words to represent the queries, and use the title words to represent the documents. However, it introduces the lexical gap between queries and documents that we try to avoid in this paper, and it is limited to the content words instead of expanding the vectors with additional related terms. Besides, it also breaks the indirect connections between the click-absent queries/documents and the documents/queries in the click graph, thus reweighting cannot be learned from the clicks.

To better estimate the vectors for click-absent queries and documents, this section proposes a novel and efficient two-step framework. We first break down queries or document titles (depending on from which side we start from in the vector propagation algorithm) into different units (e.g.,

[3] Titles are extracted from the HTML sources.

Figure 2: An example of unit vector generation. (The black thin lines are the edge of the click graph, while the edges represented by the gray thick lines indicate the pseudo clicks between units and documents.)

ngrams), and learn a vector representation for each unit based on the vectors we have already learned from the click graph. We then learn a weight for each unit by a regression model, and finally estimate the vectors for the click-absent queries and documents by a linear combination of the unit vectors. This framework connects the click-absent queries and documents to the click graph through the unit vectors and gets high-quality representations for them, thus enlarges the coverage of the vectors.

3.1 Extracting Unit Vectors

Vectors learned by the propagation algorithm keep word-level features, which provides a potential bridge to connect the click-absent queries and documents with those in the click graph. Even though we cannot exactly match a new query or document with an existing one in the search logs, the key words or phrases of these new queries and documents may be already contained in the observed queries and documents. These key terms (such as unigrams, bigrams and trigrams) can be treated as basic message units in both click-absent and existing queries and documents, and we can get these ngram units from the text content. More specifically, if the propagation starts from the query side, all the queries are broken into unigrams, bigrams and trigrams. Similarly, document contents such as titles or abstracts are decomposed to ngrams if we use document vocabulary. The set of units is denoted as $\mathcal{U}$.

The next step is to learn a vector representation for each unit. In the vector propagation algorithm (Section 2), query vectors are learned by aggregating document vectors according to their co-clicking relationship, and we can learn the unit vectors in a similar way. Let's assume the vector propagation starts from the query side and first build up the unit vectors in the query vocabulary space. For each unit u_i in $\mathcal{U}$, we find all the queries containing the unit u_i, and denote the set as O_{u_i}. We also find all the documents that are connected to any of these queries, and denote the document vector set as K_{u_i}. Next, we connect u_i with vectors in K_{u_i} based on the click information: for the k-th vector in O_{u_i} and the j-th vector in K_{u_i} (denoted as $O_{u_i}(k)$ and $K_{u_i}(j)$ respectively), if there is a click between their corresponding query and document, we say that there is a pseudo click between u_i and $K_{u_i}(j)$ through $O_{u_i}(k)$, denoted as $P_{i,k,j}$. The value $P_{i,k,j}$ equals to the query-document co-click number $C_{k,j}$. If we aggregate all the pseudo clicks between u_i and $K_{u_i}(j)$ over all queries in O_{u_i}, we get the pseudo click between u_i and $K_{u_i}(j)$ and denote it as $P_{i,j}$:

$$P_{i,j} = \sum\nolimits_{k=1}^{|O_{u_i}|} P_{i,k,j} \tag{5}$$

As the example shown in Figure 2, if u_i is "yahoo" and the propagation starts from the query side, O_{u_i} is the set of queries that contains the unit "yahoo". In this example, we have three queries in O_{u_i}, which are q_1, q_2 and q_3 respectively. d_1 and d_2 are found to be co-clicked documents for these three queries, so their vectors constitute K_{u_i}. The pseudo clicks are built between them and u_i with aggregated weights. If the unit is a bigram or trigram, we only consider the queries that contain the unit as a bigram or trigram. For example, if the unit is "yahoo finance", then queries containing "yahoo" and "finance" as separate unigrams (e.g., "yahoo news in finance") are not included.

Finally, the vector representation of u_i (denoted as U_i) is calculated by a weighted sum of vectors in K_{u_i}, normalized by $\mathcal{L}2$ norm:

$$U_i = \frac{1}{||\sum_{j=1}^{|K_{u_i}|} P_{i,j} \cdot K_{u_i}(j)||_2} \sum_{j=1}^{|K_{u_i}|} P_{i,j} \cdot K_{u_i}(j) \tag{6}$$

Similarly, if the vector propagation starts from the document side, we extract all the units from the document content. Then for each unit u_i, we find all the documents containing the unit u_i and denote the set as O_{u_i}, then find all the queries that are connected to any of these documents and denote their vectors as K_{u_i}. We then can follow the same process to build up the connections between units and the query vectors to estimate the unit vectors in the document vocabulary space.

As we can see from this process, these unit vectors are generated from the related query or document vectors that are learned by the propagation algorithm in the click graph, so click information is also embedded in them.

3.2 Learning Unit Weights

In the next step, we learn a weight per unit to capture the importance for each unit globally, which is later used for generation of vectors for click-absent queries and documents. Here we learn the weights through a linear regression model, and the vectors where the units originate from are used as training examples (named as target vectors for convenience). The basic idea is to use the linear combination of unit vectors to approximate the target vectors, and then minimize the difference between the target vector and the approximated vector which is measured by the square of Euclidean distance:

$$\min_W \sum_{i=1}^{|T|} ||T_i - \sum_{u_j \in \mathcal{U}_{T_i}^{all}} W_j \cdot U_j||_2^2 \quad (7)$$

where T is the set of target vectors and T_i is the i-th vector in T. If the units originates from queries, T consists of all the query vectors learned by the propagation algorithm; otherwise it contains all the document vectors. $\mathcal{U}_{T_i}^{all}$ is the set of all the units (unigrams, bigrams and trigrams, excluding itself) contained in the corresponding query or document content of T_i. W is the weight vector with the j-th entry W_j representing the weight for u_j in the unit set $\mathcal{U}$.

3.3 Estimating Vectors

In Section 3.1 and Section 3.2, we introduce how to generate the unit vectors and weights respectively. Given a new query or document without any click information, we can represent it by the weighted combination of unit vectors.

For a click-absent query q, we first decompose it into all possible units. If a unigram is contained in a bigram, or a bigram is contained a trigram, it is removed to avoid overlapping information. For example, given a new query, "walmart credit card", assume the set of unigrams, bigrams and trigrams contained in unit vocabulary includes {"walmart", "credit", "card", "credit card"}, then we only keep "walmart" and "credit card" in the unit set. The final unit set which is decomposed from q by the above rule is denoted as $\mathcal{U}_q$. Then the query vector q_v is calculated as a linear combination of the unit vectors in $\mathcal{U}_q$:

$$q_v = \sum\nolimits_{u_i \in \mathcal{U}_q} W_i U_i \quad (8)$$

For a click-absent document d, we can estimate its vector representation in a similar way. Any possible content of documents can be used, and here we use document titles, which are concise yet provide key information. We decompose the title of d to a unit set $\mathcal{U}_d$ according to the same rule as mentioned above, and the vector d_v is calculated as:

$$d_v = \sum\nolimits_{u_i \in \mathcal{U}_d} W_i U_i \quad (9)$$

Note that this generation algorithm estimates the vectors either in query vocabulary space or in the document vocabulary space, depending on how the unit vectors are built. Based on the vector propagation algorithm and the above vector generation algorithm, we now represent all queries and documents in the same semantic space. Relevance between any query-document pair can be measured by similarity functions such as cosine similarity, which is further used as a feature for ranking.

4. EXPERIMENTS

We apply the proposed method to a Web-scale click graph from a major commercial search engine. The learned relevance score can be either used directly to rank documents for a given query or employed as one of the features in a learning-to-rank framework. We show that the proposed method helps to improve ranking results in both cases.

4.1 Dataset

We construct the click-through bipartite graph from a major commercial search engine's search log. There are about 25 billion co-clicked query-document pairs, containing about 8 billion unique queries and 3 billion unique documents.

To investigate whether the relevance score learned by our algorithm can help to improve ranking in a learning-to-rank framework, we use another dataset that includes 63k queries and 775k query-document pairs as training examples and 16k queries with 243k query-document pairs as test set. The relevance score of each pair ("perfect", "excellent", "good", "fair" or "bad") is annotated by human annotators. 92.5% of these testing queries can be found in the search log and the others do not have click information. 78.9% of the testing documents are in the search log. For the 21.1% documents missing in the search log (about 51k documents), 91.7% of them have titles.

4.2 As an Individual Ranking Model

To give more insight into how well the proposed method captures the relevance between queries and documents, we use the relevance scores to rank documents and calculate NDCG scores to evaluate the performance. The trimming parameter K in vector propagation algorithm is set as 20.[4] We compare our methods against multiple baseline methods:

- **VPCG** is our vector propagation algorithm proposed in Section 2, and the generalized version **VPCG&VG** also predicts the vectors for the click-absent queries and documents as in Section 3. **_QUERY** and **_DOC** denote that the propagation starts from the query or document side, respectively.
- **BM25SD**, a better variation of traditional BM25 [22], uses individual words, ordered and unordered word sequences from page content to compute the score [6].
- **BM25SD_MULT**, a linear combination of BM25SD across multiple fields including page content, anchor text, and query words for which the document was clicked.
- **CTR**, a behavioral feature which measures the ratio between the impressions and the nevigational clicks in a sessions for each query-document pair, where a navigational click is defined as the only click in a session, and a session is defined as some timeout (e.g. 30 minutes) between queries for the same user. The lower bound of wilson confidence interval for this ratio in multiple sessions is used as the final feature value.
- **WMD**, a word embedding-based framework using the Word Mover's Distance [15] to measure the query-document relevance, based on a word embedding vector set trained from Google News [19].[5]

As shown in Table 1, our methods VPCG and VPCG&VG in general achieve the best performance. VPCG_QUERY performs even better than VPCG_DOC, most likely because titles sometimes contain noisy words or are not descriptive of page content. However, VPCG_QUERY and VPCG_DOC capture the query-document similarity from different viewpoints and complement each other, which is further discussed in Section 5. The generalized version VPCG&VG_QUERY

[4]Multiple experiments are done to evaluate the sensitivity of the selection of K, but it turns to be not very sensitive, thus we use $K = 20$ in this paper.

[5]The Google News word vectors are available in https://code.google.com/p/word2vec/

Table 1: Performance as an individual ranking model.

Feature	NDCG@1	NDCG@3	NDCG@5	NDCG@10
BM25SD	0.4373	0.4937	0.5460	0.6542
BM25SD_MULT	0.6132	0.6346	0.6668	0.7464
CTR	0.5769	0.5941	0.6238	0.7064
WMD	0.4585	0.5145	0.5641	0.6674
VPCG_QUERY	0.6268	0.6498	0.6797	0.7509
VPCG&VG_QUERY	**0.6344***	**0.6618***	**0.6948***	**0.7687***
VPCG_DOC	0.5648	0.6209	0.6623	0.7382
VPCG&VG_DOC	0.5668	0.6268	0.6717	0.7509

Two-tailed t-test is done for paired data where each pair is VPCG&VG_QUERY and any of the other methods, and * indicates *p-value* < 0.01 for all tests.

and VPCG&VG_DOC further improve the results of VPCG_QUERY and VPCG_DOC respectively, because the feature coverage is improved. The CTR feature used here is a very accurate predictor of relevance, but it is only available for query-document pairs that have been observed in the log, so it does not perform well on the click-absent ones.

4.3 As a Feature in a Learning-to-rank Model

A typical industrial learning-to-rank setting builds powerful nonlinear models based on a large set of high quality features [7]. Indeed, these models can often combine many weak features to outperform a single strong feature [26]. It is therefore challenging to create a new feature that significantly improves the overall model performance. Here we use a variant of the gradient boosting machine proposed in [11] to implement a learning-to-rank framework with over 2,400 features.[6]

We denote all the 2,400+ basic features as "Base". This basic feature pool contains an immense variety of features, including CTR, BM25SD and their variations, etc. We then extend the feature pool by adding new features, and the performances of the learning-to-rank model trained based on different feature pools are shown in Table 2. "Base0" is a subset of the standard feature pool which excludes CTR and BM25SD_MULT. "Base + WMD" means the standard feature pool plus WMD feature. "Base + VPCG" extends the feature pool by adding VPCG_QUERY and VPCG_DOC, and "Base + VPCG&VG" means adding VPCG&VG_QUERY and VPCG&VG_DOC to the feature pool.

As shown in Table 2, removing the powerful features CTR and BM25SD_MULT does not change the model performance much, since the remaining features in the feature pool have already contributed similar inputs to the ranking system. The result is just slightly increased by adding WMD. This is likely because WMD introduces a notion of semantic similarity between different words that is not present in most text matching features. In general, the differences between the performance of "Base0", "Base" and "Base + WMD" are all very marginal.

By contrast, we do observe a significant improvement in overall model performance after adding our features to the pool. Our features make good use of both click and content information, and bring in new information which is not presented in the existing feature set. It is interesting that the performance difference between VPCG&VG and VPCG

[6]For both space and confidentially reasons, we cannot here define the complete set of features.

Table 2: Performance as a feature in a learning-to-ranking framework.

Feature pool	NDCG@1	NDCG@3	NDCG@5	NDCG@10
Base0	0.6872	0.7024	0.7288	0.7925
Base	0.6862	0.7014	0.7281	0.7923
Base + WMD	0.6881	0.7023	0.7291	0.7934
Base + VPCG	0.7068	0.7207	0.7470	0.8080
Base + VPCG&VG	**0.7096**	**0.7256***	**0.7506***	**0.8108***

Two-tailed t-test is done for paired data where each pair is "Base + VPCG&VG" and any of the other methods, and * indicates *p-value* < 0.01 for all tests.

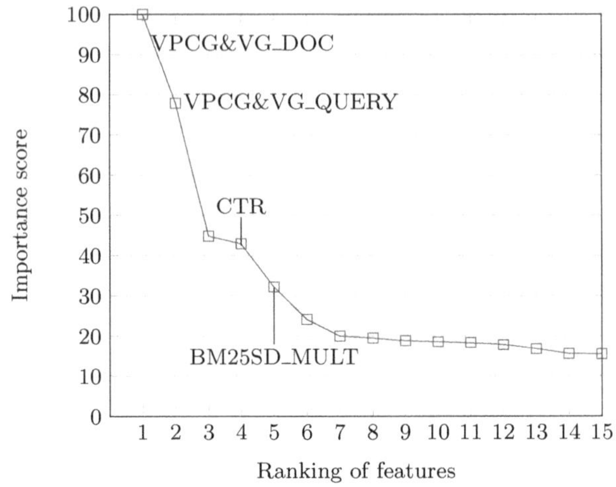

Figure 3: Importance score of the top 10 features

is narrowed in the learning-to-rank framework compared to when using them as individual ranking models (Table 1). This is because the learning-to-rank framework is able to rely on other features when the "VPCG" feature is missing. Another reason is that only a small portion (about 7.5%) of our test queries are click-absent, limiting the impact of the VG method on this data set. However, we do find click-absent queries where the ranking is significantly improved by using the VG method. More detailed discussion is provided in Section 5.

To further investigate the impact of different features, we calculate the relative importance score for all the features [11], where the most influential feature is assigned a score of 100 and the estimated scores for others are scaled accordingly. The distribution of the relative importance scores for the top 15 features are shown in Figure 3. We are not able to provide details about the features for confidentiality reasons, but we can still conclude that our features indeed play an important role in the retrieval system, since VPCG&VG_DOC and VPCG&VG_QUERY rank as the top two best features. CTR and BM25SD_MULT rank as the fourth and fifth respectively. The importance scores drop dramatically between the second and the third one, while the difference between other pairs are much smaller, indicating the superiority of our features. This is further evidence that our features significantly improve the performance both as a single feature and in the learning-to-rank models.

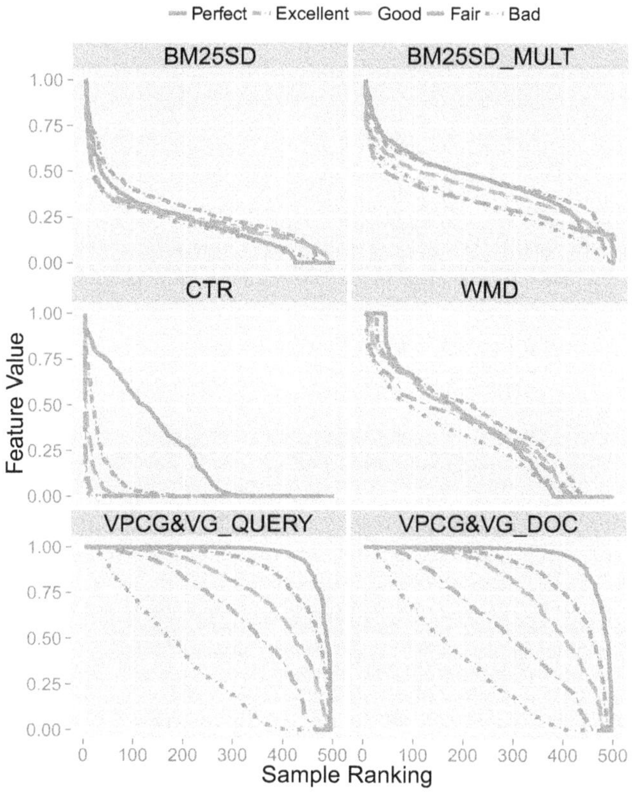

Figure 4: Separability of different features.

4.4 Separability of Features

In Section 4.2 and Section 4.3, we show significant improvement on NDCG scores by our methods in all experiment settings. In this section, we look into more details about how our features work to distinguish different documents according to their relevance to a given query.

As mentioned in Section 4.1, each document is labeled with one of the five degrees of relevance, namely "perfect", "excellent", "good", "fair" and "bad". To better evaluate the features, we measure the "separability" of the features at these five labels: we randomly sample 500 tuples (⟨query, url, feature value⟩) for each of the five labels from the test dataset, sort the tuples by their feature values, and plot them in Figure 4. Each point (x,y) in this figure corresponds to a tuple where X-coordinate is its ranking and Y-coordinate is its feature value. For the convenience of illustration, BM25SD and BM25SD_MULT are normalized by its maximal value so that it is scaled between 0 and 1. Note that the normalization does not impact the ranking.

We can see that CTR separates "perfect" from others, and WMD distinguishes "bad" from others. BM25SD is good at identifying "excellent", but its ability of distinguishing others are not as good as the enhanced version BM25SD_MULT. Compared to the baseline methods, both VPCG&VG_QUERY and VPCG&VG_DOC have a much stronger separability over all the five labels. Especially, VPCG&VG_QUERY is better at distinguishing "perfect", "excellent", "good" and "fair" from "bad", while VPCG&VG_DOC is better at seperating "perfect", "excellent" and "good" from "fair" and "bad"; and VPCG&VG_QUERY has a slightly better seperability among "perfect", "excellent" and "good", which explains why VPCG&VG_QUERY performs better as a single feature while the learning-to-rank framework benefits from the combination of them.

5. DISCUSSION

To get a better understanding about the vectors generated by our method, we study some query vectors in details and analyze how they influence the ranking result. Besides, we also further evaluate the vector generation algorithm for click-absent queries and documents, and illustrate how the generated vectors help to improve the ranking quality.

5.1 Latent Effect of Vector Propagation

The main change of query and document vectors made by our propagation method lies in two aspects: the introduction of latently related words and the re-weighting of vector terms. Introducing related words helps to explain the query or document better and re-weighting makes the key terms stand out, which facilitates tasks like disambiguation and query intent understanding.

Table 3 shows several examples of the learned query vectors (vector propagation starts from query side). We can see that keywords such as "eagles", "album" and "lyrics" can help us to distinguish the query relevant to the song named "hotel california" from an alike query "hotel california palm springs hotel" which is about a real hotel. In the third example, the meaning of "dtd amc" is hard to figure out even for a human user who is not familiar with the background knowledge. Actually "dtd" means "Downtown Disney" and the query is asking about AMC theaters in Downtown Disney. In this example, informative keywords such as "disney", "downtown", "theater" and "movie" are introduced in the learned vector. As shown in the table, ranking model trained without feature generated by the vector propagation algorithm (Base) performs very badly on this query (two of the top three are "bad"). When adding our feature, the result gets much better: both the top two retrieved documents are "good" and the third one is "fair".

5.2 Propagation Starting from Different Side

Our proposed vector propagation algorithm is very flexible to start from either query or document side, denoted as VPCG_QUERY and VPCG_DOC respectively. To study the difference between the two features and how they complement each other, we take the query "choise fm" as an example (Table 4). "choise fm" is an urban music radio station owned by Global Radio and anchored by an FM operation in London, and it is now changed to "capital xtra". Because this query is the old name of the music radio station, if we start from the query side, our algorithm propagates the old information "choise fm" to the document side and learns larger weights for "choice" and "fm". Though the relationship between "choise fm" and "capital xtra" is captured in the vector, it has much smaller weights for "capital" and "xtra". Thus the top three ranking results are all about "choise fm", and it fails to rank the perfect URL "http://www.capitalxtra.com/" in top 3. However, if we start from the document side, the document title includes the new name "capital xtra" and our algorithm propagates such information to the query side "choise fm". Thus the query vector from VPCG_DOC not only captures the relationship

Table 3: Case Study: Introduction of new words and reweighting helps ranking

Example of learned vectors		
Query	Vector	
hotel california eagles	hotel:0.675, california:0.667, eagles:0.300, **album**:0.057, **song**:0.053, **lyrics**:0.041, meaning:0.030, what:0.022, cover:0.022, youtube:0.017, about:0.016, band:0.010, video:0.010, to:0.005, songs:0.004, tyga:0.003, wiki:0.003,list:0.002, covers:0.002, art:0.002	
hotel california palm springs hotel	palm:0.596, springs:0.582, hotel:0.358, california:0.329, hotels:0.223, **ca**:0.138, resorts:0.021, spring:0.016, best:0.007, **tripadvisor**:0.006, eagles:0.005, **trip**:0.005, viceroy:0.005, resort:0.005, palms:0.004, advisor:0.003, marriott:0.003, lyrics:0.002, riviera:0.002, meaning:0.002	
dtd amc	amc:0.707, **disney**:0.475, **downtown**:0.414, island:0.158, **theater**:0.146, **movie**:0.121, **theaters**:0.121, pleasant:0.089, anaheim:0.072, pleasure:0.067, 24:0.066, orlando:0.059, movies:0.027, 12:0.024, walk:0.023, theatres:0.018, yelp:0.016, ca:0.016, dine:0.014, district:0.007	
Ranking Results for Query "dtd amc"		
Ranking	Base	Base + VPCG
1	http://acronyms.thefreedictionary.com/DTDS	http://www.yelp.com/biz/amc-downtown-disney-12-ca-anaheim
2	http://www.mydreamsofdisney.com/2014/01/saving-mr-banks-amc-fork-screen/	http://www.dadsguidetowdw.com/downtown-disney.html
3	http://www.thefreedictionary.com/DTDS	http://www.mydreamsofdisney.com/2014/01/saving-mr-banks-amc-fork-screen/

Table 4: Case Study: The vector representations from VPCG_QUERY and VPCG_DOC complement each other.

Query Vectors for Query "choise fm"		
VPCG_QUERY	**choice**:0.714, **fm**:0.666, radio:0.148, choicefm:0.110, london:0.085, nevis:0.039, **capital**:0.033, **xtra:0.027**, 3:0.024, choicefm1053:0.019, station:0.019, uk:0.016, 105:0.014, music:0.012, choicefm105:0.012, playlist:0.008, choiceradio:0.006, 3fm:0.0045, extra:0.004, 1:0.004	
VPCG_DOC	**xtra**:0.446, **capital**:0.446, urban:0.439, dance:0.438, uk:0.426, **choice**:0.112, skn:0.079, times:0.079, ltd:0.079, **fm**:0.041, radio:0.028, music:0.025, listen:0.024, online:0.020, 3:0.020, com:0.016, choiceradio:0.013, 107:0.011, 105:0.011, your:0.009	
Ranking Results for Query "choice fm"		
Ranking	Base + VPCG_QUERY	Base + VPCG_QUERY + VPCG_DOC
1	http://en.wikipedia.org/wiki/Choice_FM	http://www.capitalxtra.com/
2	http://www.choicefmnz.com/	http://en.wikipedia.org/wiki/Choice_FM
3	http://tunein.com/radio/Choice-FM-1053-s89470/	https://www.facebook.com/choicefm

Table 5: Performance of vector generation algorithm

Method	Similarity
BOW	0.4833
Unigram vector + equal weight	0.5368
Unit vector + equal weight	0.5927
VG	**0.6057**

between "choise fm" and "captial xtra", and learns more accurate weights for "capital" and "xtra". As a result, with the help from both VPCG_QUERY and VPCG_DOC, our model is able to rank the perfect URL "http://www.capitalxtra.com/" as the top 1 result. Similarly, VPCG_QUERY may capture more accurate query intent than VPCG_DOC for some queries, and due to space limit, we do not list more examples here. In general, VPCG_QUERY and VPCG_DOC complement each other and together improve the ranking results as shown in Section 4.

5.3 Evaluation of Vector Generation Algorithm

The goal of the vector generation method proposed in Section 3 is to get a good vector estimation for queries and documents that have no click information. In Section 4.2 and Section 4.3, we have already shown that those generated vectors are indeed helpful for ranking. Here we further look into these generated vector representations to see how well they approximate the target vectors.

We use the query vectors generated by the vector propagation algorithm starting from the query side as an example for the evaluation. The set is divided into two subsets, namely training set and test set. The training set is used to learn the unit vectors and their corresponding weights, based on which vectors for the test set are generated by the vector generation algorithm. The vectors learned by the vector propagation algorithm are used as ground truth. The evaluation metrics is the average of cosine similarity between the groundtruth vector and the vector generated by methods that estimate the vectors in other alternative ways.

We compare our method "VG" against several baselines, and the results are shown in Table 5. Here "BOW" is the bag-of-words model. "Unigram vector + equal weight" uses a linear combination of the vectors for each unigram with equal weights. For example, the query vector for "yahoo finance" is calculated as Q("yahoo") + Q("finance") where Q("yahoo") and Q("finance") are vectors for query "yahoo" and "finance" which are learned by the vector propagation algorithm. "Unit vector + equal weight" uses the unit vectors we introduce in Section 3. It decomposes queries into a set of units in the same way as "VG" does, but assigns equal weight to each unit instead.

From Table 5, we can see that methods making use of existing query vector information ("Unigram vector + equal weight", "Unit vector + equal weight" and "VG") outperform bag-of-words model. Using unit vectors works better than using original vectors for unigram. "VG" brings in further

Table 6: Case Study: Unit vector helps to improve ranking for click-absent queries

Unit vectors for Query "how long is into the storm"		
Unit	Weight	Vector
how long is	0.363	how:0.375, long:0.320, contagious:0.167, 5k:0.044, heat:0.039, pregnancy:0.037, eye:0.037, pink:0.036, flu:0.036, dog:0.035, dogs:0.034, does:0.030, cold:0.028, good:0.023, light:0.022, you:0.022, strep:0.022, to:0.022, many:0.020, throat:0.020
is into the	0.562	into:0.570, woods:0.303, wild:0.161, mccandless:0.118, movie:0.085, christopher:0.061, mystic:0.055, chris:0.055, storm:0.040, rncm:0.032, musical:0.028, appropriate:0.025, children:0.025, kids:0.024, van:0.020, morrison:0.020, how:0.019, rated:0.015, r:0.015, why:0.015
into the storm	1.038	storm:0.665, into:0.641, **movie**:0.159, **2014**:0.050, **watch**:0.041, online:0.040, **reviews**:0.039, free:0.034, **trailer**:0.030, torrent:0.024, black:0.017, sky:0.017, cast:0.012, **imdb**:0.011, **review**:0.010, full:0.010, tornado:0.009, rotten:0.008, tomatoes:0.008, dvd:0.007

Ranking Results for Query "how long is into the storm"		
Ranking	Base + VPCG	Base + VPCG&VG
1	http://www.rottentomatoes.com/m/into_the_storm_2014/	http://www.rottentomatoes.com/m/into_the_storm_2014/
2	http://www.ign.com/articles/2014/08/07/into-the-storm-review	https://en.wikipedia.org/wiki/Into_the_Storm_(2014_film)
3	http://science.nasa.gov/science-news/science-at-nasa/2001/ast16aug_1/	http://www.ign.com/articles/2014/08/07/into-the-storm-review

improvement compared to assigning equal weights to units. In general, our proposed generalization algorithm provides the most accurate approximation of the ground truth vector.

5.4 Query Vector Generation in Ranking

In previous sections, we have shown the quantitative analysis of the vector generation algorithm, including its performance in ranking and the quality of the estimated vectors. In this section, we continue our discussion about how it helps to improve ranking by illustrating a query example "how long is into the storm", which is about the length of a movie "Into the Storm". This query is not in the search log so we can only use the vector generation method.

To generate the query vector, "how long is into the storm" is decomposed into three units, namely "how long is", "is into the" and "into the storm", whose vectors are given in Table 6. The keyword "movie" is added to the unit vector for "into the storm" with a high weight, which increases the relevance scores of movie-related documents. Besides, our regression model successfully captures that "into the storm" is the most influential unit in this query and gives the highest weight to it. In this way, the generated query vector is more likely to be connected with documents about the corresponding movie. In our experiment, the learning-to-rank framework trained without VG (Base + VPCG) ranks a science news from NASA which is not relevant at all as a top result (number three). With the help of VG (Base + VPCG&VG), we get more reasonable results, where all the top three documents are about the movie (Table 6).

6. RELATED WORK

The most straightforward way to exploit the click log from a search engine is to aggregate statistics such as click probability and dwell time by $(query, document)$ pairs and use them as features in a learning-to-rank framework, as described by Agichtein et al. in [1].

To deal with the noise and sparsity problem in these features, there are two basic approaches. One solution is to cast it as a smoothing problem, as in [9], [13], and [29]. An alternative way is to learn a semantic representation of queries and documents, either in vocabulary space or in a latent space, as in [12], [25], and [27]. One advantage of the semantic representation approach is its flexibility. It is easier to incorporate other useful information in the learning of the semantic representation. Besides, the relevance between queries and documents only depends on the representation, so similar documents always get close relevance scores, which reduces the bias caused by the raw click-through data. The semantic approach is the one adopted in this paper.

It is common to represent a click log as a graph with edges representing clicks, an early example being Baeza-Yates and Tiberi's work [3]. Our approach is most similar to the label propagation technique of [16]. However, instead of requiring extrinsic labels or features, we propagate parts of the content information (i.e., query or document title) itself.

The semantic click models that we are aware of either make use of modeling techniques that can be difficult to scale to billions of samples, such as statistical machine translation [12], and SVD [27], or else have very many hyperparameters that are difficult to tune [12, 25]. By contrast, our method is strikingly simple and exceedingly scalable. It also has the advantage of producing a representation – a small set of weighted terms from queries or documents – that is amenable to human inspection.

Besides ranking, click-through data can be utilized for various tasks in information retrieval. Click-through history records user behavior from which user's information need can be discovered [24]. It also provides clues to discover potential relations between queries, and can be used to facilitate tasks such as query clustering [4] and query suggestion [2, 10, 17, 18]. Click-through data can also be explored for document representation and organization. In [21], the authors represent documents in the query vocabulary space, where TFIDF is used for weighting. Compared to their method, ours improves both the query and document vector representation by involving more iteractions between them.

7. CONCLUSION

This paper presents a unified approach to learn query-document relevance by utilizing both click and content information. For queries and documents in the click graph, we propagate the content information from either side on the click-through bipartite graph and represent both queries and documents as vectors in the same semantic space. For queries and documents without click information, their vector representations are generated by connecting them with the vectors learned from the click graph based on the content information. This whole process expands the vector representations with relevant new words through the propagation, and smoothes the term weights based on the click information. Besides, the sparsity and noise are also reduced during this process thus better quality and larger coverage of the vectors is guaranteed. The proposed approach works efficiently on a Web-scale click graph. The experimental results show the effectiveness of the proposed method in a ranking task. It stands out from thousands of features in a learning-to-rank framework, which is a nontrivial achievement in real practice.

Besides ranking, one potential application of our method is query and document expansion. The learned vectors usually consist of related terms propagated from their neighbors in the click graph, which can be further applied to improve automatic expansion of queries and documents in the search task.

8. REFERENCES

[1] E. Agichtein, E. Brill, S. Dumais, and R. Ragno. Learning user interaction models for predicting web search result preferences. In *Proceedings of SIGIR*, pages 3–10, 2006.

[2] R. Baeza-Yates, C. Hurtado, and M. Mendoza. Query recommendation using query logs in search engines. In *Proceedings of Workshop at EDBT*, pages 588–596, 2005.

[3] R. Baeza-Yates and A. Tiberi. Extracting semantic relations from query logs. In *Proceedings of SIGKDD*, 2007.

[4] D. Beeferman and A. Berger. Agglomerative clustering of a search engine query log. In *Proceedings of SIGKDD*, pages 407–416, 2000.

[5] M. Bendersky, D. Metzler, and W. B. Croft. Effective query formulation with multiple information sources. In *Proceedings of WSDM*, pages 443–452, 2012.

[6] A. Broder, E. Gabrilovich, V. Josifovski, G. Mavromatis, D. Metzler, and J. Wang. Exploiting site-level information to improve web search. In *Proceedings of CIKM*, pages 1393–1396, 2010.

[7] O. Chapelle and Y. Chang. Yahoo! learning to rank challenge overview. *Journal of Machine Learning*, 2011.

[8] K. Collins-Thompson and J. Callan. Query expansion using random walk models. In *Proceedings of CIKM*, pages 704–711, 2005.

[9] N. Craswell and M. Szummer. Random walks on the click graph. In *Proceedings of SIGIR*, pages 239–246, 2007.

[10] H. Deng, M. R. Lyu, and I. King. A generalized co-hits algorithm and its application to bipartite graphs. In *Proceedings of SIGKDD*, pages 239–248, 2009.

[11] J. H. Friedman. Greedy function approximation: A gradient boosting machine. *Annals of Statistics*, 29:1189–1232, 2000.

[12] J. Gao, X. He, and J. Nie. Clickthrough-based translation models for web search: from word models to phrase models. In *Proceedings of CIKM*, 2010.

[13] J. Gao, W. Yuan, X. Li, K. Deng, and J. Nie. Smoothing clickthrough data for web search ranking. In *Proceedings of SIGIR*, 2009.

[14] J. M. Kleinberg. Authoritative sources in a hyperlinked environment. *JACM*, 46(5):604–632, 1999.

[15] M. J. Kusner, Y. Sun, N. I. Kolkin, and K. Q. Weinberger. From word embeddings to document distances. In *Proceedings ICML*, 2015.

[16] X. Li, Y.-Y. Wang, and A. Acero. Learning query intent from regularized click graphs. In *Proceedings of SIGIR*, pages 339–346, 2008.

[17] H. Ma, H. Yang, I. King, and M. R. Lyu. Learning latent semantic relations from clickthrough data for query suggestion. In *Proceedings of CIKM*, pages 709–718, 2008.

[18] Q. Mei, D. Zhou, and K. Church. Query suggestion using hitting time. In *Proceedings of CIKM*, pages 469–478, 2008.

[19] T. Mikolov, K. Chen, G. Corrado, and J. Dean. Efficient estimation of word representations in vector space. In *Processings of Workshop at ICLR*, 2013.

[20] C. Müller and I. Gurevych. A study on the semantic relatedness of query and document terms in information retrieval. In *Proceedings of EMNLP*, pages 1338–1347, 2009.

[21] B. Poblete and R. Baeza-Yates. Query-sets: using implicit feedback and query patterns to organize web documents. In *Proceedings of WWW*, pages 41–50, 2008.

[22] S. E. Robertson, S. Walker, S. Jones, M. Hancock-Beaulieu, and M. Gatford. Okapi at trec-3. *Trec*, 1994.

[23] G. Salton, A. Wong, and C.-S. Yang. A vector space model for automatic indexing. *Communications of the ACM*, 18(11):613–620, 1975.

[24] X. Shen, B. Tan, and C. Zhai. Context-sensitive information retrieval using implicit feedback. In *Proceedings of SIGIR*, pages 43–50, 2005.

[25] Y. Shen, X. He, J. Gao, L. Deng, and G. Mesnil. Learning semantic representations using convolutional neural networks for web search. In *Proceeding of WWW*, 2014.

[26] K. M. Svore and C. J. Burges. A machine learning approach for improved bm25 retrieval. *Proceedings of CIKM*, 2009.

[27] W. Wu, H. Li, and J. Xu. Learning query and document similarities from click-through bipartite graph with metadata. In *Proceedings of WSDM*, pages 687–696, 2013.

[28] C. Zhai and J. Lafferty. A study of smoothing methods for language models applied to ad hoc information retrieval. In *Proceedings of SIGIR*, pages 334–342, 2001.

[29] M. Zhukovskiy and T. Khatkevich. An optimization framework for propagation of query-document features by query similarity functions. In *Proceedings of CIKM*, 2015.

Click-based Hot Fixes for Underperforming Torso Queries

Masrour Zoghi*
University of Amsterdam
Amsterdam, Netherlands
m.zoghi@uva.nl

Tomáš Tunys
Czech Technical University
Prague, Czech Republic
tunystom@fel.cvut.cz

Lihong Li
Microsoft Research
Redmond, WA
lihongli@microsoft.com

Damien Jose, Junyan Chen, Chun Ming Chin
Microsoft Bing
Bellevue, WA
{dajose, junyanch, chuchin}@microsoft.com

Maarten de Rijke
University of Amsterdam
Amsterdam, Netherlands
derijke@uva.nl

ABSTRACT

Ranking documents using their historical click-through rate (CTR) can improve relevance for frequently occurring queries, i.e., so-called head queries. It is difficult to use such click signals on non-head queries as they receive fewer clicks. In this paper, we address the challenge of dealing with *torso* queries on which the production ranker is performing poorly. Torso queries are queries that occur frequently enough so that they are not considered as tail queries and yet not frequently enough to be head queries either. They comprise a large portion of most commercial search engines' traffic, so the presence of a large number of underperforming torso queries can harm the overall performance significantly. We propose a practical method for dealing with such cases, drawing inspiration from the literature on learning to rank (LTR). Our method requires relatively few clicks from users to derive a strong re-ranking signal by comparing document relevance between pairs of documents instead of using absolute numbers of clicks per document. By infusing a modest amount of exploration into the ranked lists produced by a production ranker and extracting preferences between documents, we obtain substantial improvements over the production ranker in terms of page-level online metrics. We use an exploration dataset consisting of real user clicks from a large-scale commercial search engine to demonstrate the effectiveness of the method. We conduct further experimentation on public benchmark data using simulated clicks to gain insight into the inner workings of the proposed method. Our results indicate a need for LTR methods that make more explicit use of the query and other contextual information.

Keywords

Learning to rank; Underperforming queries

1. INTRODUCTION

An important problem in Information Retrieval (IR) is to rank the documents retrieved in response to a query such that the information need of the user is satisfied as quickly as possible. Originally, this problem was addressed by ranking documents based on their textual similarity to the query, using a feature ranker such as BM25. With the proliferation of such features, arose the problem of combining the recommendations put forth by the multitude of features. Machine learning algorithms rose to prominence as the preferred solution, and this gave rise to the field of learning to rank [32, LTR].

Despite the success of LTR, invariably the learned model performs suboptimally on certain queries, either due to the inadequacy of the features or because the query does not fit the profile of the "generic" query and since LTR methods are statistical by their very nature, they gladly sacrifice a minority of "misbehaving" queries to boost the overall performance across the full population. This problem might disappear with the introduction of new features or LTR algorithms. However, given the delay involved in the development and deployment process, it is desirable to devise a more automated and agile method for remedying underperformance. We propose a method for achieving this aim using implicit feedback from users.

We are particularly interested in improving the performance of LTR algorithms on a specific class of queries: *underperforming torso queries*. Torso queries are queries that occur less frequently than head queries, but are not so rare to be considered tail queries [33]. When sorted by frequency and split into three quantiles, queries in the second quantile are called torso queries [23]. We use a pragmatic definition that is given in absolute terms: queries that receive between 10 and 200 impressions during our two-week experimental period. Of course, the frequency of a torso query is highly dependent on the amount of traffic a search engine encounters; often, it is high enough to render our ideas practical.

A torso query is *underperforming* if the document ranking produced in response to it by the production ranker is of lower quality than the best ranking according to a page-level metric of interest [16, 27]. How can we use click feedback to improve the performance of an offline trained ranker on torso queries?

The idea of using click feedback to improve search results predates many LTR algorithms in use today. For instance, Joachims [24] proposed extracting pairwise preferences between documents for a given query, by searching through click logs produced by an already deployed ranker for skipped-clicked pairs: pairs of documents that appeared in one impression and the document that was placed in the lower position was clicked, but not the one in the higher position. Because the lower document was clicked and so inspected, assuming that the user scanned the list in descending order, we can deduce that the higher document must have also been inspected, but not clicked, so it is likely to be less relevant.

Despite the astuteness of the observation in the last paragraph,

*Part of this work was carried out when the first author was visiting Microsoft Research Redmond.

SIGIR '16, July 17 - 21, 2016, Pisa, Italy

ISBN 978-1-4503-4069-4/16/07...$15.00

DOI: http://dx.doi.org/10.1145/2911451.2911500

without some level of exploration in the ranker that was used to collect the click logs, the estimated preferences are biased and so in practice, in the absence of intervention or prior assumptions [2], this method may not be as effective as one would hope. We test the hypothesis that, with adequate exploration, the preferences expressed by users, through their clicks, can lead to significant gains in performance. We adapt an idea that has proven effective in supervised LTR to our setting: in [5], *lambda-gradients* were proposed as a method for reordering the documents used in training according to their relative relevance, where the relevances were obtained from manually-labeled assessments. Applying this idea to the click-based preferences obtained through the procedure described in the last paragraph, we arrive at our method, which we call *click-based lambdas* and describe more explicitly in §2.2.

We test the effectiveness of click-based lambdas using real users interacting with a commercial search engine (cf. §3). A key finding in §3.5 is that, given proper exploration, click-based lambdas can lead to significant improvements over existing LTR methods. The most immediate application of the findings in this paper is to remedy queries on which a production ranker is performing suboptimally. Given a set of queries that have been identified to be underperforming using one of several methods developed in recent years [16, 27, 29], they could be singled out for exploration and re-ranking without affecting the remainder of the traffic.

In addition to experiments with real users, we conduct more controlled experiments using simulated user clicks obtained from a click model in order to help us deepen our understanding of the proposed method, particularly in relation to LTR methods; see §4.1. In particular, our results show that click-based lambdas are most effective in the case of underperforming queries; see §4.4.

Importantly, our click-based lambdas method does not generalize across query-document pairs. The intended practical use case are queries on which the production ranker performs sub-optimally and for which this performance gap fails to be remedied by making modifications to the model. In such a situation, click-based lambdas can be used temporarily, as an *unsupervised*[1] *hot fix*.

We address the following research questions: (**RQ1**) Can click signals together with exploration be used to improve online performance of a commercial search engine on torso queries that receive much fewer click signals than head queries? (**RQ2**) To what extent does LambdaMART (the state-of-the-art LTR method) obtain the best ranking for each query? (**RQ3**) Can a combination of click feedback obtained from exploration and scores produced by LambdaMART lead to improvements over both methods? (**RQ4**) Is there a relationship between the effect of click-based lambdas on a query and the performance of the original LambdaMART model on it?

Our results are useful for IR researchers because they demonstrate a gap that exists between what the state-of-the-art LTR algorithms achieve and what could be achieved if one were to utilize user feedback; this presents a challenge to the researcher to invent novel methods for combining offline LTR algorithms with interaction data. Another challenge is to devise improved methods for detecting underperforming queries. Our results are useful for IR practitioners because they provide a simple yet effective solution for obtaining meaningful gains on torso queries, which comprise a large portion of the traffic, particularly in the case of underperforming queries. Given the simplicity of the proposed method, we believe it will be broadly useful in practice.

In summary, we provide an unbiased comparison of a click-based ranker against both a highly optimized, commercial search engine and the state-of-the-art LTR algorithm, LambdaMART, and demonstrate that using a small dose of exploration we can obtain improvements over both. The required exploration is small enough that the proposed method could be useful for underperforming torso queries, affecting a large segment of the traffic.

[1] By "unsupervised" we mean without the use of manually curated labels.

2. METHOD

In this section, we describe our method, click-based-lambdas, as well as the necessary background.

2.1 Background

We begin by introducing some notions and notations used in the rest of the paper. We are concerned with improving the performance of a production ranker on a fixed segment of the queries. For the sake of simplicity of the exposition, we will consider a single query in this segment, denoted q, with documents $d_1, \ldots, d_L$. The goal, then, is to order these documents so as to optimize some metric and in this paper we will assume that the metric of interest is a *page-level online metric*, which is evaluated based on the way the users react when presented with the given ranking of $d_1, \ldots, d_L$. An instance of such a metric is *page click-through rate* above a certain threshold K, i.e. the probability of receiving a click on any of the top K ranked results: we denote this by PCTR@K.

Let us point out that when considering PCTR, we may choose to limit ourselves to *satisfied* clicks if need be, where a click is deemed satisfied if the user spent 30 seconds or more reading the clicked document or if it was the last click in the session [2]. Indeed, inspired by previous work [11], this is a restriction that we impose. Other popular online metrics include time to success and session success rate. However, we use PCTR to evaluate the different methods under consideration here, since it is an online click-based metric that we could safely use in the case of both the real user data and the click model experiments.

Note that if the goal was to optimize an offline metric, such as Discounted Cumulative Gain (DCG), which is calculated based on annotated relevance judgments, then we could directly apply the many LTR algorithms in the literature. However, without assuming a particular user click model that could be used to estimate online metrics, LTR methods cannot be used to directly address the problem of optimizing an online metric; the only option is to optimize for an offline metric, such as DCG, which correlates well with the online metric of interest.

Next, we briefly review the main ideas behind the state-of-the-art LTR algorithm [7], called LambdaMART [6], which is the main source of inspiration for our proposed method. The idea is to use a succession of regression trees, each estimating the so-called *lambdas*, which are numbers that are assigned to each query-document pair (q, d_i) and indicate how much the score assigned to d_i by the previous trees needs to be modified to improve the offline metric of interest. More precisely, consider a query q and two documents d_i and d_j such that d_i has a higher relevance score for q than d_j, and suppose that the sum of the scores assigned by the regression trees grown so far to each document d_k is s_k; moreover, assume that we are interested in an offline metric M (e.g., DCG), and let ΔM_{ij} denote the difference in terms of M between the ranked list of documents sorted according to the scores s_k and the same list with the documents d_i and d_j swapped. Note that we are assuming that this quantity can be calculated, which is the case when dealing with offline metrics that can be calculated based on relevance judgments, but not so for online metrics, which is what we are concerned with in this paper. Then we define

$$\lambda_{ij} = \frac{\Delta M_{ij}}{1 + e^{\sigma(s_i - s_j)}}, \tag{1}$$

Algorithm 1 Click-based lambdas

Input: Query q, documents $d_1, \ldots, d_L$ and T impressions where q was issued to the search engine, a ranking of the documents d_i was displayed to the user and the resulting clicks were recorded

1: $\lambda_i \leftarrow 0$ for each $i = 1, \ldots, L$
2: **for** $t \in \{1, \ldots, T\}$ **do**
3: **for** (i, j) such that d_i was clicked in impression t and d_j was not clicked, but was ranked higher than the last clicked document **do**
4: $\lambda_i \leftarrow \lambda_i + 1$
5: $\lambda_j \leftarrow \lambda_j - 1$
6: **end for**
7: **end for**

Return: The documents d_i sorted in decreasing order of λ_i

where σ is a positive number that is tuned for performance in practice. Then, for each document d_i, λ_i is obtained by summing λ_{ij} over j such that document d_j is less relevant than d_i and subtracting λ_{ji} for every document d_j that is more relevant than d_i.

The general idea is that for every document that is ranked above d_i and should be ranked below it, d_i gets an "up-vote" and for every document that is ranked below d_i but should be above it, d_i gets a "down-vote" and the sum of these votes tells us whether d_i should be moved up or down in the list and how far. Then, LambdaMART fits a new regression tree to the λ_i and adds the tree to the ensemble. Although LambdaMART is known to be locally optimal for optimizing offline metrics [10], the same does not necessarily hold for online metrics that we focus on in this work.

2.2 Click-based lambdas

We propose using an online, click-based analogue of the lambdas used in LambdaMART to decide which documents should be pushed to the top. Unlike LambdaMART, our method, *click-based lambdas*, is unsupervised and only uses interaction data.

Algorithm 1 provides the pseudo-code for the method: given a query q with documents $d_1, \ldots, d_L$, a number of impressions recording the order in which these documents were presented to various users and the resulting clicks, we start out by setting $\lambda_i = 0$ for each document d_i (Line 1), and updating them as described in the following. Given an impression, suppose that the documents were presented in the order

$$\begin{array}{ll} \mathbf{d_{i_1}} & \\ \mathbf{d_{i_2}} & \checkmark \\ \mathbf{d_{i_3}} & \\ \mathbf{d_{i_4}} & \checkmark \\ \vdots & \end{array}$$

with the check mark $\checkmark$ denoting the positions where clicks were observed. Then, given a document d_i that was clicked and a document d_j that lies above the last clicked document and was not clicked (e.g., $(i, j) = (i_2, i_3)$ or (i_4, i_1)), we set $\lambda_{ij} = 1$ and $\lambda_{ji} = -1$, which is equivalent to setting σ to 0 and ΔM_{ij} to 1 in (1). Given this, we update the λ_i as follows (Lines 4 and 5):

$$\lambda_i = \lambda_i + \lambda_{ij}$$
$$\lambda_j = \lambda_j + \lambda_{ji}.$$

As the discussion of LambdaMART in §2.1 indicates, it is possible to modify the above procedure by adopting a more complex definition for λ_{ij}, but in this paper we are more interested in the question of whether or not click signals can be used to improve online performance, rather than the most optimal method for doing so.

A few comments are in order: first of all, note that there are no requirements on the ranking $d_{i_1}, d_{i_2}, \ldots$, so it could very well be provided by a deterministic ranker. However, the method benefits strongly from exploration; this is due to the following observation: consider a pair of documents d_i and d_j that are retrieved in response to a query q and consider the sum of the λ_{ij} across all impressions involving q; if these impressions presented random rankings, then this sum would be an estimate of the preference that the users have for d_i over d_j. Now, suppose that the ranker is deterministic and d_i always appears above d_j; then, the sum of the λ_{ij} could never be positive, even if d_i is strongly preferred to d_j: it can at best be equal to 0. Our experience with click-based lambdas confirms the intuition that without exploration they can lead to degradation; we do not present these negative results due to space constraints.

Given the above observations, our experiments employ two types of exploration. In the experiments with real user clicks discussed in §3, we use uniformly random shuffling of the top 5 documents ranked by the production system, while for the more flexible click model-based experiments in §4, we use a less disruptive form of exploration obtained through interleaving the existing ranker with a random one, which results in roughly half of the documents being chosen randomly. The former exploration scheme was imposed upon us due to the evaluation methodology, as discussed in §3.3.

A final comment is that our click-based lambdas method does not generalize across query-document pairs and so it is not to be thought of as a replacement for LTR methods, but as a remedy for their shortcomings, and hence should be run alongside LTR methods or as a post-processing step to such methods. See §5.

3. THE PRACTICAL IMPACT OF CLICK-BASED LAMBDAS

In this section, we address our first research question and present our experiments on real users to test the extent to which the idea of click-based lambdas can lead to improvements in practice over a production ranker in a large-scale commercial search engine. We describe our experimental setup, the data, the evaluation method and the results.

3.1 Experimental design

In order to answer **RQ1**, we use click logs collected by a popular search engine, where the results produced by the production ranker were randomized. The purpose of the randomization is twofold. First, we would like to test the hypothesis that infusing exploration into the ranked lists and using the resulting feedback can lead to improved rerankings. Secondly, and more importantly, such randomized click logs allow for a counterfactual comparison of the production ranker against the outcome of our click-based lambdas as well as a number of other baselines discussed below without the need to run numerous A/B tests on real users. In particular, we compare these methods based on their performance according to PCTR@3, as described in §2.1. Below, we detail the specifics of our experiments and evaluation methodology.

3.2 Exploration click logs

In this section, we describe the click logs that were used in the experiments aimed at answering **RQ1**. The top 5 results produced by a commercial search engine were shuffled uniformly at random before being presented to the users, and the clicks on the reshuffled ranked list were recorded. This randomization was applied to a fraction of the non-head queries that were issued to the search engine over a period of two weeks. The data was split into two parts, one for training the rankers being compared and the other for evaluation. As pointed out above, the shuffling is necessary for us to be able to conduct unbiased evaluation of our various modifications to the production ranker, without having to run expensive A/B tests.

Algorithm 2 Get Importance Probabilities

Input: Exploration log and evaluation cutoff K

for each ranking $P \in \mathcal{C}_K^L$ **do**
  $C(P) = \#\{I_j \mid I_j^{1,\ldots,K} = P\}$
end for
$IP(P) = \frac{C(P)}{\sum_Q C(Q)}$ for each $P \in \mathcal{C}_K^L$

Return: IP

The choice of 5 as the number of documents to be shuffled was motivated by the practical issue of the amount of exploration data that would be needed for us to be able to carry out our experiments. The difficulty with importance sampling, the technical core of the unbiased evaluation approach as described below, in the context of ranking is that the number of possible rankings (a.k.a. actions) grows rapidly with the length of the list. More specifically, given ranked lists of length L, in order to be able to evaluate the top L results of any ranker, we would like to have all $L!$ different impressions in our randomized logs. Since $5!$ is equal to 120, this means that less than 1% of the impressions in the exploration log can be used for evaluation. Now, given that the randomization of the results was only applied to a small fraction of the non-head traffic, shuffling even the top 6 documents would have required the randomization of a far greater portion of the traffic than was allowed by our exploration budget. It should be noted that such considerations apply to the empirical evaluation protocol we adopt here, not to the click-based lambdas approach proposed in this work.

To carry out the needed comparisons, the dataset is randomly split into two folds of equal size: one fold is reserved for the unbiased IPS evaluation (see below) and *part of* the other fold is used for training. More specifically, for a given training size, n_{imps}, we randomly select n_{imps} impressions per query in the training fold and train click-based lambdas and each of the baseline algorithms discussed above on these n_{imps} impressions and evaluate the resulting rankers using the test fold. Naturally, in the case of the production and random rankers, we skip the training part of the above procedure and only evaluate it on the test fold, since the production ranker is pre-determined by the commercial search engine and there is nothing to learn for the random ranker.

In order to avoid issues with bias, we restrict ourselves to queries such that the top 3 documents in their impressions in the test fold contain all 60 ($= 5 \times 4 \times 3$) possible ordered lists of 3 documents chosen out of the top 5 documents, which were shuffled in our dataset. Imposing this restriction leaves us with 57 queries and roughly 58,000 impressions. This restriction is put in place for the sake of our evaluation methodology: our method click-based lambdas imposes no such requirement.

The above process is repeated 1000 times for training sizes n_{imps} going between 2 and 20 impressions per query in increments of 2 and between 20 and 200 impressions in increments of 20.

3.3 Evaluation method

We set as our main metric of interest *satisfied page click-through rate on the top* 3 *positions*, which we denote by PCTR@3. This is the probability that we observe a satisfied click on one of the top 3 documents presented by the ranker, where a click is deemed satisfied if the user spent 30 seconds or more reading the clicked document or if it was the last click in the session. One important reason for this choice is that at least on some (mobile) devices the top 3 documents are visible to the users without any extra effort on their part (i.e., without having to scroll down), and so it is desirable to improve the quality of the top 3 results as much as possible. Of course, for any K, given the appropriate exploration dataset, one can replicate our experiments to evaluate for PCTR@K.

Algorithm 3 Get Importance Numerators

Input: Exploration log of length N, evaluation cutoff K and ranker R with rankings $R_1, \ldots, R_r$

$IN(P) = 0$ for all $P \in \mathcal{C}_K^L$
for $i \in \{1, \ldots, r\}$ **do**
  $IN(R_i) = \#\{I_j \mid R(I_j) = R_i\}/N$
end for

Return: IN

Algorithm 4 Evaluate $CTR@K$ of ranker

Input: Exploration log of length N, number of shuffled documents L, evaluation cutoff K and ranker R with rankings $R_1, \ldots, R_r$

Let $(d_1, \ldots, d_K) = I_1$
Let $\sigma_1, \ldots, \sigma_n \in \mathcal{C}_K^L$ be permutations on K elements such that ranking R_i orders the documents as $d_{\sigma_i(1)}, \ldots, d_{\sigma_i(K)}$
$IN =$ Get Importance Numerators$(\{I_j\}, K, R)$
$IP =$ Get Importance Probabilities$(\{I_j\}, K)$
$nM = 0$
$nCM = 0$
for $i \in \{1, \ldots, N\}$ **do**
  $P = I_i^{1,\ldots,K}$
  $nM = nM + IN(P)/IP(P)$
  if I_i received a click on the top K documents **then**
    $nCM = nCM + IN(P)/IP(P)$
  end if
end for
$CTR@K = nCM/nM$

Return: $CTR@K$

Next, we explain the Inverse Propensity Scoring (IPS) evaluator [4, 30, 31, 41] used to evaluate rankers on the exploration click logs. To understand the basic idea, let us first consider the situation with a single query, i.e., we will fix a query q and L documents $d_1, \ldots, d_L$ that need to be ranked in response to the issued query q. Let us also assume that all permutations of the L documents have been presented to users and the clicks have been logged. Then, given any ranker and any page-level metric, we can extract all impressions in our exploration log that order the L documents in the same way as our ranker and evaluate the metric on those impressions only. Such a procedure is statistically equivalent to an actual A/B test, so will give us an unbiased estimate of the metric on the given ranker; consequently, this estimate converges to the true value of the metric given enough exploration data.

This basic idea needs to be modified to address both the existence of multiple queries and the case that the ranker under consideration does not produce the same ranking of the documents $d_1, \ldots, d_L$ in every impression (e.g., due to personalization). To deal with this, we make use of importance sampling to evaluate the metric by treating the impressions in the randomized log as samples from a "source" distribution and the rankings produced by the ranker we would like to evaluate as samples from a "target" distribution. Then, we weight the contribution of each matching impression by the ratio of the probability of observing the given impression under the target and the source distributions: these probabilities are calculated from the data using Algorithms 3 and 2, respectively. These ratios are then combined as in Algorithm 4 to get the desired estimate. Since we are interested in PCTR@K, we can use impressions that match only the top K results produced by our ranker. Below, we provide the details of the IPS evaluator.

DEFINITION 1. *We denote by $\mathcal{C}_K^L$ the set of K-element ordered subsets (called "rankings") of the documents $d_1, \ldots, d_L$. Note that the size of $\mathcal{C}_K^L$ is equal to $L!/(L-K)!$.*

Suppose we are given an *exploration log*, by which we mean impressions $I_1, \ldots, I_N$, each consisting of some permutation of the documents $d_1, \ldots, d_L$, such that for each ranking $P \in \mathcal{C}_K^L$, there is one impression, I_j, in the log such that the ordered subset of top K documents (denoted by $I_j^{1,\ldots,K}$) matches P. Algorithm 2 calculates the probability of seeing each ranking P in the log.

Moreover, let R be a ranker that assigns one of the rankings $R_1, \ldots, R_r \in \mathcal{C}_K^L$ to each impression. We will denote by $R(I_j)$ the ranking that R assigns to the j-th impression. Algorithm 3 calculates the probability of encountering each R_j in the log.

Algorithm 4 loops through the N impressions and whenever there is a match between $R(I_j)$ and $I_j^{1,\ldots,K}$, it increments the number of matches (i.e. nM) by the ratio between $IN(I_j^{1,\ldots,K})$ and $IP(R(I_j))$, and if additionally there was a click on the top K documents, we also increment the number of clicked matches (i.e. nCM). The algorithm returns the ratio of the final nM and nCM.

3.4 Baselines

We compare click-based lambdas to the following baselines, which are applied to the same n_{imps} impressions used to calculate our click-based lambdas:

CTR ranker: Given a query, for each of the top 5 ranked documents, we record its click-through rate (CTR), which is equal to the number of times the document received a click divided by the number of times it was displayed (i.e., the number of times the query was issued). The CTR ranker then sorts the documents in decreasing order of their CTRs.

CTR1 ranker: Same as above with CTR replaced by CTR1, i.e., the number of times the document was clicked while at the top of the list divided by the number of times it appeared there.

Position bias corrected CTR ranker: This is a modification of the CTR ranker, where the clicks are counted as follows: given a query q appearing in impressions $I_1, \ldots, I_N$, we first count for each j the number, n_j, of impressions with clicks at the jth position; now, given an impression with a click on document d that appears at the jth position, instead of incrementing the numerator of the CTR for document d by 1 as in the CTR ranker, we add $1/n_j$. The idea is that if you are half as likely to get a click on the second position than on the first position in a collection of randomly shuffled result pages, then receiving a click on the second position is worth two clicks on the first position.

In addition to the above, we also compare against the **production** and **random** rankers, where the random ranker shuffles the top 5 results produced by the production ranker.

3.5 Results

In this section, we provide results to answer **RQ1**. We make use of the experimental setup outlined in §3.1. The average performances (determined over the 1,000 repetitions described at the end of §3.2) are depicted in Fig. 1, with 95% confidence bands drawn around each mean curve. Moreover, the results are normalized by the performance of the production ranker.

As these results illustrate, even with as few as 20 shuffled impressions per query, all four click-based methods improve significantly upon the production ranker, with three of them giving improvements even with as few as 10 impressions (click-based lambdas, CTR ranker, Bias corrected CTR ranker). Moreover, click-based lambdas give us the largest boost as the number of impressions grows.

Furthermore, inspecting the plot more closely, one can make the following observations:

- The performances of both the click-based lambdas method and the CTR1 ranker improve as the training size increases, whereas that does not seem to be the case with the CTR ranker and its position bias corrected variant.
- For training sizes that are equal to 80 impressions per query or larger, click-based lambdas significantly outperform all other methods.
- Despite the asymptotic flaw of the two CTR rankers, they appear to be very sample efficient, as even 6 randomized impressions per query suffice for them to improve upon the production ranker.
- The position bias correction employed here does not remedy the shortcomings of the CTR ranker, since the results of the two rankers (the CTR ranker and its position bias corrected version) are intertwined with each other.

The most perplexing of these observations are those involving the CTR ranker and its bias corrected variant, which seem to suggest that CTR can result in non-trivial improvements quickly, but then it hits a ceiling. We are not aware of any user models that can explain this, so we leave it as future work to come up with an explanation.

Given these results, we can answer **RQ1** in the affirmative, with the addition that relative comparisons between documents can lead to the largest improvements, as demonstrated by the click-based lambdas method. Importantly, this can be done efficiently enough to be useful for torso queries (with between 10 and 200 impressions in our exploration log), hence our click-based lambdas method has the potential to positively affect a large portion of the traffic.

4. ANALYZING THE IMPACT OF CLICK-BASED LAMBDAS

In this section, we take a closer look at the click-based lambdas method in an attempt to gain a deeper understanding of its inner workings. To this end, we conduct experiments using simulated clicks generated by a click model. This allows us to acquire a more detailed understanding of the effect of click-based lambdas and to investigate less severe forms of exploration. We opted for a more artificial experimental setup because of both the extra flexibility and the added control over the production ranker that it affords us. As we will see, in this setup we can dissect the results using quantities that cannot even be calculated in the case of real click logs.

4.1 Experimental design

The click model [8] we use for this set of experiments is a probabilistic version of the cascade click model [9, 15, 18], which inspects the documents in the result list from top to bottom and clicks on each document with a probability that depends on its relevance and abandons the search with another probability, which also depends on the current document under examination: note that we allow for more than one click on a result page. This click model is applied to the MSLR Web-30K [34] and Yahoo! Learning to Rank Challenge [7] datasets; see Table 1 for the specifics of these datasets. In particular, the documents in these datasets are assigned one of five relevance labels and we use the parameters specified by the navigational click model described in previous work [20] to set the click and abandonment probabilities, which depend on the relevance of the document being examined by the simulated user.

One important benefit of this setup is that it allows us to compute the *normalized* page click-through rate, denoted nPCTR, of a page, which we define as follows:

Table 1: The specifics of the datasets used.

Datasets	Queries	URLs	Features
MSLR-WEB30K [34]	31,531	3,771,125	136
YLR Set 1 [7]	29,921	709,877	519
YLR Set 2 [7]	6,330	172,870	596

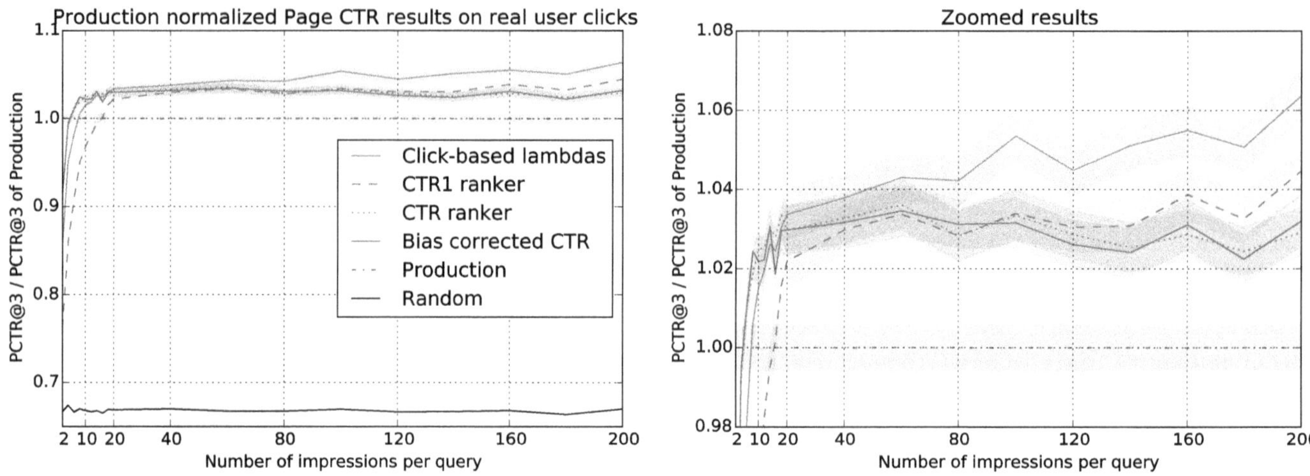

Figure 1: Page CTR@3 results for increasing numbers of impressions per query. The right plot is a zoomed version of the left one.

DEFINITION 2. *Given a click model, a query q and ranked documents* $d_1, \ldots, d_L$, *we define* nPCTR@K *of the ranked list to be equal to PCTR@K of the ranked list divided by the PCTR@K of the perfect ranking, i.e., the one obtained by sorting the documents in descending order of relevance.*

Note that PCTR is related to nPCTR in the same way that Discounted Cumulative Gain (DCG) is related to Normalized DCG (NDCG). Even though our ultimate objective is to optimize for PCTR, the utility of nPCTR is in that it gives us an indication of how suboptimal our ranked list is. Note that PCTR might be small because either there are no relevant documents to present or the ranked list is of low quality: nPCTR resolves this uncertainty by only measuring the quality of the ranker, rather than that of the documents being ranked. We will make extensive use of this metric in our click model based experiments in order to get a better understanding of the aggregate results, as explained below.

Using this setup, we carry out three sets of experiments:

1. To address **RQ2**, we consider a per query decomposition of the performance of an *offline-trained* LambdaMART model according to the nPCTR performance of each query: by an offline-trained model, we mean one that has been trained on the manually produced relevance judgments provided with our LTR datasets. This gives us a more detailed understanding of how suboptimal the performance of LambdaMART is across queries. The results are presented in §4.2.
2. To address **RQ3**, we interleave the above LambdaMART model with a random ranker for a fixed number of impressions for each query and combine the resulting click-based lambdas with the scores produced by LambdaMART in various ways and compare the performance of the resulting ranker against that of the off-line model. The results are presented in §4.3.
3. To address **RQ4** and better understand the performance changes observed in the last set of experiments, we consider a decomposition of the results into query segments according to the performance of the LambdaMART ranker on the query, where performance is measured according to nPCTR. The results are provided in §4.4.

The rationale behind the type of exploration experiment carried out in the two sets of experiments outlined above is the following: given a set of queries on which our production ranker is performing substantially worse than the ideal ranker, it might be easier to motivate an exploration scheme where a certain fraction of the top results are chosen at random, rather than a complete shuffling of the results as in the case of the exploration click log used in §3. Note that in the case of the latter, complete shuffling was necessary to facilitate offline evaluation of the re-ranking schemes investigated in this paper, but it is not necessary for the methods themselves.

4.2 Detailed analysis of the performance of LambdaMART

Given the results in §3, a natural question is how close the results produced by LTR models are to being optimal across queries. This question is interesting because it offers us a deeper understanding of whether or not there is a need for paying closer attention to individual queries. This is the purpose of **RQ2**. In order to address it, we take a closer look at the quality of the rankings produced by a parameter-tuned[2] LambdaMART model trained on two large datasets and inspect the nPCTR of the queries in the dataset, as measured using the click-model experimental setup described in §4.1. The motivation for using nPCTR, as opposed to PCTR, is that the former is a more direct indicator of the quality of the ranker, regardless of the relevance of the documents in the dataset.

More precisely, using a large parameter sweep, we train LambdaMART models using the training folds of the MSLR and Yahoo! Set 1[3] datasets; we also use the validation fold to regularize the number of trees grown by the model through early stopping of the tree growing process if no improvement on the validation set was observed after the addition of 50 consecutive trees. Given all models trained in this manner, the model with the highest nPCTR@3 performance on the validation fold is evaluated on the test fold, keeping track of the performance on individual queries.

Before proceeding to the results, let us address the issue of the target metric used by LambdaMART: we use PCTR, nPCTR and NDCG with cut-offs of 3, 5 and 10 in the training process. It turns out that the model with the highest nPCTR@3 performance uses NDCG as the training metric. This is probably because NDCG is an easier objective function to optimize than PCTR and nPCTR perhaps because of the discounting used in NDCG, which might make it a more slowly varying metric as a function of the ranking.

The plots in Fig. 2 show histograms of the nPCTR@3 performance of the parameter-tuned LambdaMART model selected as

[2]Meaning that the parameters used by LambdaMART, e.g., max tree depth, have all been tuned. In machine learning this is sometimes called "hyperparameter-tuned."

[3]For the results in this section and the ones that follow, we leave out Yahoo! Set 2 because the results of the two subsets of the Yahoo! were qualitatively similar, so we chose to leave those plots out of this presentation, in order to leave room for a more detailed discussion of the results.

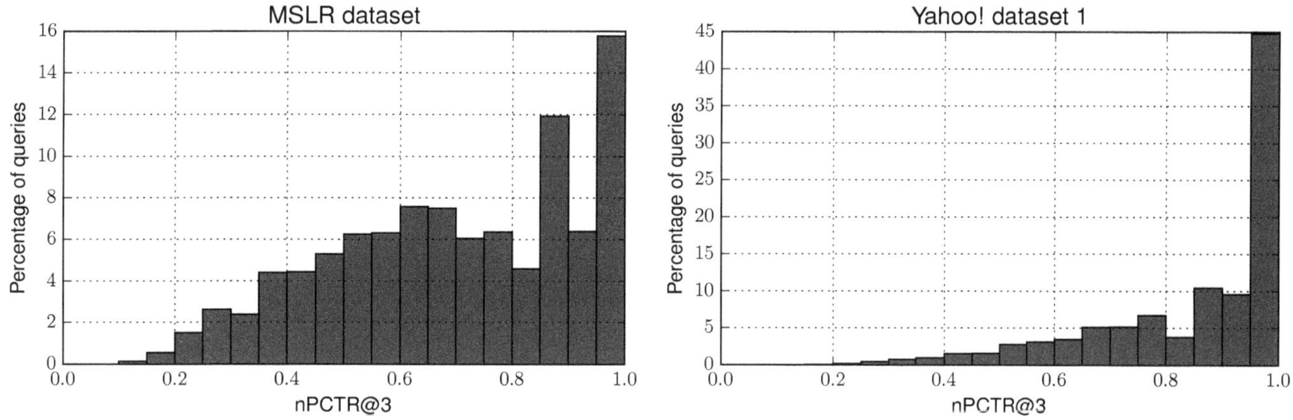

Figure 2: Histogram of the nPCTR@3 performance of LambdaMART on individual queries in the MSLR and Yahoo! datasets.

above on the individual queries in the test fold of the MSLR and Yahoo! Set 1 datasets. The most clear distinction between the two sets of results is that the ranking results produced by the model that was trained on the larger of the two datasets (i.e. MSLR) tend to be of much lower quality: in the case of the Yahoo! dataset, for roughly 55% of the queries, the PCTR@3 of our LambdaMART model is 90% of PCTR@3 of the ideal ranking (i.e. their nPCTR@3 is at least 0.9), whereas in the case of the MSLR dataset this is true of less than 23% of the queries.

We hypothesize that the above discrepancy is due to the following: even though the specific features that accompany the Yahoo! dataset are not specified, according to the overview provided by the challenge organizers [7], the feature set contains many click features, which could potentially aid in training a model that performs better on online metrics. In contrast, there are only three features among the 136 included with the MSLR dataset that pertain to clicks (cf. the feature list in [34]). Also, another potential explanation could be that the MSLR dataset has many more documents per query than the Yahoo! one, so this might hinder the ability of LambdaMART to learn the ideal ranking for each query.

Given the above observations, we see that the answer to **RQ2** depends to a large extent on the quality of the features used to train the model, but that a large fraction of the queries tend to underperform: for instance, our results for the Yahoo! dataset show that, in the case of more than 30% of the queries, the LambdaMART model attains nPCTR@3 of 0.8 or lower; in other words, there is room for a 20% improvement in the PCTR@3 of almost a third of the queries. In the case of the MSLR dataset, the same holds for more than 60% of the queries.

4.3 Click-based lambdas vs. LambdaMART

In this section, we continue using our click-model based setup to examine the effect that click-based lambdas have on page-level performance of our LambdaMART model. In particular, we interleave the offline-trained ranker against a random ranker, using the Team Draft interleaving procedure [39], and calculate click-based lambdas using the procedure described in §2.2. Please note that interleaving is used as a mechanism for introducing randomness into the ranked lists for the purpose of exploration, rather than the usual goal of comparing two rankers. This is performed for various numbers of interleaved impressions per query (denoted n_{imps}). We then consider convex combinations of the resulting click-based lambdas and the scores produced by our LambdaMART model and evaluate the resulting rankers. The reason for considering convex combinations of the LambdaMART scores and the click-based lambdas is to make use of the information provided by both methods.

The plots in Fig. 3 illustrate the results of these experiments on the MSLR and the Yahoo! datasets for 5 different values of n_{imps}. As with the results in the previous section, there are qualitative differences between the results for the two datasets:

- After 20 interleaved impressions, click-based lambdas already outperform LambdaMART in the case of the MSLR dataset: to see this, note that in the bottom curve in the left plot in Fig. 3, the right end (i.e., where $\alpha = 1$), which corresponds to click-based lambdas, is higher than the left end (i.e., $\alpha = 0$), which corresponds to LambdaMART. On the other hand, in the case of the Yahoo! dataset, we need more impressions for click-based lambdas to outperform LambdaMART on their own.
- In the case of the MSLR dataset, given 100 interleaved impressions, there is very little that is gained from combining the scores of LambdaMART with click-based lambdas over how the latter was performing, which is in contrast to the Yahoo! dataset, on which even 100 interleavings against the random ranker are not enough to render the offline model unnecessary.

We attribute these differences to the worse performance of the LambdaMART model trained on the MSLR dataset; see §4.2.

Irrespective of the difference between the results for the two datasets, what can be readily observed in both plots is that even after a small number of impressions for which the ranked results produced by LambdaMART are interleaved with a random ranker, the scores produced by LambdaMART can be modified using click-based lambdas to produce significantly improved ranked lists. Thus, the answer to **RQ3** is affirmative: using a modest amount of exploration, involving randomly selecting roughly half of the documents in 20 impressions, we can combine the resulting click-based lambdas with the LambdaMART scores to obtain substantial improvements over the LambdaMART model as well as click-based lambdas themselves.

4.4 Decomposition of the effect of click-based lambdas

Here, we inspect more closely the effect that combining click-based lambdas with LambdaMART scores has on individual queries. This is done by considering one particular value of α (as in §4.3) and investigating the change in performance, compared to the original LambdaMART model, on a per query basis. We then group the queries according to their performance under LambdaMART.

The two plots in Fig. 4 depict this decomposition for the MSLR and the Yahoo! datasets when α and n_{imps} are set to be 0.1 and 100, respectively: the value of α is set to 0.1 because in all of the curves in the two plots in Fig. 3 the value at $\alpha = 0.1$ is roughly close to the maximum, so this seems like a good practical guess for

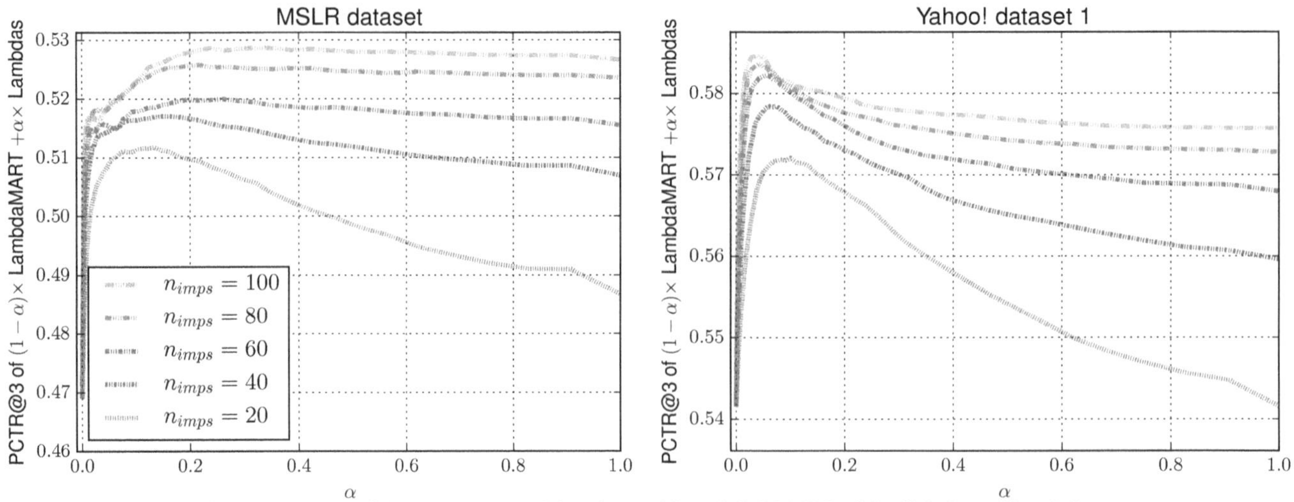

Figure 3: PCTR@3 of convex combinations of LambdaMART with click-based lambdas.

α in the absence of more detailed knowledge of the performances; moreover, we chose the number of interleaved impressions to be large to get a better understanding of the changes in the "limit" as the amount of exploration becomes large.

In both plots in Fig. 4 the horizontal axis groups queries according to nPCTR@3 of the LambdaMART model, while the vertical axis measures the change in PCTR@3 as click-based lambdas are added to the scores produced by LambdaMART. Perhaps the most prominent phenomenon in these plots is that most of the degradation caused by click-based lambdas occurs in the case of queries on which the performance of the original LambdaMART model is rather close to being optimal. This is rather obvious in the case of the Yahoo! dataset, where the majority of the degradations are caused by queries on which the nPCTR@3 of the LambdaMART model is higher than 0.975, i.e., those represented by the right-most red bar in the bottom plot in Fig. 4. However, this is also the case in the case of the MSLR dataset, although perhaps in a slightly less extreme form. We consider this finding to be a positive one, since it implies that if one can determine queries on which the production ranker's performance is close to being optimal, then we can avoid applying the ideas presented in this paper to those queries and avoid the pitfall of ruining the ranked lists produced by LambdaMART where they are performing well, leading to more effective use of the signals harvested from the exploration data.

In other words, **RQ4** can be answered in the affirmative: click-based lambdas tend to help most in the case of queries that are underperforming under the offline-trained LambdaMART model, so given an identification of such queries, it is advisable to apply the method proposed in this paper to those queries only.

4.5 Summary

The issue of underperforming queries is one that LambdaMART grapples with in most cases. Click-based lambdas used in conjunction with a small amount of exploration can lead to significant improvements, in particular when combined with the scores produced by the original LambdaMART model. This suggests that a practical solution can be devised to remedy the underperforming queries affecting our ranker's performance, which we discuss next.

5. PRACTICAL CONSIDERATIONS

In this section, we say a few words about one possible use-case for the click-based lambdas method. This is in particular relevant given the fact that all of the methods discussed in this paper are query-document specific, in the sense that the outcome is a re-ranking of a specific set of documents for each query, with no generalization across query-document pairs. This of course does not conform to the regular mold of LTR methods. However, as we describe below, our method can be used in conjunction with them. The idea is that even though eventually better features and LTR algorithms might be devised that could address the shortcomings of the existing ranker, we would like to get better results right away, rather than waiting for the invention and deployment of an

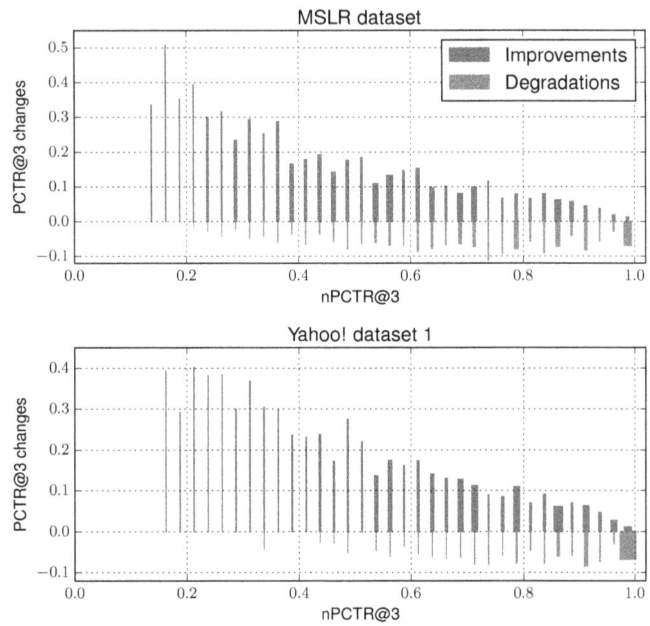

Figure 4: PCTR@3 improvements and degradations of queries if LambdaMART were to be replaced by LambdaMART + $0.1\times$ Lambdas: the queries are grouped by their nPCTR@3 under LambdaMART. The green boxes take account of queries whose PCTR@3 improves by the transition from LambdaMART to LambdaMART + $0.1\times$Lambdas, while the red boxes correspond to queries that would suffer a loss. The height of each box shows the average change in the PCTR@3 of the queries in that bin and the width measures the number of queries in the bin: so, the area of the box is an indication of the effect that the changes in the performances of the queries in the given box have on the overall performance.

improved system. We see this as a more automated alternative to rule-based patches that try to deal with specific types of queries.

Let us now address the issue of implementation in practice: given a set of underperforming queries and their corresponding ranked lists of documents provided by click-based lambdas, we can simply use the existing features to fit a (potentially large) regression tree to the lambdas. Note that the goal here is not generalizability, so the regression tree is simply a compression mechanism. Moreover, given a binary feature that singles out our underperforming queries, we can add a node to the top of the above tree to make sure it is only applied to the relevant query-document pairs. This modified tree can then be added to our existing ranker, either as a post processing step or as an additional tree in our existing ensemble of trees: in the latter case, we can modify the existing trees by adding the same underperforming query identification to the root of each tree to make sure the existing ranker is not applied to the queries for which we have click-based lambdas. In this way, we incorporate the re-rankings learned by our method into the existing ranker without the need to alter the existing infrastructure dramatically.

A natural question at this point is whether or not it is possible to use click-based lambdas to modify the LTR model globally, rather than restricting the modification to the underperforming queries. Preliminary results involving numerous attempts at augmenting the LambdaMART model resulted in no improvements in the overall performance of the ranker beyond that of the original LambdaMART model that was trained on the relevance judgments.

As the experimental results in §3.5 demonstrate, a few dozen randomized impressions is all that is required to obtain non-trivial improvements. So, given, e.g., a query that is issued a few hundred times a week, using our click-based lambdas method, obtaining improvements over the course of a month is easily within reach, even assuming that no more than 20% of the impressions can be tampered with for the purpose of exploration. In the case of many popular retrieval systems, be it web search engines or recommender systems, the rough requirements outlined above apply to torso queries.[4]

6. RELATED WORK

In addition to the work on evaluation (based, in particular, on inverse propensity scoring and click models) discussed in §3.3 and §4.1, we discuss related work on implicit feedback, exploration and online learning to rank, and ranker specialization.

6.1 Implicit feedback

Learning from user feedback has a rather long history in IR [1, 11, 22, 24, 36, 44, 45], much of it predating many of the major breakthroughs in LTR. As a result of that, many of the experimental results in the literature on this topic need to be revisited, given that the baselines used for comparison are substantially weaker than the LTR models [7] and features [42] in use today. Extensive user studies indicate that user clicks can be of great use in inferring the relative relevance of documents to a given query [25]. Given this, a natural question is whether implicit feedback can still be useful despite a decade of advances in LTR. Our results show that the answer is *yes*.

An important exception to the above criticism regarding the weakness of the baselines is [35], which is the work most closely related to ours. Like us, the authors use a commercial search engine as their main baseline. Their method corresponds to our CTR1 baseline, which our results in §3.5 show to be less efficient than click-based lambdas in learning a good ranking. Also, CTR1 only takes into account documents that appear in the first position, so it is important that each document appears in the top position relatively often. Another important difference between this work and [35] is the latter's focus on *recency ranking*, which is solely concerned with queries with shifting intent; we make no such assumption.

6.2 Exploration and online LTR

Another body of work related to ours is that of online LTR, where the goal is to balance exploration and exploitation [17, 26] while improving the ranker incrementally [14, 19, 21, 28, 37, 38, 40, 43]. This is in contrast to the "explore first" strategy investigated in this paper, where the exploration is carried out entirely before we set out to extract a ranker from the data. The advantage of the adaptive exploration scheme is in its potential ability to avoid unnecessary exploration, however such online schemes are generally very difficult to utilize in industrial applications, both for technical and business reasons. On the other hand, the exploration schemes discussed here are not as sophisticated, but they tend to be much easier use in practice. In particular, in the case of underperforming queries, where there is compelling evidence that the existing ranker is performing poorly, it is much easier to make the case for exploration.

6.3 Underperforming queries

One group of queries that have generated special attention and inspired work on ranker specialization are so-called underperforming queries [16, 27]. As discussed in §4.4, click-based lambdas are most effective in the case of underperforming queries and most harmful in the case of queries on which the production ranker is performing well, so the method would benefit greatly from prior knowledge of the quality of the existing ranker on individual queries. We have not made use of such underperforming query detection techniques for the experiments in §3 and the results presented in §3.5 are not restricted to underperforming queries. Such a restriction would of course inflate the improvements in the performance of click-based lambdas compared to the production ranker.

One solution for dealing with underperforming queries is ranker specialization [3, 12, 13, 16], where one explicitly takes into account the fact that queries vary significantly in terms of ranking and may need different treatments. The general idea is to cluster "similar" queries into different groups, based on different notions of similarity, and train a *specialized* ranker for each cluster. The main issue with this body of work is the weakness of the baselines used for comparison because the models used for the specialized rankers are linear and so are those of the baselines. It remains an interesting open question to apply the same idea with more complex models such as ensembles of trees.

7. CONCLUSION

We have investigated the use of click feedback together with exploration to improve upon learning to rank (LTR) methods. We have carried out comparisons against both a commercial search engine, using real users, and the state of the art LTR algorithm, LambdaMART, using a well-established simulated user model. Furthermore, we experimented with two different exploration schemes: random shuffling of top L documents produced by the production ranker in use, for some fixed number L, and interleaving the results of the ranker against a random ranker.

The results of these experiments demonstrate that significant improvements can be obtained in terms of page-level online metrics, in particular when employing relative comparisons between documents as with our click-based lambdas method. We provide a simple yet efficient remedy to close the gap between the online

[4]This argument also applies to head queries, but the sample efficiency demonstrated here is more likely to be of greater significance in the case of the less frequent queries.

performance of LTR methods and that of click-based methods in the case of underperforming torso queries.

We have focused on exploration methods that are simple and easily implementable. A more sophisticated exploration scheme that actively adapts to user feedback (e.g., [37]) is likely to reduce the amount of exploration needed to obtain meaningful gains, but the added complexity makes it more challenging to use. The question of what exploration scheme would lead to the largest gains while minimizing the adverse effect on user experience remains an interesting open problem. Another natural question arising out of this work is that of improved methods for detecting underperforming queries. One approach could be to use guided exploration in the presented results to detect changes in the performance of the ranker. We conjecture that the gap between the performance of the LTR methods and that of the click-based methods explored here is due to the context-insensitivity of the current state of the art, tree-based LTR algorithms, which tend not to make extensive use of query features, as well as other contextual features. If true, then a natural direction for further research would be to devise LTR algorithms that make better use of contextual information.

Acknowledgments. This research was supported by Ahold, Amsterdam Data Science, the Bloomberg Research Grant program, the Dutch national program COMMIT, Elsevier, the European Community's Seventh Framework Programme (FP7/2007-2013) under grant agreement nr 312827 (VOX-Pol), the ESF Research Network Program ELIAS, the Royal Dutch Academy of Sciences (KNAW) under the Elite Network Shifts project, the Microsoft Research Ph.D. program, the Netherlands eScience Center under project number 027.012.105, the Netherlands Institute for Sound and Vision, the Netherlands Organisation for Scientific Research (NWO) under project nrs 727.011.005, 612.001.116, HOR-11-10, 640.006.013, 612.066.-930, CI-14-25, SH-322-15, 652.002.001, 612.001.551, the Yahoo Faculty Research and Engagement Program, and Yandex. All content represents the opinion of the authors, which is not necessarily shared or endorsed by their respective employers and/or sponsors.

REFERENCES

[1] E. Agichtein, E. Brill, and S. Dumais. Improving web search ranking by incorporating user behavior information. In *SIGIR*, 2006.

[2] P. Bennett, M. Shokouhi, and R. Caruana. Implicit preference labels for learning highly selective personalized rankers. In *ICTIR*, 2015.

[3] J. Bian, X. Li, F. Li, Z. Zheng, and H. Zha. Ranking specialization for web search: A divide-and-conquer approach by using topical RankSVM. In *WWW*, 2010.

[4] L. Bottou et al. Counterfactual reasoning and learning systems: The example of computational advertising. *JMLR*, 14:3207–3260, 2013.

[5] C. Burges, R. Ragno, and Q. Le. Learning to rank with non-smooth cost functions. In *NIPS*, 2007.

[6] C. J. Burges. From RankNet to LambdaRank to LambdaMART: An overview. Techn. Report MSR-TR-2010-82, MSR, June 2010.

[7] O. Chapelle and Y. Chang. Yahoo! learning to rank challenge overview. *JMLR-Proceedings Track*, 14:1–24, 2011.

[8] A. Chuklin, I. Markov, and M. de Rijke. *Click Models for Web Search*. Morgan & Claypool, 2015.

[9] N. Craswell, O. Zoeter, M. Taylor, and B. Ramsey. An experimental comparison of click position-bias models. In *WSDM*, 2008.

[10] P. Donmez, K. M. Svore, and C. J. C. Burges. On the local optimality of LambdaRank. In *SIGIR*, 2009.

[11] S. Fox, K. Karnawat, M. Mydland, S. Dumais, and T. White. Evaluating implicit measures to improve web search. *TOIS*, 23(2): 147–168, 2005.

[12] X. Geng, T.-Y. Liu, T. Qin, A. Arnold, H. Li, and H.-Y. Shum. Query dependent ranking using k-nearest neighbor. In *SIGIR*, 2008.

[13] G. Giannopoulos, U. Brefeld, T. Dalamagas, and T. Sellis. Learning to rank user intent. In *CIKM*, 2011.

[14] A. Grotov, S. Whiteson, and M. de Rijke. Bayesian ranker comparison based on historical user interactions. In *SIGIR*, 2015.

[15] F. Guo, C. Liu, and Y.-M. Wang. Efficient multiple-click models in web search. In *WSDM*, 2009.

[16] A. Hassan, R. W. White, and Y.-M. Wang. Toward self-correcting search engines: Using underperforming queries to improve search. In *SIGIR*, 2013.

[17] K. Hofmann, S. Whiteson, and M. de Rijke. Balancing exploration and exploitation in learning to rank online. In *ECIR*, 2011.

[18] K. Hofmann, S. Whiteson, and M. de Rijke. A probabilistic method for inferring preferences from clicks. In *CIKM*, 2011.

[19] K. Hofmann, A. Schuth, S. Whiteson, and M. de Rijke. Reusing historical interaction data for faster online learning to rank for IR. In *WSDM*, 2013.

[20] K. Hofmann, S. Whiteson, and M. de Rijke. Fidelity, soundness, and efficiency of interleaved comparison methods. *TOIS*, 31(4), 2013.

[21] K. Hofmann, S. Whiteson, and M. de Rijke. Balancing exploration and exploitation in listwise and pairwise online learning to rank for information retrieval. *Information Retrieval*, 16(1):63–90, 2013.

[22] K. Hofmann, L. Li, and F. Radlinski. Online evaluation for information retrieval. *Foundations and Trends in Information Retrieval*, 2016. To appear.

[23] A. Jain and G. Mishne. Organizing query completions for web search. In *CIKM*, 2010.

[24] T. Joachims. Optimizing search engines using clickthrough data. In *KDD*, 2002.

[25] T. Joachims, L. Granka, B. Pan, H. Hembrooke, F. Radlinski, and G. Gay. Evaluating the accuracy of implicit feedback from clicks and query reformulations in Web search. *TOIS*, 25(2), 2007.

[26] M. Karimzadehgan and C. Zhai. A learning approach to optimizing exploration-exploitation tradeoff in relevance feedback. *Information Retrieval*, 16:307–330, 2013.

[27] Y. Kim, A. Hassan, R. W. White, and Y.-M. Wang. Playing by the rules: Mining query associations to predict search performance. In *WSDM*, 2013.

[28] B. Kveton, C. Szepesvari, Z. Wen, and A. Ashkan. Cascading bandits: Learning to rank in the cascade model. In *ICML*, 2015.

[29] D. Lefortier, P. Serdyukov, and M. de Rijke. Online exploration for detecting shifts in fresh intent. In *CIKM*, 2014.

[30] L. Li, W. Chu, J. Langford, and X. Wang. Unbiased offline evaluation of contextual-bandit-based news article recommendation algorithms. In *WSDM*, 2011.

[31] L. Li, S. Chen, A. Gupta, and J. Kleban. Counterfactual estimation and optimization of click metrics in search engines: A case study. In *WWW (Companion)*, 2015.

[32] T.-Y. Liu. Learning to rank for information retrieval. *Foundations and Trends in Information Retrieval*, 3(3):225–331, 2009.

[33] Z. Liu, G. Singh, N. Parikh, and N. Sundaresan. A large scale query logs analysis for assessing personalization opportunities in e-commerce sites. In *WSCD*, 2014.

[34] Microsoft Learning to Rank Datasets, 2012. http://research.microsoft.com/en-us/projects/mslr/default.aspx.

[35] T. Moon, W. Chu, L. Li, Z. Zheng, and Y. Chang. An online learning framework for refining recency search results with user click feedback. *TOIS*, 30(4):20:1–20:28, 2012.

[36] F. Radlinski and T. Joachims. Query chains: Learning to rank from implicit feedback. In *KDD*, 2005.

[37] F. Radlinski and T. Joachims. Active exploration for learning rankings from clickthrough data. In *KDD*, 2007.

[38] F. Radlinski, R. Kleinberg, and T. Joachims. Learning diverse rankings with multi-armed bandits. In *ICML*, 2008.

[39] F. Radlinski, M. Kurup, and T. Joachims. How does clickthrough data reflect retrieval quality? In *CIKM*, 2008.

[40] A. Slivkins, F. Radlinski, and S. Gollapudi. Ranked bandits in metric spaces: learning diverse rankings over large document collections. *JMLR*, 14(1):399–436, 2013.

[41] A. L. Strehl, J. Langford, L. Li, and S. M. Kakade. Learning from logged implicit exploration data. In *NIPS*, 2011.

[42] J. Teevan, D. J. Liebling, and G. Ravichandran Geetha. Understanding and predicting personal navigation. In *WSDM*, 2011.

[43] Y. Yue and T. Joachims. Interactively optimizing information retrieval systems as a dueling bandits problem. In *ICML*, 2009.

[44] M. Zoghi, S. Whiteson, M. de Rijke, and R. Munos. Relative confidence sampling for efficient on-line ranker evaluation. In *WSDM*, 2014.

[45] M. Zoghi, S. Whiteson, and M. de Rijke. MergeRUCB: A method for large-scale online ranker evaluation. In *WSDM*, 2015.

A Context-aware Time Model for Web Search

Alexey Borisov[†, ‡] alborisov@yandex-team.ru
Ilya Markov[‡] i.markov@uva.nl
Maarten de Rijke[‡] derijke@uva.nl
Pavel Serdyukov[†] pavser@yandex-team.ru

[†] Yandex, Moscow, Russia
[‡] University of Amsterdam, Amsterdam, The Netherlands

ABSTRACT

In web search, information about times between user actions has been shown to be a good indicator of users' satisfaction with the search results. Existing work uses the mean values of the observed times, or fits probability distributions to the observed times. This implies a *context-independence* assumption that the time elapsed between a pair of user actions does not depend on the context, in which the first action takes place. We validate this assumption using logs of a commercial web search engine and discover that it does not always hold. For between 37% to 80% of query-result pairs, depending on the number of observations, the distributions of click dwell times have statistically significant differences in query sessions for which a given result (i) is the first item to be clicked and (ii) is not the first. To account for this *context bias* effect, we propose a *context-aware time model* (CATM). The CATM allows us (i) to predict times between user actions in contexts, in which these actions were not observed, and (ii) to compute context-independent estimates of the times by predicting them in predefined contexts. Our experimental results show that the CATM provides better means than existing methods to predict and interpret times between user actions.

Keywords

Time modeling; User behavior; Web search

1. INTRODUCTION

Search engine logs provide a rich source of information about user browsing behavior in web search. Recently, many models have been proposed to explain and predict user clicks on search engine results [13]. While click events are the most widely logged form of user interaction, there are also other behavioral signals that need to be understood, interpreted and modeled, and that can be used for ranking or prediction purposes.

We focus on behavioral signals based on times between user actions. The ability to accurately predict (i) click dwell time (i.e., time spent by a user on the landing page of a search result), and (ii) times from submission of a query to the first/last click on the results and to the next query submission (if none of the results will be clicked) allows us to optimize search engines for constructing result pages and suggesting query reformulations that minimize time it takes users to satisfy their information needs.

SIGIR '16, July 17 - 21, 2016, Pisa, Italy

ISBN 978-1-4503-4069-4/16/07...$15.00

DOI: http://dx.doi.org/10.1145/2911451.2911504

Existing work shows that times elapsed between user actions provide means to measure user satisfaction at the result level [18, 30], session level [18, 20] and system level [10, 39]. To interpret times elapsed between user actions, existing work uses mean values of the observed times [1–3, 8, 10, 20–22, 32, 33, 36, 39], or fits probability distributions to the observed times [30, 31]. This implies a *context-independence assumption* that the time elapsed between a pair of user actions does not depend on the context in which the first action takes place.

We validate this assumption by comparing the distributions of times associated with the same user action (i.e., submitting a given query or clicking on a given result presented for a given query), but preceded by different sequences of user interactions with the search engine. We find statistically significant differences between these distributions, which we explain by a *context bias effect*, not previously reported in the literature.

To account for the context bias effect, we propose a *context-aware time model* (CATM) that allows us to predict probability distributions of times between two user actions in a given context (which we represent by a sequence of previous user interactions with the search engine). The CATM can be used (i) to predict times between user actions in contexts, in which these user actions were not observed, and (ii) to compute context-independent estimates of the times by predicting them in predefined contexts. The *context-dependent* predictions can be used for personalized ranking and personalized query suggestion. The *context-independent* predictions can be used for predicting result relevance and in other tasks that use historical times between user actions.

We evaluate the CATM on four temporal prediction tasks (i.e., tasks in which we predict the time elapsed between two user actions), and find that the CATM outperforms the standard time modeling approach that fits probability distributions to the times observed for the first user action. We test the CATM's context-independent predictions of times between consecutive clicks on a ranking task (i.e., to rank a set of results by their relevance to a query), and find that the produced rankings result in better performance in terms of relevance than the rankings produced by the standard time modeling approaches.

In summary, we make the following contributions in our work.

C1 We introduce the notion of context bias in times elapsed between user actions, which has not previously been reported in the literature, and use logs of a commercial search engine to provide empirical evidence for it.

C2 We propose a context-aware time model. Through the use of contextual information (and, in particular, previous user interactions with a search engine), it provides better means for predicting and interpreting times between user actions compared to existing time modeling techniques.

The rest of the paper is organized as follows. In §2 we specify the considered temporal prediction tasks. In §3 we propose the context-aware time model. In §4 we detail our experimental setup and in §5 we present the outcomes of our experiments. We discuss related work in §6 and conclude in §7.

2. TEMPORAL PREDICTION TASKS

We describe and motivate temporal prediction tasks that we consider in our work. In each task we aim to predict the time elapsed between a pair of user actions. The user actions can be of several types: submission of a query, click on a search result, click on an ad banner, scroll through search results, zoom in on a search result (in mobile search), etc. Here, we focus on user actions of the first two types: submission of a query (Q-action) and click on a search result (C-action), because these user actions occur in all search systems.

To define a temporal prediction task, we need to specify a set of action pairs between which we aim to predict times. When choosing these pairs, we follow two principles.

1. We select pairs of user actions for which the time elapsed between them is indicative of user satisfaction. The ability to predict times, that help to anticipate user satisfaction with search results, allows us to construct result pages that maximize user satisfaction with the search.

2. We select pairs of user actions for which the times elapsed between them have a similar nature (i.e., similar human interpretations). This is important, because times that have different human interpretations are likely to be unequally useful in practical applications, and can also be used in different scenarios. Thus, we want to be able to measure the prediction performance of each group of times separately.

We define four temporal prediction tasks: *time-to-first-click*, *time-between-clicks*, *time-to-last-click*, and *time-from-abandoned-query*. The pairs of user actions used in each task are shown in Figure 1. Below, we describe them in more detail and provide motivations

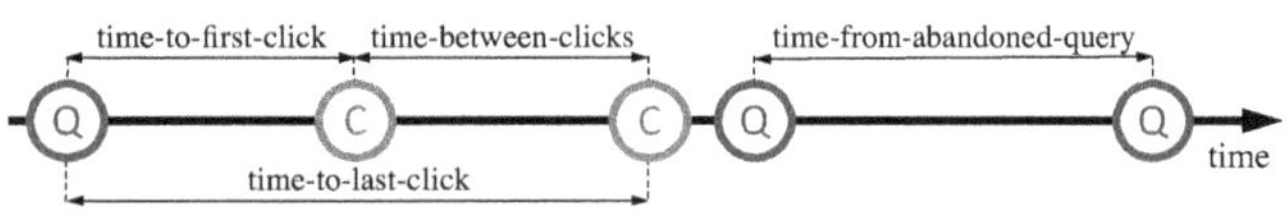

Figure 1: Times between pairs of user actions used in the considered temporal prediction tasks.

for our focus on these specific tasks.

Time-to-first-click is the time between a submission of a query and the first click on search engine results (undefined if there were no clicks on search results). Existing work shows that this time reflects the quality of result presentation: the less time it takes a user to find an attractive result, the better in terms of user experience the search engine result page (SERP) is [38]. The ability to predict time-to-first-click allows us to construct SERPs that are more intuitive to users, i.e., require less time/effort to find relevant results. Practically speaking, the predicted time can be used in any application that uses the average time-to-first-click observed in search engine logs as its more precise alternative. Existing work uses the average time-to-first-click observed for a query-result pair as a feature to predict search task difficulty [3], search goal success [20, 21], urgent information needs (e.g., how to stem a severe bleeding) [35]; and the average time-to-first-click observed for a user to cluster users based on their SERP examination strategies [7].

Time-between-clicks is the time between two consecutive clicks on search engine results (undefined for the last click on search results). We use this time as a proxy for *click dwell time* (i.e., the time spent by a user on the landing page of a search engine result), which has been shown to be a good indicator of click satisfaction [30]. The ability to predict click dwell time allows us to construct SERPs that yield more satisfied clicks, e.g., by using the predicted time-between-clicks as a feature for the search result ranker. Agichtein et al. [1, 2] use average click dwell times to improve result relevance. The Yahoo! Learning to Rank dataset [8] uses them as features for ranking. The predicted dwell times can also be utilized in most other applications that make use of the average click dwell times observed in search engine logs, which include prediction of click satisfaction [30], result usefulness [32], search task difficulty [3, 33], search goal success [20, 21], struggling vs. exploring behavior [22, 36].

Time-to-last-click is the time between a submission of a query and the last click on search engine results (undefined if there were no clicks on search results). Radlinski et al. [38] show that this time reflects the quality of search engine results: the less time it takes a user to find a relevant result, the better in terms of user experience the search engine results are. The ability to predict time-to-last-click allows us to suggest queries that require less time (effort) to satisfy user's information needs. The predicted times can be used as features for query suggestion and for other applications such as prediction of search task difficulty and search goal success (playing a similar role as the average time-to-first-click).

Time-from-abandoned-query is the time from a submission of an *abandoned query* (i.e., a query with no clicks) to the next query submission. Song et al. [41] show that this time reflects the quality of search engine results in query sessions with no clicks (thus, it is complementary to time-to-last-click, which is defined in query sessions with at least one click). A short time interval indicates user dissatisfaction (negative abandonment): the user could quickly see the problem with the presented results and it took them little time to reformulate the query. A large time interval indicates user satisfaction (positive abandonment): the user most likely could find the answer on the SERP, and it took them some time to come up with the next query. The ability to predict time-from-abandoned-query allows us to suggest queries with high chances of positive abandonment and to avoid suggesting queries that are likely to be quickly reformulated. Similar to time-to-last-click, the predicted time-from-abandoned-query can be used for query suggestion, prediction of task difficulty, search goal success, etc.

There are several other times-between-user-actions that have previously been considered in the literature, but that we do not seek to predict in this work for the reasons discussed below.

Time-between-last-click-and-next-query is the time between the last click on search engine results presented for one query and the submission of the next query. Some previous work uses both this time and the time-between-clicks as a proxy for click dwell time (called *server-side click dwell time*) [29, 30]. While both times approximate click dwell time, there are important differences between them: time-between-clicks is a sum of the actual click dwell time and the time to choose the next result to click (which is typically small and exhibits low variance), while time-between-last-click-and-next-query is a sum of the actual click dwell time and the time to formulate the next query (which is sometimes large, and exhibits high variance). Because of these differences in nature, we do not want to model time-between-clicks and time-between-last-click-and-next-query together (see principle 2). We do not create a temporal prediction task for time-between-last-click-and-next-query, as it is very similar to the time-between-clicks task, but the observed times are likely to be more noisy.

Time-to-first-satisfied-click is the time between a submission of a query and the first click classified as satisfied. This time can be seen as a generalization of time-to-first-click and time-to-last-click: if we classify all clicks as satisfied, time-to-first-satisfied-click reduces to time-to-first-click; if we classify only the last click as satisfied, time-to-first-satisfied-click reduces to time-to-last-click. Most work defines satisfied clicks as clicks with dwell times larger than a predefined threshold (e.g., 30 seconds) [18]. Kim et al. [30] propose a method to adjust this threshold individually for each search result. We do not create temporal prediction tasks for all possible definitions of satisfied clicks, because we believe that the temporal prediction tasks for time-to-first-click and time-to-last-click capture the most important phenomena.

3. METHOD

Now that we have specified the temporal prediction tasks, we describe our approach to modeling times between user actions. In §3.1 we formalize the problem and introduce the notation. In §3.2 we describe two frameworks for modeling times between user actions. In §3.3 we describe the context-aware time model (CATM).

3.1 Problem statement

Let the sequence $(a_1, t_1), \ldots, (a_n, t_n)$ be a search history, which consists of user actions $a_1, \ldots, a_n$ and their timestamps $t_1, \ldots, t_n$. We aim to design a time model for predicting times $\tau_{i \to j} = t_j - t_i$ elapsed from the action a_i to the action a_j. We consider a probabilistic formulation of this problem, where the time $\tau_{i \to j}$ is a random variable with a probability density function $f(x; \theta)$, where θ denotes a set of parameters of the probability distribution.

To describe a probabilistic time model we need to specify a probability density function $f(x; \theta)$ and an algorithm to compute its parameters θ. Common choices for $f(x; \theta)$ are the exponential, gamma and Weibull probability density functions [30, 31]; see Table 1 for their parameterizations. Below, we discuss the frameworks for computing the function parameters θ.

Table 1: Probability density functions and their parameters.

Distribution	PDF $f(x;\theta)$	Parameters θ
Exponential	ae^{-ax}	$a > 0$
Gamma	$\dfrac{x^{a-1}e^{-x/b}}{b^a\Gamma(a)}$	$a, b > 0$
Weibull	$\dfrac{a}{b}\left(\dfrac{x}{b}\right)^{a-1} e^{-(x/b)^a}$	$a, b > 0$

3.2 Time modeling frameworks

We describe two frameworks for modeling times between user actions. The first framework, called *basic time modeling framework*, makes the context-independence assumption that time between a pair of user actions depends solely on the first action ID, i.e., for submitting a query (Q-action), a unique identifier of the query string, and for clicking on a search result (C-action), an identifier of the query-result pair. The second framework, called *context-aware time modeling framework*, does not make the context-independence assumption and assumes that time between a pair of user actions depends on the first action ID and on the context in which the first action takes place.

3.2.1 Basic time modeling framework

Time models operating within the basic time modeling framework make the context-independence assumption that time $\tau_{i \to j}$ depends solely on the first action ID. We formalize this as $\tau_{i \to j} \sim f(x; \theta = \Theta(a_i))$, where Θ denotes a mapping from the space of actions $\mathcal{A}$ to the space of parameters of the probability density function $f(x; \theta)$.[1] We learn the mapping Θ by maximizing the likelihood of the observed times $\tau_{i \to j}$. The corresponding optimization problem can be formalized as follows:

$$\begin{aligned} \text{DATA} &= \{(a_i, \tau_i) \mid a_i \in \mathcal{A}, \tau_i \in [0; \infty)\}_{i=1}^{N} && (1)\\ \tau_i &\sim f(x; \theta = \Theta(a_i)) && (2)\\ \widehat{\Theta} &= \arg\max_{\Theta} \prod_{i=1}^{N} f(\tau_i; \theta = \Theta(a_i)). && (3) \end{aligned}$$

Here, we write N to denote the total number of observations, $\widehat{\Theta}$ to denote the solution of this optimization problem, and we also change τ indices to simplify the notation.

Without any constraints on the mapping $\widehat{\Theta}$, this optimization problem can be further decomposed into a set of per action ID *maximum likelihood estimation* (MLE) problems (we apply the logarithm function, which is monotonic and therefore does not change the result of the arg max operator):

$$\widehat{\Theta}(a) = \arg\max_{\theta} \sum_{i=1}^{N} \mathbf{I}_a(a_i) \log f(\tau_i; \theta), \qquad (4)$$

where $\mathbf{I}_a(x)$ denotes the indicator function, i.e., 1 if $x = a$ and 0 otherwise. For the exponential distribution, the MLE of its parameter (Table 1) is the inverse of the mean of the observed times. For the gamma and Weibull distributions, there is no closed form solution for the MLE problem. But it is possible to express one of their parameters as a function of the other one and $\tau_1, \ldots, \tau_N$, and to reduce the MLE problem to minimization of a scalar function.

Existing work on modeling click dwell times [30, 31] operates within the basic time modeling framework and follows the described approach to estimate their parameters.

3.2.2 Context-aware time modeling framework

We argue that considering only the ID of the first action is not enough to accurately model the time $\tau_{i \to j}$, and propose, in addition to using the ID of a_i, to use the context c_i in which the action a_i takes place. We formalize this as $\tau_i \sim f(x; \theta = \Theta(a_i, c_i))$, where Θ denotes a mapping from the Cartesian product of the space of actions $\mathcal{A}$ and the space of contexts $\mathcal{C}$ to the parameters of the probability density function $f(x; \theta)$.

Similar to Eqs. 1, 2 and 3, the optimization problem in the context-aware time modeling framework can be formalized as follows:

$$\begin{aligned} \text{DATA} &= \{(a_i, c_i, \tau_i) \mid a_i \in \mathcal{A}, c_i \in \mathcal{C}, \tau_i \in [0; \infty)\}_{i=1}^{N} && (5)\\ \tau_i &\sim f(x; \theta = \Theta(a_i, c_i)) && (6)\\ \widehat{\Theta} &= \arg\max_{\Theta} \prod_{i=1}^{N} f(\tau_i; \theta = \Theta(a_i, c_i)). && (7) \end{aligned}$$

However, without any additional constraints on the mapping $\widehat{\Theta}$, the solution of this optimization problem will have very poor generalization due to the sparsity of action-context pairs (a_i, c_i). Let us illustrate this using a few simple definitions of the context c_i: (i) number of previously clicked results, (ii) positions of previ-

[1]Where no confusion can arise, we write a_i to denote both the action performed by a user and the action ID.

ously clicked results, (iii) positions of previously clicked results and times between previous clicks. For these definitions of the context c_i, we list in Table 2 the number of unique action-context pairs (a_i, c_i) for which we need to estimate parameters θ. We see

Table 2: Number of unique action-context pairs (a_i, c_i) for different definitions of the context c_i; N denotes the number of results on a SERP; T denotes the number of time intervals we consider.

Context c_i	# of unique (a_i, c_i)
None	$\mathcal{O}(\lvert\mathcal{A}\rvert)$
Number of previously clicked results	$\mathcal{O}(\lvert\mathcal{A}\rvert \times N)$
Positions of previously clicked results	$\mathcal{O}(\lvert\mathcal{A}\rvert \times N^N)$
Positions of previously clicked results and times between previous clicks	$\mathcal{O}(\lvert\mathcal{A}\rvert \times (N \times T)^N)$

that the number of $\widehat{\Theta}$ parameters becomes too large to be able to estimate them using the amount of log data that can be generated by search engines.

The natural way to handle this problem is to constrain the family of mappings $\widehat{\Theta}$ in Eq. 7. In §3.3, we describe the *context-aware time model* that operates within the proposed context-aware time modeling framework and provides a way to constrain the family of mappings $\widehat{\Theta}$.

3.3 Context-aware time model

In §3.2 we introduced the context-aware time modeling framework that models times between two user actions using the ID of the first action and the context in which it takes place. To construct a model that operates within this framework, we need to specify (i) the probability density function $f(x;\theta)$, (ii) representation of the context c_i, and (iii) constraints on the mapping $\widehat{\Theta}$ (Eq. 7). We also need to describe the solution of the optimization problem (5)–(7) for the chosen constraints.

3.3.1 Probability density function $f(x;\theta)$

We follow previous work [30, 31] and use the exponential, gamma and Weibull probability density functions.

3.3.2 Context c_i

We represent the context c_i, in which the action a_i takes place, by a sequence of user interactions with a search engine that preceded the action a_i. We list the attributes that we use to describe the user interactions in Table 3.

Table 3: Attributes we use to describe user interactions with a search engine.

General	
Is Q-action	(0: no, 1: yes)
Is C-action	(0: no, 1: yes)
log (1 + observed time since previous action)	(0: undefined)
log (1 + average time since previous action)	(0: undefined)
Q-action	
Is new search session	(0: no, 1: yes)
Number of terms in issued query	(0: undefined)
BM25 (issued query, previous query)	(0: undefined)
BM25 (previous query, issued query)	(0: undefined)
C-action	
Is click on the 1st position	(0: no, 1: yes)
...	...
Is click on the 10th position	(0: no, 1: yes)

The first two attributes from the general section distinguish between Q- and C-actions. The third and fourth attributes inform us about the actual times observed between the previous actions and the average times between them. This information is useful to account for the user's reading speed, persistence, etc.

The first attribute from the Q-action section informs us about whether the query is the first in a search session or not. It is useful to distinguish between the cases (i) when a user has just started browsing, and (ii) when a user has been browsing for some time. In §5.1 we show that these cases may result in different probability distributions of times from submitting a query to the first click on the results, last click on the results and next query submission (if none of the results will be clicked). The second, third and fourth attributes from the Q-action section inform us about the query's similarity with the previous query.

The attributes from the C-action section inform us about the position of the clicked result. Existing work shows that the position of a result influences users' trust in the result's usefulness, which affects their decisions whether to click or not [13]. We allow for the possibility that the result's position might affect the time from clicking on the result to other actions.

3.3.3 Constraints on the mapping $\widehat{\Theta}(a_i, c_i)$

Without any constraints on the mapping $\widehat{\Theta}$, the solution of the optimization problem (5)–(7) will have very poor generalization due to a very large number of action-context pairs (see §3.2.2). To deal with this problem we impose additional constraints on the family of mappings $\widehat{\Theta}$. In particular, we limit the family of possible mappings $\widehat{\Theta}(a_i, c_i)$ to the ones that can be decomposed into the mappings $\widehat{\Theta}_A(a_i)$ and $\widehat{\Theta}_C(c_i)$ defined on the space of actions $\mathcal{A}$ and the space of contexts $\mathcal{C}$, respectively. Not only does this reduce the number of effective $\widehat{\Theta}$ parameters from $\mathcal{O}(|\mathcal{A}| \times |\mathcal{C}|)$ to $\mathcal{O}(|\mathcal{A}| + |\mathcal{C}|)$, but it also separates action-specific and context-specific parameters. The latter allows us (i) to estimate times between user actions in contexts in which these user action were not observed; and (ii) to estimate context-independent parameters of times between actions, which can be used for ranking and other prediction tasks that use historical times between user actions.

Now that we have described the constraints on the mapping $\widehat{\Theta}$ at the functional level, we need to explain the mapping $\widehat{\Theta}_A$, the mapping $\widehat{\Theta}_C$, and the decomposition of the mapping $\widehat{\Theta}$ into the mappings $\widehat{\Theta}_A$ and $\widehat{\Theta}_C$ in more detail.

Mapping $\widehat{\Theta}_A$. The mapping $\widehat{\Theta}_A$ is an equivalent of the mapping Θ in the basic time modeling framework. As in that setting, we treat it as a table of per action ID parameters, which we call *context-independent* parameters of the function $f(x;\theta)$. Thus, the number of parameters of the mapping $\widehat{\Theta}_A$ is $\mathcal{O}(|\mathcal{A}|)$.

Mapping $\widehat{\Theta}_C$. The mapping $\widehat{\Theta}_C$ describes how to adjust context-independent parameters computed by the mapping $\widehat{\Theta}_A$ to account for the context in which the first action takes place. We want this mapping to have $\mathcal{O}(|\mathcal{A}|)$ parameters so as not to increase the asymptotic number of parameters compared to time models that operate within the basic time modeling framework. Implementing the mapping $\widehat{\Theta}_C$ as a table of per context parameters will lead to a total of $\mathcal{O}(|\mathcal{C}|)$ parameters, which is likely to dominate $\mathcal{O}(|\mathcal{A}|)$. Thus, we decide to implement the mapping $\widehat{\Theta}_C$ using a machine learning algorithm. In particular, we implement it as a *recurrent neural network* (RNN) with *long short-term memory* (LSTM) cells [23].

We choose this architecture, because we represent the context c_i as a sequence of numerical attributes (see §3.3.2); and for tasks that involve processing sequential data, RNNs have demostrated strong performance on a wide range of tasks. See examples in language modeling [34], speech recognition [19] and machine translation [42]. By using the RNN we reduce the number of $\widehat{\Theta}$ parameters to $\mathcal{O}(N \times M)$, where N denotes the number of attributes we use to represent user interactions with the search (18 in our work) and M denotes the maximum number of units in the RNN layers (256 in our work). As $N \times M \ll |\mathcal{A}|$, we satisfy the $\mathcal{O}(|\mathcal{A}|)$ requirement.

Decomposition of $\widehat{\Theta}$ into $\widehat{\Theta}_A$ and $\widehat{\Theta}_C$. A decomposition of $\widehat{\Theta}$ into $\widehat{\Theta}_A$ and $\widehat{\Theta}_C$ describes how to compute the parameters θ of the probility density function $f(x;\theta)$ from the action-specific parameters $\widehat{\Theta}_A(a_i)$ and the context-specific parameters $\widehat{\Theta}_C(c_i)$. We want the action-specific parameters $\widehat{\Theta}_A(a_i)$ to be context-independent estimates of parameters of the probability density function $f(x;\theta)$ for the action ID a_i (see the discussion above), and the context-specific parameters $\widehat{\Theta}_C(c_i)$ to be coefficients that inform us about how to adjust $\widehat{\Theta}_A(a_i)$ to account for the context c_i. One natural way to achieve it is (i) to have two context-specific parameters α and β for each action-specific parameter θ_i, and (ii) to apply a linear transformation $g(\theta_i) = \alpha\theta_i + \beta$ to compute the context-dependent parameters of the probability density function. We formalize it as:

$$\widehat{\Theta}(a_i, c_i) = \widehat{\Theta}_A(a_i) \circ \widehat{\Theta}^0_C(c_i) + \widehat{\Theta}^1_C(c_i). \tag{8}$$

Here, $\widehat{\Theta}^0_C(c_i)$ and $\widehat{\Theta}^1_C(c_i)$ constitute the first and the last halves of the vector $\widehat{\Theta}_C(c_i)$, which contains two times more elements than $\widehat{\Theta}_A(a_i)$, and the symbol $\circ$ denotes the element-wise product.

3.3.4 *Learning the mappings $\widehat{\Theta}_A(a_i)$ and $\widehat{\Theta}_C(c_i)$*

Now, we describe an approximate solution of the optimization problem (5)–(7) with the constraints on the mapping $\widehat{\Theta}$ defined in §3.3.3. This problem does not have closed form solutions for the mappings $\widehat{\Theta}_A$ and $\widehat{\Theta}_C$. Therefore, we propose an iterative algorithm to compute them (see Algorithm 1). We use $\widehat{\Theta}(a_i, c_i) = \mathcal{F}(\widehat{\Theta}_A(a_i), \widehat{\Theta}_C(c_i))$ as a generalized version of Eq. 8.

The algorithm initializes the mapping $\widehat{\Theta}_A$ with the solution of the optimization problem (1)–(3) in the basic time modeling framework (line 1). Then it alternates between learning $\widehat{\Theta}_C$ while fixing $\widehat{\Theta}_A$ (line 3) and learning $\widehat{\Theta}_A$ while fixing $\widehat{\Theta}_C$ (line 4) until convergence. In our experiments the process converges after 5–10 iterations (i.e., passes through the loop). It is easy to show that the likelihood does not decrease between the iterations.

Algorithm 1 Learn $\widehat{\Theta}_A(\cdot), \widehat{\Theta}_C(\cdot)$

1: $\widehat{\Theta}_A \leftarrow \arg\max_{\Theta} \prod_{i=1}^{N} f(\tau_i; \theta = \Theta(a_i))$
2: **while** not $\widehat{\Theta}_A, \widehat{\Theta}_C$ converged **do**
3: $\quad \widehat{\Theta}_C \leftarrow \arg\max_{\Theta_C} \prod_{i=1}^{N} f(\tau_i; \theta = \mathcal{F}(\widehat{\Theta}_A(a_i), \Theta_C(c_i)))$
4: $\quad \widehat{\Theta}_A \leftarrow \arg\max_{\Theta_A} \prod_{i=1}^{N} f(\tau_i; \theta = \mathcal{F}(\Theta_A(a_i), \widehat{\Theta}_C(c_i)))$
5: **end while**
6: **return** $\widehat{\Theta}_A, \widehat{\Theta}_C$

To find the best $\widehat{\Theta}_C$ while fixing $\widehat{\Theta}_A$ (Algorithm 1, line 3), we use the *stochastic gradient descent* (SGD) algorithm with mini-batches, because this is the most widely used algorithm for training neural networks [4]. The learning rates for each parameter are adjusted according to the ADADELTA algorithm [44] (we use the default values of $\epsilon = 10^{-6}$ and $\rho = 0.95$). We also use the gradient clipping technique [37] to alleviate the exploding gradient problem [5] (we set the value of the threshold to 1).

To find the best $\widehat{\Theta}_A$ while fixing $\widehat{\Theta}_C$ (Algorithm 1, line 4), we decompose the optimization problem into a set of per action ID MLE problems (similar to Eq. 4):

$$\widehat{\Theta}_A(a) = \arg\max_{\theta} \sum_{i=1}^{N} \mathbf{I}_a(a_i) \log f(\tau_i; \theta = \mathcal{F}(\theta, \widehat{\Theta}_C(c_i))).$$

We solve these MLE problems using the *limited memory BFGS with bound constraints (L-BFGS-B)* algorithm [46]. We use bound constraints to ensure that the distribution parameters θ take admissible values (e.g., the values of the parameters of the exponential, gamma and Weibull distributions need to be positive).

To summarize, we predict a probability distribution over the time elapsed between a pair of user actions. Unlike existing methods, which rely solely on the first action ID, CATM also considers the context in which the first action takes place. CATM represents this context as a sequence of user interactions with a search engine that precede the first action, and employs a recurrent neural network that learns how to adjust the first action ID parameters using this context representation. CATM can be used (i) to predict the time elapsed between a pair of user actions in a context, in which these actions have not been previously observed, and (ii) to obtain a context-independent estimate of the time between two user actions by predicting it in a predefined context.

4. EXPERIMENTAL SETUP

In this section we describe our experimental setup. We start with the research questions that we seek to answer (§4.1). Then we describe the datasets that we use (§4.2) and the evaluation methodology that we follow (§4.3). Finally, we describe the experiments that we conduct to answer our research questions (§4.4).

4.1 Research questions

We address the following research questions: **(RQ1)** Can we observe the context bias effect? More precisely, can we observe a difference in time probability distributions for different contexts in which the first action takes place? **(RQ2)** Do the context-aware time models, which besides the first action ID make use of its context, provide better means to explain times between user actions than the basic time models, which make the context-independence assumption and rely solely on the first action ID? **(RQ3)** Do the context-independent predictions of the CATMs, trained on the time-between-clicks task, provide better means to rank search results than existing methods based on the observed times between clicks?

4.2 Dataset

To construct datasets for the temporal prediction tasks described in §2, we collected three months of log data from a commercial web search engine. We use the first two months of the log data to train time models and the last month to evaluate their prediction performance. In each dataset, we filter out times associated with actions IDs that occur less than 25 times in the training set. For time-to-first-click and time-from-abandoned-query, we also filter out times larger than 1 minute; for time-to-last-click and time-between-clicks, we filter out times larger than 5 minutes (this complies with actual times reported in [38]). The number of observations in the resulted datasets are shown in Table 4.

Table 4: Number of observations in the datasets for each temporal prediction task.

Time between actions	Number of observations
Time-to-first-click	30,747,733
Time-between-clicks	6,317,834
Time-to-last-click	30,446,973
Time-from-abandoned-query	11,523,351

To compare the performance of ranking models based on time-between-clicks, we also collected relevance labels for 50,137 query-result pairs that occur in our time-between-clicks dataset. The relevance labels were assigned by trained judges on a scale from 0 to 4, with 0 = bad, 1 = fair, 2 = good, 3 = excellent, 4 = perfect.

4.3 Evaluation methodology

We evaluate the performance of time models using the *log-likelihood* and the *root mean squared error* (RMSE) metrics. The log-likelihood metric shows how well a time model explains the observed times between user actions. We report the logarithm of the likelihood function, averaged over all observations in the test set. Larger values of the metric indicate better performance. The RMSE metric shows the average difference between the expected values of the time probability distributions predicted by a model and the observed times-between-actions. Lower values of the metric indicate better performance. We also evaluate the time models for predicting time-between-clicks on a ranking task (i.e., to rank a set of results by their relevance to a query). We use the NDCG metric [26], and report its scores at truncation levels 1, 3, 5 and 10. Larger values of the metric indicate better performance.

We perform significance testing in terms of all metrics using a paired t-test; the differences are considered statistically significant for p-values lower than 0.05.

4.4 Experiments

Experiment 1. To answer RQ1, for each action ID we split the observed times in two *context groups*, which correspond to different sets of previous user interactions, and run the two-sample two-sided Kolmogorov-Smirnov (KS) test [14] to determine whether the observed times were drawn from the same distribution. The null hypothesis states that the observed times were drawn from the same distribution, which means that there is no context bias effect. Rejecting it, at least for some action IDs, will prove the existence of the context bias effect for these action IDs. Not being able to reject it might happen for several reasons. First, the context bias effect may not appear for certain types of queries (e.g., navigational queries) and results (e.g., irrelevant results). Second, we may not have enough data to reject the null hypothesis. Third, we may not have chosen the best context groups.

When choosing a rule to split times-between-actions in two context groups based on the context, we give preference to easily interpretable and easily reproducible ones. For the time-to-first-click, time-to-last-click and time-from-abandoned-query, we split the observed times based on whether the query is the first in the search task or not. We say that a query is the first in the search task if it does not share terms with the previous query in the search session, or if it is the first query in the search session. For the time-between-clicks, we split the observed times based on whether the clicked result is the first item to be clicked on SERP or not.

We use the KS test, because the more popular t-test is not applicable in our setting: it requires the tested samples to be drawn from a normal distribution, which is not the case for time observations. An alternative to the KS test could be the Mann-Whitney U test [14], but following previous work [31] we use the KS test.

Without a sufficient number of observations in both context groups, the KS test would be unable to detect a difference between samples even if one exists. For this reason, we apply the KS test only to actions IDs, for which there are, at least, N observations in both context groups. Using a large value of N improves test sensitivity (increases the number of action IDs for which the null hypothesis can be rejected), but reduces the number of action IDs that we use in our experiment. Thus, we run our experiment for different values of N. In particular, we use N in the range $[25, 200]$. Table 5 shows the number of action IDs with, at least, N observations in both context groups for $N = \{25, 50, 100, 200\}$.

Table 5: Number of action IDs with at least $N = \{25, 50, 100, 200\}$ observations in each context group for different times-between-actions.

	N			
Time between actions	25	50	100	200
Time-to-first-click	60,284	24,368	7894	1545
Time-between-clicks	18,954	8335	3289	1288
Time-to-last-click	59,367	23,956	7756	1500
Time-from-abandoned-query	22,190	9180	2980	569

Experiment 2. To answer RQ2, we compare the performance in terms of log-likelihood and RMSE of the context-aware time models against the basic time models on the four temporal prediction tasks described in §2.

Experiment 3. To answer RQ3, we compare the performance in terms of NDCG of rankings models based on (i) the average values of the observed times between clicks, (ii) the expected values of the probability distributions fitted to the observed times between clicks, and (iii) the expected values of the context-independent probability distributions predicted by the CATMs trained on the time-between-clicks task. To predict the context-independent probability distributions we use the following fixed context: (i) the query is the first in the search session; (ii) the result is presented on the top position and is the first item to be clicked; (iii) the time elapsed between the query submission and the click on the result is 4 seconds (the median of the times-to-first-click observed in our dataset).

5. RESULTS

In this section we present the results of the experiments described in §4.4 and provide answers to the research questions stated in §4.1.

5.1 Experiment 1

The results of Experiment 1 are given in Figure 2. The figure shows the percentage of action IDs in each temporal prediction task, for which the Kolmogorov-Smirnov test rejected the null hypothesis ($p < 0.05$) in favor of the alternative hypothesis, which states that the times-between-actions in the chosen context groups were drawn from different probability distributions. Equivalently, the alternative hypothesis states that the context bias effect exists.

RQ1. Figure 2 shows that for each time-between-actions there is more than 5% action IDs, for which the null hypothesis is rejected. This proves the existence of the context bias effect. Indeed, if times-between-actions did not depend on previous user interactions (null hypothesis was true), the number of action IDs for which the null hypothesis would be rejected had to be 5% (significance level) of the total number of the tested action IDs.

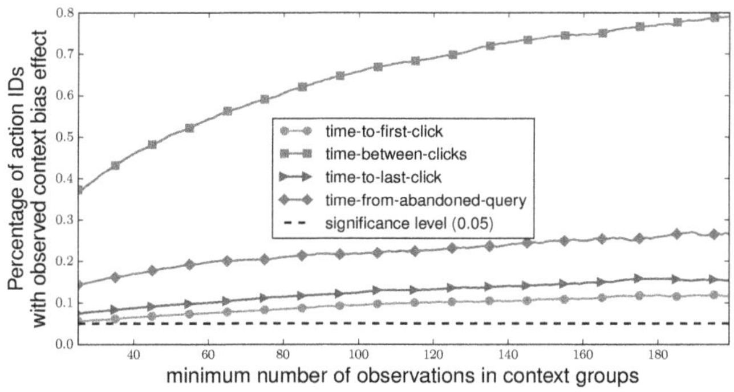

Figure 2: Percentage of actions IDs with observed context bias effect vs. minimum number of observations in context groups.

The percentage of action IDs, for which the context bias effect is detected, increases with the minimum number of observations in each context group (Figure 2). This suggests that the actual number of action IDs for which the context bias effect appears, is even larger than the number of action IDs for which we manage to detect the effect. And with more interaction data, it should be possible to detect the effect in a larger number of times-between-actions.

From the above results we conclude that there is a tangible context bias effect, which results in statistically significant differences in time-between-actions probability distributions for different contexts (in our case, for different sets of previous user interactions).

5.2 Experiment 2

The results of Experiment 2 are given in Table 6. The table shows the performance of the basic time models and the context-aware time models in terms of log-likelihood and RMSE on four temporal prediction tasks: time-to-first-click, time-between-clicks, time-to-last-click and time-from-abandoned-query (§2).

RQ2. Table 6 shows that the context-aware time models outperform the basic time models in terms of both the log-likelihood and RMSE metrics on all temporal prediction tasks. The improvements for each task and each distribution are statistically significant with $p < 0.001$. The improvements in terms of log-likelihood are comparable with the differences between the basic time models using different probability density functions, and in most cases exceed them. The improvements in terms of RMSE vary, depending on the task, between 0.98–5.32%.

To further understand the performance difference between the basic time models and the context-aware time models, we plot their performance vs. the actual times-between-actions observed in the datasets. Figures 3 and 4 show the performance on the time-between-clicks task. We start with Figure 3, which shows the performance in terms of the log-likelihood metric. Here, similar to the differences between the basic time models using different probability density functions, we observe major improvements of the context-aware time models over the basic time models for small times. In Figure 4, which shows the performance in terms of the RMSE metric, we also observe major improvements for small times.

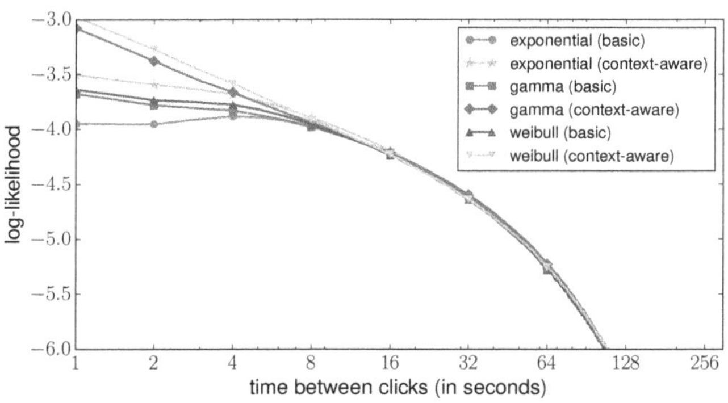

Figure 3: Time model performance in terms of the log-likelihood metric on the time-between-clicks task vs. actual times observed in the dataset.

Table 6: Performance of the basic time models and the context-aware time models on four temporal prediction tasks. Larger values of the average log-likelihood metric and lower values of the root mean squared error (RMSE) metric indicate better performance. Improvements of the context-aware time models over the basic time models using the same probability density functions (exponential, gamma, Weibull) are statistically significant ($p < 0.001$) in terms of both metrics.

Time model	Distribution	Log-likelihood	RMSE
	Time-to-first-click		
Basic	exponential	−2.9050	7.52
	gamma	−2.8399	7.51
	Weibull	−2.8970	7.52
Context-aware	exponential	−2.8715	7.29
	gamma	−2.7636	7.25
	Weibull	−2.8449	7.27
	Time-between-clicks		
Basic	exponential	−4.9219	60.73
	gamma	−4.9105	60.76
	Weibull	−4.9077	60.76
Context-aware	exponential	−4.8787	58.93
	gamma	−4.8556	58.98
	Weibull	−4.8504	58.94
	Time-to-last-click		
Basic	exponential	−3.8360	40.85
	gamma	−3.7849	40.85
	Weibull	−3.7386	40.85
Context-aware	exponential	−3.7924	40.45
	gamma	−3.7456	40.45
	Weibull	−3.7073	40.51
	Time-from-abandoned-query		
Basic	exponential	−3.5862	12.41
	gamma	−3.5422	12.41
	Weibull	−3.5560	12.41
Context-aware	exponential	−3.5210	11.75
	gamma	−3.4235	11.76
	Weibull	−3.4554	11.77

A reader might notice a drop in performance of the context-aware time models compared to the basic time models between 17 and 99 seconds in Figure 4. This is better seen in Figure 5, which plots the differences between the context-aware time models and the basic time models shown in Figure 4. Here, we see that the context-aware time models perform better for times lower than 17 seconds and larger than 99 seconds, and perform worse for times in the range of 17–99 seconds. This can be explained as follows. The average time-between-clicks in our dataset is 53.44 seconds. A naive time model that always predicts time-between-clicks to be 53.44 seconds, would have very low RMSE around 53.44 seconds and high RMSE for smaller and larger times (the overall RMSE

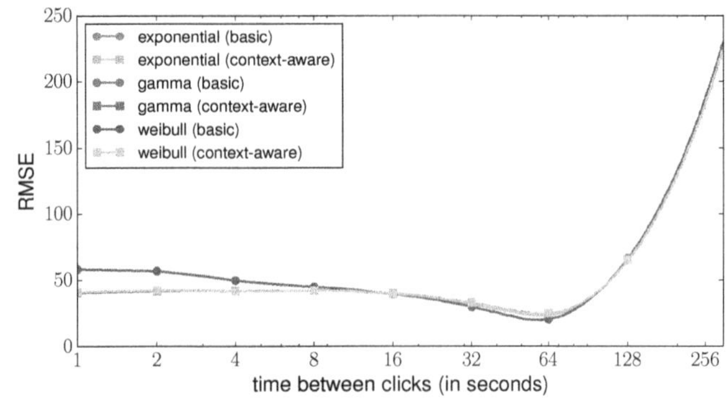

Figure 4: Time model performance in terms of the RMSE metric on the time-between-clicks task vs. actual times observed in the dataset.

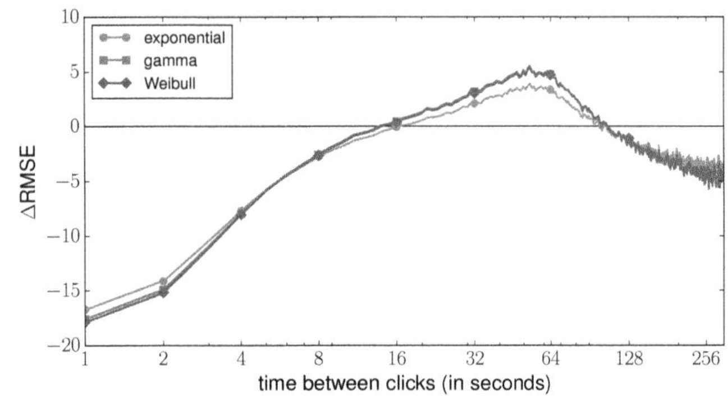

Figure 5: Performance difference in terms of the RMSE metric between the context-aware time models and the basic time models on the time-between-clicks task vs. actual times observed in the dataset.

performance of this naive approach would be low). The basic time models predict time-between-clicks across the whole time range including small and large times, and have better overall RMSE performance. However, this is achieved at the cost of having higher RMSE around the average time-between-clicks (i.e., 53.44 seconds) compared to that of the naive time model. The proposed context-aware time models, on average, predict time-between-clicks better than the basic time models (and especially so for smaller and larger times, see Figure 5). This is again achieved at the cost of having higher RMSE around the average time-between-clicks (i.e., 53.44 seconds). In fact, smaller times-between-clicks usually correspond to dissatisfied clicks, and larger times-between-clicks correspond to satisfied clicks [18]. Thus, in order to improve user satisfaction with the search, it is more important to predict small and large times-between-clicks rather than to distingush between times close to the average time-between-clicks.

From the above results we conclude that the context-aware time models, which besides the first action ID make use of its context, provide better means to explain times-between-actions that the basic time models, which rely solely on the first action ID.

5.3 Experiment 3

Table 7 shows the outcomes of Experiment 3, a comparison of the performance of ranking models based on times-between-clicks.

RQ3. Table 7 shows that the CATM-based ranking models outperform the ranking models based on the basic time models and the ranking model that scores search results by the average values of the observed times between clicks. All improvements are

Table 7: Performance of ranking models based on the time between clicks. Larger values of the NDCG metric correspond to better rankings. The improvements of the context-aware time models over the existing methods are statistically significant ($p < 0.05$).

		NDCG			
Time model	Distribution	@1	@3	@5	@10
Average	n/a	0.651	0.693	0.728	0.812
Basic	exponential	0.651	0.693	0.728	0.812
	gamma	0.646	0.693	0.728	0.812
	Weibull	0.656	0.699	0.730	0.811
Context-aware	exponential	0.668	0.710	0.743	0.820
	gamma	0.675	0.715	0.748	0.822
	Weibull	0.671	0.709	0.745	0.821

statistically significant with $p < 0.05$. Thus, we conclude that the context-independent predictions of the CATMs trained on the time-between-clicks task provide better means to rank search engine results than existing methods.

6. RELATED WORK

We discuss two types of related work: behavioral signals used to improve and evaluate web search effectiveness (§6.1); and models of user behavior used to interpret these signals (§6.2).

6.1 Behavioral information

Modern search engines log a large number of user behavioral signals to improve and evaluate their effectiveness. We classify them in two groups: behavioral signals based on user actions and behavioral signals based on times between user actions.

Behavioral signals based on user actions. User clicks provide an important source of implicit user feedback [1–3, 8–10, 20, 27, 38, 39]. They have been used (i) to infer user preferences over search results, i.e., target values for learning a ranking function [9, 27], (ii) to design features for learning a ranking function [1, 2, 8] and for other applications [3, 20], and (iii) to compare ranking functions [10, 38, 39]. Some work distinguishes different types of clicks: first click [8, 39], last click [8], long dwell time click [8], satisfied click [39] and only click [8]. Next to clicks, some recent work considers mouse cursor movements on SERPs [16, 24, 25].

Behavioral signals based on times between user actions. Click dwell time, i.e., time spent by a user on the landing page of a search result, provides valuable information about user satisfaction with the clicked result [30]. Existing work uses it as a feature for ranking [1, 2, 8] and in many tasks related to user satisfaction [3, 20–22, 30, 32, 33, 36]. Times from a submission of a query to (i) the first click [7, 10, 20, 39], (ii) the first satisfied click [39], and (iii) the last click [10] are used as features to predict user satisfaction with the clicked result [20], compare two versions of a search engine [10, 39] and to cluster users based on their SERP examination strategies [7]. Song et al. [41] use the time since a user issued an abandoned query (i.e., a query for which there were no interactions with the search results) to the next query submission for classifying the abandoned query into positively abandoned and negatively abandoned. Dupret and Lalmas [17] use times between search engine visits to compare two versions of a search engine.

6.2 Models of user behavior

Now that we have described the behavioral signals, we focus on their interpretations. To interpret a signal, we need to have a model that explains it. We start with models for explaining behavioral signals based on user actions and then discuss models for explaining behavioral signals based on times between user actions.

Modeling user actions. The simplest way to interpret click data is to compute *click-through rates* (CTRs), i.e., the ratios of the total number of clicks and the total number of impressions observed for a group of search engine results. Unfortunately, CTRs suffer from the so-called *position bias effect*, i.e., results presented at higher positions receive more clicks than results of similar quality presented at lower positions [15, 27, 28], which leads to suboptimal performance when using CTRs for ranking. To account for position bias, a large number of *click models* have been proposed [13].

Click models make a few assumptions about user interactions with search results, which ultimately allow them to obtain per query-result scores that show better correlation with relevance than CTRs. Among the most common assumptions are (i) the *linear traversal assumption* that a user scans search results from top to bottom [15]; and (ii) the *examination hypothesis* that a user clicks on a search result if, and only if, she examined the search result and is attracted by it [15]. Recently, it has been shown that patterns of user click behaviour can be learned automatically from interaction data [6]. In addition to position bias, recent work examines other types of bias including (i) *vertical bias* driven by visually salient vertical results (e.g., image results, video results, news results) [11, 12, 43]; (ii) *query bias*, which occurs if a query does not match the user's information need [45], (iii) *duplicate bias*, which occurs if a result has been examined earlier in the search task [45]; and (iv) bias driven by individual differences between users [40].

The notion of context bias, introduced in our work for times between user actions, generalizes the idea of bias in user actions (in particular, clicks and mouse hovers), and the proposed context-aware time model should be able to account for them with appropriate representations of the context.

Modeling times between user actions. The simplest way to interpret times between user actions is to compute their mean values. The average click dwell time is frequently used as a feature for ranking [1, 2, 8] and other applications [3, 20–22, 32, 33, 36]. The average time between a submission of a query to the first click is used both as a feature [20] and as an online metric for comparing two versions of a search engine [10, 39]. The average time between a submission of a query and (i) first click classified as satisfied, (ii) last click are also used as online metrics for comparing two versions of a search engine [10, 39].

A more sophisticated way to interpret times between user actions is to fit a probability distribution [30, 31]. Liu et al. [31] find that the Weibull distribution provides better goodness-of-fit to click dwell times than the exponential distribution. The authors provide an interesting interpretation for the shape parameter of the fitted Weibull distribution, which justifies the task of modeling the full probability distribution rather than just the mean of the distribution. Our work differs from their work in that we do not make the context-independence assumption that the observed times were drawn from the same probability distribution; we predict the probability distributions separately for each click using its context, and the information about click dwell times observed for the given query-result pair in other contexts. Liu et al. [31] also show that it is possible to predict parameters of the Weibull distribution for a given result using the information about the result's landing page, such as HTML tags, frequent words that occur on the page and times to download/render/parse the page. Our approach differs from their method in that we use contextual, i.e., result-independent, information; thus, our work is complementary to that of [31].

Kim et al. [30] fit gamma distributions to click dwell times, observed in a predefined click segment and labeled as satisfied or dissatisfied. The authors use the fitted distributions to classify new clicks into satisfied and dissatisfied. In particular, they compute the following features: (i) the differences between the fitted parameters of the satisfied and dissatisfied click dwell time distributions for the clicked result's segment, (ii) their expected values and the difference between them, (iii) the absolute differences between the observed click dwell time and the expected values of the satisfied and dissatisfied distributions, (iv) the log-likelihoods of the observed click dwell time according to the satisfied and dissatisfied distributions and the difference between them. The large number of features used in their work shows the advantage of modeling the full probability distribution over modeling just the mean. Similar features, computed from the probability distributions predicted in our work can potentially be used in a broad range of applications.

Our work is the first to systematically address the problem of modeling times between user actions. We introduce the notion of context bias effect and propose a context-aware time model that predicts times elapsed between user actions using both the ID of the first action (which is what existing methods rely on) and the context in which it takes place (our novelty).

7. CONCLUSION

We introduced the notion of *context bias effect* in times between user actions (i.e., a difference in probability distributions of times associated with the same user action, but observed in different contexts); and proposed a *context-aware time model* (CATM) that allows us to estimate parameters of a probability distribution of the time elapsed between user actions in a given context. CATM's ability to account for user context can be used to predict times between user actions in a context in which these actions have not previously been observed, and to obtain context-independent estimates of times between actions by predicting them in predefined contexts.

We showed that, for 37%–80% of query-result pairs (q, r), depending on the number of observations, the distributions of times elapsed between a click on the result r and the next click on the same SERP differed in sessions, in which the result r was the first item to be clicked, and in sessions, in which there were clicks on other results before the result r was clicked. Similarly, we showed that previous user interactions in a search task influence distributions of times between (i) submission of a query and the first click on a SERP, (ii) submission of a query and the last click on a SERP, and (iii) submission of an abandoned query (i.e., a query with no clicks on a SERP) and the next query submission.

We evaluated the context-aware time model on four temporal prediction tasks and a ranking task. The results on the temporal prediction tasks show that the proposed context-aware time model, which makes use of both the ID of the first action and the context in which it takes place, provides better means to explain times between user actions than existing methods, which rely solely on the first action ID. The results on the ranking task show that the context-independent estimates of times between consecutive clicks, obtained with the context-aware time model, allow us to construct rankings that result in better performance in terms of relevance than the rankings produced by the mean values of the observed times between consecutive clicks.

As to future work, we plan to consider other representations of the context. Besides using context-independent estimates of times between consecutive clicks as features for ranking, the predictions of context-aware time models can be used in a range of other applications that use the average or predicted times between user actions.

These applications include prediction of click satisfaction [30], result usefulness [32], search task difficulty [3, 33], search goal success [20, 21], urgent information needs [35], struggling vs. exploring behavior [22, 36], positive vs. negative abandonment [41] and clustering users based on their SERP examination strategies [7].

Acknowledgments. This research was supported by Ahold, Amsterdam Data Science, the Bloomberg Research Grant program, the Dutch national program COMMIT, Elsevier, the European Community's Seventh Framework Programme (FP7/2007-2013) under grant agreement nr 312827 (VOX-Pol), the ESF Research Network Program ELIAS, the Royal Dutch Academy of Sciences (KNAW) under the Elite Network Shifts project, the Microsoft Research Ph.D. program, the Netherlands eScience Center under project number 027.012.105, the Netherlands Institute for Sound and Vision, the Netherlands Organisation for Scientific Research (NWO) under project nrs 727.011.005, 612.001.116, HOR-11-10, 640.006.013, 612.066.930, CI-14-25, SH-322-15, 652.002.001, 612.001.551, and the Yahoo Faculty Research and Engagement Program. All content represents the opinion of the authors, which is not necessarily shared or endorsed by their respective employers and/or sponsors.

8. REFERENCES

[1] E. Agichtein, E. Brill, and S. Dumais. Improving web search ranking by incorporating user behavior information. In *SIGIR*, pages 19–26. ACM, 2006.

[2] E. Agichtein, E. Brill, S. Dumais, and R. Ragno. Learning user interaction models for predicting web search result preferences. In *SIGIR*, pages 3–10. ACM, 2006.

[3] J. Arguello. Predicting search task difficulty. In *Advances in Information Retrieval*, pages 88–99. Springer, 2014.

[4] Y. Bengio. Learning deep architectures for AI. *Foundations and trends in Machine Learning*, 2(1):1–127, 2009.

[5] Y. Bengio, P. Simard, and P. Frasconi. Learning long-term dependencies with gradient descent is difficult. *IEEE Transactions on Neural Networks*, 5(2):157–166, 1994.

[6] A. Borisov, I. Markov, M. de Rijke, and P. Serdyukov. A neural click model for web search. In *WWW*, pages 531–541, 2016.

[7] G. Buscher, R. W. White, S. Dumais, and J. Huang. Large-scale analysis of individual and task differences in search result page examination strategies. In *WSDM*, pages 373–382. ACM, 2012.

[8] O. Chapelle and Y. Chang. Yahoo! learning to rank challenge overview. In *Yahoo! Learning to Rank Challenge*, pages 1–24, 2011.

[9] O. Chapelle and Y. Zhang. A dynamic bayesian network click model for web search ranking. In *WWW*, pages 1–10. ACM, 2009.

[10] O. Chapelle, T. Joachims, F. Radlinski, and Y. Yue. Large-scale validation and analysis of interleaved search evaluation. *TOIS*, 30(1): 6, 2012.

[11] D. Chen, W. Chen, H. Wang, Z. Chen, and Q. Yang. Beyond ten blue links: enabling user click modeling in federated web search. In *WSDM*, pages 463–472. ACM, 2012.

[12] A. Chuklin, P. Serdyukov, and M. de Rijke. Using intent information to model user behavior in diversified search. In *Advances in Information Retrieval*, pages 1–13. Springer, 2013.

[13] A. Chuklin, I. Markov, and M. de Rijke. *Click Models for Web Search*. Morgan & Claypool Publishers, August 2015.

[14] W. J. Conover. *Practical Nonparametric Statistics*. Wiley, 1980.

[15] N. Craswell, O. Zoeter, M. Taylor, and B. Ramsey. An experimental comparison of click position-bias models. In *WSDM*, pages 87–94. ACM, 2008.

[16] F. Diaz, R. White, G. Buscher, and D. Liebling. Robust models of mouse movement on dynamic web search results pages. In *CIKM*, pages 1451–1460. ACM, 2013.

[17] G. Dupret and M. Lalmas. Absence time and user engagement: evaluating ranking functions. In *WSDM*, pages 173–182. ACM, 2013.

[18] S. Fox, K. Karnawat, M. Mydland, S. Dumais, and T. White. Evaluating implicit measures to improve web search. *TOIS*, 23(2): 147–168, 2005.

[19] A. Graves, A.-r. Mohamed, and G. Hinton. Speech recognition with deep recurrent neural networks. In *ICASSP*, pages 6645–6649. IEEE, 2013.

[20] A. Hassan. A semi-supervised approach to modeling web search satisfaction. In *SIGIR*, pages 275–284. ACM, 2012.

[21] A. Hassan, R. Jones, and K. L. Klinkner. Beyond DCG: user behavior as a predictor of a successful search. In *WSDM*, pages 221–230. ACM, 2010.

[22] A. Hassan, R. W. White, S. T. Dumais, and Y.-M. Wang. Struggling or exploring?: disambiguating long search sessions. In *WSDM*, pages 53–62. ACM, 2014.

[23] S. Hochreiter and J. Schmidhuber. Long short-term memory. *Neural computation*, 9(8):1735–1780, 1997.

[24] J. Huang, R. W. White, and S. Dumais. No clicks, no problem: using cursor movements to understand and improve search. In *SIGCHI*, pages 1225–1234. ACM, 2011.

[25] J. Huang, R. W. White, G. Buscher, and K. Wang. Improving searcher models using mouse cursor activity. In *SIGIR*, pages 195–204. ACM, 2012.

[26] K. Järvelin and J. Kekäläinen. IR evaluation methods for retrieving highly relevant documents. In *SIGIR*, pages 41–48. ACM, 2000.

[27] T. Joachims. Optimizing search engines using clickthrough data. In *KDD*, pages 133–142. ACM, 2002.

[28] T. Joachims, L. Granka, B. Pan, H. Hembrooke, and G. Gay. Accurately interpreting clickthrough data as implicit feedback. In *SIGIR*, pages 154–161. ACM, 2005.

[29] Y. Kim, A. Hassan, R. W. White, and I. Zitouni. Comparing client and server dwell time estimates for click-level satisfaction prediction. In *SIGIR*, pages 895–898. ACM, 2014.

[30] Y. Kim, A. Hassan, R. W. White, and I. Zitouni. Modeling dwell time to predict click-level satisfaction. In *WSDM*, pages 193–202. ACM, 2014.

[31] C. Liu, R. W. White, and S. Dumais. Understanding web browsing behaviors through weibull analysis of dwell time. In *SIGIR*, pages 379–386. ACM, 2010.

[32] C. Liu, J. Liu, N. Belkin, M. Cole, and J. Gwizdka. Using dwell time as an implicit measure of usefulness in different task types. *JASIST*, 48(1):1–4, 2011.

[33] J. Liu, C. Liu, M. Cole, N. J. Belkin, and X. Zhang. Exploring and predicting search task difficulty. In *CIKM*, pages 1313–1322. ACM, 2012.

[34] T. Mikolov, M. Karafiát, L. Burget, J. Cernockỳ, and S. Khudanpur. Recurrent neural network based language model. In *INTERSPEECH*, pages 1045–1048, 2010.

[35] N. Mishra, R. W. White, S. Ieong, and E. Horvitz. Time-critical search. In *SIGIR*, pages 747–756. ACM, 2014.

[36] D. Odijk, R. W. White, A. H. Awadallah, and S. T. Dumais. Struggling and success in web search. In *CIKM*. ACM, 2015.

[37] R. Pascanu, T. Mikolov, and Y. Bengio. On the difficulty of training recurrent neural networks. *arXiv preprint arXiv:1211.5063*, 2012.

[38] F. Radlinski, M. Kurup, and T. Joachims. How does clickthrough data reflect retrieval quality? In *CIKM*, pages 43–52. ACM, 2008.

[39] A. Schuth, K. Hofmann, and F. Radlinski. Predicting search satisfaction metrics with interleaved comparisons. In *SIGIR*, pages 463–472. ACM, 2015.

[40] S. Shen, B. Hu, W. Chen, and Q. Yang. Personalized click model through collaborative filtering. In *WSDM*, pages 323–332. ACM, 2012.

[41] Y. Song, X. Shi, R. White, and A. H. Awadallah. Context-aware web search abandonment prediction. In *SIGIR*, pages 93–102. ACM, 2014.

[42] I. Sutskever, O. Vinyals, and Q. V. Le. Sequence to sequence learning with neural networks. In *NIPS*, pages 3104–3112, 2014.

[43] C. Wang, Y. Liu, M. Zhang, S. Ma, M. Zheng, J. Qian, and K. Zhang. Incorporating vertical results into search click models. In *SIGIR*, pages 503–512. ACM, 2013.

[44] M. D. Zeiler. ADADELTA: An adaptive learning rate method. *arXiv preprint arXiv:1212.5701*, 2012.

[45] Y. Zhang, W. Chen, D. Wang, and Q. Yang. User-click modeling for understanding and predicting search-behavior. In *CIKM*, pages 1388–1396. ACM, 2011.

[46] C. Zhu, R. H. Byrd, P. Lu, and J. Nocedal. Algorithm 778: L-BFGS-B: Fortran subroutines for large-scale bound-constrained optimization. *TOMS*, 23(4):550–560, 1997.

Novelty based Ranking of Human Answers for Community Questions

Adi Omari
Technion IIT
Haifa,32000, Israel
omari@cs.technion.ac.il

David Carmel, Oleg Rokhlenko, Idan Szpektor
Yahoo Research
Haifa 31905, Israel
{dcarmel,olegro,idan}@yahoo-inc.com

ABSTRACT

Questions and their corresponding answers within a community-based question answering (CQA) site are frequently presented as top search results for Web search queries and viewed by millions of searchers daily. The number of answers for CQA questions ranges from a handful to dozens, and a searcher would be typically interested in the different suggestions presented in various answers for a question. Yet, especially when many answers are provided, the viewer may not want to sift through all answers but to read only the top ones. Prior work on answer ranking in CQA considered the qualitative notion of each answer separately, mainly whether it should be marked as best answer. We propose to promote CQA answers not only by their relevance to the question but also by the diversification and novelty qualities they hold compared to other answers. Specifically, we aim at ranking answers by the amount of new aspects they introduce with respect to higher ranked answers (novelty), on top of their relevance estimation. This approach is common in Web search and information retrieval, yet it was not addressed within the CQA settings before, which is quite different from classic document retrieval. We propose a novel answer ranking algorithm that borrows ideas from aspect ranking and multi-document summarization, but adapts them to our scenario. Answers are ranked in a greedy manner, taking into account their relevance to the question as well as their novelty compared to higher ranked answers and their coverage of important aspects. An experiment over a collection of Health questions, using a manually annotated gold-standard dataset, shows that considering novelty for answer ranking improves the quality of the ranked answer list.

Keywords: Community-based question answering; Novelty; Diversification

1. INTRODUCTION

Community-based Question Answering (CQA), a platform in which people can ask questions and receive answers from other people, has become a useful tool for information needs that are not answered simply by viewing a Web page, including recommendations, suggestions and homework help [26]. In popular CQA sites, such as Yahoo Answers, Baidu Zhidao, Answers.com, and Stack Overflow, hundreds of millions of answered questions have been collected. The answers to the questions are not only viewed by the asker herself, but are frequently presented as top search results for Web search queries and viewed by millions of searchers daily, in the form of a question and its corresponding answers.

The number of answers for CQA questions ranges from a handful to dozens, and even sometimes hundreds in cases of popular questions. We found that in Yahoo Answers more than 38% of the answered questions have at least 5 answers. For some questions, such as factoids, readers would be content with a single high-quality answer. However, in other types of questions, such as asking for recommendations or opinions, the asker as well as other viewers would benefit from different views or suggestions. Still, especially when many answers are provided, the reader may not want to sift through all answers but to read only the top ones. While a few works did address the task of answer ranking in CQA [22, 42, 45], they considered mainly the qualitative notions of each answer separately, its relevance to the question or whether it should be marked as best answer. These works did not address the overall quality of the ranked list of answers. Especially, they did not consider the complementary information provided by different answers.

In this paper we follow diversification approaches in Web search and Information Retrieval (IR) [13, 14] and promote CQA answers not only by their relevance to the question but also by diversification and novelty qualities they hold compared to other answers. Specifically, assuming the information need behind a CQA question can be partitioned into relevant "subtopics" or "aspects", our goal is to rank the corresponding answers not only by their relevance but also by the amount of aspects they cover (diversity), and more specifically, by the amount of new aspects they introduce with respect to higher ranked answers (novelty). Though diversification of CQA answers for input questions was considered before, it was under an IR setup, where results are retrieved from a large collection of answers [1]. To the best of our knowledge, this is the first time this task is addressed under the CQA setup, where the dozen or so answers to be ranked are manually provided by answerers directly for the target question.

There is a large body of research on document novelty and diversification for Web Search and IR [13, 4, 2, 33, 12, 43]. Yet, under a CQA setup this task bears significantly different traits. First, since the answers are provided by humans in direct response to the given question, most of these answers are relevant to the question to some extent [3]. This is a very different scenario compared to document retrieval, in which only a handful of documents are relevant out of a large list of matching documents. As a result, IR methods that incorporate novelty detection on top of relevance estimation (*e.g.*, MMR [8]) are somewhat unfitted for the CQA scenario (see Section 4). Second, CQA answers are typically much shorter than Web

SIGIR '16, July 17–21, 2016, Pisa, Italy.

DOI: http://dx.doi.org/10.1145/2911451.2911506

documents, and are therefore more condensed in terms of the content they provide. Third, IR methods aim at short ambiguous Web queries as input while CQA questions are longer and more detailed.

Another task that our CQA scenario resembles is that of summarizing different news articles on the same event [30]. In this scenario all news articles (answers) are "relevant", describing the same event (question), but may provide different views and facts (aspects) on the event by different reporters (answerers). The news articles should be summarized to provide a comprehensive view about the event. Specifically, in query-focused summarization, a typical approach is to rank sentences based on their similarity to the query and then cluster them and pick representative sentences based on the clusters [25].

While drawing similarities between news summarization and our task, the final goal is quite different, since we do not need to provide a summarization of the answers but to rank them. Furthermore, news articles are longer and well structured. This is not the case in CQA answers, which are typically short with many empty connecting unstructured sentences. Most notably in our task, many aspects may be clamped together in a single sentence, which makes the typical approach of looking at a sentence as an atomic text unit inappropriate. As an example, consider the question "*Whats your best migraine cure?*" and the provided answers "*1) Excedrine migraine, phenergan, dark room, cold compress, 8 hours of sleep*", and "*2) Take medicine, go in a dark room and sleep for at least an hour, it helps to use earplugs*". These answers contain several complementary suggestions each and they share several discussed topics: sleeping, being in a dark room, and medicine taking.

The method we propose for novelty-based answer ranking looks at syntactic propositions instead of sentences as the atomic text units. Under this view, answer 2 in the example above is decomposed into "*2.1) Take medicine*", "*2.2) go in a dark room and sleep for at least an hour*" and "*2.3) it helps to use earplugs*". We then measure the similarity between propositions and generate a hierarchical clustering of them across all answers. Finally, answers are ranked in a greedy manner based on the amount of diverse propositions they contain, taking into account each proposition's relevance to the question as well as its dissimilarity to propositions in higher ranked answers.

We tested our algorithm on a collection of health-related questions and their answers from Yahoo Answers, which were manually annotated with gold-standard aspects in each answer. We used conventional diversity-based IR evaluation metrics and also propose two novel evaluation metrics that better emphasize novelty under our settings. We compare our approach with several state-of-the-art novelty-based ranking algorithms and show that our algorithm outperforms prior work under all metrics.

Our main contributions in this paper are:

- Introducing the task of novelty-based answer ranking under the CQA setup
- Novelty-base answer ranking algorithm for CQA, which considers novelty on top of relevance
- Manually annotated dataset[1] of CQA questions together with gold-standard aspects per answer
- New evaluation metrics that emphasize diversification and novelty in CQA answer ranking

[1]Available at http://webscope.sandbox.yahoo.com

2. RELATED WORK

Novelty-based answer ranking in CQA has not attracted much attention so far. However, it is related to a several research fields. In this section we review the most related ones.

2.1 Answer Ranking

Answer ranking is essential for CQA services due to the high variance in the quality of answers. Several previous studies dealt with answer ranking for CQA sites [21, 22, 6, 27, 42, 45]. Jeon et al. [21] predicted answer quality using non-textual features of the answers. Bian et al. [6] integrated answer similarity to the question with community feedback information. Jurczyk and Agichtein [22] measured user expertise using link analysis over the question-answers graph, assuming answers given by authoritative users tend to be of high quality. Tu et al. [42] proposed an analogical reasoning-based method by measuring how valuable an answer is given its similarity to the set of best answers of similar resolved questions. Zhou et al. [45] additionally exploited three categories of user profile information – engagement-related, authority-related and level-related, for answer ranking in CQA.

Other works estimated the likelihood of an answer to be selected as best answer by the asker; an estimate that might be further used for answer ranking. Liu et. al. [27] and Shah and Pomerantz [36] trained a classifier that predicts this likelihood based on features describing the question text, category, question-answer similarity, user reputation, and user feedback. Suryanto et al. [40] studied additional features derived from the answerer expertise. The authors argued that an answerer can have different expertise levels for different topics which should be taken into account during answer quality estimation. Dalip et al. [16] proposed a learning to rank approach using a comprehensive set of eight different groups of features derived from the question-answer pair.

In this work we follow up on relevance estimation in prior work and combine it with novelty detection. We leave the integration with non-textual features such as answerer reputation and user feedback (*e.g.* votes) for future work.

2.2 Document Diversification

Novelty detection and search result diversification is an important research track in IR. Carbonel and Goldstein [8] proposed the Maximal Marginal Relevance (MMR) approach, in which documents in the result list are evaluated based on their relevance to the query as well as their difference from previously selected documents. Zhai et al. [44] studied how an interactive retrieval system can best support a user that gathers information about the different aspects of a topic. Agrawal et al. [4] selected the next document that best matches DMOZ categories that are related to a Web query but are not well covered by higher ranked documents. The xQuAD algorithm [35] measures document diversity by its relevance to sub-queries of an ambiguous Web query, which are not related to previously ranked documents. In the heart of xQuAD, a set of sub-queries that describe the different aspects of the query are assessed against each retrieved document. The sub-queries are generated using query expansion techniques or using query reformulations from search engines. Croft and Dang [15] suggested to use surface terms instead of topics as indications of aspects. They identify candidate terms as words in the vicinity of query terms that appear in retrieved documents and weigh their topicality and productiveness. However, in the CQA setup, question terms, which express information need, often do not appear in the answers, which express solutions. Therefore, a different aspect identification approach is required. We emphasize that diversification approaches for short ambiguous Web queries, whose aspects can be modeled by high level categories or additional keywords [4, 35, 17, 15], deal with scenarios that are very different from ours, in which the "query" is a detailed CQA question and its aspects are much more fine grained and very specific to the question's context.

Clarke et al. [13] proposed a framework for evaluation that systematically rewards novelty and diversity in the search results, based on cumulative gain. The task of novelty detection at the sentence level was explicitly defined at the TREC novelty track [39]: find relevant sentences for a given query; then extract only novel sentences from that list [5, 24].

Two works that are strongly related to our paper deal with diversifying user generated content. Krestel et al. [23] re-ranked user product reviews using star ratings and a latent topic model. The algorithm uses Latent Dirichlet Allocation (LDA) [7] to map different reviews of the same product to a latent topic space. It attempts to approximate the topic distribution for all reviews by selecting the top k reviews in a greedy way. Specifically, it chooses the next review to the ranked list as the one that minimizes the KL divergence between the all-reviews topic distribution and the topic distribution of the top reviews (including the new candidate). The algorithm's final goal is to construct a good summary of all reviews, assuming the reviews complement each other. This framework covers different ranking strategies based on the user need: summarizing all reviews; focusing on a particular latent topic; or focusing on sentiment aspects of the reviews.

Achananuparp et al. [1] introduced a graph ranking model for retrieving a diverse set of answers from a large answer archive given a complex input question. This algorithm constructs an ergodic directed transition matrix that combines similarities between all pairs of retrieved answers and the relevance of each answer to the question. Redundancy relations among answers are modeled in this algorithm by assigning a negative sign to the weight of edges between the answer nodes in the graph of candidate answers. The unique stationary distribution of the nodes, which is extracted via a PageRank-like approach, induces the ranking of the answers, with high probability answers on top. This algorithm showed significant improvement over prior work, including MMR. We replicated the algorithms in [1] and [23] as baselines for our study.

2.3 Multi Document Summarization

An abundance of prior work explored the task of multi-document summarization (MDS), in which a coherent summarization is generated from different documents covering similar information [28, 32, 38, 30]. We focus here on the application of these techniques in the CQA domain. Liu et al. [27] demonstrated that many open or opinion questions have multiple good answers which sometimes are better than the selected best answer. By summarizing these answers using query focused summarization techniques they were able to provide an alternative best answer. Chan et al. [9] addressed the problem of "incomplete answer", *i.e.* a best answer for a complex question that misses valuable information contained in other answers. They proposed a general Conditional Random Field (CRF) framework to create a complementary answer summary. Pande et al. [31] tackled the same incomplete answer problem by identifying a diverse set of informative threads in the user answers and summarizing each one of them.

Motivated by MDS techniques, we are interested in recognizing the important topics in an answer. Yet, in our task we are not required to generate a final summarization. Instead, we explore ways to measure the overall amount of diversity and novelty in each answer. In addition, prior work in CQA summarization operated at the sentence level. We argue that a more fine-grained analysis should be taken for aspect detection in CQA.

Excedrine migraine, phenergan, dark room, cold compress, 8 hours of sleep
Claratin and zyrtec did nothing for be then my allergist prescribed singular and it worked like a charm
try to get at least 7.5hrs of sleep and regular exercise
Id drink green tea as late as 10 pm at night but end up staying up really late, its a personal choice, you could always try a sleep aid

Table 1: Examples for single sentences in CQA answers that combine different information aspects for the question *"Whats your best migraine cure? I have the worst headache..."*.

3. NOVELTY-BASED ANSWER RANKING

In this work we propose an answer ranking solution that focuses on diversity and novelty notions of answers on top of relevance. Our goal is to rank the answers in a way that provides the reader a fast coverage of all the important aspects mentioned in the answers for the given question. Such ranking presents the user with "the whole picture" by reading only the first few answers instead of skipping repeated suggestions or opinions in order to find more relevant but diverse material.

We consider all the answers for a question to be relevant to some extent [3]. This does not mean that all the answer text is relevant to the question. Some answer parts may be irrelevant, such as emotional response (*"I am sorry to hear that Joe."*), connecting sentences (*"but let me tell you how things should really work"*) and personal agenda (*"we should blame the president for such situations"*). In addition, we do not consider all aspects as equal. Some recommendations or solutions are given in several answers, and assuming that "wisdom of the crowd" takes effect, we would like to view them as more important to the asker than others. Our task is therefore to rank higher answers that contain novel and diverse aspects, and to promote those aspects that are repeated in other answers as well.

Looking at the considerations above, we find an analogy between our task and the task of query-focused multi-document summarization [18, 41], as discussed earlier. We therefore present an algorithm that borrows ideas from textual summarization, but employ them differently for our ranking task. Similarly to extractive summarization, we focus on basic textual units as conveying the different information elements in an answer. Yet, unlike the common view of sentences as basic units, we found that often CQA answerers list several pieces of information in a single sentence. Table 1 presents such examples. We therefore focus on propositions, instead of sentences, as our basic units.

At a high level, our algorithm starts by extracting all propositions in each answer. Propositions that are irrelevant to the question are automatically filtered out based on their semantic dissimilarity from the question. The algorithm then measures the similarity between the remaining propositions as a proxy to aspect diversity, and the "importance" of each proposition is assessed based on its occurrences in different answers. Finally, a greedy procedure selects at each round the answer that best combines a set of relevant propositions that are both diverse, novel, and important. Algorithm 1 depicts this procedural overview of our algorithm. In the reminder of this section we will detail each of the steps in our algorithm.

3.1 Proposition extraction

In this step the algorithm extracts the basic semantic units, called *propositions*, which we consider as conveying coherent information given by the answerer. To this end, it starts, similarly to summarization and classic novelty detection in IR [13], by sentence splitting each answer. It then proceeds by syntactically analyzing each

```
Input: question q
Input: set of answers Ans
OrderedAns = []
/* Init                                                    */
foreach a ∈ Ans do
    Propositions[a] = extractRelevantPropositions(a, q)
    foreach p ∈ Propositions[a] do
        Novelty[p] = 1
    end
end
/* Rank                                                    */
while Ans ≠ ∅ do
    selectedAnswer = select(Ans, Novelty, Propositions)
    OrderedAns.add(selectedAnswer)
    Ans = Ans \ {selectedAnswer}
    foreach p ∈ Propositions do
        Novelty[p] =
        updateNovelty(p, Novelty, selectedAnswer)
    end
end
return OrderedAns
```

Algorithm 1: Novelty-based answer ranking overview

sentence. Specifically, the algorithm parses each sentence with the Clear[2] dependency parser [11]. It then splits the dependency tree into sub-trees based on specific edge types that indicate proposition boundaries. These edges include the following kinds of connectives: *ccomp*, *npadvmod* and *conj*. Finally, each sub-tree is turned into a text string by ordering the words in the sub-tree according to their original position in the sentence. As an example of procedure, the last sentence in Table 1 is split into "*Id drink green tea as late as 10 pm at night*", "*end up staying up really late*", "*its a personal choice*" and "*you could always try a sleep aid*".

3.2 Proposition filtering

Proposition filtering is an essential step in our algorithm, it ensures that answers will not be promoted for including irrelevant propositions like recurring empathic statements such as "*its a personal choice*" in the above example.

In order to keep only propositions relevant to the question, we rank them based on their similarity to the question. Yet, simple surface word comparison will not suffice for two reasons. First, the language used in the answer is very different from the question's language, one containing words that help express an information need and the other words that convey a solution to that need. For example, the question "*what should I see in Paris?*" and the answer "*the Eiffel tower is a must*" have no shared terms, but the answer is very relevant. Second, propositions are rather short texts while some questions may be verbose and long, containing several sentences. Therefore, surface level similarity measures such as Cosine or Jaccard will fail to identify relevant propositions.

We address these two issues by mapping the answer and question to a shared latent space and measure their similarity there. To this end, we employ a variant of the Explicit Semantic Analysis (ESA) approach [20]. Under ESA, a text is mapped to a semantic space in which each dimension is a Wikipedia page (concept). This is done by retrieving the most relevant Wikipedia documents using a search engine, given the whole text as a query. Once the vectors containing the top results for the two compared texts are retrieved, cosine similarity between the two vectors is computed to measure their similarity.

ESA is a successful semantic representation for texts. Still, standard ESA does not compensate for the difference in languages between questions and answers. To address this issue, we follow a variant of ESA, denoted *CQA-ESA*, in which instead of Wikipedia documents the latent space is defined over a collection of structured documents containing CQA questions and their best answers [37]. Each CQA document is a dimension and, as in standard ESA, the representation of a text is by retrieving the top documents in the collection. CQA-ESA differs from standard ESA in the way documents are retrieved. When representing questions, the documents are retrieved by searching only on the question field of each document, while when answers are provided as queries, documents are retrieved by searching over the answer field of each document. This way, the proper language is used for searching for each type of text, but the final latent space is shared – the document ids. We note that the underlying assumption of this approach is that the best-answer of a question is typically highly relevant to it, and therefore the two fields of a single document convey the same semantics in different "languages".

We use CQA-ESA similarity to the question for ranking the propositions in all answers. Following an empirical study over several dozen questions not in our test-set, we chose to keep the top 90% propositions similar to the question as relevant, filtering out the rest. As document collection we used a random sample of 2 million questions and their best answers from Yahoo Answers. We apply the Lucene[3] search engine, under its default settings, for searching over this collection. The search results are used for CQA-ESA representation of the queried text.

3.3 Answer Diversity and Importance

Motivation and Definitions

As discussed above, we would like to discover which relevant propositions present different aspects that appear in the answers, in order to promote answers that contain a diverse set of aspects. In addition, following the notion of "wisdom of the crowd" we would like to promote answers that include aspects that are shared with other answers as a measure of importance.

We chose to employ semantic similarity between two propositions, $sim(p, o)$, as a measure of diversity. That is, the more similar two propositions are the less diverse the aspects they convey are considered. We use proposition similarity also for importance assessment. Specifically, the more similar a proposition is to many propositions in other answers the more *support* we say it has. We describe two ways to estimate proposition support in Section 3.4.

In order to compute support and diversity we next introduce our semantic similarity function $sim(p, o)$ between two propositions.

Semantic Similarity Function

To compute the semantic similarity between two propositions we experimented with four unsupervised similarity measures:

TF-IDF. The cosine between the TF-IDF vectors of the two propositions, after stop-word removal and stemming. This is a typical surface-word similarity measure [5]. Term frequency of a term is its number of occurrences in the proposition. Document frequency of the term is counted over a collection of randomly sampled 16 million questions and their best answers from Yahoo Answers.

Word2Vec. Since propositions are short, and in general people tend to use different wordings to express the same information, we wanted to utilize measures that may overcome such differences in word selection. The following *Word2Vec* measure employs the

[2]https://code.google.com/p/clearparser/

[3]http://lucene.apache.org

Word2Vec model [29], which maps words to a low dimensional space such that semantically similar words are close to each other in this space. We used a publicly available model trained on part of Google news data-set[4] (about 100 billion words) to map words to a 500 dimension space. We then apply the following function to compute proposition similarity $sim(p, o)$:

$$Coverage(p, o) = \frac{1}{|p|} \sum_{t_p \in p} \max_{t_o \in o}[cosine(w2v(t_p), w2v(t_o))]$$

$$sim(p, o) = \sqrt{Coverage(p, o) \cdot Coverage(o, p)}$$

where p and o are propositions, t_p and t_o are terms in p and o respectively, and $w2v(t)$ is the Word2Vec representation of term t.

ESA. As another measure for semantic proposition similarly beyond surface wording, we represent each proposition with its ESA vector over the Wikipedia dump from Feb 2014, using Lucene as the search engine. The cosine between the two vectors is taken as their similarity measure.

CQA-ESA. Similarly to the ESA similarity measure, we use the CQA-ESA representation of each proposition (see Section 3.2) and compute the cosine between the two CQA-ESA vectors.

During our research we found that the performance of our similarity measures differ from one question to another. In order to get a consistently well performing similarity function we combined them in a supervised way. Specifically, we learned a classifier for predicting whether two propositions represent the same answer aspect for a given question, where the input features of each proposition pair are the four unsupervised similarity measures described above. The training set consists of pairs of propositions together with labels indicating if they capture the same aspect or not. A detailed description of this dataset is presented in Section 4. We used the SVM implementation in Weka[5] as our classifier. As a final similarity score we used the classifier's normalized output between $[0, 1]$. We note that this is the only supervised component in our algorithm.

3.4 Greedy Answer Ranking

Given a question and its corresponding set of answers, we would like to rank the answers based on the diversity and importance of their propositions. We follow a common approach in diversification literature [8, 44, 4, 35] and present a greedy ranking framework. Our algorithm iteratively selects the next answer to be added to the ranked list, (denoted by $select()$ in Algorithm 1), by considering how much each answer includes: (a) diverse aspects; (b) important aspects; (c) novel aspects that did not appear in higher ranked answers. Then, the novelty measure of all propositions is updated based on the amount of "support" they are given by the selected answer (denoted by $updateNovelty()$ in Algorithm 1). This iterative procedure continues as long as there are still answers that are not added to the ranked list, resulting in a complete ordering of all answers. We next present two methods for selecting the next answer, and for updating proposition novelty. These methods define the two variants of our overall ranking algorithm.

3.4.1 Similarity based answer selection

The first method uses the similarity between propositions directly for answer selection. The answer's score is proportional to the amount of "support" it provides for novel, yet uncovered propositions. Formally, each proposition's novelty assessment is maintained by the $Novelty[p]$ property, according to how much the aspect it represents is already represented by other propositions in higher ranked answers. We first define $Support(p, a)$, measuring how well answer a supports the information given in proposition p, based on p's similarity to the answer's propositions. Then, the score of a is determined by summing a's support over all propositions, weighted by their novelty property.

$$Support(p, a) = 1 - \prod_{p_a \in a} (1 - sim(p, p_a)) \qquad (1)$$

$$Score(a) = \sum_{p \in Propositions} Novelty[p] \cdot Support(p, a)$$

We note that $Support(p, a)$ acts as a noisy-or formulation of similarity – it is zero only when all answer's propositions are zero-similar to p, and it supports p when at least one of a's propositions is similar to p.

Once the $selectedAnswer$, the highest scoring answer, is chosen, the $Novelty$ assessment of each proposition is updated by the novelty update function

$$Novelty[p] = Novelty[p] \cdot (1 - Support(p, selectedAnswer))$$

We would like to emphasize two properties of this selection procedure. First, during the re-computation phase, the $Novelty$ property of any proposition p of the selected answer becomes 0, since $Support(p, selectedAns) = 1$. Such propositions will no longer contribute to the score of lower ranked answers in future iterations. Therefore, the $Score(a)$ formula only considers propositions in unranked answers for contribution to an answer's score.

Second, the scoring formula includes a notion of proposition importance since an important proposition is similar to many propositions that capture the same aspect. Hence, if an answer contains important propositions, many novel propositions will contribute to the answer score, more than to an answer with the same number of novel propositions which correspond to uncommon aspects.

We note that our novelty update formula resembles that of the xQuAD algorithm [35], as it downgrades the importance of aspects that are already supported by higher ranking documents. Yet, xQuAD's aspects are sub-queries, variations, or expansions of the original query, while our update model is based on the similarity measurement between answer propositions.

3.4.2 Hierarchical clustering based answer selection

Ideally, we would like to have clusters of propositions, each reflecting a single specific aspect within the answers. The size of the clusters would indicate the importance of each aspect, and the diversity of each answer could be easily derived from the number of its related clusters (aspects).

Such clustering is also in the heart of multi-document summarization, since picking a representative sentence from each cluster would generate a comprehensive yet compact summarization. However, producing high quality partitioning of propositions is not a simple task. Instead, in this method we take a "softer" approach that constructs an agglomerative hierarchical clustering (AHC) tree for the set of propositions.

The hierarchical clustering method utilizes the Cluto[6] tool to construct a hierarchical cluster tree based on the similarity matrix between propositions (using our similarity function). It then uses the resulting cluster tree structure to calculate the support of each

[4] http://tiny.cc/GoogleNews-vectors

[5] http://www.cs.waikato.ac.nz/ml/weka

[6] http://glaros.dtc.umn.edu/gkhome/software

```
Input: Selected answer selectedAnswer
Input: novelty assessment Novelty
Input: all propositions Propositions
Input: Proposition cluster tree T
/* Update propositions novelty */
foreach p_a ∈ selectedAnswer do
    n_{p_a} = findLeafNodeOf(p_a, T)
    foreach p ∈ Propositions do
        n_p = findLeafNodeOf(p, T)
        d =
        distance(n_{p_a}, nearestCommonAncestor(n_{p_a}, n_p))
        Novelty[p] = Novelty[p] · (1 − (1/2)^d)
    end
end
```

Algorithm 2: Novelty update for all propositions after selecting an answer using hierarchical clustering tree

proposition and to penalize propositions that are similar to propositions in already selected answers. The answer score function of this method is defined as follows:

$$Score_{AHC}(a) = \frac{\sum_{p \in a} Novelty[p] \cdot Depth(p, T)}{\sqrt{|a|} \cdot \left(1 + \left(1 - \frac{\sum_{p \in a} Novelty[p]}{|a|}\right)\right)} \quad (2)$$

where $Depth(p, T)$ is the distance of node p from the root of the cluster tree, and $|a|$ refers to the number of propositions in a.

We note two properties of this function. First, in contrast to Equation 1, an answer score is based only on its own propositions. However, propositions that are further down in the (unbalanced) tree are considered more important, since they are similar to more propositions, therefore the nominal part captures the average importance of the answer's proposition where each proposition is weighted by its novelty. Second, an answer with non-novel propositions will be penalized since it has a larger denominator. Therefore, this function weighs novelty and importance against each other. Finally, answer scores are normalized by the answer's number of propositions $\sqrt{|a|}$ to allow fair comparison between answers of different length.

After selecting an answer a that maximizes $Score_{AHC}(a)$ to the ranked list, we penalize all propositions that are similar to the propositions in a. Propositions are penalized according to their distance from the selected answer's propositions in the cluster tree: the further away two propositions are, the less similar they are. Specifically, for each proposition p_a in the selected answer we start from its corresponding leaf node in the tree and climb towards the tree root. At each node n on the path we penalize each proposition p for which n is its nearest common ancestor with p_a, by degrading their $Novelty$ property: $Novelty[p] = Novelty[p] \cdot (1 - \frac{1}{2}^d)$, where d is their distance to p_a. This procedure is formalized in Algorithm 2.

Similarly to the previous method, the $Novelty$ of each proposition in the selected answer is set to 0, since its distance from itself is 0. Moreover, the more similar a proposition p is to those in the selected answer, *i.e.* the closer its location is to their locations in the tree, the more p will be penalized.

4. EXPERIMENTAL SETTINGS

To assess the performance of our proposed approach, we compare our two algorithm variants and several baselines on a manually annotated gold-standard test-set. Under this evaluation setting, a gold standard annotation of the aspects in each answer is given, following the methodology in the TREC novelty track [14]. Both our algorithms and the compared baselines are evaluated according to their ability to rank higher diverse answers that contain novel aspects with respect to higher ranked answers. We compared the ranking quality using the $\alpha NDCG$ [13] and *ERR-IA* [10] measures and novel measures we propose specifically for the CQA scenario.

We next detail the gold-standard dataset construction, the compared algorithms and the novel ranking measures.

4.1 Dataset Construction

Our manually constructed dataset[7] consists of a random sample of 110 questions from the Health top category in Yahoo Answers, each with at least 10 answers. For each sampled question the authors manually split each answer into propositions and annotated those that are relevant to the question. The relevant propositions in all answers were then manually aggregated into clusters, where each cluster represents a specific aspect mentioned in the answers. This aspect cluster is referred to as the gold-standard aspect mapping for the question. From this gold standard annotation the "importance" of each aspect is taken to be the size of its cluster. Additionally, the aspect distribution in each answer is straightforwardly induced. Overall, we analyzed 1426 answers and labeled 2775 relevant propositions referring to 838 different information aspects (7.6 aspects per question on average). Interestingly, relevant propositions cover (on average) only about 30% of the answers text.

We evaluated the performance of all tested algorithms using 5-fold cross validation. The training parts were used to train our supervised similarity function (see Subsection 3.3), and to tune the parameters of the baseline algorithms.

4.2 Tested Algorithms

We implemented six baseline algorithms in order to analyze the behavior of CQA answer ranking and to compare their performance to our proposed ranking approach. The first baseline is a simple random ranking of the answers (denoted *RandomRanker*). It serves as a lower bound for the performance of the algorithms under the evaluation measures we utilize.

The second baseline, denoted *Votes*, ranks the answers by the feedback they received from other users. Specifically, we subtract the down-votes (thumbs-down) from the up-votes (thumbs-up) that each answer received. This score was viewed in prior work as an implicit quality assessment measure and was used as ground truth for learning to rank answers by their quality [16].

The next two baselines address only the relevance aspect of ranking: *BM25* [34] and *ESA* (over Wikipedia) [20]. For BM25, the query is the question's text and the documents to be ranked are the different answers. Document frequency of the terms for BM25 was estimated over a collection of 16 million question/best-answer pairs. ESA was implemented as described in Section 3.3. We note that using ESA over CQA instead of Wikipedia did not improve the results.

We are not aware of prior work that addresses novelty or diversification in answer ranking within the CQA settings (*i.e.* ranking manually provided answers for a target question). Instead, we implemented two ranking approaches from related fields as baselines (Section 2.2). The first algorithm, denoted *LDARanker*, was proposed for diversifying product reviews [23]. We implemented this algorithm including the specific ngram partitioning of the texts [19]. We learned 1000 topics for the LDA model on a collection of 1 million CQA questions from the Health top category in Yahoo Answers, in order to match our test-set domain.

The second related baseline we implemented is the answer diversification algorithm of [1], denoted *WebAnswerRanker*. Given an input complex query, this algorithm attempts to diversify the set of

[7]This dataset will be publicly available.

retrieved answers from a large answer collection, showing significant improvement over prior work (see Section 2.2). We applied this algorithm in our settings, using TF-IDF for measuring question/answer similarity and n-gram similarity for answer/answer similarity (following experiments which showed that this is the best performing configuration on our data-set).

We tested two variants of our approach against the above baselines: a) *SimRanker*, which uses Equation 1 for answer selection and the corresponding novelty update (Subsection 3.4.1); and b) *HCRanker*, which uses the hierarchical clustering based answer selection (Equation 2) and AHC-based novelty update (Subsection 3.4.2). Both variants make use of the supervised similarity function detailed in Section 3.3.

4.3 Performance Measures

Several IR metrics were proposed that consider novelty/diversity on top of relevancy. For this experiment we utilize $\alpha NDCG$ [13, 12] and the topic-aware ERR (*ERR-IA*) [10]. These two metrics were designed for typical IR scenario in which many documents are irrelevant. They therefore aim at balancing between relevance and novelty. In the CQA scenario on the other hand, most answers are relevant. Therefore, we propose two additional metrics that directly assess the effort required by a user to scan the ranked answer list through the number of redundant aspects the user would encounter. The two metrics differ in their treatment of aspect importance: one is oblivious to it while the other focuses on it.

Novelty-focused evaluation metric

This metric assesses how efficient a given answer ranking is in covering the gold-standard aspects. For each recall point r (fraction of aspects covered) a cost function is first computed:

$$NoveltyCost(A,r) = \sum_{i=1}^{m(r)} \left(1 + \beta \cdot (1 - \frac{|NovelAspects(a_i)|}{|Aspects(a_i)|})\right)$$

$$m(r) = \min_{m} \frac{|\cup_{i=1}^{m} Aspects(a_i)|}{|\cup_{a \in A} Aspects(a)|} \geq r$$

A is the ranked answer list $\{a_i\}_1^{|A|}$, $m(r)$ is the minimal rank position for which the accumulative aspects in the rank reaches recall r in terms of aspect coverage, and β controls the effect of novelty. $Aspects(a_i)$ returns the gold-standard aspects that are mentioned in the answer a_i while $NovelAspects(a_i)$ returns only those aspects in a_i that are not covered by higher ranked answers. This cost function puts emphasize on the amount of new aspects an answer introduces by penalizing answers with repeated aspects. In the extreme, a novel answer which reveals only new aspects contributes 1 to the score while an answer with no novel aspects at all contributes $(1 + \beta)$ to the score. In our experiments, we set $\beta = 0.5$.

For each question we computed the minimal possible cost for the recall point r according to the above cost function by evaluating all the permutations over the answers set. We then normalize the cost of the ranked list A as follows:

$$minNoveltyCost(A,r) = \min_{A' \in \pi(A)} [NoveltyCost(A',r)]$$

$$NormNoveltyCost(A,r) = \frac{minNoveltyCost(A,r)}{NoveltyCost(A,r)}$$

where $\pi(A)$ is the set of all permutations of the answer list A. Note that while lower $NoveltyCost(A,r)$ values correspond to a better ranking, $NormNoveltyCost(A,r)$ exhibits how good is this ranking relative to the best possible ranking, and here higher values correspond to a better ranking.

The final metric score of a ranked list A is taken as the average of all normalized costs at recall points $\{0.1, 0.2, \ldots, 1.0\}$:

$$NoveltyMetric(A) = \frac{1}{10} \sum_{r=0.1}^{r=1.0} NormNoveltyCost(A,r)$$

Support-focused evaluation metric

The novelty-focused metric views all aspects as equally important. Yet, as we discussed previously, some aspects are mentioned more than others in the answers and reflect a common recommendation or opinion. In this work we view such aspects as more "important", measuring it by the number of propositions that contain information about the aspect.

In the following proposed metric, important aspects contribute more to recall. For this purpose, recall is computed as the fraction of propositions belonging to the aspects covered by the list of answers. We follow a similar methodology as in the novelty-focused metric, by defining a cost function for a ranked list of answers A and a recall point r:

$$SupportCost(A,r) = \sum_{i=1}^{m(r)} \left(1 + \beta \cdot (1 - \frac{|Props(NovelAspects(a_i))|}{|Props(Aspects(a_i))|})\right)$$

$$m(r) = \min_{m} \frac{|\cup_{i=1}^{m} Props(Aspects(a_i))|}{|\cup_{a \in A} Props(Aspects(a))|} \geq r$$

where $Props()$ returns the list of gold-standard propositions corresponding to an input list of gold-standard aspects. The final metric is computed just like the novelty-focused metric by analogously defining *minSupportCost*, *NormSupportCost* and *SupportMetric*.

5. RESULTS

We compared the performance of all tested algorithms across the four metrics: $\alpha NDCG$, *ERR-IA*, $NoveltyMetric$ and $SupportMetric$. Table 2 summarizes the results. Statistical significance for the difference between our algorithms and the baselines is marked by the '+' sign for $p < 0.05$ using pairwise t-test. We note that the results in the table are macro averages over the parameters of each measure. Specifically, we averaged all α values in $\alpha NDCG$ metric on the range $[0, 1]$ with jumps of 0.25, and averaged all recall r values in novelty-based and support-based metrics, as discussed in Section 4.3. We used $\frac{15}{16}$ for relevant topic weight in *ERR-IA*. A more detailed analysis of the results, drawing the performance graph for each parameter range in each measure, is shown in Figures 1, 2 and 3 for $\alpha NDCG$, $NoveltyMetric$ and $SupportMetric$ respectively[8].

From the results we can see that the random baseline already places a rather high bar with respect to similar values in traditional IR tasks. This is especially true under $\alpha NDCG$ and *ERR-IA*, which supports our observation that most answers are relevant. Under our proposed metrics, which weigh novelty and diversification elements more, the random baseline is lower. This is also the reason why all systems perform similarly when considering only

[8] In all three figures our algorithms are plotted in solid lines, *Random* is plotted in dotted lines, LDA and $WebAnswer$ are plotted in mixed dashed and dots lines and *BM25*, *ESA* and *Votes* baselines are plotted in dashed lines.

Metric	$\alpha NDCG$	*ERR-IA*	Novelty	Support
RandomRanker	0.61	0.64	0.49	0.55
Votes	0.67	0.69	0.55	0.61
BM25	0.68	0.71	0.57	0.64
ESA	0.67	0.67	0.57	0.60
LDARanker	0.63	0.51	0.54	0.56
WebAnswerRanker	0.76	0.77	0.62	0.67
SimRanker	**0.80**$^+$	**0.81**	**0.68**$^+$	**0.71**
HCRanker	**0.79**	**0.81**	**0.67**$^+$	**0.71**

Table 2: Performance results of all algorithms across all metrics. $'+'$ signs mark statistically significant results between our algorithms and all the baselines.

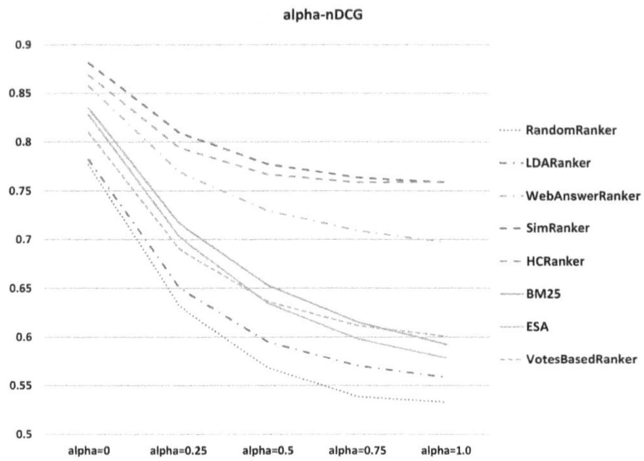

Figure 1: $\alpha NDCG$ results at different α values

relevance, under $\alpha NDCG$ with $\alpha = 0$ (Fig. 1). Yet, even under such conservative evaluation, which ignores novelty, our algorithms perform better than the baselines since they introduce more diversity in the top results. When α is increased a clearer picture is revealed. The gap between our algorithms and the baselines keeps on increasing, showing the superior ability of our proposition-based approach to recognize novel aspects in answers. This is compared to the more "global" approaches taken by *LDARanker* and *WebAnswerRanker*. At the extreme, for $\alpha = 1$, *SimRanker* and *HCRanker* achieve a relative improvement over the best performing baseline of more than 11%. A similar trend is observed under the *ERR-IA* metric.

In terms of novelty-based ranking baselines, *WebAnswerRanker* is the best performing baseline. On the other hand, *LDARanker* performs even worse than the purely-relevance-based *BM25* ranker. This result emphasizes the need to model aspects at a fine-grained textual level. In our case, the LDA model was learned over all of the Health corpus and regards only high level topics. But, typically, each question page discusses one or two such high level semantic topics, and therefore *LDARanker* cannot distinguish between answers with respect to the aspects related to the high level topic. This also shows that answer ranking is quite different than product review ranking, in which it is common to find quite a few high level topics in reviews for any specific product and therefore to rank them at this high level view.

Interestingly, all algorithms seem to arrange well the most diverse answers at the top ($r = 0.1$ in Figs. 2 and 3). But this is a phenomenon of the CQA data, not of algorithmic capabilities. It is indicated by the fact that *RandomRanker* can perform at this recall point almost as well as the best performing algorithm. On the other hand, looking at the two figures we can observe the limitation of the greedy ranking scheme that all tested algorithms use. All are doing very well at low recall points, but their performance compared to an optimal solution drops quickly. At the extreme point of $r = 1$, when compared against optimal ranking, all algorithms perform poorly. This shows that early greedy decisions are far from optimal when looking at "the whole picture", and that in general, novelty-based answer ranking, at high recall level, is far from being solved.

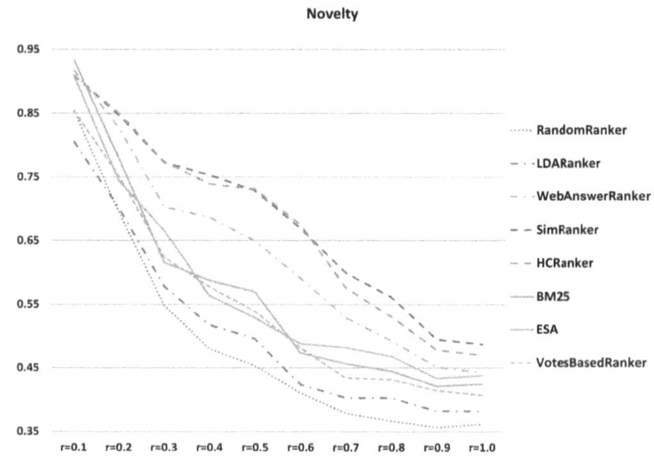

Figure 2: $NoveltyMetric$ results at different recall values

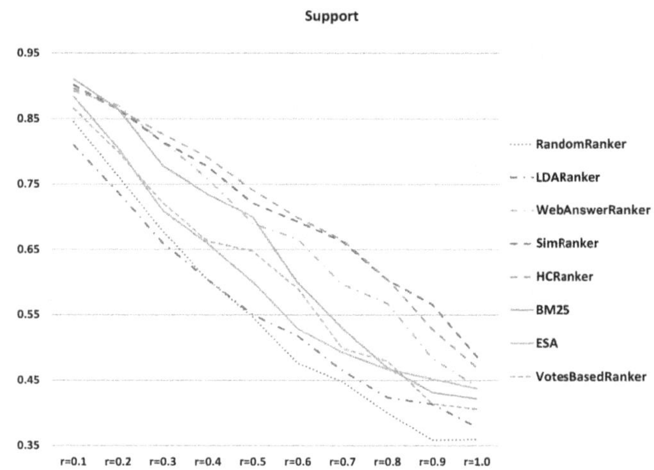

Figure 3: $SupportMetric$ results at different recall values

While at the extreme recall points all algorithms perform similarly, the overall difference between our approach and the baseline is clearly evident: both our algorithms outperform all the baselines across all four metrics under all parameter settings. This is a strong indication of the capability of our approach to promote novel and diversified answers in a robust way. In general, we see that $SimRanker$ slightly outperforms $HCRanker$, but not in a statistically significant way. Diving more deeply, the main difference between our algorithms and the baselines is at mid recall ranges ($r \in [0.3, 0.9]$). With respect to $NoveltyMetric$ (Fig. 2), a notable gap is maintained at this range with the peak reached when

Question: My alarm clock wakes me at 7 o'clock every morning. why do always wake up tired, angry and irritable?

SimRanker answers:

1: You probably are not sleeping well during the night. You might have sleep apnea which often has the same affect. [illegible]*. Also, try cutting out all caffiene, sugar and spicy foods about 4 or 5 hours before bed. Do you watch tv at night. That can make matters worse for some. Try* [illegible] *instead. And even though I am doing it right now, the computer is not good either. ... If this doesn't help,* [illegible]*. People sleep in cycles. You might be falling into an REM cycle right at 7 o'clock and those are the worst to wake up from. You might want to try resetting your internal clock by going to bed a little earlier. For me,* [illegible]*. It's a wonderful little pill...*

2: Are you watching T.V. before you go to bed? Drinking sodas, coffee, eating sugar? ... Keep your body from working too hard ... and try some soothing techniques like warm milk and reading. You wake up feeling unrested because you're not getting enough sleep, and once you are asleep, it's no fun to wake up. Just try to go to bed earlier if possible and you should slowly rotate your circadian rhythm.

3: ... Try taking a hot relaxing bath just before bed, and maybe sit reading until you feel tired in bed. ... Also try going to bed a little earlier, and try not to oversleep. Another tip would be to not have large lie ins at the weekend as this will knock your rythym out of synch...

4: well you might not be getting enough sleep and your body needs more. ... so just take a shower and it makes it better

5: Try to stay awake for 24 hours, then go to bed early. ... Also dont eat too late at night, and dont drink caffeine in the evenings.

WebAnswerRanker answers:

1: Same as #2 of SimRanker | *2: Same as #3 of SimRanker* | *3: Same as #4 of SimRanker*

4: that makes two of us, not been up too long myself and i've got a mood like a thunder storm this morning

5: Maybe you stay up too late on here. Go to bed earlier.

Figure 4: Example of a question with 2 sets of top 5 answers ordered by $SimRanker$ and $WebAnswerRanker$. The propositions of each specific information aspect are colored in a separate color (human gold-standard annotation).

half of the novel aspects are presented ($r = 0.5$). This shows that our algorithm is nicely tuned for aspect novelty.

When promoting "important" aspects via their support (Fig. 3), a more interesting result is drawn. While both our algorithms are best performing, at a significant portion of the recall spectrum *WebAnswerRanker* and more interestingly *BM25* achieve comparable results, at least with $SimRanker$. A possible reason for the relatively good performance of *BM25*, which considers only relevance, is that relevant aspects are also well supported, since answerers feel "obliged" to address these common aspects. Similarly, *WebAnswerRanker*, whose underlying target is to find answers that mostly agree with other answers, provides good results. However, to achieve recall values beyond 0.6 the ranked answers need to cover also infrequent aspects, a task that *WebAnswerRanker* and more notably *BM25* find somewhat harder to perform.

In this experiment, the quality-based baseline *Votes* performed similarly to the relevance only models *ESA* and *BM25*. As expected, user votes contain good indication of answer relevance to the question, and *Votes* scores significantly above the *Random* baseline. However, *Votes* computes a quality value for each answer separately. It therefore cannot distinguish between high quality answers with few novel aspects or that are lacking aspect diversity from those that introduce novel perspectives. For instance, users may mark similar answers as high quality, because both are appealing, but they do not contribute additional information one on top of the other. Indeed, *Votes* did not perform as well as the novelty aware algorithms. This result emphasizes the difference between the tasks of quality-based answer ranking, which was the focus of prior work, and novelty-based answer ranking, which we introduce in this paper.

As a coda, we present an example in Fig. 4, which helps to highlight the performance differences between our approach (using *SimRanker*) and the best performing baseline (*WebAnswerRanker*). In the example, 10 relevant aspects appear in the answers that were provided for the question. *SimRanker* covers 7 of them already in the first answer, adds another 2 in the second one, and another one in the third answer. *WebAnswerRanker*, also covers 7 aspects in the first answer, adds another one in the second, and doesn't cover the 2 remaining in the first 5 at all. Moreover, its forth answer doesn't contain any relevant aspects at all. In terms of support, the first answer of *SimRanker* covers 74% of all aspects, while *WebAnswerRanker* covers 77%, but after the second answer *SimRanker* covers 89% of all aspects, while *WebAnswerRanker* covers 82%. Finally, *SimRanker* covers 100% within 3 answers while *WebAnswerRanker* stays at 82%. This illustrates the capability of *SimRanker* to balance between supported aspects and novel ones, compared to *WebAnswerRanker*, which mainly addresses support.

6. DISCUSSION

Though both our ranking algorithms are based on the same approach, some differences in their performance are worth noting. The similarity-based ranker $SimRanker$ directly uses the similarity function between propositions to compute answer support. This low level usage of the similarity function makes it vulnerable to similarity value distribution issues. Specifically, we have inspected our four unsupervised similarity functions and found that their values are rarely larger than 0.2 even for highly similar propositions. While the supervised measure enabled us to normalize and leverage the different similarity perspectives captured by each individual unsupervised measure, using each of these unsupervised measures alone within $SimRanker$ provided rather poor results on our test-set. Therefore, this task would benefit from future exploration of similarity measures for very short texts that, on top of comparing their words, also leverage the immediate local context surrounding each text.

Our hierarchical clustering based ranker $HCRanker$ attempts to transform the continuous similarity score into a high-level relational semantic structure. This approach is motivated from viewing aspects as semantically separated discussion topics within answers, and it is inspired from clustering approaches in multi-document summarization [38, 30]. Yet, this transformation may suffer from information loss, since exact similarity values are not available anymore, as well as from the inherent difficulty in inducing high level semantic concepts from raw text. Specifically, observing the variance in performance, we noticed that this method is less stable and while for some questions it highly outperformed the other tested methods, in other cases its performance downgraded significantly. In the future we want to keep researching the construction and applicability of high level concept similarity graphs for text ranking in general and answer ranking specifically.

7. CONCLUSIONS

We introduced the task of novelty-based answer ranking for CQA question pages. We argued that under the CQA settings this task requires different approaches, since unlike standard document retrieval, most answers for a CQA question are relevant. We proposed a novel algorithm that looks at answer ranking as trying to cover as many aspects in a potential "summary" of all answers as possible with fewest answers. To this end, our algorithm regards syntactic propositions as the basic text units. It then computes the similarity between propositions between and within answers for assessing diversification, novelty and importance quality. We also computed each proposition's similarity to the question for assessing relevance. Finally, answers are greedily ranked based on the amount of novel propositions each answer contains, as well as their importance within all answers, taking into account their relevance to the question. To measure the performance of our algorithm we compared it to prior work that considered novelty in ranking. Under a gold standard manual evaluation, our algorithm significantly outperformed the compared works.

We would like to further investigate the importance of novelty in CQA. Specifically, which types of questions would benefit more from such ranking. In addition, we would like to incorporate novelty elements for measuring user reputation, as an additional quality notion of the answerer. Finally, we want to explore how novelty assessment can be combined with other answer quality signals such as user reputation, temporal features and writing style in order to analyze which are more important to viewers of a CQA page.

8. REFERENCES

[1] P. Achananuparp, X. Hu, T. He, C. C. Yang, Y. An, and L. Guo. Answer diversification for complex question answering on the web. In *PAKDD*, 2010.

[2] P. Achananuparp, C. C. Yang, and X. Chen. Using negative voting to diversify answers in non-factoid question answering. In *CIKM*, 2009.

[3] L. A. Adamic, J. Zhang, E. Bakshy, and M. S. Ackerman. Knowledge sharing and yahoo answers: everyone knows something. In *WWW*, 2008.

[4] R. Agrawal, S. Gollapudi, A. Halverson, and S. Ieong. Diversifying search results. In *WSDM*, 2009.

[5] J. Allan, C. Wade, and A. Bolivar. Retrieval and novelty detection at the sentence level. In *SIGIR*, 2003.

[6] J. Bian, Y. Liu, E. Agichtein, and H. Zha. Finding the right facts in the crowd: Factoid question answering over social media. In *WWW*, 2008.

[7] D. M. Blei, A. Y. Ng, and M. I. Jordan. Latent dirichlet allocation. *J. Mach. Learn. Res.*, 3:993–1022, Mar. 2003.

[8] J. Carbonell and J. Goldstein. The use of MMR, diversity-based reranking for reordering documents and producing summaries. In *SIGIR*, 1998.

[9] W. Chan, X. Zhou, W. Wang, and T.-S. Chua. Community answer summarization for multi-sentence question with group l1 regularization. In *ACL*, 2012.

[10] O. Chapelle, D. Metlzer, Y. Zhang, and P. Grinspan. Expected reciprocal rank for graded relevance. In *CIKM*, 2009.

[11] J. D. Choi and M. Palmer. Getting the most out of transition-based dependency parsing. In *ACL*, 2011.

[12] C. L. Clarke, N. Craswell, I. Soboroff, and A. Ashkan. A comparative analysis of cascade measures for novelty and diversity. In *WSDM*, 2011.

[13] C. L. Clarke, M. Kolla, G. V. Cormack, O. Vechtomova, A. Ashkan, S. Büttcher, and I. MacKinnon. Novelty and diversity in information retrieval evaluation. In *SIGIR*, 2008.

[14] C. L. A. Clarke, N. Craswell, and I. Soboroff. Overview of the TREC 2009 web track. In *TREC*, 2009.

[15] W. B. Croft and V. Dang. Term level search result diversification. In *SIGIR*, 2013.

[16] D. H. Dalip, M. A. Gonçalves, M. Cristo, and P. Calado. Exploiting user feedback to learn to rank answers in q&a forums: A case study with stack overflow. In *SIGIR*, 2013.

[17] V. Dang and W. B. Croft. Diversity by proportionality: An election-based approach to search result diversification. In *SIGIR*, 2012.

[18] H. Daumé III and D. Marcu. Bayesian query-focused summarization. In *ACL*, 2006.

[19] S. Deligne and F. Bimbot. Language modeling by variable length sequences: Theoretical formulation and evaluation of multigrams. In *ICASSP*, 1995.

[20] E. Gabrilovich and S. Markovitch. Computing semantic relatedness using wikipedia-based explicit semantic analysis. In *IJCAI*, 2007.

[21] J. Jeon, W. B. Croft, J. H. Lee, and S. Park. A framework to predict the quality of answers with non-textual features. In *SIGIR*, 2006.

[22] P. Jurczyk and E. Agichtein. Discovering authorities in question answer communities by using link analysis. In *CIKM*, 2007.

[23] R. Krestel and N. Dokoohaki. Diversifying product review rankings: Getting the full picture. In *WI*, 2011.

[24] X. Li and W. B. Croft. Improving novelty detection for general topics using sentence level information patterns. In *CIKM*, 2006.

[25] C.-Y. Lin and E. Hovy. From single to multi-document summarization: A prototype system and its evaluation. In *ACL*, 2002.

[26] Q. Liu, E. Agichtein, G. Dror, Y. Maarek, and I. Szpektor. When web search fails, searchers become askers: Understanding the transition. In *SIGIR*, 2012.

[27] Y. Liu, S. Li, Y. Cao, C.-Y. Lin, D. Han, and Y. Yu. Understanding and summarizing answers in community-based question answering services. In *COLING*, 2008.

[28] I. Mani. Multi-document summarization by graph search and matching. In *AAAI*, 1997.

[29] T. Mikolov, K. Chen, G. S. Corrado, and J. Dean. Efficient estimation of word representations in vector space, 2013.

[30] A. Nenkova and K. McKeown. A survey of text summarization techniques. In *Mining Text Data*, pages 43–76. Springer US, 2012.

[31] V. Pande, T. Mukherjee, and V. Varma. Summarizing answers for community question answer services. In I. Gurevych, C. Biemann, and T. Zesch, editors, *GSCL*, volume 8105 of *Lecture Notes in Computer Science*, pages 151–161. Springer, 2013.

[32] D. R. Radev and K. R. McKeown. Generating natural language summaries from multiple on-line sources. *Comput. Linguist.*, 24(3):470–500, 1998.

[33] D. Rafiei, K. Bharat, and A. Shukla. Diversifying web search results. In *WWW*, 2010.

[34] S. Robertson and H. Zaragoza. *The probabilistic relevance framework: BM25 and beyond*. Now Publishers Inc, 2009.

[35] R. L. Santos, C. Macdonald, and I. Ounis. Exploiting query reformulations for web search result diversification. In *WWW*, 2010.

[36] C. Shah and J. Pomerantz. Evaluating and predicting answer quality in community qa. In *SIGIR*, 2010.

[37] A. Shtok, G. Dror, Y. Maarek, and I. Szpektor. Learning from the past: Answering new questions with past answers. In *WWW*, 2012.

[38] A. Siddharthan, A. Nenkova, and K. McKeown. Syntactic simplification for improving content selection in multi-document summarization. In *COLING*, 2004.

[39] I. Soboroff and D. Harman. Novelty detection: The trec experience. In *HLT*, 2005.

[40] M. A. Suryanto, E. P. Lim, A. Sun, and R. H. L. Chiang. Quality-aware collaborative question answering: Methods and evaluation. In *WSDM*, 2009.

[41] J. Tang, L. Yao, and D. Chen. Multi-topic based query-oriented summarization. In *SDM*, 2009.

[42] X. Tu, X.-J. Wang, D. Feng, and L. Zhang. Ranking community answers via analogical reasoning. In *WWW*, 2009.

[43] D. Vallet and P. Castells. Personalized diversification of search results. In *SIGIR*, 2012.

[44] C. X. Zhai, W. W. Cohen, and J. Lafferty. Beyond independent relevance: Methods and evaluation metrics for subtopic retrieval. In *SIGIR*, 2003.

[45] Z.-M. Zhou, M. Lan, Z.-Y. Niu, and Y. Lu. Exploiting user profile information for answer ranking in cqa. In *WWW*, 2012.

That's Not My Question: Learning to Weight Unmatched Terms in CQA Vertical Search

Boaz Petersil
Dep. of Electrical Eng.
Technion, Haifa, Israel
boaz.petersil@gmail.com

Avihai Mejer
Yahoo Research
Haifa, 31905, Israel
amejer@yahoo-inc.com

Idan Szpektor
Yahoo Research
Haifa, 31905, Israel
idan@yahoo-inc.com

Koby Crammer
Dep. of Electrical Eng.
Technion, Haifa, Israel
koby@ee.technion.ac.il

ABSTRACT

A fundamental task in Information Retrieval (IR) is term weighting. Early IR theory considered both the presence or absence of all terms in the lexicon for ranking and needed to weight them all. Yet, as the size of lexicons grew and models became too complex, common weighting models preferred to aggregate only the weights of the query terms that are matched in candidate documents. Thus, unmatched term contribution in these models is only considered indirectly, such as in probability smoothing with corpus distribution, or in weight normalization by document length. In this work we propose a novel term weighting model that directly assesses the weights of unmatched terms, and show its benefits. Specifically, we propose a Learning To Rank framework, in which features corresponding to matched terms are also "mirrored" in similar features that account only for unmatched terms. The relative importance of each feature is learned via a click-through query log. As a test case, we consider vertical search in Community-based Question Answering (CQA) sites from Web queries. Queries that result in viewing CQA content often contain fine grained information needs and benefit more from unmatched term weighting. We assess our model both via manual evaluation and via automatic evaluation over a clickthrough log. Our results show consistent improvement in retrieval when unmatched information is taken into account. This holds both when only identical terms are considered matched, and when related terms are matched via distributional similarity.

Keywords: Unmatched Terms; Document Ranking; Community-based Question Answering

1. INTRODUCTION

One of the fundamental tasks in Information Retrieval (IR) is term weighting, which refers to the assessment of a weight for each term appearing in the document collection, and similarly in the input query. Early Probabilistic IR theories considered the presence or absence of all terms in the lexicon for ranking, both in the query and the documents [29, 26]. However, term weights in these models were found difficult to compute, and the main line of research around weighting models chose to consider mainly the weights of the query terms that are matched in candidate documents. Indeed, weighting schemes such as TF-IDF [31], BM25 [28] and statistical language models [33, 24, 40], as well as Learning To Rank (LTR) methods [20], are primarily based on considering the contribution of the *matched terms*, those query terms that appear also in the document. Though *unmatched terms*, i.e. terms that appear only in the query or only in the document, are not completely ignored, they are considered indirectly in these models, such as by using the document length for weight normalization or via corpus-based smoothing of maximum likelihood estimations.

As suggested by early probabilistic models we argue that analyzing directly unmatched terms may provide additional cues to the relevance of a candidate document to the query. Indeed, while the contribution of stop-words, such as determiners and modals, can be largely ignored, unmatched named entities are strong indicators of semantic differences between the query and the document. For example, for the query "*most deadliest snake*", the document title "*where can I find a list of the deadliest snakes*" is more relevant than "*which is the most deadliest snake in Russia*", though the first title is longer than the second, and second title contains all of the query terms in the right order.

Another intuition regarding direct modeling of unmatched terms refers to the percentage of query terms that are covered in the document. We would like to explicitly indicate that for two queries, a short one and a long one, if both match the same set of terms within a candidate document, this document is likely to be of less relevance for the longer query, which contains more unmatched terms, compared to the shorter one. As an example consider the queries "*most deadliest snake*" and "*most deadliest snake in Russia*" and the candidate document "*where can I find a list of the deadliest snakes*". We would like to explicitly express the lack of relevance of the document to the second query due to unmatched query terms.

We expect the subtleties between different types of unmatched terms to show especially for Web queries with fine-grained information-need. Therefore, we focus in this paper on Web queries with question intent, which constitute ~10% of the Web queries issued to a search engine [36]. Examples for such Web queries are those resulting in the searcher clicking on a question page belonging to Community-based Question Answering (CQA) sites, such as Yahoo Answers, StackExchange and Quora, and are called here *CQA queries*.

SIGIR '16, July 17-21, 2016, Pisa, Italy
© 2016 ACM. ISBN 978-1-4503-4069-4/16/07...$15.00
DOI: http://dx.doi.org/10.1145/2911451.2911496

Our retrieval scenario is vertical search [25, 2], in which content of a CQA sub-collection should be retrieved on top of general Web search.

In this work, we address this vertical search task by introducing a term weighting model that directly considers the contribution of unmatched terms for ranking. However, instead of a probabilistic framework, we utilize LTR as a ranking framework. To this end, we employ a large set of state-of-the-art features, which capture various attributes of matched terms, both statistical ones (such as variants of TF-IDF) as well as syntactic ones (such as Part-Of-Speech (POS) tags) [20, 9]. We then design "mirror" features that evaluate similar attributes, but for the unmatched terms. These novel mirror features are provided, together with the features that correspond to matched terms, as input to an LTR algorithm, which learns the relative weights of the different features using click-through training data.

Prior work in document ranking noted that, occasionally, different terms in the query and the document actually convey related meanings or even the same meaning (*e.g.* '*guy*' – '*man*', '*drink*' – '*alcohol*') and should be considered as matching for document ranking. One common approach to handle this lexical gap is via translation models, which include some similarity measure between query and document terms as part of term matching [4, 17, 39, 14]. In order to analyze the contribution of our unmatched term modeling under such "soft matching" schemes, we introduce a "soft" variant of all the features we compute for matched terms in our LTR framework, which is based on distributional similarity between terms. We then provide a similar soft variant of our unmatched-term features that complement the soft matched-term features. This should enable the unmatch-based features to better account for only semantically unmatched terms instead of terms that have similar meanings.

We conducted experiments on a vertical search setting that searches a Web query over a large collection of question pages from Yahoo Answers. The contribution of our unmatch-based features for term weighting was evaluated under two setups: a) large-scale automatic evaluation over a click-through query log; b) manual evaluation of the top retrieved documents for a set of tested queries. We compared our model to a state-of-the-art LTR model that utilizes only features that correspond to matched terms. The tested models were assessed both under the *exact* matching modeling, in which only identical terms are considered matched, and the *soft* matching modeling, where terms may be partially matched via distributional similarity. Our novel features provided consistent improvement in document ranking on both scenarios, showing the benefit of directly considering unmatched terms for term weighting.

2. RELATED WORK

Unmatched terms were addressed in prior IR ranking models in different ways, both for general search and for CQA search. We distinguish between two types of unmatched terms: a) terms that appear in the candidate document but not in the query, denoted as *excessive terms*; b) terms that appear in the query but not in the candidate document for ranking, denoted as *missing terms*.

Probabilistic information retrieval theory accounts for presence or absence of all terms in the lexicon, both in the query and in a candidate document for ranking [29]. Similarly, early reformulation of language models for IR (LMIR) [26] considered the query as a set of words, and modeled excessive terms in the document by their ability to generate terms not in the query. However, term weighting computation becomes a difficult problem under these frameworks [30, 33, 40], especially when no relevance feedback is considered. Therefore, recent ranking models, and specifically term weighting models, focus mainly on the matched terms between the query and a candidate document.

The overall ranking score of a document is typically the sum of the weights of the terms in the document that match (to some extent) the query terms. Therefore, document term weights in popular weighting schemes are non-negative and the effect of missing terms in a candidate document is considered indirectly by not contributing their weights to the document ranking score. This is the case in common probabilistic and vector space models, such as Binary Independence Model (BIM) [30], TF-IDF [31], Okapi BM25 [28], divergence from randomness [1], and multinomial language models, which view the query as a sequence of terms [33, 24, 41, 40]. Specifically, language models were extensively explored for CQA retrieval and were extended in different ways to incorporate meta data like categories [7], and the question focus and topic [13]. The same principle of scoring documents by summing matching term weights is also behind different weighting terms at the query side [3, 43].

In another line of ranking research, Learning to rank (LTR) approaches [20, 19] were introduced for learning to combine many features in a supervised way. Various learning algorithms were proposed, such as SVMRank [8] and LambdaMart [38], which may assign negative weights to some features. Still, the features themselves are typically derived for the matched terms, and therefore LTR algorithms learn the relative contribution of each feature with respect to the matched terms. Most derived features are statistical in nature, such as variants of term frequency and document frequency scores [20], and were also utilized in supervised ranking models in CQA [18, 37]. Carmel et al. [9] showed that utilizing features derived from syntactic analysis of the document title improves ranking performance for CQA queries. In a related task of answer sentence ranking within the field of Question Answering, tree kernels that incorporate semantic and syntactic features of the words provide state-of-the-art performance [34]. Still, the overall approach weigh in the number of matched sub-trees but not the unmatched ones.

Missing terms, which appear in the query but not in the document, received considerable attention within attempts to address the lexical gap problem: improving the matching between query and document terms that are not lexically identical but convey similar meaning. One common approach incorporates a translation model as part of term weighting [4, 17]. This approach was found useful also for retrieving CQA content, where translation models were used within LMIR for retrieving related questions [16, 39, 42] as well as for ranking CQA documents for Web queries [37]. Recently, lexical semantic similarity between terms via distributed representations, such as word2vec [23], was found helpful in several IR tasks, including query term weighting [43] and as features in a LTR framework for answer retrieval [10]. Ganguly et al [14] employed similarity between word embedding vectors within a translation model for LMIR as means to overcome the lexical gap between queries and documents, where it outperformed a language model extended with latent topics.

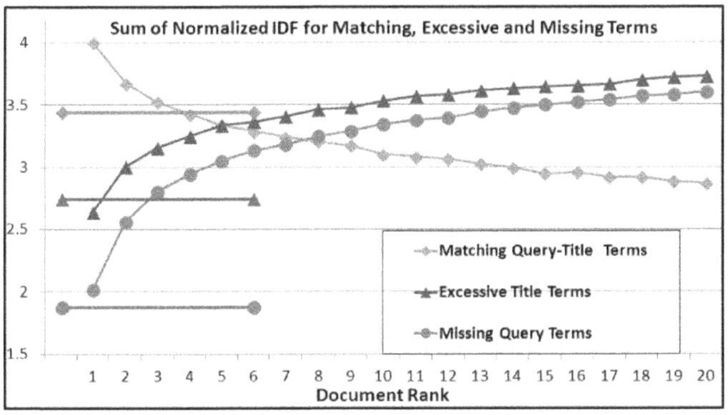

Figure 1: Sum of IDF values (normalized) for the matched, excessive and missing terms, computed separately over all non-clicked documents ranked at positions 1 to 20 (the three plots) and over the clicked documents (three horizontal lines).

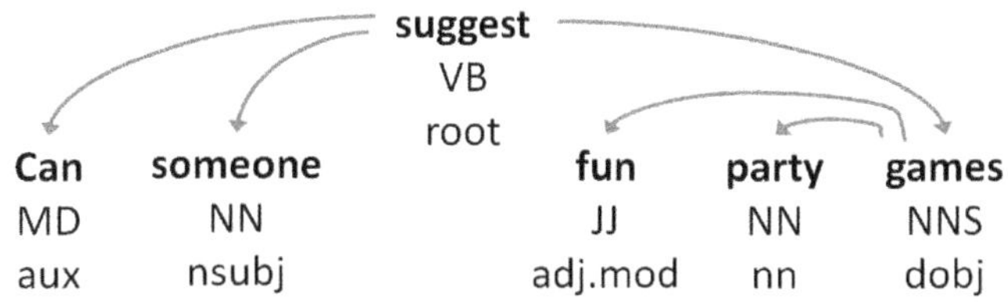

Figure 2: POS tagging and dependency parse tree for the question *Can someone suggest fun party games?*. The upper label of each token is its POS tag and the lower label is its syntactic role.

Prior work captured the effect of excessive terms (appearing only in the document) on the ranking score mainly by their contribution to overall document context or structure. Many vector space and probabilistic models (*e.g.* TF-IDF, BM25, language models) utilize the document's length as a degrading parameter for term weights, *e.g.* as the denominator of maximum likelihood estimation or in ℓ_2 vector normalization. Other models include all document terms when modeling a global latent representation for each document. One line of works uses latent topics (*e.g.* LDA [5]) as additional smoothing elements within LMIR [35]. This extension was shown useful also in retrieval of related CQA questions [6]. Another approach is to embed the document in a latent space. Latent Semantic Indexing [12] utilizes SVD to represent documents and queries within a reduced dimension space based on the main singular values of a term/document co-occurrence matrix. Lately, deep learning was shown useful for ranking by embedding the query and document texts into a shared latent space, within Web search [15] and within Question Answering [32]. Such approaches were not evaluated under the CQA vertical search setting yet, whose query length distribution and query attributes is quite distinguishable from general Web search and from question/answer datasets [9, 36].

3. YAHOO ANSWERS DATASET

In this work we perform our analysis and experiments on a large document collection taken from Yahoo Answers. Yahoo Answers is a popular CQA website containing questions about diverse topics, such as sports, healthcare, politics, science and many others. Each question page in the site consist of: a) a title, which is typically a short summary of the question, b) a body, containing a detailed description of the question, and c) all the answers provided for this question. We collected 54 million question pages from Yahoo Answers (referred to as our *corpus*) and indexed them using Lucene[1].

We also randomly sampled Web queries that were issued to a popular search engine and resulted in a click on one of the pages in our corpus by analyzing the *search log*. For each sampled query the top 100 results from our corpus were retrieved using Lucene's BM25 ranking function over all fields (title, body, answers). We retained the set of queries for which the clicked page for the query (as extracted from the search log) was found among the top 100 Lucene results. After this process, our click-based query collection consists of 136,000 queries.

Since search-engines show mostly the title of a question page on the search result page, Carmel et al. [9] reason that the relevance of the title to the query is one of the main reasons for a user to click on the page. This especially makes sense as the title is often a good summary of the question in the page. Furthermore, both title and query are concise and usually do not contain redundant information. Therefore, we expect that unmatched term weighting would help in retrieval under this scenario. Following them [9], we analyze and model unmatched terms only between the title of a Yahoo Answers question page and the target query.

4. UNMATCHED TERM ANALYSIS

To further motivate our modeling approach we analyze the properties of the unmatched terms: terms that appear in the candidate document but not in the query (*excessive*), and terms that appear in the query but not in the candidate document (*missing*). To this end, we sampled 20,000 queries[2] from our query collection and examined the matched and unmatched terms between each query and the titles of the retrieved documents (using Lucene). We compared the analysis statistics between documents that were clicked by the user who issued the query, denoted as *clicked* documents, and the other top retrieved documents, denoted as *non-clicked* documents.

4.1 IDF Distribution Analysis

First we examined the distribution of IDF values among the matched and unmatched terms. To this end, we computed the sum of IDF values for the matched terms and the excessive terms in each title (normalized by the title length). We also computed the IDF sum for the query's missing terms (normalized by the query length). These three indicators are plotted in Fig. 1, where each point in the plot represents the value averaged over all non-clicked titles ranked at the *i'th* position by the BM25 ranking, for *i=1..20.* The three horizontal lines in Fig. 1 correspond to the values of the three indicators averaged over the clicked documents. Note, higher values intuitively reflect more relevance in the matched term curve but less relevance in excessive and missing term statistics.

[1]lucene.apache.org

[2]Taken from our training set – see Sec. 5.4

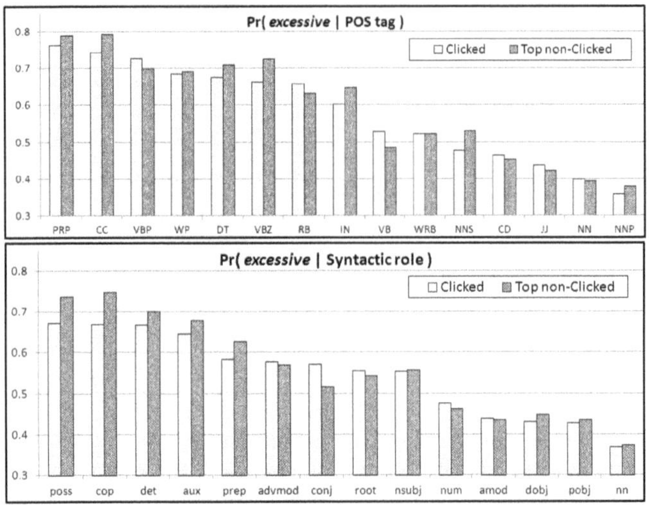

Figure 3: Probability of a term in the title not to match any query term given its POS tag (top chart) or syntactic role (bottom chart)

The matching-term IDF values (the diamond shape points) indicate that the clicked document (the horizontal line) is comparable, on average, only to the document at the $4'th$ position. This means that, with respect to matched terms, top ranked non-clicked documents usually contain as much and even more IDF volume compared to the clicked document. Yet, excessive and missing term analyses reveal complementing phenomena. First, on average, only non-clicked documents that are ranked first have the excessive term indicator lower than the value for clicked documents. This may indicate that while several non-clicked documents contain "important" (high-IDF) query terms in their title, driving them to high ranking positions, they also contain additional "important" terms that do not appear in the query and may change the meaning of the title compared to the query.

Second, the indicator for missing terms in clicked documents stands out even more, as it is lower compared to all non-clicked documents. This could indicate that in CQA queries it takes more than one term to express the gist of the information needed. While some non-clicked documents may include in their title high-IDF query terms, which correspond to "important" terms, they also tend to leave-out more "important" terms compared to the clicked document.

Assuming that click analysis is a useful approximation of relevance analysis, these results suggest that matched term statistics reveal only some aspects of the title's relevance to a searcher's information need. More relevance aspects may be further exposed by explicitly modeling unmatched terms.

4.2 Syntactic Analysis of Excessive Terms

Carmel et al. [9] showed that document terms with different syntactic properties should be weighted differently for retrieval. Hence, we examine similar syntactic properties of excessive terms, namely POS tags and dependency roles.

To this end, all titles in our corpus were syntactically analyzed using the Stanford parser[3] under the "all typed dependencies" setting. Then, for each title term in a retrieved document we extracted its POS tag and syntactic role (the dependency relation in which the term is the dependent). Fig. 2 presents an example for this analysis. Finally, for each syntactic property we counted its total occurrences in each title and its occurrences within excessive terms, and computed their ratio. The ratio of these two counts represents the probability of each syntactic property to be an excessive term. In Fig. 3 we depict two probability families, averaged across all analyzed queries: a) for all clicked documents; and b) for the three highest ranking non-clicked documents (representing the "toughest" competitors to beat for ranking the clicked documents on top of non-clicked ones). For clarity, the charts contain only the results for the 15 most common POS tags and syntactic roles, and they are sorted in decreasing order of the probability value.

Looking at Fig. 3 we observe large differences in excessive term probability between different syntactic tags. For example, in clicked items, this probability for pronouns (PRP - usually a low IDF stopword) is $\sim$0.75, while for proper nouns (NNP) it is only $\sim$0.35. Such large differences echoes previous observation [9] that there is a possible gain in modeling differently terms with different syntactic tags.

Comparing the statistics between clicked titles and the top non-clicked titles, we can see that in quite a few properties there are distinguishable differences between clicked and non-clicked titles. These differences suggest that excessive term weighting may improve if syntactic properties will be considered. As an example we look at verbs, which are important terms in a query (usually capturing the main activity asked about). The syntactic roles that are often associated with verbs in the bottom chart are '*aux*', '*cop*', '*root*' and sometimes '*conj*'. These roles can be partitioned into two groups. The first group contains '*aux*' and '*cop*', whose excessive probability is higher in non-clicked titles. The second group contains '*root*' and '*conj*', which are more likely to be excessive in clicked titles. This shows that syntactic properties can provide more fine-grained distinctions between similar terms or even for the same term when assuming different roles.

As another example, the charts in Fig. 3 also show that nouns (POS tags: NN*, Dep roles: conj, nsubj, dobj, pobj, nn) are more likely to be excessive in non-clicked documents. As nouns typically contain the main participants of a question, it is important to match all (or most) of them to align the exact semantics of the query to that of a title. Therefore, directly assessing both matched and unmatched nouns could improve retrieval. In Fig. 3 the only reverse case is with '*conj*', which is more likely to be excessive in clicked titles. Yet, conjunctive nouns, such as in the example "*good websites that stream movies and tv shows*", may be skipped (and become excessive terms) while maintaining the same semantic gist of the question.

The analysis in this section suggests that modeling statistical properties as well as syntactic properties of unmatched title terms may lead to better assessment of document relevance for CQA queries. We next explicitly construct features for unmatched terms, within a Learning To Rank (LTR) framework, which take these properties into consideration.

5. MODELING UNMATCHED TERMS

The task of our ranking algorithm is to rank a set of candidate documents D given a CQA query q. We follow a standard LTR scheme [19, 20, 9] and define a mapping function

[3] http://nlp.stanford.edu/software/lex-parser.shtml

Feature	Formulation
L_1	$\sum_{t\in q} c(t,d) \times \delta(t \in d)$
L_2	$\sum_{t\in q} \log(c(t,d)+1) \times \delta(t \in d)$
L_3	$\sum_{t\in q} \frac{c(t,d)}{\|d\|} \times \delta(t \in d)$
L_4	$\sum_{t\in q} \log\left(\frac{c(t,d)}{\|d\|}+1\right) \times \delta(t \in d)$
L_5	$\sum_{t\in q} \log\left(\frac{\|C\|}{df(t)}\right) \times \delta(t \in d)$
L_6	$\sum_{t\in q} \log\left(\log(\frac{\|C\|}{df(t)})\right) \times \delta(t \in d)$
L_7	$\sum_{t\in q} \log\left(\frac{\|C\|}{c(t,C)}+1\right) \times \delta(t \in d)$
L_8	$\sum_{t\in q} \log\left(\frac{c(t,d)}{\|d\|}\log(\frac{\|C\|}{df(t)})+1\right) \times \delta(t \in d)$
L_9	$\sum_{t\in q} c(t,d) \log\left(\frac{\|C\|}{df(t)}\right) \times \delta(t \in d)$
L_{10}	$\sum_{t\in q} \log\left(\frac{c(t,d)}{\|d\|}\frac{\|C\|}{c(t,C)}+1\right) \times \delta(t \in d)$
$G_1(p)$	$\sum_{t\in d \wedge POS(t)=p} c(t,q)$
$G_2(p)$	$\sum_{t\in d \wedge POS(t)=p} idf(t) \times c(t,q)$
$G_3(p)$	$\sum_{t\in d \wedge CPOS(t)=p} c(t,q)$
$G_4(p)$	$\sum_{t\in d \wedge CPOS(t)=p} idf(t) \times c(t,q)$
$G_5(sr)$	$\sum_{t\in d \wedge SR(t)=sr} c(t,q)$
$G_6(sr)$	$\sum_{t\in d \wedge SR(t)=sr} idf(t) \times c(t,q)$
H_1	BM25 score
H_2	log(BM25 score)
H_3	LMIR with Dirichlet smoothing parameter β

Table 1: Matched term features used in [9]; $c(t, X)$ – term frequency of t in X; $df(t)$ – document frequency of t in our corpus C; $idf(t) = log\left(\frac{|C|}{df(t)}\right)$; $|X|$ – total number of terms in X; $POS(t)$, $CPOS(t)$ and $SR(t)$ are the POS tag, coarse-POS tag and syntactic role of t respectively; $\delta()$ is the indicator function.

$\mathbf{\Phi}(q,d) \in \mathbb{R}^n$ from pairs of a query q and a candidate document d to the vector space $\mathbb{R}^n$. Our algorithm uses a weight vector $\boldsymbol{w}$ to compute a score for each $d \in D$ via the inner product $s(q,d) = \boldsymbol{w} \cdot \mathbf{\Phi}(q,d)$. Finally, the candidate documents are ranked according to the value of $s(q,d)$, where the higher the score for some document d, the higher its rank in the retrieved list. The goal of the learning algorithm is to find weights $\boldsymbol{w}$ such that more relevant documents will have high score compared to less relevant ones.

Our work focuses in the design of a new feature mapping $\mathbf{\Phi}(q,d)$ that captures both missing and excessive terms. We build on the work of Carmel et al [9] who proposed only features that consider matched terms and extend their mapping in two ways: (1) taking into account unmatched terms; (2) relaxing the notion of matched/unmatched terms, and allowing soft-matching between terms in the query and the candidate, based on distributional similarity.

We describe in Sec. 5.1 the state-of-the-art features proposed by Carmel et al [9], which are our baseline and starting point. Additionally, we present in Sec. 5.2 an abstraction of these features having in mind our goal to introduce their corresponding new features for unmatched terms. Finally, in Sec. 5.3, we incorporate soft-matching into all features presented until then. We use a previous weight learning scheme [9] (Sec. 5.4) in order to replicate their work as a baseline and have a fair comparison of our new features.

5.1 Matched Term Features

Carmel et al [9] also addressed the task of vertical search for CQA queries within an LTR framework (see Sec. 2). They proposed two types of features that analyze matched terms: standard statistical features [20], such as TF-IDF, and new syntactic-based features that collect matched term statistics for each POS tag and syntactic role separately. All these features are summarized in Tab. 1.

Carmel et al mainly analyzed the performance of the document title for matching the query, arguing that in CQA content, the title is a good summary of the question being answered within the document. Therefore, all statistics are derived only from the document's title, except for the BM25-related features (H_{1-2}) which are computed over the whole document. Under this formulation, which we follow, q and d represent the list of terms in the query and the document's title respectively. Features L_{1-10} and H_{1-3} refer to standard statistical features, while $G_{1-4}(p)$ and $G_{5-6}(sr)$ are feature families that are generated for each POS tag p and syntactic role sr, respectively. For example $G_1(IN)$ is the feature generated for the IN (preposition) POS tag and $G_5(root)$ is the feature generated for the *root* syntactic role.

Each of the features L_{1-10} and G_{1-6} can be viewed more abstractly as (possibly conditional) term summing of a product of two terms: (1) a count (or a function of it) of some event, denoted by f_{F_i}; and (2) a boolean predicate or a numeric value indicating some matching between q and d:

$$L_i(q,d) = \sum_{t\in q} f_{L_i}(t,d) \times \delta(t \in d) \quad (1)$$

$$G_i(q,d) = \sum_{t\in d \wedge cond_{G_i}(t)} f_{G_i}(t,d) \times c(t,q) \quad (2)$$

The matching indication part in L_i is $\delta(t \in d)$ – whether the query term appears in the document. The indication part of G_i is $c(t,q)$ – the occurrence count of the title term in the query, which is 0 for unmatched. Examples for instantiating these abstractions with specific statistics are: a) for L_2, $f_{L_2} := \log(c(t,d)+1)$; and b) for G_1, $f_{G_1} := 1$ and $cond_{G_1} := (POS(t) = p)$.

5.2 Unmatched Term Features

We now introduce our novel features, which induce the f_{F_i} signals in parallel to their counterpart matched term features L_{1-10} and G_{1-6}. Yet, instead for the matched terms, the new feature families do so for the set of excessive terms, denoted by EXL and EXG, and for the set of missing terms, denoted by MIL and MIG. We present the generic representations of these feature families similarly to (1) and (2):

$$EXL_i(q,d) = \sum_{t\in u(d)} f_{L_i}(t,d) \times (1 - \delta(t \in q))$$

$$EXG_i(q,d) = \sum_{t\in d \wedge cond_{G_i}(t)} f_{G_i}(t,d) \times (1 - \delta(t \in q))$$

and,

$$MIL_i(q,d) = \sum_{t\in u(q)} f_{L_i}(t,q) \times (1 - \delta(t \in d))$$

$$MIG_i(q,d) = \sum_{t\in q \wedge cond_{G_i}(t)} f_{G_i}(t,q) \times (1 - \delta(t \in d))$$

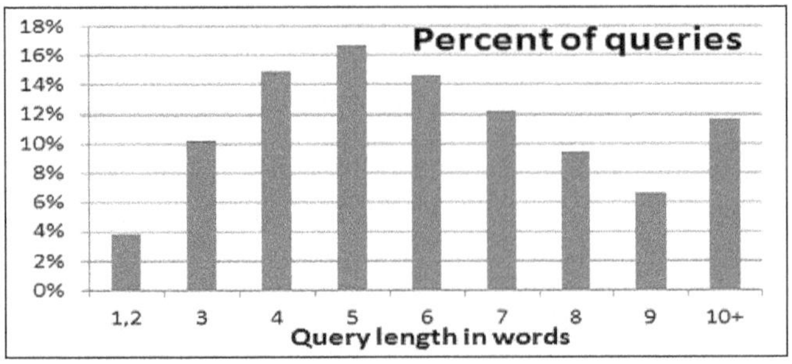

Figure 4: Percentage of queries by length

The differences between these new feature families and their matched term counterparts are in: a) the matching indicators, which turn into unmatching indicators; and b) the term sets over which the summation is performed. For example, the unmatching indicator in the excessive feature family EXL_i is $(1 - \delta(t \in q))$, which is 1 only if the document term is not in the query. In addition, the summation in EXL_i is over $u(d)$, which stands for the set of unique[4] terms in d from which we pick the excessive terms.

We note that for MIG_i, syntactic analysis of the query is required. We used the Stanford parser for query parsing as well, but found that the query dependency trees were of low quality. Therefore, in our experiments we only use the POS tags for queries, and hence only features MIG_{1-4}, leaving the reliable generation of features MIG_{5-6} for future work.

5.3 Soft Matching Formulation

As discussed in Sec. 2, some mismatches in exact matching scheme should actually be accounted as (at least partial) matches, such as in the case of synonyms or related words, *e.g. 'guitar'* and *'riff'*. We extend our proposed features and present a novel soft matching formulation of all our matched and unmatched features (except BM25-related H_{1-2}). To the best of our knowledge, this is the first formulation in the context of the standard set of LETOR features [20].

We start with a lexical similarity function $sim(t_q, t_d) \in [0, 1]$ between a query term t_q and a document term t_d. The closer the function's value is to 1 the more similar the two terms are. We follow recent successes with word embedding similarity and use in this work:

$$sim(t_q, t_d) := \max(\cos(sg(t_q), sg(d_q)), 0) \ ,$$

where $sg(t)$ is the word embedding vector of term t learned by the SkipGram algorithm [23]. We define $sim(t, t) = 1$ for every word similarity with itself and $sim(t, u) = 0$ if $t \neq u$ and either t or u are not in the lexicon.

To incorporate the similarity score $sim(t_q, t_d)$ into our features we find the best matching counterpart term for each query term and for each document term:

$$\begin{aligned} bm_d(t_q) &= \arg\max_{t_d \in d} sim(t_q, t_d) \\ bm_q(t_d) &= \arg\max_{t_q \in q} sim(t_q, t_d) \\ \delta_s(t, d) &= sim(t, bm_d(t)) \\ \delta_s(q, t) &= sim(bm_q(t), t) \ , \end{aligned}$$

[4]Term repetition is avoided since the number of occurrences of the term t in d is already counted in f_{L_i}.

where $\delta_s(t, d)$ and $\delta_s(q, t)$ are soft indicator functions that capture how well a query (document) term is matched against the document (query) via its similarity score with its best match. We note that if $sim()$ would only return 1 for exact match and 0 otherwise, $\delta_s()$ would become $\delta()$.

Finally, we extend our features using $bm()$ and $\delta_s()$:

$$\begin{aligned} L_i^s(q, d) &= \sum_{t \in q} f_{L_i}(bm_d(t), d) \times \delta_s(t, d) \\ G_i^s(q, d) &= \sum_{t \in d \wedge cond_{G_i}(t)} f_{G_i}(t, d) \times c(bm_q(t), q) \times \delta_s(q, t) \\ EXL_i^s(q, d) &= \sum_{t \in u(d)} f_{L_i}(t, d) \times (1 - \delta_s(q, t)) \\ EXG_i^s(q, d) &= \sum_{t \in d \wedge cond_{G_i}(t)} f_{G_i}(t, d) \times (1 - \delta_s(q, t)) \\ MIL_i^s(q, d) &= \sum_{t \in u(q)} f_{L_i}(t, q) \times (1 - \delta_s(t, d)) \\ MIG_i^s(q, d) &= \sum_{t \in q \wedge cond_{G_i}(t)} f_{G_i}(t, q) \times (1 - \delta_s(t, d)) \ , \end{aligned}$$

where we simply replace (or augment where necessary) the indicator function with the soft indicator variant, and instead of gathering statistics from exact match occurrences, we gather them from the occurrences of the best-match. If a query term appears as-is in the document (exact match), our feature scores are exactly as for exact matching. Yet, when a query term does not exactly appear in the document (or vice versa) instead of returning a matched feature value of zero, we resort to counting with respect to its best soft match instead. We note that a similar formulation using best-matches is utilized by Liu et al [21] for computing similarity between short documents.

5.3.1 Language Model with Soft Matching

Prior work showed that extending LMIR with some similarity notion between terms improves retrieval results [39, 14]. We therefore extend our language model feature H_3 in a similar way, following the formalism of Xue et al [39]:

$$H_3^s(q, d) = \sum_{t \in q} \log(P(t|d))$$

$$P(t|d) = \frac{|d|}{|d|+\beta}\left((1-\alpha)\frac{c(t,d)}{|d|} + \alpha P_{tt}(t|d)\right) + \frac{\beta}{|d|+\beta} P_c(t)$$

$$P_{tt}(t|d) = \sum_{t_d \in d} \frac{sim(t, t_d)}{Z(t, d)} \times \frac{c(t_d, d)}{|d|} \quad Z(t, d) = \sum_{t_d \in d} sim(t, t_d) \ ,$$

where q is the query term list; d is the document term list and $|d|$ is its length; $c(t, d)$ is the term-frequency of t in d; $P_c(t)$ is maximum likelihood estimation (MLE) of t in our corpus; Z is a probability normalizer; and α and β are hyper parameters to be tuned.

We note that H_3^s is a variant of Xue et al's language model. Instead of using a translation table as P_{tt}, we followed Ganguly et al [14], who suggested a variant of P_{tt} based on a similarity function $sim()$ (normalized into a probability distribution). Note, when $sim()$ represents exact matching, H_3^s becomes H_3.

5.4 Model Weight Learning

We learned the weights $\boldsymbol{w}$ of our ranking algorithm in a semi-supervised manner based on clickthrough data. The goal of the learning algorithm is to find a vector $\boldsymbol{w}$ such that for each query in the training data, the corresponding clicked document will be ranked as high as possible. We used the online variant of SVMRank [8] with the AROW update [11] as done before [9]. Specifically, for each training query the algorithm first re-ranks the top 100 documents retrieved by Lucene using the currently learned ranker. Then, it selects the top K ranking documents, excluding the clicked document. The algorithm then updates $\boldsymbol{w}$ such as for this query the clicked document would increase its ranking score compared to the selected K documents.

We split our query collection (see Sec. 3) into a 61,000 query training-set, a 14,000 query validation-set and a 61,000 query test-set. The validation-set was used to tune the various hyper-parameters for each tested model *separately*, namely, the number of training rounds, the value of K, and the AROW hyper-parameter r. The only hyper parameters that were tuned once for all models are $\beta = 1$, $\alpha = 0.5$ for the H_3 and H_3^s LMIR features. Specifically, β was tuned on the *LETOR* model and α was then tuned on a soft version of the *LETOR*. See Sec. 6.1 for details on the configuration of each tested model. Finally, to compute term similarity we used publicly available[5] pre-trained word embedding vectors.

6. EXPERIMENTS

We evaluated our proposed models against several baselines via two settings: first, based on a large scale clickthrough data, and second, based on manual judgments.

6.1 Tested Models

We consider six baseline models:

- *LSI*: Latent Semantic Indexing [12], where ranking score is computed as the dot product between the LSI representations of the query and the document title. We utilized the top 200 dimensions of the SVD decomposition of our corpus[6] as the latent space.
- *BIM*: Binary Independence Model [22] with unmatched probability estimation using pseudo relevance, taking the 'Relevant set' as 1, 3 or 5 top ranking documents by BM25.
- *BM25*: Using only the relevance score as provided by Lucene (feature H_1 in Tab. 1).
- *LETOR*: Using only statistical features associated with matched terms (features L_{1-10} and H_{1-3} in Tab. 1).
- *Matched*: Using all the features associated with matched terms (all features in Tab. 1).
- *SoftMatched*: Using soft-matching formulation for the matched features, *i.e.* feature families L_i^s, G_i^s and feature H_3^s (as in Sec. 5.3), and H_{1-2} from Tab. 1.

We compare the baselines to our proposed models:

- *Full*: Combining unmatched and matched features under exact matching formulation, *i.e.* all features in Tab. 1 as well as feature families EXL_i, EXG_i, MIL_i and MIG_i (described in Sec. 5.2).
- *SoftFull*: Combining unmatched and matched features under soft-matching formulation, *i.e.* feature families L_i^s, G_i^s, EXL_i^s, EXG_i^s, MIL_i^s, MIG_i^s and feature H_3^s (described in Sec. 5.3), and features H_{1-2} in Tab. 1.

We trained separately each of the LTR-based models using the algorithm in Sec. 5.4.

6.2 Automatic Evaluation

We conducted a large scale automatic evaluation using our 61,000 query test-set (see Sec. 5.4). For each query we retrieved the top 100 results from the document collection using Lucene, and then re-ranked the top results using each of the tested models. We report Mean Reciprocal Rank (MRR) and Binary Recall at position K (R@K), all derived from the rank position of the clicked document associated with each query. Fig. 4 depicts the query length distribution of our test-set. We remind the reader that CQA queries are usually longer than typical Web queries.

6.3 Manual Evaluation

We randomly sampled 1,000 queries of length 3 or more words from our test-set (shorter queries are scarce in our query collection - see Fig. 4). For each query we collected the top 10 documents as ranked by each of the tested models. Professional editors assessed the relevance of each document in the pool on three Likert-scale levels: (1) non-relevant, (2) partially-relevant, and (3) highly-relevant. Inspecting the evaluations, we found that usually only *highly-relevant* documents refer to relevant content. Hence, we report NDCG with weights of 0 for *non-relevant*, 1 for *partially-relevant* and 10 for *highly-relevant*. We also report Precision at K (P@K) taking only *highly-relevant* documents as relevant.

7. RESULTS

The results for the automatic and manual evaluations are summarized in Tab. 2 and Tab. 3, respectively. All statistical significance figures are computed using t-test. The results in both tables indicate a trend similar to the one reported by Cramel et el [9]. Namely, *LETOR* outperforms *BM25* by a large margin (*e.g.* 10.5% increase in MRR) and adding syntactic features (G_i) on top of statistical features (L_i, H_i) in the *Matched* model consistently provides additional improvement, *e.g.* 1.5% increase in MRR across all query lengths (Fig. 5). We thus refer to *Matched* as our main baseline. We note in passing that the performance of the *LSI* and *BIM* models was significantly lower than the LTR models (*e.g.* MRR of 0.202 for *LSI*, 0.164 for *BIM*) and adding them as additional features did not help either. We therefore excluded their performance report.

We next observe that adding soft term-matching to address the lexical gap between queries and documents (*SoftMatched* model) shows a nice improvement under the clickthrough automatic evaluation. For example, MRR is increased by 2.1% compared to *Matched*. In addition, manual evaluation also shows some improvement using soft matching, specifically at high rank positions. For example, P@3 is increased by 2.9% compared to *Matched*. On the other hand, the results for P@5 and P@10 are comparable to *Matched*. Analyzing our soft matching model, we found quite a few queries where exact matching provided better ranking than soft matching. For example, under the automatic evaluation setting, *SoftMatched* ranked the clicked

[5] https://code.google.com/p/word2vec/

[6] Using RedSVD: http://code.google.com/p/redsvd/

Model	MRR		R@1		R@3		R@5		R@10	
BM25	0.465	(-10.9%)	0.339	(-13.3%)	0.525	(-11.9%)	0.605	(-11.0%)	0.709	(-9.5%)
LETOR	0.514	(-1.5%)	0.386	(-1.3%)	0.581	(-2.5%)	0.663	(-2.5%)	0.763	(-2.6%)
Matched	0.522		0.391		0.596		0.680		0.783	
Full	0.537	(2.9%)	0.405	(3.6%)	0.609	(2.2%)	0.692	(1.8%)	0.792	(1.1%)
SoftMatched	0.533	(2.1%)	0.401	(2.6%)	0.604	(1.3%)	0.690	(1.5%)	0.790	(0.9%)
SoftFull	**0.543**	**(4.0%)**	**0.411**	**(5.1%)**	**0.616**	**(3.4%)**	**0.700**	**(2.9%)**	**0.800**	**(2.2%)**

Table 2: Automatic evaluation results (and percentage of change compared to *Matched* model). All differences are statistically significant at $p < 0.001$.

Model	NDCG		P@1		P@3		P@5		P@10	
BM25	0.685	(-3.9%)	0.522	(-7.9%)	0.396	(-5.5%)	0.336	(-7.9%)	0.268	(-5.6%)
LETOR	0.711	(-0.3%)	0.562	(-0.9%)	0.417	(-0.5%)	0.357	(-2.2%)	0.280	(-1.4%)
Matched	0.713		0.567		0.419		0.365		0.284	
Full	0.714	(0.1%)	0.567	(0.0%)	0.423	(1.0%)	0.366	(0.3%)	0.287*	(1.1%)
SoftMatched	0.716	(0.4%)	0.575	(1.4%)	**0.431**†	**(2.9%)**	0.366	(0.3%)	0.284	(0.0%)
SoftFull	**0.719**	**(0.8%)**	**0.577**	**(1.8%)**	**0.431**†	**(2.9%)**	**0.369**	**(1.1%)**	**0.289**†	**(1.8%)**

Table 3: Manual evaluation results (and percentage of change compared to *Matched* model). Values marked with $\star/\dagger$ indicate differences that are statistically significant at $p < 0.05$ and $p < 0.01$, respectively, compared to the *Matched* model.

query: stick a fork in it
Full: what does the phrase stick a fork in it mean? *Matched*: is it time to stick a fork in **Angels** and **Dodgers**?
query: doctorate vs phd
Full: what is the difference between phd and doctorate? *Matched*: phd in **nutrition** or **naturopathic** doctorate?
query: my family in french
Full: how do you say my family in french *Matched*: **describe** a family **member** in french?

Table 4: Examples where *Full* promoted better content at the top compared to *Matched*

document higher than *Matched* on 25% of the queries but that *Matched* ranked the clicked document higher than *SoftMatched* on 18.3% of the test-set. This may indicate that our current similarity function is noisy and could be improved in future work. While soft matching for retrieval was studied before, this is the first time it is applied in the CQA vertical search scenario. In addition, we are not aware of prior work that directly applies it to a large set of standard LTR features, specifically using similarity between word embedding vectors for lexical semantics (compared to the well studied translation models for this usage).

We now get to our main result, which is split into two parts, corresponding to the exact matching and soft matching settings. Under the exact matching setting, when adding features that directly address unmatched terms (*Full* model) we see a significant improvement in performance in the automatic evaluation compared to only using matched term features (*Matched* model). For example, MRR is increased by 2.9%, and similar trends occur for R@K. In Fig. 5 we plot MRR vs query length from which we observe that the MRR gap is maintained across all query lengths. The gap is slightly decreasing towards longer queries, perhaps because matching many of the terms for longer queries within a question title contains enough information to indicate relevant content. Under the manual evaluation, some improvement is shown. Specifically P@3 and P@10 show an increase of $\sim 1\%$ compared to *Matched* while P@1 and P@5 show comparable results. Tab. 4 shows examples where *Full* promoted better content at the top compared to *Matched*. These examples demonstrate how *Full* downgrades titles containing excessive information that changes the meaning of the title, such as '*Angles*' and '*Dodgers*' in the first example.

Both unmatched term features (*Full*) and soft matched term features (*SoftMatched*) provide a rather similar improvement over exact matching (*Matched*). However, they capture different aspects of query/document ranking, one is addressing the lexical gap between the two and the other is addressing the importance of terms that were not matched from either side. Combining both model approaches together (*SoftFull* model) shows that they convey somewhat complementing elements for ranking. Indeed, *SoftFull* is the best performing model under all metrics. Under automatic evaluation the improvement is rather additive with a nice gap in performance maintained across all query lengths from both *SoftMatched* and *Matched*. Under manual evaluation the improvement is more significant. It seems that under all metrics, but P@3, the combination of soft matching with direct unmatched term assessment is more powerful than each of its parts. This result may indicate that soft matching helps pinpointing the "true" unmatched terms and therefore improves the modeling of their contribution to ranking.

7.1 Excessive vs Missing Features

Our unmatched term features are composed of two types: a) those that address excessive terms, which occur only in the document ($EX\{L,G\}_i$); and b) those that address missing terms, which occur only in the query ($MI\{L,G\}_i$). We evaluated the contribution of each feature type independently by constructing two auxiliary models, both augmenting all matched term features (*Matched*). The first model adds only $EX\{L,G\}_i$ features, denoted *MatchedAndExces-*

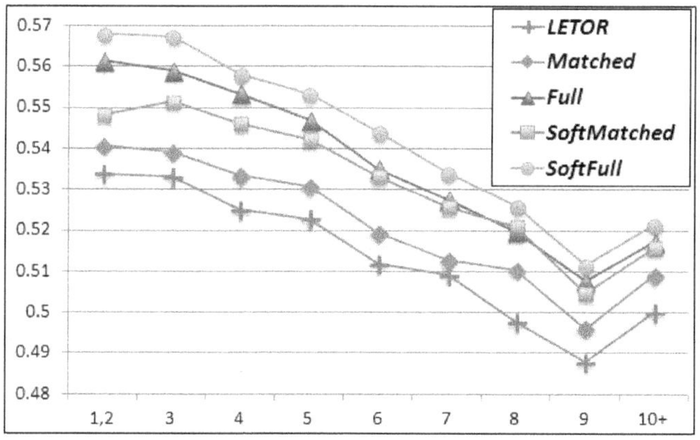

Figure 5: MRR by query length

Query	Document Title
what is candys american dream	the story "Of Mice and Men", how does the excerpt from Candy relate to the American Dream and Garden of Eden?
no virgin birth	No Virgin birth? Was the Virgin Mary really a virgin or was this a mistranslation of the Greek?
92 accord misfire	My '92 Accord misfires and loses power at about 2500 rpm. Possible causes?

Table 5: Examples where *Full* ranked a relevant clicked document low due to many excessive terms

sive, and the second model adds only the $MI\{L, G\}_i$ features, denoted *MatchedAndMissing*.

Fig. 6 presents the performance of the two new models compared to *Matched* and to *Full* on the automatic evaluation setting, measured via the MRR metric. The graph shows that while missing term features are not as strong indicators for irrelevance compared to excessive term features, they still directly improve MRR compared to *Matched*. In addition, while excessive term features contribute more to detecting irrelevant documents, a small improvement in MRR is gained when excessive and missing features are combined in the *Full* model.

Another observation from Fig. 6 is that *MatchedAndExcessive* improves over *Matched* for short queries much more than for long queries. One reason may be that for short queries there are more candidates in the corpus that contain the query terms, but many of them may have a lot of excessive information. As opposed to short web queries, in which the information need is generally wide, CQA queries tend to refer to very specific information needs even in such short queries, *e.g.* "*characteristics of enzymes*". If this hypothesis is true and our algorithm learned that a lot of excessive information indicates an irrelevant candidate, we expect the model to be particularly effective in filtering out such candidates. We note that for short queries of length 1-2 there is no improvement using missing features. This is not surprising, since there are no missing terms when matching queries of length 1, and the amount of missing information in queries of length two is at most a single term.

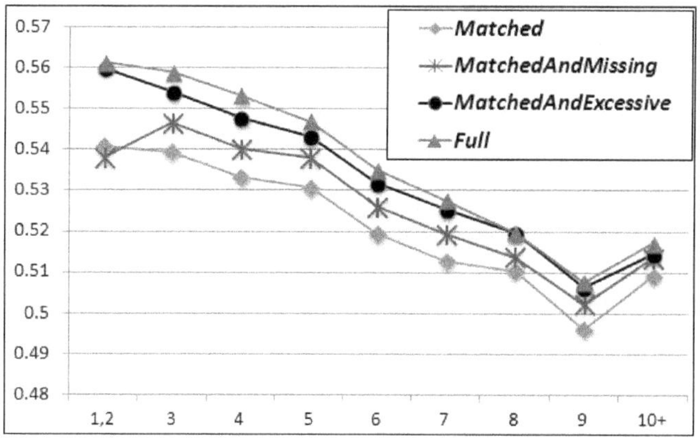

Figure 6: MRR by query length with the addition of Excessive vs. Missing Features

7.2 Error Analysis

To better understand the performance of our features, we conducted error analysis on cases in which *Full*, which considers both matched and unmatched term features, ranks a clicked document significantly lower than *Matched*, which employs only matched term features. To this end, we considered queries from our validation set in which *Matched* ranked the clicked document for the query in one of the top 3 positions while *Full* ranked it far below. We sorted the examples by the rank margin between *Matched* and *Full* and analyzed the 100 queries with the largest rank margin.

We found out that in 35 of the analyzed queries the top document ranked by *Full* was relevant and in 46 queries at least one of the top 3 documents was relevant. This is a known issue when using clickthrough logs as proxy to document relevance, as some unclicked documents may also be relevant to the query. Thus absolute model performance under such evaluation is biased. Yet, comparing ranking algorithms over a large-scale click-based gold labeling is useful for differentiating between their ranking performance [27].

Out of the 65 queries where the top candidate by *Full* was not relevant, we recognized two main reasons for this ranking failure. The most prominent reason, which occurred in 36 cases, is that some terms in the document title were not matched due to the exact-matching scheme used in *Full*, but would have considered matched under proper soft matching. Out of these 36 case, 13 queries had spelling errors and other phenomena, such as unigram/bigram variations (*e.g.* '*countertop*' vs. '*counter top*'). Such lexical variations are not recognized by our current soft term matching which uses word embedding.

The second phenomenon occurred in 16 out of the 65 queries. The clicked document title contains a lot of excessive terms, yet still fulfills the information need behind the query. Tab. 5 presents such examples. While our results show the potential in directly modeling unmatched terms, and specifically excessive terms as negative signals, a large number of such terms may accumulate into an unnecessary downgrading of the ranking score, and further research is required to develop more robust models.

8. CONCLUSIONS

In this work we proposed novel features in a Learning To Rank framework that directly assess the importance of missing and excessive terms within the task of term weighting for vertical search on CQA content. To better model truly unmatched terms we also presented a "soft matching" variant of all our features, basing it on distributional similarity between terms, where similar terms are considered partially both matched, and unmatched. Our experiments show improvement in document retrieval in all settings when unmatched information is taken into account.

In future research we plan to test whether our approach may contribute to other types of Web documents. One direction could be to explore how unmatched terms can be modeled in other parts of the document, which may require different features than the ones used in this paper.

9. ACKNOWLEDGEMENTS

The resrach was supported in part by the Yahoo Faculty Research and Engagement Program.

10. REFERENCES

[1] G. Amati, V. Rijsbergen, and C. Joost. Probabilistic models of information retrieval based on measuring the divergence from randomness. *ACM Trans. Inf. Syst.*, 20(4), Oct. 2002.

[2] J. Arguello, F. Diaz, J. Callan, and J.-F. Crespo. Sources of evidence for vertical selection. In *SIGIR*, 2009.

[3] M. Bendersky, D. Metzler, and W. B. Croft. Learning concept importance using a weighted dependence model. In *WSDM*, 2010.

[4] A. Berger and J. Lafferty. Information retrieval as statistical translation. In *SIGIR*, 1999.

[5] D. M. Blei, A. Y. Ng, and M. I. Jordan. Latent dirichlet allocation. *JMLR*, 3:993–1022, 2003.

[6] L. Cai, G. Zhou, K. Liu, and J. Zhao. Learning the latent topics for question retrieval in community qa. In *AFNLP*, 2011.

[7] X. Cao, G. Cong, B. Cui, C. S. Jensen, and C. Zhang. The use of categorization information in language models for question retrieval. In *CIKM*, 2009.

[8] Y. Cao, J. Xu, T.-Y. Liu, H. Li, Y. Huang, and H.-W. Hon. Adapting ranking svm to document retrieval. In *SIGIR*, 2006.

[9] D. Carmel, A. Mejer, Y. Pinter, and I. Szpektor. Improving term weighting for community question answering search using syntactic analysis. In *CIKM*, 2014.

[10] R.-C. Chen, D. Spina, W. B. Croft, M. Sanderson, and F. Scholer. Harnessing semantics for answer sentence retrieval. In *ESAIR Workshop*, 2015.

[11] K. Crammer, A. Kulesza, and M. Dredze. Adaptive regularization of weight vectors. *MLJ*, 91(2):155–187, 2013.

[12] S. C. Deerwester, S. T. Dumais, T. K. Landauer, G. W. Furnas, and R. A. Harshman. Indexing by latent semantic analysis. *JAsIs*, 41(6):391–407, 1990.

[13] H. Duan, Y. Cao, C.-Y. Lin, and Y. Yu. Searching questions by identifying question topic and question focus. In *ACL*, 2008.

[14] D. Ganguly, D. Roy, M. Mitra, and G. J. Jones. Word embedding based generalized language model for information retrieval. In *SIGIR*, 2015.

[15] P.-S. Huang, X. He, J. Gao, L. Deng, A. Acero, and L. Heck. Learning deep structured semantic models for web search using clickthrough data. In *CIKM*, 2013.

[16] J. Jeon, W. B. Croft, and J. H. Lee. Finding similar questions in large question and answer archives. In *CIKM*, 2005.

[17] R. Jin, A. G. Hauptmann, and C. X. Zhai. Language model for information retrieval. In *SIGIR*, 2002.

[18] Q. Liu, E. Agichtein, G. Dror, E. Gabrilovich, Y. Maarek, D. Pelleg, and I. Szpektor. Predicting web searcher satisfaction with existing community-based answers. In *SIGIR*, 2011.

[19] T.-Y. Liu. Learning to rank for information retrieval. *Found. Trends Inf. Retr.*, 3(3):225–331, Mar. 2009.

[20] T. y. Liu, J. Xu, T. Qin, W. Xiong, and H. Li. Letor: Benchmark dataset for research on learning to rank for information retrieval. In *SIGIR Workshop on Learning to Rank for Information Retrieval*, 2007.

[21] Y. Liu, C. Sun, L. Lin, Y. Zhao, and X. Wang. Computing semantic text similarity using rich features. In *PACLIC*, 2015.

[22] C. Manning, P. Raghavan, and H. Schütze. *Introduction to Information Retrieval*. Cambridge University Press, 2008.

[23] T. Mikolov, I. Sutskever, K. Chen, G. S. Corrado, and J. Dean. Distributed representations of words and phrases and their compositionality. In *NIPS*. 2013.

[24] D. R. Miller, T. Leek, and R. M. Schwartz. A hidden markov model information retrieval system. In *SIGIR*, 1999.

[25] V. Murdock and M. Lalmas. Workshop on aggregated search. *SIGIR Forum*, 42(2):80–83, Nov. 2008.

[26] J. M. Ponte and W. B. Croft. A language modeling approach to information retrieval. In *SIGIR*, 1998.

[27] F. Radlinski, M. Kurup, and T. Joachims. How does clickthrough data reflect retrieval quality? In *CIKM*, 2008.

[28] S. Robertson and H. Zaragoza. The probabilistic relevance framework: Bm25 and beyond. *Found. Trends Inf. Retr.*, 3(4):333–389, Apr. 2009.

[29] S. E. Robertson and K. S. Jones. Relevance weighting of search terms. *Journal of the American Society for Information science*, 27(3):129–146, 1976.

[30] S. E. Robertson, C. J. van Rijsbergen, and M. F. Porter. Probabilistic models of indexing and searching. In *SIGIR*, 1980.

[31] G. Salton and C. Buckley. Term-weighting approaches in automatic text retrieval. *Inf. Process. Manage.*, 24(5):513–523, Aug. 1988.

[32] A. Severyn and A. Moschitti. Learning to rank short text pairs with convolutional deep neural networks. In *SIGIR*, 2015.

[33] F. Song and W. B. Croft. A general language model for information retrieval. In *CIKM*, 1999.

[34] K. Tymoshenko and A. Moschitti. Assessing the impact of syntactic and semantic structures for answer passages reranking. In *CIKM*, 2015.

[35] X. Wei and W. B. Croft. Lda-based document models for ad-hoc retrieval. In *SIGIR*, 2006.

[36] R. W. White, M. Richardson, and W.-t. Yih. Questions vs. queries in informational search tasks. In *WWW Companion*, 2015.

[37] H. Wu, W. Wu, M. Zhou, E. Chen, L. Duan, and H.-Y. Shum. Improving search relevance for short queries in community question answering. In *WSDM*, 2014.

[38] Q. Wu, C. J. Burges, K. M. Svore, and J. Gao. Adapting boosting for information retrieval measures. *Inf. Retr.*, 13(3):254–270, June 2010.

[39] X. Xue, J. Jeon, and W. B. Croft. Retrieval models for question and answer archives. In *SIGIR*, 2008.

[40] C. Zhai. Statistical language models for information retrieval. *Synthesis Lectures on HLT*, 1(1):1–141, 2008.

[41] C. Zhai and J. Lafferty. A study of smoothing methods for language models applied to ad hoc information retrieval. In *SIGIR*, 2001.

[42] W. Zhang, Z. Ming, Y. Zhang, L. Nie, T. Liu, and T. Chua. The use of dependency relation graph to enhance the term weighting in question retrieval. In *COLING*, 2012.

[43] G. Zheng and J. Callan. Learning to reweight terms with distributed representations. In *SIGIR*, 2015.

When a Knowledge Base Is Not Enough: Question Answering over Knowledge Bases with External Text Data

Denis Savenkov
Emory University
dsavenk@emory.edu

Eugene Agichtein
Emory University
eugene@mathcs.emory.edu

ABSTRACT

One of the major challenges for automated question answering over Knowledge Bases (KBQA) is translating a natural language question to the Knowledge Base (KB) entities and predicates. Previous systems have used a limited amount of training data to learn a lexicon that is later used for question answering. This approach does not make use of other potentially relevant text data, outside the KB, which could supplement the available information. We introduce a new system, Text2KB, that enriches question answering over a knowledge base by using external text data. Specifically, we revisit different phases in the KBQA process and demonstrate that text resources improve question interpretation, candidate generation and ranking. Building on a state-of-the-art traditional KBQA system, Text2KB utilizes web search results, community question answering and general text document collection data, to detect question topic entities, map question phrases to KB predicates, and to enrich the features of the candidates derived from the KB. Text2KB significantly improves performance over the baseline KBQA method, as measured on a popular WebQuestions dataset. The results and insights developed in this work can guide future efforts on combining textual and structured KB data for question answering.

1. INTRODUCTION

It has long been recognized that searchers prefer concise and specific answers, rather than lists of document results. In particular, factoid questions have been an active focus of research for decades due to both practical importance and relatively objective evaluation criteria. As an important example, a large proportion of Web search queries are looking for entities or their attributes [19], a setting on which we focus in this work.

Two relatively separate approaches for Question Answering (QA) have emerged: text-centric, or Text-QA and knowledge base-centric, or KBQA. In the more traditional, Text-QA approach, systems use text document collections to retrieve passages relevant to a question and extract candidate answers [14]. Unfortunately, a passage of text provides a limited amount of information about the mentioned entities, which has to be inferred from the context. The KBQA approach, which evolved from the database community, relies on large scale knowledge bases, such as DBpedia [1], Freebase [9], WikiData [24] and others, which store a vast amount of general knowledge about different kinds of entities. This information, encoded as `[subject, predicate, object]` RDF triples, can be effectively queried using structured query languages, such as SPARQL.

Both approaches eventually deal with natural language questions, in which information needs are expressed by the users. While question understanding is difficult in itself, this setting is particularly challenging for KBQA systems, as it requires a translation of a text question into a structured query language, which is complicated because of the complexity of a KB schema, and many differences between natural language and knowledge representations. For example, Figure 1 shows a SPARQL query that retrieves the answer to a relatively simple question *"who was the president of the Dominican Republic in 2010?"* from Freebase.

KBQA systems must address three challenges, namely question entity identification (to anchor the query process); candidate answer generation; and candidate ranking. We will show that these challenges can be alleviated by the appropriate use of external textual data. Entity identification seeds the answer search process, and therefore the performance of the whole system greatly depends on this stage [28]. Question text is often quite short, may contain typos and other problems, that complicate entity linking. Existing approaches are usually based on dictionaries that contain entity names, aliases and some other phrases, used to refer to the entities [21]. These dictionaries are noisy and incomplete, *e.g.,* to answer the question *"what year did tut became king?"* a system needs to detect a mention *"tut"*, which refers to the entity `Tutankhamun`. If a dictionary doesn't contain a mapping *"tut"* → `Tutankhamun`, as happens for one of the state of the art systems, it will not be able to answer the question correctly. Such less popular name variations are often used along with full names inside text documents, for example, to avoid repetitions. Therefore, we propose to look into web search results to find variations of question entity names, which can be easier to link to a KB (Figure 2). This idea has been shown effective in entity linking for web search queries[1] [12].

After question entities have been identified, answer candidates need to be generated and ranked to select the best answer. A candidate query includes one or multiple triple pat-

[1]http://web-ngram.research.microsoft.com/ERD2014/

SIGIR '16, July 17-21, 2016, Pisa, Italy

DOI: http://dx.doi.org/10.1145/2911451.2911536

```
SELECT DISTINCT ?name {
    :m.027rn :government.governmental_jurisdiction.governing_officials ?gov_position .
    ?gov_position :government.government_position_held.basic_title :m.060c4 .
    ?gov_position :government.government_position_held.office_holder ?president .
    ?gov_position :government.government_position_held.from ?from_date .
    ?gov_position :government.government_position_held.to ?to_date .
    FILTER ( xsd:date(?from_date) <= "2010"^^xsd:date AND xsd:date(?to_date) >= "2010"^^xsd:date)
    ?president :type.object.name ?name
}
```

Figure 1: SPARQL query to retrieve the answer to the question *"who was the president of the dominican republic in 2010?"* from Freebase

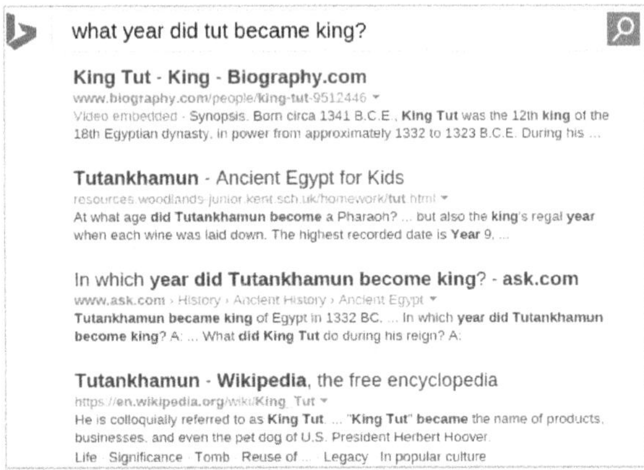

Figure 2: Search results for the question *"what year did tut became king?"*, which mention both the full name of the king and the correct answer to the question

terns with predicates, corresponding to words and phrases in the question. Existing knowledge base question answering approaches [3, 6, 7, 8, 10, 29] rely on a lexicon, learned from manually labeled training data, and supported by additional resources, such as question paraphrases [7] and weakly labeled sentences from a large text collection [30]. Such training data tends to be small compared to the number of different predicates in a KB, and therefore the coverage of these lexicons is limited. By our estimate, in a popular WebQuestions KBQA dataset, the answers to ~5.5% of test questions (112 out of 2032) involve a predicate that does not appear as a ground truth in the training set. For example, an RDF triple `[Bigos, food.dish.type_of_dish1, Stew]` answers the question *"what are bigos?"*, but no other examples in the training set involve this predicate. In addition, a lexicon needs to cover all different ways a predicate can be asked about. For example, questions *"who did jon gosselin cheat with?"* and *"who is the woman that john edwards had an affair with?"* are answered by the same KB predicate, but use different language. Therefore, presence of the first question in a training set may not help to answer the second question. On the other hand, traditional Text-QA systems benefit from the redundancy of the information on the Web, where the same facts are stated multiple times in many different ways [17]. This increases the chances of a good lexical match between a question and answer statements, which makes even some relatively simple counting-based techniques quite effective [11]. We propose to adapt these ideas from text-based question answering for KBQA. The right part of the Figure 3 shows web search results, a community question answering page, and text fragments mentioning pairs of entities, that can be useful to answer the question about John Edwards' affair.

To summarize, our contributions are three-fold:

- A novel "hybrid" knowledge base question answering system, which uses both structured data from a knowledge base and unstructured text resources. Section 3 describes the architecture of our system, and Section 4 shows that this fusion improves the performance of a state of the art KBQA system.
- Novel data sources and techniques for KBQA: enhancing question entity identification using web search results (Section 3.1); improving predicate matching by mining CQA data (Section 3.2); and improving candidate ranking by incorporating text corpus statistics (Section 3.3).
- Comprehensive empirical analysis of our system on a popular WebQuestions benchmark, demonstrating that additional text resources can improve the performance of a state-of-the-art KBQA system (Section 4). In addition, we conduct an extensive analysis of the system to identify promising directions for future improvements (Section 5).

Taken together, this work introduces novel techniques for using external text to significantly improve the performance of the KBQA approach. More broadly, our work bridges the gap between Text-QA and KBQA worlds, demonstrating an important step forward towards combining unstructured and structured data for question answering.

2. OVERVIEW OF KNOWLEDGE BASE QUESTION ANSWERING

In this section, we overview the existing approaches to Knowledge Base Question Answering (KBQA), as our approach, described in the next section, builds upon and extends some of these efforts.

Over time, KBQA systems have converged to two major approaches: *semantic parsing*, and *information extraction* (IE) [29]. The former focuses on question understanding, and attempts to parse sentences into their semantic representations, *e.g.,* logical forms [6, 7, 8]. IE approaches [3, 31, 30] are based on identifying topic entities in the question, and then, using pre-defined templates for mapping the question to predicates, explore the neighborhood of these entities in a KB. Theoretically, semantic parsing-based systems would be capable of generating any required queries, and would apply to any question, seen or unseen in training, whereas the template-based approach is less likely to generalize. In practice, however, answers to most of the questions lie within two edge traversals in a KB, making the template-based approaches quite effective.

Recent resurgence of interest in KBQA coincides with the availability of large scale knowledge bases such as Freebase and DBPedia, as well as commercial efforts from Google, Microsoft, Facebook and Yahoo; which make it possible to answer many real questions. Additionally, the creation of the WebQuestions dataset [6], provided a common benchmark which is large enough to allow both comprehensive evaluation, and training machine learning methods. In this work, we chose to extend an existing information extraction KBQA system – Aqqu [3] – which achieves one of the highest scores among publicly available systems. However, as we will show, our approach is general and can be incorporated into other IE-based systems as well.

We will first describe an information extraction approach to KBQA in more detail using Aqqu as an example. In Section 3 we present our system Text2KB, which extends this approach by incorporating external text-based data at various stages of the question answering process.

2.1 The Aqqu KBQA system

First, the system identifies question entities, which are used as sources for the answer search process. For concreteness, consider a question from the WebQuestions dataset *"who is the woman that john edwards had an affair with?"*. Here, the entity `John Edwards` with Freebase id `/m/01651q` is the main question entity. However, Freebase contains millions of entities and it can be difficult to identify the topical ones (*e.g.,* entities `Woman` and `Affair` are also present in Freebase), or to disambiguate and choose between `John Edwards` a politician (`/m/01641q`), an American racing driver (`/m/06zs089`) and other people with the same name. Aqqu considers all spans of question words under certain conditions on part of speech tags and uses an entity names lexicon [21] to map phrases to potential entities. Most reported systems, including Aqqu, do not disambiguate entities at this stage, but rather keep a set of candidates along with some information about their popularities (*e.g.,* number of mentions in the collection), and mention scores $p(entity|mention\ text)$.

At the next stage, SPARQL query candidates are generated by exploring the neighborhood of the question topic entities using a predefined set of query templates. Each query template has question entities, predicates and answer placeholders. The majority of the answers in the WebQuestions dataset can be covered by just 3 templates (q_entity - question entity, a_entity - answer entity, cvt_node - Freebase mediator node, which represent tuples with more than 2 arguments):

```
SELECT DISTINCT ?a_entity {
   <q_entity> <predicate> ?a_entity .
}
```

```
SELECT DISTINCT ?a_entity {
   <q_entity> <predicate_1> ?cvt_node .
   ?cvt_node <predicate_2> ?a_entity .
}
```

```
SELECT DISTINCT ?a_entity {
   <q_entity_1> <predicate_1> ?cvt_node .
   ?cvt_node <predicate_2> <q_entity_2> .
   ?cvt_node <predicate_3> ?a_entity .
}
```

The first template retrieves a set of entities that are directly connected to the given question entity via a certain predicate. The second template accounts for the presence of a mediator node, that groups together arguments of a multi-argument relation. And the last template looks for cases, when a question also mentions another argument of a multi-argument relation, *e.g.,* `Captain Kirk` and `Star Trek` for the question *"who played captain kirk in star trek movie?"*.

Each query candidate is represented with a set of features, that includes the scores for linked question entities, various scores for matching between question term n-grams and query predicates, the size of the results list, *etc.* The final stage of the question answering process is filtering and ranking. The Aqqu system employs a pairwise learning-to-rank model, trained on part of the dataset. For each pair of candidate answers Aqqu creates an instance, which contains 3 groups of features: features of the first, the second candidate in the pair and the differences between the corresponding features of the candidates. Specifically, a Random Forest model is used in the provided Aqqu implementation. A pair where the first candidate is better than the second belongs to class +1, and -1 otherwise. To reduce the number of pairs for the final ranking, Aqqu includes a simplified linear filtering model, which is trained to detect incorrect answers with high precision.

2.2 Basic system extensions

Before introducing our text-based improvements, we describe some basic extensions to the original Aqqu system. First, we noticed that since Aqqu does not use information about the answer entity Freebase types, in many cases it returns an answer that is incompatible with the question: *e.g.,* state instead of county *etc.* Therefore, we trained a model to return a score which measures compatibility between the question and answer entities, based on the entity notable types and question uni- and bi-grams as features, similar to Aqqu's relations score model. A second extension introduced a new date range query template, which helps solve cases like *"what team did david beckham play for in 2011?"*, where we need to look at the ranges of dates to determine whether an answer candidate satisfies the question.

```
SELECT DISTINCT ?a_entity {
   <q_entity_1> <predicate_1> ?cvt_node .
   ?cvt_node <from_predicate> ?date_from .
   ?cvt_node <to_predicate> ?date_to .
   ?cvt_node <predicate_2> ?a_entity .
   FILTER ( <question_date> >= ?date_from AND
            <question_date> <= ?date_to )
}
```

3. TEXT2KB: INCORPORATING TEXT DATA INTO KBQA

We now introduce our system, called Text2KB[2], that expands upon the basic KBQA model by incorporating external textual sources throughout the QA process. The general architecture and an example use case of Text2KB is presented on Figure 3. The left part of the figure roughly corresponds to the architecture of existing information extraction approaches to KBQA. The right part introduces additional external text data sources, namely Web search results, community question answering (CQA) data, and a collection of documents with detected KB entity mentions. We demonstrate how these data sources can help with the main challenges in KBQA, *i.e.,* question topical entity identification, predicate scoring and answer candidates ranking.

[2]http://ir.mathcs.emory.edu/projects/text2kb/

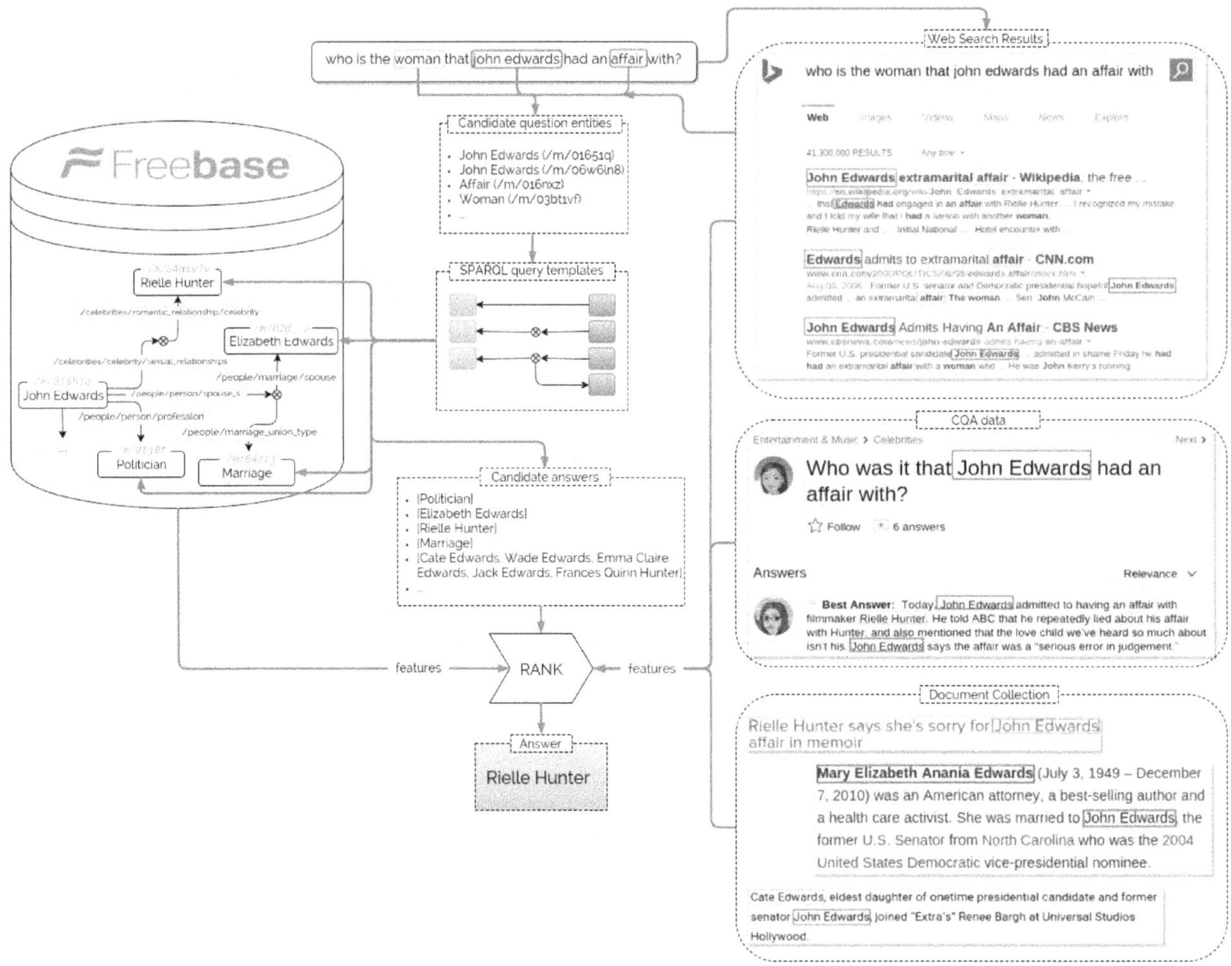

Figure 3: The architecture of our Text2KB Question Answering system

As described in detail next, this information is used to develop novel features for detecting entities and ranking candidate answers. The final ranking is performed using the same learning-to-rank method as the baseline Aqqu system [3], which uses the Random Forest model.

3.1 Web search results for KBQA

Traditional Text-QA systems rely on search results to retrieve relevant documents, which are then used to extract answers to users' questions. Relevant search results mention question entities multiple times and in various forms, which can be helpful for entity linking [12]. Furthermore, retrieved document set often contains multiple statements of the answer, which can be a strong signal for candidate ranking [17].

To obtain related web search results, Text2KB issues the question as a query to a search engine[3], extracts top 10 result snippets and the corresponding documents. Next, Text2KB uses Aqqu entity linking module to detect KB entity mentions in both snippets and documents.

Question entity identification. Question text provides only a limited context for entity disambiguation and linking; additionally, the entity name can be misspelled or an uncommon variation used. This complicates the task of entity identification, which is the foundation of KB question answering process. Fortunately, web search results help with these problems, as they usually contain multiple mentions of the same entities and provide more context for disambiguation. Text2KB uses the search result snippets to *expand* the set of detected question entities. More specifically, we count the frequencies of each entity mentioned in search snippets, and most popular ones with names similar to some of the question terms are added to the list of topical entities. The goal of this similarity condition is to keep only entities that are likely mentioned in the question text, and filter out related, but different entities. To estimate the similarity between a name and question tokens, we use Jaro-Winkler string distance. An entity is added to the list of question entities if at least one of its tokens e_t has high similarity with one of the question tokens q_t excluding stopwords (*Stop*):

$$\max_{e_t \in M \setminus Stop, q_t \in Q \setminus Stop} 1 - dist(e_t, q_t) \geq 0.8$$

Answer candidate features. The information stored in KBs can also be present in other formats, *e.g.,* text statements. For example, on Figure 2 multiple search snippets mention the date when Tutankhamun became a king. Text-QA systems use such passages to extract answer to users' questions. However, text may not provide sufficient context information about the mentioned entities, and systems have to infer the useful details, *e.g.,* entity types, which can be problematic [31]. On the other hand, KBQA systems can

[3]In our experiments we use the Bing Web Search API https://datamarket.azure.com/dataset/bing/search and local Wikipedia search using Lucene

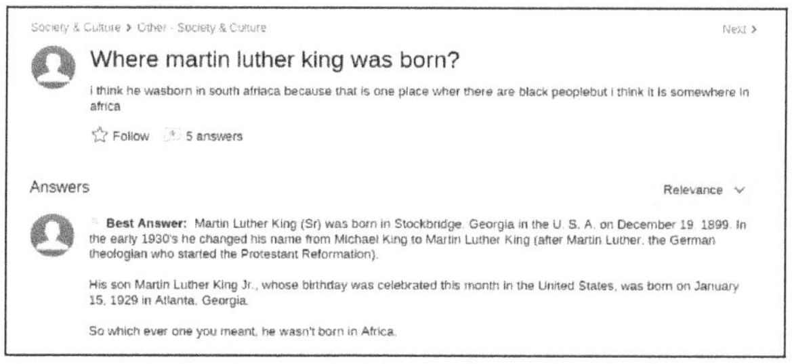

Figure 4: Example of a question and answer pair from Yahoo! Answers CQA website

utilize all the available KB knowledge about the entities in a candidate answer, and would benefit from additional text-based information to improve ranking. More specifically, Text2KB proceeds as follows:

1. Precompute term and entity IDFs. We used Google n-grams corpus to approximate terms IDF by collection frequencies and available ClueWeb Freebase entity annotations[4] to compute entity IDF scores.
2. Each snippet s_i and document d_i are represented by two TF-IDF vectors of lowercased tokens (t_{s_i} and t_{d_i}) and mentioned entities (e_{s_i} and e_{d_i}).
3. In addition, vectors of all snippets and all documents are merged together to form combined token and entity vectors: $t_{\cup s_i}$, $t_{\cup d_i}$, $e_{\cup s_i}$ and $e_{\cup d_i}$.
4. Each answer candidate a_j is also represented as TF-IDF vector of terms (from entity names), and entities: t_{a_j} and e_{a_j}
5. Cosine similarities between answer and each of 10 snippet and document vectors are computed: $\cos(t_{s_i}, t_{a_j})$, $\cos(t_{d_i}, t_{a_j})$ and $\cos(e_{s_i}, e_{a_j})$, $\cos(e_{d_i}, e_{a_j})$. We use the average score and the maximum score as features.
6. We also compute answer similarities with the combined snippet and document vectors: $\cos(t_{\cup s_i}, t_{a_j})$, $\cos(e_{\cup s_i}, e_{a_j})$, $\cos(t_{\cup d_i}, t_{a_j})$, $\cos(e_{\cup d_i}, e_{a_j})$.

3.2 CQA data for Matching Questions to Predicates

Recall that a major challenge in KBQA is that natural language questions do not easily map to entities and predicates in a KB. An established approach for this task is supervised machine learning, which requires labeled examples of questions and the corresponding answers to learn this mapping, which can be expensive to construct. Researchers have proposed to use weakly supervised methods to extend a lexicon with mappings learned from *single sentence statements* mentioning entity pairs in a large corpus [30]. However, the language used in questions to query about a certain predicate may differ from the language used in statements. A recent work [20] demonstrated how distant supervision can be applied to question-answer pairs from CQA archives for a related task of information extraction for knowledge base completion. In a similar way, we use weakly labeled collection of question-answer pairs to compute *associations* between question terms and predicates to *extend* system's lexicon (Figure 4). We emphasize that this data does not replace the mappings learned from single sentence statements, which are already used by our baseline system, but rather introduces the new ones learned from the CQA data.

For our experiments we use 4.4M questions from Yahoo! WebScope L6 dataset[5]. Question and answer texts were run through an entity linker, that detected mentions of Freebase entities. Next, we use distant supervision assumption to label each question-answer pair with predicates between entities mentioned in the question and in the answer. This labels are used to learn associations between question terms and predicates by computing pointwise mutual information scores (PMI) for each term-predicate pair. Examples of scores for some terms are given in Table 1.

Term	Predicate	PMI score
born	people.person.date_of_birth	3.67
	people.person.date_of_death	2.73
	location.location.people_born_here	1.60
kill	people.deceased_person.cause_of_death	1.70
	book.book.characters	1.55
currency	location.country.currency_formerly_used	5.55
	location.country.currency_used	3.54
school	education.school.school_district	4.14
	people.education.institution	1.70
	sports.school_sports_team.school	1.69
win	sports.sports_team.championships	4.11
	sports.sports_league.championship	3.79

Table 1: Examples of term-predicate pairs with high PMI scores, computed using distant supervision from a CQA collection

In Text2KB we evaluate candidate answer predicates by using the association (e.g., PMI) scores between predicates and the question terms (missing pairs are given a score of 0). The minimum, average and maximum of these values are used as features to represent a candidate answer. Such associations data can be sparse, we also use pretrained word2vec word embeddings[6]. We compute predicate embeddings by taking a weighted average of term vectors from predicate's PMI table. Each term vector is weighted by its PMI value (terms with negative score are skipped). Then, we compute cosine similarities between predicate vector and each of the question term vectors and take their minimum, average, maximum as features. Finally, we average embeddings of question terms and compute its cosine similarity with the predicate vector.

3.3 Estimating Entity Associations

A key step for ranking candidate answers is to estimate whether the question and answer entities are related in a way asked in the question. Existing KBQA approaches usually focus on scoring the mappings between question phrases and KB concepts from a candidate SPARQL query. However, textual data can provide another angle on the problem, as question and answer entities are likely to be mentioned together somewhere in text passages. For example, in the bottom right corner of Figure 3 we can see some passages that mention a pair of people, and the context of these mentions explains the nature of the relationships. This data can be viewed as additional edges in a KB, which connect pairs of entities, and have associated language models, estimated from text phrases, that mention these entities. Such edges do not have to coincide with the existing KB edges, and can connect arbitrary pairs of entities, that are mentioned together in text, therefore extending the KB.

[4]http://lemurproject.org/clueweb09/FACC1/

[5]https://webscope.sandbox.yahoo.com/

[6]https://code.google.com/p/word2vec/

Entity 1	Entity 2	Term counts
John Edwards	Rielle Hunter	campaign, affair, mistress, child, former ...
John Edwards	Cate Edwards	daughter, former, senator, courthouse, greensboro, eldest ...
John Edwards	Elizabeth Edwards	wife, hunter, campaign, affair, cancer, rielle, husband ...
John Edwards	Frances Quinn	daughter, john, rielle, father, child, former, paternity...

Table 2: Example of entity pairs along with the most popular terms mentioned around the entities

We use the ClueWeb12 corpus with existing Freebase entity annotations and count different terms that occur in the context of a mention of a pair of different entities (we only consider mentions within 200 characters of each other). To compute this unigram language model we use the terms separating the entities, as well as the terms within a small window (e.g., 100 characters) before and after the entity mentions. A small sample of this data is presented in Table 2.

We use this data to compute candidate ranking features as follows. Consider question words Q and an answer candidate, which contains a question entity e_1 and one or more answer entities e_2. For each answer candidate, we compute a language model score:

$$p(Q|e_1, e_2) = \prod_{t \in Q} p(t|e_1, e_2)$$

and use the minimum, average and maximum over all answer entities as features. To address the sparsity problem, we again use embeddings, *i.e.*, for each entity pair a weighted (by counts) average embedding vector of terms is computed and minimum, average and maximum cosine similarities between these vectors and question token embeddings are used as features.

3.4 Internal text data to enrich entity representation

In addition to external text data, many knowledge bases, including Freebase, contain text data as well, *e.g.*, Freebase includes a description paragraph from Wikipedia for many of its entities. These text fragments provide a general description of entities, which may include information relevant to the question [22]. For completeness, we include them in our system as well. Each entity description is represented by a vector of tokens, and a vector of mentioned entities. We compute cosine similarities between token and entity vectors of the question and description of each of the answers, and use the minimum, average and maximum of the scores as features.

4. EXPERIMENTAL RESULTS

This section reports the experimental setup, including the dataset and metrics, as well as the main methods compared for evaluating the performance of our Text2KB system. Additionally, we describe a series of ablation studies to analyze contribution of different system components.

4.1 Methods Compared

We compare our system, Text2KB, to state-of-the-art approaches, notably:

- **Aqqu**: the state-of-the-art baseline KBQA system [3], described in Section 2.
- **Text2KB(Web search)**: Our Text2KB system, using the Bing search engine API over the Web.
- **Text2KB(Wikipedia search)**: Our Text2KB system, using the standard Lucene search engine over the February 2016 snapshot of the English Wikipedia, in order to validate our system without the potential "black-box" effects of relying on a commercial Web search engine (Bing) and changing corpus (Web).
- **STAGG**: The current highest performing KBQA system [31] as measured on the WebQuestions dataset.

Additionally, other previously published results on WebQuestions are included to provide context for the improvements introduced by our Text2KB system.

4.2 Datasets

We followed the standard evaluation procedure for the WebQuestions dataset, and used the original 70-30% train-test split (3,778 training and 2,032 test instances). Within the training split, 10% was set aside for validation to tune the model parameters and only the best-performing set of parameters selected on the validation data was used to report the results on the official test split.

4.3 Evaluation Metrics

Recent papers using the WebQuestions dataset have primarily used the average F1-score as the main evaluation metric, defined as: $avg\ F1 = \frac{1}{|Q|} \sum_{q \in Q} f1(a_q^*, a_q)$

$$f1(a_q^*, a_q) = 2\frac{precision(a_q^*, a_q) recall(a_q^*, a_q)}{precision(a_q^*, a_q) + recall(a_q^*, a_q)}$$

$precision(a_q^*, a_q) = \frac{|a_q^* \cap a_q|}{|a_q|}$ and $recall(a_q^*, a_q) = \frac{|a_q^* \cap a_q|}{|a_q^*|}$, a_q^* and a_q are correct and given answers to the question q, which can be lists of entities. Additionally, we report average precision and recall, to gain better understanding of the tradeoffs achieved by different methods.

4.4 Main Results

The results of existing approaches and our Text2KB system are presented in Table 4. We should note, that text-based QA systems typically return a ranked list of answers, whereas many answers on WebQuestions dataset are lists, which complicates the comparison between KBQA and text-based systems. The result reported for YodaQA system is F1 score at position 1.

As we can see, Text2KB significantly improves over the baseline system and reaches the current best published result - STAGG [31]. We believe that this system will also benefit from the ideas of our work (Section 5).

4.5 Datasource and Features Contribution

To analyze the contribution of the features and datasources we introduced, we report results from a series of ablation studies. For convenience, we introduce the following shorthand notations for different components of our system:

- `T` - notable type score model as a ranking feature
- `DF` - date range filter-based query template
- `WebEnt` - using web search result snippets for question entity identification
- `WikiEnt` - using wikipedia search result snippets for question entity identification
- `Web` - using web search results for feature generation

System	avg Recall	avg Precision	F1 of avg P and R	avg F1
OpenQA [16]	-	-	-	0.35
YodaQA [4]	-	-	-	0.343
Jacana [30]	0.458	0.517	0.486	0.330
SemPre [6]	0.413	0.480	0.444	0.357
Subgraph Embeddings [10]	-	-	0.432	0.392
ParaSemPre [7]	0.466	0.405	0.433	0.399
Kitt AI [28]	0.545	0.526	0.535	0.443
AgendaIL [8]	0.557	0.505	0.530	0.497
STAGG [31]	0.607	**0.528**	**0.565**	**0.525**
Aqqu (baseline) [3]	0.604	0.498	0.546	0.494
Text2KB (Wikipedia search)	**0.632*** (+4.6%)	0.498	0.557* (+2.0%)	0.514* (+4.0%)
Text2KB (Web search)	**0.635*** (+5.1%)	0.506* (+1.6%)	**0.563*** (+3.1%)	**0.522*** (+5.7%)

Table 3: Performance of the Text2KB system on WebQuestions dataset compared to the existing approaches. The differences of scores marked * from the baseline Aqqu system are significant with p-value < 0.01

- `Wiki` - using wikipedia search results for feature generation
- `CQA` - using CQA-based `[question term, KB predicate]` PMI scores for feature generation
- `CW` - features, computed from entity pairs language model, estimated on ClueWeb

In our results table we will use the notation `+<comp>` for a system with a certain component added, and `-<comp>` when it is removed. For example, the baseline system will be denoted as "`Aqqu`". The same system with additional date range filter query templates and notable types score model is denoted as "`Aqqu +DF+T`", which represents the same system as "`Text2KB -WebEnt-Web-CQA-CL`" (we will call it Text2KB (base)). Our full system "`Text2KB`" can be also denoted as "`Aqqu +DF+T+WebEnt+Web+CQA+CL`".

Components: First, we analyze the improvements introduced by different components of our system (Table 4). As we can see, additional date range filters and notable types model (`Aqqu+DF+T`) are responsible for an increased recall and a drop in precision compared to the baseline model. Features generated from Wikipedia search results, CQA data and ClueWeb entity pair language models (`+Wiki+CQA+CL`) improve average F1 by 0.007 (+1.4%) compared to the base model, adding entity linking using Wikipedia search results improves results even more (+3%).

Web search results (`+Web+CQA+CL`) turned out to be more helpful than Wikipedia results (`+Wiki+CQA+CL`), which is natural since Wikipedia is a subset of the web. This was one of the reasons we didn't combine Wikipedia and Web search together. Finally, entity linking and all text-based features combined achieves an even higher score, proving that their contributions are independent.

Data Sources: We now anylize the contribution of the different data sources. We will remove a group of web search, CQA or Clueweb-based features and see how the performance of the whole system changes (Table 5). As we can see, all data sources have an impact on the system performance, and web search results based features provide the most useful signal for answer ranking.

Feature Importance for Ranking: Figure 5 plots a subset of features ranked by their Gini index-based importance scores. The figure supports the observation that web search results features are the most useful, however, other text data sources also contribute to the improvement.

In summary, Text2KB significantly outperforms the baseline system, and each of the introduced components contributes to this improvement. Web search results data turned out to be the most useful resource, and it significantly improves the quality by helping with question entity identification and candidate ranking. Next, we analyze the system performance in more detail, and investigate factors for future extension.

System	R	P	F1
`Aqqu`	0.604	0.498	0.494
`Text2KB (base) = Aqqu+DF+T`	0.617	0.481	0.499
`+Wiki+CQA+CL`	0.623	0.487	0.506
`+WikiEnt +Wiki+CQA+CL`	0.632	0.498	0.514
`+WebEnt`	0.627	0.492	0.508
`+Web+CQA+CL`	0.634	0.497	0.514
`+WebEnt +Web+CQA+CL`	0.635	0.506	0.522

Table 4: Average Recall (R), Precision (P), and F1 of Aqqu and Text2KB system with and without different components. +A means that a component A is added to the Text2KB (base) system. The list of components is given in Section 4.5.

System	R	P	F1
Text2KB (Web search)	0.635	0.506	0.522
`Text2KB -Web`	0.633	0.496	0.513
`Text2KB -CQA`	0.642	0.499	0.519
`Text2KB -CL`	0.644	0.505	0.523
`Text2KB -CQA-CL`	0.642	0.503	0.522
`Text2KB -Web-CQA`	0.631	0.498	0.514
`Text2KB -Web-CL`	0.622	0.493	0.508

Table 5: Average Recall (R), Precision (P), and F1 of Text2KB with and without features based on web search results, CQA data and ClueWeb collection.

5. ANALYSIS AND DISCUSSION

We now investigate how our system would compare to other systems on the same benchmark; then, we investigate in depth the different error modes (Section 5.1), which helps identify the areas of most substantial future improvements.

We took an existing KBQA systems and demonstrated that by combining evidence from knowledge base and external text resources we can boost the performance. A reasonable question is whether the same approach will be helpful to other systems, *e.g.,* the currently best system – STAGG [31]. STAGG differs from our baseline system Aqqu in the components: entity linking algorithm, a set of query tem-

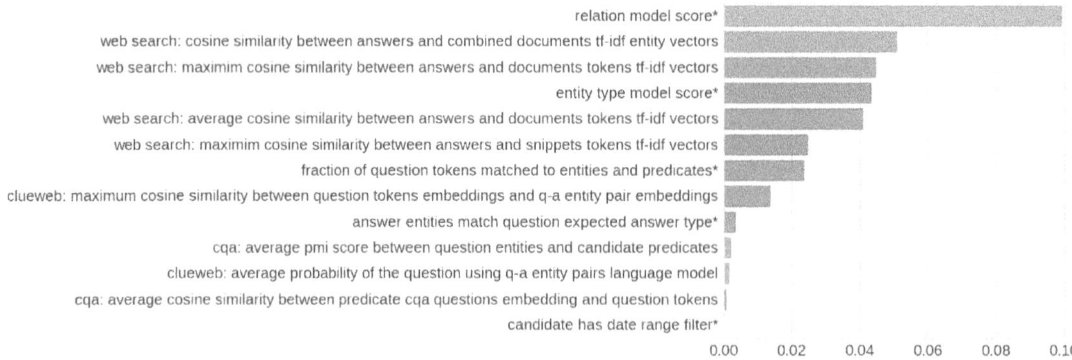

Figure 5: A plot of Gini importances of different features of our answer ranking random forest model (features marked * are not text-based and are provided for comparison)

System	F1
STAGG [31]	0.525
Text2KB + STAGG	0.532 (+1.3 %)
Text2KB + STAGG (Oracle)	0.606 (+15.4 %)

Table 6: Average F1 for combinations of Text2KB and STAGG using a simple heuristic based on the length of the answer list and Oracle upper bound

plates and ranking methods. Therefore, our approach is complementary and should be helpful for STAGG as well. To support this claim, we made an experiment to combine answers of STAGG and Text2KB. One of the advantages of the former is its set of filters, that restricts list results to entities of certain type, gender, *etc.* Therefore, we combined answers of STAGG and Text2KB using a simple heuristic: we chose to use the answer returned by STAGG if the number of answer entities is less than in the Text2KB answer, otherwise we use the answer of our approach. Table 6 gives the results of the experiment, and as we can see the combination achieves a slightly better average F1 score. Alternatively, we can look at the Oracle combination of the systems, which always selects the answer with the higher F1. As we can see such a combination results in a performance of 0.606, which is much higher than either of the systems.

As we mentioned earlier, answers to 112 of the test questions in the WebQuestions dataset involve predicates that weren't observed in the training set, which may be a problem for approaches that rely on a trained lexicon. We evaluated both systems on these questions, and indeed the performance is very low, *i.e.*, the average F1 score of Text2KB is 0.1640 compared to 0.1199 for STAGG[7].

5.1 Error analysis

To get a better insights into the problems that remain, we collected 1219 questions for which Text2KB didn't return completely correct answer, *i.e.*, F1 score < 1. We manually looked through a couple of hundreds of these examples and grouped the problems into several clusters (Figure 6).

As we can see candidate ranking is still the major problem, and it accounts for ~ 31% of the cases. The second problem is incorrect ground truth labels (almost 25% of reported errors). Another set of questions has incomplete or overcomplete ground truth answer list. Typical examples are questions asking for a list of movies, books, landmarks,

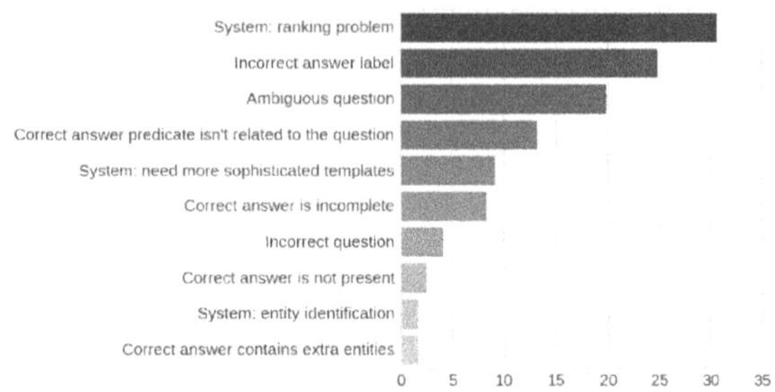

Figure 6: Distribution of problems with questions, where Text2KB returns an answer with F1<1

etc. The ground truth answer usually contains ~ 10 entities, whereas the full list is often much larger. This seems to be an artifact of the labeling process, where the answer was selected from the Freebase entity profile page, which shows only a sample of 10 entities, while the rest are hidden behind the "N values total" link. About 20% of the questions are ambiguous, *i.e.*, questions have no strict 1-1 correspondence with any of the predicates and can be answered by multiple ones without any obvious preferences. For example, the question *"what did hayes do?"* can be answered by profession, occupied position or some other achievements. Another problem is when there is no predicate that answers the question. For example, the question *"what do people in france like to do for fun?"* doesn't have a good match among the facts stored in Freebase. The ground truth entity `Cycling` comes from the list Olympic sport competitions country participated[8].

Text2KB components were quite effective in resolving some of the problems. Web search results helped identify the right question topical entity in a number of cases, *e.g.*, *"what did romo do?"* mentions only the last name of the Dallas Cowboys quarterback and the baseline system were unable to map it to the right entity. Web search results provides more than enough evidence that "*romo*" refers to `Tony Romo`. However, there are a number of loses, introduced by added unrelated entities. For example, the entity `I Love Lucy` was added for the question *"what was lucille ball?"*, because the term *lucy* had high similarity with *lucille*. A portion of these problems can be fixed by a better entity linking strategy, *e.g.*, [12]. An interesting example, when external text resources improved the performance is the question *"what ship did darwin sail around the world?"*. This is actually a hard question, because the ship entity is connected to

[7]Unfortunately, the number of questions is too low to show statistical significance (p-value=0.16) of the difference

[8]`olympics.olympic_participating_country.athletes`

the Charles Darwin entity through the "knownFor" predicate along with some other entities like Natural selection. Thus, the predicate itself isn't related to the question, but nevertheless, the name of the ship HMS Beagle is mentioned multiple times in the web search results, and entity pair model computed from ClueWeb also has high scores for the terms "ship" and "world".

There are several major reasons for the loses, introduced by features based on external text resources. Some entities often mentioned together and therefore one of them gets high values of cooccurrence features. For example, the baseline system answered the question *"when did tony romo got drafted?"* correctly, but since Tony Romo is often followed by Dallas Cowboys, Text2KB ranked the team name higher. Another common problem with our features is an artifact of entity linking, which works better for names and often skips abstract entities, like professions. For example, the correct answer to the question *"what did jesse owens won?"* is an entity with the name Associated Press Male Athlete of the Year, which is rarely mentioned or it's hard to find such mentions. Some problems were introduced by a combination of components. For example, for *"where buddha come from?"* a topical entity Buddhism was introduced from search results, and it generated Gautama Buddha as one of the answer candidates. This answer was ranked the highest due to large number of mentions in the search results.

In summary, we show that ideas behind Text2KB could be integrated into other systems and improve their performance. The error analysis suggested that even though a significant number of questions in the WebQuestions dataset have incorrect or ambiguous ground truth labels, there is still a room for improvement. In particular, the future work for Text2KB will include a better strategy for entity linking using external data sources and a better context model for entity mentions in text documents, which can put more weight on entities mentioned in the context related to the question.

6. RELATED WORK

One well known annual benchmark in knowledge base question answering is Question Answering over Linked Data (QALD), started in 2011 [23]. These benchmarks use the DBpedia knowledge base and usually provide a training set of questions, annotated with the ground truth SPARQL queries. In QALD-3 a multilingual task has been introduced, and since QALD-4 the hybrid task is included. This task asks participants to use both structured data and free form text available in DBpedia abstracts. The formulation of the hybrid task is the most relevant to our work, but there are some key differences. Questions in the hybrid track are manually created in such a way, that they can *only* be answered using a combination of RDF and free text data. Secondly, the hybrid task focuses on text data already present in a KB, whereas we are exploring external text resources. In general, because of the expensive labeling process, QALD datasets are relatively small, for example, QALD-5 training set for multilingual question answering includes 300 examples and 40 for the hybrid task, with 50 and 10 test questions correspondingly. Therefore, due to the scale of datasets and slightly different focus of tasks, we did not evaluate our techniques on the QALD benchmarks, but intend to explore it in the future.

Another benchmark dataset – WebQuestions – was introduced by Berant et al. [6]. The approaches proposed since then differ in the algorithms used for various components, and, what is more relevant to our work, the use of external datasets. WikiAnswers corpus of question clusters can be used to learn a question paraphrasing model, which helps to account for different ways a question can be formulated [7]. Another approach to learn term-predicate mappings is to mine them from a large text corpus [30], weakly labeled using distant supervision [18]. In the current paper, we build on this idea in two ways: by introducing a new data source (CQA archives), and by mining a language model for each mentioned entity pair, rather than predicates. Another approach to generate more training data is to automatically convert RDF triples to questions using entity and predicate names [10]. Finally, many systems work with distributed vector representations for words and RDF triples and use various deep learning techniques for answer selection [10, 31]. In all of these works, external resources are used to train a lexicon for matching questions to particular KB queries. In our work, we use external resources in a different way: we are targeting better candidate generation and ranking by considering the actual answer entities rather than predicates used to extract them.

In general, combining different data sources, such as text documents and knowledge bases, for question answering has been attempted before, and it has been already implemented in hybrid QA systems [2, 5]. Such systems typically have different pipelines that generate answer candidates from each of the data sources independently, and merge them to select the final answer at the end. We make a step towards integration of approaches, by incorporating text resources into the different stages of knowledge base question answering process. This is similar to the work of [22], who explored the use of entity types and descriptions from a KB for text-based question answering, and [13] explored such semantic annotations for ad-hoc document retrieval.

An alternative approach to QA is by using Open Information Extraction [15], which extract semi-structured data from text. OpenIE repositories can be queried using structured query languages, and at the same time allows keyword matching against entities and predicates [16]. In this work, we are borrowing an idea of learning about entity relationship via natural language phrases connecting them. However, since we do not need to extract clean set of relation tuples, we can keep all kinds of phrases, mentioned around entity pairs.

M. Yahya et al [27] proposed extending SPARQL triple patterns with text keywords, and using certain query relaxation techniques to improve the robustness of KBQA systems. Query relaxation drops certain triple patterns from SPARQL query and adds the corresponding question words as keywords to other triple patterns. The idea of query relaxations and using text in SPARQL queries was extended in [26], which proposed a framework for querying extended knowledge graphs, comprising of a combination of KB and OpenIE triples. These ideas are complimentary to our work, because our use of text data improves the matching between question phrases and KB concepts, whereas query relaxations are applied when a good match wasn't found. Another KB-Text hybrid approach, proposed in [25], utilizes text resources as a post-processing step for answer validation and filtering. In contrast, Text2KB integrates external textual information into all stages of question answering, resulting in more robust and overall higher performance than previously explored enhancements done in isolation.

7. CONCLUSIONS AND FUTURE WORK

Our work showed that unstructured text resources can be effectively utilized for knowledge base question answering to improve query understanding, candidate answer generation and ranking. We focused on three particular techniques and associated text information sources: web search results for query understanding and candidate ranking, community question answering data for candidate generation, and text fragments around entity pair mentions for ranking. Certainly, there are more resources that could be potential adapted, *e.g.,* entity profile pages like Wikipedia, news sources, textbooks, and many others. However, we believe that the proposed approach is general enough that it could be extended and successfully incorporate these other diverse text sources.

In the future, we plan to extend our work to the more open setup, similar to the QALD hybrid task, where questions no longer have to be answered exclusively from the KB. This would require extending the described techniques, and creating new QA benchmarks.

ACKNOWLEDGMENTS: This work was partially supported by the Yahoo Labs Faculty Research Engagement Program (FREP). We also thank the anonymous reviewers for their constructive comments.

8. REFERENCES

[1] S. Auer, C. Bizer, G. Kobilarov, J. Lehmann, R. Cyganiak, and Z. Ives. *Dbpedia: A nucleus for a web of open data.* Springer, 2007.

[2] K. Barker. Combining structured and unstructured knowledge sources for question answering in watson. In *DILS*, Lecture Notes in Computer Science. Springer, 2012.

[3] H. Bast and E. Haussmann. More accurate question answering on freebase. Proceedings of CIKM, 2015.

[4] P. Baudiš. Systems and approaches for question answering. 2015.

[5] P. Baudiš and J. Šedivỳ. Modeling of the question answering task in the yodaqa system. In *Experimental IR Meets Multilinguality, Multimodality, and Interaction.* Springer, 2015.

[6] J. Berant, A. Chou, R. Frostig, and P. Liang. Semantic parsing on freebase from question-answer pairs. In *Proceedings of EMNLP*, 2013.

[7] J. Berant and P. Liang. Semantic parsing via paraphrasing. In *Proceedings of ACL*, 2014.

[8] J. Berant and P. Liang. Imitation learning of agenda-based semantic parsers. *Transactions of the Association for Computational Linguistics*, 3, 2015.

[9] K. Bollacker, C. Evans, P. Paritosh, T. Sturge, and J. Taylor. Freebase: A collaboratively created graph database for structuring human knowledge. In *Proceedings of ICMD*, 2008.

[10] A. Bordes, S. Chopra, and J. Weston. Question answering with subgraph embeddings. In *Proceedings of EMNLP*, 2014.

[11] E. Brill, S. Dumais, and M. Banko. An analysis of the askmsr question-answering system. In *Proceedings of EMNLP*. Association for Computational Linguistics, 2002.

[12] M. Cornolti, P. Ferragina, M. Ciaramita, H. Schütze, and S. Rüd. The smaph system for query entity recognition and disambiguation. In *Proceedings of the First International Workshop on Entity Recognition and Disambiguation*, 2014.

[13] J. Dalton. *Entity-based Enrichment for Information Extraction and Retrieval.* PhD thesis, University of Massachusetts Amherst, 2014.

[14] H. T. Dang, D. Kelly, and J. J. Lin. Overview of the trec 2007 question answering track. In *Proceedings of TREC*, 2007.

[15] A. Fader, S. Soderland, and O. Etzioni. Identifying relations for open information extraction. In *Proceedings of EMNLP*, 2011.

[16] A. Fader, L. Zettlemoyer, and O. Etzioni. Open question answering over curated and extracted knowledge bases. In *Proceedings of SIGKDD*, 2014.

[17] J. Lin. An exploration of the principles underlying redundancy-based factoid question answering. *Transactions of ACM*, 25(2), Apr. 2007.

[18] M. Mintz, S. Bills, R. Snow, and D. Jurafsky. Distant supervision for relation extraction without labeled data. In *Proceedings of ACL*, 2009.

[19] J. Pound, P. Mika, and H. Zaragoza. Ad-hoc object retrieval in the web of data. In *Proceedings of WWW*, 2010.

[20] D. Savenkov, W.-L. Lu, J. Dalton, and E. Agichtein. Relation extraction from community generated question-answer pairs. In *Proceedings of NAACL: Student Research Workshop*, 2015.

[21] V. I. Spitkovsky and A. X. Chang. A cross-lingual dictionary for english wikipedia concepts. In *Proceedings of LREC*, 2012.

[22] H. Sun, H. Ma, W.-t. Yih, C.-T. Tsai, J. Liu, and M.-W. Chang. Open domain question answering via semantic enrichment. Proceedings of WWW, 2015.

[23] C. Unger, C. Forascu, V. Lopez, A.-C. N. Ngomo, E. Cabrio, P. Cimiano, and S. Walter. Question answering over linked data (qald-5). In *Proceedings of CLEF*, 2015.

[24] D. Vrandečić and M. Krötzsch. Wikidata: A free collaborative knowledgebase. *Communications of ACM*, (10), Sept. 2014.

[25] K. Xu, Y. Feng, S. Reddy, S. Huang, and D. Zhao. Enhancing freebase question answering using textual evidence. *arXiv preprint arXiv:1603.00957*, 2016.

[26] M. Yahya, D. Barbosa, K. Berberich, Q. Wang, and G. Weikum. Relationship queries on extended knowledge graphs. In *Proceedings of WSDM*, 2016.

[27] M. Yahya, K. Berberich, S. Elbassuoni, and G. Weikum. Robust question answering over the web of linked data. In *Proceedings of the CIKM*, 2013.

[28] X. Yao. Lean question answering over freebase from scratch. In *Proceedings of NAACL Demo*, 2015.

[29] X. Yao, J. Berant, and B. Van Durme. Freebase qa: Information extraction or semantic parsing? In *Proceedings of ACL*, 2014.

[30] X. Yao and B. Van Durme. Information extraction over structured data: Question answering with freebase. In *Proceedings of ACL*, 2014.

[31] W.-t. Yih, M.-W. Chang, X. He, and J. Gao. Semantic parsing via staged query graph generation: Question answering with knowledge base. In *Proceedings of ACL*, 2015.

Transfer Learning for Cross-Lingual Sentiment Classification with Weakly Shared Deep Neural Networks

Guangyou Zhou[1], Zhao Zeng[1], Jimmy Xiangji Huang[2], and Tingting He[1]
[1] School of Computer, Central China Normal University, Wuhan 430079, China
[2] School of Information Technology, York University, Toronto, Canada
{gyzhou, zhaozeng, tthe}@mail.ccnu.edu.cn jhuang@yorku.ca

ABSTRACT

Cross-lingual sentiment classification aims to automatically predict sentiment polarity (e.g., positive or negative) of data in a label-scarce target language by exploiting labeled data from a label-rich language. The fundamental challenge of cross-lingual learning stems from a lack of overlap between the feature spaces of source language data and that of target language data. To address this challenge, previous studies have been performed to make use of the translated resources for sentiment classification in the target language, and the classification performance is far from satisfactory because of the language gap between the source language and the translated target language.

In this paper, to address the above challenge, we present a novel deep neural network structure, called *Weakly Shared Deep Neural Networks* (WSDNNs), to transfer the cross-lingual information from a source language to a target language. To share the sentiment labels between two languages, we build multiple weakly shared layers of features. It allows to represent both shared inter-language features and language-specific ones, making this structure more flexible and powerful in capturing the feature representations of bilingual languages jointly. We conduct a set of experiments with cross-lingual sentiment classification tasks on multilingual Amazon product reviews. The empirical results show that our proposed approach significantly outperforms the state-of-the-art methods for cross-lingual sentiment classification, especially when label data is scarce.

Keywords

Cross-lingual; sentiment classification; auto-encoders

1. INTRODUCTION

With the development of Web 2.0, more and more user generated sentiment data have been shared on the Web. They exist in the form of user reviews on shopping or opinion sites, in posts of blogs or customer feedback in different languages. These labeled user generated sentiment data are considered as the most valuable resources for sentiment classification. However, such resources in different languages are very imbalanced. Manually labeling each individual language is a time-consuming and labor-intensive job, which makes cross-lingual sentiment classification essential for this application.

Cross-lingual sentiment classification aims to automatically predict sentiment polarity (e.g., positive or negative) of data in a label-scarce target language by exploiting labeled data from a label-rich language. The fundamental challenge of cross-lingual learning stems from a lack of overlap between the feature spaces of source language data and that of target language data. To address this challenge, previous work in the literature mainly relies on machine translation engines or bilingual resources to directly translate labeled data from source language to target language [19, 49, 46, 46, 34, 30, 50]. With the translated resources, one way is to jointly train the bi-view sentiment classifiers on labeled data from source language and their translations in target language via ensemble methods. Another way is to firstly select a subset of pivot features from source language and their translations in target language, and then use these pivot pairs to induce the language-independent features by modeling the corrections between pivot features and non-pivot features in an unsupervised fashion. Though pivot studies have been performed to make use of the translated resources for sentiment classification in target language, the methods are very straightforward by directly employing an inductive classifier, and the classification performance is far from satisfactory because of the language gap between source language and the translated target language.

Recently, many efforts have been initiated on learning feature representations with deep neural networks (DNNs) in the context of cross-lingual sentiment analysis [21, 17, 7, 22, 53, 40, 56, 18], inspired by the success of work on monolingual feature representations. Usually, the paired sentences from parallel corpora are used to learn bilingual feature representations across languages, eliminating the need of machine translation systems. By transferring the feature representations and labeling information from the source language space, we can learn a semantic-intensive target language feature representation, which can greatly improve the performance of target language sentiment classification tasks. In other words, the rich information transferred from the source language can help train the target language DNNs even with little labeled target language data. This is contrary to the popular strategy of trading the representation power of DNNs for better generalization performance in the

SIGIR '16, July 17–21, 2016, Pisa, Italy.
© 2016 ACM. ISBN 978-1-4503-4069-4/16/07...$15.00
DOI: http://dx.doi.org/10.1145/2911451.2911490

literature. In this paper, we will present how to use transferred cross-lingual information to train a powerful DNNs without sacrificing linguistic richness, which will yield much better performance for cross-lingual sentiment classification tasks.

To this end, we propose a novel DNNs that hierarchically learns to transfer the semantic knowledge from the source language to the target language, namely *Weakly Shared Deep Neural Networks* (WSDNNs). Our WSDNNs are trained in a novel way that minimizes the errors incurred by a cross-lingual information transfer process. As a hierarchically non-lineal model, WSDNNs differ from the existing shallow cross-lingual information transfer algorithms, such as cross-lingual mixture model [26], cross-lingual subspace learning [55], and cross-lingual correspondence learning [34], which learn the cross-lingual feature representations by linear mathematics models. In WSDNNs, we model two DNNs that take a pair of parallel bilingual sentences as input respectively, followed by multiple weakly-shared network layers at the top. The output of the shared layer in WSDNNs yields the translator function that can be used to transfer cross-lingual information. To the best of our knowledge, existing DNNs in the context of cross-lingual sentiment classification [7, 22, 53, 56, 18] are representation sharing. In "representation sharing structure", a set of common features are constructed, which usually overestimates the importance of language-specific features. While our weakly parameter-shared scheme makes our networks more robust of representing shared inter-language features as well as language-specific ones. To evaluate the effectiveness of the proposed approach, we conduct extensive experiments on multilingual Amazon product reviews for cross-lingual sentiment classification tasks. The empirical results show the proposed approach is effective for cross-lingual sentiment classification, and outperforms the state-of-the-art methods.

Our contribution in this paper is three-fold: (1) we propose a novel architecture of DNNs to transfer the cross-lingual information from a source language to a target language, which can adequately mitigate the problem of insufficient training data in the target language by bringing in rich sentiment labels from the source language; (2) the proposed WSDNNs are trained in a novel way that directly minimizes the loss incurred by a label transfer function via back-propagation, which can avoid unbalanced tuning of the source language and the target language DNNs; (3) we show superior results of the proposed WSDNNs on extensive experiments as compared with several strong baselines and the other state-of-the-art methods.

The remainder of this paper is organized as follows. Section 2 introduces the related work. Section 3 presents our proposed deep neural network transfer learning framework for cross-lingual sentiment classification. Section 4 presents the experimental results. Finally, we conclude the paper in Section 5.

2. RELATED WORK

Sentiment classification has gained widely interest in information retrieval (IR) and natural language processing (NLP) communities, we point the readers to recent books [31, 24] for an in-depth survey of literature on sentiment classification. Methods in the literature for sentiment classification heavily rely on quality and quantity of the label corpora, which are considered as the most valuable resources in sentiment classification task. However, such sentiment resources are imbalanced in different languages. To leverage resources in the source language to improve the sentiment classification in the target language, cross-lingual sentiment classification approaches have been investigated.

Cross-lingual sentiment classification aims to automatically predict sentiment polarity (e.g., positive or negative) of data in a label-scarce target language by exploiting labeled data from a label-rich language. The fundamental challenge of cross-lingual learning stems from a lack of overlap between the feature spaces of source language data and that of target language data.

To bridge the language gap, previous work in the literature mainly relies on machine translation engines or bilingual lexicons to directly adapt labeled data from a source language to a target language. Banea et al. [3] employed the machine translation engines to bridge the language gap in different languages for multilingual subjectivity analysis. Wan [46] proposed to use ensemble methods to train Chinese sentiment classification model on English labeled data and their Chinese translations. English labeled data are first translated into Chinese, and then the bi-view sentiment classifiers are trained on English and Chinese labeled data respectively. Pan et al. [30] proposed a bi-view non-negative matrix tri-factorization (BNMTF) model for cross-lingual sentiment classification problem. They employed machine translation engines so that both training and test data are able to have two representations, one in a source language and the other in a target language. The proposed model is derived from the non-negative matrix factorization models in both languages in order to make more accurate prediction. Prettenhofer and Stein [34] proposed a cross-lingual structural correspondence learning (CL-SCL) method to induce language-independent features. Instead of using machine translation engines to translate labeled texts, the authors first selected a subsect of pivot features in the source language to translate them into the target language, and then use these pivot pairs to induce cross-lingual representations by modeling the correlations between pivot features and non-pivot features in an unsupervised fashion. Recently, Xiao and Guo [51] used the similar idea with [34] for cross-lingual sentiment classification. Instead of in a fully unsupervised fashion, Xiao and Guo [51] performed representation learning in a semi-supervised manner by directly incorporating discriminative information with respect to the target prediction task. Li et al. [37] selected the samples in the source language that were similar to those in the target language to reduce the gap between two languages. Other similar work includes [48, 25, 1, 52, 13, 6, 12, 41, 27, 8, 23, 2, 11, 36]. All these approaches rely on machine translation or bilingual dictionary to build language connection.

Another group of studies propose to use unlabeled parallel data to fill the gap between two languages. To solve the feature coverage problem, Meng et al. [26] leveraged the unlabeled parallel data to learn unseen sentiment words. Similarly, Popat et al. [33] used the unlabeled parallel data to cluster features in order to reduce the data sparsity problem. Miao and Guo [50] formulated the cross-lingual representation as a matrix completion problem to infer unobserved feature values of the concatenated document-term matrix in the space of unified vocabulary set from the source language and target language by using unlabeled parallel bilingual data. Zhou et al. [55] proposed a subspace learning framework by leveraging the partial parallel data for cross-lingual sentiment classification. However, the parallel data is also a scarce resource. Besides, some other studies addressed the cross-lingual knowledge transferring using parallel or comparable corpora [29, 15, 28, 47, 45, 43].

Over the past few years, DNNs have gained a lot of attention from the research community and industry for their ability to automatically learn feature representations for a give task. Most recently, a number of studies leverage DNNs to learn bilingual (or multilingual) feature representations with parallel corpora. Bi-view feature representation has been successfully applied to many IR and NLP tasks, such machine translation [57], cross-lingual sentiment analysis [21, 17, 7, 53, 10, 40, 16, 55, 18, 39], cross-lingual information retrieval [20, 44], question answering [54], etc. The general idea is that they learn bilingual feature representation with aligned sentences throughout two phases: the language-specific feature representation learning phase and the shared representation learning phase. The key difference is that these existing models are "sharing representations", which usually overestimates the importance of language-specific features. While our proposed WSDNNs are "sharing parameters", which makes our networks are more robust of representing shared inter-language features as well as language-specific ones.

3. DEEP NEURAL NETWORK TRANSFER LEARNING

3.1 Task Description

Given a labeled data set $\mathcal{D}_s = \{(\mathbf{x}_i^s, y_i^s)\}_{i=1}^{N_s}$ in source language, in which $\mathbf{x}_i^s \in \mathbb{R}^m$ is a text data from the source language and $y_i^s \in \{1, 0\}$ is the positive sentiment label or negative sentiment label.[1] Our goal is to transfer the labels from the source language to the target language for sentiment classification task. To facilitate the label transfer process, we also have another co-occurrence set of parallel bilingual pairs $\mathcal{C} = \{(\bar{\mathbf{x}}_j^s, \bar{\mathbf{x}}_j^t)\}_{j=1}^{N_c}$, where $\bar{\mathbf{x}}_j^s \in \mathbb{R}^m$ and $\bar{\mathbf{x}}_j^t \in \mathbb{R}^n$ denote a data from the source language and target language respectively. By exploring this parallel bilingual set, we can reveal the alignment between the source language and target language, which will facilitate the sentiment label transfer between these two languages.

In this paper, we will jointly learn the bilingual feature representations to effectively transfer the discriminative information from the source language to the target language. The key idea of the deep neural network transfer learning is an efficient cross-lingual translator which can transfer the sentiment labels from the source language to the target language, even with the challenge of scarcely labeled target language data. By leveraging the learned deep neural network translator, we can solve the target language sentiment classification with extremely insufficient training data.

3.2 Modeling with Deep Neural Networks

An auto-encoder is an unsupervised neural network which is trained to reconstruct a given input vector from its distributed representation [4]. It can be seen as a special neural network with three layers: the input layer, the latent layer, and the reconstruction layer. An auto-encoder contains an encoder function $h(\mathbf{x}) = s_e(\mathbf{W}\mathbf{x} + \mathbf{b})$ and a counterpart decoder function $\bar{h}(\mathbf{x}) = s_d(\bar{\mathbf{W}}\mathbf{x} + \bar{\mathbf{b}})$ to minimize the reconstruction error of loss function $\mathcal{E}_r(\mathbf{x}, \bar{h}(h(\mathbf{x})))$. $s_e(\cdot)$ and $s_d(\cdot)$ are the non-linear activation function and decoder's activation function respectively. Several auto-encoders can be used as building blocks to form a Stacked Auto-Encoders (SAEs) [4, 42]. Once an auto-encoder has been trained, one can stack another auto-encoder on top of it, by training a second one which sees the latent representation of the first one as input.

[1] Besides positive and negative sentiments, there are also neural and mixed sentiments in practical applications. In this paper, we only consider binary (positive, negative) sentiment, but it is not hard to extend the proposed framework to address multi-class sentiment classification problems.

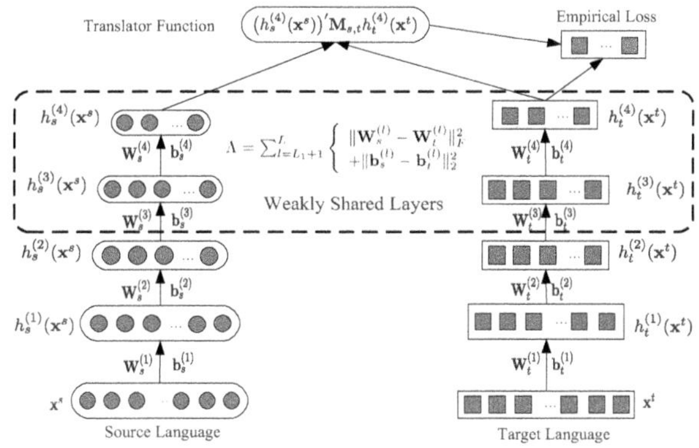

Figure 1: Weakly Shared Deep Neural Networks (WSDNNs).

Recently, many efforts have been initiated on learning feature representations with DNNs in the context of cross-lingual sentiment analysis [21, 17, 7, 22, 53, 40, 56, 18]. First, they pre-train two SAEs for the source language and the target language respectively, which output latent representations of these two languages via the multiple layers of nonlinear encoding. Assume that these two SAEs have L_1 layers, where they are structured and built separately. After the first L_1 layers, the two SAEs begin to share their structures where L_2 shared layers are constructed as shown in Figure 1. These shared layers provide a way to transfer the information across two languages represented by the two SAEs. Therefore, the input into the shared layers is the mixture of outputs of the bottom L_1 layers by the two SAEs.

However, we observe that this kind of representation sharing layers tend to over-mix the features learned from two languages. In other words, although there exist many shared features across different languages, it is difficult to completely ignore the language-specific features through the shared layers, since the source language and the target language often contain many elements that cannot be expressed by the same set of the neurons in the shared layers. In this paper, we relax such representation sharing structure, and propose a novel weakly shared deep neural networks (WSDNNs), whose structure is shown in Figure 1. The advantage of our proposed WSDNNs is the flexibility of representing shared inter-language features as well as language-specific ones, making it more powerful in modeling feature representations of bilingual languages than representation sharing layers in the literature.

Formally, there are $L + 1$ layers in WSDNNs, where $L = L_1 + L_2$. Given a pair of parallel bilingual texts $\mathbf{x}_j^s$ and

$\mathbf{x}_j^t$ respectively, we use $\mathbf{x}_{s_j}^{(l)} \in \mathbb{R}^{m_l}$ and $\mathbf{x}_{t_j}^{(l)} \in \mathbb{R}^{n_l}$ to denote the latent representation of a hidden layer l for the two SAEs respectively. At the first layer, we set $\mathbf{x}_{s_j}^{(0)} = \mathbf{x}_j^{(s)}$ and $\mathbf{x}_{t_j}^{(0)} = \mathbf{x}_j^{(t)}$ as inputs. For easy of presentation, we drop the subscripts i of $\mathbf{x}_{s_j}^{(l-1)}$ and $\mathbf{x}_{t_j}^{(l-1)}$ $(l = 1, 2, \cdots, L)$ in the following. For $l = 1, 2, \cdots, L$, the layer-wise processing of these two inputs through the whole networks are defined as follows

$$\begin{aligned} \mathbf{x}_s^{(l)} &= h_s^{(l)}(\mathbf{x}^s) = s_e(\mathbf{W}_s^{(l)}\mathbf{x}_s^{(l-1)} + \mathbf{b}_s^{(l)}) \\ \mathbf{x}_t^{(l)} &= h_t^{(l)}(\mathbf{x}^t) = s_e(\mathbf{W}_t^{(l)}\mathbf{x}_t^{(l-1)} + \mathbf{b}_t^{(l)}) \end{aligned} \quad (1)$$

where $h_s^{(l)}(\cdot)$ and $h_t^{(l)}(\cdot)$ denote the l-th layer feature representations in source language and target language SAEs respectively. $\{\mathbf{W}_s^{(l)}, \mathbf{b}_s^{(l)}\}_{l=1}^L$ and $\{\mathbf{W}_t^{(l)}, \mathbf{b}_t^{(l)}\}_{l=1}^L$ are the parameters in the source language and target language respectively.

The first L_1 layers are expected to learn the feature representations of a source language and a target language respectively, while the last L_2 layers provide shared feature representations. Under weakly-shared assumption, the parameters of the last L_2 layers should be set to be close to each other in order to trade off the shared inter-language features as well as language-specific ones. Inspired by [38], we propose the following penalty term Λ to quantify such trading-off:

$$\Lambda = \sum_{l=L_1+1}^{L} (\|\mathbf{W}_s^{(l)} - \mathbf{W}_t^{(l)}\|_F^2 + \|\mathbf{b}_s^{(l)} - \mathbf{b}_t^{(l)}\|_2^2) \quad (2)$$

Minimizing this term will minimize the difference of parameters in the last L_2 layers of two SAEs networks. It will be added to the proposed objective function in the next Subsection. A positive value of balancing coefficient will be multiplied with it in the objective function, which reflects the above trading-off for the weakly-shared layers.

3.3 Transfer Learning with DNNs

The goal of the proposed cross-lingual transfer learning is to transfer the labels annotated on the source language data set $\mathcal{D}_s$ to annotate an arbitrary test data $\mathbf{x}^t$ in the target language. Following the literature [5, 38], for an arbitrary test data $\mathbf{x}^t$ and a labeled data $\mathbf{x}_i^s$ in $\mathcal{D}_s$, we define a translator function as $(h_s^{(L)}(\mathbf{x}_i^s))'\mathbf{M}_{s,t}h_t^{(L)}(\mathbf{x}^t)$ between their weakly-shared layer outputs from the two SAEs, where $'$ denotes transpose operation in this paper, and $\mathbf{M}_{s,t}$ is the translator matrix. This translator function is used to transfer the sentiment labels from the source language to the target language as follows:

$$f(\mathbf{x}^t) = \sum_{i}^{N_s} y_i^s (h_s^{(L)}(\mathbf{x}_i^s))'\mathbf{M}_{s,t}h_t^{(L)}(\mathbf{x}^t) \quad (3)$$

which combines all the labeled data from the source language weighted by the corresponding translator functions. For the binary sentiment classification task, the distribution $f(\mathbf{x}^t)$ is the form of $[1, 0]$ for positive and $[0, 1]$ for negative, whose sign predicts the label of the target language data $\mathbf{x}^t$.

The parameters can be learned by minimizing the loss with the sentiment label transfer process, as well as minimizing the inconsistency between a set of parallel bilingual pairs to capture the cross-lingual alignment information. We model these two criteria as below:

Empirical loss on the labeled target language data set: Usually, we have a small size of labeled data $\mathcal{A}_t = \{(\mathbf{x}_i^t, y_i^t)\}_{i=1}^{N_t}$ in the target language, where $\mathbf{x}_i^t \in \mathbb{R}^{m_t}$ is the target space and $y_i^t \in \{1, 0\}$ is the sentiment label. We aim to minimize the training errors incurred by the label transfer function f on the labeled target language data set. The empirical loss on $\mathcal{A}_t$ is as follows:

$$\arg\min_\theta = \mathcal{L}_1 = \sum_{i=1}^{N_t} \ell(y_i^t \cdot f(\mathbf{x}_i^t)) \quad (4)$$

where $\ell(x) = \log(1 + \exp(-x))$ is a logistic loss function, which is used to measure the cross-lingual label transfer error. The parameters are $\theta = \{\mathbf{W}_s^{(l)}, \mathbf{b}_s^{(l)}, \mathbf{W}_t^{(l)}, \mathbf{b}_t^{(l)}, \mathbf{M}_{s,t}\}_{l=1}^L$.

Empirical loss on the parallel bilingual pairs: Given a set of parallel bilingual pairs $\mathcal{C} = \{(\bar{\mathbf{x}}_j^s, \bar{\mathbf{x}}_j^t)\}_{j=1}^{N_c}$ in the source language and target language, we wish to maximize the alignment between each pair of bilingual texts in this set, yielding a translator function that can well capture the alignment between these bilingual pairs. Specifically, we minimize the objective function as follows:

$$\arg\min_\theta = \mathcal{L}_2 = \sum_{j=1}^{N_c} \|(h_s^{(L)}(\bar{\mathbf{x}}_j^s))'\mathbf{M}_{s,t} - h_t^{(L)}(\bar{\mathbf{x}}_j^t)\|_2^2 \quad (5)$$

This loss function can be seen as a measurement of misalignment between parallel bilingual pairs caused by the translator function. Clearly, minimizing this loss function will ensure the consistency of translator function over the parallel bilingual pairs $\mathcal{C}$.

3.4 Learning Algorithm

After the above analysis, we propose the following objective function to learn the parameters of deep semantic translator as input of the top-layers of WSDNNs:

$$\arg\min_\theta = \mathcal{L} = \mathcal{L}_1 + \alpha\mathcal{L}_2 + \eta\mathcal{E}_r + \frac{\beta}{2}\Lambda + \frac{\gamma}{2}\Psi \quad (6)$$

where $\Psi = \sum_{l=1}^L (\|\mathbf{W}_s^{(l)}\|_F^2 + \|\mathbf{b}_s^{(l)}\|_2^2 + \|\mathbf{W}_t^{(l)}\|_F^2 + \|\mathbf{b}_t^{(l)}\|_2^2) + \|\mathbf{M}_{s,t}\|_F^2$ is the regularization term. The parameters α, η, β and γ weigh the importance of different term. In particular, α is the importance weight on alignment between the parallel bilingual pairs, η is the importance weight of reconstruction error, β adjusts the weakly-shared structure, and γ weights the regularization term.

To train the WSDNNs, we first pre-train each layer per time in a greedy fashion by using the unsupervised data as in conventional auto-encoder algorithms. The pre-train WSDNNs set up a good starting point that can fine tuned according to the objective function by employing the available supervision information.

We implement a back propagation process starting from the top output layers down through the whole WSDNNs to adjust all parameters. Each parameter in θ is updated by stochastic gradient descent in back-propagation algorithm below:

$$\mathbf{W}_s^{(l)} = \mathbf{W}_s^{(l)} - \delta\frac{\partial\mathcal{L}}{\partial\mathbf{W}_s^{(l)}} \quad (7)$$

$$\mathbf{b}_s^{(l)} = \mathbf{b}_s^{(l)} - \delta\frac{\partial\mathcal{L}}{\partial\mathbf{b}_s^{(l)}} \quad (8)$$

$$\mathbf{W}_t^{(l)} = \mathbf{W}_t^{(l)} - \delta\frac{\partial\mathcal{L}}{\partial\mathbf{W}_t^{(l)}} \quad (9)$$

$$\mathbf{b}_t^{(l)} = \mathbf{b}_t^{(l)} - \delta \frac{\partial \mathcal{L}}{\partial \mathbf{b}_t^{(l)}} \tag{10}$$

$$\mathbf{M}_{s,t} = \mathbf{M}_{s,t} - \delta \frac{\partial \mathcal{L}}{\partial \mathbf{M}_{s,t}} \tag{11}$$

where δ is the learning rate. These parameters can be computed based on the stochastic gradient optimization. The convergence is guaranteed when the number of iterations reaches the max or the objective function value is smaller than a predefined threshold. The overall complexity of our WSDNNs is similar with an existing SAE [4, 42].

We exploit the supervision information on the labeled target language data set $\mathcal{A}_t$ to directly tune the target language SAE. Similar to [38], we add an additional softmax layer upon the target language SAE that outputs the sentiment labels of the target language data. Then the labeled target language data in $\mathcal{A}_t$ are used to compute the back-propagated errors to tune the parameters in the target language SAE. In this paper, the back-propagated errors only arise from the target language labels that are intended to enhance the tuning of target language SAE. This can avoid unbalanced tuning of source language and target language SAEs when much more labeled data are used in label transfer process.

4. EXPERIMENTS

4.1 Data Sets

We use the multilingual sentiment classification data sets provided by Prettenhofer and Stein [34], which contain Amazon product reviews in four languages (English (E), French (F), German (G) and Japanese (J)) of three categories (Books (B), DVD (D), Music (M)). The English product reviews are sampled from previous cross-domain sentiment classification data sets, while the other three language product reviews are crawled from Amazon by the authors in November. Each category of product reviews contains a balanced training set and test set, each of which consists of 1000 positive and 1000 negative reviews for each of the language. Besides, we also collect a set of parallel bilingual reviews between English and each of the other three languages. Following the literature [50], each review is represented as a unigram bag-of-words vector representation and each entry is computed with tf-idf. Given the four languages from the three categories, we construct 18 cross-lingual sentiment classification tasks (EFB, EFD, EFM, EGB, EGD, EGM, EJB, EJD, EJM, FEB, FED, FEM, GEB, GED, GEM, JEB, JED, JEM) between English and the other three languages. For example, the task EFB uses English Books reivews as the source language and uses French Books reviews as the target language.

4.2 Compared Methods

In our experiments, we compare our proposed WSDNNs with the several strong baselines and state-of-the-art methods in the literature for cross-lingual sentiment classification:

- **TB:** This is a target bag-of-words baseline method, which trains a supervised monolingual classifier on the labeled training data from the target language without using the unlabeled parallel bilingual pairs and the source language data.
- **CL-LSA:** This is the cross-lingual learning method described in [15], which first translates each document from the source language into the target language via a bilingual dictionary to produce augmenting features, and then performs latent semantic analysis (LSA) over the augmented bilingual document-term matrix.
- **CL-SCL:** This is the cross-lingual structural correspondence learning method described in [34], which first selects some pivot features and then automatically induces the cross-lingual correspondences with a bilingual dictionary.
- **CL-MT:** This is the state-of-the-art machine translation based method described in [46], which first translates the source language to the target language, and then uses the ensembles methods to train sentiment classifiers on labeled data from the source language and their translations in the target language.
- **CL-MM:** This is the generative cross-lingual mixture model (CL-MM) described in [26], which learns previously unseen sentiment words from the large-scale bilingual parallel data to improve the vocabulary coverage. We implement this method using the 2000 unlabeled parallel reviews.
- **CL-OPCA:** This is the cross-lingual oriented principal component analysis (OPCA) method described in [32], which first learns cross-lingual representations with all data from both languages by performing OPCA and then trains a monolingual classifier with labeled data from both languages in the induced feature space.
- **CL-TS:** This is a two-step method described in [50], which formulates the cross-lingual representation as a matrix completion problem to infer unobserved feature values of the concatenated document-term matrix in the space of unified vocabulary set from the source language and target language by using the unlabeled parallel bilingual pairs.[2]
- **CL-SP:** This is the state-of-the-art multiview learning method described in [55], which is achieved by jointly learning the document-aligned review data and un-aligned data from the source language and the target language via a non-negative matrix factorization framework.

In all experiments, we train the sentiment classification model on the learned representations using the linear support vector machine (SVM) [9]. For **CL-LSA**, **CL-OPCA** and **CL-TS**, we use the same parameter setting as suggested in the paper [50]: the latent dimension is set to 50. For **CL-SCL**, we use the same parameter setting as suggested in the paper [34]: the number of pivot features is set as 450, the threshold value for selecting pivot features is 30, and the reduced dimensionality after singular value decomposition is 100. For **CL-SP**, we use the same parameter settings as suggested in the paper [55]: the shared latent dimension is set to 100 and the normalized parameter is set to 10^{-2}. We choose the above parameter values empirically because these

[2]There is a slight exception: using the same data set and parameter setting, our re-implement systems have slight differences with the results reported in [50].

Table 1: Average results (accuracy + standard derivation) for the 18 cross-lingual sentiment classification tasks. The bold formate indicates the best results, † indicates that the difference between our proposed WSDNNs and stateof-the-art CL-SP is significant with $p < 0.05$ under a McNemar paired test for labeling disagreements, and ‡ indicates the mildly significant with $p < 0.08$.

Task	TB	CL-LSA	CL-SCL	CL-MT	CL-MM	CL-OPCA	CL-TS	CL-SP	WSDNNs
EFB	66.89±0.87	79.38±0.25	79.86±0.22	78.01±0.45	69.35±0.46	76.47±0.35	81.83±0.25	82.61± 0.25	†**83.45**± 0.23
EFD	67.42±0.91	77.69±0.54	78.80±0.25	77.75±0.68	67.47±0.28	70.36±0.43	81.92±0.35	82.70± 0.45	†**83.61**± 0.33
EFM	67.55±0.50	75.26±0.43	75.95±0.31	75.86±0.51	69.12±0.38	73.43±0.37	79.06± 0.28	80.19± 0.40	†**80.97**± 0.38
EGB	67.31±0.72	77.60±0.37	77.77±0.28	77.02±0.60	70.76±0.33	74.65±0.48	79.30±0.34	79.91± 0.47	‡**81.32**± 0.36
EGD	66.54±0.73	79.16±0.26	79.93±0.23	79.75±0.58	66.93±0.38	74.47±0.56	81.27±0.26	81.86± 0.31	‡**82.40**± 0.25
EGM	67.61±0.46	73.67±0.52	73.95±0.30	73.69±0.55	69.58±0.40	74.38±0.61	79.26±0.33	79.59± 0.42	†**80.65**± 0.28
EJB	62.91±0.62	72.55±0.41	72.91±0.25	72.20±0.80	65.95±0.35	71.17±0.50	72.40±0.48	73.45± 0.27	†**74.51**± 0.40
EJD	65.33±0.58	72.51±0.32	72.82±0.28	72.68±0.56	66.20±0.37	71.70±0.45	76.51±0.37	77.06± 0.32	†**78.26**± 0.38
EJM	67.28±0.67	73.40±0.47	73.75±0.35	73.33±0.65	67.89±0.34	74.82±0.64	76.17±0.43	76.83± 0.52	‡**77.52**± 0.40
FEB	66.77±0.51	76.61±0.40	77.26±0.22	77.43±0.55	69.02±0.36	74.29±0.52	79.29±0.30	**80.48**± 0.33	80.06± 0.27
FED	65.98±0.57	76.39±0.34	76.57±0.20	76.80±0.52	66.93±0.35	72.30±0.57	77.88±0.34	78.76± 0.38	†**79.84**± 0.26
FEM	65.92±0.55	76.24±0.35	76.76±0.25	76.19±0.48	70.44±0.30	73.41±0.55	78.31±0.41	79.18± 0.33	†**80.14**± 0.31
GEB	67.05±0.68	77.43±0.26	77.85±0.27	77.50±0.66	71.13±0.31	74.66±0.42	78.45±0.29	78.61± 0.34	‡**79.23**± 0.35
GED	66.30±0.60	77.55±0.30	77.83±0.33	77.52±0.54	66.55±0.39	74.68±0.54	79.22±0.28	80.27± 0.35	‡**80.95**± 0.50
GEM	66.55±0.46	77.03±0.42	77.37±0.34	77.63±0.51	69.12±0.35	74.07±0.46	78.90±0.37	**79.80**± 0.26	79.68± 0.43
JEB	66.72±0.63	74.49±0.37	75.25±0.30	74.41±0.47	68.05±0.40	73.38±0.45	77.11±0.30	77.97± 0.35	†**79.10**± 0.48
JED	66.32±0.49	75.17±0.24	75.34±0.27	75.15±0.49	66.22±0.32	75.37±0.48	78.95±0.46	80.63± 0.38	†**81.89**± 0.52
JEM	66.48±0.55	72.29±0.45	73.21±0.33	73.16±0.50	67.55±0.41	72.55±0.61	77.13±0.51	77.78± 0.37	‡**78.22**± 0.55
avg.	66.50±0.62	75.80±0.37	76.29±0.28	75.89±0.56	68.24±0.36	73.68±0.50	78.50±0.35	79.32± 0.36	†**80.10**± 0.37

parameter settings have shown superior performance on the same benchmark [50, 34, 55].

4.3 Classification Accuracy

For each of the 18 cross-lingual sentiment classification tasks, we use all labeled data from the source language. For the target language, we use the test set as testing data while randomly choose 100 documents from the training set as labeled data. Thus, for each task, we have 2000 labeled documents from the source language, 100 labeled documents from the target language as auxiliary data ($\|\mathcal{A}_t\| = 100$) and the rest of target language as test data, as well as a set of parallel bilingual pairs. We run each experiment 10 times with different random selections of 100 labeled training documents from the target language. All parameters in our model are tuned based on a 5-fold cross-validation procedure on the training data, and the parameters are selected when the best performances are achieved. We train our model with 5-layers WSDNNs from bottom up. The last three ones are weakly shared layers. The average sentiment classification accuracies and standard deviations are presented in Table 1.

From Table 1, we can see that our proposed WSDNNs clearly outperforms the several strong baselines on 16 out of the 18 tasks. The target baseline TB performs poorly on all the 18 tasks, which indicates that 100 labeled documents from the target language is far from enough to obtain an accurate and robust sentiment classifier for sentiment classification. All the other seven cross-lingual sentiment classification methods, CL-LSA, CL-SCL, CL-MT, CL-MM, CL-OPCA, CL-TS and CL-SP, consistently outperform the baseline method TB across all the 18 tasks, which demonstrates that the labeled training data from source language is useful for classifying target language data. Among the 18 tasks, WSDNNs outperforms CL-LSA, CL-SCL, CL-MT, CL-MM, CL-OPCA and CL-TS across all the 18 tasks, outperforms CL-SP on 16 out of the 18 tasks and achieves the slight lower performance than CL-SP on the rest two tasks (FEB and GEM).

We also conduct significance tests for our proposed approach and each of the other methods using a McNemar paired test for labeling disagreements [14]. The results in bold formate indicates the best results, the overall results indicate that they are significant with $p < 0.05$. All these results demonstrate the efficacy and robustness of the proposed WSDNNs for cross-lingual sentiment classification.

Recently, many efforts have been initiated on learning feature representations with DNNs in the context of cross-lingual sentiment classification tasks [21, 17, 7, 53, 10, 40, 16, 18, 39]. However, these existing methods in the literature like bilingual SAEs [53, 55, 18] are representation sharing. While our proposed WSDNNs are weakly parameter-sharing, which makes our networks more flexible, especially when cross-lingual sentiment classification requires more language specific features are learned. In other words, by sharing parameters, we allow deviation exists between the feature representations of different languages. In contrast, in "representation sharing" structure, a set of common features are constructed, which usually overestimates the importance of language-specific features. Therefore, we also compare with the following representative representation sharing DNNs and state-of-the-art DNNs in the literature for cross-lingual sentiment classification: Chandar et al. [7] proposed a predicative auto-encoder for learning shared representation for cross-lingual tasks. Zhou et al. [53] proposed a two SAEs to learn feature representation for cross-lingual sentiment classification. Hermann and Blunsom [16] proposed to learn compositional distributed semantics for multilingual analysis. Zhou et al. [56] proposed to learn bilingual sentiment word embeddings for cross-lingual language analysis. Jain et al. [18] leveraged the sentence aligned corpora to develop a cross-lingual sentiment analysis tool. In this paper, we re-implement these representation sharing DNNs based on the original papers and train these models with a 5-fold cross-validation procedure on the training data. The average results are presented in Table 2.

From Table 2, we can see that our proposed WSDNNs significantly outperforms the state-of-the-art representation sharing DNNs in general with $p < 0.05$. Among the 18 tasks, WSDNNs achieves the best performance on 15 tasks. This

Table 2: Average results (accuracy + standard derivation) for the 18 cross-lingual sentiment classification tasks by using DNNs. The bold formate indicates the best results, † indicates that the differences between our proposed WSDNNs and other DNNs are significant with $p < 0.05$, and ‡ indicates the mildly significant with $p < 0.08$.

Task	Chandar et al. [7]	Zhou et al. [53]	Hermann and Blunsom [16]	Zhou et al. [56]	Jain et al. [18]	WSDNNs
EFB	78.75±0.37	79.68±0.27	82.47±0.34	80.37±0.38	81.33± 0.41	†**83.45**± 0.23
EFD	78.08±0.54	78.33±0.41	81.51±0.52	79.56±0.41	80.68± 0.35	†**83.61**± 0.33
EFM	76.43±0.42	78.56±0.28	79.29±0.37	77.21±0.29	79.05± 0.28	†**80.97**± 0.38
EGB	77.94±0.37	77.87±0.33	80.33±0.42	78.94±0.35	79.47± 0.56	‡**81.32**± 0.36
EGD	80.11±0.41	78.63±0.52	81.67±0.29	80.45±0.31	81.39± 0.43	‡**82.40**± 0.25
EGM	74.87±0.53	78.25±0.48	**80.73**±0.36	79.68±0.28	79.86± 0.38	80.65± 0.28
EJB	73.21±0.62	73.08±0.39	74.05±0.45	**75.53**±0.42	74.70± 0.34	74.51± 0.40
EJD	74.05±0.48	75.37±0.55	77.68±0.37	76.35±0.57	**78.43**± 0.30	78.26± 0.38
EJM	74.66±0.57	76.44±0.28	77.24±0.40	77.28±0.33	76.91± 0.36	**77.52**± 0.40
FEB	78.73±0.45	75.58±0.47	79.63±0.38	78.15±0.36	78.57± 0.47	**80.06**± 0.27
FED	77.48±0.51	77.62±0.50	78.47±0.46	76.62±0.37	78.35± 0.33	†**79.84**± 0.26
FEM	76.96±0.47	77.16±0.44	78.21±0.32	78.61±0.43	79.28± 0.40	‡**80.14**± 0.31
GEB	77.71±0.62	77.32±0.38	78.37±0.37	79.15±0.32	78.44± 0.51	**79.23**± 0.35
GED	78.64±0.55	79.05±0.33	79.15±0.44	79.44±0.38	79.61±0.32	†**80.95**± 0.50
GEM	78.02±0.39	77.31±0.51	79.07±0.35	78.87±0.27	79.14± 0.44	**79.68**± 0.43
JEB	75.59±0.44	76.67±0.47	78.27±0.45	78.05±0.35	78.20± 0.38	†**79.10**± 0.48
JED	76.16±0.48	78.73±0.38	81.20±0.39	79.33±0.34	80.93± 0.34	†**81.89**± 0.52
JEM	74.83±0.54	76.48±0.56	77.74±0.27	77.58±0.46	77.65± 0.25	‡**78.22**± 0.55
avg.	76.79±0.49	77.17±0.42	79.17±0.39	78.40±0.37	78.99± 0.38	†**80.10**± 0.37

confirms that our proposed weakly shared layers are more suitable to model the DNNs than the existing representation sharing layers.

4.4 The Impact of Number of Labeled Target Language Data

Next, we look into the performance of all eight approaches by varying the number of labeled training documents from the target language. We use the same experimental setting as before, but investigate a range of different numbers, $n_t = \{100, 200, 300, 400, 500\}$, as the number of labeled training data from the target language. Given a value n_t, we randomly select n_t documents from the training set of the target language as labeled data for each experiment. We also run the experiments on the same 2000 test data from the target language. Each experiment is repeated 10 times based on different random selection of the labeled training data from the target language. Figure 2 shows the average classification accuracies (%) vs. different numbers of labeled target language data on all the 18 tasks.[3]

From Figure 2, we can see that when the number of labeled documents from the target language is small, TB performs poorly. By increasing the number of labeled data from the target language, TB can greatly increase the classification accuracy and even outperform the CL-MM method. The CL-MM has a stable performance across the range of different numbers. The CL-LSA method has inconsistent performance across the 18 tasks. Its performance is better than TB when the labeled training data in the target language is very limited and is poor than TB when the labeled target data reaches 300 on most tasks. By using the machine translation resources, the CL-MT method outperforms TB, CL-LSA, CL-SCL and CL-MM. With a more sophisticated representation, the CL-TS, CL-SP and WSDNNs achieve the better performance than other five methods. Our proposed WSDNNs significantly outperforms all the other seven comparison methods across all experiments except on the tasks of EJB and GEM. In addition, we also observe that WSDNNs achieves high accuracies even when the number of labeled target language data is small. This is important for transferring the knowledge from a source language to a target language in order to reduce the labeling effort.

[3]In Figure 2, we do not present the results of CL-OPCA because this method has used all data from both languages in the original paper.

4.5 Parameter Analysis

In this subsection, we look into the parameters β and γ of objective function in Eq. (6). We choose $\beta \in \{0, 0.5, 1.0, 2.0\}$ and $\gamma \in \{0.1, 0.5, 1.0, 2.0\}$ via a cross-validation procedure, respectively. As usual, we set $\alpha = \eta = 1$ to equally weigh the three types of loss functions. Here, we study their impacts on the performances in Figure 3. When $\beta = 0$, the average accuracy is the lowest. The reason may be that in this case the source language and the target language SAEs are completely independent without any shared layers. This structure fails to jointly model the source language and the target language representations, and is unable of transferring sentiment labels between two languages. The accuracy increases rapidly when β becomes large. On the other hand, γ can also improve the accuracy when it is set to a proper value to regularize the model. The best accuracy on 16 cross-lingual tasks (except on the task of FEB and GEM) is achieved when $\beta = 1$ and $\gamma = 0.5$. The accuracies with different values of parameters are not varied very much, which suggests that our proposed WSDNNs are not very sensitive to the parameters.

5. CONCLUSIONS AND FUTURE WORK

In this paper, we propose a novel weakly parameter-shared deep neural networks (WSDNNs) to transfer cross-lingual information from the source language to the target language. To share the sentiment labels between two languages, we build multiple weakly shared layers of features. It allows to represent both shared inter-language features and language-specific ones, making our networks more flexible and powerful in capturing the feature representations of bilingual languages than the existing representation sharing structure. The proposed WSDNNs are trained in a novel way that directly minimizes the loss incurred by a label transfer func-

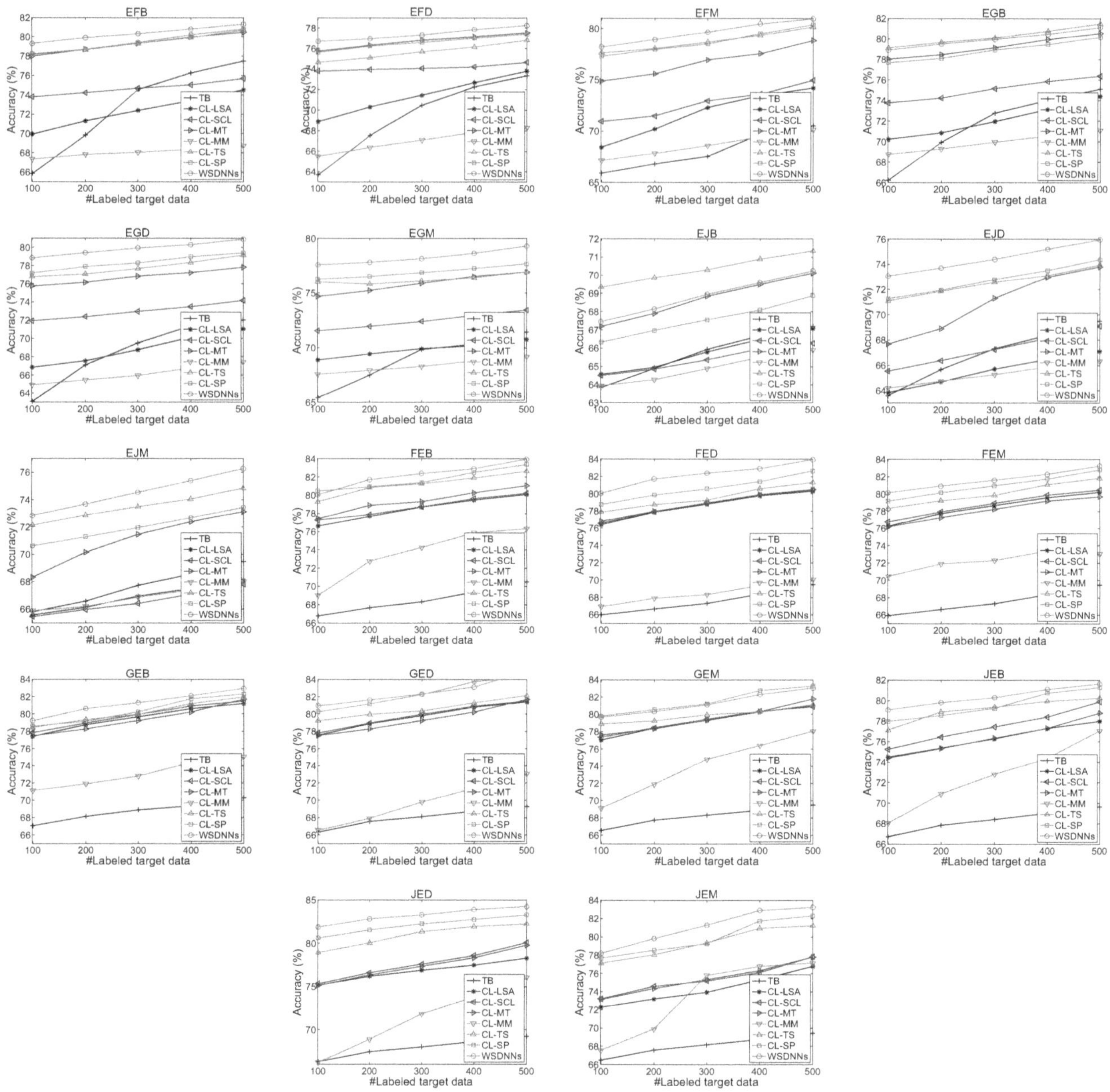

Figure 2: Average accuracies (%) vs. different numbers of labeled target language data on all the 18 tasks.

tion. This yields a fine tuning strategy to train WSDNNs from top down with via back-propagation, which can avoid unbalanced tuning of the source language and the target language. We conduct extensive experiments on 18 cross-lingual sentiment classification tasks constructed from the Amazon product reviews in four languages. The empirical results show the superior performances as compared with several strong baselines and state-of-the-art methods.

There are three research directions that we are planning to investigate in future. First, a straightforward path of the future research is to use the proposed WSDNNs for other language pairs, and apply to other tasks such as cross-lingual information retrieval [44]. Second, another straightforward extension is to replace the simple feature representations of SAE with more systematic context-aware learning methods, such as convolutional neural networks (CNNs) or recursive neural networks (RNNs). Third, inspired by the successful application of attention mechanism in multilingual neural machine translation [35], we will try to model the cross-lingual sentiment information with a shared attention mechanism.

Acknowledgments

This work was supported by the National Natural Science Foundation of China (No. 61303180, No. 61300144 and No. 61573163), the Fundamental Research Funds for the Central Universities (No. CCNU15ZD003 and No. CCNU16A02024), and also supported by a Discovery grant from the Natural Sciences and Engineering Research Council (NSERC) of

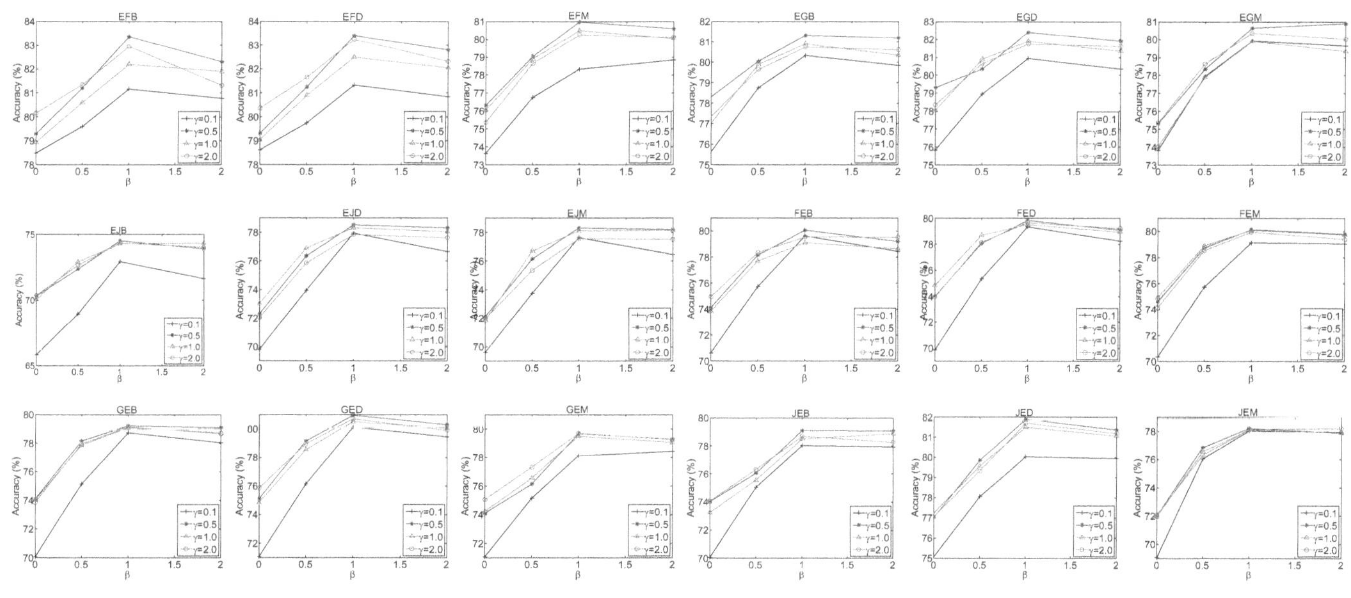

Figure 3: Average accuracies (%) vs. different values of β and γ on all the 18 tasks.

Canada and an NSERC CREATE award. We thank the anonymous reviewers for their insightful comments.

6. REFERENCES

[1] B. A., A. Joshi, and P. Bhattacharyya. Cross-lingual sentiment analysis for Indian languages using linked wordnets. In *COLING*, pages 73–82, 2012.

[2] S. Artem, J. Laura, H. Felix, and R. Stefan. Boosting cross-language retrieval by learning bilingual phrase associations from relevance rankings. In *EMNLP*, pages 1688–1699, 2013.

[3] C. Banea, R. Mihalcea, J. Wiebe, and S. Hassan. Multilingual subjectivity analysis using machine translation. In *EMNLP*, pages 127–135, 2008.

[4] Y. Bengio, P. Lamblin, D. Popovici, H. Larochelle, U. D. Montreal, and M. Quebec. Greedy layer-wise training of deep networks. In *NIPS*, pages 153–160, 2007.

[5] A. Bordes, J. Weston, and N. Usunier. Open question answering with weakly supervised embedding models. In *ECML/PKDD*, pages 165–180, 2014.

[6] G. Cao, J. Gao, J.-Y. Nie, and J. Bai. Extending query translation to cross-language query expansion with markov chain models. In *CIKM*, pages 351–360, 2007.

[7] S. Chandar A P, S. Lauly, H. Larochelle, M. Khapra, B. Ravindran, V. C. Raykar, and A. Saha. An autoencoder approach to learning bilingual word representations. In *NIPS*, pages 1853–1861. 2014.

[8] A. Chen and F. C. Gey. Multilingual information retrieval using machine translation, relevance feedback and decompounding. *Inf. Retr.*, 7(1):149–182, 2004.

[9] R. Fan, K. Chang, C. Hsieh, X. Wang, and C. Lin. Liblinear: A libary for large linear classification. *JMLR*, 9:1871–1874, 2008.

[10] M. Faruqui and C. Dyer. Improving vector space word representations using multilingual correlation. In *EACL*, pages 462–471, 2014.

[11] T. Ferhan, L. Jimmy, and D. W. Oard. Combining statistical translation techniques for cross-language information retrieval. In *COLING*, pages 2685–2702, 2012.

[12] J. Gao, E. Xun, M. Zhou, C. Huang, J.-Y. Nie, and J. Zhang. Improving query translation for cross-language information retrieval using statistical models. In *SIGIR*, pages 96–104, 2001.

[13] W. Gao, C. Niu, J.-Y. Nie, M. Zhou, J. Hu, K.-F. Wong, and H.-W. Hon. Cross-lingual query suggestion using query logs of different languages. In *SIGIR*, pages 463–470, 2007.

[14] L. Gillick and S. Cox. Some statistical issues in the comparison of speech recoginition algorithms. In *ICASSP*, pages 532–535, 1989.

[15] A. Gliozzo and C. Strapparava. Exploiting comparable corpora and bilingual dictionaries for cross-language text categorization. In *ACL*, pages 553–560, 2006.

[16] K. M. Hermann and P. Blunsom. Multilingual models for compositional distributed semantics. In *ACL*, pages 58–68, 2014.

[17] J.-T. Huang, J. Li, D. Yu, L. Deng, and Y. Gong. Cross-language knowledge transfer using multilingual deep neural network with shared hidden layers. In *ICASSP*, pages 137–140, 2013.

[18] S. Jain and S. Batra. Cross lingual sentiment analysis using modified brae. In *EMNLP*, pages 159–168, 2015.

[19] S. James, G. Gregory, Q. Yan, and E. David. Mining multilingual opinions through classification and translation. 2004.

[20] J. Kim, J. Nam, and I. Gurevych. Learning semantics with deep belief network for cross-language information retrieval. In *COLING*, pages 579–588, 2012.

[21] A. Klementiev, I. Titov, and B. Bhattarai. Inducing crosslingual distributed representations of words. In *COLING*, pages 1459–1473, 2012.

[22] T. Kočiský, K. M. Hermann, and P. Blunsom. Learning bilingual word representations by marginalizing alignments. In *ACL*, pages 224–229, 2014.

[23] W. Kraaij, J.-Y. Nie, and M. Simard. Embedding web-based statistical translation models in cross-language information retrieval. *Comput. Linguist.*, 29(3):381–419, 2003.

[24] B. Liu. Sentiment analysis and opinion mining. *Synthesis Lectures on Human Language Technologies*, 2012.

[25] B. Lu, C. Tan, C. Cardie, and B. K. Tsou. Joint bilingual sentiment classification with unlabeled parallel corpora. In *ACL*, pages 320–330, 2011.

[26] X. Meng, F. Wei, X. Liu, M. Zhou, G. Xu, and H. Wang. Cross-lingual mixture model for sentiment classification. In *ACL*, pages 572–581, 2012.

[27] S.-H. Na and H. T. Ng. Enriching document representation via translation for improved monolingual information retrieval. In *SIGIR*, pages 853–862, 2011.

[28] X. Ni, J.-T. Sun, J. Hu, and Z. Chen. Cross lingual text classification by mining multilingual topics from wikipedia. In *WSDM*, pages 375–384, 2011.

[29] J.-Y. Nie, M. Simard, P. Isabelle, and R. Durand. Cross-language information retrieval based on parallel texts and automatic mining of parallel texts from the web. In *SIGIR*, pages 74–81, 1999.

[30] J. Pan, G.-R. Xue, Y. Yu, and Y. Wang. Cross-lingual sentiment classification via bi-view non-negative matrix tri-factorization. In *PAKDD*, pages 289–300.

[31] B. Pang and L. Lee. Opinion mining and sentiment analysis. *Found. Trends Inf. Retr.*, 2(1-2):1–135, 2008.

[32] J. Platt, K. Toutanova, and W. Yih. Translingual document representations from discriminative projects. In *EMNLP*, pages 251–261, 2010.

[33] K. Popat, B. A.R, P. Bhattacharyya, and G. Haffari. The haves and the have-nots: Leveraging unlabelled corpora for sentiment analysis. In *ACL*, pages 412–422, 2013.

[34] P. Prettenhofer and B. Stein. Cross-language text classification using structural correspondence learning. In *ACL*, pages 1118–1127, 2010.

[35] I. V. Serban, A. Sordoni, Y. Bengio, A. C. Courville, and J. Pineau. Building end-to-end dialogue systems using generative hierarchical neural network models. In *AAAI*, pages 3776–3784, 2016.

[36] S. Shigehiko, H. Felix, S. Artem, and R. Stefan. Learning translational and knowledge-based similarities from relevance rankings for cross-language retrieval. In *ACL*, pages 488–494, 2014.

[37] L. Shouhan, W. Rong, L. Huanhuan, and H. Churen. Active learning for cross-lingual sentiment classification. In *NLPCC*, pages 236–246, 2013.

[38] X. Shu, G. Qi, J. Tang, and J. Wang. Weakly-shared deep transfer networks for hetergeneous-domain knowledge propagation. In *MM*, pages 35–44, 2015.

[39] G. Stephan, B. Yoshua, and C. Greg. Bilbowa: Fast bilingual distributed representations without word alignments. In *ICML*, pages 1–10, 2015.

[40] X. Tang and X. Wan. Learning bilingual embedding model for cross-language sentiment classification. In *WI*, pages 134–141, 2014.

[41] D. Trieschnigg, D. Hiemstra, F. de Jong, and W. Kraaij. A crosslingual framework for monolingual biomedical information retrieval. In *CIKM*, pages 169–178, 2010.

[42] P. Vincent, H. Larochelle, Y. Bengio, and P.-A. Manzagol. Extracting and composing robust features with denoising autoencoders. In *ICML*, pages 1096–1103, 2008.

[43] I. Vulić and M.-F. Moens. A unified framework for monolingual and cross-lingual relevance modeling based on probabilistic topic models. In *ECIR*, pages 98–109, 2013.

[44] I. Vulić and M.-F. Moens. Monolingual and cross-lingual information retrieval models based on (bilingual) word embeddings. In *SIGIR*, pages 363–372, 2015.

[45] I. Vulić, W. Smet, and M.-F. Moens. Cross-language information retrieval models based on latent topic models trained with document-aligned comparable corpora. *Inf. Retr.*, 16(3):331–368, 2013.

[46] X. Wan. Co-training for cross-lingual sentiment classification. In *ACL*, pages 235–243, 2009.

[47] Z. Wang, Z. Li, J. Li, J. Tang, and J. Z. Pan. Transfer learning based cross-lingual knowledge extraction for wikipedia. In *ACL*, pages 641–650, 2013.

[48] B. Wei and C. Pal. Cross lingual adaptation: An experiment on sentiment classifications. In *ACL*, pages 258–262, 2010.

[49] K. Wu, X. Wang, and B. liang Lu. Cross language text categorization using a bilingual lexicon. In *IJCNLP*, pages 165–172, 2008.

[50] M. Xiao and Y. Guo. A novel two-step method for cross language representation learning. In *NIPS*, 2013.

[51] M. Xiao and Y. Guo. Semi-supervised representation learning for cross-lingual text classification. In *EMNLP*, pages 1465–1475, 2013.

[52] Z. Ye, X. Huang, B. He, and H. Lin. Mining a multilingual association dictionary from wikipedia for cross-language information retrieval. *JASIST*, 63(12):2474–2487, 2012.

[53] G. Zhou, T. He, and J. Zhao. Bridging the language gap: Learning distributed semantics for cross-lingual sentiment classification. In *NLPCC*, pages 138–149, 2014.

[54] G. Zhou, T. He, J. Zhao, and P. Hu. Learning continuous word embedding with metadata for question retrieval in community question answering. In *ACL*, pages 250–259, 2015.

[55] G. Zhou, T. He, J. Zhao, and W. Wu. A subspace learning framework for cross-lingual sentiment classification with partial parallel data. In *IJCAI*, pages 1426–1432, 2015.

[56] H. Zhou, L. Chen, F. Shi, and D. Huang. Learning bilingual sentiment word embeddings for cross-language sentiment classification. In *ACL*, pages 430–440, 2015.

[57] W. Y. Zou, R. Socher, D. M. Cer, and C. D. Manning. Bilingual word embeddings for phrase-based machine translation. In *EMNLP*, pages 1393–1398, 2013.

Query to Knowledge: Unsupervised Entity Extraction from Shopping Queries using Adaptor Grammars

Ke Zhai, Zornitsa Kozareva, Yuening Hu, Qi Li and Weiwei Guo
Yahoo! Research, 701 1st Ave, Sunnyvale, CA 94089
{kzhai,kozareva,ynhu,lqi,wguo}@yahoo-inc.com

ABSTRACT

Web search queries provide a surprisingly large amount of information, which can be potentially organized and converted into a knowledgebase. In this paper, we focus on the problem of automatically identifying *brand* and *product* entities from a large collection of web queries in online shopping domain. We propose an unsupervised approach based on adaptor grammars that does not require any human annotation efforts nor rely on any external resources. To reduce the noise and normalize the query patterns, we introduce a query standardization step, which groups multiple search patterns and word orderings together into their most frequent ones. We present three different sets of grammar rules used to infer query structures and extract *brand* and *product* entities. To give an objective assessment of the performance of our approach, we conduct experiments on a large collection of online shopping queries and intrinsically evaluate the knowledgebase generated by our method qualitatively and quantitatively. In addition, we also evaluate our framework on extrinsic tasks on query tagging and chunking. Our empirical studies show that the knowledgebase discovered by our approach is highly accurate, has good coverage and significantly improves the performance on the external tasks.

1. INTRODUCTION

Queries collected by web-scale search engines provide a large amount of useful information. This information can be organized to knowledgebase [5] which can impact and improve the performance of a wide variety of applications such as parsing, coreference resolution, entity linking. Typically, researchers focus on extracting entities for movie, music, person, location, and organization names from natural language texts [22]. Others have shown that knowledgebase can be easily built from such types by consulting external resources, such as IMDB [9], DBpedia [10], or Wikipedia [24]. However, one bigger challenge is how to learn knowledgebase for more rare yet useful entity types such as *brand* and *product*. These entities are important and crucial for commercial search engines and online advertising to function properly.

Formally, we define the *brand* and *product* entity types as:

Definition 1. A **brand** entity is defined as a named entity phrase whose master[1] business is to manufacture, provide or sell one or more major products or services. It also applies to subsidiaries or even divisions that operate as a separate company and master manufacturer producing or selling their own products, for instance, "*Lexus*" (owned by "*Toyota*") and "*Chevrolet*" (owned by "*GM*").

Definition 2. A **product** entity is defined as an entity phrase specifying generic product terms, e.g., "*jeans*", "*smartphone*", "*running shoes*". Note that a product does not include any attributes, but may include necessary generic specification. For example, "*wedding dress*" and "*dress*" are considered two different products, since they are generically different products, but "*black dress*" is *not* considered a standalone product, since it is an actual product ("*dress*") with color attributes ("*black*").[2]

To the best of our knowledge, there are no publicly available knowledgebase with updated *brand* and *product* entity lists.

Fortunately, online shopping queries collected at commercial search engines provide large amount of information, which can be organized into such knowledgebase [26]. For example, the query "*calvin klein white t shirts*" contains explicit information about the *brand* ("*calvin klein*") and *product* ("*t shirts*") with arbitrary attributes or constrains ("*white*"). Utilizing this information is able to greatly reduce human annotation time and editorial labeling efforts, which can be both expensive and time consuming to acquire.

However, extracting *brand* and *product* entities from web-scale query logs in online shopping domain is fundamentally different from classic *named entity recognition* [23, NER] frameworks. Past entity extraction works focus on natural language text [22, 30] or external web resources [20, 31]. They target on identifying entity phrases, such as person, location and organization, etc, using some indicative features (e.g., capitalization), trigger words (e.g., "*Mrs*", "*Inc*") or some grammar properties (e.g., structural patterns, like a location address usually follows the pattern of *street* +

[1]The definition "master" is to distinguish the concept of *brand* from other named entity types, such as *product family* of *organization*. For example, "*nexus*" (owned by "*Google*") is **not** a *brand*, but a *product family*. It does *not* apply to branding or advertisement carriers neither, e.g., "*Manchester United*" is considered *organization*.

[2]This definition can be empirically more generic and fine-grained than the extended named entity hierarchy at nlp.cs.nyu.edu/ene/.

SIGIR '16, July 17-21, 2016, Pisa, Italy
© 2016 ACM. ISBN 978-1-4503-4069-4/16/07... $15.00
DOI: http://dx.doi.org/10.1145/2911451.2911495

city + *state*|*province* + *zip codes*). In addition, classic NER frameworks usually operate on a collection of sentences or paragraphs, which contains rich contextual information and syntactic structures, such as *part-of-speech* (POS) tagging, dependency parsing, etc.

On the other hand, online shopping queries often do not have indicative features nor do shopping entity types contain any trigger words. In terms of grammar properties, majority of web search queries consist of proper nouns or noun phrases only [3, 27], which often lacks explicit syntactic dependency structure. In addition, they are usually short and noisy (e.g., misspelling, arbitrary word ordering). All of these factors rise severe difficulties in learning *brand* and *product* entities from web query logs.

In this paper, we focus on a fundamentally challenging yet interesting problem of automatic extracting *brand* and *product* entities from web-scale online shopping queries. Ideally, the extraction framework should satisfy following:

1: It is **unsupervised** and automatic, which does not require any human annotation or external resource.
2: It is **robust** to various kinds of noise and dependency structure presented in web shopping queries.
3: It is **domain-independent**, and easily generalizable to multiple domains, e.g., apparel, electronics, etc.
4: It is **data-driven**, i.e., the numbers of *brand* and *product* entities are not known a priori. Instead, the model automatically infers the number of entities appeared in the data in a completely nonparametric fashion.

In this work, we propose a novel framework which fulfills all these requirements. Our contributions in this paper lies in the following aspects. We first formulate the entity extraction problem, in its general form, as an unsupervised shallow parsing problem with *probabilistic context-free grammars* [21, PCFG] on a collection of online shopping queries. This allows our model to be **unsupervised** and **domain-independent**, and hence easily generalizable to multiple domains. We introduce a query standardization step to reduce the sparsity of the word orderings and query patterns in data. Our proposed model relies on *adaptor grammars* [15]—a nonparametric counterpart of PCFG—which is completely **data-driven** and **robust** to noise. We subsequently propose three different grammar rule sets to regulate different pattern variants in the data. We then compare our model against strong baselines and conduct comprehensive evaluations on the extracted knowledgebase both qualitatively and quantitatively. Intrinsically, we demonstrate that our framework is able to discover high quality knowledgebase. We also extrinsically evaluate the extracted knowledgebase on applications of tagging and chunking. Our result indicates that knowledgebase generated by our method significantly improves the performance.

We organize our paper as following. In Section 2, we review the adaptor grammar model, and discuss its inference procedure using *Markov chain Monte Carlo* (MCMC) method. We introduce our unsupervised entity extraction framework based on adaptor grammars in Section 3. To give an objective assessment on our proposed method, we conduct extensive experimental analysis and empirical study on web-scale query dataset collected from online shopping domain in Section 4. In Section 5, we review some past approaches on related problem. Finally, we conclude the paper and point out some possible future research directions in Section 6.

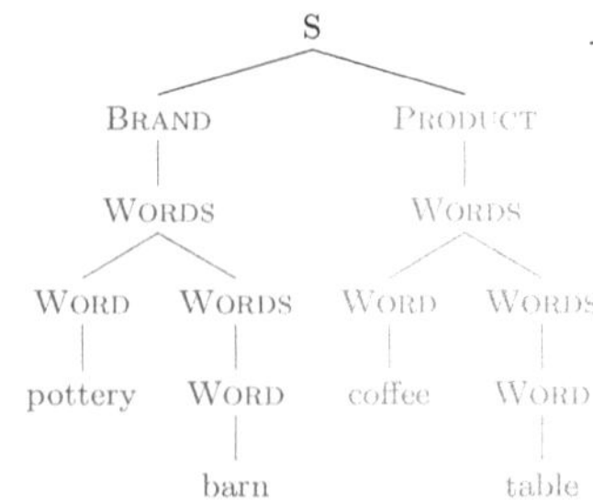

Prob	Rule
1.0	S → BRAND PRODUCT
1.0	BRAND → WORDS
1.0	PRODUCT → WORDS
0.7	WORDS → WORD WORDS
0.3	WORDS → WORD
0.1	WORD → pottery
0.1	WORD → barn
0.2	WORD → coffee
0.2	WORD → table
	...
?	BRAND → pottery barn
?	PRODUCT → coffee table

Figure 1: An example of a phrase-structure tree and underlying probabilistic context-free grammar (PCFG). PCFGs assume the set of grammar rules are defined *a priori* and fixed. Therefore, rewriting operations are independent given the nonterminal, i.e., disregarding the yields and structure of the derivation tree. For example, in the query dataset, the highlighted derivation trees may appear several times—possibly with different *brand* or *product*—such derivation trees should be cached as a *new* grammar rule. Adaptor grammars [15, AG] break this independence assumption by jointly modeling the context and grammar, i.e., a nonparametric PCFG, allow to incorporate new context-dependent grammar rules from data.

2. ADAPTOR GRAMMARS

In this section, we discuss probabilistic context-free grammars and adaptor grammars.

2.1 Probabilistic Context-free Grammars

Probabilistic context-free grammars (PCFG) define probability distributions over derivations of a context-free grammar. A PCFG $\mathcal{G}$ is defined as a set of variables $\langle \boldsymbol{W}, \boldsymbol{N}, \boldsymbol{R}, \boldsymbol{\theta} \rangle$. Given a collection of terminals $\boldsymbol{W}$ and a collection of nonterminals $\boldsymbol{N}$, $\mathcal{G}$ is described by a set of probabilistic grammar rules $\langle \boldsymbol{R}, \boldsymbol{\theta} \rangle$. Let us denote the collection of all the rules rewriting a nonterminal c is $\boldsymbol{R}(c)$. For a nonterminal c, each of the grammar rules $r \mapsto \beta \in \boldsymbol{R}(c)$—commonly referred to as a *production*—is associated with a probability $\theta_{r \mapsto \beta}$, i.e., $\sum_{r \mapsto \beta \in \boldsymbol{R}(c)} \theta_{r \mapsto \beta} = 1$.

For any given sentence, a PCFG starts with the unique *start symbol* $S \in \boldsymbol{N}$, recursively rewrites a nonterminal into its derivations according to the probabilistic grammar rules $\langle \boldsymbol{R}, \boldsymbol{\theta} \rangle$. This builds a hierarchical *derivation tree structure*, starting from a nonterminal to a sequence of terminals, i.e., leaf nodes. This sequence of terminals often referred to as the *yield* of the derivation tree. Figure 1 illustrates an example of a derivation tree, its yields and underlying probabilistic context-free grammar (PCFG). Interested readers may refer to [21] for a more detailed description of PCFGs.

2.2 Adaptor Grammars

PCFGs assume the set of grammar rules are defined *a priori* and fixed. Therefore, rewriting operations are independent given the nonterminal, i.e., disregarding the yields and structure of the derivation tree. This context-freeness assumption often can be too strong for modeling natural language. Referring to Figure 1, in the query dataset, the derivation tree BRAND ↦ $\widehat{\text{pottery barn}}$ may appear over and over again, possibly with different products. If every time, such tree is constructed from raw PCFG rules, it is both time consuming and possibly error prone.

Adaptor grammars [15] break this independence assumption by jointly modeling the context and the grammar. It

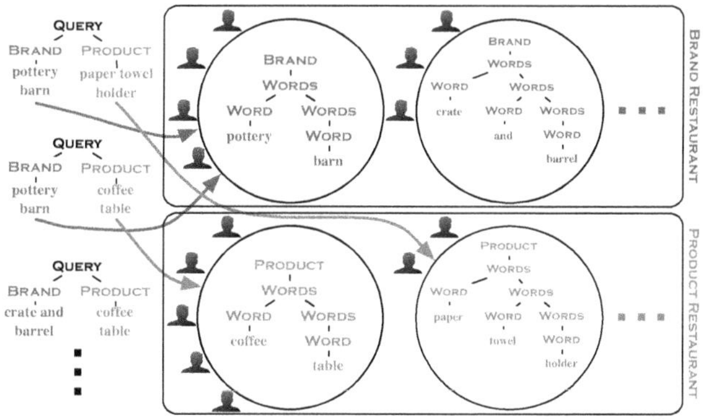

Figure 2: Illustration of the Chinese restaurant franchise.

is a nonparametric version of PCFG, which allows the model to incorporate new context-dependent grammar rules in a completely data-driven fashion. It specifies a set of adapted nonterminals, often called the *adaptors*. For each adaptor c, the model subsequently imposes a nonparametric prior on the distribution over its parse trees. This allows the model to dynamically learn more meaningful derivation trees and expand the rule set according to data. In general form, adaptor grammars use *Pitman-Yor process* [29, PYP] prior, which is also called the *Pitman-Yor adaptor grammar* (PYAG).

One realization of PYP is via the view of the *Chinese restaurant process* [13, CRP], parametrized by **scale parameter** a, **discount factor** b and **base distribution** G_c. The CRP assumes a set of tables, each of which serves a dish (a derivation tree in our context) randomly drawn from the base distribution, i.e., $z_c \sim G_c$. Each customer (an adapted nonterminal c in our context) entering the restaurant chooses a table to sit based on the choice of all previous customers (Figure 2). Let us denote K as the number of tables occupied by all past $n-1$ customers, and the sequence $x_1, \dots, x_{n-1}$ represents the table indices that they sit at, i.e., $x_i \in \{1, \dots, K\}$. The n-th customer choose to sit at table x_n

$$x_n|x_1, \dots, x_{n-1} \sim \tfrac{Kb+a}{n-1+a}\delta_{K+1} + \textstyle\sum_{k=1}^{K} \tfrac{m_k-b}{n-1+a}\delta_k, \qquad (1)$$

where m_k is the number of customers sit at table k, i.e., $\sum_{k=1}^{K} m_k = n-1$. Variable δ_{K+1} stands for the case that a new table is chosen, i.e., a new instance of derivation tree is sampled. Therefore, the n-th customer chooses to sit at a new table $K+1$ with probability $\frac{Kb+a}{n-1+a}$ and an existing table k with probability $\frac{m_k-b}{n-1+a}$.

According to exchangability and de Finetti's theorem, all customers in CRP are mutually exchangeable, and do not alter the distribution, i.e., all m_k's remain the same. Therefore, for a given distribution over number of customers per table $\boldsymbol{n} = \{n_1, \dots, n_K\}$, its probability is governed by PYP as

$$p_{\text{PYP}}(\boldsymbol{n}|a,b) = \frac{\prod_{k=1}^{K}(b(k-1)+a)\prod_{j=1}^{m_k-1}(j-b)}{\prod_{i=0}^{n-1}(i+a)}, \qquad (2)$$

where K is the number of tables occupied and n is the number of observed samples drawn from CRP, i.e., total number of customers. The CRP formulation of PYP enables us to infer the latent variables in PYAG using *Markov chain Monte Carlo* (MCMC) method, which we will discuss in Section 2.3.

Formally, a Pitman-Yor adaptor grammar PYAG $\boldsymbol{\mathcal{A}}$ extends a PCFG and defined as following variables:

1: a collection of terminals $\boldsymbol{W}$, nonterminals $\boldsymbol{N}$ and context-free grammar rule set $\boldsymbol{R}$;
2: Dirichlet prior $\boldsymbol{\alpha}_c$ for the PCFG production probabilities $\boldsymbol{\theta}_c$ of each nonterminal $c \in \boldsymbol{N}$, i.e., $\boldsymbol{\theta}_c \sim \text{Dir}(\boldsymbol{\alpha}_c)$;
3: a set of non-recursive adapted nonterminals $\boldsymbol{M} \subseteq \boldsymbol{N}$;
4: PYP parameters a_c, b_c for each adaptor $c \in \boldsymbol{M}$.

In following section, we discuss in details about the inference process using a Metropolis-Hastings sampler.

2.3 MCMC Inference

The inference process is to learn the latent variables from observed data, i.e., $p(\boldsymbol{T}|\boldsymbol{X})$. To accomplish this, we first write down the joint distribution over their derivation trees $\boldsymbol{T}$ given a collection of sentences $\boldsymbol{X}$, is

$$\begin{aligned} p(\boldsymbol{T}|\boldsymbol{\alpha},\boldsymbol{a},\boldsymbol{b}) &= \textstyle\int_{\boldsymbol{\theta},\boldsymbol{\pi},\boldsymbol{z}} p(\boldsymbol{T}|\boldsymbol{\theta},\boldsymbol{\pi},\boldsymbol{z}) \cdot p(\boldsymbol{\theta},\boldsymbol{\pi},\boldsymbol{z}|\boldsymbol{\alpha},\boldsymbol{a},\boldsymbol{b})\delta_{\boldsymbol{\theta},\boldsymbol{\pi},\boldsymbol{z}} \\ &= \textstyle\prod_{c\in \boldsymbol{N}\setminus \boldsymbol{M}} p_{\text{DIR}}(\boldsymbol{f}_c(\boldsymbol{T})|\boldsymbol{\alpha}_c) \prod_{c\in \boldsymbol{M}} p_{\text{PYP}}(\boldsymbol{n}_c(\boldsymbol{T})|a_c,b_c), \end{aligned}$$

where $\boldsymbol{n}_c(\boldsymbol{T})$ represents the frequency vector of all adapted rules for nonterminal c being observed in $\boldsymbol{T}$, and $\boldsymbol{f}_c(\boldsymbol{T})$ represents the frequency vector of all PCFG rules for nonterminal c being observed in $\boldsymbol{T}$. The posterior probability for Dirichlet $p_{\text{DIR}}(\boldsymbol{f}|\boldsymbol{\alpha})$ is

$$p_{\text{DIR}}(\boldsymbol{f}_c|\boldsymbol{\alpha}_c) = \frac{\Gamma(\sum_{k=1}^{K}\alpha_k)}{\Gamma(\sum_{k=1}^{K} f_k+\alpha_k)} \prod_{k=1}^{K} \frac{\Gamma(f_k+\alpha_k)}{\Gamma(\alpha_k)},$$

where $K = |\boldsymbol{R}(c)|$ is the number of PCFG rules associated with c, and variables $\boldsymbol{f}$ and $\boldsymbol{\alpha}$ are both vectors of size K.

Given an observation string $\boldsymbol{x}_i$, in order to compute the posterior distribution over its derivation trees, we need to normalize $p(\boldsymbol{T}|\boldsymbol{\alpha},\boldsymbol{a},\boldsymbol{b})$ over all derivation trees that has yields $\boldsymbol{x}_i$. This probability is, unfortunately, intractable to compute, so we turn to *Markov chain Monte Carlo* (MCMC) method and iteratively sample $\boldsymbol{t}_i \sim p(\boldsymbol{t}_i|\boldsymbol{x}_i, \boldsymbol{T}_{-i})$. We construct an "auxiliary" PCFG variable $\boldsymbol{\mathcal{G}}'$ that emulates the PYAG behavior, and approximate the conditional distribution with it. The PCFG approximation $\boldsymbol{\mathcal{G}}' \equiv \langle \boldsymbol{W}, \boldsymbol{N}, \boldsymbol{R}', \boldsymbol{\theta}' \rangle$ can be viewed as a static snapshot of the PYAG given all the derivation trees $\boldsymbol{T}_{-i}$. Let us assume $\boldsymbol{T}_{-i}$ are observations from a PYAG $\boldsymbol{\mathcal{A}} \equiv \langle \boldsymbol{W}, \boldsymbol{N}, \boldsymbol{R}, \boldsymbol{\alpha}, \boldsymbol{M}, \boldsymbol{a}, \boldsymbol{b} \rangle$, the rule set $\boldsymbol{R}'$ in PCFG approximation $\boldsymbol{\mathcal{G}}'$ is defined as

$$\boldsymbol{R}' = \boldsymbol{R} \cup \{c \mapsto \mathsf{yields}(z) : c \in \boldsymbol{M}, z \in \boldsymbol{z}_c\}, \qquad (3)$$

where $\boldsymbol{z}_c$ represents the set of all derivation subtrees observed in $\boldsymbol{T}_{-i}$ that rooted at c, and $\mathsf{yields}(z)$ represents the yields of derivation tree z. Their corresponding rule probability is

$$\begin{aligned} \theta'_{c\mapsto\beta} = &\left(\tfrac{m_c b_c + a_c}{n_c + a_c}\right)\left(\tfrac{f_{c\mapsto\beta}(\boldsymbol{z}_c)+\alpha_{c\mapsto\beta}}{m_c + \sum_{c\mapsto\beta\in\boldsymbol{R}(c)}\alpha_{c\mapsto\beta}}\right) \qquad (4) \\ &+ \textstyle\sum_{z\in\boldsymbol{z}_c:\mathsf{yield}(z)=\beta}\left(\tfrac{n_z-b_c}{n_c+a_c}\right), \end{aligned}$$

where $f_{c\mapsto\beta}(\boldsymbol{z}_c)$ is the frequency count of observing production $c \mapsto \beta$ in all derivation tree set $\boldsymbol{z}_c$, and n_z is the frequency count of observing a particular tree z in all $\boldsymbol{z}_c$. Variable m_c is the number of unique derivation tree, i.e., $m_c = |\boldsymbol{z}_c|$, and n_c is the frequency count of observing all derivation trees rooted at c, i.e., $n_c = \sum_{z\in\boldsymbol{z}_c} n_z$.

The approximation PCFG $\boldsymbol{\mathcal{G}}'$ offers an efficient sampling alternative using Metropolis-Hastings to generate draws from the conditional $p(\boldsymbol{t}_i|\boldsymbol{x}_i, \boldsymbol{T}_{-i})$ [11]. We use it as our proposal distribution in a Metropolis-Hastings algorithm. Let us assume $\boldsymbol{t}_i$ is the current derivation tree, and $\boldsymbol{t}'_i$ is a sample from $p(\boldsymbol{t}_i|\boldsymbol{x}_i, \boldsymbol{T}_{-i})$, we accept the proposal with probability

$$A(\boldsymbol{t}_i \to \boldsymbol{t}'_i) = \min\left(1, \tfrac{p(\boldsymbol{t}'_i,\boldsymbol{T}_{-i}|\boldsymbol{\alpha},\boldsymbol{a},\boldsymbol{b})}{p(\boldsymbol{t}_i,\boldsymbol{T}_{-i}|\boldsymbol{\alpha},\boldsymbol{a},\boldsymbol{b})} \cdot \tfrac{p(\boldsymbol{t}_i|\boldsymbol{x}_i,\boldsymbol{\mathcal{G}}')}{p(\boldsymbol{t}'_i|\boldsymbol{x}_i,\boldsymbol{\mathcal{G}}')}\right). \qquad (5)$$

informational	where, what, which, who, why, when, can, could, shall, should, will, would, how, am, is, are, do, does, ...
navigational	http, www, com, inc, org, company brand, web, site, website, ...
transactional	# best, top #, rating, cost, verse, vs, diff(erence), comparison, compare, instruction(s), before and after, ...

Table 1: Some sample patterns and words for general domain-independent query filtering and preprocessing. We ignore all queries mapping to any of these pattern to reduce sparsity and modeling noises in query dataset.

The overall inference procedure iteratively updates $\mathcal{G}'$, $\boldsymbol{\theta}'$ and $\boldsymbol{t}_i$ until convergence, which follows the standard paradigm:

1: Randomly initialize parse trees for all observations.
2: **while** model not converged **do**
3: Randomly choose observation $\boldsymbol{x}_i$ and its derivation tree $\boldsymbol{t}_i$.
4: Construct PCFG approximation $\mathcal{G}'$ from $\boldsymbol{T}_{-i}$, i.e., update the rule set and probabilities according to Equation 3 and 4.
5: Sample a parse tree $\boldsymbol{t}'_i$ from $\mathcal{G}'$ and accept the proposal according to Equation 5.
6: Adjust the associated counts with rules and grammars.

3. UNSUPERVISED ENTITY EXTRACTION

Our approach consists of three different steps. The first *preprocessing* step (Section 3.1) focuses on cleaning "out-of-domain" queries in different taxonomies (i.e., informational, navigational, and transactional queries) and regularizing the "in-domain" queries (filtering out domain-dependent stopwords). After that, we apply a *query standardization* step—which we discuss in Section 3.2—on all queries to further decrease their sparsity. Finally, in Section 3.3, we describe the grammar rules used for the adaptor grammar.

3.1 Preprocessing

One universal problem of query processing and understanding is the diversity of the queries, which introduces large amount of noise to modeling. The noise is due to possibly multiple reasons, for example, misspelling, tokenization. In addition to misspelling noise, following the general web search taxonomy [4], queries are usually of different forms, including informational (e.g., "what is gnc whey protein"), navigational (e.g., "www bobbi brown com"), and transactional (e.g., "loreal eye serum versus estee lauder eye cream" or "10 best man cologne"). Table 1 shows some of the general patterns and words for each category. In our settings, we ignore any queries matching these forms.

To reduce the noise during our modeling, we also collect some non-conventional stopwords commonly used in shopping queries. For example, marketing events (e.g., "sale", "promo", "deal"), shopping fashion (e.g., "online", "shipping"), price range (e.g., "discount", "cheap"), working condition (e.g., "used", "refurbished"), popularity (e.g., "popular", "hot", "cool"), quality control(e.g., "good", "nice"), etc. These stopwords can be applied universally on all domains, for example—in the scope of this paper—*apparel*, *electronics*, *health and beauty*, *home and garden*, and *sporting goods*. In practice, these non-conventional stopwords can be extracted using statistical methods, for instance, inverse document frequency.

Besides such preprocessing step, to further reduce the sparsity over search patterns and word orderings, we subsequently perform a query standardization step.

3.2 Query Standardization

We collect a set of online shopping queries sampled during a 9-months interval. There are large number of queries that have different word orderings despite the fact that people were searching for the same brand and/or product. For example, the queries "*florajen probiotics*" and "*probiotics florajen*" lead to the same product ("*probiotics*") from the brand ("*florajen*"). We refer to the set of queries containing exactly the same bag of words as one unique ***query family***.

Theoretically, given n words, there can be $n!$ number of unique word orderings available. However, in practice, we do not observe all possible word sequences in the search log for that particular query. In fact, we discover that the distribution over all possible word sequences for any particular query family is very sparse, regardless of different query length n. In practice, we find out that approximately more than 90% of the query families appear in exact one word ordering in our search log, and less than 2% exhibit more than two word orderings, regardless of the query length. In addition to being sparse, the distribution over the word orderings tends to be highly skewed, regardless of the query length or the number of word orderings. Namely, for a query of length n, the number of word orderings actually being observed is significantly smaller than the number of all of its possible word orderings, i.e., $n!$. For instance, significant fraction (approximately 70% to 90%) of them have one predominant word ordering which accounts for more than 60% of the total traffic against all possible word orderings. This well suggests that, in online shopping domain, one query family usually searches for one particular brand and/or product. [3]

Often, users also keep entities as continuous phrases during search, i.e., do *not* interleaving across each other. For instance, in our random sample, we observe following different word orderings for "*miracle gel*" from "*sally hansen*":[4]

sally hansen miracle gel; (96.60%)
miracle gel sally hansen; (3.37%)
sally hansen gel miracle. (0.03%)

where all other possible sequence combinations of these words do not appear in the collected search queries at all. Note that, in this case, the *product* entity "*miracle gel*" gets rewritten to "*gel miracle*" in a small fraction of queries, but it remains continuous as one product entity. Therefore, it is fairly unlikely to see queries or word orderings like "*sally miracle gel hansen*" or "*miracle sally hansen gel*", etc. The sparsity property in word orderings reveals substantial information about online search queries, and essentially enables us to model them using adaptor grammar.

However, these less frequent word orderings certainly introduce a lot of noise during modeling. To address this problem, we perform a query standardization step to reduce the sparsity and group all the word orderings in a query family to the most frequent one. The idea of query standardization is

[3] This phenomena is frequently hold within some particular domain, but not necessarily across different domains. For instance, the query "*paris hilton*" is often referred to the person in **celebrity** domain, whereas "*hilton paris*" often searches for *hilton* hotel in the city of *paris* in **travel** domain.
[4] The number after shows the probability of observing the corresponding word ordering in search logs.

summarized as following:

1: **for** every query family **do**
2: Collect distribution $\{\mathbf{w}_i : c_i\}$, where c_i is the frequency associated with word ordering $\mathbf{w}_i$.
3: Find the word ordering with highest frequency, i.e., $\hat{\mathbf{w}} = \arg\max_{w_i} c_i$, and group the query family to word ordering $\hat{\mathbf{w}}$ with frequency $\sum_i c_i$.

Take the above examples as illustrations, query standardization step reduces multiple search patterns and word orderings to their most frequent ones like following:

$$\left.\begin{array}{l} \textit{sally hansen miracle gel } (96.60\%) \\ \textit{miracle gel sally hansen } (3.37\%) \\ \textit{sally hansen gel miracle } (0.03\%) \end{array}\right\} \Rightarrow \textit{sally hansen miracle gel.}$$

It greatly reduces the sparsity in search patterns and word orderings, hence, significantly improve the parsing performance. In our experiments, our study shows that on average about half of the unique word orderings are aggregated to their predominant patterns.

3.3 Grammar Rules

As previously discussed, users tend to construct their queries in online shopping domain with continuous entity phrases (e.g., *brand*, *product*), and do not interleave them across each other. This allows us to formulate the problem into a *chunking* problem, which is also commonly referred to as the *shallow parsing* of a sentence [1]. However, there are still challenges remaining on identifying *brand* and *product* entities from online shopping queries. One particular challenge in this case, is that, unlike sentences or paragraphs, they often lack of the grammatical information or syntactic structure, since majority of them consist of proper nouns or noun phrases [3]. For instance, *part-of-speech* (POS) tagging information, in this case, is often less accurate than structured sentences or documents. Therefore, classical chunking models do not often work very well.

In addition to word orderings being sparse and highly skewed for each query family, queries often adhere to some generic patterns in online shopping domain, for example, "BRAND PRODUCT". These query search patterns are preserved from aggregated query families. Similar to the distribution over word orderings, the distribution over these patterns is also sparse and highly skewed. Out of the queries searching for the same brand and/or product, we find that significant amount of them follow the pattern of "BRAND PRODUCT", despite the variants of word ordering in each entity type. In fact, for all search queries in shopping domain, pattern "BRAND PRODUCT" is more predominant than any other patterns, such as "PRODUCT BRAND". Such a property inspires us to solve the problem with an approach akin to shallow grammar parsing, and we want our chunking model to be as "context-free" as possible.

However, as discussed in Section 2, vanilla *probabilistic context-free grammars* (PCFG) model imposes strong independence assumption between grammar rules and internal structures of derivation trees, such context-freeness hypothesis may often lead to less accurate language modeling. Unlike PCFG—its parametric counterpart—adaptor grammars constantly cache the derivation trees and dynamically expands the grammar rule set in a completely data-driven fashion. Therefore, it provides a more flexible modeling option than PCFG. In addition, it is an unsupervised method, and hence does not require any human annotation efforts to extract the *brand* and *product* entities from a large collection of online search queries.

We start with a simple grammar that decomposes a query into a BRAND, a PRODUCT or a simple combination of both:

QUERY → BRAND	PRODUCT → WORDS
QUERY → PRODUCT	WORDS → WORD WORDS
QUERY → BRAND PRODUCT	WORDS → WORD
BRAND → WORDS	WORD → ...

The underlined nonterminals refer to the adaptors, i.e., the adapted nonterminal nodes, such that derivation trees rewriting them will be cached by the framework, and subsequently added to the grammar rule set. We refer this grammar as the **chunk** grammar.

However, in practice, we found that it is not enough to capture some other common patterns with prepositional phrases, for example, "*sephora shea butter for lips*", "*chin strap to stop snoring*", "*massage oils at walgreens*", "*nail polish bottles with brush*", etc. Therefore, we propose the **chunk+prep** grammar to explicitly modeling prepositional phrases:

QUERY → BRAND	BRAND → WORDS
QUERY → PRODUCT	PRODUCT → WORDS
QUERY → BRAND PRODUCT	WORDS → WORD WORDS
QUERY → QUERY PREPPHRASE	WORDS → WORD
PREPPHRASE → PREP WORDS	WORD → ...
PREP → for|to|by|with|at|...	

These prepositional phrases are sometimes informative, such that they reveal possible *brand* entity, e.g., "*at walgreens*", "*at cvs*". On the other hand, they can also be noisy, e.g., "*at home*", "*at night*". This grammar explicitly models all prepositional phrases. We leave the study of utilizing prepositional phrases to identify *brand* and *product* entities as future work.

This grammar, again, overlooks another important information, i.e., it does not capture the modifier information about the product. These modifiers could be descriptions, but more likely are model names or product families. For example, the word "*professional*" in the query "*andis professional hair clippers*" is a general description. The phrase "*despicable me minion*" in the query "*despicable me minion hoodie*" modifies a product. The word "*hdmi*" specifies a product family in the query "*iogear wireless hdmi transmitter and receiver*". The phrase "*galaxy s1*" in the query "*samsung galaxy s1 cell phone*" is a model number. The word "*tv*" specifies the purpose of the product in the query "*ge coaxial tv cable*". To address this, we further extend it to the **chunk+prep+mod** grammar:

QUERY → BRAND	BRAND → WORDS
QUERY → MODPROD	PRODUCT → WORDS
QUERY → BRAND MODPROD	MODIFIER → WORDS
QUERY → QUERY PREPPHRASE	WORDS → WORD WORDS
MODPROD → MODIFIER PRODUCT	WORDS → WORD
PREPPHRASE → PREP WORDS	WORD → ...
PREP → for|to|by|with|at|...	

We found this grammar works best in practice. In Section 4, we conduct experimental study on the performance under different grammars, and show empirical evaluation of our approach against the vanilla PCFG approach.

4. EXPERIMENTS

In this section, we report the empirical result of our approach on a large collection of web shopping queries. To the best of our knowledge, there are no off-the-shelf unsupervised methods available to automatically identify *brand* and *product* entities from online shopping search queries. We compare our approach against the vanilla probabilistic context-free

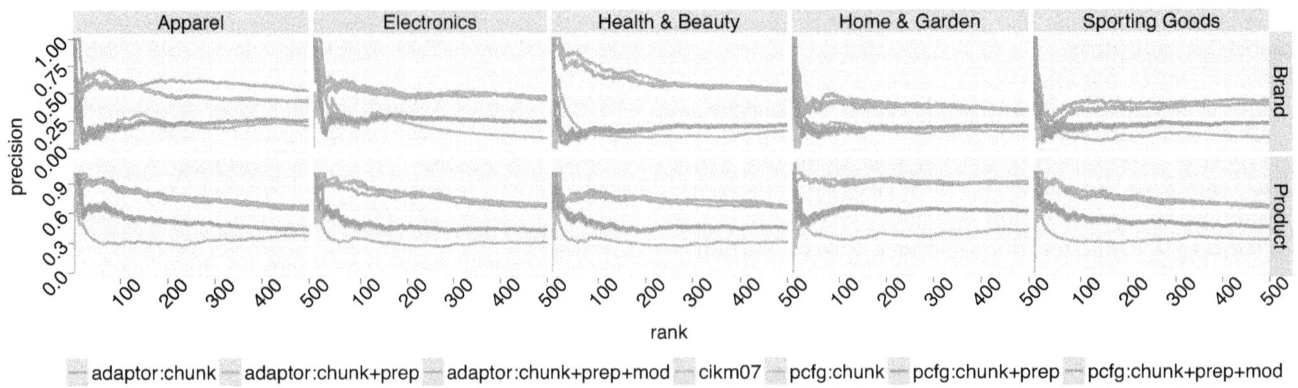

Figure 3: Precision against entity rank discovered by different approaches with different grammars regarding to 5 domains and 2 entity types. Precision is evaluated by professional editors. Our approach constantly achieves better performance.

grammar [21, PCFG] with the same parsing grammar. Different than adaptor grammars, which imposes a Pitman-Yor process prior on the distributions over grammar rules, we assume a Dirichlet distribution as the prior for PCFG. We learn the PCFG using Bayesian inference with a MCMC sampler [16]. This PCFG approach is akin to the shallow parsing approach [1] as discussed in Section 3.3, so serves as a comparable unsupervised baseline for our model. In addition, we also compare against a semi-supervised approach [25, CIKM07]. For every domain and entity type, we seed the model with a collection of 5 popular entities as suggested in [25]. The seeded list for corresponding *brand* and *product* entities for each domain are shown as below:

Apparel	*nike, michael kors, ugg, ray ban, kate spade* *shoe, dress, handbag, engagement ring, hat*
Electronics	*samsung, sony, dell, apple, canon* *printer, tablet, cell phone, remote control, laptop*
Health & Beauty	*estee lauder, gnc, urban decay, mac, opi* *supplement, shampoo, nail polish, soap, lipstick*
Home & Garden	*home depot, john deere, sears, target, lowes* *lights, chairs, curtains, lamps, pillows*
Sporting Goods	*under armour, nike, adidas, puma, kappa* *jacket, bike, pants, socks, helmet*

We first conduct intrinsic evaluation of our model against both PCFG and CIKM07 on knowledge discovery. Then, we assess the quality of the inferred knowledgebase extrinsically by using them as features on two external tasks.

4.1 Intrinsic Evaluation

The data we use are raw queries in shopping domain collected from a commercial search engine during a 9-month time interval. We retrieve all queries that have at least one online ads click, and randomly sample them. Based on the most frequent product category of their clicked ads, these queries are classified into following 5 different domains: *Apparel*, *Electronics*, *Health & Beauty*, *Home & Garden*, and *Sporting Goods*, which contains $906K$, $444K$, $625K$, $1.1M$ and $412K$ unique queries respectively. For both PCFG and our unsupervised approaches, we train them based on adaptor grammars on all available data. During our experiments, we let all MCMC samplers running for 2000 iterations to make sure all models are fully converged. For our unsupervised approach, we examine hyperparameter settings of $a = \{0.01, 0.05, 0.1\}$ and $b = \{100, 500, 1000\}$ for PYP. For the PCFG approach, recall that Dirichlet distribution is defined by its scaling parameter α, we examine different settings of $\{0.01, 0.05, 0.1\}$ in our experiments. For both unsupervised approaches, we report the performance on the model with highest data likelihood. We collect the distributions over all discovered entities and rank them according to their probabilities. For semi-supervised approach CIKM07, we rank all entities by Jensen-Shannon as suggested. We evaluate all approaches on the precision measure at different rank of the retrieved entity types.

Precision @ Rank. In order to give a comprehensive study of our approach, we looked into the precision of the retrieved entities at different rank for different approaches with different grammars. Precision measures the percentage of retrieved entities which correctly belong to an entity type. The precision is evaluated by professional editors judging if a retrieved entity belongs to the corresponding type. Figure 3 captures the performance on precision at different ranks of both *brand* and *product* entities discovered in dataset of each domain. Our approach constantly achieves better performance than CIKM07 and PCFG under all grammars. For grammars, we notice that **chunk+prep+mod** grammar yields better or comparable performance than other two grammars. We find that the semi-supervised approach CIKM07 often discovers entities in a greedy manner. For instance, in addition to "*apple*", it also ranks high on "*apple mac*" and "*hdmi cable for apple*" as *brand* names. Besides "*dress*", it also identifies "*calvin klein dress*" or "*black dress*" as *product*. In addition, we also find CIKM07 model takes much more memory resource and longer computation time to train, partly due to the large variance in search patterns. Subsampling the dataset increases the speed, but would downgrade the performance. In contrast, our proposed approach (and all PCFG-based approaches, in general) utilizes the context-free grammar rules, which are more compact, efficient and memory-friendly than flat representations. For *sporting goods* domain, all approaches yield low precision in identifying *brand* entity types. This is mainly due to the reason that our models discover a lot of sports team and club names (refer to Table 2 for examples). By our guidelines in Definition 1, even though these sport clubs are the branding or advertisement carriers for many products, they are considered *organizations*, rather than the actual *brand*. Instead, their respective sponsors—such as "*nike*", "*under armour*", etc—are.

Discovered Entities. Table 2 lists the most frequent *brands*, *products*, prepositional and modifier phrases identified by our approach based on adaptor grammars. Our approach is able to correctly identify complicated *brand* entities (e.g., "*tiffany and co*", "*at t*", "*bath and body works*", "*bed bath and beyond*"

	Apparel	Electronics	Health & Beauty	Home & Garden	Sporting Goods
Brand	michael kors	samsung	estee lauder	home depot	under armour
	north face	sony	gnc	walmart	dallas cowboys
	under armour	dell	walmart	john deere	nike
	vera bradley	samsung galaxy	urban decay	sears	green bay packers
	kate spade	apple	mac	target	denver broncos
	alex and ani	walmart	opi	lowes	chicago bears
	tiffany and co	bose	neutrogena	craftsman	seahawks
	columbia	rca	lancome	hamilton beach	notre dame
	oakley	at t	bath and body works	battery operated	orleans saints
	dooney and bourke	straight talk	too faced	bed bath and beyond	adidas
Product	running shoes	printer	supplement	lights	apparel
	wedding dresses	phone	hair products	chairs	jacket
	handbags	tablet	nail polish	curtains	accessories
	engagement ring	cell phone	soap	lamps	bike
	hats	remote control	lipstick	pillows	hoodie
	jeans	phone cases	eyeglass frames	cabinets	backpack
	necklace	cable	essential oil	bed	knife
	watch	ink cartridges	contact lenses	coffee table	pants
	rain boots	printers	protein powder	lighting fixtures	helmet
	sunglasses	adapter	shampoo and conditioner	shower curtain	socks
PrepPhrase	for toddlers	at walmart	for weight loss	at home depot	for football
	with sleeves	for laptop	for natural hair	for the home	for hunting
	for babies	with microphone	for thinning hair	for bathroom	for the money
	for teens	for mac	for plantar fasciitis	with lights	for baseball
	with pockets	with answering machine	for adults	with storage	for fishing
	for little girls	for the money	for fine hair	for living room	with wheels
	with hood	for ipad mini	at home	with wheels	for home
	with diamonds	for cars	for oily skin	with drawers	for bikes
	for school	for windows	for curly hair	by the yard	for beginners
	with rhinestones	for seniors	for babies	for crafts	for guns
Modifier	halloween	cell phone	blood pressure	dining room	football
	girls	wireless	hair	outdoor	golf
	leather	mini	natural	kitchen	pro
	gold	all in one	gel	stainless steel	fishing
	sexy	tv	weight loss	christmas	super bowl
	toddler	pro	liquid	electric	youth
	baby	phone	nail polish	christmas tree	baseball
	boys	portable	anti aging	cast iron	elite
	vintage	wifi	plus	furniture	training
	ladies	smart	pro	glass	marine

Table 2: Most frequent *brand* entities, *product* entities, prepositional and modifier phrases discovered by our approach based on adaptor grammars using ***chunk+prep+mod*** grammar for each shopping domain.

and "*green bay packers*") and *product* entities (e.g., "*engagement ring*", "*remote control*", "*shampoo and conditioner*", "*coffee table*" and "*hoodie*") of arbitrary length in a completely unsupervised data-driven fashion. One interesting observations is that our model discovers some joint phrases, such as "*samsung galaxy*", which is more like a combination of a *brand* entity ("*samsung*") with a model modifier "*galaxy*". This again is due to the nonparametric nature of the modeling framework, i.e., if the model sees a large amount of such phrases appear in the dataset, it would identify the entire phrase as a segment. On the other hand, PCFG is less capable in discovering such phrases, simply because it imposes too much independent assumption on the underlying grammar. One thing worth to note is, for the *sporting goods* category, we discover a lot of sports team names, these are due to the reason that queries fall into this domain are often looking for team jerseys, jackets, hats, etc.

In addition, our approach also discovers a lot of popular *prepositional phrases* for each shopping domain, e.g., "*for little girls*", "*with answering machine*", "*for oily skin*", "*by the yard*" and "*for beginners*", as well as some common modifier under each domain, e.g., "*halloween*", "*all in one*", "*anti aging*", "*stainless steel*" and "*super bowl*". These prepositional and modifiers phrases are modeled jointly with the *brand* and *product* entities, and provides additional information or constraints to the products.

4.2 Extrinsic Evaluation

In addition to intrinsic evaluation, we also conduct extrinsic empirical study on the quality of our discovered knowledgebase to external tasks. We use knowledgebase extracted from different approaches as features to external tasks and evaluate its effectiveness. For the purpose, we build, train and test two supervised algorithms—a query tagging model based on *conditional random fields* [18, CRF], and a query chunking model based on *maximum entropy* method [17, MAXENT].

For every category, we reserve a collection of $3K$ random samples, and manually annotate them with professional editors. In addition to *brand* and *product*, the label space also includes other entity types, such as model number, product family, attribute specification, etc. We split the labeled dataset by 80% for training and 20% for testing. For both CRF and MAXENT models, we use contextual features including words and their lemmas in a 5-word surrounding window; and lexical features including surface, pattern, shape and length of previous, current and next word. In addition, we also use the knowledgebase lookup features by examining if we find a match of the target word in any entity inside our extracted knowledgebase. We gradually increase the size of the knowledgebase, and evaluate the performance of CRF and MAXENT at different rank. We choose all parameters using 5-fold cross validation on the training data, and report the performance of the best settings.

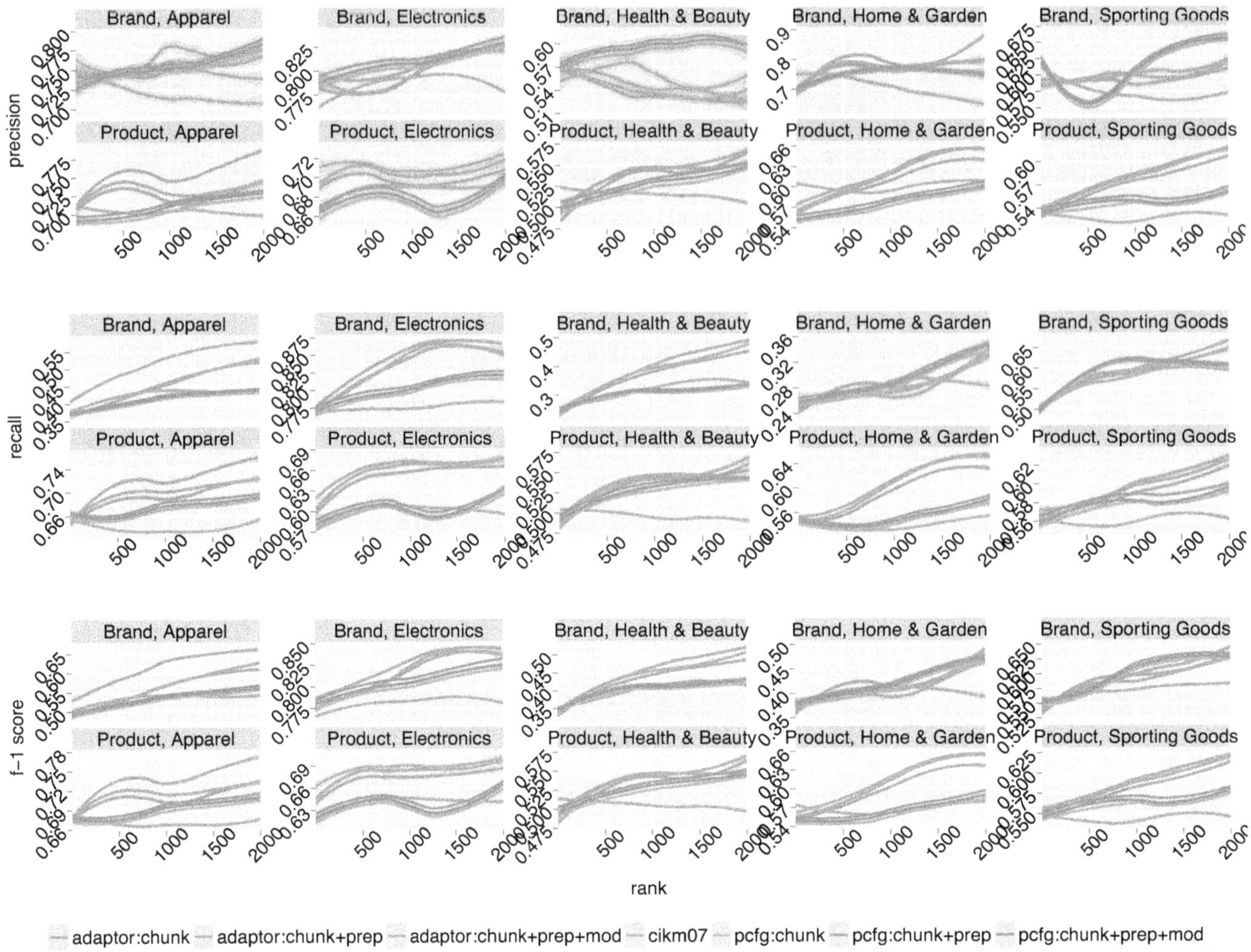

Figure 4: Precision, recall, and F_1 score of CRF tagging model on different entity types in 5 domains against the rank (size) of the knowledgebase discovered by different approaches under different grammars. Plots are smoothed to reflect clear trends. The sequence tagger constantly improves recall when we reveal more entries from the discovered knowledgebase to the model. This implies the knowledgebase discovered by our model is of good quality and provides better coverage to this tasks.

Query Tagging Model. Figure 4 shows the precision, recall, and F_1 score of CRF model on different entity types in 5 domains against the rank (size) of the knowledgebase used to generate features. These knowledgebases are extracted by different approaches with different grammars. We gradually increase the knowledgebase by the step size 50. The precision measure drops initially, but after we increase the knowledgebase to a certain threshold, which has sufficient coverage over all entity types, it starts to improve. On the recall measure, the performance of CRF tagger constantly improves when we reveal more entries from the discovered knowledgebase to the model. This implies the knowledgebase discovered by our model provides a good coverage to this tasks. The overall F_1 score demonstrates consistent improvements against entity rank. In addition, we show that the CRF sequence tagger constantly yields better performance when using knowledgebase extracted by our model based on adaptor grammar, as oppose to using the one discovered by the PCFG or CIKM07. This well indicates the knowledgebase discovered by our model is of good quality and hence can be used to improve the performance of external models.

Query Chunking Model. Figure 5 shows the precision, recall, and F_1 score of MAXENT model in 5 domains against the rank (size) of the knowledgebase used to generate features. We observe a similar behavior with previous query tagging task, such that the performance on recall and F_1 measure of MAXENT model constantly improves. This is possibly due to the reason that, as we reveal more entities from the knowledgebase discovered by our approach to the model, it establishes more sufficient coverage to the chunker. In contrast, the knowledgebases extracted by PCFG and CIKM07 models are not effective enough, and the respective performance on recall and F_1 measure does not change much. This again well implies the knowledgebase discovered by our model provides much better coverage than the ones extracted by PCFG or CIKM07 approach.

5. RELATED WORK

The objective of this work is to automatically identify *brand* and *product* entities from query logs in a complete unsupervised way. This is very different from classic *named entity recognition* (NER) problem, and can be significantly more challenging. First, unlike person names, organization titles or location labels, almost all of the products are *not*

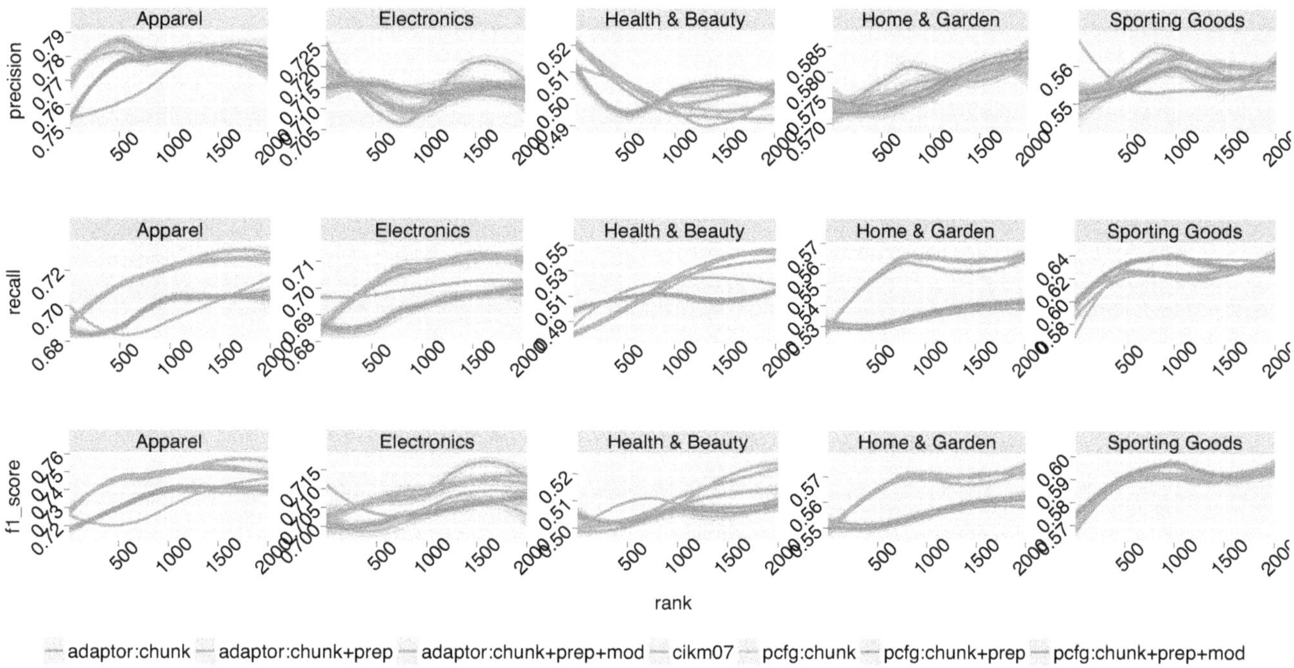

Figure 5: Precision, recall, and F_1 score of MAXENT chunking model in 5 domains against the rank (size) of the knowledgebase discovered by different approaches with different grammars. Plots are smoothed to reflect clear trends. As we reveal more entities from the discovered knowledgebase to the model, the performance over recall of MAXENT chunking model constantly improves. This indicates the knowledgebase discovered by our model is of good quality.

notable entity names. They often do not carry very indicative surface features (e.g., capitalization) nor grammar properties (e.g., structural patterns). For example, "Mr." and "Dr." may very well indicate person names; "Inc" and "Ltd" are strong indicators for organization titles; a location address usually follows the pattern of *street* + *city* + *state* or *province* + *zip codes*. Second, classic NER frameworks usually works on a collection of sentences or paragraphs, which contains rich contextual information and semantic structures. In our case, we operate the framework on a collection of web search queries, which are usually short and noisy (e.g., misspelling, arbitrary ordering, etc).

To the best of our knowledge, there have been very limited research efforts attempting to extract *brand* and *product* entities from query logs automatically. We summarize a few past approaches for NER in queries, either in a supervised or semi-supervised way.

The problem of open-domain entity recognition and extraction from web search queries is originally proposed in [25], which they rely on a seed-based weakly-supervised method. The method starts with a set of human labeled named entities—commonly referred to as seeds—and iteratively acquires new named entities explicitly from web queries. Li et al. [19] propose a semi-supervised approach based on conditional random fields method to extract entities from user queries. Guo et al. [12] introduce another weakly-supervised method, using partially labeled named entities as seeds, and train topic models on different domains. Pantel et al. [28] extend this work to jointly model user intent as latent variables in the framework. However, both of these methods are limited to the queries containing only one named entity.

Later, [14] propose a multi-stage method on different domains. The method starts with extracting named-entity candidates from query logs using surface-level properties, e.g., capitalization, etc. It then filters out the uncertain candidates and applies clustering based on different feature space. It works considerably well on domains like celebrities, cities, diseases, movies, etc, partly because queries of these domains usually carry along very indicative surface features.

In another study, Du et al. [7] focus on the domain of car models and use the entire search session as additional contextual information. They train both conditional random fields and topic models with new contextual features and demonstrate significant improvement. More recently, Alasiry et al. [2] determine named entities using grammar annotation and query segmentation with the help of additional snippets from web resources. Eiselt and Figueroa [8] propose a supervised two-step approach to identify named entities from open-domain search queries.

Unfortunately, all these works rely on semi-supervised methods with additional human annotations, which can be costly to acquire. To address this problem, we propose a completely unsupervised method based on adaptor grammar [15]. It does not require any human annotation efforts (e.g., named entity seeds or labeled data) which typically can be expensive to acquire. Our method also does not rely on additional web resources, such as query sequences in search sessions or web snippets.

6. CONCLUSION AND FUTURE WORK

Adaptor grammars [15] offer a great flexibility and modeling advantage in probabilistic context-free grammar parsing. In this paper, we apply the adaptor grammar model on a collection of queries in online shopping domain to extract *brand* and *product* entities efficiently and effectively. We propose a three step approach. The first step preprocesses the noisy query data and cleans up all stopwords. We then conduct a query standardization step, which aggregates and groups less frequent word orderings, to further reduce the noise and regularize the queries. Finally, we propose three different sets of grammar rules to infer the query structures and extract the entities in a completely data-driven fashion. We compare our model against the vanilla PCFG approach—a variant akin to the shallow parsing approach—and demonstrate significant better performance on precision measure on retrieved *brand* and *product* entities. We also evaluate the effectiveness of the discovered knowledgebase on two external supervised tasks—a query tagging model based on conditional random fields and a query chunking model based on maximum entropy model. We show that the knowledgebase discovered by our framework is of high quality and significantly improves the overall performance of both models.

We would also like to point out some possible future directions of our work. One possible extension is to use the variational Bayesian inference [6] as oppose to the MCMC method in this paper. It offers a more scalable alternative and easier amendable to online learning [33] and parallelization [32]. One limitation of our work is that we do not explicitly model the *product families* and *model numbers* during parsing. Instead, we subsume them all into the adaptor nonterminal MODIFIER. Such information can be critical for a query understanding system to better understand the constraints and prompt more desirable results to users during search and ranking. In the future, we would like to explore along this direction to jointly model these entities in adaptor grammar framework.

7. REFERENCES

[1] S. P. Abney. *Parsing by chunks*. Springer, 1992.

[2] A. Alasiry, M. Levene, and A. Poulovassilis. Detecting candidate named entities in search queries. In *SIGIR*, 2012.

[3] C. Barr, R. Jones, and M. Regelson. The linguistic structure of english web-search queries. In *EMNLP*, 2008.

[4] A. Broder. A taxonomy of web search. *SIGIR Forum*, 36(2), Sept. 2002.

[5] M. J. Cafarella, D. Downey, S. Soderland, and O. Etzioni. Knowitnow: Fast, scalable information extraction from the web. In *EMNLP*, 2005.

[6] S. B. Cohen, D. M. Blei, and N. A. Smith. Variational inference for adaptor grammars. In *NAACL*, 2010.

[7] J. Du, Z. Zhang, J. Yan, Y. Cui, and Z. Chen. Using search session context for named entity recognition in query. In *SIGIR*, 2010.

[8] A. Eiselt and A. Figueroa. A two-step named entity recognizer for open-domain search queries. In *IJCNLP*, 2013.

[9] O. Etzioni, M. Cafarella, D. Downey, A.-M. Popescu, T. Shaked, S. Soderland, D. S. Weld, and A. Yates. Unsupervised named-entity extraction from the web: An experimental study. *Artificial intelligence*, 165(1), 2005.

[10] P. Exner and P. Nugues. Entity extraction: From unstructured text to dbpedia rdf triples. In *The Web of Linked Entities Workshop (WoLE 2012)*, 2012.

[11] J. T. Goodman. *Parsing Inside-out*. PhD thesis, Cambridge, MA, USA, 1998.

[12] J. Guo, G. Xu, X. Cheng, and H. Li. Named entity recognition in query. In *SIGIR*, 2009.

[13] H. Ishwaran and L. F. James. Generalized weighted chinese restaurant processes for species sampling mixture models. *Statistica Sinica*, 13(4), 2003.

[14] A. Jain and M. Pennacchiotti. Open entity extraction from web search query logs. In *COLING*, 2010.

[15] M. Johnson, T. L. Griffiths, and S. Goldwater. Adaptor grammars: A framework for specifying compositional nonparametric Bayesian models. In *NIPS*, 2007.

[16] M. Johnson, T. L. Griffiths, and S. Goldwater. Bayesian inference for PCFGs via Markov chain Monte Carlo. In *NAACL*, 2007.

[17] R. Koeling. Chunking with maximum entropy models. In *Proceedings of the 2nd workshop on Learning language in logic and the 4th conference on Computational natural language learning-Volume 7*, 2000.

[18] J. Lafferty, A. McCallum, and F. C. Pereira. Conditional random fields: probabilistic models for segmenting and labeling sequence data. In *ICML*, 2001.

[19] X. Li, Y.-Y. Wang, and A. Acero. Extracting structured information from user queries with semi-supervised conditional random fields. In *SIGIR*, 2009.

[20] B. Liu, R. Grossman, and Y. Zhai. Mining data records in web pages. In *KDD*, 2003.

[21] C. D. Manning and H. Schütze. *Foundations of Statistical Natural Language Processing*. The MIT Press, Cambridge, MA, 1999.

[22] D. Nadeau. *Semi-supervised named entity recognition: learning to recognize 100 entity types with little supervision*. PhD thesis, 2007.

[23] D. Nadeau and S. Sekine. A survey of named entity recognition and classification. *Lingvisticae Investigationes*, 30(1), 2007.

[24] J. Nothman, J. R. Curran, and T. Murphy. Transforming wikipedia into named entity training data. In *Proceedings of the Australian Language Technology Workshop*, 2008.

[25] M. Paşca. Weakly-supervised discovery of named entities using web search queries. In *CIKM*, 2007.

[26] M. Paşca. Queries as a source of lexicalized commonsense knowledge. In *EMNLP*, October 2014.

[27] M. Paşca. Interpreting compound noun phrases using web search queries. In *NAACL*, 2015.

[28] P. Pantel, T. Lin, and M. Gamon. Mining entity types from query logs via user intent modeling. In *ACL*, 2012.

[29] J. Pitman and M. Yor. The two-parameter Poisson-Dirichlet distribution derived from a stable subordinator. *Annals of Probability*, 25(2), 1997.

[30] L. Ratinov and D. Roth. Design challenges and misconceptions in named entity recognition. In *CoNLL*, 2009.

[31] T.-L. Wong, W. Lam, and T.-S. Wong. An unsupervised framework for extracting and normalizing product attributes from multiple web sites. In *SIGIR*, 2008.

[32] K. Zhai, J. Boyd-Graber, N. Asadi, and M. L. Alkhouja. Mr. lda: A flexible large scale topic modeling package using variational inference in mapreduce. In *WWW*, 2012.

[33] K. Zhai, J. Boyd-Graber, and S. Cohen. Online adaptor grammars with hybrid inference. *TACL*, 2, 2014.

Learning for Efficient Supervised Query Expansion via Two-stage Feature Selection

Zhiwei Zhang[1]*, Qifan Wang[2], Luo Si[13], Jianfeng Gao[4]
[1]Dept of CS, Purdue University, IN, USA [2]Google Inc, Mountain View, USA
[3]Alibaba Group Inc, USA [4]Microsoft Research, Redmond, WA, USA
{zhan1187,lsi}@purdue.edu, wqfcr@google.com, jfgao@microsoft.com

ABSTRACT

Query expansion (QE) is a well known technique to improve retrieval effectiveness, which expands original queries with extra terms that are predicted to be relevant. A recent trend in the literature is Supervised Query Expansion (SQE), where supervised learning is introduced to better select expansion terms. However, an important but neglected issue for SQE is its efficiency, as applying SQE in retrieval can be much more time-consuming than applying Unsupervised Query Expansion (UQE) algorithms. In this paper, we point out that the cost of SQE mainly comes from term feature extraction, and propose a Two-stage Feature Selection framework (TFS) to address this problem. The first stage is adaptive expansion decision, which determines if a query is suitable for SQE or not. For unsuitable queries, SQE is skipped and no term features are extracted at all, which reduces the most time cost. For those suitable queries, the second stage is cost constrained feature selection, which chooses a subset of effective yet inexpensive features for supervised learning. Extensive experiments on four corpora (including three academic and one industry corpus) show that our TFS framework can substantially reduce the time cost for SQE, while maintaining its effectiveness.

Categories and Subject Descriptors

H.3.3 [**Information Search and Retrieval**]: Information Search and Retrieval

Keywords

Query Expansion; Supervised Learning; Efficiency

1. INTRODUCTION

Queries provided by users can sometimes be ambiguous and inaccurate in an information retrieval system, which may generate unsatisfactory results. Query expansion (QE) is a well known technique to address this issue, which expands the original queries with some extra terms that are predicted to be relevant [26]. It is hoped that these expanded terms can capture user's true intent that is missed in original query, thus improving the final retrieval effectiveness. In the past decades, various applications [26, 6] have proved its value.

Unsupervised QE (UQE) algorithms used to be the mainstream in the QE literature. Many famous algorithms, such as relevance model (RM) [21] and thesaurus based methods [29], have been widely applied. However, recent studies [5, 22] showed that a large portion of expansion terms selected by UQE algorithms are noisy or even harmful, which limits their performance. *Supervised Query Expansion* (SQE) is proposed to overcome this disadvantage by leveraging the power of supervised learning. Most of existing SQE algorithms [5, 22, 13, 25, 2] follow a classical machine learning pipeline: (1) utilize UQE to select initial candidate terms; (2) features of candidate terms are extracted; (3) pre-trained classifiers or rankers are utilized to select the best terms for expansion. Significant effectiveness improvement has been reported over their unsupervised counterparts, and SQE has become the new state-of-the-art.

Besides effectiveness, efficiency is another important issue in QE-involved retrieval [35]. As we will show later, UQE algorithms are usually very efficient to apply. Therefore, when UQE is adopted in retrieval, the major inefficiency comes from the second retrieval, which retrieves the entire corpus for the expanded queries. This issue is traditionally handled by indexing or documents optimization [35, 3, 30]. But recently Diaz [11] showed that simply reranking the retrieval results of original queries can already provide nearly identical performance with very low time costs, particularly for precision-oriented metrics.

However, the efficiency issue of SQE algorithms imposes new challenge beyond the UQE case. Compared with UQE algorithms, SQE requires extra time to apply supervised learning, which can incur significant time cost. Moreover, this issue is unique to SQE, and cannot be addressed by previous QE efficiency methods such as indexing optimization or reranking. Unfortunately, although important, this issue has been largely neglected in the literature.

The above observations motivate us to propose new research to address this SQE efficiency problem. In this paper, we point out that the major time cost of applying SQE algorithms comes from term feature extraction. Indeed leveraging extensive features can enhance the effectiveness of supervised learning, so that better expansion terms can be selected. However, it also inevitably decreases the efficiency. Aiming at this point, we propose a Two-stage Fea-

*Part of this work was done while the first author interned at Microsoft.

SIGIR '16, July 17-21, 2016, Pisa, Italy
© 2016 ACM. ISBN 978-1-4503-4069-4/16/07... $15.00
DOI: http://dx.doi.org/10.1145/2911451.2911539

ture Selection framework (TFS) to balance the two conflicting goals. The first stage is Adaptive Expansion Decision (AED), which predicts whether a query is suitable for SQE or not. For unsuitable queries, SQE is skipped with no features being extracted, so that the time cost is reduced most. For suitable queries, the second stage conducts Cost Constrained Feature Selection (CCFS), which chooses a subset of effective yet inexpensive features for supervised learning. We then instantiate TFS for a RankSVM based SQE algorithm. Extensive experiments on four corpora (including three academic and one industry corpus) show that our TFS framework can substantially reduce the time cost of SQE algorithm, meanwhile maintaining its effectiveness.

The rest of the paper is organized as follows: Sec. 2 introduces the preliminaries of our work, including problem analysis and literature review; Sec. 3 presents the Two-stage Feature Selection framework and its instantiation; Sec. 4 gives all experiments, and in Sec. 5 we conclude this paper.

2. PRELIMINARIES

In this section, we will thoroughly analyze the SQE efficiency problem. Meanwhile we will review the literature, and point out the difference between our work and previous works. The discussions below are presented in three subsections, each covering one specific aspect.

2.1 QE Algorithm Analysis

First we will review some basics about query epansion.

QE Formulation. Suppose we have a user query q with n terms $q = \{t_i^q|i = 1 : n\}$. Suppose m expansion terms are selected by a QE algorithm, denoted as $\{t_i^e|i = 1 : m\}$. Then the expanded query q^e is their union, i.e. $q^e = \{t^q\} \cup \{t^e\}$. Each term $t \in q^e$ is weighted by the interpolated probability

$$P(t|q^e) = (1 - \lambda)P(t|q) + \lambda P_{QE}(t) \quad (1)$$

where $P(t|q)$ is the probability of term t occurring in q (i.e. $P(t|q) = \frac{\text{frequency of term } t \text{ in } q}{\text{query length } |q|}$), $P_{QE}(t)$ is the term probability given by QE algorithm, and λ is the interpolation coefficient to be tuned. As can be seen, the key question here is how to select good expansion terms.

UQE versus SQE. Unsupervised QE (UQE) algorithms used to be the mainstream in QE literature. For example, some well known UQE algorithms include relevance model (RM) [21], positional relevance model [24], and mixture model [36]. UQE algorithms are very popular because on one hand their formulations are in general simple, and on the other hand their empirical performance is quite reasonable. However, recent works [5, 22] observed that a large portion of the expansion terms from UQE can be noisy or even harmful, which limits their performance.

SQE tackles this problem by introducing supervised learning to predict the quality of candidate expansion terms. Cao et al. [5] proposed perhaps the first SQE research, where they designed a set of term features and applied SVM for term classification (either good or bad). Later Lee et al. [22] claimed that ranking oriented term selection outperforms classification oriented methods. Gao et al. [13, 12] applied SQE to web search, where search log is utilized for candidate term generation. Some other extensions include QE robustness [25], query reformulation [2], etc. A common pipeline of SQE training and testing [5, 13] is summarized in Alg. 1. Notice here we only concern test-time efficiency, rather than the training-time efficiency.

Algorithm 1 SQE Training and Testing Pipeline

▷ Training SQE model $\mathcal{H}$
1: For training query q, record its retrieval accuracy r^q (e.g. ERR@20). Select M candidate terms $\{t_i^c|\text{i=1:M}\}$ via UQE.
2: Each time, a single candidate term t^c is appended to q, i.e. $q^c = q \cup t^c$; record its retrieval accuracy r_c^q; then $\Delta r_c^q = r_c^q - r^q$ is the label for t^c.
3: Extract term features $\mathcal{F}_t$ for all t^c, and train a classifier (based on if $\Delta r_c^q > 0$ or $\Delta r_c^q \le 0$) or train a ranker (based on the ranking order of Δr_c^q), denoted as $\mathcal{H}$.

▷ Testing (i.e. applying $\mathcal{H}$ in QE retrieval)
1: For testing query q, use UQE to select M candidate terms.
2: Extract $\mathcal{F}_t$ for all candidate terms.
3: Apply $\mathcal{H}$ to get top m terms for expansion.

2.2 QE Efficiency Analysis

Now we will analyze the efficiency issue when QE is applied in retrieval.

QE in Retrieval. The retrieval process with QE can be described as follows. Let $\mathcal{C}$ denote the target corpus upon which we will run and evaluate retrieval; denote $\mathcal{S}$ as the resource from which expansion terms are extracted. In traditional pseudo relevance feedback (PRF) scenario [6], $\mathcal{S} = \mathcal{C}$. In more general scenario, $\mathcal{S}$ is not necessarily the same as $\mathcal{C}$. For example, in web search, $\mathcal{C}$ (e.g. Clueweb09) might be too low-quality to be used for QE [1]; instead some other resources of higher quality can be used as $\mathcal{S}$ (e.g. search log [10] or Wikipedia [1]). Assuming a retrieval algorithm (e.g. BM25 or KL divergence) is utilized, then a typical process of QE in retrieval is summarized in Table 1:

Table 1: QE in retrieval with and without reranking.

(1) First Retrieval: search original query q on resource $\mathcal{S}$;
(2) Applying QE Model: select expansion terms $\{t^e\}$ from $\mathcal{S}$.
(3) Second Retrieval:
(Full) retrieve corpus $\mathcal{C}$ for expanded query q^e.
——OR——
(Reranking)
(A) If $\mathcal{C} \neq \mathcal{S}$, retrieve $\mathcal{C}$ for q, denote the results as L;
If $\mathcal{C} = \mathcal{S}$, then let the results of first retrieval as L;
(B) Rerank L for expanded query q^e.

In the above table we list two possible implementations of second retrieval. The full second retrieval is more traditional, in which the entire target corpus $\mathcal{C}$ is retrieved for expanded query q^e. This, however, is painfully time-consuming, particularly on large scale corpus. Recently Diaz [11] suggested to rerank the retrieval results of original query q as the results for q^e. Diaz pointed out that this reranking implementation can provide nearly identical performance as the full second retrieval, particularly for precision-oriented evaluation metrics. Our preliminary experiments also verified this statement. Therefore throughout this paper, we will utilize reranking as the default implementation for second retrieval. Notice in the (A) step, we present the different implementation details regarding both PRF scenario ($\mathcal{C} = \mathcal{S}$) and non-PRF scenario ($\mathcal{C} \neq \mathcal{S}$).

Existing QE Efficiency Studies. Despite the usefulness of reranking, the majority of existing works on QE efficiency still focused on how to speed up the full second retrieval. As far as we know, all of these works addressed the problem by optimizing underlying data structures such as indexing or document representation. Billerbeck et al. [3] proposed to use compact document summaries to reduce retrieval time. Lavrenko et al. [20] pre-calculated pairwise document similarities to reduce the amount of calculation

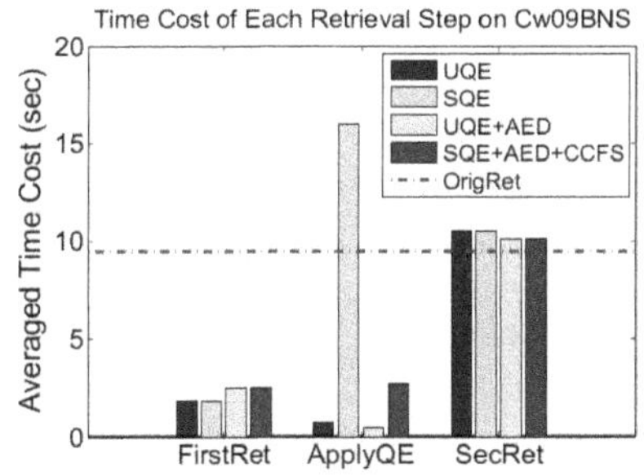

Figure 1: Comparison of the time cost of each retrieval step. AED and CCFS are the two-stages in our TFS framework, the target corpus $\mathcal{C}$ is Cw09BNS, resource $\mathcal{S}$ is Wikipedia, the number of expansion terms is 20, and the averaged time costs per query are reported by running experiments using a single-thread program on a single PC. The blue line is the averaged retrieval time cost for original query.

when searching expanded queries. Wu et al. [35] utilized a special index structure named impact-sorted indexing that improves the scoring procedures in retrieval. Theobald et al. [30] proposed the idea of merging inverted list of different terms in an incremental on-demand manner so that document scan can be delayed as much as possible. Unfortunately, our goal now is not the second retrieval, which is handled by reranking as [11] does. Nor can the inefficiency challenge of SQE be handled by the above data-level approaches.

2.3 SQE Efficiency Analysis

Now we will show why the efficiency issue of SQE is a unique and challenging problem beyond the UQE case.

Step-wise Time Cost Analysis. First let's see how UQE and SQE differs in the time cost spent on each retrieval step. On Clueweb09-B corpus, we conduct UQE (RM [21]) and SQE (applying RankSVM [19] based on Cao et al's work [5]) for QE with 20 expansion terms. As comparison, we apply our Two-stage Feature Selection framework (TFS) to SQE. Notice that although UQE does not involve term feature extraction, we can still apply adaptive expansion decision to UQE. In Figure 1, we show the time cost of each retrieval step with respect to Table 1. More experiment details can be found in Sec. 4. Here we mainly discuss the observations that motivate our research.

We can observe that, indeed applying SQE model can be much more time-consuming than applying UQE model, which supports our previous statement and validates our motivation. Notice here, step "FirstRet" and "ApplyQE" are involved in expansion term selection, while "SecRet" includes only retrieving $\mathcal{C}$ for original query q and reranking for expanded query q^e. Also notice the reranking in second retrieval only incurs very low time cost.

Feature Extraction in SQE. It is then natural to ask, which part of SQE incurs the major time cost, and why?

We argue that term feature extraction is the major inefficient part in SQE models. Recall the testing phase in Alg. 1, there are three steps to apply SQE model. The first step is essentially UQE, which is in general very efficient. The third step, which applies learned SQE model $\mathcal{H}$ for term classification or ranking, is also efficient in practice. For example, many SQE works [5, 22, 13, 2] adopted linear model, which is extremely fast yet effective. Therefore, the second step of term feature extraction forms the majority of inefficiency.

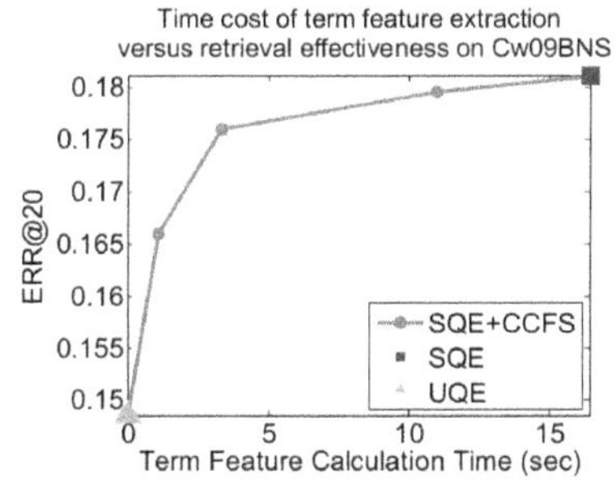

Figure 2: With more time spent, more term features are extracted, and higher retrieval accuracy is achieved.

But why would we spend much time on term feature extraction? This is because predicting the quality of terms is very challenging, so we want plenty of powerful features to enhance the learning algorithm [5, 13, 22]. In Figure 2, we show the retrieval accuracy (ERR@20) when different time cost is spent on term feature extraction. The purple triangle is UQE which does not extract any term feature (i.e. time cost equals zero); the blue rectangle is the full SQE model with all available term features (defined later). In the middle is our proposed cost constrained feature selection method. Clearly, with more time spent, more term features will be obtained, and the retrieval accuracy is higher as well. However, this inevitably degrades the efficiency.

We can further observe that, with more term features, although the retrieval accuracy of SQE is usually higher, the marginal gain becomes smaller. This motivates us to find a subset of features such that their total cost is low, meanwhile the effectiveness is reasonably maintained. This coincides with the idea of feature selection [15], although most of such methods only concern the number of selected features while ignoring their difference in time cost, which can be suboptimal.

3. TWO-STAGE FEATURE SELECTION FOR EFFICIENT SQE RETRIEVAL

Based on the above analysis, in this section we will present the proposed Two-stage Feature Selection (TFS) framework. Below we will first present TFS as a general framework, then instantiate it for an example SQE algorithm.

3.1 A General Framework

Assume the initial full set of term features are $\mathcal{F}_t$, where subscript t indicates the features are for terms. As analyzed earlier, when retrieval effectiveness is the only goal, $\mathcal{F}_t$ tends to become abundant and inefficient. Therefore, the goal of our TFS framework is to select a subset of term features $\mathcal{F}_t^*$ from $\mathcal{F}_t$, so that the effectiveness and efficiency can be optimally balanced. As mentioned earlier, the TFS framework includes the following two stages:

- Adaptive Expansion Decision (AED), which predicts whether a query is suitable for SQE or not. For unsuitable queries, SQE is skipped with no term features being extracted, which reduces the time cost most. To this end, AED builds a classifier $\mathcal{V}_{AED}$ with pre-defined query feature $\mathcal{F}_q$, so that $\mathcal{V}_{AED}(\mathcal{F}_q) < 0$ for unsuitable queries and $\mathcal{V}_{AED}(\mathcal{F}_q) > 0$ for suitable ones.
- Cost Constrained Feature Selection (CCFS), which selects a subset of effective yet inexpensive term features for SQE to apply. For those SQE-suitable queries that pass the first stage, this second stage can further reduce the time cost

Table 2: SQE in Retrieval with TFS.

(1) First retrieval:
- (1.1) Search original query q on resource $\mathcal{S}$.
- (1.2) AED: Extract query feature $\mathcal{F}_q$. If $\mathcal{V}_{AED}(\mathcal{F}_q) \leq 0$, directly go to step (3.1); otherwise continue.

(2) Apply QE model:
- (2.1) Apply UQE to generate candidate expansion terms.
- (2.2) CCFS: extract term features $\mathcal{F}_t^*$ for candidate terms.
- (2.3) Select the best terms to form expanded query q^e.

(3) Second retrieval (Reranking):
- (3.1) If $\mathcal{V}_{AED}(\mathcal{F}_q) \leq 0$: if target corpus is the resource (i.e. $\mathcal{C} = \mathcal{S}$), then return the retrieval results in step (1.1); if $\mathcal{C} \neq \mathcal{S}$, retrieve $\mathcal{C}$ for original query q. Exit.
- (3.2) If $\mathcal{V}_{AED}(\mathcal{F}_q) > 0$: if $\mathcal{C} = \mathcal{S}$, then rerank the retrieval results in step (1.1) for q^e; if $\mathcal{C} \neq \mathcal{S}$, retrieve $\mathcal{C}$ for original query q, then rerank the results for q^e. Exit.

to some extent. To this end, CCFS builds a feature selector $\mathcal{V}_{CCFS}$, which requires the time cost u_f of each term feature f, and a pre-defined overall time cost upper bound U. In this way, there is $\mathcal{F}_t^* = \mathcal{V}_{CCFS}(\mathcal{F}_t)$ and $\sum_{f \in \mathcal{F}_t^*} u_f \leq U$.

Accordingly, the complete retrieval process is shown in Table 2, which is self-evident to interpret. Below we will give more details about the two stages.

3.1.1 *Adaptive expansion decision (AED)*

Training. The training process of AED classifier $\mathcal{V}_{AED}$ is as follows. For training query q, we first retrieve corpus $\mathcal{C}$ and record its retrieval accuracy as r_q (e.g. ERR@20 value). Then we apply the SQE model $\mathcal{H}$ from Alg. 1 to get the expanded query q^e. Retrieve $\mathcal{C}$ for q^e by following the procedures in Table 2, and denote the retrieval accuracy as $r_q^{\mathcal{H}}$. Then if $r_q^{\mathcal{H}} > r_q$, we assign label $+1$ to query q, which means SQE can help improve the retrieval effectiveness for q; otherwise we assign -1 to q. Finally, we extract query features $\mathcal{F}_q$ for q, and adopt some supervised learning algorithm (e.g. SVM) to get the classifier $\mathcal{V}_{AED}$.

Discussion. The idea of AED stems from query performance prediction. It is known that query expansion may hurt the retrieval effectiveness for some queries [25, 7]. Therefore, accurately predicting those queries and avoid applying expensive SQE model to them can substantially improve the efficiency. This idea of adaptive expansion has also been applied in [18, 27, 23, 8], although their works mainly focused on retrieval effectiveness and did not report the efficiency advantage that this method might bring.

3.1.2 *Cost constrained feature selection (CCFS)*

Despite the existence of AED, queries that pass AED still face the problem of expensive term feature extraction in SQE. Now we will explain how cost constrained feature selection is designed for those SQE-suitable queries.

Algorithm Design. As mentioned, CCFS aims to select a subset of term features $\mathcal{F}_t^*$ from the complete feature set $\mathcal{F}_t$, so that the overall time cost will not exceed a pre-defined upper bound U, i.e. $\mathcal{F}_t^* = \mathcal{V}_{CCFS}(\mathcal{F}_t)$ with $\sum_{f \in \mathcal{F}_t^*} u_f \leq U$.

Our CCFS algorithm is formulated as follows. Since the SQE model $\mathcal{H}$ is used to predict the quality of expansion terms, we assume $X \in \mathbb{R}^{N*K}$ as the feature matrix for N candidate terms, where each row is a K-dimensional feature vector for each term. Denote $Y \in \mathbb{R}^{N*1}$ as the corresponding labels for terms in X, which is calculated as the Δr_c^q in Alg. 1. Assume the SQE model $\mathcal{H}$ is learned via a loss function $L_{\mathcal{H}}(X, Y|\theta)$, where θ is the model parameter. We introduce feature selector $d \in \{0, 1\}^K$, where the ith element

Algorithm 2 Cost Constrained Feature Selection

Input Learning algorithm $\mathcal{H}$, algorithm parameter θ, data $X \in \mathbb{R}^{N*K}$, label $Y \in \mathbb{R}^{N*1}$, algorithm loss function $L_{\mathcal{H}}(X, Y|\theta)$, feature cost vector $u \in \mathbb{R}^{K*1}$, final cost upper bound U, cost decrease ΔU.

Output Feature selector $d^* \in \{0, 1\}^K$ satisfying $u^T d^* \leq U$, and the learned parameter θ^*.

```
t ← 0, d* = 1_{K*1}, U^0 = u^T 1_{K*1}
do
    X ← Xd*, learn θ* = argmin_θ L_H(X, Y|θ).
    Learn d* = argmin_d L_H(Xd, Y|θ*), s.t. d ∈ {0,1}^K, u^T d ≤ U^i.
    U^{t+1} ← U^t − ΔU, t ← t + 1.
while U^i > U
```

$d_i = 1$ means the ith feature is selected. With fixed d, those unselected features in X will become invalid, which is equivalent to $X \leftarrow Xd$. Together θ and d form a revised learning objective as follows:

$$d, \theta = \arg\min L_{\mathcal{H}}(Xd, Y|\theta), \quad s.t. \quad u^T d \leq U. \qquad (2)$$

The optimization process is shown in Alg. 2, where a coordinate descent strategy is adopted to iteratively optimize w.r.t θ and d. During the iteration, we gradually decrease the cost upper bound (i.e. ΔU), so that the feature selection process can be smooth. In extreme case where $U \geq U^0$, Alg. 2 will produce the same results as vanilla $\mathcal{H}$ where no selection occurs (i.e. $d = \mathbf{1}_{K*1}$).

Discussion. Feature selection is a hot research topic in machine learning [15], and has been successfully adopted in information retrieval [13, 14, 33]. Popular methods include L1 based regularization [28, 13], cascading structure [31], feature number constraint [34], etc. Theoretically, any feature selection method can reduce time cost. But in practice we find better effectiveness can be achieved if the time cost of each feature can be explicitly considered. Unfortunately, most of previous research did not model such feature cost difference, which can be suboptimal. Wang et al. [33] proposed a greedy search algorithm for time cost aware feature selection in learning to rank. We also compare this method in our experiments, which shows our formulation outperforms this greedy design. CCFS can also be applied to the AED if necessary, which is straightforward. But due to space limitation, we simplify our experiments by only applying CCFS to term features.

3.2 Instantiation for RankSVM based SQE

So far we have elaborated all the details of TFS as a general framework. Now we will instantiate it with respect to a representative SQE algorithm, to show the implementation details. For SQE, we adopt a RankSVM based SQE method. Linear model has been widely applied in SQE literature [2, 13, 12]. Moreover, a ranking perspective has been proven to be very effective [22, 12] for SQE. Therefore, we believe RankSVM will make a representative example. Also Lavrenko's Relevance Model (RM) is utilized as the UQE model to generate candidate expansion terms, which is arguably one of the most successful UQE algorithms.

3.2.1 *AED*

The AED stage is simple to implement. Here we utilize SVM with Gaussian kernel for $\mathcal{V}_{AED}$ training. The adopted query features $\mathcal{F}_q$ are listed in Table 3, which are all well known query performance prediction features in the literature [17, 23, 16, 37].

Table 3: Query Features $\mathcal{F}_q$

Description	Formulation
Qry length	$\lvert q\rvert$
Qry Entropy	$\sum_{t\in q} -P(t\lvert D_F)log_2 p(t\lvert D_F)$
Qry Clarity 1	$\sum_{t\in q} P(t\lvert q)log\frac{P(t\lvert q)}{P(t\lvert C)}$
Qry Clarity 2	$\sum_{t\in q} -P(t\lvert D_F)log\frac{P(t\lvert D_F)}{P(t\lvert C)}$
Feedback Radius	$\frac{1}{\lvert D_F\rvert}\sum_{d\in D_F}\sum_{t\in d} P(t\lvert d)log\frac{P(t\lvert d)}{p(t\lvert \bar{d})}$, $P(t\lvert \bar{d}) = \frac{1}{\lvert D_F\rvert}\sum_{d\in D_F} P(t\lvert d)$
Qry IDF Var	$\mathrm{var}(\mathrm{idf}(t \in q))$, $idf(t) = \frac{log_2(\lvert C\rvert+0.5)/\lvert D_t\rvert}{log_2(\lvert C\rvert+1)}$
Max IDF	$\max idf(t \in q)$
AvICTF	$\frac{1}{\lvert q\rvert}log_2 \prod_{t\in q}\frac{N}{N_t}$
Qry Collection Similarity	$\sum_{t\in q}(1 + logN_t)log(1 + \frac{\lvert C\rvert}{\lvert D_t\rvert})$
Max of QCS	$\max_{t\in q}(1 + logN_t)log(1 + \frac{\lvert C\rvert}{\lvert D_t\rvert})$
Qry Variability (QVar)	$\sum_{t\in q}\sqrt{\frac{1}{\lvert D_t\rvert}\sum_{d\in D_t}(w_{d,t} - \bar{w}_t)^2}$, $\bar{w}_t = \frac{1}{\lvert D_t\rvert}\sum_{d\in D_t} w_{d,t}$, $w_{d,t} = 1 + logN_{d,t} * log(1 + \frac{\lvert C\rvert}{\lvert D_t\rvert})$
Max of QVar	$\max_{t\in q}\sqrt{\frac{1}{\lvert D_t\rvert}\sum_{d\in D_t}(w_{d,t} - \bar{w}_t)^2}$
Similar Qry Click Score	$\frac{1}{\lvert Q^{sim}\rvert}\sum_{q'\in Q^{sim}} RankScore(q', click\_doc)$
Similar Qry Click Rank	$\frac{1}{\lvert Q^{sim}\rvert}\sum_{q'\in Q^{sim}} Rank(q', click\_doc)$

Here q is the given query, t represents term, D_F is the pseudo relevant documents obtained from first retrieval of unexpanded query, C is the entire corpus, $|C|$ is the total document number in corpus, d represents document, N is the total term number in corpus, N_t is the number of term t in corpus, D_t is the set of documents containing t, $N_{d,t}$ is the number of t in doc d. The last two features are based on search log for industry dataset, which calculate the average clicked doc score/ranks of similar queries (Q^{sim}) in search log (see Sec. 4 for more details).

Table 4: Term Features $\mathcal{F}_t$

Description	Formulation
UQEScore	log score of UQE model
Term Doc Num	$log\lvert D_e\rvert$
Term Prob in Corpus	$log(N_e/N)$
Term Distribution	$log\frac{\sum_{d\in D_F} N_{d,e}}{\sum_{d\in D_F}\sum_{t\in d} N_{d,t}}$
Co-occurrence with single query term	$log\frac{1}{\lvert q\rvert}\sum_{t\in q}\frac{\sum_{d\in D_F} Win(t,e\lvert d)}{\sum_{d\in D_F}\sum_{t\in d} N_{d,t}}$
Co-occurrence with pair of query terms	$log\frac{1}{\lvert t_{i,j}\in q\rvert}\sum_{\lvert t_{i,j}\in q\rvert}\frac{\sum_{d\in D_F} Win(t_{i,j},e\lvert d)}{\sum_{d\in D_F}\sum_{t\in d} N_{d,t}}$
Term Proximity	$log\frac{\sum_{t\in q} Win(t,e)dist(t,e\lvert D_F)}{\sum_{t\in q} Win(t,e)}$
Document Number of t,e together	$log(\sum_{d\in D_F} I(t, e\lvert d) + 0.5)$
Probability in similar queries in search log	$log\frac{1}{\lvert Q^{sim}\rvert}\sum_{q\in Q} P(e\lvert q)$
Probability in docs that similar queries clicked	$log\frac{1}{\lvert D_{click}\rvert}\sum_{d\in D_{click}} P(e\lvert d)$

Here e is the target term. D_F means the working set of documents. $Win(t, e|d)$ is the co-occurrence times that term t and e appear within distance 10 in d. $Win(t_{i,j}, e|d)$ is the co-occurrence times that e appear within distance 10 with both t_i, t_j. $dist(t, e|D_F)$ is the minimal terms between t and e in doc set D_F. The last two rows are search log based term features for industry dataset, which calculate the probability of e in similar queries and their clicked documents. These two features are essentially one-step random walk features in a more general context [13]. In [5], the doc working set D_F has two choices, one is the pseudo relevant docs and the other is the entire corpus. The latter, however, is prohibitively expensive in large dataset. Therefore, we relax D_F as follows: assume the number of pseudo relevant docs is K_1, and the number of final evaluation is K_2 (actually fixed as 1000 in this paper); D_F is set as the top $\{0.5K_1, K_1, 2K_1, 2.5K_2, 5K_2\}$ docs from first retrieval.

3.2.2 CCFS

Applying Alg. 2 in practice requires a deeper insight into the SQE model itself. Nonetheless, as we show below, Alg. 2 can generate elegant solutions that are easy to implement.

Objective. For training queries q, let $x_i^q \in \mathbb{R}^{|\mathcal{F}_t|}$ be the feature vector for the ith candidate term of q. Here the term features $\mathcal{F}_t$ are adopted from [5, 13], and are listed in Table 4. Following the notations of u, U, d in Alg. 2, the objective of cost constrained RankSVM is as follows:

$$w, d = \arg\min \frac{1}{2}w^T w + \frac{G}{|\mathcal{P}|}\sum_{q,i,j\in\mathcal{P}}\gamma_{q,i,j}\xi_{q,i,j}$$
$$s.t. \forall(q, i, j) \in \mathcal{P} : w^T(x_i^q \circ d) > w^T(x_j^q \circ d) + 1 - \xi_{q,i,j}, \quad \xi_{q,i,j} \geq 0,$$
$$d \in \{0, 1\}^{|\mathcal{F}_t|}, \quad u^T d \leq U \tag{3}$$

Here $\mathcal{P}$ is the set of pairwise candidate terms (q, i, j) where $\Delta r_i^q > \Delta r_j^q$; $\circ$ is element-wise multiplication; and we add $\gamma_{q,i,j} = |\Delta r_i^q - \Delta r_j^q|$ as loss weight that emphasizes large relevance difference, which works well in practice. Notice for RankSVM, there's no need to add offset.

Eq. 3 is how Eq. 2 looks like when RankSVM objective [19] is introduced. The first three lines (if without d) of Eq. 3 constitute vanilla RankSVM (with slight modification of $\gamma_{q,i,j}$), while the feature selector d and the last line of constraints formulate the cost constrained version of RankSVM. The outcome d indicates what features are selected under cost upper bound U, and the w is the resulted RankSVM model based on the selected features.

Optimization. We solve Eq. 3 by converting it into the dual form via Lagrange multiplier [4], which gives:

$$\min_{\alpha_k, d}\sum_{k=1}^{K}\alpha_k - \frac{1}{2}\Big(\sum_{k=1}^{K}\alpha_k(\delta x_k \circ d)\Big)^T\Big(\sum_{k=1}^{K}\alpha_k(\delta x_k \circ d)\Big)$$
$$\text{s.t.} \quad 0 \leq \alpha_k \leq \frac{G\gamma_k}{K}, \quad d \in \{0, 1\}^{|\mathcal{F}_t|}, \quad u^T d \leq U \tag{4}$$

where $\forall(q, i, j)$ in Eq. 3 is re-indexed by $k = 1 : K$ with each k representing one (q, i, j) triplet; $y_k = 1$ if $\Delta r_i^q > \Delta r_j^q$, otherwise $y_k = -1$; $\delta x_k = x_i^q - x_j^q$; $\gamma_k = \gamma_{q,i,j}$. $\alpha = [\alpha_1, ..., \alpha_K]$ is the dual parameter to be learned, and we can get w as

$$w = \sum_{k=1}^{K}\alpha_k(\delta x_k \circ d) \tag{5}$$

Based on Eq. 4, now the CCFS problem can be easily optimized by iteratively solving step 3 and step 4 in Alg. 2.

(Step 3) Fix d and optimize w. When d is fixed, we can absorb d into X as $X \leftarrow X \circ d$. Under this circumstance, Eq. 3 and Eq. 4 become the standard RankSVM training problem without cost constraint, for which we can utilize existing algorithms for optimization. Considering the potential large scale of pairwise term comparison, here we adopt cutting plane method [19] for efficient optimization.

(Step 4) Fix w and optimize d. With fixed w, now we aim to find the optimal d. Notice that from step 3, we have $w = \sum_{k=1}^{K}\alpha_k\delta x_k$ (recall X is updated to absorb previous d in step 3). In this way, Eq. 4 can be reformulated as follows:

$$d^* = \arg\max\Big(\sum_{k=1}^{K}\alpha_k(\delta x_k \circ d)\Big)^T\Big(\sum_{k=1}^{K}\alpha_k(\delta x_k \circ d)\Big)$$
$$= \arg\max\Big(\big(\sum_{k=1}^{K}\alpha_k\delta x_k\big) \circ \big(\sum_{k=1}^{K}\alpha_k\delta x_k\big)\Big)^T d$$
$$= \arg\max_d (w \circ w)^T d \tag{6}$$
$$s.t. \quad d \in \{0, 1\}^{|\mathcal{F}_t|}, u^T d \leq U$$

This is a standard linear integer programming problem, for which we utilize Gurobi[1] for efficient optimization.

During iteration, the upper bound U is meant to be a tunable parameter for the users. In practice, we can set U as a portion of the overall time cost, i.e. $U = \lambda * \sum_{f\in\mathcal{F}_t} u_f$,

[1]http://www.gurobi.com/

where λ take values such as $\{1, \frac{1}{2}, \frac{1}{4}, ...\}$. ΔU controls the number of iterations. In our implementation, we set $\Delta U = \frac{\sum_{f \in \mathcal{F}_t} u_f - U}{\#Iter}$, where $\#Iter$ is the desired iteration number (e.g. $\#Iter = 5$ or 10).

4. EXPERIMENTS

So far we have elaborated all the details of the proposed TFS framework. Below we will present extensive experiments to verify its validity.

4.1 Datasets

We adopt four corpora for experiments, including three academic and one industry corpus.

Robust04. This dataset includes about 0.5 million high quality documents. 250 queries (301-450 and 601-700) provided by TREC'04 robust track [32] are utilized for the experiments. MAP is the primary evaluation metric. Notice here by primary evaluation metric, we mean the metric that is used to rank TREC competition teams.

Cw09BNS. Clueweb09 category B is used, which includes 50 million web pages. We utilize University of Waterloo's spam scores [9][2] to remove those with spam scores lower than 70, which leaves 29 million web pages. 150 queries (51 to 200 from TREC'10/11/12 web track) are examined. ERR@20 is the primary evaluation metric. We denote this dataset as Cw09BNS, as NS stands for no spam.

Cw12BNSLD. Clueweb12 category B is used, which also includes 50 million web pages. Since category B contains very few relevant documents that are labeled by TREC, we add all the labeled relevant documents into this dataset. Again University of Waterloo's spam scores [9][3] are applied to remove those spam web pages (with the same threshold 70), which leaves about 15 million documents. 50 queries from TREC'13 web track are utilized, with ERR@20 being the primary evaluation metric. We denote this dataset as Cw12BNSLD, as LD means labeled documents are added.

Industry. This is a large scale web page corpus collected from a major search engine company (i.e. Bing). We incorporate an industry corpus to diversify our experiment settings. For example, the availability of industry search log provides a new resource for query expansion, as well as the search log related features in Table 3 and Table 4. Specifically, this corpus includes about 50 million web pages and 2000 queries. NDCG@20 is the primary evaluation metric as in previous research on a similar industry corpus [13].

4.2 Settings

Now we present all the detailed experiment settings.

Corpus Preprocessing. We utilize Indri[4], one of the most popular academic search systems, to index all our corpora in the form of inverted index [38]. Krovetz stemmer is applied for stemming, and standard InQuery stopwords are removed. Except stopwords removal, we do not conduct any further pruning that might reduce document lengths.

Code & Hardware. In accordance with Indri index, all our algorithms and experiments are implemented in C++ using Lemur/Indri API. The code is compiled by GCC4.7.3 with -O3 option. The code runs in a single thread on a single lab Linux server, which is equipped with a AMD 64bit 2.0GHz quad-core CPU, 12G memory and a 3TB disk that contains all the indexed corpora.

[2]https://plg.uwaterloo.ca/~gvcormac/clueweb09spam/

[3]http://www.mansci.uwaterloo.ca/ msmucker/cw12spam/

[4]http://www.lemurproject.org/indri.php

Table 5: Examples of Search Log Records

Query	Clicked URL	Score	Rank
bloomberg news	http://www.bloomberg.com/news/	201	1
firefox com	http://www.mozilla.org/ en-US/firefox/fx/	81	2
gibson althea	http://en.wikipedia.org/ wiki/Althea_Gibson	145	3

Smaller ranks and higher scores represent a better match between queries and clicked URLs. Notice these search log queries should not be misinterpreted as the 2000 queries for QE test. They actually serve as $\mathcal{S}$ to find the relevant web pages for those 2000 queries.

QE scenarios. As mentioned in Sec. 2, we can get different QE scenarios, depending on the resource $\mathcal{S}$ upon which expansion terms are extracted. For Robust04, we apply the traditional pseudo relevance feedback (PRF) for query expansion, where resource $\mathcal{S}$ is identical to the target corpus $\mathcal{C}$. Top 20 documents retrieved for q are considered relevant, from which expansion terms are extracted.

This PRF scenario, however, did not work well on the other corpora, which include web pages of relatively low quality [9]. We find that, on Cw09BNS and Cw12BNSLD, even after filtering spams, the traditional PRF still does not work well, which is also reported in [1]. Therefore, we try the strategy of $\mathcal{S} \neq \mathcal{C}$.

For Cw09BNS and Cw12BNSLD, we follow the suggestion of Bendersky et al. in [1] to use Wikipedia as $\mathcal{S}$. Top 5 ranked Wikipedia documents of original query q are considered relevant, upon which QE is applied. On Industry corpus, we follow the idea of Gao et al. in [13] to use search log as $\mathcal{S}$. The search log is also acquired from the same search engine company, which includes one million distinct click records. Each record contains four elements: user issued query, clicked URL, the score and the rank of the clicked URL returned by the search engine. A snapshot of the search log records is shown in Table 5. For each of the 2000 queries to be experimented, we first find the top 20 similar queries from the log; then the corresponding clicked web pages are considered relevant, from which expansion terms are extracted. This is actually a one-step random walk in search log [13].

Models & Parameters. Following [5], we utilize KL divergence (KLD) as the basic retrieval model for all the experiments below. The Dirichlet coefficient is set as 1500. The UQE and SQE algorithm are the same as explained in Sec. 3.2, i.e. relevance model for UQE and RankSVM for SQE. For both of them, we empirically set the number of expansion terms as $m = 20$. Other values of m will be examined in Sec. 4.8. For SQE, the number of candidate terms are empirically set as $M = 100$. Selected expansion terms are added to the original query by probability interpolation, as introduced in Eq. 1. The interpolation coefficient λ is tuned over a finite set of values $\{0, 0.1, ..., 0.9, 1\}$ on the training/validation set.

Evaluation Metrics. Both retrieval effectiveness and efficiency will be evaluated. For effectiveness, MAP and Prec@20 are used for Robust04, and ERR@20 and NDCG@20 are utilized for the other three web page corpora. For efficiency, we report the retrieval time costs per query, which is averaged on each query set.

Training/Validation/Testing. For all the query sets, based on the order of their query IDs, we select the first 40% queries for training all the models (e.g. SQE and TFS), the

Table 6: Retrieval Performance on Robust04

	MAP(⋆)	⊖	Prec @20	⊖	Time (sec)	%
OrigRet	0.268	-	0.345	-	0.13	-
UQE	0.319	0	0.369	0	0.61	0
UQE^{α}	0.321	0.002	0.373	0.004	0.78	+27.9%
SQE	0.327	0	0.381	0	4.73	0
SQE^{α}	0.329	0.002	0.383	0.002	4.65	-1.7%
$SQE^{\beta(\frac{1}{4})}$	0.325	-0.002	0.378	-0.003	1.66	-64.9%⋄
$SQE^{\alpha\beta(\frac{1}{4})}$	0.327	0	0.380	-0.001	1.76	-62.8%⋄

Table 7: Retrieval Performance on Cw09BNS

	ERR @20(⋆)	⊖	NDCG @20	⊖	Time (sec)	%
OrigRet	0.129	-	0.169	-	9.5	-
UQE	0.149	0	0.190	0	11.3	0
UQE^{α}	0.159	0.01↑	0.194	0.004	11.67	+3.3%
SQE	0.181	0	0.197	0	27.9	0
SQE^{α}	0.187	0.006	0.191	-0.006	20.7	-25.8%⋄
$SQE^{\beta(\frac{1}{4})}$	0.176	-0.005	0.186	-0.011↓	15.6	-44.1%⋄
$SQE^{\alpha\beta(\frac{1}{4})}$	0.186	0.005	0.191	-0.006	13.8	-49.5%⋄

Table 8: Retrieval Performance on Cw12BNSLD

	ERR @20(⋆)	⊖	NDCG @20	⊖	Time (sec)	%
OrigRet	0.258	-	0.618	-	4.37	-
UQE	0.261	0	0.632	0	6.13	0
UQE^{α}	0.262	0.001	0.626	-0.006	6.27	+2.3%
SQE	0.291	0	0.660	0	23.5	0
SQE^{α}	0.292	0.001	0.664	0.004	18.1	-23%⋄
$SQE^{\beta(\frac{1}{4})}$	0.287	-0.004	0.665	0.005	10.5	-55.3%⋄
$SQE^{\alpha\beta(\frac{1}{4})}$	0.288	-0.003	0.665	0.005	9.1	-61.3%⋄

Table 9: Retrieval Performance on Industry

	NDCG @20(⋆)	⊖	ERR @20	⊖	Time (sec)	%
OrigRet	0.372	-	0.253	-	11.5	-
UQE	0.387	0	0.260	0	12.1	0
UQE^{α}	0.391	0.004	0.268	0.008	12.3	+1.7%
SQE	0.403	0	0.281	0	22.7	0
SQE^{α}	0.408	0.005	0.285	0.004	19.1	-15.8%⋄
$SQE^{\beta(\frac{1}{4})}$	0.4	-0.003	0.276	-0.005	15.1	-33.5%⋄
$SQE^{\alpha\beta(\frac{1}{4})}$	0.406	0.003	0.279	-0.002	13.9	-38.8%⋄

middle 10% queries for parameter validation, and the remaining 50% queries for testing evaluation. All experiments are repeated three times to report averaged time cost.

TFS Notation. As the two stages in TFS can be applied independently, we will utilize superscript α and β to indicate the case when AED and CCFS are applied alone, such as UQE^{α} and SQE^{β}. When the full set of TFS is applied for SQE, then we denote as $SQE^{\alpha\beta}$.

4.3 More on Time Cost

As mentioned, the time costs reported below are all obtained by running experiments using a single thread on a Linux server. The absolute value might appear larger than previous works (mainly on Cw09BNS and Cw12BNSLD), for which we feel necessary to give a full explanation.

Versus Previous Studies. The reason why previous studies such as [3, 35, 20] reported very low time costs of QE retrieval is mainly due to their selection and pre-processing upon the corpus. For example, (1) Lavrenko et al. [20] and Billerbeck et al. [3] utilized corpora that only contains $O(10^5 \sim 10^6)$ documents; in comparison our Clueweb09/12 and Industry corpora have $O(10^7)$ documents, which are at least 10 times larger. (2) Billerbeck [3] and Wu [35] reduced the document length into $20 \sim 100$ terms long, while the averaged document length for our corpora are $500 \sim 800$, which are again about $5 \sim 40$ times larger. The difference of corpus size and document length is the major reason why our reported time costs are larger than previous studies.

Versus Indri Official. With the above settings, our reported time costs are actually quite reasonable. As a proof, the Indri official website[5] reported an averaged time cost of 20 seconds per query (wall clock time) on Cw09B (50 million docs, with spam, one thread program on a 3.0GHz CPU, average query length is about 4), while ours is 9.5 seconds per query (29 million docs, no spam, 2.0GHz CPU, average query length is 2.4). After normalizing various factors[6], we can conclude that our time cost per query is very close to that reported by Indri official website. Although this is not an exact comparison, it indeed partially supports our claim.

[5]http://www.lemurproject.org/clueweb09/indri-howto.php

[6]We divide the averaged time cost per query by the number of documents (in millions) and the averaged query length, and multiply the CPU frequency (in GHz). The result can be seen as an atomic time cost for a single query term on a million documents using 1GHz CPU. In this way, the atomic time cost from official Indri website is 0.3 seconds, while ours is 0.27, which is very close.

Versus Engineering Strategy. The absolute value of time costs can be reduced by engineering strategies such as better hardware or distributed/parallel computing, which are widely adopted in commercial search engines like Bing and Google. However, such devices are usually very expensive to equip, and are not available to us. Moreover, accurately counting the time costs in distributed/parallel computing environment becomes difficult, because usually the computing resouces (e.g. CPU or memory) are automatically allocated and can vary as time passes. The advantage of us utilizing single thread program on single computer is that, the overall time costs directly reflects the amount of computation (thus the efficiency), and makes it easy to compare different retrieval methods.

4.4 Overall Performance

We first present the major results of retrieval performance on the four corpora, as shown in Table 6, 7, 8 and 9.

Comparison Methods. We conduct extensive comparison with the following retrieval configurations:

(1) Retrieval for original queries without QE (OrigRet);

(2∼3) UQE and UQE+AED (UQE^{α});

(4∼7) SQE, SQE+AED (SQE^{α}), SQE+CCFS ($SQE^{\beta(\frac{1}{4})}$), and SQE+TFS ($SQE^{\alpha\beta(\frac{1}{4})}$). Here $\beta(\frac{1}{4})$ is an example parameter for upper bound U in CCFS, which means the upper bound U is a quarter of the overall time costs of all term features, i.e. $U = \frac{1}{4}\sum_{f\in\mathcal{F}_t} u_f$. Other choices of upper bounds will be examined in Sec. 4.5.

As mentioned earlier, by default reranking (top 1000 documents) is utilized in the second retrieval to report the time costs for the above retrieval methods.

Table Explanation. We adopt evaluation metrics regarding both effectiveness (e.g. ERR@20, NDCG@20, MAP) and efficiency (Time in seconds). Here (⋆) indicates primary evaluation metric. We treat UQE and SQE as the baseline, so that we can show how AED, CCFS and TFS improve the efficiency respectively. We use column "⊖" to represent the effectiveness difference between UQE/SQE and their speedup versions, and use % for the relative time cost reduction. For example, on Cw09BNS, SQE^{α} vs SQE has ERR@20 difference 0.187-0.181=0.006; their time cost change (%, in percentage) is (20.7-27.9)/27.9=-25.8%. ↑ and ↓ label the positive and negative effectiveness difference that are statistically significant, and ⋄ means the time cost reduction upon SQE is statistically significant (t-test, $p < 0.05$).

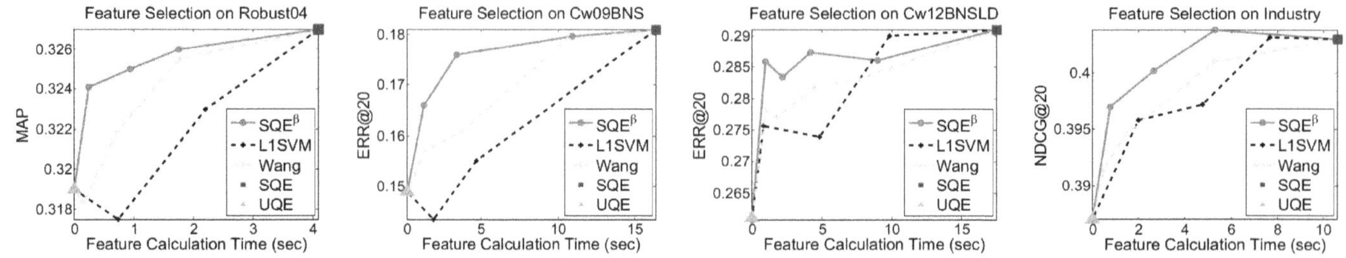

Figure 3: Comparison between different feature selection methods. The horizontal axis is the time cost for term feature extraction (excluding any retrieval time). Purple triangles at left end of curves are UQE method with no term features, and blue rectangles at right end are SQE algorithm with all available features. AED is not applied here.

Major Observations. From the tables we can draw the following two major observations.

(1) SQE is more effective but also less efficient than UQE and OrigRet. Compared with OrigRet and UQE, the retrieval effectiveness of SQE can be substantially higher. However, the time costs are also substantially larger. This verifies our motivation that the efficiency issue of SQE is an important research topic.

(2) Both AED and CCFS can substantially improve the efficiency of SQE, meanwhile only incurring insignificant effectiveness fluctuation. In the above tables, we progressively add each component to SQE, so that one can see how the efficiency is progressively improved. In general we can conclude that for SQE, CCFS achieves higher efficiency than AED, and their combination (i.e. our TFS framework) achieves the most efficiency improvement. For effectiveness, although both positive and negative changes are observed, most of them are statistically insignificant (t-test, $p<0.05$). I.e. most of the effectiveness changes are not labeled by $\uparrow$ or $\downarrow$. Therefore, we can conclude that our TFS framework can well maintain the effectiveness of SQE.

We also notice that for UQE, UQE$^{\alpha}$ has slightly increased time costs. There are two reasons for this phenomenon. First, for UQE there is no expensive term feature extraction, so that AED only skips the generation of UQE expansion terms and the reranking process in second retrieval. Since these two steps are already very fast, the reduced time cost is not substantial. Second, AED will result in some extra time costs for query feature extraction as well as the application of AED classifier. Therefore, the overall time costs of UQE$^{\alpha}$ will be slightly higher than UQE. But notice, the absolute value of such increase is very low (at most 0.37 seconds). Furthermore, as we will show in Sec. 4.9, the efficiency improvement of AED can be very substantial, if the full second retrieval is applied instead of reranking, which verifies the usefulness of AED.

Below, we will present more experiments to thoroughly investigate AED and CCFS. As CCFS will also be utilized in AED experiments, we will first analyze CCFS for sake of clear presentation.

4.5 Cost Constrained Feature Selection

In the above we have verified the validity of feature selection in speeding up SQE. Now we will investigate how our CCFS algorithm in Alg. 2 performs in this task.

Comparison Methods. The following two algorithms are compared with our CCFS algorithm.

L1-RankSVM. L1 regularization is a very popular feature selection method. When feature selection occurs, we replace the L2 regularizer in vanilla RankSVM (Eq. 3) with L1 regularizer $||w||_1$. By adjusting the coefficient G, $||w||_1$ will function to different extent, thus resulting in various combinations of features. Notice this method is unaware of the difference in the time costs of extracting each feature. L1General library[7] [28] is utilized for optimization.

Wang's method [33]. This is a greedy algorithm for cost aware feature selection, proposed by Wang et al. in [33] for learning to rank. In this algorithm, each feature is assigned a profit score, which is the ratio between feature weight and time cost. Features are sorted by profit scores; then top features are selected until the time cost upper bound is reached, which makes it a greedy selection. Different from L1-RankSVM, this is a cost aware feature selection method.

For both Alg. 2 and Wang's method, we use the same cost upper bounds as $U = \lambda \sum_{f \in \mathcal{F}_t} u_f$ as explained earlier, where we adjust λ to different values such as $\{1, \frac{1}{2}, \frac{1}{4}, ...\}$ to get all the nodes along the curves in Figure 3. For L1-RankSVM, each node represents a different G value, which is tuned on training set so that different time costs are obtained.

Overall Results. In Figure 3 we illustrate the curves of the three methods on all corpora. These curves represent the retrieval effectiveness when various feature extraction time is spent (excluding any retrieval time). The purple triangles at the left end of curves represent UQE algorithm, i.e. no term feature is extracted. The blue rectangles at the right end of curves represent SQE algorithm with all available term features. In the middle, various feature selection methods show different effectiveness-cost tradeoff. We can clearly observe that more features can produce higher retrieval accuracy, but this inevitably takes more time thus decreasing the efficiency.

CCFS performs best, particularly at low time cost. Comparing the three feature selection methods, we can see that our CCFS algorithm outperforms the others, especially when the feature cost is low. L1-RankSVM penalizes the number of selected features. That means, each feature is treated equally, ignoring the cost difference among different features. Since expensive features can be included, to reach a certain time cost, usually L1-RankSVM will over-penalizes the number of selected features, which deteriorates the retrieval effectiveness. Wang's method greedily selects features based on their profit scores, i.e. the ratio between feature weight and cost. Here the feature weights are the ones derived when all features are available. However, this selection process is suboptimal, because for a single feature, its weight will become different when fewer other features are available. Therefore, the profit score may not accurately reflect the importance of individual features, particularly when

[7] http://www.cs.ubc.ca/~schmidtm/Software/L1General.html

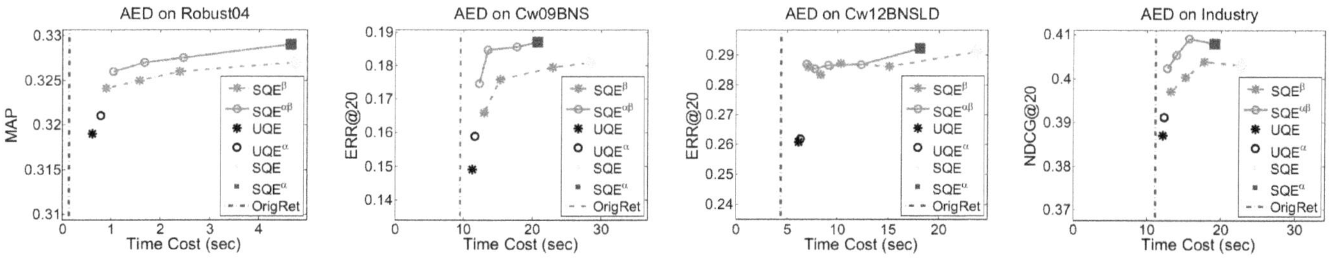

Figure 4: Experiments for AED. Red curves correspond to the SQE$^\beta$ curves in Figure 3. The UQE nodes (with zero term feature cost) are shown separately for better illustration. The horizontal axis is the overall retrieval time. The blue vertical line is the time cost of OrigRet, which is plotted as reference.

few features exist (i.e. time cost is low). In comparison, our CCFS algorithm iteratively updates learning objective, and decreases the cost upper bound smoothly. Therefore, CCFS performs better, particularly when time cost is low.

4.6 Adaptive Expansion Decision

Now we will examine how AED affects the effectiveness and efficiency of UQE and SQE retrieval. We show the performance in Figure 4, where UQE, SQE and SQE$^\beta$ algorithms are all examined before and after applying AED. For SQE$^\beta$, the CCFS curves from Figure 3 are utilized.

For both SQE and SQE$^\beta$, their performance is left-shifted after applying AED. Moreover, the SQE$^\beta$ curves shrink after AED. This means, the process of term feature extraction and second retrieval (reranking) are skipped for some of the queries (i.e. SQE-unsuitable), which makes the averaged time costs over all queries become smaller.

For UQE, the time costs of UQE$^\alpha$ is slightly higher. This has been explained in Sec. 4.4, which are due to the fast process of reranking and UQE expansion term generation, as well as the existence of AED overhead cost.

The extent of efficiency improvement of AED depends on the number of skipped queries. In Table 10 we give the detailed number of skipped queries on each corpus for SQE.

From the perspective of effectiveness, we can observe that on all corpora, for all of UQE, SQE and SQE$^\beta$, their effectiveness after applying AED is improved or at least maintained than before applying AED. This is particularly helpful in achieving a good balance between effectiveness and efficiency.

Table 10: Number of skipped queries in AED for SQE.

Dataset	#Test Query	#Skipped Query	Percentage
Robust04	125	8	6.4%
Cw09BNS	75	32	42.67%
Cw12BNSLD	25	8	32%
Industry	1000	361	36.1%

4.7 More on Step-wise Time Cost

In Figure 1 we have shown the step-wise time costs on Cw09BNS for UQE, SQE and their speedup improvements. There for CCFS we adopt the same upper bound as in Table 7 (i.e. $U = \frac{1}{4}\sum_{f \in \mathcal{F}_t} u_f$). This is a non Pseudo Relevance Feedback (PRF) scenario where $\mathcal{S}$ is Wikipedia and $\mathcal{C}$ is Cw09BNS. In this case, the time cost of second retrieval will be large because in second retrieval we need to firstly search query q on $\mathcal{C}$ then apply the reranking.

Now we further show the step-wise time costs for PRF scenario on Robust04 in Figure 5(a). In this case, $\mathcal{S} = \mathcal{C} =$ Robust04, so we only need to retrieve q once in first retrieval, and the second retrieval only needs to rerank the results of first retrieval. In this case, the cost of second retrieval will be much smaller than in non PRF scenario.

4.8 The Effect of Number of Expansion Terms

Now let's see how different number of expansion terms m affects the retrieval effectiveness and efficiency. In Figure 5(b), we show the effectiveness-cost curves when $m = \{10, 20, 30\}$ for SQE$^{\alpha\beta}$ on Industry corpus. We can see the effectiveness of $m = 20, 30$ is similar, while that of $m = 10$ is quite degraded. The time cost gap between OrigRet and SQE$^{\alpha\beta}$ curves includes the cost of first retrieval (i.e. searching $\mathcal{S}$), applying AED, extracting term features, etc. Also notice the overall time cost is not obviously affected as more expansion terms are utilized. This phenomenon is mainly due to the application of reranking. Otherwise if a full second retrieval is applied, the time cost of second retrieval will be (approximately) linear with the number of m, which can be very huge in practice (see Sec. 4.9).

4.9 Reranking vs Full Second Retrieval

Finally, for the SQE retrieval process, we compare the two strategies for second retrieval: reranking vs full second retrieval. Although we have argued the validity of reranking and have utilized it throughout the above experiments, we still feel it necessary to present a formal comparison with full second retrieval due to the following two reasons. First, as reviewed in Sec. 2.2, we find most of existing QE efficiency works [3, 35] only focused on indexing or document optimization, while ignored the value of reranking. It is only very recent that Diaz [11] pointed this out. Here we'd like to add more proof to support reranking. Second, in the above experiments for UQE and UQE$^\alpha$, we observed that pure AED may not result in substantial speedup, and point out that the application of reranking is the major reason for that. By further showing the time costs of full second retrieval, we can justify the value of AED.

In Figure 5(c) and (d), we show the performance of reranking top 1000 documents for expanded queries q^e with 20 expansion terms. We can see that for both the case of UQE and SQE, reranking does not incur obvious effectiveness loss, yet results in substantial efficiency improvement. Particularly for the UQE case, the speedup becomes obvious when full second retrieval is utilized on Cw09BNS. These observations verify our adoption of reranking instead of full second retrieval, as well as the usefulness of AED on efficiency.

5. CONCLUSION & FUTURE WORK

Supervised query expansion (SQE) has recently become the state-of-the-art in the QE literature, which usually outperforms the unsupervised counterparts. To obtain good retrieval effectiveness, SQE usually extracts many term fea-

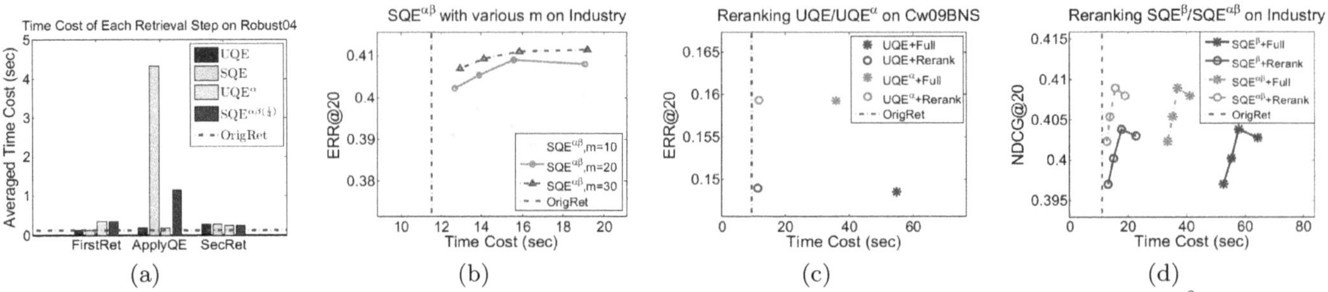

Figure 5: (a) Step-wise costs on Robust04, which is under PRF scenario. (b) Performance of SQE$^{\alpha\beta}$ on Industry with different number of expansion terms. (c) Reranking vs full second retrieval for UQE and UQE$^{\alpha}$ on Cw09BNS. (d) Reranking vs full second retrieval for SQE$^{\beta}$ and SQE$^{\alpha\beta}$ on Industry.

tures to predict the quality of expansion terms. However, this can seriously decrease its efficiency. This issue has not been studied before, nor can it be handled by previous data-level QE efficiency methods such as indexing or documents optimization. To address this problem, in this paper we propose a Two-stage Feature Selection (TFS) framework, which includes Adaptive Expansion Decision and Cost Constrained Feature Selection. Extensive experiments on four corpora show that the proposed TFS framework can significantly improve the efficiency of SQE algorithm, while maintaining its good effectiveness.

6. REFERENCES

[1] M. Bendersky, D. Fisher, and W. B. Croft. Umass at trec 2010 web track: Term dependence, spam filtering and quality bias. In *TREC*, 2010.

[2] M. Bendersky, D. Metzler, and W. B. Croft. Effective query formulation with multiple information sources. In *WSDM*, pages 443–452, 2012.

[3] B. Billerbeck and J. Zobel. Efficient query expansion with auxiliary data structures. In *Information System*, pages 573–584, 2006.

[4] C. M. Bishop. *Pattern Recognition and Machine Learning*. Springer, 2006.

[5] G. Cao, J.-Y. Nie, J. Gao, and S. Robertson. Selecting good expansion terms for pseudo-relevance feedback. In *SIGIR*, pages 243–250, 2008.

[6] C. Carpineto and G. Romano. A survey of automatic query expansion in information retrieval. In *ACM Computing Surveys*, 2012.

[7] K. Collins-Thompson. Reducing the risk of query expansion via robust constrained optimization. In *CIKM*, 2009.

[8] K. Collins-Thompson and P. N. Bennett. Predicting query performance via classification. In *ECIR*, pages 140–152, 2010.

[9] G. V. Cormack, M. D. Smucker, and C. L. A. Clarke. Efficient and effective spam filtering and re-ranking for large web datasets. *IR*, pages 441–465, 2011.

[10] H. Cui, J.-R. Wen, J.-Y. Nie, and W.-Y. Ma. Probabilistic query expansion using query logs. In *WWW*, pages 325–332, 2002.

[11] F. Diaz. Condensed list relevance models. In *ICTIR*, 2015.

[12] J. Gao, S. Xie, X. He, and A. Ali. Learning lexicon models from search logs for query expansion. In *EMNLP*, pages 666–676, 2012.

[13] J. Gao, G. Xu, and J. Xu. Query expansion using path-constrained random walks. In *SIGIR*, pages 563–572, 2013.

[14] X. Geng, T.-Y. Liu, T. Qin, and H. Li. Feature selection for ranking. In *SIGIR*, pages 407–414, 2007.

[15] I. Guyon and A. Elisseeff. An introduction to variable and feature selection. *JMLR*, pages 1157–1182, 2003.

[16] C. Hauff, D. Hiemstra, and F. de Jong. A survey of pre-retrieval query performance predictors. In *CIKM*, pages 1419–1420, 2008.

[17] B. He and I. Ounis. Query performance prediction. In *Information Systems*, pages 585–594, 2006.

[18] B. He and I. Ounis. Combining fields for query expansion and adaptive query expansion. *IPM*, pages 1294–1307, 2007.

[19] T. Joachims. Training linear svms in linear time. In *KDD*, pages 217–226, 2006.

[20] V. Lavrenko and J. Allan. Real-time query expansion in relevance models. In *Tech Report, Univ Massachusetts Amherst*, 2006.

[21] V. Lavrenko and W. B. Croft. Relevance-based language models. In *SIGIR*, pages 120–127, 2001.

[22] C.-J. Lee, R.-C. Chen, S.-H. Kao, and P.-J. Cheng. A term dependency-based approach for query terms ranking. In *CIKM*, pages 1267–1276, 2009.

[23] Y. Lv and C. Zhai. Adaptive relevance feedback in information retrieval. In *CIKM*, pages 255–264, 2009.

[24] Y. Lv and C. Zhai. Positional relevance model for pseudo-relevance feedback. In *SIGIR*, pages 579–586, 2010.

[25] Y. Lv, C. Zhai, and W. Chen. A boosting approach to improving pseudo-relevance feedback. In *SIGIR*, pages 165–174, 2011.

[26] C. D. Manning, P. Raghavan, and H. Schütze. An introduction to information retrieval. In *Cambridge University Press*, 2009.

[27] S. C.-T. ownsend Y un Zhou W. Bruce Croft. A language modeling framework for selective query expansion. In *Univ Massachusetts Amherst Tech Report*, 2004.

[28] M. Schmidt. Graphical model structure learning with l1-regularization. *Univ British Columbia PhD Thesis*, 2010.

[29] H. Schütze and J. O. Pedersen. A coocurrence-based thesaurus and two applications to information retrieval. In *IPM*, 1997.

[30] M. Theobald, R. Schenkel, and G. Weikum. Efficient and self-tuning incremental query expansion for top-k query processing. In *SIGIR*, pages 242–249, 2005.

[31] P. Viola and M. J. Jones. Robust real-time face detection. *IJCV*, pages 137–154, 2004.

[32] E. M. Voorhees. Overview of the trec 2004 robust retrieval track. In *TREC*, pages 69–77, 2004.

[33] L. Wang, D. Metzler, and J. Lin. Ranking under temporal constraints. In *CIKM*, pages 79–88, 2010.

[34] J. Weston, S. Mukherjee, O. Chapelle, M. Pontil, T. Poggio, and V. Vapnik. Feature selection for svms. In *NIPS*, pages 668–674, 2000.

[35] H. Wu and H. Fang. An incremental approach to efficient pseudo-relevance feedback. In *SIGIR*, pages 553–562, 2013.

[36] C. Zhai and J. Lafferty. Model-based feedback in the language modeling approach to information retrieval. In *CIKM*, pages 403–410, 2001.

[37] Y. Zhao, F. Scholer, and Y. Tsegay. Effective pre-retrieval query performance prediction using similarity and variability evidence. In *ECIR*, pages 52–64, 2008.

[38] J. Zobel and A. Moffat. Inverted files for text search engines. *ACM Computing Surveys*.

Leveraging Context-Free Grammar for Efficient Inverted Index Compression

Zhaohua Zhang[1] Jiancong Tong[2] Haibing Huang[1] Jin Liang[2]
Tianlong Li[2] Rebecca J. Stones[1] Gang Wang[1†] Xiaoguang Liu[1†]

[1]College of Computer and Control Engineering & College of Software, Nankai University, China
[2]Baidu, Inc.
{zhangzhaohua, jctong, hbhuang, liangjin, litianlong, becky, wgzwp, liuxg}@nbjl.nankai.edu.cn

ABSTRACT

Large-scale search engines need to answer thousands of queries per second over billions of documents, which is typically done by querying a large inverted index. Many highly optimized integer encoding techniques are applied to compress the inverted index and reduce the query processing time. In this paper, we propose a new grammar-based inverted index compression scheme, which can improve the performance of both index compression and query processing.

Our approach identifies patterns (common subsequences of docIDs) among different posting lists and generates a context-free grammar to succinctly represent the inverted index. To further optimize the compression performance, we carefully redesign the index structure. Experiments show a reduction up to 8.8% in space usage while decompression is up to 14% faster.

We also design an efficient list intersection algorithm which utilizes the proposed grammar-based inverted index. We show that our scheme can be combined with common docID reassignment methods and encoding techniques, and yields about 14% to 27% higher throughput for AND queries by utilizing multiple threads.

Keywords

Inverted index compression, context-free grammar, query processing

1. INTRODUCTION

The most widely used data structure in current search engines is the *inverted index*, which allows the operator to find documents that contain particular terms efficiently [34]. The inverted index of a commercial search engine typically occupies a large fraction of total storage, so the index is ordinarily compressed. A smaller index not only means less space is needed but also decreased transmission time between the disk and main memory.

†Corresponding authors.

SIGIR '16, July 17-21, 2016, Pisa, Italy
© 2016 ACM. ISBN 978-1-4503-4069-4/16/07...$15.00
DOI: http://dx.doi.org/10.1145/2911451.2911518

Previous work on index compression techniques [1,2,37] mainly focus on various integer encoding schemes that aim to compress the identifiers of documents (docIDs, which are integers) in the inverted index better. Since these techniques are often concerned with compressing integer sequences whose values are small on average, their resulting compression ratios depend heavily on the way in which docIDs are assigned [6,28,35].

This paper is instead dedicated to a new compression scheme which improves the compression performance by removing the duplicate data before encoding. We note that duplicate data is dominant in the inverted index, with different posting lists containing common subsequences of docIDs, which we call *patterns*. We devise an algorithm called *PISequential* (Pattern Identification Sequentially) to identify patterns in the inverted index. Like other applications of the grammar-based method in compressing non-text data, it is difficult to obtain satisfactory compression ratio and decompression speed if we encode the generated grammar directly. To improve compression performance, we design a partitioned index structure. Besides compressing the inverted index, common patterns can also be utilized to improve the efficiency of query processing by eliminating unnecessary docID comparison operations. For AND queries, we propose an efficient intersection algorithm for the grammar-based inverted index, employing document reordering methods and run-length encoding. Moreover, the proposed index structure also supports OR and WAND [7] query processing.

2. PRELIMINARIES

2.1 Inverted Index and Compression

The inverted index is a simple yet powerful data structure used in search engines. Given a collection of N documents, each document will be identified by a unique docID from 1 to N. An inverted index consists of many posting lists. Each posting list corresponds to a unique term and contains all documents where this term occurs in the collection. For a term t, the posting list $l(t)$ typically has the structure

$$\langle d_1, d_2, d_3, \ldots, d_{f_t} \rangle$$

where f_t is the number of documents that contain t, and d_i is the docID of the i-th document containing t. Since the docIDs of a posting list are generally stored in an ascending order, modern search engines usually take differences between adjacent docIDs to convert $l(t)$ into a sequence of d-gaps $l'(t)$

$$\langle d_1, d_2 - d_1, d_3 - d_2, \ldots, d_{f_t} - d_{f_t - 1} \rangle$$

and then compress $l'(t)$ instead of $l(t)$.

To skip unnecessary subregions when processing queries, posting lists are often split into blocks of, say, 128 d-gaps each, so that only the blocks that are relevant to a query need to be accessed. Although we have to store a mapping table for fast block locating, the extra space occupied by it is much smaller than that used by the inverted index itself.

In the context of a search engine, inverted index compression (encoding) is usually infrequent compared to decompression (decoding), which must be performed for every uncached query. As grammar-based compressors often need a high amount of memory and time to run, this paper not only focuses on decompression performance but also compression performance. We not only consider the compression and decompression algorithms of the docIDs, but also how to store other pertinent information needed by processing scored queries in grammar-based index, such as term frequency.

2.2 Query Processing

For a given query, which is interpreted as a set of terms, the common query operations are *conjunctive queries* and *disjunctive queries*. Conjunctive (AND) queries are used to identify the subset of documents which contain all search terms. Disjunctive (OR) queries retrieve the documents which contain at least one term in the query. In most scenarios, each result document of one query should be associated with a *relevance score*. The score indicates the relevance between the query and the document. Most search engines use the *k* highest scored documents as the final retrieval result. One of the most popular relevance ranking methods is BM25 [26], which is used in our experiments.

To illustrate, assume the query "2016 Summer Olympics" is made. The search engine will find the posting lists l_1, l_2 and l_3 for the three terms "2016", "Summer" and "Olympics", respectively, which may look like

$$l_1 = \langle 1, 2, 3, 14, 20, 21, 39, 40, 49, 51, 55\rangle,$$
$$l_2 = \langle 1, 2, 3, 9, 10, 11, 14, 21, 39, 40, 49, 55\rangle \text{ and}$$
$$l_3 = \langle 1, 2, 3, 14, 16, 39, 49, 53, 55\rangle.$$

If the query above is processed as one conjunctive query, the intersection algorithm returns

$$l_1 \cap l_2 \cap l_3 = \langle 1, 2, 3, 14, 39, 49, 55\rangle$$

and the disjunctive algorithm returns

$$l_1 \cup l_2 \cup l_3 = \langle 1, 2, 3, 9, 10, 11, 14, 16, 20, 21, 39, 40, 49, 51, 53, 55\rangle.$$

Two basic techniques for traversing posting lists are *Document-At-A-Time* (DAAT) and *Term-At-A-Time* (TAAT) [8]. DAAT maintains a pointer to the "current" posting for each list, and moves the pointers forward in parallel as the query is being processed. TAAT traverses posting lists one by one, and uses a temporary data structure to keep track of the current candidates. In our experiments, we use TAAT for Boolean conjunctive queries and disjunctive queries, while for WAND queries we use DAAT.

2.3 Grammar-based Compression

A *context-free grammar* G is a quadruple (V_T, V_N, S, P) where V_T is a finite *alphabet* whose elements are called *terminals*, V_N is the set of *non-terminals*, and S is a special non-terminal called the *start symbol*. In general, the word *symbol* refers to any terminal or non-terminal. The last component P is a set of *production rules* of the form $A \to \alpha$, where A is a non-terminal and α is a string of symbols referred to as the *definition* of A.

A production rule $A \to \alpha$ can be rewritten to a string u, by iteratively replacing each non-terminal by its definition until only terminals remain. The set of strings derived from the start symbol is denoted by $L(G)$. A grammar G is *admissible* if $|L(G)| = 1$ and for each non-terminal A, there is exactly one production rule $A \to \alpha$ defined in P. Since we use a grammar G to represent and compress a unique inverted index, this paper only considers admissible grammars. Define $|G|$ as the total length of strings on the right hand sides of all production rules.

The central idea behind grammar-based compression is to use a context-free grammar to represent the input and reduce repeating patterns captured. For example, the string "*abaababa*" could be represented by the grammar

$$(\{a, b\}, \{Q, L, S\}, S, \{Q \to aba, L \to Qab, S \to LQ\}).$$

After inferring a grammar that represents the input string, these methods [17, 18, 21, 36] often convert the grammar to a symbol stream, and then transform it into a bit stream by an entropy encoder, which affects the final size of the compressed file. A decoder simply proceeds backwards.

3. RELATED WORK

3.1 Inverted Index Compression

Inverted index compression aims not only to reduce the space consumption of index files, but also to support efficient query processing. As posting lists in the inverted index are usually represented as strictly increasing sequences of integers (i.e., docIDs) together with term's frequency, search engines utilize mathematical encoding methods to compress these lists. Since many mathematical encoding methods aim to use fewer bytes (or bits) to represent the strictly monotone sequences, *delta encoding* has been widely used to achieve a high level of compression. Most previous work on index compression usually assumes that the posting lists are turned into *d*-gap lists and mainly focuses on encoding method.

Since topics related to compressing integer sequences have been studied several decades, many solutions have been proposed for different trade-offs between compression ratio and decompression speed, while both aspects are important for inverted index compression. In this paper, however, we just limit our discussion to several established integer encoding techniques suitable for this problem. VByte [33] encodes an integer using a variable number of bytes, where each byte consists of one status bit and 7 data bits. The status bit indicates whether the current byte is the last one in the representation of the integer or not. VByte does not achieve a good compression ratio, because it is unsuitable for compressing small integers. But it allows for fast decoding as the encoding is byte-aligned, and is thus used in many systems. Stepanov et al. [32] present a variant coding method based on VByte (called Varint-G8IU) which exploits SIMD instructions in modern CPU for faster decoding.

In addition, PForDelta [38] also aims at fast decompression. It divides the list of integers into segments of length s, always divisible by 32. To encode the integers within a given segment a, it first determines the smallest b such that most integers in a (say, 90%) are less than 2^b and thus can be stored using b bits. The remaining values, called *exceptions*, are encoded separately. In the slot of each exception, it maintains a pointer to the location of the next exception, forming a linked list. One popular variant of PForDelta is OptPFD, which is introduced in [35]. Instead of setting a constant threshold of the number of exceptions per block, OptPFD makes the selection an optimization problem to achieve the best trade-off between compression ratio and decoding speed.

Simple16 (S16) is also a widely used algorithm proposed in [37] that achieves both good compression and high decompression speed.

Compared with Simple9 (S9) [2], since each case of S16 uses all data bits, it achieves slightly better compression.

As most integer encoding methods require sequential decoding, each posting list is split into blocks, where each block can be encoded and decoded independently. In most cases, the size of block is fixed, e.g. 128 or 256 integers [10, 20]. Silvestri et al. [31] introduce an optimal partition strategy for partitioning an integer sequence into blocks to get better compression ratio.

In addition to mathematical encoding methods, there are other approaches for index compression. Beskales et al. [5] propose an approach to map terms in a document collection to a new term space, thereby to generate a more compact inverted index for better compression. Giuseppe et al. [24] describe an index scheme based on dividing posting list into chunks and compressing them with Elias-Fano code, thereby forming a two-level index structure. Their method takes advantage of the local statistics of the chunk for better encoding, thus improving compression. Some works also focus on compressed indexes used in labeled graphs [14], or combined with phrase-based ranking [25], and space-time tradeoff [23].

3.2 Document Reordering

To improve inverted index compression, a number of document reordering (*docID reassignment*) methods have been developed. The key idea of this kind of approach is to actively enhance the clustering property of posting lists so that similar documents have close docIDs, thereby improving the performance of integer encoders. The approaches proposed in [6, 30] use graph structures to represent the relationship among documents and assign docIDs during a graph traversal. A much simpler yet effective approach was proposed in [29], which assigns docIDs alphabetically according to their URLs.

Recently, Arroyuelo et al. [3] proposed a reordering method based on run-length encoding which is able to create longer runs of d-gaps of 1 (or just 1s, for short). By representing each run with just two values when encoding the posting lists, they showed that space usage can be reduced. Shi et al. [27] instead achieved longer runs of 1s by reordering according to the document frequencies of terms in the inverted index. These two methods not only enhance the clustering property, but also provide more runs, thereby achieving better compression than run-length encoding. Moreover, for every occurrence of a specific run with length l, only two instead of l values need to be stored no matter how large l is, so the two methods actually reduce redundant storage for the multiple occurrences of a common docID sequence.

In this paper, we present a more general and powerful pattern identification algorithm which improves common encoding techniques and reordering methods.

3.3 List Intersection

Sorted lists intersection has been studied for several decades. There are many searching methods proposed such as linear search, interpolation search [15] and galloping search [4]. However, as the inverted lists are typically stored compactly by using the methods mentioned in Section 3.1, some special algorithms are proposed to accelerate intersection on these compact sequences. Gupta et al. [16] achieved good asymptotic performance by introducing a two-level data structure in which each level is itself searchable and compressed. Culpepper et al. [13] proposed a simpler hybrid method that can provide both compact storage and faster lists intersection. However, as described in Section 2.1, these methods need to store an auxiliary index, and decompression will be much slower than intersection when processing queries. In [3], a novel lists intersection algorithm was provided which reduces explicit decompression by directly performing range checking on the runs. Although it still stores auxiliary index, as fewer docIDs need to be decoded, it reduces the query processing time effectively.

Compared with these algorithms, the scheme presented in this paper aims at: utilizing a grammar-based index structure to reduce the redundant comparison operations, and exploiting reordering methods and encoding techniques such as run-length encoding to reduce extra overhead, e.g., random memory access overhead.

3.4 Grammar-based Compression

Grammar-based compression is an active research area with a wide variety of applications. Nevill-Manning and Witten [21, 22] proposed an on-line linear-time algorithm, called *Sequitur*, which infers a context-free grammar to losslessly represent the input. Yang and Kieffer [36] improved Sequitur to make it universal. *Re-Pair* [18], proposed by Larsson and Moffat, is an off-line algorithm that infers a dictionary by recursively creating the phrases that occur most frequently. Although these methods have shown success for many different types of data (in fact, some of them are known to be asymptotically optimal on input strings generated by finite-state sources), Charikar et al. [9] showed that many of the best-known compressors can fail dramatically. A good grammar-based compression algorithm often attempts to find the smallest possible grammar generating the input string, but a smaller grammar does not necessarily mean a smaller compression ratio as described in [36], as many practical issues are ignored.

Recently, Claude et al. [11] introduced a new compressed inverted index by using grammar-based compression for highly repetitive document collections. They use *Re-Pair* as their grammar compressor and then compress the sequence formed by concatenating all of the d-gap lists. They also add extra information to non-terminals that enables fast skipping over the compressed lists without decompressing. According to their experiments, their methods significantly reduce the space achieved by classical compression, at the price of moderated slowdowns on word and conjunctive queries. Moreover, they discuss some possible extensions in [12], such as supporting ranking capabilities within their index. Instead of the particular case of highly repetitive collections, we focus on a more general one, in which there may not be enough repetition to make up for the expansion that using a grammar causes. Therefore, in addition to making/finding more common patterns among posting lists, another important task of this paper is to reduce the overhead by using some auxiliary methods.

4. THE PROPOSED SCHEME

The key idea of the proposed compression scheme is to identify and remove repeating patterns among posting lists before encoding them. In Section 4.1, we provide the pattern identification algorithm. To illustrate, suppose the posting lists l_1, l_2, l_3 described in Section 2.2 need to be compressed. After processed by our algorithm, they are represented as a grammar G that consists of the production rules:

$$
\begin{aligned}
A &\rightarrow (1, 2, 3)\\
B &\rightarrow (21, 39, 40, 49)\\
l_1' &\rightarrow (A, 14, 20, B, 51, 55)\\
l_2' &\rightarrow (A, 9, 10, 11, 14, B, 55)\\
l_3' &\rightarrow (A, 14, 16, 39, 49, 53, 55)
\end{aligned}
$$

where A and B are the identifiers of the *patterns* found in l_1, l_2, l_3, and l_1', l_2', l_3' are the *reduced posting lists*. The identifiers of patterns and reduced posting lists together make up the set of non-terminals. For this example, the non-terminals are $\{A, B, l_1', l_2', l_3'\}$.

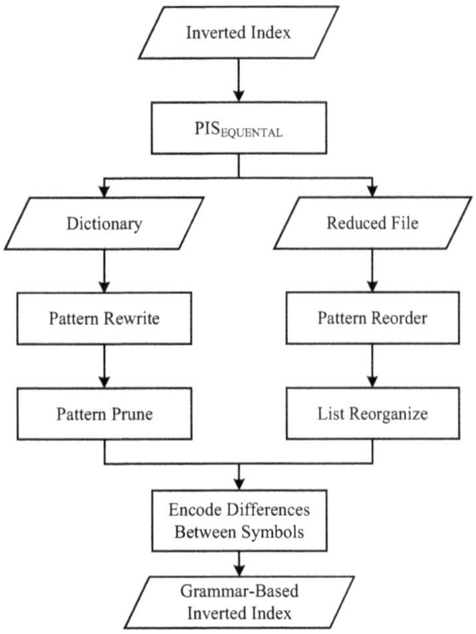

Figure 1: Flowchart of the proposed Grammar-based Compression Scheme

The remaining docIDs are terminals, which, for the above example, are $\{1, 2, 3, 9, 10, 14, \ldots, 55\}$. Since we must express distinct lists rather than a single input, this grammar has a set of start symbols rather than a single start symbol (in the example above, $\{l_1', l_2', l_3'\}$). So we represent the grammar by a quadruple $G = (DI, PI \cup RI, RI, PP \cup RP)$, where DI, PI and RI respectively denote the identifier sets of documents, patterns and reduced lists, and PP and RP denote the pattern and reduced list production sets respectively. Since the repetitions are removed, the reduced index size $|G|$ is smaller than that of the original index size $|l_1| + |l_2| + |l_3|$. The complete compression scheme is shown in Figure 1.

In our implementation, we have found that the overall memory usage for grammar generation is a critical problem. For the 12GB original index file we use, the process of pattern identification would cost more than 64GB memory. To reduce memory usage, we use a hash segmentation strategy to partition the original index into segments, where the grammar generation on each segment is independent from others. In Section 4.2, we will give the details of the index partition. Moreover, the generated grammar is unsuitable for encoding directly, so we propose some approaches to improve the compression performance. Section 4.3 introduces how we reorganize the generated grammar.

4.1 Pattern Identification

The key to grammar-based compression is to effectively find and remove repetitions occurring in the data. In this subsection, we modify a widely used grammar-based compression algorithm [36], *SEQUENTIAL*, to work on an inverted index, which we call PISEQUENTIAL.

The details of PISEQUENTIAL are shown in Algorithm 1. The function find_longest_prefix(l_i, j, PP) finds the longest prefix of the unprocessed portion of l_i beginning with $l_i[j]$ that matches the expansion of some pattern production rule in PP. If found, it returns the pattern identifier; otherwise, $l_i[j]$ is returned. In Algorithm 1, freq(p) denotes the number of times p occurs in the right-hand side of production rules in $PP \cup RP$.

Algorithm 1 PISEQUENTIAL for pattern identification

Input: Inverted index I including posting lists $\{l_1, l_2, \ldots, l_n\}$
Output: A grammar $G_0 = (DI, PI \cup RI, RI, PP \cup RP)$ that represents I
1: Initialize PI, RI, PP and RP to $\emptyset$
2: **for** each posting list l_i of I **do**
3: Create a new empty production rule $r_i \rightarrow \varepsilon$
4: **for** $j = 1$ to $|l_i|$ **do** ▷ traverse the list from left to right
5: **if** $j = 1$ **then**
6: replace $r_i \rightarrow \varepsilon$ with $r_i \rightarrow l_i[1]$
7: $j := j + 1$
8: continue
9: **end if**
10: $s :=$ find_longest_prefix(l_i, j, PP)
11: $j := j + ||s||$
▷ $||s||$ is the length of pattern rule, or 1 if not found
12: If currently $r_i \rightarrow \alpha$, set $b :=$ last_symbol$(\alpha)s$ and replace $r_i \rightarrow \alpha$ with $r_i \rightarrow \alpha s$
13: **if** b appears in y in some $x \rightarrow y \in PP \cup RP$ **then**
14: Create a new pattern $p \rightarrow b$
15: In the production rules for r_i and x, replace the occurrences of the subsequence b by p
16: Add p to PI and $p \rightarrow b$ to PP
17: **end if**
18: **end for**
19: Add r_i to RI and the production rule for r_i to RP
20: **end for**
21: **for** each pattern $p \rightarrow \delta$ in PP **do**
22: **if** freq$(p) \times (|p| - 1) < |p| + 1$ **then**
23: Replace all occurrences of p in PP and RP by δ
24: **end if**
25: **end for**
26: Make identifiers in RI consecutive and update productions in PP and RP

The main difference compared with SEQUENTIAL is that, PISEQUENTIAL processes posting lists one by one (lines 2-20) to find repeating patterns, which makes each posting list self-indexed, and separates the dictionary of found patterns from posting lists. Another important improvement happens after grammar generation. Since there's possibly upwards of millions of docIDs, most of the posting lists are relatively sparse. Therefore, the grammar-based method will naively generate a large number of short production rules, which do not combine into longer ones. In order to improve compression, PISEQUENTIAL subsequently removes some of these short production rules to improve the compression performance (lines 21-26).

After the grammar is generated, we store a dictionary containing the pattern productions PP and a file of the reduced posting list productions RP. To differentiate pattern identifiers from docIDs in posting lists, we set the most significant bit of a 32-bit word to represent a pattern identifier and use the reset bit to represent a docID.

4.2 Index Partition

In our implementation, we find that the corpora of bigrams (b on line 12 in Algorithm 1) temporarily uses at least 5.3 times more memory than the original index file, a significant constraint that also results in poor bigram search efficiency. The reason is that we need to keep a record of each possible bigram in the whole index and grammar list. Consequently, we partition the original inverted index into segments according to the most significant *K* bits of the docIDs. After this, we use Algorithm 1 to generate the grammar on each individual segment. Although some long patterns could be missed by this method, we reduce the overall memory usage when generating the context-free grammar since each segment is much smaller than the whole index. Moreover, as each segment is independent, the memory spent by the bigrams of previous segments can be reused. More details about index partition will be discussed in Section 5.2.

4.3 Grammar Reorganization

To save space, we store the gaps of docIDs instead of original values. Although there may be non-terminals in the list, we just skip them and turn each docID into the value by subtracting from the previous docID. If the preceding symbol is a non-terminal, the previous docID should be the last docID in the pattern. Take the grammar G described at the beginning of the Section 4 as an example, the grammar will be

$$\begin{aligned} &A \rightarrow (1, 1, 1) \\ &B \rightarrow (21, 18, 1, 9) \\ &l_1{}' \rightarrow (A, 11, 6, B, 2, 4) \\ &l_2{}' \rightarrow (A, 6, 1, 1, 3, B, 6) \\ &l_3{}' \rightarrow (A, 11, 2, 23, 10, 4, 2). \end{aligned}$$

Traditional integer encoding schemes are generally proposed on the assumption that the gaps are distributed according to a power-law distribution. Once the assumption does not hold, their compression performance may decline sharply. Therefore, we analyze the gap distribution of the generated grammar (G_0); see Figure 2.

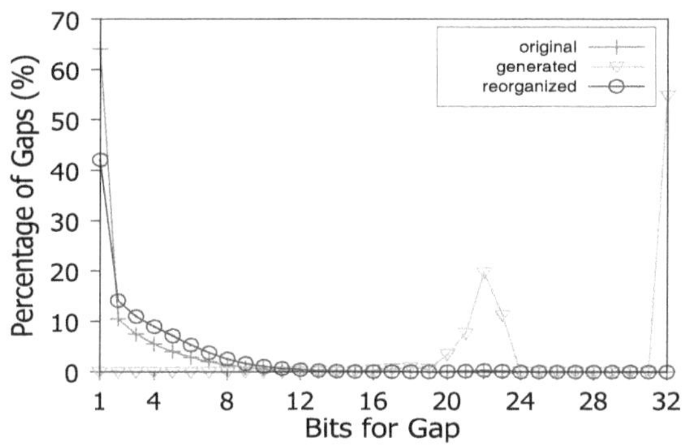

Figure 2: The proportion of gaps with a given number of bits for the *original lists*, the *generated grammar (G_0)*, and the *reorganized grammar (G_2)* on the *GOV2* data set, of which docIDs are assigned by URL.

Figure 2 shows a decided difference between the gap distribution of the generated grammar (G_0 in Algorithm 1) and that of the original lists (which display a power-law distribution). As a result, it is difficult to obtain a satisfactory compression ratio by encoding G_0 directly. Moreover, random memory accesses caused by pattern fetching significantly impacts decompression speed, so we reorganize the grammar to address these issues.

Algorithm 2 rewrites each pattern production rule to a terminal string, i.e., it eliminates hierarchies in the grammar, with the aim of reducing the memory access overhead. It also removes all patterns whose length is smaller than a preset threshold L. Although this reorganization may result in larger space requirements, it avoids many random memory accesses, and so decompression and intersection are faster.

For the reduced posting list, since each pattern identifier is represented by a 32-bit integer, indicated by setting the most significant

---

Algorithm 2 Pattern rewriting and pruning

Input: The grammar $G_0 = (DI, PI \cup RI, RI, PP \cup RP)$ generated by PISEQUENTIAL and a threshold L
Output: A grammar G_1 in which the patterns are rewritten and the corresponding lists are updated
1: **for** each pattern $p \rightarrow \alpha$ in PP **do**
2:   **while** α has non-terminal(s) **do**
3:     Replace each non-terminal in α by its definition
4:   **end while**
5:   **if** $|\alpha| \leq L$ **then** ▷ remove short patterns for performance
6:     Replace each occurrence of p by α in the right-hand side of any production rule in $PP \cup RP$
7:     Remove $p \rightarrow \alpha$ from PP and p from PI
8:   **end if**
9: **end for**
10: Remove all unreferenced patterns from PP

---

bit to 1, patterns are effectively encoded as large integers, which will result in poor compression. Algorithm 3 eliminates the indicating bit, so the integers representing pattern identifiers are smaller, and can be stored in fewer bits. Because of this, all pattern identifiers in PP are reassigned in ascending order of their patterns (line 1 in Algorithm 3) and consequently the pattern identifiers in each reduced posting list remain in ascending order, which makes it possible to store their gaps rather than the pattern identifiers themselves. We convert each non-terminal (except the first one) in a production rule of a reduced posting list to its gap value, i.e., we subtract the previous non-terminal (line 4). We store these gaps (or non-terminal for the first element in the list) with one extra integer to indicate the offset to the next non-terminal. The extra offset for the last non-terminal of the list is zero. For each list, we also have to store one extra value to indicate the position of the first non-terminal.

Algorithm 3 Pattern reordering and list reorganizing

Input: The grammar $G_1 = (DI, PI \cup RI, RI, PP \cup RP)$ generated by Algorithm 2
Output: A grammar $G_2 = (DI, PI \cup RI, RI, PP' \cup RP')$ in which the pattern identifiers are reassigned and the reduced posting lists are reorganized
1: Assign $\{1, 2, \ldots, |PP|\}$ to all pattern identifiers in PP according to the ascending order of their patterns
2: **for** each reduced posting list $l \rightarrow \beta$ in RP **do**
3:   Update non-terminals in β using new pattern identifiers
4:   Transform non-terminals in β into gap lists
5: **end for**

After these processes, the integers to be encoded are effectively decreased. In our running example, A and B will be respectively assigned the pattern identifiers 1 and 2 by Algorithm 3, and the production rules

$$\begin{aligned} &l_1{}' \rightarrow (A, 11, 6, B, 2, 4) \\ &l_2{}' \rightarrow (A, 6, 1, 1, 3, B, 6) \\ &l_3{}' \rightarrow (A, 11, 2, 23, 10, 4, 2), \end{aligned}$$

will be encoded as

$$\begin{aligned} &l_1{}'' \rightarrow (1) \uplus ((1, 3), 11, 6, (1, 0), 2, 4) \\ &l_2{}'' \rightarrow (1) \uplus ((1, 5), 6, 1, 1, 3, (1, 0), 6) \\ &l_3{}'' \rightarrow (1) \uplus ((1, 0), 11, 2, 23, 10, 4, 2) \end{aligned}$$

where patterns are replaced by the pair

(pattern identifier gap, distance to next pattern).

The pattern identifier gap is defined as the pattern identifier minus the previous pattern identifier, except for the first pattern, when it is equal to the pattern identifier. The distance to next pattern is set to 0 for the last pattern. We also preappend the location of the first non-terminal, which happens to be 1 in all three cases in our example, which we denote (1).

The gap distribution in G_2 is comparable to the distribution for the original list, as indicated in Figure 2. Moreover, experiments indicate that the compression ratio can reach around 35% after transforming G_0 into G_2. It is thus possible to use mathematical encoding methods to compress reduced lists and patterns.

4.4 Query Processing on the Grammar-based Index

In this section, we describe how we conduct processing on the grammar-based index. We consider three query operations: AND queries, OR queries and WAND queries. Here we describe boolean AND queries, but the idea applies to the other operations.

In Section 4.4.1, we present the basic intersection algorithm suitable to our index structure. To produce more patterns among lists involved in the same query, Section 4.4.2 introduces several document reordering methods. To use patterns more effectively when processing queries, in Section 4.4.3, we restrict the patterns identified by PISEQUENTIAL to common "runs" among different posting lists rather than noncontinuous sequences.

4.4.1 Intersection Algorithm

The grammar-based index consists of not only the docIDs but also the patterns. Therefore, we design a new intersection algorithm suited to process queries on grammar-based indexes, shown in Algorithm 4. This algorithm has the same skeleton as the algorithms for plain inverted index; the key difference is the function INTERSECT which perform intersections on two reduced posting lists (lines 11 to 26 in Algorithm 4).

INTERSECT scans the two lists sequentially until one of them is exhausted. For each comparison between two elements, there are three possible scenarios: (1) If the two elements are identical, INTERSECT appends p directly to the resulting list, whether or not p and q are both non-terminals or terminals (docIDs). (2) If p and q overlap and both are non-terminals, it fetches their definitions and performs an ordinary document lists intersection. (3) Otherwise, if one element is docID d and the other is pattern, it fetches the pattern's production rule from the dictionary and searches for d within it, and then appends d to the result if found (lines 19 to 22). The algorithm finally rewrites the pattern list to a terminal string and merges it with the document list.

The first situation above saves many comparison operations by placing common patterns directly in the result (i.e. both elements are non-terminals). Profiling results show an advantage of Algorithm 4 over plain lists intersection in terms of the number of comparison operations required. However, many random memory accesses come as a result of fetching pattern definitions, offsetting this advantage. Consequently, we next explore how to make more patterns and use them more effectively.

We use a "skip" strategy to avoid some unnecessary random memory accesses. Specifically, before determining whether a docID exists in a pattern, we check the next element after the pattern first. For example, on line 20 in Algorithm 4 where p is the pattern and q is the docID, the next element n is $l_i[m+1]$. If n is also a docID and q is not smaller than n, we skip p and compare q with elements after p. Otherwise, we will fetch the production rule for p and search for q in it. Experiments indicate this skip strategy can reduce random memory accesses by approximately 20%. Moreover, we utilize the prefetch CPU instruction to read production rules to hide the latency caused by cache misses, which achieves about a 13% speedup in AND query processing.

Algorithm 4 List Intersection on a grammar-based index

Input: A u-term query $(t_1, t_2, \ldots, t_u)$ and the compressed grammar G that represents inverted index I

Output: The intersection results $\bigcap_{1 \le i \le u} l(t_i)$

1: Load the dictionary into the memory
2: Re-label the u lists so that $|l(t_1)| \le |l(t_2)| \le \cdots \le |l(t_u)|$
3: $l = l(t_1)$ ▷ l keeps track of the current candidates
4: $i := 2$
5: **while** $i \le k$ **do** ▷ intersect other lists $l(t_i)$ with l one by one
6: $l' = \text{INTERSECT}(l, l(t_i))$
7: $i := i + 1$
8: $l = l'$
9: **end while**
10: **return** l

11: **procedure** INTERSECT(l_i, l_j)
12: Create an empty set $r = \emptyset$
13: **for** $m = 1$ to $|l_i|$ and $n = 1$ to $|l_j|$ **do**
14: $p := l_i[m]$ and $q := l_j[n]$
15: **if** $p = q$ **then**
16: Add p to r
17: **else if** both p and q are non-terminals **then**
18: Intersect production rules of p and q, then add result(s) to r
19: **else if** p is a non-terminal **then**
20: Search for q in p, then add q to r if found
21: **else if** q is a non-terminal **then**
22: Search for p in q, then add p to r if found
23: **end if**
24: **end for**
25: Return r
26: **end procedure**

4.4.2 Pre-grammar Document Reordering

We test two existing document reordering methods and design a new method to produce more and longer common patterns among posting lists, especially lists involved in the same query.

Intersection-Based DocID Assignment (IBDA) [3] This aims to generate longer runs in the inverted index. For a given inverted index $L = \{l_1, l_2, \ldots, l_n\}$, it computes $l_1 \cap l_2$, $l_1 \cap l_2 \cap l_3$, ..., until $|l_1 \cap l_2 \cap \cdots \cap l_{j+1}| < M$, where M is a preset threshold. Then it assigns consecutive identifiers to the documents in $l_1 \cap \cdots \cap l_j$, and then to those in $l_1 \cap \cdots \cap l_{j-1} \setminus l_j$, and so on, until to $l_1 \cap l_2 \setminus l_3$. Then it removes the documents with reassigned docIDs from L, and repeats these steps until $L = \emptyset$. A related method was also described in [3], in which the co-occurrence of term pairs mined from the query log is used to determine the processing order of the lists, which we use for the experiments in this paper.

Term sorting-based(TRM) [27] This reordering method aims to produce smaller d-gaps. It first sorts posting lists in the descending order of their length, then sorts docIDs in the order in which they appear in the lists.

Frequency-Based Reordering (FBR) Grammar-based compression will benefit from highly repetitive sequences in the dataset, resulting in long duplicated sequences and the frequencies of them are higher. So we use a two-phase reordering method. After the index partition described in Section 4.2, we reorder the docIDs inside each segment in descending order of their frequency (within all posting lists in the same segment). Since the most frequent documents are moved to the head in each posting list, we then partition these docIDs into groups, with the number of docIDs are the same for each group (say 128 elements). In each group, we use the URL reordering method to assign final consecutive docID.

4.4.3 *Run-length-based Intersection Algorithm*

The document reordering methods result in more and longer patterns. However, pattern fetching introduces a large number of random memory accesses which significantly impacts query processing performance. To address this issue, we modify PISEQUENTIAL so that it only inserts new patterns that form a run. Since each run can be represented precisely by the minimum and the maximum docIDs, the output is significantly reduced. When we check whether one docID exists in the pattern, we only need to perform two comparison operations, i.e. to check if the docID is in the range of the pattern, and no more random memory accesses are required.

While this run-based grammar index structure may have a slight impact on the compression ratio, it improves query processing performance significantly. The proposed grammar-based scheme exploits run-length encoding like IBDA and TRM, but it employs a more general and powerful common pattern (run) identification algorithm.

5. EXPERIMENTS

5.1 Experimental Setup

To compare the various index schemes, we make use of full web documents from the *GOV2* collection as our document corpus, which results in an index of approximately 12 GB without positional information and frequencies. For scored queries, there is another index of about 12 GB storing frequency information and one file about 97MB storing document sizes. The docIDs are assigned according to the lexicographic order of their URLs [29]. We choose the *TREC 2009 Efficiency query set* (*T09*), which contains 32,244 queries, as our test query set.

We carried out all experiments on a PC server with a hexa-core 2.60 GHz Intel(R) Xeon(R) CPU and 64 GB of memory, running the CentOS 6.5. All algorithms are implemented in C++ and are compiled with g++ version 4.8.2, with optimization flag -O3. In our experiments, we use the IBDA, TRM and FBR document reordering methods. We implement IBDA and TRM based on their descriptions in their corresponding papers. For the integer encoders, we use the highly-efficient implementations from [19]. In our implementation, we use OptPFD to compress the dictionary, the reduced file and term frequency information. We encode each reduced list in blocks of 128 elements (docID or non-terminal) and also store a separate array about the maximum docID of each block for fast skipping during list intersection. The term frequencies of postings are stored apart from grammar index and kept the same order to posting lists. For each non-terminal in the reduced list, we also store the offset to the next frequency in the term frquency list, since there are more than one posting in the pattern.

We make use of the state-of-art indexes from [24] as our baselines. We also use the code made available by the authors of [11] to compare our method with RePair-Skip. We find that RePair-Skip get worse results than our methods and baselines. Due to limited space, we ignore the results of RePair-Skip here. To validate grammar-based indexes against the partitioned Elias-Fano and block-based indexes, we compared the construction consumption during index building, compression ratio and query process time between our methods and baselines. We refer to the grammar-based index, Elias-Fano index and block-based index as GM, EF and BLK, respectively. GM is the index generated by PISEQUENTIAL, while GM-Run is a modified version of GM which only identifies the patterns which form a run. At the beginning of experiments of decompression and query processing, all indexes are loaded into the memory.

5.2 Memory Usage in Pattern Identification

Before comparing the performance of the different indexes, we first investigate the memory space spent on pattern identification, of which the cost is larger than other procedures when compressing the inverted index with our methods.

As described in Section 4.2, we find that memory usage for pattern identification is temporarily at least 5.3 times more than original index file. Consequently, we partition the inverted index before grammar generation. According to the most significant K bits of the docID, we split each posting list into 2^K parts (some parts may be empty), and PISEQUENTIAL will be executed on each part across different lists individually. The memory usage and space usage as K varies is shown in Figure 3.

As we would expect, as K increases, the peak value of memory usage for each segment (solid lines) becomes smaller as fewer temporary data structures need to be maintained by PISEQUENTIAL. The peak memory usage is approximately 11.5 GB for GM and 12.8 GB for GM-Run when K is 3. When K is less than 3, the memory consumption for temporary data structures exceeds 64GB, which is the physical memory capacity in our server.

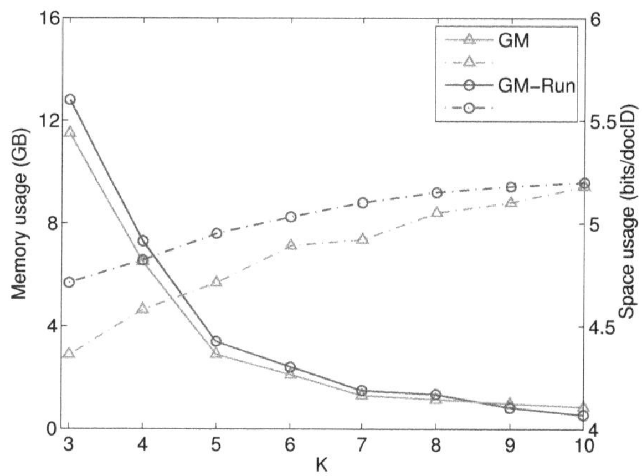

Figure 3: Peak memory usage (solid) and space usage (dashed) of GM and GM-Run.

We also find that the space usage (dashed lines in Figure 3) grows with K on both GM and GM-Run, implying the proposed method remains functional for larger indexes. As the value of K increases, more long candidate patterns have been cut off since the origin posting list becomes shorter for each segment. Based on these observation, we select $K = 3$ for our grammar-based index.

5.3 Compression and Decompression

5.3.1 *Space usage*

In Table 1 we list the compression ratio in two different formats: (a) the average number of bits required for each docID in the compressed lists, and (b) the overall space in gigabytes (without frequencies).

Table 1: Space usage of the index schemes for different document reordering methods

Index Scheme	Space (bits/int)				Space (GB)			
	URL	FBR	IBDA	TRM	URL	FBR	IBDA	TRM
EF Uniform	5.41	4.98	6.13	5.83	2.19	1.89	2.29	2.21
EF ϵ-optimal	4.77	4.38	5.98	5.68	1.83	1.66	2.24	2.13
BLK OptPFD	5.21	4.63	6.43	5.93	1.98	1.74	2.43	2.25
BLK VByte	10.32	9.83	11.24	10.20	4.12	3.81	4.47	4.01
GM	4.35	4.01	5.82	5.31	1.78	1.58	2.20	1.99
GM-Run	4.41	4.33	5.97	5.61	1.79	1.64	2.23	2.12

We make the following observations:

- Both GM and GM-Run outperform the baselines on compression. The improvement over the best baseline EF ϵ-optimal is up to 8.8%.
- The compression ratio of GM is slightly better than GM-Run. This is because GM-Run only contains the run patterns in its dictionary while some other patterns are not extracted from the inverted index.
- All schemes benefited from the use of the FBR reordering method, and the best compression ratio overall is achieved by GM with FBR reordering.

5.3.2 *Decompression speed*

To test the decompression speed, we decompress all inverted lists accessed by the queries from *T09*. In Table 2, we show the average decompression speed for the different integer encoding methods in millions of docIDs per second. Since there is no obvious decoding operation for EF indexes, we omit the decompression speed of EF indexes in Table 2.

Table 2: Decompression speed for different index schemes and document reordering methods

Index Scheme	Speed ($\times 10^6$ docs/sec)			
	URL	FBR	IBDA	TRM
BLK OptPFD	369	365	383	384
BLK VByte	498	491	492	520
GM	361	374	400	402
GM-Run	504	519	550	593

The main observations are the following:

- All index schemes achieve their best improvement on docIDs assigned by TRM, while the lowest speeds are on reordering by FBR. In all reordering methods, GM-Run achieves a better decompression speed than baselines. It yields an enhancement of 1.2% to 14% over the best baseline BLK VByte.
- The decompression speed of GM-Run outperforms GM in all document reordering methods. Unlike for GM-Run, for GM we compress the dictionary with OptPFD, and patterns in runs decompress much faster. The improvement over GM is about 38% to 48%.
- The TRM reordering method can generate longer runs in posting lists, which results in a better decompression speed for GM-Run. More longer patterns also result in fewer random memory accesses caused by pattern fetching during decompression.

From Tables 1 and 2, we can see that an index reordered by FBR can generate better a grammar-based index in terms of compression. For better decompression speed, however, the IBDA and TRM reordering methods perform better. We can conclude that the proposed grammar transformation is able to improve compression ratio by up to 8.8% and decompression speed by up to 14% vs. the baselines.

5.4 Query Processing Performance

We now focus on testing the efficiency of our methods for query processing. Since modern search engines typically utilize multi-core CPUs to boost processing, we not only conduct experiments on a single thread, but also test multi-threaded performance. For multi-threaded experiments, we report both average query processing time and throughput. Higher throughput implies that we can use less hardware resources to support the same number of users or use the same hardware resources to serve more users. For each index scheme, we batch every thousand queries for one new thread to process, while the maximum number of threads is set to 12. The average times here are measured by running the same query set 3 times.

In Table 3(a), we compare the average processing time for AND query processing. We see that grammar indexes underperform both Elias-Fano indexes and block-based indexes with a single thread. The difference between GM and EF ϵ-optimal is about 12% to 26%, while for GM-Run the difference is approximately 1.7% to 10%. Since a grammar index is divided into two parts in the main memory, frequent cache misses on random memory accesses occur during list intersection, which causes the worse performance compared to the baselines. In contrast, the speedups for grammar indexes with multiple threads are better. In this setting, GM underperforms EF ϵ-optimal by 4.3% to 7.5%, and GM-Run even outperforms ϵ-optimal about 3.3% to 15%. The reason is that the cache miss problem for grammar indexes is effectively "hidden" when utilizing multiple threads. When a cache miss occurs in one thread, the CPU instead executes another thread until the cache miss is resolved in the original thread. Therefore, the benefit of GM-Run, i.e., reducing the number of comparisons of docIDs during list intersection (e.g., the difference is about 45.7% over EF ϵ-optimal with index of which docIDs assigned by TRM), results in less query processing time.

The throughput of GM for AND query processing is closer to the baselines, while the throughput for GM-Run is much better than the EF baselines. For GM, the deficiency versus EF ϵ-optimal can be up to 7.5%, although GM slightly outperforms EF ϵ-optimal when docIDs are reassigned by TRM. The improvement of throughput of GM over BLK OptPFD is up to 26%. GM-Run achieves better throughput than most baselines, e.g. it outperforms EF ϵ-optimal by about 14% to 27% and using TRM, it outperforms the best baseline, BLK VByte, by over 5.9%. These observations indicate that the proposed grammar index can achieve higher throughput than the baselines when using multiple threads. Although the average processing time of GM and GM-Run is worse than most baselines, the difference would be insignificant to an end user (typically smaller than 1 ms).

In Tables 3(b) and 3(c), we also compare the processing time and throughput for OR and top-10 WAND queries on the different index schemes. These results indicate the proposed grammar index is not best suited to OR or WAND queries in terms of both query processing time and throughput. Unlike for AND queries, OR and WAND queries do not benefit from identifying patterns, which aims to reduce comparisons during query processing.

Table 3: Average time (ms) and throughput (queries/sec) for different query operations

(a) AND queries

Index Scheme	Avg. time, single thread				Avg. time, multiple threads				Throughput, multiple threads			
	URL	FBR	IBDA	TRM	URL	FBR	IBDA	TRM	URL	FBR	IBDA	TRM
EF Uniform	4.34	3.66	3.48	3.23	0.63	0.55	0.51	0.47	980	1026	1097	1256
EF ϵ-optimal	3.89	3.57	3.11	3.04	0.60	0.53	0.50	0.46	1104	1262	1301	1469
BLK OptPFD	4.11	3.98	3.57	3.42	0.63	0.55	0.52	0.54	1003	1026	1039	1173
BLK VByte	2.82	2.67	2.12	1.99	0.34	0.28	0.24	0.21	1305	1485	1532	1765
GM	4.37	4.04	3.89	3.82	0.64	0.57	0.53	0.48	1021	1214	1300	1483
GM-Run	3.99	3.63	3.43	3.29	0.58	0.50	0.47	0.39	1257	1465	1493	1869

(b) OR queries

Index Scheme	Avg. time, single thread				Avg. time, multiple threads				Throughput, multiple threads			
	URL	FBR	IBDA	TRM	URL	FBR	IBDA	TRM	URL	FBR	IBDA	TRM
EF Uniform	102.2	95.4	91.1	94.3	32.0	31.6	30.8	31.2	31.9	33.9	36.5	35.0
EF ϵ-optimal	104.4	97.8	92.3	96.3	33.4	32.3	30.2	32.2	29.3	32.0	35.6	33.2
BLK OptPFD	101.8	95.4	88.4	98.4	31.4	29.4	23.4	30.9	30.9	33.6	41.8	33.4
BLK VByte	98.4	90.1	86.7	92.3	30.5	28.4	23.2	29.1	34.4	37.8	44.8	37.1
GM	115.9	111.4	106.3	109.8	40.4	38.3	36.9	37.4	25.2	26.9	27.7	27.4
GM-Run	109.7	103.5	97.4	99.9	36.9	35.4	33.2	34.7	27.5	28.6	30.8	29.5

(c) Top-10 WAND queries

Index Scheme	Avg. time, single thread				Avg. time, multiple threads				Throughput, multiple threads			
	URL	FBR	IBDA	TRM	URL	FBR	IBDA	TRM	URL	FBR	IBDA	TRM
EF Uniform	17.4	14.6	13.4	14.6	4.13	3.87	3.34	3.54	263	286	315	310
EF ϵ-optimal	16.3	12.9	11.4	13.8	3.98	3.58	3.23	3.34	270	289	330	311
BLK OptPFD	14.5	12.4	11.2	13.2	3.72	3.41	3.01	3.14	274	295	321	303
BLK VByte	11.3	9.6	9.2	9.6	3.12	2.98	2.23	2.56	326	346	448	397
GM	21.4	19.3	17.6	16.4	4.32	4.56	4.42	4.33	266	281	271	290
GM-Run	18.4	17.0	14.6	14.0	4.29	4.18	3.91	3.52	259	265	284	309

6. CONCLUSIONS AND FUTURE WORK

In this paper, we propose a new compression scheme where the key idea is generating a context-free grammar to represent the inverted index succinctly and then compressing it using integer encoding. We also present approaches to query processing suited to this grammar-based index scheme.

By evaluating index compression and query processing on various index structures, the integer encoding and document reordering methods yield better general performance on the run-based grammar index structure instead of the traditional inverted index structure. On the grammar index, we obtain up to 8.8% reduction in space usage and up to 14% acceleration in index decompression speed, while still achieving a reasonable query processing performance, especially high throughput with multiple threads condition. As future work, it would be worthwhile using d-gap lists to generate grammar index, and combining grammar based compression method with Elias-Fano coding.

7. ACKNOWLEDGEMENTS

This work is partially supported by NSF of China (61373018, 11301288, 11550110491), Program for New Century Excellent Talents in University (NCET130301) and the Fundamental Research Funds for the Central Universities (65141021).

8. REFERENCES

[1] V. N. Anh and A. Moffat. Index compression using fixed binary codewords. In *Proc. 15th Australasian Database Conference*, volume 27, pages 61–67, Darlinghurst, Australia, 2004.

[2] V. N. Anh and A. Moffat. Inverted index compression using word-aligned binary codes. *Information Retrieval*, 8:151–166, 2005.

[3] D. Arroyuelo, S. González, M. Oyarzún, and V. Sepulveda. Document identifier reassignment and run-length-compressed inverted indexes for improved search performance. In *Proc. 36th International ACM SIGIR Conference*, pages 173–182, New York, NY, USA, 2013.

[4] J. L. Bentley and A. C.-C. Yao. An almost optimal algorithm for unbounded searching. *Information Processing Letters*, 5:82–87, 1975.

[5] G. Beskales, M. Fontoura, M. Gurevich, S. Vassilvitskii, and V. Josifovski. Factorization-based lossless compression of inverted indices. In *Proc. of the 20th international*

conference on Information and knowledge management, pages 327–332. ACM, 2011.

[6] D. Blandford and G. Blelloch. Index compression through document reordering. In *Proc. Data Compression Conference*, pages 342–351, Washington, DC, USA, 2002.

[7] A. Z. Broder, D. Carmel, M. Herscovici, A. Soffer, and J. Zien. Efficient query evaluation using a two-level retrieval process. In *Proc. 12th International Conference on Information and Knowledge Management*, pages 426–434. ACM, 2003.

[8] S. Büttcher, C. Clarke, and G. V. Cormack. *Information retrieval: Implementing and evaluating search engines*. MIT Press, 2010.

[9] M. Charikar, E. Lehman, D. Liu, R. Panigrahy, M. Prabhakaran, A. Sahai, and A. Shelat. The smallest grammar problem. *IEEE Transactions on Information Theory*, 51:2554–2576, 2005.

[10] J. Chen and T. Cook. Using d-gap patterns for index compression. In *Proc. of the 16th International Conference on World Wide Web*, pages 1209–1210. ACM, 2007.

[11] F. Claude, A. Fariña, M. A. Martínez-Prieto, and G. Navarro. Indexes for highly repetitive document collections. In *Proc. 20th ACM International Conference on Information and Knowledge Management*, pages 463–468, New York, NY, USA, 2011.

[12] F. Claude and J. I. Munro. Document listing on versioned documents. In *Proc. 20th International Symposium on String Processing and Information Retrieval*, pages 72–83, New York, NY, USA, 2013.

[13] J. S. Culpepper and A. Moffat. Efficient set intersection for inverted indexing. *ACM Transactions on Information Systems*, 29:1:1–1:25, 2010.

[14] P. Ferragina, F. Piccinno, and R. Venturini. Compressed indexes for string searching in labeled graphs. In *Proc. of the 24th International Conference on World Wide Web*, pages 322–332. ACM, 2015.

[15] G. H. Gonnet, L. D. Rogers, and J. A. George. An algorithmic and complexity analysis of interpolation search. *Acta Informatica*, 13:39–52, 1980.

[16] A. Gupta, W.-K. Hon, R. Shah, and J. S. Vitter. Compressed dictionaries: Space measures, data sets, and experiments. In *Proc. 5th International Conference on Experimental Algorithms*, pages 158–169, Berlin, Heidelberg, 2006.

[17] J. C. Kieffer, E.-H. Yang, G. J. Nelson, and P. Cosman. Universal lossless compression via multilevel pattern matching. *IEEE Transactions on Information Theory*, 46:1227–1245, 2000.

[18] N. J. Larsson and A. Moffat. Off-line dictionary-based compression. In *Proc. Conference on Data Compression*, pages 296–306, Washington, DC, USA, 1999.

[19] D. Lemire and L. Boytsov. Decoding billions of integers per second through vectorization. *Software: Practice and Experience*, 45(1):1–29, 2015.

[20] A. Moffat and L. Stuiver. Binary interpolative coding for effective index compression. *Information Retrieval*, 3(1):25–47, 2000.

[21] C. G. Nevill-Manning and I. H. Witten. Compression and explanation using hierarchical grammar. *The Computer Journal*, 40:103–116, 1997.

[22] C. G. Nevill-Manning and I. H. Witten. Identifying hierarchical structure in sequences: A linear-time algorithm. *Journal of Artificial Intelligence Research*, 7:67–82, 1997.

[23] G. Ottaviano, N. Tonellotto, and R. Venturini. Optimal space-time tradeoffs for inverted indexes. In *Proc. of the 8th International Conference on Web Search and Data Mining*, pages 47–56. ACM, 2015.

[24] G. Ottaviano and R. Venturini. Partitioned Elias-Fano indexes. In *Proc. 37th International ACM SIGIR Conference*, pages 273–282. ACM, 2014.

[25] M. Petri and A. Moffat. On the cost of phrase-based ranking. In *Proc. of the 38th International ACM SIGIR Conference*, pages 931–934. ACM, 2015.

[26] S. E. Robertson and K. S. Jones. Relevance weighting of search terms. *Journal of the American Society for Information Science*, 27:129–146, 1976.

[27] L. Shi and B. Wang. Yet another sorting-based solution to the reassignment of document identifiers. In *Information Retrieval Technology*, volume 7675 of *Lecture Notes in Computer Science*, pages 238–249, 2012.

[28] W.-Y. Shieh, T.-F. Chen, J.-J. Shann, and C.-P. Chung. Inverted file compression through document identifier reassignment. *Information Processing & Management*, 39:117–131, 2003.

[29] F. Silvestri. Sorting out the document identifier assignment problem. In *Proc. 29th European Conference on IR Research*, pages 101–112, Berlin, Heidelberg, 2007.

[30] F. Silvestri, S. Orlando, and R. Perego. Assigning identifiers to documents to enhance the clustering property of fulltext indexes. In *Proc. 27th International ACM SIGIR Conference*, pages 305–312, New York, NY, USA, 2004.

[31] F. Silvestri and R. Venturini. Vsencoding: efficient coding and fast decoding of integer lists via dynamic programming. In *Proc. of the 19th international conference on Information and knowledge management*, pages 1219–1228. ACM, 2010.

[32] A. A. Stepanov, A. R. Gangolli, D. E. Rose, R. J. Ernst, and P. S. Oberoi. SIMD-based decoding of posting lists. In *Proc. of the 20th international conference on Information and knowledge management*, pages 317–326. ACM, 2011.

[33] H. E. Williams and J. Zobel. Compressing integers for fast file access. *The Computer Journal*, 42:193–201, 1999.

[34] I. H. Witten, A. Moffat, and T. C. Bell. *Managing gigabytes: compressing and indexing documents and images*. Morgan Kaufmann, San Francisco, CA, USA, second edition, 1999.

[35] H. Yan, S. Ding, and T. Suel. Inverted index compression and query processing with optimized document ordering. In *Proc. 18th International Conference on World Wide Web*, pages 401–410, New York, NY, USA, 2009.

[36] E.-H. Yang and J. C. Kieffer. Efficient universal lossless data compression algorithms based on a greedy sequential grammar transform part one: without context models. *IEEE Transaction on Information Theory*, 46:755–777, 2000.

[37] J. Zhang, X. Long, and T. Suel. Performance of compressed inverted list caching in search engines. In *Proc. 17th International Conference on World Wide Web*, pages 387–396, New York, NY, USA, 2008.

[38] M. Zukowski, S. Heman, N. Nes, and P. Boncz. Super-scalar RAM-CPU cache compression. In *Proc. 22nd International Conference on Data Engineering*, pages 59–70, Washington,DC,USA, 2006.

Fast and Compact Hamming Distance Index

Simon Gog
Institute of Theoretical Informatics, Karlsruhe Institute of Technology
gog@kit.edu

Rossano Venturini
University of Pisa *and* Istella Srl
rossano.venturini@unipi.it

ABSTRACT

Searching for similar objects in a collection is a core task of many applications in databases, pattern recognition, and information retrieval. As there exist similarity-preserving hash functions like SimHash, indexing these objects reduces to the solution of the *Approximate Dictionary Queries* problem. In this problem we have to index a collection of fixed-sized keys to efficiently retrieve all the keys which are at a Hamming distance at most k from a query key.

In this paper we propose new solutions for the approximate dictionary queries problem. These solutions combine the use of succinct data structures with an efficient representation of the keys to significantly reduce the space usage of the state-of-the-art solutions without introducing any time penalty. Finally, by exploiting triangle inequality, we can also significantly speed up the query time of the existing solutions.

1. INTRODUCTION

Indexing large collections of objects for similarity search is a core task of many applications in databases, pattern recognition, and information retrieval (IR). Duplicate and near-duplicate detection in a collection of web pages or content-based retrieval in a collection of images are among the most prominent applications in IR (see e.g., [16, 22, 27] and references therein). In a general framework, each object is modelled with a vector of features and the similarity of two objects is measured by means of a similarity function, e.g., the Jaccard and the cosine similarity, on their vectors. The selection of the most appropriate set of features strictly depends on the application's domain and objectives. For example, the use of words/shingles as features for web pages is a established approach introduced by Broder et al. [5]. In image search, images are modelled as vectors of features which include color histograms, texture features, and edge orientation (see e.g., [27] and references therein). Retrieving the most similar objects by scanning and checking the whole collection is not feasible for two reasons: 1) computing the similarity function between any two objects is demanding because the vectors usually have a high-dimensionality; 2) we are dealing with collections of billions of objects and query streams of the same magnitude today. The combined use of sketching and indexing techniques is the well-established approach for addressing these two issues. Sketching reduces the dimensionality by producing succinct sketches, usually 64 bits, of the vectors, such that the similarity of objects can be estimated from their sketches. Several sketching algorithms have been proposed in the last decades; among them we mention Charikar's SimHash [7], Li and König's b-bit minwise hashing [19], and Mitzenmacher et al.'s Odd Sketches [24].

A property of most of these techniques is that if two objects are similar, the Hamming distance of their sketches is small. Thus, the problem of retrieving the most similar objects to an input one boils down to the problem of solving Hamming distance queries on a collection of fixed-length binary keys. This indexing problem is known as the *Approximate Dictionary Queries* problem and was originally formulated by Minsky and Papert [23] as follows. We are given a dictionary $D = \{K_1, K_2, \ldots, K_d\}$ of d binary keys of length m bits each, a k-query Q asks for identifying all the keys in D which are at Hamming distance at most k from Q. While there exist several theoretical solutions which provide guarantees on their space and time complexities [28, 4, 1, 2, 10, 6], the most efficient solutions in practice [22, 20, 26, 29] are based on the multi-index approach proposed by Greene et al. [14]. The main idea of the multi-index is that of splitting each key into blocks of a certain number bits. For each of these block, an index duplicates and organizes the keys in D to be able to efficiently search within the content of this block. A k-query Q is answered in two phases. The searching phase searches with all these indexes for the content of Q's blocks to identify all the keys that match these blocks, possibly up to 1 or more errors. Those keys form a set of candidates which is guaranteed to contain all the query results by properties of the above splitting. Finally, the checking phase scans all these candidates to filter out the ones with Hamming distance larger than k with Q.

Our contributions. We list here our main contributions.

1. We introduce the use of succinct data structures in the searching phase of any multi-index based solution together with a suitable representation of the keys, SIMD-based optimizations, and other tricks. This combination guarantees a space usage reduction that ranges between 18% and 40% depending on the value of k. This does not introduce any new space/time tradeoff

SIGIR '16, July 17 - 21, 2016, Pisa, Italy

ISBN 978-1-4503-4069-4/16/07...$15.00

DOI: http://dx.doi.org/10.1145/2911451.2911523

because our solution is always as fast as the best ones and always smaller. This solution is actually faster for smaller values of k ($k = \{2, 3, 4\}$) with a time improving factor that ranges between 2.1 and 3.

The description of these techniques is deferred to the experimental section (Subsection 4.2) because they are motivated and supported by experimental evidences.

2. The cost of the checking phase dominates the overall query time of any multi-index for sufficiently large values of k or dataset sizes. This is because the searching phase has only to identify large ranges of consecutive keys which may contain some query results while the checking phase has the more demanding task of explicitly checking each of these keys. In this paper we introduce the use of the triangle inequality to reduce size of this set of candidates. We propose two solutions based on this idea. The fastest one uses a two-level indexing approach. The second level stores clusters of keys which are close by the Hamming distance while the first level stores just one key to represent each cluster. At query time, all the candidates at the first level are explicitly checked but a fraction of the clusters at the second level can be safely skipped because, by triangle inequality, they cannot contain any query result. The use of this strategy reduces the set of candidates to check by a factor that ranges from 5.3 to 8.4 depending on the dataset and the value of k.

3. In an extensive empirical evaluation we explore the properties of our proposals and compare to a state-of-the-art baseline on real world datasets of sizes up to one billion objects. Overall results show that our time improvement is by a factor up to 3.4 while the space usage reduction ranges between 18% and 40%.

2. RELATED WORK

The theoretical study of the approximate dictionary queries problem has been initiated by Yao and Yao [28], who present a solution in the bit probe model restricting their attention to queries with Hamming distance one (i.e., $k = 1$). Their solution indexes D by using $O(dm \log m)$ bits and solves a query with $O(m \log \log d)$ bit probes. Subsequently, Brodal and Venkatesh [4] improve the above time complexity by a $\log \log d$ factor: their solution uses $O(dm \log d)$ bits of space and $O(m)$ bit probes. In the RAM model, the time complexity is $O(m/w)$, where w is the size of a machine word. The solution by Belazzougui [1] obtains better time and space complexities. Indeed, this solution achieves $O(m + occ)$ query time by requiring optimal $O(dm)$ bits of space. Finally, a solution by Belazzougui and Venturini [2] achieves the same time complexity but works in compressed space. We mention that some of these solutions have been experimental compared in [8].

Solving queries for larger values of k is a much more expensive task. Naïve solutions have either $\Omega(\sum_{i=0}^{k} \binom{m}{i} + \mathsf{occ}) = \Omega(\left(\frac{m}{k}\right)^k + \mathsf{occ})$ query time by using linear space or $O(m + \mathsf{occ})$ query time by using $\Omega(d\binom{m}{k}) = \Omega(d\left(\frac{m}{k}\right)^k)$ words of space, where occ is the number of reported results. In the former case, we index the dictionary to answer membership queries and, given P, we query for the membership of any key obtained by flipping at most k bits in P. In the latter case, we index the superset of keys which contains every key which is at distance at most k from any key in D. These were essentially the best solutions before the work by Cole *et al.* [10]. Their data structure significantly improves these time-space bounds by requiring $O(dm + d\frac{(c_1 \log d)^k}{k!})$ words of space and has $O(m + \frac{(c_2 \log d)^k}{k!} \log \log n + occ)$ query time, where $c_1, c_2 > 1$ are constants. The best linear space solution has $O(m^{k-1} \log n \log \log n + occ)$ query time [6]. However, we are not aware of any attempt to implement these sophisticated solutions.

We point out that there exist solutions which solve variants of this problem which, for example, ask to solve queries under the more difficult Edit distance or admit keys of variable length (i.e., strings) and drawn from larger alphabets. We refer to a survey by Boytsov [3] for a more exhaustive treatment of this topic.

The most efficient solutions in practice [14, 22, 20, 26, 29] are based on the so-called *multi-index* approach introduced by Greene et al. [14]. We defer a detailed description of these solutions to Section 3 because they are the starting point of ours.

3. HAMMING DISTANCE INDEX

In this section we first introduce the basic multi-index approach and its generalizations [14, 22, 20, 26, 29] and discuss its most important inefficiencies (Subsection 3.1).

As we will see, a query in a multi-index is solved in two phases: *searching* and *checking* phases. In the former phase, we are given substrings of the query and the goal is to find all the keys of the dictionary that match these substrings (possibly, up to one Hamming error). These keys are the candidates to be processed by the next phase which checks all of them to filter out the ones with Hamming distance larger than k with the query.

In this paper we improve the time efficiency of both phases and the overall space usage of any multi-index solution. However, in this section we only describe our improvements to the checking phase (Subsection 3.2). We defer the description of our other contributions to the experimental section (Subsection 4.2) because they are motivated, driven and supported by experimental evidences.

3.1 Multi-index approach

The multi-index approach has been introduced by Greene et al. [14] and has been popularized by Manku et al. [22] who use this index for the near-duplicate detection in a collection of Web pages showing that this approach scales with the size of the dictionary. In the following we will use multi-index to refer this approach.

The multi-index is based on a simple property: if two keys have a small Hamming distance, they must share at least a (sufficiently long) aligned substring. More precisely, consider the splitting of any two keys K and Q into $b = k + 1$ blocks of, possibly, variable length. We use $K[i]$ to denote the ith block of K in this splitting. The property is stated as follows.

PROPERTY 1. *Let $H(K, Q)$ be the Hamming distance between keys K and Q. If $H(K, Q) \le k$ and $b = k + 1$, then there must exist at least one index i, $1 \le i \le b$, such that $K[i] = Q[i]$.*

This property can be exploited by splitting each key of the dictionary D into $b = k+1$ blocks and by creating a separate

	multi-index				multi-index*	
	$b = k+1$		$b = k+2$		$b = \lfloor k/2 \rfloor + 1$	
k	idxs.	avg. cand.	idxs.	avg. cand.	idxs.	avg. cand.
2	3	3	3	> 1	2	66
3	4	262 144	10	845	2	66
4	5	3 011 244	15	24 382	3	108 908
5	6	15 853 476	21	282 248	3	108 908
6	7	53 184 325	28	1 835 008	4	4 456 448
7	8	134 217 728	36	8 089 969	4	4 456 448
8	9	279 604 801	45	27 101 194	5	41 555 165

Table 1: Number of indexes and average number of candidates for different number of erros k and fixed number of keys $d = 2^{32}$ of length $m = 64$ bits each.

index for each block; this is the reason for the name of this solution. Index I_i, for $1 \leq i \leq b$, is responsible for indexing the content of the ith block of each key. Since each of the b indexes duplicates the content of D, the overall space usage of this approach is $\Theta(b \cdot m \cdot d)$ bits.

A k-query for Q is solved in two phases: *searching* and *checking*. In the searching phase Q is first split into b blocks and, then, each of them is searched in the corresponding index to identify the subset of keys having the same block configuration. The union of these b subsets forms a set of candidates which is guaranteed by Property 1 to contain all the keys with Hamming distance at most k from Q. In the checking phase, we scan the set of candidates to identify the keys to be reported. The check of a candidate key K can be done in constant time whenever the key fits in a constant number of memory words. Indeed, the Hamming distance between K and Q equals to $H(K,Q) = \texttt{popcount}(K \oplus Q)$, where $\oplus$ denotes the bitwise XOR and popcount counts the number of bits set to one in a memory word; this instruction belongs to the instruction sets of any modern CPU.

Clearly, the overall efficiency of this approach is given by the efficiency of its two phases. As far as the searching phase is concerned, we point out that a possible solution consists in storing keys in the index I_i sorted by their ith block, so that we can use binary search to identify the range of keys which match the query block configuration. As we will see in the experiments, even if this is the most immediate approach, it is far from being the most efficient one for both time efficiency and space usage.

Storing consecutively the keys with the same ith block in the index I_i is convenient also for the cache efficiency of the second phase. Indeed this phase checks the candidates reported by the index I_i by scanning a consecutive range of keys, thus, obtaining the largest benefits from the CPU's prefetching. However, the multi-index cannot limit in any way the number of candidates to be checked so that a potentially very large fraction of the time may be wasted in filtering out false positive candidates. Observe that the number of candidates to be checked strictly depends on b which in turns is fixed by k. Indeed, we cannot have fewer than $d/2^{m/b} = d/2^{m/(k+1)}$ on average per index. Since this quantity grows rapidly with k, the query time becomes large even with relatively small values of k. For a concrete example, let us assume that D contains $d = 2^{32}$ keys of $m = 64$ bits each. Thus, each index gives $2^{16} = 65\,536$ candidates in average with $k = 3$ but this quantity becomes $2^{24} = 16\,777\,216$ with $k = 7$. The space usage is $O(4 \cdot 64 \cdot 2^{32})$ bits with $k = 3$ and $O(8 \cdot 64 \cdot 2^{32})$ bits with $k = 7$. In Table 1 we report the average number of candidates and number of indexes for different values of k.

The number of candidates can be reduced by generalizing the previous solution to let the number of blocks b be larger than $k+1$. In this generalization we build a index for every possible subset of $b-k$ block ids and each index is responsible for indexing the content of these $b-k$ blocks. Thus, we have $\binom{b}{b-k} = \binom{b}{k}$ indexes and the space usage is $O(d \cdot \binom{b}{k} \cdot m)$ bits. In the searching phase, we query each of these indexes to identify the subsets of keys having a certain configuration of each possible subset of $b-k$ blocks. As before, the checking phase processes these candidates and keeps only the query results. It is easy to see that, if the b blocks have the same length m/b, the average number of candidates identified by each index is $d/2^{(m/b)(b-k)}$. Thus, the number of candidates rapidly decreases as b increases. However, b cannot become too large because the number of indexes grows by a factor $\frac{b}{b-k}$ every time we increase b by one. In practice, the space usage of this solution on large datasets becomes prohibitive even with $b = k+2$ and, thus, this generalization may be useful only for very small datasets. We report in Table 1 the average number of candidates and number of indexes with this generalization with $b = k+2$.

A strategy used by recent papers [20, 26, 29] is able to improve both query time and space usage of multi-index by exploiting a well-known generalization of Property 1.

PROPERTY 2. *If $H(K,Q) \leq k$ and $b = \lfloor k/2 \rfloor + 1$, then there must exist at least one index i, $1 \leq i \leq b$, such that $H(K[i], Q[i]) \leq 1$.*

Essentially, this property says that, if we match blocks admitting up to 1 error, then we can reduce the number of blocks b almost by a half. This has the effect of increasing the length of the blocks and, thus, of reducing the number of candidates. We point out that Property 2 can be further generalized so that if we admit up to r errors in matching the blocks, the number of blocks can be reduced to $\lfloor k/(r+1) \rfloor + 1$.

The main idea for exploiting Property 2 is to change the searching phase of the multi-index approach. As before Q is split into b, now with $b = \lfloor k/2 \rfloor + 1$, blocks. Given the ith block in Q, the searching phase queries index I_i to identify all the keys whose ith block is at Hamming distance at most 1 with the block of Q. This can be done, for example, by using the previous binary search-based approach as follows. As before, we first search for Q's block; this gives the subset of keys which have the same block as Q. Then, if the length of the block is ℓ, we perform ℓ different searches. In each search we flip the ℓth bit of the block of Q and search for an exact match of this modified block. These ℓ searches give ℓ (possibly empty) subsets which contain all the keys whose ith block is at Hamming distance exactly 1 with the block of Q. Property 2 guarantees that the union of all the sets of candidates obtained by searching all the b indexes contains *all* the keys with Hamming distance at most k with Q. The idea is at the core of the solution in [20] and other similar approaches [26, 29]. We point out that an index using this strategy is called HEngine in [20]. However, we prefer to use multi-index* to refer to this solution to stress the fact that it is a multi-index in which the searching phase matches blocks up to 1 error.

Observe that the searching phase on multi-index* is more expensive than the one on multi-index. Indeed, we have to perform $m + b = m + \lfloor k/2 \rfloor + 1$ exact matches instead of $k + 1$ exact matches. Apart from this inefficiency, multi-index* has important benefits: 1) it has a better space usage because the number of indexes is reduced from $k + 1$ to $\lfloor k/2 \rfloor + 1$; 2) it reduces the average number of candidates to check which decreases from $d/2^{m/(k+1)}$ to $(m+b) \cdot d/(2^{m/b}) = (m + \lfloor k/2 \rfloor + 1) \cdot d/(2^{m/(\lfloor k/2 \rfloor + 1)})$. Table 1 reports these numbers for the case of a dictionary of size $d = 2^{32}$ and $m = 64$ bits.

3.2 Triangle inequality-based Multi-index

Experiments confirm that multi-index* improves significantly over multi-index on real datasets and scales with the number of errors k. Still, a large fraction of the checking phase is spent in filtering out false positive candidates. As we can see in Table 1, the average number of candidates is only 66 with $k = 3$ but this number increases rapidly to 4 456 448 with $k = 6$.

Our solution can be used indistinctly in combination with either multi-index or multi-index* and its goal is to significantly reduce the number of candidates to check. At a high level the idea consists in further subdividing the set of keys with the same block configuration into *clusters* and to exploit *triangle inequality* to avoid the check of keys of some of these clusters. The triangle inequality is stated as follows.

PROPERTY 3 (TRIANGLE INEQUALITY). *For any three keys P, K, and Q, it holds $H(Q,P) \leq H(K,Q)+H(K,P)$.*

For each cluster, we select and store a pivot P and the maximum distance δ of any key K in the cluster with P. At query time we compute the distance $H(Q,P)$ so that we can lower bound $H(K,Q)$ for any K in the cluster. Indeed, we have $H(Q,P) - \delta \leq H(K,Q)$ by triangle inequality. If the lower bound is larger than k, we can safely discard all the keys in the cluster. If it is not the case the keys in the cluster have to be explicitly checked for the presence of any query result. This general idea can lead to several different solutions which differentiate themselves with respect to the strategies used to build, layout and index the clusters. In the following we present two of them. The first solution, called Clustered multi-index, has the merit of being conceptually simple and giving an interesting speed up for sufficiently small values of k or on smaller datasets. The second one, called BoundedClustered multi-index, is more sophisticated but is able to significantly reduce the number of candidates to check. We point out that the use of pivots and triangle inequality is at the basis of the so-called Metric Indexes (see [17] and references therein). However, our objectives and, thus, the indexing strategies differ from the ones of Metric indexes. Indeed, Metric indexes deal with highly complex and large objects (e.g., video clips) and, thus, their main goal is to minimize the number of distance computations and the number of I/O to answer a query. For this reason, most of the Metric indexes use a tree structure (e.g., B-tree like) to represent the dataset in which a different set of pivots is (possibly) selected at each node of the tree.

Clustered multi-index. For any existing block configuration in index I_i, we consider the subset S of all the keys with that block configuration. The idea in this strategy is to select any pivot P and to partition S into at most $m - \ell + 1$ clusters according to the Hamming distance of the keys with P, where ℓ is the length of the block. Thus, the cluster C_j contains all the keys in S which have Hamming distance exactly j with P. At query time, we only need to check those keys that belong to at most $2k+1$ of these clusters. Indeed, let Q be the query and K be any entry, if $H(Q,K) \leq k$, then $|H(Q,P) - H(K,P)| \leq k$ by triangle inequality. This means that we only need to check clusters whose keys have a Hamming distance in the range $[H(Q,P)-k, H(Q,P)+k]$ (namely, clusters C_j with $j \in [H(Q,P) - k, H(Q,P) + k]$). Observe that we could choose a different pivot for each subset S. However, for simplicity, our implementation fixes $P = 0$ for every subset, and, thus, $H(K,P)$ is just the Hamming weight of K, i.e., the number of bits set to 1 in K.

The layout of a index I_i is as follows. We first group the keys into subsets accordingly to the content of their ith block as done by any multi-index, then we partition the keys into clusters as explained above. For each block configuration, we write its clusters sorted by their distance with P and we store pointers to the beginning of each cluster. At query time, the group of keys with the appropriate block configuration is identified in the searching phase as in any other multi-index. In the checking phase we know after computing $H(Q,P)$ that it is sufficient to check clusters with Hamming weight in $[H(Q,P) - k, H(Q,P) + k]$. An interesting feature of the layout above is that these clusters are stored one after the other. This means that the checking phase has to perform just one scan that starts at the first cluster and ends at the last one without any random access in between. However, an important drawback of this strategy is that the sizes of the obtained clusters are far from being uniformly distributed. For example, we expect that a large fraction of the keys in S belong to the cluster $C_{\frac{m}{2}}$, since it contains all the keys in S with exactly $\frac{m}{2}$ bits set to 1.

BoundedClustered multi-index. In this solution we use a two level indexing approach and we allow the selection of several pivots for each block configuration. The first level of the index stores those pivots and some additional information, including pointers to the clusters obtained with those pivots which are stored in the second level. Consider again the subset S of all the keys with a certain block configuration in index I_i. The keys in S are subdivided into clusters by using several pivots. Both pivots and clusters are chosen according to the following greedy algorithm.

The greedy algorithm works in steps. At each step it chooses a pivot and selects a subset of keys from S which form the cluster. Those keys are removed from S and the greedy algorithm continues with another step as soon as S is not empty. Consider the ith of these steps. The pivot P_i of this step is chosen at random among the most distant keys from the pivot of the preceding step which are left in S. Once the pivot P_i is selected, we can consider the subset S_j, for any $j \in [0, 64 - \ell]$, which contains all the keys in S with Hamming distance *at most* j with P_i. Since ℓ is the length of the block and all the keys in S agree on this block, the union of these subsets covers S. Moreover, S_j is contained in S_{j+1} and $S_{64-\ell} = S$. The cluster C_i at the ith step equals the subset S_{E_i} where $0 \leq E_i \leq 64 - \ell$ is the smallest index such that $|S_{E_i}| \geq \tau$ or $E_i = 64 - \ell$ whenever such a subset does not exist. Note that the latter case may happen only at the last step of the greedy algorithm. Thus, the parameter τ fixes the minimum size of all the clusters but the last one.

The index I_i is a two level index. The second level stores, the clusters of each possible block configuration while the first level stores the pivots P_i, the errors E_i and a pointer the first key of corresponding cluster in the second level.

At query time, we process the pivots P_i in their selection order. If $H(P_i, Q) \geq E_i + k + 1$, we are sure that the Hamming distance of any key in C_i to Q is larger than k and, thus, we can safely skip the whole cluster. Indeed, consider a key K in C_i. By triangle inequality, we know that $H(K, Q) \geq H(P_i, Q) - H(P_i, K)$ and, by construction, that $H(P_i, K) \leq E_i$. This means that $H(K, Q) \geq E_i + k + 1 - E_i = k + 1$ and, thus, K cannot be a query result. Instead, if $H(P_i, Q) < E_i + k + 1$, the cluster C_i may contain query results and, thus, its keys have to be explicitly checked. However, if the distance with the pivot is small enough, we can *early exit* from the checking phase. Indeed, if $H(P_i, Q) \leq E_i - k$, we are guaranteed that C_i is the last cluster to be checked because none of the subsequent ones can contain any query result. Indeed, by construction, any key K in the subsequent clusters is such that $K(P_i, K) \geq E_i + 1$ otherwise K would belong to the cluster C_i. Thus, by triangle inequality we have $H(K, Q) \geq H(P_i, K) - H(P_i, Q)$ and, since $K(P_i, K) \geq E_i + 1$ and $H(P_i, Q) \leq E_i - k$, we have $H(K, Q) \geq E_i + 1 - (E_i - k) = k + 1$.

4. EXPERIMENTS

We evaluate our indexes on four different datasets of 64-bit keys from two common application areas: similarity search in web collections and image databases. The first two datasets were generated from the ClueWeb 2009 TREC Category A test collection which consists of 503.9 million English web pages crawled in 2009. The body text of each document in the collection was extracted using Apache Tika[1], and the words lowercased and stemmed using the Porter2 stemmer. We used two different hash functions on the resulting documents and removed duplicated hashes to obtain the following datasets.

- CW09_SimHash consists of 450 806 115 unique keys (i.e., ≈ 3.7 GBytes) obtained by using SimHash [7], a Locality Preserving Hashing (LSH);
- CW09_OddSketch consists of 471 510 174 unique keys (i.e., ≈ 3.7 GBytes) obtained by using OddSketches as described in [24].

We obtained the second two datasets from the INRIA BIGANN dataset which consists of 1 billion of 128-dimensional SIFT descriptors [21] extracted from approximately 1 million images [18][2]. This dataset has been released in 2011 to evaluate high dimensional indexing algorithms on a realistic scale. The following two datasets are obtained in [26] by applying two different similarity-preserving hash functions.

- BA_Sift_Lsh consists of 949 923 339 unique keys (i.e., ≈ 7.5 GBytes) obtained by using SimHash [7]. We use the suffix Lsh to refer this dataset to be consistent with the naming in [26].
- BA_Sift_Mlh consists of 966 592 208 unique keys (i.e., ≈ 7.5 GBytes) obtained by using Minimal Loss Hashing (MLH) [25].

[1]http://tika.apache.org/
[2]http://corpus-texmex.irisa.fr/

For each dataset we generated a query set consisting of 200 000 keys which were selected as follows. The first 100 000 keys were randomly selected and removed from the original dataset while the second 100 000 keys are a subset of the remaining dataset. We performed experiments also with these two subsets of queries separately without observing any significant difference on the final results.

Testing details. All the algorithms were implemented. in C++14 and compiled with GCC 5.3 with the highest optimization settings. Our source code – which is a flexible C++ template library – and the benchmark suite, which facilitates the automatic execution of all following experiments are avaiable at https://github.com/xxsds/multi_index. The tests reported in the paper were performed on a machine with 6 Intel Xeon E5-2630 Haswell cores (12 threads) clocked at 2.80Ghz, with 64GiB RAM, running Linux 3.13.0. In addition we have run the benchmarks suite on a second machine equipped with 32 Intel Xeon E5-4640 cores (64 threads) clocked at 2.40Ghz, with 512GiB RAM, running Linux 3.13.0 to confirm the results. Note that all experiments were run in-memory.

4.1 Comparing multi-index and multi-index*

We first provide experiments similar to the ones presented in [20] to compare the time and space efficiency of multi-index and multi-index*. Even if the implementations of both index types are comparable with the one tested in [20], we obtain slightly different results. The different outcome is motivated by the fact that we run the experiments on much larger datasets: the largest dataset used in [20] contained 0.5 million keys while we scale the experimental set by three orders of magnitudes. However, our experiments further confirm the thesis in [20]: multi-index* is more convenient than multi-index.

In Figure 1 we report the average query time and space usage of multi-index and multi-index* for k ranging from 2 to 5. Due to space limitation, we report the results only for CW09_SimHash and BA_Sift_Lsh but we observed a similar behaviour also on the other datasets. Both multi-index and multi-index* use binary search in the searching phase.

As expected from our discussion in Subsection 3.1 (see Table 1), multi-index* is much more space efficient than multi-index: it improves space usage by either a factor 1.5 (for even k) or 2 (for odd k). Indeed, multi-index* uses $b = \lfloor k/2 \rfloor + 1$ indexes instead of $b = k + 1$. As far as query time is concerned, we observe that multi-index* is faster (up to a order of magnitude) than multi-index for all values of k but $k = 2$. Observe that the gap rapidly increases with the increasing of k. This is because, even if the searching phase is more demanding in multi-index*, the much smaller number of candidates to check suffices to let multi-index* outperform multi-index also regarding query time.

For $k = 2$, multi-index is faster than multi-index*. Since in this case the number of candidates is small, the more expensive searching phase in multi-index* determines the outcome. However, in the next subsection we will significantly improve the efficiency of the searching phase. This would suffice to significantly reduce, or even avoid, this effect.

The space and time inefficiency of multi-index leads us to focus our attention only to multi-index* in the remaining of the paper. Nevertheless, all the improvements we will introduce for multi-index* are also applicable to multi-index.

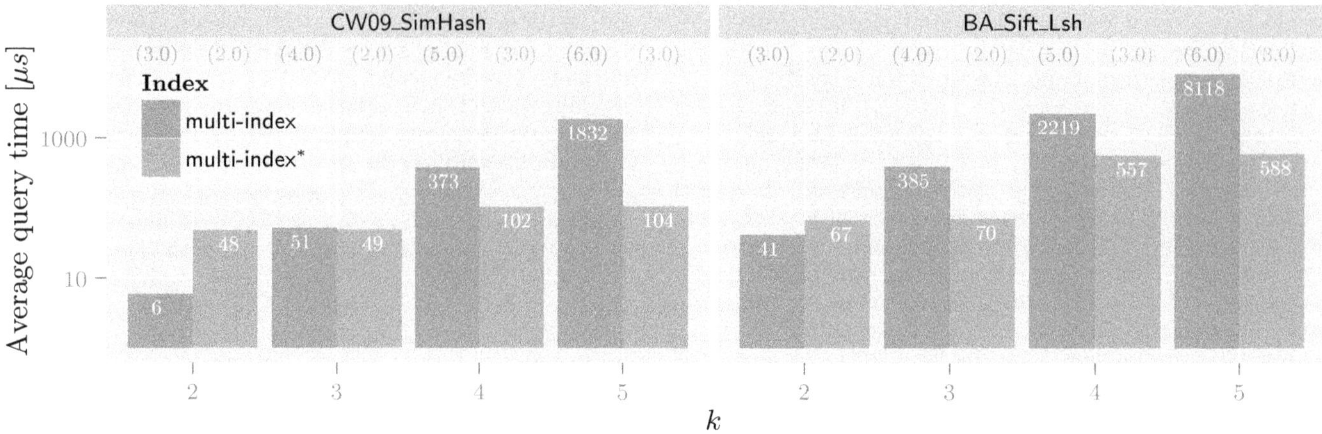

Figure 1: Average query time for multi-index and multi-index* on all data sets. The numbers in brackets denote the space usage as the increasing factor with respect to the size of the original dataset.

4.2 Improving any multi-index-based solution

In this subsection we provide an extensive experimental evaluation to measure the efficiency of both phases of the query resolution in any multi-index based solution. We first measure the efficiency of binary search in the searching phase and introduce the use of *succinct* data structures as a much better alternative for this task. This improves the efficiency of this phase up to one order of magnitude. As far as checking phase is concerned, we will first use a benchmark to estimate the time required to scan and compute Hamming distance of runs of variable-length keys. This drives the design of a novel layout for any multi-index based solution which improves the overall space usage by a factor ranging from 18% to 40% depending on the value of k, still preserving or even improving the time efficiency.

On the efficiency of the searching phase. A index I_i in the multi-index stores the keys of the dataset sorted by the content of their ith block. This way, given a certain block configuration B, the keys that have the block configuration B span a consecutive range on the sorted set of keys. The goal of the searching phase is to identify this range.

Even if the use of binary search is the simplest solution for this task, the next experiments show that it is far from being the most efficient one. A more efficient solution, that we will refer as Succinct, uses a binary vector V which is obtained as follows. We scan the sorted dataset and, for any possible block configuration, we write in unary the number of keys which have that block configuration. The binary vector V has $u = 2^\ell + n$ bits, where ℓ is the length of the block. Indeed, we have a bit set 1 for each possible block configuration (i.e., 2^ℓ bits set to 1 overall) and a bit set to 0 for each key in the dataset (i.e., n bits set to one overall). We build a data structure to answer $\mathsf{Select}_1(x)$ queries on V. A query $\mathsf{Select}_1(x)$, for any $1 \le x \le n$, returns the position of the xth bit set to 1 in V. There exists a data structure that answers any Select_1 query in $O(1)$ time by using $o(u)$ bits of additional space a part from V [9].

Note that two Select_1 queries suffice for identifying the range of keys which have a certain block configuration B. Indeed, $l = \mathsf{Select}_1(B) - B$ and $r = \mathsf{Select}_1(B+1) - B$ are the positions of the first and the last key, respectively, which have the block configuration B. Note that l equals r iff no such key exists. The space usage of this data structure is $u + o(u) = 2^\ell + n + o(2^\ell + n) < 2(2^\ell + n)$ bits and, thus, the space cost per entry of this data structure is relevant only if n is small compared to 2^ℓ. For all our datasets, n is even larger than 2^ℓ for any $k > 3$ since $\ell \le 16$, and, thus, the space usage is less than 2 bits per key. Instead, for $k \le 3$, we have $\ell = 32$ and the space usage of the data structure is less than $2 \cdot 2^{32}/n + 2$ bits per key. This data structure is not the best possible choice for any range of values of n and 2^ℓ. Indeed, if 2^ℓ is much smaller than n (i.e., $2^\ell = O(\frac{n}{\log n})$), it is better to directly tabulate the answers of all the possibile block configuration since it requires $O(2^\ell \log n)$ bits. Instead, if n is small compared to 2^ℓ, it is better to use a solution based on the Elias-Fano representation [11, 12], whose description is omitted due to space limitation. This solution uses $n \log \frac{2^\ell+n}{n} + 2n + o(n)$ bits of space and has a slightly larger query time. There exist several efficient implementation of these representations [15, 13] which provide essentially the same performance for these queries. We opted for the SDSL [13] library.

Figure 2 reports the searching time with both binary search and Succinct and the checking time for multi-index* with $k = 3$ and $k = 4$ on CW09_SimHash and BA_Sift_Lsh. Succinct is always more efficient than binary search with a factor of improvement that ranges from 3 (CW09_SimHash with $k = 3$) to 14 (BA_Sift_Lsh with $k = 4$). Apparently, the Succinct solution is space inefficient compared to binary search since the latter does not need any auxiliar information apart from the sorted dataset. However, as we will show in the next paragraph, the information stored implicitly in the data structure can be exploited to significantly reduce the overall space usage of the index.

The comparison between searching and checking time confirm our expectation: the searching phase dominates the overall query time when $k \le 3$, while it is the checking phase to become dominant when $k > 3$. Indeed, on one hand, since multi-index* performs $64 + b$ searches the cost of the searching phase only slightly increases as k increases. On the other hand, the overall expected number of candidates to check is only a small constant with $k \le 3$ but it increases rapidly with the increasing of k (see again Ta-

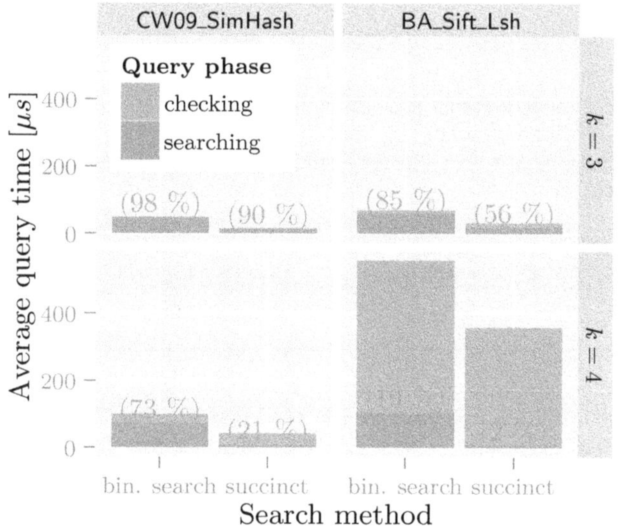

Figure 2: Searching time (resp. checking time) ratio of total time for multi-index* with $k = 3$ and $k = 4$ on CW09_SimHash and BA_Sift_Lsh

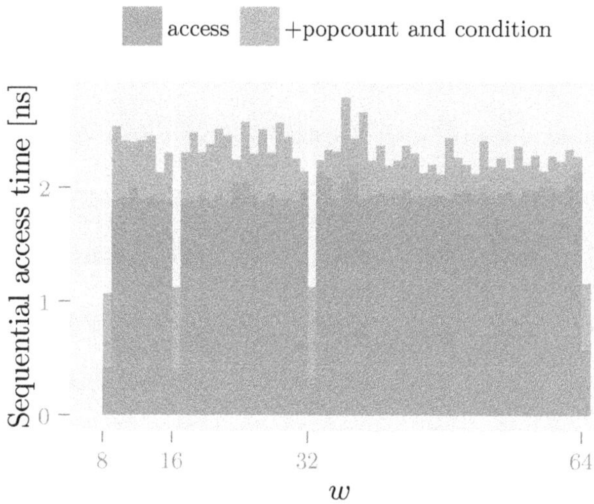

Figure 3: Average sequential processing time of a key of a vector of w-bit integers. The red part is only access, the blue part is the additional time to perform one popcount operation and branching into a condition.

ble 1). The searching phase with Succinct takes 90% on CW09_SimHash and 56% on BA_Sift_Lsh of the overall query time with $k = 3$. These percentages decrease to 21% and 2%, respectively, with $k = 4$ and further and more rapidly decrease as k increases so that the searching time becomes negligible compared to the checking time.

On the efficiency of the checking phase. Once we performed the searching phase on a index I_i, we have identified the range $R = \langle l, r \rangle$ of all the keys which have a certain block configuration B of length ℓ. The checking phase starts scanning the keys in this range and computes their Hamming distance with the query. There is a simple but crucial observation which allows us to save space in representing the keys. Indeed, we can easily note that the Succinct solution, differently from the binary search, does not need to access the ith block of the keys to identify the range R. Thus, we could store each key without its ith block by using $64 - \ell$ bits instead of 64 bits. However, since in general $64 - \ell$ is not a power of two, this would ask for storing a vector of unaligned entries which would significantly reduce the efficiency of the subsequent scanning. To measure the effect of these unaligned accesses we run a benchmark which scans a chunk of 2^{14} consecutive keys in a vector with 2^{30} keys of lengths from 8 to 64 bits each. For each processed key we also perform one `popcount` operation and a branch into a condition, thus, simulating the whole checking phase. Results (see Figure 3) show that on average accessing aligned entries is a factor 4.2 more efficient than unaligned entries. This factor reduces to 3.0 when considering the cost of the whole process because the cost of the subsequent operations does not depend on the block length.

These results discourage the use of the previous approach and motivate the design of a different representation, which, instead of using only a vector of unaligned entries, uses two different vectors: one with aligned entries and one with, possibly, unaligned ones. Consider the remaining $64 - \ell$ bits of each key. These bits are partitioned in two parts: the lower 32 bits and the remaining $64 - \ell - 32$ upper bits. We represent the keys by using two vectors L and H: the vector L stores the lower bits of the keys while H stores the upper bits. Apparently this representation does not solve the issue of the previous naïve approach: reconstructing a key still requires an access to a vector with unaligned entries. However, we can limit the overall number of accesses to unaligned entries as follows. We first compute the Hamming distance between the lower bits of the key and the query. If this Hamming distance is larger than k, we do not need to access the upper bits of the key, saving one unaligned access. Otherwise, we reconstruct the whole key and compute its Hamming distance from the query. Since 32 bits is a sufficiently large part of the key, we expect that the first check suffices for a large portion of the keys. We use SPLIT to refer to this approach.

In Figure 4 we compare SPLIT with the aligned approach and the unaligned one on BA_Sift_Lsh with $k = \{5, 7, 9\}$. We first observe that SPLIT is almost as fast as aligned and two times faster than unaligned for $k = 7$. The reason is that, for this value of k, we have $b = 4$, and, thus, entries in both H and L are aligned. For the remaining cases, SPLIT and unaligned are comparable, with the latter which is faster for larger values of k. The reason for this is that if a key has Hamming distance larger than k, the first check has to filter it out by checking only its first 32 bits. However, as k increases, there are less chances that these bits have more than k errors with the corresponding bits of the query. As the number of keys that pass this filter increases, SPLIT loses wrt unaligned because it has to access entries of two different vectors and any access at H is expensive because it is random and possibly unaligned. Experiments show that only the 1.87% of keys pass the first check for $k = 5$ but this percentage increases to 4.26% for $k = 7$, and to 8.99% for $k = 9$. To overcome this limitation we use the following trick that we refer as XOR. Given a key K, let a_K be the

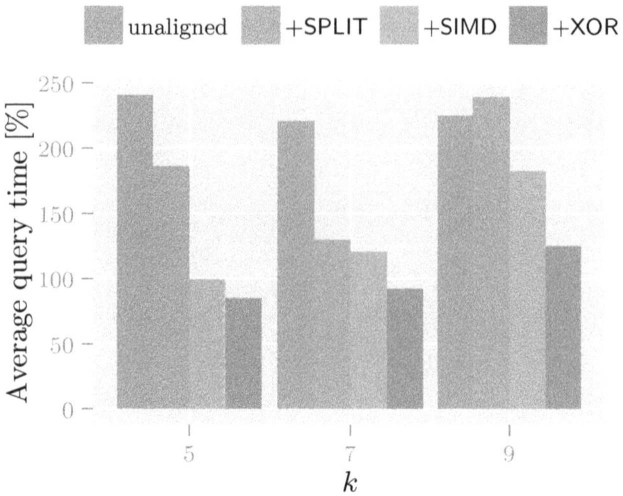

Figure 4: Average query time of the unaligned, SPLIT, SPLIT+ SIMD, and SPLIT+ SIMD+ XOR indexes as fraction of the average query time of the aligned index on BA_Sift_Lsh with $k = \{5, 7, 9\}$.

	Original		Compact	
	$[\mu s]$	$[\frac{\lvert I \rvert}{d}]$	$[\mu s]$	$[\frac{\lvert I \rvert}{d}]$
$k = 2$				
CW09_SimHash	48	2.0	17 (2.9×)	1.4 (-30%)
CW09_OddSketch	51	2.0	17 (3.0×)	1.4 (-31%)
BA_Sift_Lsh	67	2.0	25 (2.7×)	1.2 (-40%)
BA_Sift_Mlh	62	2.0	22 (2.8×)	1.2 (-40%)
$k = 3$				
CW09_SimHash	49	2.0	17 (2.9×)	1.4 (-30%)
CW09_OddSketch	49	2.0	16 (3.0×)	1.4 (-31%)
BA_Sift_Lsh	70	2.0	28 (2.5×)	1.2 (-40%)
BA_Sift_Mlh	64	2.0	25 (2.5×)	1.2 (-40%)

Table 2: Average query time and space usage of Original and Compact on all the datasets for $k = 2$ and $k = 3$. The space usage is reported as the increasing factor with respect to the size of the original dataset. We also report in brackets the improvement of Compact wrt Original.

lower 32 bits of K and b_K be its $64 - \ell - 32$ upper bits. We store $x_K = a_K \oplus b_K$ in the vector L instead of a_K. Note that x_K sketches the content of the key K in 32 bits. Clearly, given x_K and b_K, we can compute a_K. The first check now computes the Hamming distance of x_K and x_Q, where $x_Q = a_Q \oplus b_Q$ with a_Q and b_Q denoting the lower and upper bits of the query Q. This is a better estimate which allows us to reduce the number of keys that pass the first check. Experiments show that this percentage is 0.66% for $k = 5$, 1.27% for $k = 7$, and 3.02% for $k = 9$.

The use of 32-bit entries in the vector H allows a further optimization which speeds up the computation of the Hamming distance needed at the first check. Indeed, it is possible to use SIMD operations to perform 4 Hamming distance computations at once on 32-bit entries. Due to space limitations we do not enter into details of this technique, we just point out that it is not applicable to 64-bit entries. We use SIMD to refer to this optimization.

As shown in Figure 4, the combined use of SPLIT, SIMD and XOR improves the speed of the aligned representation for k up to 7 and almost cancels the gap for larger values of k. Thus, our layout uses a fraction between 0.67 (with $k = 5$) and 0.8 (with $k = 9$) of the space of the aligned representation without any time penalty.

4.3 Overall comparison

In our comparison we compare the following solutions.

- Original is an implementation of multi-index* which uses binary search in the searching phase and keys are stored in a vector with aligned 64-bit entries. We validated this implementation with the source code of the implementations in [20] and [26]. However, we were not able to compare directly with these implementations because 1) the implementation in [20] does not scale with the dataset size and, indeed, [20] tested it on a dataset with less than 0.5 million keys (i.e., three orders of magnitudes smaller than ours); 2) implementation in [26] actually solves nearest neighbor queries which is a slightly different problem. However, as far as the implementation in [26] is concerned, we point out that i) their function to compute Hamming distance is slower than ours[3] and, since these computations are the dominant cost in the checking phase, our implementation is faster; ii) our implementation is also more space efficient as, for example, their index with $b = 2$ blocks on BA_Sift_Lsh and BA_Sift_Mlh uses 28 Gbytes of space while ours uses 15 Gbytes.

- Compact is an implementation of multi-index* which uses all the time and space improvements described in Subsection 4.2, namely Succinct for the searching phase and SPLIT+ SIMD+ XOR for the checking phase.

- Clustered is an implementation which uses all the improvements of the previous implementation combined with the Clustered strategy described in Subsection 3.2.

- BoundedClustered is an implementation which uses all the improvements in Compact combined with the BoundedClustered strategy described in Subsection 3.2. The threshold τ is set to 32 for $k = \{4, 5\}$, to 64 for $k = \{6, 7\}$ and to 128 for $k = \{8, 9\}$. These thresholds have been chosen after an experimental evaluation whose results are not reported due to space limitations.

In our overall comparison we distinguish two cases based on the value of k.

The results for small values of k, namely $k = 2$ and $k = 3$, are reported in Table 2. Due to space limitations, we only report results for Original and Compact. Anyway, the higher level of sophistication of Clustered and BoundedClustered and their small improvements on the query time do not justify their use on these values of k. Indeed, their main objective is that of improving the checking phase but, as we discussed in Subsection 4.2, the time of the searching phase dominates the overall query time with these values of k.

[3] A switch statement dependent on the word length prohibits compile optimizations.

		Original		Compact		Clustered		BoundedClustered	
		[μs]	[$\lvert I\rvert/d$]	[μs]	[$\lvert I\rvert/d$]	[μs]	[$\lvert I\rvert/d$]	[μs]	[$\lvert I\rvert/d$]
CW09_SimHash	$k = 4$	102	3.0	39(2.6×)	2.1(-32%)	37(2.7×)	2.1(-31%)	41(2.5×)	2.3(-25%)
CW09_OddSketch		94	3.0	34(2.8×)	2.1(-32%)	33(2.8×)	2.1(-31%)	37(2.6×)	2.3(-25%)
BA_Sift_Lsh		557	3.0	271(2.1×)	2.0(-32%)	220(2.5×)	2.1(-31%)	163(3.4×)	2.2(-26%)
BA_Sift_Mlh		368	3.0	149(2.5×)	2.0(-32%)	126(2.9×)	2.1(-31%)	112(3.3×)	2.2(-26%)
CW09_SimHash	$k = 5$	104	3.0	42(2.4×)	2.1(-32%)	43(2.4×)	2.1(-31%)	47(2.2×)	2.3(-25%)
CW09_OddSketch		94	3.0	34(2.7×)	2.1(-32%)	35(2.7×)	2.1(-31%)	40(2.3×)	2.3(-25%)
BA_Sift_Lsh		588	3.0	329(1.8×)	2.0(-32%)	307(1.9×)	2.1(-31%)	266(2.2×)	2.2(-26%)
BA_Sift_Mlh		387	3.0	179(2.2×)	2.0(-32%)	171(2.3×)	2.1(-31%)	168(2.3×)	2.2(-26%)
CW09_SimHash	$k = 6$	871	4.0	401(2.2×)	3.1(-23%)	327(2.7×)	3.1(-23%)	286(3.1×)	3.1(-22%)
CW09_OddSketch		791	4.0	348(2.3×)	3.1(-23%)	276(2.9×)	3.1(-23%)	254(3.1×)	3.1(-22%)
BA_Sift_Lsh		4 668	4.0	3 252(1.4×)	3.1(-23%)	2 878(1.6×)	3.1(-23%)	1 465(3.2×)	3.1(-22%)
BA_Sift_Mlh		3 165	4.0	1 975(1.6×)	3.1(-23%)	1 703(1.9×)	3.1(-23%)	899(3.5×)	3.1(-22%)
CW09_SimHash	$k = 7$	875	4.0	429(2.0×)	3.1(-23%)	385(2.3×)	3.1(-23%)	358(2.4×)	3.1(-22%)
CW09_OddSketch		787	4.0	359(2.2×)	3.1(-23%)	312(2.5×)	3.1(-23%)	300(2.6×)	3.1(-22%)
BA_Sift_Lsh		4 945	4.0	4 036(1.2×)	3.1(-23%)	3 897(1.3×)	3.1(-23%)	2 488(2.0×)	3.1(-22%)
BA_Sift_Mlh		3 272	4.0	2 356(1.4×)	3.1(-23%)	2 228(1.5×)	3.1(-23%)	1 400(2.3×)	3.1(-22%)
CW09_SimHash	$k = 8$	4 737	5.0	3 930(1.2×)	4.1(-18%)	3 448(1.4×)	4.1(-18%)	2 422(2.0×)	4.1(-18%)
CW09_OddSketch		4 501	5.0	3 588(1.3×)	4.1(-18%)	3 033(1.5×)	4.1(-18%)	2 107(2.1×)	4.1(-18%)
BA_Sift_Lsh		21 936	5.0	24 148(0.9×)	4.1(-18%)	23 548(0.9×)	4.1(-18%)	12 118(1.8×)	4.1(-19%)
BA_Sift_Mlh		15 652	5.0	15 818(1.0×)	4.1(-18%)	14 881(1.1×)	4.1(-18%)	6 809(2.3×)	4.1(-19%)
CW09_SimHash	$k = 9$	4 778	5.0	4 804(1.0×)	4.1(-18%)	4 388(1.1×)	4.1(-18%)	3 218(1.5×)	4.1(-18%)
CW09_OddSketch		4 499	5.0	4 400(1.0×)	4.1(-18%)	3 871(1.2×)	4.1(-18%)	2 890(1.6×)	4.1(-18%)
BA_Sift_Lsh		24 249	5.0	31 679(0.8×)	4.1(-18%)	31 962(0.8×)	4.1(-18%)	20 929(1.2×)	4.1(-19%)
BA_Sift_Mlh		16 611	5.0	20 173(0.8×)	4.1(-18%)	19 873(0.8×)	4.1(-18%)	11 190(1.5×)	4.1(-19%)

Table 3: Average query time and space usage of all the solutions on all the datasets for $k = \{4, 5, 6, 7, 8, 9\}$. The space usage is reported as the increasing factor with respect to the size of the original dataset. We also report in brackets the improvement of our solutions wrt Original.

Results show that Compact improves the query time of Original by a factor that ranges between 2.5 and 3.0. This is mainly due to the replacement of binary search with our Succinct solution. The space usage is also improved by at least 30% and up to 40% with better results for larger datasets. This means that while the space usage of Original is two times the size of the original datasets, Compact uses slightly more space than the original datasets. Note that the space usage does not depend on k because with both values we have to use $b = 2$.

The results for larger values of k, namely k between 4 and 9, are reported in Table 3. We first observe that our solutions improve the space usage of Original by 17% up to 32% depending on the solution, the value of k and the dataset size. Note that Compact is always slightly more space efficient than Clustered and BoundedClustered. This is due to the auxiliar information stored by Clustered and BoundedClustered to describe and locate their clusters. However, the impact of this space overhead decreases with the size of the dataset and the value of k.

As far as the query time is concerned, we first observe that Compact and Clustered are faster (factor 1.4×—2.9×) than Original up to $k = 7$. For $k = \{8, 9\}$, these three solutions have a quite close time efficiency with one which is faster than the others depending on the dataset. We also observe that Clustered always outperforms Compact even if for some values of k the improvement is below the 10%. This is expected because Clustered always checks a subrange of the keys checked by Compact by using the same scanning procedure. Finally, BoundedClustered is the fastest solution with margin. Indeed, it outperforms Original by a factor that ranges between 2 and 3.4 for k up to 7. For $k = \{8, 9\}$, the factor of improvement is at least 1.5 for all datasets but BA_Sift_Lsh with $k = 9$ where it is 1.2.

k	Original or Compact	Clustered	BoundedClustered	
4	322 795	216 026(1.5×)	38 347	(8.4×)
5	322 795	253 511(1.3×)	60 151	(5.4×)
6	3 754 240	3 106 170(1.2×)	485 530	(7.7×)
7	3 754 240	3 346 000(1.1×)	701 792	(5.3×)
8	21 287 200	19 704 300(1.1×)	2 784 240	(7.6×)
9	21 287 200	20 356 400(1.0×)	3 903 500	(5.5×)

Table 4: Average number of checked candidates per query on BA_Sift_Lsh by varying the value of k. In brackets we report the reduction factor with respect to Original and Compact .

Finally, we report in Table 4 the average number of checked candidates per query on BA_Sift_Lsh. Clearly, Original and Compact always check the same set of candidates because they differ only on the representation of the keys. These numbers partially explain the time results in Table 3. It is apparent that BoundedClustered is more efficient also on this respect and, indeed, it reduces the number of checked candidates by a factor that ranges from 5.3 to 8, 4. However, these high reduction factors are not reflected on equally high speed up factors. This is due to the more predictable memory access patterns of the other solutions which scan a whole range of consecutive candidates, while BoundedClustered skips subranges of the whole range. Thus, the much smaller number of checked candidates in BoundedClustered is partially balanced by the higher benefits that the other solutions obtain by the CPU prefetching.

5. FUTURE WORK

We conclude with two interesting open questions. First, we point out that the use of the Elias-Fano representation [11, 12] to store the sorted keys of an index requires $n \log \frac{2^{64}}{n} + 2n + o(n)$ bits. This space bound implies that each key requires between 36 and 38 bits on our data. This means that it always almost halves the space usage of Original and improves the ones of the other solutions regardless the value of k. However, scanning a portion of a vector in Elias-Fano representation is much more inefficient than with the others. Thus, a solution that uses Elias-Fano would only introduce a time/space tradeoff. The design of a representation which achieves the space bound of Elias-Fano still preserving the time efficiency of the other solutions is left as a future work.

For the second one, we observe that the greedy selection of the pivots in both Clustered and BoundedClustered may be suboptimal. It would be very interesting to design an efficient optimization algorithm which selects the pivots to minimize the expected execution time of the subsequent queries. One of the challenges here is to provide a precise model to estimate the query execution time.

6. ACKNOWLEDGEMENT

This work was partially supported by the project PRA_2016_64 *Through the fog* funded by the University of Pisa and by the EU H2020 Program under the scheme *INFRAIA-1-2014-2015: Research Infrastructures* grant agreement #654024 *SoBigData: Social Mining & Big Data Ecosystem.*

7. REFERENCES

[1] D. Belazzougui. Faster and space-optimal edit distance 1 dictionary. In *CPM*, pages 154–167, 2009.

[2] D. Belazzougui and R. Venturini. Compressed string dictionary search with edit distance one. *Algorithmica*, 2016 (to appear).

[3] L. Boytsov. Indexing methods for approximate dictionary searching: Comparative analysis. *ACM Journal of Experimental Algorithmics*, 16(1), 2011.

[4] G. S. Brodal and V. Srinivasan. Improved bounds for dictionary look-up with one error. *Information Processing Letters*, 75(1-2):57–59, 2000.

[5] A. Z. Broder, S. C. Glassman, M. S. Manasse, and G. Zweig. Syntactic clustering of the web. *Computer Networks*, 29(8-13):1157–1166, 1997.

[6] H. Chan, T. W. Lam, W. Sung, S. Tam, and S. Wong. Compressed indexes for approximate string matching. *Algorithmica*, 58(2):263–281, 2010.

[7] M. Charikar. Similarity estimation techniques from rounding algorithms. In *STOC*, pages 380–388, 2002.

[8] I. Chegrane and D. Belazzougui. Simple, compact and robust approximate string dictionary. *J. Discrete Algorithms*, 28:49–60, 2014.

[9] D. Clark. *Compact Pat Trees*. PhD thesis, Department of Computer Science, University of Waterloo, 1996.

[10] R. Cole, L.-A. Gottlieb, and M. Lewenstein. Dictionary matching and indexing with errors and don't cares. In *STOC*, pages 91–100, 2004.

[11] P. Elias. Efficient storage and retrieval by content and address of static files. *J. ACM*, 21(2):246–260, 1974.

[12] R. M. Fano. On the number of bits required to implement an associative memory. *Memorandum 61, Computer Structures Group, MIT, Cambridge, MA*, 1971.

[13] S. Gog, T. Beller, A. Moffat, and M. Petri. From theory to practice: Plug and play with succinct data structures. In *SEA*, 2014.

[14] D. H. Greene, M. Parnas, and F. F. Yao. Multi-index hashing for information retrieval. In *FOCS*, pages 722–731, 1994.

[15] R. Grossi and G. Ottaviano. Design of practical succinct data structures for large data collections. In *SEA*, pages 5–17, 2013.

[16] M. Henzinger. Finding near-duplicate web pages: a large-scale evaluation of algorithms. In *SIGIR*, pages 284–291, 2006.

[17] M. L. Hetland. The basic principles of metric indexing. In *Swarm intelligence for multi-objective problems in data mining*, pages 199–232. Springer, 2009.

[18] H. Jegou, R. Tavenard, M. Douze, and L. Amsaleg. Searching in one billion vectors: Re-rank with source coding. In *ICASSP*, pages 861–864, 2011.

[19] P. Li and A. C. König. Theory and applications of b-bit minwise hashing. *Commun. ACM*, 54(8):101–109, 2011.

[20] A. X. Liu, K. Shen, and E. Torng. Large scale hamming distance query processing. In *ICDE*, pages 553–564, 2011.

[21] D. G. Lowe. Distinctive image features from scale-invariant keypoints. *International Journal of Computer Vision*, 60(2):91–110, 2004.

[22] G. S. Manku, A. Jain, and A. D. Sarma. Detecting near-duplicates for web crawling. In *WWW*, pages 141–150, 2007.

[23] M. Minsky and S. Papert. *Perceptrons*. MIT Press, Cambridge, MA, 1969.

[24] M. Mitzenmacher, R. Pagh, and N. Pham. Efficient estimation for high similarities using odd sketches. In *WWW*, pages 109–118, 2014.

[25] M. Norouzi, D. J. Fleet, and R. Salakhutdinov. Hamming distance metric learning. In *NIPS*, pages 1070–1078, 2012.

[26] M. Norouzi, A. Punjani, and D. J. Fleet. Fast exact search in hamming space with multi-index hashing. *IEEE Trans. Pattern Anal. Mach. Intell.*, 36(6):1107–1119, 2014.

[27] J. Song, Y. Yang, Y. Yang, Z. Huang, and H. T. Shen. Inter-media hashing for large-scale retrieval from heterogeneous data sources. In *SIGMOD*, 2013.

[28] A. C.-C. Yao and F. F. Yao. Dictionary look-up with one error. *Journal of Algorithms*, 25(1):194–202, 1997.

[29] X. Zhang, J. Qin, W. Wang, Y. Sun, and J. Lu. Hmsearch: an efficient hamming distance query processing algorithm. In *SSDBM*, pages 19:1–19:12, 2013.

Fast First-Phase Candidate Generation for Cascading Rankers

Qi Wang
Computer Science & Eng.
New York University
qiwang@nyu.edu

Constantinos Dimopoulos
Computer Science & Eng.
New York University
constantinos@nyu.edu

Torsten Suel
Computer Science & Eng.
New York University
torsten.suel@nyu.edu

ABSTRACT

Current search engines use very complex ranking functions based on hundreds of features. While such functions return high-quality results, they create efficiency challenges as it is too costly to fully evaluate them on all documents in the union, or even intersection, of the query terms. To address this issue, search engines use a series of cascading rankers, starting with a very simple ranking function and then applying increasingly complex and expensive ranking functions on smaller and smaller sets of candidate results. Researchers have recently started studying several problems within this framework of query processing by cascading rankers; see, e.g., [5, 13, 17, 51].

We focus on one such problem, the design of the initial cascade. Thus, the goal is to very quickly identify a set of good candidate documents that should be passed to the second and further cascades. Previous work by Asadi and Lin [3, 5] showed that while a top-k computation on either the union or intersection gives good results, a further optimization using a global document ordering based on spam scores leads to a significant reduction in quality. Our contribution is to propose an alternative framework that builds specialized single-term and pairwise index structures, and then during query time selectively accesses these structures based on a cost budget and a set of early termination techniques. Using an end-to-end evaluation with a complex machine-learned ranker, we show that our approach finds candidates about an order of magnitude faster than a conjunctive top-k computation, while essentially matching the quality.

1. INTRODUCTION

Search engines are continuously optimizing their ranking functions in order to improve result quality. This is usually achieved through more and more complex ranking functions based on large sets of features, including features derived from text, link structure, past queries, and online or proprietary data sets and knowledge bases through various data extraction and mining techniques. However, these complex ranking functions create significant performance challenges for the engines, as evaluating them on large numbers of documents is very expensive. Given the billions of queries that have to be processed each day, it would not be feasible to apply such functions directly on all documents passing the initial Boolean filter, even in the conjunctive case.

To address this challenge, all current major engines appear to be using a cascading approach to query processing that approximates the results of such ranking functions through a series of increasingly more complex intermediate functions. Thus, after query analysis and rewriting, the search engine first applies a very simple ranking function, similar to BM25 or a Cosine measure, that only uses a few features and can be very efficiently applied on large numbers of candidates. We refer to this process as the first cascade. Next, in the second cascade, a somewhat more complex function based on a larger set of features is applied to, say, the top few thousand results from the first cascade. In the third and further cascades, even more complex functions are applied to smaller and smaller sets of surviving candidates of the previous cascades. This approach was described and formalized in [51].

Thus, the goal of the cascading approach is to return (almost) the same results as we would get from applying the complex function on all candidates, at a fraction of the computational cost. Its proper implementation, however, poses several challenges that have recently received some attention in the literature [5, 13, 17, 32, 40, 51]. In particular, work has focused on four distinct challenges: (1) How to design good sequences of increasingly complex ranking functions and associated cutoffs (number of results kept for the next cascade) [51]; (2) how to efficiently apply a complex ranking function to candidates by using early-exit strategies [13]; (3) how to design ranking functions for the first cascades that preserve many good candidates for subsequent cascades, as opposed to focusing on how to order a few top results [17]; (4) how to implement the first cascade efficiently through an optimal choice of Boolean filters and various early-termination techniques [3, 5].

We focus on the last challenge, which is important as the first cascade is executed on large numbers of candidates. The results in [3, 5] indicated that for the first cascade, a conjunctive filter does essentially as well as a disjunctive one, while saving a lot of time. However, a naive attempt to use a global document ordering to avoid a complete conjunctive traversal of the index structures resulted in significant losses in end-to-end result quality.

In this paper, we propose an approach that runs about an order of magnitude faster than even highly optimized con-

SIGIR '16, July 17-21, 2016, Pisa, Italy
@ 2016 ACM. ISBN 978-1-4503-4069-4/16/07 $15.00
DOI: http://dx.doi.org/10.1145/2911451.2911515.

junctive and disjunctive top-k computations, while achieving essentially the same end-to-end result quality. More precisely, given a complex ranking function that needs to be approximated by a cascading approach, an inverted index structure for a document collection, and a training query trace, we show how to build an auxiliary layer of index structures, and how to select which parts of this layer to consult on a submitted query, in order to obtain high-quality candidates with a limited computational and space budget.

In particular, our contributions are as follows:

1. We design a framework that builds specialized single-term and pairwise index structures subject to a given space constraint. It uses limited size query traces to train query term language models and posting quality models.
2. We propose an online selection algorithm based on a cost budget that, for a given query, decides the access depth for each available structure according to the posting quality model, and present query processing and lookup strategies that further improve performance.
3. We provide an end-to-end evaluation of our proposed architecture on ClueWeb09B, and show that our approach can identify candidates about an order of magnitude faster than previous published results, with negligible quality loss.

The remainder of the paper is organized as follows: Section 2 presents some background and discusses related work. In Section 3 we give a high-level overview of our approach, and present our solutions for several components. Next, Section 4 outlines the experimental setup, and Section 5 presents the experimental evaluation of the proposed framework. Finally, Section 6 provides some concluding remarks.

2. BACKGROUND AND RELATED WORK

In this section, we provide some background on inverted indexes, query processing and early termination techniques, and cascade ranking architectures, and discuss related work.

Inverted Indexes: Commercial search engines perform query processing based on the widely used inverted index [58]. Given a collection of N documents, each document is assigned a unique identifier (docID) from 0 to N-1. The inverted index consists of a set of inverted lists and a lexicon. In particular, for each distinct term t in the collection, there is an inverted list L_t. Each L_t is a list of postings specifying the documents that t appears in. Typically, each posting contains the docID of a document containing t and the frequency of t in the document; however, there may also be other information, such as the positions of the term occurrences in the document, or a precomputed impact score. The lexicon contains for each unique term in the collection a pointer to the corresponding inverted list. Inverted index compression is crucial for search engine performance and many techniques have been proposed [6, 45].

Index Layout: There are many ways to organize the inverted lists. In document-sorted indexes, each list is sorted by docID, resulting in small delta gaps (d-gaps) between consecutive docIDs that lead to a smaller compressed size [45]. Impact-sorted indexes sort the postings in each list in decreasing order of impact scores. Thus, high-scoring query results tend to be located near the front of the lists, potentially enabling a smart query processing algorithm to skip most of the rest of the list. However, this approach leads to poor compressibility compared to document-sorted indexes, and may require random lookups into lists for docIDs that score high on one query term but low on others. Finally, impact-layered indexes split each inverted list into a small number of layers based on impact scores. Our approach uses two layers, where the first layer of high-impact postings is sorted by impact, and the second layer by docID to allow for efficient random lookups.

Index Traversal: During query processing, index structures can be traversed in different ways [50]. In Document-at-a-time (DAAT), each list has a pointer to a current posting and one document is processed at a time; then pointers are moved forward in docID space. The top results are usually maintained in a min-heap structure. In Term-at-a-time (TAAT) traversal, a list is fully traversed before accessing the next one. Partially scored documents are kept as accumulators in a hash table or other structure; this structure can be a bottleneck if it grows beyond the CPU caches. Lastly, there are hybrids between DAAT and TAAT. Note that DAAT is mainly suitable for document-sorted indexes, while TAAT works well with impact-sorted ones.

2.1 Query Processing and Early Termination

The simplest form of query processing applies a Boolean filter (AND/OR) on the inverted lists of the query terms, and then ranks all documents passing the filter. A good ranking function should (a) provide a good approximation of the relevance of a document with respect to a query and (b) be efficiently computable using the information stored in the index. Well-known examples include Cosine measures and BM25 [6]. Most of these simple ranking schemes have the property that the score of a document d for the full query q is the sum (or other simple combination) of per-term scores; i.e., $score(q, d) = \sum_{t \in q} s(t, d)$, where $s(t, d)$ is the impact score of term t in d.

Early Termination: A naïve query processing approach is inefficient, and ends up decompressing and accessing large parts of the inverted lists. To improve on this, researchers have proposed many *early termination* (ET) algorithms that try to find good results while accessing and scoring only a small part of the relevant inverted lists. ET algorithms are called *safe* if they always return the same results as an exhaustive algorithm, and *unsafe* otherwise [48]. ET techniques are widely used in commercial engines and academic systems, and include the following approaches:

- **Index Tiering:** A collection is partitioned into, say, 2 or 3, disjoint subsets of documents called *tiers*, where the first tier contains the highest-quality documents; queries are executed on the first tier and only selectively routed to other tiers [41, 42].
- **Pruning:** In static pruning, postings considered unlikely to ever be useful are deleted from the index [8, 12, 24, 37]. In dynamic pruning, inverted lists are typically organized in impact-sorted or impact-layered form, and algorithms focus on high-impact postings and only selectively access lower-impact postings for promising documents. One very widely studied example are the FA, TA, and NRA algorithms in [23].
- **Skipping:** For document-sorted indexes, there are various techniques for skipping unimportant parts of the inverted lists [10, 14, 19, 20, 21].

Our approach here is unsafe, and based on dynamic pruning with impact-layered structures for both terms and term pairs (intersections of two terms), as described later.

2.2 Cascading Ranking Architectures

In modern commercial engines, query processing is based on cascading ranking schemes [10, 13, 51], where each cascade includes a ranker that provides candidate documents to subsequent cascades. The first cascade is usually based on a very simple ranking function that is evaluated on large parts of the index structure to get an initial set of candidates. Thus, this function must be very fast, while providing a reasonably high-quality set of candidates. Subsequent cascades are executed on fewer candidates using more complex and expensive ranking functions. The challenge in designing such cascading architectures is to select a set of cascades and associated ranking functions that achieves high end-to-end quality at low cost.

Cascading setups are crucial for the performance and quality of modern commercial engines, and a number of papers have recently focused on this setup [4, 5, 13, 17, 32, 40, 51]. We focus on optimizing the efficiency of the first cascade in such architectures, a problem recently studied in [4, 5].

2.3 Comparison to Previous Work

We now discuss the relationship of our approach to previous work. The particular problem we consider is based on the setup in [5, 4, 17]. Thus, we have a two-phase cascading architecture, where the first phase obtains an initial candidate set of, say, several hundred or thousand documents, while the second phase reranks these candidates using a more sophisticated ranker based on dozens or hundreds of features. Our goal is to design very fast ET algorithms for the first phase that achieve end-to-end quality comparable to more exhaustive approaches. This is essentially the problem addressed by Asadi and Lin in [4, 5].

In particular, [5] investigates the efficiency/effectiveness trade-off for various first-phase candidates generation approaches. They experiment with conjunctive WAND [10], disjunctive WAND, and two conjunctive algorithms that first obtain the intersection and then rerank results based on BM25 or spam score, and conclude that conjunctive WAND provides the best trade-off. Work in [4] shows how to accelerate the intersection-based approaches using Bloom Filters. Our contribution here is to provide a method that achieves quality comparable to their best methods at lower cost.

Another relevant recent work [52] proposes a *document prioritization method* for selective evaluation of documents that achieves a better efficiency/effectiveness balance in the first cascade. The running times reported in [52] are significantly slower than ours, though some of the ideas could potentially be used to further optimize the lookup phase of our approach.

Our algorithm is based on a layered index organization and performs a limited-depth access to impact-sorted single-term and term-pair structures, followed by random lookups. As such, it is closely related to the well-know FA algorithm proposed by Fagin [23], and also to ET algorithms for impact-layered indexes introduced in [39]. There are many subsequent papers that further developed and often combined these approaches to solve various IR ranking problems, including, e.g., [2, 7, 9, 33, 47, 48].

We note that [28, 29] describe a number of access and lookup strategies for top-k query processing in database applications. One algorithm that is somewhat similar to our approach is the *MPro* algorithm in [28], which seeks to minimize lookup costs through sorted access. Work in [48] suggested methods for selecting the access depth into the available single-term impact-sorted lists. However, [48] focused only on single-term impact-sorted lists and did not provide cost-based query processing algorithms in the context of cascading rankers. Our approach is different from both of the above as we are proposing a framework for constructing additional impact-sorted index structures, including pairwise structures, based on query term distributions and posting quality models and subject to space constraints, plus an online depth selection algorithm and lookup strategies.

Our approach relies heavily on term-pair index structures, introduced in [34] and subsequently studied in a number of papers such as [11, 15, 26, 30, 44, 54, 56, 57]. Our work is most closely related to [30], which also applies the approach in [23] to pairwise structures. The main difference is our focus on cascading ranking schemes, and our framework for optimizing index structures and index traversals based on a limited space and access cost budget.

Also related is the work in [11], which proposes building single and pairwise impact-sorted lists that are then completely accessed during query processing. Though related, our work is different in two ways: While [11] and earlier work in [44, 54, 56, 57] assume a ranking function that directly takes proximity into account, we assume a more complex function in a cascading setup. Also, the resulting auxiliary structures in [11] are much larger than the basic index size; in contrast, our query language and posting quality models allow us to achieve high speed with only a limited increase in size. We note that our results could potentially be improved by adding special pairwise structures for terms occurring close to each other in a document, as done in [11, 54].

Finally, [1, 27] study techniques for learning better index structures given a set of documents and queries. In particular, [27] can be seen as essentially learning an ordering of index postings that is better than the "natural" impact-based ordering used, e.g., in [23]. We note that this issue is orthogonal to our approach, and could be combined to possibly yield additional benefits. Lastly, while we construct our first-layer structures using off-line preprocessing, one could also approach this via a suitable caching mechanism, such as those in [25, 38, 46] for other types of structures. Finally, our improvements are in addition to any speedups achieved through result caching, since our query traces do not have significant numbers of repeated queries.

3. PROBLEM SETUP AND APPROACH

We now define and discuss our problem setup, give a high-level description of our approach, and then provide more details about the various steps that are involved.

3.1 Problem Setup

We are given a complex ranking function CF, a simple ranking function SF used as the first cascade, and a rank cutoff c for the first cascade, meaning that only c results from the first cascade will be evaluated by the complex ranking function, which will then return the top k, $k \leq c$, results to the user. Our goal is to implement the first cascade to run as fast as possible without significantly decreasing end-to-end result quality. In our implementation, we allow unsafe early termination techniques, that is, the c results we give to CF may be different than those obtained from an exhaustive top-c computation using SF.

We measure quality in two ways: (i) *Overlap@(k,c)*, meaning how many of the top-k results that would be returned by an exhaustive application of CF (i.e., $c_{cf} = \infty$ or at least fairly large) are returned with our first cascade implementation that evaluates c candidates and (ii) *NDCG@k*, which is the normalized discounted cumulative gain that considers the order of the results.

Problem Discussion: Note that while the above definition assumes only two cascades, SF and CF, this does not really limit our approach as long as any additional intermediate cascades do a good job at approximating CF, i.e., do not lose too many good results among those nominated by SF for further processing. We believe this is a reasonable assumption in practice, and assume that subdividing the second cascade into further cascades is a separate problem. For the same reason, the reported running times are only for the first cascade, as the cost of the second cascade should only depend on c.

While an unsafe implementation of the first cascade could in principle achieve better quality than a safe disjunctive or conjunctive top-c computation using SF, this is not really expected. Thus, our goal is to do (almost) as well as these two choices, shown to be good in [3, 5], while being much faster than these and other non-safe competitors.

3.2 Our Overall Approach

We now describe our approach, which starts with an existing inverted index for the collection that could be used to run queries using SF. We then create additional auxiliary index structures to quickly identify promising candidates. We create two kinds of structures, single-term structures, and term-pair, or pairwise, structures, which together make up the *first layer* of the index, while the complete inverted index[1] makes up the second layer. For the single-term structures in the first layer, we choose, for each inverted list, some number of high-scoring postings, and arrange them by impact score in decreasing order. The pairwise structures are obtained by intersecting two inverted lists, and keeping a certain number of high-scoring two-term postings, where the score of such a posting is the sum of the impact scores of the two constituent postings. These structures are also sorted in decreasing order of impact score. We later discuss how to select which postings to put into the first layer, based on query traces and impact scores.

When a query enters, the first cascade is now executed by first selecting and accessing some prefix of the much smaller relevant structures in the first layer of the index. Afterwards, we perform a limited number of lookups into the second layer, to obtain additional scores for some promising documents for which we have found partial scores in the first layer. Finally, we identify c documents for further evaluation by CF. We show the overall index structure in Figure 1, where a query "dog cat mouse" is processed.

For our problem setup, there are various technical problems to address. In particular, when building the first layer, we need to decide how deep we should build the single-term structures, and for which pairs of terms we should build a pairwise structure and up to what depth. The goal is for the structures to be deep enough to find most good results,

[1]Except for short lists that are completely in the first layer.

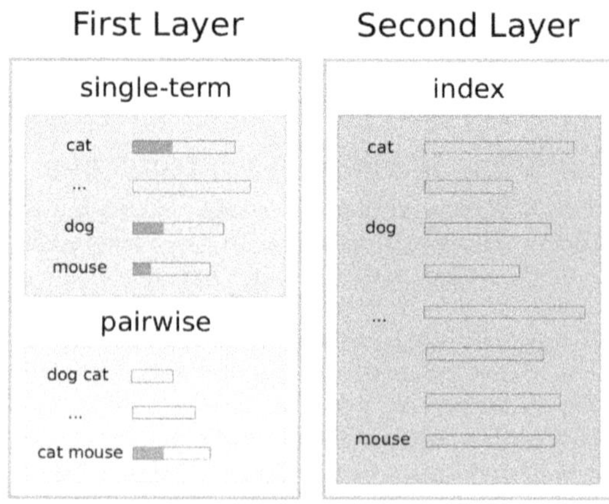

Figure 1: Our index structure, with first layer on the left and second layer on the right. In the top left are single-term structures, and in the bottom left are pairwise structures, each sorted by decreasing impact score. For a query "dog cat mouse" our method might decide to access a certain prefix (shown in red) of each relevant single-term list, and of one of the available pairwise structures (in this case, for "cat" and "mouse"), based on some access budget.

but not so deep that there is a large increase in overall index size. When a query enters, we need to decide which of the applicable index structures to consult and up to what depth – always using all potentially relevant structures in the first layer up to their full depth would not be efficient. We also need to decide what lookups into the second layer should be performed to identify the c results to be forwarded to the complex ranker for full evaluation. We later propose and evaluate solutions for all these problems.

Overall, our approach has the following steps that need to be implemented. During indexing, we have two steps:

- **Modeling:** We build two types of models by performing training on a query trace of limited size, (a) a language model for the queries that allows us to predict how frequent certain terms and combinations of terms are in the query trace, and (b) a quality model relating the rank of a posting in a first-layer structure to its likelihood of being a top result under CF.
- **Index Building:** We build the first layer based on the constructed models, by carefully choosing which structures to build and up to what depth, subject to a maximum space budget.

Later, when a query enters the system, we execute the following sequence of steps:

- **Online Greedy Depth Selection:** We consider the list of relevant structures, and decide which of them should be accessed and to what depth, based on the quality model and based on a simple model for query processing costs. In fact, costs will be modeled based on the aggregate access depth into the first-layer structures and the number of lookups into the second layer, with a certain budget available for a query.
- **Query Processing:** We throw the accessed structures and their corresponding access depths, as selected in the previous step, into a simple but fast in-memory query processor.

- **Second-Layer Lookups:** We decide for which candidate documents we should perform lookups into the second layer to get more precise scores.
- **Final Selection:** We choose the c results that should be evaluated by the complex ranker.

3.3 Index Construction

We now describe the two steps in the index construction in more detail. First, we build two models, one for query and query term distribution, and one to model the quality contributions of different parts of the index structures. These models are then stored for later use during index building and query processing.

Modeling: For the first model, we use standard Language Modeling tools, in particular the MIT Language Modeling (MITLM) toolkit[2], based on Kneser-Ney smoothing. We train these models on part of our query trace (distinct from any queries used in the evaluation), to obtain estimates of two probabilities, $p(t)$, the probability that term t occurs in a random incoming query, and $p(t_1, t_2)$, the probability that both t_1 and t_2 occur in such a query. We refer to these as our *query language models.*

For the second model, given a posting p for a term t that has rank r in its list (i.e., has the r-th highest impact score in its list), we want a rough estimate of the likelihood that the posting belongs to a top-k result under the complex ranker CF, given a random query containing t. This is done by issuing training queries and, for each posting in one of the query term lists, storing its rank, the length of its inverted list, and whether it is part of a top-k result for the query. We bucketize the list lengths and relative ranks within lists into dozens of ranges (classes) each. Then we aggregate our data into a two-dimensional table A where $A[i, j]$ estimates the probability that a posting belonging to list length class i and relative rank class j (which might, say, correspond to a list length between 1000 and 1500 and rank between 120 and 160) leads to a top-k result. This approach gives sufficiently accurate predictions, while allowing extremely fast lookups during index building and query processing to get an estimate of $p(\text{top-k}|t)$, the likelihood that a posting is part of a top-k result given that its term t is part of a query.

We then repeat the process for term intersections, where we create a table where for each posting in the intersection of two terms t_1 and t_2, we use the length of the intersection, and the rank of the posting in the intersection, to estimate $p(\text{top-k}|t_1, t_2)$, the likelihood that a pairwise posting is part of a top-k result given that both t_1 and t_2 occur in a query. We refer to these models for single lists and term intersections as *posting quality models.*

Index Building: Given a space budget, our next goal is to build a first layer containing term and term-pair postings that are likely to lead to top-k results under random queries. To do this, we allocate separate space budgets to the single-term and pairwise structures in the first layer. For single-term lists, we greedily pick postings from the highest ranks of the inverted lists to add to the first layer. That is, we try to pick postings with the highest value of $p(t) \cdot p(\text{top-k}|t)$. Since our estimate for this value based on the models is expected to be a monotonically decreasing step function in each list, we can sort each list by increasing rank, and select chunks of postings with equal value from the beginning of the lists until the budget is exhausted using a heap to decide from which list to pick.

We repeat this greedy selection process for pairwise postings. Since there is a huge number of term pairs, we first restrict the space by only considering intersections for terms t_1 and t_2 with $p(t_1, t_2) \geq \theta$ for some small θ. Then these intersections are created and sorted by impact, and we again select chunks of postings from the beginning of the intersections based on our estimates of $p(t_1, t_2) \cdot p(\text{top-k}|t_1, t_2)$, until the budget is exhausted.

All structures in the first layer are kept sorted from highest to lowest impact score. The single-term postings are of the form (docID, impact), while the term-pair posting layout is (docID, impact_{t_1}, impact_{t_2}). Note that for single-term structures, we do not remove the postings in the first layer from the second layer, but create a copy of the postings, so this uses extra space. The reason is that we only access a limited amount of the first-layer structure, and thus we need to make sure that a lookup into the second layer can retrieve all postings. An exception are very short lists, of length less than 100, where we always move the entire list into the first layer and access it fully on any query containing the term; thus, these lists do not increase space usage (though their overall size is small). We also added an additional rule that limited the depth of any selected single-term and pairwise structure to the maximum access depth for queries, typically several thousand postings, as any posting deeper than the access depth would never be used anyway.

3.4 Query Processing

We now describe the steps involved in query processing: the online greedy depth selection, the query processor, the second-layer lookups, and the final selection of candidates.

Online Greedy Depth Selection: Given a query, we first identify all relevant structures available in the first layer. This usually includes all single-term structures for the query, since our language model assigns non-zero probabilities to all terms and the first postings tend to have very high values of $p(\text{top-k}|t)$, especially for short lists. Only some of the pairwise structures will typically be available for a query.

For each query, we have a cost budget that determines how much of the relevant structures we can access. For example, we might have a budget $b = 1000$, meaning that we can only access a total of b postings from the structures. Then for each structure we select a (possibly empty) prefix of postings. This is done greedily using a heap, as during index building, except that we select chunks of postings based on $p(\text{top-k}|t)$ and $p(\text{top-k}|t_1, t_2)$, respectively, without multiplying by $p(t)$ and $p(t_1, t_2)$ (since at this point the query already contains the terms). We note that we could perform various refinements to this approach, by charging different costs for pairwise versus single-term postings, or assigning different budgets to queries based on their difficulty.

Query Processor: We now run a fast and simple query processor on the selected structures and their corresponding depths. This processor copies the selected prefixes of the first-layer structures into an array and then runs a fast Radix Sort to sort postings by docID. A subsequent scan then aggregates the impact scores for each docID, and creates a bit filter for each docID stating which terms may require lookups into the second layer. During the scan we also filter redundant lookups as follows: Suppose a posting with docID 7 and impact 2.9 was found in the prefix of the list

[2]Available at `https://code.google.com/p/mitlm/`

for "cat", and that we have also accessed all pairwise postings for the pair "cat dog" with score 2.1 or higher. Then we do not have to perform a lookup into the "dog" list in the second layer for docID 7 – if such a posting existed we would have seen it as part of a pairwise posting.

We initially implemented a TAAT query processor using a hash table for the accumulators. However, we found that the sorting-based approach was much faster, by a factor of 2 to 3. Such a sorting-based approach is possible because we fix the access depth for each structure at the start of the query.

Second Layer Lookups and Final Candidate Selection: Next, we check the candidates and their accumulated scores, where most of these scores are partial, and many may have been only seen for one of the query terms. We now decide for which of these candidates we should perform lookups into the second layer to complete their scores, subject to a budget on the number of lookups (say, a few thousand per query). This is done using the accumulated partial score, as this provides a strong signal for relevance. We select the candidates with the highest partial scores, by running a randomized approximate selection algorithm where we first draw a sample of the impact scores, sort this sample, pick a suitable threshold from the sample, and then keep all candidates with impact above this score. Finally, we perform all necessary lookups for these candidates into the second layer, and keep the c candidates with highest completed BM25 scores, to be submitted to CF.

4. EXPERIMENTAL SETUP

In this section, we describe the data sets, ranking models, evaluation metrics, and setup of our experiments.

Datasets: All our experiments were conducted on the ClueWeb09B collection, which consists of 50,220,423 documents, 86,532,822 distinct terms, and 17 billion postings. For evaluation, we used the TREC 2009 Million Query Track (40k), which we refer to as Million09. Our training set for the modeling step includes 30k queries selected at random from Million09, while the testing set for performance evaluation consists of 3k from the remaining 10k queries. Table 1 shows the query lengths for the testing query set.

Query length	2	3	4	≥5
# queries	1408	954	517	121

Table 1: Query length distribution for the 3k testing queries.

The TREC 2010 to 2012 Web Track topics (150) were used for training the machine-learned complex ranker CF. For the language models, we used linear interpolation of a model for the training queries of the query set with a model for a randomly selected sample of 1.5 million documents, using the MIT Language Modeling (MITLM) toolkit.

Ranking models: We selected the BM25 ranking scheme as our first ranker, as it is widely used as a simple ranker in the literature and satisfies the desired properties of being both computationally fast and providing a reasonable set of initial candidates.

Recent studies [31, 51] show that ranking schemes obtained using learning-to-rank methods with dozens or hundreds of features outperform traditional bag-of-words models in terms of quality. There are a number of learning-to-rank tools that are available. We decided to use LambdaMart [53] to learn our complex ranker CF, as it is considered one of the most effective learning-to-rank models [22, 35]. We trained on the 150 queries from TREC 2010 to 2012 based on standard features from the literature [5, 36, 49]. Table 2 lists a subset of these features. The anchor text features were extracted using the data from [18], while the spam and pagerank values are from [16]. The distribution feature refers to the dispersion of term occurrences across a specific document, when the document is split into pieces of fixed size, say 100 terms.

Evaluation metrics: The main aspects in the design of a scalable web search architecture include quality, time, and space. Thus, we evaluated the proposed framework on these three aspects. We measure the end-to-end quality of the proposed methods with Overlap@(k,c) and NDCG@k. In particular, the end-to-end effectiveness evaluation within the cascading ranker setup is performed as follows. In the first cascade, the top-c documents are obtained based on our method and then, in the second cascade, the CF is applied to these documents in order to return the final top-k.

For the effectiveness of the first cascade, we measure Overlap@(k,c) as the fraction of top-k documents obtained when applying CF to all top 2000 results of a safe disjunctive BM25, that are also found among the c candidates computed by our algorithm. While it was not feasible to apply the complex ranker to all documents in the union of query terms, we found in preliminary experiments that beyond the top 2000 there was little change in the final top-k. This choice is also directly supported by the recommendations in [35]. Thus, an overlap of 1.0 for a query means that all top-k results were found among the c candidates of our method. We use $k = 10$ unless stated otherwise.

We evaluated the speed of our methods using average query latency (in milliseconds) for generating the candidates. That is, we measure the time elapsed from when a query arrives until the time when the top-c candidates are ready to be evaluated by CF. (We do not count the time for applying CF as it is the same for all methods.) The space overhead was measured as the percentage of a baseline full index.

Index: The second layer was indexed and compressed using a version of PForDelta [59] proposed in [55]. The algorithms were implemented using C++ and compiled using gcc with -O3 optimization. The experiments were conducted on a single core of a 2.27Ghz Intel Xeon (E5520) CPU. All data structures and indexes are memory-resident.

Parameters: Overall, the proposed framework utilizes the following parameters: (a) the access cost budget, i.e., the number of postings to access per query, (b) the number of documents to perform lookups on, (c) the number of candidates to forward to CF, c, and (d) the space budget, i.e., the amount of additional space beyond a standard index. During selection of the term-pair structures in the first layer, we considered only pairs with probability (according to the language model of MITLM) at least $1.99 * 10^{-16}$ for the Million09 query trace. Next, we present the experimental evaluation of our approach based on these parameters.

5. EXPERIMENTAL EVALUATION

In this section, we present the experimental evaluation of our methods in terms of effectiveness, efficiency, and space.

5.1 Without Space Constraints

In the first experiment, we evaluate the proposed candi-

Textual	BM25, language model, anchor text language model [36]
Positional	absolute first position, relative first position, distribution
Query-based	query size, fraction of numbers in query, list length
Dependency Models	language model of sequential and full dependent query terms [36]
Document-based	document length, document bytes, url length, url nesting, # outlinks, position in alexa, spam and pagerank [16]

Table 2: Categories of features utilized for CF training.

date generation algorithm under the assumption that there is no space budget; i.e., all possible first layer single-term and pairwise structures are available at query time. Although this scenario is unrealistic, as the space overhead of the pairwise structures can be very large, it shows the potential of the proposed method.

We compare our method against a naïve baseline which, given a cost budget b, accesses all relevant structures of the first layer at equal depth. Thus, if there are 5 available structures for a specific query, and the cost budget is $5k$ postings, the baseline would access the first $1k$ postings in each structure. Note that this approach is similar to the *Fixed* method proposed in [48]. We evaluate three versions of this naïve approach, for the cases where only single-term, only pairwise, and both types of structures are available, to show that both types of structures give benefit. Moreover, we implemented a *clairvoyant* selection algorithm that knows apriori which of the docIDs in the postings in the first layer result in top-k results, and then selects prefixes of the structures in an optimal way, thus giving an upper bound on the quality that can be achieved with any depth-limited access scheme on impact-sorted structures. This algorithm is included to observe how close to optimal our algorithm is.

Setup: We assume unlimited space budget and use the following parameter settings and selection strategies: c is 500, the algorithms exhaustively perform lookups on all docIDs seen in the accesses of the first-layer structures (thus the number of lookups is only bounded by the access depth), and the c candidates are selected based on highest BM25.

Effectiveness: Figure 2 shows Overlap@(500, 10), i.e., the fraction of correct top-10 results preserved within the $c = 500$ candidates, as the access cost budget varies from 500 to 20000, and with the first layer consisting of different structures. Obviously, the clairvoyant algorithm achieves the best quality for all access budgets, as it is as an upper bound of our method. On the other hand, we observe that for the naïve method, having only pairwise structures consistently outperforms having only single-term ones, but having both achieves the best quality, which is 0.8864 when the cost budget is 2000. The Greedy selection algorithm outperforms all naïve methods and achieves quality close to the optimal clairvoyant one, even with moderate access budget. For instance, the quality is 0.946 for the 2000 access budget. Thus, more than 94% of the same top-10 results are returned. Finally, as the cost budget increases, quality increases for all algorithms, since we consider more postings as candidates. In particular, Greedy achieves quality really close to Clairvoyant for the 5000 access budget.

Efficiency: In Table 3, we report the average query processing time in milliseconds of the Greedy algorithm when the access budget varies from 500 to 20000. We observed that the access budget is a very good proxy for query processing time in the case of unlimited lookups, and thus we only report the time for Greedy; the numbers for the naïve and clairvoyant algorithms with the same access budget are very similar. According to Table 3, we see that it is possible

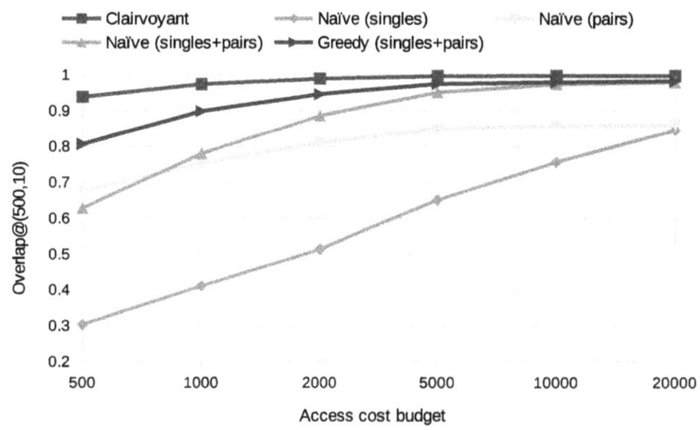

Figure 2: Effectiveness of the first-phase selection algorithms at various access cost budgets on Million09 queries, assuming no limit on space.

to achieve overlap close to 0.946 for access budget 2000, in 0.51ms. As the access budget increases, query processing becomes slower, as we process more postings. Thus, both quality and speed are very good when there is no space constraint. Next, we evaluate if comparable numbers can be obtained with limited space.

Access budget	500	1000	2000	5000	10000	20000
avg qp (ms)	0.22	0.33	0.51	0.95	1.6	2.79

Table 3: Efficiency of the Greedy algorithm with various access cost budgets on Million09 queries, assuming no limit on space.

5.2 With Space Constraints

In the next experiment, we drop the assumption of unlimited space budget and focus on more realistic scenarios. More specifically, we allow a specific percent of space overhead for the first-layer structures over the full second-layer index. Given various space budgets, we evaluate the Greedy algorithm in terms of quality and speed. In this experiment, we use the setup and parameters of the previous experiment, and assume that the first layer consists of both single-term and pairwise structures. We still do all lookups to complete the partial scores of all docIDs seen in the first layer.

Effectiveness: In Table 4, we present the effectiveness of the Greedy algorithm (measured by Overlap@(500, 10)) when a specific percentage of space overhead is allowed for the first layer structures, and the access cost budget is 2000 and 5000. For the single-term structures, we decided to keep up to 2000 and 5000 postings of every list, which correspond to 7.1% and 9.9% of the full index, respectively. On top of this small fixed space overhead, we have a limited space budget for pairwise structures that is allocated according to the Greedy allocation algorithm. The reported space in Table 4 includes only the pairwise structures in the first layer. First, we observe that our proposed method works quite well even with limited space budget, with moderate quality loss. (We look at NDCG numbers later.) Increasing the space budget of pairwise structures to more than 50% does not seem to provide significant quality gains unless a lot of space is available. When the access cost is larger, again better quality is achieved as more candidates are considered.

Space	0.1	0.3	0.5	0.7	1	∞
2000	0.8093	0.8359	0.8412	0.8426	0.8428	0.946
5000	0.8717	0.895	0.9003	0.9028	0.9037	0.9755

Table 4: Effectiveness of the Greedy algorithm (Overlap@(500, 10)) at various space budget setups, for 2000 and 5000 access budgets on the Million09 query trace.

A space overhead of 57.1% (7.1% singles and 50% pairs) for 2000 access budget, and 59.9% for 5000 is acceptable given the significant performance speedup that we achieve. For example, in the Maguro system [42], a 20x index size increase is justified for a 3x performance improvement.

Efficiency: Table 5 shows the average query processing time of the Greedy algorithm for various space budget, when access budget is 2000 or 5000. As mentioned before, the access budget provides a reliable proxy for performance and this is evident in Table 5. The Greedy algorithm requires on average 0.551ms and 1.055ms, for 2000 and 5000 access budget, respectively, still assuming no limit on lookups. As the space budget increases, the performance for both access budgets becomes better. The reason is that more high quality postings appear in the pairwise structures, which results in fewer lookups for the missing terms.

Space budget	0.1	0.3	0.5	0.7	1	∞
2000	0.581	0.56	0.558	0.556	0.555	0.5
5000	1.125	1.08	1.065	1.055	1.049	0.957

Table 5: Efficiency of the Greedy algorithm with varying space budget, for 2000 and 5000 access budgets on the Million09 query trace, measured in ms.

5.3 Lookup Selection Strategies

In the previous experiments, all algorithms exhaustively perform lookups in the second layer. However, as we will see, the lookup selection policy plays an important role in the performance. Thus, we now look at better lookup strategies.

First, we investigate how query processing costs are distributed. Table 6 shows the average time overhead of each part of the query processing cost for 5000 access budget and 3000 lookups. Recall that query processing includes the online greedy depth selection, the radix sort, the scan for aggregating scores and lookup pruning, selection by sampling, lookups into the second layer, and another selection to get the c candidates. From Table 6, it is obvious that lookups are a large part of the total cost, as they involve decompression and access to many random blocks.

Parts of Query Processing	time (in ms)
Online greedy depth selection	0.0070
Radix-sort	0.1539
Scan for merge/aggregate/filter	0.1049
Selection	0.0311
Second-layer lookups	0.5394
Second selection	0.0275
Total	0.8638

Table 6: Query processing time breakdown.

Instead of exhaustively performing all lookups, we keep only a certain number m of candidates for lookups, based on partial BM25 score. To do this, we perform a randomized approximate selection as described earlier. We evaluate the quality and the speed of this lookup strategy for access budgets of 2000 and 5000 and a 0.5 pairwise space budget on top of the single-term structures of each access budget. Figure 3 presents the Overlap@(500, 10) and the average query processing time for several configurations of m lookups, under both access budgets. More specifically, we allow lookups of $\{500, 1k, 2k, 3k, 5k\}$ candidates for access budget 5000, and $\{500, 750, 1k, 1.5k, 2k\}$ for access budget 2000 (from left to right). We see that better performance can be achieved with the proposed lookup method at the cost of some quality loss, and thus there is a trade-off between quality and time.

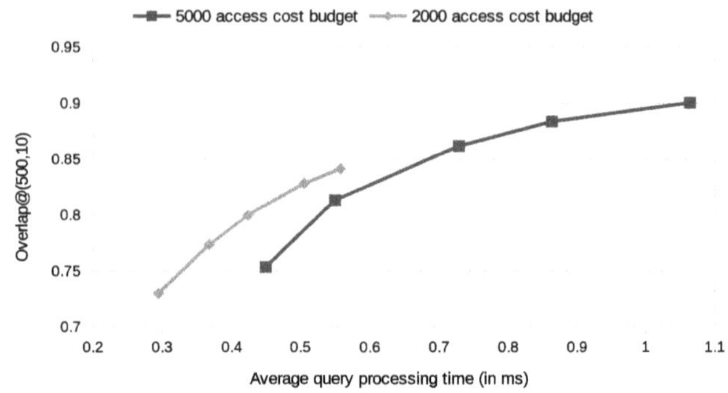

Figure 3: Effectiveness/Efficiency evaluation of our lookup strategy on Million09 queries.

Next, we compare the speed of our approach with other recently published methods. While top-10 query processing can be done in a few milliseconds [19], selecting the top 500 is much more expensive for most methods. Table 7 presents running times for different top-500 candidate generation methods. We implemented all methods in C++ and ran them on the ClueWeb09B data set. For safe methods, we pick BMW-LB, the fastest disjunctive method to our knowledge from [19], and BMA, the fastest conjunctive method from [21]. For unsafe methods, we implemented the best approach from [52], which is the tree-based Priority with pruning, and the best method from [43], BMW-CS, which uses 10% of the index as first layer. Our method with 5k-3k setup is much faster, since it only evaluates at most 5k postings, which means that less than 5k documents for each query are evaluated, while other methods usually evaluate many more documents. Both our online and offline posting selection mechanism contributes significantly to its good performance. BMA has the second fastest speed, since it is a conjunctive algorithm that only evaluates a limited number of documents. BMW-CS performs BMW on the first layer, which is the top 10 percent of the full index based on impact score. BMW-CS is different from our approach as we use pairwise structures in addition to singles in the first layer, and they do not have a fixed access budget per query or the greedy depth selection techniques. Their speed is much slower than ours, while still faster than BMW-LB. Priority is slower than BMW-LB, for top-500. For space overhead, BMA and BMW-CS both use less than 5% of the index size to store the Max-Block index. The two tiers in BMW-CS are disjoint, so the first tier takes no extra space. BMW-LB takes about 25% to cache the LB index, while priority takes no extra space. Our method with 5k-3k setup takes 59.9% extra space. Note that commercial search engines are often willing to accept significant space overheads for relatively small improvements in speed[42].

We now evaluate the effectiveness of our methods. Table 8 shows the Overlap@(500, 10) for all the methods, and for

Method	BMW-LB	BMA	BMW-CS	Priority	5k-3k
Paper	[19]	[21]	[43]	[52]	Our
Time (ms)	26.74	15.12	19.31	51.24	0.863
Space	$\sim 25\%$	<5%	<5%	0%	59.9%

Table 7: Running times and space overhead of different approaches for top-500 documents retrieval.

our approach with three different setups. BMW-LB has the best result, and BMA is almost as good, but slightly worse. This means that conjunctive query processing is almost as good as disjunctive in terms of quality, which was also shown in [5]. In Table 9, we rerank the results of all the methods according to the complex ranker. BMW-LB+CF is much better than BMW-LB, which means that the complex ranker performs well on identifying more relevant results. The 5k-3k setup achieves consistently the best quality among our methods at all cutoff levels, and it's also slightly better than the other two unsafe methods for both Overlap and NDCG. Overall, we see that under NDCG, our approach can very quickly, in less than a millisecond, identify results that are almost as good as a safe disjunctive approach (BMW-LB).

BMW-LB	BMA	BMW-CS	Priority	5k-3k	2k-2k	2k-500
0.985	0.934	0.879	0.826	0.881	0.841	0.729

Table 8: Overlap@(500,10) for different methods.

Method / cutoff	1	5	10	20	100	200
BMW-LB+CF	0.267	0.253	0.259	0.252	0.275	0.292
BMA+CF	0.261	0.253	0.253	0.247	0.270	0.290
BMW-CS+CF	0.249	0.241	0.236	0.222	0.245	0.270
Priority+CF	0.261	0.242	0.239	0.243	0.252	0.269
BMW-LB	0.143	0.162	0.161	0.174	0.225	0.256
5k-3k+CF	0.266	0.256	0.256	0.246	0.269	0.289
2k-2k+CF	0.266	0.249	0.245	0.238	0.260	0.284
2k-5k+CF	0.254	0.250	0.241	0.228	0.242	0.261

Table 9: NDCG at various cutoff levels on Million09.

5.4 Varying Query Length and Candidates

Next, we test the impact of query length on speed and quality, using various configurations of our methods. Table 10 presents the average query processing time (ms) when varying the query length, whereas Table 11 reports the corresponding Overlap@(500, 10) for each configuration. As query length increases, the query processing time also increases, since more lookups into more structures are performed. On the other hand, quality decreases, because top results in longer queries tend to be deeper inside the impact-sorted list (a basic fact in top-k query processing shown in Fagin's theoretical analysis of his algorithms [23]).

Setup	2	3	4	5	≥ 6	avg
2k-500	0.178	0.297	0.477	0.732	0.965	0.295
2k-2k	0.321	0.573	0.914	1.349	1.809	0.558
5k-3k	0.531	0.929	1.461	2.115	2.878	0.863

Table 10: Efficiency when varying query length on the Million09 queries with various setups, measured in ms.

Table 12 shows the impact of the number of candidates returned by our candidate generation algorithm (cutoff c) on Overlap@$(c, 10)$ for the 5000-3000 setup. As the cutoff c increases, the quality increases, untill flattening around 500. This justifies our choice of c = 500 throughout the paper.

Setup	2	3	4	5	≥ 6
2k-500	0.803	0.702	0.632	0.589	0.612
2k-2k	0.885	0.832	0.737	0.726	0.729
5k-3k	0.908	0.883	0.824	0.835	0.81

Table 11: Effectiveness in Overlap@(500, 10) when we vary query length on Million09 queries in various setups.

c	100	200	300	400	500	800	1200
Overlap@$(c, 10)$	0.539	0.696	0.791	0.856	0.881	0.883	0.885

Table 12: Effectiveness when we vary candidates c.

6. CONCLUSIONS AND FUTURE WORK

In this paper, we have proposed a fast first-phase candidate generation approach for cascading ranking architectures. Our framework builds an auxiliary layer of index structures (single-term and pairwise structures) based on models for query term frequency and posting quality, which is then selectively accessed at query time based on a cost budget and using early termination techniques. The experimental evaluation shows that the proposed framework can find candidates about an order of magnitude faster than conjunctive or disjunctive top-k computations, with little loss in quality.

Future work includes the addition of specialized structures for phrases and proximity into our framework. We also expect some improvements from further optimization of the query processor and lookup mechanism, e.g., by adding bit vectors, or Bloom filters as in [4], or by using more complex rules to decide which lookups to perform (possibly based on ideas similar to [52]).

Acknowledgement

This research was supported by NSF Grant IIS-1117829 "Efficient Query Processing in Large Search Engines", and by a grant from Google.

7. REFERENCES

[1] D. Agarwal and M. Gurevich. Fast top-k retrieval for model based recommendation. In *Proc. of the Fifth Int. Conf. on Web Search and Data Mining*, pages 483–492, 2012.

[2] V. N. Anh and A. Moffat. Pruned query evaluation using pre-computed impacts. In *Proc. of the 29th Annual Int. ACM SIGIR Conf. on Research and Development in Information Retrieval*, 2006.

[3] N. Asadi. *Multi-Stage Search Architectures for Streaming Documents*. PhD thesis, University of Maryland, 2013.

[4] N. Asadi and J. Lin. Fast candidate generation for two-phase document ranking: postings list intersection with bloom filters. In *Proc. of the 21st ACM Conf. Information and Knowledge Management*, 2012.

[5] N. Asadi and J. Lin. Effectiveness/efficiency tradeoffs for candidate generation in multi-stage retrieval architectures. In *Proc. of the 36th Int. ACM SIGIR Conf. on Research and Development in Information Retrieval*, 2013.

[6] R. A. Baeza-Yates and B. A. Ribeiro-Neto. *Modern Information Retrieval*. ACM Press / Addison-Wesley, 1999.

[7] H. Bast, D. Majumdar, R. Schenkel, M. Theobald, and G. Weikum. IO-Top-K: Index-access optimized top-k query processing. In *Proc. of the 32th Int. Conf. on Very Large Data Bases*, 2006.

[8] R. Blanco and A. Barreiro. Probabilistic static pruning of inverted files. *ACM Transactions on Information Systems*, 28(1), Jan. 2010.

[9] S. Brin and L. Page. The anatomy of a large-scale hypertextual web search engine. *Computer Networks*, 30(1-7):107–117, 1998.

[10] A. Z. Broder, D. Carmel, M. Herscovici, A. Soffer, and J. Y. Zien. Efficient query evaluation using a two-level retrieval process. In *Proc. of the 12th ACM Conf. on Information and Knowledge Management*, 2003.

[11] A. Broschart and R. Schenkel. High-performance processing of text queries with tunable pruned term and term pair indexes. *ACM Trans. Inf. Syst.*, 30(1):5, 2012.

[12] S. Büttcher and C. L. A. Clarke. A document-centric approach to static index pruning in text retrieval systems. In *Proc. of the 15th ACM Conf. Information and Knowledge Management*, 2006.

[13] B. B. Cambazoglu, H. Zaragoza, O. Chapelle, J. Chen, C. Liao, Z. Zheng, and J. Degenhardt. Early exit optimizations for additive machine learned ranking systems. In *Proc. of the Third Int. Conf. on Web Search and Data Mining*, 2010.

[14] K. Chakrabarti, S. Chaudhuri, and V. Ganti. Interval-based pruning for top-k processing over compressed lists. In *Proc. of the 27th Int. Conf. on Data Engineering*, 2011.

[15] S. Chaudhuri, K. W. Church, A. C. König, and L. Sui. Heavy-tailed distributions and multi-keyword queries. In *Proc. of the 30th Annual Int. ACM SIGIR Conf*, 2007.

[16] G. V. Cormack, M. D. Smucker, and C. L. A. Clarke. Efficient and effective spam filtering and re-ranking for large web datasets. *Inf. Retr.*, 14(5):441–465, 2011.

[17] V. Dang, M. Bendersky, and W. B. Croft. Two-stage learning to rank for information retrieval. In *Proc. of the 35th European Conf. on Information Retrieval*, 2013.

[18] V. Dang and W. B. Croft. Query reformulation using anchor text. In *Proc. of the Third Int. Conf. on Web Search and Data Mining*, pages 41–50, 2010.

[19] C. Dimopoulos, S. Nepomnyachiy, and T. Suel. A candidate filtering mechanism for fast top-k query processing on modern cpus. In *Proc. of the 36th Int. ACM SIGIR Conf*, 2013.

[20] C. Dimopoulos, S. Nepomnyachiy, and T. Suel. Optimizing top-k document retrieval strategies for block-max indexes. In *Proc. of the Sixth Int. Conf. on Web Search and Data Mining*, 2013.

[21] S. Ding and T. Suel. Faster top-k document retrieval using block-max indexes. In *Proc. of the 34th Int. ACM SIGIR Conf*, 2011.

[22] P. Donmez, K. M. Svore, and C. J. C. Burges. On the local optimality of lambdarank. In *Proc. of the 32th Int. ACM SIGIR Conf. on Research and Development in Information Retrieval*, 2009.

[23] R. Fagin. Combining fuzzy information: an overview. *SIGMOD Record*, 31:2002, 2002.

[24] R. Fagin, D. Carmel, D. Cohen, E. Farchi, M. Herscovici, Y. Maarek, and A. Soffer. Static index pruning for information retrieval systems. In *Proc. of the 24th Int. ACM SIGIR Conf. on Research and Development in Information Retrieval*, 2001.

[25] T. Fagni, R. Perego, F. Silvestri, and S. Orlando. Boosting the performance of web search engines: Caching and prefetching query results by exploiting historical usage data. *ACM Trans. Inf. Syst.*, 24(1):51–78, 2006.

[26] M. Fontoura, M. Gurevich, V. Josifovski, and S. Vassilvitskii. Efficiently encoding term co-occurrences in inverted indexes. In *Proc. of the 20th ACM Conf. Information and Knowledge Management*, 2011.

[27] S. Goel, J. Langford, and A. L. Strehl. Predictive indexing for fast search. In *Proc. of the 22nd Annual Conf. on Neural Information Processing Systems, Vancouver*, 2008.

[28] S. Hwang and K. C. Chang. Optimizing top-k queries for middleware access: A unified cost-based approach. *ACM Trans. Database Syst.*, 32(1):5, 2007.

[29] I. F. Ilyas, G. Beskales, and M. A. Soliman. A survey of top-k query processing techniques in relational database systems. *ACM Comput. Surv.*, 40(4), 2008.

[30] R. Kumar, K. Punera, T. Suel, and S. Vassilvitskii. Top-k aggregation using intersections of ranked inputs. In *Proc. of the Second Int. Conf. on Web Search and Data Mining*, 2009.

[31] H. Li. *Learning to Rank for Information Retrieval and Natural Language Processing*. Synthesis Lectures on Human Language Technologies. Morgan & Claypool Publishers, 2011.

[32] T. Liu. Learning to rank for information retrieval. *Foundations and Trends in Information Retrieval*, 3(3):225–331, 2009.

[33] X. Long and T. Suel. Optimized query execution in large search engines with global page ordering. In *Proc. of the 29th Int. Conf. on Very Large Data Bases*, 2003.

[34] X. Long and T. Suel. Three-level caching for efficient query processing in large web search engines. *Proc. of the 15th Int. Conf. on World Wide Web*, 9(4), 2006.

[35] C. Macdonald, R. L. T. Santos, and I. Ounis. The whens and hows of learning to rank for web search. *Inf. Retr.*, 16(5):584–628, 2013.

[36] D. Metzler. Automatic feature selection in the markov random field model for information retrieval. In *Proc. of the 16th ACM Conf. Information and Knowledge Management*, 2007.

[37] A. Ntoulas and J. Cho. Pruning policies for two-tiered inverted index with correctness guarantee. In *Proc. of the 30th Int. ACM SIGIR Conf. on Research and Development in Information Retrieval*, 2007.

[38] R. Ozcan, I. S. Altingövde, B. B. Cambazoglu, F. P. Junqueira, and Ö. Ulusoy. A five-level static cache architecture for web search engines. *Inf. Process. Manage.*, 48(5):828–840, 2012.

[39] M. Persin, J. Zobel, and R. Sacks-davis. Filtered document retrieval with frequency-sorted indexes. *Journal of the American Society for Information Science*, 47:749–764, 1996.

[40] T. Qin, T. Liu, J. Xu, and H. Li. LETOR: A benchmark collection for research on learning to rank for information retrieval. *Inf. Retr.*, 13(4):346–374, 2010.

[41] K. Risvik, Y. Aasheim, and M. Lidal. Multi-tier architecture for web search engines. In *1st LA Web Congress*, 2003.

[42] K. M. Risvik, T. M. Chilimbi, H. Tan, K. Kalyanaraman, and C. Anderson. Maguro, a system for indexing and searching over very large text collections. In *Proc. of the Sixth Int. Conf. on Web Search and Data Mining*, 2013.

[43] C. Rossi, E. S. de Moura, A. L. Carvalho, and A. S. da Silva. Fast document-at-a-time query processing using two-tier indexes. In *Proc. of the 36th Int. ACM SIGIR Conf. on Research and Development in Information Retrieval*, 2013.

[44] R. Schenkel, A. Broschart, S. Hwang, M. Theobald, and G. Weikum. Efficient text proximity search. In *Proc. of the 14th Int. Symposium on String Processing and Information Retrieval*, 2007.

[45] F. Scholer, H. E. Williams, J. Yiannis, and J. Zobel. Compression of inverted indexes for fast query evaluation. In *Proc. of the 25th Annual Int. ACM SIGIR Conf. on Research and Development in Information Retrieval*, 2002.

[46] G. Skobeltsyn, F. Junqueira, V. Plachouras, and R. A. Baeza-Yates. Resin: a combination of results caching and index pruning for high-performance web search engines. In *Proc. of the 31th Int. ACM SIGIR Conf. on Research and Development in Information Retrieval*, 2008.

[47] T. Strohman and W. B. Croft. Efficient document retrieval in main memory. In *Proc. of the 30th Annual Int. ACM SIGIR Conf*, 2007.

[48] T. Strohman, H. R. Turtle, and W. B. Croft. Optimization strategies for complex queries. In *Proc. of the 28th Annual Int. ACM SIGIR Conf. on Research and Development in Information Retrieval*, 2005.

[49] N. Tonellotto, C. Macdonald, and I. Ounis. Efficient and effective retrieval using selective pruning. In *Proc. of the Sixth Int. Conf. on Web Search and Data Mining*, 2013.

[50] H. R. Turtle and J. Flood. Query evaluation: Strategies and optimizations. *Inf. Processing and Management*, 31(6):831–850, 1995.

[51] L. Wang, J. J. Lin, and D. Metzler. A cascade ranking model for efficient ranked retrieval. In *Proc. of the 34th Annual Int. ACM SIGIR Conf. on Research and Development in Information Retrieval*, 2011.

[52] H. Wu and H. Fang. Document prioritization for scalable query processing. In *Proc. of the 23rd ACM Conf. Information and Knowledge Management*, 2014.

[53] Q. Wu, C. J. C. Burges, K. M. Svore, and J. Gao. Adapting boosting for information retrieval measures. *Inf. Retr.*, 13(3):254–270, 2010.

[54] H. Yan, S. Shi, F. Zhang, T. Suel, and J. Wen. Efficient term proximity search with term-pair indexes. In *Proc. of the 19th ACM Conf. Information and Knowledge Management*, 2010.

[55] J. Zhang, X. Long, and T. Suel. Performance of compressed inverted list caching in search engines. In *Proc. of the 17th Int. Conf. on World Wide Web*, 2008.

[56] M. Zhu, S. Shi, M. Li, and J. Wen. Effective top-k computation in retrieving structured documents with term-proximity support. In *Proc. of the 16th ACM Conf. Information and Knowledge Management*, 2007.

[57] M. Zhu, S. Shi, N. Yu, and J. Wen. Can phrase indexing help to process non-phrase queries? In *Proc. of the 17th ACM Conf. Information and Knowledge Management*, 2008.

[58] J. Zobel and A. Moffat. Inverted files for text search engines. *ACM Comput. Surveys*, 38(2), 2006.

[59] M. Zukowski, S. Heman, N. Nes, and P. Boncz. Super-scalar RAM-CPU cache compression. In *Proc. of the 22th Int. Conf. on Data Engineering*, 2006.

Learning to Rank Features for Recommendation over Multiple Categories

Xu Chen[1] Zheng Qin[2] Yongfeng Zhang[3] Tao Xu[4]

[124] School of Software,Tsinghua National Laboratory for Information Science and Technology
Tsinghua University, Beijing,10084,China
{xu-ch14,xut14,qinzh}@mails.tsinghua.edu.cn
[3] Department of Computer Science & Technology,Tsinghua University, Beijing,10084,China
yongfeng14@mails.tsinghua.edu.cn

ABSTRACT

Incorporating phrase-level sentiment analysis on users' textual reviews for recommendation has became a popular method due to its explainable property for latent features and high prediction accuracy. However, the inherent limitations of the existing model make it difficult to (1) effectively distinguish the features that are most interesting to users, (2) maintain the recommendation performance especially when the set of items is scaled up to multiple categories, and (3) model users' implicit feedbacks on the product features. In this paper, motivated by these shortcomings, we first introduce a tensor matrix factorization algorithm to **L**earn to **R**ank user **P**references based on **P**hrase-level sentiment analysis across **M**ultiple categories (LRPPM for short), and then by combining this technique with Collaborative Filtering (CF) method, we propose a novel model called LRPPM-CF to boost the performance of recommendation. Thorough experiments on two real-world datasets demonstrate that our proposed model is able to improve the performance in the tasks of capturing users' interested features and item recommendation by about 17%-24% and 7%-13%, respectively, as compared with several state-of-the-art methods.

Keywords

Recommender Systems; Sentiment Analysis; Collaborative Filtering; Tensor Factorization

1. INTRODUCTION

Emerging popularity of e-commerce has highlighted the importance of recommendation systems, with many models have been studied. Among these models, latent factor models [2, 5, 11, 20] have gained much attention from the research community and industry due to their good prediction accuracy on some benchmark datasets. However, recommendation based on these methods could hardly give

SIGIR '16, July 17-21, 2016, Pisa, Italy
© 2016 ACM. ISBN 978-1-4503-4069-4/16/07...$15.00
DOI: http://dx.doi.org/10.1145/2911451.2911549

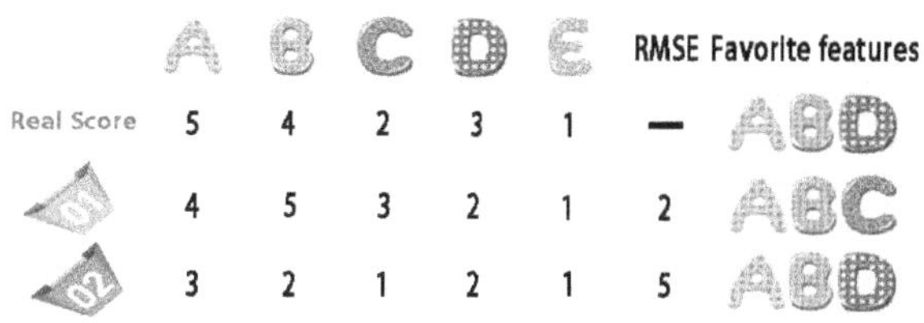

Figure 1: An example of feature ranking with ratings predicted by rating-based optimization functions.

intuitional explanations for the latent features which weakens the ability to persuade users and help users make better decisions in practical systems.

In recent years, there has been an upsurge of interest in exploiting the users' textual review information to enhance the interpretability of latent factor models. A well-known example is the HFT model [6]. By linking the latent factors leveraged in modeling user rating behavior with the topics presented in the user comments, this model directly explain the latent factors by the user mentioned topics. However, as a topic may contain products' different features and a user could express different opinions for various features in the same topic, simple topic-level analysis without more detailed natural language processing makes such approaches biased and limited.

Several attempts to construct a more explainable recommendation model have been made very recently in [17, 18]. In their models, phrase-level sentiment analysis are used to excavate products' explicit features and users' corresponding opinions.For instance, if a user purchased a phone, and made a 5 star rating with the text review "screen is perfect, but earphone is bad!" The methods proposed in [17, 18] could capture the feature-sentiment pairs like (screen, perfect) and (earphone, bad), which would provide finer-grained analysis of the textual reviews as compared with HFT, and could help to make more accurate recommendations.

Despite that encouraging improvements have been brought by these models, they still suffer from three issues. First, selecting the most interesting features is an important component in their models for user profiling, however the existing rating-based optimization target is not suitable for such an inherently ranking task. Second, they both consider a user's extent of interest towards each feature as static over all products.This setting is not practical in real-world

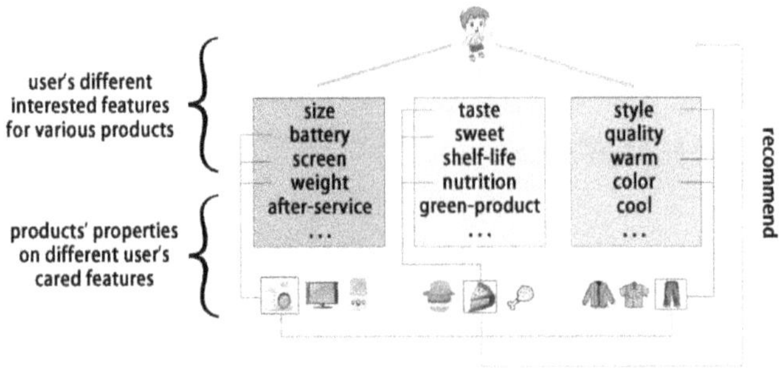

Figure 2: User's different features for various products are first extracted utilizing phrase-level sentiment analysis, and then the items which perform well on the user's cared features would be recommended.

scenarios, especially when the products are from different categories. Finally, instead of modeling users' implicit feedback(mentioned a feature in the review or not)directly, these models convert the implicit feedbacks into rating scores, which would bias it in terms of preference estimation [14].

In this paper we describe and analyze a general method to learn and infer user preferences from ratings along with textual reviews. The main building block of our proposed method is an effective tensor-matrix factorization algorithm to **L**earn to **R**ank user **P**references based on **P**hrase-level sentiment analysis across **M**ultiple categories (LRPPM). By learning to rank, we wish to make our model more suitable for ranking tasks in selecting the most interesting features for each user. By tensor-matrix factorization, we wish to capture users' different interests to various products directly from their implicit feedback, and to keep the recommendation performance even when the set of products scales up to multiple categories. Furthermore, by bridging this method with traditional Collaborative Filtering (CF) approaches, we build a novel LRPPM-CF algorithm to boost the performance of personalized recommendation.

Compared with the existing models, the key advantages of our proposed method are: (1) It introduces ranking-based optimization objective to replace rating-based target for better understanding user preferences on feature-level. In Figure 1 for instance, where our goal is to select the top-three favourite features for a user from the feature pool $\{A, B, C, D, E\}$. Suppose that the real scores the user would make on these features are $\{5, 4, 2, 3, 1\}$, and we have two strategies that predict the feature scores by $\{4, 5, 3, 2, 1\}$ and $\{3, 2, 1, 2, 1\}$, respectively. From the perspective of rating-based optimization, the former strategy is better because it gains higher prediction accuracy (lower root mean square error(RMSE)), and thus the features A, B, C would be selected. However, the latter strategy is actually more preferred because it selects A, B, D, which are the top favourite features according to the real ratings, although this strategy gains lower prediction accuracy according to RMSE. (2) It extracts the different favoured features for each user more precisely, which can further make our model more accurate when making recommendations. In Figure 2 for example, our model would value more on the screen pixel when a user is selecting digital cameras, while the style might be considered as a more important feature when he/she is looking for clothes. (3) It is able to model the user implicit feedbacks directly to capture the user preferences.

In the rest of the paper, we first review the related work in section 2, and give detailed explanation of our methods in section 3. Another rating-based tensor factorization method is explored in section 4 for model comparison. And then in section 5, we describe our experiments and analyze the effectiveness of our methods. The conclusions and outlook of this work are presented in section 6.

2. RELATED WORK

With the ever growing amount of user generated textual reviews, the problem of how to leverage such information-rich resources to construct more explainable recommendation models has received increasing attention. Until recently, a lot of recommendation algorithms [1, 3, 10, 12, 18] based on sentiment analysis of textual reviews have been proposed. In general, these algorithms are conducted on three different levels: (1) review-level, (2) sentence-level, and (3) phrase-level.

Review- or sentence-level methods. These methods take a review or a sentence as a whole, and analyze its sentiment directly. The method proposed in [1] presents three approaches to identify movie aspects which are used as features for collaborative filtering. [3] considers different sentimental orientations (SO) of similar words in different scenarios, and proposes a framework to determine the sentimental orientations. [10] focuses on the situation of user textual review without explicit rating labels, and introduces a sentiment-aware nearest neighbor model to boost the performance of existing recommendation methods. Finally, [12] constructs an opinion matrix by extracting user interests from the reviews, and combines this matrix with traditional model-based collaborative filtering to provide rating predictions.

The models mentioned above have made great contributions to the modeling of user review information in recommendation tasks. However, such review- or sentence-level approaches could not explicitly identify the product features in a review/sentence, and therefore fail to capture user preferences in a finer-grained manner towards specific features, which can be very important to generate personalized recommendations and explanations.

Phrase-level methods. A recent approach proposed in [18] utilizes phrase-level sentiment analysis to extract the explicit product features and finer-grained per feature sentiment information from user reviews. Specifically, it constructs a sentiment lexicon from a corpus of reviews, based on which to further generate an explicit user-feature attention matrix and item-feature quality matrix, where the former reflects user interests towards different features, and the latter shows the quality of each product on each feature. It then adopts matrix factorization techniques to complete these matrices by optimizing the root mean square error (RMSE). At last, this model makes recommendations by matching the most favourite features of a user with the intrinsic properties of items.

Though this model could provide more detailed user preferences and more accurate predictions, the simple matrix factorization approach to optimize RMSE as a rating-based task makes it limited in that: (1) the estimation of user-feature attentions is inherently a ranking-based task to select the favourite features, (2) it fails to distinguish users' different interests of features on different products, and (3) it converts users' implicit feedbacks on product features into explicit rating scores, which could be a step that introduces inaccuracy. In contrast, in this paper, we propose a ranking-based tensor-matrix factorization algorithm to resolve these problems, which makes more practical, explainable, and accurate recommendations.

3. THE FRAMEWORK

In this section, we describe the major components of our model. Firstly,we give a brief introduction to the extraction of feature-sentiment pairs from user textual reviews. And then we analyze the Yelp[1] dataset to verify our assumption that users usually care about different features for different product categories. Next, we elaborate the main components of our LRPPM model. At last, by combing this technique with collaborative filtering, we propose a novel framework for purchase prediction and recommendation. Specifically, we implement our framework on both product-level and category-level, respectively, so as to make it easy to compare and understand the performance of our framework.

3.1 Extracting Feature-Sentiment Pairs

In the first stage, we construct the set of feature-sentiment pairs from a corpus of textual reviews based on the state-of-art optimization approach described in [4, 18, 19] due to its high accuracy. Specifically, we first extract feature word set F from all the user textual reviews. Then for a given piece of review, we generate a set of feature-sentiment pairs (F, S) to represent this review, where S is assigned as 1 or -1 according to the sentiment polarity that the user expressed on this feature. For example, for the piece of review 'the taste is perfect, but the appearance is ugly!', the extracted feature-sentiment pairs can be (taste, +1) and (appearance, -1). Since the feature-sentiment pair extraction is not the key contribution of this paper, we refer the readers to the related literature such as [4, 18, 19], and focus our attention on the next stages of user preference prediction and recommendation.

3.2 Data Analysis and Case Studies

We adopt the Yelp dataset for analysis because it covers items from multiple categories, which matches with our research tasks. We focus our analysis on the categories of *beauty*, *entertainment*, *food*, *health*, *clothing* and *bars* due to their high co-occurrence frequencies in user transactions. To verify the hypothesis that users usually care about different features for various products, we select the most popular features in every category according to the frequencies they are mentioned in the textual reviews. In this dataset, we select top-10 most cared features for empirical analysis, as shown in Table 1. Based on simple observations we can find that:

(1) On pairwise level, only three pairs of categories contain three common features, and the others have at most two common features or no intersection at all.

(2) Among all these 47 mentioned features, only three appear in more than three categories.

These observations and case studies imply that the user interests may vary with the categories, which is an important motivation for us to model the user preferences and recommendation with the discrimination of different categories. In the next subsections, we introduce our LRPPM framework

[1]http://www.yelp.com/dataset_challenge

Table 1: The top-10 most cared features in user reviews of different categories.

category	beauty	entertainment	food
features	'hair'	'show'	'food'
	'staff'	'room'	'service'
	'job'	'rooms'	'pizza'
	'massage'	'seats'	'taste'
	'service'	'staff'	'cheese'
	'room'	'hotel'	'location'
	'salon'	'theater'	'staff'
	'nails'	'location'	'flavor'
	'spa'	'bar'	'fries'
	'location'	'tickets'	'prices'

category	health	clothing	bars
features	'staff'	'store'	'food'
	'care'	'selection'	'bar'
	'appointment'	'prices'	'service'
	'patient'	'staff'	'def'
	'doctor'	'deals'	'wait'
	'location'	'shoes'	'drinks'
	'office'	'price'	'hour'
	'paperwork'	'quality'	'music'
	'dentist'	'clothes'	'staff'
	'pain'	'items'	'table'

so as to Learn to Rank user Preferences based on Phrase-level sentiment analysis across Multiple categories, and further integrate this framework with Collaborative Filtering on both product- and category-levels.

3.3 The LRPPM model

The most direct yet naive implementation to model user interests in different categories is to conduct user/item profiling on each category independently, for example, by analyzing the reviews from each category with EFM [18] in isolation. However, with the large and ever growing number of categories, this method is practically infeasible. To alleviate the problem of both effectiveness and efficiency, we propose a unified framework based on tensor factorization in this section, and the major components of this framework would be introduced in detail in the following.

Factorizing User-Item-Feature Cube. To capture users' different favored features for various items, we should model interactions among users, items and features simultaneously, this inspires us to introduce tensor matrix factorization method, and for clear exposition, let $U = \{u_1, u_2, ...u_{|U|}\}$ be the set of users, $I = \{i_1, i_2, ...i_{|I|}\}$ be the set of items and $F = \{f_1, f_2, ...f_{|F|}\}$ be the set of features extracted from the textual reviews. Then we represent users' reviewing behavior as a set of user-item-feature triplets as follows:

$$O := \{(u, i, f) | u \in U, i \in I, f \in F, User\ u\ mentioned\ feature\ f\ in\ his/her\ review\ on\ item\ i.\} \tag{1}$$

We consider the user-item-feature relationship as an interaction cube T,where the element reflects the extent that a user is interested in a feature when he/she reviewed on an item. For more accurate modeling, we model the implicit feedback of users directly by labeling the triplets from O as observed elements in the corresponding position of cube T. Note that, instead of being converted to explicit ratings(e.g.'1'), these observed elements would be employed to construct preference pairs in the next section.

A number of techniques exist for tensor factorization [15, 16, 13], and we adopt a method similar to [15] due to its efficiency and relatively lower learning complexity. In our method, the pairwise interactions among users, items and features are modeled directly, and the scoring function which reflects $u's$ interest for $i's$ feature f is shown as follows:

$$\hat{T}_{uif} = \sum_{k=0}^{K-1} R^U_{uk} \cdot R^{UF}_{fk} + \sum_{k=0}^{K-1} R^I_{ik} \cdot R^{IF}_{fk} + \sum_{k=0}^{K-1} R^U_{uk} \cdot R^I_{ik} \tag{2}$$

where $R^U \in \mathbb{R}_+^{|U|\times K}$, $R^I \in \mathbb{R}_+^{|I|\times K}$, $\{R^{UF} \in \mathbb{R}_+^{|F|\times K}$, $R^{IF} \in \mathbb{R}_+^{|F|\times K}\}$ are the latent matrices of users, items and features respectively, and K represents the number of factors in these matrices.

Ranking-based optimization target on implicit feedback. As selecting the favourite features for each user is an inherently ranking-oriented task, we should care more about users' relative preference on different features rather than the explicit rating predictions on them, and that a ranking-based approach can be more suitable than the rating-based criterion used in [18].

In our model, we use the ranking-based criterion of Bayesian Personalized Ranking (BPR) [14] as our optimization goal. Intuitively, a user would generally review on his/her cared features, while the features not mentioned in his/her comments, in turn, are not attractive to him/her, so to conduct BPR method, we build preference pairs between the observed elements in T which correspond to interested features with the non-observed ones, we define:

$$\hat{T}_{uif_Af_B} = \hat{T}_{uif_A} - \hat{T}_{uif_B} \tag{3}$$

which reveals user $u's$ interests for feature f_A over f_B when he reviewed item i. Then we use a similar method in [14] to estimate our model parameters by maximizing a log posterior (MAP):

$$\hat{\Theta} = \arg\max_{\Theta} \sum_{u\in U} \sum_{i\in I} \sum_{f_A\in F^+_{ui}} \sum_{f_B\in F^-_{ui}} \log \sigma(\hat{T}_{uif_Af_B}) - \lambda_\Theta \|\Theta\|_F^2 \tag{4}$$

where $\sigma()$ is a logistic sigmoid function, F^+_{ui} is the set of features that were mentioned by user u for item i, F^-_{ui} is the set of features that were not mentioned, namely, $F^+_{ui} = \{f \mid (u,i,f) \in O\}$ and $F^-_{ui} = \{f|(u,i,f) \notin O\}$, Θ is the model parameter and λ_Θ is the regularization constant.

After estimating the parameters,we could rank the features according to equation (2) and select the features with top-N scores to model the user preferences on a specific item.

3.4 The Integrated LRPPM-CF Model

In this section, we incorporate both rating and reviewing information together to build a hybrid model. Specifically, we first share the latent factors used for modeling user rating behavior with the factors embedded in user reviewing behavior, and then propose a unified LRPPM-CF framework by combining our model LRPPM with model-based collaborative filtering method, which attempts to optimize the following objective:

$$\min_{\Theta} \sum_{u\in U} \sum_{i\in I} (A_{ui} - (R^U_{u\cdot})^T \cdot R^I_{i\cdot})^2 - \lambda \sum_{u\in U} \sum_{i\in I} \sum_{f_A\in F^+_{ui}} \sum_{f_B\in F^-_{ui}} ln\sigma(\hat{T}_{uif_Af_B}) + \lambda_\Theta \|\Theta\|_F^2 \tag{5}$$

where $R^U_{u\cdot}$ is the u-th row of R^U, $(R^U_{u\cdot})^T$ is the transpose of $R^U_{u\cdot}$, $R^I_{i\cdot}$ is the i-th row of R^I, Θ is the model parameter, A_{ui} is the rating that user u gives to item i, λ is the tuning parameter that balances the weight between the two types of behaviors, and λ_Θ is the regularization constant.In this expression, we model the user ratings with latent tensor factors by the first term, and further model the user preferences on features embedded in reviews through learning to rank by the second term. The parameters are regularized by a unified way in the last term.

3.4.1 Model Learning for LPRRM-CF

There is no closed-form solution for equation (8), and we introduce a stochastic gradient descent algorithm to find the optimal solution for the parameters $\Theta = \{R^U, R^I, R^{UF}, R^{IF}\}$. For convenience, we define the training set as $D_S = \{(u, i, f_A, f_B)|(u, i, f_A) \in O,\ (u, i, f_B) \notin O\}$ and the decaying parameter $l_{ui} = \frac{1}{|F^+_{ui}|*|F^-_{ui}|}$ in the optimization algorithm shown in Algorithm 1. In this algorithm, we first initialize the parameters, and then update these parameters repeatedly until convergency or reaching the maximum number of iterations.

3.4.2 Making Recommendations

Given the optimal solutions of $\{R^U, R^I, R^{UF}, R^{IF}\}$, we estimate the user-item-feature cube as $\hat{T}$ and user-item rating matrix $\hat{A}$. In order to make recommendations, we consider two aspects:(1)the direct rating that a user would score on an item and (2) the compatibility between a user's interested features and an item's high-quality features.

A user $u's$ estimated rating for item i could be readily derived as $R^{rating}_{ui} = \hat{A}_{ui}$. To evaluate the consistency between a user's favorite features and an item's intrinsic properties. We first estimate items' quality on different features. Suppose item i's quality on various features is defined as $\{s_{i1}, s_{i2}, ...s_{i|F|}\}$. Item $i's$ feature j is mentioned with sentiments $\{m_{ij1}, m_{ij2}, ...m_{ijn_j}\}$, where n_j is the number of times feature j is mentioned in all the reviews of item i, $m_{ijk} \in \{-1, 1\}$ for $k = 1, 2, ...n_j$. Then we evaluate s_{ij} by $\frac{1}{1+e^{-\sum_{l=1}^{n_j} m_{ijl}}}$ if item i is reviewed on feature j and assign it as 0 otherwise.

We assume that a user's decision about whether or not to make a purchase is based on several important product features to him or her, rather than considering all hundreds of possible features. For a given user-item pair (u, i), we could select $u's$ favorite features according to equation (2), let the indices of the n_f largest feature scores in the cube $\hat{T}$ be $INDF_{ui} = \{indf_{ui1}, indf_{ui2}, ...indf_{uin_f}\}$. Then a user's interests for an item could be derived as follows:

$$R^{feature}_{ui} = \frac{\sum_{f\in INDF_{ui}} \hat{T}_{uif} \cdot s_{if}}{\pi n_f} \tag{6}$$

where π is a rescaling parameter.Note that when implementing, we normalize every feature score to be a value in (0,1).

Algorithm 1 LPRRM-CF

Input: $A, m, n, p, K, \lambda, \lambda_\Theta, O$
Output: R^U, R^I, R^{UF}, R^{IF}

initialize
$R^U \leftarrow \mathbb{R}_+^{m\times K}$, $R^I \leftarrow \mathbb{R}_+^{n\times K}$, $R^{UF} \leftarrow \mathbb{R}_+^{p\times K}$, $R^{IF} \leftarrow \mathbb{R}_+^{p\times K}$;
iter=0
repeat
  $iter \leftarrow iter + 1$;
  draw (u, i, f_A, f_B) from D_S
  $\hat{T}_{uif_Af_B} \leftarrow \hat{T}_{uif_A} - \hat{T}_{uif_B}$
  $\delta_{ranking} \leftarrow 1 - \sigma(\hat{T}_{uif_Af_B})$
  $\delta_{rating} \leftarrow 2l_{ui}(A_{ui} - \sum_{k=0}^{K-1} \hat{R}^U_{uk}\hat{R}^I_{ik})$
  for $k \in 0, 1, ...K-1$ **do**
    $R^U_{uk} \leftarrow R^U_{uk} + learning\_rate * (\delta_{rating} \cdot R^I_{ik} + \lambda \cdot \delta_{ranking} \cdot (R^{UF}_{f_Ak} - R^{UF}_{f_Bk}) - \lambda_{R^U} \cdot R^U_{uk})$
    $R^I_{ik} \leftarrow R^I_{ik} + learning\_rate * (\delta_{rating} \cdot R^U_{uk} + \lambda \cdot \delta_{ranking} \cdot (R^{IF}_{f_Ak} - R^{IF}_{f_Bk}) - \lambda_{R^I} \cdot R^I_{ik})$
    $R^{UF}_{f_Ak} \leftarrow R^{UF}_{f_Ak} + learning\_rate * (\lambda \cdot \delta_{ranking} \cdot R^U_{uk} - \lambda_{R^{UF}} \cdot R^{UF}_{f_Ak})$
    $R^{UF}_{f_Bk} \leftarrow R^{UF}_{f_Bk} + learning\_rate * (\lambda \cdot \delta_{ranking} \cdot (-R^U_{uk}) - \lambda_{R^{UF}} \cdot R^{UF}_{f_Bk})$
    $R^{IF}_{f_Ak} \leftarrow R^{IF}_{f_Ak} + learning\_rate * (\lambda \cdot \delta_{ranking} \cdot R^I_{ik} - \lambda_{R^{IF}} \cdot R^{IF}_{f_Ak})$
    $R^{IF}_{f_Bk} \leftarrow R^{IF}_{f_Bk} + learning\_rate * (\lambda \cdot \delta_{ranking} \cdot (-R^I_{ik}) - \lambda_{R^{IF}} \cdot R^{IF}_{f_Bk})$
  end for
until Converge or iter > max_iter
return R^U, R^I, R^{UF}, R^{IF}

At last, we set the final ranking score (RS) of user u for item i as follows:

$$RS_{ui} = \alpha \cdot R^{feature}_{ui} + (1-\alpha)R^{rating}_{ui} \tag{7}$$

In our datasets, as the rating range is [1,5] and thus the maximum value of $\hat{A}_{ui}$ is 5, we set $\pi = 0.2$ to map the first part of (7) that falls in the range of (0,1) into a comparable value with $\hat{A}_{ui}$. $0 < \alpha < 1$ is a scale parameter that controls the trade off between feature-based score and direct user-item ratings. The recommendation list for user u can be constructed by ranking the items in descending order of RS_{ui}.

3.4.3 Transfer to Category-level LPRRM-CF

The LRPPM-CF model above is conducted on product-level, which is able to capture the various interested features of users for different products especially when the dataset is sufficiently dense. However, in many practical scenarios, user interactions with a single product is very sparse (usually only a single piece of review), and to make our model more robust and adaptable in such application scenarios, we further extend our LRPPM-CF approach to category-level modeling. We define the set of categories as $C = \{c_1, c_2, ...c_{NC}\}$, where NC is the number of categories and the set of user-category-feature triplets as follows:

$$O^* := \{(u,c,f)|u \in U, c \in C, f \in F, User\ u\ mentioned\ feature\ f\ when\ he(she)\ reviewed\ products\ in\ category\ c.\} \tag{8}$$

Similar to product-level LRPPM-CF, the scoring function $\hat{T}^*_{ucf}$ is computed as follows when factorizing this cube:

$$\hat{T}^*_{ucf} = \sum_{k=0}^{K-1} R^U_{uk} \cdot R^{UF}_{fk} + \sum_{k=0}^{K-1} R^C_{ck} \cdot R^{CF}_{fk} + \sum_{k=0}^{K-1} R^U_{uk} \cdot R^C_{ck} \tag{9}$$

where $R^U \in \mathbb{R}_+^{|U|\times K}$, $R^C \in \mathbb{R}_+^{|C|\times K}$, $\{R^{UF} \in \mathbb{R}_+^{|F|\times K}, R^{CF} \in \mathbb{R}_+^{|F|\times K}\}$ are the representation matrices of users, categories and features, respectively, and K is the dimension of the representations.

Suppose $R^I \in \mathbb{R}_+^{|I|\times K}$ is the representation of items. Let the products in category c be $CI_c = \{i_{c1}, i_{c2}, ...i_{cn_c}\}$. We set $R^C_{c\cdot} = \frac{1}{n_c}\sum_{i\in CI_c} R^I_{i\cdot}$ to capture the relationship between products and their categories. The integrated optimization task thus is:

$$\min_{\Theta} \sum_{u\in U}\sum_{i\in I}(A_{ui} - (R^U_{u\cdot})^T \cdot R^I_{i\cdot})^2$$
$$-\lambda \sum_{u\in U}\sum_{c\in C}\sum_{f_A\in F^+_{uc}}\sum_{f_B\in F^-_{uc}} ln\sigma(\hat{T}^*_{ucf_A} - \hat{T}^*_{ucf_B}) + \lambda_\Theta \|\Theta\|^2_F \tag{10}$$

where λ is a tuning parameter, $\Theta = \{R^U, R^I, R^{UF}, R^{IF}\}$, λ_Θ is the regularization constant. F^+_{uc} is the set of features that are mentioned by user u for category c's items, and F^-_{uc} is the set of features that are not mentioned, namely, $F^+_{uc} = \{f \mid (u,c,f) \in O^*\}$ and $F^-_{uc} = \{f|(u,c,f) \notin O^*\}$.We adopt $u's$ favourite features for $i's$ category c as the final feature list for item i. The recommendation list could be generated according equation (7), where we replace $\hat{T}_{uif}$ by $\hat{T}^*_{ucf}$.

The product-level and category-level LRPPM-CF approaches are suitable for different scenarios regarding the characteristic of the tasks (e.g., data sparsity), and they play a complementary role to each other.

3.4.4 Relations between Product-level LPRRM-CF, Category-level LPRRM-CF, and EFM

LRPPM-CF vs EFM The relationship between these two models lies in that they both attempt to model the pairwise interactions among users, items, and features. The difference is that when generating users' favourite features, a rating-based 2D-matrix factorization technique is used in EFM model to capture the static produce-irrelevant feature preferences of users. However, in our LRPPM-CF model, we designed a ranking-based tensor-matrix factorization approach to discriminate users' different interests on feature over different products.

Product- vs Category-level LRPPM-CF Obviously, if every category contains only one product, Category-level LRPPM-CF would reduce to Product-level LRPPM-CF. When the categories contain more than one products, we can bring equation (9) into (10), and rewrite the Category-level LRPPM-

CF optimization objective function as:

$$\min_{\Theta} \sum_{u\in U}\sum_{i\in I}(A_{ui} - (R^U_{u\cdot})^T \cdot R^I_{i\cdot})^2 - \lambda \sum_{u\in U}\sum_{c\in C}\sum_{f_A\in F^+_{uc}}\sum_{f_B\in F^-_{uc}} ln\sigma(\sum_{k=0}^{K-1} R^U_{uk}\cdot R^{UF}_{f_A k} + \sum_{k=0}^{K-1} R^C_{ck}\cdot R^{CF}_{f_A k} - \sum_{k=0}^{K-1} R^U_{uk}\cdot R^{UF}_{f_B k} - \sum_{k=0}^{K-1} R^C_{ck}\cdot R^{CF}_{f_B k}) + \lambda_\Theta \|\Theta\|_F^2 \quad (11)$$

$$Let \ \ H = \sum_{c\in C} ln\sigma(\sum_{k=0}^{K-1} R^U_{uk}\cdot R^{UF}_{f_A k} + \sum_{k=0}^{K-1} R^C_{ck}\cdot R^{CF}_{f_A k} - \sum_{k=0}^{K-1} R^U_{uk}\cdot R^{UF}_{f_B k} - \sum_{k=0}^{K-1} R^C_{ck}\cdot R^{CF}_{f_B k}) \quad (12)$$

and bring $R^C_{c\cdot} = \frac{1}{n_c}\sum_{i\in CI_c} R^I_{i\cdot}$ into (12) we have:

$$H = \sum_{c\in C} ln\sigma(\sum_{k=0}^{K-1} R^U_{uk}\cdot R^{UF}_{f_A k} + \sum_{k=0}^{K-1}\frac{1}{n_c}\sum_{i\in CI_c} R^I_{ik}\cdot R^{CF}_{f_A k} - \sum_{k=0}^{K-1} R^U_{uk}\cdot R^{UF}_{f_B k} - \sum_{k=0}^{K-1}\frac{1}{n_c}\sum_{i\in CI_c} R^I_{ik}\cdot R^{CF}_{f_B k})$$
$$= \sum_{c\in C} ln\sigma(\frac{1}{n_c}\sum_{i\in CI_c}\sum_{k=0}^{K-1}(R^U_{uk}\cdot R^{UF}_{f_A k} + R^I_{ik}\cdot R^{CF}_{f_A k}) - \frac{1}{n_c}\sum_{i\in CI_c}\sum_{k=0}^{K-1}(R^U_{uk}\cdot R^{UF}_{f_B k} + R^I_{ik}\cdot R^{CF}_{f_B k})) \quad (13)$$

we set $R^{CF} = R^{IF}$, and according to (3)(4), we have:

$$H = \sum_{c\in C} ln\sigma(\frac{1}{n_c}\sum_{i\in CI_c}\sum_{k=0}^{K-1}(R^U_{uk}\cdot R^{UF}_{f_A k} + R^I_{ik}\cdot R^{IF}_{f_A k} + R^U_{uk}\cdot R^I_{ik}) - \frac{1}{n_c}\sum_{i\in CI_c}\sum_{k=0}^{K-1}(R^U_{uk}\cdot R^{UF}_{f_B k} + R^I_{ik}\cdot R^{IF}_{f_B k} + R^U_{uk}\cdot R^I_{ik}))$$
$$= \sum_{c\in C} ln\sigma(\frac{1}{n_c}\sum_{i\in CI_c}(\hat{T}_{uif_A}) - \frac{1}{n_c}\sum_{i\in CI_c}(\hat{T}_{uif_B}))$$
$$= \sum_{c\in C} ln\sigma(\frac{1}{n_c}\sum_{i\in CI_c}(\hat{T}_{uif_A f_B})) \quad (14)$$

then the Category-level LRPPM-CF optimization objective function can be rewriten as:

$$\min_{\Theta}\sum_{u\in U}\sum_{i\in I}(A_{ui} - (R^U_{u\cdot})^T\cdot R^I_{i\cdot})^2 - \lambda\sum_{u\in U}\sum_{f_A\in F^+_{uc}}\sum_{f_B\in F^-_{uc}}\sum_{c\in C} ln\sigma(\frac{1}{n_c}\sum_{i\in CI_c}(\hat{T}_{uif_A f_B})) + \lambda_\Theta\|\Theta\|_F^2 \quad (15)$$

Comparing with Product-level LRPPM-CF optimization goal shown in equation (5), we see that Category-level LRPPM-CF uses all the features extracted from a category as the positive observations for its products.

4. RATING-BASED TENSOR FACTORIZATION

In our LRPPM-CF framework described above, we model the user preferences towards different features with a ranking-based approach by modeling the implicit feedbacks directly, because we believe the estimation of user preferences on features is inherently a learning to rank task, which attempts to capture the preference of a feature over another one on products- or category-levels. To verify our assumption, we also study a rating-based tensor factorization model that treats the implicit feedbacks as explicit ratings.

We define the rating user u gave to item i is defined as a_{ui}, the features extracted from user u's textual review for item i are $F_{ui} = \{f_{ui1}, f_{ui1}, ...f_{uiK_{ui}}\}$, where K_{ui} is the number of extracted features.

Similar to LRPPM-CF, we consider user-item-feature relationship as an interaction cube T^s. However, instead of modeling user's implicit behavior, the element T^s_{uik} in T^s is assigned as a score that reflects the degree of user u's interest towards item i on feature f. In this method, we assign T^s_{uik} as $\frac{a_{ui}}{K_{ui}}$ if $f_k \in F_{ui}$ with a positive sentiment polarity, $-\frac{a_{ui}}{K_{ui}}$ if $f_k \in F_{ui}$ with a negative sentiment polarity, and 0 when $f_k \notin F_{ui}$. To make fair comparison, the fitting function adopted here is the same as the method used in LRPPM-CF(equation (2)).

We adopt the least square minimization method to fit these ratings, suppose O^s is defined as:

$$O^s := \{(u,i,f)|u\in U, i\in I, f\in F, User\ u\ mentioned\ feature\ f\ in\ his/her\ review\ on\ item\ i.\} \quad (16)$$

then the optimization objective function is:

$$\min_{\Theta}\sum_{(u,i,f)\in O^s}(T^s_{uif} - \hat{T}^s_{uif})^2 + \lambda_\Theta\|\Theta\|_F^2 \quad (17)$$

where $\Theta = \{R^U, R^I, R^{UF}, R^{IF}\}$ are the model parameters.

We adapt stochastic gradient descent algorithm to learn the parameters. When making recommendation for user u, we first estimate the score u would give to the items, and then select the items with top-N highest scores to generate the recommendation list, where the score $\hat{a}_{ui}$ is computed by:

$$\hat{a}_{ui} = \sum_{k=1}^{|F|}\hat{T}^s_{uik} \quad (18)$$

Although this method tends to capture various user interests in a more compact way, it does not perform better than the LRPPM-CF approach in our experiments, which will be introduced in the following sections. The underlying reason can be that: (1) It may introduce too much noise when directly assigning T^s_{uik} as $\frac{a_{ui}}{K_{ui}}$; (2) Different features may account for different weights when deriving the rating estimations $\hat{a}_{ui}$; (3) Converting the user implicit feedback into explicit ratings may be bias and limited, which could be a shortcoming of the EFM approach, while our LRPPM-CF approach can model such implicit feedbacks directly in a learning to rank framework.

5. EXPERIMENTS

In this section, we conduct extensive experiments to evaluate our LRPPM-CF framework. We focus on the following research questions:

(1) What is the performance of our LRPPM-CF model in

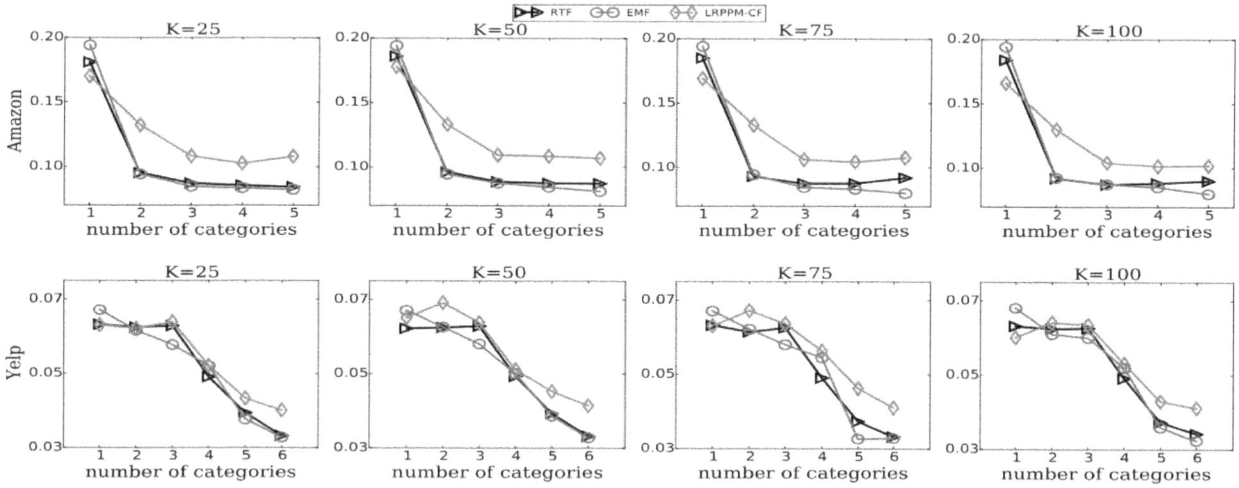

Figure 3: Performance comparison on F_1-measure of LRPPM-CF, EFM and RTF over two datasets. The number of total factors increase from 25 to 100.

Table 2: Statistics of the Amazon and Yelp datasets

	#Users	#Items	#Reviews	$\frac{\#Rviews}{\#Users}$
Amazon	965	13005	38430	39.82
Yelp	859	8750	51965	60.54

capturing various features for different products/categories. (2) What is the performance of our LRPPM-CF model in the task of item recommendation.

We begin by introducing the experimental setup, and then report and analyze the experimental results to attempt to answer the research questions.

5.1 Experimental Setup

We choose the Amazon[2][7, 8] and Yelp[3] datasets for experiments. The former dataset contains user transaction records and textual reviews from Amazon spanning May 1996 - July 2014. The latter dataset consists of user reviews on various businesses. For evaluating the properties of our models, in both of these datasets, we select the users who purchased items in at least 3 categories, and choose the items with 5 or more reviews. We randomly holdout 30% reviewed items from each user to construct the testing set, and the others are used for training. The statistics of our datasets are shown in Table 2.

5.2 Performance in Capturing Various Features

In this subsection, we investigate the performance of LRPPM-CF in capturing different features for various products/categories. We compare the predicted features with the truely mentioned features for every user-item pair in the test dataset. Two methods are selected as our baselines, which are Rating-based Tensor Factorization (RTF) proposed in section 4 and Explicit Factor Model (EFM) [18], which is the state-of-the-art approach for user preference prediction and recommendation based on explicit features from reviews. When implementing RTF, we select 5 features according to their scores in the fitted cube. When implementing EFM, in order to achieve the best performance, we tune the ratio between explicit and latent factors by fixing the total number of factors as 25, 50, 75, 100, respectively, and the weighting scalar is set as 0.85 as reported in [18]. For every user, we select 5 features for all the products according to their scores in the fitted user-feature attention matrix. When implementing LRPPM-CF, we set the dimension K as 25, 50, 75, 100, respectively, so as to ensure equal model complexity, and also select the top-5 features utilizing the method proposed in section 3.2 as the predicted results.

[2]http://jmcauley.ucsd.edu/data/amazon/

[3]http://www.yelp.com/dataset_challenge

Table 3: Statistics of the datasets containing various number of categories

	#Users	#Items	#Reviews	#Categories
Amazon_C1	749	2697	3568	1
Amazon_C2	949	5584	13004	2
Amazon_C3	965	7641	22412	3
Amazon_C4	965	8867	25242	4
Amazon_C5	965	13005	38430	5
Yelp_C1	856	1902	14274	1
Yelp_C2	858	2204	15514	2
Yelp_C3	858	2245	15607	3
Yelp_C4	859	2832	17252	4
Yelp_C5	859	8265	46059	5
Yelp_C6	859	8750	51965	6

The hyper-parameters of these methods are selected by conducting grid search and 5-fold cross-validation. We compare these models on the metric of F_1-score. In order to validate the performance under different number of categories, we construct 5 datasets for Amazon and 6 datasets for Yelp, where the n-th dataset contains products from n categories, respectively. The statistics of the datasets are shown in Table 3.

5.2.1 *Comparison between LRPPM-CF and Baselines*

The overall experimental results of comparing product-level LRPPM-CF with RTF and EFM on the task of predicting the features for a given user-item pair are shown in Figure 3. We see from the results that:

(1) When the datasets contain only one category, the EFM

method performs better than RTF and LRPPM-CF across all the choices on the number of factors. The reason may be that people tend to care about a similar and limited set of features when purchasing products in the same category, thus the RTF and LRPPM-CF approach with 25 or more factors to capture the features could face severe overfitting problems.

(2) When the datasets contain more than one categories, LRPPM-CF performs better than RTF and EFM(enhance the performance by about 17% and 24% on the Amazon dataset containing 5 categories and Yelp dataset containing 6 categories respectively), and the improvements are significantly at 0.01 level. This result is in expectation because the RTF method forcefully converts user's implicit feedbacks to ratings, which could bias the results, and that for a given user, EFM does not consider his/her different interests on features for different products. Instead, our LRPPM-CF approach models the implicit interaction between users, items, and features simultaneously and directly.

(3) With the increasing on the number of categories, LRPPM-CF maintains a satisfactory prediction accuracy compared with EFM, whose performance decrease significantly with the increase on categories.

5.2.2 *Product- and Category-level LRPPM-CF*

In this section, we further investigate the performance of LRPPM-CF by applying this model on two levels of granularities, i.e., product-level and category-level. Similar to the previous experiment, we generate 5 features for each user on each category when implementing category-level LRPPM-CF. The parameters of category-level LRPPM-CF are also selected by conducting grid search in their corresponding ranges. The models are evaluated on Amazon datasets containing 5 categories(i.e., the dataset Amazon_C5) and Yelp datasets containing 6 categories (i.e., the dataset Yelp_C6), where the statistics of the datasets can be seen in the 5th and the last line of Table 3.

Table 4: Performance comparison of Product-level and Category-level LRPPM-CF. The dimensionality is increase from 25 to 100.

dataset	dimension	25	50	75	100
Yelp	Category	0.043	0.0431	0.044	0.0432
	Product	0.040	0.0415	0.0411	0.0413
Amazon	Category	0.11	0.112	0.111	0.104
	Product	0.107	0.106	0.107	0.100

From the results shown in Table 4, we notice that category-level LRPPM-CF performs better than product-level LRPPM-CF in all dimensions, also at a significant level of 0.01. The underlying reason can be that: (1) As the implicit feedback in the user-item-feature cube on product-level is very sparse, this model fails to capture sufficiently many positive features to generate user preference pairs, which could lead to lower prediction accuracy. (2) Because all the products in a category are considered as a whole when conducting category-level LRPPM-CF, much more positive features are collected that help to alleviate the problem of data sparsity.

5.3 Performance in Item Recommendation

In this section, we investigate the LRPPM-CF model in the task of item recommendation. We analyze the model to find what and how the performance is affected by some specific parameters, and which parameters are of key importance to the users in the task.

We use the Amazon containing 5 categories and Yelp containing 6 categories for our experiments (Datasets Amazon_C5 in the 5th and Yelp_C6 in the last line of Table 3). Our product-level LRPPM-CF model is compared with the following baseline methods:

MostPopular: A static method that recommends different users with the same products according to their popularity.

PMF: The Probabilistic Matrix Factorization method proposed in [9], which is a frequently used stat-of-the-art approach for rating-based optimization and prediction. The number of latent factors is set as 50 for Yelp dataset and 20 for Amazon dataset based on cross-validation.

EFM: The state-of-art algorithm [18] in terms of making recommendations based on phrase-level sentiment analysis on textual reviews. In order to achieve the best performance, we conduct grid search on the number of each user's most cared features k in the range of [5,100], as well as the weighing scalar α in the range of (0,1]. When determining the number of explicit and latent factors, we fix the total number as 50 and tune the ratio between them to find an optimal ratio, and then we increase the total number from 10 to 100 by fixing this ratio. The parameters are finally set as $k = 5, \alpha = 0.8$, total number of factors = 20, ratio of explicit factors = 60% in the Amazon dataset, and $k = 15, \alpha = 0.85$, total number of factors = 50, ratio of explicit factors = 40% in the Yelp dataset.

RTF: The compact Rating-based Tensor Factorization method proposed in section 4. We still set the number of factors as 50 for Yelp dataset and 20 for Amazon dataset when implementing this method.

We conduct top-5 recommendation on both of the Amazon and Yelp datasets. The dimension K in our LRPPM-CF model is set as 50 for Yelp datasets and 20 for Amazon datasets to ensure equal model complexity. Grid search and five-fold cross-validation are used for parameter tuning and performance evaluation. We adopt F_1-score and Normalized Discounted Cumulative Gain (NDCG) as the measures to evaluate the performance of different models.

The experimental results are shown in Table 5. From the results we can see that: (1) Among the baseline methods PMF performs better than MostPopular because PMF takes the global information into consideration and thus provides personalized recommendations. By utilizing user review information and sentiment analysis, EFM and RTF performs better than other baseline methods, while little difference is observed between EFM and RTF. (2) Our product-level LRPPM-CF approach gains superior performance against all the baseline methods, and this is actually as expected because it captures user interests over features more precisely on a per-product level, and thus makes more accurate item recommendations.

5.3.1 *Influence of the number of most cared features n_f*

We first fix the number of most cared features $n_f = 5$ and find that the optimal value for λ is 0.3. We then fix $\lambda = 0.3$ throughout the following experiments to focus on the effect of the key parameter n_f.

Our goal is to investigate the performance of LRPPM-CF when n_f increases from 5 to the maximum possible value (100 for Amazon, and 80 for Yelp), larger n_f would lead to significant bias and the results on Yelp are shown in Figure 4. Based on performance of F_1-score we see that our LRPPM-CF model outperforms all the baseline methods when n_f

Table 5: **Comparison between LRPPM-CF and baseline methods on the Amazon and Yelp dataset. The starred values indicate significant improvements against the best baseline on 0.01 and 0.005 level, respectively.**

dataset	metric	MP	PMF	EFM	RFT	LRPPM-CF
Yelp	F1-score@5	0.0183	0.025	0.029	0.028	**0.033***
	NDCG@5	0.0111	0.012	0.0131	0.0144	**0.0186**
Amazon	F1-score@5	0.0135	0.0140	0.0142	0.0139	**0.0152***
	NDCG@5	0.0119	0.0120	0.0124	0.0132	**0.0138**

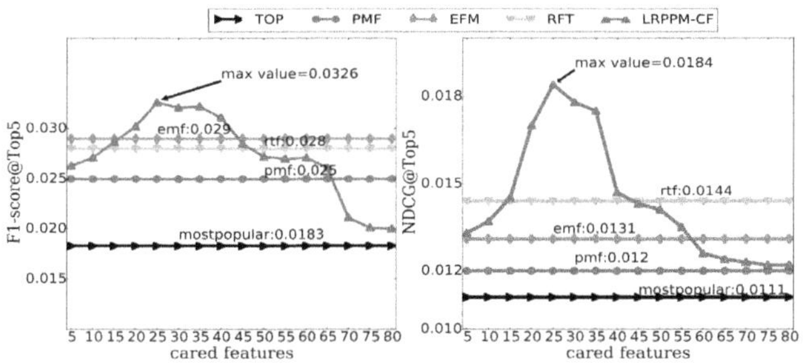

Figure 4: Influence of n_f on the Yelp dataset

ranges from 20 to 40. The best performance of LRPPM-CF with $n_f = 25$ is 11% better than EFM, which performs best among the baseline methods. From the perspective of LRPPM-CF itself, the performance continues to rise as n_f increases from 5 to 25. However, when n_f falls in the range of [25,40], the performance tends to be stable, and when n_f exceeds 40, the performance begins to drop rapidly. From the performance of NDCG@5 we see that LRPPM-CF performs better than all the baseline methods when n_f is in [15,40], and achieves its best performance when n_f arrives at 25. Similar results are observed on Amazon dataset, which are shown in Figure 5.

These observations confirm our hypothesis in section 3.3.3 that when making decisions, users usually care about several key features, and taking too many features into consideration could introduce noise into the models, which is consistent with the observations in EFM [18].

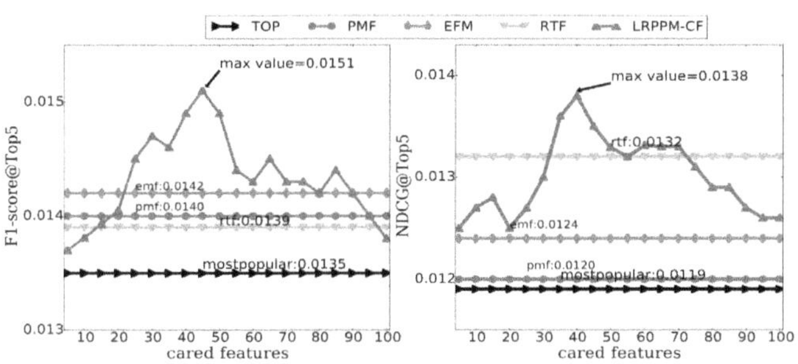

Figure 5: Influence of n_f on the Amazon dataset

5.3.2 Influence of Weighting Parameter λ

In the following set of experiments, we set $n_f = 25$ which achieves the best performance as reported above.We study how the performance (F_1-score) changes as λ increases from 0.05 to 1.2(larger λ would lead to significant bias), and the results on Yelp dataset is shown in Figure 6. We can see that:

(1) LRPPM-CF outperforms the other models when λ is in the range of [0.2, 0.5]. It confirms that our integrated model does enhance the recommendation quality as compared with the simple model of leveraging only the ratings, i.e., when $\lambda = 0$.

(2) The performance of LRPPM-CF continues to rise until λ reaches around 0.3, then after hovering approximately stable in the range of [0.3, 0.4], it begins to drop rapidly with the increase of λ. This observation indicates that although the user reviewing behavior is important in boosting the performance of recommendation, user rating behavior still helps to make accurate predictions. Besides, similar results can be seen on the Amazon dataset, which are shown in Figure 6.

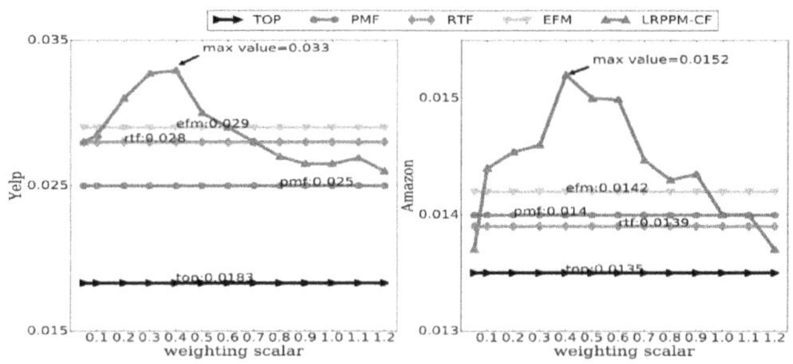

Figure 6: Influence of λ on Amazon and Yelp datasets

5.3.3 Further Analysis of Category-level LRPPM-CF

Although the results in section 5.2 show that category-level LRPPM-CF performs well in the task of capturing various features, we still want to explore whether LRPPM-CF is adequately qualified in the task of item recommendation.

In this set of experiments, we compare the performance between Category- and Product-level LRPPM-CF on the Yelp dataset. The key parameters in both of these methods are n_f and λ. For fair comparison, we tune one of these parameters by fixing the other to observe the differences between the models. For implementing, we first fix λ as 0.4, and observe the change in performance with different n_f, and then investigate the performance with various λ when $n_f = 25$. The dimensions of category- and product-level LRPPM-CF are set as 50. We still adopt F_1-score@5 for performance evaluation.

The experimental results are shown in Figure 7. It shows that category-level LRPPM-CF performs better than product-level in most cases, which indicates that a higher level LRPPM-CF may be more practically effective in personalized recommendation. The underlying reason could be that ranking and summarizing the features for users on per-category level help to alleviate the problem of data sparsity.

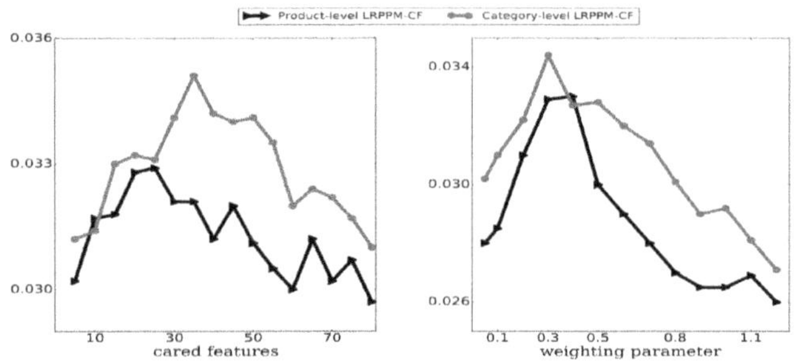

Figure 7: Performance comparison on F_1-score between Category- and Product-level LRPPM-CF in the task of item recommendation.

6. CONCLUSIONS

In this paper, we propose a learning to rank framework to model user preference on explicit features extracted from textual reviews, which is able to capture the implicit feedbacks in a direct way that promotes the accuracy. We thus propose a tensor-matrix factorization technique to learn user interests over features on both product- and category-levels. Furthermore, we integrate this technique with traditional collaborative filtering methods, and propose a unified hybrid framework for both more accurate product/category-level feature ranking and better performance on personalized recommendations, which are verified thorough extensive experiments on both Amazon and Yelp datasets.

This is a first step towards our goal in explainable recommendation on high-level feature spaces and heterogeneous cross-domain recommendation, and there is much room for further improvements. In the future, we will focus on the following research directions. Because our LRPPM approach is a framework rather than simply an algorithm, we are able to integrate more personalization models into this framework according to specific application scenarios, which may bring us more inspiring insights on the characters and performance of traditional methods from the angle of explainable recommendation. We can also adapt other machine learning methods beyond tensor factorization to capture the user-item-feature interactions, such as probabilistic graphic models and topical modeling.

7. REFERENCES

[1] N. Jakob, S. H. Weber, M. C. Müller, and I. Gurevych. Beyond the stars: exploiting free-text user reviews to improve the accuracy of movie recommendations. In *Proceedings of the 1st international CIKM workshop on Topic-sentiment analysis for mass opinion*, pages 57–64. ACM, 2009.

[2] Y. Koren, R. Bell, and C. Volinsky. Matrix factorization techniques for recommender systems. *Computer*, (8):30–37, 2009.

[3] C. W. Leung, S. C. Chan, and F.-l. Chung. Integrating collaborative filtering and sentiment analysis: A rating inference approach. In *Proceedings of the ECAI 2006 workshop on recommender systems*, pages 62–66. Citeseer, 2006.

[4] Y. Lu, M. Castellanos, U. Dayal, and C. Zhai. Automatic construction of a context-aware sentiment lexicon: an optimization approach. In *WWW*, pages 347–356. ACM, 2011.

[5] B. M. Marlin. Modeling user rating profiles for collaborative filtering. In *Advances in neural information processing systems*, page None, 2003.

[6] J. McAuley and J. Leskovec. Hidden factors and hidden topics: understanding rating dimensions with review text. In *Proceedings of the 7th ACM conference on Recommender systems*, pages 165–172. ACM, 2013.

[7] J. McAuley, R. Pandey, and J. Leskovec. Inferring networks of substitutable and complementary products. In *SIGKDD*, pages 785–794. ACM, 2015.

[8] J. McAuley, C. Targett, Q. Shi, and A. van den Hengel. Image-based recommendations on styles and substitutes. In *SIGIR*, pages 43–52. ACM, 2015.

[9] A. Mnih and R. Salakhutdinov. Probabilistic matrix factorization. In *Advances in neural information processing systems*, pages 1257–1264, 2007.

[10] N. Pappas and A. Popescu-Belis. Sentiment analysis of user comments for one-class collaborative filtering over ted talks. In *SIGIR*, pages 773–776. ACM, 2013.

[11] D. Y. Pavlov and D. M. Pennock. A maximum entropy approach to collaborative filtering in dynamic, sparse, high-dimensional domains. In *Advances in neural information processing systems*, pages 1441–1448, 2002.

[12] Š. Pero and T. Horváth. Opinion-driven matrix factorization for rating prediction. In *User Modeling, Adaptation, and Personalization*, pages 1–13. Springer, 2013.

[13] S. Rendle, L. Balby Marinho, A. Nanopoulos, and L. Schmidt-Thieme. Learning optimal ranking with tensor factorization for tag recommendation. In *SIGKDD*, pages 727–736. ACM, 2009.

[14] S. Rendle, C. Freudenthaler, Z. Gantner, and L. Schmidt-Thieme. Bpr: Bayesian personalized ranking from implicit feedback. In *Proceedings of the Twenty-Fifth Conference on Uncertainty in Artificial Intelligence*, pages 452–461. AUAI Press, 2009.

[15] S. Rendle and L. Schmidt-Thieme. Pairwise interaction tensor factorization for personalized tag recommendation. In *Proceedings of the third ACM international conference on Web search and data mining*, pages 81–90. ACM, 2010.

[16] P. Symeonidis, A. Nanopoulos, and Y. Manolopoulos. Tag recommendations based on tensor dimensionality reduction. In *Recsys*, pages 43–50. ACM, 2008.

[17] Y. Wu and M. Ester. Flame: A probabilistic model combining aspect based opinion mining and collaborative filtering. In *WSDM*, pages 199–208. ACM, 2015.

[18] Y. Zhang, G. Lai, M. Zhang, Y. Zhang, Y. Liu, and S. Ma. Explicit factor models for explainable recommendation based on phrase-level sentiment analysis. In *SIGIR*, pages 83–92. ACM, 2014.

[19] Y. Zhang, H. Zhang, M. Zhang, Y. Liu, and S. Ma. Do users rate or review?: boost phrase-level sentiment labeling with review-level sentiment classification. In *SIGIR*, pages 1027–1030. ACM, 2014.

[20] Y. Zhang, M. Zhang, Y. Liu, S. Ma, and S. Feng. Localized matrix factorization for recommendation based on matrix block diagonal forms. In *WWW*, pages 1511–1520. International World Wide Web Conferences Steering Committee, 2013.

How Much Novelty is Relevant? It Depends on Your Curiosity

Pengfei Zhao, Dik Lun Lee
Department of Computer Science and Engineering
Hong Kong University of Science and Technology
{ericzhao, dlee}@cse.ust.hk

Traditional recommendation systems (*RS*s) aim to recommend items that are relevant to the user's interest. Unfortunately, the recommended items will soon become too familiar to the user and hence fail to arouse her interest. Discovery-oriented recommendation systems (*DORS*s) complement accuracy with *discover utilities* (*DU*s) such as novelty and diversity and optimize the tradeoff between the *DU*s and accuracy of the recommendations. Unfortunately, *DORS*s ignore an important fact that different users have different appetites for *DU*s. That is, highly curious users can accept highly novel and diversified recommendations whereas conservative users would behave in the opposite manner. In this paper, we propose a curiosity-based recommendation system (*CBRS*) framework which generates recommendations with a personalized amount of *DU*s to fit the user's curiosity level. The major contribution of this paper is a computational model of user curiosity, called Probabilistic Curiosity Model (*PCM*), which is based on the curiosity arousal theory and Wundt curve in psychology research. In *PCM*, we model a user's curiosity with a curiosity distribution function learnt from the user's access history and compute a curiousness score for each item representing how curious the user is about the item. *CBRS* then selects items which are both relevant and have high curiousness score, bounded by the constraint that the amount of *DU*s fits the user's *DU* appetite. We use joint optimization and co-factorization approaches to incorporate the curiosity signal into the recommendations. Extensive experiments have been performed to evaluate the performance of *CBRS* against the baselines using a music dataset from last.fm. The results show that compared to the baselines *CBRS* not only provides more personalized recommendations that adapt to the user's curiosity level but also improves the recommendation accuracy.

Keywords

Recommendation, curiosity, psychology, personalization

1. INTRODUCTION

Traditional recommendation systems (*RS*s) based on content similarity and collaborative filtering aim to achieve high accuracy by recommending items that are relevant to the user's interest. The problem with this approach is that the recommended items are very similar to the user's interest as well as between themselves. Thus, the user will quickly find the recommended items too familiar and uninteresting for exploration. We call this the "accuracy overloading problem." To prevent accuracy from domainating the recommendations, Discovery-Oriented Recommendation Systems (*DORS*s) introduce metrics called Discovery Utilities (*DU*s) as additional dimensions besides relevance for ranking the candidate items. The ranking problem is often modeled as a multi-objective optimization problem, which seeks an optimal tradeoff between the different dimensions [16]. Many *DU*s, including novelty and diversity, have been studied in the literature [3]. Although *DORS*s can help to alleviate the accuracy overloading problem, they neglect an important fact that different users have different curiosity levels, which lead to different levels of desire to discover new things. Specifically, highly curious users would find recommendations with high *DU*s interesting but those with low *DU*s boring. The reverse is true for conservative users. We refer to this curiosity-driven, personal demand of *DU*s as *DU* appetite. Without considering the *DU* appetite of each user, *DORS*s would favor items with high *DU*s (balanced by relevance) for every user. Consequently, while highly curious users are excited about high *DU* items, conservative users would find them too overwhelming. We call this "curiosity mismatch problem."

In this paper, we present a framework for Curiosity-Based Recommendation Systems (*CBRS*s) to solve the curiosity mismatch problem. It consists of the Probabilistic Curiosity Model (*PCM*), which models a user's curiosity with a curiosity distribution function learnt from the user's access history. Thus, *each user has her own curiosity model* estimated from her access behavior. It allows us to compute a *curiousness score* for each item representing how curious the user is about the item. *CBRS* then selects items which have both high relevance and curiousness scores, bounded by the constraint that the items' *DU*s should fit the user's *DU* appetite. We note that the *CBRS* framework is general enough for incorporating different *DU*s. However, since novelty is by far the most studied *DU* in *RS* research, this paper focuses on novelty, leaving the details of modeling the other *DU*s as future research.

The Oxford dictionary defines curiosity as "a strong desire to know or learn something." According to psychology research [4], a user's appetite for novelty is influenced by her *curiosity* in that the higher/lower a user's curiosity, the bigger/smaller is her appetite for novelty. For a user with a particular curiosity level, recommendations with too much novelty will cause anxiety while too little will cause boredom.[1] To exploit this psychological phenomenon, a *RS*

SIGIR '16, July 17-21, 2016, Pisa, Italy
© 2016 ACM. ISBN 978-1-4503-4069-4/16/07...$15.00
DOI: http://dx.doi.org/10.1145/2911451.2911488

[1]This is an interesting finding in psychology. In most existing *RS* research, novelty is assumed to be the higher the better. However, we can learn from many real-life situations that this is not true. For example, *most* people going to a theme park for roller coaster rides

should select recommendations with novelty commensurate with the user's curiosity, instead of blindly maximize the novelty *for everybody*.[2]

In this paper, we address several challenges facing *CBRS*. First, we adopt the famous Wundt curve in psychology to model human curiosity [4]. The Wundt curve depicts the "inverse U-shape" relationship between an item's stimulation degree (*sd*) (i.e., stimulation generated by, say, the novelty of an item upon a user) and the user's response to the item (see Fig. 2). Briefly, given a user, as the novelty of an item increases, the user will become more and more interested in it until the novelty reaches a turning point where the interest is at a maximum; beyond this point the user will become less and less interested and will ultimately become disinterested in the item. This theory is adopted in *CBRS*. Unfortunately, Wundt curve is only a qualitative description of the relationship. In *CBRS*, we model the "inverse U-shape" with a Beta distribution and learn the distribution's parameters from the user's accessed history. Second, we use the curiosity model to compute for each candidate item a curiousness score representing how curious the user is about the item and select candidate items matching the user's curiosity based on their curiousness scores. The input to the model is the stimulation degree of the item. In the context of this paper, it is the novelty of the item. To measure an item's novelty, we propose three features, namely, the user's access frequency to the item, the recency of the accesses, and the user-specified tags of the item. These features have been confirmed to be effective by psychology research [4]. Finally, we need to integrate the curiosity and relevance aspects of the items to produce the final recommendations. We study two strategies, namely, the joint optimization of relevance and curiousness with the constraint that the novelty of the items should match the user's novelty appetite, and co-factorization of the relevance and curiousness signals associated with the item.

Throughout this paper, we use music recommendation to illustrate the ideas of *CBRS*. This is because music recommendation has been widely studied in recent years [8], and research has shown that music listening behavior is highly discovery oriented, highly personal and heavily driven by curiosity [2]. The contributions of this paper are summarized as follows.

- We propose a novel framework for Curiosity-Based Recommendation Systems (*CBRS*s) to combine relevance and curiosity in the recommendation process. Although we focus on novelty in this paper, the framework is general enough to embrace other *DU*s.
- We develop a computational model called *Probabilistic Curiosity Model* (*PCM*) to model a user's curiosity based on Wundt curve developed in psychology. On the one hand, Wundt curve forms the theoretical foundation of *PCM*. On the other hand, our work provides large-scale experimental evidence to validate the Wundt curve theory. In our opinion, this is a major and interesting contribution of our work to the psychology field.
- We propose two strategies to combine curiousness and relevance in selecting recommendations, considering the constraints that the novelty of the recommended items should match the user's curiosity level.
- We use various performance metrics, including inter-user similarity, novelty fitness and precision, to evaluate the effectiveness of *CBRS*. Experimental results show that *CBRS* not only provides personalized recommendations adapted to the user's unique curiosity but, surprisingly, also improves the recommendation precision. Further, we study the impact of including previously accessed items (i.e., non-novel items) in the recommendations and show that *CBRS* can recommend the right mix of non-novel and novel items to optimize the performance. This is an important finding because in many applications (e.g., music recommendation) users may repeatedly access some items (e.g., favorite songs).

The rest of this paper is organized as follows. We review related work in Section 2. Curiosity modeling will be introduced in Section 3. Section 4 describes the recommendation strategies, and Section 5 presents performance evaluation. Section 6 concludes our findings.

2. RELATED WORK

2.1 Discovery-Oriented RSs (DORS)

Discovery-Oriented Recommendation Systems (*DORS*s) introduce various *DU*s to complement accuracy in solving the accuracy overloading problem. Common *DU*s include novelty [7, 15, 17], diversity [18, 21] and serendipity [13, 19]. Although *DORS*s were designed to produce recommendations that are more novel, diversified, or surprising, they ignore the fact that different users would accept different amount of *DU*s, which we call the *DU* appetite, because users have different curiosity levels, causing what we call the curiosity mismatch problem described in Sec. 1. Recently, methods that personalize the *DU*s of the recommendations for individual users, termed Personalized *DORS*s or *PDORS*, have been proposed to resolve the curiosity mismatch problem.

2.2 Personalized DORSs (PDORS)

Personalization has been studied for a long time in information retrieval [6]. However, to the best of our knowledge, the only works on *PDORS*[3] were reported in [17] and [7]. [17] assumes that each user has a binary "novelty-seeking status" indicating whether the user would seek completely novel (i.e., new) items or non-novel items (previously accessed items). However, this binary assumption is too strict in many situations, e.g., user may want to receive both completely novel and non-novel items in the same recommendation list, as in Youtube which recommends both new and old items. To extend this binary assumption, [7] learns a real-value novelty preference score for each user through logistic regression. The score is then used as a parameter for balancing similarity and novelty in the top-K ranking task. We call this method personalized parameter balancing *RS* or *PPBRS*. The personalized novelty preference parameter of *PPBRS linearly* scales the novelty of all items in the final ranking process. The implication is that if a user is judged to accept novel items (large novelty preference score), then all novel items benefit equally in the ranking task. As discussed throughout this paper, linear scaling of novelty does not work for human curiosity: even for users having large novelty preference score, it does not mean that they can accept items with extremely high novelty (see Sec. 1 and Sec. 3). In our proposed *CBRS*, we model a user's novelty preference as a probability distribution rather than a single real value and verify that the distribution resembles the non-linear "inverse U-shape" Wundt curve in psychology research.

would prefer rides that are not too exciting (too thrilling) or too easy (too boring).

[2]Not explicitly mentioned here, the curiosity aspect must be balanced with the relevance of the items.

[3]Since we only consider novelty in this paper, from now on, *PDORS*s refer to delivering personalized amount of "novelty" according to the user's novelty appetite.

There are several differences between *CBRS* and existing *DORSs* and *PPBRS*. Comparing to *DORSs*, (1) curiosity in *CBRS* is not a new dimension of *DUs*; instead, it governs each user's acceptance level of *DUs*; (2) *CBRS* does not use *DUs* as ranking utility directly since a given amount of *DUs* might be attractive to one user but may turn other users away. Instead, *CBRS* transforms *DUs* into a curiousness score representing a user's curiousness about an item using the user's curiosity model and the curiousness score is then used in ranking; (3) curiosity is a human trait born with a person, but *DUs* are based on an item's property. Comparing to *PPBRS*, (1) user's novelty preference in *CBRS* is not modeled as a real value but a curiosity distribution modeling the shape of Wundt curve as a probability density function *pdf*; (2) rather than assuming that every item's *DUs* is uniformly scaled by the user's novelty preference score, *CBRS* influences the discovery ranking utility with a curiousness score that is derived for each user and each item based on the user's curiosity model.

3. CURIOSITY MODEL

3.1 Preliminaries

Due to the interdisciplinary nature of our research, it is necessary to introduce terminologies widely used in the psychological curiosity field. In psychology, **curiosity** is a human trait born with a person, driving her cognitive development through life. Since different people have different levels of curiosity, we introduce **curiousness** (cur_u^i), which is a real value, to quantify a user u's curiosity to explore an item i. *CBRS* adopts the **Curiosity Arousing Model** (*CAM*) developed in psychology research [4]. In *CAM*, a user receives stimuli and would only respond to stimuli which can arouse her curiosity. Since *CAM* describes how a user selectively responds to the stimuli, it is also referred to as the **Stimulus Selection Process** (*SSP*). For recommendation systems, each recommended item presents a **stimulus** to the user. The strength of a stimulus is quantified by the Stimulus Degree, which is a real value denoted as *sd*. Note that the same item can produce different *sds* to different users.

The *sd* of a stimulus is defined by a number of factors called **Collative Variables** (*CVs*). For this paper, *CVs* are the same as features, which are extracted from some measurable properties of a stimulus. The values of the *CVs* are called **Collative Variable Values**. As discussed, different users have different responses even if the stimulus is the same because of their difference in curiosity. We propose the **Probabilistic Curiosity Model** (*PCM*), which is a probabilistic view of *CAM*. It models a user's selected *sd*'s as a random variable, and curiosity as the probability distribution of the random variable, called **Curiosity Distribution** (C_u). In this way, a user's stimulus selection process (*SSP*) can be interpreted as drawing samples (stimuli) from the curiosity distribution under the guidance of the user's curiosity.

3.2 Curiosity Arousal Model

Berlyne interprets curiosity as the driving factor for *SSP*, that is, "when several conspicuous stimulus are introduced at once, to which stimulus will human respond" [4]. Following Berlyne's interpretation, we can take an *interior view* of curiosity, which is to consider curiosity as an internal factor of a person influencing her selection of stimulus. We can also take an *exterior view* of curiosity, that is, a person's *SSP* can reveal her curiosity inside. *CAM* points out the possibility that the interior curiosity trait can be estimated by the exterior *SSP*. To achieve this goal, we need to (1) quantify the stimulus and (2) model the curiosity. Sections 3.2 and 3.3 will discuss (1) and the remaining subsections will discuss (2).

Berlyne [4] discovered a principle set of features, named as *Collative Variables* (*CVs*), that can arouse curiosity. Four *CVs* were identified: *novelty*, *uncertainty*, *conflict* and *complexity*. Since *CVs* are dependent on user u, item i, time t, and user's access history H_u^t before time t, we use $sd_{u,i}^t(H_u^t)$ to denote item i's *sd* with respect to u at time t given u's access history H_u^t. Similarly, we use $cvv_{u,i}^t$ to denote the value of a *CV* associated with i at time t for u. Then, a stimulus can be quantified by Equation 1, where ψ is a scoring function. Since a stimulus is made up of *CVs*, it can be modeled as a (weighted) sum of *cvv*'s of the *CVs*. In this paper, we focus on novelty only, so $sd_{u,i}^t$ in Equation 1 is simplified to $Nov_{u,i}^t$, which denotes item i's novelty to user u at time t.

$$sd_{u,i}^t = \psi(u, i, t|H_u^t) = \sum_{cv} cvv_{u,i}^t \tag{1}$$

Our dataset is about the users' music listening history, in which an item corresponds to a music track. When u clicks an item i to listen to it, we say "u *accesses* i," "u accesses an artist" if u accesses at least one track performed by the artist, and u accesses a tag if at least one accessed track has the tag. From the recommendation point of view, the action that u accesses i is viewed as u's provision of a positive *feedback* on i.[4] From the curiosity point of view, u's access to i can be viewed as u *responding* to the stimulus generated by i. Thus, in this paper, we use "feedback", "access", and "response" interchangeably depending on the context.

3.3 Modeling of Novelty

In the *RS* domain, the novelty of an item reflects how much the item differs from the user's previously accessed items. In the psychology field, Berlyne suggested that novelty is inversely related to three factors [4]: (1) how often the stimulus has been experienced by the user, (2) how recent the stimulus has been experienced by the user before, and (3) how dissimilar the stimulus is to the user's previous experience. Based on the three criteria, we formally define the novelty in Equation 2,

$$Nov_{u,i}^t = \frac{1}{3} \cdot (SF_{u,i}^t + SR_{u,i}^t + Dissim_{u,i}^t) \tag{2}$$

where $SF_{u,i}^t$ denotes the scaled frequency of the user's accesses to item i before t; high frequency indicates the user's familiarity of the item, making it less novel to the user. $SR_{u,i}^t$ denotes the scaled recency of the user's access on item i w.r.t the current time t; the more recent the user's access to the item is, the less novel the item is to the user. $Dissim_{u,i}^t$ denotes the dissimilarity between item i and u's historically accessed items; a large dissimilarity indicates i is more novel to the user. Note that $SF_{u,i}$, $SR_{u,i}$ and $Dissim_{u,i}$ correspond, respectively, to Berlyne's three criteria above. In music recommendation, a user's decision to listen to a track may depend on the performing artist. For example, after picking her favorite artist, the user may play all of the tracks sequentially in the album. In this case, the reason for the user to play the tracks in the album is not the novelty of the tracks but the performing artist. Thus, we include the artist in computing a track's stimulus.

We define $SF_{u,i}^t$ formally in Equation 3:

$$SF_{u,i}^t = \frac{e^{-\rho_a \cdot |A_{u,i}^t|} + e^{-\rho_i \cdot |I_{u,i}^t|}}{2} \tag{3}$$

where $A_{u,i}^t$ is the set of u's accesses to items in the user's history H_u^t (before time t) having the same artist as i's artist, $I_{u,i}^t$ is the set of u's accesses to items i in the user's history H_u^t, $|.|$ denotes the

[4]As with most web-based applications, we only consider implicit feedback from users. A user's listening to a track indicates her preference on the track, which is a positive feedback; no negative feedback is available.

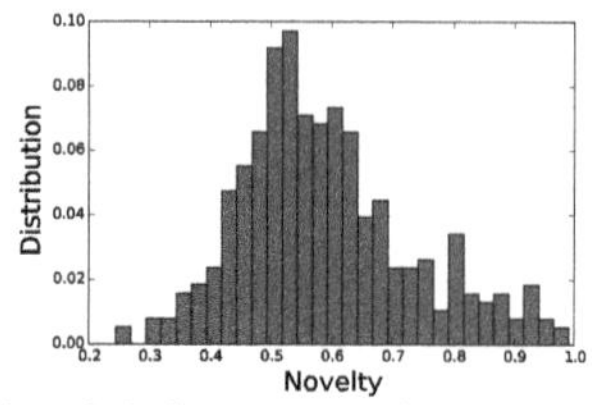

Figure 1: The global users novelty appetites distribution

cardinality of a set, and ρ_a and ρ_i are positive exponential scaling coefficients. The reason to model $SF^t_{u,i}$ based on both the frequencies of the track itself (item i) and tracks having the same artist as i's artist is that both tracks and artists are stimuli. It is clear that when $|I^t_{u,i}|$ is high, the user has accessed item i many times so i's novelty is low, and when $|A^t_{u,i}|$ is high, the user is familiar with i's artist, and so its contribution to novelty is low. Overall, a small $SF^t_{u,i}$ value means i has low novelty.

$SR^t_{u,i}$ is defined in Equation 4:

$$SR^t_{u,i} = \frac{e^{\rho_t \cdot (t - t(A^{-1}_{u,i}))} + e^{\rho_t \cdot (t - t(I^{-1}_{u,i}))}}{2} \quad (4)$$

where $t(I^{-1}_{u,i})$ and $t(A^{-1}_{u,i})$ denote, respectively, the timestamps of u's latest access in $I^t_{u,i}$ and $A^t_{u,i}$. Here, we use "day" as the time unit. ρ_t is the forgetting coefficient. Equation 3 and 4 both use the decay function with exponential forgetting rate [10] to scale frequency and recency to the 0-1 range. Note that small SR value indicates less novelty.

To model $Dissim^t_{u,i}$, for each track, we extract six tags[5] labeling the genres of the music (e.g., "pop" and "jazz") using the LastFM API. The dissimilarity is calculated based on the number of common tags between the track and the historically accessed tags, and is formally defined in Equation 5, where $Tags(i)$ denotes the set of tags associated with track i, and $I_{u,tag}$ denotes the set of accessed items in H^t_u labeled with tag. ρ_{tag} is the coefficient for tag frequency. Note that small *Dissim* value means low novelty.

$$Dissim^t_{u,i} = \frac{1}{|2 \cdot Tags(i)|} \sum_{tag}^{Tags(i)} (e^{-\rho_{tag} \cdot |I_{u,tag}|} + e^{\rho_t \cdot (t - t(I^{-1}_{u,tag}))}) \quad (5)$$

Several observations can be made from Equations 2 to 5. First, items with small *SF* (i.e., frequently accessed), small *SR* (i.e., recently accessed), and small *Dissim* (genre has been frequently and recently accessed) have small *Nov* values and thus are less novel. Second, if the user listens to a new track performed by an artist whom she has never listened to before, $SF^t_{u,i}$ and $SR^t_{u,i}$ will become 1. However, $Dissim^t_{u,i}$ may not necessarily be 1. Third, we assume that the factors in each equation are equally weighted (e.g. in Equation 2, SF, SR, $Dissim$ contribute equally to Nov). Due to space limitation, we cannot show the results for all weighting combinations and the optimal balance is application dependent anyway. Fourth, $Nov^t_{u,i}$ is defined on (u, i, t) triples and is a real value representing item i's novelty to u at time t. If we use Nov^T_u to denote the vector of $Nov^t_{u,i}$, within the time period T, when $T \to \infty$ and we omit the superscript T, then Nov_u can be viewed as a random variable representing u's inclination in accessing novel items, and each user's novelty appetite nov_u is defined as the expectation of the random variable Nov_u. Figure 1 illustrates the distribution of all users' novelty expectation. We can see that the novelty appetites of different users vary a lot. Finally, although $SF^t_{u,i}$, $SR^t_{u,i}$ and $Dissim^t_{u,i}$ are defined based on the music recommendation dataset, it is not difficult to extend them to other domains such as restaurant recommendation and movie recommendation, since user behaviors in these applications can be formulated as (u, i, t) triples.

[5]For tracks which have less than six tags, we extract all of the tags available.

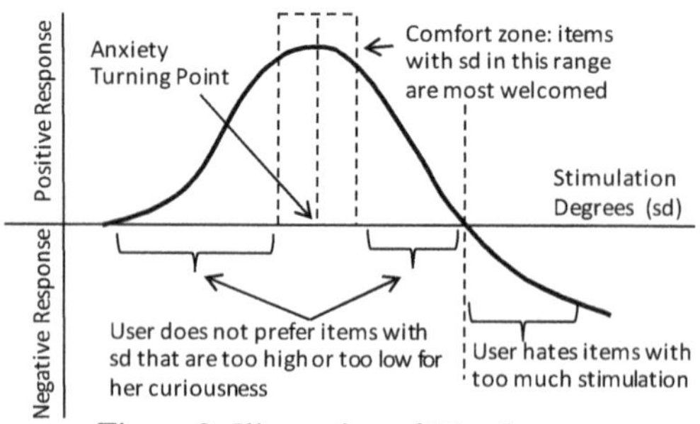

Figure 2: Illustration of Wundt curve

3.4 Wundt Curve and Probabilistic Curiosity Model

Curiosity modeling has been studied in psychology for a long time. In 1870s, Wundt introduced the theory of "optimal level of stimulation" and postulated an inverted "U-shape" relationship between stimulation level and hedonic response caused by the stimulus, which is referred to as the "Wundt curve." Figure 2 is an illustration of Wundt curve, where the x-axis denotes stimulus degrees *sd*, and the y-axis denotes the user's hedonic response. Berlyne formed the "intermediate arousal potential" (*IAP*) theory, which states that too little stimulation results in boredom while too much stimulation results in anxiety. From Fig. 2, we can see that the user's positive hedonic response increases first as *sd* increases. However, after reaching a certain threshold, the positive hedonic response will drop with further increases of *sd*. We name the turning point as user u's *anxiety turning point* (ATP_u). It means that beyond the threshold the user will become anxious due to overwhelming *sd*. An important note about applying Wundt curve to *RS* is that since we assume each of the user's interaction with an item reflects her positive feedback on the item, there is no negative feedback in our our music recommendation application, leading to a Wundt curve that is entirely above the x-axis. Since a user's curiosity can be revealed from her *SSP* and generally behaves like Wundt curve, the central task now is how to model Wundt curve.

From the probability point of view, we model each user's selected *sd*'s as a random variable and model the user's curiosity as a probability distribution of the random variable, which determines the user's *SSP*. The distribution is named *Curiosity Distribution*, denoted by C_u. In this way, *SSP* is viewed as a sampling process from the user's personal curiosity distribution, with which curiosity is able to guide *SSP*. Given a large amount of user-item interaction data and u's accessed *sd*'s, C_u can be estimated. We name our model *Probabilistic Curiosity Model* (*PCM*), which can be considered the probabilistic view of *CAM*. There are two main reasons we use *PCM* to model Wundt curve and curiosity. First, human's *SSP* behaves in a probabilistic manner. For example, a curious user may also select small *sd*'s, although the chance is small compared with a conservative user. Second, although web data lacks explicit user preference data, abundant implicit feedback data are available. By modeling curiosity probabilistically, we can utilize web-scale user interaction data for the estimation of curiosity distribution.

Figure 3 illustrates a user's *SSP* on five items with different *sd* values. According to the interior view of *CAM*, the user's *SSP* (either acceptance or rejection of an item) is guided by her curiosity. *PCM* views a user's *SSP* as continuously drawing samples from her curiosity distribution in such a way that stimuli whose *sd*'s best meet the user's curiosity have a high chance to be drawn. This ensures that the stimuli with *sd*'s that are too large or small, reflecting

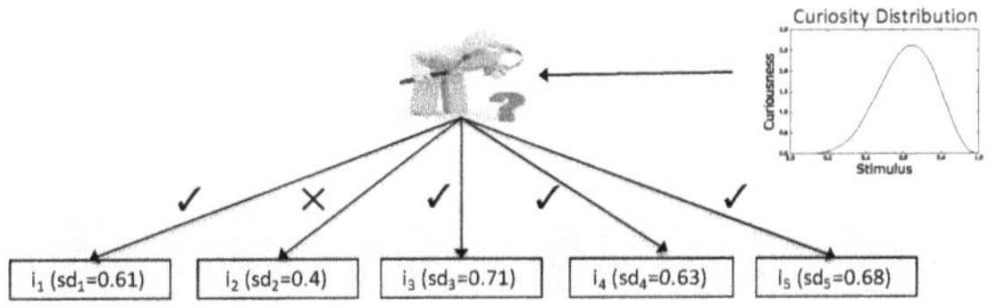

Figure 3: Illustration of the probabilistic curiosity model

the fact that the items are too novel or boring for the user, have a lower chance to be selected by the users. In the example, the user selected four items and ignored one item and the average sd of the selected items is about 0.65.

3.5 Estimation of Curiosity Distribution

Section 3.4 shows how curiosity guides a user's *SSP* from the psychology and probability points of view. In this section, we will introduce how to estimate the curiosity distribution.

Since both *CAM* from psychology and our *PCM* try to model a user's curiosity, it is natural to expect that the probability density function (*pdf*) of C_u exhibits the shape of Wundt curve. Figure 4 shows the histograms of 5 users' accessed *sd*'s, simulating the curiosity distribution. Several important findings can be obtained. First, the distribution generally fulfills the "inverted-U" shape of Wundt curve, which shows that *PCM* is suitable for modeling Wundt curve. Second, the curiosity distributions of different users are different. For example, the means for the five users are about 0.2, 0.4, 0.5 and 0.6, 0.7, respectively, showing that the users tend to show different levels of curiousness when they interact with the recommendation system. u_1 is relative more conservative compared with u_4 and u_5. Besides, the variance of the users' distributions are different. u_1 and u_2 have relative small variance while u_3 to u_5 have relative large variance. Small variance means that curiosity is stable, which means that users' curiosity tends not to change with topic or time, while large variance shows that the user's curiosity may vary with topic and time. Third, generally, there is an optimal *sd* for each curiosity distribution, indicating the *sd* has large chance to be accessed.

According to the above findings, we propose to use the Beta distribution, which has a flexible *pdf* and well studied parameter estimation techniques, to model the curiosity distribution C_u. Wundt curve's inverse U-shape can be estimated with Beta parameters α and β larger than 1. We apply the method of moments for the estimation of α and β. The red curves in Figure 4(a) to 4(e) illustrate the estimated *pdf*'s of five users' *Nov* random variable.

Once the curiosity distribution is estimated, we can obtain the likelihood that the user is curious about an item with *sd*, i.e., the user's *curiousness* on item i given its *sd*, denoted by $cur_u^i = pdf_u(sd)$, where *pdf* is the probability density function of C_u. cur_u^i can be viewed as a curiousness score mapped from an item's stimulus on the curiosity distribution. According to the psychology of interest [14], the pleasant feeling obtained from the process of exploring novel and surprising items is an important component of human interest. Thus, in addition to relevancy, the fact that an item's *sd* satisfies the user's curiosity is also a reason for the user to access an item. In the following section, we will introduce how to incorporate a user's curiousness about the items into the ranking utility of an *RS*.

4. CURIOSITY BASED RECOMMENDATION SYSTEM

4.1 Joint Optimization of Relevancy and Curiousness

We model the recommendation problem as a top-K problem, which selects the top K items to recommend based on the relevancy of the items to the user and the user's curiosity on the items. Let I be the item set of size $|I|$, and U be the user set of size $|U|$. The relevancy matrix R with dimension $|U| \times |I|$ is calculated using existing accuracy-based recommendation techniques. Each element $r_{u,i}$ in R represents the relevancy of item i to user u. We use *CR* with dimension $|U| \times |I|$ to represent the curiousness matrix, with each element $c_{u,i}$ in *CR* recording u's curiousness on i (see Section 3.5). We use *SD* with dimension $|U| \times |I|$ to represent the stimulus degree matrix, where each element $sd_{u,i}$ denotes i's stimulus degree to u. The vectors $\mathbf{R}_u$, $\mathbf{CR}_u$ and $\mathbf{SD}_u$ represent, respectively, I's relevancy to u, u's curiousness over I and I's stimulus degree to u, and correspond to one row of R, CR and SD, respectively. It is useful to represent the recommendation list $Rec \subseteq I$ using an $|I|$ dimensional indicator vector $\mathbf{y}$, such that $y(i) = 1$ if $i \in Rec$ and $y(i) = 0$ otherwise. $\mathbf{y}_u$ represents u's indicator vector, denoting the items to be recommended to u. In the *CBRS* framework, we try to recommend items which are highly relevant to the user and stimulative to her curiosity. This is bounded by the constraint that the items in the recommend list should not exceed her anxiety turning point. With these expressions, it is possible to express the tradeoffs between relevancy and curiosity as constrained optimization problems.

Given a fixed parameter $\theta \in [0,1]$, find the vector $\mathbf{y}^*$ such that

$$\begin{aligned} \max_{\mathbf{y}^*} \quad & (1-\theta)\alpha \mathbf{R}_u^T \cdot \mathbf{y} + \theta\beta \mathbf{CR}_u^T \cdot \mathbf{y} \\ \text{s.t.} \quad & \mathbf{SD}_u^T \cdot \mathbf{y} \le t_{tol} \\ & \mathbf{1}^T \cdot \mathbf{y} = K \\ & y_i \in 0, 1 \forall i \in 1, ..., |I| \end{aligned} \tag{6}$$

In this optimization problem, we seek to jointly optimize relevancy and curiosity, controlled by the parameter θ. Optimal θ can be tuned with a validation set. The final two constraints specify that $\mathbf{y}$ is a binary vector with K non-zero values. Recall that the anxiety turning point introduced in Section 3.4 is an item's optimal stimulation. If the item's stimulus exceeds this optimal stimulation, the user will feel anxious. In the constraints above, t_{tol} is the aggregate tolerance threshold of the K items. Here, we define $t_{tol} = c \cdot k \cdot ATP_u$, where c is a coefficient within [0,1], K is the number of items to be selected in the recommendation list. The constraint $\mathbf{SD}_u^T \cdot \mathbf{y} \le t_{tol}$ is referred to as the "*ATP* constraint". The *ATP* constraint tends to be more loose when c is close to 1 and more strict when c is close to 0.

4.2 Curiosity in Matrix Factorization

Matrix-factorization-based collaborative filtering (*MFCF*) has become popular in recent years due to its high accuracy [9]. From the psychology of interest [14], we know that curious emotion is an important component of interest. Thus, we believe a user's curiosity affects her choice of items and try to incorporate this additional signal into *MFCF*. There are several approaches for the incorporation, e.g. co-factorization, ensemble and regularization. Due to the space limit, we only apply the co-factorization-based method, which jointly predict the missing preferences and curiousness of the items. Other approaches will be left for future work. Specifically, *MFCF* maps both users and items to a latent space, denoted as $R \approx U^T V$, where $U \in \mathbb{R}^{l \times m}$ and $V \in \mathbb{R}^{l \times n}$ with $l < min(m, n)$, represent the users' and items' mapping to the latent space, respectively. In order to incorporate the curiosity information, we create a user-item curiousness matrix C with the same size as R, and each entry $c_{u,i}$ denotes u's curiousness about item i. Then, learning of latent factors is done by minimizing the

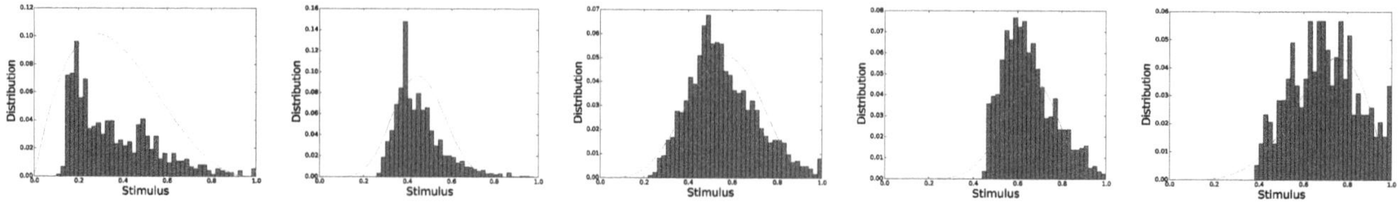

(a) User 1 (b) User 2 (c) User 3 (d) User 4 (e) User 5

Figure 4: Illustration of 5 users' stimulus degree distribution

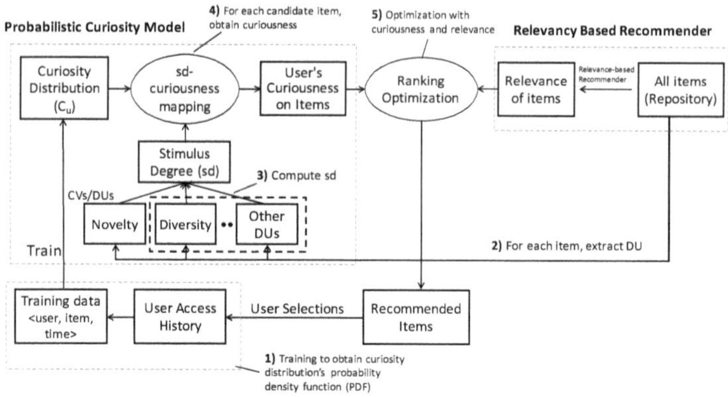

Figure 5: Illustration of CBRS framework

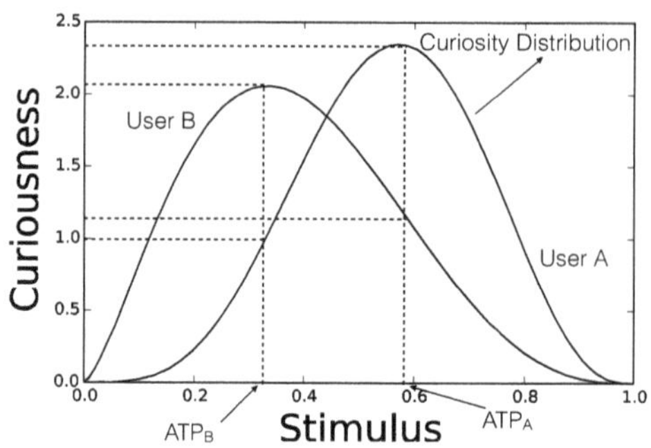

Figure 6: Illustration of two users' curiosity distribution

following sum-of-squared-errors objective functions with quadratic regularization terms:

$$\mathcal{L} = \frac{1}{2}\sum_{i=1}^{m}\sum_{j=1}^{n} I_{ij}^{R}(R_{ij} - U_i^T V_j)^2 + \frac{\lambda_C}{2}\sum_{i=1}^{m}\sum_{k=1}^{n} I_{ik}^{C}(C_{ik} - U_i^T Z_k)^2 + \frac{\lambda_U}{2}||U||_F^2 + \frac{\lambda_V}{2}||V||_F^2 + \frac{\lambda_Z}{2}||Z||_F^2, \tag{7}$$

where $\mathcal{L}$ denotes the joint loss function, I^R is the preference indicator matrix where $I_{i,j}^R = 1$ if U_i has an access on V_j in R and 0 otherwise, I_*^C is defined in the same way as the curiousness matrix C, Z denotes an item's mapping to the curiosity latent space, and $\lambda_C, \lambda_U, \lambda_V and \lambda_Z$ denote the preset coefficients. Note that this minimization task is equivalent to maximizing the log-posterior distribution over U, V, Z if Gaussian priors are assumed [11]. Since we do not have users' explicit ratings in our dataset, we use u's access frequency on i to approximate the rating $r_{i,j}$ in R. This setting is commonly used in music recommendation systems [5]. Since $C_{i,j}$ is within the range [0,1], in order to normalize R and C into the same [0,1] scale, we apply logistic function $\frac{1}{1+e^{-x}}$ to each entry of R. A local minimum of the objective function given by Eq. 7 can be found by performing gradient descent in U_i, V_j and Z_k.

$$\frac{\partial \mathcal{L}}{\partial U_i} = \sum_{j=1}^{n} I_{ij}^{R}(U_i^T V_j - R_{ij})V_j + \lambda_C \sum_{k=1}^{n} I_{ik}^{C}(U_i^T Z_k - C_{ik})Z_k + \lambda_U U_i$$

$$\frac{\partial \mathcal{L}}{\partial V_j} = \sum_{i=1}^{m} I_{ij}^{R}(U_i^T V_j - R_{ij})U_i + \lambda_V V_j$$

$$\frac{\partial \mathcal{L}}{\partial Z_k} = \lambda_C \sum_{i=1}^{m} I_{ik}^{C}(U_i^T Z_k - C_{ik})U_i + \lambda_Z Z_k \tag{8}$$

4.3 Framework

The *CBRS* framework is illustrated in Figure 5. In the training phase (Step 1), by recording a user's access history on the recommendation list, we can collect the user's responses to the stimuli (i.e., the (u, i, t) triples). The stimulus degree (sd) associated with a triple is computed as described in Section 3.3. The user's curiosity distribution is then estimated based on the selected *sd*'s. In Steps 2 and 3, for each candidate item in the item repository, we compute the *DU*s based on Equation 1.[6] In Step 4, the user's curiousness on the item is obtained by mapping the item's *sd* to the *pdf* corresponding to the user's curiosity distribution C_u. In Step 5, the recommender then integrates the user's curiousness and the relevancy (calculated by traditional accuracy-based recommendation methods) of the item by solving the optimization problem depicted in Equation 6, or formulating the co-factorization problem denoted in Equation 7. The top K items which are both relevant and with high curiousness are selected into the recommendation list.

Figure 6 shows the curiosity distributions of two users *A* and *B* to illustrate how two users with different curiosity models respond differently to the same item. According to their curiosity distributions, *A* is more curious than *B*. Now, a candidate item is recommended to both *A* and *B*, and its *sd* is high (at 0.6, denoted by ATP_A in the figure). According to the mapping, *A* will have a higher curiousness score than *B*. If the item's relevance is more or less the same to both users, the the item's high curiousness score for *A* would push the item into *A*'s recommendation but its low curiousness score for *B* may not be able to push itself into *B*'s recommendation. However, if the item has small *sd* (at 0.3, denoted by ATP_B in the figure), the situation will be reversed. *B*'s curiousness score will be higher than that of *A*, and the item will be recommended to *B* instead of *A*.

5. EXPERIMENTAL RESULTS

In this section, we first describe the dataset used in the experiment. We then apply various metrics and vary the parameters to evaluate the performances of *CBRS* and the baselines.

5.1 Dataset and Parameter Setting

We use the public dataset "Last.fm Dataset - 1K users" [1] in the experiments. The whole dataset is 2.53GB in size. It contains 19,150,868 chronologically ordered listening records of 992

[6] In this paper, only novelty is considered. Other *DU*s such as diversity and serendipity can be plugged into the framework by developing the corresponding formula to compute the *sd* of each *DU*.

Table 1: Statistics of the Dataset used in the Experiments

No. of users	937
No. of artists	83,908
No. of tracks	960,415
No. of records	16,955,328
Avg history span	762 days

unique users over several years till May 5, 2009. Each record has the format "user id, time stamp, artist id, artist name, track id, track name". The primary key is "(user id, track id, time stamp)", and we use (u, i, t) to denote the record of user u having accessed track i at time t. We remove all records without track id or artist id (every record in the dataset has a time stamp) and users with too few records for learning their curiosity distributions. The statistics of the cleaned dataset is given in Table 1.

To conduct an experiment, we need a training dataset, a historical dataset and a test dataset derived from the original dataset. The training dataset is used to learn the curiosity function for each user. The historical dataset is needed for computing the stimulation degree *sd* for each record in the training dataset, because *sd* is determined by novelty and novelty in turn depends on a user's historical accesses to the items (see below for further details). When a method is evaluated, we use the historical and training datasets to produce the recommendations and the test dataset as ground truth to evaluate the performance metrics of the recommendations.

Since the original dataset contains a large number of records, we divide it into 10 consecutive windows, $w_0, ..., w_9$, each of which contains one-tenth of the records in the dataset (denoted as $|w|$). We use three consecutive windows w_i, w_{i+1}, w_{i+2} to form, respectively, the training, historical and test datasets for one experimental run. That is, we use w_0, w_1 and w_2 in the first run, w_1, w_2 and w_3 for the second, ..., and w_7, w_8 and w_9 for the eighth run. Thus, we can perform eight experimental runs and average the results to obtain the value of a performance metric.

In the training phase, we need to compute the stimulation degree $sd^t_{u,i}$ for each (u, i, t) record in the training dataset. Given a record $r = (u, i, t)$ in the training dataset, we take the $|w|$ records preceding r as r's historical window[7] $H^t_{u,i}$, and compute r's $sd^t_{u,i}$ using Equations 1 to 5. The procedure is repeated for all records in the training dataset. At the end, each (u, i, t) record in the training dataset is associated with a $sd^t_{u,i}$ value. For each user u, we can obtain a series of sd values indicating u's accessed sd's in the training dataset and estimate u's curiosity distribution as described in Sectionrefsubsec:est.

The parameter setting in the experiments is as follows: the frequency scaling coefficients corresponding to ρ_a and ρ_i in Equation 3, and ρ_{tag} in Equation 5 are set to 0.1, the time scaling coefficient corresponding to ρ_t in Equations 4 and 5 is set to 0.01. The goal of these settings is to ensure that different novelty components ($SF^t_{u,i}$, $SR^t_{u,i}$, $sim^t_{u,i}$) are within the (0,1) scale. We set $\lambda_C, \lambda_U, \lambda_V and \lambda_Z$ in Equation 8 to 0.02. K denotes the number of items in the recommendation list, which is set to 10 by default and varied in Table 2 to study its impact on performance.

5.2 Performance Metrics

This subsection introduces the performance metrics used in the experiments.

[7]The historical window for each record r contains the same number of accessed items to avoid bias because *sd* depends on the number of accessed items in the historical window H^t_u (see Equations 3 to 5).

5.2.1 Novelty Fitness

As discussed in Section 1, a major difference between *DORS*s and *CBRS* is that *CBRS* delivers recommendations with the proper amount of novelty to suit a user's curiosity. We introduce *novelty fitness* (NF_u) to measure the fitness between the novelty of the recommended items and the user's novelty appetite nov_u (defined in Section 3.3). As defined in Equation 9, NF_u is the root-mean-square error (RMSE), where K denotes the top K recommended items and $nov_{u,i}$ denotes the novelty of the recommended item i to u. A smaller *NF* value means that the novelty of the top K recommended items has a better fit to the user's novelty appetite.

$$NF_u = \sqrt{\frac{1}{K}\sum_{i=1}^{K}(nov_{u,i} - nov_u)^2} \tag{9}$$

5.2.2 Recommendation Precision

We use precision to measure how accurate the recommendations produced by a recommendation method predict the user's future accessed items. Formally, we define precision as $\frac{1}{|U|}\sum_{u=1}^{|U|}\frac{|R_u \cap T_u|}{|R_u|}$, where U denotes the user set, R_u denotes the recommendation list for user u, T_u denotes the set of tracks that u has accessed in the test dataset (i.e., the ground truth). Note that we do not use recall as an evaluation metric, since the size of the recommendation list in Top-K recommendation is fixed.

5.2.3 Inter User Similarity

Since *CBRS* makes recommendations adapted to a user's personal curiosity, we expect its recommendations to have larger differences across users comparing to traditional *RS*s. To test the validity of this expectation, we use inter-user similarity (*IUS*) proposed in [20] to evaluate the system-wide personalization effect of a recommender. Equation 10 defines $IUS_{i,j}$ as the proportion of overlap between recommendation lists L_i and L_j received by users i and j,

$$IUS_{i,j} = \frac{|L_i \cap L_j|}{K} \tag{10}$$

The *IUS* of a *RS* is the average of $IUS_{i,j}$ over all pairs of users. A large $IUS_{i,j}$ means a high similarity between recommendation lists received by users i and j, and a large *IUS* indicates a weak personalization effect of the *RS*.

5.3 Influence of Relevancy-Curiousness Balance Weight

According to Equations 6, the selection criteria of *CBRS* is to pick the items which are both relevant and stimulative to the user's curiosity, bounded by the *ATP* constraint. The relative weight of an item's relevancy and the user's curiousness on the item is controlled by θ. A large θ promotes items with high curiousness, while a small θ favors items with high relevance. In this subsection, we investigate the effect of θ on the performance of a recommendation system in terms of the three metrics introduced in the preceding subsections. Since the optimization task for all items is very time consuming, we take the top 50 items as candidate items for each baseline recommender. Then, the top-K recommendation task is to select K items from the candidates.

To facilitate comparison, we pick two sets of recommenders, non-curiosity-aware (*non-CBRS*) and curiosity-aware (*CBRS*). For *non-CBRS*, we pick three baseline recommenders, namely, Popularity, Item-based collaborative filtering (Item-CF) and ranking ma-

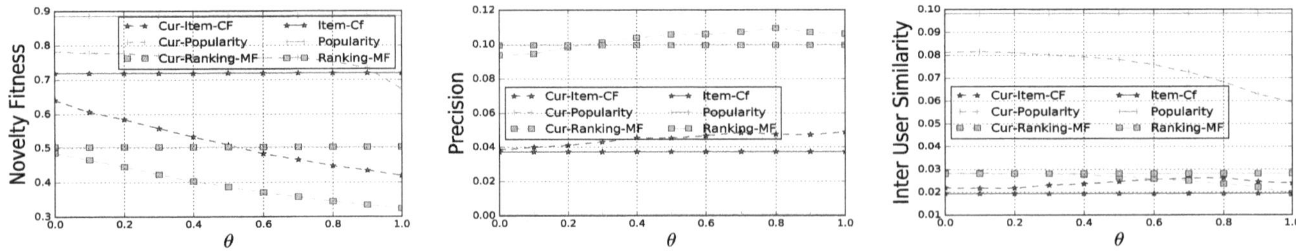

(a) Novelty Fitness, small better (b) Precision, large better (c) Inter User Similarity, small better

Figure 7: Variation of θ in joint optimization (Equation 6)

trix factorization (Ranking-MF).[8] For *CBRS*, we incorporate curiosity into the three baselines by solving the joint optimization problem in Equation 6. The *CBRS* recommenders are denoted as *Cur-Popularity*, *Cur-Item-CF* and *Cur-Ranking-MF*.

Figure 7 illustrates the influence of θ on the performance metrics. A general observation for all three metrics is that as θ becomes larger (i.e., curiousness plays a more important role in recommendation), the performance of the recommenders generally increases. In Fig. 7(a), a small *NF* means a better fit between the novelty of the recommendations and the users' novelty appetite. We can observe that *CBRS* has lower *NF* (i.e., better) than *non-CBRS*, because *non-CBRS* does not consider curiosity at all and hence cannot optimize the recommendations for novelty. This also explains why the *NF* of *non-CBRS* is flat w.r.t θ. Further, the *NF* of *CBRS* improves as θ increases, because as θ increases *CBRS* will bias towards curiosity, thus producing recommendations with better novelty fitness. Finally, for both *CBRS* and *non-CBRS*, Ranking MF is better than Item-CF, which in turn is better than Popularity in terms of *NF*. It is interesting to note that even for *non-CBRS*, which does not consider curiosity, Popularity has the worst *NF*, because popular items have less novelty.

In Fig. 7(b), we can observe the same relative performance as in Fig. 7(a), that is, Ranking-MF has higher precision than item-CF, which in turn has higher precision than Popularity for both *CBRS* and *non-CBRS*. It is interesting to note that although *CBRS* is designed to balance relevance with curiousness, its precision not only has not suffered but is better than *non-CBRS*. This can be attributed to the fact that *CBRS* optimizes novelty according to *each user*'s curiosity distribution. For example, if a user has low curiosity, *CBRS* would favor items that are less novel (i.e., more familiar) to the user. Since conservative users tend to listen to familiar tracks, precision is improved. In Fig. 7(c), a small *IUS* indicates a large difference and hence higher personalization effect between the recommendation lists received by the users. Again, Popularity (both *CBRS* and *non-CBRS*) performs the worst because it favors hot items and thus its recommendations to different users tend to be more similar. We can also see that Item-CF has the lowest *IUS* among all recommenders because it does not recommend non-novel items. Further, its *IUS* is also lower than Cur-Item-CF because the latter would consider non-novel items (which could be hot items) if the user is judged to be conservative.

From the previous experiments, we can see that optimal performance is reached when $\theta = 1.0$. This is equivalent to re-ranking the 50 candidate items purely based on the user's curiousness on the items (see Equation 6) with the *ATP* constraint. This is because the candidate items produced by the recommenders already have very high relevance so further optimizing the items' relevance has much smaller effect than re-ranking the items based on their curiousness scores. Thus, in the remainder of this paper, when we perform recommendation with the joint optimization method discussed in Section 4.1, we use $\theta = 1.0$. In summary, take the best performer *Ranking-MF* as an example, *CBRS* produces 35.6%, 6.6%, 31.3% improvement in *NF*, precision, and *IUS*, respectively, compared to *non-CBRS* when $\theta = 1.0$. It demonstrates the superior effectiveness of *CBRS*.

5.4 Comparing to DORS

From Section 2, we know that existing *DORS*s have proposed various *DU*s to complement accuracy. However, they suffer from the curiosity mismatch problem. In contrast, *CBRS* believes a user's need of novelty is non-linear and depends on her curiosity. In this section, we compare the performance of *CBRS* and *DORS*s. Figure 8 illustrates the result.

To setup the experiment, we pick the best performers *Ranking-MF* and *Cur-Ranking-MF* in Section 5.3 as baselines. Our proposed method is labeled as *Pure* and *Rel-Cur-ATP* in Figure 8, representing, respectively, pure application of *Ranking-MF* and joint optimization according to Equation 6, which considers an item's relevancy, curiousness and the *ATP* constraint. *Rel-Nov* performs joint optimization between relevancy and novelty as specified in Equation 6 without the *ATP* constraint, reflecting the implementation of traditional *DORS*s. *Rel-Nov-ATP* is the same as *Rel-Nov* except the addition of the *ATP* constraint. From the comparison between *Pure* and *Rel-Nov*, we can find that with novelty complementing relevancy, *IUS* decreases, indicating the users' recommendation lists become less similar to each other. This is an advantage of *DORS*s. However, recommendation precision is sacrificed and the recommendations deviate more from the user's real novelty appetite (i.e., novelty fitness score increases). This trade-off is a common phenomenon in many *DORS*s. From the comparison between *Rel-Nov* and *Rel-Nov-ATP*, we can observe that with the *ATP* constraint, *Rel-Nov-ATP* can retain the benefit of small *IUS* in *DORS*s without suffering from decreased precision. The novelty fitness is even better compared to *Pure*. This could be attributed to the incorporation of the *ATP* constraint, which models individual user's personalized novelty appetite. From the comparison between *Rel-Nov-ATP* and *Rel-Cur-ATP*, we can observe the importance of modeling a user's personalized non-linear novelty appetite, since novelty fitness and precision are improved about 33% and 29%, respectively at $\theta = 1.0$, while retraining the improvement of *IUS*.

5.5 Incorporate Previously Accessed Items

Most existing *RS*s aim to recommend completely novel (new)

[8]Popularity and Item-CF denote methods based on item popularity and similarity, respectively. Ranking-MF denotes the factorization machine approach [12]. An overview and implementation details of the three recommenders can be obtained from Dato Graphlab (https://dato.com/) API.

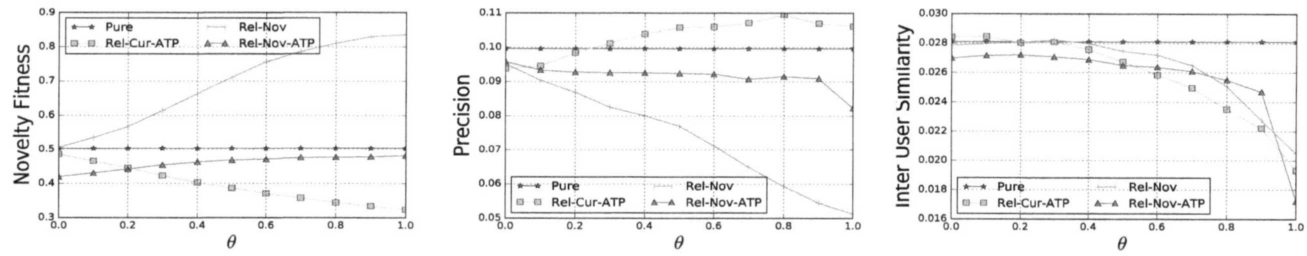

Figure 8: Compare *CBRS* to *DORS*, proving the importance of modeling user's personalized needs of novelty

items, because they assume that users will not be interested in items they have accessed before. This assumption is reasonable in some applications such as movie recommendation, but in some applications such as music listening users may repeatedly access previously accessed items. It is important to note that novelty in *CBRS* is not binary. Instead, novelty is a continuous value affected by many factors. For example, a music track that the user has listened to can still have high novelty to the user if she listened to the track or similar tracks only occasionally and a long time ago. In this subsection, we will study how the inclusion/exclusion of previously accessed items in recommendations affects performance. We use the same experiment setting as in Section 5.3, except that in addition to the 50 candidate items we randomly add N items that the user has previously accessed (*old items*). Now the recommendation problem is to pick the top K items for each user from these $N+50$ candidates. We set $K = 10$, and vary N from 2 to 20.

The result is shown in Figure 9, from which several observations can be made. First, with the additional N old items, both *non-CBRS* and *CBRS* have improved performance in all of the three performance metrics. This can be attributed to the users' habit of listening to their favorite songs frequently, and adding old items in the recommendations will capture this user behavior. Second, although the performance of both *non-CBRS* and *CBRS* is improved, *CBRS* produces much larger improvement than *non-CBRS*. For example, compared with *Ranking-MF*, the best performer *Cur-Ranking-MF* achieves 85.5%, 166.7%, and 77.9% improvement on *NF*, precision, and *IUS*, respectively, when $N = 20$. This is attributed to *CBRS*'s ability to capture a user's unique novelty appetite. That is, if a user likes to listen to old songs, *CBRS* will model her as a conservative listener and recommend old songs to her and the contrary is also true. Thus, *CBRS* can better utilize the N old items to satisfy the user's preference on old songs. This is a significant contribution of this paper since very few works, if any, have discussed the importance of non-novel items to the users and how to incorporate them into a recommendation list. Third, even when $N = 0$, i.e., only new items are recommended, *CBRS* still outperforms *non-CBRS* even though the improvement is not as much as when old items are included. This can be attributed to the fact that new items still have different degrees of novelty to the user because of their properties (e.g. a new track may have low novelty to a user when the user is familiar with the genre or performer of the track). Finally, with N becomes larger, the performance difference among the *CBRS* recommenders narrows down. As discussed, users would listen to their favorite tracks repeatedly. Thus, as N increases, *CBRS* recommenders would recommend more from the N old items. This would greatly improve their performance and thus narrow down their performance gap. This is indeed an advantage of *CBRS*, since curiosity can be incorporated into any specific recommender to make it curiosity-aware and improve its performance.

5.6 Overall Performance Comparison

From Sections 5.3 to 5.5, all recommendations are based on Equation 6, which performs joint optimization between relevancy and curiousness. In this subsection, we will compare *CBRS* to other state-of-the-art *PDORS* methods. As introduced in Section 2, the only two works on *PDORS* are [17] and [7]. We choose the *PPBRS* method proposed in [7] as the baseline, because it is more recent and closer to our work. *PPBRS* learns a personalized novelty preference score for each user by logistic regression. For comparison, we use *Ranking-MF* as the reference recommender, instead of the Item-based collaborative filtering in [7]. We also choose the standalone *Ranking-MF* as another baseline, because it performs best among the traditional accuracy-based recommenders (shown in Figure 7) and does not consider curiosity. As introduced in Sections 4.1 and 4.2, we propose two ways to incorporate curiosity information into an *RS*. Thus, our proposed *CBRS* methods are Cur-Ranking-MF and Cur-MFCF, corresponding to Equations 6 and 7, respectively. The results are shown in Table 2.

Comparing the two baselines *PPBRS* and *Ranking-MF*, we can see that although *PPBRS* can provide more personalized novelty to the users (small *NF* score), it is limited in enhancing precision. This is because although *PPBRS* learns a personalized "relevancy-novelty" balance parameter, it applies the parameter to *all items* in the same way. That is, if the parameter favors novelty, then all items' novelty scores will be emphasized in the same way. This may result in some recommended items overly novel to the user because they may already have high novelty scores and amplifying them further will make them too novel for the user's curiosity level. For the same reason, some recommended items could become too boring to the user. Comparing *PPBRS* and *CBRS* (*Cur-Ranking-MF* and *Cur-MFCF*), we can see that *CBRS* performs better in both novelty fitness and precision (e.g. *Cur-Ranking-MF* achieves 32.1%, 7.8%, 18.8% improvement over *PPBRS* on *NF*, precision, *IUS*, respectively, when $K = 10$) because it is able to capture a user's non-linear novelty appetite. Between the two *CBRS* recommenders, *Cur-Ranking-MF* performs better than *Cur-MFCF*. This might be attributed to the ability of explicit joint optimization to combine an item's relevancy and the user's novelty appetite more optimally. Detailed study on how to better incorporate the curiosity signal into the traditional recommendation framework is beyond the scope of this paper and will be treated in future work.

6. CONCLUSION

Various Discovery-Oriented Recommendation Systems (*DORS*s) have been proposed to address the accuracy overloading problem of traditional recommendation systems. They introduce Discovery Utilities (*DU*s) such as novelty, diversity and serendipity as additional ranking dimensions to ensure that recommendations are not dominated by accuracy. However, *DORS*s do not consider the fact that different users have different appetite for *DU*s and suffer

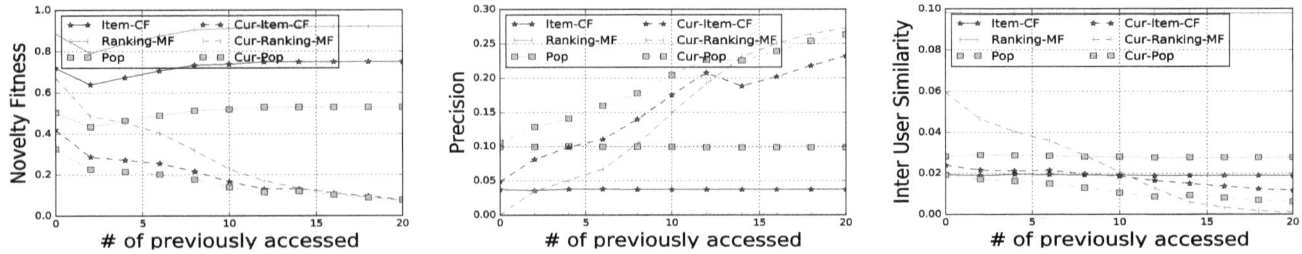

Figure 9: Performance when previously accessed items are included

Table 2: Performance comparison between *CBRS* and *PPBRS*

Model	NF			Precision			IUS		
	k=5	k=10	k=20	k=5	k=10	k=20	k=5	k=10	k=20
Ranking-MF	0.455	0.503	0.463	0.105	0.0973	0.0857	0.0220	0.0281	0.0392
PPBRS	0.417	0.477	0.449	0.0995	0.0983	0.0961	0.0209	0.0238	0.0262
Cur-MFCF	0.324	0.368	0.361	0.112	0.106	0.101	0.0195	0.0208	0.0223
Cur-Ranking-MF	0.278	0.324	0.268	0.120	0.106	0.113	0.0170	0.0193	0.0244

from the curiosity mismatch problem. In this paper, we present the Curiosity-based Recommendation System (*CBRS*) framework for integrating the curiosity and relevance aspects of recommendations. The Probabilistic Curiosity Model (*PCM*) models a user's unique appetite for novelty. *PCM* is formulated based on the curiosity arousal theory and Wundt curve in psychology [4]. It uses the Beta Distribution to model Wundt curve representing a user's non-linear desire of novelty. With *PCM*, for each user we can obtain a curiousness score for each candidate item. Joint optimization and matrix factorization methods are used to incorporate the curiosity signal into *RS*s. Experimental results show that *CBRS* significantly outperforms the baselines in various performance metrics. An important finding is that *CBRS* can provide personalized recommendations adapted to an individual user's curiosity and at the same time improve the recommendation accuracy. We also study the impact of allowing previously access items (i.e., non-novel items) in the recommendations and show that *CBRS* can recommend the right mix of non-novel and novel items to optimize the performance. This is an important finding because in many applications (e.g., music recommendation) users may repeatedly access some items (e.g., favorite songs).

For future work, we plan to study other *DU*s such as diversity and surprisal and integrate curiosity and social relationship into the *CBRS* framework. Finally, we recognize the mutual benefit between our work and psychology research and plan to apply web-scale data in the study of human's psychological curiosity behavior.

Acknowledgement

Research reported in this paper was supported by the Research Grants Council, HKSAR, GRF No. 615113.

7. REFERENCES

[1] Lastfm homepage, 2015.

[2] A. Anglade, O. Celma, B. Fields, P. Lamere, and B. McFee. Womrad: 2nd workshop on music recommendation and discovery. 2011.

[3] I. Avazpour, T. Pitakrat, L. Grunske, and J. Grundy. Dimensions and metrics for evaluating recommendation systems. Springer Berlin Heidelberg, 2014.

[4] D. Berlyne. *Conflict, Arousal and Curiosity*. McGraw-Hill, 1960.

[5] E. Bernhardsson. Collaborative filtering at spotify, 2013.

[6] W. Fan, M. D. Gordon, and P. Pathak. Personalization of search engine services for effective retrieval and knowledge management. ICIS '00.

[7] K. Kapoor, J. A. Kumar, and P. Schrater. "i like to explore sometimes": Adapting to dynamic user novelty preferences. RecSys '15.

[8] P. Knees and M. Schedl. Music retrieval and recommendation: A tutorial overview. SIGIR '15.

[9] Y. Koren, R. Bell, and C. Volinsky. Matrix factorization techniques for recommender systems. *Computer*, 2009.

[10] X. Li and W. B. Croft. Time-based language models. CIKM '03.

[11] H. Ma, Yang, and I. King. Sorec: Social recommendation using probabilistic matrix factorization. CIKM '08.

[12] S. Rendle. Factorization machines. ICDM '10.

[13] G. Shani and A. Gunawardana. Evaluating recommendation systems. *Recommender Systems Handbook*, 2011.

[14] P. J. Silvia. Interest the curious emotion. *Current Directions in Psychological Science*, 2008.

[15] P. Vargas, Castells. Rank and relevance in novelty and diversity metrics for recommender systems. RecSys '11.

[16] S. Vargas. Novelty and diversity enhancement and evaluation in recommender systems and information retrieval. SIGIR '14.

[17] F. Zhang, K. Zheng, Yuan, and X. Zhou. A novelty-seeking based dining recommender system. WWW '15.

[18] M. Zhang and N. Hurley. Avoiding monotony: Improving the diversity of recommendation lists. RecSys '08.

[19] Y. C. Zhang and T. Jambor. Auralist: Introducing serendipity into music recommendation. WSDM '12.

[20] Y. Zhou, T.and Zhang. Solving the apparent diversity-accuracy dilemma of recommender systems. *Proceedings of the National Academy of Sciences*, 2010.

[21] C.-N. Ziegler and G. Lausen. Improving recommendation lists through topic diversification. WWW '05.

Discrete Collaborative Filtering

Hanwang Zhang[1] Fumin Shen[2] Wei Liu[3] Xiangnan He[1] Huanbo Luan[4] Tat-Seng Chua[1]
[1]School of Computing, National University of Singapore
[2]School of Computer Science and Engineering, University of Electronic Science and Technology of China
[3]Didi Research, [4]Department of Computer Science & Technology, Tsinghua University
{hanwangzhang,fumin.shen,xiangnanhe,luanhuanbo}@gmail.com; wliu@ee.columbia.edu; dcscts@nus.edu.sg

ABSTRACT

We address the efficiency problem of Collaborative Filtering (CF) by hashing users and items as latent vectors in the form of binary codes, so that user-item affinity can be efficiently calculated in a Hamming space. However, existing hashing methods for CF employ binary code learning procedures that most suffer from the challenging discrete constraints. Hence, those methods generally adopt a two-stage learning scheme composed of relaxed optimization via discarding the discrete constraints, followed by binary quantization. We argue that such a scheme will result in a large quantization loss, which especially compromises the performance of large-scale CF that resorts to longer binary codes. In this paper, we propose a principled CF hashing framework called Discrete Collaborative Filtering (DCF), which directly tackles the challenging discrete optimization that should have been treated adequately in hashing. The formulation of DCF has two advantages: 1) the Hamming similarity induced loss that preserves the intrinsic user-item similarity, and 2) the balanced and uncorrelated code constraints that yield compact yet informative binary codes. We devise a computationally efficient algorithm with a rigorous convergence proof of DCF. Through extensive experiments on several real-world benchmarks, we show that DCF consistently outperforms state-of-the-art CF hashing techniques, *e.g.*, though using only 8 bits, DCF is even significantly better than other methods using 128 bits.

Keywords

Recommendation; Discrete Hashing; Collaborative Filtering

1. INTRODUCTION

Over the past decades, we have witnessed continued efforts in increasing the accuracy and efficiency of Recommender Systems, which have been widely known as one of the key technologies for the thrift of Web services like Facebook, Amazon and Flickr. However, their ever-growing scales make today's recommendations even more challenging. Taking a typical Flickr user as an example, a practical recommender system should quickly prompt to recommend photos in a billion-scale collection by exploring extremely sparse user history; and, there are millions of such users[1]!

Collaborative Filtering (CF), more specifically, latent factor based CF (*e.g.*, matrix factorization), has been demonstrated to achieve a successful balance between accuracy and efficiency in real-world recommender systems [4, 16, 1]. Such CF methods factorize an $m \times n$ user-item rating matrix of m users and n items into an r-d low-dimensional latent vector (*a.k.a.* feature) space. Then the predictions for user-item ratings can be efficiently estimated by inner products between the corresponding user and item vectors. In this way, recommendation by CF naturally falls into a similarity search problem—top-K item recommendation for a user can be cast into finding the top-K similar items queried by the user [30, 3, 12]. When m or n is large, storing user (or item) vectors of the size $\mathcal{O}(mr)$ (or $\mathcal{O}(nr)$) and similarity search of the complexity $\mathcal{O}(n)$ will be a critical efficiency bottleneck, which has not been well addressed in recent progress on recommender efficiency [23].

Fortunately, hashing has been widely shown as a promising approach to tackle fast similarity search [29]. First, by encoding real-valued data vectors into compact binary codes, hashing makes efficient in-memory storage of massive data feasible. Second, as similarity calculation by inner product in a vector space is replaced by bit operations in a proper Hamming space, the time complexity of linear scan is significantly reduced and even constant time search is made possible by exploiting lookup tables [28, 31]. Recently, several works have brought the advance of hashing into collaborative filtering for better recommendation efficiency [18, 33, 32]. However, those works essentially divide the hashing into two independent stages: real-valued optimization and binary quantization. More specifically, due to the discrete constraints imposed on the corresponding binary code learning procedure which is generally NP-hard [11], they resort to simply solving relaxed optimization problems by discarding the discrete constraints and then rounding off [32] or rotating [18, 33] the obtained continuous solutions to target binary codes. We argue that these "two-stage" approaches oversimplify original discrete optimization, resulting in a large quantization loss. Here, we refer to "quantization loss"

[1]https://www.flickr.com/photos/franckmichel/6855169886

SIGIR '16, July 17-21, 2016, Pisa, Italy
© 2016 ACM. ISBN 978-1-4503-4069-4/16/07... $15.00
DOI: http://dx.doi.org/10.1145/2911451.2911502

as the accumulated deviations of the binary bits originating from thresholding real values to integers; unsurprisingly, large deviations will violate the original data geometry in the continuous vector space (*e.g.*, intrinsic user-item relations). As we can foresee, in real-world large-scale applications which require longer codes for accuracy, such accumulated errors will inevitably deteriorate the recommendation performance.

In this paper, we propose a principled approach for efficient collaborative filtering, dubbed Discrete Collaborative Filtering (DCF), which has not been addressed yet. As illustrated in Figure 1, instead of choosing an erroneous two-stage approach, we directly tackle the challenging discrete optimization that should have been treated adequately in hashing. Our formulation is directly based on the loss function of traditional CF, where the user/item features are replaced by binary codes and the user-item inner product is replaced by Hamming similarity (cf. Eq. (2)). By doing so, the proposed DCF explicitly optimizes the binary codes that fit the intrinsic user-item similarities and hence the quantization error is expected to be smaller than those of two-stage approaches. Besides, we explicitly impose the balanced and uncorrelated bits on the codes. Though these two constraints make DCF even more challenging, they are crucial for achieving compact yet informative codes [31]. To tackle the discrete optimization of DCF in a computationally tractable manner, we develop an alternating optimization algorithm which consists of iteratively solving mixed-integer programming subproblems. In particular, we provide efficient solutions that require fast bit-wise updates and eigen–decompositions for small matrices, and therefore they can easily scale up to large-scale recommendations. We evaluate the proposed DCF on three real-world datasets in various million-scale applications including movies, books and business recommendations.

Our contributions are summarized as follows:

- We propose an efficient CF approach called Discrete Collaborative Filtering (DCF). To the best of our knowledge, DCF is the first principled framework that directly learns user-item binary codes via discrete optimization.

- We develop an efficient algorithm for solving DCF. The convergence of our algorithm is rigorously guaranteed.

- Through extensive experiments performed on three real-world datasets, we show that DCF consistently surpasses several state-of-the-art CF hashing techniques.

2. RELATED WORK

We first review efficient Collaborative Filtering (CF) algorithms using latent factor models, and then discuss recent advance in discrete hashing techniques. For comprehensive reviews of CF and hashing, please refer to [5] and [29], respectively.

2.1 Efficient Collaborative Filtering

One line of research towards efficient CF includes designing scalable online methods such as preference ranking [10], matrix factorization [20], and regression [2]. In particular, our out-of-sample hashing scheme for new users/items (cf. Section. 4.2) follows a similar spirit of [25, 8], which projects new samples onto a learned factor space. However, these

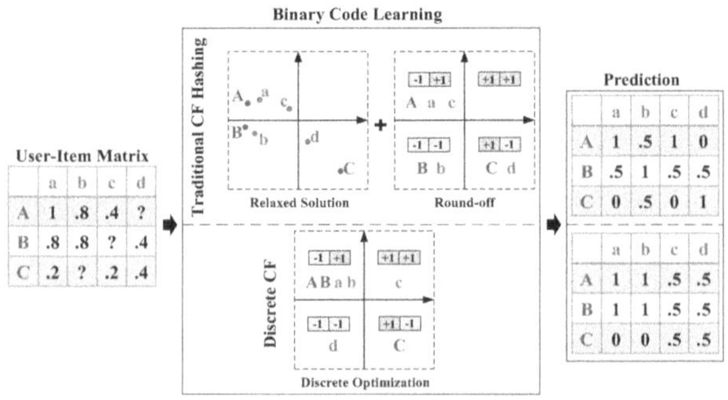

Figure 1: Illustration of the key difference between existing hashing methods for CF (top) and our proposed DCF (bottom). DCF directly learns binary codes that preserve the user-item similarity discovered from the user-item matrix (with missing entries denoted as "?"); while traditional methods first relax the discrete problem and then round-off the real-valued results to binary codes. As can be seen, such a rounding-off quantization step causes errors when two points are quite close but assigned to different bits (*e.g.*, A and B); while two points are quite far away but assigned to the same bits (*e.g.*, C and d). However, DCF can preserve the intrinsic user-item geometry, so it predicts user-item ratings (normalized Hamming similarity, cf. Eq. (2)) with a lower error, *e.g.*, the squared loss of DCF is only half of those of traditional methods.

works neglect that CF is essentially a similarity search problem, where even linear time complexity is prohibitive for large-scale recommendation tasks. Therefore, another line of research focuses on encoding users and items into binary codes, *e.g.*, hashing for the purpose of significant efficiency. As a pioneering work, Das *et al.* [6] used Locality-Sensitive Hashing (LSH) [7] to generate hash codes of Google news users based on an item-sharing similarity. Karatzoglou *et al.* [14] learned user-item features with traditional CF and then randomly projected the features to acquire hash codes. Similarly, Zhou and Zha [33] rotated their learned features by running ITQ [9] to generate hash codes. Liu *et al.* [18] imposed the uncorrelated bit constraints on the traditional CF objective for learning user-item features and then rounded them to produce hash codes. Zhang *et al.* [32] argued that inner product is not a proper similarity, which is nevertheless the fundamental assumption about hashing, so subsequent hashing may harm the accuracy of preference predictions. To this end, they proposed to regularize the user/item features to compute their cosine similarities, and then quantized them by respectively thresholding their magnitudes and phases.

One can easily sum up that the aforementioned hashing techniques for CF are essentially "two-stage" approaches, where hash codes for users and items are obtained through two independent steps: relaxed user-item feature learning and binary quantization (cf. Figure 1). As we will review next, such a two-stage relaxation is well-known to suffer from a large quantization loss, which is the main challenge we tackle in this paper.

2.2 Discrete Hashing

In order to reduce quantization errors caused by the oversimplifying rounding-off step, discrete hashing—direct bi-

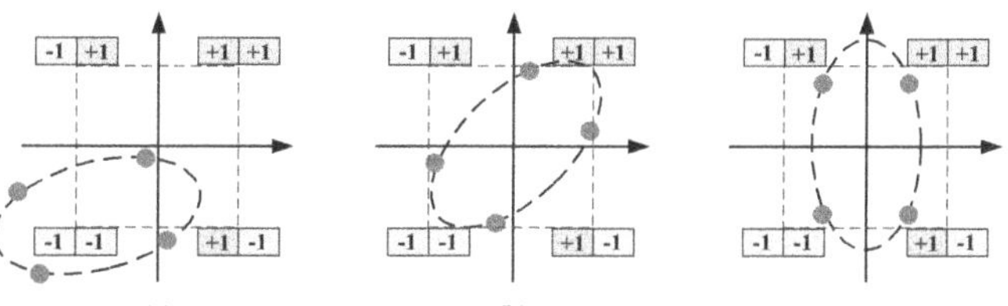

Figure 2: Illustration of the effectiveness of the balance and decorrelation constraints in DCF. The ellipse represents an intrinsic user-item relation manifold and the red dots denote four distinct real-valued user/item vectors that should be separated in Hamming space. (a) Three points are encoded as $(-1,-1)$ and the other one as $(-1,+1)$, which are not discriminative. However, after (b) balancing and (c) decorrelation, the codes are optimized to preserve the user-item relations.

nary code learning by discrete optimization—is becoming popular recently. The most widely used discrete hashing technique is perhaps Iterative Quantization (ITQ) [9], which minimizes the quantization loss by alternatively learning the binary codes and hash functions. However, it has two drawbacks. First, ITQ requires the hash functions to use orthogonal projections, which is not a generic assumption; second, ITQ can also be considered as a two-stage approach since it first learns relaxed solutions and then treats quantization as an independent post-processing, which does not necessarily capture the intrinsic data geometry. Thus, ITQ is suboptimal. Latest improvements on joint optimizations of quantization losses and intrinsic objective functions can be found in Discrete Graph Hashing [17] and Supervised Discrete Hashing [26], which demonstrate significant performance gain over the above two-stage hashing methods. Our work is also an advocate of such a joint discrete optimization but focused on CF which is fundamentally different from the above objectives. To the best of our knowledge, DCF is a research gap that we fill in this paper; and due to the generic matrix factorization formulations in CF, we believe that DCF will have a high potential in plenty of machine learning and information retrieval tasks other than recommendations [18].

3. PROBLEM FORMULATION

3.1 Preliminaries

We use bold uppercase and lowercase letters as matrices and vectors, respectively; In particular, we use $\mathbf{a}_i$ as the i-th row vector of matrix $\mathbf{A}$, A_{ij} as the entry at the i-th row and j-th column of $\mathbf{A}$; alternatively, we rewrite A_{ij} as a_{ij} to highlight the j-th entry of vector $\mathbf{a}_i$. We denote $\|\cdot\|_F$ as the Frobenius norm of a matrix and $\mathrm{tr}(\cdot)$ as the matrix trace. We denote $\mathrm{sgn}(\cdot): \mathbb{R} \rightarrow \{\pm 1\}$ as the round-off function.

We focus on discussing matrix factorization CF models, which has been successfully applied in many recommender systems [16]. CF generally maps both users and items to a joint low-dimensional latent space where the user-item similarity (or preference) is estimated by vector inner product. Formally, suppose $\mathbf{u}_i \in \mathbb{R}^r$ is the i-th user vector and $\mathbf{v}_j \in \mathbb{R}^r$ is the j-th item vector, the rating of user i for item j is approximated by $\mathbf{u}_i^T\mathbf{v}_j$. Thus, the goal is to learn user vectors $\mathbf{U} = [\mathbf{u}_1, ..., \mathbf{u}_m] \in \mathbb{R}^{r\times m}$ and item vectors $\mathbf{V} = [\mathbf{v}_1, ..., \mathbf{v}_n] \in \mathbb{R}^{r\times n}$, where $r \ll \min(m, n)$ is the feature dimension, and $\mathbf{U}^T\mathbf{V}$ is expected to reconstruct the observed ratings as well as predict the unobserved ones. The objective is to minimize the following regularized squared loss on observed ratings:

$$\underset{\mathbf{U},\mathbf{V}}{\mathrm{argmin}} \sum_{i,j\in\mathcal{V}} (S_{ij} - \mathbf{u}_i^T\mathbf{v}_j)^2 + \alpha\|\mathbf{U}\|_F^2 + \beta\|\mathbf{V}\|_F^2, \tag{1}$$

where S_{ij} is the observed rating, whose index set is $\mathcal{V}$. Since the number of observed ratings is sparse, we should properly regularize $\mathbf{U}$ and $\mathbf{V}$ by $\alpha, \beta > 0$ in order to prevent from overfitting. After we obtain the optimized user and item vectors, recommendation is then reduced to a similarity search problem. For example, given a "query" user $\mathbf{u}_i$, we recommend items by ranking the predicted ratings $\mathbf{V}^T\mathbf{u}_i \in \mathbb{R}^n$; when n is large, such similarity search scheme is apparently an efficiency bottleneck for practical recommender systems [33, 32].

To this end, we are interested in hashing users and items into binary codes for efficient recommendation since the user-item similarity search can be efficiently conducted in Hamming space. Denote $\mathbf{B} = [\mathbf{b}_1, ..., \mathbf{b}_m] \in \{\pm1\}^{r\times m}$ and $\mathbf{D} = [\mathbf{d}_1, ..., \mathbf{d}_n] \in \{\pm1\}^{r\times n}$ respectively as r-length user and item binary codes, the Hamming similarity between $\mathbf{b}_i$ and $\mathbf{d}_j$ is defined as [33]:

$$\begin{aligned} \mathrm{sim}(i,j) &= \frac{1}{r}\sum_{k=1}^{r}\mathbb{I}(b_{ik} = d_{jk}) \\ &= \frac{1}{2r}\left(\sum_{k=1}^{r}\mathbb{I}(b_{ik} = d_{jk}) + r - \sum_{k=1}^{r}\mathbb{I}(b_{ik} \neq d_{jk})\right) \\ &= \frac{1}{2r}\left(r + \sum_{k=1}^{r} b_{ik}d_{jk}\right) = \frac{1}{2} + \frac{1}{2r}\mathbf{b}_i^T\mathbf{d}_j \end{aligned} \tag{2}$$

where $\mathbb{I}(\cdot)$ denotes the indicator function that returns 1 if the statement is true and 0 otherwise. We can easily verify that $sim(i,j) = 0$ if all the bits of $\mathbf{b}_i$ and $\mathbf{d}_j$ are different and $sim(i,j) = 1$ if $\mathbf{b}_i = \mathbf{d}_j$.

Similar to the problem of conventional CF in Eq. (1), the above similarity score should reconstruct the observed user-item ratings. Therefore, the problem of the proposed Discrete Collaborative Filtering (DCF) is formulated as:

$$\begin{aligned} &\underset{\mathbf{B},\mathbf{D}}{\mathrm{argmin}} \sum_{i,j\in\mathcal{V}} \left(S_{ij} - \mathbf{b}_i^T\mathbf{d}_j\right)^2, \\ &s.t.\ \mathbf{B} \in \{\pm1\}^{r\times m}, \mathbf{D} \in \{\pm1\}^{r\times n} \\ &\underbrace{\mathbf{B}\mathbf{1} = 0, \mathbf{D}\mathbf{1} = 0}_{\text{Balanced Partition}},\ \underbrace{\mathbf{B}\mathbf{B}^T = m\mathbf{I}, \mathbf{D}\mathbf{D}^T = n\mathbf{I}}_{\text{Decorrelation}}. \end{aligned} \tag{3}$$

where we slightly abuse the notation S_{ij} as a scaled score in $[-r, r]$ as $\mathbf{b}_i^T\mathbf{d}_j \in \{-r, -r+2, ..., r-2, r\}$[2]. Due to the binary constraints in DCF, the regularization $\|\mathbf{B}\|_F^2 + \|\mathbf{D}\|_F^2$ as in Eq. (1) is constant and hence is canceled; however, DCF imposes two additional constraints on the binary codes in order to maximize the information encoded in short code length [31]. First, we require that each bit to split the dataset as balanced as possible. This will maximize the information entropy of the bit. Second, each bit should be as independent as possible, *i.e.*, the bits are uncorrelated and the variance is maximized. This removes the redundancy among the bits. Figure 2 illustrates how binary code learning benefits from the two constraints. Note that other latent

[2]Suppose the original $S_{ij} \in [0, 1]$, then we scale $S_{ij} \leftarrow 2rS_{ij} - r$.

models with various objective functions such as ranking [24] and regression [2] can be applied in this work with simple algebraic operations.

3.2 Learning Model

It is worth noting that the proposed DCF in Eq. (3) has two key advantages over related work [33, 32]. First, we strictly enforce the binary constraint while theirs relax discrete binary codes to continuous real values. Thus, DCF is expected to minimize the quantization loss during learning. Second, we require the binary codes to be balanced and uncorrelated. Therefore, DCF hashes users and items in a more informative and compact way. However, solving DCF in Eq. (3) is a challenging task since it is generally NP-hard that involves $\mathcal{O}(2^{(m+n)r})$ combinatorial search for the binary codes [11]. Next, we introduce a learning model that can solve DCF in a computationally tractable manner. We propose to solve DCF in Eq. (3) by softening the balance and decorrelation constraints, since strictly imposing them may cause the original DCF infeasible. Let us define two sets: $\mathcal{B} = \{\mathbf{X} \in \mathbb{R}^{r\times m} | \mathbf{X1} = 0, \mathbf{XX}^T = m\mathbf{I}\}$, $\mathcal{D} = \{\mathbf{Y} \in \mathbb{R}^{r\times n} | \mathbf{Y1} = 0, \mathbf{YY}^T = n\mathbf{I}\}$ and distances $d(\mathbf{B}, \mathcal{B}) = \min_{\mathbf{X}\in\mathcal{B}} \|\mathbf{B}-\mathbf{X}\|_F$, $d(\mathbf{D}, \mathcal{D}) = \min_{\mathbf{Y}\in\mathcal{D}} \|\mathbf{D}-\mathbf{Y}\|_F$. Therefore, we can soften the original DCF in Eq. (3) as:

$$\begin{aligned}&\underset{\mathbf{B},\mathbf{D}}{\text{argmin}} \sum_{i,j\in\mathcal{V}} \left(S_{ij} - \mathbf{b}_i^T\mathbf{d}_j\right)^2 + \alpha d^2(\mathbf{B}, \mathcal{B}) + \beta d^2(\mathbf{D}, \mathcal{D})\\ &s.t., \ \mathbf{B} \in \{\pm 1\}^{r\times m}, \mathbf{D} \in \{\pm 1\}^{r\times n}\end{aligned} \tag{4}$$

where $\alpha > 0$ and $\beta > 0$ are tuning parameters. The above Eq (4) allows a certain discrepancy between the binary codes (*e.g.*, $\mathbf{B}$) and delegate continuous values (*e.g.*, $\mathbf{X}$), to make the constraints computationally tractable. Note that if the constraints in Eq. (3) is feasible, we can enforce the distances $d(\mathbf{B}, \mathcal{B}) = d(\mathbf{D}, \mathcal{D}) = 0$ in Eq. (4) by imposing very large tuning parameters.

By noting the decorrelation constraints imposed on $\mathbf{B}$, $\mathbf{D}$, $\mathbf{X}$ and $\mathbf{Y}$, Eq. (4) is equivalent to:

$$\begin{aligned}&\underset{\mathbf{B},\mathbf{D},\mathbf{X},\mathbf{Y}}{\text{argmin}} \sum_{i,j\in\mathcal{V}} \left(S_{ij} - \mathbf{b}_i^T\mathbf{d}_j\right)^2 - 2\alpha tr(\mathbf{B}^T\mathbf{X}) - 2\beta tr(\mathbf{D}^T\mathbf{Y})\\ &s.t., \mathbf{X1} = 0, \mathbf{XX}^T = m\mathbf{I}, \mathbf{Y1} = 0, \mathbf{YY}^T = n\mathbf{I},\\ &\quad \mathbf{B} \in \{\pm 1\}^{r\times m}, \mathbf{D} \in \{\pm 1\}^{r\times n},\end{aligned} \tag{5}$$

which is the proposed learning model for DCF. It is worth noting that we do not discard the binary constraint $\mathbf{B} \in \{\pm 1\}^{r\times m}, \mathbf{D} \in \{\pm 1\}^{r\times n}$ and directly optimize discrete $\mathbf{B}$ and $\mathbf{D}$. Through joint optimization for the binary codes and the delegate real variables, we can obtain nearly balanced and uncorrelated hashing codes for users and items. Next, we will introduce an efficient solution for the mixed-integer optimization problem in Eq. (5).

4. SOLUTION

We alternatively solving four subproblems for DCF model in Eq. (5): $\mathbf{B}$, $\mathbf{D}$, $\mathbf{X}$ and $\mathbf{Y}$. In particular, we show that 1) $\mathbf{B}$ and $\mathbf{D}$ can be efficiently updated by parallel discrete optimization; and 2) $\mathbf{X}$ and $\mathbf{Y}$ can be efficiently updated by small-scale Singular Value Decomposition (SVD).

4.1 Alternating Optimization

It is worth highlighting that the following $\mathbf{B}/\mathbf{D}$-subproblem seeks binary latent features that preserves the intrinsic user-item relations due to the observed loss in Eq. (5); while $\mathbf{X}/\mathbf{Y}$-subproblem attempts to regularize the learned binary codes should be as balanced and uncorrelated as possible.

B-subproblem. In this subproblem, we update $\mathbf{B}$ with fixed $\mathbf{D}$, $\mathbf{X}$ and $\mathbf{Y}$. Since the objective function in Eq. (5) is based on summing over independent users, we can update $\mathbf{B}$ by updating $\mathbf{b}_i$ in parallel according to

$$\underset{\mathbf{b}_i\in\{\pm 1\}^r}{\text{argmin}} \ \mathbf{b}_i^T(\sum_{j\in\mathcal{V}_i} \mathbf{d}_j\mathbf{d}_j^T)\mathbf{b}_i - 2(\sum_{j\in\mathcal{V}_i} S_{ij}\mathbf{d}_j^T)\mathbf{b}_i - 2\alpha\mathbf{x}_i^T\mathbf{b}_i, \tag{6}$$

where $\mathcal{V}_i$ is the observed rating set for user i.

Due to the binary constraints, the above minimization is generally NP-hard, we propose to use Discrete Coordinate Descent (DCD) to update binary codes $\mathbf{b}_i$ *bit by bit* [26]. Denote b_{ik} as the k-th bit of $\mathbf{b}_i$ and $\mathbf{b}_{i\bar{k}}$ as the rest codes excluding b_{ik}, DCD will update b_{ik} while fixing $\mathbf{b}_{i\bar{k}}$. Thus, the DCD update rule for user binary codes $\mathbf{b}_i$ can be derived as:

$$b_{ik} \leftarrow \text{sgn}\left(K(\hat{b}_{ik}, b_{ik})\right), \tag{7}$$

where $\hat{b}_{ik} = \sum_{j\in\mathcal{V}_i}\left(S_{ij} - \mathbf{d}_{j\bar{k}}^T\mathbf{b}_{i\bar{k}}\right) d_{jk} + \alpha x_{ik}$.[3], $\mathbf{d}_{j\bar{k}}^T$ is the rest set of item codes excluding d_{jk}, and $K(x, y)$ is a function that $K(x, y) = x$ if $x \neq 0$ and $K(x, y) = y$ otherwise, *i.e.*, when $\hat{b}_{ik} = 0$, we do not update b_{ik}. In this way, $\mathbf{b}_i$ is iteratively updated bit by bit in several passes until convergence (*e.g.*, no more flips of bits). Detailed derivation of Eq. (7) is given in Appendix.

D-subproblem. In this subproblem, we update $\mathbf{D}$ with fixed $\mathbf{B}$, $\mathbf{X}$ and $\mathbf{Y}$. Similar to the B-subproblem, we can update $\mathbf{D}$ by updating $\mathbf{d}_i$ in parallel according to

$$\underset{\mathbf{d}_j\in\{\pm 1\}^r}{\text{argmin}} \ \mathbf{d}_j^T(\sum_{i\in\mathcal{V}_j} \mathbf{b}_i\mathbf{b}_i^T)\mathbf{d}_j - 2(\sum_{i\in\mathcal{V}_j} S_{ij}\mathbf{b}_i^T)\mathbf{d}_j - 2\beta\mathbf{y}_j^T\mathbf{d}_j. \tag{8}$$

where $\mathcal{V}_j$ is the observed rating set for item j. Denote d_{jk} as the k-th bit of $\mathbf{d}_j$ and $\mathbf{d}_{j\bar{k}}$ as the rest codes excluding d_{jk}, the DCD update for d_{jk} is given as:

$$d_{jk} \leftarrow \text{sgn}\left(K(\hat{d}_{jk}, d_{jk})\right), \tag{9}$$

where $\hat{d}_{jk} = \sum_{i\in\mathcal{V}_j}\left(S_{ij} - \mathbf{b}_{i\bar{k}}^T\mathbf{d}_{j\bar{k}}\right) b_{ik} + \beta y_{jk}$.

X-subproblem. When $\mathbf{B}$, $\mathbf{D}$ and $\mathbf{Y}$ are fixed in Eq. (6), the $\mathbf{X}$-subproblem is:

$$\underset{\mathbf{X}}{\text{argmax}} \ tr(\mathbf{B}^T\mathbf{X}), s.t. \ \mathbf{X1} = 0, \mathbf{XX}^T = m\mathbf{I} \tag{10}$$

It can be solved with the aid of SVD. Denote $\overline{\mathbf{B}}$ is a row-wise zero-mean matrix, where $\overline{B}_{ij} = B_{ij} - \frac{1}{m}\sum_j B_{ij}$. By SVD, we have $\overline{\mathbf{B}} = \mathbf{P}_b\mathbf{\Sigma}_b\mathbf{Q}_b^T$, where $\mathbf{P}_b \in \mathbb{R}^{r\times r'}$ and $\mathbf{Q}_b \in \mathbb{R}^{m\times r'}$ are left and right singular vectors corresponding to the r' ($\leq r$) positive singular values in the diagonal matrix $\mathbf{\Sigma}_b$. In practice, we first apply eigendecomposition for the small $r \times r$ matrix $\overline{\mathbf{B}}\,\overline{\mathbf{B}}^T = [\mathbf{P}_b \ \widehat{\mathbf{P}}_b]\begin{bmatrix}\mathbf{\Sigma}_b^2 & \mathbf{0}\\ \mathbf{0} & \mathbf{0}\end{bmatrix}[\mathbf{P}_b \ \widehat{\mathbf{P}}_b]^T$, where $\widehat{\mathbf{P}}_b$ are the eigenvectors of the zero eigenvalues. Therefore, by

[3] If linear algebra boosting library is available (*e.g.*, Matlab), the first term of $\hat{b}_{ik}$ can be rewritten in matrix form: $(\mathbf{D}_i\mathbf{s}_i)_k - \left(\mathbf{D}_i\mathbf{D}_i^T\right)_k^T\hat{\mathbf{b}}_i$, where $\mathbf{D}_i$ is the subset of $\mathbf{D}$ selected by rows $j \in \mathcal{V}_i$, $\mathbf{s}_i$ is as $s_{ij} = S_{ij}$, and $\widehat{\mathbf{b}}_i$ is as $\hat{b}_{ik} = 0$. Similar form can be obtained for $\hat{d}_{jk}$ in Eq. (9).

the definition of SVD, we have $\mathbf{Q}_b = \overline{\mathbf{B}}^T \mathbf{P}_b \mathbf{\Sigma}_b^{-1}$. In order to satisfy the constraint $\mathbf{X1} = \mathbf{0}$, we further obtain additional $\widehat{\mathbf{Q}}_b \in \mathbb{R}^{m \times (r-r')}$ by Gram-Schmidt orthogonalization based on $[\mathbf{Q}_b\ \mathbf{1}]$, thus, we have $\widehat{\mathbf{Q}}_b^T \mathbf{1} = \mathbf{0}$. The fact $\mathbf{Q}_b^T \mathbf{1} = \mathbf{0}$ is detailed in Appendix.

Now we are ready to obtain a closed-form update rule for the $\mathbf{X}$-subproblem in Eq. (10):

$$\mathbf{X} \leftarrow \sqrt{m}[\mathbf{P}_b\ \widehat{\mathbf{P}}_b][\mathbf{Q}_b\ \widehat{\mathbf{Q}}_b]^T. \tag{11}$$

Y-subproblem. When $\mathbf{B}$, $\mathbf{D}$ and $\mathbf{X}$ are fixed in Eq. (5), the $\mathbf{Y}$-subproblem is:

$$\underset{\mathbf{Y}}{\operatorname{argmax}}\ tr(\mathbf{D}^T \mathbf{Y}),\ s.t.\ \mathbf{Y1} = \mathbf{0}, \mathbf{YY}^T = n\mathbf{I} \tag{12}$$

According to the above analysis, we can derive a closed form update rule for $\mathbf{Y}$ as:

$$\mathbf{Y} \leftarrow \sqrt{n}[\mathbf{P}_d\ \widehat{\mathbf{P}}_d][\mathbf{Q}_d\ \widehat{\mathbf{Q}}_d]^T, \tag{13}$$

where $\mathbf{P}_d$ and $\mathbf{Q}_d$ are the left and right singular vectors of the row-centered matrix $\overline{\mathbf{D}}$, $\widehat{\mathbf{P}}_d$ are the left singular vectors corresponding to zero singular values, and $\widehat{\mathbf{Q}}_d$ are the vectors obtained by Gram-Schimidt process based on $[\mathbf{Q}_d\ \mathbf{1}]$.

4.2 Out-of-Sample Extension

When new users, items and the corresponding ratings come in, it is impractical to retrain DCF for obtaining hashing codes of these out-of-sample data. Instead, an economical way is to learn ad-hoc codes for new data online and then update for the whole data offline when possible [25, 8].

Without loss of generality, we only discuss the case when a new user comes in. Denote $\{s_j | j \in \mathcal{N}\}$ as the set of observed ratings for existing items by the new user, whose binary codes are $\mathbf{b}$. For a single user, it is too expensive and unnecessary to impose the global balance and decorrelation constraints as batch DCF in Eq. (5). Therefore, we only focus on minimizing the rating prediction loss:

$$\underset{\mathbf{b} \in \{\pm 1\}^r}{\operatorname{argmin}} \sum_{j \in \mathcal{N}} (s_j - \mathbf{b}^T \mathbf{d}_j)^2 \tag{14}$$

It is easy to see that Eq. (14) is a special case of $\mathbf{B}$-subproblem in Eq. (6). Therefore, we can quickly develop the DCD update rule for the k-th bit b_k of $\mathbf{b}$ as:

$$b_k \leftarrow \operatorname{sgn}\left(K(\hat{b}_k, b_k)\right), \tag{15}$$

where $\hat{b}_k = \sum_{j \in \mathcal{N}} \left(s_j - \mathbf{d}_{j\bar{k}}^T \mathbf{b}_{\bar{k}}\right) d_{jk}$.

Similarly, for a new item, whose ratings are $\{s_i | i \in \mathcal{N}\}$ made by existing users, the update rule for the k-th bit d_k of the new item codes $\mathbf{d}$ is:

$$d_k \leftarrow \operatorname{sgn}\left(K(\hat{d}_k, d_k)\right), \tag{16}$$

where $\hat{d}_k = \sum_{i \in \mathcal{N}} \left(s_i - \mathbf{b}_{i\bar{k}}^T \mathbf{d}_{\bar{k}}\right) b_{ik}$.

5. ALGORITHMIC ANALYSIS

We summarize the solution for DCF in Algorithm 1. We will discuss the convergence, complexity and initialization issues in this section.

Algorithm 1: Discrete Collaborative Filtering

Input : $\{S_{ij} | i, j \in \mathcal{V}\}$: observed user-item ratings,
r: code length,
α and β: trade-off parameter
Output: $\mathbf{B} \in \{\pm 1\}^{r \times m}$: user codes,
$\mathbf{D} \in \{\pm 1\}^{r \times n}$: item codes

1 **Initialization**: $\mathbf{B}$, $\mathbf{D}$, $\mathbf{X} \in \mathbb{R}^{r \times m}$ and $\mathbf{Y} \in \mathbb{R}^{r \times n}$ by Eq. (18)
2 **repeat**
  `// B-subproblem, parallel outer for loop`
3   **for** i=1 **to** m **do**
4   **repeat**
5   **for** k=1 **to** r **do**
6         $\hat{b}_{ik} \leftarrow \sum_{j \in \mathcal{V}_i} \left(S_{ij} - \mathbf{d}_{j\bar{k}}^T \mathbf{b}_{i\bar{k}}\right) d_{jk} + \alpha x_{ik}$;
7         $b_{ik} \leftarrow \operatorname{sgn}\left(K(\hat{b}_{ik}, b_{ik})\right)$;
8   **end**
9   **until** *converge*;
10   **end**
  `// D-subproblem, parallel outer for loop`
11   **for** j=1 **to** n **do**
12   **repeat**
13   **for** k=1 **to** r **do**
14         $\hat{d}_{jk} \leftarrow \sum_{i \in \mathcal{V}_j} \left(S_{ij} - \mathbf{b}_{i\bar{k}}^T \mathbf{d}_{j\bar{k}}\right) b_{ik} + \beta y_{jk}$;
15         $d_{jk} \leftarrow \operatorname{sgn}\left(K(\hat{d}_{jk}, d_{jk})\right)$;
16   **end**
17   **until** *converge*;
18   **end**
  `// X-subproblem`
19   $\left([\mathbf{P}_b \widehat{\mathbf{P}}_b], \mathbf{Q}_b\right) \leftarrow \mathrm{SVD}(\overline{\mathbf{B}})$, $\widehat{\mathbf{Q}}_b \leftarrow \mathrm{GramSchmidt}\left([\mathbf{Q}_b \mathbf{1}]\right)$;
20   $\mathbf{X} \leftarrow \sqrt{m}[\mathbf{P}_b\ \widehat{\mathbf{P}}_b][\mathbf{Q}_b\ \widehat{\mathbf{Q}}_b]^T$;
  `// Y-subproblem`
21   $\left([\mathbf{P}_d \widehat{\mathbf{P}}_d], \mathbf{Q}_d\right) \leftarrow \mathrm{SVD}(\overline{\mathbf{D}})$, $\widehat{\mathbf{Q}}_d \leftarrow \mathrm{GramSchmidt}\left([\mathbf{Q}_d \mathbf{1}]\right)$;
22   $\mathbf{Y} \leftarrow \sqrt{n}[\mathbf{P}_d\ \widehat{\mathbf{P}}_d][\mathbf{Q}_d\ \widehat{\mathbf{Q}}_d]^T$;
23 **until** *converge*;
24 **return** $\mathbf{B}$, $\mathbf{D}$

5.1 Convergence

The convergence of the proposed DCF algorithm is guaranteed by the following theorem.

Theorem 1 (CONVERGENCE OF ALGORITHM 1). *The sequence $\{\mathbf{B}^{(t)}, \mathbf{D}^{(t)}, \mathbf{X}^{(t)}, \mathbf{Y}^{(t)}\}$ generated by Algorithm 1 monotonically decreases the objective function L of Eq. (5); the objective function sequence $\{L\left(\mathbf{B}^{(t)}, \mathbf{D}^{(t)}, \mathbf{X}^{(t)}, \mathbf{Y}^{(t)}\right)\}$ converges; the sequence $\{\mathbf{B}^{(t)}, \mathbf{D}^{(t)}, \mathbf{X}^{(t)}, \mathbf{Y}^{(t)}\}$ converges.*

In nutshell, we need to prove two key facts. First, we show that the updating steps in Step 7, 15, 20 and 22 monotonically decreases the objective function in Eq. (5), which is proved to be bounded below. Then, we use the fact that $L(\mathbf{B}, \mathbf{D})$ has finite values to show that $\{\mathbf{B}^{(t)}, \mathbf{D}^{(t)}\}$ converges. See Appendix for detailed proof.

5.2 Initialization

Since DCF deals with mixed-integer non-convex optimization, initialization is crucial for better convergence and local optimum. Here, we suggest an efficient initialization heuristic, which essentially relaxed the binary constraints

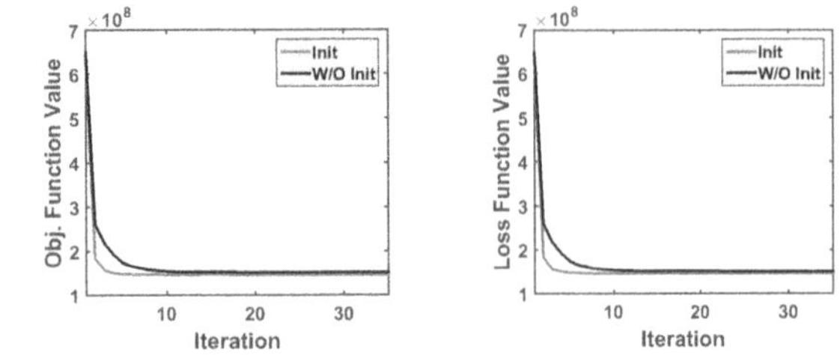

Figure 3: Convergence curve of the overall objective function value (left) and the squared loss value (right) using DCF with/without initializations on Yelp ($\alpha = \beta = 0.001$). We can see that the proposed initialization strategy helps to achieve faster convergence and lower objective/loss values.

in Eq. (5) as:

$$\begin{aligned} \underset{\mathbf{U},\mathbf{V},\mathbf{X},\mathbf{Y}}{\text{argmin}} \sum_{i,j\in\mathcal{V}} (S_{ij} - \mathbf{u}_i^T\mathbf{v}_j)^2 + \alpha\|\mathbf{U}\|_F^2 + \beta\|\mathbf{V}\|_F^2 \\ - 2\alpha tr(\mathbf{U}^T\mathbf{X}) - 2\beta tr(\mathbf{V}^T\mathbf{Y}) \quad (17) \\ s.t., \mathbf{X1} = 0, \mathbf{XX}^T = m\mathbf{I}, \mathbf{Y1} = 0, \mathbf{YY}^T = n\mathbf{I}. \end{aligned}$$

In fact, we can consider the above initialization as traditional CF in Eq. (1) with balance and decorrelation constraints imposed on real-valued $\mathbf{U}$ and $\mathbf{V}$. A possible explanation for why Eq. (17) may offer better initialization is illustrated in Figure 2, where the two constraints can restrict real-valued results within a subspace with small quantization error.

To solve Eq. (17), we can further initialize real-valued $\mathbf{U}$ and $\mathbf{V}$ randomly and find feasible initializations for $\mathbf{X}$ and $\mathbf{Y}$ by solving $\mathbf{X}/\mathbf{Y}$-subproblems in Section 4. Then, the optimization can be done alternatively by solving $\mathbf{U}$ and $\mathbf{V}$ by traditional CF in Eq. (1), and solving $\mathbf{X}$ and $\mathbf{Y}$ by $\mathbf{X}/\mathbf{Y}$-subproblem. Suppose the solutions are $(\mathbf{U}^*, \mathbf{V}^*, \mathbf{X}^*, \mathbf{Y}^*)$, we can initialize Algorithm 1 as:

$$\mathbf{B} \leftarrow \text{sgn}(\mathbf{U}^*), \mathbf{D} \leftarrow \text{sgn}(\mathbf{V}^*), \mathbf{X} \leftarrow \mathbf{X}^*, \mathbf{Y} \leftarrow \mathbf{Y}^*. \quad (18)$$

It is easy to see that the initializations above are feasible to Eq. (5). The effectiveness of the proposed initialization is illustrated in Figure 3.

5.3 Complexity

For space complexity, Algorithm 1 requires $\mathcal{O}(|\mathcal{V}|)$ for storing $\{S_{ij}\}$ and $\mathcal{O}(r \cdot \max(m,n))$ for $\mathbf{B}$, $\mathbf{D}$, $\mathbf{X}$ and $\mathbf{Y}$. As r is usually less than 256 bits, we can easily store the above variables at large-scale in memory.

We first analyze the time complexity for each of the subproblems. For $\mathbf{B}$-subproblem, it takes $\mathcal{O}(r^2|\mathcal{V}_i|T_s)$ for completing the inner loop of updating $\mathbf{b}_i$, where T_s is the number of iterations needed for convergence (Step 4 to 8). Further, suppose we have p computing threads, then the overall complexity for $\mathbf{B}$-subproblem is $\mathcal{O}(r^2T_s|\mathcal{V}|/p)$. Similarly, the overall complexity for $\mathbf{D}$-subproblem is also $\mathcal{O}(r^2T_s|\mathcal{V}|/p)$. In practice, T_s is usually 2∼5. For $\mathbf{X}$-subproblem, it requires $\mathcal{O}(r^2m)$ to perform the SVD and Gram-Schimdt orthogonalization in Step 19, and $\mathcal{O}(r^2m)$ matrix multiplication in Step 20. Similarly, it takes $\mathcal{O}(r^2n)$ for solving $\mathbf{Y}$-subproblem. Suppose the entire algorithm requires T iterations for convergence, the overall time complexity for Algorithm 1 is $\mathcal{O}\left(Tr^2\left(T_s|\mathcal{V}|\frac{1}{p} + m + n\right)\right)$, where we observe that T is usually 10∼20. In summary, training DCF is efficient since it scales linearly with the size of the data, *e.g.*, $|\mathcal{V}|$ and $m+n$.

6. EXPERIMENTS

As the proposed DCF fundamentally tackles the problem of quantization loss caused by traditional hashing methods of CF, the goal of our experiments is to answer the following three research questions:

RQ1 How does DCF perform as compared to other state-of-the-art hashing methods?

RQ2 Does DCF generalize well to new users? If yes, how much training overhead is needed?

RQ3 How do the discrete, balanced and uncorrelated constraints contribute to the overall effectiveness of DCF?

Table 1: Statistics of datasets in evaluation.

Dataset	Rating#	User#	Item#	Density
Yelp	696,865	25,677	25,815	0.11%
Amazon	5,057,936	146,469	189,474	0.02%
Netflix	100,480,507	480,189	17,770	1.18%

6.1 Datasets

We used three publicly available datasets from various real-world online websites:

Yelp: This is the latest Yelp Challenge dataset[4]. It originally includes 366,715 users, 60,785 items (*e.g.*, restaurants and shopping malls), and 1,569,264 ratings.

Amazon: This is a collection of user ratings on Amazon products of Book category [21], which originally contains 2,588,991 users, 929,264 items and 12,886,488 ratings.

Netflix: This is the classic movie rating dataset used in the Netflix challenge[5]. We use the full dataset that contains 480,189 users, 17,770 items and 100,480,507 ratings.

Due to the severe sparsity of Yelp and Amazon original datasets, we follow the convention in evaluating CF algorithms [24] by removing users and items that have less than 10 ratings[6]. When a user rates an item multiple times, we merge them into one rating by averaging the duplicate rating scores. Table 1 summarizes the filtered, experimental datasets. For each user, we randomly sampled 50% ratings as training and the rest 50% as testing. We repeated for 5 random splits and reported the averaged results.

6.2 Setups

6.2.1 Evaluation Metrics

As practical recommender systems usually generate a ranked list of items for user, we diverge from the error-based measure (*e.g.*, RMSE [15]), which is a suboptimal to recommendation task [3]. Instead, we treat it as a ranking problem, evaluating the ranking performance on test ratings with NDCG (Normalized Discounted Cumulative Gain), which is a widely used measure for evaluating recommendation algorithms [30, 3], owing to its comprehensive consideration of both ranking precisions and the positions of ratings.

[4] http://www.yelp.com/dataset_challenge

[5] http://www.netflixprize.com

[6] Note the similar filtering was conducted to Netflix dataset [15], so we use the Netflix dataset as-it-is.

6.2.2 Search Protocols

We adopted two search protocols which are widely used in search with binary codes. We used code length within $\{8, 16, 32, 64, 128, 256\}$.

Hamming Ranking: Items are ranked according to their Hamming distance (or similarity) from the query user. Although the search complexity of Hamming ranking is still linear, it is very fast in practice since the Hamming distance (or similarity) calculation can be done by fast bit operations and the sorting is constant time due to integer distance.

Hashtable Lookup: A lookup table is constructed using the item codes and all the items in the buckets that fall within a small Hamming radius (*e.g.*, 2) of the query user are returned. Therefore, search is performed in constant time. However, a single table would be insufficient when the code length is larger than 32 since it would require over $\mathcal{O}(2^{32})$ space to store the table in memory. We adopted Multi-Index Hashing (MIH) table [22], which builds one table for each code subsegment. Items are aggregated by all the tables and then conducted Hamming ranking for the items. By doing this, the search time is significantly reduced to sublinear—linear scan a short returned list. We empirically set the substring length as $\{1, 1, 2, 2, 4, 4\}$ for bit size $\{8, 16, 32, 64, 128, 256\}$ as suggested in [32].

It is worth mentioning that the above two search protocols focus on different characteristics of hashing codes. Hamming ranking provides a better measurement of the learned Hamming space, *i.e.*, the accuracy upper bound that the codes can achieve since it linearly scans the whole data. Hashtable lookup, on the other hand, emphasizes the practical speed of large-scale search. However, a common issue in this protocol is that it may not return sufficient items for recommendation, as a query lookup may miss due to the sparse Hamming space. In our experiments, if a query user returns no items, we treated as a failed query with an NDCG of zero.

6.2.3 Compared Methods

We benchmark the performance using the traditional real-valued CF method, comparing with several state-of-the-art hashing-based CF methods:

MF: This is the classic Matrix Factorization based CF algorithm [16], which learns user and item latent vectors in Euclidean space. We used MF as a baseline to show the performance gap between real values and binary codes. We adopt the ALS algorithm suggested by [34]. Note that it is beyond the scope of this paper to further investigate other popular variants of MF [15, 19].

BCCF: This is a two-stage Binary Code learning method for Collaborative Filtering [33]. At the relaxation stage, it imposes a balanced code regularization instead of the ℓ_2-norm regularization of MF; at quantization stage, it applies orthogonal rotation to user and item features, which is essentially an ITQ method [9].

PPH: This is a two-stage Preference Preserving Hashing [32]. At the relaxation stage, different from MF, it encourages the latent feature norm to reach the maximum ratings and hence smaller discrepancy between inner product (preference preserving) and cosine similarity (hashing friendly) is expected. At quantization stage, PPH quantizes each feature vector into $(r-2)$-bit phase codes and 2-bit magnitude codes. Therefore, in order to keep the code length consistent to other methods, we only learned $(r-2)$-dim latent features at relaxation stage.

CH: Collaborative Hashing [18] is also a two-stage approach, where the relaxation stage is based on full-matrix factorization, *i.e.*, unobserved ratings are considered as zeros. Since the original CH is formulated for visual features, we implemented CH for collaborative filtering as: $\arg\min_{\mathbf{U},\mathbf{V}} \|\mathbf{S} - \mathbf{U}^T\mathbf{V}\|_F^2$, *s.t.*, $\mathbf{U}\mathbf{U}^T = m\mathbf{I}, \mathbf{V}\mathbf{V}^T = n\mathbf{I}$, where $\mathbf{S}$ is the scaled rating matrix where $S_{ij} = 0$ if (i, j) is not observed, *i.e.*, $i, j \notin \mathcal{V}$. By several algebraic transformations, the above problem can be cast into alternating solving SVDs for $\mathbf{US}$ and $\mathbf{VS}^T$, which is analogous to our $\mathbf{X}/\mathbf{Y}$-subproblem. Then, the binary quantization is simply $\text{sgn}(\mathbf{U})$ and $\text{sgn}(\mathbf{V})$.

We also compared the following two settings of DCF to investigate its effectiveness:

MFB: This is the MF results with round-off binary quantization. We used this as a baseline to show how quantization loss degrades performance.

DCFinit: This is the Initialization problem of DCF in Eq. (17), whose binary codes are given in Eq. (18). By comparing with MFB, we can investigate whether the balance and decorrelation constraints are useful for binary quantization. Moreover, DCFinit can be considered as a relaxed two-stage version of DCF. Compared with DCF, we can see whether discrete optimization is effective.

All the hyper-parameters (*e.g.*, α and β) of DCF and the above methods were tuned within $\{1e^{-4}, 1e^{-3}, ..., 1e^{2}\}$ by 5-fold cross validation on the training split. We used MATLAB with mex C for algorithm implementations and we run them on a cluster of 9 machines, each of which has 6-core 2.4GHz CPU and 48GB RAM.

6.3 Result Analysis

6.3.1 Comparison with State-of-The-Arts (RQ1)

Figure 6 shows the performances (NDCG@K) of DCF and the three state-of-the-art hashing methods in terms of Hamming ranking and table lookup. We can have the following key observations:

1). The proposed DCF considerably outperforms all the state-of-the-art methods. For example, as shown in Table 2, in most cases, DCF can even achieve significantly better performance by using only 8 bits as compared to the most competitive CH using 128 bits. This suggests that DCF can reduce a huge amount of memory and time cost as compared to the state-of-the-art methods. One possible reason why CH outperforms BCCF and PPH is that it incorporates the uncorrelated codes constraints during joint optimization, which is beneficial for the subsequent quantization. DCF, on the other hand, minimizing the quantization loss directly by joint discrete optimization with balanced and uncorrelated code constraints, resulting in better performance than CH.

2). When using lookup tables, the performances of all the methods are not as stable as those by using ranking, specifically, at larger K positions on smaller datasets like Yelp and Amazon. This is due to that zero item is returned when lookup misses—Hamming ranking treats the entire items as candidates, while lookup table only indexes a small fraction of items as candidate. This is why NDCG at smaller K positions does not significantly decrease as compared to Hamming ranking. Therefore, as we can observe that DCF considerably outperforms other methods, we can infer that the codes generated by DCF have less lookup misses.

3). As the bit size increases, the performance gap between DCF and other methods becomes larger, especially when

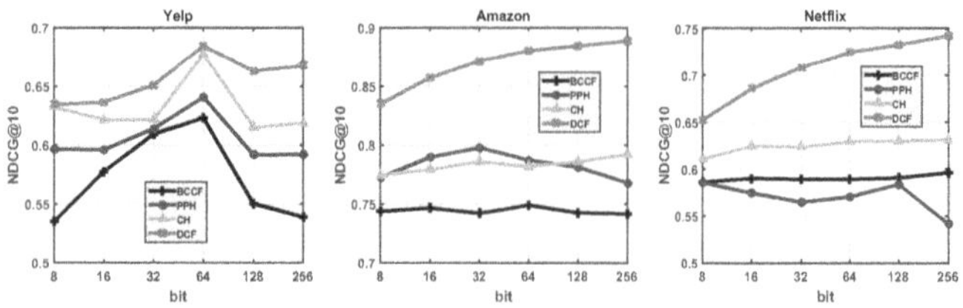

Figure 4: Recommendation performance (NDCG@10) on 50% held-out "new" users (RQ 2).

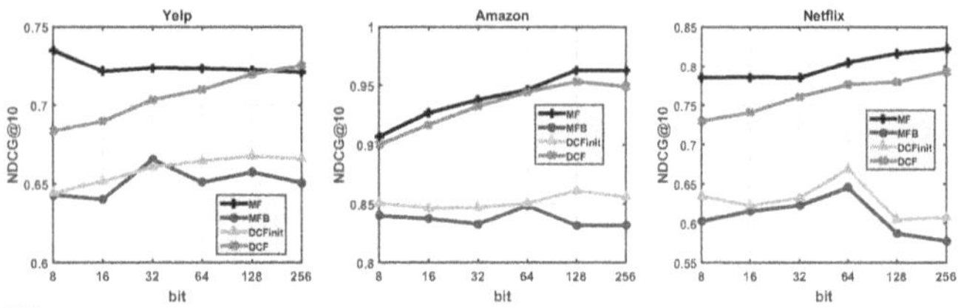

Figure 5: Recommendation performance (NDCG@10) of CF and DCF variants (RQ 3).

using lookup. This demonstrates that the two-stage approaches (BCCF, PPH and CH) increasingly suffer from quantization loss as code length increases.

6.3.2 Generalization to New Users (RQ2)

In this study, we performed the strong generalization test. Following [27], we trained all models on 50% of randomly sampled users with full history; the remaining 50% of users are the new users for testing. In the testing phase, we fed 50% ratings of the test users into the model for an out-of-sample update (cf. Section 4.2), obtaining the hashing codes for test users. The performance was then evaluated against the remaining 50% ratings for the test users. In this way, we simulated the online learning scenario, where a full re-training is prohibitive and the model needs to be instantly refreshed to better serve new users.

Figure 4 shows the performance of the generalization test. We can see that DCF consistently outperforms other methods. The key reason is that the out-of-sample hashing by DCF preserves the original binary separations of the Hamming space by directly performing discrete optimization. On the other hand, since BCCF, PPH and CH are all two-stage approaches, the latent vectors of new users are first approximated with fixed item vectors. As a result, the subsequent quantization loss will be more severe. We can also see that the performances drop of DCF caused by less training data is acceptable, *e.g.*, only 7% NDCG@10 drop as compared to the results obtained by original data.

Table 2: Performance (NDCG@10) of various methods (#bit) using two search protocols on three datasets. * denotes the statistical significance for $p < 0.05$.

Protocol	Hamming Ranking			Table Lookup		
Dataset	Yelp	Amazon	Netflix	Yelp	Amazon	Netflix
BCCF(128)	0.623	0.827	0.633	0.268	0.300	0.262
PPH(128)	0.643	0.841	0.587	0.626	0.799	0.566
CH(128)	0.655	**0.922***	0.693	0.647	0.815	0.680
DCF(8)	**0.684***	0.890	**0.730***	**0.674***	**0.825***	**0.710***

To show the training overhead, we show the time cost for hashing new users of the largest dataset Netflix in Table 3. First, we see CH requires the least hashing time, followed by our DCF method. The efficiency of CH is owing to its simple design — which adopts the conventional SVD and only needs to apply a matrix multiplication operation for hashing new users. Although the proposed DCF is about tens of times slower than CH, we believe this overhead is acceptable since DCF considerably generalizes better than CH. Comparing with BCCF and PPH, our DCF is about 20 times faster. The reason is that both BCCF and PPH need to iteratively solve least square problems, which involve the expensive matrix inverse. In addition, BCCF requires two matrix multiplications after least square, *i.e.*, PCA projection and ITQ rotation, and hence needs more time. In contrast, our DCF only requires Tr matrix multiplications in total, where T is 2∼5 and r is the code length.

Table 3: Time cost (s) of various methods hashing 240,094 new users of Netflix using a single 6-core CPU.

Method/#Bits	8	16	32	64	128	256
BCCF	51.3	64.5	78.0	$1.21e^2$	$4.81e^2$	$2.69e^3$
PPH	51.2	64.3	77.5	$1.21e^2$	$4.81e^2$	$2.69e^3$
CH	$2.12e^{-1}$	$4.11e^{-1}$	$8.37e^{-1}$	1.66	3.34	6.71
DCF	2.25	3.16	5.18	9.52	29.6	93.4

6.3.3 Impact of Discrete, Balanced and Uncorrelated Constraints (RQ3)

As shown in Figure 5, it is not surprising that real-valued user/item features—MF outperforms other user/item binary codes. However, if we simply quantize MF features to MFB binary codes, significant performance drop can be observed, especially as the bit size increases. As analyzed above, this is due to the quantization loss caused by the two-stage approaches. Interestingly, by adding the balanced and uncorrelated constraints, DCFinit generally outperforms MFB. An intuitive explanation is illustrated in Figure 2 that the two constraints can shift and rotate the real-valued features to a new user-item manifold that is beneficial for the binary split of the original vector space into Hamming space, and thus less quantization loss is expected. Moreover, we can see that DCF significantly outperforms DCFinit. This demonstrates the superiority of the proposed joint discrete optimization over the two-stage approaches.

7. CONCLUSIONS

In this paper, a novel hashing approach dubbed Discrete Collaborative Filtering (DCF) was proposed to enable efficient collaborative filtering. In sharp contrast to existing collaborative filtering hashing methods which are generally in a two-stage fashion, DCF directly learns binary codes for users and items according to the Hamming similarity induced rating loss. Through extensive experiments carried out on three benchmarks, we demonstrated that the main disadvantage of those two-stage hashing methods is the severe quantization loss caused by the inconsistency between input real-valued features and subsequent binary quantization. Beyond conventional two-stage methods that are not entirely optimized for hashing, our proposed DCF completes discrete optimization inherent to hashing and therefore achieves considerable performance gain over state-of-the-art collaborative filtering hashing techniques.

To the best of our knowledge, DCF is the first principled learning-to-hash framework for accelerating CF, so we believe that it has a great potential to advance real-world recommendation systems since DCF can effectively compress

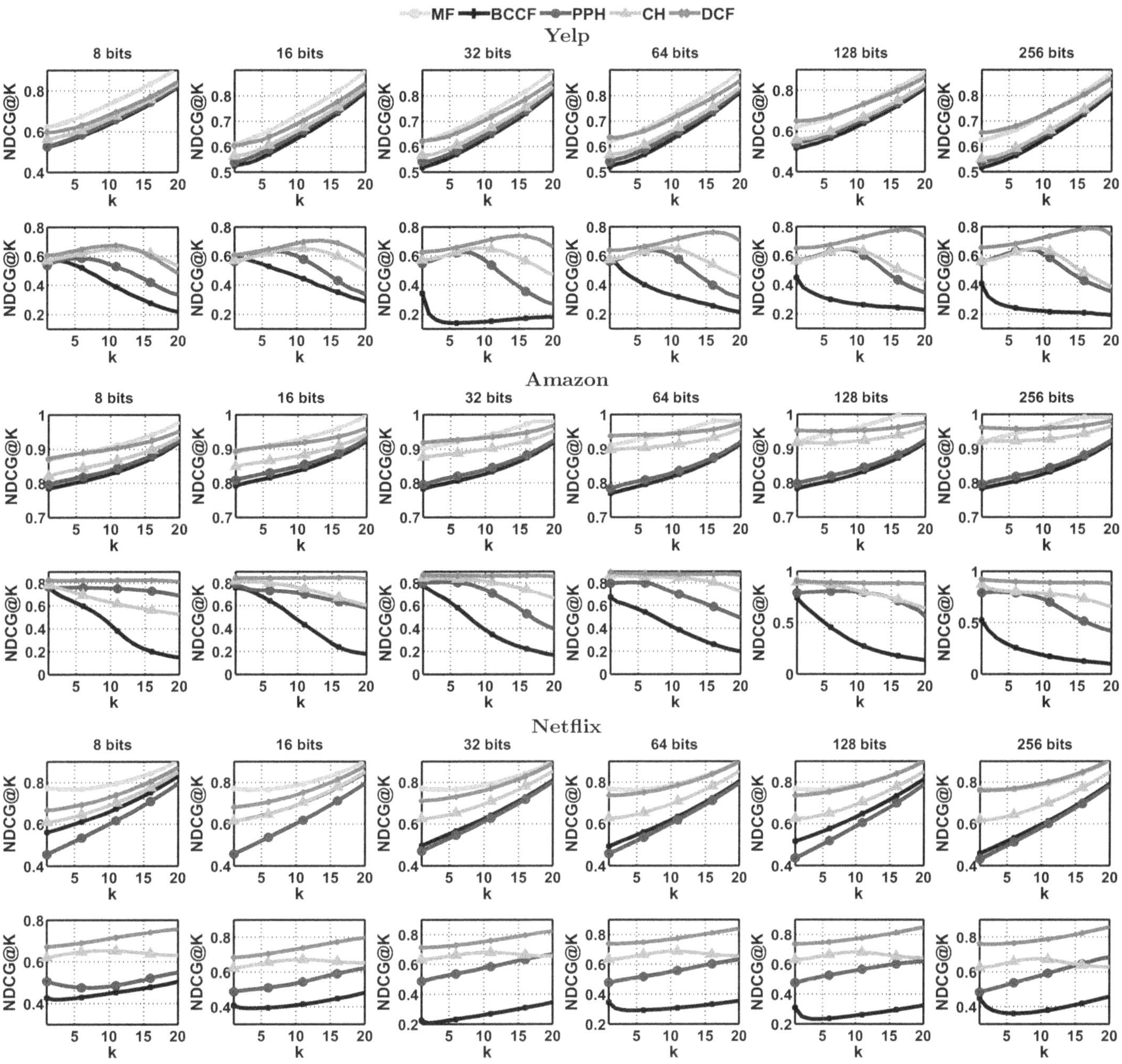

Figure 6: Item recommendation performance (NDCG@K) of all the CF hashing methods of various code lengths. For each dataset, the top row is the performance by Hamming ranking and the bottom row is by table lookup (RQ 1). As MF is continuous, we used cosine ranking and table lookup is not applied.

gigantic users/items to compact binary codes. As moving forward, we are going to apply DCF to various CF applications [27, 13] as well as more generic feature-based factorization approaches [23].

Acknowledgements

NExT research is supported by the National Research Foundation, Prime Minister's Office, Singapore under its IRC@SG Funding Initiative.

8. REFERENCES

[1] G. Adomavicius and A. Tuzhilin. Toward the next generation of recommender systems: A survey of the state-of-the-art and possible extensions. *TKDE*, 2005.

[2] D. Agarwal, B.-C. Chen, and P. Elango. Fast online learning through offline initialization for time-sensitive recommendation. In *KDD*, 2010.

[3] S. Balakrishnan and S. Chopra. Collaborative ranking. In *WSDM*, 2012.

[4] J. Bennett and S. Lanning. The netflix prize. In *KDD*, 2007.

[5] J. Bobadilla, F. Ortega, A. Hernando, and A. Gutiérrez. Recommender systems survey. *Knowledge-Based Systems*, 2013.

[6] A. S. Das, M. Datar, A. Garg, and S. Rajaram. Google news personalization: scalable online collaborative filtering. In *WWW*, 2007.

[7] A. Gionis, P. Indyk, R. Motwani, et al. Similarity search in high dimensions via hashing. In *VLDB*, 1999.

[8] K. Goldberg, T. Roeder, D. Gupta, and C. Perkins. Eigentaste: A constant time collaborative filtering algorithm. *Information Retrieval*, 2001.

[9] Y. Gong, S. Lazebnik, A. Gordo, and F. Perronnin. Iterative quantization: A procrustean approach to learning binary codes for large-scale image retrieval. *TPAMI*, 2013.

[10] E. F. Harrington. Online ranking/collaborative filtering using the perceptron algorithm. In *ICML*, 2003.

[11] J. Håstad. Some optimal inapproximability results. *JACM*, 2001.

[12] X. He, T. Chen, M.-Y. Kan, and X. Chen. Trirank: Review-aware explainable recommendation by modeling aspects. In *CIKM*, 2015.

[13] X. H. He, H. Zhang, M.-Y. Kan, and T.-S. Chua. Fast matrix factorization for online recommendation with implicit feedback. In *SIGIR*, 2016.

[14] A. Karatzoglou, M. Weimer, and A. J. Smola. Collaborative filtering on a budget. In *AISTAT*, 2010.

[15] Y. Koren. Collaborative filtering with temporal dynamics. In *KDD*, 2009.

[16] Y. Koren, R. Bell, and C. Volinsky. Matrix factorization techniques for recommender systems. *Computer*, 2009.

[17] W. Liu, C. Mu, S. Kumar, and S.-F. Chang. Discrete graph hashing. In *NIPS*, 2014.

[18] X. Liu, J. He, C. Deng, and B. Lang. Collaborative hashing. In *CVPR*, 2014.

[19] H. Ma, D. Zhou, C. Liu, M. R. Lyu, and I. King. Recommender systems with social regularization. In *WSDM*, 2011.

[20] J. Mairal, F. Bach, J. Ponce, and G. Sapiro. Online learning for matrix factorization and sparse coding. *JMLR*, 2010.

[21] J. McAuley and J. Leskovec. Hidden factors and hidden topics: Understanding rating dimensions with review text. In *RecSys*, 2013.

[22] M. Norouzi, A. Punjani, and D. J. Fleet. Fast search in hamming space with multi-index hashing. In *CVPR*, 2012.

[23] S. Rendle. Scaling factorization machines to relational data. *VLDB*, 2013.

[24] S. Rendle, C. Freudenthaler, Z. Gantner, and L. Schmidt-Thieme. Bpr: Bayesian personalized ranking from implicit feedback. In *UAI*, 2009.

[25] B. Sarwar, G. Karypis, J. Konstan, and J. Riedl. Item-based collaborative filtering recommendation algorithms. In *WWW*, 2001.

[26] F. Shen, C. Shen, W. Liu, and H. T. Shen. Supervised discrete hashing. In *CVPR*, 2015.

[27] M. Volkovs and G. W. Yu. Effective latent models for binary feedback in recommender systems. In *SIGIR*, 2015.

[28] J. Wang, S. Kumar, and S.-F. Chang. Semi-supervised hashing for large-scale search. *TPAMI*, 2012.

[29] J. Wang, W. Liu, S. Kumar, and S.-F. Chang. Learning to hash for indexing big data: A survey. *Proceedings of the IEEE*, 2016.

[30] M. Weimer, A. Karatzoglou, Q. V. Le, and A. Smola. Maximum margin matrix factorization for collaborative ranking. *NIPS*, 2007.

[31] Y. Weiss, A. Torralba, and R. Fergus. Spectral hashing. In *NIPS*, 2009.

[32] Z. Zhang, Q. Wang, L. Ruan, and L. Si. Preference preserving hashing for efficient recommendation. In *SIGIR*, 2014.

[33] K. Zhou and H. Zha. Learning binary codes for collaborative filtering. In *KDD*, 2012.

[34] Y. Zhou, D. Wilkinson, R. Schreiber, and R. Pan. Large-scale parallel collaborative filtering for the netflix prize. In *AAIM*, 2008.

APPENDIX

Derivation of Eq. (7). Without loss of generality, suppose $\mathbf{b}_i = [\mathbf{b}_{i\bar{k}}^T \ b_{ik}]^T$ and $\mathbf{d}_j = [\mathbf{d}_{j\bar{k}}^T \ d_{jk}]^T$, the quadratic term in Eq. (6) w.r.t b_{ik} can be rewritten as:

$$\begin{aligned}&\mathbf{b}_i^T(\sum_{j\in\mathcal{V}_i}\mathbf{d}_j\mathbf{d}_j^T)\mathbf{b}_i = \sum_{j\in\mathcal{V}_i}(\mathbf{d}_j^T\mathbf{b}_i)^2 = \\ &2b_{ik}\sum_{j\in\mathcal{V}_i}\left(\mathbf{d}_{j\bar{k}}^T\mathbf{b}_{i\bar{k}}d_{jk}\right) + \underbrace{\sum_{j\in\mathcal{V}_i}\left((\mathbf{d}_{j\bar{k}}^T\mathbf{b}_{i\bar{k}})^2 + (d_{jk}b_{ik})^2\right)}_{\text{constant}},\end{aligned} \tag{19}$$

and the rest two linear terms w.r.t. b_{ik} can be rewritten as:

$$\begin{aligned}&2(\sum_{j\in\mathcal{V}_i}S_{ij}\mathbf{d}_j^T)\mathbf{b}_i - 2\alpha\mathbf{x}_i^T\mathbf{b}_i = \\ &-2b_{ik}\sum_{j\in\mathcal{V}_i}S_{ij}d_{jk} - 2\alpha x_{ik}b_{ik} - \underbrace{2\sum_{j\in\mathcal{V}_i}S_{ij}\mathbf{d}_{j\bar{k}}^T\mathbf{b}_{i\bar{k}} - 2\alpha\mathbf{x}_{i\bar{k}}^T\mathbf{b}_{i\bar{k}}}_{\text{constant}}.\end{aligned} \tag{20}$$

Therefore, we can derive a set of bit-wise minimizations:

$$\underset{\mathbf{b}_{ik}\in\{\pm1\}}{\operatorname{argmin}} \quad -\hat{b}_{ik}b_{ik}, \tag{21}$$

where $\hat{b}_{ik} = \sum_{j\in\mathcal{V}_i}\left(S_{ij} - \mathbf{d}_{j\bar{k}}^T\mathbf{b}_{i\bar{k}}\right)d_{jk} + \alpha x_{ik}$. It is easy to see that the optimized b_{ik} should be the sign of $\hat{b}_{ik}$. Therefore, the update rule for b_{ik} can be given in Eq. (7). Tthe update rule for d_{jk} in Eq. (9) can be derived in a similar way.

Proof of Theorem 1. We prove the three parts of Theorem 1 one by one.

Part 1. It is easy to see that $\{\mathbf{B}^{(t)}, \mathbf{D}^{(t)}\}$ generated by the DCD Step 7 and Step 15 monotonically decreases the objective functions of $\mathbf{B}$-subproblem and $\mathbf{D}$-subproblem in Eq. (6) and Eq. (8), respectively. Without loss of generality, we show that $\{\mathbf{X}^{(t)}\}$ generated by Step 20 monotonically decreases the objective function of $\mathbf{X}$-subproblem in Eq. (10). In particular, denote $\mathbf{X}'$ as the updated $\mathbf{X}$ at each step, we show that $\mathbf{X}'$ maximizes the $\mathbf{X}$-subproblem.

We first show that $\mathbf{X}'$ is feasible, *i.e.*, $\mathbf{X}' \in \mathcal{B}$. Note that $\overline{\mathbf{B}} = \mathbf{BJ}$, where $J = \mathbf{I} - \frac{1}{m}\mathbf{1}\mathbf{1}^T$. Since $\overline{\mathbf{B}}^T$ and $\mathbf{Q}_b$ has the same row space, we have $\mathbf{Q}_b^T\mathbf{1} = 0$ due to $\overline{\mathbf{B}}\mathbf{1} = 0$. As we construct $\widehat{Q}_b$ such that $\mathbf{1}^T\widehat{\mathbf{Q}}_b = \mathbf{0}$, we have $\mathbf{1}^T[\mathbf{Q}_b\widehat{\mathbf{Q}}_b] = \mathbf{1}$, which implies $\mathbf{X}'\mathbf{1} = \mathbf{0}$. Moreover, it is easy to show that $\mathbf{X}\mathbf{X}^T = m[\mathbf{P}_b\widehat{\mathbf{P}}_b][\mathbf{Q}_b\widehat{\mathbf{Q}}_b]^T[\mathbf{Q}_b\widehat{\mathbf{Q}}_b][\mathbf{P}_b\widehat{\mathbf{P}}_b]^T = m\mathbf{I}$. Therefore, $\mathbf{X}'$ is feasible. As SVD $\mathbf{BJ} = [\mathbf{P}_b \ \widehat{\mathbf{P}}_b]\begin{bmatrix}\mathbf{\Sigma}_b & \mathbf{0}\\ \mathbf{0} & \mathbf{0}\end{bmatrix}[\mathbf{Q}_b \ \widehat{\mathbf{Q}}_b]^T$, we have $tr(\mathbf{X}'\overline{\mathbf{B}}^T) = \sqrt{m}\sum_{k=1}^r\sigma_k$, where σ_k is diagonal eigenvalues of $\mathbf{\Sigma}_b$. $\forall\mathbf{X}\in\mathcal{B}$, by using von Neumann's trace inequality, we have $tr(\mathbf{X}\overline{\mathbf{B}}^T) \le \sqrt{m}\sum_{k=1}^r\sigma_k$. Due to $\mathbf{X}\mathbf{1} = \mathbf{0}$, we have $\mathbf{XJ} = \mathbf{X}$. So, $\mathbf{X}'$ is a maximizer. Thus far, we have $tr(\mathbf{X}\mathbf{B}^T) = tr(\mathbf{X}\overline{\mathbf{B}}^T) \le tr(\mathbf{X}'\overline{\mathbf{B}}^T) = tr(\mathbf{X}'\mathbf{B}^T)$.

Part 2. We show that the loss function $L(\mathbf{B},\mathbf{D},\mathbf{X},\mathbf{Y})$ in Eq. (5) is lower bounded. By Cauchy-Schwartz inequality $tr(B^T\mathbf{X}) \le \|\mathbf{B}\|_F\|\mathbf{X}\|_F$, we have

$$\begin{aligned}L(\mathbf{B},\mathbf{D},\mathbf{X},\mathbf{Y}) &\ge 0 - 2\alpha\|\mathbf{B}\|_F\|\mathbf{X}\|_F - 2\beta\|\mathbf{D}\|_F\|\mathbf{Y}\|_F \\ &\ge -2\alpha\sqrt{mr}\sqrt{mr} - 2\beta\sqrt{nr}\sqrt{nr} = -2\alpha mr - 2\beta nr.\end{aligned} \tag{22}$$

Thus, together with the monotonic decrease proved in Part 1, we can conclude that $\{L(\mathbf{B}^{(t)},\mathbf{D}^{(t)},\mathbf{X}^{(t)},\mathbf{Y}^{(t)})\}$ converges.

Part 3. It is easy to see that $L(\mathbf{X},\mathbf{Y},\mathbf{B},\mathbf{D})$ is Lipschitz continuous w.r.t. $\mathbf{X}$ and $\mathbf{Y}$, thus, $\{\mathbf{X}^{(t)},\mathbf{Y}^{(t)}\}$ converges. Therefore, it is sufficient to prove $\{\mathbf{B}^{(t)},\mathbf{D}^{(t)}\}$ converges.

Without loss of generality, we drop the subscript i and only show that $\exists T$ such that $\forall k$, $t > T$, $b_k^{(t+1)} = b_k^{(t)}$. Suppose there is a k' such that $b_{k'}^{(t+1)} \ne b_{k'}^{(t)}$, due to the update rule in Eq. (7), $\hat{b}_{k'} \ne 0$, which implies a strict decrease for the objective function $L(\mathbf{b})$. Since $\mathbf{b}$ is binary valued, $L(\mathbf{b})$ has finite values. If such k' exists, it will lead to infinite values, which contradicts the fact. Therefore, we conclude that $\{\mathbf{B}^{(t)}\}$ converges. Moreover, since $L(\mathbf{B},\mathbf{D})$ has finite values, there exists $\mathbf{B}^{(t+1)}$ such that $\mathbf{D}^{(t+1)} = \mathbf{D}^{(t)}$. Therefore, $\{\mathbf{B}^{(t)},\mathbf{D}^{(t)}\}$ converges and so does $\{\mathbf{B}^{(t)},\mathbf{D}^{(t)},\mathbf{X}^{(t)},\mathbf{Y}^{(t)}\}$. □

Understanding Information Need: an fMRI Study

Yashar Moshfeghi
School of Computing Science
University of Glasgow
Glasgow, UK
Yashar.Moshfeghi@glasgow.ac.uk

Peter Triantafillou
School of Computing Science
University of Glasgow
Glasgow, UK
Peter.Triantafillou@glasgow.ac.uk

Frank E. Pollick
School of Psychology
University of Glasgow
Glasgow, UK
Frank.Pollick@glasgow.ac.uk

ABSTRACT

The raison d'etre of IR is to satisfy human information need. But, do we really understand information need? Despite advances in the past few decades in both the IR and relevant scientific communities, this question is largely unanswered. We do not really understand how an information need emerges and how it is physically manifested. Information need refers to a complex concept: at the very initial state of the phenomenon (i.e. at a visceral level), even the searcher may not be aware of its existence. This renders the measuring of this concept (using traditional behaviour studies) nearly impossible. In this paper, we investigate the connection between an information need and brain activity. Using functional Magnetic Resonance Imaging (fMRI), we measured the brain activity of twenty four participants while they performed a Question Answering (Q/A) Task, where the questions were carefully selected and developed from TREC-8 and TREC 2001 Q/A Track. The results of this experiment revealed a distributed network of brain regions commonly associated with activities related to information need and retrieval and differing brain activity in processing scenarios when participants knew the answer to a given question and when they did not and needed to search. We believe our study and conclusions constitute an important step in unravelling the nature of information need and therefore better satisfying it.

Keywords: Anomalous States of Knowledge, Information Need, Information Retrieval, fMRI Study

1. INTRODUCTION

The main goal of Information Retrieval (IR) systems is to satisfy searchers' information need (IN). Given the core and fundamental role IN plays in an information seeking and retrieval process, over the last several decades much research has been dedicated to better understand this concept in both information retrieval and other relevant scientific communities. As a result of such research, seminal theories, models, and findings have been published, shaping the foundations of current IR systems. A few examples of such influential works are Wilson's Information Seeking Behaviour model [46], Kuhlthau's Information Seeking Process (ISP) model [28], Ingwersen's Cognitive IR Theory [21], and Belkin's Anomalous States of Knowledge (ASK) model [8]. These works are mainly based on *behavioural studies of searchers* while they engaged in an Information Retrieval and Seeking process, mainly through questionnaires/interviews [28], or by observing and studying searchers interaction with IR systems via their submitted queries and their reformulation [26], or via their interaction with retrieved results [44]. Despite their invaluable contributions, they have all investigated the phenomenon of IN indirectly, via some sort of mediator. Therefore, important research questions remain unanswered, such as:

- **RQ1:** "What is the nature of IN from a neuropsycology perspective?";
- **RQ2:** "Is there a clear, detectable, physical manifestation (i.e. neural correlate) of IN in human brains?";
- **RQ3:** "Can such manifestations be identified in an early stage of an information seeking and retrieval process?"; and
- **RQ4:** "Do such manifestations differ when an anomaly in the user's state of knowledge has been experienced? i.e., when searchers choose not to engage in a search process (Don't know – Don't search Scenario), compared to a scenario where they engage in a search process (Don't know – Do Search Scenario)?".

An answer to these questions will definitely improve our understanding and lead to robust definitions of the IN concept. And, fundamentally, it will play a key role in opening new doors to the design and implementations of novel IR techniques which will be enabled to better (and even proactively) satisfy searchers' need. The research described in this paper represents our efforts towards this direction. In particular, in this paper we focus on discovering and mapping the brain mechanisms of IN realisation, within an information retrieval process performed by humans engaged in a Question Answering (Q/A) retrieval task. Our central aims are to identify: (i) the brain regions associated with an IN realisation (in its earliest state) and (ii) contrast the scenarios where individuals engage in search or simply state the

SIGIR '16, July 17–21, 2016, Pisa, Italy.

ACM ISBN 978-1-4503-4069-4/16/07..
DOI: http://dx.doi.org/10.1145/2911451.2911534

need to search. We are focusing on the time period in which the brain exhibits the highest activity with regards to the process of IN realisation, from the moment of observing a question, i.e. recognising an ASK. The identification of the brain regions involved in an IN realisation (in particular in an early state) and observing the period of time in which there is a clear association of the activation of brain regions where there exists an Information Need, can be the basis to detect an IN in a Q/A task.

Our experiments rely on measuring Blood Oxygenation Level Dependent (BOLD) signals and the fact that BOLD signals can be analysed to detect significant brain activities in the process of realising an IN in a Q/A task. In particular, we aim to identify the time frame in which significant activity appears in users' brains, while they are realising an IN. In this spirit, this paper reports the results of an fMRI based user study on Q/A search. In particular, we have monitored, by an MRI device, the brain activities of twenty four participants engaged in a Q/A search task for a predefined set of questions with respect to a predefined set of relevant and non-relevant documents. In order to do so, we devised an experiment consisting of collecting data via a 3T MRI scanner in a lab-based user study, and analysed the collected data off-line. Our hypothesis is that there are brain regions in which the BOLD signals would be different for No-IN scenarios (i.e., "know the answer") versus IN scenarios (i.e., "don't know an answer and need to search"). Moreover, this difference would be sensitive to whether individuals engage in search or simply state the need to search.

The remainder of the paper is organised as follows: Section 2 presents related work and the background. Section 3 discusses at length the experimental methodology. Section 4 presents and analyses our results. Finally, Section 5 presents our key conclusions.

2. RELATED WORK

2.1 IN Complexity and the IN-Query Gap

IN is an essential concept and at the core of the information retrieval processes. When searchers realise an information need, they experience an anomaly in their current state of knowledge (ASK) [8]. As a result, search processes are initiated: Searchers transform their IN into a query and submit it to an IR system. In turn, the IR system retrieves potentially relevant documents, aiming to satisfy the IN. Subsequently, searchers evaluate retrieved documents, accumulating relevant information which leads them to satisfy their IN. Often, however, searchers are not satisfied with the results obtained in response to their initial query formulation [42], and thus must engage in further interaction with the system to resolve their need. Therein lies the complexity associated with the concept of IN.

The complexity of IN rests in its paradoxical nature [12]: Unlike other primary human need (e.g., physiological ones), it is often unknown to the individual beforehand what information is required to satisfy the IN. Research indicates that this is because an IN is "intangible and visceral" and therefore "unknowable and non-specifiable" – thus, how can one express an IN using a query to an IR system? [8, 12] Hence, the very nature of IN inherently makes it nearly impossible for searchers to correctly map their IN to a IR query [8, 9, 20, 12, 40]. This produces a gap between how an IN is represented (i.e. the formulated query) and the actual IN, because the formulated query is not guaranteed to provide an exact description required to retrieve the relevant documents [45]. In other words, expressing an IN using a set of query keywords is considered to be uncertain and noisy [41], as it can only vaguely approximate the actual IN [40]. The problem becomes even more pronounced when an IN is *ill-defined*: i.e., when the searcher only knows "fringes of a gap in [his/her] knowledge" [12] making it extremely difficult for the searcher to identify and describe the IN [7, 8, 11]. Therefore, it is possible that a given query may not sufficiently define the characteristics of relevant documents, or even any relevant information, since a searcher cannot form an appropriate initial state from which to form a query [13].

Taylor's [40] classic four-level theory of IN theorised the complex nature of IN as follows: (i) a search begins with a process based on an area of doubt or a gap in understanding, which is a compromised expression of the need (Taylor calls this the Q4 level). The searcher, as a result of searching, can subsequently frame an IN, borrowing generic knowledge frames from adjacent areas in memory; at a certain point, a transformational event of information use leads to the IN being actualised, resulting in the information search becoming focused. This transformation in the use of information causes the searcher's Q4 compromised level of need to access deeper levels of the need, i.e. the formal expression of the need (Taylor calls this the Q3 level), the conscious "within brain" description of the need (Taylor calls this the Q2 level) and finally the deepest level of the need is the "visceral" (i.e., instinctual) level (Taylor calls the Q1 level) [40, 12]. What is of particular interest to the current paper are the lower levels in Taylor's conceptualisation of IN, namely the unconscious, visceral information need (which the user cannot know and therefore cannot specify to the IR system) leading to the "within brain" description of the IN. Ingwersen [21] in his Cognitive theory of IR explains that, based on the perspective of cognitive science, theories of information and empirical evidence, an appropriate approach to understanding IR is first to examine the mental formation of the information need and use this as the starting point for IR interaction. This formulation is a central issue in IR. This paper takes substantial motivation from this vein of research, arguing that IR systems that can detect and understand INs, starting from their Q1 levels, can better satisfy them.

2.2 Closing the IN-Query Gap

Typically, IR systems rely on a progressive disambiguation of the user's information need through an interactive and iterative process known as the relevance feedback cycle. Relevance feedback is central to the IR system's efforts to construct a better representation of the users' IN. Relevance feedback may be gathered through explicit [27], implicit [43], and/or affective feedback [2]. Explicit feedback is viewed as a robust method to improve retrieval effectiveness [27]. However, it is not always applicable due to the cognitive burden that it places on users [44]. Enter implicit feedback, in which relevance is inferred from the interactional data in an indirect and unobtrusive manner [22]. For example, researchers try to understand how task [43], dwell time [25] and click-through [22] relate to relevance. However, a problem occurs when actions are taken as an indication of relevance without sufficient evidence to support their effectiveness [36]. For example, Kelly and Belkin [24] show that the implicit feedback measures based on user interaction with the full content of documents can often be unreliable, and difficult to measure or interpret. Recently, affective feedback has been proposed [2] which relies on capturing facial expression [5], eye tracking [30], and physiological signals [3, 33] (such as skin temperature) and uses them as implicit relevance judgements. However, these methods can only help researchers to understand the concept of relevance to a certain level and are not considered to be very effective. Implicit feedback IR systems, albeit noisy, can collect several distinct signals of the user's interests through the analysis of both user's actions and user generated contents [44]. Recently, affective and physiological features have been considered as a valid ground to define implicit feedback techniques [2, 35, 33]. For example, Arapakis et al., studied the role of emotions in information retrieval, and introduced a number of models [2, 4]. In their subsequent work, the authors have shown that emotional features can be effectively included in building implicit feedback systems [4], and they can also be used to personalise search [2]. Similarly, the work by Moshfeghi et al. demonstrated that, in addition to emotional features [34], physiological features can also be used to model relevance and they can also be used to predict task types [33].

2.3 Neuropsychology and IR

Recent research has begun to examine IR from a neuroscience perspective, using techniques of brain imaging to reveal the brain activity related to the underlying neural activity of a user. One particular area of emphasis to this research has been to examine the concept of relevance. Results of Moshfeghi et al. [35] showed, using fMRI, that it is possible to identify brain regions activated by the process of judging relevance of an image. The brain regions they reported included the inferior parietal lobe, inferior temporal gyrus and superior frontal gyrus; the activation of these regions during relevance assessment was significantly higher when evaluating relevant items.

Another example is a study conducted by Eugster et al. [17] that used EEG to show that the frequency content of the EEG signal as well as Event Related Potentials (ERPs) can be used effectively as a set of features to decode the relevance of a text. Similarly, Allegretti et al. [1] reported on EEG results that indicated that within 500 ms EEG signals begin to appear that differentiate between viewing a relevant and a non relevant image. Likewise, Kauppi et al. [23] used magnetoencephalography (MEG) to show that the frequency content of the MEG signal, along with eye movement data can be used for decoding relevance of images. These studies have used the relative strength of the different measurement techniques to make great progress and to indicate where in the brain relevance judgments are happening and what the time course is of these neural processes that determine relevance.

However, the above studies have not investigated the wider view of how IN emerges. In this paper we take an important step to understanding the neural processes involved with primary stages when an IN emerges.

3. EXPERIMENTAL METHODOLOGY

3.1 Research Questions and Hypothesis

This paper studies the concept of information need from a neuropsychological perspective by investigating brain activity during periods in which an information need was induced. In particular, we implemented two different scenarios to create information need, in both scenarios participants were asked a multiple choice question, but in the first scenario when participants confronted an ASK they only had the option to acknowledge that they needed to search, they could not act on this IN. In the second scenario when participants confronted an ASK they were able to engage in a search process. Our hypothesis was that there exists brain regions for which the activation levels are different depending on the state of information need and that the regions found for these two scenarios would provide measurement data of brain states to complement our theoretical understanding of IN.

Related to our hypotheses there are several considerations on the design and analysis of fMRI data [35, 14]. Of particular importance are several factors that were critical in guiding our research plans. Firstly, the fMRI scanning environment is restrictive in that a participant must lay supine with their head kept still, and that only limited response/interactive devices can be in this scanning environment without causing signal or safety issues. This constraint led to the use of multiple choice questions for a task since it was possible to provide response using an MRI-compatible button box. Another constraint is that while fMRI provides the ability to localise activity to within millimetres, the temporal resolution of fMRI (the time to take a single measurement of the entire brain) is on the order of around 2 seconds. This relatively slow rate of data acquisition is compounded by the fact that the Blood Oxygenation Level Dependent (BOLD) signal measured is related to the underlying neural signal in a complex way that introduces further delays [18]. To address these delays it was necessary to time the events of the different scenarios at a rate that was compatible with our fMRI measurements. To achieve a suitable design for our questions about IN we adapted the methods used in related work in problem solving [47] which examined neural correlates of insight by comparing brain activity when a multiple choice response showed insight, to brain activity when a multiple choice response did not show insight.

3.2 Design

A "within-subjects" design was used in this study. The independent variable was the information need (with two levels: information need, and no information need), which was controlled by responding to questions viewed on the screen. The set of questions were designed so that averaged across all participants there would be an equal number of responses expressing an answer and expressing a need for search. The dependent variable was brain activity revealed by the BOLD signal.

3.3 Task

Each participant completed two different search scenarios.

Question-Response (QR) Task: In the first scenario, which we term Question-Response (QR), participants were first presented with a question for 4 seconds, then for 4 seconds four possible responses were provided while the question stayed on the screen (Figure 1). Participants could not make a response until after the 4 seconds of observing the possible responses. This was done so that brain activity related to the motor response of pressing the button would not be contained in the model of brain activity, which only considered these first 8 seconds. After the 8 seconds participants were able to respond and in this QR scenario the experiment progressed directly on to the next trial. Of the four possible responses, one was always the correct answer and one of them was always "need to search". The position of the four alternatives was randomised for each trial and the response given by pressing one of the four buttons available on the button box that each participant had in their right hand. The time to respond was left free so that participants were not under time pressure to respond. The order of the questions was randomised for each participant.

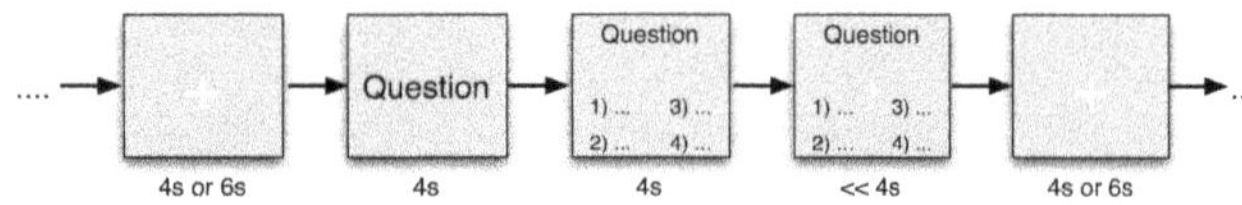

Figure 1: A schematic representation of Scenario 1

Question-Response-Search (QRS) Task: In the second scenario, which we term Question-Response-Search (QRS), participants performed the same task as in the QR scenario except that if the answer "need to search" was provided then they entered an additional stage where they formulated a search query (and submitted it verbally into a noise-cancelling microphone), received a document and evaluated this document. In the present study we do not investigate brain activity during the search and document evaluation periods. Instead we focus only on the brain activity in response to the the presentation of the question and the possible responses. The difference between the two scenarios is that in Scenario 1 participants do not engage in a search process, while in the second scenario they do engage in a search process. This is important from the conceptual stance that in Scenario 1 stating the need to search is the endpoint of the entire process, while for Scenario 2 it is a transition to the start of a search.

3.4 Question Answering Dataset

In order to perform the two task scenarios mentioned in Section 3.3, we created a Question Answering dataset[1]. To develop this standard set of questions, we used previous runs of TREC Q/A Track, in particular we carefully selected a set of 80 questions from the TREC-8 and TREC-2001 Question Answering Tracks - Main Task[2]. We chose these two Tracks since they were the first and last tracks where the questions presented there were (i) independent from one another, in contrast to other Tracks that share a relationship, and (ii) they also provided the correct answer to the questions.

We then manually examined all the questions presented in these two tracks and selected a subset of questions that (i) were not longer than one line, and (ii) the correct answer to the question was not longer than 5 words. This constraint is due to the limitation of presenting the questions and options to the participants in an fMRI settings. An additional constraint was that there were at least two relevant and non-relevant answers in their QRel. We then removed the questions that were ambiguous or were time dependent, e.g. Who is the president of Stanford University? (TREC-8, Topic 51), making the answers provided in the Track not appropriate. The answers of all these questions were then checked by current search engines to make sure that the answers are still valid and correct. We also created two wrong answers for each question that were in the domain of the question, e.g. "What is supernova?" (TREC-2001, Topic 1067) the correct answer is "An exploding star" and we created two other wrong answers i.e. "A newborn star" and "A dead star". We also made sure that the questions covered a wide range of topics, e.g. history, politics, science, etc. This was done in order to reduce any bias that might occur from emphasis of a particular type of question.

Over this set of questions, two annotators separately judged the difficulty of the questions (i.e. hard or easy) and then selected a subset of 80 questions where both annotators agreed upon their difficulties, i.e. 40 of them were hard and 40 were easy questions. For Scenario 1, 40 questions out of these 80 questions were selected where 20 were easy and 20 were hard questions. The remainder of the questions were used for Scenario 2. Since Scenario 2 was divided into two runs, additional care was made to further divide the questions across the runs so that they both had 10 easy and 10 hard questions covering a variety of topics. The goal of this procedure was to control the set of questions such that on average there was an equal chance of experiencing ASK and knowing the answer.

Another extra step for Scenario 2 was to prepare the documents that were shown to the subjects once they engaged in a search process. This took the form of simulating a snippet answer that is returned by current search engine such as Google when a question is submitted. For this purpose we selected two relevant and two non-relevant documents from QRel. The length of the answers provided in TREC-8 and TREC 2001 were incompatible. In order to keep the size of the results consistent, for those answers that were too short, we found the original source file and selected sentences around the answer so that all snippets had the same length. The average length of the answers shown to the participants for first and second run of Scenario 2 were 39.47 words (SD of 3.33) and 39.65 words (SD of 3.285) respectively. This was done in order to reduce any potential confounding effect of snippet size on the brain activity results.

3.5 Procedure

This section outlines the flow of the study, from beginning to end. Ethical permission for the study was obtained from the Ethics Committee of the College of Science and Engineering, University of Glasgow. Participants were recruited from the participant database at Centre for Cognitive Neuroimaging, University of Glasgow. Participants were instructed of the duration of the experiment, which included approximately 50 minutes to perform all tasks examining information need, and approximately 10 minutes to obtain a scan of their anatomical structure. They were informed that they could leave at any point in time during the experiment and would still receive payment (the payment rate was £6/hr). They were then asked to sign a consent form. Before participating, participants underwent a safety check to guarantee that they did not possess any metal items inside or outside of their body, or any other contraindications for scanning, such as certain tattoo inks. They were

[1] The Question Answering dataset is available upon request.

[2] For more information please visit http://trec.nist.gov/data/qa/t8_qadata.html and http://trec.nist.gov/data/qa/2001_qadata/main_task.html

then provided with gear (similar to a training suit) to wear for the duration of the experiment to avoid interference from any metal objects in their clothes with the fMRI signal.

Next, as a training process they were given an example task and a corresponding set of example questions in order to familiarise themselves with the procedure. Once they had successfully completed their training task, participants entered the fMRI machine and the experimenter adjusted the settings of the machine to maximise their comfort and vision. While being scanned, each participant first participated in one run of the QR scenario, which contained 40 questions. They then participated in two separate runs of the QRS scenario, with each run comprised of 20 questions. Two runs were chosen to give the participants a further break to relax during the scanning and to prevent fatigue on the QRS task, which consumed more time. After the functional runs were complete the anatomical data of each participant was obtained.

After completion of scanning participants were asked to fill out an exit questionnaire that provided further demographic and qualitative descriptions of their experience during the experiment. They also filled out the Edinburgh handedness questionnaire [37] which provides evaluation of whether the participant was right-, left- or mixed-handed. Handedness information was obtained since lateralization of brain function is influenced by handedness and we wished to ensure that our sample of participants approximated the general population.

Apparatus: The images were presented using Presentation® software[3], and projected using a LCD projector onto a translucent screen, while participants watched them in an angled mirror in the MRI scanner.

fMRI Data Acquisition: All fMRI data was collected using a 3T Tim Trio Siemens scanner and 32-channel head coil at the Centre for Cognitive Neuroimaging, University of Glasgow. A functional T2*-weighted MRI run was acquired for the single run of the QR scenario and the two runs of the QRS scenario (TR 2000ms; TE 30ms; 32 Slices; $3mm^3$ voxel; FOV of 210, imaging matrix of 70×70).

An anatomical scan was performed at the end of the scanning session that comprised a high-resolution T1-weighted anatomical scan using a 3D magnetisation prepared rapid acquisition gradient echo (ADNI- MPRAGE) T1-weighted sequence (192 slices; $1mm^3$ voxel; Sagittal Slice; TR = 1900ms; TE = 2.52; 256×256 image resolution).

Questionnaires: At the end of the experiment, the participants were introduced to an *exit questionnaire*, which gathered background and demographic information. It also enquired about previous experience with fMRI type user studies as well as participants general comments for the user study. Finally, it also included questions to ascertain participants' subjective experience of performing the experiment.

Pilot Studies: Prior to running the actual user study, a pilot study was performed using two participants to confirm that the process worked correctly and smoothly. A number of changes were made to the experimental paradigm based on feedback from the pilot study. After the pilot, it was determined that the participants were able to complete the user study without problems and that the system was correctly logging participants' interaction data.

[3]Presentation® software (Neurobehavioral systems, Inc.), http://www.neurobs.com.

4. RESULTS

A study with the procedure explained in Section 3.5 was conducted over 15 days from 7 December, 2015 to 22 December, 2015. Participants consisted of 24 healthy individuals with 11 males and 13 females. All participants were under the age of 44, with the largest group between the ages of 18-23 (54.1%) followed by a group between the ages of 30-35 (20.8%). The handedness survey indicated that 79.1% were right-handed, 12.5% were left-handed and 8.33% were mixed-handed. Participants tended to have a postgraduate degree (20.8%), bachelors (33.33%) or other qualifications (45.8%). They were primarily students (54.1%), though there were a number of individuals who were self-employed (20.8%), not employed (4.16%) or employed by a company or organisation (20.8%). Participants were primarily native speakers (79.1%) or had an advanced level of English (20.8%). They all had experience in searching, with an average of 11.66 years (SD of 3.58) experience.

Task Perception: At the end of the procedure an exit questionnaire was performed that included questions about participants' overall subjective experience of performing the tasks. These questions specifically addressed participants' perception of their performed tasks in terms of the difficulty of the task, the familiarity of the participant with the task and the extent to which they found the task stressful, clear, successful, and satisfactory. Namely, participants were given the following questions *"The tasks we asked you to perform were [easy/stressful/familiar/clear/Satisfactory] (answer: 1: "Strongly Disagree", 2: "Disagree", 3: "Neutral", 4: "Agree", 5: "Strongly Agree")"*. Descriptive statistics of these responses are shown by box plots in Figure 2, which show five key statistics: the minimum, first, second (median), third, and maximum quartiles.[4]. These results indicate that participants found the tasks difficult (not easy) and stressful, familiar, clear, successful, and satisfactory.

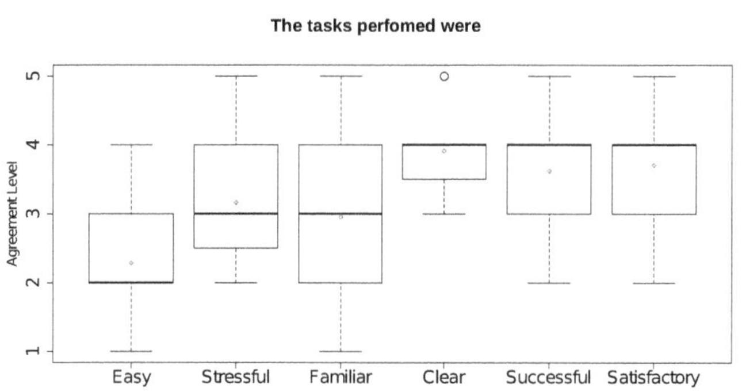

Figure 2: Box plot of the task perception based on the information gathered from the questionnaires of 24 participants. The red diamond represents the mean value.

Log Analysis: The fMRI analysis for both Scenario 1 and Scenario 2 relied upon a participant's response of the question to code whether a trial was IN or No-IN. This raised two considerations: firstly, for examination of brain data within a scenario it is important to have approximately an equal response rate for IN and No-IN responses. Secondly, comparison across scenarios is strengthened by having similar response rates since this argues against the possibility

[4]Further information can be found in [31].

that any difference found was due to simply response bias. Thus, it was important to examine the average response rates for whether the number of IN and No-IN responses were approximately balanced for each scenario and whether there was a difference between scenarios. In Scenario 1 the average number of IN responses was 18.45 (SD of 4.59) and the average number of No-IN responses was 21.42 (SD of 4.41). A paired t-test revealed that there was no difference between the type of responses (p-value = 0.12). In Scenario 2 the average number of IN responses was 17.5 (SD of 5.91) and the average number of No-IN responses was 22.5 (SD of 5.91). A paired t-test revealed a marginal difference between the type of responses (p-value = 0.05). An examination of the response rates across scenarios using paired t-tests revealed no significant difference between scenarios for either IN responses (p-value = 0.24) or No-IN responses (p-value = 0.19).

fMRI Data Preprocessing: The fMRI data were preprocessed using Brain Voyager QX[5]. A standard pipeline of pre-processing of the data was performed for each participant [19]. This involved slice scan time correction using trilinear interpolation based on information about the TR and the order of slice scanning. Three-dimensional motion correction was performed to detect and correct for small head movements by spatial alignment of all the volumes of a participant to the first volume by rigid body transformations. In addition, linear trends in the data were removed and high pass filtering with a cutoff of 0.0025 Hz performed to reduce artefact from low frequency physiological noise. The functional data were then coregistered with the anatomic data and spatially normalised into the common Talairach space [39]. Finally, the functional data of each individual underwent spatial smoothing using a Gaussian kernel of 6mm to facilitate analysis of group data.

4.1 General Linear Model (GLM) Analysis

Analysis began with a first-level analysis on the data of individual participants using multiple linear regression of the BOLD-response time course in each voxel, using two predictors for the different Response Type (respond need to search, respond with answer). To achieve this, for each participant's data a BrainVoyager protocol file (PRT) was derived that represented the onset and duration of the 8s total time that the question (4s) and question and possible responses (4s) were available. Predictors' time courses were adjusted for the hemodynamic response delay by convolution with a hemodynamic response function. Group data were statistically tested with a second-level analysis using a random effects analysis of variance using Response Type as a within-participants factor. To address the issue of multiple statistical comparisons across all voxels, activations are reported using False Discovery Rate (FDR) at a threshold of $q < 0.01$ [10]. Using FDR we control for the number of false positive voxels among the subset of voxels labelled as significant.

Main Results: The key findings which emerged from the results are that the analysis of fMRI brain data revealed differences in brain activity due to whether participants experienced IN or not. These differences appeared sensitive to whether or not the IN was associated with actually making a search or simply deciding that a search would be necessary. Although several brain regions showed differential activity with IN, our results point to a particular region of the brain known as the posterior cingulate which is known to be a critical hub area involved in coordinating brain activity between the internal and external environment.

Analysis of Scenario 1 (RQ): In Scenario 1 we investigated brain activity when participants were presented with questions and possible responses, and they needed to decide that they knew the answer already or would need to search. For all participants we contrasted brain activity when they provided an answer versus when they provided the response that they needed to search. We hypothesised that this contrast would reveal brain regions associated with successful memory retrieval and working memory when they responded with an answer, signifying No-IN. When the response was that there was a need to search we expected activity in regions associated with IN.

The results, based on all 24 participants, for the effect of the factor Type of Response are shown for Scenario 1 in Figure 3 plotted on an average brain and in Table 1. To evaluate whether the effect of the Type of Response indicated higher or lower activity when a search was requested the average beta weights for each cluster were obtained and these are presented in bar charts for each of the clusters. Results showed that 4 of the 5 clusters had higher activation for the No-IN condition. This included thalamus, extending into the left head of caudate, right head of caudate, the left caudate body and an extensive cluster in the right inferior frontal gyrus (also known as the dorsolateral prefrontal cortex). These regions are known to have anatomical connectivity [16] and have been implicated in processes of memory retrieval [32], working memory [6], and decision making [15]. The only cluster showing greater activation for the ASK condition was found in the the ventral aspect of the posterior cingulate cortex. This region has often been associated with what is known as the default mode network [38] which shows decreased activation when a task is performed and increased activity when mind-wandering. We will return to discussion of the posterior cingulate later in the paper.

An interesting finding is that the situation when an answer could be provided, and thus an information need did not exist, provided 4 of the 5 clusters. Moreover, these clusters can be considered a network involving memory retrieval, information accumulation and working memory, all functions we would expect when a participant can provide an answer to the question. The remaining cluster in ventral posterior cingulate provides us with a putative brain region where activity reflects IN. Activity in this region has been hypothesised [29] to reflect a narrow focus of attention on internal information, and this is consistent with the "need to search" response in Scenario 1. Here, the response can be generated by assessing internally only that it was not possible to provide an answer; for success in the task there is no need to modify behaviour or to broaden the focus of attention.

Analysis of Scenario 2 (RQS): In Scenario 2 we investigated brain activity when participants were presented with questions and possible responses and if they responded that a search was needed then they would subsequently engage in a search. For all participants we contrasted brain activity when they provided an answer versus when they provided the response that they needed to search. Again we hypothesised that this contrast would reveal brain regions associ-

[5] http://www.BrainVoyager.com

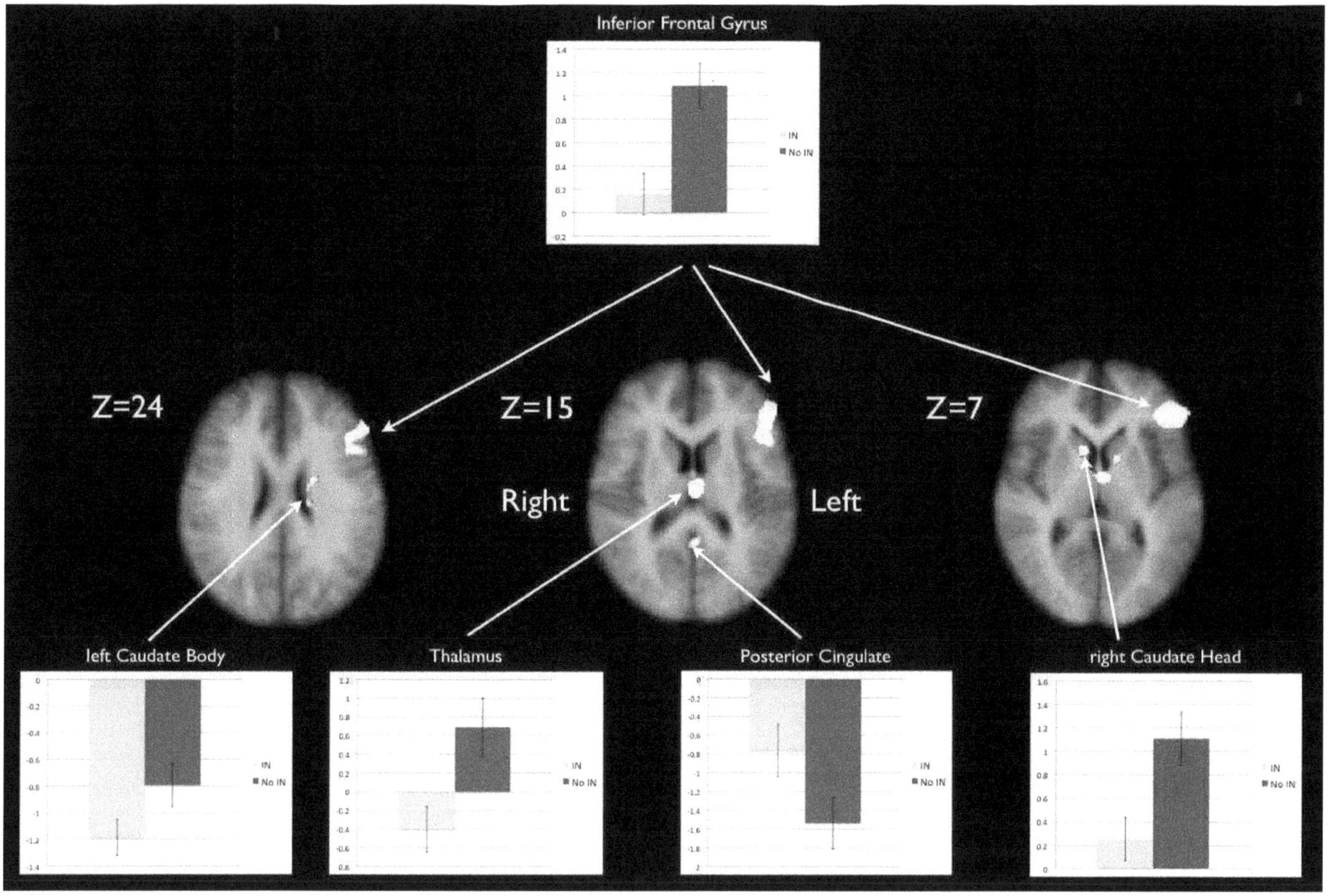

Figure 3: The five activation clusters from Scenario 1 are projected onto the average anatomical structure for three transverse sections. Note that the brains are in radiological format where the left side of the brain is on the right side of the image.

Table 1: Details of Scenario 1 activations, including their anatomic label, location, Brodmann Area (BA), effect size and volume.

		Talairach Coordinates				Effect size		Number of voxels
Brain Area	Hemisphere	X	Y	Z	BA	F(1,23)	p-value	mm^3
Caudate Head	Right	11	10	3	-	42.91	0.000001	427
Thalmus	Left	-1	-11	12	-	52.39	<0.000001	2017
ventral Posterior Cingulate	Left	-4	-44	12	29	33.09	0.000007	263
Caudate Body	Left	-19	-17	21	-	39.03	0.000002	282
Inferior Frontal Gyrus	Left	-46	31	6	46	107.63	<0.000001	8024

ated with successful memory retrieval and working memory when they responded with an answer, signifying No-IN. In contrast to Scenario 1, such a result was not obtained. Instead we only found regions where brain activity was greater for IN, including a region of the posterior cingulate known as the dorsal posterior cingulate.

The results, based on all 24 participants, for the effect of the factor Type of Response are shown for Scenario 2 in Figure 4 plotted on an average brain and in Table 2. Again, to help assess the direction of the effect, parameter estimates are displayed as bar charts for each cluster. All clusters including the fusiform gyrus, the dorsal posterior cingulate and the cuneus (extending into the precuneus) showed greater activation for the IN condition. As both the precuneus and posterior cingulate clusters have been associated with the default mode network, it is perhaps not surprising that deactivations are apparent for these regions.

The fusiform gyrus is often associated with high level visual processing and it is possible that this cluster reflects greater visual activity when participants were in the state of IN.

The fact that the posterior cingulate was again identified as a region where activity was greater for the IN condition further raises the possibility that monitoring activity in this area could provide a useful brain signal for identifying information need. The fact that it was the dorsal posterior cingulate is important from a theoretical perspective. It has been hypothesised that the dorsal posterior cingulate is involved when there is brain activity directed towards external sources and broad attention is used [29]. This is consistent with the need to search as the individual must transition from a state of accessing internal information to one where they are engaging with the collection of new information from external sources.

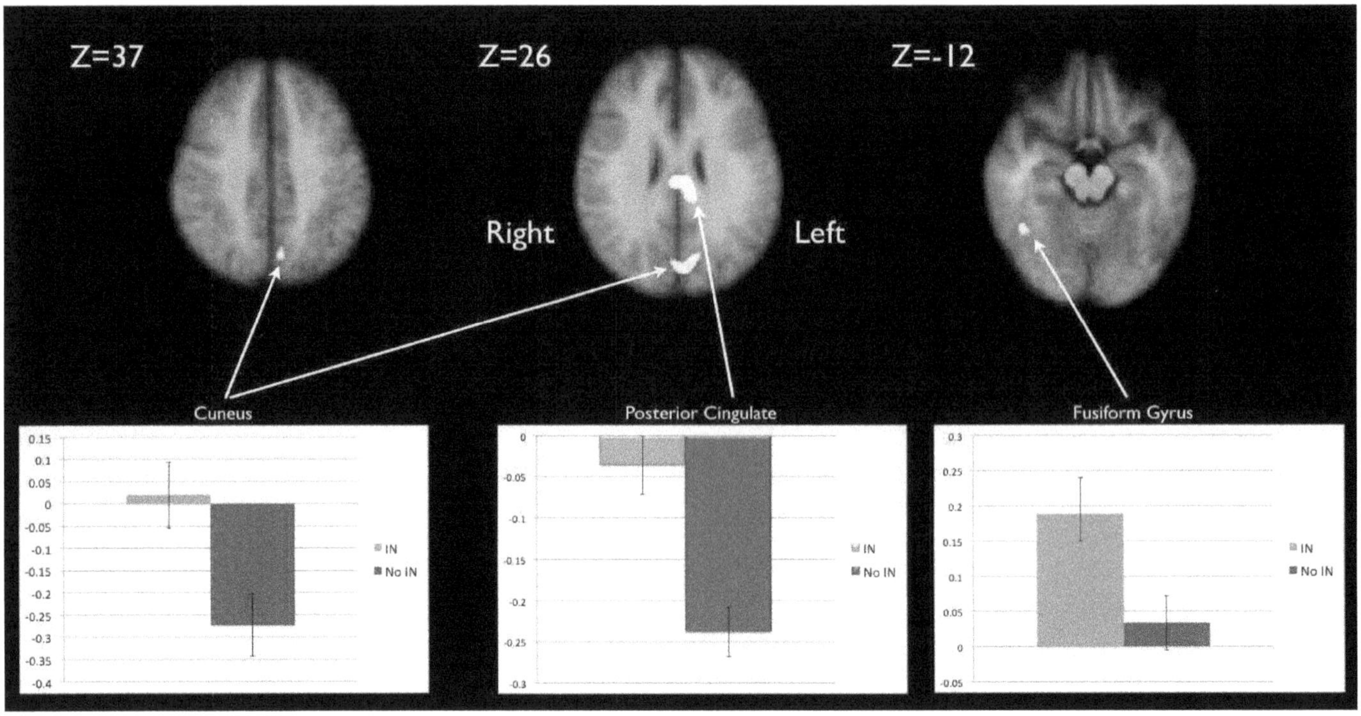

Figure 4: The three activation clusters from Scenario 2 are shown projected onto the average anatomical structure for three transverse sections. Note that the brains are in radiological format where the left side of the brain is on the right side of the image.

Table 2: Details of Scenario 2 activations, including their anatomic label, location, Brodmann Area (BA), effect size and volume.

		Talairach Coordinates				Effect size		Number of voxels
Brain Area	Hemisphere	X	Y	Z	BA	F(1,23)	p-value	mm^3
Fusiform Gyrus	Right	41	-50	-12	37	31.29	0.000011	266
Cuneus	Left	-7	-74	24	18	38.64	0.000002	3453
dorsal Posterior Cingulate	Left	-10	-29	27	23	60.35	<0.000001	2147

Significance of the Posterior Cingulate: As we have discussed in relation to the current results, both the greater activation during IN and the switch between ventral and dorsal regions when an actual search is performed provide a unique signature for IN. In this regard it is useful to review that the posterior cingulate is thought to be what is known as a "hub" area. Such areas are known to be densely connected with many different brain regions and to be involved in the coordination of large scale brain networks. One function of the posterior cingulate appears to be in the balance between directing brain activity towards either internal or external sources and this role resonates with the requirements of detecting IN in that detecting the switch between internal and external processing is synonymous with search.

5. DISCUSSION AND CONCLUSION

This paper investigated the concept of information need from a neuropsychological perspective by investigating brain activity during periods in which an information need was induced. The raison d'etre of IR is to satisfy human information needs. Despite advances in the past few decades in both the IR and relevant scientific communities, we do not really understand how an information need emerges and how it is physically manifested. Information need refers to a complex concept: at the very initial state of the phenomenon (i.e. at a visceral level), even the searcher may not be aware of its existence. This renders the measuring of this concept (using traditional behaviour studies) nearly impossible. Using functional Magnetic Resonance Imaging (fMRI), we measured the brain activity of twenty four participants while they performed a Question Answering (Q/A) Task. In order to do so, we devised a "within-subjects" design experiment where the independent variable was the information need (with two levels: Information Need, and No-Information Need), which was controlled by responding to questions viewed on the screen. A set of questions were designed for a typical participant to respond equally between expressing an information need to answer the question or expressing a need to search for more information to answer the question using TREC-8 and TREC 2001 Q/A Tracks. The dependent variable was brain activity revealed by the BOLD signal.

We implemented two different task scenarios to create information need, in both scenarios participants were asked a multiple choice question, but in the first scenario when participants confronted an ASK they only had the option to acknowledge that they needed to search, they could not act on this IN (i.e. QR Task). In the second scenario when participants confronted an ASK they were able to engage in a search process (i.e. QRS Task). Our hypothesis was that there exists brain regions for which the activation levels are different depending on the state of information need and that the regions found for these two scenarios would provide measurement data of brain states to complement our theoretical understanding of IN.

The key findings which emerged from the results are that the analysis of fMRI brain data revealed differences in brain activity due to whether participants experienced IN or not (addressing **RQ2**). These differences were obtained from modelling brain activity during the presentation of the question and possible responses and thus precede the actual decision to search (addressing **RQ3**). These differences appeared sensitive to whether or not the IN was associated with actually making a search or simply deciding that a search would be necessary (addressing **RQ4**). Although several brain regions showed differential activity with IN, our results point to a particular region of the brain known as the posterior cingulate which is known to be a critical hub area involved in coordinating brain activity between the internal and external environment. We speculate that this hub nature of switching between large scale brain networks that involve either internal or external processing could be an essential component of IN (addressing some issues raised by **RQ1**).

The results for the QR task of Scenario 1 and the QRS task of Scenario 2 provided strikingly different results. In the QR task of Scenario 1 the contrast of brain activation between the IN and No-IN conditions revealed greater activity for the IN condition in one brain area (posterior cingulate) and greater activity for the No-IN condition in four of the five areas obtained. These four areas can be associated with recalling information and making a decision. Relating this to IR we see evidence for the neural substrate involved with successfully recovering internal knowledge, a situation that relieves the need for information. However, a primary interest of the current research is to explore what brain regions are associated with IN. Thus, the results of the QRS task of Scenario 2 are of interest since we see that all three regions reported had greater activity for the IN condition. In particular, the dorsal posterior cingulate provides results similar to that found for the ventral posterior cingulate found in Scenario 1.

These differences between dorsal and ventral activation of posterior cingulate can be related to theories of the posterior cingulate and its special role in brain function [29]. The posterior cingulate is known to be an area that is metabolically active, using substantial energy and serving as a hub that regulates cognitive activity. It is especially involved in regulating brain resources between engaging in internal or external processes and the Arousal, Balance and Breadth of Attention (ABBA) model provides an explanation of the differences between the IN conditions in Scenarios 1 and 2. The model holds that activation in ventral posterior cingulate is consistent with a narrow internal focus while activation in dorsal posterior cingulate is consistent with a broad external focus. Thus, in Scenario 1, when participants need only to focus on the fact that they need to search (not what they need to search or mechanisms of search) the pattern of results in posterior cingulate shows a narrow and internal focus. However, in Scenario 2, when participants need to engage in a subsequent search task the pattern of results in posterior cingulate shows a broad and external focus. The implication for IR is that the differential patterns of activation in the posterior cingulate provide a window into how cognitive processes are being directed and switching state from a narrow internal focus to a broad external focus can be used as a sign of a searcher needing to gather information from external sources.

Regarding the pattern of activity in posterior cingulate several aspects deserve further investigation. One is whether this general difference of activity found between IN and no-IN is unique, the posterior cingulate is a complicated and densely connected brain region and other differences in cognitive states might reveal similar patterns of BOLD activity. This could be explained by heterogeneity of function in the posterior cingulate, or possibly by some more basic, and yet undetermined, mechanism that is common to IN and other cognitive processes. One possible way forward to studying this would for more detailed analysis of the spatiotemporal pattern of activity in posterior cingulate to determine the encoding of IN. Research in these directions would potentially aid in ways to exploit this neural signal in retrieval systems.

While our present interpretation of brain activity provides a parsimonious account of how IN is represented in the brain, further study is needed to advance this interpretation. One possible way forward is to perform a more detailed analysis of the spatiotemporal pattern of activity in posterior cingulate to see whether multivariate techniques of machine learning could provide a means to decode IN directly from brain activity, rather than to infer it from univariate comparison of brain activity during IN and no-IN states. Such a result could pave the way, as brain measuring technology advances, to monitor the IN state of an individual and to exploit this knowledge in a search engine system. Prerequisites to achieve this would be to confirm that this pattern of activity in posterior cingulate is robust across different IN scenarios as well as being unique to IN.

Our present results indicating differences between the QR and QRS tasks show the importance of task on brain activation. Thus, a meaningful research direction to pursue would be to investigate similar research questions in the context of other information retrieval and interaction tasks. This could provide converging evidence and would advance our neurotheoretical understanding of IN leading to exploitation of such signals in functioning IR systems.

In conclusion, the results of this experiment revealed a distributed network of brain regions commonly associated with information retrieval and produced novel results about the neural bases of information need. These results have implications both for theories explaining information need and the potential to design systems that could detect information need. Finally, we believe our study and conclusions constitute an important step in unravelling the nature of information need and therefore better satisfying it.

Acknowledgement: This work was supported by the Economic and Social Research Council [grant number ES/L011921/1].

6. REFERENCES

[1] M. Allegretti, Y. Moshfeghi, M. Hadjigeorgieva, F. E. Pollick, J. M. Jose, and G. Pasi. When relevance judgement is happening?: An eeg-based study. In *SIGIR '15*, New York, NY, USA, 2015. ACM.

[2] I. Arapakis, K. Athanasakos, and J. M. Jose. A comparison of general vs personalised affective models for the prediction of topical relevance. In *SIGIR '10*, pages 371–378, 2010.

[3] I. Arapakis, I. Konstas, and J. M. Jose. Using facial expressions and peripheral physiological signals as implicit

indicators of topical relevance. In *MM ' 09*, pages 461–470, 2009.

[4] I. Arapakis, Y. Moshfeghi, H. Joho, R. Ren, D. Hannah, and J. M. Jose. Enriching user profiling with affective features for the improvement of a multimodal recommender system. *CIVR '09*, 2009.

[5] I. Arapakis, Y. Moshfeghi, H. Joho, R. Ren, D. Hannah, and J. M. Jose. Integrating facial expressions into user profiling for the improvement of a multimodal recommender system. In *ICME '09*, pages 1440–1443, 2009.

[6] A. K. Barbey, M. Koenigs, and J. Grafman. Dorsolateral prefrontal contributions to human working memory. *Cortex*, 49(5):1195–1205, 2013.

[7] M. J. Bates. Indexing and access for digital libraries and the internet: Human, database, and domain factors. *JASIST*, 49(13):1185–1205, 1998.

[8] N. Belkin, R. Oddy, and H. Brooks. ASK for information retrieval: Part I. Background and theory. *Journal of Documentation*, 38(2):61–71, 1982.

[9] N. J. Belkin, R. N. Oddy, and H. M. Brooks. ASK for information retrieval: Part II. Results of a design study. *Journal of documentation*, 38(3):145–164, 1982.

[10] Y. Benjamini and Y. Hochberg. Controlling the false discovery rate: a practical and powerful approach to multiple testing. *Journal of the Royal Statistical Society. Series B (Methodological)*, pages 289–300, 1995.

[11] C. L. Borgman. *From Gutenberg to the global information infrastructure: access to information in the networked world.* Mit Press, 2000.

[12] C. Cole. A theory of information need for information retrieval that connects information to knowledge. *JASIST*, 62(7):1216–1231, 2011.

[13] C. Cole, C.-A. Julien, and J. E. Leide. An associative index model for hypertext internet search based on vannevar bushâĂŹs memex machine: An exploratory case study. *Information Research*, 15(3):15–3, 2010.

[14] A. Dimoka. How to conduct a functional magnetic resonance (fmri) study in social science research. *MIS Quarterly*, 36(3):811–840, 2012.

[15] L. Ding and J. I. Gold. Caudate encodes multiple computations for perceptual decisions. *The Journal of Neuroscience*, 30(47):15747–15759, 2010.

[16] B. Draganski, F. Kherif, S. Klöppel, P. A. Cook, D. C. Alexander, G. J. Parker, R. Deichmann, J. Ashburner, and R. S. Frackowiak. Evidence for segregated and integrative connectivity patterns in the human basal ganglia. *The Journal of Neuroscience*, 28(28):7143–7152, 2008.

[17] M. J. Eugster, T. Ruotsalo, M. M. Spapé, I. Kosunen, O. Barral, N. Ravaja, G. Jacucci, and S. Kaski. Predicting term-relevance from brain signals. In *SIGIR'14*, pages 425–434. ACM, 2014.

[18] K. Friston, C. Buechel, G. Fink, J. Morris, E. Rolls, and R. Dolan. Psychophysiological and modulatory interactions in neuroimaging. *NeuroImage*, 6:218–229, 2007.

[19] R. Goebel. *BrainVoyager QX, Vers.2.1, Brain Innovation B.V.* Maastricht, Netherlands.

[20] B. Hjørland. The foundation of the concept of relevance. *JASIST*, 61(2):217–237, 2010.

[21] P. Ingwersen. Cognitive perspectives of information retrieval interaction: elements of a cognitive ir theory. *Journal of documentation*, 52(1):3–50, 1996.

[22] T. Joachims, L. Granka, B. Pan, H. Hembrooke, and G. Gay. Accurately interpreting clickthrough data as implicit feedback. In *SIGIR '05*, pages 154–161, 2005.

[23] J. P. Kauppi, M. Kandemir, V. M. Saarinen, L. Hirvenkari, L. Parkkonen, A. Klami, R. Hari, and S. Kaski. Towards brain-activity-controlled information retrieval: Decoding image relevance from MEG signals. *NeuroImage, in press*, 2015.

[24] D. Kelly and N. Belkin. A user modeling system for personalized interaction and tailored retrieval in interactive ir. *ASIST*, 39(1):316–325, 2005.

[25] D. Kelly and N. J. Belkin. Display time as implicit feedback: understanding task effects. In *SIGIR '04*, pages 377–384, New York, NY, USA, 2004. ACM.

[26] D. Kelly and X. Fu. Eliciting better information need descriptions from users of information search systems. *Inf. Process. Manage.*, 43(1):30–46, Jan. 2007.

[27] J. Koenemann and N. J. Belkin. A case for interaction: a study of interactive information retrieval behavior and effectiveness. In *SIGCHI '96*, pages 205–212. ACM, 1996.

[28] C. C. Kuhlthau. A principle of uncertainty for information seeking. *Journal of Documentation*, 49(4):339–355, 1993.

[29] R. Leech and D. J. Sharp. The role of the posterior cingulate cortex in cognition and disease. *Brain*, 137(1):12–32, 2014.

[30] L. Lorigo, M. Haridasan, H. Brynjarsdóttir, L. Xia, T. Joachims, G. Gay, L. Granka, F. Pellacini, and B. Pan. Eye tracking and online search: Lessons learned and challenges ahead. *JASIST*, 59(7):1041–1052, 2008.

[31] R. McGill, J. W. Tukey, and W. A. Larsen. Variations of box plots. *American Statistician*, 32(1):12–16, 1978.

[32] A. S. Mitchell and S. Chakraborty. What does the mediodorsal thalamus do? *Frontiers in systems neuroscience*, 7, 2013.

[33] Y. Moshfeghi and J. M. Jose. An effective implicit relevance feedback technique using affective, physiological and behavioural features. In *SIGIR '13*, pages 133–142, 2013.

[34] Y. Moshfeghi and J. M. Jose. On cognition, emotion, and interaction aspects of search tasks with different search intentions. In *WWW*, pages 931–942, 2013.

[35] Y. Moshfeghi, L. R. Pinto, F. E. Pollick, and J. M. Jose. Understanding relevance: An fmri study. In *ECIR*, pages 14–25, 2013.

[36] D. M. Nichols. Implicit rating and filtering. In *Proceedings of the Fifth DELOS Workshop on Filtering and Collaborative Filtering*, pages 31–36, 1997.

[37] R. C. Oldfield. The assessment and analysis of handedness: the edinburgh inventory. *Neuropsychologia*, 9(1):97–113, 1971.

[38] M. E. Raichle, A. M. MacLeod, A. Z. Snyder, W. J. Powers, D. A. Gusnard, and G. L. Shulman. A default mode of brain function. *Proceedings of the National Academy of Sciences*, 98(2):676–682, 2001.

[39] J. Talairach and P. Tournoux. *Co-planar stereotaxic atlas of the human brain*, volume 147. Thieme New York:, 1988.

[40] R. S. Taylor. Question-negotiation and information seeking in libraries. *College & research libraries*, 29(3):178–194, 1968.

[41] P. I. und Kalervo Järvelin. *The Turn: Integration of Information Seeking and Retrieval in Context.* Springer, 2005. xiv, 448 S. ISBN 1-4020-3850-X, 2006.

[42] C. van Rijsbergen. (invited paper) A new theoretical framework for information retrieval. In *SIGIR*, pages 194–200. ACM, 1986.

[43] R. White and D. Kelly. A study on the effects of personalization and task information on implicit feedback performance. In *CIKM*, pages 297–306, 2006.

[44] R. W. White. *Implicit Feedback for Interactive Information Retrieval.* PhD thesis, University of Glasgow, 2004.

[45] R. W. White, J. M. Jose, and I. Ruthven. A task-oriented study on the influencing effects of query-biased summarisation in web searching. *IPM '03*, 39(5):707–733, 2003.

[46] T. D. Wilson. On user studies and information needs. *Journal of documentation*, 37(1):3–15, 1981.

[47] Q. Zhao, Z. Zhou, H. Xu, S. Chen, F. Xu, W. Fan, and L. Han. Dynamic neural network of insight: a functional magnetic resonance imaging study on solving chinese 'chengyu' riddles. *PloS one*, 8(3):e59351, 2013.

User Behavior in Asynchronous Slow Search

Ryan Burton
University of Michigan School of Information
105 S. State St.,
Ann Arbor MI, 48109
ryb@umich.edu

Kevyn Collins-Thompson
University of Michigan School of Information
105 S. State St.,
Ann Arbor MI, 48109
kevynct@umich.edu

ABSTRACT

Conventional Web search is predicated on returning results to users as quickly as possible. However, for some search tasks, users have reported a willingness to wait for the perfect set of results. In this work, we present the first study to analyze users' willingness to wait and their search success, when given a Web search system that embodies characteristics of *slow search*, where speed can be traded for an improvement in quality. We conducted a between-subjects user study involving tasks that required multiple queries to complete, providing a Web search system that gave users the option to additionally issue asynchronous queries for which results improve in relevance over time as users continued working. We analyze the resulting survey results and interaction log data to investigate how users spent their time while waiting, and how behavior and search outcomes changes when users are given the option of using a system with asynchronous slow search capabilities. We find that when given a slow search system, users are able to perceive the improvement in quality over time, and find tasks to be easier compared to a baseline conventional Web search system. Additionally, we find that users continue to issue their own queries and examine additional documents while the slow search queries are processed in the background, and use the slow search feature more effectively as they gain exposure to its behavior across tasks. Our study significantly advances our understanding of the benefits and tradeoffs involved in providing slow search scenarios for Web search.

Keywords

Search behavior; interactive information retrieval; user interfaces; slow search

1. INTRODUCTION

Current search systems are heavily optimized for speed: commercial search engines often conspicuously display the fraction of a second that it takes to return the list of results to a query. Traditional systems take numerous shortcuts for efficiency, such as making simplifying linguistic assumptions for query processing, document matching and ranking [16, 12]. As a result, much semantic richness is discarded in the process of retrieval, and much of the potential in terms of relevance quality may not be realized. The implicit time budget to which system developers must adhere also limits the scope and effectiveness of creative and useful extensions that may be considered for search processing and interfaces, such as enhanced personalization or novel ways of diversifying or summarizing results [10].

Slow search – the notion that a system may be able to "take its time" to process results for increased effectiveness – has been proposed, but only at the level of advancing the concept and exploring user attitudes to waiting for queries [16, 17, 8]. In this paper, we present a study that investigates the effect that an actual slow search system that supports asynchronous (background) query processing has on user behavior.

Search that focuses on speed, sometimes at the expense of quality, may be underserving users with particular needs or devices. For instance, the growth of mobile phone usage is outpacing that of desktop PCs—especially in developing countries—but there is a capability gap not only between phones and PCs, but between different phones as well. This may lead to lower levels of information seeking and engagement [14]. This study would therefore be useful to search engine implementers and interface designers targeting developing regions. Demonstrating the feasibility of this new slow search paradigm would also encourage implementers of conventional search engines to further explore the importance of the time–quality tradeoff, potentially leading to more systems that can automatically adjust their performance along a scale that effectively trades off urgency and quality.

The contributions we present in this paper include an extensive analysis of a search system that embodies characteristics of slow search. We are primarily interested in the practical value of trading speed for quality. To that end, we developed a novel system which improves the topic relevance of a query asynchronously over time while the user continues to work. This allows us to investigate the types of tasks for which users are willing to tolerate a delay in processing for more relevant search results. Using log data, we show how users behave when given asynchronous slow search capabilities and compare it to a baseline without these features. We also trained a logistic regression classifier to predict task success depending on the capabilities given to the user and interaction features. We also contribute an anonymized data set[1] to allow for analysis by other researchers.

As the primary purpose of this work is concerned with understanding patterns of interaction behavior when users have the ability to run a slow search in the background, we consider the following research questions:

[1]http://umich.edu/~ryb/slow

SIGIR '16, July 17-21, 2016, Pisa, Italy
 ISBN 978-1-4503-4069-4/16/07...$15.00
DOI: http://dx.doi.org/10.1145/2911451.2911541

RQ1: What are the types of queries for which users initially report they would have a willingness to wait?
RQ2: How much time will users typically wait for results from a slow query?
RQ3: In terms of search activity, how do users spend their time while waiting for a slow query to finish?
RQ4: How does typical user behavior change when provided with the ability to run a slow query?
RQ5: Do users perform search tasks more effectively with slow search?

We address RQ1 in Section 3.2, and RQ2–RQ5 in Section 4.

2. RELATED WORK

The concept of slow search was introduced to the literature by Dörk et al. [8] and Teevan et al. [16]. With inspiration from other "slow" movements, including slow food, slow travel, and slow technology, the authors posit the changes in how individuals and groups approach the process of search if a system emphasized slowness over speed. Poirier and Robinson [15] described a model of how slow principles may be applicable to information behavior. These initial papers provide insight in how proposed slow systems might be built, or survey-based results on how users might be willing to use such systems.

Previous work has shown that users would be willing to engage in slow search for certain kinds of queries and tasks. A study by Teevan et al. [16] based on user surveys and empirical analysis of search query logs found that, while increased load times for search results led to increased abandonment for typical queries, for tasks in which result quality was poor, users were willing to wait for better results or try alternative methods of finding information. However, none of this previous work built or studied a working slow search system with real users: to our knowledge, our paper represents the first study of how users interact with an actual Web search scenario providing slow search features.

Asynchronous search has been studied previously, but primarily in the context of bandwidth limitations and without recognition to the notion of improving search results [5]. Prior work has examined the relationship between time delays and user behavior [3, 16, 13], but these were in the context of conventional search systems, where users have the expectation of rapid responses, and with no benefit to waiting.

Slow search also has parallels with question answering systems. Aperjis et al. [2] found that users wait longer to get an additional answer after receiving a small number of responses on Yahoo! Answers. By analogy, a user performing a search may be willing to repeatedly check in on the results of a slow search as it builds a final result set, and decide whether to stop the search or continue waiting. However, the authors do not show how the number of answers for a question relate to their quality or the times in which they arrive. Liu et al. [11] demonstrated in a field experiment that the frequency, quality and time of solutions to tasks on the crowdsourcing site Taskcn reflect strategic decisions depending on the reward level, the existence of a reserve (i.e., a prior high-quality solution), and expertise of crowdworkers. The authors however do not investigate the waiting behavior of the requester in light of the solutions. In other words, for slow search, we are interested in a mix of the two—examining when a user believes the information received is "good enough" to stop waiting for additional information.

Büttcher et al. [4] compared the effectiveness of different systems while accounting for the CPU time involved in query processing. Generally, the systems that used more CPU time showed better results in effectiveness. In the efficiency task, comparing each system's best run to its fastest run, the differences in ms/query can be quite appreciable. This shows that there is often a benefit to extra processing time, and a system that takes advantage of this time when appropriate could satisfy users better, provided they are willing to wait.

There is also increasing recognition of time as an important factor in the evaluation of search systems. Clarke and Smucker [6] proposed a metric of time-based gain to measure an information retrieval system's effectiveness to reflect the value that a user gains over time in interacting with the system. For slow search, this metric is applicable to the value gained from waiting as the system works to provide better results. A recent user study by Crescenzi et al. looked at a design somewhat contrary to ours, namely, the effect on search behavior when users were given *less* time to search [7].

Compared to the existing literature, this work presents a working system that embodies the principles of slow search and directly improves the relevance of search results, while investigating the relationship between types of tasks, user impatience, and quality improvement over time.

3. METHOD

To measure user behavior characteristics, we designed an extension for the Chrome Web browser that works in conjunction with Web search engines to capture the current query and send it to a server for extended processing when the user clicks a "Work Harder" button to the right of the main search editbox on the search engine page, as shown in Figure 1. Doing this adds the query to a sidebar (a) on the search engine result page, which shows a progress bar (b) as well as the top three results at any given time (c). We call this extended-time background query a 'slow' query. The user may click on the "(more results)" link (d) at the bottom of the sidebar to view the full list of re-ranked results, as they are improved and updated asynchronously by potentially adding new documents to the list and re-ranking them. This page also displays a progress bar, and may be left open while the user continues to search on the main search page.

This 'slow' query processing occurs as a background process, during which users are free to continue performing their own searching and query reformulations in the main interface while the 'slow' query completes. In this study, we allow at most one slow query at a time, which may be cancelled before its progress is complete and removed from the sidebar. The extension also serves to log interaction through queries, clicks, and mouse movements.

3.1 Study participants

Our study consisted of 44 participants (18 Male, 26 Female; mean age = 23.5 SD = 5.9), recruited through the University of Michigan School of Information. Most were undergraduates (n = 18) or holders of an undergraduate degree (n = 12). The majority reported being very experienced with search engines: we asked about their familiarity on a scale from one to five; the mean response was 4.6 (SD = 0.6). Additionally, 38 reported using search engines more than once per day, while 5 reported using them more than once per week. The remaining participant reported using them more than once per month. We also asked participants to report their confidence in their abilities to find the information they need while searching on a scale from one to five; the mean response was 4.36 (SD = 0.65).

3.2 Background Survey

To better understand tasks for which people might be willing to wait for a better answer (RQ1), we asked participants to provide a description of the last search task they performed in which they failed in satisfying their information need. We report these tasks as well as their anticipated willingness to wait for the perfect results below.

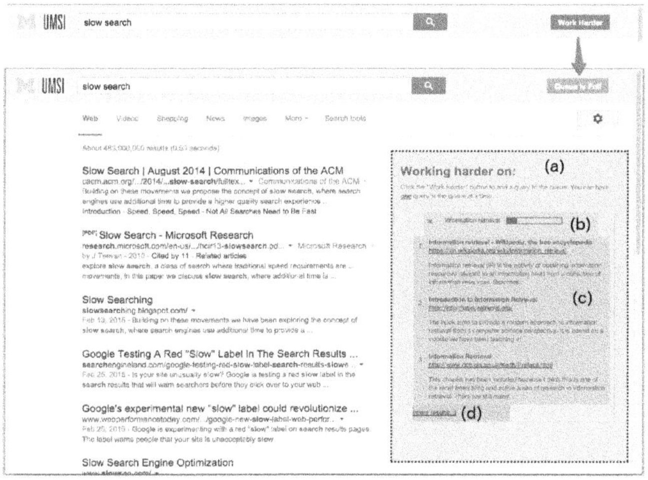

Figure 1: Interface with "Work Harder" button and sidebar (a). Colors added for illustration. Clicking the "Work Harder" button in the upper right adds the current query to the queue (b). The top three results at any moment are presented below (c), and a full list of re-ranked results is available by clicking on (d). These interface additions are always present.

3.2.1 Prior tasks users reported as difficult

We first asked participants the following question:

Think back to the last time you had trouble finding information with a Web search engine. What was the information that you were trying to find? Please be as specific as you can, as best as you can remember.

We coded responses by topic, summarized in Table 1. As most participants were students, the majority had issues finding information for classes or assignments. The common trends for difficult education-related needs involve finding new and novel information (e.g., finding articles on a topic that has not been seen before), finding reliable scholarly articles on a topic, and expressing the problem in the right way for the search engine to yield useful results ("It was difficult to search for because I wasn't sure what I was searching for.").

For other topics, users had difficulty finding a specific item, such as a person, product, or song, most commonly among the Career, Entertainment, and Shopping topics. The main issue in these cases involved expressing the right criteria to find these items. For instance, one subject tried to find a particular drawer slide, but was not able to use the right search terms. Instead, he had to iteratively search related topics in order to pick up more useful search terms.

Topic	Count
Education	16
Shopping	6
Entertainment	5
Health	5
Career	3
Technology/Troubleshooting	3
Food	2
Sports	2

Table 1: Topics of tasks reported as difficult.

We also categorized participants' reported tasks according to the nature of information they were seeking. Overall, 16/44 (36%) of difficult/unsatisfied needs involved searching for specific items or facts that satisfied multiple attributes; 10/44 (22%) were questions seeking a specific factual answer; 4/44 (9%) needs were for the latest version of information; 4/44 (9%) involved searching for a person. The remaining needs involved more vaguely-defined needs, more exploratory research needs, or procedural information on how to solve a problem. This predominance of multi-attribute search needs, the nature of which we can find examined in [10], motivated our design of tasks for slow search as described in Sec. 3.3.1.

3.2.2 User willingness to wait

As part of studying the time-quality tradeoffs that users might find acceptable in a search engine (RQ2), we asked participants:

Given your experience, if a search system was able to provide the perfect results, how long would you be willing to wait for the search engine to process your query while you did other tasks and you were notified when it found these results?

We are interested in what users self-report as acceptable, not only to calibrate our experiment, but also to see if their actual behavior matches the expected behavior (which we compare in Sec. 4.1). Users reported a willingness to wait 9.5 minutes on average (SD = 13.2). An exponential decay in acceptable waiting time is evident from our analysis: with the survey response data, we fitted an exponential decay model $w = \exp(-at)$ to estimate the empirical probability w that a typical user would be willing to wait at least t minutes. The fitted exponential parameter was $a = 0.11$, meaning that for every additional minute of waiting time, about 10% of remaining users were not willing to continue waiting. We note that this rate of decay 'impatience factor' is in accord with that reported by Teevan et al. [16] that asked a similar question about willingness to wait for perfect results.

3.3 Experiment Design

For the purpose of this study, we focused on investigating the effects of an improvement in relevance for multi-attribute tasks. To that end, we implemented a server that communicates with the Chrome extension to simulate an improvement in relevance over the course of five minutes for each slow query submitted. For each task that a user may choose to tackle, we manually selected five to ten high-quality documents and snippets that, collectively, allow a participant to correctly solve the problem posed by the task. When the "Work Harder" button is used, the server selects documents from the pool to insert into the ranking every twenty seconds. Similarly, another process on the server periodically moves high-quality documents closer to the top of the ranking over the course of the five minute period, until these documents reach the top of the ranking.

We randomly assigned participants to one of three conditions. In the baseline condition ($n = 16$), the interface resembles a conventional Web search engine, with no "Work Harder" button or sidebar. In the "*static gain*" condition ($n = 15$), the interface adds a persistent "Work Harder" button and sidebar to the conventional interface. Furthermore, the system inserts highly-relevant documents in the middle of the ranking "below the fold" of the re-ranked results page and the rank position of these documents stays the same over the course of the five minutes. Finally, in the "*dynamic gain*" condition ($n = 13$), the interface is the same as in the "*static gain*" condition, but the system inserts documents at the last position of the re-ranked list and then continuously increases the position of documents at 20 second intervals, over the five minute time window, until they finish at the top of the ranking. In this study, we used a dynamic gain that was linear with respect to time. With this design, we introduce the two new capabilities of an improved result list and a dynamic ranking. We chose to contrast the "*static gain*" condition with the "*dynamic gain*" condition to determine whether users actually perceived the improved relevance as well as to study the effect of the dynamic ranking.

3.3.1 Description of Search Tasks

Participants were presented with a list of four topics, with each topic having three tasks within it. Each participant was required to select one task from two separate topics. We allowed participants to choose tasks and topics of interest to them with the goal of increasing their intrinsic motivation to complete each task.

We prepared the total set of twelve tasks such that each task was presented in the form of a question to be answered, and each task called for the participant to find five items that satisfy multiple attributes specified within the problem. We did this to control the cognitive effort required for each task – users were expected to find a set of candidate answers and verify that each of them satisfied all constraints in order to receive the full reward. For any particular item that the user submitted in their answer, we considered it "correct" if and only if it satisfied all of the required constraints. We believed that having a slow search system which reduced this high expected effort would encourage use of that capability when available.

Local Businesses (32 tasks completed)
Name five I.T. companies in Ann Arbor with at least 50 employees.
Entertainment (28 tasks completed)
Name five video games in which Pharrell Williams's music has been featured.
Education (21 tasks completed)
Who are the five most influential professors in the United States in the field of sociology?
Shopping (7 tasks completed)
What are five smartphones that are thinner than a standard No. 2 pencil and usable on AT&T?

Table 2: Examples of search tasks and their topics.

In Table 2 we present examples of search tasks for each of the four topics, along with the number of task completions by topic. Local Businesses had the most interest, with its tasks being chosen 32 times in total. Conversely, Shopping received the least attention, which users choosing these tasks only 7 times.

3.3.2 Study Procedure

The user study took place in a laboratory setting at the University of Michigan School of Information. Participants volunteered to attend one of eight study sessions, with each session lasting a maximum of 90 minutes. Each participant was placed at a computer set up with the Chrome extension, which in turn was randomly associated with one of the three study conditions (Baseline, *static gain*, and *dynamic gain*). Participants completed two search tasks, with each task lasting a maximum of thirty minutes.

To introduce participants to the capabilities of the system before they began the first task, users were asked to perform an exploratory search task—in this case to explore the topic 'snow leopards' —as a warmup for five to ten minutes.

As motivation to finish the task within the allotted thirty minutes, we compensated users based on their performance in answering each question, which called for an answer that addressed each attribute of the problem, as well as three relevant documents that they found useful in solving the problem. This gave us a way of verifying whether participants found the documents inserted into the ranking, and explicit relevance feedback of these documents. An answer that perfectly met the criteria of the task led to a bonus of $2 with partial credit being possible, and giving relevant documents led to a bonus of $1 per URL – this served as motivation to give explicit relevance feedback.

3.4 Data Preparation

Missing Data. For each request made by the extension to log interaction data, the system associated a session ID with a particular interaction event, with this session ID being linked to the user's ID, which is randomly generated when a user begins the study. After the data collection was complete, there were 34 out of 1149 clicks without session IDs in our log database, and hence, we were unable to associate these clicks with a task, user ID, or condition. We therefore manually inspected the click data in an attempt to re-associate each click with a session ID. We were able to re-associate all clicks but one due to ambiguity in candidate tasks: 13 of 34 clicks were recoverable from session IDs included in page URLs, and 20 of 34 clicks could be manually recovered based on analyzing clicks with session IDs from closely associated contemporaneous queries.

Relevance Judgements. As a part of completing the task, we asked users to provide three relevant documents that helped in answering the task's question. We made final judgements on these documents in the process of calculating bonuses – if the document indeed provides information relevant to answering the question correctly, then the document was deemed relevant for the bonus. Otherwise, we considered the document not relevant.[2]

4. EXPERIMENT RESULTS

In this section we conduct an analysis of user activity, addressing the remaining research questions (RQ2–RQ5) and examining users' behavior in more detail.

4.1 How Long Participants Waited For Results

Our second research question (RQ2) concerns the amount of time users typically wait for results. In our background questionnaire described in Section 3.2.2, our participants expressed a mean willingness to wait 9.5 minutes for the perfect results for their difficult information needs. Our system imposes a maximum wait time of five minutes, which was not explicitly communicated to our participants. Five minutes was selected in order to give users more time to submit multiple slow queries within a single task session. 2/15 participants in the *static gain* condition and 2/13 participants in the *dynamic gain* condition explicitly mentioned without prompting that the waiting time was too long when asked about their impressions of using the system in post-task questionnaires.

Analyzing the behavioral data, we find that in both the *dynamic gain* and *static gain* conditions, approximately twice as many participants used slow search in the second task ($n = 11$) compared to the first task ($n = 5$). Table 3 presents expected wait times for each condition and task, representing the time for which each slow query is processed until

[2] If the document only provides information that would result in answering the question incorrectly, as, for example, only providing a Web page for a coffee shop outside of the location we ask, the page was considered not relevant.

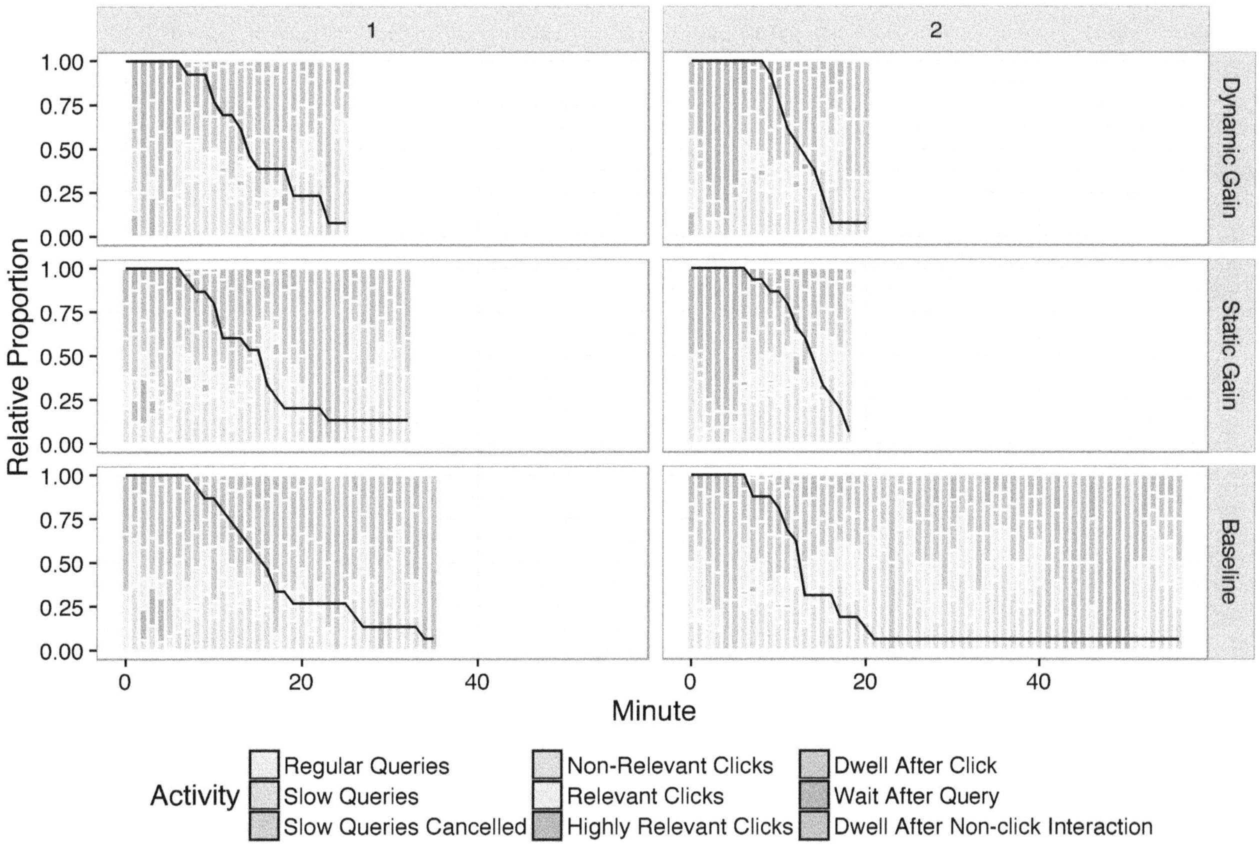

Figure 2: The actions that users perform over the course of the two tasks by condition. The black lines show the proportion of remaining participants in the session.

Condition	Task	Query Processing Time (sec)	SD	Users
dynamic gain	1	227.3	109.8	4/13
dynamic gain	2	227.2	82.4	3/13
static gain	1	136.1	145.6	5/15
static gain	2	266.6	85.0	1/15

Table 3: Mean slow query processing times by task, with standard deviation (SD) and fraction of users who cancelled their slow query.

either completion, or cancellation by a user. Users in the *dynamic gain* condition waited an average of 227 seconds in both tasks 1 and 2. By comparison, for users in the *static gain* condition, their wait times increased from an expected 136.1 seconds to 266.6 seconds: participants cancelled more queries in the first task than in the *dynamic gain* condition, but by the second task, these users cancelled fewer than in the *dynamic gain* condition, which likely contributed to the increase in mean slow processing time observed for the static gain condition. An independent two-group t-test shows that the difference between the mean wait time in the first and second tasks of the *static gain* condition is statistically significant ($t(9.7949) = -2.318$, $p < 0.05$).

4.2 How Participants Spent Their Time

To obtain an overview of user activity as participants progressed through each task, we aggregated the actions that users performed and averaged across users for each minute of activity. The resulting plot of these aggregated actions is shown in Figure 2. Generally, participants took slightly longer to complete their first task than their second (944 seconds vs. 804 seconds on average). For the two tasks, the users in the dynamic gain condition had the shortest completion times (879 seconds for the first task, and 735 seconds for the second task). These differences were not statistically significant.

Differences between first and second session. In general, there appeared to be a period of slight acclimatisation as users in the slow search conditions made and cancelled slow queries throughout the session. By comparison, in the second task, users started by making slow queries and committed more to this decision rather than cancelling and restarting. More precisely, in the *static gain* condition, users made an average of 0.53 slow queries and cancelled 0.33 of them in the first task. By the second task, they made 0.93 slow queries and cancelled 0.07 of them. Similarly, in the *dynamic gain* condition, they made an average of 0.62 slow queries in their first task and cancelled 0.23 of them; by their second task, they made 1 slow query and cancelled 0.08 of them. Potentially, this small number of slow queries could reflect an optimal interaction strategy, which we will discuss further in Section 4.4. We present the results for comparison in Table 4.

Document assessment over time. In Figure 3, we plot the mean cumulative clicks performed during each task as time progressed. We can see that the conditions began with

Condition	Task	Submitted	Cancelled
dynamic gain	1	0.62	0.23
dynamic gain	2	1.00	0.08
static gain	1	0.53	0.33
static gain	2	0.93	0.07

Table 4: Slow queries submitted/cancelled by task.

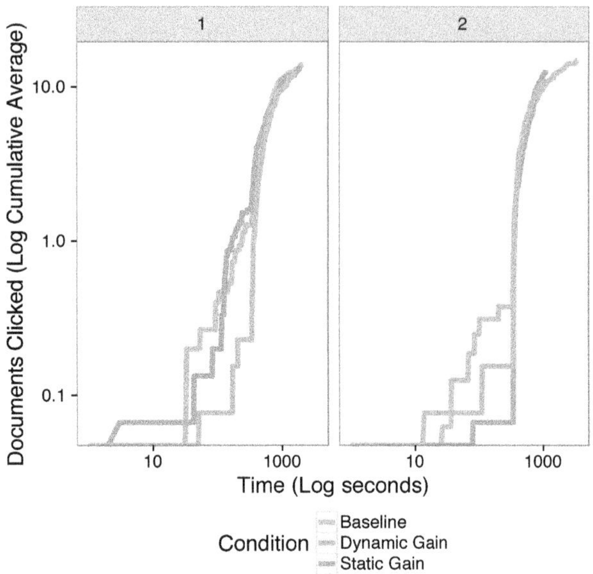

Figure 3: Average time-click curves by task. This includes non-relevant clicks.

rather different click trajectories at the beginning of each task, but eventually converged as the task continued. Users in the *dynamic gain* condition begin examining documents slightly later than in the baseline and *static gain* conditions in the first task. Comparing this to the second task, users in the three conditions examined fewer documents in the corresponding period at the beginning of the first task. Additionally, users in the baseline condition began examining more documents sooner than in the slow conditions.

4.2.1 *Behavior While Waiting*

Our third research question (RQ3) pertains to activity while waiting for slow search results to finish processing. To answer this question, we looked at how users continued to interact with the system after submitting a slow query. We note that for the conditions with the slow search button, many users spent their time waiting after submitting a slow query. This was especially pronounced in their first five minutes of each task, where more users waited on average after making a query than at subsequent time periods, Comparing the two slow search conditions in the first task, we see in Figure 2 that more users spend time waiting after querying in the first five minutes of *dynamic gain* than in *static gain*. However, the profiles are more similar by the second task: in both groups, users made heavy use of the "Work Harder" button initially, waiting before eventually clicking on results.

Figure 4 shows the activities that users performed while slow queries were processing for the *dynamic gain* and *static gain* conditions, i.e. after a slow query was submitted, and before the query either finished processing or was cancelled.

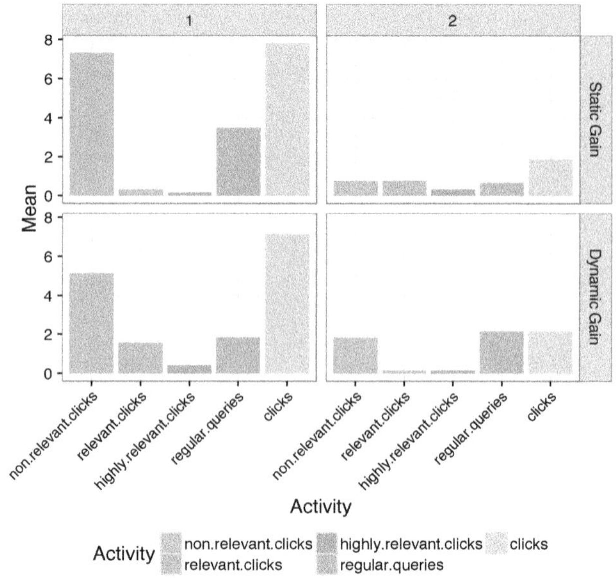

Figure 4: How users spend their time while waiting for slow queries to finish.

Most activity in this interval is focused on examining documents: the number of clicks is relatively high in the first task (6.6 for *static gain* and 7.6 for *dynamic gain*). In comparison, the number of queries is relatively low (2.2 for *static gain* and 3.8 for *dynamic gain*). By the second task, users do less in this interval, perhaps relying on the system more than examining documents and conducting additional queries themselves. In both conditions, the average number of queries and clicks both decrease (*static gain*: Queries = 1.55, Clicks = 3; *dynamic gain*: Queries = 0.91, Clicks = 3.09). Of additional note is that for *static gain*, the number of relevant clicks dropped from 1.2 to 0.18, while the number of highly relevant clicks stayed relatively consistent (0.6 in task 1 and 0.55 in task 2). This may indicate that users' time was better spent in the second task with regards to finding the most relevant documents to solving the given task. We can compare this to *dynamic gain*, where the number of relevant clicks increased (0.4 to 0.73), and also the number of highly relevant clicks increased from 0 to 0.36. Thus, while the number of non-relevant clicks and queries decreased, users made better use of their time in finding helpful documents.

4.3 Feature Analysis of Search Behavior

To investigate research questions RQ4 and RQ5, we computed a list of features characterizing search behavior, as inspired by previous studies such as [1]. The features we calculated are outlined in Table 5 and Table 6.

Dwell time (C_{IT}) was determined by calculating the time between a click and any subsequent interaction with a search page (mouse movements, scrolling, keyboard events, queries, or clicks). As we ask users to provide five correct items that satisfy multiple attributes for each task, we calculate Precision as the proportion of items included in their answer for a task that satisfy all attributes.

4.3.1 *Behavioral Analysis of Searchers by Condition*

For our fourth research question (RQ4), we investigate the types of changes seen in users' behavior when given asynchronous slow search capabilities. Having randomly assigned

Feature	SG	DG	Baseline	U Test
Baseline features				
Session length ($\Sigma\Delta t$*, sec.)	839.47	807.23	961.00	-
Regular queries ($CntQ_R$)	6.50	4.58	8.81	-
Regular queries/sec (Q_RPS)	0.01	0.01	0.01	-
Slow features				
Slow queries ($CntQ_S$)	0.73	0.81	0.00	SG > B*; DG > B*
Slow queries per second (Q_SPS)	9.03×10^{-4}	9.99×10^{-4}	0.00	-
Slow queries cancelled ($CntQ_SC$)	0.33	0.35	0.00	SG > B*; DG > B*
Slow queries cancelled per second (Q_SCPS)	3.86×10^{-4}	3.65×10^{-4}	0.00	SG > B*; DG > B*
Query features				
Query word length (QWL)	4.48	5.20	5.72	-
Query character length (QCL)	27.14	31.20	34.88	-
Click features				
Pages in session ($CntR$)	13.27	11.62	14.48	-
Clicks per query (CPQ)	3.14	3.23	2.37	-
Time to first click (sec.) (Q_{DT})	24.93	25.53	24.46	-
Dwell Time (sec.) (C_{IT})	234.36	276.28	358.86	-
Outcomes				
Reward ($)	4.21	4.04	4.16	-
Reward Variance ($)	1.13	1.12	2.14	-
Precision	0.85	0.72	0.83	-
Click Relevance	4.03	3.08	3.55	-

Table 5: Comparison of behavioral features across conditions. SG = *Static Gain*; DG = *Dynamic Gain*. *p<0.05; **p<0.01; ***p<0.001.

users into a condition either with or without such capabilities, we compare the session-level features for each condition. We present the values of these features in Table 5.

Compared to the two slow search conditions, users in the baseline condition on average were the slowest in completing a session ($\Sigma\Delta t = 961$ seconds), issued the highest number of queries ($CntQ_R = 8.81$) and the longest queries ($QWL = 5.72$; $QCL = 34.88$), and had the longest dwell time ($C_{IT} = 358.86$). These differences were not statistically significant, but they may reflect a greater degree of effort for users in this condition, as users take more time to examine and possibly evaluate documents, and conduct more queries to address the various facets of the problem. We also found that users did indeed make use of slow search when given the option: features that quantify the use of slow search such as $CntQ_S$, Q_SPS, $CntQ_SC$, and Q_SCPS were significantly greater than zero in the *dynamic gain* and *static gain* conditions ($p < 0.05$). For most of these features (that is, $CntQ_S$, Q_SPS, and $CntQ_SC$), the values were highest in *dynamic gain*, though not significantly more so than in *static gain*. In contrast, Q_SCPS was highest in the *static gain* condition, though this was not statistically significant. No other differences were significant (with all tests here based on paired Mann-Whitney U tests with Bonferroni correction). Cognitive factors such as the evolving degree of user trust in result quality for the slow search conditions may contribute to these cross-condition differences and exploring these is a topic for future work.

Feature	NS	S	U Test
Baseline features			
Session length ($\Sigma\Delta t$*, sec.)	847.69	891.10	NS < S*
Regular queries ($CntQ_R$)	7.53	6.20	-
Regular queries/sec (Q_RPS)	0.01	0.01	-
Slow query features			
Slow queries ($CntQ_S$)	0.39	0.57	-
Slow queries per second (Q_SPS)	5.22×10^{-4}	6.72×10^{-4}	-
Slow queries cancelled ($CntQ_SC$)	0.14	0.27	-
Slow queries cancelled/sec (Q_SCPS)	2.97×10^{-4}	1.65×10^{-4}	-
Query features			
Query word length (QWL)	5.01	5.23	-
Query character length (QCL)	28.90	32.67	-
Click features			
Pages in session ($CntR$)	12.44	13.75	-
Clicks per query (CPQ)	2.55	3.14	-
Dwell Time (sec.) (C_{IT})	284.20	296.36	-
Time to first click (sec.) (Q_{DT})	13.65	32.86	NS < S*
Outcomes			
Reward ($)	3.23	4.74	-
Reward Variance ($)	1.70	0.36	-
Precision	0.52	1.00	NS < S***
Click Relevance	3.42	3.69	-

Table 6: Comparison of behavioral features by success level. NS = Not Successful; S = Successful. *p<0.05; **p<0.01; ***p<0.001.

4.3.2 Behavioral Analysis of Successful Searchers

Our fifth and final research question (RQ5) investigates whether users perform tasks more effectively with the help of slow search. As Table 5 shows, users in the *dynamic gain* condition received the smallest reward, and had the lowest precision. This raised the question of what factors played a part in increased performance. We compared user features for successfully completed tasks to those of the remaining tasks. We define success as a precision of 1 for a particular task, such that the answers given satisfied all the criteria set by the task's question. We present the features computed based on success in Table 6. We performed Mann-Whitney U tests to determine whether there were significant differences by success.

We found significant differences in session length ($\Sigma\Delta t$; $p < 0.05$) and time to first click ($p < 0.05$). The average session length for successful tasks (891.10 seconds) was significantly higher than that for less successful tasks (847.69 seconds). Despite this, the number of queries issued is not significantly different, though the average time to first click is significantly higher for the successful (343 seconds) than for the less successful (260.44 seconds). This indicates that the time spent examining the search results was a major factor in success, as we also notice that the dwell times were not significantly different. We also investigated click relevance, as described in Section 4.2. Users who were successful had an expected click relevance of 3.69, compared to a click relevance of 3.42 for the rest of the users. However, this difference was not statistically significant.

We also performed logistic regression to predict user success using the above feature set. We found that the intercept ($\beta = -6.524$) and the clicks per query ($\beta = 0.887$) were significant predictors of success ($p < 0.05$). For the intercept, a participant is not likely to be successful, with all other predictors held constant. An additional click per query increases the odds of success by 143%. Other predictors that were marginally significant ($p < 0.1$) include the rate of regular queries (Q_RPS, $\beta = -0.009$, $p < 0.1$) and the effect of session length when the condition is *static gain* ($\beta = -0.009$, $p = 0.1$). In the case of the query rate, an increase in this rate predicts an increase in the odds of success, whereas an increase in the session length in the *static gain* condition predicts a decrease in the odds of success. No other terms were significant predictors.

Overall, the logistic regression analysis shows that making good use of one's time is the main factor in success. That is, searching and examining documents in a short period of time usually means that the user will be successful. The interaction between the session length and using the *static gain* system also suggests that, as a longer session length implies difficulty in satisfying an information need, not being able to take adequate advantage of the system's assistance decreases the likelihood of success.

4.4 Analysis of Interaction Strategies

Because the ability to perform a slow search was a new feature for participants – the training period built into the start of the study not withstanding – we examined how participants' choice of search strategies changed across sessions as users became more familiar with the feature.

In particular, we were interested in how users in the two slow conditions adapted their decision-making and use of the feature in relation to more optimal strategies. Each of the slow conditions could be considered to have an optimal strategy in terms of the number of regular queries issued, the number of snippets examined, the time taken to invoke the "Work Harder" button for the first time, and the waiting time for slow processing.

For the *dynamic gain* condition, we consider one optimal strategy to be the following: 1. Issue a query; 2. Click "Work Harder"; 3. Wait for 5 minutes as the results automatically improve to maximum effectiveness; 4. Examine the first 10 slow results[3]. In comparison, the *static gain* condition has a very different strategy: 1. Issue a query; 2. Click "Work Harder" 3. Examine the first 30 slow results immediately. The differences stem from the fact that the *static gain* condition happens to improve relevance immediately, but to a much lesser degree than in the *dynamic gain* condition at 100% completion. Thus, for the *static gain* condition, it is in the user's best interest not to wait, but this is not evident from the interface.

To examine how behavior changed relative to these strategies, we analyzed whether these strategic components shifted toward optimality from the first task to the second task, in each condition. To do this, we estimated the number of snippets examined by using time on page from our baseline condition to determine the time to examine one snippet (8s), and used the time on page from the improved results page with slow results with the assumption that the times to examine a snippet are comparable. This value is capped at the number of results on the page (50). We employed a bootstrap hypothesis testing procedure [9], and present our findings in Tables 7 and 8.

Table 7 shows for that for *static gain* users, the time it took for users to first use slow search significantly decreased from the first to second task: from 386 s to 130 s ($p < 0.01$).

[3]The times taken for each step would be as short as possible, and a user might elect to do other things, including regular searches, during the waiting interval.

[4]Insufficient data due to lack of use of this feature during the session.

Component	Task 1	Task 2	p-value
Queries	6.4	6.6	0.479
Time to "Work Harder" (sec.)	386	130.1	0.005 **
Wait time (sec.)	136.1	277.3	0.002 **
Snippets examined	NA[4]	22.5	

Table 7: Changes in interaction in relation to optimal strategies for *static gain*. The number of snippets examined is estimated. *p<0.05; **p<0.01; ***p<0.001.

Component	Task 1	Task 2	p-value
Queries	5.38	3.68	0.131
Time to "Work Harder" (sec.)	190.8	135.9	0.04 *
Wait time (sec.)	266.6	277.1	0.048 *
Snippets examined	21.2	20.1	0.5

Table 8: Changes in interaction in relation to optimal strategies for *dynamic gain*. The number of snippets examined is estimated. *p<0.05; **p<0.01; ***p<0.001.

Wait time increased significantly from 136.1 s to 277.3 s ($p < 0.01$). We see users moving closer to the optimal strategy for when to invoke slow search, but not for wait time. The number of queries did not change significantly, but increased slightly from 6.4 to 6.6. This could suggest that users did not know to take advantage of the fact that the preselected documents were always in the middle of the ranking, and continued to search on their own even as they waited more for an effect.

Table 8 shows that in the *dynamic gain* condition, users invoked slow search much sooner for the second task (190.8 s to 135.9 s; $p < 0.05$), and significantly increased their waiting time (266.6 s to 277.1 s; $p < 0.05$). Additionally, although not statistically significant, we notice a decrease in the number of queries issued (5.38 to 3.68). This seems to suggest that these users had begun adjusting their behaviors toward the optimal strategy, as they developed a better mental model of how the system responded to their use of the "Work Harder" button.

4.5 Post-task Survey Results

After each task, we asked users about their experience using the system. We also asked participants in conditions having the "Work Harder" button to give their impressions on whether the button made the task easier, whether they noticed an improvement in the quality of results, as well as to write about their thoughts on the usefulness and ease of use of the system.

Figure 5 shows the mean ratings on a five point Likert scale of participants' experiences of using the system by condition. The error bars represent the standard errors of the means. We performed ANOVAs on these results to see if exposure to the different conditions affected the ratings given to whether they were able to find the information they were looking for, their productivity, the effort extended, if they liked using the system, if the button made the task easier, if the button improved the quality of results, if the progress bars were useful, and if the ability to check the intermediate results was useful. Of these, we saw significant differences between conditions in response to the button making the task easier ($F(1,54) = 5.324$, $p < 0.05$), the button improving the quality of the results ($F(1,54) = 4.529$, $p < 0.05$), and the progress bars being useful ($F(1,54) = 5.146$, $p < 0.05$).

In general, users' perceptions of the slow search features (the latter four in Figure 5) were higher in the *dynamic gain*

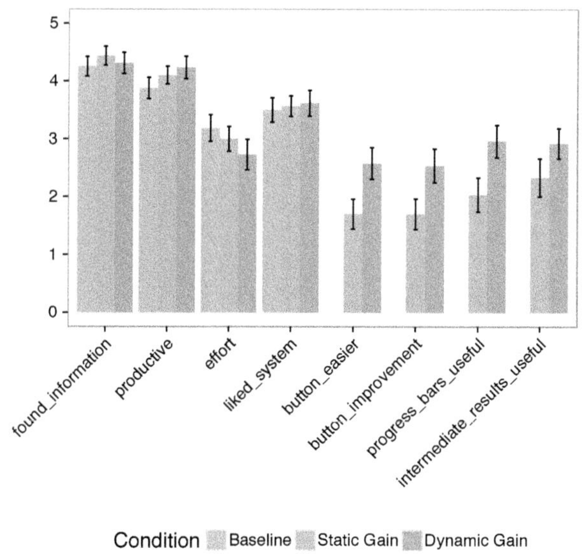

Figure 5: Post-task survey scores by condition.

condition than in the *static gain* condition. Among the more general experiential questions (the former four), we see that users in the *static gain* condition gave the highest rating for whether they found the information they were looking for (M = 4.43, SD = 0.90), while in the *dynamic gain* condition they gave the lowest rating (M = 4, SD = 1.17). For productivity, we see that having the button improved users' perceptions over the baseline (M = 3.88, SD = 1.04), with the *static gain* condition having the slight edge (M = 4.1, SD = 0.84) over the *dynamic gain* condition (M = 4.07, SD = 1.01). Users in the baseline condition also reported exerting the most effort (M = 3.19, SD = 1.31), which might have been reflected in their interactions, with users in this condition taking longer on average to complete tasks, perform more queries, and examine documents. Compared to the other conditions, users in the *static gain* condition reported liking the system the most (M = 3.57, SD = 0.97). Indeed, among these former four questions, the *static gain* condition has the highest ratings, though, once again, the differences were not statistically significant.

5. DISCUSSION AND IMPLICATIONS

Our study provides insights about how users engaged with a slow search system that provided an asynchronous query capability with improvements in search result quality over time. We now discuss our main findings and implications.

Users are willing to wait for multi-attribute queries (RQ1). We found through our background survey that many of the tasks and queries that users typically have trouble with are multi-attribute queries in which various constraints of a query must be satisfied (Section 3.2.1). This justifies our use of such queries in our study, and the use of slow search after users gain familiarity with the system shows that multi-attribute queries are a good fit for a slow search system.

Users will typically wait for results (RQ2). Our background survey revealed that users reportedly are willing to wait for a mean of 9.5 minutes for "perfect" results (Section 3.2.2). Placing users under time pressure and imposing a maximum time of five minutes for query processing also led to users waiting, as was seen in Section 4.1. Interestingly, in both *dynamic gain* and *static gain* conditions, users typically submitted more slow queries, waited more, and cancelled fewer slow queries by the second task. A future study may manipulate the processing time for these slow queries to examine users' tolerance for waiting, and whether users will wait under tighter time constraints. Future studies may also look at impatience under greater uncertainty.

Users spent time looking for additional documents while waiting (RQ3). As illustrated in Section 4.2, users in both the *dynamic gain* and *static gain* conditions spent their time performing queries and clicking on documents in the interval while a slow query was processing. By the second task, these activities were reduced, but not in a statistically significant sense. We also showed that users in both of these conditions performed more slow queries in the second task and also waited more after performing these queries instead of clicking on documents or cancelling. This may indicate that users could still have been learning to use the system by the second task despite the training period and using the system for the first task. The reasons why users appeared to make more effective use of slow search by the second task require further study: the change could be due simply to their experience with the system in the first task, or it could be due to their increased awareness of the feature due to our explicitly asking users about their experience in using the "Work Harder" button between tasks. A future study may extend the training period to ensure that users are not only familiar with the system, but that they are also confident in predicting what the system will do. We also plan to do a longer-term online study in which users interact with the system for an extended period of time, which will help us to determine how long it takes for user behavior to stabilize and what it looks like when it does. Such a study will also help to understand usage in different scenarios without artificial constraints.

User search behavior did not significantly change with additional slow search capabilities (RQ4). Our analysis in Section 4.3.1 showed that user behavior in terms of search interactions was similar across conditions, with users in the two slow conditions making significant use of the "Work Harder" button. We observed that users in the baseline condition took longer to complete sessions, conducted more and longer queries, and clicked on fewer documents per query (Table 5). Users, by the end of the study, may have still not yet fully understood the capabilities of the system. However, these results may also indicate that slow search systems should cater to similar types of queries as current search systems, and support the kinds of interactions that users have grown accustomed to. A future study may serve to tease out these differences by looking at users who have become familiar with the system and users without such a system.

Users did not achieve higher final effectiveness with slow search, but showed evidence of higher efficiency (RQ5). For the tasks we evaluated, users achieved comparable final rewards across the three conditions, with the *baseline condition* showing slightly higher average reward, but overall differences were not statistically significant. However, as we note above, users obtained these rewards in less overall time for both slow search conditions compared to the baseline condition, giving some evidence of higher efficiency. In addition, users in the *dynamic gain* condition did indeed report that they noticed more of a difference in the improvement in search results than users in the *static gain* condition, and gave higher ratings for the usefulness of the progress bars. This may have been because it would have been clearer in the *dynamic gain* condition that the results were changing, and continued to change during the five minute duration. In contrast, users in the *static gain* condition may have not noticed the change between the unmodified and the modified results. Regardless, this shows that users are able to notice the difference when the results change, suggesting there is some utility in having future systems expose progressive improvements in ranking to users.

We note that users found slightly fewer relevant documents on average in the *dynamic gain* condition compared to the *static gain* condition. One explanation for this difference is that in the *static gain* condition, the system inserts all of the same documents that would have been inserted in the *dynamic gain* condition, but in the lower quarter of the ranking. As a result, *static gain* users had the opportunity to gain access to these documents more quickly if they were willing to look for them in the ranking. In the *dynamic gain* condition, however, users had to wait longer to see the same highly relevant results, since the system begins with those documents at the bottom of the initial ranking and improves their position steadily over the course of five minutes.

While our dataset and corresponding analysis has allowed us to gain insight into the research questions we posed, we also recognize a number of limitations in our current study. Our findings, particularly that of RQ1, would be more robust with a larger sample of users. A future study in a more natural setting may also reduce experimental demand effects that might have influenced user behavior, and users' choices of tasks may have also affected their performance.

For future work, there are multiple possible avenues in exploring user interaction with slow search systems The 'Work Harder' button might be removed altogether and replaced with a background process that can automatically find and attempt to improve results for failed or abandoned search sessions. A user with low time pressure and a high degree of trust in a slow search system may submit a query to be processed in the background while performing non-search tasks, especially in the transition between devices, in which case supporting the examination of intermediate results or performing more queries in the interim would not be vital. In another instance, a user may use the system as as a supporting agent in a search task: the system would gather additional relevant documents and present them to the user as they continue to search. The participants' tendency in this study to continue searching shows that this is a useful capability to have.

The concept of "slowness" could additionally be applied to many different scenarios in which other aspects of retrieval 'quality' may be improved. This study focused on improving relevance for multi-attribute queries—a difficult class of queries for many existing systems, but in principle a system could also improve intrinsic diversity, employ crowdsourcing to augment algorithms, or summarize and organize results.

6. CONCLUSION

We reported on a user study that investigated five research questions about user interaction with a slow search system that offered users the option of running a 'slow' query in the background, showing progressive results in a sidebar. Using surveys and log data, we analyzed users who interacted with the system in one of three between-subjects conditions: a 'dynamic gain' condition that steadily improved search result quality of the optional slow query over the course of five minutes, a 'static gain' slow query that inserted relevant documents immediately with no additional ranking improvements over time, or a baseline condition giving conventional Web search results. Our findings suggest that users elected to perform slow search queries when given the opportunity. Additionally, we show that users are willing to wait for multi-attribute queries (RQ1), users will indeed wait for results when using slow search (RQ2), and users continued to search while waiting for results (RQ3). User behavior did not significantly change with additional slow search capabilities (RQ4), and users did not achieve higher final effectiveness with slow search, but did finish in less time (RQ5) on the tasks we evaluated. Followup studies may explore different mechanisms to improve quality for slow search and further investigate the nature of time-quality tradeoffs and user choice.

Acknowledgements. We thank Eytan Adar, Yan Chen, and the anonymous reviewers for their feedback.

References

[1] M. Ageev, Q. Guo, D. Lagun, and E. Agichtein. Find it if you can: a game for modeling different types of web search success using interaction data. In *Proceedings of SIGIR 2011*, pages 345–354. ACM, 2011.

[2] C. Aperjis, B. A. Huberman, and F. Wu. Human speed-accuracy tradeoffs in search. In *System Sciences (HICSS), 2011 44th Hawaii International Conference on*, pages 1–10. IEEE, 2011.

[3] J. Brutlag. Speed matters for Google web search. *Google*, June 2009. URL http://bit.ly/1Oonkyz.

[4] S. Büttcher, C. L. Clarke, and I. Soboroff. The TREC 2006 Terabyte track. In *TREC 2006 Notebook*, volume 6, page 39. NIST Special Publication, 2006.

[5] J. Chen, S. Amershi, A. Dhananjay, and L. Subramanian. Comparing web interaction models in developing regions. In *Proceedings of the First ACM Symposium on Computing for Development*, page 6. ACM, 2010.

[6] C. L. Clarke and M. D. Smucker. Time well spent. In *Proceedings of the 5th Information Interaction in Context Symposium*, pages 205–214. ACM, 2014.

[7] A. Crescenzi, D. Kelly, and L. Azzopardi. Time pressure and system delays in information search. In *Proceedings of SIGIR 2015*, pages 767–770, New York, NY, USA, 2015. ACM.

[8] M. Dörk, P. Bennett, and R. Davies. Taking our sweet time to search. In *Proceedings of CHI 2013 Workshop on Changing Perspectives of Time in HCI*, 2013.

[9] R. Gould. Bootstrap hypothesis testing. *Stats 110A*, 2002. URL http://bit.ly/1ncz67z.

[10] Y. Kim, K. Collins-Thompson, and J. Teevan. Using the crowd to improve search result ranking and the search experience. *ACM TIST: Special Issue on the Crowd in Intelligent Systems*, 7(4):50, 2016.

[11] T. X. Liu, J. Yang, L. A. Adamic, and Y. Chen. Crowdsourcing with all-pay auctions: A field experiment on Taskcn. *Proceedings of the American Society for Information Science and Technology*, 48(1):1–4, 2011.

[12] M. L. Mauldin. Retrieval performance in FERRET: A conceptual information retrieval system. In *Proceedings of SIGIR 1991*, pages 347–355. ACM, 1991.

[13] D. Maxwell and L. Azzopardi. Stuck in traffic: how temporal delays affect search behaviour. In *Proceedings of the 5th Information Interaction in Context Symposium*, pages 155–164. ACM, 2014.

[14] P. M. Napoli and J. A. Obar. The emerging mobile internet underclass: A critique of mobile internet access. *The Information Society*, 30(5):323–334, 2014.

[15] L. Poirier and L. Robinson. Informational balance: slow principles in the theory and practice of information behaviour. *Journal of Documentation*, 70(4):687–707, 2014. . URL http://dx.doi.org/10.1108/JD-08-2013-0111.

[16] J. Teevan, K. Collins-Thompson, R. W. White, S. T. Dumais, and Y. Kim. Slow search: Information retrieval without time constraints. In *Proceedings of HCIR 2013*, page 1. ACM, 2013.

[17] J. Teevan, K. Collins-Thompson, R. W. White, and S. Dumais. Slow search. *Communications of the ACM*, 57 (8):36–38, 2014.

Going back in Time: An Investigation of Social Media Re-finding

Florian Meier
I:IMSK
University of Regensburg
Germany
florian.meier@ur.de

David Elsweiler
I:IMSK
University of Regensburg
Germany
david@elsweiler.co.uk

ABSTRACT

Social Media (SM) has become a valuable information source to many in diverse situations. In IR, research has focused on real-time aspects and as such little is known about how long SM content is of value to users, if and how often it is re-accessed, the strategies people employ to re-access and if difficulties are experienced while doing so. We present results from a 5 month-long naturalistic, log-based study of user interaction with Twitter, which suggest re-finding to be a regular activity and that Tweets can offer utility for longer than one might think. We shed light on re-finding strategies revealing that remembered people are used as a stepping stone to Tweets rather than searching for content directly. Bookmarking strategies reported in the literature are used infrequently as a means to re-access. Finally, we show that by using statistical modelling it is possible to predict if a Tweet has future utility and is likely to be re-found. Our findings have implications for the design of social media search systems and interfaces, in particular for Twitter, to better support users re-find previously seen content.

1. INTRODUCTION

Information re-finding is the behaviour exhibited to access previously seen or possessed information [27]. People regularly re-find items of different kinds including documents [12], emails [50], photos and web pages [42, 5, 44] and in these contexts re-finding can be a frustrating, time consuming and expensive task [27]. It is less clear if re-finding is so pervasive and challenging within social media applications (SMA) where the focus is often on real-time information [47] and information exchange [33] and where much of the content has been identified as disposable, "mindless babble" [25].

Nevertheless, some SMAs have features explicitly designed to prolong content lifespans. Examples include retweeting (RT) and the heart icon (formerly star) on Twitter. A RT allows users to forward Tweets to their followers and places these amongst the user's sent messages - a separate space from which a Tweet may be located. The heart icon labels a Tweet as a "favourite" (FAV) and again places the message in a separate space. Studies have confirmed that both features are indeed used with the intention of preserving [3, 32]. New features have recently been added to SMAs to help users return to previously viewed content e.g. Facebook has the "read it later" button and Whatsapp has introduced a star icon. Moreover, as of November 2014 Twitter offers users the ability to search over the complete dataset of Tweets, unrestricted by age. Investigations of Twitter search behaviour do provide some evidence of re-finding [15]. Nevertheless, in transaction log studies of SM search behaviour, interactions often associated with re-finding (e.g. repeated queries) have been attributed instead to monitoring behaviour due to the perception of SM posts as a shallow, ephemeral media [47].

Thus there is uncertainty in the literature with respect to the frequency with which SM content is re-found and the lifespans of posts for individual users. Moreover little is known about how users re-find content on SMAs, the difficulties they experience or the support they require. In this paper we contribute by reporting the results of a naturalistic, log-based investigation of user interactions with the Twitter website. Our specific contributions are as follows:

- We present a dataset of click stream interactions with the Twitter website, revealing patterns of user behaviour not possible with data collected via the API.
- We identify re-finding behaviour using specific interaction sequences as a proxy. This indicates that re-finding occurs and that the life-cycle of many Tweets is longer than the literature suggests.
- We examine the relationship between FAV-ing, RT-ing and re-finding and discover that if people are trying to bookmark Tweets for future use as the literature suggests, they are not doing so with any great success.
- We investigate re-finding strategies by studying the features of Twitter used to re-access messages.
- Finally, based on our initial discoveries we test several groups of predictive features to determine that it is possible to predict with reasonable accuracy which Tweets will be re-found in the future.

2. RELATED WORK

We overview three research areas of relevance to our work: (i) Twitter behaviour studies informing on the life-cycle of Tweets. (ii) Re-finding behaviour in disparate domains as

SIGIR'16, July 17-21, 2016, Pisa, Italy

DOI: http://dx.doi.org/10.1145/2911451.2911524.

well as related personal information management (PIM) activities. (iii) Studies investigating PIM behaviour on Twitter, which links (i) and (ii) and motivates our specific research questions.

(i) Insights into Life-cycle of Tweets: Twitter is used for diverse purposes including conversing [22], sharing thoughts [33], monitoring topics for up-to-date information [29], establishing social capital [24] and even political mobilisation [6]. None of these use cases, however, suggest that the distributed content holds any long-term utility for Tweet consumers and Twitter's emphasis on the present, the popular and the ephemeral has been well documented [38]. Twitter creator Jack Dorsey underlined the ephemerality of his service, stating: "[I] don't go back in time. You're kind of as good as your last update."[1].

The RT feature can extend the *global life-cycle* of a Tweet by propagating it over the network [29]. This means that even very old content can enter a user's timeline in the same way as new Tweets. Although half of all RTs occur within a day, 10% of RTs do take place at least one month later [29] with the probability decreasing with time from the Tweet's arrival in a user's Timeline [29, 21]. One reason for this is that a Tweet's visibility to a user decreases rapidly - a major barrier to information propagation leading to short Tweet life-cycles overall [21]. Several other features have been identified as good predictors for whether or not a Tweet will be RT'd including social attributes of the users involved, e.g. number of followers, number of followees and how often the user has been added to lists; as well as presence of URLs and hashtags in Tweets [36, 23, 41]. Thus, although the life-cycle of Tweets is typically short, Tweets can have long life-cycles over several Twitter users[2], but it is unclear how long Tweets are useful for individual users.

(ii) Personal Information Management (PIM) is the field concerned with behaviours related to the management of information [27]. Those most pertinent to our work are 1) re-finding, for which the literature describes strategies people employ, identifies patterns in re-finding behaviour, difficulties they have and the system features that can help and 2) the keeping decision, which influences what people will remember about their information and consequently, how it will be re-found [42, 12, 44, 14, 4].

Prominent re-finding strategies are *orienteering* and *teleporting* [1, 37, 45]. The former utilises recognition by navigating spatially or by using contextual information to narrow in on the sought-after information. It can consist of a series of different browsing and searching actions. The latter involves recalling detailed information about an item to navigate to it directly e.g. typing the URL of a web page into the browser or submitting elaborate search queries. The strategy employed will be influenced by numerous factors including the type of item (e.g. email vs web page), elapsed time between access and re-access and previously applied keeping decisions and re-finding actions [7].

The decision to keep information can be error prone as it depends on a user's ability to anticipate personal future information needs [4] and the value of encountered information is often only realised long after it has been initially seen (post-valued recall) [49]. Although keeping actions can support later re-finding, often users decide not to keep and rely on search systems for re-access and this can be problematic [5]. Keeping information is not a guaranteed solution either, however, as people often forget that they did so [26], cannot recall where they stored the information or the organisational structures fail [50, 12, 14]. Re-finding can be supported algorithmically [39, 8] or with interactive features, such as search histories [28], changes to the appearance or ordering of results [43, 46] or different organisational structures based on e.g. tagging [9].

(iii) PIM on Twitter: Only recently have researchers turned to Twitter as an object of study in PIM. An investigation of motivations for RTing showed that the feature is important not only for message propogation, but also for extending a Tweet's *personal life-cycle* with users reporting RTing to preserve Tweets [3]. A similar study of favouriting revealed 25 motivations including bookmarking, either with an anticipated need in mind or with the aim of building a personal collection [32]. Researchers have also attempted to predict whether a favourited Tweet was for liking, bookmarking, self-promotion, as part of a conversation or gratitude [18].

Re-finding on Twitter can be frustrating, primarily for very active users who follow many accounts and who typically take steps to preserve Tweets of interest [31]. Teevan et al. [47] analysed Twitter search query logs captured via the Bing toolbar. Repeated queries - which in other contexts are attributed to re-finding - were interpreted as monitoring. However, the same authors later note that older posts can be of value to users, but as the Twitter search only returns the most recent Tweets, searching for older Tweets occurs infrequently [13]. A long term diary study found that 40% of users reported reasons for using the search function are related to finding previously viewed information [15].

With Twitter now a valuable source of information to many a certain research deficit exists as we lack a detailed understanding of keeping and re-finding practices on this platform. Our study aims to address this by investigating personal Tweet life-cycles, keeping and re-finding strategies, and features of Tweets that make them candidates for re-finding.

3. STUDY METHODOLOGY

Although the Twitter API offers a simple and cost-effective way to source behavioural data, the data is limited to traces resulting from *active engagement* with certain features of the service e.g. RTing. In this work, we collect a much richer and complete naturalistic data-set by also accounting for more *latent* Twitter usage e.g. stream consumption (reading and clicking Tweets) and sub-page navigation.

3.1 Chrome Extension

We developed a Chrome web-browser extension to collect user interactions with the Twitter website. The extension logged metadata from Tweets viewed or interacted with (moused-over, clicked on, FAV'd, RT'd etc.) and the context in which the interaction took place (i.e. personal timeline (*Timline Event*), another user's profile page (*User-Profile Event*), search results page (*Search Event*), on the favourite's list (*Favourites Event*) etc.). Interactions, such as search queries, mouse movement and scrolling were also recorded.

[1]http://latimesblogs.latimes.com/technology/2009/02/jack-dorsey-on.html

[2]Even the first ever Tweet posted featured in our logs.

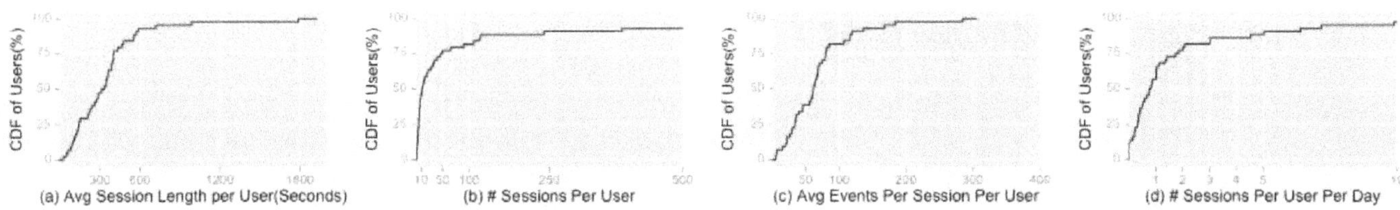

Figure 1: Overview on session behaviour for users

(n=27)	min	max	mean	median
Tweets(n)	0	73 780	5637	59
Following Count(n)	4	1041	203	57
Follower Count(n)	0	1139	202.5	39
Favourites Count(n)	0	44520	1796	18.50
Registered (years) (NA=12)	2	6	4.6	5

Table 1: Participant account properties

3.2 Setup and Participants

Participants were recruited in various ways including advertising on Twitter, mailing lists and posts on diverse Internet fora. Over a five month period, lasting from the end of March to the end of August 2015, 44 Twitter users downloaded and installed the extension. We could establish background information for 27 of these users as we were able to reliably map these to an Twitter account[3]. However all 44 subjects feature in the analyses.

Achieving a representative sample of Twitter users with this kind of study is close to impossible. Our aim was rather to achieve a sample as large and diverse as possible to provide insight into the re-finding practices of a relatively heterogeneous group of users. Table 1 summarises basic participant account statistics, indicating a reasonably diverse sample in terms of how and how often they use Twitter. Although we did not survey participants for demographic information, examining their accounts reveals divergent educational backgrounds, work situations and users based in many countries, prominently in Germany, USA and the UK.

4. GENERAL TWITTER BEHAVIOUR

Applying 5 minutes inactivity as session threshold as in previous social media studies [40] resulted in a total of 4573 sessions for all users. The number of events per session ranges from 2 to 2155 (median=11, IQR=31). A session lasted on average slightly over 4 minutes but the longest session lasted over 3 hours (median=83sec, IQR=270sec). These figures are in line with session characteristics reported in other social media log studies [40, 2]. The number of events per session and session duration are highly correlated (Pearson r=0.90) indicating that participants were typically very engaged when using Twitter.

Figures 1(a)-(d) present an overview of general session behaviour: (a) examines the average session length per user and shows that for 50% of users the average session lasted 320sec or longer. (b) shows that the number of sessions per user varies greatly; the sharp slope indicating a heavy long-tailed distribution. 75% of participants completed 46 sessions or less. For about 80% of participants, the average number of events per session completed (shown in (c)) was below 100 events and peaks at around 300. Finally (d) indicates that 40% of participants performed 1 session per day on average, a quarter of participants completed 2 or more sessions and the maximum number of sessions per day was 10. These plots underline very different patterns of usage across participants.

Most events occurred in the context of participants' home timeline (72.40%). The second most common context was the profile site of other users (10.10%) followed by the notifications page (7.50%). Other contexts/event categories featured infrequently. Only 3.05% of events were search events or occurred on the Twitter SERP page and even fewer come from favourites lists (0.30%). In fact only 8 participants (18.20%) visited their favourites list at all. This aligns with the findings of a previous study where users reported rarely or never examining their favourites [32].

In total 143,721 unique Tweets appear in the logs. 273,550 references to these were collected, of which 146,735 are unique user-tweets (i.e. the same Tweet was counted twice if it appeared in the logs of two users). Of such Tweets, 3.76% received a special interaction (FAV=3.10%, RT=0.24%, RT+FAV=0.35%). Again, stark differences in behaviour can be observed across users. 23 (52.27%) participants FAV'd or RT'd. Twitter feature usage can be heavily skewed, e.g. 4,186 (83.00%) favouriting actions were performed by a single, dominant user. The same user had by a considerable margin the highest number of favourited Tweets (Table 1).

The average age of a viewed Tweet was 28.1 hours (median=1.44 hours, max=80667 hours (9 years), IQR=11.02 hours). These statistics indicate that Twitter is perhaps not as real-time as people may think. Figure 2 plots the age of Tweets when viewed, showing that 52,340 (19.13%) Tweets were not viewed within a day of being posted. Although the vast majority of Tweets are fresh (orange points) - as would be expected with a real-time platform - a good number of Tweets are in fact relatively old when viewed. This is a first hint that certain Tweets may have an extended life-cycle.

The analyses in this section demonstrate: 1) diverse behaviour across participants, 2) that users spend most time on their own timelines and rarely access their favourites list or own profile, 3) that users interact with old Tweets - a first clue that re-finding may occur.

[3]Identification required the user to visit their own profile page. Participants consented to establishing background information via the API.

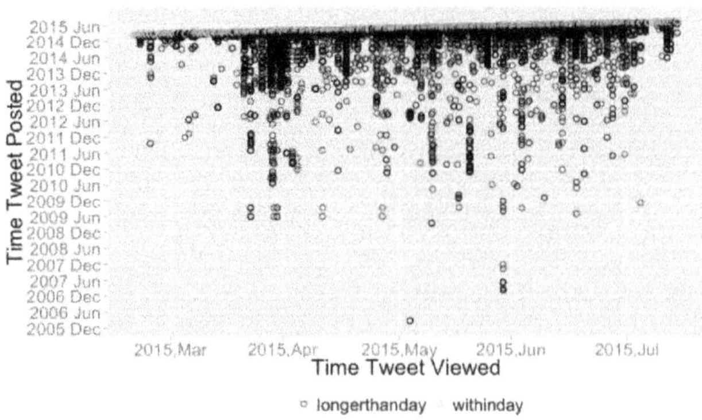

Figure 2: Age of viewed Tweets

5. INVESTIGATING RE-FINDING

The following sections analyse various aspects of re-finding. First, by comparing different proxies for the behaviour, we examine its frequency and how it varies across the participants. Next we look at temporal patterns in Tweet re-access. Finally, we look at re-finding behaviour in detail by examining the differences between re-finding and non-re-finding sessions and analysing the steps involved.

5.1 Re-finding Frequency

Several methods for identifying re-finding behaviour in naturalistic log data have been reported in the literature: using interaction sequences as a proxy [44, 48, 19], supervised learning approaches with a manually annotated training set [16] and pairing repeated session goals as produced by a classifier [39]. We employ the approach taken in equivalent early studies in web search, that is we utilise particular interaction patterns as a proxy for re-finding [44, 48]. We investigate several proxies before settling on the conservative approach of examining instances of repeated clicks on Tweets.

Table 2 shows that only ~30% of all Tweets that appeared on the participants' timeline were interacted with explicitly and 12% of these receive a special interaction. This could mean that many Tweets are never read or that the content of many Tweets requires no mouse-over or click in order to be consumed. Interpreting the logs in this second manner would mean that many of the older Tweets in Figure 2 could be treated as re-finding, although it is difficult to say which. Classifying viewed Tweets older than the median age would result in 25.30% of all seen as being re-found with 93.18% of participants doing this at some point during the study. This is an extremely liberal proxy and would very likely over-estimate the frequency with which re-finding occurs.

A more accurate proxy is to consider Tweets that were explicitly interacted with multiple times across sessions. 11% of the interacted-with Tweets were interacted with again in a future session. Taking cross-session interactions as a proxy for re-finding means that 34 (77%) participants can be considered to have re-found at some point in the study with the proportion of their Tweets being re-found varying from 0.43% to 30%. On average 10.13% of Tweets are interacted-with across sessions. Again this probably over-estimates the frequency of re-finding. For instance users with a low

unique user-tweets 146735	Tweets interacted	Tweets interacted with SI	Re-interacted Tweets without SI	Re-interacted Tweets with SI
Hover or Click	40486 (27.59%)	4847 (11.97%)	375 (7.73%)	3996 (11.21%)
Click only	8320 (5.67%)	4743 (57.00%)	134 (3.75%)	85 (1.79%)

Table 2: The proxies re-interacted and re-click in detail. SI stands for special interaction i.e. Tweets that got RT'd or FAV'd.

number of followers may implicitly mouse-over older Tweets due to a lack of new content in their stream and several re-interactions may result from a single re-finding intention.

A further method of identifying re-finding in the logs is to use a repeated click pair across sessions as has been used in web [44, 48], email [19] and desktop search contexts [12]. In streamed data like Twitter, where there is a heavy focus on the newest information, it is also a comparatively conservative proxy as it is very unlikely that users accidentally click on an older message that they have previously clicked on as part of general interactions with the service.

Using this proxy 17 participants (38.64%) re-find and they do so with varying frequency (1.29% - 15.35% of clicked Tweets are re-clicked in a future session). Using re-clicks as a proxy results in 276 re-finding actions of 219 unique Tweets across 176 different sessions. This indicates that re-finding sessions can contain multiple instances of re-finding and some Tweets (55) can be re-accessed several times across multiple sessions (median=2, max=3).

We have presented three different proxies that can be used to identify re-finding. Figure 3 summarises what these show regarding the frequency of re-finding sessions, tweets and users. The most conservative proxy reduces false positives, but comes at the cost of missing many potential re-finding actions as 95% of Tweets were not clicked at all and thus cannot be identified as being re-found using this approach. The true re-finding frequency probably lies within the range suggested by the three proxies. Nevertheless we focus on repeated clicks beyond sessions in the remainder of the paper as when describing re-finding behaviour, we want to be as sure as possible that what we are describing is indeed re-finding. Figure 3 shows that taking re-clicks as a proxy dramatically reduces the number of re-finding instances to

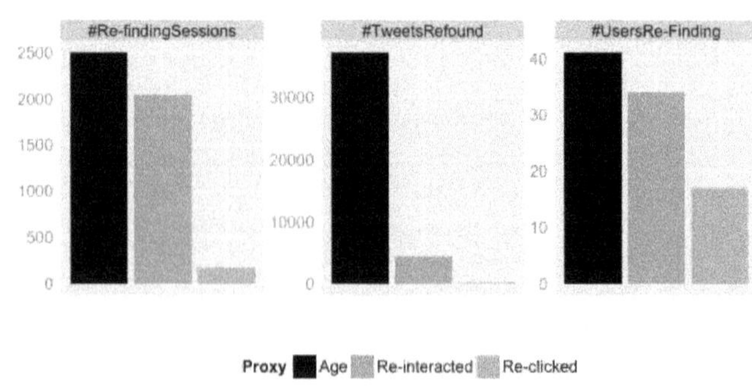

Figure 3: The three proxies (age, re-interaction across sessions and re-click across sessions) in comparison of number of re-finding sessions, Tweets refound and users re-finding.

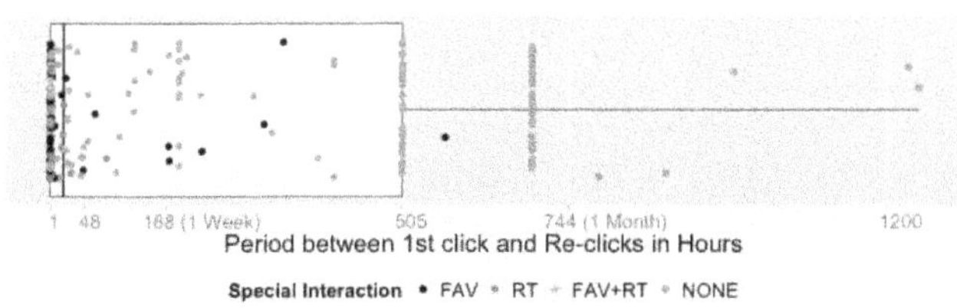

Figure 4: Temporal Patterns of Re-clicks

investigate. Nevertheless, even this conservative proxy suggests re-finding to be a pervasive activity affecting over one third of the users.

5.2 Personal Tweet Life-cycles

The period between the first click and a re-click on a Tweet sheds light on the personal life-cycle of re-accessed Tweets i.e. the period for which the Tweet or its content has utility to an individual user. Figure 4 shows that the personal life-cycle of a Tweet is typically short: half of all re-finding actions happen within a day (median time between click and re-click = 18.8 hours, mean=217 hours (9 days)). The longest personal life-cycle in our logs was 52 days, which we find surprisingly long for a medium known as ephemeral and suggests that Twitter content can hold utility several weeks after it is first encountered. Many repeated clicks happen within one day, yet the period between 1 day and 1 week shows far fewer clicks. Once a period of a week has past the frequency of re-clicks rises again. Moreover Figure 4 illustrates how special interactions and re-finding period relate. Different point colours show whether or not re-clicked Tweets were FAV'd or RT'd. The percentage of specially interacted Tweets is very high in the short re-click period group (61.60%), whereas in the long re-click period group this is not the case (10.44%).

Previous work has suggested that both RT and FAV are signs of relevance [36] and used as a means to "bookmark" a Tweet for future use. Intuitively, therefore, one would assume that Tweets interacted with in these ways would be more likely to be re-found across a longer time period compared to Tweets not marked as a FAV or RT'd. Figure 4 indicates the opposite to be the case. The proportion of Tweets (61.60%) with special interaction amongst Tweets with a short re-click period (<median) is much higher than the proportion among Tweets (10.44%) that are re-clicked after a long period (>median). A chi-square test confirms this relationship, showing a highly significant effect of special interaction on re-click period (χ^2=77.18, df=1, $p<0.05$, ϕ=0.536, Odds-Ratio: 14). The odds ratio indicates the chance of a Tweet being re-clicked after a long re-click period is 14 times higher for Tweets which have not been FAV'd and/or RT'd. The results suggest that users seem to favourite and/or re-tweet a Tweet whose relevance is immediately obvious and short-term, but struggle with assessing the future utility of encountered Tweets over longer periods.

5.3 Re-finding Behaviour

We examine re-finding behaviour in 3 stages. We start by comparing re-finding with non-re-finding sessions. Next we investigate re-finding strategies by analysing the contexts in which Tweets are re-clicked. Here we discover that re-finding via user profile pages is a common strategy. Therefore, in a final step, we look more closely at how participants navigate to user profiles. This provides insight into what people remember about sought-after Tweets and how they make use of these recollections when re-finding.

5.3.1 Examining re-finding sessions

To discover how re-finding differs from typical Twitter usage we compare the 176 re-finding sessions with 176 randomly sampled non-re-finding sessions. Using appropriate (Bonferroni corrected) non-parametric tests revealed 34 session features with significantly differing distributions. Re-finding sessions are longer in terms of session duration (492 secs vs 76), have more events in general (75.81 vs 29.66) and more search interactions (2.17 vs 0.37). Moreover, interactions were more likely to be in contexts other than the home timeline. During re-finding sessions more Tweets were viewed (75.51 vs 28.70), hovered over (16.24 vs 9.35) and clicked (5.14 vs 1.24). Also, relating to heavy downward scrolling (10416.44 px vs 5322.73) and mouse movement, participants tended to view Tweets much deeper in the timeline (25.62 vs 11.87) and consequently encounter older Tweets. The average age of a Tweet viewed in a re-finding session was typically much older than in non-refinding sessions (11.60 days vs 7.50). Finally, during re-finding sessions more user profiles are visited (0.75 vs 0.28) raising the questions of why this is the case and how users achieve this.

In summary, re-finding sessions are longer and contain more extensive and more varied behaviour. The analyses paint the picture of re-finding being much harder work than normal Twitter use.

5.3.2 Examining re-finding strategies

Here we characterise re-finding by looking at the different contexts in which re-clicks on Tweets occur. This relates to the strategies people employ.

As in Section 5.2, we divide the re-clicked Tweets in short re-click period (<median) and long re-click period (>median) and examine the URL in which the re-clicks take place. Figure 5 shows the distribution of re-click contexts. In short re-click periods the dominant context is the Timeline (65%), illustrating that often users need not leave their own stream to re-access content. This also means, however, that if a

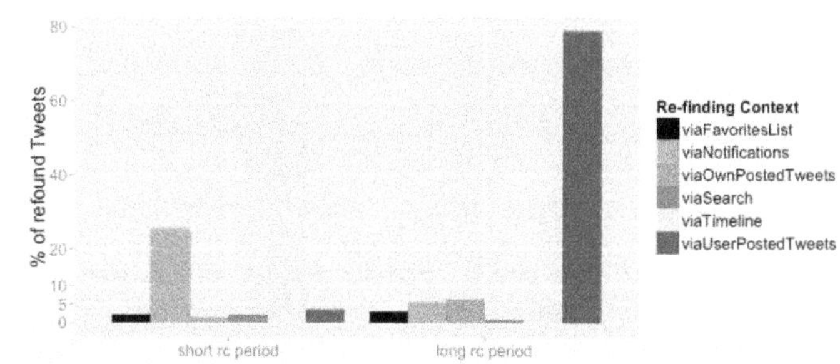

Figure 5: Comparison of different re-click contexts corresponding to re-finding strategies for short and long re-click periods.

large number of active users are followed and if some time has passed since the Tweet was last seen, the user will be required to scroll a lot. This aligns with the findings in Section 5.3.1 where re-finding sessions were shown to contain significantly more scrolling. 25% of Tweets are re-accessed via the *Notifications* page. Other re-access strategies, such as keyword search (2.1%) or strategies that require certain preserving behaviour upfront e.g. FAVing (2.1%) or RTing (1.4%) are infrequently used. Thus, even if people are able to correctly predict they will need a Tweet in the future and bookmark - which Section 5.2 suggests to sometimes be the case for short time periods - they rarely make use of the bookmark when re-accessing.

The pattern changes dramatically for Tweets with a long re-click period. Re-finding via the notifications page or the Timeline decrease to ~5%. Re-finding Tweets via the favourites list (2.9%) stays fairly constant, whereas search drops below 1%. In contrast re-finding via the own posted Tweets increases to about 5%. The context in which almost all Tweets get re-clicked, however, is another user's profile page with 78.9% of re-accesses occurring in this context. This is of note as it suggests users associate Tweets with the author or poster of a Tweet or at least have a vague idea of who might have posted it. The fact that the author or sender of an information item is well remembered is known from previous PIM studies [12, 16] including on Twitter [10].

Surprisingly, it seems features designed to prolong Tweet life-cycles, such as FAVing and RTing are not the contexts in which Tweets are re-found. Instead Tweets tend to be re-accessed by scrolling either on the home timeline (after short periods) or another user's timeline (after long periods).

5.3.3 Re-finding Paths

Next, we look more closely at the paths people take to re-access Tweets. We do this by examining bi-gram events, i.e. two consecutive actions occurring prior to a user profile visit which, as we saw previously, was the most common context in which Tweets were re-accessed after longer time periods.

Table 3 shows the top 5 bi-gram events preceding a user profile event in re-finding sessions. The most frequent bi-gram is a home timeline visit followed by a search query. 30% of profile visits are proceeded by a search event. This suggests that although re-clicks did not occur in search contexts, search is still important as it is used to locate people associated with the sought-after information. Users exhibit orienteering behaviour, narrowing down on the information source by searching for the user, before browsing through the user's posted Tweets to re-find the desired Tweet. This fits the well known phenomenon in information seeking that people prefer to locate information via other people [20].

The remaining bi-grams all share one common event: the profile summary view.[4] By clicking on a mention or the Tweet author name the profile summary view is the link leading a participant to a user's complete profile and his posted Tweets. This shows participants' use of navigational links i.e. orienteering to get to user profiles. Overall 70% of bi-grams can be attributed as link-based orienteering solely relying on a browsing strategy.

[4]In September 2015 (shortly after our study ended) the profile summary view of users was replaced with a hover effect showing user details.

Top 5 bi-grams (N=33)	
1. Home site visit, Search	24% (N=8)
2. PSV, Click on user name	15% (N=5)
3. PSV, Click on user profile picture	15% (N=5)
4. PSV, Click on author of recent Tweet	9% (N=3)
5. PSV, Click on "complete profile" button	9% (N=3)

Table 3: Top 5 bi-grams events preceding a user profile event. PSV stands for profile summary viewed.

5.3.4 Summary

Section 5.1 showed that even on SMAs, which focus on real-time information, the re-finding of older information is prevalent and Tweets can offer utility for long time periods. The literature suggests that regardless of domain, re-finding can be challenging and frustrating [14, 31, 39] and the results in Section 5.3.1 seem to support this. Section 5.3.3 showed that *teleporting* strategies (e.g. searching directly to re-find Tweets) are almost never applied. Instead *orienteering* is preferred to narrow down on desired content. Orienteering can be *search-based*, where users submit queries to navigate to a specific context before browsing or *link-based*, where existing hypertext links are followed to navigate stepwise.

6. PREDICTING RE-FINDING

As users struggle with assessing the future utility of Tweets, we wanted to test how effective automated algorithms can be at predicting which Tweets will be re-clicked in the future.

6.1 Experimental Setup

We perform modelling experiments framed as a binary classification problem where the positive class consists of 217 of the re-clicked Tweets analysed above[5]. To attain 217 Tweets in the negative class we first randomly draw 100 clicked Tweets from each user who re-clicked a Tweet during the study. This is important as we do not want to bias the sample by including too many clicks from users who did not re-click at all. We then sample 217 non-re-clicked Tweets randomly from this set.

15 models are compared with varying degrees of complexity, in terms of the number of predictive features and the costs incurred in obtaining these features. 10-fold-cross-validation is performed on every iteration using a Random Forest classifier, as it has proven to be robust for classification problems [17]. We also experimented with other classifiers including SVM, but none of these resulted in better performance. Therefore only results from the Random Forest experiments are reported, specifying F1, accuracy and the area under the ROC curve (AUC).

6.2 Features

In our modelling we used four groups of predictive features (listed in detail in Table 4):

Tweet features describe general characteristics of Tweets with respect to their text (*CharCount, WordCount*), part of speech information (*POSTags*) [35] and use of Twitter features (*HashtagCount, MentionCount, LinkCount, maxFAVCount, maxRTCount*). Moreover we algorithmically as-

[5]2 of the Tweets were deleted and it is impossible to derive many of the features detailed below

sessed a Tweet's sentiment[6] (*sentiment.score*) and readability[7] (*readability.score*), as well as its type as established by human coders (Cohens Kappa: 0.48). The five content categories were slightly adapted from [11]: Conversational, Status Message, News Providing, Broadcasting, Unclassifiable & Spam.

Sender-related features: As senders were shown to play an important role in re-finding, we investigate a range of features describing a Tweet's sender and the relationship between the participant and the sender. This group encompasses a sender's general account information (*SenderTweetsPosted, SenderFollowerCount* etc.) and several heuristics derived from the literature (*TweetsRT*) to determine whether the sender posts primarily about themselves ("meformers") or about more broader topics ("informers") [34]. The user-sender-relation was captured by how many of a sender's Tweets were received, clicked or specially interacted with by the participant (*TweetsPerSender, TweetsClickedPerSender, TweetsSIPerSender* etc.).

Session features characterise a user's behaviour during the session in which a Tweet was clicked for the first time. These include high-level session characteristics such as (*Duration, EventsTotal*), events per event categories (e.g. *TimelineEvents, UserProfileEvents*), features with respect to Tweets (*TweetsHover, TweetsClick, TweetsBuffer*) information about Tweets on global level (*RTCount, FAVCount*) as well as information on a Tweet's age and click-position (*TweetAge, TweetPosition*). Moreover a wide range of features related to mouse movement (*ScrollSummary, DownScrollTotal, UpScrollTotal, MouseMoveCount* etc.) are part of this feature group. Finally, again with respect to the importance of senders, we integrate information regarding how many profiles are visited during the session (*ProfileVisits, TotalProfileTime*).

User features describe a participant's overall Twitter behaviour as recorded by the extension e.g. number of sessions in total, number of sessions per day (*SessionCount, SessionsPerUserPerDay* etc.) and account information (*UserTweetsPosted, UserFollowerCount* etc.).

Some of the described features cost more to obtain than others. For example, Tweet features are freely available, given a reference to the clicked Tweet. Session-features can be recorded during regular Twitter use and not stored, if no Tweet was clicked. Finally, long term information about a user's overall behaviour (user feature group) and her relation to other senders (user-sender-relation feature group) complete the picture, but are expensive in that they involve monitoring user behaviour over time and storing this in some way.

Name	Description
Tweet Features	
TweetAge	Age of Tweet at time of click
TweetPosition	Position in stream at time of click
TweetVistime	Period of visibility till time of click
SpecialInteraction	Special interaction if any
FAVCount	Number of FAVs at time of click
RTCount	Number of RTs at time of click
MentionCount	Number of @-mentions in a Tweet
LinkCount	Number of links in a Tweet
HashtagCount	Number of hashtags in a Tweet
maxFAVCount	Overall maximum number of FAV
maxRTCount	Overal maximum number of RT
CharCount	Number of characters in a Tweet
WordCount	Number of words in a Tweet
avgWordLength	Average word length
POSTags	21 part of speech features e.g. noun count
POC	If Tweet was part of a conversation
sentiment.score	Positive or negative sentiment of a Tweet
readability.score	Flesch-Reading-Ease-Score
content.cat	Tweet Category by human coder approach
User-Sender-Relation Features	
TweetsPerSender	Number of Tweets received by user from sender x
TweetsClickedPerSender†	Clicked Tweets of received Tweets from sender x
TweetsSIPerSender†	Tweets specially interacted with of Tweets from sender x
SpecialInteractionNorm	Normalization of special interaction
FracTweetsMentions	Fraction of Tweets with mentions from sender x
FracTweetsHashtags	Fraction of Tweets with hashtags from sender x
FracTweetsLinks	Fraction of Tweets with links from sender x
TweetsRT†	Number and Fraction of Tweets that are RTs by sender x
SenderTweetsPosted	Number of Tweets posted by sender x
SenderFollowerCount	Number of followers of sender x
SenderFollowingCount	Number sender x is following
SenderFAVCount	Number of FAV'd Tweets by sender x
SenderCreated	Time since registration
SenderListedCount	Number of lists sender x is listed
UserClass	Meformer or Informer
Session Features	
EventsTotal	Number of events per session
Duration	Session duration in seconds
BusynessIndex	Number of events per duration
TimelineEvents†	Number of events per context Timeline
NotificationsEvents†	Number of events per context Notifications
UserProfileEvent†	Number of events on user profiles
OwnProfileEvent†	Number of events on own profile
FFMRelationsEvents†	Number of events for Following-Follower-Mention
SearchEvents†	Number of events per context search/number of search events
FavouritesEvents†	Number of events per context favourites list
SingleTweetEvents†	Number of events per single Tweet view
TweetingEvents†	Number of Tweets posted per session
DirectmessageEvents†	Number of direct message interactions
ListEvents†	Number of events on lists
OtherEvents†	Number of events on other sub-pages (e.g. Twitter API site)
TweetsSeen	Number of Tweets seen by user in session
MUR	Message uncertainty ratio (Tweets clicked/distinct Tweets clicked)
RTCountSession*	Average and maximum number of RTs observed over all Tweets seen
FAVCountSession*	Average and maximum number of FAVs observed over all Tweets seen
TweetPosition*	Average and maximum position observed over all Tweets seen
TweetAge*	Average and maximum age of Tweet observed over all Tweets seen
TweetVistime*	Average and maximum Tweet visibility till click
TweetsBuffer†	Number of Tweets added to stream while scrolling
TweetsClick†	Number of Tweets clicked
TweetsHover†	Number of Tweets hovered
ScrollSummary	Number of continuous scrolling activities
DownScrollTotal	Down scroll distance in px
UpScrollTotal	Up scroll distance in px
ScrollIndex	Total pixels scrolled/scroll summary events
MouseMoveCount	Number of distinct mouse movements
MouseDistance*	Average and maximum distance covered by cursor in px
AvgMouseActivityIndex	Site area (square px) covered by number of mouse movements
ProfileVisits	Number of user profile sites visited
TotalProfileTime	Number of time spent on user profiles
DistinctProfilesVisited	Number of distinct user profiles visited
PUR	Person uncertainty ratio
User Features	
MeanSessionDuration	Average session duration for user
SessionCount	Number of sessions for user
AvgEventPerSession	Average events per session per user
SessionsPerUserPerDay	Number of sessions per user per day
UserTweetsPosted	Number of Tweets posted by user
UserFollowerCount	Number of followers a users has
UserFollowingCount	Number of accounts a user is following
UserFAVCount	Number of FAV'd Tweets for user
UserCreated	Time since registration
UserMediaSent	Number of Tweets with media posted by user

Table 4: Features used in the prediction task classified by feature group. Features tagged with † have absolute and relative values. Features tagged with * have average and max values.

6.3 Prediction Results

Table 5 shows the results of the prediction experiments. The performance of all models is generally very good with only small gains in F1 and accuracy over the baseline model based only on (cheap to obtain) Tweet-features. The best model is a complicated model consisting of 115 features from three feature groups (Tweet + User-Sender-Relation + Session) and in practice would require long term observation.

To understand which features contribute most to model accuracy and whether it is possible to reduce the feature space, we applied a cross validation function[8] for feature selection, which assesses prediction performance of different models by reducing the number of predictors in a stepwise

[6]https://github.com/trinker/sentimentr

[7]https://cran.r-project.org/web/packages/koRpus/

[8]We used the rfcv function from the R package *randomForest* (https://cran.r-project.org/web/packages/randomForest/)

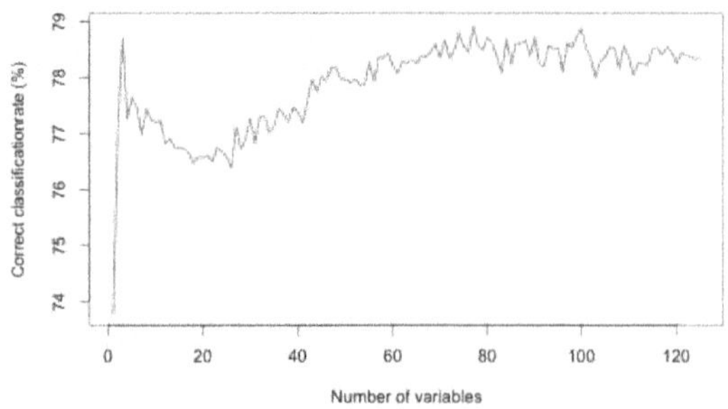

Figure 6: Accuracy vs #predictors. 3 top features obtain a similar performance to 80 or more.

	Feature Groups	F1-Score	Accuracy	AUC	# of Features
1	Tweet + User-Sender-Relation + Session	0.80	0.79	0.88	115
2	Top 3 features identified	0.79	0.80	0.86	3
3	Tweet + Session	0.79	0.78	0.87	97
4	Session	0.76	0.76	0.85	58
5	User	0.75	0.75	0.82	10
6	User-Sender-Relation	0.75	0.74	0.82	18
7	Tweet	0.74	0.72	0.78	39

Table 5: Prediction performance for models with different feature groups sorted by F1.

manner. Figure 6 shows that with the three features contributing most to model accuracy a random forest model can achieve a similar result as it would with 80 features or more. These features are: *SessionCount*, *SessionsPerUserPerDay* and *TweetsClickedPerSender*. All three are related to long-term behaviour and are costly to acquire. These features underline, however, that frequent Twitter users do seem to use Twitter as an information silo.

As we want models that work well for all users and don't base predictions largely on detecting active users, we also tested variants which only utilise easily obtainable features and do not model long-term user behaviour at all. Removing such behavioural features from the process still results in a model with many features (97), but achieves a high performance overall (*Tweet + Session* F1: 0,79, Acc: 0,78).

Figure 7 shows the importance of the top 25 features in the *Tweet + Session* model as determined by the decrease in accuracy if the feature is dropped. The plot shows a dominance of variables from session group. However, two features from the Tweet-feature group (if a Tweet was part of a conversation (*POC*) and/or specially interacted with) are both good predictors for future clicks.

7. SUMMARY AND DISCUSSION

When summarising our findings it is important to concede that we only had access to a small sample of Twitter users and moreover only to interactions with the Twitter website via Chrome. A large proportion of Twitter usage is mobile/app-based[9] and these interactions were missing in our analyses. Nevertheless, in a way this makes our findings even more striking:

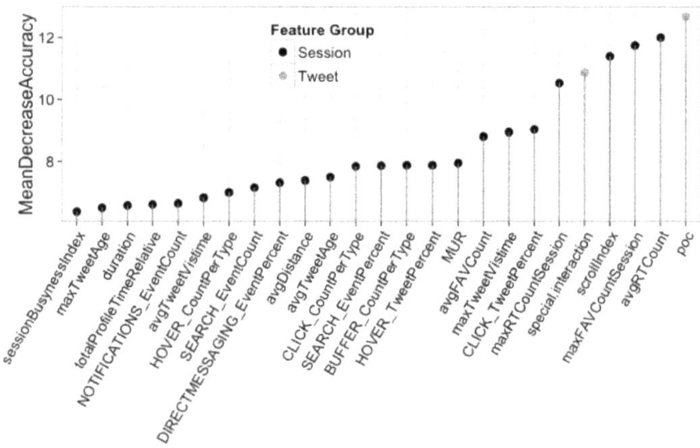

Figure 7: Top 25 features according to their mean decrease in accuracy of the model using only Tweet and session features. Each feature is colour-coded to show which feature group it belongs to.

(i) Using a conservative proxy and missing cross-device interactions we can be certain we are under-estimating the frequency of re-finding, yet our results still indicate it is prevalent and the personal life-cycle of Tweets is longer than one might expect. Moreover, the data reveal that many older Tweets were interacted with, showing that Tweets can still be of value even after years have passed.

(ii) Although participants were able to predict some short-term re-finding and bookmark these Tweets, hardly any of the longer-term re-accesses were RT'd or FAV'd. This suggests that it is only later - induced by a then current information need - that the user becomes aware of the Tweet's value (post-valued recall). This phenomenon has been observed in other PIM contexts [30, 49]. Even when participants did correctly predict a Tweet's future utility and bookmark it, they tended not to use the bookmark to re-access. Forgetting about bookmarks due to an "out of sight, out of mind" problem has also been reported in the PIM literature [26].

(iii) Search is not used as IR-researchers might hope. Rather than searching for content directly (*teleporting*), participants first narrowed the space by searching for a person, then scrolled to re-access. This was one of two *orienteering* strategies revealed and is most similar to the behaviour seen in email search [14]. The second *orienteering* strategy was link-based and reminiscent of the spatial navigation often preferred when re-finding computer files [1]. The lack of teleporting strategies supports Teevan and colleagues' decision not to classify repeated queries as re-finding behaviour.

(iv) We showed that future re-accesses can be predicted with reasonable accuracy. Different kinds of features are helpful, including long-term behavioural clues, which are costly to attain. Good performance can be attained, however, using only predictors derived from Tweet content and meta-data.

(v) Many of our analyses underline the importance of people in re-finding on Twitter: Re-finding sessions have more user profile requests, re-finding Tweets via the sender's profile page is the most common strategy for Tweets older than a day and some of the most powerful predictive features for

[9]According to Twitter 80% of active users access via a mobile device (https://about.twitter.com/company).

future re-access describe the relationship between the participant and the sender. Predictive models may offer utility in several ways as we outline below.

8. DESIGN IMPLICATIONS

We have shown that some Tweets can offer relevance for longer than the period in which they are visible on the user's timeline. Although Twitter is already taking steps to avoid the decaying visibility of Tweets by giving a recap of top Tweets via the "While you were away..." feature[10], the platform could do more to further help users return to relevant, older Tweets. We propose design implications for the two orienteering strategies observed in our study, but first make suggestions with respect to teleporting behaviour, which was not observed but is known from re-finding studies in other domains.

Support for teleporting: Although teleporting would be a more direct strategy to re-access Tweets, it is perhaps unsurprising that it wasn't used. Twitter provides no obvious means to apply search queries only to Tweets, which have appeared in the user's own timeline. The one exception being CTRL+F in the browser over the currently loaded Tweets. Twitter search queries can be restricted to return only Tweets posted by a specified user with the @-syntax, but we did not observe this in our data. It could be that users are unaware of the function. The auto-complete function also biases behaviour by immediately suggesting a user-profile page. Based on what we have learned, we believe users would benefit from making the @-operator more prominent and allowing additional query terms to make the feature more usable for immediate re-finding.

There is also scope for improving the Twitter search algorithm directly to support re-finding. The features identified as effective in the prediction task, may also offer utility in a "learning to rank" approach to search. Similar to recent approaches for email search a decay function combined with behavioural features might lead to enhanced performance [8]. Our data could be used to run experiments similar to those in [8].

Support for orienteering: Support for re-finding via orienteering could be implemented via various different SUI features that support history mechanisms and help users return to previously viewed Tweets. One helpful change might be to subtly alter the colour of Tweets predicted to have future utility. This would make them easier to identify during the scrolling behaviour we identified as being typical of re-finding sessions. This change could be applied on home timelines and on the profile pages of other users. Another approach would be to allow such Tweets to re-appear amongst new Tweets. This idea has been shown to be effective for web-page re-finding [43] and Facebook has started to do something similar with "memories", but several user studies would be required to determine how many older Tweets to show, how to show them etc., as well as determine user tolerance for such an approach.

9. CONCLUSIONS AND FUTURE WORK

Analysing log data has proven very fruitful for IR research in recent years. We have used this technique to learn about information re-access and re-finding on Twitter. We have shed light on several aspects, demonstrating that re-finding is pervasive. That is, contrary to Jack Dorsey's comments, people do "go back in time" and Tweets do sometimes prove useful for longer than they are typically visible in the service. We have investigated re-finding strategies applied and in doing so highlighted limitations of bookmarking strategies, both in terms of the accuracy in choosing which Tweets to bookmark and re-using them when they exist. A later step showed that automatic algorithms might be more effective at predicting future utility. Based on our findings we made a number of design suggestions. In future work we hope to implement and evaluate some of the features we suggested. Nevertheless a deeper understanding of specific aspects would also be useful. For example we know from our analyses that people are important, but we don't know which people are important nor why. Future studies might want to investigate what makes a person salient. Our next step, however, will be to think about how to perform algorithmic experiments similar to those described in [8] as mentioned above.

[10]https://blog.twitter.com/2015/while-you-were-away-0

10. REFERENCES

[1] D. Barreau and B. A. Nardi, *Finding and reminding: File organization from the desktop*, SIGCHI Bull. **27** (1995), no. 3, 39–43.

[2] F. Benevenuto, T. Rodrigues, M. Cha, and V. Almeida, *Characterizing user behavior in online social networks*, Proc. IMC, ACM, 2009, pp. 49–62.

[3] d. boyd, S. Golder, and G. Lotan, *Tweet, tweet, retweet: Conversational aspects of retweeting on twitter*, Proc. HICSS, IEEE, 2010, pp. 1–10.

[4] H. Bruce, *Personal, anticipated information need*, Information Research **10(3)** (2005), no. 232.

[5] H. Bruce, W. Jones, and S. Dumais, *Information behaviour that keeps found things found*, Information Research **10** (2004), no. 1.

[6] R. Buettner and K. Buettner, *A systematic literature review of twitter research from a socio-political revolution perspective*, Proc. HICSS, IEEE, 2016.

[7] R. Capra and M. Perez-Quinones, *Using web search engines to find and refind information*, Computer **38** (2005), no. 10, 36–42.

[8] D. Carmel, G. Halawi, L. Lewin-Eytan, Y. Maarek, and A. Raviv, *Rank by time or by relevance?: Revisiting email search*, Proc. CIKM, 2015, pp. 283–292.

[9] A. Civan, W. Jones, P. Klasnja, and H. Bruce, *Better to organize personal information by folders or by tags?: The devil is in the details*, Proc. ASIST **45** (2008), no. 1, 1–13.

[10] S. Counts and K. Fisher, *Taking it all in? visual attention in microblog consumption.*, Proc. ICWSM, The AAAI Press, 2011.

[11] S. Dann, *Twitter content classification*, First Monday **15** (2010), no. 12.

[12] S. Dumais, E. Cutrell, JJ Cadiz, G. Jancke, R. Sarin, and D. C. Robbins, *Stuff i've seen: A system for personal information retrieval and re-use*, Proc. SIGIR, 2003, pp. 72–79.

[13] S. Dumais, R. Jeffries, D. M. Russell, D. Tang, and J. Teevan, *Understanding user behavior through log data and analysis*, Ways of Knowing in HCI, 2014, pp. 349–372.

[14] D. Elsweiler, M. Baillie, and I. Ruthven, *What makes re-finding information difficult? a study of email re-finding*, Proc. ECIR, 2011, pp. 568–579.

[15] D. Elsweiler and M. Harvey, *Engaging and maintaining a sense of being informed: Understanding the tasks motivating twitter search*, JASIST (2014).

[16] D. Elsweiler, M. Harvey, and M. Hacker, *Understanding re-finding behavior in naturalistic email interaction logs*, Proc. SIGIR, 2011, pp. 35–44.

[17] M. Fernández-Delgado, E. Cernadas, S. Barro, and D. Amorim, *Do we need hundreds of classifiers to solve real world classification problems?*, J. Mach. Learn. Res. **15** (2014), no. 1.

[18] G. Gorrell and K. Bontcheva, *Classifying twitter favorites: Like, bookmark, or thanks?*, JASIST (2015).

[19] M. Harvey and D. Elsweiler, *Exploring query patterns in email search*, Proc. ECIR, 2012, pp. 25–36.

[20] M. Hertzum, *People as carriers of experience and sources of commitment: Information seeking in a software design project*, New Rev. Inf. Behav. Res. **1** (2000), no. January, 135–149.

[21] N. Hodas and K Lerman, *How visibility and divided attention constrain social contagion*, SocialCom-PASSAT'12, 2012, pp. 249–257.

[22] C. Honeycutt and S. C. Herring, *Beyond microblogging: Conversation and collaboration via twitter*, Proc. HICSS, 2009, pp. 1–10.

[23] L. Hong, O. Dan, and B. D. Davison, *Predicting popular messages in twitter*, Proc. WWW, ACM, 2011, pp. 57–58.

[24] C.J. Hutto, S. Yardi, and E. Gilbert, *A longitudinal study of follow predictors on twitter*, Proc. SIGCHI, 2013, pp. 821–830.

[25] A. Java, X. Song, T. Finin, and B. Tseng, *Why we twitter: Understanding microblogging usage and communities*, Proc. WebKDD/SNA-KDD, 2007, pp. 56–65.

[26] W. Jones, A. J. Phuwanartnurak, R. Gill, and H. Bruce, *Don't take my folders away!: Organizing personal information to get ghings done*, SIGCHI, 2005, pp. 1505–1508.

[27] W. Jones and J. Teevan (eds.), *Personal information management*, University of Washington Press, 2007.

[28] A. Komlodi, D. Soergel, and G. Marchionini, *Search histories for user support in user interfaces*, JASIST **57** (2006), no. 6, 803–807.

[29] H. Kwak, C. Lee, H. Park, and S. Moon, *What is twitter, a social network or a news media?*, Proc. WWW '10, ACM, 2010, pp. 591–600.

[30] M. Lansdale, *The psychology of personal information management*, App. Ergonomics **19** (1988), no. 1, 55–66.

[31] F. Meier and D. Elsweiler, *Tweets i've seen: Analysing factors influencing re-finding frustration on twitter*, Proc. IIiX, 2014, pp. 287–290.

[32] F. Meier, D. Elsweiler, and M. L. Wilson, *More than liking and bookmarking? towards understanding twitter favouriting behaviour*, Proc. ICWSM, The AAAI Press, 2014.

[33] M. R. Morris, J. Teevan, and K. Panovich, *What Do People Ask Their Social Networks, and Why? A Survey Study of Status Message Q&A Behavior*, Proc. CHI, 2010, pp. 1739–1748.

[34] M. Naaman, J. Boase, and C-H. Lai, *Is it really about me? message content in social awareness streams*, Proc. CSCW, 2010, pp. 189–192.

[35] O. Owoputi, B. O'Connor, C. Dyer, K. Gimpel, N. Schneider, and N. A. Smith, *Improved part-of-speech tagging for online conversational text with word clusters*, Proc. NAACL-HLT, 2013, pp. 380–390.

[36] S. Petrovic, M. Osborne, and V. Lavrenko, *RT to Win! Predicting Message Propagation in Twitter*, Proc. ICWSM, 2011.

[37] P. Ravasio, S. G. Schär, and H. Krueger, *In pursuit of desktop evolution: User problems and practices with modern desktop systems*, ACM Trans. Comput.-Hum. Interact. **11** (2004), no. 2, 156–180.

[38] R. Rogers, *Debanalizing twitter: The transformation of an object of study*, Proc. WebSci, 2013, pp. 356–365.

[39] S. Sadeghi, R. Blanco, P. Mika, M. Sanderson, F. Scholer, and D. Vallet, *Predicting re-finding activity and difficulty*, Proc. ECIR, 2015, pp. 715–727.

[40] F. Schneider, A. Feldmann, B. Krishnamurthy, and W. Willinger, *Understanding online social network usage from a network perspective*, Proc. IMC, 2009, pp. 35–48.

[41] B. Suh, L. Hong, P. Pirolli, and Ed H. Chi, *Want to be retweeted? large scale analytics on factors impacting retweet in twitter network*, Proc. SOCIALCOM, 2010, pp. 177–184.

[42] L. Tauscher and S. Greenberg, *Revisitation patterns in world wide web navigation*, Proc. CHI, ACM, 1997, pp. 399–406.

[43] J. Teevan, *The re:search engine: Simultaneous support for finding and re-finding*, Proc UIST, ACM, 2007, pp. 23–32.

[44] J. Teevan, E. Adar, R. Jones, and M. A. S. Potts, *Information re-retrieval: Repeat queries in yahoo's logs*, Proc. SIGIR, 2007, pp. 151–158.

[45] J. Teevan, C. Alvarado, M. S. Ackerman, and D. R. Karger, *The perfect search engine is not enough: A study of orienteering behavior in directed search*, Proc. CHI, ACM, 2004, pp. 415–422.

[46] J. Teevan, E. Cutrell, D. Fisher, S. M. Drucker, G. Ramos, P. André, and C. Hu, *Visual snippets: Summarizing web pages for search and revisitation*, Proc. CHI, 2009, pp. 2023–2032.

[47] J. Teevan, D. Ramage, and M. R. Morris, *#twittersearch: A comparison of microblog search and web search*, Proc. WSDM, 2011, pp. 35–44.

[48] S. K. Tyler and J. Teevan, *Large scale query log analysis of re-finding*, Proc. WSDM, 2010, pp. 191–200.

[49] J. Wen, *Post-valued recall web pages: User disorientation hits the big time*, IT & Society **1** (2003), 184–194.

[50] S. Whittaker and C. Sidner, *Email overload: Exploring personal information management of email*, Proc. CHI, ACM, 1996, pp. 276–283.

R-Susceptibility: An IR-Centric Approach to Assessing Privacy Risks for Users in Online Communities

Joanna Asia Biega[1], Krishna P. Gummadi[2], Ida Mele[3],
Dragan Milchevski[1], Christos Tryfonopoulos[4], Gerhard Weikum[1]

[1]Max Planck Institute for Informatics, Germany [2]Max Planck Institute for Software Systems, Germany
[3]Università della Svizzera Italiana, Switzerland [4]University of Peloponnese, Greece

{jbiega, dmilchev, weikum}@mpi-inf.mpg.de,
gummadi@mpi-sws.org, ida.mele@usi.ch, trifon@uop.gr

ABSTRACT

Privacy of Internet users is at stake because they expose personal information in posts created in online communities, in search queries, and other activities. An adversary that monitors a community may identify the users with the most sensitive properties and utilize this knowledge against them (e.g., by adjusting the pricing of goods or targeting ads of sensitive nature). Existing privacy models for structured data are inadequate to capture privacy risks from user posts.

This paper presents a ranking-based approach to the assessment of privacy risks emerging from textual contents in online communities, focusing on sensitive topics, such as being depressed. We propose ranking as a means of modeling a rational adversary who targets the most afflicted users. To capture the adversary's background knowledge regarding vocabulary and correlations, we use latent topic models. We cast these considerations into the new model of R-Susceptibility, which can inform and alert users about their potential for being targeted, and devise measures for quantitative risk assessment. Experiments with real-world data show the feasibility of our approach.

Keywords

Privacy Risk Assessment, Online Communities

1. INTRODUCTION

1.1 Motivation and Background

The goal of this paper is to provide privacy risk assessments for users in online communities. An online post may directly or indirectly disclose personal information, such as gender, age, political affiliation, or interests. An adversary can combine such observations with his background knowledge of correlations between different attributes to infer privacy-sensitive information and discriminate against users. We argue that existing privacy models for structured data, such as k-anonymity [33], l-diversity [24], t-closeness [22], membership privacy [23] and differential privacy [10], are inherently inappropriate to capture these situations. One reason is that user posts in social media are mostly of textual form, inducing a high-dimensional data space of word-level or phrase-level features. A second reason is that users might not want to be prevented from posting contents, but instead be selectively warned about emerging privacy risks. In our setting, certain assumptions also differ from the assumptions of prior work on privacy-preserving data publishing [13]: users do want to post information, but they should be aware of possible exposure and targeting risks. For these reasons, this paper pursues an IR-centric approach to privacy, making novel use of topic models and ranking.

Scenario: To understand why adversaries and user risks are different from the privacy concerns for structured databases, consider the following scenario. An unscrupulous drug company wishes to advertise its new anxiety-reducing drug to Facebook users. It decides to target ads at a million users that are most susceptible to be afflicted by depression within the 1 billion population of Facebook. The company plans to infer users' demographics by text mining their posts and combine it with the background knowledge correlating demographics and certain vocabulary usage with depression, obtained from text mining an archive of medical journals. In such a scenario, how can a Facebook user estimate her risk of being targeted? Similar issues arise also within specialized online communities such as `healthboards.com` or `patient.co.uk`. Although these have a much smaller scale, a smart adversary would still target only a subset of highly susceptible users to avoid the impression of mass spamming.

Targeted ads of sensitive nature constitute one kind of risk, but there are even more severe threats with real cases reported: scoring users for financial credit worthiness or insurance payments, factoring a user's social-media posts in assessing her job application, and more (e.g., [7, 12]). Despite these being big trends, most users do not need hard guarantees regarding privacy (e.g., preventing de-anonymization by all means), and perfect anonymity cannot be guaranteed without severely diminishing the utility of social media. For example, someone who always posts using a one-off anonymous identity cannot build up a reputation as a credible information source. Conversely, even making all posts under a pseudonym is insufficient to prevent tracking-and-rating companies (e.g., `www.spokeo.com`) from linking user accounts across different social platforms. Therefore, we fo-

SIGIR '16, July 17-21, 2016, Pisa, Italy

© 2016 ACM. ISBN 978-1-4503-4069-4/16/07... $15.00

DOI: `http://dx.doi.org/10.1145/2911451.2911533`

cus on the assessment of privacy *risks* and on alerting users to support their awareness, rather than pursuing the elusive goal of enforcing privacy.

Existing privacy models fail to capture theses issues, along the following dimensions:

- *Data model*: Privacy models like k-anonymity or differential privacy are primarily geared for structured data or content that can be cast into low-dimensional feature spaces. Capturing risks from textual contents in online communities faces the problem of high-dimensional feature vectors (e.g., word bigrams). Prior work that coped with text focused on specific settings, such as predicting sensitive posts [30], sanitizing the information from query logs (e.g., [6, 28]), or publishing high-dimensional datasets [9]. Our goal, on the other hand, is to be able to quantify privacy risks from text in a generic way.
- *Adversary's background knowledge:* Prior work on privacy assumes computationally powerful adversaries, but disregards or makes special assumptions about the background knowledge that an adversary may have beyond the dataset at hand. However, adversaries may easilly tap into many datasets including large text corpora, thus obtaining a model of the typical vocabulary used by potential targets as well as semantic dependencies or statistical correlations between topics.
- *Disclosure vs. discrimination risk:* Existing privacy models focus on limiting information disclosure, but they do not capture the exposure within a community with regard to sensitive properties. Standing out in a community this way may result in discriminatory treatment, such as being rejected for loans or job applications, or receiving ads of sensitive nature.

1.2 Approach and Challenges

This paper introduces *R-Susceptibility*: a ranking-based privacy risk model for assessing users' privacy risks in online communities, accompanied by IR-style risk measures for quantifying risks from textual contents. The model is very versatile: in this paper we demonstrate how it can capture user posts or search queries, but it can also be used with click streams, and other online activities. Semantic dependencies and statistical correlations among words and sensitive topics are represented using latent topic models, such as LDA [5] or Skip-grams [25]. This way, we anticipate adversaries with rich background knowledge. Adversaries are assumed to be rational: they target only a fraction of "promising" users. Therefore, we model the risk of a user as the ranking position in the community when all the users are ordered by the relevance of their contents to sensitive topics, such as pregnancy, depression, financial debts, etc. This ranking-based model is meant to alert the users whenever critical situations arise. We posit that users might be then guided to selectively post anonymously.

Our model addresses several technical challenges:

- *Sensitive vs. general topics:* A trained latent topic model does not indicate which of the topics are privacy-sensitive. We carried out a crowdsourcing study to identify sensitive topics. Our study differs from the prior work of [30] as the latter relied on explicit categories.
- *Personal vs. professional interest:* A user who posts about a sensitive topic may merely have a professional or educational interest without being personally afflicted. To be able to rank such users lower, our model introduces the notion of topical *breadth* of interest, complementing the user's strength of interest in a sensitive topic.
- *Personal interest vs. curiosity:* A user may become interested in a topic out of curiosity, perhaps prompted by an external event (e.g., a celebrity scandal). To be able to rank such non-critical users lower, our model also considers the *temporal variation* of interest in a topic.

The paper's salient contributions are:

- a novel approach to privacy risks focusing on exposure in user rankings within online communities, and emphasizing risk awareness;
- a framework for quantifying privacy risks from textual contents in online communities, based on latent topic models and user rankings;
- measures for computing risk scores with regard to sensitive topics based on users' posts or search queries.

2. R-SUSCEPTIBILITY MODEL

2.1 Sensitive states and adversaries

We assess the risk of a user being perceived as afflicted by a *sensitive state*, such as depression, pregnancy, or financial debts. An adversary in our model attempts to find the most susceptible users, that is, the users who are most exposed with regard to a sensitive state. For instance, an adversarial insurance company might want to identify the users who are likely afflicted by certain diseases, an adversarial HR department of a company might want to screen for the users with likely drug or alcohol problems, while a seller of illegal anti-depressants might want to find the users most likely to be depressed, and thus prospective customers.

We therefore propose *ranking* as a means of modeling a rational adversary trying to identify the most susceptible users. To rank the users with respect to a given sensitive state, an adversary needs to choose a measure of quantitative risk assessment based on the contents of user profiles. We discuss several such measures in Section 3.

2.2 Sensitive topics

We associate sensitive states with a vocabulary distribution, i.e., distributional vectors of related words. For example, the topic *financial debts*, could be captured by related words and phrases like *loan, mortgage, money, problem, sorrows*, or *sleepless night.* Such salient phrases related to a sensitive state can be obtained by unsupervised or semi-supervised training of latent topic models over external datasets such as news archives, digital libraries or large crawls of social media. This way we capture the adversaries' background knowledge about the vocabulary for a topic and about semantic dependencies and correlations.

Sensitive states might manifest themselves in the online contents of users. User posts can also be characterized as distributional vectors of salient words. Then, the similarity between the distributional vectors of the user's posts and a sensitive topic can be used to assess the user's susceptibility to being exposed with regard to that topic.

2.3 Background knowledge

An adversary in our model is assumed to be interested in a sensitive state and aims to target a fraction of the most afflicted users. The adversary has *background knowledge*, characterized by statistical language and topic models. This is a natural form of useful knowledge for a rational adversary who wants rank the users based on the textual contents, and to bound the cost of his targeting efforts.

In this paper, we consider three versions of adversary's background knowledge. The basic version is the knowledge of the most salient words for different topics, which is assumed in all the solutions we explore. The more advanced version assumes that the adversary is able to compute similarities between words, in the sense of semantic relatedness. Finally, in some of the solutions, we assume an adversary is able to assign latent topics to broader thematic domains, e.g., the topic of depression to the domain of psychiatry.

We believe that this model reflects a wide class of adversaries whose goal is to discriminate and target the most susceptible users in online communities.

2.4 R-Susceptibility

We propose R-Susceptibility (Rank-Susceptibility) as a measure of a user's privacy risk. To measure R-Susceptibility with respect to a sensitive topic, we first rank all users within an online community based on their decreasing susceptibility of being exposed with regard to a sensitive topic (as described above) and then compute the position where the user is ranked.

Intuitively, the R-Susceptibility model could also have the following IR interpretation: we rank the users according to the relevance of their posts to a query containing the words of a sensitive topic, and choose the top-ranked, who should be the most likely to be personally afflicted.

3. RISK ASSESSMENT MEASURES

Risk measures are plug-in components in the framework and orthogonal to the idea of R-Susceptibility. In this paper, we begin by investigating three kinds of risk scores, leaving an extended risk-measure study as future work.

The first two of the risk scores are baselines, inspired by standard measures in privacy research, namely, the entropy of attribute value distributions (as used in the t-closeness model) and the changes in the global probability distributions of attribute values incurred by the inclusion of an individual user's data (as used in the differential privacy model). The third measure is a novel IR-centric score based on topic models, capturing lexical correlations and three different characteristics of user interest in a topic: the strength of interest, the breadth of interest, and the temporal variation of interest.

Desired properties. By considering the community and interpreting risk with respect to a user's rank in the community, our framework does not impose any restrictions on the absolute values or the value domains of valid risk measures. Intuitively, for the framework to function, we expect a good measure to correlate with human assessments on the sensitivity of user profiles: the more human observers agree that a user might be in a senitive state, the higher the value of the risk score should be.

3.1 Entropy baseline measure

The entropy baseline measure is inspired by comparing a global probability distribution (for an entire community) against a local distribution (for an individual user) using relative entropy (aka KL divergence). We apply this measure to textual data as follows.

Let X be a sensitive topic, and $\{x_1, ..., x_j\}$ be the salient words and phrases of X. The knowledge of this vocabulary for different topics is assumed to be a part of the adversarial background knowledge (e.g., derived from latent topic models). We treat $x_1, ..., x_j$ as database attributes and represent users as database records where the value of an attribute x_i equals to 1 if the word appears in the user's contents, and to 0 otherwise.

Let U_0 be the user for whom we wish to compute the risk score with respect to X, and $U = \{U_1, .., U_k\}$ be the set of other users in the community. Let further be $U^* = \{U_0\} \cup U$, and let P_U, P_{U^*} denote the distributions of attribute values for U and U^*, respectively.

We compute the risk score by averaging the relative entropy of the univariate distributions P_U, P_{U^*} for the individual attributes $\{x_1, ..., x_j\}$. Note that measuring the relative entropy over the multivariate joint distributions of attributes could be an alternative, but we do not pursue this here because of the data sparseness that we would face.

Definition 1 (Entropy baseline risk score of topic X for U_0). *The entropy baseline risk score of the user U_0 with respect to a topic X is:*

$$risk_{\text{ENT}}(U_0, X) = \frac{1}{j} \sum_i \sum_{v=\{0,1\}} P_U[x_i = v] log(\frac{P_U[x_i = v]}{P_{U^*}[x_i = v]}).$$

The ranking method based on this definition is being referred to as ENT.

Measure properties. It holds that $risk_{\text{ENT}}(U_0, X) \geq 0$. The lowest value of 0 is reached when the user does not have any of the topic's salient attributes in her observable contents. Otherwise, the risk score is lowest when half of the community's users exhibit an attribute in their contents and highest when all or none of the users have the attribute.

3.2 Differential-privacy baseline measure

The differential-privacy-based measure is inspired by the definition of differential privacy, that is calculating the changes of attribute probabilities incurred by the inclusion of a user's data. Let X, $\{x_1, ..., x_j\}$, U_0, U, U^*, P_U, and P_{U^*} be defined as in the previous section. The differential privacy principle requires that

$P_U[x_i] \leq 2^\epsilon P_{U^*}[x_i]$ and $P_{U^*}[x_i] \leq 2^\epsilon P_U[x_i]$

for some small $\epsilon > 0$. To give an ϵ-differential-privacy guarantee, existing methods would perturb the data by Laplacian noise if the inequalities are not already satisfied. However, our "attributes" are words in user posts that the user intentionally chose and our goal is to quantify risk rather than perturb the data. We thus aim to determine the best possible value of ϵ for which the guarantee holds without perturbation. This is the minimum ϵ for each x_i, but the guarantee is only as strong as the weakest x_i, leading to the following formulation:

Definition 2 (Differential-privacy baseline risk score of topic X for U_0). *The differential-privacy baseline risk score of the user U_0 with respect to a topic X is:*

$$risk_{\text{D-P}}(U_0, X) = \max_{x_i} \left(\max \left(log \left(\frac{P_U[x_i]}{P_{U^*}[x_i]} \right), log \left(\frac{P_{U^*}[x_i]}{P_U[x_i]} \right) \right) \right).$$

The ranking method based on this definition is being referred to as DIFF-PRIV.

Measure properties. It holds that $risk_{\text{D-P}}(U_0, X) \geq 0$. The risk value is lowest for a user who does not have any of the sensitive topic's salient attributes in her contents and highest for a user who has a critical attribute that is not present in the contents of any other user.

3.3 Topical risk measure

The third measure we consider is IR-style and based on topic models. To this end, we construct a distributional representation of each of the sensitive topics X (e.g., financial debts), user contents U (e.g., from an online community such as `quora.com`), and each post P the user authors in the online community. We model X, P and U as vectors in a distributional vector space.

3.3.1 *Distributional vectors for topics and users*

Topic vectors. Topics are represented as vocabulary distributions found by collecting word statistics over suitably chosen corpora.

Definition 3 (Sensitive Topic Vector). *For sensitive topic X, the topic vector is a distributional vector $\vec{X}$ constructed using words or bigrams weighted by topic relevance.*

For example, *hiv* and *positive* are salient for the topic of hiv infection. Such topics and their salient phrases can be automatically extracted by applying latent topic analysis to large, thematically broad text corpora.

User vectors. To be able to relate posts and users to topics, we map each user U and post P created by the user in an online community to a vector.

Definition 4 (User Post and User Vectors). *The content of a post P of a user U is modeled as a distributional vector $\vec{P}$. User U in the context of a topic X is modeled as a distributional vector $\vec{U}$ defined as:*

$$\vec{U} = \max_{P \in U} cos(\vec{P}, \vec{X}).$$

Vector construction. The exact mapping of topics and posts to vectors depends on the vector space in which we are operating. We use three different configurations in our experiments: i) a bag-of-words model (BOW), ii) an LDA model (LDA), and iii) a Skip-gram model (W2V).

Note that the use of LDA here is to construct a lower-dimensional vector space; this is orthogonal to using LDA for obtaining topics with their salient phrases, which we discussed above.

In the BOW vector space, we create topic vectors directly over the characteristic topic words with binary scoring; we also use these words as features with tf-scoring for user and post vectors.

In the LDA model, topic vectors are indicator vectors of for the latent dimensions. Users and posts are treated as documents that LDA maps into its low-dimensional latent space.

The third technique that we consider, `w2v`, is a model based on learning word relatedness, which can be trained over large text corpora [25]. To create the topic vectors in this word-centric vector space, we compute a weighted sum of words from the previously computed sensitive topic distributions. Since there is no natural mapping of documents to vectors in this setting, the procedure for posts is similar. However, to discount the impact of words unrelated to the topics at hand, we introduce a topic-dependent weighting scheme for user vectors. Namely, for a topic X and a post containing the set of words $\{v_1, v_2, \dots\}$, the post vector is $\vec{P} = \sum_j cos(\vec{v_j}, \vec{X}) \cdot \vec{v_j}$.

Risk scoring. Given these vectors, we can now compare a user posting history against a sensitive topic by vector-based similarity measures, like the cosine similarity. An advantage of this risk measure is that, unlike the ENTROPY or DIFF-PRIV measures, it does not require any community-level data, as the risk score of a user is independent of other users' data. Thus, each user can compute her score locally and privately, and send the value to a server to obtain an R-Susceptibility rank.

In addition to quantifying the *strength* of user interest in a sensitive topic, we also capture the *breadth* and *temporal variation* of that interest. This is crucial to avoid erroneously ranking higher those users who have a professional interest in a topic without being personally afflicted, or are temporarily interested out of curiosity. In our previous preliminary work in this area, we identified these two components to be crucial for reducing classification error in a similar setup [4].

3.3.2 *Strength of Interest*

Having a vector representation of a user U, we can now compute the similarity between U and a topic vector X.

Definition 5 (Topic-aware risk score). *The strength-of-interest risk score for a user U with respect to a topic X is:*

$$risk(U, X) = \cos\left(\vec{U}, \vec{X}\right).$$

We further refer to methods based on this definition as BOW, LDA, and W2V.

Measure properties. It holds that $-1 \leq risk(U, X) \leq 1$. A high value of this measure means the user has at least one post with vocabulary related to the topic. Thus, the strength of interest is reflected by the presence of the topic's salient vocabulary in user posts.

3.3.3 *Breadth of Interest*

When ranking users, an adversary might want to distinguish between users who show a focused interest in a topic and users who show a broad interest in many topics within a domain, ranking the former higher than the latter. Applying this strategy could help, for instance, to capture users who are not personally afflicted but rather showing educational, hobbyist or professional interest in a topic. For example, for the topic of financial debts, a bank agent or finance hobbyist could offer advice in Q&A communities; similarly, a medical doctor or student could engage herself in health forums.

The posts of a user with a broad interest should exhibit a diversity of topics within their respective domain. We aim to capture this behavior, by means of distributional vectors, assigning each topic X to a broader domain, like finance, medicine, psychology, etc.

Definition 6 (Domain Vectors). *A domain D is a set of topics $X_1, ..., X_{|D|}$ and its vector representation is a set of corresponding topic vectors $(\vec{X}_1, ..., \vec{X}_{|D|})$.*

To assess the risk taking into account whether a user U has a focused or a broad interest in a topic X, we compute:

1. how similar $\vec{U}$ is to $\vec{X}$ and

2. how dissimilar $\vec{U}$ is to the domain D by computing the distances between $\vec{U}$ and $\vec{X}_j$ for $j = 1..|D|$ and taking the $\lceil k * |D| \rceil$-th largest value, for some $0 < k \leq 1$.

If both of these measures are high, then we conclude that U is personally afflicted by topic X.

Definition 7 (Domain-aware risk score). *The domain-aware risk score for a user U with respect to a topic X from the domain D is:*

$$risk_{\mathrm{D}}(U, X) = \cos\left(\vec{U}, \vec{X}\right) - max_{\lceil k*|D| \rceil}\{\cos\left(\vec{U}, \vec{X}_j\right) |\}_{j=1..|D|}.$$

We further refer to methods based on this definition as BOW-D, LDA-D, and W2V-D.

Measure properties. It holds that $-2 \leq risk_{\mathrm{D}}(U, X) \leq 2$. The value would be high for a user who has a post containing topic's salient vocabulary, but whose contents do not exhibit any vocabulary from other topics in the respective domain. A low value occurs in a situation where the user has not written any posts related to the topic at hand, but has contents related to other topics in the domain. Studying the relative importance of the two components in different online communities is an interesting topic of future work.

The intuition for parameter k is that a personally afflicted user would not have high posting activities in k-fraction of different topics within the same domain. The value of the parameter controls how large the domain coverage should be for the users to be considered broadly interested. In practice, setting this parameter requires the knowledge of the breadth of topics discussed in a particular community.

3.3.4 Temporal Variation of Interest

Being interested in users most likely afflicted by a given state, we would like to rank the users who exhibit recurring activity regarding a topic X higher than the non-afflicted (possibly curious or exploratory) users exhibiting a short-term interest in the topic. Such a bursty activity might be prompted by prominent news related to X, be it sex scandals in the press, or social campaigns about depression.

To capture this issue, rather than computing a user vector $\vec{U}$ over the entire user history, we divide the history into time buckets and compute a sequence of vectors $\vec{U_i}$ using the contents from each bucket i separately. In our model, bucketization may be realized at different granularity levels depending on the user observation period and the characteristics of the community.

We then identify the top-m time buckets with the highest risk level, representing m different time periods (such as days or weeks). Let us denote these buckets of the user model as $U_1^*, \ldots, U_m^*$. A user whose interest in X is clearly above the level of a bursty interest (signifying occasional curiosity) would consistently have high risk scores in all of the top-m buckets. This leads us to our next definition of a user's privacy risk regarding topic X.

Definition 8 (Time-aware risk score). *The time-aware risk score for a user U in time period i with respect to a topic X is:*

$$risk_{\mathrm{T}}(U, X) = \mathrm{avg}_{i=1..m}\left\{\cos\left(\vec{U_i^*}, \vec{X}\right)\right\}.$$

We further refer to methods based on this definition as BOW-T, LDA-T, and W2V-T.

Measure properties. It holds that $-1 \leq risk_{\mathrm{T}}(U, X) \leq 1$. The value would be high for a user whose posts contain relevant topic vocabulary in at least m observation buckets, and low for a user who does not exhibit topic's vocabulary in their contents.

The choice of a particular value of the m parameter depends on the available observation timeline and the characteristics of a given community. The parameter controls how often the activity regarding a topic should occur in order to not be considered occasional.

3.3.5 Combining Domain- and Time-Awareness

The final measure we introduce combines all the aforementioned dimensions of interest. Note that we use bucketized user contents for computing the temporal variation component, but the breadth-of-interest component is computed over the full contents.

Definition 9 (Domain- and time-aware risk score). *The risk of user U in time period i for topic X in domain D is:*

$$risk_{\mathrm{DT}}(U, X) = \mathrm{avg}_{i=1..m}\left\{\cos\left(\vec{U_i^*}, \vec{X}\right)\right\} - \cos\left(\vec{U}, \left(\vec{D} - \vec{X}\right)\right).$$

We further refer to methods based on this definition as BOW-DT, LDA-DT, and W2V-DT.

4. IDENTIFYING SENSITIVE TOPICS

To complete our framework, we need to train a background knowledge model and answer the remaining question of how to identify sensitive topics. Although our model is applicable to any topic irrespective of its sensitivity, in practice users would only be interested in their R-Susceptibility ranks for truly sensitive topics. There is indeed a systematic way of gathering such information in a reasonably inter-subjective manner: training a latent topic model on a background corpus and crowdsourcing sensitivity judgments for each topic. This section presents our results along these lines.

4.1 Experiments on topic sensitivity

Datasets. We trained 3 LDA models, using the Mallet topic modeling toolkit: i) with 500 topics, on 600K Quora posts we crawled ii) with 200 topics, on 3M posts from health Q&A online forums, and iii) with 500 topics, on a sample of 700K articles from the New York Times (NYT) news archive.

Crowdsourcing sensitivity and domain judgements. We collected human judgements regarding the sensitivity and the domains of topics using Amazon Mechanical Turk (AMT), employing only master workers from the USA, and collecting 7 judgements per topic. For each of the topics, the workers were shown the 20 most salient words computed by LDA, and asked whether they would consider a post in social media containing these words privacy-sensitive. We explained that by privacy-sensitive we mean that a person uses these words because he/she is in a privacy-sensitive situation (e.g, alcohol addicted), or that the usage of these words might lead to a privacy-sensitive situation (e.g., political extremism). The first condition can capture, for instance, words related to diseases, the second can capture words related to political or religious positions.

We computed Fleiss' Kappa to measure the inter-annotator agreement for this task, obtaining 0.241 for the Quora topics, 0.294 for the HF topics, and 0.157 for the NYT topics. These low values confirm that sensitivity is rather subjective. However, there is a considerable number of topics in all of these corpora, which were unanimously or almost unanimously rated as sensitive. These were mostly related to

Table 1: #topics with #judges agreeing on being sensitive topics.

#judges	#topics Quora	#topics NYT	#topics HF
7	29	8	38
6	43	27	32
5	48	60	30
4	56	84	21
3	68	73	22
2	99	90	28
1	106	111	23
0	51	47	6

Table 2: Examples: vocabulary of sensitive topics.

Topic	Vocabulary
clinical depression	depression depress suicide feel depressed suffer suicidal commit
drug addiction	drug addiction addict cocaine heroin substance meth addictive
pregnancy	baby birth pregnancy pregnant mother woman born child
hiv and viral diseases	hiv disease aids virus spread infection cure vaccine
financial debts	debt loan pay student interest payment money owe

health, private relationships, political and religious convictions, personal finance, legal problems and others. Table 1 shows the numbers of topics on which certain numbers of judges agree on their sensitivity.

The judges were also asked to assign a topic to one of seven high-level categories. Six of these, potentially containing some sensitive topics, were chosen based on the top-level Microsoft Academic Search categories. The annotators could also choose a generic category *other*.

Topics for evaluation in Section 5. For our further experiments, to make the much more laborious and costly evaluation of user profiles feasible, we leverage the above study to restrict the evaluation to 5 topics from the group of the most sensitive topics. The choice of particular topics is guided by the reported cases of social media screening by insurance companies, employers, and credit companies mentioned in Section 1. These are: *clinical depression*, *drug addiction*, *hiv*, *pregnancy*, and *financial debts*, assigned to the domains of *psychology*, *medicine*, and *finance&economy*. Table 2 shows the most prominent words for each of the chosen topics from the Quora topic model.

5. EXPERIMENTAL EVALUATION

5.1 Setup

5.1.1 Data sources

To test our methods in a variety of scenarios, we constructed three datasets using online communitites of different nature. As a first data source, we used the AOL query log collected between March and May 2006. The resulting data source amounts to around $107K$ users and more than $13M$ queries. The second data source consisted of over 5M posts spanning 13 years (2000-2013) from `healthboards` and `ehealthforum` Q&A health communities. We also collected data from the Quora Q&A community over a period of three months, between February and May 2015. The crawl focused on Quora users who were active in categories related to the considered sensitive topics and their domains, and comprised more than 200K users and 1.3M posts.

Ethics. To adhere to ethical standards concerning incorporation of user data into research, we decided to only use data that is publicly available – either as online profiles (Quora, Health Q&A), or as datasets used in numerous other studies (AOL). We never attempted to identify the individuals whose profiles we analyzed.

5.1.2 User sampling

We created our datasets by sampling the users from the data sources described above. However, we encounter a technical challenge, as the number of sensitive users for a given topic is very small when compared to the size of the whole community. Sampling users uniformly would not constitute a good benchmark for risk scoring methods. For example, we could achieve high accuracy, in a misleading way, by the simplistic prediction that all users are non-sensitive.

What we want, though, is ranking evaluation – our goal is to see how sensitive the users are in different ranking regions. Therefore, our sampling method is non-uniform and proceeds as follows. We first rank all users for each of the datasets using our basic strength-of-interest method from Section 3.3.2, and then sample users from this ranking. To pick a user, the sampling procedure orders users by their score, then computes prefix sums Σ_i for all users up to user i, with Σ_n being the score sum for all users. Then we draw a random number between 0 and Σ_n. If the number falls between Σ_i and Σ_{i+1}, we choose user $i+1$ (with users numbered from 1 to n. However, given that risk scores are extremely skewed, this sampling does still not yield good coverage of all the ranking regions. Therefore, we transform the original risk score q into a^q, where constant a needs to be determined based on the score skew in a data source. The intuition is to give a higher probability of being sampled to users with higher scores, so that the final sample set has good coverage of users with both high and low scores. Figure 1 depicts the depression risk scores of our 100 samples from the AOL data vs. the scores of the original dataset of 170K users.

In our case, a value of $a = 10^2$ for the Health Q&A, and a value of $a = 10^3$ for the AOL were reasonable to compensate the skew. For each of these datasets, we sampled 100 users for each sensitive topic. We did not perform this kind of sampling for Quora, as our dataset was based on a focused crawl in the first place with focus on sensitive discussion threads. Since evaluating sizeable Quora profiles requires much more effort, for this data source we constructed smaller datasets with 40 users per topic. In total, our datasets comprised 1100 user profiles: personal histories of posts or queries.

5.1.3 User study for ground-truth labels

To assign sensitivity labels for user-topic pairs as ground truth, we used crowdsourcing and asked human judges to examine user profiles with chronologically ordered textual posts. Specifically, we asked whether based on the content

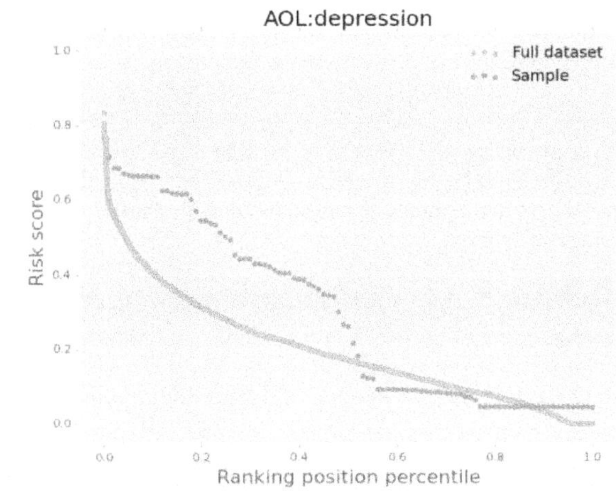

Figure 1: Example comparison of risk scores of sample vs. full data.

Table 3: Number of sensitive users according to judges' assessments (x/y means x sensitive users out of y in total).

	AOL	HF	Quora
depression	24	42	20
drugs	22	31	11
pregnancy	15	42	21
hiv	14	19	5
debts	24	n/a	11
TOTAL	99/500	134/400	68/200

of the profile, the judge suspects that the user (or a family member) is in a given sensitive state.

To evaluate the AOL and Health Q&A datasets, we employed AMT master workers from the USA and collected 5 judgements for each of the profiles. Since the majority of Quora profiles contain hundreds of posts, to ensure that proper care is given to evaluating them, we collected the judgements employing 19 students from our institutions.

We computed Fleiss' Kappa to quantify the global inter-annotator agreement across all the topics. The respective values for the AOL, Health Forums and Quora datasets were 0.442, 0.444, and 0.468 respectively, all corresponding to a moderate agreement. Table 3 shows the number of users who were marked by the human judges as sensitive by a majority vote.

5.1.4 *Configuration of methods*

To evaluate the topic-model-based method, we used three different distributional vector spaces: a bag-of-word vector space, as well as two 500-dimensional vector spaces trained with (i) the LDA implementation from the Mallet toolkit and (ii) `word2vec`[1] tool [25]. The latter two models were trained on NYT and Quora corpora described in Section 4.

In the breadth-of-interest model from Section 3.3.3, we set the parameter k to 0.3, i.e. we want a user of a broad interest in a domain to have at least a 30% coverage of topics from the domain.

[1]`https://code.google.com/p/word2vec/`

In the temporal-variance-of-interest models described in Section 3.3.4, we compute the results using weekly time buckets and set the number of buckets parameter m to 3.

We later analyze the robustness of the ranking methods with respect to these parameters.

5.1.5 *Ranking effectiveness metrics*

- **R-Precision.** For a given sensitive topic, where r users were identified by the judges as sensitive, we compute the precision@r. When computing the average precision over all sensitive topics, we report both micro and macro average scores (summing over individual samples, and summing over topic precisions, respectively). To apply this measure, for each of the profiles we have to cast the five collected judgements to a binary score. We assume that an average of more than 0.5 classifies a user as sensitive. Note that r-precision imitates an adversary who, for instance, knowing that 1% of the population is depressed, ranks the users according to a depression-risk measure and chooses the top 1% of the users for further investigation.
- **Mean Average Precision (MAP).** For a given sensitive topic, we compute the average precision computed at the ranking positions of sensitive users.
- **Normalized Discounted Cumulative Gain (NDCG).** To asses the effectiveness of our methods using the actual non-binary judge assessments, we employ NDCG, which compares the rankings our methods yield with a perfect ranking obtained using the crowdsourced scores.

5.1.6 *Significance testing*

The number of topics in our experiments is too small to perform significance tests over macro-averaged metrics. We thus resort to performing a paired t-test over r-precision differences on individual test samples within a dataset, marking the significance in the micro-averaged r-precision columns in the result tables. The $*$ symbols denote the case when the gain of a given ranking method over the baseline (ENT and DIFF-PRIV in Table 4, strength-of-interest baselines within a block of results for a given vector space in Table 5) is statistically significant with a p-value < 0.05. This lets us conclude that a good r-precision score of a ranking method does not likely depend on the particular choice of user profiles.

5.1.7 *Research questions*

The remainder of the experimental section seeks to answer the following research questions.

RQ 1: Do the proposed topical risk measures perform better than the ENTROPY and DIFF-PRIV methods in predicting human risk judgements? (Sec. 5.2.)

RQ 2: Does the topical risk scoring measure perform better when extended with the breadth and temporal dimensions of user interest? (Sec. 5.3.)

RQ 3: How robust is the proposed method against changes in the parameter configuration and the background knowledge of the adversary? (Sec. 5.4.)

5.2 Traditional vs. IR risk scoring

We begin the risk scoring methods analysis by comparing the effectiveness of the baseline (ENTROPY, DIFF-PRIV) and

Table 4: **Average metrics over all sensitive topics for different risk assessment measures**

	R-precision		Prec@5	MAP	NDCG
	micro	macro			
			AOL		
ENTROPY	0.495	0.496	**0.760**	0.524	0.819
DIFF-PRIV	0.475	0.465	0.480	0.492	0.789
W2V	**0.556***	**0.533**	0.720	**0.589**	**0.836**
			Health Forums		
ENTROPY	0.560	0.537	**0.750**	0.613	0.870
DIFF-PRIV	0.560	0.559	0.500	0.542	0.794
W2V	**0.664***	**0.634**	**0.750**	**0.696**	**0.894**
			Quora		
ENTROPY	0.239	0.205	0.240	0.317	0.632
DIFF-PRIV	0.239	0.223	0.200	0.310	0.623
W2V	**0.343***	**0.341**	**0.280**	**0.352**	**0.637**

the strength-of-interest topical risk scoring methods. Here, we choose the baseline IR-based methods for comparison, while exteding the measures with dimensions of interest will be addressed in the sections to follow.

Table 4 shows that the LDA risk scoring outperforms the alternatives (similar observation holds for W2V), which confirms that these methods are not naturally applicable to textual data in the context of risk scoring. The relatively good Precision@5 of these measures indicates that the most sensitive users tend to use highly salient words. However, operating on explicitly given salient attributes for each topic, the baseline measures do not capture any lexical correlations, an important prerequisite to capture users manifesting their sensitivity in a less direct way. This result validates the need to design new privacy risk measures better tuned to textual contents.

5.3 Risk scoring with dimensions of interest

We posited that extending the topical risk measures with the breadth and the temporal-variation dimensions of interest can help to predict sensitivity judgements better. Table 5 shows the evaluation results averaged over all topics, confirming that incorporating breadth and temporal variation into the risk score indeed improves the ranking performance.

We observe that breadth-of-interest is especially important for Quora, which is a Q&A community with a very wide variety of topics. Many Quora users seem to frequently post replies prompted by others rather than by their personal situation; hence the lower impact of the temporal component. Contrary, in AOL the temporal component takes over. With merely implicit cues in the form of queries, the temporal dimension is an important indicator of user sensitivity (also for the annotators). The breadth-of-interest component performs worse for AOL, possibly due to the short time span of the query log (3 months).

Note that in case of the proposed breadth-of-interest score, an underlying assumption is that an adversary is able to assign latent topics to broader thematic domains. Thus the best performing -DT methods imply a stronger background knowledge of an adversary.

Risk scoring for different topics.

Table 6 shows the values of r-precisions split by the topic, for different variants of LDA-based risk scoring. The trends observed in the results averaged over all topics can be seen here as well - there are consistent improvements across topics when incorporating the temporal and breadth dimensions. These results constitute anecdotal evidence that the proposed methods are general enough to be potentially applied to a variety of topics.

5.4 Robustness to configuration changes

Model changes. The BOW vector space models only an adversarial knowledge of salient words for different topics, whereas the latent vector spaces additionally enable an adversary to compute similarities between arbitrary words. The results presented in Table 5 show that this has a direct consequence in the risk ranking performance. The methods with the latent models as the background knowledge outperform the methods with the BOW background knowledge, while being comparable with each other. Thus the model seems resilient to rational background knowledge model changes, capturing a wide class of adversaries - the rational, cost-aware adversaries adopting latent models.

Training corpus changes. The results presented in the experimental section were obtained using the Quora topic model as the background knowledge model. We ran additional experiments using the NYT topic model described in section 4.1, and noticed that for the topics which were captured in the other latent model as well, we observe similar trends and dependencies in the results. This would suggest that an adversary has the freedom to choose among the inputs where his topics of interest are well captured.

Parameter changes in risk measures. The topical risk measures introduce two parameters: k for coverage of domain topics, and m for the number of (weekly) time buckets. Observing the values of r-precision and NDCG obtained when varying these parameters between $k = \{0.1, 0.2, ..., 1.0\}$, and $m = \{1, 2, ..., 12\}$, yields the following observations. First, when the parameters are set to values from the lower half of the ranges, we still observe improvements over the baseline strength-of-interest measure. Second, when the parameters are set to higher values, the results tend to deteriorate, possibly due to the incompleteness of user profiles in our datasets. Third, we observe higher sensitivity to parameters when a given dimension of interest is important for a given community (e.g. temporal for AOL, breadth for Quora). This result suggests that there is room for improvement within the framework of R-Susceptibility in that community-specific risk measures could be employed.

5.5 Discussion

The presented experimental results suggest that R-Susceptibility with appropriate risk measures is able to identify sensitive users with reasonable accuracy. The topical risk measures that quantify a user's exposure with respect to different topics work well, especially when the domain- and time-awareness components are included.

The R-Susceptibility framework allows the plugging of different risk measures, and in the future more advanced measures could be studied to address some of the limitations of this work. These could, for instance, model semi-experts, subtle vocabulary correlations, user contexts, or specific characteristics of a community.

Table 5: Results averaged over all sensitive topics.

	AOL				Health Forums				Quora			
	R-prec		MAP	NDCG	R-prec		MAP	NDCG	R-prec		MAP	NDCG
	micro	macro			micro	macro			micro	macro		
BOW	0.434	0.420	0.459	0.759	**0.642**	**0.625**	0.620	0.833	0.284	0.262	0.319	0.605
BOW-D	0.364	0.358	0.394	0.700	0.612	0.580	0.610	0.832	0.418*	0.398	0.400	0.672
BOW-T	**0.556***	**0.546**	**0.574**	**0.843**	0.582	0.574	0.619	0.873	0.284	0.285	0.317	0.605
BOW-DT	0.374	0.372	0.441	0.758	0.612	0.597	**0.667**	**0.894**	**0.463***	**0.444**	**0.440**	**0.688**
W2V	0.556	0.533	0.589	0.836	0.664	0.634	0.696	0.894	0.343	0.341	0.352	0.637
W2V-D	0.414	0.395	0.427	0.738	0.642	0.600	0.647	0.874	**0.493***	**0.465**	**0.532**	**0.776**
W2V-T	**0.586**	**0.580**	**0.645**	0.859	0.619	0.616	0.643	0.884	0.313	0.312	0.401	0.695
W2V-DT	0.545	0.530	0.601	**0.860**	**0.687**	**0.678**	**0.768**	**0.939**	0.463*	0.434	0.489	0.763
LDA	0.525	0.518	0.557	0.796	0.649	0.636	0.724	0.913	0.358	0.362	0.428	0.715
LDA-D	0.566	0.563	0.557	0.803	**0.716***	0.703	0.772	0.921	**0.493***	**0.485**	**0.489**	**0.752**
LDA-T	0.576	0.567	**0.655**	**0.879**	0.709	0.704	0.748	0.925	0.299	0.264	0.378	0.669
LDA-DT	**0.616***	**0.616**	0.649	0.859	**0.716***	**0.709**	**0.825**	**0.957**	0.418	0.389	0.481	0.751

Table 6: Comparison of r-precision of LDA, LDA-D, LDA-T and LDA-DT for different topics.

	AOL				Health Forums				Quora			
	LDA	LDA-D	LDA-T	LDA-DT	LDA	LDA-D	LDA-T	LDA-DT	LDA	LDA-D	LDA-T	LDA-DT
depression	0.542	0.542	0.625	**0.667**	0.762	0.762	**0.833**	0.762	**0.650**	0.550	**0.650**	0.600
drugs	0.545	**0.636**	0.591	**0.636**	0.710	**0.806**	0.677	0.774	0.364	**0.545**	0.273	0.364
pregnancy	0.533	0.667	0.533	**0.733**	0.571	**0.667**	0.619	**0.667**	0.095	**0.429**	0.095	0.381
hiv	0.429	0.429	**0.500**	**0.500**	0.526	0.579	**0.684**	**0.632**	**0.400**	**0.400**	0.200	**0.400**
debts	0.542	0.542	**0.583**	0.542	n/a	n/a	n/a	n/a	0.300	**0.500**	0.100	0.200

5.5.1 *User guidance*

The R-susceptibility model and risk measures can work on a user history in a streaming manner, considering all contents up to a given point and periodically or continuously repeating the risk assessment. These methods could also be embedded in a privacy advisor tool that would help users assess their privacy risk, raising an alert when they become too exposed with regard to a sensitive topic.

6. RELATED WORK

Data-centric privacy. Methods for privacy-preserving data publising [13] aim at preventing the disclosure of individuals' sensitive attribute values, while maintaining data utility, e.g., for data mining [3], using concepts like k-anonymity [33], l-diversity [24], t-closeness [22], and membership privacy [23]. All these models are geared for and limited to dealing with structured data, and this holds also for the most powerful and versatile privacy model, differential privacy [10]. In the field of Private Information Retrieval the goal of retrieving data from a database without revealing the query is mainly addressed by query encryption/obfuscation [36]. Generating dummy queries to obscure user activity is another intensively studied technique (e.g., [29]).

Sensitivity prediction. There is little research on characterizing what consitutes a sensitive topic. The recent work of [30] analyzed features of posts and user behavior in Quora, and developed a classifier that can predict the sensitivity of individual posts. However, the solution is largely based on explicit categories (rather than latent embeddings) and the "go anonymous" posting option that users may choose. In contrast, our work aims to understand the sensitivity of any latently represented topic, and provide assessment for risk understood as topical exposure in a community.

Query log sanitization. This line of work tackles the challenge of an adversary using session information to infer user identities from queries [2]. A variety of techniques have been proposed for anonymizing query logs, e.g., hashing tokens, removing identifiers, deleting infrequent queries, shortening sessions, and more [8, 11, 16, 20, 21]. [15] compared different methods for publishing frequent keywords, queries and clicks, and showed that most methods are vulnerable to information leakage.

User-centric privacy. Stochastic privacy [32] is one of the few works that focus on users rather than data. This model introduces a user-defined threshold for sharing data to be obeyed by the platform provider. Closest in spirit to our approach is [4], which uses probabilistic graphical models to infer sensitive user properties, but is very limited in scope.

Linkability and de-anonymization. Privacy research for social networks has demonstrated the feasibility of linking user profiles across different communities [14] and de-anonymizing users [26, 27, 37]. To prevent such attacks, a family of methods (e.g., [34]) eliminates joinable attributes from published datasets.

User behavior modeling. It has been shown that search queries can often be used to predict identity of users, as well as their gender, location, and other demographic attributes [18, 17, 35]. Such information can be harnessed for personalization but may also incur privacy threats. [31] analyzed Twitter profiles and network information to predict the political affiliation and race of users.

Expertise identification and trust analysis. Expert and trustworthy users can be identified based on their questions/answers contents and community votes [1] or by analyzing user interaction graphs [19, 38]. Unlike in these works, our aim is not to identify experts, but to push the users who have a broad interest in a domain down the privacy risk ranking.

7. CONCLUSION

This paper proposes a framework for quantifying privacy risks from textual contents of user profiles in online communities. By employing IR techniques such as ranking and latent topic models, it specifically addresses the risk of exposure with respect to sensitive topics and targeting by a rational adversary with rich background knowledge about topic vocabulary and word correlations.

Although more large scale studies of adversarial risk scoring strategies are needed, our experiments constitute a proof of concept that the approach is a viable basis for privacy risk assessment for users who want to post about sensitive topics but would like to be warned when the risk of being targeted becomes high.

In the future, R-Susceptibility can be extended to incorporate other forms of online activities, and be integrated in a framework for risk mitigation through appropriately guided user actions. Our vision is a trusted personal privacy advisor which assesses risks, alerts the user when critical situations arise, and guides her in appropriate countermeasures.

8. REFERENCES

[1] L. A. Adamic et al. Knowledge sharing and yahoo answers: Everyone knows something. *WWW'08.*

[2] E. Adar. User 4xxxxx9: anonymizing query logs. *Workshop on Query Log Analysis, WWW'07.*

[3] E. Bertino, D. Lin, W. Jiang: A Survey of Quantification of Privacy Preserving Data Mining Algorithms. In: *Privacy-Preserving Data Mining,* Springer 2008.

[4] J. Biega, I. Mele, G. Weikum. Probabilistic Prediction of Privacy Risks in User Search Histories. *Workshop on Privacy and Security of Big Data, CIKM'14.*

[5] D. Blei, A. Ng, M. Jordan. Latent Dirichlet Allocation. *JMLR'03.*

[6] C. Carpineto, G. Romano. Kθ-affinity privacy: Releasing infrequent query refinements safely. Information Processing & Management '15.

[7] Chicago Tribune Online: Social media activity might affect your credit score. `www.chicagotribune.com/lifestyles/sns-201511020000--tms--kidmoneyctnsr-cc20151102-20151102-story.html`, accessed on 2016/01/21.

[8] A. Cooper. A survey of query log privacy-enhancing techniques from a policy perspective. *TWeb'08.*

[9] W. Day, N. Li. Differentially Private Publishing of High-dimensional Data Using Sensitivity Control. *ASIACCS'15.*

[10] C. Dwork. Differential Privacy: A Survey of Results. *TAMC'08.*

[11] L. Fan et al. Monitoring Web Browsing Behavior with Differential Privacy. *WWW'14.*

[12] Forbes Online: How Social Media Can Help (or Hurt) Your Job Search. `www.forbes.com/sites/jacquelynsmith/2013/04/16/how-social-media-can-help-or-hurt-your-job-search/`, accessed on 2016/01/21.

[13] B. Fung et al. Privacy-preserving data publishing: A survey of recent developments. *ACM Comput. Surv. 42(4), 2010.*

[14] O. Goga et al. Exploiting Innocuous Activity for Correlating Users Across Sites. *WWW'13.*

[15] M. Gotz et al. Publishing search logs – a comparative study of privacy guarantees. *TKDE'12.*

[16] Y. Hong et al. Differentially Private Search Log Sanitization with Optimal Output Utility. *EDBT'12.*

[17] J. Hu et al. Demographic prediction based on user's browsing behavior. *WWW'07.*

[18] R. Jones et al. "i know what you did last summer": Query logs and user privacy. *CIKM'07.*

[19] P. Jurczyk, E. Agichtein. Discovering authorities in question answer communities by using link analysis. *CIKM'07.*

[20] A. Korolova et al. Releasing search queries and clicks privately. *WWW'09.*

[21] R. Kumar et al. On anonymizing query logs via token-based hashing. *WWW'07.*

[22] N. Li, T. Li, S. Venkatasubramanian. t-Closeness: Privacy Beyond k-Anonymity and l-Diversity. *ICDE'07.*

[23] N. Li et al. Membership privacy: a unifying framework for privacy definitions. *CCS'13.*

[24] A. Machanavajjhala et al. L-diversity: Privacy beyond k-anonymity. *TKDD'07.*

[25] T. Mikolov et al. Distributed Representations of Words and Phrases and their Compositionality. *NIPS'13.*

[26] A. Narayanan et al. On the Feasibility of Internet-Scale Author Identification. *SP'12.*

[27] A. Narayanan, V. Shmatikov. De-anonymizing Social Networks. *SP'09.*

[28] G. Navarro-Arribas et al. User k-anonymity for privacy preserving data mining of query logs. *Information Processing & Management '12.*

[29] H. Pang, X. Xiao, J. Shen. Obfuscating the Topical Intention in Enterprise Text Search. *ICDE'12.*

[30] S. T. Peddinti et al. Cloak and swagger: Understanding data sensitivity through the lens of user anonymity *IEEE S&P '14.*

[31] M. Pennacchiotti, A.-M. Popescu. A machine learning approach to twitter user classification. *ICWSM'11.*

[32] A. Singla et al. Stochastic Privacy. *AAAI'14.*

[33] L. Sweeney. k-Anonymity: A Model for Protecting Privacy. *J. of Uncertainty, Fuzziness and Knowledge-Based Systems '02.*

[34] D. Vatsalan, P. Christen, V. Verykios. A taxonomy of privacy-preserving record linkage techniques. *IS'13.*

[35] I. Weber, C. Castillo. The demographics of web search. *SIGIR'10.*

[36] S. Yekhanin. Private Information Retrieval. *CACM'10.*

[37] A. Zhang et al. Privacy Risk in Anonymized Heterogeneous Information Networks. *EDBT'14.*

[38] J. Zhang, M. S. Ackerman, L. Adamic. Expertise networks in online communities: Structure and algorithms. *WWW'07.*

Scalable Semantic Matching of Queries to Ads in Sponsored Search Advertising

Mihajlo Grbovic, Nemanja Djuric, Vladan Radosavljevic, Fabrizio Silvestri, Ricardo Baeza-Yates
Yahoo Labs, Sunnyvale, CA, USA
{mihajlo, nemanja, vladan, silvestr, rby}@yahoo-inc.com

Andrew Feng, Erik Ordentlich, Lee Yang, Gavin Owens
Yahoo Hadoop Group, Sunnyvale, CA, USA
{afeng, eord, leewyang, gowens}@yahoo-inc.com

ABSTRACT

Sponsored search represents a major source of revenue for web search engines. This popular advertising model brings a unique possibility for advertisers to target users' immediate intent communicated through a search query, usually by displaying their ads alongside organic search results for queries deemed relevant to their products or services. However, due to a large number of unique queries it is challenging for advertisers to identify all such relevant queries. For this reason search engines often provide a service of advanced matching, which automatically finds additional relevant queries for advertisers to bid on. We present a novel advanced matching approach based on the idea of semantic embeddings of queries and ads. The embeddings were learned using a large data set of user search sessions, consisting of search queries, clicked ads and search links, while utilizing contextual information such as dwell time and skipped ads. To address the large-scale nature of our problem, both in terms of data and vocabulary size, we propose a novel distributed algorithm for training of the embeddings. Finally, we present an approach for overcoming a cold-start problem associated with new ads and queries. We report results of editorial evaluation and online tests on actual search traffic. The results show that our approach significantly outperforms baselines in terms of relevance, coverage, and incremental revenue. Lastly, we open-source learned query embeddings to be used by researchers in computational advertising and related fields.

Keywords

Sponsored search; ad retrieval; word embeddings.

1. INTRODUCTION

The remarkable growth of the Internet in the last decades has brought huge benefits to its users, allowing easy, one-click access to all kinds of information and services. However, along with the increase in size and variety of the web there inevitably came the increase in its complexity, which left many users lost in the immense digital jungle of web content. To mitigate the situation, very early in the web's existence there appeared search engines such as Altavista, AOL, or Lycos, that allowed users to easily browse and discover webpages of interest. The service has evolved and improved significantly since these beginnings, and today search engines represent one of the most popular web services.

Advertisers are interested in making use of the vast business potential that the search engines offer. Via issued search query users communicate a very clear intent that allows for effective ad targeting. This idea is embodied in the sponsored search model [19], where advertisers *sponsor* the top search results in order to redirect user's attention from original (or *organic*) search results to ads that are highly relevant to the entered query. Sponsored search drives significant portions of traffic to websites, and accounted for 46% of overall online advertising spend of astonishing $121 billion in 2014 alone[1]. Moreover, with the advent of handheld devices the sponsored search also made a successful transition to mobile platforms. Here, it equally shares the advertising market with display ad formats, and is projected to reach $12.85 billion spend in 2015[2].

The booking process for ad campaigns in sponsored search is typically self-served. This means that the advertisers create their own ads by providing ad creative to be shown to the users (comprising concise title, description, and display URL), along with ancillary ad parameters that are visible only to the web search publisher. These include the list of bid terms (i.e., queries for which advertisers wish to show their ad) and their bid values (i.e., monetary amounts they are willing to pay if the ad is shown and clicked). In the model currently used by most major search engines, in a case that multiple advertisers are competing for the same query the selected ads enter a generalized second price (GSP) auction [10], where the winner pays the runner-up's bid value when a user clicks on the shown ad.

The principal strategy for ad selection is based on explicit matching of user search queries to all the bid terms in the system, referred to as *exact match*. Provided that the advertiser-defined bid terms are indeed relevant to the ad, exact match ensures that advertisers interact only with the relevant audience. However, as it is nearly impossible for advertisers to explicitly list all commercially relevant bid

[1]zenithoptimedia.com, accessed January 2016
[2]emarketer.com, accessed January 2016

SIGIR '16, July 17-21, 2016, Pisa, Italy

DOI: http://dx.doi.org/10.1145/2911451.2911538

Table 1: Examples of variant and broad match queries

Ad title	Host a Fun Murder Mystery Party
Ad description	Huge selection of fun murder mystery games for all ages, groups. #1 site for instant downloads and boxed sets of exciting murder mystery party games!
Bid term	murder mystery party
Variant matches	murder mystery parties murder mistery party
Broad matches	murder mystery dinner murder mystery parties at home murder mystery dinner party how to host a mystery party friends game night detective games murder mystery games for parties

terms, it may also limit user reach and lead to lower traffic volume for the advertiser [14]. This can clearly result in lost opportunities and revenue for both the search engine and the advertisers. To address this problem a service of *advanced matching* is usually offered to the advertisers.

More specifically, with advertiser's permission search engines attempt to match ads to related queries not explicitly provided by the advertisers, by implementing *variant* and *broad* match techniques (illustrated in Table 1). Variant match looks for slight variations of the bid term (e.g., typos, inflections), typically by leveraging Levenshtein distance [24]. Broad match is a more involved process of matching queries to advertiser-provided bid terms that do not necessarily have any words in common, yet have same or similar meaning (e.g., query "running machine" and bid term "elliptical trainer"). Existing techniques include expanding user query to find similar queries that can be matched exactly to existing bid terms, commonly referred to as query rewriting [4, 15], or computing similarity between query and text in ad title and description. Query rewriting approaches are limited to matching only against defined bid terms and may not be suitable in cases when advertisers do not provide relevant bid terms to begin with. On the other hand, matching queries to ads based solely on textual information is problematic in case when no common words can be found.

In this paper we describe a novel broad match technique that was recently deployed in sponsored search system of Yahoo Search, which effectively and efficiently addresses the shortcomings of the existing broad match techniques. Motivated by recent advances in distributed neural language models [2, 8, 25, 28], we aim at learning low-dimensional continuous representations of queries and ads in a common vector space. To do so we rely on the search sessions, defined as sequences of queries, ad clicks and search link clicks performed by a particular user, and leverage surrounding context of queries and ads in a session to learn vectors that best describe them. As a result ads and queries which occurred in similar contexts will have similar representations, and finding relevant ads for a specific query amounts to a simple K nearest neighbor search in the learned embedding space, without ever considering the text in queries and ads.

Compared to our previous work [15], novel contributions of this paper are summarized below:

- **Implicit negatives**. We incorporated implicit negative signal (in terms of skipped, non-clicked ads) into the training procedure, leading to higher quality broad matches compared to training with random negatives;
- **Dwell time weights**. We integrated dwell time (i.e., time spent on the advertiser's page following an ad click) into the training procedure, allowing us to weight short and long clicks differently, according to a strength of the interest signal;
- **Large-scale training**. To address the scalability problems due to training data size and the need for large vocabulary (amounting to hundreds of millions of unique queries and ads), we proposed a novel distributed algorithm for training embeddings using parameter server framework that results in 10x training time speedup and over 5x bigger vocabulary compared to single machine training described in [25];
- **Cold-start ad embeddings**. We solved an important problem of computing embeddings for ads that were not observed in training, such that newly booked ads can be instantly matched to user queries;
- **Cold-start query embeddings**. We proposed a procedure for calculating high-quality embeddings for new and tail queries using embeddings of head queries;
- **Experiments on real search traffic**. We provide insights on how different state-of-the-art algorithms perform when applied to actual search traffic;
- **Open-source vectors**. As part of this work we open-sourced a portion of query embeddings for research purposes.

We trained a search embedding model using more than 9 billion search sessions, resulting in ad and query representations of very high quality. Extensive evaluation on real-world search traffic showed that the proposed approach significantly outperformed the existing state-of-the-art broad match methods on a number of critical performance measures, including relevance, reach, and click-through rate (CTR).

2. RELATED WORK

In the following we introduce related work on advanced query-ad matching in sponsored search, and recent advances in neural language models and distributed embeddings.

2.1 Neural language models

It has been shown that a number of problems in Natural Language Processing (NLP) domain can be effectively solved by defining a probability distribution over word sequences, shown to perform well in chunking, parsing, or sentiment analysis, to name a few. For this reason researchers have proposed a number of methods called language models to mathematically represent generation of language, aimed to capture statistical characteristics of written language [1, 22]. Classic methods for language modeling represented words as high-dimensional, sparse vectors using one-hot representation. Using this approach word vectors have dimensionality equal to the size of the entire vocabulary, with zero values everywhere except for the element corresponding to the given word. However, the approach often gives suboptimal results due to sparsity issues and curse of dimensionality.

In order to mitigate the problems with word representations in high-dimensional spaces, neural language models have been introduced. Unlike classical approaches, these methods learn distributed, low-dimensional representations of words through the use of neural networks [2, 8, 28]. The networks are trained by directly taking into account the word order and their co-occurrence, based on the assumption that words frequently appearing together in the sentences also share more statistical dependence.

Despite their effectiveness, training a large number of parameters of neural network-based approaches has been a serious obstacle to wider use of the neural models. In particular, a single parameter update requires iteration over the entire vocabulary, which can grow prohibitively large for many practical applications. However, with the recent advances in the NLP domain, and in particular with the development of highly scalable continuous bag-of-words (CBOW) and skip-gram (SG) language models for word representation learning [25], the models have been shown to obtain state-of-the-art performance on many traditional language tasks after training on large-scale textual data sets.

2.2 Broad match in sponsored search

Broad match is a well established, often used approach in sponsored search advertising, responsible for billions of dollars of search engine revenue. In addition to exact and variant match, which typically have the highest click-through rates, many advertisers use broad match to increase the reach to relevant queries that were not explicitly provided, entrusting search engines with this task.

Most of the existing broad match techniques rely on query rewriting to rewrite an unmatched user query to several similar queries, in expectation that one of the rewrites will match an advertiser-provided bid term, resulting in retrieval of ads that bidded on that term. A basic query rewriting approach involves representing queries as bag-of-words using tf-idf weighting, and calculating similarity between the query and all other queries in order to find good rewrite candidates. However, the bag-of-words representation of queries is extremely sparse, which makes it impossible to find related queries that do not share common words. Moreover, it can lead to false positives when queries share common words that have different meanings in different contexts, e.g. "house music" and "house prices". To mitigate these issues some researchers proposed to enrich query representation using text from web search results [7]. Others proposed to extend query rewriting beyond string matching by applying graph-based methods, such as Query Flow Graph (QFG) [4], where similar queries are found by a random walk over a bipartite graph of queries and link clicks [11], or neural networks [15], where query feature representations are learned from web search data. However, none of these methods can overcome an inherent limitation of the query rewriting approach. More specifically, once the query is rewritten it can only be matched to ads that have the resulting rewrites as bid terms, potentially overlooking other relevant ads.

Alternative methods aim to address this issue by directly retrieving ads by calculating similarity between bag-of-words representation of queries and bag-of-words representation of ads obtained from ad title and description. Even though it reduces sparsity, this approach does not completely solve the vocabulary mismatch problem [26] and may even introduce additional issues, especially in the case of *templated* ad creatives where majority of phrases in titles and descriptions have little to do with the advertised product (e.g., "free shipping", "best prices", "buy now").

Finally, to rank the ads by relevance (e.g., in the case too many ads are retrieved via query rewriting), it is common to apply the learning-to-rank approach [16] that learns weights for query and ad features based on editorially-labeled training set. These methods typically require enormous amounts of accurate editorial grades for (query, ad) matches that are often very expensive to obtain.

In this paper we go beyond query rewriting and supervised learning-to-rank, and propose to learn query and ad embeddings from search data in an unsupervised manner, followed by directly matching and ranking ads for queries based on the distances in the learned embedding space.

3. METHODOLOGY

To address the shortcomings of existing broad match algorithms in sponsored search, we propose to take a new approach to this task, motivated by the recent success of distributed language models in NLP applications [25, 28]. In the context of NLP, distributed models are able to learn word representations in a low-dimensional continuous vector space using a surrounding context of the word in a sentence, where in the resulting embedding space semantically similar words are close to each other [25]. Our objective is to take advantage of this property for the task of query-ad matching in sponsored search, and to learn query and ad representations in a low-dimensional space where queries would be close to related ads. This would allow direct matching of queries to ads, instead of taking the longer route of query rewriting. Clearly, such approach reduces the complex broad match task to a trivial K-nearest-neighbor (K-nn) search between queries and ads in the joint embedding space.

Finding distributed query and ad representation, as opposed to finding word representations, brings very unique challenges. For example, while the basic unit for learning word representations is a sentence $s = (w_1, \dots, w_M)$ consisting on M words $w_m, m = 1, \dots, M$, in our proposed approach the basic unit for learning query and ad representations are user actions within a search session $s = (a_1, \dots, a_M)$, where in the simplest case an action can be a search query or an ad click. Moreover, search sessions have a number of additional contexts that can be used to improve quality of the final model. For instance, search sessions typically contain link clicks. Even though we are only interested in query and ad embeddings, link clicks can provide additional context. In essence, the query and ad embeddings will be affected by the co-click behavior between queries and search link clicks, resulting in an improved model. In addition, ad dwell time can be leveraged to distinguish between good ad clicks and unsatisfactory or accidental clicks [21], and can provide useful context for training better quality embeddings. Finally, ads that are skipped in favor of a click on a lower positioned ad can be used as implicit negative signal and serve as negative context during training to improve the resulting model.

To formalize the training procedure, let us assume we are given a set $\mathcal{S}$ of S search sessions obtained from N users, where each session $s = (a_1, \dots, a_M) \in \mathcal{S}$ is defined as an uninterrupted sequence of M user actions comprising queries, ad clicks, and link clicks. A new session is initiated whenever there is a time gap of more than 30 minutes between two consecutive user actions [12]. Then, the learning objective is to find D-dimensional real-valued representation $\mathbf{v}_{a_m} \in \mathbb{R}^D$ of each unique user action a_m.

The proposed search embedding model (called *search2vec*) learns user search action representations using the skip-gram model [25] by maximizing the objective function $\mathcal{L}$ over the entire set $\mathcal{S}$ of search sessions, defined as follows,

$$\mathcal{L} = \sum_{s \in \mathcal{S}} \sum_{a_m \in s} \sum_{-b \leq i \leq b, i \neq 0} \log \mathbb{P}(a_{m+i}|a_m). \quad (3.1)$$

Probability $\mathbb{P}(a_{m+i}|a_m)$ of observing a neighboring user action a_{m+i} given the current action a_m is defined using the soft-max function,

$$\mathbb{P}(a_{m+i}|a_m) = \frac{\exp(\mathbf{v}_{a_m}^\top \mathbf{v}'_{a_{m+i}})}{\sum_{a=1}^{|\mathcal{V}|} \exp(\mathbf{v}_{a_m}^\top \mathbf{v}'_a)}, \quad (3.2)$$

where $\mathbf{v}_a$ and $\mathbf{v}'_a$ are the input and output vector representations of user action a, hyperparameter b is defined as a length of the relevant context for action sequences, and $\mathcal{V}$ is a vocabulary defined as a set of unique actions in the data set comprising queries, ads, and links. From (3.1) and (3.2) we see that search2vec models temporal context of action sequences, where actions with similar contexts (i.e., with similar neighboring actions) will have similar representations.

Time required to compute gradient $\nabla\mathcal{L}$ of the objective function in (3.1) is proportional to the vocabulary size, which may be computationally infeasible in practical tasks as $|\mathcal{V}|$ could easily reach hundreds of millions. As an alternative we used negative sampling approach proposed in [25], which significantly reduces computational complexity. Negative sampling can be formulated as follows. We generate a set $\mathcal{D}_p$ of pairs (a, c) of user actions a and their contexts c (i.e., actions within a window of length b that either precede or follow action a), and a set $\mathcal{D}_n$ of negative pairs (a, c) of user actions and n randomly sampled actions from the entire vocabulary. The optimization objective then becomes,

$$\underset{\theta}{\operatorname{argmax}} \sum_{(a,c) \in \mathcal{D}_p} \log \frac{1}{1 + e^{-\mathbf{v}'_c \mathbf{v}_a}} + \sum_{(a,c) \in \mathcal{D}_n} \log \frac{1}{1 + e^{\mathbf{v}'_c \mathbf{v}_a}}, \quad (3.3)$$

where parameters θ to be learned are $\mathbf{v}_a$ and $\mathbf{v}'_c$, $a, c \in \mathcal{V}$. The optimization is done via stochastic gradient ascent.

Visual representation of the search2vec model is presented in Figure 1. As discussed previously, and as depicted in Figure 1, we propose to utilize additional context specific to sponsored search domain, namely implicit negatives and dwell-time. In the experimental section we explore this approach and empirically evaluate their benefits in detail.

Leveraging ad dwell time. Let us assume that a user performed a search query q_1, followed by an ad click ad_1. We define *ad dwell time* as the time that the user spent on the ad landing page. When the user stayed longer on the ad landing page, it is usually interpreted as a positive engagement signal, as opposed to the user immediately bouncing back from the advertiser's website. There also exists a notion of accidental ad clicks with dwell time of only a few seconds, which is especially apparent on mobile phone devices. To incorporate this signal into our learning framework we propose to weight query-ad pairs with higher dwell times more, while penalizing shorter dwell times.

More specifically, when optimizing the objective function in (3.3), we introduce an additional weight $\eta_t = \log(1 + t)$ for each element of the first sum, where t denotes the dwell

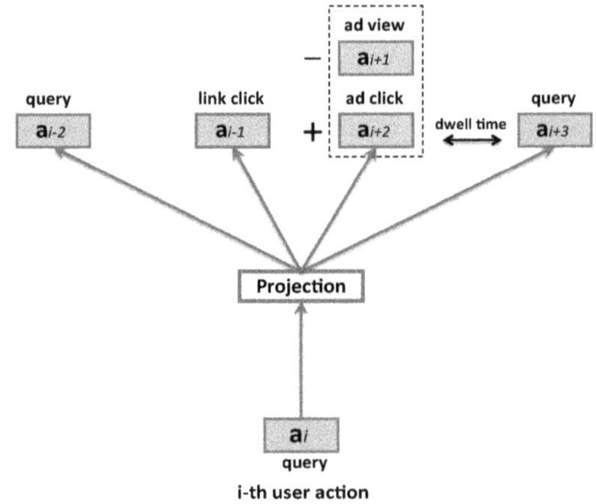

Figure 1: search2vec: dwell-time implicit negative skip-gram

time in minutes. For dwell times above 10 minutes we set $\eta_t = 1$. Moreover, we use this approach to compute weight only when updating the ad vector with the immediately preceding query and when updating the query vector with the immediately succeeding ad, otherwise we set $\eta_t = 1$.

Leveraging implicit negative signals. Unlike in the NLP domain, in the domain of sponsored search there does exist an implicit negative signal in a form of ads that the user decided to skip in favor of a click on a lower positioned ad, which can be utilized during training. In particular, given an issued user query q_1, let us assume that after the GSP auction a total of k ads, $ad_1, ad_2, \ldots, ad_k$, were shown at different positions on the page, with ad_1 being shown at the top position in the page followed by the remaining $k - 1$ ads below. Note that the top position has the highest value to the advertisers, as it has been shown to have the highest probability of being clicked, especially on mobile devices due to limited screen sizes. We adopt an assumption that if the user scrolls down the page and clicks on a lower positioned ad, all the ads ranked higher were of no interest to him and can be treated as negative signal for query q_1. We consider implicit negatives only on top $k = 3$ positioned ads, and only in cases where user had a single ad click in the session with dwell time of over 10 seconds.

We formulate the use of implicit negatives in the following way. In addition to sets $\mathcal{D}_p$ and $\mathcal{D}_n$, we generate a set $\mathcal{D}_{in}$ of pairs (q, ad) of user queries q and the ads ad at higher positions which were shown to the user, and skipped over in favor of a click on ad at one of the lower positions. The new optimization objective then becomes as follows,

$$\underset{\theta}{\operatorname{argmax}} \sum_{(a,c) \in \mathcal{D}_p} \log \frac{1}{1 + e^{-\mathbf{v}'_c \mathbf{v}_a}} + \sum_{(a,c) \in \mathcal{D}_n} \log \frac{1}{1 + e^{\mathbf{v}'_c \mathbf{v}_a}} + \sum_{(q,ad) \in \mathcal{D}_{in}} \log \frac{1}{1 + e^{\mathbf{v}'_{ad} \mathbf{v}_q}}, \quad (3.4)$$

where parameters θ to be learned remain the same as before.

Inference. Given learned query and ad embeddings, ad retrieval for a given query q is performed by calculating cosine similarity between its vector $\mathbf{v}_q$ and all ad vectors $\mathbf{v}_{ad}$ in the vocabulary. The K ads with the highest similarity are retrieved as broad matches. For large vocabularies, efficient K-nn search can be done via locality-sensitive hashing [13].

3.1 Scalable training algorithm

To realize the full potential of the proposed approach, we found it necessary to train embeddings for several hundred million of actions (i.e., *words* in the "vocabulary"), which include queries, ads, and links comprising the search session data. Existing implementations for training word embeddings were found to fall short for our vocabulary size target, as they require that all of the input and output vectors fit in the memory of a single machine. For example, a vocabulary of 200 million words with 300-dimensional vectors requires 480GB of RAM memory, which is beyond the capacity of typical machines. To address this issue, we developed a novel distributed word embedding training algorithm based on a variation of the parameter server paradigm.

A parameter server (PS) [9] is a high-performance, distributed, in-memory key-value store specialized for machine learning applications, typically used to store latest values of model parameters throughout the course of training. A PS-based training system includes a number of PS shards that store model parameters and a number of clients that read different portions of the training data from a distributed file system (e.g., Hadoop Distributed File System).

In the conventional PS system, the word embedding training can be implemented as follows. Each PS shard stores input and output vectors for a portion of the words from the vocabulary. Each client reads a subset of training data in minibatches (e.g., 200 lines at a time), and after each minibatch performs the vector updates of words found in the minibatch and randomly sampled negative words. The updates are achieved by transmitting the IDs of the words to all the PS shards, which will, as a result, send back the corresponding vectors to the client. The client calculates the gradient descent updates with respect to the minibatch restriction of the objective (3.3) and transmits them to the PS shards where the actual updates happen.

However, due to transmission costs of the actual word vectors over the network, the conventional PS-based implementation of word embedding training requires too much network bandwidth to achieve acceptable training throughput. For this reason we propose a different distributed system architecture that requires significantly less network bandwidth. The proposed algorithm, illustrated in Figure 2, features the following contributions with respect to the conventional PS-based training approach:

- Column-wise partitioning of vectors among PS shards;
- No transmission of word vectors across the network;
- PS shard-side negative sampling and computation of partial vector dot products.

In our algorithm, each PS shard stores distinct portion of vector dimensions for *all* words from the vocabulary $\mathcal{V}$, as opposed to previously described word-wise partitioning where each PS shard stores entire vectors for a subset of words. For example, assuming a vector dimension $d = 300$ and 10 PS shards, shard $s \in \{0, \ldots, 9\}$ would store 30 dimensions of input vectors $\mathbf{v}(w)$ and output vectors $\mathbf{v}'(w)$ with indices i in the range $30s \leq i < 30s + 30$ for all vocabulary words.

Since each PS shard now stores the entire vocabulary (i.e., different vector dimensions of *all* words), we can implement the random sampling step and the dot product calculation step to the PS shards themselves. In this way we avoid transmission costs of the actual vectors. Each client still processes

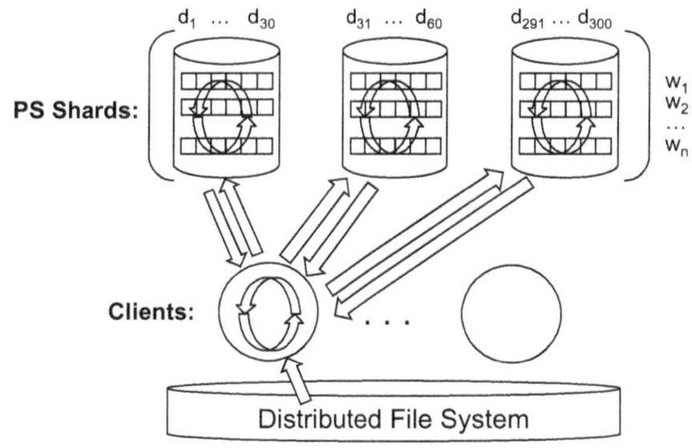

Figure 2: Scalable word2vec on Hadoop

data in minibatches, and sends to the PS shards the indices of (word, context) pairs that need to be updated. In addition, the client broadcasts common random number generator seeds, such that all shards can sample the same negative context words. Each PS shard then calculates the partial dot products with respect to their local dimensions for each of the positive and negative (word, context) pairs and sends the result to a client that made the request. Finally, the client aggregates local dot products it received from all PS shards and calculates the global coefficient needed for gradient updates. The single client's minibatch step ends by sending the global coefficients to all PS shards, where input and output vectors are updated correspondingly, without any locking or synchronization mechanism.

In a typical at-scale run of the algorithm, the above process is carried out by multiple client threads running on each of a few hundred cluster nodes, all interacting with the PS shards in parallel. The dataset is iterated over multiple times, and after each iteration the learning rate α is reduced. The distributed implementation handles implicit negatives in the same manner as positive contexts only with negative multiplier in the gradient update, and can handle dwell-time weights seamlessly. In comparison to [25], our system was found to be up to 10x faster depending on the load on the shared cluster, training set, and vocabulary size.

3.2 Cold start ad embeddings

Contrary to everyday language where new words come into existence occasionally, in ad serving business new ads are introduced to the system every day. Matching service is required to find good query candidates for these new ads even before they are shown to users. In this section we propose a method that addresses this problem by producing cold start ad embeddings of good quality, which are then used to find relevant queries for that ad.

Given a newly booked ad, in absence of ad clicks that could be used to learn a context vector, we must rely on its textual content, including the bid term, ad title, and description. In particular, in the process of learning query context vectors V_q we learned embeddings for a large number of words and phrases, many of which appear in ad titles and descriptions. In addition, the bid term context vector is likely to be available (in 80% of cases by our evaluation).

The bid term context vector itself could be a good choice for the cold start ad embedding. However, even though the bid term should summarize the message being conveyed in the ad, oftentimes advertisers bid on general terms, such as "shoes", "fitness", or "sports", to maximize their traffic po-

Data: ad title, ad description, ad URL, bid term b, threshold τ_c, set of context query vectors V_q
Initialization: $\tau_c = 0.45$, get bid term vector $\mathbf{v}_b$ from V_q, set $\mathbf{v}_{ad} = \mathbf{v}_b$, create ad document $\mathbf{d}_{ad}$ from all n-grams ($n = 1, .., 10$) in ad title, description, URL;
forall the *phrases p in ad document* $\mathbf{d}_{ad}$ **do**
    if $\mathbf{v}_p$ *exists in* V_q **then**
        if *sim*($\mathbf{v}_b$,$\mathbf{v}_p$)$> \tau$ **then**
            $\mathbf{v}_{ad} = \mathbf{v}_{ad} + \mathbf{v}_p$;
        end
    end
end
Result: ad content vector $\mathbf{v}_{ad}$

Algorithm 1: content search2vec

tential. Evidently, one could find additional useful phrases in the ad title and description, whose vectors, in combination with the bid term vector, could produce an embedding that is closer to more specific query matches for that ad.

To compute a content-based ad vector we propose to extract relevant words and phrases from ad content and compute the linear combination of their context vectors,

$$\mathbf{v}_{ad} = \sum_{t=1:T_a} \mathbf{v}_{p_t}, \tag{3.5}$$

where T_a is the number of extracted words and phrases with vectors $\mathbf{v}_{p_t}$ in V_q. The resulting ad vector is of the same dimensionality and in the same feature space as the query context vectors. Consequently, the same retrieval procedure as the one used for context ad vectors can be used to find relevant broad match queries for the cold-start ads.

The most challenging part of this procedure is extracting relevant words and phrases from the textual ad information. For example, let us consider an ad with title "Visit Metropolitan Opera House in New York" and bid term "performing arts". While phrases "opera house" and "metropolitan opera house" are relevant in the context of this ad, other phrases such as "visit", "house", or "house in new york" do not carry any useful information or have completely different meaning from what is communicated in the ad. For example, phrase "visit" is too general and "house in new york" refers to real-estate in New York with no connections to performing arts. In addition, ads often contain generic phrases such as "free shipping", "buy now", "30% off", and "best deals on", which if used in the final sum (3.5) may cause the resulting vector to diverge from relevant queries in the embedding space, leading to poor broad matches.

To decide which n-grams should be formed from words in short text, a typical approach is to use a CRF segmentation model [20]. However, CRF models have their limitations: 1) they require a large training set with human-annotated examples of correct text segmentations, which needs to be constantly updated to account for new entities; 2) they cannot automatically detect phrases that should not be considered and would require creating a blacklist of terms that should be excluded from (3.5). Similar shortcomings are present in the paragraph2vec model [23] that suggests simply using all words in a document to learn its embedding.

To this end we propose an *anchor phrases* model, summarized in Algorithm 1, that uses search context vectors to automatically filter out stopwords and non-relevant phrases and keep only the ones closely related to the *anchor*. The choice of the anchor falls on the advertiser-defined bid term, as that is the one phrase we know is related to the ad. In rare cases when anchor context vector is not available, one can be constructed as described in Section 3.3. The algorithm uses context vectors of queries learned from search sessions. It initializes the content ad vector to the context vector of the bid term. Next, it creates a textual ad document from all possible n-gram phrases contained in the ad title, description, and URL. Finally, it considers all phrases from the ad document for which a context vector exists and has a high enough cosine similarity to the bid term vector (above threshold τ_c). These relevant phrases are then added to the ad vector to further focus its representation. The resulting ad vector lies in the same embedding space as the search queries. Therefore, relevant broad match query candidates can be found via K-nearest neighbor search. We refer to this method as *content search2vec*.

3.3 Cold start query embeddings

Quality of the query embedding is contingent on the number of times it was observed in the training data. Therefore, even though our scalable training procedure allows us to train vectors for several hundred millions of queries, we are still limited by the frequency of queries in search sessions. Following the procedure from [25] we train context vectors for queries that occur at least 10 times. Considering that frequency of queries in search logs follows a power low distribution [27], a large number of queries will not meet this frequency requirement. They are referred to as *tail* queries, as opposed to *head* and *torso* queries that occupy the portion of the power law curve for which a context vector can be learned. While individually rare, *tail* queries make up a significant portion of the query volume. For this reason, these queries have significant potential for advertising revenue.

Most major search engines pre-compute broad matches for a large number of *head* and *torso* queries. This table T_b is then cached for fast access and retrieval. The nonexistence or lack of presence in search sessions makes *tail* queries much harder to match against ads [6], as they lack useful contexts of surrounding web activities to help in matching. Matching them to ads solely based on textual information results in matches of low quality, primarily due to the so-called vocabulary mismatch problem [26]. Finally, short text in queries introduces limitations into producing query embeddings based on their content.

To address this problem we propose to expand the head queries from table T_b with K nearest neighbor queries in the learned embedding space and build an *inverted index* to be used for efficient matching against tail queries. In the online phase, when a new user query arrives that has no matched ads we use the inverted index to map the query into related previously-seen queries that have ads associated with them. Finally, the user query inherits ads of the top matched query. To illustrate the matching procedure, in Table 2 we show examples of tail queries and top matched queries, obtained via inverted index. Bolded words are the ones matched against the user query. We refer to this method as *elastic search2vec*.

Previous attempts at building an inverted index of head queries for dealing with tail queries were based on features extracted directly from words of the head query [6] or from words of queries that co-occurred in the same sessions as the head query [5], such as typos and reformulations. While words from query are good representations of its syntax, they fail to accurately represent its semantics. On the other

Table 2: Demonstration of elasting search2vec

User search query (not present in V_q)	Matched query-document	Query-document features (K-nn queries)
metropolitan opera house that is in new york city	metropolitan opera house	**metropolitan opera house**, ny **opera** **new york opera, new york opera house** **metropolitan opera**, nyc **opera house**
best flight deals that travel to paris france	best flight tickets to paris	**best flight** tickets to **paris**, cheap flights to **paris** cheap tickets to **paris**, **best flight** fares to **paris** cheap airfare **paris france**, **travel to paris france**
what is the best stock ticker trading app in appstore	best stock ticker apps	**best stock ticker** apps, **stock** tracker **app in appstore** **best stock** apps in **appstore**, **stock ticker** apps **best trading** apps, real time stocks on the **app** store

hand, words from co-occurring queries may not be the best choice as semantically similar queries often have similar contexts (e.g., same link and ad clicks), but do not necessarily appear in the same session. For this reason, we build the inverted index by considering words of semantically similar queries obtained by K-nn search in the embedding space V_q. As our experiments confirm, this leads to more accurate cold-start query embeddings and better quality ad matches.

4. EXPERIMENTS

In this section we describe the training data set and give empirical evaluation of the proposed search2vec method. The performance was evaluated in terms of relevance on editorially judged set of (query, ad) pairs, as well as in terms of click-through rates from a live bucket tests on Yahoo Search traffic. We compared several variations of our method discussed in the previous sections, as well as a number of baseline approaches. Finally, we conducted experiments to evaluate the proposed models for cold-start ad and query embeddings that address the limitations of the context models by allowing us to produce matches for new queries and ads.

Search2vec training. In order to learn query and ad embeddings we organized our search data into sessions, or uninterrupted sequences of user's web search activities: queries, ad clicks, and search link clicks. Each ad impression was uniquely identified by its creative ID and bid term ID. Search sessions that contained only 1 user action were discarded. We discarded from the vocabulary all activities that occurred less than 10 times in the search sessions. The most frequent actions were downsampled with threshold of 10^{-5} as in [25]. The dimensionality of the embedding space was set to $d = 300$, the window size was set to 5 and the number or random negative samples per vector update was set to 5.

We learned embeddings for more than 126.2 million unique queries, 42.9 million unique ads, and 131.7 million unique links, using one of the largest search data set reported so far, comprising over 9.1 billion search sessions collected on Yahoo Search. End-to-end search2vec training via parameter server using 10 iteration over the data set takes about 30 hours to complete. In comparison, multi-threaded single machine implementation [25] on 256GB RAM box with 24 threads and same training parameters takes more than a week to complete and can train only up to 80 million vectors.

4.1 Broad match models

1) word2vec model uses publicly available word vectors[3] trained on Google News data set. Query vectors were generated by summing vectors of word tokens within a query, and ad vectors were generated by summing vectors of word tokens from title, description, bid term, and display URL. English stopwords were not considered in the summation.

2) TF-IDF model generates broad match candidates by computing the cosine similarity between bag-of-words representation of queries and ads (constructed from ad title, description, bid term, and display URL, excluding stopwords).

3) QFG model was trained using a click-flow graph constructed from search sessions data set $\mathcal{S}$. Broad matches were produced by query rewriting of the ad bid term.

4) search2vec model was trained using search sessions data set $\mathcal{S}$ composing of search queries, ads and links. Broad match candidates for a query were generated by calculating cosine similarity between the query vector and all ad vectors.

5) search2vec$_{dwell,in}$ is a variation of search2vec method with dwell time weights, and implicit negatives added to the training data. We combined dwell time and implicit negative enhancements under one framework as both of them aim at reducing the effect of bad clicks.

6) content search2vec is tailored for the cold-start case (i.e. ads that do not appear in search sessions). Broad match candidates are found by calculating cosine similarity between the context query vector the content ad vectors.

7) elastic search2vec aims at finding ads for tail queries by matching against an inverted index of context queries that already have ad matches.

Our evaluation did not include topic models such as LDA [3] or PLSA [17], as a number of researchers [18] found that they obtain suboptimal performance on short texts.

[3]https://code.google.com/p/word2vec, accessed Jan. 2016

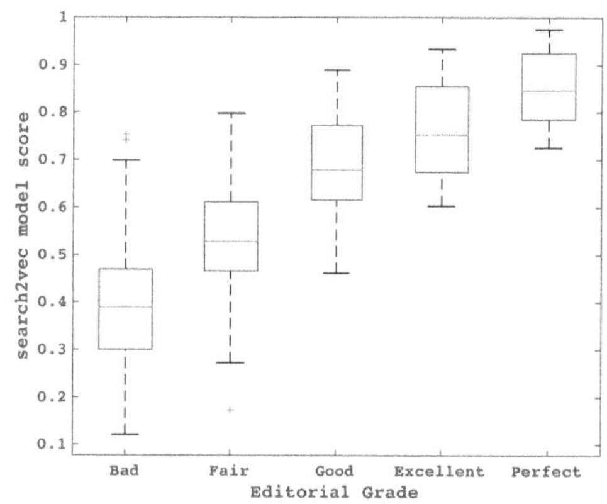

Figure 3: Box plot of editorial grades vs. search2vec scores

4.2 Offline relevance results

In the first set of experiments we used editorial judgments of query-ad pairs to compare broad match methods in terms of relevance. For this purpose we used an in-house

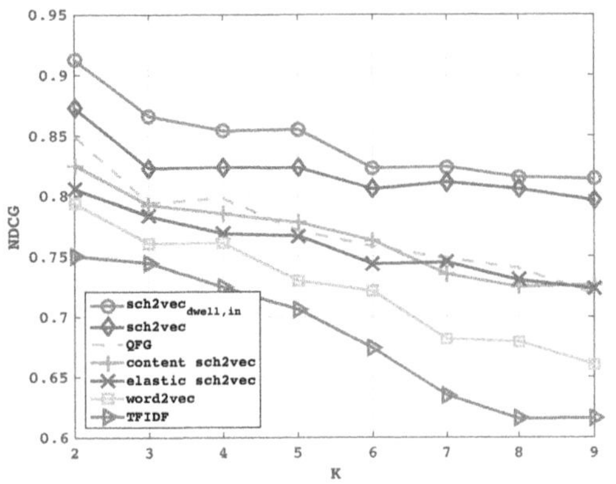

Figure 4: NDCG@K for different models

Table 3: Comparison of different methods on editorial data

Method	oAUC	Macro NDCG
word2vec	0.6573	0.7308
TF-IDF	0.6407	0.6983
QFG	0.6928	0.7848
search2vec	0.7254	0.8303
search2vec$_{dwell,in}$	**0.7392**	**0.8569**
content search2vec	0.6881	0.7758
elastic search2vec	0.6805	0.7612

dataset consisting of a query-ad pairs that were graded editorially. The editors were instructed to grade more than 24,000 query-ad pairs as either *Bad*, *Fair*, *Good*, *Excellent*, or *Perfect* match. For each ad, the editors had access to bid term, ad title, description, and display URL to help them reach their judgment. Note that the candidate query-ad pairs were not generated by any of the tested methods. For each query there were up to 9 judged ads, allowing us to evaluate ranking of ads in addition to relevance.

Using each of the compared methods we generated query features and ad features for each judged pair. Then, to calculate score for a particular pair, we calculated cosine similarity between the query vector and the ad vector. In case of QFG query rewriting model, the query-ad relevance score was calculated between the query and the ad bid term. In case of elastic search2vec model, query vector was obtained by inverse index search that excluded the searched query and calculating the cosine similarity of the top retrieved context query vector and the ad context vector.

There are several questions one could ask regarding algorithm relevance. First, how well can the algorithm score distinguish between good and bad query-ad pairs. Second, how well can the ads be ranked based on the algorithm score, and how much does this ranking deviate from ranking based on editorial grades. For this purpose we concentrated on the following two metrics to measure relevance:

1) oAUC Ordinal AUC measures how well the cosine similarity scores computed by the trained model can discriminate between editorial grades, by computing the average AUC (area under ROC curve) across four classifiers: perfect-and-above vs. below-perfect, excellent-and-above vs. below excellent, good-and-above vs. below good, and lastly fair-and-above vs. below fair.

2) Macro NDCG measures how well the ranked scores align with the ranked editorial grades. Given numerical grades (1 for Bad, 2 for Fair, 3 for Good, 4 for Excellent and 5 for Perfect) we used $(2^{grade} - 1)$ as NDCG labels and position discounting of log(position in ranked list). Finally, we average the metric across all queries. Unlike oAUC, this performance measure incurs a greater penalty for mistakes found at the top of the list.

In Table 3 we report the averaged oAUC and Macro NDCG of editorial query-ad pairs for different methods. In addition, to get a sense of how different models compare at a particular rank we show the NDCG metric at values of rank ranging from 2 to 9 in Figure 4.

Several conclusions can be drawn. First, we can see that the models that did not utilize search sessions (i.e., word2vec and TF-IDF) perform worse than the models that use historical search logs (i.e., QFG and search2vec). Second, search2vec embedding method performs better than QFG graph method. This can be explained by the fact that QFG only makes use of the co-occurrence of user actions in search sessions, while search2vec also accounts for similarity of their contexts. Third, introduction of dwell time and implicit negatives improves relevance over baseline search2vec model.

Interestingly, the increase in oAUC of search2vec$_{dwell,in}$ over search2vec was not as large as the improvement in Macro NDCG. This higher improvement in ranking measure can be explained by the fact that search2vec$_{dwell,in}$ leverages ad views in addition to ad clicks. Therefore, if two ads have the same number of clicks but one of them was viewed an order of magnitude more frequently, search2vec$_{dwell,in}$ will rank it lower than the ad which was shown less times, thus obtaining a better result. Finally, relevance based on cold-start query and ad embeddings produces reasonable results, indicating that they can be successfully used until context vectors can be learned from sessions.

To better characterize the search2vec method, in Figure 3 we show a box plot of cosine similarities between editorially judged queries and ads for search2vec$_{dwell,in}$ model, grouped by different editorial grades. We can see that the cosine similarity scores correlate well with the editorial judgments, indicating a strong potential of the learned embeddings for the task of retrieval of high-quality query-ad pairs.

4.3 Online test results

Following successful offline evaluation of the proposed broad match methods, in the second set of experiments we conducted tests on live Yahoo Search traffic. Five buckets with five different broad match techniques were set up (QFG, search2vec, search2vec$_{dwell,in}$, content search2vec and elastic search2vec), all on 5% of overall search traffic and compared against control bucket, which employed a broad match model currently used in production. Note that, although the buckets used different broad match techniques, all of them still included the same exact match and variant match techniques. The online test was run for 7 days, and was performed on a subset of active sponsored search ads.

Different search2vec methods produced broad matches by finding $K = 30$ nearest ads in the embedding space for each search query from our 126.2M vocabulary, and keeping only ads with cosine similarity above $\tau = 0.65$. The threshold was chosen based on editorial results from Figure 3, where it can be observed that threshold of 0.65 captures most Good, Excellent, and Perfect query-ad pairs while discarding most of

Table 4: Comparison of broad match methods in A/B test

Method	CTR	Coverage
QFG	-	-
elastic search2vec	−4.81%	+43.79%
content search2vec	−1.24%	+35.61%
search2vec	+6.21%	+26.44%
search2vec$_{dwell,in}$	**+10.64%**	**+19.95%**

Table 5: Comparison of ad cold-start methods

Method	Average	STD
bid term vector	0.731	0.128
words	0.574	0.059
anchor words	0.688	0.077
phrases	0.665	0.067
CRF phrases	0.604	0.075
anchor phrases	**0.792**	**0.077**

Fair and Bad ones. While search2vec and search2vec$_{dwell,in}$ were restricted to only ads for which we previously observed clicks in historical search logs, content search2vec generated embeddings for all active ads, and it is expected to have higher ad coverage. In the case of QFG method, the retrieval was done via query rewriting. For each query we determined the most relevant bid terms, and retrieved all ad creatives with that bid term, up to $K = 30$ ads per query.

The results of the test in terms of CTR and coverage are summarized in Table 4. For CTR we measured the number of clicks on particular broad match ads, divided by the total number of shown ads by that broad match model. Then, for each broad match model we report a relative improvement of CTR over QFG method, as well as relative change in coverage, defined as a number of ad impressions.

Considering the results, we can conclude that search2vec$_{dwell,in}$ is the best choice among the competing method as it achieves the highest CTR while maintaining a large coverage. When dwell time and implicit negatives were incorporated in search2vec training we observed a large improvement in CTR, with slight coverage drop, which can be explained by the fact that some ad candidates were eliminated due to low dwell time of high number of skips. Content search2vec and elastic search2vec produced a large increase in coverage since they are not restricted to only clicked ads or queries that appeared in search sessions. At the same time they had satisfactory CTR, indicating that they are good alternatives to search2vec$_{dwell,in}$.

One of the highlights of the A/B test with the control bucket was that more than 80% of broad matches produced by search2vec$_{dwell,in}$ were unique to that method (i.e., not found by the production model) while retaining high CTR, which can directly lead to incremental gains in revenue. Our search2vec$_{dwell,in}$ combined with cold start ad embeddings was launched in production and it is currently serving more than 30% of all broad matches.

4.4 Cold start experiments

To evaluate different algorithms for cold start ad embeddings we conducted the following experiment. We used search2vec$_{dwell,in}$ context vectors of queries to construct ad content vectors based on available textual information: title, description, display URL and bid term. To achieve this task, we tested several methods that use different strategies to extract the most relevant keywords from ad text and calculate the embedding as a linear combination of their vectors (3.5). To this end, we evaluated the following techniques: 1) *bid term vector*, which uses the vector of a bid term query as the ad vector 2) *words*, similar to [23] the sum (3.5) uses vectors of all words in the document 3) *phrases*, which uses vectors of all possible n-grams from the ad texr, $n = 1, .., 10$ 4) *CRF phrases*, which uses vectors of phrases obtained by CRF segmentation [20] 5) *anchor phrases*, which is explained in Algorithm 1 and 6) *anchor words*, which is the Algorithm 1 that uses words instead of phrases. In all above-mentioned algorithms, except *anchor* algorithms, a hand curated collection of stopwords (e.g., "free shipping" and "best prices") were dropped to improve performance. The performance was measured in terms of cosine similarity between the ad context vector and its corresponding content vector. High similarity indicates that the cold-start method can produce a vector that is close enough to the one that would be learned from sessions, and could therefore be matched to relevant queries in the embedding space. In Table 5 we show results on a subset of 2M ads. We can observe that *anchor phrases*, which automatically discards uninformative phrases, outperformed the competing baselines by a large margin.

We repeat a similar procedure for queries. Specifically, we test how well the vectors of last 50M queries in our vocabulary could be generated using vectors of 40M head queries. It should be noted that generating query content vectors is much more challenging as we have less content (i.e., text) to work with and no concept of *anchor* point that could help in extraction. To address this issue we proposed *elastic search2vec* described in Section 3.3. We evaluate 3 different sizes of query expansions when creating the inverted index: K= 5, 10 and 100. In addition to previously mentioned baselines, we also test an inverted index approach similar to [5], where index is generated based on words from K= 10 top co-occurring queries. In Table 6 we summarize the results, where we can observe that the proposed approach with K= 10 achieved the best performance.

Table 6: Comparison of query cold-start methods

Method	Average	STD
words	0.452	0.101
phrases	0.574	0.120
CRF phrases	0.514	0.119
elastic co-occurred queries, K=10	0.621	0.084
elastic search2vec, K=5	0.685	0.085
elastic search2vec, K=10	**0.717**	**0.091**
elastic search2vec, K=100	0.693	0.089

4.5 Open-source query embeddings

As part of this research, we open-sourced 8M query vectors trained using search2vec[4]. The vectors may serve as a testbed for query rewriting task as well as to word and sentence similarity task, which are common problems in NLP research. We would like for researchers to be able to produce query rewrites based on these vectors and test them against other state-of-the-art techniques. In addition, we provide an

[4]http://webscope.sandbox.yahoo.com/catalog.php?datatype=l&did=73

Table 7: Comparison of query rewriting methods

Method	oAUC	Macro NDCG@5
word2vec	0.817	0.929
search2vec	**0.880**	**0.959**

editorially judged set of 4016 query rewrites, on which we compared search2vec performance against word2vec. The results are summarized in Table 7.

5. CONCLUSIONS AND FUTURE WORK

We proposed a novel broad match method based on neural language models. The method learns low-dimensional representations of search queries and ads based on contextual co-occurrence in user search sessions. To better leverage available web search contexts, we incorporate link clicks, dwell time and implicit negative signals into the training procedure. We evaluated the proposed method using both editorial data and online test on live search traffic. When compared to the baseline approaches, we showed that proposed search2vec model generated the most relevant broad matches between queries and ads, and had the highest CTR. Moreover, we found that in the case of new queries and ads the proposed cold-start embeddings are a good substitute for the learned ones. The results clearly indicate significant advantages of search2vec model over the existing broad match algorithms, and suggest high monetization potential in sponsored search. Finally, to address the scalability issues with regards to data and vocabulary size, we propose a novel distributed algorithm that can achieve 10x training speedup and train 5x larger vocabularies, compared to a single machine algorithm. In our future work we plan to make use of additional search contexts to further improve search2vec ad ranking, including user's age, gender and geo location.

6. REFERENCES

[1] R. Baeza-Yates and B. Ribeiro-Neto. *Modern information retrieval*, volume 463. ACM press, 1999.

[2] Y. Bengio, H. Schwenk, J.-S. Senécal, F. Morin, and J.-L. Gauvain. Neural probabilistic language models. In *Innovations in Machine Learning pp. 137-186*. 2006.

[3] D. M. Blei, A. Y. Ng, and M. I. Jordan. Latent dirichlet allocation. *JMLR*, 3:993–1022, 2003.

[4] P. Boldi, F. Bonchi, C. Castillo, D. Donato, A. Gionis, and S. Vigna. The query-flow graph: Model and applications. CIKM '08, pages 609–618, 2008.

[5] D. Broccolo, L. Marcon, F. M. Nardini, R. Perego, and F. Silvestri. Generating suggestions for queries in the long tail with an inverted index. *Inf. Process. Manage.*, 48(2):326–339, Mar. 2012.

[6] A. Broder, P. Ciccolo, E. Gabrilovich, V. Josifovski, D. Metzler, L. Riedel, and J. Yuan. Online expansion of rare queries for sponsored search. WWW '09, pages 511–520, New York, NY, USA, 2009. ACM.

[7] A. Z. Broder, P. Ciccolo, M. Fontoura, E. Gabrilovich, V. Josifovski, and L. Riedel. Search advertising using web relevance feedback. In *CIKM 2008*.

[8] R. Collobert, J. Weston, L. Bottou, M. Karlen, K. Kavukcuoglu, and P. Kuksa. Natural language processing (almost) from scratch. *The Journal of Machine Learning Research*, 12:2493–2537, 2011.

[9] J. Dean, G. S. Corrado, R. Monga, K. Chen, M. Devin, Q. V. Le, M. Z. Mao, M. Ranzato, A. Senior, P. Tucker, K. Yang, and A. Y. Ng. Large scale distributed deep networks. In *NIPS*, 2012.

[10] B. Edelman, M. Ostrovsky, and M. Schwarz. Internet advertising and the generalized second price auction: Selling billions of dollars worth of keywords. In *National Bureau of Economic Research*, 2005.

[11] A. Fuxman, P. Tsaparas, K. Achan, and R. Agrawal. Using the wisdom of the crowds for keyword generation. In *WWW 2008*.

[12] D. Gayo-Avello. A survey on session detection methods in query logs and a proposal for future evaluation. *Inf. Sci.*, 179(12):1822–1843, May 2009.

[13] A. Gionis, P. Indyk, R. Motwani, et al. Similarity search in high dimensions via hashing. In *VLDB*, volume 99, pages 518–529, 1999.

[14] S. Goel, A. Broder, E. Gabrilovich, and B. Pang. Anatomy of the long tail: ordinary people with extraordinary tastes. In *WSDM 2010*.

[15] M. Grbovic, N. Djuric, V. Radosavljevic, F. Silvestri, and N. Bhamidipati. Context-and content-aware embeddings for query rewriting in sponsored search. In *SIGIR*, pages 383–392. ACM, 2015.

[16] L. Hang. A short introduction to learning to rank. *IEICE Transactions on Information and Systems*, 94(10):1854–1862, 2011.

[17] T. Hofmann. Probabilistic latent semantic indexing. In *SIGIR*, pages 50–57. ACM, 1999.

[18] L. Hong and B. D. Davison. Empirical study of topic modeling in twitter. In *Proceedings of the First Workshop on Social Media Analytics*. ACM, 2010.

[19] B. J. Jansen and T. Mullen. Sponsored search: An overview of the concept, history, and technology. *International Journal of Electronic Business*, 6(2):114–131, 2008.

[20] J. Lafferty, A. McCallum, and F. C. Pereira. Conditional random fields: Probabilistic models for segmenting and labeling sequence data. 2001.

[21] M. Lalmas, J. Lehmann, G. Shaked, F. Silvestri, and G. Tolomei. Promoting positive post-click experience for in-stream yahoo gemini users. In *SIGKDD 2015*.

[22] V. Lavrenko and W. B. Croft. Relevance based language models. In *SIGIR*. ACM, 2001.

[23] Q. V. Le and T. Mikolov. Distributed representations of sentences and documents. 2014.

[24] V. Levenshtein. Binary codes capable of correcting deletions, insertions, and reversals. In *Soviet Physics-Doklady*, volume 10, 1966.

[25] T. Mikolov, I. Sutskever, K. Chen, G. S. Corrado, and J. Dean. Distributed representations of words and phrases and their compositionality. In *NIPS*, 2013.

[26] B. Ribeiro-Neto, M. Cristo, P. B. Golgher, and E. Silva de Moura. Impedance coupling in content-targeted advertising. In *SIGIR 2005*.

[27] A. Spink, D. Wolfram, M. B. Jansen, and T. Saracevic. Searching the web: The public and their queries. *Journal of the American society for information science and technology*, 52(3):226–234, 2001.

[28] J. Turian, L. Ratinov, and Y. Bengio. Word representations: a simple and general method for semi-supervised learning. In *ACL 2010*, pages 384–394.

Retrieving Non-Redundant Questions to Summarize a Product Review

Mengwen Liu*
College of Computing and Informatics
Drexel University
Philadelphia 19104, PA, USA
ml943@drexel.edu

Yi Fang*
Department of Computer Engineering
Santa Clara University
Santa Clara 95053, CA, USA
yfang@scu.edu

Dae Hoon Park
Department of Computer Science
University of Illinois at Urbana-Champaign
Urbana, IL 61801, USA
dpark34@illinois.edu

Xiaohua Hu
College of Computing and Informatics
Drexel University
Philadelphia 19104, PA, USA
xh29@drexel.edu

Zhengtao Yu
Kunming University of Science and Technology
Kunming, China
ztyu@bit.edu.cn

ABSTRACT

Product reviews have become an important resource for customers before they make purchase decisions. However, the abundance of reviews makes it difficult for customers to digest them and make informed choices. In our study, we aim to help customers who want to quickly capture the main idea of a lengthy product review before they read the details. In contrast with existing work on review analysis and document summarization, we aim to retrieve a set of real-world user questions to summarize a review. In this way, users would know what questions a given review can address and they may further read the review only if they have similar questions about the product. Specifically, we design a two-stage approach which consists of question retrieval and question diversification. We first propose probabilistic retrieval models to locate candidate questions that are relevant to a review. We then design a set function to re-rank the questions with the goal of rewarding diversity in the final question set. The set function satisfies submodularity and monotonicity, which results in an efficient greedy algorithm of submodular optimization. Evaluation on product reviews from two categories shows that the proposed approach is effective for discovering meaningful questions that are representative for individual reviews.

*The first two authors made equal contributions to this paper

SIGIR '16, July 17-21, 2016, Pisa, Italy

DOI: http://dx.doi.org/10.1145/2911451.2911544

CCS Concepts

•Information systems → Summarization; *Information retrieval diversity;*

Keywords

Review summarization; Question retrieval; Diversification

1. INTRODUCTION

With the rapid growth of online review sites, more people rely on advices from fellow users before they make purchase decisions. Unfortunately, finding relevant information from large quantities of user reviews in a short time is a huge challenge. Thus, review analysis with the goal of extraction of useful information has become an important way to improve user experience of online shopping.

Existing techniques for review analysis include review rating prediction [33, 17], sentiment polarity classification [13, 22], and aspect-based review summarization [11, 32, 28]. The first two techniques aim to predict numerical ratings and sentiment orientations of reviews. They do not summarize the main points discussed in reviews. Review summarization is beneficial for aggregating user opinions towards a product through the generation of a short summary from a set of product reviews. However, the generated summary may not be of interest to end users since it may contain little relevant information that addresses the specific questions that are in the user's mind.

In our study, we seek an approach to help customers quickly comprehend a product review through questions. Questions are often more attractive for customers to read than plain opinion sentences are. In other words, we aim to find a concise set of questions that are addressed by a given review as well as cover the main points of it. Many users have certain questions about a product in mind and want to look at online reviews to see if their questions can be answered; but examining all lengthy reviews is too time-consuming. Given the concise set of questions for a review, users can quickly understand the review and may further read it only if they have similar questions in their minds.

Directly synthesizing such questions is too intimidating. Thanks to the emergence of Community Question Answering (CQA), large e-commerce websites now offer CQA services for their products. A notable example is Amazon's Customer Questions & Answers service[1]. In this paper, our goal is to retrieve real-world user questions to summarize individual reviews. Take the following segment of a real-world review[2] from Amazon as an example:

> autofocus. Its still worse than most cameras on the market, but its certainly better than the shot ruining autofocus of the first version. I like to use the DJI Ronin stabilizer and so autofocus is vital to me. I can't count how many times the a7s couldn't keep up with a subject simply walking forward. This camera does a much better job tracking subjects, although still far from perfect.

As we can see, this segment of review describes some personal experience with the camera's *autofocus* feature and compares it with another camera *a7s*. On the other hand, a real relevant question[3] was asked and answered on Amazon's CQA service as shown below:

> **Q:** Does it have a fast autofocus?
> **A:** Autofocus is in the middle of the pack I'd say. The a7rii has faster autofocus, (so does the a6000 for that matter, a $500 camera) but this is better than the first a7s.

This question asked about *autofocus* feature and can well represent the semantic of the segment of the above review. Meanwhile, since it is a question, users with similar questions in their minds would be very interested in further reading the review if they see this question as part of the summary of the review. Thus, this question would be a good candidate to retrieve for this review. Moreover, directly retrieving this question could be challenging given the short length of the question, but we can exploit the answers of the question. For example, this particular answer also discussed the comparison with *a7s*. Using it would be helpful to measure the relevance between the question and review.

This task of summarizing a product review through user questions is a challenging task. First of all, user generated reviews are usually long, ranged from hundreds to thousands of words, while questions are much shorter. Directly matching questions to a review may lead to unsatisfactory results. Second, a product review often discusses multiple aspects of a product. The set of retrieved questions for a given review should cover as many aspects as possible so that customers have a comprehensive understanding of the review. Last but not the least, the questions should not be redundant.

To tackle these challenges, we develop a two-stage framework to achieve the goal of retrieving a set of non-redundant questions to represent a product review. We first employ a probabilistic retrieval model to retrieve candidate questions based on their relevance scores to a review. We further leverage answers to a question to bridge the vocabulary gap between a review and a question. To remove redundancy in the candidate question set, we propose a set function that is used to re-rank the retrieved questions with the goal of diversifying the questions. Particularly, the set function satisfies monotone submodularity such that it can be efficiently optimized by a greedy algorithm. The main contributions of this paper can be summarized as follows:

- We introduce a new task of summarizing a product review by real-world user questions. To the best of our knowledge, no prior work has been done, as the existing work on review summarization focuses on extracting opinion sentences from product reviews.
- We propose a two-stage approach consisting of question retrieval and question diversification. Questions are retrieved based on query likelihood language models by incorporating query priors and answers.
- Question diversification is based on submodular optimization by considering both question coverage and non-redundancy. The choice of monotone submodular functions enables an efficient greedy algorithm for question diversification.
- We create and annotate a dataset for evaluation by manually locating and editing relevant questions for reviews in two product categories. We will make the data publicly available, which can be used for similar research. We conduct thorough experiments on the dataset and demonstrate the effectiveness of our proposed approach.

2. RELATED WORK

2.1 Review Summarization

Automatic review summarization has been a hot research topic over the past decade. Different from standard text summarization [7], which aims to generate a concise summary for a single [31] or multi-document [8], review summarization aims to integrate users' opinions for a large collection of reviews with respect to a product [23, 36]. The key idea is to identify the key specifications of a product and opinion sentences towards each specification. Detailed analysis of state-of-the-art literature can be found in [26, 14, 21]. Our problem of aligning questions to a review is similar to text summarization problem, with the goal of finding relevant and non-redundant questions (summary) for a review (document). It is also similar to review summarization, but the difference is that opinion-based summarization focuses on sentence or phrase extraction from reviews, while ours focuses on using relevant questions to represent the main points discussed in a review. By doing this, we are able to create more "relevant" summaries of reviews for potential buyers.

2.2 Question Retrieval

Our goal of finding a set of representative questions to summarize reviews is similar to question retrieval in the field of community question answering (CQA). The key problem is to quantify the similarity between newly generated user

[1]http://www.amazon.com/gp/forum/content/qa-guidelines.html
[2]http://www.amazon.com/Sony-ILCE7SM2-Full-Frame-Mirrorless-Interchangeable/product-reviews/B0158SRJVQ/
[3]http://www.amazon.com/Sony-ILCE7SM2-Full-Frame-Mirrorless-Interchangeable/dp/B0158SRJVQ/

questions and curated questions so that corresponding answers can be used to answer those newly generated questions. Examples of work include Zhou et al. [39] who firstly proposed a context-aware model for addressing the lexical gap problem between questions; and Zhou et al. [40] who designed an elegant study to model the question representations with metadata powered deep neural networks. However, question retrieval in CQA is different from our problem in two aspects. First, newly generated user questions and historical questions are "parallel texts", while user reviews and questions are highly asymmetric on the information they convey. Second, newly generated questions that are used to retrieve similar questions are usually short (i.e., less than 20 words), while user reviews are longer (usually more than 100 words).

Our problem also relates to automatic question generation from text data. Zhao et al., [38] developed a method to automatically generate questions from short user queries in CQA. Chali et al., [4] developed a method to generate all possible questions in regards a topic. One limitation of these studies is that questions are generated based on template, so they might not be representative of real user questions. Our study is different, as we aim to select relevant questions that can be used to summarize user reviews from real-user question archives.

2.3 Text Retrieval with Verbose Queries

As our goal is to use long reviews to find short representative questions as summaries, our problem relates to the problem of information retrieval with verbose queries [10]. Due to term redundancy, query sparsity, and difficulty in identifying key concepts, verbose queries often result in null results. In tackling these challenges, recent studies have developed techniques to re-compose queries. Examples include query reduction [15, 12], query reformulation [5, 35], and query segmentation [1, 27]. However, the errors accumulated during the query transformation process cannot be corrected during the retrieval phase. In our study, we do not split long reviews into sentences or phrases, and use the text chunks to retrieve relevant questions. Instead, we utilize a two-stage framework: 1) use the entire review as a query to retrieve relevant questions; and 2) after retrieving a set of questions, we employ a diversity objective function to encourage question diversity. To the best of our knowledge, no existing work attempts to retrieve non-redundant questions to summarize a product review.

3. PROBLEM CHARACTERIZATION

3.1 Problem Statement

Our task is to use a set of questions to summarize a product review. The review in turn is supposed to contain the answers to those questions. Introducing this feature to e-commerce platforms is beneficial for customers who want to quickly capture the main idea of lengthy reviews before reading the details. Consider a product database with m products. Each product i is associated with a set of reviews $R^{(i)} = \{r_1^{(i)}, ..., r_{m_i}^{(i)}\}$ where m_i is the number of reviewers for product i. Each review can be represented by a bag of words. Meanwhile, we have a question database/corpus $Q = \{q^{(1)}, ..., q^{(n)}\}$ where the questions are crawled from Community Question Answering (CQA) sites. Given a review $r_j^{(i)}$ of product i, our task is to select a small subset of questions $S \subseteq Q$ to summarize the review.

Similar to other text summarization tasks [24], the quality of selected questions can be quantified by a set function $\mathcal{F} : 2^Q \to \mathbb{R}$. In addition, the selected subset S should satisfy certain constraints. Formally, our task is to find the optimal question subset S^* defined as the following combinatorial optimization problem:

$$\begin{aligned} S^* &= \arg\max_{S \subseteq Q} \mathcal{F}(S) \\ s.t. &: \sum_{q \in S} c(q) \leq b, \end{aligned} \tag{1}$$

where $c(\cdot)$ is a constraint function defined on q, and $b \geq 0$ is a constant threshold. For example, if we want to enforce that the total length of all the selected questions should not exceed 50 words, we can define $c(\cdot)$ as a function to calculate the length of each question and set $b = 50$. Similarly, we can define a constraint to restrain the total number of questions in the set.

The set function $\mathcal{F}$ in Eqn.(1) measures the quality of the selected question subset S. The choice of $\mathcal{F}$ depends on the property of the questions that we desire. In general, Eqn.(1) would be an NP-hard problem. Fortunately, if $\mathcal{F}$ satisfies non-decreasing submodular [6], the optimization problem can be solved by efficient greedy algorithms with a close approximation. We introduce the background on submodular functions in Section 3.2.

It is worth noting that we do not solve Eqn.(1) directly over all the possible questions in the database. Otherwise, it would be too time-consuming given the sheer size of all available questions on CQA. Instead, we retrieve a set of potentially relevant questions first by using information retrieval techniques, e.g., obtaining the top 100 questions based on their relevance to a given review. We will introduce the question retrieval models in Section 4.2. Given these questions, we then apply Eqn.(1) to select a few questions (e.g., 5) as the final results by considering both question coverage and diversity. Thus, this module can be viewed as re-ranking for achieving diversified results. We present our formulation of Eqn.(1) in Section 4.3.

3.2 Submodular Functions

Submodular functions are discrete functions that model laws of diminishing returns [30]. They have been used in a wide range of applications such as sensor networks [16], information diffusion [9], and recommender systems [29]. Recently, it has been explored in multi-document summarization [19, 20]. Following the notations introduced in the previous section, some basic definitions of submodular functions are given as follows.

Definition 1. A set function $\mathcal{F} : 2^Q \to \mathbb{R}$ is submodular if for any subset $S, T \subseteq Q$,

$$\mathcal{F}(S) + \mathcal{F}(T) \geq \mathcal{F}(S \cap T) + \mathcal{F}(S \cup T).$$

Definition 2. A set function $\mathcal{F} : 2^Q \to \mathbb{R}$ is modular if for any subset $S, T \subseteq Q$,

$$\mathcal{F}(S) + \mathcal{F}(T) = \mathcal{F}(S \cap T) + \mathcal{F}(S \cup T).$$

Modular set functions also satisfy submodularity according to Definition 1.

DEFINITION 3. A set function $\mathcal{F} : 2^Q \rightarrow \mathbb{R}$ is monotone, if for any subset $S \subseteq T \subseteq Q$,

$$\mathcal{F}(S) \leq \mathcal{F}(T).$$

The class of submodular functions enjoys a good property with concave functions as follows.

THEOREM 1. *If $\mathcal{F} : 2^Q \rightarrow \mathbb{R}$ is a submodular function, $g(S) = \phi(\mathcal{F}(S))$, where $\phi(\cdot)$ is a concave function, is also a submodular function* [30].

In Section 4.3, we discuss the construction of $\mathcal{F}(S)$ and demonstrate that it is submodular and monotone based on Theorem 1. These properties enable efficient greedy approximation algorithms [25] for the optimization problem.

4. METHODS

4.1 Overview

In order to provide customers with "hints" of a review, the questions should be representative of the review. For example, if a review discusses *image quality* and *battery life* of a camera, relevant questions would be related to these two features, e.g., *"Does the camera take high quality macro images?"* or *"How many days of battery life can you get with this camera?"*. In addition, the questions are expected to be dissimilar to each other such that there is little redundant information covered in the question set. For example, the question *"How is the battery life?"* is redundant as it contains similar semantic information with the aforementioned question related to *battery life*.

With the dual goal of relevancy and diversity, we design a two-stage framework to find a set of questions that can be used to summarize a review. We first utilize a probabilistic retrieval model to select a smaller set of candidate questions that are relevant to a given review from a large pool of questions crawled from the CQA website. Considering the possible semantic mismatch between the review and question corpus, we incorporate answers into the retrieval model to resolve the vocabulary gap between them. After obtaining the top ranked relevant questions, we design a set function to re-rank questions in the candidate list with the goal of removing redundant questions. The final question set is derived through the measurement of a trade-off between the relevance of selected questions to the review as well as the diversity of the questions.

In the following sections, we present the query likelihood language models to generate a candidate question list (Section 4.2) and introduce our set function to re-rank candidate questions (Section 4.3) with an efficient greedy algorithm (Section 4.4) for optimization.

4.2 Question Retrieval

4.2.1 Query Likelihood Language Model

To retrieve candidate questions that are relevant to a given review, we employ query likelihood language model [2]. We assume that before drafting a review, a user would think about what questions he/she would like to answer. Therefore, the relevance score of a question q retrieved by a review r is computed as the log-likelihood of the conditional probability $P(q|r)$ of the question given the review:

$$\text{score}(r, q) = \log P(q|r) \tag{2}$$

Similar to other text retrieval tasks, a review can be regarded as a sample drawn from a language model built on a question pool. Formally, using the Bayes' theorem, the conditional probability can be calculated by:

$$\begin{aligned} P(q|r) &= \frac{P(r|q)P(q)}{P(r)} \\ &\propto P(r|q)P(q) \end{aligned} \tag{3}$$

In Eqn.(3), $P(r)$ denoted the probability of the review r, which can be ignored for the purpose of ranking questions because it is a constant for all questions. Thus, we only need to compute $P(r|q)$ and $P(q)$. $P(r|q)$ represents the conditional probability of review r given question q. We can apply the unigram language model to calculate $P(r|q)$:

$$P(r|q) = \prod_{w \in r} P(w|q) \tag{4}$$

where $P(w|q)$ is the probability of observing word w in a question q. The word probability can be estimated based on maximum likelihood estimation (MLE) with Jelinek-Mercer smoothing [37] to avoid zero probabilities of unseen words in q:

$$P(w|q) = (1 - \lambda)P_{ml}(w|q) + \lambda P_{ml}(w|C) \tag{5}$$

where λ is a smoothing parameter and C denotes the whole question corpus. The MLE estimates for $P_{ml}(w|q)$ and $P_{ml}(w|Q)$ are:

$$P_{ml}(w|q) = \frac{\text{count}(w, q)}{|q|} \tag{6}$$

$$P_{ml}(w|C) = \frac{\text{count}(w, C)}{|C|} \tag{7}$$

where $\text{count}(w, q)$ and $\text{count}(w, C)$ denote the term frequency of w in q and C, respectively. $|\cdot|$ denotes the total number of words in q or C.

$P(q)$ in Eqn.(3) denotes the prior probability of the question q regardless of review. It can encode our prior preference about questions. In order to summarize a review, we prefer shorter questions so that users can digest information faster. Hence, we reward shorter questions by making the prior probability inversely proportional to the length of the question as follows:

$$P(q) \propto \frac{1}{|q|} \tag{8}$$

$P(q)$ can also be computed by other ways. For example, if there exists rating information of the questions on the CQA website, we can use it to prefer questions with higher ratings.

By plugging Eqn.(4) and Eqn.(8) into Eqn.(3), we can obtain the relevance scores for all questions in the question corpus.

4.2.2 Incorporating Answers

Since questions and reviews are not "parallel texts", there exists vocabulary gap between the two corpus. As shown in the real-world example in Section 1, directly retrieving this question could be challenging given the short length of the question. To address this issue, we incorporate the corresponding answers of the question corpus to estimate the parameters in the language model defined in Eqn.(5) [34]. After including all the answers a of question q, the relevance score becomes:

$$\text{score}\big(r, (q, a)\big) = \log P\big((q, a)|r\big). \tag{9}$$

Based on the Bayes' theorem, we have:

$$\begin{aligned} P((q,a)|r) &= \frac{P(r|(q,a))P(q,a)}{P(r)} \\ &\propto P(r|(q,a))P(q,a) \\ &= P(r|(q,a))P(a|q)P(q) \\ &\propto P(r|(q,a))P(q) \end{aligned} \tag{10}$$

The above derivation is based on the following reasoning. Similar to Eqn.(3), $P(r)$ is a constant for all the questions, and thus it can be ignored. We further assume the probability of answers a given a question q is uniform, and thus $p(q,a)$ is proportional to $p(q)$.

We then leverage both question and answers to estimate $P(r|(q,a))$:

$$\begin{aligned} P(r|(q,a)) &= \prod_{w\in r} P(w|(q,a)) \\ &= \prod_{w\in r} (1-\lambda)P_{mx}(w|(q,a)) + \lambda P_{ml}(w|C') \end{aligned} \tag{11}$$

where C' denotes the whole question and answe corpus, and $P_{ml}(w|C')$ is the collection language model which is estimated based on Eqn.(7). λ is a smoothing parameter. $P_{mx}(w|(q,a))$ denotes the word probability estimated from the question and answers. It takes a weighted average of maximum-likelihood estimates from question and answers, respectively:

$$\begin{aligned} P_{mx}(w|(q,a)) &= (1-\alpha)P_{ml}(w|q) + \alpha P_{ml}(w|a) \\ &= (1-\alpha)\frac{\text{count}(w,q)}{|q|} + \alpha\frac{\text{count}(w,a)}{|a|} \end{aligned} \tag{12}$$

where $\alpha \in [0,1]$ is a trade-off cofficient.

The prior probability $P(q)$ can be calculated in the same way as in Eqn.(8). By plugging $P(r|(q,a))$ and $P(q)$ in Eqn.(10), we can obtain the relevance scores in Eqn.(9). The top-k questions are then retrieved as candidates and to be re-ranked by promoting diversity among them.

4.3 Question Diversification

Similar to other text summarization tasks, the final questions presented to users should avoid redundancy as much as possible. At the same time, these questions are still relevant to the review and can convey the main information in the review. In other words, we aim to achieve a dual goal in the final question set: relevancy and diversity. Mathematically, we formulate our objective function as a combinatorial optimization problem by following Eqn.(1) as follows:

$$\begin{aligned} &\arg\max_{S\subseteq V} \mathcal{F}(S) = \mathcal{L}(S) + \eta\mathcal{R}(S) \\ &\qquad s.t. \sum_{q\in S} \text{length}(q) \leq b \end{aligned} \tag{13}$$

where V is the candidate question set obtained by the question retrieval component. $\mathcal{L}(S)$ measures the relevance of the final question set S with respect to the review. $\mathcal{R}(S)$ measures the diversity of the final question set. η is a constant for diversity regularization. The constraint $\sum_{q\in S}$ length$(q) \leq b$ requires that the word count of all the questions is less than a threshold b, which is usually a small number because a concise summary is desirable for users.

The set function $\mathcal{L}(S)$ is defined to encourage the selection of questions with high relevance scores. Specifically, we use the logarithm of sum of offset relevance scores of questions in the final question set S. Formally,

$$\mathcal{L}(S) = \log\big(\sum_{q\in S} \text{score}(q) - c\big) \tag{14}$$

where score(q) is the relevance score of question q. It can be calculated based on the query likelihood language models without (Eqn.(2)) or with (Eqn.(9)) incorporating answers (for convenience of presentation, we omit argument r and a). $c = \min_{q\in V}(\text{score}(q))$ is a constant to ensure the argument of $\log(\cdot)$ is always positive.

The set function $\mathcal{R}(S)$ is designed to select as "diverse" questions as possible. The function will score a set of questions high if those questions do not semantically overlap with each other. Formally,

$$\mathcal{R}(S) = \sum_{i=1}^{T} \log(\epsilon + \sum_{q\in P_i\cap S} r_q), \tag{15}$$

where $P_i, i = 1, ..., T$ indicates a partition of the candidate question set V into T disjoint clusters, and r_q indicates the reward of selecting question q in the final summary set. Specifically, $r_q = \frac{1}{|V|}\sum_{v\in V} w_{qv}$, where w_{qv} is the similarity score between question q and v [20]. Applying the logarithm function will make one cluster have diminishing gain if one question has been chosen from it. In this way, $\mathcal{R}(S)$ rewards question selection from a cluster in which none of the questions have been selected. Addition of a small positive value ϵ to the argument of the logarithm function guarantees the argument is positive.

THEOREM 2. *Both $\mathcal{L}(S)$ and $\mathcal{R}(S)$ are monotone submodular functions.*

PROOF. The logarithm function is non-decreasing concave function. The functions inside each logarithm function are non-negative modular functions (see Definition 2), so they are monotone (see Definition 3). Applying the logarithm function, which is a concave function, to non-decreasing modular functions yield submodular functions (see Theorem 1). For $\mathcal{R}(S)$, the summation of submodular functions results in a submodular function as well. Hence, the set function $\mathcal{F}(S)$ satisfies monotonicity and submodularity. □

4.4 Greedy Algorithm

The submodular optimization problem in Eqn.(13) is still NP-hard, but Nemhauser et al. [25] has proven that the approximated solution achieved by a greedy algorithm is guaranteed to be within $(1-1/e)$ of the optimal solution. It is worth noting that this is a worst case bound, and in most cases the quality of the solution obtained would be much better than this bound suggests. Hence, we describe an efficient approximation algorithm by utilizing monotone submodular properties of $\mathcal{F}(S)$. Algorithm 1 shows a greedy algorithm that finds approximation solution to the optimization problem in Eqn.(13). The algorithm selects the best question q^* that brings maximum increase in $\mathcal{F}(S)$ at stage i, as long as the total length of questions l in the selected question set S does not exceed the threshold b. It terminates when none of the questions in the candidate set V satisfy the length threshold constraint $l + \text{length}(q) < b$.

Algorithm 1: The Greedy Algorithm

```
input  : candidate question set V with relevance
         scores, length threshold b, diversity
         trade-off η
output: selected question set S, total length l
initialization S ← ∅, A ← ∅, l ← 0
for i = 1 to |V| do
    for q ∈ V\S do
        if l + length(q) < b then
            S_q ← S ∪ {q}
            L(S_q) ← log ( Σ_{q∈S_q} score(q) − c)
            R(S_q) ←
            Σ_{t=1}^{T} log(ε + Σ_{q∈S_q} (1/|V|) Σ_{v∈V} w_{qv})
            F(S_q) ← L(S_q) + ηR(S_q)
            A ← A ∪ {q}
        end
    end
    if A = ∅ then
        return S, l
    end
    q* ← arg max_{q∈A} F(S_q)
    S ← S ∪ {q*}
    l ← l + length(q*)
    A ← ∅
end
return S, l
```

5. EXPERIMENTS

5.1 Data Collection and Annotation

One of the fundamental challenges is the lack of ground-truth data available for evaluating the quality of retrieved questions. Since the proposed task is a document summarization problem, we follow the same evaluation method and metric that are used for text summarization task in NIST Document Understanding Conferences (DUC)[4].

We choose to focus on products from Amazon[5], as it displays various kinds of products with associated reviews and question and answering (QA) data contributed by real end users. We first decide on which product category to focus in our experiment. We select products from two categories, camera and TV, and download their QA data. We rely on NLTK[6] to preprocess the content of the data, including sentence segmentation, word tokenization, lemmatization and stopword removal. We remove meaningless questions whose lengths are shorter than 3 words. We also discard questions that are longer than 25 words, which are supposed to convey detailed information, as they might not be general to summarize many product reviews. The preprocessing step yields 331 products in the digital camera category and 226 in the TV category. Table 1 summarizes the questions and answers of products for each category.

After obtaining the QA data, we need to create a review dataset for evaluation. We first select the top 100 products retrieved from the two product categories, each for 50 products. For each product, we select the top 5 reviews ranked by Amazon's *Helpfulness* voting system, and retain

[4]http://duc.nist.gov/duc2004/
[5]http://www.amazon.com/
[6]http://www.nltk.org/

Table 1: Statistics of Question Data for Camera and TV Category

	Camera	TV
Number of Products	331	226
Number of Questions	8,781	12,926
Average Question Length	11.898	11.179
Vocabulary Size of Questions	1,196	1,318
Vocabulary Size of Answers	2,948	2,541
Vocabulary Size in Total	2,987	2,668

only reviews whose length is between 200 and 2,000. After obtaining the 500 reviews for the two product categories, we follow the guidelines for summary generation of NIST DUC[7]. Specifically, we request 10 graduate students to read the reviews and generate questions for each of them. The questions, which is regarded as a summary, should cover all the product features that are discussed in a product review, but not overlap with each other with respects to product features. To ensure the generated questions are representative for real-user questions, we ask students to first select questions from the question pool obtained through the crawling process. If no question can be selected, they are allowed to write their own questions. For each review, a student can generate up to 10 questions. The maximum of total length of all questions is 100. In order to accomplish the annotation task, 10 students are equally divided into two groups. The students from the first group select or write questions for 100 reviews, and the students from another group examine the quality of questions. The students from the two groups will do one more round of annotation together to resolve any conflicts. It usually takes 50 minutes to finish question generation and examination for a single review, which is a very time-consuming process since the annotators should consider both relevancy and diversity. We apply the same preprocessing steps (as we did for the QA data) to process the annotated review data. The averaged review length for camera dataset is 814.976 and the averaged review length for TV dataset is 582.932.

5.2 Retrieval/Summarization Systems

In order to evaluate the performance of our proposed approach, we implement the following six summarization systems based on the variant of our approach:
(1) Query Likelihood Model: The query generation probability is estimated based on question corpus (Eqn.(3)).
(2) Combined Query Likelihood Model: The query generation probability is estimated based on question and answer corpus (Eqn.(10)).
(3) Query Likelihood Model with Maximal Marginal Relevance (MMR): re-rank retrieved questions by query likelihood model (system (1)) using MMR [3], which is designed to remove redundancy while preserving the relevance by using a trade-off parameter σ. Note that MMR is non-monotone submodular, so a greedy algorithm is not theoretically guaranteed to be a constant factor approximation algorithm [20].
(4) Combined Query Likelihood Model with Maximal Marginal Relevance: re-rank retrieved questions by combined query likelihood model (system (2)) using MMR.
(5) Query Likelihood Model with Submodular Function: re-rank retrieved questions by query likelihood model (system

[7]http://duc.nist.gov/duc2004/t1.2.summarization.instructions

(1)) using submodular function (Eqn.(13)).
(6) Combined Query Likelihood Model with Submodular Function: re-rank retrieved questions by combined query likelihood model (system (2)) using submodular function.

For system (1) and (2), we choose the Jelinek-Mercer smoothing parameter λ between 0.1 and 0.3 (Eqn.(5)). For system (3) and (4), we choose the trade-off parameter σ between 0.1 and 1.0. For system (5) and (6), we set the number of questions in the candidate set V (Eqn.(13)) as 100, the length threshold b as 50, 75, and 100, and the number of clusters (Eqn.(15)) as 10. We rely on K-means clustering algorithm to partition V, which leverages IDF-weighted term vector for each question. We also experiment with different settings of smoothing parameter α (Eqn.(12)) and diversity regularizer η (Eqn.(13)), which will be shown in Section 6.3.

5.3 Evaluation Metrics

We follow the evaluation of conventional summarization systems to measure the performance of the aforementioned six systems for finding questions to summarize a product review. Specifically, we rely on ROUGE [18] (Recall-Oriented Understudy for Gisting Evaluation), which measures how well a system-generated summary matches the content in a human-generated summary based on n-gram co-occurrence. In our experiment, we compare unigram and bigram-based ROUGE scores.

One limitation of ROUGE score is that it assumes all words play equally important roles in a document. However, the words related to product aspects such as "image" or "screen" are more important than stopwords such as "does" or "it", which are frequently occurred in questions. Therefore, we also use TFIDF cosine similarity, which rewards important words by inverse document frequency. The definition of cosine similarity function can be found in [20].

6. RESULTS

6.1 Qualitative Analysis

We first show the feasibility of our method to retrieve non-redundant questions that can be used to summarize a review. We take one review[8] from the digital camera category from Amazon as an example. The review length is around 700 tokens after preprocessing. The following segment shows the main aspects that the author talks about:

> ...Highlights: 14 bit uncompressed RAW, 4k video internal recording, new 50% quiet shutter rated at 500,000 cycles, 5-axis stabilization, better EVF, better signal to noise ratio...

Table 2 shows the questions edited by a human annotator. The first five questions are selected from the question corpus, while the last two are created by the annotator. Basically, the questions correspond to the top features highlighted in the review segment, and covers all the aspects that are discussed in the review, including RAW files, 4K recording, shutter, stabilization, EVF, low light performance, and sensor. The last two aspects are not mentioned in the segment but are discussed in the main body. Table 3 shows the top-10 questions retrieved by query likelihood language model smoothed by answers. They cover the following aspects, camera's performance in low light (the 1st, 3rd, 5th, and 7th question), comparison between different camera models (the 2nd question), lens adaption (the 4th question), video recording (6th question), shutter (the 9th and 10th question), and a general one (the 8th question). It shows that three of the top-5 results are redundant with respect to low light performance, and the last two questions overlap with each other with respect to shutter noise.

Table 4 shows the top-10 questions selected by the submodular function. The re-ranked questions cover the following aspects: camera's performance in low light (the 1st, 6th, 8th, and 10th question), comparison between different camera models (the 2nd question), shutter (the 3rd and 9th question), video recording (4th question), lens adaption (the 5th question), and RAW files (7th question). Com-

[8]http://www.amazon.com/gp/customer-reviews/R360W96STA0KUI?ASIN=B0158SRJVQ

Table 2: Human Annotation

(1) How does this camera take videos in low light?
(2) Does this camera provide RAW Image format?
(3) Does this camera record 4K internally?
(4) Does this camera have image stabilization?
(5) How would you describe the shutter noise?
(6) Does the EVF work well in bright conditions?
(7) Is there much of a difference in term of sensor?

Table 3: Questions Retrieved by Query Likelihood Model

(1) What were the improvements to the low light capabilities of the sensor?
(2) What are the key differences between the a7, the a7r and the a7s?
(3) How is the camera for indoor low light? I've had Sony point and shoots in the past and the interior shots had so much noise.
(4) What lens adapter would allow someone to use canon ef lenses on the a7s and a7s ii with reasonable autofocus performance?
(5) One review claims the camera has very poor low light performance for video, lots of video noise. Comments from videographers?
(6) Do you need a special external recorder for 4k video like it is with α7s?
(7) Very curious to see how it does in low light. did sony really solve the noise problem??
(8) Where is it better? or is it?
(9) Does the a7II have a silent electronic shutter like the a7s?
(10) Is the shutter noise less pronounced than the a7?

Table 4: Questions Reranked by Submodular Function

(1) What were the improvements to the low light capabilities of the sensor?
(2) What are the key differences between the a7, the a7r and the a7s?
(3) Is the shutter noise less pronounced than the a7?
(4) Does sony a7r ii have the maximum aperture of f3.5 when video recording as other sony camera?
(5) What lens adapter would allow someone to use canon ef lenses on the a7s and a7s ii with reasonable autofocus performance?
(6) How is the camera for indoor low light? I've had Sony point and shoots in the past and the interior shots had so much noise.
(7) Raw files, Would I see higher noise in the raw files?
(8) One review claims the camera has very poor low light performance for video, lots of video noise. Comments from videographers?
(9) Does the a7II have a silent electronic shutter like the a7s?
(10) Very curious to see how it does in low light. did sony really solve the noise problem??

pared with questions retrieved by query likelihood model, even though there still exist four questions that are relevant to low light performance, three of the related questions are demoted from the top due to their redundancy with the top-1 question. The questions asking camera model comparison and shutter noise are promoted because they are semantically dissimilar to the top-1 question. There are non-redundant questions in top-5 positions of the re-ranked list. The re-ranking function is able to promote one question related to RAW files, which is not included in the candidate question set retrieved by query likelihood model. In addition, it also demotes the general question which was ranked at the 8th position, because it is not representative of questions asking product aspects.

By comparing the human annotation with retrieved/ranked question set, there are overlaps such as low light performance, RAW files, 4K video recording, and shutter noise. Still, there are three aspects annotated by annotator that are not covered in the reranked question list: image stabilization, sensor, and EVF. It is not surprising that the retrieved questions do not cover the last two aspects, sensor and EVF, as the annotator does not select relevant questions from the question pool either. Meanwhile, the questions related to comparison between different models and adaption of lenses are not selected by annotator. However, if we take a close look at the review, we can find some relevant sentences that can be used to answer the retrieved questions regarding the two questions:

> ...Sony, having already introduced 2nd gen versions on the A7 and A7R, is now applying the same treatment to the A7S. The A7S II blends and combines a variety of features from the two aforementioned cameras... The 7S II can record internally, thus eliminating the additional cost of an external recorder which in turn can allow one to spend the money on additional lenses...

Considering the nature that summarizing a review is highly subjective, the questions generated by the proposed automatic retrieval and reranking method are reasonable and cover most of the aspects discussed in a product review.

6.2 Quantitative Analysis

The results on the two datasets (introduced in Section 5.1) achieved by different summarization systems (introduced in Section 5.2) are shown in Table 5 and 6. We set the total length threshold as 50, 75, and 100, respectively. Boldface stands for the best performance per column with respect to each length threshold. We conduct paired t-test for all comparisons of results achieved by two different methods. † indicates the corresponding method outperforms the simple query likelihood baseline statistically significantly, and ‡ indicates the corresponding method outperforms all the other methods significantly.

On the TV dataset, the combined query likelihood language model ($\text{QL}(Q, A)$) yields better results than simple query likelihood language model ($\text{QL}(Q)$) does in terms of all evaluation metrics for different length threshold settings. Using MMR to rerank questions achieves competitive results against $\text{QL}(Q, A)$ and $\text{QL}(Q)$ do. Using the submodular function to re-rank the questions retrieved by simple and combined query likelihood language model (denoted as $\text{QL}(Q)$ +sub and $\text{QL}(Q, A)$ + sub, respectively) show better results over corresponding retrieval models for all evaluation metrics. $\text{QL}(Q, A)$ + sub achieves significant better results than all the other systems do at 0.01 level for all evaluation metrics, except for bigram-ROUGE precision score when $b = 50$ and TFIDF cosine similarity score when $b = 100$.

On the camera dataset, unfortunately, incorporating answer corpus in the query likelihood language model does not bring improvement on the ROUGE and TFIDF cosine similarity scores. One possible reason is that the vocabulary size of answer collections for the camera category is larger than that of the TV category according to Table 1. Incorporating an answer collection might add many irrelevant words to the language model, such that the results retrieved by $\text{QL}(Q, A)$ contain more noises than that by $\text{QL}(Q)$. After promoting diversity in the retrieved question set using MMR, $\text{QL}(Q)$ + MMR is able to achieve slightly higher or competitive results against $\text{QL}(Q)$ except for bigram ROUGE scores when $b = 100$; but $\text{QL}(Q, A)$ + MMR yields slightly inferior results against $\text{QL}(Q, A)$.

Even though the combined retrieval model does not help increase the ROUGE and TFIDF cosine similarity scores, $\text{QL}(Q, A)$ + sub yields the highest unigram-ROUGE scores. The precision and F_1 scores are significantly higher than that by $\text{QL}(Q)$ ($p < 0.01$). $\text{QL}(Q)$ + sub achieves the best TFIDF cosine similarity scores without significant difference with that by $\text{QL}(Q)$. The results on bigram-ROUGE scores are mixed. The highest bigram-ROUGE scores achieved by either $\text{QL}(Q)$ or $\text{QL}(Q, A)$ are significantly better than the score achieved by simple query likelihood at level 0.01, except the bigram-ROUGE recall score and F_1 score when b is set to 100.

In summary, query likelihood model incorporating answers is able to yield better summarization performance when the vocabulary size of the answer collection is moderate. The results achieved by query likelihood models with the submodular function are promising compared with conventional diversity promotion technique. The combined query likelihood model with submodular function yields significantly better performance on the TV dataset for both ROUGE and TFIDF cosine similarity metrics. This model also shows the potential ability to correct the order of a question list by promoting diversified results on the camera dataset.

6.3 Parameter Analysis

In order to examine the impact of the smoothing parameter α of the answer collection (Eqn.(12)) and diversity regularizer η for the sumbodular function (Eqn.(13)), we examine the summarization performance achieved by system (2) and (6) (introduced in Section 5.2) with different settings of α and η on the TV and camera datasets. Figure 1 shows the unigram ROUGE F_1 scores achieved by different α between 0 and 1 with an interval of 0.1 when the length threshold is set to 50. The ROUGE curves achieved with other threshold settings follow similar patterns so we leave them out. For the TV dataset, as shown in the previous section, incorporating answers benefits the simple query likelihood language model estimated on the question collection. When α is between 0 and 0.3, the unigram ROUGE F_1 scores increase with the benefit of the integration of the answer collection. After that, the scores decrease when α is getting larger, meaning that imposing too much weights on the estimates from the answer collection is harmful to the performance of retrieval model. For the camera dataset, results have shown

Table 5: Summarization Results on TV Dataset

L	Method	COSINE	ROUGE1-R	ROUGE1-P	ROUGE1-F_1	ROUGE2-R	ROUGE2-P	ROUGE2-F_1
50	QL(Q)	0.191	0.248	0.177	0.192	0.0440	0.0281	0.0313
	QL(Q, A)	0.211	0.267	0.190	0.205	0.0447	0.0303	0.0329
	QL + MMR	0.191	0.250	0.181	0.195	0.0443	0.0290	0.0320
	QL(Q, A) + MMR	0.207	0.263	0.189	0.204	0.0414	0.0292	0.0312
	QL(Q) + sub	0.219	0.268	0.190	0.206	0.0440	0.0302	0.0330
	QL(Q, A) + sub	**0.241**‡	**0.288**‡	**0.209**‡	**0.225**†	**0.0601**‡	**0.0409**	**0.0446**‡
75	QL(Q)	0.190	0.324	0.157	0.199	0.0590	0.0261	0.0335
	QL(Q, A)	0.199	0.334	0.161	0.203	0.0605	0.0273	0.0347
	QL(Q) + MMR	0.188	0.326	0.158	0.200	0.0580	0.0260	0.0330
	QL(Q, A) + MMR	0.199	0.336	0.162	0.205	0.0630	0.0290	0.0370
	QL(Q) + sub	0.208	0.332	0.161	0.203	0.0612	0.0274	0.0352
	QL(Q, A) + sub	**0.222**‡	**0.353**‡	**0.175**‡	**0.220**‡	**0.0797**‡	**0.0361**‡	**0.0462**‡
100	QL(Q)	0.179	0.372	0.137	0.190	0.0696	0.0237	0.0333
	QL(Q, A)	0.190	0.380	0.140	0.194	0.0746	0.0255	0.0355
	QL(Q) + MMR	0.177	0.376	0.139	0.192	0.0700	0.0240	0.0340
	QL(Q, A) + MMR	0.191	0.386	0.142	0.196	0.0800	0.0270	0.0370
	QL(Q) + sub	0.200	0.382	0.140	0.194	0.0757	0.0254	0.0357
	QL(Q, A) + sub	**0.206**†	**0.401**‡	**0.150**‡	**0.207**‡	**0.0921**‡	**0.0315**‡	**0.0441**‡

Table 6: Summarization Results on Camera Dataset

L	Method	COSINE	ROUGE1-R	ROUGE1-P	ROUGE1-F_1	ROUGE2-R	ROUGE2-P	ROUGE2-F_1
50	QL(Q)	0.111	0.218	0.260	0.227	0.0463	0.0520	0.0467
	QL(Q, A)	0.091	0.211	0.258	0.223	0.0406	0.0497	0.0427
	QL(Q) + MMR	0.111	0.218	0.263	0.229	0.0469	0.0531	0.0474
	QL(Q, A) + MMR	0.090	0.210	0.259	0.223	0.0401	0.0491	0.0422
	QL(Q) + sub	**0.112**	0.223	0.231	0.236	**0.0484**†	0.0585	0.0507
	QL(Q, A) + sub	0.093	**0.225**	**0.275**†	**0.238**†	0.0477	**0.0605**†	**0.0511**†
75	QL(Q)	0.109	0.286	0.231	0.245	0.0626	0.0474	0.0516
	QL(Q, A)	0.090	0.277	0.228	0.240	0.0530	0.0433	0.0455
	QL(Q) + MMR	0.110	0.288	0.234	0.248	0.0634	0.0482	0.0523
	QL(Q, A) + MMR	0.090	0.277	0.229	0.241	0.0528	0.0435	0.0456
	QL(Q) + sub	**0.116**	0.295	0.241	0.254	**0.0648**†	**0.0511**†	**0.0546**†
	QL(Q, A) + sub	0.102	**0.297**	**0.242**†	**0.256**†	0.0617	0.0509	0.0532
100	QL(Q)	0.110	0.342	0.209	0.249	0.0785	0.0447	0.0545
	QL(Q, A)	0.094	0.333	0.207	0.246	0.0661	0.0410	0.0484
	QL(Q) + MMR	0.110	0.344	0.211	0.251	0.0773	0.0445	0.0541
	QL(Q, A) + MMR	0.094	0.331	0.207	0.245	0.0656	0.0406	0.0481
	QL(Q) + sub	**0.116**	0.350	0.216	0.257	**0.0786**	0.0467	**0.0562**
	QL(Q, A) + sub	0.106	**0.352**	**0.217**†	**0.258**†	0.0759	**0.0474**†	0.0558

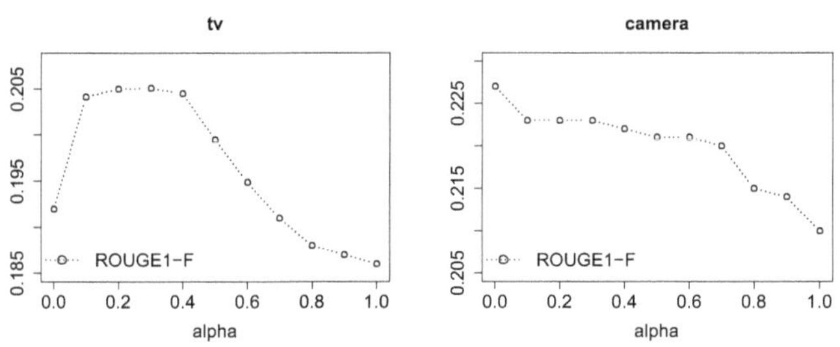

Figure 1: ROUGE-1 F_1 Scores on TV and Camera Datasets with different Weights of Answer Collection when $b = 50$

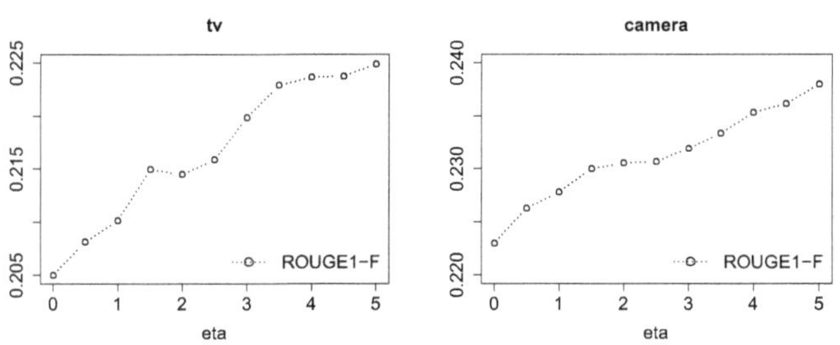

Figure 2: ROUGE-1 F_1 Scores on TV and Camera Datasets with Different Diversity Regularizer when $b = 50$

that the answer collection does not help increase the unigram ROUGE F_1 scores. With larger α values, the scores are getting smaller.

Figure 2 shows the impact of diversity regularizer η on the combined query likelihood language model. With the increasing η values, the unigram ROUGE F_1 scores increase on both datasets. These figures are consistent with previous findings that adding submodular function to retrieval models will improve the summarization results. It shows that $\eta = 5.0$ is a good choice for both datasets.

7. CONCLUSIONS AND FUTURE WORK

This paper addresses a new task: summarizing a review through questions. Questions are often more attractive for customers to read than plain opinion sentences. They can serve as "hints" for customers to decide whether they want to further read the review. To the best of our knowledge, no prior work has studied this task. We propose a two-stage approach consisting of question retrieval and question diversification. Submodular optimization is used to consider both question coverage and non-redundancy. To evaluate the proposed approach, we create and annotate a dataset by manually locating and editing questions for reviews in two product categories. The experiments demonstrate the proposed approach can effectively find relevant questions for review summarization.

This work is an initial step towards a promising research direction. In future work, we will utilize more information about products such as product specifications and question ratings to enrich the proposed question retrieval component. Regarding question diversification, we will explore other submodular functions. We also would like to deploy the proposed method to a real-world review system and measure the satisfaction of real users.

8. ACKNOWLEDGMENTS

The authors would like to thank Miao Jiang for data collection, anonymous reviewers for valuable comments, and TCL Research America for generous funding support.

9. REFERENCES

[1] M. Bendersky, W. B. Croft, and D. A. Smith. Joint annotation of search queries. In *ACL*, pages 102–111, 2011.

[2] A. Berger and J. Lafferty. Information retrieval as statistical translation. In *SIGIR*, pages 222–229, 1999.

[3] J. Carbonell and J. Goldstein. The use of mmr, diversity-based reranking for reordering documents and producing summaries. In *SIGIR*, pages 335–336, 1998.

[4] Y. Chali and S. A. Hasan. Towards automatic topical question generation. In *COLING*, pages 475–492, 2012.

[5] V. Dang and B. W. Croft. Query reformulation using anchor text. In *WSDM*, pages 41–50, 2010.

[6] S. Fujishige. *Submodular functions and optimization*, volume 58. Elsevier, 2005.

[7] J. Goldstein, M. Kantrowitz, V. Mittal, and J. Carbonell. Summarizing text documents: sentence selection and evaluation metrics. In *SIGIR*, pages 121–128, 1999.

[8] J. Goldstein, V. Mittal, J. Carbonell, and M. Kantrowitz. Multi-document summarization by sentence extraction. In *NAACL-ANLP Workshop on Automatic Summarization*, pages 40–48, 2000.

[9] M. Gomez Rodriguez, J. Leskovec, and A. Krause. Inferring networks of diffusion and influence. In *SIGKDD*, pages 1019–1028, 2010.

[10] M. Gupta and M. Bendersky. Information retrieval with verbose queries. In *SIGIR*, pages 1121–1124, 2015.

[11] M. Hu and B. Liu. Mining opinion features in customer reviews. In *AAAI*, volume 4, pages 755–760, 2004.

[12] S. Huston and W. B. Croft. Evaluating verbose query processing techniques. In *SIGIR*, pages 291–298, 2010.

[13] Y. Jo and A. H. Oh. Aspect and sentiment unification model for online review analysis. In *WSDM*, pages 815–824, 2011.

[14] H. D. Kim, K. Ganesan, P. Sondhi, and C. Zhai. Comprehensive review of opinion summarization. *UIUC Technical Report*, 2011.

[15] G. Kumaran and V. R. Carvalho. Reducing long queries using query quality predictors. In *SIGIR*, pages 564–571, 2009.

[16] J. Leskovec, A. Krause, C. Guestrin, C. Faloutsos, J. VanBriesen, and N. Glance. Cost-effective outbreak detection in networks. In *SIGKDD*, pages 420–429, 2007.

[17] F. Li, N. Liu, H. Jin, K. Zhao, Q. Yang, and X. Zhu. Incorporating reviewer and product information for review rating prediction. In *IJCAI*, volume 11, pages 1820–1825, 2011.

[18] C.-Y. Lin. Rouge: A package for automatic evaluation of summaries. In *Text summarization branches out: Proceedings of the ACL-04 workshop*, volume 8, 2004.

[19] H. Lin and J. Bilmes. Multi-document summarization via budgeted maximization of submodular functions. In *NAACL*, pages 912–920, 2010.

[20] H. Lin and J. Bilmes. A class of submodular functions for document summarization. In *ACL*, pages 510–520, 2011.

[21] B. Liu. Sentiment analysis and opinion mining. *Synthesis Lectures on Human Language Technologies*, 5(1):1–167, 2012.

[22] C.-L. Liu, W.-H. Hsaio, C.-H. Lee, G.-C. Lu, and E. Jou. Movie rating and review summarization in mobile environment. *IEEE Transactions on Systems, Man, and Cybernetics, Part C: Applications and Reviews*, 42(3):397–407, 2012.

[23] D. K. Ly, K. Sugiyama, Z. Lin, and M.-Y. Kan. Product review summarization from a deeper perspective. In *ACM/IEEE joint conference on Digital ibraries*, pages 311–314, 2011.

[24] I. Mani and M. T. Maybury. *Advances in automatic text summarization*, volume 293. MIT Press, 1999.

[25] G. L. Nemhauser, L. A. Wolsey, and M. L. Fisher. An analysis of approximations for maximizing submodular set functions-i. *Mathematical Programming*, 14(1):265–294, 1978.

[26] B. Pang and L. Lee. Opinion mining and sentiment analysis. *Foundations and trends in information retrieval*, 2(1-2):1–135, 2008.

[27] N. Parikh, P. Sriram, and M. Al Hasan. On segmentation of ecommerce queries. In *CIKM*, pages 1137–1146, 2013.

[28] D. H. Park, H. D. Kim, C. Zhai, and L. Guo. Retrieval of relevant opinion sentences for new products. In *SIGIR*, pages 393–402, 2015.

[29] L. Qin and X. Zhu. Promoting diversity in recommendation by entropy regularizer. In *IJCAI*, pages 2698–2704. AAAI Press, 2013.

[30] R. W. Shephard and R. Färe. *The law of diminishing returns*. Springer, 1974.

[31] K. M. Svore, L. Vanderwende, and C. J. Burges. Enhancing single-document summarization by combining ranknet and third-party sources. In *EMNLP-CoNLL*, pages 448–457, 2007.

[32] I. Titov and R. T. McDonald. A joint model of text and aspect ratings for sentiment summarization. In *ACL*, volume 8, pages 308–316, 2008.

[33] H. Wang, Y. Lu, and C. Zhai. Latent aspect rating analysis on review text data: a rating regression approach. In *SIGKDD*, pages 783–792, 2010.

[34] X. Xue, J. Jeon, and W. B. Croft. Retrieval models for question and answer archives. In *SIGIR*, pages 475–482, 2008.

[35] X. Xue, Y. Tao, D. Jiang, and H. Li. Automatically mining question reformulation patterns from search log data. In *ACL*, pages 187–192, 2012.

[36] K. Yatani, M. Novati, A. Trusty, and K. N. Truong. Analysis of adjective-noun word pair extraction methods for online review summarization. In *IJCAI*, volume 22, page 2771, 2011.

[37] C. Zhai and J. Lafferty. A study of smoothing methods for language models applied to information retrieval. *ACM Transactions on Information Systems (TOIS)*, 22(2):179–214, 2004.

[38] S. Zhao, H. Wang, C. Li, T. Liu, and Y. Guan. Automatically generating questions from queries for community-based question answering. In *IJCNLP*, pages 929–937, 2011.

[39] G. Zhou, L. Cai, J. Zhao, and K. Liu. Phrase-based translation model for question retrieval in community question answer archives. In *ACL*, pages 653–662, 2011.

[40] G. Zhou, T. He, J. Zhao, and P. Hu. Learning continuous word embedding with metadata for question retrieval in community question answering. In *ACL*, pages 250–259, 2015.

Modeling Document Novelty with Neural Tensor Network for Search Result Diversification

Long Xia Jun Xu* Yanyan Lan Jiafeng Guo Xueqi Cheng
CAS Key Lab of Network Data Science and Technology,
Institute of Computing Technology, Chinese Academy of Sciences
xialong@software.ict.ac.cn, {junxu, lanyanyan, guojiafeng, cxq}@ict.ac.cn

ABSTRACT

Search result diversification has attracted considerable attention as a means to tackle the ambiguous or multi-faceted information needs of users. One of the key problems in search result diversification is *novelty*, that is, how to measure the novelty of a candidate document with respect to other documents. In the heuristic approaches, the predefined document similarity functions are directly utilized for defining the novelty. In the learning approaches, the novelty is characterized based on a set of handcrafted features. Both the similarity functions and the features are difficult to manually design in real world due to the complexity of modeling the document novelty. In this paper, we propose to model the novelty of a document with a neural tensor network. Instead of manually defining the similarity functions or features, the new method automatically learns a nonlinear novelty function based on the preliminary representation of the candidate document and other documents. New diverse learning to rank models can be derived under the relational learning to rank framework. To determine the model parameters, loss functions are constructed and optimized with stochastic gradient descent. Extensive experiments on three public TREC datasets show that the new derived algorithms can significantly outperform the baselines, including the state-of-the-art relational learning to rank models.

Keywords

search result diversification; neural tensor network; relational learning to rank

1. INTRODUCTION

In web search, it has been widely observed that a large fraction of queries are ambiguous or multi-faceted. Search result diversification has been proposed as a way to tackle this problem and diverse ranking is one of the central problems. The goal of diverse ranking is to develop a ranking model that can sort documents based on their relevance to the given query as well as the *novelty* of the information in the documents. Thus, how to measure the novelty of a candidate document with respect to other documents becomes a key problem in the designing of the diverse ranking models.

Methods for search result diversification can be categorized into heuristic approaches and learning approaches. The heuristic approaches construct diverse rankings with heuristic rules [3, 8, 14, 24, 25, 26]. As a representative model, the maximal marginal relevance (MMR) [3] formulates the construction of a diverse ranking as a process of sequential document selection. At each iteration the document with the highest marginal relevance is selected. The marginal relevance consists of the relevance score and novelty score. The novelty score is calculated based on a predefined document similarity function. Thus, the selection of the document similarity function becomes a critical issue for MMR. Different choices of the similarity functions result in different ranking lists. Usually it is difficult to define an appropriate similarity function in a real application.

Recently, machine learning models have been proposed and applied to the task of search result diversification [17, 20, 23, 28, 32]. The basic idea is to automatically learn a diverse ranking model from the labeled training data. Relational learning to rank is one of the representative framework in this field. In relational learning to rank, the novelty of a document with respect to the previously selected documents is encoded as a set of handcrafted novelty features. Several algorithms have been developed under the framework and state-of-the-art performances have been achieved [28, 32]. However, it is still an unsolved problem to define a set of novelty features which can effectively capture the complex document relationship. Unlike the designing of relevance features in conventional learning to rank, it is much more difficult to extract novelty features for search result diversification. Currently, a very limited number of novelty features can be utilized when constructing a diverse ranking model. For example, in R-LTR [32] and PAMM [28], the novelty of a document is characterized with only seven novelty features. Most of the features are based on the cosine similarities of two documents represented with tf-idf vectors or topic vectors. Thus, it is very difficult, if not impossible, for users to handcraft an optimal set of novelty features for search result diversification.

To address above problems and inspired by the neural models for relation classification [27], we propose to model the document novelty for search result diversification using a neural tensor network (NTN). Unlike existing methods

*Corresponding author: Jun Xu.

SIGIR '16, July 17–21, 2016, Pisa, Italy.
© 2016 ACM. ISBN 978-1-4503-4069-4/16/07... $15.00
DOI: http://dx.doi.org/10.1145/2911451.2911498

which manually define the document similarity functions or novelty features, the method automatically learns a non-linear document novelty function from the training data. It first generates the novelty signals with a nonlinear tensor layer, through interacting the candidate document with other documents. Then, a max-pooling operation is applied to select the most effective novelty signals. Finally, the selected signals are combined linearly to form the final document novelty score.

New diverse ranking models, then, can be proposed under the relational learning to rank framework. The marginal relevance in relational learning to rank, which is used for selecting the best document at each step, is calculated as a sum of the query-document relevance score and document novelty score. Modeling the document novelty score with the proposed neural tensor network, we can achieve new diverse ranking models. On the basis of existing relational learning to rank algorithms of R-LTR and PAMM, two new loss functions are constructed and optimized, achieving two novel diverse ranking algorithms of R-LTR-NTN and PAMM-NTN.

To evaluate the effectiveness of the proposed algorithms, we conducted extensive experiments on three public TREC benchmark datasets. The experimental results showed that our proposed algorithms, including R-LTR-NTN and PAMM-NTN, can significantly outperform the state-of-the-art baselines including heuristic approaches of MMR, and learning approaches of SVM-DIV [29], R-LTR, and PAMM. Analysis showed that the proposed approaches achieved better results through learning better document dissimilarities in terms of distinguishing the documents with different subtopics. Thus, the proposed algorithms have the ability to improve the queries with high ambiguity.

Contributions of the paper include: 1) We proposed to model the document novelty with a neural tensor network, which enables us to get rid of the manually defined similarity functions or handcrafted novelty features in search result diversification; 2) Based on the new document novelty model, two diverse ranking algorithms were derived under the framework of relational learning to rank; 3) The effectiveness of the proposed algorithms were verified based on public benchmark datasets.

The rest of the paper is organized as follows. After a summary of related work in Section 2, we present the neural tensor network model for measuring document novelty in Section 3. Section 4 presents the two derived diverse ranking algorithms under the relational learning to rank framework. Experimental results and discussions are given in Section 5. Section 6 concludes the paper and gives future directions.

2. RELATED WORK

This paper concerns about the ranking models for search result diversification. Existing methods can be categorized into heuristic approaches and learning approaches. One of the central problems in both of these two approaches is novelty, that is, how to model the novelty information of a document with respect to other documents.

2.1 Heuristic approaches

It is a common practice to use heuristic rules to construct a diverse ranking list in search. Usually, the rules are created based on the observation that in diverse ranking a document's novelty depends on not only the document itself but also the documents ranked in previous positions. Carbonell and Goldstein [3] proposed the maximal marginal relevance criterion to guide the design of diverse ranking models. The criterion is implemented with a process of iteratively selecting the documents from the candidate document set. At each iteration, the document with the highest marginal relevance score is selected, where the score is a linear combination of the query-document relevance and the maximum distance of the document to the documents in current result set, in another word, novelty. The marginal relevance score is then updated in the next iteration as the number of documents in the result set increases by one. A number of methods have been developed under the criterion. PM-2 [8] treats the problem of finding a diverse search result as finding a proportional representation for the document ranking. xQuAD [26] directly models different aspects underlying the original query in the form of sub-queries, and estimates the relevance of the retrieved documents to each identified sub-query. Hu et al. [14] proposed a diversification framework that explicitly leverages the hierarchical intents of queries and selects the documents that maximize diversity in the hierarchical structure. See also [2, 4, 10, 11, 12, 22]

All of these heuristic approaches rely on a predefined document similarity (or distance) function to measure the novelty of a document. Thus, the selection of the similarity function is critical for the ranking performances. Usually it is hard to design an optimal similarity function for a specific task. In this paper, we focus on the learning approaches to estimate the novelty scores of documents.

2.2 Learning approaches

Machine learning techniques have been applied to construct ranking models for search result diversification. In these approaches, the relevance features and novelty features are extracted for characterizing the relevance and novelty information of a document, respectively. The ranking score is usually a linear combination of these features and the parameters can be automatically estimated from the training data. Some promising results have been obtained. For example, Zhu et al. [32] proposed the relational learning to rank framework in which the diverse ranking is constructed with a process of sequential document selection. The training of a relational learning to rank model thus amounts to optimizing the object function based on the ground-truth rankings. With different definitions of the object functions and optimization techniques, different diverse ranking algorithms have been derived [28, 32]. Radlinski et al. [23] proposed online learning algorithms that directly learn a diverse ranking of documents based on users' clicking behaviors. More works please refer to [17, 20, 30].

Most learning approaches depend on a set of handcrafted novelty features to represent the novelty of a document. Construction of such features is usually difficult and time consuming in real applications. In real world, we have a very limited number of novelty features, which greatly limits the usability of these diverse ranking models. In this paper, we propose to automatically learn the novelty with a neural tensor network and enhance the usability of the diverse ranking algorithms.

3. MODELING DOCUMENT NOVELTY WITH NEURAL TENSOR NETWORK

Inspired by the neural models for relation classification, in

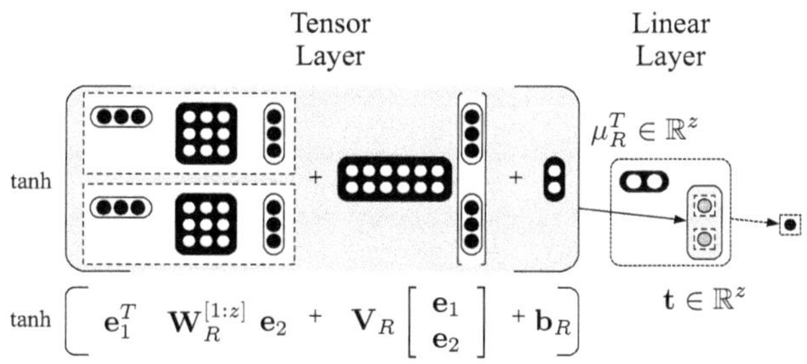

Figure 1: Visualization of the neural tensor network for relation classification. Each dashed box represents one slice of the tensor, in this case there are $z = 2$ slices.

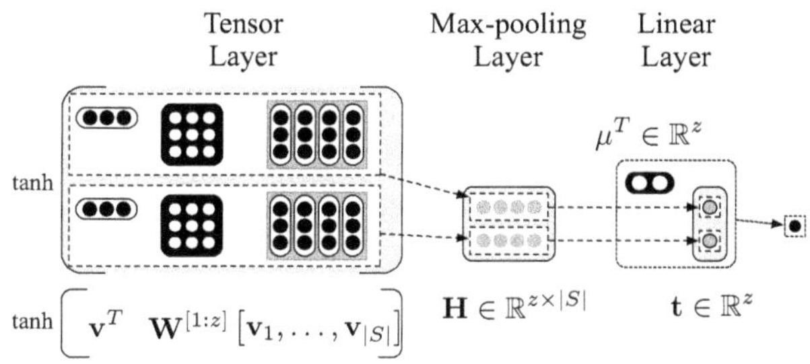

Figure 2: Visualization of the neural tensor network for modeling document novelty ($z = 2$).

this paper we propose to use neural tensor network to model the novelty of a document w.r.t. a set of other documents.

3.1 Neural tensor network

In deep learning literature, neural tensor networks (NTN) is originally proposed to reason the relationship between two entities in knowledge graph [27]. Given two entities $(\mathbf{e}_1, \mathbf{e}_2)$ represented with $l_\mathbf{e}$ dimensional features, the goal of NTN is to predict whether they have a certain relationship R. Specifically, NTN computes a score of how likely it is that these two entities are in certain relationship R by the following function:

$$g(\mathbf{e}_1, R, \mathbf{e}_2) = \mu_R^T \tanh\left(\mathbf{e}_1^T \mathbf{W}_R^{[1:z]}\mathbf{e}_2 + \mathbf{V}_R \begin{bmatrix} \mathbf{e}_1 \\ \mathbf{e}_2 \end{bmatrix} + \mathbf{b}_R\right),$$

where $\mathbf{e}_1, \mathbf{e}_2 \in \mathbb{R}^{l_\mathbf{e}}$ are the vector representations of two entities, $\mathbf{W}_R^{[1:z]} \in \mathbb{R}^{l_\mathbf{e}\times l_\mathbf{e}\times z}$ is a tensor and the bilinear tensor product $\mathbf{e}_1^T\mathbf{W}_R^{[1:z]}\mathbf{e}_2$ results in a vector $\mathbf{h} \in \mathbb{R}^z$, where each entry of $\mathbf{h}$ is computed by one slice i ($i = 1, \cdots, z$) of the tensor: $h_i = \mathbf{e}_1^T\mathbf{W}_R^{[i]}\mathbf{e}_2$. The other parameters for relation R are the standard form of a neural network: $\mathbf{V}_R \in \mathbb{R}^{z\times 2l_\mathbf{e}}$, $\mu_R \in \mathbb{R}^z$, and $\mathbf{b}_R \in \mathbb{R}^z$. Figure 1 illustrates the neural tensor network with two slices for entity relationship reasoning.

3.2 Modeling document novelty with neural tensor network

Intuitively, the neural tensor networks model the relationships between two entities with a bilinear tensor product. The idea can be naturally extended to model the novelty relation of a document with respect to other documents for search result diversification. That is, we can represent the novelty information of a candidate document as a bilinear tensor product of the document and other documents, as shown in Figure 2.

More specifically, suppose that we are given a set of M documents $X = \{d_j\}_{j=1}^M$, where each document d_j can be characterized with its preliminary representation $\mathbf{v}_j \in \mathbb{R}^{l_\mathbf{v}}$, e.g., the topic distribution [9, 13] of d_j or the document vector generated with a doc2vec [15] model. Given a candidate document $d \in X$ with its preliminary presentation $\mathbf{v}$, and a set of documents $S \subseteq X \setminus \{d\}$ with their preliminary representations $\{\mathbf{v}_1, \cdots, \mathbf{v}_{|S|}\}$, the novelty score of d with respect to the documents in S can be defined as a neural tensor network with z hidden slices:

$$g_n(\mathbf{v}, S) = \mu^T \max\left\{\tanh\left(\mathbf{v}^T\mathbf{W}^{[1:z]}\left[\mathbf{v}_1, \ldots, \mathbf{v}_{|S|}\right]\right)\right\},$$

where each column in matrix $\left[\mathbf{v}_1, \ldots, \mathbf{v}_{|S|}\right] \in \mathbb{R}^{l_\mathbf{v}\times|S|}$ stands for the preliminary representation vector of the corresponding document in S, $\mathbf{W}^{[1:z]} \in \mathbb{R}^{l_\mathbf{v}\times l_\mathbf{v}\times z}$ is a tensor, and $\mu \in \mathbb{R}^z$ the weights correspond to the slices of the tensor. As shown in Figure 2, the neural tensor network consists of a tensor layer, a max-pooling layer, and a linear layer.

Tensor Layer: The tensor layer takes the preliminary representations of the documents as inputs. The interactions between the document d and documents in S are represented as a bilinear product followed by a nonlinear operation:

$$\mathbf{H} = \begin{bmatrix} \mathbf{h}_1^T \\ \vdots \\ \mathbf{h}_z^T \end{bmatrix} = \begin{bmatrix} \tanh\left(\mathbf{v}^T\mathbf{W}^{[1]}\left[\mathbf{v}_1, \ldots, \mathbf{v}_{|S|}\right]\right) \\ \vdots \\ \tanh\left(\mathbf{v}^T\mathbf{W}^{[z]}\left[\mathbf{v}_1, \ldots, \mathbf{v}_{|S|}\right]\right) \end{bmatrix}, \qquad (1)$$

where $\mathbf{h}_i \in \mathbb{R}^{|S|}$ is computed by one slice of the tensor.

Compared with the original neural tensor network in Section 3.1, the tensor in Equation (1) models the relationship between one document and *multiple documents* simultaneously. Thus, the output of Equation (1) is a $z \times |S|$ matrix rather than a z-dimensional vector. Also, since the number of documents in S varies in different document selection iterations, the term $\mathbf{V}_R \begin{bmatrix} \mathbf{e}_1 \\ \mathbf{e}_2 \end{bmatrix}$ in the original tensor neural network is ignored. Moreover, in ranking we cares about the order of the documents rather than the ranking scores. Thus, the bias term $\mathbf{b}_R$ is also ignored.

Max-pooling Layer: In the max-pooling layer, the matrix outputted by the tensor layer is mapped to a z-dimensional vector with the max operation:

$$\mathbf{t} = \left[\max(\mathbf{h}_1^T), \cdots, \max(\mathbf{h}_z^T)\right]^T. \qquad (2)$$

Intuitively, the pooling layer aggregates individual novelty signal learned at each tensor layer $\mathbf{h}_i^T$. Max-pooling extracts the most significant signals among them. Thus, vector $\mathbf{t}$ can be considered as a the z-dimensional novelty features and each dimension is defined by one slice of the tensor.

Linear Layer: Finally, the novelty score of the document is calculated as a linear combination of the novelty signals outputted by the max-pooling layer: $\mu^T\mathbf{t}$, where μ is an z-dimensional parameter vector.

4. DIVERSE RANKING ALGORITHMS BASED ON NEURAL TENSOR NETWORK

New diverse ranking algorithms can be derived based on the proposed neural tensor network for modeling document novelty. In this paper, we propose two algorithms under the framework of relational learning to rank.

Algorithm 1 Ranking via maximizing marginal relevance

Input: documents X and novelty features R
Output: ranking of documents Y
1: $S_0 \leftarrow$ empty set
2: **for** $r = 1, \cdots, M$ **do**
3: $\quad Y(r) \leftarrow \arg\max_{j:\mathbf{x}_j \in X \setminus S_{r-1}} f(\mathbf{x}_j, R_j, S_{r-1})$
4: $\quad S_r \leftarrow S_{r-1} \cup \{\mathbf{x}_{Y(r)}\}$
5: **end for**
6: **return** Y

4.1 Relational learning to rank

The relational learning to rank framework [32] formalizes the ranking of documents as a process of sequential document selection and defines the marginal relevance as linear combination of the relevance score and the novelty score. Formally, let $X = \{d_1, \cdots, d_M\}$ denotes the set of documents retrieved by a query q. For each query-document pair (q, d_i), relevance feature vector $\mathbf{x}_i \in \mathbb{R}^{l_\mathbf{x}}$ is extracted. Let $R \in \mathbb{R}^{M \times M \times K}$ denotes a 3-way tensor representing relationships between the documents, where R_{ijk} stands for the k-th feature of relationship between documents d_i and d_j. Assuming that a set of documents S have been selected in the previous iterations, the marginal relevance of the i-th candidate document with respect to S, denoted as $f(\mathbf{x}_i, R_i, S)$, is then defined as the combination of the relevance score and the novelty score:

$$f(\mathbf{x}_i, R_i, S) = \omega_r^T \mathbf{x}_i + \omega_n^T h_S(R_i), \forall \mathbf{x}_i \in X \backslash S, \quad (3)$$

where $\omega_r^T \mathbf{x}_i$ stands for the relevance score and ω_r is the relevance weight vector, $\omega_n^T h_S(R_i)$ stands for the novelty score of the document with respect to S and ω_n is the diversity weight vector, R_i stands for the *matrix* of relationships between document $\mathbf{x}_i$ and other documents, and $h_S(R_i)$ stands for the aggregation function on R_i which aggregates the matrix R_i into a novelty feature vector. Usually, h_S can be one of the operations of max, min, or average.

According to the maximal marginal relevance criterion, sequential document selection process can be used to create a diverse ranking, as shown in Algorithm 1. The algorithm initializes S_0 as an empty set, and then iteratively selects the documents from the candidate set. At iteration r ($r = 1, 2, \cdots, M$), the document with the maximal marginal relevance score $f(\mathbf{x}_j, R_j, S_{r-1})$ is selected and ranked at position r. At the same time, the selected document is inserted into S_{r-1}.

Given a set of training instances which consist of queries, documents, and their relevance labels, the model parameters can be learned from the training data. The process amounts to optimizing an objective function based on the training data. Different definitions of the objective functions and optimization techniques lead to different relational learning to rank algorithms. For example, in algorithm R-LTR [32], the likelihood of the training queries is maximized using stochastic gradient descent. In algorithm PAMM [28], the loss function upper bounding the diversity evaluation measure is constructed and optimized with structured Perceptron.

Relational learning to rank models depend on a set of handcrafted features for characterizing the novelty of a document. However, how to design the features that can effectively capture the complex document relationship is still an unsolved problem. Unlike the conventional learning to rank in which a large number effective relevance features have been developed [21], it is much harder to find novelty features for search result diversification. As a result, the relational learning to rank algorithms of R-LTR and PAMM utilized only seven features in their experiments, as have listed in Table 1. We can see that most of these features are calculated based on the predefined similarities of two documents (represented as tf-idf vectors or topic distributions), and respectively applied to the document fields of title, body, and anchor.

Table 1: Novelty features used in R-LTR.

Name	Explanation
Subtopic diversity	document distance based on PLSA [13]
Text diversity	one minus cosine similarity of the tf-idf vectors on body text
Title diversity	text novelty feature based on title
Anchor text diversity	text novelty feature based on anchor
ODP-Based diversity	categorical distance based on ODP[1] taxomony
Link-based diversity	link similarity based on inlink/outlink
URL-based diversity	whether the two URLs belong to the same domain/site

In real world applications, the performances of the ranking algorithms heavily depend on the effectiveness of these handcrafted features and different ranking tasks need different features. It is necessary to develop a method that can learn the document novelty automatically and release people from the handcrafted novelty features.

4.2 Relational learning to rank algorithms based on neural tensor network

In this subsection, based on the technique of modeling the document novelty with neural tensor network, we develop two new relational learning to rank algorithms that can learn the document novelty function automatically.

4.2.1 The ranking model

Following the notations used in Section 3.2 and Section 4.1, let $X = \{d_1, \cdots, d_M\}$ denotes the set of documents retrieved by a query q. Each query-document pair (q, d) is represented with the relevance feature vector $\mathbf{x} \in \mathbb{R}^{l_\mathbf{x}}$. Each document $d \in X$ is characterized with its preliminary representation vector $\mathbf{v} \in \mathbb{R}^{l_\mathbf{v}}$. Assuming that at one iteration of the sequential document selection, a set of documents S have been selected. We define the marginal relevance score of a candidate document d as:

$$\begin{aligned} f(d, S) =& g_r(\mathbf{x}) + g_n(\mathbf{v}, S) \quad (4)\\ =& \omega^T \mathbf{x} + \mu^T \max\left\{\tanh\left(\mathbf{v}^T \mathbf{W}^{[1:z]} \left[\mathbf{v}_1, \ldots, \mathbf{v}_{|S|}\right]\right)\right\}, \end{aligned}$$

where $g_r(\mathbf{x})$ is the relevance of d w.r.t. query q, which is further defined as a linear combination of the relevance features; $g_n(\mathbf{v}, S)$ is the novelty of d w.r.t. the documents in S, which is further defined as a neural tensor network, as have been shown in Section 3.2. The model parameters ω, μ, and $\mathbf{W}^{[1:z]}$ can be learned with the training data.

In the online ranking, a diverse ranking can created with the sequential document selection process, similar to the procedure shown in Algorithm 1.

[1] http://www.dmoz.org

The main advantage of using neural tensor network to model document novelty is that the tensor can relate the candidate document and the selected documents multiplicatively, instead of only through a predefined similarity function (as that of in heuristic approaches) or through a linear combination of novelty features (as that of in learning approaches and shown in Equation (3)). Intuitively, the model can be explained that each slice of the tensor is responsible for one aspect or subtopic of a query. Each tensor slice settles the diversity relationship between the candidate document and the selected documents set differently. Thus, with multiple tensor slices, the model calculates the novelty scores based on multiple diversity aspects.

4.2.2 General loss function

The parameters of the ranking model can be determined with supervised learning methods, which amounts to optimizing the objective function built upon the labeled training data.

In training procedure, given the labeled data with N queries as: $(X^{(1)}, J^{(1)}), (X^{(2)}, J^{(2)}), \cdots, (X^{(N)}, J^{(N)})$, where $X^{(n)} = \{d_j^{(n)}\}_{j=1}^{M^{(n)}}$, where $M^{(n)}$ denotes the number of documents related with the n-th query. Let $\mathbf{x}_j^{(n)} \in \mathbb{R}^{l_\mathbf{x}}$ denote the relevance feature vector for the n-th query and document $d_j^{(n)}$, $\mathbf{v}_j^{(n)} \in \mathbb{R}^{l_\mathbf{v}}$ the preliminary representation of document $d_j^{(n)}$, and $J^{(n)}$ the human labels on documents which is in the form of a binary matrix. $J_{js}^{(n)} = 1$ if document $d_j^{(n)}$ contains the s-th subtopic of the query and 0 otherwise[2]. The learning process amounts to minimizing the total loss with respect to the given training data:

$$\min_{f \in \mathcal{F}} \sum_{n=1}^{N} \ell\left(\pi\left(X^{(n)}, f\right), J^{(n)}\right),$$

where $\pi\left(X^{(n)}, f\right)$ denotes the ranking generated by the ranking model f in Equation (4), for the documents in $X^{(n)}$. The generated ranking π is then compared with the human labels $J^{(n)}$ by the loss function ℓ. Intuitively, the learning process can be interpreted as finding an optimal ranking model f from some functional space $\mathcal{F}$ so that for each training query the difference between the generated permutation π and the human labels J is minimal.

Different objective functions and optimization techniques lead to different algorithms. In this section, based on the relational learning to rank algorithms of R-LTR [32] and PAMM [28], we construct two novel algorithms in which the document novelty is modeled with a neural tensor network, referred to as R-LTR-NTN and PAMM-NTN, respectively.

4.2.3 R-LTR-NTN

Based on the loss function defined for R-LTR [32], we derive the loss function of R-LTR-NTN, which is a negative logarithm likelihood of the training queries:

$$L^{\text{R-LTR-NTN}}(f) = -\sum_{n=1}^{N} \log \Pr\left(Y^{(n)} | X^{(n)}\right),$$

where $Y^{(n)}$ is the ground-truth ranking generated from the human label $J^{(n)}$. For any query, the probability $\Pr(Y|X)$ can be further defined as

$$\begin{aligned} \Pr(Y|X) &= \Pr(d_{Y(1)} d_{Y(2)} \cdots d_{Y(M)} | X) \\ &= \prod_{r=1}^{M-1} \Pr(d_{Y(r)} | X, S_{r-1}) \\ &= \prod_{r=1}^{M-1} \frac{\exp\{f(d_{Y(r)}, S_{r-1})\}}{\sum_{k=r}^{M} \exp\{f(d_{Y(k)}, S_{r-1})\}}, \end{aligned} \quad (5)$$

where $Y(r)$ denotes the index of the document ranked at the r-th position in Y, $S_{r-1} = \{d_{Y(k)}\}_{k=1}^{r-1}$ is the documents ranked at the top $r-1$ positions in Y, $f(d_{Y(r)}, S_{r-1})$ is the marginal relevance score of document $d_{Y(r)}$ w.r.t. the selected documents in S_{r-1}, as defined in Equation (4), and S_0 is an empty set.

Stochastic gradient descent is adopted to conduct the optimization. Given a query q, the retrieved documents $X = \{d_j\}_{j=1}^{M}$, and the ranking Y generated by the ground-truth labels, the gradient of the model parameters can be written as

$$\nabla\omega = \sum_{r=1}^{M-1} \left\{ \frac{\sum_{k=r}^{M} \{\exp\{f(d_{Y(k)}, S_{r-1})\} \mathbf{x}_{Y(k)}\}}{\sum_{k=r}^{M} \exp\{f(d_{Y(k)}, S_{r-1})\}} - \mathbf{x}_{Y(r)} \right\}, \quad (6)$$

$$\nabla\mu = \sum_{r=1}^{M-1} \left\{ \frac{\sum_{k=r}^{M} \{\exp\{f(d_{Y(k)}, S_{r-1})\} \mathbf{t}_{Y(k)}\}}{\sum_{k=r}^{M} \exp\{f(d_{Y(k)}, S_{r-1})\}} - \mathbf{t}_{Y(r)} \right\}, \quad (7)$$

$$\nabla\mathbf{W}^{[i]} = \sum_{r=1}^{M-1} \left\{ \frac{\sum_{k=r}^{M} \{\exp\{f(d_{Y(k)}, S_{r-1})\} \mu_i \Omega_{Y(k)}\}}{\sum_{k=r}^{M} \exp\{f(d_{Y(k)}, S_{r-1})\}} - \mu_i \Omega_{Y(r)} \right\}, \quad (8)$$

where $\mathbf{t}$ is defined in Equation (2), and

$$\Omega_{Y(r)} = \left\{1 - \tanh^2\left(\mathbf{v}_{Y(r)}^T \mathbf{W}^{[i]} \mathbf{v}_{\tau_i}\right)\right\} \mathbf{v}_{Y(r)} \mathbf{v}_{\tau_i}^T, \quad (9)$$

where $\Omega \in \mathbb{R}^{l_\mathbf{v} \times l_\mathbf{v}}$ and $\tau_i (1 \le \tau_i \le |S|)$ stands for the output of the max-pooling position for the i-th $(1 \le i \le z)$ tensor slice.

Algorithm 2 shows the pseudo code of the R-LTR-NTN.

Algorithm 2 The R-LTR-NTN Algorithm

Input: training data $\{(X^{(n)}, J^{(n)})\}_{n=1}^{N}$ and learning rate η
Output: model parameter $(\omega, \mu, \mathbf{W}^{[1:z]})$

initialize $\{\omega, \mu, \mathbf{W}^{[1:z]}\} \leftarrow$ random values in $[0, 1]$
repeat
  Shuffle the training data
  for $n = 1, \cdots, N$ **do**
    calculate $\nabla\omega^{(n)}$, $\nabla\mu^{(n)}$ and $\nabla\mathbf{W}^{[1:z](n)}$
    {Equation (6), Equation (7), and Equation (8)}
    $\omega \leftarrow \omega - \eta \times \nabla\omega^{(n)}$
    $\mu \leftarrow \mu - \eta \times \nabla\mu^{(n)}$
    $\mathbf{W}^{[1:z]} \leftarrow \mathbf{W}^{[1:z]} - \eta \times \nabla\mathbf{W}^{[1:z](n)}$
  end for
until convergence
return $(\omega, \mu, \mathbf{W}^{[1:z]})$

4.2.4 PAMM-NTN

Based on the loss function defined for PAMM [28], we derive the loss function of PAMM-NTN, which is directly

[2]In this paper we assume that all labels are binary.

defined over a diversity evaluation measure:

$$\sum_{n=1}^{N} 1 - E\left(\pi\left(X^{(n)}, f\right), J^{(n)}\right), \tag{10}$$

where $E(\cdot,\cdot) \in [0,1]$ is a diversity evaluation measure such as α-NDCG or ERR-IA etc. It can be proved that the Equation (10) is upper bounded by

$$L^{\text{PAMM-NTN}}(f) = \sum_{n=1}^{N} \sum_{\substack{Y^+ \in \mathcal{Y}^{(n)+};\\ Y^- \in \mathcal{Y}^{(n)-}}} \left[\!\left[\left(\Pr(Y^+|X^{(n)}) - \Pr(Y^-|X^{(n)})\right) \right.\right.$$
$$\left.\left. \leq \left(E(Y^+,J^{(n)}) - E(Y^-,J^{(n)})\right)\right]\!\right].$$

where $\mathcal{Y}^{(n)+}$ and $\mathcal{Y}^{(n)-}$ are the sets of positive and negative rankings generated from human labels $J^{(n)}$, respectively. $[\![\cdot]\!]$ is one if the condition is satisfied otherwise zero. $\Pr(\cdot|\cdot)$ stands for the probability of the ranking, as defined in Equation (5).

Also, stochastic gradient descent is adopted to conduct the optimization. At each iteration, we are given a query q, the retrieved documents $X = \{d_j\}_{j=1}^{M}$, a positive ranking Y^+, and a negative ranking Y^-. For convenience of calculation, we resort to the optimization problem of $\max \log \frac{\Pr(Y^+|X)}{\Pr(Y^-|X)}$. Thus, the gradients of the parameters can be written as

$$\nabla\omega = \sum_{r=1}^{M-1} \left\{ \frac{\sum_{k=r}^{M}\left\{\exp\left\{f(d_{Y^+(k)}, S_{r-1})\right\}\mathbf{x}_{Y^+(k)}\right\}}{\sum_{k=r}^{M}\exp\left\{f(d_{Y^+(k)}, S_{r-1})\right\}} - \frac{\sum_{k=r}^{M}\left\{\exp\left\{f(d_{Y^-(k)}, S_{r-1})\right\}\mathbf{x}_{Y^-(k)}\right\}}{\sum_{k=r}^{M}\exp\left\{f(d_{Y^-(k)}, S_{r-1})\right\}} - \mathbf{x}_{Y^+(r)} + \mathbf{x}_{Y^-(r)} \right\}, \tag{11}$$

$$\nabla\mu = \sum_{r=1}^{M-1} \left\{ \frac{\sum_{k=r}^{M}\left\{\exp\left\{f(d_{Y^+(k)}, S_{r-1})\right\}\mathbf{t}_{Y^+(k)}\right\}}{\sum_{k=r}^{M}\exp\left\{f(d_{Y^+(k)}, S_{r-1})\right\}} - \frac{\sum_{k=r}^{M}\left\{\exp\left\{f(d_{Y^-(k)}, S_{r-1})\right\}\mathbf{t}_{Y^-(k)}\right\}}{\sum_{k=r}^{M}\exp\left\{f(d_{Y^-(k)}, S_{r-1})\right\}} - \mathbf{t}_{Y^+(r)} + \mathbf{t}_{Y^-(r)} \right\}, \tag{12}$$

$$\nabla\mathbf{W}^{[i]} = \sum_{r=1}^{M-1} \left\{ \frac{\sum_{k=r}^{M}\left\{\exp\left\{f(d_{Y^+(k)}, S_{r-1})\right\}\mu_i\Omega_{Y^+(k)}\right\}}{\sum_{k=r}^{M}\exp\left\{f(d_{Y^+(k)}, S_{r-1})\right\}} - \frac{\sum_{k=r}^{M}\left\{\exp\left\{f(d_{Y^-(k)}, S_{r-1})\right\}\mu_i\Omega_{Y^-(k)}\right\}}{\sum_{k=r}^{M}\exp\left\{f(d_{Y^-(k)}, S_{r-1})\right\}} - \mu_i\Omega_{Y^+(r)} + \mu_i\Omega_{Y^-(r)} \right\}, \tag{13}$$

where $\mathbf{t}$ is defined in Equation (2), and Ω is defined in Equation (9). Algorithm 3 shows the pseudo code of the PAMM-NTN algorithm.

4.2.5 *Time complexities*

We analyzed time complexities of R-LTR-NTN and PAMM-NTN. The learning process of R-LTR-NTN (Algorithm 2) is of order $\mathcal{O}(T \cdot N \cdot M^2 \cdot (l_{\mathbf{x}} + l_{\mathbf{v}} \cdot Z))$, where T denotes the number of iterations, N the number of queries in training data, M the maximum number of documents per training query, $l_{\mathbf{x}}$ the number of relevance features, $l_{\mathbf{v}}$ the dimensions of the preliminary document representation, and Z the number of tensor slices. The learning process of PAMM-NTN (Algorithm 3) is of order $\mathcal{O}(T \cdot N \cdot \tau^+ \cdot \tau^- \cdot M^2 \cdot (l_{\mathbf{x}} + l_{\mathbf{v}} \cdot Z))$, where τ^+ denotes the number of positive rankings per query and τ^- the number of negative rankings per query.The time complexity of online ranking prediction (Algorithm 1) is of order $\mathcal{O}(M \cdot K \cdot (l_{\mathbf{x}} + l_{\mathbf{v}} \cdot Z))$, where M is the number of candidate documents for the query and K denotes the number documents need to be ranked.

Algorithm 3 The PAMM-NTN algorithm

Input: training data $\{(X^{(n)}, J^{(n)})\}_{n=1}^{N}$,
  parameter: learning rate η, diversity evaluation measure E, number of positive/negative rankings per query τ^+/τ^-.
Output: model parameter $(\omega, \mu, \mathbf{W}^{[1:z]})$
for $n = 1$ **to** N **do**
  $PR^{(n)} \leftarrow$ Sample positive rankings {[28]}
  $NR^{(n)} \leftarrow$ Sample negative rankings {[28]}
end for
initialize $(\omega, \mu, \mathbf{W}^{[1:z]}) \leftarrow$ random values in $[0,1]$
repeat
  for $n = 1$ **to** N **do**
    for all $\{Y^+, Y^-\} \in PR^{(n)} \times NR^{(n)}$ **do**
      $\Delta P \leftarrow \Pr(Y^+|X^{(n)}) - \Pr(Y^-|X^{(n)})$
      {$\Pr(Y|X)$ is defined in Equation (5)}
      if $\Delta P \leq E(Y^+,J^{(n)}) - E(Y^-,J^{(n)})$ **then**
        calculate $\nabla\omega$, $\nabla\mu$ and $\nabla\mathbf{W}^{[1:z]}$
        {Equation (11), Equation (12), and Equation (13)}
        $\omega \leftarrow \omega + \eta \times \nabla\omega$
        $\mu \leftarrow \mu + \eta \times \nabla\mu$
        $\mathbf{W}^{[1:z]} \leftarrow \mathbf{W}^{[1:z]} + \eta \times \nabla\mathbf{W}^{[1:z]}$
      end if
    end for
  end for
until convergence
return $(\omega, \mu, \mathbf{W}^{[1:z]})$

5. EXPERIMENTS

5.1 Experimental settings

We conducted experiments to test the performances of R-LTR-NTN and PAMM-NTN using three TREC benchmark datasets for diversity task: TREC 2009 Web Track (WT2009), TREC 2010 Web Track (WT2010), and TREC 2011 Web Track (WT2011). Each dataset consists of queries, corresponding retrieved documents, and human judged labels. Each query includes several subtopics identified by the TREC assessors. The document relevance labels were made at the subtopic level and the labels are binary[3]. Statistics on the datasets are given in Table 2.

All the experiments were carried out on the ClueWeb09 Category B data collection[4], which comprises of 50 million English web documents. Porter stemming, tokenization, and stop-words removal (using the INQUERY list) were applied to the documents as preprocessing. We conducted 5-fold cross-validation experiments on the three datasets. For each dataset, we randomly split the queries into five even subsets.

[3]The graded judgements in WT2011 was treated as binary.
[4]http://boston.lti.cs.cmu.edu/data/clueweb09

Table 2: Statistics on WT2009, WT2010 and WT2011.

Dataset	#queries	#labeled docs	#subtopics per query
WT2009	50	5149	$3 \sim 8$
WT2010	48	6554	$3 \sim 7$
WT2011	50	5000	$2 \sim 6$

At each fold three subsets were used for training, one was used for validation, and one was used for testing. The results reported were the average over the five trials.

The TREC official evaluation metrics for the diversity task were used in the experiments, including the ERR-IA [5], α-NDCG [6], and NRBP [7]. They measure the diversity of a result list by explicitly rewarding novelty and penalizing redundancy observed at every rank. Following the default settings in official TREC evaluation program, the parameters α and β in these evaluation measures are set to 0.5. We also used traditional diversity measures of Precision-IA (denoted as "Pre-IA") [1], and Subtopic Recall (denoted as "S-recall") [31]. All of the measures are computed over the top-k search results ($k = 20$).

We compared R-LTR-NTN and PAMM-NTN with several types of baselines. The baselines include three heuristic approaches to search result diversification.

MMR [3] : a heuristic approach in which the document ranking is constructed via iteratively selecting the document with the maximal marginal relevance.

xQuAD [26] : a representative heuristic approach to search result diversification which explicitly accounts for the various aspects associated to an under-specified query.

PM-2 [8] : a method of optimizing proportionality for search result diversification.

Note that these baselines require a prior relevance function to implement their diversification steps. In our experiments, ListMLE [16, 18] was chosen as the relevance function.

The baselines also include state-of-the-art learning approaches to search result diversification.

SVM-DIV [29] : a learning approach in which structural SVMs was used to optimize the subtopic coverage.

R-LTR [32] : a state-of-the-art learning approach developed in the relational learning to rank framework.

PAMM [28] : another state-of-the-art learning algorithm that directly optimizes diversity evaluation measure.

Following the practice in [32], for the baseline of R-LTR, we used the results of R-LTR$_{\text{min}}$ in which the relation function $h_S(R)$ was defined as the minimal distance of the candidate document to the selected documents.

For the baseline PAMM (and our approach PAMM-NTN), we configure them to directly optimize α-NDCG@20 because it is one of the most widely used performance measures. Thus, the baseline of PAMM is denoted as PAMM(α-NDCG). Following the practice in [28], we set the number of sampled positive rankings per query $\tau^+ = 5$ and the number of sampled negative rankings per query $\tau^- = 20$.

5.2 Relevance features and preliminary document representations

As for the relevance features, we adopted the features used in R-LTR experiments [21], including the typical weighting models (e.g., TF-IDF, BM25, LM) and term dependency model [19]. Table 3 summarized the relevance features. For all the query-document matching features, they were applied in five fields: body, anchor, title, URL, and the whole document, resulting in 5 features in total. Note that the MRF feature has two variations: ordered phrase and unordered phrase [19]. Thus the total number of MRF features becomes 10.

Table 3: Relevance features used in the experiments. Each of the first 4 features is applied to the fields of body, anchor, title, URL, and the whole documents. [32]

Name	Description	# Features
TF-IDF	The tf-idf model	5
BM25	BM25 with default parameters	5
LMIR	LMIR with Dirichlet smoothing	5
MRF [19]	MRF with ordered/unordered phrase	10
PageRank	PageRank score	1
#inlinks	number of inlinks	1
#outlinks	number of outlinks	1

The neural tensor network need preliminary representations of the documents as its inputs. In the experiments, we used the document vector generated by the topic model of probabilistic latent semantic analysis (PLSA) [13] or the deep learning model of doc2vec [15], both are trained on all of the documents in ClueWeb09 Category B data collection and the number of latent dimensions are set to 100. For training the doc2vec model, we used the distributed bag of words (DBOW) model[5]. In all of the experiments, the learning rate is set to 0.025 and the window size is set to 8.

Our approaches (R-LTR-NTN and PAMM-NTN) with the settings of using the PLSA or doc2vec as document representations are denoted with the corresponding subscripts. For example, the R-LTR-NTN that using PLSA as document representations is denoted as R-LTR-NTN$_{\text{plsa}}$. Thus, in all of the experiments, our approaches include R-LTR-NTN$_{\text{plsa}}$, R-LTR-NTN$_{\text{doc2vec}}$, PAMM-NTN(α-NDCG)$_{\text{plsa}}$, and PAMM-NTN(α-NDCG)$_{\text{doc2vec}}$. Please note in all of the experiments, PAMM-NTN was configured to direct optimize the evaluation measure of α-NDCG@20.

5.3 Experimental results

Table 4, Table 5, and Table 6 report the performances of the proposed methods and baselines in terms of 5 diversity metrics (ERR-IA@20, α-NDCG@20, NRBP@20, Pre-IA@20, and S-recall@20) on the datasets of WT2009[6], WT2010, and WT2011, respectively. Boldface indicates the highest score among all runs. For all of our approaches, the number of tensor slices z is set to 7.

From the results we can see that, on all of the three datasets and in terms of the five diversity evaluation metrics, our approaches (R-LTR-NTN$_{\text{plsa}}$, R-LTR-NTN$_{\text{doc2vec}}$, PAMM-NTN(α-NDCG)$_{\text{plsa}}$, and PAMM-NTN(α-NDCG)$_{\text{doc2vec}}$) can outperform all of the baselines. We conducted significant testing (t-test) on the improvements of our approaches over the baselines. The results indicate that the improvements of R-LTR-NTN$_{\text{plsa}}$ and R-LTR-NTN$_{\text{doc2vec}}$ over R-LTR are significant (p-value < 0.05), in terms of all of the

[5]http://radimrehurek.com/gensim/models/doc2vec.html

[6]The performances of XQuAD reported in Table 4 are different to that of reported in [26]. It may caused by the different splitting of the dataset in cross validation.

Table 4: Performance comparison of all methods for WT2009.

Method	ERR-IA@20	α-NDCG@20	NRBP@20	Pre-IA@20	S-recall@20
MMR	0.2022	0.3083	0.1715	0.0918	0.4698
xQuAD	0.2316	0.3437	0.1956	0.0984	0.4931
PM-2	0.2294	0.3369	0.1788	0.0949	0.4876
SVM-DIV	0.2408	0.3526	0.2073	0.1075	0.5101
R-LTR	0.2714	0.3964	0.2339	0.1233	0.5511
R-LTR-NTN$_{\text{plsa}}$	0.3015	0.4444	0.2563	0.1588	0.5743
R-LTR-NTN$_{\text{doc2vec}}$	0.3117	0.4503	0.2578	0.1670	**0.5910**
PAMM(α-NDCG)	0.2842	0.4271	0.2411	0.1265	0.5612
PAMM-NTN(α-NDCG)$_{\text{plsa}}$	0.3081	0.4377	**0.2642**	0.1661	0.5755
PAMM-NTN(α-NDCG)$_{\text{doc2vec}}$	**0.3135**	**0.4555**	0.2626	**0.1745**	0.5772

Table 5: Performance comparison of all methods for WT2010.

Method	ERR-IA@20	α-NDCG@20	NRBP@20	Pre-IA@20	S-recall@20
MMR	0.2735	0.4036	0.2252	0.1722	0.6444
xQuAD	0.3278	0.4445	0.2872	0.1883	0.6732
PM-2	0.3296	0.4478	0.2901	0.1885	0.6749
SVM-DIV	0.3331	0.4593	0.2934	0.1925	0.6774
R-LTR	0.3647	0.4924	0.3293	0.2042	0.6893
R-LTR-NTN$_{\text{plsa}}$	0.3876	0.5311	0.3333	0.2341	0.6912
R-LTR-NTN$_{\text{doc2vec}}$	**0.3932**	0.5376	**0.3623**	**0.2418**	0.6994
PAMM(α-NDCG)	0.3802	0.5249	0.3431	0.2111	0.6832
PAMM-NTN(α-NDCG)$_{\text{plsa}}$	0.3898	0.5379	0.3479	0.2264	0.7006
PAMM-NTN(α-NDCG)$_{\text{doc2vec}}$	0.3901	**0.5407**	0.3553	0.2386	**0.7032**

Table 6: Performance comparison of all methods for WT2011.

Method	ERR-IA@20	α-NDCG@20	NRBP@20	Pre-IA@20	S-recall@20
MMR	0.4284	0.5302	0.3913	0.3176	0.7567
xQuAD	0.4753	0.5645	0.4274	0.3299	0.7683
PM-2	0.4873	0.5786	0.4318	0.3405	0.7743
SVM-DIV	0.4898	0.5910	0.4475	0.3468	0.7750
R-LTR	0.5389	0.6297	0.4982	0.3921	0.8512
R-LTR-NTN$_{\text{plsa}}$	0.5483	0.6537	0.5050	0.4011	0.8543
R-LTR-NTN$_{\text{doc2vec}}$	0.5538	0.6555	**0.5223**	0.4125	**0.8590**
PAMM(α-NDCG)	0.5417	0.6433	0.5012	0.3955	0.8518
PAMM-NTN(α-NDCG)$_{\text{plsa}}$	0.5496	0.6469	0.5111	0.4169	0.8524
PAMM-NTN(α-NDCG)$_{\text{doc2vec}}$	**0.5554**	**0.6566**	0.5212	**0.4177**	0.8533

performance measures. The results also indicate that the improvements of PAMM-NTN(α-NDCG)$_{\text{plsa}}$ and PAMM-NTN(α-NDCG)$_{\text{doc2vec}}$ over all of the baselines are significant, in terms of all of the performance measures. The results indicate that the neural tensor network is effective for modeling the document novelty information, and thus can improve the performances.

5.4 Discussions

We conducted experiments to show the reasons that our approaches outperformed the baselines and impacts of different parameter settings, using the results of R-LTR-NTN$_{\text{plsa}}$ and R-LTR-NTN$_{\text{doc2vec}}$ on WT2009 dataset as examples.

5.4.1 Ability to learn better document dissimilarities

We found that the learned neural tensor network can help to distinguish the relevant documents in terms of different subtopics, by learning a better dissimilarity (novelty) function for documents. That is one of the reasons why our approaches can outperform the baselines.

Specifically, the dissimilarities between two documents can be calculated based on the preliminary document representations, either using the Euclidean distance or using the learned neural tensor network (the novelty score of a document w.r.t. another document). That is, given two documents represented with the preliminary presentations $\mathbf{v}_i$ and $\mathbf{v}_j$, the dissimilarity score can calculated either based on the Euclidean distance:

$$d_e(\mathbf{v}_i, \mathbf{v}_j) = \|\mathbf{v}_i - \mathbf{v}_j\|_2,$$

or based on the learned neural tensor network:

$$d_n(\mathbf{v}_i, \mathbf{v}_j) = g_n(\mathbf{v}_i, \{\mathbf{v}_j\}) = \mu^T \tanh\left(\mathbf{v}_i^T \mathbf{W}^{[1:z]} \mathbf{v}_j\right)$$

where μ and $\mathbf{W}^{[1:z]}$ are learned with the R-LTR-NTN algorithms. Here we can ignore the max operation because there is only one document $\mathbf{v}_j$ at the righthand of $\mathbf{W}^{[1:z]}$.

Suppose we are given a set of queries and the associated relevant documents. For each query, the relevant documents can be grouped into several clusters, each corresponds a subtopic of the query. Thus, all of the associated documents from all queries are grouped into different clusters, each corresponds to a subtopic. We calculated the ratio of average inter-cluster documents dissimilarities to average intra-cluster document dissimilarities. It is obvious that in search result diversification, a good document dissimilarity function would get large inter-cluster document dissimilarities and small intra-cluster document dissimilarities (large ratio value). This is because such a dissimilarity function could discriminate the subtopics well.

Table 7 shows the ratios calculated based on different dissimilarity definitions and different preliminary document representations. From the results, we can see that the ratio of "d_n with PLSA" (documents represented with PLSA topics and dissimilarities are calculated with neural tensor

Table 7: **Ratio of average inter-cluster documents dissimilarities to average intra-cluster document dissimilarities. The documents are grouped according to their associated subtopics.**

Method	average dissimilarity ratio
d_e with PLSA	1.65
d_n with PLSA	**2.73**
d_e with doc2vec	2.10
d_n with doc2vec	**4.32**

network) is larger than the ratio of "d_e with PLSA" (documents represented with PLSA topics and dissimilarities are calculated as Euclidean distance), and the ratio of "d_n with doc2vec" is larger than the ratio of "d_e with doc2vec". The results indicates that the dissimilarity functions learned by the tensor neural network are better than the Euclidean distances, in terms of discriminating the query subtopics.

The conclusion is quite intuitive and nature because the parameters of neural tensor network are determined based on the labeled data and thus can be adapted to the specific dataset and task, while the Euclidean distance is a predefined function for all datasets and tasks. Therefore, we can conclude that R-LTR-NTN (and also PAMM-NTN) can improve the performances through learning a better document dissimilarity function which distinguishes the documents with different subtopics effectively.

5.4.2 *Ability to improve queries with high ambiguity*

We also conducted experiments to show on which kinds of queries our approaches can perform well. Specifically, in each fold of the experiments on WT2009, we trained an R-LTR-NTN$_{\text{doc2vec}}$ model, an R-LTR, and a PAMM(α-NDCG) model on the training data and tested them on the test data. We then grouped the queries in the test datasets according to the number of subtopics they associated. We compared the performances of these three models in terms of α-NDCG@20 on each of the query groups and the results are shown in Figure 3. Boldface indicates the number of associated subtopics by the candidate documents, and the numbers in the parentheses indicate the proportion of queries in that group to the number of all queries. Please note that in Figure 3 some queries associated with only one or two subtopics while in Table 2 all queries have at least 3 subtopics associated. This is because we used the Indri[7] toolkit to retrieve the top 1000 documents as the candidates. Some labeled documents may not be ranked at top 1000 and thus be eliminated from the candidate set.

From the results reported in Figure 3, we can see that for those queries that associated with only one or two subtopics, R-LTR-NTN performed worse than the baselines of R-LTR and PAMM(α-NDCG). However, for those queries that associated with three or more subtopics (queries with high ambiguity), R-LTR-NTN outperformed the baselines. We also observed the trends that larger improvements R-LTR-NTN can achieve on the queries with more subtopics. The results is also intuitive because the document relations are more complex for ambiguous queries and neural tensor network can model the complex document relationship better. Thus, we can conclude that R-LTR-NTN can improve the baselines through improving the high ambiguity queries.

[7]http://lemurproject.org/indri

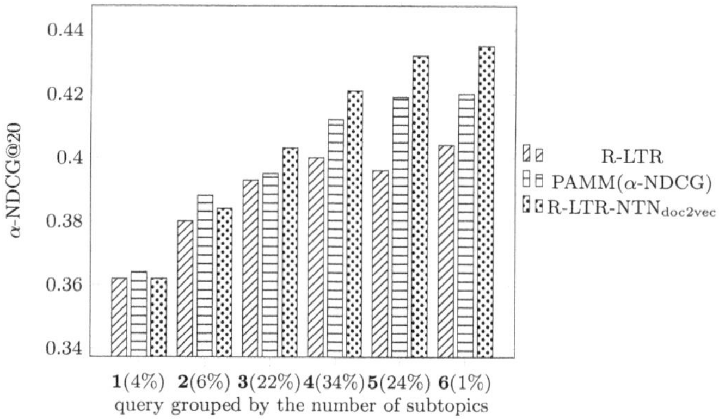

Figure 3: Performances with respect to query groups with different number of subtopics. The numbers in the parentheses indicate the proportion of queries in that group to the number of all queries.

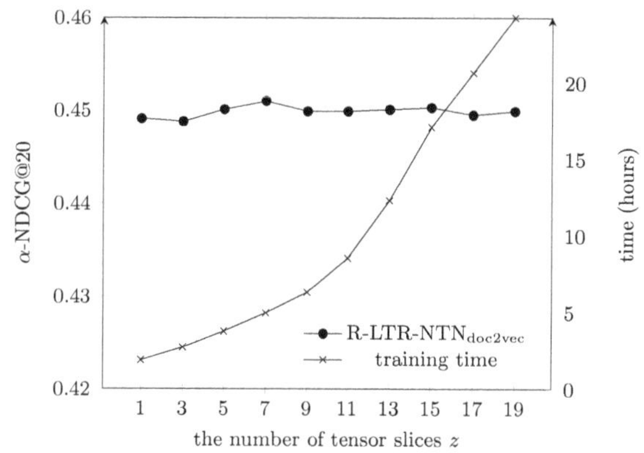

Figure 4: Ranking accuracies and training time with respect to the number of tensor slices z.

5.4.3 *Effects of the number of tensor slices*

Finally, we conducted experiments to test if the proposed algorithms are sensitive to the model parameters. One of the most important parameters in the proposed method is the number of tensor slices z. Thus, in the experiments we tested if R-LTR-NTN$_{\text{doc2vec}}$ is sensitive to different settings of z values. Specifically, we tuned z by varying the values of parameter z from 1 to 19, with step 2 and fixing other model parameters to the default or optimal values. Figure 4 shows the performances of R-LTR-NTN$_{\text{doc2vec}}$ with respect to number of slices z, in terms of α-NDCG@20. The training time (in hours) with respect to z are also shown in the figure.

From the results, we can see that the performances did not change much with different z values, which indicates R-LTR-NTN$_{\text{doc2vec}}$ (and other proposed algorithms) are robust and not sensitive to the parameter settings. In all of the experiments the number of tensor slices was set to the optimal value 7.

One of the negative effects of increasing z values is that the training time increased dramatically with the creased z values, as shown in Figure 4. This is because much more operations are needed for training the model if z is increased. Please refer to Section 4.2.5 for the time complexities of the proposed algorithms.

6. CONCLUSIONS

How to model the *novelty* of a candidate document with respect to other documents is one of the key problems in search result diversification. Existing approaches have been hurt from the necessaries of predefining a document similarity function or a set of novelty features, which are usually hard in real applications. In this paper we proposed to model the novelty of a document with a neural tensor network, which enables us to automatically learns a nonlinear novelty function based on the preliminary representations of the candidate document and other documents. Under the framework of relational learning to rank, new diverse learning to rank models have been derived, by replacing the novelty term in the original objective function with the neural tensor network. Experimental results based on three benchmark datasets showed that the proposed models significantly outperformed the baseline methods, including the state-of-the-art relational learning to rank models. Experimental results also showed that the proposed algorithms can improve the baselines via learning a document dissimilarity function that matches well with the query subtopics. The results also showed that more improvements can be achieved on the queries with high ambiguity.

As future work, we would like to verify the effectiveness of the proposed algorithms on applications other than search result diversification such as multi-document summarization etc. We also want to study the approaches to learning the relevance features and novelty features simultaneously.

7. ACKNOWLEDGMENTS

The work was funded by the 973 Program of China under Grants No. 2014CB340401 and 2012CB316303, the 863 Program of China under Grants No. 2014AA015204, the National Natural Science Foundation of China (NSFC) under Grants No. 61232010, 61472401, 61433014, 61425016, and 61203298, the Key Research Program of the Chinese Academy of Sciences under Grant No. KGZD-EW-T03-2, and the Youth Innovation Promotion Association CAS under Grants No. 20144310 and 2016102.

8. REFERENCES

[1] R. Agrawal, S. Gollapudi, A. Halverson, and S. Ieong. Diversifying search results. In *Proceedings of ACM WSDM '09*, pages 5–14, 2009.

[2] S. Bhatia. Multidimensional search result diversification: Diverse search results for diverse users. In *Proceedings of ACM SIGIR '11*, pages 1331–1332, 2011.

[3] J. Carbonell and J. Goldstein. The use of mmr, diversity-based reranking for reordering documents and producing summaries. In *Proceedings of ACM SIGIR '98*, pages 335–336, 1998.

[4] B. Carterette and P. Chandar. Probabilistic models of ranking novel documents for faceted topic retrieval. In *Proceedings of ACM CIKM '09* pages 1287–1296, 2009.

[5] O. Chapelle, D. Metlzer, Y. Zhang, and P. Grinspan. Expected reciprocal rank for graded relevance. In *Proceedings of ACM CIKM '09*, pages 621–630, 2009.

[6] C. L. Clarke, M. Kolla, G. V. Cormack, O. Vechtomova, A. Ashkan, S. Büttcher, and I. MacKinnon. Novelty and diversity in information retrieval evaluation. In *Proceedings of ACM SIGIR '08*, pages 659–666, 2008.

[7] C. L. Clarke, M. Kolla, and O. Vechtomova. An effectiveness measure for ambiguous and underspecified queries. In *Proceedings of ICTIR '09*, pages 188–199, 2009.

[8] V. Dang and W. B. Croft. Diversity by proportionality: An election-based approach to search result diversification. In *Proceedings of ACM SIGIR '12*, pages 65–74, 2012.

[9] S. Deerwester, S. T. Dumais, G. W. Furnas, T. K. Landauer, and R. Harshman. Indexing by latent semantic analysis. *JASIS*, 41(6):391–407, 1990.

[10] S. Gollapudi and A. Sharma. An axiomatic approach for result diversification. In *Proceedings ofWWW '09*, pages 381–390, 2009.

[11] S. Guo and S. Sanner. Probabilistic latent maximal marginal relevance. In *Proceedings ofACM SIGIR '10*, pages 833–834, 2010.

[12] J. He, V. Hollink, and A. de Vries. Combining implicit and explicit topic representations for result diversification. In *Proceedings of ACM SIGIR '12*, pages 851–860, 2012.

[13] T. Hofmann. Probabilistic latent semantic indexing. In *Proceedings of ACM SIGIR '99*, pages 50–57, 1999.

[14] S. Hu, Z. Dou, X. Wang, T. Sakai, and J.-R. Wen. Search result diversification based on hierarchical intents. In *Proceedings of ACM CIKM '15*, pages 63–72, 2015.

[15] Q. V. Le and T. Mikolov. Distributed Representations of Sentences and Documents. *ArXiv e-prints*, May 2014.

[16] H. Li. *Learning to rank for information retrieval and natural language processing; 2nd ed.* Synthesis Lectures on Human Language Technologies. Morgan & Claypool Publ., San Rafael, CA, 2014.

[17] L. Li, K. Zhou, G.-R. Xue, H. Zha, and Y. Yu. Enhancing diversity, coverage and balance for summarization through structure learning. In *Proceedings of WWW '09*, pages 71–80, 2009.

[18] T.-Y. Liu. Learning to rank for information retrieval. *Found. Trends Inf. Retr.*, 3(3):225–331, Mar. 2009.

[19] D. Metzler and W. B. Croft. A markov random field model for term dependencies. In *Proceedings of ACM SIGIR '05*, pages 472–479, 2005.

[20] L. Mihalkova and R. Mooney. Learning to disambiguate search queries from short sessions. In W. Buntine, M. Grobelnik, D. MladeniÄĞ, and J. Shawe-Taylor, editors, *Machine Learning and Knowledge Discovery in Databases*, volume 5782 of *Lecture Notes in Computer Science*, pages 111–127. Springer Berlin Heidelberg, 2009.

[21] T. Qin, T.-Y. Liu, J. Xu, and H. Li. Letor: A benchmark collection for research on learning to rank for information retrieval. *Inf. Retr.*, 13(4):346–374, Aug. 2010.

[22] F. Radlinski and S. Dumais. Improving personalized web search using result diversification. In *Proceedings of ACM SIGIR '06*, pages 691–692, 2006.

[23] F. Radlinski, R. Kleinberg, and T. Joachims. Learning diverse rankings with multi-armed bandits. In *Proceedings of ACM ICML '08*, pages 784–791, 2008.

[24] D. Rafiei, K. Bharat, and A. Shukla. Diversifying web search results. In *Proceedings of WWW '10*, pages 781–790, 2010.

[25] K. Raman, P. Shivaswamy, and T. Joachims. Online learning to diversify from implicit feedback. In *Proceedings of ACM SIGKDD '12*, pages 705–713, 2012.

[26] R. L. Santos, C. Macdonald, and I. Ounis. Exploiting query reformulations for web search result diversification. In *Proceedings of WWW '10*, pages 881–890, 2010.

[27] R. Socher, D. Chen, C. D. Manning, and A. Ng. Reasoning with neural tensor networks for knowledge base completion. In C. Burges, L. Bottou, M. Welling, Z. Ghahramani, and K. Weinberger, editors, *Advances in Neural Information Processing Systems 26*, pages 926–934. Curran Associates, Inc., 2013.

[28] L. Xia, J. Xu, Y. Lan, J. Guo, and X. Cheng. Learning maximal marginal relevance model via directly optimizing diversity evaluation measures. In *Proceedings of ACM SIGIR '15*, pages 113–122, 2015.

[29] Y. Yue and T. Joachims. Predicting diverse subsets using structural svms. In *Proceedings of ACM ICML '08*, pages 1224–1231, 2008.

[30] Y. Yue and T. Joachims. Interactively optimizing information retrieval systems as a dueling bandits problem. In *Proceedings of ACM ICML '09*, pages 1201–1208, 2009.

[31] C. X. Zhai, W. W. Cohen, and J. Lafferty. Beyond independent relevance: Methods and evaluation metrics for subtopic retrieval. In *Proceedings of ACM SIGIR '03*, pages 10–17, 2003.

[32] Y. Zhu, Y. Lan, J. Guo, X. Cheng, and S. Niu. Learning for search result diversification. In *Proceedings of ACM SIGIR '14*, pages 293–302, 2014.

ScentBar: A Query Suggestion Interface Visualizing the Amount of Missed Relevant Information for Intrinsically Diverse Search

Kazutoshi Umemoto*, Takehiro Yamamoto, and Katsumi Tanaka
Kyoto University, Yoshida Honmachi, Sakyo, Kyoto, 606-8501, Japan
{umemoto,tyamamot,tanaka}@dl.kuis.kyoto-u.ac.jp

ABSTRACT

For intrinsically diverse tasks, in which collecting extensive information from different aspects of a topic is required, searchers often have difficulty formulating queries to explore diverse aspects and deciding when to stop searching. With the goal of helping searchers discover unexplored aspects and find the appropriate timing for search stopping in intrinsically diverse tasks, we propose ScentBar, a query suggestion interface visualizing the amount of important information that a user potentially misses collecting from the search results of individual queries. We define the amount of missed information for a query as the additional gain that can be obtained from unclicked search results of the query, where gain is formalized as a set-wise metric based on aspect importance, aspect novelty, and per-aspect document relevance and is estimated by using a state-of-the-art algorithm for subtopic mining and search result diversification. Results of a user study involving 24 participants showed that the proposed interface had the following advantages when the gain estimation algorithm worked reasonably: (1) ScentBar users stopped examining search results after collecting a greater amount of relevant information; (2) they issued queries whose search results contained more missed information; (3) they obtained higher gain, particularly at the late stage of their sessions; and (4) they obtained higher gain per unit time. These results suggest that the simple query visualization helps make the search process of intrinsically diverse tasks more efficient, unless inaccurate estimates of missed information are visualized.

Keywords

query suggestion interface; intrinsic diversity; search stopping

1. INTRODUCTION

Searchers often issue more than one query and browse multiple documents in exploratory search tasks [31]. These tasks can be characterized as open-ended and multi-faceted, requiring searchers to collect multiple relevant documents [32]. Many people conduct exploratory searches in the medical and health domains [4]. Take, as an example, a searcher who investigates the effect of smoking through Web searches in order to decide whether to continue smoking or not. This search topic contains various aspects such as diseases caused by smoking, increases in the price of cigarettes, and how smoking affects mental health. To fully understand this topic and make appropriate decisions, the searcher needs to collect extensive information covering different aspects. Such tasks are called *intrinsically diverse* search tasks in the literature [25].

Figure 1: Our concept of visualizing missed information.

There are several problems common to intrinsically diverse tasks. First, searchers often cannot easily come up with effective queries for collecting documents that cover diverse aspects. They have to issue more queries to complete the tasks if search engines return few documents relevant to unexplored aspects. Second, deciding when to stop searching is also difficult for searchers. Quitting the tasks too early without in-depth exploration prevents searchers from finding essential information; on the other hand, if they have already obtained extensive information, continuing these tasks for too long wastes time and effort, as they will not be able to acquire much more gain. The above problems are primarily due to the fact that (1) searchers may not know what aspects exist in the search topic and how important they are and (2) they cannot guess how much important information on each aspect is available on the Web and how much of the information remains unexplored.

The present study proposes a query suggestion interface, which we call ScentBar, with the goal of helping searchers discover unexplored aspects and find the appropriate timing for search stopping in intrinsically diverse tasks. As shown in Figure 1, ScentBar visualizes, for both the search query and suggestion queries, the amount of missed information[1] important to the current search topic in the form of a stacked bar chart so that users can grasp their search progress visually. We define the amount of missed information for a query as the additional gain that can be obtained from unclicked search results of the query. Gain is formalized as a set-wise metric based on aspect importance, aspect novelty, and per-aspect docu-

*Currently at the University of Tokyo and at the National Institute of Information and Communications Technology

[1] We use the phrase "missed information" to refer to information that has been retrieved by the system but that the searcher misses collecting, similar to the definition by Mansourian and Ford [20].

SIGIR '16, July 17–21, 2016, Pisa, Italy

ISBN 978-1-4503-4069-4/16/07...$15.00
DOI: http://dx.doi.org/10.1145/2911451.2911546

ment relevance and is estimated by using a state-of-the-art algorithm [30] for subtopic mining and search result diversification.

We conducted a user study involving 24 participants to investigate how ScentBar affected their search strategies and search outcomes. Post-hoc analyses revealed that ScentBar had the following advantages when the gain estimation algorithm worked reasonably: (1) ScentBar users stopped examining search results after collecting a greater amount of relevant information; (2) they issued queries whose search results contained more missed information; (3) they obtained higher gain, particularly at the late stage of their sessions; and (4) they obtained higher gain per unit time. These results suggest that the simple query visualization helps make the search process of intrinsically diverse tasks more efficient, unless inaccurate estimates of missed information are visualized.

The main contributions of this paper are as follows.

- We formalized an intent-aware metric for evaluating the gain that searchers acquire from a set of their collected documents and provided the explanation of its relation to other metrics for search result diversification.
- We proposed ScentBar, which visualizes the amount of missed information estimated as the additional gain searchers can obtain, and conducted a user study involving 24 participants to investigate the effect of ScentBar on their search strategies and outcomes (*e.g.*, query formulation and search stopping).

2. RELATED WORK

Existing studies related to this work cover the following research areas: (1) search interfaces showing information scent, (2) understanding and modeling searchers' stopping behavior, and (3) subtopic mining for search result diversification.

2.1 Search Interfaces

The concept of *information scent* was introduced in Information Foraging Theory [22], which explains the information seeking behavior of human beings by making an analogy to the food foraging behavior of animals. In this theory, information scent indicates proximal cues from which searchers perceive the value of distal information sources [6]. As summarized in Hearst's book [12], considerable research has been conducted on developing search interfaces that show users information scent [11, 13, 17] with the objective of gaining a better understanding of users' search behavior and/or making their searches more effective.

To help searchers make quick relevance assessments, Hearst [11] proposed the TileBars interface visualizing the query term occurrence as a rectangle for each search result, where the horizontal bar represents the document length and the vertical one represents the query terms. Iwata *et al.* [15] also proposed a tile-based visualization interface, called AspecTiles, which was designed to help users issue queries with multiple aspects. Zha *et al.* [37] proposed an interface that suggests queries with their representative images so that users can efficiently convey their specific search intents. Aiming to help searchers understand inter-query relationships, Kato *et al.* [16] proposed SParQS, which presents query suggestions classified into automatically generated categories.

One of the studies closest to ours is the query preview interface proposed by Qvarfordt *et al.* [24]. Their interface visualizes three kinds of information on the search results of the current search query in the form of a stacked bar chart: (1) the number of newly retrieved search results, (2) the number of re-retrieved but not clicked ones, and (3) the number of re-retrieved ones that have already been clicked by the searcher. While both interfaces provide query-level proximal cues, ScentBar is designed to help searchers conduct intrinsically diverse tasks, where the click information alone is, we think, less informative as they need to collect extensive information covering a variety of different aspects. Therefore, given the complexity of intrinsically diverse tasks, we consider aspect-level factors when formalizing the amount of missed information.

2.2 Search Stopping

Much effort has been devoted to understanding how users decide when to stop searching [20, 23, 33, 35] and to modeling searchers' stopping behavior [18]. Most studies have been based on interviews that clarify the qualitative characteristics of search stopping. Prabha *et al.* [23], for example, interviewed people in academia to analyze how much information is enough to meet their information needs. They reported that study participants had qualitative criteria for search stopping, including whether they feel that sufficient information has been collected (the sense of "good enough" [35]).

Toms and Freund's work [29] is one of the few quantitative studies on search stopping. They analyzed the characteristic actions that preceded people stopping their searches. Wu *et al.* [34] conducted a user study in which they varied the number and distribution of relevant search results and found that these factors had different effects on when searchers left the search engine results pages (SERPs). There have also been attempts to mathematically model search stopping behavior [2]. Maxwell *et al.* [21] very recently investigated different search stopping rules to find which one approximated actual search behavior most closely.

Dostert and Kelly [8] demonstrated through a user study the gap between cognitive and actual recall: while the study participants believed that they had found about 51–60% of relevant documents when they stopped their search tasks, the actual recall they obtained was less than 10% on average. These results suggest that searchers have difficulty in accurately estimating the amount of relevant information they have (or have not) found.

2.3 Subtopic Mining

Researchers have proposed various search result diversification algorithms [1, 9, 27] to satisfy different user intents behind ambiguous or underspecified queries. Most of these algorithms depend on subtopic mining, which is a technique for mining the intents underlying a given query, in order to find a set of documents that cover as many important intents as possible. Approaches to subtopic mining can be classified into two categories: subtopics that are modeled explicitly or implicitly [10]. Maximal Marginal Relevance (MMR) proposed by Carbonell and Goldstein [3] is based on the implicit modeling of subtopics; it iteratively selects a document that is relevant to a given query and dissimilar from already selected documents as the next element of a diversified document list. Approaches belonging to explicit subtopic modeling include IA-Select proposed by Agrawal *et al.* [1], who defined the problem of search result diversification as discovering a set of documents covering important subtopics.

Tsukuda *et al.* [30] proposed one of the state-of-the-art algorithms for explicitly mining subtopics. Their algorithm utilizes different resources to collect subtopics for a given query and clusters the resulting subtopics to identify intents behind the query. We use their algorithm to identify aspects underlying intrinsically diverse tasks. The resulting aspects are used to estimate the amount of missed information for individual queries. We also use the MMR algorithm to diversify search results returned by a search engine.

3. PROPOSED INTERFACE

In this section, we illustrate how ScentBar works through an example and describe the research questions addressed in this work.

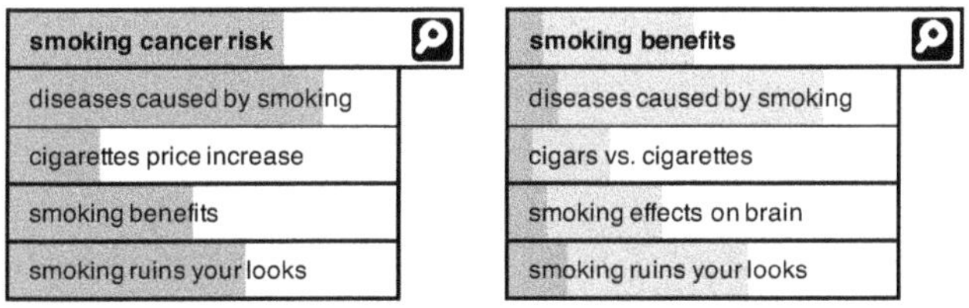

(a) At beginning of search task (b) At end of search task

Figure 2: How ScentBar works. The state of missed information after the initial search is shown in Figure 1.

3.1 How It Works

When a user is typing a search query, ScentBar visualizes the amount of *missed information* for both the search query and suggestion queries in the form of a stacked bar chart. To be precise, missed information for a query represents information that (1) can be obtained from the search results of the query, (2) is important to the search topic, and (3) the user has not yet obtained.

Take the search topic described in Section 1 as an example again. Figure 2a illustrates the state of ScentBar visualization when a user starts his/her search task with the query "smoking cancer risk" to learn the effect of smoking. At the beginning of this task, the amount of missed information for a query can be interpreted as the total amount of important information that the user can obtain from the search results of this query. For example, the user can infer from Figure 2a that the queries "smoking cancer risk" and "diseases caused by smoking" return search results containing more important information than those such as "cigarettes price increase".

When the user has obtained sufficient important information from the returned documents, the amount of missed information for the search query decreases, as shown in Figure 1. The length of the bar for the search query (indicated in deep pink) is much shorter than its initial length (indicated in light pink), which suggests this query contains only a small amount of missed information. Note that the bar for the suggestion query "diseases caused by smoking" also has a short length compared to the initial state. This is because the suggestion query shares with the search query a certain amount of important information. In contrast, the visualized bars for other suggestion queries (*e.g.*, "smoking ruins your looks") remain almost unchanged from the initial ones, which suggests great amounts of important information are still unexplored for these queries.

When the user has exhaustively collected important information on the search topic from a variety of angles through several query reformulations, the amount of missed information considerably decreases for any query related to the topic. Figure 2b illustrates the state of ScentBar visualization at the end of the search task. As suggested in the figure, there is little important information left for either the search query or the suggestion queries.

3.2 Research Questions

In the present study, we investigate the effect of displaying missed information on searchers' strategies and outcomes. More specifically, we address the five research questions listed below.

In intrinsically diverse tasks, searchers are more likely to issue multiple queries to exhaustively collect relevant information from different angles. Thus, we frame the following two research questions on individual searches (*i.e.*, after a query is issued before another one is issued or the session ends):

RQ1 *How does ScentBar affect users' decisions on when to stop the current search?*

RQ2 *How does ScentBar affect users' decisions on which query to use for the next search?*

We expect our visualization enables searchers to utilize more rational strategies in individual searches. For example, ScentBar users may be able to stop the current search after collecting a sufficient amount of important information by monitoring the bar visualization for the search query. Missed information may also affect searchers' query formulation strategies; ScentBar users may use a more effective query for the subsequent search by comparing the visualized bars for suggestion queries.

The remaining three research questions relate to the overall search sessions of intrinsically diverse tasks:

RQ3 *How does ScentBar affect the temporal change in gain that users acquire through their search process?*

RQ4 *How does ScentBar affect users' decisions on when to stop their task sessions?*

RQ5 *How does ScentBar affect the relationship between the effort that users expend and the gain that they obtain?*

Missed information may affect searchers' strategies and outcomes at the session level as well as at the query level. For example, ScentBar users may acquire high gain at any point in their sessions. Analogous to **RQ1**, ScentBar may also enable users to rationally decide when to stop the task sessions[2]. It can also be hypothesized that ScentBar makes users' search processes more cost-effective: they may be able to collect a sufficient amount of important information from a variety of angles without expending much effort.

4. MISSED INFORMATION ESTIMATION

In this section, we first introduce *gain*, a metric for evaluating search outcomes in intrinsically diverse tasks, and then define the amount of *missed information* by using the gain metric. We then describe our algorithm of estimating the gain components.

4.1 Gain

Let us consider how searchers can obtain gain in intrinsically diverse tasks. As described in Section 1, these tasks require searchers to collect extensive information covering a variety of different aspects. Considering this characteristic, it would be natural to assume that the gain they obtain through their searches is independent of their browsing order of documents. Thus, we formalize gain as a set-wise metric, whose relation to other metrics is discussed in Section 4.2. We also derive from this characteristic the following requirements that the gain metric should satisfy:

Importance Documents relevant to a central aspect of the search topic produce higher gain than those relevant to a peripheral one.

Relevance Highly relevant documents produce higher gain than partially relevant ones.

Novelty Documents relevant to an unexplored aspect produce higher gain than those relevant to a fully explored aspect.

First, we decompose the gain metric from the topic level to the aspect level in an intent-aware manner [1]. More specifically, given a topic t, we formulate the topic-level gain $\text{Gain-IA}_t(D)$ that can be obtained from a set of documents $D = \{d_1, d_2, \dots\}$ as

$$\text{Gain-IA}_t(D) = \sum_{a \in A_t} \Pr(a \mid t) \cdot \text{Gain}_a(D)\,,$$

where A_t is a set of aspects for t, $\Pr(a \mid t)$ is a probability mass function representing the importance of an aspect a to t, and $\text{Gain}_a(D)$ is the per-aspect gain that can be obtained from the documents D with respect to a. To satisfy the first requirement, the above formula puts greater value on the per-aspect gain for highly important aspects when calculating the topic-level gain.

[2] As in the literature [21], we refer to stopping behavior regarding **RQ1** as *query stopping* and that regarding **RQ4** as *session stopping*. *Search stopping* is used as the generic phrase for these two.

Next, the per-aspect gain is calculated by

$$\mathrm{Gain}_a(D) = \sum_{i=1}^{|D|} \mathrm{Rel}_a(d_i) \cdot \mathrm{Disc}_a(\{d_1, \ldots, d_{i-1}\}),$$

where $\mathrm{Rel}_a(d) \in [0, 1]$ denotes the degree of relevance of a document d to the aspect a. To satisfy the second requirement, this formula sums up the per-aspect relevance degrees of individual documents and returns a high value if D contains many documents that are highly relevant to a. Note that $\mathrm{Gain}_a(\emptyset) = 0$.

The other term $\mathrm{Disc}_a(\cdot)$ in the above formula is a function designed to satisfy the third requirement; it discounts the degree of per-aspect document relevance $\mathrm{Rel}_a(d_i)$ when the aspect a is well covered by a set of documents $\{d_1, \ldots, d_{i-1}\}$ that have already been browsed. We define the discount function as

$$\mathrm{Disc}_a(D') = \prod_{d'_j \in D'} (1 - \mathrm{Rel}_a(d'_j)) .$$

When D' contains many documents that are highly relevant to the aspect a, the above formula returns a value of nearly zero. In this case, newly browsed documents relevant to a receive high discounts from this formula and therefore contribute little to the per-aspect gain for a. Note that $\mathrm{Disc}_a(\emptyset) = 1$.

4.2 Relation of Gain to Others

Gain-IA, the intent-aware gain metric defined above, apparently looks similar to the intent-aware version of Expected Reciprocal Rank (ERR-IA) [5], which is an evaluation metric for diversified search results. The only difference between ERR-IA and Gain-IA is that the latter does not have any reciprocal rank factor. As ERR-IA evaluates the effectiveness of *ordered* search results, it discounts the value of lower-ranked documents. Unlike ERR-IA, our objective is to evaluate the gain that searchers can obtain from *unordered* documents, separately from their expended effort. Thus, we designed Gain-IA to be a set-wise metric that is affected by neither the rank of nor the browsing order of documents. This is obvious from the fact that Gain-IA has the following equivalent form:

$$\text{Gain-IA}_t(D) = \sum_{a \in A_t} \Pr(a \mid t) \cdot \left[1 - \prod_{d \in D} (1 - \mathrm{Rel}_a(d))\right],$$

which is derived from the following lemma[3]:

LEMMA 1. $\mathrm{Gain}_a(D) = 1 - \mathrm{Disc}_a(D)$.

Note that the rewritten Gain-IA is exactly the same as the objective function formulated by Agrawal *et al.* [1] for search result diversification. Assuming that $\mathrm{Rel}_a(d)$ represents the probability that a document d satisfies a searcher who believes an aspect a is as important to a topic t as $\Pr(a \mid t)$, this function can be viewed as the probability that the searcher gains satisfaction with the topic t by browsing a set of documents D.

4.3 Missed Information

Using the above-mentioned gain metric, we define the amount of *missed information* for a query as the additional gain that can be obtained from unclicked search results of the query. Let D_u be a set of documents that a user u has already browsed in the current task on a topic t and D_q^K be a set of top-K documents returned for a query q. Then, $\mathrm{MI}_{u,t}(q)$, the amount of missed information for q, is defined as

$$\mathrm{MI}_{u,t}(q) = \text{Gain-IA}_t(D_u \cup D_q^K) - \text{Gain-IA}_t(D_u) .$$

Under situations where the above formula behaves ideally, a high value of $\mathrm{MI}_{u,t}(q)$ indicates that unclicked documents $D_q^K \setminus D_u$ contains a large amount of information important to the topic t that the user u misses collecting from the search results of the query q.

[3] Due to space limitation, we omit the proof of Lemma 1, which can be accomplished by mathematical induction.

4.4 Gain Components

The following three components are required to calculate the gain and the amount of missed information on a topic t: (1) A_t, a set of aspects for t; (2) $\Pr(a \mid t)$, a probability representing the importance of an aspect a to t; and (3) $\mathrm{Rel}_a(d)$, the degree of relevance of a document d to a. As for the parameter K (*i.e.*, the number of search results to be fetched), which is also required to calculate the amount of missed information, we report the value used in our experiment in Section 5. We describe below our algorithm of estimating these three components. Note that, if the topic is known beforehand, these components can be estimated before ScentBar users conduct their searches.

As overviewed in Section 2.3, existing approaches to explicitly mining subtopics have the same task of estimating the above components. Thus, we decided to use one of the state-of-the-art explicit subtopic mining algorithms developed by Tsukuda *et al.* [30] to perform this estimation task. Their algorithm, which is easy to implement, achieved the second-best performance among 14 submissions in the Subtopic Mining subtask of the NTCIR-10 INTENT-2 task [26]. In what follows, we describe the outline of the algorithm and clarify some differences from theirs[4]. As described hereinafter, this algorithm relies on a search engine to fetch search results for given queries. The search engine for the algorithm is identical to the one for our search interface (see Section 5 for more details).

Topic Aspects. To estimate a set of aspects A_t for a given topic t, we first mine a set of subtopics S_t for t using three resources, following Tsukuda *et al.* [30]. The first resource consists of query suggestions (*i.e.*, related queries and auto-completion queries) returned by Web search engines in response to the topic query t. Each suggested query is regarded as a subtopic of t. The second resource is query logs, from which queries starting from t are extracted as subtopics. The last resource is the search results for the topic query. The clustering algorithm proposed by Zeng *et al.* [36] is applied to the search results for extracting key phrases as subtopics from individual clusters. Once S_t is mined in this way, Ward's method is applied to S_t for obtaining a set of subtopic clusters $\mathcal{C}_t$, each of which is regarded as belonging to an aspect of the topic t.

As described in Section 5, the search topics used in our experiment were selected from tasks in past NTCIR workshops. Thus, we utilized the resources distributed to the task participants to mine subtopics for these topics.

Aspect Importance. To estimate the importance probability of an aspect of a topic t, we first estimate $\mathrm{Imp}_t(s)$, the importance of a subtopic s to t, by using $\mathrm{Imp}_t(s) = \sum_{d \in D_s^N \cap D_t^N} 1/\mathrm{Rank}_t(d)$, as with Tsukuda *et al.* [30], where $\mathrm{Rank}_t(d)$ denotes the rank of a document d returned for the topic query t. Next, we select a representative subtopic a from each cluster $C \in \mathcal{C}_t$ by using $a = \arg\max_{s \in C} \mathrm{Imp}_t(s)$. The selected subtopic a is regarded as a member of the aspect set A_t for the topic t. Finally, we estimate the importance probability $\Pr(a \mid t)$ of each aspect $a \in A_t$ to t by

$$\Pr(a \mid t) = \frac{\mathrm{Imp}_t(a)}{\sum_{a' \in A_t} \mathrm{Imp}_t(a')} .$$

Per-Aspect Document Relevance. The algorithm proposed by Tsukuda *et al.* [30] performs the relevance estimation only for top-N documents returned for each aspect query $a \in A_t$. This is probably because their objective is to obtain diversified search results comprising about ten documents. However, searchers are expected to browse many more documents in intrinsically diverse tasks. To obtain more accurate estimates of missed information,

[4] We use parameter values reported in the original paper [30].

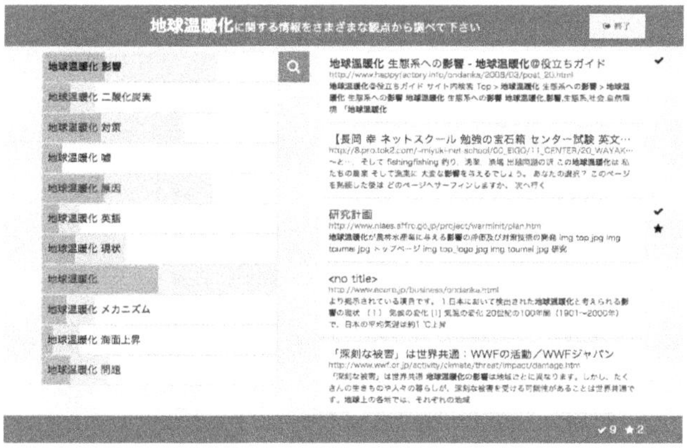

Figure 3: Screenshot of ScentBar (topic: "global warming").

the relevance should be estimated for as many related documents as possible. Thus, we expand the target of the relevance estimation with respect to an aspect a to $D_a = \bigcup_{s \in C_a} D_s^N$, where $C_a \in \mathcal{C}_t$ is a cluster of subtopics belonging to a. In light of the subtopic importance, we estimate $\mathrm{Rel}_a(d)$, the relevance degree of a document $d \in D_a$ to an aspect $a \in A_t$, by

$$\mathrm{Rel}_a(d) = \frac{\sum_{s \in C_a} \mathrm{Imp}_t(s) \cdot \mathrm{Rel}_s(d)}{\sum_{s \in C_a} \mathrm{Imp}_t(s)},$$

where $\mathrm{Rel}_s(d)$ is d's relevance degree to a subtopic s and is estimated by $\mathrm{Rel}_s(d) = 1/\sqrt{\mathrm{Rank}_s(d)}$, as with Tsukuda *et al.* [30].

5. EXPERIMENTAL DESIGN

We conducted a user study in a laboratory setting to investigate the research questions listed in Section 3.2. The details of the experimental design are described below.

5.1 Interfaces

We designed the type of interfaces was to be a within-subjects factor in our user study, where we compared two search interfaces: (1) *w/ scent*, *i.e.*, the proposed interface ScentBar, which visualizes missed information for individual queries; and (2) *w/o scent*, *i.e.*, a baseline interface without missed information visualization.

Figure 3 shows the screenshot of ScentBar for the sample search topic "global warming". Note that the baseline interface has the same appearance as ScentBar except for the query visualization. The brief description of the current search topic is shown at the top of these interfaces. While a user is typing a query into the search box (at the upper left), the interfaces obtain at most ten auto-completion queries through the Google Suggest API[5] and show them at the bottom of the search box. ScentBar also visualizes missed information for these queries in the form of a stacked bar chart. The suggested auto-completion queries remain at the same place even after the user issues the current query to our search system. This behavior allows the user to easily reformulate his/her search query by clicking the bar of a suggestion query. The top K search results returned for the query are shown on the right side of the interfaces. When the user clicks the title of a search result, a document viewer is displayed within the interfaces and the user can browse the landing page on the viewer. The interfaces also have a feature for bookmarking Web pages displayed on the document viewer and present the information on which search results have already been clicked and bookmarked for the current query (on the right side of each search result) and on how many documents have already been clicked and bookmarked through the current search task (at the bottom of the interfaces).

[5] http://www.google.com/complete/search

5.2 Search System

Both interfaces described above used the same internal search system to fetch search results in response to queries. We built the search system on Apache Solr and indexed documents in ClueWeb09-JA, the Japanese portion of the ClueWeb09 collection[6], into this system. We utilized the Okapi BM25 algorithm with default Solr parameters (*i.e.*, $k_1 = 1.2$ and $b = 0.75$) to rank documents.

When testing our implemented interfaces, however, we found that near-duplicate documents sometimes occupied high positions in the search results, which would prevent users from exhaustively collecting information from multiple aspects. To deal with this problem, we decided to diversify the search results by applying the MMR algorithm [3] to R_q^K, the top-K documents retrieved by BM25 for a query q. More precisely, MMR selects d_k, a document ranked at the k-th position, by using

$$d_k = \mathop{\arg\max}_{d \in R_q^K \setminus S^{k-1}} \left[\lambda \cdot \mathrm{Rel}_q^{\mathrm{BM25}}(d) - (1 - \lambda) \max_{d' \in S^{k-1}} \mathrm{Sim}(d, d') \right],$$

where S^{k-1} denotes a set of $k-1$ documents that MMR has already selected and $\mathrm{Rel}_q^{\mathrm{BM25}}(d)$ returns a document d's relevance score[7] that BM25 calculates for a query q. As for $\mathrm{Sim}(\cdot, \cdot)$, we used the cosine similarity between tf-idf vectors, each of which was constructed from a set of terms appearing in the title and snippet areas.

In this way, the resulting list of top-K diversified documents D_q^K was returned to the experimental interfaces in response to a query q. The control parameter was set to $\lambda = 0.3$, following Tsukuda *et al.* [30] and Dou *et al.* [9]. The number of search results to be fetched was set to $K = 100$, following Qvarfordt *et al.* [24].

5.3 Search Topics

As the topic source, we decided to use the NTCIR INTENT-1 [28], INTENT-2 [26], and IMine-1 [19] tasks, where the aspects of each topic and their imporance are provided for evaluating search result diversification. We selected four topics that satisfied the characteristics of intrinsically diverse tasks (*i.e.*, having diverse documents relevant to different aspects). These topics are listed in Table 1. Two of them were selected from the medical domain, in which people often conduct exploratory searches to collect diverse information from multiple sources [4], while the remaining two were from non-medical domains. Table 1 also shows a subset of *oracle* aspects for these topics, which were provided by the NTCIR task organizers. As shown in this table, there are a number of different aspects in these topics (the mean number of oracle aspects per topic was 10.50), and multiple relevant documents may be needed to cover each aspect.

We used these topics to design four types of intrinsically diverse search tasks. More specifically, the following description was given to the participants of our user study for the search task on a topic t:

> *You were given the assignment of submitting a thorough report on the topic t. To fully understand t, collect relevant information on this topic from a number of different aspects that you think is important. You may end this search task when you feel there is little important information left.*

5.4 Procedure

We recruited study participants via the recruiting Web site of our university. As a result, we had 24 participants (4 females and 20 males) in our user study: 16 undergraduate students, 6 graduate students, and 2 researchers. Their mean age was 23.29 (SD = 3.67)

[6] http://www.lemurproject.org/clueweb09.php

[7] We normalized $\mathrm{Rel}_q^{\mathrm{BM25}}(\cdot)$ to $[0, 1]$ by using the BM25 score of a document ranked at the first position for a query q.

Table 1: Search topics (with oracle aspects) used in our user study (translated from Japanese).

ID	Topic	Aspects
T1	symptoms of diabetes	causes, early symptoms, terminal illness, subjective symptoms, prevention, complicating diseases, drowsiness, ...
T2	clinical depression	symptoms, work, society, communication, treatment
T3	dress codes for wedding ceremony	males, females, families and relatives, hairstyles, after-party, invited guests, wedding reception, ...
T4	dinosaurs	fossils, extinction, pictorial books, species, museums, Jurassic period, images, ...

and their fields of study included informatics (six participants), engineering (four), law (four), science (three), *etc.* At the end of the experiment, they received bookstore gift cards (equivalent to $16 per person) as a reward for participating. Prior to the actual tasks, participants were assigned a training task (on the topic of global warming) to get familiar with the tasks and interfaces. During the training task, we provided participants with detailed instructions on how to use the interfaces and on what they were expected to do in our experiment. The training task took approximately 15 minutes.

A demographic questionnaire was administered at the beginning of the experiment. After filling out the questionnaire, participants worked on the four tasks one by one (two tasks with ScentBar and two with the baseline interface). The order of interfaces and tasks was determined with a Graeco-Latin square to remove the ordering effect of these variables. All tasks followed the same procedure. First, participants read the task description and completed a pre-task questionnaire asking about their knowledge on the topic and their estimated difficulty of the task. Next, they started the task with the assigned interface. To make the search process as realistic as possible, they were allowed to freely formulate search queries and were asked to use the bookmark feature provided by both interfaces when they found documents useful for completing the task. We did not allow them to follow links in the landing page because we could not guarantee that the linked pages were stored in ClueWeb09-JA, the document corpus used by our search system. After completing the task, participants filled out a post-task questionnaire asking about task-level feedback (*e.g.*, their experienced difficulty). Finally, we administered an exit questionnaire at the end of the experiment to gather feedback on both interfaces.

As mentioned above, we asked the participants to finish each task when they felt they had exhaustively collected relevant information from various aspects of the search topic (*i.e.*, each task had no time limit). We did not tell them the total number of tasks so as to avoid its effect on their stopping decisions, since they knew in advance from the recruitment information that the maximum amount of time required for our experiment was two hours. Instead, we instructed them that there were a certain number of tasks and that the experiment would finish when they had completed all tasks or two hours had passed from the beginning of the experiment. Note that, in a pilot study, every task was completed within 20 minutes. In fact, all participants completed the whole experiment within two hours.

6. RESULTS

This section reports the results of our user study and attempts to answer the research questions listed in Section 3.2. As normality was not guaranteed for the experimental data, we used non-parametric significance tests in our post-hoc analyses. Significant effects are reported on the significance level $\alpha = 0.05$.

6.1 Ground-Truth Data

To evaluate gain that participants obtained, we prepared the ground-truth data for each search topic used in our user study. As described in Section 4.4, the following three components are required to calculate the gain and the amount of missed information: (1) a set of aspects for the search topic, (2) the importance of each aspect, and (3) per-aspect document relevance. As these topics were selected from the NTCIR tasks, we used oracle data provided by the task organizers as for the first two components.

Table 2: Correlations between oracle and estimated gains. The top three values for each measure are shown in bold face.

Topic	Pearson's r	Spearman's ρ	Kendall's τ
T1	**0.834**	**0.851**	**0.683**
T2	**0.845**	**0.860**	**0.678**
T3	**0.824**	**0.862**	**0.713**
T4	0.710	0.702	0.529

Relevance Assessment. To prepare the remaining ground-truth data (*i.e.*, per-aspect document relevance), three assessors judged the relevance of each document that had been browsed by participants. A four-grade scale was used to assess the relevance of a document for each oracle aspect: irrelevant (= 0), partially relevant (= 1), highly relevant (= 2), and perfect (= 3). The following criteria were shared between assessors to make the assessed relevance as consistent and reliable as possible: documents covering (1) less than 30%, (2) at least 30% but less than 60%, (3) at least 60% but less than 90%, and (4) more than 90% of the information on a certain aspect should be respectively labeled as (1) irrelevant, (2) partially relevant, (3) highly relevant, and (4) perfect for that aspect. The resulting relevance grade $g_{a,d} \in \{0, 1, 2, 3\}$ of a document d for an aspect a was converted into the oracle relevance degree by $\mathrm{Rel}^*_a(d) = (2^{g_{a,d}} - 1)/2^3$. This conversion is often used when calculating evaluation metrics, such as ERR [5], and guarantees that the resulting relevance degree is any of $\{0, 0.125, 0.375, 0.875\}$.

Accuracy of Gain Estimation. The amount of missed information is defined as the additional gain, which is estimated by the algorithm mentioned in Section 4.4. If the estimated gain is far different from the oracle one, our interface ends up showing searchers missed information that is unrealistic and unreliable, which may have a negative effect on their searches. Thus, we decided to investigate the gap between the gain estimated by our algorithm and that calculated using the ground-truth data, before conducting post-hoc analyses. The former is referred to as *estimated gain* and the latter as *oracle gain* hereinafter.

To this end, we calculated the estimated and oracle gain scores at each point where participants browsed documents and measured correlations for pairs of gain scores using Pearson's r, Spearman's ρ, and Kendall's τ. Note that strong correlation for a topic indicates high consistency between the change in estimated gain and that in oracle gain, which suggests the gain algorithm works reasonably for that topic. Table 2 shows the values of these three correlation measures calculated for each topic.

As shown in this table, quite high correlation was observed for all topics except T4 ("dinosaurs"), which suggests that ScentBar users who conducted searches on the topic T4 might have experienced unexpected changes in visualized missed information. When analyzing the possible causes of the inaccurate gain estimation for T4, we found that aspects mined by our algorithm as important to this topic included "merchandising sales" and "skeleton models selling". As can be seen in Table 1, none of these were contained in the oracle aspects for this topic. We also found that many documents retrieved by the query "dinosaurs" at high positions tended to be

Table 3: **Mean change (with SD) in oracle missed information at the query level. Significant differences from the baseline interface at $p < 0.05$ are shown in bold face.**

	All topics		HC topics		LC topic	
	w/o scent	w/ scent	w/o scent	w/ scent	w/o scent	w/ scent
ΔMI	0.109 (0.110)	**0.138** (0.134)	0.128 (0.120)	**0.186** (0.147)	0.069 (0.073)	0.071 (0.072)

less relevant to the oracle aspects. As described in Section 4.4, the gain estimation algorithm relies on aspect mining and document ranking. Thus, the aspect mismatch and poor document ranking would cause the estimated gain to be inaccurate for the topic T4.

As noted above, inaccurate gain estimation could have an undesirable effect on participants' fulfilling search tasks; they might get confused by seeing unreliable missed information and quit searching at an inappropriate point. To investigate the effect of the accuracy of the estimated gain, the analyses reported in the remainder of this section were conducted at the following three topic levels: (1) all topics; (2) *HC topics*, which comprise T1, T2, and T3, where the estimated gain had high correlation with the oracle one; and (3) *LC topic*, which comprises T4, where low correlation was observed between the estimated gain and the oracle one.

6.2 Query Stopping

To answer **RQ1**, we investigated the effect of missed information on query stopping (*i.e.*, the point at which a user stops examining search results for the current query). We hypothesized that ScentBar users would stop the current search once they had exhaustively collected relevant documents from the search results. If this is the case, query stopping should occur when the amount of missed information for the query greatly decreases from its initial value. Thus, for each query issued by participants, we calculated the change in the amount of oracle missed information between the beginning of the task and the query stopping point. A large change indicates that the searcher obtained a great amount of relevant information from the current search.

Table 3 shows the mean change (with SD) in the amount of oracle missed information at the query level. As for all topics, the amount of oracle missed information decreased greatly when participants used ScentBar. The difference from the baseline interface was shown to be significant by the Mann-Whitney U test ($p = 0.001$). The greater difference was observed for the HC topics ($p < 0.001$). In contrast, the change in oracle missed information was quite small for the LC topic ($p = 0.683$). These results indicate that when gain was estimated reasonably accurately, ScentBar users collected a greater amount of relevant information through individual searches than the baseline interface users, which supports our hypothesis on query stopping. When inaccurate estimates were presented to participants, however, ScentBar had no effect on the amount of collected information at the query level.

6.3 Query Selection

To answer **RQ2**, we investigated the effect of missed information on users' query selection decisions in the subsequent search. We hypothesized that ScentBar would help users issue queries whose search results contained much missed relevant information. To test this hypothesis, we calculated, for each query issued by participants, the amount of oracle missed information on query issuing.

Table 4 shows the mean (with SD) of the amount of oracle missed information on query issuing. On average, queries with large amounts of oracle missed information were issued through ScentBar rather than through the baseline interface for all topics. The Mann-Whitney U test revealed a significant difference between these interfaces

Table 4: Mean (with SD) of oracle missed information on query issuing. Significant differences from the baseline interface at $p < 0.05$ are shown in bold face.

	All topics		HC topics		LC topic	
	w/o scent	w/ scent	w/o scent	w/ scent	w/o scent	w/ scent
MI	0.211 (0.194)	**0.241** (0.191)	0.238 (0.214)	**0.298** (0.210)	0.155 (0.126)	0.162 (0.123)

($p = 0.002$). While a clearer trend was observed for the HC topics ($p < 0.001$), the difference was insignificant for the LC topic ($p = 0.521$). These results indicate that when the gain was estimated reasonably, ScentBar users issued queries more effective for exhaustively collecting relevant information than the baseline interface users. This supports our hypothesis on query selection. When the gain estimation was inaccurate, however, queries issued through the two interfaces differed little from one another in terms of the amount of oracle missed information on query issuing.

6.4 Gain Change

To answer **RQ3**, we investigated the effect of missed information on the change in gain over time. More specifically, we split participants' task sessions into one-minute segments and calculated the (cumulative) oracle gain they had obtained at each cutoff time point. Note that when calculating the gain at a time point, we excluded participants who had completed the task before that time.

Figure 4 shows the gain curves averaged over the individual interfaces. The two gain curves for all topics (Figure 4a) behaved similarly until seven minutes had passed from the task initiation. After that, the oracle gain for ScentBar outperformed that for the baseline interface at nearly every time point. The difference between the interfaces widened for the HC topics (Figure 4b) while the gain curve for ScentBar underperformed that for the baseline interface at most time points (Figure 4c). These results indicate that when the gain estimation was accurate enough, ScentBar users obtained as much gain at an early time of their task sessions as, and higher gain after that time than, the baseline interface users. In contrast, when ScentBar presented inaccurate estimates to participants, they obtained less gain than the baseline interface users who spent the same amount of time or more searching.

6.5 Session Stopping

To answer **RQ4**, we investigated the effect of missed information on session stopping (*i.e*, the point at which a user completed the current search task). As in the case of our analysis on query stopping (reported in Section 6.2), we hypothesized that ScentBar users would complete the current task after exhaustively collecting information relevant to the search topic. If this is the case, session stopping should occur when the amount of oracle missed information for most queries related the task greatly decreases from the initial values. Thus, for each query issued by participants, we calculated the change in the amount of oracle missed information between the beginning and end of the task. In addition, we also calculated the (total) oracle gain obtained from the documents that individual participants had collected through their task sessions.

In Table 5, the mean change (with SD) in the amount of oracle missed information at the session level is shown at the top, and the mean (with SD) of the oracle gain obtained through task sessions is at the bottom. As for the former measure, the amount of oracle missed information decreased greatly for all topics when participants used ScentBar. The Mann-Whitney U test revealed a significant difference from the baseline interface ($p = 0.002$). The larger difference was observed for the HC topics ($p < 0.001$), while there was no significant difference for the LC topic ($p = 0.845$). As for

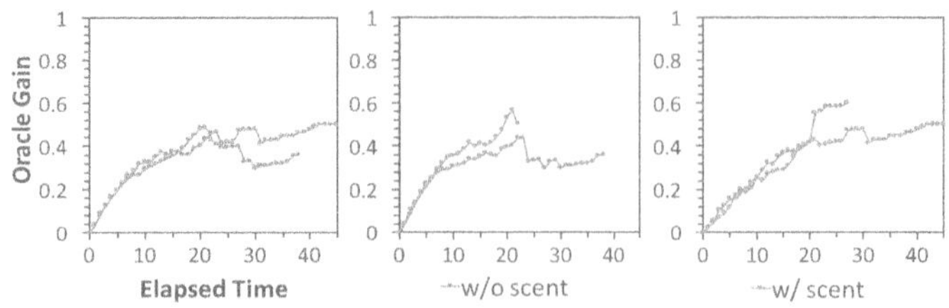

(a) All topics (b) HC topics (c) LC topic

Figure 4: Mean change in oracle gain over time.

Table 5: Top: mean change (with SD) in oracle missed information at the session level. Bottom: mean (with SD) of oracle gain obtained through task sessions. Significant differences from the baseline interface at $p < 0.05$ are shown in bold face.

	All topics		HC topics		LC topic	
	w/o scent	w/ scent	w/o scent	w/ scent	w/o scent	w/ scent
ΔMI	0.162 (0.132)	**0.195** (0.151)	0.188 (0.143)	**0.256** (0.158)	0.106 (0.080)	0.110 (0.086)
Gain	0.358 (0.132)	0.404 (0.147)	0.370 (0.133)	0.415 (0.150)	0.322 (0.129)	0.371 (0.138)

the latter measure, the mean oracle gain for ScentBar was higher for all topics than that for the baseline interface. While the same trend was observed for both the HC and LC topics, we could not find any significant differences between the two interfaces ($p = 0.097$ for all topics, $p = 0.191$ for the HC topics, and $p = 0.410$ for the LC topic). These results partially support our hypothesis on session stopping: when the gain estimation algorithm worked reasonably, ScentBar users completed their tasks after collecting greater amounts of relevant information from the SERPs of their issued queries. However, the resulting total gain obtained through ScentBar did not show statistically significant improvement compared to the baseline interface, which implies some users of ScentBar might complete their tasks earlier than others who used the baseline interface. The analysis related to this issue is reported in Section 6.6.

6.6 Relationship Between Effort and Gain

To answer **RQ5**, we investigated the effect of missed information on the relationship between expended effort and acquired gain. In the present study, the time that participants spent completing the tasks was regarded as the effort that they expended. We plotted scatter charts in which the x-axis represented the task completion time (in minutes) and the y-axis represented the oracle gain that participants obtained through their task sessions. We also performed a linear regression analysis to better understand the relationship between the effort (modeled as the explanatory variable) and the gain (as the response variable).

Figure 5 shows the scatter charts and regression lines of the effort-gain data. As can be seen in Figure 5a, little difference existed between the two interfaces for all topics. In fact, the slope β of both regression lines was almost the same: $\beta = 0.008$ ($R^2 = 0.187$) for ScentBar and $\beta = 0.007$ ($R^2 = 0.158$) for the baseline interface. As for the HC topics (Figure 5b), the great improvement was observed for ScentBar ($\beta = 0.014$, $R^2 = 0.281$), while the slope was nearly unchanged for the baseline interface ($\beta = 0.006$, $R^2 = 0.120$). In contrast, for the LC topic (Figure 5c), the slope of the regression line for ScentBar ($\beta = 0.007$, $R^2 = 0.310$) was lower than that for the baseline interface ($\beta = 0.012$, $R^2 = 0.416$). These results indicate that when the gain estimation was accurate enough, ScentBar users obtained higher gain per unit time than the baseline users. However, the former users could not obtain gain as effective as the latter ones when ScentBar displayed inaccurate estimates. Figure 4 also demonstrates that some ScentBar

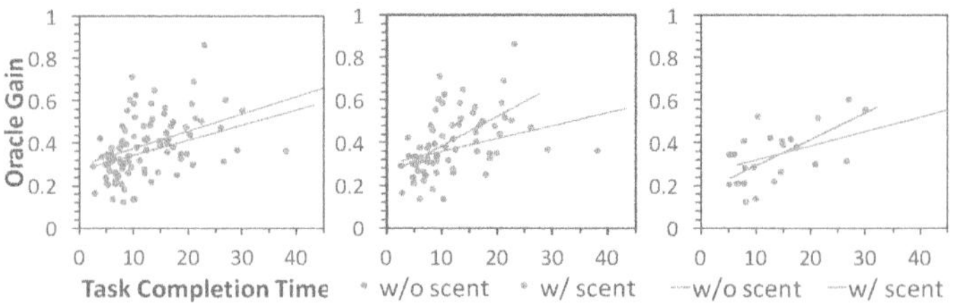

(a) All topics (b) HC topics (c) LC topics

Figure 5: Relationship between effort and gain.

Table 6: Results of search interaction analysis. The mean (with SD) values are reported. Significant differences from the baseline interface at $p < 0.05$ are shown in bold face.

		All topics		HC topics		LC topic	
		w/o scent	w/ scent	w/o scent	w/ scent	w/o scent	w/ scent
search behavior	**#Queries**	10.417 (6.523)	11.563 (10.886)	9.444 (6.381)	8.944 (7.131)	13.333 (6.315)	19.417 (15.963)
	%Sugg Queries	0.376 (0.230)	0.480 (0.275)	0.355 (0.238)	**0.505** (0.279)	0.437 (0.201)	0.405 (0.259)
	#Clicks LastRel-Q	0.156 (0.494)	0.164 (0.511)	0.165 (0.543)	0.175 (0.465)	0.133 (0.342)	0.142 (0.596)
	#Clicks LastRel-S	0.208 (0.617)	0.563 (1.610)	0.278 (0.701)	0.389 (0.871)	0.000 (0.000)	1.083 (2.875)
	#Docs	22.333 (14.961)	25.729 (15.284)	22.667 (13.980)	24.972 (15.242)	21.333 (18.252)	28.000 (15.857)
search outcomes	**Precision**	0.714 (0.126)	0.723 (0.106)	0.685 (0.114)	0.729 (0.111)	0.801 (0.124)	0.705 (0.091)
	Recall	0.078 (0.050)	**0.093** (0.057)	0.078 (0.047)	0.095 (0.061)	0.076 (0.060)	0.088 (0.043
	Aspect Coverage	0.718 (0.154)	0.757 (0.157)	0.731 (0.162)	0.756 (0.162)	0.677 (0.125)	0.760 (0.146)

users completed tasks earlier without expending much effort while others spent longer to obtain much more gain.

6.7 Search Interaction

We analyzed participants' interaction data to investigate how ScentBar affects their search behavior in intrinsically diverse tasks. To investigate its effect on query selection, we calculated the number of queries issued by participants (#Queries) and the fraction of suggestion queries selected by them (%SuggQueries). As document-related measures, we calculated the number of, precision of, and recall of documents browsed by participants (#Docs, Precision, and Recall, respectively) and the fraction of aspects covered by their browsed documents (AspectCoverage). We also calculated the number of clicks after the last relevant document both at query and session levels (#ClicksLastRel-Q and -S) for analyzing search stopping behavior. While Precision, Recall, and AspectCoverage are interaction metrics related to search outcomes, the other metrics are related to search behavior.

Table 6 shows the results of our analysis based on these measures. On average, more than ten queries were issued through both interfaces for all topics. While the difference in #Queries between the interfaces was not significant according to the Mann-Whitney U test, ScentBar users issued significantly more suggestion queries in the HC topics ($p = 0.017$). We also calculated some query complexity measures (*e.g.*, query length), but did not find any clear trends. As for the document-related measures, ScentBar users, on average, browsed more documents covering more aspects, although the difference was not statistically significant. Remarkably, ScentBar users obtained significantly higher recall than baseline interface users ($p = 0.048$), which demonstrates the advantage of ScentBar because recall is one of the most desired properties in intrinsically diverse tasks. Last but not least, no significant difference was observed for the number of irrelevant document clicks just before search stopping. This result was contrary to our expectation that ScentBar could prevent searchers from continuing tasks when no additional gain would be obtained. We discuss this issue in more detail in Section 7.

6.8 Questionnaires

Finally, we report the results of the post-task and exit questionnaires, which are summarized in Table 7. Note that the per-interface results of the exit questionnaire for the HC and LC topics in the table were calculated from the ratings given by participants who addressed those topics with that interface.

The results for the questions Q1 and Q2 indicate that most participants faced difficulty exhaustively collecting relevant information in the LC topic. The question Q3 suggests that the low quality of search results presented by the search system would be a possible cause of this difficulty. As unreliable missed information was displayed in this topic (Q10 and Q11), ScentBar did not guide participants in effective decision-making on search stopping (Q7 and Q9). In fact, The Mann-Whitney U test revealed that the baseline interface was rated significantly better than ScentBar for the question Q2 ($p = 0.039$), which indicates that the inaccurate estimation had harmful effects on the subjective efficiency for ScentBar, as well as the objective one (Section 6.6). The results for the questions Q7–Q11 indicate that the ratings for missed information improved in the HC topics. As for usability, ScentBar was much more preferred by participants than the baseline interface (Q12–Q14). The differences between the two interfaces for these questions were shown to be significant by the Wilcoxon signed-rank test ($p < 0.001$ for Q12, $p < 0.001$ for Q13, and $p = 0.004$ for Q14).

7. DISCUSSION

Our user study uncovered how ScentBar affected users' search strategies and search outcomes. This section discusses the implications of our experimental results and the limitations of this work.

7.1 Implications

Our results demonstrated that ScentBar had the following advantages when the gain estimation algorithm worked reasonably: (1) ScentBar users stopped individual searches after collecting much relevant information from the SERPs (Section 6.2); (2) they issued search queries whose search results contained much missed information (Section 6.3); (3) they obtained high gain, particularly at the late stage of their sessions (Section 6.4); and (4) they obtained high gain per unit time (Section 6.6). Our post-hoc analysis of search interaction data revealed that query suggestion was more frequently used by ScentBar users (Section 6.7), which implies that suggesting queries with missed information affected searchers' query formulation strategies and thus enabled them to conduct intrinsically diverse tasks more efficiently.

The search interaction analysis also revealed that displaying missed information did not affect the number of irrelevant document clicks just before search stopping. A possible explanation for this phenomenon is that seeing visualized missed information made participants more cautious about making decisions on search stopping. In fact, ScentBar users spent, on average, longer completing the tasks (13.6 minutes) than the baseline interface users (11.8 minutes), although the difference was not statistically significant. These results suggest that additional features would be needed for supporting searchers' decision-making on search stopping. While ScentBar suggests which queries have much missed information, it does not provide any clues about which search results users should assess to obtain additional gain. Possible solutions to this issue include visualizing the per-aspect relevance for each search result, like AspecTiles [15], and/or re-ranking search results containing much missed information at high positions, both of which can be incorporated with ScentBar. Another approach could be notifying searchers of the effort they have expended so far as well as their missed information. This could help searchers more rationally decide whether they should conduct additional searches to obtain more gain or stop searching to avoid wasting time. Techniques for quantifying search cost (*e.g.*, [2]) would be useful for implementing this idea.

Another finding from our user study is that ScentBar worsened rather than improved search performance when missed information was estimated inaccurately. More specifically, the gain per unit time obtained by ScentBar users was lower than that by the baseline interface users. This is probably because unconvincing visualization of missed information and its unexpected change prevented searchers from making rational decisions on query selection and search stopping. Our results suggest that the accuracy of gain estimation is critical for ScentBar to produce intended effects.

7.2 Limitations

This work has several limitations that we should acknowledge. First, while we formalized gain as an intent-aware metric, as with other evaluation metrics like ERR-IA [5], this approach has a drawback in that the content overlap among documents is not taken into account when the gain is evaluated. Thus, this metric has the potential to give a high score to documents with high overlap. While we tried to prevent participants from collecting overlapped documents by presenting diversified search results to them, this is an ad-hoc solution, not an optimal one. Ideally speaking, gain should be modeled on the basis of more fine-grained units, such as nuggets [7]. Thus, for more accurate evaluation, our gain formalization and estimation algorithm would require further improvement by, for example, modeling and mining aspects hierarchically [14].

Second, we used only four search topics to evaluate the effectiveness of ScentBar in intrinsically diverse tasks. Limiting the number of topics was necessary given that the interfaces were designed to be the within-subject factor in our user study (*i.e.*, every participant used both interfaces) and that we could not use a predefined length of task execution time as our research questions included the effect of ScentBar on session stopping. To validate the generality of our claim about the effectiveness of ScentBar, we would need to conduct additional experiments with more search topics and more diverse participants in the future.

Third, we selected a simple interface as the baseline in our user study while various interfaces showing information scent have been proposed. As outlined in Section 2.1, the query preview interface proposed by Qvarfordt *et al.* [24] provides a similar functionality as ours: their interface visualizes the number of (un)clicked search results for the current query. To estimate its effectiveness in intrinsically diverse tasks, we measured correlations between the number of unclicked search results and the oracle missed information scent in a manner similar to the gain accuracy estimation (Section 6.1). The correlation coefficient was 0.334 even in the best topic. Given the fact that ScentBar worsened the search performance for the LC topic, this suggests that such simple visualization could be less effective for intrinsically diverse tasks, while direct comparison in a user study setting would be needed to gain more insights.

8. CONCLUSIONS

In this paper, we proposed ScentBar, a query suggestion interface visualizing the amount of missed information for individual queries. We defined the amount of missed information for a query as the additional gain that can be obtained from unclicked search

Table 7: Mean rating scores (with SD) of post-task and exit questionnaires in which five-point scale was used for each question. Significant differences from the baseline interface at $p < 0.05$ are shown in bold face.

		Question	All topics		HC topics		LC topic	
			w/o scent	w/ scent	w/o scent	w/ scent	w/o scent	w/ scent
post-task	Q1	Was it difficult to exhaustively collect relevant information?	3.10 (1.32)	3.13 (1.31)	2.72 (1.23)	2.69 (1.19)	4.25 (0.87)	4.42 (0.67)
	Q2	Did you exhaustively collect relevant information in an efficient manner?	3.25 (1.21)	3.02 (1.34)	3.56 (1.16)	3.50 (1.18)	2.33 (0.89)	**1.58** (0.51)
	Q3	Were you satisfied with the quality of the search results?	2.92 (1.18)	2.88 (1.35)	3.17 (1.08)	3.31 (1.19)	2.17 (1.19)	1.58 (0.90)
	Q4	Were you satisfied with the quality of the suggestion queries?	3.04 (1.15)	3.33 (1.06)	3.33 (1.04)	3.47 (1.00)	2.17 (1.03)	2.92 (1.16)
	Q5	Were you satisfied with the information you collected?	3.43 (1.15)	3.29 (1.30)	3.78 (0.99)	3.75 (1.11)	2.42 (1.00)	1.92 (0.79)
	Q6	How much relevant information do you think was left unexplored?	3.38 (1.38)	3.25 (1.18)	2.97 (1.28)	2.89 (1.09)	4.58 (0.90)	4.33 (0.65)
	Q7	Was missed information useful for your decision on query stopping?	—	3.04 (1.35)	—	3.28 (1.32)	—	2.33 (1.23)
	Q8	Was missed information useful for your decision on query selection?	—	3.33 (1.24)	—	3.39 (1.27)	—	3.17 (1.19)
	Q9	Was missed information useful for your decision on session stopping?	—	3.15 (1.32)	—	3.44 (1.32)	—	2.25 (0.87)
exit	Q10	Was the amount of missed information convincing?	—	2.96 (0.91)	—	3.08 (1.00)	—	2.83 (0.83)
	Q11	Did missed information change as you expected?	—	2.50 (0.83)	—	2.58 (0.90)	—	2.42 (0.79)
	Q12	Was this interface useful for exhaustively collecting relevant information?	2.96 (0.86)	**3.79** (1.06)	2.75 (0.87)	**3.92** (0.90)	3.17 (0.83)	3.67 (1.23)
	Q13	Was this interface easy to use?	2.96 (0.95)	**3.88** (0.95)	3.00 (0.85)	**3.92** (0.90)	2.92 (1.08)	**3.83** (1.03)
	Q14	Do you want to use this interface again?	2.50 (1.14)	**3.50** (1.06)	2.67 (1.30)	**3.42** (1.24)	2.33 (0.98)	3.58 (1.44)

results of the query. Results of our user study involving 24 participants showed the following advantages of our interface for search topics where gain was estimated reasonably accurately: (1) ScentBar users stopped SERP examination after collecting more relevant information; (2) they issued queries whose search results contained more missed information; (3) they obtained higher gain, particularly at the late stage of their sessions; and (4) they obtained higher gain per unit time. These results suggest that unless inaccurate estimates of missed information were visualized, ScentBar enabled users to utilize effective query formulation strategies, while it had little noticeable effect on their search stopping behavior.

Future directions of this work include exploring ways for utilizing missed information. While ScentBar visualizes what is left for browsing (*i.e.*, the visualization decreases as searchers obtain gain), showing how much searchers have browsed might have a different effect on their search behavior. Providing the visualization in different places and/or at different timing would also be worth exploring. Missed information could also be incorporated with query suggestion algorithms to rank suggestion queries from which searchers would be able to obtain much additional gain at high positions.

9. ACKNOWLEDGMENTS

This work was supported in part by JSPS Grants-in-Aid for Scientific Research (Nos. 13J06404, 15H01718, and 16K16156).

10. REFERENCES

[1] R. Agrawal, S. Gollapudi, A. Halverson, and S. Ieong. Diversifying search results. In *WSDM*, pages 5–14, 2009.

[2] L. Azzopardi and G. Zuccon. An analysis of theories of search and search behavior. In *ICTIR*, pages 81–90, 2015.

[3] J. Carbonell and J. Goldstein. The use of MMR, diversity-based reranking for reordering documents and producing summaries. In *SIGIR*, pages 335–336, 1998.

[4] M.-A. Cartright, R. W. White, and E. Horvitz. Intentions and attention in exploratory health search. In *SIGIR*, pages 65–74, 2011.

[5] O. Chapelle, D. Metlzer, Y. Zhang, and P. Grinspan. Expected reciprocal rank for graded relevance. In *CIKM*, pages 621–630, 2009.

[6] E. H. Chi, P. Pirolli, K. Chen, and J. Pitkow. Using information scent to model user information needs and actions and the web. In *CHI*, pages 490–497, 2001.

[7] C. L. Clarke, M. Kolla, G. V. Cormack, O. Vechtomova, A. Ashkan, S. Büttcher, and I. MacKinnon. Novelty and diversity in information retrieval evaluation. In *SIGIR*, pages 659–666, 2008.

[8] M. Dostert and D. Kelly. Users' stopping behaviors and estimates of recall. In *SIGIR*, pages 820–821, 2009.

[9] Z. Dou, S. Hu, K. Chen, R. Song, and J.-R. Wen. Multi-dimensional search result diversification. In *WSDM*, pages 475–484, 2011.

[10] J. He, V. Hollink, and A. de Vries. Combining implicit and explicit topic representations for result diversification. In *SIGIR*, pages 851–860, 2012.

[11] M. A. Hearst. TileBars: Visualization of term distribution information in full text information access. In *CHI*, pages 59–66, 1995.

[12] M. A. Hearst. *Search User Interfaces*. Cambridge University Press, 2009.

[13] O. Hoeber and X. D. Yang. A comparative user study of web search interfaces: Hotmap, concept highlighter, and google. In *WI*, pages 866–874, 2006.

[14] S. Hu, Z. Dou, X. Wang, T. Sakai, and J.-R. Wen. Search result diversification based on hierarchical intents. In *CIKM*, pages 63–72, 2015.

[15] M. Iwata, T. Sakai, T. Yamamoto, Y. Chen, Y. Liu, J.-R. Wen, and S. Nishio. AspecTiles: Tile-based visualization of diversified web search results. In *SIGIR*, pages 85–94, 2012.

[16] M. P. Kato, T. Sakai, and K. Tanaka. Structured query suggestion for specialization and parallel movement: Effect on search behaviors. In *WWW*, pages 389–398, 2012.

[17] D. Kelly, A. Cushing, M. Dostert, X. Niu, and K. Gyllstrom. Effects of popularity and quality on the usage of query suggestions during information search. In *CHI*, pages 45–54, 2010.

[18] D. Kraft and T. Lee. Stopping rules and their effect on expected search length. *IPM*, 15(1):47–58, 1979.

[19] Y. Liu, R. Song, M. Zhang, Z. Dou, T. Yamamoto, M. Kato, H. Ohshima, and K. Zhou. Overview of the NTCIR-11 IMine task. In *NTCIR-11*, 2014.

[20] Y. Mansourian and N. Ford. Search persistence and failure on the web: a "bounded rationality" and "satisficing" analysis. *JDoc*, 63(5):680–701, 2007.

[21] D. Maxwell, L. Azzopardi, K. Järvelin, and H. Keskustalo. Searching and stopping: An analysis of stopping rules and strategies. In *CIKM*, pages 313–322, 2015.

[22] P. Pirolli. *Information Foraging Theory: Adaptive Interaction with Information*. Human Technology Interaction Series. Oxford University Press, 2007.

[23] C. Prabha, L. S. Connaway, L. Olszewski, and L. R. Jenkins. What is enough? satisficing information needs. *JDoc*, 63(1):74–89, 2007.

[24] P. Qvarfordt, G. Golovchinsky, T. Dunnigan, and E. Agapie. Looking ahead: Query preview in exploratory search. In *SIGIR*, pages 243–252, 2013.

[25] K. Raman, P. N. Bennett, and K. Collins-Thompson. Toward whole-session relevance: Exploring intrinsic diversity in web search. In *SIGIR*, pages 463–472, 2013.

[26] T. Sakai, Z. Dou, T. Yamamoto, Y. Liu, M. Zhang, and R. Song. Overview of the NTCIR-10 INTENT-2 task. In *NTCIR-10*, 2013.

[27] R. L. Santos, C. Macdonald, and I. Ounis. Exploiting query reformulations for web search result diversification. In *WWW*, pages 881–890, 2010.

[28] R. Song, M. Zhang, T. Sakai, M. P. Kato, Y. Liu, M. Sugimoto, Q. Wang, and N. Orii. Overview of the NTCIR-9 INTENT task. In *NTCIR-9*, 2011.

[29] E. G. Toms and L. Freund. Predicting stopping behaviour: A preliminary analysis. In *SIGIR*, pages 750–751, 2009.

[30] K. Tsukuda, T. Sakai, Z. Dou, and K. Tanaka. Estimating intent types for search result diversification. In *AIRS*, pages 25–37, 2013.

[31] R. W. White and R. A. Roth. Exploratory Search: Beyond the Query-Response Paradigm. *Synthesis Lectures on Information Concepts, Retrieval, and Services*, 1(1):1–98, 2009.

[32] B. M. Wildemuth and L. Freund. Assigning search tasks designed to elicit exploratory search behaviors. In *HCIR*, pages 4:1–4:10, 2012.

[33] W.-C. Wu and D. Kelly. Online search stopping behaviors: An investigation of query abandonment and task stopping. In *ASIS&T Annual Meeting*, 2014.

[34] W.-C. Wu, D. Kelly, and A. Sud. Using information scent and need for cognition to understand online search behavior. In *SIGIR*, pages 557–566, 2014.

[35] L. Zach. When is "enough" enough? modeling the information-seeking and stopping behavior of senior arts administrators. *JASIST*, 56(1):23–35, 2005.

[36] H.-J. Zeng, Q.-C. He, Z. Chen, W.-Y. Ma, and J. Ma. Learning to cluster web search results. In *SIGIR*, pages 210–217, 2004.

[37] Z.-J. Zha, L. Yang, T. Mei, M. Wang, and Z. Wang. Visual query suggestion. In *MM*, pages 15–24, 2009.

Evaluating Search Result Diversity using Intent Hierarchies

Xiaojie Wang[1,2], Zhicheng Dou[*,1,2], Tetsuya Sakai[3], and Ji-Rong Wen[1,2,4]
[1]School of Information, Renmin University of China
[2]Beijing Key Laboratory of Big Data Management and Analysis Methods, China
[3]Department of Computer Science and Engineering, Waseda University
[4]Key Laboratory of Data Engineering and Knowledge Engineering, MOE, China
[2]{wangxiaojie,dou}@ruc.edu.cn, [3]tetsuyasakai@acm.org, [4]jirong.wen@gmail.com

ABSTRACT

Search result diversification aims at returning diversified document lists to cover different user intents for ambiguous or broad queries. Existing diversity measures assume that user intents are independent or exclusive, and do not consider the relationships among the intents. In this paper, we introduce intent hierarchies to model the relationships among intents. Based on intent hierarchies, we propose several hierarchical measures that can consider the relationships among intents. We demonstrate the feasibility of hierarchical measures by using a new test collection based on TREC Web Track 2009-2013 diversity test collections. Our main experimental findings are: (1) Hierarchical measures are generally more discriminative and intuitive than existing measures using flat lists of intents; (2) When the queries have multilayer intent hierarchies, hierarchical measures are less correlated to existing measures, but can get more improvement in discriminative power; (3) Hierarchical measures are more intuitive in terms of diversity or relevance. The hierarchical measures using the whole intent hierarchies are more intuitive than only using the leaf nodes in terms of diversity and relevance.

Keywords

Ambiguity; Diversity; Evaluation; Novelty; Hierarchy

1. INTRODUCTION

Nowadays, people tend to meet their daily information needs by typing keywords into search engines like Google and Bing. However, these keywords, also known as queries, are often ambiguous or broad [14, 15, 28, 10]. The queries usually have several interpretations or aspects, also known as subtopics or user intents. When users submit the same query to retrieval systems, they may want different information returned to fulfill their information needs. This poses a challenge to search engines when the targeted user intent cannot be known in advance.

To tackle this problem, a wide range of search result diversification algorithms ([1, 2, 5, 13, 18, 26, 27, 31, 25, 12, 11]) have been proposed over the past years. They aim at returning a diversified ranked document list that covers different intents of the queries. In the meantime, some researchers have introduced a variety of diversity measures, such as I-rec [22], α-nDCG [9], Intent-Aware measures [1], D♯-measures [24], etc. These measures evaluate ranked lists in terms of both diversity and relevance, and indicate which diversification algorithms are better to use. Existing diversity measures assume that the users' information need could be represented by a single layer of intents and these intents are either independent or exclusive. However, some of the intents are not independent and are related to each other.

We use the query "bobcat", which is a topic (No. 77) in Text Retrieval Conference(TREC) 2010 Web Track [8], as an example. This query is ambiguous because of the polysemy of "bobcat": one interpretation is a company called "bobcat company" whose core business is about tractors; another interpretation is a kind of wild animals called "wild bobcat." We show its official intents, marked by i_1-i_4, in Figure 1(a). The figure shows that except intent i_2 that is about "wild bobcat," the remaining ones, i_1, i_3, and i_4, are all about "bobcat company." This indicates that i_1, i_3, and i_4 are more related to each other, but are less related to i_2. Even within the three intents about "bobcat company," i_1 and i_3 are closer because they are about the trade involving tractors of the company, whereas i_4 is about homepage the company. We argue that this kind of relationships among intents should be modeled when evaluating search result diversity. However, none of existing measures considers this.

Specifically, we find two submitted runs for the query, cmuFuTop10D and THUIR10DvNov, in TREC Web Track 2010 diversity task. cmuFuTop10D covers i_1, i_3, and i_4, while THUIR10DvNov covers i_1, i_2, and i_4 in their top ten ranks. Since i_1, i_3, and i_4 are all about "bobcat company," cmuFuTop10D misses another interpretation of bobcat, i.e. "wild bobcat," but THUIR10DvNov covers both interpretations. In this sense, the latter is more diversified but I-rec [22] treats them as equally good because they cover the same number of intents. Some other existing measures also have similar problems, which will be illustrated in Section 3.3.1. We think that this is due to their lack of recognition of the relationships among intents.

In light of the above observation, we introduce intent hierarchies to represent the relationships among intents. We

*Corresponding author

SIGIR '16, July 17 - 21, 2016, Pisa, Italy

ISBN 978-1-4503-4069-4/16/07...$15.00
DOI: http://dx.doi.org/10.1145/2911451.2911497

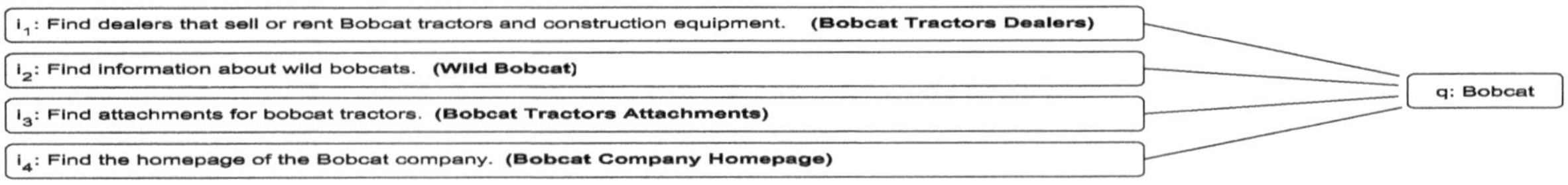

(a) Official intents of the query "bobcat".

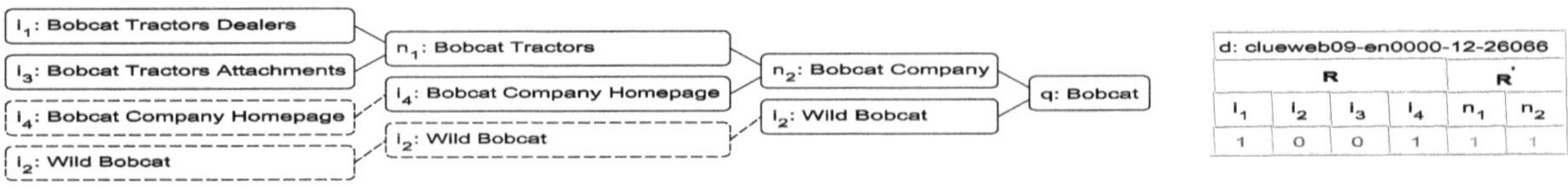

(b) LEFT: Intent Hierarchies OIH and EIH. OIH is comprised of the solid boxes, whereas EIH includes both solid and dashed nodes. RIGHT: An example showing relevance assessments for the added nodes (under $\mathbf{R}'$ in red) derived from relevance assessments for the official intents (under $\mathbf{R}$ in blue).

Figure 1: The official intents, original intent hierarchy (OIH), and extended intent hierarchy (EIH) of No. 77 query "bobcat" in TREC Web Track 2010.

design hierarchical measures using the intent hierarchies to solve the problems mentioned above. The main contributions of this paper are:

(1) To the best of our knowledge, this is the first work on modeling user intents as intent hierarchies and using the intent hierarchies for evaluating search result diversity.

(2) We propose hierarchical measures using intent hierarchies, including Layer-Aware measures, N-rec, LD♯-measures, LAD♯-measures, and HD♯-measures. We show several cases where hierarchical measures outperform existing measures in terms of discriminative power and intuitiveness.

(3) We present a method for creating intent hierarchies from existing diversity test collections, and reusing the relevance assessments. We create a new dataset based on the TREC Web Track 2009-2013 diversity test collections. The new dataset can be assessed online [1].

(4) We compare our measures with existing measures. We find that (i) Hierarchical measures are generally more discriminative and intuitive than existing measures, especially when using the intent hierarchies whose leaf nodes have the same depth; (ii) When the queries have multilayer intent hierarchies, hierarchical measures are less correlated to existing measures, but can get more improvement in discriminative power; (iii) The hierarchical measures using the whole intent hierarchies are more intuitive than only using the leaf nodes in terms of diversity and relevance.

The remainder of this paper is organized as follows. Section 2 describes some existing diversity measures and the methods for testing evaluation measures. In Section 3, we introduce intent hierarchies, and our method for creating a new test collection based on TREC Web Track 2009-2013 diversity test collections. We then propose several new diversity measures that can utilize the intent hierarchies. Section 4 describes experimental results and analysis. We conclude our work in Section 5.

2. RELATED WORK

Given a query q, most existing measures evaluate a ranked document list by modeling users' information need as a flat list of intents $\{i\}$. Some measures can handle intent probability $Pr(i|q)$ and graded relevance assessments but some cannot. In this section, we briefly summarize the previous work on designing and testing diversity measures.

[1] http://www.playbigdata.com/dou/heval/

2.1 Diversity Measures

2.1.1 Intent Recall

Intent recall(I-rec) [22], also known as subtopic recall [30] is the proportion of intents covered by a ranking list. Let d_r denote the document at rank r, and let $I(d_r)$ denote the set of intents to which document d_r is relevant. Then, *I-rec* for a certain cutoff K can be expressed as:

$$I\text{-}rec@K = \frac{|\bigcup_{r=1}^{K} I(d_r)|}{|\{i\}|} \tag{1}$$

Note that I-rec does not take the positions of relevant documents into account, and cannot handle intent probability and graded relevance assessments.

2.1.2 α-nDCG

In order to balance both relevance and diversity of ranked lists, $\alpha\text{-}nDCG$ [9] is defined as:

$$\begin{aligned} \alpha\text{-}nDCG@K &= \frac{\sum_{r=1}^{K} NG(r)/\log(r+1)}{\sum_{r=1}^{K} NG^*(r)/\log(r+1)} \\ NG(r) &= \sum_{i\in\{i\}} J_i(r)(1-\alpha)^{C_i(r-1)} \end{aligned} \tag{2}$$

where $NG^*(r)$ is $NG(r)$ in the ideal ranked list; $J_i(r)$ is 1 if the document at rank r is relevant to intent i, and 0 otherwise; $C_i(r) = \sum_{k=1}^{r} J_i(k)$ is the number of relevant documents to intent i within top r; and α is a parameter. α-nDCG tends to disregard unpopular intents and hence can be counterintuitive sometimes [24].

2.1.3 Intent-Aware measures

Intent-Aware measures (IA $measures$) [1] is a general framework to evaluate ranked document lists. Assuming that $\sum_{i\in\{i\}} Pr(i|q) = 1$, $M\text{-}IA$ can be computed as:

$$M\text{-}IA@K = \sum_{i\in\{i\}} Pr(i|q) M_i@K \tag{3}$$

where M_i is the per-intent version of measure M. Measure M can be nDCG [16], ERR [4], nERR [7], etc.

2.1.4 D♯-measures

D♯-measures [24] aim to boost intent recall, and to reward documents that are highly relevant to more popular intents. Assume that $g_i(r)$ is the gain value of the document at rank

r for intent i, and $g_i(r)$ is calculated based on per-intent relevance assessments. Then the global gain at rank r is given by:

$$GG(r) = \sum_{i \in \{i\}} Pr(i|q) g_i(r) \quad (4)$$

Let $CGG(r) = \sum_{k=1}^{r} GG(k)$, which is the cumulative global gain at rank r. Further, let $GG^*(r)$ and $CGG^*(r)$ denote the global gain and the cumulative global gain respectively at rank r in the ideal ranked list. The ideal list is obtained by listing up all relevant documents in descending order of global gains. Let $J(r) = 1$ if the document at rank r is relevant to any of the intents $\{i\}$, and $J(r) = 0$ otherwise. Let $C(r) = \sum_{k=1}^{r} J(k)$, which is the number of relevant documents within top r. *D-nDCG* and *D-Q* at document cutoff K are defined as:

$$D\text{-}nDCG@K = \frac{\sum_{r=1}^{K} GG(r)/\log(r+1)}{\sum_{r=1}^{K} GG^*(r)/\log(r+1)} \quad (5)$$

$$D\text{-}Q@K = \frac{1}{\min(K, R)} \sum_{r=1}^{K} J(r) \frac{C(r) + \beta CGG(r)}{r + \beta CGG^*(r)} \quad (6)$$

where R is the number of judged relevant documents. Then *D♯-measure* is defined as:

$$D\sharp\text{-}measure@K = \gamma I\text{-}rec@K + (1-\gamma) D\text{-}measure@K \quad (7)$$

where *D-measure* can be D-nDCG or D-Q, and γ is a parameter controlling the tradeoff between diversity and relevance. D♯-measures are free of the under-normalization problem of α-nDCG and IA measures.

The diversity measures mentioned above are widely used in several tasks of TREC Web Track [2] or NII Testbeds and Community for Information access Research (NTCIR) [3], *but they do not take the relationships among intents into con sideration*, which is what we aim to deal with in this paper.

2.2 Measure Evaluation

Given a certain significance level, *discriminative power* measures the stability of measures across queries and experiments based on significance tests, e.g. paired bootstrap test [20], Tukey's Honestly Significant Differences(HSD) [3] test, etc. Discriminative power can be used to estimate the performance difference required to achieve statistical significance between two retrieval systems [21].

oncordance test [21] is proposed to quantify the intuitiveness of diversity measures. In concordance test, one or more gold standard measures are chosen and assumed to truly represent intuitiveness. Given two diversity measures M_1 and M_2, the relative intuitiveness of M_1 (or M_2) is measured in terms of preference agreement with the gold standard measures. The preference agreement is that M_1 (or M_2) agrees with the gold standard measure(s) about which one of two ranked lists should be preferred.

ank correlation compares two rankings, which are two ranked system lists in our case. Kendall's τ [17] is a widely-used statistic to measure rank correlation. However τ lacks the property of top heaviness, which means the exchanges near the top of a ranked list and those near the bottom are treated equally, even though the swaps near the top is generally more important in the context of IR evaluation. τ_{ap} [29] is proposed to deal with the problem. Note that τ is symmetric but τ_{ap} is not. However, a symmetric τ_{ap} can be obtained by averaging two τ_{ap} values when each list is treated as the former one. Both τ and τ_{ap} range from -1, which implies two ranked lists perfectly disagree, to 1, which implies two ranked lists are identical.

In this paper, we use discriminative power, concordance test, and rank correlation to evaluate diversity measures.

3. PROPOSED METHODS

In this section, we define two types of intent hierarchies to represent the relationships among user intents and discuss their properties. We then introduce our method for creating such intent hierarchies and obtaining relevance assessments for the intent hierarchies based on TREC Web Track 2009-2013 diversity test collections. Last, we propose several diversity measures based on intent hierarchies, and demonstrate that in some cases, the new measures outperform their corresponding existing measures.

3.1 Intent Hierarchies

Given a query q, the users' information need is represented as a set of intents $\{i\}$. We assume these intents cannot be further subdivided, and refer to them as *atomic intents*. We aim to build an *intent hierarchy* based on the semantic similarity or relatedness of the intents. The intent hierarchy should possess some basic properties as follows:

roperty 1 The intent hierarchy is in a tree structure, where every child has only one parent.

roperty 2 The root of intent hierarchy is denoted by q itself, which stands for the user's information need as a whole. The root is a dummy node only for the completeness of the tree, and is not considered in our measures.

roperty 3 When q is broad, the intent hierarchy is built in such a way that a parent node refers to a more general concept than its children, and a child node refers to one aspect of its parent. When q is ambiguous, each child node of the root is one interpretation of the query, and each of its subtrees is built in the same way as a broad query.

roperty 4 These atomic intents, i.e. $\{i\}$, correspond one to one with leaves of the intent hierarchy. This means the number of leaves in the intent hierarchy is the same as the number of the atomic intents.

We call an intent hierarchy that satisfies the properties specified above is called an *original intent hierarchy* (*OIH*). OIH can be extended so as to satisfy an extra property as:

roperty 5 These atomic intents are in the same layer of the intent hierarchy. In other words, all leaf nodes of the intent hierarchy have the same depth because the atomic intents correspond to leaves of the intent hierarchy (see Property 4).

An intent hierarchies that satisfies all five properties are called an *extended intent hierarchy* (*EIH*). If a query's OIH satisfies Property 5, then its EIH is the same as the OIH.

We consider the root of an intent hierarchy as the zeroth layer, the child nodes of the root as the first layer and so forth. If an intent hierarchy only has the zeroth layer and the first layer, the height of the intent hierarchy is one. In the paper, a *single layer intent hierarchy* refers to an intent hierarchy whose height is one, while a *multilayer intent hierarchy* refers to that whose height is greater than one.

[2]http://plg.uwaterloo.ca/~trecweb/

[3]http://research.nii.ac.jp/ntcir/index-en.html

3.2 Creating Intent Hierarchies

In this paper, we create intent hierarchies based on TREC Web Track 2009-2013 diversity test collections. Note that for each query in TREC Web Track 2010-2013, the description of its first intent is the same as the description of the query itself. We find that although the descriptions are the same, if a query has several different interpretations, the first intent is just one of these interpretations. A query's first intent does not refer to a more general concept than the other intents. So we do not treat the first intent differently.

We use the official intents as atomic intents to avoid reassessing relevance of the documents. First we create original intent hierarchies (OIH) by manually grouping the official intents based on their semantic similarity or relatedness. Then, we extend them to extended intent hierarchies (EIH). Figure 1 illustrates how we create OIH and EIH for the query "bobcat" in TREC 2010 Web Track. It can be seen from Figure 1(a) that this query has four official intents and intent i_1 and i_3 are related to the trade involving tractors of the "bobcat company." So we create a new node n_1 that stands for "bobcat tractors" as their parent node. Similarly, n_1 and i_4 are related to "bobcat company," hence we create another new node n_2 representing "bobcat company" as their parent. Finally, since n_2 ("bobcat company") and i_2 ("wild bobcat") are two distinct interpretations of query "bobcat," they are considered as the child nodes of the root node. The resultant OIH is shown in solid boxes in the left of Figure 1(b). Further, we extend the OIH by adding more child nodes to i_2 and i_4 to make sure that all the leaf nodes have the same height. The resultant EIH is shown in solid boxes plus dashed boxes in the left of Figure 1(b).

For a leaf node, we use its original weight of the corresponding official intent as its initial weight. For an intermediate node, we set its original weight to the sum of its child node weights. We then normalize the weights for each layer to make sure that these weights sum to 1. For TREC Web Track 2009-2013 test collections, because of the lack of official intent weights, we assume that each official intent for a query is equally important.

As for the OIH or EIH shown in Figure 1(b): (1) It is in a tree structure (Property 1); (2) Its root is query "bobcat" itself (Property 2); (3) The query is ambiguous, so the child nodes of root are its two different interpretations, i.e. "bobcat company" and "wild bobcat." A parent node refers to a more general concept than its children (Property 3), e.g. "bobcat company" is more general than "bobcat company homepage;" (4) The leaf nodes are exactly the official intents of query "bobcat" (Property 4). Further, the depth of all the leaf nodes in EIH is three (Property 5).

Note that we only have document relevance assessments for the original intents appeared in TREC Web Track diversity test collections. In other words, for the intent hierarchies we create, document relevance judgments are just available for their leaf intents. We do not have document relevance assessments for intermediate intents. As assessing document relevance is usually very time-consuming, it is not desirable to reassess the documents for intermediate nodes of the intent hierarchies. Fortunately, according to Property 3, a parent node of an intent hierarchy stands for a more general concept than its child nodes. Hence it is reasonable to assume that if a document is relevant to a node, it would be relevant to the node's parent. This means that we can derive relevance assessments for the intermediate nodes starting from the leaves. In this paper, we simply let:

$$L_d(n) = \max_{c \in C(n)} L_d(c) \tag{8}$$

where $L_d(n)$ is the relevance rating assigned to document d for node n, and $C(n)$ is the set of child nodes of n.

We show an actual document (denoted by d in the following) from TREC Web Track 2010 diversity test collection in Figure 1(b). In the table, the officially provided relevance assessments are marked in blue, e.g. the relevance rating of d for i_1 is 1. Firstly, node n_1 has two child nodes, i_1 and i_3, and the relevance ratings of d for them are 1 and 0. According to Equation (8), the relevance rating of d for n_1 is 1. Similarly, we can derive the relevance rating for n_2 based on its child node i_4 and n_1. These derived relevance assessments are shown in red in the table of Figure 1(b).

To conclude, we create a new dataset containing intent hierarchies by manually grouping the official intents from TREC Web track test collections. The good news is that we do not need to reassess document relevance with regards to the intent hierarchies. We directly leverage document relevance assessments for the leaf intents, and automatically assign relevance ratings for the intermediate intents. This also implies that when we want to create hierarchical intents for evaluating diversity, we just need to assess document relevance for the leaf nodes or atomic intents.

The new test collection has 250 queries, and 105 topics have multilayer intent hierarchies. Most of the time of creating the new dataset is spent on grouping the original intents. On average, we spend about three minutes per query mainly in understanding the original intents with the assistance of search engines such as Bing and Google.

3.3 Hierarchical Measures

3.3.1 Layer-Aware measures

Given a query q and its intent hierarchy, our first proposal for evaluating a ranked list is to first evaluate the ranked list for each layer using existing measures, then combine the evaluation scores.

Let H denote the height of the intent hierarchy, and let $L = \{l_1, l_2, ..., l_H\}$ denote its first layer to the last layer. We define Layer-Aware measures (*LA measures*) at document cutoff K as the follows.

$$M\text{-}LA@K = \sum_{i=1}^{H} w_i * M_i@K \tag{9}$$

Here, w_i is the weight of layer l_i, where $\sum_{i=1}^{H} w_i = 1$, and M_i is the evaluation score of measure M by using the intents of layer l_i. For example, ERR-IA-LA is computed as follows: (1) For each layer, compute the per-layer scores of ERR-IA; (2) Compute the weighted average of the per-layer scores using Equation (9).

We find that the combination of measures over layers of intent hierarchies could outperform the original measures using a flat list of intents. We use the query "defender", which is a topic (No. 20) in TREC Web Track 2009 [6], as an example. We choose this query because it has a relatively simple intent hierarchy. Its extended intent hierarchy (EIH) is shown in the left of Figure 2(b). Suppose we have three documents, d_1-d_3, and each of them can be viewed as a ranked list containing only one document. Their relevance assessments for the EIH are displayed in blue in the right of

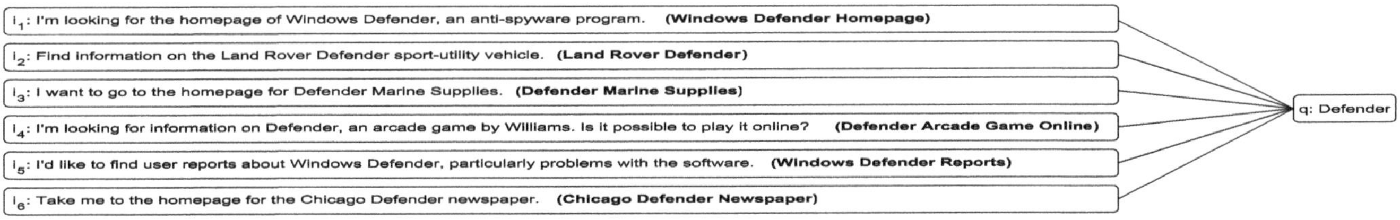

(a) Official intents of the query "defender".

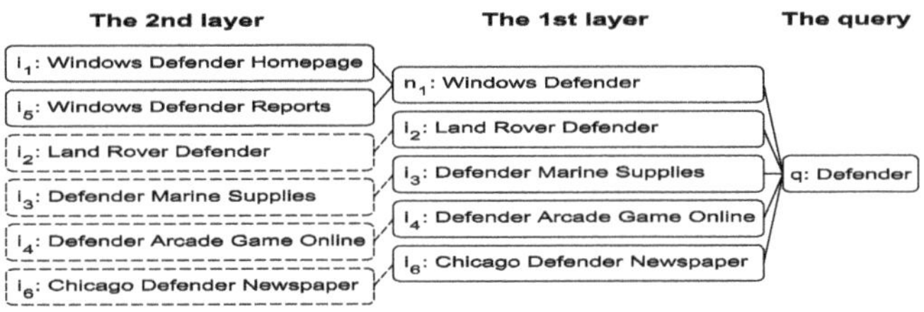

	R			R'	S						
	i_1	i_4	i_5	n_1	D#-nDCG$_1$@1	D#-nDCG$_2$@1	D#-nDCG-LA$_E$@1	I-rec$_1$@1	I-rec$_2$@1	N-rec$_E$@1	N-rec$_O$@1
d_1	1	1	0	1	0.70	0.67	0.68	0.40	0.33	0.36	0.43
d_2	1	0	1	1	0.35	0.67	0.51	0.20	0.33	0.27	0.43
d_3	1	0	0	1	0.35	0.33	0.34	0.20	0.17	0.18	0.29
d^*	1	1	1	1	(Note that these measures are computed at rank 1)						

(b) LEFT: Intent Hierarchies OIH and EIH. OIH is comprised of the solid boxes, whereas EIH includes both solid and dashed nodes. RIGHT: 1st column: document IDs (d^*: the ideal one), each document is equal to a ranked list of length 1. 2nd to 5th column (**R** and **R**$'$): relevance assessments for the official intents (in red) and derived relevance assessments for added nodes (in blue). 6th to 12th column (**S**): the measures are computed at rank 1 (subscript $_1$ means only using the first layer of EIH and subscript $_2$ means only using the second layer. subscript $_O$ means using OIH and subscript $_E$ means using EIH.), e.g. d_2 get 0.35 when using D♯-nDCG on the first layer of EIH. Note that the original D♯-nDCG is equal to D♯-nDCG$_2$ and the original I-rec is equal to I-rec$_2$.

Figure 2: The official intents, original intent hierarchy (OIH), and extended intent hierarchy (EIH) of No. 20 query "defender" in TREC Web Track 2009. In the right table, if two documents have the same scores under a measure (in green below), it means that this measure cannot tell which one is better, e.g. D♯-nDCG$_1$@1 treats d_2 and d_3 as equally good, but d_3 is better because of its relevance to an extra intent i_5.

Figure 2(b). Note that the nodes that receive no relevant documents within the documents are not displayed to save space. Assume d^* is the first document within the ideal rank list and it is relevant to every node displayed. In the right of Figure 2(b), D♯-nDCG$_1$@1 is the evaluation score when only using the first layer of the EIH, D♯-nDCG$_2$@1 means only using the second layer, and D♯-nDCG-LA$_E$@1 is the average of D♯-nDCG$_1$@1 and D♯-nDCG$_2$@1. Note that the original D♯-nDCG is equal to D♯-nDCG$_2$. We use the measures to score d_1 to d_3, which is equivalent of evaluating at document cutoff 1. We show the evaluation results in Figure 2(b), e.g. d_2 gets 0.35 when using D♯-nDCG$_1$@1.

We find that $d_1 > d_2 = d_3$ in terms of D♯-nDCG$_1$@1, $d_1 = d_2 > d_3$ in terms of D♯-nDCG$_2$@1, whereas $d_1 > d_2 > d_3$ in terms of D♯-nDCG-LA$_E$@1. Here, ">" means the former document is preferred compared with the latter when evaluating them at rank 1, and "=" means neither is preferred. The real preference should be $d_1 > d_2 > d_3$. This is because (1) d_1 is more diversified than d_2 because d_1 refers to two interpretations of query "defender", i.e. "windows defender" and "defender arcade game online," while d_2 only refers to the former; (2) d_2 is more diversified than d_3 because d_2 refers to two aspects of "windows defender", i.e. "windows defender homepage" and "windows defender reports" while d_3 just refers to the former. Here, only D♯-nDCG-LA$_E$@1 is consistent with the real preference. D♯-nDCG$_1$@1 fails to tell the difference between d_2 and d_3, whereas D♯-nDCG$_2$@1 fails to tell the difference between d_1 and d_2. This indicates that the combination over layers has higher potential to reflect real user satisfaction than the use of a flat list of intents in some cases.

3.3.2 Node Recall

Given a query q, let V denote the nodes in its intent hierarchy except for its root. Let d_r denote the document at rank r, and let $N(d_r)$ denote the set of nodes in V to which d_r is relevant. Given a document cutoff K, we define node recall (*N-rec*) as:

$$N\text{-}rec@K = \frac{|\bigcup_{r=1}^{K} N(d_r)|}{|V|} \tag{10}$$

which is the proportion of nodes in the hierarchy covered by the top K documents. N-rec is a natural generalization of I-rec when using the intent hierarchy rather than a flat list of intents. They both are rank-insensitive and cannot handle graded relevance assessments.

We use an example to show that N-rec is able to outperform I-rec in terms of discriminative power. In the right of Figure 2(b), I-rec$_1$@1 means only using the first layer, I-rec$_2$@1 means only using the second layer, and N-rec$_E$@1 means using the extended intent hierarchy (EIH) when computing N-rec. These measures are computed at rank 1. Note that the original I-rec is equal to I-rec$_2$. We find that $d_1 > d_2 = d_3$ according to I-rec$_1$@1, $d_1 = d_2 > d_3$ according to I-rec$_2$@1, whereas $d_1 > d_2 > d_3$ according to N-rec$_E$@1. As we discussed in Section 3.3.1, The real preference should be $d_1 > d_2 > d_3$. I-rec$_1$@1 fails to tell the difference between d_2 and d_3, while I-rec$_2$@1 fails to distinguish between d_1 and d_2. Only N-rec$_E$@1 can tell the difference between the three documents, and thus is more discriminative than I-rec.

Another point worth noting is that the types of intent hierarchies are crucial to N-rec. In the right of Figure 2(b), N-rec$_O$@1 means using the original intent hierarchy (OIH) instead of EIH. We find that N-rec$_O$@1 cannot determine which one of d_1 and d_2 is better because they have exactly the same score. This indicates that using EIH has higher discriminative power than using OIH.

We aim to retrieve documents that cover as many nodes of intent hierarchies as possible. At the same time, we prefer the documents that are highly relevant to more popular nodes and layers. N-rec mainly rewards wide coverage of different nodes of intent hierarchies in the top ranks. In the following, we discuss some measures to complement N-rec.

3.3.3 LD♮-measures

We use the leaf nodes of intent hierarchies to compute D-measures. Then, *LD♮-measure* is defined as:

$$LD\natural\text{-}measure@K = \gamma N\text{-}rec@K + (1-\gamma) D\text{-}measure@K \quad (11)$$

where γ is a parameter controlling the tradeoff between diversity and relevance. Since D-measures only use the leaves of intent hierarchies, LD♮-measures reward high relevance with more popular leaves, but do not reward high relevance with more popular intermediate nodes. Also, LD♮-measures cannot handle the weights of layers. To tackle these, we propose HD♮-measures and LAD♮-measures in the next section.

3.3.4 HD♮-measures and LAD♮-measures

Inspired by D♮-measures, we define the global gain for an intent hierarchy at rank r as:

$$GG_h(r) = \sum_{i=1}^{H} w_i * GG_i(r) \quad (12)$$

where w_i is the weight of layer l_i and $GG_i(r)$ is the global gain for layer l_i at rank r. Let $CGG_h(r) = \sum_{k=1}^{r} GG_h(k)$, which is the cumulative global gain for the intent hierarchy at rank r. Further, let $GG_h^*(r)$ and $CGG_h^*(r)$ denote the global gain and the cumulative global gain for the intent hierarchy at rank r in the ideal ranked list. The ideal list is obtained by listing up all the judged documents in descending order of global gains for the intent hierarchy. Let $J(r) = 1$ if the document at rank r is relevant to the intent hierarchy, and $J(r) = 0$ otherwise. Let $C(r) = \sum_{k=1}^{r} J(k)$. We define *HD-nDCG* and *HD-Q* at document cutoff K as:

$$HD\text{-}nDCG@K = \frac{\sum_{r=1}^{K} GG_h(r)/\log(r+1)}{\sum_{r=1}^{K} GG_h^*(r)/\log(r+1)} \quad (13)$$

$$HD\text{-}Q@K = \frac{1}{\min(K,R)} \sum_{r=1}^{K} J(r) \frac{C(r) + \beta CGG_h(r)}{r + \beta CGG_h^*(r)} \quad (14)$$

where R is the number of judged documents relevant to the intent hierarchy. We define *HD♮-measure* as:

$$HD\natural\text{-}measure@K = \gamma N\text{-}rec@K + (1-\gamma) HD\text{-}measure@K \quad (15)$$

where *HD-measure* can be HD-nDCG or HD-Q, and γ is a parameter controlling the tradeoff between diversity and relevance. Besides, We define *LAD♮-measure* as:

$$LAD\natural\text{-}measure@K = \gamma N\text{-}rec@K + (1-\gamma) D\text{-}measure\text{-}LA@K \quad (16)$$

where γ is a parameter balancing diversity with relevance, and D-measure-LA is the LA version of D-measure.

To measure the relevance of ranked lists, HD♮-measures use HD-measures, while LAD♮-measures use D-measures-LA. HD-measures and D-measures-LA reward high relevance to more popular nodes, and can handle layer weights. The difference between them is what to combine over layers: HD-measures combine the global gain for each layer while D-measures-LA combine D-measures for each layer. Take HD-nDCG and D-nDCG-LA as an example:

$$HD\text{-}nDCG@K = \frac{\sum_{r=1}^{K} [\sum_{i=1}^{H} w_i * GG_i(r)]/\log_2(r+1)}{\sum_{r=1}^{K} [\sum_{i=1}^{H} w_i * GG_i^*(r)]/\log_2(r+1)}$$

$$D\text{-}nDCG\text{-}LA@K = \sum_{i=1}^{H} w_i * D\text{-}nDCG_i@K$$

where $GG_i(r)$ is the global gain for layer l_i at rank r, and $D\text{-}nDCG_i$ means only using the nodes of layer l_i.

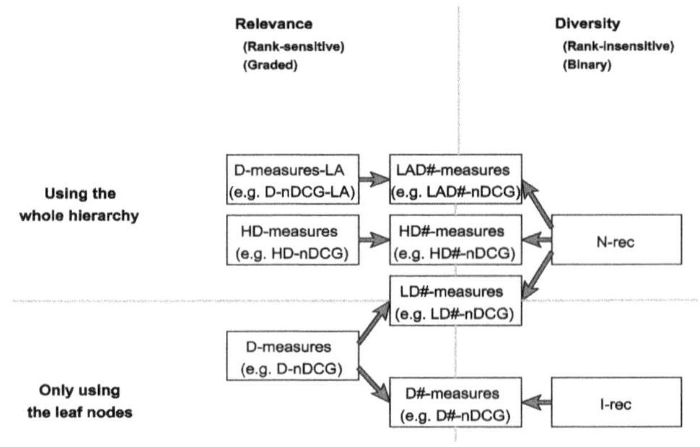

Figure 3: Relationships of D♮-measures, LD♮-measures, HD♮-measures, and LAD♮-measures.

3.3.5 Summarization

Since our measures use intent hierarchies, we call them *hierarchical measures*. Each of D♮-measures, LD♮-measures, HD♮-measures and LAD♮-measures is a linear combination of two measures: one measure mainly rewards the diversity of ranked lists, whereas another measure mainly rewards the relevance. We show their relationships in Figure 3. It can be seen that (1) To reward the diversity, LD♮-measures, HD♮-measures and LAD♮-measures use the whole intent hierarchy, whereas D♮-measures only use the leaf nodes; (2) To reward the relevance, HD♮-measures and LAD♮-measures use the whole intent hierarchy, whereas D♮-measures and LD♮-measures only use the leaf nodes.

4. EXPERIMENTS

4.1 Settings

We experiment with the proposed measures on the TREC Web Track 2009-2013 diversity test collections and the new test collection mentioned in Section 3.2. The new test collection has two types of intent hierarchies, i.e. the original intent hierarchies (OIH), and the extended intent hierarchies (EIH). The results of our measures using OIH are different from those using EIH. In the following, subscript $_O$ means using the OIH, while subscript $_E$ means using the EIH.

We use uniform probabilities for official intents like in TREC Web Track 2009-2013 diversity task. We use uniform layer weights when computing our measures, and leave the investigation of nonuniform weights to future. Unless stated otherwise, we use document cutoff $K = 20$ for all measures, and $\gamma = 0.5$ in Equation (7, 11, 15, and 16).

4.2 Discriminative Power Results

Following the previous work [19, 20, 23, 24, 21], we use the paired bootstrap test and set $B = 1,000$ (B is the number of bootstrap samples). When the queries have single-layer intent hierarchies: (1) LA measures are reduced to their corresponding existing measures. For example, D♮-measures-LA are reduced to D♮-measures; (2) LD♮-measures, HD♮-measures, and LAD♮-measures are reduced to D♮-measures. We conduct the experiments as follows: (1) Sampling 20 submitted runs every year (2009-2013), which produces 950 pairs of

Table 1: Discriminative power and performance Δ of diversity measures based on the paired bootstrap test at $\alpha = 0.05$. The leftmost column shows existing measures' results; the middle column shows their corresponding LA measures' results using original intent hierarchies (denoted by subscript $_O$); the rightmost column shows their corresponding LA measures' results using extended intent hierarchies (denoted by subscript $_E$). For each row, the greatest value is in bold.

(a) 250 queries in TREC Web Track 2009-2013								
existing measures			measures based on OIH			measures based on EIH		
measure	disc.power	required Δ	measure	disc.power	required Δ	measure	disc.power	required Δ
I-rec	49.1%	0.14	I-rec-LA$_O$	48.5%	0.13	I-rec-LA$_E$	**49.7%**	0.13
α-nDCG	**56.8%**	0.11	α-nDCG-LA$_O$	56.4%	0.12	α-nDCG-LA$_E$	56.0%	0.11
ERR-IA	52.0%	0.12	ERR-IA-LA$_O$	51.1%	0.14	ERR-IA-LA$_E$	**52.1%**	0.14
nDCG-IA	53.4%	0.07	nDCG-IA-LA$_O$	52.4%	0.06	nDCG-IA-LA$_E$	**53.5%**	0.06
Q-IA	43.1%	0.06	Q-IA-LA$_O$	42.7%	0.06	Q-IA-LA$_E$	**43.5%**	0.06
D♯-nDCG	55.1%	0.09	D♯-nDCG-LA$_O$	54.4%	0.10	D♯-nDCG-LA$_E$	**55.3%**	0.09
D♯-Q	52.7%	0.09	D♯-Q-LA$_O$	52.7%	0.09	D♯-Q-LA$_E$	**53.7%**	0.08
(b) 105 queries that have multilayer intent hierarchies (out of 250)								
I-rec	36.4%	0.23	I-rec-LA$_O$	33.4%	0.26	I-rec-LA$_E$	**36.6%**	0.26
α-nDCG	**38.7%**	0.22	α-nDCG-LA$_O$	37.8%	0.26	α-nDCG-LA$_E$	37.9%	0.18
ERR-IA	31.9%	0.19	ERR-IA-LA$_O$	31.2%	0.23	ERR-IA-LA$_E$	**32.9%**	0.21
nDCG-IA	29.9%	0.11	nDCG-IA-LA$_O$	29.2%	0.13	nDCG-IA-LA$_E$	**32.3%**	0.13
Q-IA	20.2%	0.14	Q-IA-LA$_O$	20.3%	0.13	Q-IA-LA$_E$	**22.4%**	0.14
D♯-nDCG	38.9%	0.17	D♯-nDCG-LA$_O$	36.4%	0.19	D♯-nDCG-LA$_E$	**39.7%**	0.18
D♯-Q	38.7%	0.17	D♯-Q-LA$_O$	36.3%	0.16	D♯-Q-LA$_E$	**39.3%**	0.16

Table 2: Discriminative power (shown in columns A) and performance Δ (shown in columns B) of diversity measures ranked by their discriminative power based on the paired bootstrap test at $\alpha = 0.05$. Baseline measures are marked by *.

(a) 250 queries in TREC Web Track 2009-2013					
measure	A	B	measure	A	B
HD♯-nDCG$_E$	55.9%	0.11	HD♯-Q$_E$	53.4%	0.09
LD♯-nDCG$_O$	55.5%	0.10	LAD♯-Q$_O$	53.4%	0.09
LD♯-nDCG$_E$	55.3%	0.09	LD♯-Q$_O$	53.3%	0.09
LAD♯-nDCG$_E$	55.2%	0.10	HD♯-Q$_O$	53.1%	0.09
*D♯-nDCG	55.1%	0.09	LAD♯-Q$_E$	52.9%	0.10
HD♯-nDCG$_O$	54.7%	0.10	LD♯-Q$_E$	52.7%	0.09
LAD♯-nDCG$_O$	54.5%	0.10	*D♯-Q	52.7%	0.09
(b) 105 queries that have multilayer intent hierarchies (out of 250)					
HD♯-nDCG$_E$	40.5%	0.16	LD♯-Q$_E$	39.4%	0.19
LD♯-nDCG$_E$	40.0%	0.17	LAD♯-Q$_E$	39.4%	0.19
LAD♯-nDCG$_E$	39.1%	0.19	HD♯-Q$_E$	38.9%	0.17
*D♯-nDCG	38.9%	0.17	*D♯-Q	38.7%	0.17
LD♯-nDCG$_O$	38.1%	0.19	HD♯-Q$_O$	38.1%	0.17
LAD♯-nDCG$_O$	36.8%	0.21	LD♯-Q$_O$	37.3%	0.19
HD♯-nDCG$_O$	36.5%	0.17	LAD♯-Q$_O$	37.1%	0.15

sampled runs in total; (2) With the 950 pairs of sampled runs, computing the discriminative power and performance Δ using all 250 queries in TREC Web Track 2009-2013 diversity test collections; (3) With the 950 pairs of sampled runs, computing the discriminative power and performance Δ using the 105 queries that have multilayer intent hierarchies. Performance Δ is the required value to achieve statistical significance, and is computed following [21]. The results are shown in Table 1 and Table 2.

By comparing the discriminative power scores of existing measures and their corresponding LA measures based on OIH or EIH in each row of Table 1, we find that: (1) Except α-nDCG-LA, LA measures using EIH are more discriminative than their corresponding existing measures, especially in the case of IA measures. For example, when experimenting with 105 queries that have multilayer intent hierarchies, Q-IA-LA$_E$ (22.4%) outperforms Q-IA (20.2%) in terms of discriminative power; (2) The measures using OIH are less discriminative than the measures using EIH. For example, nDCG-IA-LA$_O$ is 29.2% while nDCG-IA-LA$_E$ is 32.3% when experimenting with 105 queries that have multilayer intent hierarchies.

By comparing the discriminative power results of D♯-measures, LD♯-measures, HD♯-measures, and LAD♯-measures (each block in Table 2), we find that: (1) The measures using EIH are generally more discriminative than the measures using OIH; (2) When using EIH, LD♯-measures, HD♯-measures and LAD♯-measures are better than (or at least as good as) D♯-measures in terms of discriminative power.

By comparing the results using all 250 queries in TREC Web Track 2009-2013 (shown in Table 1(a) or Table 2(a)) and the results only using the queries that have multilayer intent hierarchies (shown in Table 1(b) or Table 2(b)), we find that hierarchical measures have greater improvement of discriminative power than existing measures for queries that have multilayer intent hierarchies. This is reasonable because our measures have potential to recognize the difference between ranked lists by utilizing the hierarchies whereas existing measures cannot. Another justification is that our measures are equivalent to existing measures when the queries only have single-layer intent hierarchies.

The above observations suggest that it is preferable to use EIH when computing hierarchical measures. We think that the hierarchical measures using EIH have higher discriminative power than the hierarchical measures using OIH. For example, Figure 2(b) shows that d_1 is more diversified than d_2 because d_1 refers to two interpretations of the query, while d_2 only refers to one of them. N-rec$_E$ agrees with this but N-rec$_O$ cannot tell which one is more diversified.

4.3 Intuitiveness

4.3.1 Difference between using OIH and EIH

The hierarchical measures using EIH are more intuitive than using OIH in terms of diversity. Following the previous work [21], we use I-rec as the gold standard measure for the diversity because it does not depend on intent hierarchies OIH and EIH. Table 3 shows the intuitiveness when using all the queries in TREC Web Track 2009-2013 diversity test collections. We find that for a document cutoff $K = 10$, the hierarchical measures using EIH are more intuitive than using OIH. For a document cutoff $K = 20$, there is only one exception (LD♯-nDCG@20).

This is because the hierarchical measures using OIH may reward high relevance to some official intents, and fail to

Table 3: Intuitiveness based on preference agreement with I-rec. For each measure pair (using OIH or EIH), the higher score is shown in bold and the numbers of disagreements between this pair are shown in parentheses below.

(a) Document cutoff $K = 10$. Gold standard measure: I-rec

	ERR-IA-LA	nDCG-IA-LA	Q-IA-LA	LD♯-nDCG	HD♯-nDCG	LAD♯-nDCG
OIH	.663	.624	.653	.802	.025	.753
EIH	**.724**	**.748**	**.696**	**.841**	**.999**	**.886**
	(4973)	(5492)	(4660)	(2601)	(3421)	(4948)

(b) Document cutoff $K = 20$. Gold standard measure: I-rec

	ERR-IA-LA	nDCG-IA-LA	Q-IA-LA	LD♯-nDCG	HD♯-nDCG	LAD♯-nDCG
OIH	.692	.656	.677	**.821**	.823	.827
EIH	**.732**	**.748**	**.729**	.739	**.837**	**.840**
	(5362)	(6688)	(5273)	(2511)	(5329)	(5645)

reward wide coverage of the official intents. Take the OIH in Figure 2 as an example. Since we assume that the documents that are relevant to a node are relevant to its parent node, the relevance assessments for intent i_1 or i_5 are reflected in the relevance assessments for their parent node n_1. Though the first layer of the OIH excludes i_1 or i_5, it indirectly considers them through their parent node n_1. By including the other four intents, the first layer considers all six official intents, but the second layer of the OIH only has i_1 or i_5. When combining the two layers, the relevance assessments for i_1 or i_5 are considered twice, once in the first layer and again in the second layer. However, the relevance assessments for the other four intents are only considered once in the first layer. This means that when using the OIH, hierarchical measures mainly reward higher relevance to i_1 and i_5 than other intents. The EIH in Figure 2 solves this problem by extending i_2, i_3, i_4, and i_6 to the second layer so that every official intent can be considered in each layer when evaluating the ranking quality.

In the remaining part of the section, we will only report experimental results using EIH due to space limitation. In most experiments, using EIH yields higher discriminative power and intuitiveness than OIH.

4.3.2 Intuitiveness of Hierarchical Measures

In Section 4.2, we show that LD♯-nDCG$_E$, HD♯-nDCG$_E$, and LAD♯-nDCG$_E$ are highly discriminative among hierarchical measures. In this section, we further compare their intuitiveness with some existing measures, including α-nDCG, ERR-IA, and D♯-nDCG. We do the concordance test based on all the queries in TREC Web Track 2009-2013 diversity test collections, and show the results in Table 4. In Table 4(a) and Table 4(b), we use N-rec$_E$ and Precision as the gold standard measure respectively, whereas in Table 4(c), both N-rec$_E$ and Precision are used as the gold standard measures. We use N-rec$_E$ as a gold standard measure in terms of the diversity because: (1) It is a simple binary measures; (2) It measures diversity better than I-rec, which is traditionally used as the gold standard measure for diversity.

Table 4 shows that (1) In terms of the diversity, LD♯-nDCG$_E$, HD♯-nDCG$_E$, and LAD♯-nDCG$_E$ are more intuitive than existing measures. This is expected because these hierarchical measures directly depend on N-rec$_E$ by means of Equation (11) and the like; (2) In terms of diversity, LD♯-nDCG$_E$ is most intuitive; (3) In terms of relevance, HD♯-nDCG$_E$ is most intuitive; (4) In terms of both diversity and relevance, LAD♯-nDCG$_E$ is the most intuitive measure.

Table 4 shows that using the whole intent hierarchies instead of only using the leaf nodes can improve the intuitiveness of measures. HD♯-nDCG$_E$ and LAD♯-nDCG$_E$ use the

Table 4: Intuitiveness based on preference agreement with gold standard measures. For each measure pair, the higher score is shown in bold and the numbers of disagreements between this pair are shown in parentheses below.

(a) Gold standard measure: N-rec$_E$ ("diversity")

	ERR-IA	D♯-nDCG	LD♯-nDCG$_E$	HD♯-nDCG$_E$	LAD♯-nDCG$_E$
α-nDCG	**.988**/.362 (14215)	.661/**.983** (43908)	.656/**.986** (44098)	.663/**.984** (44522)	.661/**.984** (44444)
ERR-IA	-	.577/**.987** (56060)	.573/**.991** (56011)	.578/**.990** (56245)	.577/**.990** (56209)
D♯-nDCG	-	-	.428/**.612** (2124)	.700/**.741** (3822)	.677/**.738** (3586)
LD♯-nDCG$_E$	-	-	-	**.898**/.799 (2356)	**.895**/.811 (2026)
HD♯-nDCG$_E$	-	-	-	-	.724/**.915** (330)

(b) Gold standard measure: Precision ("relevance")

	ERR-IA	D♯-nDCG	LD♯-nDCG$_E$	HD♯-nDCG$_E$	LAD♯-nDCG$_E$
α-nDCG	**.749**/.345 (14215)	.359/**.746** (43908)	.358/**.749** (44098)	.358/**.751** (44522)	.357/**.751** (44444)
ERR-IA	-	.348/**.754** (56060)	.346/**.756** (56011)	.345/**.758** (56245)	.345/**.758** (56209)
D♯-nDCG	-	-	.488/**.592** (2124)	.502/**.625** (3822)	.499/**.625** (3586)
LD♯-nDCG$_E$	-	-	-	.523/**.629** (2356)	.518/**.633** (2026)
HD♯-nDCG$_E$	-	-	-	-	**.603**/.552 (330)

(c) Gold standard measures: N-rec$_E$ and Precision

	ERR-IA	D♯-nDCG	LD♯-nDCG$_E$	HD♯-nDCG$_E$	LAD♯-nDCG$_E$
α-nDCG	**.738**/.085 (14215)	.156/**.731** (43908)	.154/**.735** (44098)	.159/**.734** (44522)	.157/**.735** (44444)
ERR-IA	-	.126/**.742** (56060)	.124/**.747** (56011)	.127/**.748** (56245)	.127/**.749** (56209)
D♯-nDCG	-	-	.036/**.217** (2124)	.267/**.371** (3822)	.247/**.368** (3586)
LD♯-nDCG$_E$	-	-	-	.432/**.438** (2356)	.424/**.449** (2026)
HD♯-nDCG$_E$	-	-	-	-	.370/**.476** (330)

whole intent hierarchy to measure both diversity and relevance of ranked lists. LD♯-nDCG$_E$ uses the whole intent hierarchy to measure the diversity but only uses the leaf nodes to measure the relevance. D♯-nDCG only uses the leaf nodes to measure the diversity and relevance. Table 4 shows that LD♯-nDCG$_E$, HD♯-nDCG$_E$ and LAD♯-nDCG$_E$ are more intuitive than D♯-nDCG in terms of diversity. HD♯-nDCG$_E$ and LAD♯-nDCG$_E$ are more intuitive than D♯-nDCG and LD♯-nDCG$_E$ in terms of relevance. We get the same result when both diversity and relevance are considered.

4.3.3 Case Studies

D♯-nDCG, LD♯-nDCG$_E$, HD♯-nDCG$_E$, and LAD♯-nDCG$_E$ are closely related (shown in Section 3.3.5 and Section 4.4). We examine their differences in terms of intuitiveness by looking at some real examples from the submitted runs in TREC Web Track 2009-2013 diversity task.

Specifically, we select five pairs of real ranked lists from TREC Web Track diversity runs in Table 5, and refer to them as **Case A-E**. For example, **Case A** stands for two runs cmuFuTop10D and THUIR10DvNov for No. 77 query; The middle column shows the relevance assessments of the top ten documents in each run (e.g. the first document retrieved by cmuFuTop10D is relevant to intent i_4 with a relevance rating 1); The last four columns show the Δ's for each query (e.g. score of cmuFuTop10D minus that of THUIR10DvNov) where arrows indicate which run has higher score under each measure. Note that in this section, the measures are computed for a document cutoff $K = 10$ because we only have space to show top 10 documents in Table 5. We categorize five cases into two classes from the viewpoint of diversity (**Case A-C**) or relevance (**Case D-E**).

Table 5: Five ranked list pairs from TREC Web Track 2009-2013 diversity test collections, document cutoff $K = 10$. 1st column: case IDs (query IDs). 2nd column: run IDs. 3rd column: number of official intents covered by each run. 4th column: number of nodes in extended intent hierarchies covered by each run. 5th column: relevance ratings for each intent at ranks 1-10. The rightmost column: performance differences using each measure and arrows point to its preferred run.

				Document rank (i: official intents) 1	2	3	4	5	6	7	8	9	10	Δ in D♯-nDCG	Δ in LD♯-$nDCG_E$	Δ in HD♯-$nDCG_E$	Δ in LAD♯-$nDCG_E$
A (77)	cmuFuTop10D	3	6	i_4L1				i_3L1					i_1L1	0.0013 ⇑	-0.1098 ⇓	-0.0977 ⇓	-0.0988 ⇓
	THUIR10DvNov	3	8	i_4L1					i_1L1				i_2L1				
B (77)	THUIR10DvQEW	2	5	i_4L1					i_3L1					0.0300 ⇑	-0.0256 ⇓	0.0011 ⇑	-0.0019 ⇓
	UAMSD10aSRfu	2	6						i_4L1			i_2L1					
C (77)	msrsv2div	3	8	i_4L1			i_2L1	i_2L1	i_2L1			i_3L1	i_2L1	-0.0329 ⇓	0.0226 ⇑	-0.0115 ⇓	-0.0085 ⇓
	qirdcsuog3	3	7	i_3L1			i_1L1 i_3L1	i_1L1		i_1L1 i_3L1	i_1L1	i_2L1					
D (117)	qutir11a	3	5	i_1L1 i_2L1	i_2L1	i_2L1 i_3L1	i_1L1 i_3L1	i_1L2 i_2L1 i_3L1	i_2L1	i_1L2 i_2L2	i_1L3 i_2L1	i_2L1	i_2L1	-0.0030 ⇓	-0.0030 ⇓	0.0171 ⇑	0.0148 ⇑
	uwBBadhoc	3	5	i_1L3 i_2L2 i_3L3	i_3L1								i_1L1 i_2L2 i_3L1				
E (128)	2011SiftR2	3	5	i_1L2 i_2L2 i_3L1			i_1L2 i_3L2							0.0087 ⇑	0.0087 ⇑	-0.0005 ⇓	0.0004 ⇑
	UWatMDSdm	3	5	i_1L1 i_2L1	i_1L1		i_1L1 i_3L1		i_1L1	i_1L2 i_2L2			i_1L2 i_2L2				

In **Case A**, we argue that D♯-nDCG is less intuitive than the other three. THUIR10DvNov covers both "bobcat company" and "wild bobcat" while cmuFuTop10D only covers the former (Please refer to the detailed description for the official intents of No. 77 query shown in Figure 1) although both runs cover three leaf intents. In this sense, THUIR10DvNov is more diversified than cmuFuTop10D and should be preferred. Note that this is also a case where I-rec cannot tell which run is better but N-rec_E can. The rightmost column of Table 5 shows that only D♯-nDCG disagrees with this intuition. In **Case B**, we argue that D♯-nDCG and HD♯-$nDCG_E$ are less intuitive than the other two. Similar to **Case A**, UAMSD10aSRfu covers both "bobcat company" and "wild bobcat," whereas THUIR10DvQEW fails to cover the latter. So UAMSD10aSRfu should be preferred, and only LAD♯-$nDCG_E$ and LD♯-$nDCG_E$ agree with this. In **Case C**, we argue that LD♯-$nDCG_E$ is the most intuitive among the four measures. In this case, both msrsv2div and qirdcsuog3 cover "bobcat company" and "wild bobcat". However, Figure 1 shows that msrsv2div covers both "bobcat tractors" and "bobcat company homepage," which are sub intents of "bobcat company," while qirdcsuog3 does not cover "bobcat company homepage." Because of this, msrsv2div should be preferred and only LD♯-$nDCG_E$ agrees with this.

In summary, from the viewpoint of diversity, LD♯-$nDCG_E$ is the most intuitive measure. HD♯-$nDCG_E$ is less intuitive than LAD♯-$nDCG_E$, but is more intuitive than D♯-nDCG.

The two runs in **Case D** and in **Case E** have the same I-rec and N-rec_E, hence the measures' preference is determined by their Precision part (e.g. D-nDCG if it is D♯-nDCG, and HD-$nDCG_E$ if it is HD♯-$nDCG_E$). In **Case D**, we argue that D♯-nDCG and LD♯-$nDCG_E$ are less intuitive than the other two. No matter whether measuring by I-rec or by N-rec_E, qutir11a and uwBBadhoc are equally good in terms of diversity. However, qutir11a should be preferred because its top ten documents are all relevant, whereas uwBBadhoc only has three. From the rightmost column of Table 5, we find that D♯-nDCG and LD♯-$nDCG_E$ fail to reflect this. In **Case E**, we argue that HD♯-$nDCG_E$ is the most intuitive among the four measures. UWatMDSdm should be preferred because it returns much more relevant documents than 2011SiftR2. In this case, only HD♯-$nDCG_E$ successfully recognizes this.

Table 6: Kendall's τ / Symmetric τ_{ap} by averaging over TREC Web track 2009-2013. Values greater than .950 are shown in bold.

(a) 250 queries in TREC Web Track 2009-2013	ERR-IA	D♯-nDCG	LD♯-$nDCG_E$	HD♯-$nDCG_E$	LAD♯-$nDCG_E$
α-nDCG	.923/.870	.840/.796	.845/.796	.843/.792	.844/.793
ERR-IA	-	.772/.699	.780/.706	.779/.704	.779/.706
D♯-nDCG	-	-	**.976/.959**	**.976/.957**	**.977/.960**
LD♯-$nDCG_E$	-	-	-	**.991/.988**	**.995/.993**
HD♯-$nDCG_E$	-	-	-	-	**.995/.994**
(b) 105 queries that have multilayer intent hierarchies (out of 250)	**ERR-IA**	**D♯-nDCG**	**LD♯-$nDCG_E$**	**HD♯-$nDCG_E$**	**LAD♯-$nDCG_E$**
α-nDCG	.872/.802	.812/.747	.821/.755	.821/.758	.822/.759
ERR-IA	-	.701/.609	.714/.624	.712/.626	.714/.628
D♯-nDCG	-	-	**.964**/.941	**.959**/.933	**.958**/.932
LD♯-$nDCG_E$	-	-	-	**.984/.977**	**.986/.981**
HD♯-$nDCG_E$	-	-	-	-	**.996/.995**

Generally, from the viewpoint of relevance, LAD♯-$nDCG_E$ is more intuitive than LD♯-$nDCG_E$. LAD♯-$nDCG_E$ is able to measure the relevance of ranked lists more accurately by considering the whole intent hierarchy, and thus make the measures more consistent with Precision than LD♯-$nDCG_E$.

4.4 Rank Correlation Results

We compute Kendall's τ and τ_{ap} for different pairs of measures to check the correlation between these measures. Results are shown in Table 6. The table shows that: (1) LD♯-$nDCG_E$, HD♯-$nDCG_E$ and LAD♯-$nDCG_E$ are less correlated to existing measures, especially when only using the queries that have multilayer intent hierarchies. This is because our measures are able to recognize the subtle difference between ranked lists when multilayer intent hierarchies are used, whereas the existing measures may not. This indicates that our measures are useful and could be supplementary to the existing measures; (2) LD♯-$nDCG_E$, HD♯-$nDCG_E$, as well as LAD♯-$nDCG_E$ are more correlated to D♯-nDCG than α-nDCG and ERR-IA. This is because they are different kinds of extensions of D♯-nDCG. Similar to D♯-nDCG, they model diversity and relevance in different components separately. They yield the same evaluation results when the queries only have single-layer intent hierarchies. (3) LD♯-$nDCG_E$ and HD♯-$nDCG_E$ are less correlated. As discussed in 4.3, LD♯-$nDCG_E$ prefers highly diversified ranked lists, whereas HD♯-$nDCG_E$ prefers highly relevant ranked lists.

5. CONCLUSIONS AND FUTURE WORK

In this paper, we argued that user intents of a query could be hierarchical. We described the concept of hierarchical intents and proposed hierarchical measures that could work with intent hierarchies. We created a new test collection containing intent hierarchies based on the existing TREC Web Track 2009-2013 diversity test collections by grouping the official intents into original intent hierarchies and extending them to extended intent hierarchies. Our experimental results showed that our proposed hierarchical measures can be more discriminative than existing measures which use a flat list of intents and assume the independence among intents. We revealed that LD♯-nDCG should be used when the diversity of search results is more valued than the relevance, whereas HD♯-nDCG should be used when the relevance is more important. LAD♯-nDCG is a better choice when both diversity and relevance are important.

In this paper, we simply assume that the official intents provided in TREC Web Track 2009-2013 diversity test collections are atomic intents. It is possible that some of these intents can be further divided into sub intents. We will investigate this in the future.

6. ACKNOWLEDGMENTS

This work was supported by the National Key Basic Research Program (973 Program) of China under grant No. 2014CB340403, and the Fundamental Research Funds for the Central Universities, the Research Funds of Renmin University of China No. 15XNLF03, the National Natural Science Foundation of China (Grant No. 61502501, 61502502, and 61502503)

7. REFERENCES

[1] R. Agrawal, S. Gollapudi, A. Halverson, and S. Ieong. Diversifying search results. In *WSD* , 2009.

[2] J. Carbonell and J. Goldstein. The use of MMR, diversity-based reranking for reordering documents and producing summaries. In *S* , 1998.

[3] B. A. Carterette. Multiple testing in statistical analysis of systems-based information retrieval experiments. *S*, 2012.

[4] O. Chapelle, D. Metlzer, Y. Zhang, and P. Grinspan. Expected reciprocal rank for graded relevance. In , 2009.

[5] H. Chen and D. R. Karger. Less is more: probabilistic models for retrieving fewer relevant documents. In *S* , 2006.

[6] C. L. Clarke, N. Craswell, and I. Soboroff. Overview of the trec 2009 web track. In , 2009.

[7] C. L. Clarke, N. Craswell, I. Soboroff, and A. Ashkan. A comparative analysis of cascade measures for novelty and diversity. In *WSD* , 2011.

[8] C. L. Clarke, N. Craswell, I. Soboroff, and G. V. Cormack. Overview of the trec 2010 web track. In , 2010.

[9] C. L. Clarke, M. Kolla, G. V. Cormack, O. Vechtomova, A. Ashkan, S. Büttcher, and I. MacKinnon. Novelty and diversity in information retrieval evaluation. In *S* , 2008.

[10] C. L. Clarke, M. Kolla, and O. Vechtomova. An effectiveness measure for ambiguous and underspecified queries. In , 2009.

[11] V. Dang and B. W. Croft. Term level search result diversification. In *S* , 2013.

[12] V. Dang and W. B. Croft. Diversity by proportionality: an election-based approach to search result diversification. In *S* , 2012.

[13] Z. Dou, S. Hu, K. Chen, R. Song, and J.-R. Wen. Multi-dimensional search result diversification. In *WSD* , 2011.

[14] Z. Dou, R. Song, and J.-R. Wen. A large-scale evaluation and analysis of personalized search strategies. In *WWW*, 2007.

[15] B. J. Jansen, A. Spink, and T. Saracevic. Real life, real users, and real needs: a study and analysis of user queries on the web. *n ormation rocessing & anagement*, 2000.

[16] K. Järvelin and J. Kekäläinen. Ir evaluation methods for retrieving highly relevant documents. In *S* , 2000.

[17] M. G. Kendall. A new measure of rank correlation. *Biometrika*, 1938.

[18] F. Radlinski and S. Dumais. Improving personalized web search using result diversification. In *S* , 2006.

[19] T. Sakai. Bootstrap-based comparisons of ir metrics for finding one relevant document. In *S*, 2006.

[20] T. Sakai. Evaluating evaluation metrics based on the bootstrap. In *S* , 2006.

[21] T. Sakai. Evaluation with informational and navigational intents. In *WWW*, 2012.

[22] T. Sakai, N. Craswell, R. Song, S. Robertson, Z. Dou, and C.-Y. Lin. Simple evaluation metrics for diversified search results. In *V* , 2010.

[23] T. Sakai and S. Robertson. Modelling a user population for designing information retrieval metrics. In *V* , 2008.

[24] T. Sakai and R. Song. Evaluating diversified search results using per-intent graded relevance. In *S* , 2011.

[25] R. L. Santos, C. Macdonald, and I. Ounis. Exploiting query reformulations for web search result diversification. In *WWW*, 2010.

[26] R. L. Santos, C. Macdonald, and I. Ounis. Selectively diversifying web search results. In , 2010.

[27] R. L. Santos, C. Macdonald, and I. Ounis. Intent-aware search result diversification. In *S* , 2011.

[28] C. Silverstein, H. Marais, M. Henzinger, and M. Moricz. Analysis of a very large web search engine query log. *S orum*, 1999.

[29] E. Yilmaz, J. A. Aslam, and S. Robertson. A new rank correlation coefficient for information retrieval. In *S* , 2008.

[30] C. X. Zhai, W. W. Cohen, and J. Lafferty. Beyond independent relevance: methods and evaluation metrics for subtopic retrieval. In *S* , 2003.

[31] X. Zhu, A. B. Goldberg, J. Van Gael, and D. Andrzejewski. Improving diversity in ranking using absorbing random walks. In *N* , 2007.

Robust and Collective Entity Disambiguation through Semantic Embeddings

Stefan Zwicklbauer
University of Passau
Passau, Germany
szwicklbauer@acm.org

Christin Seifert
University of Passau
Passau, Germany
christin.seifert@uni-passau.de

Michael Granitzer
University of Passau
Passau, Germany
michael.granitzer@uni-passau.de

ABSTRACT

Entity disambiguation is the task of mapping ambiguous terms in natural-language text to its entities in a knowledge base. It finds its application in the extraction of structured data in RDF (Resource Description Framework) from textual documents, but equally so in facilitating artificial intelligence applications, such as Semantic Search, Reasoning and Question & Answering. We propose a new collective, graph-based disambiguation algorithm utilizing semantic entity and document embeddings for robust entity disambiguation. Robust thereby refers to the property of achieving better than state-of-the-art results over a wide range of very different data sets. Our approach is also able to abstain if no appropriate entity can be found for a specific surface form. Our evaluation shows, that our approach achieves significantly (>5%) better results than all other publicly available disambiguation algorithms on 7 of 9 datasets without data set specific tuning. Moreover, we discuss the influence of the quality of the knowledge base on the disambiguation accuracy and indicate that our algorithm achieves better results than non-publicly available state-of-the-art algorithms.

CCS Concepts

•**Information systems** → **Information extraction;** *Information systems applications;*

Keywords

Entity Disambiguation; Neuronal Networks; Embeddings

1. INTRODUCTION

Entity disambiguation refers to the task of linking phrases in a text, also called surface forms, to a set of candidate meanings, referred to as the knowledge base (KB), by resolving the correct semantic meaning of the surface form. It is an essential task in combining unstructured with structured or formal information; a prerequisite for artificial intelligence applications such as Semantic Search, Reasoning and Question & Answering. While entity disambiguation systems have been well-researched so far [19, 14, 5, 12, 15], most approaches have been optimised to work on a particular type of disambiguation task, like for example on short Twitter messages [2], web pages [12, 28], news documents [10, 15], encyclopedias [16, 11, 5], RSS-Feeds [9] etc. While most authors report to outperform other entity disambiguation algorithms on their domain/data set, they do not achieve comparable accuracy on other domains. So their approaches could be considered as not being very robust against different types of data sets.

In our work, we focus on robust entity disambiguation, where robustness is defined as achieving high accuracy over a large set of different domains. The only assumption we make is to disambiguate entities collectively, i.e. we disambiguate all entities in a given textual document at once. Our approach is based on creating a k-partite relatedness graph between all entity candidates for all given surface forms in a document. The relatedness between entity candidates is determined using semantic embeddings, i.e. real-valued n-dimensional vectors capturing the semantics of entities. We use two types of semantic embeddings, namely embeddings capturing the meaning on the word (entity) level and semantic embeddings capturing the meaning on the document level. As we show, both embeddings are important for our approach.

In particular, we provide the following contributions:

- We present a new state-of-the-art approach for collective entity disambiguation that emphasizes robustness, i.e. achieving high accuracy over different kinds of data sets. Our approach is based on semantic embeddings that capture entity and document contexts and utilizes a sequence of graph algorithms to eliminate wrong candidates.
- We evaluate our algorithm against 5 strong, publicly available entity disambiguation systems on 9 data sets and show that our approach outperforms all other system by a significant margin on nearly all data sets.
- We discuss the influence of the quality of the underlying KB on the entity disambiguation accuracy and indicate that our algorithm achieves better results than non-publicly available current state-of-the-art algorithms.
- We provide our entity disambiguation system as well as the underlying KB as open source solution. These resources allow a fair comparison between future entity disambiguation algorithms and our approach that are not biased by the KB.

The remainder of the paper is structured as follows: In Section 2, we review related work. Section 3 introduces the problem formally and outlines our approach. Sections 4 and 5 explain the process of generating semantic embeddings and our approach. In Section 6 and 7, we describe the experimental setup and the results achieved on 9 data sets. We conclude our paper in Section 8.

SIGIR '16, July 17 - 21, 2016, Pisa, Italy

ISBN 978-1-4503-4069-4/16/07...$15.00

DOI: http://dx.doi.org/10.1145/2911451.2911535

2. RELATED WORK

Entity disambiguation has been studied extensively in the past 10 years. One of the first works defined a similarity measure to compute the cosine similarity between the text around the surface form and the referent entity candidate's Wikipedia page [4]. The publicly available framework DBpedia Spotlight [19] for disambiguating Linked Data Resources is also based on the vector space model and cosine similarity. Cucerzan et al. introduced topical coherence for entity disambiguation [7]. The authors used the referent entity candidate and other entities within the same context to compute topical coherence by analyzing the overlap of categories and incoming links in Wikipedia. Milne and Witten [22] improved the exploitation of topical coherence using Normalized Google Distance and unambiguous entities in the context only. A well-known publicly available system is Wikifier [25, 5] from 2013. It incorporates, along with statistical methods, richer relational analysis of the text. In 2014, the authors Guo et al. [10] proposed the use of a probability distribution resulting from a random walk with restart over a suitable entity graph to represent the semantics of entities and documents in a unified way. Their algorithm updates the semantic signature of the document as surface forms are disambiguated.

Other works explicitly make use of topic models to link surface forms to a KB. For instance, Kataria et al. [16] proposed a topic model that uses all words of Wikipedia to learn entity-word associations and the Wikipedia category hierarchy to capture co-occurrence patterns among entities. The authors of [11] also propose a generative approach which jointly models context compatibility, topic coherence and its correlation.

Several other work focus on graph-based algorithms. For instance, publicly available, graph-based disambiguation approaches are AIDA [14], Babelfy [23], WAT [24] and AGDISTIS [28]. AIDA is based on the YAGO2 KB and relies on sophisticated graph algorithms. This approach uses dense sub-graphs of the underlying KB to identify coherent surface forms using a greedy algorithm. In 2014, Babelfy [23] has been presented to the community. It is based on random walks and densest subgraph algorithms. In contrast to our work, Babelfy differentiates between word sense disambiguation, i.e., resolution of polysemous lexicographic entities like play, and entity disambiguation. The WAT [24] system is a redesign of TagMe [8] components and introduces two disambiguation families: graph-based algorithms for collective entity disambiguation and vote-based algorithms for local entity disambiguation [29]. Finally, AGDISTIS [28] is based on string similarity measures and the graph-based Hypertext-Induced Topic Search algorithm. AGDISTIS disambiguates named entities only and exclusively relies on RDF-KBs like DBpedia or YAGO2. All these collective disambiguation approaches rely on graph algorithms but mostly compute the coherence measure with the help of relations between entities within KBs (i.e. DBpedia, YAGO2).

Another graph-based approach was presented by Alhelbawy et al. [1], who applied the PageRank algorithm to a disambiguation graph. To compute the edge weights between entity candidates the authors either used a boolean relation whether two entities refer to each other or estimated a probability of both entities appearing in the same sentence. The authors Han et al. [12] proposed the graph-based representation called Referent Graph, which models the global interdependence between different disambiguation decisions. Then, they proposed a collective inference algorithm, which can jointly infer the referent entities of all name surface forms by exploiting the interdependence captured in the Referent Graph.

Semantic embeddings have also been used for entity disambiguation. In 2013, He et al. [13] proposed an entity disambiguation model, based on Deep Neural Networks. The model learns a context-entity similarity measure for entity disambiguation. The intermediate representations are learned leveraging large-scale an- notations of Wikipedia. The most recent approach of semantic embeddings is presented by Huang et al. [15] in 2015. The authors present a new entity semantic relatedness model for topical coherence modeling. Similar to our approach the model can be directly trained on large-scale knowledge graphs. It maps heterogeneous types of knowledge of an entity from knowledge graphs to numerical feature vectors in a feature space such that the distance between two semantically-related entities is minimized. Unfortunately, the approach is only evaluated on two data sets and, thus, the robustness properties of this approach are debatable.

3. PROBLEM STATEMENT & APPROACH

The goal of entity disambiguation is to find the correct semantic mapping between surface forms in a document and entities in a KB. More formally, let $M =< m_1, ..., m_K >$ be a tuple of K surface forms in a document D, and $\Omega = \{e_1, ..., e_{|\Omega|}\}$ be a set of target entities in a KB. Let Γ be a possible entity configuration $< t_1, ..., t_K >$ with $t_i \in \Omega$, where t_i is the target entity for surface form m_i. Here, we assume that each entity in Ω is a candidate for surface form m_i. The goal of collective entity disambiguation can then be formalized as finding the optimal configuration Γ^* [25]:

$$\Gamma^* = \underset{\Gamma}{\operatorname{argmin}} \sum_{i=1}^{K} \phi(m_i, t_i) + \Psi(\Gamma) \tag{1}$$

Different to [25] we do **not** pose the optimization problem as maximizing the sum of the scores of a locality function ϕ and a coherence function Ψ (cf. Equation 1), which has been proven to be NP-hard [7]. We approximate the solution using the PageRank (PR) algorithm with priors [3, 30] on specially constructed graphs which encompass the locality and the coherence function (still NP-hard). Our locality function reflects the likelihood that a target entity t_i is the correct disambiguation for m_i, whereas the coherence function computes a score describing the coherence between entities in Γ^*.

The PR algorithm is a well-researched, link-based ranking algorithm simulating a random walk on graphs and reflecting the importance of each node. It has been shown to provide good performance in many applications [31], also in disambiguation tasks [12, 1].

The graphs we construct consist of nodes for all entity candidates per surface form and one node, the topic node, that represents the current predominant topic of already disambiguated entities. This topic node allows us to include a-priori information from previous steps into the structure of the graph and, hence, influence the PR algorithm. The edge weights are based on similarities between **entity embeddings** as well as similarities between **entity-context embeddings** and the surface forms' surrounding context. In our work, an entity embedding is a trained vector that is used to compute the semantic similarity between entities. Moreover, an entity-context embedding is a trained context vector of an entity to compute a matching how good this entity fits to the context of a surface form.

Abstaining is an important task if no appropriate entity can be found in the entity set Ω. In this case, our disambiguation algorithm returns the pseudo-entity *NIL*. In our work, a surface form is linked to *NIL* if one of the following cases occurs: 1. when the surface form has no candidate entities, or 2. the algorithm is uncertain about the relevant entity after the last PR application.

4. SEMANTIC EMBEDDINGS

Embeddings are n-dimensional vectors of concepts which describe the similarities between these concepts using the cosine similarity. This has already been well researched for words [20, 21] and documents [18] in literature. In this work, we make use of both embedding types in form of entity embeddings (Word2Vec) and entity-context embeddings (Doc2Vec) to improve entity disambiguation. First, we briefly introduce Word2Vec, a set of models that are used to produce word embeddings, and Doc2Vec, a modification of Word2Vec to generate document embeddings, in Section 4.1. Second, we describe how we create corpora that serve as input for the Word2Vec and Doc2Vec algorithms in Section 4.2.

4.1 Learning Semantic Embeddings

Word2Vec is a group of state-of-the-art, unsupervised algorithms for creating word embeddings from (textual) documents [20]. To train these embeddings, Word2Vec uses a two-layer neural network to process non-labeled documents. The neuronal network architecture is based either on the continuous bag-of-words (CBOW) or the skip-gram architecture. Using CBOW, the input to the model for a word w_i are the words preceding and succeeding this word, e.g. $w_{i-2}, w_{i-1}, w_{i+1}, w_{i+2}$ when using two words before and after the current word. The output of the network is the probability of w_i being the correct word. The task can be described as predicting a word given its context. The skip-gram model works vice-versa: the input to the model is a word w_i and Word2Vec predicts the surrounding context words $w_{i-2}, w_{i-1}, w_{i+1}, w_{i+2}$. In contrast to other natural language neuronal network models, Word2Vec models can be trained very fast and can be further significantly improved by using parallel training [26].

An important property of Word2Vec is that it groups the vectors of similar words together in the vector space. If sufficient data is used for training, Word2Vec makes highly accurate guesses about a word's meaning based on its context words in the training corpus. The resulting word embeddings capture linguistic regularities, for instance the vector operation vec("President") $-$ vec("Power") $\approx$ vec("Prime Minister"). The semantic similarity between two words, which is important in the context of our work, denotes the cosine similarity between the words' Word2Vec vectors.

Since our approach considers only the semantic similarity between entities (and not words), we treat entities similar to words. This means, we build entity embeddings with the help of an entity corpus instead of a textual corpus containing sentences and paragraphs (cf. Section 4.2). Our evaluation of the influence of the specific architecture in Section 7.3 shows that the skip-gram model outperforms CBOW in our disambiguation setting. Thus, for all other experiments in this paper, the skip-gram model is used.

Doc2Vec, a modification of Word2Vec, learns fixed-length embeddings from variable-length pieces of texts like documents [18]. It addresses some of the key weaknesses of bag-of-word models by incorporating more semantics and considering the word order within a small context. As an example for the semantic embedding, the Doc2Vec model embeds the word "powerful" closer to "strong" than to "Paris", which is not the case in bag-of-word models.

The architecture is either based on the distributed memory model (PV-DM), which is similar to the CBOW model of Word2Vec, or on the distributed bag-of-words model (PV-DBOW), which is similar to the skip-gram model. Using PV-DM, the context words' corresponding document vector d_i (vector of the document which contains the context words) is added as an input in the neural net. Thus, the input becomes d_i, w_{j-1}, w_{j+1}, meaning that the document vector with the two context vectors is used to predict the word w_j. For more details on calculating the document vector see [18].

Similar to the skip-gram model in Word2Vec, the intention of PV-DBOW is to ignore the context words in the input, but force the model to predict words randomly sampled from the document in the output. A disadvantage is, that it ignores the word sequence.

The authors of Doc2Vec report consistently better results with the PV-DM architecture. PV-DM also outperforms PV-DBOW in the context of our disambiguation algorithm (cf. Section 7.3). Since we want to compute the similarity between an entity-context embedding and the surrounding context of a surface form, one needs to perform an inference step to compute the surrounding context vector. The Doc2Vec model is trained on the entity-context corpus yielding the entity-context embeddings (see next section), and the same model is later used to generate the surface-form-context embeddings. For a detailed introduction to Word2Vec and Doc2Vec, we refer the reader to the original works [20, 21, 18].

4.2 Corpus Creation

Word2Vec typically accepts a set of corpora containing natural language text as input and trains its word vectors according to the words' order in the corpora. Since we want to learn **entity representations** (entity embeddings) only, we have to create an appropriate Word2Vec input corpus file that exclusively comprises entities. The entities' order in the corpus file should be retained as given in the entity-annotated document KBs. For this purpose, we iterate over all documents in these corpora and replace all available, linked surface forms with its respective target entity identifier. Further, all non-entity identifiers like words and punctuations are removed so that all documents consist of entity identifiers separated by whitespaces only. However, the collocation of entities is maintained as given by the original document, but the distance between the annotations is ignored. All resulting documents are concatenated to create a single Word2Vec corpus file. Details are provided in [32].

To generate **entity-context embeddings** with Doc2Vec, any natural language source can be used that offers sufficient descriptions of the entities. To generate embeddings, the source needs to be either already a single document, or needs to be aggregated to a single document. These documents describe the respective entities as detailed as possible. A well-known example for entity describing documents are Wikipedia pages, which are used in our experiments.

5. DISAMBIGUATION ALGORITHM

Our disambiguation algorithm accepts documents that contain one or multiple surface forms that should be linked to entities. It disambiguates all surface forms within a document using a graph-based collective approach. Algorithm 1 gives an overview of the disambiguation process, which is explained in the following. The first step in the disambiguation chain is the *Candidate Generation*. The goal is to reduce the number of possible entity candidates for each input surface form m_i by determining a set of relevant target entities, the candidate set CS_{m_i}. Details of our candidate generation process are described in Section 5.1. Given these candidates we disambiguate surface forms with none or one candidate and initialize the entity set E_d with the entities of unambiguous surface forms or already disambiguated surface forms (Lines 2-7).

Our second step *Semantic Embedding Candidate Filter* filters entity candidates that fit to the general topic described by the already disambiguated entities (Lines 8-17) requiring at least 3 already assigned entities. The underlying assumption is, that all entities in a paragraph are somehow topically related. To infer this general topic, we create a topic vector $tv = \sum_{e \in E_d} v(e)$, with E_d being the set of already disambiguated entities, and $v(e)$ the entity embedding of entity e (Word2Vec vector). Next, we compute the semantic similarity (cosine similarity) between the general topic vector tv and the entity candidates of all not yet disambiguated surface forms. If the similarity exceeds the a-priori given *CandidateFilter* threshold, the entity candidate remains in the candidate list of the respective surface form. If no candidate of a specific surface form

Algorithm 1: Our graph-based disambiguation algorithm

input : $M =< m_1, ..., m_K >$, Threshold λ, $margin_1$, $margin_2$
output: Assignment $\Gamma^* =< t_1, ..., t_K >$, with t_i being the entity of m_i

1 configuration $\Gamma^* = tuple()$; dis. entities $E_d = \emptyset$; candidate set $CS_{m_i} = \emptyset$
// Candidate Generation
2 **for** $m_i \in M$ **do**
3 $\quad CS_{m_i}$ = generateCandidates(m_i)
4 $\quad$ **if** $|CS_{m_i}| = 0$ **then**
5 $\quad\quad \Gamma(i) = NIL$
6 $\quad$ **else if** $|CS_{m_i}| = 1$ **then**
7 $\quad\quad \Gamma^*(i) = e \in CS_{m_i}; E_d = E_d \cup CS_{m_i}$
// Semantic Embedding Candidate Filter
8 **if** $|E_d| > 2$ **then**
9 $\quad$ **for** $m_i \in M$ *and* $|CS_{m_i}| > 1$ **do**
10 $\quad\quad set = \emptyset$
11 $\quad\quad$ **for** $e_j \in CS_{m_i}$ **do**
12 $\quad\quad\quad$ **if** $cosineSim(sumEmbeddings(E_d), e) > \lambda$ **then**
13 $\quad\quad\quad\quad set = set \cup e$
14 $\quad\quad$ **if** $set \neq \emptyset$ **then**
15 $\quad\quad\quad CS_{m_i} = set$
16 $\quad\quad$ **if** $|set| = 1$ **then**
17 $\quad\quad\quad \Gamma^*(i) = CS_{m_i}; E_d = E_d \cup CS_{m_i}$
// High Probability Candidate Disambiguation
18 CreateDisambiguationGraphAndSolvePageRank(CS_{m_i}, E_d)
19 Rank candidates.
20 Select highest PR score h, second highest PR score s, average PR score avg.
21 **for** $m_i \in M$ *and* $|CS_{m_i}| > 1$ **do**
22 $\quad dynThreshold = h - margin_2 \cdot (h - avg)$
23 $\quad$ **if** $s < dynThreshold$ **then**
24 $\quad\quad \Gamma^*(i) = h; E_d = E_d \cup h; C_{m_i} = h$
25 $\quad$ **else**
26 $\quad\quad CS_{m_i} = selectTop4RankedCandidates$
// Final Disambiguation and Abstaining
27 CreateDisambiguationGraph(CS_{m_i}, E_d)
28 **for** $m_i \in M$ *and* $|CS_{m_i}| > 1$ **do**
29 $\quad$ Perform PR and rank candidates.
30 $\quad$ Select highest PR score h, second highest PR score s, average PR score avg.
31 $\quad abstainingThreshold = margin_2 \cdot (h - avg)$
32 $\quad$ **if** $s < abstainingThreshold$ **then**
33 $\quad\quad \Gamma^*(i) = h; E_d = E_d \cup h; C_{m_i} = h$
34 $\quad$ **else**
35 $\quad\quad \Gamma^*(i) = NIL; C_{m_i} = \emptyset$
36 $\quad$ updateGraph(CS_{m_i}, E_d)

exceeds the threshold, the candidate set for this surface forms remains unchanged. We note that this filter is a crucial step towards fast and accurate entity disambiguation. Omitting this step results in a significantly lower performance combined with decreasing results ($\approx$ 2 to 5 percentage points F1, depending on the data set).

The third step *High Probability Candidate Disambiguation* comprises the PageRank (PR) application on a disambiguation graph to disambiguate high probability candidates (Lines 18-26). Detailed information for graph construction and PR can be found in Section 5.2. Next, we rank the entity candidates for each surface form according to their relevance score given by PR in descending order. Additionally, we select the highest PR score h, second-highest PR score s and average PR score avg across all entities that belong to the same surface form. Given these parameters, we define a threshold $dynT$ for determining the certainty in the ranking based on the differences between the first and the second ranked candidate:

$$dynT = h - margin_1 \cdot (h - avg) \quad (2)$$

whereas details on the parameter $margin_1$ are discussed in Section 6.2. We use this threshold as a certainty criterion, indicating whether the top-ranked entity candidate of a surface form is the correct disambiguation target. More specific, if the PR score s of the second ranked candidate does not exceed the threshold $dynT$, the highest ranked entity denotes the target entity of its surface form. In other words, if the relevance score margin between the highest ranked candidate and the other candidates is large, then the likelihood of the top-ranked candidate being the correct target entity is also high. If the threshold is exceeded, we reduce the candidate set of the respective surface form to the top 4 ranked entity candidates.

The last step *Final Disambiguation and Abstaining* disambiguates the remaining entities or abstains if the algorithm is uncertain about the correct target entity (Lines 27-36). We first create a disambiguation graph (cf. Section 5.2) and, then, iteratively disambiguate the entities of the remaining surface forms. For this purpose, every iteration applies the PR to the underlying graph and ranks the candidate entities of each surface form in descending order. The scores h, s, and avg are calculated as in the previous step. The abstaining threshold *abstainingThreshold* is calculated using formula 2 with a different margin parameter ($margin_2$). If the second ranked entity candidate exceeds the abstaining threshold *abstainingThreshold*, the algorithm returns the *NIL* identifier for the respective surface form. Otherwise, the top ranked entity candidate denotes the target entity. After every iteration, we update the graph according to the changes in candidates and disambiguated entities and proceed until all surface form have been processed.

We note, that we apply the PR only once in step 3 due to performance reasons. The disambiguation graph in step 4 usually does not include many entity candidates and, thus, we apply the PR in every iteration, also to provide the maximum accuracy in the abstaining task. The $margin$ parameter to compute the *high probability threshold* and *abstaining threshold* varies in both steps. Information about the parameter choice is presented in Section 6.2.

5.1 Candidate Generation

In the first step, the goal is to reduce the number of possible entity candidates for each input surface form m_i by determining a set of relevant target entities. We proceed as follows:

First, we search for all those entities that have already been annotated with m_i in a corpus. All entities that provide an exact surface form matching serve as entity candidate. To perform this task our algorithm relies on a pre-built index, which has to be created before entities can be disambiguated (cf. Section 6.1). If the candidate set is empty, we additionally use the candidate generation approach proposed by Usbeck et al. for AGDISTIS [28], which includes String normalization and String comparison via trigram similarity. The corresponding parameters are adopted from the default settings in the AGDISTIS framework[1].

Gathering all relevant entity candidates might result in a long list of candidates. To keep the list short and to improve the efficiency, we prune noisy candidates according to the following three criteria:

1. **Prior probability:** Some entities (e.g. Influenza) occur more frequently than others in documents (e.g. the IIV3-011L gene). Thus, these popular entities have a higher probability to reoccur in other documents. In our work, the prior probability [19] $p(e_i|m)$ estimates the probability of seeing an entity with a given surface form. We select the top x entities as the candidates to keep the popular candidates.
2. **Context similarity:** We select the top x entities ranked by their context matching. To this end, we compute the cosine similarity between the entity-context embeddings and the Doc2Vec inferred context vector of the surface form.

[1] http://aksw.org/Projects/AGDISTIS.html

3. **Entity-topic similarity:** If a document contains at least two surface forms that have already been disambiguated ($|E_d| > 1$), we create a topic vector $tv = \sum_{e \in E_d} v(e)$, with $v(e)$ denoting the entity embedding of e, and E_d is the set of already disambiguated entities. In the following, we select those remaining candidates of each surface form where the cosine similarity between the entity candidate embedding and tv exceeds the *CandidateFilter* threshold (cf. Section 1).

For all criteria we use $x = 8$, which is enough to capture the relevant entity candidates. An experimental increase of x, results in a negligibly higher recall of the candidate generation task, but significantly decreases disambiguation performance.

5.2 Disambiguation Graph and PageRank

In our approach, we generate a disambiguation graph twice in order to disambiguate high probability candidate entities first and to perform abstaining afterwards. On this graph we perform a random walk and determine the entity relevance which can be seen as the average amount of its visits. The random walk is simulated by a PR algorithm that permits edge weights and non-uniformly-distributed random jumps [3, 30].

First, we create a **complete, directed** K-partite graph whose set of nodes V is divided in K disjoint subsets $V_0, V_1, ..., V_K$. K denotes the amount of surface forms and V_i is the set of generated entity candidates $\{e_1^i, ..., e_{|V_i|}^i\}$ for surface form m_i. We define m_0 as pseudo surface form and use the subset $V_0 = \{e_1^0\}$ to contain the topic node. The topic node represents the average topic of all already disambiguated entities in E_d. Hence, the edge weight between an entity e_a^i and the topic node e_1^0 represents the relatedness between e_a^i and all already disambiguated entities. Since our graph is K-partite, there are only directed, weighted edges between entity candidates that belong to different surface forms. Connecting the entities that belong to the same surface form would be wrong since the correct target entities of surface forms are determined by the other surface forms' entity candidates (coherence).

The edge weights in our graph represent entity transition probabilities (ETP) which describe the likelihood to walk from a node to the adjacent node. We compute these probabilities by first computing the *Transition Harmonic Mean* (THM) between two nodes. The THM is the harmonic mean between two nodes' **semantic similarity** and the **context similarity** of the target entity (cf. Equation 3).

The semantic similarity between two nodes is the cosine similarity (cos) of the entities' semantic embeddings (vectors) $v(e_a^i)$ and $v(e_b^j)$. The semantic embedding of our topic node e_1^0 is the sum of all entity embeddings in E_d (i.e. $v(e_1^0) = \sum_{e \in E_d} v(e)$). The context similarity between the target entity e_b^j and the surrounding context of its surface form m_j is the cosine similarity of e_b^j's entity-context embedding $cv(e_b^j)$, and the inferred surrounding context vector $cv(m_j)$ of m_j. In case, the target entity is our topic node the context similarity equals 0. The ETB is computed by normalizing the respective THM value (cf. Equation 4).

$$THM(e_a^i, e_b^j) = \frac{2 \cdot cos(v(e_a^i), v(e_b^j)) \cdot cos(cv(e_b^j), cv(m_j))}{cos(v(e_a^i), v(e_b^j)) + cos(cv(e_b^j), cv(m_j))} \quad (3)$$

$$ETP(e_a^i, e_b^j) = \frac{THM(e_a^i, e_b^j)}{\sum_{k \in (V \setminus V_i)} THM(e_a^i, k)} \quad (4)$$

Given the current graph, we additionally integrate a possibility to jump from any node to any other node in the graph during the random walk with probability α. Typical values for α (according to the original paper [30]) are in the range $[0.1, 0.2]$. We compute

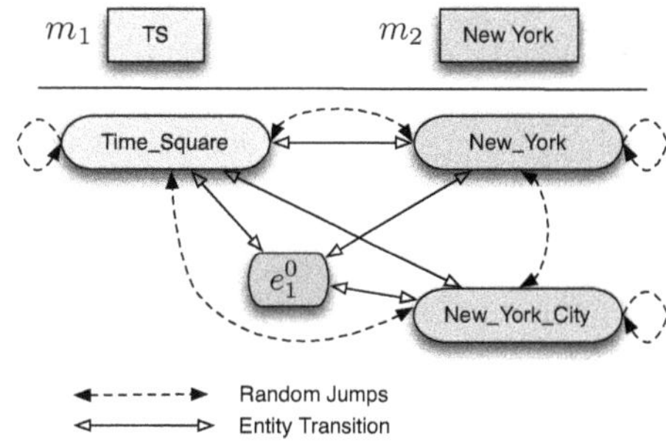

Figure 1: Entity candidate graph with candidates for the surface forms "TS" and "New York".

a probability for each entity candidate being the next jump target. We employ the prior probability as jump probability for each node (entity). The probability to jump to or from the topic node equals 0. Combining the prior probability and context similarity instead leads to decreasing results of ≈ 3 percentage points F1 on average.

Figure 1 shows a possible entity candidate graph. The surface form "TS" has only one entity candidate and consequently has already been linked to the entity "Time Square". The surface form "New York" is still ambiguous, providing two candidates. The topic node e_1^0 comprises the already disambiguated surface form "Time Square". We omit the edge weights and jump probabilities in the figure to improve visualization.

After constructing the disambiguation graph, we apply the PR algorithm and compute a relevance score for each entity candidate. Depending on the disambiguation task, our approach decides which entity candidate is the correct target entity or abstains if no appropriate candidate is available (cf. Algorithm 1).

6. EXPERIMENTAL SETUP

Our disambiguation algorithm is fully-implemented in Java and is embedded in our publicly available disambiguation system *DoSeR*[2] (**D**isambiguation **o**f **Se**mantic **R**esources) which is being developed continuously. For the Word2Vec and Doc2Vec algorithms we chose Gensim [26], a robust and efficient framework to realize unsupervised semantic modeling from plain text. Before we report the disambiguation results in detail, we first describe the preprocessing details in Section 6.1, important parameter settings and evaluation measures in Section 6.2 and 9 test data sets in Section 6.3.

6.1 Preprocessing

Before our algorithm is able to disambiguate entities, we first have to perform some preprocessing steps. First, we choose a KB whose entities define our target entity set Ω. In the context of this work, we make use of the current version of DBpedia 2015-04 as entity data base, which reflects information from the last years Wikipedia version. Overall, we extract $\approx 4.1M$ entities (all entities belonging to the *owl:thing* class) out of DBpedia that we would like to disambiguate in our work.

Next, we select Wikipedia ($\approx 81M$ annotations) and the Google Wikilinks Corpus[3] ($\approx 40M$ annotations) as entity-annotated document KB that serve as training data for our semantic entity embeddings (Word2Vec). To create the Doc2Vec entity-context embeddings, we parse the entities' Wikipedia pages and remove all Wikipedia syntax elements as well as tables. The resulting natural-language texts serve as input for the Doc2Vec algorithm.

[2]https://github.com/quhfus/DoSeR
[3]https://code.google.com/p/wiki-links/

In the following, we learn entity embeddings and entity-context embeddings with Word2Vec and Doc2Vec. To train the entity embeddings with Word2Vec, we define a feature space of $d = 400$ dimensions and employ the skip-gram architecture that performs better with infrequent words [20]. In terms of Doc2Vec we use a feature space of $d = 1000$ dimensions and employ the PV-DM learning architecture. An experimental comparison between the architectures and various settings for parameter d is presented in Section 7.3. The Word2Vec training time takes ≈ 90 minutes on our personal computer with a 4x3.4GHz Intel Core i7 processor and 16 GB RAM (1 corpus iteration). The training time for Doc2Vec takes $\approx 11/2$ days since we performed 5 iterations overall.

Next, we create a disambiguation index with each entry defining an entity. The index comprises the following three entity describing information which are relevant for our disambiguation algorithm:

1. **Labels:** By default, we extract the *rdfs:label* attributes of DBpedia, which are used by the candidate generation approach proposed by Usbeck et al. [28] (cf. Section 5.1).
2. **Surface Forms:** We gather and generate surface forms from DBpedia and Wikipedia and store them separately in a surface form field. Additionally, we store the amount of occurrences how often a surface form has been annotated with an entity to compute the prior probability (cf. Section 5.1).
3. **Semantic Entity Embeddings:** We store the semantic embeddings created with Word2Vec and Doc2Vec in our index to provide fast access.

Our manually-constructed disambiguation index is publicly available on the GitHub page.

6.2 Parameters and Evaluation Measures

Our approach offers several parameters to tweak the disambiguation results. In the following, we will mention only those that have the most impact on the results. An overview of all parameters can be found on the GitHub page.

- **Surrounding Context:** For Doc2Vec we use a surrounding context of 75 words, which denotes that 75 words before and after the surface forms form the context. Using more context words, results in less meaningful query vectors. However, the best context size also depends on the domain of the input documents and should be adapted accordingly (e.g. tables).
- **Candidate Filter:** The cosine similarity ranges from -1 (unequal) to 1 (equal). A reasonable way to tune λ is to sweep the value between $0.25 < \lambda < 0.8$ (necessary similarity). We select the value $\lambda = 0.57$ according to the best averaged F1 values throughout the experiments.
- **PageRank:** We perform 100 PR iterations since the overall results do not change with more iterations. In terms of the PR jump probability α, we choose $\alpha = 0.1$ in algorithm step 3 (according to the original paper [30]). In algorithm step 4 we choose $\alpha = 0.2$ to increase the prior influence (i.e. a robust baseline) since the correct entity could not been determined with the help of topical coherence in the steps before. In the disambiguation step, *High Probability Candidate Disambiguation*, we determined the parameter $margin_1 = 0.5$ by sweeping the value between $0.2 < margin_1 < 0.6$. Again, the best value is selected according to the best averaged F1 values throughout the experiments.
- **Abstaining:** We note that abstaining is disabled by default using a $margin_2 = -\infty$. To provide the best abstaining results we chose $margin_2 = 0.3$ by sweeping the value between $0.2 < margin_2 < 0.6$ as described above.

Table 1: Statistics of our test corpora.

Data Set	Topic	#Doc.	#Ent.	Ent./Doc.	Annotation
ACE2004	news	57	253	4.44	voting
AIDA TestB	news/web	231	4458	19.40	voting
AQUAINT	news	50	727	14.50	voting
DBpedia Spot.	news	58	330	5.69	domain experts
MSNBC	news	20	658	32.90	domain experts
N3-Reuters	news	128	650	5.08	voting
IITB	news/web	103	11245	109.01	domain experts
Microposts	tweets	1165	1440	1.24	domain experts
N3-RSS 500	RSS-feeds	500	524	1.05	domain experts

In our evaluation, we use the well-known standard measures: *recall* ρ, *precision* π, *F1* and *accuracy* a. Given the ground truth G and the output of an entity disambiguation system O, in which G_{ent} and O_{ent} are the sets of surface forms that link to entities, and G_{nil} and O_{nil} are the sets of surface forms that link to NIL ($G = G_{\text{ent}} \cup G_{\text{nil}}$, $O = O_{\text{ent}} \cup O_{\text{nil}}$, and $|G| = |O|$):

$$\rho = \frac{|G_{ent} \cap O_{ent}|}{|G_{ent}|}, \quad \pi = \frac{|G_{ent} \cap O_{ent}|}{|O_{ent}|}, \quad F1 = \frac{2 * \pi * \rho}{\rho + \pi}$$

$$a = \frac{|G_{ent} \cap O_{ent}| + |G_{nil} \cap O_{nil}|}{|G|}$$

6.3 Data Sets

An often occurring problem in evaluating entity disambiguation systems is that authors often download available data sets and ignore those entity ground truth annotations that are not available in their underlying KB [12, 14, 13]. Thus, results often slightly differ due to different data set queries across literature. To avoid this problem, the authors of Uzbeck et al. [29] proposed GERBIL - General Entity Annotator Benchmark, an easy-to-use platform for the agile comparison of annotators using multiple data sets and uniform measuring approaches. Being a web-based platform it can be also used to publish the disambiguation results. The reported results of our approach and competitive systems are based on this platform and serve as comparable results for future systems.

In the following, we present nine well-known and publicly available data sets which are integrated in GERBIL and are used in our evaluation. All data sets provide different characteristics in form of surface form frequency and length of surrounding context (cf. Table 1). We evaluate our algorithm on all these data sets to demonstrate the robustness across different documents/data sets.

1. **ACE2004:** This data set from Ratinov et al. [25] is a subset of the ACE2004 coreference documents and contains 57 news articles comprising 253 surface forms.
2. **AIDA/CO-NLL-TestB:** The original AIDA data set [14] was derived from the CO-NLL 2003 shared task and contains 1.393 news articles. Cornolti et al. [6] subdivided this corpus into a training and two test corpora. The AIDA/CO-NLL-TestB data set has 231 documents with 19.40 entities on average. We note that this data set comprises several table-similar documents which mostly lack natural-language text.
3. **AQUAINT:** Compiled by Milne and Witten [22], the data set contains 50 documents and 727 surface forms from a news corpus from the Xinhua News Service, the New York Times, and the Associated Press.
4. **DBpedia Spotlight:** The DBpedia Spotlight corpus was released with the Spotlight system [19] and served as it's benchmark data set. It also contains several non-named entities (e.g. home). With 5.69 entities per document the corpus provides enough entities for collective entity disambiguation.

5. **MSNBC:** The corpus was presented by Cucerzan et al. [7] in 2007 and contains 20 news documents with 32.90 entities per document. The data set contains a wide range of entities which are linked via direct relations in DBpedia. Thus, many (simple) approaches achieve decent results.
6. **N3-Reuters128:** This corpus is based on the Reuters-21578 corpus which contains economic news articles. Roeder et al. proposed this corpus in [27] which contains 128 short documents with 4.85 entities on average.
7. **IITB:** This manually created data set by Kulkarni et al. [17] with 103 documents displays the highest entity/document-density of all data sets ($\approx$ 109 entities/document on average). Additionally, the documents are similar to Wikipedia pages and contain sufficient textual context.
8. **Microposts-2014 Test:** The tweet data set [2] was introduced for the "Making Sense of Microposts" challenge and has very few entities per document on average [29]. As usual in tweet data, the amount of textual context is very limited.
9. **N3 RSS-500:** This corpus has been published by Gerber et al. [9] and is one of the N3 data sets [27]. It consists of data collected from 1,457 RSS feeds. The list includes all major worldwide newspapers and a wide range of topics, e.g. World, U.S., Business etc. A subset of this corpus has been created by randomly selecting 1% of the contained sentences. Finally, domain experts annotated 500 sentences manually.

All ground truth annotations in these data sets either refer to entities in DBpedia or Wikipedia. Both KBs contain the same entities whose URLs can be easily converted to the other KB URL. Thus, we simply always return DBpedia URLs to GERBIL, which automatically processes the URLs according to the underlying data sets. We note that the GERBIL version that we use does not consider *NIL* annotations when computing the F1, recall and precision values. If our service returns a *NIL* annotation, GERBIL treats it like "not annotated". Thus, for our abstaining experiment we manually evaluate the accuracy on the IITB data set, which also considers *NIL* annotations.

7. EVALUATION

In the following, we compare the results of our approach with those attained by other disambiguation frameworks. To this end, we use GERBIL v1.1.4 and evaluate the approaches on the D2KB (i.e. link to a KB) task. In Section 7.1 we directly compare the approaches on the basis of its results achieved with GERBIL. In Section 7.2 we discuss our results in contrast to other works that are not publicly available. Section 7.3 provides a parameter study of the semantic embeddings and in Section 7.4 we evaluate the abstaining mechanism of our approach.

7.1 Results

In the following, we directly compare our approach to publicly available, state-of-the-art entity disambiguation systems, which disambiguate Wikipedia, DBpedia or YAGO entities, via GERBIL. These are the currently available versions of DBpedia Spotlight [19], AIDA [14] (new disambiguation index), Babelfy [23], WAT [24] and Wikifier [25, 5]. To the best of our knowledge, Wikifier is the current state-of-the-art entity disambiguation system which is publicly available. Wikifier and WAT use Wikipedia as underlying KB and link surface forms directly to Wikipedia pages. Babelfy also returns Wikipedia entities but uses BabelNet as KB, which was automatically created by linking Wikipedia to WordNet. In contrast, DBpedia Spotlight and AIDA rely on the RDF-KBs DBpedia and YAGO2, while additionally making use of Wikipedia knowledge.

Table 2: Micro-averaged F1, π and ρ of DoSeR on 9 data sets.

Data Set	F1	π	ρ
ACE2004	0.907	0.912	0.901
AIDA/CONLL-TestB	0.784	0.784	0.784
AQUAINT	0.842	0.85	0.838
DBpedia Spotlight	0.810	0.814	0.806
MSNBC	0.911	0.913	0.908
N3-Reuters128	0.850	0.856	0.844
IITB	0.741	0.744	0.738
Microposts-2014 Test	0.750	0.783	0.719
N3 RSS-500	0.751	0.752	0.750

Since entities within these three KBs (DBpedia, Wikipedia and YAGO2) provide sameAs relations, GERBIL maps the systems' output to the corresponding ground truth URLs. For all systems we choose the best configurations according to the authors. In addition to these frameworks, we define the strong baseline *PriorProb* which links surface forms to the entities with the highest prior probability (cf. Section 5.1). We also present the results when excluding entity-context embeddings (*DoSeR -Doc2Vec*). We investigate how well the approach performs with entity-embeddings as semantic relatedness feature only. In this case, we use the entity embeddings directly to compute the ETP (cf. Section 5.2). Table 2 lists the results on nine data sets in terms F1, precision and recall, aggregated across surface forms (micro-averaged). Table 3 shows the F1 values in comparison to the competitor systems on all data sets. The corresponding GERBIL result sheet is available on the GERBIL website[4] and can be used to make comparisons to our approach in future evaluations.

Overall, our approach attains the best averaged F1 value of all systems. Thereby, it outperforms Wikifier by 5 F1 percentage points on average. Additionally, we significantly outperform the other systems as well as the PriorProb baseline by up to 25 F1 percentage points on average. On the data sets ACE2004, MSNBC, Microposts2014-Test and N3-Reuters128 our approach performs exceptionally well (up to 12 F1 percentage points in advance). We note that our PriorProb baseline outperforms Wikifier on the Microposts-2014-Test data set because of using a newer version of DBpedia/Wikipedia. The Micropost2014-Test data set was released in 2014 and obviously queries some very new (or changed) entities. On the DBpedia Spotlight and N3 RSS-500 data sets our approach also performs best with F1 values of ≈ 0.81 (DBpedia Spotlight) and ≈ 0.75 (N3 RSS-500) respectively. Considering the AIDA/CONLL-TestB data set, our approach performs slightly better than Wikifier but performs comparatively poor with a F1 value of ≈ 0.78 compared to ≈ 0.84 by the WAT system. The reasons for this are two-fold: First, the underlying data set is still annotated with entities whose identifiers have been changed over the years with updates. Thus our service returns wrong entity URLs according to the ground truth. The same problem occurs in the AIDA system when using the newer AIDA entity index. In this case, the F1 value drops from 0.82 to 0.77. In an experiment where we disambiguate the original AIDA entities, our system achieves a F1 value of ≈ 0.84. Second, a more detailed analysis of the surface forms' textual context is necessary to perform even better. Nevertheless, our algorithm outperforms the other systems and also AIDA which was optimized on this data set. Regarding AQUAINT and IITB, Wikifier leads DoSeR by 2 percentage points F1 on both data sets.

[4]http://dx.doi.org/10.5281/zenodo.51250

Table 3: **Comparing micro-averaged F1 values of DoSeR, DoSeR without Doc2Vec, the prior probability baseline as well as the publicly available entity disambiguation systems Wikifier, Spotlight, AIDA, Babelfy and WAT on nine data sets.**

Data Set	DoSeR	DoSeR (-Doc2Vec)	PriorProb	Wikifier	Spotlight	AIDA	Babelfy	WAT
ACE2004	**0.907**	0.872	0.831	0.834	0.713	0.815	0.561	0.800
AIDA/CONLL-TestB	0.784	0.754	0.661	0.777	0.593	0.774	0.592	**0.843**
AQUAINT	0.842	0.842	0.803	**0.862**	0.713	0.532	0.652	0.768
DBpedia Spotlight	**0.810**	0.775	0.745	0.797	0.789	0.508	0.522	0.652
MSNBC	**0.911**	0.876	0.711	0.851	0.511	0.782	0.607	0.777
N3-Reuters128	**0.850**	0.810	0.700	0.703	0.577	0.596	0.534	0.644
IITB	0.741	0.738	0.711	**0.766**	0.447	0.270	0.470	0.611
Microposts-2014 Test	**0.750**	0.704	0.630	0.586	0.453	0.453	0.473	0.595
N3 RSS-500	**0.751**	0.713	0.678	0.732	0.622	0.716	0.630	0.682
Average	**0.816**	0.787	0.718	0.768	0.602	0.605	0.560	0.708

In *summary*, we state that our approach significantly outperforms other publicly available disambiguation approaches. Overall, our approach disambiguates the entities highly accurate and attains state-of-the-art or nearly state-of-the-art results on all nine data sets. Hence, our approach is very well suited for all kinds of documents available in the web (e.g. tweets, news, etc.). We emphasize that despite the huge amount of training data used to improve disambiguation robustness, our approach attains nearly identical results on all data sets with entity embeddings trained on Wikipedia only. Our results proposed in [32] show that a simple graph algorithm using entity embeddings based on Wikipedia already performs exceptionally well. In terms of performance, our approach annotates roughly as fast as the Wikifier and WAT annotation system but is slower compared to Spotlight and AIDA. The Babelfy system is the slowest and takes too much time, especially on the IITB data set. Our system has the advantage to accept multiple queries in parallel, but is not yet optimized for high-performance disambiguation.

7.2 Discussion

Comparing our results to those of other state-of-the-art approaches that are not publicly available is not an easy task. Reimplementing the respective algorithms is not an absolutely fair method to compare the approaches with our KB: Usually crucial implementation details remain unknown in the original publications, since the focus mostly lies on the algorithm instead of the implementation.

Anyhow, we use the work of Guo et al. [10] as an entry point in the following. Their approach was exclusively evaluated and optimized on the ACE2004, MSNBC and AQUAINT data sets on which the authors achieve state-of-the-art results. A direct comparison of our results and the results of [10] shows that both works perform equally well on the MSNBC data set. Furthermore, our approach performs better on the ACE2004 data set (0.906 vs. 0.877 F1) but loses on the AQUAINT data set (0.842 vs. 0.907 F1). The problem with a pure number-based comparison, however, lies in the uncertainty in the underlying KB used in the experiments. If the underlying KB has a lower number of entities, the average likelihood of a wrong disambiguation is also reduced. In order to compare our algorithm with the approach in [10], we introduce the concept of the Surface Form Ambiguity Degree (SFAD). The SFAD is based on two assumptions: First, both approaches are able to disambiguate all entities in the ground truth data set, i.e. the KB covers the entities in the data sets and contains similar entity occurrences resulting from a given corpus (important for prior computation). Second, the candidate entities retrieved from the KB contain the correct entity, i.e. the error introduced by candidate selection is zero. Under these assumptions, a varying prior probability of an entity defines the degree of ambiguity, the SFAD, for that surface form. So the SFAD describes how many entities are potentially relevant for a specific surface form. Since our approach has a (significantly) lower prior probability on these data sets, the SFAD is higher, respectively. In Table 4 we compare the differences of the best result and the result achieved with the prior alone for our approach and the Guo et al. approach. Overall, our disambiguation index contains more entities that are relevant for a surface form on average and hints that our core-algorithm (without KB and candidate selection) is more robust than the approach from Guo et al. [10]. Another evidence is that the authors reimplemented the approach used in Wikifier and achieved significantly better results on their KB as we achieved with GERBIL with Wikifier's original KB. Guo et al. also report the results of former, well-known state-of-the-art approaches (e.g. Cucerzan [7], Han et al. [12], Glow [25]), but we do not discuss the results in detail because these approaches perform worse than Wikifier and the approach of Guo et al.

Considering the IITB data set, the system by Han et al. [11] performs best with a micro F1 value of 0.80. The authors did not evaluate their system on other data sets. However, their topic model approach is fully-trained on Wikipedia and takes all words into account. Since, the IITB data set consists of long documents very similar to those in Wikipedia, the system performs best on it.

In 2014, the Micropost2014-Test data set was created in the context of the workshop challenge *Making Sense of Microposts* [2]. The best system in the workshop was proposed by Microsoft which attains a micro F1 value of 0.70. To the best of our knowledge, this has been the best disambiguation approach on this data set so far, but is outperformed by our approach by ≈ 5 percentage points.

Considering the CONLL-TestB data set, the current state-of-the-art approach has been presented by Huang et al. [15] and attains a micro F1 value of 0.866. Similar to our approach, the authors learn semantic embeddings with a deep neuronal network approach from DBpedia and Wikipedia (but not with Word2Vec and Doc2Vec). Again, the approach was only evaluated on the CONLL-TestB data set as well as on a tweet data set. Experiments show that we can also further improve our results on this data set to a micro F1 value of 0.850 by (i) reducing entity candidates (lower SFAD), (ii) training the semantic embeddings on DBpedia instead of Wikipedia and (iii) using an older entity index. However, since our main goal was to create a **robust** disambiguation approach which performs well on several data sets with varying underlying document properties, we do not optimize the DoSeR algorithm on a single data set.

Table 4: Differences of the best result and the prior DoSeR and Guo et al. [10] on 3 data sets.

Approach	ACE2004	MSNBC	AQUAINT
DoSeR F1(best) - F1(prior)	0.076	0.200	0.039
Guo et al. F1(best) - F1(prior)	0.022	0.049	0.035
Δ in F1 percentage points	**5.4**	**15.1**	**0.4**

In summary, we state that a pure number-based result comparison is not always easy since multiple factors play an important role (e.g. disambiguation index, data set queries). However, the results give the hint that our approach achieves comparable accuracy, while being robust on other data sets at the same time.

7.3 Semantic Embeddings Parameter Study

The accuracy of our approach depends on a number of parameters, foremost the parameters of the semantic embeddings. In order to analyze this sensitivity, we conducted experiments in which we vary the dimension number of our semantic embeddings and report the results for both Word2Vec and Doc2Vec architectures (CBOW vs. Skip-gram and PV-DM vs. PV-DBOW).

Figure 2 (top) depicts the average micro F1 value (across all data sets) of our approach when using either the CBOW or skip-gram Word2-Vec architecture and a specific amount of dimensions. During this experiment the corresponding Doc2Vec architecture is set to PV-DM since it is better suited as we will see in the following. Basically, in our experiments, the skip-gram architecture consistently creates better entity embeddings then CBOW. This might be due to skip-gram performs better with infrequent words (entities) in the training corpus [20]. However, the difference between both architectures is $\approx 1-2$ percentage points F1. On $d = 400$ the result margin between both architectures is maximized and the average F1-value reaches its peak. It is interesting to see that even more dimensions slightly decrease the result values. We assume that this leads to some kind of overfitting and, thus, the optimal number of dimensions for entity embeddings probably depends on the number of entities and amount of training data.

We conduct the same experiment for our entity-document embeddings (Doc2Vec). In this particular case, we use the skip-gram architecture as baseline training algorithm for the entity embeddings (Word2Vec). Figure 2 (bottom) depicts the corresponding average micro F1 values for various dimensions and both Doc2Vec architectures. The PV-DM architecture for Doc2Vec performs better if the number of dimensions is higher than $d = 400$. We assume that the context consideration in the PV-DM architecture leads to an advance. However, the best average F1 value is achieved with $d = 1000$, whereby the difference between PV-DBOW and PV-DM is maximal ≈ 2 percentage points F1.

In *summary*, we state that the skip-gram architecture for Word2-Vec and the PV-DM architecture for Doc2Vec perform best. It is interesting to see that the number of optimal dimensions for entity embeddings must be geared to the underlying corpora.

7.4 Abstaining

Abstaining is an important task in disambiguation algorithms when it comes to disambiguating surface forms whose referent entity is not in the entity set Ω. It is also used if there is uncertainty about the correct entity due to insufficient context information.

In this experiment, our algorithm returns the pseudo-entity *NIL* in the following situations: (i) if no entity candidates can be found during the candidate generation step (cf. Section 5.1), and (ii) if the algorithm is uncertain about the correct entity after the last PR iteration (cf. Algorithm 1). For experimental purpose, we downloaded the original IITB data set (information on our GitHub page), which additionally contains 7652 *NIL* annotations in addition to the default annotations (18897 annotations overall), and report the disambiguation *accuracy*. We also rerun the GERBIL experiments with abstaining to investigate to what extent the results decrease on data sets which do not provide *NIL* ground truth annotations.

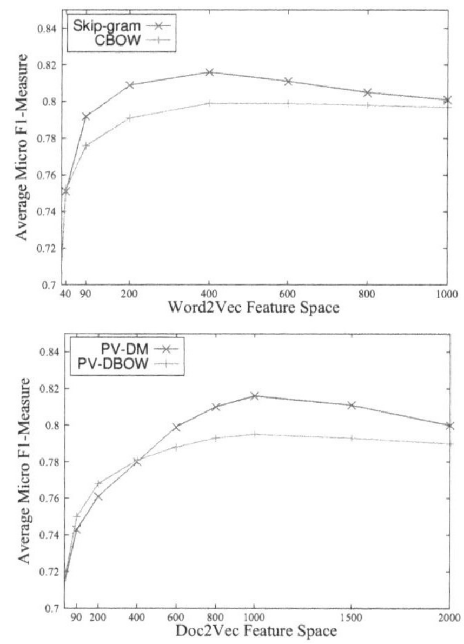

Figure 2: Comparison of Word2Vec and Doc2vec architectures with various feature-space dimensions.

Conducting the experiment on the manually downloaded IITB data set results in a disambiguation accuracy of 0.757 (micro-averaged). With returning 6120 *NIL* annotations overall, our algorithm does not find candidates for surface forms in 3823 cases ($\approx 62.5\%$) and abstains 2297 surface forms ($\approx 37.5\%$). When we tune our abstaining parameter to abstain more aggressive, our overall accuracy slightly decreases. Unfortunately, the authors of the topic-model, state-of-the-art approach [11] on this data set do not provide abstaining results for comparison in their work.

However, Table 5 reports the micro F1 values of our algorithm with abstaining on all data sets in the GERBIL evaluation. As a result of GERBIL not querying surface forms with *NIL* annotations in the ground truth, our results (slightly) decrease. Nevertheless, the amount of abstained surface forms is very limited and, thus, our approach still outperforms Wikifier on 6 out of 9 data sets. On the Microposts2014-Test data set the F1 decrease is the highest with 7 percentage points F1. Obviously, our algorithm is sometimes uncertain about the correct entity and abstains, which is due a small amount of surface forms per document. In other words, our algorithm lacks sufficient evidence about the correct entity and, hence, abstains due to exceeding the abstaining threshold. In *summary*, we state that our algorithm is able to successfully abstain entity annotations if evidence of the correct entity is missing. Our abstaining mechanism performs well even if data sets do not provide *NIL* annotations (as simulated by GEBRIL).

8. CONCLUSION AND FUTURE WORK

In this work, we present a new collective, graph-based entity disambiguation approach that utilizes semantic entity and entity-context embeddings for robust entity disambiguation. Robust there-

Table 5: Micro F1 values of our approach with abstaining on data sets without *NIL* annotations.

Data Set	F1	Change in F1 percentage points
ACE2004	0.892	-1.65
AIDA/CONLL-TestB	0.782	-0.26
AQUAINT	0.820	-2.61
DBpedia Spotlight	0.773	-4.57
MSNBC	0.906	-0.55
N3-Reuters128	0.809	-4.82
IITB	0.722	-2.56
Microposts-2014 Test	0.607	-7.07
N3 RSS-500	0.738	-1.73

by refers to the property of achieving (better than) state-of-the-art results over a wide range of very different data sets. Our approach is also able to abstain if no appropriate entity can be found for a specific surface form. We evaluate our approach against 5 strong, publicly available entity disambiguation systems on 9 data sets and show that our approach outperforms all other system by a significant margin on nearly all data sets. We also discuss the influence of the quality of the underlying knowledge base on the disambiguation accuracy and compare our results to those of other non-publicly available state-of-the-art algorithms. We also provide our approach as well as the underlying knowledge base as open source solution.

Future work includes the evaluation of non-collective disambiguation. This is important if queries provide only a single surface form to disambiguate. We also want to optimize the disambiguation performance and provide in-depth performance tests.

9. ACKNOWLEDGMENTS

The presented work was developed within the EEXCESS project funded by the European Union Seventh Framework Programme FP7/2007-2013 under grant agreement number 600601. Additionally, it was partially funded by the IRYXYS Research Center.

10. REFERENCES

[1] A. Alhelbawy and R. J. Gaizauskas. Collective named entity disambiguation using graph ranking and clique partitioning approaches. In *Proc. of the 25th Int. Conf. on Computational Linguistics, Technical Papers*, pages 1544–1555, 2014.

[2] A. E. C. Basave, G. Rizzo, A. Varga, M. Rowe, M. Stankovic, and A.-S. Dadzie. Making sense of microposts named entity linking challenge. volume 1141 of *CEUR*, pages 54–60, 2014.

[3] S. Brin and L. Page. The anatomy of a large-scale hypertextual web search engine. In *7th WWW*, pages 107–117, Amsterdam, The Netherlands, 1998. Elsevier Science Publishers B. V.

[4] R. Bunescu and M. Pasca. Using encyclopedic knowledge for named entity disambiguation. In *Proc. of the 11th Conf. of the European Association for Computational Linguistics (EACL-06)*, pages 9–16, Trento, Italy, 2006.

[5] X. Cheng and D. Roth. Relational inference for wikification. In *Proc. of the Conf. on Empirical Methods in NLP*, EMNLP '13, 2013.

[6] M. Cornolti, P. Ferragina, and M. Ciaramita. A framework for benchmarking entity-annotation systems. In *Proc. of the 22nd Int. Conf. on World Wide Web*, WWW '13, pages 249–260, Republic and Canton of Geneva, Switzerland, 2013. International World Wide Web Conferences Steering Committee.

[7] S. Cucerzan. Large-scale named entity disambiguation based on wikipedia data. In *EMNLP-CoNLL*, volume 7, pages 708–716, 2007.

[8] P. Ferragina and U. Scaiella. Fast and accurate annotation of short texts with wikipedia pages. *IEEE Softw.*, 29(1):70–75, Jan. 2012.

[9] D. Gerber, A.-C. Ngonga Ngomo, S. Hellmann, T. Soru, L. Bühmann, and R. Usbeck. Real-time RDF extraction from unstructured data streams. In *Proceedings of ISWC*, 2013.

[10] Z. Guo and D. Barbosa. Robust entity linking via random walks. In *Proc. of the 23rd ACM Int. Conf. on Information and Knowledge Management*, CIKM '14, pages 499–508, New York, NY, USA, 2014. ACM.

[11] X. Han and L. Sun. An entity-topic model for entity linking. In *Proc. of the 2012 Joint Conf. on Empirical Methods in Natural Language Processing and Computational Natural Language Learning*, EMNLP-CoNLL '12, pages 105–115, Stroudsburg, PA, USA, 2012. ACL.

[12] X. Han, L. Sun, and J. Zhao. Collective entity linking in web text: A graph-based method. In *Proceedings of the 34th International ACM SIGIR Conference on Research and Development in Information Retrieval*, SIGIR '11, pages 765–774, New York, NY, USA, 2011. ACM.

[13] Z. He, S. Liu, M. Li, M. Zhou, L. Zhang, and H. Wang. Learning entity representation for entity disambiguation. In *ACL*, 2013.

[14] J. Hoffart, M. A. Yosef, I. Bordino, H. Fürstenau, M. Pinkal, M. Spaniol, B. Taneva, S. Thater, and G. Weikum. Robust disambiguation of named entities in text. In *Proc. of the Conf. on Empirical Methods in Natural Language Processing*, EMNLP '11, pages 782–792, Stroudsburg, PA, USA, 2011. ACL.

[15] H. Huang, L. Heck, and H. Ji. Leveraging deep neural networks and knowledge graphs for entity disambiguation. *CoRR*, abs/1504.07678, 2015.

[16] S. S. Kataria, K. S. Kumar, R. R. Rastogi, P. Sen, and S. H. Sengamedu. Entity disambiguation with hierarchical topic models. In *Proc. of the 17th ACM SIGKDD international Conf. on Knowledge Discovery and Data Mining*, KDD '11, pages 1037–1045, New York, NY, USA, 2011. ACM.

[17] S. Kulkarni, A. Singh, G. Ramakrishnan, and S. Chakrabarti. Collective annotation of wikipedia entities in web text. In *Proceedings of the 15th ACM SIGKDD International Conference on Knowledge Discovery and Data Mining*, KDD '09, pages 457–466, New York, NY, USA, 2009. ACM.

[18] Q. V. Le and T. Mikolov. Distributed representations of sentences and documents. In *Proc. of the 31th Int. Conf. on Machine Learning, ICML 2014, Beijing, China, 21-26 June 2014*, pages 1188–1196, 2014.

[19] P. N. Mendes, M. Jakob, A. García-Silva, and C. Bizer. Dbpedia spotlight: Shedding light on the web of documents. In *Proceedings of the 7th International Conference on Semantic Systems*, I-Semantics '11, pages 1–8, New York, NY, USA, 2011. ACM.

[20] T. Mikolov, K. Chen, G. Corrado, and J. Dean. Efficient estimation of word representations in vector space. *CoRR*, abs/1301.3781, 2013.

[21] T. Mikolov, I. Sutskever, K. Chen, G. S. Corrado, and J. Dean. Distributed representations of words and phrases and their compositionality. In *Advances in Neural Information Processing Systems 26: 27th Annual Conference on Neural Information Processing Systems 2013. Proceedings of a meeting held December 5-8, 2013, Lake Tahoe, Nevada, United States.*, pages 3111–3119, 2013.

[22] D. Milne and I. H. Witten. Learning to link with wikipedia. In *Proceedings of the 17th ACM Conference on Information and Knowledge Management*, CIKM '08, pages 509–518, New York, NY, USA, 2008. ACM.

[23] A. Moro, A. Raganato, and R. Navigli. Entity linking meets word sense disambiguation: a unified approach. *TACL*, 2:231–244, 2014.

[24] F. Piccinno and P. Ferragina. From tagme to wat: A new entity annotator. In *First Int. Workshop on Entity Recognition/Disambiguation*, ERD '14, pages 55–62, NY, USA, 2014. ACM.

[25] L. Ratinov, D. Roth, D. Downey, and M. Anderson. Local and global algorithms for disambiguation to wikipedia. In *Proceedings of the 49th Annual Meeting of the Association for Computational Linguistics: Human Language Technologies - Volume 1*, HLT '11, pages 1375–1384, Stroudsburg, PA, USA, 2011. Association for Computational Linguistics.

[26] R. Řehůřek and P. Sojka. Software Framework for Topic Modelling with Large Corpora. In *Proceedings of the LREC 2010 Workshop on New Challenges for NLP Frameworks*, pages 45–50, Valletta, Malta, May 2010. ELRA.

[27] M. Röder, R. Usbeck, S. Hellmann, D. Gerber, and A. Both. N3 - a collection of datasets for named entity recognition and disambiguation in the nlp interchange format. In *The 9th edition of the Language Resources and Evaluation Conference, 26-31 May, Reykjavik, Iceland*, 2014.

[28] R. Usbeck, A.-C. Ngonga Ngomo, M. Röder, D. Gerber, S. A. Coelho, S. Auer, and A. Both. Agdistis - graph-based disambiguation of named entities using linked data. In *14th ISWC*, pages 457–471, New York, NY, USA, 2014. Springer-Verlag New York, Inc.

[29] R. Usbeck, M. Röder, A.-C. Ngonga Ngomo, C. Baron, A. Both, M. Brümmer, D. Ceccarelli, M. Cornolti, D. Cherix, B. Eickmann, P. Ferragina, C. Lemke, A. Moro, R. Navigli, F. Piccinno, G. Rizzo, H. Sack, R. Speck, R. Troncy, J. Waitelonis, and L. Wesemann. Gerbil: General entity annotator benchmarking framework. In *Proc. of the 24th Int. Conf. on World Wide Web*, WWW '15, pages 1133–1143, Republic and Canton of Geneva, Switzerland, 2015. International World Wide Web Conferences Steering Committee.

[30] S. White and P. Smyth. Algorithms for estimating relative importance in networks. In *Proceedings of the Ninth ACM SIGKDD International Conference on Knowledge Discovery and Data Mining*, KDD '03, pages 266–275, New York, NY, USA, 2003. ACM.

[31] W. Xie, D. Bindel, A. Demers, and J. Gehrke. Edge-weighted personalized pagerank: Breaking a decade-old performance barrier. In *21th SIGKDD*, pages 1325–1334, NY, USA, 2015. ACM.

[32] S. Zwicklbauer, C. Seifert, and M. Granitzer. Doser - a knowledge-base agnostic framework for entity disambiguation using semantic embeddings. In *The Semantic Web. Latest Advances and New Domains*, ESWC '16. Springer, 2016.

Parameterized Fielded Term Dependence Models for Ad-hoc Entity Retrieval from Knowledge Graph

Fedor Nikolaev
Department of Computer Science
Wayne State University
Detroit, Michigan 48202
fedor@wayne.edu

Kazan Federal University
35 Kremlyovskaya Street
Kazan, Russia 420008
feanikolaev@kpfu.ru

Alexander Kotov*
Department of Computer Science
Wayne State University
Detroit, Michigan 48202
kotov@wayne.edu

Nikita Zhiltsov
Kazan Federal University
35 Kremlyovskaya Street
Kazan, Russia 420008
nzhilcov@kpfu.ru

ABSTRACT

Accurate projection of terms in free-text queries onto structured entity representations is one of the fundamental problems in entity retrieval from knowledge graph. In this paper, we demonstrate that existing retrieval models for ad-hoc structured and unstructured document retrieval fall short of addressing this problem, due to their rigid assumptions. According to these assumptions, either all query concepts of the same type (unigrams and bigrams) are projected onto the fields of entity representations with identical weights or such projection is determined based only on one simple statistic, which makes it sensitive to data sparsity. To address this issue, we propose the Parametrized Fielded Sequential Dependence Model (PFSDM) and the Parametrized Fielded Full Dependence Model (PFFDM), two novel models for entity retrieval from knowledge graphs, which infer the user's intent behind each individual query concept by dynamically estimating its projection onto the fields of structured entity representations based on a small number of statistical and linguistic features. Experimental results obtained on several publicly available benchmarks indicate that PFSDM and PFFDM consistently outperform state-of-the-art retrieval models for the task of entity retrieval from knowledge graph.

CCS Concepts

•**Information systems** → **Structured text search;**

Keywords

Entity Retrieval; Structured Document Retrieval; Feature-based Models; Learning-to-rank Models; Knowledge Graph

*The first two authors provided equal contribution.

SIGIR '16, July 17 - 21, 2016, Pisa, Italy

ISBN 978-1-4503-4069-4/16/07...$15.00

DOI: http://dx.doi.org/10.1145/2911451.2911545

1. INTRODUCTION

Recent studies [16, 22] indicate that more than 75% of queries issued to Web search systems aim at finding information about entities, which could be material objects or concepts that exist in the real world or fiction (e.g. people, products, scientific papers, colors). Most common information needs underlying this type of queries include finding a certain entity (e.g. *"Einstein relativity theory"*), a particular attribute or property of an entity (e.g. *"Who founded Intel?"*) or a list of entities satisfying a certain criteria (e.g. *"Formula 1 drivers that won the Monaco Grand Prix"*). Such information needs can be efficiently addressed by presenting the target entity or a list of entities, either directly as search results or in addition to the ranked list of documents. This scenario gives rise to the problem of ad-hoc entity retrieval from knowledge graph, when the output of retrieval models is a list of entities given their (potentially verbose) textual description.

Recent successes in the development of Web information extraction methods have resulted in the emergence of a number of large-scale publicly available and proprietary knowledge repositories, such as DBpedia[1], Freebase[2], Google's Knowledge Graph and Microsoft's Satori. All these repositories adopt a simple knowledge representation model based on subject-predicate-object triples that can be conceptualized as a directed labeled multi-graph (commonly referred to as a knowledge graph), in which the nodes correspond to entities and the edges denote typed relations between entities. This model makes knowledge graphs a natural choice for addressing different types of entity-centric information needs. However, since the structure of knowledge graphs has been optimized for automated reasoning and answering structured graph pattern queries, finding entities in knowledge graphs that conceptually match unstructured free-text queries presents certain challenges to existing retrieval models.

First, since entities in knowledge graphs are designated only by an identifier (e.g. machine ID */m/0jcx*, in the case of Freebase, or URI *http://dbpedia.org/page/Albert_Einstein*,

[1]http://dbpedia.org
[2]http://freebase.com

in the case of DBpedia), there is no notion of document in this retrieval scenario. A simple workaround for this issue used in recent work is to aggregate the objects and predicates in all the triples, which include each distinct entity as a subject, into the fields of a structured document for that entity. Such aggregation can be done by predicate type [21], according to the importance weights manually assigned to predicates [6], based on a flat structure with fixed number of fields (e.g. title and content [19] or entity name, attributes, categories, similar and related entity names [33]) or a two-level hierarchy, in which the first level corresponds to predicate types, while the second level corresponds to individual predicates [18]. Accurately matching unstructured keyword queries with such structured entity representations, however, is another fundamental theoretical problem, which has received much less research attention.

In particular, existing retrieval models are based on a set of rigid assumptions, which limit their effectiveness for retrieval of structured entity documents. On one hand, retrieval models incorporating term dependencies, such as Sequential Dependence Model [17] (which allows to assign different importance weights to matching query concepts of different type), Weighted Sequential Dependence Model (WSDM) [4] (which estimates the importance of each matching query concept individually) and retrieval model based on copulas [10] disregard entity document structure by considering the matches of the same query concept in different fields of entity documents as equally important. On the other hand, although existing models for ad-hoc structured document retrieval, such as the Mixture of Language Models (MLM) [20] and BM25F [23], factor in document structure when determining the degree of relevance of queries to documents, they do not take into account term dependencies (i.e. are agnostic to bigram query concepts). Furthermore, these models calculate the retrieval score of a structured document as a sum of the matching scores of each query term in a linear combination of the language models (LMs) for each document field. As a result, the field weights in this linear combination, which effectively determine the projection of query terms onto document fields, are the same for all query terms. Although the recently proposed Fielded Sequential Dependence Model (FSDM) [33] partially addressed this limitation by allowing different importance weights to the matches of a query concept in different fields of structured entity documents, such parametrization still lacks flexibility, as those weights are the same for all query concepts of the same type (unigrams, ordered and unordered bigrams). This can create a problem, which is illustrated by an example query *"capitals in Europe which were host cities of summer Olympic games"*. First, contrary to the assumption of FSDM, query concepts of the same type in this query should be projected onto different fields of relevant entity documents (e.g. *"capitals"* should be mapped onto the *categories* field, while *"Europe"* should be mapped onto the *attributes* field). Incorrect projection of any query concept (e.g. mapping *"Europe"* and *"Olympic games"* to the *entity names* field) is likely to substantially degrade the accuracy of retrieval results for this query. Probabilistic Retrieval Model for Semistructured Data (PRMS) [14] is a unigram bag-of-words model for ad-hoc structured document retrieval that learns a simple statistical relationship between the intended mapping of terms in free-text queries and their frequency in different document fields. Robust estimation of this relationship, however, requires query terms to have a non-uniform distribution across document fields and is negatively affected by data sparsity, particularly in the case of entity representations with a large number of fields. As a result, PRMS has inferior performance on entity retrieval tasks not only relative to FSDM [33], but also to both MLM and BM25F [2, 33].

To overcome the limitations of existing retrieval models, we propose the Parametrized Fielded Sequential Dependence Model (PFSDM) and the Parametrized Fielded Full Dependence Model (PFFDM), two novel feature-based retrieval models, which *infer the user's intent behind each individual query concept (unigram or bigram) by dynamically estimating its probabilistic mapping onto the fields of structured entity representations* using a small number of statistical and linguistic features. We also provide a learning-to-rank algorithm to learn the weights of these features that maximize the target retrieval metric from the training data. The key contributions of this work are as follows:

1. We proposed PFSDM and PFFDM, two *novel feature-based models for structured document retrieval*, which account for sequential and full term dependencies as well as provide flexible parametrization allowing to dynamically project each query concept onto document fields. To the best of our knowledge, there are no previous studies of feature-based models for structured document retrieval, in general, and ad-hoc entity retrieval from knowledge graph, in particular;
2. We propose a set of statistical and linguistic features of query concepts that enable their accurate projection onto the fields of structured entity documents;
3. We experimentally demonstrate that, for the task of ad-hoc entity retrieval from knowledge graph, dynamic projection of query concepts onto entity representations is more effective than dynamic estimation of their importance. We also found out that retrieval models accounting for all dependencies between query terms provide more accurate retrieval results for this task than the models that account only for sequential dependencies.

The rest of this paper is organized as follows. Section 2 provides a brief overview of previous research along the directions relevant to the present work. Ranking functions of PFSDM and PFFDM, features to estimate the mapping of query concepts onto the fields of entity documents along with the method to learn the weights of those features are presented in Section 3. Experimental results are reported and analyzed in Section 4, while Section 5 concludes the paper and outlines the directions for future work.

2. RELATED WORK

In this section, we provide an overview of the recent work in ad-hoc entity retrieval from knowledge graph as well as term dependence and feature-based retrieval models, the three research directions most closely related to this work.

Ad-hoc Entity Retrieval from Knowledge Graph. Every information access task involving knowledge graphs requires finding entities matching a keyword query, either as an intermediate step or a final goal. Entity retrieval *methods* are typically designed to address one particular entity-centric information need, such as entity search [29, 32, 33], list search [7] or entity-based question answering [26, 31], and consist of two stages. Entities retrieved in the first stage of those methods using a standard retrieval model, such as BM25 [2, 29], BM25F [6, 11, 29] or MLM [18, 32], are re-ranked or expanded in the second stage with their immediate neighbors in the knowledge graph, which can be obtained using SPARQL queries [29] or through random walk [24].

In particular, Tonon et al. [29] proposed a hybrid method combining IR and structured graph search that starts by retrieving an initial set of entities using BM25 retrieval model and then extends it using SPARQL queries with the entities that are directly related to the ones in the initial search results. Zhiltsov and Agichtein [32] proposed a learning-to-rank method for re-ranking the results of MLM using query term and structural entity similarity features calculated in latent space. The SemSets method [7] proposed for entity list search utilizes the relevance of entities to automatically constructed categories (i.e. semantic sets) measured according to structural and textual similarity. This approach combines a basic TF-IDF retrieval model with spreading activation over the link structure of a knowledge graph and evaluation of membership in semantic sets. Sawant and Chakrabarti [25] proposed a learning-to-rank method for handling Web queries aimed at finding entities that belong to a particular category. Several approaches that translate free-text questions into structured SPARQL queries have been proposed for question answering over linked data [26, 31]. The proposed *retrieval models* can be leveraged in the first stage of the above *methods* to improve their overall performance. Models designed specifically for ad-hoc entity retrieval can also be leveraged to obtain a set of entities related to a keyword query (a process known as entity linking [12]), which is an important step for the methods utilizing knowledge bases for query expansion in ad-hoc document retrieval [9, 15, 30].

Several entity representation schemes, in which the objects from RDF triples involving an entity are grouped into the fields of a structured entity document based on the predicates in those triples, have also been proposed [6, 18, 19]. In [6], objects are grouped into three fields based on manually designated predicate type (important, neutral, and unimportant). A simple scheme, in which the entities are represented as documents with two fields (title and content) was proposed in [19]. Experimental comparison of a structured entity representation scheme based on four fields with an unstructured and more complicated hierarchical scheme indicated superior performance of a simple structured representation [18].

Term Dependence and Feature-based Retrieval Models. Markov Random Fields (MRF) based retrieval framework [17], proposed by Metzler and Croft, provided a theoretical foundation for incorporating term dependencies (in the form of query bigrams and unordered two-word phrases) into retrieval models. Sequential Dependence Model (SDM), which only considers two-word sequences of query terms, and Full Dependence Model (FDM), which considers all possible two-word combinations of query terms, are the two most popular variants of the MRF retrieval models for ad-hoc document retrieval. Subsequent work along this direction [1, 8] demonstrated strong positive effect of accounting for query term dependencies and proximity on both ad-hoc and Web document retrieval.

SDM was later extended into WSDM by Bendersky et al. [4]. WSDM estimates the relative importance of query concepts as a linear combination of statistical features based on the frequency of occurrence of these concepts in the collection and external resources. Superior retrieval performance of different variants of WSDM for ad-hoc document retrieval has been demonstrated through extensive experimental evaluation in [13]. The utility of linguistic analysis for accurate processing of verbose queries in ad-hoc document retrieval has been demonstrated in [3]. While feature-based retrieval models have been shown to be effective for weighting concepts in verbose queries [4, 5], this work examines their effectiveness for ad-hoc entity retrieval from knowledge graph.

3. APPROACH

In this section, we introduce the ranking functions of Parameterized Fielded Sequential Dependence (PFSDM) and the Parameterized Fielded Full Dependence (PFFDM) retrieval models, the features used by these models to determine the projection of query concepts onto the fields of entity documents along with an algorithm to learn the weights of those features that maximize the target retrieval metric.

3.1 PFSDM and PFFDM

The quality of retrieval results for entity-centric free-text queries depends on the correctness of inference of implicit query structure and the accuracy of matching the intent behind each query concept with different aspects of semantics of relevant entities encoded in their structured representations. However, the ambiguity of natural language can lead to many plausible interpretations of a keyword query, which combined with the requirement to accurately project those interpretations onto entity representations, makes entity retrieval from knowledge graph a challenging IR problem.

PFSDM is a parametric extension of FSDM [33], a recently proposed MRF-based entity retrieval model, which takes into account *both term dependencies and document structure*. FSDM uses the following function to score each entity profile E with respect to a given keyword query Q:

$$\begin{aligned} P_\Lambda(E|Q) \stackrel{rank}{=} & \lambda_T \sum_{q \in Q} \tilde{f}_T(q_i, E) + \\ & \lambda_O \sum_{q \in Q} \tilde{f}_O(q_i, q_{i+1}, E) + \\ & \lambda_U \sum_{q \in Q} \tilde{f}_U(q_i, q_{i+1}, E) \end{aligned} \quad (1)$$

where $\tilde{f}_T(q_i, E)$, $\tilde{f}_O(q_i, q_{i+1}, E)$, $\tilde{f}_U(q_i, q_{i+1}, E)$ are the potential functions and λ_T, λ_O, λ_U are the relative importance weights for unigram, ordered and unordered bigram query concepts, respectively. The potential function for unigrams is defined as:

$$\tilde{f}_T(q_i, E) = \log \sum_{j=1}^{F} w_j^T P(q_i|\theta_j^E) = \log \sum_{j=1}^{F} w_j^T \frac{tf_{q_i,E_j} + \mu_j \frac{cf_{q_i,j}}{|C_j|}}{|E_j| + \mu_j}$$

where F is the number of fields in structured entity documents, θ_j^E is the language model of field j in structured document for entity E smoothed using the field-specific Dirichlet prior μ_j; $|E_j|$ is the length of field j in E and w_j^T are the field weights for unigrams with the following constraints: $\sum_{j=1}^{F} w_j^T = 1, w_j^T \geq 0$; tf_{q_i,E_j} is the frequency of query unigram q_i in field j of E; $cf_{q_i,j}$ is the frequency of q_i in the field j across structured documents for all entities in the collection; $|C_j|$ is the total number of terms in field j across all entity documents in the collection. The potential function for ordered bigrams is defined as:

$$\tilde{f}_O(q_{i,i+1}, E) = \log \sum_{j=1}^{F} w_j^O \frac{tf_{\#1(q_{i,i+1}),E_j} + \mu_j \frac{cf_{\#1(q_{i,i+1}),j}}{|C_j|}}{|E_j| + \mu_j}$$

while the potential function for unordered bigrams is defined as:

$$\tilde{f}_U(q_{i,i+1}, E) = \log \sum_{j=1}^{F} w_j^U \frac{tf_{\#uw_n(q_{i,i+1}),E_j} + \mu_j \frac{cf_{\#uw_n(q_{i,i+1}),j}}{|C_j|}}{|E_j| + \mu_j}$$

where $tf_{\#1(q_{i,i+1}),E_j}$ is the frequency of query bigram q_iq_{i+1} in field j of structured document for entity E, $cf_{\#1(q_{i,i+1}),j}$ is the collection frequency of q_iq_{i+1} in field j and $tf_{\#uw_n(q_{i,i+1}),E^j}$ is the number of times the terms q_i and q_{i+1} co-occur within a window of n words in field j of E, regardless of their order.

In the case of entity descriptions with F fields, FSDM has $3 * F + 3$ parameters: F field mapping weights plus λ_T, λ_O and λ_U. We believe that this parametrization lacks the necessary degrees of freedom, which can potentially limit the accuracy of this retrieval model. We propose to address this issue by dynamically estimating $w^T_{q_i,j}$, the relative contribution of each individual query unigram q_i, and $w^{O,U}_{q_{i,i+1},j}$, the relative contribution of each individual query bigram $q_{i,i+1}$, that are matched in field j of structured entity document for E towards the retrieval score of this entity, as a weighted linear combination of features:

$$w^T_{q_i,j} = \sum_k \alpha^U_{j,k} \phi_k(q_i, j)$$

$$w^{O,U}_{q_{i,i+1},j} = \sum_k \alpha^B_{j,k} \phi_k(q_{i,i+1}, j)$$

under the following set of constraints:

$$\sum_j w^T_{q_i,j} = 1, w^T_{q_i,j} \geq 0, \alpha^U_{j,k} \geq 0, 0 \leq \phi_k(q_i, j) \leq 1$$

$$\sum_j w^{O,U}_{q_{i,i+1},j} = 1, w^{O,U}_{q_{i,i+1},j} \geq 0, \alpha^B_{j,k} \geq 0, 0 \leq \phi_k(q_{i,i+1}, j) \leq 1$$

where $\phi_k(q_i, j)$ and $\phi_k(q_{i,i+1}, j)$ are the values of the k-th non-negative feature function for query unigram q_i and bigram $q_{i,i+1}$ in field j of entity document, respectively. $w^T_{q_i,j}$ and $w^{O,U}_{q_{i,i+1},j}$, which can also be considered as posteriors $p(E_j|q_i)$ and $p(E_j|q_{i,i+1})$, provide probabilistic projection of query unigram q_i and bigram $q_{i,i+1}$ onto the fields of structured entity representations (to reduce the number of parameters in the model, we set $w^O_{q_{i,i+1},j} = w^U_{q_{i,i+1},j}$). PFSDM determines this projection based on multiple features, unlike PRMS [14], which estimates it directly from the data based only on the total number of occurrences of a query term in a particular field across all documents in a collection. Feature-based estimation of this projection increases its robustness by overcoming the issues of sparsity and uniform distribution of occurrences of a query concept across the fields of entity documents.

PFFDM is different from PFSDM in that it accounts for all dependencies between the query terms, rather than only sequential ones.

3.2 Features

The features of different type that we propose to estimate the projection of a query concept κ onto field j of structured entity representations are presented in Table 1. In particular, PFSDM and PFFDM use two types of features: the ones whose value depends on a query concept and a field of entity representation and the ones that depend only on a query concept itself. The intuition behind also having the latter type of features is that the relation between them and the fields will be learned in the process of estimating their weights. For example, one can expect that the weight of a feature indicating whether a query concept is plural non-proper noun (NNS) will be higher in the *categories* field than in all other fields. For the features that depend on a field, one can expect that the value of the feature in that field will indicate the likelihood of a concept to be mapped to it. Nevertheless, we still learn the weights for these features, since: (1) ranges of values for particular features can be different in different fields and optimizing their weights is one of the ways to perform adequate scaling (2) contribution of the feature to the relevance of a field can be different for different fields.

Two of the features (FP, TS) depend on the collection statistics of a particular field. During optimization and retrieval, these two real-valued features (FP, TS) were rescaled to $[0, 1]$ range. The FP feature was rescaled logarithmically.

The other group of field mapping features (NNP, NNS, JJS, NPP, NNO) are binary and take particular values based on the output of Standford POS Tagger or Parser. NNP takes positive values for the query concepts that are proper nouns (e.g. entity names) and, thus, should be mapped to the *names*, *similar entity names* and *related entity names* fields. The NNS, NPP, and NNO features take positive values for the concepts that designate a broader class or type of the desired entities and, therefore, should be mapped to the *categories* field, while the JJS feature should project superlative adjectives to the *attributes* field. Constant feature (INT), which has the same value for all concepts, is known to be useful for mapping bigrams concepts.

3.3 Parameter estimation

In total, PFSDM and PFFDM have $F * U + F * B + 3$ parameters ($F * U + F * B$ feature weights as well as λ_T, λ_O and λ_U), where F is the number of fields, while U and B are the number of field mapping features for unigrams and bigrams, respectively. An efficient two-stage block optimization algorithm for learning the parameters of PFSDM and PFFDM with respect to the target retrieval metric is presented in Algorithm 1.

Algorithm 1 An algorithm for learning the feature weights in PFSDM and PFFDM.

```
1: Q ← Train queries
2: e_U = {1,0,0}, e_B = {0,1,1}
3: for s ∈ {U,B} do
4:     λ = e_s
5:     α̂_s ← CA(Q, λ)
6: end for
7: λ̂ ← CA(Q, α̂_U, α̂_B)
```

In the first stage (lines 3-6), the algorithm optimizes field mapping feature weights α separately for unigrams and bigrams. During optimization of the feature weights for un-

Table 1: **Features to estimate the contribution of query concept κ matched in field j towards the retrieval score of E. Column CT designates the type of query concept that a feature is used for (UG stands for unigrams, BG stands for bigrams).**

Source	Feature	Description	CT
Collection statistics	$FP(\kappa, j)$	Posterior probability $P(E_j\|w)$ obtained through Bayesian inversion of $P(w\|E_j)$, as defined in [14].	UG BG
	$TS(\kappa, j)$	Retrieval score of the top document according to SDM [17], when concept κ is used as a query and only the jth fields of entity representations are used as documents.	BG
Stanford POS Tagger[3]	$NNP(\kappa)$	Is concept κ a proper noun (singular or plural)?	UG
	$NNS(\kappa)$	Is concept κ a plural non-proper noun? We consider a bigram as plural when at least one of its terms is plural.	UG BG
	$JJS(\kappa)$	Is concept κ a superlative adjective?	UG
Stanford Parser[4]	$NPP(\kappa)$	Is concept κ part of a noun phrase?	BG
	$NNO(\kappa)$	Is concept κ the only singular non-proper noun in a noun phrase?	UG
	INT	Intercept feature, which has value 1 for all concepts.	UG BG

igrams, the feature weights for bigrams are not considered and vice versa. This is achieved by setting the corresponding λ weights to 0. After the algorithm is finished with optimizing the α weights, it proceeds to optimize the weights of MRF potential functions for different query concept types (λ_T, λ_O and λ_U in Eq. 1).

4. EXPERIMENTS

4.1 Experimental setup

Experimental results reported in this work were obtained on a publicly available benchmark developed by Balog and Neumayer [2], which uses DBpedia as the knowledge graph. For fair comparison, we used the same five field entity representation scheme and the same query sets as in [33] (SemSearch ES consisting primarily of named entity queries, ListSearch consisting primarily of entity list search queries, QALD-2 consisting of entity-focused natural language questions, and INEX-LD containing a mix of entity-centric queries of different type). We pre-processed both entity documents and queries by applying the Krovetz stemmer and removing the stopwords in the INQUERY stopword list.

4.2 Feature analysis

First, to evaluate the effectiveness of the proposed features, we performed an exploratory analysis of distributions of their values (for the features whose values depend on document fields) or frequencies of their occurrences (for the features whose values are independent of document fields) in different fields of entity representations. Specifically, we manually annotated each concept in all queries according to the user's intent with respect to a particular aspect of target entities as an *attribute* concept, *entity* concept, *relation* concept, or *type* concept. Our intuition is that the *attribute* query concepts (e.g. when a user is searching for an entity attribute rather than an entity itself) should be frequently occurring or have relatively higher feature values in the *attributes* field of entity representations. Query terms or phrases marked as *entity* concepts (e.g. when a user is searching for a particular named entity) should be primarily occurring in the *names* and *similar entity names* fields, while the *relation* concepts (when a query is about a relation between the two named entities) should be primarily occurring in the *similar entity names* and *related entity names* fields of entity representations. Finally, query concepts marked as *type* (when a query is about several entities with the same type) should be frequently occurring or have relatively greater feature values in the *categories* field.

Figure 1 visualizes the distributions of values of the Field Probability (FP) and Top Score (TS) features for the query concepts of different types in different fields of structured entity representations. As can be observed in Figure 1 (left), the median values of the FP feature for the query concepts of type *entity* in all three *entity* fields (*entity names*, *similar entity names* and *related entity names*) are significantly greater than the median values of the same feature for the query concepts of the same type in both the *attributes* and *categories* fields. The median values of the FP feature for the query concepts of type *attribute* in the *attributes* and *categories* fields are significantly greater than the median values of the same feature for the query concepts of the same type in all three *entity* fields. Furthermore, for the *type* and *relation* query concepts, the median values of the same feature in the *categories* and *related entity names* fields, respectively, are significantly greater than the median values of this feature in all other fields. It can also be observed in Figure 1 (right), that the median values of the TS feature for the query concepts of type *entity* in the *similar entity names* and *related entity names* fields are significantly greater than the median values of the same feature for the query concepts of the same type in all other fields. Furthermore, the median values of the TS feature for the *type* and *attribute* query concepts in the *attributes* field are greater than the median values of the same feature in all other fields.

To formally validate these observations, we conducted statistical significance tests. In particular, the Kruskal-Wallis

[3]http://nlp.stanford.edu/software/tagger.html
[4]http://nlp.stanford.edu/software/lex-parser.html

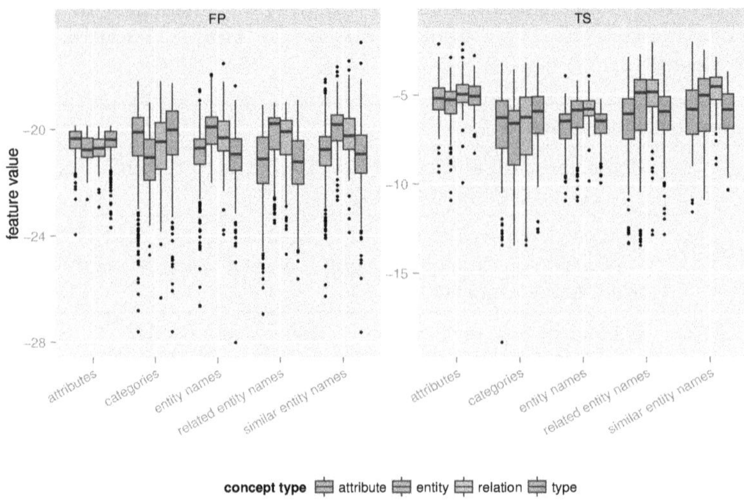

Figure 1: Boxplots for the distributions of values of real-valued features for the query concepts of different types in different fields of entity documents.

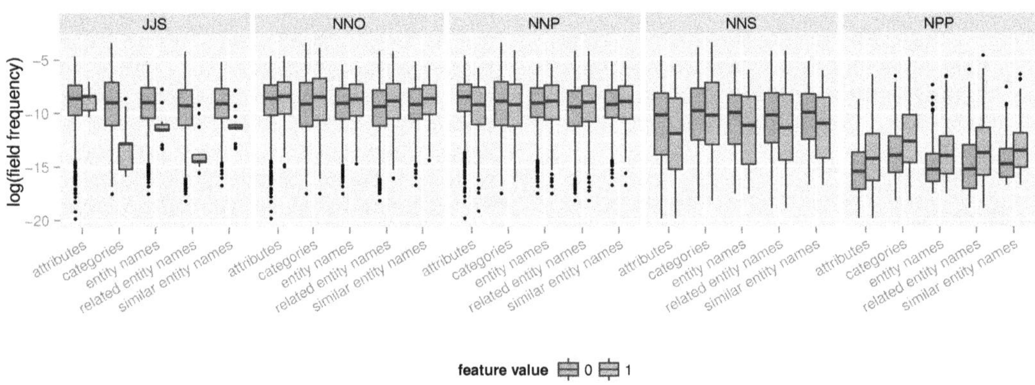

Figure 2: Boxplots for the distributions of normalized frequencies of query concepts with negative and positive feature values in different fields of entity documents.

test [27] indicated that the null hypothesis of the FP and TS feature values having the same median in different fields of entity representations for all concept types should be rejected ($p < 0.05$). Following the Kruskal-Wallis test, we performed a multiple comparison test (kruskalmc), which besides confirming the above empirical observations, indicated other statistically significant differences in feature values. In particular, the values of the TS feature for the query concepts of type *relation* in the *related entity names* field are different from its values in the *categories* and all three *entity* fields. This test also indicated that for all concept types the values of the FP feature in all three *entity* fields (*entity names, similar entity names* and *related entity names*) are significantly different from the values of the same feature in both *attributes* and *categories* fields, which in turn are significantly different from each other for the query concepts of type *relation*.

Figure 2 visualizes the distributions of normalized frequencies of query concepts with negative and positive values of the features that do not depend on a field in different fields of structured entity representations. Examining the properties of these distributions for concepts with positive and negative feature values in the same field as well as across different fields can give us an intuition about whether the concepts having positive values for a particular feature are more likely to occur in certain fields of entity representations than in the others. This in turn can give us an insight about whether certain linguistic properties of query concepts are indicative of the user's intent with respect to the projection of those concepts onto specific aspects of relevant entities. As follows from Figure 2, the query concepts that are superlative adjectives (JJS is true) much more frequently occur in the *attributes* field and are very likely to designate the attributes of relevant entities; plural non-proper unigrams and bigrams (NNS is true), bigrams (NPP is true) or singular non-proper nouns (NNO is true) that are part of a noun phrase are more likely to represent the categories of relevant entities, while singular or plural proper nouns (NNP is true) more frequently occur in three *entity* fields, than in any other field of entity documents and, thus, typically

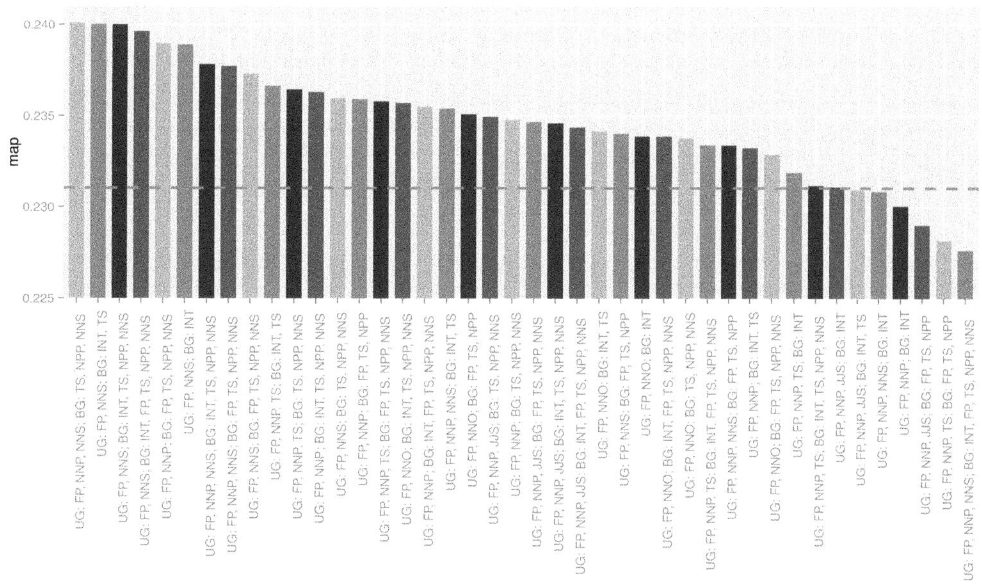

Figure 3: MAP of PFSDM on DBpedia knowledge graph and the benchmark in [2] depending on different combinations of field mapping features for unigram and bigram query concepts. Dashed red line represents the performance of FSDM [33].

designate the target entities directly. These observations indicate that entity-centric keyword queries have an implicit structure, with each element in that structure designating a particular aspect in multi-fielded representation of relevant entities.

4.3 Feature effectiveness

To determine the combination of features, which results in the best performance of PFSDM and PFFDM, we conducted a feature selection study. First, we determined the combinations of only unigram and only bigram features (using simplified versions of PFSDM that consider only unigrams or bigrams, respectively), which result in the best retrieval performance in terms of MAP (target retrieval metric). In particular, we identified 6 most effective unigram and 7 most effective bigram feature sets. Then we evaluated the performance of PFSDM using each possible combination of unigram and bigram feature sets to determine the best performing combined feature set. Retrieval effectiveness of different feature combinations for PFSDM is illustrated in Figure 3. As follows from Figure 3, most feature combinations result in higher MAP than FSDM. PFSDM achieves the highest MAP of 0.240 in conjunction with FP, NNS, NNP features for unigram query concepts and TS, NNS, NPP features for bigram ones. The weights of these features that result in the highest MAP of PFSDM are presented in Table 3.

From Table 3, it follows that the learned feature weights are similar to the distribution of frequencies of manually marked up query concept types across the fields of structured entity representation.

4.4 Comparison with baselines

Retrieval accuracy of PFSDM and PFFDM using the best feature combination is compared with that of state-of-the-art retrieval models for ad-hoc document (SDM [17] and WSDM [4] with *cf* and *df* features) and structured document (BM25F [23], PRMS [14], MLM [20] and FSDM [33]) retrieval in Table 2. Parameters of both the proposed retrieval models and the baselines have been optimized using 5-fold cross validation (except PRMS, which does not require optimization).

Several important conclusions can be made based on the results in Table 2. First, WSDM shows minor improvement and, on some query sets, is even worse than SDM, which indicates that feature-based query concept importance weighting is less effective for entity retrieval than for document retrieval. On the other hand, dynamic feature-based estimation of relative importance of matching query concepts in different fields of entity documents provides significant improvement of retrieval accuracy on verbose queries, such as the ones in QALD-2 query set. Second, the relatively small difference in performance between PFSDM and FSDM on SemSearch ES and ListSearch query sets can be explained by the fact that all concepts in those query sets map to only a few fields. In particular, most concepts in SemSearch ES queries map onto the *entity* field, while most concepts in ListSearch queries map onto the *categories* and *attributes* fields. In such cases, estimating field mapping degenerates to estimating relative importance of matching concepts in a particular field of entity representation, which nullifies the advantages of PFSDM. We can also observe that taking into account all dependencies between query terms can partially mitigate this problem, as evidenced by superior performance of PFFDM on both ListSearch and INEX-LD query sets. Third, although it can be seen that PFSDM achieves improvement over FSDM in terms of MAP, MRR and NDCG@5 at the expense of decreased P@10, taking into account all dependencies between the query terms allows PFFDM to achieve consistent improvement over both FSDM and FFDM in terms of all retrieval metrics.

Table 4 compares the retrieval accuracy of PFSDM and PFFDM with the same baselines on the knowledge graph

Table 2: Performance of retrieval models on DBpedia knowledge graph and the benchmark in [2]. Relative improvement over PRMS and FSDM is shown in parenthesis, while "*" and "†" indicate statistically significant improvement over the same baselines, according to the Fisher's randomization test ($\alpha = 0.05$) [28].

	SemSearch ES			
	MAP	**P@10**	**MRR**	**NDCG@5**
SDM	0.254 (+10.5%)	0.202 (+14.4%)	0.520 (−5.3%)	0.306 (−3.5%)
WSDM	0.246 (+7.2%)	0.201 (+13.5%)	0.507 (−7.7%)	0.298 (−5.9%)
BM25F-tc [2]	0.334 (+45.3%)	0.263 (+48.7%)	0.705 (+28.4%)	0.453 (+42.9%)
PRMS	0.230	0.177	0.549	0.317
MLM	0.320 (+39.3%)	0.250 (+41.3%)	0.680 (+23.9%)	0.423 (+33.3%)
FSDM	0.386 (+68.1%)	0.286 (+61.7%)	0.737 (+34.3%)	0.476 (+50.3%)
PFSDM	0.394* (+71.4%/+1.9%)	0.286* (+61.7%/0.0%)	0.757* (+38.0%/+2.7%)	0.494*† (+55.9%/+3.7%)
FFDM	0.389* (+69.3%/+0.7%)	0.286* (+61.7%/0.0%)	0.734* (+33.8%/−0.4%)	0.479* (+51.3%/+0.6%)
PFFDM	0.380* (+65.3%/−1.7%)	0.286* (+61.7%/0.0%)	0.739* (+34.6%/+0.2%)	0.477* (+50.6%/+0.2%)
	ListSearch			
	MAP	**P@10**	**MRR**	**NDCG@5**
SDM	0.197 (+78.3%)	0.252 (+63.8%)	0.463 (+30.5%)	0.282 (+60.1%)
WSDM	0.194 (+75.4%)	0.257 (+66.7%)	0.457 (+28.8%)	0.280 (+58.7%)
BM25F-tc [2]	0.159 (+43.9%)	0.221 (+43.5%)	0.390 (+9.8%)	0.217 (+23.2%)
PRMS	0.111	0.154	0.355	0.176
MLM	0.190 (+71.7%)	0.252 (+63.8%)	0.439 (+23.5%)	0.280 (+58.5%)
FSDM	0.203 (+83.9%)	0.256 (+66.1%)	0.447 (+25.8%)	0.274 (+55.2%)
PFSDM	0.201* (+81.8%/−1.1%)	0.253* (+64.4%/−1.0%)	0.443* (+24.8%/−0.8%)	0.278* (+57.5%/+1.5%)
FFDM	0.226*† (+104.4%/+11.2%)	0.282*† (+83.1%/+10.2%)	0.499*† (+40.6%/+11.7%)	0.313*† (+77.2%/+14.2%)
PFFDM	0.228*† (+106.4%/+12.3%)	0.286*† (+85.9%/+11.9%)	0.487* (+37.2%/+9.1%)	0.302*† (+71.3%/+10.4%)
	INEX-LD			
	MAP	**P@10**	**MRR**	**NDCG@5**
SDM	0.117 (+83.5%)	0.258 (+77.9%)	0.567 (+38.7%)	0.341 (+57.4%)
WSDM	0.118 (+85.3%)	0.257 (+77.2%)	0.549 (+34.4%)	0.341 (+57.4%)
BM25F-tc [2]	0.117 (+83.0%)	0.249 (+71.7%)	0.559 (+36.7%)	0.341 (+57.4%)
PRMS	0.064	0.145	0.409	0.216
MLM	0.102 (+60.2%)	0.238 (+64.1%)	0.530 (+29.7%)	0.306 (+41.3%)
FSDM	0.111 (+74.4%)	0.263 (+81.4%)	0.546 (+33.7%)	0.322 (+48.7%)
PFSDM	0.116* (+81.7%/+4.2%)	0.259* (+78.6%/−1.5%)	0.579* (+41.5%/+5.9%)	0.341* (+57.6%/+6.0%)
FFDM	0.122*† (+91.3%/+9.7%)	0.273* (+88.3%/+3.8%)	0.560* (+37.0%/+2.5%)	0.345*† (+59.5%/+7.3%)
PFFDM	0.121*† (+89.9%/+8.9%)	0.274* (+89.0%/+4.2%)	0.556* (+36.0%/+1.8%)	0.343* (+58.7%/+6.7%)
	QALD-2			
	MAP	**P@10**	**MRR**	**NDCG@5**
SDM	0.184 (+52.9%)	0.106 (+35.5%)	0.287 (+52.0%)	0.215 (+46.5%)
WSDM	0.183 (+52.8%)	0.112 (+42.7%)	0.288 (+52.6%)	0.214 (+45.7%)
BM25F-tc [2]	0.107 (−11.1%)	0.062 (−20.9%)	0.158 (−16.0%)	0.117 (−20.6%)
PRMS	0.120	0.079	0.188	0.147
MLM	0.152 (+26.3%)	0.103 (+30.9%)	0.215 (+14.0%)	0.170 (+15.7%)
FSDM	0.195 (+62.7%)	0.136 (+73.6%)	0.283 (+50.0%)	0.229 (+55.7%)
PFSDM	0.218*† (+81.9%/+11.7%)	0.140* (+78.2%/+2.6%)	0.308* (+63.2%/+8.8%)	0.253*† (+72.5%/+10.8%)
FFDM	0.200* (+66.5%/+2.3%)	0.139* (+76.4%/+1.6%)	0.292* (+54.9%/+3.3%)	0.237* (+61.6%/+3.8%)
PFFDM	0.219*† (+82.1%/+11.9%)	0.147* (+87.3%/+7.9%)	0.310* (+64.2%/+9.5%)	0.267*† (+81.5%/+16.6%)
	All queries			
	MAP	**P@10**	**MRR**	**NDCG@5**
SDM	0.192 (+41.5%)	0.198 (+45.0%)	0.449 (+21.3%)	0.281 (+31.5%)
WSDM	0.189 (+39.6%)	0.200 (+46.5%)	0.441 (+19.1%)	0.278 (+30.2%)
BM25F-tc [2]	0.182 (+34.3%)	0.192 (+40.8%)	0.442 (+19.5%)	0.277 (+29.5%)
PRMS	0.136	0.136	0.370	0.214
MLM	0.196 (+44.3%)	0.206 (+50.6%)	0.458 (+23.7%)	0.292 (+36.4%)
FSDM	0.231 (+70.4%)	0.231 (+69.2%)	0.498 (+34.5%)	0.325 (+52.0%)
PFSDM	0.240*† (+77.1%/+3.9%)	0.231* (+68.9%/−0.2%)	0.516*† (+39.5%/+3.7%)	0.342*† (+59.9%/+5.2%)
FFDM	0.241*† (+77.5%/+4.2%)	0.240*† (+75.7%/+3.8%)	0.515*† (+39.2%/+3.4%)	0.342*† (+60.1%/+5.3%)
PFFDM	0.244*† (+79.9%/+5.6%)	0.244*† (+78.4%/+5.4%)	0.518*† (+39.9%/+4.0%)	0.347*† (+62.5%/+6.9%)

from the 2009 Billion Triple Challenge (BTC-2009). This knowledge graph consists of 1.14 billion RDF triples and contains entities from other knowledge bases besides DBpedia. For this experiment, we used the queries from the Entity Search (ES) track of 2010[5] and 2011[6] Yahoo! Sem-

[5]http://km.aifb.kit.edu/ws/semsearch10/
[6]http://km.aifb.kit.edu/ws/semsearch11/

Table 3: **Optimized weights of the best performing features for PFSDM (averaged over all folds).**

concept type	feature	attributes	categories	names	related entity names	similar entity names
Unigram	*FP*	0.147	0.109	0.026	0.020	0.041
	NNS	0.110	0.141	0.019	0.023	0.014
	NNP	0.116	0.092	0.025	0.060	0.057
Bigram	*TS*	0.065	0.153	0.029	0.043	0.087
	NNS	0.039	0.183	0.028	0.046	0.057
	NPP	0.091	0.073	0.000	0.075	0.042

Table 4: Comparison of retrieval models on SemSearch ES queries and BTC-2009 knowledge graph.

	MAP	P@10	MRR	NDCG@5
SDM	0.102 (+4.4%)	0.210 (+6.0%)	0.518 (−4.9%)	0.248 (−8.0%)
WSDM	0.100 (+2.6%)	0.214 (+8.2%)	0.495 (−9.1%)	0.230 (−14.7%)
PRMS	0.098	0.198	0.545	0.269
MLM	0.121 (+23.6%)	0.243 (+22.8%)	0.588 (+8.0%)	0.312 (+16.0%)
FSDM	0.171 (+75.3%)	0.323 (+63.3%)	0.631 (+15.8%)	0.358 (+32.9%)
PFSDM	$0.182^{*}_{\dagger}$ (+87.0%/+6.7%)	0.335^{*} (+69.4%/+3.7%)	$0.657^{*}_{\dagger}$ (+20.7%/+4.2%)	0.371^{*} (+37.8%/+3.7%)
FFDM	$0.180^{*}_{\dagger}$ (+84.8%/+5.4%)	$0.330^{*}_{\dagger}$ (+66.9%/+2.2%)	0.647^{*} (+18.8%/+2.6%)	$0.373^{*}_{\dagger}$ (+38.6%/+4.3%)
PFFDM	0.187^{*} (+91.8%/+9.4%)	$0.342^{*}_{\dagger}$ (+72.6%/+5.7%)	0.650^{*} (+19.4%/+3.1%)	0.377^{*} (+40.2%/+5.5%)

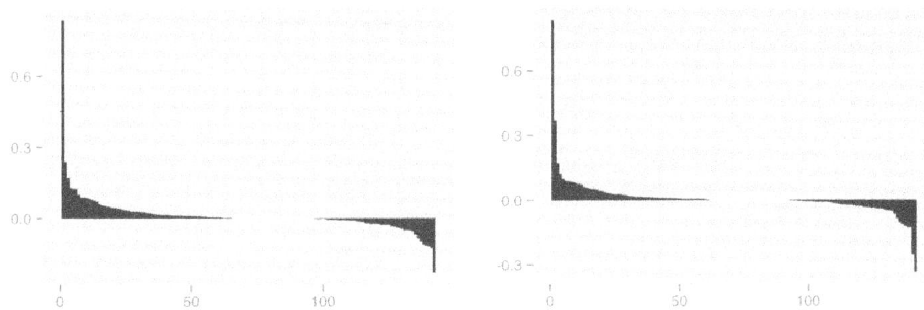

(a) (b)

Figure 4: Topic-level differences in average precision on BTC-2009: a) between PFSDM and FSDM; b) between PFFDM and FFDM.

Search Challenge and publicly available relevance judgments for those queries[7]. We used the same 5-field entity representation scheme for this knowledge graph, as we did for the DBpedia one. As can be seen in Table 4, PFSDM and PFFDM demonstrate significant and consistent improvement relative to PRMS, as well as FSDM and FFDM, respectively.

From Figures 4a and 4b, it also follows that parameterizing the field importance weights in PFSDM and PFFDM results in more improved topics and greater magnitude of improvements than using static weights in FSDM and FFDM.

4.5 Success/Failure Analysis

Next, we provide a brief qualitative analysis of sample queries illustrating the strengths and weaknesses of PFSDM and PFFDM. The ability to map query concepts of the same type onto different fields of entity documents allows PFSDM to promote the correct entities for verbose and question queries. For example, for the query *"Who produces Orangina?"*, PFSDM returns the correct result *A.G. Barr* at the top, unlike FSDM, which ranks it as the 18th result. For this query, PFSDM correctly assigns higher weights to the matches of the query term *produce* in the *attributes* (0.49) and *categories* (0.41) fields, of the query term *Orangina* in the *related entity names* field (0.55) and of the bigram *produce Orangina* in the *categories* (0.45) field, unlike FSDM, which uses the same field weighting scheme (0.40 for *attributes*, 0.20 for *categories*, 0.30 for *related entity names* and 0.10 for *similar entity names* fields) for all query unigrams. The correct field mapping weights for these query concepts are determined by the FP and NNP features. The same effect was observed for the query *"Who is the governor of Texas?"*. PFSDM promoted *Rick Perry*, the only correct answer for this query, from the second to the first position by boosting the matches of query concepts *governor* (captured by the FP and NNP features) and *governor Texas* (captured by the TS feature) in the *categories* field.

Another type of queries with the highest relative MAP

[7]https://github.com/nzhiltsov/YSC-relevance-data

gain of PFSDM over FSDM are list search queries, such as *"Give me a list of all American inventions"* (from 0.032 to 0.232), *"Tom Hanks movies where he plays a leading role"* (from 0.073 to 0.181) and *"Give me all companies in Munich"* (from 0.114 to 0.252). For the first query, PFSDM promotes the correct entities *Aberdeen Chronograph*, *Lisp programming language* by boosting their matching scores in the *categories* field, while FSDM ranks *The Heroic Age of American Invention*, a science book for children, as the highest entity, by not taking into account the absence of an important term *invention* in its *categories* field.

We also observed that the common causes of PFSDM failures are assignment of uniform field weights to query concepts and a lack of concept statistics. For example, for the query *"Give me all people that were born in Vienna and died in Berlin"*, PFSDM underestimates the importance of relatively rare concepts *Vienna* and *Berlin*, but overestimates the importance of very popular concepts *born* and *die*. The issue can be addressed by using a minimum support matching strategy or by introducing additional features.

5. CONCLUSION

In this paper, we proposed two novel models for ad-hoc entity retrieval from knowledge graph, which account for term dependencies and perform feature-based projection of query concepts onto the fields of entity documents. By demonstrating the possibility of inferring implicit structure of keyword queries using linguistic attributes and simple field statistics of query concepts, the proposed models constitute an important step in the evolution of models for structured document retrieval. We hypothesize that the proposed models can be effective in other structured information retrieval scenarios, such as product and social graph search, and leave verification of this hypothesis to future work.

Acknowledgments

This work was partially supported by the subsidy from the government of the Russian Federation to support the program of competitive growth of Kazan Federal University and by the Russian Foundation for Basic Research (grants # 15-07-08522, 15-47-02472).

6. REFERENCES

[1] J. Bai, Y. Chang, H. Cui, Z. Zheng, G. Sun, and X. Li. Investigation of Partial Query Proximity in Web Search. In *Proceedings of the 17th WWW*, pages 1183–1184, 2008.

[2] K. Balog and R. Neumayer. A Test Collection for Entity Search in DBpedia. In *Proceedings of the 36th ACM SIGIR*, pages 737–740, 2013.

[3] M. Bendersky and W. B. Croft. Discovering Key Concepts in Verbose Queries. In *Proceedings of the 31st ACM SIGIR*, pages 491–498, 2008.

[4] M. Bendersky, D. Metzler, and W. B. Croft. Learning Concept Importance Using a Weighted Dependence Model. In *Proceedings of the 3rd ACM WSDM*, pages 31–40, 2010.

[5] M. Bendersky, D. Metzler, and W. B. Croft. Parameterized Concept Weighting in Verbose Queries. In *Proceedings of the 34th ACM SIGIR*, pages 605–614, 2011.

[6] R. Blanco, P. Mika, and S. Vigna. Effective and Efficient Entity Search in RDF Data. In *Proceedings of the 10th ISWC*, pages 83–97, 2011.

[7] M. Ciglan, K. Nørvåg, and L. Hluchý. The SemSets Model for Ad-hoc Semantic List Search. In *Proceedings of the 21st WWW*, pages 131–140, 2012.

[8] R. Cummins and C. O'Riordan. Learning in a Pairwise Term-term Proximity Framework for Information Retrieval. In *Proceedings of the 32nd ACM SIGIR*, pages 251–258, 2009.

[9] J. Dalton, L. Dietz, and J. Allan. Entity Query Feature Expansion Using Knowledge Base Links. In *Proceedings of the 37th ACM SIGIR*, pages 365–374, 2014.

[10] C. Eickhoff, A. P. de Vries, and T. Hoffman. Modelling Term Dependencies with Copulas. In *Proceedings of the 38th ACM SIGIR*, pages 783–786, 2015.

[11] B. Fetahu, U. Gadiraju, and S. Dietze. Improving Entity Retrieval on Structured Data. In *Proceedings of the 14th ISWC*, pages 474–491, 2015.

[12] F. Hasibi, K. Balog, and S. E. Bratsberg. Entity Linking in Queries: Tasks and Evaluation. In *Proceedings of the 1st ACM ICTIR*, pages 171–180, 2015.

[13] S. Huston and W. B. Croft. A Comparison of Retrieval Models using Term Dependencies. In *Proceedings of the 23rd ACM CIKM*, pages 111–120, 2014.

[14] J. Y. Kim, X. Xue, and W. B. Croft. A Probabilistic Retrieval Model for Semistructured Data. In *Proceedings of the 31st ECIR*, pages 228–239, 2009.

[15] A. Kotov and C. Zhai. Tapping into Knowledge Base for Concept Feedback: Leveraging ConceptNet to Improve Search Results for Difficult Queries. In *Proceedings of the 5th WSDM*, pages 403–412, 2012.

[16] T. Lin, P. Pantel, M. Gamon, A. Kannan, and A. Fuxman. Active Objects Actions for Entity Centric Search. In *Proceedings of the 21st WWW*, pages 589–598, 2012.

[17] D. Metzler and W. B. Croft. A Markov Random Field Model for Term Dependencies. In *Proceedings of the 28th ACM SIGIR*, pages 472–479, 2005.

[18] R. Neumayer, K. Balog, and K. Nørvåg. On the Modeling of Entities for Ad-hoc Entity Search in the Web of Data. In *Proceedings of the 34th ECIR*, pages 133–145, 2012.

[19] R. Neumayer, K. Balog, and K. Nørvåg. When Simple is (more than) Good Enough: Effective Semantic Search with (almost) no Semantics. In *Proceedings of the 34th ECIR*, pages 540–543, 2012.

[20] P. Ogilvie and J. Callan. Combining Document Representations for Known-item Search. In *Proceedings of the 26th ACM SIGIR*, pages 143–150, 2003.

[21] J. R. Pérez-Aguera, J. Arroyo, J. Greenberg, J. P. Iglesias, and V. Fresno. Using BM25F for Semantic Search. In *Proceedings of the 3rd SemSearch Workshop*, 2010.

[22] J. Pound, P. Mika, and H. Zaragoza. Ad-hoc Object Retrieval in the Web of Data. In *Proceedings of the 19th WWW*, pages 771–780, 2010.

[23] S. Robertson, H. Zaragoza, and M. Taylor. Simple BM25 Extension to Multiple Weighted Fields. In *Proceedings of the 13th ACM CIKM*, pages 42–49, 2004.

[24] C. Rocha, D. Schwabe, and M. P. de Argão. A Hybrid Approach for Searching in the Semantic Web. In *Proceedings of the 13th WWW*, pages 374–383, 2004.

[25] U. Sawant and S. Chakrabarti. Learning Joint Query Interpretation and Response Ranking. In *Proceedings of the 22nd WWW*, pages 1099–1110, 2013.

[26] S. Shakarpour, A.-C. N. Ngomo, and S. Auer. Question Answering on Interlinked Data. In *Proceedings of the 22nd WWW*, pages 1145–1156, 2013.

[27] S. C. Siegel and J. Castellan. Nonparametric Statistics for the Behavioral Sciences. *McGraw-Hill*, 1998.

[28] M. D. Smucker, J. Allan, and B. Carterette. A Comparison of Statistical Significance Tests for Information Retrieval Evaluation. In *Proceedings of the 16th ACM CIKM*, pages 623–632, 2007.

[29] A. Tonon, G. Demartini, and P. Cudré-Mauroux. Combining Inverted Indices and Structured Search for Ad-hoc Object Retrieval. In *Proceedings of the 35th ACM SIGIR*, pages 125–134, 2012.

[30] C. Xiong and J. Callan. Query Expansion with Freebase. In *Proceedings of the 1st ACM ICTIR*, pages 111–120, 2015.

[31] M. Yahya, K. Berberich, S. Elbassuoni, and G. Weikum. Robust Question Answering over the Web of Linked Data. In *Proceedings of the 22nd ACM CIKM*, pages 1107–1116, 2013.

[32] N. Zhiltsov and E. Agichtein. Improving Entity Search over Linked Data by Modeling Latent Semantics. In *Proceedings of the 22nd ACM CIKM*, pages 1253–1256, 2013.

[33] N. Zhiltsov, A. Kotov, and F. Nikolaev. Fielded Sequential Dependence Model for Ad-Hoc Entity Retrieval in the Web of Data. In *Proceedings of the 38th ACM SIGIR*, pages 253–262, 2015.

Hierarchical Random Walk Inference in Knowledge Graphs

Qiao Liu
qliu@uestc.edu.cn

Liuyi Jiang
harperliuyi@gmail.com

Minghao Han
hanmhao@gmail.com

Yao Liu
liuyao@uestc.edu.cn

Zhiguang Qin
qinzg@uestc.edu.cn

School of Information and Software Engineering
University of Electronic Science and Technology of China
Chengdu 610054, China

ABSTRACT

Relational inference is a crucial technique for knowledge base population. The central problem in the study of relational inference is to infer unknown relations between entities from the facts given in the knowledge bases. Two popular models have been put forth recently to solve this problem, which are the latent factor models and the random-walk models, respectively. However, each of them has their pros and cons, depending on their computational efficiency and inference accuracy. In this paper, we propose a hierarchical random-walk inference algorithm for relational learning in large scale graph-structured knowledge bases, which not only maintains the computational simplicity of the random-walk models, but also provides better inference accuracy than related works. The improvements come from two basic assumptions we proposed in this paper. Firstly, we assume that although a relation between two entities is syntactically directional, the information conveyed by this relation is equally shared between the connected entities, thus all of the relations are semantically bidirectional. Secondly, we assume that the topology structures of the relation-specific subgraphs in knowledge bases can be exploited to improve the performance of the random-walk based relational inference algorithms. The proposed algorithm and ideas are validated with numerical results on experimental data sampled from practical knowledge bases, and the results are compared to state-of-the-art approaches.

CCS Concepts

•**Information systems** → **Retrieval tasks and goals;** •**Computing methodologies** → **Knowledge representation and reasoning;** *Machine learning algorithms;*

Keywords

Relational inference; Random walk model; Statistical relational learning; Knowledge base; Knowledge graphs

SIGIR '16, July 17 - 21, 2016, Pisa, Italy

ISBN 978-1-4503-4069-4/16/07...$15.00

DOI: http://dx.doi.org/10.1145/2911451.2911509

1. INTRODUCTION

The goal of relational inference research is to infer new knowledge (facts) from the existed knowledge bases[6]. This paper considers the problem of relational inference on large-scale *graph-structured knowledge bases* (**GKBs**, a.k.a. *knowledge graphs*), such as Freebase, YAGO and DBpedia, which stores factual information in the form of <entity-relation-entity> triplets. Currently, relational inference remains a challenge as the knowledge bases are plagued with incompleteness and ambiguity. For example, most of the basic information about the public figures that one would think typically available, such as the "Place of Birth"and the "Parents" attributes, are still missing in the latest version of Freebase and alike knowledge bases at this time[14].

However, research on statistical relational learning (SRL) reveals that the existing knowledge in GKBs contain useful information about the latent relations between entities, which can be effectively explored by using statistical learning methods[18]. Current research efforts are largely focused on developing relational learning models that can scale to massive GKBs, among which the latent factor model (**LFM**) and the random-walk model (**RWM**) are the most heavily studied, and some related algorithms have been introduced (instantly) into practical usage[14]. For instance, the *Never-Ending Language Learning* (NELL) project takes the RWM based *path ranking algorithm* (PRA) as their relation reasoning module. While in the Google's *Knowledge Vault* project, a hybrid solution that combines the LFM and the RWM is implemented for knowledge evaluation tasks[20].

Each of these two models has its benefits and limitations. Generally speaking, the RWMs are more computationally efficient than the LFMs, because the LFMs inherently involve a matrix factorization operation over the GKBs, which is difficult to be parallelized. In contrast the RWMs are naturally parallelized, which makes it more scalable for large-scale GKBs. However, according to our empirical studies (see Sec. 4.3), the performance of the RWM solutions are not as competitive as those of some LFM solutions, in terms of inferential accuracy and recall rate. Since both of the efficiency and the accuracy are crucial to the success of relational learning tasks in practice, we present in this study for the first time a comprehensive investigation of the potential benefits of the random-walk model, with the purpose of determining whether it can outperform the most competitive LFM solutions, thus providing new insights into the mechanisms that underlie graph based relational inference.

The principle contribution of this paper is the development of a new random-walk based learning algorithm, called the ***Hi**erarchical **R**andom-walk **i**nference* (**HiRi**) algorithm, for relational inference on GKBs. Specifically, we describe a two-tier random-walk mechanism for relational retrieval, wherein the upper-tier of the model corresponds to the *relation sequence* pattern recognition and learning process in a global perspective, the lower-tier is designed to capture useful information from inside the relation-specific subgraphs in GKBs (which means that each subgraph only represents one specific type of relation). The proposed HiRi algorithm outperforms widely used PRA on two benchmark data sets sampled from real GKBs, achieving an improvement in MRR score of up to 79.5%, and in Hits@1 score of up to 79.2%. The proposed algorithm also outperforms some state-of-the-art LFM based algorithms on all of the data sets.

Another contribution of this paper is that we propose two basic assumptions for relational inference model building:

(1) Since the relations between entities are semantically bidirectional, the knowledge graphs can be modeled with undirected graphs in relational learning tasks.

(2) The reciprocal information transfer between the head and tail entities within the relation-specific cliques of a GKB is of special value in relational learning tasks.

The first assumption is in accordance with intuition, but is in direct conflict with the basic assumption universally accepted by scholars, which represent the GKBs as directed graphs so as to make it consistent with the logical structure of the facts stored in GKBs. The second assumption explains why the latent factor models consistently outperform the random walk models with respect to recall and accuracy, thus it also helps explaining why a hierarchical random-walk mechanism is necessary for RWM-alike solutions. Experimental results are shown to agree with our assumptions, we hope this may shed some light on better understanding the existing methods, and on further study of this problem.

The rest of this paper is organized as follows. We first provide a brief literature review of the related work in Section 2, and then we present a detailed description of our methodology in Section 3. Experiments and discussions are provided in Section 4, and Section 5 concludes this paper.

2. RELATED WORK

Statistical relational learning (SRL) has received a lot of attention in information retrieval and artificial intelligence communities[6]. Methods from SRL research have also been applied to develop link prediction models and context-aware recommender systems[3, 13]. There is an extensive amount of literature available, hence we will only give a very brief overview of the closely related work in this section.

For relational learning in graph-structured knowledge bases, the most commonly-used research method in the past two decades was to develop probabilistic inference models, such as the Markov logic networks[18] and the Bayesian networks[11], based on the first-order logic rules, to infer new facts from existing facts[5]. However, such approaches suffer from the **scalability** problem (due to the computational expense associated with the rule learning process) and the **generalization** problem (caused by the brittleness of the logical rules), which limits their usefulness for relational learning on large-scale GKBs[17]. To catch up with the rapid expansion of the industrial GKBs, several new approaches have been devised, among which the latent factor models (LFMs) and the random-walk models (RWMs) have been in the forefront of academic efforts in recent years[16, 7].

The basic idea of the latent factor models is to obtain a vectorized *representation* for each of the entities and/or relations stored in the GKBs, by transforming it into a low-dimensional subspace, and then infer the missing facts from such *representations*[14]. Depending on the different approximate factorization schemes adopted, the LFMs are also called *tensor decomposition* models[16] or *structured embedding* models[2]. For instance, the RESCAL algorithm tries to represent the relation-specific subgraph of a GKB with a third-order tensor model, in which entities and their relation are mapped into different tensor spaces[15]. While the TransE algorithm treats a relation as a *translating operation* between the corresponding *head* and *tail* entities, thus in TransE, both of the relation and the associated entities are mapped into the same embedding space[1].

The TransH algorithm further improves the TransE by representing relations as hyperplanes, rather than vectors, in an embedding space, which enables an entity to have distinct representations when involved in different type of relations[21]. Both of the TransE and the TransH algorithms were trying to mapping the entities and relations into the same embedding concept space, however, Lin et. al. proposed in TransR model that the entities and relations should be treated differently, because they are conceptually different types of objects, thus should be mapped into different concept spaces, and they claimed that the (inferential) translation should only be performed in the relation space[9].

Another line of research that has also drawn increasing attention are the random-walk based relational learning models. Studies of the RWMs were originally inspired by the idea of the *First Order Inductive Learner* (FOIL), which is a supervised relational learning algorithm based on the Horn clause rules extracted from the GKBs[19]. The seminal work of the RWM for relational learning is the *Path Ranking Algorithm* (PRA), which extends the idea of the FOIL by searching through the GKB for *path features* instead of Horn clause rules[8]. The merits of the PRA algorithm are that its inference results are easily interpretable, and it is inherently parallelizable. In contrast, the meanings of the latent factor models (i.e. the embedding spaces) are hard to be explained. Furthermore, since the LFM solutions require a computational extensive matrix factorization process during the model training stage, it is difficult to be parallelized efficiently. For more details about the recent advances in theories and applications of the LFMs and the RWMs in this area, a good review can be found in [14].

The merits of PRA make it a promising candidate not only for research but also for industrial applications as well. In fact, it has already been used successfully in some large-scale GKB projects, such as the *Knowledge Vault* project of Google, and the *Never-Ending Language Learning* (NELL) project of Carnegie Mellon University[10]. However, according to the comparative study made in this paper, the random-walk based PRA algorithm is obviously at a disadvantage compared with the best performed LFM solutions, in terms of both the inferential accuracy and the recall rate.

Therefore the motivation of this work was to extend the existing studies by addressing the following question: is it possible to design a relational learning model that not only

Table 1: **Meanings of notations.**

def.	**Meanings of notations**
$\boldsymbol{G}$	symbol of the knowledge graph
N	number of the SPO triplets in $\boldsymbol{G}$
$\boldsymbol{R}$	set $\boldsymbol{R}$ contains all of the relation types in $\boldsymbol{G}$
n	number of the relation types in $\boldsymbol{R}$
$\boldsymbol{E}$	set $\boldsymbol{E}$ contains all of the unique entities in $\boldsymbol{G}$
m	number of the entities in $\boldsymbol{E}$
r_i	the i-th element in $\boldsymbol{R}$
$\boldsymbol{G}_i$	subgraph of $\boldsymbol{G}$ that only contains relation r_i
$\boldsymbol{H}_i$	set $\boldsymbol{H}_i$ contains all of the *head* entities in $\boldsymbol{G}_i$
$\boldsymbol{T}_i$	set $\boldsymbol{T}_i$ contains all of the *tail* entities in $\boldsymbol{G}_i$
$<h, r, t>$	SPO triplet, the unit of knowledge (fact)
$<h, t>$	ordered entity pair extracted from $<h, r, t>$

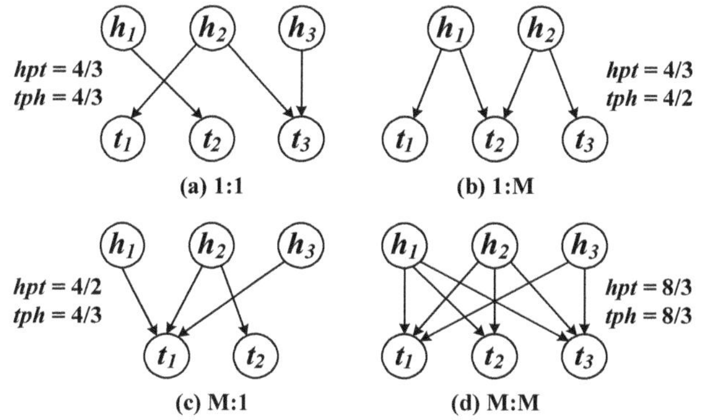

Figure 1: Illustration of the four relation categories.

maintains the efficiency of the RWMs, but also keeps the accuracy of the LFMs? The proposed HiRi algorithm is a pure random-walk based relational learning algorithm, this is markedly distinct from the efforts of developing hybrid models (the blending of RWMs and LFMs), which has become a major focus of the research community[4, 12].

The most related work to ours is the PRA algorithm, both of them rely on the same pattern discovery strategy and path feature learning framework for relational retrieval modeling from the global perspective. However, there are two significant differences: firstly, the path feature discovery process of HiRi is based on the undirected graph representation of the GKB, although the PRA algorithm also does allow the inverse of a relation to be considered in its path feature discovery process, but only limited to some of the *non-functional* predicates (relations). Secondly, HiRi contains a local inference mechanism, which makes it capable of utilizing the inferable information conveyed in the relation-specific cliques to enhance the performance of the global inference procedure, which is not considered by the PRA algorithm. Experimental results demonstrate the effectiveness of HiRi and the validity of the underlying assumptions, which also provides a positive answer to the above question.

3. THE HIRI ALGORITHM

In this section, we start by introducing some preliminary background and the symbol system used in this paper, then we discuss the intuition and algorithmic framework of the proposed HiRi algorithm. The detailed implementation of the HiRi algorithm is divided into three parts, which will be described in Section 3.3 to 3.5, respectively.

3.1 Preliminary And Notation

Knowledge graphs (KGs) represent facts in the form of binary relations, in particular <*subject, predicate, object*> triplets, where *subject* and *object* are entities and *predicate* is the type of a relation. For simplicity and in accordance with previous studies[9, 20], we will use the notation $<h, r, t>$ to represent the SPO triplets, in which h and t represent the *head* (subject) and *tail* (object) entities and r is the relation between them. The meanings of the major notations used in this paper are given in Table 1. According to previous research, the relation types in a knowledge graph can be artificially classified into four categories by means of the *heads-per-tail* ratio (*hpt*) and *tails-per-head* ratio (*tph*):

$$hpt_i = \frac{\#\ triplets_i}{\#\ tails_i};\quad tph_i = \frac{\#\ triplets_i}{\#\ heads_i}. \tag{1}$$

where $\#\ triplets_i$ denotes the number of SPO triplets in subgraph $\boldsymbol{G}_i$, $\#\ heads_i$ and $\#\ tails_i$ represents the number of *head* and *tail* entities in $\boldsymbol{G}_i$. Then a particular type of relation can be assigned to one of the four categories: one-to-one (1:1), one-to-many (1:M), many-to-one (M:1) and many-to-many (M:M), according to the following criteria.

$$\begin{cases} hpt_i < \delta \text{ and } tph_i < \delta \Rightarrow \text{1:1 relations} \\ hpt_i < \delta \text{ and } tph_i \geq \delta \Rightarrow \text{1:M relations} \\ hpt_i \geq \delta \text{ and } tph_i < \delta \Rightarrow \text{M:1 relations} \\ hpt_i \geq \delta \text{ and } tph_i \geq \delta \Rightarrow \text{M:M relations} \end{cases} \tag{2}$$

where $\delta \geq 1$ is an empirical parameter proposed in [1]. In this paper we follow the same approach as in [1] and [21], and choose $\delta = 1.5$ as the classification criteria. Figure 1 depicts four simple examples in an illustrative manner to facilitate intuitive understanding of this classification method.

3.2 Assumptions And Framework

The basic idea of the HiRi algorithm is simple: figure out why exactly the RWM solutions systematically perform worse than the LFM solutions, and try to fix it. For this purpose, we begin by comparing the performance of two typical algorithms that have attracted considerable attentions recently, which are the RWM based PRA algorithm[8], and the LFM based TransE algorithm[1]. Table 2 provides the comparison of the performance between PRA and TransE by use of the FB15k data sets, the test sets were split into four parts according to Eq. (2). For more details about the experimental settings and protocols, please refer to Sec. 4.

Roughly speaking, the Hits@10 score represents the averaged *hits* ratio on the top 10 prediction results of the corresponding algorithms. From Table 2, one can see that the TransE algorithm clearly performs better than the PRA algorithm on 1:M and M:M relations. Since similar situations are also observed in comparing PRA with other LFM solutions (see Section 4.5), we believe that the presence of such a recurring pattern worth further investigation.

Firstly, notice that the PRA performs comparable to the TransE algorithm on M:1 relations, which is in contrast with the results observed upon 1:M relations. Since if we ignore the directionality of the edges, the topological structures of the entity-relation graphs corresponding to 1:M and M:1 re-

Table 2: Comparison test: Hits@10 on FB15k

Algorithm	1:1	1: M	M:1	M:M
TransE	71.5%	49.0%	85.0%	72.9%
PRA	63.3%	20.4%	81.4%	32.6%

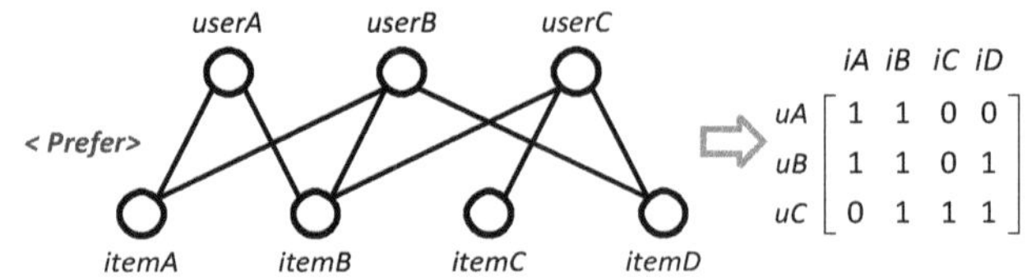

Figure 2: Inference on relation-specific cliques.

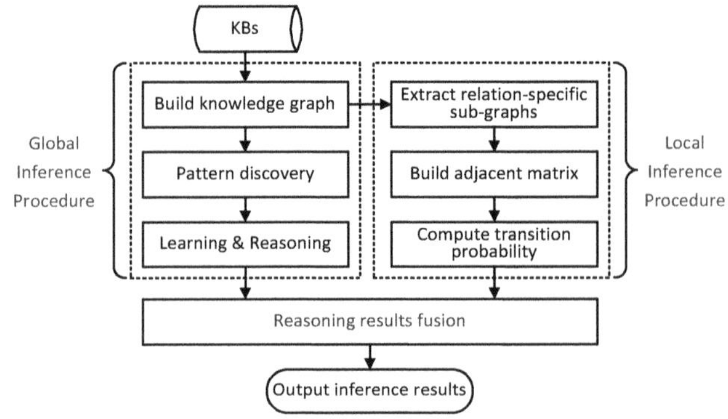

Figure 3: Flow chart of the HiRi algorithm.

lations are very similar to each other (see Figure 1(b) and 1(c)), we suggest that the reason for the different behavior of PRA on these relations is due to the "*directed relation*" assumption made by PRA. PRA models the KBs with directed graphs, and its *path feature* discovery process is a mimic of the logical inference process based on first order Horn clause rules[8]. This assumption is reasonable to some extent, in that it is in accordance with the logical and syntactic constraints of the natural languages. However, a potential problem with this assumption is that it probably underestimates the diversity of the syntax patterns used for relation expressions, and the incompleteness and imbalance of the facts stored in GKBs. This leads to our first assumption:

Assumption I. The semantic information of a relation is reciprocally shared between the connected entities, so it is reasonable to model the knowledge graphs with undirected graphs for relational learning tasks.

Secondly, based on the comparison results on M:M relations, we suggest that the *path feature* discovery process used in PRA is not efficient in utilizing the inferrable information contained in richly connected relation-specific cliques to make inference. Take Figure 2 for example, a collection of the <user-*prefer*-item> triplets is represented by a bipartite graph, the relation "*prefer*" is a typical M:M relation. One can see that since *userA* prefers *itemB*, and *itemB* is preferred by *userB* and *userC*, so it is reasonable to anticipate that *userA* may also be interested in *itemD*, because both of *userB* and *userC* prefer it. For the same reason, we could also anticipate that *userA* might prefer *itemC*, but with less confidence, since we have only one piece of evidence <*userC-prefer-itemC*> to support this inference. From the perspective of PRA, in both of above situations, the inference rule used are the same *path feature*: "$r_i \rightarrow r_i^{-1} \rightarrow r_i$", in which r_i^{-1} denotes the inverse of the relation $r_i \in \boldsymbol{R}$.

The problem with this *path feature* is that it cannot tell the difference between these two situations, and such information should not be ignored. In contrast, the latent factor models (such as TransE) can make full use of such information, by decomposing it into the vector representation of the relations and entities. This explains why TransE performs significantly better than PRA on M:M relations in FB15k data set. From this observation we conclude that some relations are more *reciprocal* and *transitive* than other relations. From the perspective of RWMs, *reciprocal* means that the inverse of the relation is effective in bridging the inference path from the *tail* entities back to the related *head* entities. *Transitive* means that the specified relation is inferable from the *path feature* of the form "$r_i \rightarrow r_i^{-1} \rightarrow \cdots \rightarrow r_i$", which can be modeled with an odd-hop random-walk model. This leads us to the second assumption:

Assumption II. The topological structure of the relation-specific cliques may convey useful information for relation inference, which can be employed to enhance the performance of the random-walk based relational learning algorithms.

In designing of the problem-solving algorithm, we propose a hierarchical structured random-walk model based on above assumptions, a schematic flow chart of the proposed HiRi algorithm is illustrated in Figure 3. Basically, the inference process of HiRi consists of the following steps, greater details of the implementation are given in subsequent sections.

(1) **Global inference procedure**: For each $r_i \in \boldsymbol{G}$, we learn an global inference model $f(h, r_i, t)$ with a revised PRA algorithm from the global knowledge graph $\boldsymbol{G}$, in which $f(h, r_i, t)$ denotes the probability of the random event that there exists a relation r_i between the entity pair <h, t> from the global perspective.

(2) **Local inference procedure**: For each $r_i \in \boldsymbol{G}$, we calculate a 3-hop transition probability matrix from the relation-specific clique $\boldsymbol{G}_i$, so that for any given <h, r_i, t>, we could easily compute the probability (denoted by $g(h, r_i, t)$) of the random event that there exists a relation r_i between <h, t>, from the local perspective.

(3) **Results fusion procedure**: We merge the results from the aforementioned two steps with a linear model. For any given triplet <h, r_i, t>, the final output is a relevance score, denoted by $score(h, r_i, t)$, which indicates the relevance of the entity pair <h, t> with regard to r_i.

3.3 Learning Model For Global Inference

In this paper, we use a revised PRA algorithm for recognizing *path features* and for learning the global inference models for each r_i from $\boldsymbol{G}$. As mentioned above, the major difference between PRA and our implementation is that we use undirected graph for *path feature* discovery. The direct effect is to increase the chance of finding more plausible *features*. Another difference is that we abandon the *importance weight* parameter assigned to each facts to save labor costs.

For completeness, a brief review of the essentials of the PRA algorithm is given in the following, more details can be found in [7] and [8]. For any given relation r_i, PRA tries to find out all of the path sequences within 3-hop from each $h \in \boldsymbol{H}_i$ to its direct neighborhood t, subject to $t \in \boldsymbol{T}_i$. Some additional constraints are also imposed over the random-walkers, such as the first move can not choose r_i.

The qualified path sequences are called the *path features*, which will be used to build a learning model for relational inference on r_i. Let Π_i denotes the *path feature set* of r_i, $\mathbf{x}$ denotes the feature vector of entity pair $<h,t>$, which is an instance of Π_i, $x_j \in \mathbf{x}$ represents the j-th element of $\mathbf{x}$, which is defined as the probability of a random-walker started from entity h, after the path sequence $\pi_j \in \Pi^i$, reached entity t. Let Θ_i represent the corresponding coefficients vector to the feature vector Π_i, $\theta_j \in \Theta_i$ denotes the j-th element of Θ_i. Let $f(h, r_i, t)$ denotes the strength of the possibility that there exists relation r_i in between entity pair $<h,t>$. The global inference model can be represented as:

$$f(h, r_i, t) = \mathbf{x}^T \cdot \Theta_i = \sum_{j=1}^{|\Theta_i|} x_j \theta_j \tag{3}$$

where $|\Theta_i|$ denotes the number of elements in Θ_i. The parameter estimation process is described as follows. Firstly, for each relation $r_i \in \boldsymbol{R}$, we construct a training dataset $\mathbf{Dat}_i = \{(\boldsymbol{x}_k, y_k)\}$ from $\boldsymbol{G}$, where $\boldsymbol{x}_k$ is an instance of Π_i, each $\boldsymbol{x}_k$ is corresponding to a node pair $<h_k,t_k>$ in $\boldsymbol{G}$, $y_k = 1$ if $<h_k, r_i, t_k> \in G_i$, else $y_k = 0$. Secondly, the parameter vector Θ_i is estimated by fitting a penalized logistic regression model, the target function is defined as:

$$\Theta_i = \underset{\Theta_i}{\operatorname{argmax}}(\mathcal{L}(\mathbf{x}, \Theta_i) - \lambda_1 \|\Theta_i\|_1, -\lambda_2 \|\Theta_i\|_2). \tag{4}$$

where $\lambda_1 > 0$ and $\lambda_2 > 0$ are ℓ_1-norm and ℓ_2-norm penalty factors, the ℓ_1 penalty encourages sparsity in the coefficients of Θ_i, while the ℓ_2 penalty shrinks the coefficients to prevent over-fitting. $\mathcal{L}(\mathbf{x}, \Theta)$ is the likelihood function, defined as:

$$\mathcal{L}(\mathbf{x}, \Theta) = \sum_{k=0}^{|\mathbf{Dat}_i|} (y_k \ln q_k + (1 - y_k) \ln(1 - q_k)). \tag{5}$$

where q_k denotes the probability $p(y_k = 1|\mathbf{x}_k; \Theta_i)$, which is defined with the following sigmoid function:

$$q_k = 1/(1 + \exp(-\mathbf{x}_k^T \cdot \Theta_i)) \tag{6}$$

After getting the coefficients vector Θ^i, for any given entity pairs $<h,t>$, we can compute the *score of global relevance* of $<h, r_i, t>$ with Eq. (3), by constructing a feature vector $\mathbf{x}$ for $<h,t>$ from searching through the global knowledge graph $\boldsymbol{G}$. Next, we are going to compute the *score of local relevance* of $<h, r_i, t>$, according to the second assumption.

3.4 Random Walk For Local Inference

In this section, the scope of inference is limited to the relation-specific clique $\boldsymbol{G}_i$. Our objective is to infer new beliefs from current beliefs by using of the first order Horn clause rule, defined as follows:

$$r_i(h, t') \wedge r_i^{-1}(t', h') \wedge r_i(h', t) \Rightarrow r_i(h, t) \tag{7}$$

where $r_i(h,t)$ denotes the triplet $<h, r_i, t>$ to be evaluated, $r_i(h, t')$, $r_i(h', t')$, and $r_i(h', t)$ are *triplets* existed in $\boldsymbol{G}_i$. Our idea is that, if the inference rule (7) is applicable to a relation r_i with respect to entity pair $<h,t>$, it should be reflected by the *relation pattern* of the facts existed in $\boldsymbol{G}_i$. The more evidence it provides, the more likely the inference results are valid. A 3-hop random-walk model would be sufficient to capture all such evidence in $\boldsymbol{G}_i$, and the transition probability of the random-walker from h to t can be taken as the measure of the strength of the feasibility of $r_i(h,t)$.

In order to compute the transition probability efficiently for all of the entity pairs in $\boldsymbol{G}_i$, we resort to the transition matrix representation of graph $\boldsymbol{G}_i$. Firstly, we construct an adjacent matrix $\mathbf{A}_i$ from $\boldsymbol{G}_i$ (as shown in right part of Fig. 2), in which each row is corresponding to a *head* entity in $\boldsymbol{G}_i$, and each column is corresponding to a *tail* entity in $\boldsymbol{G}_i$. Secondly, we construct two diagonal matrices $\mathbf{D}_h$ and $\mathbf{D}_t$ for the *head* and *tail* entities in $\boldsymbol{G}_i$, respectively. The diagonal elements of $\mathbf{D}_h$ and $\mathbf{D}_t$ are the degrees of the corresponding entities in $\boldsymbol{G}_i$. The 3-hop transition matrix between the *head* and *tail* entities of $\boldsymbol{G}_i$ can be computed as follows:

$$\mathbf{M}_i = (\mathbf{D}_h^{-1}\mathbf{A}_i)(\mathbf{D}_t^{-1}\mathbf{A}_i^T)(\mathbf{D}_h^{-1}\mathbf{A}_i) \tag{8}$$

in which $\mathbf{M}_i[h,t]$ represents the probability of a random-walker started from entity $h \in \boldsymbol{G}_i$, after three moves along the paths in $\boldsymbol{G}_i$, finally appeared in entity $t \in \boldsymbol{G}_i$. Based on previous discussion, the *score of local relevance* of entity pair $<h,t>$ with regard to relation r_i is defined as:

$$g(h, r_i, t) = \mathbf{M}_i[h, t] \tag{9}$$

Given an entity pair $<h,t>$ and a relation r_i, we can compute two relevant scores according to Eq. (3) and (9), in which $f(h, r_i, t)$ is derived from the global structure of the knowledge graph $\boldsymbol{G}$ based on our first assumption. $g(h, r_i, t)$ is derived from the local structure of the relation-specific clique $\boldsymbol{G}_i$ based on the second assumption. Next, we describe how to combine these estimators into a single measure of relevance for entity pairs (with respect to specific r_i).

3.5 Combine The Inference Results

In this section, we describe how to combine the strength of the two inferential systems proposed in previous sections. According to Eq. (3), $f(h, r_i, t)$ can be seen as a linear combination of probabilities (recall that each $x_j \in \mathbf{x}$ represents the probability of the random event that a random walker moves along the *path* π_j from h to t on graph $\boldsymbol{G}$). Since $g(h, r_i, t)$ is also a probability of the same type, so that they are additive. Which naturally leads to the following linear equation for results fusion :

$$score(h, r_i, t) = f(h, r_i, t) + \alpha \cdot g(h, r_i, t) \tag{10}$$

in which $\alpha > 0$ is a weighting factor that indicates the relative importance of the local inference results. Note that Eq. (3) is linear, thus the Eq. (10) can be rewritten as:

$$score(h, r_i, t) = \left(g(h, r_i, t), \mathbf{x}^T\right) \cdot \begin{pmatrix} \alpha \\ \Theta_i \end{pmatrix} \tag{11}$$

Eq. (11) should raise some doubt about the necessity of the local inference process, because under the *undirected graph assumption*, for most of the relation $r_i \in \boldsymbol{R}$ (especially the M:M relations), it is highly possible that the *path feature* of the form "$r_i \rightarrow r_i^{-1} \rightarrow r_i$" has already been included in the *path feature set* Π_i, which is exactly the same as the situation considered the local inference process.

However, as we found by experiments, excluding the local inference results from Eq. (10) will actually decrease the performance of HiRi (see Section 4.3), which indicates that the effects of the information transitivity within a relation-specific clique should be taken into account individually when modeling the relation from GKBs. For ease of investigation and interpretation, we rewrite the Eq. (10) as:

$$score(h, r_i, t) = \frac{e^{f(h,r_i,t)}}{1 + e^{f(h,r_i,t)}} + \alpha \cdot g(h, r_i, t) \quad (12)$$

In this equation, the contribution of all the global path features are considered as a whole by using sigmoid function, and the $f(h, r_i, t)$ score is mapped to range $(0, 1)$. Since now the value ranges of the transformed $f(h, r_i, t)$ scores are comparable to the $g(h, r_i, t)$ scores, it will be much easier to investigate the effects of the local inference results to the relational learning model proposed above, and to interpret the relative importance of the local and global inferential process by varying the value of the weighting factor α.

4. EXPERIMENTS AND DISCUSSION

To evaluate the performance of the proposed algorithm, we compared it with four representative algorithms proposed for the relational inference tasks on large-scale GKBs, namely PRA [8], RESCAL [15], TransE[1], and TransR[9].

The PRA algorithm is the most representative random-walk based relational learning algorithm, which has been successfully used in some large-scale GKB projects.

The other candidates belong to the latent factor models family, in which RESCAL is a classical tensor factorization algorithm which can be treated as a benchmark. TransE and TransR are two of the most competitive structured embedding algorithms at this time.

Besides, in order to test the validity of the assumptions involved in the HiRi algorithm, we take the global inference module individually as the **baseline** for comparison with the proposed hierarchical random-walk scheme.

4.1 Data Sets

The evaluation is performed on two data sets extracted from Wordnet and Freebase[1], which were created by A. Bordes et al.[1], and have been frequently used in recent research for performance comparison and evaluation[21, 9]. In order to be in accordance with related works, these data sets will be denoted as WN18 and FB15k in the rest of this section. The statistics of the data sets are summarised in Table 3.

The FB15k data sets are sampled from the Freebase (a practical large-scale knowledge base), which cover the facts from almost all aspects of the physical world. Comparing with WN18 data sets, which are sampled from a dictionary-alike GKB, the knowledge distributions and structures of FB15k are more close to reality and more comparable to other industrial GKB products. For this reason, our discussion will mainly focus on this data set. To further explore the relation structure of FB15k, we manually split all of the relations into four categories according to Eq. (2). Detailed statistics are given in Table 4 and Table 5, respectively.

From Table 3, 4 and 5 one can see that there are 1,345 types of relations contained in FB15k, which are evenly distributed across four categories, however the distribution of the number of triplets (i.e. edges of the knowledge graph) are extremely unbalanced. The triplets with one-to-many and

[1]https://everest.hds.utc.fr/doku.php?id=en:transe

Table 3: Statistics of the data sets

Data set	WN18	FB15k
#entities	40,943	14,951
#relation types	18	1,345
#triplets in training set	141,442	483,142
#triplets in validation set	5,000	50,000
#triplets in test set	5,000	59,071

Table 4: Distribution of the relations of FB15k

Categories	**1:1**	**1: M**	**M:1**	**M:M**
Training set	27.36%	22.97%	29.29%	20.38%
Test set	25.50%	23.27%	28.92%	22.31%

Table 5: Distribution of the facts (triplets) of FB15k

Categories	**1:1**	**1: M**	**M:1**	**M:M**
Training set	1.57%	9.48%	15.88%	73.07%
Testing set	1.48%	9.54%	15.12%	73.86%

many-to-many relations add up to 90% of the total number of triplets in FB15k, which indicates that effectively dealing with relation types belonging to these categories is critical to the overall performance of the algorithm.

4.2 Experimental Setup

We follow the evaluation protocol used in [1] and [8]. Firstly, for each triplet $<h, r_i, t>$ in the test set, the *head* entity h is replaced by each of the entities in the training set, then we remove from this corrupted triplets set (denoted by C) of all the triplets that appear in the training, validation and test set, except the test triplet of interest. For each of the triplets in C, we compute its relevance score by using the algorithms on trial, after that the relevance scores are sorted by ascending order to form a recommendation list. The rank of the correct fact in this list is denoted by $Rank(?, r_i, t)$.

Secondly, repeat this procedure while this time removing the *tail* entity t instead of h, and record the rank of the correct fact in this new list (of the ordered corrupted triplets) as $Rank(h, r_i, ?)$. The rank of a test triplet $<h, r_i, t>$ reported in this paper is the average of above two rank numbers:

$$Rank(h, r_i, t) = \frac{Rank(?, r_i, t) + Rank(h, r_i, ?)}{2} \quad (13)$$

Based on this definition, we report three measures of performance in the tests, namely *Hits@1*, *Hits@10*, and the *mean reciprocal rank* (MRR), explained as follows. The Hits@1 score denotes the proportion of correct facts which were ranked first by the algorithms on trial. Similarly, the Hits@10 score is the average proportion of correct facts ranked in the top 10 position. Empirically speaking, the Hits@1 score can be seen as the measure of *predictive accuracy* of the inferential algorithm, while the Hits@10 score reflects the *recall rate* of the algorithms (since in many real-world expert systems, top 10 recommendation is a psychological boundary of the acceptable length of the recommendation list for manual inspections). The MRR score is defined as:

Table 6: Experimental results on WN18 dataset

Algorithms	MRR	Hits@1	Hits@10
HiRi	**0.691**	**79.1%**	90.8%
Baseline	0.667	65.4%	67.9%
PRA	0.458	42.2%	48.1%
Rescal	0.431	10.2%	52.8%
TransE	0.495	11.3%	89.2%
TransR	0.605	33.5%	**91.7%**

Table 7: Experimental results on FB15k dataset

Algorithms	MRR	Hits@1	Hits@10
HiRi	**0.603**	**54.3%**	70.3%
Baseline	0.515	49.7%	54.3%
PRA	0.336	30.3%	39.2%
Rescal	0.354	23.5%	44.1%
TransE	0.463	29.7%	**73.4%**
TransR	0.346	21.8%	65.5%

$$MRR = \frac{1}{N} \sum_{<h,r_i,t>\in \boldsymbol{G}} \frac{1}{Rank(h, r_i, t)} \tag{14}$$

where $\boldsymbol{G}$ refers to the test set, N denotes the number of triplets in $\boldsymbol{G}$. The MRR is a normalized score of range $[0, 1]$, an increase in its value reflects that the majority "hits" will appear higher higher in the ranking order of the recommendation list, which indicates a better performance of the corresponding relational inference algorithm.

4.3 Overall Performance

For experiments with HiRi, we selected the optimal configurations by grid search, the penalty factors λ_1 and λ_2 were set to 0.001 and 0.001 for all of the tests in this section. For all data sets, the weighting factor α is varied from 0.0 to 12.0 with step size 0.1, the best models were selected by early stopping using the MRR score on the validation sets.

The test performance of the different algorithms on both data sets are reported in Table 6 and Table 7 for comparison purposes, in which the best results of each column are highlighted in boldface. We first compare our work with other related works (except the Baseline algorithm). The test results show that HiRi consistently outperforms PRA and those three LFM algorithms in terms of both MRR and Hits@1. However, there are two exceptions when considering the Hits@10 scores. In these cases, HiRi is found to perform comparable to TransR (on WN18) and TransE (on FB15k), respectively, but the difference is neither significant nor consistent (this issue will be further discussed later).

To sum up, the comparison between HiRi and other alternative algorithms indicates that the *recall rate* of HiRi is consistently in accordance with the best performed methods, while its MRR and Hits@1 scores are notably better than alternative methods. Since MRR represents the (inverse) average ranking position of the correct facts in the recommendation list, and Hits@1 means the *first round hit* probability, all these improvements can offer considerable benefits for practical applications and better user experiences.

Next, we further investigate the difference between HiRi and other two RWM algorithms by looking at their respective performance on each data set. Experimental results show that on both data sets, the Baseline algorithm consistently and significantly outperforms PRA. Meantime, it was outperformed consistently and significantly by HiRi. Since the Baseline algorithm can be seen as the *undirected graph* based PRA, a direct conclusion obtained from above results is that the *undirect graph* assumption made in this paper is effective in promoting the performance of the random-walk models, but this is not enough for a successful inference algorithm. The obtained solution can be further improved by imposing the local structure information on the algorithm.

4.4 Fine-Grained Analysis

In this section, we take a closer look at the impacts of the localized inference to the overall performance of HiRi, by tuning the weighting factor α and inspecting respectively the test results on each category of relations. Since there are only 18 relations contained in the WN18, the FB15k data set was used for all the tests in the following discussion.

We first test the impact of α on each of the three performance measures used in this paper, the numeric results are depicted in Figure 4. Simulations are done for α varying in the range $[0, 12]$ with step size 0.1. The dash lines represent the performance of the Baseline algorithm, which is equivalent to setting $\alpha = 0$ in the HiRi algorithm.

As shown in Figure 4(a), 4(b), and 4(c), almost the same behavior can be observed for all of the three measures, an inflection point appears at $\alpha = 0.5$ for all observations. In comparing with the Baseline, the value of MRR, Hits@1, and Hits@10 with respect to the peak point achieves an improvement of approximately 17.09%, 10.06% and 29.47%, respectively. These results reveal that the reasoning ability of the random-walk model can be further enhanced by introducing a localized inferential mechanism into the system. More than that, the numerical results also indicate that in practice, there exists an appreciable amount of relations that can be inferred from their local structures.

Figure 4 also shows that, after reaching the peak value at $\alpha = 0.5$, all of the three performance indicators started to decrease as the weighting factor α increased. Among which the MRR and Hits@1 score seemed to be affected more seriously, and eventually at $\alpha \geq 9.0$, the Hits@1 score even dropped below the Baseline level of performance. This indicates that the results of the global and local inference procedures are complementary to each other, both of them are necessary to the random-walk inference models.

We also notice that in Figure 4, the Hits@10 score decreases slightly with the increase of α, and its value remained above 70% for all $\alpha \in [0.5, 12]$. This is in contrast to the rapid decrease behavior observed in MRR, which indicates that the increment of α will likely result in a substantial downgrading of the ranks of the correct results, in which about 30% of the relations will be significantly affected in FB15k test set. In order to understand the reason of this discrepancy in between the recall rate of different relations, we manually partitioned the 1,345 relations in FB15k test set into four categories, then perform tests on each of them with the HiRi algorithm, the results are depicted in Figure 5. Some conclusions can be drawn from Figure 5 as follows.

Firstly, The MRR scores of HiRi are highly and positively

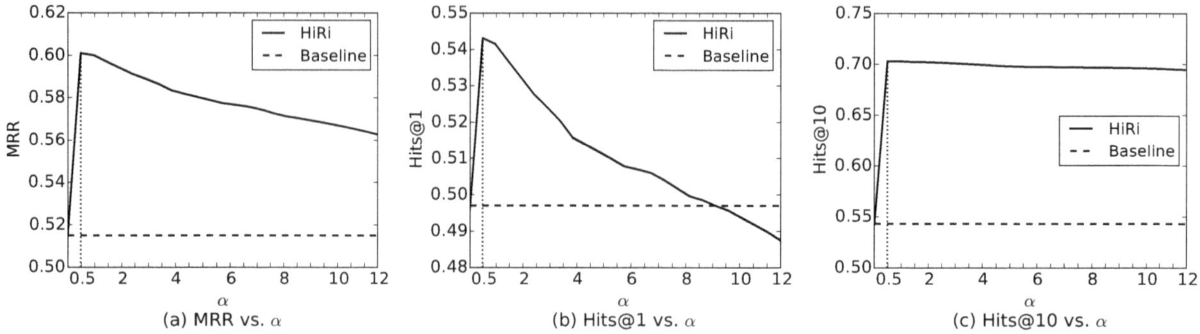

Figure 4: Evaluation of the impacts of α in HiRi on FB15k test set

correlated with its *predictive accuracy* (measured by Hits@1 scores) on all the four category of relations, and both of them declined steadily after the peak value has been reached, which indicates that the inference accuracy of HiRi depends on both of the global and local inference results. However, the Hits@10 recall rate of HiRi are found to be quite insensitive to the variation of α on all of the relation categories after the peak value had been reached, except on M:1 relations it shows a clear downward trend in the recall rate at $\alpha \geq 3.5$. The stability of the Hits@10 scores indicates that the inference results provided by both of the two inference procedures of HiRi are largely consistent with each other, while the variation of MRR and Hits@1 (and Hits@10 on M:1 relations) reflects that there exists some differences between the resulting list of the local and global inference procedures, indicating that both of them provide a one-sided view of the general patterns of the relationships between entities, and can be fine-tuned by varying the value of α to provide better performance than either method alone. These results clearly support our second assumption about the effectiveness of making use of the connection structures in relation-specific cliques to improve and to enhance the performance of the relational retrieval models.

Secondly, each of the performance curves displayed in Figure 5(b) and Figure 5(d) possesses a clear flex point at approximately $\alpha = 0.5$, which suggests that the incorporated local inference procedure is especially helpful in cases of reasoning on 1:M and M:M relations. This also reveals that the global random-walk inference model can not make full use of the information available in these relation-specific cliques. However, as can be seen from the variation of the MRR and Hits@1 scores in Figure 5(a) and Figure 5(c), incorporating a local inference procedure into the HiRi algorithm may only cause a slight decrease in the predictive accuracy. The most plausible explanation of this phenomenon is that the first order Horn clause rule of the specific form "$r_i \rightarrow r_i^{-1} \rightarrow r_i$" might not be suitable for relational inference in such cases.

Thirdly, we notice that both of the MRR and the Hits@1 scores of HiRi are less sensitive to the variance of α on 1:1 and 1:M relations than on other two category of relations, which indicates that the inference results of the global and local inference procedures of HiRi are relatively more consistent with each other on 1:1 and 1:M relations than on other relations. This observation suggests that the reasoning power of random-walk models on 1:1 and 1:M relations is mainly coming from the internal structures of the relation-specific cliques, which can be modeled effectively by use of the proposed local inference method. However, since the interconnections between relation-specific cliques are deliberately neglected by the local inference procedure, it can not capture the inferrable relation sequence patterns other than of the form "$r_i \rightarrow r_i^{-1} \rightarrow r_i$", thus a global inference mechanism is a necessary requirement for capturing such information from the data, this again verifies the validity of the proposed hierarchical random-walk inference scheme.

Finally, as can be seen from Figure 5(b) and Figure 5(c), the performance of HiRi exhibits clear differences with the increase in α on 1:M and M:1 relations. Perhaps the only explanation that can be put forward for this observation is that, the directionality of the relations might play a role in affecting the performance of HiRi, which seems in conflict with our first assumption that the GKBs should be modeled with undirected graphs. In order to justify the validity of this assumption, and to seek a deeper understanding of the reasoning power of the random-walk models, we perform tests on each category of relations on FB15k respectively. Results and discussions are presented in the next section.

4.5 Further Investigation

In this section, we provide more evidence on the validity of our solution by taking into consideration the directionality of the relations in the experiments. The tests are performed on each category of relations respectively with four selected algorithms. Since our HiRi algorithm significantly outperforms other related approaches in terms of Hit@1 and MRR, hence for clarity of presentation in the paper, we only focus our discussion on Hit@10 scores of the tests in this section. The numerical results are reported in Table 8.

Firstly, test results show that the Baseline algorithm performs better on three category of relations (1:1, 1:M, and M:1) compared with PRA. Further, comparing the Baseline algorithm with HiRi, one could see that the differences of their performance are trivial, which suggests that the superior performance of HiRi with regard to PRA is mainly resulting from our first assumption. It is worth noting that the most significant improvement was found in dealing with 1:M relations, both of the *undirected* RWM algorithms outperform PRA with improvements of approximately 200%, which provides a solid evidence for our first assumption.

Secondly, by comparing the performance of HiRi with PRA and Baseline algorithms on M:M relations in Table 8, it is clear to see that through adopting the *undirected graph* as-

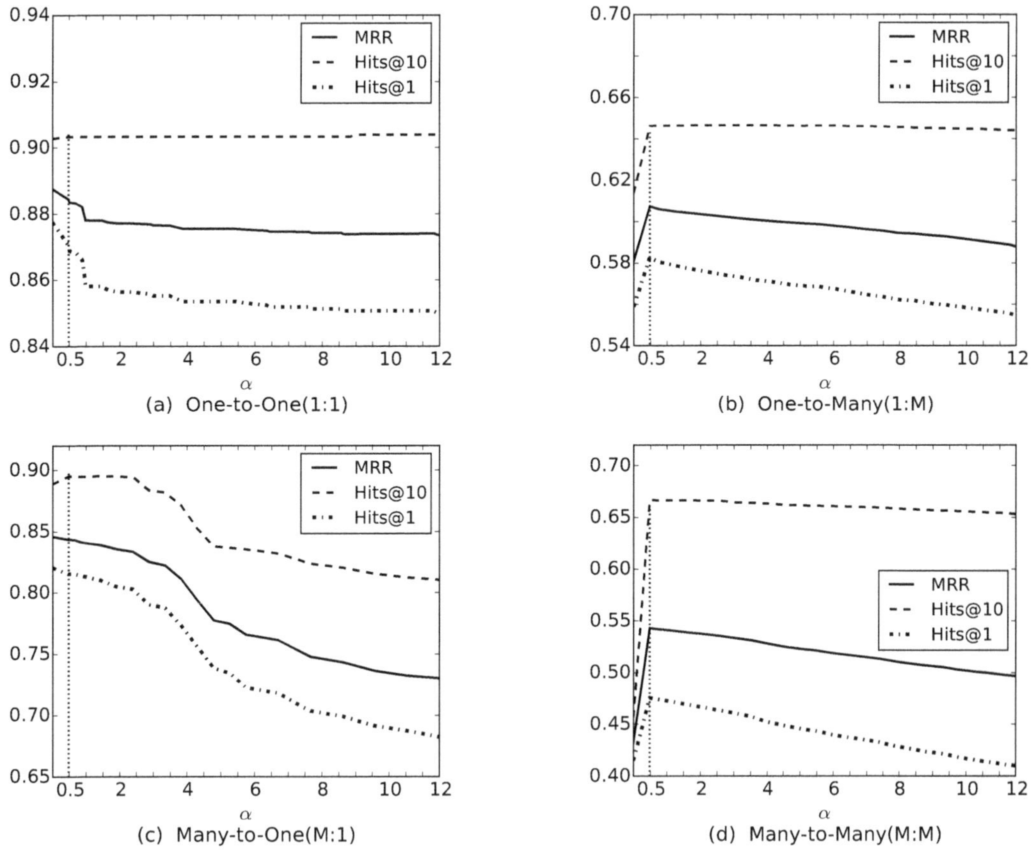

Figure 5: Evaluation of the impacts of α on Hits@10 of HiRi, on four category of relations in FB15k test set

sumption, the Hits@10 score was improved by 40.49% (Baseline vs. PRA), while after incorporating the local inference results into the inference model, the Hits@10 score was improved again by 54.15% (HiRi vs. Baseline). This helps in verifying the validity of our second assumption, which claims that some type of relations are more inferrable than other relations, such information can be modeled and learned from the structure of the relation-specific cliques, to enhance the inference ability of the random-walk based models.

Lastly, Table 8 shows that HiRi outperforms TranseE on three of the four category of relations, except on M:M relations (with a 3.26% discrepancy), combining with the observation that the local inference mechanism only helps in improving the recall rate of HiRi on M:M relations, which suggests that the major advantage of the latent factor models is that they can make full use of the structure information of GKBs by using of the matrix factorization techniques, while such information can not be utilized sufficiently in PRA through learning from the *path features* extracted from the global knowledge graph. However, on the other hand, this "advantage" can also become a disadvantage of the latent factor model, in that it tends to fit the data too closely, and thus resulted in a loss of generalization ability. In fact, this may seriously affect the accuracy of the inference results provided by such approaches, especially in dealing with incomplete and unbalanced knowledge graphs. In contrast, the random-walk models are less affected by this problem, because the focus of RWMs is to discover the inferrable relation patterns to build inference rules. We also notice that the parameter estimation process of the RWMs are based on supervised learning techniques, which means that their generalization ability will largely depend on the learning model and the training data.

However, it is still reasonable to expect that the RWM solutions are more flexible than the LFM solutions, in that they are not restricted to *perfectly fit* of all of the facts existed in the training data (as required in LFMs). As can be seen from Table 8, the generalization ability of HiRi is confirmed by the fact that it achieves better *recall rate* than TransE on most of the relations (more than 78%, according to Table 4). Combining with the results reported in Table 7, we could conclude that by adopting the undirected graph assumption, and by introducing a local inference mechanism into the model, the random-walk models can be superior to the latent factor models in terms of both the accuracy and the recall rate, which makes it a promising candidate for further investigation and application.

5. CONCLUSIONS

We propose in this paper a novel hierarchical random-walk inference algorithm (HiRi) based on two assumptions drawn from our empirical studies. There were two important findings in this study. First, we found that since the relations

Table 8: Evaluation of Hits@10 on FB15k test set

Categories	1:1	1: M	M:1	M:M
HiRi	**89.5%**	**60.5%**	**92.3%**	70.6%
Baseline	89.5%	60.0%	91.4%	45.8%
PRA	63.3%	20.4%	81.4%	32.6%
TransE	71.5%	49.0%	85.0%	**72.9%**

are semantically bidirectional, the undirected graph representation of the knowledge graph can be effectively used for learning the first order Horn clause rules from the GKB-s, which we believe to be essential for better understanding the existing methods and for designing new models. Second, we found that the path feature of the form "$r \rightarrow r^{-1} \rightarrow r$" is of special importance to relational learning for some specific type of relations, and we work out a simple but very effective solution for utilizing such information in a RWM framework. Regarding future work, our plan is to further explore the performance of the HiRi algorithm on more large-scale data sets, to examine the practical consistency of the proposed inference model, and to further improve the algorithm performance, then make it publicly available to the community.

6. ACKNOWLEDGMENTS

This work was supported by NSFC under grant 61133016, 61502087, and U1401257, and by the Fundamental research funds for the central universities under grant ZYGX2014J066.

7. REFERENCES

[1] A. Bordes, N. Usunier, A. Garcia-Duran, J. Weston, and O. Yakhnenko. Translating embeddings for modeling multi-relational data. In *Proc. of the 27th NIPS*, pages 2787–2795, 2013.

[2] A. Bordes, J. Weston, R. Collobert, and Y. Bengio. Learning structured embeddings of knowledge bases. In *Proc. of the 25th AAAI Conference on Artificial Intelligence*, pages 301–306, 2011.

[3] J. Cheng, T. Yuan, J. Wang, and H. Lu. Group latent factor model for recommendation with multiple user behaviors. In *Proc. of the 37th ACM SIGIR*, pages 995–998, 2014.

[4] M. Gardner, P. Talukdar, J. Krishnamurthy, and T. Mitchell. Incorporating vector space similarity in random walk inference over knowledge bases. In *Proc. of the 2014 EMNLP*, pages 397–406, 2014.

[5] L. Getoor and L. Mihalkova. Learning statistical models from relational data. In *Proc. of the 2011 ACM SIGMOD*, pages 1195–1198, 2011.

[6] L. Getoor and B. Taskar. *Introduction to Statistical Relational Learning*. The MIT Press, 2007.

[7] N. Lao and W. W. Cohen. Relational retrieval using a combination of path-constrained random walks. *Machine Learning*, 81(1):53–67, 2010.

[8] N. Lao, T. Mitchell, and W. W. Cohen. Random walk inference and learning in a large scale knowledge base. In *Proc. of the 2011 EMNLP*, pages 529–539, 2011.

[9] Y. Lin, Z. Liu, M. Sun, Y. Liu, and X. Zhu. Learning entity and relation embeddings for knowledge graph completion. In *Proc. of the 29th AAAI Conference on Artificial Intelligence*, pages 2181–2187, 2015.

[10] T. M. Mitchell, W. W. Cohen, E. R. H. Jr., P. P. Talukdar, J. Betteridge, A. Carlson, B. D. Mishra, M. Gardner, B. Kisiel, J. Krishnamurthy, N. Lao, K. Mazaitis, T. Mohamed, N. Nakashole, E. A. Platanios, A. Ritter, M. Samadi, B. Settles, R. C. Wang, D. T. Wijaya, A. Gupta, X. Chen, A. Saparov, M. Greaves, and J. Welling. Never-ending learning. In *Proc. of the 29th AAAI Conference on Artificial Intelligence*, pages 2302–2310, 2015.

[11] S. Natarajan, T. Khot, K. Kersting, B. Gutmann, and J. Shavlik. Gradient-based boosting for statistical relational learning: The relational dependency network case. *Machine Learning*, 86(1):25–56, 2011.

[12] A. Neelakantan, B. Roth, and A. McCallum. Compositional vector space models for knowledge base inference. In *Proc. of the 53rd ACL-IJCNLP 2015*, pages 156–166, 2015.

[13] T. V. Nguyen, A. Karatzoglou, and L. Baltrunas. Gaussian process factorization machines for context aware recommendations. In *Proc. of the 37th ACM SIGIR*, pages 63–72, 2014.

[14] M. Nickel, K. Murphy, V. Tresp, and E. Gabrilovich. A review of relational machine learning for knowledge graphs. *Proceedings of the IEEE*, 104(1):11–33, 2016.

[15] M. Nickel, V. Tresp, and H.-P. Kriegel. A three-way model for collective learning on multi-relational data. In *Proc. of the 28th ICML*, pages 809–816, 2011.

[16] M. Nickel, V. Tresp, and H.-P. Kriegel. Factorizing yago: Scalable machine learning for linked data. In *Proc. of the 21st International Conference on World Wide Web*, pages 271–280, 2012.

[17] F. Niu, C. Zhang, C. Re, and J. Shavlik. Scaling inference for markov logic via dual decomposition. In *Proc. of the 12th IEEE ICDM*, pages 1032–1037, 2012.

[18] M. Richardson and P. Domingos. Markov logic networks. *Machine Learning*, 62(1):107–136, 2006.

[19] S. Schoenmackers, O. Etzioni, D. S. Weld, and J. Davis. Learning first-order horn clauses from web text. In *Proc. of the EMNLP*, pages 1088–1098, 2010.

[20] C. Wang, Y. Song, A. El-Kishky, D. Roth, M. Zhang, and J. Han. Incorporating world knowledge to document clustering via heterogeneous information networks. In *Proc. of the 21th ACM SIGKDD*, pages 1215–1224, 2015.

[21] Z. Wang, J. Zhang, J. Feng, and Z. Chen. Knowledge graph embedding by translating on hyperplanes. In *Proc. of the 28th AAAI Conference on Artificial Intelligence*, pages 1112–1119, 2014.

When Watson Went to Work - Leveraging Cognitive Computing in the Real World

Aya Soffer
IBM Research - Haifa
Mount Carmel, Haifa 31905
ayas@il.ibm.com

David Konopnicki
IBM Research - Haifa
Mount Carmel, Haifa 31905
davidko@il.ibm.com

Haggai Roitman
IBM Research - Haifa
Mount Carmel, Haifa 31905
haggai@il.ibm.com

1. INTRODUCTION

In February 2011, the world was introduced to Watson, IBM's cognitive computing system [1] that defeated Ken Jennings and Brad Rutter at Jeopardy! It was the first widely seen demonstration of cognitive computing, and it marked the end of the so-called "AI winter." Watson's ability to answer subtle, complex, pun-laden questions made clear that a new era of computing was at hand. An era where computers can start making sense of the vast amount of unstructured data in the world and apply this understanding not only to answer trivia questions, but also to tackle some of the world's pressing problems and change how people interact with computers.

Indeed, since Jeopardy!, Watson has tackled increasingly complex data sets, and developed understanding, reasoning, and learning. Specifically, we have identified five core capabilities of Cognitive Computing: 1. They create deeper human engagement; 2. They scale and elevate expertise; 3. They infuse products and services with cognition; 4. They enable cognitive processes and operations; 5. They enhance exploration and discovery. The true potential of the Cognitive Era will be realized by combining the data analytics, and statistical reasoning of machines with uniquely human qualities, such as self-directed goals, common sense, and ethical values. This is what Watson was built to do, and is in fact already doing. Banks are analyzing customer requests and financial data to surface insights to help them make investment recommendations. Companies in heavily regulated industries are querying the system to keep up with ever-changing legislation and standards of compliance. And oncologists are testing ways in which cognitive systems can help interpret cancer patients' clinical information and identify individualized, evidence-based treatment options that leverage specialists' experience and research. Customer and technical support are in particular being re-invented, relying more on cognitive systems for self-help and for agent assist.

In this talk, we highlight some of the applications of Watson that are being pursued by IBM. These include applications in customer and technical support, in Finance, in Legal and more. We also elaborate on some of the underlying technologies that are available via APIs on the Watson Developer Cloud[1]. Finally, we discuss some of the challenges of applying this technology in real-world use cases. We specifically discuss two challenges that we face in leveraging Watson for tech support and customer support in some more detail. The first is in the area of technical support, where Watson is being used to find solutions for relatively complex technical support issues. In this case, we developed extensions to Watson's state of the art techniques that can take into account the format and the richness of the problem definition.

The second is in the area of customer support, where Watson is being used to answer customer queries about products and services. In this case, the sentiment of the person dialoging with the system as well as the system's responses are found to be important in being able to satisfy the customer's information need.

SIGIR '16 July 17-21, 2016, Pisa, Italy

ACM ISBN 978-1-4503-4069-4/16/07.
DOI: http://dx.doi.org/10.1145/2911451.2926724

2. FINDING ANSWERS TO COMPLEX TECHNICAL SUPPORT QUESTIONS

As a concrete example, in one of the technical support use cases, Watson handles problem management records (PMRs) submitted by various clients and aims to discover technical notes (technote) that contain potential solutions to their technical problems. Each such record may describe several aspects of the client's problem expressed in natural language. For example, a PMR may include multiple problem related issues describing the problem, the impact on the client's business, the client's system characteristics, etc. Figure 1 depicts an example of a real PMR query and its matching technote (both represented in JSON format). PMR descriptions are highly ambiguous, verbose in most cases, multi-lingual and their quality spans from detailed problem descriptions to computer generated error log traces. On the other hand, technotes (documents) in the corpus describe technical details of various problem solutions, and may include multiple searchable fields that may be relevant for solving a PMR.

PMRs processing is a challenging task, and Watson's original question-answering paradigm which is geared more towards factoid queries is insufficient here. In order for find a relevant solution, the system needs to search over multiple combinations of PMR problem aspects and technical document and find the best match(es). Alternative solutions to this challenging problem were explored using a "TREC-

[1] https://www.ibm.com/smarterplanet/us/en/ibmwatson/developercloud/

```
PMR:
{
  id:"*****-***-***_***-**-**",
  product_desc:"TIVOLI FEDERATED IDENTITY MGR",
  component_desc:"SAM WEBSEAL",
  os:"Appliance Firmware",
  business_impact:"Trying to simplify management
   of our WebSEAL environments.",
  problem_title:"Curl/JSON scripting assistance",
  problem_desc:"I am looking for information and best
   practices around using Curl and JSON scripts to do
   administrative tasks on WebSEAL..."
}

Technote:
{
  url:http://www-01.ibm.com/support/docview.wss?uid=swg21663434
  title:"IBM Security Access Manager for Web API documentation"
}
```

Figure 1: Example of a PMR query and its relevant technote

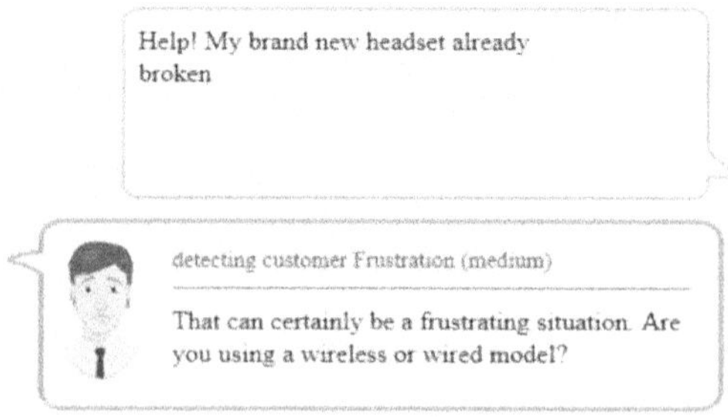


```
...
Customer: The mic is not working
Agent: (detecting customer anger - medium) I'm sorry to hear
that. Could you please try to install the Skype app and run an
echo test? ...
Customer: what is an echo test?
Agent: (detecting customer confusion - low) Apologies for the
confusion. Here are some instructions...
```

Figure 2: Example of an affective dialog. The actual UI followed by the rest of the conversation

like" competition, where several different research and development teams within IBM have explored various retrieval approaches including those that employ both state-of-the-art and novel QA, NLP, deep-learning and learning-to-rank techniques.

To handle such complex retrieval task, based on one of the leading retrieval strategies that were developed, Watson employs several state-of-the-art IR and question-answering methods, spanning from verbose query processing and pseudo-relevance feedback to techniques that utilize query performance prediction for selecting ranking strategies and their fusion. Furthermore, a new "multi-field" retrieval approach developed as part of this approach further allows Watson to consider all possible PMR–technote (cross product) querying options, while intelligently focus only on those combinations that are predicted to be the most important for answering the complex information need expressed in the PMR. Overall, Watson's retrieval quality for this domain has been boosted by more than 30%.

3. ADDING AFFECT TO CUSTOMER SUPPORT

One domain in which the concept of Watson has evolved since Jeopardy! is the domain of *dialog*. Originally, IBM Watson was conceived as a question answering system in which interactions with users were limited to question-answer pairs. When Watson technology was deployed in different domains, it became evident that more advanced dialog capabilities are necessary in order to handle more complex tasks e.g. in order to obtain clarifications from users about their questions. In this case, Watson becomes a dialog engine with which users can converse and relies on its question answering capabilities when necessary as a conversation evolves.

One of the most common implementations of Watson's conversation engine is in the area of customer support. In this case, in addition to being able to converse with the user, it becomes important to understand the sentiment of the user as well as tailor the engine's response based on this sentiment. In other words, as users start to converse with computers in very natural ways, they expect computers not only to address their information needs but also their emotional needs.

In such a case, computers should identify user emotions and then take those emotions into account when replying. Effectively, a computer involved in dialog should be able to thank, apologize, and be empathetic similar to a human agent. Such a dialog between a human and a Watson-based support agent is provided as an example in Figure 2 (showing which emotions have been detected).

This example is focused on textual interactions between the user and Watson but clearly other input modalities like speech and video offer even more opportunities to detect and act upon user emotions.

In addition to emotions which are naturally transient, Watson provides capabilities to analyze more static aspects of a user's personality based on the language being used. By combining personality and emotional aspects, the goal in the longer term is to automatically craft a digital personality personalized to interact with a particular user.

In a recent study, we examined emotions being expressed in Twitter service conversations between humans [2]. We show that customer's and agent's personality traits combined with the emotion being expressed in the first turn of a conversation are good predictors of user satisfaction at the end of the conversation: specifically, our model shows an improvement of 30% in the F1-score for predicting dissatisfaction. This result enables automatically matching the best agents to a particular user in a given context.

4. REFERENCES

[1] David Ferrucci, Eric Brown, Jennifer Chu-Carroll, James Fan, David Gondek, Aditya A Kalyanpur, Adam Lally, J William Murdock, Eric Nyberg, John Prager, et al. Building watson: An overview of the deepqa project. *AI magazine*, 31(3):59–79, 2010.

[2] Jonathan Herzig, Guy Feigenblat, Michal Shmueli-Scheuer, David Konopnicki, and Anat Rafaeli. Predicting customer satisfaction in customer support conversations in social media using affective features. In *To be published in: User Modeling, Adaptation, and Personalization*, 2016.

Ask Your TV: Real-Time Question Answering with Recurrent Neural Networks

Ferhan Ture
Comcast Labs
1110 Vermont Ave NW Washington, DC 20005
ferhan_ture@cable.comcast.com

Oliver Jojic
Comcast Labs
1110 Vermont Ave NW Washington, DC 20005
oliver_jojic@cable.comcast.com

Voice-based interfaces are very popular in today's world, and Comcast customers are no exception. Usage stats show that our new X1 TV platform receives millions of voice queries per day. As a result, expanding the coverage of our voice interface provides a critical competitive advantage, allowing customers to speak freely instead of having to stick to a rigid set of commands. The ultimate objective is to provide a more natural user experience and increase access to our knowledge graph (KG) and entertainment platform.

We describe a real-time factoid question answering (QA) system, using our internal KG for training (i.e., generating labeled example question-answer pairs) and for retrieval at test time. We hope that this will inspire other companies to take advantage of readily available unlabeled data, machine learning and search technologies to build products that can improve customer experiences. Our approach consists of two steps: First, two neural network models are trained to *predict* a structured query from the free-form input question. Then, a *search* through all facts in the KG retrieves answers consistent with the structured query.

Related work: Iyyer et al. [3] assume the answer is an entity, treating QA as classification, which cannot scale to millions of entities. Also, this does not cover cases where the answer is not a named entity. Dong et al. [2] search for answers within two hops of the target node in a KG, but they assume that the target entity is provided to them. Entity resolution is, in our experience, the most difficult part of factoid QA, especially when the question consists largely of a title and/or name. Memory Networks and variations have worked quite well on QA benchmark datasets, scaling up to similar-sized KGs [1]. However, the main focus is to rerank candidate facts with respect to a given question. Candidate facts are generated based on an n-gram match between question and named entities in the KG. Instead, we train a model to extract entity text from the question, which reduces latency and decouples entity detection from the KG. A KG in the entertainment domain is likely to be dominated by the relation type denoting that a person took part in a watchable (e.g., actress appeared in movie). Due to this, simply visiting all nodes within K hops of an entity might increase latency significantly. We train a separate model to predict the relation type(s).

From Question to Structured Query: Our internal database is converted into a *knowledge graph*, consisting of a large set of *facts* — a binary [subject, relation, object] or ternary [subject, relation, attribute, object] relationship. We focus on *first-order questions*, where the answer can be retrieved from a single fact (e.g., "How old is Tom Hanks?" can be answered by the fact [Tom Hanks,birthDate,7/9/1956]).

Our approach is based on converting the input question into a structured query, which can be ran against the knowledge graph to retrieve the fact(s) that answer(s) the question (e.g., the question above would be converted to [Tom Hanks, birthDate, ?]). This process can be modularized into two parts: *entity detection* and *relation prediction*. In the former, the objective is to *tag* whether each question word is part of an entity, and optionally further divide into *subject*, *object*, and *attribute* classes. In the latter, the objective is to *classify* the question into one of the K relation types.

We used recurrent neural networks (RNN) to tackle both tasks, hence dependencies across words in the question are naturally modeled without the need for feature engineering. Certain variations of RNNs, such as long short-term memory (LSTM), can theoretically learn contextual features that are useful for the task, while ignoring irrelevant parts. RNNs' effectiveness in exploiting wide textual context for classification or tagging has been shown in numerous cases.

Each question word passes through an embedding lookup layer before the recurrent layer(s). We fixed this layer based on the pre-trained 300-dimensional Google News embedding,[1] which is followed by one or more recurrent layers. In tagging, for each question word, output of the last RNN layer is projected to one of the 4 tags (subject, object, attribute, none) via a fully connected layer. In classification, words are processed through recurrent units sequentially, and the question is classified at the end, with the hidden layer from the entire question as part of the input. In both cases, parameters are learned via stochastic gradient descent, using categorical cross-entropy as objective. In order to handle variable-length input, we limit to 15 tokens and prepend a special pad word if input has fewer.

A large training set is key to success with RNNs — this is especially expensive for QA, since domain-relevant questions need to be generated and annotated with tags at the word-level, as well as a relation type at the question-level. In

[1]word2vec.googlecode.com Out-of-vocabulary (OOV) words are randomly sampled from a uniform distribution.

SIGIR '16 July 17-21, 2016, Pisa, Italy

ACM ISBN 978-1-4503-4069-4/16/07.
DOI: http://dx.doi.org/10.1145/2911451.2926729

practice, such data is rarely available at development time. As a solution to this cold start problem, we generated training data directly from the KG in a synthetic manner, and augmented further to improve robustness. After identifying the set of relation types in the KG, we manually created question templates for each. For example, for the `birthDate` relation, one such template is "How old is *subj*?". Using these templates, we can generate questions for each fact in the KG, by instantiating the variables (e.g., *subj*="Tom Hanks"). This process requires significantly less labor than annotating millions of training examples.[2]

Synthetic data is easy to create, but the lack of lexical diversity might cause overfitting, especially with complex models. For example, an RNN will learn that questions *always* follow a certain template, and therefore fail even with a slight variation at test time. This aspect of QA is often ignored in academic publications, and we are not aware of benchmark datasets that focus on noisy factoid questions. For our product, this is especially critical, since many utterances are not well-formed. In order to tackle this, we expand certain domain-specific words with their synonyms, simply by using a dictionary. Additionally, we add noise by randomly (a) switching the plurality of nouns, (b) changing the tense of verbs, and (c) dropping context words. We experiment with different ratios of synonym and noise expansion.

Searching the Knowledge Graph: In order to make our KG searchable (given a structured query), we build multiple indexes: an inverted index for each entity type I_{subj}, I_{obj}, I_{attr} scores all n-grams of an entity using BM25 (e.g., "lost world" is a 2-gram for the entity "Lost World: Jurassic Park", so the index creates a mapping from the former to the latter with an associated score). A separate index I_{reach} maps each entity node s to all nodes e' that are reachable (a single hop away). Search for QA works as follows: Given a new question, we run the two RNN models to construct the structured query q (e.g., {*rel*=director, *subj*=lost world}). We go through all entity n-grams t' (starting from the entire text "lost world"), and find all matching entity nodes through $I_{\text{subj}}(t')$ (e.g., ["The Lost World", "Lost World: Jurassic Park", ...]). For each matching node q_e, we find all nodes reachable from it, $I_{\text{reach}}(q_e)$, and filter out ones where the path is not consistent with q Remaining nodes are candidate answers, scored by $BM25(t, q_e)$.

Evaluation: Our KG was constructed incrementally, first initialized with all direct facts about the most popular 64K entities. This was expanded twice, to include all indirect facts (i.e., direct facts about neighbor entities). As a result, we have 18.6M facts about 3.9M entities, from which 13.9M synthetic training examples were generated, as well as 4.5M/9.8M more through synonym/noise addition.

The KG is indexed into two files, each around 2GB, which is easily stored in memory. This allows very high latency — below 100ms per question on a research server running an Intel Xeon 2.66GHz processor. Each model takes around 40ms to predict, and the remaining time is used for search.

A challenge related to the entertainment domain is the large number of rarely used and foreign named entity words. Even with the 3 million pre-trained word embeddings, our training set has a 48% OOV rate. How much this impacts the end task, and whether there is a good solution to train embeddings for these words, are still open questions.

[2]There are 55 relation types in our entertainment KG.

We experimented with a variety of parameters and tested both tasks on held-out data, using the open-source deep learning toolkit Keras (http://keras.io). Due to space limitations, we will mention few key findings. With only synthetic questions, both tasks only make mistakes for the few ambiguous questions (e.g., author vs screenwriter vs writer). A more realistic case is when we add noise — in this case, classification accuracy drops to 96.2% (single LSTM layer with 20% drop out) while tagging accuracy remains to be almost 100% F1-score (two LSTM layers with 20% drop out). To simulate the worst-case scenario in which the test set is not just a noisy variation of an observed question type, but a completely new form of question, we separated the synthetic question templates into train, validation, and test sets. Classification accuracy decreased all the way down to 52.2%, using a single bidirectional LSTM with 10% drop out. The tagging model must have better generalization properties, since it was able to obtain an F1 of 91% for the *attribute* tag, and 88% for *subject* tags. The 45% F-score on *object* was due to a single type of unseen question — while this is a good exercise to understand the weakness of our approach, continuing the training process with new synthetic examples of the incorrect question type will easily fix the problem.

Conclusions and Future work: We described a simple yet effective approach for factoid question answering: a low-latency, scalable, and generalizable approach using minimal labor (no time spent on feature engineering!), based on a publicly available free machine learning toolkit and relatively cheap hardware. Our system is in the development phase, as it is being tested for quality assurance. We are hoping to bring it into production in the near future, and provide an innovative way for our customers to engage with their TV. We anticipate that our solution will add business value to our company, while building motivation for future research in the IR/NLP/ML space.

Next step is to handle questions where there are multiple entities, connected by various relations (e.g., "Which action movie did Tom Cruise and Meg Ryan both appear in?"). We would need to modify the structured query and expand search to more than one hop. Another important extension is to train a separate model to learn-to-rank the answers output by the current approach. This could especially help with personalization. We are also eager to find out how we can take advantage of deeper networks for the purpose of QA. Ensemble methods can provide improvements, since many times two variations of the model make complementary predictions. On the other hand, deeper models can implicitly learn the equivalent of an ensemble model. A key feature of our approach is that the knowledge search is separated from structured prediction. However, incorporating what we know into the model can provide higher accuracy.

1. REFERENCES

[1] A. Bordes, N. Usunier, S. Chopra, and J. Weston. Large-scale simple question answering with memory networks. *CoRR*, abs/1506.02075, 2015.

[2] L. Dong, F. Wei, M. Zhou, and K. Xu. Question answering over freebase with multi-column convolutional neural networks. In *ACL*, 2015.

[3] M. Iyyer, J. L. Boyd-Graber, L. M. B. Claudino, R. Socher, and H. Daumé. A neural network for factoid question answering over paragraphs. In *EMNLP*, 2014.

Amazon Search: The Joy of Ranking Products

Daria Sorokina
A9.com
130 Lytton, Palo Alto, CA, US
dariasor@a9.com

Erick Cantú-Paz
A9.com
130 Lytton, Palo Alto, CA, US
cantupaz@a9.com

ABSTRACT

Amazon is one of the world's largest e-commerce sites and Amazon Search powers the majority of Amazon's sales. As a consequence, even small improvements in relevance ranking both positively influence the shopping experience of millions of customers and significantly impact revenue. In the past, Amazon's product search engine consisted of several hand-tuned ranking functions using a handful of input features. A lot has changed since then. In this talk we are going to cover a number of relevance algorithms used in Amazon Search today. We will describe a general machine learning framework used for ranking within categories, blending separate rankings in All Product Search, NLP techniques used for matching queries and products, and algorithms targeted at unique tasks of specific categories — books and fashion.

1. RANKING MODELS

Ranking models are responsible for a function that, given a customer's query, returns a sorted list of products in a match set. A single ranking model usually covers a combination of a category and a marketplace, e.g., Books in Japan.

For training the ranking models we use labels based on customers actions, such as purchases, add-to-basket, or clicks.

We use the search engine to collect our training sets. Several times per day we compute the unique set of keywords issued for each context of interest. The context can be a combination of marketplace, category, and some user features. Then we re-issue these queries in their context requesting feature values for all items in the match set. This feature collection runs regularly, so that the feature vector collected is as close as possible to the one observed when the query was originally issued by customers.

To train ranking models, we construct training, validation, and test sets by collecting data from several days of customer traffic. Test sets are constructed from dates after the training set dates. We choose impressions that resulted in either click or purchase as positive examples. There are two types of negative example impressions: seen, corresponding to items which were displayed to a customer, and unseen, corresponding to items which matched the query terms but were never shown due to pagination. To manage the size of the training set, we sample unseen examples.

Gradient boosted trees[1] are our method of choice in ranking because they can discover complex feature interactions, can handle categorical and real-valued features, are robust in the presence of missing values, and work well even without significant tuning. For ranking problems, we use models trained with pairwise objectives and nDCG as the default objective function.

We do feature selection in two stages. First, with fixed values of tree depth and learning rate, we train a "kitchen sink" model allowing all features available. We then discard the features which end up being ranked lower than random features and use the remaining features to grow the final feature set in a forward selection process. Once the feature set is chosen, we perform a grid search over the pairs of values for tree depth and learning rate, choosing the model which has the highest offline score on the validation set.

Finally, the model is evaluated through an A/B test. We look at a large variety of metrics, including the number of converting customers, the number of products they purchase and the overall revenue.

2. BEHAVIORAL FEATURES

When training ranking models we use many features. Some of them measure intrinsic properties of products (e.g., sales, reviews). Others reflect properties of the queries or the context in which the query is issued (e.g., query specificity, customer status). Other features provide different measures of textual similarity. However in product search, hundreds of products might share very similar descriptions and seem to be equally relevant to a particular query. But some of those products are more popular than others and should be ranked higher. That's why behavioral features drive the rankings in Amazon Search to a much larger extent than they do in Web Search. Typically, they account for most of the variance reduction in gradient-boosted trees.

It is well-known that users tend to click more often on results on the top of a search result page. To correct for that, we have tried to use classical versions of click-over-expected-clicks features[3]. However, since more relevant documents tend to appear higher in the ranking, the observed click-through rate at a given position captures not only the position bias, but also the typical relevance at this position. This problem is more pronounced for a product

SIGIR '16 July 17-21, 2016, Pisa, Italy

ACM ISBN 978-1-4503-4069-4/16/07.
DOI: http://dx.doi.org/10.1145/2911451.2926725

search engine, compared to web search or advertising, as more products on average are relevant to a single query, and more clicks on average happen at higher position. To correct for that, we developed a scheme that adapts the bias correction from day to day.

3. MATCHING PRODUCTS AND QUERIES

A major problem in understanding queries in product search is determining whether a word or phrase in the query refers to a product type. For example, recognizing that "dress" in the query "casual dress" refers to a product type and not a modifier as in "dress shoes" or "dress socks" allows the systematic exclusion of non-dress products from the search results.

We treat each query as a noun phrase and consider the head of the noun phrase to be the core product type and all other words in the query to be modifiers. This is expressed as a probabilistic context-free grammar (PCFG), which is trained in an unsupervised manner using Variational Bayes. Limited supervision is inserted into the model by using brands from the Amazon catalog as well as other common modifiers such as color and gender. The set of product types observed in the training set under this model is extended to incorporate multiword expressions which encompass the product types (like "t shirt"), and the model is retrained with this augmented set of possible product types.

The second part of the task is to assign each product all the product-type expressions that properly describe it. For example, if the product is a tshirt, we want to label it "tshirt","shirt","clothing". This problem is naturally framed as a multilabel classification problem and the predictor can be trained as a series of logistic regression models. We represent the multilabel structure by a hypernym-synonym graph over the various product types and use it to enforce consistency constraints on the final predictions.

We use detected product types in queries and product descriptions to create powerful features in ranking models.

4. FINDING PREFERRED EDITION

Some of the product categories present unique problems. For example, books come in a variety of different editions (e.g. hardcover, paperback, digital, audiobook, etc). In search results we surface only a single, representative preferred edition in order to avoid overwhelming the user. Customers can then select a specific variation of the product on the details page. We use a separate combination of gradient boosted tree models to predict the face out edition for each book. These models are using only query-independent features, such as publication date or binding format, and most of the score is precalculated offline.

5. RANKING IN FASHION

Ranking in Amazon Fashion presents several unique challenges due to a large and varied product catalog, users with diverse fashion preferences, and business requirements to make the store appear fashionable and fresh.

We found that optimizing for an individual target (such as click, add-to-cart, or purchase) does not achieve the desired outcome. For example, while customers tend to purchase discounted items, they often browse and click on the items that are high-end fashion. We discovered that optimizing for a fused target that combines purchases with clicks often satisfies users' information need better in the Fashion Store.

An interesting challenge in the Fashion Store is the discrepancy between what the majority of customers actually buy and what they want to see on top of the page. The item most commonly bought for the query "diamond ring" might be a cheap zirconium ring. However, if we show the zirconium ring as a first result, our search will be perceived as broken. Besides, our Fashion Store would look like a flea market, instead of a classic department store where the latest collections meet you at the entrance.

To approach this problem, we identify strategic categories of fashionable customers — customers who bought or added to cart fashion brand products — and significantly amplify their influence while designing the training set.

6. BLENDING ACROSS CATEGORIES

Ranking models provide rankings within categories, but customers often use the "Search All" option on the search box. One of the biggest challenges in this case is to provide a blend of results from different categories. For example, for the query "game of thrones" customers may be looking for a book, a DVD, or a board game. The ordering of results returned by any ranking model is not changed, we only interleave results from individual categories based on an estimate of the probability that a given query is associated with a particular category. For the most common queries, this probability is based on observed user actions following that query. For tail queries, we predict category intent using an n-gram based language model. We use all queries with clicks on products from a given category over the last 90 days as text corpus for this category. Then, the affinity for a given query and a category is the probability of the query text to be observed in the category corpus. We use trigram language model with Modified Kneser-Ney smoothing[2] for this task.

7. ACKNOWLEDGEMENTS

This talk provides description of a number of past and current projects in Amazon Search. As such, this paper has a large number of authors, including, but probably not limited to, **Praveen Arasada, William Headden, François Huet, Anish Nair, Anil Sewani, Sheng Peng, Stefan Schroedl, Chris Varano, Bing Yin**.

8. REFERENCES

[1] J. Friedman. Greedy Function Approximation: a Gradient Boosting Machine. *Annals of Statistics*, 29:1189–1232, 2001.

[2] F. James. Modified Kneser-Ney Smoothing of N-gram Models. Technical report, 2000.

[3] W. V. Zhang and R. Jones. Comparing click logs and editorial labels for training query rewriting. In *WWW'07 workshops*.

Learning to Rank Personalized Search Results in Professional Networks

Viet Ha-Thuc
LinkedIn
2029 Stierlin Court
Mountain View, CA, USA
vhathuc@linkedin.com

Shakti Sinha
LinkedIn
2029 Stierlin Court
Mountain View, CA, USA
ssinha@linkedin.com

ABSTRACT

LinkedIn search is deeply personalized - for the same queries, different searchers expect completely different results. This paper presents our approach to achieving this by mining various data sources available in LinkedIn to infer searchers' intents (such as hiring, job seeking, etc.), as well as extending the concept of homophily to capture the searcher-result similarities on many aspects. Then, learning-to-rank is applied to combine these signals with standard search features.

Keywords

Learning-to-Rank; Personalization; Federation

1. INTRODUCTION

LinkedIn has evolved over past few years to become a platform containing various professional information sources - including 400+ million member profiles, 6+ million active jobs, millions of professional groups and 18+ million presentations. As the number of sources and their document volumes increase, the problem of serving the right results to fulfill each individual information need becomes increasingly challenging. Moreover, compared to typical information retrieval systems (such as generic Web search), LinkedIn search is deeply personalized. For instance, if a member enters the query "software engineer", depending on whether he or she is a recruiter, job seeker or professional content consumer, the member expects to see very different results: software engineers' profiles, software engineer jobs or slideshows on the topic, respectively. Even within a single vertical like Job search, for the query above, if the searcher happens to be an information retrieval expert, he or she is much more likely to be interested in software engineer jobs related to the field rather than software engineer jobs focusing on, say, software QA. For these reasons, we use rich information from the professional network - such as the searchers' identity, profile, network and behavior - to understand their interests and intent, and serve a deeply personalized, relevant search experience.

SIGIR '16 July 17-21, 2016, Pisa, Italy

ACM ISBN 978-1-4503-4069-4/16/07.

DOI: http://dx.doi.org/10.1145/2911451.2927018

With this context, we present our approach to personalize search ranking, leveraging the information available on LinkedIn. At the vertical level, we extend the concept of *homophily* to construct personalized features. Traditionally, the main idea of homophily is that in a social network, people tend to connect or interact with similar people. In the context of LinkedIn, we hypothesize that searchers tend to be interested in results similar or related to them. For example, in People search, searchers are often interested in people in the same or similar industries or companies and people with similar expertise. In Job search, searchers are usually interested in jobs at similar companies, jobs at nearby locations and jobs requiring expertise similar to their own. In particular, for *expertise homophily*, we propose an approach incorporating members' profiles, skill-endorsement graphs and skill co-occurrence patterns to estimate their expertise scores for the skills listed on their profiles, as well as the skills we infer they have. To combine these personalized features with traditional IR features, we apply learning-to-rank (LTR) techniques to learn ranking functions.

Given results from multiple verticals, a federated model blends them into a single search result page. To personalize the federated model, we mine members' profiles and their recent activities at a large scale to understand their *intents*, such as, hiring intent, job seeking intent or content consuming intent, etc. Then, the federated model is learnt to couple this insight with other signals, including the ones from verticals, to select verticals and to aggregate vertical results into a single ranking that is personally relevant to each of our members.

2. SEARCH RANKING

2.1 Expertise Homophily

On LinkedIn, skills are an integral part of members' profiles that showcase their expertise. A challenge on estimating member expertise is that many members do not explicitly list all skills they have. To overcome this, we employ a two-step approach (Figure 1). In the first step, we use a supervised learning algorithm combining various signals on LinkedIn, such as skill-endorsement graph page rank, skill-profile textual similarity, member seniority, etc., to estimate the expertise scores, i.e., $p(expert|member, skill)$. After this step, the expertise matrix (E_0) is very sparse since we can be certain about expertise scores only for a small percentage of the pairs. In the second step, we factorize the matrix into member and skill matrices in K-dimensional latent space. Then, we compute the dot-product of the matrices to fill in

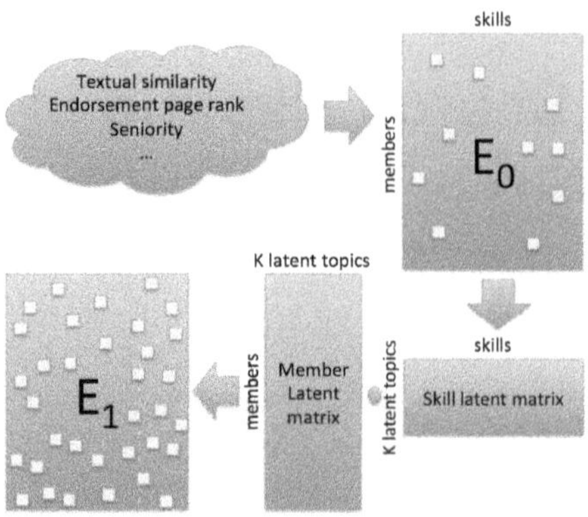

Figure 1: Member-skill expertise estimation

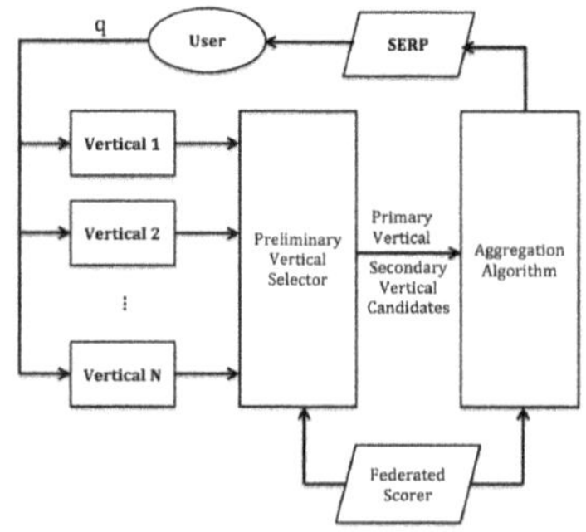

Figure 2: Federated Search

the "unknown" cells. The intuition for this can be illustrated as follows: if a member has "machine learning" and "information retrieval" skills, based on skill co-occurrence patterns from all of our member base, we could infer that the member is likely to also know "learning-to-rank". Interested readers can refer to our recent work [3, 2] for more details. The expertise homophily is then estimated by the cosine similarity between the searcher's and results' scores.

2.2 Learning

We apply an LTR approach to combine expertise homophily with more traditional search features. In deeply personalized settings like LinkedIn search, editorial judgement does not work well since result relevance strongly depends on individual searchers. Labels derived from search logs containing searchers' actions on results, on the other hand, are personalized by nature. However, the logs have both position and sample selection biases. To avoid position bias, we collect labels from a small traffic fraction that randomizes top-K results. The labeled data is then augmented with *easy negatives*, which are sampled from the tails of rankings to reduce sample bias. The labeled data collection approach is described in [2].

3. FEDERATION

3.1 Overall Framework

Given a pair of *(query, searcher)*, the federator selects a primary vertical and a set of secondary verticals, then ranks the primary individual results and the secondary vertical blocks in a single ranked list. The overall framework is described in Figure 2. When a member issues a query q, the query is passed to verticals and triggers the corresponding vertical search engines to get the top K results for each. In preliminary vertical selection phase, the federated scorer extracts features and computes a relevance score for each of the verticals. The top vertical is selected as the primary and the rest are selected as *candidates* for secondary verticals. Then, in aggregation phase, these candidates compete with individual results in the primary vertical to form the final ranking. Note that these candidates are not guaranteed to show up in the ranking. Instead, depending on queries, searchers and vertical results, all, some or none of these candidates could be selected. A critical feature used in the federated scorer is searcher intent, which is described in the next subsection.

3.2 Searcher Intent

LinkedIn searchers' information needs constitute a very diverse set of intents. For instance, members actively looking for jobs are likely to be more interested in job results than other verticals. Similarly, members hiring new employees should consider people results to be more important. Given this, we personalize search federation by using the searcher's profile and past activity to infer their *intents*. If a member's job title is recruiter, he is likely to have hiring intent. If a member recently searched for or applied to jobs, he is likely to have job seeking intent. We train machine-learned models combining all of the signals to predict intents for all searchers daily. It is worth noting that a member could have multiple intents at the same time.

The impact of the intents can vary significantly between different verticals. For example, knowing that a searcher has job seeking intent has much more importance for results that are jobs. We address this variation by constructing *composite features*, capturing both searcher intent and result type. In the example below, the feature is activated only if the searcher has job seeking intent and the result is job. We create combinations of all intents and result categories and learn their weights in our models. In essence, we let the learning algorithm associate evidence with the verticals, and normalize across all verticals from training data. More details can be found in [1].

$$f = \begin{cases} 1 & \text{if searcher is a job seeker AND the result is job} \\ 0 & \text{otherwise} \end{cases}$$

4. CONCLUSIONS

We have described how vastly differing intents for the same query arising from different searchers makes LinkedIn search unique and presented the approaches we use to personalize both vertical ranking and federation to deliver a relevant experience to all our searchers.

5. REFERENCES

[1] D. Arya, V. Ha-Thuc, , and S. Sinha. Personalized federated search at linkedin. In *ACM CIKM*, 2015.

[2] V. Ha-Thuc, G. Venkataraman, M. Rodriguez, S. Sinha, S. Sundaram, and L. Guo. Personalized expertise search at linkedin. In *IEEE Big Data*, 2015.

[3] V. Ha-Thuc, Y. Xu, S. P. Kanduri, X. Wu, V. Dialani, Y. Yan, A. Gupta, and S. Sinha. Search by ideal candidates: Next generation of talent search at linkedin. In *ACM WWW*, 2016.

When does Relevance Mean Usefulness and User Satisfaction in Web Search?

Jiaxin Mao[†], Yiqun Liu[†*], Ke Zhou[⋆], Jian-Yun Nie[#], Jingtao Song[†], Min Zhang[†], Shaoping Ma[†], Jiashen Sun[‡], Hengliang Luo[‡]
[†]Tsinghua National Laboratory for Information Science and Technology, Department of Computer Science & Technology, Tsinghua University, Beijing, China
[⋆]Yahoo! Research, London, U.K.
[#]Université de Montréal
[‡]Samsung R&D Institute China - Beijing
yiqunliu@tsinghua.edu.cn

ABSTRACT

Relevance is a fundamental concept in information retrieval (IR) studies. It is however often observed that relevance as annotated by secondary assessors may not necessarily mean usefulness and satisfaction perceived by users. In this study, we confirm the difference by a laboratory study in which we collect relevance annotations by external assessors, usefulness and user satisfaction information by users, for a set of search tasks. We also find that a measure based on usefulness rather than relevance annotated has a better correlation with user satisfaction. However, we show that external assessors are capable of annotating usefulness when provided with more search context information. In addition, we also show that it is possible to generate automatically usefulness labels when some training data is available. Our findings explain why traditional system-centric evaluation metrics are not well aligned with user satisfaction and suggest that a usefulness-based evaluation method can be defined to better reflect the quality of search systems perceived by the users.

Keywords

Relevance; Usefulness; User satisfaction; Evaluation

1. INTRODUCTION

Relevance, which "expresses a criterion for assessing effectiveness in retrieval of information, or of objects potentially conveying information" [37], is a central concept in IR and plays an important role in search engine evaluation. It is well known that this notion involves multiple aspects. In the traditional system evaluation paradigm [10, 43], in order to compare the performances of different search systems, we typically rely on a test collection that consists of a document corpus, a set of predefined statements of information needs, and a set of *relevance judgements*. Based on the relevance judgements of query - document pairs, evaluation metrics, such as MAP, NDCG [21], and ERR [7], are computed for the ranked lists returned by different systems. Each of these measures is defined according to a different user model, which describes how the user interacts with the ranked list [33], and links the document-level relevance judgments with an estimation of the query-level user satisfaction [1, 28].

Conceptually, the relevance judgements are expected to represent users' opinions about whether the retrieved documents are relevant and meet users' information needs [43, 44] and should be made by the users themselves. However in practice, it is usually hard to collect relevance feedbacks directly from actual search users, especially in Web search. We therefore ask external (secondary) assessors to make the relevance judgements instead. In this case, there is a high risk that the collected relevance judgments may not necessarily reflect the user-perceived *usefulness* of retrieved documents. This is due to several reasons. On the one hand, in general, the assessors do not originate the information needs themselves and thus may not fully understand what the user actually wants. It has been indeed questioned whether the search intent can always be captured by the assessors [42]. On the other hand, conventionally the relevance judgments are made in a much simplified environment in which the assessor is asked to judge the relevance relation between each query-document pair independently. The assessor does not have access to much contextual information that may affect relevance judgment, such as the queries the user issued previously in the session, the documents examined or clicked by the user, and so on. In addition, the assessor is only provided with a single short query, which may hardly describe accurately the user's information need. In reality, the Web search engine users often issue multiple queries in a search session [38], especially for exploratory and struggling search tasks [19]. It has been well documented that there are dependency and redundancy among the result documents [5, 9] . When all these contextual factors are ignored, it is very difficult for the assessor to put herself in the shoe of the user to make correct relevance judgment.

The lack of contextual information and accurate description of the information need often leads the assessor to limit herself to judge the *topical* aspect of relevance, which is different from the highly *situational*, *subjective*, user-perceived usefulness. This difference can be easily observed when the relevance judgment of the assessor is compared to the usefulness feedback from the user. Table 1 shows a search session collected in our experimental study in which we collect assessor's relevance judgments and user's usefulness feedback (see Section 3 for more details). Given a search task, a user issued two queries and viewed several results. For the first query, `baggage restrictions`, the user clicked on two results in order. The contents of these two documents are very similar and both are topically related to the query. The assessor judged both document to be "highly relevant". However, the user judged the first document to be more useful than the second. This may be due to the fact that the second result does not contain

*Yiqun Liu is the corresponding author.

SIGIR '16, July 17-21, 2016, Pisa, Italy
© 2016 ACM. ISBN 978-1-4503-4069-4/16/07... $15.00
DOI: http://dx.doi.org/10.1145/2911451.2911507

Table 1: An example session showing the difference between user's feedbacks on usefulness and assessor's relevance labels.

Search Task:	
You are going to US by air, so you want to know what restrictions there are for both checked and carry-on baggage during air travel.	
Query Logs:	
Query #1	`baggage restrictions`
Click #1	Checked baggage policy - American Airlines
	Relevance: 4(Highly) Usefulness: 3(Fairly)
Click #2	Air Canada - BaggageInformation
	Relevance: 4(Highly) Usefulness: 2(Somewhat)
Query #2	`carry-on baggage liquids`
...	
Click #3	The Best Way to Pack a Suitcase
	Relevance: 2(Somewhat) Usefulness: 4(Very)

much novel information after reading the first one. As for the second query, the user clicked on the result titled `The Best Way to Pack a Suitcase`. From the assessor's point of view, this document is not so relevant to the query `carry-on baggage liquids`, but the user finds it very useful when he or she is preparing for an air trip (this is part of the task specification missing in the short query). In these examples, we clearly spot that the usefulness of a document is dependent on previously read contents and on the accurate specification of the search task, and therefore, is different from its topical relevance. In this paper, the difference on relevance judgments between the user and the assessors will be further analyzed.

A number of existing studies have noticed the differences between users' and external assessors' relevance labels. Vakkari and Sormunen found that the relevance criterion of some users is more liberal than that used by TREC assessors [41]. Al-Maskari et al. [2] also compared the differences in relevance labeling process between users and TREC assessors, and observed that various factors, such as the number of retrieved relevant documents and the ranking of relevant documents (i.e. context of the current document), contribute to the differences. Although these previous studies show that users' judgements are different from the assessors', they do not attempt to propose a new way to evaluate systems to better correspond to user's perception. Yilmaz et al. [47] compared document usefulness for users (called utility in their paper) with relevance annotation by assessors, which is in line with our work. They come to an interesting conclusion that some of the differences between user's usefulness and assessor's relevance are caused by the amount of effort required to find the relevant information in a document. They used dwell time as a sign of usefulness. In our work, we collect users' explicit feedback information, which is expected to be more reliable than implicit behavior signals. The idea of replacing relevance-based measurements with usefulness-based ones is also proposed by Belkin et al. [3] and Cole et al. [13]. However, the idea has not been implemented and no experimental study has been carried out so far on realistic data.

In this paper, we examine the relationship between relevance, usefulness and user satisfaction in a realistic Web search setting. In particular, we design a protocol to collect data [1] containing both (1) user's explicit feedbacks on document usefulness and user satisfaction, which will be considered as ground truth; and (2) external assessor's relevance judgments. Based on the collected data, we examine the following research questions in order to see if usefulness should be used for system evaluation rather than annotated relevance:

RQ1 What is the difference between user's perceived usefulness and the external assessor's relevance annotation?

RQ2 How do document's usefulness perceived by the user and relevance annotated by the assessors correlate with user's satisfaction?

[1] This dataset and the detailed instructions used to construct the dataset are publicly available on https://github.com/THUIR/UsefulnessUserStudyData

However, in a practical Web search setting, it is impossible to ask users to provide explicit feedback on usefulness. We have to resort to an alternative approach. This motivates us to examine the following two additional research questions:

RQ3 Can we rely on external assessors to make reliable and valid assessments for the document-level usefulness?

RQ4 Can we automatically generate usefulness labels based on user behavior and search context features?

Regarding **RQ3** and **RQ4**, we propose two approaches that can collect usefulness labels in practical Web search settings. The first approach relies on manual labeling by external assessors who are provided with more information about the search task and the search context. We will show that the usefulness annotation in this case is reasonably close to estimate user-perceived usefulness. The second approach goes a step further by utilizing machine learning techniques based on user behavior data to automatically generate usefulness labels. We show that this approach is feasible when a small amount of training data is available. Such an automatic usefulness labeling approach can help save the tedious work of manual labeling.

By answering these research questions, we aim to propose a new evaluation framework in which usefulness, instead of the current simplified relevance, is used. Based on manually labeled or automatically generated usefulness labels, evaluation metrics in this new framework are expected to better correlate with users' feelings of satisfaction, which will be confirmed in our experiments. We do not hope to fully replace the current practice of relevance judgment with usefulness assessment in all situations. Instead, we hope to show that in certain circumstances where usefulness information can be collected or deduced, evaluation based on usefulness assessment can better reflect users' opinions.

The rest of this paper is organized as follows: Related studies are discussed in Section 2. In Section 3, we describe the experiment design and the data collecting procedure. In Section 4, we compare user's usefulness feedback with assessor's relevance annotation to answer **RQ1**. In Section 5, we characterize the relationship between document-level measures and user satisfaction, and answer **RQ2**. To answer **RQ3** and **RQ4**, we propose and test two approaches for acquiring usefulness labels, manually or automatically, in Section 6. Finally we draw conclusions and provide future work directions in Section 7.

2. RELATED WORK

Our work is related to a broad range of IR evaluation studies.

In the traditional system-centric Cranfield-style evaluation [10, 43], most evaluation metrics are based on an implicit user model describing how the user interacts with a SERP [33]. They assess and summarize the effectiveness at *query* level. Recent studies extend the Cranfield-style evaluation paradigms to (1) cope with the redundancy and diversity of documents [9, 35]; (2) assess the overall effectiveness in a search session [6, 22, 25].

On the other hand, the user-centric evaluation draws more and more attention along with the emergence of Web search engines. It has been argued for a long time that instead of relevance, usefulness (or utility) should be used as a measure of retrieval effectiveness [13, 14]. Using the user behavior information that can be implicitly collected at a large scale, the utility or usefulness of a document (sometimes referred to as click satisfaction or intrinsic relevance) are estimated [4, 8, 24, 46]. These studies are based on the assumption that there are correlations between user behaviors and usefulness of documents. We will further investigate these correlations in Section 6.2. Our work is complementary to the existing work in the following ways: (1) instead of relying on natural log data from a search engine, we collect explicit usefulness feedbacks as well as comprehensive user behavior and search context information in a laboratory user study, which allow us to investigate the correlations between different notions. (2) Different from the studies that focus on predicting user satisfaction and search success at query- or

Table 2: Descriptions of major measures used in this work.

Concepts	Measures	Descriptions
Relevance	Relevance annotation (R)	4-level graded relevance annotations made by external assessors in Stage II.1 (see Figure 1 and Section 3.2).
Usefulness	Usefulness feedbacks (U_u)	4-level graded usefulness feedbacks collected in Stage I.4 (see Figure 1 and Section 3.2). We use them as the ground truth labels for usefulness.
	Usefulness annotation (U_a)	4-level graded usefulness annotations made by external assessors reviewing augmented search logs in Stage II.2 (see Figure 1 and Section 3.2).
	Usefulness prediction or predicted usefulness (U_Q, U_{Q+S}, etc.)	Predicted usefulness labels. We utilize a machine learning method and different combinations of features to predict usefulness (See Section 6.2).
Query-level Satisfaction	Query-level satisfaction feedbacks ($QSAT_u$)	5-level graded satisfaction feedbacks for each issued query collected in Stage I.4 (see Figure 1 and Section 3.2).
	Query-level satisfaction annotation ($QSAT_a$)	5-level graded satisfaction annotations made by external assessors in Stage II.2 (see Figure 1 and Section 3.2).
Task-level Satisfaction	Task-level satisfaction feedbacks ($TSAT_u$)	5-level graded satisfaction feedbacks for each search task collected in Stage I.4 (see Figure 1 and Section 3.2). .
	Task-level satisfaction annotation ($TSAT_a$)	5-level graded satisfaction annotations made by external assessors in Stage II.2 (see Figure 1 and Section 3.2).

task-level in Web search [18, 23, 32, 34], our primary goal in this study is to exploit the possible correlations between *document*-level measures and *query*- and *task*-level user satisfaction so that (1) we can understand the relationship between document utility and user satisfaction; and (2) we can derive appropriate usefulness measures.

Some existing studies investigated the relation between the system-centric and user-centric evaluation by comparing the system-centric evaluation metrics, usually based on relevance, with user performance, satisfaction, or preference [1, 20, 28, 36, 40]. In a recent work, Yilmaz et al. [47] compared document utility with document relevance. They showed that the required effort plays an important role in the degree of document utility perceived by a real search user. Our work also extensively compares document usefulness with its annotated relevance, and extends their work as follows: (1) instead of relying on the dwell time as a surrogate for utility, we collect user's explicit feedbacks of usefulness; (2) in addition to the required effort and dwell time, we also consider other factors, such as the the current search task and the redundancy with previous documents read by the user, as they have been shown to influence document usefulness perceived by the user.

Usefulness and satisfaction are both subjective. Therefore, our work is also indirectly related to the field of personalized search [15, 39]. As personalized search aims to take into account the diverse and volatile information needs from different users, to make our study more reliable, we control this variability by designing predefined and clearly stated search tasks for the participants, which differentiate our work from most personalized search studies.

3. DATA COLLECTION

As shown in Figure 1, the data collection procedure consists of two parts: I. User Study and II. Data Annotation. The first part is collected in a laboratory environment. We collected users' behavior logs and their explicit feedbacks for both usefulness and satisfaction. In the second step, we hired external assessors to generate corresponding relevance annotations. To investigate **RQ3** and **RQ4**, we also asked the assessors to provide their usefulness and satisfaction annotations. We use these feedbacks and annotations as *measures* for relevance, usefulness or satisfaction. Table 2 provides a summary of these measures.

Table 3: Examples of search tasks. The TREC topic indexes are given in parentheses ().

Init. Query	Description
baggage restrictions	You are going to US by air, so you want to know what restrictions there are for both checked and carry-on baggage during air travel. (2010-7)
long-term care insurance	You just learned about the existence of long-term care insurance and want to know about it: costs / premiums, companies that offer it, types of policies, people's opinion about long term care insurance; what are the differences between long term care and health insurance? (2013-8)
quit smoking	Your friend would like to quit smoking. You would like to provide him with relevant information about: the different ways to quit smoking, benefits of quitting smoking, second effects of quitting smoking. (2013-12)

3.1 User Study Design

In the laboratory user study, each participant was asked to complete 12 search tasks using an experiment search engine system. Compared with collecting data from real search logs [23, 34], or by browser plugins [16, 45], the laboratory user study had a smaller scale, but enabled us to fully control the variabilities in search tasks and information needs as well as to collect explicitly the information needed.

To simulate a real Web search environment, we built an experimental search engine that can access the open Web. As shown in Figure 1(I.3), this experimental search engine has an interface similar to common Web search engines, and supports query reformulation and pagination. When the user issues a query, or clicks a pagination link, the experimental search system will forward the request to a commercial search engine in real time, and retrieve the corresponding search engine result page (SERP). To control the variability in presentation styles, all query suggestions, ads, sponsor search results, and vertical results in the retrieved SERP are removed, only the remaining organic results are returned to the user. We also store these organic results in our system, not only for further annotation and analysis, but also to make sure that if another participant issues the same query, he or she will be shown the same SERP. A javascript plugin was injected into the returned SERP to log users' search behaviors including query reformulation, click, scrolling, tab switching and mouse movement.

12 search tasks were selected from the topics of TREC Session Track 2010-2014[2]. Several criteria were considered when selecting the search tasks. Firstly, a search task should be clearly stated so that different participants could interpret the task description in the same way. Secondly, the difficulty and complexity of a search task should be appropriate. The search task should be neither too time-consuming, nor so easy that only requires one query and a few clicks on top results to complete. A pilot experiment was conducted to test whether these criteria were met. Based on the result of the pilot experiment, we made necessary modifications to the original TREC task descriptions to adjust the difficulties and complexities. We further provided an initial query for each search task. While providing initial query might threaten the ecological validity of our experiment, it can make sure that all participants will see the same initial SERP for each search task, and thus effectively prevent potential topic drifts. Table 3 shows some examples of the selected search tasks.

We recruited 29 undergraduate students, via emails and online social networks, to take part in the user study. 15 participants were female and 14 were male. The ages of participants range from 18 to 26. The distribution of their major is: 15 in engineering, 10 in humanities and social sciences, and 4 in designs and arts. All the participants were familiar with basic usage of Web search engines, and most of them reported using Web search engines daily.

Each participant was asked to complete all of the 12 search tasks in a random order. As shown in Figure 1(I), to make sure that every participant was familiar with the experiment procedure,

[2]http://trec.nist.gov/data/session.html

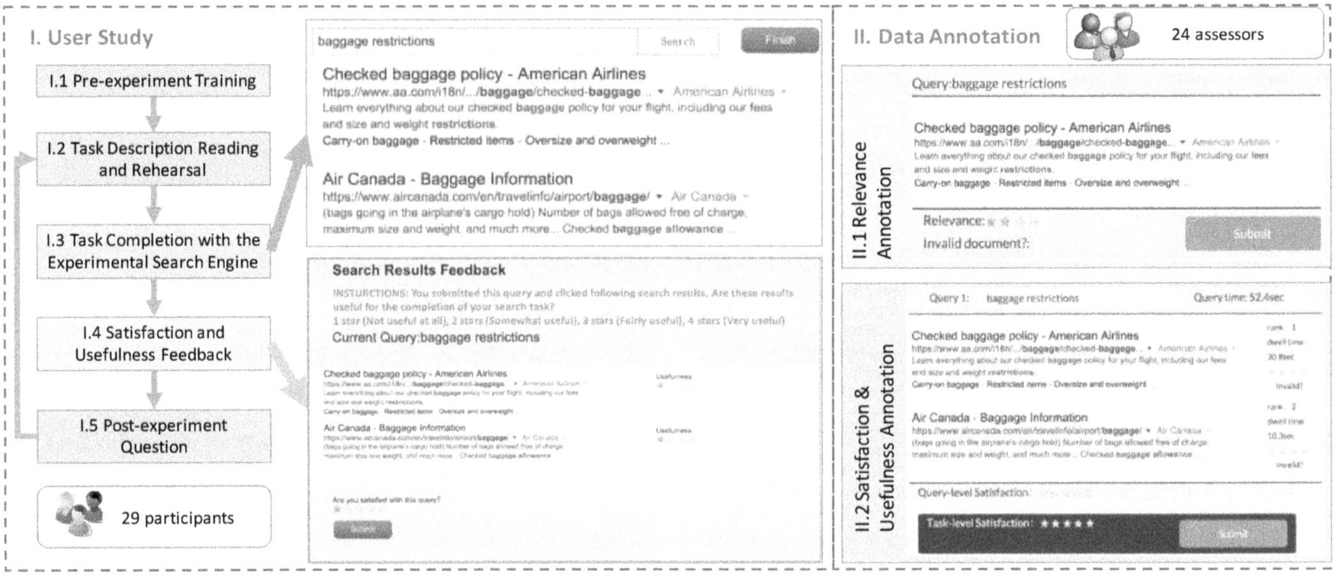

Figure 1: Data collection procedure. With enrolled participants, we collected behavior logs and feedback data in I. User Study. With hired external assessors, we generated relevance, usefulness and satisfaction annotation data in II. Data Annotation.

an example task was used for demonstration in the Pre-experiment Training stage (I.1). For each search task, the participant had to go through 4 different stages (I.2-I.5). Firstly, the participant should read and memorize the task description (note that the complete task description is provided to the participant). After that, s/he was required to re-input the task description without viewing it again during searching (I.2). Then s/he would be redirected to the SERP of the initial query, and start completing the search task (I.3). The participant could click on the results and submit new queries freely, just like using a normal Web search engine. While no task time limits were imposed, s/he could stop searching and click the finish button when s/he thought the task was completed, or no more helpful information would be found. After the task completion stage, the participant was required to review the search process and provide explicit feedbacks (I.4). Figure 1(I.4) shows the interface for collecting usefulness and query-level satisfaction feedbacks. We used a 4-level graded usefulness feedback (U_u, 1: not useful at all; 2: somewhat useful; 3: fairly useful; 4: very useful) since we aim to compare it against 4-level graded relevance annotation [26]. We used a 5-level graded *query-level satisfaction* feedback. The 5-level satisfaction scale and instructions are in accordance with those introduced by Liu et al. [32]. We only collected usefulness feedbacks for documents that were clicked by that particular participant in the task completion stage. After reviewing all issued queries, the participant would further submit a 5-level *task-level satisfaction* feedback ($TSAT_u$). The explicit feedback stage was immediately after, but did not interfere with, the search process. We believe such an experiment design could collect most accurate feedbacks while introduce a minimal interference to users' search behavior. A question answering stage was put at the end of each search task (I.5). The participant must answer a question related to the search task (e.g. "Please provide three suggestions for quitting smoking." for the task "quit smoking") in voice. In the pilot test we found that the voice question answering introduces much less cognitive cost than requiring the participants to use keyboard to input the answers, and it can effectively ensure that the participants indeed put some effort in finishing the search task.

3.2 Data Annotation

After collecting the search behavior logs and user feedbacks in the user study, we hired external assessors to generate: (1) relevance annotations (R) for all the documents that were clicked by users or shown in the top 5 positions of a SERP; (2) usefulness annotations (U_a) for all clicked documents; (3) query-level satisfaction annotations ($QSAT_a$) for all issued queries; and (4) task-level satisfactions ($TSAT_a$) for all search sessions.

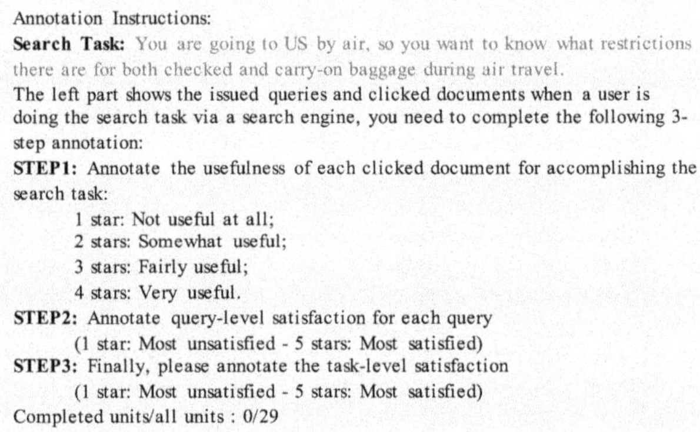
Annotation Instructions:
Search Task: You are going to US by air, so you want to know what restrictions there are for both checked and carry-on baggage during air travel.
The left part shows the issued queries and clicked documents when a user is doing the search task via a search engine, you need to complete the following 3-step annotation:
STEP1: Annotate the usefulness of each clicked document for accomplishing the search task:
1 star: Not useful at all;
2 stars: Somewhat useful;
3 stars: Fairly useful;
4 stars: Very useful.
STEP2: Annotate query-level satisfaction for each query
(1 star: Most unsatisfied - 5 stars: Most satisfied)
STEP3: Finally, please annotate the task-level satisfaction
(1 star: Most unsatisfied - 5 stars: Most satisfied)
Completed units/all units : 0/29

Figure 2: Annotation instructions shown to assessors.

Figure 1(II.1) shows the interface for relevance annotation. A relevance annotation unit consists of a query-document pair. For each unit, we showed the short query and the snippet of the document, in a single page, to the assessors. The assessors were required to click and examine the document and make a 4-level graded relevance judgment (1: irrelevant; 2: somewhat relevant; 3: fairly relevant; 4: highly relevant). The relevance scale and annotation instructions are similar to those introduced by Kekäläinen et al. [26] and are also consistent with the current practice in Web search. Some documents were not accessible during the annotation process because the page had been removed or deleted. So we asked the assessor to check the `Invalid document?` checkbox when s/he could not access the document.

The annotation unit of usefulness and satisfaction annotation is a search session in which a participant completed a single search task (with full task description). As shown in Figure 1(II.2), for each annotation unit, we showed an augmented search log, along with the instruction and the search task description (see Figure 2), to the assessor. All queries and clicked documents in the log were presented in the same order as when the participant issued and clicked them in the user study. To imitate the search process and reproduce the search context, the assessors were instructed to inspect the search session and judge the document-level

Table 4: Statistics of behavior logs.

#tasks	#participants	#sessions	#queries	#clicks
9	25	225	935	1,512

Table 5: Statistics of annotation data.

	R_{nc}	R_c	U_a	$QSAT_a$	$TSAT_a$
#Annotations	1,944	1,161	1,512	935	225
Weighted κ	0.344	0.413	0.530	0.535	0.274

usefulness, query-level satisfaction and task-level satisfaction sequentially. Similar to the laboratory user study, we used the same 4-level graded scale for usefulness, and 5-level graded scale for satisfaction. We also showed behavioral information including the query dwell time, click dwell time and the ranks of clicked documents to the assessors. The above annotation approaches are consistent with the existing studies [23, 29, 32] on user satisfaction.

24 assessors were enrolled in the data annotation tasks. They were all graduate, or senior undergraduate students. We *randomly* assigned 9 of them to complete the relevance annotation task, and 15 of them the usefulness and satisfaction annotation task.

3.3 Quality Control and Data Filtering

To make sure the data annotations are *reliable*, we ensured that each unit was judged by at least 3 different assessors. As the annotations are *ordinal*, we applied Cohen's Weighted κ [11] to assess the inter-assessor agreements. This requires a weight matrix W to indicate how severe a disagreement is. We chose to use the difference on the ordinal scale as the values in W.

After a careful inspection of the annotation data, we filtered out three search tasks: one search task which contained a considerable number of invalid documents; and two other search tasks for which there were many documents with commercial intents, and the assessors had difficulties in determining whether they were spams or not. While these tasks represent real search situations, we judge that the collected judgments are not reliable enough to serve as ground truth, so they are discarded. We also examined the search log collected in the user study, and removed the data generated by 4 participants who did not put sufficient effort in search tasks. They completed search tasks in a significantly shorter time than other participants, and gave very vague answers in the question answering stage.

Summary

Through the user study, data annotation and filtering, we collected user behavior logs, users' explicit feedbacks for usefulness and satisfaction, and a set of corresponding annotation data from external assessors. The statistics of the behavior logs are shown in Table 4. The number of collected relevance, usefulness and satisfaction annotations are shown in Table 5. We separate the assessor's relevance annotations R into two groups: R_c and R_{nc}. R_c are the relevance annotations for clicked documents, which will be compared with usefulness measures. R_{nc} are the relevance annotations for the documents that were among the top 5 results of a query, but never clicked by a user. We also list the average Weighted κ for each kind of annotations. According to Landis et al. [30] [3] , fair inter-assessor agreements between assessors are reached for R_{nc} and $TSAT_a$, and moderate agreements are reached for R_c, U_a, and $QSAT_a$, which indicates the annotation data are of reasonable quality.

4. USEFULNESS V.S. RELEVANCE

Based on the data collected, we first investigate the difference and relationship between assessor's relevance and user's usefulness to answer **RQ1**. In this work, we use usefulness feedbacks (U_u) as the ground truth labels for usefulness, to which the relevance annotation (R) for each clicked document, will be compared.

[3]Landis et al. [30] characterize κ values < 0 as no agreement, $0 - 0.20$ as slight, $0.21 - 0.40$ as fair, $0.41 - 0.60$ as moderate, $0.61 - 0.80$ as substantial, and $0.81 - 1$ as almost perfect agreement.

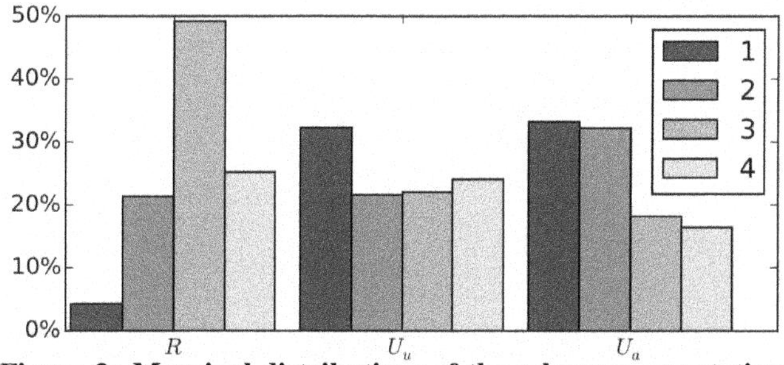

Figure 3: Marginal distributions of the relevance annotations (R), usefulness feedbacks (U_u) and usefulness annotations (U_a) for the clicked documents. The values from 1 to 4 mean respectively not relevant/useful, somewhat relevant/useful, fairly relevant/useful, very relevant/useful.

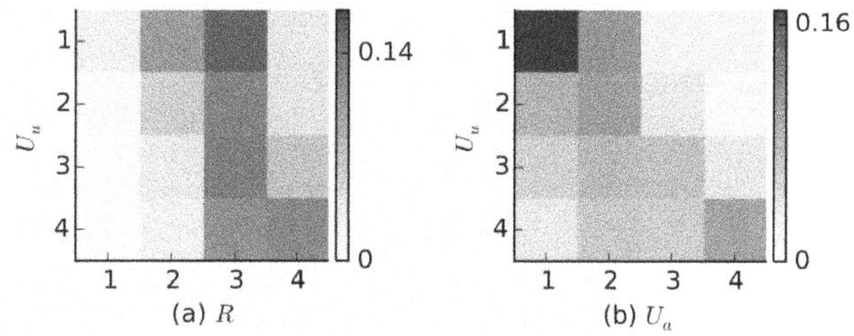

Figure 4: Joint distributions of document-level measures for clicked documents. Darker color indicates a higher frequency. (a) joint distribution of relevance annotations (R) and usefulness feedbacks (U_u); (b) joint distribution of usefulness annotations (U_a) and usefulness feedbacks (U_u).

The marginal distribution of R and U_u are shown in Figure 3. Note that the distributions are computed per click, so only the relevance annotations of clicked documents (R_c in Section 3.3) are used. We can see an obvious difference between these two distributions (Chi-Square test, $\chi^2(3, N = 1,512) = 874$, $p < 0.001$). For relevance R, nearly 50% of clicked documents are annotated as fairly relevant ($R = 3$). This is not surprising because all these documents ranked in high positions by a commercial search engine are topically related to the short query. Meanwhile, for usefulness feedbacks U_u, we spot a nearly uniform distribution with a little more clicks with $U_u = 1$, which implies that the user knows clearly whether an examined document is useful or not. As there are only a few clicks on the document with $R = 1$ (4.3%), and a considerable number of clicks (32.3%) are reported as $U_u = 1$, we can conclude that a large proportion of the documents considered relevant by the assessors may not be useful to users.

To study the correlation between U_u and R, we compute Pearson's correlation coefficient r and Cohen's Weighted κ between these two document-level measures. A moderate positive correlation is detected, $r(1,510) = 0.332$[4], $p < 0.001$, two tails. The computed Weighted κ is 0.209 ($\sigma_\kappa = 0.017$), just reaching a fair agreement level [30]. We plot the heat map for the joint distribution of U_u and R in Figure 4 (a) and find that R and U_u are not aligned well. Except for the document with perfect relevance ($R = 4$), other documents are likely to be not useful at all ($U_u = 1$). Even for the clicks on documents with fair relevancy ($R = 3$), 29.3% are not useful from the users' perspective. However, only a few clicked documents have low relevance ($R \leq 2$) and high usefulness ($U_u \geq 3$), suggesting that high relevance is a necessary condition for high usefulness. This finding may explain why some implicit signals for high usefulness (e.g. long dwell time [4, 46], and last click [8, 24]) could be used as positive implicit relevance feedbacks in previous studies.

We are now interested in understanding why U_u and R are not aligned. We manually inspected the clicks with low relevance

[4]The degree of freedom is given by $\#clicks - 2$

Table 6: Correlations with query-level satisfaction feedback $QSAT_u$.

All correlations (measured in Pearson's r) are significant at $p < 0.001$. *(or **) indicates the difference is significant at $p < 0.05 (p < 0.01)$, comparing to the same metric based on relevance annotation R.

	All Queries ($df = 933$)		Queries with only top 5 clicks ($df = 635$)	
	U_u	R	U_u	R
cCG	0.572**	0.425	0.647**	0.499
cDCG	0.724**	0.498	0.747**	0.535
cMAX	0.751**	0.563	0.759**	0.599
cCG/#clicks	0.733**	0.551	0.751**	0.587
MAP@5	-	0.192	-	0.255
DCG@5	-	0.295	-	0.363
ERR@5	-	0.258	-	0.332
Weighted Rel. [20]	-	0.229	-	0.273

($R \leq 2$) and high usefulness ($U_u \geq 3$), and the clicks with high relevance ($R \geq 3$) and low usefulness ($U_u \leq 2$). We find that the major reason for the users reporting that a document with low relevance is actually very useful, is that the document is useful for the overall search task but not so relevant to the current issued query (e.g. Click 3 that we showed in Table 1). On the other hand, the users will report low usefulness for some relevant documents because (1) the document is redundant in content with previously seen documents in the search session [5]; (2) the dwell time on the document is short, the user might not read it as carefully as the assessors did in relevance annotation process [47]. These observations confirm once again that the query-level relevance judgments are unable to fully capture user's perceived usefulness.

Summary

To summarize, regarding **RQ1**, we find that although there is a moderate positive correlation between assessor's relevance annotation R and user's usefulness feedback U_u, there is a significant gap between these two document-level measures in our dataset. High relevance seems to be a necessary but not sufficient condition for high usefulness, which explains the success of the previous approaches using positive usefulness feedback as positive relevance feedback. The differences observed between assessor's relevance annotations and user's usefulness judgments also suggest that a system evaluation directly based on usefulness may be more appropriate.

5. RELEVANCE, USEFULNESS AND USER SATISFACTION

As stated by Kelly [27], "satisfaction can be understood as the fulfillment of a specified desire or goal". Satisfaction attempts to gauge users' actual feelings about the system. It is becoming an important criterion in the user-centric evaluation for Web search engines [1, 20]. As we observed in Section 4 that at document -level, user reported usefulness U_u is not well aligned with annotator's relevance annotation R, we further investigate their correlations with query-level and task-level user satisfaction ($QSAT_u$ and $TSAT_u$) to answer **RQ2**.

To do this, first we need to introduce some evaluation metrics to link document-level measures with query-level and task-level user satisfaction. In traditional batch evaluation paradigm, evaluation metrics, such as NDCG, MAP, and ERR, are used to summarize document-level relevance annotations to estimate query-level satisfactions. We refer to these classic metrics as *rank-based* metrics. On the other hand, the *click-sequence-based* metrics are computed based on the click sequences and document-level measures (i.e. usefulness or relevance) of clicked documents. We believe that this latter type of measure can better capture user satisfaction.

5.1 Correlation with Query-level Satisfaction

For query-level satisfaction, we use four click-sequence-based metrics: *cCG*, *cDCG*, *cMAX*, and *cCG/#clicks*. Click cumulated gain (*cCG*) for a query measures the total information gain, or utility, after submitting the query and viewing all the clicked documents in sequence. It is computed by summing up the document-level measures for all clicks under that query [23, 32]:

$$cCG(CS, M) = \sum_{i=1}^{|CS|} M(d_i)$$

Here, $CS = (d_1, d_2, \ldots, d_{|CS|})$ is the click sequence in which each element d_i is a clicked document. $M(d_i)$ is the document-level measure for document d_i. In this section, M can be either relevance annotation R or usefulness feedback U_u. *cCG/#clicks* is the average gain per click. Click discounted cumulative gain (*cDCG*) is defined as:

$$cDCG(CS, M) = \sum_{i=1}^{|CS|} \frac{M(d_i)}{log_2(i+1)}$$

cMAX assumes that the user's satisfaction is largely dependent on the most relevant or useful document s/he finds. It is given by:

$$cMAX(CS, M) = \max(M(d_1), M(d_2), \ldots, M(d_{|CS|}))$$

We also use four rank-based metrics: *MAP@5*, *DCG@5*, *ERR@5* and Weighted Relevance introduced by Huffman et al. [20]. All these metrics use cut-off at rank 5, because we only collected relevance annotations for top 5 documents in the relevance annotation stage (see Section 3.2). We do not use *nDCG* [21] here, because the computation of ideal *DCG* is biased when we do not have an exhaustive list of relevant documents.

As we only have usefulness measures for clicked document, we compare the click-sequence-based metrics based on usefulness feedback U_u with those based on relevance annotation R. We compute their correlations with query-level satisfaction $QSAT_u$, and use the rank-based metrics based on relevance annotation R as references. In order to compare two correlation coefficients (rs), we construct a t-statistic to test the significance of the difference between dependent r's [12]. As the cut-off of 5 for rank-based metrics may affect their correlations with satisfaction, especially when the user goes deeper than rank 5, we further compute and report the correlations for 637 queries that only has clicks among top 5 results.

The correlations are shown in Table 6. First, we can see that the correlations between $QSAT_u$ and the click-sequence-based metrics (shown in upper part of Table 6) are stronger than those between $QSAT_u$ and rank-based metrics (shown in the lower part of Table 6). The best rank-based metric is *DCG@5* with $r(933) = 0.295$ (the degrees of freedom is given by $\#queries - 2$). However, all the click-sequence-based metrics are more positively correlated with $QSAT_u$ than rank-based metrics, with all differences being significant at $p < 0.001$, two-tailed. Second, the click-sequence -based metrics based on U_u are more correlated with $QSAT_u$ than those based on R, with all the differences between two counterparts being significant at $p < 0.01$, two-tailed. $cCG(U_u)$, $cDCG(U_u)$ and $cCG(U_u)$ are strongly correlated with $QSAT_u$, with $r(933) > 0.7$. This result shows that user usefulness feedback is a much better indicator of user satisfaction than assessor's relevance annotations. Third, for the queries with only top 5 results clicked, the correlations between $QSAT_u$ and the rank-based metrics are slightly stronger than those for all queries; but they are still much weaker than those between click-sequence-based metrics and $QSAT_u$, with all differences being significant at $p < 0.01$, two-tailed. This suggests that click-based metrics can better capture user perceived satisfaction.

5.2 Correlation with Task-level Satisfaction

For task-level satisfaction, we only use four click-sequence-based metrics: *sCG*, *sCG/#queries*, *sCG/#clicks*, and *sDCG*. *sCG* is defined as the sum of each query's gain [22]. We use *cCG* to measure a query q_j's gain. So *sCG* is computed by:

$$sCG(M) = \sum_{j=1}^{n} gain(q_j) = \sum_{j=1}^{n} cCG(CS_j, M)$$

Table 7: Correlations with task-level satisfaction feedback $TSAT_u$.

Measured in Pearson's $r(df=223)$. The darker and lighter shadings indicate the correlation is significant at $p<0.01$ and 0.05. *(or **) indicates the difference is significant at $p<0.05(p<0.01)$, comparing to the same metric based on relevance annotation R.

	U_u	R
sCG	0.110**	-0.046
sCG/#queries	0.437**	0.330
sCG/#clicks	0.525**	0.320
sDCG	0.317**	0.142

Here n is the number of queries in the session. CS_j is the click sequence for q_j. *sCG/#queries* and *sCG/ #clicks* measure average gain per query and per click. *sDCG* [22] discounts the gains for later queries in a search session:

$$sDCG(M)=\sum_{j=1}^{n}\frac{gain(q_j)}{1+log(j)}=\sum_{j=1}^{n}\frac{cCG(CS_j,M)}{1+log(j)}$$

The correlations between these click-sequence-based metrics and the task-level satisfaction feedbacks $TSAT_u$ are shown in Table 7. Except for *sCG*, the other metrics significantly correlate with $TSAT_u$. The click-sequence-based metrics based on U_u are significantly more correlated with $TSAT_u$ than their counterparts based on R (with $p<0.01$, two-tailed). $sCG(U_u)/\#clicks$ is moderately correlated with task-level satisfaction $TSAT_u$, with $r(223)=0.525$.

Summary

In this section, regarding **RQ2**, we compare a variety of evaluation metrics based on either user's usefulness feedbacks U_u or assessor's relevance annotation R with query-level satisfaction feedbacks $QSAT_u$ and task-level satisfaction feedbacks $TSAT_u$. Comparing to the rank-based metrics, the click-sequence-based metrics are more related to users' query-level satisfaction feedbacks. Comparing to relevance, usefulness has a stronger correlation with user satisfaction in all metrics. These empirical results further suggest that: (1) when the click sequence is known, we can exploit click-sequence-based metrics to make a better user-oriented evaluation; (2) usefulness can better reflect user's real feelings in Web search than assessor's relevance.

6. COLLECTING USEFULNESS LABELS

In Section 4 and 5, we showed that there is a significant difference between assessor's relevance and user's usefulness. Although usefulness may be more suited for evaluating the Web search engine, it is unrealistic to collect explicit usefulness feedback from users. We have to resort to alternative approaches to assess and acquire document-level usefulness labels. In this section, with regard to **RQ3** and **RQ4**, we test two such approaches. The first one is to rely on external assessors to review augmented search logs and make document-level usefulness annotations. The second one uses a machine learning method and features extracted from behavior logs to estimate usefulness.

We evaluate these two usefulness estimation approaches in terms of their *reliability* and *validity*. As stated by Kelly [27] (p. 176), reliability is "the extent to which the method and measures yield consistent findings", and validity is "the extent to which methods and measures allow a researcher to get at the essence of whatever it is that is being studied". Reliability is a necessary condition for validity, and when combined together, these two criteria measure the extent to which the usefulness labels produced by theses two approaches can reflect the user-perceived usefulness of documents.

For usefulness annotation approach, we assess its reliability by calculating the inter-assessor agreement, and its validity by comparing usefulness annotations U_a with usefulness feedbacks from users U_u and correlating them with query-level satisfaction feedbacks $QSAT_u$. For usefulness prediction approach, we also

Table 8: Correlations with usefulness feedbacks U_u.

*(or **) indicates difference is significant at $p<0.05(p<0.01)$, comparing to the same metric related to R

	Pearson's r	*MSE*	*MAE*	Weighted κ
U_a	0.413**	1.51**	0.852**	0.321**
R	0.332	1.79	1.020	0.209

Table 9: Correlations with query-level satisfactions $QSAT_u$.

* (or **) indicates the difference between U_a and R is significant at $p<0.05(p<0.01)$. $^{\triangledown}$ (or $^{\blacktriangledown}$) indicates the difference between U_a and U_u is significant at $p<0.05(p<0.01)$. The darker and lighter shadings indicate the difference between U_a and $QSAT_a$ is significant at $p<0.01$ and 0.05.

	Pearson's $r(df=933)$			Pref. agreement ratio		
	U_a	U_u	R	U_a	U_u	R
cCG	.466▼/*	.572	.425	.701▼/**	.751	.669
cDCG	.518▼/*	.724	.498	.742▼/**	.826	.698
cMAX	.580▼/*	.751	.563	.681▼/**	.779	.632
cCG/#clicks	.548▼	.733	.551	.716▼/*	.807	.689
$QSAT_a$	.508			.584		

assess its validity by comparing the predicted usefulness scores with U_u and $QSAT_u$, and we use cross-validations and significance tests to ensure the results are reliable.

6.1 Usefulness Annotation

The detailed procedure of usefulness annotation is described in Section 3.2. So here we only describe and discuss the reliability and validity of collected usefulness annotations U_a.

To measure the reliability of usefulness annotation, we use Cohen's Weighted κ to assess the agreement between different assessors. As shown in Table 5, the κ for U_a ($\kappa_{U_a}=0.530$, $\sigma_{\kappa_{U_a}}=0.008$) is larger than those for R_c ($\kappa_{R_c}=0.413$, $\sigma_{\kappa_{R_c}}=0.010$) and R_{nc} ($\kappa_{R_{nc}}=0.344$, $\sigma_{\kappa_{R_{nc}}}=0.008$). The standard error of weighted κs are computed by the method introduced by Cohen [11]. The difference between κ_{U_a} and κ_{R_c} and the difference between κ_{U_a} and $\kappa_{R_{nc}}$ are both significant at $p<0.001$ (two-tailed independent t-tests). These results suggest that, measuring at the inter-assessor agreement level, the usefulness annotations are more *reliable* than the conventional relevance annotations. The possible reason is that providing search context and behavioral information (e.g. the full search task, search session and dwell times) to assessors may help them make judgments more consistently with the users. This is corroborated to some extent by the marginal distribution of U_a shown in Figure 3: unlike the relevance distribution concentrated on $R=3$, the distribution of U_a is a more similar to U_u than R, which indicates that, with the help of search context and user behavior information, the assessors can detect low usefulness clicks and make more discriminative judgements.

To assess the validity of usefulness annotation, we first compare U_a with the usefulness feedbacks U_u, which are used as the ground truth labels for usefulness. The correlations are measured in Pearson's r, Mean Squared Error (*MSE*), Mean Absolute Error (*MAE*), and Cohen's Weighted κ. The results are shown in Table 8. A moderate positive correlation ($r(1,510)=0.412$, $p<0.001$, two tailed) and a fair agreement ($\kappa=0.321$, $\sigma_\kappa=0.017$) between U_u and U_a are detected. The correlation between U_a and U_u is significantly stronger than that between R and U_u. We also show the joint distribution of U_u and U_a in Figure 4(b). The diagonal blocks are the darkest block in almost every rows and columns, showing a fair agreement between U_u and U_a. From the correlation metrics and the joint distribution we can see that although U_u and U_a are not perfectly aligned, comparing to relevance annotation, usefulness annotation can better reflect the user-perceived usefulness.

As shown in Section 5.1, a strong correlation exists between usefulness feedbacks and query-level satisfaction. Therefore, a valid assessment of usefulness should also correlate well with query-level satisfaction feedbacks $QSAT_u$. We use usefulness annotations U_a to compute four click-sequence-based metrics defined in Section 5.1: *cCG*, *cDCG*, *cMAX*, and *cCG/#clicks*, and correlate them with $QSAT_u$. Beside computing the Pearson's r for these correlations, we also conduct a naturalistic pairwise preference test. In the preference test, we extract 1,455 query pairs (q_i, q_j), where q_i and q_j belong to the same search session, and $QSAT_u(q_i) > QSAT_u(q_j)$. For each query pair, if an evaluation metric also indicates the same relative preference, then we say the evaluation metric agrees with $QSAT_u$ on that query pair. A similar method is used by Sanderson et al. [36]. As we only extract query pairs from the same search sessions, the preference test can effectively reduce the variabilities introduced by different users and different search tasks.

We report the correlations with $QSAT_u$, measured in Pearson's r and the agreement ratios in the preference test, in Table 9. We compare the correlations related to U_a to those related to relevance R (baseline) and usefulness feedbacks U_u (oracle performance). We also use the query-level satisfaction annotation from external assessors ($QSAT_a$) as another baseline. The results show that, although usefulness annotations U_a do not correlate with query-level satisfaction feedbacks $QSAT_u$ as well as usefulness feedbacks U_u from users (all the differences are significant at $p < 0.01$), most click-sequence-based metrics based on U_a outperform their counterparts based on R, in terms of correlation with $QSAT_u$. It is also interesting to observe that query-level satisfaction annotations from external assessors ($QSAT_a$) are quite different from query-level satisfaction feedbacks from users ($QSAT_u$), which is also observed by Liu et al. [32]. Some of click-sequence-based metrics based on U_a are significantly better than satisfaction annotations ($QSAT_a$), which suggests that document-level usefulness annotation may be more valid than query-level satisfaction annotation.

6.2 Usefulness Prediction

As previous studies show that there are substantial correlations between the user behavior signals (e.g. long dwell time [4, 31, 46], last click in a query [8, 24], and query position and reformulation types [34]) and evaluation-related measures like document relevance, search success, and user satisfaction, we attempt to use a regression model based on user behavior features and search context features to (1) automatically generate document-level usefulness labels, and (2) improve and enhance the document-level annotations (both R and U_a) so as to make them more aligned to users' usefulness feedbacks U_u.

Features

We list the features extracted from behavior logs in Table 10. We categorize these features into three groups: Query features (Q), Session features (S) and User features (U). Query features are the features related to a single query. With user behavior features, such as click numbers and dwell time included, they mainly describe how the user interacted with the search engine. Session features depend on the whole search session, and include short-term search context features like query position and query reformulation types. To compute User features, we need the long-term search history of that user. For (1) automatic usefulness label generation, only query features, session features and user features are involved (Q+S+U or referred to as All for simplicity). For (2) annotation enhancement, we extract relevance annotation features (R) and usefulness annotation features (A) from the annotation data. In particular, we use the document-level annotation itself, and the four interactive evaluation metrics computed by the document-level annotations, as relevance annotation features (R) and usefulness annotation features (A).

Prediction Models

We frame the usefulness prediction as a supervised regression problem, and use usefulness feedbacks (U_u) for clicked documents as the target value of the regression model. We perform five-fold cross-validation over search sessions to ensure the results are reliable. All the user features are computed on the training set. Since the cross-validation are performed over sessions, each session belongs to either the training set or the test set, the query and session features for a test document will not be present in the training set. We use a Gradient Boosting Regression Tree (GBRT) [17] as our regression model, because it can naturally handles mixed types of features, has a good predictive power, and is robust to outliers. A variety of feature combinations are tested. Similar to usefulness annotation studied in Section 6.1, we evaluate the validity of usefulness predictions in terms of their correlations with usefulness feedbacks (U_u), and their correlations with query-level satisfaction feedbacks ($QSAT_u$).

Table 10: Features to predict usefulness, extracted from the behavior logs.

Query features(Q)	
rank	The rank of clicked document in result list
#clicks	The number of clicks in the query
query length	The length of the query, in words and in characters
click position	Whether the click is the first/last/intermediate click in a query with more than one click, and whether the query has only one click
dwell time	click dwell time and query dwell time
Session features(S)	
#queries	The number of queries in the search session
#queries w/o click	The number of queries without click in session
query position	Whether the query is the first/last/intermediate query in a session with more than one query, and whether the session has only one query
time to completion	The total time spent on this search session
query reformulation	Whether the query is generated from a specification/ generalization/ parallel reformulation, and whether the query leads to a specification/ generalization/ parallel reformulation
User features(U)	
user #clicks	The average/max/min/standard deviation of #clicks per query of the user
user #queries	The average/max/min/standard deviation of #queries per session of the user
user #dwell time	The average/max/min/standard deviation of query/click dwell time of the user

Prediction Results

We measure the correlations between predicted usefulness scores and usefulness feedbacks from users (U_u) in Pearson's r, *MSE* and *MAE*. The results are shown in Table 11. We use subscripts to indicate the feature groups used in usefulness prediction, for examples, U_{Q} refers to the predicted usefulness based on the query features and U_{All} refers to the predictions based on all the features extracted from the behavior logs (i.e. Q+S+U). Both relevance annotation R and usefulness annotation U_a are used as baselines.

The results show that, as we add more behavior features, the performance of usefulness prediction increases, which proves that search context features (Q) and user-specific features (U) are useful in usefulness prediction. Comparing to R, all the predicted usefulness scores $U_{(\cdot)}$ are significantly more correlated with users' usefulness feedbacks, which once again demonstrates the gap between relevance and user-perceived usefulness. When we combine all the features extracted from the behavior logs, the resulting U_{All} establishes a comparable or stronger correlation with U_u, than usefulness annotation U_a does. This result suggests that when some usefulness feedbacks from users U_u are available for training, instead of relying on external assessors to generate usefulness annotation U_a, we can automatically generate document-level usefulness labels U_{All} of at least equal validity to U_a, based on the features that can be implicitly collected from behavior logs.

On the other hand, for (2) annotation enhancement, when we combined behavior features (All) with document-level annotations (A or R), significant improvements over the annotation-based baselines (U_a and R) are found. While it is not surprising to see $U_{\mathrm{All+A+R}}$ achieving the best performance, it is interesting to observe that $U_{\mathrm{All+R}}$ is better than $U_{\mathrm{All+A}}$. A possible reason for

Table 11: Results for usefulness prediction.

Measured in the correlations with usefulness feedback U_u. *(or **) indicates the difference between $U_{(\cdot)}$ and R is significant at $p < 0.05 (p < 0.01)$. The darker / lighter shadings indicates the difference between $U_{(\cdot)}$ and U_a is significant at $p < 0.05/0.01$.

	Pearson's r	*MSE*	*MAE*
U_{Q}	0.398*	1.198**	0.894**
U_{Q+S}	0.410**	1.186**	0.889**
U_{All}	0.461**	1.103**	0.851**
U_{All+A}	0.467**	1.105**	0.845**
U_{All+R}	0.519**	1.021**	0.815**
$U_{All+A+R}$	0.521**	1.023**	0.803**
U_a	0.413	1.512	0.852
R	0.332	1.786	1.020

Table 12: Correlations with query-level satisfactions $QSAT_u$.

Measured in Pearson's $r(df = 933)$. *(or **) indicates the difference between $U_{(\cdot)}$ and U_a is significant at $p < 0.05 (p < 0.01)$. $^{\triangledown}$(or $^{\blacktriangledown}$) indicates the difference between $U_{(\cdot)}$ and U_u is significant at $p < 0.05 (p < 0.01)$. The darker and lighter shadings indicate the difference between $U_{(\cdot)}$ and Jiang et al. [23] is significant at $p < 0.01$ and 0.05.

	U_{All}	$U_{All+A+R}$	U_a	U_u
cCG	0.459$^{\blacktriangledown}$	0.490$^{**/\blacktriangledown}$	0.466	0.572
cDCG	0.580$^{**/\blacktriangledown}$	0.612$^{**/\blacktriangledown}$	0.518	0.724
cMAX	0.601$^{\blacktriangledown}$	0.635$^{**/\blacktriangledown}$	0.580	0.751
cCG/#clicks	0.571$^{\blacktriangledown}$	0.608$^{**/\blacktriangledown}$	0.548	0.733
$QSAT_a$	0.508			
Jiang et al. [23]	0.539			

this is that while usefulness annotations inevitably depend on some behavior features like dwell time, the relevance annotations of documents are in some sense more complementary to the behavior features than usefulness annotations, thus U_{All+R} has a broader coverage of useful features than U_{All+A}.

Correlations with Query-level Satisfaction

We further demonstrate the validity of usefulness prediction approach by showing the correlations between predicted usefulness labels and query-level satisfaction feedbacks $QSAT_u$. Due to the lack of space, we only show the correlations in Pearson's r, since the preference test gives similar results. Usefulness annotation U_a and usefulness feedback U_u are used as document-level baselines; query-level satisfaction annotation $QSAT_a$ and a graded satisfaction prediction method based on user behavior features developed by Jiang et al. [23] are used as query-level baselines. Although our goal is not to predict satisfaction, we use this method as a baseline because we share similar behavior features, and the performance of a recently proposed satisfaction prediction model sets up a relatively high standard about how well one can predict satisfaction based on these features.

The results (Table 12) show the following facts: Firstly, because the correlations related to U_{All} are comparable or stronger when compared to those related to U_a, the usefulness predictions based on behavior features are at least as valid as usefulness annotations. Secondly, the usefulness predictions based on both behavior features and annotation features $U_{All+A+R}$ are significantly better than U_a (therefore better than R). We can thus use behavior features to enhance usefulness and relevance annotation. Finally, although there is still a significant gap between usefulness predictions (U_{All} and $U_{All+A+R}$) and usefulness feedbacks (U_u), the click-sequence-based metrics based on document-level usefulness predictions outperforms the query-level satisfaction prediction baselines in terms of correlations with $QSAT_u$, which indirectly proves that these usefulness predictions indeed reflect users' opinions and perception to some extent.

Summary

In this section, we proposed two usefulness labeling methods: usefulness annotation and automatic usefulness prediction, and conducted analyses to demonstrate their reliability ad validity. With regards to **RQ3**, we find that usefulness annotations are more reliable than conventional relevance annotations. The assessors in usefulness annotation process can detect low usefulness clicks effectively. The usefulness annotations collected in this process are shown to be valid due to their consistence with usefulness feedbacks and query-level satisfaction feedbacks from users. With regards to **RQ4**, we show that using behavior features, we can automatically generate valid usefulness labels, and improve existing document-level annotations so as to make them more aligned to usefulness feedbacks.

To summarize, we can collect reliable and valid usefulness labels by different approaches. When there is no usefulness feedback from any users at all, we can hire external assessors to generate usefulness annotation when provided with sufficient search context information. When there are some usefulness feedbacks from real users, we can use machine learning techniques and features extracted from behavior logs, to generate usefulness labels for other search sessions. We can also combine manual annotations from assessors and features from behavior logs to better estimate usefulness. In this case, if the cost of the additional annotations is taken into account, it is better to ask the assessors to make relevance judgments instead of usefulness annotations.

7. CONCLUSIONS AND DISCUSSIONS

In this work, through a carefully designed user study and dedicated annotation processes, we collected a comprehensive dataset that consists of behavior logs, user feedback data, and corresponding annotation data. Based on this dataset, we first investigated the difference and relationship between two document-level measures: the system-centric, highly-independent, relevance assessed by assessors, and the user-centric, situational, and subjective usefulness assessed by users. The results suggest that high relevance by assessors is a necessary but not sufficient condition for high usefulness for users, thus, in general, these two document-level measures are not aligned well. We further studied the correlations between relevance, usefulness, and user satisfaction, and found that usefulness is potentially of a great value in the evaluation of Web search engines since it is highly correlated with query-level satisfaction feedbacks. These findings partially explain why traditional system-centric evaluation metrics are not well aligned with user satisfaction. Finally, we proposed two approaches to collect usefulness labels in practical Web search settings, and evaluate them in terms of their reliability and validity.

Our findings and conclusions are based on a laboratory user study in which a set of predefined tasks are used and 29 participants are treated as real search users. Compared to a naturalist study based on real search logs, a laboratory user study has its limitations in its scale and the ecological validity of the collected data could be questioned. However, the laboratory study has the advantage to be able to control the variabilities that lie in the different information needs from different users. To enhance the ecological validity and ensure our findings can generalize, we carefully chose the search tasks and designed the experimental search system to simulate practical Web search scenarios.

The main focus of this paper is contrasting usefulness perceived by users with relevance annotations by assessors. Although we showed that it may be better to use the former in system evaluation rather than the latter, we do not expect the replacement can be done in all situations. Traditional relevance annotations have the advantage to be reusable, thus can be used to evaluate the system *in prior to* its deployment; while usefulness is suited in a more user-centric *post hoc* evaluation.

Our study makes a first step towards a new user-centric evaluation framework. A variety of click-sequence-based evaluation metrics (e.g. *cCG* and *cDCG*) are shown to be better suited for user-centric evaluations in this work. Their properties, and the assumptions and user models behind them are worth being investigated in the future. To fully establish a new evaluation framework based on usefulness and these metrics, more user studies that involve multiple search systems and more users are required in the future.

8. ACKNOWLEDGMENTS

This work was supported by Tsinghua University Initiative Scientific Research Program(2014Z21032), National Key Basic Research Program (2015CB358700), Natural Science Foundation (61532011, 61472206) of China and Tsinghua-Samsung Joint Laboratory for Intelligent Media Computing.

9. REFERENCES

[1] A. Al-Maskari, M. Sanderson, and P. Clough. The relationship between ir effectiveness measures and user satisfaction. In *Proc. SIGIR '07*, pages 773–774, New York, NY, USA, 2007. ACM.

[2] A. Al-Maskari, M. Sanderson, and P. Clough. Relevance judgments between trec and non-trec assessors. In *Proc. SIGIR '08*, pages 683–684, New York, NY, USA, 2008. ACM.

[3] N. J. Belkin, M. Cole, and R. Bierig. Is relevance the right criterion for evaluating interactive information retrieval. In *Proc. SIGIR '08 Workshop on Beyond Binary Relevance: Preferences, Diversity, and Set-Level Judgments.*, 2008.

[4] G. Buscher, L. van Elst, and A. Dengel. Segment-level display time as implicit feedback: A comparison to eye tracking. In *Proc. SIGIR '09*, pages 67–74, New York, NY, USA, 2009. ACM.

[5] J. Carbonell and J. Goldstein. The use of mmr, diversity-based reranking for reordering documents and producing summaries. In *Proc. SIGIR '98*, pages 335–336, New York, NY, USA, 1998. ACM.

[6] B. Carterette, E. Kanoulas, M. Hall, and P. Clough. Overview of the trec 2014 session track. 2013.

[7] O. Chapelle, D. Metlzer, Y. Zhang, and P. Grinspan. Expected reciprocal rank for graded relevance. In *Proc. CIKM '09*, pages 621–630, New York, NY, USA, 2009. ACM.

[8] O. Chapelle and Y. Zhang. A dynamic bayesian network click model for web search ranking. In *Proc. WWW '09*, pages 1–10, 2009.

[9] C. L. Clarke, M. Kolla, G. V. Cormack, O. Vechtomova, A. Ashkan, S. Büttcher, and I. MacKinnon. Novelty and diversity in information retrieval evaluation. In *Proc. SIGIR '08*, pages 659–666, 2008.

[10] C. Cleverdon. The cranfield tests on index language devices. In *Aslib proceedings*, volume 19, pages 173–194. MCB UP Ltd, 1967.

[11] J. Cohen. Weighted kappa: Nominal scale agreement provision for scaled disagreement or partial credit. *Psychological bulletin*, 70(4):213, 1968.

[12] J. Cohen and P. Cohen. *Applied multiple regression/correlation analysis for the behavioral sciences*, chapter 2, pages 53–54. Lawrence Erlbaum Associates, 1975.

[13] M. Cole, J. Liu, N. Belkin, R. Bierig, J. Gwizdka, C. Liu, J. Zhang, and X. Zhang. Usefulness as the criterion for evaluation of interactive information retrieval. *Proc. HCIR*, pages 1–4, 2009.

[14] W. S. Cooper. On selecting a measure of retrieval effectiveness. *JASIS*, 24(2):87–100, 1973.

[15] Z. Dou, R. Song, and J.-R. Wen. A large-scale evaluation and analysis of personalized search strategies. In *Proc. WWW '07*, pages 581–590, New York, NY, USA, 2007. ACM.

[16] S. Fox, K. Karnawat, M. Mydland, S. Dumais, and T. White. Evaluating implicit measures to improve web search. *ACM TOIS*, 23(2):147–168, 2005.

[17] J. H. Friedman. Greedy function approximation: a gradient boosting machine. *Annals of statistics*, pages 1189–1232, 2001.

[18] A. Hassan, R. Jones, and K. Klinkner. Beyond dcg: User behavior as a predictor of a successful search. In *Proc. WSDM '10*, pages 221–230, 2010.

[19] A. Hassan, R. W. White, S. T. Dumais, and Y.-M. Wang. Struggling or exploring?: Disambiguating long search sessions. In *Proc. WSDM '14*, pages 53–62, New York, NY, USA, 2014. ACM.

[20] S. Huffman and M. Hochster. How well does result relevance predict session satisfaction? In *Proc. SIGIR '07*, pages 567–574, 2007.

[21] K. Järvelin and J. Kekäläinen. Cumulated gain-based evaluation of ir techniques. *ACM TOIS*, 20(4):422–446, Oct. 2002.

[22] K. Järvelin, S. L. Price, L. M. Delcambre, and M. L. Nielsen. Discounted cumulated gain based evaluation of multiple-query ir sessions. In *Advances in Information Retrieval*, pages 4–15. 2008.

[23] J. Jiang, A. Hassan Awadallah, X. Shi, and R. W. White. Understanding and predicting graded search satisfaction. In *Proc. WSDM '15*, pages 57–66, New York, NY, USA, 2015. ACM.

[24] S. Jung, J. L. Herlocker, and J. Webster. Click data as implicit relevance feedback in web search. *Information Processing & Management*, 43(3):791–807, 2007.

[25] E. Kanoulas, B. Carterette, P. Clough, and M. Sanderson. Evaluating multi-query sessions. In *Proc. SIGIR '11*, pages 1053–1062, 2011.

[26] J. Kekäläinen and K. Järvelin. Using graded relevance assessments in ir evaluation. *JASIST*, 53(13):1120–1129, 2002.

[27] D. Kelly. Methods for evaluating interactive information retrieval systems with users. *Foundations and Trends in Information Retrieval*, 3(1—2):1–224, 2009.

[28] D. Kelly, X. Fu, and C. Shah. Effects of rank and precision of search results on users' evaluations of system performance. *University of North Carolina*, 2007.

[29] Y. Kim, A. Hassan, R. W. White, and I. Zitouni. Modeling dwell time to predict click-level satisfaction. In *Proc. WSDM '14*, pages 193–202, New York, NY, USA, 2014. ACM.

[30] J. R. Landis and G. G. Koch. The measurement of observer agreement for categorical data. *biometrics*, pages 159–174, 1977.

[31] C. Liu, J. Liu, N. Belkin, M. Cole, and J. Gwizdka. Using dwell time as an implicit measure of usefulness in different task types. *Proc. ASIST*, 48(1):1–4, 2011.

[32] Y. Liu, Y. Chen, and et. al. Different users, different opinions: Predicting search satisfaction with mouse movement information. In *Proc. SIGIR '15*, pages 493–502, 2015.

[33] A. Moffat, P. Thomas, and F. Scholer. Users versus models: What observation tells us about effectiveness metrics. In *Proc. CIKM '13*, pages 659–668, New York, NY, USA, 2013. ACM.

[34] D. Odijk, R. W. White, A. Hassan Awadallah, and S. T. Dumais. Struggling and success in web search. In *Proc. CIKM '15*, pages 1551–1560, New York, NY, USA, 2015. ACM.

[35] T. Sakai and R. Song. Evaluating diversified search results using per-intent graded relevance. In *Proc. SIGIR '11*, pages 1043–1052.

[36] M. Sanderson, M. L. Paramita, P. Clough, and E. Kanoulas. Do user preferences and evaluation measures line up? In *Proc. SIGIR '10*, pages 555–562, New York, NY, USA, 2010. ACM.

[37] T. Saracevic. Relevance reconsidered. In *the Second Conference on Conceptions of Library and Information Science*, volume 1, pages 201–218, 1996.

[38] M. Shokouhi, R. W. White, P. Bennett, and F. Radlinski. Fighting search engine amnesia: Reranking repeated results. In *Proc. SIGIR '13*, pages 273–282, New York, NY, USA, 2013. ACM.

[39] J. Teevan, S. T. Dumais, and E. Horvitz. Personalizing search via automated analysis of interests and activities. In *Proc. SIGIR '05*, pages 449–456, New York, NY, USA, 2005. ACM.

[40] A. Turpin and F. Scholer. User performance versus precision measures for simple search tasks. In *Proc. SIGIR '06*, pages 11–18, 2006.

[41] P. Vakkari and E. Sormunen. The influence of relevance levels on the effectiveness of interactive information retrieval. *JASIST*, 55(11):963–969, 2004.

[42] S. Verberne, M. Heijden, M. Hinne, M. Sappelli, S. Koldijk, E. Hoenkamp, and W. Kraaij. Reliability and validity of query intent assessments. *JASIST*, 64(11):2224–2237, 2013.

[43] E. M. Voorhees. The philosophy of information retrieval evaluation. In *the Second Workshop of the Cross-Language Evaluation Forum on Evaluation of Cross-Language Information Retrieval Systems*, CLEF '01, pages 355–370, 2002.

[44] E. M. Voorhees and D. Harman. Overview of trec 2001. In *Trec*, 2001.

[45] R. W. White and S. M. Drucker. Investigating behavioral variability in web search. In *Proc. WWW '07*, pages 21–30, 2007.

[46] R. W. White and D. Kelly. A study on the effects of personalization and task information on implicit feedback performance. In *Proc. CIKM '06*, pages 297–306, New York, NY, USA, 2006. ACM.

[47] E. Yilmaz, M. Verma, N. Craswell, F. Radlinski, and P. Bailey. Relevance and effort: An analysis of document utility. In *Proc. CIKM '14*, pages 91–100, New York, NY, USA, 2014. ACM.

How Many Workers to Ask? Adaptive Exploration for Collecting High Quality Labels

Ittai Abraham * Omar Alonso Vasilis Kandylas Rajesh Patel Steven Shelford
Aleksandrs Slivkins †

ABSTRACT

Crowdsourcing has been part of the IR toolbox as a cheap and fast mechanism to obtain labels for system development and evaluation. Successful deployment of crowdsourcing at scale involves adjusting many variables, a very important one being the number of workers needed per human intelligence task (HIT). We consider the crowdsourcing task of learning the answer to simple multiple-choice HITs, which are representative of many relevance experiments. In order to provide statistically significant results, one often needs to ask multiple workers to answer the same HIT. A stopping rule is an algorithm that, given a HIT, decides for any given set of worker answers to stop and output an answer or iterate and ask one more worker. In contrast to other solutions that try to estimate worker performance and answer at the same time, our approach assumes the historical performance of a worker is known and tries to estimate the HIT difficulty and answer at the same time. The difficulty of the HIT decides how much weight to give to each worker's answer. In this paper we investigate how to devise better stopping rules given workers' performance quality scores. We suggest adaptive exploration as a promising approach for scalable and automatic creation of ground truth. We conduct a data analysis on an industrial crowdsourcing platform, and use the observations from this analysis to design new stopping rules that use the workers' quality scores in a non-trivial manner. We then perform a number of experiments using real-world datasets and simulated data, showing that our algorithm performs better than other approaches.

Keywords: Crowdsourcing; label quality; ground truth; assessments; adaptive algorithms; multi-armed bandits.

1. INTRODUCTION

Crowdsourcing has become a central tool for improving the quality of search engines and many other large scale on-line services that require high quality assessments or labels. In this usage of crowdsourcing, a task or parts thereof are broadcast to multiple independent, relatively inexpensive workers, and their answers are aggregated. Automation and optimization of this process at a large scale allows to significantly reduce the costs associated with setting up, running, and analyzing experiments that contain such tasks.

In a typical industrial scenario that we consider in this paper, a *requester* has a collection of HITs, where each HIT has a specific, simple structure and involves only a small amount of work. We focus on multiple-choice HITs, that is, a HIT that contains a question with several possible answers. The goal of the requester is to learn the preference of the crowd on each of the HITs. For example, if a HIT asks whether a particular URL should be labeled as spam and most workers believe it should, then the requester would like to learn this. This abstract scenario with multiple-choice HITs covers important industrial applications such as relevance assessment and other optimizations for a web search engine and construction of training sets for machine learning algorithms. Obtaining high quality labels is not only important for both model training and development but also for quality evaluation.

The requester has two goals: extract high-quality information from the crowd (i.e., reduce the error rate), and minimize costs (e.g., in terms of money and time spent). There is a tension between these two goals; we will refer to it as the *quality-cost trade-off*. In practice, it is assumed that there is some noise from the crowd, so the requester defines in advance how many workers are needed per assignment for the whole task. This approach may not always be the right thing to do. For example, assessing the relevance of the query-URL pair (`facebook`, `www.facebook.com`) should need no more than one or two workers for such popular destination. In contrast, the pair (`solar storms`, `solarstorms.org`) would require more workers as the topic may not be familiar to some. Using a fixed number of workers may result in wasting resources for cases that are not needed or in not pooling more answers in assignments that require more power. Wouldn't it be useful if there is a flexible mechanism for adjusting the number of workers?

For cost-efficiency, one needs to take into account the heterogeneity in task difficulty and worker skills: some tasks are harder than others, and some workers are more skilled than others. Further, workers' relative skill level may vary from one task to another. In general, it is desirable to (1) use less aggregation for easier tasks, (2) use more skilled workers. The crowdsourcing system initially has a very limited knowledge of task difficulty, and possibly also of worker skills, but both can, in principle, be learned over time.

A common application that stems from the assessment scenario is the generation of ground truth or gold standard, usually called *gold* HITs or *honey pots*. These gold HITs are a set of HITs where the associated answers are known in advance. They can be a very effective mechanism to measure the performance of workers and data quality. Gold HITs are usually generated manually, typically

*VMware. Email: `ittaia@gmail.com`.
†All: Microsoft. `{omalonso, vakandyl, rajeshpa, steven.shelford, slivkins}@microsoft.com`.

SIGIR '16, July 17 - 21, 2016, Pisa, Italy

ISBN 978-1-4503-4069-4/16/07...$15.00

DOI: http://dx.doi.org/10.1145/2911451.2911514

by hired domain experts. This approach is not scalable: it is expensive, time consuming and error prone. We believe that much more automated systems should be available, whereby a requester starts with a relatively small gold HIT set for bootstrapping, and uses the crowd to generate arbitrarily larger gold HIT sets of high quality. A central challenge in designing a mechanism for automated gold HIT creation is cost-efficient quality control. With error-prone workers, one needs to aggregate the answers of several workers to obtain a statistically robust answer for a gold HIT.

We make the following contributions: (1) data analysis of HITs from a production platform, (2) design of two new stopping rule algorithms and (3) automatic generation of ground truth at scale. We now describe the specifics insights and improvements.

1. Data analysis of a crowdsourcing platform. We collected and analyzed a real-world data set from logs of UHRS, a large in-house crowdsourcing platform operated by a comercial search engine. We note that our data set cannot be easily replicated on a publicly accessible crowdsourcing platform such as Amazon Mechanical Turk. Indeed, this is a much larger data set (250,000 total answers) than one could realistically collect via targeted experiments (i.e., without access to platform's logs) because of budget and time limitations. Moreover, using realistic HITs in an open experiment tends to be difficult because of trade secrets.

Analysing the data, we make two empirical observations. First, we find that the difficulty of a random HIT is distributed near-uniformly across a wide range. Second, we investigate the interplay between HIT difficulty and worker quality, and we find that the high-quality workers are significantly better than the low-quality workers for the relatively harder tasks, whereas there is very little difference between all workers for the relatively easy tasks. These observations motivate our algorithms and allow us to construct realistic simulated workloads.

The above observations are based on a large-scale data analysis, which makes them valuable even if they may seem intuitive to one's common sense (albeit perhaps counterintuitive to someone else's). UHRS, Amazon Mechanical Turk, CrowdFlower, and others have similar architectural characteristics (e.g., HITs, task templates, payment system, etc.) so our data should be comparable to other platforms. Due to the proprietary nature of UHRS, this is the best information that we can share with the community.

2. Adaptive stopping rule algorithms. We consider obtaining a high-quality answer for a single HIT. We investigate a natural *adaptive* approach in which the platform adaptively decides how many workers to use before stopping and choosing the answer. The core algorithmic question here is how to design a *stopping rule*: an algorithm that at each round decides whether to stop or to ask one more worker. An obvious quality-cost trade-off is that using more workers naturally increases both costs and quality. In view of our empirical observation, we do not optimize for a particular difficulty level, but instead design *robust* algorithms that provide a competitive cost-quality trade-off for the entire range of difficulty.

As a baseline, we consider a scenario where workers are "anonymous", in the sense that the stopping rule cannot tell them apart. We design and analyze a simple stopping rule algorithm for this scenario, and optimize its parameters.

As workers vary in skill and expertise, one can assign quality scores to workers based on their past performance (typically, as measured on gold HITs). We investigate how these quality scores can help in building better stopping rules. While an obvious approach is to assign a fixed "voting weight" to each worker depending on the quality score, we find that more nuanced approaches perform even better. Given our empirical observations, we would like to utilize all workers for easy tasks, while giving more weight to better workers on harder tasks. As the task difficulty is not known a priori, we use the stopping time as a proxy: we start out believing that the task is easy, and change the belief in the "harder" direction over time as we ask more workers. We design a new adaptive stopping rule algorithm optimized for this setting. We conduct simulations based on the real workload, and conclude that this approach performs better than the "fixed-weight" approach.

We focus on the workers' quality scores that are given externally. This is for a practical reason: it is extremely difficult to design the entire crowdsourcing platform as a single algorithm that controls everything. Instead, one is typically forced to design the system in a modular way. In particular, while different requesters may want to have their own stopping rules, the crowdsourcing system may have a separate module that maintains workers' quality scores over different requesters.

3. Scalable gold HIT creation. Creating gold HITs presents additional challenges compared to the normal HITs. As the quality of the entire application (or successful experiment) hinges on the correctness of gold HITs, it is feasible and in fact desirable to route gold HITs to more reliable workers on the crowdsourcing platform. Worker quality is typically estimated via performance on the gold HITs that are already present in the system, so the estimates may be very imprecise initially, and gradually improve over time as more gold HITs are added. To find answers for individual HITs in a cost-efficient manner, one can use stopping rules as described above.

We tackle these challenges using ideas from *multi-armed bandits*, a problem space focused on sequentially choosing between a fixed and known set of alternatives with a goal to increase the cumulative reward and/or converge on the best alternative. A multi-armed bandit algorithm needs to trade off *exploration*, trying out various alternatives in order to gather information probably at the expense of short-term gains, and *exploitation*, choosing alternatives that perform well based on the information collected so far.

We consider a stylized model in which HITs arrive one by one, and the system sequentially assigns workers to a given HIT until it concludes that the answer is known with sufficient confidence. In particular, such system needs to "explore" the available workers in order to estimate their quality. We incorporate an insight from multi-armed bandits called *adaptive exploration*: not only the exploitation decisions, but also the exploration schedule itself can be adapted to the data points collected so far (e.g., we can give up early on low-performing alternatives). To implement adaptive exploration, we take a well-known approach from prior work on multi-armed bandits and tailor it to our setting, connecting it with the stopping rules described above. Our algorithm performs significantly better than the baseline uniform assignment of workers.

For algorithm evaluation we used the UHRS dataset discussed above, and also two previously published data sets from [26, 16]. Since the UHRS dataset is somewhat sensitive, we have been required to sanitize our results, and in particular we only evaluate on simulated data parameterized by the key properties of that dataset. One advantage of using a simulated workload is that one can replicate our algorithm evaluation (after choosing some values for the first column in Table 1). Also, we have been able to generate as much simulated data as needed for the experiments, whereas the available number of workers in the original data set was insufficient for some HITs.

The paper is organized as follows. Section 2 summarizes the related work on this area. We describe preliminary background in Section 3. We provide an analysis using data from an industrial crowdsourcing platform in Section 4. The design of a stopping rule for anonymous workers and its evaluation are described in Section 5. Similarly, the case for non-anonymous workers is described in Section 6. The gold HIT creation method is described in Section 7. Finally, conclusions and future work are outlined in Section 8.

2. RELATED WORK

The use of crowdsourcing as a cheap, fast and reliable mechanism for gathering labels was demonstrated in the areas of natural language processing [26], machine translation [8] and information retrieval [2] by running HITs on Amazon Mechanical Turk or CrowdFlower and comparing the results against an existing ground truth. While early publications have shown that majority voting is a reasonable approach to achieve good results, new strategies have emerged in the last few years. Jointly with that, several papers consider *task allocation*, the problem of allocating tasks to workers.

Oleson et al. [21] propose to use the notion of *programmatic gold*, a technique that employs manual spot checking and detection of bad work, in order to reduce the amount of manual work. Ground truth creation is a problem for new evaluation campaigns when no gold standard is available. Blanco et al. [6] rely on manual creation of gold answers for monitoring worker quality in a semantic search task. Scholer et al. [23] study the feasibility of using duplicate documents as ground truth in test collections.

Sheng et al. [24] design an algorithm that adaptively decides how many labels to use on a given HIT based on the distribution of all previously encountered HITs. Crucially, they assume that all HITs have the same difficulty for a given worker. However, our empirical evidence shows that HITs have widely varying difficulty levels; our algorithms are tailored to deal with this heterogeneity. Also, they optimize the quality of an overall classification objective, rather than the error rate.

Other approaches use the EM algorithm to estimate the workers' accuracy and the final HIT result at the same time [12]. The work presented in [16] is another algorithm based on EM, with several improvements. EM-based solutions use information from all the HITs in the data set and assume that a worker is answering many (or all) of these HITs and with more or less similar performance across them. Our approach is to consider each HIT individually and without using information from previously answered HITs. Because of this, we do not need to make the assumption that all the HITs are of similar difficulty. Additionally, it is not necessary to have the same workers answer multiple HITs. In fact, each HIT could be answered by a completely new set of workers. In a later section of this paper we make the additional assumption that we have knowledge of the overall quality of the workers, but we still consider that HITs could have varying (and unknown) difficulties.

Vox Populi [13] is a data cleaning algorithm that prunes low quality workers with the goal of improving a training set. The technique uses the aggregate label as an approximate ground truth and eliminates the workers that tend to provide incorrect answers.

Karger et al. [19] optimize task allocation given budgets. Unlike ours, their solution is non-adaptive, in the sense that the task allocation is not adapted to the answers received so far. Further, [19] assume known Bayesian prior on both tasks and judges, whereas we do not.

From a methodology perspective, CrowdSynth [18] focuses on addressing consensus tasks by leveraging supervised learning.

Parameswaran et al. [22] consider a setting similar to our stopping rules for HITs with two possible answers. Unlike us, they assume that all HITs have the same difficulty level, and that the (two-sided) error probabilities are known to the algorithm. They focus designing algorithms for computing an optimal stopping rule.

Settings similar to stopping rules for anonymous workers, but incomparable on a technical level, were considered in prior work, e.g. [4], [17], [5], [11], [20], [1].

For scalable gold HIT creation, our model emphasizes explore-exploit trade-off, and as such is related to multi-armed bandits; see [9, 7] for background on bandits and [25] for a discussion of explore-exploit problems that arise in crowdsourcing markets. Our algorithm builds on a bandit algorithm from Auer et al. [3].

Ho et al. [15], Abraham et al. [1] and Chen et al. [10] consider models for adaptive task assignment with heterogeneity in task difficulty levels and worker skill that are technically different from ours. In [15], the interaction protocol is "inverted": workers arrive one by one, and the algorithm sequentially and adaptively assigns tasks to each worker before irrevocably moving on to the next one. The exploration schedule in [15] is non-adaptive, unlike ours, in the sense that it does not depend on the observations already collected. The solution in [1] focuses on a single HIT. The algorithm in [10] develops an approach based on Bayesian bandits that requires exact knowledge of the experimentation budget and the Bayesian priors.

3. PRELIMINARIES

A HIT is a question with a set of S of possible answers. For each HIT we assume that there exists one answer which is the correct answer (more on this below under "probabilistic assumptions"). A requester has a collection of HITs, which we call a *workload*. The goal of the requester is to learn what is the correct answer for each HIT. The requester has access to a crowdsourcing system.

We model a stylized crowdsourcing system that operates in rounds. In each round the crowdsourcing systems chooses one HIT from the workload and a worker arrives, receives the HIT, submits her answer and gets paid a fixed amount for her work. The crowdsourcing system needs to output an answer for each HIT in the workload. The algorithm can adaptively decide for each HIT how many workers to ask for answers. We mostly focus on a single HIT. In each round, a worker arrives and submits an answer to this HIT. The algorithm needs to decide whether to stop (stopping rule) and if so, which answer to choose (selection rule).

There are two measures to be minimized in such an algorithm: (1) the *error rate* for this workload (the percentage of HITs for which the algorithm outputs the wrong answer), and (2) the *average cost* for this workload (the average cost per HIT paid to the workers by the algorithm). Formally this is a bi-criteria optimization problem. If all workers are paid equally, the average cost is simply the average number of rounds.

Probabilistic Assumptions. We model each worker's answer as a random variable over S, and assume that these random variables are mutually independent. We assume that the most probable answer is the same for each worker. For the purposes of this paper, the "correct answer" is just the most probable answer, and this is the answer that we strive to learn.The difference between the probability of the most probable answer and the second most probably answer is called the *bias* of a given worker on a given HIT. This quantity, averaged over all workers, is the *bias* of a given HIT. A large bias (close to 1) corresponds to our intuition that the HIT is very easy: the error rate is very small, whereas a small bias (close to 0) implies that the HIT is hard, in the sense that it is very difficult to distinguish between the two most probable options. Here, our notion of easy/hard HITs is objective (reflecting agreement with majority), rather than subjective (reflecting workers' sentiments). Hereafter we use the bias of a HIT as a measure of its hardness. In particular, we say that HIT A is *harder* than HIT B if the bias of A is smaller than the bias of B.

4. DATA ANALYSIS

We performed our analysis using data from UHRS, a large in-house crowdsourcing platform operated by Microsoft. UHRS is used by many different internal groups for evaluation, label collection, and machine learning applications. The tasks range from TREC-like evaluations to domain specific labeling and experimentation. In particular, UHRS is used to gather training and evaluation data for various aspects of the search engine.

Using the logs of UHRS, we collected a data set from a variety of tasks and workers. In that data set, we selected all tasks that contained at least 50 HITs, and all HITs with at least 50 answers. These HITs have been used for training and/or quality control, which explains an unusually large number of answers per HIT. This large number has been essential for our purposes. We considered all HITs in all these tasks. This gave us a data set containing 20 tasks, 3,000 workers, 2,700 HITs, and 250,000 total answers. For each HIT we computed the majority answer, which we considered as the "correct" answer. Details of the different types of HITs, design templates, and other specific metrics are left out due to proprietary information.

Empirical Biases of HITs. Workers' replies to a given HIT are, at first approximation, IID samples from some fixed distribution $\mathcal{D}$. A crucial property of $\mathcal{D}$ is the difference between the top two probabilities, which we call bias of this HIT; note that the bias completely defines $\mathcal{D}$ if there are only two answers. Informally, larger bias corresponds to easier HIT. We study the distribution over biases in our workload. For each HIT, we consider the empirical frequencies of answers, and define "empirical bias" as the difference between the top two frequencies. We plot the CDF for empirical biases in Figure 1.

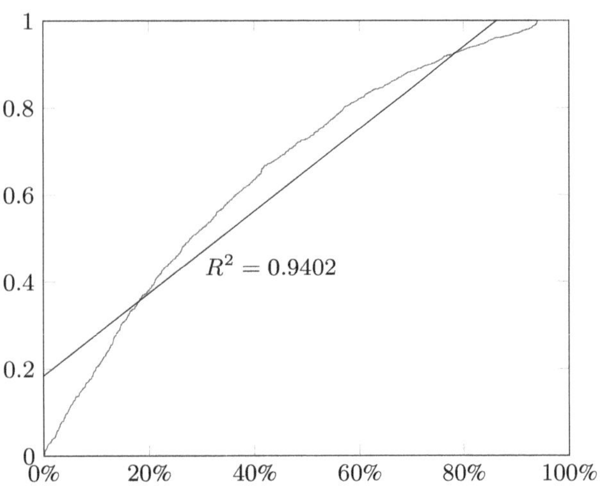

Figure 1: CDF for the empirical bias of HITs.

We conclude that HITs have a wide range of biases: some are significantly more difficult than others. In particular, tailoring a decision rule to HITs with a specific narrow range of biases is impractical. Further, we observe that the empirical distribution is, roughly, near-uniform. We use this observation to generate the simulated workload in the next section.

Error Rates. For each worker, we compute the average error rate across all HITs that she answered. According to that, we split all workers into 9 equally sized groups, from best-performing (W_0) to worst-performing (W_8). Similarly, for each HIT we compute the average error rate across all workers that answered it. We split all HITs into 9 equally-sized groups, from easiest (H_0) to most difficult (H_8). Let $\texttt{error}(W_i, H_j)$ be the average error rate of the workers in the worker group W_i when answering the HITs in the HIT group H_j.

To make our main finding clearer, and also because our data set is somewhat sensitive, we report a 9-by-8 table (see Table 1): for each HIT group $H_i, i = 0 \dots 8$ and each worker group $W_j, j = 1 \dots 8$, the corresponding cell contains the difference

$$\texttt{error}(W_i, H_j) - \texttt{error}(W_0, H_j). \quad (1)$$

The table is also visualized as a heat map in Figure 2.

%	W_1	W_2	W_3	W_4	W_5	W_6	W_7	W_8
H_0	0	0	0	1	1	1	2	4
H_1	1	1	2	2	3	4	6	15
H_2	1	3	3	4	6	8	11	20
H_3	1	4	4	7	7	11	16	27
H_4	4	7	8	12	13	17	23	36
H_5	5	9	11	14	18	20	26	43
H_6	7	11	15	18	22	25	30	47
H_7	11	14	19	21	25	26	33	48
H_8	19	24	27	29	31	35	39	50

Table 1: Error rates for different worker/HIT groups. The cell (W_i, H_j) contains the difference (1), in percent points.

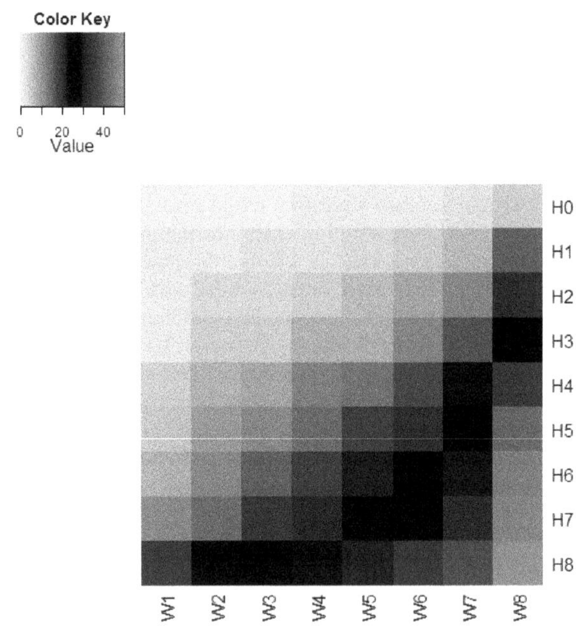

Figure 2: Error rates for different worker/HIT groups.

Findings. From Table 1, we make the following observations. For difficult tasks ($H_6 \dots H_8$) the set of good judges ($W_0 \dots W_2$) is significantly better (has a lower error rate) than the set of bad judges ($W_6 \dots W_8$). For easy tasks ($H_0 \dots H_2$) there is very little difference between *all judges* (expect perhaps for the very worst judges).

These observations are robust to changing the number of HIT and worker groups (from 5 to 9). To summarize, *the difference in performance between good and bad workers is much more significant for harder HITs than for easier HITs.* Accordingly, we devise algorithms that tend to use all workers for easier HITs, and favor better workers for more difficult HITs.

5. STOPPING RULE FOR ANONYMOUS WORKERS

We start with a simpler case when workers are anonymous, in the sense that there is no prior information on which workers are better than others. Absent such information, we treat all workers equally: essentially, we give each worker's vote the same weight.

5.1 Algorithm

For simplicity, let us assume there are only two answers for a HIT: A and B. In each round t, let $V_{A,t}$ and $V_{B,t}$ be the number of workers that vote for A and B, respectively. Note that $t = V_{A,t} + V_{B_t}$. Our stopping rule is as follows:

$$\text{Stop if } |V_{A,t} - V_{B,t}| \geq C\sqrt{t} - \epsilon t. \tag{2}$$

Here $\epsilon \geq 0$ and $C \geq 0$ are parameters that need to be chosen in advance. After the algorithm stops, the selection rule is simply to select the most frequent answer. Note that the right-hand side is not an integer, so we can randomly round it to one of the two closest integers in a way that is proportional to the fractional part.

Discussion. Our intuition is that each worker's reply is drawn IID from some fixed distribution over answers; recall that the bias of a HIT is the difference between the top two probabilities in this distribution. For two answers:

$$\texttt{bias} = |\Pr[A] - \Pr[B]|$$

Informally, the meaning of parameter ϵ is that we are willing to tolerate a higher error rate for HITs with $\texttt{bias} \leq \epsilon$, in order to improve the error-cost trade-off for the entire workload. We find in our simulations that a small value of ϵ performs better than $\epsilon = 0$.

Parameter C controls the error-cost trade-off: increasing it increases the average cost and decreases the error rate. In practice, the parameters (C, ϵ) should be adjusted to typical workloads to obtain the desirable error-cost trade-off.

Analysis. For the sake of analysis, let us consider a slight modification of algorithm (2) in which parameter C is proportional to $\log t$ (we view this dependence as minor compared to the $\sqrt{t}$ term).

We prove that our algorithm returns a correct answer with high probability if $\texttt{bias} \geq \epsilon$. We consider two hypotheses:

(H1) The correct answer is A and $\texttt{bias} \geq \epsilon$,

(H2) The correct answer is B and $\texttt{bias} \geq \epsilon$.

Effectively, if one hypothesis is right, our algorithm rejects the other with high probability.

With $\epsilon = 0$, the expected cost (stopping time) is on the order of $\texttt{bias}^{-2}$, in line with standard results on biased coin tossing. Using $\epsilon > 0$ relaxes this to $(\epsilon + \texttt{bias})^{-2}$.

Lemma 5.1 *Fix $\delta \in (0,1)$. Consider the algorithm (2) with parameters $\epsilon > 0$ and $C = C_t = \sqrt{\log(t^2/\delta)}$. Suppose this algorithm is applied to a HIT with* $\texttt{bias} = \epsilon_0$.

(a) *If $\epsilon_0 \geq \epsilon$ then the algorithm returns a correct answer with probability at least $1 - O(\delta)$.*

(b) *The expected cost (stopping time) is at most $O\left(\rho^{-2} \log \frac{1}{\delta\rho}\right)$, where $\rho = \epsilon + \epsilon_0$.*

PROOF. W.l.o.g., suppose $\Pr[A] \geq \Pr[B]$. Consider the difference $Z_t = V_{A,t} - V_{B,t} - \epsilon_0 t$, where t ranges over rounds. The increments $Z_t - Z_{t-1}$ are independent random variables with mean 0 and values ± 1, so Z_t is a random walk. Therefore for each t:

$$\Pr[|Z_t| \leq C_t\sqrt{t}] \geq 1 - O(\delta/t^2). \tag{3}$$

by a standard application of the *Azuma-Hoeffding Inequality*. Taking the Union Bound over all t, it follows that

$$\Pr\left[|Z_t| \leq C_t\sqrt{t} \quad \text{for all } t\right] \geq 1 - O(\delta). \tag{4}$$

For part (a) assume that hypothesis (H1) holds, i.e. that $\epsilon_0 \geq \epsilon$, but the algorithm returns an incorrect answer, i.e. stops at some round t so that answer B is chosen. We show this cannot happen if the high-probability event in (4) holds. Indeed, at such round t:

$$V_{B,t} - V_{A,t} > C_t\sqrt{t} - \epsilon t$$
$$Z_t < (\epsilon - \epsilon_0)t - C_t\sqrt{t} < -C_t\sqrt{t}.$$

The latter contradicts the high-probability event in (4).

For part (b), let T be the stopping time. Consider round t such that $t \geq (2C_t/\rho)^2$. For any such round, the high-probability event $\{Z_t > -C_t\sqrt{t}\}$ implies that

$$V_{A,t} - V_{B,t} > -C_t\sqrt{t} + \epsilon_0 t \geq C_t\sqrt{t} - \epsilon t,$$

so the algorithm stops at round t or earlier, i.e., $T \leq t$. By (3), we conclude that $\Pr[T > t] < O(\delta/t^2)$. Now, there exists $t_0 = O(\rho^{-2} \log \frac{1}{\delta\rho})$ such that $t \geq (2C_t/\rho)^2$ for all $t \geq t_0$. Therefore:

$$\mathbb{E}[T] = \textstyle\sum_{t=1}^{\infty} \Pr[T > t] \leq t_0 + \sum_{t>t_0} \delta/t^2 = t_0 + O(\delta).$$

So the expected stopping time $\mathbb{E}[T]$ is as small as we claimed. □

Extension to multiple answers. One can extend the stopping rule (2) to more than two answers in an obvious way. At time t, let $A^*(t)$ and $B^*(t)$ be the answers with the largest and second-largest number of votes, respectively. The stopping rule is

$$\text{Stop if } V_{A^*(t),t} - V_{B^*(t),t} \geq C\sqrt{t} - \epsilon t. \tag{5}$$

The selection rule is to select the most frequent answer.

Lemma 5.1 easily carries over to multiple answers. (The proof considers a separate random walk for each pair of answers A, B:

$$Z_t^{A,B} = V_{A,t} - V_{B,t} - t(\Pr[A] - \Pr[B]),$$

obtains high-probability event $\{|Z_t^{A,B}| \leq C_t\sqrt{t}\}$ as in (3), and then conditions on the intersection of all such events.)

5.2 Experimental Results

We used a simulated workload, consisting of 100,000 HITs, each with two answers. For each HIT, the bias towards the correct answer (the difference between the probabilities of the two answers) was chosen uniformly at random in the interval $[0.1, 0.6]$. This closely matches an empirical distribution of biases, as we have found in the previous experiments. For each worker answering this HIT, the answer was chosen independently at random with the corresponding bias.

For each pair (ϵ, C) of parameters, running our algorithm on a single HIT gives a two-fold outcome: the cost and whether the correct answer was chosen. Thus, running our algorithm on all HITs in our workload results in two numbers: average cost and error rate (over all HITs). We plot these pairs of numbers on a coordinate plane where the axes are average cost and error rate. Thus, fixing ϵ and varying C we obtain a curve on this plane, which we call the *varying-C curve*.

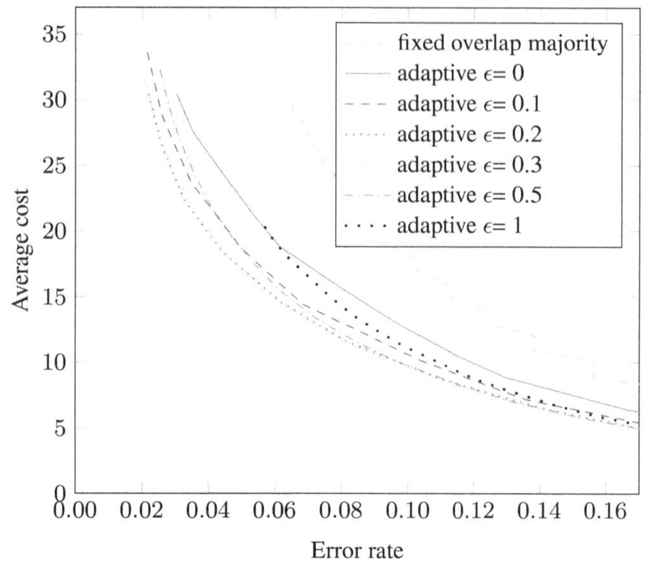

Figure 3: Cost-quality trade-off for fixed overlap majority and the adaptive algorithm on a simulated data set.

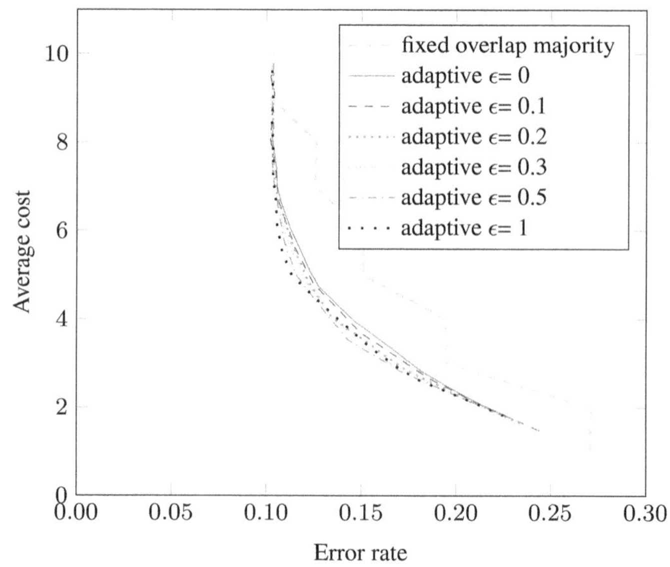

Figure 4: Cost-quality trade-off for fixed overlap majority and the adaptive algorithm on the RTE data set.

We consider several values for ϵ, ranging from 0 to 1. For each value of ϵ, we plot the corresponding varying-C curve (Figure 3). We also plot, as baseline, the fixed overlap majority algorithm, which uses a fixed number of annotations per HIT (we vary from 1 to 30) and uses simple majority voting (breaking ties randomly). This technique is used in [26]. Surprisingly, we find that, up to some minor noise, for any two varying-C curves it holds that one lies below another. This did not have to be the case, as two curves could criss-cross. If one varying-C curve lies below another varying-C curve, this means that the ϵ parameter for the former curve is always better: for any C, it gives better average cost for the same error rate. Thus, we find that for any two significantly different values of parameter ϵ, one value is better than another, regardless of the C. From Figure 3, we find that the most promising range for ϵ is $[.2, .3]$. We have omitted the less interesting values for clarity.

We repeat the same experiment with the NLP RTE data set from [26]. The RTE data set contains 800 HITs and 10 annotations per HIT. For the fixed overlap majority algorithm we randomly sampled a fixed number of worker labels per HIT (varying the fixed number to produce the curve), whereas for the other algorithms we randomly permuted the order of the worker labels. The results we report are the averages of the error rates and costs over 100 runs (Figure 4). As with the simulated data set, the adaptive algorithm performs better than the fixed overlap majority. Because of the 10 annotations per HIT, it is impossible to do better than the minimum error rate of about 0.11, which is achieved when all available annotations are used. However, the adaptive algorithm can achieve approximately the same error with much lower average cost (about 6 instead of 10).

Finally, we repeat the same experiment with the adult data set from [16]. This data set contains classifications of web pages into four categories (G, PG, R, X), depending on the adult content on the page. There are 500 web pages with approximately 100 labels per page. We were unable to obtain from the authors the original gold labels of the web pages that they used for their experiments, therefore we computed the majority answer per web page and treated that as gold. Using the same adult data set, we also run the EM-based algorithm from [16], known as Get Another Label (GAL). The original algorithm also contains a majority voting step that can be used to break ties using label priors (we call GAL with this step GAL majority vote). For GAL, GAL majority vote and the fixed overlap majority algorithms we randomly sampled a fixed number of worker labels per HIT (varying the fixed number to produce the curves), whereas for the other algorithms we randomly permuted the order of the worker labels. The results we report are the averages of the error rates and costs over 100 runs (Figure 5). We have omitted some curves for the adaptive algorithm for clarity. The performance of the adaptive algorithm is better than fixed overlap majority and GAL. This is not too surprising, considering that both GAL and fixed overlap majority use a fixed number of labels for every HIT so they cannot really decrease the cost by stopping early like adaptive does. The GAL majority vote algorithm performs comparably to the fixed overlap majority which is expected as they only differ on how they break ties. Somewhat surprisingly, GAL performed worse than the GAL majority vote. We believe this was caused by the way we generated the ground truth. Since we could not obtain the original ground truth of the adult data set, we used the majority answer as ground truth and this may have impacted the results.

6. STOPPING RULE FOR NON-ANONYMOUS WORKERS

Depending of the task and qualifications required, some workers may be better than others, and one can often estimate who is better by looking at the past performance. We assume workers have a one-dimensional personal measure of *expertise* or skill level, which influences their error rate on HITs. Further, we assume we have access to a *reputation system* which can (approximately and coarsely) rank workers by their expertise level. We develop a weighted version of the stopping rule from Section 5 that is geared to take advantage of such a reputation system. We begin by describing a general weighted stopping rule, then detail how we use it.

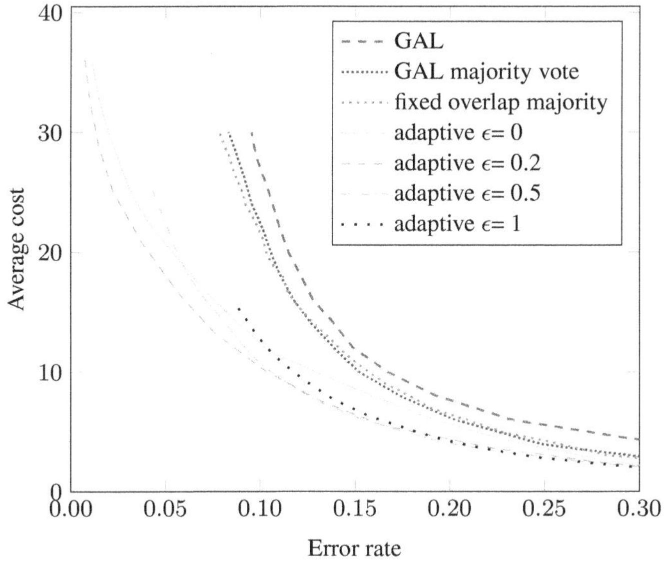

Figure 5: Cost-quality trade-off for fixed overlap majority, Get Another Label (GAL) and the adaptive algorithm on the adult data used by Get Another Label.

6.1 Algorithm

In each round t, the worker is assigned weight w_t. In general, the weights may depend on the available information about the worker and the task. Also, the stopping rule can update the next worker's weight depending on the number t itself. For now, we do not specify *how* the weights are assigned. Absent any prior information on the workers, all weights are 1. Such stopping rules will be called *unweighted*; we have discussed them in Section 5.

Fix some round t. The weighted vote $V_{A,t}$ for a given answer A is defined as the total weight of all workers that arrived up to (and including) round t and chose answer A. For simplicity, assume there are only two answers: A and B. Our stopping rule is as follows:

$$\text{Stop if } |V_{A,t} - V_{B,t}| \geq C\sqrt{\textstyle\sum_{s=1}^{t} w_s^2} - \epsilon \textstyle\sum_{s=1}^{t} w_s. \quad (6)$$

Here $C > 0$ and $\epsilon \in [0, 1)$ are parameters that need to be chosen in advance. Note that in the unweighted case ($w_t \equiv 1$), this reduces to Equation (2). Our default selection rule is to choose the answer with the largest weighted vote. We call this the *deterministic* selection rule.

Discussion. The goal for weighted stopping rule is identical to the unweighted case: among the two hypotheses (H1) and (H2), reject the one that is wrong.

Letting $W_{t,q} = (\sum_{s=1}^{t} w_s^q)^{1/q}$, we can re-write the stopping rule (6) more compactly as

$$\text{Stop if } |V_{A,t} - V_{B,t}| \geq C\,W_{t,2} - \epsilon W_{t,1}. \quad (7)$$

The meaning of the right-hand side is as follows. $Z_t = V_{A,t} - V_{B,t}$ can be viewed as a biased random walk: its increments $Z_t - Z_{t-1}$ are independent random variables with values $\pm w_t$ and mean $\epsilon_0 = \Pr[A] - \Pr[B]$. The expected drift of this random walk is $\mathbb{E}[Z_t] = \epsilon_0\, W_{t,1}$. Thus, the term $\epsilon W_{t,1}$ in (7) is a lower bound on the expected drift assuming either (H1) or (H2) holds. The meaning of the $C\,W_{t,2}$ term in (7) is that $W_{t,2}$ is the best available upper bound on the standard deviation of Z_t.

Extension to multiple answers. It is easy to extend the stopping rule (6) to more than two answers. Let A and B be the answers with the largest and second-largest weighted vote, respectively. The stopping rule is

$$\text{Stop if } V_{A,t} - V_{B,t} \geq C\,W_{t,2} - \epsilon W_{t,1}. \quad (8)$$

Defining the weights. We restrict our attention to *coarse* quality scores. This is because a reputation system is likely to be imprecise in practice, especially in relation to a specific HIT. So more fine-grained quality scores, especially continuous ones, are not likely to be meaningful.

Suppose each worker is assigned a coarse quality score $\texttt{qty}$, e.g. $\texttt{qty} \in \{\texttt{good}, \texttt{average}, \texttt{bad}\}$. Our general approach, which we call *reputation-dependent exponentiation*, is as follows. For each possible quality score $\texttt{qty}$ we have an initial weight $\lambda_{\texttt{qty}}$ and the multiplier $\gamma_{\texttt{qty}}$. If in round t a worker with quality score $\texttt{qty}$ is asked, then her weight is

$$w_t = \lambda_{\texttt{qty}}\, \gamma_{\texttt{qty}}^{t-1}$$

A notable special case is *time-invariant weights*: $\gamma_{\texttt{qty}} = 1$.

The intuition is that we want to gradually increase the weight of the better workers, and gradually decrease the weight of the worse workers. The gradual increase/decrease may be desirable because of the following heuristic argument. As we found empirically (see Table 1), the difference in performance between good and bad workers is more significant for hard HITs, whereas for very easy HITs all workers tend to perform equally well. Therefore we want to make the difference in *weights* between the good and bad workers to be more significant for harder HITs. While we do not know a priori how difficult a given HIT is, we can estimate its difficulty as we get more answers. One very easy estimate is the number of answers so far: if we asked many workers and still did not stop, this indicates that the HIT is probably hard. Thus, we increase/decrease weights gradually over time.

6.2 Experimental Results

Simulated workload. We use the real data 9-by-9 table of error rates for different worker and HIT groups to generate a simulated workload that consists of 100,000 HITs, all with two answers, and 100 workers that answer all these HITs. We split workers uniformly across worker groups, and split HITs uniformly among HIT groups. For each worker and each HIT, the correct answer is chosen with the probability given by the corresponding cell in the table. We define a coarse quality score depending on the worker group: the best three worker groups were designated *good*, the middle three *average* and the last three *bad*. This quality score is given as input to the algorithm.

Algorithms tested. We tested several "reputation-dependent exponentiation" algorithms. Recall that the weights in each such algorithm are defined by the initial weights $\lambda_{\texttt{qty}}$ and the multipliers $\gamma_{\texttt{qty}}$ for each quality score $\texttt{qty} \in \{\texttt{good}, \texttt{average}, \texttt{bad}\}$. For convenience, we denote the initial weights $\vec{\lambda} = (\lambda_{\texttt{good}}, \lambda_{\texttt{average}}, \lambda_{\texttt{bad}})$ and likewise the multipliers $\vec{\gamma} = (\gamma_{\texttt{good}}, \gamma_{\texttt{average}}, \gamma_{\texttt{bad}})$. We experimented with many assignments for $(\vec{\lambda}, \vec{\gamma})$. Below we report on several paradigmatic versions:

1. No weights (all weights are set to 1, $\vec{\lambda} = (1, 1, 1)$):
   - *Fixed overlap majority:* Same as section 5.2, uses a fixed number of annotations (i.e. overlap) per HIT and computes the simple majority answer. Ties are broken randomly. We vary the overlap parameter to produce the cost-error curve.

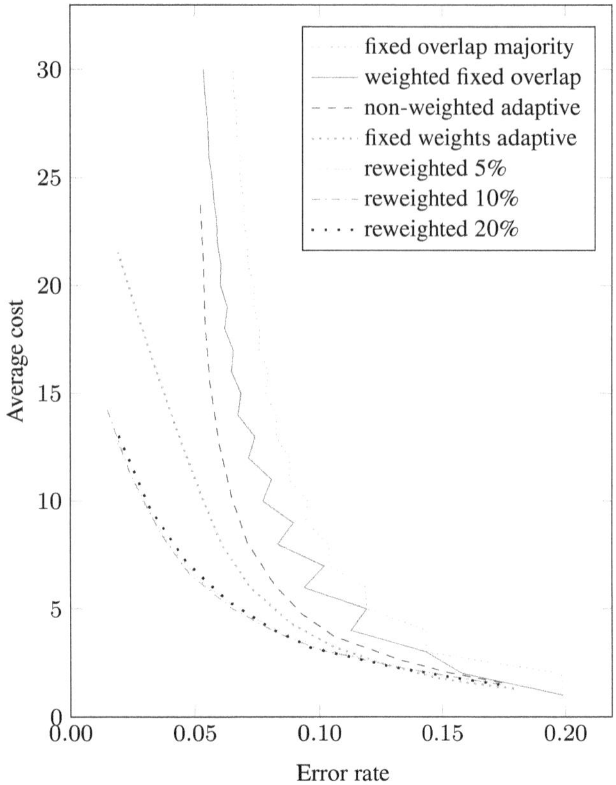

Figure 6: Cost-error trade-off for weighted stopping rules. (For all varying-C curves, $\epsilon = 0.2$.)

- *Non-weighted adaptive:* The adaptive algorithm from the previous section, which assumes all the workers are anonymous.

2. Time-invariant weights (multipliers are set to 1, $\vec{\gamma} = (1, 1, 1)$):

   - *Weighted fixed overlap:* Same as the fixed overlap majority algorithm, but the majority is weighted, using weights $\vec{\lambda} = (1.2, 1, 0.8)$.
   - *Fixed weights adaptive:* Similar to the adaptive algorithm, but uses the weighted stopping rule with weights $\vec{\lambda} = (1.2, 1, 0.8)$. The weights do not change during execution.

3. Time-varying weights. All weights start equal to 1 ($\vec{\lambda} = (1, 1, 1)$), but they increase/decrease by certain multipliers per round. We consider different multipliers $\vec{\gamma}$, so that weights change as follows.

   - *Reweighted adaptive 5%:* The weights change by 5% per round with multipliers $\vec{\gamma} = (1.05, 1, 0.95)$.
   - *Reweighted adaptive 10%:* The weights change by 10% per round with multipliers $\vec{\gamma} = (1.1, 1, 0.9)$.
   - *Reweighted adaptive 20%:* The weights change by 20% per round with multipliers $\vec{\gamma} = (1.2, 1, 0.8)$.

For each assignment of $(\vec{\lambda}, \vec{\gamma})$, we consider several values for the parameter ϵ, and for each ϵ we plotted a varying-C curve in the error rate vs. expected cost plane. To showcase our findings, some representative choices are shown in Figure 6.

Our findings. As in the previous section, we find that (up to some minor noise) for any two varying-C curves, one lies below another. This enables comparisons between different algorithms that are valid for all choices of parameter C. We conclude:

- Using weights is better than not. The weighted fixed overlap algorithm performs better than the non-weighted version. Similarly, the adaptive algorithm performs better with weights (fixed or time-varying) than in the non-weighted (anonymous workers) case.
- The adaptive algorithm performs better than the fixed overlap majority, even if the adaptive does not use weights, and the fixed overlap does.
- For the adaptive, it is better to update the weights per round, rather than keeping them fixed.
- How much the weights get updated does not have a big effect in performance (for the range of 5% to 20% that was tested).
- It is better to use $\epsilon > 0$. The best value for ϵ is usually in the range $[.2, .3]$, and the effect of changing ϵ within this range is usually very small. This follows from experiments not shown in figure 6, but also supported in the experiments of the previous section and Figure 3.

We also experimented with various other combinations of weight updating schemes and multiplier values, which are not shown in the figure. We tried updating the weights every four rounds rather than every round (updating by $\gamma^4_{\texttt{qty}}$, accordingly, for each quality score $\texttt{qty}$), and we found that updating every round performs better. We also tried updating only the weights of the good workers (or only the weights of the bad workers) and the differences were very small.

Further, we investigated the effect of the magnitude of the multipliers $\vec{\gamma}$. We tried the previously mentioned weighted adaptive algorithm with multipliers that modify the worker weights by 5%, 10%, 20%, 30%, 40% and 50% (for example, $\vec{\gamma} = (1.3, 1, 0.7)$ for 30% weight updates). We found the differences to be very small, with the updates of 5% and 10% to be very slightly better.

7. SCALABLE GOLD HIT CREATION

We turn to the problem of scalable gold HIT creation, as described in the Introduction. We consider a stylized model with heterogeneity in worker quality but not in HIT difficulty. The system processes a stream of HITs, possibly in parallel. Each HIT is assigned to workers, sequentially and adaptively, at unit cost per worker, until the gold HIT answer is generated with sufficient confidence or the system gives up. Worker skill levels are initially not known to the algorithm, but can be estimated over time based on past performance. The goal is to minimize the total cost while ensuring low error rate.

Algorithm. We adopt the following idea from prior work on multi-armed bandits: for each worker, combine exploration and exploitation in a single numerical score, updated over time, and at each decision point choose a worker with the highest current score [27, 14, 3]. This score, traditionally called an *index*, takes into account both the average skill observed so far (to promote exploitation) and the uncertainty from insufficient sampling (to promote exploration). Over time, the algorithm zooms in on more skilled workers.

We use a simple algorithm which builds on [3, 1]. For each worker i, let t_i be the number of performed HITs for which the algorithm has generated a gold HIT answer, and let t_i^+ be the number of those HITs where the worker's answer coincides with the gold HIT. If $t_i \geq 1$, we define this worker's index as

$$\texttt{Index}_i = \frac{t_i^+}{t_i} + \frac{1}{\sqrt{t_i}}.$$

Note that $\texttt{Index}_i \le 2$. For initialization, we set $\texttt{Index}_i = 2$.

Now that we've defined $\texttt{Index}_i$, the algorithm is very simple:

- At each time step, pick a worker with the highest index, breaking ties arbitrarily.
- For each HIT, use the unweighted stopping rule (5) to decide whether to stop processing this HIT. Then the gold HIT answer is defined as the majority answer.

Experimental setup. To study the empirical performance of our index-based algorithm, we use a simulation parameterized by real data as follows. We focus on HITs with binary answers. We have $1,000$ workers and each worker generates a correct answer for each HIT independently, with some fixed probability (*success rate*) which reflects her skill level. The success rate of each worker is drawn independently from a realistic "quality distribution" $\mathcal{D}_{\texttt{qty}}$.

We determined $\mathcal{D}_{\texttt{qty}}$ by examining a large set ($> 1,500$) of real workers from our internal platform (cf. Section 4), and computing their average success rates over several months. Thus we obtained an empirical quality distribution, which we approximate by a low degree polynomial (see Figure 7).

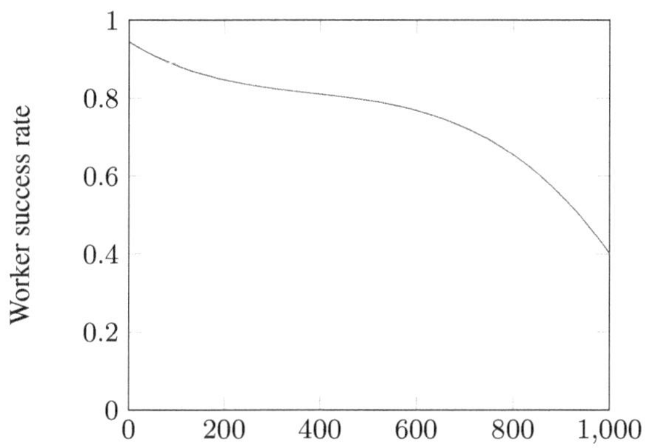

Figure 7: Worker quality distribution $\mathcal{D}_{\texttt{qty}}$.

We compare our index-based algorithm to a naive algorithm, called Random, which assigns each HIT to a random worker. Both algorithms use the same unweighted stopping rule (5). In our simulation, each algorithm processes HITs one by one (but in practice the HITs could be processed in parallel).

Recall that the stopping rule comes with two parameters, ϵ and C. We consider three different values of ϵ, namely $\epsilon = 0$, $\epsilon = 0.05$ and $\epsilon = 0.1$. (Recall that according to our simulations in Section 5, $[0.05, 2]$ is the most promising range for ϵ.) For each algorithm and each value of ϵ, we vary the parameter C to obtain different cost vs. quality trade-offs. For each value of C, we compute 5K gold HITs using each algorithm. Thus, for each algorithm and each value of ϵ we obtain a varying-C curve. The simulation results are summarized in Figure 8. The main finding is that our index-based algorithm reduces the per-HIT average cost by 35% to 50%, compared to Random with the same error rate. Recall that the cost here refers to the number of workers, which in practical terms translates to both time and money. Thus, we suggest adaptive exploration, and particularly index-based algorithms, as a very promising approach for automated gold HIT creation.

8. DISCUSSION AND CONCLUSIONS

In this paper, we mainly focus on the issue of deciding how many workers to ask for a given HIT. The number of workers asked defines a trade-off between the cost of the HIT and the error rate of the

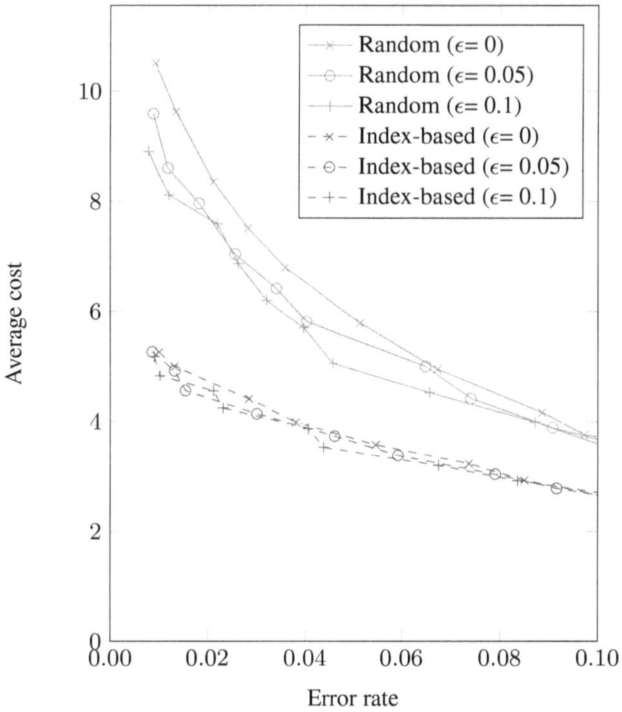

Figure 8: Simulation results.

final answer. We propose an adaptive stopping rule which, every time a worker is asked, decides whether to stop or continue asking another worker. The stopping rule takes into account the differences in the workers' answers and the uncertainty from the limited number of these answers. This allows asking few workers for easy HITs, where their answers are mostly identical, and thus incurring low cost. On the other hand, for harder HITs, more workers are asked in order to maintain a low error rate. A simpler scheme that uses a fixed number of workers per HIT wastes answers on the easy HITs and lacks enough answers on the harder HITs.

If workers' skill levels are approximately known from their past performance, we can improve the stopping rule to take the skill levels into account. The difficulty of a new HIT is, as before, assumed to be unknown. From our data analysis we know that all workers tend to perform well on easy HITs, whereas on harder HITs the skill level of the workers tends to make a big difference. We can thus estimate the HIT difficulty by the number of answers when the stopping rule decided to stop. We use this information to re-weight the answers of the workers according to their known skill, so that for harder HITs we rely more on the better workers. With other EM-based algorithms, the assumption is that we do not know much about the workers and we try to assign a score to them that corresponds to how good they are (e.g., spammers get a low score, whereas workers that are giving correct answers get a high score). The EM-based algorithms try to estimate the worker scores at the same time as estimating the HIT answers. If workers give answers that agree with the estimated ones, then they tend to get high scores. Our adaptive algorithm instead assumes that we know how good or bad the workers are. What it tries to estimate is how easy or hard the HIT is, and what should be the HIT answer. The idea is that for easy HITs, even poorly performing workers are quite reliable So, if we can figure out that a HIT is easy we can rely on pretty much every worker, whereas if a HIT is hard we should discount the answers of the bad workers. The adaptive algorithm estimates the difficulty of the HIT based on how much the workers agree or disagree and then assigns a weight to each worker's answer that relies on both the estimated difficulty of the HIT and the worker quality. This also means that the worker weights differ from HIT to HIT.

One can envision an approach where the worker skill is not known beforehand but can be learned algorithmically. For example, after the stopping rule decides to stop and produce a final answer for the HIT, we could compare the worker's answer to the final answer. If their answer matches, we can assume they gave a correct answer. This approach is particularly suitable to the problem of scalable gold HIT creation. However, further research is required to establish if this can produce accurate results in practice or if it leads to "self-fulfilling loops" where the workers who are considered skilled provide the same wrong answer. Such answer is then interpreted as the "correct" answer by the system, which in turn reinforces the belief that these workers are highly skilled.

While our stopping rules return a single answer for a given HIT, they can be extended to HITs with *several* correct answers. For example, if the vote difference is small between the top two answers, but large between the second and the third answer, then we could stop and output the top two answers as both being correct. With similarly simple modifications, the rules can be expanded to deal with HITs in which the answers correspond to specific numerical values. In that case, it is not only the vote difference that matters but also the difference between the corresponding numerical values. These extensions are the subject of future research.

Acknowledgments. We thank Jennifer Wortman Vaughan for providing valuable feedback.

9. REFERENCES

[1] Ittai Abraham, Omar Alonso, Vasilis Kandylas, and Aleksandrs Slivkins. Adaptive crowdsourcing algorithms for the bandit survey problem. In *26th COLT*, 2013.

[2] Omar Alonso and Stefano Mizzaro. Using crowdsourcing for TREC relevance assessment. *Inf. Process. Manage.*, 48(6):1053–1066, 2012.

[3] Peter Auer, Nicolò Cesa-Bianchi, and Paul Fischer. Finite-time analysis of the multiarmed bandit problem. *Machine Learning*, 47(2-3):235–256, 2002.

[4] R. E. Bechhofer, S. Elmaghraby, and N. Morse. A single-sample multiple decision procedure for selecting the multinomial event which has the highest probability. *Annals of Mathematical Statistics*, 30:102–119, 1959.

[5] R. E. Bechhofer and D. Goldsman. Truncation of the bechhofer-kiefer-sobel sequential procedure for selecting the multinomial event which has the largest probability. *Communications in Statistics – Simulation and Computation*, B14:283–315, 1985.

[6] Roi Blanco, Harry Halpin, Daniel M. Herzig, Peter Mika, Jeffrey Pound, Henry S. Thompson, and Duc Thanh Tran. Repeatable and reliable search system evaluation using crowdsourcing. In *34th SIGIR*, 2011.

[7] Sébastien Bubeck and Nicolo Cesa-Bianchi. Regret Analysis of Stochastic and Nonstochastic Multi-armed Bandit Problems. *Foundations and Trends in Machine Learning*, 5(1):1–122, 2012.

[8] Chris Callison-Burch. Fast, cheap, and creative: Evaluating translation quality using amazon's mechanical turk. In *EMNLP*, pages 286–295, 2009.

[9] Nicolò Cesa-Bianchi and Gábor Lugosi. *Prediction, learning, and games*. Cambridge Univ. Press, 2006.

[10] Xi Chen, Qihang Lin, and Dengyong Zhou. Optimistic knowledge gradient for optimal budget allocation in crowdsourcing. In *30th ICML*, 2013.

[11] Paul Dagum, Richard M. Karp, Michael Luby, and Sheldon M. Ross. An optimal algorithm for monte carlo estimation. *SIAM J. on Computing*, 29(5):1484–1496, 2000.

[12] Alexander Philip Dawid and Allan M Skene. Maximum likelihood estimation of observer error-rates using the em algorithm. *Applied statistics*, pages 20–28, 1979.

[13] Ofer Dekel and Ohad Shamir. Vox populi: Collecting high-quality labels from a crowd. In *22nd COLT*, 2009.

[14] J. C. Gittins. Bandit processes and dynamic allocation indices (with discussion). *J. Roy. Statist. Soc. Ser. B*, 41:148–177, 1979.

[15] Chien-Ju Ho, Shahin Jabbari, and Jennifer Wortman Vaughan. Adaptive task assignment for crowdsourced classification. In *30th ICML*, 2013.

[16] Panagiotis Ipeirotis, Foster Provost, and Jing Wang. Quality Management on Amazon Mechanical Turk. In *HCOMP*, 2010.

[17] J. T. Ramey Jr. and K. Alam. A sequential procedure for selecting the most probable multinomial event. *Biometrica*, 66:171–173, 1979.

[18] Ece Kamar, Severin Hacker, and Eric Horvitz. Combining human and machine intelligence in large-scale crowdsourcing. In *11th AAMAS*, 2012.

[19] David R. Karger, Sewoong Oh, and Devavrat Shah. Iterative learning for reliable crowdsourcing systems. In *25th NIPS*, pages 1953–1961, 2011.

[20] Volodymyr Mnih, Csaba Szepesvári, and Jean-Yves Audibert. Empirical bernstein stopping. In *25th ICML*, pages 672–679, 2008.

[21] David Oleson, Alexander Sorokin, Greg Laughlin, Vaughn Hester, John Le, and Lukas Biewald. Programmatic gold: Targeted and scalable quality assurance in crowdsourcing. In *Human Computation Workshop*, 2011.

[22] Aditya G. Parameswaran, Hector Garcia-Molina, Hyunjung Park, Neoklis Polyzotis, Aditya Ramesh, and Jennifer Widom. Crowdscreen: algorithms for filtering data with humans. In *ACM SIGMOD*, pages 361–372, 2012.

[23] Falk Scholer, Andrew Turpin, and Mark Sanderson. Quantifying test collection quality based on the consistency of relevance judgements. In *Proceeding of the 34th International ACM SIGIR*, pages 1063–1072, 2011.

[24] Victor S. Sheng, Foster J. Provost, and Panagiotis G. Ipeirotis. Get another label? improving data quality and data mining using multiple, noisy labelers. In *14th KDD*, 2008.

[25] Aleksandrs Slivkins and Jennifer Wortman Vaughan. Online decision making in crowdsourcing markets: Theoretical challenges. *SIGecom Exchanges*, 12(2), December 2013.

[26] Rion Snow, Brendan O'Connor, Daniel Jurafsky, and Andrew Y. Ng. Cheap and fast - but is it good? evaluating non-expert annotations for natural language tasks. In *EMNLP*, pages 254–263, 2008.

[27] William R. Thompson. On the likelihood that one unknown probability exceeds another in view of the evidence of two samples. *Biometrika*, 25(3-4):285–294, 1933.

Risk-Sensitive Evaluation and Learning to Rank using Multiple Baselines

B. Taner Dinçer[1], Craig Macdonald[2], Iadh Ounis[2]

[1] Sitki Kocman University of Mugla, Mugla, Turkey

[2] University of Glasgow, Glasgow, UK

dtaner@mu.edu.tr[1],{craig.macdonald, iadh.ounis}@glasgow.ac.uk[2]

ABSTRACT

A robust retrieval system ensures that user experience is not damaged by the presence of poorly-performing queries. Such robustness can be measured by risk-sensitive evaluation measures, which assess the extent to which a system performs worse than a given baseline system. However, using a particular, single system as the baseline suffers from the fact that retrieval performance highly varies among IR systems across topics. Thus, a single system would in general fail in providing enough information about the real baseline performance for every topic under consideration, and hence it would in general fail in measuring the real risk associated with any given system. Based upon the Chi-squared statistic, we propose a new measure Z_{Risk} that exhibits more promise since it takes into account multiple baselines when measuring risk, and a derivative measure called GeoRisk, which enhances Z_{Risk} by also taking into account the overall magnitude of effectiveness. This paper demonstrates the benefits of Z_{Risk} and GeoRisk upon TREC data, and how to exploit GeoRisk for risk-sensitive learning to rank, thereby making use of multiple baselines within the learning objective function to obtain effective yet risk-averse/robust ranking systems. Experiments using 10,000 topics from the MSLR learning to rank dataset demonstrate the efficacy of the proposed Chi-square statistic-based objective function.

1. INTRODUCTION

The classical evaluation of information retrieval (IR) systems has focused upon the arithmetic mean of their effectiveness upon a sample of queries. However, this does not address the *robustness* of the system, i.e. its effectiveness upon the worst performing queries. For example, while some retrieval techniques (e.g. query expansion [2, 8]) perform effectively for some queries, they can orthogonally cause a decrease in effectiveness for other queries. To address this, various research into robust and *risk-sensitive* measures has taken place. For instance, in the TREC Robust track, systems were measured by geometric mean average precision [23, 25] to determine the extent to which they perform well on all queries. More recently, the notion of risk-sensitivity has been introduced, in that an evaluation measure should consider per-query losses and gains compared to a particular baseline technique [11]. Within this framework, measures such as U_{Risk} [27] and T_{Risk} [13] have been proposed. Both measures can be adapted to integrate with the state-of-the-art LambdaMART learning to rank technique.

Since risk-sensitive measures compare to a specific baseline, such measures are most naturally applied in experiments using a *before-and-after* design, where different treatments are applied to a particular baseline system, e.g. query expansion. However, when simply considering a single baseline, a full knowledge of the difficulty of a particular query cannot be obtained. For instance, a single baseline system may perform lowly for a query that other systems typically perform well. For this reason, the inference of risk based upon a population of baseline systems is attractive. One can easily draw an analogy with the building of ranking methods that combine multiple weighting models, such as data fusion or learning to rank, to obtain a more effective final ranking. Moreover, the use of multiple baselines permits a deployed search engine to evaluate the risk of an alternative retrieval approach not only with respect to its own baseline, but also to other competitor systems.

In this paper, we show how a risk-sensitive evaluation based on the Chi-square test statistic permits the consideration of multiple baselines, unlike the existing measures U_{Risk} & T_{Risk} which can only consider a single baseline. In doing so, we argue that a robust system should not be less effective for a given topic than an *expectation* of performance given a population of other (baseline) systems upon that topic. In particular, this paper contributes: a new risk-sensitive evaluation measure, namely Z_{Risk}, based on Chi-square test statistic, and a derivative called GeoRisk that enhances Z_{Risk} by also taking into account the overall magnitude of effectiveness; Moreover, we demonstrate the use of Z_{Risk} and GeoRisk upon a TREC comparative evaluation of Web retrieval systems; Finally, we show how to directly and effectively integrate GeoRisk within the state-of-the-art LambdaMART learning to rank technique.

This paper is organised as follows: Section 2 provides a background on robust and risk-sensitive evaluation; Section 3 defines Z_{Risk} based upon Chi-squared statistic, as well as the GeoRisk derivative; Section 4 & Section 5 demonstrate the proposed measures upon synthetic & real TREC data, while Section 6 shows the integration of GeoRisk within the LambdaMART learning to rank technique; Related work and concluding remarks follow in Sections 7 & 8.

2. RISK-SENSITIVE EVALUATION

Risk-sensitive evaluation [11] aims at quantifying the trade-off between risk and reward for any given retrieval strat-

SIGIR '16, July 17–21, 2016, Pisa, Italy.

DOI: http://dx.doi.org/10.1145/2911451.2911511

egy. Information retrieval performance, which is usually measured by a given retrieval effectiveness measure (e.g. NDCG@20, ERR@20 [9]) over a set of topics Q, can be expressed in terms of risk and reward as a risk function. Such a risk function takes into account the downside-risk of a new system s with respect to a given baseline system b (i.e. a loss: performing a topic q worse than the baseline according to the effectiveness measure, $s_q < b_q$) and an orthogonal reward function that takes into account the upside-risk (i.e. a win: performing a topic better than the baseline, $s_q > b_q$).

A single measure, U_{Risk} [27], which allows the tradeoff between risk and reward to be adjusted, is defined as:

$$\mathrm{U}_{Risk} = \frac{1}{c}\left[\sum_{q\in Q_+}\delta_q + (1+\alpha)\sum_{q\in Q_-}\delta_q\right], \quad (1)$$

where $c = |Q|$ and $\delta_q = s_q - b_q$. The left summand in the square brackets, which is the sum of the score differences δ_q for all q where $s_q > b_q$ (i.e. $q \in Q_+$), gives the total win (or upside-risk) with respect to the baseline. On the other hand, the right summand, which is the sum of the score differences δ_q for all q where $s_q < b_q$, gives the total loss (or downside-risk). The risk sensitivity parameter $\alpha \geq 0$ controls the tradeoff between reward and risk (or win and loss): $\alpha = 0$ calculates the average change in effectiveness between s and b, while for higher α, the penalty for under-performing with respect to the baseline is increased: typically $\alpha = 1, 5, 10$ [12] to penalise risky systems, where $\alpha = 1$ doubles the emphasis of down-side risk compared to $\alpha = 0$.

Recently, Dinçer et al. [13] introduced a statistically-grounded risk-reward tradeoff measure, T_{Risk}, as a generalisation of U_{Risk}, for the purposes of hypothesis testing:

$$\mathrm{T}_{Risk} = \frac{\mathrm{U}_{Risk}}{SE(\mathrm{U}_{Risk})}, \quad (2)$$

where $SE(\mathrm{U}_{Risk})$ is the *standard error* in the risk-reward tradeoff score U_{Risk}. Here, T_{Risk} is a linear monotonic transformation of U_{Risk}. This transformation is called *studentisation* in statistics (c.f., t-scores) [16], and T_{Risk} can be used as the test statistic of the Student's t-test. Moreover, the aforementioned work shows that T_{Risk} permits a state-of-the-art learning to rank algorithm (LambdaMART) to focus on those topics that lead to a significant level of risk in order to learn effective yet risk-averse ranking systems.

On the other hand, the comparative risk-sensitive evaluation of different IR systems is challenging, as the systems may be based upon a variety of different (base) retrieval models – such as learning to rank or language models – or upon different IR platforms (Indri, Terrier etc.). It has been shown that using a particular system as the baseline in a comparative risk-sensitive evaluation of a set of diverse IR systems – as attempted by the TREC 2013 and 2014 Web track – yields biased risk-reward tradeoff measurements [14], especially when the systems under evaluation are not variations of the provided baseline system. To address this, the use of the within-topic mean system performance was proposed as an unbiased baseline (as well as the within-topic median system performance and the within-topic maximum system performance). Given a particular topic q and a set of r systems, the arithmetic mean of the r performance scores according to an evaluation measure observed on q is the unbiased baseline score:

$$\mathrm{Mean}_q = \frac{1}{r}\sum_{i=1}^{r} s_i(q), \quad (3)$$

where $s_i(q)$ is the performance score of system i on topic q measured by a given evaluation measure (e.g. ERR@20) for $i = 1, 2, \ldots, r$. Since the arithmetic mean gives equal weight to every retrieval strategy in determining the within-topic mean system performance, a baseline system that is determined by the Mean_q scores will be unbiased with respect to the retrieval strategies yielding the r system scores.

However, as shown in [14], the use of Mean_q exposes a problem about the validity of the comparative risk-sensitive evaluation of different IR systems. This issue is related to the risk-based rankings of the systems obtained using Mean_q. Indeed, such a comparison of the risk-sensitive performances of different IR systems actually implies the comparison of the retrieval effectiveness of the individual systems based on the underlying effectiveness measure, i.e. ERR-@20 [14]. That is, the ranking of the systems obtained by using the underlying effectiveness measure will be the same as the risk-based ranking of the systems obtained using the unbiased baseline Mean_q, irrespective of the value of the risk sensitivity parameter α.

Most importantly, the previously proposed risk measures are only sensitive to the mean and the variance of the observed losses and wins, i.e. U_{Risk} is sensitive to mean and T_{Risk} is sensitive to mean and variance (c.f. $SE(\mathrm{U}_{Risk})$). However in a comparative risk-sensitive evaluation, we argue that it is necessary to be sensitive to the shape of the score distributions, as well as the mean and the variance. As such, in the next section, we propose the Z_{Risk} measure, which satisfies the aforementioned variance and shape requirements of a comparative risk-sensitive IR evaluation, while the derivative GeoRisk measure enhances Z_{Risk} by naturally incorporating the overall effectiveness of the considered system.

3. MEASURES OF RISK FROM CHI-SQUARE

Each existing robust and risk-sensitive evaluation measure each encodes properties about what a good (or bad) IR system should exhibit. Firstly, the classical mean measure (e.g. MAP or mean NDCG) stipulates that a good system should perform well on a population of topics on average; The geometric mean (e.g. as proposed in [24] for Mean Average Precision as GMAP) says that a good system should avoid performing lowly on any topics, while comparing GMAP values permits identifying improvements in low performing topics, in contrast to mean, which gives equal weight to absolute changes in per-topic scores, regardless of the relative size of the change [4]. Risk-sensitive evaluation measures such as U_{Risk} and T_{Risk} use the notion of a baseline - a good system should perform well, but preferably no worse than the given baseline. Hence U_{Risk} responds to changes in the mean effectiveness of the system, but emphasises those worse than the baseline. Building upon U_{Risk}, T_{Risk} is also sensitive to the variance exhibited by a system across the population of topics. These attributes are highlighted in Table 1.

In this section, we argue for a risk measure that considers the 'shape' of a system's performance across topics. In particular, we consider that the distribution of the effectiveness scores of a set of baseline systems across the topics, mapped to the same overall mean effectiveness as the system at hand, represents an expected performance for each topic that the system should not underperform. In other words, we calculate the *expectation* of the system's performance for each topic, by considering the overall performance of the current system and the observed performances of other baseline systems. This allows to determine topics that the system should be performing better on. It follows that our proposal encap-

Measure	Baseline	Penalty of low topics	Sensitive to: Mean	Var.	Shape
Mean AP	None	None	✔	✗	✗
Geo. MAP	None	Focus on lowest topics	✔	✗	✗
U_{Risk}	Single	$1+\alpha$	✔	✗	✗
T_{Risk}	Single	$1+\alpha$	✔	✔	✗
Z_{Risk}	Multiple	$1+\alpha$	✗	✔	✔
GeoRisk	Multiple	$1+\alpha$	✔	✔	✔

Table 1: Comparison of existing and proposed robustness/risk-sensitive measures.

$\mathbf{X} =$

Systems	$\mathbf{t}_1$	$\mathbf{t}_2$	$\mathbf{t}_3$	...	$\mathbf{t}_c$	Total
$\mathbf{s}_1$	x_{11}	x_{12}	x_{13}	...	x_{1c}	S_1
$\mathbf{s}_2$	x_{21}	x_{22}	x_{23}	...	x_{2c}	S_2
$\mathbf{s}_3$	x_{31}	x_{32}	x_{33}	...	x_{3c}	S_3
⋮	⋮	⋮	⋮	⋮	⋮	⋮
$\mathbf{s}_r$	x_{r1}	x_{r2}	x_{r3}	...	x_{rc}	S_r
Total	T_1	T_2	T_3	...	T_c	N

Table 2: Data matrix for an IR experiment.

sulates two separate measures: Z_{Risk}, introduced in Section 3.1, which measures the shape of the system's performance irrespective of the overall magnitude of effectiveness; and later in Section 3.2 we show how to create a risk-measure responsive to mean effectiveness called GeoRisk. The subsequent Section 4 & Section 5 demonstrate the Z_{Risk} and GeoRisk measures upon artificial and TREC data.

The first measure, Z_{Risk}, is inspired by the Chi-square statistic used in the Chi-square test for goodness-of-fit, which is one of the well-established nonparametric hypothesis tests in categorical data analysis [1]. In statistics, goodness-of-fit tests are used to decide whether two distributions are significantly different from each other in shape/form. In relation to risk-sensitive evaluation, this means that, given a sample of topics, a risk measure based on Chi-square statistic permits quantifying the difference in the performance profiles of two IR systems across the topics. As mentioned above, none of the previously proposed risk measures are sensitive to the score distributions of IR systems on topics. However, risk-sensitive evaluation, by nature, should take into account all of shape, mean and variance, while Z_{Risk} is independent of overall mean effectiveness. Hence, building upon Z_{Risk}, we propose the GeoRisk measure, which covers all of the aforementioned aspects including the overall mean effectiveness of the system at hand, as highlighted in Table 1.

3.1 The Chi-square Statistics & $\mathrm{Z}_{\mathrm{Risk}}$

Z_{Risk} is best explained by deriving it directly from the Chi-square statistic used in the Chi-square test for goodness-of-fit. In particular, the Chi-square statistic is calculated over a data matrix of $r \times c$ cells, called the contingency table. The result of an IR experiment involving r systems and c topics can be represented by a $r \times c$ data matrix $\mathbf{X}$, whose rows and columns correspond respectively to the r systems and c topics, where the cells x_{ij} (for $i = 1, 2, \ldots, r$ and $j = 1, 2, \ldots, c$) contain the observed performances of the corresponding systems for the associated topics, measured by an effectiveness measure such as ERR@20. Table 2 provides a graphical portrayal of data matrix $\mathbf{X}$.

For such a data matrix, the row and the column marginal totals are given by $S_i = \sum_{j=1}^{c} x_{ij}$ and $T_j = \sum_{i=1}^{r} x_{ij}$ respectively, and the grand total is given by $N = \sum_{i=1}^{r} \sum_{j=1}^{c} x_{ij}$. The average effectiveness of a system i over c topics is given by S_i/c and similarly, the within-topic mean system effectiveness is given by T_j/r.

Given a data matrix $\mathbf{X}$, the Chi-square statistic, G^2, can be expressed as

$$G^2 = \sum_{i=1}^{r} \sum_{j=1}^{c} \frac{(x_{ij} - e_{ij})^2}{e_{ij}}, \tag{4}$$

where the expected value for cell (i, j), e_{ij}, is given by

$$e_{ij} = \frac{S_i \times T_j}{N} = S_i \times \frac{T_j}{N} = S_i \times p_j. \tag{5}$$

In Equation (5), $p_j = \frac{T_j}{N}$ can be described as the density or mass of column j, for $j = 1, 2, \ldots, c$. If a row total S_i is distributed on columns proportional to the column masses p_j, then the Chi-squared differences of the associated cell values from the corresponding expected values will sum up to zero, i.e. $\sum_{j=1}^{c}(x_{ij} - e_{ij})^2 = 0$. Note that $e_{ij} = x_{ij}$ when $r = 1$, where $p_j = x_{ij}/S_i$ since $N = S_i$. Intuitively, when there is only one IR system, the expected system performance for any topic j will be equal to the score observed for that system. When $r = 1$, $G^2 = 0$, meaning that the observed score distribution of the system across topics is perfectly fit to itself. Thus, G^2 values that are greater than zero indicate a discordance between two distributions, above or below expectations. This makes G^2 not directly applicable as a risk-sensitive evaluation measure, since it equally and uniformly penalises both downside (losses) *and* upside risk (wins). In contrast, risk-sensitive measures should favour wins and orthogonally penalise losses. Hence, we propose below a measure derived from G^2 that addresses this limitation.

For large samples, the Pearson's Chi-square statistic G^2 in Eq. (4) follows a Chi-square distribution with $(r-1)(c-1)$ degrees of freedom and the observed cell values x_{ij} follow a *Poisson* distribution with mean e_{ij} and variance e_{ij} [1]. This means that the Chi-square statistic can also be expressed as the sum of the square of standard normal deviates [1]:

$$G^2 = \sum_{i=1}^{r} \sum_{j=1}^{c} z_{ij}^2 \quad \text{where} \quad z_{ij} = \frac{x_{ij} - e_{ij}}{\sqrt{e_{ij}}}.$$

The square root of the components of Chi-square statistic, z_{ij}, gives the *standardised* deviation in cell (i, j) from the expected value e_{ij} (i.e. z-scores). Thus, for large samples, the distribution of z_{ij} values on the population can be approximated by the *standard normal* distribution with zero mean and unit variance.

It follows that a risk-reward tradeoff measure can be expressed in terms of the standard normal deviates from the expected effectiveness, as given by:

$$\mathrm{Z}_{Risk} = \left[\sum_{q \in Q_+} z_{iq} + (1+\alpha) \sum_{q \in Q_-} z_{iq} \right], \tag{6}$$

for any system i, $i = 1, 2, \ldots, r$. Q_+ (Q_-) is the set of queries where $z_{iq} > 0$ ($z_{iq} < 0$, respectively), determined by whether system i outperforms its expectation on topic j (c.f. $x_{ij} - e_{ij}$).

Z_{Risk} takes the classical form of a risk-sensitive evaluation measure, in that upside risk is rewarded and the effectiveness penalty of downside risk is amplified by α - i.e. the higher the Z_{Risk}, the more safe and less risky a system is. In addition, Z_{Risk} calculates the risk of a system in relation to the shape of effectiveness across topics exhibited by multiple baselines. In this way, Z_{Risk} brings a new dimension to the measurement of robustness, originally defined by

Voorhees [24] as *"the ability of the system to return reasonable results for every topic"*, in that for Z_{Risk}, robustness is measured compared to a per-topic expectation calculated from a population of baseline systems.

3.2 GeoRisk

As noted before, a limitation of Z_{Risk} is that it measures robustness irrespective of the mean effectiveness of IR systems. Indeed, one may consider that the baseline for any given system i is composed of the expected per-topic scores of the system, e_{ij}, such that the sum of expected per-topic scores is equal to the sum of the observed per-topic scores of the system, i.e. $\sum_j e_{ij} = S_i$. This means that Z_{Risk} measures robustness using individual baselines for every system, each of which is derived on the basis of the observed total effectiveness of the system (i.e. S_i) and the observed topic masses (i.e. T_j). This makes the robustness/risk measurements of Z_{Risk} independent of the observed mean effectiveness of the systems, i.e. $\sum_j x_{ij} = \sum_j e_{ij}$ for $i = 1, 2, \ldots, r$.

On the other hand, for the purposes of the comparative risk-sensitive evaluation of different IR systems, we combine the risk measure with the effectiveness measure in use, Z_{Risk} and ERR@20 for example, into a final measure. A natural method for such a combination is the *geometric mean*, which is expressed as the nth root of the product of n numbers. The geometric mean is a type of average, like arithmetic mean, that represents the central tendency in a given set of numbers. In contrast to the arithmetic mean, the geometric mean normalises the ranges of the variables, so that each datum has an equal impact on the resulting geometric mean. Hence, the geometric mean of the ERR@20 scores and the Z_{Risk} scores represents, evenly, both the effectiveness and the robustness of system s_i under evaluation:

$$\text{GeoRisk}\,(s_i) = \sqrt{S_i/c \times \Phi(Z_{Risk}/c)}, \tag{7}$$

where $0 \leq \Phi() \leq 1$ is the cumulative distribution function of the standard normal distribution. In this way, we use $\Phi()$ to normalise Z_{Risk} into [0,1], because $-\infty \leq Z_{Risk}/c \leq \infty$.

4. DEMONSTRATION

To illustrate Z_{Risk} and GeoRisk introduced in Section 3, Table 3 presents an example data matrix X composed of 8 systems and 5 topics. The effectiveness scores of the example systems are artificially determined so that the resulting performance profiles of the systems across the topics serve as a basis to exemplify some potential differences in performance profiles of IR systems in relation to their mean effectiveness. Figure 1 shows the performance profiles of the 8 systems, which can be characterised as follows:

- Systems $\mathbf{s}_1$ and $\mathbf{s}_2$ have the same mean effectiveness over the 5 topics (i.e. 0.3000) but the scores of $\mathbf{s}_1$ are monotonically increasing in magnitude across the topics, whereas, the scores of $\mathbf{s}_2$ are monotonically decreasing. That is, $\mathbf{s}_1$ and $\mathbf{s}_2$ have *contrasting* performance profiles across the topics, with respect to the same mean effectiveness score of 0.3000.
- Systems $\mathbf{s}_3$ and $\mathbf{s}_4$ have constant scores across the topics that are equal to their respective mean effectiveness scores. In other words, these systems have *constant* performance profiles, while system $\mathbf{s}_3$ has the same mean effectiveness as both $\mathbf{s}_1$ and $\mathbf{s}_2$.
- Systems $\mathbf{s}_5$ and $\mathbf{s}_6$ again have the same mean effectiveness as systems $\mathbf{s}_1$ and $\mathbf{s}_2$, but have alternating scores across the topics, such that one has a higher score in magnitude than the other for one topic and vice versa for the next topic. We describe such systems as having *alternating* performance profiles across the topics.
- Systems $\mathbf{s}_7$ and $\mathbf{s}_8$ have different mean effectiveness scores from each other and also from that of the other systems. Their performance profiles are visually parallel to each other, and *concordant* with the profile of the mean topic scores, i.e. the row "Mean" of Table 3.

	$\mathbf{t}_1$	$\mathbf{t}_2$	$\mathbf{t}_3$	$\mathbf{t}_4$	$\mathbf{t}_5$	S_i	Mean
$\mathbf{s}_1$	0.0500	0.1500	0.3000	0.4500	0.5500	1.5000	0.3000
$\mathbf{s}_2$	0.4000	0.3500	0.3000	0.2500	0.2000	1.5000	0.3000
$\mathbf{s}_3$	0.3000	0.3000	0.3000	0.3000	0.3000	1.5000	0.3000
$\mathbf{s}_4$	0.2500	0.2500	0.2500	0.2500	0.2500	1.2500	0.2500
$\mathbf{s}_5$	0.4000	0.1500	0.4000	0.1500	0.4000	1.5000	0.3000
$\mathbf{s}_6$	0.2000	0.4500	0.2000	0.4500	0.2000	1.5000	0.3000
$\mathbf{s}_7$	0.2542	0.2629	0.2802	0.2975	0.3061	1.4009	0.2802
$\mathbf{s}_8$	0.2918	0.2994	0.3147	0.3301	0.3378	1.5738	0.3148
T_j	2.1460	2.2123	2.3449	2.4776	2.5440	11.7248	
Mean	0.2683	0.2765	0.2931	0.3097	0.3180		

Table 3: Example data matrix X.

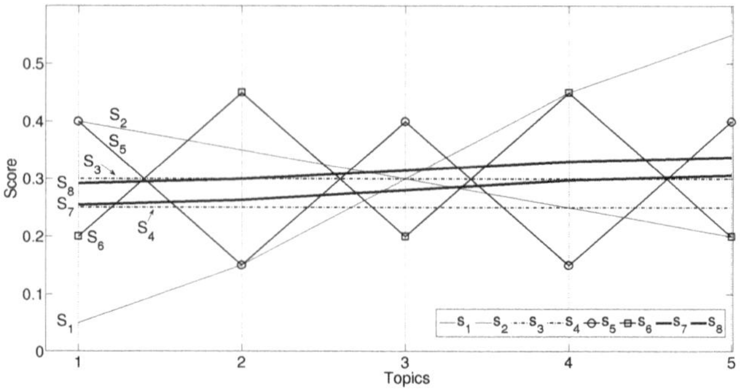

Figure 1: Example systems' performance profiles.

4.1 Single Baseline

Measuring the level of risk associated with a given IR system s with respect to a particular single baseline system b means that, in total, there are two systems under consideration, i.e. $r = 2$. For such a risk-sensitive evaluation, the Chi-square statistic G^2 is given by

$$G^2 = \sum_{j=1}^{c} \left[\frac{(x_{sj} - e_{sj})^2}{e_{sj}} + \frac{(x_{bj} - e_{bj})^2}{e_{bj}} \right],$$

and, under the null hypothesis that the observed score distributions of both systems follow a common distribution with mean μ and variance σ^2, it can be expressed as

$$\sum_{j=1}^{c} \frac{(x_{sj} - x_{bj})^2}{x_{sj} + x_{bj}}, \tag{8}$$

where x_{sj} is the observed score of the system s for topic j, and x_{bj} is the observed score of the baseline system b. Note that, when there are only two systems, $T_j = x_{sj} + x_{bj}$, and hence $x_{bj} = T_j - x_{sj}$ and $x_{sj} = T_j - x_{bj}$. Here,

$$\begin{aligned} e_{sj} &= \frac{S_s \times T_j}{N} = \frac{S_s}{N} \times (x_{sj} + x_{bj}) \\ e_{bj} &= \frac{S_b \times T_j}{N} = \frac{N - S_s}{N} \times (x_{sj} + x_{bj}) \end{aligned}$$

where $N = S_s + S_b$.

In fact, given two IR systems, the level of risk associated with any one of the two systems can be measured by taking the other system as the baseline, as implied by Eq. (8). Most importantly, Eq. (8) suggests, in this respect, that, if the

$\alpha=0$	t_1	t_2	t_3	t_4	t_5	Z_{Risk}
s_2 vs. s_1	0.3689	0.2000	0.0000	-0.1690	-0.2858	0.1141
s_1 vs. s_2	-0.3689	-0.2000	0.0000	0.1690	0.2858	-0.1141
s_3 vs. s_1	0.2988	0.1581	0.0000	-0.1225	-0.1917	0.1427
s_1 vs. s_3	-0.2988	-0.1581	0.0000	0.1225	0.1917	-0.1427
s_4 vs. s_1	0.3077	0.1599	0.0000	-0.1209	-0.1884	0.1583
s_1 vs. s_4	-0.2809	-0.1460	0.0000	0.1103	0.1720	-0.1445
s_5 vs. s_1	0.3689	0.0000	0.0845	-0.2739	-0.1088	0.0708
s_1 vs. s_5	-0.3689	0.0000	-0.0845	0.2739	0.1088	-0.0708
s_6 vs. s_1	0.2121	0.2739	-0.1000	0.0000	-0.2858	0.1002
s_1 vs. s_6	-0.2121	-0.2739	0.1000	0.0000	0.2858	-0.1002
s_7 vs. s_1	0.2799	0.1422	0.0000	-0.1057	-0.1669	0.1496
s_1 vs. s_7	-0.2705	-0.1374	0.0000	0.1021	0.1613	-0.1446
s_8 vs. s_1	0.2792	0.1445	-0.0001	-0.1097	-0.1732	0.1408
s_1 vs. s_8	-0.2860	-0.1480	0.0001	0.1123	0.1774	-0.1442

Table 4: Single baseline example.

systems show an equal mean performance over a given set of c topics (i.e. $S_s = S_b$), the measured level of risk will be the same for both systems. In risk-sensitive evaluations, a baseline system defines what is a *robust* system, so that risk can be quantified as the degree of divergence from that baseline. However, given a set of IR systems, taking every system as a baseline, actually contributes information for the qualification of a robust (i.e. not 'risky' or safe) system on the population of topics. In this regard, multiple baselines can provide more information about the real level of risk associated with any IR system.

Let system s_1 in Table 3 be the baseline system. The level of risk associated with system s_2, which has the same mean performance with s_1, is $Z_{Risk} = 0.1141$, while the level of risk associated with s_1 for baseline s_2 is the same in magnitude but different in sign, i.e. -0.1141. The sign of the Z_{Risk} scores indicates the direction of the observed level of risk-reward tradeoff, where minus indicates down-side risk and plus indicates up-side risk. Table 4 shows the calculated values of Z_{Risk} at $\alpha = 0$ for each system $i = 2, 3, \ldots, 8$. As can be seen, for those systems whose mean performances are equal to the mean performance of s_1, only the sign of the calculated Z_{Risk} values changes when the baseline is swapped.

Based on the calculated Z_{Risk} values when the baseline is s_1, system s_4 is the least 'risky' system among the 8 example runs with the highest Z_{Risk} value of 0.1583 (i.e. the s_4 vs. s_1 row of the table). However, as can be seen in Figure 1, s_3, s_7, or s_8 are relatively less 'risky' than s_4. That is, those three systems have performance profiles that are concordant/parallel with that of s_1 and also they have relatively higher mean effectiveness scores than s_4: thus, s_4 could not be considered less "risky" than s_3, s_7, or s_8. The reason behind this counter-intuitive result is two-fold. Firstly, baseline system s_1 has performance scores that are monotonically increasing in magnitude across the topics. Thus, as a baseline, it suggests that the expected system performance on the population of topics that is represented by the sample topic t_1 would be low, and for the population of topics represented by t_2 it would be relatively higher than that of t_1, and so on. However, as seen from Figure 1, considering the observed scores of the other systems, it would appear that the expected per-topic system performances are in general different from those that the system s_1 suggests, i.e. the 'mean' row of Table 3. Secondly, the risk that is measured by Z_{Risk} is related to the distribution of the total system performance S_i on topics with respect to the expected per-topic system performances, and is not dependent on the magnitude of the mean performance of the systems across topics.

These two issues explain the above counter-intuitive result that s_4 is declared as the least 'risky' system. Indeed, the former issue can be resolved by employing multiple baselines as shown in the following Section 4.2, and the latter issue of independence from the magnitude of mean effectiveness can be resolved as shown in Section 4.3, where the risk measure Z_{Risk} and the measure of effectiveness are combined into a single measure of effectiveness, GeoRisk.

		$\alpha=0$		$\alpha=1$		$\alpha=5$		$\alpha=10$	
	Mean	Z_{Risk}	Geo	Z_{Risk}	Geo	Z_{Risk}	Geo	Z_{Risk}	Geo
s_1	0.300	-0.049	0.386	-0.727	0.364	-3.442	0.271	-6.835	0.160
s_2	0.300	0.026	0.388	-0.312	0.378	-1.668	0.333	-3.362	0.274
s_3	0.300	0.006	0.387	-0.069	0.385	-0.368	0.376	-0.742	0.364
s_4	0.250	0.005	0.354	-0.063	0.352	-0.336	0.344	-0.677	0.334
s_5	0.300	0.006	0.387	-0.541	0.370	-2.727	0.296	-5.460	0.203
s_6	0.300	0.005	0.387	-0.539	0.370	-2.718	0.297	-5.442	0.204
s_7	0.280	-0.001	0.374	-0.008	0.374	-0.036	0.373	-0.072	0.372
s_8	0.315	0.001	0.397	-0.010	0.396	-0.052	0.395	-0.106	0.393

Table 5: Z_{Risk} and GeoRisk for the example systems.

4.2 Multiple Baselines

Chi-square statistic allows the use of all systems in data matrix $\mathbf{X}$ as multiple baselines for risk-reward tradeoff measurements using Z_{Risk}. Recall that the expected value for cell (i, j), e_{ij}, is given by

$$e_{ij} = S_i \times \frac{T_j}{N} = S_i \times p_j.$$

For the case of a single baseline system b, given a particular system s, to calculate the mass or density p_j of topic j, the within topic total performance score T_j is taken as $x_{sj} + x_{bj}$, i.e. $p_j = (x_{sj} + x_{bj})/N$. Similarly, given a set of baselines, the topic masses can be calculated as

$$p_j = \frac{1}{N} \sum_{i=1}^{r} x_{ij},$$

for each topic $j = 1, 2, \ldots, c$. Intuitively this means that, given a set of r systems, the level of risk associated with every system is measured by taking the remaining $(r-1)$ systems as the baseline. Compared to the case of taking a particular system as the baseline, as the number of baseline systems increases, the accuracy of the estimates of expected system performance for each topic increases, and hence the accuracy of the estimates of real risk increases.

Table 5 shows the calculated Z_{Risk} values for each of the 8 example runs at $\alpha = 0, 1, 5, 10$. We observe from the table that, as the risk sensitivity parameter α increases, example systems s_7 and s_8 exhibit the lowest levels of risk relative to the other systems, (i.e. $\alpha = 1, 5, 10$), while s_1 exhibits the highest level of risk ($Z_{Risk} = -6.835$ at $\alpha = 10$). As can be seen, using multiple baselines resolves the effect of the lack of information about the expected per-topic system performance in assessing the risk levels of systems, i.e. s_4 vs. s_7 and s_4 vs s_8. In the following section, we show how to combine Z_{Risk} with mean system effectiveness in order to solve the last issue about Z_{Risk}, i.e. the counter-intuitive case of s_4 vs. s_3, where the measured level of risk for s_3 is higher than that of s_4 (e.g. the Z_{Risk} score of s_3 is -0.368 and it is -0.336 for s_4 at $\alpha = 5$), while s_3 has higher effectiveness score than s_4 (i.e. 0.300 vs. 0.250) and it has also a performance profile concordant with that of s_4.

4.3 Effectiveness vs. Risk

Table 5 shows the calculated GeoRisk values for each of the 8 example runs. As can be seen, for the case of s_4 vs. s_3, the issue of the independence of Z_{Risk} measurements from the magnitude of the mean effectiveness of IR systems is solved. The example system s_3 is now measured as less

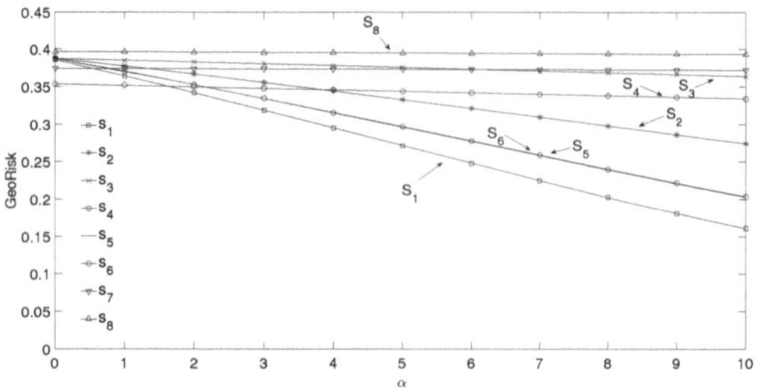

Figure 2: Example systems' GeoRisk as $0 \leq \alpha \leq 10$.

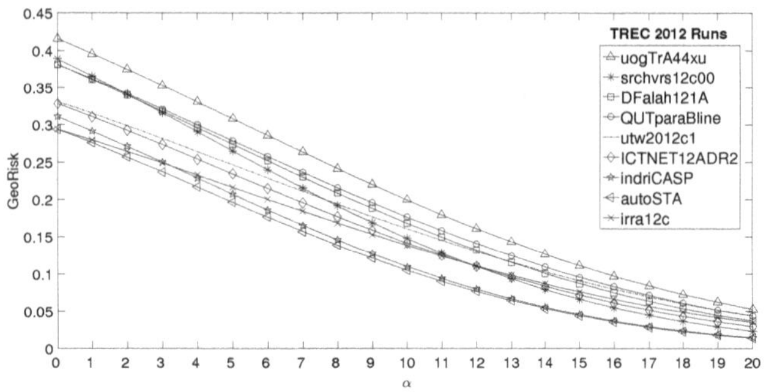

Figure 3: GeoRisk plot for 8 TREC 2012 runs.

'risky' than s_4, as suggested by the magnitude of the observed mean effectiveness scores.

Figure 2 shows the plot of GeoRisk scores for each example system for $\alpha = 0, 1, 2, \dots, 10$, where the systems with lines sloping downward along the increasing values of α (i.e. x-axis) are those that exhibit a risk of abject failure, (i.e. s_1, s_2, s_5, and s_6) while, in contrast, the robust systems such as s_3, s_4, s_7 and s_8 have nearly a straight, horizontal lines.

In summary, the GeoRisk measure takes into account both the mean effectiveness of IR systems and the difference in the shapes of their performance profiles. As a result, GeoRisk is sensitive to mean (i.e. the component S_i/c), variance and the shape of the observed effectiveness scores across topics (i.e. the Z_{Risk} component).

5. ANALYSIS OF TREC DATA

In this section, we demonstrate the use of the risk-reward tradeoff measure derived from the Chi-square statistic, Z_{Risk}, and the aggregate measure GeoRisk, on real systems submitted to the TREC 2012 Web track [10][1], in comparison with the existing measures U_{Risk} and T_{Risk}. In the subsequent year of the Web track [12], a standard baseline called *indriCASP* and based on the *Indri* retrieval platform was provided. Similar to [13, 14], we use the same indriCASP system as the nominal single baseline on the 2012 Web track topics.

In particular, out of the 48 runs submitted to TREC 2012, we select the top runs of the highest 8 performing groups, based on the mean ERR@20 score, While we omit other submitted runs for brevity, the following analysis would be equally applicable to them. For each run, we report the risk-reward tradeoff scores obtained using the official TREC 2012 evaluation measure, ERR@20.

[1]Although our analysis is equally applicable to the TREC 2013 Web track, due to the lack of space, we report results from TREC 2012, which are also directly comparable to that of previous works [13, 14].

Table 6 lists the U_{Risk}, T_{Risk}, T^*_{Risk}, Z_{Risk} and GeoRisk risk-reward tradeoff scores for the 8 runs. For the measures U_{Risk} and T_{Risk}, the baseline run is *indriCASP*; for the measures Z_{Risk} and GeoRisk, we use as multiple baselines all 48+1 TREC 2012 runs including *indriCASP*; T^*_{Risk} denotes T_{Risk} calculated using the per-topic mean effectiveness of the 49 runs as the baseline, i.e. Mean_q in Eq. (3). Note that Dinçer et al. [13] showed that T_{Risk} is inferential, i.e. the T_{Risk} scores correspond to scores of the Student's t statistic. For this reason, for the U_{Risk} scores in TREC 2012 in Table 6 (where $c = 50$), $\mathrm{T}_{Risk} > \pm 2$ indicates that the observed U_{Risk} score exhibits a significant level of risk.

Table 6 shows in general that the notion of risk quantified by the Chi-square statistic-based risk measure Z_{Risk} differs from that of the U_{Risk}, T_{Risk} and T^*_{Risk} measures, as illustrated by the contrasting systems' rankings (the column R next to each measure) for Z_{Risk}. In particular, at $\alpha = 0$, U_{Risk} and T_{Risk} agree with the effectiveness measure ERR@20 on the rankings of the 8 TREC 2012 runs. However, at $\alpha = 5$, although U_{Risk} and T_{Risk} still agree with each other, they both diverge from the agreement with ERR@20. On the other hand, the risk measure Z_{Risk} agrees neither with ERR@20 nor with the risk measures U_{Risk} and T_{Risk}. Note that, except for the determination of baselines, the three risk measures U_{Risk}, T_{Risk}, and Z_{Risk} rely on the same notion of risk and reward, i.e. down-side risk and up-side risk. Thus, comparing Z_{Risk} with U_{Risk} and T_{Risk}, it follows that multiple baselines (i.e. 49 TREC 2012 runs) provide information that is different from the information provided by the single baseline system *indriCASP*.

According to Z_{Risk}, the most robust run is "uogTrA44xu" with a Z_{Risk} value of 0.962 at $\alpha = 0$, and the next is "irra12c" with $\mathrm{Z}_{Risk} = 0.265$, and so on, given the expected per-topic performance scores representing the baselines for each system. Based on the definition of Z_{Risk}, it is expected that "uogTrA44xu" would perform any given topic with an ERR@20 score that is better than or equal to the expected score for that topic on a population of systems with mean ERR@20 scores equal to 0.3406. Conversely, the least robust or most 'risky' run is "srchvrs12c00" with a $\mathrm{Z}_{Risk} = -0.912$.

Recall that Z_{Risk} is independent of the observed mean effectiveness scores of the systems, which is, by definition, inappropriate for the purpose of a comparative IR evaluation. Thus, as an aggregate measure, GeoRisk, the geometric mean of Z_{Risk} and ERR@20, can be used to tackle this challenge. As can be seen in Table 6, GeoRisk agrees with ERR@20 at $\alpha = 0$ on the rankings of the 8 TREC 2012 runs. Here, GeoRisk gives equal weights to ERR@20 and Z_{Risk}, and similarly, at $\alpha = 0$, Z_{Risk} gives equal weights to down-side risk and up-side risk. Thus, the observed agreement between GeoRisk and ERR@20 implies that the measured Z_{Risk} scores for each of the 8 TREC 2012 runs at $\alpha = 0$ are negligible compared to the observed differences in effectiveness between the runs. In other words, every TREC 2012 run exhibits risk, to a certain extent, but none of the measured risk levels are high enough to compensate for the observed difference in mean effectiveness between two systems, so that a swap between risk and reward for a given topic is likely to occur for two systems on the population of topics. Note that the agreements of T_{Risk}, as well as U_{Risk}, at $\alpha = 0$, with ERR@20 also give support in favour of the same conclusion, i.e. the practical insignificance of the measured levels of risk at $\alpha = 0$.

On the other hand, as α increases (i.e. as the emphasis of down-side risk increases in Z_{Risk} measurements), GeoRisk

		$\alpha = 0$							$\alpha = 5$										$\alpha = 20$	
	ERR	U_{Risk}	T_{Risk}	T^*_{Risk}	Z_{Risk}	R	Geo	R	U_{Risk}	R	T_{Risk}	R	T^*_{Risk}	R	Z_{Risk}	R	Geo	R	Geo	R
uogTrA44xu	0.3406	0.146	$\underline{2.822}$	4.833	0.962	1	0.4158	1	-0.130	2	-0.798	2	2.767	1	-29.255	1	0.308	1	0.053	1
srchvrs12c00	0.3067	0.112	$\underline{2.332}$	2.985	-0.912	9	0.3887	2	-0.100	1	-0.673	1	-0.678	2	-37.069	7	0.265	4	0.024	7
DFalah121A	0.2920	0.097	$\underline{2.290}$	2.895	-0.328	7	0.3811	3	-0.156	3	-0.981	3	-0.861	3	-32.635	5	0.274	3	0.037	4
QUTparaBline	0.2901	0.095	$\underline{2.130}$	2.870	0.004	4	0.3809	4	-0.189	4	-1.112	4	-1.006	4	-30.966	4	0.279	2	0.044	3
utw2012c1	0.2203	0.026	0.561	0.917	-0.172	6	0.3314	5	-0.388	6	$\underline{-2.046}$	6	-2.987	5	-29.807	2	0.246	5	0.044	2
ICT...DR2	0.2149	0.020	0.487	0.569	0.233	3	0.3284	6	-0.329	5	-1.994	5	-3.238	6	-32.887	6	0.234	6	0.030	6
indriCASP	0.1947	*	*	-0.120	-0.339	8	0.3111	7	*	*	*		*	*	-38.619	9	0.207	8	0.014	8
autoSTA	0.1735	-0.021	-0.498	-0.968	-0.143	5	0.2942	8	-0.509	8	$\underline{-2.518}$	7	-4.195	7	-38.215	8	0.196	9	0.014	9
irra12c	0.1723	-0.022	-0.545	-1.214	0.265	2	0.2942	9	-0.501	7	$\underline{-2.634}$	8	-4.510	8	-30.410	3	0.216	7	0.035	5

Table 6: U_{Risk}, T_{Risk}, T^*_{Risk} and Z_{Risk} risk-reward tradeoff scores for the top 8 TREC 2012 runs, along with GeoRisk at $\alpha = 0, 1, 5, 10, 20$. For U_{Risk} and T_{Risk} the baseline is *indriCASP*, and for T^*_{Risk} it is Mean_q in Eq. (3) over all $48 + 1$ TREC 2012 runs including *indriCASP*, and for Z_{Risk} and GeoRisk, the baselines are estimated for the 8 runs over the same set of 49 runs and 50 Web track topics. The underlined T_{Risk} scores correspond to those U_{Risk} scores for which a two-tailed paired t-test gives significance with p-value < 0.05 - i.e. $T_{Risk} > \pm 2$.

diverges from ERR@20 and ranks the 8 TREC 2012 runs in a way that is different from all of the risk measures under consideration including Z_{Risk} (for example, $\alpha = 5$), and at a high value of α, it converges to an agreement with Z_{Risk}, e.g. the systems' rankings in Table 6 at $\alpha = 20$ for GeoRisk and at $\alpha = 5$ for Z_{Risk}. The tendency of GeoRisk towards Z_{Risk} as α increases is expected from the definition of GeoRisk.

Figure 3 plots the GeoRisk scores calculated for each run at $\alpha = 0, 1, \ldots, 20$. As can be seen, each of the 8 TREC 2012 runs has a decreasing GeoRisk score in magnitude, as the risk sensitivity parameter α increases. This means in general that - to a varying extent - every run under evaluation is subject to the risk of committing an abject failure, as the importance of getting a reasonable result for every topic increases. In particular, the runs "uogTrA44xu" and "ICTNET12ADR2" keep their relative positions in the observed rankings across all α values, while the ranks of the other runs considerably change. For example, the rank of "srchvrs12c00" changes from 2 at $\alpha = 0$ to 7 at $\alpha = 5$. At $\alpha = 0$, the run with rank 7 is *indriCASP*. However, the calculated risk for "srchvrs12c00" at any level of α cannot be considered as empirical evidence to favour *indriCASP* over "srchvrs12c00" for any given topic from the population, since the mean effectiveness of "srchvrs12c00" is significantly higher than the mean effectiveness of *indriCASP* ($p < 0.0239$, paired t-test).

Note that, for two IR systems whose mean effectiveness scores are significantly different from each other, a measured risk level could have no particular meaning from a user perspective. This is because the system with higher mean effectiveness would be the one that can fulfil the users' information needs better than the other on average, no matter what level of risk is associated with it. The system with significantly low mean effectiveness would, on average, fail to return a "reasonable" result for any given topic, compared to the other system's effectiveness. For a declared significance with a p-value of 0.05, a swap in scores between the two systems for a topic (i.e. a transition from risk to reward or vice versa between the systems) is likely to occur 5% of the time on average [26].

Nevertheless, the same case is not true for runs "DFalah121A" and "QUTparaBline", whose observed mean effectiveness scores are not significantly different from the mean effectiveness of "srchvrs12c00". The paired t-test, which is performed at a significance level of 0.05, fails to give significance to the observed difference in mean effectiveness between "DFalah121A" and "srchvrs12c00" with a p-value of 0.7592, and similarly for "QUTparaBline" with a p-value of 0.7003. This means that, for a given topic, a transition from risk to reward, or vice versa, between the runs "DFalah121A" and "srchvrs12c00", or between runs "QUTparaBline" and "srchvrs12c00", is highly likely to occur on the population of topics. Thus, both systems can be considered less "risky" or more robust than "srchvrs12c00".

In summary, this analysis of the TREC 2012 Web track runs demonstrates the suitability of GeoRisk for balancing risk-sensitivity and overall effectiveness, and the importance of using multiple baselines within the appropriate statistical framework represented by Z_{Risk}. The analysis performed for the 8 TREC runs shows overall that, in a comparative IR evaluation effort, relying only on the observed mean effectiveness of the systems may be misleading, even for a best performer system like "srchvrs12c00", where the risk associated with such a system is high enough that it can cause an over-estimation of the real performance of the system. However, we showed that GeoRisk provides a solution for identifying systems exhibiting such risks.

6. RISK-SENSITIVE OPTIMISATION

In this section, we show how GeoRisk can be integrated within the state-of-the-art LambdaMART learning to rank technique [7, 28]. Indeed, Wang et al. [27] showed how their U_{Risk} measure could be integrated within LambdaMART. Similarly, Dinçer et al. [13] proposed variants of T_{Risk} that resulted in learned models that exhibited less risk.

The method of integration of risk-sensitive measures into LambdaMART requires adaptation of its objective function. In short, LambdaMART's objective function is a product of (i) the derivative of a cross-entropy that was originally defined in the RankNet learning to rank technique [6], based on the scores of two documents a and b, and (ii) the absolute change ΔM_{ab} in an evaluation measure M due to the swapping of documents a and b [28]. Various IR measures (e.g. NDCG) can be used as M, as long as the measure is *consistent*: for each pair of documents a and b with differing relevance labels, making an *"improving swap"* (moving the higher labelled document above the lesser) must result in $\Delta M_{ab} \geq 0$, and orthogonally for *"degrading swaps"*.

In adapting LambdaMART to be more robust within a risk-sensitive setting, the ΔM is replaced by a variant $\Delta M'$ that considers the change in risk observed by swapping documents a and b, according to the underlying evaluation measure M, e.g. NDCG. In the following, we summarise existing instantiations of $\Delta M'$ arising from U_{Risk} and T_{Risk} (called U-CRO, T-SARO and T-FARO), followed by our proposed instantiation of GeoRisk within LambdaMART.

U-CRO: Constant Risk Optimisation based upon the U_{Risk} measure [27] (U-CRO) maintains a constant risk-level, regardless of the topic. In particular, let M_m define the effectiveness of the learned model m according to measure M, and let M_b define the effectiveness of the baseline b. Correspondingly, $M_m(j)$ ($M_b(j)$) is the effectiveness of the learned model (baseline) for query j, then:

$$\Delta M' = \begin{cases} \Delta M & \text{if } M_m(j) + \Delta M \geq M_b(j); \\ \Delta M \cdot (1+\alpha) & \text{otherwise.} \end{cases} \quad (9)$$

T-SARO & T-FARO: Adaptive Risk-sensitive Optimisation makes use of the fact that T_{Risk} can identify queries that exhibit real (significant) levels of risk [13] compared to the baseline b. Dinçer et al. [13] proposed two *Adaptive* Risk-sensitive Optimisation adaptations of LambdaMART, namely T-SARO and T-FARO, which use this observation to focus on improving those risky queries. Indeed, in U-CRO, ΔM is multiplied by $(1+\alpha)$, for a static $\alpha \geq 0$. In T-SARO and T-FARO, α is replaced by a variable α', which varies according to the probability of observing a query with a risk-reward score greater than that observed. By modelling this probability using the standard normal cumulative distribution function $Pr\left(Z \geq \mathrm{T}_{R_j}\right) \approx 1 - \Phi\left(\mathrm{T}_{R_j}\right)$, T-SARO replaces the original α in Eq. (9) with α' as:

$$\alpha' = \left[1 - \Phi\left(\mathrm{T}_{R_j}\right)\right] \cdot \alpha, \quad (10)$$

where $\mathrm{T}_{R_j} = \delta_j / SE(\mathrm{U}_{Risk})$ determines the level of risk exhibited by topic j. T-SARO and T-FARO contrast on the topics for which α' is adjusted – while T-SARO only adjusts topics with downside risk as per Eq. (9), T-FARO adjusts all topics:

$$\Delta M' = \Delta M \cdot (1 + \alpha')$$

The experiments in [13] found that T-FARO exhibited higher effectiveness than T-SARO, thus we compare GeoRisk to only U-CRO and T-FARO in our experiments.

GeoRisk: Our adaptation of ΔM for the newly proposed GeoRisk is more straightforward than the T_{Risk} Adaptive Risk-sensitive Optimisations, in that we use GeoRisk directly as the measure within LambdaMART.

$$\begin{aligned} \Delta M' &= GeoRisk(M_m + \Delta M) - GeoRisk(M) \\ &= \sqrt{(S_i + \Delta M)/c \times \Phi(Z_{Risk}/c)} - GeoRisk(M) \end{aligned}$$

Indeed, GeoRisk is suitable for LambdaMART as it exhibits the consistency property: an improving 'swap' will increase both the left factor (Si/c) and the right factor Z_{Risk} and therefore the value of GeoRisk for $M_m + \Delta M$ will likewise increase. Moreover, as ΔM is calculated repeatedly during the learning process, the speed of the implementation is critical for efficient learning. In this respect, it is important to note that retaining the values of the separate z_{ij} summands for each query in the Z_{Risk} calculation (see Equation (6)) allows the new Z_{Risk} value to be calculated by only recomputing the z_{ij} for the query affected, then recalculating GeoRisk.

Recall from Section 3 that z_{ij} encapsulates differential weighting of downside and upside risks, but with respect to the expected performance on the topic. Hence, by using GeoRisk, the objective function of LambdaMART will favour learned models that make improving swaps of documents on topics where the learned model performs below expectation as calculated on the set of baselines.

Naturally, the instantiation of GeoRisk within a learning to rank setting depends on the set of baselines $\mathbf{X}$, to allow the estimation of the topic expectations e_{ij} (see Eq. (5)). The choice of baselines to provide for learning can impact upon which topics the learner aims to improve. Previous works on risk-sensitive learning [13, 27] have used the performance of a single BM25 retrieval feature as the baseline. Indeed, single weighting models such as BM25 are typically used to identify the initial set of documents, which are then re-ranked by the learned model [19, 20], and hence it is a baseline that the learner should outperform. However, it does not represent the typical performance of a learned approach upon the queries, as it cannot encapsulate the effectiveness of refined ranking models using many other features.

Hence, instead of using GeoRisk to learn a model more effective than a set of BM25-like baselines, we argue for the use of state-of-the-art baselines, which portray representative estimations of query difficulty to the learner. Such baselines are more akin to the systems submitted to TREC (which themselves have been trained on previous datasets), rather than a single weighting model feature. In a deployed search engine, such state-of-the-art-baselines could represent the effectiveness of the currently deployed search engine, or other deployed search engines for the same query. In an experimental setting, such as in this paper, we use held-out data to pre-learn several learned models before conducting the main comparative experiments. Finally, for comparison purposes, we also deploy T*-FARO in our experiments, where the *mean* performance of the state-of-the-art baselines for each topic is used as the *single* learning baseline.

6.1 Experimental Setup

Our experiments use the open source Jforests learning to rank tool [15][2], which implements U-CRO, and T-FARO, as well as plain LambdaMART. Our implementations of T*-FARO & GeoRisk are also built upon Jforests[3]. As baselines, in addition to LambdaMART, we also deploy a plain gradient boosted regression trees learner (also implemented by Jforests), and two linear learned models, Automatic Feature Selection (AFS) [21] & AdaRank [19, Ch. 4].

We conduct experiments using the MSLR-Web10k dataset[4]. This learning to rank dataset contains 136 query-dependent and query-independent feature values for documents retrieved for 10,000 queries, along with corresponding relevance labels. As highlighted above, our baselines require separate training. For this reason, we hold out 2000 queries for initial training (two thirds) and validation (one third). The remaining 8000 queries are then split into 5 folds, each with a balance of 60% queries for training, 20% for validation, and 20% for testing. Hence, our reported results are not comparable to previous works using all 10000 queries of the MSLR dataset, but instead performances for LambdaMART, U-CRO & T-FARO are presented on the 8000 queries. The underlying evaluation measure M in each learner is NDCG.

For GeoRisk & T*-FARO, the multiple baselines are evaluated for each query in the main 5 folds, which represent 'unseen' queries for those systems. For U-CRO, T-SARO and T-FARO, the baseline is depicted by the performance of the `BM25.wholedocument` feature.

Finally, we note that LambdaMART has several hyperparameters, namely the minimum number of documents in each leaf m, the number of leaves l, the number of trees in the ensemble nt and the learning rate r. Our experiments use a uniform setting for all parameters across all folds, namely $m = 1500$, $l = 50$, $nt = 500$, $l = 0.1$, which are similar to those reported in [27] for the same dataset.

6.2 Results

In Table 7, we report the NDCG@10 effectiveness and robustness for LambdaMART, U-CRO, T-FARO, T*-FARO

[2]https://github.com/yasserg/jforests

[3]We have contributed GeoRisk as open source to Jforests.

[4]http://research.microsoft.com/en-us/projects/mslr/

and GeoRisk for $\alpha = \{1, 5\}$[5]. The table is split into two halves: comparison to the effectiveness of the single BM25 baseline, and comparison viz. the 4 baseline learned models. For each of the baselines, we report the reward to risk ratio (denoted "Reward/Risk"), which measures the gain over the effectiveness of the baseline. Similarly, the win to loss ratio (denoted "W/L") measures the number of queries that the risk-sensitive optimisation contributed to reward against risk. Finally, the number of queries that each model wins or looses relative to the baseline are also shown for each α value, along with the number of queries that experience a relative loss greater than 20% NDCG@10. For clarity, the header of Table 7 denote arrows to show the favourable direction of each measure, e.g. $\uparrow$ means that higher is better.

On analysis of the top half of Table 7, we observe that GeoRisk generates the highest mean NDCG effectiveness, marginally improving over LambdaMART. This is also observable for the Reward measure, in comparison to the BM25 baseline. However, for the risk measures, T-FARO and U-CRO obtain the best values. For α, $\alpha = 1$ is deemed the appropriate setting across all risk-sensitive learners, which has the effect of doubling the penalty of a query underperforming the corresponding baseline for that learner.

In the bottom half of Table 7, we examine the performance profiles of the different learners compared to the effectiveness of the 4 learned model baselines - the measures reported are the macro-average, i.e. the mean when each measure is calculated with respect to each learned baseline in turn (rather than compared to the micro-averaged effectiveness of the 4 learned baselines). In this half of the table, we note that, for $\alpha = 1$, GeoRisk demonstrates the highest Reward and number of Wins and lowest Losses (and the resulting best Reward/Risk & Win/Loss ratios (the latter is a 2.7% improvement over LambdaMART). These improvements in the risk profile of the systems are achieved while still attaining the highest mean NDCG effectiveness among the systems. All differences are statistically significant ($n = 8000$ queries).

Finally, we note that the effectiveness and risk profiles attained by T*-FARO are markedly different, with T*-FARO attaining the lowest Reward/Risk & Win/Loss ratios. This verifies that the use of expected topic performance by GeoRisk rather than a mean per-topic performance (as used by T*-FARO) results in a learned model more attuned to the normal performances of state-of-the-art baseline systems.

Overall, this empirical evidence confirms our claim that the new risk-sensitive objective function GeoRisk for the LambdaMART learning to rank technique allows effective yet robust learned models to be obtained using multiple baselines. Moreover, we would highlight the more impressive risk-profiles attained in the bottom half of Table 7, which demonstrate that given a set of state-of-the-art baselines, using GeoRisk can generate an effective model that is as effective as LambdaMART with better risk profiles, and allows learning-to-rank to benefit from natural incremental improvements as practiced in real deployment settings.

7. RELATED WORK

One aspect of this paper is the assessment of the robustness of IR systems, initiated first by the TREC Robust track [24] based on the geometric mean average precision measure [23, 25], and developed further by the introduction of new measures of risk/robustness, such as U_{Risk} [27] and T_{Risk} [13]. In this respect, while Dinçer et al. [13] investigated the use of the Student's t-test for risk-sensitive evaluation, this is the first work to investigate the use of Pearson's Chi-square statistic for risk-sensitive evaluation, thereby facilitating the use of multiple baselines. Instead, previous usages of the Chi-square statistic has encompassed index term weighing [18] and document classification [22].

In IR experimentation, Armstrong et al. [3] noted that many papers appeared to show improvement upon older, weaker baselines. More recent work by Kharazmi et al. [17] showed that testing upon state-of-the-art baselines is necessary to demonstrate an advance. Similarly, this paper advocates the use of multiple state-of-the-art baselines, both in experimental and learning settings.

We also note several attempts to develop robust learning to rank techniques: of note, the AdaRank technique [19, Ch. 4] focuses on improving hard queries using boosting. Since then, risk-sensitive optimisation techniques such as U-CRO [27], T-SARO & T-FARO [13] have aimed to adapt the LambdaMART technique by identifying risky topics with respect to a single baseline. Our work goes further by making use of multiple state-of-the-art baseline systems when calculating risk-estimation in the learning to rank objective function. Finally, Bennett et al.[5] take a different route, by developing personalised risk-averse ranking strategies upon the LambdaMART technique. As they build upon U-CRO, it may be possible to combine both approaches in the future.

8. CONCLUSIONS

This is the first paper that thoroughly investigated the use of multiple baselines in risk-sensitive evaluation. It argued for a new definition of risk-sensitivity related to the expected performance upon a given topic, calculated from a population of existing baseline systems. In particular, the paper introduced two new risk-sensitive evaluation measures, Z_{Risk} and GeoRisk that are based upon the Chi-square statistic. Moreover, while Z_{Risk} estimates risk independent of the overall mean retrieval effectiveness, GeoRisk enhances Z_{Risk} by additionally accounting for overall effectiveness.

Our new measures were demonstrated on the results of a comparative system evaluation from the TREC Web track. Finally, the paper showed how the proposed GeoRisk measure can be directly integrated within the objective function of the state-of-the-art LambdaMART learning to rank technique. Experiments upon 8000 queries from a learning to rank dataset showed that the resulting learned models were as effective as LambdaMART, but also more risk-averse when compared to four learned baselines.

9. ACKNOWLEDGMENTS

This work is partially supported by TUBITAK, The Scientific and Technological Research Council of Turkey (Project No: 114E558). All opinions are that of the authors.

10. REFERENCES

[1] A. Agresti. *Categorical Data Analysis.* Wiley, 2002.
[2] G. Amati, C. Carpineto, and G. Romano. Query difficulty, robustness, and selective application of query expansion. In *Proceedings of ECIR*, 2004.
[3] T. Armstrong, A. Moffat, W. Webber, and J. Zobel. Improvements that don't add up: ad-hoc retrieval results since 1998. In *Proceedings of ACM CIKM*, 2009.
[4] S. Beitzel, E. Jensen, and O. Frieder. GMAP. In L. Liu and M. Özsu, eds., *Encyclopedia of Database Systems*, pp 1256–1256, 2009.

[5] α=0 is equivalent to the normal LambdaMART algorithm.

	α	NDCG↑	Reward↑	Risk↓	Reward/Risk↑	Wins↑	Losses↓	W/L↑	L > 20%↓
				Compared to BM25 Baseline					
L'MART	0	0.4578	0.195	0.036	5.401	5892	1715	3.44	982
U-CRO	1	0.4558	0.192	0.035	5.472	5913	1684	3.51	965
U-CRO	5	0.4461	0.180	**0.032**	5.552	5913	**1666**	**3.55**	**880**
T-FARO	1	0.4576	0.194	0.035	**5.568**	**5928**	1671	**3.55**	963
T-FARO	5	0.4569	0.194	0.036	5.435	5889	1719	3.43	995
T*-FARO	1	0.4557	0.194	0.037	5.25	5857	1753	3.34	1016
T*-FARO	5	0.4562	0.194	0.037	5.26	5861	1737	3.37	999
GeoRisk	1	**0.4581**	**0.196**	0.037	5.327	5868	1732	3.39	992
GeoRisk	5	0.4557	0.195	0.038	5.179	5876	1728	3.40	1037
				Compared to 4 Learned Models Baselines					
L'MART	0	0.4578	**0.061**	0.053	1.138	3978.3	3669.0	1.12	1722.5
U-CRO	1	0.4558	0.059	0.053	1.103	3954.5	3690.0	1.11	1718.8
U-CRO	5	0.4461	0.051	0.056	0.941	3748.8	3887.3	1.01	1825.8
T-FARO	1	0.4576	0.059	**0.052**	1.137	3965.5	3674.3	1.12	**1677.0**
T-FARO	5	0.4569	0.059	**0.052**	1.121	3967.3	3676.5	1.12	1692.0
T*-FARO	1	0.4557	0.042	0.051	0.820	3562.0	4079.5	0.87	1821.5
T*-FARO	5	0.4562	0.041	0.053	0.823	3539.0	4099.5	0.86	1783.5
GeoRisk	1	**0.4581**	**0.061**	0.054	**1.142**	**4017.0**	**3628.8**	**1.15**	1709.8
GeoRisk	5	0.4557	0.060	0.055	1.095	3974.0	3674.0	1.12	1756.5

Table 7: Learning to rank results, with risk results calculated w.r.t. BM25 & the 4 learned models. All differences are statistically significant over the $n = 8000$ queries.

[5] P. N. Bennett, M. Shokouhi, and R. Caruana. Implicit preference labels for learning highly selective personalized rankers. In *Proceedings of ACM ICTIR*, 2015.

[6] C. Burges, T. Shaked, E. Renshaw, A. Lazier, M. Deeds, N. Hamilton, and G. Hullender. Learning to rank using gradient descent. In *Proceedings of ICML*, 2005.

[7] C. J. Burges. From RankNet to LambdaRank to LambdaMART: An overview. Technical Report MSR-TR-2010-82, Microsoft Research, 2010.

[8] D. Carmel, E. Farchi, Y. Petruschka, and A. Soffer. Automatic query refinement using lexical affinities with maximal information gain. In *Proceedings of ACM SIGIR*, 2002.

[9] O. Chapelle, D. Metlzer, Y. Zhang, and P. Grinspan. Expected reciprocal rank for graded relevance. In *Proceedings of ACM CIKM*, 2009.

[10] C. L. A. Clarke, N. Craswell, and E. Voorhees. Overview of the TREC 2012 Web track. In *Proceedings of TREC*, 2012.

[11] K. Collins-Thompson. Reducing the risk of query expansion via robust constrained optimization. In *Proceedings of ACM CIKM*, 2009.

[12] K. Collins-Thompson, P. Bennett, F. Diaz, C. Clarke, and E. M. Voorhees. Overview of the TREC 2013 Web track. In *Proceedings of TREC*, 2013.

[13] B. T. Dinçer, C. Macdonald, and I. Ounis. Hypothesis testing for the risk-sensitive evaluation of retrieval systems. In *Proceedings of ACM SIGIR*, 2014.

[14] B. T. Dinçer, I. Ounis, and C. Macdonald. Tackling biased baselines in the risk-sensitive evaluation of retrieval systems. In *Proceedings of ECIR*, 2014.

[15] Y. Ganjisaffar, R. Caruana, and C. Lopes. Bagging gradient-boosted trees for high precision, low variance ranking models. In *Proceedings of ACM SIGIR*, 2011.

[16] D. Hoaglin, F. Mosteller, and J. Tukey, eds. *Understanding robust & exploratory data analysis.* Wiley, 1983.

[17] S. Kharazmi, F. Scholer, D. Vallet and M. Sanderson. Examining Additivity and Weak Baselines. *TOIS*, to appear, 2016.

[18] I. Kocabaş, B. T. Dinçer, and B. Karaoğlan. A nonparametric term weighting method for information retrieval based on measuring the divergence from independence. *Information Retrieval*, 17(2):153–176, 2014.

[19] T.-Y. Liu. Learning to rank for information retrieval. *Foundation and Trends in Information Retrieval*, 3(3):225–331, 2009.

[20] C. Macdonald, R. L. Santos, and I. Ounis. The whens and hows of learning to rank for web search. *Information Retrieval.*, 16(5):584–628, 2013.

[21] D. A. Metzler. Automatic feature selection in the markov random field model for information retrieval. In *Proceedings of ACM CIKM*, 2007.

[22] M. Oakes, R. Gaaizauskas, H. Fowkes, A. Jonsson, V. Wan, and M. Beaulieu. A method based on the chi-square test for document classification. In *Proceedings of ACM SIGIR*, 2001.

[23] S. Robertson. On GMAP - and other transformations. In *Proceedings of ACM CIKM*, 2006.

[24] E. M. Voorhees. Overview of the TREC 2003 Robust retrieval track. In *Proceedings of TREC*, 2003.

[25] E. M. Voorhees. The TREC Robust retrieval track. *SIGIR Forum*, 39(1):11–20, June 2005.

[26] E. M. Voorhees and C. Buckley. The effect of topic set size on retrieval experiment error. In *Proceedings of ACM SIGIR*, 2002.

[27] L. Wang, P. N. Bennett, and K. Collins-Thompson. Robust ranking models via risk-sensitive optimization. In *Proceedings of ACM SIGIR*, 2012.

[28] Q. Wu, C. J. C. Burges, K. M. Svore, and J. Gao. Ranking, boosting, and model adaptation. Technical Report MSR-TR-2008-109, Microsoft, 2008.

Event Digest: A Holistic View on Past Events

Arunav Mishra*
*Max Planck Institute for Informatics
Saarbrücken, Germany
{amishra,kberberi}@mpi-inf.mpg.de

Klaus Berberich*,†
†htw saar
Saarbrücken, Germany
klaus.berberich@htwsaar.de

ABSTRACT

For a general user, easy access to vast amounts of online information available on past events has made retrospection much harder. We propose a problem of automatic event digest generation to aid effective and efficient retrospection. For this, in addition to text, a digest should maximize the reportage of time, geolocations, and entities to present a holistic view on the past event of interest.

We propose a novel divergence-based framework that selects excerpts from an initial set of pseudo-relevant documents, such that the overall relevance is maximized, while avoiding redundancy in text, time, geolocations, and named entities, by treating them as independent dimensions of an event. Our method formulates the problem as an Integer Linear Program (ILP) for global inference to diversify across the event dimensions. Relevance and redundancy measures are defined based on JS-divergence between independent query and excerpt models estimated for each event dimension. Elaborate experiments on three real-world datasets are conducted to compare our methods against the state-of-the-art from the literature. Using Wikipedia articles as gold standard summaries in our evaluation, we find that the most holistic digest of an event is generated with our method that integrates all event dimensions. We compare all methods using standard Rouge-1, -2, and -SU4 along with Rouge-NP, and a novel weighted variant of Rouge.

CCS Concepts

•**Information systems → Retrieval tasks and goals; Summarization;** *Probabilistic retrieval models; Information retrieval diversity;*

Keywords

Linking; Event digest; Diversification; Semantic annotations

1. INTRODUCTION

Today, in this era of digitization, the World Wide Web plays an integral role as an effective and efficient digital medium for providing information on events of global as well as local importance. Large volumes of online news data are generated by media houses and other independent providers as they report eagerly on current events or those that have happened in the past. Contributing to the volume, variety, and velocity of the data, social media is also proving to be a new popular medium of news propagation across the globe. On one hand, this change from traditional print media to publishing online news has given rise to less polarizing and more democratic journalism. On the other hand, from the perspective of a general user, vast amounts of information with a high degree of redundancy have made it difficult to connect the dots and get a holistic understanding on past events with large ramifications.

State-of-the-art vertical news search engines, like Google News, are among the first choices of a general user when seeking information on past events. However, these search engines are keyword based and retrieve a large ranked list of news articles, all of which are temporally biased to the query issuing time. It is hard for a user to sift through all retrieved news articles so as to get a holistic view on a past event. For such an information need, it would be useful if a system could automatically generate an *event digest* by extracting text from retrieved news articles. With such a digest given, the user can first get a broader view on the event and then, if desired, refer to individual documents to get necessary details. A concrete example of an event digest is given in Table 1. For further motivation consider this scenario: A journalist, Laura Lang, wants to quickly get a holistic view on the event of East Timor's independence, illustrated in Table 1. She uses Google News and issues the keyword query {*East*, *Timor*, *votes*, *independence*, *Indonesia*, *referendum*}. Not to her surprise, she finds that the system retrieves numerous (more than one thousand) news articles published by different news agencies. To get a good understanding of the event, she tediously sifts through many articles, most of which contain redundant information. However, with a concise digest given, she can first get an overview of the event, and then jump into news articles connected to the *excerpts* in the digest to get necessary details.

One plausible solution to the information overloading problem is to link orthogonal sources of information on past events [20, 22, 25]. With a similar goal, in a recent work [19, 20], we investigated a linking task that leveraged semantic annotations to identify relevant news articles that can be linked to excerpts from Wikipedia articles. We motivate that Wikipedia articles summarize past events by often abstracting from fine-grained details, and on the other hand, online news are published as the events happen and cover all angles with necessary details. Individually, they both fall short in providing a full picture due to context missing from news articles, and fine-grained details omitted from Wikipedia articles. However, connections can facilitate navigation between them and help in getting a larger picture. One drawback of such a linking task is that for an excerpt from Wikipedia that represents an event with long ramifications, like the one in our example, many news articles get linked

SIGIR '16, July 17-21, 2016, Pisa, Italy

DOI: http://dx.doi.org/10.1145/2911451.2911526

Figure 1: Example of an event digest.

Event Query

Description: East Timor votes for independence from Indonesia in a referendum
Time: August 30, 1999
Geolocations: 1643084; 1623843; 7289708;
Entities: East_Timor; Indonesia; 1999_East_Timorese_crisis;

Event Digest (with chronological ordering on publication dates)

- **Publication Date:** *July 20, 1999* **Source Link:** *http://goo.gl/rJYDiZ*
(1) Indonesia is preparing to relinquish control of East Timor after 23 years of occupation and it believes that independence advocates are highly likely to win a referendum next month says an authentic internal government report that has been made available to reporters by advocates of independence. **(2)** Late next month estimated 400 000 East Timorese are to choose between broad autonomy within Indonesia option 1 or independence option 2.
- **Publication Date:** *August 29, 1999* **Source Link:** *http://goo.gl/Cz6Jkk*
(3) Former president Jimmy Carter whose human rights and diplomacy organization the Carter Center is monitoring the referendum here said this this month some top representatives of the government of Indonesia have failed to fulfill their main obligations with regard to public order and security.
- **Publication Date:** *November 21, 1999* **Source Link:** *http://goo.gl/hdqYm8*
(4) The last time it was East Timor which voted for independence from Indonesia in August only to be plunged into a spasm of violence that required an Australian led international military force to quell it. **(5)** Acehs latest push for independence began with the fall of President Suharto in May 1998 and accelerated after the East Timor referendum.
- **Publication Date:** *September 24, 2000* **Source Link:** *http://goo.gl/AijWVY*
(6) East Timor has been under a transitional United Nations administration since the Aug. 30 independence vote last year. **(7)** The groups pillaged East Timor after last year's independence vote which freed the territory from military control.
- **Publication Date:** *August 24, 2001* **Source Link:** *http://goo.gl/EAGBxC*
(8) This vote like the referendum in 1999 is being organized by the United Nations which has continued to administer East Timor a former Portuguese colony annexed by Indonesia as it struggles to its feet economically and politically.

Figure 2: Different views on a past event.

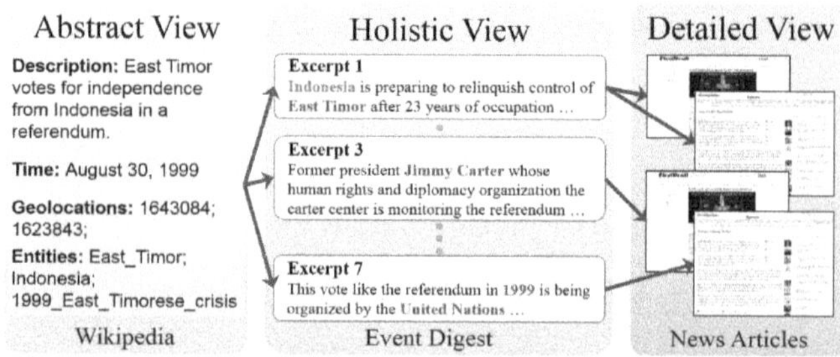

to it. An event digest in such a case becomes an intermediate level of linking that presents a *holistic view*. Excerpts from Wikipedia, an *abstract view*, are connected to excerpts in the digest which are in-turn connected to news articles that give a *detailed view* as illustrated in Figure 2. As other use cases, since event digests are generated with a fixed length, smaller digests can be considered as *sneak peaks* (snippets) into news articles, retrieved as a search result. Longer digests can be treated as automatically generated reports for deeper analysis of an event's ramifications.

In this paper, we propose to address the following problem: *given an event from Wikipedia along with a time interval indicating its occurrence period, automatically generate a digest that presents a holistic view on the event.* As input, we consider: **1)** an *event query* that comes with a short textual description, and a time interval indicating when the event happened; and **2)** a set of textually *pseudo-relevant documents* retrieved using a standard retrieval model with a keyword query generated from the event description. As output, our goal is to return a diverse set of excerpts from news articles to compose an *event digest* with its total length under a given length budget such that it presents a holistic view on the event in the query.

Traditional multi-document extractive summarization tasks [4, 12, 14, 16, 18, 21, 31] focus on generating textual summaries from filtered relevant documents such that they are as close as possible to a manually created summary. Unsupervised methods in this realm, consider only text to maximize relevance and reduce redundancy in the generated summaries. However, we define an event to be a joint distribution over independent *text*, *time*, *geolocation*, and *entity* dimensions, indicating the time period, geographic locations, and entities affected by its ramifications. To present a holistic view on an event, we motivate that relevant information along all four dimensions has to be diversified. For the example in Figure 1, diversifying across time will result in information on *causality* (excerpt 1 and 2), *effects during happening* (excerpts 3 to 5), and *after-math* (excerpts 6 to 8) of the event. Similarly, diversifying across geolocations will give information on the entire geographical scope, and diversifying across entities will give information on all persons, places, and organizations involved. We refer to such a view as an *event digest* that contrasts from a traditional notion of a summary.

Challenges. Leveraging text, time, geolocation, and entity dimensions of an event to automatically generate an event digest becomes a challenge. Further, we note that the event descriptions are verbose. Thus, it becomes a challenge to deal with verbosity to select relevant excerpts into the digest.

Contributions made by this paper are the following: **1)** we propose the new problem of event digest creation. **2)** We present a novel method that uses a *divergence-based framework*, and formulates the problem as an integer linear program (ILP) to perform global inference for the event digest creation. To the best of our knowledge, we are the first to present a *unified method* to explicitly diversify across text, time, geolocations, and entities using query modeling approaches. **3)** We present an experimental evaluation on three real-world datasets by treating Wikipedia articles central to an event query as a gold standard.

Organization. In Section 2 we review the literature; Section 3 gives details of our approach. Conducted experiments and their results are described in Section 4. We conclude in Section 5.

2. RELATED WORK

We contrast the event digest generation problem defined in this paper from prior works along the following five lines.

Extractive Summarization focuses on selecting sentences from a single or multiple input documents to create a summary. This line of research has received much attention in the past [4, 12, 14, 16, 18, 21, 31]. It was also investigated at the Document Understanding (DUC) and Text Analysis Conferences (TAC). From various subclasses of extractive summarization, we identify three that seem to be most related to our task: *multi-document summarization*, *query focused multi-document summarization*, and *timeline generation*. In the realm of unsupervised summarization techniques, MMR [4] stands as the most popular approach that defines an objective function rewarding relevance and penalizing redundancy. McDonald et al. [18] proposed an ILP formulation with a slight change to the original MMR objective function. Litvak and Last [16], and Riedhammer et al. [21] proposed to use key phrases to summarize news articles and meetings. Gillick et al. [8] maximized the coverage of the salient terms in input documents to generate summaries. However, in the problems investigated by all above mentioned works, there is no notion of a user query. This stands as a difference to our problem where we have to generate a digest for a given event query. Further, we incorporate additional semantics to identify informational excerpts for the digest. However, in our approach, we incorporate the formulation given by Riedhammer et al. [21] to develop our text-only method.

Query-Focused Multi-Document Summarization takes into consideration a topic that is input as a user query to generate a topic-focused summary. For this task, supervised approaches have recently proved to be effective [12, 14, 31]. However, they require labeled data for training. Firstly, these approaches focus on short queries, like TREC adhoc topics used in TAC, whereas in our problem, event queries are verbose textual descriptions of events. Secondly, we present an unsupervised approach that formulates an ILP for event digest generation.

Timeline Generation as a subclass that focuses on events, has also received attention [1, 5, 28]. The main goal is to generate a time-stamped list of updates as sentences, key phrases, etc., covering different facets of an event. As an early approach, Allan et al. [1] proposed clustering-based approaches on entities and noun phrases to generate a timeline for a given event. Chieu et al. [5] leveraged burstiness as a ranking metric to identify sentences to be included into a timeline. McCreadie et al. [17] proposed an incremental update summarization task and presented supervised methods to address it. Recently, in a different direction, Shahaf et al. [22] addressed the information overloading problem by presenting a map of connected news articles that captures the story development of a given event. Timeline generation and incremental update summarization tasks aim at presenting a concise ordered summary of events. This is different from our task in two ways: firstly, we do not focus on the ordering of the excerpts in a digest; and secondly, we focus on generating a holistic view by explicitly diversifying across different dimensions of a past event to aid retrospection.

Search Result Diversification problem originally aimed at identifying documents from a relevant set that catered to different information needs of a user query. Further, we look into prior novelty-based strategies to diversify search results. MRR [4] is among the first formulations that penalized documents based on redundancy. This was extended by Zhai et al. [30] for language models and they proposed a risk minimization framework to diversify search results. Wang et al. [26] proposed a mean-variance analysis (MVA) diversification objective. A recent work that becomes interesting is presented by Dou et al. [6] as they attempt to diversify across multiple implicit sub topics by treating them as dimensions of the query. All the methods above cater only to text, and extending them to time, geolocations, and entity dimensions is not straightforward.

Passage Retrieval tasks have been well studied in the past. Systems retrieving passages have been proven to be effective for IR tasks when the documents are long or contain diverse topics. One popular way to define a passage is based on the document structure [3, 9, 23]. Another example of passages are windows consisting of a fixed number of words. These can be further classified into overlapping [3] or non-overlapping windows [13]. The traditional passage retrieval tasks do not take diversity of the passages into consideration. However, we find that the definitions of the passages to be complementary to our excerpts.

3. APPROACH

We present our approach to create a concise digest for a given event that presents a holistic view by describing as many aspects as possible. Intuitively, while selecting excerpts from the input documents, if the reportage of time, geolocations, and entities associated with the input event is maximized then a holistic view can be developed. We propose a novel *divergence-based framework* for event digest creation. Under this framework, our method estimates independent query and excerpt models, and maximizes the relevance while avoiding inter-excerpt redundancy based on the KL-divergence between the models. We define an event as a joint distribution over text, time, geolocation, and entity dimensions. Our method extends the divergence-based retrieval framework, and formulates a single *unified* linear problem to perform global inference across the event dimensions. We design an ILP with appropriate binary indicator variables and constraints.

3.1 Definitions

We begin by defining our notations and representations.

Event Query q is derived from a given Wikipedia event that comes with a short textual description and a time interval indicating its occurrence period. We assume that an event is a joint distribution over four independent dimensions: text, time, geolocation, and entity. Thus, from a given query we derive the following four parts from the textual description: query-text part q_{text} as a bag of textual terms; query-time part q_{time} as a bag of explicit temporal expressions; query-space part q_{space} as a bag of geolocations; and query-entity part q_{entity} as a bag of entity mentions.

Excerpt ε is a single unit of an input document that gives information on an event. In this work, we fix an excerpt as a single sentence, however other definitions may be adopted depending on the application. Analogous to the query, each excerpt has four parts: text ε_{text}, time ε_{time}, geolocation ε_{space}, and entity ε_{entity} part.

In our method, we sometimes use the entire collection as a single coalesced document and refer to its corresponding parts as C_{text}, C_{time}, C_{space}, and C_{entity}.

Time dimension is modeled as a two-dimensional space $T \times T$, as proposed by Berberich et al. [2]. We normalize a temporal expression to an interval $[tb, te]$ with begin time tb and end time te. Further, each interval is described as a quadruple $[tb_l, tb_u, te_l, te_u]$ where tb_l gives the lower bound, and tb_u gives the upper bound for the begin time tb of the interval. Analogously, te_l and te_u give the bounds for the end time te. A *time unit* or *chronon* t indicates the time passed (to pass) since (until) a reference date such as the UNIX epoch. We fix the granularity of a time unit to a single day.

Geolocation dimension is modeled using the geodetic system in terms of $latitude \times longitude$. A geolocation s is represented by its minimum bounding rectangle (MBR). Each MBR is described as quadruple $[tp, lt, bt, rt]$, where point (tp, lt) is the top-left corner and (bt, rt) is the bottom-right corner of the MBR. A geolocation unit g refers to a geographical point in our two-dimensional grid. Further, we empirically set a minimum resolution $resol_{lat} \times resol_{long}$ of the grid to smooth out noisy annotations at a very high granularity (like streets and avenues).

Entity e refers to a location, person, or organization. Our entity dimension represents all entities in the YAGO2 [10] knowledge base. We use the YAGO URI of an entity, as its unique identifier while estimating query- and excerpt-entity models.

3.2 Query and Excerpt Models

The divergence-based framework with the independence assumption between the dimensions allows us to estimate the corresponding query models uniquely. For this, we first expand the original parts of a query (other than text) with the given input set of the documents, thus treating them as pseudo-relevant. Intuitively, by expanding the query parts, we cope with overly specific annotations in the original query. We refer to our prior work [20] for more detailed explanation. We estimate the independent query models from corresponding expanded parts as follows.

Query-Text Model Q_{text}. Query modeling for text is a well-studied problem. The main intuition is that the query-text model should capture the true intent of the query in the text dimension. In our approach, we treat the set of excerpts R in the input documents as pseudo-relevant, and estimate a feedback model. We then combine the feedback model with the empirical query model, estimated from q_{text}, to boost salient terms for the event in the query. Since the best way combining is through linear interpolation [29], we define the generative probability of a term $\mathcal{W}$ as,

$$P(\mathcal{W} \mid Q_{text}) = (1-\theta) \cdot P(\mathcal{W}|q_{text}) + \theta \cdot \sum_{\varepsilon \in R} P(\mathcal{W}|\mathcal{E}_{text}). \quad (1)$$

A term $\mathcal{W}$ is generated from the feedback model with θ probability and from the original query with $(1-\theta)$ probability. Since we use a subset of the available terms, we finally re-normalize as,

$$\hat{P}(\mathcal{W} \mid Q_{text}) = \frac{P(\mathcal{W} \mid Q_{text})}{\sum_{\mathcal{W}' \in V} P(\mathcal{W}' \mid Q_{text})} . \quad (2)$$

Query-Time Model Q_{time} can be understood as a probability distribution in our time domain $T \times T$ that captures the true temporal scope of an input event. We assume that the time part q_{time} of a query is sampled from Q_{time}. The generative probability of a time unit t from the query-time model Q_{time} is estimated by iterating over all the time intervals $[tb, te] \in q_{time}$ as,

$$P(t \mid Q_{time}) = \sum_{[tb,te] \in q_{time}} \frac{\mathbb{1}(t \in [tb_l, tb_u, te_l, te_u])}{|[tb_l, tb_u, te_l, te_u]|} \quad (3)$$

where $\mathbb{1}(\cdot)$ function returns 1 if there is an overlap between a time unit t and interval $[tb_l, tb_u, te_l, te_u]$. If a time unit overlaps with a time interval then we add a probability mass proportional to the inverse of the interval's area in the space. Intuitively, this assigns higher probability to time units that overlap with a layer of specific (smaller area) intervals in q_{time}. For computation of areas and intersections of temporal intervals we refer to [2]. To handle *near misses* [20] perform an additional two-dimensional Gaussian smoothing that blurs the boundaries of Q_{time} by spilling some probability mass to adjacent time units. With this, the new generative probability is estimated as,

$$\hat{P}(t \mid Q_{time}) = \sum_{t \in T \times T} G_\sigma(t) \cdot P(t \mid Q_{time}) \quad (4)$$

where G_σ denotes a 2-D Gaussian kernel that is defined as,

$$G_\sigma(t) = \frac{1}{2\pi\sigma^2} \cdot exp\left(-\frac{(tb_l, tb_u)^2 + (te_l, te_u)^2}{2\sigma^2}\right) .$$

Finally, we re-normalize similar to Equation 2.

Query-Space Model Q_{space}. Analogous to time, the query-space model is a probability distribution from which the geolocation part of a given query is sampled. It captures the true geographical scope of the event described in the query. The generative probability of a geolocation unit g from the query-space model Q_{space} by iterating over all $[tp, lt, bt, rt] \in q_{space}$ is estimated as,

$$P(g \mid Q_{space}) = \sum_{(tp,lt,bt,rt) \in q_{space}} \frac{\mathbb{1}(g \in [tp, lt, bt, rt])}{|[tp, lt, bt, rt]|} . \quad (5)$$

The $\mathbb{1}(\cdot)$ functions indicates an overlap between a space unit l and a MBR $[tp, lt, bt, rt]$. Since we normalize with the area of the MBR, a geolocation unit gets higher probability if it overlaps with many specific geolocations (MBR with smaller area) in q_{space}. Area of a MBR, $|[tp, lt, bt, rt]|$ can easily be computed as $(rt - lt + resol_{lat}) * (tp - bt + resol_{long})$. To avoid the issue of near misses we estimate $\hat{P}(l|Q_{Space})$ with additional Gaussian smoothing as described in Equation 4, and finally re-normalize as per Equation 2.

Query-Entity Model Q_{entity} is a probability distribution over our entity space and captures the entities that are salient to the event in a given query. To estimate the Q_{entity} from q_{entity}, we follow a similar process as described for the query-text model, by combining the empirical entity model with a feedback model estimated from the pseudo-relevant excerpt set R. The generative probability of an entity e is estimated as,

$$P(e|Q_{entity}) = (1-\theta) \cdot P(e|q_{entity}) + \theta \cdot \sum_{\varepsilon \in R} P(e|\mathcal{E}_{entity}) \quad (6)$$

where $P(e \mid q_{entity})$ and $P(e \mid \mathcal{E}_{entity})$ are the likelihoods of generating the entity from the original query and pseudo-relevant excerpts $\varepsilon \in R$ respectively. We finally re-normalize as in Equation 2.

Excerpt Model in each dimension is estimated by following a similar methodology as for the query modeling. However, we additionally add Dirichlet smoothing [29] to the excerpt models with the collection C as a background model. For the text dimension, the excerpt-text model $\mathcal{E}_{text}$ is formally estimated as,

$$P(\mathcal{W} \mid \mathcal{E}_{text}) = \frac{\hat{P}(\mathcal{W} \mid \mathcal{E}_{text}) + \mu \cdot P(\mathcal{W} \mid C_{text})}{\mid \mathcal{E}_{text} \mid + \mu} \quad (7)$$

where $\hat{P}(\mathcal{W}|\mathcal{E}_{text})$ is computed according to Equation 1 and μ is set as the average excerpt length of our collection [29]. Similarly, for time, geolocations, and entity models we follow Equation 3, 5, and 6 respectively. However for estimating $\mathcal{E}_{time}$ and $\mathcal{E}_{space}$, we do not employ the Gaussian smoothing (Equation 4) as this tends to introduce additional information into the excerpts artificially.

3.3 ILP Formulation

After estimating necessary query and excerpt models, we next describe our ILP designed for the event digest generation. With our assumptions in mind, we first specify our exact requirements. A digest should portray the following characteristics:

i) contain relevant excerpts to a given event query;
ii) avoid redundancy;
iii) maximize the reportage of the temporal scope, geolocations, and entities;
iv) length in words should not be more than a given budget L.

To design an ILP, we define the following binary indicator variables: S_i indicates if a candidate excerpt ε_i is finally selected into the digest; for a given excerpt ε_i, M_{ij} indicates the single most redundant excerpt ε_j that is already selected into the digest; T_{it} indicates if there is an overlap with $t \in Q_{time}$; G_{ig} indicates if there is an overlap with $g \in Q_{space}$; E_{ie} indicates if there is an overlap with $e \in Q_{entity}$. Using the above definitions, we can now precisely formulate our ILP as illustrated in Algorithm 1.

Algorithm 1 ILP to generate an event digest.

Maximize:

$$\sum_i \Bigg[\alpha\Big(\lambda \cdot rel_i S_i - (1-\lambda)\cdot \sum_{j\neq i} red_{ij} M_{ij}\Big) + \frac{\beta}{N_t}\sum_{t\in Q_{time}} w_{it}T_{it} + \frac{\gamma}{N_g}\sum_{g\in Q_{space}} w_{ig}G_{ig} + \frac{\psi}{N_e}\sum_{e\in Q_{entity}} w_{ie}E_{ie}\Bigg]$$

Subject to:

Constraints on text:

1) $\sum_j m_{ij} = s_i \quad \forall\ i$

2) $m_{ij} \leqslant s_i \quad \forall\ i$

3) $m_{ij} \leqslant s_j \quad \forall\ j$

4) $m_{ik} \geqslant s_k - (1-s_i) - \sum_{j:red_{ij}\geqslant red_{ik}} s_j \quad \forall i \neq k$

Constraints on time:

5) $\sum_i T_{it} \geqslant 1 \quad \forall\ t \in Q_{time}$

6) $T_{it} \geqslant s_i \cdot o_{it} \quad \forall\ i,\ t \in Q_{time}$

7) $T_{it} \leqslant s_i \quad \forall\ i,\ t \in Q_{time}$

Constraints on geolocation:

8) $\sum_i G_{ig} \geqslant 1 \quad \forall\ g \in Q_{space}$

9) $G_{ig} \geqslant s_i \cdot o_{ig} \quad \forall\ i,\ g \in Q_{space}$

10) $G_{ig} \leqslant s_i \quad \forall\ i,\ g \in Q_{space}$

Constraints on entity:

11) $\sum_i E_{ie} \geqslant 1 \quad \forall\ e \in Q_{entity}$

12) $E_{ie} \geqslant s_i \cdot o_{ie} \quad \forall\ i,\ e \in Q_{entity}$

13) $E_{ie} \leqslant s_i \quad \forall\ i,\ e \in Q_{entity}$

Objective Function can be explained as four parts: text, time, geolocation, and entity. In the text part, rel_i function computes the relevance between an excerpt ε_i and query q. Each excerpt is penalized with the maximum textual redundancy score red_{ij} with the already selected excerpts into the digest. The parameter λ balances textual relevance and redundancy estimates.

To explain the rest of the formulation, let us consider the time part in isolation. For each excerpt, the following steps are followed: first, identify the time units that overlap with the given Q_{time}. Second, weights w_{it} of the time units are summed and assigned as temporal scores. The rest of the parts, i.e., space and entity, are handled similar to time. To specify the global importance of the dimensions, four parameters, α, β, γ, and ψ are introduced into the objective function. Finally, we normalize the time, geolocations, and entity parts with the size of their corresponding query models denoted as N_t, N_g, and N_e respectively.

Constraints defined for our ILP are categorized into the four parts corresponding to the objective function. Constraints on text are defined on the binary indicator variable M_{ij}. Constraints 1-3 enforce that exactly one excerpt in the digest is selected for consideration as most redundant. Constraint 4 is to ensure that if $M_{ik} = 1$ then ε_j is most redundant to ε_i and they both are selected into the final digest. Constraints 5, 8, and 11 ensure that each unit in the query model is covered by at least one excerpt in the digest, thus maximizing total coverage of the query units in the digest. Constraints 6, 9, and 12 specify that if an excerpt is selected then overlapping units across the dimensions are covered. For these constraints, we introduce an additional binary variable o_{ik} that indicates if there is an overlap between a kth unit in query with excerpt ε_i model. Finally, constraints 7, 10, and 13 are required as sanity check that a unit can be covered only if an overlapping excerpt is selected.

Textual relevance rel between a given query q and excerpt ε in the objective function is estimated by computing the KL-divergence KLD between their language models, denoted as Q_{text} and $\mathcal{E}_{text}$ respectively. Formally, this is given as,

$$rel_i = -KLD(Q_{text}||\mathcal{E}_{i\ text})\ . \tag{8}$$

Textual Redundancy red between any two excerpts can be simply interpreted as the similarity between them. For this, we compute the Jensen-Shannon divergence JSD which is the symmetric variant of the KLD and a popularly used distance metric. In this case, lower divergence indicates higher redundancy between the excerpts. Formally, this is defined as,

$$red_{ij} = -JSD(\mathcal{E}_{i\ text}||\mathcal{E}_{j\ text}) \tag{9}$$

Weights w_{it}, w_{ig}, and w_{ie} specify the importance of the time t, geolocation g, and entity unit e respectively for an excerpt ε_i. Under our divergence-based framework, we define the weights as the negative KL-divergence between the generative probability of a unit from the query and excerpt models. Formally, we define weights for all dimensions analogous to time as,

$$w_{it} = -KLD\big(P(t|Q_{time})||P(t|\mathcal{E}_{i\ time})\big)\ . \tag{10}$$

For a single dimension considered in isolation, summing over the weights gives the overall divergence between excerpt and query models in that dimension. For example, in the time dimension the divergence $KLD(Q_{time}||\mathcal{E}_{i\ time})$ can be computed by summing over query time units as $\sum_{t\in Q_{time}} w_{it}T_{it}$. Intuitively, objective is maximized by globally minimizing the overall divergence of a query with entire digest. However, since the KL-divergence scores are not bounded, we normalize the weights across all excerpts as,

$$\frac{KLD - KLD_{min}}{KLD_{max} - KLD_{min}}\ .$$

In our divergence framework, the redundancies in time, geolocations, and entity dimensions are minimized implicitly by maximizing the coverage of the units in query models. However, at the same time, the relevance of excerpts in these dimensions are also considered. The ILP solver first selects excerpts that cover most important units (receiving high probability in query model) with the lowest divergence scores as indicated by their weights.

4. EXPERIMENTS

Next, we give details on the conducted experiments. For reproducibility, we make the experimental data publicly available[1].

4.1 Setup

We begin by describing our test collections, query set, gold standards, and measures used in the experimental setup.

Test Collections. We perform experiments on three real-world datasets: **1)** The New York Times Annotated Corpus (NYT) with about 2 million news articles published between 1987 and 2007; **2)** English Gigaword corpus with about 9 million news articles published between 1991 and 2010; and **3)** ClueWeb12-B13 (CW12) corpus with about 50 million web pages crawled in 2012. We process the queries in our test set with a standard query likelihood document retrieval model. Top-10 retrieved documents from each dataset are considered pseudo-relevant and input into our methods.

[1]http://resources.mpi-inf.mpg.de/d5/eventDigest/

Test Queries are generated from the *timeline of modern history*[2] in Wikipedia that contains the most prominent news events in the past. We randomly sample 100 events occurring between 1987 and 2007 as test queries. Each query comes with a short textual description and a time interval indicating when the event happened. Further, we automatically annotate each query with time, geolocations, and entities by disambiguating mentions in their descriptions.

Gold Standard. We consider a Wikipedia article that describes the specific event in a query as its human-generated or *gold standard digest* created by Wikipedians. Since these articles on past events are elaborate and cover most of the important aspects, they are apt for evaluating our task. For this, we manually identify Wikipedia articles that are central to an event query.

Measures. We use the following measures:

• *Rouge-1*, *Rouge-2*, and *Rouge-SU4* measures [15] are well established for evaluating method-generated against gold standard (human-generated) summaries.

• *Rouge-NP*: We introduce a new measure that takes into consideration only the noun phrases overlap. Generally, noun phrases represent the key concepts in a gold standard, and a larger overlap indicates better information coverage in the digest. This is further motivated by Taneva et al. [24] in their experimental evaluation.

• *weighted-Rouge (w-Rouge)*: The above rouge measures evaluate how close a method-generated digest is to the gold standard. However, due to the disparate quantity of text between a method-generated digest and the gold standard, these measures are not indicative of the diversity of excerpts in a digest. Thus, we introduce w-Rouge that computes Rouge-1 score of a method-generated digest S with each paragraph p of the corresponding gold standard GS. The individual Rouge-1 scores are weighted with the normalized length of each paragraph $\frac{|p|}{|GS|}$. To get the final score for a method, we average over all queries q in query set QS. Formally,

$$\textit{w-Rouge} = \frac{1}{|QS|} \sum_{q \in QS} \sum_{p \in GS} \frac{|p|}{|GS|} \text{Rouge-1}(S, p) \quad (11)$$

Additionally, we also report the mean variance ($MVar$) of the w-Rouge across all the queries. Formally, this is given as,

$$MVar = \frac{1}{|QS|} \sum_{q \in QS} \frac{1}{N} \sum_{p \in GS} \left[\textit{w-Rouge}(S,p) - \textit{w-Rouge}(S,GS)\right]^2$$

where N is the number of paragraphs in GS. We assume that in a long Wikipedia article, each paragraph describes an aspect of the central event. Thus, a method-generated summary that gives diverse information should show overlap with more number of paragraphs in the gold standard Wikipedia article. A method that generates a digest that is closer to the gold standard by covering more aspects of the given event should have a higher mean F1 score and mean variance of w-Rouge.

Implementation. All the methods are implemented in Java. For the temporal annotation, we use Stanford CoreNLP toolkit [3]. To annotate geolocations, we use an open-source gazetteer-based tool[4] that extracts locations and maps them to the GeoNames[5] knowledge base. For entity annotations, we use the AIDA [11] system. We use the Gurobi ILP solver[6] in our experiments.

[2]https://en.wikipedia.org/wiki/Timeline_of_modern_history
[3]http://stanfordnlp.github.io/CoreNLP/
[4]https://github.com/geoparser/geolocator
[5]http://www.geonames.org/
[6]http://www.gurobi.com

4.2 Methods

We next describe the different methods that are compared in our experiments. We distinguish three frameworks that use integer linear programs for global inference: **1)** maximum marginal relevance [4, 18, 21], **2)** coverage-based [7, 8, 27], and **3)** divergence-based methods. While the first two are derived from literature as state-of-the-art frameworks for unsupervised methods, the third divergence-based framework is proposed in this paper. We extend the frameworks to incorporate time, geolocations, and entities, and design methods that leverage different combination of the dimensions under each framework. All our methods formulate the event digest problem as solvable ILPs.

Maximum Marginal Relevance [4] is arguably the most popular unsupervised framework for generating document summaries. We compare the following two methods that fall under this framework:

• *Mcd*: As first method, we consider the summarizer presented by McDonald et al. [18] that uses an ILP for global inference in summarization. Though they follow the MMR [4] style formulation, they make a slight change to the global objective function by introducing linear approximation. This results in candidates being penalized with the average redundancy to the already selected excerpts. Their objective is defined as,

$$Maximize: \sum_i \left[\lambda \cdot rel_i S_i - (1-\lambda) \cdot \sum_{j \neq i} red_{ij} S_{ij}\right]. \quad (12)$$

We refer to [18] for the full set of constraints. The generalized ILP framework allows us to define the rel and red functions using language modeling methods as described in Equation 8 and 9.

• *Rdh:* More recently, Riedhammer et al. [21] propose an ILP formulation that got rid of the linear approximation in the global objective function of *Mcd*, thus giving an optimal solution. In their formulation, they introduce an additional binary variable M_{ij} to indicate the maximum redundancy of an excerpt to the already selected excerpts in the digest. Further, they have additional constraints that are defined on this variable which leads to efficient convergence to the optimal value. Their global objective function is defined as,

$$Maximize: \sum_i \left[\lambda \cdot rel_i S_i - (1-\lambda) \cdot \sum_{j \neq i} red_{ij} M_{ij}\right]. \quad (13)$$

We refer to [21] for full set of constraints. Similar to *Mcd*, we use the definitions for rel and red as given in Equations 8 and 9.

Coverage-Based Framework [8] is also popular in the summarization community as an unsupervised global inference method. It follows the idea of implicitly reducing the redundancy in the final summary by maximizing the coverage of textual units. Prior works [7, 27] propose various definitions for such units in context of different tasks. This framework remains state of the art, and approaches have shown to work well in comparison to other unsupervised global inference methods. At large, the framework is general enough and can easily be extended to our event dimensions. Their global objective function is defined as,

$$Maximize: \sum_i w_i \cdot C_i , \quad (14)$$

where w_i is defined as $P(c \mid Q_{text})$ probability of generating a term from query-text model, and C_i is a binary indicator variable that marks the occurrence of a term c in an excerpt ε_i. Using this framework, we design the following methods that consider different subsets of the four event dimensions:

• *Cov-txtEM* and *Cov-txtQM*: As text-only methods, *Cov-txt* maximizes the coverage of the salient terms associated with an event. In their original work, Gillick et al. [8] relied heavily on preprocessing the documents to be summarized including key-phrase extraction. For this work, we do not do any preprocessing. In contrast, we make use of a query-text model Q_{text} to capture salient textual terms for the event in the query. We motivate that this makes their method more query-focused and stronger as a baseline. To demonstrate the advantage of incorporating a query model, we compare two methods: *Cov-txtEM* that uses only the empirical terms (after stop words removal), and *Cov-txtQM* that estimates a query model by expanding the query with terms from the pseudo-relevant documents as shown in Equation 1.

• *Cov-T*, *Cov-S*, *Cov-E*, *Cov-ST*, and *Cov-EST*: In principle, the coverage-based method can easily be extended to time, geolocations, and entity dimensions. In the time dimension, we adapt the objective function in Equation 14, such that it selects excerpts by maximizing the global coverage of all time units $\tau \in Q_{time}$. We label this method as *Cov-T*. Similarly, *Cov-S*, and *Cov-E* maximize the coverage of geolocation units $l \in Q_{space}$ and entities $e \in Q_{entity}$ respectively. We motivate that *Cov-E* method is similar to the original approach proposed by Gillick et al. that maximizes concepts, which in our case are entities. It is not hard to think of methods that maximize a combination of the dimensions in their objective functions. *Cov-ST* maximizes the coverage of geolocations and time, and *Cov-EST* additionally combines entities.

In all the above methods, weights w_i as in Equation 14, are generative probabilities from query models described in Section 3.2.

Divergence-Based Framework, discussed in Section 3, takes into consideration the divergence between query and excerpt models in all the dimensions. We note that the text-only method under this framework is equivalent to *Rdh* that defines its rel and red functions in Equation 13 based on the KL-divergence between corresponding text models. We design the following methods:

• *Div-T*, *Div-S*, *Div-E*, *Div-ST*, *Div-txtST*, *Div-EST*, and *Div-txtEST*: In Section 3, we present a unified divergence-based framework that maximizes the textual relevance and minimizes the redundancy across text, time, geolocations, and entities. We label this as the *Div-txtEST* method. However, one can think of methods that consider only a subset of the dimension. We thus design *Div-T*, *Div-S*, *Div-E*, *Div-ST*, *Div-txtST*, and *Div-EST* methods that leverage a combination of text (*txt*), time (*T*), space (*S*), and entities (*E*) as indicated by the suffixes in their labels.

Random. Finally, we consider the *Rand* method that selects excerpts at uniformly random from the input top-10 pseudo-relevant documents until the length constraint is satisfied.

Parameters of the methods were tuned by varying one parameter at a time while keeping the others fixed to observe the change in the overall result quality as described in [28]. We have two groups of parameters, first denoted by λ that balances the relevance rel with redundancy red. Second, that specifies the importance of text, time, geolocations, and entities with parameters, α, β, γ, and ψ respectively. For NYT, Gigaword, and CW12 datasets, we set λ to 0.85, 0.90 , and 0.95 respectively. In the second group of parameters, we tune β, γ, and ψ while fixing $\alpha = 1 - (\beta + \gamma + \psi)$. We empirically observe that setting the three parameters too high leads to a deterioration of the results. For NYT, Gigaword, and CW12, we set $\beta = [0.10, 0.10, 0.10]$, $\gamma = [0.05, 0.01, 0.01]$, and $\psi = [0.01, 0.30, 0.01]$. Finally, for the query models in Equation 1, 3, 5, and 6, we use settings described in [20].

Table 1: Results on The New York Times dataset.

Methods	Rouge 1			Rouge 2			Rouge NP			Rouge SU4		
	P	R	F1	P	R	F1	P	R	F1	P	R	F1
Rand	0.618	0.073	0.113	0.155	0.014	0.024	0.084	0.007	0.012	0.209	0.025	0.039
Mcd	0.652	0.078	0.121	0.192	0.019	0.030	0.086	0.008	0.013	0.205	0.026	0.039
Rdh	0.662	0.078	0.121	0.203	0.019	0.031	0.088	0.008	0.013	0.210	0.026	0.040
Cov-txtEM	0.652	0.051	0.085	0.180	0.011	0.020	0.091	0.005	0.009	0.219	0.017	0.029
Cov-txtQM	0.646	0.079	0.122	0.190	0.018	0.030	0.086	0.009	0.014	0.204	0.026	0.039
Cov-T	0.544	0.023	0.041	0.188	0.007	0.012	0.079	0.003	0.006	0.182	0.008	0.014
Cov-S	0.464	0.027	0.043	0.154	0.006	0.011	0.058	0.003	0.005	0.149	0.009	0.014
Cov-E	0.666	0.069	0.110	0.215	0.018	0.031	0.076	0.007	0.011	0.213	0.023	0.036
Cov-ST	0.647	0.038	0.062	0.214	0.010	0.017	0.087	0.005	0.008	0.212	0.013	0.021
Cov-EST	0.666	0.073	0.115	0.214	0.019	0.032	0.078	0.008	0.012	0.214	0.024	0.038
Div-T	0.647	0.068	0.110	0.195	0.017	0.028	0.088	0.008	0.013	0.211	0.023	0.037
Div-S	0.653	0.072	0.113	0.199	0.018	0.030	0.090	0.008	0.013	0.212	0.025	0.038
Div-E	0.652	0.077	0.120	0.195	0.019	0.031	0.091	0.008	0.014	0.213	0.026	0.041
Div-ST	0.662	0.081	0.124	0.210	0.020	0.033	0.090	0.008	0.014	0.215	0.027	0.041
Div-txtST	0.667	0.082	0.125	0.214	0.021	0.034	0.090	0.009	0.014	0.214	0.027	0.041
Div-EST	0.649	0.080	0.122	0.196	0.020	0.031	0.087	0.008	0.013	0.211	0.027	0.041
Div-txtEST	0.675	0.084	**0.127**	0.219	0.022	**0.035**	0.089	0.010	**0.016**	0.219	0.028	**0.042**

Table 2: Results on the Gigaword dataset.

Methods	Rouge 1			Rouge 2			Rouge NP			Rouge SU4		
	P	R	F1	P	R	F1	P	R	F1	P	R	F1
Rand	0.643	0.069	0.109	0.191	0.016	0.027	0.163	0.017	0.028	0.242	0.026	0.041
Mcd	0.663	0.073	0.113	0.204	0.019	0.030	0.191	0.020	0.032	0.255	0.028	0.043
Rdh	0.654	0.075	0.119	0.201	0.019	0.031	0.190	0.021	0.034	0.247	0.028	0.045
Cov-txtEM	0.676	0.052	0.086	0.204	0.013	0.022	0.184	0.012	0.021	0.257	0.020	0.033
Cov-txtQM	0.652	0.078	0.122	0.197	0.019	0.031	0.178	0.021	0.033	0.242	0.029	0.045
Cov-T	0.372	0.015	0.027	0.120	0.004	0.007	0.127	0.005	0.008	0.150	0.006	0.010
Cov-S	0.509	0.021	0.036	0.167	0.005	0.008	0.164	0.006	0.011	0.206	0.008	0.013
Cov-E	0.664	0.070	0.111	0.212	0.018	0.030	0.173	0.017	0.028	0.255	0.027	0.042
Cov-ST	0.553	0.028	0.048	0.169	0.007	0.012	0.180	0.008	0.014	0.214	0.011	0.018
Cov-EST	0.665	0.071	0.112	0.214	0.018	0.030	0.174	0.017	0.028	0.257	0.027	0.043
Div-T	0.650	0.077	0.120	0.198	0.019	0.031	0.191	0.022	0.035	0.244	0.029	0.045
Div-S	0.647	0.071	0.112	0.201	0.017	0.028	0.191	0.020	0.033	0.245	0.026	0.042
Div-E	0.646	0.077	0.121	0.190	0.018	0.029	0.189	0.022	0.035	0.241	0.029	0.045
Div-ST	0.668	0.045	0.074	0.212	0.011	0.019	0.201	0.013	0.021	0.260	0.017	0.028
Div-txtST	0.655	0.081	0.125	0.201	0.020	0.033	0.192	0.023	0.036	0.248	0.031	0.047
Div-EST	0.619	0.074	0.116	0.189	0.018	0.030	0.182	0.022	0.034	0.233	0.028	0.044
Div-txtEST	0.655	0.081	**0.126**	0.205	0.021	**0.034**	0.192	0.022	**0.036**	0.248	0.031	**0.048**

Table 3: Results on the ClueWeb12-B13 dataset.

Methods	Rouge 1			Rouge 2			Rouge NP			Rouge SU4		
	P	R	F1	P	R	F1	P	R	F1	P	R	F1
Rand	0.604	0.058	0.095	0.173	0.013	0.022	0.135	0.011	0.018	0.248	0.021	0.035
Mcd	0.642	0.058	0.095	0.197	0.014	0.024	0.157	0.011	0.019	0.269	0.021	0.036
Rdh	0.630	0.063	0.101	0.193	0.015	0.026	0.156	0.012	0.020	0.261	0.023	0.038
Cov-txtEM	0.649	0.052	0.084	0.209	0.012	0.022	0.167	0.011	0.018	0.278	0.019	0.032
Cov-txtQM	0.650	0.065	0.105	0.206	0.016	0.028	0.164	0.014	0.022	0.277	0.024	0.040
Cov-T	0.410	0.011	0.020	0.155	0.004	0.007	0.140	0.003	0.006	0.186	0.005	0.009
Cov-S	0.375	0.014	0.026	0.131	0.004	0.008	0.112	0.004	0.007	0.168	0.006	0.010
Cov-E	0.628	0.060	0.097	0.199	0.015	0.026	0.140	0.012	0.020	0.260	0.022	0.036
Cov-ST	0.532	0.019	0.036	0.191	0.006	0.011	0.170	0.005	0.010	0.237	0.008	0.015
Cov-EST	0.634	0.060	0.097	0.203	0.015	0.026	0.146	0.012	0.020	0.265	0.022	0.037
Div-T	0.608	0.070	0.110	0.173	0.016	0.026	0.124	0.011	0.018	0.248	0.024	0.039
Div-S	0.568	0.055	0.092	0.163	0.013	0.022	0.117	0.009	0.015	0.235	0.019	0.033
Div-E	0.617	0.073	0.114	0.174	0.016	0.026	0.119	0.011	0.017	0.253	0.025	0.040
Div-ST	0.654	0.045	0.069	0.215	0.010	0.017	0.171	0.008	0.013	0.284	0.016	0.025
Div-txtST	0.614	0.072	0.113	0.172	0.017	0.027	0.122	0.011	0.019	0.249	0.025	0.041
Div-EST	0.613	0.073	0.113	0.170	0.016	0.026	0.115	0.011	0.017	0.248	0.025	0.041
Div-txtEST	0.632	0.075	**0.117**	0.192	0.018	**0.030**	0.152	0.014	**0.023**	0.264	0.027	**0.044**

4.3 Results

We compare the quality of event digests generated from the three different datasets. We also compare the variance of weighted-Rouge measure that we propose to highlight the diversification effect of each method.

Rouge score analysis. Table 1, Table 2, and Table 3 show the results of generating an event digest of length 250 words from NYT, Gigaword, CW12 documents respectively. We compare the digest generated by different methods against Wikipedia articles as gold standards, and report Rouge-1, Rouge-2, Rouge-NP, and Rouge-SU4 scores. We find that across all the three datasets the best quality digest is generated by the *Div-txtEST* method.

Firstly, we note that the random method *Rand* already achieves a decent F1 score. Across the three datasets, selecting excerpts randomly from the top-10 input pseudo-relevant NYT and Giga-

Table 4: Statistical significance test with two tailed paired t test at three α levels: 0.01 (▲/▼), 0.05 (△/▽), and 0.10(∧/∨); of all against the text-only methods. Three symbols in each cell denote increase (up), decrease (down), or no change (–) in Rouge-1, -2, and -SU4, respectively.

Datasets	Methods	Mcd	Rdh	Cov–txtQM	Cov–T	Cov–S	Cov–E	Cov–ST	Cov–EST	Div–T	Div–S	Div–E	Div–ST	Div–txtST	Div–EST	Div–txtEST
NYT	Mcd	– – –	▲ △ △	– – –	▼ ▼ ▼	▼ ▼ –	▼ – ▽	▼ ▼ –	▼ ∧ –	▼ ▼ –	▼ – –	– – ∧	– ▲ –	▲ ▲ ▲	– – ▲	▲ ▲ ▲
	Rdh	▼ ▽ ▽	– – –	▲ ▽ –	▼ ▼ ▼	▼ ▼ ▼	▼ – ▽	▼ ▼ ▼	▼ – ▽	▼ ▼ ▽	▼ ∨ ▽	▼ ∨ ▲	△ – ▲	– ▲ ∧	▲ – ▲	– ▲ ▲
	Cov–txtQM	– – –	▼ △ –	– – –	▼ ▼ ∨	▼ ▼ –	▼ – ∨	▼ ▼ –	▼ △ –	▼ ▽ –	∨ – –	– – △	– ▲ ∧	▲ ▲ ▲	– – △	▲ ▲ ▲
Giga	Mcd	– – –	▲ ▲ △	▲ △ △	▼ ▼ ▼	▼ ▼ ▼	– – –	▼ ▼ ▼	– – –	▲ – –	– – –	▲ – –	▼ ▼ ▼	▲ ▲ ▲	▲ – –	▲ ▲ ▲
	Rdh	▼ ▼ ▽	– – –	– – –	▼ ▼ ▼	▼ ▼ ▼	▼ – ▼	▼ ▼ ▼	▼ – ▼	– – –	– – –	– – –	▼ ▼ ▼	▲ – △	– – –	▲ ▲ ▲
	Cov–txtQM	▼ ▽ ▽	– – –	– – –	▼ ▼ ▼	▼ ▼ ▼	▼ ▽ ▼	▼ ▼ ▼	▼ – ▼	– – –	▽ ∨ –	– ▽ –	▼ ▼ ▼	– – △	– – –	– ∧ ∧
CW12	Mcd	– – –	▲ ▲ –	▲ ▲ ∧	▼ ▼ ▼	▼ ▼ ▼	– – –	▼ ▼ ▼	– ∧ –	▲ ∧ ▲	∨ – –	▲ ▲ ▲	▼ ▼ ▼	▲ △ ▲	▲ △ ▲	▲ ▲ ▲
	Rdh	▼ ▼ –	– – –	– – –	▼ ▼ ▼	▼ ▼ ▼	▽ – –	▼ ▼ ▼	∨ – –	– – –	– – –	△ – –	▼ ▼ ▼	△ – –	△ – –	▲ ▲ –
	Cov–txtQM	▼ ▼ ∨	– – –	– – –	▼ ▼ ▼	▼ ▼ ▼	∨ ∨ –	▼ ▼ ▼	∨ – –	△ – –	– ∨ –	▲ – –	▼ ▼ ▼	▲ – –	▲ – –	▲ △ ∧

Table 5: Comparison of methods in Weighted-Rouge1.

	NYT			GIGA			CW12		
	F1	**MVar**	**MSD**	**F1**	**MVar**	**MSD**	**F1**	**MVar**	**MSD**
Rand	0.022	1.87E-03	0.032	0.031	1.90E-03	0.030	0.025	1.51E-03	0.026
Mcd	0.023	2.10E-03	0.034	0.033	2.27E-03	0.031	0.026	1.47E-03	0.026
Rdh	0.023	2.07E-03	0.034	0.032	2.34E-03	0.033	0.026	1.58E-03	0.027
Cov-txtQM	0.023	2.19E-03	0.034	0.033	2.30E-03	0.033	0.029	1.72E-03	0.028
Cov-T	0.009	5.55E-04	0.012	0.008	3.95E-04	0.008	0.005	1.93E-04	0.005
Cov-S	0.010	7.29E-04	0.013	0.011	5.52E-04	0.011	0.006	2.59E-04	0.007
Cov-E	0.022	1.93E-03	0.032	0.031	1.97E-03	0.030	0.026	1.48E-03	0.026
Cov-ST	0.013	8.95E-04	0.018	0.014	8.28E-04	0.014	0.008	3.90E-04	0.010
Cov-EST	0.023	2.06E-03	0.033	0.031	2.00E-03	0.030	0.027	1.44E-03	0.026
Div-T	0.021	1.89E-03	0.032	0.033	2.47E-03	0.033	0.029	1.93E-03	0.030
Div-S	0.022	1.92E-03	0.032	0.029	2.28E-03	0.031	0.020	1.33E-03	0.024
Div-E	0.023	2.05E-03	0.034	0.033	2.36E-03	0.032	0.030	2.00E-03	0.030
Div-ST	0.023	2.22E-03	0.035	0.025	1.39E-03	0.021	0.022	1.28E-03	0.019
Div-txtST	0.023	2.16E-03	0.035	0.034	2.47E-03	0.033	0.030	1.99E-03	0.030
Div-EST	0.023	2.09E-03	0.034	0.031	2.40E-03	0.031	0.030	1.99E-03	0.030
Div-txtEST	**0.024**	**2.30E-03**	**0.036**	**0.034**	**2.49E-03**	**0.033**	**0.031**	**2.07E-03**	**0.031**

word news articles generate better digests as compared to CW12 web pages. The text-only methods, *Mcd*, *Rdh*, and *Cov-txtQM* perform significantly better than *Rand*, as expected. Among the text-only methods, *Rdh* and *Cov-txtQM* show significant improvements over *Mcd* in terms of Rouge scores. At the same time, *Rdh* and *Cov-txtQM* follow different frameworks and prove to have overall similar performance. However, *Cov-txtQM* method proves to be better for Gigaword, and CW12 datasets while for NYT, *Cov-txtQM* gets significantly lower Rouge-2 F1 score. *Cov-txtEM* that uses only the empirical query terms proves to be the worst text-only method, thus highlighting the advantage of incorporating our query-text model. Next, we look at the methods that extend the coverage based framework into the different dimensions. *Cov-T* and *Cov-S* do not prove to be effective in any dataset. The *Cov-E* gets significantly higher score from its contemporary methods considering only time and geolocations. This method gets the highest gain over its contemporaries in the CW12 dataset. However, it always performs significantly worse than the text-only methods as shown in Table 4. The coverage-based methods in the time, geolocations, and entity dimensions get worse scores than the *Rand* due to relatively shorter digest generated. Later in the section, we discuss this in detail. Our proposed divergence-based methods perform better that the coverage-based methods across all three datasets. This is because *Div-T*, *Div-S*, *Div-E*, *Div-ST*, and *Div-STE* always perform better than the *Cov-T*, *Cov-S*, *Cov-E*, *Cov-ST*, and *Cov-STE* methods. Next we analyze the different combinations of dimensions in the divergence framework. The text-only method under this framework is equivalent to *Rdh* that performs significantly better than *Div-T*, *Div-S*, and *Div-E*. However, different combinations of the time, geolocations, and entities as *Div-ST* and *Div-STE* perform better than the text-only method. Finally, the *Div-txtSTE* with highest score proves to be the best method for our task.

Variance Analysis. From our experiments so far what is clear is that event digests generated by the *Div-txtEST* method are closest to the gold standard Wikipedia articles. However, we perform an extended evaluation using the proposed w-Rouge measure that computes the mean Rouge-1 F1 score with respect to individual paragraphs in the Wikipedia articles. Firstly, we assume that each paragraph describes some aspect of the event. Thus, a larger mean with high variance in the weighted F1 score indicates higher coverage of the Wikipedia paragraphs, and hence better diversity in the generated digest. As shown in Table 5, all methods get higher mean and variance from *Rand* across all three datasets. We find that the *Div-txtEST* method proves to be the method that generates most diversified digest by achieving the highest mean and MVar scores. The next best method is *Div-txtST*.

Varying Digest Length. Next we analyze the effect on the quality of the digest by varying the digest *length budget*. Table 6 compares the *Div-txtEST* method with the text-only methods, *Cov-txtQM* and *Rdh*, in terms of Rouge-2. What we find is that for smaller length budget, *Cov-txtQM* performs better than other methods. We also find that both *Cov-txtQM* and *Div-txtEST* perform better than the *Rdh* across all the length budgets in Gigaword and CW12 datasets. The poor performance of the *Rdh* as compared to *Cov-txtQM* can easily be understood by analyzing their formulation. For very small budget of only 50 words, on average only two excerpts are selected into the digest by all the methods. *Rdh* first selects the most relevant excerpt, and then as the next it selects the one that is least redundant from the first. This causes the Precision to fall and an overall decrease in the F1 score. On the other hand, *Cov-txtQM* attempts to cover as many important terms with high probability in the Q_{text} to maximize the coverage. This generates a better digest for the smaller length budget. However, in the NYT dataset, for larger length budgets, *Cov-txtQM* suffers due to the lesser redundancy in the news articles. Thus, as it tries to maximize term coverage, the Precision falls resulting in lower F1 scores as compared to *Rdh*. The effect of diversifying across time, geolocations, and entities in the *Div-txtEST* method is evident when the length budget is larger than 100.

Discussion. As the first point, we discuss the poor performance of the coverage framework in time, geolocation, and entity dimensions. The coverage-based framework selects excerpts such that the maximum number of *units* (of time, geolocations, or entities) in a given query are covered. The associated weights, as described in Equation 14, denote the importance of the units for a given query, thus forcing the ILP solver to cover more important units first. As a drawback, this framework does not take into consideration the importance of the units for the excerpts. This causes selection of excerpts that may not be relevant. Moreover, in the dimensions other than text, excerpts that do not come with explicit annotations are

Table 6: Varying the length budget of methods.

Datasets	Length	Rdh P	Rdh R	Rdh F1	Cov-txtQM P	Cov-txtQM R	Cov-txtQM F1	Div-txtEST P	Div-txtEST R	Div-txtEST F1
NYT	50	0.166	0.003	0.006	0.231	0.005	**0.009**	0.236	0.004	0.008
	100	0.222	0.009	**0.016**	0.211	0.008	0.015	0.223	0.008	0.015
	200	0.208	0.016	0.027	0.194	0.015	0.026	0.213	0.016	**0.027**
	300	0.199	0.022	0.036	0.184	0.021	0.034	0.205	0.023	**0.036**
	400	0.194	0.029	0.044	0.176	0.026	0.040	0.199	0.029	**0.044**
	500	0.189	0.034	0.050	0.169	0.032	0.046	0.194	0.035	**0.051**
Giga	50	0.146	0.003	0.005	0.268	0.006	**0.010**	0.242	0.005	0.009
	100	0.225	0.009	0.016	0.236	0.010	**0.018**	0.227	0.009	0.017
	200	0.209	0.016	0.027	0.206	0.016	0.027	0.209	0.017	**0.028**
	300	0.196	0.022	0.036	0.193	0.022	0.035	0.200	0.024	**0.037**
	400	0.189	0.028	0.043	0.186	0.028	0.043	0.191	0.030	**0.044**
	500	0.184	0.033	0.049	0.182	0.034	0.049	0.186	0.035	**0.051**
CW12	50	0.192	0.004	0.007	0.265	0.006	**0.010**	0.198	0.005	0.009
	100	0.189	0.007	0.013	0.223	0.009	**0.016**	0.187	0.009	0.016
	200	0.184	0.012	0.021	0.191	0.016	0.026	0.185	0.016	**0.027**
	300	0.187	0.017	0.028	0.176	0.021	0.032	0.176	0.022	**0.035**
	400	0.185	0.021	0.032	0.168	0.026	0.039	0.172	0.028	**0.041**
	500	0.183	0.023	0.035	0.164	0.030	0.044	0.169	0.033	**0.046**

automatically disregarded. Since a single temporal or geographical expression can represent a large time interval (e.g., a century) or geographic area (e.g., a continent) respectively, the coverage of query units are easily maximized by selecting few excerpts. For example, the entire temporal scope of query in Figure 1 is covered by excerpt 8. This causes the *Cov-T* and *Cov-S* methods to generate digests with fewer excerpts. Hence, they receive a worse Rouge score than the *Rand* which simply benefits from generating longer digest. On the other hand, the divergence-based framework additionally regards the importance (higher generative probability) of a unit for the individual excerpts. While generating the digest, the ILP solver first selects excerpts which cover important query units with higher probability, thus lowering the overall divergence of the digest to the query. Moreover, since each excerpt is associated with an independent smoothed model for each dimension, no excerpt is disregarded for digest generation.

Next, we discuss the diversification of excerpts in the digest achieved by each method. We note that Wikipedia articles as gold standard digests are textually larger than the system generated digests. We assume that Wikipedia articles cover most aspects of a given event as a query. To get a better insight into the diversification of the excerpts, we compare the methods using w-Rouge, proposed by us. The *Div-txtEST* gets the highest mean and variance scores, and proves that it achieves the best diversification.

We next discuss the individual dimensions. Text is clearly the most important dimension in all our methods. However, we find that the text-only methods heavily rely on the query modeling techniques. Using only the empirical query terms leads to worse performance as shown by the *Cov-txtEM* method. The *Cov-E* method uses only entities instead of all terms, as motivated by Gillick et al., is not able to beat text-only methods in Rouge-2 scores. Time and geolocations are important indicators of identifying event-related excerpts and work well as a combination. Individually, we run into sparsity problems with very few annotations in excerpts. This is more pronounced in the CW12 dataset. Combination of text, time, and geolocations as the *Div-txtST* proves to be the second best method in the news datasets where we get comparatively more annotations. This is also due to the fact that every excerpt from a news article is also annotated with the publication date of the source article. Entities are more prominent in the CW12 documents and help to reinforce the text model. However, across all the datasets, combination of all four dimensions proves to be most effective.

Gain/Loss analysis. Rouge measures assume that higher n-gram overlap with gold standard implies more relevant excerpts in the digest. Thus, to get insights into the overall quality of digests, we manually identify relevant excerpts (highlighted in green) by referring to their source documents. We look at queries for which *Div-txtEST* shows the highest gain and worst loss in w-Rouge scores, when compared to the best among the text-only methods.

It achieves the highest gain in w-Rouge from the best text-only method for the query:

January 26, 2001: An earthquake hits Gujarat, India, killing almost 20,000.

For this query, the best text-only method proves to be *Cov-txtQM*. Let us compare the digest generated by both methods:

Event Digest by the *Div-txtEST* method:
• In 1988 a devastating earthquake struck northern Armenia, killing 25,000 people, and in 1990 50,000 were killed by an earthquake that struck Rasht, Iran. • AP, 10405 2005 Oct 8, A 7.6-magnitude earthquake hit Kashmir near the Pakistan-India border reaching to Afghanistan. • Reuters, 725052005 Jul 24, A 7.2 earthquake hit Indias southern Andaman and Nicobar Islands and part of Indonesia. • **Shobha De, The Week, February 18, 2001 The story of the devastating earthquake in Gujarat is the story of women.** • **Scientists are already working to prepare earthquake probability map.** • **Skyscrapers need special construction to make them earthquake resistant.** • **This earthquake was not felt in Amreli, Junagarh or Porbander districts.** • **Leaders called for greater cooperation within the region to deal with the aftermath of disasters like the Kashmir earthquake and last year's devastating tsunami.** • **Additional Info The earthquake was centred 4.5 kms E of Gandhidham Gujarat, India.** • The Herald,India – was affected by the December 26, 2004 earthquake and subsequent tsunamis. • **Exactly a month ago, 18,122 people were killed in a deadly earthquake in the Kutch district.** • **The earthquake was felt strongly in parts of east-central Kachchh near the towns of Bachau and Vondh.** • Quito, now the capital of Ecuador, was shaken by an earthquake in 1797, and more than 40,000 people died. • **Almost four weeks after the earthquake, Gujarat is still coming to terms with what was and what is.** • The newly reopened Peace Bridge linking the Indian and Pakistani portions of disputed Kashmir nearly collapsed during the earthquake.

Event Digest by the *Cov-txtQM* method:
• 543 AD - Disastrous earthquakes shaked much of the world; 803 AD - Fierce storms lashed the west coast of Ireland, killing close to 1,000; 851 AD - Rome had a violent earthquake that damaged Pope Leos 4-year-old Leonine Wall and further destroyed the Colosseum; 856 AD - an earthquake at Corinth killed an estimated 45,000 Greeks; 856 AD - an earthquake at Damghan, Iran killed an estimated 200,000; 893 AD - an earthquake at Ardabil, Iran killed about 150,000 people1138 AD - an earthquake at Aleppo, Syria claimed lives of aprox 230,000 people; 1290 AD - an earthquake at Chihli, China killed about 100,000 people; 1319 AD - an Armenian earthquake shatters the city of Ani. • By Dear Anonymous As far as policymakers go, it is an ardous task to make them understand the dangers of exploiting all our...By Scientists suggest local-level mapping as India upgrades its seismic map. • The earthquake that hit Sikkim on September 18, killing some 150 people and devastating the Himalayan state, was unexpected. • 1976 AD - an earthquake and tidal wave hit Mindanao, Philippines; 1976 AD - an earthquake hit Guatemala; 1978 AD - an earthquake destroyed Tabas a city in eastern Iran; 1985 AD - a magnitude 8.1 earthquake devastated part of Mexico City and three coastal states1: 985 AD - Nevada del Ruiz errupted, 85 mi northwest of Bogot. • In North America, the San Francisco earthquake of 1906 caused extensive damage and claimed about 700 lives. • **Almost four weeks after the earthquake, Gujarat is still coming to terms with what was and what is.**

We note that the *Div-txtEST* method selects more relevant excerpts. The *Cov-txtQM* method maximizes the coverage of the textual terms in the query-text model which leads to selection of irrelevant excerpts that enlist past earthquakes. These are however not selected by *Div-txtEST* due to their large divergence with query-time and -space models. Thus, due to combined diversification across the time, geolocations, and entities, *Div-txtEST* generates better quality digest with more relevant excerpts and a wider coverage.

The *Div-txtEST* method gets the worst loss in w-Rouge from the best text-only method, *Cov-txtQM*, for query:

November 22, 1995: Rosemary West is sentenced to life for killing 10 women and girls, including her daughter and stepdaughter, after the jury returns a guilty verdict at Winchester Crown Court. The trial judge recommends that she should never be released from prison, making her only the second woman in British legal history to be subjected to a whole life tariff (the other is Myra Hindley).

Let us compare the digest generated by both methods:

Event Digest by the *Div-txtEST* method:
• An Orange County jury found Miller guilty in November, and on Nov. 27 see voted 11-1 to recommend the death sentence. • A Pasco County jury found Partin guilty of 1st-degree murder in March. • In July, a jury found Ballard, 67, white, guilty of the 1st-degree murder of Traub. • The same jury found Abdool guilty of first-degree murder last week for the Feb. 25, 2006 death of 17-year-old Amelia Sookdeo. • Last month, on March 5 see, a jury voted 7-5 to recommend a death sentence for Smith. • The sentence followed an 11-1 jury recommendation that Wade receive the death penalty. • The judge may override the jury decision. • Albright Gregory Murphy, 45, was convicted of the 1st-degree premeditated killing in a March jury trial. • The points in Welchs appeal, he challenged his sentence on the basis of jury selection. • The jury voted 7 to 5 to recommend the killer receive a death sentence. • The jury voted 10 to 2. • **She was found guilty of murder and sentenced to life imprisonment.** • The jury recommended by a 9-3 vote that Ballard be executed. • Judges typically follow jury recommendations, so Teppers ruling was somewhat surprising. • On Sept. 26 the same jury that found him guilty, unanimously recommended the death penalty. • After a bench trial, JudgeBurge found Kovarbasich guilty of voluntary manslaughter on April 29, 2010. • A life sentence was recommended by Florida prosecutors. • Watson vacated the sentence in 2005. • The sentence is determined by a jury.

Event Digest by the *Cov-txtQM* method:
• An Orange County jury found Miller guilty in November, and on Nov. 27 see voted 11-1 to recommend the death sentence. • It is a very difficult case, but it is the verdict of the jury, he said. • The sentence is determined by a jury. • Albright Gregory Murphy, 45, was convicted of the 1st-degree premeditated killing in a March jury trial. • As he had during the verdict, Riley showed little emotion as his sentence was imposed. • On Sept. 26 the same jury that found him guilty, unanimously recommended the death penalty. • But next week vital and previously withheld testimony from one of her children could overturn the sentence By Tracy McVeigh • **A battered wife serving life imprisonment for killing her husband may soon be freed following evidence from her traumatize daughter which was held back from the original jury.** • **The jury was unanimous West was guilty of ten murders, and the judge, Mr Justice Mantell, sentenced her to life imprisonment with a recommendation that she should serve at least 25 years.** • The jury voted 10 to 2. • Miscarriage of justice and womens groups have been campaigning on Donna's behalf since the verdict two years ago. • After a three-day trial and only two and a half hours of deliberation, a jury of five men and one woman convicted Wade of second-degree murder. • Circuit Judge Lynn Tepper sentenced Smith, 30, to life in prison for killing Robert Crawford in 1999, breaking with a split jurys recommendation that Smith be sentenced to death.

Both methods select few relevant excerpts into the digest. However, the text-only method selects excerpts based on term matching that leads to better Rouge scores. *Div-txtEST* method suffers due to the sparsity of annotations in the event dimensions.

5. CONCLUSION

We proposed the problem of generating a digest that presents a holistic view on a given Wikipedia event. We proposed a novel divergence-based framework for selecting excerpts from pseudo-relevant input news articles such that the global divergence between the digest and the query is minimized. The problem was formulated as an ILP for global inference to maximize the overall relevance of the digest to the input event query, while reducing inter-excerpt redundancies in text, time, geolocations, and entity dimensions. In experimental evaluation, we compared several methods, and found that our divergence-based method that considers all dimensions of an event proves to be most appropriate for event digest generation.

References

[1] J. Allan, R. Gupta, and V. Khandelwal. Temporal summaries of new topics. *SIGIR* 2001.

[2] K. Berberich, S. J. Bedathur, O. Alonso, and G. Weikum. A language modeling approach for temporal information needs. *ECIR* 2010.

[3] J. P. Callan. Passage-level evidence in document retrieval. *SIGIR* 1994.

[4] J. Carbonell and J. Goldstein. The use of mmr, diversity-based reranking for reordering documents and producing summaries. *SIGIR* 1998.

[5] H. L. Chieu and Y. K. Lee. Query based event extraction along a timeline. *SIGIR* 2004.

[6] Z. Dou, S. Hu, K. Chen, R. Song, and J. R. Wen. Multi-dimensional search result diversification. *WSDM* 2009.

[7] E. Filatova. Event-based extractive summarization. *ACL Workshop on Summarization* 2004.

[8] D. Gillick and B. Favre. A scalable global model for summarization. *ILP* 2009.

[9] M. A. Hearst and C. Plaunt. Subtopic structuring for full-length document access. *SIGIR* 1993.

[10] J. Hoffart, F. M. Suchanek, K. Berberich, and G. Weikum. YAGO2: A spatially and temporally enhanced knowledge base from Wikipedia. *AAAI Press* 2013.

[11] J. Hoffart. Discovering and Disambiguating Named Entities in Text. *SIGMOD/PODS Ph.D. Symposium* 2013.

[12] P. Hu, D. H. Ji, H. Wang, and C. Teng. Query-focused multi-document summarization using co-training based semi-supervised learning. *PACLIC* 2009.

[13] M. Kaszkiel and J. Zobel. Effective ranking with arbitrary passages. *Journal of the American Society for Information Science and Technology*, 52(4) 2001.

[14] Y. Li and S. Li. Query-focused multi-document summarization: Combining a topic model with graph-based semi-supervised learning. *COLING* 2014.

[15] C. Y. Lin. Rouge: A package for automatic evaluation of summaries. *ACL Workshop* 2004.

[16] M. Litvak and M. Last. Graph-based keyword extraction for single-document summarization. *ACL* 2008.

[17] R. McCreadie, C. Macdonald, and I. Ounis. Incremental update summarization: Adaptive sentence selection based on prevalence and novelty. *CIKM* 2014.

[18] R. McDonald. A Study of Global Inference Algorithms in Multi-document Summarization. *Springer Berlin-Heidelberg* 2007.

[19] A. Mishra and K. Berberich. Linking Wikipedia Events to Past News. *TAIA* 2014.

[20] A. Mishra and K. Berberich. Leveraging Semantic Annotations to Link Wikipedia and News Archives. *ECIR* 2016.

[21] K. Riedhammer, B. Favre, and D. Hakkani-Tür. Long story short–global unsupervised models for keyphrase based meeting summarization. *Speech Communication*, 52(10) 2010.

[22] D. Shahaf, C. Guestrin, E. Horvitz, J. Leskovec. Effective ranking with arbitrary passages. *Communications of the ACM*, 58(11) 2015.

[23] G. Salton, J. Allan, and C. Buckley. Approaches to passage retrieval in full text information systems. *SIGIR* 1993.

[24] B. Taneva , G .Weikum. Gem-based entity-knowledge maintenance. *ECIR* 2013.

[25] M. Tsagkias, M. de Rijke, and W. Weerkamp. Linking online news and social media. *WSDM* 2011.

[26] X. Wang, H. Fang, and C. Zhai. A study of methods for negative relevance feedback. *SIGIR* 2008.

[27] K. Woodsend and M. Lapata. Multiple aspect summarization using integer linear programming. *EMNLP-CoNLL* 2012.

[28] R. Yan, X. Wan, J. Otterbacher, L. Kong, X. Li, and Y. Zhang. Evolutionary timeline summarization: a balanced optimization framework via iterative substitution. *SIGIR* 2011.

[29] C. Zhai and J. D. Lafferty. Two-stage language models for information retrieval. *SIGIR* 2002.

[30] C. X. Zhai, W. W. Cohen, and J. Lafferty. Beyond independent relevance: methods and evaluation metrics for subtopic retrieval. *SIGIR* 2003.

[31] S. H. Zhong, Y. Liu, B. Li, and J. Long. Query-oriented unsupervised multi-document summarization via deep learning model. *Expert Systems with Applications*, 42(21) 2015.

Terms over LOAD: Leveraging Named Entities for Cross-Document Extraction and Summarization of Events

Andreas Spitz
spitz@informatik.uni-heidelberg.de

Michael Gertz
gertz@informatik.uni-heidelberg.de

Institute of Computer Science, Heidelberg University
Im Neuenheimer Feld 205, 69120 Heidelberg, Germany

ABSTRACT

Real world events, such as historic incidents, typically contain both spatial and temporal aspects and involve a specific group of persons. This is reflected in the descriptions of events in textual sources, which contain mentions of named entities and dates. Given a large collection of documents, however, such descriptions may be incomplete in a single document, or spread across multiple documents. In these cases, it is beneficial to leverage partial information about the entities that are involved in an event to extract missing information. In this paper, we introduce the LOAD model for cross-document event extraction in large-scale document collections. The graph-based model relies on co-occurrences of named entities belonging to the classes *locations*, *organizations*, *actors*, and *dates* and puts them in the context of surrounding *terms*. As such, the model allows for efficient queries and can be updated incrementally in negligible time to reflect changes to the underlying document collection. We discuss the versatility of this approach for event summarization, the completion of partial event information, and the extraction of descriptions for named entities and dates. We create and provide a LOAD graph for the documents in the English Wikipedia from named entities extracted by state-of-the-art NER tools. Based on an evaluation set of historic data that include summaries of diverse events, we evaluate the resulting graph. We find that the model not only allows for near real-time retrieval of information from the underlying document collection, but also provides a comprehensive framework for browsing and summarizing event data.

Keywords

Event extraction; event representation; document indexing; named entities; entity linking; summarization; ranking

1. INTRODUCTION

The description of events is one of the core concepts of human communication, as we desire to not only speak about the way things *are*, but also about how they *change*. It thus comes as no surprise that the detection, extraction and analysis of events plays a pivotal role in natural language processing. As a result, a lot of research has already been devoted to these tasks, and existing works focus on the extraction of events and temporal facts from more or less unstructured textual sources such as news articles [24, 27], social media [16], Twitter [3, 32], Wikipedia articles [13, 28, 41] or even Wikipedia edits [19, 25]. Some authors take the opposite approach and link Wikipedia events to historic news articles [29]. The breadth of these applications is reflected in the number of different definitions for the term *event* in the literature. Here, we view an event in analogy to the definition given for the TDT task [8] as *"something that happens at a given place and time between a group of actors."* Thus, we regard events as something at the intersection of *time*, *location* and involved *actors*, either individually or in *organizations* of multiple persons. In these cases, the void of structural information in unstructured textual sources is one of the greatest challenges, albeit one that can be ameliorated by focussing on the structure of the events themselves. On a language level, this is reflected in the original ACE definition of event detection [10] and has been utilized for tasks such as event threading [30] and incident threading [12]. On a higher level and across documents, however, with prior knowledge of already extracted named entities that are not necessarily contained within the sentences that correspond to the traditional definition of events, a local approach alone is not sufficient.

Given the definition of an event through the involved entities, the information pertaining to a specific event may be spread across several pages and not provided in one single context. Consider, for example, the documentation of the Olympic Games in Wikipedia. For each iteration of the games, there are pages that go into great detail about the games themselves, along with a multitude of pages about individual athletes. However, not all information about events at the games can be found on the central page, while the pages of individual athletes may be lacking important information such as exact dates or even the location, and merely reference to the Olympic Games of a given year. Thus, only the combination of data from multiple pages allows the reconstruction of all pieces of an event, including the place, time, and involved participants. As a result, the tasks of event extraction and summarization are closely tied to named entity extraction and entity linking. For large document collections, such a global approach thus requires the inclusion of efficient indexing strategies of the involved entities and documents in the process.

SIGIR '16, July 17-21, 2016, Pisa, Italy
© 2016 ACM. ISBN 978-1-4503-4069-4/16/07... $15.00
DOI: http://dx.doi.org/10.1145/2911451.2911529

When considering events as the co-occurrences of named entities of different types, we are also no longer bound by the concepts of *one sense per discourse* [15] or *one sense per collocation* [42]. While these have been shown to be valid in most situations and thus acceptable assumptions, they leave room for improvement as the task of disambiguation becomes less taxing when multiple entities of differing classes are involved in a given context. Given the close link between event detection and named entity extraction, a representation of the data that accounts for this seems sensible, especially if it enables queries to the data in a similar fashion. This approach is supported by recent research into web query evaluation, where the importance of the distinction between so called *content words* and *intent words* has been highlighted [34]. We find that this concept can be applied to the browsing of event data, where membership of query entities to a certain class is known at query formulation time. By using a structure for queries that reflects the structure of the event data itself, we can leverage this information that would otherwise be lost.

While numerous systems and approaches exist that enable browsing of extracted information or query results based on temporal characteristics as a timeline [3, 26, 35, 40], there are others that allow browsing on a spatial dimension instead [2]. With regard to events, however, we argue that the temporal, geographic and social components are inextricably interwoven and retain their full semantic meaning only within this entire context. Any method for the extraction and representation of events should therefore include all of these components (or *entities*) and assign to them equal importance in the underlying model. Here, we provide an important step in this direction and demonstrate the flexibility of such an approach, not just for event extraction but also for related tasks such as summarization and the generation of timelines.

Contributions. Our contributions are twofold. **(i)** We define the LOAD model for the representation and indexing of named entities for the task of event retrieval and description, which is versatile and well suited to related tasks such as event and entity summarization or entity linking. **(ii)** We provide an instantiation of our model on the English Wikipedia, which we make available to the research community[1], including the code for creating and using such a graph, as well as the evaluation data sets.

Structure. In Section 2, we discuss prior and related work, before we present our model in detail in Section 3. Afterwards, we discuss implementation strategies and an application of the model to the English Wikipedia in Section 4. In Section 5, we evaluate the LOAD graph for Wikipedia against a ground truth that is based on a *This Day in History* data set. We give a summary and outlook in Section 6.

2. RELATED WORK

Related work can be split into two broad categories, namely the extraction of events or temporal facts and graph-based information retrieval frameworks.

Extraction of temporal facts and events. Temporal information is prevalent in many documents across domains and provides a method of inducing structure in unstructured document collections due to the ordering aspects of time. Thus, exploiting temporal information extracted from documents has become an important part of information retrieval [6], which has recently seen a lot of advances in this regard. Therefore, the following list is focussed on works that are based on linking temporal and entity information for event retrieval and description.

Using a news archive, Setty et al. generate timelines highlighting important dates for a specific user query (e.g., about persons or events) [35]. Their approach exploits the document creation times of news articles under the assumption that the top-k time-travel query result for the topic of interest changes significantly at important times. Huet et al. use structured data in the form of a knowledge base to mine temporal trends or assess the importance of entities [22]. In an approach that is also based on an external knowledge base of news articles, Gupta and Berberich identify time intervals of interest for given keyword queries based on pseudo-relevant documents [21]. They employ a probabilistic approach for the selection of suitable documents for a given query and generate a time interval from the contained temporal expressions. Kanhabua and Nejdl analyse temporal anchor texts extracted from Wikipedia's edit history to track and detect the evolution of entities and events [25]. As in the approaches described above, temporal metadata (in this case, the edit history) is used to discover time-related knowledge.

In contrast to these approaches, our method uses only a document collection and exploits the temporal information that is available in the unstructured content of the documents. Articles that are similar in this respect include the analysis by Filannino and Nenadic, who extract temporal footprints of objects, persons, or historic periods from encyclopedic descriptions of Wikipedia articles [13]. Abujabal and Berberich also address the problem of extracting events from semantically annotated document collections. Based on methods from frequent itemset mining, they identify and rank events with relation to named entities [1]. In contrast to our approach, however, they consider events to be represented by sentences and thus cannot extract events that are spread across multiple documents. Kanhabua et al. assess the importance of temporal expressions to events based on entities and features [26]. They extract events based on the co-occurrence of entities and locations, but restrict co-occurrences to those within documents and single sentences.

While these approaches are similar to our work in exploiting temporal information described in the documents' text, we do not analyse single Wikipedia pages or use concept templates, but rather study the relationship between dates and content (e.g., entities, events, or keywords) in a general and global way. For this, we consider the full document collection at once without limiting our knowledge extraction to specific concepts. In addition, our model can be used for a multi-way summarization approach for points in time, entities and concepts.

There are also a number of systems for building knowledge bases of temporal information or timelines. One such system, CATE, extracts the context of entities (e.g., persons) and presents them in a timeline structure [40]. Kuzey and Weikum provide a framework for the extraction of temporal facts and events from the content and structure of Wikipedia articles by means of patterns and rules [28]. A similar approach is used to extend YAGO to include temporal knowledge [41]. Unlike these systems, we do not aim

[1]The Wikipedia LOAD graph, a Java implementation of our algorithm and interface, and the evaluation data can be found at `http://dbs.ifi.uni-heidelberg.de/?id=load`

to provide a knowledge base but a method of exploring and browsing a previously unknown document collection of unstructured text with respect to not only time but all entities that participate in real-world events.

Graph-based information retrieval. Das Sarma et al. build an *entity dynamic relation graph* to identify specific entities that participate in trending events, but do not consider locations [9]. Jatowt et al. use a time-term association graph in an estimation of the focus time of entire documents [23]. This graph is constructed from information that is extracted from an external corpus of news articles. Based on this association information, they identify discriminative time-term associations and employ these to estimate the focus time of given documents. Dutta and Weikum perform cross document co-reference resolution based on spectral graph clustering of mentions [11]. In a study of query methods, Bendersky and Croft use hypergraphs to model the occurrence of arbitrary classes of entities in queries [4]. However, this model is only applied to the queries themselves and not to the underlying data representation of the documents. The two works that are likely the most similar to our approach with respect to the model are based on graph representations of documents that facilitate Information Retrieval tasks. Blanco and Lioma explore a graph-based approach that models terms as nodes in a graph and weights their connections based on co-occurrence counts [5]. Based on this approach, they analyse the fitness of structural graph metrics for document ranking, but do not include named entities. Similarly, Rousseau and Vazirgiannis use an unweighted but directed graph to account for term order in text representation, the so called *graph-of-word* model [33]. In contrast to our work, they focus on the sentence level and do not include entities, which limits the possibilities of this model in event extraction. A third paper that uses a method similar to ours is from the field of citation analysis, where Chakraborty et al. suggest a system for finding communities in citation networks that uses a tripartite graph approach of authors, venues and papers [7], which is similar in semantics to our definition of actors, locations, and times.

The significant difference between our model and the above mentioned approaches is the proximity-based method of representing the co-occurrences of entities in the documents. This factor has been shown to play a major role in the quality of the retrieved information [39] and has recently been used by Geiß et al. to extract semantically meaningful networks of relations between entities of identical types from Wikipedia [17, 18]. In this paper, we combine this concept of text-based proximity with graph-based indexing of entities that has been employed for the modelling of terms and temporal expressions in a bipartite model [36]. We extend this concept to a multi-partite approach that includes all classes of entities that are of relevance to the task of event extraction. To this end, we provide an efficient representation of co-occurring entities that allows for both ad-hoc browsing of the entire data and real-time updates of the database in the case of changes to the underlying document collection, and take a step towards obtaining some of the functionality behind Google's Knowledge Graph for previously unseen document collections without an external knowledge base.

3. MODEL

With the main task being the identification and representation of events that emerge from the joint occurrence of named entities and temporal expressions, we base our model on the relationship between distinct classes of such entities that can be found in document collections. The most prominent class of involved entities are the *actors* in an event. Generally, these correspond to the named entity type of *persons*, but we use the more general term to also include non-person actors in possible fictional settings, to which the model is equally applicable. The underlying assumption is that actors are singular individuals. In contrast, we consider groups of people to be *organizations*, meaning that in this model, an organization may describe a company, a political party or even a rock band. To represent the geographic component, we include *locations*, which in the most general formulation are points or areas in space at which events take place. Finally, the temporal dimension is included by *dates*. Here, we only consider dates and not intervals, although a refinement of the model in such a way that it includes a set of temporally ordered, discrete dates as an interval is certainly possible. Since we are interested in modelling and ultimately extracting the relationship between these entities, a graph is a natural choice for the model as described in the following.

3.1 The LOAD graph model

Let P be a collection of documents (or *pages*) for which we define the model. Each document $p \in P$ consists of a number of sentences $s \in p$. With S we denote the set of all sentences in all documents, i.e., $S := \bigcup_{p \in P} \{s \in p\}$. Note that, while two sentences may have identical content, we consider them to be separate entities under this model. We define an ordering $\tau : S \to \mathbb{N}$ that maps a sentence to its index in the document that contains it. Assuming an underlying bag-of-words model, we can now treat a sentence as a collection of words, which we partition into several classes in accordance to the motivation given in Section 1. Note that we do not make a distinction between words and expressions that may consist of multiple words. For the purpose of this paper, we consider words to be units within a text that has already been tagged for named entities and dates. Specifically, we distinguish between the classes *locations* L, *organizations* O, *actors* A, and *dates* D, hence the acronym *LOAD*. Any word in a sentence that is neither of the aforementioned is considered to be a *term*. Thus, we define the set of terms T as

$$T := \bigcup_{s \in S} \{w \in s \mid w \notin L \cup O \cup A \cup D\}. \qquad (1)$$

A sentence can thus be considered to be a multiset of entities $s \in (L \cup O \cup A \cup D \cup T)^*$. In the following, we refer to the set of actors, locations, organizations, dates and terms as *entities*. Based on these seven classes, we define their union $V := L \cup O \cup A \cup D \cup T \cup S \cup P$ along with a function $\sigma : V \to \{L, O, A, D, T, S, P\}$ that maps each element $v \in V$ to its original class $\sigma(v)$. Note that we do not consider ambiguities at this stage. Therefore, if a word has two meanings (e.g., Washington, which could be a person's name or a location), we consider these meanings to be represented by two distinct elements of V that belong to different classes.

To obtain an undirected graph representation $G = (V, E)$ of the co-occurrences of these entities, sentences and pages, we introduce a set of edges as defined in the following. Since G is undirected, we do not make a distinction in notation between the edges (v, w) and (w, v). To retain the seven partitions of V, we disallow edges between nodes in the same set, i.e., G is a multi-partite graph, such that for all $e = (v, w) : e \in E \Rightarrow \sigma(v) \neq \sigma(w)$. Since there exists a surjection from S to P, we also exclude direct edges between P and all further sets, as they are not necessary. Thus, we obtain for all $(v, w) \in E : w \in P \Rightarrow v \in S$. A schematic representation of the resulting graph structure is shown in Figure 1.

To generate weights $\omega : E \to \mathbb{R}$ for the edges of the graph, we introduce the concept of *Instances* I of entities. An instance describes a distinct occurrence of an entity in a sentence (and thus a page) and there exist surjective mappings $m : I \to V$ from instances to entities and $m_s : I \to S$ from instances to sentences. For example, if an entity v occurs twice on a given page p, there exist instances i and j along with sentences $s_i, s_j \in p$ such that $m_s(i) = s_i$ and $m_s(j) = s_j$ as well as $m(i) = m(j) = v$. With I_v we denote the set of all instances of entity v, i.e., $I_v := \{i \in I \mid m(i) = v\}$. To generate edge weights based on these instances, we furthermore distinguish between two different types of relationships. The first type of relationship occurs between sentences, pages and entities and describes a type of inclusion. For the inclusion of entities v in sentences s, we simply use the number of occurrences as a weight, i.e. we set

$$\omega(v, s) := |\{i \in I \mid m(i) = v \wedge m_s(i) = s\}| \qquad (2)$$

We define the weight between sentences and pages analogously, but note that the weight always equals 1 iff the page contains the sentence and 0 if it does not. The second type of relationship occurs between multiple entities and describes a co-occurrence within sentences and pages. To arrive at a definition of weights in this case, we first define the distance δ between two instances as

$$\delta(i, j) := |\tau(m_s(i)) - \tau(m_s(j))| \qquad (3)$$

i.e., the distance equals the number of sentences between the instances, or 0 if they occur in the same sentence. If i and j do not occur on the same page, we set $\delta(i, j) := \infty$. Based on this distance, we define the weight of edges between two entities v and w as

$$\omega(v, w) := \sum_{\substack{i \in I_v \\ j \in I_w}} \exp(-\delta(i, j)) \qquad (4)$$

i.e., we assign to all co-occurrences of instances of v and w a weight that diminishes exponentially with the distance between the two instances and derive the total edge weight as the sum of weights for all instances. Without loss of generality, we may treat edges with a weight of 0 as non-existing in the resulting graph to obtain a sparser and more efficient representation for the subsequent analysis. We thus define the binary adjacency matrix of G with dimension $|V|^2$ as $A_{vw} := 1$ iff $\omega(v, w) > 0$ and $A_{vw} := 0$ otherwise. We call the number of edges that are adjacent to a node v the degree of v and write $deg(v)$. Analogously, we define the class-specific degree $deg_x(v)$ of a node v as the number of edges from v to other nodes w for which $\sigma(w) = x$.

3.2 Hierarchical completeness conditions

For some of the entities that we consider in this context, there exist hierarchies that can be beneficial to include in the graph representation. One type of hierarchy is given by the granularity of dates, which includes years, months or days. To account for these differences in granularity, we consider dates to be sets of time points for which an inclusion hierarchy exists. That is, each day is included in a month and the same relation holds between months and years. As a result, we partition D into three subsets $D = D_y \cup D_m \cup D_d$. This hierarchy can be reflected in the graph by requiring that for all edges $(d, v) \in E$, if there exists a $d' \in D$ such that $d \subset d'$, then we also have $(d', v) \in E$ and we adjust the edge weight by setting $\omega(d', v) = \omega(d', v) + \omega(d, v)$, e.g., an edge between a day and another entity or sentence also induces an edge between this entity and both the month and year that include the day. An analogous hierarchical completeness condition can be formulated for locations if a geographic hierarchy of places is known.

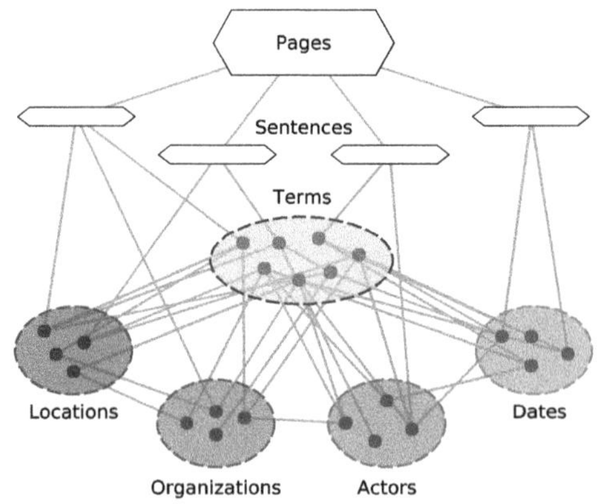

Figure 1: Schematic view of terms over the LOAD model along with their connections to the original sentences and documents.

A second kind of hierarchy can be defined for person names. Here, we observe that persons are frequently referred to by only parts of their full name, such as the first or last name. As an example, Alan Turing may be referred to as Alan Turing, Turing, etc. However, all mentions refer to the same person and induce co-occurrence relationships. Thus, we employ an approach that is reciprocal to the inclusion condition for dates and split a name n into components $n_1, ..., n_k$, for which we require that if there exists an edge $(n, v) \in E$ between the full name and some other entity v, then we also include edges $(n_1, v), ..., (n_k, v)$ and adjust the edge weight accordingly. While it is possible to apply this scheme to the names of organizations, these generally do not follow the same naming conventions as persons. However, an application to the names of locations is possible in cases where geographic hierarchy information is missing.

3.3 Ranking functions

To leverage the graph representation and extract information from the co-occurrences of entities in the document collection, we employ ranking functions. For any given entity, we can rank adjacent nodes in the graph representation by the importance of their co-occurrences to obtain the most relevant related entities. In other words, we obtain a ranking of nodes in one set, depending on the strength of their connections to nodes in other sets. The benefit of this approach is the possibility of computing relevant neighbours efficiently due to the graph representation, despite the overall size of the document collection.

First, we consider a binary ranking function between two sets of nodes. Thus, let $X, Y \in \{L, O, A, D, T\}$ be two classes of entities such that $X \neq Y$. We define a binary ranking function as $r_{XY} : X \rightarrow \mathbb{R}^{|Y|}$, i.e., we map a node $v \in X$ to a vector of ranking scores such that each node in Y is assigned a relevance score with regard to v. Thus, we can determine the most relevant neighbours of a query entity v.

In order to instantiate the ranking function, we want to find a way of ranking relevant nodes efficiently on a local level, i.e., by using only the neighbourhood of that node. Therefore, we employ a graph adaptation of the *tf-idf* score that has been shown to work well in a bipartite graph setting for ranking temporal expressions and terms [36], which we further modify to include the distance-based weight between entities instead of simple co-occurrence counts. As a measure of the relevance of co-occurrences between two specific nodes, we build upon the analogy to terms that are contained in a document by equating nodes $y \in Y$ with documents that "contain" the nodes $x \in X$ they are connected to (i.e., the entities they co-occur with). We then observe that the weight $\omega(x, y)$ in the graph corresponds to the overall strength of co-occurrences between x and y in the document collection, meaning that it represents a kind of term frequency (*tf*). Similarly, the class-specific degree of a node (i.e., the number of adjacent edges that lead to nodes of the respective class) is equivalent to the frequency with which it appears alongside entities of that particular class. As such, it is a kind of document frequency and can be used to compute an inverse document frequency (*idf*). By combining the two, we arrive at a version of the *tf-idf* score that is adapted to the graph representation:

$$tf\text{-}idf(x, y) := \frac{1}{f}\omega(x, y) \log \frac{|Y|}{deg_Y(x)} \tag{5}$$

To obtain a normalized ranking in the interval $[0, 1]$, we divide the resulting scores by a normalization factor f, which is chosen as the maximum local *tf-idf* score:

$$f := \max_{y' \in Y}(tf\text{-}idf(x, y')) \tag{6}$$

By ranking all entities that are connected to a query entity according to their normalized *tf-idf* scores, we obtain the desired ranking. Since there is no difference between the partitions of the graph from a graph-theoretic point of view, we may input any of the classes as X and Y in any combination. We are, however, not limited to binary ranking functions. In the case of events that have a geographic and temporal aspect and pertain to actors and locations (or both), it may be required to rank the importance of entities in one set with regard to entities from multiple other sets. With the inclusion of terms, we thus need a function that is of higher arity, i.e., we require a function $r : X^n \rightarrow \mathbb{R}^{|Y|}$, where the X_i are pairwise disjoint with Y. Here, we can use a ranking that consists of a combination of the individual rankings as defined in Equation 5, i.e.

$$r(\vec{x}, y) := \frac{1}{n}\eta(\vec{x}, y) \sum_{i=1}^{n} r(x_i, y) \tag{7}$$

for a query vector $\vec{x} \in X^n$. The parameter η enforces a local cohesion, i.e., it ensures that only those candidate entities count towards the ranking that are connected to at least two query entities. Formally,

$$\eta(\vec{x}, y) := \begin{cases} 1 & \text{if } \sum_{i=1}^{n} \sum_{j>i}^{n} A_{yx_i} A_{yx_j} > 1 \\ 0 & \text{otherwise} \end{cases} \tag{8}$$

In regard to summarization as an application, it is possible to extract a description of entities or a combination of entities as a ranking of adjacent terms with respect to the entity (or entities). However, it may be more convenient to directly extract entire sentences that are relevant to the provided entities instead of just keywords. Similarly, with respect to the task of entity linking, it may be pertinent to recommend well suited pages (i.e., documents) for a combination of entities. Thus, the ranking of sentences and documents is also of interest and can be achieved easily within the graph model. Formally, this requires a function $r : X^n \rightarrow \mathbb{R}^{|Y|}$, where the $X_i \in \{L, O, A, D, T\}$ and $Y \in \{S, P\}$. Here, we employ a straightforward instantiation of this ranking function as a proof-of-concept, although more involved measures are certainly possible within the model. To do this, we count the number of nodes in the query set that are connected to a sentence (i.e., entities that are contained in the sentence) or to all sentences within a page, respectively. For sentences s, we thus arrive at the following instantiation of a ranking:

$$r(\vec{x}, s) := \sum_{i=1}^{n} A_{sx_i} \tag{9}$$

For pages p, we can use the fact that the edges between sentences and pages are 0-1-valued to count the occurrences of all query terms in sentences of a page and obtain

$$r(\vec{x}, p) := \sum_{s \in S} \sum_{i=1}^{n} A_{sx_i} A_{sp} \tag{10}$$

Complexity. A key consideration for large document collections is the running time. The ranking functions as defined in Equations 5 and 7 can be computed efficiently in $\mathcal{O}(\langle deg_X Y \rangle \langle deg_Y X \rangle)$, where $\langle deg_X Y \rangle$ is the average set-specific degree of nodes in X with respect to set Y. For sparse graphs, these average degrees are smaller than the number of nodes by orders of magnitude, thus making these measures very efficient for the analysis of large document collections. Given the size of graphs that are obtained for larger document collections, this is a critical feature as we show in Section 4, where these ranking functions allow for ad-hoc ranking of neighbouring nodes. Beyond the presented ranking functions, the graph representation can serve as an index for further approaches based on entity co-occurrences.

4. APPLICATION AND EXPLORATION

In the following, we describe the technical details that are relevant to the implementation of our model. We then apply it to the English Wikipedia and discuss the resulting graph as well as query performance.

4.1 Document processing

Based on the model presented in the previous section, the implementation of a LOAD graph is fairly straightforward by extracting named entities from sentences and connecting them in a graph structure based on their distances in the text. However, we note at this point that the title of this paper was chosen due to the combinatorial explosion in the number of edges that result from fully connecting all entities that occur on a page, a process which creates a graph that is prohibitively large for large document collections. While the theory of the model is based on the assumption that entities on the same page share some connection, regardless of their distance in the text, long-distance connections are very weak and mostly negligible due to the exponential decay in edge weights. Therefore, we include a cut-off parameter c in the algorithm that excludes edges if the distance between the two instances is too large. Similarly, terms are less likely to be related to entities outside of their own sentence, so we limit the edges between terms and entities to those that appear in the same sentence. Based on these considerations, we arrive at the LOAD algorithm for constructing a graph representation of a document collection (see Algorithm 1). In the following, we discuss a number of aspects of practical importance to the implementation.

Term extraction. The extraction of terms is not as straightforward as it initially appears. Since terms are defined as everything that is left over after entities have been removed from a sentence, the deletion of entities is key. Ideally, entities should not overlap, which would enable a structured deletion of entities from a sentence. In practice, overlaps happen, especially if several annotation tools are used. We find the simplest solution to be the use of a bitmap for characters in a sentence to mark the covered text of entities for deletion. Afterwards, marked parts of a sentence are removed and the remainder is considered for term generation. Stop words are removed to prevent high frequency noise from masking the co-occurrences of content words.

Stemming. To reduce the size of the graph and group related terms into one node for improved recall in query answering, we recommend the use of a stemmer for term processing. This makes it much easier to match semantically similar words in a query on the resulting graph. While lemmatization would be preferable during the document processing phase, it would not be compatible with queries on the graph, as lemmatization is hardly possible on query terms that are used outside of sentences.

Algorithm 1 Creation of the LOAD graph based on the output of NER, temporal tagger and sentence splitter. The set function σ and distance function δ are defined in Section 3. The *update* function adds a new edge if it is not yet contained in E or adds the value to the existing weight ω if it already is. The cut-off parameter limits the number of co-occurrences.

Input: Documents D, cut-off parameter c

Initialize $V \leftarrow \emptyset$, $E \leftarrow \emptyset$ and $\omega(i,j) \leftarrow 0 \; \forall i,j$
for $d \in D$ **do**
    $S_d \leftarrow$ sentences in d
    $N_d \leftarrow$ entities in d
    $V \leftarrow V \cup S_d \cup N_d \cup \{d\}$
    for $s \in S_d$ **do**
        update E with $(s, d, 1)$
        $N_s \leftarrow s \cap N_d$
        $T_s \leftarrow s \setminus N_s$
        $V \leftarrow V \cup T_s$
        for $t \in T_s$ **do**
            update E with $(t, s, 1)$
            for $n \in N_s$ **do**
                update E with $(n, t, 1)$
    for $n_1 \in N_d$ **do**
        $N_d \leftarrow N_d \setminus \{n_1\}$
        for $n_2 \in N_d$ **do**
            if $\sigma(n_1) \neq \sigma(n_2)$ and $\delta(n_1, n_2) \leq c$ **then**
                $w \leftarrow \exp(-\delta(n_1, n_2))$
                update E with (n_1, n_2, w)

Output: $G = (V, E, \omega)$

Implementation architecture. As the resulting graph can be quite large, we consider two architectures. A purely memory-based approach is possible through the representation of the graph as a list of nodes with five types of adjacency lists, i.e., one adjacency list per adjacent class (thus, six lists in the case of nodes representing sentences and one for pages). Edge weights are stored in an identical structure. While such a representation is highly efficient with regard to query answering, it also requires large maps for the lookup of entity names, which tend to take up large amounts of memory. Alternatively, an external database can be used to store most of the information. With efficient indexing, the retrieval of node neighbourhoods is then slower but still possible. Hybrid approaches between the two architecture solutions are viable. For our experiments, we store only the sentences in an external database, as these are equivalent in size to the entire original document collection.

4.2 LOADing Wikipedia

To test the model on a large-scale document collection, we use the English Wikipedia dump of June 2, 2015, as input. Since the algorithm is designed to extract information from unstructured text, we exclude info boxes, tables, references, and pages of lists and thus only use the raw text without any links or pre-existing annotations. For the tokenization, sentence-splitting, POS-tagging, lemmatization and named entity recognition we use the Stanford Named Entity Recognizer [14]. We employ the 3-class model trained for CoNLL data to extract persons, organizations and locations per our definition of LOAD. As temporal tagger we use Heideltime [38] instead of StanfordNER, since Wikipedia articles largely follow a narrative structure and we therefore need a domain sensitive temporal tagger that distinguishes between the news and narrative domains [37]. For stemming terms, we use the Snowball stemmer that is an implementation of the Porter stemming algorithm [31]. We set the cut-off parameter for the distance between entities to $c = 5$, since this value allows the use of 32 bit single precision floating point numbers for storing the exponentially diminishing edge weights without loss of precision, which helps in keeping the graph size manageable. We use the hierarchical completeness condition for dates and the inclusion by splitting for the names of persons and locations.

In the annotation phase, we find that there are about 4.6M English Wikipedia articles that contain at least one annotation. The pages can be split into a total of 91.4M sentences, 53.5M of which contain at least one annotation. We find a total of 137.0M instances of entities, which are divided into 27.0M of class date, 44.2M of class location, 44.4M of class person and 21.3M that are annotated as organizations. After the extraction of co-occurrences and the aggregation of parallel edges, we obtain the LOAD graph, for which we give the metrics in Table 1. We observe that the number of distinct dates is by far the smallest due to the selected granularities year, month, and day. However, the coverage of dates in Wikipedia is above 50% for dates after the middle of the 16th century and perfect for dates after 1800 [36], meaning that each such date is mentioned at least once. The large number of terms can be explained by the presence of technical terms, mismatched names or loca-

class	L	O	A	D	T	S	P
L	0						
O	90.8	0					
A	275.8	105.7	0				
D	83.0	45.5	127.6	0			
T	182.8	93.9	316.6	57.3	0		
S	71.3	20.9	84.4	38.3	412.2	0	
P	0	0	0	0	0	53.5	0
nodes	2.7	3.4	7.1	0.2	4.9	53.5	4.5

Table 1: Number of edges (top) and nodes (bottom) of the LOAD graph constructed from the English Wikipedia (in millions).

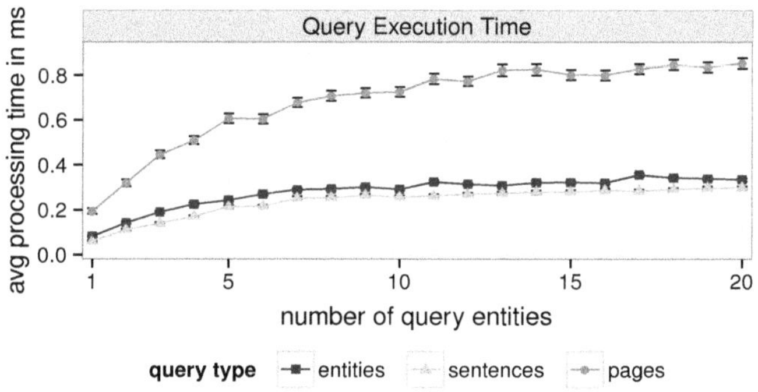

Figure 2: Processing speeds of the three query types with respect to the number of entities in the query. Results were averaged over 1000 samples, error bars denote the standard mean error.

tions and numeric data, which we did not model as separate entities (although it is a possible extension of the model).

The annotation of the data required approximately 4 days on a dual Intel Xeon E5-2650 CPU with 20 physical cores and 256GB main memory. The LOAD graph construction took 46 hours with a serial algorithm that is in theory trivially parallelizable for future approaches. The resulting graph has an uncompressed size of about 70GB on disk when edges are stored in one direction or 110GB if they are duplicated for faster initialization of the query interface. Despite these expensive initial computations, the resulting graph allows for near real-time information retrieval and browsing of relations as shown in Figure 2. Even for higher counts of entities in a query, the processing takes less than a millisecond on average (queries on multiple highly connected entities may take up to a second), due to the representation of the sparse graph in adjacency list format. Queries on page recommendations (i.e., for entity linking) take slightly longer since the connections between entities from all sentences on the page must be considered. For sentence queries, the shown time does not include the lookup of the actual sentences in the external database. In summary, we find that the processing time of information retrieval is insignificant given the size of the document collection and is thus competitive with search engine speeds, especially since queries are processed only serially in the current implementation.

4.3 Experimental results

Based on the LOAD graph of Wikipedia, we include a number of example applications. Due to the versatility of the system with regard to the classes of entities that can be used in a query, we only present a selection of possible application scenarios. However, we invite the reader to download the graph alongside our query interface and explore the data themselves or implement further ranking scores (see Section 1 for a link). For the following examples and the subsequent evaluation, we introduce the concept of a subquery. Here, this means that input strings for entities of classes *location* and *actor* in a query are split into their components which are then included in the query as well. The queries thus benefit from the completeness condition of the graph as defined in Section 3. In the following, we use the syntax $\langle OC : (IC, value)^{*} \rangle$ to describe queries, where $OC, IC \in \{L, O, A, D, T, S, P\}$ are the desired output class and the classes of input entities, respectively, while *value* is the name of the query entity.

Browsing. The most straightforward application of the graph is the ability to browse the connections between actors, locations, dates, and organizations. In Table 2, we show the top-ranked results of three queries centred on *Edward Snowden*. By including Snowden as the only query entity, we obtain a list of organizations that are closely tied to him, including the *NSA* and *USIS*, the company that vetted Snowden. Duplicate entries for the different spellings of the NSA are caused by the NER step, which suggests that the LOAD approach can be used as a tool for disambiguation or co-reference resolution. If we include *Barack Obama* as a second query entity, the focus of the results shifts from security agencies to politics, where the incident was discussed. Such browsing can thus be used as a tool in following connections and co-occurrences of entities through the data to explore events, much like a knowledge graph.

Summarization. Based on the relationships of entities and terms in the graph, extracting descriptions for entities is no different from asking for any other entity (see Table 2, right). However, we can also query for sentences that contain the relevant entities directly. For example, the resulting sentences for the query $\langle S : (A, \text{Edward Snowden}), (O, \text{NSA}) \rangle$ is *"In early 2013, thousands of thousands of classified documents were disclosed by NSA contractor Edward Snowden"*, which summarizes the relationship nicely. While the current approach of locating sentences that contain the specified entities is straightforward, more intricate summarization metrics can be adapted to the existing graph structure.

Entity and concept linking. Since we built the graph on Wikipedia, we can also use it to recommend Wikipedia pages for entities. The query $\langle P : (A, \text{Edward Snowden}) \rangle$ unsurprisingly yields Snowden's Wikipedia page as the highest ranked result. However, we can link concepts as well, for example with $\langle P : (A, \text{Edward Snowden}), (T, \text{Surveillance}) \rangle$. For this query, the Wikipedia page for *Global surveillance disclosures since 2013* is placed ahead of Snowden's page in the ranking, since it lists the surveillance activities that Snowden reported about in greater detail. In this context, the concept of subqueries is helpful, since persons are rarely referred to repeatedly by their full name on their own page. For example, the query $\langle P : (A, \text{Albert Einstein}) \rangle$ ranks the page for the *Albert Einstein Transfer Vehicle* highest, which was used to supply the International Space Station. The reason for this is that it is always referred to by the full name, while Albert Einstein himself is more often referred to as Einstein. Allowing subqueries fixes this and results in the physicist's page being top ranked. While the transport vehicle never should have been tagged as a person during NER, our findings indicate that the model is able to detect such problems.

query:	$\langle O : (A, \text{Edward Snowden})\rangle$		$\langle O : (A, \text{Edward Snowden}), (A, \text{Barack Obama})\rangle$		$\langle T : (A, \text{Edward Snowden})\rangle$	
rank	organizations	score	organizations	score	terms	score
1	nsa	1.000	nsa	0.546	surveil	1.000
2	national security agency	0.288	senate	0.503	leak	0.985
3	gchq	0.182	congress	0.340	document	0.610
4	us national security agency	0.083	republican	0.290	whistleblow	0.532
5	usis	0.043	democratic party	0.283	contractor	0.496

Table 2: Top 5 highest ranked results for three queries centred on *Edward Snowden*. Weights are given as the normalized adapted *tf-idf* weights or their combination in queries with multiple entities. Terms are stemmed.

5. EVALUATION

In the following, we present two data sets of historic events and use them to evaluate the LOAD graph of Wikipedia.

5.1 Evaluation data

Since we constructed the LOAD graph on Wikipedia data, we cannot turn to the Wikipedia event pages that are frequently used for evaluation in this context. To our knowledge, there are no data sets that have already been annotated for entities and are suitable for an evaluation of Wikipedia content, so we annotated it ourselves. To avoid using Wikipedia data, we obtained a list of events from the World History Project, which provides trivia about events *On This Day in History* [20]. These websites contain lists of historic events for each day of the year as well as dates of birth and dates of death of more or less famous persons. The site has information about 6558 dates of birth with a short mention of the person's job and 1483 dates of death along with a sentence about that person's accomplishments or circumstances of death. There are 5805 diverse historic events from scientific discoveries to famous events. We describe the preparation and annotation in the following.

Historic Events. As historic events we view the set of dates that remain when dates of birth and dates of death are removed. For these events, we also have a date of granularity day and one sentence that describes the event. We randomly chose 500 such events and annotated them by hand for persons, locations, organizations, and remaining terms. An example is shown in Table 3. It is evident that this data is very diverse in both structure and content. Structurally, events consist of differing numbers of entities of different classes and have varying numbers of terms. Based on content, the data can be categorized into various areas of life and ranges from well known world events to minor descriptions, such as the patent on a bicycle crank. We specifically chose this set of random events instead of hand picked events to exclude further bias and provide a more challenging evaluation data set than the dates of death baseline.

Dates of death. The dates of death serve as a baseline since they are likely represented by a single sentence in Wikipedia. Since they end with the word *died*, we use pattern matching to remove them from the historic events. Afterwards, we manually annotate the data to strip titles from names, split the description from the name and separate multiple names and nicknames. For example, the sentence *"H(oward) P(hillips) Lovecraft, horror writer, died."* yields the information that Lovecraft was a horror writer, which we can use as terms to describe him, but it also provides the alias *H.P. Lovecraft* in addition to his full name. We store this information together with the provided dates for a total of 1483 persons.

data	method	found	miss	cor@1	prc@1
dates of death	LOAD	869	613	122	0.082
	LOADsq	1326	156	**207**	**0.140**
	LOADTsq	1374	108	125	0.084
	LOADTsq+	**1443**	**39**	13	0.009
	BASEw	869	613	206	0.140
	BASEr	869	613	63.25	0.043
historic events	LOAD	290	210	39	0.078
	LOADsq	341	159	**40**	**0.080**
	LOADTsq	**414**	**86**	33	0.066
	BASEw	290	210	19	0.038
	BASEr	290	210	0.48	0.001

Table 4: Evaluation results for both data sets. Shown are the used methods and the two baselines, the number of identified dates, the number of missing dates (not identified), the number of top ranked dates that were in the evaluation data sets (cor@1), and the resulting precision at rank 1 (prc@1).

5.2 Date prediction

To evaluate the performance of the LOAD model on Wikipedia based on the two event data sets, we use the description of events as query input and evaluate the resulting ranking of dates with respect to the known date. We chose this approach since there exists exactly one date of granularity day per event in the evaluation data set, and the coverage of dates in Wikipedia is very good for the considered time frame [36], which reduces the chance of evaluating the completeness of Wikipedia or the NER tool. For the ranking, we only consider days since this is the granularity in the evaluation data sets. We test several possible methods based on the LOAD approach. With *LOAD*, we denote the basic method of inputting all query entities and ranking dates according to the combined *tf-idf* ranking. For *LOADsq*, we allow subqueries. For *LOADTsq*, we use the descriptive terms of events in the query in addition to the entities. *LOADTsq+* is a special query in which we also include the terms *death* and *died*. Additionally, we use two baseline approaches. For *BASEr*, we rank dates that are connected to any query entity at random (this is iterated 1000 times and averaged). *BASEw* on the other hand ranks dates by their weighted connection ω to any entity in the query.

In Table 4, we show the results for both evaluation sets. Independent of the data set, we find that the LOAD methods are able to locate a higher number of correct dates and include it at some position in their ranking. The number rises as we include more entities and terms in the queries. In the case of death dates, the LOAD approach outperforms the randomized baseline but is strongly correlated with the weighted baseline. Since we only have one class of query entity in this case, this result is expected. Here, the *LOADsq* approach with subqueries performs best with regard to the

date	event	type	locs	orgs	actors	terms
1918-07-08	*Ernest Hemingway*, `Red Cross` volunteer, wounded in **Italy**.	war	1	1	1	2
1966-09-08	"Star Trek" debuted (`NBC`).	cul	0	1	0	3
1973-10-06	**Israel** attacked by **Egypt** and **Syria**.	war	3	0	0	1
1866-11-20	Bicycle with a rotary crank patented (*Pierre Lallemont*).	sci	0	0	1	4
1960-08-19	*Francis Gary Powers*, U2 spy plane pilot, convicted in a **Moscow** court.	pol	1	0	1	6

Table 3: Examples of events from the evaluation data set that are annotated for *actors*, locations and `organizations` together with the date on which the event took place. For each event, the number of entities by class is listed. Note that these events are not necessarily represented by a single sentence in Wikipedia.

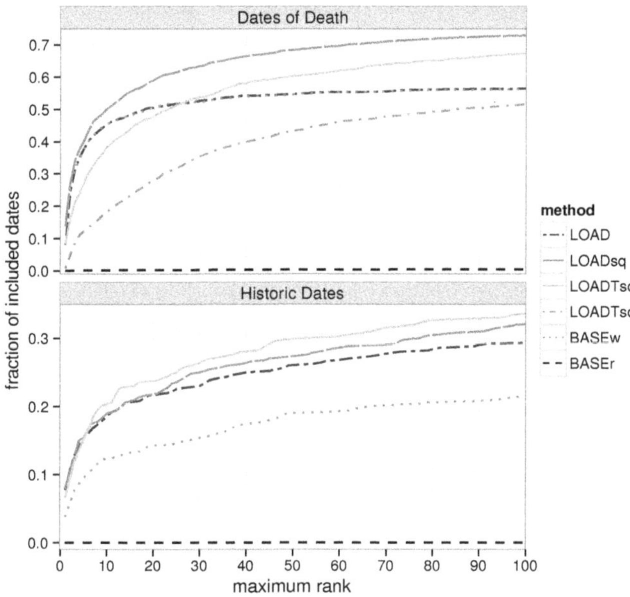

Figure 3: Prediction of dates based on event data. Shown is the number of identified correct dates in the top k ranks versus the rank k.

number of correct dates that are ranked at top position. The results are similar for the historical event data, although the weighted baseline performs much poorer with the addition of further query entities. Interestingly, the inclusion of terms in the query helps with the overall recall but not with the precision of the results. In order to evaluate the browsing potential of the method when used as a kind of search engine, we also consider the number of correctly identified dates with progressing rank in the list, as shown in Figure 3.

Here, we find that *LOADsq* performs best for the date of death data, for which it includes 50% of the correct dates in the first 10 positions of the ranking. The performance of *LOADTsq* is worse and even though it and *LOADTsq+* ultimately include the most correct dates, this happens at a point in the ranking where it is of little relevance, unless this were to be used as a pre-selection step for a further analysis. For either data set, the LOAD methods with subqueries perform significantly better than either baseline. For the historic event data, the inclusion of terms leads to a further improvement over the other LOAD methods, which emphasizes the need for terms in the model that may be important or even the only known features of an event.

6. CONCLUSION & ONGOING WORK

In this paper, we presented the graph-based LOAD model for the representation of named entities, dates and terms in the context of a document collection for the purpose of event extraction, browsing and indexing. We demonstrated the versatility of the system, pointed out further applications, and evaluated the system on two data sets of historic events.

A point that is worth discussing is the dependence of the LOAD model on the quality of the NER phase. While StanfordNER is a state-of-the-art system, certain topics on Wikipedia are simply too far removed from the training data to achieve good performance. For example, a query for entities related to the term *Klingon* yields results that will be familiar to any fan of Star Trek. However, the classes of such entities are assigned randomly, since Stanford is for obvious reasons unable to handle fictional Klingon names. This is unlikely to be an issue for smaller corpora of news articles, but for diverse document collections, further considerations are necessary. As such, we see a number of areas where the model can be improved in practical applications. Most prominent is the selection of terms, which can be reduced to a given set of parts-of-speech, based on the POS tags that are assigned in the NER phase. Doing so would allow for a more finely nuanced selection of terms. Different parts of speech such as verbs could then also be used to distinguish or describe certain kinds of events as composites of entities A second possibility is the inclusion of further classes of named entities, such as StanfordNER's *money* or *percent* classes. With regard to the model itself, the distinction between different classes of entities in the edge creation step (i.e., the multi-partiteness) is geared towards event extraction. For different applications, however, relationships between entities of the same class could be included. For example, a measure of similarity between persons might help to improve the quality of queries by accounting for synonyms and co-references.

We conclude with the observation that we tested the approach on Wikipedia, primarily because it is an enormous and free source of unstructured text that can be cleaned to remove noise. However, the LOAD model itself is useful for any document collection, since it makes no assumptions about document structure or origin. An application to a streaming or online setting is possible, where the model stands to benefit profoundly from the underlying graph representation, which allows incremental updates of any kind. The addition of new entire documents is possible in real-time, simply by processing the document and adding the resulting subgraph to the main graph structure. Even addition to or deletions from individual sections of a document can easily be accounted for, since the adjustment of edge weights happens locally within the graph structure. Thus, the model is able to handle the processing of frequently edited document collections like Wikipedia or news feeds.

Ongoing work. We are currently working on combining NER, temporal tagger, LOAD algorithm, query interface, and word embedding for terms into a standalone version that can be applied to any document collection to facilitate efficient event browsing. Given the quality issues in the output of NER on Wikipedia, we are also working on the extraction of named entities from Wikipedia based on internal links, with the aim of constructing a more accurate version of the Wikipedia LOAD graph as a community resource.

7. REFERENCES

[1] A. Abujabal and K. Berberich. Important events in the past, present, and future. In *WWW*, 2015.

[2] B. Adams, G. McKenzie, and M. Gahegan. Frankenplace: Interactive thematic mapping for ad hoc exploratory search. In *WWW*, 2015.

[3] O. Alonso and K. Shiells. Timelines as summaries of popular scheduled events. In *TempWeb*, 2013.

[4] M. Bendersky and W. B. Croft. Modeling higher-order term dependencies in information retrieval using query hypergraphs. In *SIGIR*, 2012.

[5] R. Blanco and C. Lioma. Graph-based term weighting for information retrieval. *Information Retrieval*, 2012.

[6] R. Campos, G. Dias, A. M. Jorge, and A. Jatowt. Survey of temporal information retrieval and related applications. *ACM Computing Surveys*, 2014.

[7] T. Chakraborty and A. Chakraborty. OverCite: Finding overlapping communities in citation network. In *ASONAM*, 2013.

[8] C. Cieri, S. Strassel, D. Graff, N. Martey, K. Rennert, and M. Liberman. Corpora for topic detection and tracking. In *Topic Detection and Tracking*. Springer, 2002.

[9] A. Das Sarma, A. Jain, and C. Yu. Dynamic relationship and event discovery. In *WSDM*, 2011.

[10] G. R. Doddington, A. Mitchell, M. A. Przybocki, L. A. Ramshaw, S. Strassel, and R. M. Weischedel. The automatic content extraction (ACE) program-tasks, data, and evaluation. In *LREC*, 2004.

[11] S. Dutta and G. Weikum. Cross-document co-reference resolution using sample-based clustering with knowledge enrichment. *TACL*, 3:15–28, 2015.

[12] A. Feng and J. Allan. Finding and linking incidents in news. In *CIKM*, 2007.

[13] M. Filannino and G. Nenadic. Mining temporal footprints from Wikipedia. *COLING*, 2014.

[14] J. R. Finkel, T. Grenager, and C. Manning. Incorporating non-local information into information extraction systems by Gibbs sampling. In *ACL*, 2005.

[15] W. A. Gale, K. W. Church, and D. Yarowsky. One sense per discourse. In *Proceedings of the workshop on Speech and Natural Language*, 1992.

[16] A. Gattani, D. S. Lamba, N. Garera, M. Tiwari, X. Chai, S. Das, S. Subramaniam, A. Rajaraman, V. Harinarayan, and A. Doan. Entity extraction, linking, classification, and tagging for social media: a Wikipedia-based approach. *PVLDB*, 6(11), 2013.

[17] J. Geiß, A. Spitz, and M. Gertz. Beyond friendships and followers: The Wikipedia social network. In *ASONAM*, 2015.

[18] J. Geiß, A. Spitz, J. Strötgen, and M. Gertz. The Wikipedia location network - overcoming borders and oceans. In *GIR*, 2015.

[19] M. Georgescu, N. Kanhabua, D. Krause, W. Nejdl, and S. Siersdorfer. Extracting event-related information from article updates in Wikipedia. In *Advances in Information Retrieval*. Springer, 2013.

[20] A. Guisepi. History world: On this day in history. `http://history-world.org/ontd.htm` (2015-10-02).

[21] D. Gupta and K. Berberich. Identifying time intervals of interest to queries. In *CIKM*, 2014.

[22] T. Huet, J. Biega, and F. M. Suchanek. Mining history with Le Monde. In *AKBC*, 2013.

[23] A. Jatowt, C.-M. Au Yeung, and K. Tanaka. Estimating document focus time. In *CIKM*, 2013.

[24] S. Julinda, C. Boden, and A. Akbik. Extracting a repository of events and event references from news clusters. *COLING*, 2014.

[25] N. Kanhabua and W. Nejdl. On the value of temporal anchor texts in Wikipedia. In *TAIA*, 2014.

[26] N. Kanhabua, S. Romano, and A. Stewart. Identifying relevant temporal expressions for real-world events. In *TAIA*, 2012.

[27] E. Kuzey, J. Vreeken, and G. Weikum. A fresh look on knowledge bases: Distilling named events from news. In *CIKM*, 2014.

[28] E. Kuzey and G. Weikum. Extraction of temporal facts and events from Wikipedia. In *TempWeb*, 2012.

[29] A. Mishra, D. Milchevski, and K. Berberich. Linking Wikipedia events to past news. In *TAIA*, 2014.

[30] R. Nallapati, A. Feng, F. Peng, and J. Allan. Event threading within news topics. In *CIKM*, 2004.

[31] M. F. Porter. An algorithm for suffix stripping. *Program*, 14(3):130–137, 1980.

[32] A. Ritter, Mausam, O. Etzioni, and S. Clark. Open domain event extraction from Twitter. In *KDD*, 2012.

[33] F. Rousseau and M. Vazirgiannis. Graph-of-word and TW-IDF: new approach to ad hoc IR. In *CIKM*, 2013.

[34] R. S. Roy, R. Katare, N. Ganguly, S. Laxman, and M. Choudhury. Discovering and understanding word level user intent in web search queries. *Web Semantics*, 30:22–38, 2015.

[35] V. Setty, S. Bedathur, K. Berberich, and G. Weikum. InZeit: Efficiently identifying insightful time points. In *VLDB*, 2010.

[36] A. Spitz, J. Strötgen, T. Bögel, and M. Gertz. Terms in time and times in context: A graph-based term-time ranking model. In *TempWeb*, 2015.

[37] J. Strötgen and M. Gertz. Temporal tagging on different domains: Challenges, strategies, and gold standards. In *LREC*, 2012.

[38] J. Strötgen and M. Gertz. Multilingual and cross-domain temporal tagging. *Language Resources and Evaluation*, 47(2):269–298, 2013.

[39] T. Tao and C. Zhai. An exploration of proximity measures in information retrieval. In *SIGIR*, 2007.

[40] T. A. Tuan, S. Elbassuoni, N. Preda, and G. Weikum. CATE: context-aware timeline for entity illustration. In *WWW*, 2011.

[41] Y. Wang, M. Zhu, L. Qu, M. Spaniol, and G. Weikum. Timely YAGO: harvesting, querying, and visualizing temporal knowledge from Wikipedia. In *EDBT*, 2010.

[42] D. Yarowsky. One sense per collocation. In *HLT*, 1993.

GeoBurst: Real-Time Local Event Detection in Geo-Tagged Tweet Streams

Chao Zhang[1], Guangyu Zhou[1], Quan Yuan[1], Honglei Zhuang[1], Yu Zheng[2,3], Lance Kaplan[4], Shaowen Wang[1], and Jiawei Han[1]
[1]Dept. of Computer Science, University of Illinois at Urbana-Champaign, Urbana, IL, USA
[2]Microsoft Research, Beijing, China
[3]Shenzhen Institutes of Advanced Technology, Chinese Academy of Sciences
[4]U.S. Army Research Laboratory, Adelphi, MD, USA
[1]{czhang82, gzhou6, qyuan, hzhuang3, shaowen, hanj}@illinois.edu
[2]yuzheng@microsoft.com [4]lance.m.kaplan.civ@mail.mil

ABSTRACT

The real-time discovery of local events (*e.g.*, protests, crimes, disasters) is of great importance to various applications, such as crime monitoring, disaster alarming, and activity recommendation. While this task was nearly impossible years ago due to the lack of timely and reliable data sources, the recent explosive growth in geo-tagged tweet data brings new opportunities to it. That said, how to extract quality local events from geo-tagged tweet streams *in real time* remains largely unsolved so far.

We propose GEOBURST, a method that enables effective and real-time local event detection from geo-tagged tweet streams. With a novel authority measure that captures the geo-topic correlations among tweets, GEOBURST first identifies several *pivots* in the query window. Such pivots serve as representative tweets for potential local events and naturally attract similar tweets to form candidate events. To select truly interesting local events from the candidate list, GEOBURST further summarizes continuous tweet streams and compares the candidates against historical activities to obtain spatiotemporally bursty ones. Finally, GEOBURST also features an updating module that finds new pivots with little time cost when the query window shifts. As such, GEOBURST is capable of monitoring continuous streams in real time. We used crowdsourcing to evaluate GEOBURST on two real-life data sets that contain millions of geo-tagged tweets. The results demonstrate that GEOBURST significantly outperforms state-of-the-art methods in precision, and is orders of magnitude faster.

Keywords

Twitter; tweet; local event; event detection; social media

1. INTRODUCTION

A local event (*e.g.*, protest, crime, disaster, sport game) is an unusual activity bursted in a local area and within specific duration while engaging a considerable number of participants. The real-time detection of local events was nearly impossible years ago due to the lack of timely and reliable data sources, yet the recent explosive growth in geo-tagged tweet data brings new opportunities to it. With the ubiquitous connectivity of wireless networks and the wide proliferation of mobile devices, more than 10 million geo-tagged tweets are created in the Twitterverse every day [1]. Each geo-tagged tweet, which contains a text message, a timestamp, and a geo-location, provides a unified 3W (*what, when*, and *where*) view of the user's activity. Even though the geo-tagged tweets account for only about 2% of the entire tweet stream [16], their sheer size, multi-faceted information, and real-time nature make them an invaluable source for detecting local events. For example, when the tragic 2011 Tohoku Earthquake hit Japan on March 11th 2011, thousands of related geo-tagged tweets were created instantly; and when the Baltimore Riot took place in April 2015, many people posted geo-tagged tweets to broadcast it right on the spot.

We aim to achieve *real-time local event detection* from geo-tagged tweet streams. This task is important as it can underpin various applications. Take disaster alarming as an example. By detecting emergent disasters (*e.g.*, earthquakes, fires) in real time, we can send alarms to the populace at the very first moment when these disasters outbreak. Such alarms can be much faster than traditional news media [9, 24, 30], and thus allow for timely response that avoids huge life and economic losses. As another example, the detected local events can be easily filtered by a few keywords for activity recommendation. Consider a user who is interested in sport games, movies, and music festivals. With proper filtering keywords, the detector can continuously feed the user with such activities in the city. As such, she can easily learn about what is happening around and decide what to do.

Despite its practical importance, real-time local event detection in the geo-tagged tweet stream is nontrivial because it introduces several unique challenges: (1) *Integrating diverse types of data.* The geo-tagged tweet stream involves three different data types: location, time, and text. Considering the totally different representations of those data types and the complicated correlations among them, how to effectively integrate them for local event detection is challenging. (2) *Extracting interpretable events from overwhelming noise.* Existing studies have revealed that about 40% tweets are just pointless babbles [2], and even those event-related tweets are mostly short and noisy. As truly interesting local events are buried in massive irrelevant tweets, it is nontrivial to accurately identify them and describe in an interpretable way. (3) *On-line and real-time detection.* When a local event outbreaks, it is key to report the event instantly to allow for timely actions. As massive geo-tagged

SIGIR '16, July 17-21, 2016, Pisa, Italy
© 2016 ACM. ISBN 978-1-4503-4069-4/16/07...$15.00
DOI: http://dx.doi.org/10.1145/2911451.2911519

tweets stream in, the detector should work in an on-line and real-time manner instead of a batch-wise and inefficient one.

A number of studies [6, 12, 13, 28, 17, 5] have investigated event detection in Twitter. Although these techniques have demonstrated inspiring results in detecting global events, they are inapplicable to detecting local events. Unlike global events that are bursty in the entire stream, local events are "bursty" in a small geographical region and involve a limited number of tweets. Such local bursts cannot be readily captured by global event detection methods. Recently, a few methods tailored for local event detection [15, 10, 7, 3] have been introduced. The state-of-the-art method EVENTTWEET [3] extracts the keywords that are both temporally bursty and spatially localized, and then clusters those keywords into events based on spatial distributions. Unfortunately, the quality of the result events is limited because it does not model the semantic correlations between keywords. Furthermore, EVENTTWEET cannot detect local events in real time, because it partitions the stream into fixed-width time windows and the detection is triggered only when the current window is saturated.

We propose GEOBURST, an effective and real-time local event detector. Our key insight is that, a local event usually leads to a considerable number of geo-tagged tweets around the occurring place (*e.g.*, many participants of a protest may post tweets on the spot). As such tweets are geographically close and semantically coherent, we call them a geo-topic cluster and consider it as a potential local event. Nevertheless, not necessarily does every geo-topic cluster correspond to a local event because (1) the activity could be just routine in that region instead of an unusual event, *e.g.*, many shopping-related tweets are posted on the 5th Avenue in New York every day; and (2) the activity may be geographically scattered instead of localized, *e.g.*, a popular TV show may result in several geo-topic clusters in different regions. Hence, we should also carefully measure the spatiotemporal burstiness of each geo-topic cluster to identify true local events.

Motivated by the above, the first step of GEOBURST finds all geo-topic clusters in the query window as candidate events. Specifically, we compute a tweet's geo-topic authority by combining the geographical and semantic contributions from its similar tweets, where the geographical side is measured using a kernel function, and the semantic side is captured using random walk on a keyword co-occurrence graph. We then design an authority ascent process to identify all pivot tweets, which are essentially authority maxima in the geo-topic space. Such pivot tweets naturally attract similar tweets to form geo-topic clusters.

The second step of GEOBURST ranks all the candidates based on spatiotemporal burstiness. For this purpose, we continuously summarize the stream and store the summaries in a space-efficient structure called activity timeline. The stored summaries, which describe the typical activities in different regions, serve as background knowledge to measure the spatiotemporal burstiness of geo-topic clusters and select out local events.

Besides extracting local events from an ad-hoc query window, GEOBURST also features an updating module that enables continuous monitoring of the stream. As new geo-tagged tweets stream in, GEOBURST can shift the query window and update the results in real time. The updating incurs little time cost because authority computation, which is the most time-consuming operation in the framework, can be completed by subtracting the contributions of outdated tweets and emphasizing the contributions of new ones.

To summarize, we make the following contributions:

1. We design GEOBURST for local event detection in the geo-tagged tweet stream. The effectiveness of GEOBURST is underpinned by a novel pivot seeking process that generates candidate events, along with a ranking module that measures spatiotemporal burstiness based on stream summarization.
2. With the additive property of the authority score, we design an updating module for GEOBURST. It fast updates the event list when the query window shifts, and thus enables real-time and continuous local event detection.
3. We perform extensive experiments on millions of geo-tagged tweets in two different cities, and evaluate the results using a crowdsourcing platform. Our results demonstrate that GEOBURST significantly outperforms state-of-the-art methods in precision, and runs orders of magnitude faster.

2. RELATED WORK

Global Event Detection. Global event detection aims at extracting events that are bursty and unusual in the entire tweet stream. Existing approaches to this end can be classified into two categories: *document-based* and *feature-based*.

Document-based approaches consider each document as a basic unit and group similar documents to form events. Allan *et al.* [6] perform single-pass clustering of the stream, and use a similarity threshold to determine whether a new document should form a new topic or be merged into an existing one. Aggarwal *et al.* [5] also detect events by continuously clustering the tweet stream, but their similarity measure considers both tweet content relevance and user proximity. Sankaranarayanan *et al.* [25] train a Naïve Bayes filter to identify news-related tweets, and cluster them based on TF-IDF similarity. They also enrich each piece of news with location information by extracting geo-entities.

Feature-based approaches [12, 13, 21, 28, 17] identify a set of bursty features (*e.g.*, keywords) from the stream and cluster them into events. Fung *et al.* [12] model feature occurrences with binomial distribution to extract bursty features. He *et al.* [13] construct the time series for each feature and perform Fourier Transform to identify bursts. Weng *et al.* [28] use wavelet transform and auto-correlation to measure word energy and extract high-energy words. Li *et al.* [17] segment each tweet into meaningful phrases and extract bursty phrases based on frequency, which are clustered into candidate events and further filtered using Wikipedia.

The above methods are all designed for detecting global events that are bursty in the entire stream. As aforementioned, a local event is usually bursty in a small geographical region instead of the entire stream. Hence, directly applying these methods to the geo-tagged tweet stream would miss many local events.

There has also been work [24, 22, 19] on detecting specific types of events. Sakaki *et al.* [24] investigate real-time earthquake detection. A classifier is trained to judge whether an incoming tweet is related to earthquake or not, and an alarm is released when the number of earthquake-related tweets is large. Li *et al.* [19] detect crime and disaster events (CDE) with a self-adaptive crawler that dynamically retrieves CDE-related tweets. Different from those studies, we aim to detect all kinds of local events from the stream.

Local Event Detection. Foley *et al.* [11] use distant supervision to extract local events from Web pages, but the proposed method can only extract local events that are well advertised in advance on the Web. Watanabe *et al.* [27] and Quezada *et al.* [23] study location-aware events in the social media, but their major focus is on geo-locating tweets/events, whereas we aim to automatically extract local events from raw geo-tagged tweets.

Krumm *et al.* [15] propose the detection of spatiotemporal spikes in the tweet stream as local events. Nevertheless, their approach can only detect events for pre-defined rigid time windows (*e.g.*, 3-6 pm, 6-9 pm), because it discretizes time and compares the number of tweets in the same bin across different days. It supports neither ad-hoc query windows nor real-time detection.

Chen *et al.* [7] extract events from geo-tagged Flickr photos. By converting the spatiotemporal distribution of each tag into a 3-dimensional signal, they perform wavelet transform to extract spatiotemporally bursty tags, and clusters those tags into events based on co-occurrence as well as spatiotemporal distributions. Such a method, however, can only detect local events in batch manner.

The most relevant work to our task is by Abdelhaq *et al.* [3]. They propose EVENTWEET, which detects local event in a time window with four steps: (1) examine several previous windows to extract bursty words; (2) compute the spatial entropy of each bursty word and select localized words; (3) cluster localized words based on spatial distribution; and (4) rank the clusters based on features such as burstiness and spatial coverage. Unfortunately, EVENTWEET suffers from two drawbacks. First, the clustering of localized keywords is merely based on spatial distribution without considering tweet content. It results in irrelevant keywords in the same cluster, and cannot distinguish different events that occur at the same location. Second, although EVENTWEET is an online method, it is incapable of detecting local events in real time, as the detection is triggered only when the current window is saturated.

3. PRELIMINARIES

In this section, we formulate the real-time local event detection problem, and then explore several of its characteristics, which motivate the design of GEOBURST.

Problem description. Let $\mathcal{D} = (d_1, d_2, \ldots, d_n, \ldots)$ be a continuous stream of geo-tagged tweets that arrive in chronological order. Each tweet d is a tuple $\langle t_d, l_d, E_d \rangle$, where t_d is its post time, l_d is its geo-location, and E_d is a bag of keywords. For each tweet, we use an off-the-shelf tool[1] to extract entities and noun phrases as its keywords. Note that such preprocessing does not affect the generality of our method, and one can also represent each tweet message as a bag of uni-grams for simplicity.

Consider a query time window $Q = [t_s, t_e]$ where t_s and t_e are the start and end timestamps satisfying $t_{d_1} \leq t_s < t_e \leq t_{d_n}$. The local event detection problem consists of two sub-tasks: (1) extract from $\mathcal{D}$ all the local events that occur during Q; and (2) monitor the continuous stream $\mathcal{D}$ and update the local event list in real time as Q shifts continuously.

GEOBURST overview. In practice, a local event often results in a considerable number of relevant tweets around its occurring location. Take Figure 1 as an example. Suppose a protest occurs on the 5th Avenue in New York, many participants may post tweets on the spot to express their attitude, with keywords such as "protest" and "rights". We call such a set of tweets a *geo-topic cluster* as they are geographically close and semantically coherent.

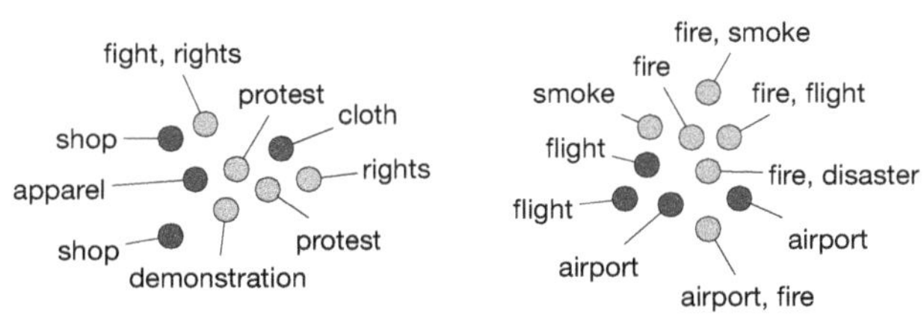

Figure 1: An illustration of geo-topic clusters.

Nevertheless, not necessarily does every geo-topic cluster correspond to a local event even if the cluster has a large size. First, the activity can be just routine in that region. Continue with the example in Figure 1. On almost every day, we can observe many shopping-related tweets on the 5th Avenue. Although such tweets also form a geo-topic cluster, they do not reflect any unusual activities. Second, the cluster may correspond to a global event instead of a local one. For instance, when a popular TV show like "Game of Thrones" goes online, we can observe geo-topic clusters discussing about it in different regions. Such geo-topic clusters do not correspond to local events as well. We thus define *a local event as a geo-topic cluster that shows clear spatiotemporal burstiness.*

Based on the above observations, we first detect all geo-topic clusters in the query window and regard them as candidates — this step ensures high coverage of the underlying local events. The discovery of geo-topic clusters, however, poses several challenges: how to combine the geographical and semantic similarities in a reasonable way? how to capture the correlations between different keywords? and how to generate quality clusters without knowing the suitable number of clusters in advance? To address these challenges, we perform a novel pivot seeking process to identify the centers of geo-topic clusters. Our key insight is that: the spot where the event occurs acts as a pivot that produces relevant tweets around it; the closer we are to the pivot, the more likely we observe relevant tweets. Therefore, we define a geo-topic authority score for each tweet, where the geographical influence among tweets is captured by a kernel function, and the semantic influence by a random walk on a keyword co-occurrence graph. With this authority measure, we develop an authority ascent procedure to retrieve authority maxima as pivots; and each pivot naturally attracts similar tweets to form a quality geo-topic cluster. After discovering the candidate events, we rank them by spatiotemporal burstiness. To this end, we continuously cluster the stream to obtain summaries of regional activities at different timestamps, and store the summaries in a space-efficient structure called activity timeline. The stored summaries serve as background knowledge that enables us to measure the spatiotemporal burstiness of any candidate.

GEOBURST also includes a module that updates the result list in real time as the query window shifts. It will be shown shortly that, the authority score satisfies an additive property. Hence, instead of finding new pivots from scratch when the query window shifts, we can identify them by simply updating the authority scores and then performing fast authority ascent.

We summarize the framework of GEOBURST in Figure 2. As shown, GEOBURST offers two detection modes. The first is the batch mode, which uses the candidate generator and the ranker to detect local events in a fixed query window. The second is the online mode, at the core of which is an updater that updates pivots in real time as the query window shifts. Meanwhile, the ranker is underpinned by the activity timeline structure, which continuously summarizes the stream to obtain background knowledge.

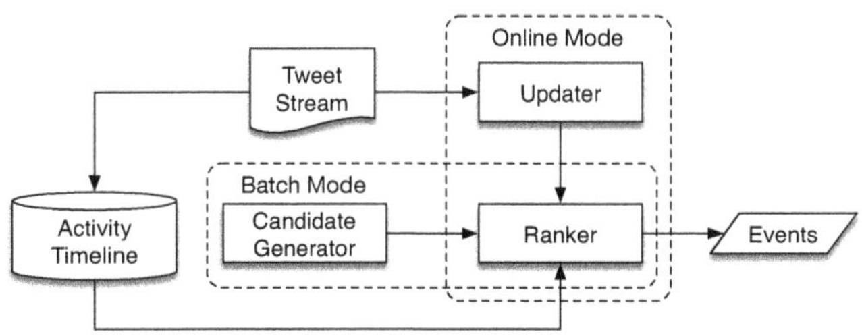

Figure 2: The framework of GEOBURST.

4. THE BATCH MODE

In this section, we describe the batch mode of GEOBURST. As

[1] https://github.com/aritter/twitter_nlp

aforementioned, given a query window Q, the batch mode detects local events in Q by first generating geo-topic clusters as candidate events, and then ranking the candidates by spatiotemporal burstiness. In the sequel, we present the details of these two steps in Sections 4.1 and 4.2, respectively.

4.1 Candidate Event Generation

Let D_Q be the set of tweets falling in Q. The task of candidate generation is to divide D_Q into several geo-topic clusters, such that the tweets in each cluster are geographically close and semantically coherent. As motivated in Section 3, our idea is to view the occurring spot of an event as a pivot and assign each tweet to its corresponding pivot. Below, we introduce a novel geo-topic authority score to define *pivot*, and then develop an authority ascent procedure for pivot seeking.

4.1.1 Pivot

Geographical impact. Given two tweets d and d', we measure the geographical impact of d' to d as

$$G(d' \to d) = K(\|l_d - l_{d'}\|/h),$$

where $K(\cdot)$ is a kernel function, $\|l_d - l_{d'}\|$ is the geographical distance between d and d', and h is the kernel bandwidth. While various kernel functions can be used, we choose the Epanechnikov kernel here due to its simplicity and optimality in terms of bias-variance tradeoff [8]. With the Epanechnikov kernel, $G(d' \to d)$ becomes

$$G(d' \to d) = \begin{cases} c(1 - \|l_d - l_{d'}\|^2/h^2) & \text{if } \|l_d - l_{d'}\| < h \\ 0 & \text{otherwise,} \end{cases}$$

where c is a scaling constant of the Epanechnikov kernel.

Semantic impact. As each tweet message is represented by a bag of keywords, a very straightforward idea for measuring semantic impact is to compute the vector similarity between two tweet messages. Nevertheless, the effectiveness of vector similarity is limited, not only because tweets are short in nature, but also that the dimensions (keywords) are correlated instead of independent. To overcome these drawbacks, we propose a random-walk-based approach to capture semantic impact more effectively.

DEFINITION 1 (KEYWORD CO-OCCURRENCE GRAPH). *The keyword co-occurrence graph for D_Q is an undirected graph $G = (V, E)$ where: (1) V is the set of all keywords in D_Q; and (2) E is the set of edges between keywords, and the weight of an edge (e_i, e_j) is the number of tweets in which e_i and e_j co-occur.*

The keyword co-occurrence graph can be easily built from D_Q. With such a graph, we employ *random walk with restart (RWR)* to define keyword similarity, as it uses the holistic graph structure to capture node correlations. Consider a surfer who starts RWR from the keyword $x_0 = u$. Suppose the surfer is at keyword $x_t = i$ at step t, she returns to u with probability α $(0 < \alpha < 1)$ and continues surfing with probability $1 - \alpha$. If continuing, she randomly moves to i's neighbor j with probability $\mathbf{P}_{ij}$, where $\mathbf{P}$ is the transition matrix of the graph. The stationary distribution of such a process defines the RWR scores from u to all the keywords in V, and the score from u to keyword v, denoted as $r_{u \to v}$, is the probability that the surfer resides on v.

Now, given two tweets d and d', we start RWR from the keywords of d', and define the semantic impact of d' to d as the average probability that the random walk resides on d [20, 29]. Formally, let $E_d = \{e_1, e_2, \dots, e_m\}$ be the keyword set of d, and $E_{d'} = \{e'_1, e'_2, \dots, e'_n\}$ the keyword set of d', then the semantic impact from d' to d is

$$S(d' \to d) = \frac{1}{mn} \sum_{e \in E_d} \sum_{e' \in E_{d'}} r_{e' \to e}. \qquad (1)$$

Geo-topic authority. Based on geographical and semantic impacts, we measure the *geo-topic authority* of a tweet as follows.

DEFINITION 2 (NEIGHBOR). *Given a tweet d, we say d' is a neighbor of d if d' satisfies $G(d' \to d) > 0$ and $S(d' \to d) > \delta$, where $0 < \delta < 1$ is a pre-specified threshold.*

DEFINITION 3 (AUTHORITY). *Given a tweet $d \in D_Q$, let $N(d)$ be the set of d's neighbors in D_Q. The authority of d is*

$$A(d) = \sum_{d' \in N(d)} G(d' \to d) \cdot S(d' \to d). \qquad (2)$$

Given a tweet d, d' is a neighbor of d if it resembles d both geographically and semantically. The set of all neighbors in D_Q form d's neighborhood and contribute to d's authority. We could interpret Equation 2 as follows: an amount of $G(d' \to d)$ energy is distributed from d' to d through random walk on the graph, $G(d' \to d) \cdot S(d' \to d)$ is the amount that successfully reaches d; and d's authority is the total amount of energy that d receives from its neighbors.

Pivot. With Definition 3, we define a *pivot* as an authority maximum.

DEFINITION 4 (PIVOT). *Given a tweet $d \in D_Q$ and its neighborhood $N(d)$, d is a pivot if $A(d) = \max_{d' \in N(d)} A(d')$.*

Consider a local event that occurs at location l. If d is a tweet discussing about that event at l, then d is likely to be surrounded by relevant tweets to become the pivot for that event. The notion of neighborhood plays an important role in Definition 4: it ensures the supporting tweets are both geographically close and semantically relevant. This property leads to different pivots that can distinguish different-semantics events happening at the same location, as well as same-semantics events happening at different locations.

4.1.2 Authority ascent for pivot seeking

Now our task is to find all pivots in D_Q and assign each tweet to its corresponding pivot. We develop an authority ascent procedure for this purpose. As shown in Figure 3, starting from a tweet d_1 as the initial center, we perform step-by-step center shifting. Assuming the center at step t is tweet d_t, we find d_t's neighborhood $N(d_t)$, and the *local pivot* $l(d_t)$ — the tweet having the largest authority in $N(d_t)$. Then we regard $l(d_t)$ as our new center, *i.e.*, $d_{t+1} = l(d_t)$. As we continue such an authority ascent process, the center is guaranteed to converge to an authority maximum. It is because every shift operation increases the authority of the current center, and the authority is upper bounded (there are only a finite number of tweets in D_Q).

Candidate Event Generation. Algorithm 1 depicts the process of finding the pivot for every tweet in D_Q. As shown, we first compute the neighborhood for each tweet $d \in D_Q$ (lines 1-2). Subsequently, we compute the authority of each tweet (lines 3-4), and obtain its local pivot (lines 5-6). So long as the local pivots are obtained, we perform authority ascent to identify the pivot each tweet belongs to. Finally, the tweets having the same pivot are grouped into one geo-topic cluster and returned as a candidate event.

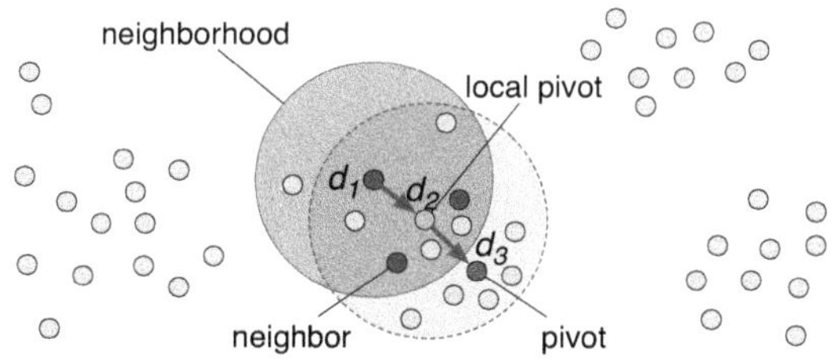

Figure 3: An illustration of the authority ascent process.

Algorithm 1: Pivot seeking.

Input: The tweet set D_Q, the kernel bandwidth h, the semantic threshold δ.
Output: The pivot for each tweet in D_Q.

```
// Neighborhood computation.
foreach d ∈ D_Q do
    N(d) ← {d'|d' ∈ D_Q, G(d' → d) > 0, S(d' → d) > δ};
// Authority computation.
foreach d ∈ D_Q do
    A(d) ← d's authority score computed from N(d);
// Find local pivot for each tweet.
foreach d ∈ D_Q do
    l(d) ← arg max_{d' ∈ N(d)} A(d');
// Authority ascent.
foreach d ∈ D_Q do
    Perform authority ascent to find the pivot for d;
```

Fast RWR score computation. In Algorithm 1, while it is easy to compute geographical impact based on tweet location, the challenge is how to compute semantic impact efficiently. A naïve idea is to obtain the RWR score between any two keywords, but such an idea is not efficient as the keyword co-occurrence graph can be large. To address this challenge, we leverage the locality of RWR: given a keyword q, we observe that only a limited number of keywords falling in q's vicinity have large values, while most keywords have extremely small RWR scores. We thus introduce the concept of *keyword vicinity*, which keeps only large enough RWR scores by exploring a small neighborhood around q. Below, we demonstrate how to fast compute the keyword vicinity based on the *Decomposition Theorem* [14].

THEOREM 1. *For a keyword u, let $\mathcal{O}_u$ be the set of u's out-neighbors in G. Given a keyword q, the RWR from u to q satisfies*

$$r_{u \to q} = \begin{cases} (1-\alpha) \sum_{v \in \mathcal{O}_u} \mathbf{P}_{uv} r_{v \to q} & \text{if } u \neq q \\ (1-\alpha) \sum_{v \in \mathcal{O}_u} \mathbf{P}_{uv} r_{v \to q} + \alpha & \text{if } u = q. \end{cases} \quad (3)$$

Theorem 1 says that, the RWR from u to q can be derived by linearly combining the RWR scores of u's out-neighbors, with extra emphasis on q itself. With this theorem, we use a local computation algorithm [20] to obtain q's vicinity. Starting from an initial vicinity, we gradually expand the vicinity and propagate RWR scores among the keywords falling inside. The RWR approximation becomes tighter and tighter as the vicinity expansion continues, and terminates when an error bound ϵ ($0 < \epsilon \ll \delta$) is guaranteed. Algorithm 2 depicts the detailed vicinity computation process. To compute q's vicinity, we maintain two quantities for any keyword u: (1) $s(u)$ is the current RWR score from u to q; and (2) $p(u)$ is the score that needs to be propagated. We use a priority queue to keep $p(u)$ for all the keywords. Every time we pop the keyword

Algorithm 2: Approximate RWR score computation.

Input: The keyword co-occurrence graph G, a keyword q, the restart probability α, an error bound ϵ.
Output: q's vicinity V_q.

```
s(q) ← α, p(q) ← α, V_q ← φ;
Q ← a priority queue that keeps p(u) for the keywords in G;
while Q.peek() ≥ αε do
    u ← Q.pop();
    for v ∈ I(u) do
        Δs(v) = (1 − α) p_vu p(u);
        s(v) ← s(v) + Δs(v);
        V_q[v] ← s(v);
        Q.update(v, p(v) + Δs(v));
    p(u) ← 0;
return V_q;
```

u that has the largest to-propagate score, and update the score and to-propagate score for each in-neighbor of u. After that, we set $p(u)$ to zero to avoid redundant propagation. The algorithm terminates when the max element in the priority queue is less than $\alpha\epsilon$, and returns all the keywords that have non-zero RWR scores as q's vicinity. Any keyword u not in q's vicinity must satisfy $r_{u \to q} < \epsilon$.

THEOREM 2. *Let $\hat{r}_{u \to q}$ be the approximate RWR score computed by Algorithm 2, then $\hat{r}_{u \to q}$ satisfies $|r_{u \to q} - \hat{r}_{u \to q}| \le \epsilon$. The time complexity of Algorithm 2 is $O(D_q/\alpha \log 1/(\epsilon\alpha))$, where* $D_q = \sum_{u: s_{u \to q} > \alpha\epsilon} (|I(u)| + \log |V|)$.

PROOF. See [20] for details. □

4.2 Candidate Ranking

Up to now, we have obtained a set of geo-topic clusters in the query window as candidate events. Nevertheless, as discussed in Section 3, not necessarily does every candidate correspond to a local event because it can be either routine in that region or a global event. In this subsection, we describe GEOBURST's ranking module, at the core of which is the activity timeline structure to facilitate ranking candidates by spatiotemporal burstiness. In what follows, we describe activity timeline construction in Section 4.2.1, and present the ranking function in Section 4.2.2.

4.2.1 Activity timeline construction

The activity timeline aims at summarizing the stream to unveil typical activities in different regions during different time periods. For this purpose, we design a structure called *tweet cluster* (TC), and extend CluStream [4], an effective stream clustering algorithm.

Let S be a set of tweets that are geographically close, its TC maintains the following statistics:

1) $n = |S|$: the number of tweets.
2) $m_l = \sum_{d \in S} l_d$: the sum vector of locations.
3) $m_{l^2} = \sum_{d \in S} l_d \circ l_d$: the squared sum vector of locations.
4) $m_t = \sum_{d \in S} t_d$: the sum of timestamps.
5) $m_{t^2} = \sum_{d \in S} t_d^2$: the squared sum of timestamps.
6) $m_e = \sum_{d \in S} E_d$: the sum dictionary of keywords.

The TC essentially provides a where-when-what summary for S: (1) where: with n, m_l, and m_{l^2}, one can easily compute the mean location and spatial variance for S; (2) when: with n, m_t, and m_{t^2}, one can easily compute the mean time and temporal variance for S; and (3) what: m_e keeps the number of occurrences for each keyword. As we shall see shortly, those fields enable us to estimate the number of keyword occurrences at any location. Moreover, TC satisfies the additive property, *i.e.*, the fields can be easily incremented if a new tweet is absorbed. Based on this property, we adapt CluStream to continuously clusters the stream into a set of TCs. When a new tweet d arrives, it finds the TC m that is geographically closest to d. If d is within m's boundary (computed from n, m_l, and m_{l2}, see [4] for details), it absorbs d into m and updates its fields; otherwise it creates a new TC for d. Meanwhile, we employ two strategies [26] to limit the maximum number of TCs: (1) deleting the TCs that are too old and contain few tweets; and (2) merging closest TC pairs until the number of remaining TCs is small enough.

The *activity timeline* is a sequence of clustering snapshots produced by CluStream at different timestamps. As storing the snapshot of every timestamp is unrealistic, we use the pyramid time frame (PTF) structure [4] to achieve both good space efficiency and high coverage of the stream history. The PTF structure imposes finer granularity for recent snapshots and coarser granularity for old ones. It involves two integer parameters: $b > 1$ and $l > 0$. Given a tweet stream $\mathcal{D}$, assume the start timestamp is 0 and the most recent timestamp is T. PTF creates $\lceil \log_b T \rceil$ layers: $0, 1, \ldots\ldots \log_b T$. Each layer i stores the snapshots for the timestamps that can be divided by b^i. If a timestamp matches multiple layers, it is stored in the highest possible layer to avoid redundancy. Further, every layer has a capacity of $b^l + 1$ so that only the latest $b^l + 1$ snapshots are stored. As such, the total number of snapshots in PTF is no larger than $(b^l + 1)\lceil \log_b(T) \rceil$.

EXAMPLE 1. *Suppose the start timestamp of the stream is 0 and the most recent timestamp is 25. Then the maximum layer in the corresponding PTF is $\lfloor \log_2 25 \rfloor = 4$, and the capacity of each layer is 5. The snapshots stored in different layers are:*

Layer 0 : 25 23 21 19 17;
Layer 1 : 22 18 14 10 6;
Layer 2 : 20 12 4;
Layer 3 : 24 8;
Layer 4 : 16.

4.2.2 The ranking function

The snapshots stored in the activity timeline serve as background knowledge for ranking candidate events. To derive the ranking score of candidate C, we quantify the spatiotemporal burstiness of each keyword in C, and then aggregate the burstiness of all the keywords as C's final ranking score.

Temporal burstiness. First, we measure how temporally bursty a keyword $k \in C$ is at the pivot location l_C, by vertically comparing C against the historical activities at l_C. As shown in Figure 4, we retrieve the snapshots in a reference time window R that right precedes the query window Q. Each pair of consecutive snapshots in R corresponds to a *historical activity*, defined as follows.

DEFINITION 5 (HISTORICAL ACTIVITY). *Let s_1 and s_2 be two snapshots at timestamp t_{s_1} and t_{s_2} ($t_{s_1} < t_{s_2}$). The historical activity during the time interval $[t_{s_1}, t_{s_2}]$ is the set of TCs obtained by subtracting s_1 from s_2.*

Let us use an example in Figure 4 to illustrate how we acquire historical activities in the reference window R. As shown, the snapshots s_1, s_2, s_3, s_4 fall in R. For each pair of consecutive snapshots, *i.e.*,$[s_1, s_2]$, $[s_2, s_3]$, $[s_3, s_4]$, we perform snapshot subtraction to obtain the historical activity during the respective time interval. For instance, for the snapshot pair $[s_1, s_2]$, we subtract s_1 from s_2 and obtain the historical activity, represented as a set of TCs: $\{m_1, m_2, m_4, m_6, m_7, m_8\}$. Note that the subtraction of two snapshots can be easily done by matching TC ids and subtracting the fields.

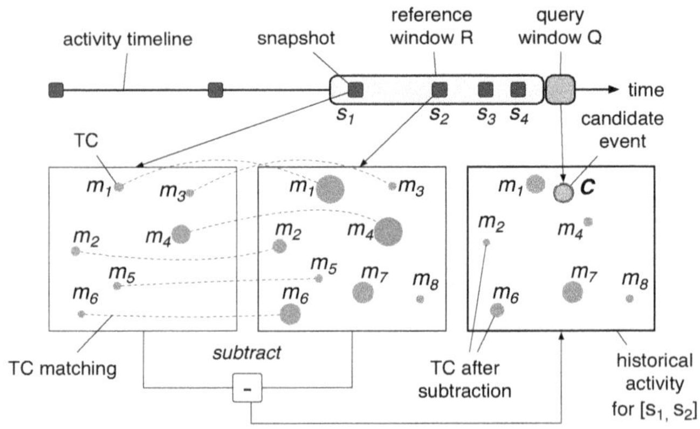

Figure 4: Retrieving historical activities from activity timeline.

Using each historical activity, we can employ kernel density estimation to infer the expected number of occurrences of keyword k at location l_C. Consider the query time window $Q = [t_s, t_e]$ and the historical activity in $[t'_s, t'_e]$. Denote the set of TCs in $[t'_s, t'_e]$ as $\{m_1, m_2, \ldots, m_n\}$. We estimate the number of occurrences of keyword k at location l_C as:

$$N_l(k) = \frac{t_e - t_s}{t_{e'} - t_{s'}} \sum_{i=1}^{n} K(\frac{\|l_C - l_{m_i}\|}{h}) N_{m_i}(k),$$

where $N_{m_i}(k)$ is the number of k's occurrences in m_i, l_{m_i} is the mean location of m_i, and h is the kernel bandwidth. As R contains multiple historical activities, and each can generate an estimation of keyword k's occurrences at location l_C, we obtain a set of estimations, denoted as $\Omega_t = \{\hat{N}_1(k), \hat{N}_2(k), \ldots, \hat{N}_c(k)\}$. Then we use z-score to quantify k's temporal burstiness at l_C:

$$z_t(k) = \frac{N(k) - \mu_{\Omega_t}}{\sigma_{\Omega_t}},$$

where $N(k)$ is k's actual number of occurrences in C, and μ_{Ω_t} and σ_{Ω_t} are the mean and standard deviation of Ω_t.

Spatial burstiness. To measure spatial burstiness, we horizontally compare all the candidates in Q. The rationale is that, among the spatially scattered candidates, a keyword k in candidate C is spatially bursty if k's proportion in C is significantly higher than in other candidates. Given n candidate events $C_1, C_2, \ldots, C_n$, let P_i denote the keyword probability distribution of candidate C_i. With $\Omega_s = \{P_1(k), P_2(k), \ldots, P_n(k)\}$, we compute the spatial burstiness of keyword k in candidate C_i as:

$$z_s(k) = \frac{P_i(k) - \mu_{\Omega_s}}{\sigma_{\Omega_s}},$$

where μ_{Ω_s} and σ_{Ω_s} are the mean and standard deviation of Ω_s.

Ranking function. For each keyword k in a candidate C, we have used vertical comparison against the historical activities to measure its temporal burstiness, and horizontal comparison with the other candidates to measure its spatial burstiness. As the final step, we compute the ranking score of candidate C by aggregating the burstiness of all the keywords in C:

$$s(C) = \sum_{k \in C} w_C(k)(\eta z_t(k) + (1 - \eta) z_s(k)),$$

where η ($0 < \eta < 1$) is a factor balancing the spatial and temporal burstiness; and $w_C(k)$ is the TF-IDF weight of keyword k.

5. THE ONLINE MODE

In this section, we present the online mode of GeoBurst. Consider a query window Q, let Q' be the new query window after Q shifts. Instead of finding local events in Q' from scratch, the online mode leverages the results in Q and updates the event list with little cost. The updated event list is guaranteed to be the same as directly running batch-mode detection on Q'.

In GeoBurst's two steps, the candidate generation step has a dominating time cost. At the core of the online mode is thus an updating module that finds new pivots in the new window Q' with little overhead. Let D_Q be the tweets falling in Q and D'_Q be the tweets in Q'. We denote by R_Q the tweets removed from D_Q, *i.e.*, $R_Q = D_Q - D'_Q$; and by I_Q the tweets inserted into D_Q, *i.e.*, $I_Q = D'_Q - D_Q$. In the sequel, we design a strategy that finds pivots in D'_Q by just processing R_Q and I_Q.

Recall that, the pivot seeking process first computes the local pivot for each tweet and then performs authority ascent via a path of local pivots. So long as the local pivot information is correctly maintained for each tweet, the authority ascent can be fast completed. The key to avoiding finding pivots from scratch is that, as D_Q is changed to D'_Q, only a number of tweets have their local pivots changed. We call them mutated tweets and identify them by analyzing the influence of R_Q and I_Q.

Definition 6 (Mutated Tweet). *A tweet $d \in D'_Q$ is a mutated tweet if d's local pivot in D'_Q is different from its local pivot in D_Q.*

For any tweet, it can become a mutated tweet only if at least one of its neighbors has authority change. Therefore, we take a *reverse search* strategy to find mutated tweets. We first identify in D'_Q all the tweets whose authorities have changed. Then for each authority-changed tweet t, we retrieve the tweets that regard t as its neighbor, and update their local pivots. Hence, the key becomes how to find authority-changed tweets. In what follows, we handle R_Q and I_Q to this end.

Handling deletions. The deletion of a tweet $d \in R_Q$ can cause authority change in two ways. First, for the tweets having d as a neighbor in D_Q, their authorities decrease. Second, the keyword co-occurrence graph may evolve because of deleting d. As a result, the vicinities of certain keywords need to be recomputed and the authorities of corresponding tweets may change. The first case can be easily handled due to the additive property of authority. When d is deleted, we simply retrieve the tweets having d as a neighbor in D_Q. For each of those tweets, we subtract d's contribution from the authority score. For the second case, the key is to identify the keywords that need vicinity recomputation. Let us look at an example in Figure 5. If d contains two keywords e_1 and e_2, deleting d would decrease the weight of the edge $[e_1, e_2]$. For any other keywords having e_1 or e_2 in their old vicinities (e_3 and e_4 in this example), we mark them as to-recompute keywords. However, we defer the computation of their vicinities until I_Q is handled to identify the complete set of to-recompute keywords.

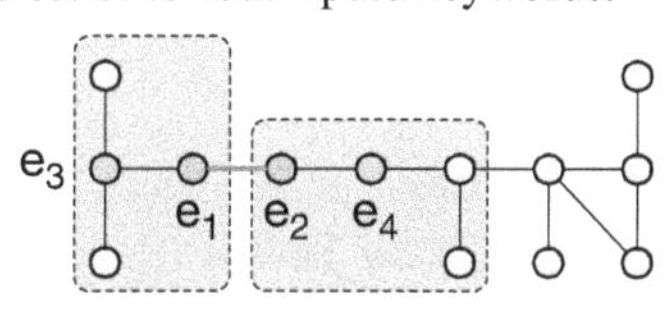

Figure 5: Updating the keyword co-occurrence graph and keyword vicinities.

Handling insertions. A new tweet $d \in I_Q$ can also cause authority changes in two ways: (1) increasing the authority of the tweets that regard d as a neighbor; and (2) making the keyword co-occurrence graph evolve. Here, we need to first deal with the second case to ensure authority computation in the first case is based on the updated keyword vicinities. Similarly, we identify the keywords whose attaching edges have weight change, and mark other keywords that include such keywords in their vicinities. After all the to-recompute keywords are identified, we call Algorithm 2 to obtain their new vicinities. Once the keyword vicinities are updated, we retrieve the affected tweet pairs and update the corresponding authority scores. For the second case, now that the keyword vicinities have already been updated, for the inserted tweet d, we simply find which other tweets having d as their neighbor, and then add d's contribution to their authorities.

6. EXPERIMENTS

We evaluate the empirical performance of GeoBurst in this section. All the algorithms were implemented in JAVA and the experiments were conducted on a computer with Intel Core i7 2.4Ghz CPU and 8GB memory.

6.1 Experimental Setup

Data Set. Our experiments are based on two real-life data sets, both of which are crawled using Twitter Streaming API[2] during 2014.08.01 — 2014.11.30. The first data set, referred to as NY, consists of 9.5 million geo-tagged tweets in New York. After removing the tweets having no entities or noun phrases, we obtain 2.4 million tweets. The second data set, referred to as LA, consists of 9.9 million geo-tagged tweets in Los Angeles, and there are 2.8 million tweets that have entities and/or noun phrases. The reason we choose these two cities is because they have quite different population distributions — the populace of New York is relatively concentrated in Manhattan and Brooklyn, while the populace of Los Angeles is spread out in many different districts.

Compared methods. For comparison, we implemented two existing local event detection methods. The first is EventTweet [3], which extracts bursty and localized keywords as features, and then clusters those features based on their spatial distributions. The second is Wavelet [7], which uses wavelet transform to identify spatiotemporally bursty keywords and then clusters them by considering both co-occurrence and spatiotemporal distribution.

Parameters. There are four major parameters in GeoBurst: (1) the kernel bandwidth h; (2) the restart probability α; (3) the RWR similarity threshold δ; and (4) the ranking parameter η for balancing spatial and temporal burstiness. Unless stated explicitly, we set $h = 0.01, \alpha = 0.2, \delta = 0.02$, and $\eta = 0.5$. EventTweet partitions the whole space into $N \times N$ small grids. We find N is EventTweet's most sensitive parameter, and set $N = 50$ after tuning. For Wavelet, the most sensitive parameters are the granularities for constructing the spatiotemporal signal. After tuning, we set the space partitioning granularity to $\delta_x = 0.1, \delta_y = 0.1$; and the time granularity to $\delta_t = 3$ hours.

6.2 Effectiveness Study

To evaluate effectiveness, we randomly generate 80 query time windows that are non-overlapping during 2014.08.01 — 2014.11.30. Among them, there are 20 3-hour windows, 20 4-hour ones, 20 5-hour ones, and 20 6-hour ones. As all the three methods require a reference window, we use a 5-day reference window right preceding each query. For every query, we run the three methods to retrieve top-5 local events on the two data sets, and upload the results

[2]https://dev.twitter.com/streaming/overview

to CrowdFlower[3], a popular crowdsourcing platform, for evaluation. For GEOBURST, we ran both its batch mode and online mode to detect local events in the query window, and found these two modes produce exactly the same results. Thus, we only upload the results produced by the online mode and report its effectiveness.

On CrowdFlower, we represent each event with 5 most representative tweets as well as 10 representative keywords, and ask three CrowdFlower workers to judge whether the event is indeed a local event or not. To ensure the quality of the workers, we label 10 queries for groundtruth judgments on each data set, such that only the workers who can achieve no less than 80% accuracy on the groundtruth can submit their answers. Finally, we use majority voting to aggregate the workers' answers.

The representative tweets and keywords are selected as follows: (1) For GEOBURST, each event is a cluster of tweets, we select the 5 tweets having the largest authority scores, and the 10 keywords having the largest TF-IDF weights. (2) EVENTWEET represents each event as a group of keywords. We select top-10 keywords in each event. Then we regard the group of keywords as a query to retrieve the top-5 most similar tweets in the query window using the BM25 retrieval model. (3) WAVELET represents an event with both keywords and matching tweets. We simply select the top-5 tweets and the top-10 keywords.

6.2.1 *Quantitative analysis*

After gathering judgments from CrowdFlower, we compute the precision for each method. Figure 6 shows the precisions of the three methods on NY and LA when K and query interval vary. One may notice that the overall precision is not high for all the three methods. This phenomenon is reasonable because the query time windows are generated randomly. There are chances that some query windows fall in a time period (*e.g.*, early morning) during which no local events happened in the city.

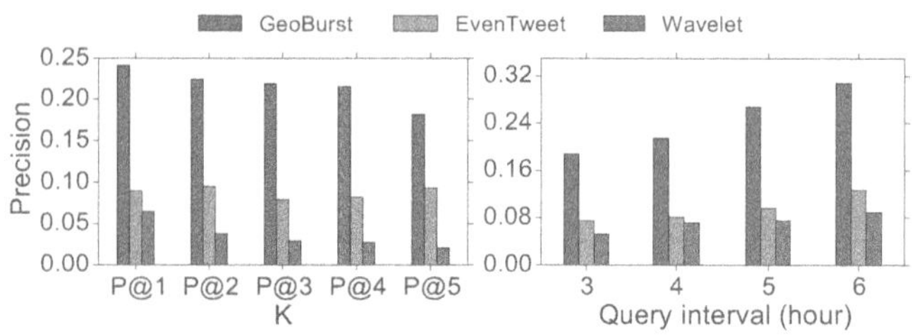

(a) Precision comparison (NY).

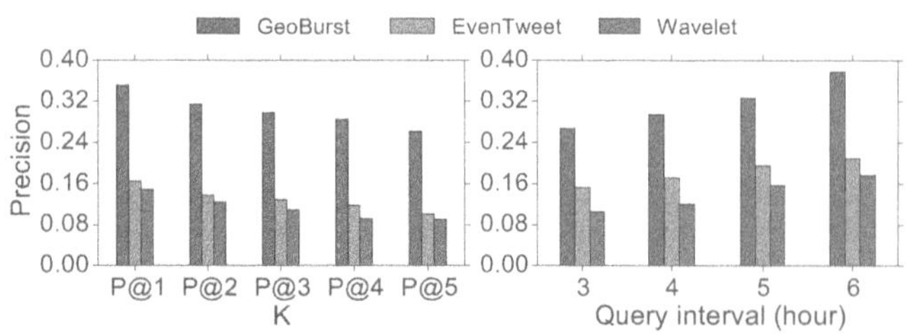

(b) Precision comparison (LA).

Figure 6: Precision comparison of GEOBURST, EVENTWEET, and WAVELET.

Comparing the three methods, we find that GEOBURST significantly outperforms EVENTWEET and WAVELET on both data sets. The huge improvements indicate the superiority of GEOBURST's two-step scheme: (1) the candidate generation step ensures a good coverage of all potential local events; and (2) the ranking step effectively identifies true local events by carefully measuring spatiotemporal burstiness.

We also observe that the precisions of the three methods all increase with the query interval. It is because a larger query interval is more likely to cover a time period in which certain local events have taken place.

6.2.2 *Illustrative cases*

Now we perform a case study on NY to compare the local events detected by the three methods. We choose the query window to be 7 – 10pm on November 7th 2014 and show the top-3 local events detected by different methods in Figure 7. For each event, we show the messages of the top-3 tweets, highlight the representative keywords, and plot the locations of the member tweets.

Examining the results of GEOBURST, one can see the generated geo-topic clusters are of high quality: the tweets in each cluster are both geographically compact and semantically coherent. Interestingly, GEOBURST can group the tweets that discuss about the topic using different keywords (*e.g.*, "Thai Restaurant" and "Asian Dishes"). This is because the RWR measure effectively captures the subtle semantic correlations between keywords. Another interesting observation is that, the pivot tweet of each cluster is highly interpretable. This is because such high-quality tweets mention most important keywords about the topic and locate closely to the occurring spot, thereby receiving high authority scores.

For the given query, the top two clusters produced by GEOBURST correspond to two local events: (1) the New York Festival of Light, which is held under the Manhattan Bridge; and (2) the basketball game between two NBA teams — Brooklyn Nets and New York Knicks. The third cluster is a group of tweets discussing about dinner instead of any interesting local events. Nevertheless, our investigation into its z-score reveals that there is a huge score gap (16.23 versus 0.73) between the second cluster and the third one. This suggests that one can easily use a z-score threshold to rule out non-event clusters in practice.

EVENTWEET also successfully detects the basketball game between Nets and Knicks. Nevertheless, the interpretability of the result event is not satisfactory, because it just groups bursty keywords based on their spatial distributions. As a result, the keywords in the same cluster may not be semantically coherent. One may notice that there exist geographically faraway tweets in the same cluster. This is because EVENTWEET is a feature-based method that uses only keywords to represent an event. As the matching tweets are retrieved based on keyword similarity, it is possible that some tweets are geographically faraway even if they use the same keywords.

For WAVELET, it also reports the basketball game event, but misses the event of New York Festival of Light. The result clusters are of high quality as WAVELET considers both keyword co-occurrence information and spatiotemporal distribution during the clustering process. Nevertheless, the major drawback of WAVELET is that it tends to miss many local events in the query window. Using wavelet transform for bursty keyword identification, WAVELET is more suitable for extracting influential local events on a tweet collection that spans a long time period, rather than real-time local event detection in an ad-hoc query window.

6.3 Efficiency Study

To study the efficiency of the three methods, we generate 200 random queries with different lengths. For every query, we run each method for 10 times and report the average running time.

6.3.1 *Running time comparison*

In the first set of experiments, we compare the running time of

[3]http://www.crowdflower.com/

	GeoBurst	Is event?
# 1	1. **Festival of Light**! **#nyfol** (@ **The Archway** under the **Manhattan Bridge** in **Brooklyn, NY**) 2. **#Lasers and beats** under the **Manhattan Bridge**! **#NewYorkFestivalofLight #NYFOL @ DUMBO** 3. **New York Festival of Lights #nyfol #dumbo @ DUMBO, Brooklyn**	Yes
# 2	1. **Knicks** vs. **Nets** at **Barclays Center**. @ Barclays Center http://t.co/PILk1xK3Tn 2. **Brooklyn** go hard @ **Barclays Center** http://t.co/iVUsJJ5TNG 3. Let's go **Knicks**! #NETS1107 (@ **Barclays Center** - @brooklynnets for @nyknicks vs @BrooklynNets)	Yes
# 3	1. **#Thai Restaurant** #spicythaifood (@ 104 **2nd Avenue** in **New York, NY**) 2. The **ASIAN DISHES** here are always my favorite. @ **Ugly Kitchen** 3. **Dinner time** with my family. Suuuuper Nice **Indian RESTAURANT**! @ Malai Marke **Indian Cuisine**.	No
	EvenTweet	**Is event?**
# 1	1. I practiced... Almost time for **Amy Schumer**. **Jennifer** (@ **Carnegie Hall**) https://t.co/HfqfTLmK2y 2. **2014 Gold Glove Awards Ceremony** with **Hall of Famers**, **All-Stars Jay Leno** @ **The Plaza Hotel** 3. My best attempt at a **selfie** with **Hugh Jackman** after **The River at CITS** @ **The River on Broadway**	No
# 2	1. **Knicks** vs. **Nets** at **Barclays Center**. @ **Barclays Center** http://t.co/PILk1xK3Tn 2. **Budweiser** brings everyone together #family #nonewfriends @ **Alchemy Tavern, Brooklyn** 3. **#Knicks** vs **#nets** with my best gal. @ **Barclays Center Brooklyn** http://t.co/eXXMUKxpIs	Yes
# 3	1. **#katespade** @ **Kate Spade / Jack Spade HQ** http://t.co/g6jiFwyc4M 2. Inspiring **keynote** by **Twitter CEO**, **Dick Costolo** @GirlsWhoCode Gala. http://t.co/yEGh803CuT 3. I wonder if **Jake** from **Statefarm** covers **Jumanji**?	No
	Wavelet	**Is event?**
# 1	1. **Spike**'s face says it all. Sorry **Knicks** fans maybe next time. **@Brooklynnets #Nets** @ **Barclays Center** 2. **#Knicks** vs **#nets** with my best gal. @ **Barclays Center Brooklyn** http://t.co/eXXMUKxpIs 3. **Brooklyn** go hard @ **Barclays Center** http://t.co/hPooLfa9pQ	Yes
# 2	1. **#BEMF** (at **@VerbotenNewyork** in **Brooklyn**, NY) https://t.co/uVgTHNZzSP 2. Starting the **weekend** right. (at **@VerbotenNewyork** in **Brooklyn, NY**) https://t.co/cRiPHK1Qdy 3. What a **NIGHT**!! @ **Irving Plaza**	No
# 3	1. **Alex** from target isn't even cute... 2. Thank you **Alex** and **Eric** and **chief Alex** and @nyysteak dad loves his **long bone**. 3. So here I am in **NYC** alone without **Alex**. but I know who i am I'm in the right **direction**.	No

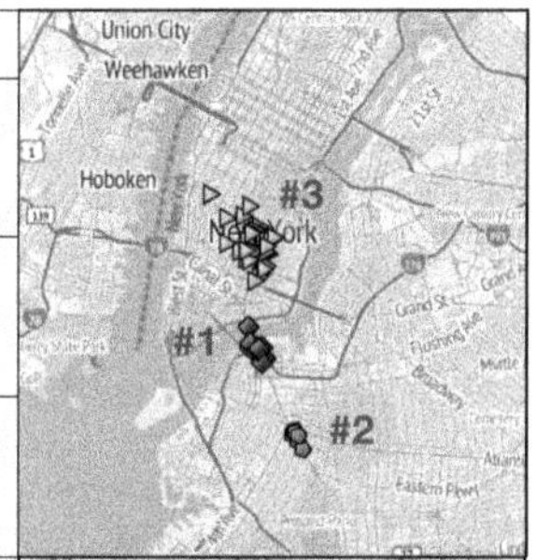

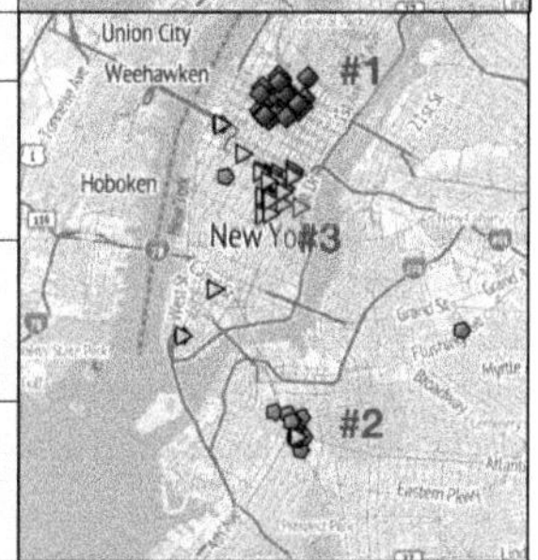

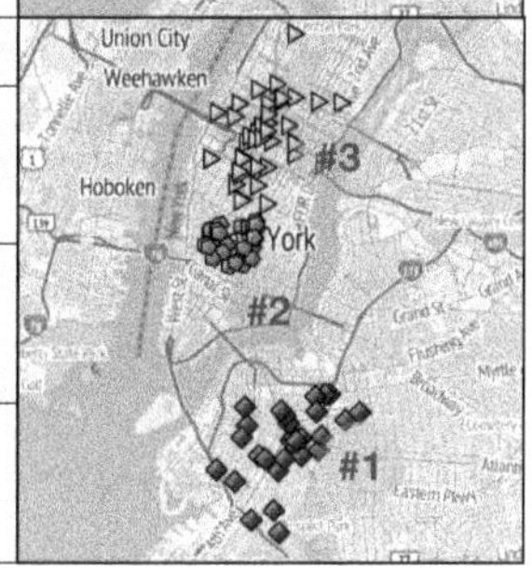

Figure 7: Top-3 local events detected by different methods in New York during 7 – 10pm, November 7th 2014.

GEOBURST against EVENTWEET and WAVELET. We run GEOBURST in both batch mode and online mode. Given a query window Q, the batch mode performs candidate generation and ranking in Q; the online mode considers a window Q' that precedes Q by 10 minutes, and finds local events in Q by updating the results in Q'.

Figure 8 shows the running time of the three methods on NY and LA. We observe that GEOBURST is much more efficient than EVENTWEET and WAVELET even when in the batch mode. This phenomenon is explained by two facts. First, in the candidate generation step, the approximate RWR computation strategy can effectively speed up the pivot seeking process. Second, in the ranking step, GEOBURST just uses a number of historical activities to compute z-scores, which is very efficient (we found that the running time of the ranking step accounts for less than 1% of GEOBURST's total running time). Meanwhile, the online mode is even much faster than the batch mode. This is expected as the online mode does not need to find pivots from scratch in the time-consuming candidate generation step, but just needs to process the updated tweets and can achieve excellent efficiency.

The major overhead of EVENTWEET and WAVELET is due to their space partitioning strategy. Specifically, EVENTWEET needs to compute spatial entropy to select localized keywords and perform clustering based on keyword spatial distributions; WAVELET needs to perform wavelet transform on the spatiotemporal signal and compute the spatiotemporal KL-divergence between keywords. One may propose to partition the space at a coarser granularity to improve the running time of the two methods, but that comes with the price of being much less effective. Note that the running time of

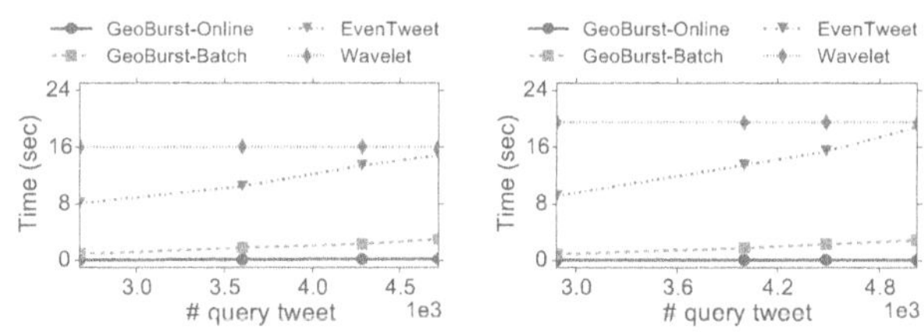

(a) Running time (NY). (b) Running time (LA).

Figure 8: Running time v.s. # tweets in the query window.

WAVELET remains almost unchanged when the number of tweets increases. The reason is WAVELET finds events in an augmented window that includes both reference and query tweets. As our queries are at the same scale of several hours, we fixed the length of the reference window to 5 days. Accordingly, the running time of WAVELET is not affected much by the length of the query interval.

6.3.2 *Throughput Study*

In Figure 9, we report the scalability of GEOBURST's online mode when the number of updates varies:

$$\#\text{updates} = \#\text{deleted tweets} + \#\text{inserted tweets}.$$

To this end, we choose a 3-hour query window Q. Then we use a window Q' that precedes Q by 1, 2, ..., 8, 9, 10 minutes, respectively, and update the results in Q'. One can observe that the running time of the online mode shows good scalability with the number of updates. For example, when there are as many as 212 updates, the online mode takes just 0.282 second to finish on the

NY data set. Such performance suggests that, GEOBURST's online mode is capable of continuously monitoring the stream and realizing real-time detection.

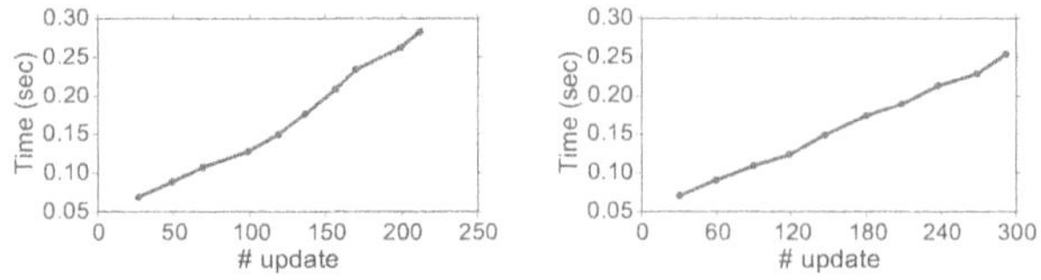

(a) Time v.s. # update (NY). (b) Time v.s. # update (LA).

Figure 9: Throughput of GEOBURST's online mode.

We proceed to study the throughput of GEOBURST for constructing the activity timeline. We apply GEOBURST to construct activity timeline on NY and LA and periodically record the number of tweets processed so far and the running time. As shown in Figure 10, GEOBURST finished constructing activity timeline for 2.4 million tweets in 341.35 seconds on NY, and 2.8 million tweets in 330.82 seconds on LA, and it scales well with the number of tweets.

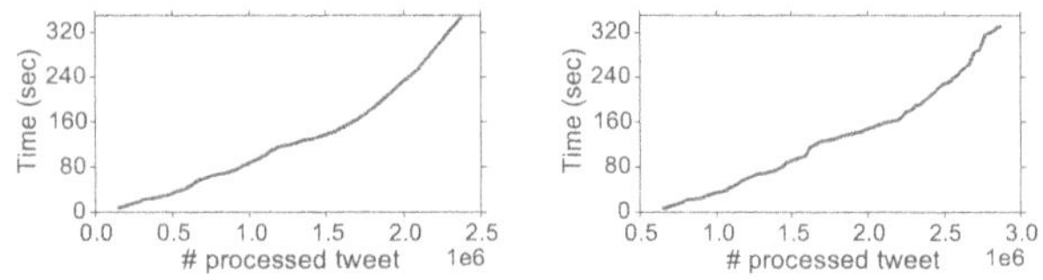

(a) Time v.s. # tweet (NY). (b) Time v.s. # tweet (LA).

Figure 10: Throughput of activity timeline construction.

7. CONCLUSION

We studied the problem of real-time local event detection in the geo-tagged tweet stream. We proposed the GEOBURST detector. To the best of our knowledge, GEOBURST is the first method that is capable of extracting highly interpretable local events in real time. GEOBURST first generates candidate events based on a novel pivot seeking process, and then leverages the continuous summarization of the stream as background knowledge to rank the candidates. Our extensive experiments have demonstrated that GEOBURST is highly effective and efficient. The usage of GEOBURST is not limited to Twitter. Rather, any geo-textual social media stream (*e.g.*, Instagram photo tags, Facebook posts) can use GEOBURST to extract interesting local events as well. For future work, it is interesting to extend GEOBURST for handling the tweets that mention geo-entities but do not include exact GPS coordinates. We plan to pursue this direction by augmenting GEOBURST with existing geo-locating techniques [18, 27].

8. ACKNOWLEDGEMENTS

This work was sponsored in part by the U.S. Army Research Lab. under Cooperative Agreement No. W911NF-09-2-0053 (NSCTA), National Science Foundation IIS-1017362, IIS-1320617, and IIS-1354329, HDTRA1-10-1-0120, NSFC (Grant No. 61572488), and Grant 1U54GM114838 awarded by NIGMS through funds provided by the trans-NIH Big Data to Knowledge (BD2K) initiative (www.bd2k.nih.gov), and MIAS, a DHS-IDS Center for Multimodal Information Access and Synthesis at UIUC. The views and conclusions contained in this document are those of the author(s) and should not be interpreted as representing the official policies of the U.S. Army Research Laboratory or the U.S. Government. The U.S. Government is authorized to reproduce and distribute reprints for Government purposes notwithstanding any copyright notation hereon.

9. REFERENCES

[1] http://goo.gl/GQF38b.

[2] http://goo.gl/i0Gdol.

[3] H. Abdelhaq, C. Sengstock, and M. Gertz. Eventweet: Online localized event detection from twitter. *PVLDB*, 6(12):1326–1329, 2013.

[4] C. C. Aggarwal, J. Han, J. Wang, and P. S. Yu. A framework for clustering evolving data streams. In *VLDB*, pages 81–92, 2003.

[5] C. C. Aggarwal and K. Subbian. Event detection in social streams. In *SDM*, pages 624–635, 2012.

[6] J. Allan, R. Papka, and V. Lavrenko. On-line new event detection and tracking. In *SIGIR*, pages 37–45, 1998.

[7] L. Chen and A. Roy. Event detection from flickr data through wavelet-based spatial analysis. In *CIKM*, pages 523–532, 2009.

[8] D. Comaniciu and P. Meer. Mean shift analysis and applications. In *ICCV*, pages 1197–1203, 1999.

[9] S. Doan, B.-K. H. Vo, and N. Collier. An analysis of twitter messages in the 2011 tohoku earthquake. In *Electronic Healthcare*, pages 58–66. Springer, 2012.

[10] W. Feng, C. Zhang, W. Zhang, J. Han, J. Wang, C. Aggarwal, and J. Huang. Streamcube: Hierarchical spatio-temporal hashtag clustering for event exploration over the twitter stream. In *ICDE*, pages 1561–1572, 2015.

[11] J. Foley, M. Bendersky, and V. Josifovski. Learning to extract local events from the web. In *SIGIR*, pages 423–432, 2015.

[12] G. P. C. Fung, J. X. Yu, P. S. Yu, and H. Lu. Parameter free bursty events detection in text streams. In *VLDB*, pages 181–192, 2005.

[13] Q. He, K. Chang, and E.-P. Lim. Analyzing feature trajectories for event detection. In *SIGIR*, pages 207–214, 2007.

[14] G. Jeh and J. Widom. Scaling personalized web search. In *WWW*, pages 271–279, 2003.

[15] J. Krumm and E. Horvitz. Eyewitness: Identifying local events via space-time signals in twitter feeds. In *SIGSPATIAL*, 2015.

[16] K. Leetaru, S. Wang, G. Cao, A. Padmanabhan, and E. Shook. Mapping the global twitter heartbeat: The geography of twitter. *First Monday*, 18(5), 2013.

[17] C. Li, A. Sun, and A. Datta. Twevent: segment-based event detection from tweets. In *CIKM*, pages 155–164, 2012.

[18] G. Li, J. Hu, J. Feng, and K.-l. Tan. Effective location identification from microblogs. In *ICDE*, pages 880–891, 2014.

[19] R. Li, K. H. Lei, R. Khadiwala, and K.-C. Chang. Tedas: A twitter-based event detection and analysis system. In *ICDE*, pages 1273–1276, 2012.

[20] P. Lofgren and A. Goel. Personalized pagerank to a target node. *arXiv:1304.4658*, 2013.

[21] M. Mathioudakis and N. Koudas. Twittermonitor: trend detection over the twitter stream. In *SIGMOD*, pages 1155–1158, 2010.

[22] S. Phuvipadawat and T. Murata. Breaking news detection and tracking in twitter. In *WI-IAT*, pages 120–123, 2010.

[23] M. Quezada, V. Peña-Araya, and B. Poblete. Location-aware model for news events in social media. In *SIGIR*, pages 935–938, 2015.

[24] T. Sakaki, M. Okazaki, and Y. Matsuo. Earthquake shakes twitter users: real-time event detection by social sensors. In *WWW*, pages 851–860, 2010.

[25] J. Sankaranarayanan, H. Samet, B. E. Teitler, M. D. Lieberman, and J. Sperling. Twitterstand: news in tweets. In *GIS*, pages 42–51, 2009.

[26] L. Shou, Z. Wang, K. Chen, and G. Chen. Sumblr: continuous summarization of evolving tweet streams. In *SIGIR*, pages 533–542, 2013.

[27] K. Watanabe, M. Ochi, M. Okabe, and R. Onai. Jasmine: a real-time local-event detection system based on geolocation information propagated to microblogs. In *CIKM*, pages 2541–2544, 2011.

[28] J. Weng and B.-S. Lee. Event detection in twitter. In *ICWSM*, pages 401–408, 2011.

[29] C. Zhang, S. Jiang, Y. Chen, Y. Sun, and J. Han. Fast inbound top-k query for random walk with restart. In *ECML/PKDD*, pages 608–624. 2015.

[30] Y. Zheng, L. Capra, O. Wolfson, and H. Yang. Urban computing: Concepts, methodologies, and applications. *ACM TIST*, 5(3):38:1–38:55, 2014.

Building a Self-Learning Search Engine: From Research to Business

Manos Tsagkias
manos@904labs.com
904Labs, Amsterdam, The Netherlands

Wouter Weerkamp
wouter@904labs.com
904Labs, Amsterdam, The Netherlands

ABSTRACT

904Labs B.V. was founded in 2014 by Wouter Weerkamp, Manos Tsagkias, and Maarten de Rijke to commercialize state-of-the-art search engine technology. 904Labs' strategic product is a self-learning search engine for online retailers, which uses some of the most recent scientific developments in machine learning and search engine evaluation. 904Labs has raised about 200K in funding and has signed pilots with large international and national companies. Since its start, 904Labs has grown with two developers and two experienced business people. In this presentation we tell how to go from research to business and the challenges it brings along?

1. FROM RESEARCH TO BUSINESS

In our talk we take you on a journey that starts at a university and ends owning a search technology company that is still in its early stages. We describe this journey in several steps, including the lessons learned after each step. We explain the current state of the company and the future plans and opportunities, and conclude by listing some of the major challenges.

1.1 Setting off

The journey of 904Labs starts at the University of Amsterdam. Witnessing a growing number of organizations knocking on the university's door to ask for help with their "scientifically interesting" problems, which turned out to be not of interest to the university, we saw an opportunity for a business entity to jump in and help these organizations solve their problems. 904Labs was born, and we thought of it much like an extension of the research group from which it originates. As one can imagine, the problems organizations face are as diverse as the research done within the research group, ranging from entity extraction and linking, via text summarization, to more regular search issues. Offering all these solutions is infeasible as a startup for three reasons: (1) there is limited manpower, you cannot do everything; (2) it is unclear to the outside world what the company actually offers; and (3) there is no scalable business model in developing custom-made software solutions.

Lessons learned: Focus. Do not try to solve everything, but pick one problem and design your solution around it. Think of it as writing one paper. What is the core problem you are trying to solve and focus on that particular problem. Ignore the rest, as interesting as it might be, you might add it in a later paper.

SIGIR '16 July 17-21, 2016, Pisa, Italy

ACM ISBN 978-1-4503-4069-4/16/07.
DOI: http://dx.doi.org/10.1145/2911451.2926728

1.2 Choosing a path

Working under the assumption that most businesses were by now at a reasonable level when it comes to implementing search solutions (e.g., use Elasticsearch or Solr), we figured that the world was ready to meet self-learning search. Self-learning search is a fancy name for online learning to rank, which is learning to rank tightly coupled with interleaving, which allows real-time learning and experimenting with new search algorithms.

After initial talks with a few potential clients (i.e., large e-commerce sites), it became clear that these organizations are not looking to replace their current systems with yet another solutions. Also, the search engines running at their sites are part of very complex product and customer management systems, in which we are not interested. On the other hand, these large sites could potentially benefit a lot from self-learning search, given the amount of traffic and the revenue deriving from search. Taking everything into consideration, we decided to offer self-learning search as-a-service, a middleware layer sitting between the e-commerce site and the client's existing search infrastructure. It allows for quick easy integration.

Many months later, after talks with yet other potential clients, we found out that SaaS solutions have their own problems (e.g., latency, reliability), keeping large organizations from buying. Implementing self-learning search as plugins for major search solutions (Elasticsearch, Solr) is now another viable direction we are exploring.

Lessons learned: Test assumptions. You cannot do this enough (and we actually did not do it enough). Which problems are your clients facing? What do they want? How do they want it? Ask, ask, ask. Do not sell, but learn. It is like testing the research waters with a small workshop paper before working on the full SIGIR submission. If no one cares about the workshop paper, do not bother writing the full paper.

1.3 En route

The direction has been determined, now how to actually go there? Being confident researchers, we thought implementing well-known methods into a working system should be a matter of weeks. Selling it would, of course, be easy, because who would not want to have such a cool system? So we would be making money within a few months, meaning that until then we could do without funding.

Wrong. Building a product takes time. A lot of it. Selling takes at least an equal amount of time, and probably more when you are not a natural-born salesperson. This means that you will not see any money coming in from product sales any time soon. Unless you get more people on board, for which you need … money. With a growing need for revenue, it becomes hard to say no to consultancy projects, which take up much of your time and distract from developing your own product. We finally figured out that money is a necessity and applied for various grants, receiving 175K euro. The money gave us the opportunity to hire developers, speed up product development, and focus on business development instead of consultancy jobs.

Lessons learned: Take care of the financials. And stay on track. Try to find grants (e.g., from your university) or investors so that you do not get sidetracked by consultancy jobs. It is like working on your final technical thesis chapter, while you have already started as a postdoc somewhere else. You get paid, but cannot do the work you should be doing.

1.4 Getting lost and finding the way

Being en route does not mean you cannot change directions anymore. Or that you will not get lost. From a business perspective, finding the right client segment is a challenge, and one that continually changes. Your marketing depends on your client segment, your website depends on the marketing strategy, grants have milestones that should fit product development, which in itself is dependent on the problems faced by your potential clients. And how do you convince clients to buy your product? We might have PhDs in search technology, but why would potential clients care? They do not. Being convinced of your product is one thing, but selling it is another. After trying to get pilots and clients, with mixed success, and doing so without a clear strategy, we decided that it was time to acknowledge our weaknesses. We are not experienced business men and you do need those to find your way. We have reached out to potential investors who, instead of investing money, have jumped on board in hands on positions related to business development, marketing, and sales. Having experienced people taking care of this side of running a company helps immensely and allows us to focus on the things we are good at.

Lessons learned: Take care of the team. Make sure you have (experienced) people at the important positions in the team; you cannot do everything yourself. Sales and marketing is a very different beast. Think of writing a paper, scrapping all technical sections, and leaving only the main result and original problem ("Web search is hard. We improve MAP by 10%"). No one cares how you do it.

1.5 What the future may bring

We have a first version of our product, self-learning search as-a-service. We have pilot agreements with several companies, like Elsevier, WizeNoze, and Autostyle. We have a team that includes developers, business people, and ourselves. And we have a buffer of money. Now we need sales. Hardcore sales. We are in the money-making business, so let us try that. After money comes in, we can focus on improving the product by thinking about faceted search and online learning to rank, personalized online learning to rank, and delayed feedback.

1.6 Conclusion

Are you thinking of entering the startup arena with a brilliant idea that has proven itself in research? Do it! It is a fun ride. But do keep in mind that business is not research. People do not care about the technical and theoretical details, they want to know which problems it solves and what it brings them. So, (1) talk to potential clients, find out what their problems are; (2) Focus on one problem and create a solution for it; (3) Get funding to hire people and avoid distractions, and (4) take care of the business side of things.

Sedano: A News Stream Processor for Business

Ugo Scaiella, Giacomo Berardi, Giuliano Mega, Roberto Santoro
Spaziodati, Italy
{scaiella,berardi,mega,santoro}@spaziodati.eu

ABSTRACT

We present SEDANO, a system for processing and indexing a continuous stream of business-related news. SEDANO defines pipelines whose stages analyze and enrich news items (e.g., newspaper articles and press releases). News data coming from several content sources are stored, processed and then indexed in order to be consumed by Atoka, our business intelligence product. Atoka users can retrieve news about specific companies, filtering according to various facets. SEDANO features both an entity-linking phase, which finds mentions of companies in news, and a classification phase, which classifies news according to a set of business events. Its flexible architecture allows SEDANO to be deployed on commodity machines while being scalable and fault-tolerant.

Keywords

business intelligence; news retrieval; entity linking; text classification

1. INTRODUCTION

Nowadays a deluge of news articles and press releases often bewilders readers; this explains why news aggregators have surged in popularity. While news aggregators do a good job for readers in general, they may not be enough if someone is interested in specific business-related news and events, e.g.: which are the news where a particular company is mentioned? Which news recently talked about company events, like lay-offs or mergers and acquisitions? Which are the interesting events regarding a specific company? For this reason we created SEDANO, a system that is able to ingest, process and enrich news stream in a scalable manner. The news are indexed and offered via a RESTful API, in order to be consumed by our end-user product Atoka[1], a semantic tool for *lead generation*, but also by other business clients that integrate the information provided by SEDANO in their products.

[1]http://atoka.io

SIGIR '16 July 17-21, 2016, Pisa, Italy

ACM ISBN 978-1-4503-4069-4/16/07.
DOI: http://dx.doi.org/10.1145/2911451.2926730

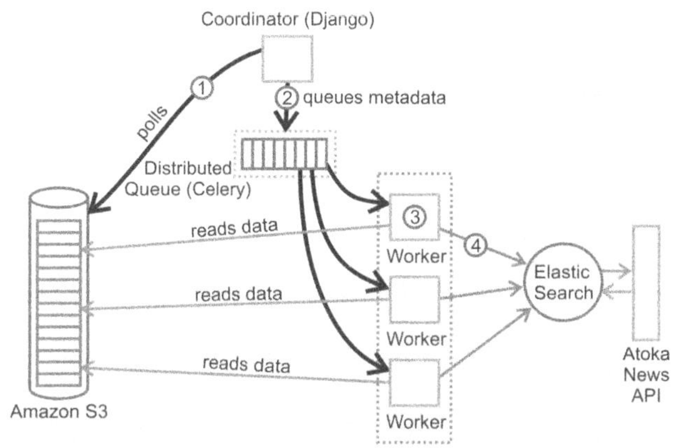

Figure 1: Sedano's base architecture.

2. ARCHITECTURE

SEDANO is based on a simple distributed architecture, depicted in Figure 1. It leverages Amazon's S3[2] for high aggregated throughput, and the Celery[3] distributed queue for control messages. Data is stored in S3 as a collection of *data chunks*, i.e., S3 objects containing *news items*. Processing in SEDANO is triggered by a *coordinator node*, which (1) periodically (i.e., every minute) polls S3 for new chunks and, (2) enqueues *work orders* referring to chunks that require processing into Celery. Once into Celery, work orders become visible to *worker nodes* who then dequeue them, (3) download the corresponding chunks in parallel from S3, and process them independently. At the end of the processing, the resulting news items are (4) indexed into an ElasticSearch[4] cluster. Basic fault tolerance is achieved by having Amazon's Elastic Container Service (ECS)[5] supervise individual components, respawning them into available machines in the event of crashes.

Processing at worker nodes takes place as a series of sequential stages that make up SEDANO's *processing pipelines*. Pipelines are composed of three major steps, discussed next.

Cleansing and normalization. The first step at every pipeline deals with content cleansing and normalization—we extract the relevant content from each news item by processing the HTML in which they are represented, and compute several measures (e.g. the length of an article or if its con-

[2]http://aws.amazon.com/s3
[3]http://www.celeryproject.org
[4]http://www.elastic.co
[5]https://aws.amazon.com/ecs

tent is well-structured) which later help us understand if that news item is "good" or not (and therefore whether or not it should be served to certain clients).

Deduplication. News items are then deduplicated. Since finding duplicates by comparing new documents with previously indexed ones would be costly, we adopt a more scalable on-line approach, based on a novel Locality-Sensitive Hashing (LSH) algorithm which mixes the Solr[6] approach with the Nilsimsa algorithm[7] to hash similar news items into the same code. A news item is then tagged as a duplicate if and only if another news item with the same hash code is known to have been processed before. To keep this information consistent across worker nodes, we rely on a scalable key-value store with strong consistency guarantees.

Enrichment. The remainder of this section discusses the two main enrichment components in the SEDANO pipelines: the *Dandelion Company API* (Section 2.1), an entity linking platform focused on the identification of company mentions in news, and *Selino* (Section 2.2), an ensemble of linear multi-label text classifiers whose classes are business events of interest.

2.1 Dandelion Company API

Dandelion API[8] is a platform for text-analytics as a service: it is the evolution of TAGME [1], a state-of-the-art entity linking system based on a knowledge graph extracted from Wikipedia, whose main benefits are its performance on short texts and its speed. Our partnership with Cerved[9], the leader of business information in Italy, gave us access to data of all Italian companies. We used this data to specialize the entity linking system into the Dandelion Company API for identifying company mentions. It includes information on almost 3M companies, which are added as new entities to our knowledge graph. Despite the huge number of entities that have been added, the system preserves its speed.

Since the new entities do not have cleaned data like Wikipedia ones, they may introduce noise. For this reason we added a new layer, based on a Named Entity Recognition (NER) classifier, which is able to identify named entities of type "company". The result of the NER classifier is used as an additional feature for the subsequent disambiguation step[10], in order to better identify company entities.

We carried out several tests with data sets created by means of crowd-sourced annotations, and we yield a F_1 of 60%. However, for each annotation we also compute a confidence score; setting a threshold for this score can be used to balance prevision vs. recall. Since for this kind of product we are mainly interested in precision, we decided to set the threshold to maximize the $F_{0.5}$, yielding a precision of $\sim 80\%$ and a recall of $\sim 45\%$.

2.2 Selino

Selino is a component of the SEDANO pipeline dedicated to the automatic classification of news according to a predefined set of categories. The categories we are interested in are business events with negative connotation (i.e.: layoffs, strikes, shutdowns, material damages, financial losses, frauds and legal issues) plus other generic events (mergers and acquisitions, new product launches and management changes).

We first built a training set for each category. Given the small size of the taxonomy we created an independent data set for each category; we chose CrowdFlower[11] as crowdsourcing platform for the manual annotation of news. Instead of randomly sampling news for each annotation job, we selected sets of articles ($\sim 12K$ samples per category) through a boolean retrieval model. Each category query was made by expanding a seed query of event related terms. The expansion was performed by (a) creating a vector space model of Italian word semantics using Word2Vec [2], (b) identifying the most similar words to the seeds, (c) manually selecting words for defining the query. This approach allowed us to minimize the manual annotation work and to obtain balanced training sets (each one is made of $\sim 30\%$ positive samples).

Our approach to event detection is through supervised learning: we chose a logistic regression algorithm as text classifier. This linear model has proven to be effective for text classification [3] and it is also reasonably fast. We evaluated the classifiers through 3-fold cross validation, obtaining good results (i.e. an average precision of 0.8 and an average recall of 0.6), especially on precision. The latter is our critical evaluation measure, since a false positive on a negative event can produce unpleasant image damages to the companies cited in an article.

3. CONCLUSIONS

SEDANO is an effective system for processing news and extracting rich information about companies and interesting signals for the business domain. We have shown its design and components, among which the main ones are the entity linking system for identifying company mentions and the events detection classifier. SEDANO has proven to be reliable and scalable, analyzing and indexing hundreds of thousands of Italian news items every day.

We plan to improve further this application by:

- Integrating new components, such as a clustering algorithm to group together related news.
- Moving from the current static event-detection models to an on-line active learning approach, in which we sample news with "ambiguous" classifications and we annotate them through CrowdFlower.
- Extracting specific facts about events from textual contents, employing more sophisticated event detection techniques.

4. REFERENCES

[1] P. Ferragina and U. Scaiella. Tagme: on-the-fly annotation of short text fragments (by wikipedia entities). In *CIKM*, pp 1625–1628, 2010.

[2] T. Mikolov, I. Sutskever, K. Chen, G. Corrado, and J. Dean. Distributed Representations of Words and Phrases and their Compositionality. In *NIPS*, pp 3111–3119, 2013.

[3] T. Zhang and F.J. Oles. Text Categorization Based on Regularized Linear Classification Methods. *Information Retrieval*, 4(1):5-31, 2001.

[6] http://lucene.apache.org/solr

[7] https://en.wikipedia.org/wiki/Nilsimsa_Hash

[8] https://dandelion.eu

[9] https://www.cerved.com

[10] Refer to [1] for further details and terminology

[11] http://www.crowdflower.com

Ranking Financial Tweets

Diego Ceccarelli
Bloomberg LP
dceccarelli4@bloomberg.net

Francesco Nidito
Bloomberg LP
fnidito@bloomberg.net

Miles Osborne
Bloomberg LP
mosborne29@bloomberg.net

ABSTRACT

Recently Twitter has complemented traditional newswire as a source of valuable Financial information. Although there is a rich body of published research dealing with the task of ranking tweets, there has been little published research dealing with ranking tweets within a Financial context. Here we consider whether popularity factors within Twitter can be used as a signal for popularity within the domain of financial experts. Our results suggest that what interests Finance is not the same as what interests the users of Twitter.

1. INTRODUCTION

Financial market participants constantly need new information when decision making, with news being an important signal. Financially-relevant news is traditionally divided into a number of broad topics such as securities (equities, foreign exchange, fixed income, commodities, derivatives), mergers and acquisitions, regulation and compliance. News can concern broad macro-level events (for example, a central bank raising interest rates or the UK leaving the EU) as well as staples of traditional news, such as natural disasters.

Relatively recently Twitter has gained importance within Finance. In part this is due to the US Securities and Exchange Commission allowing companies to use Social Media to communicate company announcements,[1] along with a growing awareness that it is becoming a source of breaking news [4]. Rumour and speculation on Twitter can be informative as this can reflect investor mood and outlook. Given the massive volume of tweets published each day (upwards of 500 Million posts), how can we effectively rank Financially relevant tweets so that Markets can react to them?

2. RANKING TWEETS

The Bloomberg Terminal allows a user to browse/search tweets that are relevant for Financial professionals. Users can perform simple topic search (e.g., "find me tweets about Oil") and get a mix of tweets and news articles, as well as more traditional search. In both scenarios *ranked lists* of results are produced. Bloomberg has signed a long-term data agreement with Twitter and ingests more than one million newswire articles per day.[2] [3]

Tweets typically are ingested as a stream and ranking needs to take into account factors such as novelty and relevance. Here we focus on relevance and how it relates to *popularity* within Twitter. Ranking microblog posts is a well studied problem [2, 5], with a dedicated TREC track that started in 2011 [3]. Usually in social media popularity is seen as being correlated with relevance and many learning to rank retrieval models are trained using, *inter alia*, social signals such as the number of followers or the number of retweets [1]. Does author popularity (when measured using the number of followers) or community popularity (when measured using the number of times a given post was reported or *retweeted*) have any bearing on ranking within a Financial setting?

3. SOCIAL AND FINANCIAL IMPORTANCE

We carried-out a small scale experiment in order to explore our question: for each tweet that we made available to Bloomberg users for 25 days in 2016 we recorded the number of recorded *user views* (a user view is a client reading a post in Bloomberg) together with post statistics such the number of author followers and the number of times a post was retweeted.[4] We collected the top 100 tweets ranked by the number of views. Our assumption here is that the number of user views made by Financial professionals is a good proxy of relevance within Finance as a whole.

For each of these tweets we considered the extent to which retweeting rates and author followers are correlated with the number of views. We computed the correlation coefficient ρ for these variables. We found a good correlation between retweets and followers ($\rho = .76$, statistically significant) but a very low correlation between views and retweets, and views and followers (resp. $\rho = .12$, $\rho = .14$). This suggests that the number of retweets and followers are not direct proxies for relevance in the financial setting.

Given that news covers a broad range of topics, we considered whether perhaps certain types of news better corre-

[1] http://www.bloomberg.com/news/articles/2013-04-02/sec-approves-social-media-use-for-companies-material-disclosure

[2] https://blog.twitter.com/2015/bloomberg-twitter-data

[3] https://youtu.be/oMOV7DB4gnA?t=271

[4] We recorded the number of retweets for each post after the census period.

SIGIR '16, July 17-21, 2016, Pisa, Italy
ACM 978-1-4503-4069-4/16/07.
http://dx.doi.org/10.1145/2911451.2926727

lated with external popularity. For example, news about a major company might be popular both within Twitter and also within the Financial community. We manually categorized the top tweets into five categories: *news about a company* (40 tweets), *governance* (12 tweets), *news about pharma industry* (14 tweets), *merging and acquisitions* (24 tweets) *miscellanea* (10 tweets). We computed the ρ for the news categories obtaining ρ values similar to the previous: for example on companies we measured $\rho = .79$ between views and retweets, while $\rho = .19$ for views and retweets and $\rho = .18$ for views and followers. This suggests that external popularity does not carry over to individual Financial categories.

4. EXAMPLES OF POPULAR TWEETS

We selected the mostly highly viewed tweets and analysed why they were popular. Topics included (numbers after each post indicate the number of times the corresponding tweet was retweeted):

1. An unauthorised comment on advertising spending declining (15).
2. Notification of a company defaulting (91).
3. News of an ongoing bribery scandal affecting a hedge fund (4).
4. News about a biotech company having a potential buyer (37).
5. Speculation on the valuation of a company (1).

Three of these stories appeared in first place on Twitter and were posted on the Terminal minutes before news about the same facts produced by more traditional news sources. We also note that rumours are favoured. As expected, within Finance, core financial stories are highly viewed. Twitter complements traditional news in that we see speculation (Example 5) as well as off-the-cuff reporting (Example 1). We see that important Financial tweets are not necessarily highly retweeted (Examples 5 and 3). None of these stories used hashtags (though two used cashtags[5]). None mentioned other Twitter users and only two posts had an image in them. Not within these examples, we also observed that the authors of highly viewed tweets need not always have many Twitter followers. One story was written by an account with less than one hundred followers.

5. WHAT ABOUT UNPOPULAR TWEETS?

We also randomly sampled 50 tweets that received only one view during the same period and analysed them in the same way. We noticed that some tweets that were not relevant for the Financial professionals exhibit a large number of retweets (> 100). In particular we found:

1. A story about a probable terrorist attack in Paris (410).
2. A rumour about a large acquisition of a company (190).
3. A story about governance, not in English (192).
4. A story about a major phishing attack, posted by a major news company with more than 10 million followers (42).

[5] A *cashtag* is a hashtag-like symbol for a traded company.

We were surprised by the fact that Example 2 was not considered relevant in our financial context. On closer inspection, there were other newswire stories about that company that we made available two minutes before –probably at that point the Twitter story was no longer temporally relevant for the users. This again suggests that novelty is a major characteristic of relevant news: in this case the story was on-topic for Finance, but the fact that a similar, non-Twitter story was published and surfaced two minutes prior made the otherwise topical Twitter story no longer interesting.

6. COMMENTS

Ranking tweets for the Financial Community is different to standard ranking for micro-blogs. Initial evidence suggests that novelty is important and that what counts as being popular within Finance is not necessarily the same as popularity within Twitter. Crucially, 'novelty' is with respect to the totality of *all* news and not just news as found in Twitter. Successfully ranking tweets for Finance must also take account of temporally relevant newswire stories. It does not suffice to rank tweets in isolation. For Finance, speculation, capture of fleeting information and core financial topics are all important and complement more traditional news content.

7. REFERENCES

[1] Y. Duan, L. Jiang, T. Qin, M. Zhou, and H.-Y. Shum. An empirical study on learning to rank of tweets. In *Proceedings of the 23rd International Conference on Computational Linguistics*, pages 295–303. Association for Computational Linguistics, 2010.

[2] R. Nagmoti, A. Teredesai, and M. De Cock. Ranking approaches for microblog search. In *Web Intelligence and Intelligent Agent Technology (WI-IAT), 2010 IEEE/WIC/ACM International Conference on*, volume 1, pages 153–157. IEEE, 2010.

[3] I. Ounis, C. Macdonald, J. Lin, and I. Soboroff. Overview of the trec-2011 microblog track. In *Proceeddings of the 20th Text REtrieval Conference (TREC 2011)*, volume 32, 2011.

[4] S. Petrovic, M. Osborne, R. McCreadie, C. Macdonald, I. Ounis, and L. Shrimpton. Can twitter replace newswire for breaking news? In *Seventh International AAAI Conference on Weblogs and Social Media*, 2013.

[5] I. Soboroff, D. McCullough, J. Lin, C. Macdonald, I. Ounis, and R. McCreadie. Evaluating real-time search over tweets. *Proc. ICWSM*, pages 943–961, 2012.

Contextual Bandits in A Collaborative Environment

Qingyun Wu[1], Huazheng Wang[1], Quanquan Gu[2], Hongning Wang[1]
[1]Department of Computer Science
[2]Department of Systems and Information Engineering
University of Virginia, Charlottesville VA, 22904 USA
{qw2ky,hw7ww,qg5w,hw5x}@virginia.edu

ABSTRACT

Contextual bandit algorithms provide principled online learning solutions to find optimal trade-offs between exploration and exploitation with companion side-information. They have been extensively used in many important practical scenarios, such as display advertising and content recommendation. A common practice estimates the unknown bandit parameters pertaining to each user independently. This unfortunately ignores dependency among users and thus leads to suboptimal solutions, especially for the applications that have strong social components.

In this paper, we develop a collaborative contextual bandit algorithm, in which the adjacency graph among users is leveraged to share context and payoffs among neighboring users while online updating. We rigorously prove an improved upper regret bound of the proposed collaborative bandit algorithm comparing to conventional independent bandit algorithms. Extensive experiments on both synthetic and three large-scale real-world datasets verified the improvement of our proposed algorithm against several state-of-the-art contextual bandit algorithms.

CCS Concepts

•Information systems → Recommender systems; •Theory of computation → Regret bounds; •Computing methodologies → Sequential decision making;

Keywords

Collaborative contextual bandits; online recommendations; reinforcement learning

1. INTRODUCTION

Satisfying users with personalized information plays a crucial role for online service providers to succeed in market. However, the rapid appearance of new information and new users together with the ever-changing nature of content popularity make traditional recommendation approaches, e.g., collaborative filtering [7, 25], incompetent. Modern information service systems now adopt online learning solutions to adaptively find good mappings between available content and users. During online learning, the need to focus on information that raises user interest and, simultaneously, the need to explore new information for globally improving user experience create an explore-exploit dilemma. Significant research attention has been paid on multi-armed bandit algorithms [16, 19, 4, 5], which provide a principled solution of the dilemma. Intuitively, bandit algorithms designate a small amount of traffic to collect user feedback while improving their estimation qualities in realtime.

With the available side information about users or items to be presented, contextual bandits have become a reference solution [3, 10, 21, 14]. Specifically, contextual bandits assume the expected payoff is determined by a conjecture of unknown bandit parameters and given context, which is represented as a set of features extracted from both users and recommendation candidates. Such algorithms are especially advantageous when the space of recommendation is large but the payoffs are interrelated. They have been successfully applied in many important applications, e.g., content recommendation [21, 6] and display advertising [11, 23].

However, a common practice in contextual bandit algorithms estimates the unknown bandit parameters pertaining to each user independently. This unfortunately ignores dependency among users. Due to the existence of social influence [13], e.g., content and opinions sharing among friends in a social network, exploiting the dependency among users raises new challenges and opportunities in personalized information services. For example, in many real-world applications, e.g., content recommendation in Facebook or Twitter, because of the mutual influence among friends and acquaintances, one user's click decision on the recommended items might be greatly influenced by his/her peers. This indicates the knowledge gathered about the interest of a given user can be leveraged to improve the recommendation to his/her friends, i.e., collaborative learning. In other words, the observed payoffs from a user's feedback might be a compound of his/her own preference and social influence he/she receives, e.g., social norms, conformity and compliance. As a result, propagating the knowledge collected about the preference of one user to his/her related peers can not only capitalize on additional information embedded in the dependency among users, which is not available in the context vectors; but also helps conquer data sparsity issue by reducing the sample complexity of preference learning (e.g., known as cold-start in recommender systems [26]). Failing to recognize such information among users will inevitably lead to a suboptimal solution.

In this work, we develop a collaborative contextual bandit algorithm that explicitly models the underlying dependency among users. In our solution, a weighted adjacency graph is constructed, where each node represents a contextual bandit deployed for a single user and the weight on each edge indicates the influence between a pair of users. Based on this dependency structure, the observed payoffs on each user are assumed to be determined by a mixture of neighboring users in the graph. We then estimate the bandit parameters over all the users in a collaborative manner: both

SIGIR '16, July 17-21, 2016, Pisa, Italy

DOI: http://dx.doi.org/10.1145/2911451.2911528

context and received payoffs from one user are prorogated across the whole graph in the process of online updating. The proposed collaborative bandit algorithm establishes a bridge to share information among heterogenous users and thus reduce the sample complexity of preference learning. We rigorously prove that our collaborative bandit algorithm achieves a remarkable reduction of upper regret bound with high probability, comparing to the linear regret with respect to the number of users if one simply runs independent bandits on them. Extensive experiment results on both simulations and large-scale real-world datasets verified the improvement of the proposed algorithm compared with several state-of-the-art contextual bandit algorithms. In particular, our algorithm greatly alleviates the cold-start challenge, in which encouraging performance improvement is achieved on new users and new items.

2. RELATED WORK

Multi-armed bandit algorithms provide principled solutions to the explore/exploit dilemma, which exists in many real-world applications, such as display advertisement selection [11, 23], recommender systems [21, 6], and search engine systems [24, 28]. As opposed to the traditional K-armed bandit problems [5, 4, 16, 19], feature vectors in contextual bandits are created to infer the conditional expected payoff of an action [3, 12, 20, 21]. The setting for contextual bandit with linear payoffs was first introduced in [3], where the expectation of payoff for each action is assumed to be a linear function of its context vector. In the follow-up research [21, 12], LinUCB is introduced to use ridge regression to compute the expected payoff of each action and corresponding confidence interval. Later on, generalized linear models are introduced to parameterize bandit algorithms for non-linear payoffs [14]. Comparing to their context-free counterparts, contextual bandits have achieved superior performance in various application scenarios [21, 14].

The idea of modeling dependency among bandits has been explored in prior research [8, 9, 10, 15, 17]. Studies in [2, 27] explore contextual bandits with assumptions about probabilistic dependencies on the product space of context and actions. Hybrid-LinUCB [21] is such an instance, which uses a hybrid linear model to share observations across users. Social network structures are explored in bandit algorithms for introducing possible dependencies [9, 15]. In [8], parallel context-free K-armed bandits are coupled by the social network structure among the users, where the observed payoffs from neighboring nodes are shared as side-observations to help estimate individual bandits. Besides utilizing existing social networks for modeling relatedness among bandits, there is also work automatically estimates the bandit parameters together with the dependency relation among them, such as clustering the bandits via the learned model parameters during online updating [15]. Some recent work incorporates collaboration among bandits via matrix factorization based collaborative filtering techniques: Kawale et al. preformed online matrix factorization based recommendation via Thompson sampling [18], and Zhao et al. studied interactive collaborative filtering via probabilistic matrix factorization [29].

The most similar work to ours studied in this paper is the GOB.Lin algorithm introduced in [10]. GOB.Lin requires connected users in a network to have similar bandit parameters via a graph Laplacian based model regularization. As a result, GOB.Lin explicitly requires the learned bandit parameters across related users to be close to each other. In our algorithm, we do not have such strong assumption about each individual bandit, but we make explicit assumptions about the reward generation via an additive model: neighboring users' judgements of the recommendations will be shared across, i.e., word-of-mouth, to explain the observed payoffs in different users. This gives us the flexibility in capturing the heterogeneity of preferences among different users in practice, and leads to both theoretically and empirically improved results.

3. METHODOLOGY

We develop a contextual bandit algorithm in a collaborative environment, where the adjacency graph among users is leveraged to share context and payoffs between neighboring bandits during online update. We provide rigorous proof of the resulting upper regret bound, which has a significant regret reduction comparing to running independent bandit algorithms on the same collection of users. In the following discussions, we will first describe the notations and our model assumptions about the collaborative bandit problem, then carefully illustrate our developed bandit algorithm and corresponding regret analysis.

3.1 Bandits in a Collaborative Setting

We consider a contextual bandit problem with a finite, but possibly large, number of arms, which correspond to the candidate item set to be presented (e.g., articles in a content recommendation system). We denote the arm set as $\mathcal{A}$ and the cardinality of $\mathcal{A}$ as K. There are N different users in this collection. At each trial t, a learner observes a given user u_t from user collection and a subset of arms from $\mathcal{A}$, where each arm a is associated with a feature vector $\mathbf{x}_{a_t,u_t} \in \mathbb{R}^d$ summarizing the information of both user u_t and arm a_t at trial t. The learner displays an arm a_t to u_t and receives the corresponding payoff r_{a_t,u_t} from the user. The goal of the learner is to update its arm-selection strategy with respect to the new observations, such that after T trials its *regret* with respect to the oracle arm selection strategy is minimized. In particular, the accumulated T-trial regret for all users is defined formally as,

$$\mathbf{R}(T) = \sum_{t=1}^{T} R_t = \sum_{t=1}^{T}(r_{a_t^*,u_t} - r_{a_t,u_t}) \quad (1)$$

where a_t^* is the best arm to display to user u_t at trial t according to the oracle strategy, $r_{a_t^*,u_t}$ is the corresponding optimal payoff, and R_t is the regret from all users at trial t.

In standard linear contextual bandit problems, the payoffs of each arm with respect to different users are assumed to be governed by a noisy version of an unknown linear function of the context vectors [3, 21]. Specifically, each user i is assumed to associate with an unknown parameter $\boldsymbol{\theta}_i \in \mathbb{R}^d$ (with $\|\boldsymbol{\theta}_i\| \leq 1$), which determines the payoff of a_t by $r_{a_t,i} = \mathbf{x}_{a_t,i}^{\mathsf{T}}\boldsymbol{\theta}_i + \epsilon_t$, where ϵ_t is drawn from a Guassian distribution $N(0, \sigma^2)$. $\boldsymbol{\theta}$s are independently estimated based on the observations from each individual user. However, due to the existence of mutual influence among users, an isolated bandit can hardly explain all the observed payoffs even for a single user. For example, the context vectors fail to encode such dependency. To capitalize on the additional information embedded in the dependency structure among users (i.e., $\boldsymbol{\theta}$ for different users), we propose to study contextual bandit problems in a collaborative setting.

In this collaborative environment, we place the bandit algorithms on a weighted graph $G = (V, E)$, which encodes the affinity relationship among users. Specifically, each node $v_i \in \{V_1, ..., V_N\}$ in G hosts a bandit parameterized by $\boldsymbol{\theta}_i$ for user i; and the edges in E represent the affinity relation over pairs of users. This graph can be described as an $N \times N$ stochastic matrix $\mathbf{W}$. In this matrix, each element w_{ij} is nonnegative and proportional to the influence that user j has on user i in determining the payoffs of different arms. $w_{ij} = 0$ if and only if user j has no influence on user i. $\mathbf{W}$ is column-wise normalized such that $\sum_{j=1}^{N} w_{ij} = 1$ for $i \in \{1, ..., N\}$. In this work, we assume $\mathbf{W}$ is time-invariant and known to the learner beforehand.

Based on the graph G, collaboration among bandits happens when determining the payoff of a particular arm with respect to a given user. To denote this, we define a $d \times N$ matrix $\boldsymbol{\Theta}$, which consists of parameters from all the bandits in the graph: $\boldsymbol{\Theta} = (\boldsymbol{\theta}_1, \ldots, \boldsymbol{\theta}_N)$. Accordingly, we define a context feature matrix

Algorithm 1 Collaborative LinUCB

Inputs: $\alpha \in \mathbb{R}_+, \lambda \in [0,1]$, $\mathbf{W} \in \mathbb{R}^{N \times N}$
Initialize: $\mathbf{A}_1 \leftarrow \lambda\mathbf{I}, \mathbf{b}_1 \leftarrow \mathbf{0}, \hat{\boldsymbol{\vartheta}}_1 \leftarrow \mathbf{A}_1^{-1}\mathbf{b}_1, \mathbf{C}_1 \leftarrow (\mathbf{W}^\mathsf{T} \otimes \mathbf{I})\mathbf{A}_1^{-1}(\mathbf{W} \otimes \mathbf{I})$,
for $t = 1$ to T **do**
  Receive user u_t
  Observe context vectors, $\mathbf{x}_{a_t,u_t} \in \mathbb{R}^d$ for $\forall a \in \mathcal{A}$
  Take action $a_t = \arg\max_{a \in \mathcal{A}} \mathring{\mathcal{X}}_{a_t,u_t}^\mathsf{T} vec(\widehat{\boldsymbol{\Theta}}_t \mathbf{W}) + \alpha\sqrt{\mathring{\mathcal{X}}_{a_t,u_t}^\mathsf{T} \mathbf{C}_t \mathring{\mathcal{X}}_{a_t,u_t}}$
  Observe payoff r_{a_t,u_t}
  $\mathbf{A}_{t+1} \leftarrow \mathbf{A}_t + vec(\mathring{\mathbf{X}}_{a_t,u_t}\mathbf{W}^\mathsf{T})vec(\mathring{\mathbf{X}}_{a_t,u_t}\mathbf{W}^\mathsf{T})^\mathsf{T}$
  $\mathbf{b}_{t+1} \leftarrow \mathbf{b}_t + vec(\mathring{\mathbf{X}}_{a_t,u_t}\mathbf{W}^\mathsf{T})r_{a_t,u_t}$
  $\mathbf{C}_{t+1} \leftarrow (\mathbf{W}^\mathsf{T} \otimes \mathbf{I})\mathbf{A}_{t+1}^{-1}(\mathbf{W} \otimes \mathbf{I})$
  $\hat{\boldsymbol{\vartheta}}_{t+1} \leftarrow \mathbf{A}_{t+1}^{-1}\mathbf{b}_{t+1}$
end for

$\mathbf{X}_t = (\mathbf{x}_{a_{t,1}}, \ldots, \mathbf{x}_{a_{t,N}})$, where the ith column is the context vector $\mathbf{x}_{a_{t,i}}$ for arm a at trial t selected for user i. The collaboration among bandits characterized by the influence matrix $\mathbf{W}$ results in a new bandit parameter matrix $\bar{\boldsymbol{\Theta}} = \boldsymbol{\Theta}\mathbf{W}$, which determines the payoff r_{a_t,u_t} of arm a_t for user u_t at trial t by,

$$r_{a_t,u_t} - diag_{u_t}(\mathbf{X}_t^\mathsf{T}\boldsymbol{\Theta}\mathbf{W}) \sim N(0, \sigma^2) \tag{2}$$

where $diag_{u_t}(\mathbf{X})$ is the operation returning the u_t-th element in the diagonal of matrix $\mathbf{X}$. Eq (2) postulates our *additive* assumption about reward generation in this collaborative environment: the reward r_{a_t,u_t} is not only determined by user u_t's own preference on the arm a_t (i.e., $w_{u_t u_t}\mathbf{x}_{a_t,u_t}^\mathsf{T}\boldsymbol{\theta}_{u_t}$), but also by the judgements from the neighbors who have influence on u_t (i.e., $\sum_{j \neq u_t} w_{u_t j}\mathbf{x}_{a_t,j}^\mathsf{T}\boldsymbol{\theta}_j$). This enables us to distinguish a user's intrinsic preference of the recommended content from his/her neighbors' influence, i.e., personalization. In addition, the linear payoff assumption in our model is to simplify the discussion in this paper; and it can be relaxed via a generalized linear model [14] to deal with nonlinear rewards.

We should note that our model assumption about the collaborative bandits is different from that specified in the GOB.Lin model [10]. In GOB.Lin, connected users in the graph are required to have similar underlying bandit parameters, i.e., via graph Laplacian regularization over the learned bandit parameters. And their assumption about reward generation follows conventional contextual bandit settings, i.e., rewards are independent across users. In our setting, neighboring users do not have to share similar bandit parameters, but they will generate influence on their neighbors' decisions. This assumption is arguably more general, and it leads to an improved upper regret bound and practical performance. Theoretical comparison between these two algorithms will be rigorously discussed in Section 3.3.

3.2 Collaborative Linear Bandit Algorithm

To simplify the notations in our following discussions, we define two long context feature vectors and a long bandit parameter vector based on the vectorize operation $vec(\cdot)$. We define $\mathcal{X}_{a_t} = vec(\mathbf{X}_{a_t}) = (\mathbf{x}_{a_t,1}^\mathsf{T}, \ldots, \mathbf{x}_{a_t,N}^\mathsf{T})^\mathsf{T}$, which is a concatenation of context feature vectors of the chosen arm a_t at trial t for all the users. And we define $\mathring{\mathcal{X}}_{a_t,u_t} = vec(\mathring{\mathbf{X}}_{a_t,u_t})$, in which $\mathring{\mathbf{X}}_{a_t,u_t}$ is a special case of $\mathbf{X}_{a_t}$: only the column corresponding to the user u_t at time t is set to $\mathbf{x}_{a_t,u_t}^\mathsf{T}$, and all the other columns are set to zero. This corresponds to the situation that at trial t the learner only needs to interact with one user. Correspondingly, we define $\boldsymbol{\vartheta} = vec(\boldsymbol{\Theta}) = (\boldsymbol{\theta}_1^\mathsf{T}, \boldsymbol{\theta}_2^\mathsf{T}, ..., \boldsymbol{\theta}_N^\mathsf{T})^\mathsf{T} \in \mathbb{R}^{dN}$ as the concatenation of bandit parameter vectors over all the users.

With the collaborative assumption about the expected payoffs defined in Eq (2), we appeal to ridge regression for estimating the unknown bandit parameter $\boldsymbol{\theta}$ for each user. In particular, we simultaneously estimate the global bandit parameter matrix $\boldsymbol{\Theta}$ for all the users as follows,

$$\widehat{\boldsymbol{\Theta}} = \arg\max_{\boldsymbol{\Theta}} \frac{1}{2}\sum_{t=1}^{T}(\mathring{\mathcal{X}}_{a_t,u_t}^\mathsf{T} vec(\boldsymbol{\Theta}_t\mathbf{W}) - r_{a_t,u_t})^2 + \frac{\lambda}{2}tr(\boldsymbol{\Theta}^\mathsf{T}\boldsymbol{\Theta}) \tag{3}$$

where $\lambda \in [0,1]$ is a trade-off parameter of $l2$ regularization in ridge regression.

Since the objective function defined in Eq (3) is quadratic with respect to $\boldsymbol{\Theta}$, we have a closed-form estimation of $\boldsymbol{\Theta}$ as $\hat{\boldsymbol{\vartheta}}_t = \mathbf{A}_t^{-1}\mathbf{b}_t$, in which $\hat{\boldsymbol{\vartheta}} = vec(\widehat{\boldsymbol{\Theta}})$ and $\mathbf{A}_t$ and $\mathbf{b}_t$ are computed as,

$$\mathbf{A}_t = \lambda\mathbf{I} + \sum_{t'=1}^{t} vec(\mathring{\mathbf{X}}_{a_{t'},u_{t'}}\mathbf{W}^\mathsf{T})vec(\mathring{\mathbf{X}}_{a_{t'},u_{t'}}\mathbf{W}^\mathsf{T})^\mathsf{T} \tag{4}$$

$$\mathbf{b}_t = \sum_{t'=1}^{t} vec(\mathring{\mathbf{X}}_{a_{t'},u_{t'}}\mathbf{W}^\mathsf{T})r_{a_{t'},u_{t'}} \tag{5}$$

where $\mathbf{I}$ is a $dN \times dN$ identity matrix.

The effect of collaboration among bandits is clearly depicted in the above estimation of $\boldsymbol{\Theta}$. Matrix $\mathbf{A}_t$ and vector $\mathbf{b}_t$ store global information shared among all the bandits in the graph. More specifically, the context vector $\mathbf{x}_{a_t,u_t}$ and payoff r_{a_t,u_t} observed in user u_t at trial t can be propagated through the whole graph via the relational matrix $\mathbf{W}$ to other users. To understand this, note that $vec(\mathring{\mathbf{X}}_{a_t,u_t}\mathbf{W}^\mathsf{T})$ is a dense vector with projected context vectors on every user, while the original $\mathring{\mathcal{X}}_{a_t,u_t}$ is a sparse vector with observations only at active users u_t. Because of this information sharing, at certain trial t, although some users might have not generate any observation yet (i.e., cold-start), they can already start from a non-random initialization of their bandit parameters $\boldsymbol{\theta}_i$. It is easy to verify that when $\mathbf{W}$ is an identity matrix, i.e., users have no influence among each other, the estimation of $\boldsymbol{\Theta}$ degenerates to independently computing N different $\boldsymbol{\theta}$s (since $vec(\mathring{\mathbf{X}}_{a_t,u_t}\mathbf{W}^\mathsf{T}) = \mathring{\mathcal{X}}_{a_t,u_t}$). And the mutual influence will be maximized when $\mathbf{W}$ is a uniform matrix, i.e., all the users have equivalent influence to each other. We have to emphasize that the benefit of this collaborative estimation of $\boldsymbol{\Theta}$ is not to just simply compute the $\boldsymbol{\theta}$s in an integrated manner; but because of the collaboration among users, the estimation uncertainty of all $\boldsymbol{\theta}$s can be quickly reduced comparing to simply running N independent bandit algorithms. This in turn leads to an improved regret bound. We will elaborate the effect of collaboration in online bandit learning with more theoretical justifications in Section 3.3.

The estimated bandit parameters $\widehat{\boldsymbol{\Theta}}$ predict the expected payoff of a particular arm for each user according to the observed context feature matrix $\mathbf{X}_t$. To complete an adaptive bandit algorithm, we need to design the exploration strategy for each user. Our collaborative assumption in Eq (2) implies that r_{a_t,u_t} across users are independent given $\mathbf{X}_t$ and $\mathbf{W}$. As a result, for any σ, i.e., the standard deviation of Gaussian noise in Eq (2), the following inequality holds with probability at least $1 - \delta$,

$$|r_{a_t^*,u_t} - r_{a_t,u_t}| \leq \alpha_t\sqrt{vec(\mathring{\mathbf{X}}_{u_t}\mathbf{W}^\mathsf{T})^\mathsf{T}\mathbf{A}_t^{-1}vec(\mathring{\mathbf{X}}_{u_t}\mathbf{W}^\mathsf{T})} \tag{6}$$

where α_t is a parameter in our algorithm defined in Lemma 1 of Section 3.3 and δ is embedded in the computation of α_t. The proof of this inequality can be found in the Appendix.

The inequality specified in Eq (6) gives us a reasonably tight upper confidence bound (UCB) for the expected payoff of a particular arm over all the users in the graph G, from which a UCB-style arm-selection strategy can be derived. In particular, at trial t, we choose an arm for user u_t according to the following arm-selection strategy,

$$a_{t,u_t} = \arg\max_{a \in \mathcal{A}} \Big(\mathring{\mathcal{X}}_{a_{t,u_t}}^\mathsf{T} vec(\widehat{\Theta}_t \mathbf{W}) \qquad (7)$$
$$+ \alpha_t \sqrt{vec(\mathring{\mathbf{X}}_{u_t} \mathbf{W}^\mathsf{T})^\mathsf{T} \mathbf{A}_t^{-1} vec(\mathring{\mathbf{X}}_{u_t} \mathbf{W}^\mathsf{T})} \Big)$$

We name this resulting algorithm as Collaborative Linear Bandit, or CoLin in short. The detailed description of CoLin is illustrated in Algorithm 1, where we use the property that $vec(\mathring{\mathbf{X}}_{u_t} \mathbf{W}^\mathsf{T}) = (\mathbf{W} \otimes \mathbf{I}) vec(\mathring{\mathbf{X}}_{u_t}) = (\mathbf{W} \otimes \mathbf{I}) \mathring{\mathcal{X}}_t$ to simplify Eq (7).

Another evidence of the benefit from collaboration among users is demonstrated in Algorithm 1. When estimating the confidence interval of the expected payoff for action a_t in user u_t at trial t, CoLin not only considers the prediction confidence from bandit u_t, but also that from its neighboring bandits (as described by the Kronecker product between $\mathbf{W}$ and $\mathbf{I}$). When $\mathbf{W}$ is an identity matrix, such effect disappears. Clearly, this collaborative confidence interval estimation will help the algorithm quickly reduce estimation uncertainty, and thus leads to the optimal solution more rapidly.

One potential issue with CoLin is its computational complexity: matrix inverse has to be performed on $\mathbf{A}_t$ at every trial. First, because of the rank one update of matrix $\mathbf{A}_t$ (8th step in Algorithm 1), quadratic computation complexity is possible via applying the Sherman-Morrison formula. Second, we may compute $\mathbf{A}_t^{-1}$ in a mini-batch manner to further reduce computation with some extra penalty in regret. We will leave this as our future research.

3.3 Regret Analysis

In this section, we provide detailed regret analysis of our proposed CoLin algorithm. We first prove that the estimation error of bandit parameters $\widehat{\Theta}$ is upper bounded in Lemma 1.

Lemma 1: *For any $\delta > 0$, with probability at least $1 - \delta$, the estimation error of bandit parameters in CoLin is bounded by,*

$$\|\hat{\vartheta}_t - \vartheta^*\|_{\mathbf{A}_t} \leq \sqrt{dN \ln\Big(1 + \frac{\sum_{t'=1}^{t}\sum_{j=1}^{N} w_{u_{t'}j}^2}{\lambda dN}\Big) - 2\ln(\delta)} + \sqrt{\lambda}\|\vartheta^*\|$$

in which $\|\hat{\vartheta}_t - \vartheta^*\|_{\mathbf{A}_t} = \sqrt{(\hat{\vartheta}_t - \vartheta^*)^\mathsf{T} \mathbf{A}_t (\hat{\vartheta}_t - \vartheta^*)}$, i.e., the matrix norm induced by the positive semidefinite matrix $\mathbf{A}_t$

Based on Lemma 1, we have the following theorem about the upper regret bound of the CoLin algorithm.

Theorem 1: With probability at least $1 - \delta$, the cumulated regret of CoLin algorithm satisfies,

$$\mathbf{R}(T) \leq 2\alpha_T \sqrt{2dNT \ln\Big(1 + \frac{\sum_{t=1}^{T}\sum_{j=1}^{N} w_{u_t j}^2}{\lambda dN}\Big)} \qquad (8)$$

in which α_T is the upper bound of $\|\hat{\vartheta}_T - \vartheta^*\|_{\mathbf{A}_T}$ and it can be explicitly calculated based on Lemma 1. The detailed proof of this theorem is provided in the Appendix.

As shown in Theorem 1, the graph structure plays an important role in the upper regret bound of our CoLin algorithm. Consider two extreme cases. First, when $\mathbf{W}$ is an identity matrix, i.e., no influence among users, the upper regret bound degenerates to $O(N\sqrt{T}\ln\frac{T}{N})$. Second, when the graph is fully connected and uniform, i.e., $\forall i, j, w_{ij} = \frac{1}{N}$, such that users have homogeneous influence among each other, and the upper regret bound of CoLin decreases to $O(N\sqrt{T}\ln\frac{T}{N^2})$. That means via collaboration, CoLin achieves an $O(\sqrt{T}\ln N)$ regret reduction for every single user in the graph comparing to the independent case.

Note that the our regret analysis in Theorem 1 is in a very general form, in which we did not make any assumption about the order or frequency that each user will be served. To illustrate the relationship between the proposed collaborative bandit algorithm and conventional independent bandit algorithms in a more intuitive way, we can make a very specific assumption about how a sequential learner interacts with a set of users. Assuming all the users are evenly served by CoLin, i.e., each user interacts with the learner $\bar{T} = \frac{T}{N}$ times. When $\mathbf{W}$ is an identity matrix, the regret bound of CoLin degenerates to the case of running N independent LinUCB, whose upper regret bound is $O(N\sqrt{\bar{T}}\ln\bar{T})$. When $\mathbf{W}$ is uniform, the regret bound reduces to $O(N\sqrt{\bar{T}}\ln\frac{\bar{T}}{N})$, where we achieves an $O(\sqrt{\bar{T}}\ln N)$ regret reduction comparing to running N independent LinUCBs on each single user. The proof of regret bound in this special case is given in the Appendix.

It is necessary to compare the derived upper regret bound of CoLin with that in the GOB.Lin algorithm [10], which also exploits the relatedness among a set of users. In GOB.Lin, the divergence among every pair of bandits (if connected in the graph) is measured by Euclidean distance between the learned bandit parameters. In its upper regret bound, such divergence is accumulated throughout the iterations. In extreme case where users are all connected but associate with totally distinct bandit parameters, GOB.Lin's upper regret bound could be much worse than running N independent bandits, due to this additive pairwise divergence. While in our algorithm, such divergence is controlled by the multiplicative factor $\sum_{t=1}^{T}\sum_j w_{u_t j}^2 \leq T$. We can rigorously prove the following inequalities between the upper regret bound of CoLin ($R_C(T)$) and GOB.Lin ($R_G(T)$) always holds,

$$0 \leq R_G^2(T) - R_C^2(T) \leq 16TN\ln\Big(1 + \frac{2T}{dN^2}\Big) \sum_{(i,j)\in E} \|\boldsymbol{\theta}_i^* - \boldsymbol{\theta}_j^*\|^2$$

It is clear to notice that if there is no influence between the users in the collection, i.e., no edge in G, these two algorithms' regret bound touches (both degenerate to N independent contextual bandits). Otherwise, GOB.Lin will always lead to a worse and faster growing regret bound than our CoLin algorithm.

In addition, limited by the use of graph Laplacian, GOB.Lin can only capture the binary connectivity relation among users. CoLin differentiates the strength of connections with a stochastic relational graph. This makes CoLin more general when modeling the relatedness among bandits and provides a tighter upper regret bound. This effect is also empirically verified by our extensive experiments on both synthetic and real-world data sets.

4. EXPERIMENTS

We performed empirical evaluations of our CoLin algorithm against several state-of-the-art contextual bandit algorithms, including N independent LinUCB [21], hybrid LinUCB with user features [21], GOB.Lin [10], and online cluster of Bandits (CLUB) [15]. Among these algorithms, hybrid LinUCB exploits user dependency via a set of hybrid linear models over user features, GOB.Lin encodes the user dependency via graph-based regularization over the learned bandit parameters, and CLUB clusters users during online learning to enable model sharing. In addition, we also compared with several popularly used context-free bandit algorithms, including EXP3 [5], UCB1 [4] and ϵ-greedy [4]. But their performance is much worse than the contextual bandits, and thus we do not include their performance in the following discussions.

We tested all the algorithms on a synthetic data set via simulations, a large collection of click stream from Yahoo! Today Module dataset [21], and two real-world dataset extracted from the social bookmarking web service Delicious and music streaming service LastFM [10]. Extensive experiment comparisons confirmed the advantage of our proposed CoLin algorithm against all the baselines. More importantly, comparing to the baselines that also exploit user dependencies, CoLin performs significantly better in identifying

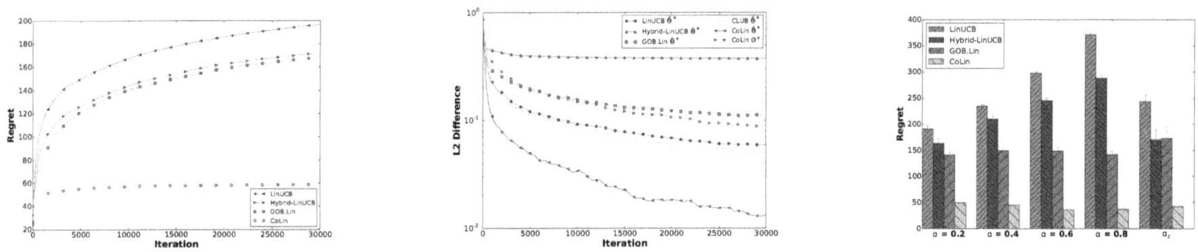

(a) Convergence of cumulated regret (b) Accuracy of bandit parameter estimation (c) The effect of α

Figure 1: Analysis of regret, bandit parameter estimation and parameter tuning.

users' preference on less popular items (items that are only observed among a small group of users). This validates that with the proposed collaborative learning among users, CoLin better alleviates the cold-start challenge comparing to the baselines.

4.1 Experiments on synthetic dataset

In this experiment, we compare the bandit algorithms based on simulations and use the accumulated regret and bandit parameter estimation accuracy as the performance metrics.

4.1.1 Simulation Setting

In simulation, we generate N users, each of which is associated with a d-dimensional parameter vector $\boldsymbol{\theta}^*$, i.e., $\boldsymbol{\Theta}^* = (\boldsymbol{\theta}_1^*, \ldots, \boldsymbol{\theta}_N^*)$. Each dimension of $\boldsymbol{\theta}_i^*$ is drawn from a uniform distribution $U(0,1)$ and normalized to $\|\boldsymbol{\theta}_i^*\| = 1$. $\boldsymbol{\Theta}^*$ is treated as the ground-truth bandit parameters for reward generation, and they are unknown to bandit algorithms. We then construct the golden relational stochastic matrix $\mathbf{W}$ for the graph of users by defining $w_{ij} \propto \langle \boldsymbol{\theta}_i^*, \boldsymbol{\theta}_j^* \rangle$, and normalize each column of $\mathbf{W}$ by its L1 norm. The resulting $\mathbf{W}$ is disclosed to the bandit algorithms. In the end, we generate a size-K action pool $\mathcal{A}$. Each action a in $\mathcal{A}$ is associated with a d-dimensional feature vector $\mathbf{x}_a$, each dimension of which is drawn from $U(0,1)$. We also normalize $\mathbf{x}_a$ by its L1 norm. To construct user features for hybrid LinUCB algorithm, we perform Principle Component Analysis (PCA) on the relational matrix $\mathbf{W}$, and use the first 5 principle components to construct the user features.

To simulate the collaborative reward generation process among users, we first compute $\bar{\Theta}^* = \boldsymbol{\Theta}^*\mathbf{W}$ and then compute the payoff of action a for user i at trial t as $r_{a_{t,i}} = diag_i(\mathbf{X}_t^\mathsf{T}\bar{\Theta}^*) + \epsilon_t$, where $\epsilon_t \sim N(0, \sigma^2)$. To increase the learning complexity, at each trial t, our simulator only discloses a subset of actions in $\mathcal{A}$ to the learning algorithms for selection, e.g., randomly select 10 actions from $\mathcal{A}$ without replacement. In simulation, based on the known bandit parameters $\bar{\Theta}^*$, the optimal action $a_{t,i}^*$ and the corresponding payoff $r_{a_{t,i}^*}$ for each bandit i at trial t can be explicitly computed.

Under this simulation setting, we compared hybrid LinUCB, N independent LinUCB, GOB.Lin, CLUB and CoLin. At each trial, the same set of actions are presented to all the algorithms; and the Gaussian noise ϵ_t is fixed for all those actions at trial t. In our experiments, we fixed the feature dimension d to 5, article pool size K to 1000, and set the trade-off parameter λ for L2 regularization to 0.2 in all the algorithms. We compared the regret of different bandit algorithms during adaptive learning. Furthermore, since the ground-truth bandit parameters are available in the simulator, we also compared the quality of learned parameters in each contextual bandit algorithm. This unveils the nature of each bandit algorithm, e.g., how accurately they can recover a user's true preference.

4.1.2 Results & Analysis

We first set the user size N to 100 and fix the standard deviation σ to 0.1 in the Gaussian noise for reward generation. All the contextual bandit algorithms are executed up to 300 iterations per user in this experiment. We report the cumulated regret as defined in Eq (1) and the Euclidean distance between the learnt bandit parameters from different algorithms and the ground-truth in Figure 1. To reduce randomness in simulation-based evaluation, we reported the mean and standard deviation of final regret from different algorithms after 30,000 iterations over 5 independent runs for results in all following experiments. To increase visibility, we did not plot error bars in Figure 1 (a) and (b).

As we can find in Figure 1 (a), simply running N independent LinUCB algorithm gives us the worst regret, which is expected. Hybrid LinUCB, which exploits user dependency via a set of hybrid linear models over user features performed better than LinUCB, but still much worse than CoLin. Although GOB.Lin also exploits the graph structure when estimating the bandit parameters, its assumption about the dependency among bandits is too restrictive to well capture the information embedded in the interaction with users. We should note that in our simulation, by multiplying the relational matrix $\mathbf{W}$ with the ground-truth bandit parameter matrix $\boldsymbol{\Theta}^*$, the resulting bandit parameters $\bar{\Theta}^*$ align with GOB.Lin's assumption, i.e., neighboring bandits are similar. And $\bar{\Theta}^*$ is used in reward generation. Therefore, our simulation does not produce any bias against GOB.Lin. In Figure 1 (a) we did not include CLUB, whose regret grew linearly. After looking into the selected arms from CLUB, we found because of the aggregated decisions from users in the automatically constructed user clusters, CLUB always chose suboptimal arms, which led to a linearly increasing regret.

In Figure 1 (b), we compared accuracy of the learnt bandit parameters from different algorithms. Because of their distinct modeling assumptions, LinUCB, hybrid LinUCB, CLUB and GOB.Lin cannot directly estimate $\boldsymbol{\Theta}^*$, i.e., the true bandit parameters for each user. Instead, they can only estimate $\bar{\Theta}^*$, which directly governs the generation of observed payoffs. Only CoLin can estimate both $\bar{\Theta}^*$ and $\boldsymbol{\Theta}^*$. As we can find in the results, CoLin gave the most accurate estimation of $\bar{\Theta}^*$, which partially explains its superior performance in regret. We also find that LinUCB actually achieved a more accurate estimation of $\bar{\Theta}^*$ than GOB.Lin, but its regret is much worse. To understand this, we looked into the actual execution of LinUCB and GOB.Lin, and found that because of the graph Laplacian regularization in GOB.Lin, it better controlled exploration in arm selection and therefore picked the optimal arm more often than LinUCB. Hyrbid LinUCB's estimation of $\bar{\Theta}^*$ is the worst, but it is expected: hybird LinUCB uses a shared model and a personalized model to fit the observations. Comparing to CoLin's estimation quality of $\bar{\Theta}^*$, its estimation of $\boldsymbol{\Theta}^*$ is much worse. The main reason is that CoLin has to decipher $\boldsymbol{\Theta}$ from the estimated $\bar{\Theta}$ based on $\mathbf{W}$, where noise is accumulated to prevent accurate estimation. Nevertheless, this result demonstrates the possibility of discovering each individual user's true preference from their compound feedback. This is meaningful for many practical applications, such as user modeling and social influence analysis.

We also notice that although CLUB's estimated $\bar{\Theta}^*$ is almost as good as LinUCB's (as shown in Figure 1 (b)), its regret is the

Table 1: Cumulated regret with different bandit size (σ=0.1).

Bandit Size (N)	40	80	100	200
LinUCB	75.31±5.11	168.42±9.90	191.53±6.18	355.56±7.23
HybridLinUCB	59.12±2.11	150.09±5.29	164.11±9.19	311.43±11.59
GOB.Lin	58.49±5.04	143.42±5.28	141.96±6.36	275.32±10.51
CoLin	21.78±12.84	47.73±4.31	49.83±6.55	77.38±20.59

Table 2: Cumulated regret with different noise level (N=100).

Noise (σ)	0.01	0.05	0.1	0.3
LinUCB	92.72±2.56	116.53±3.07	191.53 ±6.18	830.47±69.48
HybridLinUCB	69.47±2.12	91.48±1.94	164.11±9.19	759.93±39.15
GOB.Lin	58.85±6.25	82.33±1.53	141.96±6.36	708.13±43.73
CoLin	41.69±6.95	40.95±4.43	49.83±6.55	83.98±8.57

Table 3: Cumulated regret with different noise level on matrix W (N=100).

matrix noise (δ)	0	0.01	0.03	0.05
HybridLinUCB	164.11±9.19	171.74±7.67	171.51±13.31	163.93±9.19
GOB.Lin	141.96±6.36	163.28±5.63	164.36±6.66	169.87±11.89
CoLin	49.83±6.55	54.42±2.45	101.39±6.01	239.88±13.86

Table 4: Cumulated regret with different matrix sparsity level.

Sparsity (M/N)	20/100	40/100	60/100	80/100
HybridLinUCB	135.98±5.11	141.15±4.82	150.49±4.58	160.12±7.55
GOB.Lin	133.30±3.98	126.13±5.59	143.29±6.49	143.42±5.82
CoLin	39.74±8.80	30.76±3.66	37.29±3.55	49.56±8.88

worst. As we described earlier, CLUB's aggregated decision at user cluster level constantly forced the algorithm to choose sub-optimal arms; but the reward generation for each arm in our simulator follows that defined in Eq (2), which still provides validate information for CLUB to estimate $\bar{\Theta}^*$ with reasonable accuracy.

In Figure 1 (c), we investigated the effect of exploration parameter α_t's setting in different algorithms. The last column indexed by α_t represents the theoretical values of α computed from the algorithms' corresponding regret analysis. As shown from results, the empirically tuned α yields comparable performance to the theoretical values, and makes online computation more efficient. As a result, in all our following experiments we use a fixed α instead of a computed α_t.

To further investigate the convergence property of different bandit algorithms, we examined the following four scenarios: 1) various user sizes N, 2) different noise level σ, 3) a corrupted affinity matrix $\mathbf{W}$, and 4) a sparse affinity matrix $\mathbf{W}$, in reward generation. We report the results in Table 1 to 4. Because of its poor performance, we did not include CLUB in those tables.

Firstly, in Table 1, we fixed the noise level σ to 0.1 and varied the user size N from 40 to 200. We should note in this experiment the total number of iterations varies as every user will interact with the bandit learner 300 times. The regret in LinUCB goes linearly with respect to the number of users, since no information is shared across them. Via model sharing, hybrid LinUCB achieved some regret reduction compared with LinUCB; but its regret still increases linearly with the number of users. Compared with the independent bandits, we can clearly observe the regret reduction in CoLin with increasing number of users. As we discussed in Section 3.3, although GOB.Lin exploits the dependency among users, its regret might be even worse than running N independent LinUCBs, especially when the divergence between users is large.

Secondly, in Table 2, we fixed N to 100 and varied the noise level σ from 0.01 to 0.3. We can notice that CoLin is more robust to noise in the feedback: its regret grows much slower than all baselines. Our current regret analysis does not consider the effect of noise in reward, as long as it has a zero mean and finite variance. It would be interesting to incorporate this factor in regret analysis to provide more insight of collaborative bandit algorithms.

Thirdly, in CoLin, we have assumed the adjacency matrix $\mathbf{W}$ is known to the algorithm beforehand. However, in reality one might not precisely recover this matrix from noisy observations, e.g., via social network analysis. It is thus important to investigate the robustness of collaborative bandit algorithms to a noisy $\mathbf{W}$. We fixed the user size N to 100 and corrupted the ground-truth adjacency matrix $\mathbf{W}$: add Gaussian noise $N(0, \delta)$ to w_{ij} and normalize the resulting matrix. We refer to this noisy adjacency matrix as $\mathbf{W}_0$. The simulator still uses the true adjacency matrix $\mathbf{W}$ to compute the reward of each action for a given user; while the noisy matrix $\mathbf{W}_0$ will be provided to the bandit algorithms, i.e., CoLin and GOB.Lin. This newly introduced Gaussian noise is different from the noise in generating the rewards as described in Eq (2).

From the cumulated regret shown in Table 3, we can find that under moderate noise level, CoLin performed much better than GOB.Lin; but CoLin is more sensitive to noise in $\mathbf{W}$ than GOB.Lin. Because CoLin utilizes a weighted adjacency graph to capture the dependency among users, it becomes more sensitive to the estimation error in $\mathbf{W}$. While in GOB.Lin, because only the graph connectivity is used and the random noise is very unlikely to change the graph connectivity, its performance is more stable. Further theoretical analysis of how an inaccurate estimation of $\mathbf{W}$ would affect the resulting regret will be an interesting future work yet to explore.

Finally, the regret analysis of CoLin shows that its upper regret bound is related with the graph structure through the term $\sum_{t=1}^{T}\sum_{j=1}^{N} w_{u_t j}^2$ and GOB.Lin's regret bound is related to the graph connectivity [10]. We designed another set of simulation experiments to verify the effect of graph structure on CoLin and GOB.Lin. In this experiment, we set the user size N to 100 and controlled the graph sparsity as follows: for each user in graph G, we only included the edges from his/her top M most influential neighbors (measured by the edge weight in $\mathbf{W}$) in the adjacency matrix, and normalized the resulting adjacency matrix to a stochastic matrix. No noise is added to $\mathbf{W}$ in this experiment (i.e., $\delta = 0$).

As shown in Table 4, the regret of all bandit algorithms increases as $\mathbf{W}$ becomes sparser, i.e., less information can be shared across

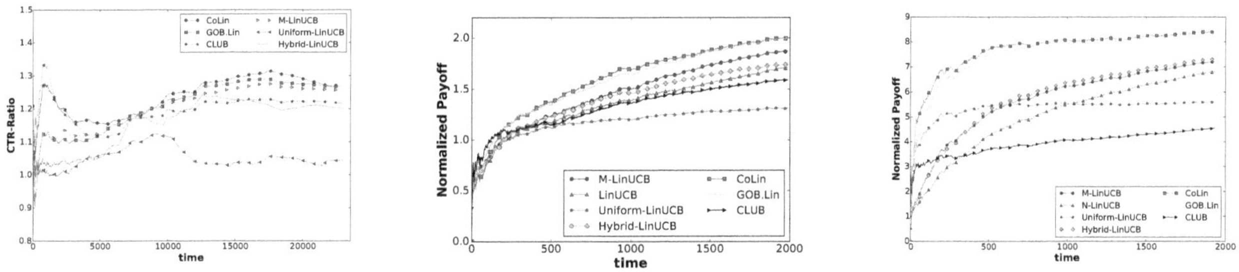

(a) Yahoo dataset (b) Delicious dataset (c) LastFM dataset

Figure 2: Normalized reward on three real-world datasets

users. We can observe that the regret of CoLin increases faster than that in GOB.Lin, since more information becomes unavailable to CoLin. The results empirically verified that CoLin's regret bound is directly related to the graph structure described by the term $\sum_{t=1}^{T}\sum_{j=1}^{N} w_{u_t j}^2$ and GOB.Lin's regret bound is only related to the graph connectivity.

4.2 Experiments on Yahoo! Today Module

In this experiment, we compared our CoLin algorithm with LinUCB, hybrid LinUCB, GOB.Lin and CLUB on a large collection of ten days' real traffic data from Yahoo! Today Module [21] using the unbiased offline evaluation protocol proposed in [22].

The dataset contains 45,811,883 user visits to the Today Module in a ten-day period in May 2009. For each visit, both the user and each of the 10 candidate articles are associated with a feature vector of six dimensions (including a constant bias feature), constructed by a conjoint analysis with a bilinear model [21]. However, this data set does not contain any user identity. This forbids us to associate the observations with individual users. To address this limitation, we first clustered all users into user groups by applying K-means algorithm on the given user features. Each observation is assigned to its closest user group. The weight in the adjacency matrix $\mathbf{W}$ is estimated by the dot product between the centroids from K-means' output, i.e., $w_{ij} \propto \langle u_i, u_j \rangle$. The CoLin and GOB.Lin algorithms are then executed over those identified user groups. For LinUCB baseline, we tested two variants: one is individual LinUCBs running over the identified user groups and it is denoted as M-LinUCB; another one is a uniform LinUCB shared by all the users, i.e., it does not distinguish individual users, and it is denoted as Uniform-LinUCB.

In this experiment, click-through-rate (CTR) was used to evaluate the performance of all bandit algorithms. Average CTR is computed in every 2000 observations (not the cumulated CTR) for each algorithm as the performance metric based on the unbiased offline evaluation protocol proposed in [22, 21]. Following the same evaluation principle used in [21], we normalized the resulting CTR from different bandit algorithms by the logged random strategy's CTR. We report the normalized CTR from different contextual bandit algorithms over the 160 derived user groups in Figure 2 (a).

CoLin outperformed all baselines on this real-world data set, except CLUB on the first day. Results from other user cluster sizes (40 and 80) showed consistent improvement as demonstrated in Figure 2 (a) with 160 user clusters; but due to space limit, we did not include those results on cluster size of 40 and 80. As we can find CLUB achieved the best CTR on the first day; but as some popular news articles became out-of-date, CLUB cannot correctly recognize their decreased popularity, and thus provided degenerated recommendations. But in CoLin, because of the collaborative preference learning, it better controlled exploration-exploitation trade-off and thus timely recognized the change of items' popularity. However, one potential limitation of CoLin algorithm is its computational complexity: because the dimension of global statistic matrix $\mathbf{A}_t$ defined in Eq (4) is $dN \times dN$, the running time of CoLin scales quadratically with the number of users. It makes CoLin less attractive in practical applications where the size of users is large. One potential solution is to enforce sparsity in the estimated $\mathbf{W}$ matrix such that distributed model update is possible, i.e., only share information within the connected users. The simulation study in Table 4 confirms the feasibility of this direction and we will explore it in our future work.

4.3 Experiments on LastFM & Delicious

The LastFM dataset is extracted from the music streaming service Last.fm (http://www.last.fm), and the Delicious data set is extracted the social bookmark sharing service website Delicious (https://delicious.com). These two datasets were generated by the Information Retrieval group at Universidad Autonomade Madrid for the HetRec 2011 workshop with the goal of investigating the usage of heterogeneous information in recommendation system[1]. The LastFM dataset contains 1892 users and 17632 items (artists). We used the information of "listened artists" of each user to create payoffs for bandit algorithms: if a user listened to an artist at least once, the payoff is 1, otherwise 0. The Delicious dataset contains 1861 users and 69226 items (URLs). We generated the payoffs using the information about the bookmarked URLs for each user: the payoff is 1 is the user bookmarked a particular URL, otherwise 0. Both of these two data sets contain the users' social network graph, which makes them a perfect testbed for collaborative bandits.

Following the same settings in [10], we pre-processed these two datasets in order to fit them into the contextual bandit setting. Firstly, we used all tags associated with a single item to create a TF-IDF feature vector, which uniquely represents the item. Then we used PCA to reduce the dimensionality of the feature vectors. In both datasets, we only retained the first 25 principle components to construct the context vectors, i.e., the feature dimension $d = 25$. We then generate the candidate arm pool as follows: we fix the size of candidate arm pool to be $K = 25$; for a particular user u, we pick one item from those nonzero payoff items for user u according to the whole observations in the dataset, and randomly pick the other 24 from those zero-payoff items for user u.

User relation graph is naturally extracted from the social network information provided by the datasets. In order to make the graph denser and make the algorithms computationally feasible, we performed graph-cut to cluster users into M clusters (following the same setting as in [10]). Users in the same clusters are assumed to have the same bandit parameters. In our experiments, M was set to be 50, 100, and 200. Our reported results are from the setting of $M = 200$, and similar results were achieved in other settings of M. After user clustering, a weighted graph can be generated: the nodes are the clusters of the original graph; and the edges between differ-

[1]Datasets and their full description is available at http://grouplens.org/datasets/hetrec-2011

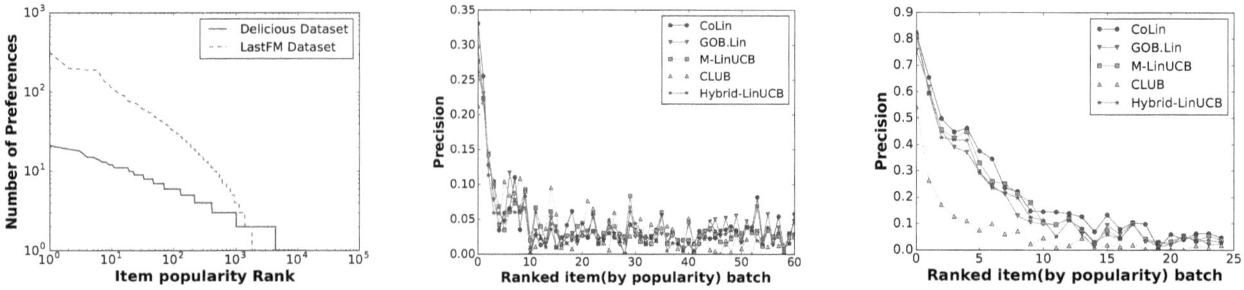

(a) Item popularity of the two datasets (b) Item-based Precision on Delicious (c) Item-based Precision on LastFM

Figure 3: Item-based analysis on Delicious and LastFM datasets

ent clusters are weighted by the number of inter-cluster edges in the original graph. In CoLin, we also need the diagonal elements in $\mathbf{W}$, which is undefined in a graph-cut based clustering algorithm. We computed the diagonal elements based on the derived regret bound of CoLin. Specifically, we first set $w_{ij} \propto c(i,j)$, where $c(i,j)$ is the number of edges between cluster i and j; then we optimize $\{w_{ii}\}_{i=1}^{N}$ which minimizes the term $\sum_i^N \sum_j^N w_{ij}^2$.

We included three variants of LinUCB, hybrid LinUCB, GOB.Lin and CLUB as our baselines. The three variants of LinUCB include: 1) LinUCB that runs independently on each user, denoted as N-LinUCB; 2) LinUCB that is shared in each user cluster, denoted as M-LinUCB (M is the number of clusters); 3) LinUCB that is shared by all the users, denoted as Uniform-LinUCB. Following the setting it [10], GOB.Lin also operates at the user cluster level and it takes the connectivity among clusters as input. We normalized the cumulated reward in each algorithm by a random strategy's cumulated reward, and compute the average accumulated normalized reward in every 50 iterations. Note that user features required by hybrid LinUCB are not given in these two datasets. We construct the user features by applying PCA on CoLin's adjacency matrix $\mathbf{W}$ and retained the first 25 principle components.

From the results shown in Figure 2 (b) and (c), we can find that CoLin outperforms all the baselines on both Delicious and LastFM datasets. It's worth noting that these two datasets are structurally different, as shown in Figure 3 (a), the popularity of items on these two data sets differs significantly: on LastFM dataset, there are a lot more popular artists whom everybody listens to than the popular websites which everyone bookmarks on Delicious dataset. Thus the highly skewed distribution of item popularity makes recommendation on Delicious dataset much more challenging. Because most of items are only bookmarked by a handful of users, exploiting the relatedness among users to propagate feedback become vital. While on LastFM since there are much more popular items that most users would like, most algorithms can easily recognize the quality of items. In order to better understand this difference, we performed detailed item-level analysis to examine the effectiveness of different algorithms on items with varied popularity. Specifically, we first ranked all the items in these two datasets in a descending order of item popularity and then examined the item-based recommendation precision from all the bandit algorithms, e.g., percentage of item recommendations that are accepted by the users. In order to better visualize the results, we further grouped ranked items into different batches and report the average recommendation precision over each batch in Figure 3 (b) and Figure 3 (c).

From the item-based recommendation precision results, we can clearly find that on the LastFM dataset, CoLin achieved superior performance against all the baselines in every category of items, given the popularity of items in this data set is more balanced. On Delicious dataset, CoLin achieved superior performance on top-ranked items, however, because of the skewness of item popularity distribution, less popular items are still challenging for all the compared algorithms.

This analysis motivates us to further analyze the user-level recommendation performance of different bandit algorithms, especially to understand the effectiveness of collaboration among bandits in alleviating the cold-start problem. To quantitatively evaluate this, we first ranked the user clusters in a descending order with respect to the number of observations in it. We then selected top 50 clusters as group 1. From the bottom 100 user clusters, we select 50 of them who are mostly connected to the users in group 1, as refer to them as group 2. The first group of users is called "learning bucket" and the second group is called "testing bucket". Based on this separation of user clusters, we designed two different experiment settings: one is warm-start, another one is cold-start. In the warm-start setting, we first run all the algorithms on the learning bucket to estimate parameters for both group of users, such as $\mathbf{A}_t$ and $\mathbf{b}_t$ in CoLin. However, because user group 2 does not have any observation in the learning bucket, their model parameters can only be updated via collaboration among bandits, i.e., in CoLin and GOBLin. Then with the model parameters estimated from the learning bucket, we run and evaluate different algorithms on the deployment bucket. Correspondingly, in the cold-start setting, we directly run and evaluate the bandit algorithms on the deployment bucket. It is obvious that since LinUCB assume users are independent and there is no sharing parameters among users, LinUCB's performance will not change under warm-start and cold start setting. While in CoLin, GOB.Lin and CLUB, because of the collaboration among users, model parameters are shared among users. In this case, user preference information learned from the learning bucket can be propagated to the deployment bucket.

We report the performance on the first 10% observations in the deployment bucket instead of the whole observations in order to better simulate the cold-start situation (i.e., all the algorithms do not have sufficient observations to confidently estimate model parameters). In Figure 4 (a) and (b) we report the gap of cumulated rewards from CoLin GOB.Lin, and CLUB between warm-start setting and cold-start setting, normalized by rewards obtained from LinUCB. From Figure 4(a) we can notice that on Delicious dataset, although at the very beginning of the warm-start setting both GOB-Lin and CoLin performed worse than the cold-start setting, both algorithms in warm-start quickly improved and outperformed the cold-start setting. One possible explanation is that the algorithms might take the first several iterations to adapt the model propagated from user group 1 to user group 2. In particular, from Figure 4 (a), it is clear that once both algorithm are adapted, the improvement between warm-start and cold-start on CoLin is larger than that on GOB.Lin. This verified CoLin's effectiveness in address the cold-start challenge. From Figure 4 (b), we can find that warm-start helps both algorithms immediately at the first several iterations on LastFM dataset. This might be caused by the flat distribution of item popularity in this data set: users in group 2 also prefer the

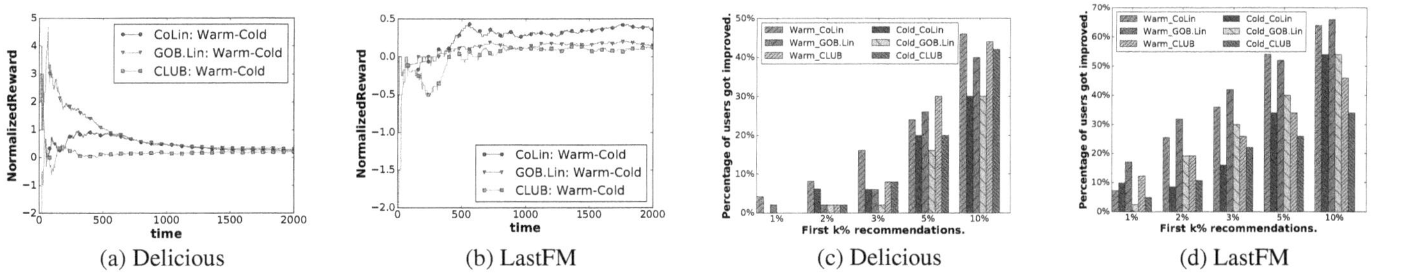

(a) Delicious (b) LastFM (c) Delicious (d) LastFM

Figure 4: Effectiveness of collaboration and User-based analysis

items liked by user group 1. We should note that the larger gap from GOB.Lin than that from CoLin between warm-start and cold-start settings does not mean CoLin is worse than GOB.Lin; but it indicates the cold-start CoLin learned faster than the cold-start GOB.Lin on this data set. And the final performance of both cold-start and warm-start CoLin was better than GOB.Lin in the corresponding settings. We can also notice that cold-start CLUB performed very similarly as warm-start CLUB. It means the user clusters automatically constructed in CLUB does not help collaborative learning. This experiment confirms that appropriate observation sharing among users indeed helps address the cold-start problem in recommendation.

Furthermore, we performed a user-based analysis to examine how many users will benefit from the collaborative bandits setting. We define an improved user as the user who is served with improved recommendations from a collaborative bandit algorithm (i.e. CoLin, GOB.Lin and CLUB) than those from isolated LinUCBs. We report the percentage of improved users in the first 1%, 2%, 3%, 5%, and 10% observations during online learning process. Figure 4 (c) and (d) demonstrate that on all collaborative bandit algorithms, the warm-start setting benefits much more users than in the cold-start setting. This result further supports our motivation of this research that collaboration among bandits can help alleviate the cold-start challenge.

5. CONCLUSIONS

In this paper, we developed CoLin algorithm to study contextual bandit problem in a collaborative environment. In CoLin, context and payoffs are shared among the neighboring bandits during online update, and it helps reduce the preference learning complexity (i.e., requires less observations to achieve satisfactory prediction performance) and leads to reduced overall regret. We religiously proved a reduced upper regret bound comparing to independent bandit algorithms. Experimental results based on extensive simulations and three real-world datasets consistently confirmed the improvement of the proposed collaborative bandit algorithm against several state-of-the-art contextual bandit algorithms.

In our current setting, we have assumed the graph structure among users is known to the algorithm beforehand. It is meaningful to study how to dynamically estimate the graph structure during online update with provable regret bound. The computation complexity in CoLin is now expensive. Utilizing the sparse graph structure to decentralize the computation is an important and interesting research direction. Besides, CoLin should not be only limited to linear payoffs; various types of link functions and regret definitions can be explored as our future work.

6. ACKNOWLEDGMENTS

We thank the anonymous reviewers for their insightful comments. This paper is based upon work supported by the National Science Foundation under grant IIS-1553568.

7. REFERENCES

[1] Y. Abbasi-yadkori, D. Pál, and C. Szepesvári. Improved algorithms for linear stochastic bandits. In *NIPS*, pages 2312–2320. 2011.

[2] K. Amin, M. Kearns, and U. Syed. Graphical models for bandit problems. *Proceedings of UAI 2011*, 2011.

[3] P. Auer. Using confidence bounds for exploitation-exploration trade-offs. *Journal of Machine Learning Research*, 3:397–422, 2002.

[4] P. Auer, N. Cesa-Bianchi, and P. Fischer. Finite-time analysis of the multiarmed bandit problem. *Mach. Learn.*, 47(2-3):235–256, May 2002.

[5] P. Auer, N. Cesa-Bianchi, Y. Freund, and R. E. Schapire. Gambling in a rigged casino: The adversarial multi-armed bandit problem. In *Foundations of Computer Science, 1995. Proceedings., 36th Annual Symposium on*, pages 322–331, 1995.

[6] D. Bouneffouf, A. Bouzeghoub, and A. L. Gançarski. A contextual-bandit algorithm for mobile context-aware recommender system. In *Neural Information Processing*, pages 324–331. 2012.

[7] J. S. Breese, D. Heckerman, and C. Kadie. Empirical analysis of predictive algorithms for collaborative filtering. Technical Report MSR-TR-98-12, Microsoft Research, May 1998.

[8] S. Buccapatnam, A. Eryilmaz, and N. B. Shroff. Multi-armed bandits in the presence of side observations in social networks. In *Decision and Control (CDC), 2013 IEEE 52nd Annual Conference on*, pages 7309–7314. IEEE, 2013.

[9] S. Buccapatnam, A. Eryilmaz, and N. B. Shroff. Stochastic bandits with side observations on networks. *SIGMETRICS Perform. Eval. Rev.*, 42(1):289–300, June 2014.

[10] N. Cesa-Bianchi, C. Gentile, and G. Zappella. A gang of bandits. *In Pro. NIPS*, 2013.

[11] O. Chapelle and L. Li. An empirical evaluation of thompson sampling. In *Advances in Neural Information Processing Systems*, pages 2249–2257, 2011.

[12] W. Chu, L. Li, L. Reyzin, and R. E. Schapire. Contextual bandits with linear payoff functions. In *International Conference on Artificial Intelligence and Statistics*, pages 208–214, 2011.

[13] R. B. Cialdini and M. R. Trost. Social influence: Social norms, conformity and compliance. 1998.

[14] S. Filippi, O. Cappe, A. Garivier, and C. Szepesvári. Parametric bandits: The generalized linear case. In *NIPS*, pages 586–594, 2010.

[15] C. Gentile, S. Li, and G. Zappella. Online clustering of bandits. In *Proceedings of the 31st International Conference on Machine Learning (ICML-14)*, pages 757–765, 2014.

[16] J. C. Gittins. Bandit processes and dynamic allocation indices. *Journal of the Royal Statistical Society. Series B (Methodological)*, pages 148–177, 1979.

[17] S. Kar, H. Poor, and S. Cui. Bandit problems in networks: Asymptotically efficient distributed allocation rules. In *Decision and Control and European Control Conference (CDC-ECC), 2011 50th IEEE Conference on*, pages 1771–1778, Dec 2011.

[18] J. Kawale, H. H. Bui, B. Kveton, L. Tran-Thanh, and S. Chawla. Efficient thompson sampling for online matrix-factorization recommendation. In *Advances in Neural Information Processing Systems*, pages 1297–1305, 2015.

[19] T. L. Lai and H. Robbins. Asymptotically efficient adaptive allocation rules. *Advances in applied mathematics*, 6(1):4–22, 1985.

[20] J. Langford and T. Zhang. The epoch-greedy algorithm for multi-armed bandits with side information. In *NIPS*, pages 817–824. 2008.

[21] L. Li, W. Chu, J. Langford, and R. E. Schapire. A contextual-bandit approach to personalized news article recommendation. In *Proceedings of 19th WWW*, pages 661–670. ACM, 2010.

[22] L. Li, W. Chu, J. Langford, and X. Wang. Unbiased offline evaluation of contextual-bandit-based news article recommendation algorithms. In *Proceedings of 4th WSDM*, pages 297–306. ACM, 2011.

[23] W. Li, X. Wang, R. Zhang, Y. Cui, J. Mao, and R. Jin. Exploitation and exploration in a performance based contextual advertising system. In *Proceedings of 16th SIGKDD*, pages 27–36. ACM, 2010.

[24] F. Radlinski, R. Kleinberg, and T. Joachims. Learning diverse rankings with multi-armed bandits. In *Proceedings of 25th ICML*, pages 784–791. ACM, 2008.

[25] B. Sarwar, G. Karypis, J. Konstan, and J. Riedl. Item-based collaborative filtering recommendation algorithms. In *Proceedings of 10th WWW*, pages 285–295. ACM, 2001.

[26] A. I. Schein, A. Popescul, L. H. Ungar, and D. M. Pennock. Methods and metrics for cold-start recommendations. In *Proceedings of 25th SIGIR*, pages 253–260. ACM, 2002.

[27] A. Slivkins. Contextual bandits with similarity information. *The Journal of Machine Learning Research*, 15(1):2533–2568, 2014.

[28] Y. Yue and T. Joachims. Interactively optimizing information retrieval systems as a dueling bandits problem. In *Proceedings of 26th ICML*, pages 1201–1208. ACM, 2009.

[29] X. Zhao, W. Zhang, and J. Wang. Interactive collaborative filtering. In *Proceedings of the 22nd CIKM*, pages 1411–1420. ACM, 2013.

APPENDIX

Proof of Lemma 1:

Consider the objective function of ridge regression defined in Eq (3). By taking the gradient of $L(\boldsymbol{\Theta})$ with respect to $\boldsymbol{\Theta}$ and applying our model assumption specified in Eq (2), we have,

$$\mathbf{A}_t(\hat{\boldsymbol{\vartheta}}_t - \boldsymbol{\vartheta}^*) = \sum_{t'=1}^{t} vec(\mathring{\mathbf{X}}_{a_{t'},u'_t}\mathbf{W}^\top)\epsilon_{t'} - \lambda\boldsymbol{\vartheta}^*$$

in which $\epsilon_{t'}$ is the Gaussian noise at time t' in reward generation.

Define $\mathbf{S}_t = \sum_{t'=1}^{t} vec(\mathring{\mathbf{X}}_{a_{t'},u'_t}\mathbf{W}^\top)\epsilon_{t'}$, we have,

$$\hat{\boldsymbol{\vartheta}}_t - \boldsymbol{\vartheta}^* = \mathbf{A}_t^{-1}(\mathbf{S}_t - \lambda\boldsymbol{\vartheta}^*)$$

Because $\mathbf{S}_t$ is a martingale, according to Theorem 1 and 2 in [1],

$$\|\hat{\boldsymbol{\vartheta}}_t - \boldsymbol{\vartheta}^*\|_{\mathbf{A}_t} \le \sqrt{2\ln\Big(\frac{det(\mathbf{A}_t)^{1/2}det(\lambda\mathbf{I})^{-1}}{\delta}\Big)} + \sqrt{\lambda}\|\boldsymbol{\vartheta}^*\| \quad (9)$$

Since $\|\mathbf{x}_{a_{t,i}}\| \le 1$, $trace(\mathbf{A}_t) \le \lambda dN + \sum_{t'=1}^{t}\sum_{j=1}^{N} w^2_{u'_t j}$, we have $det(\mathbf{A}_t) \le (\frac{trace(\mathbf{A}_t)}{dN})^{dN} \le (\lambda + \frac{\sum_{t'=1}^{t}\sum_{j=1}^{N} w^2_{u'_t j}}{dN})^{dN}$. Similarly, we have $det(\lambda\mathbf{I}_{dN}) \le \lambda^{dN}$. Putting all these into Eq (9), we have,

$$\|\hat{\boldsymbol{\vartheta}}_t - \boldsymbol{\vartheta}^*\|_{\mathbf{A}_t} \le \sqrt{dN\ln\Big(1 + \frac{\sum_{t'=1}^{t}\sum_{j=1}^{N} w^2_{u'_t j}}{\lambda dN}\Big) - 2\ln(\delta)} + \sqrt{\lambda}\|\boldsymbol{\vartheta}^*\|$$

□

Proof of Theorem 1:

According to the definition of regret in Eq (1), the regret of CoLin at time t can be written as,

$$\begin{aligned}
R_t &= r_{a_t^*,u_t} - r_{a_t,u_t}\\
&= vec(\mathring{\mathbf{X}}^*_{u_t}\mathbf{W}^\top)^\top\boldsymbol{\vartheta}^* - vec(\mathring{\mathbf{X}}_{u_t}\mathbf{W}^\top)^\top\boldsymbol{\vartheta}^*\\
&\le vec(\mathring{\mathbf{X}}_{u_t}\mathbf{W}^\top)^\top\hat{\boldsymbol{\vartheta}}_{t-1} + \alpha_t\|vec(\mathring{\mathbf{X}}_{u_t}\mathbf{W}^\top)\|_{\mathbf{A}_{t-1}^{-1}} - vec(\mathring{\mathbf{X}}_{u_t}\mathbf{W}^\top)^\top\boldsymbol{\vartheta}^*\\
&\le \|vec(\mathring{\mathbf{X}}_{u_t}\mathbf{W}^\top)\|_{\mathbf{A}_{t-1}^{-1}}\|\hat{\boldsymbol{\vartheta}}_{t-1} - \boldsymbol{\vartheta}^*\|_{\mathbf{A}_{t-1}} + \alpha_t\|vec(\mathring{\mathbf{X}}_{u_t}\mathbf{W}^\top)\|_{\mathbf{A}_{t-1}^{-1}}\\
&\le 2\alpha_t\|vec(\mathring{\mathbf{X}}_{u_t}\mathbf{W}^\top)\|_{\mathbf{A}_{t-1}^{-1}}
\end{aligned}$$

where the first inequality is based on the following two inequalities,

(1) Based on CoLin's arm selection strategy, if arm $\mathbf{X}_t$ is chosen at time t, it must satisfy,

$$\begin{aligned}
&vec(\mathring{\mathbf{X}}_{u_t}\mathbf{W}^\top)^\top\hat{\boldsymbol{\vartheta}}_{t-1} + \alpha_t\|vec(\mathring{\mathbf{X}}_{u_t}\mathbf{W}^\top)\|_{\mathbf{A}_{t-1}^{-1}}\\
&\ge vec(\mathring{\mathbf{X}}^*_{u_t}\mathbf{W}^\top)^\top\hat{\boldsymbol{\vartheta}}_{t-1} + \alpha_t\|vec(\mathring{\mathbf{X}}^*_{u_t}\mathbf{W}^\top)\|_{\mathbf{A}_{t-1}^{-1}}
\end{aligned}$$

(2) Based on Cauchy-Schwarz inequality, we have,

$$\begin{aligned}
&vec(\mathring{\mathbf{X}}^*_{u_t}\mathbf{W}^\top)^\top\hat{\boldsymbol{\vartheta}}_{t-1} + \alpha_t\|vec(\mathring{\mathbf{X}}^*_{u_t}\mathbf{W}^\top)\|_{\mathbf{A}_{t-1}^{-1}} - vec(\mathring{\mathbf{X}}^*_{u_t}\mathbf{W}^\top)^\top\boldsymbol{\vartheta}^*\\
&\ge -\|vec(\mathring{\mathbf{X}}^*_{u_t}\mathbf{W}^\top)^\top\|_{\mathbf{A}_{t-1}^{-1}}\|\hat{\boldsymbol{\vartheta}}_{t-1} - \boldsymbol{\vartheta}^*\|_{\mathbf{A}_{t-1}} + \alpha_t\|vec(\mathring{\mathbf{X}}^*_{u_t}\mathbf{W}^\top)\|_{\mathbf{A}_{t-1}^{-1}}\\
&\ge -\alpha_{t-1}\|vec(\mathring{\mathbf{X}}^*_{u_t}\mathbf{W}^\top)\|_{\mathbf{A}_{t-1}^{-1}} + \alpha_t\|vec(\mathring{\mathbf{X}}^*_{u_t}\mathbf{W}^\top)\|_{\mathbf{A}_{t-1}^{-1}}\\
&\ge 0
\end{aligned}$$

and therefore, we have

$$vec(\mathring{\mathbf{X}}^*_{u_t}\mathbf{W}^\top)^\top\hat{\boldsymbol{\vartheta}}_{t-1} + \alpha_t\|vec(\mathring{\mathbf{X}}^*_{u_t}\mathbf{W}^\top)\|_{\mathbf{A}_{t-1}^{-1}} \ge vec(\mathring{\mathbf{X}}^*_{u_t}\mathbf{W}^\top)^\top\boldsymbol{\vartheta}^*$$

And according to Lemma 11 in [1], we have,

$$\ln\Big(\frac{det(\mathbf{A}_T)}{det(\lambda\mathbf{I})}\Big) \le \sum_{t=1}^{T}\|vec(\mathring{\mathbf{X}}_{u_t}\mathbf{W}^\top)\|^2_{\mathbf{A}_{t-1}^{-1}} \le 2\ln\Big(\frac{det(\mathbf{A}_T)}{det(\lambda\mathbf{I})}\Big)$$

Thus the accumulated regret at time T in CoLin can be bounded by,

$$\begin{aligned}
\mathbf{R}(T) &\le \sqrt{T\sum_{t=1}^{T} R_t^2} \le \sqrt{T4\alpha_T^2\sum_{t=1}^{T}\|vec(\mathring{\mathbf{X}}_{u_t}\mathbf{W}^\top)\|^2_{\mathbf{A}_{t-1}^{-1}}}\\
&= \sqrt{T8\alpha_T^2\ln\Big(\frac{det(\mathbf{A}_T)}{det(\lambda\mathbf{I})}\Big)}\\
&\le 2\alpha_T\sqrt{2dNT\ln\Big(\frac{\sum_{t=1}^{T}\sum_{j=1}^{N} w^2_{u_t j}}{\lambda dN} + 1\Big)}
\end{aligned}$$

□

Analysis for the special case of evenly served users :

If we assume users are evenly served, say each user is served $\bar{T} = T/N$ times. With this assumption, the regret of CoLin can be further written as,

$$\begin{aligned}
\mathbf{R}(T) &\le \sum_{i=1}^{N}\sqrt{\bar{T}\sum_{t=\bar{T}(i-1)+1}^{t'=\bar{T}i} R_t^2}\\
&\le \sum_{i=1}^{N}\sqrt{\bar{T}\Big(\ln^2\Big(\frac{det(\mathbf{A}_{t'})}{det(\mathbf{A}_t)}\Big) + \lambda\|\boldsymbol{\vartheta}^*\|\ln\Big(\frac{det(\mathbf{A}_{t'})}{det(\mathbf{A}_t)}\Big)\Big)}
\end{aligned} \quad (10)$$

(1) In the extreme case that W is identity matrix, the $\mathbf{A}$ matrix in CoLin becomes a block diagonal matrix, which consists of $\mathbf{A}^{u_i}$, $i \in 1,..,N$. Using the block diagonal matrix's property that $det(\mathbf{A}) = \prod_i^N det(\mathbf{A}^{u_i})$, the regret can be further simplified as,

$$\begin{aligned}
\mathbf{R}(T) &\le \sum_{i=1}^{N}\sqrt{\bar{T}\Big(\ln^2\big(det(\mathbf{A}^{u_i})\big) + \lambda\|\boldsymbol{\vartheta}^*\|\ln(det(\mathbf{A}^{u_i}))\Big)}\\
&\le N\sqrt{\bar{T}\Big(d^2\ln^2(1 + \frac{\bar{T}}{d}) + \lambda\|\boldsymbol{\vartheta}^*\| d\ln(1 + \frac{\bar{T}}{d})\Big)}
\end{aligned} \quad (11)$$

which is $O\big(N\ln(\bar{T})\sqrt{\bar{T}}\big)$ and is identical with N independent LinUCB.

(2) In the extreme case where W is uniform, we have,

$$\mathbf{A}'_t = \mathbf{A}_t + \bar{T}vec(\mathring{\mathbf{X}}\mathbf{W}^\top)vec(\mathring{\mathbf{X}}\mathbf{W}^\top)^\top$$

such that,

$$det(\mathbf{A}'_t) = det(\mathbf{A}_t)(1 + \bar{T}\|vec(\mathring{\mathbf{X}}\mathbf{W}^\top)\|^2_{\mathbf{A}_t^{-1}}) \quad (12)$$

By applying Eq(12) and according to Eq (10) the regret bound of CoLin can be written as,

$$\mathbf{R}(T) \le N\sqrt{\bar{T}\Big(\ln^2(1 + \frac{\bar{T}}{\lambda N}) + \lambda\|\boldsymbol{\vartheta}^*\|\ln(1 + \frac{\bar{T}}{\lambda N})\Big)}$$

which is $O\big(N\ln(\frac{\bar{T}}{N})\sqrt{\bar{T}}\big)$.

Collaborative Filtering Bandits

Shuai Li
University of Insubria, Italy
shuaili.sli@gmail.com

Alexandros Karatzoglou
Telefónica Research, Spain
alexk@tid.es

Claudio Gentile
University of Insubria, Italy
claudio.gentile@uninsubria.it

ABSTRACT

Classical collaborative filtering, and content-based filtering methods try to learn a static recommendation model given training data. These approaches are far from ideal in highly dynamic recommendation domains such as news recommendation and computational advertisement, where the set of items and users is very fluid. In this work, we investigate an adaptive clustering technique for content recommendation based on exploration-exploitation strategies in contextual multi-armed bandit settings. Our algorithm takes into account the collaborative effects that arise due to the interaction of the users with the items, by dynamically grouping users based on the items under consideration and, at the same time, grouping items based on the similarity of the clusterings induced over the users. The resulting algorithm thus takes advantage of preference patterns in the data in a way akin to collaborative filtering methods. We provide an empirical analysis on medium-size real-world datasets, showing scalability and increased prediction performance (as measured by click-through rate) over state-of-the-art methods for clustering bandits. We also provide a regret analysis within a standard linear stochastic noise setting.

Keywords

Filtering and Recommending; Recommender Systems; Online Learning; Collaborative Filtering; Clustering; Bandits; Regret; Computational Advertising

1. INTRODUCTION

Recommender Systems are an essential part of many successful on-line businesses, from e-commerce to on-line streaming, and beyond. Moreover, Computational Advertising can be seen as a recommendation problem where the user preferences highly depend on the current *context*. In fact, many recommendation domains such as Youtube video recommendation or news recommendation *do not* fit the classical description of a recommendation scenario, whereby a set of users with essentially fixed preferences interact with a fixed set of items. In this classical setting, the well-known *cold-start* problem, namely, the lack of accumulated interactions by users on items, needs to be addressed, for instance, by turning to *hybrid* recommendation methods (e.g., [19]). In practice, many relevant recommendation domains are dynamic, in the sense that user preferences and the set of active users change with time. Recommendation domains can be distinguished by how much and how often user preferences and content universe change (e.g., [24]). In highly dynamic recommendation domains, such as news, ads and videos, active users and user preferences are fluid, hence classical collaborative filtering-type methods, such as Matrix or Tensor-Factorization break down. In these settings, it is essential for the recommendation method to adapt to the shifting preference patterns of the users.

Exploration-exploitation methods, a.k.a. multi-armed bandits, have been shown to be an excellent solution for these dynamic domains (see, e.g., the news recommendation evidence in [23]). While effective, standard contextual bandits do not take collaborative information into account, that is, users who have interacted with similar items in the past will not be deemed to have similar taste based on this fact alone, while items that have been chosen by the same group of users will also not be considered as similar. It is this significant limitation in the current bandit methodology that we try to address in this work. Past efforts on this problem were based on using online clustering-like algorithms on the graph or network structure of the data in conjunction with multi-armed bandit methods (see Section 3).

Commercial large scale search engines and information retrieval systems are examples of highly dynamic environments where users and items could be described in terms of their membership in some preference cluster. For instance, in a music recommendation scenario, we may have groups of listeners (the users) clustered around music genres, with the clustering changing across different genres. On the other hand, the individual songs (the items) could naturally be grouped by sub-genre or performer based on the fact that they tend to be preferred by the same group of users. Evidence has been collected which suggests that, at least in specific recommendation scenarios, like movie recommendation, data are well modeled by clustering at both user and item sides (e.g., [31]).

In this paper, we introduce a Collaborative Filtering based stochastic multi-armed bandit method that allows for a flexible and generic integration of information of users and items interaction data by alternatively clustering over both user and item sides. Specifically, we describe and analyze an

SIGIR '16, July 17-21, 2016, Pisa, Italy
© 2016 ACM. ISBN 978-1-4503-4069-4/16/07...$15.00
DOI: http://dx.doi.org/10.1145/2911451.2911548

adaptive and efficient clustering of bandit algorithm that can perform collaborative filtering, named COFIBA (pronounced as "coffee bar"). Importantly enough, the clustering performed by our algorithm relies on sparse graph representations, avoiding expensive matrix factorization techniques. We adapt COFIBA to the standard setting of sequential content recommendation known as (contextual) multi-armed bandits (e.g., [5]) for solving the canonical exploration vs. exploitation dilemma.

Our algorithm works under the assumption that we have to serve content to users in such a way that each content *item* determines a clustering over users made up of relatively few groups (compared to the total number of users), within which users tend to react similarly when that item gets recommended. However, the clustering over users need not be the same across different items. Moreover, when the universe of items is large, we also assume that the items might be clustered as a function of the clustering they determine over users, in such a way that the number of *distinct* clusterings over users induced by the items is also relatively small compared to the total number of available items.

Our method aims to exploit collaborative effects in a bandit setting in a way akin to the way co-clustering techniques are used in batch collaborative filtering. Bandit methods also represent one of the most promising approaches to the research community of recommender systems, for instance in tackling the cold-start problem (e.g., [25]), whereby the lack of data on new users leads to suboptimal recommendations. An exploration approach in these cases seems very appropriate.

We demonstrate the efficacy of our dynamic clustering algorithm on three benchmark and real-world datasets. Our algorithm is scalable and exhibits significant increased prediction performance over the state-of-the-art of clustering bandits. We also provide a regret analysis of the $\sqrt{T}$-style holding with high probability in a standard stochastically linear noise setting.

2. LEARNING MODEL

We assume that the user behavior similarity is encoded by a family of clusterings depending on the specific feature (or context, or item) vector $\boldsymbol{x}$ under consideration. Specifically, we let $\mathcal{U} = \{1, \dots, n\}$ represent the set of n users. Then, given $\boldsymbol{x} \in \mathbb{R}^d$, set $\mathcal{U}$ can be partitioned into a small number $m(\boldsymbol{x})$ of clusters $U_1(\boldsymbol{x}), U_2(\boldsymbol{x}), \dots, U_{m(\boldsymbol{x})}(\boldsymbol{x})$, where $m(\boldsymbol{x})$ is upper bounded by a constant m, independent of $\boldsymbol{x}$, with m being much smaller than n. (The assumption $m << n$ is not strictly required but it makes our algorithms more effective, and this is actually what we expect our datasets to comply with.) The clusters are such that users belonging to the same cluster $U_j(\boldsymbol{x})$ tend to have similar behavior w.r.t. feature vector $\boldsymbol{x}$ (for instance, they both like or both dislike the item represented by $\boldsymbol{x}$), while users lying in different clusters have significantly different behavior. The mapping $\boldsymbol{x} \to \{U_1(\boldsymbol{x}), U_2(\boldsymbol{x}), \dots, U_{m(\boldsymbol{x})}(\boldsymbol{x})\}$ specifying the actual partitioning of the set of users $\mathcal{U}$ into the clusters determined by $\boldsymbol{x}$ (including the number of clusters $m(\boldsymbol{x})$ and its upper bound m), as well as the common user behavior within each cluster are *unknown* to the learning system, and have to be inferred based on user feedback.

For the sake of simplicity, this paper takes the simple viewpoint that clustering over users is determined by linear functions $\boldsymbol{x} \to \boldsymbol{u}_i^\top \boldsymbol{x}$, each one parameterized by an unknown vector $\boldsymbol{u}_i \in \mathbb{R}^d$ hosted at user $i \in \mathcal{U}$, in such a way that if users i and i' are in the same cluster w.r.t. $\boldsymbol{x}$ then $\boldsymbol{u}_i^\top \boldsymbol{x} = \boldsymbol{u}_{i'}^\top \boldsymbol{x}$, while if i and i' are in different clusters w.r.t. $\boldsymbol{x}$ then $|\boldsymbol{u}_i^\top \boldsymbol{x} - \boldsymbol{u}_{i'}^\top \boldsymbol{x}| \geq \gamma$, for some (unknown) gap parameter $\gamma > 0$, independent of $\boldsymbol{x}$.[1] As in the standard linear bandit setting (e.g., [5, 23, 12, 3, 13, 21, 30, 34, 16, 1], and references therein), the unknown vector $\boldsymbol{u}_i$ determines the (average) behavior of user i. More concretely, upon receiving context vector $\boldsymbol{x}$, user i "reacts" by delivering a payoff value

$$a_i(\boldsymbol{x}) = \boldsymbol{u}_i^\top \boldsymbol{x} + \epsilon_i(\boldsymbol{x}) \ ,$$

where $\epsilon_i(\boldsymbol{x})$ is a conditionally zero-mean and bounded variance noise term so that, conditioned on the past, the quantity $\boldsymbol{u}_i^\top \boldsymbol{x}$ is indeed the expected payoff observed at user i for context vector $\boldsymbol{x}$. Notice that the unknown parameter vector $\boldsymbol{u}_i$ we associate with user i is supposed to be time invariant in this model.[2]

Since we are facing sequential decision settings where the learning system needs to continuously adapt to the newly received information provided by users, we assume that the learning process is broken up into a discrete sequence of rounds: In round $t = 1, 2, \dots$, the learner receives a user index $i_t \in \mathcal{U}$ to serve content to, hence the user to serve may change at every round, though the same user can recur many times. We assume the sequence of users $i_1, i_2, \dots$ is determined by an exogenous process that places nonzero and independent probability to each user being the next one to serve. Together with i_t, the system receives in round t a set of feature vectors $C_{i_t} = \{\boldsymbol{x}_{t,1}, \boldsymbol{x}_{t,2}, \dots, \boldsymbol{x}_{t,c_t}\} \subseteq \mathbb{R}^d$ encoding the content which is currently available for recommendation to user i_t. The learner is compelled to pick some $\bar{\boldsymbol{x}}_t = \boldsymbol{x}_{t,k_t} \in C_{i_t}$ to recommend to i_t, and then observes i_t's feedback in the form of payoff $a_t \in \mathbb{R}$ whose (conditional) expectation is $\boldsymbol{u}_{i_t}^\top \bar{\boldsymbol{x}}_t$. The goal of the learning system is to maximize its total payoff $\sum_{t=1}^T a_t$ over T rounds. When the user feedback at our disposal is only the click/no-click behavior, the payoff a_t is naturally interpreted as a binary feedback, so that the quantity $\frac{\sum_{t=1}^T a_t}{T}$ becomes a clickthrough rate (CTR), where $a_t = 1$ if the recommended item was clicked by user i_t, and $a_t = 0$, otherwise. CTR is the measure of performance adopted by our comparative experiments in Section 5.

From a theoretical standpoint (Section 6), we are instead interested in bounding the cumulative *regret* achieved by our algorithms. More precisely, let the regret r_t of the learner at time t be the extent to which the average payoff of the best choice in hindsight at user i_t exceeds the average payoff of the algorithm's choice, i.e.,

$$r_t = \left(\max_{\boldsymbol{x} \in C_{i_t}} \boldsymbol{u}_{i_t}^\top \boldsymbol{x}\right) - \boldsymbol{u}_{i_t}^\top \bar{\boldsymbol{x}}_t \ .$$

We are aimed at bounding with high probability the cumulative regret $\sum_{t=1}^T r_t$, the probability being over the noise variables $\epsilon_{i_t}(\bar{\boldsymbol{x}}_t)$, and any other possible source of randomness, including i_t – see Section 6.

[1]As usual, this assumption may be relaxed by assuming the existence of two thresholds, one for the within-cluster distance of $\boldsymbol{u}_i^\top \boldsymbol{x}$ to $\boldsymbol{u}_{i'}^\top \boldsymbol{x}$, the other for the between-cluster distance.

[2]It would in fact be possible to lift this whole machinery to time-drifting user preferences by combining with known techniques (e.g., [11, 28]).

The kind of regret bound we would like to contrast to is one where the latent clustering structure over $\mathcal{U}$ (w.r.t. the feature vectors $\boldsymbol{x}$) is somehow known beforehand (see Section 6 for details). When the content universe is large but known a priori, as is frequent in many collaborative filtering applications, it is often desirable to also group the items into clusters based on similarity of user preferences, i.e., two items are similar if they are preferred by many of the same users. This notion of "two-sided" clustering is well known in the literature; when the clustering process is simultaneously grouping users based on similarity at the item side and items based on similarity at the user side, it goes under the name of "co-clustering" (see, e.g., [14, 15]). Here, we consider a computationally more affordable notion of collaborate filtering based on adaptive two-sided clustering.

Unlike previous existing clustering techniques on bandits (e.g., [1, 29]), our clustering setting only applies to the case when the content universe is large but known a priori (yet, see the end of Section 4). Specifically, let the content universe be $\mathcal{I} = \{\boldsymbol{x}_1, \boldsymbol{x}_2, \ldots, \boldsymbol{x}_{|\mathcal{I}|}\}$, and $P(\boldsymbol{x}_h) = \{U_1(\boldsymbol{x}_h), U_2(\boldsymbol{x}_h), \ldots, U_{m(\boldsymbol{x}_h)}(\boldsymbol{x}_h)\}$ be the partition into clusters over the set of users $\mathcal{U}$ induced by item $\boldsymbol{x}_h$. Then items $\boldsymbol{x}_h, \boldsymbol{x}_{h'} \in \mathcal{I}$ belong to the same cluster (over the set of items $\mathcal{I}$) if and only if they induce the same partition of the users, i.e., if $P(\boldsymbol{x}_h) = P(\boldsymbol{x}_{h'})$. We denote by g the number of distinct partitions so induced over $\mathcal{U}$ by the items in $\mathcal{I}$, and work under the assumption that g is *unknown* but significantly smaller than $|\mathcal{I}|$. (Again, the assumption $g << |\mathcal{I}|$ is not strictly needed, but it both makes our algorithms effective and is expected to be satisfied in relevant practical scenarios.)

Finally, in all of the above, an important special case is when the items to be recommended do not possess specific features (or do not possess features having significant predictive power). In this case, it is common to resort to the more classical non-contextual stochastic multiarmed bandit setting (e.g., [6, 4]), which is recovered from the contextual framework by setting $d = |\mathcal{I}|$, and assuming the content universe $\mathcal{I}$ is made up of the d-dimensional vectors $\boldsymbol{e}_h, h = 1, \ldots, d$, of the canonical basis of $\mathbb{R}^d$, As a consequence, the expected payoff of user i on item h is simply the h-th component of vector $\boldsymbol{u}_i$, and two users i and i' belong to the same cluster w.r.t. to h if the h-th component of $\boldsymbol{u}_i$ equals the h-th component of $\boldsymbol{u}_{i'}$. Because the lack of useful annotation on data was an issue with all datasets at our disposal, it is this latter modeling assumption that motivates the algorithm we actually implemented for the experiments reported in Section 5.

3. RELATED WORK

Batch collaborative filtering neighborhood methods rely on finding similar groups of users and items to the target user-item pair, e.g., [33], and thus in effect rely on a dynamic form of grouping users and items. Collaborative Filtering-based methods have also been integrated with co-clustering techniques, whereby preferences in each co-cluster are modeled with simple statistics of the preference relations in the co-cluster, e.g., rating averages [18].

Beyond the general connection to co-clustering (e.g., [14, 15]), our paper is related to the research on multi-armed bandit algorithms for trading off exploration and exploitation through dynamic clustering. We are not aware of any specific piece of work that combines bandits with co-clustering based on the scheme of collaborative filtering; the papers which are most closely related to ours are [16, 27, 29, 8, 22, 1, 2]. In [16], the authors work under the assumption that users are defined using a feature vector, and try to learn a low-rank hidden subspace assuming that variation across users is low-rank. The paper combines low-rank matrix recovery with high-dimensional Gaussian Process Bandits, but it gives rise to algorithms which do not seem practical for sizeable problems. In [27], the authors analyze a non-contextual stochastic bandit problem where model parameters are assumed to be clustered in a few (unknown) types. Yet, the provided solutions are completely different from ours. The work [29] combines (k-means-like) online clustering with a contextual bandit setting, but clustering is only made at the user side. The paper [8] also relies on bandit clustering at the user side (as in [27, 29]), with an emphasis on diversifying recommendations to the same user over time. In [22], the authors propose cascading bandits of user behavior to identify the k most attractive items, and formulate it as a stochastic combinatorial partial monitoring problem. Finally, the algorithms in [1, 2, 26] can be seen as a special case of COFIBA when clustering is done only at the user side, under centralized [1, 26] or decentralized [2] environments.

Similar in spirit are also [7, 9, 10, 20]: In [7], the authors define a transfer learning problem within a stochastic multi-armed bandit setting, where a prior distribution is defined over the set of possible models over the tasks; in [9], the authors rely on clustering Markov Decision Processes based on their model parameter similarity. In [10], the authors discuss how to choose from n unknown distributions the k ones whose means are largest by a certain metric; in [20] the authors study particle Thompson sampling with Rao-Blackwellization for online matrix factorization, exhibiting a regret bound in a very specific case of $n \times m$ rank-1 matrices. Yet, in none of above cases did the authors make a specific effort towards item-dependent clustering models applied to stochastic multi-armed bandits.

Further work includes [25, 32]. In [25], an ensemble of contextual bandits is used to address the cold-start problem in recommender systems. A similar approach is used in [32] to deal with cold-start in recommender systems but based on the probability matching paradigm in a parameter-free bandit strategy, which employs online bootstrap to derive the distribution of the estimated models. In contrast to our work, in neither [25] nor [32] are collaborative effects explicitly taken into account.

4. THE ALGORITHM

COFIBA, relies on upper-confidence-based tradeoffs between exploration and exploitation, combined with adaptive clustering procedures at both the user and the item sides. COFIBA stores in round t an estimate $\boldsymbol{w}_{i,t}$ of vector $\boldsymbol{u}_i$ associated with user $i \in \mathcal{U}$. Vectors $\boldsymbol{w}_{i,t}$ are updated based on the payoff feedback, as in a standard linear least-squares approximation to the corresponding $\boldsymbol{u}_i$. Every user $i \in \mathcal{U}$ hosts such an algorithm which operates as a linear bandit algorithm (e.g., [12, 3, 1]) on the available content C_{i_t}. More specifically, $\boldsymbol{w}_{i,t-1}$ is determined by an inverse correlation matrix $M_{i,t-1}^{-1}$ subject to rank-one adjustments, and a vector $\boldsymbol{b}_{i,t-1}$ subject to additive updates. Matrices $M_{i,t}$ are initialized to the $d \times d$ identity matrix, and vectors $\boldsymbol{b}_{i,t}$ are initialized to the d-dimensional zero vector. Matrix $M_{i,t-1}^{-1}$ is also used to define an upper confidence bound $\text{CB}_{i,t-1}(\boldsymbol{x})$ in the approximation of $\boldsymbol{w}_{i,t-1}$ to $\boldsymbol{u}_i$ along direction $\boldsymbol{x}$. Based on the local information encoded in the weight vectors $\boldsymbol{w}_{i,t-1}$ and the confidence bounds $\text{CB}_{i,t-1}(\boldsymbol{x})$, the algorithm also maintains and updates a family of clusterings of the set of users $\mathcal{U}$, and a single clustering over the set of items $\mathcal{I}$. On both sides, such clusterings are represented through connected components of undirected graphs (this is in the same vein as in [1]), where nodes are either users or items. A pseudocode description of our algorithm is contained in Figures 1, 2, and 3, while Figure 4 illustrates the algorithm's behavior through a pictorial example.

At time t, COFIBA receives the index i_t of the current user to serve, along with the available item vectors $\boldsymbol{x}_{t,1}, \ldots, \boldsymbol{x}_{t,c_t}$, and must select one among them. In order to do so, the algorithm computes the c_t *neighborhood sets* N_k, one per item $\boldsymbol{x}_{t,k} \in C_{i_t}$ based on the current aggregation of users (clusters "at the user side") w.r.t. item $\boldsymbol{x}_{t,k}$. Set N_k should be regarded as the current approximation to the cluster (over the users) i_t belongs to when the clustering criterion is defined by item $\boldsymbol{x}_{t,k}$. Each neighborhood set then defines a compound weight vector $\bar{\boldsymbol{w}}_{N_k,t-1}$ (through the aggregation of the corresponding matrices $M_{i,t-1}$ and vectors $\boldsymbol{b}_{i,t-1}$) which, in turn, determines a compound confidence bound[3] $\text{CB}_{N_k,t-1}(\boldsymbol{x}_{t,k})$. Vector $\bar{\boldsymbol{w}}_{N_k,t-1}$ and confidence bound $\text{CB}_{N_k,t-1}(\boldsymbol{x}_{t,k})$ are combined through an upper-confidence exploration-exploitation scheme so as to commit to the specific item $\bar{\boldsymbol{x}}_t \in C_{i_t}$ for user i_t. Then, the payoff a_t is received, and the algorithm uses $\bar{\boldsymbol{x}}_t$ to update $M_{i_t,t-1}$ to $M_{i_t,t}$ and $\boldsymbol{b}_{i_t,t-1}$ to $\boldsymbol{b}_{i_t,t}$. Notice that the update is only performed at user i_t, though this will affect the calculation of neighborhood sets and compound vectors for other users in later rounds.

After receiving payoff a_t and computing $M_{i_t,t}$ and $\boldsymbol{b}_{i_t,t}$, COFIBA updates the clusterings at the user side and the (unique) clustering at the item side. In round t, there are multiple graphs $G^U_{t,h} = (\mathcal{U}, E^U_{t,h})$ at the user side (hence many clusterings over $\mathcal{U}$, indexed by h), and a single graph $G^I_t = (\mathcal{I}, E^I_t)$ at the item side (hence a single clustering over $\mathcal{I}$). Each *clustering* at the user side corresponds to a single *cluster* at the item side, so that we have g_t *clusters* $\hat{I}_{1,t}, \ldots, \hat{I}_{g_t,t}$ over items and g_t *clusterings* over users – see Figure 4 for an example. On both user and item sides, updates take the form of edge deletions. Updates at the user side are only performed on the graph $G^U_{t,\widehat{h}_t}$ pointed to by the selected item $\bar{\boldsymbol{x}}_t = \boldsymbol{x}_{t,k_t}$. Updates at the item side are only made if it is likely that the neighborhoods of user i_t has significantly changed when considered w.r.t. two previously deemed similar items. Specifically, if item $\boldsymbol{x}_h$ was directly connected to item $\bar{\boldsymbol{x}}_t$ at the beginning of round t and, as a consequence of edge deletion at the user side, the set of users that are now likely to be close to i_t w.r.t. $\boldsymbol{x}_h$ is no longer the same as the set of users that are likely to be close to i_t w.r.t. $\bar{\boldsymbol{x}}_t$, then this is taken as a good indication that item $\boldsymbol{x}_h$ is not inducing the same partition over users as $\bar{\boldsymbol{x}}_t$ does, hence edge $(\bar{\boldsymbol{x}}_t, \boldsymbol{x}_h)$ gets deleted. Notice that this need not imply that, as a result of this deletion, the two items are now belonging to different clusters over $\mathcal{I}$, since these two items may still be indirectly connected.

[3]The one given in Figure 1 is the confidence bound we use in our experiments. In fact, the theoretical counterpart to CB is significantly more involved, same efforts can also be found in order to close the gap, e.g., in [4, 1].

Input:
- Set of users $\mathcal{U} = \{1, \ldots, n\}$;
- set of items $\mathcal{I} = \{\boldsymbol{x}_1, \ldots, \boldsymbol{x}_{|\mathcal{I}|}\} \subseteq \mathbb{R}^d$;
- exploration parameter $\alpha > 0$, and edge deletion parameter $\alpha_2 > 0$.

Init:
- $\boldsymbol{b}_{i,0} = \boldsymbol{0} \in \mathbb{R}^d$ and $M_{i,0} = I \in \mathbb{R}^{d \times d}$, $i = 1, \ldots n$;
- *User* graph $G^U_{1,1} = (\mathcal{U}, E^U_{1,1})$, $G^U_{1,1}$ is connected over $\mathcal{U}$;
- Number of *user* graphs $g_1 = 1$;
- No. of *user* clusters $m^U_{1,1} = 1$;
- *Item* clusters $\hat{I}_{1,1} = \mathcal{I}$, no. of *item* clusters $g_1 = 1$;
- *Item* graph $G^I_1 = (\mathcal{I}, E^I_1)$, G^I_1 is connected over $\mathcal{I}$.

for $t = 1, 2, \ldots, T$ **do**

Set

$$\boldsymbol{w}_{i,t-1} = M^{-1}_{i,t-1}\boldsymbol{b}_{i,t-1}, \qquad i = 1, \ldots, n \ ;$$

Receive $i_t \in \mathcal{U}$, and get items $C_{i_t} = \{\boldsymbol{x}_{t,1}, \ldots, \boldsymbol{x}_{t,c_t}\} \subseteq \mathcal{I}$;
For each $k = 1, \ldots, c_t$, determine which cluster (within the current user clustering w.r.t. $\boldsymbol{x}_{t,k}$) user i_t belongs to, and denote this cluster by N_k;
Compute, for $k = 1, \ldots, c_t$, aggregate quantities

$$\bar{M}_{N_k,t-1} = I + \sum_{i \in N_k} (M_{i,t-1} - I),$$

$$\bar{\boldsymbol{b}}_{N_k,t-1} = \sum_{i \in N_k} \boldsymbol{b}_{i,t-1},$$

$$\bar{\boldsymbol{w}}_{N_k,t-1} = \bar{M}^{-1}_{N_k,t-1}\bar{\boldsymbol{b}}_{N_k,t-1} \ ;$$

Set

$$k_t = \operatorname*{argmax}_{k=1,\ldots,c_t} \left(\bar{\boldsymbol{w}}^\top_{N_k,t-1}\boldsymbol{x}_{t,k} + \text{CB}_{N_k,t-1}(\boldsymbol{x}_{t,k})\right),$$

where $\text{CB}_{N_k,t-1}(\boldsymbol{x}) = \alpha\sqrt{\boldsymbol{x}^\top \bar{M}^{-1}_{N_k,t-1}\boldsymbol{x}\,\log(t+1)}$;
Set for brevity $\bar{\boldsymbol{x}}_t = \boldsymbol{x}_{t,k_t}$;
Observe payoff $a_t \in \mathbb{R}$, and update weights $M_{i,t}$ and $\boldsymbol{b}_{i,t}$ as follows:

- $M_{i_t,t} = M_{i_t,t-1} + \bar{\boldsymbol{x}}_t\bar{\boldsymbol{x}}_t^\top$,
- $\boldsymbol{b}_{i_t,t} = \boldsymbol{b}_{i_t,t-1} + a_t\bar{\boldsymbol{x}}_t$,
- Set $M_{i,t} = M_{i,t-1}$, $\boldsymbol{b}_{i,t} = \boldsymbol{b}_{i,t-1}$ for all $i \neq i_t$,

Determine $\widehat{h}_t \in \{1, \ldots, g_t\}$ such that $k_t \in \hat{I}_{\widehat{h}_t,t}$;
Update *user* clusters at graph $G^U_{t,\widehat{h}_t} = (\mathcal{U}, E^U_{t,\widehat{h}_t})$ by performing the steps in Figure 2;
For all $h \neq \widehat{h}_t$, set $G^U_{t+1,h} = G^U_{t,h}$;
Update *item* clusters at graph $G^I_t = (\mathcal{I}, E^I_t)$ by performing the steps in Figure 3 .

end for

Figure 1: The COFIBA algorithm.

Update *user* clusters at graph $G^U_{t,\widehat{h}_t}$ as follows:
- Delete from $E^U_{t,\widehat{h}_t}$ all (i_t, j) such that
$$|\boldsymbol{w}^\top_{i_t,t}\bar{\boldsymbol{x}}_t - \boldsymbol{w}^\top_{j,t}\bar{\boldsymbol{x}}_t| > \text{CB}_{i_t,t}(\bar{\boldsymbol{x}}_t) + \text{CB}_{j,t}(\bar{\boldsymbol{x}}_t) ,$$
where $\text{CB}_{i,t}(\boldsymbol{x}) = \alpha_2\sqrt{\boldsymbol{x}^\top M^{-1}_{i,t}\boldsymbol{x}\,\log(t+1)}$;
- Let $E^U_{t+1,\widehat{h}_t}$ be the resulting set of edges, set $G^U_{t+1,\widehat{h}_t} = (\mathcal{U}, E^U_{t+1,\widehat{h}_t})$, and compute associated clusters $\hat{U}_{1,t+1,\widehat{h}_t}, \hat{U}_{2,t+1,\widehat{h}_t}, \ldots, \hat{U}_{m^U_{t+1,\widehat{h}_t},t+1,\widehat{h}_t}$ as the connected components of $G^U_{t+1,\widehat{h}_t}$.

Figure 2: User cluster update in the COFIBA

Update *item* clusters at graph G_t^I as follows:

- For all ℓ such that $(\bar{\boldsymbol{x}}_t, \boldsymbol{x}_\ell) \in E_t^I$ build neighborhood $N_{\ell,t+1}^U(i_t)$ as:
$$N_{\ell,t+1}^U(i_t) = \Big\{ j \,:\, j \neq i_t\,, |\boldsymbol{w}_{i_t,t}^\top \boldsymbol{x}_\ell - \boldsymbol{w}_{j,t}^\top \boldsymbol{x}_\ell| \le \mathrm{CB}_{i_t,t}(\boldsymbol{x}_\ell) + \mathrm{CB}_{j,t}(\boldsymbol{x}_\ell) \Big\}\,;$$
- Delete from E_t^I all $(\bar{\boldsymbol{x}}_t, \boldsymbol{x}_\ell)$ such that $N_{\ell,t+1}^U(i_t) \neq N_{k_t,t+1}^U(i_t)$, where $N_{k_t,t+1}^U(i_t)$ is the *neighborhood* of node i_t w.r.t. graph $G_{t+1,\widehat{h}_t}^U$;
- Let E_{t+1}^I be the resulting set of edges, set $G_{t+1}^I = (\mathcal{I}, E_{t+1}^I)$, compute associated *item* clusters $\hat{I}_{1,t+1}, \hat{I}_{2,t+1}, \ldots, \hat{I}_{g_{t+1},t+1}$ through the connected components of G_{t+1}^I;
- For each new item cluster created, allocate a new connected graph over users representing a single (degenerate) cluster $\mathcal{U}$.

Figure 3: Item cluster update in the COFIBA

It is worth stressing that a naive implementation of COFIBA would require memory allocation for maintaining $|\mathcal{I}|$-many n-node graphs, i.e., $\mathcal{O}(n^2\,|\mathcal{I}|)$. Because this would be prohibitive even for moderately large sets of users, we make full usage of the approach of [1], where instead of starting off with complete graphs over users each time a new cluster over items is created, we randomly sparsify the complete graph by drawing an Erdos-Renyi initial graph, still retaining with high probability the underlying clusterings $\{U_1(\boldsymbol{x}_h), \ldots, U_{m(\boldsymbol{x}_h)}(\boldsymbol{x}_h)\}$, $h = 1, \ldots, |\mathcal{I}|$, over users. This works under the assumption that the latent clusters $U_i(\boldsymbol{x}_h)$ are not too small – see the argument in [1], where it is shown that in practice the initial graphs can have $\mathcal{O}(n \log n)$ edges instead of $\mathcal{O}(n^2)$. Moreover, because we modify the item graph by edge deletions only, one can show that with high probability (under the modeling assumptions of Section 2) the number g_t of clusters over items remains upper bounded by g throughout the run of COFIBA, so that the actual storage required by the algorithm is indeed $\mathcal{O}(ng \log n)$. This also brings a substantial saving in running time, since updating connected components scales with the number of edges of the involved graphs. It is this graph sparsification techniques that we used and tested along the way in our experimentation parts.

Finally, despite we have described in Section 2 a setting where $\mathcal{I}$ and $\mathcal{U}$ are known a priori (the analysis in Section 6 currently holds only in this scenario), nothing prevents in practice to adapt COFIBA to the case when new content or new users show up. This essentially amounts to adding new nodes to the graphs at either the item or the user side, by maintaining data-structures via dynamic memory allocation. In fact, this is precisely how we implemented our algorithm in the case of very big item or user sets (e.g., the Telefonica and the Avazu dataset in the next section).

5. EXPERIMENTS

We compared our algorithm to standard bandit baselines on three real-world datasets: one canonical benchmark dataset on news recommendations, one advertising dataset from a living production system, and one publicly available advertising dataset. In all cases, no features on the items have been used. We closely followed the same experimental setting as in previous work [12, 1], thereby evaluating prediction performance by click-through rate.

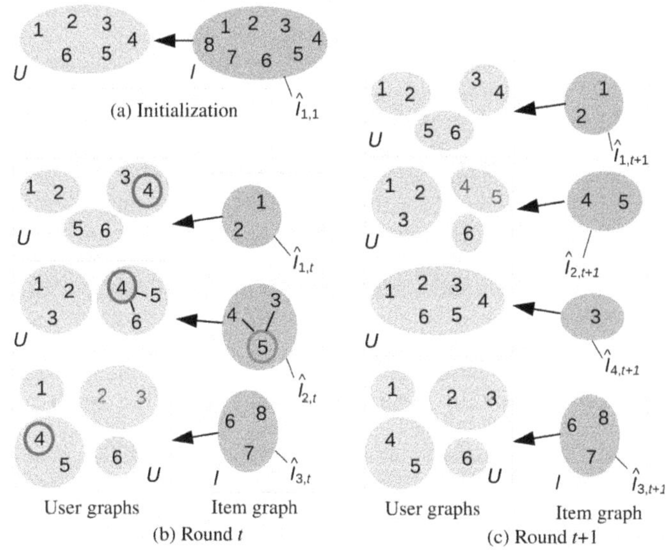

Figure 4: In this example, $\mathcal{U} = \{1, \ldots 6\}$ and $\mathcal{I} = \{\boldsymbol{x}_1, \ldots, \boldsymbol{x}_8\}$ (the items are depicted here as $1, 2, \ldots, 8$). (a) At the beginning we have $g_1 = 1$, with a single item cluster $\hat{I}_{1,1} = \mathcal{I}$ and, correspondingly, a single (degenerate) clustering over $\mathcal{U}$, made up of the unique cluster $\mathcal{U}$. (b) In round t we have the $g_t = 3$ item clusters $\hat{I}_{1,t} = \{\boldsymbol{x}_1, \boldsymbol{x}_2\}$, $\hat{I}_{2,t} = \{\boldsymbol{x}_3, \boldsymbol{x}_4, \boldsymbol{x}_5\}$, $\hat{I}_{3,t} = \{\boldsymbol{x}_6, \boldsymbol{x}_7, \boldsymbol{x}_8\}$. Corresponding to each one of them are the three clusterings over $\mathcal{U}$ depicted on the left, so that $m_{t,1}^U = 3$, $m_{t,2}^U = 2$, and $m_{t,3}^U = 4$. In this example, $i_t = 4$, and $\bar{\boldsymbol{x}}_t = \boldsymbol{x}_5$, hence $\widehat{h}_t = 2$, and we focus on graph $G_{t,2}^U$, corresponding to user clustering $\{\{1,2,3\},\{4,5,6\}\}$. Suppose in $G_{t,2}^U$ the only neighbors of user 4 are 5 and 6. When updating such user clustering, the algorithm considers therein edges $(4,5)$ and $(4,6)$ to be candidates for elimination. Suppose edge $(4,6)$ is eliminated, so that the new clustering over $\mathcal{U}$ induced by the updated graph $G_{t+1,2}^U$ becomes $\{\{1,2,3\},\{4,5\},\{6\}\}$. After user graph update, the algorithm considers the item graph update. Suppose $\boldsymbol{x}_5$ is only connected to $\boldsymbol{x}_4$ and $\boldsymbol{x}_3$ in G_t^I, and that $\boldsymbol{x}_4$ is not connected to $\boldsymbol{x}_3$, as depicted. Both edge $(\boldsymbol{x}_5, \boldsymbol{x}_4)$ and edge $(\boldsymbol{x}_5, \boldsymbol{x}_3)$ are candidates for elimination. The algorithm computes the neighborhood N of $i_t = 4$ according to $G_{t+1,2}^U$, and compares it to the the neighborhoods $N_{\ell,t+1}^U(i_t)$, for $\ell = 3, 4$. Assume $N \neq N_{3,t+1}^U(i_t)$, because the two neighborhoods of user 4 are now different, the algorithm deletes edge $(\boldsymbol{x}_5, \boldsymbol{x}_3)$ from the item graph, splitting the item cluster $\{\boldsymbol{x}_3, \boldsymbol{x}_4, \boldsymbol{x}_5\}$ into the two clusters $\{\boldsymbol{x}_3\}$ and $\{\boldsymbol{x}_4, \boldsymbol{x}_5\}$, hence allocating a new cluster at the item side corresponding to a new degenerate clustering $\{\{1,2,3,4,5,6\}\}$ at the user side. (c) The resulting clusterings at the beginning of round $t+1$. (In this picture it is assumed that edge $(\boldsymbol{x}_5, \boldsymbol{x}_4)$ was not deleted from the item graph at time t.)

5.1 Datasets

Yahoo!. The first dataset we use for the evaluation is the freely available benchmark dataset which was released in the "ICML 2012 Exploration & Exploitation Challenge"[4]. The aim of the challenge was to build state-of-the-art news article recommendation algorithms on Yahoo! data, by building an algorithm that learns efficiently a policy to serve news articles on a web site. The dataset is made up of random traffic records of user visits on the "Today Module" of Yahoo!, implying that both the visitors and the recommended news article are selected randomly. The available options (the items) correspond to a set of news articles available for recommendation, one being displayed in a small box on the visited web page. The aim is to recommend an interesting article to the user, whose interest in a given piece of news is asserted by a click on it. The data has 30 million visits over a two-week time stretch. Out of the logged information contained in each record, we used the user ID in the form of a 136-dimensional boolean vector containing his/her features (index i_t), the set of relevant news articles that the system can recommend from (set C_{i_t}); a randomly recommended article during the visit; a boolean value indicating whether the recommended article was clicked by the visiting user or not (payoff a_t). Because the displayed article is chosen uniformly at random from the candidate article pool, one can use an unbiased off-line evaluation method to compare bandit algorithms in a reliable way. We refer the reader to [1] for a more detailed description of how this dataset was collected and extracted. We picked the larger of the two datasets considered in [1], resulting in $n \approx 18K$ users, and $d = 323$ distinct items. The number of records ended up being $2.8M$, out of which we took the first $300K$ for parameter tuning, and the rest for testing.

Telefonica. This dataset was obtained from Telefonica S.A., which is the number one Spanish broadband and telecommunications provider, with business units in Europe and South America. This data contains clicks on ads displayed to user on one of the websites that Telefonica operates on. The data were collected from the back-end server logs, and consist of two files: the first file contains the ads interactions (each record containing an impression timestamp, a user-ID, an action, the ad type, the order item ID, and the click timestamp); the second file contains the ads metadata as item-ID, type-ID, type, order-ID, creative type, mask, cost, creator-ID, transaction key, cap type. Overall, the number n of users was in the scale of millions, while the number d of items was approximately 300. The data contains $15M$ records, out of which we took the first $1,5M$ for parameter tuning, and the rest for testing. Again, the only available payoffs are those associated with the items served by the system. Hence, in order to make the procedure be an effective estimator in a sequential decision process (e.g., [13, 17, 1, 23]), we *simulated* random choices by the system by generating the available item sets C_{i_t} as follows: At each round t, we stored the ad served to the current user i_t and the associated payoff value a_t (1 ="clicked", 0 ="not clicked"). Then we created C_{i_t} by including the served ad along with 9 extra items (hence $c_t = 10\ \forall t$) which were drawn uniformly at random in such a way that, for any item $\boldsymbol{e}_h \in \mathcal{I}$, if $\boldsymbol{e}_h$ occurs in some set C_{i_t}, this item will be the one served by the system 1/10 of the times. The random selection was done independent of the available payoff values a_t. All our experiments on this dataset were run on a machine with 64GB RAM and 32 Intel Xeon cores.

Avazu. This dataset was prepared by Avazu Inc,[5] which is a leading multinational corporation in the digital advertising business. The data was provided for the challenge to predict the click-through rate of impressions on mobile devices, i.e., whether a mobile ad will be clicked or not. The number of samples was around $40M$, out of which we took the first $4M$ for parameter tuning, and the remaining for testing. Each line in the data file represents the event of an ad impression on the site or in a mobile application (app), along with additional context information. Again, payoff a_t is binary. The variables contained in the dataset for each sample are the following: ad-ID; timestamp (date and hour); click (boolean variable); device-ID; device IP; connection type; device type; ID of visited App/Website; category of visited App/Website; connection domain of visited App/Website; banner position; anonymized categorical fields (C1, C14-C21). We pre-processed the dataset as follows: we cleaned up the data by filtering out the records having missing feature values, and removed outliers. We identified the user with device-ID, if it is not null. The number of users on this dataset is in the scale of millions. Similar to the Telefonica dataset, we generated recommendation lists of length $c_t = 20$ for each distinct timestamp. We used the first $4M$ records for tuning parameters, and the remaining $36M$ for testing. All data were transferred to Amazon S3, and all jobs were run through the Amazon EC2 Web Service.

5.2 Algorithms

We compared COFIBA to a number of state-of-the-art bandit algorithms:

- LINUCB-ONE is a single instance of the UCB1 [6] algorithm, which is a very popular and established algorithm that has received a lot of attention in the research community over the past years;
- DYNUCB is the dynamic UCB algorithm of [29]. This algorithm adopts a "K-means"-like clustering technique so as to dynamically re-assign the clusters on the fly based on the changing contexts and user preferences over time;
- LINUCB-IND [1] is a set of independent UCB1 instances, one per user, which provides a fully personalized recommendation for each user;
- CLUB [1] is the state-of-the-art online clustering of bandits algorithm that dynamically cluster users based on the confidence ellipsoids of their models;
- LINUCB-V [4] is also a single instance of UCB1, but with a more sophisticated confidence bound; this algorithm turned out to be the winner of the "ICML 2012 Challenge" where the Yahoo! dataset originates from.

We tuned the optimal parameters in the training set with a standard grid search as indicated in [13, 1], and used the test set to evaluate the predictive performance of the algorithms. Since the system's recommendation need not coincide with the recommendation issued by the algorithms we tested, we only retained the records on which the two recommendations were indeed the same. Because records are discarded on

[4]https://explochallenge.inria.fr/category/challenge

[5]https://www.kaggle.com/c/avazu-ctr-prediction

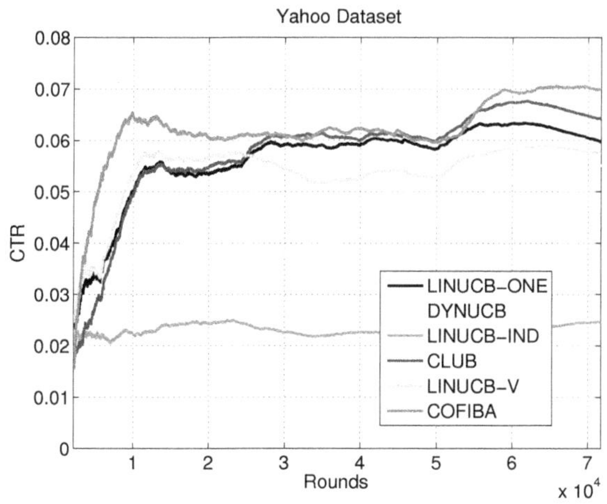

Figure 5: Results on the Yahoo dataset.

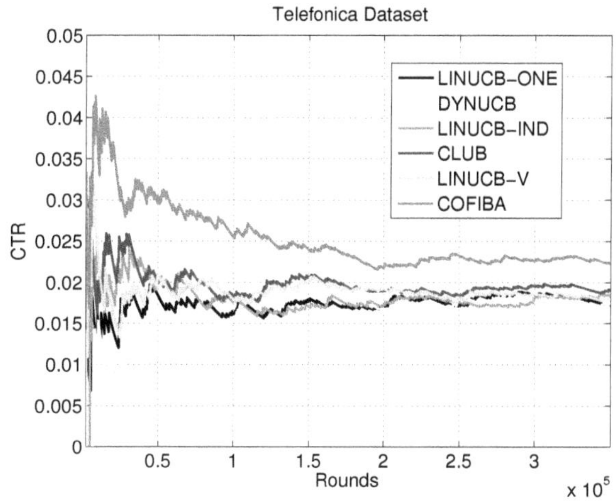

Figure 6: Results on the Telefonica dataset.

the fly, the actual number T of retained records ("Rounds" in the plots of the next subsection) changes slightly across algorithms; T was around $70K$ for the Yahoo! data, $350K$ for the Telefonica data, and $900K$ for the Avazu data. All experimental results we report were averaged over 3 runs (but in fact the variance we observed across these runs was fairly small).

5.3 Results

Our results are summarized in Figures 5, 6, and 7. Further evidence is contained in Figure 8. In Figures 5–7, we plotted click-through rate ("CTR") vs. retained records so far ("Rounds"). All these experiments are aimed at testing the performance of the various bandit algorithms in terms of prediction performance, also in cold-start regimes (i.e., the first relatively small fraction of the time horizon in the x-axis). Our experimental setting is in line with previous ones (e.g., [12, 1]) and, by the way the data have been prepared, gives rise to a reliable estimation of actual CTR behavior under the same experimental conditions as in [12, 1]. Figure 8 is aimed at supporting the theoretical model of Section 2, by providing some evidence on the kind of clustering statistics produced by COFIBA at the end of its run.

Whereas the three datasets we took into consideration are all generated by real online web applications, it is worth pointing out that these datasets are indeed different in the way customers consume the associated content. Generally speaking, the longer the lifecycle of one item the fewer the items, the higher the chance that users with similar preferences will consume it, and hence the bigger the collaborative effects contained in the data. It is therefore reasonable to expect that our algorithm will be more effective in datasets where the collaborative effects are indeed strong.

The users in the Yahoo! data (Figure 5), are likely to span a wide range of demographic characteristics; on top of this, this dataset is derived from the consumption of news that are often interesting for large portions of these users and, as such, do not create strong polarization into subcommunities. This implies that more often than not, there are quite a few specific hot news that all users might express interest in, and it is natural to expect that these pieces of news are intended to reach a wide audience of consumers. Given this state of affairs, it is not surprising that on the Yahoo! dataset both LINUCB-ONE and LINUCB-V (serving the same news to all users) are already performing quite well, thereby making the clustering-of-users effort somewhat less useful. This also explains the poor performance of LINUCB-IND, which is

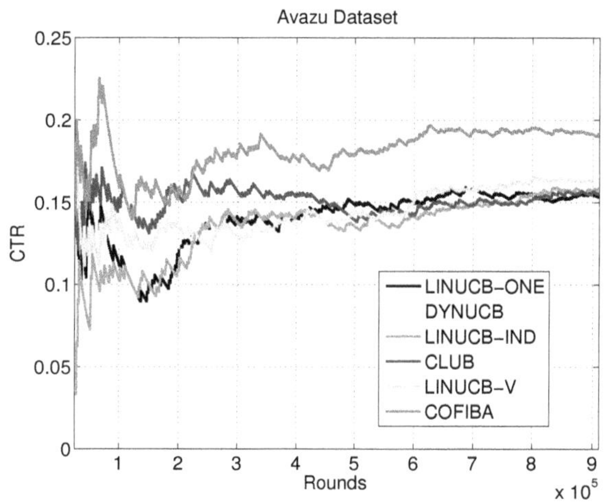

Figure 7: Results on the Avazu dataset.

not performing any clustering at all. Yet, even in this non-trivial case, COFIBA can still achieve a significant increased prediction accuracy compared, e.g., to CLUB, thereby suggesting that simultaneous clustering at both the user and the item (the news) sides might be an even more effective strategy to earn clicks in news recommendation systems.

Most of the users in the Telefonica data are from a diverse sample of people in Spain, and it is easy to imagine that this dataset spans a large number of communities across its population. Thus we can assume that collaborative effects will be much more evident, and that COFIBA will be able to leverage these effects efficiently. In this dataset, CLUB performs well in general, while DYNUCB deteriorates in the initial stage and catches-up later on. COFIBA seems to surpass all other algorithms, especially in the cold-start regime, all other algorithms being in the same ballpark as CLUB. Finally, the Avazu data is furnished from its professional digital advertising solution platform, where the customers click the ad impressions via the iOS/Android mobile apps or through websites, serving either the publisher or the advertiser which leads to a daily high volume internet traffic. In this dataset, neither LINUCB-ONE nor LINUCB-IND displayed a competitive cold-start performance. DYNUCB is underperforming throughout, while LINUCB-V demonstrates a relatively high CTR. CLUB is strong at the beginning, but then its CTR performance degrades. On the

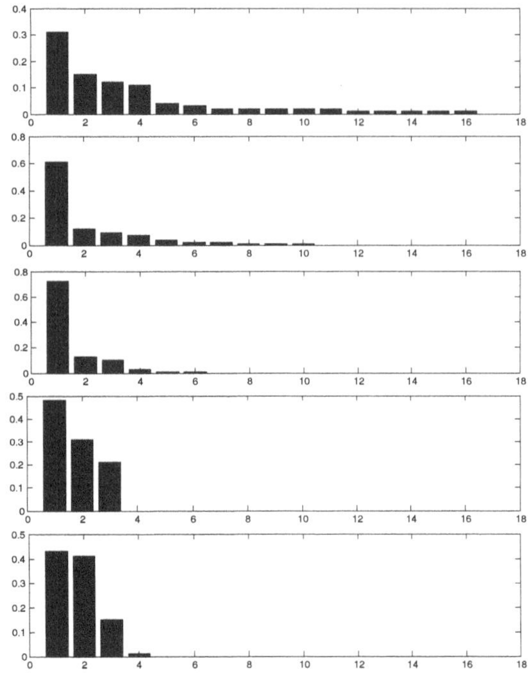

Figure 8: A typical distribution of cluster sizes over users for the Yahoo dataset. Each bar plot corresponds to a cluster at the item side. We have 5 plots since this is the number of clusters over the items that COFIBA **ended up with after sweeping once over this dataset in the run at hand. Each bar represents the fraction of users contained in the corresponding cluster. For instance, the first cluster over the items generated 16 clusters over the users (bar plot on top), with relative sizes 31%, 15%, 12%, etc. The second cluster over the items generated 10 clusters over the users (second bar plot from top) with relative sizes 61%, 12%, 9%, etc. The relative size of the 5 clusters over the items is as follows: 83%, 10%, 4%, 2%, and 1%, so that the clustering pattern depicted in the top plot applies to 83% of the items, the second one to 10% of the items, and so on.**

other hand, COFIBA seems to work extremely well during the cold-start, and comparatively best in all later stages.

In Figure 8 we give a typical distribution of cluster sizes produced by COFIBA after at the end of its run.[6] The emerging pattern is always the same: we have few clusters over the items with very unbalanced sizes and, corresponding to each item cluster, we have few clusters over the users, again with very unbalanced sizes. This recurring pattern is in fact the motivation behind our theoretical assumptions (Section 2), and a property of data that the COFIBA algorithm can provably take advantage of (Section 6). These bar plots, combined with the comparatively good performance of COFIBA, suggest that our datasets do actually possess clusterability properties at both sides.

To summarize, despite the differences in the three datasets, the experimental evidence we collected on them is quite consistent, in that in all the three cases COFIBA significantly outperforms all other competing methods we tested. This is especially noticeable during the cold-start period, but the same relative behavior essentially shows up during the whole time window of our experiments. COFIBA is a bit involved to implement, as contrasted to its competitors, and is also somewhat slower to run (unsurprisingly slower than, say, LINUCB-ONE and LINUCB-IND). On the other hand, COFIBA is far more effective in exploiting the collaborative effects embedded in the data, and still amenable to be run on large datasets.

6. REGRET ANALYSIS

The following theorem is the theoretical guarantee of COFIBA, where we relate the cumulative regret of COFIBA to the clustering structure of users $\mathcal{U}$ w.r.t. items $\mathcal{I}$. For simplicity of presentation, we formulate our result in the one-hot encoding case, where $\boldsymbol{u}_i \in \mathbb{R}^d$, $i = 1, \ldots, n$, and $\mathcal{I} = \{\boldsymbol{e}_1, \ldots, \boldsymbol{e}_d\}$. In fact, a more general statement can be proven which holds in the case when $\mathcal{I}$ is a generic set of feature vectors $\mathcal{I} = \{\boldsymbol{x}_1, \ldots, \boldsymbol{x}_{|\mathcal{I}|}\}$, and the regret bound depends on the geometric properties of such vectors.[7]

In order to obtain a provable advantage from our clusterability assumptions, extra conditions are needed on the way i_t and C_{i_t} are generated. The clusterability assumptions we can naturally take advantage of are those where, for most partitions $P(\boldsymbol{e}_h)$, the relative sizes of clusters over users are highly unbalanced. Translated into more practical terms, cluster unbalancedness amounts to saying that the universe of items $\mathcal{I}$ tends to influence users so as to determine a small number of major common behaviors (which need neither be the same nor involve the same users across items), along with a number of minor ones. As we saw in our experiments, this seems like a frequent behavior of users in some practical scenarios.

THEOREM 1. *Let the* COFIBA *algorithm of Figure 1 be run on a set of users* $\mathcal{U} = \{1, \ldots, n\}$ *with associated profile vectors* $\boldsymbol{u}_1, \ldots, \boldsymbol{u}_n \in \mathbb{R}^d$, *and set of items* $\mathcal{I} = \{\boldsymbol{e}_1, \ldots, \boldsymbol{e}_d\}$ *such that the h-th induced partition* $P(\boldsymbol{e}_h)$ *over* $\mathcal{U}$ *is made up of* m_h *clusters of cardinality* $v_{h,1}, v_{h,2}, \ldots, v_{h,m_h}$, *respectively. Moreover, let* g *be the number of* distinct *partitions so obtained. At each round* t, *let* i_t *be generated uniformly at random*[8] *from* $\mathcal{U}$. *Once* i_t *is selected, the number* c_t *of items in* C_{i_t} *is generated arbitrarily as a function of past indices* $i_1, \ldots, i_{t-1}$, *payoffs* $a_1, \ldots, a_{t-1}$, *and sets* $C_{i_1}, \ldots, C_{i_{t-1}}$, *as well as the current index* i_t. *Then the sequence of items in* C_{i_t} *is generated i.i.d. (conditioned on* i_t, c_t *and all past indices* $i_1, \ldots, i_{t-1}$, *payoffs* $a_1, \ldots, a_{t-1}$, *and sets* $C_{i_1}, \ldots, C_{i_{t-1}}$*) according to a given but unknown distribution* $\mathcal{D}$ *over* $\mathcal{I}$. *Let payoff* a_t *lie in the interval* $[-1, 1]$, *and be generated as described in Section 2 so that, conditioned on history, the expectation of* a_t *is* $\boldsymbol{u}_{i_t}^\top \bar{\boldsymbol{x}}_t$. *Finally, let parameters* α *and* α_2 *be suitable functions of* $\log(1/\delta)$. *If* $c_t \le c$ $\forall t$ *then, as* T *grows large, with probability at least*

[6]Without loss of generality, we take the first Yahoo dataset to provide statistics, for similar shapes of the bar plots can be established for the remaining ones.

[7]In addition, the function CB should be modified so as to incorporate these properties.

[8]Any distribution having positive probability on each $i \in \mathcal{U}$ would suffice here.

$1 - \delta$ *the cumulative regret satisfies*[9]

$$\sum_{t=1}^{T} r_t = \widetilde{\mathcal{O}}\left(\left(\mathbb{E}[S] + \sqrt{c\sqrt{mn}\,\text{VAR}(S)} + 1\right)\sqrt{\frac{dT}{n}}\right),$$

where $S = S(h) = \sum_{j=1}^{m_h} \sqrt{v_{h,j}}$, *h is a random index such that* $\boldsymbol{e}_h \sim \mathcal{D}$, *and* $\mathbb{E}[\cdot]$ *and* $\text{VAR}(\cdot)$ *denote, respectively, the expectation and the variance w.r.t. this random index.*

To get a feeling of how big (or small) $\mathbb{E}[S]$ and $\text{VAR}[S]$ can be, let us consider the case where each partition over users has a single big cluster and a number of small ones. To make it clear, consider the extreme scenario where each $P(\boldsymbol{e}_h)$ has one cluster of size $v_{h,1} = n - (m-1)$, and $m-1$ clusters of size $v_{h,j} = 1$, with $m < \sqrt{n}$. Then it is easy to see that $\mathbb{E}[S] = \sqrt{n-(m-1)} + m - 1$, and $\text{VAR}(S) = 0$, so that the resulting regret bound essentially becomes $\widetilde{\mathcal{O}}(\sqrt{dT})$, which is the standard regret bound one achieves for learning a *single* d-dimensional user (aka, the standard noncontextual bandit bound with d actions and no gap assumptions among them). At the other extreme lies the case when each partition $P(\boldsymbol{e}_h)$ has n-many clusters, so that $\mathbb{E}[S] = n$, $\text{VAR}(S) = 0$, and the resulting bound is $\widetilde{\mathcal{O}}(\sqrt{dnT})$. Looser upper bounds can be achieved in the case when $\text{VAR}(S) > 0$, where also the interplay with c starts becoming relevant. Finally, observe that the number g of distinct partitions influences the bound only indirectly through $\text{VAR}(S)$. Yet, it is worth repeating here that g plays a crucial role in the computational (both time and space) complexity of the whole procedure.

PROOF OF THEOREM 1. The proof sketch builds on the analysis in [1]. Let the true underlying clusters over the users be $V_{h,1}, V_{h,2}, \ldots, V_{h,m_h}$, with $|V_{h,j}| = v_{h,j}$. In [1], the authors show that, because each user i has probability $1/n$ to be the one served in round t, we have, with high probability, $\boldsymbol{w}_{i,t} \to \boldsymbol{u}_i$ for all i, as t grows large. Moreover, because of the gap assumption involving parameter γ, all edges connecting users belonging to different clusters at the user side will eventually be deleted (again, with high probability), after each user i is served at least $O(\frac{1}{\gamma^2})$ times. By the way edges are disconnected at the item side, the above is essentially independent (up to log factors due to union bounds) of which graph at the user side we are referring to. In turn, this entails that the current user clusters encoded by the connected components of graph $G^U_{t,h}$ will eventually converge to the m_h true user clusters (again, independent of h, up to log factors), so that the aggregate weight vectors $\bar{\boldsymbol{w}}_{N_k,t-1}$ computed by the algorithm for trading off exploration vs. exploitation in round t will essentially converge to $\boldsymbol{u}_{i_t}$ at a rate of the form[10]

$$\mathbb{E}\left[\frac{1}{\sqrt{1 + T_{h_t,j_t,t-1}/d}}\right], \qquad (1)$$

where h_t is the index of the true cluster over *items* that $\bar{\boldsymbol{x}}_t$ belongs to, j_t is the index of the true cluster over *users* that i_t belongs to (according to the partition of $\mathcal{U}$ determined by h_t), $T_{h_t,j_t,t-1}$ is the number of rounds so far where we happened to "hit" cluster V_{h_t,j_t}, i.e.,

$$T_{h_t,j_t,t-1} = |\{s \le t-1 \,:\, i_s \in V_{h_t,j_t}\}|,$$

and the expectation is w.r.t. both the (uniform) distribution of i_t, and distribution $\mathcal{D}$ generating the items in C_{i_t}, conditioned on all past events. Since, by the Azuma-Hoeffding inequality, $T_{h_t,j_t,t-1}$ concentrates as

$$T_{h_t,j_t,t-1} \approx \frac{t-1}{n} v_{h_t,j_t},$$

we have

$$(1) \approx \mathbb{E}_{\mathcal{D}}\left[\sum_{j=1}^{m_{h_t}} \frac{v_{h_t,j}}{n} \frac{1}{\sqrt{1 + \frac{t-1}{dn} v_{h_t,j}}}\right].$$

It is the latter expression that rules the cumulative regret of COFIBA in that, up to log factors:

$$\sum_{t=1}^{T} r_t \approx \sum_{t=1}^{T} \mathbb{E}_{\mathcal{D}}\left[\sum_{j=1}^{m_{h_t}} \frac{v_{h_t,j}}{n} \frac{1}{\sqrt{1 + \frac{t-1}{dn} v_{h_t,j}}}\right]. \qquad (2)$$

Eq. (2) is essentially (up to log factors and omitted additive terms) the regret bound one would obtain by knowning beforehand the latent clustering structure over $\mathcal{U}$.

Because $h_t \in C_{i_t}$ is itself a function of the items in C_{i_t}, we can eliminate the dependence on h_t by the following simple stratification argument. First of all, notice that

$$\sum_{j=1}^{m_{h_t}} \frac{v_{h_t,j}}{n} \frac{1}{\sqrt{1 + \frac{t-1}{dn} v_{h_t,j}}} \approx \sqrt{\frac{d}{nt}} \sum_{j=1}^{m_{h_t}} \sqrt{v_{h_t,j}}.$$

Then, we set for brevity $S(h) = \sum_{j=1}^{m_h} \sqrt{v_{h,j}}$, and let $h_{t,k}$ be the index of the true cluster over items that $\boldsymbol{x}_{t,k}$ belongs to (recall that $h_{t,k}$ is a random variable since so is $\boldsymbol{x}_{t,k}$). Since $S(h_{t,k}) \le \sqrt{mn}$, a standard argument shows that

$$\begin{aligned}\mathbb{E}_{\mathcal{D}}\left[S(h_t)\right] &\le \mathbb{E}_{\mathcal{D}}\left[\max_{k=1,\ldots,c_t} S(h_{t,k})\right] \\ &\le \mathbb{E}_{\mathcal{D}}[S(h_{t,1})] + \sqrt{c\sqrt{mn}\,\text{VAR}_{\mathcal{D}}(S(h_{t,1}))} + 1,\end{aligned}$$

so that, after some overapproximations, we conclude that $\sum_{t=1}^{T} r_t$ is upper bounded with high probability by

$$\widetilde{\mathcal{O}}\left(\left(\mathbb{E}_{\mathcal{D}}[S(h)] + \sqrt{c\sqrt{mn}\,\text{VAR}_{\mathcal{D}}(S(h))} + 1\right)\sqrt{\frac{dT}{n}}\right),$$

the expectation and the variance being over the random index h such that $\boldsymbol{e}_h \sim \mathcal{D}$. □

7. CONCLUSIONS

We have initiated an investigation of collaborative filtering bandit algorithms operating in relevant scenarios where multiple users can be grouped by behavior similarity in different ways w.r.t. items and, in turn, the universe of items can possibly be grouped by the similarity of clusterings they induce over users. We carried out an extensive experimental comparison with very encouraging results, and have also given a regret analysis which operates in a simplified scenario. Our algorithm can in principle be modified so as to be combined with any standard clustering (or co-clustering) technique. However, one advantage of encoding clusters as connected components of graphs (at least at the user side) is

[9] The $\widetilde{\mathcal{O}}$-notation hides logarithmic factors in n, m, g, T, d, $1/\delta$, as well as terms which are independent of T.

[10] Because $\mathcal{I} = \{\boldsymbol{e}_1, \ldots, \boldsymbol{e}_d\}$, the minimal eigenvalue λ of the process correlation matrix $\mathbb{E}[X\,X^\top]$ in [1] is here $1/d$. Moreover, compared to [1], we do not strive to capture the geometry of the user vectors $\boldsymbol{u}_i$ in the regret bound, hence we do not have the extra $\sqrt{m}$ factor occurring in their bound.

that we are quite effective in tackling the so-called *cold start* problem, for the newly served users are more likely to be connected to the old ones, which makes COFIBA in a position to automatically propagate information from the old users to the new ones through the aggregate vectors $\bar{w}_{N_k,t}$. In fact, so far we have not seen any other way of adaptively clustering users and items which is computationally affordable on sizeable datasets and, at the same time, amenable to a regret analysis that takes advantage of the clustering assumption.

All our experiments have been conducted in the setup of one-hot encoding, since the datasets at our disposal did not come with reliable/useful annotations on data. Yet, the algorithm we presented can clearly work when the items are accompanied by (numerical) features. One direction of our future research is to compensate for the lack of features in the data by first *inferring* features during an initial training phase through standard matrix factorization techniques, and subsequently applying our algorithm to a universe of items $\mathcal{I}$ described through such inferred features. Another line of experimental research would be to combine different bandit algorithms (possibly at different stages of the learning process) so as to roughly get the best of all of them in all stages. This would be somewhat similar to the meta-bandit construction described in [25]. Another one would be to combine with matrix factorization techniques as in, e.g., [20].

8. ACKNOWLEDGMENTS

We would like to thank the anonymous reviewers for their helpful and constructive comments. The first author thanks the support from MIUR and QCRI-HBKU. Also, the first and the third author acknowledge the support from Amazon AWS Award in Machine Learning Research Grant. The work leading to these results has received funding from the European Union's Seventh Framework Programme (FP7/ 2007-2013) under CrowdRec Grant Agreement n° 610594.

9. REFERENCES

[1] C. Gentile, S. Li, and G. Zappella. Online clustering of bandits. In *ICML*, 2014.

[2] N. Korda, B. Szorenyi, and S. Li, Distributed Clustering of Linear Bandits in Peer to Peer Networks. In *ICML*, 2016.

[3] Y. Abbasi-Yadkori, D. Pál, and C. Szepesvári. Improved algorithms for linear stochastic bandits. 2011.

[4] J.-Y. Audibert, R. Munos, and C. Szepesvári. Exploration-exploitation tradeoff using variance estimates in multi-armed bandits. *Theoretical Computer Science*, 410(19):1876–1902, 2009.

[5] P. Auer. Using confidence bounds for exploration-exploitation trade-offs. *Journal of Machine Learning Research*, 3:397–422, 2002.

[6] P. Auer, N. Cesa-Bianchi, and P. Fischer. Finite-time analysis of the multiarmed bandit problem. *Machine Learning*, 2001.

[7] M. G. Azar, A. Lazaric, and E. Brunskill. Sequential transfer in multi-armed bandit with finite set of models. In *NIPS*, pages 2220–2228, 2013.

[8] G. Bresler, G. Chen, and S. D. A latent source model for online collaborative filtering. In *NIPS*. MIT Press, 2014.

[9] E. Brunskill and L. Li. Sample complexity of multi-task reinforcement learning. In *UAI*, 2013.

[10] W. Cao, J. Li, Y. Tao, and Z. Li. On top-k selection in multi-armed bandits and hidden bipartite graphs. In *NIPS*, 2015.

[11] G. Cavallanti, N. Cesa-Bianchi, and C. Gentile. Tracking the best hyperplane with a simple budget perceptron. *Machine Learning*, 69/2:143–167, 2007.

[12] W. Chu, L. Li, L. Reyzin, and R. E. Schapire. Contextual bandits with linear payoff functions. In *AISTATS*, 2011.

[13] K. Crammer and C. Gentile. Multiclass classification with bandit feedback using adaptive regularization. In *ICML*, 2011.

[14] I. S. Dhillon. Co-clustering documents and words using bipartite spectral graph partitioning. In *7th KDD*, pages 269–274. ACM, 2001.

[15] I. S. Dhillon, S. Mallela, and D. S. Modha. Information-theoretic co-clustering. In *9th KDD*, pages 89–98, New York, NY, USA, 2003. ACM.

[16] J. Djolonga, A. Krause, and V. Cevher. High-dimensional gaussian process bandits. In *NIPS*, pages 1025–1033, 2013.

[17] M. Dudik, D. Erhan, J. Langford, and L. Li. Sample-efficient nonstationary-policy evaluation for contextual bandits. In *UAI*, 2012.

[18] T. George and S. Merugu. A scalable collaborative filtering framework based on co-clustering. In *5th ICDM*, pages 625–628. IEEE Computer Society, 2005.

[19] F. Hao, S. Li, G. Min, H. Kim, S. Yau, and L. Yang, An Efficient Approach to Generating Location-Sensitive Recommendations in Ad-hoc Social Network Environments. *IEEE Transactions on Services Computing*, 8:3, pp. 520–533, 2015.

[20] J. Kawale, H. Bui, B. Kveton, L. Thanh, and S. Chawla. Efficient thompson sampling for online matrix-factorization recommendation. In *NIPS*, 2015.

[21] A. Krause and C. Ong. Contextual gaussian process bandit optimization. In *25th NIPS*, 2011.

[22] B. Kveton, C. Szepesvari, Z. Wen, and A. Ashkan. Cascading bandits: Learning to rank in the cascade model. In *ICML*, 2015.

[23] L. Li, W. Chu, J. Langford, and R. Schapire. A contextual-bandit approach to personalized news article recommendation. In *WWW*, pages 661–670, 2010.

[24] S. Li, F. Hao, M. Li, and H.C. Kim. Medicine Rating Prediction and Recommendation in Mobile Social Networks. In *International Conference on Green, Pervasive and Cloud Computing*, 2013.

[25] L. Tang, Y. Jiang, L. Li, and T. Li. Ensemble contextual bandits for personalized recommendation. In *RecSys*, 2014.

[26] S. Li, C. Gentile, and A. Karatzoglou. Graph clustering bandits for recommendation. *arXiv*:1605.00596.

[27] O. Maillard and S. Mannor. Latent bandits. In *ICML*, 2014.

[28] E. Moroshko, N. Vaits, and K. Crammer. Second-order non-stationary online learning for regression. *Journal of Machine Learning Research*, 16:1481–1517, 2015.

[29] T. T. Nguyen and H. W. Lauw. Dynamic clustering of contextual multi-armed bandits. In *23rd CIKM*, pages 1959–1962. ACM, 2014.

[30] Y. Seldin, P. Auer, F. Laviolette, J. Shawe-Taylor, and R. Ortner. Pac-bayesian analysis of contextual bandits. In *NIPS*, pages 1683–1691, 2011.

[31] I. Sutskever, R. Salakhutdinov, and J. Tenenbaum. Modelling relational data using bayesian clustered tensor factorization. In *NIPS*, pages 1821–1828. MIT Press, 2009.

[32] L. Tang, Y. Jiang, L. Li, C. Zeng, and T. Li. Personalized recommendation via parameter-free contextual bandits. In *SIGIR*. ACM, 2015.

[33] K. Verstrepen and B. Goethals. Unifying nearest neighbors collaborative filtering. In *RecSys*, 2014.

[34] Y. Yue, S. A. Hong, and C. Guestrin. Hierarchical exploration for accelerating contextual bandits. In *ICML*, 2012.

Fast Matrix Factorization for Online Recommendation with Implicit Feedback*

Xiangnan He Hanwang Zhang Min-Yen Kan Tat-Seng Chua
School of Computing, National University of Singapore
{xiangnan, hanwang, kanmy, chuats}@comp.nus.edu.sg

ABSTRACT

This paper contributes improvements on both the effectiveness and efficiency of *Matrix Factorization* (MF) methods for implicit feedback. We highlight two critical issues of existing works. First, due to the large space of unobserved feedback, most existing works resort to assign a uniform weight to the missing data to reduce computational complexity. However, such a uniform assumption is invalid in real-world settings. Second, most methods are also designed in an offline setting and fail to keep up with the dynamic nature of online data.

We address the above two issues in learning MF models from implicit feedback. We first propose to weight the missing data based on item popularity, which is more effective and flexible than the uniform-weight assumption. However, such a non-uniform weighting poses efficiency challenge in learning the model. To address this, we specifically design a new learning algorithm based on the **e**lement-wise **A**lternating **L**east **S**quares (eALS) technique, for efficiently optimizing a MF model with variably-weighted missing data. We exploit this efficiency to then seamlessly devise an incremental update strategy that instantly refreshes a MF model given new feedback. Through comprehensive experiments on two public datasets in both offline and online protocols, we show that our eALS method consistently outperforms state-of-the-art implicit MF methods. Our implementation is available at https://github.com/hexiangnan/sigir16-eals.

Keywords

Matrix Factorization, Implicit Feedback, Item Recommendation, Online Learning, ALS, Coordinate Descent

1. INTRODUCTION

User personalization has become prevalent in modern recommender system. It helps to capture users' individualized preferences and has been shown to increase both satisfaction for users and revenue for content providers. Among its various methods, matrix factorization (MF) is the most popular and effective technique that characterizes users and items by vectors of latent factors [15, 32]. Early work on MF algorithms for recommendation [14, 27] have largely focused on explicit feedback, where users' ratings that directly reflect their preference on items are provided. These works formulated recommendation as a rating prediction problem for which the large volume of unobserved ratings (*i.e.*, missing data) are assumed to be extraneous for modeling user preference [12]. This greatly reduces the modeling workload, and many sophisticated methods have been devised, such as SVD++ [15] and timeSVD [14].

However, explicit ratings are not always available in many applications; more often, users interact with items through **implicit feedback**, *e.g.*, users' video viewing and product purchase history. Compared to explicit ratings, implicit feedback is easier to collect for content providers, but more challenging to utilize due to the natural scarcity of negative feedback. It has been shown that modeling only the observed, positive feedback results in biased representations in user profiles [4, 12]; *e.g.*, Marlin *et al.* [18] finds that users listen to music they expect to like and avoid the genres they dislike, leading to a severe bias in the observed data.

To solve the problem of lacking negative feedback (also known as the one-class problem [21]), a popular solution is to model all the missing data as negative feedback [12]. However, this adversely degrades the learning efficiency due to the full consideration of both observed and missing data. More importantly, the low efficiency makes it even more difficult to deploy implicit MF method **online** [29]. In practical recommender systems where new users, items and interactions are continuously streaming in, it is crucial to refresh the underlying model in real-time to best serve users. In this work, we concern the above two challenging problems of the MF method — implicit feedback and online learning. We note that we are not the first to consider both aspects for MF, as a recent work by Devooght *et al.* [4] has proposed an efficient implicit MF method for learning with dynamic data. However, we argue that Devooght's method [4] models missing data in an unrealistic, suboptimal way. Specifically, it assigns a uniform weight to the missing data, assuming that the missing entries are equally likely to be negative feedback. However, such an assumption limits model's fidelity and flexibility for real applications. For example, content providers usually know which items have been frequently featured to users but seldom clicked; such items are more likely to be

*NExT research is supported by the National Research Foundation, Prime Minister's Office, Singapore under its IRC@SG Funding Initiative.

SIGIR '16, July 17-21, 2016, Pisa, Italy
© 2016 ACM. ISBN 978-1-4503-4069-4/16/07...$15.00
DOI: http://dx.doi.org/10.1145/2911451.2911489

true negative assessments and should be weighted higher than others. In addition, Devooght's method learns parameters through gradient descent, requiring an expensive line search to determine the best learning rate at each step.

We propose a new MF method aimed at learning from implicit feedback effectively while satisfying the requirement of online learning. We develop a new learning algorithm that efficiently optimizes the implicit MF model without imposing a uniform-weight restriction on missing data. In particular, we assign the weight of missing data based on the popularity of items, which is arguably more effective than the previous methods [4, 12, 23, 30, 31] that are limited by the uniformity assumption. Our eALS algorithm is fast in accounting for missing data — analytically K times faster than ALS [12] where K denotes number of latent factors — the same time complexity with the recent dynamic MF solution [4]. This level of efficiency makes eALS suitable for learning online, for which we develop an incremental update strategy that instantly refreshes model parameters given new incoming data. Another key advantage of eALS is that it works without learning rate, bypassing the well-known difficulty for tuning gradient descent methods such as [4] and *Stochastic Gradient Descent* (SGD) [25].

We summarize our key contributions as follows.

1. We propose an item popularity-aware weighting scheme on the full missing data that effectively tailors the MF model for learning from implicit feedback.
2. We develop a new algorithm for learning model parameters efficiently and devise an incremental update strategy to support real-time online learning.
3. We conduct extensive experiments with both offline and online protocols on two real-world datasets, showing that our method consistently outperforms state-of-the-art implicit MF methods.

2. RELATED WORK

Handling missing data is obligatory for learning from implicit data due to the lack of negative feedback. To this end, two strategies have been proposed — **sample based learning** [21, 25] that samples negative instances from missing data, or **whole-data based learning** [12, 30] that treats all missing data as negative. Both methods have pros and cons: sample-based methods are more efficient by reducing negative examples in training, but risk decreasing the model's predictiveness; whole-based methods model the full data with a potentially higher coverage, but inefficiency can be an issue. To retain model's fidelity, we persist in the whole-data based learning, developing a fast ALS-based algorithm to resolve the inefficiency issue.

For existing whole-data based methods [4, 12, 23, 30, 31], one major limitation is in the uniform weighting on missing entries, which favors algorithm's efficiency but limits model's flexibility and extensibility. The only works that have considered non-uniform weighting are from Pan *et al.* [20, 21]; however their cubic time complexity *w.r.t.* K makes it unsuitable to run on large-scale data [23], where a large number of factors needs to be considered to gain improved performance [31].

To optimize MF, various learners have been investigated, including SGD [14, 25], *Coordinate Descent* (CD) [4, 32], and *Markov Chain Monto Carlo* (MCMC) [26]. SGD is the most popular one owing to the ease of derivation, however, it is unsuitable for whole-data based MF [12] due to the large amount of training instances (the full user–item interaction matrix is considered). ALS can be seen as an instantiation of CD and has been widely used to solve the whole-based MF [12, 20, 21, 30]; however, its inefficiency is the main obstacle for practical use [23, 31]. To resolve this, [23] describes an approximate solution to ALS. Recently, [4] employs the *Randomized block Coordinate Descent* (RCD) learner [28], reducing the complexity and applying it to a dynamic scenario. Similarly, [31] enriches the implicit feedback matrix with neighbor-based similarly, followed by applying unweighted SVD. Distinct from previous works, we propose an efficient element-wise ALS solution for the whole-data based MF with non-uniform missing data, which has never been studied before.

Another important aspect for practical recommender system lies in handling the dynamic nature of incoming data, for which timeliness is a key consideration. As it is prohibitive to retrain the full model online, various works have developed incremental learning strategies for neighbor-based [13], graph-based [9], probabilistic [3] and MF [4, 5, 17, 27] methods. For MF, different learners have been studied for online updating, including SGD [5, 27], RCD [4] and dual-averaging [17]. To our knowledge, this work is the first attempt to exploit the ALS technique for online learning.

3. PRELIMINARIES

We first introduce the whole-data based MF method for learning from implicit data, highlighting the inefficiency issue of the conventional ALS solution [12, 21]. Then we describe eALS, an element-wise ALS learner [26] that can reduce the time complexity to linearity *w.r.t.* number of factors. Although the learner is generic in optimizing MF with all kinds of weighting strategies, the form introduced is costly in accounting for all missing data and is thus unrealistic for practical use. This defect motivates us to further develop eALS to make it suitable for learning from implicit feedback (details in Section 4.2).

3.1 MF Method for Implicit Feedback

We start by introducing some basic notation. For a user–item interaction matrix $\mathbf{R} \in \mathbb{R}^{M\times N}$, M and N denote the number of users and items, respectively; $\mathcal{R}$ denotes the set of user–item pairs whose values are non-zero. We reserve the index u to denote a user and i to denote an item. Vector $\mathbf{p}_u$ denotes the latent feature vector for u, and set $\mathcal{R}_u$ denotes the set of items that are interacted by u; similar notations for $\mathbf{q}_i$ and $\mathcal{R}_i$. Matrices $\mathbf{P} \in \mathbb{R}^{M\times K}$ and $\mathbf{Q} \in \mathbb{R}^{N\times K}$ denote the latent factor matrix for users and items.

Matrix factorization maps both users and items into a joint latent feature space of K dimension such that interactions are modeled as inner products in that space. Mathematically, each entry r_{ui} of $\mathbf{R}$ is estimated as:

$$\hat{r}_{ui} = < \mathbf{p}_u, \mathbf{q}_i > = \mathbf{p}_u^T \mathbf{q}_i. \quad (1)$$

The item recommendation problem is formulated as estimating the scoring function $\hat{r}_{ui}$, which is used to rank items. Note that this basic model subsumes the biased MF [14], commonly used in modeling explicit ratings:

$$\hat{r}_{ui} = b_u + b_i + < \mathbf{p}_u^B, \mathbf{q}_i^B >,$$

where b_u (b_i) captures the bias of user u (item i) in giving (receiving) ratings. To recover it, set $\mathbf{p}_u \leftarrow [\mathbf{p}_u^B, b_u, 1]$ and

$\mathbf{q}_i \leftarrow [\mathbf{q}_i^B, 1, b_i]$. As such, we adopt the basic MF model to make notations simple and also to enable a fair comparison with baselines [4, 12] that also complied with the basic model.

To learn model parameters, Hu *et al.* [12] introduced a weighted regression function, which associates a confidence to each prediction in the implicit feedback matrix $\mathbf{R}$:

$$J = \sum_{u=1}^{M}\sum_{i=1}^{N} w_{ui}(r_{ui} - \hat{r}_{ui})^2 + \lambda(\sum_{u=1}^{M} ||\mathbf{p}_u||^2 + \sum_{i=1}^{N} ||\mathbf{q}_i||^2), \quad (2)$$

where w_{ui} denotes the weight of entry r_{ui} and we use $\mathbf{W} = [w_{ui}]_{M\times N}$ to represent the weight matrix. λ controls the strength of regularization, which is usually an L_2 norm to prevent overfitting. Note that in implicit feedback learning, missing entries are usually assigned to a zero r_{ui} value but non-zero w_{ui} weight, both crucial to performance.

3.2 Optimization by ALS

Alternating Least Square (ALS) is a popular approach to optimize regression models such as MF and graph regularization [10]. It works by iteratively optimizing one parameter, while leaving the others fixed. The prerequisite of ALS is that the optimization sub-problem can be analytically solved. Here, we describe how Hu's work [12] solves this problem.

First, minimizing J with respect to user latent vector $\mathbf{p}_u$ is equivalent to minimizing:

$$J_u = ||\mathbf{W}^u(\mathbf{r}_u - \mathbf{Q}\mathbf{p}_u)||^2 + \lambda||\mathbf{p}_u||^2,$$

where $\mathbf{W}^u$ is a $N \times N$ diagonal matrix with $W_{ii}^u = w_{ui}$. The minimum is where the first-order derivative is 0:

$$\begin{aligned} \frac{\partial J_u}{\partial \mathbf{p}_u} &= 2\mathbf{Q}^T\mathbf{W}^u\mathbf{Q}\mathbf{p}_u - 2\mathbf{Q}^T\mathbf{W}^u\mathbf{r}_u + 2\lambda\mathbf{p}_u = 0 \\ \Rightarrow \quad \mathbf{p}_u &= (\mathbf{Q}^T\mathbf{W}^u\mathbf{Q} + \lambda\mathbf{I})^{-1}\mathbf{Q}^T\mathbf{W}^u\mathbf{r}_u, \end{aligned} \quad (3)$$

where $\mathbf{I}$ denotes the identity matrix. This analytical solution is also known as the *ridge regression* [23]. Following the same process, we can get the solution for $\mathbf{q}_i$.

3.2.1 *Efficiency Issue with ALS*

As we can see, in order to update a latent vector, inverting a $K \times K$ matrix is inevitable. Matrix inversion is an expensive operation, usually assumed $O(K^3)$ in time complexity [12]. As such, updating one user latent vector takes time $O(K^3 + NK^2)$. Thus, the overall time complexity of one iteration that updates all model parameters once is $O((M+N)K^3 + MNK^2)$. Clearly, this high complexity makes the algorithm impractical to run on large-scale data, where there can be millions of users and items and billions of interactions.

Speed-up with Uniform Weighting. To reduce the high time complexity, Hu *et al.* [12] applied a uniform weight to missing entries; *i.e.*, assuming that all zero entries in $\mathbf{R}$ have a same weight w_0. Through this simplification, they can speed up the computation with memoization:

$$\mathbf{Q}^T\mathbf{W}^u\mathbf{Q} = w_0\mathbf{Q}^T\mathbf{Q} + \mathbf{Q}^T(\mathbf{W}^u - \mathbf{W}^0)\mathbf{Q}, \quad (4)$$

where $\mathbf{W}^0$ is a diagonal matrix that each diagonal element is w_0. As $\mathbf{Q}^T\mathbf{Q}$ is independent of u, it can be pre-computed for updating all user latent vectors. Considering the fact that $\mathbf{W}^u - \mathbf{W}^0$ only has $|\mathcal{R}_u|$ non-zero entries, we can compute Eq. (4) in $O(|\mathcal{R}_u|K^2)$ time. Thus, the time complexity of ALS is reduced to $O((M+N)K^3 + |\mathcal{R}|K^2)$.

Even so, we argue that the $O((M+N)K^3)$ term can be a major cost when $(M+N)K \geq |\mathcal{R}|$. In addition, the $O(|\mathcal{R}|K^2)$ part is still much higher than in SGD [25], which only requires $O(|\mathcal{R}|K)$ time. As a result, even with the acceleration, ALS is still prohibitive for running on large data, where large K is crucial as it can lead to better generalizability and thus better prediction performance. Moreover, the uniform weighting assumption is usually invalid in real applications and adversely degrades model's predictiveness. This thus motivates us to design an efficient implicit MF method not subject to uniform-weights.

3.3 Generic Element-wise ALS Learner

The bottleneck of the previous ALS solution lies in the matrix inversion operation, which is due to the design that updates the latent vector for a user (item) as a whole. As such, it is natural to optimize parameters at the element level — optimizing each coordinate of the latent vector, while leaving the others fixed [26]. To achieve this, we first get the derivative of objective function Eq. (2) with respect to p_{uf}:

$$\frac{\partial J}{\partial p_{uf}} = -2\sum_{i=1}^{N}(r_{ui} - \hat{r}_{ui}^f)w_{ui}q_{if} + 2p_{uf}\sum_{i=1}^{N} w_{ui}q_{if}^2 + 2\lambda p_{uf},$$

where $\hat{r}_{ui}^f = \hat{r}_{ui} - p_{uf}q_{if}$, *i.e.*, the prediction without the component of latent factor f. By setting this derivative to 0, we obtain the solution of p_{uf}:

$$p_{uf} = \frac{\sum_{i=1}^{N}(r_{ui} - \hat{r}_{ui}^f)w_{ui}q_{if}}{\sum_{i=1}^{N} w_{ui}q_{if}^2 + \lambda}. \quad (5)$$

Similarly, we can get the solver for an item latent factor:

$$q_{if} = \frac{\sum_{u=1}^{M}(r_{ui} - \hat{r}_{ui}^f)w_{ui}p_{uf}}{\sum_{i=1}^{M} w_{ui}p_{uf}^2 + \lambda}. \quad (6)$$

Given the closed-form solution that optimizes one parameter with other fixed, the algorithm iteratively executes it for all model parameters until a joint optimum is reached. Due to the non-convexity of the objective function, critical points where gradients vanish can be local minima.

Time Complexity. As can be seen, by performing optimization at the element level, the expensive matrix inversion can be avoided. A raw implementation takes $O(MNK^2)$ time for one iteration, directly speeding up ALS by eliminating the $O(K^3)$ term. Moreover, by pre-computing $\hat{r}_{ui}$ [26], we can calculate $\hat{r}_{ui}^f$ in $O(1)$ time rather than $O(K)$. As such, the complexity can be further reduced to $O(MNK)$, which is the same magnitude with evaluating all the user–item predictions.

4. OUR IMPLICIT MF METHOD

We first propose an item-oriented weighting scheme on the missing data, and follow with a popularity-aware weighting strategy, which is arguably more effective than the uniform weighting for the recommendation task. Then, we develop a fast eALS algorithm to optimize the objective function that significantly reduces learning complexity comparing with the conventional ALS [12] and generic element-wise ALS learner [26]. Lastly, we discuss how to adjust the learning algorithm for real-time online learning.

4.1 Item-Oriented Weighting on Missing Data

Due to the large space of items, the missing entries for a user are a mixture of negative and unknown feedback. In specifying the weight w_{ui} of missing entries, it is desired to assign a higher weight to the negative feedback. However, it is a well-known difficulty to differentiate the two cases. In addition, as the interaction matrix $\mathbf{R}$ is usually large and sparse, it will be too consuming to store each zero entry an individualized weight. To this end, existing works [4, 12, 23, 30, 31] have applied a simple uniform weight on missing entries, which are, however, suboptimal and non-extendable for real applications.

Considering the ease of content providers in accessing negative information of the item side (*e.g.,* which items have been promoted to users but receive little interaction), we believe it is more realistic to weight missing data based on some item property. To capture this, we devise a more fine-grained objective function as follows:

$$L = \sum_{(u,i)\in\mathcal{R}} w_{ui}(r_{ui} - \hat{r}_{ui})^2 + \sum_{u=1}^{M}\sum_{i\notin\mathcal{R}_u} c_i\hat{r}_{ui}^2 + \lambda(\sum_{u=1}^{M}||\mathbf{p}_u||^2 + \sum_{i=1}^{N}||\mathbf{q}_i||^2), \tag{7}$$

where c_i denotes the confidence that item i missed by users is a true negative assessment, which can serve as a means to encode domain knowledge from practitioners. It is clear that the first term denotes the prediction error of the observed entries, which has been widely adopted in modeling explicit ratings [15, 27]. The second term accounts for the missing data, which acts as the role of negative instances and is crucial for recommendation from implicit feedback [12, 25]. Next, we present a domain-independent strategy to determine c_i by leveraging a ubiquitous feature of modern Web 2.0 systems.

4.1.1 Popularity-aware Weighting Strategy

Existing visual interfaces of many Web 2.0 systems showcase popular items in their recommendations. All other factors being equal, popular items are more likely to be known by users in general [10], and thus it is reasonable to think that a miss on a popular item is more probable to be truly irrelevant (as opposed to unknown) to the user. To account for this effect, we parametrize c_i based on item's popularity:

$$c_i = c_0 \frac{f_i^\alpha}{\sum_{j=1}^{N} f_j^\alpha}, \tag{8}$$

where f_i denotes the popularity of item i, given by its frequency in the implicit feedback data: $|\mathcal{R}_i|/\sum_{j=1}^{N}|\mathcal{R}_j|$, and c_0 determines the overall weight of missing data. Exponent α controls the significance level of popular items over unpopular ones — when $\alpha > 1$ the weights of popular items are promoted to strengthen the difference against unpopular ones; while setting α within the lower range of $(0, 1)$ suppresses the weight of popular items and has a smoothing effect. We empirically find $\alpha = 0.5$ usually leads to good results. Note that the uniform weighting is a special case by setting α to 0 with $w_0 = c_0/N$.

Relationship to Negative Sampling. Our proposed popularity-aware weighting strategy has the same intuition with Rendle's popularity-based oversampling [24] for learning BPR, which basically samples popular items as negative feedback with a higher probability. However, [24] empirically shows the oversampling method underperforms the basic uniform sampler. We suspect the reason comes from the SGD learner, which will result in more gradient steps on popular items, due to oversampling. As a result, popular items may be over-trained locally at the expense of less popular items which would then be under-trained. To resolve this, tricks like subsampling frequent items [19] and adaptive learning rates like Adagrad [6] have been adopted in other domains. As the focus of this paper is on whole-data based implicit MF, we do not further explore the details of SGD. It is worth pointing out that our proposed eALS learner avoids these learning issues by an exact optimization on each model parameter.

4.2 Fast eALS Learning Algorithm

We can speed up learning by avoiding the massive repeated computations introduced by the weighted missing data. We detail the derivation process for p_{uf}; where the counterpart for q_{if} is achieved likewise.

First, we rewrite the p_{uf} update rule Eq. (5) by separating the observed data part:

$$p_{uf} = \frac{\sum_{i\in\mathcal{R}_u}(r_{ui} - \hat{r}_{ui}^f)w_{ui}q_{if} - \sum_{i\notin\mathcal{R}_u}\hat{r}_{ui}^f c_i q_{if}}{\sum_{i\in\mathcal{R}_u} w_{ui}q_{if}^2 + \sum_{i\notin\mathcal{R}_u} c_i q_{if}^2 + \lambda}.$$

Clearly, the computational bottleneck lies in the summation over missing data portion, which requires a traversal of the whole negative space. We first focus on the numerator:

$$\begin{aligned}\sum_{i\notin\mathcal{R}_u}\hat{r}_{ui}^f c_i q_{if} &= \sum_{i=1}^{N} c_i q_{if}\sum_{k\neq f} p_{uk}q_{ik} - \sum_{i\in\mathcal{R}_u}\hat{r}_{ui}^f c_i q_{if} \\ &= \sum_{k\neq f} p_{uk}\sum_{i=1}^{N} c_i q_{if} q_{ik} - \sum_{i\in\mathcal{R}_u}\hat{r}_{ui}^f c_i q_{if}.\end{aligned} \tag{9}$$

By this reformulation, we can see that the major computation — the $\sum_{i=1}^{N} c_i q_{if} q_{ik}$ term that iterates over all items — is independent of u. However, a naïve implementation repeatedly computes it unnecessarily, when updating the latent factors for different users. Clearly, we can achieve a significant speed-up by memoizing it.

We define the $\mathbf{S}^q$ cache as $\mathbf{S}^q = \sum_{i=1}^{N} c_i \mathbf{q}_i \mathbf{q}_i^T$, which can be pre-computed and used in updating the latent factors for all users. Then, Eq. (9) can be evaluated as:

$$\sum_{i\notin\mathcal{R}_u}\hat{r}_{ui}^f c_i q_{if} = \sum_{k\neq f} p_{uk} s_{fk}^q - \sum_{i\in\mathcal{R}_u}\hat{r}_{ui}^f c_i q_{if}, \tag{10}$$

which can be done in $O(K + |\mathcal{R}_u|)$ time.

Similarly, we can apply the cache to speed up the calculation of denominator:

$$\sum_{i\notin\mathcal{R}_u} c_i q_{if}^2 = \sum_{i=1}^{N} c_i q_{if}^2 - \sum_{i\in\mathcal{R}_u} c_i q_{if}^2 = s_{ff}^q - \sum_{i\in\mathcal{R}_u} c_i q_{if}^2. \tag{11}$$

To summarize the above memoization strategy, we give the update rule for p_{uf} with the use of $\mathbf{S}^q$ cache:

$$p_{uf} = \frac{\sum_{i\in\mathcal{R}_u}[w_{ui}r_{ui} - (w_{ui} - c_i)\hat{r}_{ui}^f]q_{if} - \sum_{k\neq f} p_{uk}s_{kf}^q}{\sum_{i\in\mathcal{R}_u}(w_{ui} - c_i)q_{if}^2 + s_{ff}^q + \lambda}. \tag{12}$$

Algorithm 1: Fast eALS Learning algorithm.

```
   Input: R, K, λ, W and item confidence vector c;
   Output: Latent feature matrix P and Q;
1  Randomly initialize P and Q ;
2  for (u,i) ∈ R do  r̂_ui ← Eq. (1) ;                    ▷ O(|R|K)
3  while Stopping criteria is not met do
       // Update user factors
4      S^q = Σ_{i=1}^{N} c_i q_i q_i^T ;                   ▷ O(MK^2)
5      for u ← 1 to M do                                 ▷ O(MK^2 + |R|K)
6          for f ← 1 to K do
7              for i ∈ R_u do r̂^f_ui ← r̂_ui − p_uf q_if ;
8              p_uf ← Eq. (12) ;                          ▷ O(K + |R_u|)
9              for i ∈ R_u do r̂_ui ← r̂^f_ui + p_uf q_if ;
10         end
11     end
       // Update item factors
12     S^p ← P^T P ;                                      ▷ O(NK^2)
13     for i ← 1 to N do                                 ▷ O(NK^2 + |R|K)
14         for f ← 1 to K do
15             for u ∈ R_i do r̂^f_ui ← r̂_ui − p_uf q_if ;
16             q_if ← Eq. (13) ;                          ▷ O(K + |R_i|)
17             for u ∈ R_i do r̂_ui ← r̂^f_ui + p_uf q_if ;
18         end
19     end
20 end
21 return P and Q
```

Table 1: Time complexity of implicit MF methods.

Method	Time Complexity
ALS (Hu *et al.*[12])	$O((M+N)K^3 + \|\mathcal{R}\|K^2)$
BPR (Rendle *et al.*[25])	$O(\|\mathcal{R}\|K)$
IALS1 (Pilászy *et al.*[23])	$O(K^3 + (M+N)K^2 + \|\mathcal{R}\|K)$
ii-SVD (Volkovs *et al.*[31])	$O((M+N)K^2 + MN \log K)$
RCD (Devooght *et al.*[4])	$O((M+N)K^2 + \|\mathcal{R}\|K)$
eALS (Algorithm 1)	$O((M+N)K^2 + \|\mathcal{R}\|K)$

$|\mathcal{R}|$ denotes the number of non-zeros in user–item matrix $\mathbf{R}$.

Similarly, we can derive the update rule for q_{if}:

$$q_{if} = \frac{\sum_{u \in \mathcal{R}_i}[w_{ui} r_{ui} - (w_{ui} - c_i)\hat{r}^f_{ui}] p_{uf} - c_i \sum_{k \neq f} q_{ik} s^p_{kf}}{\sum_{u \in \mathcal{R}_i}(w_{ui} - c_i) p^2_{uf} + c_i s^p_{ff} + \lambda}, \tag{13}$$

where s^p_{kf} denotes the $(k,f)^{th}$ element of the $\mathbf{S}^p$ cache, defined as $\mathbf{S}^p = \mathbf{P}^T\mathbf{P}$.

Algorithm 1 summarizes the accelerated algorithm for our element-wise ALS learner, or **eALS**. For convergence, one can either monitor the value of objective function on training set or check the prediction performance on a hold-out validation data.

4.2.1 *Discussion*

Time Complexity. In Algorithm 1, updating a user latent factor takes $O(K + |\mathcal{R}_u|)$ time. Thus, one eALS iteration takes $O((M+N)K^2 + |R|K)$ time. Table 1 summarizes the time complexity (of one iteration or epoch) of other MF algorithms that are designed for implicit feedback.

Comparing with the vector-wise ALS [12, 21], our element-wise ALS learner is K times faster. In addition, our proposed eALS has the same time complexity with RCD [4], being faster than ii-SVD [31], another recent solution. RCD is a state-of-the-art learner for whole-data based MF, which performs a gradient descent step on a randomly chosen latent vector. Since it requires a good learning rate, the work [4] adaptively determines it by a line search in each gradient step, which essentially chooses the learning rate that leads to the steepest descent among pre-defined candidates. A major advantage of eALS has over RCD is that it avoids the need for a learning rate by an exact optimization in each parameter update, arguably more effective and easier to use than RCD. The most efficient algorithm is BPR, which applies the SGD learner on sampled, partial missing data only.

Computing the Objective Function. Evaluating the objective function is important to check the convergence of iterations and also to verify the correctness of implementation. A direct calculation takes $O(MNK)$ time, requiring a full estimation on the $\mathbf{R}$ matrix. Fortunately, with the item-oriented weighting, we can similarly exploit the sparseness of $\mathbf{R}$ for acceleration. To achieve this, we reformulate the loss of the missing data part that causes the major cost:

$$\sum_{u=1}^{M} \sum_{i \notin \mathcal{R}_u} c_i \hat{r}^2_{ui} = \sum_{u=1}^{M} \mathbf{p}_u^T \mathbf{S}^q \mathbf{p}_u - \sum_{(u,i) \in \mathcal{R}} c_i \hat{r}^2_{ui}. \tag{14}$$

By reusing $\mathbf{S}^q$ and the prediction cache $\hat{r}_{ui}$, we can calculate the objective function in $O(|\mathcal{R}| + MK^2)$ time, much faster than with direct calculation.

Parallel Learning. The iterations of eALS can be easily parallelized. First, computing the $\mathbf{S}$ caches (line 4 and 12) is the standard matrix multiplication operation, for which modern matrix toolkits provide very efficient and parallelized implementation. Second, in updating the latent vectors for different users (line 5-11), the shared parameters are either independent with each other (*i.e.,* $\hat{r}_{ui}$) or remaining unchanged (*i.e.,* $\mathbf{S}^q$). This nice property means that an exact parallel solution can be obtained by separating the updates by users; that is, letting different workers update the model parameters for disjoint sets of users. The same parallelism can also be achieved in updating item latent vectors.

This is an advantage over the commonly-used SGD learner, which is a stochastic method that updates model parameters given a training instance. In SGD, different gradient steps can influence with each other and there is no exact way to separate the updates for workers. Thus, sophisticated strategies are required to control the possible losses introduced by parallelization [7]. Our proposed eALS solution optimizes by coordinate descent where in each step a dedicated parameter is updated, making the algorithm embarrassingly parallel without any approximate loss.

4.3 Online Update

In practice, after a recommender model is trained offline on historical data, it will be used online and will need to adapt to best serve users. Here, we consider the online learning scenario that refreshes model parameters given a new user–item interaction.

Incremental Updating. Let $\hat{\mathbf{P}}$ and $\hat{\mathbf{Q}}$ denote the model parameters learnt from offline training, and (u,i) denotes the new interaction streamed in. To approximate the model parameters in accounting for the new interaction, we perform optimization steps for $\mathbf{p}_u$ and $\mathbf{q}_i$ only. The underlying assumption is that the new interaction should not change $\hat{\mathbf{P}}$ and $\hat{\mathbf{Q}}$ too much from a global perspective, while it should

Algorithm 2: Online Incremental Updates for eALS.

Input: $\hat{\mathbf{P}}$, $\hat{\mathbf{Q}}$, new interaction (u, i) and its weight w_{new}
Output: Refreshed parameters $\mathbf{P}$ and $\mathbf{Q}$;

1 $\mathbf{P} \leftarrow \hat{\mathbf{P}}$; $\mathbf{Q} \leftarrow \hat{\mathbf{Q}}$; ;
2 **If** u is a new user **do** Randomly initialize $\mathbf{p}_u$;
3 **If** i is a new item **do** Randomly initialize $\mathbf{q}_i$;
4 $r_{ui} \leftarrow 1$; $\hat{r}_{ui} \leftarrow Eq. (1)$; $w_{ui} \leftarrow w_{new}$;
5 **while** *Stopping criteria is not met* **do**
  `// Line 6-10 of Algorithm 1`
6   update_user(u); ; $\triangleright\ O(K^2 + |\mathcal{R}_u|K)$
7   update_cache(u, $\mathbf{S}^p$); ; $\triangleright\ O(K^2)$
  `// Line 14-18 of Algorithm 1`
8   update_item(i); ; $\triangleright\ O(K^2 + |\mathcal{R}_i|K)$
9   update_cache(i, $\mathbf{S}^q$); ; $\triangleright\ O(K^2)$
10 **end**
11 **return** ***P*** *and* ***Q***

change the local features for u and i significantly. Particularly, when u is a new user, executing the local updates will force $\mathbf{p}_u$ close to $\mathbf{q}_i$, which meets the expectation of latent factor model. The new item case is similar.

Algorithm 2 summarizes the incremental learning strategy for eALS. For the stopping criteria, our empirical study shows that one iteration is usually sufficient to get good results. Moreover, it is important to note that after updating a latent vector, we need to update the $\mathbf{S}$ cache accordingly.

Weight of New Interactions. In an online system, new interactions are more reflective of a user's short-term interest. Comparing to the historical interactions used in offline training, fresh data should be assigned a higher weight for predicting user's future action. We assign a weight w_{new} to each new interaction (line 4 of Algorithm 2) as a tunable parameter. Later in Section 5.3, we investigate how the setting of this parameter impacts online learning performance.

Time Complexity. The incremental update for a new interaction (u, i) can be done in $O(K^2 + (|\mathcal{R}_u| + |\mathcal{R}_i|)K)$ time. It is worth noting that the cost depends on the number of observed interactions for u and i, while being independent with number of total interactions, users and items. This localized complexity make the online learning algorithm suitable to deployment in industrial use, as the complex software stack that deals with data dependencies [29] can be avoided.

5. EXPERIMENTS

We begin by introducing the experimental settings. Then we perform an empirical study with the traditional offline protocol, followed by a more realistic online protocol.

5.1 Experimental Settings

Datasets. We evaluate on two publicly accessible datasets: Yelp[1] and Amazon Movies[2]. We transform the review dataset into implicit data, where each entry is marked as 0/1 indicating whether the user reviewed the item. Since the high sparsity of the original datasets makes it difficult to evaluate recommendation algorithms (*e.g.,* over half users have only one review), we follow the common practice [25] to filter out users and items with less than 10 interactions. Table 2 summarizes the statistics of the filtered datasets.

Table 2: Statistics of the evaluation datasets.

Dataset	Review#	Item#	User#	Sparsity
Yelp	731,671	25,815	25,677	99.89%
Amazon	5,020,705	75,389	117,176	99.94 %

Methodology. We evaluate using two protocols:

- **Offline Protocol**. We adopt the *leave-one-out* evaluation, where the latest interaction of each user is held out for prediction and the models are trained on the remaining data. Although it is a widely used evaluation protocol in the literature [9, 25], we point out that it is an artificial split that does not correspond to the real recommendation scenario. In addition, the new users problem is averted in this evaluation, as each test user has a training history. Thus this protocol only evaluates an algorithm's capability in providing one-shot recommendation for existing users by leveraging the static history data.

- **Online Protocol**. To create a more realistic recommendation scenario, we simulate the dynamic data stream. We first sort all interactions in chronological order, training models on the first 90% of the interactions and holding out the last 10% for testing. In the testing phase, given a test interaction (*i.e.,* a user–item pair) from the hold-out data, the model first recommends a ranked list of items to the user; the performance is judged based on the ranked list. Then the test interaction is fed into the model for an incremental update. Note that with the global split by time, 14% and 57% test interactions are from new users for the Yelp and Amazon dataset, respectively. Overall this protocol evaluates an online learning algorithm's effectiveness in digesting the dynamic new data.

To assess the ranked list with the ground-truth (GT) item that user actually consumed, we adopt *Hit Ratio* (HR) and *Normalized Discounted Cumulative Gain* (NDCG). We truncate the ranked list at 100 for both metrics. HR measures whether the ground truth item is present on the ranked list, while NDCG accounts for the position of hit [9]. We report the score averaged by all test interactions.

Baselines. We compare with the following methods:

- **ALS** [12]. This is the conventional ALS method that optimizes the whole-data based MF. Due to the high time complexity, this method is infeasible in a real-time dynamic updating scenario, so we only evaluate it with the offline protocol.

- **RCD** [4]. This is the state-of-the-art implicit MF method that has the same time complexity with eALS and is suitable for online learning. For the line search parameters, we use the suggested values in the authors' implementation[3].

- **BPR** [25]. This is a sample-based method that optimizes the pair-wise ranking between the positive and negative samples. It learns by SGD, which can be adjusted to online incremental learning by [27]. We use a fixed learning rate, varying it and reporting the best performance.

Parameter Settings. For the weight of observed interactions, we set it uniformly as 1, a default setting by previous works [4, 25]. For regularization, we set λ as 0.01 for all methods for a fair comparison. All methods are implemented in Java and running on the same machine (Intel

[1]We used the Yelp Challenge dataset downloaded on October 2015 that contained 1.6 million reviews: http://www.yelp.com/dataset_challenge

[2]http://snap.stanford.edu/data/web-Amazon-links.html

[3]https://github.com/rdevooght/MF-with-prior-and-updates

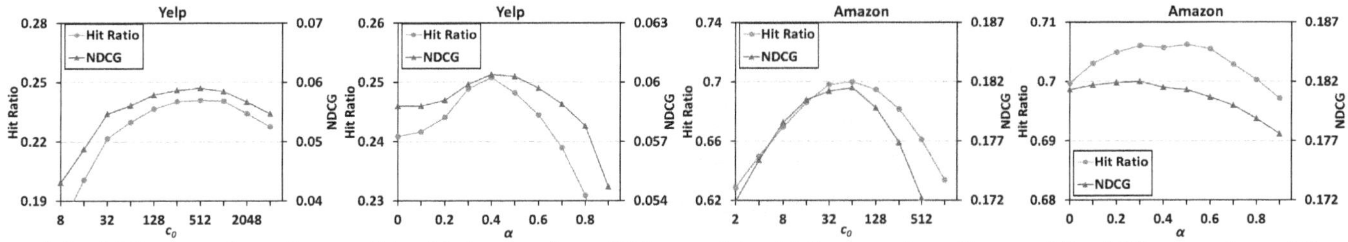

(a) eALS vs. c_0 ($\alpha = 0$) (b) eALS vs. α ($c_0 = 512$) (c) eALS vs. c_0 ($\alpha = 0$) (d) eALS vs. α ($c_0 = 64$)

Figure 1: Impact of weighting parameters c_0 and α on eALS's performance evaluated by offline protocol.

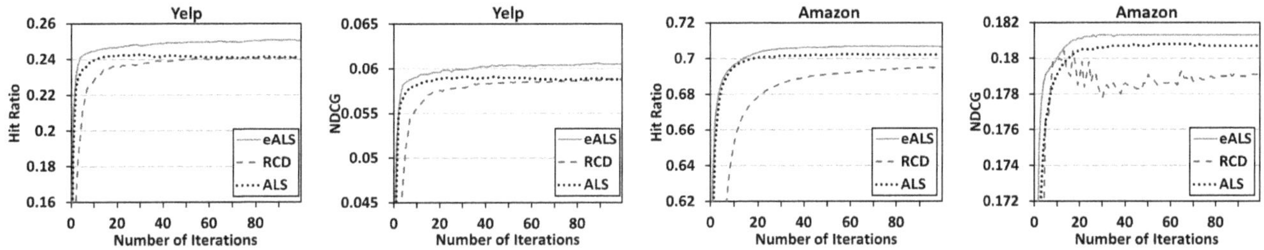

(a) Iterations vs. HR (b) Iterations vs. NDCG (c) Iterations vs. HR (d) Iterations vs. NDCG

Figure 2: Prediction accuracy of three whole-data based MF methods in each iteration ($K = 128$).

Xeon 2.67GHz CPU and 24GB RAM) in a single-thread for a fair comparison on efficiency. As the findings are consistent across the number of factors K, without any particular outlier, we only show the results of $K = 128$, a relatively large number that maintains good accuracy.

5.2 Offline Protocol

We first study how does the weighting scheme on missing data impact eALS's performance. Then we compare with the whole-data based implicit MF methods ALS and RCD, as well as the sample-based ranking method BPR.

5.2.1 *Weight of Missing Data*

In Section 4.1, we propose an item popularity-aware weighting strategy, which has two parameters: c_0 determines the overall weight of missing data and α controls the weight distribution. First, we set a uniform weight distribution (*i.e.*, $\alpha = 0$), varying c_0 to study how does the weight of missing data impact the performance. For Yelp (Figure 1a), the peak performance is achieved when c_0 is around 512, corresponding to that the weight of each zero entry is 0.02 ($w_0 = c_0/N$); similarly for Amazon (Figure 1c), the optimal c_0 is around 64, corresponding to $w_0 = 0.0001$. When c_0 becomes smaller (where w_0 is close to 0), the performance degrades significantly. This highlights the necessity of accounting for the missing data when modeling implicit feedback for item recommendation. Moreover, when c_0 is set too large, the performance also suffers. Based on this observation, we believe the traditional SVD technique [2] that treats all entries equally weighted will be suboptimal here.

Then, we set c_0 to the best value (in the case of $\alpha = 0$), varying α to check the performance change. As can be seen from Figure 1b and 1d, the performance of eALS is gradually improved with the increase of α, and the best result is reached around 0.4. We further conducted the one-sample paired t-test, verifying that the improvements are statistically significant (p-value < 0.01) for both metrics on the two datasets. This indicates the effectiveness of our popularity-biased weighting strategy. Moreover, when α is larger than 0.5, the performance starts to drop significantly. This reveals the drawback of over-weighting popular items as negative instances, thus the importance of accounting for less popular items with a proper weight.

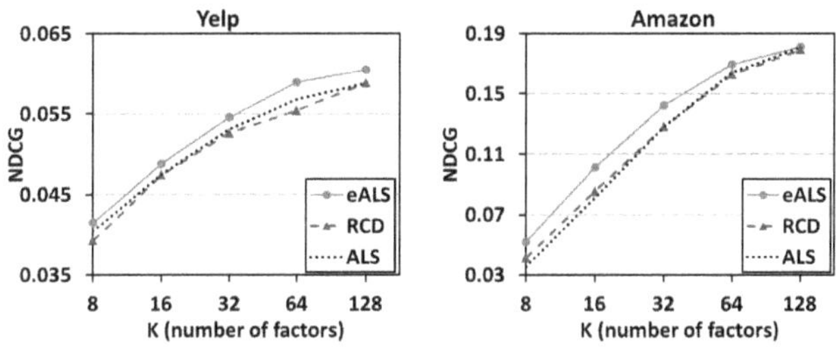

Figure 3: NDCG of whole-data based MF across K.

In the following experiments, we fix c_0 and α according to the best performance evaluated by HR, *i.e.*, $c_0 = 512, \alpha = 0.4$ for Yelp and $c_0 = 64, \alpha = 0.5$ for Amazon.

5.2.2 *Compare Whole-data based MF Methods*

We performed the same grid search of w_0 for RCD and ALS and reported the best performance.

Convergence. Figure 2 shows the prediction accuracy with respect to number of iterations. First, we see that eALS achieves the best performance after converge. All improvements are statistically significant evidenced by the one-sample paired t-test ($p < 0.01$). We believe the benefits mainly come from the popularity-aware objective function, as both ALS and RCD apply a uniform weighting on the unknowns. Second, eALS and ALS converge faster than RCD. We think the reason is that (e)ALS updates a parameter to minimize the objective function of the current status, while RCD updates towards the direction of the negative gradient, which can be suboptimal. On Amazon, RCD shows high but turbulent NDCG in early iterations, while the low hit ratio and later iterations indicate the high NDCG is unstable. Finally, we point out that in optimizing the same objective function, ALS outperforms RCD in most cases, demonstrating the advantage of ALS over the gradient descent learner.

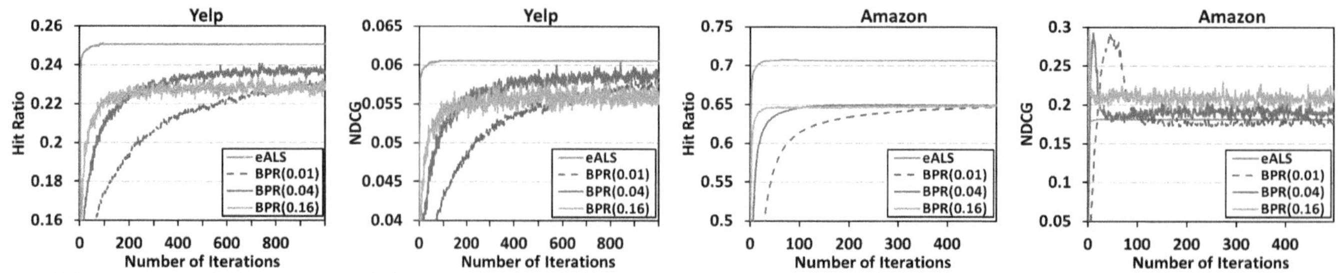

(a) Iterations vs. HR (b) Iterations vs. NDCG (c) Iterations vs. HR (d) Iterations vs. NDCG

Figure 4: Accuracy and convergence comparison of eALS with BPR of different learning rate.

Accuracy vs. Number of Factors. Figure 3 shows the prediction accuracy with varying number of factors K. We only show the evaluation by NDCG as HR admits the same trend. First, eALS consistently outperforms ALS and RCD across K, demonstrating the effectiveness of our eALS method (*n.b.* although the three methods seem to perform on par for Amazon at $K = 128$, their difference can be clearly seen in Figure 2d). Second, all methods can be improved significantly with a larger K. Although a large K might have the risk of overfitting, it can increase model's representation ability thus better prediction. Especially for large datasets that can have millions of users and billions of interactions, a large K is particularly important for the accuracy of MF methods.

Efficiency. Analytically, ALS's time complexity is $O((M+N)K^3 + |\mathcal{R}|K^2)$, while eALS and RCD are K times faster. To compare their efficiency empirically, we show the actual training time per iteration in Table 3.

Table 3: Training time per iteration of different whole-based MF methods with varying K.

	Yelp			Amazon		
K	eALS	RCD	ALS	eALS	RCD	ALS
32	1s	1s	10s	9s	10s	74s
64	4s	3s	46s	23s	17s	4.8m
128	13s	10s	221s	72s	42s	21m
256	1m	0.9m	23m	4m	2.8m	2h
512	2m	2m	2.5h	12m	9m	11.6h
1024	7m	11m	25.4h	54m	48m	74h

s, *m*, and *h* denote seconds, minutes and hours, respectively.

As can be seen, with the increase of K, ALS takes much longer time than eALS and RCD. Specifically, when K is 512, ALS requires 11.6 hours for one iteration on Amazon, while eALS only takes 12 minutes. Although eALS does not empirically show K times faster than ALS due to the more efficient matrix inversion implementation (we used the fastest known algorithm [1] with time complexity around $O(K^{2.376})$), the speed-up is already very significant. Moreover, as RCD and eALS have the same analytical time complexity, their actual running time are in the same magnitude; the minor difference can be caused by some implementation details, such as the data structures and caches used.

5.2.3 *eALS vs. BPR (sample-based)*

Figure 4 plots the performance of BPR with different learning rates[4] in each iteration. Note that we only run eALS for 100 iterations, which are enough for eALS to converge. First, it is clear that BPR's performance is subjected to the choice of learning rate — Figure 4a and 4b show that a higher learning rate leads to a faster convergence, while the final accuracy may be suffered. Second, we see that eALS significantly outperforms BPR on the Yelp dataset evaluated by both measures ($p < 0.001$). For Amazon, eALS obtains a much higher hit ratio but a lower NDCG score, indicating that most hits occur at a relatively low ranks for eALS. Comparing with the performance of other whole-based MF methods ALS and RCD (Figure 2), we draw the conclusion that BPR is a weak performer in terms of the prediction recall, while being a strong performer in terms of the precision at top ranks. We think BPR's strength in ranking top items is due to its optimization objective, which is a pairwise ranking function tailored for ranking correct item high. In contrast, the regression-based objective is not directly optimized for ranking; instead, by account for all missing data in regression, it better predicts user's preference on unconsumed items, leading to a better recall. This is consistent with [2]'s finding in evaluating top-K recommendation.

We notice that BPR shows unusual NDCG spike in early iterations on the Amazon dataset, however the performance is unstable and goes down with more iterations. The same phenomenon was also observed for another gradient descent method RCD on the same dataset (see Figure 2d). We hypothesize that it might be caused by some regularities in the data. For example, we find some Amazon users review on a movie multiple times[5]. In early iterations, BPR ranks these repeated items high, leading to a high but unstable NDCG score. There might be other reasons responsible for this, and we do not further explore here.

5.3 Online Protocol

In the evaluation of online protocol, we hold out the latest 10% interactions as the test set, training all methods on the remaining 90% data with the best parameter settings evidenced by the offline evaluation. We first study the number of online iterations required for eALS to converge. Then we show how does the weight of new interactions impact the performance. Lastly, we compare with dynamic MF methods RCD and BPR in the online learning scenario.

5.3.1 *Number of Online Iterations*

Figure 6 shows how does eALS's accuracy change with number of online iterations. Results at the 0-th iteration benchmark the performance of the offline trained model, as no incremental update is performed. First, we can see that the offline trained model performs very poorly, highlight-

[4] We have also tried other intermediate values of learning rates, and the findings are consistent. Thus, to make the figure more clear, we only show three selected values.

[5] Due to user's repeat consumption behaviours, we do not exclude training items when generating recommend list.

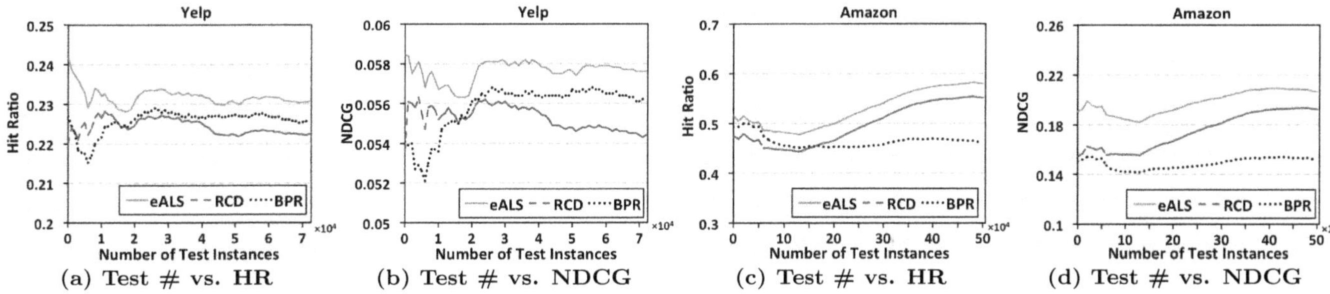

(a) Test # vs. HR (b) Test # vs. NDCG (c) Test # vs. HR (d) Test # vs. NDCG

Figure 5: Performance evolution of eALS and other dynamic MF methods in online learning.

ing the importance of refreshing recommender model for an online system with dynamic data. Second, we find most performance gain comes from the first iteration, and more iterations do not further improve. This is due to the fact that only the local features regarding to the new interaction are updated, and one eALS step on a latent factor can find the optimal solution with others fixed. Thus, one iteration is enough for eALS to learn from a new interaction incrementally, making eALS very efficient for learning online.

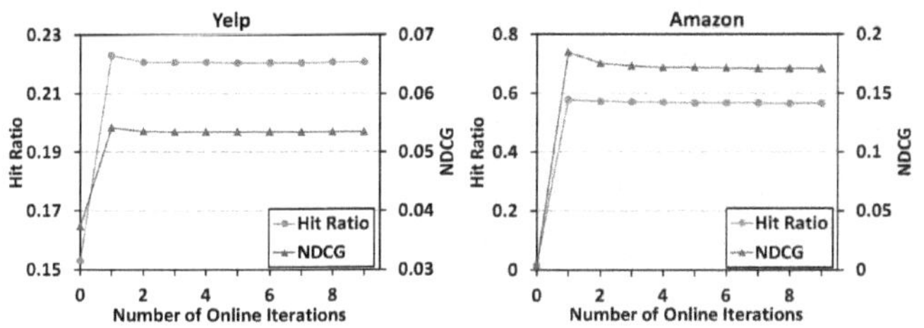

Figure 6: Impact of online iterations on eALS.

We have also investigated number of online iterations required for baselines RCD and BPR. RCD shows the same trend that good prediction is obtained in the first iteration. While BPR requires more iterations, usually 5-10 iterations to get a peak performance and more iterations will adversely hurt the performance due to the local over-training.

5.3.2 *Weight of New Interactions*

To evaluate how does the weight of new interactions effect the online learning algorithms, we also apply the same weight w_{new} on RCD. Note that the original RCD paper [4] does not consider the weight of interactions; we encode w_{new} the same way with eALS, revising the RCD learner to optimize the weighted regression function.

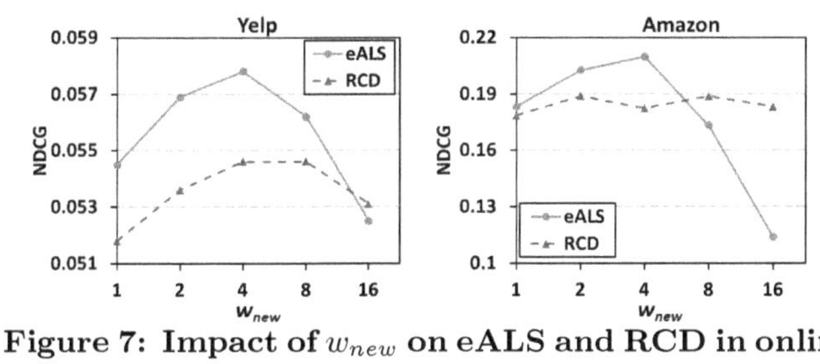

Figure 7: Impact of w_{new} on eALS and RCD in online learning evaluated by NDCG.

Figure 7 shows the performance evaluated by NDCG (results of HR show the same trend thus omitted for space). Setting w_{new} to 1 signifies that new interaction is assigned a same weight with the old training interaction. As expected, with a modest increasing on w_{new}, the prediction of both models is gradually improved, demonstrating the usefulness of strengthening user's short-term interest. The peak performance is obtained around 4, where eALS shows better prediction than RCD. Overly increasing w_{new} will adversely hurt the performance, admitting the utility of user's historical data used in offline training. Overall, this experiment indicates the importance of balancing user's short-term and long-term interest for quality recommendation.

5.3.3 *Performance Comparison*

With the simulated data stream, we show the performance evolution with respect to number of test instances in Figure 5. First, eALS consistently outperforms RCD and BPR evidenced by both measures, and one-sample paired t-test verifies that all improvements are statistically significant with $p < 0.001$. BPR betters RCD for Yelp, while underperforms for Amazon. Second, we observe the trend that the performance of dynamic learning first decreases, and then increases before becoming stable. This is caused by the new users problem — when there are few feedback for a user, the model can not personalize the user's preference effectively; with more feedbacks streaming in, the model can adapt itself to improve the preference modeling accordingly. To show this, we further breakdown the results of eALS by number of past interactions of test user in Figure 8.

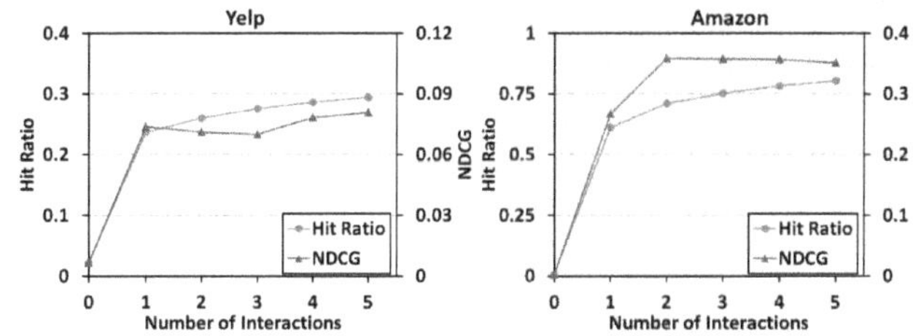

Figure 8: Results breakdown of eALS by # of past interactions of test user. Note: Interaction # > 0 denotes the performance for non-cold-start users.

It is clear that when there are no historical feedback for a test user (*i.e.*, user cold-start cases), the performance is very poor — no better than random. After the first interaction streams in, the prediction is significantly improved; and with more interactions, the performance is further improved. This highlights the importance of incorporating instantaneous user feedback into the model, especially for cold-start or sparse users that have few history in training.

6. CONCLUSION AND FUTURE WORK

We study the problem of learning MF models from implicit feedback. In contrast to previous work that applied a uniform weight on missing data, we propose to weight missing data based on the popularity of items. To address the key efficiency challenge in optimization, we develop a new learning algorithm — eALS — which effectively learns parameters by performing coordinate descent with memoization. For online learning, we devise an incremental update strategy for eALS to adapt dynamic data in real-time. Experiments with both offline and online protocols demonstrate promising results. Importantly, our work makes MF more practical to use for modeling implicit data, along two dimensions. First, we investigate a new paradigm to deal with missing data which can easily incorporate prior domain knowledge. Second, eALS is embarrassingly parallel, making it attractive for large-scale industrial deployment.

We plan to study the optimal weighting strategy for online data as a way to explore user's short-term interest. Along the technical line, we explored the element-wise ALS learner in its basic MF form and solved the efficiency challenge in handling missing data. To make our method more applicable to real-world settings, we plan to encode side information such as user social contexts [8] and reviews [9] by extending eALS to more generic models, such as collective factorization [11] and Factorization machines [26]. In addition, we will study binary coding for MF on implicit data, since a recent advance [32] has shown that discrete latent factors are beneficial to collaborative filtering for explicit ratings.

The strength of eALS can be applied to other domains, owing to the universality of factorizing sparse data matrices. For example, recent advances in natural language processing [16] have shown the connection between neural word embeddings and MF on the word–context matrix. This bridge nicely motivates several proposals to use MF to learn word embeddings; however, when it comes to handling missing data, they have either ignored [22] or equally weighted the missing entries, similar to traditional SVD [16]. It will be interesting to see whether eALS will also improve these tasks.

Acknowledgement

The authors would like to thank the additional discussion and help from Steffen Rendle, Bhargav Kanagal, Immanuel Bayer, Tao Chen, Ming Gao and Jovian Lin.

7. REFERENCES

[1] D. Coppersmith and S. Winograd. Matrix multiplication via arithmetic progressions. *J. Symb. Comput.*, 9(3):251–280, 1990.

[2] P. Cremonesi, Y. Koren, and R. Turrin. Performance of recommender algorithms on top-n recommendation tasks. In *RecSys 2010*, pages 39–46.

[3] A. S. Das, M. Datar, A. Garg, and S. Rajaram. Google news personalization: Scalable online collaborative filtering. In *WWW 2007*, pages 271–280.

[4] R. Devooght, N. Kourtellis, and A. Mantrach. Dynamic matrix factorization with priors on unknown values. In *KDD 2015*, pages 189–198.

[5] E. Diaz-Aviles, L. Drumond, L. Schmidt-Thieme, and W. Nejdl. Real-time top-n recommendation in social streams. In *RecSys 2012*, pages 59–66.

[6] J. Duchi, E. Hazan, and Y. Singer. Adaptive subgradient methods for online learning and stochastic optimization. *J. Mach. Learn. Res.*, 12:2121–2159, 2011.

[7] R. Gemulla, E. Nijkamp, P. J. Haas, and Y. Sismanis. Large-scale matrix factorization with distributed stochastic gradient descent. In *KDD 2011*, pages 69–77.

[8] X. Geng, H. Zhang, J. Bian, and T.-S. Chua. Learning image and user features for recommendation in social networks. In *ICCV 2015*, pages 4274–4282.

[9] X. He, T. Chen, M.-Y. Kan, and X. Chen. Trirank: Review-aware explainable recommendation by modeling aspects. In *CIKM 2015*, pages 1661–1670.

[10] X. He, M. Gao, M.-Y. Kan, Y. Liu, and K. Sugiyama. Predicting the popularity of web 2.0 items based on user comments. In *SIGIR 2014*, pages 233–242.

[11] X. He, M.-Y. Kan, P. Xie, and X. Chen. Comment-based multi-view clustering of web 2.0 items. In *Proc. of WWW '14*, pages 771–782, 2014.

[12] Y. Hu, Y. Koren, and C. Volinsky. Collaborative filtering for implicit feedback datasets. In *ICDM 2008*, pages 263–272.

[13] Y. Huang, B. Cui, W. Zhang, J. Jiang, and Y. Xu. Tencentrec: Real-time stream recommendation in practice. In *SIGMOD 2015*, pages 227–238.

[14] Y. Koren. Collaborative filtering with temporal dynamics. In *KDD 2009*, pages 447–456.

[15] Y. Koren and R. Bell. Advances in collaborative filtering. In *Recommender systems handbook*, pages 145–186. Springer, 2011.

[16] O. Levy and Y. Goldberg. Neural word embedding as implicit matrix factorization. In *NIPS 2014*, pages 2177–2185.

[17] G. Ling, H. Yang, I. King, and M. R. Lyu. Online learning for collaborative filtering. In *IJCNN 2012*, pages 1–8.

[18] B. M. Marlin, R. S. Zemel, S. Roweis, and M. Slaney. Collaborative filtering and the missing at random assumption. In *UAI 2007*, pages 267–276.

[19] T. Mikolov, I. Sutskever, K. Chen, G. S. Corrado, and J. Dean. Distributed representations of words and phrases and their compositionality. In *NIPS 2013*, pages 3111–3119.

[20] R. Pan and M. Scholz. Mind the gaps: Weighting the unknown in large-scale one-class collaborative filtering. In *KDD 2009*, pages 667–676.

[21] R. Pan, Y. Zhou, B. Cao, N. Liu, R. Lukose, M. Scholz, and Q. Yang. One-class collaborative filtering. In *ICDM 2008*, pages 502–511.

[22] J. Pennington, R. Socher, and C. D. Manning. Glove: Global vectors for word representation. In *EMNLP 2014*, pages 1532–1543.

[23] I. Pilászy, D. Zibriczky, and D. Tikk. Fast als-based matrix factorization for explicit and implicit feedback datasets. In *RecSys 2010*, pages 71–78.

[24] S. Rendle and C. Freudenthaler. Improving pairwise learning for item recommendation from implicit feedback. In *WSDM 2014*, pages 273–282.

[25] S. Rendle, C. Freudenthaler, Z. Gantner, and L. Schmidt-Thieme. Bpr: Bayesian personalized ranking from implicit feedback. In *UAI 2009*, pages 452–461.

[26] S. Rendle, Z. Gantner, C. Freudenthaler, and L. Schmidt-Thieme. Fast context-aware recommendations with factorization machines. In *SIGIR 2011*, pages 635–644.

[27] S. Rendle and L. Schmidt-Thieme. Online-updating regularized kernel matrix factorization models for large scale recommender systems. In *RecSys 2008*, pages 251–258.

[28] P. Richtárik and M. Takáč. Iteration complexity of randomized block-coordinate descent methods for minimizing a composite function. *Math. Prog.*, 2014.

[29] D. Sculley, G. Holt, D. Golovin, E. Davydov, T. Phillips, D. Ebner, V. Chaudhary, and M. Young. Machine learning: The high interest credit card of technical debt. In *SE4ML (NIPS 2014 Workshop)*, 2014.

[30] H. Steck. Training and testing of recommender systems on data missing not at random. In *KDD 2010*, pages 713–722.

[31] M. Volkovs and G. W. Yu. Effective latent models for binary feedback in recommender systems. In *SIGIR 2015*, pages 313–322.

[32] H. Zhang, F. Shen, W. Liu, X. He, H. Luan, and T.-S. Chua. Discrete collaborative filtering. In *SIGIR 2016*.

Leveraging User Interaction Signals for Web Image Search

Neil O'Hare
Yahoo Research
Sunnyvale, CA
nohare@yahoo-inc.com

Paloma de Juan
Yahoo
New York, NY
pdjuan@yahoo-inc.com

Rossano Schifanella
University of Turin
Turin, Italy
schifane@di.unito.it

Yunlong He
Yahoo Research
Sunnyvale, CA
yunlong@yahoo-inc.com

Dawei Yin
Yahoo Research
Sunnyvale, CA
daweiy@yahoo-inc.com

Yi Chang
Yahoo Research
Sunnyvale, CA
yichang@yahoo-inc.com

ABSTRACT

User interfaces for web image search engine results differ significantly from interfaces for traditional (text) web search results, supporting a richer interaction. In particular, users can see an enlarged image preview by hovering over a result image, and an 'image preview' page allows users to browse further enlarged versions of the results, and to click-through to the referral page where the image is embedded. No existing work investigates the utility of these interactions as implicit relevance feedback for improving search ranking, beyond using clicks on images displayed in the search results page. In this paper we propose a number of implicit relevance feedback features based on these additional interactions: hover-through rate, 'converted-hover' rate, referral page click through, and a number of dwell time features. Also, since images are never self-contained, but always embedded in a referral page, we posit that clicks on other images that are embedded on the same referral webpage as a given image can carry useful relevance information about that image. We also posit that query-independent versions of implicit feedback features, while not expected to capture topical relevance, will carry feedback about the quality or attractiveness of images, an important dimension of relevance for web image search. In an extensive set of ranking experiments in a learning to rank framework, using a large annotated corpus, the proposed features give statistically significant gains of over 2% compared to a state of the art baseline that uses standard click features.

CCS Concepts

•Information systems → Web search engines; Content ranking; Image search;

Keywords

Web Image Search, User Behavior, Ranking

SIGIR '16, July 17-21, 2016, Pisa, Italy

DOI: http://dx.doi.org/10.1145/2911451.2911532

1. INTRODUCTION

Although multimedia search in general, and image search in particular, have been very active research areas for well over a decade, there has been relatively little work in understanding how user behavior, based on interactions with image search engine interfaces, the traces of which are stored in search engine logs, can be used to provide implicit relevance feedback that can improve the rankings for commercial image search engines. Instead, standard approaches, developed with general web search in mind, are applied to multimedia search without any effort to adapt them to the special case of image search and the rich, and unique, user interactions that the interfaces of commercial image search engines facilitate. On the other hand, image search has been shown to be very important within web search: for example, a recent study shows that queries showing image intent were second only to the navigational intent[1] queries on desktops and tablets, and they were the most popular (42%) for mobile phone devices [22].

In this work, we address this gap by leveraging the rich user interactions with web image search results to extract implicit relevance feedback information and improve search engine rankings. Interaction features that are found in image search, but not in general web search, include: (1) 'hovering' over result images to see a preview; (2) browsing enlarged previews of many images after a click on a search result, via next/previous buttons; (3) the ability to further click through, from this image preview, to the host webpage where the image is embedded. In this work, we propose a number of novel implicit user feedback features for image search based on the above interface features, and evaluate their usefulness for image search ranking on a large annotated image search corpus, showing an improvement in relevance over a strong baseline based on click data.

The main contributions of this paper are as follows:

- We propose a 'hover' rate feature based on an image-specific interaction on the *Search Results Page.*
- We propose two sets of user behavior features based on user interactions with the image *Preview Page*: (i) click-through from the preview page to the host/referral page where the image is embedded, and (ii) a set of dwell time features.

[1] navigational queries = queries that seek a single website or web page of a single entity

- We propose propagating the user behavior features beyond the *query-image url* level to the *query-referral page url* level, and also to the *query-independent* level.
- We evaluate these novel features in a learning to rank framework using a large scale annotated corpus, and show that they achieve significant improvements over a strong baseline based on standard click features.

Although other work has explored dwell time, to the best of our knowledge this is the first work to use dwell time for a large scale, general search relevance task.

The rest of the paper is organized as follows: in the next Section we introduce the related work, before going on to describe the unique features of web image search user interfaces in Section 3. In Section 4 we introduce novel implicit relevance feedback features for web image search. In Section 5 we describe the data that we use in our experiments, and then we go on to describe our experiments and results in Section 6. Finally, we conclude the paper in Section 7.

2. RELATED WORK

Click information from the search engine logs has long been used as an implicit relevance feedback signal to improve relevance for web search. Features like click-through rate are calculated from the log data and used as a signal for relevance, under the assumption that relevant documents have more clicks than non-relevant ones [12, 13, 1]. Agichtein et al. [1], for example, show that adding such implicit user behavior information can give as much as a 30% improvement for relevance in web search. Other work tries to better understand user behavior by creating click models that aim to account for biases caused by the display position and other factors [5]. While most of this has focused on web search, and treats the results as a simple ranked list, at least one recent work studied aggregated search on a web search results page, where video and image results, among others, are displayed alongside traditional web results [25].

There has been relatively little work that has aimed at leveraging user behavior information to improve results for multimedia search, either for images or videos. Craswell et al. [4] explore random walk models on the click graph for propagating click information to URLs which have not been clicked. They are not specifically interested in image search, however, but use image data because it has features that suit the research questions on that paper. They show that 75% of clicked images are relevant to the query, which means that basic click data is a very strong indicator of relevance for image search. Jain & Varma [9] use click data to train query-dependent re-ranking models, but do not focus on exploiting click data as a feature for ranking. Smith & Ashman [21] study click-through data for image search and, consistently with Craswell et al., showed that it was 'considerably more accurate in general than document based search click-through data', although the reliability of the clicks was shown to be dependent on factors such as query type and the quality (in terms of precision) of the results shown. Tsikrika *et al.* [24] have used image clicks to automatically create ground truth labels for training visual classifiers, while other work has combined click data and visual features for image ranking [30]. Other researchers have studied web image search interaction logs to understand how interaction with image search engines differs from general search, without exploring the utility of these interactions as implicit relevance information [10, 2, 17, 19].

In traditional web search, beyond standard clicks on the *Search Results Page* (SRP), some researchers have explored post-SRP clicks for improving relevance [3, 26], although this work relies on user-installed browser toolbars to log the post SRP-click user trails, while other work has explored user branching behavior using tabs [8]. Some recent work has investigated using dwell time on search result pages to model user satisfaction [15], although they do not use dwell time as a signal to predict relevance. Other work has explored using dwell time for personalization of web search results [28, 27], while Liu et al. [16] showed that dwell time is a good indicator of document usefulness for a variety of tasks. Yi *et al.* use dwell time as a novel feature in a learning to rank framework for recommendation [29]. With respect to images, Trevisiol et al. [23] leveraged extended user browsing traces on the Flickr photo sharing platform to create a query independent image authority measure.

This work focuses on novel features for implicit relevance feedback beyond the standard SRP clicks. While 'hovers', and clicks from the image *Preview Page* to the image *Referral Page*, are totally unexplored due to their uniqueness to image search, our use of dwell time features is related to the work cited above. We emphasize, however, that the rich interaction with multiple search results *after* an SRP click, but still within the search engine experience (and therefore these interactions are stored in the search engine logs), are unique to image search, providing much more dwell time data than would be available in general web search. Also, we note that we explore propagating click data beyond the *query image url* level, again unique to image search and to this work. To the best of our knowledge, the is the first work to use dwell time features extracted from large scale log data for a search relevance ranking task (although Yi *et al.* [29] did so for a recommendation task).

3. IMAGE SEARCH USER INTERACTION

Image search interfaces differ greatly from traditional web search, supporting a number of interactions not associated with traditional search. Figure 1 (first row) shows the *Search Results Page* for the three major U.S. search engines (Bing, Yahoo and Google). The main section of the layout presents a grid of clickable thumbnails. Two out of the three search engines allow a form of interaction that is specific to image search: the 'hover' (see pointer 1 in Figure 1). After hovering the mouse cursor on a search result image for about 1-2 seconds, the user can see an enlarged version of the thumbnail with some additional information about the context of the image (e.g., the website it was crawled from, the image resolution).

When the user clicks on a thumbnail (or its enlarged version), the *Preview Page* is loaded (see Figure 1, second row). This page is generally displayed as a new view, or it can unfold from the thumbnail. In either case, the *Preview Page* extends over the whole width of the screen, and shows a larger version of the image, not necessarily in the original size. In addition to a link to the actual image (i.e., a full size version hosted in its original server), a *Preview Page* typically provides other elements for interaction:

- **Thumbnails** (see pointer 2 in Figure 1): The user can jump to a specific image by clicking on a thumbnail,

Figure 1: *Search Results Page* (SRP) and *Preview Page* from the three major search engines.

without leaving the *Preview Page*. The thumbnails show neighboring results from the *Search Results Page* (following the original ranking).

- **Navigation** (see pointer 3): By clicking on previous/next buttons, the user can switch to the previous and next images from the thumbnail list without leaving the *Preview Page*.
- **Referral Page** (see pointer 4): Contextual information (title and URL of the *Referral Page* that the image was crawled from, and sometimes a text snippet from the same page) is shown to the user, who can click on a link to go to that *Referral Page*.

The user can additionally 'close' the *Preview Page* to go back to the *Search Results Page*.

3.1 Context of Images in Web

Images are not standalone content items on the web, but instead they are embedded in web pages, that link to the servers where the images are actually hosted. Images are typically discovered by search engine crawlers in the context of the web pages in which they are embedded, and the search engines will store details of that page along with the details of the image. Also, images are not canonical resources pages link to, which means that there is a very high level of replication. Two identical images can be hosted in two different servers (and hence have two different URLs), and any of those locations can be linked to by any number of websites. Additionally, images do not carry any information about what they represent, so search engines need to extract this information from their context, i.e., the surrounding text in the website they are linked from. This means that the information that an image is associated with is heavily dependent on the content of its *Referral Page*.

As the same image (in terms of content or location) can be embedded in different contexts, it is important to take into account the website the image was crawled from when it is shown to the user as a result for a particular query. In other words, much of the information we have available to decide on the relevance of an image to a given query depends heavily on the textual content and metadata of its *Referral Page*, and its power to accurately describe what the image depicts. This means that, when considering implicit user feedback, we should also consider the relevance of the image *referral page* since, when a user interacts with an image result, they are not only validating the relevance of the image to the query, but also indirectly validating the relevance of its *Referral Page* to that same query.

3.2 Relevance Requirements for Image Search

Work on user expectations for relevance in image search in commercial web search engines has shown that, in addition to *topical relevance*, users consider *image quality*, or *attractiveness*, to be of paramount importance. Geng et al [7] have shown that all of the top requirements for image search results are directly related to attractiveness or quality: 'high quality', 'colorful', 'sharp', 'beautiful', 'appealing', 'vivid'. These aspects were actually rated as *more important* than relevance although, as the authors note, this is likely due to the design of the study, where the users were presented with the top results from commercial search engines. In that setting, there were unlikely to be any problems with *topical relevance*, and so these users did not identify this as a major issue. Nevertheless, that work clearly emphasizes that image quality and attractiveness are, alongside topical relevance, the most important user requirements in image search. For this reason, in this paper we will focus our evaluation of image search ranking algorithms on topical relevance and image quality (we use quality in the general sense, to capture objective image quality, beauty and appealingness).

4. IMPLICIT FEEDBACK FEATURES FOR IMAGE SEARCH

In this section we introduce new implicit relevance feedback features for Image Search, first describing features extracted from the *Search Results Page* and the image *Preview Page*, and then describing how we propagate these features to the *Referral Page* level and the *query-independent* level.

4.1 Implicit Feedback Features from the Image Search Results Page

The standard way to exploit user behavior in web search is to use the click-through rate (or click probability) on the *Search Results Page* (SRP). This is calculated by dividing the number of times an image has been clicked for a given query by the number of times it has been displayed, or viewed, for that query:

$$CTR = \frac{clicks(image\ url, query)}{views(image\ url, query)} \tag{1}$$

In Section 3.1 we also described how some web image search engines also support a 'hover' event, where leaving the mouse hovering over an image for a number of seconds results in an enlarged version of the image being displayed (see Figure 1). Park et al. [19] have shown that image search interfaces elicit 8 to 10 times more hover interactions than clicks, and that the images that are hovered on are moderately to highly correlated with the images that are clicked on. This suggests that, although potentially more noisy than clicks, this noise could be compensated by the larger volume, and hovers could be a strong additional signal for relevance. To exploit the interaction for improving relevance, we propose the hover-through rate (HTR) feature, as follows:

$$HTR = \frac{hovers(image\ url, query)}{views(image\ url, query)} \tag{2}$$

Also, in many sessions, the display of an enlarged 'hover' image may be followed by a standard click on the image, if the user wants to see a bigger version of the image in the *Preview Page*[2]. We can interpret this interaction as the user first inspecting the enlarged images for relevance and, if they judge this image as being relevant, they then click through to the image *Preview Page*. Based on this, we also propose a new feature, which we call *converted hover rate* (CHR), the proportion of hover events that are followed by clicks the same session (i.e. hovers that are 'converted' to clicks):

$$CHR = \frac{converted\ clicks(image\ url, query)}{hovers(image\ url, query)} \tag{3}$$

4.2 Implicit Feedback Features from the Image Preview Page

From the image *Preview Page*, we derive two types of features: (i) features based on clicks from the image *Preview Page* to the original *Referral Page* where the image is hosted, and (ii) features on the dwell time on images in this page. Interactions with this page can be very important, since users often interact with images in this view that they did not click on in the *Search Results Page*: one recent study [19] showed that, for each click on an image from the *Search Results Page* (which opens the *Preview Page*), an average of 17 additional images are viewed by the user in the *Preview Page* via navigation using the previous/next buttons.. Given this, we propose that these interactions carry much additional implicit relevance information.

4.2.1 Referral Page Click-through

All of the major U.S. search engines provide, in the *Image Preview* page, a link to the original *referral page* where the image was crawled from, allowing the user to view the image in its original context. We posit that this deeper method of interaction should be strongly correlated with relevance, and that it can be used as a feature for image relevance. We can calculate the *Referral Page Click-through Rate* (RP-CTR), as follows:

$$RP\text{-}CTR = \frac{referral\ page\ clicks(image\ url, query)}{preview\ page\ views(image\ url, query)} \tag{4}$$

4.2.2 Dwell Time Features

Given that a number of images are consumed on each user visit to the *Preview Page*, we know the time when the user started viewing an image (when they clicked through from the *Search Results Page*, or when they accessed it via the *next* button), and when they finished viewing the image (when they clicked the *next/previous* button, or exiting the *Preview Page*). With this information, we calculate the amount of time that the user spent viewing each image, or the image *dwell time*. Previous work has shown that dwell time can be a strong indicator of user satisfaction for many tasks [16, 15], and it has been used successfully as a feature to improve recommendation [29]. We hypothesize that larger dwell times on a individual images indicates a deeper interaction with results, reflecting higher quality and/or topical relevance. Once we know the dwell time on an individual image, we can calculate a number of features based on it. We calculate three main types of *dwell time* features (see Table 1 for a complete list):

- *Absolute* dwell time features: the dwell time in seconds, and the log of the dwell time.
- *Normalised* dwell time features. Previous work [14] has shown that dwell time can be dependent on both the user and the task. To correct for both of these factors, we normalize the dwell time with respect to other images viewed in the same *Preview Page* session. We define such a session as starting when a user clicks on a result in the *Search Results Page* to enter *Preview Page* mode, and ends when the user exits the image *Preview Page*. This within-session normalization naturally controls for both user and task. Normalised features are calculated by normalizing against the total session duration, the dwell time of previous/subsequent images, etc.
- Binary *categorical* dwell time features calculated relative to the rest of the *preview page* session, such as whether the dwell time is the longest, shortest, greater than the median/mean, less than the median/mean, for that *preview page* session.

To create our final representation of the dwell time features, we calculate the average value of each feature across all sessions.

4.3 Propagating Implicit Feedback Features

Normally, click-through data is calculated at the query-URL level. That is, when a user clicks on a result, the click is associated with the URL of that result. In web image search, this is the URL of the image result. In image search, however, each image is also hosted in the context of the referral webpage where it has been shown, and this webpage can also exhibit relevance to the query; it could be an article or fanpage dedicated to the topic of the query, for example, and may contain multiple images relevant to the query. For this reason, unique to image search, there are two separate

[2]Note that, although these clicks may take place very soon after a hover, the search logging instrumentation is very reliable at successfully logging, and distinguishing, both events.

Feature	Type	Description
		Absolute
DT	Int	Dwell time, in seconds.
$log(DT)$	Float	The log of the dwell time.
		Normalised
$\frac{DT}{\mu}$	Float	Dwell time divided by the mean dwell time (μ) for that session.
$\frac{DT}{median}$	Float	Dwell time divided by the median dwell time for that session.
DT z-score	Float	$\frac{DT-\mu}{\sigma}$ where μ is the mean dwell time for the session and σ its standard deviation.
$\frac{DT}{total}$	Float	Dwell time divided by the total dwell time for the session.
$\frac{DT}{min}$	Float	Dwell time divided by the minimum dwell time for any image in the session.
$\frac{DT}{max}$	Float	Dwell time divided by the maximum dwell time for any image in the session.
$\frac{DT}{next}$	Float	Dwell time divided by the dwell time of the next image in the session.
$\frac{DT}{prev}$	Float	Dwell time divided by the dwell time of the previous image in the session.
$\frac{DT}{meanNext}$	Float	Dwell time divided by the mean dwell time of all subsequent images in the session.
$\frac{DT}{medianNext}$	Float	Dwell time divided by the median dwell time of all subsequent images in the session.
$\frac{DT}{meanPrev}$	Float	Dwell time divided by the mean dwell time of all previous images in the session.
$\frac{DT}{medianPrev}$	Float	Dwell time divided by the median dwell time of all previous images in the session.
		Categorical
skipped	Binary	If the dwell time is less than a threshold (0.5 sec), the image is considered to be skipped.
isLast	Binary	The last image viewed in the session.
isSingleImage	Binary	The first and last image viewed in the session.
isMax	Binary	The longest dwell time of all images in the session.
isMin	Binary	The shortest dwell time of all images in the session.
gtMean	Binary	Dwell time is greater than the mean for the session.
ltMean	Binary	Dwell time is less than the mean for the session.
eqMean	Binary	Dwell time is equal to the mean for the session.
gtMedian	Binary	Dwell time is greater than the median for the session.
ltMedian	Binary	Dwell time is less than the median for the session.
eqMedian	Binary	Dwell time is equal to the median for the session.

Table 1: Definition of Dwell time features. Binary features are 1 if true, 0 if false. Features where the denominator is based on previous (or next) images are not defined for the first (or last) image in the session.

URLs that we can associate search result clicks with: the *image URL* and the *referral page URL*. In Sections 4.1 and 4.2 we proposed new features at the *image URL* level. We now propose to propagate these features to the *referral page URL* level or, equivalently, to associate clicks with the *referral page URL* instead of the *image URL*. This should capture referral page relevance information, and also increase coverage of the implicit feedback features for images which have not been clicked, but for which other images from the same *Referral Page* have been clicked. So, in Equations 2, 3 and 4, this simply means replacing (*image url*, *query*) with (*referral page url, query*). Similarly, for this version of the dwell time features, we associate the features with the *referral page URL* rather than the *image URL*.

It is also possible to ignore the query completely, and consider the user behavior features at the *query-independent* level. Unlike propagating to the *Referral Page* level, this is not strictly unique to image search. However, we propose that query independent features will capture the *quality* of images, independent of topical relevance. As discussed in Section 3, Geng et al. [7] previously showed that image attractiveness or quality very important for image search. Given this, we posit that propagating click features to the query independent level will capture implicit user feedback about image quality, and so we also calculate all of our proposed features independent of the query.

In summary, we have three levels of propagation for the user behavior features:

- *Q-URL.* The query is associated with the image URL for the clicked/viewed image: this is our default setting and, if not otherwise stated, this version of the implicit feedback features is being used.
- *Q-Refpage.* The query is associated with the URL of the referral page where the image is embedded.
- *Q-Independent.* The features are calculated for the image url, independently of the query.

5. DATA

We take the complete search engine log data, covering all queries across all device types (mobile, desktop, etc) from the Yahoo search engine, covering a 6 month period from

July 2014 to December 2014[3]. From this log, we extract all user interaction events from the *Search Results Page* and the image *Preview Page*.

We extract the following fields from each entry in the log: session id, timestamp, query string, anonymous user identifier, page type, and event type (i.e. pageview, click). For pageview events we extract the URLs of all thumbnail result images (and their referral pages) displayed on the page. For click events, we have information about the type of click (e.g. click, hover) and the URL of the clicked images and their referral pages. We then aggregate this data and calculate all of the features described in Section 4 for all *query-url* pairs, *query-referral page* pairs, and all *image urls* in the data.

5.1 Corpus for Web Image Search

To create a corpus that we can use to train and evaluate web image search ranking models, we take a traffic based query sample. That is, we calculate the query volume (the number of times the query was issued) for each query in the logs, and sort the queries by volume. Since in this work we are interested in head and torso queries, for which user behavior information is available in the log data, we restrict our corpus to queries from the top 50% of this traffic distribution (i.e. the most popular queries, covering 50% of the overall traffic volume), taking as our sample a total of 9,272 queries from the top 50% of queries.

5.1.1 Relevance Annotations for Image Web Search

The two main facets of relevance for web image search are *topical relevance* and *image quality/attractiveness* [7]. In order to measure each of these facets separately, for candidate image URLs for each query, we gather separate judgements for topical relevance and quality. All of these annotations are carried out by professional editors, trained to use the topical relevance and quality scales outlined below.

For *topical relevance*, we gather judgements on a 3 point-scale:

- *Relevant.* The main subject of the image is the main subject of the query, and is clearly visible.
- *Moderately Relevant.* The image is only partially relevant to the query. Either the subject of the query is fully depicted, but is only the partial focus of the image, or else it is not depicted clearly enough.
- *Non Relevant.* The image fails to match the subject of the query, or matches it so poorly as to be not useful.

For image quality, we gather judgements on the following 5-point scale:

- *Exceptional.* Very appealing images, showing both outstanding professional quality (photographic and/or editing techniques) and high artistic value.
- *Professional.* Professional-quality images (flawless framing, focus, and lightning), which should also be somewhat attractive/appealing.
- *Good.* Standard quality images without technical flaws (subject well framed, in focus, and easily recognizable), and without any artistic value.
- *Fair.* Low quality images with some technical flaws (slightly blurred, slightly over/underexposed, incorrectly framed), which are not very appealing

[3]We do not reveal further details about this initial dataset (e.g. size, etc) as such information is commercially sensitive.

- *Bad.* Extremely low quality, out of focus, underexposed, badly framed images.

Finally, we create a single combined *relevance + quality* judgement that incorporates both topical relevance and quality, and maps to a standard 5-point PEGFB scale (Perfect, Excellent, Good, Fair, Bad). We do this using a simple heuristic which gives precedence to topical relevance:

- *Non Relevant* images map to *bad*, regardless of quality.
- *Moderately Relevant* images map to *fair*, regardless of quality.
- For *Relevant* images only, the quality score is considered in the final mapping, as follows: *bad* → *bad*, $fair \rightarrow fair$, *good* → *good*, $professional \rightarrow excellent$, $exceptional \rightarrow perfect$.

5.1.2 Image URL Sampling

To avoid biasing our sample towards the features of the images ranked highly by the ranking algorithm used, we take a sample of a 15 images per query from the top 500 results of a baseline ranking algorithm, and have these annotated by editors. After this initial round of annotation, a preliminary analysis showed that some frequent queries had few or no negatively annotated (i.e. moderately/non relevant) images. For these cases, to ensure a good balance of annotations in our corpus, we identified queries for which the initial annotations suffered from this bias, and sampled additional image URLs to be annotated for these queries. This gave a variable number of image URLs annotated per query, resulting in a total of 221,920 annotations over the 9,272 queries in our sample, an average of almost 24 image URLs per query, with the labels (from the combined mapping) distributed as follows: 1,195 *Perfect*, 46,926 *Excellent*, 30,571 *Good*, 67,669 *Fair* and 75,559 *Bad*.

5.2 Feature Coverage in Corpus

Using the corpus described in the previous subsection, Table 2 shows the coverage of each feature in terms of the percentage of judged query-url paris in the corpus for which we have a non-null value, or a positive (i.e., non-zero) value. In order to remove noise from sparse data, when calculating the implicit feedback features, we treat them as undefined if they are based on less than a minimum number of impressions in the *Search Results Page* or the *Preview Page* (we set the threshold at 20). In Table 2, a non-null value indicates that the corresponding feature can be calculated, whereas a null value means there are too few impressions to calculate the feature reliably, so we treat it as undefined (for the feature vectors used in MLR models, undefined features are assigned the value -1). While the *absolute* coverage values are influenced by the amount of log data available for processing and by the method used to sample image urls for each query, we are mostly interested in the *relative* gain in coverage from adding new features and from propagating those features, which should be quite robust against these factors. The coverage of HTR is slightly lower than that of CTR due to the fact that the impressions accounted for the former are desktop-only, since there is no hover action on mobile. The coverage of the Dwell Time (DT) and the RP-CTR features is based on the number of impressions on the *Preview Page*, which must always be preceded by a click on the *Search Results Page*. DT has slightly lower coverage because the dwell time can not be computed for those im-

Features	Query-URL		Query-Refpage		Query-Independent	
	Non-null (%)	Non-zero (%)	Non-null (%)	Non-zero (%)	Non-null (%)	Non-zero (%)
CTR	24.93	17.13	29.67	20.37	59.19	36.78
DT	6.35	-	6.96	-	10.40	-
HTR	21.32	**18.28**	26.03	**22.19**	52.58	**43.52**
CHR	7.24	6.64	8.69	7.96	13.93	12.72
RP-CTR	7.05	2.78	8.48	3.24	13.27	6.02
All	24.93	**20.44**	29.68	**24.43**	59.19	**46.51**

Table 2: Feature coverage for implicit feedback features: *non-null* coverage calculated as the proportion of the dataset for which the features can be calculated, *non-zero* calculated as the proportion of the corpus for which the feature has non-zero values.

ages viewed at the end of the session (e.g., if the users closes the browser or navigates away from the *Preview Page*).

The non-zero coverage shows the proportion of query-URLs in the corpus with non-zero values for this metric: that is, there has been at least one click, so this is potentially a positive relevance signal (the non-zero coverage does not apply to the DT features, since by definition the dwell time, if defined, will always be non-zero). Here HTR has a higher coverage than CTR, despite of the fact that it does not include interactions on mobile devices. We can also see that the overall coverage (last row, calculated as proportion of the corpus where at least one of the features is non-zero) increases when we consider all implicit feedback features, and that corpus coverage increases significantly when propagating features. In fact, we see that the coverage increases for all the features with the adoption of the propagation schemes, and it doubles at the query-independent level compared with the query-URL level. This is important because is shows that by adding new features, and propagating them, the number of image URLs that can potentially benefit from these features increases significantly. This also emphasizes how the introduction of image specific user feedback signals can better capture the peculiarities of user behavior in image search, compared with generic web search.

6. EVALUATION

To evaluate our proposed features we adopt a learning to rank framework. We employ the state of the art *GBRank* ranking algorithm [31], which uses a pairwise loss function based on Gradient Boosting Regression Trees (GBDT), as our ranking function. We convert the combined *relevance + quality* judgements to a numeric learning target as follows: Perfect - 4, Excellent -3, Good - 2, Fair - 1, Bad - 0.

We calculate over 2,000 features as input to the learning algorithm to train two separate baseline models, **B1** and **B2**. We evaluate the effectiveness of our proposed features by adding them as additional features on top of each of the baselines, and measure their effect on search ranking. We compare against the first baseline to confirm that our proposed features carry significant relevance information, and against the second to show that our methods can outperform a strong baseline based on standard click features:

- **B1**: The first set of features is purely content-based, as it does not include information about user interactions. The features used for this baseline are:
  - *Query Features*: Query length, query frequency, query category, etc.
  - *Text Matching*: Features based on the *document text* and *anchor text*. For image search, we extract the title and URL of the referral page, keywords and file name from the image URL, the image 'alt' text, the text surrounding the image, and the anchor text. Each of these is indexed into a separate field, and a number of query-URL level text-based similarity scores are calculated for each field. For each of these fields, basic features are computed and then aggregated to form new composite features. The match score can be as simple as a count or can be more complex such as BM25 [20]. Counts include the number of occurrences in the document, the number of missing query terms or the number of extra terms. Other features measure proximity and order of query terms within the document [18].
  - *Referral Page*: We calculate page authority features for the page where the image is embedded using random walk based methods, host level authority, domain level authority, URL authority, etc.
- **B2**: The second baseline includes *CTR* for query-URL pairs, in addition to all the features from baseline **B1**.

Partition	Queries	Judgements
Training	7,418	177,736
Tuning	463	10,917
Test	1,391	33,267
Total	*9,272*	*221,920*

Table 3: Basic statisistics for the Web Image Search training and evaluation corpus.

We use Normalized Discounted Cumulative Gain (NDCG) as the metric to assess search relevance performance. NDCG has been widely used to assess relevance in the context of search engines [11]. For a ranked list of N documents, Discounted Cumulative Gain (DCG) is calculated as follows:

$$\mathrm{DCG}_N = \sum_{i=1}^{N} \frac{G_i}{\log_2(i+1)}$$

where G_i represents the weight assigned to the label of the document at position i, i.e., 10 for Perfect, 7 for Excellent, 3 for Good, 0.5 for Fair, and 0 for Bad. NDCG normalizes DCG by dividing it by the ideal DCG that would be

Features	NDCG1	NDCG3	NDCG5	NDCG10
B1	0.661	0.664	0.668	0.721
B2	0.735††	0.731††	0.738††	0.775††
B1 + HTR	0.709††	0.717††	0.727††	0.764††
B1 + CHR	0.676	0.682††	0.685††	0.727†
B1 + RP-CTR	0.660	0.655	0.664	0.712
B1 + DT	0.689††	0.687††	0.687††	0.728†
B2 + HTR	0.752‡	0.738‡‡	0.746‡‡	0.778‡‡
B2 + CHR	0.748	0.738‡	0.745‡‡	0.778‡‡
B2 + RP-CTR	0.74	0.739‡	0.747‡‡	0.779‡‡
B2 + DT	0.745‡	0.740‡‡	0.746‡‡	0.779‡‡
B2 + All	0.753‡‡	0.737‡	0.747‡‡	0.779‡‡
B2 + All (Q-URL + Q-Refpage)	0.747	0.739‡	0.748‡‡	0.785‡‡
B2 + All (Q-URL + Q-Independent)	0.746	0.739‡	0.747‡‡	0.781‡‡
B2 + All (Q-URL + Q-Refpage + Q-Independent)	**0.755‡‡**	**0.745‡‡**	**0.754‡‡**	**0.790‡‡**

Table 4: Relevance + Quality NDCG Results for Image Search with Implicit Feedback features. †- significantly better than B1. ††- highly significantly better than B1. ‡: significantly better than B2. ‡‡: highly significantly better than B2.

obtained from a perfect ranking: NDCG has the advantage that it is easier to interpret, in that its score always falls between 0 and 1, with 1 indicating a perfect ranking. We use the symbol $\overline{NDCG}$ to indicate the average of this value over a set of testing queries in our experiments. In the following sections, we will report NDCG1, NDCG3, NDCG5 and NDCG10, referring to NDCG calculated for the top 1 ranked document only (NDCG1), the top 3 ranked documents only (NDCG3), etc. For our main evaluation metric, we calculate NDCG based on the combined *relevance + quality* scale. For a supplemental evaluation, we use the *topical relevance* labels only, on a 3-point scale, where we map *relevant* to Good, *moderately relevant* to Fair, and *non-relevant* to Bad, and calculate NDGC based on this.

Taking the set of annotated queries described in Section 5.1, we partition them into training, tuning and testing sets. The partitioning is query-based (i.e., all judgements for a given query will be assigned to the same partition) as follows: 80% training, 5% tuning, and 15% test. More details of the evaluation corpus can be found in Table 3. The training partition is used to train the models, the tuning partition is used to conduct a parameter search for the optimal parameters of the *GBRank* algorithm (i.e., the parameter set with the best NDCG score on the tuning partition is selected), and then the model trained with these optimal parameters is tested against the test set to produce our evaluation results.

6.1 Results

6.1.1 Relevance + Quality NDCG

The NDCG results for *Relevance+Quality* are shown in Table 4. Firstly, we can see that all of the proposed features, except for the RP-CTR, give significant improvements over **B1**. For NDCG5, for example, this improvement is 8.2% for the HTR, 2.5% for the CHR, and 2.8% for the DT, and all of these differences are highly statistically significant ($p < 0.01$). The B2 + HTR model outperforms B2 by over 2% for NDCG1, showing a highly significant improvement over B2 for NDCG3, NDCG5 and NDCG10. In fact, all of the proposed new features show at least significant improvements ($p < 0.05$) over B2 of around 1% for NDCG3, highly significant improvements of around 1% for NDCG5, and smaller, but highly significant, improvements for NDCG10. It is also noteworthy that the RP-CTR, which did not improve over **B1**, achieves improvements over **B2** that are comparable with the other proposed features. We hypothesize that the lack of coverage for this feature means that it is not a reliable signal for relevance in the absence of other click data, but since it provides complementary information to *Search Results Page* clicks, this feature can improve relevance in combination with other features. We can also see that the combination of all features gives the best overall performance, even though the improvement gained by adding each of the individual features to **B2** is relatively minor.

Features	NDCG1	NDCG5	NDCG10
B2	0.735	0.738	0.775
With Hover Features			
B2 + All	0.753‡‡	0.747‡‡	0.779‡
B2 + All (propagated)	**0.755‡‡**	**0.754‡‡**	**0.790‡‡**
Without Hover Features			
B2 + All	0.747	0.748‡‡	0.780‡‡
B2 + All (propagated)	0.752‡	0.752‡‡	0.788‡‡

Table 5: Relevance + Quality NDCG Results for Image Search with and without hover-based Implicit Feedback features. †- significantly better than B1. ††- highly significantly better than B1. ‡: significantly better than B2. ‡‡: highly significantly better than B2.

These results show that the proposed features can give significant improvements over the strong, state of the art baseline (B2) although the improvements are relatively small at approximately 1% or less for most metrics, with the exception of NDCG1 which shows an improvement of over 2%. Looking at the results for the propagated features, we get further improvements, with all metrics showing highly significant improvements over **B2** of 2% or greater. This confirms that propagating the click features also gives important improvements for image search relevance, and the fact that these improvements can be seen at a greater ranking depth

(NDCG10) also shows that these features will give more robust ranking at depth, which is important in image search, where users explore search results much more deeply than in web search, often examining several pages of results [2, 19].

Relative importance of dwell time features.

To understand which among the 25 proposed dwell time features are most useful, we take the relative importance score of each feature in the best *B1 + DT* model, which is calculated by accumulating decrease of loss of each tree splitting point [6]. From this, we find that the following, in order of importance, are the most important dwell time features for this model: *gtMedian*, *DT z-score*, *DT/Mean*, *DT/Total*, *DT/Median*. Four of these features are normalised features, and one is a categorical features. These results seem to confirm that our proposed normalized and categorical dwell time features are important if we are to make the best use of dwell time information.

6.1.2 Topical Relevance only NDCG

We use NDCG for *Relevance+Quality* as our main evaluation metric because we believe that it captures topical relevance while also boosting the scores for methods that give higher rank to the most attractive, high-quality images. However, to verify that the improvements in quality do not come at the expense of topical relevance, we also report, in Table 6, results for topical relevance only NDCG. The results in Table 6 show very similar improvements over the baselines: the best method shows around 1.5% improvement for NDCG1, NDCG5 and NDCG10, and this improvement is highly significant for NDCG5 and NDCG10. These results demonstrate that, whether we focus on *topical relevance* only, or *relevance + quality*, our proposed features for image search ranking give non-trivial, and highly significant improvements over a strong baseline.

6.1.3 Removing the Hover Features

At the time of the study, two of the three major U.S search engines had a 'hover' interaction in their web image search SRP interface. Since then, one of these removed this feature, meaning that only one of these three search engine now supports this interaction, which raises questions as to whether the results reported so far in this paper are generalizable, or whether they are dependent on transient user interface features. The other web image search user interaction features highlighted in Section 3 on which our proposed features are based, however, have been stable features of all of these search engines for a number of years now, and this can be expected to continue. Table 5 shows results for our methods without the hover-based features, as the results without these features are based on more stable, and therefore more generalizable, features. We can see that removing the hover-based features has a relatively small impact on the NDCG; the improvement over the baseline is still more than 2% (and statistically significant) better than **B2** for NDCG1, and it is highly significantly, and over 1.5% better, for NDCG5 and NDCG10.

7. CONCLUSIONS

In this paper we have proposed a number of novel user behavior features for improving web image search ranking: (1) hover-through rate based on 'hovers' in the *Search Results Page*; (2) click-through from the image *Preview Page* to the *Referral Page* where the images are embedded; (3) dwell time features from the image *Preview Page*; and (4) propagating user behavior features to the query-referral page and the query-independent level. We created a large scale corpus to evaluate the usefulness of these features in a learning to rank framework, and show that the new features achieve highly statistically significant improvements of over 2% beyond a strong, state of the art baseline based on standard click-based features.

While this study focused on image search, many of the user interactions discussed here are shared by web video search interfaces, and so we plan to explore the usefulness of the same features for video search. Also, the latest image search interfaces now support clicking through from the *Preview Page* directly to a full size view of the image. This was not available at the time of our study, but we expect that it will provide similar relevance information as click through from the *Preview Page* to the *Referral Page*, and plan to explore this in the future.

Features	NDCG1	NDCG5	NDCG10
B1	0.818	0.782	0.785
B2	0.893††	0.850††	0.836††
B2 + All	0.905	0.857‡‡	0.839‡‡
B2 + All (propagated)	0.906	**0.862**‡‡	**0.849**‡‡

Table 6: Topical Relevance NDCG Results for Image Search with Implicit Feedback features. †- significantly better than B1. ††- highly significantly better than B1. ‡: significantly better than B2. ‡‡: highly significantly better than B2.

8. REFERENCES

[1] E. Agichtein, E. Brill, and S. Dumais. Improving web search ranking by incorporating user behavior information. In *Proceedings of the 29th Annual International ACM SIGIR Conference on Research and Development in Information Retrieval*, SIGIR '06, pages 19–26, New York, NY, USA, 2006. ACM.

[2] P. Andre, E. Cutrell, D. S. Tan, and G. Smith. Designing novel image search interfaces by understanding unique characteristics and usage. In *INTERACT 2009*, pages 340–353. Springer-Verlag, 2009.

[3] M. Bilenko and R. W. White. Mining the search trails of surfing crowds: Identifying relevant websites from user activity. In *Proceedings of the 17th International Conference on World Wide Web*, WWW '08, pages 51–60, New York, NY, USA, 2008. ACM.

[4] N. Craswell and M. Szummer. Random walks on the click graph. In *Proceedings of the 30th Annual International ACM SIGIR Conference on Research and Development in Information Retrieval*, SIGIR '07, pages 239–246, New York, NY, USA, 2007. ACM.

[5] N. Craswell, O. Zoeter, M. Taylor, and B. Ramsey. An experimental comparison of click position-bias models. In *Proceedings of the 2008 International Conference on Web Search and Data Mining*, WSDM '08, pages 87–94, New York, NY, USA, 2008. ACM.

[6] J. H. Friedman. Greedy function approximation: A gradient boosting machine. *Annals of Statistics*, 29:1189–1232, 2000.

[7] B. Geng, L. Yang, C. Xu, X.-S. Hua, and S. Li. The role of attractiveness in web image search. In *Proceedings of the 19th ACM International Conference on Multimedia*, MM '11, pages 63–72, New York, NY, USA, 2011. ACM.

[8] J. Huang, T. Lin, and R. W. White. No search result left behind: branching behavior with browser tabs. In *WSDM*, 2012.

[9] V. Jain and M. Varma. Learning to re-rank: Query-dependent image re-ranking using click data. In *Proceedings of the 20th International Conference on World Wide Web*, WWW '11, pages 277–286, New York, NY, USA, 2011. ACM.

[10] B. J. Jansen, A. Spink, and J. O. Pedersen. The effect of specialized multimedia collections on web searching. *J. Web Eng.*, 3(3-4):182–199, 2004.

[11] K. Järvelin and J. Kekäläinen. Cumulated gain-based evaluation of ir techniques. *ACM TOIS*.

[12] T. Joachims. Optimizing search engines using clickthrough data. In *Proceedings of the Eighth ACM SIGKDD International Conference on Knowledge Discovery and Data Mining*, KDD '02, pages 133–142, New York, NY, USA, 2002. ACM.

[13] T. Joachims, L. Granka, B. Pan, H. Hembrooke, and G. Gay. Accurately interpreting clickthrough data as implicit feedback. In *Proceedings of the 28th Annual International ACM SIGIR Conference on Research and Development in Information Retrieval*, SIGIR '05, pages 154–161, New York, NY, USA, 2005. ACM.

[14] D. Kelly and N. J. Belkin. Display time as implicit feedback: Understanding task effects. In *Proceedings of the 27th Annual International ACM SIGIR Conference on Research and Development in Information Retrieval*, SIGIR '04, pages 377–384, New York, NY, USA, 2004. ACM.

[15] Y. Kim, A. Hassan, R. W. White, and I. Zitouni. Modeling dwell time to predict click-level satisfaction. In *Proceedings of the 7th ACM International Conference on Web Search and Data Mining*, WSDM '14, pages 193–202, New York, NY, USA, 2014. ACM.

[16] C. Liu, J. Liu, N. Belkin, M. Cole, and J. Gwizdka. Using dwell time as an implicit measure of usefulness in different task types. *Proceedings of the American Society for Information Science and Technology*, 2011.

[17] S. Maniu, N. O'Hare, L. Aiello, L. Chiarandini, and A. Jaimes. Search behaviour on photo sharing platforms. In *ICME 2013*, pages 1–6, 2013.

[18] D. Metzler and W. B. Croft. A markov random field model for term dependencies. In *Proceedings of the 28th Annual International ACM SIGIR Conference on Research and Development in Information Retrieval*, SIGIR '05, pages 472–479, New York, NY, USA, 2005. ACM.

[19] J. Y. Park, N. O'Hare, R. Schifanella, A. Jaimes, and C.-W. Chung. A large-scale study of user image search behavior on the web. In *Proceedings of the 33rd Annual ACM Conference on Human Factors in Computing Systems*, CHI '15, pages 985–994, New York, NY, USA, 2015. ACM.

[20] S. Robertson and H. Zaragoza. The probabilistic relevance framework: Bm25 and beyond. *Found. Trends Inf. Retr.*, 3(4):333–389, Apr. 2009.

[21] G. Smith and H. Ashman. Evaluating implicit judgements from Image search interactions. In *Proceedings of the WebSci'09: Society On-Line*, Mar. 2009.

[22] Y. Song, H. Ma, H. Wang, and K. Wang. Exploring and exploiting user search behavior on mobile and tablet devices to improve search relevance. In *Proceedings of the 22Nd International Conference on World Wide Web*, WWW '13, pages 1201–1212, Republic and Canton of Geneva, Switzerland, 2013. International World Wide Web Conferences Steering Committee.

[23] M. Trevisiol, L. Chiarandini, L. M. Aiello, and A. Jaimes. Image ranking based on user browsing behavior. In *Proceedings of the 35th International ACM SIGIR Conference on Research and Development in Information Retrieval*, SIGIR '12, pages 445–454, New York, NY, USA, 2012. ACM.

[24] T. Tsikrika, C. Diou, A. P. de Vries, and A. Delopoulos. Image annotation using clickthrough data. In *Proceedings of the ACM International Conference on Image and Video Retrieval*, CIVR '09, pages 14:1–14:8, New York, NY, USA, 2009. ACM.

[25] C. Wang, Y. Liu, M. Zhang, S. Ma, M. Zheng, J. Qian, and K. Zhang. Incorporating vertical results into search click models. In *Proceedings of the 36th International ACM SIGIR Conference on Research and Development in Information Retrieval*, SIGIR '13, pages 503–512, New York, NY, USA, 2013. ACM.

[26] R. W. White and J. Huang. Assessing the scenic route: Measuring the value of search trails in web logs. In *Proceedings of the 33rd International ACM SIGIR Conference on Research and Development in Information Retrieval*, SIGIR '10, pages 587–594, New York, NY, USA, 2010. ACM.

[27] S. Xu, H. Jiang, and F. C. M. Lau. Mining user dwell time for personalized web search re-ranking. In *Proceedings of the Twenty-Second International Joint Conference on Artificial Intelligence - Volume Volume Three*, IJCAI'11, pages 2367–2372. AAAI Press, 2011.

[28] S. Xu, Y. Zhu, H. Jiang, and F. C. M. Lau. A user-oriented webpage ranking algorithm based on user attention time. In *Proceedings of the Twenty-Third AAAI Conference on Artificial Intelligence, AAAI 2008, Chicago, Illinois, USA, July 13-17, 2008*, pages 1255–1260, 2008.

[29] X. Yi, L. Hong, E. Zhong, N. N. Liu, and S. Rajan. Beyond clicks: Dwell time for personalization. In *Proceedings of the 8th ACM Conference on Recommender Systems*, RecSys '14, pages 113–120, New York, NY, USA, 2014. ACM.

[30] J. Yu, D. Tao, M. Wang, and Y. Rui. Learning to rank using user clicks and visual features for image retrieval. *IEEE Trans. Cybernetics*, 45(4):767–779, 2015.

[31] Z. Zheng, K. Chen, G. Sun, and H. Zha. A regression framework for learning ranking functions using relative relevance judgments. In *Proceedings of SIGIR '07*.

Self-Paced Cross-Modal Subspace Matching

Jian Liang[1], Zhihang Li[1], Dong Cao[1], Ran He[1,2*], Jingdong Wang[3]
[1] Center for Research on Intelligent Perception and Computing,
National Laboratory of Pattern Recognition, Institute of Automation,
Chinese Academy of Sciences (CAS), Beijing 100190, China
[2] Center for Excellence in Brain Science and Intelligence Technology, CAS, Shanghai 200031, China
[3] Microsoft Research, Beijing 100190, China
{jian.liang, zhihang.li, dong.cao, rhe}@nlpr.ia.ac.cn, jingdw@microsoft.com

ABSTRACT

Cross-modal matching methods match data from different modalities according to their similarities. Most existing methods utilize label information to reduce the semantic gap between different modalities. However, it is usually time-consuming to manually label large-scale data. This paper proposes a Self-Paced Cross-Modal Subspace Matching (SCSM) method for unsupervised multimodal data. We assume that multimodal data are pair-wised and from several semantic groups, which form hard pair-wised constraints and soft semantic group constraints respectively. Then, we formulate the unsupervised cross-modal matching problem as a non-convex joint feature learning and data grouping problem. Self-paced learning, which learns samples from 'easy' to 'complex', is further introduced to refine the grouping result. Moreover, a multimodal graph is constructed to preserve the relationship of both inter- and intra-modality similarity. An alternating minimization method is employed to minimize the non-convex optimization problem, followed by the discussion on its convergence analysis and computational complexity. Experimental results on four multimodal databases show that SCSM outperforms state-of-the-art cross-modal subspace learning methods.

Keywords

Cross-Modal Matching; Heterogeneous Data; Unsupervised Subspace Learning; Self-Paced Learning

1. INTRODUCTION

Nowadays, multimodal data spring up as the popularity of social network on the Internet. People would like to upload personalized content through various forms such as text, image, audio and video simultaneously, this phenomenon urgently pushes the need for heterogeneous content retrieval. Compared with unimodal retrieval, cross-modal retrieval exploiting heterogeneous feature representations to discover optimal heterogeneous content for a given user query, is more and more frequently utilized. Although search engines also provide such services, e.g., text-image search, they mainly rely on homogeneous contents associated with heterogeneous contents within the same web pages or tweets. The main challenge in cross-modal matching is how to bridge the semantic gap between heterogeneous modalities (e.g., different distributions, different dimensionalities). In this literature, some promising approaches [31, 37, 44] have been developed to alleviate this gap. Probability based learning algorithms [28, 16] along with subspace based learning algorithms [12, 29, 37, 18, 22] are even more favored and widely applied for cross-modal learning applications, e.g., image annotation and cross-language information retrieval.

Topic models, such as Latent Dirichlet Allocation (LDA) [6], have proved effective at describing the underlying topics in one single modality. Following researches [5, 28] focused on correlating topics among different modalities, and extended it to the multi-modal case. While [5] assumed a one-to-one correspondence between the topics of each modality, and [28] assumed a regression module between two sets of topics instead of one-to-one correspondence, and achieved better performance with more freedom allowed. [16] further defined a Markov random field to capture the relationships between different topic sets in every modality. Besides traditional topic models, [35] adopted deep Boltzmann machines to learn a generative model, and [27] proposed an effective nonparametric Bayesian framework based on the Indian Buffet Process (IBP) for integrating multimodal data in a latent space. Besides, some recent work [1, 19] exploited deep models for cross-modal matching. And [38] further investigated the impact of deep features on cross-modal retrieval.

In contrast, subspace based cross-modal methods seem attractive due to its efficiency. They aimed to learn a latent common subspace to make all modalities of data to be close to each other. In this literature, Canonical Correlation Analysis (CCA) [12] is the most popular one to obtain such a common space. CCA tries to find two linear projections to maximally preserve the mutual correlations among multimodal data. Owing to its simplicity and effectiveness, CCA has been widely applied to the cross-modal retrieval [7], face recognition [21] and word embedding [8, 9]. Another popular method is the Partial Least Squares (PLS) [31] that learns orthogonal score vectors by maximizing the covariance between different multimodal data. Although both CCA and PLS are able to solve cross-modal subspace matching, the valuable label information

*Corresponding Author.

SIGIR '16, July 17-21, 2016, Pisa, Italy

DOI: http://dx.doi.org/10.1145/2911451.2911527

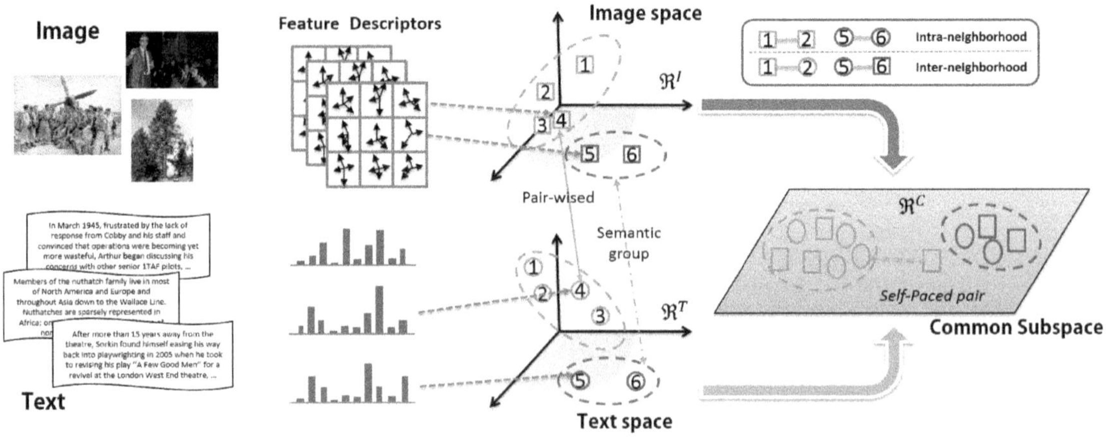

Figure 1: Overview of the proposed SCSM for unsupervised cross-modal matching. Handling hard pair-wised constraints and soft semantic group constraints (labels are unknown) simultaneously, SCSM is formulated as a non-convex joint feature learning and data grouping problem. Self-paced learning is further introduced to refine the grouping result so that we can train a model from 'easy' pairs to 'complex' pairs. Moreover, a novel multimodal similarity graph is leveraged to preserve the local intra- and inter- neighborhoods in the common subspace $\mathcal{R}^C$. (Best viewed in colors).

has not been fully utilized to reduce the semantic gap between text and image modalities.

Since label information potentially reduces the semantic gap between the low-level image features and high-level document descriptions, supervised methods have drawn considerable attentions in cross-modal subspace learning. A generalized multi-view framework [33] was presented to learn a discriminative common space. Built on CCA, [11] proposed to incorporate the third view (label information) to capture the high-level semantics. To select relevant and discriminative features simultaneously, [37] developed a coupled linear regression framework. Moreover, the authors of [13] seek the common structure hidden in heterogeneous modalities via the pairwise constraint. Hashing methods have been also used successfully in multimodal problem [24, 39] and cross-modal problem [40, 43, 41]. While [40] utilized discriminative coupled dictionaries to learn better hash functions, [43] exploited matrix factorization to learn the hash functions. Despite the improvement brought by these supervised cross-modal methods, they will suffer from unlabeled data exceedingly.

To address these above problems, we propose a self-paced joint learning framework (as shown in Figure 1) for the unsupervised cross-modal matching problem by considering feature learning and data grouping simultaneously, which result in a non-convex objective. First, we assume that multimodal data are pair-wised and from several semantic groups, which form hard pair-wised constraints and soft semantic group constraints respectively. For these hard pair-wised constraints, two linear projections are learned to map different modalities into a common space respectively. For the soft semantic group constraints, self-paced learning strategy [20, 42] is applied to refine the grouping results so that we can train a model from 'easy' pairs to 'complex' pairs. Second, the projection regularization is employed for feature learning. A graph-based regularization term preserves the relationship of both inter- and intra- modality similarities. Finally, we present an alternating algorithm to cope with this optimization problem. Extensive experimental results on four benchmark databases demonstrate that our approach is highly effective.

The contributions of this paper are summarized as follows:

1) We propose a general framework for unsupervised cross-modal subspace learning that can handle hard pair-wised constraints and soft semantic group constraints simultaneously. A joint feature learning and data grouping formulation is accordingly developed and results in a non-convex problem.

2) Self-paced learning is used to alleviate the inaccurate estimation of soft semantic group so that we can gradually include sample pair sequences from 'easy' to 'complex'. Multimodal graph, preserving the inter-modality and intra-modality similarity, is then utilized to better explore unsupervised multimodal data.

3) An alternating minimization method is put forward to efficiently minimize the proposed non-convex optimization problem. Experimental results validate that our method outperforms state-of-the-art unsupervised subspace learning methods or even better than some supervised ones.

The remainder of the paper is organized as follows. In Section 2, we will illustrate the details of our SCSM method. Experimental results are presented in Section 3. Finally, the conclusion is summarized in Section 4.

2. SELF-PACED CROSS-MODAL SUBSPACE MATCHING

In this section, we will present our SCSM in details and use two modalities for example in this paper. Note that SCSM can be easily extended to cover the case for more than two modalities.

2.1 Notation and Problem Definition

We start with a brief introduction to some notations. For a matrix $\mathbf{M} \in \mathbb{R}^{n \times m}$, its i-th row, j-th column are denoted by $\mathbf{m}_i$, $\mathbf{m}^j$ respectively, and $M_{i,j}$ lies in the i-th row and j-th column. The Frobenius norm of the matrix $\mathbf{M}$ is defined as $||\mathbf{M}||_F = \sqrt{\sum_{i=1}^{n} ||\mathbf{m}_i||_2^2}$, and the trace of the square matrix M is defined as $Tr(M) = \sum_i M_{i,i}$.

Assume that we have two sets of features from different modalities (e.g., image and text), $\mathbf{X}_a = [\mathbf{x}_1^a, \mathbf{x}_2^a, \ldots, \mathbf{x}_n^a] \in \mathbb{R}^{d_1 \times n}$, $\mathbf{X}_b = [\mathbf{x}_1^b, \mathbf{x}_2^b, \ldots, \mathbf{x}_n^b] \in \mathbb{R}^{d_2 \times n}$, where d_i is the dimensionality of the i-th modality, n is the amount of training image-text pairs. And each pair $\{\mathbf{x}_i^a, \mathbf{x}_i^b\}$ has the same underlying content and belongs to the same class, i.e., the hard pair-wised constraint. However, the concrete label of each pair is unknown here.

The goal of cross-modal matching is to obtain two subspaces $\mathbf{S}_p = \mathbf{U}_p^T \mathbf{X}_p \in \mathbb{R}^{c \times n}, p \in \{a, b\}$ with the same dimensionality, where $\mathbf{U}_p \in \mathbb{R}^{d_p \times c}, p \in \{a, b\}$ denote two projection matrices for these two modalities $\mathbf{X}_p, p \in \{a, b\}$, respectively. Cross-modal matching tasks usually include: 1) using texts to match the related images, and 2) using images to match the related texts.

Here, we mainly focus on the case that one retrieved result is a good matching only when it shares the same semantic label with the given user query.

2.2 Self-Paced Learning Revisit

Curriculum learning [4] and self-paced learning [20] have been attracting increasing attention in machine learning, computer vision and multimedia analysis fields. The philosophy under these concepts is to simulate the learning process of humans/animals, i.e., humans/animals generally start with learning easier aspects of a learning task, and then gradually take more complex examples into consideration [25]. Instead of using the aforementioned heuristic strategies in curriculum learning, self-paced learning automatically includes training samples from 'easy' to 'complex' in a purely self-paced way.

Given a training dataset $\mathbb{D} = \{(x_i, y_i)\}_{i=1}^n$, in which $\{x_i, y_i\}$ denotes the i-th observed sample and its label, then let $L(y_i, g(x_i, w))$ be the loss function, w is the model parameter inside the decision function g. Generally, the objective of self-paced learning consists of two parts, i.e., a weighted loss term on all samples and a general self-paced regularizer imposed on sample weights, is expressed as:

$$\min_{w, v \in [0,1]^n} E(w, v; \lambda) = \sum_{i=1}^{n} (v_i L(y_i, g(x_i, w)) + f(v_i, \lambda)), \quad (1)$$

where λ is the age parameter for controlling the learning rate, and $f(v, \lambda)$ is the self-paced regularizer. A formal definition is given in [17, 42]. This strategy, as supported by empirical evaluation, has proved helpful in alleviating the local optimum problem in non-convex optimization [3].

2.3 Model Formulation

In Figure 1, multimodal data are firstly pair-wised, further supposed to come from several latent semantic groups, which form hard pair-wised constraints and soft semantic group constraints respectively.

Latent Discriminative Subspace Learning For the cross-modal problem, a CCA-like objective function expressed as

$$\min_{\mathbf{U}_a, \mathbf{U}_b} \|\mathbf{U}_a^T \mathbf{X}_a - \mathbf{U}_b^T \mathbf{X}_b\|_F^2 + \Phi(\mathbf{U}_a, \mathbf{U}_b), \quad (2)$$

where $\Phi(\cdot)$ is a regularizer imposed on the projection matrices, is exploited frequently to discover the optimal common subspace. Then we consider the following objective,

$$\min_{\mathbf{U}_a, \mathbf{U}_b, \mathbf{Y}} \sum_{p \in \{a,b\}} \|\mathbf{U}_p^T \mathbf{X}_p - \mathbf{Y}\|_F^2 + \Phi(\mathbf{U}_a, \mathbf{U}_b), \quad (3)$$

as a relaxed candidate for that in Eq.(2), owing to the basic inequality $\|A - C\|_F^2 + \|B - C\|_F^2 \geq \frac{\|A-B\|_F^2}{2}$.

Since multimodal data are separated into several groups in the latent subspace, we further strict the latent variable $\mathbf{Y}$ lying in the discrete space $\{0, 1\}^{c \times n}$, revealing the group/cluster membership, where c is the amount of latent groups. Obviously, $\mathbf{1}_c \mathbf{Y} = \mathbf{1}_n$, where $\mathbf{1}_c$ and $\mathbf{1}_n$ denote the constant vectors of all one, of dimensions c and n respectively. Let $\Phi(\mathbf{U}_a, \mathbf{U}_b) = \beta \left(\|\mathbf{U}_a\|_F^2 + \|\mathbf{U}_b\|_F^2\right)$ as [2], we can write the multimodal feature learning term as follows:

$$\begin{aligned} &\min_{\mathbf{U}_a, \mathbf{U}_b, \mathbf{Y}} \sum_{p \in \{a,b\}} \|\mathbf{U}_p^T \mathbf{X}_p - \mathbf{Y}\|_F^2 + \beta \|\mathbf{U}_p\|_F^2, \\ &s.t. \ \mathbf{Y} \in \{0, 1\}^{c \times n}, \sum_i^c Y_{i,j} = 1, \forall j \in [1, n], \end{aligned} \quad (4)$$

where each $\mathbf{X}_p$ is the feature representation matrix, $\mathbf{U}_p$ is the corresponding projection matrix, and $\|\mathbf{U}_p\|_F^2$ is a regularizer imposed on project matrices to avoid trivial solutions.

Cluster indicator $\mathbf{Y}$ is a discrete variable, which easily involves the optimization method in a local optimum. Fortunately, the learning process from 'easy' to 'complex' proposed in self-paced learning can effectively avoid the local optimum. Thus we incorporate self-paced learning model in Eq.(1) into Eq.(4), resulting in the following form:

$$\begin{aligned} &\min_{\mathbf{U}_a, \mathbf{U}_b, \mathbf{v}, \mathbf{Y}} \sum_{p \in \{a,b\}} \sum_{i=1}^{n} v_i \ell_i + \beta \sum_{p \in \{a,b\}} \|\mathbf{U}_p\|_F^2 + f(\mathbf{v}; k) \\ &s.t. \ \mathbf{Y} \in \{0, 1\}^{c \times n}, \sum_i^c Y_{i,j} = 1, \forall j \in [1, n], \end{aligned} \quad (5)$$

where the i-th loss of sample is defined as $\ell_i = \|(\mathbf{U}_p^T \mathbf{x}_p^i - \mathbf{y}^i)\|_F^2$ above.

Multimodal Locality Preserving The term in Eq.(4) mainly focuses on the similarities among pair-wised heterogeneous data. Local similarity in each modality may vanish in the process of feature learning. We then take locality preserving into consideration, which has also proven effective in [14], the projected features in the common subspace $\mathcal{R}^C$ should inherit the similar local structure to it in these two original feature spaces. Then for each projected modality, we try to minimize the following objective function:

$$\sum_{i,j} (z_p^i - z_p^j)^2 \mathbf{W}_{ij}, \quad (6)$$

where $Z_p = \mathbf{U}_p^T \mathbf{X}_p$ are the projected feature matrices, and W_{ij} is the intra-similarity between the i-th and the j-th sample. We adopt the Gaussian kernel function $d(\mathbf{x}_p^i, \mathbf{x}_p^j) = e^{\frac{-\|\mathbf{x}_p^i - \mathbf{x}_p^j\|^2}{2\sigma^2}}$ to measure the local similarity:

$$W_{ij}^p = \begin{cases} d(\mathbf{x}_p^i, \mathbf{x}_p^j) & \text{if } \mathbf{x}_p^i \in N_r(\mathbf{x}_p^j) \text{ or } \mathbf{x}_p^j \in N_r(\mathbf{x}_p^i), \\ 0 & \text{otherwise}, \end{cases} \quad (7)$$

where $N_r(\cdot)$ is the set of r-nearest samples. The total intra-similarity preserving term in Eq.(6) for each modality can be formulated as:

$$\mathcal{L}_{intra} = \sum_{p \in \{a,b\}} Tr(\mathbf{Z}_p \mathbf{L}_p \mathbf{Z}_p^T), \quad (8)$$

where $\mathbf{L}_p = \mathbf{D}^p - \mathbf{W}^p$ is the Laplacian matrix and $\mathbf{D}^p$ is a diagonal matrix, where $D_{i,i}^p = \sum_j W_{i,j}^p$.

Moreover, a novel similarity preserving term is introduced to maximize the similarity between data from one identical latent cluster. Given the cluster indicator $\mathbf{Y}$ instead of the missing semantic labels in [36], $W^{ab} = W^{ba} = \mathbf{Y}^T\mathbf{Y}$ can be seen as the inter-similarity matrix. Apparently, only paired data from the same cluster are treated as similar pair, the similarity of coupled data from different clusters equals to 0, otherwise. We can define a inter-similarity preserving term akin to the intra-similarity term above, expressed as:

$$\mathcal{L}_{inter} = Tr(\mathbf{Z}_a\mathbf{L}_{ab}\mathbf{Z}_b^T). \quad (9)$$

Then we introduce a new joint similarity matrix as below:

$$\mathbf{W} = \begin{bmatrix} \gamma W^a & W^{ab} \\ W^{ba} & \gamma W^b \end{bmatrix}. \quad (10)$$

Combining these two locality-preserving terms $\mathcal{L}_{intra}$ and $\mathcal{L}_{inter}$ together, we further obtain the following term:

$$\begin{aligned} \mathcal{L}(\mathbf{U}_a, \mathbf{U}_b) &= \mathcal{L}_{inter} + \gamma\mathcal{L}_{intra} \\ &= \sum_{p,q\in\{a,b\}} Tr(\mathbf{U}_p^T\mathbf{X}_p\mathbf{L}_{pq}\mathbf{X}_q^T\mathbf{U}_q), \end{aligned} \quad (11)$$

where $\mathbf{L}_{pq}$ is the corresponding block of the Laplacian matrix $\mathbf{L}$, and γ is a trade-off parameter to balance the intra- and inter- similarity preserving terms.

Associating discriminative subspace learning with local similarity preserving together, we obtain the overall objective function for SCSM:

$$\begin{aligned} \min_{\mathbf{U}\{a,b\},\mathbf{v},\mathbf{Y}} &\sum_{p\in\{a,b\}}\sum_{i=1}^{n} v_i\ell_i + \alpha\mathcal{L}(\mathbf{U}_a, \mathbf{U}_b) \\ &+\beta\sum_{p\in\{a,b\}}||\mathbf{U}_p||_F^2 + f(\mathbf{v};k) \\ s.t.\ \ &\mathbf{Y}\in\{0,1\}^{c\times n}, \sum_i^c Y_{i,j} = 1, \forall j\in[1,n]. \end{aligned} \quad (12)$$

2.4 Optimization Algorithm

In this subsection, a fast iterative optimization algorithm is developed to find the optimal solution of Eq.(12). Regarding the self-paced regualrizer $f(\cdot)$, we adopt the same strategy utilized in [20]: $f(\mathbf{v};k) = -\frac{1}{k}\sum_i v_i$, where $\mathbf{v}\in\mathbb{R}^n$ denotes the weights imposed on the loss term, which is a binary vector. When age parameter k is given in each iteration, the current indicator variable v_i can be defined for each sample x_i as:

$$v_i = \begin{cases} 1 & \text{if } \ell_i \le \frac{1}{k}, \\ 0 & \text{if } \ell_i > \frac{1}{k}. \end{cases} \quad (13)$$

Besides, we rewrite Eq.(12) into the following form:

$$\begin{aligned} \min_{\mathbf{U}\{a,b\},\mathbf{v},\mathbf{Y}} &\sum_{p\in\{a,b\}} ||(\mathbf{U}_p^T\mathbf{X}_p - \mathbf{Y})diag(\mathbf{v})||_F^2 \\ &+\alpha\sum_{p\in\{a,b\}} Tr(\mathbf{U}_p^T\mathbf{X}_p\mathbf{L}_{pq}\mathbf{X}_q^T\mathbf{U}_q) \\ &+\beta\sum_{p\in\{a,b\}}||\mathbf{U}_p||_F^2 - \frac{1}{k}\sum_i v_i \\ s.t.\ \ &\mathbf{Y}\in\{0,1\}^{c\times n}, \sum_i^c Y_{i,j} = 1, \forall j\in[1,n]. \end{aligned} \quad (14)$$

Since the matrix $\mathbf{Y}\in\{0,1\}^{c\times n}$ is limited to discrete values, i.e., a non-convex set, Eq.(14) is a non-convex problem. We employ an alternating minimization algorithm for Eq.(14), the involved parameters include $\mathbf{U}_a, \mathbf{U}_b, \mathbf{v}$ and $\mathbf{Y}$.

1) Solve $\mathbf{U}_a, \mathbf{U}_b$ when $\mathbf{Y}, \mathbf{v}$ are fixed. Optimizing the objective function(14) is equal to minimizing the following problem:

$$\begin{aligned} \min_{\mathbf{U}_p} &||(\mathbf{U}_p^T\mathbf{X}_p - \mathbf{Y})\mathbf{V}||_F^2 \\ &+\alpha\sum_p\sum_q Tr(\mathbf{U}_p^T\mathbf{X}_p\mathbf{L}_{pq}\mathbf{X}_q^T\mathbf{U}_q) + \beta||\mathbf{U}_p||_F^2, \end{aligned} \quad (15)$$

where $\mathbf{V}$ is a diagonal matrix whose entries correspond to the elements in v. Differentiating the objective function in Eq.(15) with respect to $\mathbf{U}_p$ and setting it to zero, we have the following equation:

$$\begin{aligned} &(\mathbf{X}_p\mathbf{V}\mathbf{V}^T\mathbf{X}_p^T + \alpha\mathbf{X}_p\mathbf{L}_{pp}\mathbf{X}_p^T + \beta\mathbf{I})\mathbf{U}_p \\ &\quad = \mathbf{X}_p\mathbf{V}\mathbf{V}^T\mathbf{Y}^T - \alpha\mathbf{X}_p\mathbf{L}_{pq}\mathbf{X}_q^T\mathbf{U}_q \end{aligned} \quad (16)$$

Then, the optimal solution of Eq.(16) can be computed via solving the above linear system problem.

2) Solve $\mathbf{Y}$ when $\mathbf{U}_a, \mathbf{U}_b, \mathbf{v}$ are fixed. Optimizing the objective function in Eq.(14) is equal to optimizing the following problem:

$$\begin{aligned} \min_{\mathbf{Y}} &\sum_{p\in\{a,b\}} ||(\mathbf{U}_p^T\mathbf{X}_p - \mathbf{Y})\mathbf{V}||_F^2 + 2\alpha Tr(\mathbf{U}_a^T\mathbf{X}_a\mathbf{Y}^T\mathbf{Y}\mathbf{X}_b^T\mathbf{U}_b) \\ s.t.\ \ &\mathbf{Y}\in\{0,1\}^{c\times n}, \sum_i^c Y_{i,j} = 1, \forall j\in[1,n]. \end{aligned} \quad (17)$$

It is challenging to directly minimize the above objective function w.r.t $\mathbf{Y}$ due to the discrete constraints, resulting in a NP hard problem. Inspired by [34], we can optimize $\mathbf{Y}$ column by column, i.e., optimize one column of $\mathbf{Y}$ with all the other columns fixed. So we can iteratively learn one column at one time. Then Eq.(17) is equivalent to:

$$\begin{aligned} \min_{\mathbf{Y}} \ &Tr(\mathbf{V}^T\mathbf{Y}^T\mathbf{Y}\mathbf{V}) + \alpha Tr(\mathbf{E}\mathbf{Y}^T\mathbf{Y}\mathbf{F}^T) \\ &- Tr(\mathbf{G}\mathbf{Y}^T) - Tr(\mathbf{H}\mathbf{Y}^T) \\ s.t.\ \ &\mathbf{Y}\in\{0,1\}^{c\times n}, \sum_i^c Y_{i,j} = 1, \forall j\in[1,n], \end{aligned} \quad (18)$$

where $\mathbf{E} = \mathbf{U}_a^T\mathbf{X}_a$, $\mathbf{F} = \mathbf{U}_b^T\mathbf{X}_b$, $\mathbf{G} = \mathbf{U}_a^T\mathbf{X}_a\mathbf{V}\mathbf{V}^T$, $\mathbf{H} = \mathbf{U}_b^T\mathbf{X}_b\mathbf{V}\mathbf{V}^T$.

The objective in Eq.(18) can be further attributed to minimizing two following general cases, i.e., $Tr(\mathbf{A}\mathbf{Y}^T\mathbf{Y}\mathbf{B}^T)$ and $Tr(\mathbf{C}\mathbf{Y}^T)$. Let $\mathbf{y}$ be the i-th column of $\mathbf{Y}$, $i = 1,\cdots,n$, and $\widetilde{\mathbf{Y}}$ the matrix $\mathbf{Y}$ of excluding $\mathbf{y}$ where $\mathbf{y}$ is one of all n samples. Similarly, denote by $\mathbf{a}$ the i-th column of $\mathbf{A}$, $\widetilde{\mathbf{A}}$ the matrix of $\mathbf{A}$ excluding $\mathbf{a}$, $\mathbf{b}$ the i-th column of $\mathbf{B}$, and $\widetilde{\mathbf{B}}$ the matrix of $\mathbf{B}$ excluding $\mathbf{b}$ and $\mathbf{c}$ the i-th column of $\mathbf{C}$ and $\widetilde{\mathbf{C}}$ the matrix of $\mathbf{C}$ excluding $\mathbf{c}$. Then we have the following form:

$$\begin{aligned} Tr(\mathbf{A}\mathbf{Y}^T\mathbf{Y}\mathbf{B}^T) &= Tr((\mathbf{a}\mathbf{y}^T + \widetilde{\mathbf{A}}\widetilde{\mathbf{Y}}^T)(\mathbf{y}\mathbf{b}^T + \widetilde{\mathbf{Y}}\widetilde{\mathbf{B}}^T)) \\ &= const + Tr(\mathbf{a}\mathbf{y}^T\mathbf{y}\mathbf{b}^T) + \mathbf{y}^T\widetilde{\mathbf{Y}}\widetilde{\mathbf{B}}^T\mathbf{a} + \mathbf{y}^T\widetilde{\mathbf{Y}}\widetilde{\mathbf{A}}^T\mathbf{b} \\ &= const + \mathbf{y}^T\widetilde{\mathbf{Y}}\widetilde{\mathbf{B}}^T\mathbf{a} + \mathbf{y}^T\widetilde{\mathbf{Y}}\widetilde{\mathbf{A}}^T\mathbf{b}. \end{aligned} \quad (19)$$

Here $Tr(\mathbf{a}\mathbf{y}^T\mathbf{y}\mathbf{b}^T) = Tr(\mathbf{a}\mathbf{b}^T) = const$. Similarly, we have:

$$Tr(\mathbf{C}\mathbf{Y}^T) = Tr(\mathbf{c}\mathbf{y}^T) + Tr(\widetilde{\mathbf{C}}\widetilde{\mathbf{Y}}^T) = const + \mathbf{y}^T\mathbf{c}. \quad (20)$$

According to Eq.(19) and Eq.(20), we can formulate Eq.(18) as follows:

$$\begin{aligned} &\min_{\mathbf{y}} \ \mathbf{y}^T(2\widetilde{\mathbf{Y}}\widetilde{\mathbf{V}}^T\mathbf{v} + \alpha\widetilde{\mathbf{Y}}\widetilde{\mathbf{F}}^T\mathbf{e} + \alpha\widetilde{\mathbf{Y}}\widetilde{\mathbf{E}}^T\mathbf{f} - \mathbf{g} - \mathbf{h}) \\ &s.t. \ \ \mathbf{y} \in \{0,1\}^{c\times 1}, \sum_i^c \mathbf{y}_i = 1, \end{aligned} \quad (21)$$

where $\mathbf{e}, \mathbf{f}, \mathbf{g}, \mathbf{h}$ are the i-th column of $\mathbf{E}$,$\mathbf{F}$,$\mathbf{G}$,$\mathbf{H}$ and $\widetilde{\mathbf{E}}$,$\widetilde{\mathbf{F}}$,$\widetilde{\mathbf{G}}$,$\widetilde{\mathbf{H}}$ are the matrices of $\mathbf{E}, \mathbf{F}, \mathbf{G}, \mathbf{H}$ excluding $\mathbf{e}, \mathbf{f}, \mathbf{g}, \mathbf{h}$ respectively.

Thus, this subproblem can be easily solved as:

$$\mathbf{y}_i = \begin{cases} 1 & \mathrm{i} = \mathrm{h}(\mathbf{m}) \\ 0 & \text{otherwise}, \end{cases} \quad (22)$$

where $\mathbf{m} = 2\widetilde{\mathbf{Y}}\widetilde{\mathbf{V}}^T\mathbf{v} + \alpha\widetilde{\mathbf{Y}}\widetilde{\mathbf{F}}^T\mathbf{e} + \alpha\widetilde{\mathbf{Y}}\widetilde{\mathbf{E}}^T\mathbf{f} - \mathbf{g} - \mathbf{h}$, and $\mathrm{h}(\mathbf{m})$ returns the index of the minimum value of $\mathbf{m}$. After $2 \sim 3$ inner iterations, we can obtain a optimal complete $\mathbf{Y}$.

3) Solve $\mathbf{v}$ *when* $\mathbf{U}_a, \mathbf{U}_b, \mathbf{Y}$ *are fixed.* The loss of each sample can be directly computed, thus we can obtain $\mathbf{v}$ by Eq.(13).

Algorithm 1 Self-Paced Cross-Modal Subspace Matching (SCSM)

Input: The matrices of unlabeled data $\mathbf{X}_p \in \mathbb{R}^{d_p \times n}, p \in \{a, b\}$;

Output: The projection matrices $\mathbf{U}_p \in \mathbb{R}^{d_p \times c}, p \in \{a, b\}$;

1: Initialize $\mathbf{Y}$ by K-means clustering, and compute the Laplacian matrix of the multimodal graph $\mathbf{L}$, and initialize $t = 0, \mathbf{U}_p, p \in \{a, b\}$ as identity matrix;

2: **repeat**

3: Compute $\mathbf{v}^t$ according to Eq.(13);

4: Compute $\mathbf{U}_p^t, p \in \{a, b\}$ by solving the linear system problems in Eq.(16);

5: Compute $\mathbf{Y}^t$ according to Eq.(21) and Eq.(22);

6: Compute $\mathbf{W}^t$ according to Eq.(10);

7: $t = t + 1$;

8: **until** Convergence;

Algorithm 1 summarizes the alternate minimization procedure to optimize Eq.(14). Firstly, the label information $\mathbf{Y}$ is obtained by K-means clustering on the text modality and the multimodal Laplacian matrix is constructed in Step 1; Then, Step $3 \sim 6$ is an alternate procedure of iteratively updating each of $\mathbf{U}\{a, b\}, \mathbf{v}, \mathbf{Y}$ one by one in a loop.

2.5 Computational Complexity Analysis

Here we try to discuss the time complexity of the proposed SCSM. For each outer iteration, we need $\mathcal{O}(nd_1^2 + nd_2^2)$ to solve $\mathbf{U}_a$ and $\mathbf{U}_b$, $\mathcal{O}(nc^2)$ to solve $\mathbf{Y}$, and $\mathcal{O}(ncd_1 + ncd_2)$ for solving v. Thus, the overall time complexity is $\mathcal{O}(nd^2 + n^2c)$ for SCSM, where c is the dimension of the common subspace and d is the larger original dimensionality for each modality.

3. EXPERIMENT

In this section, we comprehensively compare SCSM and other existing cross-modal approaches on four benchmark datasets, the Pascal VOC [15, 10], the Wikipedia [29], and the LabelMe [32, 26] dataset, which are widely adopted for cross-modal matching tasks.

3.1 Evaluation Criteria & Baseline Methods

There are several widely used evaluation criteria for cross-modal subspace matching algorithms [29, 33, 37]. During the testing phase, multimodal data are mapped into a common subspace via the learned projection matrices for each modality. Then in the subspace, we take one type of modality as a query set to match another type of modality. Like [29, 37, 18], the cosine distance is utilized to measure the similarity of projected features. The simple goal is that given a query from one modality, we can return the top k closest matches in another modality via subspace learning.

The mean average precision (MAP) metric is a classical performance evaluation criterion in the information retrieval circle. The higher MAP indicates the better performance. Besides the MAP, we also exploit the precision-scope curve [30] and precision-recall curve [29] to intensively evaluate the effectiveness of different methods, where the scope K is specified by the number of the top-ranked texts/images presented to users.

With regards to baseline methods, CCA [12], PLS [31] and GMBLM [33] are three unsupervised methods, which merely use the hard pair-wised information to learn a common latent subspace. In contrast, supervised methods such as CDFE [23], GMLDA [33], GMMFA [33], LCFS [37] and recent JFSSL [36] all take the semantic class information into account, and they are also compared here. Despite the improved performance, semantic labels are usually expensive and time-consuming to obtain for supervised methods. To further study the effect of initial clustering result, we further assume the clustering result as pseudo semantic labels, and attain the matching performance of above supervised methods, referred as UCDFE, UGMLDA and UGMMFA.

3.2 Performance on Cross-Modal Matching

3.2.1 Results on the Pascal VOC dataset

The Pascal VOC dataset [15] is a commonly used dataset, it consists of 9,963 image-text pairs from 20 categories, including 5,011 training and 4,952 testing image-text pairs. Since some of the images have multiple labels, we select the images with only one label [33, 37]. As a result, we obtain 2808 training and 2841 testing data samples that correspond to 20 categories. The image and text features are 512-dimensional Gist [26] features and 399-dimensional word frequency features, respectively.

We first use the Principal Component Analysis (PCA) to remove the redundancy in features. 95% information energy is preserved by the PCA before evaluation. The MAP scores of the cross-modal retrieval results are shown in Table 1.

From Table 1, we can observe that the proposed SCSM achieves the best performance on both the image-to-text and text-to-image matching tasks. Obviously, supervised methods (i.e., CDFE, GMLDA and GMMFA) outperform their unsupervised versions by 10%, and earn bigger advantages over CCA and PLS. This is because supervised methods rely on semantic labels to reduce the semantic gap of different modalities, but unsupervised methods only use pair-wised information. However, our unsupervised method not only surpasses the unsupervised methods,

Dataset & Methods	Pascal VOC			Wiki			Wiki++			LabelMe		
	Image	Text	Avg	Image	Text	Avg	Image	Text	Avg	Image	Text	Avg
CCA	0.250	0.212	0.231	0.251	0.199	0.225	0.347	0.310	0.329	0.268	0.236	0.252
PLS	0.256	0.241	0.249	0.262	0.174	0.218	0.304	0.329	0.317	0.522	0.435	0.478
GMBLM	0.312	0.232	0.272	0.255	0.204	0.229	0.347	0.318	0.333	0.515	0.466	0.490
UCDFE	0.279	0.209	0.244	0.224	0.184	0.204	0.333	0.301	0.317	0.570	0.594	0.582
UGMMFA	0.298	0.232	0.265	0.269	0.211	0.240	0.340	0.310	0.325	0.512	0.499	0.505
UGMLDA	0.301	0.239	0.270	0.272	0.215	0.244	0.340	0.318	0.325	0.542	0.536	0.539
CDFE	0.306	0.227	0.267	0.260	0.209	0.234	0.397	0.344	0.370	0.685	**0.725**	0.705
GMMFA	0.327	0.259	0.293	0.273	0.219	0.246	0.409	0.362	0.386	**0.719**	0.724	**0.722**
GMLDA	0.324	0.260	0.292	0.273	0.218	0.246	0.409	0.362	0.386	0.716	0.720	0.718
LCFS [36]	0.344	0.267	0.306	0.280	0.214	0.247	0.413	0.384	0.404	-	-	-
JFSSL [36]	**0.361**	**0.280**	**0.320**	**0.306**	**0.228**	**0.267**	**0.428**	**0.396**	**0.412**	-	-	-
SCSM	**0.375**	**0.282**	**0.329**	**0.274**	**0.217**	**0.245**	**0.423**	**0.381**	**0.402**	**0.641**	**0.672**	**0.656**

Table 1: MAP scores of *unsupervised* SCSM and other methods on the Pascal VOC, Wiki, Wiki++ and LabelMe datasets, while CDFE, GMMFA, GMLDA, LCFS and JFSSL are *supervised* methods.

but outperforms several supervised methods, achieving the state-of-the-art performance.

Figure 2 shows the corresponding precision-recall curves and precision-scope curves. The scope, i.e., the top K retrieved items, varies from $K = 50$ to 1000. It can be observed from Figure 2 that SCSM consistently outperforms other unsupervised methods for both Image query vs. Text database and Text query vs. Image database, regardless of precision-scope curves and precision-recall curves. Note that GMBLM only performs inferior to SCSM, due to its consideration of intra-similarity.

Class	Tags queries	True Image	Matching Images
aeroplane	aeroplane grass door window wheel		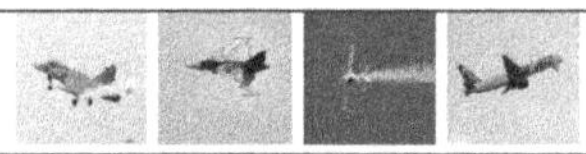
boat	boat rigging water sky wave	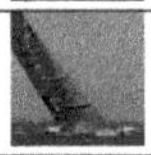	
bird	bird tree sky	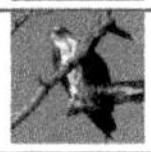	
train	train rope railroad pole tree		

Table 2: Retrieval examples by user tags queries on the Pascal VOC database by the proposed SCSM. For each tags query (second column), the top several retrieved images are shown in the fourth column. The first column represents the ground truth class of each corresponding tags query, and the third column shows the ground truth Image with the queries. (Best viewed in colors.)

3.2.2 Results on the Wiki dataset

The Wiki image-text dataset [29] generated from Wikipedia articles, is a fundamental dataset for cross-modal matching. It is composed of 2,866 image-text pairs from 10 semantic classes, with image features being 128-dimensional SIFT feature and the text feature being 10-dimensional Latent Dirichlet allocation (LDA) feature. We split it into a training set of 1,300 pairs and a testing set of 1,566 pairs in the experiment [37]. We directly carry out the experiment with the provided datasets owing to the low dimensional image and text features. The MAP scores obtained by SCSM and other approaches are shown in Table 1.

From Table 1, we can see that SCSM achieves similar results to GMLDA and GMMFA, and is just inferior to JFSSL. However, it continues to be the best algorithm for unsupervised cross-modal subspace learning. The reason for these results is that the dimension of the features in this database is generally low so that the feature learning hardly takes effect. In the next subsection, we will show our improved performances with the help of better feature representations.

The corresponding precision-recall curves (a) and precision-scope curves (b) are also plotted for both forms of cross-modal retrieval tasks in Figure 3. We observe that, for an image query, SCSM obtains similar and even inferior performance, while for the text query, it performs the best among these unsupervised algorithms.

3.2.3 Results on the Wiki++ dataset

The Wiki++ dataset [36] is built on the famous Wiki dataset [29]. They share all but feature representations. 4,096-dimensional Convolutional Neural Network (CNN) features are extracted for images by Caffe[1], and 5,000-dimensional BOW feature vectors are learned based on the basic tf-idf features. We also split the entire dataset into a 1,300 training set and a 1,566 testing set. Specifically, PCA is also performed on the features, and 95% information energy preserved for both views.

From Table 1, it is obvious that the proposed SCSM algorithm achieves the best performance with average MAP 40.2% among unsupervised methods. Even though SCSM performs a little lower than JFSSL, it still can beat other supervised methods such as GMLDA and LCFS. Compared with performances obtained in the Wiki dataset, all methods achieve better results when using CNN visual features in spite of the image query or the text query. This is because the CNN features have proven effective for image feature representation. In the high and sparse dimensional feature setting, SCSM shrinks the distance with the best-performing JFSSL from 2.2% to 1%, offers the great potentials when better features are provided.

SCSM obtains the best performance in terms of precision-

[1] http://caffe.berkeleyvision.org/.

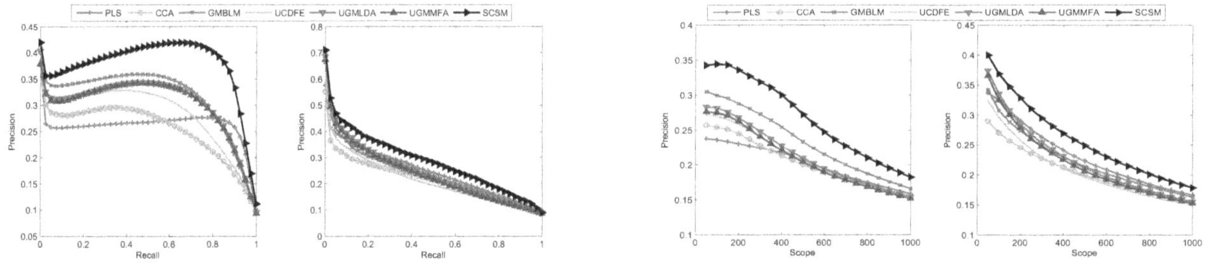

(a) precision-recall curve (b) precision-scope curve

Figure 2: Performance of various *unsupervised* methods on the **Pascal VOC** dataset, based on precision-recall curve(a) for $K = 50$ to 1000 and precision-scope curve(b). The performances for image query are shown in the left sub-figures.

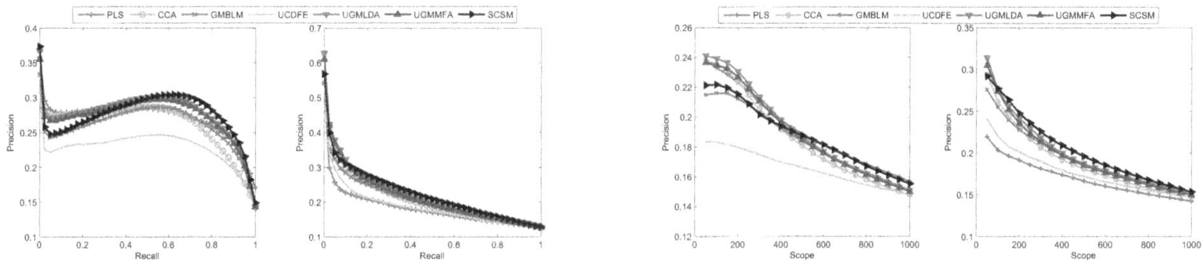

(a) precision-recall curve (b) precision-scope curve

Figure 3: Performance of various *unsupervised* methods on the **Wiki** dataset, based on precision-recall curve(a) for $K = 50$ to 1000 and precision-scope curve(b). The performances for image query are shown in the left sub-figures.

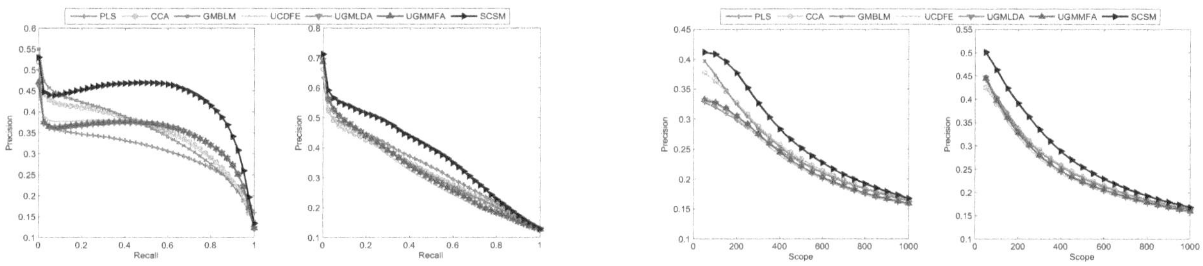

(a) precision-recall curve (b) Precision-scope curve

Figure 4: Performance of various *unsupervised* methods on the **Wiki++** dataset, based on precision-recall curve(a) for $K = 50$ to 1000 and precision-scope curve(b). The performances for image query are shown in the left sub-figures.

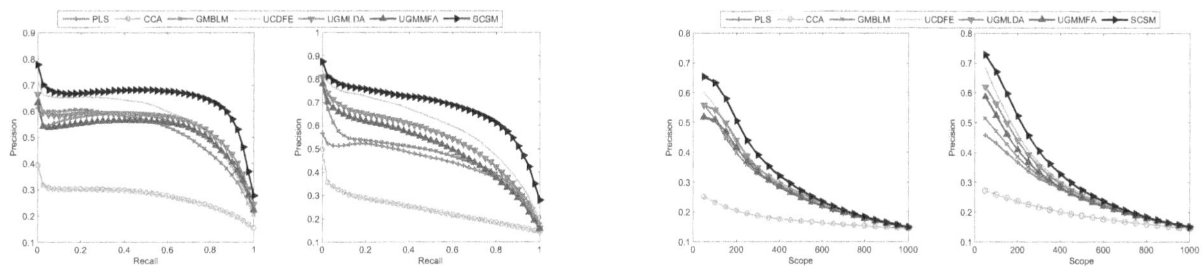

(a) precision-recall curve (b) precision-scope curve

Figure 5: Performance of various *unsupervised* methods on the **LabelMe** dataset, based on precision-recall curve(a) for $K = 50$ to 1000 and precision-scope curve(b). The performances for image query are shown in the left sub-figures.

recall curves for both image query and text query, as shown in Figure 4(a). From the precision-scope curves in Figure 4(b), SCSM discovers more good matches in the top K documents than its several counterparts.

To further study the difference between SCSM and other methods (here we ignore the unsupervised versions of supervised methods due to the space limit) in Figure 6. From the figure, we can find that SCSM takes the first space for 5 classes, all these classes are easily distinguished. For the rest 5 classes, SCSM is a bit lower than supervised methods but higher than CCA, PLS and GMBLM. It can be concluded that SCSM can achieve a comprehensively better performance among unsupervised methods.

Methods	Matching Images
SCSM	
GMLDA	
CCA	
GMBLM	

Table 3: Retrieval examples by text query "In 1994, Angus and Malcolm invited Rudd to several *jam sessions* ..." on the Wiki database by the proposed method. Red border indicates an incorrect matching result. (Best viewed in colors.)

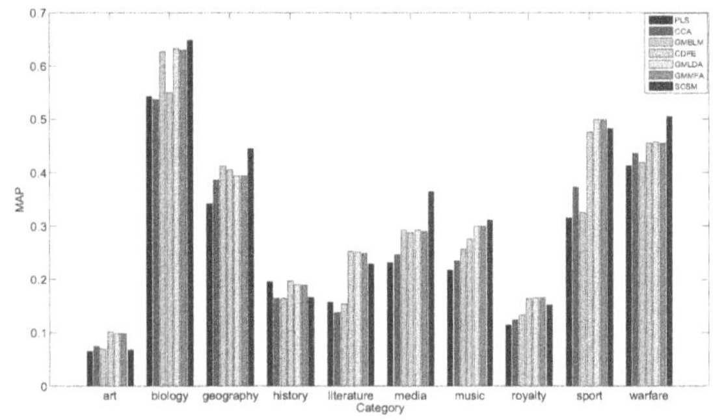

Figure 6: MAP of different methods on the Wiki++ dataset with respect to each category. (Best viewed in colors.)

3.2.4 Results on the LabelMe dataset

The LabelMe Outdoor dataset [32, 18] consists of 2,688 fully annotated outdoor images from 8 categories, i.e., "coast", "forest", "highway", "inside city", "mountain", "open country" and "tall building". For the text modality, we generate the object account vector via the LabelMe[2] toolbox. We randomly select 200 samples from each category for training, resulting in 1,600 image-text pairs for the training set and the remaining 1,086[3] image-text pairs for the testing set. There are total 789 unique words with frequencies varying from one time to more than 2000 times. We select the word frequencies that are more than one time. As a result, the image and text features are 512-dimensional Gist features and 470-dimensional word frequency features, respectively.

From Table 1, SCSM obtains the best average score 65.6% among the unsupervised methods, however, it performs worse than some supervised methods. It may be because the word frequency features contain massive noises, such as misspelling and duplicated words, make it hard for unsupervised methods to do feature learning without semantic labels. However, the advanced performances from the Wiki to the Wiki++ database indicate that SCSM can probably approach the supervised methods with deep features for the LabelMe database.

Regarding the precision-recall and precision-scope curves, SCSM still obtains the best performances in both image query and text query tasks. The gap between SCSM and second-best performing UCDFE is apparent, thus we can conclude that SCSM is distinguished, even other algorithms share the same initial pseudo semantic labels.

Class	Tags queries	True Image	Matching Images
coast	sky sea water sand beach	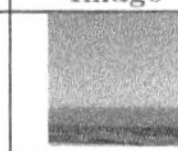	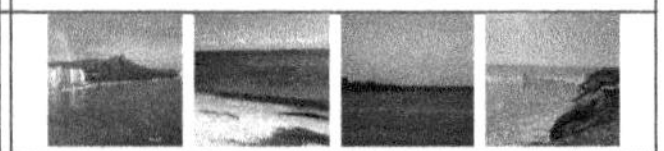
insidecity	building staircase window flag balcony		
mountain	clouds mountain land river water island		
street	tree sidewalk cars side road streetlight		

Table 4: Retrieval examples by tags queries on the LabelMe database by the proposed method. For each tags query (second column), the top several retrieved images are shown in the fourth column. The first column represents the ground truth class of each corresponding tags query, and the third column shows the ground truth Image with the queries. (Best viewed in colors.)

Image queries	SCSM	GMLDA
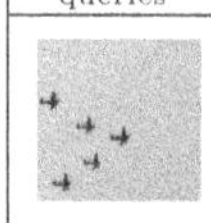	"aeroplane tree grass insect navy", "aeroplane leaves tail building sky light", "sky aeroplane cable", "aeroplane sky branch"	"sky aeroplane cable", "aeroplane letter wing moon star door tail sky", "bicyclehandle wheel clothes pedal leaves ground stairstep", "aeroplane radiotower cart cone"
	"car tree road sky stone grass", "pole wire sign trafficlight road fence", "car ground road hill road", "car road sky grass tree"	"house tree sky grass curb street car tag", "car street grass tree house sky", "car decoration grill carlight", "bus debris trash house house"
	"foot leg clothes had tabletop", "rock water waterfall person ground", "person arm hand foot clothes", "person clothes water shoe glasses wall"	"sign building trash wall person", "person ribbon clothes slide fence", "clothes ground junk", "frame clothes watch bracelet person"

Table 5: Retrieval examples by image queries on the Pascal VOC database. For each image query (second column), the top several retrieved tags are shown in the second column for the proposed **unsupervised** SCSM and third column for **supervised** GMLDA.

3.3 Convergence & Parameter Analysis

It is obvious to prove that the employed alternative minimization strategy can converge to a local optimum. However, under the self-paced framework, our learning algorithm is hard to guarantee the global convergence. On the other hand, the experimental results in Figure 8 on all four datasets can demonstrate the objective, $\sum_{p\in\{a,b\}} ||(\mathbf{U}_p^T\mathbf{X}_p - \mathbf{Y})diag(\mathbf{v})||_F^2 + \alpha Tr(\mathbf{U}_p^T\mathbf{X}_p\mathbf{L}_{pq}\mathbf{X}_q^T\mathbf{U}_q)$, decreases as the iteration number increases.

With regards to the parameters α and β in SCSM, we conduct an experiment to study the influence of different

[2]http://labelme.csail.mit.edu/Release3.0/browserTools/php/matlabtool_box.php.

[3]Two instances are dropped due to its missing tags (refrred as text).

Image queries	SCSM	GMLDA
	"water sea building sky sand beach mountain rainbow", "sand beach water sea sky", "sky mountain ocean water water sea sand beach trees", "water sea sky waves"	"sky mountain field river water trees", "sea water sky sand beach building tree", "sky buildings sea water", "sky buildings sea water"
	"sky field road tree shrub", "sky desert ground trees hill", "sky snowy mountain hill buildings", "sky mountain field grass cow"	"sky path shrub trees stone", "sky mountain field river water trees", "sky mountain field desert shrub plant", "sky desert ground trees hill"
	"sky skyscraper building", "building trees sidewalk road bus", "sky buildings skyscraper", "sky skyscraper building"	"sky building wall step person walking", "sky building car box plants", "sky skyscraper buildings car side sidewalk", "city river water building skyscraper dock"

Table 6: Retrieval examples by image queries on the LabelMe database. For each image query (second column), the top several retrieved tags are shown in the second column for the proposed **unsupervised** SCSM and third column for **supervised** GMLDA.

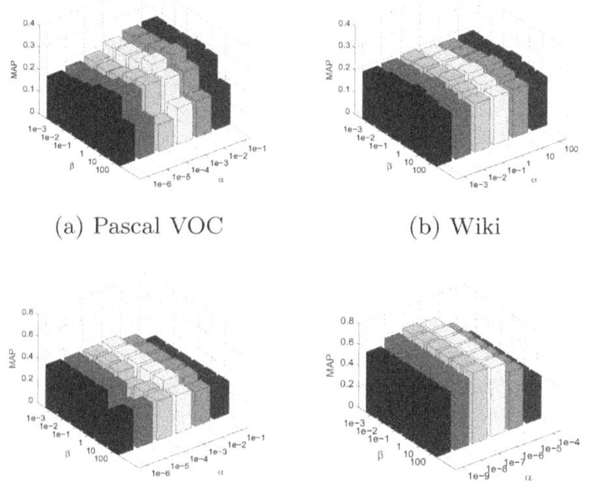

(a) Pascal VOC (b) Wiki

(c) Wiki++ (d) LabelMe

Figure 7: Performance variation for the average MAP with respect to α and β with γ fixed as 1.

choices. Note that in our experiment, γ is set as 1 while α varies with the training data size n and feature length d, and β varies from $[1e^{-3}, 1e^{-2}, \cdots, 1e^{2}]$. The analysis on parameter sensitivity shows that SCSM is very robust to model parameters which can achieve stable and superior performance under a wide range of parameter values.

For fair comparisons, we tune the parameter of subspace dimensionality for subspace based cross-modal approaches, and adopt the best-performing dimensionality for comparison. For LCFS, JFSSL and our SCSM, the subspace dimensionality is fixed as the number of semantic classes (e.g., $c = 20$ for the Pascal VOC dataset). Besides, the width parameter σ for Gaussian kernel in Eq.(7) is fixed as 1 for following experiments.

3.4 Discussion

Experimental results show that, our SCSM not only surpasses the unsupervised methods (e.g., CCA, GMBLM), but also outperforms some supervised methods (e.g., CDFE, GMLDA, and LCFS), in the Pascal VOC and Wiki++ datasets. As an unsupervised method, the reasons for the better performance of our SCSM may lie in twofold.

First, images often contain several semantic concepts, potentially belonging to several semantic groups, their labels may be inaccurate for some challenging datasets. Hence the grouping results may be a complementary for the missing label information when feature representations are enough powerful. Second, the pseudo group label obtained by canonical clustering methods is inaccurate. Since clustering is a non-convex problem, we introduce self-paced learning to avoid the local minima and refine the grouping results. Besides, the projection matrices are computed by two regression-like analyses on the pseudo label, and the multimodal graph preserving the inter- and intra- similarities is also constructed.

Moreover, we observe that all methods, especially SCSM, perform better in the Wiki++ dataset. Because the deep features in the Wiki++ dataset are high-dimensional and discriminative, SCSM can more effectively learn features, and estimate the latent semantic group more accurately. However, our method in the Wiki and LabelMe dataset is inferior to the supervised state-of-the-art method proposed by [36], much effort still needs to be taken to improve the performance when the features contain massive noises.

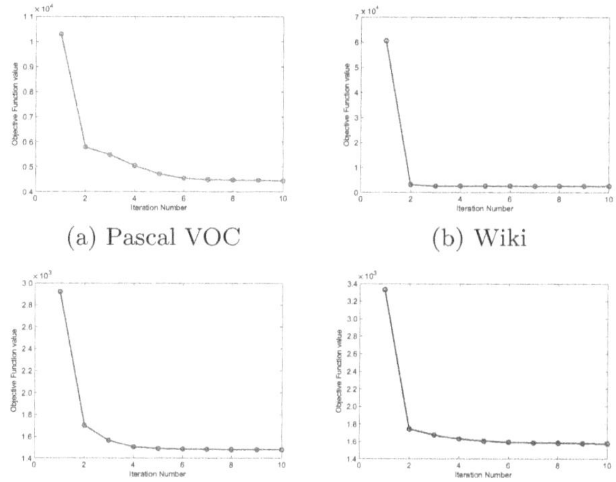

(a) Pascal VOC (b) Wiki

(c) Wiki++ (d) LabelMe

Figure 8: Convergence curve of the proposed SCSM.

4. CONCLUSION

In this paper, we have proposed a novel *unsupervised* method for cross-modal subspace matching. We have introduced hard pair-wised constraints and soft semantic group constraints for multi-modal data, which are potentially effective for unsupervised learning. A joint feature learning and data grouping formulation has been accordingly developed. For an accurate estimation of the semantic group, self-paced learning has been incorporated into the non-convex loss. Moreover, multimodal graph is included to preserve the inter- and intra- modality similarity. To minimize this joint learning problem, we have presented an alternating minimization solution. Experimental results on four multimodal databases demonstrate that the effectiveness of the proposed method for unsupervised multimodal data. For future work, the proposed method will be extended for multi-label cross-modal matching problem.

Acknowledgments

This work was supported by the National Basic Research Program of China (Grant No. 2012CB316300), the Youth Innovation Promotion Association of the Chinese Academy of Sciences (CAS) (Grant No. 2015190) and the National Natural Science Foundation of China (Grant No. 61473289). Jian Liang and Zhihang Li contributed equally to this work and should be considered co-first authors.

5. REFERENCES

[1] G. Andrew, R. Arora, J. Bilmes, and K. Livescu. Deep canonical correlation analysis. In *ICML*, pages 1247–1255, 2013.

[2] F. Bach and Z. Harchaoui. Diffrac: a discriminative and flexible framework for clustering. In *NIPS*, pages 49–56, 2008.

[3] S. Basu and J. Christensen. Teaching classification boundaries to humans. In *AAAI*, pages 109–115, 2013.

[4] Y. Bengio, J. Louradour, R. Collobert, and J. Weston. Curriculum learning. In *ICML*, pages 41–48. ACM, 2009.

[5] D. M. Blei and M. I. Jordan. Modeling annotated data. In *SIGIR*, pages 127–134, 2003.

[6] D. M. Blei, A. Y. Ng, and M. I. Jordan. Latent dirichlet allocation. *JMLR*, 3:993–1022, 2003.

[7] J. Costa Pereira, E. Coviello, G. Doyle, N. Rasiwasia, G. R. Lanckriet, R. Levy, and N. Vasconcelos. On the role of correlation and abstraction in cross-modal multimedia retrieval. *IEEE TPAMI*, 36(3):521–535, 2014.

[8] P. Dhillon, D. P. Foster, and L. H. Ungar. Multi-view learning of word embeddings via cca. In *NIPS*, pages 199–207, 2011.

[9] P. S. Dhillon, J. Rodu, D. P. Foster, and L. H. Ungar. Two step cca: A new spectral method for estimating vector models of words. In *ICML*, pages 1551–1558, 2012.

[10] M. Everingham, L. Van Gool, C. K. Williams, J. Winn, and A. Zisserman. The pascal visual object classes (voc) challenge. *IJCV*, 88(2):303–338, 2010.

[11] Y. Gong, Q. Ke, M. Isard, and S. Lazebnik. A multi-view embedding space for modeling internet images, tags, and their semantics. *IJCV*, 106(2):210–233, 2014.

[12] D. R. Hardoon, S. Szedmak, and J. Shawe-Taylor. Canonical correlation analysis: An overview with application to learning methods. *Neural Computation*, 16(12):2639–2664, 2004.

[13] R. He, M. Zhang, L. Wang, Y. Ji, and Q. Yin. Cross-modal subspace learning via pairwise constraints. *IEEE TIP*, 24(12):5543–5556, 2015.

[14] X. He and P. Niyogi. Locality preserving projections. In *NIPS*, pages 153–160, 2003.

[15] S. J. Hwang and K. Grauman. Reading between the lines: Object localization using implicit cues from image tags. *IEEE TPAMI*, 34(6):1145–1158, 2012.

[16] Y. Jia, M. Salzmann, and T. Darrell. Learning cross-modality similarity for multinomial data. In *ICCV*, pages 2407–2414, 2011.

[17] L. Jiang, D. Meng, T. Mitamura, and A. G. Hauptmann. Easy samples first: Self-paced reranking for zero-example multimedia search. In *MM*, pages 547–556, 2014.

[18] C. Kang, S. Xiang, S. Liao, C. Xu, and C. Pan. Learning consistent feature representation for cross-modal multimedia retrieval. *IEEE TMM*, 17(3):370–381, 2015.

[19] R. Kiros, Y. Zhu, R. R. Salakhutdinov, R. Zemel, R. Urtasun, A. Torralba, and S. Fidler. Skip-thought vectors. In *NIPS*, pages 3276–3284, 2015.

[20] M. P. Kumar, B. Packer, and D. Koller. Self-paced learning for latent variable models. In *NIPS*, pages 1189–1197, 2010.

[21] A. Li, S. Shan, X. Chen, B. Ma, S. Yan, and W. Gao. Cross-pose face recognition by canonical correlation analysis. *arXiv preprint: 1507.08076*, 2015.

[22] J. Liang, R. He, Z. Sun, and T. Tan. Group-invariant cross-modal subspace learning. In *IJCAI*, 2016.

[23] D. Lin and X. Tang. Inter-modality face recognition. In *ECCV*, pages 13–26. 2006.

[24] J. Masci, M. M. Bronstein, A. Bronstein, and J. Schmidhuber. Multimodal similarity-preserving hashing. *IEEE TPAMI*, 36(4):824–830, 2014.

[25] D. Meng and Q. Zhao. What objective does self-paced learning indeed optimize? *arXiv preprint:1511.06049*, 2015.

[26] A. Oliva and A. Torralba. Modeling the shape of the scene: A holistic representation of the spatial envelope. *IJCV*, 42(3):145–175, 2001.

[27] B. Ozdemir and L. S. Davis. A probabilistic framework for multimodal retrieval using integrative indian buffet process. In *NIPS*, pages 2384–2392, 2014.

[28] D. Putthividhy, H. T. Attias, and S. S. Nagarajan. Topic regression multi-modal latent dirichlet allocation for image annotation. In *CVPR*, pages 3408–3415, 2010.

[29] N. Rasiwasia, J. Costa Pereira, E. Coviello, G. Doyle, G. R. Lanckriet, R. Levy, and N. Vasconcelos. A new approach to cross-modal multimedia retrieval. In *MM*, pages 251–260, 2010.

[30] N. Rasiwasia, P. J. Moreno, and N. Vasconcelos. Bridging the gap: Query by semantic example. *IEEE TMM*, 9(5):923–938, 2007.

[31] R. Rosipal and N. Krämer. Overview and recent advances in partial least squares. In *Subspace, Latent Structure and Feature Selection*, pages 34–51. Springer, 2006.

[32] B. C. Russell, A. Torralba, K. P. Murphy, and W. T. Freeman. Labelme: a database and web-based tool for image annotation. *IJCV*, 77(1-3):157–173, 2008.

[33] A. Sharma, A. Kumar, H. Daume III, and D. W. Jacobs. Generalized multiview analysis: A discriminative latent space. In *CVPR*, pages 2160–2167, 2012.

[34] F. Shen, C. Shen, W. Liu, and H. Tao Shen. Supervised discrete hashing. In *CVPR*, pages 37–45, 2015.

[35] N. Srivastava and R. R. Salakhutdinov. Multimodal learning with deep boltzmann machines. In *NIPS*, pages 2222–2230, 2012.

[36] K. Wang, R. He, L. Wang, W. Wang, and T. Tan. Joint feature selection and subspace learning for cross-modal retrieval. *IEEE TPAMI*, 2015. doi:10.1109/TPAMI.2015.2505311.

[37] K. Wang, R. He, W. Wang, L. Wang, and T. Tan. Learning coupled feature spaces for cross-modal matching. In *ICCV*, pages 2088–2095, 2013.

[38] Y. Wei, Y. Zhao, C. Lu, S. Wei, L. Liu, Z. Zhu, and S. Yan. Cross-modal retrieval with cnn visual features: A new baseline. *IEEE TCYB*, 2016. doi:10.1109/TCYB.2016.2519449.

[39] B. Wu, Q. Yang, W.-S. Zheng, Y. Wang, and J. Wang. Quantized correlation hashing for fast cross-modal search. In *IJCAI*, pages 3946–3952, 2015.

[40] Z. Yu, F. Wu, Y. Yang, Q. Tian, J. Luo, and Y. Zhuang. Discriminative coupled dictionary hashing for fast cross-media retrieval. In *SIGIR*, pages 395–404, 2014.

[41] T. Zhang and J. Wang. Collaborative quantization for cross-modal similarity search. In *CVPR*, 2016.

[42] Q. Zhao, D. Meng, L. Jiang, Q. Xie, Z. Xu, and A. G. Hauptmann. Self-paced learning for matrix factorization. In *AAAI*, pages 3196–3202, 2015.

[43] J. Zhou, G. Ding, and Y. Guo. Latent semantic sparse hashing for cross-modal similarity search. In *SIGIR*, pages 415–424, 2014.

[44] Y. T. Zhuang, Y. F. Wang, F. Wu, Y. Zhang, and W. M. Lu. Supervised coupled dictionary learning with group structures for multi-modal retrieval. In *AAAI*, pages 1070–1076, 2013.

Composite Correlation Quantization for Efficient Multimodal Retrieval*

Mingsheng Long†, Yue Cao†, Jianmin Wang†, and Philip S. Yu‡♯
†School of Software, Tsinghua National Laboratory (TNList), Tsinghua University, Beijing, China
‡Institute for Data Science, Tsinghua University ♯University of Illinois at Chicago, IL, USA
{mingsheng, jimwang}@tsinghua.edu.cn, caoyue10@gmail.com, psyu@uic.edu

ABSTRACT

Efficient similarity retrieval from large-scale multimodal database is pervasive in modern search engines and social networks. To support queries across content modalities, the system should enable cross-modal correlation and computation-efficient indexing. While hashing methods have shown great potential in achieving this goal, current attempts generally fail to learn isomorphic hash codes in a seamless scheme, that is, they embed multiple modalities in a continuous isomorphic space and separately threshold embeddings into binary codes, which incurs substantial loss of retrieval accuracy. In this paper, we approach seamless multimodal hashing by proposing a novel Composite Correlation Quantization (CCQ) model. Specifically, CCQ jointly finds correlation-maximal mappings that transform different modalities into isomorphic latent space, and learns composite quantizers that convert the isomorphic latent features into compact binary codes. An optimization framework is devised to preserve both intra-modal similarity and inter-modal correlation through minimizing both reconstruction and quantization errors, which can be trained from both paired and partially paired data in linear time. A comprehensive set of experiments clearly show the superior effectiveness and efficiency of CCQ against the state of the art hashing methods for both unimodal and cross-modal retrieval.

Keywords

Hashing, quantization, multimodal retrieval, correlation analysis

1. INTRODUCTION

While big data with large volume, high dimensions, and multiple modalities are ubiquitous in search engines and social networks, it has attracted increasing attention to distill the correlation structures across heterogenous data modalities. For example, an uploaded image on Flickr is usually annotated with some relevant descriptions or tags, while a featured article on Wikipedia may consist of some correlative images. As relevant data from different modalities may endow semantic correlations, it is desirable to support *multimodal search*, which retrieves semantically-relevant results of all modals in response to a unimodal query. Taking Flickr as an example, when a query image is given, the system should return both relevant tags and images. Due to large volume and semantic gap [18], effective and efficient retrieval of multimodal data remains a challenge.

In the case that the reference database is large-scale or that the distance calculation between query item and database item is costly, an efficient solution to enabling similarity search is hashing based methods [22], which perform approximate nearest neighbor (ANN) search with both computation efficiency and acceptable accuracy. The principle of hashing is to transform high-dimensional data into compact binary codes and generate similar binary codes for similar data items. The seminal work includes Locality Sensitive Hashing (LSH) [1] and Spectral Hashing (SH) [25]. However, traditional *unimodal* hashing methods cannot support multimodal search as ANN cannot be directly computed across different modalities.

Recently, several useful attempts have been made to *multimodal hashing*, which builds correlation structures across multiple modalities in the process of hash function learning and index multimodal data in a common Hamming space [5, 29, 13, 32, 33, 34, 20, 24, 27, 28, 8, 26, 16]. These methods generally work in two-step pipeline: first, embed multiple data modalities into a *continuous* isomorphic latent space by maximizing inter-modal correlations, and second, quantize the isomorphic embeddings into binary hash codes by sign thresholding. While showing promising performance, the two-step pipeline may encounter two limitations: first, conversion from real-valued features to discrete codes may incur substantial information loss, making the continuous latent space suboptimal for binary coding and the binary codes suboptimal for retrieval [24, 10]; second, directly binarizing latent features may lead to unbalanced encoding schemes [32, 33]. Fundamentally, by continuous relaxation of the binary constraints, most methods solve an optimization problem which may deviate significantly from the hashing objective as the quantization error is not accounted for in the optimization process. This somewhat contradicts the motivation of multimodal hashing. Hence, how to learn isomorphic hash codes for multimodal data in a seamless optimization framework remains an open problem.

In this paper, we propose Composite Correlation Quantization (CCQ), a novel model towards seamless multimodal hashing. Technically, CCQ jointly finds correlation-maximal mappings that transform different modalities into an isomorphic latent space, and learns composite quantizers that convert the isomorphic latent features into compact binary codes. The flowcharts of CCQ and prior work are shown in Figure 1. To create a seamless optimization framework, we are inspired by Latent Semantic Analysis (LSA) [7] and decompose each datum into three latent factors, namely, correlation-maximal mapping, similarity-preserving codebook, and compact binary code. The three latent factors are jointly learned through an optimization problem, which preserves both intra-modal similarity

*Corresponding authors: Jianmin Wang and Mingsheng Long.

SIGIR '16, July 17–21, 2016, Pisa, Italy
© 2016 ACM. ISBN 978-1-4503-4069-4/16/07...$15.00
DOI: http://dx.doi.org/10.1145/2911451.2911493

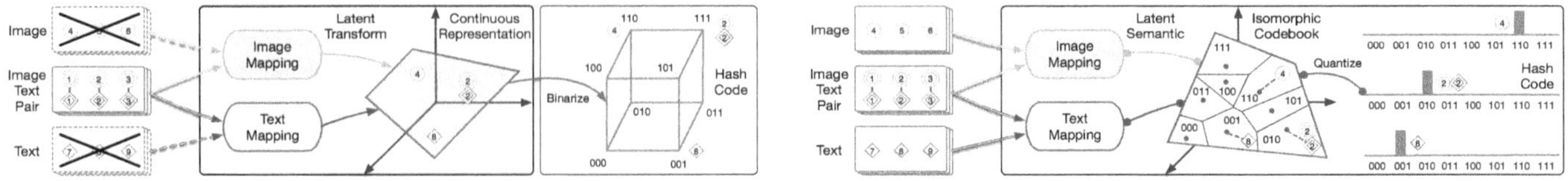

Figure 1: Flowcharts of prior work (left) and CCQ (right). Prior work is a two-step pipeline: first map image-text pairs to isomorphic latent space (denoted as polygon) and then binarize the continuous representation to hash codes (denoted as vertices of hypercube) by *sign thresholding*. CCQ is a seamless optimization framework: jointly map both paired/unpaired images and texts to isomorphic latent space (denoted as polygon) and learn hash codes by *composite quantization*. The quantization model learns isomorphic codebook (denoted as Voronoi digram) and binary codes (denoted as histograms) by minimizing the quantization error, which suffices to assign each latent representation to M-nearest codewords (denoted as Voronoi cells) and assignment indices are used as hash codes.

and inter-modal correlation while minimizing both reconstruction and quantization errors. The CCQ model can construct extremely compressed and balanced binary codes to enable efficient multimodal search, can readily handle a ubiquitous semi-paired scenario where only a fraction of input data are multimodal, and can scale linearly to large sample size. Comprehensive empirical evidence on large-scale datasets confirms that the CCQ model exhibits superior performance in both effectiveness and efficiency on both unimodal and cross-modal search against state of the art hashing methods.

The subsequent paper is organized as follows. We review related works in Section 2. We formally present our model in Section 3 and algorithm with analysis in Section 4. Empirical evaluations are reported in Section 5, while conclusions are enclosed in Section 6.

2. RELATED WORK

Recently, hashing-based multimodal search is a prevalent research focus in machine learning and information retrieval communities [5, 13, 34, 20, 27, 8, 10, 28, 26, 23, 31], which enables approximate similarity search on multimedia database with significant speedup and acceptable accuracy. Refer to [22] for a comprehensive survey.

Existing multimodal hashing methods can be organized into two categories: supervised methods and unsupervised methods. CMSSH [5], SCM [28], QCH [26], and SePH [14] are supervised hashing methods that require labeled pairs to indicate if the objects from different modalities are similar (positive) or dissimilar (negative). As supervised information is usually unavailable in many applications, the deployment of these methods may be severely restricted. CVH [13], IMH [20], MSAE [24] and CorrAE [8] are unsupervised hashing methods applicable to the most general multimodal retrieval case given that paired data are available, while our proposed CCQ model falls into this category. IMH [20] is an extension of spectral hashing [25] to multimodal data, which is restricted by the training burden since constructing and eigendecomposing the similarity matrices require $O(N^2)$. While CVH [13] tackles the scalability issue, it does not jointly maximize cross-modality correlation and preserve intra-modality similarity. MSAE [24] and CorrAE [8] can capture both intra-modal similarity and inter-modal correlation by deep autoencoders, but they require spectral hashing or sign thresholding for obtaining binary codes from the continuous embeddings, which will give rise to uncontrollable quantization errors [9, 12].

A crucial problem with existing methods is that they essentially work in a separated two-step pipeline: first embed multimodal data into a common *continuous* latent space and then threshold the continuous embeddings into binary codes of the Hamming space. Such conversion from real-valued features to discrete codes may result in substantial information loss, making the continuous latent space suboptimal for the binary codes and the binary codes suboptimal for retrieval [30]. Furthermore, directly binarizing latent representation may lead to unbalanced encoding schemes, as shown in [32, 33]. Although IMVH [10] learns multimodal hash functions using a graph-cut quantizer instead of the sign thresholding, the quantizer solves a fast approximation of energy function with orthogonal constraints and recurs large quantization error and unbalanced codes. CCQ approaches this problem by learning the modality-consistent latent space and balanced binary codes in a principled framework.

3. COMPOSITE CORRELATION QUANTIZATION

3.1 Problem Statements

In the multimodal search system, the database and query consist of objects from different modalities. We only use image and text as two modalities to explain our approach, but the approach is formulated to support any number V of modalities. Let $\mathbf{X}^1 \in \mathbb{R}^{P_1 \times N_1}$ be an image set of N_0 images with tags and the rest $\bar{N}_1$ images without tags, where $N_1 = N_0 + \bar{N}_1$ and each image is represented by P_1-dimensional feature vector. Let $\mathbf{X}^2 \in \mathbb{R}^{P_2 \times N_2}$ be a text set of N_0 documents of the image tags and additional $\bar{N}_2$ documents, where $N_2 = N_0 + \bar{N}_2$ and each text is represented by P_2-dimensional feature vector. Note that the proposed approach can handle *semi-paired* data where only a fraction $N_0/(N_1 + N_2)$ of objects are multimodal, and is more realistic than typical multimodal methods.

An efficient approach to calculating the distance between image and text is to map images and texts to modality-isomorphic binary codes in which different modalities of the objects are comparable. In this paper, we will approach this problem by a joint optimization framework, dubbed Composite Correlation Quantization (CCQ).

DEFINITION 1 (CCQ). *Given an image $\mathbf{x}_n^1 \in \mathbb{R}^{P_1}$ and a text $\mathbf{x}_n^2 \in \mathbb{R}^{P_2}$, learn two correlation-maximal mappings $f^1 : \mathbb{R}^{P_1} \mapsto \mathbb{R}^D$ and $f^2 : \mathbb{R}^{P_2} \mapsto \mathbb{R}^D$ that transform images and texts into a D-dimensional isomorphic latent space, and jointly learn two composite quantizers $q^1 : \mathbb{R}^D \mapsto \{0,1\}^H$ and $q^2 : \mathbb{R}^D \mapsto \{0,1\}^H$ that quantize latent embeddings into compact H-bits binary codes.*

In the common H-bits binary space, image and text can be easily comparable such that both intra-modal and cross-modal search can be readily supported. After mappings f^1, f^2 and quantizers q^1, q^2 have been learned, the multimodal search problem can be converted into classical approximate nearest neighbor (ANN) search problem.

3.2 Composite Correlation Quantization

The main idea of CCQ is to jointly learn a correlation-maximal latent space and a similarity-preserving composite quantization in a unified optimization framework. To achieve this mission, we are inspired by Latent Semantic Analysis (LSA) [7] and decompose each input datum (image or text) $\mathbf{x}_n^v$ into three latent factors $\mathbf{R}^v$, $\mathbf{C}^v$, $\mathbf{b}_n^v$, that is, $\mathbf{x}_n^v \approx \mathbf{R}^v\mathbf{C}^v\mathbf{b}_n^v$. While sharing similar formation as LSA, our formulation endows these latent factors with different semantics and thus constrains them with different conditions. More specifically, $\mathbf{R}^v$ is correlation-maximal mapping, $\mathbf{C}^v$ is similarity-preserving codebook, and $\mathbf{b}_n^v$ is the compact binary code of $\mathbf{x}_n^v$. We present how to formulate the CCQ approach under these semantics.

3.2.1 Intra-Modality Similarity Quantization

To represent inputs with compact binary codes, two mainstream paradigms are sign thresholding in Hamming embedding methods [25], and vector quantization in codebook-based encoding methods [12]. As sign thresholding cannot guarantee minimal quantization error, we therefore adopt the vector quantization paradigm. CCQ is based on a set of M codebooks $\mathbf{C}^v = [\mathbf{C}_1^v, \ldots, \mathbf{C}_M^v]$, where each codebook $\mathbf{C}_m^v$ contains K codewords $\mathbf{C}_m^v = [\mathbf{C}_{m1}^v, \ldots, \mathbf{C}_{mK}^v]$, and each codeword $\mathbf{C}_{mk}^v$ is a D-dimensional vector like the cluster centroid in kmeans clustering. Corresponding to the M codebooks, we partition the binary codewords assignment vector $\mathbf{b}_n^v$ into M 1-of-K indicator vectors $\mathbf{b}_n^v = [\mathbf{b}_{1n}^v; \ldots; \mathbf{b}_{mn}^v]$, and each indicator vector $\mathbf{b}_{mn}^v$ indicates which one (and only one) of the K codewords in the mth codebook is selected to approximate the nth data point. The CCQ model encodes each $\mathbf{x}_n^v$ as the sum of M codewords, one codeword per codebook, each indicated by the binary assignment vector $\mathbf{b}_n^v$. This yields a novel and more accurate composite approximation scheme $\mathbf{x}_n^v \approx \mathbf{R}^v \sum_{m=1}^{M} \mathbf{C}_m^v \mathbf{b}_{mn}^v$. Consistent with LSA and kmeans, the sum of squared loss between all $\mathbf{x}_n^v$'s and the sum of selected codewords after transformed by $\mathbf{R}^v$, is minimized,

$$\begin{aligned} \min_{\mathbf{R}^v, \mathbf{C}^v, \mathbf{B}^v} & \sum_{n=1}^{N_v} \left\| \mathbf{x}_n^v - \mathbf{R}^v \sum_{m=1}^{M} \mathbf{C}_m^v \mathbf{b}_{mn}^v \right\|_2^2 \\ \text{s.t.} \quad & \|\mathbf{b}_{mn}\|_0 = 1, \mathbf{b}_{mn} \in \{0,1\}^K \\ & m = 1 \ldots M, n = 1 \ldots N_v, \end{aligned} \tag{1}$$

where $\|\cdot\|_0$ denotes the ℓ_0-norm that simply counts the number of the vector's nonzero elements. The constraint guarantees that only one codeword in each codebook can be activated to approximate the input data, hence it can lead to compact binary codes. As the binary constraints are directly imposed to the learning objective and are valid throughout the optimization procedure, the derived binary codes are much more accurate than sign thresholding binary codes. The rationale of using M codebooks instead of single codebook to approximate each input datum is to further minimize quantization error, as the latter is shown to yield significantly lossy compression and incur evident performance drop [30, 3]. Quantization based on multiple codebooks yields balanced composite binary codes which are more effective than Hamming embedding binary codes [12, 17].

3.2.2 Inter-Modality Correlation Maximization

The most desirable value of multimodal retrieval is to enable transfer of knowledge across different modalities so that cross-modal retrieval performance can be improved. A fundamental assumption for multimodal retrieval is that by mapping objects in a modality-consistent latent space, the latent space representations of semantically relevant inter-modal pairs should be consistent. More specifically, for each input object with both image modality $\mathbf{x}_n^1$ and text modality $\mathbf{x}_n^2$, after being transformed by $\mathbf{R}^1$ and $\mathbf{R}^2$ in Equation (1), the latent space representations for image modality $\mathbf{C}^1\mathbf{b}_n^1$ and text modality $\mathbf{C}^2\mathbf{b}_n^2$ should be similar. To our knowledge, most prior work adopts the coupling strategy to minimize $\left\|\mathbf{C}^1\mathbf{b}_n^1 - \mathbf{C}^2\mathbf{b}_n^2\right\|_2^2$. In this paper, we propose to maximize cross-modal correlation by sharing codebooks $\{\mathbf{C}_m\}_{m=1}^M$ for different modalities and sharing binary codes $\{\mathbf{b}_n\}_{n=1}^{N_0}$ for semantically relevant inter-modal pairs. While for the data points with only one modality, the multimodal sharing strategy does not apply. Hence, the proposed condition that the modality-consistent latent space should satisfy is formulated as

$$\mathbf{C}_m^v = \mathbf{C}_m \ \text{ and } \ \delta\left(\mathbf{b}_{mn}^v\right) = \begin{cases} \mathbf{b}_{mn}, & n = 1 \ldots N_0 \\ \mathbf{b}_{mn}^v, & \text{otherwise}, \end{cases} \tag{2}$$

where $\delta(\cdot)$ distinguishes multimodal objects from unimodal ones. Different from most prior methods [20, 8], our modality-consistent condition requires identical code $\mathbf{b}_n^1 = \mathbf{b}_n^2$, instead of minimized distance $\left\|\mathbf{b}_n^1 - \mathbf{b}_n^2\right\|$, for the semantically relevant inter-modal pairs. There are two advantages of our approach. First, since our learning objective keeps the binary constraint valid throughout optimization procedure, it is very difficult to require minimized distance between two binary codes as their nonzero elements may differ significantly. Note that prior methods simply drop the binary condition and solve a continuous problem, which leads to uncontrollable quantization error with the post-step sign thresholding. Second, integrating the minimized distance condition in the learning objective as existing methods may introduce a trade-off term, or parameter, that is hard to tune since its magnitude is very different from learning loss (1).

3.2.3 Joint Optimization Framework

To approach CCQ, which jointly learns a similarity-preserving composite quantization and a correlation-maximal latent space in a unified optimization framework, we jointly require the codebooks $\{\mathbf{C}_m\}_{m=1}^M$ subject to minimizing the quantization error of all modalities as Equation (1), and the mappings $\mathbf{R}^v$ subject to maximizing the correlations between semantically relevant inter-modal pairs as Equation (2) while jointly minimizing the reconstruction error of input data as LSA. This leads to a joint optimization framework as

$$\begin{aligned} \min_{\mathbf{R}^v, \mathbf{C}, \mathbf{B}^v} & \sum_{v=1}^{V} \sum_{n=1}^{N_v} \lambda_v \left\| \mathbf{x}_n^v - \mathbf{R}^v \sum_{m=1}^{M} \mathbf{C}_m \delta\left(\mathbf{b}_{mn}^v\right) \right\|_2^2 \\ \text{s.t.} \quad & \mathbf{R}^{v\mathsf{T}}\mathbf{R}^v = \mathbf{I}_{D\times D}, \mathbf{R}^v \in \mathbb{R}^{P_v \times D} \\ & \left\|\delta\left(\mathbf{b}_{mn}^v\right)\right\|_0 = 1, \delta\left(\mathbf{b}_{mn}^v\right) \in \{0,1\}^K \\ & \delta\left(\mathbf{b}_{mn}^v\right) = \begin{cases} \mathbf{b}_{mn}, & n = 1 \ldots N_0 \\ \mathbf{b}_{mn}^v, & \text{otherwise} \end{cases} \\ & v = 1 \ldots V, m = 1 \ldots M, n = 1 \ldots N_v, \end{aligned} \tag{3}$$

where λ_v is the weight parameter for each modality, and in bimodal problems with $V = 2$, we can simplify the notations by denoting $\lambda_1 = 1$ and $\lambda_2 = \lambda$, while such notations are used throughout this paper. $\mathbf{R}^v$ is the transformation matrix that maps the inputs of each modality to a D-dimensional modality-consistent latent space. The orthogonal constraints are motivated by LSA, which can turn latent factors $\mathbf{R}^v$ into transformation matrices for efficient out-of-sample quantization. The binary codes $\mathbf{b}_n^v$ are $M \times K$-dimensional, fortunately however, each $\mathbf{b}_{mn}^v$ is 1-of-K encoding with only one nonzero element and can be represented using $\log_2 K$ bits, hence the final hash codes $\mathbf{b}_n^v$ can be compacted into $H = M\log_2 K$ bits, which is independent on the dimensions of input or latent spaces. To fit each $\mathbf{b}_{mn}^v$ into one byte, $K = 256$ is a good choice [12, 30]. We simply set $D = \min(\{P_v\}_{v=1}^V, H)$, in the sense that an H-bit binary code can reconstruct a D-dimensional vector accurately.

Formally, we derive correlation-maximal mappings $f^v\left(\mathbf{x}_n^v\right) = \mathbf{R}^{v\mathsf{T}}\mathbf{x}_n^v$ and similarity-preserving quantizers $q^v\left(f^v\left(\mathbf{x}_n^v\right)\right) = \mathbf{b}_n^v$. There are several advantages of the CCQ approach. First, CCQ jointly learns a correlation-maximal latent space and a similarity-preserving composite encoding, which can minimize the quantization loss and guarantee search quality. Second, CCQ explores both paired and unpaired data in a semi-paired quantization paradigm, which can benefit from semi-supervised learning in that paired data consolidate inter-modality correlation and unpaired data enhance intra-modality quantization. Third, CCQ is formulated with only two easy-tuning model parameters D and λ, where D can be set as simply as LSA to retain most covariance information, and λ can be selected by trading off different modalities using prior information. In particular, the proposed sharing of codebooks and binary codes across modalities (2) enables joint learning of latent semantics that are maximally correlated in the isomorphic feature space, which contributes most significantly to the efficacy of the CCQ approach.

3.3 Approximate Nearest Neighbor Search

Approximate nearest neighbor (ANN) search based on Euclidean distance is a powerful task for quantization techniques [12]. Given a database of CCQ hash codes $\{\mathbf{b}_n^v\}_{n=1}^{N_v}$, we follow [12, 17] and use *Asymmetric Quantizer Distance* (AQD) as similarity metric that computes the distance between query $\mathbf{q}^{\bar{v}}$ and database point $\mathbf{x}_n^v$ as

$$\begin{aligned} \text{AQD}\left(\mathbf{q}^{\bar{v}}, \mathbf{x}_n^v\right) &= \left\|\mathbf{q}^{\bar{v}} - \mathbf{R}^{\bar{v}} \sum\nolimits_{m=1}^{M} \mathbf{C}_m \mathbf{b}_{mn}^v\right\|_2^2 \\ &= -2\sum\nolimits_{m=1}^{M} \left\langle \tilde{\mathbf{q}}^{\bar{v}}, \mathbf{C}_m \mathbf{b}_{mn}^v \right\rangle + \left\|\sum\nolimits_{m=1}^{M} \mathbf{C}_m \mathbf{b}_{mn}^v\right\|_2^2 \\ &\quad + \left\|\tilde{\mathbf{q}}^{\bar{v}}\right\|_2^2 + \left\|\mathbf{R}_{\perp}^{\bar{v}\mathsf{T}} \mathbf{q}^{\bar{v}}\right\|_2^2, \end{aligned} \tag{4}$$

where $\tilde{\mathbf{q}}^{\bar{v}} = \mathbf{R}^{\bar{v}\mathsf{T}} \mathbf{q}^{\bar{v}}$ is the transformed query. In the second row, the first term computes the inner products between $\tilde{\mathbf{q}}^{\bar{v}}$ and M codewords selected by $\mathbf{b}_n^v$. Given a query, these inner products for all M codebooks $\{\mathbf{C}_m\}_{m=1}^M$ and all K possible values of $\mathbf{b}_{mn}^v$ can be pre-computed and stored in a query-specific $M \times K$ lookup table, which is used to compute AQD between the query and all database points, each entails M table lookups and additions and is slightly more costly than Hamming distance. The second term computes the squared norm of decoded database point, which is independent on the query and can be encoded using one byte by quantizing these scale values on held-out dataset [3]. At quantization, we augment CCQ code with the norm byte, which costs one more lookup and one more byte per database point. We can eliminate this norm byte by composite quantization [30], but will leave it to our future work.

4. ALGORITHM AND ANALYSIS

4.1 Learning Algorithm

The CCQ optimization problem (3) consists of three variables, $\mathbf{R}^v$, $\mathbf{C}$, and $\mathbf{B}^v$. We adopt alternating optimization [12, 17, 3, 30] which iteratively updates one variable with the rest variables fixed.

4.1.1 Update $\mathbf{R}^v$

We update $\mathbf{R}^v$ by fixing $\mathbf{C}$ and $\mathbf{B}^v$ as known variables, and write Equation (3) with $\mathbf{R}^v$ as unknown variables in matrix formulation,

$$\begin{aligned} &\min\nolimits_{\mathbf{R}^v} \left\|\mathbf{X}^v - \mathbf{R}^v \mathbf{C}\delta\left(\mathbf{B}^v\right)\right\|_F^2 \\ &\text{s.t.} \quad \mathbf{R}^{v\mathsf{T}} \mathbf{R}^v = \mathbf{I}_{D \times D}. \end{aligned} \tag{5}$$

This is equivalent to the Orthogonal Procrustes problem [19] and can be solved exactly using SVD. More specifically, we perform SVD as $\mathbf{X}^v [\mathbf{C}\delta(\mathbf{B}^v)]^{\mathsf{T}} = \mathbf{USV}^{\mathsf{T}}$, then we achieve $\mathbf{R}^v = \mathbf{UV}^{\mathsf{T}}$.

4.1.2 Update $\mathbf{C}$

We update $\mathbf{C}$ by fixing $\mathbf{R}^v$ and $\mathbf{B}^v$ as known variables, and write Equation (3) with $\mathbf{C}$ as unknown variables in matrix formulation,

$$\min_{\mathbf{C}} \sum\nolimits_{v=1}^{V} \left\|\mathbf{R}^{v\mathsf{T}} \mathbf{X}^v - \mathbf{C}\delta\left(\mathbf{B}^v\right)\right\|_F^2. \tag{6}$$

Algorithm 1: CCQ: Composite Correlation Quantization

Input: Data $\{\mathbf{X}^v\}_{v=1}^V$; latent dimension D, modal weight λ.
Output: Mappings $\{\mathbf{R}^v\}$, codebook $\mathbf{C}$, binary codes $\{\mathbf{B}^v\}$.

```
Initialize {R^v} by identity, C randomly, {B^v} by NN search.
repeat
    Update {R^v} by Orthogonal Procrustes as Eqn. (5).
    Update C by Quadratic Optimization as Eqn. (6).
    for n ← 1 to N_v do
        Update {b_n^v} by ICM or greedy algorithm as Eqn. (7).
    end
until Convergence
```

This is an unconstrained quadratic problem with analytic solution $\mathbf{C} = \left[\sum_{v=1}^{V} \lambda_v \mathbf{R}^{v\mathsf{T}} \mathbf{X}^v \delta\left(\mathbf{B}^v\right)^{\mathsf{T}}\right] \left[\sum_{v=1}^{V} \lambda_v \delta\left(\mathbf{B}^v\right) \delta(\mathbf{B}^v)^{\mathsf{T}}\right]^{-1}$. Algorithms such as L-BFGS can be used to speed up computation.

4.1.3 Update $\mathbf{B}^v$

It is obvious that each $\mathbf{b}_n^v$ is independent on $\{\mathbf{b}_{n'}^v\}_{n' \neq n}$, then the optimization problem for $\mathbf{B}^v$ is decomposed to N_v subproblems,

$$\begin{aligned} &\min_{\mathbf{b}_n^v} \sum\nolimits_{v=1}^{V} \lambda_v \left\|\mathbf{R}^{v\mathsf{T}} \mathbf{x}_n^v - \sum\nolimits_{m=1}^{M} \mathbf{C}_m \delta\left(\mathbf{b}_{mn}^v\right)\right\|_2^2 \\ &\text{s.t.} \quad \left\|\delta\left(\mathbf{b}_{mn}^v\right)\right\|_0 = 1, \delta\left(\mathbf{b}_{mn}^v\right) \in \{0, 1\}^K. \end{aligned} \tag{7}$$

This optimization problem is generally NP-hard. As shown in [30], this problem is essentially high-order Markov Random Field (MRF) problem and can be solved by the Iterated Conditional Modes (ICM) algorithm [4] which solves M indicators $\{\mathbf{b}_{mn}^v\}_{m=1}^M$ alternatively. Given $\{\mathbf{b}_{m'n}^v\}_{m' \neq m}$ fixed, we update $\mathbf{b}_{mn}^v$ by exhaustively checking all the codeword in codebook $\mathbf{C}_m$, finding the codeword such that the objective in (7) is minimized, and setting the corresponding entry of $\mathbf{b}_{mn}^v$ as 1 and the rest as 0. The algorithm is guaranteed to converge, and can be terminated if maximum iterations are reached. To accelerate quantization, we can explore hierarchical structure of codebooks $\{\mathbf{C}_m\}$ and update $\{\mathbf{b}_{mn}^v\}$ by a new greedy algorithm. Specifically, after updating $\{\mathbf{b}_{m'n}^v\}_{m' < m}$, we can update $\mathbf{b}_{mn}^v$ by encoding residual $\mathbf{R}^{v\mathsf{T}} \mathbf{x}_n^v - \sum_{m'=1}^{m-1} \mathbf{C}_{m'} \delta\left(\mathbf{b}_{m'n}^v\right)$ with codebook $\mathbf{C}_m$. The overall learning procedure is summarized in Algorithm 1.

4.2 Large-Scale Implementation

Batch algorithms are memory-inefficient for large-scale datasets, hence we formulate CCQ optimization into mini-batch algorithms for large-scale problems [24]. The main idea is to split the training set into mini-batches and load a fraction of data points into memory each time. Hence, the memory usage stays constant when the size of the training set increases. The update of $\mathbf{B}^v$ in Equation (7) is already mini-batch in that update of each data point is independent on the other data points. To update $\mathbf{R}^v$ in mini-batch, we notice that the matrix for SVD is $\mathbf{X}^v [\mathbf{C}\delta\left(\mathbf{B}^v\right)]^{\mathsf{T}} \in \mathbb{R}^{P_v \times D}$, which if given, the SVD can be solved in $O(P_v^2 D)$, independent on the number of data points. We thus formulate the matrix for SVD in a point-wise summation form as $\sum_{n=1}^{N_v} \mathbf{x}_n^v [\mathbf{C}\delta\left(\mathbf{b}_n\right)]^{\mathsf{T}}$, then it can be computed by traversing all data points in a mini-batch paradigm. Similarly, the update of $\mathbf{C}$ can also be formulated in a summation form for mini-batch implementation. Note that we can allocate all available memory to mini-batch and trade off memory and disk reading costs.

4.3 Computational Complexity

We analyze the cost of each iteration to show CCQ scales linearly to sample size N_v. To update $\mathbf{R}^v$, it takes $O\left(N_v P_v D + N_v D M\right)$ to prepare the problem and $O\left(P_v^2 D + D^3\right)$ to compute the SVD.

To update $\mathbf{C}$, it takes $O\left(N_v P_v D + N_v DM + N_v M^2\right)$ to prepare the problem and $O\left(DM^2K^2 + M^3K^3\right)$ to compute the quadratic optimization. To update $\mathbf{B}^v$, it takes $O\left(N_v P_v D + N_v DMKT_i\right)$, where T_i is the number of iterations and $T_i = 3$ in ICM algorithm or $T_i = 1$ in greedy algorithm can obtain satisfactory performance. As a rule of thumb, $D = H$ and $K = 256$ are good choices for most applications. For longer codes, update of $\mathbf{C}$ is inefficient, in which case we can adopt the online L-BFGS algorithm for speedup.

4.4 Approximation Error Analysis

Given a query $\mathbf{q}^{\bar{v}}$ and a database point $\mathbf{x}_n^v$, after transformed by correlation-maximal mappings $\tilde{\mathbf{q}}^{\bar{v}} = \mathbf{R}^{\bar{v}\mathsf{T}}\mathbf{q}^{\bar{v}}$ and $\tilde{\mathbf{x}}_n^v = \mathbf{R}^{v\mathsf{T}}\mathbf{x}_n^v$, they can be comparable in the modality-consistent latent space, and their Euclidean distance is computed as $d\left(\tilde{\mathbf{q}}^{\bar{v}}, \tilde{\mathbf{x}}_n^v\right) = \left\|\tilde{\mathbf{q}}^{\bar{v}} - \tilde{\mathbf{x}}_n^v\right\|_2$. As computing Euclidean distance on real-valued vectors is too costly for large-scale search, we compute AQD (4) on binary codes. Hence, we need to analyze the error bound of using AQD to approximate real-valued distance. Denote $\hat{\mathbf{x}}_n^v = \sum_{m=1}^{M} \mathbf{C}_m \mathbf{b}_{mn}^v$ the decoded vector of $\mathbf{x}_n^v$, then AQD $\left(\mathbf{q}^{\bar{v}}, \mathbf{x}_n^v\right) = d\left(\tilde{\mathbf{q}}^{\bar{v}}, \hat{\mathbf{x}}_n^v\right) + \epsilon$, ϵ is a constant.

THEOREM 1 (BOUND). *The error is bounded by learning loss*

$$\left|d\left(\tilde{\mathbf{q}}^{\bar{v}}, \tilde{\mathbf{x}}_n^v\right) - d\left(\tilde{\mathbf{q}}^{\bar{v}}, \hat{\mathbf{x}}_n^v\right)\right| \leqslant \left\|\mathbf{x}_n^v - \mathbf{R}^v \sum_{m=1}^{M} \mathbf{C}_m \mathbf{b}_{mn}^v\right\|_2. \tag{8}$$

PROOF. From the triangle inequality, $\left|d\left(\tilde{\mathbf{q}}^{\bar{v}}, \tilde{\mathbf{x}}_n^v\right) - d\left(\tilde{\mathbf{q}}^{\bar{v}}, \hat{\mathbf{x}}_n^v\right)\right| \leqslant d\left(\tilde{\mathbf{x}}_n^v, \hat{\mathbf{x}}_n^v\right)$. Then

$$\begin{aligned} d^2\left(\tilde{\mathbf{x}}_n^v, \hat{\mathbf{x}}_n^v\right) &= \left\|\mathbf{R}^{v\mathsf{T}}\mathbf{x}_n^v - \sum_{m=1}^{M} \mathbf{C}_m \mathbf{b}_{mn}^v\right\|_2^2 \\ &\leqslant \left\|\mathbf{R}^{v\mathsf{T}}\mathbf{x}_n^v - \sum_{m=1}^{M} \mathbf{C}_m \mathbf{b}_{mn}^v\right\|_2^2 + \left\|\mathbf{R}_\perp^{v\mathsf{T}}\mathbf{x}_n^v\right\|_2^2 \\ &= \left\|\mathbf{x}_n^v - \mathbf{R}^v \sum_{m=1}^{M} \mathbf{C}_m \mathbf{b}_{mn}^v\right\|_2^2, \end{aligned} \tag{9}$$

where $\mathbf{R}_\perp^v$ is an orthogonal complement of $\mathbf{R}^v$, $\mathbf{R}^{v\mathsf{T}}\mathbf{R}_\perp^v = \mathbf{0}$. □

The theorem confirms that the error of using AQD to approximate real-valued distance is statistically bounded by CCQ learning loss. Hence, CCQ is more accurate than sign thresholding methods [25]. An important advantage of CCQ in Equation (9) is that mapping $\mathbf{R}^v$ is learned by a joint optimization of canonical correlation analysis (CCA) and principal component analysis (PCA) corresponding to the first and second terms of Line 2 in Equation (9). This can be much more effective than most CCA-based methods [13, 28, 26].

5. EXPERIMENTS

We conduct extensive evaluation of CCQ against state of the art methods on three public multimodal datasets. We investigate both effectiveness and efficiency in terms of search precision, recall, and time. The codes, data, and configurations will be available online.

5.1 Datasets

The evaluation is conducted on three datasets: NUS-WIDE [6], Wiki [18], and Flickr1M [11], with statistics depicted in Table 1. We preprocess all datasets by applying ZCA [24] to normalize each dimension of image/text features to be zero mean and unit variance.

Table 1: The Statistics of Three Datasets

Dataset	NUS-WIDE	Wiki	Flickr1M
Complete Set	195,834	2,866	1,000,000
Labeled Set	195,834	2,866	25,000
Query Set	2,000	693	1,000
Database	193,834	2,173	24,000
Training Set	10,000	2,173	975,000

NUS-WIDE[1] is a Web image dataset containing 269,648 images downloaded from Flickr, each associated with 6 tags on average. There are 81 ground truth concepts manually annotated for search evaluation. Following prior works [34, 24], we prune the original NUS-WIDE to form a new dataset consisting of 195,834 image-text pairs by keeping the pairs that belong to one of the 21 most frequent concepts. The images are represented by 500-dimensional bag-of-words vectors extracted from the SIFT features using k-means, and the texts are represented by 1,000-dimensional vectors extracted from the tag occurrence features using PCA. A query set of 2,000 image-text pairs are randomly sampled from the dataset, while the remaining 193,834 image-text pairs are serving as the database. The hash models are learned on the training set containing 10,000 image-text pairs randomly sampled from the database [34, 20].

Wiki[2] contains 2,866 image-text pairs selected from Wikipedia's featured articles comprised of multiple sections of images and texts. Every image-text pair is labeled by one of the 10 concepts in the article categories. Each image is represented by a 128-dimensional bag-of-words vector extracted from SIFT features, and each text is represented by the probability distribution over 10 topics learned by a latent Dirichlet allocation (LDA) model. The dataset is released with a query set of 693 pairs and a database of 2,173 pairs, and the whole database is used as the training set for hash coding [18, 34].

Flickr1M comprises 1,000,000 images associated with tags from Flickr, in which 25,000 are labeled with 38 concepts while the remaining 975,000 are unlabeled. The public available preprocessed dataset[3] is employed for evaluation, in which each image is represented by a 3,857-dimensional vector concatenated by local SIFT feature, global GIST feature, etc [21]. Each text is represented by a 2,000-dimensional vector extracted from tag occurrences. The query set contains 1,000 image-text pairs randomly sampled from the 25,000 labeled pairs, and the rest 24,000 labeled pairs are used as the database. In scalability test of CCQ (Section 5.7), all 975,000 unlabeled pairs are used as the training set for learning hash codes.

5.2 Comparison Methods

We compare CCQ against many state of the art hashing methods.

- **Unsupervised hashing:** Cross-View Hashing (**CVH**)[6] [13] and Inter-Media Hashing (**IMH**)[4] [20] are unsupervised hashing methods that extend spectral hashing to exploit the local structure of multimodal data for learning binary codes.
- **Deep hashing:** Correspondence Auto-Encoders (**CorrAE**)[5] [8] learns latent features via unsupervised deep auto-encoders, which captures both intra-modal and inter-modal correspondences, and binarizes latent features via sign thresholding.
- **Supervised hashing:** Cross-Modal Similarity-Sensitive Hashing (**CMSSH**)[6] [5], Semantic Correlation Maximization (**SCM**) [28], and Quantized Correlation Hashing (**QCH**) are supervised hashing methods which embed multimodal data into a common Hamming space using supervised metric learning.

[1] http://lms.comp.nus.edu.sg/research/NUS-WIDE.htm

[2] http://www.svcl.ucsd.edu/projects/crossmodal

[3] http://www.cs.toronto.edu/~nitish/multimodal

[4] http://staff.itee.uq.edu.au/shenht/UQ_IMH

[5] https://github.com/fangxiangfeng/deepnet

[6] http://www.cse.ust.hk/~dyyeung/code/mlbe.zip

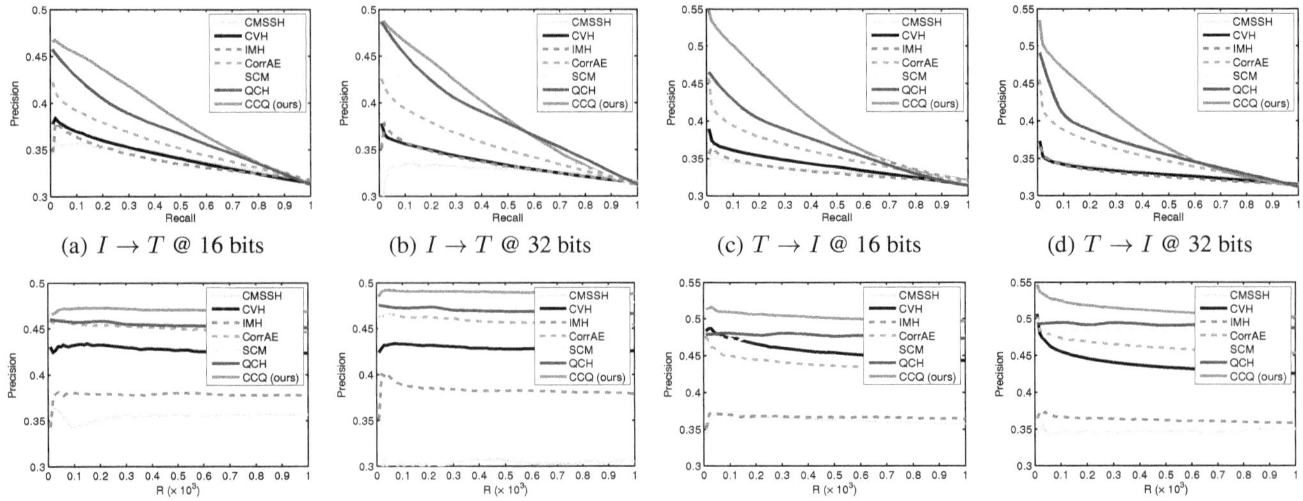

(a) $I \to T$ @ 16 bits (b) $I \to T$ @ 32 bits (c) $T \to I$ @ 16 bits (d) $T \to I$ @ 32 bits

(e) $I \to T$ @ 16 bits (f) $I \to T$ @ 32 bits (g) $T \to I$ @ 16 bits (h) $T \to I$ @ 32 bits

Figure 2: Precision-recall curves (top) and precision@R curves (bottom) on NUS-WIDE cross-modal search tasks @ 16 and 32 bits.

5.3 Evaluation Protocols

We perform four types of multimodal retrieval schemes: (1) $I \to I$: use image queries to retrieve relevant images; (2) $T \to T$: use text queries to retrieve relevant texts; (3) $I \to T$: use image queries to retrieve relevant texts; and (4) $T \to I$: use text queries to retrieve relevant images. The first two tasks are intra-modal retrieval and the last two tasks are cross-modal retrieval. As CCQ can also handle multimodal search where both modalities are available for the database, we show the results of multimodal retrieval schemes where each image-text pair is quantized into a unified hash code by fusing knowledge of different modalities: (5) $I \to IT$: use image queries to retrieve relevant image-text pairs; (6) $T \to IT$: use text queries to retrieve relevant image-text pairs. The baseline methods do not support multimodal search because they do not use shared coding for different modalities of the same object. Given a query, the ground truth is defined as: if a result shares at least one common concept with the query, it is relevant; otherwise it is irrelevant.

We adopt *Mean Average Precision* (MAP) to measure the effectiveness of multimodal search [20, 34, 24, 27, 8]. Given a set of queries, we first calculate Average Precision (AP) of each query as

$$\mathrm{AP@}R = \frac{\sum_{r=1}^{R} P(r)\,\delta(r)}{\sum_{r'=1}^{R} \delta(r')}, \tag{10}$$

where R is the number of retrieved documents, $P(r)$ denotes the precision of the top r retrieved results, and $\delta(r) = 1$ if the r-th retrieved result is a true neighbor of the query, otherwise $\delta(r) = 0$. Then MAP is computed as the mean of all the queries' average precision, and the larger the MAP, the better the retrieval performance. In the experiments, we follow [15, 27, 24] to report MAP@R = 50. We also report another two standard retrieval criteria, *precision-recall* curves and *precision@top-R* curves of all retrieval tasks. In addition to effectiveness, we report *time and memory* costs as the efficiency measures for query processing and model training.

The CCQ approach involves two model parameters: dimension of modality-consistent subspace D and modality trade-off weight λ. In principle, CCQ is almost immune to different choices of D, as long as D is large enough to retain the majority amount of covariance information as LSA. While no prior knowledge is available, we can simply set equal weights $\lambda = 1$ for different modalities, which can already achieve satisfactory performance. Nonetheless, for image-text bimodal search, the text modality usually carry more semantic information, hence we equip CCQ with the flexibility for selecting the optimal λ to encode such important prior knowledge. Given annotation ground truths as in the evaluation datasets, we can automatically select D and λ using cross-validation. However, we choose to blindly fix $\lambda = 5$ throughout the comparative study. This is desirable as cross-validation may be impossible in the pervasive unsupervised multimodal search. We will study parameter sensitivity in Section 5.8 to validate that CCQ can consistently outperform the state of the arts with a wide range of parameter configurations.

For the comparison methods, we adopt cross-validation to select their optimal parameters, respectively. As cross-validation requires annotation ground truths, this further confirms CCQ's superior parameter stability. Subject to computation burden, it is too costly to train CMSSH and IMH on the complete Flickr1M dataset, hence we randomly sample 10,000 image-text pairs to train these models. Each experiment repeats ten runs and the average result is reported.

5.4 Experimental Results

We compare CCQ with state of the art methods in terms of MAP and precision-recall on 4 multimodal retrieval tasks ($I \to I, T \to T, I \to T, T \to I$) of three datasets (NUS-WIDE, Wiki, and Flickr1M).

5.4.1 *Results on NUS-WIDE*

We evaluate CCQ against state of the arts with different lengths of hash codes, i.e. 8, 16, 32, and 64 bits, and report the MAP results in Table 2. For all multimodal retrieval tasks, CCQ achieves significantly better performance than all unsupervised hashing methods CVH, IMH, and CorrAE, and generally outperforms the state of the art supervised hashing methods CMSSH, SCM, QCH in most cases. It is very worth noting that, CCQ is an *unsupervised* hashing method that does not require labeled similarity information. Hence CCQ is particularly beneficial when labeled information is unavailable, which is the most common scenario in big data era. A notable limitation of orthogonal constrained methods CVH and IMH is that longer codes do not necessarily improve performance in cross-modal tasks $I \to T$ and $T \to I$. The reason is that these methods learn uncorrelated hash bits via eigenvalue decomposition on similarity matrix, which leads to unbalanced hash codes with the first k eigenvectors (hash bits) dominating the whole hash codes. CCQ

Table 2: Mean Average Precision (MAP) Comparison of Six Multimodal Retrieval Tasks on Three Standard Datasets

Task	Method	NUS-WIDE				Wiki				Flickr1M			
		8 bits	16 bits	32 bits	64 bits	8 bits	16 bits	32 bits	64 bits	8 bits	16 bits	32 bits	64 bits
$I \to I$	CVH [13]	0.3954	0.4542	0.4759	0.4780	0.1988	0.1969	0.2042	0.2058	0.6050	0.6328	0.6615	0.6712
	IMH [20]	0.4313	0.4545	0.4155	0.4005	0.1910	0.1963	0.1937	0.1935	0.5239	0.5725	0.5736	0.5748
	CorrAE [8]	0.4223	0.4478	0.4587	0.4796	0.2055	0.2086	0.2188	0.2194	0.6145	0.6397	0.6588	0.6654
	CMSSH [5]	0.3776	0.4060	0.4356	0.4490	0.1987	0.1979	0.2007	0.2126	0.5738	0.6304	0.6587	0.6932
	SCM [28]	0.4258	0.4578	0.4695	0.4831	0.2048	0.2103	0.2177	0.2212	0.5926	0.6257	0.6615	0.6801
	QCH [26]	0.4289	0.4557	0.4786	0.4898	0.2087	0.2155	0.2198	0.2252	0.6165	0.6586	0.6787	0.6885
	CCQ (ours)	**0.4711**	**0.4859**	**0.4921**	**0.4932**	**0.2226**	**0.2265**	**0.2373**	**0.2386**	**0.6714**	**0.7092**	**0.7318**	**0.7451**
$T \to T$	CVH [13]	0.5825	0.6485	0.6837	**0.7189**	0.4049	0.5506	0.6075	0.6239	0.5812	0.6085	0.6242	0.6337
	IMH [20]	0.4531	0.4740	0.5421	0.6202	0.3805	0.4623	0.5773	0.5989	0.5585	0.5973	0.6360	0.6436
	CorrAE [8]	0.5501	0.5856	0.6344	0.6678	0.5765	0.5889	0.6045	0.6123	0.6060	0.6176	0.6389	0.6443
	CMSSH [5]	**0.5911**	0.5968	0.6215	0.6613	0.5503	0.6065	0.6188	0.6232	0.5487	0.5573	0.5583	0.5614
	SCM [28]	0.5524	0.6315	0.6606	0.6736	0.5814	0.6051	0.6189	0.6324	0.5924	0.6320	0.6410	0.6485
	QCH [26]	0.5706	**0.6586**	0.6796	0.6855	0.6002	0.6128	0.6226	0.6355	0.6022	0.6427	**0.6554**	**0.6686**
	CCQ (ours)	**0.5913**	0.6481	**0.6917**	0.7069	**0.6017**	**0.6286**	**0.6366**	**0.6422**	**0.6090**	**0.6433**	0.6541	0.6550
$I \to T$	CVH [13]	0.4588	0.4713	0.4743	0.4740	0.1673	0.1877	0.1716	0.1696	0.6091	0.6225	0.6364	0.6199
	IMH [20]	0.4345	0.4399	0.4203	0.4115	0.1734	0.1896	0.1714	0.1601	0.5449	0.5646	0.5936	0.5539
	CorrAE [8]	0.4398	0.4522	0.4699	0.4964	0.1929	0.1982	0.2033	0.2155	0.6301	0.6329	0.6357	0.6401
	CMSSH [5]	0.3950	0.4052	0.4076	0.3516	0.1672	0.1727	0.1750	0.1759	0.5076	0.5272	0.5357	0.5219
	SCM [28]	0.4693	0.4648	0.4619	0.4851	0.2258	0.2372	0.2381	0.2378	0.6361	0.6493	0.6495	0.6440
	QCH [26]	0.4765	0.4895	0.5050	0.5125	0.2288	0.2343	0.2368	**0.2402**	0.6452	0.6523	0.6685	0.6721
	CCQ (ours)	**0.5124**	**0.5161**	**0.5165**	**0.5372**	**0.2338**	**0.2349**	**0.2371**	0.2374	**0.6879**	**0.7081**	**0.7183**	**0.7176**
$I \to IT$	CCQ (ours)	0.5074	0.5411	0.5414	0.5441	0.2512	0.2513	0.2529	0.2587	0.7063	0.6894	0.6989	0.6996
$T \to I$	CVH [13]	**0.5598**	0.5217	0.5129	0.4875	0.2309	0.2219	0.2214	0.2350	0.5972	0.6032	0.5738	0.5794
	IMH [20]	0.4380	0.4582	0.4186	0.4051	0.2394	0.2227	0.2333	0.1896	0.5374	0.5536	0.5513	0.5583
	CorrAE [8]	0.4303	0.4501	0.4634	0.4880	0.2688	0.2928	0.3478	0.3566	0.6142	0.6198	0.6247	0.6431
	CMSSH [5]	0.3783	0.3499	0.3944	0.4015	0.2926	0.2991	0.2537	0.2582	0.5868	0.5732	0.6176	0.6323
	SCM [28]	0.4449	0.4859	0.5105	0.5259	0.3157	0.3698	0.4239	0.4369	0.6037	0.5998	0.5805	0.6078
	QCH [26]	0.5020	0.5195	**0.5489**	**0.5622**	0.3426	0.3753	**0.4411**	**0.4565**	0.6258	0.6425	0.6485	0.6528
	CCQ (ours)	0.5359	**0.5410**	**0.5413**	0.5556	**0.3885**	**0.4000**	0.4222	0.4178	**0.6548**	**0.7026**	**0.7165**	**0.7266**
$T \to IT$	CCQ (ours)	0.6022	0.6925	0.7131	0.7153	0.6355	0.6351	0.6394	0.6405	0.6942	0.7151	0.7190	0.7416

via composite quantization in isomorphic space can learn balanced binary codes, hence its performance improves with longer codes.

It is interesting to observe that the performances of cross-modal search task $I \to T$ is generally better than that of intra-modal search task $I \to I$, while this observation does not hold for the counterparts $T \to I$ and $T \to T$. This seems abnormal at first sight as cross-modal search tasks are often more challenging than intra-modal search tasks due to semantic gap [18]. However, in general, text retrieval is much easier than image retrieval, making different modalities of the objects contribute differently the cross-modal retrieval performance. We believe that $T \to T$ is much easier than $T \to I$, but $I \to T$ may be easier than $I \to I$ because image-to-image retrieval is often the most difficult task. In the case of cross-modal task $I \to T$, the knowledge of text modality is transferred to image modality, making cross-modal retrieval easier. This shows cross-modal retrieval can be improved by knowledge transfer.

The precision-recall curves and the precision@top-R curves [34, 24] are illustrated in Figure 2. For space limitation, only the results of cross-modal tasks $I \to T$ and $T \to I$ are presented, while similar trends of results are observed on intra-modal tasks $I \to I$ and $T \to T$. CCQ shows the best cross-modal retrieval performance on all recall levels and top-R ranks. This validates that CCQ is capable for diverse retrieval scenarios, which may emphasize higher precision at smaller number of top-R retrieved results, i.e. Web search, or higher recall tolerating fairly lower precision, i.e. vertical search.

5.4.2 *Results on Wiki*

Table 2 also compares the search performance of CCQ and the state of the art methods on the Wiki dataset, which shows that CCQ significantly outperforms the unsupervised hashing methods CVH, IMH, and CorrAE, and performs comparably to supervised hashing methods SCM and QCH. A notable observation is that the MAPs are much smaller than those on the NUS-WIDE dataset. This is reasonable as the images of Wiki are of low-quality (low-resolution) and high-diversity, i.e. the text can well describe the semantics of the image-text pair while the image may not be well related to the semantics of the image-text pair, which makes it more challenging to capture the semantic correlations between image query and text database. Note that the texts of Wiki are featured articles which are well edited by experts and rich in semantic information, hence it is fairly easy to correlate a text query with the multimodal database.

The precision-recall curves and the precision@top-R curves [34, 24] are demonstrated in Figure 3. Again, CCQ is among the top-performing methods on all recall levels and all top-R ranks. A noticeable performance drop can be examined from the precision-recall curves to the precision@top-R curves. And this is because the Wiki dataset is very small-scale with only 2,173 database items, hence all relevant results will be retrieved at small R and no more relevant results can be further retrieved when R grows too large. This highlights the importance of evaluation with different metrics.

A crucial superiority of CCQ over the comparison methods lies in that CCQ jointly learns the isomorphic latent space and compact binary codes by minimizing both correlation and quantization errors in a unified optimization framework, while comparison methods merely learn the isomorphic space and binary codes in a separated two-step pipeline. As examined by CorrAE [8], the quality of searching with binary codes using Hamming distance is evidently inferior to searching with continuous features using Euclidean distance, due to substantial information loss by converting continuous features to binary codes without minimizing the quantization error. The search quality loss due to binarization is shown in Figure 5(a), and for CCQ, we use $\mathbf{R}^{v\mathsf{T}}\mathbf{x}_n^v$ for continuous features and $\mathbf{C}\mathbf{b}_n^v$ for

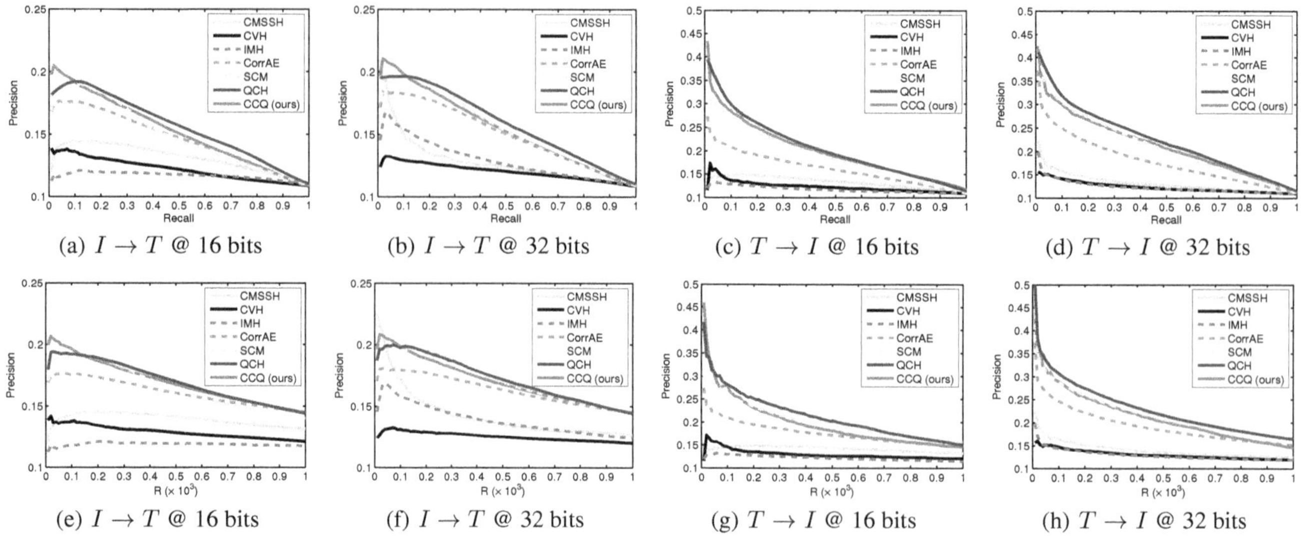

Figure 3: Precision-recall curves (top) and precision@R curves (bottom) on Wiki cross-modal search tasks @ 16 and 32 bits.

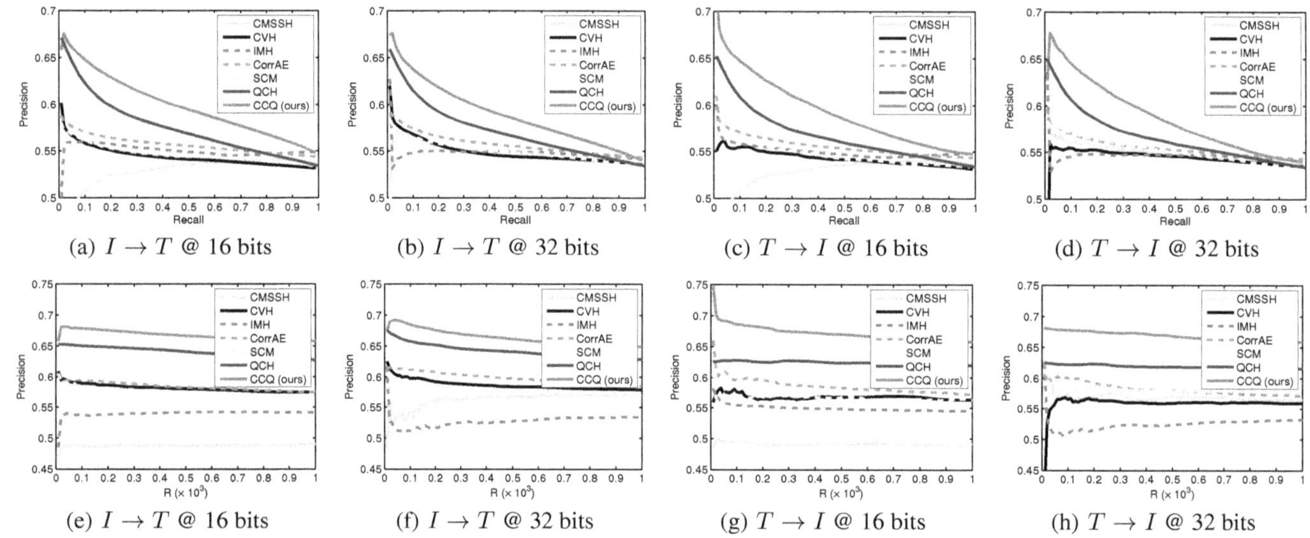

Figure 4: Precision-recall curves (top) and precision@R curves (bottom) on Flickr1M cross-modal search tasks @ 16 and 32 bits.

binary codes. We see that IMH and CorrAE suffer from substantial MAP loss (similar trends are observed from other methods) while CCQ is almost lossless to binarization. In other words, by jointly minimizing the correlation error and quantization error, CCQ can circumvent information loss and learn more accurate binary codes.

5.4.3 Results on Flickr1M

In practical retrieval systems, it is crucial to process large-scale datasets in both training and testing phases, and thus we compare CCQ with state of the art methods on large-scale Flickr1M dataset. We report the MAP results in Table 2 and illustrate the detailed precision-recall curves and precision@top-R curves in Figure 4. As mentioned before, we randomly select 10,000 image-text pairs as training set to learn hash functions if it is computationally too demanding to train these methods on the complete Flickr1M dataset. We can observe that CCQ significantly outperforms the comparison methods on all retrieval tasks and performs better with longer codes. This validates the superiority of CCQ in processing large-scale datasets, as the experimental setting on Flickr1M is consistent with real-word system setting where a sufficiently accurate model needs to be derived on a sufficiently large training set. We will examine CCQ's ability to process real semi-paired data in the sequel.

5.5 Semi-Paired Data Quantization

Most of the existing methods, including the ones in comparison, require full correspondences between different modalities. In other words, the multimodal data objects are fully paired, e.g. image-text pairs. As a result, these methods are unable to tackle more realistic scenarios in which only a limited number of paired data points are available. CCQ explores the idea of semi-supervised learning and can leverage both paired data (all modalities of the objects are available) and unpaired data (partial modalities of the objects are available) to boost the search quality when paired data are limited. To verify this, we consider the NUS-WIDE and Flickr1M datasets and for each dataset, we randomly sample as the training set 1) 10,000 images without text modality, 2) 10,000 texts without image modality, and 3) different numbers, i.e. $[0.5, 1, 2, 4, 8] \times 10^3$, of image-text pairs. We train CCQ with these semi-paired data and evaluate the search performance in terms of MAP @ 32 bits.

The search performances of CCQ on NUS-WIDE and Flickr1M

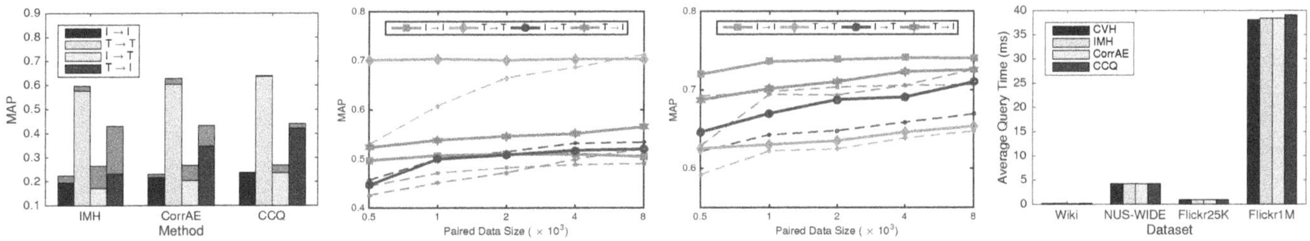

(a) MAP Loss (b) NUS-WIDE (c) Flickr1M (d) Search Efficiency

Figure 5: Effectiveness and efficiency experiments: (1) Loss of search quality in MAP (by red bars) due to conversion from continuous features to binary codes on Wiki. (b)–(c) the MAP of CCQ w.r.t. different numbers of paired data points (the number of unpaired data points is fixed to $10,000$). Solid lines indicate training with both paired and unpaired data, and dashed lines indicate training with only paired data. (d) Average search time (ms) for each query via lookup tables on Wiki, NUS-WIDE, Flickr25K, and Flickr1M.

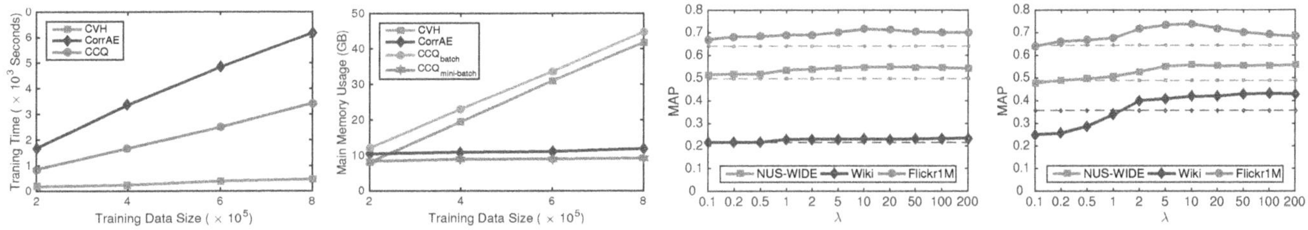

(a) Time (b) Memory (c) $I \to T$ @ 32 bits (d) $T \to I$ @ 32 bits

Figure 6: Efficiency verification experiments: (a)–(b) Training time and memory costs of different methods on the complete Flickr1M dataset. CCQ with batch (mini-batch) training scales linearly (constantly) to the sample size. (c)–(d) The MAP of CCQ @ 32 bits versus parameter $\lambda \in [0.1, 200]$ for cross-modal retrieval tasks $I \to T$ and $T \to I$ on the NUS-WIDE, Wiki, and Flickr1M datasets.

are demonstrated in Figures 5(b) and 5(c) respectively, where solid lines indicate training with both paired and unpaired data, and dashed lines indicate training with only paired data. We can observe that when the number of paired data points is small, CCQ trained with both paired and unpaired data significantly outperforms CCQ trained with only paired data on most of the multimodal search tasks; when the number of paired data points increases, the search performance of CCQ will gradually saturate while the search quality of the two training paradigms will finally match. This clearly shows that CCQ can effectively leverage both paired and unpaired data (partial multimodal data) to boost search quality in a semi-paired data scenario.

An unexpected phenomenon is that semi-paired training slightly deteriorates search performance on task $I \to T$. We conjecture the plausible reason is that searching text database with image queries significantly relies on maximizing the image-text correlations to bridge the semantic gap between low-level image features and high-level image semantics, i.e. its associated texts. When the number of paired data points is obviously smaller than the number of unpaired data points, semi-paired training may tend to weaken correlation learning from image-text pairs and incur performance degradation.

5.6 Search Efficiency

To search for approximate nearest neighbors (ANN) in database for a given query, all methods in comparison perform linear scan using symmetric or asymmetric distance. Specifically, to compare a query vector with a database vector, CVH, IMH, and CorrAE all compute symmetric Hamming distance via lookup tables, and CCQ constructs a distance lookup table for each query that stores the Euclidean distances between the query and the multiple codebooks. As a result, CVH, IMH, CorrAE, and CCQ compute exactly the same number of table lookups for linear scan, while their costs of computing the query-codebook distance lookup tables are slightly different, which can be negligible as they are infinitesimal w.r.t. the cost of linear scan. For example, the cost of computing the distance lookup table for CCQ takes only less than 1% of the cost for linear scan on Flickr1M. The average search time of each query by CVH, IMH, CorrAE, and CCQ on the Wiki, NUS-WIDE, Flickr25K, and Flickr1M datasets is illustrated in Figure 5(d), from which we can observe that the search efficiency are comparable for all methods. While it is beyond the scope of this paper, we want to note that one can adopt a Multi-Index [2] approach to achieve sub-linear search complexity on the binary codes and further boost search efficiency.

5.7 Training Complexity

The training time and memory costs of CCQ scale linearly with the training sample size and hence can process large-scale dataset. To verify this, we follow [24] and use the complete Flickr1M dataset to evaluate the consumptions of training time and memory. CMSSH and IMH are not compared in this study since they require $O(N^2)$ complexity and run out of either time or memory on this dataset.

The comparison of training time costs is illustrated in Figure 6(a). We can observe that the training time of CCQ increases linearly with respect to the sample size. Due to multiple iterations between three sets of variables, i.e. transformation matrices $\mathbf{R}^v$, quantizer codebook $\mathbf{C}$, and modal-specific binary codes $\mathbf{B}^v$, CCQ is not as efficient as CVH. However, CCQ performs much more efficiently in time than CorrAE, which is a deep learning based method solving a time-demanding non-convex nonlinear optimization problem.

The training memory consumptions are compared in Figure 6(b). Both batch and mini-batch (large-scale) implementations of CCQ store the model parameters in memory, which are independent of training dataset size. For the batch implementation, all training data is loaded in memory, while for the mini-batch implementation, the training data is partitioned into multiple mini-batches while only one mini-batch is loaded in memory each time. Hence in the mini-batch (large-scale) implementation, the memory cost stays constant when training dataset size increases. We can flexibly allocate memory to each mini-batch to trade off memory and disk reading costs.

5.8 Parameter Sensitivity

Towards unsupervised multimodal retrieval, CCQ is designed to involve only two parameters, dimension of modality-isomorphic subspace D and modality trade-off weight λ, and the performance is expected to be stable against parameter variations. Since we have fixed $D = \min(\{P_v\}_{v=1}^{V}, H)$, we only inspect the sensitivity of λ.

We compute MAP @ 32 bits on both cross-modal retrieval tasks by varying λ between 0.1 and 200. The performance of CCQ w.r.t. parameter λ is shown in Figure 6(c) and 6(d). We see that CCQ can consistently outperform all the unsupervised baseline methods by a large margin with λ varying between 1 and 200. This validates that CCQ is robust against parameter selection and is applicable to unsupervised multimodal retrieval with easily-configured parameters.

6. CONCLUSION AND FUTURE WORK

In this paper, we have formally approached seamless multimodal hashing through a novel composite correlation quantization (CCQ). It integrates multimodal correlation and composite quantization into a seamless latent semantic analysis (LSA) framework, which yields compact binary codes that encode both intra-modal similarity and inter-modal correlation. The sharing of codebooks and binary codes across modalities enables joint learning of latent semantics that are maximally correlated in the isomorphic feature space, which serves as the key contributor to the efficacy of the proposed CCQ method.

In the future, we plan to equip our model with a deep learning architecture which can learn highly abstract nonlinear representations to better distill the correlation structures across multiple modalities.

7. ACKNOWLEDGMENTS

The authors would like to thank Dr Jingdong Wang for insightful comments. This work was supported by National Natural Science Foundation of China (61325008, 61502265), China Postdoctoral Science Foundation (2015T80088), National Science&Technology Supporting Program (2015BAH14F02), NSF grant III-1526499, and Tsinghua TNList Lab Fund for Big Data Science and Technology.

8. REFERENCES

[1] A. Andoni and P. Indyk. Near-optimal hashing algorithms for approximate nearest neighbor in high dimensions. In *FOCS*. IEEE, 2006.

[2] A. Babenko and V. Lempitsky. The inverted multi-index. In *CVPR*, pages 3069–3076. IEEE, 2012.

[3] A. Babenko and V. Lempitsky. Additive quantization for extreme vector compression. In *CVPR*. IEEE, 2014.

[4] J. Besag. On the statistical analysis of dirty pictures. *Journal of the Royal Statistical Society*, 48(3):259–320, 1986.

[5] M. Bronstein, A. Bronstein, F. Michel, and N. Paragios. Data fusion through cross-modality metric learning using similarity-sensitive hashing. In *CVPR*. IEEE, 2010.

[6] T.-S. Chua, J. Tang, R. Hong, H. Li, Z. Luo, and Y.-T. Zheng. Nus-wide: A real-world web image database from national university of singapore. In *CIVR*. ACM, 2009.

[7] S. Deerwester, S. T. Dumais, G. W. Furnas, T. K. Landauer, and R. Harshman. Indexing by latent semantic analysis. *Journal of the American Society for Information Science*, 41(6):391–407, 1990.

[8] F. Feng, X. Wang, and R. Li. Cross-modal retrieval with correspondence autoencoder. In *MM*. ACM, 2014.

[9] Y. Gong and S. Lazebnik. Iterative quantization: A procrustean approach to learning binary codes. In *CVPR*, 2011.

[10] Y. Hu, Z. Jin, H. Ren, D. Cai, and X. He. Iterative multi-view hashing for cross media indexing. In *MM*. ACM, 2014.

[11] M. J. Huiskes and M. S. Lew. The mir flickr retrieval evaluation. In *ICMR*. ACM, 2008.

[12] H. Jegou, M. Douze, and C. Schmid. Product quantization for nearest neighbor search. *TPAMI*, 33(1):117–128, Jan 2011.

[13] S. Kumar and R. Udupa. Learning hash functions for cross-view similarity search. In *IJCAI*, 2011.

[14] Z. Lin, G. Ding, M. Hu, and J. Wang. Semantics-preserving hashing for cross-view retrieval. In *CVPR*, 2015.

[15] X. Lu, F. Wu, S. Tang, Z. Zhang, X. He, and Y. Zhuang. A low rank structural large margin method for cross-modal ranking. In *SIGIR*. ACM, 2013.

[16] L. Ma, Z. Lu, L. Shang, and H. Li. Multimodal convolutional neural networks for matching image and sentence. In *ICCV*, 2015.

[17] M. Norouzi and D. J. Fleet. Cartesian k-means. In *CVPR*. IEEE, 2013.

[18] J. C. Pereira, E. Coviello, G. Doyle, N. Rasiwasia, G. R. G. Lanckriet, R. Levy, and N. Vasconcelos. On the role of correlation and abstraction in cross-modal multimedia retrieval. *TPAMI*, 36(3):521–535, 2014.

[19] P. H. Schönemann. A generalized solution of the orthogonal procrustes problem. *Psychometrika*, 31(1):1–10, 1966.

[20] J. Song, Y. Yang, Y. Yang, Z. Huang, and H. T. Shen. Inter-media hashing for large-scale retrieval from heterogeneous data sources. In *SIGMOD*. ACM, 2013.

[21] N. Srivastava and R. Salakhutdinov. Multimodal learning with deep boltzmann machines. *JMLR*, 15:2949–2980, 2014.

[22] J. Wang, H. T. Shen, J. Song, and J. Ji. Hashing for similarity search: A survey. Arxiv, 2014.

[23] Q. Wang, L. Si, and B. Shen. Learning to hash on partial multi-modal data. In *IJCAI*, pages 3904–3910, 2015.

[24] W. Wang, B. C. Ooi, X. Yang, D. Zhang, and Y. Zhuang. Effective multi-modal retrieval based on stacked auto-encoders. In *VLDB*. ACM, 2014.

[25] Y. Weiss, A. Torralba, and R. Fergus. Spectral hashing. In *NIPS*, 2009.

[26] B. Wu, Q. Yang, W.-S. Zheng, Y. Wang, and J. Wang. Quantized correlation hashing for fast cross-modal search. In *IJCAI*, 2015.

[27] Z. Yu, F. Wu, Y. Yang, Q. Tian, J. Luo, and Y. Zhuang. Discriminative coupled dictionary hashing for fast cross-media retrieval. In *SIGIR*. ACM, 2014.

[28] D. Zhang and W.-J. Li. Large-scale supervised multimodal hashing with semantic correlation maximization. In *AAAI*, 2014.

[29] D. Zhang, F. Wang, and L. Si. Composite hashing with multiple information sources. In *SIGIR*. ACM, 2011.

[30] T. Zhang, C. Du, and J. Wang. Composite quantization for approximate nearest neighbor search. In *ICML*. ACM, 2014.

[31] F. Zhao, Y. Huang, L. Wang, and T. Tan. Deep semantic ranking based hashing for multi-label image retrieval. In *CVPR*, 2015.

[32] Y. Zhen and D.-Y. Yeung. Co-regularized hashing for multimodal data. In *NIPS*, 2012.

[33] Y. Zhen and D.-Y. Yeung. A probabilistic model for multimodal hash function learning. In *SIGKDD*. ACM, 2012.

[34] X. Zhu, Z. Huang, H. T. Shen, and X. Zhao. Linear cross-modal hashing for efficient multimedia search. In *MM*. ACM, 2013.

Principles for the Design of Online A/B Metrics

Widad Machmouchi
Bing, Microsoft, USA
widadm@microsoft.com

Georg Buscher
Bing, Microsoft, USA
georgbu@microsoft.com

ABSTRACT
In this paper, we describe principles for designing metrics in the context of A/B experiments. We share some issues that comes up in designing such experiments and provide solutions to avoid such pitfalls.

Keywords
A/B measurement; controlled experiments; metric design principles.

1. INTRODUCTION
Online experimentation is becoming more and more popular. Controlled experiments with thousands or even millions of users are applied to establish causal relationships between a new treatment and a change in user behavior. Such A/B experimentation is used widely now in industries related to social media, e-commerce, online publishing, search engines, etc., which try to optimize for engagement, revenue, user success, among other aspects [2]. One of the key factors in evaluating online controlled experiments are metrics. They help discern whether the treatment effect on users was desired or not and therefore guide ship decisions of the teams building the new treatments. For that reason, good A/B metrics are of critical importance in order to make sound data-driven decisions.

Yet, it is very easy to build A/B metrics that suffer from undetected weaknesses and which eventually point in the wrong direction leading to – unknowingly – incorrect ship decisions. Therefore, great care has to be devoted to proper design of A/B metrics that are expressive, robust, and trustworthy.

In this paper we report a few important lessons learnt while designing A/B ship metrics for the large search engine Bing.com. Based on many years of experience, we elaborate on a number of important aspects that should be taken into account when designing online A/B metrics, specifically having user satisfaction metrics in mind.

2. THE A/B METRIC PROBLEM
The eventual purpose of A/B metrics, particularly OECs (Overall Evaluation Criterion) is to tell whether the treatment user group A demonstrated more desirable behavior than the control user group B. In the context of web search, this often means measuring whether treatment users had an improved or impaired search experience in terms of user satisfaction.

SIGIR '16, July 17-21, 2016, Pisa, Italy
ACM 978-1-4503-4069-4/16/07.
http://dx.doi.org/10.1145/2911451.2926731

When designing an A/B metric, a question of critical importance is: How do you know you found a good metric?

Traditionally, in research, this question has been framed and treated as a prediction problem. Given logs with recorded user behavior, and given ground truth labels for the successfulness / outcome of the logged user interactions, build a predictor (classifier) that ingests signals from the logs and optimizes precision/recall/etc. against the ground truth labels [1,2]. Then, the assumption often is that the best predictor will also result in the best A/B metric.

While this type of evaluation is a reasonable first step in designing a good A/B metric, it can easily yield something ineffective and flawed for the following reasons.

1) Insensitivity to changes the metric is supposed to measure: When designing a metric, one needs to be cognizant of the nature of treatment changes it is supposed to measure and be sensitive to. Even a very good predictor might not pick up certain user behavior changes and therefore miss measuring an A/B difference. This can happen particularly for rare user interaction patterns that a predictor might, e.g., prune away to avoid over-fitting. Yet, a particular treatment might change the occurrence of this specific rare user interaction pattern, and not much else, and hence the predictor would be "blind" to the change.

2) The usage of endogenous signals: Search engine logs usually contain information on how the search results page served to the user looked like, and how the user interacted with the page. A predictor might use signals based on both types of information, yet only the latter type of information is generally safe to use when the application is an A/B metric. We call the former type of signals "endogenous signals" which encode the system response from the search engine, and the latter type "exogenous signals" which encode the user response. Using endogenous signals in the predictor opens it up for loopholes that can seriously affect its trustworthiness as an A/B metric. As an obvious example, if a predictor declares user success whenever the weather forecast element is displayed on the search results page (e.g., for the query "weather" that could make sense), then this predictor would be in favor of showing the weather forecast on every single results page, no matter what query, and it would not guard against showing a broken forecast or a forecast for the wrong location to the user, all of which is certainly undesired.

Hence, rather than treating the initial question as a prediction problem, it should be treated as an A/B measurement problem: given an experiment corpus, i.e., a set of controlled A/B experiments with ground truth labels specifying whether an entire experiment is considered an improvement or a regression, design an A/B metric that directionally aligns best with the ground truth labels. Ground truth labels for entire experiments can be attained from a panel of experts that don't only take a large collection of metrics into account, but also deep-dive to get a detailed technical understanding of the treatment change and how it could affect the user experience. It is critical to cover a diverse set of experiments in the experiment corpus, and ideally include representative experiments for all types of changes to the search engine that need to be evaluated by the metric, since otherwise the metric might have "blind spots" regarding certain treatments. Based on such an experiment corpus, the best metric should both have the best directional alignment with the labels as well as be most sensitive to the treatment effects (statistical sensitivity in terms of, e.g., t-value of a t-test).

3. DESIGNING A METRIC SYSTEM

No metric is perfect – all of them have weaknesses or loopholes and incorrectly move for certain treatments they are not designed for. Hence, it is important to design a good metric system for making ship decisions, i.e., a collection of metrics that measure treatment effects from various different angles, so that based on their entirety it is possible to get a comprehensive understanding of the implications of the experiment. The challenge with having a large number of metrics, though, is that 1) some metrics will move statistically significantly by chance (for independent metrics typically 1 in 20 with a pval threshold of 0.05), and 2) for strong treatment effects many metrics will move, some of them in seemingly contradictory ways. As a consequence, experimenters might be allured to cherry-pick the metrics that are most in-line with their intuition, which can easily lead to seemingly data-driven yet unsound ship decisions.

To address these challenges, we generally design metric systems in a hierarchical way. At the top are the most robust metrics, in our case a metric like "sessions per user". They are defined at the user-level, have the fewest built-in assumptions on user behavior interpretation, yet are usually are the least sensitive. On the next level come session-level metrics such as Session Success Rate. They have built-in assumptions on what success looks like, therefore are less robust, yet more sensitive. On the third level, there are many feature-specific metrics, often on the impression level, such as Web Result Success Click Rate, etc. These have even more assumptions on how user success will show up for certain experiments, are least robust, yet most sensitive.

As part of this hierarchy, such a system should have metrics that covers different areas of the page. This is what defines the scope of a metric. A metric that measures the change in user behavior on a specific feature is a feature-level metric, e.g. Web Result Success Click Rate. A metric that measures success across all the page is a page-level metric and has a higher scope than feature-level metrics, e.g. Page Click Through Rate. Similarly, we can define metrics that consider success across one session of the user, or even across all their traffic during the experiment. A metric system that targets all the different scopes guarantees that experiments are not missing global effects of their changes that cannot be captured by the feature-level metrics.

When interpreting a scorecard, we would look at metrics in a top-down fashion. Particularly when metrics on the first or second level are moving already, then metrics on the third level have to be interpreted very carefully due to, e.g., denomination effects as explained in the next section.

4. METRIC DEFINITIONS

There are few very important aspects to keep in mind when working on concrete metric definition formulas.

1) When counting events, time, or anything that doesn't have an upper bound, then using plain counts in the metric can introduce large amounts of noise making the metric less sensitive. For a metric like "time to click" where time from the page request to the first click is measured, variance is usually very high due to outliers. Effective ways to address this are to apply truncation (i.e., treating any value > x as x), or functional transformation (e.g., using the log function reducing effects from outliers).

2) The metric can be invalid if it changes due to denominator movements. Figure 1 shows an example where the objective is to measure user engagement in the form of clicks. Depending on which denominator is used, the metrics can move in contradictory directions or not at all, and this can be very confusing for experimenters making ship decisions. Generally, the more fine-grained the denominator, the higher the sensitivity of the metric, yet the higher the chance that the denominator moves on its own. Our guidance is to use the metric with the most fine-grained denominator which doesn't yet move on its own. In the figure below that would be Clicks/Session.

Sensitivity increase ↑

Metric	delta	pValue	valid
#Clicks/#Pages	-3.73%	0.000001	✖
#Clicks/#Sessions	5.84%	0.0006	✔
#Clicks	-	0.2	✔

Denominators	delta	pValue
#Pages	2.20%	0.009
#Sessions	-	0.6

Figure 1: Denominator changes can lead to invalid and contradictory metric movements.

5. DEBUGGABLITY

Once an A/B metric system is developed, experimenters will rely on the movements in the metric to decide whether to ship the change they are testing. However, even if these changes are localized to a specific feature, they can affect users' behavior outside these features and influence their interaction with the rest of the page.

Due to these effects, it is important for an online metric system to be easily debuggable and its movements clearly understood. A metric need to be easily decomposable to the different signals and user behavior that contributes to its movements. Simple linear functions that combine basic features representing users' interactions guarantee that experimenters are able to pinpoint to the main drivers behind a metric movement. Compare that with machine-learned metrics that can easily become a black box, where the inner workings of the metric are opaque. This would make debugging the metric movements and identifying the failings of the change being tested hard for the experimenters.

6. ACKNOWLEDGMENTS

The authors would like to thank Aidan Crook, Anand Oka, Siamak Faridani and Victor Hu for interesting discussions on the topic of this paper.

7. REFERENCES

[1] H. Feild et al. 2010. Predicting searcher frustration. In *SIGIR'10*: 34–41.

[2] Hassan. 2012. A semi-supervised approach to modeling web search satisfaction. In *SIGIR'12*: 275–284.

[3] Ron Kohavi, Alex Deng, Brian Frasca, Roger Longbotham, Toby Walker, and Ya Xu. Trustworthy online controlled experiments: Five puzzling outcomes explained. Proceedings of the 18th Conference on Knowledge Discovery and Data Mining, 2012.

Visual Recommendation Use Case for an Online Marketplace Platform - allegro.pl

Anna Wróblewska
Allegro Group
Warszawa, Poland
anna.wroblewska@allegrogroup.com

Łukasz Rączkowski
Allegro Group
University of Warsaw
Toruń, Poland
lukasz.raczkowski@allegrogroup.com

ABSTRACT
In this paper we describe a small content-based visual recommendation project built as part of the Allegro online marketplace platform. We extracted relevant data only from images, as they are inherently better at capturing visual attributes than textual offer descriptions. We used several image descriptors to extract color and texture information in order to find visually similar items. We tested our results against available textual offer tags and also asked human users to subjectively assess the precision. Finally, we deployed the solution to our platform.

Keywords
visual search; image search; content-based recommendations; e-commerce; online auctions; image processing; LIRE; OpenCV; Elasticsearch; CBIR

1. INTRODUCTION
Content based image retrieval (CBIR) has slowly but steadily been growing in importance as a means to improve search experience in e-commerce. Several prominent companies have already deployed their own image retrieval solutions. Pinterest developed an image search platform and thus they showed that content recommendation powered by visual search improves user engagement [10]. At eBay it's been proven that image-based information can be used to quantify image similarity, which can be used to discern products with different visual appearances [2]. Finally, Yahoo built a visual similarity-based interactive search system, which led to more refined product recommendations [8].

At Allegro [1] our main goal is the satisfaction of our users, so in order to further push for that objective, we've decided to try our hand at visual recommendations. The aim of the project was to develop a system that returns product offers that are visually similar to the given input image. That similarity is determined based on several features extracted from offer images. Low-level image information like that is particularly useful in product categories for which visual aspects are important and also for categories that contain products which are hard to describe with words, e.g. fashion or jewellery items.

SIGIR'16, July 17–21, 2016, Pisa, Italy.
© 2016 ACM. ISBN 978-1-4503-4069-4/16/07…$15.00.
DOI: http://dx.doi.org/10.1145/2911451.2926722

We started our project in a very small agile team consisting of a data scientist, a software engineer, a UX designer and a product owner. From the very start our main objective was to create a data-driven product and deploy it within the Allegro platform. We were given a strict deadline to deliver business value, so we've decided to utilize readily available open-source projects.

In the following sections, we describe these topics in detail: presentation of available offer data stored in the Allegro platform (section 2), software architecture of our solution, used tools, image features and similarity metrics (section 3), variety of techniques to test the solution based on available data (section 4). In the last section we conclude the paper and discuss future work.

2. CHARACTERISTICS OF OFFER DESCRIPTIONS
Offers listed in our marketplace platform can be described by a limited set of well-defined attributes, short title and a long description that contains unstructured data with a lot of additional information, e.g. seller addresses or tailored recommendations. Each offer is categorized and each should include at least one photo that shows the offered product.

Usually text parameters of offers in our service are high-level abstractions and as such are not very precise, e.g. a dotted pattern may describe a large spectrum of dot sizes and configurations. Furthermore, our traditional textual color tags have only around 10 very general values, e.g. shades of yellow or shades of brown. In spite of the fact that color and pattern attributes are obligatory, our sellers often specify them ambiguously as "other color", "other pattern" or "multicolor". Thus recommendations based only on text attributes are sometimes quite vague and not precise. A cursory data analysis in a single fashion category (Figure 1) shows that a large fraction of fashion items listed online lacks precise color information.

Having such a huge disparity in attribute quality drove us to hypothesize that by extracting image features we can get a better understanding of offers in our service.

The quality of images attached to product offers varies greatly. In some categories they're quite bad, and in others they're very professional. To overcome this quality hurdle in the beginning of our work, we've decided to test our algorithms only on images from a special part of Allegro called Brand Zone. These images usually have a bright background and the main object/product is in the middle. Thanks to this we were able to easily crop the essential part of every image.

We came to this conclusion last year, when we tested the offer image quality in a single fashion product category using our dedicated tool – Nigel - that marks image quality on the scale from 0 (bad quality) to 1 (the best quality). In Figure 2 we show a density distribution plot that showcases how Nigel scores images in the Brand Zone versus Allegro as a whole.

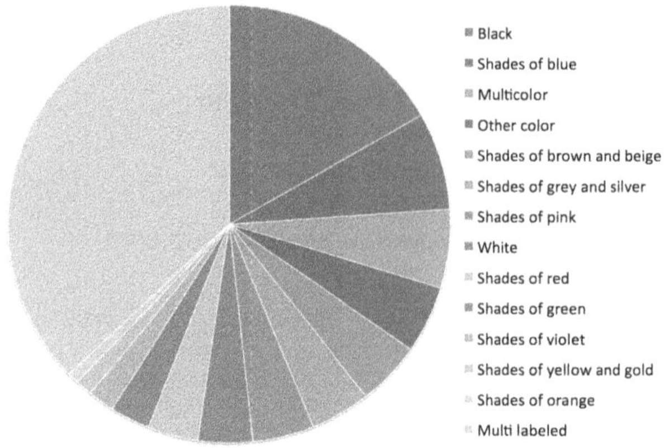

Figure 1. Color attributes distribution in the dresses category. Almost 50% of offers have multi-labeled assignments or values like multicolor / other color.

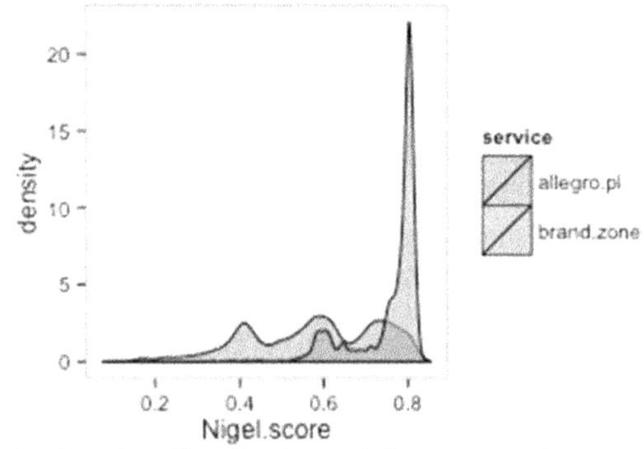

Figure 2. Density distribution of image quality assessment with the Nigel tool.

3. TOOLS AND METHODS

3.1 Solution Architecture

We developed our product in two stages. First, we created the necessary backend for the image retrieval system and also a test web application, which we affectionately named Imagator (Figure 3). In the development of the backend we utilized the following open-source projects: Elasticsearch (ES) [6], LIRE (Lucene Image Retrieval) [11], OpenCV [4] and elasticsearch-image [5]. Elasiticsearch serves as a database for image feature vectors and also as a search engine. The image features can be incorporated into ES index thanks to the elasticsearch-image plugin and LIRE. The latter piece of software includes a set of numeric descriptors based on MPEG-7 edge detection and color histogram algorithms. We extended LIRE with new image features and mixed them with an image-cropping utility, which was possible thanks to OpenCV. We used OpenCV because of its efficient algorithms and also with the hope that in the future we'd be able utilize GPGPU functionality within it. Imagator's user interface was created as a single-page web application in AngularJS. It was used to test a variety of image features, regions of interest and similarity metrics.

The second part of the project was to prepare a production-ready system. This required the development of two additional components: an indexer service and a public API (Figure 4).

Figure 3. Our test application - Imagator

The indexer service is a subscriber in our internal events queue. It receives all events pertaining to new, deleted and changed offers. We filter out unnecessary categories and offers outside of the Brand Zone and then index the images into our ES index.

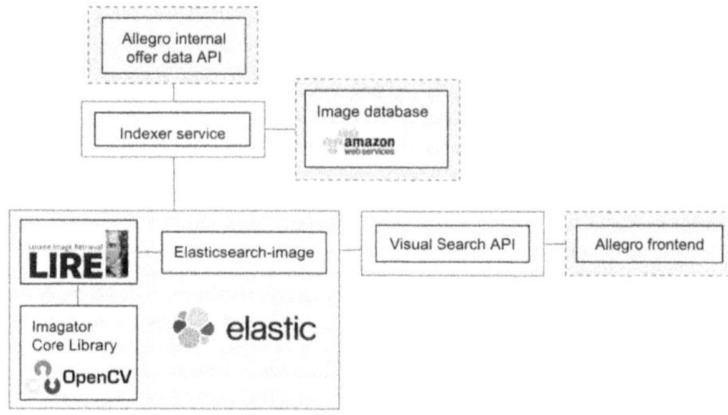

Figure 4. Architecture of our production-ready system.

A public visual recommendation API was needed to interface between the image retrieval backend and recommendation boxes in the Allegro frontend. The results from our visual search API are shown in a separate layer after clicking on a *Show similar* button in a recommendation box (Figure 5).

Figure 5. Screenshot showing the system in action within Allegro's production environment.

3.2 Image features and similarity metrics

The LIRE library contains an extensive suite of image features, focusing both on color and pattern extraction. In this work we spotlight the following ones:

- auto color correlogram (ACC) [9]
- edge histogram (EH) [14]
- binary patterns pyramid (BPP) [3][11]
- joint histogram (JH) [11]

Additionally, we implemented a new feature, palette power (PP), as described in [2].

Extracting data from an image is only a first part of the equation. In order to compare images and assess their similarity, we need to compare the results that we get from the above image features. We tried several distance comparison metrics and in the end settled for three that gave the best results: Tanimoto Distance [12], Earth Mover's Distance [13] and Hellinger Distance [7].

4. TESTS

To measure the precision of our image-based search, we conducted both automatic and user-focused tests. The effects of the deployment to production can be quantified thanks to the CTR (click through rate) metric.

4.1 Automatic tests based on textual tags

To assess the difference between descriptors (and also between similarity metrics), we performed automatic tests using textual color tags as a benchmark on a set of about 1300 images from a category containing dresses. We measured the mean average precision (MAP) for positions 1 through 5 in our search listing. Top N selected images similar to the query image are marked as a good choice when they have the same text benchmark parameter. We conducted tests for different sets of text benchmark parameters. We chose among color, pattern or style parameters. However, it's worth mentioning that the results are not very precise and may be too high because of the low quality of textual offer parameters and their low relevance to real visual product descriptions, which was mentioned in section 2.

This automatic test results ranged from 100% for MAP@1 to 60-70% for MAP@5 (Figures 6-8).

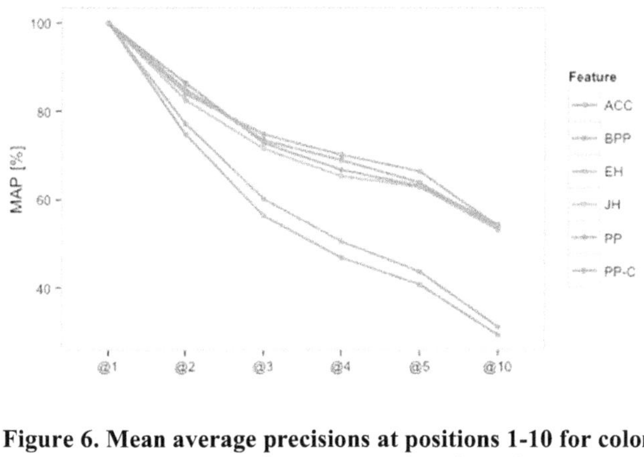

Figure 6. Mean average precisions at positions 1-10 for color parameter values as a text benchmark.

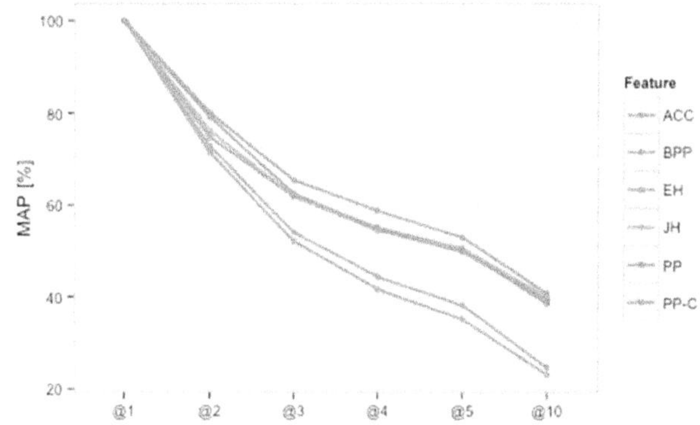

Figure 7. Mean average precisions at positions 1-10 for color and pattern parameter values as a text benchmark.

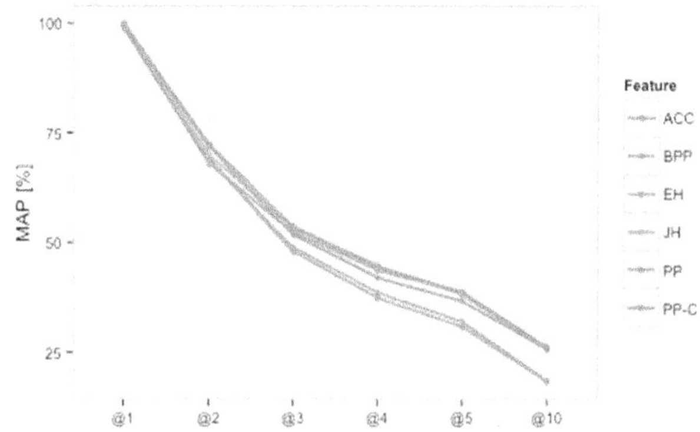

Figure 8. Mean average precisions at positions 1-10 for color, pattern and style parameter values as a text benchmark.

4.2 Subjective user assessments

Imagator shows a view with a large main image and 5 smaller images (Figure 3), deemed as similar by our system (5 images having the highest ranking in ES). We showed this app to about 10 people. We gave the users a simple task to assess the visual similarity of smaller images to the main image using a 5 point scale, where 1 means no correspondence between the main image and the small one and 5 – very similar products in both pictures.

These subjective tests were performed many times - we wanted to gather as much data as possible in order to make decisions on design strategies, i.e. which image features are the most suitable for a particular domain and which segmentation technique is the best. We chose 66 images as main test images. Each of them was used as input in the ES query to find similar images amongst all 1166 indexed images. The main test images were chosen so that their color and pattern parameters must have had similar distribution as the distribution of parameters in all active offers in the dresses category (within the Brand Zone).

Results for different image descriptors settled in the range 2.8 - 3.2 (Table 1, Figure 9).

Many of the users remarked that although the association was not perfect, most of the time there were some similar aspects, e.g. similar tone of color or a comparable pattern. They also said that such recommendations could be very attractive for users who would browse through offers in our service with an intention to buy a roughly similar product.

Table 1. User subjective assessments (UA) for different feature descriptors (-C suffix denotes a central ROI).

Test features	Average UA	UA StdDev	UA Number
1st test phase			
ACC-C users assessed only color similarity	2.82	1.09	990
ACC	3.26	1.27	750
EH-C users assessed only pattern similarity	2.90	1.23	990
ACC-C + EH-C users assessed both characteristics (color and pattern similarity)	2.8	1.04	990
2nd test phase			
JH	3.32	1.05	330
PP	3.08	1.44	465
JH+PP	3.05	1.26	575
BPP+JH	2.41	1.41	655

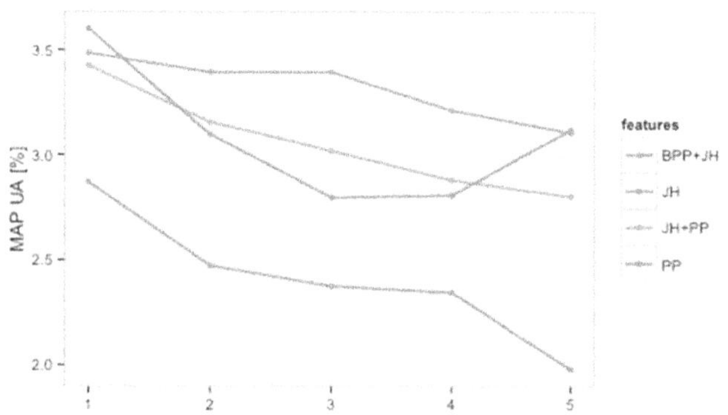

Figure 9. Mean average precision of user assessments (MAP UA) at 1-5 position for 4 feature combinations in subjective tests.

4.3 Production results and discussion

Finally, after analyzing our test results after the 1st phase of tests, we've chosen the best image descriptor (ACC) and similarity metric for Brand Zone images and decided to deploy our solution to operate in a production environment. We integrated it with a recommendation box on the offer description page. Initial A/B tests performed on small user traffic show click through rate results comparable to other techniques based only on textual tags (taking into account the same category).

The subjective results from the 2nd test phase and numbers taken from the production environment show that our product has a great potential to improve, especially when we consider combining the image–based features with textual offer tags.

5. CONCLUSION

Thanks to existing open-source tools it is easy to create an image recommendations system from scratch. The insight of our team members allowed us to fully utilize this opportunity, which resulted in giving Allegro users a new way to browse the service. However, there are still a few challenges ahead of us. We need a way to automatically measure the image quality, which will in turn allow us to appropriately adjust the image matching methods. We are also considering mixing textual descriptions with numeric features extracted from images. Finally, we would like to develop more sophisticated deep learning methods to find visual similarity between our offers.

6. ACKNOWLEDGEMENTS

We would like to sincerely thank Monika Cierzniak (our product owner) and Maria Borowy (our UX designer) for helping us with the deployment to production and with the UX design of Imagator respectively, as well as for all the great ideas and insights.

7. REFERENCES

[1] Allegro online marketplace platform: *http://allegro.pl*.

[2] Bhardwaj, A., Das Sarma, A., Di, W., Hamid, R., Piramuthu, R. and Sundaresan, N. 2013. Palette power: enabling visual search through colors. *Proceedings of the 19th ACM SIGKDD International Conference on Knowledge Discovery and Data Mining* (2013), 1321–1329.

[3] Bosch, A., Zisserman, A. and Munoz, X. 2007. Representing shape with a spatial pyramid kernel. *Proceedings of the 6th ACM international conference on Image and video retrieval* (2007), 401–408.

[4] Bradski, G. 2000. The OpenCV Library. *Dr. Dobb's Journal of Software Tools*. 25, 11 (Nov. 2000), 120–126.

[5] Elasticsearch content-based image retrieval plugin: *https://github.com/kzwang/elasticsearch-image*.

[6] Elasticsearch search engine: *https://www.elastic.co*.

[7] Hazewinkel, M. 2002. *Encyclopaedia of mathematics*. Springer-Verlag.

[8] Hsiao, J.-H. and Li, L.-J. 2014. On visual similarity based interactive product recommendation for online shopping. *2014 IEEE International Conference on Image Processing (ICIP)* (Oct. 2014), 3038–3041.

[9] Jing Huang, Kumar, S.R., Mitra, M., Wei-Jing Zhu and Zabih, R. 1997. Image indexing using color correlograms. *Proceedings of IEEE Computer Society Conference on Computer Vision and Pattern Recognition* (1997), 762–768.

[10] Jing, Y., Liu, D., Kislyuk, D., Zhai, A., Xu, J., Donahue, J. and Tavel, S. 2015. Visual Search at Pinterest. *Proceedings of the 21th ACM SIGKDD International Conference on Knowledge Discovery and Data Mining* (2015), 1889–1898.

[11] Lux, M. 2011. Content based image retrieval with LIRE. *Proceedings of the 19th ACM International Conference on Multimedia* (2011), 735–738.

[12] Rogers, D.J. and Tanimoto, T.T. 1960. A Computer Program for Classifying Plants. *Science*. 132, 3434 (Oct. 1960), 1115–1118.

[13] Rubner, Y., Tomasi, C. and Guibas, L.J. 1998. A metric for distributions with applications to image databases. *Proceedings of the Sixth International Conference on Computer Vision* (1998), 59–66.

[14] Won, C.S.W., Park, D.K.P. and Park, S.-J.P. 2002. Efficient Use of MPEG-7 Edge Histogram Descriptor. *ETRI Journal*. 24, 1 (Feb. 2002), 23–30.

AOL's Named Entity Resolver: Solving Disambiguation via Document Strongly Connected Components and Ad-Hoc Edges Construction

Roni Wiener
AOL Relegence
Tel-Aviv, Israel
roni.wienner@teamaol.com

Yonatan Ben-Simhon
AOL Relegence
Tel-Aviv, Israel
yoni.ben-simhon@teamaol.com

Anna Chen
AOL Relegence
Tel-Aviv, Israel
anna.chen@teamaol.com

ABSTRACT
Named Entity Disambiguation is the task of disambiguating named entity mentions in unstructured text and linking them to their corresponding entries in a large knowledge base such as Freebase. Practically, each text match in a given document should be mapped to the correct entity out of the corresponding entities in the knowledge base or none of them if no correct entity is found (Empty Entry). The case of an empty entry makes the problem at hand more complex, but by solving it, one can successfully cope with missing and erroneous data as well as unknown entities. In this work we present AOL's Named Entity Resolver which was designed to handle real life scenarios including empty entries. As part of the automated news analysis platform, it processes over 500K news articles a day, entities from each article are extracted and disambiguated. According to our experiments, AOL's resolver shows much better results in disambiguating entities mapped to Wikipedia or Freebase compared to industry leading products.

Keywords
Named entity resolution; Named entity disambiguation.

1. INTRODUCTION
The ability to identify named entities [1] and link them to entries in knowledge bases (KB) [4] is a popular task in Information Retrieval and NLP communities. In this article we will address the final stage in the process of selecting the best fitting entities to the text from a set of given text matches plus the empty match. In the presence of an entity name in an article, the common practice of entity resolvers is to match the mention to the most probable entity in the KB, even when the entity in the article is clearly not one of the existing options [2]. Formally, the option of an empty entry for each text match extends the traditional entity disambiguation definition. The extended disambiguation needs to match the most probable entity in the KB or none of them if it's more probable. Humans are usually much better than machines at tasks of news articles entity disambiguation, probably because humans can exploit a priori domain and world knowledge which helps identifying the correct context at hand. In many cases, the article's author leaves contextual and disambiguation hints aimed to help human readers to quickly identify and understand the article's domain and context (e.g.: The famous *anthropologist* Michael Jackson.). We believe this ability is very helpful for the human disambiguation process. AOL's Named Entity Resolver tries to mimic the human entity disambiguation process, while leveraging the author's hints and language logic (true ambiguities are dealt by the author, e.g. "New York City" and "New York State" will be mentioned at least once in full form in order to help readers disambiguate). We rely on a World Knowledge Graph derived from data sources such as Wikipedia to represent readers' a priori domains knowledge, and a Document Graph to represent the article at hand along with the author's hint.

SIGIR '16, July 17-21, 2016, Pisa, Italy.
ACM 978-1-4503-4069-4/16/07.
DOI: http://dx.doi.org/10.1145/2911451.2926721

2. NAMED ENTITIES RESOLUTION
In this section we present our entity resolution approach. We first describe the algorithm's input. Then we lay out the data preparation and data structures built in order to support the disambiguation process. Finally the iterative disambiguation process is described.

2.1 Available Data for Entity Resolution
The data for the resolution process contains the document text, all possible entity matches from our KB where each entity has a known type (Person, Location etc.) and its known relations to other entities in the KB. In addition, the inferred article categories are given to the resolver as well (Sports, Politics, etc.). A priori global data such as term frequencies, lists of given names and surnames are available as well.

2.2 Building the Document Graph
As a first stage we build a document graph that represents all the possible resolution permutations. This document graph is the corresponding subgraph derived from the knowledge graph incorporating all the possible entities for the given document augmented with additional nodes and edges representing inferred data as described below.

2.2.1 Graph Nodes
At first, all possible entities from the document are added as entity nodes. Categories inferred from the document are added as category nodes. Predefined textual tokens (e.g. "TV", "actor") appearing in the document are added as text nodes if exist. Heuristics nodes such as high frequency tokens, common names and stop words are added as well. Finally we add nodes for entities that have no match in the document itself, but are highly connected to several entities in the document as context nodes (e.g. "The Beatles" when John Lennon, Paul McCartney & Ringo Starr are present).

2.2.2 Graph Edges

Positively weighted edges are drawn between entity nodes according to their relations in the KB. Additional edges are drawn between entity nodes and other node types (categories, heuristic, text) according to predefined weights or correlation with entity types (e.g. the word "author" will have positive weight to the Harry Potter book entity and negative weight to the Harry Potter movie entity). Ad-hoc positive edges are drawn between entities in the article that share several context nodes when the nodes are not connected in the KB. These ad-hoc edges can be thought of as indicating the paired entities as more probable in term of document context.

2.3 Entity Resolution

Once the document graph is constructed, the entity resolution process commences. As a first stage, graph nodes are weighted according to the sum of their edges weights.

2.3.1 Non-Positive Nodes

Negatively weighted nodes are filtered out at this stage as there are more negative indicators regarding their correctness than positive ones. Nodes with zero weight, usually those nodes without edges in the graph, are put aside at this stage as their polarity is unclear. These will be analyzed at the end of the disambiguation process when the document context is clearer.

2.3.2 Graph Strongly Connected Components

Solely remaining with positively weighted entity nodes to resolve, two groups of nodes are formed. The first "solved" group consists of all text and category nodes as well as entity nodes without ambiguity (positively weighted entity with no other entity text matches). This group's nodes are considered positively resolved. The second "unsolved" group consists of all entity nodes with some ambiguity. Strongly Connected Components (SCCs) [3] are now constructed to identify context regions in each one of the groups. As SCC has paths from each node to another, it represents a common domain.

2.3.3 Resolving Inner SCCs Ambiguities

In cases where there is a KB edge between entities with the same text match, ambiguities exist among the SCC's nodes. In order for the process to properly converge, inner SCCs ambiguities must be resolved first. On each SCC with inner ambiguity the entities with the max scores *S(n)* as depicted in equation 1 are kept, and their ambiguous nodes (nodes competing on the same text matches) are filtered out. Entities scores are based on their edges to each of the solved group SCCs and their weights e_w.

$$S(n) = \left(\sum_{e}^{edges} e_w \cdot |scc| \right) + \left(1 + \frac{|uccs|}{|sscc|}\right) \quad (1)$$

Here $|scc|$ represents the connected SCC size, $|uccs|$ is the number of unique solved SCCs connected to the node and $|sscc|$ is the number of all solved SCCs. Correlations of types and categories are used as a tie breaker. After this stage, all ambiguities exist between separate SCCs in the "unsolved" group.

2.3.4 Resolving Outer SCCs Ambiguities

Our goal is to iteratively move entities from the unsolved group to the solved one. Instead of trying to solve ambiguities on the entity level, at this stage we solve them on the SCC level (previous stage assures that this is possible as each SCC is devoid of internal ambiguities). On each iteration, nodes from the SCC with the max score *S(scc)* are joined to the solved group and their ambiguous nodes are filtered out.

$$S(scc) = \sum_{n}^{scc} S(n) \quad (2)$$

Since entity nodes where filtered out, weights of the remaining ones may become negative, and may be filtered out too. Note that after each iteration the node-groups change and SCCs are recomputed.

2.3.5 Resolve Zero Weight Nodes

At this stage all the nodes in the solved group are considered as correct. But a resolution for zero weighted nodes should still take place. Having confidence in the resolved SCCs and their corresponding context regions, nodes correlating to these regions are considered correct, where the rest are filtered out. The correlation to the context regions is based on the entities types and categories. Any node with no signal what so ever is filtered out.

2.4 Empty Entries

During the entity resolution process nodes are filtered out. Usually empty entries are filtered out at the first and last stages as negative or zero weight nodes, due to lack of corroborative information regarding their inclusion in the document context.

3. CONCLUSION

In this work we demonstrated the document graph and how to merge a priori knowledge with dynamic data and signals residing on a given document. The construction of ad-hoc disambiguating edges between nodes in the document graph, yields denser document context regions. These regions improve the disambiguation accuracy and the ability to handle empty entry cases, even on sparse document graphs. The process was empirically tested on real life scenarios on large scale dynamic news articles sets (not shown). The process shows significant improvements both on our own entity extractor and on similar state of the art commercial and open source products.

4. REFERENCES

[1] Cucerzan, S., 2007, June. *Large-Scale Named Entity Disambiguation Based on Wikipedia Data.* In EMNLP-CoNLL (Vol. 7, pp. 708-716).

[2] Dredze, M., McNamee, P., Rao, D., Gerber, A. and Finin, T., 2010, August. *Entity disambiguation for knowledge base population.* In Proceedings of the 23rd International Conference on Computational Linguistics (pp. 277-285). Association for Computational Linguistics.

[3] Tarjan, R., 1972. *Depth-first search and linear graph algorithms.* SIAM journal on computing, 1(2), pp.146-160.

[4] Zheng, Z., Si, X., Li, F., Chang, E.Y. and Zhu, X., 2012, December. *Entity disambiguation with freebase.* In Proceedings of the The 2012 IEEE/WIC/ACM International Joint Conferences on Web Intelligence and Intelligent Agent Technology-Volume 01 (pp. 82-89). IEEE Computer Society.

The Data Stack in Information Retrieval

Omar Alonso
Microsoft
omalonso@microsoft.com

ABSTRACT
I propose to look at information retrieval applications from the perspective of the data stack infrastructure that is needed in research prototypes and production systems.

Keywords
Data science, big data, small data, infrastructure, applications.

1. INTRODUCTION
Every day millions of users rely on web search engines and social networks to search for information and learn about current events. While the user interface of those services is intuitive and easy to use, the amount of data being collected, mined, analyzed, and indexed for presenting relevant information is quite large. At the same time, large data sets are used internally by service providers for measuring user satisfaction and testing improvements with large scale experimentation. In this talk, I will present the notion of the *data stack*, an alternative way of looking at information retrieval applications.

The database community is focused on data and systems for storing, organizing, and querying all sorts of data [1]. The information retrieval community promotes research and development in the areas of search and information access and has, traditionally, been focused on metrics and modeling and not so much on data analysis and exploration as a core principle [2]. Given the massive adoption of different types of search services, information retrieval is becoming a more data-driven and data-intensive area. Besides the large scale of the Web and social networks that require systems to crawl and ingest such data, users also leave enormous amounts of new data in the form of search query logs, clicks, and generated content that are used to improve relevance and for predictive modeling.

Almost a decade ago, Jim Gray proposed to start thinking in terms data-intensive research and discovery, known as the *Fourth Paradigm*, a new way of doing science that uses data as one of the main pillars [3]. The goal is for scientists to turn to discovery through data analysis making use of massive data sets. With the *data science* role now taking a central part in the software industry and the on-going cross-pollination with other disciplines, data is currently perceived as the new oil.

SIGIR '16, July 17-21, 2016, Pisa, Italy
ACM 978-1-4503-4069-4/16/07.
http://dx.doi.org/10.1145/2911451.2926726

The focus on data analysis and exploration is causing developers to include a number of tools and languages (e.g., MapReduce, R, Spark, etc.) for managing the increasing variety and volume of data. In software development, there is the notion of a full-stack developer, that is, a person who can work on back-end and front-end with everything in the middle. LAMP (Linux, Apache, MySQL, and PHP) has been one of the most popular development stacks for many years. Search practitioners are now expected to master a wide range of data problems at different levels where the assumption of an individual database that contains everything and a single language for data processing is unlikely. Is there a *data stack* equivalent? If so, how does it look like and what are the main characteristics? As a driving example and in the context of IR, I propose to look at the following data stack:

1. Ingestion and processing of raw data. Examples: crawling, data cleaning, near-duplicate detection, etc.
2. Annotation for augmenting the ingested data. Examples: named-entity detection, information extraction, metadata generation, content classification, etc.
3. Indexing and ranking of high quality content. Examples: efficient data structures, feature engineering, etc.
4. Behavioral data for capturing user activity. Examples: search query logs, clicks, link sharing, etc.
5. Experimentation and analysis infrastructure for evaluation and exploration. Examples: Sampling, interleaving, A-B testing, crowdsourcing, etc.

The data stack presents new challenges and opportunities to perform research and development at different levels with the goal of improving current systems and user satisfaction.

2. REFERENCES
[1] Daniel Abadi *et al.* "The Beckman Report on Database Research", *Comm. of the ACM*, 59(2), pp. 92-99, 2016.

[2] James Allan, W. Bruce Croft, Alistair Moffat, and Mark Sanderson. "Frontiers, challenges, and opportunities for information retrieval: Report from SWIRL 2012 the second strategic workshop on information retrieval in Lorne". *SIGIR Forum*, 46(1):2-32, 2012.

[3] Tony Hey, Stewart Tansley, and Kristin Tolle (Eds.). *The Fourth Paradigm*, Microsoft Research, 2009.

Predicting User Engagement with Direct Displays Using Mouse Cursor Information

Ioannis Arapakis*
Eurecat
Barcelona, Spain
arapakis.ioannis@gmail.com

Luis A. Leiva†
Sciling
Valencia, Spain
llt@acm.org

ABSTRACT

Predicting user engagement with direct displays (DD) is of paramount importance to commercial search engines, as well as to search performance evaluation. However, understanding within-content engagement on a web page is not a trivial task mainly because of two reasons: (1) engagement is subjective and different users may exhibit different behavioural patterns; (2) existing proxies of user engagement (e.g., clicks, dwell time) suffer from certain caveats, such as the well-known position bias, and are not as effective in discriminating between useful and non-useful components. In this paper, we conduct a crowdsourcing study and examine how users engage with a prominent web search engine component such as the knowledge module (KM) display. To this end, we collect and analyse more than 115k mouse cursor positions from 300 users, who perform a series of search tasks. Furthermore, we engineer a large number of meta-features which we use to predict different proxies of user engagement, including attention and usefulness. In our experiments, we demonstrate that our approach is able to predict more accurately different levels of user engagement and outperform existing baselines.

CCS Concepts

•Information systems → Task models; •Human-centered computing → User studies;

Keywords

web search; knowledge module; direct displays; mouse cursor tracking; user engagement

*Work conducted while affiliated with Yahoo Labs.

†Work partially conducted while affiliated with the PRHLT Research Center at the Universitat Politècnica de València.

SIGIR '16, July 17 - 21, 2016, Pisa, Italy

ISBN 978-1-4503-4069-4/16/07...$15.00

DOI: http://dx.doi.org/10.1145/2911451.2911505

Figure 1: The KM display (in red border) and video snippets (in orange border) on the Yahoo SERP for the query "interstellar".

1. INTRODUCTION

In recent years, direct displays (DDs) have become a standard component on the search engine result pages (SERPs) of all major web search engines, where they display vertical search results, i.e., focused, specific content. One such prominent example is the knowledge module (KM) display (Fig. 1), which provides users with information about the named entities they are searching for as part of their search tasks. The content presented in the KM display is typically obtained in a semi-structured format from curated entity databases, such as Freebase or Wikipedia, and often includes both quantitative and qualitative information (e.g., domain-specific knowledge) about the queried entity. This raw information can be further enriched by the search engine, e.g., by showing a ranking of related entities, accompanied with explanations of their relationship. Often, the KM display is complemented with additional content, such as multimedia or social media content associated with the entity, typically obtained from third-party data sources.

In practice, DDs serve two main purposes. First, they provide the users with a well-structured summary of information which, otherwise, would be difficult or time-consuming to access. That is, the information is made available within the SERP itself and thus the user is not required to actively look for it and navigate away from the SERP. Second, DDs help tidy up the SERP section that contains the universal search results (i.e., the mix of main web search results, vertical search results and various DDs). For example, image and video results can now be displayed under the KM display, making the interaction with textual results an easier task.

In this context, most research has focused on general backend system tasks, the most important being knowledge base construction [6, 11, 14, 24, 41], or more specific backend tasks, such as related entity recommendation [9, 10]. With the exception of a recent query log analysis on exploratory search [34], so far little has been done to understand the way web search users interact with the frontend system and the embedded DDs. Our work attempts to understand how users engage with a prominent DD like the KM display in entity-centric search tasks. In particular, we are interested in predicting user engagement with a DD in the absence of explicit feedback (e.g., self-report data). To this end, we consider three proxies of engagement with online content: (1) attention, (2) usefulness and (3) perceived task duration, which all together reflect relevant cognitive and emotional processing.

Existing modelling techniques make a simplifying assumption when analysing web search log data: the user is assumed to be equally engaged with all parts of the SERP. However, in practice this assumption is not always true. For example, a user may click on certain links on the page, but not all links. Similarly, she may read a certain result snippet in the SERP, but not necessarily the entire list of results. She may even ignore the SERP content completely and focus only on the images shown in the KM display or other DDs. In sum, user interests inferred from the parts of the SERP the user did not engage with may not reflect the true reason for user's interests in the SERP. We believe that the users' interests can be better captured by analysing their within-content activity and, for this reason, we need to go beyond the existing user modelling techniques that assume a uniform user engagement with the page content. To meet this objective, one potential approach is to analyse the mouse cursor data of the user to identify the DDs that captured user's attention and lead to a deeper engagement with the SERP content. The proposed method relies on the use of simple yet highly discriminative features that lack the computational complexity of other methods, such as those that necessitate the extraction of cursor motifs. More importantly, it offers better granularity of user interactions, on a DD-level basis, especially in the absence of explicit user feedback (e.g., clicks or dwell time).

2. RELATED WORK

There has been an enormous body of research investigating user interactions from mouse cursor data. Mouse cursor tracking is considered today as a low-cost yet scalable proxy for user's attention, and so we focus our review of related work in this research area. Concretely, we will focus on web search and interaction mining as foundational precursors of user engagement research.

Early works considered simple, coarse-grained features derived from mouse cursor data to be surrogate measurements of user interest, such as amount of cursor movements [17, 39] or cursor travel time [12]. More recently, fine-grained cursor features have been taking into consideration, which have been proved more useful. For example, Guo and Agichtein [18] found differences in cursor travel distances between informational and navigational queries, and could classify the query type using cursor movements more accurately than using clicks. Guo and Agichtein [19] also used interactions such as cursor movement, hovers and scrolling to accurately infer search intent and interest in search results. They focused on automatically identifying a searcher's research or purchase intent based on features of the interaction. Huang et al. [26] sought to understand result relevance and search abandonment by mining cursor behaviour on SERPs. This work was extended by Diriye et al. [13] to investigate the use of cursor interactions for classifying the reason why a user abandoned a query, whether it was because they were satisfied because they found the information they were seeking or dissatisfied at the point of abandonment. Finally, Huang et al. [25] and Speicher et al. [40] modelled user cursor interactions on SERPs by extending click models to compute more accurate relevance judgments for the search results.

Mouse cursor data have also been used for more practical tasks. For example, to investigate the usability of online forms [5], prototype website redesigns [4, 28] cluster documents according to users' interactions [30] and predict page-level measurements such as dwell time, number of clicks or scroll reach [31].

In sum, previous approaches that relied on mouse cursor feature engineering have been directed at predicting general-purpose web search tasks like document relevance [20], search success [21] or searcher's frustration [16]. However, little work has been done on predicting user engagement within page content. The following are the most prominent works in this regard. Arapakis et al. [1, 2] extracted mouse *gestures* to measure within-content engagement on news pages and predict reading experiences, and Arapakis et al. [3] conducted a preliminary study which revealed the potential benefits of the KM display and its overall utility w.r.t. user experience. Lagun et al. [27] introduced the concept of frequent cursor subsequences (namely *motifs*) in the estimation of result relevance, which is a more general approach but does not address the problem user engagement prediction. Finally, Liu et al. [32] have applied the motifs concept to SERPs in order to predict search result utility, searcher effort and satisfaction at a search task level. However, it has been always assumed a uniform engagement with all parts of the page. In contrast, our work is the first to investigate user engagement within particular components of SERPs, in this case the KM display.

3. CROWDSOURCING STUDY

To understand how web search users engage with DDs like the KM display, we conducted a crowdsourcing study and collected feedback from participants who performed short, entity-centric search tasks using the Yahoo web search engine. With this study, we aim to predict: (1) when a user notices the KM display on the SERP, (2) if it is perceived as a useful aid to their search tasks and (3) whether interacting with the KM display alters the users' perception of how fast they complete the search tasks.

Crowdsourcing offers several advantages not available in other experimental settings [33], such as access to a large and diverse pool of participants with stable availability, as well as collection and analysis of real usage data at a large scale. Another advantage of crowdsourcing is the low cost of the tasks, which makes it a preferable solution over the more expensive laboratory-based experiments. On the downside, a limited range of parameters can be explored in a controlled manner and experimenters have to account for potential threats to ecological validity, distractions in the physical environment of the user, and privacy issues, to name a few.

Table 1: Examples of search query patterns. Asterisks represent multi-answer questions to increase the difficulty of the search tasks.

Category	Question Pattern	Question Example	Suggested Query
People	Who is X <wife | husband | sons>	Who is X's husband|wife?	Who is Orlando Bloom's wife?
People	What is X doing now	What is X's current occupation?	What is Gisele Bundchen doing now?
People	Where was X born	Where was X born?	Where was Ernest Hemingway born?
*People	X movies	Name two movies that X plays in	Peter Seller's movies
Movies	How long is the movie X	How long is the movie X?	How long is the movie Tron?
Movies	When is X coming out	When is movie X coming out?	When is Mad Max Fury Road coming out?
Movies	What is X rated	What is movie X rated?	What is Anchorman rated?
Movies	What is X about	What is movie X about?	What is Taxi Driver about?
Athletes	X salary	What is X's salary?	Lebron James salary
Athletes	X draft	What is X's draft?	Andrian Peterson draft
Athletes	X weight	What is X's weight?	Jimmy Graham weight
Athletes	X team	In which team X plays?	Joe Thomas team
Sport Teams	X head coach	Who is the head coach of the team X?	Miami Heat head coach
*Sport Teams	X players	Name two players of the team X	Houston Rockets players
Sport Teams	X official website	What is the official website of the team X?	Sacramento Kings official website
Sport Teams	X record	What is the record of the team X?	Oakland Raiders record

```
cursor timestamp xpos ypos event xpath attrs extras
0 1405605225834 390 195 mousemove /html/body/p[2] {"P":{}} {"tr":451,"tl":277,"br":473,"bl":313,"mid":317}
...
```

Figure 2: Example of a mouse cursor log, including the distance of the cursor to 5 control points of the KM display: `tr` (top right corner), `tl` (top left corner), `br` (bottom right corner), `bl` (bottom left corner), `mid` (center).

In our study, we used the Amazon Mechanical Turk service. All of the aforementioned limitations were taken into consideration and preventive measures were put into practice to discount low-quality responses. Also, strict selection criteria were applied to exclude unsuitable participants (e.g., HIT approval rate $\geq$ 98%, number of HITs approved $\geq$ 1,000).

3.1 Experimental Design

The experiment had a repeated measures design with one independent variable: KM display (with two levels: "visible" or "hidden"). The KM display visibility was controlled with client-side scripting, removing the KM display from the SERP in the "hidden" condition. The dependent variables (Section 3.4) were: (i) KM display noticeability, (ii) KM display usefulness and (iii) perceived task accomplishment speed. The experiment consisted of two short search tasks that were completed using the Yahoo search engine, one task with the KM display on the SERP and one without it. To control for order effects, we counterbalanced task assignments using a Latin square design.

Participants accessed the search engine through a custom proxy which did not alter the original look and feel of the SERPs. This allowed us to instrument the browsed pages on the fly and capture user interactions with the SERP without interfering with the actual web search engine interface in production. The proxy had a common entry page for all participants. For each search task, participants were presented with a question and were suggested a search query to begin with. The suggested queries were all picked from a pool of queries that triggered the KM display on the SERP, independent of the KM display visibility (Section 3.2).

3.2 Search Query Sample

Our query set consisted of 32 unique query patterns that were selected after a large-scale query log analysis. All queries would trigger the KM display on the Yahoo SERP, so we could ensure that in all tasks the KM display would be displayed on the SERP, thus allowing us to choose between leaving it visible or hiding it, depending on the control (hidden) and experimental (visible) conditions.

The selected query patterns belonged to four different topics (celebrities, movies, athletes, sport teams) and required either single or multiple answers. An example of a single-answer query is "Who is the head coach of the team X?" while an example of a multi-answer query is "Who are X's children?". To diversify our search query pool, we produced three questions per query pattern, as can be seen in Table 1, while we introduced some additional multi-answer questions (marked with *) to increase the difficulty of the search tasks. In total, our query set included 144 different queries.[1] In the study, the query set was repeated as many times as needed to accommodate all participants. Each query was answered under each condition by at least two participants and at most six participants.

3.3 Mouse Cursor Tracking

As previously stated, all users performed the search tasks through a web proxy. This allowed us to automatically instrument all browsed pages with mouse cursor tracking. For this, we used EVTRACK,[2] an open source JavaScript event tracking library that is part of the smt2ϵ system [31]. EVTRACK makes it possible to specify what browser events should be captured and *how* they should be captured, i.e., via event listeners (the event is captured as soon as it is fired) or via event polling (the event is captured at fixed-time intervals). Concretely, we captured all regular browser events (e.g., `load`, `click`, `scroll`) via event listeners and only `mousemove` via event polling (at 150 ms), since this event may introduce unnecessary overhead both while recording on the client side and while transmitting the data to the server [29].

Whenever an event was recorded, we logged the following information (Fig. 2): cursor id (0 for desktop browsers, a number identifying the touch point for mobile browsers), mouse cursor position (x and y coordinates), timestamp,

[1] `http://personales.upv.es/luileito/kme/queries.tsv`
[2] `https://github.com/luileito/evtrack`

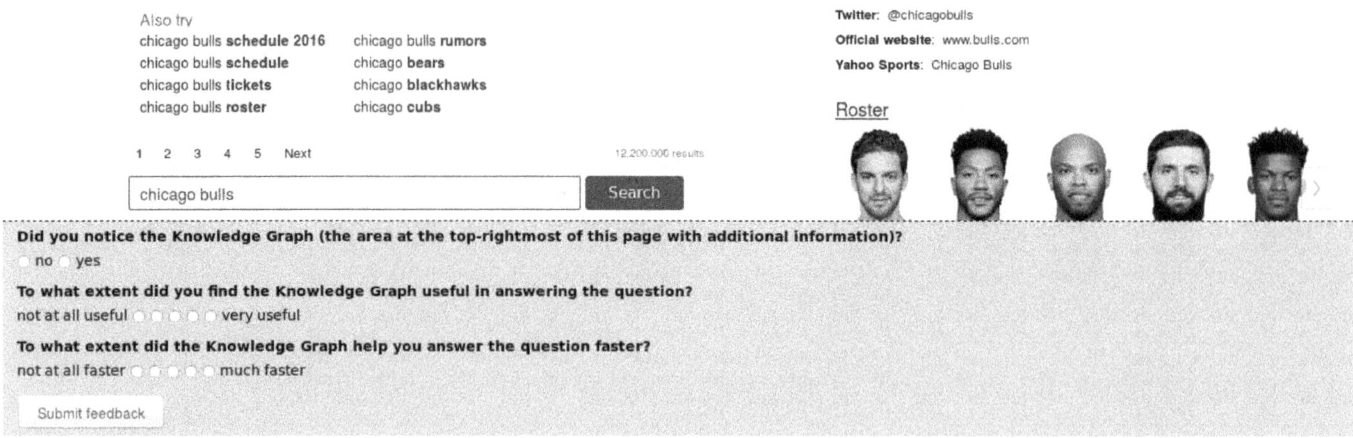

Figure 3: Example of the mini-questionnaire inserted at the bottom of the instrumented SERPs.

event name, xpath of the DOM element that relates to the event, DOM element attributes, and the Euclidean distance to 5 control points of the KM display (Fig. 2). The data were saved as CSV files, one browsed page at a time.

3.4 Self-Reported Measures of Engagement

In addition to recording mouse cursor data, the web proxy inserted a mini-questionnaire on the SERPs where the KM display was visible (experimental condition), in order to gather ground truth labels for the mouse cursor data; see Fig. 3. The mini-questionnaire was initially hidden, in order not to interfere with regular browsing, and was shown to the user just before leaving the SERP. The mini-questionnaire comprised 3 questions:

1. *Did you notice the knowledge module?* [yes/no]
2. *To what extent did you find the knowledge module useful in answering the question?* [1–5 Likert-type scale]
3. *To what extent did the knowledge module help you answer the question faster?* [1–5 Likert-type scale]

The labels of Likert-type scale was 1: not at all useful/faster, ..., 5: very useful/faster (Fig. 3).

Our ground truth thus consists of three user engagement proxies, all of them being considered intrinsic components of engagement, as traditionally measured using questionnaires [36].

3.5 Participants

We recruited 612 participants through Amazon Mechanical Turk. From this initial sample, we approved assignments for 533 participants (female = 226, male = 307), aged from 18 to 66. Participants were of mixed nationality (e.g., American, Belgian, British, Finnish, German) and had varying educational backgrounds: 29.98% had a high school diploma, 18.98% had a college diploma, 41.56% had a BSc degree, 7.97% had an MSc and 1.52% had a PhD. All participants were proficient in English, 98.31% being native speakers. Finally, the majority were full-time (60.41%) or part-time (9.76%) employees while the remaining were either full-time students (7.69%), pursuing further studies while working (10.69%), performing home duties (6.75%) or other (4.69%).

3.6 Procedure

To begin, participants were informed about the terms and conditions of the study, followed by a short description of the SERP. The study had to be done in a single session. Participants could opt out at any moment, in which case they would not be compensated. Participants were asked to "evaluate two different backend systems of Yahoo web search by performing two search tasks". For each task, participants had to answer a question by searching for relevant information on the proxified search engine. As previously mentioned, in one task the KM display would be hidden (control condition) and in the other task it would be visible (experimental condition). The order of the tasks was randomized for each participant. Participants were also presented with a suggested query to begin their search, although they were free to submit additional queries (e.g., if the suggested query did not lead to the answer) and examine as many results as necessary to complete the search task. We used informational, entity-centric queries to introduce a common starting point across all participants. Upon finishing each task, participants were instructed to submit their answer and complete a post-task questionnaire. The study concluded with a demographics questionnaire. The payment for participation was $1.20 and each participant could take the study only once.

4. MODELLING USER ENGAGEMENT

In this section, we present our methodological approach for predicting the three user engagement proxies discussed in Section 3.4. By demonstrating that we can successfully model within-content interactions with DDs, using an inexpensive and scalable feedback like mouse cursor information, will allow us to derive more accurate and valid signals for predicting user engagement. In addition, with the proposed method we could infer with higher granularity which parts of a SERP or a web page the user truly notices and engages with, while lacking the additional cost of computationally expensive techniques for mouse cursor analysis.

4.1 Mouse Cursor Data

From our initial sample of 533 participants, we conclude to a subset of 300 participants, after excluding those cases which had incomplete mouse cursor logs. Our final dataset consists of 115,699 cursor positions, collected during 600 search task sessions. Out of those 600 search task sessions, we further analyse the 300 cases that correspond to the experimental condition with the visible KM (Section 3.1) in the SERP. We note that cases are generally balanced, with 176 users having reported noticing the KM display. As a last step,

Table 2: Features used in the classification task to predict user engagement.

Base features	Meta-features	Aggregate functions*
Viewport (width, height)	# Moves (towards, away) KM	$x_{\min}$, $x_{\max}$
Cursor positions and timestamps	# Moves (towards, away) KM within dist. d	Σ, μ, $\tilde{x}$
Unique cursor positions	# Clicks (inside, outside) KM	σ^2, $\sigma_{\bar{X}}$, SST
Normalised viewport positions	Time to first click on KM	$\sum$ intra-distances of cursor positions w.r.t. KM
Unique normalised viewport pos.	# Preceding clicks to KM	Shannon entropy
Subsequent points' distance	# Hovers over KM	Permutation entropy ($w \in \{2,\ldots,5\}$)
Subsequent points' duration	# Hovers over other elements	Weighted Permutation entropy ($w \in \{2,\ldots,5\}$)
Cursor distance from KM	# Hovers over KM vs. other elements	Approximate entropy ($w \in \{2,\ldots,5\}$)
Cursor speed	# Preceding hovers over other elements	FFT: i_{th} most powerful frequency ($i \in \{1,\ldots,5\}$)
Cursor normalised speed	Time to first hover (KM, other elements)	Multivariate KL div. (symmetric, non-symmetric)
Cursor acceleration	Time hovering (KM, other elements)	Earth mover's distance
Cursor normalised acceleration	Distance traversed overall	Hausdorff distance
Cursor position status wrt. KM	Distance traversed (inside, outside) KM	
Vector angles	Distance from KM (corners, center)	
	# Cursor positions within distance d from KM	

* These functions are computed for most base and meta-features.

we normalise the values for each computed feature in the range [0, 1] so that feature values that fall in greater numeric ranges do not dominate those in smaller numeric ranges.

4.2 Feature Engineering

Our task is to predict user engagement solely on the basis of inexpensive, easy-to-acquire user interaction signals. To this end, we explored a large number of basic as well as high-level meta-features that we engineered from the mouse cursor data we collected. We treated each data sequence as a time series and examined the statistical, spectral and temporal properties through the application of a number of aggregate functions. Each mouse cursor log was encoded as a feature vector of 638 components. In Table 2 we summarise these features under different categories and also list the aggregate functions applied to them. In what follows, we provide a brief description of the most important feature categories.

Temporal. Previous works [22, 35] have shown that accounting for the temporal characteristics of mouse cursor interactions can improve user profiling and prediction methods. Similarly, we considered the temporal dimension and measured (in milliseconds) the duration of cursor movements, the duration of hovering events and the total time up to the first click or hover, among others, both inside and outside of the KM display.

Spatial. Spatial features include the distance that the cursor has traveled overall. We considered both the Euclidean distance and the per-pixel travel distance on the x and y axes. In addition, we recorded the Euclidean distance of the mouse cursor to five reference points of the KM (Section 3.3). Finally, we recorded the status of the cursor position with respect to the KM display (inside, outside).

Direction. For every three subsequent mouse cursor positions, we determined the vectors they form and computed their angle in degrees. We also computed the direction of the mouse cursor movement with respect to the KM display.

Speed. The speed of mouse cursor movements has discriminative characteristics and can help disambiguate user intent [20]. For example, slow movements may indicate that the cursor is resting while the user is engaged in a cognitively demanding task such as reading carefully. On the other hand, ballistic movements suggest that the user is performing a quick scan to locate an information of interest in the text. In our analysis, we computed the speed for the distance that the mouse cursor travelled between subsequent pairs of positions. We considered both the Euclidean distance and the per-pixel travel distance on the x and y axes.

Acceleration. We also measured the acceleration for the distance that the mouse cursor travelled between three subsequent positions. As previously, we considered both the Euclidean distance and the pixel travel distance on the x and y axes.

Clicks. We considered the number of clicks performed inside and outside of the KM display, their ratio, as well as the number of preceding clicks prior to the first click on the KM display. The number of clicks has been used extensively in web search for decades, and is considered one of the most prominent features in user engagement research.

Descriptive statistics. This type of statistics provide simple, quantitative summaries of the data, such that patterns can emerge. In our analysis, we employed two general categories of descriptive statistics: measures of central tendency and measures of spread, motivated by the visualisations of the gathered mouse cursor trails (Figs. 4 and 5). The first category describes the central position of a frequency distribution for a dataset. Such examples in our feature set are the mean and the median. The second category describes how spread the scores in a dataset are distributed. To determine this spread, we computed the variance, sum of squares, standard deviation, kurtosis and skewness. Finally, we considered other simpler statistics, like the min, max and sum of values for each mouse cursor trail.

Distribution. These features include the sum of the mouse cursor positions' intra-distances, both inside and outside the KM display as well as overall, which indicate how compact or dispersed is the distribution of mouse cursor positions.

Shannon entropy. In information theory, entropy measures the disorder or uncertainty associated with a discrete, random variable, i.e., the expected value of the information in a message. The Shannon entropy [38] allows to estimate the average minimum number of bits needed to encode a string of symbols in binary form (if log base is 2) based on the alphabet size and the frequency of the symbols. Given

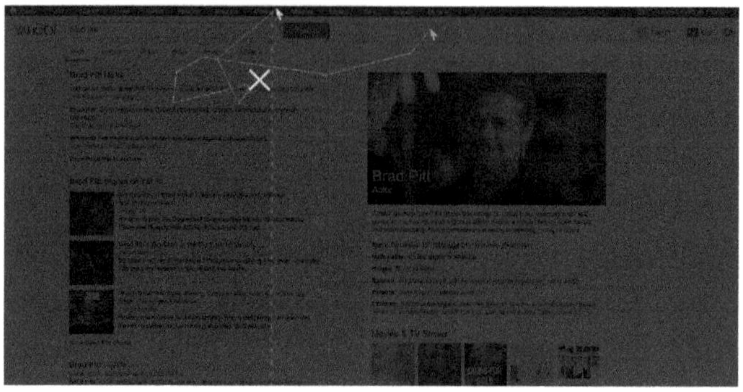

(a) Did not notice the KM display

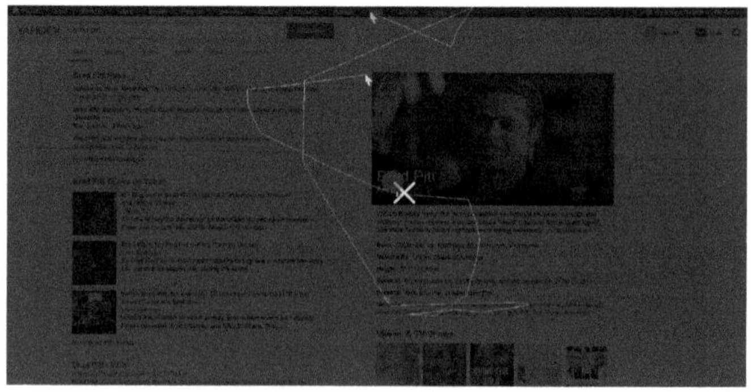

(b) Noticed the KM display

Figure 4: Examples of the mouse cursor data by a user who did not notice the KM display (a) and a user who noticed the KM display (b). Green cursors represent the entry coordinate (first point of the mouse cursor trail). Red cursors represent the exit coordinate (last point of the mouse cursor trail). White crosses represent the centroid of the mouse cursor trail. Blue circles represent clusters of interacted areas.

a finite time series $X(t) = (x_t \colon 1 \leq t \leq T)$, the Shannon entropy can be expressed as

$$H(X) = -\sum_t p(x_t) \log p(x_t), \tag{1}$$

In our prediction task, we used Equation 1 to characterise the complexity of our mouse cursor trails and applied it to several meta-features. As we demonstrate later, this feature is useful in discriminating between engaged vs. non-engaged users, depending on the level of uncertainty exhibited by the mouse cursor data.

Permutation entropy. Permutation entropy [7] provides a fast and robust method for estimating the complexity of time series, by considering the temporal order of the values. More specifically, it calculates the variety of different permutations appearing at the components of a time series such as our mouse cursor trails.

Denoting S_n the set of all possible $n!$ permutations π of order n for a time series $X(t)$, the relative frequency for each $\pi \in S_n$ is defined as

$$p(\pi) = \frac{\#\{t \mid 0 \leq t \leq T-n, (x_{t+1}, \ldots, x_{t+n}) \text{ has type } \pi\}}{T-n+1} \tag{2}$$

Then, the permutation entropy of order $n \geq 2$ is defined as

$$H(n) = -\sum_{\pi \in S_n} p(\pi) \log p(\pi) \tag{3}$$

This feature can be calculated for arbitrary real-world time series, and particularly in the presence of dynamical and observational noise. We computed the entropy for all permutations of order $n = 2, \ldots, 5$.

Weighted Permutation entropy. The Weighted Permutation entropy [15] extends the concept of Permutation entropy and addresses certain limitations such as its inability to differentiate between distinct patterns and their sensitivity.

This feature is computed in two steps. First, the weighted relative frequencies for each mouse cursor trail:

$$p_w(\pi_i^{n,\tau}) = \frac{\sum_{j \leq N} 1_{u:\text{type}(u)=\pi_i}(X_j^{n,\tau}) \cdot w_j}{\sum_{j \leq N} 1_{u:\text{type}(u)\in\Pi}(X_j^{n,\tau}) \cdot w_j} \tag{4}$$

where $1_A(u)$ denotes the indicator function of set A defined as $1_A(u) = 1$ if $u \in A$ and $1_A(u) = 0$ if $u \notin A$. The Weighted Permutation entropy is then computed as

$$H_w(n,\tau) = -\sum_{i:\pi_i^{n,\tau}\in\Pi} p_w(\pi_i^{n,\tau}) \log p_w(\pi_i^{n,\tau}) \tag{5}$$

where n and τ denote respectively the embedding dimension and time delay. The Weighted Permutation entropy is different from the Permutation entropy in the sense that the former is suitable for cursor trails with considerable amplitude information. For the range of trails that do not satisfy this property, the Permutation entropy might be a better alternative. We computed the entropy for all permutations of order $n = 2, \ldots, 5$.

Approximate entropy. The approximate entropy [37] expresses the (logarithmic) likelihood of similar patterns to be followed by similar observations. In other words, it quantifies the amount of regularity and the unpredictability of fluctuations in a time series. A low entropy indicates that the time series is deterministic, whereas a high value indicates randomness.

Denoting m the length of the compared data and r a filter factor (vector-wise comparison distance), we can define the approximate entropy ApEn of a time series $X(t)$ as

$$\text{ApEn}(m,r) = \Phi_m(r) - \Phi_{m+1}(r) \tag{6}$$

We computed the entropy for $m = 2, \ldots, 5$. We set $r = 0.2\,\text{SD}$, where SD is the standard deviation of the sequence values. The approximate entropy can be computed for any time series, chaotic or otherwise, at a low computational cost, and even for small data samples ($T < 50$).

Fast Fourier Transform. We performed a spectral analysis to determine the frequency components of our time series data. We used the fast Fourier transform (FFT), which is a more efficient way to compute the discrete Fourier transform (DFT). Given a time series $X(t)$ of length T and assuming a period T, the FFT computes two $T/2+1$ point frequency domain signals

$$X_k = \sum_t x_t \, e^{-i2\pi k \frac{t}{T}}, \quad k = 0 : T-1 \tag{7}$$

(a) Did not notice the KM display　　(b) Noticed the KM display

Figure 5: Heatmaps of mouse movements for all users who did not notice the KM display (a) and all users who noticed the KM display (b). The SERP shown here is an example to illustrate its parts and structure.

The two signals in the frequency domain are the real part and the imaginary part, and hold the amplitudes of the cosine and sine waves respectively. This frequency representation indicates how much of the variability of the data is due to low or high frequencies. In our analysis, we computed the amplitudes of all frequencies in our time series data and used their rankings as features, i.e., first most powerful frequency, second most powerful frequency, and so on.

Multivariate Kullback-Leibler divergence. We computed the multivariate Kullback-Leibler (MKL) divergence between 2 joint distributions:

$$D_{KL}(\mathcal{N}_1 \| \mathcal{N}_2) = \frac{1}{2}\Bigg[\log\frac{|\Sigma_1|}{|\Sigma_2|} + \mathrm{tr}(\Sigma_1^{-1}\Sigma_2) + (\mu_1 - \mu_2)^T\Sigma_1^{-1}(\mu_1 - \mu_2) - l\Bigg] \tag{8}$$

where μ is the mean vector, l is the length of the mean vector and Σ is the covariance matrix. The way we employed the multivariate KL divergence in our experiments is as follows. Initially, we used a set of training data (see Section 4.3) to learn the joint distributions of x and y mouse cursor positions for both engaged and non-engaged users. The browser viewport was normalised in $[0, 1]$ and discretised into 20 bins of size 0.05. This way, the cursor positions were split across the bins so that we could derive their distributions. Next, we computed the symmetric and non-symmetric KL distances between these two joint distributions and the training examples. Finally, we used these KL distances as features in our prediction task.

Earth Mover's Distance. Another feature we considered is the Earth Mover's distance (EMD), which is a measure of distance between two probability distributions. More specifically, the distributions are sets of weighted features that capture the distributions and the EMD is defined as the minimum amount of work needed to change one sequence into another. The notion of work is based on a unit of ground distance. Similarly to the KL divergence, we computed the EMD between the normalised mouse cursor positions in our training examples and the distributions of both engaged and non-engaged users.

Hausdorff Distance. The Hausdorff distance (HD) is the maximum distance of a set to the nearest point in the other set. More formally, the HD from set X to set Y is a maximin function defined as

$$d_H(A, B) = \max\Big\{\sup_{x\in X}\inf_{y\in Y} d(x, y),\ \sup_{y\in Y}\inf_{x\in X} d(x, y)\Big\} \tag{9}$$

where sup is the supremum (least upper bound of a set), inf is the infimum (greatest lower bound of a set), x and y are coordinates of sets X and Y respectively and $d(x, y)$ can be any distance function (e.g., Euclidean) between these coordinates. We computed the HD for the different distributions of mouse cursor positions in the same manner as described in the previous two features.

4.3 Prediction Task

In this section we demonstrate that our modelling approach can predict successfully the three proxies of user engagement discussed in Section 3.4, and that it outperforms the standard baseline methods. The value of our prediction task lies in the fact that we use highly discriminative yet low-cost features. For each user engagement proxy, we trained a random forest (RF) classifier using the feature set described in Section 4.2.

As a first step, we performed a correlation analysis and excluded from our feature set those features that are highly correlated ($r \geq .80, p < .05$) and/or linearly dependent. Then, prior to training our models, we performed feature selection using a wrapper method that uses recursive feature elimination until finding the optimal feature set that maximises model's performance. To get performance estimates that account for the variation due to feature selection, we applied a 10-fold cross-validation and used the Area Under Curve (AUC) as the performance measure to optimise. By applying this step, we avoided overfitting our models and excluded noisy features that would not contribute to the accurate prediction of our classes.

Table 3: Top-10 features of each user engagement proxy according to the mean decrease in accuracy (MDA).

Attention (52 feat.)	MDA	Usefulness (103 feat.)	MDA	Task Duration (81 feat.)	MDA
CD_minCursorDistFromKGMiddle	.0105	CD_medianCursorDistFromKGTopRight	.0056	CD_meanCursorDistFromKGMiddle	.0063
CD_minCursorDistFromKGBottomRight	.0066	CD_meanCursorDistFromKGMiddle	.0054	E_consecutivePointsDistXYAPE2	.0053
H_noHoversKGOverNoHoversOtherElements	.0062	emd_None	.0042	CD_medianCursorDistFromKGTopRight	.0049
CD_cursorDistYOverCursorDistXYInsKG	.0061	emd_Notice	.0041	CD_meanCursorDistFromKGTopRight	.0044
CD_minCursorDistFromKGTopRight	.0057	S_sdCursorSpeed	.0033	H_noHoversKGOverNoHoversOtherElements	.0039
H_timeHoverKG	.0049	CD_cursorDistX	.0032	DL_noMovesTowardsKGWithinDistX	.0038
CP_noCursorPosInsKGOverNoCursorPosOutKG	.0045	E_consecutivePointsDistXYAPE2	.0031	emd_Notice	.0033
CD_cursorDistXOverCursorDistYInsKG	.0042	MKL_SymmetricNoneIn	.0030	MKL_SymmetricNoticeIn	.0024
H_timeHoverKGOverHoverOtherElements	.0042	MKL_SymmetricNoticeIn	.0028	E_consecutivePointsDistXYAPE4	.0021
S_medianCursorSpeedInsKG	.0041	S_meanCursorSpeedOutKG	.0026	MKL_SymmetricNoneIn	.0021

Next, we performed a 10-fold cross-validation using stratified sampling, to create balanced splits of the data that preserve the overall class distribution. In each fold, we used 90% of the data for training and 10% for testing. Additionally, we held out a validation set from the training set for fine-tuning the classifier's hyperparameters (e.g., ϵ-threshold, number of trees). We then applied the optimal parameter values to our final model and evaluated its performance against the test set, and in comparison to several baselines.

Our choice of baselines was informed by existing research as well as current practices in industry [19, 20, 25, 26, 42]. More specifically, we considered if the user has clicked on the KM display (`hasClickedKM`, binary classifier), if the mouse cursor has hovered over the KM display (`hasHoveredKM`, binary classifier), and the time spent on the page (`dwellTime`) as a feature to the same **RF** classifier. For assessing the models' performance, we considered the standard IR metrics of precision, recall and accuracy. Traditionally, the most frequently used metrics are accuracy and error rate. However, metrics like accuracy can be deceiving in certain situations and are highly sensitive to changes in data [23]. Therefore, we also computed the F-Measure, which combines precision and recall as a measure of the effectiveness of classification in terms of the weighted importance on either recall or precision as determined by the β coefficient (we use $\beta = 1$). Last, because F-Measure is sensitive to data distribution, we used as an additional performance criterion the AUC.

4.4 Results

In what follows, we report the results of our prediction task for each user engagement proxy. A Kruskal-Wallis test for stochastic dominance was statistically significant in all cases. We therefore conducted a *post-hoc* analysis involving multiple pairwise comparisons, for which we corrected the level of significance to control the false discovery rate by using the Benjamini-Hochberg correction [8]. We note that the final performance values reported in Table 4 are the macro-averages across all ten folds. We highlight all cases where our model performs significantly better than the different baselines and provide the corresponding Z statistic.

4.4.1 *Attention*

The first proxy of user engagement we predicted is the noticeability of the KM display. More specifically, we were interested in detecting accurately if the KM display captures the user attention even at the absence of events such as clicks or hovers. For training our model, we used a subset of 52 features (some examples are shown in Table 3) from our initial feature set of 638 features. The top section of Table 4 reports the performance of our classification model in comparison to the different baselines. As we can observe, our model's predictive performance is better than any of the competitor baselines. This improvement is evident across all performance metric that we considered, but more importantly with respect to F-Measure, where our model introduces an improvement over all baselines of 13.8% (`hasClickedKM`), 15.6% (`hasHoveredKM`), 24.6% (`dwellTime`) and 9% (joint model) respectively. Another encouraging result is our model's performance with respect to the AUC which, given existing research conventions, can be considered as excellent/good. On the other hand, the AUC achieved by the baselines indicates no discrimination between the predicted classes.

4.4.2 *Usefulness*

The next proxy of user engagement that we considered is the usefulness of the KM display. The highly subjective nature of this engagement metric suggests that it is a more challenging task, something which is made evident by the overall performance degradation observed in the `hasClickedKM` baseline. Nevertheless, our model appears to be the best performer in comparison to the other baselines and maintains its advantage (using an extended set of 103 features shown in Table 3), as indicated by the reported measures. From the results shown in the middle section of Table 4, we can see that the difference between our model and the other baselines in terms of F-Measure is widened to 44.1% (`hasClickedKM`), 9.8% (`hasHoveredKM`), 7.2% (`dwellTime`) and 2% (joint model) respectively.

4.4.3 *Perceived Task Duration*

We conclude our prediction task with a final proxy of user engagement: the perceived task duration. Here, we aimed to predict whether users felt that they completed their task faster, given that this belief is attributed to the examined DD (in our case the KM display). For this task, we learned a **RF** model using the 81 top-ranked features shown in Table 3. We performed the same 10-fold cross-validation to ensure that our model's performance is not over-optimistic. As shown in the bottom section of Table 4, the performance of our model did not change much despite the prediction challenge that the targeted concept posses. The differences in the F-Measure scores between our model and the baselines (39% for `hasClickedKM`, 14.3% for `hasHoveredKM`, 9.5% for `dwellTime` and 10% for the model that combines all baselines) indicate once more the capacity of the proposed method to capture this aspect of engagement and provide accurate predictions on future user engagement for a DD.

4.5 Computational Complexity

As a side contribution, we comment on the computational complexity of recent approaches to mouse cursor analysis, in terms of temporal cost, and compare them with our proposed method. On the one hand, the Mouse Gestures technique [2]

Table 4: **Performance metrics for the proposed method and the different baselines. Scores in parentheses are Dunn's pairwise Z statistic. A bold typeface denotes the best result in a row.**

	Performance Metric	Our method	hasClickedKM	hasHoveredKM	dwellTime	All baselines
Attention	(Weighted Avg.) Precision	**.77**	.62 (3.08)**	.67 (1.96)	.50 (4.81)***	.74 (0.56)
	(Weighted Avg.) Recall	**.76**	.62 (3.21)*	.61 (3.58)***	.52 (5.38)***	.69 (1.57)
	(Weighted Avg.) F-Measure	**.76**	.58 (3.86)***	.60 (3.48)***	.51 (5.23)***	.68 (1.53)
	(Weighted Avg.) Accuracy	**.76**	.62 (3.21)*	.61 (3.58)***	.52 (5.36)***	.67 (1.51)
	AUC	**.86**	.42 (5.31)***	.51 (4.18)***	.53 (3.59)***	.72 (1.51)
Usefulness	(Weighted Avg.) Precision	**.74**	**.74** (0.43)	.69 (0.86)	.62 (2.76)*	.65 (2.23)
	(Weighted Avg.) Recall	**.74**	.33 (4.86)***	.61 (3.02)**	.73 (0.39)	**.74** (0.64)
	(Weighted Avg.) F-Measure	**.74**	.30 (5.56)***	.64 (2.78)**	.66 (2.07)	.68 (2.05)
	(Weighted Avg.) Accuracy	**.74**	.33 (4.86)***	.61 (3.02)**	.73 (0.39)	**.74** (0.64)
	AUC	**.71**	.45 (4.80)***	.58 (2.22)*	.57 (2.47)*	.60 (2.24)*
Task Dur.	(Weighted Avg.) Precision	.74	**.77** (-0.96)	.63 (1.88)	.62 (2.01)	.64 (1.55)
	(Weighted Avg.) Recall	**.73**	.40 (4.77)***	.57 (2.81)**	.70 (0.86)	.66 (1.28)
	(Weighted Avg.) F-Measure	**.73**	.34 (5.46)***	.59 (2.67)**	.64 (2.16)*	.63 (2.16)*
	(Weighted Avg.) Accuracy	**.73**	.40 (4.77)***	.57 (2.81)**	.70 (0.86)	.66 (1.28)
	AUC	**.77**	.41 (5.60)***	.55 (3.41)**	.62 (2.25)*	.59 (2.76)**

Significance levels (two tails, corrected for multiple comparisons): $^{*}p < .05$; $^{**}p < .01$; $^{***}p < .001$.

relies on principal component analysis (PCA) preprocessing and k-means clustering. The cost of PCA is $\mathcal{O}(p^2N + p^3)$ (covariance matrix computation + eigen value decomposition) with p features and N data points, whereas k-means has $\mathcal{O}(i\,c\,N)$ with i iterations and c clusters. On the other hand, the algorithms used in Cursor Motifs [27, 32] use both dynamic time warping (DTW), which has cost $\mathcal{O}(N^2)$, and k-nearest neighbours (kNN), which has cost $\mathcal{O}(N^2k^2)$ with k neighbours. Our method has computations of $\mathcal{O}(N)$ (linear) or $\mathcal{O}(N \log N)$ (quasilinear) cost, instead of the cubic and quadratic cost associated to the other approaches. Most important, our method is straightforward to implement and highly discriminative. As such, we expect that it may be of practical value in several problems that make use of mouse cursor analysis.

5. DISCUSSION AND CONCLUSIONS

With the rising presence of direct answers in search results where no click is required to acquire relevant information, the need to understand the utility of within-page interactions becomes critical. Whether a DD like the KM display is useful is hard to determine, particularly if the information the user is seeking is on the module itself. To this end, this work has examined the impact of DDs in web search, providing empirical evidence of their overall utility. We conducted a crowdsourcing study that revealed the potential benefits of using mouse cursor data to predict user engagement with DDs. In particular, we showed that our feature selection model outperforms the standard baselines to measure three user engagement proxies with the KM display.

With respect to the noticeability proxy, our initial results clearly suggest that it is possible to predict when the user attention is captured by a DD like the KM display using only a simple, yet highly discriminative, set of features derived from mouse cursor activity. This is an important finding considering that existing online user engagement metrics assume a uniform engagement with the web page content and do not distinguish well enough between attended and ignored DDs. If we can predict accurately if a DD was truly noticed although it was not clicked or hovered, then we can be more confident that the user engaged with it and improve our *true negative* prediction rate. On the other hand, if we can predict when a DD was indeed not noticed, although it was clicked or hovered, we can reduce our *false negative* rate.

Regarding our second user engagement proxy, usefulness of the KM display, we observe that the `dwellTime` model managed, to some extent, to capture how users engage with the DDs by considering the amount of time they spend on the page. In fact, the model that combines the three baselines performs equally good as ours in terms of accuracy and recall. However, it lacks the precision of our model. In other words, when that model predicts the positive class it will be less often correct and, as a result, will not provide trustworthy judgements. Our model's ability to predict more accurately when a user finds a DD useful has important implications on the methodology for understanding the impact of launching a new DD, modifying its existing design, and how that change may affect web search UIs.

In the final proxy of user engagement, perceived task duration, our model was able to discriminate more accurately than any baseline when users felt that they have completed their task faster, given that this belief is attributed to the examined DD. This information, combined with the previous grounds truths that we predicted successfully allows us to understand better, for example, how users engage with ads, images or videos; something which existing click-based models do not address adequately due to their current biases and limitations.

While our prediction tasks may be useful for descriptive analysis, the main practical use of our models is perhaps to automatically select or lay out the DDs. This is an interesting research avenue, because DDs are optional for the SERPs and so the user behaviour could provide signals about whether DDs should be shown or not in particular queries. Ultimately, modelling user engagement with DDs has wide-ranging applications in web search ranking, evaluation and interface design. Therefore we anticipate that further research on this topic may have an important impact on future web search interfaces.

Acknowledgments

We thank B. Barla Cambazoglu and Marios Koulakis for fruitful discussions. This work was partially supported by the International Excellence VLC/CAMPUS program.

6. REFERENCES

[1] I. Arapakis, M. Lalmas, B. B. Cambazoglu, M.-C. Marcos, and J. M. Jose. User engagement in online news: Under the scope of sentiment, interest, affect, and gaze. *JASIST*, 65(10), 2014.

[2] I. Arapakis, M. Lalmas, and G. Valkanas. Understanding within-content engagement through pattern analysis of mouse gestures. In *Proc. CIKM*, 2014.

[3] I. Arapakis, L. A. Leiva, and B. B. Cambazoglu. Know your onions: Understanding the user experience with the knowledge module in web search. In *Proc. CIKM*, 2015.

[4] E. Arroyo, S. Sullivan, and T. Selker. CarCoach: A polite and effective driving coach. In *Proc. CHI EA*, 2006.

[5] R. Atterer, M. Wnuk, and A. Schmidt. Knowing the User's Every Move - User Activity Tracking for Website Usability Evaluation and Implicit Interaction. In *Proc. WWW*, 2006.

[6] S. Auer, C. Bizer, G. Kobilarov, J. Lehmann, R. Cyganiak, and Z. Ives. DBpedia: A nucleus for a web of open data. In *Proc. ISWC*, 2007.

[7] C. Bandt and B. Pompe. Permutation entropy: A natural complexity measure for time series. *Phys. Rev. Lett.*, 88, Apr 2002.

[8] Y. Benjamini and Y. Hochberg. Controlling the false discovery rate - a practical and powerful approach to multiple testing. *Journal of the Royal Statistical Society, Series B*, 57(1):289–300, 1995.

[9] B. Bi, H. Ma, B.-J. P. Hsu, W. Chu, K. Wang, and J. Cho. Learning to recommend related entities to search users. In *Proc. WSDM*, 2015.

[10] R. Blanco, B. B. Cambazoglu, P. Mika, and N. Torzec. Entity recommendations in web search. In *Proc. ISWC*. 2013.

[11] K. Bollacker, C. Evans, P. Paritosh, T. Sturge, and J. Taylor. Freebase: A collaboratively created graph database for structuring human knowledge. In *Proc. SIGMOD*, 2008.

[12] M. Claypool, P. Le, M. Wased, and D. Brown. Implicit interest indicators. In *Proc. IUI*, 2001.

[13] A. Diriye, R. W. White, G. Buscher, and S. Dumais. Leaving so soon?: understanding and predicting web search abandonment rationales. In *Proc. CIKM*, 2012.

[14] X. Dong, E. Gabrilovich, G. Heitz, W. Horn, N. Lao, K. Murphy, T. Strohmann, S. Sun, and W. Zhang. Knowledge vault: A web-scale approach to probabilistic knowledge fusion. In *Proc. SIGKDD*, 2014.

[15] B. Fadlallah, B. Chen, A. Keil, and J. Príncipe. Weighted-permutation entropy: A complexity measure for time series incorporating amplitude information. *Phys. Rev. E*, 87(2), 2013.

[16] H. A. Feild, J. Allan, and R. Jones. Predicting searcher frustration. In *Proc. SIGIR*, 2010.

[17] J. Goecks and J. Shavlik. Learning users' interests by unobtrusively observing their normal behavior. In *Proc. IUI*, 2000.

[18] Q. Guo and E. Agichtein. Exploring mouse movements for inferring query intent. In *Proc. SIGIR*, 2008.

[19] Q. Guo and E. Agichtein. Ready to buy or just browsing? Detecting web searcher goals from interaction data. In *Proc. SIGIR*, 2010.

[20] Q. Guo and E. Agichtein. Beyond dwell time: estimating document relevance from cursor movements and other post-click searcher behavior. In *Proc. WWW*, 2012.

[21] Q. Guo, D. Lagun, and E. Agichtein. Predicting web search success with fine-grained interaction data. In *Proc. CIKM*, 2012.

[22] Q. Guo, D. Lagun, D. Savenkov, and Q. Liu. Improving relevance prediction by addressing biases and sparsity in web search click data. In *WSCD Workshop*, 2012.

[23] H. He and E. A. Garcia. Learning from imbalanced data. *IEEE TKDE*, 21(9):1263–1284, 2009.

[24] J. Hoffart, F. M. Suchanek, K. Berberich, and G. Weikum. Yago2: A spatially and temporally enhanced knowledge base from Wikipedia. *Artif. Intell.*, 194, 2013.

[25] J. Huang, R. W. White, G. Buscher, and K. Wang. Improving searcher models using mouse cursor activity. In *Proc. SIGIR*, 2012.

[26] J. Huang, R. W. White, and S. Dumais. No clicks, no problem: using cursor movements to understand and improve search. In *Proc. CHI*, 2011.

[27] D. Lagun, M. Ageev, Q. Guo, and E. Agichtein. Discovering common motifs in cursor movement data for improving web search. In *Proc. WSDM*, 2014.

[28] L. A. Leiva. Restyling website design via touch-based interactions. In *Proc. MobileHCI*, 2011.

[29] L. A. Leiva and J. Huang. Building a better mousetrap: Compressing mouse cursor activity for web analytics. *Inf. Process. & Manage.*, 51(2), 2015.

[30] L. A. Leiva and E. Vidal. Assessing user's interactions for clustering web documents: a pragmatic approach. In *Proc. Hypertext*, 2010.

[31] L. A. Leiva and R. Vivó. Web browsing behavior analysis and interactive hypervideo. *ACM TWEB*, 7(4), 2013.

[32] Y. Liu, Y. Chen, J. Tang, J. Sun, M. Zhang, S. Ma, and X. Zhu. Different users, different opinions: Predicting search satisfaction with mouse movement information. In *Proc. SIGIR*, 2015.

[33] W. Mason and S. Suri. Conducting Behavioral Research on Amazon's Mechanical Turk. *Behav. Res. Methods*, 44(1), 2010.

[34] I. Miliaraki, R. Blanco, and M. Lalmas. From "Selena Gomez" to "Marlon Brando": Understanding explorative entity search. In *Proc. WWW*, 2015.

[35] V. Navalpakkam and E. Churchill. Mouse tracking: measuring and predicting users' experience of web-based content. In *Proc. CHI*, 2012.

[36] H. L. O'Brien and E. G. Toms. The development and evaluation of a survey to measure user engagement. *JASIST*, 61(1), 2010.

[37] S. M. Pincus. Approximate entropy as a measure of system complexity. *PNAS*, 88(6), 1991.

[38] C. Shannon. A mathematical theory of communication. *Bell Syst. Tech.*, 27(3), 1948.

[39] B. Shapira, M. Taieb-Maimon, and A. Moskowitz. Study of the usefulness of known and new implicit indicators and their optimal combination for accurate inference of users interests. In *Proc. SAC*, 2006.

[40] M. Speicher, A. Both, and M. Gaedke. Tellmyrelevance! predicting the relevance of web search results from cursor interactions. In *Proc. CIKM*, 2013.

[41] F. M. Suchanek, G. Kasneci, and G. Weikum. Yago: A core of semantic knowledge. In *Proc. WWW*, 2007.

[42] D. Warnock and M. Lalmas. An exploration of cursor tracking data. In *arXiv:1502.00317*, 2015.

Search Result Prefetching Using Cursor Movement

Fernando Diaz*
fdiaz@microsoft.com
Microsoft Research

Qi Guo†
qiguo@google.com
Google

Ryen W. White
ryenw@microsoft.com
Microsoft Research

ABSTRACT

Search result examination is an important part of searching. High page load latency for landing pages (clicked results) can reduce the efficiency of the search process. Proactively prefetching landing pages in advance of clickthrough can save searchers valuable time. However, prefetching consumes resources that are wasted unless the prefetched results are requested by searchers. Balancing the costs in prefetching particular results against the benefits in reduced latency to searchers represents the search result prefetching challenge. We present methods that leverage searchers' cursor movements on search result pages in real time to dynamically estimate the result that searchers will request next. We demonstrate through large-scale log analysis that our approach significantly outperforms three strong baselines that prefetch results based on (i) the search engine result ranking, (ii) past clicks from all searchers for the query, or (iii) past clicks from the current searcher for the query. Our promising findings have implications for the design of search support that makes the search process more efficient.

1. INTRODUCTION

Search result selection is a core part of the Web search experience. Following the generation of a search engine result page (SERP) comprised of candidate results, searchers must select results of interest and wait for them to load. While the latency in SERP generation has been well studied and shown to impact measures of the search experience (e.g., higher SERP generation latency leads to higher dissatisfaction and reduced SERP engagement) [2, 38], the relationship between latency and the loading of landing pages is less well understood. Despite a lack of research on this topic in the Web search community, general research on latencies in interactions with computer systems [39] and interactions with Web pages in particular [32] suggests that it has a significant impact on the overall experience. Methods to proactively fetch the content of particular search results before they are selected could benefit searchers, while balancing the costs involved in downloading content that is never viewed; we define this as the *search result prefetching challenge*.

*Author order alphabetical.

†Work conducted while at Microsoft.

SIGIR '16, July 17-21, 2016, Pisa, Italy

DOI: http://dx.doi.org/10.1145/2911451.2911516

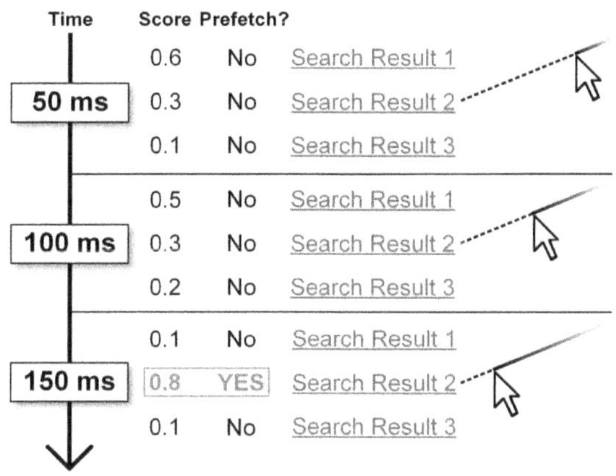

Figure 1: Example of cursor-based prefetching. The model estimate of whether the searcher will select one of the top three results over time (at 50ms, 100ms, 150ms) is shown alongside each link (as *Score*). These estimates change as a function of the searcher's cursor movements. The cursor trail and the trajectory towards the second result are highlighted in the figure with solid and dashed lines respectively. When the model score for a result reaches a certain threshold (0.8 for Search Result 2), that result is prefetched.

To address this challenge, the prefetching system needs to predict which result the user will select next. In previous research, such predictions are usually made via static estimates learned from historic usage data [13, 14, 22, 26, 45]. For example, search engines prefetch the top result for queries where there is little variation in intent (primarily navigational queries [1]). However, these methods are only applied for small sets of queries where the dominant intent is clearly defined and observable via prior click patterns.

In contrast, we propose to address this challenge by dynamically updating the estimates of likelihood of each result being selected during interaction with a SERP; when the system is confident that a link will be selected, the page is prefetched (Figure 1). Our method leverages the mouse cursor movements on the SERP (which can now be collected in a scalable manner [8, 20]), contextualized by the query, the results, and the searcher's historic activity to make *real-time predictions*. If we can correctly prefetch early enough, we can save people significant time–this is especially important for those accessing the Web on low-bandwidth connections, who may need to be more selective about the results that they view. Indeed, on average, our methods save searchers 650ms per query for the 65% of queries where we correctly prefetch the clicked result.

We make the following contributions with our research:

- Introduce the search result prefetching challenge and estimate the scope of its potential impact on searchers and their search experience (in terms of the fraction of query volume and average time savings per query of our method);
- Develop machine-learned models that leverage a rich array of features to prefetch search results pre-click;
- Experiment with large-scale logs and demonstrate gains over strong baselines, including variations for different query types. We also identify the important feature classes in the learned models via ablation experiments, and;
- Present implications of result prefetching for search system design and for society (e.g., enabling more rapid information access for those on slower Internet connections).

The remainder of this paper is structured as follows. Section 2 describes related work in areas such as prefetching, the impact of response latency on user engagement, and mouse cursor monitoring. Section 3 motivates our research by demonstrating the potential impact of our prefetching system. Section 4 presents a formal description of the search result prefetching challenge. Section 5 describes the prefetching approach, including the data used, the features generated, and the models that result. In Section 6, we describe our experimental setup, including datasets and evaluation. In Section 7, we present the results of our experiments, demonstrating the effectiveness of our method compared to baselines. Section 8 discusses our findings, their limitations given the data and the problem setting, and their implications for the design of search systems. We conclude in Section 9 and present opportunities for future work.

2. RELATED WORK

The following areas are relevant: (a) latency effects in human-computer interaction and SERP generation, (b) methods to reduce latency during search, and (c) using cursor movements collected in laboratory settings and at scale.

2.1 Latency Effects

Since the early days of human computer interaction, researchers have studied the influence of system response time on the success, speed, and satisfaction of interactions [31, Chapter 5]. These studies have found that rapid responses (i.e., less than a second) are preferred and can increase user productivity [31]. Shneiderman [39] reviewed the literature on computer response time and recommended that computers should respond immediately, in part based on limitations in human short-term memory [27]. Web page download time is affected by factors such as browser performance, Internet connection speed, local network traffic, load on the remote host, and the structure and format of requested content. Download speeds are an important aspect of the user experience [32]. Studies have examined the interplay between page load time and the user experience, including tolerable wait times [30] and their psychological impact [36].

Intensive research and engineering efforts have been devoted to achieving low latency in large, complex computing systems such as search engines [10]. Modern Web search engines deliver results rapidly because fast results are perceived as being of higher quality and searchers engage more with them. For example, Google conducted online experiments where they intentionally injected server-side delays, ranging from 100 to 400 milliseconds, into the search results to observe changes to people's behavior. They found that increasing the load time of the SERP by as little as 100 milliseconds decreased the number of searches per person. These differences increased over time and persisted even after the experiment ended [38]. In similar experiments, Bing added server delays ranging from 50 to 2000 milliseconds. They observed decreases in queries and clicks, and an increase in time to click, with larger effects with more delay [38]. Arapakis et al. employed user studies and large-scale log analysis, and showed that response latencies of 500ms were noticeable by searchers [2]. Recognizing the importance of speed to searchers, Google added site speed (i.e., how quickly a Website responds to requests) as a relevance signal in search ranking [40]. Recent work on slow search discusses the cost-benefit tradeoffs in retrieving search results quickly, and what could be accomplished given more time [41]. Beyond just making search faster (or slower), there are other reasons why page load latency matters, e.g., to address network bandwidth constraints [14].

2.2 Reducing Latency

To address latency in query responses, researchers have designed caches to rapidly serve results [5], including ways to leverage historic search behavior [13, 22, 26]. These methods limit the set of documents searched in response to queries, incurring increased infrastructure costs. Search engines already try to reduce time to click by promoting popular results [1]. Since repeat visits to the same result is common [43], search engines have promoted results that are likely to be selected; reducing the time for searchers to locate these results on SERPs. The Bing search engine already uses new browser capabilities to prefetch results that are highly likely to be selected [35]. This can enhance the search experience by reducing latency beyond SERP creation.

Moving beyond search engine support for latency reduction, Padbanabham and Mogul [33] use N-hop Markov models based on surfing patterns for improving pre-fetching strategies for Web caches. Fan *et al.* [14] leverage a user's historic surfing activity and a Markov predictor tree to predict future page accesses. Yang et al. [45] mined frequent sequences from Website access logs and employed them to derive association rules that could be used in prefetching decisions. More recently, White et al. [44] used recent search interactions and other contextual signals (e.g., incoming hyperlinks) to predict searchers' future topical interests given a Web page. Research on *continual computation* [18] proposed decision-theoretic methods for the ideal use of idle time for computational problem solving. These methods have been applied for selective (utility-directed) content prefetching, including the partial prefetching of specific Web page elements, while balancing associated costs and benefits.

To be successful, all of these methods rely on popularity data and/or the sequence of visited Web pages. This may be reasonable for popular queries/pages or active users, but less applicable for other scenarios with less data (e.g., tail queries). The methods that leverage browsing data relies on being able to track sequences of Web page visits, which can require significant infrastructure, especially at scale across many Websites. It is also not clear the extent to which such an approach applies in search scenarios, where the results returned for a query are dynamically generated and the set of prefetching candidates may change over time [6].

2.3 Leveraging Cursor Movements

We are focused on dynamically prefetching search result content once a query has been issued. Retrieving the top result for all queries or all results for all queries incurs a high cost in terms of resource consumption (primarily network bandwidth but also battery power on mobile devices). We hypothesize that by monitoring searcher attention in real-time on SERPs we can perform better prefetching than these crude methods. Lee et al. [25] performed prefetching of video materials via models learned from eye-gaze and cursor movements. They did so in a laboratory setting with access to gaze tracking technology. Recent research has shown that there is a strong association between gaze and cursor position [16, 20], especially around the time of a click [19]. This can be used to predict attention and intentions from cursor movement data [16, 19] in laboratory environments. Beyond controlled settings, recent work has shown that such methods can be deployed at scale online [8, 20]. This facilitates a better understanding of search behavior [8], and enables predictions of SERP examination activity [11], improved relevance estimation [19], and ranking [23] based on common patterns in cursor signals. From this data we learn models to predict which results will be clicked *in real time*, and evaluate our models in a natural setting.

Human-computer interaction (HCI) researchers have predicted aspects of cursor movement termination, focusing on endpoint prediction (i.e., predicting the terminal location of the cursor) and target prediction (i.e., deciding between multiple targets). Within HCI, these have traditionally been used in applications to expedite the acquisition of targets.

Simple versions of target prediction leverages distance from the mouse cursor [24] or consider angles between the movement vector and vectors for the target positions [29]. More sophisticated methods build probabilistic models based on previous clicks [46], or using kinematic template matching [34]. Although there are similarities between this work and ours, experiments in this area are generally conducted in carefully-controlled, artificial environments. On SERPs, there are many results to choose from, there are many aspects of the page competing for searcher attention in addition to the results (e.g., advertisements, related searches), and there are preconceived biases that affect where people click in the result list, irrespective of content (e.g., positional biases [21]). All of these factors make the task of real-time click prediction on SERPs quite challenging, especially if searchers' clicks disagree with the query's aggregate click distribution.

2.4 Contributions Over Previous Work

Our research extends previous work in a number of ways. First, we focus on prefetching in dynamic environments where the list of targets can change over time, even for the same query. Most prefetching methods rely on static predictions and transition probabilities learned from historic data. Second, many of the studies of end-point prediction focus on carefully controlled studies in laboratory settings. In contrast, we operate in a non-controlled environment with cursor movements with multiple targets, potential distractions, and biases that can affect behaviors irrespective of the relevance of the results retrieved by the search engine. Third, by leveraging cursor movements and other features our approach can better adapt to the current search situation and less common informational queries. Many current prefetching methods within Websites and search engines focus only on providing this support for popular pages. Finally, since we propose a model that is learned offline from many searchers' behavior, there is no need for searchers to calibrate the model to accommodate their search activity before the first use (as is the case in other models, e.g., [4]).

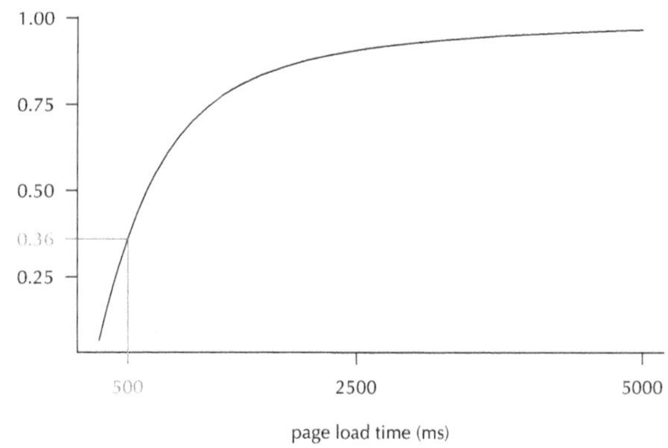

Figure 2: Cumulative distribution function of landing page load times for result clicks on SERPs.

3. MOTIVATION

Before proceeding, it is important to quantify the potential gains from prefetching in a Web search setting. If all landing pages were to load instantly then there would be no benefit from prefetching. Obviously this is not the case given the computational differences in the machines serving and accessing online content, and the network transport pipeline. To better understand the potential of prefetching in Web search settings we analyzed six months of search-click logs from millions of consenting users of Internet Explorer in 2013. From these data, we obtained a distribution of page load times for hyperlink clicks on SERPs from a popular Web search engine. The mean and median landing page load times (PLTs) were 1282ms and 672ms respectively. The empirical cumulative distribution of PLTs from 200ms to five seconds or more is shown in Figure 2. Given that searchers start to notice PLT delays at 500ms [2] (or even earlier [3]), the figure suggests that, if we could make an accurate prediction about which results to prefetch, we could noticeably improve the search experience for at least 64% of SERP clicks (as highlighted in red in Figure 2). These findings serve as a strong motivation for developing the prefetching model introduced and evaluated in this paper.

4. PROBLEM DEFINITION

Let $\mathcal{U}$ be a set of algorithmic results. Each result is associated with a specific SERP region or *area of interest* (AOI), comprising the region spanning the result title, snippet, and URL. Given that the SERP was presented to the searcher at time 0 and the searcher clicks on $u^* \in \mathcal{U}$ at time T, we would like to fetch u^* at some point before T. Decision-making is online: starting at time 0, the system observes a sequence of interactions (cursor movements in our case) which might inform its decision-making. Once a decision to fetch has been made, the system may not fetch another page until the searcher clicks on u^*. This budget represents a conservative estimate of the cost, in terms of time and bandwidth, of prefetching the result, and considers all clicks equally, e.g., for simplicity the size of the page is not considered in the evaluation, even though prefetching a large/media-rich document costs more than prefetching a smaller resource.

5. ALGORITHMS

We regard the search result prefetching challenge as a ranking problem. We model probability of clicking on a result as a function of static features of the result (e.g., position) as well as dynamic features of the result (e.g., proximity of the cursor to the result AOI). Our model computes this relevance score throughout the searcher's interaction with the SERP. If the score exceeds a threshold τ, then the landing page content is fetched. In this section, we will describe the features and model that we developed for this challenge.

5.1 Features

Our features can be divided into *static* and *dynamic* based on whether they are the same across all cursor movements for a query impression (static) or change as the searcher moves the cursor (dynamic). Each group can be further divided into *global* and *local*. Global features of the SERP are the same over all AOIs (e.g., SERP includes an advertisement). Local features refer to properties unique to each result AOI (e.g., Euclidean distance between cursor and AOI). Features are computed every time the cursor positon is sampled (i.e., after 250ms have passed or the cursor has moved at least eight pixels) for each of the result AOIs, since the goal is to predict the result AOI that will be selected.

Previous research has shown that modeling differences with the normative behavior for each searcher can help better estimate document relevance [17]. As such, we include the normalized version for each feature for each searcher using the deviations from average for the $\langle$searcher, feature$\rangle$ pair. User deviation is defined as the difference between the feature value at the current cursor position and the the average feature value for that searcher computed over all their historic actions. User deviation variants are included for *Dynamic Global* and *Dynamic Local* features (Table 1).

5.1.1 Static Global Features

Query Features comprise query frequency and query click entropy (as defined in [12]). Searchers may interact differently for different query classes, e.g., navigational queries vs. informational queries, as shown previously [9].

SERP Features capture the presence of non-target elements such as advertisements and related searches, which may influence the click behavior on the target organic search results. Binary features for SERP has advertisements and SERP has related searches are included.

5.1.2 Dynamic Global Features

Global Cursor Features capture the dynamics of cursor movements up to the cursor sample in question. Features include velocity, acceleration, jerk (i.e., rate of acceleration change) and changes from previous cursor sample. These also include features that capture where the cursor was located on the SERP, such as its horizontal and vertical coordinates, the maximum vertical coordinate reached by the

Table 1: Features used in prefetching model. Coordinates are relative to upper-left corner of the SERP. Distances, coordinates, and areas measured in pixels. Features with maxima or totals (denoted *) are computed since SERP load.

Feature name	Description
Static Global	
Query frequency	Frequency of the query
Query click entropy	Result click entropy of the query (as in [12])
SERP has advertisements	SERP has advertisement(s)? (binary)
SERP has related searches	SERP has related searches? (binary)
Dynamic Global	
Cursor xcoord	X-coordinate of cursor
Cursor ycoord	Y-coordinate of cursor
Cursor delta	Distance cursor moved since it was last sampled
Num non hyperlink clicks	Number of cursor clicks on SERP that are not on hyperlinks, e.g., for text selections
Cursor is reading	Reading behavior (i.e., following text with cursor [37])
Cursor max ycoord*	Max y coordinate of cursor
Cursor max AOI rank*	Max AOI rank of cursor
Cursor total distance*	Total cursor move distance
Cursor total time*	Total time moved
Cursor time delta	Time since cursor position was last sampled
Static Local	
AOI area	Area of result AOI
AOI width	Width of result AOI
AOI height	Height of result AOI
AOI rank	Rank position of result AOI
AOI xcoord	X-coordinate of result AOI
AOI ycoord	Y-coordinate of result AOI
AOI has card	AOI has special image (e.g., a brand logo) and/or additional result information such as deep links? (binary)
AOI has answer	AOI has answer? (binary)
Dynamic Local	
AOI is visible	AOI in viewport? (binary)
AOICursor hover	Cursor over AOI? (binary)
AOICursor distance	Euclidean distance from the cursor position to the center of the AOI
AOICursor angle	Angle between direction vector center of result AOI. AOI with least deviation receives 1, otherwise 0
AOICursor proximity	Proximity changes of cursor with respect to AOI. 2 = moving away from AOI, 1 = moving toward AOI, 0 = same distance from AOI
AOICursor speed	Speed of cursor movement toward AOI
AOICursor acceleration	Acceleration toward AOI
AOICursor jerk	Rate of cursor acceleration change toward AOI
AOICursor on target	On track to visit AOI. Project least squares line through last five cursor movements. Return 1 if it intersects the AOI, otherwise 0
AOICursor xdistance	Horizontal distance between cursor and AOI
AOICursor ydistance	Vertical distance between cursor and AOI
AOICursor dwell	Cursor dwell time in AOI
AOICursor title dwell	Cursor dwell time in result title of AOI

cursor and maximum AOI rank that the cursor is observed passing over, and the number of non-hyperlink clicks the impression has received up to the cursor sample. The rationale for these features is to capture the different stages of the cursor movements. A directed, rapid movement may mean that the searcher has found content of potential value; slow, undirected movements may suggest that they are still searching. Determining the maximum vertical position of the cursor offers insight into the number of search results considered. Finally, to explicitly model reading behavior using cursor as an aid [37] (which could be an indicator of interest in a landing page), a binary feature captures whether two consecutive left-right cursor movements are observed.

5.1.3 Static Local Features

AOI Features characterize rhe target AOIs (in our case, each search result). For each AOI, specific features include the rank position of the AOI, horizontal and vertical coordinates, width, height, area of the AOI, and the type of the AOI (e.g., whether AOI is an aggregated result). The rationale here is that behavior is highly influenced by the presentation of the AOIs, for example, higher ranked AOIs may be more likely to receive clicks while bigger AOIs and AOIs with cards (e.g., brand logos) may be more likely to attract searcher attention and result in clicks [11].

5.1.4 Dynamic Local Features

Local Cursor Features capture the interaction between cursor movements and each AOI, in particular, to capture if the cursor is moving towards the AOI for a potential click. Features include the overall, vertical, horizontal distances, between the AOI and the cursor, the angle between the moving direction of the cursor and the AOI, and, in turn, the proximity between the two (2 = moving away from AOI, 1 = moving toward AOI, 0 = same distance from AOI), as well as whether the AOI is on target per the cursor trajectory (i.e., draw a least squares line through last five cursor movements and return true/false on whether it intersects each AOI). We also compute the dwell time the cursor hover on the AOI and the title of the AOI, respectively, as they may be strong indicators of a potential click on the AOI.

View Features capture whether the AOI is visible in the viewport. Invisible AOIs cannot be selected by searchers.

5.2 Model

We train a regression model to predict which result will be clicked. The training procedure builds an ensemble of decision trees based on gradient boosting [7]. This technique has been shown to provide state-of-the-art performance for various applications. In the context of learning to rank, we treat each cursor sample as a query and each u as a document. The objective of the model is to predict u^*. At test time, for each cursor sample, we featurize and score each $u \in \mathcal{U}$. If the score of one or more results is above τ, we fetch u with the highest score.

6. METHODS

We now define the methods employed in training and evaluating our prefetching models, starting with the log data.

6.1 Data

To record searcher interactions with the Bing SERP at scale without the need to install any browser plugins, we used an efficient and scalable approach [8]. JavaScript-based logging functions were embedded into the HTML source code of the SERP. To obtain a detailed understanding of user interactions with the SERP, we recorded information on mouse cursor movements, clicks, scrolling, text selection events, focus gain and loss events of the browser window, as well as bounding boxes of several AOIs on the SERP and the browser's viewport size. We optimize our implementation and run large-scale live experiments to ensure no significant delay in PLT for SERPs with this logging enabled.

The JavaScript function for logging mouse cursor positions checked the cursor's horizontal and vertical coordinates relative to the top-left corner of the SERP every 250 milliseconds. Whenever the cursor moved more than eight pixels away from its previously logged position, its new coordinates were sent to the remote Web server. Eight pixels correspond to approximately the height of half a line of text on the SERP. We used this approach rather than recording every cursor movement since we wanted to minimize the data gathered and transmitted so as to not adversely affect the user experience with delays associated with log data capture and data uploads to the remote server. Since cursor tracking was relative to the document, we captured cursor alignment to SERP content regardless of how the user reached that position (e.g., by scrolling or keyboard).

Mouse clicks were recorded using the JavaScript `onMouseDown` event handling method. The backend server received log entries with location coordinates for every mouse click, including clicks that occurred on a hyperlink as well as those that occurred elsewhere on the SERP (even on white space containing no content). To identify clicks on hyperlinks and differentiate them from clicks on inactive page elements, we logged unique hyperlink identifiers embedded in the SERP.

The width and height of the browser viewport in pixels at SERP load time were also logged. This told us which AOIs were visible. Browser window resizing during SERP interaction was not accounted for. We also recorded the current scroll position, i.e., the vertical coordinate of the uppermost visible pixel of the SERP in the browser viewport. This coordinate was checked three times per second and was recorded whenever it had changed by more than 40 pixels compared to the last logged scrolling position. This corresponds to approximately the height of two lines of text.

Simply logging the text of what was displayed on the SERP is insufficient for reconstructing its layout since SERPs vary per query (depending on whether vertical results are shown, etc.), font sizes, and other browser preferences.

To reconstruct the exact SERP layout as it was rendered in the user's browser, we recorded the positions and sizes of AOIs. We use the method from [8] to identify and record the exact position of AOIs on SERP loading. The specific AOIs recorded were: (i) top and bottom search boxes, (ii) left rail and its contained related searches, search history, and query refinement areas, (iii) mainline results area and its contained result entries, including advertisements and answers, and (iv) right rail. Some of these AOIs are visualized in Figure 3. For each AOI bounding box, we determined and logged the coordinates of its upper left corner as well as its width and height in pixels. Using this information, we map cursor positions and clicks to AOIs. Although we record the position all AOIs shown in Figure 3, we focus only on predicting clicks on one of the ten result AOIs.

The final, processed dataset consists of batches of instances

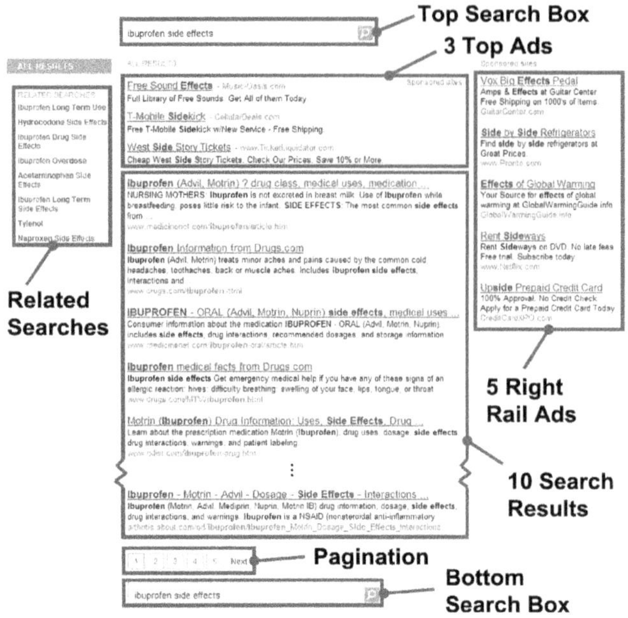

Figure 3: Segmentation of a search engine results page (SERP) by areas of interest (AOI). Each of the 10 search result captions (title, snippet, URL) is regarded as its own AOI. These 10 result AOIs are our click prediction targets.

of the form: $\langle \sigma, t, u, \phi, y \rangle$ where σ is a unique identifier for this impression, encoding information about the user and query, t denotes the timestamp (relative to 0) of the measurement, u is a unique identifier for the AOI, ϕ represents all of the feature values computed as discussed in Section 5.1, and y is a boolean variable indicating whether u was clicked during the session σ. We focus on impressions with exactly one detected click [1] and at least five detected cursor positions (73.8% of all query impressions). Running experiments with a smaller number of minimum cursor positions resulted in no performance differences relative to our baselines. This is because when cursor data is missing (<10% of all query impressions), our model effectively fall back to the strongest baseline of original search result ranking (as it is part of our model), and our gains over the baseline would just be slightly diluted by including this small fraction of traffic but findings and conclusions would remain the same.

We recorded the SERP interactions from the Microsoft Bing Web search engine. Log data were gathered from searchers in the control groups (i.e., with no experimental treatments on frontend or backend) of multiple experiments on the search engine in the U.S. English geographic locale, run between May 2011 and June 2012, during external experiments on small fractions of user traffic. For the duration of the experiments, all queries from searchers in the control groups (which is a representative sample of the overall search traffic) are recorded along with their cursor movements.

6.2 Training

We selected a random set of 100K users (and their 1M queries) from our dataset. We split the set by searcher and time with 80% for training and 20% for testing. That is, all tuples belonging to the same searcher–and therefore impression–were in the same split. The prediction targets are set to 4 for clicked hyperlinks and 0 for hyperlinks that were not clicked. Our model outputs a score for each hyperlink at each cursor movement, stopping and prefetching a link when its score exceeds a threshold τ. Instead of optimizing for a fixed τ, we present precision-recall curves to demonstrate performance at different operating points.

[1] The comparison on impressions without a click is not very relevant since they do not impact the user experience.

6.3 Evaluation

We focus evaluation on prefetching algorithmic search results. As discussed in Section 3, the page load time can vary dramatically. We therefore want to test our algorithm under various regimes. For a given score τ, we evaluate our algorithm when given at least ℓ milliseconds to fetch a page before the click. So, for example, if ℓ is 500 ms and the user took 2000 ms to investigate the page before clicking, then we can observe the user's behavior for 1500 ms before losing our chance to get any benefit from prefetching. We compute precision and recall for $\ell \in \{500, 5000\}$ to demonstrate regimes of normal and severely-limited bandwidth. For a given ℓ, the true positive (TP) is defined as the prefetching decision made for the link that was actually clicked at least ℓ time later. A negative (TN) occurs when the system accurately predicts that no clicks on any links occurred during the impression. The prefetching on an unclicked target link is considered false positive (FP) while prefetching made with lead time shorter than ℓ is considered as late positive (LP). A false negative (FN) is an impression where the model did not select any link, even though the user eventually clicked one. We evaluate the performance of our models (and the baselines described in the next subsection) using precision and recall. With the above definitions, the precision is then defined as $TP/(TP+FP)$ while recall is defined as $TP/(TP+LP+FN)$. Notice that a random prefetching system will achieve precision of $\frac{1}{|\mathcal{U}|}$.

6.4 Baselines

We employed three strong baselines: (i) the original search engine ranking, (ii) historic clicks from all searchers for the query, and (iii) historic clicks from the current searcher for the query. These baselines, in particular the latter two, are similar to prefetching methods proposed in prior research, in which, prefetching is determined by static estimates of likelihood of future content access from historic usage data [1, 13, 22, 26]. The baselines are defined as:

Search engine ranking: This baseline always prefetches the top-ranked result for the query as returned by the Bing search engine at the time the logs were collected. Note that this baseline is expected to be very strong since commercial search engines rank results by leveraging a variety of sources of evidence, including content and historic usage data, and the top-ranked search result often receives most clicks.

Historic clicks (all users) (denoted $p(click_{all})$): Selects the most popular clicked URL for the query. Multi-year click logs from a separate data source (same search engine, but not the cursor-tracking flights) were used to compute the probability of selecting a particular URL given the current query. The separate dataset was much larger than the set of data collected during the online cursor tracking experiments. This enabled broader query coverage and more reliable click predictions. The result that is most likely to be clicked based on this historic data was prefetched if it appeared in the current result ranking. To improve coverage, all URLs were normalized to remove trailing slashes, lowercase, and collapse https and http protocols.

Historic clicks (current user) (denoted $p(click_{user})$): Applies the personal navigation algorithm [43] to prefetch the result that was visited by the current searcher historically for the current query. Specifically, if the searcher has visited the same result for the previous two instances of the query, then that result will be prefetched for the current (third) instance of the query if it appears in the result ranking. URLs were normalized as with the previous baseline.

7. RESULTS

We now present our experimental results, starting with the descriptive statistics of the cursor movement data.

7.1 Descriptive Statistics

In this section, we characterize the features proposed in the previous subsection for building the prefetching models. Since our goal is to prefetch clicked results, we wanted to understand whether certain features could indicate future clicks. We report analysis across 41.6 million cursor samples from 186k unique query impressions used for training our model. The results are summarized in Table 2 and the discussions are organized by the feature group. We focus on the two classes of cursor samples with clicked AOI and unclicked AOI to understand the changes of feature values across the two groups. Features in the two global groups are impacting at the impression-level, i.e., features that impact overall clickthrough for the entire impression would, in turn, impact clickthrough for individual AOIs on the SERP. In contrast, the features in the two local groups impact directly regarding the AOI in question.

Static Global: All the features in this group are significantly different among the two groups. Interestingly, the queries with less clicks have higher frequencies, which may be due to the more likely presence of answer results – this hypothesis is further supported by the averaged higher value of the *has answer* feature in the *StaticLocal* group.

Dynamic Global: Almost all the features in this group are significantly different among the two groups except for cursor ycoord and cursor total time. The total cursor distance of cursor for the unclicked impressions is higher, as is the number of non-hyperlink clicks (often associated with text selections) and evidence of reading behavior, which suggest that people are exploring and more deeply engaged with examining the SERP (rather than clicking).

Static Local: All the features in this group are significantly different among the two classes. As we can see, certain types of AOIs are indeed more likely to attract more clicks. For example, the clicked class has larger *AOI area*, which makes sense, as larger AOI may be more likely to attract user attention. Other examples include the rate of AOI having the card attribute (e.g., additional information such as brand logo and/or deep links) which may increase both user confidence in document quality as well as attractiveness, resulting in more chance of clickthrough. In contrast, having answer directly in the AOI, as discussed earlier, reduces the chance of the AOI being clicked due to "good abandonment" [20]. Also, as expected, the clicked AOI tends to have lower rank (demonstrated by both lower *AOI rank* and *AOI ycoord*).

Dynamic Local: There are interesting differences in this group's features. Cursor hovers on the AOI are a significant indicator of an impending click, as is dwell time on the AOI (which is much higher when a click is observed). The speed and acceleration toward the AOI suggests that the searcher is performing a focused movement before the click. This is also supported by the higher value of *AOICursor ontarget*.

Table 2: Descriptive statistics of the proposed features for the two classes of cursor sample with clicked AOI and unclicked AOI. The differences between the two classes are statistically significant for the majority of the features based on Welch's t-test ($p < 0.05$) except for features that are noted with *. (s) denotes seconds, (px) denotes pixels.

Feature name	Mean (Standard deviation) Unclicked	Clicked
Static Global		
Query frequency	79K (408K)	74K (389K)
Query click entropy	1.697 (1.218)	1.630 (1.186)
SERP has advertisements	0.330 (0.470)	0.322 (0.467)
SERP has related searches	0.739 (0.439)	0.795 (0.403)
Dynamic Global		
Cursor xcoord (px)	457 (277)	468 (272)
Cursor ycoord (px)*	334 (224)	334 (228)
Cursor delta (px)	89 (123)	87 (121)
Num non hyperlink clicks	0.122 (0.010)	0.103 (0.010)
Cursor is reading	0.081 (0.273)	0.074 (0.261)
Cursor max ycoord (px)	396 (246)	397 (253)
Cursor max AOI rank	3.10 (2.25)	3.21 (2.10)
Cursor total distance (px)	773 (918)	765 (918)
Cursor total time (s)*	47 (54)	47 (55)
Cursor time delta (s)	6.17 (15.70)	5.93 (13.70)
Static Local		
AOI area (px^2)	58510 (35340)	75177 (51117)
AOI width (px)	682 (195)	632 (86)
AOI height (px)	89 (56)	120 (81)
AOI rank	5.75 (2.72)	2.57 (2.27)
AOI xcoord (px)	148 (75)	177 (39)
AOI ycoord (px)	515 (414)	354 (261)
AOI has card	0.002 (0.043)	0.192 (0.394)
AOI has answer	0.375 (0.484)	0.136 (0.343)
Dynamic Local		
AOI is visible	0.527 (0.499)	0.755 (0.430)
AOICursor hover	0.002 (0.107)	0.319 (0.466)
AOICursor distance (px)	558 (331)	367 (283)
AOICursor angle	4.21 (65.41)	16.39 (11.23)
AOICursor proximity	1.28 (0.84)	1.23 (0.61)
AOICursor speed	4.77 (36.47)	7.03 (39.04)
AOICursor acceleration	-0.104 (96.88)	0.667 (98.62)
AOICursor jerk*	2.45 (1010.79)	3.42 (977.76)
AOICursor ontarget	0.110 (0.372)	0.136 (0.455)
AOICursor xdistance (px)	316 (270)	299 (265)
AOICursor ydistance (px)	389 (312)	155 (176)
AOICursor dwell (s)	0.08 (0.64)	1.03 (2.50)
AOICursor title dwell (s)	0.03 (0.37)	0.34 (1.46)

7.2 Prefetching Experiments

We present the results of our prefetching experiments for different lead times in the precision-recall curves in Figure 4. As we can see from these curves, for comparable recall levels, we achieve substantial improvements over prefetching based on all cursor-agnostic methods. Although performance drops when we require a conservative five second leadtime, our algorithm still outperforms baselines by a significant margin. We present the results of significance tests in Table 3 for a high precision model (with a high value of τ) and a high recall model (with a low value of τ).

7.2.1 Effect of Query Type

One might suspect that pre-fetching decisions for naviga-

Table 3: Comparison with baselines. Superscripts denote statistically significant improvements over a competing run using a Student's t-test ($p < 0.05$) with respect to rank (r), $p(click_{all})$ (a), $p(click_{user})$ (u), high precision model (P), or high recall model (R).

Model	Precision	Recall
rank	0.605^{a}	0.602^{auP}
$p(click_{all})$	0.399	0.326^{u}
$p(click_{user})$	0.697^{ar}	0.032
high recall	0.723^{aur}	0.670^{aurP}
high precision	0.877^{aurR}	0.567^{au}

Table 4: The effectiveness of prefetching models trained suppressing the specified feature groups against the full model trained with all features the score threshold τ of 3 and a leadtime ℓ of 500 ms. * represents statistically significant *decreases* in performance with respect to using all features using a Student's t-test ($p < 0.05$).

Suppressed	Precision	Recall
-	0.877	0.567
Static Global	0.865*	0.566
Static Local	0.875	0.531*
All Static	0.819*	0.547*
Dynamic Global	0.877	0.563
Dynamic Local	0.876	0.464*
All Dynamic	0.831*	0.432*
User Deviation	0.880	0.563

tional queries, because they have a single target result, can be made without cursor information. To test this, we examined the performance of our algorithm on queries defined as navigational (i.e., with a click entropy less than or equal to one, as in [42]). Figure 4b demonstrates the higher performance of all methods, including baselines. The differences in performance are statistically significant ($p < 0.05$). We similarly investigated the performance of our model when evaluating only on informational queries (i.e., queries with a click entropy of two or more (again, as in [42]). These queries involve more thorough examination of the ranked list. This behavior can result from either multiple intents, poor retrieval performance, or higher recall intent. Because of the diversity of the click patterns, we suspect that our baselines will perform less well on these queries. The results (Figure 4c) demonstrate the lower performance of all runs, including our model. Nevertheless, the model-based approach significantly improves over the baselines ($p < 0.05$).

7.2.2 Feature Ablation

We present the feature ablation experiments in Table 4, where we remove one feature group at a time to examine the effectiveness of each of them in the presence of other feature groups. To do this, we use the high precision model, whose overall results are reported in Table 3. Static features, taken as a whole, contribute substantially (removing them results in a 6.6% drop in precision and a 3.5% drop in recall). This reflects the importance of visual layout and attractiveness in successful prefetching. Importantly, the degradation is not observed when suppressing global or local features alone, suggesting that static features perform best when using conjunctions of local and global features. Dynamic features, taken as a whole, also provide significant information (removing them results in a 5.2% drop in precision and a 23.8% drop in recall). The majority of this contribution comes from local features, suggesting that information about the AOI with respect to the cursor are critical to high performance. The local features are important in recall since they provide signals about each of the AOIs that may be missed in general SERP-level analysis. For the high precision model, user deviation features appear to add no value over the other features, in combination.

Table 5: Feature importance. Five most and least important features and weights. Weights are normalized to be in unit range with respect to the most important feature (AOICursor hover from the *Dynamic Local* class).

Feature name	Importance
AOICursor hover	1.000000
AOI has card	0.443321
AOI rank	0.373836
Cursor max AOI rank	0.228811
Query frequency	0.077288
⋮	⋮
USERDEV AOICursor acceleration	0.000066
AOICursor jerk	0.000062
USERDEV AOICursor jerk	0.000062
AOICursor on target	0.000061
Cursor is reading	0.000000

7.2.3 Feature Importance

Finally, we wanted to understand feature importance. We present the most and least informative features in Table 5. Unsurprisingly, hovering over an AOI is a strong signal that a click is imminent. Other *Dynamic Local* features, such as AOICursor ydistance, are also important but are not in the top five. While features such as the rank position of the result AOI and the distance between the cursor and the AOI might seem obvious, others are less so. The presence of a card suggests that the visual attractiveness of an AOI may result in a higher clickthrough rate. Variations in searcher attention as a function of caption attractiveness have been noted in previous studies (e.g., [11]). Conversely, query click entropy appears to help the model distinguish between more predictable behavior connected to navigational intentions and less predictable behaviors for informational intent. The less informative features involve more granular cursor movements (e.g., jerk, acceleration), suggesting that in order to perform effectively our prefetching model only requires a coarse model of search interaction behavior.

8. DISCUSSION AND IMPLICATIONS

We have introduced the search result prefetching challenge and real-time prefetching methods to address it based primarily on cursor movements. Our approach significantly outperforms three strong baselines leveraging result rankings and historic clicks to prefetch search results. Analysis of the differences between the prefetch time and click time reveals that on average, our method could save searchers around 650ms per query for the 65% of queries where our model correctly prefetches the clicked result. The average prefetch lead time is 6-7 seconds (depending on τ), but we

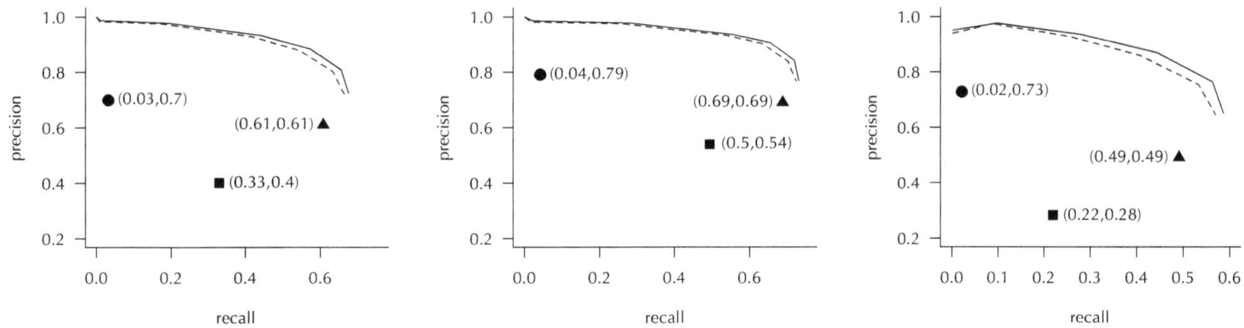

(a) All (b) Navigational (c) Informational

Figure 4: Click precision and recall. The solid line indicates performance as a function of the score threshold τ for a leadtime ℓ of 500ms. The dashed line indicates the performance for a leadtime ℓ of 5s. The points indicate the performance of baselines prefetching based on rank position (▲), the probability of click (all users) (■), and probability of click (current user) (●).

cap our time savings to the median landing page load time from earlier (672ms). 650ms in time savings per accurate prediction is a sizable efficiency increase, especially at Web scale, where prefetching could benefit millions of searchers.

Our findings showed that we can achieve strong prediction accuracy. As with other studies [8, 9] we noted evidence of task effects (e.g., our models do better for navigational queries, where search behavior is more predictable). We break out our findings by query type, but not by searcher type. Variability in interactions between searchers is high [8] and differences in model performance per individual or cohort should be considered. This could inform decisions about the selective application of cursor-based prefetching.

There are some limitations in this study. First, we consider prefetching only one result per SERP. In the future, we plan to extend our method to handle prefetching of multiple results during SERP examination. Second, in our evaluation we represent cost as the action of prefetching a result. In practice, cost is more nuanced: there is a variable cost associated with prefetching, depending on the nature of the prefetched page (e.g., size, content types). Third, we have not fully explored the trade-off between client-side code optimization and its impact on prefetching performance. In the current implementation, we optimize our client-side code to ensure no significant delay on PLT for SERPs with the logging enabled. This includes lazy loading of the logging code, enforcing mouse sampling (i.e., every 250ms or 8px of movement), and optimizing our prediction latency in both feature extraction (i.e., constant time in the number of cursor samples) and model execution (i.e., using decision trees, which can be turned into heavily optimized binaries). However, we do not know whether these optimizations are truly optimal and plan to further explore this in future work. Finally, we focused on desktop devices (e.g., PCs) in this study. We will extend our methods to mobile devices (e.g., smartphones, tablets), where multi-touch interactions and viewport dynamics would replace the mouse cursor. Bandwidth may be more limited in mobile settings and result prefetching could prove to be more valuable therein.

Looking ahead, the ability to prefetch visited resources has a number of implications. People on slow network connections (e.g., in developing countries or remote locations in developed countries) can benefit from faster landing page loading, as would those engaged in time-critical tasks [28]. Accurately prefetching clicked results also allows search engines to offer enhanced interaction capabilities such as augmenting landing pages to better support transitions from SERPs (e.g., clickable snippets [15]). More broadly, our prefetching methods could help reduce latency in any Website, especially those with low traffic or large amounts of dynamically-generated content; both of which can hinder the use of historic activity in prefetching decisions.

9. CONCLUSIONS AND FUTURE WORK

We presented a dynamic framework for prefetching Web pages in response to SERP interaction behavior. Previous models have focused on static prediction using historic data. We show that incorporating aspects of the SERP visual layout and dynamic on-SERP behavior, such as cursor movement, can substantially improve the accuracy of real-time prefetching decisions and may improve searcher efficiency. In future work, we will experiment with more sophisticated models to better capture the temporal dynamics and personal nature of cursor movements. While our technique generalizes beyond SERPs, optimal performance may require task-specific models. We will extend our analysis to a diverse range of non-SERP Web pages. Finally, we will adapt our models to mobile devices where viewport and touch interactions can be leveraged in place of cursor movements.

10. REFERENCES

[1] E. Agichtein and Z. Zheng. Identifying "best bet" web search results by mining past user behavior. *SIGKDD*, 902–908, 2006.

[2] I. Arapakis, X. Bai, and B.B. Cambazoglu. Impact of response latency on user behavior in web search. *SIGIR*, 103–112, 2014.

[3] M. Barreda-Ángeles et al. Unconscious physiological effects of search latency on users and their click behaviour. *SIGIR*, 203–212, 2015.

[4] T. Asano, E. Sharlin, Y. Kitamura, K. Takashima, and F. Kishino. Predictive interaction using the delphian desktop. *UIST*, 133–141, 2005.

[5] R. Baeza-Yates et al. The impact of caching on search engines. *SIGIR*, 183–190, 2007.

[6] R. Blanco et al. Caching search engine results over incremental indices. *SIGIR*, 82–89, 2010.

[7] C.J. Burges. From ranknet to lambdarank to lambdamart: An overview. Technical Report MSR-TR-2010-82, Microsoft Research, 2010.

[8] G. Buscher et al. Large-scale analysis of individual and task differences in search result page examination strategies. *WSDM*, 373–382, 2012.

[9] E. Cutrell and Z. Guan. What are you looking for?: An eye-tracking study of information usage in web search. *SIGCHI*, 407–416, 2007.

[10] J. Dean and L.A. Barroso. The tail at scale. *CACM*, 56(2):74–80, 2013.

[11] F. Diaz et al. Robust models of mouse movement on dynamic web search results pages. *CIKM*, 1451–1460, 2013.

[12] Z. Dou, R. Song, and J.-R. Wen. A large-scale evaluation and analysis of personalized search strategies. *WWW*, 581–590, 2007.

[13] T. Fagni et al. Boosting the performance of web search engines: Caching and prefetching query results by exploiting historical usage data. *TOIS*, 24(1):51–78, 2006.

[14] L. Fan et al. Web prefetching between low-bandwidth clients and proxies: Potential and performance. *SIGMETRICS*, 178–187, 1999.

[15] H. Feild, R.W. White, and X. Fu. Supporting orientation during search result examination. *SIGCHI*, 2999–3008, 2013.

[16] Q. Guo and E. Agichtein. Towards predicting web searcher gaze position from mouse movements. *SIGIR*, 3601–3606, 2010.

[17] Q. Guo and E. Agichtein. Beyond dwell time: estimating document relevance from cursor movements and other post-click searcher behavior. *WWW*, 569–578, 2012.

[18] E. Horvitz. Continual computation policies for utility-directed prefetching. *CIKM*, 175–184, 1998.

[19] J. Huang, R.W. White, and G. Buscher. User see, user point: Gaze and cursor alignment in web search. *SIGCHI*, 1341–1350, 2012.

[20] J. Huang, R.W. White, and S. Dumais. No clicks, no problem: using cursor movements to understand and improve search. *SIGCHI*, 1225–1234, 2011.

[21] T. Joachims et al. Accurately interpreting clickthrough data as implicit feedback. *SIGIR*, 154–161, 2005.

[22] S. Jonassen, L. Granka, and F. Silvestri. Prefetching Query Results and Its Impact on Search Engines. *SIGIR*, 631–640, 2012.

[23] D. Lagun et al. Discovering common motifs in cursor movement data for improving web search. *WSDM*, 183–192, 2014.

[24] D.M. Lane et al. A process for anticipating and executing icon selection in graphical user interfaces. *Int. J. Human-Computer Inter.*, 19(2):241–252, 2005.

[25] S. Lee, J. Yoo, and G. Han. Gaze-assisted user intention prediction for initial delay reduction in web video access. *Sensors*, 15:14679–14700, 2015.

[26] R. Lempel and S. Moran. Predictive caching and prefetching of query results in search engines. *WWW*, 19–28, 2003.

[27] R.B. Miller. Response time in man-computer conversational transactions. *AFIPS*, 267–277, 1968.

[28] N. Mishra et al. Time-critical search. *SIGIR*, 747–756, 2014.

[29] A. Murata. Improvement of pointing time by predicting targets in pointing with a pc mouse. *Int. J. Human-Computer Interaction*, 10(1):23–32, 1998.

[30] F.F. Nah. A study on tolerable waiting time: how long are Web users willing to wait? *Behaviour & Information Technology*, 23(3):153–163, 2004.

[31] J. Nielsen. *Usability Engineering.* Morgan Kaufmann, 1993.

[32] J. Nielsen. User interface directions for the web. *CACM*, 42(1):65–72, 1999.

[33] V.N. Padmanabhan and J.C. Mogul. Using predictive prefetching to improve world wide web latency. *SIGCOMM Comput. Commun. Rev.*, 26(3):22–36, 1996.

[34] P.T. Pasqual and J.O. Wobbrock. Mouse pointing endpoint prediction using kinematic template matching. *SIGCHI*, 743–752, 2014.

[35] J. Psaroudakis and M. Khambatti. A deeper look at task completion. blogs.bing.com/search/2013/10/14/a-deeper-look-at-task-completion, 2013.

[36] J. Ramsay, A. Barbesi, and J. Preece. A psychological investigation of long retrieval times on the world wide web. *Interacting with Computers*, 10(1):77–86, 1998.

[37] K. Rodden et al. Eye-mouse coordination patterns on web search results pages. *SIGCHI EA*, 2997–3002, 2008.

[38] E. Schurman and J. Brutlag. Performance related changes and their user impact. *Velocity*, 2009.

[39] B. Shneiderman. Response time and display rate in human performance with computers. *ACM Comput. Surv.*, 16(3):265–285, 1984.

[40] A. Singhal and M. Cutts. Using site speed in web search ranking. googlewebmastercentral.blogspot.com/2010/04/using-site-speed-in-web-search-ranking.html, 2010.

[41] J. Teevan et al. Slow search. *CACM*, 57(8):36–38, 2014.

[42] J. Teevan, S.T. Dumais, and D.J. Liebling. To personalize or not to personalize: Modeling queries with variation in user intent. *SIGIR*, 163–170, 2008.

[43] J. Teevan, D.J. Liebling, and G. Ravichandran Geetha. Understanding and predicting personal navigation. *WSDM*, 85–94, 2011.

[44] R.W. White, P. Bailey, and L. Chen. Predicting user interests from contextual information. *SIGIR*, 363–370, 2009.

[45] Q. Yang, H.H. Zhang, and T. Li. Mining web logs for prediction models in www caching and prefetching. *SIGKDD*, 473–478, 2001.

[46] B. Ziebart, A. Dey, and J.A. Bagnell. Probabilistic pointing target prediction via inverse optimal control. *IUI*, 1–10, 2012.

Predicting Search User Examination with Visual Saliency

Yiqun Liu[†], Zeyang Liu[†], Ke Zhou[‡], Meng Wang[⋆], Huanbo Luan[†], Chao Wang[†],
Min Zhang[†], Shaoping Ma[†],
[†]Tsinghua National Laboratory for Information Science and Technology, Department of Computer Science & Technology, Tsinghua University, Beijing, China
[‡]Yahoo! Research, London, U.K.
[⋆]School of Computer and Information, HeFei University of Technology, Hefei, China
yiqunliu@tsinghua.edu.cn

ABSTRACT

Predicting users' examination of search results is one of the key concerns in Web search related studies. With more and more heterogeneous components federated into search engine result pages (SERPs), it becomes difficult for traditional position-based models to accurately predict users' actual examination patterns. Therefore, a number of prior works investigate the connection between examination and users' explicit interaction behaviors (e.g. click-through, mouse movement). Although these works gain much success in predicting users' examination behavior on SERPs, they require the collection of large scale user behavior data, which makes it impossible to predict examination behavior on newly-generated SERPs. To predict user examination on SERPs containing heterogenous components without user interaction information, we propose a new prediction model based on visual saliency map and page content features. Visual saliency, which is designed to measure the likelihood of a given area to attract human visual attention, is used to predict users' attention distribution on heterogenous search components. With an experimental search engine, we carefully design a user study in which users' examination behavior (eye movement) is recorded. Examination prediction results based on this collected data set demonstrate that visual saliency features significantly improve the performance of examination model in heterogeneous search environments. We also found that saliency features help predict internal examination behavior within vertical results.

Keywords

User behavior analysis; Visual saliency; Eye tracking

1. INTRODUCTION

Web search has reached a level at which a good understanding of user interactions may significantly impact its quality. Among all kinds of user interactions, examination is an important one that are studied by many research works. Our understanding on how users allocate their limited attention to search engine result pages (SERPs) can contribute to improving search UI design, result ranking, performance evaluation, ad delivery and many other research issues in Web search. It also plays a central role in the *Examination Hypothesis* [9, 40], which is the basis of most search engine click model construction efforts [6, 8, 44].

One of the most frequently adopted information sources in search examination studies is the eye movement data collected by eye-tracking devices. According to the findings in cognitive psychological studies, vision appears to be blurred during saccades and new information is only acquired during eye fixations in the reading process [36]. Therefore, eye fixation sequence on SERP is usually adopted as a strong signal of search examination behavior according to the *strong eye-mind hypothesis* [27], that there is no appreciable lag between what is fixated on and what is processed.

Although eye tracking studies are able to offer rich detailed information about users' examination behaviors, the high cost and inconvenience of eye tracking devices limit the application of this methodology.[1] Therefore, some prior studies [15, 19] try to use mouse interaction information (e.g. click, movement and scroll) as a cheap surrogate to model and predict users' examination behaviors. These works reveal a strong correlation between eye fixation and mouse positions. However, these mouse-interaction-based researches also have their limitations. In these research works, users' mouse interaction data is required to predict search examination behaviors. It means that it is impossible for us to predict examination behavior on newly generated SERPs which are not shown to users yet. Firstly, considering the fact that there are a large number of long-tailed queries which are only submitted by one or few search users [38], modeling examination behaviors on their corresponding SERPs becomes rather difficult. Secondly, more and more heterogenous components are federated into SERPs and many of them contain highly dynamic information (e.g. news verticals). It makes it rather questionable whether examination behavior predicted based on a previous SERP can be adopted to the current one since the contents may have partially changed. Therefore, a more practical examination prediction method should rely on static (cold-start) information of SERPs and avoid the usage of user interaction information.

One of the key concerns in click model construction researches is to infer users' examination probabilities on search results. Therefore, most existing click models propose their assumptions in how users examine results on SERPs. Some of these assumptions (e.g. in Cascade model [9], DCM [14], DBN [6], UBM [12]) regard the results as homogeneous and take the position factor into consideration. Meanwhile, some recent proposed models also try to model users' behavior on heterogeneous SERPs (e.g. FCM [7], VCM [44])

[1] Although some inexpensive eye-tracking solutions such as the eye tribe (https://theeyetribe.com) exist, they still require each user to equip one on the PC and calibrate each time before usage, which makes it impossible for large scale user behavior data collection.

SIGIR '16, July 17-21, 2016, Pisa, Italy
© 2016 ACM. ISBN 978-1-4503-4069-4/16/07...$15.00
DOI: http://dx.doi.org/10.1145/2911451.2911517

and thus incorporate presentation style information as well. Since models that only consider position information may not perform well for SERPs that contain heterogeneous components [44], the assumptions in click models that can deal with vertical results should be adopted in practical examination prediction tasks. However, these click models also suffer from the same problem as mouse interaction based works: they cannot be adopted to previously unseen SERPs because they rely on users' click-through information to infer the examination behavior.

To shed light on the research question and propose an effective examination prediction method which relies only on static features (features that can be collected without user interaction), we propose to predict user examination with visual saliency information on SERPs. Visual saliency[2], as a measure of the likelihood of a location to attract human visual attention, has been widely adopted in the communities of Computer Vision (CV) and Human Computer Interaction (HCI). Many research efforts [22, 23] have revealed a strong connection between human attention and saliency map. Considering the existence of attractiveness bias in user behavior on SERPs with heterogeneous components [7, 29, 34, 44], saliency features may be suitable to model the influence of these components whose presentation styles are different from organic search results.

Take the two SERP samples in Figure 1 for example, the figures 1(a), 1(b) and 1(c) are corresponding to a SERP with only organic results while figures 1(d), 1(e) and 1(f) are corresponding to a SERP with an image vertical result ranked at the 5th position. The left, middle and right figures show users' eye fixation heatmaps (a, d), mouse hover positions (b, e) and the SERP images' visual saliency maps (c, f), respectively. From these figures we can see that the mouse hover positions correlate well with users' eye fixation positions, which validates previous findings in [11, 15, 19] that mouse movement data can serve as a surrogate for search users' fixation behaviors. We also noticed that the visual saliency maps are similar with eye fixation maps in certain parts of the SERPs. Particularly, the salient points in Figure 1(f) are quite similar with the eye fixation points in Figure 1(d), which are both located close to the image vertical result. Salient points in Figure 1(c) do not accord so well with eye fixation points in Figure 1(a) but they still provide some traces of the fixation points at lower-ranked results (e.g. the 4th and 5th results).

From Figure 1, we find that visual saliency information may provide some insights into users' examination behaviors, especially when mouse movement information (those recorded in Figure 1(b) and (e)) is absent. The salient points may not reflect well the position bias phenomena (i.e. the golden triangle) because top-ranked results do not necessarily contain visually salient components. However, it helps provide information on the modeling of attractiveness of search results, which is particularly important for SERPs with heterogeneous components [7, 34, 44]. It makes us believe that a prediction framework based on traditional position factors and the newly proposed visual saliency information may be a better way than existing solutions in modeling the examination behavior of search users.

To our best knowledge, we are among the first to adopt visual saliency information in predicting search examination behavior. A recent work [30] also propose to incorporate content salience into predicting user attention on SERPs. Their proposed MICS method (Mixture of Interactions and Content Salience) is adopted to predict users' eye-fixation points on multiple popular types of Web content pages and gains much success. We believe that their work and

[2]In this paper, we use the term *visual saliency* to describe a computational model of users' observed examination behavior.

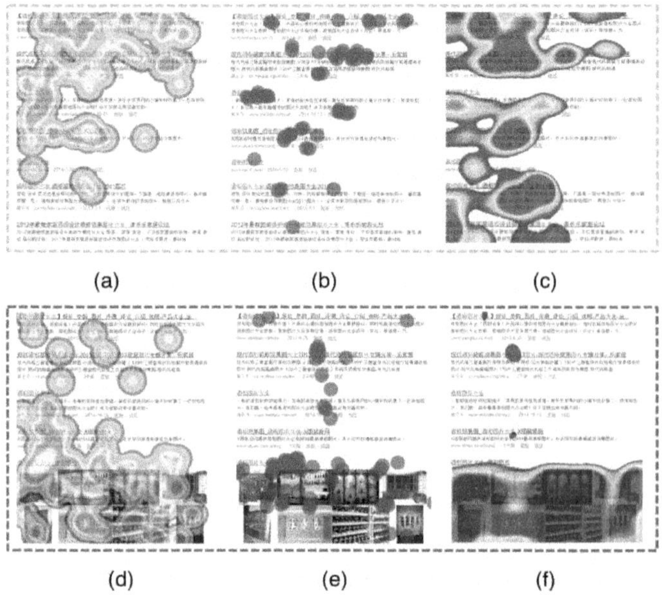

Figure 1: **Heatmaps of eye fixation (a, d), mouse hover (b, e) and visual saliency (c, f) on two search result pages (a, b, c: a SERP with only organic results; d, e, f: a SERP with both organic and image vertical results).**

our proposed method share a similar idea of incorporating salience information into examination models, but there are still many important differences. Firstly, their proposed method depends on user interaction behavior (e.g. mouse movement) in the prediction process. Therefore, it does not only rely on static features as our method and may also encounter the problem of inapplicability for newly-generated SERPs as other mouse-interaction-based methods do. Secondly, the MICS method in [30] uses page structure information (e.g. font size, image size, etc.) to calculate the salient points on Web pages, which means that it does not directly take the visual content information into consideration. Different from MICS, we are the first to use visual saliency maps derived from image content to predict users' examination behaviors. It makes it possible for us to take the influence of images with different color tones, edge densities and contrasts into consideration. Last but not least, our proposed method does not require the collection of extra user behavior data such as mouse movement information like in MICS. Experimental results in Section 5.5 also show that the visual saliency map extraction process can be quite efficient. Therefore, the proposed method is a relatively "cheap" solution for examination behavior prediction tasks.

Our contributions in this paper are three-fold: 1) We propose a novel examination prediction method that only utilizes the static information of SERPs, which makes it much more applicable to practical Web search environment than existing user-interaction-based solutions, especially for long-tailed queries. 2) By taking visual saliency map into consideration, the proposed method can be adopted to both homogeneous and heterogeneous search environment. 3) Besides page-level result examination behavior prediction, the proposed method can also model the internal examination behavior patterns of results within the vertical blocks.

The rest of the paper is organized as follows. Section 2 presents an overview of the related work. Then we introduce the experimental design for collecting user behavior data in Section 3. In Section 4 and 5 respectively, we describe the implementation of the saliency model, and discuss the results on using our model to predict search users' examination. We conclude the paper in Section 6.

2. RELATED WORK

Three lines of researches are closely related to the search user examination and attention prediction problem we describe in this paper: Web search eye-tracking studies, eye-mouse coordination, and visual saliency model.

2.1 Eye-tracking studies in Web search

The application of eye-tracking devices to Web search has received a considerable amount of attention from both academic and industrial researchers. Eye-tracking devices allow researchers to record users' real-time eye movement information, which helps better understand how users examine results on SERPs.

Granka et al. [13], Richardson et al. [40] and Joachims et al. [24, 25] used eye-tracking devices to analyze users' eye fixation distributions on SERPs and examination sequences throughout search tasks. Cutrell et al. [10] further investigated how users' eye movement behavior varies with different search intents. Recent work [34, 44] found that different result appearances might create different biases on eye movement behavior for both vertical and organic results on SERPs. Navalpakkam et al. [37] found that the flow of user attention on nonlinear page layouts is different from the widely believed top-down linear examination order of search results.

Based on these findings, a number of generative click models [6, 8, 9, 12, 44] have been constructed to model users' behavior during the search process. Most of these studies follow the strong eye-mind hypothesis [27] and regard eye fixation sequences to be the same as users' examination sequences.

2.2 Eye-Mouse Coordination in Web search

While eye movements during a search process can give us much insight into users' examination behavior, it is not applicable at large-scale in practice due to the high expense of eye-tracking devices. Therefore, many researchers turn to mouse movement information, which can be collected at large scale to simulate eye movements. Rodden et al. [41] identified multiple patterns of eye-mouse coordination, including the mouse following behavior in both vertical and horizonal directions while the eye inspected results. They also found a general correlation between eye and mouse positions, where the centers of the distribution of the eye/mouse distances are quite close to each other. Huang et al. [19] extended these findings by investigating variations in eye-mouse distances over time. They found that the distance between eye fixated points and cursors peaked approximately 600 ms after page loading and decreased over time. They also found that the mouse tended to be behind eye gaze by approximately 700 ms on average. These findings show that mouse movements may not be a good indicator for the current eye fixation position. However, in the whole session level it can help us identify which results are ever fixated by users.

Huang et al. [21] found correlations between result relevance and the cursor hovering behavior on the SERP. They incorporated mouse hover and scroll information as additional signals into click models to improve click prediction performance and gain promising results [20]. Guo et al. [16] analyzed the relationship between examination patterns and result relevance from post-click behaviors including cursor movements on landing pages. They constructed a predictive model to capture these patterns in order to improve search result ranking. Although mouse movements can be collected inexpensively in large-scale experiments, it is still difficult for commercial search engine to collect this kind of information in practical environment because it leads to extra burden for front-end servers. Considering the existence of the situations where users' behavior information is unavailable (e.g. on newly-generated pages), it is difficult for these models to predict users' behavior. Using static features of Web pages makes it possible to address this problem and predict users' examination without collecting users' interaction information.

2.3 Saliency-based Model

The idea of identifying salient items in search process has been investigated in a number of existing researches such as [2], in which "salient result" is defined as the one that users should examine or click in the next round of actions according to a theoretical framework (e.g. Search Economic Theory). However, in this paper, we focus on the concept of visual saliency of results on SERPs. Koch and Ullman [28] were among the first to introduce the concept of a saliency map, which is an explicit two-dimensional map that describes the saliency of objects or regions in the visual environment. Based on the idea of saliency map construction, Itti et al. [22] proposed an algorithmatic implementation to model saliency-based visual attention. They presented a bottom-up model to describe the pre-attentive selection mechanism, which works in three steps. Firstly, visual features (e.g. color, intensity and orientation) are extracted from the input image in the scene. Secondly, saliency features compete with each other in each feature map according to a certain strategy (e.g. winner-take-all). Finally, these different feature maps are combined at each location and summed into an unique saliency map. Inspired by the architecture of this saliency model, many saliency-based models have been proposed. For example, GBVS model [17], which is a complete bottom-up saliency model, creates feature maps applying Itti's method and perform their normalization and combination process with graph-based approaches. By extending from traditional saliency framework, some prior work [26, 31, 42] incorporated middle-level or high-level image features into attention models and performed a supervised training to predict eye fixations on images. The results of these work indicated that higher level features may be more effective in the attention prediction tasks.

Because the mechanism of selective visual attention may direct our gaze rapidly towards objects of interest in our visual field [23], saliency maps are usually applied to help analyze and predict users attention distributions. For example, Peters et al. [39] proposed an extension of saliency model to predict users' attention while they are playing video games. Carmi et al. [5] applied saliency models in dynamic scenes. Some existing studies also develop attention prediction models based on saliency information, such as [30]. However, to our best knowledge, the visual saliency model has not been adopted in predicting search examination behavior in Web search scenario. Our study indicates that saliency features can improve the performance of examination models and play an important role in predicting users' examination in Web search.

3. COLLECTING USER BEHAVIOR

3.1 Collection Procedure

To investigate the relationship between examination behavior and visual saliency features, we perform a user study to collect examination behavior on SERPs with the help of eye-tracking device (i.e. eye saccades and fixations on different areas of the SERPs). Considering that the presentation style of vertical result may have a strong effect on examination behavior [7, 34, 44], we implement an experimental search engine system to control the ranking position of both organic and vertical results.

With the experimental system, the user study is performed in the following steps. Firstly, we prepare two warm-up tasks to ensure that each participant is familiar with the experimental procedure and search system. In this step, each participant is told that his/her

Table 1: **Example search tasks in the user study**

Task Initial Query	Incorporated Vertical Result
Ancient Greek Architectural style	Textual
The 9th zone (movie)	Encyclopedia
Nike basketball shoes	Image-only
iTunes download	Application
Ebola virus mutation	News

eye movements will be recorded while they are performing a few search tasks so that we can design better search systems. After the two warm-up tasks, participants are asked to go through calibration processes with the eye tracking device. Then they are instructed to finish the same set of 30 search tasks. All of the search tasks adopted in this study are selected from real-world commercial search logs so that they contain the practical users' search intention (some example tasks are shown in Table 1). To make sure that all participants see the same SERP in each search task, we provided a fixed initial query and its corresponding first result page from a popular commercial search engine (the same one which provides search logs) for each task.

Participants are allowed to click on any result link and visit the landing page for as long as they wish. The purpose of this design is to simulate the realistic search scenario in an experimental environment. At the end of the experiment, participants were required to provide some feedback about their search experiences and compensated with about US$10.

3.2 SERP Generation

In order to thoroughly investigate the influence of saliency features in practical search scenario, both organic-only and federated search pages were taken into consideration in our experiment. All the results of these pages, including both organic and vertical results, are crawled from the same commercial search engine and the original ranking of these organic results were preserved in the SERP generation process. The same protocol was also adopted in our previous work [34]. Since prior studies [1, 3, 7, 34, 44, 45] reveal that different factors of verticals lead to different behavior biases in heterogeneous search environment, we also take three aspects of federated search into account:

- Vertical type. We choose the same set of vertical result types as in some existing works [34, 44], including textual, encyclopedia, image, application-download and news verticals.
- Vertical position. Each vertical result is placed at the 1st, 3rd or 5th position of an SERP shown to participants (corresponding to the top, middle or bottom of the first viewport, respectively).
- Vertical relevance. For each search query, we collect both a relevant vertical and an irrelevant one from the search engine. The irrelevant vertical was collected by revising the original query to a related but different query so that it is actually not relevant to the user query. It is worth noting that these two verticals are all presented in the same layouts and presentation styles on SERPs.

Therefore, we generate six different federated SERPs (relevant or irrelevant vertical at 3 position options) per search task. Each federated SERP comprises one specific vertical and nine organic results. When a participant starts a certain task, one of the corresponding vertical results is randomly integrated into the SERP at the 1st, 3rd or 5th position. Following the pre-procedure steps above, we finally generated 180 (30 search tasks $\times$ 3 positions options $\times$ 2 vertical relevance) federated pages and 30 organic-only SERPs in total. To make sure that all tasks are completed with equal opportunities in each SERP condition, we used a Graeco-Latin square design [4, 18] to show tasks and conditions to participants. All the generated SERPs can be found in the public available dataset (see Section 5.1 for more details) to prompt reproductivity of the findings in the work.

4. EXAMINATION PREDICTION WITH VISUAL SALIENCY

With the information collected from the procedure described in Section 3, we aim to verify in this section the assumption that visual saliency information is useful in the examination prediction task. We start by describing the saliency model adopted in our study, and then present the features and our prediction models.

4.1 Visual Saliency Modeling on SERPs

Saliency map is an explicit two-dimensional map that encodes the saliency or conspicuity of objects in the visual scene. Most saliency models [17, 22, 23] were biologically inspired and based on a bottom-up computational model, which assumes that competition among neurons in saliency map causes a single winning location that corresponds to the next users' attention. Typically, there are three main steps in the generation of saliency models. Firstly, the input image is decomposed into multiple low-level visual features (e.g. color, intensity and orientation) and transferred to a set of static feature maps based on these pre-attentive features. After that, saliency models combine all the feature maps into a unique saliency map after neurons in each feature map compete for salience. This is the key step in the generation procedure and different competitive strategies may significantly affect the performance of saliency models. In the last step, models detect the most salient location and predict user next attend target based on winner-take-all network.

Considering the fact that vertical results are more likely to attract users' visual attention, we believe that the saliency model may also be appropriate to describe the implicit bias of user examination in search scenario, especially in federated search environment. In other words, saliency models can help capture the salient sections of pages and model the examination bias caused by verticals or other heterogeneous elements.

To predict users' examination behavior on SERPs, we selected one traditional and two state-of-the-art saliency models to generate the static saliency features. The traditional saliency model is presented by Itti et al. [22] in 2000, which model has been adopted by many works [23, 26] to predict the first few seconds of user attention on a wide range of images. Besides the traditional model, two state-of-the-art saliency models were also selected. The first one is the Graph-Based Visual Saliency (GBVS) model proposed in [17], which is one of the best performers in the evaluation benchmark of MIT300[3]. The second adopted state-of-the-art model is the TIP model proposed in [32]. This model is based on intermediate features between the low-level and the object-level features, and show promising results in multiple benchmarks. In our experiment, we deploy these three models to generate saliency maps of SERP pages (with color information) and extract saliency features from the corresponding saliency map. Considering the scrolling behavior may cause modification of salience distribution, we only focus on the examination behavior in the first viewport (containing first five or six search results of the SERP in general). It means that we construct static saliency maps based on the first viewport and predict users' examination in the first viewport of pages. Since most visual saliency models are designed to predict the first few fixation

[3]http://saliency.mit.edu/results.html

points of users, it is reasonable to focus on the first viewport. From the practical application's point of view, the prediction of examination behavior on the first viewport is also most important because users pay much attention on this set of results due to the existence of position bias [13, 24] (i.e. users tend to examine the search results from top to bottom of the ranking list while the probability of examination decreases dramatically as the ranking position increases).

4.2 Extraction of Saliency-based Features

The aim of our study is to develop a general model to predict user examination which only relies on static information of the SERPs. We mainly take two kinds of static features into account: content features and visual saliency features (shown in Table 2).

Similar to content feature group in the MICS method [30], we also concentrate on both layout information about results' positions, sizes of area, font sizes, and content information such as the number of child elements and area of images. These features are regarded as content features in experiment and many of them are believed to contain content saliency information according to [30].

Table 2: **Content and saliency features in examination models**

Feature Name	Feature Description
Content	Position of the given element
	Type of the given element
	Number of links and images
	Left, top, width, height
	Number of child elements
	Area of text and image
	Text space divided by the element's area
	Font size of the element's text
Saliency	Sum, mean and variance of the given element
	Histogram vector of the given element

To extract visual saliency features, we firstly calculate the salience value for each pixel in the target image using the saliency models as introduced in section 4.1. It is worth noting that different input images lead to completely different saliency maps. As mentioned, in our study, we take the first viewport of pages as the input images of saliency models. Then we compute the statistic information such as sum, mean and variance of each result block with the salience value of generated saliency maps. In addition, to further record the distribution of salient points in result blocks, we generated a histogram of salience values (in 5 equal bins) in the target images as features. The boundaries of each bin depend on the minimum and maximum salience values in the target image.

4.3 Prediction Models

We utilize machine learning models for the purpose of predicting examination behavior. Specifically, machine learning models consist of three types of variants: the learning target, the feature set used to represent the data and the learning model used for training, which we describe respectively as below.

4.3.1 Learning Targets

Considering the application of prediction results in practical Web search engines, we are mainly interested in predicting the examination behavior of search users in three scenarios:

- **Organic only SERP**: the search engine result page with only organic Web search results (i.e. traditional ten blue links);
- **SERP with a single vertical**: the search engine result page where a single vertical result block is embedded within the organic results (i.e. federated search page);

Figure 2: **An example vertical block which consists of a title part and four image components.**

- **The vertical block**: the search result vertical block while an example of block for the image vertical is shown in Figure 2.

For each of these three scenarios, we mainly concentrate on two particular learning targets:

- **Attention Regression**: regress to the actual examination duration of each search results based on their total fixation duration obtained from eye-tracking devices;
- **Binary Examination**: classify the search results into two class: examined or not examined.

In order to obtain the fixation duration for the attention regression, we exclude all the saccade events and aggregate the eye fixation events for each search result in the SERP. To obtain the binary examination label (i.e. whether a given search result was examined or not), we deem all the search results that were fixated by users for at least 100ms as positive examples (examined) and treat the rest as negative examples. We tune various fixation thresholds (e.g. 100ms, 200ms, etc.) and found similar results in terms of the effectiveness ranking of models with different feature set. Therefore, in the rest of the paper, all our reported results on binary classification is based on the threshold of 100ms in users' fixations.

4.3.2 Features and Models

To thoroughly investigate the implicit effects of static (cold-start) features, we plan to compare different combinations of content and visual saliency features, which is shown in Table 3. Our baseline feature group is the one with Group ID = 1 which only contains content features (see section 4.2). This baseline can be regarded as an implementation of the cold-start MICS model [30] because they are based on the same static feature set.

Feature group SF only involves saliency features. Because result position plays an important role in users' examination processes, in feature group PSF we also consider the combination of position and visual saliency features. Feature group CSF is the union group of both content and visual saliency features, which contains all the static features of SERPs.

Note that we also report group 0 (PF), which only relies on the position of the given element (one of the content features) for comparison (but we do not use this as the baseline to compare against). Position bias is modeled in most existing click modeling efforts and we use this as a reference in order to track how we can improve over this. With respect to the vertical blocks, the ranking sequence is defined either from top to bottom or from left to right (e.g. image vertical block shown in Figure 2) in our experiment.

To predict users' examination of results with the proposed feature groups, we experiment with five different learning methods that are widely-adopted in related studies: SVM, Logistic Regression (LR), Random Forrest (RF), Decision Tree (DT) and gradient boosting regression tree (GBRT). The implementation of scikit-learn toolkit[4] was adopted for these methods.

[4]http://scikit-learn.org/stable/

Table 3: **Feature groups in the examination models**

Group ID	Group Name	Features
0	PF	Position of the given element
1	CF	Content features
2	SF	Saliency features
3	PSF	Position and Saliency features
4	CSF	Content and Saliency features

5. EXPERIMENTAL RESULTS

5.1 Experimental Setup

With the data collection procedure described in Section 3, we constructed an experimental dataset with users' eye movement information during the 30 search tasks. The dataset involves 35 undergraduate students (aged 18 to 25, mean = 18.8) as participants, all of whom were recruited from a wide range of majors of a university. Because of the calibration problems with the eye tracker, not all participants' eye movement data were available and 32 of them were finally taken into account. Therefore, we have altogether 32*30=960 search sessions in the dataset[5].

Considering that head-free eye trackers may make the collected interaction more natural and realistic, a Tobii X2-30 eye tracker was used to capture participants' eye movements and deployed the search system on a 17-inch LCD monitor whose resolution is 1366*768. Internet Explorer 11 browser was used to display the pages of search system. To identify users' examination behaviors, we detect fixations using built-in algorithms from Tobii Studio. In this dataset, users' fixation data on both organic only SERPs and SERPs with five different kinds of verticals (textual, encyclopedia, image-only, application, news) were collected and used as ground truth for the prediction experiments.

In our study, we not only systematically investigate the effects of saliency features in the prediction process on page level, but also focus on the prediction performance of internal examination within vertical blocks. For the prediction of internal examination, we need to identify which element is examined by users and extract the static features from these elements. To this end, we follow the methodology described in [30] by manually segmenting verticals into HTML DOM elements and selecting a subset of these elements as features. For the ranking of internal components within verticals, we assume that users prefer to examine vertical blocks from top to bottom and left to right. Therefore, we can label these segmented elements as a ranked list and take the rank of the elements as position features.

We use a variety of evaluation metrics to measure the performance of the trained model. Specifically, for binary classification (examined or not), we adopt the evaluation metrics of precision, recall, F-measure, accuracy and Matthews' correlation coefficient (MCC) score [35]. For attention regression, we mainly report in terms of the Pearson correlation and MSE (mean square error).

The prediction performance of the different methods is compared based on a five-fold cross validation and we report the average performance on the test folds.

5.2 Comparison of Machine Learning Models

We first compare the performance of different machine learning methods for the examination prediction task. Table 4 presents the comparison results of the five learning models as described in Sec.4.3.2. The baseline is corresponding to a naive majority judgment method in which we predict all results as examined ones (majority baseline). We just report a binary classification results due to limited space but the regression results follow a similar trend.

Table 4: **Examination prediction results of different learning methods in our dateset using both Content and Saliency Features (the saliency model of Itti [22] was adopted, bolded results are the best in corresponding columns, ** represents p-value < 0.01 compared with baseline)**

Model	Precision	Recall	F-measure	MCC	Accuracy
Baseline	0.618	1.000	0.764	0.000	0.618
GBRT	0.766**	0.783**	**0.775****	**0.401****	**0.719****
SVM	0.717**	**0.819****	0.764	0.316**	0.688**
LR	0.744**	0.798**	0.770**	0.364**	0.705**
RF	0.732**	0.791**	0.765	0.370**	0.701**
DT	**0.775****	0.693**	0.732**	0.360**	0.686**

From the results of Table 4, we can see that almost all learning frameworks outperform the majority baseline significantly in terms of F-measure, MCC and Accuracy. Especially, GBRT performs the best in most metrics. Therefore, we select GBRT as our machine learning model for training and prediction in the subsequent steps.

5.3 Comparison of Saliency Models

With the selected learning method, we focus on the contribution of visual saliency features generated by the three different models, i.e. Itti [22], GBVS [17] and TIP model [31] (see Section 4.1 for more details). To save space, we only report the results for the binary classification in Table 5 while we obtain similar results on the attention regression task.

Table 5: **Examination prediction results with visual saliency features generated by different saliency models**

	Organic only SERP		SERP with Vertical	
	F-measure	Accuracy	F-measure	Accuracy
Itti [22]	0.74	0.66	0.76	0.65
GBVS [17]	0.75	0.68	0.76	0.65
TIP [31]	0.73	0.64	0.77	0.65

From Table 5 we can see that the three visual saliency models do not lead to much differences in examination prediction performance. The TIP model works slightly better while being applied on SERPs with verticals but a little worse on the organic only SERPs. For the rest of the paper, we adopt TIP as the saliency feature generation model as we are more interested in the performance of heterogeneous search pages.

5.4 Examination Prediction Results

In this section, we report the examination prediction results of different feature groups on three different scenarios (as described in Section 4.3.1): page-level prediction on organic only SERPs, page-level prediction on SERPs with verticals and block-level prediction within vertical results. Due to space limitation, we only report two main evaluation metrics for each task: Pearson correlation and MSE for the attention regression task, F-measure and Accuracy for the examination binary classification task.

5.4.1 *Prediction on Organic only SERPs*

We start by reporting the prediction results on organic only SERPs. From the example shown in Figure 1(a), 1(b) and 1(c), we assume that the position features may be good enough for the prediction task due to the existence of position bias on these SERPs. Visual

[5]The dataset is available to download for research purposes at http://www.thuir.cn/group/~yqliu/publications/sigir2016Liu.zip.

saliency and content features may not be so useful in this circumstance because all results seem to be homogeneous ones (without the involvement of verticals). From the experimental results presented in Table 6, we verify our above assumptions with the following findings:

Firstly, the model that uses only the ranking position (PF) perform reasonably well while the content feature based baseline (CF) do not improve over the ranking position based baseline. This implies that on organic only SERPs, the font, area size and other content based features do not matter so much and users' attention is generally affected by the position factor.

Secondly, the saliency feature based model (SF) performs the worst, especially in the task of predicting attention duration (regression). This is as expected since on organic only SERPs, the results can be regarded as homogeneous ones and do not vary so much in terms of visual saliency. The only difference of saliency among the search results is that some results may contain more query terms (which are shown as bold and colored as red). In some cases, the top ranked results may have more exact matches and are therefore a bit more salient. However, this effect seems not so significant on the organic only SERPs.

Thirdly, when adding saliency and other content features in addition to the ranking position feature (CSF), we still can not improve over PF. This implies that it is difficult to outperform the position feature based model with the content and visual saliency features in the organic only search environment.

Table 6: **Prediction Performance on Organic only SERPs. Two-tailed t-test is performed to detect any significant changes against the prediction performance of content features (CF) (* represents p-value < 0.05 and ** represents p-value < 0.01)**

	Regression		Classification	
	Pearson	MSE	F-measure	Accuracy
PF	0.48	2.00E+06	0.77	0.72
CF	0.48	2.01E+06	0.77	0.72
SF	0.23**	2.40E+06*	0.73**	0.64**
PSF	0.48	2.04E+06	0.74**	0.68**
CSF	0.47	2.09E+06*	0.74**	0.68**

We also report the feature importance of the CSF model in Table 7. Due to space limitation again, we only report the prediction results of binary classification (examined or not). Not surprisingly, the ranking position (rank) and top result's position in pixel (top) are the two most important features in determining whether a given search result is examined or not. Interestingly, the saliency histogram information (e.g. saliency_hist4) that captures visual saliency on the pixel level can be helpful, while saliency_hist4 represents the fraction of level4 saliency pixels of this result against the whole SERP (1 means least salient and 5 means most salient). In addition, the saliency_var (saliency variance) feature, which quantifies the "saliency contrastness" of the result, is also useful. Note that not as we expected, we do not find that the area of the text, which quantifies the size of the each result, contribute much to the examination prediction task.

5.4.2 Prediction on SERPs with Verticals

As for the prediction task on SERPs with verticals, we believe that visual saliency features may be more effective since the SERPs are heterogeneous while vertical results maintain different presentation styles. Some vertical results may be more visually salient than others and this factor can affect users' examination process. The prediction performance of different feature groups on SERPs with verticals is shown in Table 8 and it also verifies our thoughts.

Table 7: **Feature Importance of the CSF Model while Predicting Examination on Organic only SERPs**

Top 1-5 Features		Top 6-10 Features	
Feature	**Weight**	**Feature**	**Weight**
rank	0.14	saliency_hist1	0.11
top	0.14	saliency_hist3	0.09
saliency_hist4	0.13	saliency_sum	0.05
saliency_var	0.13	saliency_ave	0.05
saliency_hist2	0.13	saliency_hist5	0.04

Table 8: **Model Performance on SERPs with Vertical. Two-tailed t-test is performed to detect any significant changes against the performance of CF model (* represents p-value < 0.05 and ** represents p-value < 0.01)**

	Regression		Classification	
	Pearson	MSE	F-measure	Accuracy
PF	0.36	2.02E+06**	0.76**	0.71
CF	0.43	1.87E+06	0.77	0.71
SF	0.39	1.94E+06**	0.77	0.65**
PSF	0.45	1.83E+06*	0.78**	0.72*
CSF	0.45	1.83E+06**	0.78**	0.72*

Firstly, position based features (PF) do not gain so promising results as on organic only SERPs, comparing all metrics of PF in Table 8 with those in Table 6. We can also find that the prediction performance of content features (CF) is better than that of PF and the difference is significant for MSE and F-measure. Comparing to the scenario of organic only SERPs, saliency based model (SF) performs better. It outperforms PF and is comparable to CF (although the performance differences in terms of MSE and Accuracy are still significant).

Secondly, especially in terms of MSE metric, adding visual saliency information to content based features (CSF) can further improve over the content based baseline (CF) and the difference is significant. For example, we found that PSF and CSF significantly (with paired two-tailed t-test) outperform CF with p-value < 0.05 and 0.01 respectively.

To investigate the performance of different features in the prediction process, we further show the feature importance of the CSF prediction model on SERPs with verticals in Table 9. We can observe that: again, the ranking position factors (rank and top) are very important in determining the examination behavior. Meanwhile, the "saliency contrastness" (saliency_var) and saliency histogram of medium levels (saliency_hist3 and saliency_hist2) become more important compared with the results in Table 7.

Table 9: **Feature Importance of the CSF Model while Predicting Examination on SERPs with Verticals**

Top 1-5 Features		Top 6-10 Features	
Feature	**Weight**	**Feature**	**Weight**
top	0.24	saliency_ave	0.08
saliency_var	0.16	saliency_sum	0.06
rank	0.14	saliency_hist4	0.04
saliency_hist3	0.09	saliency_hist1	0.04
saliency_hist2	0.08	saliency_hist5	0.03

5.4.3 Prediction within Vertical Results

After investigating the page-level prediction results, we also look into the component-level prediction within vertical results, e.g. to predict which images are examined or paid much more attention in the image vertical block. From the results in Table 10 we can see that: Firstly, when predicting the examination of components within the vertical blocks, the ranking position features (PF) cannot compete with the content based features (CF). For all evaluation metrics, the results of PF model are worse than the CF model and the differences are significant with $p<0.01$.

Secondly, adding visual saliency features to position features (PSF) can help improve the prediction performance of PF. This improvement is reasonable considering the existence of multimedia components (e.g. images within the image vertical) and the heterogeneity nature (e.g. both image and text in the news vertical) of the vertical blocks. Thirdly, content feature based baseline (CF) performs the best, and significantly outperforms PF and SF, which show that the cold-start MICS model proposed in [30] is effective for predicting examination behavior within vertical results.

Table 10: **Model Performance on Internal Vertical Block.Two-tailed t-test is performed to detect any significant changes aganist the performance of CF model (* represents p-value < 0.05 and ** represents p-value < 0.01)**

	Regression		Classification	
	Pearson	MSE	F-measure	Accuracy
PF	0.22**	5.16E+05**	0.58**	0.65**
CF	0.39	4.65E+05	0.64	0.70
SF	0.33**	4.86E+05**	0.59**	0.67**
PSF	0.36*	4.81E+05**	0.62*	0.69**
CSF	0.38	4.70E+05	0.63*	0.69**

By examining the feature importance scores in Table 11, we can also obtain some insights why content feature based baseline performs so well. We can observe that the most important feature is the area_text, which represents the area size of a component within the vertical results. Not surprisingly, when users examine the items within the vertical blocks, the size of the area plays a vital part in attracting users' attentions. Meanwhile, the ranking position of the results (top) and the "saliency contrastness" (saliency_var) as well as saliency histogram of medium levels (saliency_hist3 and saliency_hist2) are also helpful in the prediction.

Table 11: **Feature Importance of the CSF Model while Predicting Examination within Vertical Results**

Top 1-5 Features		Top 6-10 Features	
Feature	**Weight**	**Feature**	**Weight**
area_text	0.19	saliency_hist4	0.06
top	0.15	saliency_sum	0.05
saliency_hist3	0.12	saliency_ave	0.05
saliency_var	0.07	left	0.05
saliency_hist2	0.06	saliency_hist1	0.05

5.5 Accuracy vs. Efficiency

From the experimental results in Sections 5.3 and 5.4, we find that visual saliency information helps improve prediction performance of users' examination behaviors. However, the feature groups that include saliency features (SF and CSF) require the processing of visual content information and may increase computational cost. To adopt this method in practical applications, we also want to find out whether the cost of saliency feature extraction is acceptable and how we can improve the efficiency if the cost is too much.

Considering that the TIP model outperforms the other two saliency models according to Table 5 in the federated SERPs, we just show the computational cost of TIP for generating saliency maps of federated SERPs in Figure 3. According to the figure, we can see that the average time for generating saliency map is around 44 seconds, which makes the extraction process almost impossible for practical applications when huge number of SERPs are processed. Therefore, we have to find a way to improve the efficiency of the feature extraction process.

Table 12: **Prediction Model Performance (CSF) with Different Resize Resolution Ratios**

resolution	F-measure	Accuracy
82×46(6%)	0.77	0.72
95×54(7%)	0.77	0.71
109×61(8%)	0.77	0.71
122×69(9%)	0.77	0.71
136×77(10%)	0.77	0.71
272×154(20%)	0.77	0.71
544×307(40%)	0.78	0.72
816×461(60%)	0.78	0.72
1366×768(100%)	0.78	0.72

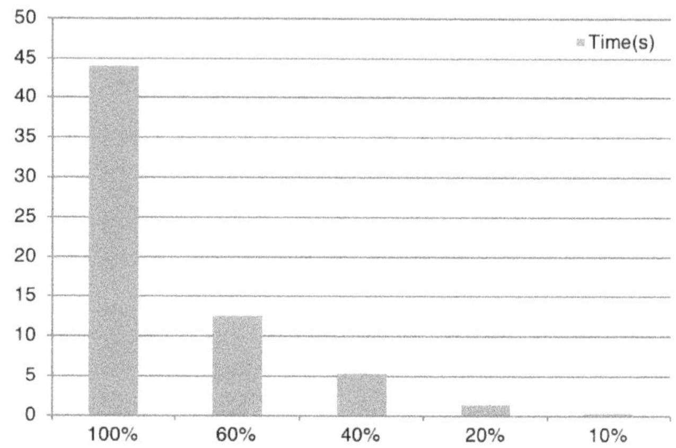

Figure 3: **Average computational cost (in Seconds) of generating saliency maps for the experimental data set.**

According to the selective attention theory [43] in cognitive psychology studies, human attention consists of two functionally independent, hierarchical stages: An early, pre-attentive stage that operates without capacity limitation and in parallel across the entire visual field, followed by a later, attentive limited-capacity stage that can deal with only one item (or at most a few items) at a time. Liu et. al. [33] show that in Web search examination process, a similar two-stage mechanism also applies. These existing research shows that search users will firstly allocate their attention in a skimming stage, in which no actual content is carefully read and understood. It reveals the possibility that low-resolution visual saliency features may also help in the examination prediction task.

To find out whether we can improve the efficiency of visual saliency model without loss of performance, we test the performance of visual saliency features extracted from SERP images with different resolutions. We resize the SERP image to different resolutions with the Matlab imresize function using default interpolation method and antialiasing. After that, we test the computational cost of extraction for each resolution and corresponding performances for examination prediction. Since Table 8 shows that the CSF feature set performs best among all feature combinations, we test the classification results on SERPs with verticals using the CSF model. The experimental results are shown in Table 12 and Figure 3, respectively. Please be noted that we do not test the performance with resolution ratio less than 6% because that is the lowest allowed input for the imresize function.

According to the experimental results shown in Table 12, we can see that the model performance remain stable with different resize resolution ratios. Even when the image is resized to a resolution of 82×46, which is only 6% of the original image, the model performs almost as well as the original one. It indicates that although visual saliency features help improve examination prediction performance, there is no need to use the high-resolution image of SERPs. This phenomena is probably due to the fact that users just rely on the visual content to make a rough judgment of the possible interesting areas on SERP in the skimming stage of examination.

From Figure 3, we can find that the computational cost for resized images are greatly reduced. It only costs about 360 ms to generate the visual saliency map with a resized resolution rate of 10%. It makes the efficiency of the extraction process acceptable and shows that our proposed prediction model based on visual saliency features is applicable for practical Web search applications.

6. CONCLUSIONS AND FUTURE WORK

In this paper, we present a novel examination model based on static information of SERPs, which has more practical applications in search scenario than existing user-interaction-based models. To our best knowledge, we are the first to use visual saliency maps in search scenario. With an in-depth study to analyze the impacts of saliency features in search environment, we demonstrate visual saliency features have a significant improvement on the performance of examination prediction. Importantly, saliency features, which contain the information of image content (e.g., color, brightness intensity), make it possible to predict user examination in complex search environment, especially in heterogeneous federated search. Without the information of user interaction, our model could offer good examination prediction only depending on the cold-start static information of pages. This could be quite valuable for the situations which lack users' behavior information, such as the evaluation of newly generated pages or in the new context (e.g. mobile). Further, we also confirm the positive effects of saliency features in the prediction of internal examination in vertical blocks. Our findings show that the proposed method can be also adopted to model the internal examination behavior patterns within vertical results. This may be particularly beneficial to the design of vertical layout.

Interesting directions for future work will include extending this work to construct click models based on static features of pages to improve search ranking performance. Moreover, inspired by the mechanism of inhibition of return in saliency map [22, 23] in cognitive psychology, we also plan to model the examination sequence depending on *dynamic* saliency maps in search environment.

7. ACKNOWLEDGEMENT

We thank Mr. Ming Liang and Dr. Xiaoling Hu for providing their visual saliency extraction implementations. This work is supported by Tsinghua University Initiative Scientific Research Program (2014Z21032), National Key Basic Research Program (2015CB358700), Tsinghua-Samsung Joint Laboratory for Intelligent Media Computing and Natural Science Foundation (61532011, 61472206) of China.

8. REFERENCES

[1] J. Arguello and R. Capra. The effects of vertical rank and border on aggregated search coherence and search behavior. In *Proceedings of the 23rd ACM International Conference on Conference on Information and Knowledge Management*, pages 539–548. ACM, 2014.

[2] L. Azzopardi and G. Zuccon. An analysis of theories of search and search behavior. In *Proceedings of the 2015 International Conference on The Theory of Information Retrieval*, pages 81–90, 2015.

[3] J. Bar-Ilan, K. Keenoy, M. Levene, and E. Yaari. Presentation bias is significant in determining user preference for search results—a user study. *Journal of the American Society for Information Science and Technology*, 60(1):135–149, 2009.

[4] G. Buscher, S. T. Dumais, and E. Cutrell. The good, the bad, and the random: an eye-tracking study of ad quality in web search. In *Proceedings of the 33rd international ACM SIGIR conference on Research and development in information retrieval*, pages 42–49. ACM, 2010.

[5] R. Carmi and L. Itti. Visual causes versus correlates of attentional selection in dynamic scenes. *Vision research*, 46(26):4333–4345, 2006.

[6] O. Chapelle and Y. Zhang. A dynamic bayesian network click model for web search ranking. In *Proceedings of the 18th international conference on World wide web*, pages 1–10. ACM, 2009.

[7] D. Chen, W. Chen, H. Wang, Z. Chen, and Q. Yang. Beyond ten blue links: enabling user click modeling in federated web search. In *Proceedings of the fifth ACM international conference on Web search and data mining*, pages 463–472.

[8] A. Chuklin, I. Markov, and M. d. Rijke. Click models for web search. *Synthesis Lectures on Information Concepts, Retrieval, and Services*, 7(3):1–115, 2015.

[9] N. Craswell, O. Zoeter, M. Taylor, and B. Ramsey. An experimental comparison of click position-bias models. In *Proceedings of the 2008 International Conference on Web Search and Data Mining*, pages 87–94. ACM, 2008.

[10] E. Cutrell and Z. Guan. What are you looking for?: an eye-tracking study of information usage in web search. In *Proceedings of the SIGCHI conference on Human factors in computing systems*, pages 407–416. ACM, 2007.

[11] F. Diaz, R. White, D. Liebling, and G. Buscher. Robust models of mouse movement on dynamic web search results pages. In *Proceedings of the 22nd ACM international conference on Information and Knowledge Management (CIKM2013)*, pages 1451–1460.

[12] G. E. Dupret and B. Piwowarski. A user browsing model to predict search engine click data from past observations. In *Proceedings of the 31st annual international ACM SIGIR conference on Research and development in information retrieval*, pages 331–338. ACM, 2008.

[13] L. A. Granka, T. Joachims, and G. Gay. Eye-tracking analysis of user behavior in www search. In *Proceedings of the 27th annual international ACM SIGIR conference on Research and development in information retrieval*, pages 478–479. ACM, 2004.

[14] F. Guo, C. Liu, and Y. M. Wang. Efficient multiple-click models in web search. In *Proceedings of the Second ACM International Conference on Web Search and Data Mining*, pages 124–131. ACM, 2009.

[15] Q. Guo and E. Agichtein. Towards predicting web searcher gaze position from mouse movements. In *CHI'10 Extended Abstracts on Human Factors in Computing Systems*, pages 3601–3606. ACM, 2010.

[16] Q. Guo and E. Agichtein. Beyond dwell time: estimating document relevance from cursor movements and other post-click searcher behavior. In *Proceedings of the 21st World Wide Web Conference 2012, WWW 2012, Lyon, France, April 16-20, 2012*, pages 569–578, 2012.

[17] J. Harel, C. Koch, and P. Perona. Graph-based visual saliency. In *Advances in neural information processing systems*, pages 545–552, 2006.

[18] K. Hofmann, B. Mitra, F. Radlinski, and M. Shokouhi. An eye-tracking study of user interactions with query auto completion. In *Proceedings of the 23rd ACM International Conference on Conference on Information and Knowledge Management*, pages 549–558. ACM, 2014.

[19] J. Huang, R. White, and G. Buscher. User see, user point: gaze and cursor alignment in web search. In *Proceedings of the SIGCHI Conference on Human Factors in Computing Systems*, pages 1341–1350. ACM, 2012.

[20] J. Huang, R. W. White, G. Buscher, and K. Wang. Improving searcher models using mouse cursor activity. In *the 35th international ACM SIGIR conference on Research and development in information retrieval*, pages 195–204, 2012.

[21] J. Huang, R. W. White, and S. Dumais. No clicks, no problem: using cursor movements to understand and improve search. In *the SIGCHI Conference on Human Factors in Computing Systems*, pages 1225–1234, 2011.

[22] L. Itti and C. Koch. A saliency-based search mechanism for overt and covert shifts of visual attention. *Vision research*, 40(10):1489–1506, 2000.

[23] L. Itti and C. Koch. Computational modelling of visual attention. *Nature reviews neuroscience*, 2(3):194–203, 2001.

[24] T. Joachims, L. Granka, B. Pan, H. Hembrooke, and G. Gay. Accurately interpreting clickthrough data as implicit feedback. In *Proceedings of the 28th annual international ACM SIGIR conference on Research and development in information retrieval*, pages 154–161. ACM, 2005.

[25] T. Joachims, L. Granka, B. Pan, H. Hembrooke, F. Radlinski, and G. Gay. Evaluating the accuracy of implicit feedback from clicks and query reformulations in web search. *ACM Transactions on Information Systems (TOIS)*, 25(2):7, 2007.

[26] T. Judd, K. Ehinger, F. Durand, and A. Torralba. Learning to predict where humans look. In *Computer Vision, 2009 IEEE 12th international conference on*, pages 2106–2113, 2009.

[27] M. A. Just and P. A. Carpenter. A theory of reading: from eye fixations to comprehension. *Psychological review*, 87(4):329, 1980.

[28] C. Koch and S. Ullman. Shifts in selective visual attention: towards the underlying neural circuitry. In *Matters of intelligence*, pages 115–141. Springer, 1987.

[29] D. Lagun and E. Agichtein. Effects of task and domain on searcher attention. In *Proceedings of the 37th international ACM SIGIR conference on Research & development in information retrieval*, pages 1087–1090. ACM, 2014.

[30] D. Lagun and E. Agichtein. Inferring searcher attention by jointly modeling user interactions and content salience. In *Proceedings of the 38th International ACM SIGIR Conference on Research and Development in Information Retrieval*, pages 483–492. ACM, 2015.

[31] M. Liang and X. Hu. Feature selection in supervised saliency prediction. *Cybernetics, IEEE Transactions on*, 45(5):900–912, 2015.

[32] M. Liang and X. Hu. Predicting eye fixations with higher-level visual features. *Image Processing, IEEE Transactions on*, 24(3):1178–1189, 2015.

[33] Y. Liu, C. Wang, K. Zhou, J. Nie, M. Zhang, and S. Ma. From skimming to reading: A two-stage examination model for web search. In *Proceedings of the 23rd ACM International Conference on Conference on Information and Knowledge Management*, pages 849–858. ACM, 2014.

[34] Z. Liu, Y. Liu, K. Zhou, M. Zhang, and S. Ma. Influence of vertical result in web search examination. In *Proceedings of the 38th International ACM SIGIR Conference on Research and Development in Information Retrieval*, pages 193–202, 2015.

[35] B. W. Matthews. Comparison of the predicted and observed secondary structure of t4 phage lysozyme. *Biochimica et Biophysica Acta (BBA)-Protein Structure*, 405(2):442–451, 1975.

[36] G. W. McConkie and K. Rayner. The span of the effective stimulus during a fixation in reading. *Perception & Psychophysics*, 17(6):578–586, 1975.

[37] V. Navalpakkam, L. Jentzsch, R. Sayres, S. Ravi, A. Ahmed, and A. Smola. Measurement and modeling of eye-mouse behavior in the presence of nonlinear page layouts. In *Proceedings of the 22nd international conference on World Wide Web*, pages 953–964, 2013.

[38] S. Pandey, K. Punera, M. Fontoura, and V. Josifovski. Estimating advertisability of tail queries for sponsored search. In *Proceedings of the 33rd international ACM SIGIR conference on Research and development in information retrieval*, pages 563–570. ACM, 2010.

[39] R. J. Peters and L. Itti. Applying computational tools to predict gaze direction in interactive visual environments. *ACM Transactions on Applied Perception (TAP)*, 5(2):9, 2008.

[40] M. Richardson, E. Dominowska, and R. Ragno. Predicting clicks: estimating the click-through rate for new ads. In *Proceedings of the 16th international conference on World Wide Web*, pages 521–530. ACM, 2007.

[41] K. Rodden, X. Fu, A. Aula, and I. Spiro. Eye-mouse coordination patterns on web search results pages. In *CHI'08 Extended Abstracts on Human Factors in Computing Systems*, pages 2997–3002. ACM, 2008.

[42] T. Shi, M. Liang, and X. Hu. A reverse hierarchy model for predicting eye fixations. In *Computer Vision and Pattern Recognition (CVPR), 2014 IEEE Conference on*, pages 2822–2829. IEEE, 2014.

[43] J. Theeuwes. Visual selective attention: A theoretical analysis. *Acta psychologica*, 83(2):93–154, 1993.

[44] C. Wang, Y. Liu, M. Zhang, S. Ma, M. Zheng, J. Qian, and K. Zhang. Incorporating vertical results into search click models. In *Proceedings of the 36th international ACM SIGIR conference on Research and development in information retrieval*, pages 503–512. ACM, 2013.

[45] K. Zhou, R. Cummins, M. Lalmas, and J. M. Jose. Evaluating aggregated search pages. In *Proceedings of the 35th international ACM SIGIR conference on Research and development in information retrieval*, pages 115–124, 2012.

A Comparison of Cache Blocking Methods for Fast Execution of Ensemble-based Score Computation

Xin Jin, Tao Yang, Xun Tang
University of California at Santa Barbara, CA 93106, USA
{xin_jin, tyang, xtang}@cs.ucsb.edu

ABSTRACT

Machine-learned classification and ranking techniques often use ensembles to aggregate partial scores of feature vectors for high accuracy and the runtime score computation can become expensive when employing a large number of ensembles. The previous work has shown the judicious use of memory hierarchy in a modern CPU architecture which can effectively shorten the time of score computation. However, different traversal methods and blocking parameter settings can exhibit different cache and cost behavior depending on data and architectural characteristics. It is very time-consuming to conduct exhaustive search for performance comparison and optimum selection. This paper provides an analytic comparison of cache blocking methods on their data access performance with an approximation and proposes a fast guided sampling scheme to select a traversal method and blocking parameters for effective use of memory hierarchy. The evaluation studies with three datasets show that within a reasonable amount of time, the proposed scheme can identify a highly competitive solution that significantly accelerates score calculation.

Categories and Subject Descriptors

H.3.3 [**Information Storage and Retrieval**]: Information Search and Retrieval

Keywords

Ensemble methods; query processing; cache locality

1. INTRODUCTION

Ensemble-based machine learning techniques have been proven to be effective for dealing data-intensive applications with complex features and document ranking is a representative application benefiting from use of the large number of ensembles. For example, in the Yahoo! learning-to-rank challenge [7], all winners have used some forms of gradient boosted regression trees, e.g. [8]. The total number of trees reported for ranking can be upto 3,000 to 20,000 [10, 5, 11], or even 300,000 or more using bagging method [13]. Ranking for large ensembles is expensive. As reported in [14], it takes more than 6 seconds to rank the top-2000 results for a query processing a 8,051-tree ensemble and 519 features per document on an AMD 3.1 GHz core. If such an algorithm is used to compute scores for a large number of vectors in applications such as classification, the total job is also very time consuming.

The previous work addressed the speedup of runtime execution for ensemble-based ranking in several aspects including tree trimming [3] for a tradeoff of ranking accuracy and performance, earlier exit [6], and loop unrolling [4], and ensemble restructuring for a tree-based model [12]. Memory access can be 100x slower than L1 cache and un-orchestrated slow memory access incurs significant cost, dominating the entire computation. The work shown in [14, 12] proposes a cache-conscious blocking method for better cache locality. However, there are other block methods to select and it is an open problem how to identify the best cache blocking method and parameter settings given different data and architecture characteristics. Experimentally determining this choice can be extremely time-consuming and the comparative result may not be valid any more with a change of underlying feature vector structure or architecture. This paper provides an analysis of multiple blocking methods with different data traversal orders, which provides better insight on program execution performance and leads a fast approximation to select the optimized structure.

Here, we consider the fast computation of ensemble-based scoring that aggregates and derives final scores for n feature vectors using m ensembles. For testing and comparing performance in ranking q sampled queries, the time cost for searching through all combinations can be as high as $O(m^2 * n^2 * q)$. The main contribution of this work is to develop an analytic framework to compare memory access performance of data traversal under multi-level caches to find the fastest program execution with effective use of memory hierarchy. Our scheme results in a much smaller complexity with $O(m * n * q)$. Our experiments with three datasets corroborate the effectiveness of search cost reduction while the guided approximation identifies a highly competitive blocking choice. We also demonstrate the use of this scheme with QuickScorer [12] and for batched query processing.

The rest of the paper is organized as follow. Next, we describe the background information and related work. Section 3 discusses the design considerations. Section 4 gives a comparative analysis on different blocking methods. Section

SIGIR '16, July 17 - 21, 2016, Pisa, Italy

ISBN 978-1-4503-4069-4/16/07...$15.00

DOI: http://dx.doi.org/10.1145/2911451.2911520

5 presents evaluation results. Finally, Section 6 concludes the paper.

2. BACKGROUND AND RELATED WORK

Given n feature vectors and an ensemble model that contains m scorers, these vectors and scorers fit in memory. The ensemble computation calculates a score for each feature vector and each scorer contributes a subscore to the overall score for a vector. For example, for ranking a document set with an additive regression tree model [8, 5], each document is represented as a feature vector and each tree can be stored in a compact array-based format [4]. Following the notation in [6], Algorithm 1 shows the DS method with the two-loop standard execution order. At each out loop iteration i, all scorers are used to gather subscores for a vector before moving to another vector. The dominating cost is slow memory accesses when scorers read feature vector values and update partial values.

Algorithm 1: DS standard method for score calculation.

```
for i = 1 to n do
    for j = 1 to m do
        Update score for vector i with scorer j.
```

Tang et. al [14] proposed a 2D cache blocking structure called SDSD as depicted in Algorithm 2 which partitions the program in Algorithm 1 into four nested loops. The inner two loops process d feature vectors with s trees. To simplify the presentation, we assume n/d and m/s are integers. By fitting the inner block in fast cache, this method can be much faster than DS. There are other possible cache blocking methods with different data traversal orders and it is an unanswered question on how to choose among them. Also, in [14] there is no cost analysis on how to set a proper parameter for the size of blocking in terms of s and d values. While choices of their values can be restricted to fit in the fast cache, they can still be fairly large. For example, s and d can still reach upto 3,276 and 11,440 respectively in some of our experiments shown in Section 5. Assume m and n are smaller than these upper bound numbers, s ranges from 1 to m and d ranges from 1 to n and there are $m * n$ combinations to compare as they all fit in different levels of cache. Since running each test query takes $O(n * m * q)$, the total cost is $O(m^2 * n^2 * q)$. For instance, given $n = 10,000$, $m = 3,000$, $q = 1000$, the total time takes over 1,141 years with one core, assuming it takes 40 nanoseconds to compute a partial score for a vector with a scorer. If we sample each of s and d values with step gap 100, the total one-core time is over 41 days without knowing if such sampling finds a solution competitive to the optimum. While running such a sampling can be fully parallelized, we still need a faster scheme with well-guided approximation.

Algorithm 2: 2D blocking with SDSD structure.

```
for j = 0 to m/s − 1 do
    for i = 0 to n/d − 1 do
        for jj = 1 to s do
            for ii = 1 to d do
                Update score for vector i × d + ii with
                scorer j × s + jj.
```

There are other performance speedup techniques proposed in the previous work to speedup fast ranking score computation, which can be summarized into two categories. The first category is to achieve a tradeoff between ranking efficiency and accuracy. In [6], an early exit optimization was developed to reduce scoring time while retaining a good ranking accuracy. In [16, 17], ranking is optimized to seek the tradeoff between efficiency and effectiveness. Asadi et.al [3] considered the fact that compact, shallow, and balanced trees yield faster computation and generated such trees with trimming technique. The second category is to improve efficiency given a fixed model. The work in [4] proposed an architecture-conscious solution called VPred that converts control dependence of code to data dependence and employs loop unrolling with vectorization. Lucchese et.al proposed the QuickScorer (QS) algorithm [12] which traverses multiple trees in an interleaved manner and accelerates with bit-wise operations. They propose a block-wise variant of QS (called BWQS) by partitioning trees into blocks and applying QS to each block of trees. Given different dataset characteristics, it is an open problem how to find the optimal partitioning. Also there are other ways to arrange blocking and our work is complementary and can be used to compare different options.

3. DESIGN CONSIDERATION AND COST MODEL

There are six ways of loop blocking depending on the order of data traversal: DSD, SDS, DSDS, DSSD, SDDS, and SDSD. Following the naming in [15], symbol D here stands for a loop control over feature vectors and S stands for a loop control over scorers. For example, DSDS means that feature vector traversal is controlled by the outermost and the third outermost loops while scorer traversal is controlled by the second and the innermost loops. The inner two loops access d vectors and s scorers.

Figure 1 illustrates the execution and data traversal order of these methods. Figure 1(a) shows that DSD initially visits one scorer and d vectors. Then it visits another scorer and the same d vectors. Figure 1(b) depicts that SDS initially visits one vector and s scorers. Then it visits another vector and the same s scorers. Figure 1(c) illustrates DSDS which visits scorers and vectors block by block and row by row. Figure 1(f) illustrates SDSD which visits scorers and vectors block by block and column by column.

Our objective is to compare these blocking methods and find a value for s and d to minimize the time cost of score computation under a constraint $1 \leq s \leq m$, $1 \leq d \leq n$. We have the following considerations.

- For DSD, when the inner most loop uses $d = 1$, it becomes a special case DS which is the same as the traditional loop structure DS shown in Algorithm 1. For SDS, when the inner loop uses $s = 1$, it becomes a special case SD.
- The traversal order of DSSD during execution is the same as that of DSD as illustrated in Figure 1(a) and (d). Thus DSD can represent both during our analysis. Similarly, the traversal order of SDDS is the same as that of SDS as shown in Figure 1(b) and (e). As a result of the above argument, the six types of control are reduced to four.

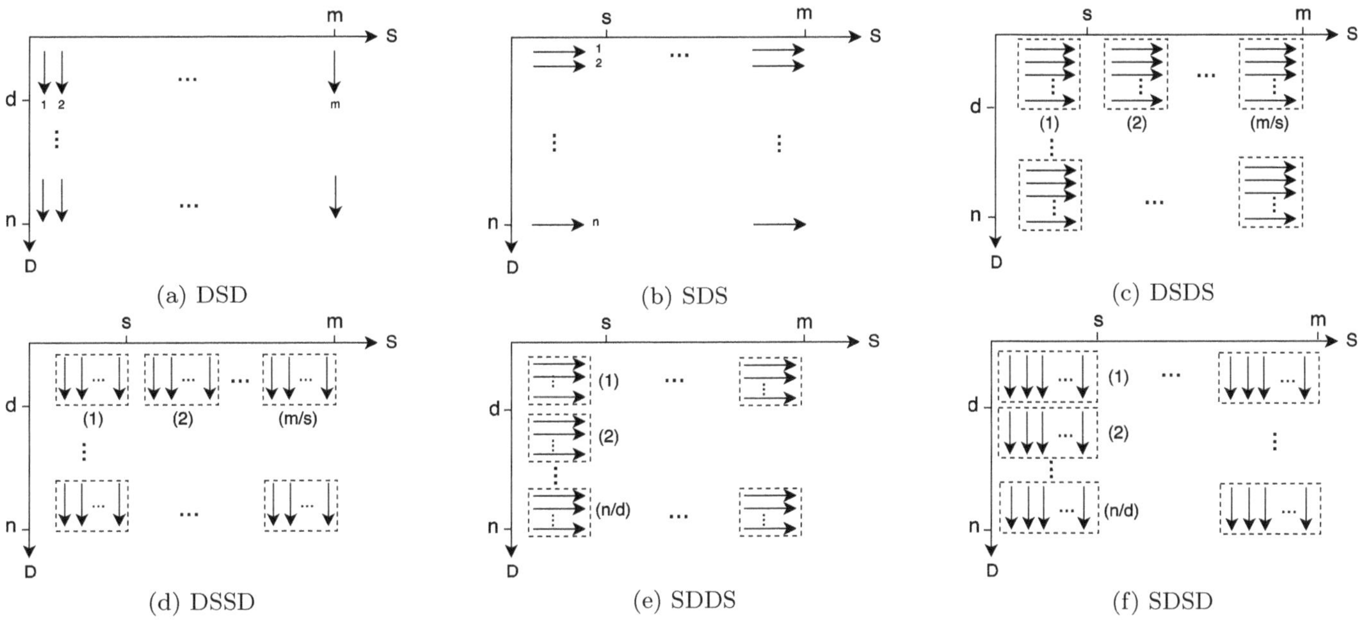

(a) DSD (b) SDS (c) DSDS (d) DSSD (e) SDDS (f) SDSD

Figure 1: Data traversal order of cache blocking methods during execution

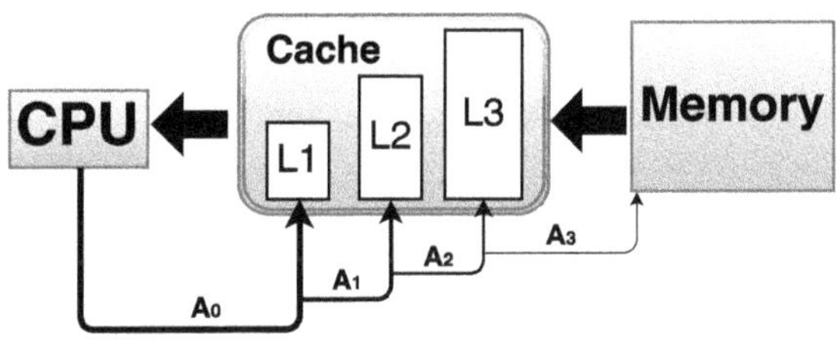

Figure 2: Data access flow of CPU with memory hierarchy.

The following parameters are used in assessing the average memory access cost of processing n feature vectors with m scorers. We assume that CPU has three levels of caches: L1, L2, and L3 and the three level setting is popular in the currently available processors from Intel and AMD. Let δ_1 be the read or write cost of accessing L1 and cost for accessing other cache is δ_1 multiplied by a constant ratio. Namely $c_2\delta_1$ is the cost of accessing L2, $c_3\delta_1$ is the cost of accessing L3, and $c_4\delta_1$ is the cost of accessing memory.

Our analysis separates the cost for accessing feature vectors and scorers. Without losing the generality, let A_i be the total amount of data access to feature vectors at cache level $i+1$ while ηA_i be the total amount of accesses to scorers at cache level $i+1$ and η is the average frequency ratio between access of feature vectors and scorers during computation.

The total data access cost is the summation of the cost of accessing each level of memory hierarchy:

$$\begin{aligned} Cost = & A_0\delta_1(1 + \alpha_D c_2 + \alpha_D\beta_D c_3 + \alpha_D\beta_D\gamma_D c_4) \\ & + \eta(A_0\delta_1(1 + \alpha_S c_2 + \alpha_S\beta_S c_3 + \alpha_S\beta_S\gamma_S c_4)). \end{aligned}$$

where α_S, β_S, γ_S, α_D, β_D, and γ_D are the miss rates of L1, L2 and L3 to access scorers and feature vectors respectively. Data accesses flow from CPU to memory for feature vectors is illustrated in Figure 2. $A_1 = A_0\alpha_D$ is the total number of feature data access to L2 due to their misses to L1; $A_2 = A_0\alpha_D\beta_D$ is the total number of feature data access to L3. $A_3 = A_0\alpha_D\beta_D\gamma_D$ is the total number of data access to memory.

Then the time cost divided by $A_0\delta_1$ is defined as

$$T = \frac{Cost}{\delta_1 A_0} = \eta T_S + T_D$$

where $T_D = 1 + \alpha_D c_2 + \alpha_D\beta_D c_3 + \alpha_D\beta_D\gamma_D c_4$ and $T_S = 1 + \alpha_S c_2 + \alpha_S\beta_S c_3 + \alpha_S\beta_S\gamma_S c_4$.

Since A_0 and δ_1 are constants, in the rest of the analysis, we focus on computing the above data access cost ratio T.

Notice that once data is brought from memory hierarchy, the arithmetic computing cost of all four methods is the same. Thus we just need to analyze and compare the data access cost ratio T for the four traversal methods. In practice, data access cost often weights more than arithmetic cost.

Due to the restriction on the paper length, we first present the analysis of cache performance for DSD and then list the result of DSDS, SDSD, and SDS as the case subdivision and cost derivation process are similar. Finally we describe an approximate scheme to select the best structure by taking advantages of the derived data access cost ratio for the four methods.

4. COST ANALYSIS AND COMPARISON

4.1 Time cost for DSD

4.1.1 Cases under consideration

Algorithm 3: The program structure of DSD method.

```
for all vector blocks do
    for i in all scorers do
        for j in a vector block do
            Update score for vector j with scorer i.
```

Algorithm 3 lists the program control structure of DSD and a vector block contains d vectors. Once a scorer s_i is loaded to cache, it will be used by d vectors in the inner most loop. Then the next scorer s_{i+1} will go through the same d vectors. If we choose d properly such that d vectors fit in cache, we do not need to load them from memory for each scorer. Figure 3 illustrates how the cost of score computation could change when value d increases from 1 to n. The impact of d value on the cost is segmented with respect to the size of L1, L2, and L3. When d is small, the d vectors can fit in L1 cache, and there is an advantage of reusing these d vectors within L1 cache. Thus d should be as large as possible. When d value becomes too big, the benefit of leveraging L1 cache decreases because d vectors may not fit in L1 any more and therefore the access cost can increase with larger d value. We can reason similarly when d vectors fit or do not fit in L2 and L3 caches.

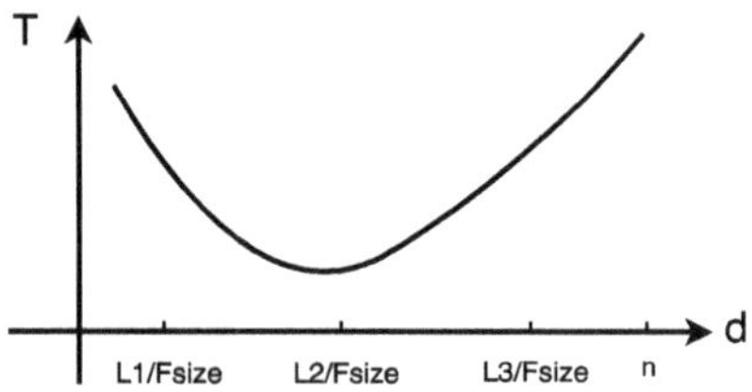

Figure 3: Performance under different values of d.

We will clarify the tradeoff of increasing d value when we derive a more concrete analysis. Let $Fsize$ be the average data size of each feature vector. Without introducing more symbols, we also let $L1, L2$ and $L3$ represent the size of L1 cache, L2 cache and L3 cache respectively in a formula expression. To assess the impact of increasing d values, we divide the increasing range into four parts as illustrated in Figure 3.

- d vectors fits in L1 cache. Namely $d \leq \frac{L1}{Fsize}$
- d vectors do not fit in L1 cache, but fit in L2 cache. $\frac{L1}{Fsize} < d \leq \frac{L2}{Fsize}$
- d vectors do not fit in L2 cache, but fit in L3 cache. $\frac{L2}{Fsize} < d \leq \frac{L3}{Fsize}$
- d vectors exceed L3 cache and but fit in memory. $\frac{L3}{Fsize} < d \leq n$.

The cache access behavior of inner most loop in Algorithm 3 is affected by the average size of each scorer. For example, a larger scorer footprint leaves little space for L1 to host feature vectors. Figure 4 illustrates that we need to consider the following four scenarios and for each scenario, we need to further consider the four d range cases discussed above. Let $Ssize$ represent the average data size of each scorer and the four scenarios corresponding to the root branches in Figure 4 are defined as follows.

- **Scenario 1:** $Ssize \leq L1$. When a scorer can fit in L1 cache, there are four cases for the d vectors: the vector block fits in L1 cache, L2 cache, L3 cache or memory.
- **Scenario 2:** $L1 < Ssize \leq L2$. When a scorer size is between L1 and L2 cache sizes, the vector block can only fit in a higher level of cache (say L2 or L3 cache). Otherwise, old vectors will be kicked out from L1 cache by the scorer and the vector block could not stay in L1 cache. Thus there are only three cases for the d vectors as depicted in the second root branch of Figure 4: the vector block fits in L2 cache, L3 cache or memory.
- **Scenario 3:** $L2 < Ssize \leq L3$. When a scorer size is inbetween L2 and L3 cache size, there are two cases for the d vectors: the vector block fits in L3 cache or memory.
- **Scenario 4:** $Ssize > L3$. When a scorer cannot fit in L3 cache, the d feature vectors will not be able to fit in L3 cache also and they can only fit in memory.

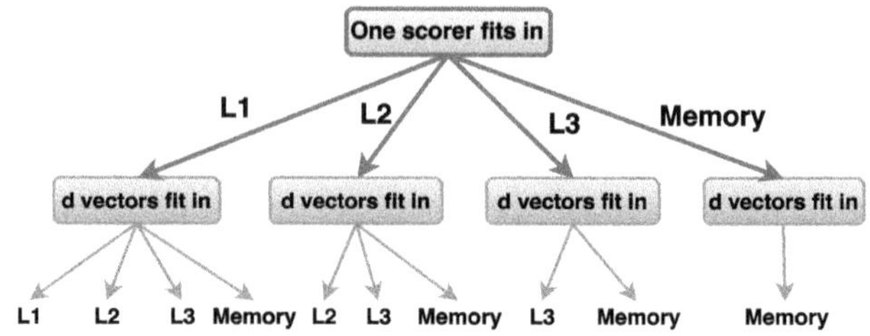

Figure 4: Range cases of d considered under different scenarios for DSD.

To simplify the analysis, we assume that m and n are sufficiently large so that m scorers do not fit in L3 cache, and also n feature vectors do not fit in L3 cache.

4.1.2 DSD under Scenario 1

Under Scenario 1, we first compute T_S as follows. Since each scorer is loaded once for the inner loop most and will reused d times for computing the subscores for d vectors in the inner most loop. Then the L1 cache miss ratio $\alpha_S \approx 1/d$. If there is an L1 cache miss for a scorer, L2 cache miss and L3 cache miss can occur with a high chance because the unseen new scorer has not been used ever and thus it is fetched from memory. Thus $\beta_S \approx 1$ and $\gamma_S \approx 1$.

$$T_S \approx 1 + \frac{c_2}{d} + \frac{1}{d}(c_3 + c_4) \approx 1 + \frac{c_4}{d}$$

We shall estimate T_D under 4 different ranges of d values following Figure 3. We call these 4 range cases under DSD as DSD_i where $1 \leq i \leq 4$. The total cost ratio of accessing scorers for DSD is

$$T_{DSD_i} = \frac{Cost}{\delta_1 A_0} = \eta T_S + T_D \approx \eta + \frac{\eta c_4}{d} + T_D$$

where

$$T_D = 1 + c_2\alpha_i + \alpha_i\beta_i(c_3 + c_4\gamma_i) \quad (1)$$

and α_i, β_i and γ_i are cache miss rates for accessing feature vectors under range case i. Note that in differentiating these miss rate of different cases, we use script "i" instead of "D, i" in order to simplify the presentation. Table 1 summarizes the cost of DSD for Scenario 1 when each scorer fits in L1 cache on average.

Range Case DSD_1**:** d vectors fit in L1. Once a scorer is loaded to L1, the inner most loop load d feature vectors to L1 and these vectors stay and will be available in L1 when a new scorer is fetched to L1. Given m scorers, each feature vector in L1 is accessed m times and there is one 1 miss initially and the rest of $m-1$ accesses will hit L1. Thus the L1 cache miss ratio with respect to feature vectors is $\alpha_1 \approx 1/m$. If there is an L1 cache miss for a feature vector, there must be an L2 cache miss and L3 cache miss. Thus, $\beta_1 \approx 1$ and $\gamma_1 \approx 1$. Plugging into Equation 1, we get the total cost ratio:

$$T_D \approx 1 + \frac{c_2}{m} + \frac{1}{m} \cdot (c_3 + c_4).$$

Range case DSD_2**:** d vectors fits in L2. Once a scorer is loaded to L1, the inner most loop can load a feature vector and keep it at least at L2 when a new scorer is loaded. Given there are m scorers, $A_2/A_0 \approx 1/m$. Namely $\alpha_2\beta_2 = A_2/A_0 \approx 1/m$. Since L2 can hold d vectors needed for inner most loop, $A_2 \approx A_3$. Thus $\gamma_2 = A_3/A_2 \approx 1$.

$$T_D \approx 1 + \alpha_2 \cdot c_2 + \frac{1}{m} \cdot (c_3 + c_4).$$

Range case DSD_3**:** d vectors fit in L3. Once a scorer is loaded to L1, the inner most loop can load a feature vector and keep it at least at L3 when a new scorer is loaded. Given there are m scorers, $A_3/A_0 \approx 1/m$. Namely $\alpha_3\beta_3\gamma_3 = A_3/A_0 \approx 1/m$.

$$T_D \approx 1 + \alpha_3 \cdot c_2 + \alpha_3\beta_3 \cdot c_3 + \frac{1}{m} \cdot c_4.$$

Range case DSD_4**:** d vectors donot not fit in L3. In this case, $A_0 \approx A_1 \approx A_2 \approx A_3$. In this case, actually we put n documents in the inner loop. It's obvious to see that L1, L2 and L3's cache miss ratio are all 1 because comparing to the memory size, even L3 cache size is too small.

$\alpha_4 \approx 1$, $\beta_4 \approx 1$ and $\gamma_4 \approx 1$.

$$T_D \approx 1 + c_2 + c_3 + c_4.$$

Cases	d vectors fit in	$T_{DSD_i} = \eta T_s + T_D \approx$
DSD_1	L1	$\eta + \eta\frac{c_4}{d_1} + 1 + \frac{c_2+c_3+c_4}{m}$
DSD_2	L2	$\eta + \eta\frac{c_4}{d_2} + 1 + \alpha_2 c_2 + \frac{c_3+c_4}{m}$
DSD_3	L3	$\eta + \eta\frac{c_4}{d_3} + 1 + \alpha_3 c_2 + \alpha_3\beta_3 c_3 + \frac{c_4}{m}$
DSD_4	memory	$\eta + \eta\frac{c_4}{d_4} + 1 + c_2 + c_3 + c_4$

Table 1: Cost of DSD when 1 scorer fits in L1.

4.1.3 *Other Scenarios of DSD*

For Scenario 2 when a scorer fits in L2 on average, there are only 3 range cases: DSD_2, DSD_3, and DSD_4. L1 miss rate in T_D becomes 1 and T_S adds c_2 as $T_S \approx 1 + c_2 + \frac{c_4}{d}$. For Scenario 3 where a scorer fits in L3, there are only 2 possible cases to consider: DSD_3 and DSD_4. L1 and L2 miss rates in T_D become 1 and T_S adds c_3 as $T_S \approx 1+c_3+\frac{c_4}{d}$. For Scenario 4 where a scorer fits memory only, there is one case to consider: DSD_4. Its T_D does not change while $T_S \approx 1 + c_4$.

4.2 Cost Comparison of the Four Methods

The data access cost for SDS, DSDS, and SDSD is listed in Appendix A. There is a total of 28 range cases considered in these four methods: DSD_i, SDS_i, DSD_iS_j, and SDS_iD_j where $1 \le i, j \le 4$. The cost results of these 28 cases can be used in the following two aspects.

- Identify the approximated optimum selection from 28 cases instead of exhaustive search of all combinations. The selection algorithm goes through 28 cases and runs the average time performance sampling through a benchmark of q queries.

  From Tables 1, Tables 8, Tables 9, and Tables 10, increasing d or s under its range limit decreases the time cost. Thus d and s should be chosen to be as large as possible. On the other hand, scorers and vectors share each level of cache and we set a constraint that vectors and scorers accessed in the inner most loop of DSD and SDS or in the two inner most loops of DSDS and SDSD fit in the corresponding cache. For example, as a midpoint approximation, we let d vectors occupy upto half of each cache level and s scorers occupy upto half of each cache level. Namely, for $1 \le i \le 3$, d and s are chosen for each range case as: $d_i = \frac{0.5Li}{Fsize}$, $s_i = \frac{0.5Li}{Ssize}$. As all n vectors and m scorers fit in memory, $d_4 = n$ and $s_4 = m$.

- Narrow the search scope when characteristics of a dataset or targeted machine architecture is given because many of 28 cases may be eliminated. That facilitates the reduction of search space and allows more sampling points at each range case selected as long as time complexity permits. For example, the above midpoint sampling for each range case after elimination can be expanded as follows. Since each scorer may only access a fraction of a feature vector and a fraction of the scorer data structure for computation, we choose sampling points as $d_i = \frac{0.5Li}{\mu Fsize}$, $s_i = \frac{0.5Li}{\mu Ssize}$. Coefficient μ represents the average data usage of a vector or a scorer during computation and for example, we sample more points with μ as 1, 0.75, 0.5, and 0.25.

To illustrate the second point above, we show that the following proposition is true and can narrow the search scope from 28 to 4 range cases.

PROPOSITION 1. *When each feature vector fits in L1 and each score fits in L1 on average, and* $\frac{\eta c_4}{d_2} \ll 1$, $\frac{c_4}{s_2} \ll 1$, *the candidates with the lowest access cost are among range cases* DSD_2, DSD_2S_1, SDS_2D_2, *and* SDS_2D_1.

A proof is listed in Appendix B. Yahoo!, MS, and MQ datasets discussed in Section 5 fall into the condition of this proposition when each regression tree used is not too big (e.g. containing upto 50 leaves). The range of d and s values for these datasets is listed in Table 3 and Table 2 of Section 5. When a regression tree contains 150 leaves, ratio c_4/s_2 is getting close to 1, cases SDS_3D_1 and SDS_3D_2 can be competitive as a best candidate. Thus with such a condition, we can search for 6 cases instead of 28 cases.

In summary, a guided sampling scheme conducts the following steps. 1) Identify data and architecture parameters. When possible, apply Proposition 1 or its variation to eliminate some of 28 range cases from the cost analysis of DSD, SDS, DSDS, and SDSD. 2) For each of selected range cases, choose blocking factor d_i and s_i under a constraint that vectors and scorers accessed in the inner most loop of DSD and SDS or in the two inner most loops of DSDS and SDSD fit in the corresponding level of cache. One approach is to choose $d_i = \frac{0.5Li}{\mu Fsize}$ $s_i = \frac{0.5Li}{\mu Ssize}$ with a number of sampled μ values. 3) Run and collect the average query response time with m

scorers and n vectors from each sampled case. Select the case and parameter setting with the lowest response time. The total complexity of this scheme with q test queries is $O(m * n * q)$.

4.3 Discussions

Integration with the QuickScorer method. When the ensemble computation uses the original computing algorithm for gradient boosted regression trees (e.g. [8, 5]), the main data structure of each scorer is a tree. To use the BWQS algorithm [12], we treat each scorer as the application of QS on a block of trees. The following parameters are involved: the size of a scorer changes when different partitioning is adopted while the number of inner-loop scorers (s) and inner-loop vectors (d) can vary too for different blocking methods. Thus we add a partitioning search loop on the top of the aforementioned comparison and sampling scheme to select the best partitioning.

Batched query processing. When the ensemble score computation is used for query processing where n is small, d value of the inner most loop limited by n can be insufficient to explore the cache locality and the effectiveness of blocking degrades. When batch processing is allowed, we can boost the cache utilization by processing feature vectors from multiple queries in fast cache, which essentially raises n values. One application of such batched processing is to conduct an offline experiment to assess the ranking performance of an algorithm in answering a large number of queries and there is no need to output ranking results immediately.

For an online ranking application, the ranking results need to be produced promptly. While reaching a high throughput, batching a large number of queries can increase the average waiting time of batched queries and affect the response time. With this constraint in mind, we set a limit on the largest waiting time allowed in choosing a batch size for a higher throughout with a modest increase of response time.

5. EVALUATIONS

5.1 Settings

This section provides an experimental comparison of different cache blocking methods and validates the effectiveness of the selected method with unoptimized ones. The evaluation tasks are listed as follows: (1) Illustrate the fast comparison of the 28 range cases for using DSD, SDS, SDSD and DSDS with guided sampling. (2) Integrate our cache blocking selection algorithm with the QS algorithm [12] for tree-based ranking. (3) Assess the batched query processing in improving the throughput when n is small.

We implement the blocking methods using C compiled with GCC optimization flag -O3. Experiments are conducted on a Linux CentOS 6.6 server with 8 cores of 3.1GHz AMD Bulldozer FX8120 and 16GB memory. FX8120 has 16KB of L1. We set $L2 \approx 1MB$ as 2MB L2 cache is shared by two cores. Its 8MB L3 cache is shared by 8 cores and since L3 hosts tree data useful for multiple queries, we set $L3 \approx 2MB$. The cache line is of size 64 bytes. For AMD Bulldozer, c_2 is around 7.3, c_3 is around 25.1, and c_4 is around 80.9. We have also conducted experiments in a 24-core Intel Xeon E5-2680v3 2.5 GHz server with $L1 = 32KB$, $L2 = 256KB$,, and $L3 \approx 2.5MB$ per core. The Intel results are similar and thus we mainly report the AMD numbers.

The following learning-to-rank datasets are used as evaluation benchmarks. (1) Yahoo! dataset [7] with 700 features per document feature vector. (2) MSLR-30K dataset [2] with 136 features per document vector. (3) MQ2007 dataset [1] with 46 features per document vector. Table 2 shows the range of d values when fitting d vectors in different cache levels for these 3 datasets.

d vectors fit in	Yahoo!	MS	MQ
L1	$d \leq 5$	$d \leq 30$	$d \leq 89$
L2	$d \leq 373$	$d \leq 1928$	$d \leq 5720$
L3	$d \leq 747$	$d \leq 3856$	$d \leq 11440$
Memory	$d \leq n$	$d \leq n$	$d \leq n$

Table 2: The vector counts for fitting in differnt cache levels.

We use LambdaMART [5] for ranking with additive tree ensembles and derive tree ensembles using the open-source jforests [9] package. To assess score computation in presence of a large number of trees, we have also used a bagging method [13] to combine multiple ensembles and each ensemble contains additive boosting trees. Because the size of a scorer affects the cache performance and parameter choices, we generate the size of each tree with several settings: 10 leaves per tree, 50 leaves per tree, and 150 leaves per tree. Table 3 shows the range of s values when fitting s scorers in different cache levels under three choices of the regression tree size. The η value is about 1 because the basic access operation of a scorer is to fetch 1 tree node and then a document feature. Each of them fits in one cache line. The default total number of trees used is about 20,000 for Yahoo! dataset, 10,000 for MS, and 4,000 for MQ. We also use other numbers of trees in our experiments. When using the QS method [12], each scorer is a meta tree merged from multiple trees and η value is around 4 because the basic access operation of a scorer fetches elements from 4 data structures and then a document feature.

s scorers fit in	10 leaves	50 leaves	150 leaves
L1	$s \leq 25$	$s \leq 5$	$s = 1$
L2	$s \leq 1638$	$s \leq 327$	$s \leq 109$
L3	$s \leq 3276$	$s \leq 655$	$s \leq 218$
Memory	$s \leq m$	$s \leq m$	$s \leq m$

Table 3: The tree counts for fitting different cache levels.

The above data sets contain 23 to 120 documents per query with labeled relevancy judgment. In practice, a search system with a large dataset ranks thousands or tens of thousands of top results after a preliminary selection. To evaluate the score computation in such a setting, we synthetically generate more matched document vectors for each query. In this process, we generate relatively more vectors that bear similarity to those with low labeled relevance scores, because a large percentage of matched results per query are less relevant in practice. The number of vectors per query including synthetically generated vectors varies from 3,000 to 10,000 for Yahoo! dataset, from 2,000 to 6,000 for MS, and from 1,000 to 4,000 for MQ.

Metrics. We mainly report the average time of computing a subscore for each vector under one tree. With n matched vectors scored using an m-tree model, this scoring time multiplied by n and m is the scoring time per query. The throughput is the number of feature vectors scored per second. The number reported here is measured in a multi-core environment where each query is executed in a single core.

5.2 A comparison of cache blocking methods

Table 4 shows the score computing time of a vector per tree in nanoseconds under different cache blocking cases for Yahoo!, MS and MQ datasets. "Y! 10" means Yahoo! dataset and each regression tree has 10 leaves. Row 2 is the scoring time of DS without cache blocking. The cost of all 28 cases under 4 cache blocking methods using guided sampling are listed, starting from Row 3. Under Proposition 1, our scheme searches the optimum only from four cases DSD_2, DSD_2S_1, SDS_2D_1, and SDS_2D_2. The corresponding entries in this table are marked in a gray color. For Yahoo! dataset with 150 leaves per tree, as we discussed in Section 4.2, extra two cases SDS_3D_1, and SDS_3D_2 are also compared and thus marked in a gray color. For each column from column 2, entry marked '$\star$' indicates the smallest value is found and this entry is considered to be highly competitive. Our comparison scheme selects DSD_2 as the best range case with $d = 373$ for Yahoo! dataset under all three tree size settings, $d = 1928$ for MS 50 leaves case and $d = 5720$ for MQ 10 leaves case. It selects SDS_2D_2 with $d = 1928$ and $s = 1638$ for MS 10 leaves case.

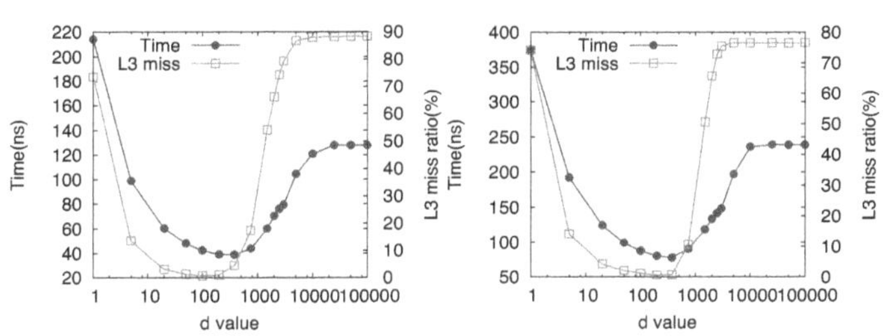

(a) Yahoo! 50 leaves (b) Yahoo! 150 leaves

Figure 5: Time cost and cache miss of DSD as d varies.

The running cost of the above guided sampling in CPU hours with one core is shown the second row of Table 5 and can be completed within about 10 hours using a 8-core server. We have also conducted exhaustive search with greatly-increased sampling points to obtain an estimated optimum solution. The best cases identified in the estimated optimum are listed in the third row of Table 5 and exactly match what has been selected by our guided sampling scheme. The fourth row of the Table 5 shows the sample error which is the cost difference ratio between the optimum solution and the solution approximated by our scheme. The difference is within 2.2%. The fifth and sixth rows are the best cases and difference ratio obtained on the Intel machine. The error is within 2.4% while all best cases of the estimated optimum match those of the approximated solution. The above result shows that our guided sampling can find a highly competitive blocking solution within reasonable hours using a modest server and such a solution can result in upto 6.57x response time reduction compared to DS without cache blocking.

Impact of blocking size on time cost and cache miss rate. In Section 4, we have used Figure 3 to illustrate the correlation between data access time cost and blocking

	Y! 10	Y! 50	Y! 150	MS 10	MS 50	MQ 10
DS	59.83	214.29	374.56	59.67	206.98	34.89
DSD_1	33.04	99.00	193.95	17.34	47.79	9.82
DSD_2	14.09$\star$	39.11 $\star$	78.11$\star$	14.37	31.49$\star$	8.52$\star$
DSD_3	25.51	71.45	143.55	25.95	49.72	13.84
DSD_4	54.06	126.32	241.47	42.37	77.75	20.13
DSD_1S_1	41.56	125.44	237.35	24.46	63	13.67
DSD_2S_1	21.55	50.41	84.87	17.31	38.61	11.4
DSD_3S_1	25.71	77.75	141.07	18.1	40.38	11.6
DSD_4S_1	40.13	120.84	235.36	19.93	52.93	11.83
DSD_2S_2	29.77	72.42	123.3	30.38	67.33	19.5
DSD_3S_2	30.49	72.79	124.16	31.25	67.71	19.88
DSD_4S_2	29.73	72.74	123.07	31.35	68.45	19.85
DSD_3S_3	39.58	79.73	131.6	40.73	76.2	22.39
DSD_4S_3	46.13	105.91	157.47	46.2	100.58	28.16
DSD_4S_4	59.81	217.14	375.24	59.09	210.08	34.95
SDS_1D_1	60.67	149.17	267.69	23.67	62.61	10.99
SDS_2D_1	23.75	58.28	102.93	16.28	40.53	9.52
SDS_3D_1	27.08	72.31	130.48	16.85	43.22	9.6
SDS_4D_1	31.58	98.72	192.1	17.47	48.65	9.83
SDS_2D_2	14.5	39.75	82.26	13.21$\star$	32.23	8.68
SDS_3D_2	15.71	42.68	88.05	15.09	37.30	10.12
SDS_4D_2	15.55	45.46	88.45	15.07	34.52	10.03
SDS_3D_3	20.76	59.03	120.15	21.55	50.02	13.04
SDS_4D_3	26.28	73.81	143.4	26.28	52.29	13.93
SDS_4D_4	54	131.58	250.17	42.46	81.7	20.13
SDS_1	42.96	113.73	240.89	21.39	50.83	12.62
SDS_2	30.91	72.22	122.22	31.65	67.28	20.27
SDS_3	46.11	107.19	156.67	46.56	100.75	28.78
SDS_4	59.83	214.29	374.56	59.67	206.98	34.89

Table 4: Scoring time of one vector per tree in nanoseconds for different cache blocking range cases.

size in deriving the cost for DSD. Figure 5 shows the experimental result to validate. This figure shows time cost curve of DSD and L3 miss rate measured using Linux tool perf when d value varies for Yahoo! dataset with 50 leaves (a) and 150 leaves (b) per tree. When d is too small, cache is not fully utilized and the cost of T_S for DSD derived in Section 4.1.2 is large. When d is too big which falls into case DSD_3 or DSD_4, the cost curve matches the analysis in Appendix A that $T_{DSD_4} > T_{DSD_3} > T_{DSD_2}$.

There is also a correlation between the overall time cost and L3 cache miss when d varies. For small d, the coefficient for L3 cost c_3 in T_S is big. For large d, there is more L3 cache miss, making T_D bigger as shown in Section 4.

Impact of m and n values on time cost. Figure 6 shows the time cost per tree per document when m changes from 2,000 to 20,000 for all datasets. In this experiment, we generate extra trees for MS and MQ datasets. It shows that with sufficiently large value of m, the cache behavior does not change much and the processing cost is about the same for different m values.

	Y! 10	Y! 50	Y! 150	MS 10	MS 50	MQ 10
Comp. time	10.67h	27.09h	81.86h	2.719h	6.349h	0.424h
Best AMD	DSD_2	DSD_2	DSD_2	SDS_2D_2	DSD_2	DSD_2
Error AMD	0.21%	0.15%	0.10%	0.61%	2.2%	0.47%
Best Intel	DSD_2	SDS_2D_2	SDS_2D_2	DSD_2	SDS_2D_2	DSD_2
Error Intel	1.4%	2.4%	0.64%	0.18%	0.52%	0.14%

Table 5: CPU hours for comparison, sampling errors, and best cases.

Figure 7 shows the time cost per tree per vector when n changes from 1 to 100,000. When n is smaller than 100, the performance drops significantly and cache is not fully utilized. When n is larger than 1000, the cost becomes stable

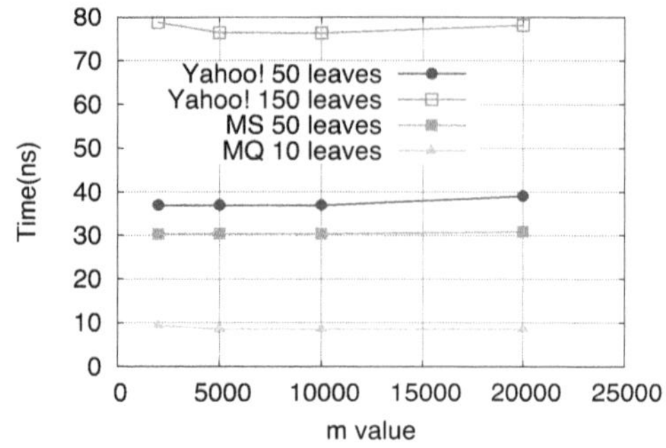

Figure 6: Scoring time per vector per tree when m changes.

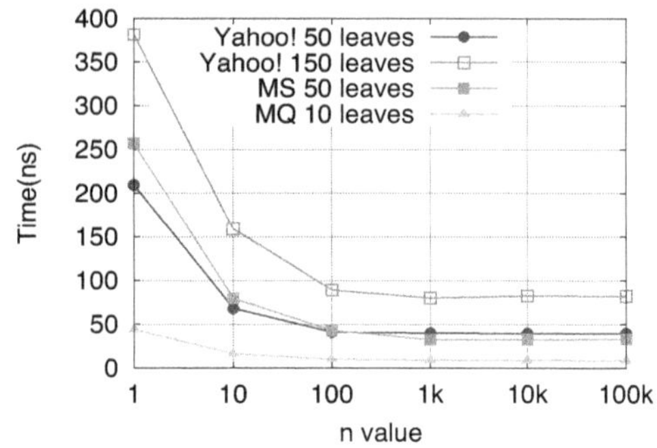

Figure 7: Scoring time per vector per tree when n changes.

and there is no much reduction. We will discuss the experiment results when batched query processing is allowed shortly.

5.3 Selective cache blocking for QuickScorer

We integrate our scheme with the BWQS algorithm [12] as follows. Step 1: Given m trees and let τ be the number of trees that will be merged to use the QS method. The number of scorers is $m' = m/\tau$. Step 2: Given m' scorers and n vectors, use our scheme to find the best blocking method and parameters. Step 3: Repeat Step 1 and Step 2 for a different sampling choice of τ. Step 4: The τ with the smallest time cost yields the best overall performance.

Figure 8 shows the BWQS results under the different number of scorers m' where m is fixed as 20,000 and m' varies from 1 to 20,000. Notice that when m' is small, each scorer contains many trees and does not fit in L1 or even L2. The

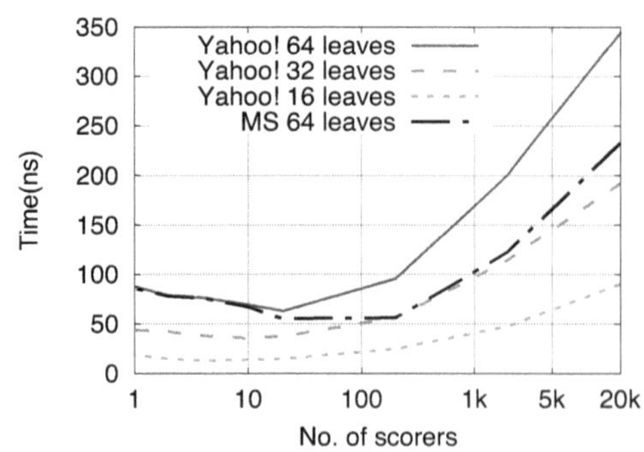

Figure 8: Scoring time of a vector per tree when varying the number of BWQS scorers.

Time(ns)	Tree scorers	BWQS scorers
Yahoo! 10	14.09	11.24
Yahoo! 50	39.11	52.88
Yahoo! 150	78.11	2869.29
MS 50	31.49	44.64
MQ 10	8.52	7.39

Table 6: Use of the comparison and selection scheme with BWQS scorers and with the original regression tree scorers.

best m' found for Y!64, Y!32, Y!16 and MS64 are 20, 10, 4 and 200, respectively. For Y!64, when $m' = 20$, case DSD_3 with $d = 75$ reaches the best performance with 62.89ns scoring time. If d is chosen as 1, the scoring time would be 89.33ns. Here the constraint to derive d value is explained as follow. Let F be the number of features in each document vector and L be the number of leaves in each tree. Following [12], the size of d document vectors is $4dF$ bytes and the QS data structure is composed of 6 parts: the result bit vectors with size $d\tau \cdot \frac{L}{8}$, the thresholds with size $4\tau L$, the offsets with size $4F$, the tree ids with size $4\tau L$, the bitvectors with size $\frac{\tau \cdot L^2}{8}$, and leaves with size $4\tau L$. The total size of d vectors and QS data structure is $4F(d+1) + (d \cdot \frac{L}{8} + (12 + \frac{L}{8})L) \cdot \tau$, which needs to fit in L3 cache because one BWQS scorer may not fit in $L2$. For Yahoo! dataset with $F = 700$, when $L = 64$ and $\tau = 1000$, we can derive $d = 75.4$ with $L3 \approx 2MB$.

Table 6 shows the scoring time per vector per tree when applying cache blocking with our comparison and selection scheme to the original tree scorer and to the BWQS scorer. This comparison shows that when the number of leaves per tree is small(10), BWQS performs better. When the number of leaves per tree increases to 150, BWQS becomes fairly slow. Our explanation is listed as follows. The core QS scheme has a complexity sensitive to the number of tree nodes detected as "false" nodes because bit-wise operations need to be conducted for all such nodes. When the number of "false" nodes is large and linear to L, the overall time cost grows at linearly to increasing of L for small L. When $L > 64$, the bit operation has to be carried by multiple 64-bit instructions and there is additional overhead for managing this complexity. For a large tree with many false nodes, QuickScorer can become very expensive. On the other other hand, the original regression tree algorithm has a complexity logarithmically proportional to L. It should be mentioned that the scoring time per vector per tree reported here seems to be slower than what was reported in [12] for $L = 64$. That can be caused by a difference in dataset characteristics, our code implementation, and test platform. We will investigate this issue in the future work.

5.4 Batched Query Processing

We illustrate the benefit of batched query processing when n is small. Table 7 shows the throughput under different batch sizes when ranking only 10 document vectors ($n = 10$). The throughput is defined as the number of queries processed per second. The last row shows the throughput when DS without cache blocking is used. When batch size is 10, for MS 50, the average processing time is reduced from 79.79ns to 42.93ns. When the batch size becomes much bigger, the benefit is not significant any more while there is an increase of waiting time. Thus a modest batch size is sufficient in

Batch size	Y! 50	Y! 150	MS 50	MQ 10
10k	125.79	60.78	310.27	2880.2
1k	125.60	60.64	304.88	2805.8
100	125.00	60.37	308.45	2673.8
10	121.54	56.03	232.94	2460.6
1	73.53	31.40	125.33	1505.1
DS	23.87	13.12	38.89	565.6

Table 7: Throughput under different batch size when $n = 10$.

this case to reach upto 1.86x throughput performance improvement.

6. CONCLUSIONS

The main contribution of this paper is a fast comparison and selection scheme to find an optimized cache blocking method with guided sampling. Our analysis estimates the data access cost of different methods approximately, which provides a foundation to select sampling points in comparing different methods and in narrowing search space.

The evaluation studies with 3 datasets show that different blocking methods and parameter values can exhibit different cache and cost behavior and our guided sampling can identify a highly competitive solution among DSD, SDS, DSDS, and SDSD methods in a reasonable amount of hours using a modest multi-core server. The difference between the selected solution and the estimated optimum is within 2.4% and the response time of this solution can be 6.57x faster than DS without cache blocking. The analytic cost analysis shows that the search space for datasets such as Yahoo!, MS, and MQ can be greatly narrowed by taking advantages of data and architectural characteristics. When the number of feature vectors per query is small, cache utilization is affected and if allowed, batched query processing can bring upto 1.86x performance improvement. The evaluation demonstrates that our scheme can be used to find the optimized partitioning for QuickScorer.

Acknowledgments. We thank the anonymous referees for their thorough comments. This work is supported in part by NSF IIS-1528041 and IIS-1118106. Any opinions, findings, conclusions or recommendations expressed in this material are those of the authors and do not necessarily reflect the views of the NSF.

APPENDIX

A. COST ANALYSIS FOR SDS, DSDS, AND SDSD

Similar to the analysis of DSD in Section 4, this appendix section estimates the data access cost of SDS, DSDS, and SDSD. We skip the details on how the results are derived and summarize them in the following tables. We use a similar naming of range cases for these 3 methods: SDS_i, DSD_iS_j, and SDS_iD_j where $1 \leq i, j \leq 4$. Notation D_i in each range case name means that d vectors fit in cache level i, but not $i-1$. Level $i = 4$ refers to memory. Notation S_i means that s scorers fit in cache level i, but not $i-1$.

Table 8 lists the access cost ratio of SDS for the scenario when a feature vector fits in L1. For the scenario when one vector fits in L2 only, there are 3 range cases to consider: SDS_2, SDS_3, and SDS_4. Formula T_S is the same while T_D adds c_2 as: $T_D = 1 + c_2 + \frac{c_4}{s}$. For the scenario when a vector fits in L3 only, there are only 2 cases to consider: SDS_3, and SDS_4. Formula T_S is the same while T_D adds c_3 as $T_D = 1 + c_3 + \frac{c_4}{s}$. For the scenario when a vector fits in memory only: there is one case to consider: SDS_4. T_S is the same while T_D changes as $T_D = 1 + c_4$.

Cases	s scorers fit in	$T_{SDS_i} = T_D + \eta T_S \approx$
SDS_1	L1	$1 + \frac{c_4}{s_1} + \eta + \eta\frac{c_4}{n}$
SDS_2	L2	$1 + \frac{c_4}{s_2} + \eta + \eta c_2$
SDS_3	L3	$1 + \frac{c_4}{s_3} + \eta + \eta c_3$
SDS_4	memory	$1 + \frac{c_4}{s_4} + \eta + \eta c_4$

Table 8: Cost of SDS when 1 feature vector fits in L1.

Table 9 lists the data access cost ratio of DSDS for the scenario when a feature vector fits in L1. For the scenario when one vector fits in L2, there are only 6 range cases to consider: DSD_2S_2, DSD_3S_2, DSD_4S_2, DSD_3S_3, DSD_4S_3 and DSD_4S_4. Formula T_S does not change while T_D adds an extra c_2 term. For the scenario when one vector fits in L3, there are only 3 cases to consider: DSD_3S_3, DSD_4S_3 and DSD_4S_4. Formula T_S does not change while T_D adds an extra c_3 term. For the scenario when one vector fits in memory only, there is only one case to consider: DSD_4S_4. Formula T_S does not change while T_D adds an extra c_4 term.

Cases	d vectors fit in	s scorers fit in	$T_{DSD_iS_j} = T_D + \eta T_S \approx$
DSD_1S_1	L1	L1	$1 + \frac{c_4}{m} + \eta + \eta\frac{c_4}{d_1}$
DSD_2S_1	L2	L1	$1 + \frac{c_2}{s_1} + \eta + \eta\frac{c_4}{d_2}$
DSD_3S_1	L3	L1	$1 + \frac{c_3}{s_1} + \eta + \eta\frac{c_4}{d_3}$
DSD_4S_1	memory	L1	$1 + \frac{c_4}{s_1} + \eta + \eta\frac{c_4}{d_4}$
DSD_2S_2	L2	L2	$1 + \frac{c_2}{s_2} + \eta + \eta c_2 + \eta\frac{c_4}{d_2}$
DSD_3S_2	L3	L2	$1 + \frac{c_3}{s_2} + \eta + \eta c_2 + \eta\frac{c_4}{d_3}$
DSD_4S_2	memory	L2	$1 + \frac{c_4}{s_2} + \eta + \eta_2 + \eta\frac{c_4}{d_4}$
DSD_3S_3	L3	L3	$1 + \frac{c_3}{s_3} + \eta + \eta c_3 + \eta\frac{c_4}{d_3}$
DSD_4S_3	memory	L3	$1 + \frac{c_4}{s_3} + \eta + \eta c_3 + \eta\frac{c_4}{d_4}$
DSD_4S_4	memory	memory	$1 + \frac{c_4}{s_4} + \eta + \eta c_4$

Table 9: Cost of DSDS when 1 feature vector fits in L1.

Table 10 lists the data access time ratio for SDSD when a feature vector fits in L1. Symbol $\alpha_{i,j}$ denotes L1 cache miss rate in the corresponding case SDS_iD_j; Symbol $\beta_{i,j}$ is the corresponding L2 miss rate.

For the scenario 2 when one scorer fits in L2, there are 6 range cases to consider: SDS_2D_2, SDS_3D_2, SDS_4D_2, SDS_3D_3, SDS_4D_3 and SDS_4D_4. α in T_D becomes 1 and T_S adds an extra c_2 term. For the scenario when one scorer fits in L3, there are 3 cases to consider: SDS_3D_3, SDS_4D_3 and SDS_4D_4. α and β in T_D becomes 1 and T_S adds an extra c_3 term. For the scenario when one scorer does not fit L3, there is only one case to consider: SDS_4D_4. Its T_D does not change while T_S adds an extra c_4 term.

B. PROOF FOR PROPOSITION 1

For each of DSD, SDS, DSDS, and SDSD methods, we eliminate its range cases that do not qualify for the best candidate as follows.

Cases	$T_{SDS_iD_j} = \eta T_S + T_D \approx$
SDS_1D_1	$\eta + \eta\frac{c_4}{n} + 1 + \frac{c_4}{s_1}$
SDS_2D_1	$\eta + \eta\frac{c_2}{d_1} + 1 + \frac{c_4}{s_2}$
SDS_3D_1	$\eta + \eta\frac{c_3}{d_1} + 1 + \frac{c_4}{s_3}$
SDS_4D_1	$\eta + \eta\frac{c_4}{d_1} + 1 + \frac{c_4}{s_4}$
SDS_2D_2	$\eta + \eta\frac{c_2}{d_2} + 1 + \alpha_{2,2}c_2 + \frac{c_4}{s_2}$
SDS_3D_2	$\eta + \eta\frac{c_3}{d_2} + 1 + \alpha_{3,2}c_2 + \frac{c_4}{s_3}$
SDS_4D_2	$\eta + \eta\frac{c_4}{d_2} + 1 + \alpha_{4,2}c_2 + \frac{c_4}{s_4}$
SDS_3D_3	$\eta + \eta\frac{c_3}{d_3} + 1 + \alpha_{3,3}c_2 + \alpha_{3,3}\beta_{3,3}c_3 + \frac{c_4}{s_3}$
SDS_4D_3	$\eta + \eta\frac{c_4}{d_3} + 1 + \alpha_{4,3}c_2 + \alpha_{4,3}\beta_{4,3}c_3 + \frac{c_4}{s_4}$
SDS_4D_4	$\eta + \eta\frac{c_4}{d_4} + 1 + c_4$

Table 10: Cost of SDSD when one scover fits in L1.

- For DSD cases listed in Table 1, case DSD_4 is excluded from the best case list as term c_4 in DSD_4 cost dominates the weight. Thus $T_{DSD_4} > T_{DSD_3}$, $T_{DSD_4} > T_{DSD_2}$, and $T_{DSD_4} > T_{DSD_1}$. We also drop DSD_1 because $T_{DSD_1} > T_{SDS_2D_1}$.

  Now we compare DSD_2 and DSD_3. Since $\frac{\eta c_4}{d_2} \ll 1$, $\frac{\eta c_4}{d_3} \ll 1$, and these two terms can be dropped approximately from the cost expressions. Note that $\alpha_3\beta_3 = \frac{1}{m\gamma_3} \geq \frac{1}{m}$, and c_3 is much larger than c_2. Also $\alpha_2 < \alpha_3$ since the inner most loop of DSD_2 accesses less vectors. This makes $T_{DSD_3} > T_{DSD_2}$.

- Now we compare SDS cases listed in Table 8. Since $\frac{c_4}{s_2} \ll 1$, this leads to $\frac{c_4}{s_3} \ll 1$, and $\frac{c_4}{s_4} \ll 1$, and $\frac{c_4}{m} \ll 1$. Therefore $T_{SDS_4} > T_{SDS_3} > T_{SDS_2}$. Thus we drop cases SDS_3 or SDS_4.

  We drop case SDS_2 because $T_{SDS_2} > T_{DSD_2S_2}$. We also drop case SDS_1 because $T_{SDS_1} > T_{DSD_2S_1}$ given $\frac{\eta c_4}{d_2} \ll 1$.

- For DSDS, since $\frac{\eta c_4}{d_2} \ll 1$, $T_{DSD_2S_1} \approx 1 + \eta + \frac{c_2}{s_1}$. Then $T_{DSD_2S_1} < T_{DSD_3S_1}$ and $T_{DSD_2S_1} < T_{DSD_4S_1}$. Thus we drop cases DSD_2S_1 and DSD_4S_1.

  Since $\frac{c_4}{s_2} \ll 1$, $\frac{c_2}{s_2} \ll 1$. Then $T_{DSD_2S_2} \approx 1 + \eta + \eta c_2$. Then $T_{DSD_2S_2}$ is smaller than any of $T_{DSD_3S_2}$, $T_{DSD_4S_2}$, $T_{DSD_3S_3}$, $T_{DSD_4S_3}$, and $T_{DSD_4S_4}$. We drop all cases in DSDS except DSD_1S_1, DSD_2S_1, and DSD_2S_2.

  Since $T_{DSD_2S_2} > 1 + \eta + \eta\frac{c_2}{d_1} \approx T_{SDS_2D_1}$ given $\frac{\eta c_4}{s_2} \ll 1$, we can further drop case DSD_2S_2. Then $T_{DSD_1S_1} > T_{DSD_2S_1}$ and we can further drop case DSD_1S_1.

- For SDSD, we drop case SDS_1D_1 because $T_{SDS_1S_1} \approx 1 + \eta + \frac{c_4}{s_1} > T_{DSD_2S_1}$ given $\frac{\eta c_4}{d_2} \ll 1$. We drop Case SDS_3D_1 because $T_{SDS_3S_1} \approx 1 + \eta + \eta \cdot \frac{c_3}{d_1} > T_{SDS_2S_1}$. We drop Case SDS_4D_1 because $T_{SDS_4S_1} \approx 1 + \eta + \eta \cdot \frac{c_4}{d_1} > T_{SDS_2S_1}$.

  Note that $T_{SDS_2S_2} \approx 1 + \eta + \alpha_{2,2}c_2$ because $\frac{\eta c_4}{s_2} \ll 1$ and $\frac{\eta c_2}{d_2} < \frac{\eta c_4}{d_2} \ll 1$. Then we drop SDS_4D_4 because $T_{SDS_2D_2} < T_{SDS_4D_4}$. Also, $T_{SDS_2D_2}$ is smaller than any of $T_{SDS_3D_2}$, $T_{SDS_4D_2}$, $T_{SDS_3D_3}$, and $T_{SDS_4D_3}$. That is because $\alpha_{2,2} < \alpha_{3,2}, \alpha_{4,2}, \alpha_{3,3}, \alpha_{4,3}$ due to the fact that s scorers fits in the smaller cache in Case SDS_2D_2 than other cases compared here. Thus only SDS_2D_2 and SDS_2D_1 qualify for the best candidates.

C. REFERENCES

[1] Lector 4.0 datasets. http://research.microsoft.com/en-us/um/beijing/projects/letor/letor4dataset.aspx.

[2] Microsoft learning to rank datasets. http://research.microsoft.com/en-us/projects/mslr/.

[3] Nima Asadi and Jimmy Lin. Training Efficient Tree-Based Models for Document Ranking. In *ECIR*, pages 146–157, 2013.

[4] Nima Asadi, Jimmy Lin, and Arjen P De Vries. Runtime Optimizations for Tree-Based Machine Learning Models. *IEEE TKDE*, pages 1–13, 2013.

[5] Christopher J. C. Burges, Krysta Marie Svore, Paul N. Bennett, Andrzej Pastusiak, and Qiang Wu. Learning to rank using an ensemble of lambda-gradient models. In *J. of Machine Learning Research*, pages 25–35, 2011.

[6] B. Barla Cambazoglu, Hugo Zaragoza, Olivier Chapelle, Jiang Chen, Ciya Liao, Zhaohui Zheng, and Jon Degenhardt. Early exit optimizations for additive machine learned ranking systems. WSDM '10, pages 411–420, 2010.

[7] Olivier Chapelle and Yi Chang. Yahoo! Learning to Rank Challenge Overview. *J. of Machine Learning Research*, pages 1–24, 2011.

[8] Jerome H. Friedman. Greedy function approximation: A gradient boosting machine. *Annals of Statistics*, 29:1189–1232, 2000.

[9] Yasser Ganjisaffar, Rich Caruana, and Cristina Lopes. Bagging Gradient-Boosted Trees for High Precision, Low Variance Ranking Models. In *SIGIR*, pages 85–94, 2011.

[10] Pierre Geurts and Gilles Louppe. Learning to rank with extremely randomized trees. *J. of Machine Learning Research*, 14:49–61, 2011.

[11] Andrey Gulin, Igor Kuralenok, and Dmitry Pavlov. Winning the transfer learning track of yahoo!'s learning to rank challenge with yetirank. *J. of Machine Learning Research*, 14:63–76, 2011.

[12] Claudio Lucchese, Franco Maria Nardini, Salvatore Orlando, Raffaele Perego, Nicola Tonellotto, and Rossano Venturini. Quickscorer: A fast algorithm to rank documents with additive ensembles of regression trees. In *SIGIR*, pages 73–82, 2015.

[13] Dmitry Yurievich Pavlov, Alexey Gorodilov, and Cliff A. Brunk. Bagboo: a scalable hybrid bagging-the-boosting model. In *CIKM*, pages 1897–1900, 2010.

[14] Xun Tang, Xin Jin, and Tao Yang. Cache-conscious runtime optimization for ranking ensembles. SIGIR '14, pages 1123–1126, 2014.

[15] Jiancong Tong, Gang Wang, and Xiaoguang Liu. Latency-aware strategy for static list caching in flash-based web search engines. In *CIKM*, pages 1209–1212, 2013.

[16] Lidan Wang, Jimmy Lin, and Donald Metzler. Learning to efficiently rank. SIGIR '10, pages 138–145, 2010.

[17] Lidan Wang, Jimmy Lin, and Donald Metzler. A cascade ranking model for efficient ranked retrieval. SIGIR '11, pages 105–114, 2011.

Improved Caching Techniques for Large-Scale Image Hosting Services

Xiao Bai
Yahoo Research
Sunnyvale, USA
xbai@yahoo-inc.com

B. Barla Cambazoglu
Independent Researcher
Barcelona, Spain
barla@berkantbarlacambazoglu.com

Archie Russell
Yahoo Inc.
San Francisco, USA
archie@yahoo-inc.com

ABSTRACT

Commercial image serving systems, such as Flickr and Facebook, rely on large image caches to avoid the retrieval of requested images from the costly backend image store, as much as possible. Such systems serve the same image in different resolutions and, thus, in different sizes to different clients, depending on the properties of the clients' devices. The requested resolutions of images can be cached individually, as in the traditional caches, reducing the backend workload. However, a potentially better approach is to store relatively high-resolution images in the cache and resize them during the retrieval to obtain lower-resolution images. Having this kind of on-the-fly image resizing capability enables image serving systems to deploy more sophisticated caching policies and improve their serving performance further.

In this paper, we formalize the static caching problem in image serving systems which provide on-the-fly image resizing functionality in their edge caches or regional caches. We propose two gain-based caching policies that construct a static, fixed-capacity cache to reduce the average serving time of images. The basic idea in the proposed policies is to identify the best resolution(s) of images to be cached so that the average serving time for future image retrieval requests is reduced. We conduct extensive experiments using real-life data access logs obtained from Flickr. We show that one of the proposed caching policies reduces the average response time of the service by up to 4.2% with respect to the best-performing baseline that mainly relies on the access frequency information to make the caching decisions. This improvement implies about 25% reduction in cache size under similar serving time constraints.

1. INTRODUCTION

Commercial image hosting services (e.g., Flickr, Facebook) rely on image serving systems that are geographically distributed in nature. A typical image serving system involves at least one data center, some cache proxies, and a number of edge caches. The main storage system is located in the data center(s) and hosts at least one copy of all available images. Cache proxies are located in different geographical regions and have relatively smaller storage systems that host images requested by the clients in their region.[1] Finally, edge caches are general-purpose storage systems located at the network entry points of the image hosting service and may store images as well as other kinds of files.

The data centers, cache proxies, and edge caches form parts of a storage system hierarchy that is distributed over the network. When a client of the hosting service requests a particular image, the request is first tried to be resolved by looking up the image in the closest edge cache in the network. If the requested image is not found in the edge cache, the request is forwarded to the regional cache proxy responsible for the client's region. If the requested image is found in the regional cache proxy, the image is served by the cache. If the requested image itself is not available, it may still be possible to obtain and serve the image by resizing a higher resolution version of the image previously cached in the proxy [9]. If both attempts fail (i.e., a cache miss), the request is finally forwarded to a data center, which is guaranteed to have the requested image, and the image is served by the backend image storage in that data center.

When designing and constructing cache hierarchies like the one mentioned above, an important optimization objective is to minimize the miss rate of regional caches.[2] This is usually achieved by storing, in the respective regional cache, images that are frequently and/or recently requested by the clients of a particular region. Reducing the miss rate of regional caches relieves the request workload of the backend storage systems in data centers. Moreover, due to the close proximity of such caches to the clients, considerable reduction can be achieved in the serving latency if more images are served by these caches. This, in turn, may make a positive impact on users' engagement with the image hosting service, especially when the user-perceived response latency values (in case of no regional caches) are beyond the range tolerable by the users. In practice, the financial cost of constructing these regional caches often forms a constraint for image hosting companies. Therefore, a regional cache can have storage capacity (memory and disk) that is sufficient to cache only a limited portion of the image collection.

Our paper investigates the static caching problem in geographically distributed image hosting services. Despite the

SIGIR '16, July 17-21, 2016, Pisa, Italy

DOI: http://dx.doi.org/10.1145/2911451.2911513

[1]Here, the client may refer to a real user, a crawling bot, or some automated software.

[2]In the rest of the paper, we refer to cache proxies and edge caches together as regional caches.

dynamic nature of the request streams, previous research [1] has revealed that static caches, which serve highly frequent requests, play an important role in building effective caching systems with high hit rates. Small dynamic caches usually lead to lower hit rates than static caches of similar size, and a combined static/dynamic cache always has its dynamic part built on top of its static part.[3] In this work, we particularly focus on static caching, which is a more fundamental problem than dynamic caching. Adding a dynamic cache to serve images that are not found in the static cache is complementary to our problem.

The objective in our static caching problem is to select images to be stored in a fixed-capacity regional cache (in an offline manner) such that the average response time for future image retrieval requests is minimized. This particular caching problem is slightly different from the static caching problem in similar domains (e.g., page caching in web proxies or result caching in web search engines) because the same image is often stored in many different resolutions.[4] As a result, a cache hit does not necessarily lead to similar response time as in web search, rendering the cache hit rate not an ideal optimization target. In our case, it is possible to serve a retrieval request by generating the requested image after resizing one of its higher resolution versions previously stored in the cache [9]. Hence, a cache hit may be possible even if the requested resolution of the image is not found in the cache. As we will discuss, this difference leads to a slightly more complex cost model when caching images.

The contributions of this paper are as follows. We first provide a system model and a cost model, both guided by real-life observations, for the static caching problem in large-scale image hosting services. We then provide a formal definition for the static image caching problem where the optimization objective is to minimize the average serving time of the image hosting system under a cache capacity constraint. As a solution for this problem, we provide some frequency-based heuristics and propose two gain-based heuristics that aim to reduce the average serving time. We conduct extensive experiments using real-life access logs obtained from Flickr. Under the same cache capacity constraint, the average response time achieved by one of the proposed heuristics is up to 4.2% less than that of the best-performing baseline. This is equivalent to a cache size reduction of 25% under similar serving time constraints.

The rest of the paper is organized as follows. In Section 2, we formally define the static caching problem that we investigate after presenting a realistic system model and a cost model. In Section 3, we provide some heuristic solutions for the problem. The experimental setting and results are presented in Sections 4 and 5, respectively. The related work is surveyed in Section 6. We conclude the paper in Section 7.

2. STATIC IMAGE CACHING

2.1 System Model

We assume an image collection $\{I_1, \ldots, I_n\}$ containing n images each with a unique id (referred to as logical images).

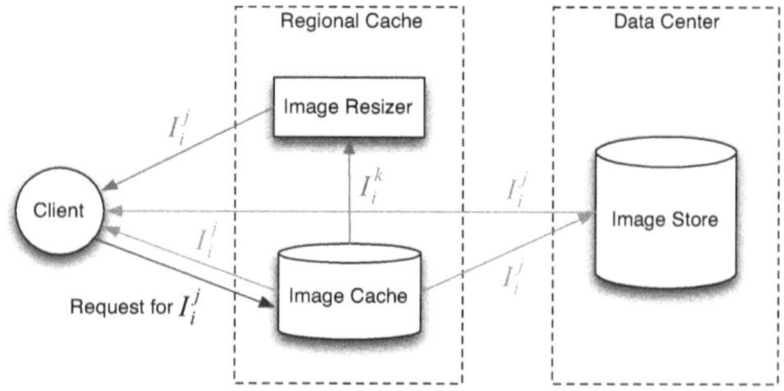

Figure 1: Architecture of an image serving system.

Every logical image I_i in the collection is available in exactly m different resolutions $\{I_i^1, \ldots, I_i^m\}$ (referred to as physical images). We denote by $S(I_i^j)$ the size of a physical image I_i^j (in bytes). For convenience, we assume that $S(I_i^k) > S(I_i^j)$ if and only if $k > j$, for all i.

Without loss of generality, we consider an abstract serving architecture composed of a single data center D and a single regional cache R. Data center D stores at least one copy of all physical images in the collection. Regional cache R can store a much smaller and fixed subset $\mathcal{R}$ of physical images. As we will discuss in Section 2.3, the selection of images to be stored on R forms the focus of our static caching problem. We illustrate the system architecture in Fig. 1.

The client requests are redirected to one of the nearby regional caches (e.g., using the IP addresses) in a quasi-deterministic way to ensure low network latency. Therefore, each regional cache has its own stream of requests and the related images to manage. Moreover, regional caches do not communicate with each other due to their high geographical (and network) distance. Communicating with a single data center or several data centers only affects the cost of fetching an image from the backend as we will discuss shortly. Therefore, using this abstract serving architecture does not affect the design of caching policy.

A request issued by some client c to retrieve a physical image I_i^j is resolved in the following order.

- Physical cache hit: The request first reaches regional cache R. If I_i^j exists in $\mathcal{R}$, it can be immediately served to client c by regional cache R (the green edge in Fig. 1).

- Logical cache hit: Occasionally, I_i^j does not exist in $\mathcal{R}$, but a higher resolution physical image I_i^k, such that $j < k \leq m$, may exist in $\mathcal{R}$. In that case, I_i^k is resized on-the-fly by the image resizer that is co-located with the cache servers to obtain I_i^j, which is then served to client c by regional cache R (the blue edges in Fig. 1).

- Cache miss: If both attempts fail, the request for I_i^j is forwarded to the backend image store in data center D. I_i^j is then transferred over the network from data center D to regional cache R and then served to client c (the red edges in Fig. 1).

2.2 Cost Model

Given a regional cache R with its image collection $\mathcal{R}$ and a physical image I_i^j, we compute the end-to-end response latency, $T(\mathcal{R}, I_i^j)$, as

[3]In general, the items in a static cache are updated periodically, e.g., on a daily basis, and those in a dynamic cache may be updated upon a cache miss.

[4]This is mainly because client devices differ in terms of their resolution (e.g., a desktop computer versus a mobile phone).

$$T(\mathcal{R}, I_i^j) = \begin{cases} T_{\text{PCH}}(I_i^j), & I_i^j \in \mathcal{R}; \\ T_{\text{LCH}}(I_i^j, I_i^k), & I_i^j \notin \mathcal{R}, \exists k, j < k \leq m, I_i^k \in \mathcal{R}; \\ T_{\text{CM}}(I_i^j), & \text{otherwise.} \end{cases} \quad (1)$$

Here, T_{PCH}, T_{LCH}, and T_{CM} denote the response latency in the case of a physical cache hit, a logical cache hit, and a cache miss, respectively.

In the case of a physical cache hit, the latency is simply computed as

$$T_{\text{PCH}}(I_i^j) = T_{\text{read}}(I_i^j) + T_{Rc}(I_i^j), \quad (2)$$

where $T_{\text{read}}(I_i^j)$ denotes the time to read image I_i^j from the memory or disk (depending on where the image is stored in the cache) and $T_{Rc}(I_i^j)$ denotes the time to send image I_i^j from regional cache R to client c. Both times are positively correlated with the size of image I_i^j. $T_{Rc}(I_i^j)$ is also correlated with the distance between R and c.

For a logical cache hit, the latency is computed as

$$T_{\text{LCH}}(I_i^j, I_i^k) = T_{\text{read}}(I_i^k) + T_{\text{resize}}(I_i^k, I_i^j) + T_{Rc}(I_i^j), \quad (3)$$

where $T_{\text{resize}}(I_i^k, I_i^j)$ denotes the time required to obtain the requested image I_i^j by resizing a higher resolution image I_i^k available in $\mathcal{R}$. This cost increases with both $S(I_i^k)$ and $S(I_i^j)$. We note that, if there are multiple images that have higher resolution than I_i^j, we always use the one that leads to the least time for resizing, i.e., the one closest to I_i^j in terms of resolution.

Finally, for a cache miss, the latency is computed as

$$T_{\text{CM}}(I_i^j) = T_{\text{read}}(I_i^j) + T_{DR}(I_i^j) + T_{Rc}(I_i^j), \quad (4)$$

where $T_{\text{read}}(I_i^j)$ denotes the time it takes to read image I_i^j from the disk (of the backend image store), and $T_{DR}(I_i^j)$ denotes the time to transfer image I_i^j from data center D to regional cache R over the network.

We note that this cost model assumes that conversion from I_i^k to I_i^j is time-wise cheaper than fetching I_i^j from the backend image store in data center D, i.e., logical cache hits are always cheaper than cache misses. In practice, however, there may be cases where it is more beneficial to retrieve I_i^j from data center D instead of resizing at regional cache R (especially when the resolution difference between I_i^k and I_i^j is too large). In Section 4.4, we provide more detail for the computation of the costs given in Eqs. (2), (3), and (4).

2.3 Problem Definition

We are given a sequence $\mathcal{I}$ of image retrieval requests. We denote by $f(I_i^j)$ the frequency of requests in $\mathcal{I}$ for physical image I_i^j. Given a statically cached image collection $\mathcal{R}$, the average response latency for serving the requests in $\mathcal{I}$ can be computed as

$$T(\mathcal{R}, \mathcal{I}) = \frac{\sum_{I_i^j \in \mathcal{I}} f(I_i^j) \times T(\mathcal{R}, I_i^j)}{\sum_{I_i^j \in \mathcal{I}} f(I_i^j)}. \quad (5)$$

The objective of our static image caching problem is to fill a fixed-capacity static cache with a selected subset $\mathcal{R}^*$ of images so that the average response latency is minimized for a given sequence $\mathcal{I}$ of image retrieval requests. More formally, the objective is to find

$$\mathcal{R}^* = \underset{\mathcal{R}}{\operatorname{argmin}}\, T(\mathcal{R}, \mathcal{I}) \quad (6)$$

without violating the cache capacity constraint

$$\sum_{I_i^j \in \mathcal{R}^*} S(I_i^j) \leq C, \quad (7)$$

where C denotes the storage capacity of the cache (in bytes).

3. STATIC CACHING HEURISTICS

In this section, we introduce some heuristic solutions for the problem given in Section 2.3. All of the presented heuristics are greedy in nature. The basic idea behind them is to sort logical or physical images according to a greedy choice property and select images to be cached in that sorted order. The selection of images continues as long as the cache capacity constraint given in Eq. (7) is not violated. The heuristics differ mainly in the way they define the greedy choice property. Herein, we present the heuristics under two headings: frequency-based and gain-based heuristics.

3.1 Frequency-Based Heuristics

In this line of heuristics, the greedy choice property relies on the frequency with which images will be requested from the image hosting service. Since the future request frequency of an image is unknown, it is estimated using the image's observed request frequency in a past time period. As in most other static caching problems, the fundamental assumption here is that the past and future request frequencies of images are highly correlated. We denote by $f'(I_i)$ the past request frequency of a logical image I_i and compute it as

$$f'(I_i) = \sum_{j=1}^{j=m} f'(I_i^j), \quad (8)$$

where $f'(I_i^j)$ denotes the past request frequency of physical image I_i^j. We next present three frequency-based heuristics.

Largest requested (LR). Logical images are sorted in decreasing order of their past frequency values ($f'(I_i)$) and we iterate on images in this order. For each logical image I_i that is currently under consideration, we select its largest physical image that was requested at least once in the past, i.e., we cache a single physical image I_i^k such that $f'(I_i^k) \geq 1$ and $S(I_i^k) \geq S(I_i^j)$, for all I_i^j, where $1 \leq j \leq m$.[5] This heuristic aims to increase the logical cache hit rate at the expense of more aggressive cache space consumption at each caching decision.

Most requested (MR). Similar to LR, logical images are considered in decreasing order of their past frequency values. For each logical image currently being considered, we select the most frequently requested physical image associated with that logical image, i.e., we cache a single physical image I_i^k such that $f'(I_i^k) \geq f'(I_i^j)$, for all I_i^j, where $1 \leq j \leq m$. This heuristic aims to increase the physical cache hit rate while preserving high logical cache hit rates for physical images with lower resolutions (i.e., smaller sizes).

Most requested per byte (MRPB). Physical images are sorted in decreasing order of their size-normalized past frequency values ($f'(I_i^j)/S(I_i^j)$) and are admitted to the cache in this order. Normalizing frequency values with image sizes enables more efficient use of available cache space. Similar heuristics were previously used in other problem contexts, such as posting list caching [1], result caching [7, 14], and document replication [6, 10] for web search engines.

[5] The ties are broken arbitrarily.

Algorithm 1 Gain-based caching heuristic (LGPB)

1. **Input:** Image collection $\{I_1, ..., I_n\}$
2. **Output:** Set $\mathcal{R}^*$ of images to be placed in the cache
3. **for** each logical image I_i in $\{I_1, ..., I_n\}$ **do**
4. cacheCandidates $\leftarrow \emptyset$
5. imageCandidates $\leftarrow \{I_i^1, ..., I_i^m\}$
6. **while** imageCandidates $\neq \emptyset$ **do**
7. timeGains $\leftarrow \emptyset$
8. **for** each physical image I_i^j in imageCandidates **do**
9. timeGains $\leftarrow$ timeGains $\cup \{ \langle I_i^j, G(\mathcal{R}_i, I_i^j)/S(I_i^j)\rangle\}$
10. **end for**
11. get image $I_i^{j^*}$ having the highest $G(\mathcal{R}_i, I_i^{j^*})/S(I_i^{j^*})$ in timeGains
12. $\mathcal{R}_i \leftarrow \mathcal{R}_i \cup \{I_i^{j^*}\}$
13. imageCandidates $\leftarrow$ imageCandidates $\setminus \{I_i^{j^*}\}$
14. cacheCandidates $\leftarrow$ cacheCandidates $\cup \{ \langle I_i^{j^*}, G(\mathcal{R}_i, I_i^{j^*})/S(I_i^{j^*})\rangle\}$
15. **end while**
16. **end for**
17. sort the images in cacheCandidates in decreasing order of $G(R_i, I_i^j)/S(I_i^j)$
18. select images for $\mathcal{R}^*$ until $\sum_{I_i^j \in \mathcal{R}^*} S(I_i^j) > C$
19. **return** $\mathcal{R}^*$

3.2 Gain-Based Heuristic

In this line of heuristics, instead of mainly relying on the observed request frequency of images, the greedy choice property prefers to select images that can ensure low response time, which is more inline with the objective of the static image caching problem defined in Section 2.3. Herein, we propose two gain-based heuristics. We note that different gain-based heuristics were proposed before in the context of web search result caching [7, 14].

Largest gain per byte (LGPB). When making caching decisions, this heuristic prefers images that are expected to bring the largest reduction in response time over all image requests. Given a set $\mathcal{R}$ of statically cached images and a physical image I_i^j, we can estimate the total response time gain, $G(\mathcal{R}, I_i^j)$, achieved by caching I_i^j as

$$G(\mathcal{R}, I_i^j) = \sum_{k=1}^{m} f'(I_i^k) \times (T(\mathcal{R}, I_i^k) - T(\mathcal{R} \cup \{I_i^j\}, I_i^k)). \quad (9)$$

Here, we essentially compute the expected response time gain by only considering logical image I_i. This is because caching physical image I_i^j may affect only the response time of requests for physical images (I_i^k, for $1 \leq k \leq m$) associated with logical image I_i. The response times of requests for other physical images remain the same as none of those images can be obtained by resizing I_i^j. However, caching a physical image I_i^j may affect the response time gains estimated for other physical images associated with logical image I_i. To be more specific, when the set $\mathcal{R}$ of cached images does not contain any physical image associated with logical image I_i, the estimated response time gain for caching image I_i^k for image I_i^j ($j < k$) is $T_{\text{CM}}(I_i^j) - T_{\text{LCH}}(I_i^j, I_i^k)$ (Eq. (1)). Once image I_i^ℓ ($\ell > k$) is cached in $\mathcal{R}$, the estimated response time gain of caching image I_i^k for image I_i^j becomes $T_{\text{LCH}}(I_i^j, I_i^\ell) - T_{\text{LCH}}(I_i^j, I_i^k)$. Therefore, we compute the response time gain for each image in an iterative way, considering physical images previously estimated to have higher priority (i.e., those with larger estimated response time gains) for the corresponding logical image.

Similar to MRPB, the LGPB heuristic selects the images in decreasing order of their estimated response time gains normalized by the image size ($G(\mathcal{R}, I_i^j)/S(I_i^j)$) to enable more efficient use of the available cache space. The pseudo-code given in Algorithm 1 shows how the LGPB heuristic updates the estimated response time gain for each image and how it selects the images admitted to the cache. For every logical image I_i, we first compute the size-normalized response time gain for each of the physical images associated with I_i (Lines 3–10) and assign the largest gain to the corresponding image I_i^j (Lines 11–14). $\mathcal{R}_i$ denotes the set of physical images that have been estimated to have high priority to be added to the cache for logical image I_i. We then recompute the response time gains for every image I_i^k, where $1 \leq k \leq m$ and $k \neq j$, given that I_i^j has been added to $\mathcal{R}_i$ (by repeating Lines 6–15). We keep assigning the largest (updated) response time gain to the corresponding image and recomputing the gain values for the rest of images whose gain values have not been assigned yet. We continue this process until a gain value is assigned to each of the physical images associated with the logical image (by repeating Lines 3–16).

The size-normalized response time gains for m physical images associated with a logical image can be computed by performing $\frac{m \times (m-1)}{2}$ updates. Therefore, the overall complexity to compute the response time gain for all n logical images is $O(m^2 \times n)$. Since an image usually has a dozen of different resolutions in an image hosting service while a large-scale service may receive requests for millions of images every day, we typically have $m \ll n$. Therefore, in practice, the complexity of the LGPB heuristic is comparable to the complexity ($O(n)$) of the frequency-based heuristics presented in Section 3.1.

Largest gain per byte with frequency adjustment (LGPB-FA). This heuristic is a variant of LGPB. Its key difference with LGPB, as well as the frequency-based heuristics, is in the way it estimates the future frequency of each request. The motivation stems from the observation that the past frequency of requests is not always strongly correlated with their future frequency, especially in the case of infrequent requests [7]. Table 1 shows the Pearson correlation coefficient between the frequency of the physical image requests in the past (the training period of the experiments reported in Section 4.2) and the frequency of the same physical image requests in the future (the testing period of the experiments). As the request frequency follows a heavily skewed distribution, we group the requests according to their frequencies in the past and compute the Pearson correlation coefficient for each group respectively. We observe that the future frequency of a request is more correlated with its past frequency if it is a frequent query, and there is little correlation when a request only occurs a handful of times in the past. We further observe from Fig. 2 that the reason for the decreasing correlation at low frequency range is mainly because the likelihood of not observing the infrequent requests in the future increases. In the figure, the requests with high frequencies are grouped by frequency to ensure each group has at least 100 requests to compute the probability. The adjacent two x-axis values represent the frequency range of the corresponding group.

To take this into account, we adjust the frequency estimation for computing the response time gain of caching image I_i^j, i.e., $G(\mathcal{R}, I_i^j)$ in Eq. (9), as follows. Instead of using the past frequency of each request directly in Eq. (9), we multiply $f'(I_i^k)$ by the probability of the requests whose past fre-

Table 1: Correlation between past and future frequencies of physical image requests

Frequency range	Percent of requests	Correlation coefficient
$[1, 10)$	97.6307	0.0775
$[10, 100)$	2.2864	0.1587
$[100, 1000)$	0.0786	0.5480
$[1000, 10000)$	0.0041	0.6024
$[10000, \infty]$	0.0002	0.9806

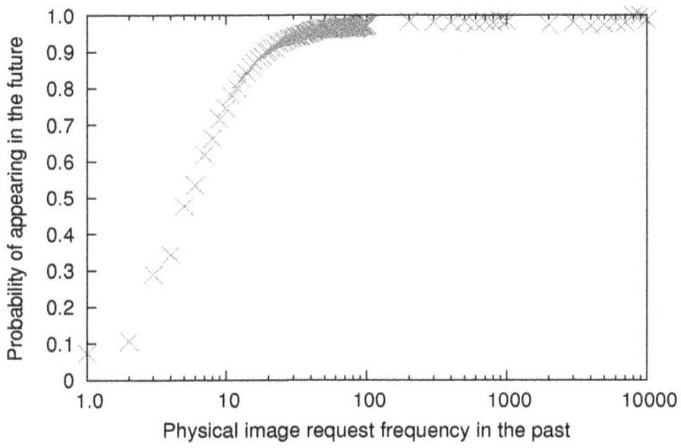

Figure 2: The probability of a past request to reappear in the future with respect to its past frequency.

quencies fall into the same frequency range $[a, b)$ as $f'(I_i^k)$, appearing in the future. The total response time gain due to caching of image I_i^j is now computed as

$$G(\mathcal{R}, I_i^j) = \sum_{k=1}^{m} p(\widehat{f}(I_i^k) > 0 \mid f'(I_i^k) \in [a, b)) \times f'(I_i^k) \times (T(\mathcal{R}, I_i^k) - T(\mathcal{R} \cup \{I_i^j\}, I_i^k)), \quad (10)$$

where $\widehat{f}(I_i^k)$ denotes the future frequency of request for image I_i^k. The underlying intuition for this adjustment is that an image is only beneficial to maintain in the cache if it will appear again in the future.

The images to fill the cache are selected in the same way as `LGPB` (Algorithm 1) with the total response time gain of caching image I_i^j computed using Eq. (10). We note that, as shown in Fig. 2, the probability of a request appearing at least 100 times in the past also appearing in the future is close to 1, we only need to compute the probability $p(\widehat{f}(I_i^k) > 0 \mid f'(I_i^k) \in [a, b))$ for a limited number of frequency ranges. For instance, if we compute one probability for each frequency range $[10^x, 10^{x+1})$ for $x \geq 2$, one probability for each frequency range $[10x, 10(x + 1))$ for $1 \leq x < 10$, and one probability for each frequency range $[x, x + 1)$ for each $1 \leq x < 10$, at most 30 precomputed probabilities are enough to compute the largest gain with frequency adjustment. This adds a constant lookup overhead when computing the response time gain per byte and does not increases the overall complexity of the gain-based heuristics, i.e., the complexity of `LGPB-FA` is still $O(m^2 \times n)$.

4. EXPERIMENTAL SETTING

4.1 Dataset

As the dataset, we use an access log containing image download requests issued to an edge cache of Flickr during a period of three consecutive days. The entire log contains about 530 million requests. For each request, the access log contains the id of the requested image (logical image), the id of the requested image resolution, the size of the requested image (in bytes), the timestamp of the request, and the IP address of the user who issued the request. We note that the id of the requested image and the id of the requested image resolution, together, uniquely identify a physical image.

Table 2: Available physical image resolutions

Symbol	Name	Resolution (in pixels)
s_1	Square 75	75×75
s_2	Thumbnail	100×67
s_3	Square 150	150×150
s_4	Small 240	$240 \times W$
s_5	Small 320	$320 \times W$
s_6	Medium 500	$500 \times W$
s_7	Medium 640	$640 \times W$
s_8	Medium 800	$800 \times W$
s_9	Large 1024	$1024 \times W$
s_{10}	Large 1600	$1600 \times W$
s_{11}	Large 2048	$2048 \times W$

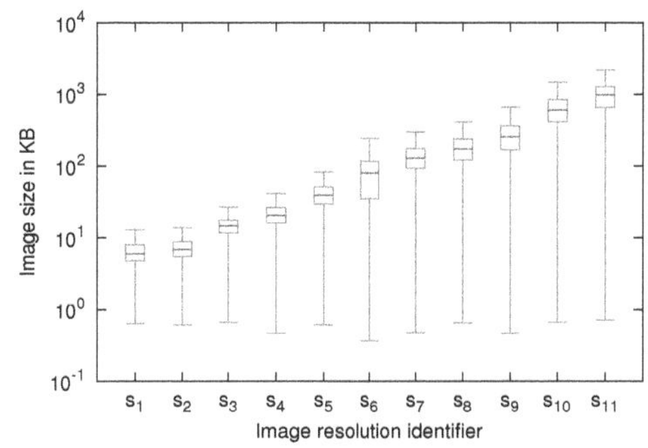

Figure 3: Distribution of image sizes in bytes for each image resolution id.

Each logical image is associated with 11 physical images. Different image resolutions are denoted by ids $s_1, s_2, \ldots, s_{11}$. All physical images are obtained by resizing the original image uploaded by the user and stored in the backend image store. Table 2 shows the name and resolution information associated with each id. Since the aspect ratio of the original image is preserved during resizing, images with ids from s_4 to s_{11} may have variable pixel widths, which we denote by W.

The storage size of an image (in bytes) depends on the way the color is represented and the format of the image (e.g., PNG, JPG, etc.). In our case, all physical images are stored in JPG format, which uses lossy compression. Therefore, the storage requirement of images may be very different even if their resolution is the same.

The box plot in Fig. 3 provides information about the distribution of image sizes (in KB) for each resolution id. The blue lines in the plot indicate the median storage sizes. The median values vary from several KBs to one MB in increasing order of ids. The boxes extend to the first and third quartiles while the whiskers extend to the 10th and 90th percentiles.

The bar chart in Fig. 4 shows the fraction of download requests with a particular image resolution id observed in the access log. According to the figure, about half of the requests are for s_6 (medium resolution images with a length of 500 pixels), which is the default resolution when serving

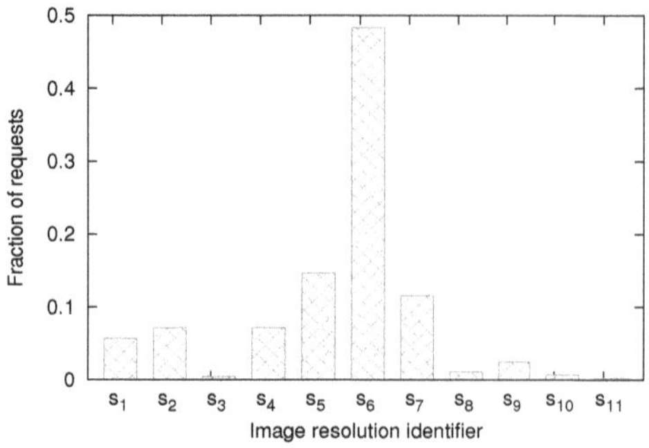

Figure 4: Number of requests for each resolution id.

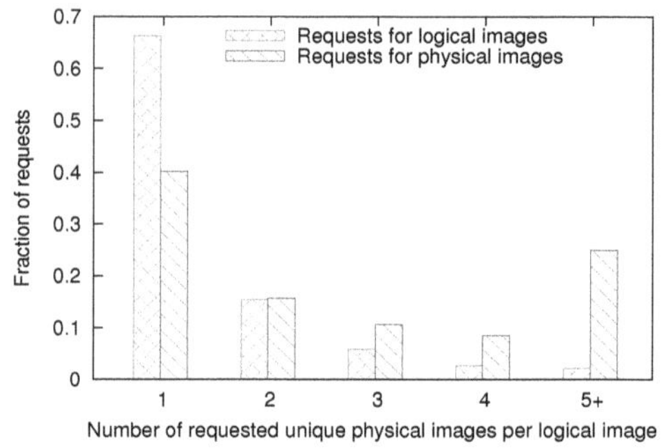

Figure 5: Distribution of requests with respect to the number of unique physical images requested per logical image.

images. The requests for other resolutions are usually due to the variation in user devices, the resolution of screens, particular user requirements on image quality, and available network bandwidth.

Fig. 5 shows the distribution of requests for logical and physical images with respect to the number of different physical image resolutions requested for a logical image. We observe that, for more than 33% of logical images, at least two different physical image sizes are requested. The number of requests for such images accounts for 60% of the total number of requests (for physical images). This implies that when on-the-fly resizing is enabled in the cache, it is possible to improve the system performance for the requests for different physical images of the same logical image by caching well-selected resolutions of that image rather than all possible physical images.

4.2 Methodology

We use the first two days (training period) of the access log to compute the frequency of requests for each physical image. The probability of a past request in a given frequency range appearing in the future is computed by considering the first day as the past and the second day as the future. We then execute our heuristics using the corresponding frequency information to fill the cache with images. The requests in the third day (test period) are used to evaluate the performance of the caching heuristics. The test set contains about 155 million requests.

Our access log contains the size (in bytes) of each requested physical image. As shown in Fig. 5, often there are physical image resolutions that were not requested for a logical image. This means that for physical images that were not requested before, we need a mechanism to estimate their actual size in bytes. To this end, we use the following heuristic. If only one resolution s_j of a (logical) image I_i was requested, the number of bytes for resolution s_k $(k \neq j)$ of I_i^k is estimated as

$$S(I_i^k) = \frac{S(I_i^j) \times \sum_i S(I_i^k)/n_k}{\sum_i S(I_i^j)/n_j}, \qquad (11)$$

where n_k denotes the number of images with resolution s_k in the log. If more than one resolution of an image was requested, we use resolution s_j whose index j is the closest to index k to estimate $S(I_i^k)$ with the same equation. Our preliminary experiments show that using the closest index gives the most accurate estimation of the actual image size.

We define the cache size as a percentage of the total number of bytes available in the backend image store. This definition takes into account the fact that a cache can be distributed over a number of servers according to the backend size to make the system scalable. We assume that the cache is composed of an in-memory cache and a disk cache, which is widely used in modern caching systems. The cache size thus represents the total size of both caches. In our experiments, we assume that the backend image store maintains all 11 physical images associated with each logical image requested in the first two days of the access log. This results in a backend size of 287TB. Note that this assumption underestimates the size of the backend as the backend usually stores all images that were uploaded to the system in the past and is not limited to two days. Caching heuristics first fill the in-memory cache and then the on-disk cache until both caches are full.

We evaluate the performance of the caching heuristics using a simulator written in Java. The simulator runs in a server with Quad-core 2.4GHz CPU and 48GB RAM. The information used by the simulator for selecting images to fill the cache (e.g., response time gain, frequency, sizes, etc.) is obtained by processing the training log using MapReduce jobs on Hadoop. This computation takes less than an hour for our training log and for each of the caching heuristics.

4.3 Metrics

We use three different metrics to evaluate the performance of the proposed caching heuristics.

- Cache hit rate: This metric measures the fraction of requests that are served by the cache. Since the system has an in-memory cache and a disk cache, and on-the-fly resizing is used to compress images in both caches, we measure additional hit ratios: memory physical hit rate, disk physical hit rate, memory logical hit rate, and disk logical hit rate.

- Response time: This metric measures the time it takes for the system to resolve a request, i.e., the time it takes before sending the requested image to the user after the request is received. The time between the user and the image hosting service (i.e., T_{Rc} in Eqs. (2), (3), and (4)) is excluded since this depends on other factors (e.g., user's location, device, and bandwidth) that are not in the focus of this work. In addition, this time is the same for different caching heuristics given the same request issued by the same user, and thus

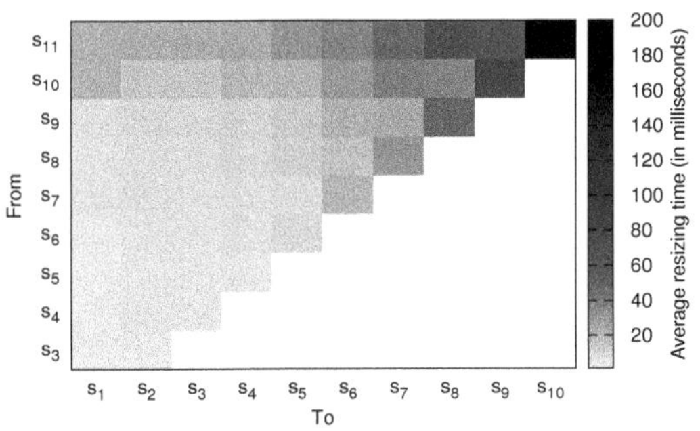

Figure 6: Average image resizing cost.

does not help to contrast the difference among caching heuristics.

- Backend workload: This metric measures the number of bytes fetched from the backend to serve a requested image. In other words, it measures the communication cost incurred due to cache misses.

4.4 Parameters

An important variable in the experiments is the cache capacity. We set this parameter to 0.2%, 0.4%, 0.6%, 0.8%, and 1.0% of the total size of the backend image store. We set the sizes of the in-memory and on-disk caches as 1% and 99% of the cache capacity, respectively. This is a realistic setting since a cache server usually has tens of GBs of RAM and a few TBs of disk storage. In fact, given a fixed cache capacity, increasing the relative size of the in-memory cache does not change the overall miss rate of the cache, but only slightly reduces the response time for certain requests. Our preliminary experiments show that having a 10% in-memory cache reduces the average response time of a 1% in-memory cache by only 0.7%.

We compute the average time for resizing an image from size s_i to size s_j as follows: (i) download all 11 sizes of 100 random images from Flickr; (ii) repeat resizing each image from resolution s_i to resolution s_j 100 times for every (s_i, s_j) pair with $i > j$; and (iii) compute the average time to resize the image from resolution s_i to size s_j.[6] The I/O times for reading the input image of resolution s_i and writing the output image of resolution s_j are not taken into account.

Fig. 6 shows the average time to resize an image from resolution s_i to resolution s_j. Images with resolution s_2 cannot be resized to resolution s_1 since these images are not large enough in width (see Table 2). The average resizing time varies between 2ms and 186ms depending on input and output resolutions. We note that by using more advanced hardware, such as GPU, the resizing time can be reduced to less than 30ms. This increases the response time difference between logical cache hits and cache misses. We evaluate the caching heuristics without assuming the use of such advanced hardware. Therefore, the reported performance results are more likely to be lower bounds.

We use a cost model similar to those described in [13, 18] to compute the time for reading an image from the cache, i.e., $T_{\text{read}}(I_i^k)$ in Eqs. (2), (3), and (4). In the case of the in-memory cache, $T_{\text{read}}(I_i^k)$ is simply equal to the cache lookup cost (set to 40ns). In the case of the on-disk cache, $T_{\text{read}}(I_i^k)$ is computed as

$$T_{\text{read}}(I_i^k) = D_{\text{seek}} + D_{\text{rotation}} + \lceil S(I_i^k)/D_{\text{block}} \rceil \times D_{\text{read}}, \quad (12)$$

where D_{seek} is the disk seek time (set to 5.80ms), D_{rotation} is the rotational latency (set to 4.17ms), D_{block} is the size of a disk block in bytes (set to 512 bytes), and D_{read} is the average time to read a block from the disk (set to 4.883ns). The parameters are set to the same values as in [13] that are determined either empirically or by consulting the literature.

The time to transfer an image from the backend image store to the cache, i.e., $T_{DR}(I_i^j)$ in Eq. (4), is computed as

$$2 \times N_{\text{latency}} + S(I_i^k)/N_{\text{bandwidth}}, \quad (13)$$

where N_{latency} denotes the network latency between the backend image store and the cache and $N_{\text{bandwidth}}$ denotes the network bandwidth between them. In the simulations, we assume that the backend is located in the U.S. and the regional cache is located in the U.S., Europe, or Asia. For these cache locations, we set the network latency between them and the backend to 25ms, 50ms, and 100ms, respectively. We also set the network bandwidth between the backend and the cache to different values: 0.1MB/s, 1MB/s, and 10MB/s. Table 3 shows the average response time, the 95th-percentile response time, and the 99th-percentile response time for the LGPB heuristic. Since a regional cache is more useful when placed in remote locations that are not close to the backend and the combination of 50ms network latency and 1MB/s bandwidth results in reasonable response times, we focus on this setting in our experiments.

5. EXPERIMENTAL RESULTS

5.1 Hit Rate

In Fig. 7, we first compare the memory physical hit rate, disk physical hit rate, memory logical hit rate, and disk logical hit rate metrics for every caching heuristic and for varying cache capacity values. We observe that MRPB achieves the highest memory physical hit rate and disk physical hit rate. This is not surprising as MRPB is among the best policies in the literature in achieving high hit rates. MR also achieves high hit rates as it selects the most frequently requested physical images to fill the cache. Yet, given that several physical images of the same logical image may be requested frequently and with similar likelihood, caching only one of them misses some potential hits and thus results in lower memory/disk physical hit rates than those of MRPB. The decrease in the hit rates of MR is partially compensated by resizing the cached physical images in both in-memory and on-disk caches as shown in the figure. In contrast, LR results in the highest memory and disk logical hit rates, but the lowest memory and disk physical hit rates among all heuristics. This is because LR selects the largest requested physical image of the most frequently requested logical images to increase the likelihood of obtaining most of the requested physical images of these logical images in the cache (through on-the-fly resizing) rather than in the backend image store. Different from all these baseline policies, the proposed caching policy LGPB and LGPB-FA achieve more balanced physical and logical hit rates between the two extremes that target high physical hit rates and high logical hit rates, respectively. LGPB-FA is slightly more in favor of

[6] To resize the images, we use Ymagine, an open-source high-performance CPU-based tool.

Table 3: Response time (in ms) for the LGPB heuristic (cache size: 0.2%)

	Bandwidth (MB/s)								
	0.1			1.0			10.0		
Latency (ms)	Avg.	95th	99th	Avg.	95th	99th	Avg.	95th	99th
25	620	2028	4032	99	259	461	46	81	101
50	651	2063	4099	130	310	514	77	130	151
100	716	2186	4201	192	411	617	139	230	252

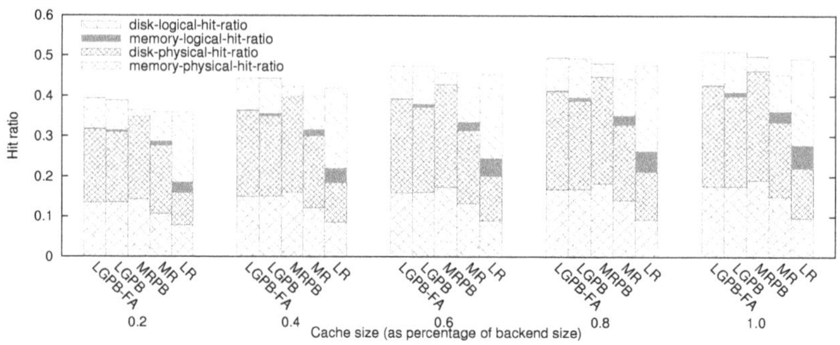

Figure 7: Hit rates for different caching heuristics and cache capacity values.

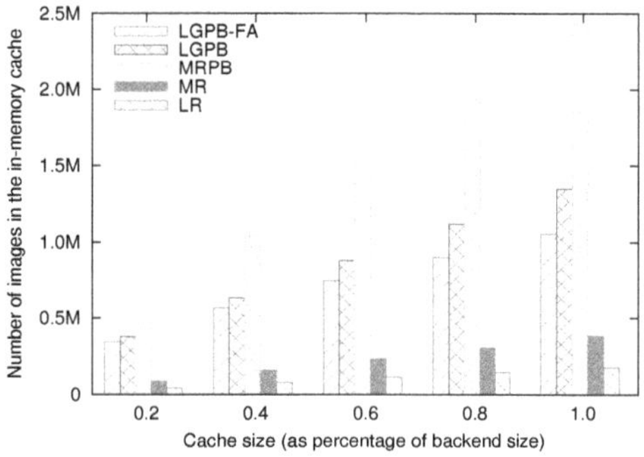

Figure 8: Number of images in the in-memory cache for different caching heuristics and different cache capacity values.

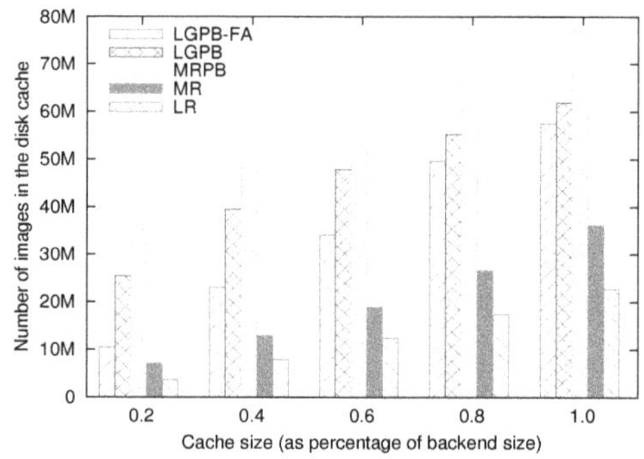

Figure 9: Number of images in the on-disk cache for different caching heuristics and different cache capacity values.

cache hits than resizing as the past frequencies of infrequent requests, which are more likely to benefit from resizing, are discounted more by the likelihood they may appear in the future. Depending on the size of the cache, from 39% to 51% of all requests can be served by the cache, being physical or logical hits, using LGPB-FA. This is up to 9.7% higher than the amount of requests that can be served by a static cache constructed using the best frequency-based caching heuristic.

Figs. 8 and 9 further show the number of physical images stored in the in-memory and on-disk caches, respectively. We observe from both figures that, given the same cache capacity, LGPB-FA, LGPB, and MRPB admit much more images into the cache than MR and LR. This is because when selecting images with LGPB-FA, LGPB, or MRPB, the response time gain or frequency of each image is divided by its size. They are thus more likely to add small images into the cache given the same response time gain or frequency. LGPB-FA feeds the cache with fewer images than LGPB. Since the frequency of each image is adjusted by its likelihood of appearing in the future, only images that have high likelihood of appearing again and high past frequency are selected. LGPB-FA thus ensures more effective use of the cache capacity than LGPB.

5.2 Response Time

In Fig. 10, we first compare the average response time of each caching heuristic for varying cache capacity values. As shown in the figure, by using the proposed caching heuristics LGPB-FA and LGPB, the average response time is reduced by up to 5.4% and 4.3%, respectively, compared to MRPB. In fact, independent of the cache capacity, LGPB-FA and LGPB consistently perform better than the best frequency-based heuristic and reduce its average response time by up to 4.2% and 3.1%, respectively. LGPB-FA leads to lower average response time than LGPB especially when the cache capacity is low. This conveys the effectiveness of the frequency adjustment as selecting the right images is more crucial under lower-capacity constraint. More importantly, while achieving similar average response time (e.g., around 115ms), LGPB-FA and LGPB considerably reduce the capacity of the cache (by about 25%). This implies a large reduction in the hardware investment needed for the caching system without any degradation in response latency and hence user experience.

Fig. 11 shows the cumulative distribution of response time for different caching heuristics for a fixed cache capacity (set to 0.4%). We observe that MR and LR result in more requests to be served within 30ms, but fewer requests are

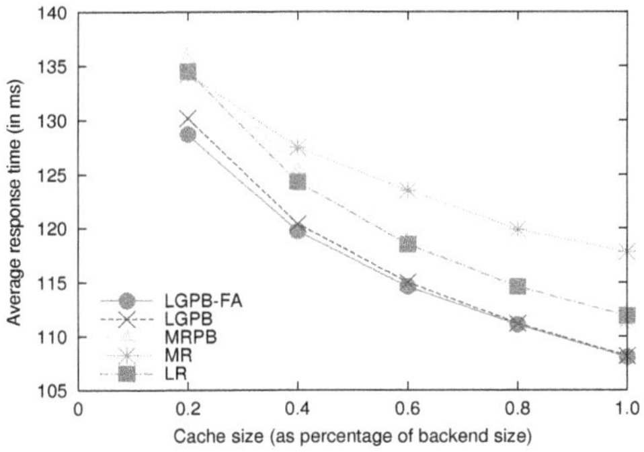

Figure 10: Average response time for different caching heuristics and cache capacity values.

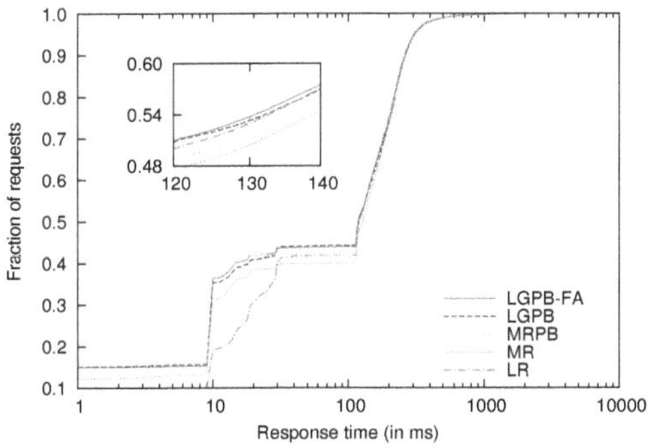

Figure 11: Cumulative distribution of response time for different caching heuristics (cache capacity: 0.4%).

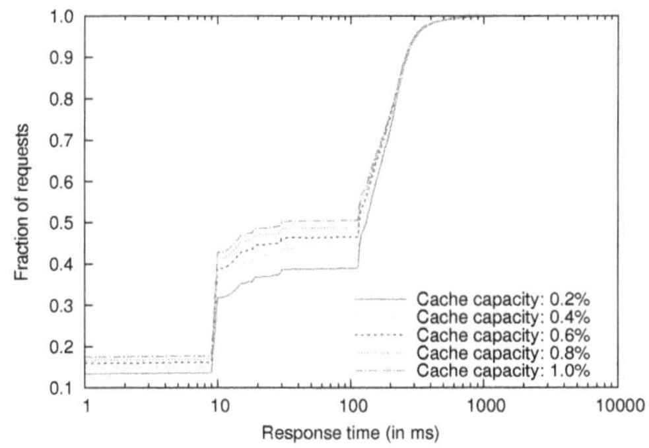

Figure 12: Cumulative distribution of response time for LGPB-FA with varying cache capacity values.

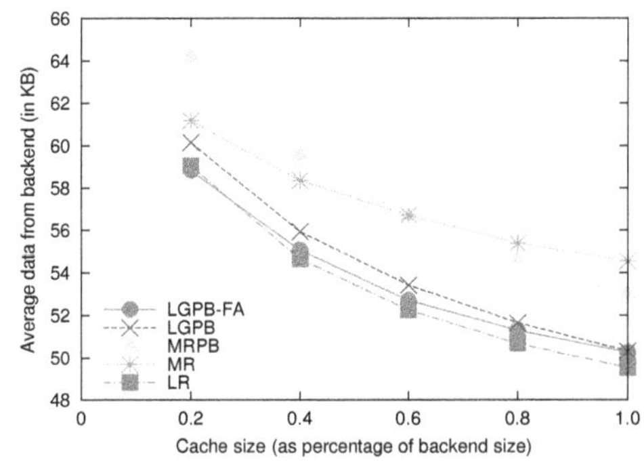

Figure 13: Backend communication cost for different caching heuristics and different cache capacity values.

served between 30ms and 100ms, compared to the proposed gain-based caching heuristics LGPB-FA and LGPB. As shown in Fig. 7, this is because MR prefers to select images that lead to direct hits in the cache while LR prefers to select large images to fill the cache so that more requests can be served through resizing. Although both physical hits and logical hits usually take less time than cache misses, the limited number of images in the cache filled by these two heuristics (Figs. 8 and 9) forces more images to be fetched from the backend, leading to high response time for more requests than LGPB-FA and LGPB. Finally, we observe in the inner plot in Fig. 11 that LGPB-FA and LGPB serve 57.5% and 56.9% of the requests under 140ms, respectively, outperforming all frequency-based caching heuristics.

Fig. 12 shows the cumulative distribution of response time for the LGPB-FA heuristic for varying cache capacity values. We observe that larger cache capacity values lead to lower response times. For instance, by using a cache capacity of 1.0%, more than 30% of the requests can be served under 100ms compared to using a cache capacity of 0.2%.

5.3 Backend Workload

We quantify the cost of the backend communication using the amount of data transferred between the cache and the backend image store. Fig. 13 shows the average number of bytes fetched from the backend to serve a request. We observe that LR always incurs the lowest communication overhead, and on average, it fetches at most 2.3% less bytes from the backend for each request than the gain-based caching heuristics LGPB-FA and LGPB. This is because, with LR, the requests for different physical images associated with the most frequently requested logical images can be resized on-the-fly in the cache rather than being forwarded to the backend. Despite its lower backend communication cost, as we have observed in Fig. 10, it takes more time to serve a request. This is because resizing a large image may itself be very costly (e.g., converting an image from resolution s_{11} to resolution s_{10} as shown in Fig. 6). Finally, we observe that LGPB-FA and LGPB incur up to 8.9% and 7.0% lower communication overhead than the other frequency-based caching heuristics MR and MRPB, respectively.

6. RELATED WORK

Caching has been an active research topic for many years, and hence the previous work on caching is vast. While earlier works were focused on more fundamental areas, such as operating systems [16] and databases [5], more recent works in the Web era have investigated the use of caching in applications such as web servers [15, 19] and search engines [4, 13]. Media access patterns in the Internet were investigated in [8]. Herein, we prefer to keep our survey brief and limit it to the related work on static caching and image caching.

Static caching has found application especially in web search engines [1, 11, 13]. Cost-based heuristics were proposed for static caching of web search results, aiming to reduce the query workload of backend search systems [7, 14]. The gain-based heuristics we proposed in this work differ from earlier cost-based heuristics in the way they try to reduce the average response latency. Moreover, their implementation requires iterative computation of the gains since the response times depend on which images are already cached. A brief survey of caching techniques used in web search engines can be found in [3].

Regarding image caching, the only work we are aware of is [9], which presents the photo serving stack of Facebook. According to [9], Facebook has a highly distributed infrastructure involving client-side caches, edge caches, origin caches, and data centers.[7] This architecture is slightly different from the architecture we presented in this paper due to the presence of client-side caches and lack of regional proxies. While the hit rate of client-side caches is reported to be 65.5% for Facebook, the contribution of these caches is negligible in our application (as most client-side hits of Facebook come from the cached profile photos of users' friends) and hence they are omitted. Another difference is that the work in [9] considers dynamic caching techniques while we explore static caching heuristics. More importantly, in terms of cache performance when using image resizing, their objective is to improve the cache hit rate, which may not be ideal as the cost of responding to an image request upon a cache hit may be very different (in contrast to result caching in web search engines). Indeed, as our experiments indicate, high hit rates do not always ensure low response times. For interested reader, some detail on the backend photo storage system of Facebook can be found in [2]. Facebook's newer large binary object storage system is introduced in [12]. A recent work on photo caching in flash storage systems of Facebook is available in [17].

7. CONCLUSIONS

In this work, we formalized the static caching problem for large-scale image serving systems and proposed two caching heuristics that aim to improve the average response time. Extensive experiments using real-life access logs obtained from Flickr demonstrated that the proposed heuristics reduce the image serving time and the system workload in terms of backend communication cost compared to simpler, frequency-based caching heuristics. More importantly, the proposed heuristics were shown to require much lower cache capacity than the baseline heuristics to achieve comparable response times, potentially leading to significant hardware savings when building image caching systems. A possible extension that may further improve the performance of such systems would be to investigate the request dynamics and propose similar heuristics for dynamic caching.

8. REFERENCES

[1] R. Baeza-Yates, A. Gionis, F. P. Junqueira, V. Murdock, V. Plachouras, and F. Silvestri. Design trade-offs for search engine caching. *ACM Transactions on the Web*, 2(4):20:1–20:28, 2008.

[2] D. Beaver, S. Kumar, H. C. Li, J. Sobel, and P. Vajgel. Finding a needle in haystack: Facebook's photo storage. In *Proc. 9th USENIX Conf. Operating Systems Design and Implementation*, pages 1–8, 2010.

[3] B. B. Cambazoglu and R. A. Baeza-Yates. *Scalability Challenges in Web Search Engines*. Synthesis Lectures on Information Concepts, Retrieval, and Services. Morgan & Claypool Publishers, 2015.

[4] B. B. Cambazoglu, F. P. Junqueira, V. Plachouras, S. Banachowski, B. Cui, S. Lim, and B. Bridge. A refreshing perspective of search engine caching. In *Proc. 19th Int'l Conf. World Wide Web*, pages 181–190, 2010.

[5] W. Effelsberg and T. Haerder. Principles of database buffer management. *ACM Transactions on Database Systems*, 9(4):560–595, 1984.

[6] G. Francès, X. Bai, B. B. Cambazoglu, and R. Baeza-Yates. Improving the efficiency of multi-site web search engines. In *Proc. 7th ACM Int'l Conf. Web Search and Data Mining*, pages 3–12, 2014.

[7] Q. Gan and T. Suel. Improved techniques for result caching in web search engines. In *Proc. 18th Int'l Conf. World Wide Web*, pages 431–440, 2009.

[8] L. Guo, E. Tan, S. Chen, Z. Xiao, and X. Zhang. The stretched exponential distribution of Internet media access patterns. In *Proc. 27th ACM Symp. Principles of Distributed Computing*, pages 283–294, 2008.

[9] Q. Huang, K. Birman, R. van Renesse, W. Lloyd, S. Kumar, and H. C. Li. An analysis of Facebook photo caching. In *Proc. 24th ACM Symp. Operating Systems Principles*, pages 167–181, 2013.

[10] E. Kayaaslan, B. B. Cambazoglu, and C. Aykanat. Document replication strategies for geographically distributed web search engines. *Information Processing & Management*, 49(1):51–66, 2013.

[11] E. P. Markatos. On caching search engine query results. *Computer Communications*, 24(2):137–143, 2001.

[12] S. Muralidhar, W. Lloyd, S. Roy, C. Hill, E. Lin, W. Liu, S. Pan, S. Shankar, V. Sivakumar, L. Tang, and S. Kumar. F4: Facebook's warm BLOB storage system. In *Proc. 11th USENIX Conf. Operating Systems Design and Implementation*, pages 383–398, 2014.

[13] R. Ozcan, I. S. Altingovde, B. B. Cambazoglu, F. P. Junqueira, and O. Ulusoy. A five-level static cache architecture for web search engines. *Information Processing & Management*, 48(5):828–840, 2012.

[14] R. Ozcan, I. S. Altingovde, and O. Ulusoy. Cost-aware strategies for query result caching in web search engines. *ACM Transactions on the Web*, 5(2):9:1–9:25, 2011.

[15] S. Podlipnig and L. Böszörmenyi. A survey of web cache replacement strategies. *ACM Computing Surveys*, 35(4):374–398, 2003.

[16] A. J. Smith. Cache memories. *ACM Computing Surveys*, 14(3):473–530, 1982.

[17] L. Tang, Q. Huang, W. Lloyd, S. Kumar, and K. Li. RIPQ: Advanced photo caching on flash for Facebook. In *Proc. 13th USENIX Conf. File and Storage Technologies*, pages 373–386, 2015.

[18] A. Trotman. Compressing inverted files. *Information Retrieval*, 6(1):5–19, 2003.

[19] J. Wang. A survey of web caching schemes for the Internet. *SIGCOMM Computer Communication Review*, 29(5):36–46, 1999.

[7] The origin cache is distributed across the data centers.

Author Index

www.ingramcontent.com/pod-product-compliance
Ingram Content Group UK Ltd.
Pitfield, Milton Keynes, MK11 3LW, UK
UKHW051419290926
15471UKWH00009B/1678